For Reference Use On

```
Ref.
O 650.14 Vocationa 1992
Vocational careers
sourcebook.
Gale Research,
c1992-
```

DATE DUE

MYNDERSE LIBRARY

Seneca Falls, N.Y.

Mynderse Library
Discard

Supported by Federal Services and Construction Act
Title I Funds, granted by The New York State Library

MAY 1 8 1999

VOCATIONAL CAREERS SOURCEBOOK

Career Research Resources— Step by Step

Step 1: Beginning Your Career Search	Step 2: Planning Your Career	Step 3: Finding the Job You Want

Occupational Outlook Handbook (OOH)

Describes careers in detail:
   nature of work
   working conditions
   employment statistics
   job outlook
   earnings
   job training, qualifications, and advancement
Provides additional information sources:
   associations, organizations, unions, and governmental agencies
   publications

Vocational Careers Sourcebook (VCS) and Professional Careers Sourcebook (PCS)

Provide concise job descriptions noting:
   employment outlook
   salaries
Offer descriptive listings:
   directories and catalogs of educational programs
   special training programs
   standards/certification agencies
Expand *OOH*'s additional information sources:
   complete information on professional associations and related organizations
   comprehensive entries for professional reference works and trade periodicals
Provide extensive listings for other categories of resources:
   career guides
   test guides
   awards, scholarships, grants, and fellowships
   meetings and conventions

Job Hunter's Sourcebook (JHS)

Features profiles of job-hunting information for specific careers:
   sources of help-wanted ads
   placement and job referral services
   employer directories and networking lists
   handbooks and manuals
   employment agencies and executive search firms
   other leads
Identifies sources of general job-hunting information:
   reference works
   newspapers, magazines, and journals
   audio/visual resources
   online services
   software
   other sources
Includes an essay offering tips on using the public library as a career information center.

ISSN 1060-5630

VOCATIONAL CAREERS SOURCEBOOK

Where to find help planning careers in skilled, trade, and nontechnical vocations

FIRST EDITION

Kathleen M. Savage and Karen Hill, Editors

Joseph M. Palmisano, Associate Editor

Compiled in cooperation with InfoPLACE, the Job, Career, and Education Service of the Cuyahoga County Public Library, Cleveland, Ohio

 Gale Research Inc. • DETROIT • LONDON

Kathleen M. Savage and Karen Hill, *Editors*
Joseph M. Palmisano, *Associate Editor*
Ned Burels and Joyce Jakubiak, *Assistant Editors*
Aided by: Cynthia Grayson
Annette Novallo, *Contributing Editor*
Linda S. Hubbard, *Senior Editor*

Victoria B. Cariappa, *Research Manager*

Lisa Lantz, Mary Beth McElmeel, and Joseph R. Schroeder, *Editorial Associates*

Melissa E. Brown, Brian Escamilla, Charles A. Jewell, Julie K. Karmazin, and Julie A. Synkonis, *Editorial Assistants*

Mary Beth Trimper, *Production Manager*
Mary Winterhalter, *Production Assistant*

Arthur Chartow, *Art Director*
Bernadette M. Gornie, *Graphic Designer*

Benita L. Spight, *Data Entry Supervisor*
Edgar Jackson and Nancy Aiuto, *Data Entry Associates*

Theresa A. Rocklin, *Supervisor of Systems and Programming*
Charles Beaumont, *Programmer*

While every effort has been made to ensure the reliability of the information presented in this publication, Gale Research Inc. does not guarantee the accuracy of the data contained herein. Gale accepts no payment for listing; and inclusion in the publication of any organization, agency, institution, publication, service, or individual does not imply endorsement of the editors or publishers.

Errors brought to the attention of the publisher and verified to the satisfaction of the publisher will be corrected in future editions.

The paper used in this publication meets the minimum requirements
of American National Standard for Information Sciences—Permanence
Paper for Printed Library Materials, ANSI Z39.48-1984. ∞™

Copyright © 1992
Gale Research Inc.
835 Penobscot Bldg.
Detroit, MI 48226-4094

ISBN 0-810-3-8405-1
ISSN 1060-5630

Printed in the United States of America

Published simultaneously in the United Kingdom
by Gale Research International Limited
(An affiliated company of Gale Research Inc.)

MYNDERSE LIBRARY
31 Fall Street
Seneca Falls, New York 13148

Contents

Highlights vii
Preface ix
Introduction xi
User's Guide xiii
Master List of Profiled Careers xvii
Career Profiles 1

Marketing and Sales Occupations
Cashiers 5
Counter and Rental Clerks 11
Insurance Sales Workers 17
Manufacturers' and Wholesale Sales
    Representatives 31
Real Estate Agents, Brokers, and
    Appraisers 39
Retail Sales Workers 55
Securities and Financial Services Sales
    Representatives 65
Services Sales Representatives 75
Travel Agents 83

Administrative Support Occupations, Including Clerical
Adjusters, Investigators, and Collectors ...97
Bank Tellers 105
Clerical Supervisors and Managers 113
Computer and Peripheral Equipment
    Operators 119
Credit Clerks and Authorizers 129
Financial Records Processors 135
    Billing Clerks 139
    Bookkeeping, Accounting, and
        Auditing Clerks 143
    Payroll and Timekeeping Clerks 151
General Office Clerks 155
Information Clerks 161
    Hotel and Motel Desk Clerks 165
    Interviewing and
        New Accounts Clerks 171
    Receptionists 177
    Reservation and Transportation
        Ticket Agents and Travel Clerks ..183
Mail Clerks and Messengers 191
Material Recording, Scheduling,
    Dispatching, and
    Distributing Occupations 195
    Dispatchers 199
    Stock Clerks 205
    Traffic, Shipping, and
        Receiving Clerks 209
Postal Clerks and Mail Carriers 215
Record Clerks 225
    Brokerage Clerks and
        Statement Clerks 229
    File Clerks 233
    Library Assistants and Bookmobile
        Drivers 239
    Order Clerks 245
    Personnel Clerks 249
Secretaries 255
Stenographers 267
Teacher Aides 277

Telephone, Telegraph, and Teletype
    Operators 283
Typists, Word Processors, and
    Data Entry Keyers 289

Service Occupations

Protective Service Occupations 301
Correction Officers 301
Firefighting Occupations 309
Guards 321
Police, Detectives, and Special Agents 327

Food and Beverage Preparation and Service Occupations 347
Chefs, Cooks, and
    Other Kitchen Workers 347
Food and Beverage Service
    Occupations 363

Health Service Occupations 377
Dental Assistants 377
Medical Assistants 387
Nursing Aides and Psychiatric Aides ...397

Personal Service and Building and Grounds Service Occupations 405
Animal Caretakers, Except Farm 405
Barbers 415
Childcare Workers 421
Cosmetologists and Related Workers ...429
Flight Attendants 439
Gardeners and Groundskeepers 445
Homemaker-Home Health Aides 455
Janitors and Cleaners 461
Private Household Workers 467

Agriculture, Forestry, Fishing, and Related Occupations
Farm Operators and Managers 475
Fishers, Hunters, and Trappers 495
Timber Cutting and Logging Workers ..509

Mechanics, Installers, and Repairers
Aircraft Mechanics and
    Engine Specialists 523
Automotive Body Repairers 529
Automotive Mechanics 539
Commercial and Industrial Electronic
    Equipment Repairers 551
Communications Equipment
    Mechanics 559
Computer and Office Machine
    Repairers 565

Diesel Mechanics 573
Electronic Home Entertainment
  Equipment Repairers 581
Elevator Installers and Repairers 589
Farm Equipment Mechanics 595
General Maintenance Mechanics 601
Heating, Air-conditioning, and
  Refrigeration Mechanics 607
Home Appliance and Power Tool
  Repairers 617
Industrial Machinery Repairers 623
Line Installers and Cable Splicers 629
Millwrights 635
Mobile Heavy Equipment Mechanics .. 639
Motorcycle, Boat, and Small Engine
  Mechanics 645
Musical Instrument Repairers and
  Tuners 651
Telephone Installers and Repairers 659
Vending Machine Servicers and
  Repairers 665

**Construction Trades and Extractive
  Occupations**
Bricklayers and Stonemasons 671
Carpenters 681
Carpet Installers 691
Concrete Masons and
  Terrazzo Workers 697
Drywall Workers and Lathers 707
Electricians 715
Glaziers 725
Insulation Workers 733
Painters and Paperhangers 741
Plasterers 749
Plumbers and Pipefitters 757
Roofers 769
Roustabouts 777
Sheet-metal Workers 783
Structural and Reinforcing Ironworkers.. 793
Tilesetters 801

Production Occupations

Assemblers 807
Precision Assemblers 807

Blue-collar Worker Supervisors 813

Food Processing Occupations 819
Butchers and Meat, Poultry, and Fish
  Cutters 819

Inspectors, Testers, and Graders 825

**Metalworking and Plastic-working
  Occupations 831**
Boilermakers 831
Jewelers 837

Machinists 845
Metalworking and Plastic-working
  Machine Operators 851
    Metalworking Machine Operators ... 851
    Plastic-working Machine Operators .. 857
    Steel Workers 863
Numerical-control Machine-tool
  Operators 867
Tool and Die Makers 873
Welders, Cutters, and Welding Machine
  Operators 879

Plant and Systems Operators 887
Electric Power Generating Plant
  Operators and Power Distributors
  and Dispatchers 887
Stationary Engineers 895
Water and Wastewater Treatment Plant
  Operators 901

Printing Occupations 909
Bindery Workers 909
Compositors and Typesetters 915
Lithographic and Photoengraving
  Workers 921
Printing Press Operators 927

**Textile, Apparel, and Furnishings
  Occupations 933**
Apparel Workers 933
Shoe and Leather Workers and
  Repairers 941
Textile Machinery Operators 947
Upholsterers 953

Woodworking Occupations 959

**Miscellaneous Production
  Occupations 967**
Dental Laboratory Technicians 967
Ophthalmic Laboratory Technicians ... 973
Painting and Coating Machine
  Operators 979
Photographic Process Workers 985

**Transportation and Material
  Moving Occupations**
Busdrivers 995
Material Moving Equipment
  Operators 1003
Rail Transportation Occupations 1011
Truckdrivers 1021
Water Transportation Occupations 1035

**Handlers, Equipment Cleaners,
  Helpers, and Laborers 1047**

**Job Opportunities in the
  Armed Forces 1059**

Appendixes
Appendix I: State Occupational and Professional Licensing Agencies 1071
Appendix II: Employment Growth Rankings and Statistics 1077
Index to Information Sources 1083

Highlights

Students, jobseekers, career changers, and counselors involved with vocational guidance can turn first to *Vocational Careers Sourcebook* to locate essential career planning sources.

VCS identifies and pulls together a broad spectrum of resources used to explore vocational career opportunities. It profiles 135 vocational occupations, ranging from aircraft mechanic and animal caretaker to welder and woodworker. Each profile lists up to 11 categories of career information:

- Job Descriptions
- Career Guides
- Associations
- Standards/Certification Agencies
- Test Guides
- Educational Directories and Programs
- Awards, Scholarships, Grants, and Fellowships
- Basic Reference Guides and Handbooks
- Periodicals
- Meetings and Conventions
- Other Sources of Information

Each entry includes, as appropriate and available:

- Organization, association, or publication name
- Contact information, including address and phone
- Author/editor, dates, and frequency
- Brief description of purpose, services, or content
- Toll-free and facsimile numbers

Also included in *VCS*:

A Master List of Profiled Careers referencing vocational occupations by job titles, alternate names, popular names, and synonymous and related names

State Occupational and Vocational Licensing Agencies listings

Employment Growth Rankings and Statistics of profiled careers

Index to Information Sources listed in *VCS*

Compiled in Cooperation With Career Information Center

Many of the sources listed in *VCS* were selected from the career collection of InfoPlace, the job, career, and education service of the Cuyahoga County Public Library, and are used daily to develop career planning strategies and provide answers to career-related questions.

Preface

Each of us possesses a unique set of values and abilities, and the ideal job complements these qualities. Someone well suited to a career enjoys not just financial rewards, but personal satisfaction as well. Not everyone is willing or able to go to college or pursue advanced technical training to land a job, but this need not mean a disappointing work life. Many careers do not require advanced education, yet have good growth prospects and offer comfortable living standards. The first step in successfully selecting and developing a career is to become familiar with the opportunities available.

Today's Job Market

As economists continue to search for signs of the long-awaited economic recovery, the job market remains difficult in many areas and uncertain in others. This affects not only those looking for their first full-time job, but workers at all levels displaced by downsizing and company closings. Achieving a management position no longer guarantees security. In retailing, for example, according to the 1991 edition of *U.S. Employment Opportunities*, "The farther you get away from the customer, the more difficult it will be to justify your salary in a time of declining sales." And increasingly, workers decide to make a career change as they find their goals or needs change.

In addition to economic and personal factors, the evolution of the business community and society as a whole will play an important role in the near-term job market. The Department of Labor reports that seven out of ten workers are now found in service industries. A growing population and increased demand for services of all types are spurring the continued expansion of the service-producing sector, according to the federal government's *Occupational Outlook Handbook, 1990-91*. This will open doors in such vocational occupations as food service, cashiering, and clerical work, along with many more skilled careers. Opportunities for data processors and repair and maintenance workers are also expected to increase, with technical skills often the best hedge in getting and keeping a job.

Making Good Career Choices

Understanding economic trends can doubtless aid someone looking for security and growth in a career, but many important questions are much more specific to the job and the person. Clear knowledge of one's own skills, aptitudes, interests, and goals is crucial to achieving job satisfaction. Coupling that with knowledge of a particular occupation makes it possible to evaluate a career choice on such key factors as:

- Will the work offer personal satisfaction?
- Are special skills or training needed?
- What is the outlook for future growth?
- How are the working conditions?
- What is the typical salary range?

Vocational Careers Sourcebook (*VCS*) helps jobseekers answer just these types of questions for 135 occupational categories. It provides both a quick summary of specific careers that do not require an advanced degree and a comprehensive list of resources for evaluating and pursuing each one. In today's complex arena of career resources, *VCS* fills a gap in vocational career information in a uniquely accessible way. Those new to the job market, career changers, counselors, and information professionals all will find it a valuable resource.

Introduction

The U.S. Bureau of Labor Statistics predicts that 80% of the occupations traditionally classified as vocational will grow in the next decade, bringing the total employed in these job categories to nearly 72,000,000 workers by the year 2000. A job is usually considered vocational when employment in that occupation does not depend upon a degree from a college or other institution for higher education. Examples of these occupations include construction, clerical, and food service workers; machine operators; mechanics; and salespeople.

Although an advanced degree is not required, many of the better-paying, more stimulating, and more secure vocational careers do require some training. It often begins in high school, where classes in office procedures or automotive mechanics can give graduating students a practical edge in looking for a job. This type of education can also foster an interest in additional training at a technical or trade school. Cosmetology schools and culinary institutes are examples of specialized schools that offer certificate programs denoting a certain level of achievement or training. Still other vocational jobs, such as postal clerks, require applicants to pass a standard examination before they are considered for employment.

Comprehensive Tool for Career Planning

With such diversity in vocational occupations and training requirements, careful research and planning plays an essential role preparing for a career. *Vocational Careers Sourcebook (VCS)* was published to support these activities. *VCS* compiles comprehensive information about 135 specific vocational careers and presents it in a single, easy-to-use volume. Arranged by job type, *VCS* can be used by students, jobseekers, career changers, career librarians, employment and guidance counselors, and others to:

- Research occupations. Brief career descriptions summarize the duties and responsibilities that each job entails, complete with salary levels and growth potentials for each.

- Explore vocational careers. Specific job categories are described in the listed career guides, including books, articles, kits, pamphlets, and brochures—materials that are often difficult to identify or locate quickly.

- Find vocational or certification test guides. Students and jobseekers can locate information on test guides and handbooks designed to assist with preparing for vocational or certification examinations.

- Identify career-enhancing resources. *VCS* identifies newsletters, magazines, newspapers, trade journals, and other serials that are used by individuals employed in the profiled careers. Valuable resources such as manuals, textbooks, directories, dictionaries, encyclopedias, films, videocassettes, and other significant reference materials are also identified.

- Target associations and organizations for networking. *VCS* lists organizations and other resources that will assist individuals seeking advice on career planning, development, and networking, including:

    Trade and professional associations and unions

    Standards and certification agencies

    State vocational and occupational licensing agencies

    Meetings, conventions, trade shows, and conferences within given fields

    Awards and financial support programs that encourage students and jobseekers to further pursue a given career

Easy access to information on specific occupations is facilitated by the Master List of Profiled Careers. This definitive guide to *VCS* contents lists the job titles used in *VCS* to identify each occupation, popular names, and synonymous or related terms. The Index to Information Sources alphabetically lists publication titles and organization names represented in the directory.

Please consult the User's Guide for more information about the arrangement, content, and indexing of the information sources cited in *VCS*.

VCS Complements the *Occupational Outlook Handbook*

Owing to the importance of career information to students, parents, counselors, and librarians, *VCS* is designed as a companion to today's foremost career resource—the Department of Labor's *Occupational Outlook Handbook (OOH)*. The *OOH* provides detailed descriptions of some 250 occupations, covering areas such as the nature of the work, working conditions, job outlook, earnings, job training, qualifications, and advancement. It also offers selected sources of additional information for each of the occupations covered, listing the names and addresses of associations, organizations, unions, government agencies, and publications.

VCS has been designed to complement—not replace—*OOH* by augmenting the information about the 135 careers generally defined as "vocational" and found in the 1990-91 edition of the *OOH*. *VCS* greatly expands the Additional Sources of Information sections in each *OOH* chapter by offering complete information about associations and related organizations and providing comprehensive entries for reference works and periodicals. In addition, *VCS* has extensive listings of career guides, test guides, awards, scholarships, grants, fellowships, meetings and conventions, and more. *VCS* career profiles are arranged in the same order as *OOH* chapters on the covered job categories, allowing the books to be used in tandem to create a complete career research program.

VCS Compiled in Cooperation With
Career Information Center

Many of the information sources included in this edition of *VCS* were selected from the more than 3,000 books, pamphlets, newspapers, and periodicals that comprise the career collection of InfoPLACE, the highly regarded job, career, and education service of the Cuyahoga County Public Library in Cleveland, Ohio. Kathleen M. Savage, the InfoPLACE information librarian, selected career resources that have been successfully used by patrons and counselors at InfoPLACE. InfoPLACE also conducts individual consultations and sponsors workshops such as "Career Decisions" for career planning and "Career Realities" for job hunters seeking professional positions.

Additional information contained in *VCS* was compiled through direct contact with selected associations, agencies, and organizations; from career collections of other major public libraries; and from selected material from other Gale databases.

Comments and Suggestions Are Welcome

Libraries, associations, career counseling firms, agencies, publishers, and other organizations active in career planning and research are encouraged to submit material about their programs, activities, publications, or other resources for use in future editions of *VCS*. Other comments and suggestions from users of this directory also are appreciated. Please contact:

Editors
Vocational Careers Sourcebook
Gale Research Inc.
835 Penobscot Bldg.
Detroit, MI 48226-4094
Toll-free: 800-347-GALE
Facsimile: (313)961-6815
Telex: 810 221 7087

User's Guide

Vocational Careers Sourcebook (VCS) consists of:

Master List of Profiled Careers
135 Career Profiles
State Occupational and Vocational Licensing Agencies
Employment Growth Rankings and Statistics
Index to Information Sources

Master List of Profiled Careers

The Master List of Profiled Careers, following this guide, lists in a single alphabetic sequence the job titles used to identify the 135 careers profiled in *VCS*, as well as alternate, popular, synonymous, and related job titles and names, and occupation names contained within job titles. "See" references lead from alternate names to the appropriate career profiles and their beginning page numbers.

Content and Arrangement of Career Profiles

The order of the 135 career profiles contained in *VCS* reflects the arrangement used in the *Occupational Outlook Handbook*, as listed on the Contents pages. Profiles are organized into ten major sections by general vocation type (which are further subdivided into more specific occupation types in some cases) and are then listed alphabetically.

Each profile contains up to 11 categories of information sources, as described below. Within each category, individual entries are organized alphabetically by name or title. The organizations, publications, and other sources listed are fully cited in all relevant chapters and categories, providing the user with a complete selection of information resources for each career in a single, convenient location. Entries are numbered and arranged sequentially, beginning with the first entry in the first profile.

Categories of Information in Career Profiles

- **Job Descriptions.** Each profile contains a summary explaining the duties and responsibilities that a particular occupation or vocation entails, including educational and training requirements, if available. The description abstracts the 1990-1991 *Occupational Outlook Handbook* (*OOH*). Salaries and growth potential for an occupation also will be noted, with the following phrases used as defined by the *OOH*:

If employment growth reads . . .	then *OOH* predicts
Faster than average	20 percent or more increase
Average	11 to 19 percent increase
Slower than average	4 to 10 percent increase
More slowly than average	3 percent or less increase

- **Career Guides.** This section lists books, articles, kits, pamphlets, brochures, and other materials that describe a given vocation. Often these works will be part of a career/vocational series. Entries in this section will include the source's title; name, address, and phone number of its publisher or distributor; name of the editor or author; publication date or frequency; description of contents; arrangement; indexes; toll-free or additional phone numbers; and facsimile numbers, when applicable. Publication, videocassette, and film titles appear in italics.

- **Associations.** This category of information covers trade and professional associations that offer career-related information and services. Entries note the association's name, address, and phone number; membership; purpose and objectives; publications; toll-free or additional phone numbers; and facsimile numbers, when known. Publication titles are rendered in italics. In some cases, the publications mentioned in these entries are described in greater detail as separate entries in the Career Guides, Basic Reference Guides and Handbooks, and Periodicals categories.

- **Standards/Certification Agencies.** This section offers information about accrediting agencies, certification examinations, national or vocational standards programs, or association-sponsored certification and testing programs. Entries in this section provide the certifying agency or program's name, address, and phone number; a description; publication titles; toll-free or additional phone numbers; and facsimile numbers, when available.

- **Test Guides.** This section lists guides and handbooks designed to assist in preparing for vocational or certification examinations; for instance, instruction booklets on how to prepare for the Civil Service Exam will appear in this section. The entries include the guide's title; its publisher's or distributor's name, address, and phone number; editor's or author's name; publication date or frequency; description of contents; arrangement; indexes; toll-free or additional phone numbers; and facsimile numbers, when available. Publication titles appear in italics.

- **Educational Directories and Programs.** This category notes directories, catalogs, and other publications that list career-related course offerings of schools, associations, and other organizations. Association and special school programs exclusively for the profiled career may be listed here as well. Entries for directories and other publications will offer the title; name, address, and phone number of the publisher or distributor; name of the editor or author; publication date or frequency; description of contents; arrangement; indexes; toll-free or additional phone numbers; and facsimile numbers, when known. Entries for programs will offer the name, address, and phone number of the institution; a description of course offerings; toll-free or additional phone numbers; and facsimile numbers, when available. Publication titles appear in italics.

- **Awards, Scholarships, Grants, and Fellowships.** This section lists awards given in recognition of vocational achievement and financial support programs that aid students and other individuals in fulfilling or continuing their education in a given career. Entries in this section include the name of the award or program; the name, address, and phone number of the sponsoring organization; a description; toll-free or additional phone numbers; and facsimile number, when applicable.

- **Basic Reference Guides and Handbooks.** This category provides information about manuals, textbooks, directories, dictionaries, encyclopedias, films and videocassettes, and other published reference material used by individuals working in the profiled career. Entries offer the resource's title; the name, address, and phone number of its publisher or distributor; the editor's or author's name; publication date or frequency; description of contents; arrangement; indexes; toll-free and additional phone numbers; and facsimile numbers, when applicable. Publication and film titles are rendered in italics.

- **Periodicals.** This section lists newsletters, magazines, newspapers, trade journals, and other serials that offer information to individuals in the profiled career. Entries note the resource's title; the name, address, and phone number of the publisher; the editor's name; frequency; description of contents; toll-free and additional phone numbers; and facsimile numbers, when available. Publication titles appear in italics.

- **Meetings and Conventions.** This section includes trade shows, conferences, conventions, and meetings that provide opportunities for networking and vocational development. Entries feature the event's name; the name, address, and phone number of the event's organizer or sponsor; the frequency of the event and forthcoming dates and locations; toll-free and additional phone numbers; and facsimile numbers, when known.

- **Other Sources of Information.** This category lists online databases, compilations of performance standards, statistical sources, sources of supply, special reference works, films and videocassettes, annual reviews, or other miscellaneous material that might be of interest to individuals working in the given vocation. (Material routinely used by individuals in a profiled career will be found in the Basic Reference Guides and Handbooks category.) Entries for sources of information feature the title; the name, address, and phone number of the publisher or distributor; editor's or author's name; publication date or frequency;

description of contents; arrangement; indexes; toll-free and additional phone numbers; and facsimile numbers, when known. Publication and film titles appear in italics.

Appendixes Enhance the Usefulness of Career Profiles

Appendix I: State Occupational and Vocational Licensing Agencies covers state government agencies responsible for granting professional and occupational licenses. Entries are arranged alphabetically by state and include the state agency's or department's name, address, and phone number.

Appendix II: Employment Growth Rankings and Statistics provides Bureau of Labor Statistics figures indicating the job growth for occupations covered in this edition of *VCS*.

Index to Information Sources

VCS includes a comprehensive Index to Information Sources that lists all associations, organizations, agencies, publications, database services, and information sources cited in the Career Profiles and State Occupational and Professional Licensing Agencies. Entries are arranged alphabetically and are referenced by their entry numbers. Publication and film titles are rendered in italics.

Master List of Profiled Careers

This list outlines references to covered occupations and professions by job titles, alternate names, occupation names contained within job titles, popular names, and synonymous and related names. Beginning page numbers for each occupation's profile are provided. Titles of profiles appear in boldface.

Able seamen *See* Water transportation occupations 1035
Accident prevention squad police officers *See* Police, detectives, and special agents 327
Accordion repairers *See* Musical instrument repairers and tuners 651
Account analysts *See* Bookkeeping, accounting, and auditing clerks 143
Account information clerks *See* Bookkeeping, accounting, and auditing clerks 143
Acid tank liners *See* Bricklayers and stonemasons 671
Adjusters, investigators, and collectors 97
Advertising sales representatives *See* Services sales representatives 75
Air and hydronic balancing technicians *See* Heating, air conditioning, and refrigeration mechanics 607
Air-conditioning mechanics *See* Heating, air conditioning, and refrigeration mechanics 607
Air-conditioning window unit installer-repairers *See* Home appliance and power tool repairers 617
Air Force *See* Job opportunities in the Armed Forces 1059
Airbrush artists *See* Photographic process workers 985
Aircraft accessories mechanics *See* Aircraft mechanics and engine specialists 523
Aircraft body repairers *See* Aircraft mechanics and engine specialists 523
Aircraft mechanics and engine specialists 523
Aircraft rigging and controls mechanics *See* Aircraft mechanics and engine specialists 523
Airline security representatives *See* Guards 321
Airplane charter clerks *See* Counter and rental clerks 11
Airplane flight attendants *See* Flight attendants 439
Alarm operators *See* Dispatchers 199
Animal breeders *See* Farm operators and managers 475
Animal caretakers, except farm 405
Animal keepers *See* Animal caretakers, except farm 405
Animal nursery workers *See* Animal caretakers, except farm 405
Animal trappers *See* Fishers, hunters, and trappers 495
Apparel workers 933
Appliance repairers *See* Home appliance and power tool repairers 617
Appointment clerks *See* Receptionists 177
Appraisers, real estate *See* Real estate agents, brokers, and appraisers 39
Aquarists *See* Animal caretakers, except farm 405
Arc welders *See* Welders, cutters, and welding machine operators 879

Armed Forces *See* Job opportunities in the Armed Forces 1059
Armored car guards and drivers *See* Guards 321
Army *See* Job opportunities in the Armed Forces 1059
Artificial-breeding distributors *See* Farm operators and managers 475
Artificial glass-eye makers *See* Ophthalmic laboratory technicians 973
Artificial plastic-eye makers *See* Ophthalmic laboratory technicians 973
Assembler brazers *See*
 Precision assemblers 807
 Welders, cutters, and welding machine operators 879
Assistant chief train dispatchers *See* Dispatchers 199
Audio-video repairers *See* Electronic home entertainment equipment repairers 581
Audiovisual program productions sales representatives *See* Services sales representatives 75
Audit clerks *See* Bookkeeping, accounting, and auditing clerks 143
Auto body repairers *See* Automotive body repairers 529
Automated equipment engineer technicians *See* Millwrights 635
Automatic developers *See* Photographic process workers 985
Automatic equipment technicians *See* Communications equipment mechanics 559
Automatic gluing machine operators *See* Bindery workers 909
Automatic mounters *See* Photographic process workers 985
Automatic print developers *See* Photographic process workers 985
Automobile accessories installers *See* Automotive mechanics 539
Automobile body customizers *See* Automotive body repairers 529
Automobile rental clerks *See* Counter and rental clerks 11
Automobile upholsterers *See* Upholsterers 953
Automotive body repairers 529
Automotive generator and starter repairers *See* Automotive mechanics 539
Automotive leasing sales representatives *See* Services sales representatives 75
Automotive mechanics 539
Auxiliary equipment operators *See* Electric power generating plant operators and plant distributors and dispatchers 887

VOCATIONAL CAREERS SOURCEBOOK, 1st Edition

Avionics technicians *See* Communications equipment mechanics 887
Bakers *See* Chefs, cooks, and other kitchen workers 347
Bank messengers *See* Mail clerks and messengers 191
Bank tellers 105
Bar attendants *See* Food and beverage service occupations 363
Bar waiters/waitresses *See* Food and beverage service occupations 363
Barbecue cooks *See* Chefs, cooks, and other kitchen workers 347
Barbers 415
Barge captains *See* Water transportation occupations 1035
Bartenders *See* Food and beverage service occupations 363
Battalion chiefs *See* Firefighting occupations 309
Beekeepers *See* Farm operators and managers 475
Billing clerks 139
Billing machine operators *See* Billing clerks 139
Bindery workers 909
Bird trappers *See* Fishers, hunters, and trappers 495
Birth attendants *See* Nursing aides and psychiatric aides 397
Blood donor recruiters *See* Services sales representatives 75
Blood donor recruiters supervisors *See* Services sales representatives 75
Blower insulators *See* Insulation workers 733
Blue collar worker supervisors 813
Blueprinting machine operators *See* Lithographic and photoengraving workers 921
Boat mechanics *See* Motorcycle, boat, and small engine mechanics 645
Boatswains *See* Water transportation occupations 1035
Body make-up artists *See* Cosmetologists and related workers 429
Bodyguards *See* Guards 321
Boilerhouse mechanics *See* Boilermakers 831
Boilermakers 831
Bonded structures repairers *See*
Aircraft mechanics and engine specialists 523
Automotive body repairers 529
Book binders *See* Bindery workers 909
Book repairers *See* Bindery workers 909
Book sewing machine operators *See* Bindery workers 909
Book trimmers *See* Bindery workers 909
Booking clerks *See* Traffic, shipping and receiving clerks ...209
Booking police officers *See* Police, detectives, and special agents 327
Bookkeepers *See* Bookkeeping, accounting, and auditing clerks 143
Bookkeeping, accounting, and auditing clerks 143
Bookmobile drivers *See* Library assistants and bookmobile drivers 239
Border guards *See* Police, detectives, and special agents 327
Bouncers *See* Guards 321
Braille and talking books clerks *See* Library assistants and bookmobile drivers 239
Brake adjusters *See* Automotive mechanics 539
Brake holders *See* Rail transportation occupations 1011
Bricklayers and stonemasons 671
Bridge carpenters *See* Carpenters 681
Brokerage clerks and statement clerks 229
Broker's floor representatives *See* Securities and financial services sales representatives 65
Brush clearing laborers *See* Timber cutting and logging workers 509
Buckers *See* Timber cutting and logging workers 509

Buffet waiters/waitresses *See* Food and beverage service occupations 363
Building maintenance repairers *See* General maintenance mechanics 601
Burnishers and bumpers *See* Aircraft mechanics and engine specialists 523
Busdrivers 995
Business services sales agents *See* Services sales representatives 75
Butchers and meat, poultry, and fish cutters 819
Cable ferryboat operators *See* Water transportation occupations 1035
Cable installer-repairers *See* Line installers and cable splicers 629
Cable splicers *See* Line installers and cable splicers 629
Cadmium burners *See* Steel workers 863
Cafeteria attendants *See* Food and beverage service occupations 363
Cancellation clerks *See* Adjusters, investigators, and collectors 97
Canteen operators *See* Food and beverage service occupations 363
Car barn laborers *See* Rail transportation occupations 1011
Car checkers *See* Traffic, shipping, and receiving clerks 209
Car hops *See* Food and beverage service occupations 363
Car retarder operators *See* Rail transportation occupations 1011
Carbide operators *See* Tool and die makers 873
Career guidance technicians *See* General office clerks 155
Carpenters 681
Carpet installers 691
Carvers *See* Chefs, cooks, and other kitchen workers 347
Case making machine operators *See* Bindery workers 909
Casers *See* Bindery workers 909
Cash grain farmers *See* Farm operators and managers 475
Cash register servicers *See* Computer and office machine repairers 565
Cashiers 5
Casters *See* Steel workers 863
Casting-in-line setters *See* Bindery workers 909
Cement masons *See* Concrete masons and terrazzo workers 697
Cemetery workers *See* Gardeners and groundskeepers 445
Central office operators *See* Telephone, telegraph, and teletype operators 283
Chainsaw operators *See* Timber cutting and logging workers 509
Charge account clerks *See* Interviewing and new accounts clerks 171
Chasers *See* Timber cutting and logging workers 509
Check cashiers *See* Cashiers 5
Chefs, cooks, and other kitchen workers 347
Chefs de froid *See* Chefs, cooks, and other kitchen workers 347
Chicken and fish butchers *See* Butchers and meat, poultry, and fish cutters 819
Chief deputy sheriffs *See* Police, detectives, and special agents 327
Chief jailers *See* Police, detectives, and special agents 327
Childcare workers 421
Children's institution attendants *See* Childcare workers 421
Chimney repairers *See* Bricklayers and stonemasons 671
Chimney sweeps *See* Janitors and cleaners 461

xviii

Master List of Profiled Careers

Chip tuners *See* Welders, cutters, and
welding machine operators 879
Chiropractic assistants *See* Medical assistants 387
Choke setters *See* Timber cutting and
logging workers 509
Christmas tree farm managers *See* Farm operators and
managers 475
Civil service clerks *See* Personnel clerks 249
Claims adjusters *See* Adjusters, investigators, and
collectors 97
Claims clerks *See* Adjusters, investigators, and collectors 97
Claims examiners *See* Adjusters, investigators, and
collectors 97
Clarifying plant operators *See* Water and wastewater
treatment plant operators 901
Classification clerks *See* File clerks 233
Classification control clerks *See* Bookkeeping, accounting,
and auditing clerks 143
Cleaners *See* Janitors and cleaners 461
Clerical supervisors and managers 113
Clerks *See* specific types
Clerk-typists *See* Typists, word processors, and data entry
keyers 289
Coating machine operators *See* Painting and coating
machine operators 979
Cobblers *See* Shoe and leather workers and
repairers 941
Coin machine service repairers *See* Vending machine
servicers and repairers 665
Collators *See* Bindery workers 909
Collection and exchange tellers *See* Bank teller 105
Collectors *See* Adjusters, investigators, and
collectors 97
Color printer operators *See* Photographic
process workers 985
**Commercial and industrial electronic equipment
repairers** 551
Commercial or institutional cleaners *See*
Janitors and cleaners 461
Commodity loan clerks *See* Bookkeeping, accounting, and
auditing clerks 143
Communication center operators *See* Telephone, telegraph,
and teletype operators 283
Communications consultants *See* Services sales
representatives 75
Communications equipment mechanics 559
Community relations police lieutenants *See* Police,
detectives, and special agents 327
Community service officers *See* Police, detectives, and
special agents 327
Complaint evaluation officers *See* Police, detectives, and
special agents 327
Composition stone applicators *See* Bricklayers and
stonemasons 671
Compositors and typesetters 915
Computer and office machine repairers 565
Computer and peripheral equipment operators 119
Computer operators *See* Computer and peripheral
equipment operators 119
Concrete masons and terrazzo workers 697
Concrete-mixing truck operators *See* Truckdrivers 1021
Concrete rubbers *See* Concrete masons and terrazzo
workers 697
Concrete stone finishers *See* Concrete masons and terrazzo
workers 697
Congressional district aides *See* General office clerks ...155
Construction equipment mechanics *See* Mobile heavy
equipment mechanics 639
Construction equipment operators *See* Material moving
equipment operators 1003

Contact lens blockers and cutters *See* Ophthalmic laboratory
technicians 973
Contact lens lathe operators *See* Ophthalmic laboratory
technicians 973
Contingents supervisors *See* Personnel clerks 249
Cook apprentices *See* Chefs, cooks, and
other kitchen workers 347
Cooks *See* Chefs, cooks, and other kitchen workers 347
Coppersmiths *See* Plumbers and pipefitters 757
Copy messengers *See* Mail clerks and messengers 191
Corn seed production managers *See* Farm operators and
managers 475
Correction officers 301
Cosmetologists and related workers 429
Counter and rental clerks 11
Court deputies *See* Police, detectives, and special agents ...327
Crash, fire, and rescue firefighters *See* Firefighting
occupations 309
Crating and moving estimators *See* Services sales
representatives 75
Credit authorizers *See* Credit clerks and
authorizers 129
Credit clerks and authorizers 129
Credit reference clerks *See* Credit clerks and authorizers ...129
Crime prevention police officers *See* Police, detectives, and
special agents 327
Criminal and patrol division deputy sheriffs *See* Police,
detectives, and special agents 327
Cruisers *See* Timber cutting and logging workers 509
Cupola patchers *See* Bricklayers and stonemasons 671
Customer complaint clerks *See* Adjusters, investigators,
and collectors 97
Customs patrol officers *See* Police, detectives, and special
agents 327
Cutting and printing machine operators *See* Lithographic
and photoengraving workers 921
Cutting machine operators *See* Bindery workers 909
Dairy equipment repairers *See* Farm equipment
mechanics 595
Dairy farm managers *See* Farm operators and managers ...475
Data coder operators *See* Typists, word processors, and
data entry keyers 289
Data entry keyers *See* Typists, word processors, and data
entry keyers 289
Data processing auxiliary-equipment operators *See* Computer
and peripheral equipment operators 119
Data processing services sales representatives *See* Services
sales representatives 75
Data typists *See* Typists, word processors, and data entry
keyers 289
Day-haul or farm charter busdrivers *See* Busdrivers 995
Deckhands *See* Water transportation occupations 1035
Deep submergence vehicle operators *See* Water
transportation occupations 1035
Deli cutter-slicers *See* Chefs, cooks, and
other kitchen workers 347
Dental assistants 377
Dental ceramists *See* Dental laboratory technicians 967
Dental laboratory technicians 967
Denture contour wire specialists *See*
Dental laboratory technicians 967
Derrick boat captains *See* Water transportation
occupations 1035
Desk officers *See* Police, detectives, and
special agents 327
Detective chiefs *See* Police, detectives, and special agents ..327
Detectives *See* Police, detectives, and
special agents 327
Developers *See* Photographic process workers 985

VOCATIONAL CAREERS SOURCEBOOK, 1st Edition

Dictating/transcribing machine servicers *See* Computer and office machine repairers 565
Die makers *See* Tool and die makers 873
Diesel engine erectors *See* Diesel mechanics 573
Diesel engine pipefitters *See* Plumbers and pipefitters 757
Diesel engine testers *See* Diesel mechanics 573
Diesel mechanics 573
Diesel plant operators *See* Electric power generating plant operators and plant distributors and dispatchers 887
Digitizer operators *See* Computer and peripheral equipment operators 119
Dining car waiters/waitresses *See* Food and beverage service occupations 363
Dining room attendants *See* Food and beverage service occupations 363
Dinkey operators *See* Rail transportation occupations 1011
Direct mail clerks *See* Mail clerks and messengers 191
Directory assistance operators *See* Telephone, telegraph, and teletype operators 283
Disbursement clerks *See* Credit clerks and authorizers 129
Dispatchers 199
Diving fishers *See* Fishers, hunters, and trappers 495
Dog groomers *See* Animal caretakers, except farm 405
Dog licensers *See* Adjusters, investigators, and collectors ..97
Dredge captains *See* Water transportation occupations 1035
Dredge mates *See* Water transportation occupations 1035
Drip pumpers *See* Truckdrivers 1021
Driver-utility workers *See* Truckdrivers 1021
Drivers *See* Truckdrivers 1021
Drywall applicators *See* Drywall workers and lathers 707
Drywall workers and lathers 707
Dulsers *See* Fishers, hunters, and trappers 495
Dump truck operators *See* Truckdrivers 1021
Electric organ inspectors and repairers *See* Musical instrument repairers and tuners 651
Electric power generating plant operators and power distributors and dispatchers 887
Electric powerline examiners *See* Line installers and cable splicers 629
Electric track and switch maintainers *See* Communications equipment mechanics 559
Electrical appliance servicers and repairers *See* Home appliance and power tool repairers 617
Electrical, plumbing, mechanical installers *See* Electricians 715
Plumbers and pipefitters 757
Electrician apprentices *See* Electricians 715
Electricians 715
Electrologists *See* Cosmetologists and related workers .429
Electron beam photo mask makers *See* Lithographic and photoengraving workers 921
Electron beam welding machine operators *See* Welders, cutters, and welding machine operators 879
Electron beam welding machine setters *See* Welders, cutters, and welding machine operators 879
Electronic home entertainment equipment repairers 581
Electronic organ technicians *See* Musical instrument repairers and tuners 651
Electronic sales and service technicians *See* Commercial and industrial electronic equipment repairers 551
Electronic typesetting machine operators *See* Compositors and typesetters 915
Electronics mechanics *See* Commercial and industrial electronic equipment repairers 551
Computer and office machine repairers 565
Electroslag welding machine operators *See* Welders, cutters, and welding machine operators 879

Elevator constructors *See* Elevator installers and repairers 589
Elevator examiners and adjusters *See* Elevator installers and repairers 589
Elevator installers and repairers 589
Elevator repairers *See* Elevator installers and repairers 589
Elevators, escalators, and dumbwaiters service representatives *See* Services sales representatives 75
Employment clerks *See* Personnel clerks 249
Endless track vehicle mechanics *See* Mobile heavy equipment mechanics 639
Environmental control system installer-servicers *See* Heating, air-conditioning, and refrigeration mechanics 607
Equipment cleaners *See* Handlers, equipment cleaners, helpers, and laborers 1047
Equipment installers *See* Communications equipment mechanics 559
Escort vehicle drivers *See* Truckdrivers 1021
Ethnic specialty cooks *See* Chefs, cooks, and other kitchen workers 347
Evaporative cooler installers *See* Heating, air-conditioning, and refrigeration mechanics 607
Exchange clerks *See* Bank tellers 105
Expedition supervisors *See* Fishers, hunters, and trappers ..495
Explosion welders *See* Welders, cutters, and welding machine operators 879
Explosives transporters *See* Truckdrivers 1021
Express clerks *See* Mail clerks and messengers 191
Fallers *See* Timber cutting and logging workers 509
Farm equipment mechanics 595
Farm machinery set-up mechanics *See* Farm equipment mechanics 595
Farm managers *See* Farm operators and managers 475
Farm operators and managers 475
Fast-foods workers *See* Food and beverage service occupations 363
Feeder switchboard operators *See* Electric power generating plant operators and plant distributors and dispatchers 887
Ferryboat captains *See* Water transportation occupations ..1035
Field crop farmers *See* Farm operators and managers 475
Field engineers *See* Commercial and industrial electronic equipment repairers 551
Field horticultural specialty growers *See* Farm operators and managers 475
Field service technicians *See*
Commercial and industrial electronic equipment repairers 551
Millwrights 635
File clerks 233
Film developers *See* Photographic process workers 985
Film or tape librarians *See* Stock clerks 205
Film laboratory technicians *See* Photographic process workers 985
Film printers *See* Photographic process workers 985
Film processing utility workers *See* Photographic process workers 985
Financial records processors (*See also* Billing clerks; Bookkeeping, accounting, and auditing clerks; Payroll and timekeeping clerks) 135
Financial report service sales agents *See* Services sales representatives 75
Fingernail formers *See* Cosmetologists and related workers 429
Fingerprint clerks *See* File clerks 233
Fire captains *See* Firefighting occupations 309
Fire chief's aides *See* Firefighting occupations 309
Fire extinguisher sprinkler inspectors *See* Firefighting occupations 309
Fire inspectors *See* Firefighting occupations 309
Fire investigation lieutenants *See* Firefighting occupations ..309

Master List of Profiled Careers

Fire lookouts *See* Firefighting occupations 309
Fire marshals *See* Firefighting occupations 309
Fire prevention bureau captains *See* Firefighting
    occupations 309
Fire rangers *See* Firefighting occupations 309
Fire wardens *See* Firefighting occupations 309
Firebrick and refractory tile bricklayers *See* Bricklayers
    and stonemasons 671
Firefighters *See* Firefighting occupations 309
Firefighting equipment specialists *See* General maintenance
    mechanics 601
Firefighting occupations 309
First aid attendants *See* Nursing aides and
    psychiatric aides 397
Fish cleaners *See* Butchers and meat, poultry, and fish
    cutters 819
Fish farmers *See* Farm operators and managers 475
Fishers, hunters, and trappers 495
Fishing vessel workers *See*
    Fishers, hunters, and trappers 495
    Water transportation occupations 1035
Flight attendants 439
Flight test shop mechanics *See* Aircraft mechanics and
    engine specialists 523
Floor waxers *See* Janitors and cleaners 461
Folding machine workers *See* Bindery workers 909
Food and beverage service occupations 363
Food service drivers *See* Truckdrivers 1021
Foreign exchange position clerks *See* Bookkeeping,
    accounting, and auditing clerks 143
Form builders *See* Carpenters 681
Formal waiters/waitresses *See* Food and beverage service
    occupations 363
Forwarders *See* Bindery workers 909
Fountain servers *See* Food and
    beverage service occupations 363
Frame repairers *See* Automotive body repairers 529
Frame wirers *See* Communications equipment mechanics .. 559
Franchise sales representatives *See* Services sales
    representatives 75
Freight rate analysts *See* Billing clerks 139
Fretter instrument repairers *See* Musical instrument
    repairers and tuners 651
Friction welding machine operators *See* Welders, cutters,
    and welding machine operators 879
Fuel injection servicers *See* Diesel mechanics 573
Fuel-oil clerks *See* Stock clerks 205
Fund raisers *See* Services sales representatives 75
Fur farmers *See* Farm operators and managers 475
Furnace installers *See* Heating, air conditioning, and
    refrigeration mechanics 607
Furnace operators *See* Steel workers 863
Furnace tenders *See* Steel workers 863
Furniture upholsterers *See* Upholsterers 953
Game bird farmers *See* Farm operators and managers 475
Game breeding farm managers *See* Farm operators and
    managers 475
Game preserve managers *See* Farm operators and
    managers 475
Garbage truck operators *See* Truckdrivers 1021
Gardeners and groundskeepers 445
Gas appliance servicers *See* Home appliance and power
    tool repairers 617
Gas engine operators *See* Stationary engineers 895
Gas main fitters *See* Plumbers and pipefitters 757
Gas welders *See* Welders, cutters, and welding machine
    operators 879
Gate agents *See* Reservation and transportation ticket
    agents and travel clerks 183
Gate tenders *See* Guards 321

Gathering machine feeders *See* Bindery workers 909
General accounting systems operators *See* Bookkeeping,
    accounting, and auditing clerks 143
General ledger bookkeepers *See* Bookkeeping, accounting,
    and auditing clerks 143
General maintenance mechanics 601
General office clerks 155
Geriatric nurse assistants *See* Nursing aides and psychiatric
    aides 397
Glass installers *See* Glaziers 725
Glass tinters *See* Painters and paperhangers 741
Glaziers 725
Golf course rangers *See* Guards 321
Grain elevator clerks *See* Traffic, shipping, and
    receiving clerks 209
Graphic art sales representatives *See* Services sales
    representatives 75
Greasers *See* Farm equipment mechanics 595
Greenskeepers *See* Gardeners and groundskeepers 445
Groundskeepers *See* Gardeners and groundskeepers 445
Guards 321
Gun welders *See* Welders, cutters, and welding machine
    operators 879
Hair stylists *See* Cosmetologists and related workers .. 429
Hand collators *See* Bindery workers 909
Hand etchers *See* Lithographic and photoengraving
    workers 921
Hand stitchers *See* Bindery workers 909
Hand thermal cutters *See* Welders, cutters, and welding
    machine operators 879
Handlers, equipment cleaners, helpers, and laborers ... 1047
Harbor police launch commanders *See* Police, detectives,
    and special agents 327
Harness makers *See* Shoe and leather workers and
    repairers 941
Harp regulators *See* Musical instrument repairers and
    tuners 651
Heaters *See* Steel workers 863
Heating, air-conditioning, and refrigeration mechanics ... 607
Heavy repairers *See* Automobile mechanics 539
Heavy truck operators *See* Truckdrivers 1021
Helpers *See* Handlers, equipment cleaners, helpers, and
    laborers 1047
Herbicide service sales representatives *See* Services sales
    representatives 75
Highway patrol pilots *See* Police, detectives, and
    special agents 327
Home appliance and power tool repairers 617
Home health technicians *See* Homemaker-home
    health aides 455
Homemaker-home health aides 455
Homicide squad commanding officers *See* Police,
    detectives, and special agents 327
Horseshoers *See* Animal caretakers, except farm 405
Horticultural specialty growers *See* Farm operators and
    managers 475
Horticulture superintendents *See* Farm operators and
    managers 475
Hospital-admitting clerks *See* Interviewing and new
    accounts clerks 171
Hospital cleaners *See* Janitors and cleaners 461
Hospital food service workers *See* Food and beverage
    service occupations 363
Hostlers *See*
    Rail transportation occupations 1011
    Truckdrivers 1021
Hot top liners *See* Bricklayers and stonemasons 671
Hotel and motel desk clerks 165
Hotel services sales representatives *See* Services sales
    representatives 75

House repairers *See* Carpenters 681
Housecleaners *See* Janitors and cleaners 461
Household appliance installers *See* Home appliance and power tool repairers 617
Household workers *See* Private household workers 467
Housekeeping cleaners *See* Janitors and cleaners 461
Hunters *See* Fishers, hunters, and trappers 495
Hydroelectric station operators *See* Electric power generating plant operators and power distributors and dispatchers ...887
Ice cream chefs *See* Chefs, cooks, and other kitchen workers 347
Identification and communications supervisors *See* Police, detectives, and special agents 327
Identification and records commanders *See* Police, detectives, and special agents 327
Identification clerks *See* Personnel clerks 249
Identification officers *See* Police, detectives, and special agents 327
In-file operators *See* Receptionists 177
Industrial cleaners *See* Janitors and cleaners 461
Industrial-commercial groundskeepers *See* Gardeners and groundskeepers 445
Industrial gas fitters *See* Plumbers and pipefitters 757
Industrial machinery repairers 623
Industrial maintenance repairers *See* General maintenance mechanics 601
Industrial sweeper-cleaners *See* Janitors and cleaners 461
Industrial truck mechanics *See* Diesel mechanics 573
Information clerks (*See also* Hotel and motel desk clerks; Interviewing and new accounts clerks; Receptionists) 161
Inspectors, testers, and graders 825
Insulation power unit tenders *See* Insulation workers 733
Insulation workers 733
Insurance clerks *See*
  Adjusters, investigators, and collectors 97
  Billing clerks 139
  Personnel clerks 249
Insurance sales workers 17
Internal affairs investigators *See* Police, detectives, and special agents 327
Interstate bus dispatchers *See* Dispatchers 199
Interviewing and new accounts clerks 171
Inventory clerks *See* Stock clerks 205
Investigation division commanding officers *See* Police, detectives, and special agents 327
Invoicing systems operators *See* Billing clerks 139
Irish moss bleachers/gatherers *See* Fishers, hunters, and trappers 495
Ironworkers *See* Structural and reinforcing ironworkers ...793
Jailers *See* Correction officers 301
Janitors and cleaners 461
Jewelers 837
Job opportunities in the Armed Forces 1059
Job printers *See* Compositors and typesetters 915
Job setters *See* Plastic working machine operators 857
Joggers *See* Bindery workers 909
Joiners *See* Carpenters 681
Kelp cutters *See* Fishers, hunters, and trappers 495
Keypunch operators *See* Typists, word processors, and data entry keyers 289
Kitchen food assemblers *See* Chefs, cooks, and other kitchen workers 347
Laborers *See* Handlers, equipment cleaners, helpers, and laborers 1047
Ladle pourers *See* Steel workers 863
Landscape laborers *See* Gardeners and groundskeepers 445
Larder cooks *See* Chefs, cooks, and other kitchen workers 347
Laser beam color scanner operators *See* Lithographic and photoengraving workers 921

Laser beam machine operators *See* Welders, cutters, and welding machine operators 879
Lathers *See* Drywall workers and lathers 707
Lawn service workers *See* Gardeners and groundskeepers ..445
Layboy tenders *See* Bindery workers 909
Layout technicians *See* Ophthalmic laboratory technicians ..973
Lead burners *See* Welders, cutters, and welding machine operators 879
Leather workers *See* Shoe and leather workers and repairers 941
Legal secretaries *See* Secretaries 255
Lens and frames prescription clerks *See* Stock clerks 205
Lens mould setters *See* Ophthalmic laboratory technicians ..973
Lens mounters *See* Ophthalmic laboratory technicians 973
Library assistants and bookmobile drivers 239
Light truck operators *See* Truckdrivers 1021
Line erectors *See* Line installers and cable splicers 629
Line fishers *See* Fishers, hunters, and trappers 495
Line installers and cable splicers 629
Line maintainers *See* Line installers and cable splicers ...629
Line repairers *See* Line installers and cable splicers 629
Linotype operators *See* Compositors and typesetters 915
Liquid fertilizer servicers *See* Truckdrivers 1021
Lithographic and photoengraving workers 921
Livestock ranchers *See* Farm operators and managers 475
Load dispatchers *See* Electric power generating plant operators and plant distributors and dispatchers 887
Loan closers *See* Credit clerks and authorizers 129
Lock tenders *See* Rail transportation occupations 1011
Locket makers *See* Jewelers 837
Locomotive engineers *See* Rail transportation occupations 1011
Locomotive firers *See* Rail transportation occupations ..1011
Locomotive operator helpers *See* Rail transportation occupations 1011
Log markers and sorters *See* Timber cutting and logging workers 509
Log truck operators *See* Truckdrivers 1021
Loggers *See* Timber cutting and logging workers 509
Logging tractor operators *See* Timber cutting and logging workers 509
Looseleaf binder coverers *See* Bindery workers 909
Luggage makers and repairers *See* Shoe and leather workers and repairers 941
Machine lead burners *See* Welders, cutters, and welding machine operators 879
Machinery erectors *See* Millwrights 635
Machinists 845
Magazine keepers *See* Stock clerks 205
Magazine repairers *See* Bindery workers 909
Magnetic tape composer operators *See* Compositors and typesetters 915
Magnetic tape typewriter operators *See* Typists, word processors, and data entry keyers 289
Magneto repairers *See* Motorcycle, boat, and small engine mechanics 645
Maids *See*
  Janitors and cleaners 461
  Private household workers 467
Mail carriers *See* Postal clerks and mail carriers 215
Mail censors *See* Mail clerks and messengers 191
Mail clerks and messengers 191
Mail handlers *See* Postal clerks and mail carriers 215
Mailers *See* Mail clerks and messengers 191
Make-up arrangers *See* Compositors and typesetters 915
Make-up artists *See* Cosmetologists and related workers ..429
Manicurists *See* Cosmetologists and related workers 429
Manufacturers' and wholesale sales representatives 31
Manufacturers' service representative *See* Millwrights 635
Marble setters *See* Bricklayers and stonemasons 671

Master List of Profiled Careers

Margin clerks *See* Brokerage clerks and statement clerks ...229
Marine oilers *See* Water transportation occupations 1035
Marines *See* Job opportunities in the Armed Forces 1059
Material moving equipment operators 1003
Material recording, scheduling, dispatching, and distributing occupations (*See also* Dispatchers; Stock clerks; Traffic, shipping, and receiving clerks) 195
Meat butchers *See* Butchers and meat, poultry, and fish cutters 819
Meat cutters *See* Butchers and meat, poultry, and fish cutters 819
Mechanics *See* Specific types
Medical assistants 387
Medical secretaries *See* Secretaries 255
Membership secretaries *See* Secretaries 255
Mental retardation aides *See* Nursing aides and psychiatric aides 397
Merchandise distributors *See* Stock clerks 205
Merchant patrollers *See* Guards 321
Mess attendants *See* Food and beverage service occupations 363
Mess cooks *See* Chefs, cooks, and other kitchen workers 347
Messengers *See* Mail clerks and messengers 191
Metal building assemblers *See* Structural and reinforcing ironworkers 793
Metal pourers *See* Steel workers 863
Metal reclamation kettle tenders *See* Steel workers 863
Metal reed tuners *See* Musical instrument repairers and tuners 651
Metalworking machine operators 851
Milk drivers *See* Truckdrivers 1021
Millwrights 635
Mobile heavy equipment mechanics 639
Mobile lounge drivers *See* Busdrivers 995
Mold carpenters *See* Carpenters 681
Molding plasterers *See* Plasterers 749
Money counters *See* Cashiers 5
Monotype keyboard operators *See* Compositors and typesetters 915
Morgue librarians *See* File clerks 233
Mortgage accounting clerks *See* Bookkeeping, accounting, and auditing clerks 143
Mortgage processing clerks *See* Credit clerks and authorizers 129
Mortuary beauticians *See* Cosmetologists and related workers 429
Motion picture equipment machinists *See* Machinists 845
Motor boat mechanics *See* Motorcycle, boat, and small engine mechanics 645
Motor room controllers *See* Electric power generating plant operators and power distributors and dispatchers 887
Motor vehicle dispatchers *See* Dispatchers 199
Motorcycle, boat, and small engine mechanics 645
Motorcycle subassembly repairers *See* Motorcycle, boat, and small engine mechanics 645
Motorized squad commanding officers *See* Police, detectives, and special agents 327
Muffler installers *See* Automotive mechanics 539
Musical instrument repairers and tuners 651
Narcotics investigators *See* Police, detectives, and special agents 327
Navy *See* Job opportunities in the Armed Forces 1059
Neon sign servicers *See* Electricians 715
Net fishers *See* Fishers, hunters, and trappers 495
Net repairers *See* Fishers, hunters, and trappers 495
New accounts clerks *See* Interviewing and new accounts clerks 171
Notereaders *See* Typists, word processors, and data entry keyers 289

Numerical-control machine-tool operators 867
Nursery managers *See* Farm operators and managers 475
Nursery school attendants *See* Childcare workers 421
Nursing aides and psychiatric aides 397
Office clerks *See* General office clerks 155
Office helpers *See* Mail clerks and messengers 191
Office machine repairers and servicers *See* Computer and office machine repairers 565
Oil burner servicers and installers *See* Heating, air-conditioning, and refrigeration mechanics 607
Oil dispatchers *See* Dispatchers 199
Ophthalmic laboratory technicians 973
Optical effects layout persons *See* Photographic process workers 985
Optical element coaters *See* Ophthalmic laboratory technicians 973
Optical instrument assemblers *See* Ophthalmic laboratory technicians 973
Opticians *See* Ophthalmic laboratory technicians 973
Optometric assistants *See* Medical assistants 387
Order clerks 245
Order fillers *See* Stock clerks 205
Orderlies *See* Nursing aides and psychiatric aides 397
Ordinary seamen *See* Water transportation occupations ...1035
Organ pipe voicers *See* Welders, cutters, and welding machine operators 879
Orthodontic technicians *See* Dental laboratory technicians ..967
Orthopedic boot and shoe designers and makers *See* Shoe and leather workers and repairers 941
Outboard motor mechanics *See* Motorcycle, boat, and small engine mechanics 645
Outdoor advertising leasing agents *See* Services sales representatives 75
Outpatient admitting clerks *See* Interviewing and new accounts clerks 171
Outside deliverers *See* Mail clerks and messengers 191
Oxygen furnace operators *See* Steel workers 863
Oyster floaters *See* Fishers, hunters, and trappers 495
Pad hands *See* Shoe and leather workers and repairers 941
Painters and paperhangers 741
Painting and coating machine operators 979
Pantographers *See* Lithographic and photoengraving workers 921
Pantry goods makers *See* Chefs, cooks, and other kitchen workers 347
Paperhangers *See* Painters and paperhangers 741
Parcel post clerks *See* Mail clerks and messengers 191
Parts clerks *See* Stock clerks 205
Passenger barge masters *See* Water transportation occupations 1035
Passenger car conductors *See* Rail transportation occupations 1011
Passenger train brakers *See* Rail transportation occupations 1011
Paste-up copy camera operators *See* Compositors and typesetters 915
Lithographic and photoengraving workers 921
Pastry cooks *See* Chefs, cooks, and other kitchen workers 347
Patch workers *See* Janitors and cleaners 461
Patchers *See* Bricklayers and stonemasons 671
Patrol officers *See* Police, detectives, and special agents 327
Patrol police lieutenants *See* Police, detectives, and special agents 327
Paymasters of purses *See* Cashiers 5
Payroll and timekeeping clerks 151
Percussion instrument repairers *See* Musical instrument repairers and tuners 651
Perforating machine operators *See* Bindery workers 909

Personnel clerks 249
Pest control service sales agents *See* Services sales
   representatives 75
Photocomposing machine operators *See* Compositors and
   typesetters 915
Photoengravers *See* Lithographic and
   photoengraving workers 921
Photoengraving apprentices *See* Lithographic and
   photoengraving workers 921
Photoengraving etchers *See* Lithographic and
   photoengraving workers 921
Photoengraving finishers *See* Lithographic and
   photoengraving workers 921
Photoengraving photographers *See* Lithographic and
   photoengraving workers 921
Photoengraving printers *See* Lithographic and
   photoengraving workers 921
Photoengraving proofers *See* Lithographic and
   photoengraving workers 921
Photoengraving retouchers *See* Lithographic and
   photoengraving workers 921
Photoengraving sketch makers *See* Lithographic and
   photoengraving workers 921
Photofinishing laboratory workers *See* Photographic
   process workers 985
Photograph retouchers *See* Photographic process workers ...985
Photographic process workers 985
Photographic spotters *See* Photographic process workers ...985
Photography colorists *See* Photographic process workers ...985
Photolettering machine operators *See* Compositors and
   typesetters 915
Photolithographic photographers *See* Lithographic and
   photoengraving workers 921
Photolithographic strippers *See* Lithographic and
   photoengraving workers 921
Phototypesetter operators *See* Compositors
   and typesetters 915
Phototypesetting equipment monitors *See* Compositors
   and typesetters 915
Piano technicians *See* Musical instrument repairers and
   tuners 651
Pie makers *See* Chefs, cooks, and other kitchen workers ...347
Pipe coverers and insulators *See* Insulation workers 733
Pipe cutters *See* Plumbers and pipefitters 757
Pipe organ tuners and repairers *See* Musical instrument
   repairers and tuners 651
Pipefitters *See* Plumbers and pipefitters 757
Pizza makers *See* Chefs, cooks, and other
   kitchen workers 347
Plant and maintenance technicians *See* Communications
   equipment mechanics 559
Plant propagators *See* Farm operators and managers 475
Plasterers 749
Plastic working machine operators 857
Plastics heat welders *See* Welders, cutters, and welding
   machine operators 879
Playroom attendants *See* Childcare workers 421
Pleasure craft sailors *See* Water transportation
   occupations 1035
Plumbers and pipefitters 757
Podiatric assistants *See* Medical assistants 387
Police academy program coordinators *See* Police,
   detectives, and special agents 327
Police, detectives, and special agents 327
Police district switchboard operators *See* Telephone,
   telegraph, and teletype operators 283
Police officers *See* Correction officers 301
Police reserves commanders *See* Police, detectives,
   and special agents 327
Policy information clerks *See* Receptionists 177

Poser operators *See* Electric power generating plant
   operators and plant distributors and dispatchers 887
Postal clerks and mail carriers 215
Pot fishers *See* Fishers, hunters, and trappers 495
Poultry breeders *See* Farm operators and managers 475
Poultry cutters *See* Butchers and meat, poultry, and
   fish cutters 819
Power plant operators *See* Electric power generating plant
   operators and power distributors and dispatchers 887
Power reactor operators *See* Electric power generating plant
   operators and plant distributors and dispatchers 887
Power saw mechanics *See* Motorcycle, boat, and small
   engine mechanics 645
Power tool repairers *See* Home appliance and power tool
   repairers 617
Power truck operators *See* Truckdrivers 1021
Practical nurses *See* Nursing aides and psychiatric aides 397
Precinct police captains *See* Police, detectives, and special
   agents 327
Precinct police sergeants *See* Police, detectives, and special
   agents 327
Precision assemblers 807
Precision lens centerers and edgers *See* Ophthalmic
   laboratory technicians 973
Precision lens grinders and polishers *See* Ophthalmic
   laboratory technicians 973
Predatory animal hunters *See* Fishers, hunters, and
   trappers 495
Pressers *See* Bindery workers 909
Pressure sealers and testers *See* Aircraft mechanics and
   engine specialists 523
Printed circuit board reworkers *See* Commercial and
   industrial electronic equipment repairers 551
Printing press operators 927
Printing sales representatives *See* Services sales
   representatives 75
Private branch exchange installers and repairers *See*
   Communications equipment mechanics 559
Private household workers 467
Probe test card, semiconductor wafers repairers *See*
   Commercial and industrial electronic
   equipment repairers 551
Process artists *See* Lithographic and photoengraving
   workers 921
Process strippers *See* Lithographic and photoengraving
   workers 921
Production line welders *See* Welders, cutters, and welding
   machine operators 879
Production repairers *See*
   Commercial and industrial electronic equipment
   repairers 551
   Communications equipment mechanics 559
   Electronic home entertainment equipment repairers 581
Projection printers *See* Photographic process workers 985
Proofsheet correctors *See* Compositors and typesetters 915
Prop makers *See* Carpenters 681
Protective officers *See* Police, detectives, and
   special agents 327
Protective signal installers and repairers *See* Electricians 715
Psychiatric aides *See* Nursing aides and psychiatric aides 397
Psychiatric hospital cooks *See* Chefs, cooks, and other
   kitchen workers 347
Public address servicers *See* Communications equipment
   mechanics 559
Public safety officers *See* Police, detectives, and
   special agents 327
Public utilities sales representatives *See* Services sales
   representatives 75
Pullman conductors *See* Rail transportation occupations ...1011
Pulp pilers *See* Timber cutting and logging workers 509

Master List of Profiled Careers

Quality control clerks *See* Stock clerks 205
Radio and television time sales representatives *See*
  Services sales representatives 75
Radio dispatchers *See* Dispatchers 199
Radio electricians *See* Communications equipment
  mechanics 559
Radio interference investigators *See* Line installers and
  cable splicers 629
Radio mechanics *See* Communications equipment
  mechanics 559
Radio repairers *See* Electronic home entertainment
  equipment repairers 581
Radioactive waste disposal dispatchers *See* Dispatchers 199
Radioactivity instrument maintenance technicians *See*
  Commercial and industrial electronic equipment
  repairers 551
Rafters *See* Timber cutting and logging workers 509
Rail carpenters *See* Carpenters 681
Rail tractor operators *See* Rail transportation occupations ..1011
Rail transportation occupations 1011
Railroad car letterers *See* Painters and paperhangers 741
Railroad cooks *See* Chefs, cooks, and other
  kitchen workers 347
Raw shellfish preparers *See* Chefs, cooks, and other
  kitchen workers 347
Real estate agents, brokers, and appraisers 39
Real estate appraisers *See* Real estate agents, brokers,
  and appraisers 39
Receptionists 177
Reclamation workers *See* Aircraft mechanics and engine
  specialists 523
Reconcilement clerks *See* Bookkeeping, accounting, and
  auditing clerks 143
Reconsignment clerks *See* Traffic, shipping, and
  receiving clerks 209
Record clerks (*See also* Brokerage clerks and statement
  clerks; File clerks; Library assistants and bookmobile
  drivers; Order clerks; Personnel clerks) 225
Records custodians *See* Record clerks 225
Rectification printers *See* Photographic process workers 985
Referral and information aides *See* Receptionists 171
Refrigeration mechanics *See* Heating, air-conditioning, and
  refrigeration mechanics 607
Refrigeration plant cork insulators *See* Insulation workers ..733
Registered mail clerks *See* Mail clerks and messengers 191
Registrars *See* Receptionists 177
Registration clerks *See* Hotel and motel desk clerks 165
Reinforcing metal workers *See* Structural and reinforcing
  ironworkers 793
Relay dispatchers *See* Dispatchers 199
Rental clerks *See* Counter and rental clerks 11
Repeat chiefs *See* Lithographic and
  photoengraving workers 921
Repeat photocomposing machine operators *See*
  Lithographic and photoengraving workers 921
Repossessors *See* Adjusters, investigators, and collectors 97
Reproduction technicians *See* Photographic process
  workers 985
Reptile farmers *See* Farm operators and managers 475
Rescue firefighters *See* Firefighting occupations 309
**Reservation and transportation ticket agents and travel
  clerks** 183
Resistance welding machine operators *See* Welders,
  cutters, and welding machine operators 879
Resistance welding machine setters *See* Welders, cutters,
  and welding machine operators 879
Restaurant hosts/hostesses *See* Food and beverage service
  occupations 363
Retail sales workers 55
Reviewers *See* Adjusters, investigators, and collectors 97
Riggers *See* Communications equipment mechanics 559
Rigging slingers *See* Timber cutting and logging workers 509
Ring makers *See* Jewelers 837
Riverboat masters *See* Water transportation occupations ...1035
Rivers *See* Timber cutting and logging workers 509
Road freight break couplers *See* Rail transportation
  occupations 1011
Road freight conductors *See* Rail transportation
  occupations 1011
Rocket engine mechanics *See* Machinists 845
Roller print tenders *See* Lithographic and photoengraving
  workers 921
Roofer applicators *See* Roofers 769
Roofers 769
Room service waiters/waitresses *See* Food and beverage
  service occupations 363
Rough carpenters *See* Carpenters 681
Rounding and backing machine operators *See* Bindery
  Workers 909
Roustabouts 777
Saddle and side wire stitchers *See* Bindery workers 909
Saddle makers *See* Shoe and leather workers and repairers ..941
Saddle stitching machine operators *See* Bindery workers 909
Safety instruction police officers *See* Police, detectives,
  and special agents 327
Salad makers *See* Chefs, cooks, and other kitchen
  workers 347
Sales representatives *See* Services sales representatives 75
Sales promotion representatives *See* Services sales
  representatives 75
Sandblaster paint sprayers *See* Automotive body repairers ..529
Sandwich makers *See* Chefs, cooks, and other kitchen
  workers 347
Satellite communications antenna installers *See*
  Communications equipment mechanics 559
Saw makers *See* Tool and die makers 873
Scalp treatment operators *See* Cosmetologists and related
  workers 429
Scanner operators *See* Lithographic and photoengraving
  workers 921
Schedulers *See* Receptionists 177
School cafeteria cooks *See* Chefs, cooks, and other kitchen
  workers 347
School secretaries *See* Secretaries 255
Scullions *See* Chefs, cooks, and other kitchen workers 347
Sealers *See* Fishers, hunters, and trappers 495
Second cooks and bakers *See* Chefs, cooks, and other
  kitchen workers 347
Secretaries 255
Securities and financial services sales representatives ...65
Securities clerks *See*
  Bookkeeping, accounting, and auditing clerks 143
  Brokerage clerks and statement clerks 229
Securities traders *See* Securities and financial services
  sales representatives 65
Security systems sales representatives *See* Services sales
  representatives 75
Seed corn production managers *See* Farm operators and
  managers 475
Service mechanics *See* Automotive body repairers 529
Service representatives *See* Adjusters, investigators, and
  collectors 97
Services sales representatives 75
Sextons *See* Janitors and cleaners 461
Sheet-metal workers 783
Sheetrock applicators *See* Drywall workers and lathers 707
Shellfish growers *See* Farm operators and managers 475
Ship carpenters *See* Carpenters 681
Ship masters *See* Water transportation occupations 1035
Ship mates *See* Water transportation occupations 1035

Ship pilots *See* Water transportation occupations 1035
Ship runners *See* Traffic, shipping, and receiving clerks 209
Shipping and receiving clerks *See* Traffic, shipping, and receiving clerks 209
Shipping checkers *See* Traffic, shipping, and receiving clerks 209
Shipping services sales representatives *See* Services sales representatives 75
Shipwrights *See* Carpenters 681
Shipyard painters *See* Painters and paperhangers 741
Shoe and leather workers and repairers 941
Shoe repairers *See* Shoe and leather workers and repairers .. 941
Shoemakers *See* Shoe and leather workers and repairers 941
Shop estimators *See* Automotive body repairers 529
Short order cooks *See* Chefs, cooks, and other kitchen workers 347
Shorthand reporters *See* Stenographers 267
Side stitching machine operators *See* Bindery workers 909
Silversmiths *See* Jewelers 837
Singing messengers *See* Mail clerks and messengers 191
Sketch makers *See* Lithographic and photoengraving workers 921
Skiff operators *See* Fishers, hunters, and trappers 495
Smoke jumper supervisors *See* Firefighting occupations 309
Social secretaries *See* Secretaries 255
Solar energy system installers *See* Heating, air-conditioning and refrigeration mechanics 607
Song pluggers *See* Services sales representatives 75
Sound technicians *See* Communications equipment mechanics 559
Space and storage clerks *See* Stock clerks 205
Special agents *See* Police, detectives, and special agents 327
Specialty cooks *See* Chefs, cooks, and other kitchen workers 347
Spiral binders *See* Bindery workers 909
Sponge clippers and hookers *See* Fishers, hunters, and trappers 495
Sprinkler/irrigation equipment mechanics *See* Farm equipment mechanics 595
Stable attendants *See* Animal caretakers, except farm 405
State police officers *See* Police, detectives, and special agents 327
Stationary engineers 895
Steam service inspectors *See* Plumbers and pipefitters 757
Steel post installers *See* Line installers and cable splicers 629
Steel workers 863
Stencil machine operators *See* Lithographic and photoengraving workers 921
Stenographers 267
Stenotype operators *See* Stenographers 267
Stitching machine feeder offbearers *See* Bindery workers .. 909
Stitching machine setters *See* Bindery workers 909
Stock clerks 205
Stone repairers *See* Bricklayers and stonemasons 671
Stonemasons *See* Bricklayers and stonemasons 671
Storekeepers *See* Stock clerks 205
Streetcar operators *See* Rail transportation occupations 1011
Strippers *See* Lithographic and photoengraving workers ... 921
Structural steel workers *See* Steel workers 863
Stucco masons *See* Plasterers 749
Structural and reinforcing ironworkers 793
Submarine cable equipment technicians *See* Communications equipment mechanics 559
Substation operators *See* Electric power generating plant operators and plant distributors and dispatchers 887
Supply clerks *See* Stock clerks 205
Survey workers *See* Interviewing and new accounts clerks .. 171
Switch inspectors *See* Electricians 715
Tack welders *See* Welders, cutters, and welding machine operators 879

Take-down sorters *See* Photographic process workers 985
Take-out waiters/waitresses *See* Food and beverage service occupations 363
Tanbark laborers *See* Timber cutting and logging workers ... 509
Tank builders and erectors *See* Carpenters 681
Tank setters *See* Structural and reinforcing ironworkers 793
Tank truck operators *See* Truckdrivers 1021
Tape recorder repairers *See* Electronic home entertainment and equipment repairers 581
Tapers *See* Drywall workers and lathers 707
Tariff inspectors *See* Adjusters, investigators, and collectors 97
Taxicab coordinators *See* Dispatchers 199
Teacher aides 277
Telecommunicators *See* Dispatchers 199
Telegraph office telephone clerks *See* Mail clerks and messengers 191
Telegraph operators *See* Telephone, telegraph, and teletype operators 283
Telegraph plant maintainers *See* Communications equipment mechanics 559
Telephone answering service operators *See* Telephone, telegraph, and teletype operators 283
Telephone installers and repairers 659
Telephone maintenance mechanics *See* Telephone installers and repairers 659
Telephone operators *See* Telephone, telegraph, and teletype operators 283
Telephone, telegraph, and teletype operators 283
Teletype operators *See* Telephone, telegraph, and teletype operators 283
Television and radio repairers *See* Electronic home entertainment equipment repairers 581
Television cable service sales representatives *See* Services sales representatives 75
Television installers *See* Electronic home entertainment equipment repairers 581
Tellers *See*
  Bank tellers 105
  Cashiers 5
Temporary-help agency referral clerks *See* Personnel clerks 249
Terrapin fishers *See* Fishers, hunters, and trappers 495
Terrazzo workers *See* Concrete masons and terrazzo workers 697
Textile machinery operators 947
Thermit welding machine operators *See* Welders, cutters, and welding machine operators 879
Third cooks *See* Chefs, cooks, and other kitchen workers ... 347
Third riggers *See* Timber cutting and logging workers 509
Ticket agents *See* Reservation and transportation ticket agents and travel clerks 183
Ticketing clerks *See* Reservation and transportation ticket agents and travel clerks 183
Tilesetters 801
Timber cutting and logging workers 509
Timber framers *See* Carpenters 681
Timekeepers *See* Payroll and timekeeping clerks 151
Tippers *See* Bindery workers 909
Toll collectors *See* Cashiers 5
Tool and die makers 873
Tool crib attendants *See* Stock clerks 205
Tooth clerks *See* Stock clerks 205
Torch straighteners and heaters *See* Welders, cutters, and welding machine operators 879
Tow truck operators *See* Truckdrivers 1021
Tower erectors *See* Line installers and cable splicers 629
Tower operators *See* Rail transportation occupations 1011
Trackmobile operators *See* Rail transportation occupations 1011

Master List of Profiled Careers

Tractor trailer truck operators *See* Truckdrivers 1021
Traffic lieutenants *See* Police, detectives, and special agents 327
Traffic or system dispatchers *See* Dispatchers 199
Traffic rate clerks *See* Traffic, shipping, and receiving clerks 209
Traffic sergeants *See* Police, detectives, and special agents ..327
Traffic, shipping, and receiving clerks 209
Trailer rental clerks *See* Counter and rental clerks 11
Transfer table operators *See* Rail transportation occupations 1011
Trappers *See* Fishers, hunters, and trappers 495
Travel agents 83
Travel clerks *See* Reservation and transportation ticket agents and travel clerks 183
Tree cutters *See* Timber cutting and logging workers 509
Tree, fruit, and nut crops farmers *See* Farm operators and managers 475
Tree shear operators *See* Timber cutting and logging workers 509
Tree trimmers *See* Timber cutting and logging workers 509
Truck mechanics *See*
   Automotive mechanics 539
   Diesel mechanics 573
Truckdrivers 1021
Tugboat captains *See* Water transportation occupations 1035
Tugboat dispatchers *See* Dispatchers 199
Tugboat mates *See* Water transportation occupations 1035
Tune-up mechanics *See* Automotive mechanics 539
Turbine operators *See* Electric power generating plant operators and power distributors and dispatchers 887
Type proof reproducers *See* Compositors and typesetters ...915
Typesetters *See* Compositors and typesetters 915
Typesetting machine tenders *See* Compositors and typesetters 915
Typewriter aliners and repairers *See* Computer and office machine repairers 565
Typists, word processors, and data entry keyers 289
Ultrasonic welding machine operators *See* Welders, cutters, and welding machine operators 879
Underwater hunter-trappers *See* Fishers, hunters, and trappers 495
Upholsterers 953
Upholstery and furniture repair sales representatives *See* Services sales representatives 75
Van drivers *See* Truckdrivers 1021
Varitype operators *See* Typists, word processors, and data entry keyers 289

Vegetable farmers *See* Farm operators and managers 475
Vehicle fuel systems converters *See* Automotive mechanics 539
Vending machine attendants *See* Vending machine servicers and repairers 665
Vending machine servicers and repairers 665
Vice investigators *See* Police, detectives, and special agents 327
Vine fruit crops farmers *See* Farm operators and managers ..475
Violin repairers *See* Musical instrument repairers and tuners 651
Waiters *See* Food and beverage service occupations 363
Waitresses *See* Food and beverage service occupations 363
Wall cleaners *See* Janitors and cleaners 461
Wastewater treatment plant operators *See* Water and wastewater treatment plant operators 901
Water and wastewater treatment plant operators 901
Water softener servicers and installers *See* Plumbers and pipefitters 757
Water transportation occupations 1035
Water treatment operators *See* Water and wastewater treatment plant operators 901
Waterworks pump station operators *See* Water and wastewater treatment plant operators 901
Weir fishers *See* Fishers, hunters, and trappers 495
Welder-assemblers *See* Welders, cutters, and welding machine operators 879
Welder-fitters *See* Welders, cutters, and welding machine operators 879
Welders, cutters, and welding machine operators 879
Welding machine tenders *See* Welders, cutters, and welding machine operators 879
Wheelwrights *See* Automotive mechanics 539
Wholesale sales representatives *See* Manufacturers' and wholesale sales representatives 31
Wig dressers *See* Cosmetologists and related workers 429
Wind instrument repairers *See* Musical instrument repairers and tuners 651
Window cleaners *See* Janitors and cleaners 461
Wine stewards *See* Food and beverage service occupations 363
Wood boatbuilders *See* Carpenters 681
Woodworking occupations 959
Word-processing machine operators *See* Typists, word processors, and data entry keyers 289
Worm growers *See* Farm operators and managers 475
Yacht masters *See* Water transportation occupations 1035
Yard engineers *See* Rail transportation occupations 1011

Career Profiles

Marketing and Sales Occupations

Cashiers

Cashiers are employed by supermarkets, department stores, movie theaters, restaurants, and many other businesses to facilitate the sale of merchandise. Cashiers total bills, receive money, make change, fill out charge forms, and give receipts. Cashiers traditionally have rung up customers' purchases using a cash register, manually entering the price of each product the consumer was buying. An increasing number of establishments are now using more sophisticated equipment such as scanners and computer terminals. Other workers with similar duties include bank tellers, counter and rental clerks, postal clerks, sales clerks, and food counter clerks.

$alaries

Earnings for cashiers range from the minimum wage to several times that amount. Wages tend to be higher in unionized establishments and in areas where there is intense competition for workers.

Lowest 10 percent	$130/week or less
Median	$151-269 /week
Top 10 percent	$400/week and up.

Employment Outlook

Growth rate until the year 2000: Average.

Cashiers

Career Guides

★1★
Cashier
Careers, Inc.
PO Box 135
Largo, FL 34649-0135　　　　Phone: (813)584-7333
1991. Two-page job guide card describing duties, working conditions, personal qualifications, training, earnings and hours, employment outlook, places of employment, related careers and where to write for more information.

★2★
"Cashier" in *Marketing and Distribution,* **Volume 10 of Career Information Center** (pp. 41-42)
Glencoe/Macmillan
15319 Chatsworth St.
Mission Hills, CA 91345　　　　Phone: (818)898-1391
Richard Lidz and Dale Anderson, editorial directors. Fourth edition, 1990. For 600 occupations, describes job duties, entry-level requirements, education and training needed, advancement possibilities, employment outlook, earnings and benefits. The set is divided into 12 volumes. Each volume includes jobs related under a broad career field. Volume 13 is the index. **Facsimile Number:** (818)365-5489.

★3★
"Cashier" in *Occu-Facts: Information on 565 Careers in Outline Form* (p. 11.22)
Careers, Inc.
P.O. Box 135
1211 Tenth St., S.W.
Largo, FL 33640　　　　Phone: (813)584-7333
Elizabeth Handville. Biennial, 1989-90 edition. Each one-page occupational profile describes duties, working conditions, physical surroundings and demands, aptitudes, temperament, educational requirements, employment outlook, earnings, and places of employment.

★4★
"Cashiers" in *Occupational Outlook Handbook* (pp. 227-228)
Superintendent of Documents
U.S. Government Printing Office
Washington, DC 20402　　　　Phone: (202)783-3238
Biennial; latest edition, 1990-91. Encyclopedia of careers describing more than 250 occupations and comprising about 86 percent of all jobs in the economy. Occupations that require lengthy education or training are given the most attention. For each occupation, the handbook describes job duties, working conditions, training, educational preparation, personal qualities, advancement possibilities, job outlook, earnings, and sources of additional information.

★5★
"Cashiers" in *Travel Agent* (pp. 171-172)
Arco/Prentice Hall Press
1 Gulf & Western Plaza
New York, NY 10023　　　　Phone: (212)373-8500
Wilma Boyd. 1989. Introduction to the travel business. Covers U.S. and foreign travel, time zones, ticketing, world geography, and airline, railroad, and tour bus connections, and accommodations. Outlines entry-level positions in the airline, car rental, and hospitality industries as well as in travel agencies and related travel services. Explains travel agency operations, sales techniques, and the use of computers in travel services. Gives job hunting advice and sales tips.

★6★
"Cashiers" in Volume 1 of *Career Discovery Encyclopedia* (pp. 164-165)
J.G. Ferguson Publishing Co.
200 W. Monroe
Chicago, IL 60606　　　　Phone: (312)580-5480
E. Russell Primm, editor-in-chief. 1990. Contains two-page articles on 504 occupations. Each article describes job duties, earnings, and educational and training requirements.

★7★
"Cashiers" in Volume 3 of *The Encyclopedia of Careers and Vocational Guidance* (pp. 8-12)
J.G. Ferguson Publishing Co.
200 W. Monroe
Chicago, IL 60606　　　　Phone: (312)580-5480
William E. Hopke, editor-in-chief. Eighth edition, 1990. Four-volume set that profiles 500 occupations and describes job trends in 76 industries. Includes career description, educational requirements, history of the job, methods of entry, advancement, employment outlook, earnings, working conditions, social and psychological factors, and sources of additional information.

★8★
Cashiers and Checkers
Chronicle Guidance Publications, Inc.
PO Box 1190
Moravia, NY 13118-1190　　　　Phone: (315)497-0330
1991. This career brief describes the nature of the work, working conditions, hours and earnings, education and training, licensure, certification, unions, personal qualifications, social and psychological factors, employment outlook, entry methods, advancement, and related occupations. **Toll-free/Additional Phone Number(s):** 800-622-7284.

★9★

"Cashiers/Retail Clerk" in *The American Almanac of Jobs and Salaries* (p. 531)
Avon Books
105 Madison Avenue
New York, NY 10016   Phone: (212)481-5600
John Wright and Edward J. Dwyer. Revised and updated, 1990. A comprehensive guide to the wages of hundreds of occupations in a wide variety of industries and organizations.

★10★
Grocery Checker
Careers, Inc.
PO Box 135
Largo, FL 34649-0135   Phone: (813)584-7333
1991. Two-page job guide card describing duties, working conditions, personal qualifications, training, earnings and hours, employment outlook, places of employment, related careers and where to write for more information.

★11★
"Grocery Checker" in *Occu-Facts: Information on 565 Careers in Outline Form* (p. 11.23)
Careers, Inc.
P.O. Box 135
1211 Tenth St., S.W.
Largo, FL 33640   Phone: (813)584-7333
Elizabeth Handville. Biennial, 1989-90 edition. Each one-page occupational profile describes duties, working conditions, physical surroundings and demands, aptitudes, temperament, educational requirements, employment outlook, earnings, and places of employment.

★12★
"Hospitality Cashier" in *Hospitality and Recreation, Volume 8 of Career Information Center* (pp. 49-50)
Glencoe/Macmillan
15319 Chatsworth St.
Mission Hills, CA 91345   Phone: (818)898-1391
Richard Lidz and Dale Anderson, editorial directors. Fourth edition, 1990. For 600 occupations, describes job duties, entry-level requirements, education and training needed, advancement possibilities, employment outlook, earnings and benefits. The set is divided into 12 volumes. Each volume includes jobs related under a broad career field. Volume 13 is the index. **Facsimile Number:** (818)365-5489.

★13★
Jobs in Shops & Stores
Beekman Publishers, Inc.
Rte. 212
PO Box 888
Woodstock, NY 12498   Phone: (914)679-2300
Carole Chester. 1990.

★14★
Supermarket Cashier
Vocational Biographies, Inc.
PO Box 31, Dept. VF10
Sauk Centre, MN 56378   Phone: (612)352-6516
1990. This pamphlet profiles a person working in the job. Includes information about job duties, working conditions, places of employment, educational preparation, labor market outlook, and salaries. **Toll-free/Additional Phone Number(s):** 800-255-0752.

★15★
Video Career Library - Clerical & Administrative Support
Careers, Inc.
1211 10th St., SW
PO Box 135
Largo, FL 34649-0135   Phone: (813)584-7333
Videocassette. 1990. 26 mins. Part of the Video Career Library covering 165 occupations. Shows actual workers on the job. Includes secretaries, cashiers, receptionists, bookkeepers and audit clerks, telephone operators, postal clerks/carriers/supervisors, insurance investigators, bank tellers, data entry keyers, and court reporters.

────── Associations ──────

★16★
United Food and Commercial Workers International Union (UFCW)
Suffridge Bldg.
1775 K St. NW
Washington, DC 20006   Phone: (202)223-3111
Membership: AFL-CIO. **Purpose:** Maintains 1500 volume library. **Publications:** *UFCW Action*, bimonthly. • *UFCW Leadership Update*, monthly.

────── Test Guides ──────

★17★
Assistant Cashier
National Learning Corp.
212 Michael Dr.
Syosset, NY 11791   Phone: (516)921-8888
Jack Rudman. Part of the Career Examination Series No. 1. All examination guides in this series contain questions with answers. **Facsimile Number:** (516)921-8743. **Toll-free/Additional Phone Number(s):** 800-645-6337.

★18★
Cashier
National Learning Corp.
212 Michael Dr.
Syosset, NY 11791   Phone: (516)921-8888
Jack Rudman. Part of the Career Examination Series No. 1. All examination guides in this series contain questions with answers. **Facsimile Number:** (516)921-8743. **Toll-free/Additional Phone Number(s):** 800-645-6337.

★19★
Cashier-Cashier I
National Learning Corporation
212 Michael Dr.
Syosset, NY 11791   Phone: (516)921-8888
Jack Rudman. 1989. Part of Career Examination Series.

★20★
Cashier II
National Learning Corporation
212 Michael Dr.
Syosset, NY 11791   Phone: (516)921-8888
Jack Rudman. 1989. Part of Career Examination Series.

★21★
NCR No. 3100 Operator
National Learning Corporation
212 Michael Dr.
Syosset, NY 11791   Phone: (516)921-8888
Jack Rudman. 1989. Part of Career Examination Series.

★22★
Principal Cashier
National Learning Corp.
212 Michael Dr.
Syosset, NY 11791   Phone: (516)921-8888
Jack Rudman. Part of the Career Examination Series No. 1. All examination guides in this series contain questions with answers. **Facsimile Number:** (516)921-8743. **Toll-free/Additional Phone Number(s):** 800-645-6337.

★23★
Senior Cashier
National Learning Corp.
212 Michael Dr.
Syosset, NY 11791   Phone: (516)921-8888
Jack Rudman. Part of the Career Examination Series No. 1. All examination guides in this series contain questions with answers. **Facsimile Number:** (516)921-8743. **Toll-free/Additional Phone Number(s):** 800-645-6337.

★24★
Supervising Cashier
National Learning Corporation
212 Michael Dr.
Syosset, NY 11791   Phone: (516)921-8888
Jack Rudman. 1989. Part of Career Examination Series.

Basic Reference Guides and Handbooks

★25★
Math on the Job: Cashier
National Center for Research in Vocational Education
Ohio State University
1900 Kenry Rd.
Columbus, OH 43210   Phone: (614)292-4353
1985.

Periodicals

★26★
UFCW Action (UFCW)
United Food and Commercial Workers International Union (UFCW)
Suffridge Bldg.
1775 K St. NW
Washington, DC 20006   Phone: (202)223-3111
Bimonthly. Magazine covering union activities, political and legislative matters, and consumer news.

★27★
UFCW Leadership Update (UFCW)
United Food and Commercial Workers International Union (UFCW)
Suffridge Bldg.
1775 K St. NW
Washington, DC 20006   Phone: (202)223-3111
Monthly.

Meetings and Conventions

★28★
United Food and Commercial Workers International Union (UFCW)
Suffridge Bldg.
1775 K St. NW
Washington, DC 20006   Phone: (202)223-3111
Frequency: Quinquennial - 1993 Jul. or Aug.

Counter and Rental Clerks

Counter and rental clerks are responsible for answering questions, taking orders, receiving payments, and accepting returns. Specific duties vary by establishment, and can be very general, or very specialized. Typical employers for counter and rental clerks include drycleaning and laundry establishments, video rental and grocery stores, automobile rental firms, leasing services, and equipment rental firms. Regardless of where they work, counter and rental clerks must be knowledgeable about the company's services, policies, and procedures. When taking orders, counter and rental clerks use various types of equipment. In some establishments, they write out tickets and order forms. In others, they use computers and scanners. Other workers with similar duties includee food counter clerks, bank tellers, cashiers, retail sales workers, postal service clerks, and toll collectors.

$alaries

Earnings for counter and rental clerks often start at the minimum wage, but in areas with intense competition for workers, wages are often much higher. In addition some receive commissions based on the number of contracts they complete or services they sell.

Lowest 10 percent	$138/week or less
Median	$164-296/week
Top 10 percent	$443/week and up.

Employment Outlook

Faster than average.

Counter and Rental Clerks

Career Guides

★29★
"Car or Truck Rental Agent" in *Transportation* (pp. 69-73)
Franklin Watts, Inc.
387 Park Avenue, S.
New York, NY 10016　　　　　Phone: (212)686-7070
Marjorie Rittenberg Schulz. 1990. Surveys the transportation industry including air, water, and rail services. Provides job description, training, salary, and employment outlook. Offers job hunting advice.

★30★
"Car Rental Agent" in *Transportation*, Volume 12 of *Career Information Center* (pp. 44-46)
Glencoe/Macmillan
15319 Chatsworth St.
Mission Hills, CA 91345　　　Phone: (818)898-1391
Richard Lidz and Dale Anderson, editorial directors. Fourth edition, 1990. For 600 occupations, describes job duties, entry-level requirements, education and training needed, advancement possibilities, employment outlook, earnings and benefits. The set is divided into 12 volumes. Each volume includes jobs related under a broad career field. Volume 13 is the index. **Facsimile Number:** (818)365-5489.

★31★
Car Rental Agents
Chronicle Guidance Publications, Inc.
PO Box 1190
Moravia, NY 13118-1190　　　Phone: (315)497-0330
1988. This career brief describes the nature of the work, working conditions, hours and earnings, education and training, licensure, certification, unions, personal qualifications, social and psychological factors, employment outlook, entry methods, advancement, and related occupations. **Toll-free/Additional Phone Number(s):** 800-622-7284.

★32★
"Car Rental Agents" in Volume 1 of *Career Discovery Encyclopedia* (pp. 158-159)
J.G. Ferguson Publishing Co.
200 W. Monroe
Chicago, IL 60606　　　　　Phone: (312)580-5480
E. Russell Primm, editor-in-chief. 1990. Contains two-page articles on 504 occupations. Each article describes job duties, earnings, and educational and training requirements.

★33★
"Car Rental Agents" in Volume 3 of *The Encyclopedia of Careers and Vocational Guidance* (pp. 136-139)
J.G. Ferguson Publishing Co.
200 W. Monroe
Chicago, IL 60606　　　　　Phone: (312)580-5480
William E. Hopke, editor-in-chief. Eighth edition, 1990. Four-volume set that profiles 500 occupations and describes job trends in 76 industries. Includes career description, educational requirements, history of the job, methods of entry, advancement, employment outlook, earnings, working conditions, social and psychological factors, and sources of additional information.

★34★
Career Insights
RMI Media Productions, Inc.
2807 West 47th St.
Shawnee Mission, KS 66205　　Phone: (913)262-3974
Videocassette series. 1987. This videotape series describes 50 occupations, including skill requirements and interviews with people employed in these fields. Occupations include: flight service, air transportation/ground services, data processing, carpentry, clerk in banking/insurance/business, cosmetic personal grooming, firefighting, roofing, material handling, photographic processing, plumbing, secretarial services, tool and die operations.

★35★
"The Center of the Travel Industry - Getting Started in Car Rental" in *Travel and Hospitality Career Directory* (pp. 41-46)
Career Press, Inc.
PO Box 34
62 Beverly Rd.
Hawthorne, NJ 07507　　　　Phone: (201)427-0229
Ronald W. Fry, editor. 1989. Offers advice on career planning and job hunting in hotel, travel, and related industries. Lists companies offering entry level positions in airlines, convention and visitors' bureaus, foreign tourist boards, hotels, travel agencies, car rental firms, and cruise lines. Lists travel and hospitality associations and trade publications.

★36★
"Counter and Rental Clerks" in *America's 50 Fastest Growing Jobs* (pp. 100-101)
JIST Works, Inc.
720 N. Park Ave.
Indianapolis, IN 46202　　　Phone: (317)264-3720
Michael J. Farr, compiler. 1991. Describes the 50 fastest growing jobs within major career clusters such as technicians, and marketing and sales. Each job profile explains the nature of

the work, skills and abilities required, employment outlook, average earnings, related occupations, education and training requirements, and employment opportunities. Also contains career planning information and job search tips.

★37★
"Counter and Rental Clerks" in *Occupational Outlook Handbook* **(pp. 228-230)**
Superintendent of Documents
U.S. Government Printing Office
Washington, DC 20402   Phone: (202)783-3238

Biennial; latest edition, 1990-91. Encyclopedia of careers describing more than 250 occupations and comprising about 86 percent of all jobs in the economy. Occupations that require lengthy education or training are given the most attention. For each occupation, the handbook describes job duties, working conditions, training, educational preparation, personal qualities, advancement possibilities, job outlook, earnings, and sources of additional information.

★38★
"Counter and Retail Clerks" in Volume 3 of *The Encyclopedia of Careers and Vocational Guidance* **(pp. 23-26)**
J.G. Ferguson Publishing Co.
200 W. Monroe
Chicago, IL 60606   Phone: (312)580-5480

William E. Hopke, editor-in-chief. Eighth edition, 1990. Four-volume set that profiles 500 occupations and describes job trends in 76 industries. Includes career description, educational requirements, history of the job, methods of entry, advancement, employment outlook, earnings, working conditions, social and psychological factors, and sources of additional information.

★39★
"Counter and Retail Clerks" in Volume 2 of *Career Discovery Encyclopedia* **(pp. 68-69)**
J.G. Ferguson Publishing Co.
200 W. Monroe
Chicago, IL 60606   Phone: (312)580-5480

E. Russell Primm, editor-in-chief. 1990. Contains two-page articles on 504 occupations. Each article describes job duties, earnings, and educational and training requirements.

★40★
Counter Worker
Careers, Inc.
PO Box 135
Largo, FL 34649-0135   Phone: (813)584-7333

1992. Two-page job guide card describing duties, working conditions, personal qualifications, training, earnings and hours, employment outlook, places of employment, related careers and where to write for more information.

★41★
"Equipment Rental and Leasing Service Agent" in *Marketing and Distribution,* **Volume 10 of** *Career Information Center* **(pp. 48-49)**
Glencoe/Macmillan
15319 Chatsworth St.
Mission Hills, CA 91345   Phone: (818)898-1391

Richard Lidz and Dale Anderson, editorial directors. Fourth edition, 1990. For 600 occupations, describes job duties, entry-level requirements, education and training needed, advancement possibilities, employment outlook, earnings and benefits. The set is divided into 12 volumes. Each volume includes jobs related under a broad career field. Volume 13 is the index. **Facsimile Number:** (818)365-5489.

★42★
Internships Volume 4: The Travel and Hospitality Industries
Career Press, Inc.
PO Box 34
62 Beverly Rd.
Hawthorne, NJ 07507   Phone: (201)427-0229

Ronald W. Fry, editor-in-chief. 1989. Offers advice on obtaining internships with airlines, hotels, cruise ships, convention and visitors centers, car rental companies, and travel agencies. Each company listing includes name, address, phone number, contact person, paid or unpaid internships, duration, qualifications, application procedures, and deadlines.

★43★
Jobs in Shops & Stores
Beekman Publishers, Inc.
Rte. 212
PO Box 888
Woodstock, NY 12498   Phone: (914)679-2300

Carole Chester. 1990.

★44★
Laundromat Attendant
Careers, Inc.
PO Box 135
Largo, FL 34649-0135   Phone: (813)584-7333

1988. Two-page job guide card describing duties, working conditions, personal qualifications, training, earnings and hours, employment outlook, places of employment, related careers and where to write for more information.

★45★
"Laundromat Attendant" in *Occu-Facts: Information on 565 Careers in Outline Form* **(p. 11.21)**
Careers, Inc.
P.O. Box 135
1211 Tenth St., S.W.
Largo, FL 33640   Phone: (813)584-7333

Elizabeth Handville. Biennial, 1989-90 edition. Each one-page occupational profile describes duties, working conditions, physical surroundings and demands, aptitudes, temperament, educational requirements, employment outlook, earnings, and places of employment.

★46★
"Rental Clerk" in *Travel Agent* **(p. 168)**
Arco/Prentice Hall Press
1 Gulf & Western Plaza
New York, NY 10023   Phone: (212)373-8500

Wilma Boyd. 1989. Introduction to the travel business. Covers U.S. and foreign travel, time zones, ticketing, world geography, and airline, railroad, and tour bus connections, and accommodations. Outlines entry-level positions in the airline, car rental, and hospitality industries as well as in travel agencies and related travel services. Explains travel agency operations, sales techniques, and the use of computers in travel services. Gives job hunting advice and sales tips.

★47★
Retailing & Merchandising
Morris Video
2730 Monterey St. #105
Monterey Business Park
Torrance, CA 90503   Phone: (213)533-4800

Videocassette. 1987. 15 mins. A look at the variety of career opportunities available in the world of retail.

Counter and Rental Clerks

★48★
Vehicle Leasing Agent
Vocational Biographies, Inc.
PO Box 31, Dept. VF10
Sauk Centre, MN 56378   Phone: (612)352-6516
1988. This pamphlet profiles a person working in the job. Includes information about job duties, working conditions, places of employment, educational preparation, labor market outlook, and salaries. **Toll-free/Additional Phone Number(s):** 800-255-0752.

★49★
Wings and Wheels
Walter J. Klein Company, Ltd.
6311 Carmel Rd.
Post Office Box 2087
Charlotte, NC 28247   Phone: (704)542-1403
Videocassette. 1980. 15 mins. The concept of renting a car has been in existence since the 1920's. The history of automobile rentals is told from its inception to today's "rent it here, leave it there" era.

Associations

★50★
United Food and Commercial Workers International Union (UFCW)
Suffridge Bldg.
1775 K St. NW
Washington, DC 20006   Phone: (202)223-3111
Membership: AFL-CIO. **Purpose:** Maintains 1500 volume library. **Publications:** *UFCW Action*, bimonthly. • *UFCW Leadership Update*, monthly.

Test Guides

★51★
Senior Clerical Series
Prentice Hall Press
Simon & Schuster Inc.
200 Old Tappan Rd.
Old Tappan, NJ 07675
Hy Hammer. Fourth edition, 1983. Complete test preparation for the following senior grade positions: clerk, typist, stenographer, account clerk, file clerk, statistics clerk, stenographer (law), mail and supply clerk, and stores clerk. **Toll-free/Additional Phone Number(s):** 800-223-2348.

★52★
Stores Clerk
National Learning Corp.
212 Michael Dr.
Syosset, NY 11791   Phone: (516)921-8888
Jack Rudman. Part of the Career Examination Series No. 1. All examination guides in this series contain questions with answers. **Facsimile Number:** (516)921-8743. **Toll-free/Additional Phone Number(s):** 800-645-6337.

Periodicals

★53★
Auto Rental News
Quist Publishing Inc.
210 Madison Ave., No. 1108
New York, NY 10016-3802
David Kearney, Managing Editor. Monthly (not published in August).

★54★
Counterman
Babcox Publications
11 S. Forge St.
Akron, OH 44304   Phone: (216)535-6117
Gary A. Molinaro, Editor. Monthly. Magazine devoted to improving the effectiveness of professional counter-sales personnel. **Facsimile Number:** (216)535-0874.

★55★
UFCW Action
United Food and Commercial Workers International Union (UFCW)
Suffridge Bldg.
1775 K St. NW
Washington, DC 20006   Phone: (202)223-3111
Bimonthly. Magazine covering union activities, political and legislative matters, and consumer news.

★56★
UFCW Leadership Update
United Food and Commercial Workers International Union (UFCW)
Suffridge Bldg.
1775 K St. NW
Washington, DC 20006   Phone: (202)223-3111
Monthly.

Meetings and Conventions

★57★
United Food and Commercial Workers International Union (UFCW)
Suffridge Bldg.
1775 K St. NW
Washington, DC 20006   Phone: (202)223-3111
Frequency: Quinquennial - 1993 Jul. or Aug.

Insurance Sales Workers

Insurance sales workers (agents and brokers) sell policies that provide financial protection against loss to individuals and businesses. They plan for the financial security of individuals, families, and businesses; advise about insurance protection for automobiles, homes, businesses, or other properties; prepare reports and maintain records; and help policyholders settle insurance claims. Insurance sales workers sell one or many types of insurance. Life insurance agents offer policies that pay survivors when a policyholder dies. Casualty insurance agents sell policies that protect individuals and businesses from financial loss as a result of automobile accidents, fire, theft, or other losses. Health insurance sales workers sell health insurance policies covering the costs of hospital and medical care or loss of income due to illness or injury.

$alaries

Salaries for insurance sales workers vary by level of experience.

Lowest 10 percent	$13,900/year or less
Median	$25,000/year
Top 10 percent	$52,000/year or more

Employment Outlook

Growth rate until the year 2000: Average.

Insurance Sales Workers

Career Guides

★58★
All Pro
BNA Communications, Inc.
9439 Key West Ave.
Rockville, MD 20850   Phone: (301)948-0540
Videocassette. 1981. 29 mins. Conversations with five top sales professionals. They discuss their careers and the traits that make a top professional.

★59★
Business and Finance Career Directory
Career Press, Inc.
PO Box 34
62 Beverly Rd.
Hawthorne, NJ 07507   Phone: (201)427-0229
Ronald W. Fry, editor. 1989. Chapters are written by practitioners in accounting, securities, financial planning and insurance. Describes job duties, educational preparation required, entry into the field, and earnings. Identifies internship opportunities and lists companies actively hiring at entry level.

★60★
Business Insurance: A Sales Skills Introduction
R & R Newkirk
520 Dearborn St.
Chicago, IL 60610   Phone: (312)836-4400
Videocassette. 19??. 28 mins. This program is designed to develop the vital sales skills an agent needs to make a smooth transition into the lucrative area of business insurance.

★61★
Career Success Series
Cambridge Career Products
90 MacCorkle Ave., SW
South Charleston, WV 25311   Phone: (304)744-9323
Videocassette. 1986. 15 mins. A series, available separately, outlining various career choices for students. Occupations include: flight service, air transportation/ground service, data processing, carpentry, clerk in banking/insurance, commodity sales, cosmetic personal grooming, fire fighting, forestry services, home economics, insulation/roofing, material handling, mechanics, photographic processing, pipefitting and plumbing, police science, printing, secretarial services, and utilities equipment operator.

★62★
Careers in Insurance: Property and Casualty
Insurance Information Institute
110 William St.
New York, NY 10038   Phone: (212)669-9200
1987. This 12-page booklet explores careers in property and casualty insurance and covers job duties and training.

★63★
Consider a Career as an Insurance Agent
Professional Insurance Agents
National Association
400 N. Washington St.
Alexandria, VA 22314   Phone: (703)836-9340
This six-panel brochure offers career information and advice. Covers qualifications, job duties, future opportunities, and entry into the field.

★64★
Explore Your Future: A Career in Life Insurance Sales
National Association of Life Underwriters
1922 F St., N.W.
Washington, DC 20006-4387   Phone: (202)331-6000
This six-panel brochure describes opportunities, qualifications, and training.

★65★
Hot Tips, Sneaky Tricks, and Last Ditch Tactics: An Insider's Guide to Getting Your First Corporate Job
John Wiley & Sons, Inc.
605 Third Ave.
New York, NY 10158   Phone: (212)850-6000
Jeff B. Speck. 1989. Written for college graduates who are looking for jobs in banking, consulting, accounting, insurance, real estate or the Fortune 500. Offers tips on surviving the standardized selection process used by large companies.

★66★
"Insurance" in Jobs '91 (pp. 309-316)
Prentice Hall Press
1 Gulf & Western Plaza
New York, NY 10023   Phone: (212)373-8500
Kathryn Petras and Ross Petras. Annual, 1991. Discusses employment prospects and trends for 15 professional careers and 29 industries. Lists leading companies, associations, directories, and magazines.

★67★
"Insurance" in *Major Decisions: A Guide to College Majors* (p. 91)
Orchard House, Inc.
112 Balls Hill Rd.
Concord, MA 01742   Phone: (508)369-0467
Richard A. Blumenthal and Joseph A. Despres. 1990. Provides a one-page description of 155 college majors. Included under each major is a description, the plan of study, typical major courses, high school courses and career possibilities. **Facsimile Number:** (508)369-9472.

★68★
"Insurance" in *The Black Woman's Career Guide* (pp. 288-294)
Doubleday & Co., Inc.
666 Fifth Avenue
New York, NY 10103   Phone: (212)984-7561
Beatryce Nivens. Revised edition, 1987. Offers career planning and job hunting advice. Contains information on 20 different career areas and profiles women working in the field. Each occupational profile describes the work, career paths and earning potential.

★69★
"Insurance" in Volume 1 of *The Encyclopedia of Careers and Vocational Guidance* (pp. 243-249)
J.G. Ferguson Publishing Co.
200 W. Monroe
Chicago, IL 60606   Phone: (312)580-5480
William E. Hopke, editor-in-chief. Eighth edition, 1990. Four-volume set that profiles 500 occupations and describes job trends in 76 industries. Includes career description, educational requirements, history of the job, methods of entry, advancement, employment outlook, earnings, working conditions, social and psychological factors, and sources of additional information.

★70★
"Insurance Agent" in *Top Professions: The 100 Most Popular, Dynamic, and Profitable Careers in America Today* (pp. 8-9)
Peterson's Guides, Inc.
202 Carnegie Center
PO Box 2123
Princeton, NJ 08543-2123   Phone: (609)243-9111
Nicholas Basta. 1989. Includes occupations requiring a college or advanced degree. Describes job duties, earnings, some typical job titles, career opportunities at different degree levels, and lists related associations.

★71★
"Insurance Agent and Broker" in *Marketing and Distribution*, Volume 10 of *Career Information Center* (pp. 71-73)
Glencoe/Macmillan
15319 Chatsworth St.
Mission Hills, CA 91345   Phone: (818)898-1391
Richard Lidz and Dale Anderson, editorial directors. Fourth edition, 1990. For 600 occupations, describes job duties, entry-level requirements, education and training needed, advancement possibilities, employment outlook, earnings and benefits. The set is divided into 12 volumes. Each volume includes jobs related under a broad career field. Volume 13 is the index. **Facsimile Number:** (818)365-5489.

★72★
"Insurance Agent and Broker" in *VGM's Careers Encyclopedia* (pp. 222-225)
National Textbook Co.
4255 W. Touhy Ave.
Lincolnwood, IL 60646   Phone: (312)679-5500
Third edition, 1991. Contains two- to five-page descriptions of 200 managerial, professional, technical, trade and service occupations. Includes job duties, places of employment, qualifications, educational preparation, training, employment potential, advancement, income, and additional sources of information.

★73★
"Insurance Agent and Broker" in *VGM's Handbook of Business and Management Careers* (pp. 47-50)
National Textbook Co.
4255 W. Touhy Ave.
Lincolnwood, IL 60646   Phone: (312)679-5500
Craig T. Norback. 1990. Contains 43 two-page occupational profiles describing job duties, places of employment, working conditions, qualifications, education, employment outlook, and income.

★74★
Insurance Agent/Broker, Life
Careers, Inc.
PO Box 135
Largo, FL 34649-0135   Phone: (813)584-7333
1989. Eight-page brief offering the definition, history, duties, working conditions, personal qualifications, educational requirements, earnings, hours, employment outlook, advancement possibilities, and related occupations.

★75★
Insurance Agent, Property and Liability
Careers, Inc.
PO Box 135
Largo, FL 34649-0135   Phone: (813)584-7333
1988. Two-page occupational summary card describing duties, working conditions, personal qualifications, training, earnings and hours, employment outlook, places of employment, related careers and where to write for more information.

★76★
"Insurance Agent/Property & Liability" in *Occu-Facts: Information on 565 Careers in Outline Form* (p. 11.3)
Careers, Inc.
P.O. Box 135
1211 Tenth St., S.W.
Largo, FL 33640   Phone: (813)584-7333
Elizabeth Handville. Biennial, 1989-90 edition. Each one-page occupational profile describes duties, working conditions, physical surroundings and demands, aptitudes, temperament, educational requirements, employment outlook, earnings, and places of employment.

★77★
Insurance Agents and Brokers
Chronicle Guidance Publications, Inc.
PO Box 1190
Moravia, NY 13118-1190   Phone: (315)497-0330
1989. This career brief describes the nature of the work, working conditions, hours and earnings, education and training, licensure, certification, unions, personal qualifications, social and psychological factors, employment outlook, entry methods, advancement, and related occupations. **Toll-free/Additional Phone Number(s):** 800-622-7284.

Insurance Sales Workers

★78★
"Insurance Agents and Brokers" in *Jobs! What They Are...Where They Are...What They Pay* (p. 285)
Simon & Schuster, Inc.
Simon & Schuster Bldg.
1230 Avenue of the Americas
New York, NY 10020   Phone: (212)698-7000
Robert O. Snelling and Anne M. Snelling. Revised edition, 1989. Profiles 241 occupations, describing duties and responsibilities, educational preparation, earnings, employment opportunities, training, and qualifications.

★79★
"Insurance Agents and Brokers" in *101 Careers: A Guide to the Fastest-Growing Opportunities* (pp. 17-20)
John Wiley & Sons, Inc.
605 Third Ave.
New York, NY 10158   Phone: (212)850-6000
Michael Harkavy. 1990. Each occupational profile includes a job description, job titles, work environment, employment outlook, qualifications, personal skills, and earnings.

★80★
"Insurance Agents and Brokers" in Volume 3 of *The Encyclopedia of Careers and Vocational Guidance* (pp. 144-153)
J.G. Ferguson Publishing Co.
200 W. Monroe
Chicago, IL 60606   Phone: (312)580-5480
William E. Hopke, editor-in-chief. Eighth edition, 1990. Four-volume set that profiles 500 occupations and describes job trends in 76 industries. Includes career description, educational requirements, history of the job, methods of entry, advancement, employment outlook, earnings, working conditions, social and psychological factors, and sources of additional information.

★81★
"Insurance Agents and Brokers: Making It in a Premium Career" in *Careers for Women Without College Degrees* (pp. 239-245)
McGraw-Hill Publishing Co.
11 W. 19th St.
New York, NY 10011   Phone: (212)337-6010
Beatryce Nivens. 1988. Career planning and job hunting guide containing information on decision-making, skills assessment, and resumes for career changers. Profiles careers with the best occupational outlook. Describes the work, educational preparation, employment outlook, salaries, and required skills.

★82★
"Insurance is Fun!" in *Internships Volume 3: Accounting, Banking, Brokerage, Finance & Insurance* (pp. 55-61)
Career Press, Inc.
PO Box 34
62 Beverly Rd.
Hawthorne, NJ 07507   Phone: (201)427-0229
Ronald W. Fry, editor-in-chief. 1989. Offers advice about obtaining internships with accounting, brokerage and investment banking firms, banks, and insurance companies. Lists companies offering internships and includes the contact person, duration, duties, qualifications, and application procedures and deadlines.

★83★
"Insurance, Sales" in *Career Choices for the 90's for Students of Business* (pp. 163-164)
Walker and Co.
720 Fifth Ave.
New York, NY 10019   Phone: (212)265-3632
1990. Describes jobs in different industries and includes interviews with people working in related occupations. Presents employment outlook, preferred geographic location, entry-level opportunities, career paths, job responsibilities, advancement, personal and professional qualifications, salaries, working conditions, material for further reading, and associations.

★84★
"Insurance Sales" in *Career Choices for the 90's for Students of Communications and Journalism* (pp. 171-172)
Walker and Co.
720 Fifth Ave.
New York, NY 10019   Phone: (212)265-3632
1990. Describes jobs in different industries and includes interviews with people working in related occupations. Presents employment outlook, preferred geographic location, entry-level opportunities, career paths, job responsibilities, advancement, personal and professional qualifications, salaries, working conditions, material for further reading, and associations.

★85★
"Insurance, Sales" in *Career Choices for the 90's for Students of Economics* (pp. 72-74)
Walker and Co.
720 Fifth Ave.
New York, NY 10019   Phone: (212)265-3632
1990. Describes jobs in different industries and includes interviews with people working in related occupations. Presents employment outlook, preferred geographic location, entry-level opportunities, career paths, job responsibilities, advancement, personal and professional qualifications, salaries, working conditions, material for further reading, and associations.

★86★
"Insurance, Sales" in *Career Choices for the 90's for Students of Mathematics* (pp. 97-99)
Walker and Co.
720 Fifth Ave.
New York, NY 10019   Phone: (212)265-3632
1990. Describes jobs in different industries and includes interviews with people working in related occupations. Presents employment outlook, preferred geographic location, entry-level opportunities, career paths, job responsibilities, advancement, personal and professional qualifications, salaries, working conditions, material for further reading, and associations.

★87★
"Insurance Sales" in *Career Choices for the 90's for Students of Political Science & Government* (pp. 172-173)
Walker and Co.
720 Fifth Ave.
New York, NY 10019   Phone: (212)265-3632
1990. Describes jobs in different industries and includes interviews with people working in related occupations. Presents employment outlook, preferred geographic location, entry-level opportunities, career paths, job responsibilities, advancement, personal and professional qualifications, salaries, working conditions, material for further reading, and associations.

★88★

★88★
"Insurance Sales" in *Career Choices for the 90's for Students of Psychology* (pp. 192-193)
Walker and Co.
720 Fifth Ave.
New York, NY 10019   Phone: (212)265-3632

1990. Describes jobs in different industries and includes interviews with people working in related occupations. Presents employment outlook, preferred geographic location, entry-level opportunities, career paths, job responsibilities, advancement, personal and professional qualifications, salaries, working conditions, material for further reading, and associations.

★89★
"Insurance Sales" in *Fast-Track Careers: A Guide to the Highest-Paying Jobs* (pp. 152-153)
John Wiley & Sons, Inc.
605 Third Ave.
New York, NY 10158   Phone: (212)850-6000

William Lewis and Nancy Schuman. 1987. Profiles eight glamourous and high paying careers describing entry-level opportunities, earnings, personal qualities, types of companies, educational preparation and training, and employment outlook. Lists prominent companies in each industry, typical jargon, and professional associations.

★90★
"Insurance Sales" in *Transitions: Military Pathways to Civilian Careers* (pp. 141-142)
Rosen Publishing Group, Inc.
29 E. 21st St.
New York, NY 10010   Phone: (212)777-3017

Robert W. MacDonald. 1988. Describes how to make the best use of your military service to create a civilian career. Describes skills needed in civilian employment and compares them to skills acquired in the military. Covers career planning, job search, resume writing, and starting a small business. Lists many resources.

★91★
"Insurance Sales Workers" in *Occupational Outlook Handbook* (pp. 230-232)
Superintendent of Documents
U.S. Government Printing Office
Washington, DC 20402   Phone: (202)783-3238

Biennial; latest edition, 1990-91. Encyclopedia of careers describing more than 250 occupations and comprising about 86 percent of all jobs in the economy. Occupations that require lengthy education or training are given the most attention. For each occupation, the handbook describes job duties, working conditions, training, educational preparation, personal qualities, advancement possibilities, job outlook, earnings, and sources of additional information.

★92★
"Insurance Salesperson" in *College Board Guide to Jobs and Career Planning* (pp. 134-136)
College Entrance Examination Board
45 Columbus Ave.
New York, NY 10023-6992   Phone: (212)713-8000

Joyce Slayton Mitchell. 1990. Career planning guide written for high school and college students. Covers 100 careers in 15 occupational groups. Provides job description, educational preparation needed, salaries, related careers, and sources of additional information. Includes information about the 90's labor market.

★93★
"Insurance Salespersons" in *Opportunities in Vocational and Technical Careers* (pp. 61-63)
National Textbook Co.
4255 W. Touhy Ave.
Lincolnwood, IL 60646   Phone: (312)679-5500

Adrian A. Paradis. 1987. Describes careers which can be prepared for by attending a private vocational or proprietary school—office employee, sales worker, service worker, health services, mechanic, craftworker, and technician. Covers employment outlook, job duties, and salaries. Offers career planning advice.

★94★
"Life Insurance Agent/Broker" in *Occu-Facts: Information on 565 Careers in Outline Form* (p. 11.2)
Careers, Inc.
P.O. Box 135
1211 Tenth St., S.W.
Largo, FL 33640   Phone: (813)584-7333

Elizabeth Handville. Biennial, 1989-90 edition. Each one-page occupational profile describes duties, working conditions, physical surroundings and demands, aptitudes, temperament, educational requirements, employment outlook, earnings, and places of employment.

★95★
"Life Insurance Agents and Brokers" in Volume 4 of *Career Discovery Encyclopedia* (pp. 28-29)
J.G. Ferguson Publishing Co.
200 W. Monroe
Chicago, IL 60606   Phone: (312)580-5480

E. Russell Primm, editor-in-chief. 1990. Contains two-page articles on 504 occupations. Each article describes job duties, earnings, and educational and training requirements.

★96★
"Marine Insurance Careers" in *Opportunities in Marine and Maritime Careers* (pp. 111-112)
National Textbook Co.
4255 W. Touhy Ave.
Lincolnwood, IL 60646   Phone: (312)679-5500

William Ray Heitzmann. 1988. Includes careers related by their proximity to water: cruise ships, oceanography, marine sciences, fishing, commercial diving, maritime transportation, shipbuilding, Navy, Coast Guard. Covers qualifications, job outlook, job duties, educational preparation, and training. Lists associations and schools.

★97★
"Property and Casualty Insurance Agents and Brokers" in Volume 5 of *Career Discovery Encyclopedia* (pp. 92-93)
J.G. Ferguson Publishing Co.
200 W. Monroe
Chicago, IL 60606   Phone: (312)580-5480

E. Russell Primm, editor-in-chief. 1990. Contains two-page articles on 504 occupations. Each article describes job duties, earnings, and educational and training requirements.

★98★
"Sales" in *Opportunities in Insurance Careers* (pp. 34-36)
National Textbook Co.
4255 W. Touhy Ave.
Lincolnwood, IL 60646   Phone: (312)679-5500

Robert M. Schrayer. 1987. Explores the history and career opportunities of the insurance industry. Describes educational requirements, certification, licensing, salaries, and employment outlook.

Insurance Sales Workers

★107★

★99★
"Sales (Insurance)" in *The Encyclopedia of Career Choices for the 1990s: A Guide to Entry Level Jobs* (pp. 442-444)
Walker and Co.
720 Fifth Ave.
New York, NY 10019　　　　　　　Phone: (212)265-3632
1991. Describes entry-level opportunities in 42 career fields for college graduates. Each chapter covers a single career field, including an overview, employment outlook, major employers, tips on entering the field, international job opportunities, functional job areas with personal and professional qualifications, career paths, job responsibilities, advancement possibilities, salaries, and working conditions. Lists related sources of information.

★100★
Video Career Library - Marketing and Sales
Careers, Inc.
1211 10th St., SW
PO Box 135
Largo, FL 34649-0135　　　　　　Phone: (813)584-7333
Videocassette. 1990. Part of the Video Career Library covering 165 occupations. Shows actual workers on the job. Includes insurance salespersons.

Associations

★101★
American Society of CLU and ChFC (ASCLU & ChFC)
270 Bryn Mawr Ave.
Bryn Mawr, PA 19010　　　　　　Phone: (215)526-2500
Membership: Professional society of insurance agents and financial services professionals who hold Chartered Life Underwriter (CLU) or Chartered Financial Consultant (ChFC) designations. **Purpose:** Conducts week-long graduate-level educational sessions (CLU Institutes); one-day seminars with experts lecturing on subjects such as law, taxation, estate planning, and business life insurance; symposia and clinics; research. Offers scholarship. **Publications:** *Assets: A Business, Tax, and Financial Newsletter*, bimonthly. • *Financial Monitor*, bimonthly. • *Journal of the American Society of CLU & ChFC*, bimonthly. • *Keeping Current*, quarterly. • *Query: Questions and Answers About Managing Your Money*, monthly. • *Society Page*, bimonthly. • Also publishes case studies; produces audio- and videotape recordings on taxes, trusts, estate planning, and other financial topics. **Facsimile Number:** (215)527-4010; teleconferencing.

★102★
Health Insurance Association of America (HIAA)
1025 Connecticut Ave. NW, Ste. 1200
Washington, DC 20036　　　　　　Phone: (202)223-7780
Membership: Accident and health insurance firms. **Purpose:** To promote development of voluntary insurance against loss of income and financial burdens resulting from accident and sickness. Holds individual insurance forums. **Publications:** *Bulletin*, periodic. • *Directory*, annual. • *Executive Report*, monthly. • *Sourcebook of Health Insurance Data*, biennial. • Also publishes statistical studies, law digests, and regulations.

★103★
Independent Insurance Agents of America (IIAA)
127 Peyton
Alexandria, VA 22314　　　　　　Phone: (703)683-4422
Membership: Sales agencies handling fire, casualty, and surety insurance. **Purpose:** Organizes technical and sales courses for new and established agents. Sponsors Insurance Youth Golf Classic. **Publications:** *IIAAction News*, monthly. • *Independent Agent*, monthly. • *Management Service*, bimonthly. • Also publishes pamphlets, reports, guides, and handbooks.

★104★
National Association of Health Underwriters (NAHU)
1000 Connecticut Ave. NW, Ste. 1111
Washington, DC 20036　　　　　　Phone: (202)223-5533
Membership: Insurance agencies and individuals engaged in the promotion, sale, and administration of disability income and health insurance. **Purpose:** Sponsors advanced health insurance underwriting and research seminars at universities. Testifies before federal and state committees on pending health insurance legislation. Presents numerous awards, including annual Harold R. Gordon Memorial Award, the health insurance industry's Man of the Year Award, and distinguished service awards to industry leaders; sponsors leading producers roundtable awards and health insurance quality awards for leading salesmen. Grants RHU certification to qualified Registered Disability Income and Health Insurance Underwriters. Is organizing a speakers' bureau and a political action committee. **Boards:** Disability Insurance Training Council; Leading Producers Round Table. **Publications:** *Health Insurance Underwriter*, 10/year.

★105★
National Association of Life Underwriters (NALU)
1922 F St. NW
Washington, DC 20006　　　　　　Phone: (202)331-6001
Membership: Federation of state (50) and local associations (950) representing 138,000 life insurance agents, general agents, and managers; associate members are home office officials of life companies, life insurance teachers, journalists, and others. **Purpose:** Objectives are: to support and maintain the principles of legal reserve life insurance and health insurance; to promote high ethical standards; to inform the public, render community service, and promote public goodwill. Sponsors public service programs. Offers educational programs. Bestows annual awards. **Publications:** *LeaderLine Newsletter*, monthly. • *Life Association News*, monthly.

★106★
Professional Insurance Agents (PIA)
400 N. Washington St.
Alexandria, VA 22314　　　　　　Phone: (703)836-9340
Membership: Independent property and casualty agents. **Purpose:** Activities are educational, representative, and service-oriented. Sponsors over 200 educational programs and seminars each year on all aspects of property and casualty insurance, ranging from the novice to specialist level. Bestows awards; compiles statistics; offers consulting, testing, and evaluation services; conducts research programs; develops products/services unique to independent agencies. Maintains 600 volume insurance library. **Publications:** *PIACTION*, monthly. • *Professional Agent*, monthly. • Also publishes public service and consumer brochures on insurance.

Standards/Certification Agencies

★107★
National Association of Health Underwriters (NAHU)
1000 Connecticut Ave. NW, Ste. 1111
Washington, DC 20036　　　　　　Phone: (202)223-5533
Grants RHU certification to qualified Registered Disability Income and Health Insurance Underwriters.

Test Guides

★108★
Actuarial Clerk
National Learning Corp.
212 Michael Dr.
Syosset, NY 11791   Phone: (516)921-8888
Jack Rudman. Part of the Career Examination Series No. 1. All examination guides in this series contain questions with answers. **Facsimile Number:** (516)921-8743. **Toll-free/Additional Phone Number(s):** 800-645-6337.

★109★
Insurance Salesman
National Learning Corp.
212 Michael Dr.
Syosset, NY 11791   Phone: (516)921-8888
Jack Rudman. Part of the Career Examination Series No. 1. All examination guides in this series contain questions with answers. **Facsimile Number:** (516)921-8743. **Toll-free/Additional Phone Number(s):** 800-645-6337.

Awards, Scholarships, Grants, and Fellowships

★110★
Health and Disability Insurance Sales Achievement
National Association of Health Underwriters
c/o Patricia Hannaway
1000 Connecticut Ave., N.W., Ste. 1111
Washington, DC 20036   Phone: (202)223-5533
To recognize health and disability income insurance agents who reach their full potential in professional development, technical competence and sales performance. Applications may be submitted by March 31. Leading Producers Round Table Annual Sales Achievement certificates are awarded annually. Established in 1942.

★111★
National Quality Award
National Association of Life Underwriters
c/o Phyllis A. Smith
1922 F St., N.W.
Washington, DC 20006   Phone: (202)331-6050
To promote and recognize the maintenance of quality business, as reflected by a high persistency standard of insurance sales to benefit the industry and the public. Members of the NALU are eligible. A certificate or a plaque are awarded annually. Established in 1944. Co-sponsored by the Life Insurance Marketing and Research Association.

★112★
National Sales Achievement Award
National Association of Life Underwriters
c/o Phyllis A. Smith
1922 F St., N.W.
Washington, DC 20006   Phone: (202)331-6050
To honor successful life underwriters who, during a particular year, excel in placing a substantial amount of life insurance on a large number of lives. Members of local affiliates of NALU are eligible. A certificate or a plaque are awarded annually. Established in 1966.

Basic Reference Guides and Handbooks

★113★
HIAA Directory
Health Insurance Association of America (HIAA)
1025 Connecticut Ave. NW, Ste. 1200
Washington, DC 20036   Phone: (202)223-7780
Annual.

Periodicals

★114★
AAIS Viewpoint
American Association of Insurance Services (AAIS)
1035 S. York Rd.
Bensenville, IL 60106   Phone: (708)595-3225
Editor(s): Carol Poynter. Quarterly. Contains news of current insurance issues, AAIS activities, insurance legislation, and other subjects of interest. **Facsimile Number:** (708)595-4647.

★115★
American Salesman
National Research Bureau, Inc.
424 N. 3rd St.
Burlington, IA 52601-5224   Phone: (319)752-5415
Barbara Boeding, Editor. Monthly. Salesmanship magazine. **Facsimile Number:** (319)752-3421.

★116★
ASCLU & ChFC Financial Monitor
American Society of CLU and ChFC (ASCLU & ChFC)
270 Bryn Mawr Ave.
Bryn Mawr, PA 19010   Phone: (215)526-2500
Bimonthly. Newsletter of clients of CLUs and ChFCs covering investments, estate planning, life insurance, annuities, disability, business planning, and personal business.

★117★
Assets: A Business, Tax, and Financial Newsletter (ASCLU & ChFC)
American Society of CLU and ChFC (ASCLU & ChFC)
270 Bryn Mawr Ave.
Bryn Mawr, PA 19010   Phone: (215)526-2500
Bimonthly. Covers life insurance, tax, business, and other financial planning topics. Includes question and answer column dealing with financial planning topics.

★118★
CLAIMS
Insurance Week, Inc.
1001 4th Ave. Plaza, Ste. 3029
Seattle, WA 98154   Phone: (206)624-6965
Bill Thorness, Editor. Monthly. Magazine for the property-casualty insurance claims industry. **Facsimile Number:** (206)624-5021.

Insurance Sales Workers

★119★
CPCU Journal
The Society of CPCU
PO Box 3009
720 Providence Rd.
Malvern, PA 19355-0709   Phone: (215)251-2728
Lisa A. Fittipaldi, Managing Editor. Quarterly. Journal covering insurance and related fields. **Facsimile Number:** (215)251-2761.

★120★
Degree of Honor Review
Degree of Honor Protective Assn.
325 Cedar St.
Degree of Honor Bldg.
Saint Paul, MN 55101   Phone: (612)224-7436
Wilma A. Williams, Editor. Quarterly. Fraternal life insurance magazine.

★121★
Excess Express
Merritt Company, Inc.
1661 9th St.
PO Box 955
Santa Monica, CA 90406   Phone: (213)450-7234
Editor(s): Dr. William R. Feldhaus. Monthly. Covers events and trends related to the insurance industry and specialty insurance. Discusses strategies for ensuring total insurance coverage and offers legislative commentaries. Recurring features include case studies, company and personnel items, and letters to the editor.

★122★
HIAA Bulletin (HIAA)
Health Insurance Association of America (HIAA)
1025 Connecticut Ave. NW, Ste. 1200
Washington, DC 20036   Phone: (202)223-7780
Periodic.

★123★
HIAA Executive Report (HIAA)
Health Insurance Association of America (HIAA)
1025 Connecticut Ave. NW, Ste. 1200
Washington, DC 20036   Phone: (202)223-7780
Monthly.

★124★
IIA Action News (IIAA)
Independent Insurance Agents of America (IIAA)
127 Peyton
Alexandria, VA 22314   Phone: (703)683-4422
Monthly.

★125★
Independent Agent
Independent Insurance Agents of America, Inc.
127 S. Peyton St.
Alexandria, VA 22310   Phone: (703)683-4422
Howard P. Hoskins, Editor. Monthly. Trade magazine featuring information on property/casualty, and life insurance. **Facsimile Number:** (703)683-7556.

★126★
The Insurance Advocate
Chase Communications Group Ltd.
25-35 Beechwood Ave.
Mount Vernon, NY 10053   Phone: (212)233-3768
Emanuel Levy, Editor. Weekly (Sat.). Magazine reporting legislative, regulatory, judicial, and industry news for the insurance industry. **Facsimile Number:** (914)699-2025.

★127★
Insurance Industry Newsletter
Insurance Field Company
PO Box 3006
Savannah, GA 31402-3006   Phone: (912)355-4117
Editor(s): George V.R. Smith. Weekly. Provides news and comment on the insurance industry in the U.S. Contains information on legislation and regulation, trends, promotions, and new products. Recurring features include book reviews, news of research, statistics, obituaries, and meetings in the fields of liability, property, life, and health insurance.

★128★
Insurance Journal
Wells Publishing
80 S. Lake Ave., Ste. 550
Pasadena, CA 91101-2610   Phone: (818)793-7717
John McCann, Editor. Every other week. Insurance magazine. **Facsimile Number:** (818)793-1462.

★129★
The Insurance Record
Record Publishing Co.
PO Box 225770
Dallas, TX 75222-5770   Phone: (214)630-0687
Glen E. Hargis, Editor. Every other week. Insurance trade magazine. **Facsimile Number:** (214)631-2476.

★130★
Insurance Review
Insurance Information Institute
110 William St.
New York, NY 10038   Phone: (212)669-9200
Olga Badillo-Sciortino, Editor. Monthly. Magazine for insurance agents and brokers, insurance company executives, risk managers, and others interested in the property/casualty insurance business. **Facsimile Number:** (212)267-9591.

★131★
Insurance Sales
The Rough Notes Co., Inc.
1200 N. Meridian St.
PO Box 564
Indianapolis, IN 46206   Phone: (317)634-1541
Raymond E. Werner, Editor. Monthly. Trade magazine on life and health insurance sales. **Facsimile Number:** (317)634-1041.

★132★
International Insurance Monitor
Chase Communications Group Ltd.
25-35 Beechwood Ave.
Mount Vernon, NY 10550   Phone: (914)699-2020
Stephen H. Acunto, Editor and Publisher. Monthly (July/August and November/December combined issues). Magazine covering insurance topics worldwide.

★133★
Journal of the American Society of CLU & ChFC (ASCLU & ChFC)
American Society of CLU and ChFC (ASCLU & ChFC)
270 Bryn Mawr Ave.
Bryn Mawr, PA 19010   Phone: (215)526-2500
Bimonthly. Provides information on insurance and financial planning. Includes book reviews.

★134★
Keeping Current
American Society of CLU and ChFC (ASCLU & ChFC)
270 Bryn Mawr Ave.
Bryn Mawr, PA 19010   Phone: (215)526-2500
Quarterly.

★135★
LeaderLine Newsletter
National Association of Life Underwriters (NALU)
1922 F St. NW
Washington, DC 20006   Phone: (202)331-6001
Monthly.

★136★
Life Association News
National Association of Life Underwriters (NALU)
1922 F St. NW
Washington, DC 20006   Phone: (202)331-6001
Monthly. Magazine featuring industry news and instructional articles on sales techniques and business management. Includes book reviews and legislative reviews.

★137★
Management Service
Independent Insurance Agents of America (IIAA)
127 Peyton
Alexandria, VA 22314   Phone: (703)683-4422
Bimonthly.

★138★
The National Gleaner Forum
Gleaner Life Insurance Society
5200 W. U.S. 223
Adrian, MI 49221   Phone: (517)263-2244
Noel Loveland, Editor. 4x/yr. Fraternal insurance magazine. **Facsimile Number:** (517)265-7745.

★139★
National Underwriter Property and Casualty/Risk and Benefits Management
National Underwriter Co.
505 Gest St.
Cincinnati, OH 45203-1716   Phone: (513)721-2140
Thomas Slattery, Editor. Weekly (Mon.). News magazine for agents, brokers, executives, and managers in risk and benefit insurance. **Facsimile Number:** (513)721-0126.

★140★
PIACTION
Professional Insurance Agents (PIA)
400 N. Washington St.
Alexandria, VA 22314   Phone: (703)836-9340
Monthly.

★141★
Professional Agent
Professional Insurance Agents (PIA)
400 N. Washington St.
Alexandria, VA 22314   Phone: (703)836-9340
Monthly. Magazine concerned with educating and informing independent property and casualty insurance agents. Includes tax adviser and insurance policy columns.

★142★
Professional Insurance Agents
PIA Management Services Inc.
PO Box 997
Glenmont, NY 12077-0997   Phone: (518)434-3111
Mary Morrison Vanniere, Editor. 11x/yr. Insurance trade magazine. **Facsimile Number:** (518)434-2342.

★143★
Query: Questions and Answers About Managing Your Money
American Society of CLU and ChFC (ASCLU & ChFC)
270 Bryn Mawr Ave.
Bryn Mawr, PA 19010   Phone: (215)526-2500
Monthly. Newsletter covering insurance, estate, tax, business, and financial planning topics.

★144★
Resource
Life Office Management Association (LOMA)
5770 Powers Ferry Rd., NW
Atlanta, GA 30327   Phone: (404)951-1770
Monthly. Magazine.

★145★
Rough Notes
Rough Notes Co., Inc.
PO Box 564
Indianapolis, IN 46206   Phone: (317)634-1541
Tom Al McCoy, Editor. Monthly. Sales/management magazine for property/casualty insurance agents and brokers. **Facsimile Number:** (317)634-1041.

★146★
Salesman's Insider
Marv Q. Modell Associates
6009 Montgomery Corner
San Jose, CA 95135-1431   Phone: (408)270-4526
Editor(s): Marv Q. Modell. Monthly. Concerned with selling techniques and methodology in all sales areas. Tracks new sales developments, trends, and profit opportunities. Details negotiatineg process with "tips that work".

★147★
Smart's Insurance Bulletin
Darrell Heppner Risk Management Services, Inc.
2203 Los Angeles Ave.
Berkeley, CA 94707   Phone: (415)524-8682
Editor(s): James Whitaker. 48/yr. Discusses insurance, including risk management, property and casualty insurance, and workers' compensation. Reports on significant aspects of case law and on legislative developments. Recurring features include statistics, book reviews, reports of current industry trends, special issues, and summaries of court cases.

Insurance Sales Workers

★148★
Society Page
American Society of CLU and ChFC (ASCLU & ChFC)
270 Bryn Mawr Ave.
Bryn Mawr, PA 19010   Phone: (215)526-2500
Bimonthly. Membership newsletter for insurance and financial planning practitioners.

★149★
Southern Insurance
2535 Beechwood Ave., No. 9001
Mount Vernon, NY 10552
A.J. Davis, Editor and Publisher. Monthly. Insurance industry magazine.

★150★
The Weekly Insider
Independent Insurance Agents and Brokers of California (IIABC)
101 Market St., Ste. 702
San Francisco, CA 94105   Phone: (415)957-1212
Editor(s): Theresa Whitmarsh. Weekly. Carries insurance industry news, legislative developments, insurance technical reviews of workers compensation and commercial and personal lines. Recurring features include interviews, a calendar of events, and legislative and legal reports. **Toll-free/Additional Phone Number(s):** 800-772-8998.

Meetings and Conventions

★151★
Alliance of American Insurers
1501 Woodfield Rd., Ste. 400 W
Schaumburg, IL 60173   Phone: (708)330-8500
Frequency: Annual. **Facsimile Number:** (708)330-8602.

★152★
American Association of Managing General Agents Trade Mart
American Association of Managing General Agents
9140 Ward Pkwy.
Kansas City, MO 64114   Phone: (816)444-3500
1992; May 27-31; White Sulphur, WV • 1993; Apr. 18-24; Palm Desert, CA • 1994; May 15-19; Orlando, FL. **Facsimile Number:** (816)444-0330.

★153★
American Society of Chartered Life Underwriters National Conference
American Society of Chartered Life Underwriters
270 Bryn Mawr Ave.
Bryn Mawr, PA 19010   Phone: (215)526-2500
1992; Oct. 11-14; Orlando, FL • 1993; Oct. 06-09; Kansas City, KS • 1994; Oct. 09-12; Seattle, WA • 1995; Oct. 15-18; Atlanta, GA. **Facsimile Number:** (215)527-4010.

★154★
Carolinas Association of Professional Insurance Agents Annual Convention
Carolinas Association of Professional Insurance Agents
3109 Charles B. Root Wynd
Raleigh, NC 27612   Phone: (919)782-5807
Frequency: Always held in June. 1992; Jun. Charleston, SC • 1993; Jun. Asheville, NC • 1994; Jun. Hilton Head Island, SC • 1995; Jun. Myrtle Beach, SC.

★155★
Independent Insurance Agents of America Annual Convention and Exhibit
Independent Insurance Agents of America
127 S. Peyton St.
Alexandria, VA 22314   Phone: (703)683-4422
1992.

★156★
Insurance Accounting and Systems Association Annual Conference and Business Show
Insurance Accounting and Systems Association, Inc.
PO Box 51340
Durham, NC 27717   Phone: (919)489-0991
1992.

★157★
National Association of Life Underwriters (NALU)
1922 F St. NW
Washington, DC 20006   Phone: (202)331-6001
Frequency: Annual, with exhibits.

★158★
Professional Insurance Agents Convention and Trade Show
Professional Insurance Agents
400 N. Washington St.
Alexandria, VA 22314   Phone: (703)836-9340
1992; Nov. 08-11; Boston, MA. **Facsimile Number:** (703)836-1279.

★159★
Risk and Insurance Management Society Annual Conference
Risk and Insurance Management Society, Inc.
205 E. 42nd St.
New York, NY 10017   Phone: (212)286-9292
1992; Mar. 29-03; Anaheim, CA • 1993; Apr. 25-30; Orlando, FL • 1994; Apr. 17-22; New Orleans, LA. **Facsimile Number:** (212)986-9716.

★160★
Society of Actuaries Convention
Society of Actuaries
475 N. Martingale Rd., Ste. 800
Schaumburg, IL 60173-2226   Phone: (708)706-3500
1992; Oct. 25-28; Washington, DC • 1993; Oct. 17-20; New York, NY. **Facsimile Number:** (708)706-3599.

★161★
Society of Chartered Property and Casualty Underwriters Annual Meeting and Seminar
Society of Property and Casualty Underwriters
PO Box 3009
Malvern, PA 19355-0709   Phone: (215)251-2742
1992; Oct. 11-14; San Francisco, CA • 1993; Oct. 24-27; Baltimore, MD • 1994; Sep. 25-29; Chicago, IL • 1995; Oct. 08-11; Honolulu, HI. **Facsimile Number:** (215)251-2761.

Manufacturers' and Wholesale Sales Representatives

Firms employ manufacturers' and wholesale sales representatives to market their products to manufacturers, wholesale and retail establishments, government agencies, and other institutions. The primary job of these sales representatives is to interest wholesale and retail buyers and purchasing agents in their merchandise. Manufacturers' and wholesale sales representatives spend much of their time traveling to and visiting with prospective buyers, to inform these potential customers about prices, availability, and how their products can save money and improve productivity. Prospecting for new clients is an important component of this job. Sales representatives whose products are not in wide distribution follow leads generated by other clients, from advertisements in trade journals, and participation in trade shows and conferences. Other duties include analyzing sales statistics, preparing reports, and handling administrative duties, such as filing expense account reports, scheduling appointments, and making travel plans.

$alaries

Compensation methods are usually a combination of salary and commission or salary plus bonus. Median annual salaries are as follows:

Lowest 10 percent	$14,400/year or less
Middle 50 percent	$19,000-41,400/year
Top 10 percent	$51,700/year or more.

Employment Outlook

Growth rate until the year 2000: Faster than average.

Manufacturers' and Wholesale Sales Representatives

────────── **Career Guides** ──────────

★162★
According to Hoyle
Commonwealth Films, Inc.
223 Commonwealth Ave.
Boston, MA 02116　　　　　Phone: (617)262-5634
Videocassette. 1988. 30 mins. An entire business deal is enacted, from the purchasing of goods to the sales.

★163★
All Pro
BNA Communications, Inc.
9439 Key West Ave.
Rockville, MD 20850　　　　Phone: (301)948-0540
Videocassette. 1981. 29 mins. Conversations with five top sales professionals. They discuss their careers and the traits that make a top professional.

★164★
American Professionals Series
Cambridge Career Products
90 MacCorkle Ave., SW
South Charleston, WV 25311　Phone: (304)744-9323
Videocassette. 1984. 30 mins. In this series of twenty-one half hour programs, various occupations are examined in depth, including a day in the life of each worker. Included are: fireman, farmer, oil driller, fisherman, horse trainer, and auto assembly repairman.

★165★
Career Success Series
Cambridge Career Products
90 MacCorkle Ave., SW
South Charleston, WV 25311　Phone: (304)744-9323
Videocassette. 1986. 15 mins. A series, available separately, outlining various career choices for students. Occupations include: flight service, air transportation/ground service, data processing, carpentry, clerk in banking/insurance, commodity sales, cosmetic personal grooming, fire fighting, forestry services, home economics, insulation/roofing, material handling, mechanics, photographic processing, pipefitting and plumbing, police science, printing, secretarial services, and utilities equipment operator.

★166★
Careers Working With Animals
Acropolis Books
11741 Bowman Greene Dr.
Reston, VA 22090　　　　　Phone: (703)709-0006
Guy R. Hodge. 1979. **Facsimile Number:** (703)709-0942.

★167★
"Getting Started in Industrial Sales" in *Marketing and Sales Career Directory* (pp. 18-22)
Career Press, Inc.
PO Box 34
62 Beverly Rd.
Hawthorne, NJ 07507　　　　Phone: (201)427-0229
Ronald W. Fry, editor. Third edition, 1990. Guide to career planning and job hunting in a marketing or sales capacity at a major corporation, market research company, or public relations agency. Lists hundreds of employers seeking entry level employees. Includes job description, work environments, educational preparation, career advancement, earnings, and trends.

★168★
How Food Brokers Serve You
National Food Brokers Association
1010 Massachusetts Ave., N.W.
Washington, DC 20001　　　Phone: (202)789-2844
This four-page brochure describes the work of food brokers.

★169★
"Industrial (Business-to-Business) Marketing" in *Opportunities in Marketing Careers* (pp. 36-37)
National Textbook Co.
4255 W. Touhy Ave.
Lincolnwood, IL 60646　　　Phone: (312)679-5500
Margery Steinberg. 1988. Defines marketing and surveys marketing fields such as research and retailing. Covers employment outlook, educational and training requirements, and the financial and other rewards of marketing. Offers job hunting advice for this field.

★170★
"Industrial Sales and Wholesaling" in *Careers in Marketing* (pp. 52-55)
National Textbook Co.
4255 W. Touhy Ave.
Lincolnwood, IL 60646　　　Phone: (312)679-5500
Lila B. Stair. 1991. Surveys career opportunities in marketing and related areas such as marketing research, product development, and sales promotion. Includes a description of the work, places of employment, employment outlook, trends, educational preparation, organizational charts, and salaries. Offers job hunting advice.

★171★
"Instrument Sales Representative" in *Career Opportunities in the Music Industry* (pp. 95-96)
Facts on File, Inc.
460 Park Avenue, S.
New York, NY 10016   Phone: (212)683-2244
Shelly Field. Second edition, 1991. Describes more than 70 music related jobs. Each occupational profile covers job duties, employment outlook, career paths, salaries, skills, and educational preparation. Offers tips for entering the field.

★172★
Making 70,000 Plus a Year as a Self-Employed Manufacturer's Representative
Ten Speed Press
PO Box 7123
Berkeley, CA 94707   Phone: (415)845-8414
Leigh Silliphant and Sureleigh Silliphant. Revised and updated edition, 1988. Covers deciding what to sell, negotiating with the manufacturer and determining compensation. Offers advice on how to sell, locating outlets and clients, and traveling.

★173★
"Manufactured Products" in *Career Choices for the 90's for Students of Communications and Journalism* (pp. 175-178)
Walker and Co.
720 Fifth Ave.
New York, NY 10019   Phone: (212)265-3632
1990. Describes jobs in different industries and includes interviews with people working in related occupations. Presents employment outlook, preferred geographic location, entry-level opportunities, career paths, job responsibilities, advancement, personal and professional qualifications, salaries, working conditions, material for further reading, and associations.

★174★
"Manufactured Products" in *Career Choices for the 90's for Students of Political Science & Government* (pp. 178-181)
Walker and Co.
720 Fifth Ave.
New York, NY 10019   Phone: (212)265-3632
1990. Describes jobs in different industries and includes interviews with people working in related occupations. Presents employment outlook, preferred geographic location, entry-level opportunities, career paths, job responsibilities, advancement, personal and professional qualifications, salaries, working conditions, material for further reading, and associations.

★175★
"Manufactured Products" in *Career Choices for the 90's for Students of Psychology* (pp. 198-201)
Walker and Co.
720 Fifth Ave.
New York, NY 10019   Phone: (212)265-3632
1990. Describes jobs in different industries and includes interviews with people working in related occupations. Presents employment outlook, preferred geographic location, entry-level opportunities, career paths, job responsibilities, advancement, personal and professional qualifications, salaries, working conditions, material for further reading, and associations.

★176★
"Manufactured Products (Sales)" in *The Encyclopedia of Career Choices for the 1990s: A Guide to Entry Level Jobs* (pp. 780-783)
Walker and Co.
720 Fifth Ave.
New York, NY 10019   Phone: (212)265-3632
1991. Describes entry-level opportunities in 42 career fields for college graduates. Each chapter covers a single career field, including an overview, employment outlook, major employers, tips on entering the field, international job opportunities, functional job areas with personal and professional qualifications, career paths, job responsibilities, advancement possibilities, salaries, and working conditions. Lists related sources of information.

★177★
"Manufactured Sales" in *Career Choices for the 90's for Students of Business* (pp. 169-172)
Walker and Co.
720 Fifth Ave.
New York, NY 10019   Phone: (212)265-3632
1990. Describes jobs in different industries and includes interviews with people working in related occupations. Presents employment outlook, preferred geographic location, entry-level opportunities, career paths, job responsibilities, advancement, personal and professional qualifications, salaries, working conditions, material for further reading, and associations.

★178★
The Manufacturers' Agent
Manufacturers' Agents National Association
23016 Mill Creek Rd.
PO Box 3467
Laguna Hills, CA 92654   Phone: (714)859-4040
This five-page leaflet covers duties, personal qualifications, working conditions, education, training, earnings, and employment outlook.

★179★
"Manufacturers' and Wholesale Sales Representatives" in *Occupational Outlook Handbook* (pp. 232-234)
Superintendent of Documents
U.S. Government Printing Office
Washington, DC 20402   Phone: (202)783-3238
Biennial; latest edition, 1990-91. Encyclopedia of careers describing more than 250 occupations and comprising about 86 percent of all jobs in the economy. Occupations that require lengthy education or training are given the most attention. For each occupation, the handbook describes job duties, working conditions, training, educational preparation, personal qualities, advancement possibilities, job outlook, earnings, and sources of additional information.

★180★
Manufacturer's Representative
Careers, Inc.
PO Box 135
Largo, FL 34649-0135   Phone: (813)584-7333
1992. Eight-page brief offering the definition, history, duties, working conditions, personal qualifications, educational requirements, earnings, hours, employment outlook, advancement possibilities, and related occupations.

Manufacturers' and Wholesale Sales Representatives

★181★
"Manufacturer's Representative/Sporting Good or Equipment Company" in *Career Opportunities in the Sports Industry* (pp. 172-174)
Facts on File, Inc.
460 Park Avenue, S.
New York, NY 10016   Phone: (212)683-2244
Shelly Field. 1991. Describes various jobs in the sports industry. Each occupational profile covers job duties, employment outlook, career paths, salaries, skills, and educational preparation. Offers tips for entering the field.

★182★
Manufacturer's Representatives
Chronicle Guidance Publications, Inc.
PO Box 1190
Moravia, NY 13118-1190   Phone: (315)497-0330
1988. This career brief describes the nature of the work, working conditions, hours and earnings, education and training, licensure, certification, unions, personal qualifications, social and psychological factors, employment outlook, entry methods, advancement, and related occupations. **Toll-free/Additional Phone Number(s):** 800-622-7284.

★183★
Manufacturers Sales Representative
Vocational Biographies, Inc.
PO Box 31, Dept. VF10
Sauk Centre, MN 56378   Phone: (612)352-6516
1991. This pamphlet profiles a person working in the job. Includes information about job duties, working conditions, places of employment, educational preparation, labor market outlook, and salaries. **Toll-free/Additional Phone Number(s):** 800-255-0752.

★184★
"Manufacturer's Sales Representative" in *VGM's Careers Encyclopedia* (pp. 257-259)
National Textbook Co.
4255 W. Touhy Co.
Lincolnwood, IL 60646   Phone: (312)679-5500
Third edition, 1991. Contains two- to five-page descriptions of 200 managerial, professional, technical, trade, and service occupations. Each profile includes job duties, places of employment, qualifications, educational preparation, training, employment potential, advancement, income, and additional sources of information.

★185★
"Manufacturer's Sales Representative" in *VGM's Handbook of Business and Management Careers* (pp. 59-61)
National Textbook Co.
4255 W. Touhy Ave.
Lincolnwood, IL 60646   Phone: (312)679-5500
Craig T. Norback, editor. 1990. Contains 43 two-page occupational profiles describing job duties, places of employment, working conditions, qualifications, education, employment outlook, and income.

★186★
"Manufacturers' Sales Representatives" in *Jobs! What They Are...Where They Are...What They Pay* (p. 281)
Simon & Schuster, Inc.
Simon & Schuster Bldg.
1230 Avenue of the Americas
New York, NY 10020   Phone: (212)698-7000
Robert O. Snelling and Anne M. Snelling. Revised edition, 1989. Profiles 241 occupations, describing duties and responsibilities, educational preparation, earnings, employment opportunities, training, and qualifications.

★187★
"Manufacturers' Sales Representatives" in Volume 4 of *Career Discovery Encyclopedia* (pp. 52-53)
J.G. Ferguson Publishing Co.
200 W. Monroe
Chicago, IL 60606   Phone: (312)580-5480
E. Russell Primm, editor-in-chief. 1990. Contains two-page articles on 504 occupations. Each article describes job duties, earnings, and educational and training requirements.

★188★
"Manufacturers' Sales Worker" in *Marketing and Distribution*, Volume 10 of *Career Information Center* (pp. 73-74)
Glencoe/Macmillan
15319 Chatsworth St.
Mission Hills, CA 91345   Phone: (818)898-1391
Richard Lidz and Dale Anderson, editorial directors. Fourth edition, 1990. For 600 occupations, describes job duties, entry-level requirements, education and training needed, advancement possibilities, employment outlook, earnings and benefits. The set is divided into 12 volumes. Each volume includes jobs related under a broad career field. Volume 13 is the index. **Facsimile Number:** (818)365-5489.

★189★
"Manufacturers' Sales Workers" in *Opportunities in Vocational and Technical Careers* (pp. 68-69)
National Textbook Co.
4255 W. Touhy Ave.
Lincolnwood, IL 60646   Phone: (312)679-5500
Adrian A. Paradis. 1987. Describes careers which can be prepared for by attending a private vocational or proprietary school—office employee, sales worker, service worker, health services, mechanic, craftworker, and technician. Covers employment outlook, job duties, and salaries. Offers career planning advice.

★190★
"Manufacturers' Sales Workers" in Volume 3 of *The Encyclopedia of Careers and Vocational Guidance* (pp. 153-158)
J.G. Ferguson Publishing Co.
200 W. Monroe
Chicago, IL 60606   Phone: (312)580-5480
William E. Hopke, editor-in-chief. Eighth edition, 1990. Four-volume set that profiles 500 occupations and describes job trends in 76 industries. Includes career description, educational requirements, history of the job, methods of entry, advancement, employment outlook, earnings, working conditions, social and psychological factors, and sources of additional information.

★191★
"Manufacturer's Salespeople: Selling Goods" in *Careers for Women Without College Degrees* (pp. 250-253)
McGraw-Hill Publishing Co.
11 W. 19th St.
New York, NY 10011 Phone: (212)337-6010

Beatryce Nivens. 1988. Career planning and job hunting guide containing information on decision-making, skills assessment, and resumes for career changers. Profiles careers with the best occupational outlook. Describes the work, educational preparation, employment outlook, salaries, and required skills.

★192★
"Manufacturer's Salesperson" in *College Board Guide to Jobs and Career Planning* (pp. 137-138)
College Entrance Examination Board
45 Columbus Ave.
New York, NY 10023-6992 Phone: (212)713-8000

Joyce Slayton Mitchell. 1990. Career planning guide written for high school and college students. Covers 100 careers in 15 occupational groups. Provides job description, educational preparation needed, salaries, related careers, and sources of additional information. Includes information about the 90's labor market.

★193★
"Manufacturing Reps" in *The New York Times Career Planner* (pp. 237-240)
Times Books
201 E. 50th St.
New York, NY 10022 Phone: (213)751-2600

Elizabeth M. Fowler. 1987. Offers career planning and job hunting advice for the college graduate. Surveys labor market trends. Contains "inside" information on professional careers including educational preparation, employment opportunities, and salaries.

★194★
Medical Equipment Sales
Vocational Biographies, Inc.
PO Box 31, Dept. VF10
Sauk Centre, MN 56378 Phone: (612)352-6516

1989. This pamphlet profiles a person working in the job. Includes information about job duties, working conditions, places of employment, educational preparation, labor market outlook, and salaries. **Toll-free/Additional Phone Number(s):** 800-255-0752.

★195★
Opportunities in Sales Careers
National Textbook Co.
4255 W. Touhy Ave.
Lincolnwood, IL 60646 Phone: (312)679-5500

Ralph M. Dahm and James Brescoli. 1988. Surveys jobs in sales and describes the skills needed to succeed. Covers the nature of the work, employment outlook, educational preparation, and training, salary, and rewards of the work.

★196★
"Pharmaceutical Sales Representative" in *Opportunities in Pharmacy Careers* (pp. 106-108)
National Textbook Co.
4255 W. Touhy Ave.
Lincolnwood, IL 60646 Phone: (312)679-5500

Fred B. Gable. 1990. Surveys the wide variety of career options available to pharmacists including community, industrial, and public pharmacy. Covers job duties, licensure, and salaries. Provides in-depth information about pharmaceutical education including high school preparation, and pharmacy school admissions and curriculum.

★197★
"Sales Representative, Wholesale Distribution" in *Occu-Facts: Information on 565 Careers in Outline Form* (p. 11.13)
Careers, Inc.
P.O. Box 135
1211 Tenth St., S.W.
Largo, FL 33640 Phone: (813)584-7333

Elizabeth Handville. Biennial, 1989-90 edition. Each one-page occupational profile describes duties, working conditions, physical surroundings and demands, aptitudes, temperament, educational requirements, employment outlook, earnings, and places of employment.

★198★
Sales Representatives, Wholesale Distribution
Careers, Inc.
PO Box 135
Largo, FL 34649-0135 Phone: (813)584-7333

1992. Eight-page brief offering the definition, history, duties, working conditions, personal qualifications, educational requirements, earnings, hours, employment outlook, advancement possibilities, and related occupations.

★199★
Video Career Library - Marketing and Sales
Careers, Inc.
1211 10th St., SW
PO Box 135
Largo, FL 34649-0135 Phone: (813)584-7333

Videocassette. 1990. Part of the Video Career Library covering 165 occupations. Shows actual workers on the job. Includes sales representatives.

★200★
"Wholesale and Retail Trade" in *The Encyclopedia of Career Choices for the 1990s: A Guide to Entry Level Jobs* (pp. 242-243)
Walker and Co.
720 Fifth Ave.
New York, NY 10019 Phone: (212)265-3632

1991. Describes entry-level opportunities in 42 career fields for college graduates. Each chapter covers a single career field, including an overview, employment outlook, major employers, tips on entering the field, international job opportunities, functional job areas with personal and professional qualifications, career paths, job responsibilities, advancement possibilities, salaries, and working conditions. Lists related sources of information.

★201★
"Wholesale Sales Worker" in *Marketing and Distribution*, Volume 10 of *Career Information Center* (pp. 65-67)
Glencoe/Macmillan
15319 Chatsworth St.
Mission Hills, CA 91345 Phone: (818)898-1391

Richard Lidz and Dale Anderson, editorial directors. Fourth edition, 1990. For 600 occupations, describes job duties, entry-level requirements, education and training needed, advancement possibilities, employment outlook, earnings and benefits. The set is divided into 12 volumes. Each volume includes jobs related under a broad career field. Volume 13 is the index. **Facsimile Number:** (818)365-5489.

Manufacturers' and Wholesale Sales Representatives

★202★
"Wholesale Sales Workers" in Volume 6 of *Career Discovery Encyclopedia* (pp. 158-159)
J.G. Ferguson Publishing Co.
200 W. Monroe
Chicago, IL 60606　　　　　　　　　Phone: (312)580-5480
E. Russell Primm, editor-in-chief. 1990. Contains two-page articles on 504 occupations. Each article describes job duties, earnings, and educational and training requirements.

★203★
"Wholesale Trade Sales Representative" in *Guide to Careers Without College* (pp. 23-25)
Franklin Watts, Inc.
387 Park Avenue, S.
New York, NY 10016　　　　　　　　Phone: (212)686-7070
Kathleen S. Abrams. 1988. Discusses careers that do not require a college degree in fields such as health care, sales and marketing, and the building trades. Describes the work, employment opportunities, and training.

★204★
"Wholesale Trade Sales Representatives" in *Jobs! What They Are. . .Where They Are. . .What They Pay* (p. 284)
Simon & Schuster, Inc.
Simon & Schuster Bldg.
1230 Avenue of the Americas
New York, NY 10020　　　　　　　　Phone: (212)698-7000
Robert O. Snelling and Anne M. Snelling. Revised edition, 1989. Profiles 241 occupations, describing duties and responsibilities, educational preparation, earnings, employment opportunities, training, and qualifications.

★205★
"Wholesale Trade Sales Workers" in *Opportunities in Vocational and Technical Careers* (pp. 66-68)
National Textbook Co.
4255 W. Touhy Ave.
Lincolnwood, IL 60646　　　　　　　Phone: (312)679-5500
Adrian A. Paradis. 1987. Describes careers which can be prepared for by attending a private vocational or proprietary school—office employee, sales worker, service worker, health services, mechanic, craftworker, and technician. Covers employment outlook, job duties, and salaries. Offers career planning advice.

★206★
"Wholesale Trade Sales Workers" in Volume 3 of *The Encyclopedia of Careers and Vocational Guidance* (pp. 189-193)
J.G. Ferguson Publishing Co.
200 W. Monroe
Chicago, IL 60606　　　　　　　　　Phone: (312)580-5480
William E. Hopke, editor-in-chief. Eighth edition, 1990. Four-volume set that profiles 500 occupations and describes job trends in 76 industries. Includes career description, educational requirements, history of the job, methods of entry, advancement, employment outlook, earnings, working conditions, social and psychological factors, and sources of additional information.

★207★
Wholesalers and Distributors
Quiet Advantage
1949 South Manchester St. 34
Anaheim, CA 92802　　　　　　　　Phone: (714)748-1840
Videocassette. 1991. 28 mins. Defines and differentiates the duties and qualifications of wholesalers and distributors.

Associations

★208★
Bureau of Wholesale Sales Representatives
1819 Peachtree Rd. NE, Ste. 210
Atlanta, GA 30309　　　　　　　　　Phone: (404)351-7355
Membership: Professional organization for sales representatives of apparel, accessories, and western wear. **Purpose:** Emphasizes professional education, development, and image of members, and advocates legislative positions on their behalf. Local groups sponsor trade shows for retailers.

★209★
Distributive Education Clubs of America (DECA)
1908 Association Dr.
Reston, VA 22091　　　　　　　　　Phone: (703)860-5000
Membership: High school juniors and seniors; junior college students interested in the field of marketing and distribution (retailing and wholesaling) as a vocation. **Publications:** *DECA Advisor*, 5/year. ● *DECA Guide*, annual. ● *New Dimensions*, quarterly.

★210★
Manufacturers' Agents National Association (MANA)
23016 Mill Creek Rd.
PO Box 3467
Laguna Hills, CA 92654　　　　　　　Phone: (714)859-4040
Membership: Manufacturers' agents in all fields representing two or more manufacturers on a commission basis; associate members are manufacturers and others interested in improving the agent-principal relationship. **Purpose:** Maintains code of ethics and rules of business and professional conduct; maintains list of attorneys and accountants experienced in agency matters; issues model standard form of agreement. **Publications:** *Agency Sales Magazine*, monthly. ● *Annual Directory of Members*. ● *Confidential Newsletter*, quarterly. ● *Financial Fax*, monthly. ● *MANA Membership Directory of Manufacturers' Sales Agencies*, annual. ● *Manufacturers' Agents National Association—Special Report*, periodic. ● Also publishes special announcements.

Standards/Certification Agencies

★211★
Manufacturers' Agents National Association (MANA)
23016 Mill Creek Rd.
PO Box 3467
Laguna Hills, CA 92654　　　　　　　Phone: (714)859-4040
Maintains code of ethics and rules of business and professional conduct; issues model standard form of agreement.

Basic Reference Guides and Handbooks

★212★
DECA Guide
Distributive Education Clubs of America (DECA)
1908 Association Dr.
Reston, VA 22091　　　　　　　　　Phone: (703)860-5000
Annual. Resource guide covering insurance, membership, and competitive events programs; catalog of instructional materials; scholarship information.

Periodicals

★213★
Agency Sales Magazine
Manufacturers' Agents National Assn.
23016 Mill Creek Rd.
PO Box 3467
Laguna Hills, CA 92654　　　　　Phone: (714)859-4040
Bert Holtje, Editor. Monthly. Magazine for manufacturers' agents & manufacturers. Includes tax developments and tips; management aids for manufacturers and agents; legal bulletins; trend-identifying market data; classified ads; industry trade show calendar, and new product information.

★214★
American Salesman
National Research Bureau, Inc.
424 N. 3rd St.
Burlington, IA 52601-5224　　　　Phone: (319)752-5415
Barbara Boeding, Editor. Monthly. Salesmanship magazine. **Facsimile Number:** (319)752-3421.

★215★
ARW Counterline
Air-Conditioning and Refrigeration Wholesalers Association
6360 NW 5th Way, Ste. 202
Ft. Lauderdale, FL 33309-6128　　Phone: (305)771-1000
Editor(s): Charles L. Willits. Quarterly. Carries informational and motivational articles to help sales personnel generate customer loyalty, handle customer complaints, and to increase sales. **Facsimile Number:** (305)491-8100.

★216★
ARW Wholesaler News
Air-Conditioning and Refrigeration Wholesalers Association (ARW)
6360 NW 5th Way, No. 202
Ft. Lauderdale, FL 33309-6128　　Phone: (305)771-1000
Editor(s): N.F. Aramino. Bimonthly. Focuses on association news and industry information of concern to member wholesalers and suppliers. Recurring features include information on Association programs and services, notices of educational materials available, a calendar of events, and news of members. **Facsimile Number:** (305)491-8100.

★217★
Bureau News
Bureau of Wholesale Sales Representatives
1819 Peachtree Rd. NE, Ste. 210
Atlanta, GA 30309　　　　　　　Phone: (404)351-7355
Monthly. Newspaper (tabloid) presenting organizational and legislative news pertinent to wholesale apparel sales reps. **Facsimile Number:** (404)352-5298.

★218★
Bureau of Wholesale Sales Representatives News
1819 Peachtree St., Ste. 210
Atlanta, GA 30309　　　　　　　Phone: (404)351-7355
Juanna Harper, Editor. Monthly Clothing industry newspaper. **Facsimile Number:** (404)352-5298.

★219★
DECA Advisor
Distributive Education Clubs of America (DECA)
1908 Association Dr.
Reston, VA 22091　　　　　　　Phone: (703)860-5000
5/year. Newsletter on teaching aids, surveys, corporation support, scholarships, and special events. Includes teaching guide.

★220★
Health of the Rep Newsletter
United Association of Manufacturers' Representatives (UAMR)
PO Box 3407
Laguna Hills, CA 92654　　　　　Phone: (714)859-6363
Editor(s): Karen Kittrell Mazzola. Monthly. Provides manufacturers' representatives "the latest tips on how to stay healthy." Carries information on various diseases and a list of related publications. **Facsimile Number:** (714)859-9131.

★221★
Idea Source Guide
Bramlee, Inc.
PO Box 366
Devon, PA 19333
Editor(s): Fred Davis. Monthly. Supplies ideas for premiums, incentives, sales promotions and merchandising.

★222★
MANA Agency Sales Magazine
Manufacturers' Agents National Association (MANA)
23016 Mill Creek Rd.
PO Box 3467
Laguna Hills, CA 92654　　　　　Phone: (714)859-4040
Monthly. Contains how-to articles for manufacturers' agents and manufacturers. Includes book reviews, industry calendar, and *RepLetter* a monthly supplemental newsletter.

★223★
MANA Confidential Newsletter
Manufacturers' Agents National Association (MANA)
23016 Mill Creek Rd.
PO Box 3467
Laguna Hills, CA 92654　　　　　Phone: (714)859-4040
Quarterly.

★224★
MANA Financial Fax
Manufacturers' Agents National Association (MANA)
23016 Mill Creek Rd.
PO Box 3467
Laguna Hills, CA 92654　　　　　Phone: (714)859-4040
Monthly. Tax information newsletter covering all facets of accounting situations of manufacturers' agencies.

★225★
Manufacturers Representatives of America—Newsline
Manufacturers Representatives of America
PO Box 150229
Arlington, TX 76015-6229　　　　Phone: (817)465-5511
Editor(s): William R. Bess. Quarterly. Published for member independent manufacturers' representatives handling sanitary supplies and paper and plastic disposable products. Carries articles to help improve agent sales skills, market coverage, and customer service, and to help establish more effective agent/principal communications. Recurring features include news of members, a calendar of events, job listings, notices of publications available, news of educational opportunities, and a column titled President's Report.

★226★
NAW Report
National Association of Wholesaler-Distributors (NAW)
1725 K St. NW, 7th Fl.
Washington, DC 20006   Phone: (202)872-0885
Editor(s): Philip B. Jaffa. Monthly. Publishes information on government issues and actions affecting wholesaler-distributors specifically and the business community generally. Recurring features include reports on federal legislative and regulatory developments; legal and insurance trends; industry research and statistics; and business services offered through the association's group purchasing program.

★227★
New Dimensions
Distributive Education Clubs of America (DECA)
1908 Association Dr.
Reston, VA 22091   Phone: (703)860-5000
Quarterly. Magazine for high school and college students of marketing, merchandising, and management.

★228★
Personal Selling Power
Personal Selling Power, Inc.
1127 International Pkwy.
PO Box 5467
Fredericksburg, VA 22403   Phone: (703)752-7000
L.B. Gschwandtner, Editor. Gerhard Gschwandtner, Publisher. 8x/yr. Magazine presenting motivational and sales skills and techniques for sales and marketing executives. **Facsimile Number:** (703)752-7001.

★229★
The Rep Travel Newsletter
United Association of Manufacturers' Representatives (UAMR)
133 Terrace Trail, W.
Lake Quivira, KS 66106   Phone: (913)268-9466
Editor(s): Charles A. Kittrell. Monthly. Provides business and vacation travel tips for manufacturers' representatives. Includes information on tours and travel discounts.

★230★
Rep World
Albee-Campbell, Inc.
806 Penn Ave.
Sinking Spring, PA 19608   Phone: (215)678-3361
Editor(s): Thomas C. Reinhart. Quarterly. Helps manufacturers' representatives "locate and appoint qualified Rep agencies according to geographic territory and product line compatibility." Shares ideas on direct mail, public relations, telemarketing, imprinted advertising specialities, and company brochures. Also concerned with trade shows, media advertising, line cards, and lead follow-up. Recurring features include book reviews and news of seminars.

★231★
RepLetter
Manufacturers' Agents National Association (MANA)
23016 Mill Creek Rd.
PO Box 3467
Laguna Hills, CA 92654   Phone: (714)859-4040
A monthly supplemental newsletter for sales executives who use manufacturers agents.

★232★
Retailing News
Martin Stanley Publishing, Inc.
248 W. Cerritos Ave.
Anaheim, CA 92805   Phone: (714)635-9774
Martin Barsky, Editor and Publisher. Monthly. Trade magazine (tabloid) reaching dealers, retailers, manufacturers, manufacturing reps, and distributors in the consumer electronics and major appliance industries.

★233★
RWDSU Record
Retail, Wholesale and Dept. Store Union—AFL-CIO
30 E. 29th St.
New York, NY 10016   Phone: (212)684-5300
Stuart Applebaum, Editor. 6x/yr. Labor union newspaper.

★234★
Sales & Marketing Training
National Society of Sales Training Executives
Executive Business Media, Inc.
825 Old Country Rd.
PO Box 1500
Westbury, NY 11590   Phone: (708)990-0555
Robert Moran, Editor. Quarterly. Professional magazine. **Facsimile Number:** (516)334-3059.

★235★
Salesman's Insider
Marv Q. Modell Associates
6009 Montgomery Corner
San Jose, CA 95135-1431   Phone: (408)270-4526
Editor(s): Marv Q. Modell. Monthly. Concerned with selling techniques and methodology in all sales areas. Tracks new sales developments, trends, and profit opportunities. Details negotiatineg process with "tips that work".

★236★
Salesmanship
Dartnell Corp.
4660 Ravenswood
Chicago, IL 60640   Phone: (312)561-4000
Editor(s): R.S. Minor. Biweekly. Offers sales ideas and inspiration, samples of letters designed to promote sales, and articles on topics related to sales training. Recurring features include sections titled Objections Clinic and Sales Letters Clinic. **Toll-free/Additional Phone Number(s):** 800-621-5463. **Facsimile Number:** (312)561-3801.

★237★
Supply House Times
Horton Publishing Co.
7574 N. Lincoln Ave.
Skokie, IL 60077   Phone: (708)677-2707
Greg Cassel, Editor. Monthly. Trade magazine for wholesalers in plumbing, heating, cooling, piping, and water systems. Areas of major emphasis include: warehousing, materials handling, inventory control, accounting, data processing, merchandising, salesmanship and general management. **Facsimile Number:** (708)677-5003.

★238★
UAMR Confidential Bulletin
United Association of Manufacturers' Representatives (UAMR)
133 Terrace Trail, W.
Lake Quivira, KS 66106   Phone: (913)268-9466
Editor(s): H. Keith Kittrell and Karen Mazzola. Monthly. Covers product lines offered for representation in all fields. Provides details of the company and product, type of accounts

to be serviced, and the areas open for representation. **Facsimile Number:** (714)859-9131.

★239★
UAMR Newsletter
United Association of Manufacturers' Representatives (UAMR)
133 Terrace Trail, W.
Lake Quivira, KS 66106　　　　Phone: (913)268-9466
Editor(s): H. Keith Kittrell. Monthly. Discusses topics of interest to manufacturers' representatives, "with particular emphasis on selling, tax advantages, world conditions and happenings in Washington.". Recurring features include news of members and the association.

Meetings and Conventions

★240★
Bureau of Wholesale Sales Representatives
1819 Peachtree Rd. NE, Ste. 210
Atlanta, GA 30309　　　　Phone: (404)351-7355
Frequency: Annual conference. **Facsimile Number:** (404)728-1520.

★241★
Distributive Education Clubs of America Career Development Conference (DECA)
1908 Association Dr.
Reston, VA 22091　　　　Phone: (703)860-5000
Frequency: Annual.

★242★
International Mass Retail Association Convention and Exhibits
International Mass Retail Association
1901 Pennsylvania Ave., NW, Ste. 1000
Washington, DC 20006-3455　　　　Phone: (202)861-0774
1992; May 16-20; Orlando, FL • 1993; May 01-05; Orlando, FL.

★243★
Manufacturers' Agents National Association (MANA)
23016 Mill Creek Rd.
PO Box 3467
Laguna Hills, CA 92654　　　　Phone: (714)859-4040
Frequency: Quarterly seminar usually held in February, May, September, and November.

★244★
National Agri-Marketing Association Conference
Agri Marketing
6201 Howard St.
Niles, IL 60648　　　　Phone: (708)647-1200
1992; Apr. 05-08; Kansas City, MO • 1993; Apr. 09-22; Kissimmee, FL • 1994; Apr. 06-09; Indianapolis, IN. **Facsimile Number:** (708)647-7055.

★245★
Sales and Marketing Show and Conference
Flagg Management, Inc.
369 Lexington Ave.
New York, NY 10017　　　　Phone: (212)286-0333
Facsimile Number: (212)286-0086.

Real Estate Agents, Brokers, and Appraisers

Real estate agents, brokers, and appraisers assist people in the purchase or sale of a home, or an investment property. They have a thorough knowledge of the housing market in their community, which neigborhoods will best fit their clients' budgets, local zoning and tax laws, and where to obtain financing for the purchase. They also may act as a medium for price negotiations between buyer and seller. Brokers are independent business people who not only sell real estate owned by others, but also rent and manage properties and develop new building projects. Real estate agents are generally independent sales workers who provide their services to a licensed broker on a contract basis. In return, the broker pays agents a portion of the commission earned from property sold through the firm by the agent. Agents' and brokers' jobs involve more than just selling. They must have property to sell to begin with, so spend much time obtaining "listings" (owner agreements to place properties for sale with the firm). Real estate appraisers, objective experts with no vested interest in the property, give unbiased estimates of the quality, value, and best use of a specific property. They do this by compiling information on a property's construction, condition, functional design, and by searching public records of sales, leases, assessments, and other transactions.

$alaries

Commissions on sales are the main source of earnings of real estate brokers and agents. Few receive a salary.

Median gross income of real estate brokers (after expenses)	$41,000/year
Broker associates (licensed brokers who do not have their own firm)	$28,500/year

Employment Outlook

Growth rate until the year 2000: Average.

Real Estate Agents, Brokers, and Appraisers

Career Guides

★246★
Agents and Brokers
Quiet Advantage
1949 South Manchester St. 34
Anaheim, CA 92802   Phone: (714)748-1840
Videocassette. 1991. 28 mins. Defines and differentiates agents and brokers, their techniques and duties.

★247★
"Appraisal" in *Career Choices for the 90's for Students of Mathematics* (pp. 142-144)
Walker and Co.
720 Fifth Ave.
New York, NY 10019   Phone: (212)265-3632
1990. Describes jobs in different industries and includes interviews with people working in related occupations. Presents employment outlook, preferred geographic location, entry-level opportunities, career paths, job responsibilities, advancement, personal and professional qualifications, salaries, working conditions, material for further reading, and associations.

★248★
"Appraisal" in *Opportunities in Real Estate Careers* (pp. 81-85)
National Textbook Co.
4255 W. Touhy Ave.
Lincolnwood, IL 60646   Phone: (312)679-5500
Mariwyn Evans. 1988. Surveys the real estate industry and its jobs and related careers. Covers the work, academic preparation, future employment outlook, licensing, and financial compensation. Offers information about choosing a firm and job hunting.

★249★
"Appraisal" in *The Encyclopedia of Career Choices for the 1990s: A Guide to Entry Level Jobs* (pp. 750-752)
Walker and Co.
720 Fifth Ave.
New York, NY 10019   Phone: (212)265-3632
1991. Describes entry-level opportunities in 42 career fields for college graduates. Each chapter covers a single career field, including an overview, employment outlook, major employers, tips on entering the field, international job opportunities, functional job areas with personal and professional qualifications, career paths, job responsibilities, advancement possibilities, salaries, and working conditions. Lists related sources of information.

★250★
"Appraiser" in *Career Choices for the 90's for Students of Economics* (pp. 130-132)
Walker and Co.
720 Fifth Ave.
New York, NY 10019   Phone: (212)265-3632
1990. Describes jobs in different industries and includes interviews with people working in related occupations. Presents employment outlook, preferred geographic location, entry-level opportunities, career paths, job responsibilities, advancement, personal and professional qualifications, salaries, working conditions, material for further reading, and associations.

★251★
"Appraiser" in *Consumer, Homemaking, and Personal Services*, Volume 5 of *Career Information Center* (pp. 95-96)
Glencoe/Macmillan
15319 Chatsworth St.
Mission Hills, CA 91345   Phone: (818)898-1391
Richard Lidz and Dale Anderson, editorial directors. Fourth edition, 1990. For 600 occupations, describes job duties, entry-level requirements, education and training needed, advancement possibilities, employment outlook, earnings and benefits. The set is divided into 12 volumes. Each volume includes jobs related under a broad career field. Volume 13 is the index. **Facsimile Number:** (818)365-5489.

★252★
"Assessors and Appraisers" in Volume 1 of *Career Discovery Encyclopedia* (pp. 64-65)
J.G. Ferguson Publishing Co.
200 W. Monroe
Chicago, IL 60606   Phone: (312)580-5480
E. Russell Primm, editor-in-chief. 1990. Contains two-page articles on 504 occupations. Each article describes job duties, earnings, and educational and training requirements.

★253★
"Assessors and Appraisers" in Volume 2 of *The Encyclopedia of Careers and Vocational Guidance* (pp. 44-48)
J.G. Ferguson Publishing Co.
200 W. Monroe
Chicago, IL 60606   Phone: (312)580-5480
William E. Hopke, editor-in-chief. Eighth edition, 1990. Four-volume set that profiles 500 occupations and describes job trends in 76 industries. Includes career description, educational requirements, history of the job, methods of entry, advancement, employment outlook, earnings, working conditions, social and psychological factors, and sources of additional information.

★254★
Associate Real Estate Broker
Vocational Biographies, Inc.
PO Box 31, Dept. VF10
Sauk Centre, MN 56378   Phone: (612)352-6516

1988. This pamphlet profiles a person working in the job. Includes information about job duties, working conditions, places of employment, educational preparation, labor market outlook, and salaries. **Toll-free/Additional Phone Number(s):** 800-255-0752.

★255★
"Business Realtors" in *The New York Times Career Planner* (pp. 139-141)
Times Books
201 E. 50th St.
New York, NY 10022   Phone: (213)751-2600

Elizabeth M. Fowler. 1987. Offers career planning and job hunting advice for the college graduate. Surveys labor market trends. Contains "inside" information on professional careers including educational preparation, employment opportunities, and salaries.

★256★
Career Opportunities
American Inst. of Real Estate Appraisers of the National Assoc. of Realtors
430 N. Michigan Ave.
Chicago, IL 60611-4088   Phone: (312)329-8559

1989. This eight-page booklet describes the work, needed skills, qualifications, educational requirements, income, and working conditions in real estate careers.

★257★
Careers in Real Estate
National Association of Realtors
430 N. MI Ave.
Chicago, IL 60611-4087   Phone: (312)329-8387

1990. This 30-page booklet explores the varied opportunities in real estate sales. Covers educational preparation, licensing requirements, continuing education, preferred skills and personal characteristics, places of employment, and employment outlook.

★258★
Hot Tips, Sneaky Tricks, and Last Ditch Tactics: An Insider's Guide to Getting Your First Corporate Job
John Wiley & Sons, Inc.
605 Third Ave.
New York, NY 10158   Phone: (212)850-6000

Jeff B. Speck. 1989. Written for college graduates who are looking for jobs in banking, consulting, accounting, insurance, real estate or the Fortune 500. Offers tips on surviving the standardized selection process used by large companies.

★259★
"Opportunities in Marketing & Sales" in *Travel and Hospitality Career Directory* (pp. 66-68)
Career Press, Inc.
PO Box 34
62 Beverly Rd.
Hawthorne, NJ 07507   Phone: (201)427-0229

Ronald W. Fry, editor. 1989. Offers advice on career planning and job hunting in hotel, travel, and related industries. Lists companies offering entry level positions in airlines, convention and visitors' bureaus, foreign tourist boards, hotels, travel agencies, car rental firms, and cruise lines. Lists travel and hospitality associations and trade publications.

★260★
Opportunities in Real Estate Careers
National Textbook Co.
4255 W. Touhy Ave.
Lincolnwood, IL 60646   Phone: (312)679-5500

Mariwyn Evans. 1988. Surveys the real estate industry and its jobs and related careers. Covers the work, academic preparation, future employment outlook, licensing, and financial compensation. Offers information about choosing a firm and job hunting.

★261★
"Real Estate" in *Career Choices for the 90's for Students of Business* (pp. 131-154)
Walker and Co.
720 Fifth Ave.
New York, NY 10019   Phone: (212)265-3632

1990. Describes jobs in different industries and includes interviews with people working in related occupations. Presents employment outlook, preferred geographic location, entry-level opportunities, career paths, job responsibilities, advancement, personal and professional qualifications, salaries, working conditions, material for further reading, and associations.

★262★
"Real Estate" in *Career Choices for the 90's for Students of Economics* (pp. 122-145)
Walker and Co.
720 Fifth Ave.
New York, NY 10019   Phone: (212)265-3632

1990. Describes jobs in different industries and includes interviews with people working in related occupations. Presents employment outlook, preferred geographic location, entry-level opportunities, career paths, job responsibilities, advancement, personal and professional qualifications, salaries, working conditions, material for further reading, and associations.

★263★
"Real Estate" in *Career Choices for the 90's for Students of Mathematics* (pp. 134-157)
Walker and Co.
720 Fifth Ave.
New York, NY 10019   Phone: (212)265-3632

1990. Describes jobs in different industries and includes interviews with people working in related occupations. Presents employment outlook, preferred geographic location, entry-level opportunities, career paths, job responsibilities, advancement, personal and professional qualifications, salaries, working conditions, material for further reading, and associations.

★264★
"Real Estate" in *Major Decisions: A Guide to College Majors* (p. 142)
Orchard House, Inc.
112 Balls Hill Rd.
Concord, MA 01742   Phone: (508)369-0467

Richard A. Blumenthal and Joseph A. Despres. 1990. Provides a one-page description of 155 college majors. Included under each major is a description, the plan of study, typical major courses, high school courses and career possibilities. **Facsimile Number:** (508)369-9472.

Real Estate Agents, Brokers, and Appraisers

★265★
"Real Estate" in *The Black Woman's Career Guide* (pp. 295-302)
Doubleday & Co., Inc.
666 Fifth Avenue
New York, NY 10103   Phone: (212)984-7561

Beatryce Nivens. Revised edition, 1987. Offers career planning and job hunting advice. Contains information on 20 different career areas and profiles women working in the field. Each occupational profile describes the work, career paths and earning potential.

★266★
"Real Estate" in Volume 1 of *The Encyclopedia of Careers and Vocational Guidance* (pp. 401-406)
J.G. Ferguson Publishing Co.
200 W. Monroe
Chicago, IL 60606   Phone: (312)580-5480

William E. Hopke, editor-in-chief. Eighth edition, 1990. Four-volume set that profiles 500 occupations and describes job trends in 76 industries. Includes career description, educational requirements, history of the job, methods of entry, advancement, employment outlook, earnings, working conditions, social and psychological factors, and sources of additional information.

★267★
"Real Estate Agent/Broker" in *VGM's Careers Encyclopedia* (pp. 395-397)
National Textbook Co.
4255 W. Touhy Ave.
Lincolnwood, IL 60646   Phone: (312)679-5500

Third edition, 1991. Contains two- to five-page descriptions of 200 managerial, professional, technical, trade, and service occupations. Each profile includes job duties, places of employment, qualifications, educational preparation, training, employment potential, advancement, income, and additional sources of information.

★268★
"Real Estate Agent/Broker" in *VGM's Handbook of Business and Management Careers* (pp. 81-83)
National Textbook Co.
4255 W. Touhy Ave.
Lincolnwood, IL 60646   Phone: (312)679-5500

Craig T. Norback, editor. 1990. Contains 43 two-page occupational profiles describing job duties, places of employment, working conditions, qualifications, education, employment outlook, and income.

★269★
"Real Estate Agents" in *Opportunities in Home Economics Careers* (pp. 95-96)
National Textbook Co.
4255 W. Touhy Ave.
Lincolnwood, IL 60646   Phone: (312)679-5500

Rhea Shields and Anna K. Williams. 1988. Describes the history of home economics and current trends affecting the field. Explores related careers in interior design, family relations, and home management. Covers the nature of the work, educational preparation, skills, employment outlook, places of employment, and salaries. Lists professional organizations and offers job hunting advice.

★270★
"Real Estate Agents" in *Opportunities in Vocational and Technical Careers* (pp. 64-66)
National Textbook Co.
4255 W. Touhy Ave.
Lincolnwood, IL 60646   Phone: (312)679-5500

Adrian A. Paradis. 1987. Describes careers which can be prepared for by attending a private vocational or proprietary school—office employee, sales worker, service worker, health services, mechanic, craftworker, and technician. Covers employment outlook, job duties, and salaries. Offers career plannning advice.

★271★
Real Estate Agents and Brokers
Chronicle Guidance Publications, Inc.
PO Box 1190
Moravia, NY 13118-1190   Phone: (315)497-0330

1989. This career brief describes the nature of the work, working conditions, hours and earnings, education and training, licensure, certification, unions, personal qualifications, social and psychological factors, employment outlook, entry methods, advancement, and related occupations. **Toll-free/Additional Phone Number(s):** 800-622-7284.

★272★
"Real Estate Agents and Brokers" in *Jobs! What They Are...Where They Are...What They Pay* (p. 286)
Simon & Schuster, Inc.
Simon & Schuster Bldg.
1230 Avenue of the Americas
New York, NY 10020   Phone: (212)698-7000

Robert O. Snelling and Anne M. Snelling. Revised edition, 1989. Profiles 241 occupations, describing duties and responsibilities, educational preparation, earnings, employment opportunities, training, and qualifications.

★273★
"Real Estate Agents and Brokers" in *101 Careers: A Guide to the Fastest-Growing Opportunities* (pp. 48-51)
John Wiley & Sons, Inc.
605 Third Ave.
New York, NY 10158   Phone: (212)850-6000

Michael Harkavy. 1990. Each occupational profile includes a job description, job titles, work environment, employment outlook, qualifications, personal skills, and earnings.

★274★
"Real Estate Agents and Brokers" in *The American Almanac of Jobs and Salaries* (pp. 552-553)
Avon Books
105 Madison Avenue
New York, NY 10016   Phone: (212)481-5600

John Wright and Edward J. Dwyer. Revised and updated, 1990. A comprehensive guide to the wages of hundreds of occupations in a wide variety of industries and organizations.

★275★
"Real Estate Agents and Brokers" in Volume 5 of *Career Discovery Encyclopedia* (pp. 132-133)
J.G. Ferguson Publishing Co.
200 W. Monroe
Chicago, IL 60606   Phone: (312)580-5480

E. Russell Primm, editor-in-chief. 1990. Contains two-page articles on 504 occupations. Each article describes job duties, earnings, and educational and training requirements.

★276★

★276★
"Real Estate Agents and Brokers" in Volume 3 of *The Encyclopedia of Careers and Vocational Guidance* (pp. 162-167)
J.G. Ferguson Publishing Co.
200 W. Monroe
Chicago, IL 60606   Phone: (312)580-5480
William E. Hopke, editor-in-chief. Eighth edition, 1990. Four-volume set that profiles 500 occupations and describes job trends in 76 industries. Includes career description, educational requirements, history of the job, methods of entry, advancement, employment outlook, earnings, working conditions, social and psychological factors, and sources of additional information.

★277★
"Real Estate Agents and Brokers: Sellers of the Land" in *Careers for Women Without College Degrees* (pp. 245-250)
McGraw-Hill Publishing Co.
11 W. 19th St.
New York, NY 10011   Phone: (212)337-6010
Beatryce Nivens. 1988. Career planning and job hunting guide containing information on decision-making, skills assessment, and resumes for career changers. Profiles careers with the best occupational outlook. Describes the work, educational preparation, employment outlook, salaries, and required skills.

★278★
"Real Estate Agents, Brokers, and Appraisers" in *Occupational Outlook Handbook* (pp. 234-236)
Superintendent of Documents
U.S. Government Printing Office
Washington, DC 20402   Phone: (202)783-3238
Biennial; latest edition, 1990-91. Encyclopedia of careers describing more than 250 occupations and comprising about 86 percent of all jobs in the economy. Occupations that require lengthy education or training are given the most attention. For each occupation, the handbook describes job duties, working conditions, training, educational preparation, personal qualities, advancement possibilities, job outlook, earnings, and sources of additional information.

★279★
"Real Estate and Construction" in *Jobs '91* (pp. 349-359)
Prentice Hall Press
1 Gulf & Western Plaza
New York, NY 10023   Phone: (212)373-8500
Kathryn Petras and Ross Petras. Annual, 1991. Discusses employment prospects and trends for 15 professional careers and 29 industries. Lists leading companies, associations, directories, and magazines.

★280★
Real Estate Appraiser
Careers, Inc.
PO Box 135
Largo, FL 34649-0135   Phone: (813)584-7333
1989. Two-page occupational summary card describing duties, working conditions, personal qualifications, training, earnings and hours, employment outlook, places of employment, related careers and where to write for more information.

★281★
"Real Estate Appraiser" in *Career Choices for the 90's for Students of Business* (pp. 139-141)
Walker and Co.
720 Fifth Ave.
New York, NY 10019   Phone: (212)265-3632
1990. Describes jobs in different industries and includes interviews with people working in related occupations. Presents employment outlook, preferred geographic location, entry-level opportunities, career paths, job responsibilities, advancement, personal and professional qualifications, salaries, working conditions, material for further reading, and associations.

★282★
"Real Estate Appraiser" in *Marketing and Distribution*, Volume 10 of *Career Information Center* (pp. 98-99)
Glencoe/Macmillan
15319 Chatsworth St.
Mission Hills, CA 91345   Phone: (818)898-1391
Richard Lidz and Dale Anderson, editorial directors. Fourth edition, 1990. For 600 occupations, describes job duties, entry-level requirements, education and training needed, advancement possibilities, employment outlook, earnings and benefits. The set is divided into 12 volumes. Each volume includes jobs related under a broad career field. Volume 13 is the index. **Facsimile Number:** (818)365-5489.

★283★
"Real Estate Appraiser" in *Occu-Facts: Information on 565 Careers in Outline Form* (p. 11.4)
Careers, Inc.
P.O. Box 135
1211 Tenth St., S.W.
Largo, FL 33640   Phone: (813)584-7333
Elizabeth Handville. Biennial, 1989-90 edition. Each one-page occupational profile describes duties, working conditions, physical surroundings and demands, aptitudes, temperament, educational requirements, employment outlook, earnings, and places of employment.

★284★
"Real Estate Appraiser" in *VGM's Careers Encyclopedia* (pp. 399-400)
National Textbook Co.
4255 W. Touhy Ave.
Lincolnwood, IL 60646   Phone: (312)679-5500
Third edition, 1991. Contains two- to five-page descriptions of 200 managerial, professional, technical, trade, and service occupations. Each profile includes job duties, places of employment, qualifications, educational preparation, training, employment potential, advancement, income, and additional sources of information.

★285★
"Real Estate Appraiser" in *VGM's Handbook of Business and Management Careers* (pp. 84-86)
National Textbook Co.
4255 W. Touhy Ave.
Lincolnwood, IL 60646   Phone: (312)679-5500
Craig T. Norback, editor. 1990. Contains 43 two-page occupational profiles describing job duties, places of employment, working conditions, qualifications, education, employment outlook, and income.

Real Estate Agents, Brokers, and Appraisers

★286★
Real Estate Appraisers
Chronicle Guidance Publications, Inc.
PO Box 1190
Moravia, NY 13118-1190 Phone: (315)497-0330
1990. This career brief describes the nature of the work, working conditions, hours and earnings, education and training, licensure, certification, unions, personal qualifications, social and psychological factors, employment outlook, entry methods, advancement, and related occupations. **Toll-free/Additional Phone Number(s):** 800-622-7284.

★287★
"Real Estate Appraisers" in *The New York Times Career Planner* (pp. 283-285)
Times Books
201 E. 50th St.
New York, NY 10022 Phone: (213)751-2600
Elizabeth M. Fowler. 1987. Offers career planning and job hunting advice for the college graduate. Surveys labor market trends. Contains "inside" information on professional careers including educational preparation, employment opportunities, and salaries.

★288★
"Real Estate Broker" in *Top Professions: The 100 Most Popular, Dynamic, and Profitable Careers in America Today* (pp. 68-69)
Peterson's Guides, Inc.
202 Carnegie Center
PO Box 2123
Princeton, NJ 08543-2123 Phone: (609)243-9111
Nicholas Basta. 1989. Includes occupations requiring a college or advanced degree. Describes job duties, earnings, some typical job titles, career opportunities at different degree levels, and lists related associations.

★289★
"Real Estate Careers" in *Transitions: Military Pathways to Civilian Careers* (pp. 137-140)
Rosen Publishing Group, Inc.
29 E. 21st St.
New York, NY 10010 Phone: (212)777-3017
Robert W. MacDonald. 1988. Describes how to make the best use of your military service to create a civilian career. Describes skills needed in civilian employment and compares them to skills acquired in the military. Covers career planning, job search, resume writing, and starting a small business. Lists many resources.

★290★
"Real Estate" in *The Career Connection II: A Guide to Technical Majors and Their Related Careers* (pp. 113-114)
ERIS
PO Box 7509
University Station
Provo, UT 84602-0509
Fred A. Rowe. 1988. Contains technical majors, such as automotive technology. Describes the major and the job. Lists high school and postsecondary school courses. Includes occupations related to the major, employment outlook, and starting salary.

★291★
"Real Estate" in *The Encyclopedia of Career Choices for the 1990s: A Guide to Entry Level Jobs* (pp. 742-765)
Walker and Co.
720 Fifth Ave.
New York, NY 10019 Phone: (212)265-3632
1991. Describes entry-level opportunities in 42 career fields for college graduates. Each chapter covers a single career field, including an overview, employment outlook, major employers, tips on entering the field, international job opportunities, functional job areas with personal and professional qualifications, career paths, job responsibilities, advancement possibilities, salaries, and working conditions. Lists related sources of information.

★292★
"Real Estate Sales" in *Career Choices for the 90's for Students of Business* (pp. 164-167)
Walker and Co.
720 Fifth Ave.
New York, NY 10019 Phone: (212)265-3632
1990. Describes jobs in different industries and includes interviews with people working in related occupations. Presents employment outlook, preferred geographic location, entry-level opportunities, career paths, job responsibilities, advancement, personal and professional qualifications, salaries, working conditions, material for further reading, and associations.

★293★
"Real Estate Sales" in *Career Choices for the 90's for Students of Communications and Journalism* (pp. 172-175)
Walker and Co.
720 Fifth Ave.
New York, NY 10019 Phone: (212)265-3632
1990. Describes jobs in different industries and includes interviews with people working in related occupations. Presents employment outlook, preferred geographic location, entry-level opportunities, career paths, job responsibilities, advancement, personal and professional qualifications, salaries, working conditions, material for further reading, and associations.

★294★
"Real Estate Sales" in *Opportunities in Property Management Careers* (pp. 101-105)
National Textbook Co.
4255 W. Touhy Ave.
Lincolnwood, IL 60646 Phone: (312)679-5500
Mariwyn Evans. 1990. Describes the past, present, and future of property management, job duties, entering the field, licensure, educational preparation, salary, and related careers. Lists books, periodicals, and associations.

★295★
"Real Estate Sales" in *The Encyclopedia of Career Choices for the 1990s: A Guide to Entry Level Jobs* (pp. 775-778)
Walker and Co.
720 Fifth Ave.
New York, NY 10019 Phone: (212)265-3632
1991. Describes entry-level opportunities in 42 career fields for college graduates. Each chapter covers a single career field, including an overview, employment outlook, major employers, tips on entering the field, international job opportunities, functional job areas with personal and professional qualifications, career paths, job responsibilities, advancement possibilities, salaries, and working conditions. Lists related sources of information.

★296★
"Real Estate Sales Worker and Broker" in *Marketing and Distribution*, Volume 10 of *Career Information Center* (pp. 75-76)
Glencoe/Macmillan
15319 Chatsworth St.
Mission Hills, CA 91345			Phone: (818)898-1391
Richard Lidz and Dale Anderson, editorial directors. Fourth edition, 1990. For 600 occupations, describes job duties, entry-level requirements, education and training needed, advancement possibilities, employment outlook, earnings and benefits. The set is divided into 12 volumes. Each volume includes jobs related under a broad career field. Volume 13 is the index. **Facsimile Number:** (818)365-5489.

★297★
Real Estate Salesperson
Careers, Inc.
PO Box 135
Largo, FL 34649-0135			Phone: (813)584-7333
1991. Two-page occupational summary card describing duties, working conditions, personal qualifications, training, earnings and hours, employment outlook, places of employment, related careers and where to write for more information.

★298★
"Real Estate Salesperson" in *College Board Guide to Jobs and Career Planning* (pp. 138-140)
College Entrance Examination Board
45 Columbus Ave.
New York, NY 10023-6992			Phone: (212)713-8000
Joyce Slayton Mitchell. 1990. Career planning guide written for high school and college students. Covers 100 careers in 15 occupational groups. Provides job description, educational preparation needed, salaries, related careers, and sources of additional information. Includes information about the 90's labor market.

★299★
"Real Estate Salesperson" in *Occu-Facts: Information on 565 Careers in Outline Form* (p. 11.5)
Careers, Inc.
P.O. Box 135
1211 Tenth St., S.W.
Largo, FL 33640			Phone: (813)584-7333
Elizabeth Handville. Biennial, 1989-90 edition. Each one-page occupational profile describes duties, working conditions, physical surroundings and demands, aptitudes, temperament, educational requirements, employment outlook, earnings, and places of employment.

★300★
"Real Estate: What's Hot, What's Not" in *Fast-Track Careers: A Guide to the Highest-Paying Jobs* (pp. 99-121)
John Wiley & Sons, Inc.
605 Third Ave.
New York, NY 10158			Phone: (212)850-6000
William Lewis and Nancy Schuman. 1987. Profiles eight glamourous and high paying careers describing entry-level opportunities, earnings, personal qualities, types of companies, educational preparation and training, and employment outlook. Lists prominent companies in each industry, typical jargon, and professional associations.

★301★
Video Career Library - Marketing and Sales
Careers, Inc.
1211 10th St., SW
PO Box 135
Largo, FL 34649-0135			Phone: (813)584-7333
Videocassette. 1990. Part of the Video Career Library covering 165 occupations. Shows actual workers on the job. Includes real estate agents and brokers.

★302★
Your Successful Real Estate Career
AMACOM
135 W. 50th St.
New York, NY 10020			Phone: (212)903-8089
Kenneth W. Edwards. 1987. Describes the work of real estate agents and brokers, skills needed, earnings, and licensure. Offers advice about job hunting and choosing a company. Surveys real estate related careers.

Associations

★303★
American Society of Appraisers (ASA)
PO Box 17265
Washington, DC 20041			Phone: (703)478-2228
Membership: Professional appraisal teaching, testing, and certifying society concerned with all property. **Purpose:** "To maintain recognition that members are qualified, objective, unbiased appraisers and advisors of property values; establish members' status as expert witnesses before courts, administrative tribunals, agencies, and other governmental and municipal authorities; attain recognition of the profession of value determination in property economics by educational and governmental institutions and bodies." Awards professional designation of A.S.A. to senior members of legal age, with at least five years' valuation experience, who have successfully passed written and oral examinations and other criteria; presents the F.A.S.A. designation to Fellows chosen from among the senior members by the society's board of governors in recognition of outstanding services to the society and the appraisal profession. Sponsors mandatory Recertification Program for all senior members. Offers a consumer information service to the public. **Publications:** *Business Valuation*, annual. • *Certified Professional Property Appraisers*, annual. • *Newsline*, bimonthly. • *Professional Appraisal Services*, annual. • *Valuation Journal*, semiannual. • Also publishes monographs, pamphlets, bibliography of appraisal literature, and manuals; also produces cassettes.

★304★
Appraisal Institute (AI)
225 N. Michigan Ave., Ste. 724
Chicago, IL 60601-7601			Phone: (312)819-2400
Membership: Professional society of real estate appraisers. **Purpose:** Awards designations of MAI to specialists in the appraisal of all types of properties and SRA to specialists in residential appraisals. Enforces standards of professional practice and ethics. Sponsors courses in preparation for state certification and licensing; offers continuing education programs for members. **Publications:** *Appraisal Institute Directory of Members*, annual. **Toll-free/Additional Phone Number(s):** (800)331-7732. **Facsimile Number:** (312)819-2360.

Real Estate Agents, Brokers, and Appraisers

★305★
National Association of Realtors (NAR)
430 N. Michigan Ave.
Chicago, IL 60611-4087 Phone: (312)329-8200
Membership: Federation of 50 state associations and 1848 local real estate boards whose members are called Realtors and Realtor-Associates. **Purpose:** Terms are registered by the association in the U.S. Patent and Trademark Office and in the states. Promotes education, high professional standards, and modern techniques in specialized real estate work such as brokerage, appraisal, property management, land development, industrial real estate, farm brokerage, and counseling. Conducts research programs. Sponsors a program of Realtor involvement in service projects in their communities. Maintains library of 20,000 books, 700 periodicals, and vertical file on real estate subjects. **Publications:** *The Executive Officer*, 5/year. • *Existing Home Sales*, monthly. • *National Association of Realtors—National Roster of Realtors*, annual. • *The Real Estate Index*, periodic. • *Real Estate Today*, 9/year. • *Realtor News*, biweekly. • Also publishes and produces *Subject Headings for Real Estate*, *Library Manual for Boards of Realtors*, booklets, statistical reports, lecture outlines, and promotional materials. **Facsimile Number:** (312)329-8576.

Standards/Certification Agencies

Real estate agents and brokers must be licensed in every state. All states require applicants to be high school graduates and at least 18 years old. Most states require additional classroom instruction. Real estate appraisers must also be licensed in each state, and must be "certified" to appraise federally-related transactions over $1,000,000. Certification usually involves appraisal experience and passing a written exam.

★306★
American Society of Appraisers (ASA)
PO Box 17265
Washington, DC 20041 Phone: (703)478-2228
Awards professional designation of A.S.A. to senior members of legal age, with at least five years' valuation experience, who have successfully passed written and oral examinations and other criteria. Sponsors mandatory Recertification Program for all senior members.

★307★
Appraisal Institute (AI)
225 N. Michigan Ave., Ste. 724
Chicago, IL 60601-7601 Phone: (312)819-2400
Awards designations of MAI to specialists in the appraisal of all types of properties and SRA to specialists in residential appraisals. Enforces standards of professional practice and ethics. Sponsors courses in preparation for state certification and licensing; offers continuing education programs for members.

★308★
The MAI Appraiser
Appraisal Institute
875 N. Michigan Ave., Ste. 2400
Chicago, IL 60611-1980 Phone: (312)335-4100
1991. Booklet describing requirements for certification for commercial and industrial real estate appraisers.

★309★
The SRA Appraiser
Appraisal Institute
875 N. Michigan Ave., Ste. 2400
Chicago, IL 60611-1980 Phone: (312)335-4100
This booklet describes requirements for certification for residential real estate appraisers.

Test Guides

★310★
Appraisal Investigator
National Learning Corp.
212 Michael Dr.
Syosset, NY 11791 Phone: (516)921-8888
Jack Rudman. Appraiser and Appraisal Investigator are two of the many guides that are part of the Career Examination Series No. 1. All examination guides in this series contain questions with answers. **Facsimile Number:** (516)921-8743. **Toll-free/Additional Phone Number(s):** 800-645-6337.

★311★
Appraiser
National Learning Corp.
212 Michael Dr.
Syosset, NY 11791 Phone: (516)921-8888
Jack Rudman. Part of the Career Examination Series No. 1. All examination guides in this series contain questions with answers. **Facsimile Number:** (516)921-8743. **Toll-free/Additional Phone Number(s):** 800-645-6337.

★312★
Assistant Real Estate Agent
National Learning Corp.
212 Michael Dr.
Syosset, NY 11791 Phone: (516)921-8888
Jack Rudman. Part of the Career Examination Series No. 1. All examination guides in this series contain questions with answers. **Facsimile Number:** (516)921-8743. **Toll-free/Additional Phone Number(s):** 800-645-6337.

★313★
Assistant Real Estate Appraiser
National Learning Corp.
212 Michael Dr.
Syosset, NY 11791 Phone: (516)921-8888
Jack Rudman. Part of the Career Examination Series No. 1. All examination guides in this series contain questions with answers. **Facsimile Number:** (516)921-8743. **Toll-free/Additional Phone Number(s):** 800-645-6337.

★314★
How to Prepare for Real Estate Licensing Examinations—Salesperson and Broker
Barron's Educational Series, Inc.
PO Box 8040
250 Wireless Blvd.
Hauppauge, NY 11788 Phone: (516)434-3311
J. Bruce Lindeman and Jack P. Friedman. Fourth edition. Applicable for all 50 states, this study guide contains over 1,000 questions, five practice tests, and special tests for contracts, closing statements, and the Rectangular survey. **Toll-free/Additional Phone Number(s):** 800-645-3476. (In NY call 800-257-5729).

★315★
Math Review for Real Estate License Examinations
Prentice Hall Press
Simon & Schuster Inc.
200 Old Tappan Rd.
Old Tappan, NJ 07675

Susan A. Shulman. Third edition, 1990. Includes over 100 practice problems with answers, coverage of the math of real estate financing, and two practice math exams with solutions. **Toll-free/Additional Phone Number(s):** 800-223-2348.

★316★
Q & A on the Real Estate License Examinations (RE)
National Learning Corp.
212 Michael Dr.
Syosset, NY 11791   Phone: (516)921-8888

Jack Rudman. Part of the Admission Test Series No. 3. Books in this series provide test practice and drill for actual professional certification and licensure tests. **Facsimile Number:** (516)921-8743. **Toll-free/Additional Phone Number(s):** 800-645-6337.

★317★
Real Estate Agent
National Learning Corp.
212 Michael Dr.
Syosset, NY 11791   Phone: (516)921-8888

Jack Rudman. Part of the Career Examination Series No. 1. All examination guides in this series contain questions with answers. **Facsimile Number:** (516)921-8743. **Toll-free/Additional Phone Number(s):** 800-645-6337.

★318★
Real Estate Aide
National Learning Corp.
212 Michael Dr.
Syosset, NY 11791   Phone: (516)921-8888

Jack Rudman. Part of the Career Examination Series No. 1. All examination guides in this series contain questions with answers. **Facsimile Number:** (516)921-8743. **Toll-free/Additional Phone Number(s):** 800-645-6337.

★319★
Real Estate Appraiser
National Learning Corp.
212 Michael Dr.
Syosset, NY 11791   Phone: (516)921-8888

Jack Rudman. Part of the Career Examination Series No. 1. All examination guides in this series contain questions with answers. **Facsimile Number:** (516)921-8743. **Toll-free/Additional Phone Number(s):** 800-645-6337.

★320★
Real Estate Assistant
National Learning Corp.
212 Michael Dr.
Syosset, NY 11791   Phone: (516)921-8888

Jack Rudman. Part of the Career Examination Series No. 1. All examination guides in this series contain questions with answers. **Facsimile Number:** (516)921-8743. **Toll-free/Additional Phone Number(s):** 800-645-6337.

★321★
Real Estate Broker
National Learning Corp.
212 Michael Dr.
Syosset, NY 11791   Phone: (516)921-8888

Jack Rudman. Part of the Career Examination Series No. 1. All examination guides in this series contain questions with answers. **Facsimile Number:** (516)921-8743. **Toll-free/Additional Phone Number(s):** 800-645-6337.

★322★
Real Estate Broker (REB)
National Learning Corp.
212 Michael Dr.
Syosset, NY 11791   Phone: (516)921-8888

Jack Rudman. Part of the Admission Test Series No. 3. Books in this series provide test practice and drill for actual professional certification and licensure tests. **Facsimile Number:** (516)921-8743. **Toll-free/Additional Phone Number(s):** 800-645-6337.

★323★
Real Estate License Examinations
Prentice Hall Press
Simon & Schuster Inc.
200 Old Tappan Rd.
Old Tappan, NJ 07675

Joseph H. Martin and Eve P. Steinberg. Third edition, 1990. Revised and expanded guide for nationwide real estate salesperson and broker exams. Covers all three national exams (ETS, ACT, and ASI). Includes five practice tests with answer keys and solutions to all math problems. **Toll-free/Additional Phone Number(s):** 800-223-2348.

★324★
Real Estate Salesman (RES)
National Learning Corp.
212 Michael Dr.
Syosset, NY 11791   Phone: (516)921-8888

Jack Rudman. Part of the Admission Test Series No. 3. Books in this series provide test practice and drill for actual professional certification and licensure tests. **Facsimile Number:** (516)921-8743. **Toll-free/Additional Phone Number(s):** 800-645-6337.

★325★
Senior Real Estate Agent
National Learning Corp.
212 Michael Dr.
Syosset, NY 11791   Phone: (516)921-8888

Jack Rudman. Part of the Career Examination Series No. 1. All examination guides in this series contain questions with answers. **Facsimile Number:** (516)921-8743. **Toll-free/Additional Phone Number(s):** 800-645-6337.

★326★
Senior Real Estate Appraiser
National Learning Corp.
212 Michael Dr.
Syosset, NY 11791   Phone: (516)921-8888

Jack Rudman. Part of the Career Examination Series No. 1. All examination guides in this series contain questions with answers. **Facsimile Number:** (516)921-8743. **Toll-free/Additional Phone Number(s):** 800-645-6337.

★327★
SuperCourse for Real Estate Licensing
Prentice Hall Press
Simon & Schuster Inc.
200 Old Tappan Rd.
Old Tappan, NJ 07675

Julie Garton-Good. First edition, 1990. Features include in-depth review of real estate principles and practices, strategies for both state and multistate exams, hundreds of practice questions, and seven full-length practice tests for salespersons

Real Estate Agents, Brokers, and Appraisers

and brokers; answers included. **Toll-free/Additional Phone Number(s):** 800-223-2348.

Educational Directories and Programs

★328★
Real Estate Schools Directory
American Business Directories, Inc.
American Business Information, Inc.
5711 S. 86th Circle
Omaha, NE 68127   Phone: (402)593-4600
Annual. 1,303. Entries include: Name, address, phone, size of advertisement, name of owner or manager, number of employees, year first in "Yellow Pages." Arrangement: Geographical. **Facsimile Number:** (402)331-1505.

Awards, Scholarships, Grants, and Fellowships

★329★
Commercial Transaction of the Year Award
Realtors National Marketing Institute - Residential Sales Council
430 N. Michigan Ave.
Chicago, IL 60611-4092   Phone: (312)670-3780
For recognition of the member of the Institute who helped to negotiate the most creative and outstanding commercial sales or lease transaction. The Campbell Trophy, donated by Realtor William J. Campbell of Kansas City, Missouri, is awarded annually. Administered by the Commercial-Investment Council of the Institute.

★330★
Distinguished Service Award
National Association of Realtors
Public Affairs Division
c/o Ms. Valerie Allridge
777 14th St., N.W.
Washington, DC 20005-3271   Phone: (202)383-1195
To recognize outstanding public service by a realtor over a period of years to the real estate industry and the community at the national, state and local levels. The person may not have served as president of the Association. An engraved statuette and jewelled lapel pin are awarded annually. Established in 1980. Additional information is available from the National Association of Realtors, Public Relations Division, c/o Dolores Rodgers, 430 N. Michigan Ave., Chicago, IL 60611-4087, phone: (312) 329-8874.

★331★
Exchange of the Year Award
Realtors National Marketing Institute - Residential Sales Council
430 N. Michigan Ave.
Chicago, IL 60611-4092   Phone: (312)670-3780
For recognition of the realtor who has negotiated the most outstanding commercial exchange of the year. Members of the Institute are eligible. The Snyder Trophy, donated by Realtor Clinton B. Snyder of Jersey City, New Jersey, is awarded annually. Administered by the Commercial-Investment Council of the Institute.

★332★
Realtor of the Year
National Association of Realtors
Public Affairs Division
c/o Ms. Valerie Allridge
777 14th St., N.W.
Washington, DC 20005-3271   Phone: (202)383-1195
For recognition of the most successful realtor in each of the 50 states of the United States, the District of Columbia, Puerto Rico, the Virgin Islands, and Guam. Awarded annually at a special luncheon during the national convention of the Association. Additional information is available from the National Association of Realtors, Public Relations Division, c/o Dolores Rodgers, 430 N. Michigan Ave., Chicago, IL 60611-4087, phone: (312) 329-8874.

★333★
Percy and Betty Wagner Award
American Institute of Real Estate Appraisers
430 N. Michigan Ave., 9th Fl.
Chicago, IL 60611-4088   Phone: (312)329-8559
To foster the training of persons in the science of real estate appraising and related subjects; to encourage improvements of appraisal techniques; to provide for needed research in the field of real estate valuation; to award scholarships to deserving students interested in the study of real estate valuation and related subjects; to give recognition to authors of published articles, writings, papers, or the like, which enhance or advance education and knowledge in appraising; and for any other purpose which the Trustees deem worthy to improve the image of the professional appraiser or which would further the work of the Institute. A monetary award of $1,000 and a plaque are presented annually at the November meeting. Established in 1972 in honor of Percy Wagner for his lifelong dedication to real estate and appraisal education, and for the support provided by his wife Betty.

Basic Reference Guides and Handbooks

★334★
ASA Business Valuation
American Society of Appraisers (ASA)
PO Box 17265
Washington, DC 20041   Phone: (703)478-2228
Annual. Directory.

★335★
Certified Professional Property Appraisers
American Society of Appraisers (ASA)
PO Box 17265
Washington, DC 20041   Phone: (703)478-2228
Annual. Directory.

★336★
How to Succeed As a Real Estate Salesperson: A Comprehensive Training Guide
Betterway Publications, Inc.
Box 219
Crozet, VA 22932   Phone: (804)823-5661
Lowell Hodgkings. 1990.

★337★
Library Manual for Boards of Realtors
National Association of Realtors (NAR)
430 N. Michigan Ave.
Chicago, IL 60611-4087   Phone: (312)329-8200

★338★
National Real Estate Directory
Real Estate Publications, Inc.
Box 20027
Tampa, FL 33622   Phone: (813)237-0484
Thomas J. Lucier, editor. Annual. About 22,500 federal and state agencies, offices, and departments related to the regulation of real estate; real estate associations, publications, and organizations. Entries include: Agency, association, department, or publication name, address, phone. Arrangement: Classified by type of organization, then geographical. **Toll-free/Additional Phone Number(s):** (800)356-2317.

★339★
Retirement Housing: Step by Step Guide for Investors, Developers, Accountants, & Other Professionals
John Wiley & Sons, Inc.
605 3rd Ave.
New York, NY 10158   Phone: (212)850-6000
Laughlin. 1989. Part of Real Estate for Professional Practitioners Series. **Facsimile Number:** (212)850-6088.

Periodicals

★340★
The Appraisal Journal
Appraisal Institutes
430 N. Michigan Ave.
Chicago, IL 60611-4088   Phone: (312)329-8559
Mark Harris, Managing Editor. Quarterly. Real estate appraisal magazine. **Facsimile Number:** (312)329-8354.

★341★
The Appraisal Review
National Assn. of Independent Fee Appraisers
7501 Murdoch Ave.
St. Louis, MO 63119   Phone: (314)781-6688
Donna Walter, Publications Editor. Quarterly.

★342★
Appraiser Gram
National Association of Independent Fee Appraisers
7501 Murdoch
St. Louis, MO 63119   Phone: (314)781-6689
Editor(s): Donna J. Walter. Monthly. Publishes information of interest to real estate appraisers, including news of association activities.

★343★
Appraiser News
Appraisal Institute
875 N. Michigan Ave., Ste. 2400
Chicago, IL 60611-1980   Phone: (312)335-4100
Editor(s): Grace Hayek. Semimonthly. Covers current news and trends in the real estate appraisal field. **Facsimile Number:** (312)335-4400.

★344★
ASA Newsline
American Society of Appraisers (ASA)
PO Box 17265
Washington, DC 20041   Phone: (703)478-2228
Bimonthly.

★345★
Commercial Investment Real Estate Journal
Realtors National Marketing Institute
430 N. Michigan Ave., Ste. 500, 5th Fl.
Chicago, IL 60611-4092   Phone: (312)670-3780
Lorene Norton, Editor. Quarterly. Professional development magazine for commercial and investment realtors and allied personnel. **Facsimile Number:** (312)329-8882.

★346★
The Commercial Record
435 Buckland Rd.
South Windsor, CT 06074-0902   Phone: (203)644-3484
Nena Groskind, Editor. Weekly (Fri.). Real estate and financial newspaper. **Facsimile Number:** (203)644-7363.

★347★
Corporate Real Estate Executive
NACORE
440 Columbia Dr., Ste. 100
West Palm Beach, FL 33409-6685   Phone: (407)683-8111
Kathleen B. Dempsey, Editor. 9x/yr. Real estate magazine. **Facsimile Number:** (407)697-4853.

★348★
The Corridor Real Estate Journal
Journal Two Publishing, Inc.
1020 N. Fairfax St., Ste. 400
Alexandria, VA 22314   Phone: (703)548-0850
Robert Hickey, Publisher. Weekly. Real estate magazine. **Facsimile Number:** (703)683-3687.

★349★
The Executive Officer
National Association of Realtors (NAR)
430 N. Michigan Ave.
Chicago, IL 60611-4087   Phone: (312)329-8200
5/year. Magazine.

★350★
Existing Home Sales
National Association of Realtors (NAR)
430 N. Michigan Ave.
Chicago, IL 60611-4087   Phone: (312)329-8200
Monthly.

★351★
Journal of Property Management
Institute of Real Estate Management
PO Box 109025
Chicago, IL 60610   Phone: (312)661-1930
Mariwyn Evans, Editor. 6x/yr. Magazine serving real estate managers. **Facsimile Number:** (312)661-0217.

★352★
The Journal of Real Estate Development
Federal Research Press
210 Lincoln St.
Boston, MA 02111   Phone: (617)423-0978
Susan B. Hodgson, Editor. Quarterly. Real estate journal.

★353★
Journal of Real Estate Taxation
Warren, Gorham & Lamont, Inc.
1 Penn Plaza, 40th Fl.
New York, NY 10119   Phone: (212)971-5194
Eugene Krader, Editor. Quarterly. Real estate tax journal. **Facsimile Number:** (212)971-5025.

Real Estate Agents, Brokers, and Appraisers

★354★
National Real Estate Investor
Communication Channels, Inc.
6255 Barfield Rd.
Atlanta, GA 30328   Phone: (404)256-9800
Paula Stephens, Editor/Assoc. Publisher. Monthly. Magazine on real estate investment and development. **Facsimile Number:** (404)256-3116.

★355★
National Relocation and Real Estate
The Relocation Information Service, Inc.
113 E. Post Rd., No. 2
Westport, CT 06880-3410   Phone: (203)227-3800
Peter S. Featherston, Editor. 6x/yr Trade magazine focusing on the real estate and corporate relocation market **Facsimile Number:** (203)227-7108.

★356★
New Homes Magazine
MDM Publications
3151 Airway Ave., Ste. D-1
Costa Mesa, CA 92626   Phone: (714)751-5813
Jim Trumbull, Mng. Editor. 6x/yr. Real estate magazine. **Facsimile Number:** (714)755-5500.

★357★
Prime Real Estate
Prime Publishing Co.
4141 State St., No. E-14
Santa Barbara, CA 93110-1814 Phone: (805)967-3663
Michael Colin, Editor. 6x/yr. Magazine featuring displays of luxury residential property ($500,000 and up) for sale; including feature editorials on exclusive towns, neighborhoods, and resort areas where homes are located. **Facsimile Number:** (805)683-7645.

★358★
Real Estate Business
PO Box 300
Wheaton, IL 60189   Phone: (708)752-0500
Pierce Hollingsworth, Publisher. Quarterly. Trade magazine for real estate brokers and residential sales personnel. **Facsimile Number:** (708)752-0525.

★359★
Real Estate Center Journal
Real Estate Center
Texas A&M University
College Station, TX 77843-2115 Phone: (409)845-0369
David S. Jones, Editor. Quarterly. Journal covering real estate research.

★360★
Real Estate Finance
Federal Research Press
155 Federal St.
Boston, MA 02110   Phone: (617)423-0978
Barbara Grzincic, Esq., Editor. Quarterly Journal covering commercial and industrial real estate finance for lenders, investors, and developers. **Facsimile Number:** (617)482-7820.

★361★
The Real Estate Finance Journal
Warren, Gorham and Lamont, Inc.
1 Penn Plaza, 40th Fl.
New York, NY 10119   Phone: (212)971-5225
William Zucker, Editor. Quarterly. Magazine contains articles by industry practitioners on new financing techniques, case studies, issues of interest to the real estate industry, as well as general columns. **Facsimile Number:** (212)971-5024.

★362★
Real Estate Finance Today
Mortgage Bankers Assn.
PO Box 37236
Washington, DC 20013   Phone: (202)861-6500
Janet R. Hewitt, Editor-in-Chief. Weekly. Tabloid tracing economic trends and government actions that affect mortgage lenders. **Facsimile Number:** (202)872-0186.

★363★
Real Estate Forum
12 W. 37th St.
New York, NY 10018   Phone: (212)563-6460
Harold Kelman, Editor. Monthly. Magazine providing national coverage of real estate investment and development news. **Facsimile Number:** (212)967-1498.

★364★
Real Estate News
2600 W. Peterson Ave.
Chicago, IL 60659   Phone: (312)465-5151
Donna Proske, Assoc. Publisher. Monthly. **Facsimile Number:** (312)465-7218.

★365★
Real Estate News
Toronto Real Estate Board
1400 Don Mills Rd.
Don Mills, ON, Canada M3B 3N1 Phone: (416)443-8113
Leslie A. Gordon, Editor. Weekly (Fri.). Real estate newspaper. **Facsimile Number:** (416)443-9185.

★366★
Real Estate Outlook
Warren, Gorham and Lamont, Inc.
1 Penn Plaza, 40th Fl.
New York, NY 10119   Phone: (212)971-5225
Janis L. Gibson, Editor. Quarterly. Newspaper for real estate professionals. **Facsimile Number:** (212)971-5024.

★367★
Real Estate Record and Builders Guide
Real Estate Data, Inc.
475 5th Ave., Ste. 1901
New York, NY 10017   Phone: (212)532-2705
Venice Kelly, Editor. Weekly (Sat.). Real estate reports magazine.

★368★
Real Estate Review
Warren, Gorham and Lamont, Inc.
1 Penn Plaza, 40th Fl.
New York, NY 10119   Phone: (212)971-5225
Alvin I. Arnold, Editor. Quarterly. Real estate magazine. **Facsimile Number:** (212)971-5024.

★369★
Real Estate Today
National Assn. of Realtors
430 N. Michigan Ave.
Chicago, IL 60611-4087   Phone: (312)329-8275
Maureen Glass, Editor. 10x/yr. (combined Jan/Feb and Nov/Dec issues). Applications-oriented magazine featuring how-to approach to aspects of residential real estate sales, brokerage management, and commercial real estate. **Facsimile Number:** (312)329-5978.

★370★
Real Estate Weekly
Hagedorn Publishing Co., Inc.
1 Madison Ave.
New York, NY 10010　　　　Phone: (212)679-1234
Charles G. Hagedorn, Executive Editor. Weekly. Real estate newspaper. **Facsimile Number:** (212)689-2267.

★371★
Real Estate West
Grier & Co.
444 17th St., Ste. 918
Denver, CO 80202-0918　　　　Phone: (303)825-6269
Doug Gill, Editor. 6x/yr. Magazine (tabloid) for corporate real estate executives, developers, building owners and managers, commercial and industrial retail brokers, investors, appraisers, and financial institutions.

★372★
Realtor News
National Association of Realtors (NAR)
430 N. Michigan Ave.
Chicago, IL 60611-4087　　　　Phone: (312)329-8200
Biweekly.

★373★
Realtor News - All Member Issue
National Assn. of Realtors
430 N. Michigan Ave.
Chicago, IL 60611-4087　　　　Phone: (312)329-8461
William Adkinson, Editor. 2x/mo. Real estate newspaper.

★374★
Realtor News-Broker Issue
National Assn. of Realtors
430 N. Michigan Ave.
Chicago, IL 60611-4087　　　　Phone: (312)329-8461
William Adkinson, Editor. 2x/mo. Real estate newspaper. **Facsimile Number:** (312)324-8576.

★375★
REALTORS Land Institute
National Assn. of Realtors
430 N. Michigan Ave.
Chicago, IL 60611　　　　Phone: (312)329-8446
J. Gregory Wiezorek, Editor. 11x/yr. Newsletter and journal.

★376★
Realty
80-34 Jamaica
Woodhaven, NY 11421　　　　Phone: (516)378-5221
Lester Sobel, Editor. Every other week (Tues.). Real estate trade newspaper.

★377★
Right of Way
International Right of Way Assn.
13650 Gramercy Pl.
Gardena, CA 90249　　　　Phone: (213)538-0233
Ken Rose, Editor. 6x/yr. Trade magazine offering technical articles on right of way management and acquisition, real estate appraisal, and property management. **Facsimile Number:** (213)538-1471.

★378★
S/F (Square Foot)
Mass Tech Times, Inc.
755 Mt. Auburn St.
Watertown, MA 02172　　　　Phone: (617)924-5100
Douglas Green, Publisher. 6x/yr. Real estate magazine. **Facsimile Number:** (617)923-3008.

★379★
Sea Shelters
PO Box 150
Accomac, VA 23301
Darel LaPrade, Editor. Monthly. Real estate magazine.

★380★
Society of Real Estate Appraisers—Briefs
Society of Real Estate Appraisers
225 N. Michigan Ave., Ste. 724
Chicago, IL 60601-7601　　　　Phone: (312)819-2400
Editor(s): Jan Seefeldt. Biweekly. Provides information on topics of interest to real estate appraisal or analysis professionals, especially on governmental, economic, and social factors which affect property values. Includes news of Society activities. **Toll-free/Additional Phone Number(s):** 800-331-7732 **Facsimile Number:** (312)819-2360.

★381★
Southeast Real Estate News
Communication Channels, Inc.
6255 Barfield Rd.
Atlanta, GA 30328　　　　Phone: (404)256-9800
Coles McKagen, Editor. Monthly. Magazine covering commercial and industrial real estate transactions. **Facsimile Number:** (404)256-3116.

★382★
Southwest Real Estate News
Communications Channels, Inc.
18601 LBJ Fwy., No. 240
Mesquite, TX 75150　　　　Phone: (214)270-6651
James Mitchell, Editor. 6x/yr. Commercial real estate tabloid. **Facsimile Number:** (214)681-8391.

★383★
Valuation Journal
American Society of Appraisers (ASA)
PO Box 17265
Washington, DC 20041　　　　Phone: (703)478-2228
Semiannual.

──────── Meetings and Conventions ────────

★384★
American Real Estate and Investment Show
Miller Marketing Network Ltd.
119 W. 57th St.
New York, NY 10019　　　　Phone: (212)247-6060
1992; Apr. London, England ● 1993; Apr. Paris, France ● 1994; Cannes, France. **Facsimile Number:** (212)586-5446.

★385★
American Society of Appraisers (ASA)
PO Box 17265
Washington, DC 20041　　　　Phone: (703)478-2228
Frequency: Holds annual conference, with exhibits. 1992; New Orleans; LA ● 1993; Reno, NV.

Real Estate Agents, Brokers, and Appraisers

★386★
Appraisal Institute (AI)
225 N. Michigan Ave., Ste. 724
Chicago, IL 60601-7601   Phone: (312)819-2400
Frequency: Holds annual conference. **Toll-free/Additional Phone Number(s):** (800)331-7732. **Facsimile Number:** (312)819-2360.

★387★
International Real Estate Institute International Real Estate Trade Show and Exhibition
International Real Estate Institute
8383 E. Evans Rd.
Scottsdale, AZ 85260-3614   Phone: (602)998-8267
1992. **Facsimile Number:** (602)998-8022.

★388★
National Association of Realtors Annual Trade Exposition
National Association of Realtors
430 N. Michigan Ave.
Chicago, IL 60614   Phone: (312)329-8886
Frequency: Always held in November. 1992; Nov. 12-17; Honolulu, HI • 1993; Nov. 11-16; Miami, FL • 1994; Nov. 03-08; Anaheim, CA • 1995; Nov. 09-14; Atlanta, GA • 1996; Nov. 14-19; San Francisco, CA. **Facsimile Number:** (312)329-8576.

★389★
National Association of Realtors Midyear Trade Exposition
National Association of Realtors
430 N. Michigan Ave.
Chicago, IL 60611   Phone: (312)329-8886
Frequency: Always held during April at the Sheraton in Washington, D.C. 1992; Apr. 24-29; Washington, DC • 1993; Apr. 23-28; Washington, DC • 1994; Apr. 22-27; Washington, DC. **Facsimile Number:** (312)329-8576.

★390★
National Association of Review Appraisers and Mortgage Underwriters Convention
National Association of Review Appraisers and Mortgage Underwriters
8383 E. Evans Rd.
Scottsdale, AZ 85260   Phone: (602)998-3000
1992. **Facsimile Number:** (602)998-8022.

Other Sources of Information

★391★
Guide to Appraising for Federal Agencies   Real estate industry
Society of Real Estate Appraisers
225 N. Michigan Ave., Ste. 724
Chicago, IL 60601   Phone: (312)819-2400
J. Seefeldt, editor. Irregular; latest edition 1987. Nearly 20 federal agencies that employ or use the services of real estate appraisers. Entries include: Agency headquarters name, address, phone, addresses and phone numbers of regional offices, annual volume of appraisal work, basis of determining fees, appraisal forms used, condemnation requirements, application procedure, description of projects requiring independent appraisers. Arrangement: Alphabetical. **Toll-free/Additional Phone Number(s):** (800)331-7732. **Facsimile Number:** (312)819-2360.

★392★
The Real Estate Index
National Association of Realtors (NAR)
430 N. Michigan Ave.
Chicago, IL 60611-4087   Phone: (312)329-8200
Periodic.

★393★
Subject Headings for Real Estate
National Association of Realtors (NAR)
430 N. Michigan Ave.
Chicago, IL 60611-4087   Phone: (312)329-8200

Retail Sales Workers

Retail sales workers are employed by virtually every type of retailer to assist customers in the selection and purchase of merchandise. A sales worker's primary job is to interest customers in the product by describing its construction, demonstrating its use, or showing various models or colors. Most retail sales workers also make out sales checks; receive cash, check, and charge payments; and give change and receipts. They may also handle returns and exchanges, perform gift wrapping services, and monitor inventory. A knowledge of the store's policies, procedures, and promotions is essential, in addition to familiarity with the store's security practices. With increased competition and heavy emphasis on pleasing the customer, a store's sales force becomes more important. Sales workers must offer superior service, ensuring customer satisfaction.

$alaries

Compensation systems vary by type of establishment and merchandise being sold. Some sales workers receive salary plus commissions, others are paid only on a salary or commission basis. The starting wage for many part-time positions is the going Federal minimum wage.

Employment Outlook

Growth rate until the year 2000: Faster than average.

Retail Sales Workers

---------- **Career Guides** ----------

★394★
According to Hoyle
Commonwealth Films, Inc.
223 Commonwealth Ave.
Boston, MA 02116   Phone: (617)262-5634
Videocassette. 1988. 30 mins. An entire business deal is enacted, from the purchasing of goods to the sales.

★395★
All Pro
BNA Communications, Inc.
9439 Key West Ave.
Rockville, MD 20850   Phone: (301)948-0540
Videocassette. 1981. 29 mins. Conversations with five top sales professionals. They discuss their careers and the traits that make a top professional.

★396★
"Art Supply Salesperson" in *Career Opportunities in Art* (p. 155)
Facts on File, Inc.
460 Park Avenue, S.
New York, NY 10016   Phone: (212)683-2244
Susan H. Haubenstock and David Joselit. 1988. Profiles more than 75 art-related jobs. Each occupational profile covers job duties, employment outlook, career paths, salaries, skills, and educational preparation. Offers tips for entering the field.

★397★
"Auto and Car-Parts Sales Representatives" in *Jobs! What They Are...Where They Are...What They Pay* (pp. 277-278)
Simon & Schuster, Inc.
Simon & Schuster Bldg.
1230 Avenue of the Americas
New York, NY 10020   Phone: (212)698-7000
Robert O. Snelling and Anne M. Snelling. Revised edition, 1989. Profiles 241 occupations, describing duties and responsibilities, educational preparation, earnings, employment opportunities, training, and qualifications.

★398★
"Auto Parts Counter Worker" in *Marketing and Distribution*, Volume 10 of *Career Information Center* (pp. 37-38)
Glencoe/Macmillan
15319 Chatsworth St.
Mission Hills, CA 91345   Phone: (818)898-1391
Richard Lidz and Dale Anderson, editorial directors. Fourth edition, 1990. For 600 occupations, describes job duties, entry-level requirements, education and training needed, advancement possibilities, employment outlook, earnings and benefits. The set is divided into 12 volumes. Each volume includes jobs related under a broad career field. Volume 13 is the index. **Facsimile Number:** 818-365-5489.

★399★
"Auto Sales Worker" in *Marketing and Distribution*, Volume 10 of *Career Information Center* (pp. 39-41)
Glencoe/Macmillan
15319 Chatsworth St.
Mission Hills, CA 91345   Phone: (818)898-1391
Richard Lidz and Dale Anderson, editorial directors. Fourth edition, 1990. For 600 occupations, describes job duties, entry-level requirements, education and training needed, advancement possibilities, employment outlook, earnings and benefits. The set is divided into 12 volumes. Each volume includes jobs related under a broad career field. Volume 13 is the index. **Facsimile Number:** 818-365-5489.

★400★
"Automobile Sales Workers" in Volume 1 of *Career Discovery Encyclopedia* (pp. 92-93)
J.G. Ferguson Publishing Co.
200 W. Monroe
Chicago, IL 60606   Phone: (312)580-5480
E. Russell Primm, editor-in-chief. 1990. Contains two-page articles on 504 occupations. Each article describes job duties, earnings, and educational and training requirements.

★401★
"Automobile Sales Workers" in Volume 3 of *The Encyclopedia of Careers and Vocational Guidance* (pp. 134-136)
J.G. Ferguson Publishing Co.
200 W. Monroe
Chicago, IL 60606   Phone: (312)580-5480
William E. Hopke, editor-in-chief. Eighth edition, 1990. Four-volume set that profiles 500 occupations and describes job trends in 76 industries. Includes career description, educational requirements, history of the job, methods of entry, advancement, employment outlook, earnings, working

★402★
Automobile Salespeople
Chronicle Guidance Publications, Inc.
PO Box 1190
Moravia, NY 13118-1190   Phone: (315)497-0330
1991. This career brief describes the nature of the work, working conditions, hours and earnings, education and training, licensure, certification, unions, personal qualifications, social and psychological factors, employment outlook, entry methods, advancement, and related occupations. **Toll-free/Additional Phone Number(s):** 800-622-7284.

★403★
"Automobile Salesperson" in *College Board Guide to Jobs and Career Planning* (pp. 132-134)
College Entrance Examination Board
45 Columbus Ave.
New York, NY 10023-6992   Phone: (212)713-8000
Joyce Slayton Mitchell. 1990. Career planning guide written for high school and college students. Covers 100 careers in 15 occupational groups. Provides job description, educational preparation needed, salaries, related careers, and sources of additional information. Includes information about the 90's labor market.

★404★
"Automotive Parts Specialists" in *Opportunities in Automotive Service Careers* (pp. 39-44)
National Textbook Co.
4255 W. Touhy Ave.
Lincolnwood, IL 60646   Phone: (312)679-5500
Robert M. Weber. 1989. Describes the work of the automobile mechanic and related occupations such as service station attendant and automobile body repairer. Covers working conditions, places of employment, qualifications, training, apprenticeships, certification, advancement opportunities, employment outlook, tools needed, and earnings.

★405★
Basic Retail Selling Skills
American Media, Inc.
1454 30th St.
West Des Moines, IA 50265   Phone: (515)224-0919
Videocassette. 1988. 26 mins. A step-by-step approach that will improve the performance of a sales team.

★406★
Basic Retail Selling Skills
United Learning, Inc.
6633 West Howard St.
Niles, IL 60648   Phone: (708)647-0600
Videocassette. 1984. 14 mins. This video, originally developed for Walgreen, stresses the basics of selling goods in the retail marketplace.

★407★
"Career Profile: Interview with a Personal Computer Salesman" in *Exploring Careers in the Computer Field* (pp. 95-101)
Rosen Publishing Group, Inc.
29 E. 21st St.
New York, NY 10010   Phone: (212)777-3017
Joseph Weintraub. 1990. Surveys the newest growth areas in the computer industry including artificial intelligence, desktop publishing, and personal computers. Discusses entry into the field, salaries, future trends and offers job search advice.

conditions, social and psychological factors, and sources of additional information.

Contains interviews with five people who describe their real-life experiences working in computer related jobs. Lists organizations and colleges.

★408★
Career Success Series
Cambridge Career Products
90 MacCorkle Ave., SW
South Charleston, WV 25311   Phone: (304)744-9323
Videocassette. 1986. 15 mins. A series, available separately, outlining various career choices for students. Occupations include: flight service, air transportation/ground service, data processing, carpentry, clerk in banking/insurance, commodity sales, cosmetic personal grooming, fire fighting, forestry services, home economics, insulation/roofing, material handling, mechanics, photographic processing, pipefitting and plumbing, police science, printing, secretarial services, and utilities equipment operator.

★409★
Careers in a Department Store
Lerner Publications Co.
241 First Ave., N.
Minneapolis, MN 55401
Jennifer Brooks Dean. 1973. Describes the varied careers possible in a department store including sales clerk, sales manager, and many others. **Toll-free/Additional Phone Number(s):** 800-328-4920. **Facsimile Number:** (612)332-7615.

★410★
Careers in Computer Sales
Rosen Publishing Group, Inc.
29 E. 21st St.
New York, NY 10010   Phone: (212)777-3017
Lawrence Epstein. 1990. Describes working in computer hardware and software sales, the skills needed, educational preparation, work environments, and salaries. Offers job hunting advice and lists computers, computer related products, magazines, and companies.

★411★
Careers in Fashion Retailing
Rosen Publishing Group, Inc.
29 E. 21st St.
New York, NY 10010   Phone: (212)777-3017
Pat Koester. 1990. Describes fashion retailing, industry structure, career paths, and typical jobs such as sales, management, and buying. Profiles persons working in the field and discusses educational preparation. Lists schools that offer programs in fashion retailing.

★412★
"Department Store Retailing" in *The Encyclopedia of Career Choices for the 1990s: A Guide to Entry Level Jobs* (pp. 252-272)
Walker and Co.
720 Fifth Ave.
New York, NY 10019   Phone: (212)265-3632
1991. Describes entry-level opportunities in 42 career fields for college graduates. Each chapter covers a single career field, including an overview, employment outlook, major employers, tips on entering the field, international job opportunities, functional job areas with personal and professional qualifications, career paths, job responsibilities, advancement possibilities, salaries, and working conditions. Lists related sources of information.

★413★
"Direct Sales Worker" in *Marketing and Distribution, Volume 10* of *Career Information Center* (pp. 46-48)
Glencoe/Macmillan
15319 Chatsworth St.
Mission Hills, CA 91345　　　　Phone: (818)898-1391
Richard Lidz and Dale Anderson, editorial directors. Fourth edition, 1990. For 600 occupations, describes job duties, entry-level requirements, education and training needed, advancement possibilities, employment outlook, earnings and benefits. The set is divided into 12 volumes. Each volume includes jobs related under a broad career field. Volume 13 is the index. **Facsimile Number:** 818-365-5489.

★414★
Direct Selling: An Income Opportunity for You
Direct Selling Association
1776 K St. NW, Ste. 600
Washington, DC 20006　　　　Phone: (202)293-5760
1987. This eight-panel brochure describes the nature of direct selling and skills required to succeed.

★415★
"Door to Door Sales Workers" in Volume 3 of *The Encyclopedia of Careers and Vocational Guidance* (pp. 140-143)
J.G. Ferguson Publishing Co.
200 W. Monroe
Chicago, IL 60606　　　　Phone: (312)580-5480
William E. Hopke, editor-in-chief. Eighth edition, 1990. Four-volume set that profiles 500 occupations and describes job trends in 76 industries. Includes career description, educational requirements, history of the job, methods of entry, advancement, employment outlook, earnings, working conditions, social and psychological factors, and sources of additional information.

★416★
"Door-to-Door Sales Workers" in Volume 2 of *Career Discovery Encyclopedia* (pp. 122-123)
J.G. Ferguson Publishing Co.
200 W. Monroe
Chicago, IL 60606　　　　Phone: (312)580-5480
E. Russell Primm, editor-in-chief. 1990. Contains two-page articles on 504 occupations. Each article describes job duties, earnings, and educational and training requirements.

★417★
Fact Sheet: Facts About Direct Selling
Direct Selling Association
1776 K St. NW, Ste. 600
Washington, DC 20006　　　　Phone: (202)293-5760
1987. This two-page leaflet describes the industry, the jobs of salespeople, customers, and products.

★418★
"Health and Fitness Retail Sales" in *Careers in Health and Fitness* (pp. 71-73)
Rosen Publishing Group, Inc.
29 E. 21st St.
New York, NY 10010　　　　Phone: (212)777-3017
Jackie Heron. 1990. Describes careers related to sports and fitness. Covers job duties, pros and cons, equipment used, employment outlook, educational preparation, certification, licensing, and salaries.

★419★
Hobby Supply Salesperson
Vocational Biographies, Inc.
PO Box 31, Dept. VF10
Sauk Centre, MN 56378　　　　Phone: (612)352-6516
1989. This pamphlet profiles a person working in the job. Includes information about job duties, working conditions, places of employment, educational preparation, labor market outlook, and salaries. **Toll-free/Additional Phone Number(s):** 800-255-0752.

★420★
Jobs in Shops & Stores
Beekman Publishers, Inc.
Rte. 212
PO Box 888
Woodstock, NY 12498　　　　Phone: (914)679-2300
Carole Chester. 1990.

★421★
"Music Shop Salesperson" in *Career Opportunities in the Music Industry* (pp. 89-90)
Facts on File, Inc.
460 Park Avenue, S.
New York, NY 10016　　　　Phone: (212)683-2244
Shelly Field. Second edition, 1991. Describes more than 70 music related jobs. Each occupational profile covers job duties, employment outlook, career paths, salaries, skills, and educational preparation. Offers tips for entering the field.

★422★
Musical Instrument Salesperson
Vocational Biographies, Inc.
PO Box 31, Dept. VF10
Sauk Centre, MN 56378　　　　Phone: (612)352-6516
1990. This pamphlet profiles a person working in the job. Includes information about job duties, working conditions, places of employment, educational preparation, labor market outlook, and salaries. **Toll-free/Additional Phone Number(s):** 800-255-0752.

★423★
"Personal Computer Salesperson" in *Straight Talk on Careers: 80 Pros Take You Into Their Professions* (pp. 8-10)
Garrett Park Press
PO Box 190
Garrett Park, MD 20896　　　　Phone: (301)946-2553
Mary Barbera-Hogan. 1987. Written for readers in high school and college. Contains candid interviews from professionals who discuss what their days are like and the pros and cons of their occupations.

★424★
"Record Shop Clerk" in *Career Opportunities in the Music Industry* (pp. 93-94)
Facts on File, Inc.
460 Park Avenue, S.
New York, NY 10016　　　　Phone: (212)683-2244
Shelly Field. Second edition, 1991. Describes more than 70 music related jobs. Each occupational profile covers job duties, employment outlook, career paths, salaries, skills, and educational preparation. Offers tips for entering the field.

★425★
"Retail Industry" in *Footsteps in the Ocean: Careers in Diving* (pp. 37-42)
Lodestar Books
2 Park Avenue
New York, NY 10016   Phone: (212)725-1818
Denise V. Lang. 1987. Explores employment opportunities in sport and commercial diving, science and research, in the military, and police work. Describes the work and training. Lists schools. **Facsimile Number:** (212)532-6568.

★426★
"Retail Sales" in *Careers in Marketing* (pp. 66-68)
National Textbook Co.
4255 W. Touhy Ave.
Lincolnwood, IL 60646   Phone: (312)679-5500
Lila B. Stair. 1991. Surveys career opportunities in marketing and related areas such as marketing research, product development, and sales promotion. Includes a description of the work, place of employment, employment outlook, trends, educational preparation, organizational charts, and salaries. Offers job hunting advice.

★427★
Retail Sales Power
Professional Development, Inc.
27955 Clemens Rd.
Westlake, OH 44145   Phone: (216)892-0770
Videocassette. 1986. 30 mins. A two-part program for retail clerks, dealing with customer relations, theft and business decisions.

★428★
"Retail Sales Worker" in *VGM's Careers Encyclopedia* (pp. 409-411)
National Textbook Co.
4255 W. Touhy Ave.
Lincolnwood, IL 60646   Phone: (312)679-5500
Third edition, 1991. Contains two- to five-page descriptions of 200 managerial, professional, technical, trade, and service occupations. Each profile includes job duties, places of employment, qualifications, educational preparation, training, employment potential, advancement, income, and additional sources of information.

★429★
"Retail Sales Worker" in Volume 5 of *Career Discovery Encyclopedia* (pp. 156-157)
J.G. Ferguson Publishing Co.
200 W. Monroe
Chicago, IL 60606   Phone: (312)580-5480
E. Russell Primm, editor-in-chief. 1990. Contains two-page articles on 504 occupations. Each article describes job duties, earnings, and educational and training requirements.

★430★
"Retail Sales Workers" in *Occupational Outlook Handbook* (pp. 236-238)
Superintendent of Documents
U.S. Government Printing Office
Washington, DC 20402   Phone: (202)783-3238
Biennial; latest edition, 1990-91. Encyclopedia of careers describing more than 250 occupations and comprising about 86 percent of all jobs in the economy. Occupations that require lengthy education or training are given the most attention. For each occupation, the handbook describes job duties, working conditions, training, educational preparation, personal qualities, advancement possibilities, job outlook, earnings, and sources of additional information.

★431★
"Retail Sales Workers" in *Opportunities in Vocational and Technical Careers* (pp. 63-64)
National Textbook Co.
4255 W. Touhy Ave.
Lincolnwood, IL 60646   Phone: (312)679-5500
Adrian A. Paradis. 1987. Describes careers which can be prepared for by attending a private vocational or proprietary school—office employee, sales worker, service worker, health services, mechanic, craftworker, and technician. Covers employment outlook, job duties, and salaries. Offers career planning advice.

★432★
"Retail Sales Workers" in Volume 3 of *The Encyclopedia of Careers and Vocational Guidance* (pp. 167-171)
J.G. Ferguson Publishing Co.
200 W. Monroe
Chicago, IL 60606   Phone: (312)580-5480
William E. Hopke, editor-in-chief. Eighth edition, 1990. Four-volume set that profiles 500 occupations and describes job trends in 76 industries. Includes career description, educational requirements, history of the job, methods of entry, advancement, employment outlook, earnings, working conditions, social and psychological factors, and sources of additional information.

★433★
"Retail Salespeople" in *Jobs! What They Are...Where They Are...What They Pay* (pp. 272-273)
Simon & Schuster, Inc.
Simon & Schuster Bldg.
1230 Avenue of the Americas
New York, NY 10020   Phone: (212)698-7000
Robert O. Snelling and Anne M. Snelling. Revised edition, 1989. Profiles 241 occupations, describing duties and responsibilities, educational preparation, earnings, employment opportunities, training, and qualifications.

★434★
"Retail Store Sales Worker" in *Marketing and Distribution*, Volume 10 of *Career Information Center* (pp. 53-54)
Glencoe/Macmillan
15319 Chatsworth St.
Mission Hills, CA 91345   Phone: (818)898-1391
Richard Lidz and Dale Anderson, editorial directors. Fourth edition, 1990. For 600 occupations, describes job duties, entry-level requirements, education and training needed, advancement possibilities, employment outlook, earnings and benefits. The set is divided into 12 volumes. Each volume includes jobs related under a broad career field. Volume 13 is the index. **Facsimile Number:** 818-365-5489.

★435★
"Retail Store Salesperson" in *The Complete Computer Career Guide* (pp. 57-58)
Tab Books, Inc.
Blue Ridge Summit, PA 17294-0850   Phone: (717)794-2191
Judith Norback. 1987. Offers career planning tips and describes the educational preparation needed, employment outlook, industry trends, and certification. Offers job search advice. A separate section includes opportunities for women and minorities.

Retail Sales Workers

★448★

★436★
Retailing & Merchandising
Morris Video
2730 Monterey St. #105
Monterey Business Park
Torrance, CA 90503   Phone: (213)533-4800
Videocassette. 1987. 15 mins. A look at the variety of career opportunities available in the world of retail.

★437★
"Salesclerk" in *Guide to Careers Without College* (pp. 20-21)
Franklin Watts, Inc.
387 Park Avenue, S.
New York, NY 10016   Phone: (212)686-7070
Kathleen S. Abrams. 1988. Discusses careers that do not require a college degree in fields such as health care, sales and marketing, and the building trades. Describes the work, employment opportunities, and training.

★438★
Salespeople, Household Appliance
Chronicle Guidance Publications, Inc.
PO Box 1190
Moravia, NY 13118-1190   Phone: (315)497-0330
1988. This career brief describes the nature of the work, working conditions, hours and earnings, education and training, licensure, certification, unions, personal qualifications, social and psychological factors, employment outlook, entry methods, advancement, and related occupations. **Toll-free/Additional Phone Number(s):** 800-622-7284.

★439★
Salespeople, Retail
Chronicle Guidance Publications, Inc.
PO Box 1190
Moravia, NY 13118-1190   Phone: (315)497-0330
1988. This career brief describes the nature of the work, working conditions, hours and earnings, education and training, licensure, certification, unions, personal qualifications, social and psychological factors, employment outlook, entry methods, advancement, and related occupations. **Toll-free/Additional Phone Number(s):** 800-622-7284.

★440★
"Salesperson" in *Occu-Facts: Information on 565 Careers in Outline Form* (pp. 11.14, 11.15, 11.16, 11.17, 11.18, 11.19, 11.20, 11.27)
Careers, Inc.
P.O. Box 135
1211 Tenth St., S.W.
Largo, FL 33640   Phone: (813)584-7333
Elizabeth Handville. Biennial, 1989-90 edition. Each one-page occupational profile describes duties, working conditions, physical surroundings and demands, aptitudes, temperament, educational requirements, employment outlook, earnings, and places of employment.

★441★
Salesperson, Automobile
Careers, Inc.
PO Box 135
Largo, FL 34649-0135   Phone: (813)584-7333
1991. Two-page occupational summary card describing duties, working conditions, personal qualifications, training, earnings and hours, employment outlook, places of employment, related careers and where to write for more information.

★442★
Salesperson, Automotive Parts
Careers, Inc.
PO Box 135
Largo, FL 34649-0135   Phone: (813)584-7333
1991. Two-page occupational summary card describing duties, working conditions, personal qualifications, training, earnings and hours, employment outlook, places of employment, related careers and where to write for more information.

★443★
Salesperson, Camera Store
Careers, Inc.
PO Box 135
Largo, FL 34649-0135   Phone: (813)584-7333
1988. Two-page occupational summary card describing duties, working conditions, personal qualifications, training, earnings and hours, employment outlook, places of employment, related careers and where to write for more information.

★444★
Salesperson, Drugstore
Careers, Inc.
PO Box 135
Largo, FL 34649-0135   Phone: (813)584-7333
1988. Two-page occupational summary card describing duties, working conditions, personal qualifications, training, earnings and hours, employment outlook, places of employment, related careers and where to write for more information.

★445★
Salesperson, Grocery Products
Careers, Inc.
PO Box 135
Largo, FL 34649-0135   Phone: (813)584-7333
1990. Two-page occupational summary card describing duties, working conditions, personal qualifications, training, earnings and hours, employment outlook, places of employment, related careers and where to write for more information.

★446★
Salesperson, Hardware Store
Careers, Inc.
PO Box 135
Largo, FL 34649-0135   Phone: (813)584-7333
1990. Two-page occupational summary card describing duties, working conditions, personal qualifications, training, earnings and hours, employment outlook, places of employment, related careers and where to write for more information.

★447★
Salesperson, Music Store
Careers, Inc.
PO Box 135
Largo, FL 34649-0135   Phone: (813)584-7333
1991. Two-page occupational summary card describing duties, working conditions, personal qualifications, training, earnings and hours, employment outlook, places of employment, related careers and where to write for more information.

★448★
Salesperson, Retail
Careers, Inc.
PO Box 135
Largo, FL 34649-0135   Phone: (813)584-7333
1992. Two-page occupational summary card describing duties, working conditions, personal qualifications, training, earnings and hours, employment outlook, places of employment, related careers and where to write for more information.

VOCATIONAL CAREERS SOURCEBOOK, 1st Edition

★449★

★449★
Selling Direct: Choosing the Right Opportunity
Direct Selling Association
1776 K St. NW, Ste. 600
Washington, DC 20006   Phone: (202)293-5760
1987. Explains direct selling and offers guidelines for choosing a product to sell.

★450★
Shoe Salesperson
Vocational Biographies, Inc.
PO Box 31, Dept. VF10
Sauk Centre, MN 56378   Phone: (612)352-6516
1991. This pamphlet profiles a person working in the job. Includes information about job duties, working conditions, places of employment, educational preparation, labor market outlook, and salaries. **Toll-free/Additional Phone Number(s):** 800-255-0752.

★451★
So You Want to Be a Success at Selling?
Video Arts, Inc.
Northbrook Tech Center
4088 Commercial Ave.
Northbrook, IL 60062   Phone: (708)291-1008
Videocassette. 1982. 25 mins. A lesson on the fundamental skills of selling, from the initial research to the close.

★452★
"Sporting Goods Salesperson" in *Career Opportunities in the Sports Industry* (pp. 178-180)
Facts on File, Inc.
460 Park Avenue, S.
New York, NY 10016   Phone: (212)683-2244
Shelly Field. 1991. Describes various jobs in the sports industry. Each occupational profile covers job duties, employment outlook, career paths, salaries, skills, and educational preparation. Offers tips for entering the field.

★453★
Take this Job and Love It!
United Learning, Inc.
6633 West Howard St.
Niles, IL 60648   Phone: (708)647-0600
Videocassette. 1987. 9 mins. This video orients and motivates new retail employees.

★454★
Video Career Library - Marketing and Sales
Careers, Inc.
1211 10th St., SW
PO Box 135
Largo, FL 34649-0135   Phone: (813)584-7333
Videocassette. 1990. Part of the Video Career Library covering 165 occupations. Shows actual workers on the job. Includes retail salespersons.

★455★
"Video Sales Clerk" in *Career Opportunities in Television, Cable, and Video* (pp. 194-195)
Facts on File, Inc.
460 Park Avenue, S.
New York, NY 10016   Phone: (212)683-2244
Third edition, 1990. Describes 100 media-related jobs. Each occupational profile covers job duties, employment outlook, career paths, salaries, skills, and educational preparation. Offers tips for entering the field.

★456★
Your Career in Business-to-Business Direct Marketing
Direct Marketing Educational Foundation, Inc.
3 E 43rd St.
New York, NY 10017   Phone: (212)689-4977
This 12-page booklet explains business-to-business direct marketing, and lists the types of companies engaged in businesses-to-business direct marketing. Lists career opportunities and offers advice on entry into the field.

Associations

★457★
National Retail Federation (NRF)
100 W. 31st St.
New York, NY 10001   Phone: (212)244-8780
Membership: Department, chain, mass merchandise, and specialty stores retailing men's, women's, and children's apparel and home furnishings. **Purpose:** Conducts conferences and workshops; provides extensive group of manuals, bulletins, promotional materials, and advisory services on all phases of retailing, including financial planning and cash management, taxation, economic forecasting, expense planning, shortage control, credit, electronic data processing, telecommunications, merchandise management, buying, traffic, security, supply, materials handling, store planning and construction, personnel administration, recruitment and training, and advertising and display. Presents awards; maintains a library of 1000 volumes on retail management and fashion merchandising. **Publications:** *AD Pro*, monthly. • *Employee Relations Bulletin*, monthly. • *Retail Control*, 10/year. • *STORES Magazine*, monthly. **Facsimile Number:** (212)594-0487.

Test Guides

★458★
Sales Store Worker
National Learning Corp.
212 Michael Dr.
Syosset, NY 11791   Phone: (516)921-8888
Jack Rudman. Part of the Career Examination Series No. 1. All examination guides in this series contain questions with answers. **Facsimile Number:** (516)921-8743. **Toll-free/Additional Phone Number(s):** 800-645-6337.

Awards, Scholarships, Grants, and Fellowships

★459★
NRMA Gold Medal Award
National Retail Merchants Association
c/o Charles A. Binder, Executive Vice President
100 W. 31st St.
New York, NY 10001   Phone: (212)244-8780
To recognize an individual for distinguished service to the craft of retailing. An engraved gold medal is awarded annually. Established in 1929.

Periodicals

★460★
American Salesman
National Research Bureau, Inc.
424 N. 3rd St.
Burlington, IA 52601-5224   Phone: (319)752-5415
Barbara Boeding, Editor. Monthly. Salesmanship magazine. **Facsimile Number:** (319)752-3421.

★461★
AudioVideo International
Dempa Publications, Inc.
400 Madison Ave.
New York, NY 10017   Phone: (212)752-3003
Nancy Klosek, Mng. Editor. Monthly. Magazine for domestic retailers of consumer electronics products. Feature stories include trends and developments in audio, hi-fi, TV, video, car stereo, and home and personal electronics products. **Facsimile Number:** (212)752-3289.

★462★
Inside Retailing
Lebhar-Friedman, Inc.
425 Park Ave.
New York, NY 10022   Phone: (212)756-5017
Editor(s): David Mahler. Biweekly. Provides up-to-date information on what is happening in the retail industry and how current economic conditions affect retailing. Summarizes actions, acquisitions, and policies of major retail chains across the U.S. Discusses problems facing retail operations, i.e., shoplifting and retaining customer loyalty. **Facsimile Number:** (212)838-9487.

★463★
NRF Employee Relations Bulletin
National Retail Federation (NRF)
100 W. 31st St.
New York, NY 10001   Phone: (212)244-8780
Monthly. Newsletter providing information on personnel/human resources for retail personnel and employee relations executives.

★464★
Personal Selling Power
Personal Selling Power, Inc.
1127 International Pkwy.
PO Box 5467
Fredericksburg, VA 22403   Phone: (703)752-7000
L.B. Gschwandtner, Editor. Gerhard Gschwandtner, Publisher. 8x/yr. Magazine presenting motivational and sales skills and techniques for sales and marketing executives. **Facsimile Number:** (703)752-7001.

★465★
Retail Control
National Retail Federation (NRF)
100 W. 31st St.
New York, NY 10001   Phone: (212)244-8780
10/year. Journal providing retail financial information.

★466★
Retail Merchandising
Canadian Engineering Publications Ltd.
111 Peter, Ste. 411
Toronto, ON, Canada M5V 2W2   Phone: (416)596-1624
T. Burley, Editor. 6x/yr. General merchandising magazine (tabloid).

★467★
Retailing News
Martin Stanley Publishing, Inc.
248 W. Cerritos Ave.
Anaheim, CA 92805   Phone: (714)635-9774
Martin Barsky, Editor and Publisher. Monthly. Trade magazine (tabloid) reaching dealers, retailers, manufacturers, manufacturing reps, and distributors in the consumer electronics and major appliance industries.

★468★
RIS News
Edgell Enterprises, Inc.
21 Hilltop Circle, Ste. 150
Brookside, NJ 07926   Phone: (201)543-4762
Georgia Colichio, Editor. 10x/yr. Retail Information Systems News. **Facsimile Number:** (201)543-5753.

★469★
RWDSU Record
Retail, Wholesale and Dept. Store Union—AFL-CIO
30 E. 29th St.
New York, NY 10016   Phone: (212)684-5300
Stuart Applebaum, Editor. 6x/yr. Labor union newspaper.

★470★
Sales & Marketing Training
National Society of Sales Training Executives
Executive Business Media, Inc.
825 Old Country Rd.
PO Box 1500
Westbury, NY 11590   Phone: (708)990-0555
Robert Moran, Editor. Quarterly. Professional magazine. **Facsimile Number:** (516)334-3059.

★471★
Salesman's Insider
Marv Q. Modell Associates
6009 Montgomery Corner
San Jose, CA 95135-1431   Phone: (408)270-4526
Editor(s): Marv Q. Modell. Monthly. Concerned with selling techniques and methodology in all sales areas. Tracks new sales developments, trends, and profit opportunities. Details negotiatineg process with "tips that work".

★472★
STORES Magazine
National Retail Federation (NRF)
100 W. 31st St.
New York, NY 10001   Phone: (212)244-8780
Monthly. Provides retail executives and other retail personnel with information on current trends, concepts, and promotional innovations in the retail industry; includes association news and activities.

★473★
Supply House Times
Horton Publishing Co.
7574 N. Lincoln Ave.
Skokie, IL 60077　　　　　　　　Phone: (708)677-2707
Greg Cassel, Editor. Monthly. Trade magazine for wholesalers in plumbing, heating, cooling, piping, and water systems. Areas of major emphasis include: warehousing, materials handling, inventory control, accounting, data processing, merchandising, salesmanship and general management. **Facsimile Number:** (708)677-5003.

Meetings and Conventions

★474★
International Mass Retail Association Convention and Exhibits
International Mass Retail Association
1901 Pennsylvania Ave., NW, Ste. 1000
Washington, DC 20006-3455　　　Phone: (202)861-0774
1992; May 16-20; Orlando, FL • 1993; May 01-05; Orlando, FL.

★475★
National Retail Federation Convention and Exposition
National Retail Federation
100 W. 31st St.
New York, NY 10001　　　　　　Phone: (212)244-8780
Frequency: Always held in New York City during January.

★476★
Southern Apparel Exhibitors Shows
Southern Apparel Exhibitors, Inc.
Miami International Merchandise Mart
777 NW 72nd Ave., Ste. Lobby 18
Miami, FL 33126　　　　　　　　Phone: (305)261-2021
Frequency: Held five times per year in Miami, Florida at the Radisson Mart Plaza Hotel. 1992. **Facsimile Number:** (305)267-0513.

Other Sources of Information

★477★
Who's Who in Direct Selling
Direct Selling Association
1776 K St. NW, Ste. 600
Washington, DC 20006　　　　　Phone: (202)293-5760
1988. Lists companies which are members of the Direct Selling Association. Includes address, phone number, contact person, and indicates product sold.

Securities and Financial Services Sales Representatives

Securities sales representatives, sometimes called registered representatives, account executives, or brokers, assist investors in the buying or selling of stocks, bonds, shares in mutual funds, insurance annuities, certificates of deposit, or other financial products. Securities sales representatives may explain the meaning of stock market terms and trading practices, offer financial counseling, devise an individual financial portfolio for the client, and offer advice on the purchase or sale of particular securities. An important part of their job is building a customer base. Beginning securities sales representatives must search for clients, relying heavily on phone solicitation and business contacts. Sometimes they may inherit the clients of representatives who have retired. Financial services sales representatives call on various businesses to solicit applications for loans and new deposit accounts for banks or savings and loan associations. They also locate and contact prospective customers to present their bank's financial services and to determine the customer's banking needs.

$alaries

Average earnings for securities sales representatives are listed below.

Beginning securities sales representatives	$28,000/year
Full-time, experienced securities sales representatives who serve individual investors	$71,000/year
Sales representatives who handle institutional accounts	$240,000/year

Employment Outlook

Growth rate until the year 2000: Faster than average.

Securities and Financial Services Sales Representatives

Career Guides

★478★
All Pro
BNA Communications, Inc.
9439 Key West Ave.
Rockville, MD 20850 Phone: (301)948-0540
Videocassette. 1981. 29 mins. Conversations with five top sales professionals. They discuss their careers and the traits that make a top professional.

★479★
"Banking and Financial Services" in Volume 1 of *The Encyclopedia of Careers and Vocational Guidance* (pp. 54-64)
J.G. Ferguson Publishing Co.
200 W. Monroe
Chicago, IL 60606 Phone: (312)580-5480
William E. Hopke, editor-in-chief. Eighth edition, 1990. Four-volume set that profiles 500 occupations and describes job trends in 76 industries. Includes career description, educational requirements, history of the job, methods of entry, advancement, employment outlook, earnings, working conditions, social and psychological factors, and sources of additional information.

★480★
"Breaking into Sales & Trading on Wall Street" in *Internships Volume 3: Accounting, Banking, Brokerage, Finance & Insurance* (pp. 49-53)
Career Press, Inc.
PO Box 34
62 Beverly Rd.
Hawthorne, NJ 07507 Phone: (201)427-0229
Ronald W. Fry, editor-in-chief. 1989. Offers advice about obtaining internships with accounting, brokerage and investment banking firms, banks, and insurance companies. Lists companies offering internships and includes the contact person, duration, duties, qualifications, and application procedures and deadlines.

★481★
"Broker" in *Careers in Banking and Finance* (pp. 27-33)
Rosen Publishing Group, Inc.
29 E. 21st St.
New York, NY 10010 Phone: (212)777-3017
Patricia Haddock. 1990. Describes more than 20 jobs at all levels in banking and finance. Contains information about the types of financial organizations where the jobs are found, educational requirements, job duties, and salaries. Offers advice on job hunting.

★482★
"Brokers" in *The American Almanac of Jobs and Salaries* (pp. 420-421)
Avon Books
105 Madison Avenue
New York, NY 10016 Phone: (212)481-5600
John Wright and Edward J. Dwyer. Revised and updated, 1990. A comprehensive guide to the wages of hundreds of occupations in a wide variety of industries and organizations.

★483★
"Brokers: Steady As It Goes" in *Getting Into Money: A Career Guide* (pp. 58-73)
Ballantine Books
201 E. 50th St.
New York, NY 10022 Phone: (212)751-2600
Cheri Fein. 1988. Describes careers related to finance, what it takes to succeed in the field, and income potential. Contains interviews with people working in the field and offers job hunting tips.

★484★
Business and Finance Career Directory
Career Press, Inc.
PO Box 34
62 Beverly Rd.
Hawthorne, NJ 07507 Phone: (201)427-0229
Ronald W. Fry, editor. 1989. Chapters are written by practitioners in accounting, securities, financial planning and insurance. Describes job duties, educational preparation required, entry into the field, and earnings. Identifies internship opportunities and lists companies actively hiring at entry level.

★485★
Careers in the Investment World
Chelsea House Publishers
1974 Sproul Rd., Ste. 400
Broomall, PA 19008 Phone: (215)353-5166
Rachel S. Epstein. 1988. **Facsimile Number:** (215)359-1439.

★486★
Commodities Trader
Vocational Biographies, Inc.
PO Box 31, Dept. VF10
Sauk Centre, MN 56378 Phone: (612)352-6516
1991. This pamphlet profiles a person working in the job. Includes information about job duties, working conditions, places of employment, educational preparation, labor market outlook, and salaries. **Toll-free/Additional Phone Number(s):** 800-255-0752.

★487★
"Commodities Traders: Upping the Stakes" in *Getting Into Money: A Career Guide* **(pp. 91-107)**
Ballantine Books
201 E. 50th St.
New York, NY 10022   Phone: (212)751-2600

Cheri Fein. 1988. Describes careers related to finance, what it takes to succeed in the field, and income potential. Contains interviews with people working in the field and offers job hunting tips.

★488★
"Commodity Trader" in *Careers in Banking and Finance* **(pp. 37-39)**
Rosen Publishing Group, Inc.
29 E. 21st St.
New York, NY 10010   Phone: (212)777-3017

Patricia Haddock. 1990. Describes more than 20 jobs at all levels in banking and finance. Contains information about the types of financial organizations where the jobs are found, educational requirements, job duties, and salaries. Offers advice on job hunting.

★489★
"Financial Services" in *Jobs '91* **(pp. 269-278)**
Prentice Hall Press
1 Gulf & Western Plaza
New York, NY 10023   Phone: (212)373-8500

Kathryn Petras and Ross Petras. Annual, 1991. Discusses employment prospects and trends for 15 professional careers and 29 industries. Lists leading companies, associations, directories, and magazines.

★490★
"Floor Brokers, Traders, and Commodity Traders" in *Jobs! What They Are. . .Where They Are. . .What They Pay* **(pp. 119-120)**
Simon & Schuster, Inc.
Simon & Schuster Bldg.
1230 Avenue of the Americas
New York, NY 10020   Phone: (212)698-7000

Robert O. Snelling and Anne M. Snelling. Revised edition, 1989. Profiles 241 occupations, describing duties and responsibilities, educational preparation, earnings, employment opportunities, training, and qualifications.

★491★
"Institutional Broker" in *Careers in Banking and Finance* **(pp. 54-55)**
Rosen Publishing Group, Inc.
29 E. 21st St.
New York, NY 10010   Phone: (212)777-3017

Patricia Haddock. 1990. Describes more than 20 jobs at all levels in banking and finance. Contains information about the types of financial organizations where the jobs are found, educational requirements, job duties, and salaries. Offers advice on job hunting.

★492★
"Launching a Career on Wall Street" in *Internships Volume 3: Accounting, Banking, Brokerage, Finance & Insurance* **(pp. 23-33)**
Career Press, Inc.
PO Box 34
62 Beverly Rd.
Hawthorne, NJ 07507   Phone: (201)427-0229

Ronald W. Fry, editor-in-chief. 1989. Offers advice about obtaining internships with accounting, brokerage and investment banking firms, banks, and insurance companies. Lists companies offering internships and includes the contact person, duration, duties, qualifications, and application procedures and deadlines.

★493★
No Experience Necessary: Make 100,000 a Year as a Stockbroker
Simon & Schuster, Inc.
Simon & Schuster Bldg.
1230 Avenue of the Americas
New York, NY 10020   Phone: (212)698-7000

Bruce Eaton. 1987. Explains a day in the life of a stockbroker including the work, training, entry into the profession, how to get a job, how to succeed, and earning potential. Offers career planning and job hunting advice.

★494★
"Options Traders" in *The New York Times Career Planner* **(pp. 261-263)**
Times Books
201 E. 50th St.
New York, NY 10022   Phone: (213)751-2600

Elizabeth M. Fowler. 1987. Offers career planning and job hunting advice for the college graduate. Surveys labor market trends. Contains "inside" information on professional careers including educational preparation, employment opportunities, and salaries.

★495★
Salesperson, Securities
Careers, Inc.
PO Box 135
Largo, FL 34649-0135   Phone: (813)584-7333

1989. Two-page occupational summary card describing duties, working conditions, personal qualifications, training, earnings and hours, employment outlook, places of employment, related careers and where to write for more information.

★496★
"Securities" in *Career Choices for the 90's for Students of Business* **(pp. 173-193)**
Walker and Co.
720 Fifth Ave.
New York, NY 10019   Phone: (212)265-3632

1990. Describes jobs in different industries and includes interviews with people working in related occupations. Presents employment outlook, preferred geographic location, entry-level opportunities, career paths, job responsibilities, advancement, personal and professional qualifications, salaries, working conditions, material for further reading, and associations.

★497★
"Securities" in *Career Choices for the 90's for Students of Economics* **(pp. 146-167)**
Walker and Co.
720 Fifth Ave.
New York, NY 10019   Phone: (212)265-3632

1990. Describes jobs in different industries and includes interviews with people working in related occupations. Presents employment outlook, preferred geographic location, entry-level opportunities, career paths, job responsibilities, advancement, personal and professional qualifications, salaries, working conditions, material for further reading, and associations.

Securities and Financial Services Sales Representatives

★498★
"Securities" in *Career Choices for the 90's for Students of M.B.A.* (pp. 176-197)
Walker and Co.
720 Fifth Ave.
New York, NY 10019   Phone: (212)265-3632
1990. Describes jobs in various industries and contains interviews with people working in related occupations. Presents employment outlook, best geographic location, entry-level opportunities, career paths, job responsibilities, advancement possibilities, personal and professional qualifications, salaries, working conditions, material for further reading, and associations.

★499★
"Securities" in *Career Choices for the 90's for Students of Mathematics* (pp. 158-179)
Walker and Co.
720 Fifth Ave.
New York, NY 10019   Phone: (212)265-3632
1990. Describes jobs in different industries and includes interviews with people working in related occupations. Presents employment outlook, preferred geographic location, entry-level opportunities, career paths, job responsibilities, advancement, personal and professional qualifications, salaries, working conditions, material for further reading, and associations.

★500★
"Securities and Exchange Commission" in *Career Choices for the 90's for Students of Law* (pp. 23-24)
Walker and Co.
720 Fifth Ave.
New York, NY 10019   Phone: (212)265-3632
1990. Describes jobs in different industries and includes interviews with people working in related occupations. Presents employment outlook, preferred geographic location, entry-level opportunities, career paths, job responsibilities, advancement, personal and professional qualifications, salaries, working conditions, material for further reading, and associations.

★501★
"Securities and Financial Services Sales Representatives" in *America's 50 Fastest Growing Jobs* (pp. 101-104)
JIST Works, Inc.
720 N. Park Ave.
Indianapolis, IN 46202   Phone: (317)264-3720
Michael J. Farr, compiler. 1991. Describes the 50 fastest growing jobs within major career clusters such as technicians, and marketing and sales. Each job profile explains the nature of the work, skills and abilities required, employment outlook, average earnings, related occupations, education and training requirements, and employment opportunities. Also contains career planning information and job search tips.

★502★
"Securities and Financial Services Sales Representatives" in *Occupational Outlook Handbook* (pp. 238-240)
Superintendent of Documents
U.S. Government Printing Office
Washington, DC 20402   Phone: (202)783-3238
Biennial; latest edition, 1990-91. Encyclopedia of careers describing more than 250 occupations and comprising about 86 percent of all jobs in the economy. Occupations that require lengthy education or training are given the most attention. For each occupation, the handbook describes job duties, working conditions, training, educational preparation, personal qualities, advancement possibilities, job outlook, earnings, and sources of additional information.

★503★
"Securities and Financial Services Sales Representatives" in Volume 3 of *The Encyclopedia of Careers and Vocational Guidance* (pp. 175-177)
J.G. Ferguson Publishing Co.
200 W. Monroe
Chicago, IL 60606   Phone: (312)580-5480
William E. Hopke, editor-in-chief. Eighth edition, 1990. Four-volume set that profiles 500 occupations and describes job trends in 76 industries. Includes career description, educational requirements, history of the job, methods of entry, advancement, employment outlook, earnings, working conditions, social and psychological factors, and sources of additional information.

★504★
"Securities Broker" in *Administration, Business, and Office*, Volume 1 of *Career Information Center* (pp. 139-141)
Glencoe/Macmillan
15319 Chatsworth St.
Mission Hills, CA 91345   Phone: (818)898-1391
Richard Lidz and Dale Anderson, editorial directors. Fourth edition, 1990. For 600 occupations, describes job duties, entry-level requirements, education and training needed, advancement possibilities, employment outlook, earnings and benefits. The set is divided into 12 volumes. Each volume includes jobs related under a broad career field. Volume 13 is the index. **Facsimile Number:** 818-365-5489.

★505★
"Securities Brokerage" in *How to Get the Hot Jobs in Business & Finance* (pp. 117-130)
HarperCollins Inc.
10 E. 53rd St.
New York, NY 10022   Phone: (212)207-7000
Mary E. Calhoun. Revised edition, 1988. Job hunting and career guide written for the college graduate. Surveys the highest paying jobs on Wall Street. Each chapter describes the work, certification or licensure, and entry into the field. Lists 500 financial institutions.

★506★
"Securities Brokers" in *Jobs! What They Are...Where They Are...What They Pay* (p. 121)
Simon & Schuster, Inc.
Simon & Schuster Bldg.
1230 Avenue of the Americas
New York, NY 10020   Phone: (212)698-7000
Robert O. Snelling and Anne M. Snelling. Revised edition, 1989. Profiles 241 occupations, describing duties and responsibilities, educational preparation, earnings, employment opportunities, training, and qualifications.

★507★
"Securities" in *The Encyclopedia of Career Choices for the 1990s: A Guide to Entry Level Jobs* (pp. 784-804)
Walker and Co.
720 Fifth Ave.
New York, NY 10019   Phone: (212)265-3632
1991. Describes entry-level opportunities in 42 career fields for college graduates. Each chapter covers a single career field, including an overview, employment outlook, major employers, tips on entering the field, international job opportunities, functional job areas with personal and professional qualifications, career paths, job responsibilities, advancement possibilities, salaries, and working conditions. Lists related sources of information.

★508★
"Securities Sales" in *Career Choices for the 90's for Students of Business* (pp. 160-163, 180-182)
Walker and Co.
720 Fifth Ave.
New York, NY 10019   Phone: (212)265-3632
1990. Describes jobs in different industries and includes interviews with people working in related occupations. Presents employment outlook, preferred geographic location, entry-level opportunities, career paths, job responsibilities, advancement, personal and professional qualifications, salaries, working conditions, material for further reading, and associations.

★509★
"Securities Sales" in *Career Choices for the 90's for Students of Communications and Journalism* (pp. 169-171)
Walker and Co.
720 Fifth Ave.
New York, NY 10019   Phone: (212)265-3632
1990. Describes jobs in different industries and includes interviews with people working in related occupations. Presents employment outlook, preferred geographic location, entry-level opportunities, career paths, job responsibilities, advancement, personal and professional qualifications, salaries, working conditions, material for further reading, and associations.

★510★
"Securities Sales" in *Career Choices for the 90's for Students of Political Science & Government* (pp. 169-172)
Walker and Co.
720 Fifth Ave.
New York, NY 10019   Phone: (212)265-3632
1990. Describes jobs in different industries and includes interviews with people working in related occupations. Presents employment outlook, preferred geographic location, entry-level opportunities, career paths, job responsibilities, advancement, personal and professional qualifications, salaries, working conditions, material for further reading, and associations.

★511★
"Securities Sales" in *Career Choices for the 90's for Students of Psychology* (pp. 189-191)
Walker and Co.
720 Fifth Ave.
New York, NY 10019   Phone: (212)265-3632
1990. Describes jobs in different industries and includes interviews with people working in related occupations. Presents employment outlook, preferred geographic location, entry-level opportunities, career paths, job responsibilities, advancement, personal and professional qualifications, salaries, working conditions, material for further reading, and associations.

★512★
"Securities Sales Agents" in *Transitions: Military Pathways to Civilian Careers* (pp. 140-141)
Rosen Publishing Group, Inc.
29 E. 21st St.
New York, NY 10010   Phone: (212)777-3017
Robert W. MacDonald. 1988. Describes how to make the best use of your military service to create a civilian career. Describes skills needed in civilian employment and compares them to skills acquired in the military. Covers career planning, job search, resume writing, and starting a small business. Lists many resources.

★513★
"Securities Sales" in *The Encyclopedia of Career Choices for the 1990s: A Guide to Entry Level Jobs* (pp. 771-774)
Walker and Co.
720 Fifth Ave.
New York, NY 10019   Phone: (212)265-3632
1991. Describes entry-level opportunities in 42 career fields for college graduates. Each chapter covers a single career field, including an overview, employment outlook, major employers, tips on entering the field, international job opportunities, functional job areas with personal and professional qualifications, career paths, job responsibilities, advancement possibilities, salaries, and working conditions. Lists related sources of information.

★514★
Securities Sales Representatives
Chronicle Guidance Publications, Inc.
PO Box 1190
Moravia, NY 13118-1190   Phone: (315)497-0330
1990. This career brief describes the nature of the work, working conditions, hours and earnings, education and training, licensure, certification, unions, personal qualifications, social and psychological factors, employment outlook, entry methods, advancement, and related occupations. **Toll-free/Additional Phone Number(s):** 800-622-7284.

★515★
"Securities Sales Representatives (Stockbrokers)" in *101 Careers: A Guide to the Fastest-Growing Opportunities* (pp. 32-35)
John Wiley & Sons, Inc.
605 Third Ave.
New York, NY 10158   Phone: (212)850-6000
Michael Harkavy. 1990. Each occupational profile includes a job description, job titles, work environment, employment outlook, qualifications, personal skills, and earnings.

★516★
"Securities Sales Worker (Stockbroker)" in *VGM's Careers Encyclopedia* (pp. 427-429)
National Textbook Co.
4255 W. Touhy Ave.
Lincolnwood, IL 60646   Phone: (312)679-5500
Third edition, 1991. Contains two- to five-page descriptions of 200 managerial, professional, technical, trade, and service occupations. Each profile includes job duties, places of employment, qualifications, educational preparation, training, employment potential, advancement, income, and additional sources of information.

★517★
"Securities Sales Worker (Stockbroker)" in *VGM's Handbook of Business and Management Careers* (pp. 90-92)
National Textbook Co.
4255 W. Touhy Ave.
Lincolnwood, IL 60646   Phone: (312)679-5500
Craig T. Norback. 1990. Contains 43 two-page occupational profiles describing job duties, places of employment, working conditions, qualifications, education, employment outlook, and income.

Securities and Financial Services Sales Representatives ★528★

★518★
"Securities Salesperson" in *Occu-Facts: Information on 565 Careers in Outline Form* (p. 11.6)
Careers, Inc.
P.O. Box 135
1211 Tenth St., S.W.
Largo, FL 33640 Phone: (813)584-7333
Elizabeth Handville. Biennial, 1989-90 edition. Each one-page occupational profile describes duties, working conditions, physical surroundings and demands, aptitudes, temperament, educational requirements, employment outlook, earnings, and places of employment.

★519★
"Security Sales Workers and Brokers" in *Opportunities in Financial Careers* (pp. 54-61)
National Textbook Co.
4255 W. Touhy Ave.
Lincolnwood, IL 60646 Phone: (312)679-5500
Michael Crist Sumichrast. 1991. Describes job opportunities in banking, financial services, corporate and industrial finance, and accounting. Provides job duties, working conditions, educational requirements, earnings, and industry trends. Lists associations, periodicals, and major employees in finance and banking.

★520★
"Services Sales Representatives" in Volume 6 of *Career Discovery Encyclopedia* (pp. 18-19)
J.G. Ferguson Publishing Co.
200 W. Monroe
Chicago, IL 60606 Phone: (312)580-5480
E. Russell Primm, editor-in-chief. 1990. Contains two-page articles on 504 occupations. Each article describes job duties, earnings, and educational and training requirements.

★521★
Stockbroker
Vocational Biographies, Inc.
PO Box 31, Dept. VF10
Sauk Centre, MN 56378 Phone: (612)352-6516
1990. This pamphlet profiles a person working in the job. Includes information about job duties, working conditions, places of employment, educational preparation, labor market outlook, and salaries. **Toll-free/Additional Phone Number(s):** 800-255-0752.

★522★
"Stockbroker" in *College Board Guide to Jobs and Career Planning* (pp. 142-144)
College Entrance Examination Board
45 Columbus Ave.
New York, NY 10023-6992 Phone: (212)713-8000
Joyce Slayton Mitchell. 1990. Career planning guide written for high school and college students. Covers 100 careers in 15 occupational groups. Provides job description, educational preparation needed, salaries, related careers, and sources of additional information. Includes information about the 90's labor market.

★523★
"Stockbroker" in *Top Professions: The 100 Most Popular, Dynamic, and Profitable Careers in America Today* (pp. 1-3)
Peterson's Guides, Inc.
202 Carnegie Center
PO Box 2123
Princeton, NJ 08543-2123 Phone: (609)243-9111
Nicholas Basta. 1989. Includes occupations requiring a college or advanced degree. Describes job duties, earnings, some typical job titles, career opportunities at different degree levels, and lists related associations.

★524★
"Stockbrokers" in *The New York Times Career Planner* (pp. 308-310)
Times Books
201 E. 50th St.
New York, NY 10022 Phone: (213)751-2600
Elizabeth M. Fowler. 1987. Offers career planning and job hunting advice for the college graduate. Surveys labor market trends. Contains "inside" information on professional careers including educational preparation, employment opportunities, and salaries.

★525★
"Stockbrokers" in Volume 6 of *Career Discovery Encyclopedia* (pp. 66-67)
J.G. Ferguson Publishing Co.
200 W. Monroe
Chicago, IL 60606 Phone: (312)580-5480
E. Russell Primm, editor-in-chief. 1990. Contains two-page articles on 504 occupations. Each article describes job duties, earnings, and educational and training requirements.

★526★
"Trader" in *Careers in Banking and Finance* (pp. 67-72)
Rosen Publishing Group, Inc.
29 E. 21st St.
New York, NY 10010 Phone: (212)777-3017
Patricia Haddock. 1990. Describes more than 20 jobs at all levels in banking and finance. Contains information about the types of financial organizations where the jobs are found, educational requirements, job duties, and salaries. Offers advice on job hunting.

★527★
"Traders" in *The American Almanac of Jobs and Salaries* (pp. 421-422)
Avon Books
105 Madison Avenue
New York, NY 10016 Phone: (212)481-5600
John Wright and Edward J. Dwyer. Revised and updated, 1990. A comprehensive guide to the wages of hundreds of occupations in a wide variety of industries and organizations.

★528★
"Traders: Dealing With Uncertainty" in *Getting Into Money: A Career Guide* (pp. 74-90)
Ballantine Books
201 E. 50th St.
New York, NY 10022 Phone: (212)751-2600
Cheri Fein. 1988. Describes careers related to finance, what it takes to succeed in the field, and income potential. Contains interviews with people working in the field and offers job hunting tips.

★529★
Traders: the Jobs, the Products, the Markets
New York Institute of Finance
2 Broadway
New York, NY 10004-2207

David M. Weiss. 1990. Provides an overview of the securities industry. Describes the work and procedures of many different types of trades in many different marketplaces.

★530★
"Wall Street Bond Broker" in ***Straight Talk on Careers: 80 Pros Take You Into Their Professions*** (pp. 21-24)
Garrett Park Press
PO Box 190
Garrett Park, MD 20896 Phone: (301)946-2553

Mary Barbera-Hogan. 1987. Written for readers in high school and college. Contains candid interviews from professionals who discuss what their days are like and the pros and cons of their occupations.

★531★
"Wall Street: Building a Career in Finance" in ***Fast-Track Careers: A Guide to the Highest-Paying Jobs*** (pp. 17-39)
John Wiley & Sons, Inc.
605 Third Ave.
New York, NY 10158 Phone: (212)850-6000

William Lewis and Nancy Schuman. 1987. Profiles eight glamourous and high paying careers describing entry-level opportunities, earnings, personal qualities, types of companies, educational preparation and training, and employment outlook. Lists prominent companies in each industry, typical jargon, and professional associations.

Associations

★532★
Securities Industry Association (SIA)
120 Broadway
New York, NY 10271 Phone: (212)608-1500

Membership: Investment bankers, securities underwriters, and dealers in stocks and bonds. **Purpose:** To represent and serve all segments of the securities industry and provide a unified voice in legislation, regulation, and public information. Conducts studies and compiles statistics on investment, securities markets, and related matters. Sponsors management development programs; conducts roundtables. Maintains offices in New York City, Washington, DC, and Albany, NY. **Publications:** *International Capital Markets Review*, periodic. • *Securities Industry Association—Directory and Guide*, annual. • *Securities Industry Association—Foreign Activity Report*, quarterly. • *Securities Industry Association—Yearbook*. • *Securities Industry Trends*, monthly. • *SIA Washington Report*, bimonthly. • *SOURCES: The Securities Executive's Guide to Products and Services*, annual. • *Tax Briefs from SIA*, periodic. **Facsimile Number:** (212)608-1604.

Standards/Certification Agencies

Securities sales representatives must meet state licensing requirements, usually by passing an exam and furnishing a personal bond. To qualify as a registered representative, applicants must pass the General Securities Registered Representative Examination administered by the National Association of Securities Dealers as well as the Uniform Securities Agents State Law Examination administered by each state.

Basic Reference Guides and Handbooks

★533★
Glossary of Financial Services Terminology
Institute of Financial Education
111 E. Wacker Dr.
Chicago, IL 60601-4389 Phone: (312)644-3100

Fourth edition. 1990. **Facsimile Number:** (312)856-0497.

★534★
Sales Management in Financial Services: How to Build a Competitive Sales Team
Bank Administration Institute
60 Gould Center
Rolling Meadows, IL 60008

Jeff Sucec. 1990. **Toll-free/Additional Phone Number(s):** 800-323-8552.

★535★
Setting Up & Running Financial Systems
Butterworth Legal Publishers
289 E. 5th St.
St. Paul, MN 55101 Phone: (612)227-4200

Steve Ives. 1989.

★536★
Smart Selling: Successful Sales Techniques for Bankers
Bank Administration Institute
60 Gould Center
Rolling Meadows, IL 60008

Judith A. Pennington. 1990. **Toll-free/Additional Phone Number(s):** 800-323-8552.

Periodicals

★537★
American Salesman
National Research Bureau, Inc.
424 N. 3rd St.
Burlington, IA 52601-5224 Phone: (319)752-5415

Barbara Boeding, Editor. Monthly. Salesmanship magazine. **Facsimile Number:** (319)752-3421.

★538★
Bank Auditing and Accounting Report
Warren, Gorham & Lamont, Inc.
One Penn Plaza
New York, NY 10119 Phone: (212)971-5201

Editor(s): Stephen Collins. Monthly. Provides information on developments, practices, and techniques in bank accounting, auditing, and financial controls. Covers such topics as procedures for preventing embezzlement, improving management information systems, audit planning and supervision, and electronic data processing developments.

★539★
Bank Director's Report
Warren, Gorham & Lamont, Inc.
One Penn Plaza
New York, NY 10119 Phone: (212)971-5000

Editor(s): Margaret Murray. Monthly. Provides information on economics, regulations, law, and competition in the banking

Securities and Financial Services Sales Representatives ★552★

industry. Reports on current developments that affect banks, such as interstate banking, competition with nonfinancial institutions, purchasing new banks, and director's liability insurance. Covers the activities of federal financial institutions. Recurring features include news of research and a column titled Bank Director's Legal Report.

★540★
Bank Insurance & Protection Bulletin
American Bankers Association (ABA)
1120 Connecticut Ave. NW
Washington, DC 20036   Phone: (202)663-5305
Editor(s): C. Howie Hodges, II. Monthly. Monitors the latest trends in risk management, insurance, and security for banks. Reports on current bank crime statistics, methods of deterrence, and other "state of the art information.". Recurring features include news of research, notices of publications available, a calendar of events, meeting reports, and news of educational opportunities.

★541★
Bank Operations Report
Warren, Gorham & Lamont, Inc.
One Penn Plaza
New York, NY 10119   Phone: (212)971-5000
Editor(s): Pat Durner. Monthly. Focuses on electronic data processing control, check processing, record keeping, cost control, Federal regulation, credit and debit cards, electronic funds transfer system, physical security, and office automation, computer, and systems applications.

★542★
Bank Security Report
Warren, Gorham & Lamont, Inc.
One Penn Plaza
New York, NY 10119   Phone: (212)971-5000
Editor(s): Pat Durner. Monthly. Compiles news, information, case histories, suggestions, and advice on bank security equipment and procedures, forgeries, check alterations, identifications, kiting, counterfeiting, internal controls, and new federal announcements on bank security.

★543★
Banking Expansion Reporter
Law and Business, Inc.
Prentice-Hall, Inc.
910 Sylvan Ave.
Englewood Cliffs, NJ 07632   Phone: (201)894-8538
Semimonthly. Discusses new strategies, techniques, and developments in the financial services industry. **Facsimile Number:** (201)894-8666.

★544★
Credit
American Financial Services Assn.
1101 14th St. NW
Washington, DC 20005   Phone: (202)289-0400
Barbara E. Van Gorder Editor. 6x/yr. Financial services magazine. **Facsimile Number:** (202)842-4342.

★545★
Gold Mining Stock Report
Robert Bishop
PO Box 1217
Lafayette, CA 94549   Phone: (510)283-4848
Editor(s): Bob Bishop. Monthly. Offers analysis and specific recommendations for investors interested in gold mining stocks, emphasizing junioe companies. Carries discussions of market strategy. Recurring features include news of research and interviews. **Toll-free/Additional Phone Number(s):** 800-759-7677 **Facsimile Number:** (510)283-8901.

★546★
Independent Operations
American Financial Services Association
1101 14th St. NW, Ste. 400
Washington, DC 20005   Phone: (202)289-0400
Editor(s): Glen Kaup. Quarterly. Furnishes members with news of the financial services industry, small business, and other areas of concern to the members of the Association's Section on Independent Operations. Includes news of current legislation, regulations, and individual/company profiles. Recurring features include letters to the editor, interviews, reports of meetings, news of association events and conferences, and notices of publications available. **Toll-free/Additional Phone Number(s):** 800-843-3280 **Facsimile Number:** (202)842-4342.

★547★
International Capital Markets Review
Securities Industry Association (SIA)
120 Broadway
New York, NY 10271   Phone: (212)608-1500
Periodic. Newsletter covering U.S. investments in foreign markets, as well as foreign investments in the United States; includes statistics.

★548★
Investment Vision
Independent Investor Publications, Inc.
82 Devonshire St.
Boston, MA 02109   Phone: (617)570-7000
Susan Feldman, Editor-in-Chief. 6x/yr Investment and personal finance magazine.

★549★
The Journal of Portfolio Management
Institutional Investor
488 Madison Ave.
New York, NY 10022   Phone: (212)303-3300
Frank J. Fabozzi. Quarterly. Magazine focusing on portfolio management and investment systems.

★550★
Moody's Bond Survey
99 Church St.
New York, NY 10007   Phone: (212)553-0402
Robert Thompson, Editor. Weekly (Mon.). Magazine focusing on the bond market.

★551★
OTC Chart Manual
Standard & Poor's
25 Broadway
New York, NY 10004   Phone: (212)208-8000
Kenneth Lutz, Editor. 6x/yr. Charts on over-the-counter stocks.

★552★
Over-The-Counter Stock Reports
Standard & Poor's
25 Broadway
New York, NY 10004   Phone: (212)208-8000
S. Vallance, Editor. Daily. Analytical reports on companies. **Facsimile Number:** (212)412-0299.

★553★
Salesman's Insider
Marv Q. Modell Associates
6009 Montgomery Corner
San Jose, CA 95135-1431   Phone: (408)270-4526
Editor(s): Marv Q. Modell. Monthly. Concerned with selling techniques and methodology in all sales areas. Tracks new sales developments, trends, and profit opportunities. Details negotiatineg process with "tips that work".

★554★
Securities Industry Trends
Securities Industry Association (SIA)
120 Broadway
New York, NY 10271   Phone: (212)608-1500
Monthly. Report covering trends within the securities industry and on economic developments affecting securities firms; includes statistics.

★555★
Securities Regulation Law Journal
Warren, Gorham and Lamont, Inc.
1 Penn Plaza
New York, NY 10019   Phone: (212)971-5000
Jayne Allen, Mng. Editor. Quarterly. Securities law journal. **Facsimile Number:** (212)971-5025.

★556★
Security Management
America Society for Industrial Security
1655 N. Fort Myer Dr., Ste. 1200
Arlington, VA 22209   Phone: (703)522-5800
Mary Alice Crawford, Editor-in-Chief/Publisher. Monthly. Loss prevention and security magazine. **Facsimile Number:** (703)243-4954.

★557★
SIA Washington Report
Securities Industry Association (SIA)
120 Broadway
New York, NY 10271   Phone: (212)608-1500
Bimonthly. Bulletin informing members of legislative and regulatory developments in Washington pertinent to the industry.

★558★
Tax Briefs from SIA (SIA)
Securities Industry Association (SIA)
120 Broadway
New York, NY 10271   Phone: (212)608-1500
Periodic. Newsletter informing firms of important tax issues affecting day-to-day operations.

——— Meetings and Conventions ———

★559★
Securities Industry Association Sales and Marketing Conference
120 Broadway
New York, NY 10271   Phone: (212)608-1500
Frequency: Annual. **Facsimile Number:** (212)608-1604.

★560★
Securities Industry Institute
Securities Industry Association (SIA)
120 Broadway
New York, NY 10271   Phone: (212)608-1500
Frequency: Annual. **Facsimile Number:** (212)608-1604.

Services Sales Representatives

Services sales representatives sell a wide variety of services. Sales representatives for data processing services may sell services like payroll processing, and financial reporting. Sales representatives for hotels may contact government, business, and social groups in an effort to solicit convention business for the hotel. Other representatives sell sell advertising, automotive leasing, printing, and management consulting services. They must establish a client base through use of business directories and personal referrals. Services sales representatives must fully understand and be able to discuss the services their company offers. Often literature or demonstrations are used to describe their company's services. If they fail to make a sale on the first visit, they may follow up with more visits, letters, and phone calls. If a sale is made, representatives call on their customers to ensure that everything is satisfactory. A sales representative's job can vary with the kind of service being sold. In general, highly technical services require more complex and lengthy sales processes. The job may also vary with the size of the company and territory. Those working for large companies usually are more specialized and assigned territorial boundaries.

$alaries

Sales representatives work on different types of compensation plans. Some get a straight salary, others are paid on a commission basis or a combination of both. The median annual earnings of full-time advertising sales representatives are about $23,100. Representatives selling other business services earn $23,700.

Employment Outlook

Growth rate until the year 2000: Faster than average.

Services Sales Representatives

Career Guides

★561★
"Advertising Sales" in *Careers in Fashion Retailing* (pp. 80-82)
Rosen Publishing Group, Inc.
29 E. 21st St.
New York, NY 10010　　　　Phone: (212)777-3017
Pat Koester. 1990. Describes fashion retailing, industry structure, career paths, and typical jobs such as sales, management, and buying. Profiles persons working in the field and discusses educational preparation. Lists schools that offer programs in fashion retailing.

★562★
"Advertising Sales Person" in *VGM's Handbook of Business and Management Careers* (pp. 11-14)
National Textbook Co.
4255 W. Touhy Ave.
Lincolnwood, IL 60646　　　　Phone: (312)679-5500
Craig T. Norback. 1990. Contains 43 two-page occupational profiles describing job duties, places of employment, working conditions, qualifications, education, employment outlook, and income.

★563★
"Advertising Sales Representatives" in *Jobs! What They Are...Where They Are...What They Pay* (pp. 275-276)
Simon & Schuster, Inc.
Simon & Schuster Bldg.
1230 Avenue of the Americas
New York, NY 10020　　　　Phone: (212)698-7000
Robert O. Snelling and Anne M. Snelling. Revised edition, 1989. Profiles 241 occupations, describing duties and responsibilities, educational preparation, earnings, employment opportunities, training, and qualifications.

★564★
"Advertising Sales, Television" in *Career Choices for the 90's for Students of Communications and Journalism* (pp. 189-191)
Walker and Co.
720 Fifth Ave.
New York, NY 10019　　　　Phone: (212)265-3632
1990. Describes jobs in different industries and includes interviews with people working in related occupations. Presents employment outlook, preferred geographic location, entry-level opportunities, career paths, job responsibilities, advancement, personal and professional qualifications, salaries, working conditions, material for further reading, and associations.

★565★
"Advertising Sales (Television)" in *The Encyclopedia of Career Choices for the 1990s: A Guide to Entry Level Jobs* (pp. 828-830)
Walker and Co.
720 Fifth Ave.
New York, NY 10019　　　　Phone: (212)265-3632
1991. Describes entry-level opportunities in 42 career fields for college graduates. Each chapter covers a single career field, including an overview, employment outlook, major employers, tips on entering the field, international job opportunities, functional job areas with personal and professional qualifications, career paths, job responsibilities, advancement possibilities, salaries, and working conditions. Lists related sources of information.

★566★
"Advertising Sales Workers" in Volume 1 of *Career Discovery Encyclopedia* (pp. 20-21)
J.G. Ferguson Publishing Co.
200 W. Monroe
Chicago, IL 60606　　　　Phone: (312)580-5480
E. Russell Primm, editor-in-chief. 1990. Contains two-page articles on 504 occupations. Each article describes job duties, earnings, and educational and training requirements.

★567★
"Advertising Salesperson" in *Career Opportunities in Television, Cable, and Video* (pp. 110-111)
Facts on File, Inc.
460 Park Avenue, S.
New York, NY 10016　　　　Phone: (212)683-2244
Third edition, 1990. Describes 100 media-related jobs. Each occupational profile covers job duties, employment outlook, career paths, salaries, skills, and educational preparation. Offers tips for entering the field.

★568★
"Advertising Space Sales" in *Career Choices for the 90's for Students of Business* (pp. 155-158)
Walker and Co.
720 Fifth Ave.
New York, NY 10019　　　　Phone: (212)265-3632
1990. Describes jobs in different industries and includes interviews with people working in related occupations. Presents employment outlook, preferred geographic location, entry-level opportunities, career paths, job responsibilities, advancement, personal and professional qualifications, salaries, working conditions, material for further reading, and associations.

★569★
"Advertising Space Sales" in *Career Choices for the 90's for Students of Political Science & Government* (pp. 164-167)
Walker and Co.
720 Fifth Ave.
New York, NY 10019   Phone: (212)265-3632
1990. Describes jobs in different industries and includes interviews with people working in related occupations. Presents employment outlook, preferred geographic location, entry-level opportunities, career paths, job responsibilities, advancement, personal and professional qualifications, salaries, working conditions, material for further reading, and associations.

★570★
"Advertising Space Sales" in *The Encyclopedia of Career Choices for the 1990s: A Guide to Entry Level Jobs* (pp. 610-613, 766-769)
Walker and Co.
720 Fifth Ave.
New York, NY 10019   Phone: (212)265-3632
1991. Describes entry-level opportunities in 42 career fields for college graduates. Each chapter covers a single career field, including an overview, employment outlook, major employers, tips on entering the field, international job opportunities, functional job areas with personal and professional qualifications, career paths, job responsibilities, advancement possibilities, salaries, and working conditions. Lists related sources of information.

★571★
"Advertising Space Sales, Newspaper Publishing" in *Career Choices for the 90's for Students of Communications and Journalism* (pp. 104-106)
Walker and Co.
720 Fifth Ave.
New York, NY 10019   Phone: (212)265-3632
1990. Describes jobs in different industries and includes interviews with people working in related occupations. Presents employment outlook, preferred geographic location, entry-level opportunities, career paths, job responsibilities, advancement, personal and professional qualifications, salaries, working conditions, material for further reading, and associations.

★572★
"Advertising Space Sales, Newspaper Publishing" in *Career Choices for the 90's for Students of Political Science & Government* (pp. 110-113)
Walker and Co.
720 Fifth Ave.
New York, NY 10019   Phone: (212)265-3632
1990. Describes jobs in different industries and includes interviews with people working in related occupations. Presents employment outlook, preferred geographic location, entry-level opportunities, career paths, job responsibilities, advancement, personal and professional qualifications, salaries, working conditions, material for further reading, and associations.

★573★
"Advertising Space Salesperson" in *Occu-Facts: Information on 565 Careers in Outline Form* (p. 11.7)
Careers, Inc.
P.O. Box 135
1211 Tenth St., S.W.
Largo, FL 33640   Phone: (813)584-7333
Elizabeth Handville. Biennial, 1989-90 edition. Each one-page occupational profile describes duties, working conditions, physical surroundings and demands, aptitudes, temperament, educational requirements, employment outlook, earnings, and places of employment.

★574★
All Pro
BNA Communications, Inc.
9439 Key West Ave.
Rockville, MD 20850   Phone: (301)948-0540
Videocassette. 1981. 29 mins. Conversations with five top sales professionals. They discuss their careers and the traits that make a top professional.

★575★
"A Bright Future in Classified Ad Sales" in *Newspapers Career Directory* (pp. 17-19)
Career Press, Inc.
PO Box 34
62 Beverly Rd.
Hawthorne, NJ 07507   Phone: (201)427-0229
Ronald W. Fry, editor. Third edition, 1990. Separate chapters written by practitioners describe newspaper careers in classified and retail ad sales, editorial cartooning, circulation, editing, librarianship, production and promotion. Explains job duties, entry into the field, educational preparation, trends, career paths, and skills needed. Lists associations, publications, and companies actively seeking entry level employees.

★576★
"A Career in Outdoor Advertising Sales" in *Advertising Career Directory* (pp. 61-64)
Career Press, Inc.
PO Box 34
62 Beverly Rd.
Hawthorne, NJ 07507   Phone: (201)427-0229
Ronald W. Fry, editor. Fourth edition, 1990. Provides an overview of the advertising industry and describes what agencies do, and four areas of specialization including account management, and the creative, media, and research functions. Lists companies that offer entry-level job opportunities.

★577★
Classified Sales Representative
Careers, Inc.
PO Box 135
Largo, FL 34649-0135   Phone: (813)584-7333
1989. Two-page occupational summary card describing duties, working conditions, personal qualifications, training, earnings and hours, employment outlook, places of employment, related careers and where to write for more information.

★578★
"Customer Services Sales" in *Careers in Marketing* (pp. 68-69)
National Textbook Co.
4255 W. Touhy Ave.
Lincolnwood, MI 60646   Phone: (312)679-5500
Lila B. Stair. 1991. Surveys career opportunities in marketing and related areas such as marketing research, product development, and sales promotion. Includes a description of the work, places of employment, employment outlook, trends, educational preparation, organizational charts, and salaries. Offers job hunting advice.

★579★
Exploring Careers in Computer Sales
Rosen Publishing Group, Inc.
29 E. 21st. St.
New York, NY 10010	Phone: (212)777-3017
Lawrence Epstein. 1990. Part of Career Series. **Toll-free/Additional Phone Number(s): 800-237-9932. Facsimile Number:** (212)777-0277.

★580★
"Getting Started in Retail Ad Sales" in *Newspapers Career Directory* (pp. 21-24)
Career Press, Inc.
PO Box 34
62 Beverly Rd.
Hawthorne, NJ 07507	Phone: (201)427-0229
Ronald W. Fry, editor. Third edition, 1990. Separate chapters written by practitioners describe newspaper careers in classified and retail ad sales, editorial cartooning, circulation, editing, librarianship, production and promotion. Explains job duties, entry into the field, educational preparation, trends, career paths, and skills needed. Lists associations, publications, and companies actively seeking entry level employees.

★581★
"Magazine Advertising Sales" in *Career Choices for the 90's for Students of Business* (pp. 167-169)
Walker and Co.
720 Fifth Ave.
New York, NY 10019	Phone: (212)265-3632
1990. Describes jobs in different industries and includes interviews with people working in related occupations. Presents employment outlook, preferred geographic location, entry-level opportunities, career paths, job responsibilities, advancement, personal and professional qualifications, salaries, working conditions, material for further reading, and associations.

★582★
"Magazine Advertising Sales" in *Career Choices for the 90's for Students of Political Science & Government* (pp. 176-178)
Walker and Co.
720 Fifth Ave.
New York, NY 10019	Phone: (212)265-3632
1990. Describes jobs in different industries and includes interviews with people working in related occupations. Presents employment outlook, preferred geographic location, entry-level opportunities, career paths, job responsibilities, advancement, personal and professional qualifications, salaries, working conditions, material for further reading, and associations.

★583★
"Magazine Advertising Sales" in *Career Choices for the 90's for Students of Psychology* (196-198)
Walker and Co.
720 Fifth Ave.
New York, NY 10019	Phone: (212)265-3632
1990. Describes jobs in different industries and includes interviews with people working in related occupations. Presents employment outlook, preferred geographic location, entry-level opportunities, career paths, job responsibilities, advancement, personal and professional qualifications, salaries, working conditions, material for further reading, and associations.

★584★
"Magazine Advertising Sales" in *The Encyclopedia of Career Choices for the 1990s: A Guide to Entry Level Jobs* (pp. 778-780)
Walker and Co.
720 Fifth Ave.
New York, NY 10019	Phone: (212)265-3632
1991. Describes entry-level opportunities in 42 career fields for college graduates. Each chapter covers a single career field, including an overview, employment outlook, major employers, tips on entering the field, international job opportunities, functional job areas with personal and professional qualifications, career paths, job responsibilities, advancement possibilities, salaries, and working conditions. Lists related sources of information.

★585★
"Marketing and Sales, Hotel Management" in *Career Choices for the 90's for Students of Psychology* (pp. 101-103)
Walker and Co.
720 Fifth Ave.
New York, NY 10019	Phone: (212)265-3632
1990. Describes jobs in different industries and includes interviews with people working in related occupations. Presents employment outlook, preferred geographic location, entry-level opportunities, career paths, job responsibilities, advancement, personal and professional qualifications, salaries, working conditions, material for further reading, and associations.

★586★
"Marketing and Sales" in *The Encyclopedia of Career Choices for the 1990s: A Guide to Entry Level Jobs* (pp. 407-409)
Walker and Co.
720 Fifth Ave.
New York, NY 10019	Phone: (212)265-3632
1991. Describes entry-level opportunities in 42 career fields for college graduates. Each chapter covers a single career field, including an overview, employment outlook, major employers, tips on entering the field, international job opportunities, functional job areas with personal and professional qualifications, career paths, job responsibilities, advancement possibilities, salaries, and working conditions. Lists related sources of information.

★587★
"Marketing/Sales" in *Career Choices for the 90's for Students of Business* (pp. 99-101)
Walker and Co.
720 Fifth Ave.
New York, NY 10019	Phone: (212)265-3632
1990. Describes jobs in different industries and includes interviews with people working in related occupations. Presents employment outlook, preferred geographic location, entry-level opportunities, career paths, job responsibilities, advancement, personal and professional qualifications, salaries, working conditions, material for further reading, and associations.

★588★
"Newspaper and Magazine Advertising Sales Representative" in *Career Opportunities in Advertising and Public Relations* (pp. 224-226)
Facts on File, Inc.
460 Park Avenue, S.
New York, NY 10016	Phone: (212)683-2244
Shelly Field, 1990. Contains more than 80 jobs related to advertising and public relations in the private, public, and nonprofit sectors. Each occupational profile describes job

duties, salary, employment outlook, career paths, advancement prospects, educational preparation, training, and skills. Offers tips for entering the field.

★589★
"Opportunities in Marketing & Sales" in *Travel and Hospitality Career Directory* (pp. 66-68)
Career Press, Inc.
PO Box 34
62 Beverly Rd.
Hawthorne, NJ 07507 Phone: (201)427-0229
Ronald W. Fry, editor. 1989. Offers advice on career planning and job hunting in hotel, travel, and related industries. Lists companies offering entry level positions in airlines, convention and visitors' bureaus, foreign tourist boards, hotels, travel agencies, car rental firms, and cruise lines. Lists travel and hospitality associations and trade publications.

★590★
"Radio Advertising Salesperson" in *Career Opportunities in Advertising and Public Relations* (pp. 128-130)
Facts on File, Inc.
460 Park Avenue, S.
New York, NY 10016 Phone: (212)683-2244
Shelly Field, 1990. Contains more than 80 jobs related to advertising and public relations in the private, public, and nonprofit sectors. Each occupational profile describes job duties, salary, employment outlook, career paths, advancement prospects, educational preparation, training, and skills. Offers tips for entering the field.

★591★
"Radio, Television, and Print Advertising Sales Workers" in Volume 3 of *The Encyclopedia of Careers and Vocational Guidance* (pp. 158-162)
J.G. Ferguson Publishing Co.
200 W. Monroe
Chicago, IL 60606 Phone: (312)580-5480
William E. Hopke, editor-in-chief. Eighth edition, 1990. Four-volume set that profiles 500 occupations and describes job trends in 76 industries. Includes career description, educational requirements, history of the job, methods of entry, advancement, employment outlook, earnings, working conditions, social and psychological factors, and sources of additional information.

★592★
"Sales Opportunities in Service Industries" in *Opportunities in Sales Careers* (pp. 123-131)
National Textbook Co.
4255 W. Touhy Ave.
Lincolnwood, IL 60646 Phone: (312)679-5500
James Brescoll and Ralph M. Dahm. 1988. Surveys jobs in sales and describes the skills needed to succeed. Covers the nature of the work, employment outlook, educational preparation, and training, salary, and rewards of the work.

★593★
Salesperson, Advertising Space
Careers, Inc.
PO Box 135
Largo, FL 34649-0135 Phone: (813)584-7333
1988. Two-page occupational summary card describing duties, working conditions, personal qualifications, training, earnings and hours, employment outlook, places of employment, related careers and where to write for more information.

★594★
Selling Services
United Learning, Inc.
6633 West Howard St.
Niles, IL 60648 Phone: (708)647-0600
Videocassette. 1986. 17 mins. This video is designed for people who sell services as opposed to goods.

★595★
Service Marketing
Quiet Advantage
1949 South Manchester St. 34
Anaheim, CA 92802 Phone: (714)748-1840
Videocassette. 1991. 28 mins. Defines the service industry and its produts.

★596★
"Service Sales Representatives" in *America's 50 Fastest Growing Jobs* (pp. 104-106)
JIST Works, Inc.
720 N. Park Ave.
Indianapolis, IN 46202 Phone: (317)264-3720
Michael J. Farr, compiler. 1991. Describes the 50 fastest growing jobs within major career clusters such as technicians, and marketing and sales. Each job profile explains the nature of the work, skills and abilities required, employment outlook, average earnings, related occupations, education and training requirements, and employment opportunities. Also contains career planning information and job search tips.

★597★
"Service Sales Representatives" in Volume 3 of *The Encyclopedia of Careers and Vocational Guidance* (pp. 177-181)
J.G. Ferguson Publishing Co.
200 W. Monroe
Chicago, IL 60606 Phone: (312)580-5480
William E. Hopke, editor-in-chief. Eighth edition, 1990. Four-volume set that profiles 500 occupations and describes job trends in 76 industries. Includes career description, educational requirements, history of the job, methods of entry, advancement, employment outlook, earnings, working conditions, social and psychological factors, and sources of additional information.

★598★
"Services Sales Representatives" in *Occupational Outlook Handbook* (pp. 240-242)
Superintendent of Documents
U.S. Government Printing Office
Washington, DC 20402 Phone: (202)783-3238
Biennial; latest edition, 1990-91. Encyclopedia of careers describing more than 250 occupations and comprising about 86 percent of all jobs in the economy. Occupations that require lengthy education or training are given the most attention. For each occupation, the handbook describes job duties, working conditions, training, educational preparation, personal qualities, advancement possibilities, job outlook, earnings, and sources of additional information.

★599★
So You Want to Be a Success at Selling?
Video Arts, Inc.
Northbrook Tech Center
4088 Commercial Ave.
Northbrook, IL 60062 Phone: (708)291-1008
Videocassette. 1982. 25 mins. A lesson on the fundamental skills of selling, from the initial research to the close.

Services Sales Representatives ★610★

★600★
"Television Advertising Representative" in *Career Opportunities in Advertising and Public Relations* (pp. 137-139)
Facts on File, Inc.
460 Park Avenue, S.
New York, NY 10016   Phone: (212)683-2244
Shelly Field, 1990. Contains more than 80 jobs related to advertising and public relations in the private, public, and nonprofit sectors. Each occupational profile describes job duties, salary, employment outlook, career paths, advancement prospects, educational preparation, training, and skills. Offers tips for entering the field.

★601★
"Television Advertising Sales Assistant" in *Career Opportunities in Advertising and Public Relations* (pp. 140-142)
Facts on File, Inc.
460 Park Avenue, S.
New York, NY 10016   Phone: (212)683-2244
Shelly Field, 1990. Contains more than 80 jobs related to advertising and public relations in the private, public, and nonprofit sectors. Each occupational profile describes job duties, salary, employment outlook, career paths, advancement prospects, educational preparation, training, and skills. Offers tips for entering the field.

★602★
Video Career Library - Marketing and Sales
Careers, Inc.
1211 10th St., SW
PO Box 135
Largo, FL 34649-0135   Phone: (813)584-7333
Videocassette. 1990. Part of the Video Career Library covering 165 occupations. Shows actual workers on the job. Includes sales representatives.

Associations

★603★
National Association for Professional Saleswomen (NAPS)
PO Box 2606
Novato, CA 94948   Phone: (415)898-2606
Membership: Women actively involved or interested in professional sales and marketing careers. **Purpose:** Conducts seminars, surveys, and research projects. Participates in television and radio programs. Maintains 450 volume library on business and sales. Operates speakers' bureau. Compiles statistics; sponsors competitions; bestows awards.

★604★
National Council of Salesmen's Organizations (NCSO)
303 5th Ave., Rm. 1303
New York, NY 10016   Phone: (718)835-4591
Membership: Wholesale commissioned salesmen in all industries. **Purpose:** Monitors and reports legislation affecting commissioned salesmen; provides members with arbitration and mediation machinery in disputes with employers.

Basic Reference Guides and Handbooks

★605★
The AMA Handbook of Marketing for the Service Industries
AMACOM
135 W. 50th St.
New York, NY 10020   Phone: (212)903-8089
Carole A. Congram, editor. 1990.

★606★
Managing for Quality in the Service Sector
Basil Blackwell, Inc.
3 Cambridge Center
Cambridge, MA 02142   Phone: (617)225-0430
Willem Mastenbroek, editor. 1991.

★607★
Marketing Your Services: A Step-by-Step Guide for Small Businesses & Professionals
John Wiley & Sons
605 3rd Ave.
New York, NY 10158   Phone: (212)850-6000
Anthony O. Putnam. 1990. **Facsimile Number:** (212)850-6088.

★608★
Multinational Service Firms
Routledge, Chapman & Hall, Inc.
29 W. 35th St.
New York, NY 10001-2291   Phone: (212)244-3336
Peter Enderwick, editor. 1989. **Facsimile Number:** (212)563-2269.

★609★
Strategic Trends in Services: An Inquiry into the Global Service Economy
HarperCollins Inc.
10 E. 53rd St.
New York, NY 10022   Phone: (212)207-7000
Albert Bressand, editor. 1989.

Periodicals

★610★
AACS News
Association of Accredited Cosmetology Schools (AACS)
5201 Leesburg Pike, Ste. 205
Falls Church, VA 22041   Phone: (703)845-1333
Editor(s): Seda Gelenian. Bimonthly. Presents news about government legislation, regulatory agency actions, and association activities involving cosmetology schools. Recurring features include news of research and new products, a calendar of events, and President's and Chairman's columns. **Facsimile Number:** (703)845-1336.

★611★
American Salesman
National Research Bureau, Inc.
424 N. 3rd St.
Burlington, IA 52601-5224   Phone: (319)752-5415
Barbara Boeding, Editor. Monthly. Salesmanship magazine. **Facsimile Number:** (319)752-3421.

★612★
Idea Source Guide
Bramlee, Inc.
PO Box 366
Devon, PA 19333

Editor(s): Fred Davis. Monthly. Supplies ideas for premiums, incentives, sales promotions and merchandising.

★613★
Personal Selling Power
Personal Selling Power, Inc.
1127 International Pkwy.
PO Box 5467
Fredericksburg, VA 22403   Phone: (703)752-7000
L.B. Gschwandtner, Editor. Gerhard Gschwandtner, Publisher. 8x/yr. Magazine presenting motivational and sales skills and techniques for sales and marketing executives. **Facsimile Number:** (703)752-7001.

★614★
Retailing News
Martin Stanley Publishing, Inc.
248 W. Cerritos Ave.
Anaheim, CA 92805   Phone: (714)635-9774
Martin Barsky, Editor and Publisher. Monthly. Trade magazine (tabloid) reaching dealers, retailers, manufacturers, manufacturing reps, and distributors in the consumer electronics and major appliance industries.

★615★
Sales & Marketing Training
National Society of Sales Training Executives
Executive Business Media, Inc.
825 Old Country Rd.
PO Box 1500
Westbury, NY 11590   Phone: (708)990-0555
Robert Moran, Editor. Quarterly. Professional magazine. **Facsimile Number:** (516)334-3059.

★616★
Salesman's Insider
Marv Q. Modell Associates
6009 Montgomery Corner
San Jose, CA 95135-1431   Phone: (408)270-4526
Editor(s): Marv Q. Modell. Monthly. Concerned with selling techniques and methodology in all sales areas. Tracks new sales developments, trends, and profit opportunities. Details negotiatineg process with "tips that work".

★617★
Salesmanship
Dartnell Corp.
4660 Ravenswood
Chicago, IL 60640   Phone: (312)561-4000
Editor(s): R.S. Minor. Biweekly. Offers sales ideas and inspiration, samples of letters designed to promote sales, and articles on topics related to sales training. Recurring features include sections titled Objections Clinic and Sales Letters Clinic. **Toll-free/Additional Phone Number(s):** 800-621-5463. **Facsimile Number:** (312)561-3801.

Meetings and Conventions

★618★
National Agri-Marketing Association Conference
Agri Marketing
6201 Howard St.
Niles, IL 60648   Phone: (708)647-1200
1992; Apr. 05-08; Kansas City, MO ● 1993; Apr. 09-22; Kissimmee, FL ● 1994; Apr. 06-09; Indianapolis, IN. **Facsimile Number:** (708)647-7055.

★619★
National Council of Salesmen's Organizations (NCSO)
303 5th Ave., Rm. 1303
New York, NY 10016   Phone: (718)835-4591
Frequency: Annual, always held first Monday in December.

★620★
Sales and Marketing Show and Conference
Flagg Management, Inc.
369 Lexington Ave.
New York, NY 10017   Phone: (212)286-0333
Facsimile Number: (212)286-0086.

Other Sources of Information

★621★
Seventh Annual Services Marketing Conference Proceedings: Designing a Winning Service Strategy
American Marketing Association
250 S. Wacker Dr.
Chicago, IL 60606   Phone: (312)648-0536
Mary J. Bitner. 1989. **Facsimile Number:** (312)993-7542.

Travel Agents

Travel agents give advice on destinations, make arrangements for transportation, hotel accommodations, car rentals, tours, and recreation. They may also advise on weather conditions, restaurants, and tourist attractions. Travel agents also provide information on customs regualations, required papers like passports and visas, and currency exchange rates. Travel agents use a variety of published and computer-based sources for information on departure and arrival times, fares, and hotel accommodations.

$alaries

Experience, sales ability, and size and location of the agency determine the salary of a travel agent.

Beginning travel agents	$12,000/year
Experienced travel agents	$21,000/year
Managers	$30,000/year

Employment Outlook

Growth rate until the year 2000: Faster than average.

Travel Agents

Career Guides

★622★
Career in Air Transport Ground Services
Morris Video
2730 Monterey St. #105
Monterey Business Park
Torrance, CA 90503   Phone: (213)533-4800
Videocassette. 198?. 15 mins. Discover the different jobs available in ground services from air traffic controller to ramp attendant.

★623★
Communication Skills
Travel Text Associates
12605 State Fair
Detroit, MI 48205   Phone: (313)527-6971
Chris Hoosen. 1989. Part of Travel Agent Training Series.

★624★
Exploring Careers in the Travel Industry
Rosen Publishing Group, Inc.
29 E. 21st St.
New York, NY 10010   Phone: (212)777-3017
Edgar Grant. 1989. Provides an overview of the travel and tourism industries. Describes the work of the travel agent, skills, training, pay, and employment outlook. Offers job hunting advice.

★625★
Flying High in Travel: A Complete Guide to Careers in the Travel Industry
John Wiley and Sons, Inc.
605 3rd Ave.
New York, NY 10158   Phone: (212)850-6000
Karen Rubin. 1986. **Facsimile Number:** (212)850-6088.

★626★
Getting Down to Business: Travel Agency
American Institutes for Research
PO Box 11131
Palo Alto, CA 94302   Phone: (415)493-3550
Rachel L. Rassen. 1981. **Facsimile Number:** (415)858-0958.

★627★
How to Get a Job with A Cruise Line: Adventure-Travel-Romance - How to Sail Around the World on Cruise Ships & Get Paid for It
Ticket to Adventure, Inc.
PO Box 47622
St. Petersburg, FL 33743   Phone: (813)544-0066
Mary F. Miller. 1990.

★628★
How to Open and Run a Money-Making Travel Agency
John Wiley and Sons, Inc.
605 3rd Ave.
New York, NY 10158   Phone: (212)850-6000
Pamela Fremont. 1983. **Facsimile Number:** (212)850-6088.

★629★
"Professionalism - Certified Travel Counselor" in *The Travel Agent: Dealer in Dreams* (pp. 21-22)
Prentice Hall Press
1 Gulf & Western Plaza
New York, NY 10023   Phone: (212)373-8500
Aryear Gregory. Third edition, 1989. Comprehensive guide for those interested in the travel industry. Covers the work of the travel agent, agency problems, techniques, and promotion. Describes various jobs within the travel industry including travel consultant, agency manager, and tour operators. Explains the knowledge, skills, training, and educational preparation needed to succeed.

★630★
"Travel Agencies" in *Opportunities in Travel Careers* (pp. 77-90)
National Textbook Co.
4255 W. Touhy Ave.
Lincolnwoodq, IL 60646   Phone: (312)679-5500
Robert Scott Milne. 1991. Explores job opportunities in many travel related fields including the airlines, resorts, travel agencies, recreation, and tourism. Covers the work, salaries, educational preparation and training, and advancement possibilities.

★631★
Travel Agent
Arco/Prentice Hall Press
1 Gulf & Western Plaza
New York, NY 10023   Phone: (212)373-8500
Wilma Boyd. 1989. Introduction to the travel business. Covers U.S. and foreign travel, time zones, ticketing, world geography, and airline, railroad, and tour bus connections, and accommodations. Outlines entry-level positions in the airline,

car rental, and hospitality industries as well as in travel agencies and related travel services. Explains travel agency operations, sales techniques, and the use of computers in travel services. Gives job hunting advice and sales tips.

★632★
Travel Agent
Careers, Inc.
PO Box 135
Largo, FL 34649-0135   Phone: (813)584-7333

1990. Two-page occupational summary card describing duties, working conditions, personal qualifications, training, earnings and hours, employment outlook, places of employment, related careers and where to write for more information.

★633★
Travel Agent
Vocational Biographies, Inc.
PO Box 31, Dept. VF10
Sauk Centre, MN 56378   Phone: (612)352-6516

1989. This pamphlet profiles a person working in the job. Includes information about job duties, working conditions, places of employment, educational preparation, labor market outlook, and salaries. **Toll-free/Additional Phone Number(s):** 800-255-0752.

★634★
"Travel Agent" in *College Board Guide to Jobs and Career Planning* (pp. 144-146)
College Entrance Examination Board
45 Columbus Ave.
New York, NY 10023-6992   Phone: (212)713-8000

Joyce Slayton Mitchell. 1990. Career planning guide written for high school and college students. Covers 100 careers in 15 occupational groups. Provides job description, educational preparation needed, salaries, related careers, and sources of additional information. Includes information about the 90's labor market.

★635★
"Travel Agent" in *Guide to Careers Without College* (pp. 25-26)
Franklin Watts, Inc.
387 Park Avenue, S.
New York, NY 10016   Phone: (212)686-7070

Kathleen S. Abrams. 1988. Discusses careers that do not require a college degree in fields such as health care, sales and marketing, and the building trades. Describes the work, employment opportunities, and training.

★636★
"Travel Agent" in *Hospitality and Recreation*, Volume 8 of *Career Information Center* (pp. 118-122)
Glencoe/Macmillan
15319 Chatsworth St.
Mission Hills, CA 91345   Phone: (818)898-1391

Richard Lidz and Dale Anderson, editorial directors. Fourth edition, 1990. For 600 occupations, describes job duties, entry-level requirements, education and training needed, advancement possibilities, employment outlook, earnings and benefits. The set is divided into 12 volumes. Each volume includes jobs related under a broad career field. Volume 13 is the index. **Facsimile Number:** 818-365-5489.

★637★
"Travel Agent" in *Occu-Facts: Information on 565 Careers in Outline Form* (p. 11.28)
Careers, Inc.
P.O. Box 135
1211 Tenth St., S.W.
Largo, FL 33640   Phone: (813)584-7333

Elizabeth Handville. Biennial, 1989-90 edition. Each one-page occupational profile describes duties, working conditions, physical surroundings and demands, aptitudes, temperament, educational requirements, employment outlook, earnings, and places of employment.

★638★
"Travel Agent" in *Opportunities in Vocational and Technical Careers* (pp. 59-61)
National Textbook Co.
4255 W. Touhy Ave.
Lincolnwood, IL 60646   Phone: (312)679-5500

Describes careers which can be prepared for by attending a private vocational or proprietary school—office employee, sales worker, service worker, health services, mechanic, craftworker, and technician. Covers employment outlook, job duties, and salaries. Offers career planning advice.

★639★
"Travel Agent" in *Top Professions: The 100 Most Popular, Dynamic, and Profitable Careers in America Today* (pp. 57-59)
Peterson's Guides, Inc.
202 Carnegie Center
PO Box 2123
Princeton, NJ 08543-2123   Phone: (609)243-9111

Nicholas Basta. 1989. Includes occupations requiring a college or advanced degree. Describes job duties, earnings, some typical job titles, career opportunities at different degree levels, and lists related associations.

★640★
"Travel Agent" in *Travel & Tourism* (pp. 27-31)
Franklin Watts, Inc.
387 Park Avenue, S.
New York, NY 10016   Phone: (212)686-7070

Marjorie Rittenberg Schulz. 1990. Surveys employment opportunities in the travel and tourism industry. Provides job description, educational preparation, training, salary, employment outlook, and sources of additional information. Offers job hunting advice.

★641★
"Travel Agent" in *VGM's Careers Encyclopedia* (pp. 468-470)
National Textbook Co.
4255 W. Touhy Ave.
Lincolnwood, IL 60646   Phone: (312)679-5500

Third edition, 1991. Contains two- to five-page descriptions of 200 managerial, professional, technical, trade, and service occupations. Each profile includes job duties, places of employment, qualifications, educational preparation, training, employment potential, advancement, income, and additional sources of information.

★642★
"Travel Agent" in *VGM's Handbook of Business and Management Careers* (pp. 97-99)
National Textbook Co.
4255 W. Touhy Ave.
Lincolnwood, IL 60646

Craig T. Norback. 1990. Contains 43 two-page occupational profiles describing job duties, places of employment, working conditions, qualifications, education, employment outlook, and income.

★643★
The Travel Agent: Dealer in Dreams
Prentice Hall Press
1 Gulf & Western Plaza
New York, NY 10023   Phone: (212)373-8500

Aryear Gregory. Third edition, 1989. Comprehensive guide for those interested in the travel industry. Covers the work of the travel agent, agency problems, techniques, and promotion. Describes various jobs within the travel industry including travel consultant, agency manager, and tour operators. Explains the knowledge, skills, training, and educational preparation needed to succeed.

★644★
Travel Agents
Chronicle Guidance Publications, Inc.
PO Box 1190
Moravia, NY 13118-1190   Phone: (315)497-0330

1988. This career brief describes the nature of the work, working conditions, hours and earnings, education and training, licensure, certification, unions, personal qualifications, social and psychological factors, employment outlook, entry methods, advancement, and related occupations. **Toll-free/Additional Phone Number(s):** 800-622-7284.

★645★
"Travel Agents" in *Jobs! What They Are...Where They Are...What They Pay* (pp. 171-172)
Simon & Schuster, Inc.
Simon & Schuster Bldg.
1230 Avenue of the Americas
New York, NY 10020   Phone: (212)698-7000

Robert O. Snelling and Anne M. Snelling. Revised edition, 1989. Profiles 241 occupations, describing duties and responsibilities, educational preparation, earnings, employment opportunities, training, and qualifications.

★646★
"Travel Agents" in *101 Careers: A Guide to the Fastest-Growing Opportunities* (pp. 319-322)
John Wiley & Sons, Inc.
605 Third Ave.
New York, NY 10158   Phone: (212)850-6000

Michael Harkavy. 1990. Each occupational profile includes job description, job titles, work environment, employment outlook, qualifications, personal skills, and earnings.

★647★
"Travel Agents" in *The American Almanac of Jobs and Salaries* (pp. 554-556)
Avon Books
105 Madison Avenue
New York, NY 10016   Phone: (212)481-5600

John Wright and Edward J. Dwyer. Revised and updated, 1990. A comprehensive guide to the wages of hundreds of occupations in a wide variety of industries and organizations.

★648★
"Travel Agents" in Volume 6 of *Career Discovery Encyclopedia* (pp. 130-131)
J.G. Ferguson Publishing Co.
200 W. Monroe
Chicago, IL 60606   Phone: (312)580-5480

E. Russell Primm, editor-in-chief. 1990. Contains two-page articles on 504 occupations. Each article describes job duties, earnings, and educational and training requirements.

★649★
"Travel Agents" in Volume 3 of *The Encyclopedia of Careers and Vocational Guidance* (pp. 185-189)
J.G. Ferguson Publishing Co.
200 W. Monroe
Chicago, IL 60606   Phone: (312)580-5480

William E. Hopke, editor-in-chief. Eighth edition, 1990. Four-volume set that profiles 500 occupations and describes job trends in 76 industries. Includes career description, educational requirements, history of the job, methods of entry, advancement, employment outlook, earnings, working conditions, social and psychological factors, and sources of additional information.

★650★
"Travel Agents" in *America's 50 Fastest Growing Jobs* (pp. 106-107)
JIST Works, Inc.
720 N. Park Ave.
Indianapolis, IN 46202   Phone: (317)264-3720

Michael J. Farr, compiler. 1991. Describes the 50 fastest growing jobs within major career clusters such as technicians, and marketing and sales. Each job profile explains the nature of the work, skills and abilities required, employment outlook, average earnings, related occupations, education and training requirements, and employment opportunities. Also contains career planning information and job search tips.

★651★
"Travel Agents: Plotters of Unforgettable Trips" in *Careers for Women Without College Degrees* (pp. 234-238)
McGraw-Hill Publishing Co.
11 W. 19th St.
New York, NY 10011   Phone: (212)337-6010

Beatryce Nivens. 1988. Career planning and job hunting guide containing information on decision-making, skills assessment, and resumes for career changers. Profiles careers with the best occupational outlook. Describes the work, educational preparation, employment outlook, salaries, and required skills.

★652★
"Travel and Tourism" in *The Career Connection II: A Guide to Technical Majors and Their Related Careers* (pp. 129-130)
ERIS
PO Box 7509
University Station
Provo, UT 84602-0509

Fred A. Rowe. 1988. Contains technical majors, such as automotive technology. Describes the major and the job. Lists high school and postsecondary school courses. Includes occupations related to the major, employment outlook, and starting salary.

★653★
Travel Career Development
Houghton Mifflin Co.
1 Beacon St.
Boston, MA 02108 Phone: (617)725-5000
Nona Starr. Fourth edition, 1990.

★654★
***"The Travel Consultant" in The Travel Agent: Dealer in Dreams* (pp. 13-24)**
Prentice Hall Press
1 Gulf & Western Plaza
New York, NY 10023 Phone: (212)373-8500
Aryear Gregory. Third edition, 1989. Comprehensive guide for those interested in the travel industry. Covers the work of the travel agent, agency problems, techniques, and promotion. Describes various jobs within the travel industry including travel consultant, agency manager, and tour operators. Explains the knowledge, skills, training, and educational preparation needed to succeed.

★655★
Travel Free: How to Start and Succeed in Your Own Travel Consultant Business
Prima Publishing and Communications
4970 Topaz Ave., PO Box 1260
Rocklin, CA 95677 Phone: (916)624-5718
Ben Dominitz. 1984.

★656★
Travel Industry Career Directory
Career Press, Inc.
62 Beverly Rd.
PO Box 34
Hawthorne, NJ 07507 Phone: (201)427-0229
1989. **Facsimile Number:** (201)427-2037.

★657★
Travel Industry Guidelines for Employment
Travel Text Associates
12605 State Fair
Detroit, MI 48205 Phone: (313)527-6971
Chris Hoosen. 1990. Part of Travel Agent Training Series.

★658★
Travel Training Workbook, 1991. Section 1: Introduction to Travel & Geography
Solitaire Publishing
216 S. Bungalow Park Ave.
Tampa, FL 33609 Phone: (813)876-0286
Claudine L. Dervaes. Fifth revised edition, 1990. **Toll-free/Additional Phone Number(s):** 800-226-0286.

★659★
What is a Travel Agent?
American Society of Travel Agents
1101 King St., Ste. 200
Alexandria, VA 22314 Phone: (703)739-2782
This six-panel brochure describes industry outlook, education, training, job duties, and working conditions.

Associations

★660★
American Society of Travel Agents (ASTA)
1101 King St.
Alexandria, VA 22314 Phone: (703)739-2782
Membership: Travel agents; allied members are representatives of carriers, hotels, resorts, sightseeing and car rental companies, official tourist organizations, and other travel interests. **Purpose:** Purposes are to: promote and encourage travel among people of all nations; to promote the image and encourage the use of professional travel agents worldwide; serve as an information resource for the travel industry worldwide; promote and represent the views and interests of travel agents to all levels of government and industry; promote professional and ethical conduct in the travel agency industry worldwide; facilitate consumer protection and safety for the traveling public. Maintains biographical archives and travel hall of fame. Sponsors competitions; bestows awards; conducts research and education programs. **Publications:** *ASTA Educational System Catalog*, annual. • *ASTA Stat*, monthly. • *ASTA Travel Agency Management Magazine*, monthly. • *AstaNotes*, weekly. • *ASTA Officials Directory*, annual. • *ASTA Stat*, monthly. • *Membership Directory*, annual. • *Travel Industry Honors*, periodic. • Also publishes pamphlets.

★661★
Institute of Certified Travel Agents (ICTA)
148 Linden St.
PO Box 82-56
Wellesley, MA 02181 Phone: (617)237-0280
Membership: Individuals who have been accredited as Certified Travel Counselors (CTC) after meeting the institute's requirements (5 years' travel industry experience, 4 travel management courses, 4 examinations, and an original research project). **Purpose:** Seeks to increase the level of competence in the travel industry. Provides educational guidance, continuing education, and examination and certification program; conducts workshops and executive management seminars. Operates Travel Career Development Program to increase skills of pre-management personnel and Destination Specialist Program to enhance the geographical knowledge of sales agents. Organizes study groups of instruction with enrolled student bodies in most major cities. Maintains library on travel agency management and travel reference topics. **Publications:** *CTCs Newsletter*, monthly. • *ICTA News*, monthly. • *Institute of Certified Travel Agents—Directory*, annual. • *Travel Trainers Network*, semiannual. • Also publishes catalog and books. **Facsimile Number:** (617)237-3860.

Standards/Certification Agencies

★662★
American Society of Travel Agents (ASTA)
1101 King St.
Alexandria, VA 22314 Phone: (703)739-2782
Promotes and represents the views and interests of travel agents to all levels of government and industry. Promotes professional and ethical conduct in the travel agency industry worldwide. Sponsors competitions; bestows awards; conducts research and education programs.

Travel Agents

★663★
Institute of Certified Travel Agents (ICTA)
148 Linden St.
PO Box 82-56
Wellesley, MA 02181　　　　　Phone: (617)237-0280
Provides certification program.

★664★
Travel Agents
Institute of Certified Travel Agents
148 Linden St.
PO Box 82-56
Wellesley, MA 02181　　　　　Phone: (617)237-0280
1991. This 31 page booklet describes the services, programs, and courses offered by this nonprofit organization to its members. Explains requirements and procedures to become a Certified Travel Consultant or Destination Specialist.

Educational Directories and Programs

★665★
ASTA Educational System Catalog
American Society of Travel Agents (ASTA)
1101 King St.
Alexandria, VA 22314　　　　　Phone: (703)739-2782
Annual. Contains information on ASTA programs including programs in accounting, automation, geography, group travel, law, and management.

★666★
Travel Agent—Focus 500 Directory Issue
Universal Media, Inc.
801 2nd Ave.
New York, NY 10017　　　　　Phone: (212)370-5050
Annual. Lists of attractions, restaurants, convention and visitor bureaus, hotel chains and management companies, cruise lines, state tourism offices, travel trade associations, tourist railways; coverage includes Canada. Entries include: Company, agency, or center name, address, phone, name and title of contact. Arrangement: Geographical. Indexes: Attraction/activity, location of national comnpany or association headquarters, contact name.

Awards, Scholarships, Grants, and Fellowships

★667★
Outstanding International Travel Agent of the Year
Association of Community Travel Clubs
c/o Abe Solomon, Sr.
2330 S. Brentwood Blvd.
St. Louis, MO 63144-2096　　　　　Phone: (314)961-2300
For recognition of contributions in the field of tourism. Selection is by nomination. A plaque is awarded annually at the convention. Established in 1948.

★668★
Joseph W. Rosenbluth Memorial Award
American Society of Travel Agents
c/o Diane Marques
1101 King St.
Alexandria, VA 22314　　　　　Phone: (703)739-2782
To recognize the travel agent who has made the greatest contribution to the travel industry and whose outstanding influence and activity have advanced the professional status of the agency business. A crystal piece is presented annually at the World Travel Congress. Established in 1970 in memory of Joseph W. Rosenbluth, a dedicated member of ASTA. Formerly: Joseph W. Rosenbluth Memorial Travel Agent of the Year Award.

Basic Reference Guides and Handbooks

★669★
Africa's Top Wildlife Countries
Global Travel Publishers, Inc.
First Union Bank Bldg.
1620 S. Federal Hwy., Ste. 900
Pompano Beach, FL 33062　　　　　Phone: (305)781-3933
Mark W. Nolting, President, editor. Biennial, April of even years. List of parks, accommodations, banks, tourist camps and offices, and automobile associations and clubs in 14 African countries; African embassies; airlines that fly to Africa. Entries include: Name, address, phone, services. Arrangement: Classified by service. Indexes: Product/service, geographical. **Toll-free/Additional Phone Number(s):** (800)882-9453. **Facsimile Number:** (305)781-0984.

★670★
American Bus Association's Motorcoach Marketer: Complete Directory of the Intercity Bus & Travel/Tourism Industry
American Bus Association
1015 15th St. NW, No. 250
Washington, DC 20005　　　　　Phone: (202)842-1645
Tom Jackson, Publisher, editor. Annual, September. Over 2,000 hotels and sightseeing services, convention information centers, visitors' centers, and similar businesses and organizations of interest to motorcoach tour organizers; includes about 1,000 companies which operate intercity scheduled and charter buses; coverage includes Canada. Entries include: Company name, address, phone, name and title of contact. Arrangement: Classified by line of business. **Toll-free/Additional Phone Number(s):** (800)283-2877. **Facsimile Number:** (202)842-0850.

★671★
American Express Pocket Guides
American Express Publishing Corp.
1120 Avenue of the Americas
New York, NY 10036　　　　　Phone: (212)382-5600
Series of guides that list hotels, restaurants, and shopping and entertainment centers throughout the world, including guides to England, Mexico, Paris, Spain, and Venice. Entries include: Business name, address, phone, days and hours of operation; travel access to hotels, restaurants, shops; highlighted descriptions of all major cities and points of interest. Indexes: Product/service, subject, trade name.

★672★
ASTA Officials Directory
American Society of Travel Agents (ASTA)
1101 King St.
Alexandria, VA 22314　　　　　Phone: (703)739-2782
Annual. Lists information on committee, council, and task force activities and members. Includes antitrust compliance guidelines, code of ethics, and bylaws.

★673★
Budget Vacationers Guidebook—Western U.S.
Glastonbury Press
12816 E. Rose Dr.
Whittier, CA 90601   Phone: (213)698-4243
Michael J. Studebaker, President, editor. Irregular; latest edition 1986. About 3,300 tourist attractions, campgrounds, budget lodgings, and restaurants located in 11 Western states. Entries include: For attractions*Name, address or location, mileage from nearest town, description, admission cost. For campgrounds*Name, address or location from town, altitude, fees, period of operation, number of campsites, phone, facilities. For lodgings*Name, address, toll free and local phone numbers, rates. For restaurants*Name, address, phone, type of food served. Arrangement: Geographical.

★674★
Business of Travel: Agency Operations & Administration
Macmillan Publishing Company, Inc.
866 3rd Ave.
New York, NY 10022   Phone: (212)702-2000
Dennis L. Foster. 1990.

★675★
Condominiums for Rent in Resort Areas – Database
Information Resource Consultants
12015 Manchester Rd., Ste. 150
St. Louis, MO 63131   Phone: (314)822-7072
Information on over 1,000 condominiums available for rent in resort areas.

★676★
Defense Science—Directory of Validated Ada Compilers Issue
Rush Franklin Publishing, Inc.
PO Box 33619
Indialantic, FL 32903-0619   Phone: (407)773-5711
Jim Martin, editor. Annual, February. List of suppliers of Ada language software compilers that have passed United States Department of Defense validation testing. Entries include: Company name, address, phone, contact name. Arrangement: Subdivided into native & cross compilers. **Facsimile Number:** (408)370-1212.

★677★
Travel Agency Communications Reports—North American Edition
Cabell Travel Publications
2235 E. Flamingo Rd., No. 100-F
Las Vegas, NV 89119   Phone: (702)796-0040
Quarterly. Travel agents, wholesale tour operators, motor coach-sightseeing companies, airlines, steamships, railroads, car rental companies, foreign auto sales, state and government tourist offices, foreign consulates, hotel/motel chains and systems, hotel and travel representatives, and special service companies throughout North America. Entries include: Company name, address, phone, fax, telex, cable address, association memberships, number of employees, head office, location, names of executives. Arrangement: By type of business, then geographical. Indexes: Alphabetical index of travel agencies; classified index of wholesale tour operators by destination areas.

★678★
Travel Agent—Domestic Tour Manual Issue
American Traveler, Inc., Division
Fairchild Publications
Capital Cities Media, Inc.
7 W. 34th St., 6th Fl.
New York, NY 10003   Phone: (212)630-3880
Annual. Lists of leading motorcoach tour companies offering over 500 escort vacation tours with 9,000 departures throughout the U.S. and Canada. Entries include: For tour companies*Name, address, phone. For tours*Dates offered, name of tour, costs, number of days. Arrangement: Alphabetical. Indexes: Chronological, destination.

★679★
Travel and Tourism Research and Marketing Directory
Travel and Tourism Research Association (TTRA)
Box 58066
Salt Lake City, UT 84158-0066   Phone: (801)581-3351
Mari Lou Wood, editor. Irregular; 1990. More than 200 organizations engaged in research and consulting on travel and tourism, including government agencies, university departments and private firms. Entries include: Company name, address, phone, fax, date founded, chief officer, name of member, type of organization, number of employees, services available, publications. Arrangement: Alphabetical. Indexes: Alphabetical, geographical, company cagegory. **Facsimile Number:** (801)581-3354.

★680★
Travel & Vacation Discount Guide
Pilot Books
103 Cooper St.
Babylon, NY 11702   Phone: (516)422-2225
Paige Palmer, author. 1990. Nearly 335 sponsors of discount travel programs, including discount travel clubs, hotels, airlines, and other travel industry firms; also lists tourist information agencies in the United States and abroad. Entries include: Sponsor name, address, phone, description of program. Arrangement: Alphabetical.

★681★
Travel Industry Association of America—International Travel News Directory
Travel Industry Association of America (TIA)
2 Lafayette Center
1133 21st St., NW
Washington, DC 20036   Phone: (202)293-1433
Shawn Flaherty, editor. Biennial. Travel editors of major newspapers, magazines, and broadcast outlets; consumer and travel industry magazines and publications, including guide books, in-flight publications, in-room publications; news and photo services; international coverage for travel trade and consumer travel editors. Entries include: Generally, publication title, address, phone, fax, telex, names of editorial and advertising contacts, target audience, editorial and advertising deadlines. Arrangement: Classified by media, then in separate section for United States and international. Indexes: Media title, geographical. **Facsimile Number:** (202)293-3155.

★682★
Worldwide Travel Information Contact Book
Gale Research Inc.
835 Penobscot Bldg.
Detroit, MI 48226-4094   Phone: (313)961-2242
Burkhard Herbote, author. Biennial, September of even years; first edition 1990. Approximately 25,000 contacts and sources for travel information including: travel agents, associations, tourist authorities, tour operators, lodging associations, and publications. Entries include: Name, address, phone, fax, telex.

Arrangement: Geographical, then by subject heading. Indexes: Travel destination. **Toll-free/Additional Phone Number(s):** (800)877-GALE. **Facsimile Number:** (313)961-6083.

Periodicals

★683★
Airline, Ship & Catering
International Publishing Co. of America
PO Box 188
Hialeah, FL 33011   Phone: (305)887-1701
Jim O'Neal, Editor. 8x/yr. Travel magazine. **Facsimile Number:** (305)885-1923.

★684★
ARTAFACTS
Association of Retail Travel Agents (ARTA)
1745 Jefferson Davis Pkwy., Ste. 300
Arlington, VA 22202-3402   Phone: (703)553-7777
Monthly. Reviews developments in the travel industry for retail travel agents. Covers topics such as ethics, tour operations, transportation services, educational opportunities, commissions, and political action in pertinent issues. Includes chapter and association news. **Toll-free/Additional Phone Number(s):** 800-969-6069 **Facsimile Number:** (703)486-0228.

★685★
ASTA Agency Management
Yankee Publications
666 5th Ave.
New York, NY 10103   Phone: (212)765-5454
Patrick Arton, Editor. Monthly. Magazine reporting and analyzing the business of the travel industry with special reference to travel agency profitability.

★686★
ASTA Stat
American Society of Travel Agents (ASTA)
1101 King St.
Alexandria, VA 22314   Phone: (703)739-2782
Monthly. Newsletter containing current travel industry statistics.

★687★
ASTA Travel Agency Management Magazine
American Society of Travel Agents (ASTA)
1101 King St.
Alexandria, VA 22314   Phone: (703)739-2782
Monthly.

★688★
AstaNotes
American Society of Travel Agents (ASTA)
1101 King St.
Alexandria, VA 22314   Phone: (703)739-2782
Weekly. Newsletter.

★689★
Atterbury Letter
Kirby and Renee Atterbury
PO Box 1197
Bethel Island, CA 94511   Phone: (510)684-3142
Editor(s): Kirby and Renee Atterbury. 6/yr. Carries personal opinions from readers and writers on their experience in various locales integrating wine, dining, and travel. Reports on travel fares, accommodations, conditions, tours, restaurants, and vineyards. Recurring features include specific recommendations, off-beat travel ideas, and discussions of seasonal differences in prices and services.

★690★
CTCs Newsletter
Institute of Certified Travel Agents (ICTA)
148 Linden St.
PO Box 82-56
Wellesley, MA 02181   Phone: (617)237-0280
Monthly.

★691★
CTO News for Travel Agents
Caribbean Tourism Organization (CTO)
20 E. 46th St.
New York, NY 10017   Phone: (212)682-0435
6/yr. Instructs travel agents on how to effectively sell the Caribbean for greater profit. Reviews developments in Caribbean tourism, providing information on air flights, hotels, restaurants, and other attractions. Recurring features include editorials, news of members, and a calendar of events. **Facsimile Number:** (212)697-4258.

★692★
The Hideaway Report
Harper Associates, Inc.
PO Box 50
Sun Valley, ID 83353-0050   Phone: (208)622-3183
Editor(s): Andrew Harper. Monthly. Provides informative critiques on small, secluded resorts and executive retreats around the world. Composed of 12-15 hotel descriptions per issue. Recurring features include Hideaway of the Year Awards in December issue and columns titled Reader Requests and Hotel & Travel Watch.

★693★
Hotel & Travel Index
500 Plaza Dr.
Secaucus, NJ 07096   Phone: (201)902-1600
Melinda Bush, Publisher. Quarterly. Magazine serving as a worldwide hotel directory. **Facsimile Number:** (201)319-1628.

★694★
ICTA News
Institute of Certified Travel Agents (ICTA)
148 Linden St.
PO Box 56
Wellesley, MA 02181-0503   Phone: (617)237-0280
Editor(s): Dawn Ringel. 10/yr. Covers the educational activities of the Institute, which grants the Certified Travel Counselor (CTC) designation to travel industry personnel. Offers special news stories on topics relevant to the travel industry. Recurring features include news of members, management tips, and names of newly certified agents. **Toll-free/Additional Phone Number(s):** 800-542-4282 **Facsimile Number:** (617)237-3860.

★695★
Lodging Briefing
Walter Mathews Associates, Inc.
28 W. 38th St.
New York, NY 10018   Phone: (212)921-4314
Editor(s): Walter Mathews. 10/yr. Remarks on industry developments, consumer trends, and economic performance in the area of travel. Carries information to help travel agents increase their sales, develop their promotional techniques, and to better manage both their employees and finances. Recurring features include travel price indexes. **Facsimile Number:** (212)719-9382.

★696★
Motel/Hotel Insider
Magna Publishing
2718 Dryden
Madison, WI 53704　　　　　　　　　Phone: (608)249-2455
Editor(s): Robert Reis. Weekly. Covers motel/hotel management, travel and vacation trends, business travel, new products and services for the hospitality market, motel/hotel chains, and trends and changes in the lodging industry.

★697★
North American Edition OAG Business Travel Planner
Official Airline Guides
2000 Clearwater Dr.
Oak Brook, IL 60521　　　　　　　　　Phone: (708)574-6000
Richard A. Nelson, Publisher. Quarterly. Official lodging directory of the American Hotel and Motel Association includes city destination information, hotel listings, airport diagrams, city, metro, resort area and country maps, travel basics, and reservation directories. **Facsimile Number:** (708)574-6667.

★698★
Official Airline Guide, Worldwide Edition
Official Airline Guides
2000 Clearwater Dr.
Oak Brook, IL 60521　　　　　　　　　Phone: (708)574-6000
Richard A. Nelson, Publisher. Monthly. Guide containing schedules of airlines operating throughout the world (excluding North America and Caribbean), published as a service for the airlines, travel agents, and volume users of air transportation. **Facsimile Number:** (708)574-6667.

★699★
Official Tour Directory
Thomas Publishing Company
5 Penn Plaza
New York, NY 10001　　　　　　　　　Phone: (212)629-2175
Ester Reiter, editor. Lists 2,000 tour operators that offer tours and vacation packages to over 700 destinations worldwide. **Facsimile Number:** (212)629-1544.

★700★
PATA Travel News (Americas Edition)
Baxter Publications, Inc.
310 Dupont St.
Toronto, ON, Canada M5R 1V9　　　　　Phone: (416)968-7252
Timothy Baxter, Editor. Monthly. Magazine for the travel trade, emphasizing travel to the Pacific-Asia region. Includes news from the Pacific Asia Travel Association and its 35 chapters in the Americas.

★701★
Recommend
Worth International Communications Corp.
5979 NW, 151 St., Ste. 120
Miami Lakes, FL 33014　　　　　　　　Phone: (305)828-0123
Hal Herman, Pres./Editor-in-Chief. Monthly. Travel industry magazine. **Facsimile Number:** (305)826-6950.

★702★
Southeast Travel Professional
1200 NW 78th Ave., Ste. 201
Miami, FL 33126　　　　　　　　　　　Phone: (305)592-6133
Larry Cafiero, Editor. Monthly. Travel magazine (tabloid). **Facsimile Number:** (305)592-9741.

★703★
Travel Industry Honors
American Society of Travel Agents (ASTA)
1101 King St.
Alexandria, VA 22314　　　　　　　　　Phone: (703)739-2782
Periodic.

★704★
Travel Trainers Network
Institute of Certified Travel Agents (ICTA)
148 Linden St.
PO Box 82-56
Wellesley, MA 02181　　　　　　　　　Phone: (617)237-0280
Semiannual. Newsletter providing information of interest to those teaching travel courses.

★705★
Winston's Travel Discoveries
Winston's Travel Discoveries
PO Box C
Sausalito, CA 94966　　　　　　　　　Phone: (415)332-9612
Editor(s): Isabella Winston. Bimonthly. Features "refreshingly critical" reviews of the better resorts, hotels, and restaurants in the U.S. and abroad, with all establishments being reviewed anonymously and in-person by the editor. Recurring features include "travel planners," for particular areas, which carry data on typical weather conditions, major airlines, and tourist information sources.

――――――― Meetings and Conventions ―――――――

★706★
American Society of Travel Agents World Travel Congress
American Society of Travel Agents
1101 King St.
Alexandria, VA 22314　　　　　　　　　Phone: (703)739-2782
1992; Sep. 20-26; Cairo, Egypt ● 1993; Nov. 07-11; Lisbon, Portugal ● 1995; Nov. 12-18. **Facsimile Number:** (703)684-8319.

★707★
Institute of Certified Travel Agents Forum (ICTA)
148 Linden St.
PO Box 82-56
Wellesley, MA 02181　　　　　　　　　Phone: (617)237-0280
Frequency: Annual. **Facsimile Number:** (617)237-3860.

★708★
International Travel Industry Expo (ITIX)
The Interface Group, Inc.
300 1st Ave.
Needham, MA 02194　　　　　　　　　Phone: (617)449-6600
1992. **Facsimile Number:** (617)449-6953.

――――――― Other Sources of Information ―――――――

★709★
Choosing the Right Travel School
American Society of Travel Agents
1101 King St., Ste. 200
Alexandria, VA 22314　　　　　　　　　Phone: (703)739-2782
1989. This four-panel brochure offers a list of questions to help prospective students evaluate a travel agent training program.

Travel Agents

★710★
Eurail Guide: How to Travel Europe and All the World by Train
Eurail Guide Annual
27540 Pacific Coast Hwy.
Malibu, CA 90265   Phone: (213)457-7286

Kathryn S. Turpin and Marvin L. Saltzman, editor. Annual, January. Rail trips for tourists in 112 countries. Entries include: Departure times, arrival times, on board services (eating, sleeping, air conditioning facilities), and notable scenery en route. Arrangement: Geographical.

★711★
Europe by Train: The Complete Guide to Inter Railing
HarperCollins
10 E. 53rd St.
New York, NY 10022   Phone: (212)207-7000

Katie Wood and George McDonald, author. Annual, March. Hotels, inns, hostels, and restaurants near European train stations that are recommended by the editors as being reasonably priced; also includes attractions and sites. Arrangement: Geographical. **Toll-free/Additional Phone Number(s):** (800)2HA-RPER. **Facsimile Number:** (717)343-3611 (orders only).

★712★
Fodor's Guides
Fodor's Travel Publications, Inc.
Random House, Inc.
201 E. 50th St.
New York, NY 10022   Phone: (212)872-8254

Annual. This series of travel guides now comprises approximately 140 titles; prospective travelers may select coverage at the continental, regional, national, or local scale. The guides offer detailed information about sights and accomodations, as well as general travel advice and commentary. **Toll-free/Additional Phone Number(s):** (800)733-3000.

★713★
Travel Industry—Trade Show Directory
Travel Industry Publications, Inc.
1681 E. 34th St.
Brooklyn, NY 11234   Phone: (718)375-0244

W. G. Christopher, editor. Annual. More than 500 domestic and international trade shows for the travel industry, including about 100 detailed trade show profiles. Entries include: For all shows: Name, location, dates. In detailed profiles: Event name, location, dates, frequency, sponsor, fee, target audience, previous and expected attendance, exhibitor information and fees, contact name, address, phone. Arrangement: Detailed profiles are alphabetical; separate section lists all shows chronologically. Indexes: Geographical.

Administrative Support Occupations, Including Clerical

Adjusters, Investigators, and Collectors

Adjusters, investigators, and collectors act as intermediaries between an organization and its clients. Claim representatives investigate claims, negotiate settlements, and authorize payments to claimants. To expedite the precessing, minor claims filed by automobile or homeowner policy holders are usually handled by inside adjusters or telephone adjusters. These workers contact claimants by telephone or by mail to get information on repair costs, medical expenses, or other records needed by the company. More complex cases are referred to a claim adjuster or outside adjuster. Claim adjusters plan and schedule the work required to process a claim. Material damage adjusters inspect automobile damage and prepare estimates of the damage. Claim adjusters sometimes testify in court on contested claims. Claim examiners investigate questionable claims or those exceeding a designated amount. Examiners are authorized to investigate and approve payments on all claims up to a certain limit; larger claims are referred to a senior examiner. Policy processing clerks process new policies, modifications to existing policies, and claims. Claim clerks, also called claim interviewers, obtain information from policy-holders regarding claims, prepare reports, and review insurance claim forms. Adjustment clerks investigate and resolve customers' complaints about merchandise, service, billing, or credit rating. Sometimes they are called customer service representatives, customer complaint clerks, or adjustment correspondents. Bill and account collectors, sometimes called collection correspondents, are responsible for ensuring that customers pay their overdue accounts. This may involve meeting with customers to offer payment advice or review the terms of the original sale, service or credit contract. Welfare eligibility workers and interviewers— sometimes referred to as intake workers, eligibility determination workers, eligibility specialists, or income maintenance specialists— determine who can receive welfare and other types of social assistance. Adjusters, investigators, and collectors often work for insurance companies, real estate firms, department stores, manufacturing firms, banks and other financial institutions, telephone companies, and credit reporting and collection agencies.

$alaries

Earnings of adjusters, investigators, anc collectors vary significantly.

Inside adjusters	$22,300/year
Senior inside adjusters	$26,700/year
Outside adjusters	$24,800/year
Senior outside adjusters	$33,200/year
Technical specialist claims adjusters	$39,800/year
Claim examiners	$29,900/year
Senior claim examiners	$33,600/year
Claim supervisors	$36,600/year
Claim managers	$47,100/year
Automobile damage appraisers	$28,800/year
Policy processing clerks	$16,400/year
Interviewers	$15,000/year

Bill and account collectors	$16,600
Adjustment clerks employed in department stores	$9,000-$13,800/year
Customer service representatives	$17,000/year
Welfare eligibility workers and interviewers	$17,600/year

Employment Outlook

Growth rate until the year 2000: Average.

Adjusters, Investigators, and Collectors

Career Guides

★714★
"Adjusters" in *Opportunities in Insurance Careers* (pp. 42-43)
National Textbook Co.
4255 W. Touhy Ave.
Lincolnwood, IL 60646   Phone: (312)679-5500
Robert M. Schrayer. 1987. Explores the history of the insurance industry and career opportunities. Describes educational requirements, certification, licensing, salaries, and employment outlook.

★715★
"Adjusters, Investigators, and Collectors" in *Occupational Outlook Handbook* (pp. 244-248)
Superintendent of Documents
U.S. Government Printing Office
Washington, DC 20402   Phone: (202)783-3238
Biennial; latest edition, 1990-91. Encyclopedia of careers describing more than 250 occupations and comprising about 86 percent of all jobs in the economy. Occupations that require lengthy education or training are given the most attention. For each occupation, the handbook describes job duties, working conditions, training, educational preparation, personal qualities, advancement possibilities, job outlook, earnings, and sources of additional information.

★716★
"Benefits Claims Examiner" in *Opportunities in Insurance Careers* (p. 39)
National Textbook Co.
4255 W. Touhy Ave.
Lincolnwood, IL 60646   Phone: (312)679-5500
Robert M. Schrayer. 1987. Explores the history of the insurance industry and career opportunities. Describes educational requirements, certification, licensing, salaries, and employment outlook.

★717★
Bill Collector
Careers, Inc.
PO Box 135
Largo, FL 34649-0135   Phone: (813)584-7333
1989. Two-page occupational summary card describing duties, working conditions, personal qualifications, training, earnings and hours, employment outlook, places of employment, related careers and where to write for more information.

★718★
"Bill Collector" in *Occu-Facts: Information on 565 Careers in Outline Form* (p. 12.44)
Careers, Inc.
P.O. Box 135
1211 Tenth St., S.W.
Largo, FL 33640   Phone: (813)584-7333
Elizabeth Handville. Biennial, 1989-90 edition. Each one-page occupational profile describes duties, working conditions, physical surroundings and demands, aptitudes, temperament, educational requirements, employment outlook, earnings, and places of employment.

★719★
Bill Collectors
Chronicle Guidance Publications, Inc.
PO Box 1190
Moravia, NY 13118-1190   Phone: (315)497-0330
1990. This career brief describes the nature of the work, working conditions, hours and earnings, education and training, licensure, certification, unions, personal qualifications, social and psychological factors, employment outlook, entry methods, advancement, and related occupations. **Toll-free/Additional Phone Number(s):** 800-622-7284.

★720★
Careers in Insurance: Property and Casualty
Insurance Information Institute
110 William St.
New York, NY 10038   Phone: (212)669-9200
1987. This 12-page booklet explores careers in property and casualty insurance and covers job duties and training.

★721★
Careers in Life and Health Claims
International Claim Association
Mississippi River at 17th St.
Rock Island, IL 61201   Phone: (309)786-6481
This booklet describes jobs in insurance claims. Covers salaries and future trends.

★722★
"Claim Adjuster" in *Administration, Business, and Office*, Volume 1 of *Career Information Center* (pp. 72-74)
Glencoe/Macmillan
15319 Chatsworth St.
Mission Hills, CA 91345   Phone: (818)898-1391
Richard Lidz and Dale Anderson, editorial directors. Fourth edition, 1990. For 600 occupations, describes job duties, entry-level requirements, education and training needed,

advancement possibilities, employment outlook, earnings and benefits. The set is divided into 12 volumes. Each volume includes jobs related under a broad career field. Volume 13 is the index. **Facsimile Number:** 818-365-5489.

★723★
"Claim Agent" in *Careers in Trucking* (pp. 75-76)
Rosen Publishing Group, Inc.
29 E. 21st St.
New York, NY 10010   Phone: (212)777-3017
Donald D. Schauer. 1987. Describes employment in the trucking industry including driving, operations, sales, and administration. Covers qualifications, training, future outlook, and salaries. Offers career planning and job hunting advice.

★724★
"Claim Examiner" in *Administration, Business, and Office*, Volume 1 of *Career Information Center* (pp. 74-75)
Glencoe/Macmillan
15319 Chatsworth St.
Mission Hills, CA 91345   Phone: (818)898-1391
Richard Lidz and Dale Anderson, editorial directors. Fourth edition, 1990. For 600 occupations, describes job duties, entry-level requirements, education and training needed, advancement possibilities, employment outlook, earnings and benefits. The set is divided into 12 volumes. Each volume includes jobs related under a broad career field. Volume 13 is the index. **Facsimile Number:** 818-365-5489.

★725★
"Claim Representative" in *VGM's Careers Encyclopedia* (pp. 107-111)
National Textbook Co.
4255 W. Touhy Ave.
Lincolnwood, IL 60646   Phone: (312)679-5500
Third edition, 1991. Contains two- to five-page descriptions of 200 managerial, professional, technical, trade, and service occupations. Each profile includes job duties, places of employment, qualifications, educational preparation, training, employment potential, advancement, income, and additional sources of information.

★726★
"Claim Representative" in *VGM's Handbook of Business and Management Careers* (pp. 31-34)
National Textbook Co.
4255 W. Touhy Ave.
Lincolnwood, IL 60646   Phone: (312)679-5500
Craig T. Norback. 1990. Contains 43 two-page occupational profiles describing job duties, places of employment, working conditions, qualifications, education, employment outlook, and income.

★727★
"Claim Representatives" in *Jobs! What They Are...Where They Are...What They Pay* (pp. 129-130)
Simon & Schuster, Inc.
Simon & Schuster Bldg.
1230 Avenue of the Americas
New York, NY 10020   Phone: (212)698-7000
Robert O. Snelling and Anne M. Snelling. Revised edition, 1989. Profiles 241 occupations, describing duties and responsibilities, educational preparation, earnings, employment opportunities, training, and qualifications.

★728★
Claims Adjusters (Insurance)
Chronicle Guidance Publications, Inc.
PO Box 1190
Moravia, NY 13118-1190   Phone: (315)497-0330
1988. This career brief describes the nature of the work, working conditions, hours and earnings, education and training, licensure, certification, unions, personal qualifications, social and psychological factors, employment outlook, entry methods, advancement, and related occupations. **Toll-free/Additional Phone Number(s):** 800-622-7284.

★729★
"Claims Representatives" in *Opportunities in Insurance Careers* (p. 37)
National Textbook Co.
4255 W. Touhy Ave.
Lincolnwood, IL 60646   Phone: (312)679-5500
Robert M. Schrayer. 1987. Explores the history of the insurance industry and career opportunities. Describes educational requirements, certification, licensing, salaries, and employment outlook.

★730★
Clerks, Insurance
Careers, Inc.
PO Box 135
Largo, FL 34649-0135   Phone: (813)584-7333
1992. Two-page occupational summary card describing duties, working conditions, personal qualifications, training, earnings and hours, employment outlook, places of employment, related careers and where to write for more information.

★731★
"Collection Workers" in Volume 3 of *The Encyclopedia of Careers and Vocational Guidance* (pp. 15-18)
J.G. Ferguson Publishing Co.
200 W. Monroe
Chicago, IL 60606   Phone: (312)580-5480
William E. Hopke, editor-in-chief. Eighth edition, 1990. Four-volume set that profiles 500 occupations and describes job trends in 76 industries. Includes career description, educational requirements, history of the job, methods of entry, advancement, employment outlook, earnings, working conditions, social and psychological factors, and sources of additional information.

★732★
"Collection Workers" in Volume 2 of *Career Discovery Encyclopedia* (pp. 28-29)
J.G. Ferguson Publishing Co.
200 W. Monroe
Chicago, IL 60606   Phone: (312)580-5480
E. Russell Primm, editor-in-chief. 1990. Contains two-page articles on 504 occupations. Each article describes job duties, earnings, and educational and training requirements.

★733★
"Collectors" in *Jobs! What They Are...Where They Are...What They Pay* (pp. 126-127)
Simon & Schuster, Inc.
Simon & Schuster Bldg.
1230 Avenue of the Americas
New York, NY 10020   Phone: (212)698-7000
Robert O. Snelling and Anne M. Snelling. Revised edition, 1989. Profiles 241 occupations, describing duties and responsibilities, educational preparation, earnings, employment opportunities, training, and qualifications.

Adjusters, Investigators, and Collectors

★734★
"Credit Collector" in *Administration, Business, and Office*, Volume 1 of *Career Information Center* (pp. 51-52)
Glencoe/Macmillan
15319 Chatsworth St.
Mission Hills, CA 91345   Phone: (818)898-1391
Richard Lidz and Dale Anderson, editorial directors. Fourth edition, 1990. For 600 occupations, describes job duties, entry-level requirements, education and training needed, advancement possibilities, employment outlook, earnings and benefits. The set is divided into 12 volumes. Each volume includes jobs related under a broad career field. Volume 13 is the index. **Facsimile Number:** 818-365-5489.

★735★
"Customer Service Assistant" in *Career Opportunities in Art* (p. 135)
Facts on File, Inc.
460 Park Avenue, S.
New York, NY 10016   Phone: (212)683-2244
Susan H. Haubenstock and David Joselit. 1988. Profiles more than 75 art-related jobs. Each occupational profile covers job duties, employment outlook, career paths, salaries, skills, and educational preparation. Offers tips for entering the field.

★736★
"Customer Service Representative" in *Career Opportunities in Television, Cable, and Video* (pp. 170-171)
Facts on File, Inc.
460 Park Avenue, S.
New York, NY 10016   Phone: (212)683-2244
Third edition, 1990. Describes 100 media-related jobs. Each occupational profile covers job duties, employment outlook, career paths, salaries, skills, and educational preparation. Offers tips for entering the field.

★737★
"Customer Service Representative" in *Careers in Trucking* (pp. 21-23)
Rosen Publishing Group, Inc.
29 E. 21st St.
New York, NY 10010   Phone: (212)777-3017
Donald D. Schauer. 1987. Describes employment in the trucking industry including driving, operations, sales, and administration. Covers qualifications, training, future outlook, and salaries. Offers career planning and job hunting advice.

★738★
"Customer Service Representative" in *Jobs! What They Are. . .Where They Are. . .What They Pay* (pp. 207-208)
Simon & Schuster, Inc.
Simon & Schuster Bldg.
1230 Avenue of the Americas
New York, NY 10020   Phone: (212)698-7000
Robert O. Snelling and Anne M. Snelling. Revised edition, 1989. Profiles 241 occupations, describing duties and responsibilities, educational preparation, earnings, employment opportunities, training, and qualifications.

★739★
"Field Representatives" in *Opportunities in Insurance Careers* (pp. 42-43)
National Textbook Co.
4255 W. Touhy Ave.
Lincolnwood, IL 60646   Phone: (312)679-5500
Robert M. Schrayer. 1987. Explores the history of the insurance industry and career opportunities. Describes educational requirements, certification, licensing, salaries, and employment outlook.

★740★
Insurance Adjuster
Careers, Inc.
PO Box 135
Largo, FL 34649-0135   Phone: (813)584-7333
1991. Two-page occupational summary card describing duties, working conditions, personal qualifications, training, earnings and hours, employment outlook, places of employment, related careers and where to write for more information.

★741★
"Insurance Adjuster" in *Occu-Facts: Information on 565 Careers in Outline Form* (p. 12.43)
Careers, Inc.
P.O. Box 135
1211 Tenth St., S.W.
Largo, FL 33640   Phone: (813)584-7333
Elizabeth Handville. Biennial, 1989-90 edition. Each one-page occupational profile describes duties, working conditions, physical surroundings and demands, aptitudes, temperament, educational requirements, employment outlook, earnings, and places of employment.

★742★
"Insurance Claims Representatives" in Volume 3 of *Career Discovery Encyclopedia* (pp. 152-153)
J.G. Ferguson Publishing Co.
200 W. Monroe
Chicago, IL 60606   Phone: (312)580-5480
E. Russell Primm, editor-in-chief. 1990. Contains two-page articles on 504 occupations. Each article describes job duties, earnings, and educational and training requirements.

★743★
"Insurance Claims Representatives" in Volume 2 of *The Encyclopedia of Careers and Vocational Guidance* (pp. 323-326)
J.G. Ferguson Publishing Co.
200 W. Monroe
Chicago, IL 60606   Phone: (312)580-5480
William E. Hopke, editor-in-chief. Eighth edition, 1990. Four-volume set that profiles 500 occupations and describes job trends in 76 industries. Includes career description, educational requirements, history of the job, methods of entry, advancement, employment outlook, earnings, working conditions, social and psychological factors, and sources of additional information.

★744★
"Insurance Clerks" in *Occu-Facts: Information on 565 Careers in Outline Form* (p. 12.25)
Careers, Inc.
P.O. Box 135
1211 Tenth St., S.W.
Largo, FL 33640   Phone: (813)584-7333
Elizabeth Handville. Biennial, 1989-90 edition. Each one-page occupational profile describes duties, working conditions, physical surroundings and demands, aptitudes, temperament,

educational requirements, employment outlook, earnings, and places of employment.

★745★
"Insurance Policy Processing Occupations" in Volume 3 of *Career Discovery Encyclopedia* (pp. 154-155)
J.G. Ferguson Publishing Co.
200 W. Monroe
Chicago, IL 60606   Phone: (312)580-5480

E. Russell Primm, editor-in-chief. 1990. Contains two-page articles on 504 occupations. Each article describes job duties, earnings, and educational and training requirements.

★746★
"Insurance Policy Processing Occupations" in Volume 3 of *The Encyclopedia of Careers and Vocational Guidance* (pp. 52-55)
J.G. Ferguson Publishing Co.
200 W. Monroe
Chicago, IL 60606   Phone: (312)580-5480

William E. Hopke, editor-in-chief. Eighth edition, 1990. Four-volume set that profiles 500 occupations and describes job trends in 76 industries. Includes career description, educational requirements, history of the job, methods of entry, advancement, employment outlook, earnings, working conditions, social and psychological factors, and sources of additional information.

★747★
Secrets of Locating Past Due Debtors
International Collection Training Institute
735 East Hartman Rd.
Post Office Box 880
Anderson, IN 46015   Phone: (317)649-0608

Videocassette. 1986. 42 mins. For training debt collectors, how to track down welchers.

★748★
Video Career Library - Clerical & Administrative Support
Careers, Inc.
1211 10th St., SW
PO Box 135
Largo, FL 34649-0135   Phone: (813)584-7333

Videocassette. 1990. 26 mins. Part of the Video Career Library covering 165 occupations. Shows actual workers on the job. Includes secretaries, cashiers, receptionists, bookkeepers and audit clerks, telephone operators, postal clerks/carriers/supervisors, insurance investigators, bank tellers, data entry keyers, and court reporters.

Associations

★749★
Alliance of American Insurers
1501 Woodfield Rd., Ste. 400 W
Schaumburg, IL 60173   Phone: (708)330-8700

Membership: Property and casualty insurance companies. **Publications:** *Journal of American Insurance*, quarterly. **Facsimile Number:** (708)330-8602.

★750★
American Collectors Association (ACA)
4040 W. 70th St.
PO Box 39106
Minneapolis, MN 55439-0106   Phone: (612)926-6547

Membership: Collection services handling overdue accounts for retail, professional, and commercial credit grantors. **Purpose:** Maintains Healthcare Client Services Program, which provides services for members who work with the health care industry and providers. Bestows awards; maintains museum; conducts research. Offers specialized education; compiles statistics. Operates 400 volume library. **Publications:** *American Collectors Association—Membership Roster*, annual. • *Collector*, monthly. • *Cred-Alert*, monthly. • *Public Affairs Review*, monthly.

★751★
Insurance Information Institute (III)
110 William St.
New York, NY 10038   Phone: (212)669-9200

Membership: Property and liability insurance companies. **Purpose:** To provide information and educational services to mass media, educational institutions, trade associations, businesses, government agencies, and the public. Conducts public opinion surveys. Sponsors seminars and briefings on insurance, safety, research, public policy, and economic topics. Bestows insurance leadership awards. Maintains 1400 volume library on property and casualty insurance and related topics. **Publications:** *Data Base News*, 5/week. • *Data Base Reports*, monthly. • *Educators Letter*, monthly. • *Executive Letter*, weekly. • *Insurance Facts*, annual. • *Insurance Pulse*, quarterly. • *Insurance Review*, monthly. • *Insurance Update*, bimonthly. • Also publishes books, monographs, pamphlets, and brochures; makes available filmstrips, slides, films, and videotapes. **Toll-free/Additional Phone Number(s):** 800-221-4954 (Consumer hot line). **Facsimile Number:** (212)732-1916.

★752★
Life Office Management Association (LOMA)
5770 Powers Ferry Rd., NW
Atlanta, GA 30327   Phone: (404)951-1770

Membership: Life and health insurance companies in the U.S. and Canada; associate members are life insurers in 33 countries; affiliate members are firms that provide professional support to member companies. Provides research, information, and educational activities in areas of operations and systems, human resources, and financial planning and control. Administers FLMI Insurance Education Program, which awards FLMI (Fellow, Life Management Institute) designation to life and health insurance company employees and others who complete the ten-examination program. Maintains library of research materials relating to company operations. Maintains speakers' and writers' bureaus; compiles statistics. **Publications:** *Annual Report*. • *LOMA Membership Directory*, annual. • *Resource*, monthly. • Also publishes reports, surveys, case studies, proceedings, manuals, index of publications, and price list of information materials; produces video- and audiocassette programs. **Facsimile Number:** (404)984-0441.

★753★
National Association of Public Insurance Adjusters (NAPIA)
300 Water St., Ste. 400
Baltimore, MD 21202   Phone: (301)539-4141

Membership: Professional society of public insurance adjusters. **Purpose:** Sponsors seminars and certification and professional education programs. **Publications:** *Bulletin*, quarterly. • *Directory*, biennial. • Also publishes brochures and charts. **Facsimile Number:** (301)659-9491.

Standards/Certification Agencies

Most states require adjusters to be licensed. Applicants usually must comply with one or more of the following: Pass a written examination covering the fundamentals of adjusting; complete an approved course in insurance or loss adjusting; furnish character references; be at least 20 or 21 years of age and a resident of the state; and file a surety bond. The Insurance

Institute of America, a nonprofit organization, offers educational programs and professional certification to persons in the property-liability insurance industry. The organization offers an Associate in Claims designation upon successful completion of six examinations. The International Claim Association offers a program on life and health insurance claims administration. Completion of the five-examination program leads to the professional designation, Associate, Life and Health Claims. The Life Office Management Association (LOMA) offers a comprehensive 10-course life and health insurance educational program that leads to the professional designation, Fellow, Life Management Institute. LOMA also offers the Master Fellow Program designed for life and health insurance professionals.

★754★
Life Office Management Association (LOMA)
5770 Powers Ferry Rd., NW
Atlanta, GA 30327   Phone: (404)951-1770
Administers FLMI Insurance Education Program, which awards FLMI (Fellow, Life Management Institute) designation to life and health insurance company employees and others who complete the ten-examination program.

★755★
National Association of Public Insurance Adjusters (NAPIA)
300 Water St., Ste. 400
Baltimore, MD 21202   Phone: (301)539-4141
Sponsors seminars and certification and professional education programs.

Test Guides

★756★
Assessment Assistant
National Learning Corp.
212 Michael Dr.
Syosset, NY 11791   Phone: (516)921-8888
Jack Rudman. Part of the Career Examination Series No. 1. All examination guides in this series contain questions with answers. **Facsimile Number:** (516)921-8743. **Toll-free/Additional Phone Number(s):** 800-645-6337.

★757★
Assessment Clerk
National Learning Corp.
212 Michael Dr.
Syosset, NY 11791   Phone: (516)921-8888
Jack Rudman. Part of the Career Examination Series No. 1. All examination guides in this series contain questions with answers. **Facsimile Number:** (516)921-8743. **Toll-free/Additional Phone Number(s):** 800-645-6337.

★758★
Associate Claim Examiner
National Learning Corp.
212 Michael Dr.
Syosset, NY 11791   Phone: (516)921-8888
Jack Rudman. Part of the Career Examination Series No. 1. All examination guides in this series contain questions with answers. **Facsimile Number:** (516)921-8743. **Toll-free/Additional Phone Number(s):** 800-645-6337.

★759★
Chief Investigator
National Learning Corp.
212 Michael Dr.
Syosset, NY 11791   Phone: (516)921-8888
Jack Rudman. Part of the Career Examination Series No. 1. All examination guides in this series contain questions with answers. **Facsimile Number:** (516)921-8743. **Toll-free/Additional Phone Number(s):** 800-645-6337.

★760★
Claims Clerk
National Learning Corp.
212 Michael Dr.
Syosset, NY 11791   Phone: (516)921-8888
Jack Rudman. Part of the Career Examination Series No. 1. All examination guides in this series contain questions with answers. **Facsimile Number:** (516)921-8743. **Toll-free/Additional Phone Number(s):** 800-645-6337.

★761★
Claims Investigator
National Learning Corp.
212 Michael Dr.
Syosset, NY 11791   Phone: (516)921-8888
Jack Rudman. Part of the Career Examination Series No. 1. All examination guides in this series contain questions with answers. **Facsimile Number:** (516)921-8743. **Toll-free/Additional Phone Number(s):** 800-645-6337.

★762★
Credit and Collection Coordinator
National Learning Corp.
212 Michael Dr.
Syosset, NY 11791   Phone: (516)921-8888
Jack Rudman. Part of the Career Examination Series No. 1. All examination guides in this series contain questions with answers. **Facsimile Number:** (516)921-8743. **Toll-free/Additional Phone Number(s):** 800-645-6337.

★763★
Investigator/Claim Examiner
Prentice Hall Press
Simon & Schuster Inc.
200 Old Tappan Rd.
Old Tappan, NJ 07675
John Czukor. First edition, 1990. Complete preparation for the qualifying test for civil service Investigators/Claim Examiners. Includes five practice tests with answers. **Toll-free/Additional Phone Number(s):** 800-223-2348.

Awards, Scholarships, Grants, and Fellowships

★764★
NAFI Man of the Year
National Association of Fire Investigators
20 E. Jackson Blvd., Ste. 1000
Chicago, IL 60604-2210   Phone: (312)939-6050
To recognize significant contributions to the fire investigation profession and NAFI. Firemen, policemen, attorneys, insurance adjusters, claimsmen, fire experts, fire marshals in the military, or full-time fire investigators may be nominated. An engraved plaque is awarded annually when merited. Established in 1969. Formerly: Fire Investigator of the Year.

Basic Reference Guides and Handbooks

★765★
Adjusters Reference Guide
Insurance Field Co.
PO Box 18630
Louisville, KY 40218   Phone: (502)459-7910
R.W. Bourne, Jr., Editor. Quarterly. Reference guide for insurance adjusters. Contains claim information and specimen policies. **Facsimile Number:** (502)458-0616.

★766★
Directory
National Association of Public Insurance Adjusters (NAPIA)
300 Water St., Ste. 400
Baltimore, MD 21202   Phone: (301)539-4141
Biennial.

Periodicals

★767★
AMA Public Affairs Review
American Collectors Association (ACA)
4040 W. 70th St.
PO Box 39106
Minneapolis, MN 55439-0106   Phone: (612)926-6547
Monthly. Legislative bulletin for professionals in the industry.

★768★
American Agent & Broker
Commerce Publishing Co.
408 Olive St.
Saint Louis, MO 63102   Phone: (314)421-5445
George Williams, Editor. Monthly. Magazine for independent agents in fire, casualty, and surety insurance businesses. **Facsimile Number:** (314)421-1070.

★769★
Collector
American Collectors Association (ACA)
4040 W. 70th St.
PO Box 39106
Minneapolis, MN 55439-0106   Phone: (612)926-6547
Monthly. Magazine covering the consumer debt collection industry. Includes regulation, agency management, and collection techniques information. Contains annual index.

★770★
Cred-Alert
American Collectors Association (ACA)
4040 W. 70th St.
PO Box 39106
Minneapolis, MN 55439-0106   Phone: (612)926-6547
Monthly. Industry bulletin for credit grantors and collectors.

★771★
Data Base News
Insurance Information Institute (III)
110 William St.
New York, NY 10038   Phone: (212)669-9200
5/week.

★772★
Data Base Reports
Insurance Information Institute (III)
110 William St.
New York, NY 10038   Phone: (212)669-9200
Monthly.

★773★
Educators Letter
Insurance Information Institute (III)
110 William St.
New York, NY 10038   Phone: (212)669-9200
Monthly.

★774★
III Executive Letter
Insurance Information Institute (III)
110 William St.
New York, NY 10038   Phone: (212)669-9200
Weekly.

★775★
Insurance Pulse
Insurance Information Institute (III)
110 William St.
New York, NY 10038   Phone: (212)669-9200
Quarterly.

★776★
Insurance Review
Insurance Information Institute (III)
110 William St.
New York, NY 10038   Phone: (212)669-9200
Monthly.

★777★
Insurance Update
Insurance Information Institute (III)
110 William St.
New York, NY 10038   Phone: (212)669-9200
Bimonthly.

★778★
NAPIA Bulletin
National Association of Public Insurance Adjusters (NAPIA)
300 Water St., Ste. 400
Baltimore, MD 21202   Phone: (301)539-4141
Quarterly.

★779★
Southern Insurance
2535 Beechwood Ave., No. 9001
Mount Vernon, NY 10552
A.J. Davis, Editor and Publisher. Monthly. Insurance industry magazine.

Other Sources of Information

★780★
Insurance Facts
Insurance Information Institute (III)
110 William St.
New York, NY 10038   Phone: (212)669-9200
Annual.

Bank Tellers

Bank tellers cash customers' checks and process deposits and withdrawals from checking and savings accounts. Larger banks employ tellers with more specialized duties such as selling savings bonds, handling foreign currency, or computing interest on savings accounts. In most banks, tellers use computer terminals to keep accurate records of all transactions. Although they work independently, bank tellers are closely supervised and work directly with the public.

$alaries

Earnings for bank tellers vary according to responsibility, experience, and size and location of bank.

Lowest 10 percent	$9,200/year
Median	$12,800/year
Top 10 percent	$20,300/year

Employment Outlook

Growth rate until the year 2000: More slowly than average.

Bank Tellers

Career Guides

★781★
Bank Teller
Careers, Inc.
PO Box 135
Largo, FL 34649-0135   Phone: (813)584-7333
1990. Two-page occupational summary card describing duties, working conditions, personal qualifications, training, earnings and hours, employment outlook, places of employment, related careers and where to write for more information.

★782★
Bank Teller
Vocational Biographies, Inc.
PO Box 31, Dept. VF10
Sauk Centre, MN 56378   Phone: (612)352-6516
1991. This pamphlet profiles a person working in the job. Includes information about job duties, working conditions, places of employment, educational preparation, labor market outlook, and salaries. **Toll-free/Additional Phone Number(s):** 800-255-0752.

★783★
"Bank Teller" in *Administration, Business, and Office, Volume 1 of Career Information Center* (pp. 42-44)
Glencoe/Macmillan
15319 Chatsworth St.
Mission Hills, CA 91345   Phone: (818)898-1391
Richard Lidz and Dale Anderson, editorial directors. Fourth edition, 1990. For 600 occupations, describes job duties, entry-level requirements, education and training needed, advancement possibilities, employment outlook, earnings and benefits. The set is divided into 12 volumes. Each volume includes jobs related under a broad career field. Volume 13 is the index. **Facsimile Number:** 818-365-5489.

★784★
"Bank Teller" in *Careers in Banking and Finance* (pp. 21-26)
Rosen Publishing Group, Inc.
29 E. 21st St.
New York, NY 10010   Phone: (212)777-3017
Patricia Haddock. 1990. Describes more than 20 jobs at all levels in banking and finance. Contains information about the types of financial organizations where the jobs are found, educational requirements, job duties, and salaries. Offers advice on job hunting.

★785★
"Bank Teller" in *Guide to Careers Without College* (pp. 53-56)
Franklin Watts, Inc.
387 Park Avenue, S.
New York, NY 10016   Phone: (212)686-7070
Kathleen S. Abrams. 1988. Discusses careers that do not require a college degree in fields such as health care, sales and marketing, and the building trades. Describes the work, employment opportunities, and training.

★786★
"Bank Teller" in *Occu-Facts: Information on 565 Careers in Outline Form* (p. 12.45)
Careers, Inc.
P.O. Box 135
1211 Tenth St., S.W.
Largo, FL 33640   Phone: (813)584-7333
Elizabeth Handville. Biennial, 1989-90 edition. Each one-page occupational profile describes duties, working conditions, physical surroundings and demands, aptitudes, temperament, educational requirements, employment outlook, earnings, and places of employment.

★787★
"Bank Teller" in *VGM's Careers Encyclopedia* (pp. 60-61)
National Textbook Co.
4255 W. Touhy Ave.
Lincolnwood, IL 60646   Phone: (312)679-5500
Third edition, 1991. Contains two- to five-page descriptions of 200 managerial, professional, technical, trade, and service occupations. Each profile includes job duties, places of employment, qualifications, educational preparation, training, employment potential, advancement, income, and additional sources of information.

★788★
"Bank Tellers" in *Jobs! What They Are...Where They Are...What They Pay* (pp. 125-126)
Simon & Schuster, Inc.
Simon & Schuster Bldg.
1230 Avenue of the Americas
New York, NY 10020   Phone: (212)698-7000
Robert O. Snelling and Anne M. Snelling. Revised edition, 1989. Profiles 241 occupations, describing duties and responsibilities, educational preparation, earnings, employment opportunities, training, and qualifications.

★789★
"Bank Tellers" in *Occupational Outlook Handbook* (pp. 248-250)
Superintendent of Documents
U.S. Government Printing Office
Washington, DC 20402　　　　　　　Phone: (202)783-3238

Biennial; latest edition, 1990-91. Encyclopedia of careers describing more than 250 occupations and comprising about 86 percent of all jobs in the economy. Occupations that require lengthy education or training are given the most attention. For each occupation, the handbook describes job duties, working conditions, training, educational preparation, personal qualities, advancement possibilities, job outlook, earnings, and sources of additional information.

★790★
"Bank Tellers" in Volume 1 of *Career Discovery Encyclopedia* (pp. 110-111)
J.G. Ferguson Publishing Co.
200 W. Monroe
Chicago, IL 60606　　　　　　　Phone: (312)580-5480

E. Russell Primm, editor-in-chief. 1990. Contains two-page articles on 504 occupations. Each article describes job duties, earnings, and educational and training requirements.

★791★
Career Success Series
Cambridge Career Products
90 MacCorkle Ave., SW
South Charleston, WV 25311　　　　　Phone: (304)744-9323

Videocassette. 1986. 15 mins. A series, available separately, outlining various career choices for students. Occupations include: flight service, air transportation/ground service, data processing, carpentry, clerk in banking/insurance, commodity sales, cosmetic personal grooming, fire fighting, forestry services, home economics, insulation/roofing, material handling, mechanics, photographic processing, pipefitting and plumbing, police science, printing, secretarial services, and utilities equipment operator.

★792★
Careers in the Investment World
Chelsea House Publishers
1974 Sproul Rd., Ste. 400
Broomall, PA 19008　　　　　　　Phone: (215)353-5166

Rachel S. Epstein. 1988. **Facsimile Number:** (215)359-1439.

★793★
Clerk: Bank, Insurance and Commerce
Morris Video
2730 Monterey St. #105
Monterey Business Park
Torrance, CA 90503　　　　　　　Phone: (213)533-4800

Videocassette. 1981. 15 mins. The many and varied duties of the clerk are examined.

★794★
"Financial Institution Tellers" in Volume 3 of *The Encyclopedia of Careers and Vocational Guidance* (pp. 41-45)
J.G. Ferguson Publishing Co.
200 W. Monroe
Chicago, IL 60606　　　　　　　Phone: (312)580-5480

William E. Hopke, editor-in-chief. Eighth edition, 1990. Four-volume set that profiles 500 occupations and describes job trends in 76 industries. Includes career description, educational requirements, history of the job, methods of entry, advancement, employment outlook, earnings, working conditions, social and psychological factors, and sources of additional information.

★795★
"Tellers and Clerks (Bank)" in *The American Almanac of Jobs and Salaries* (pp. 415-417)
Avon Books
105 Madison Avenue
New York, NY 10016　　　　　　　Phone: (212)481-5600

John Wright and Edward J. Dwyer. Revised and updated, 1990. A comprehensive guide to the wages of hundreds of occupations in a wide variety of industries and organizations.

★796★
Tellers, Financial Institution
Chronicle Guidance Publications, Inc.
PO Box 1190
Moravia, NY 13118-1190　　　　　Phone: (315)497-0330

1990. This career brief describes the nature of the work, working conditions, hours and earnings, education and training, licensure, certification, unions, personal qualifications, social and psychological factors, employment outlook, entry methods, advancement, and related occupations. **Toll-free/Additional Phone Number(s):** 800-622-7284.

★797★
Tellers—How Important Are They?
1st Financial Video Network
1701 East Woodfield Rd.
Suite 412
Schaumburg, IL 60173-5133　　　　Phone: (708)605-0222

Videocassette. 1987. 23 mins. The importance of tellers and other platform personnel is the thrust of this program.

★798★
Video Career Library - Clerical & Administrative Support
Careers, Inc.
1211 10th St., SW
PO Box 135
Largo, FL 34649-0135　　　　　　Phone: (813)584-7333

Videocassette. 1990. 26 mins. Part of the Video Career Library covering 165 occupations. Shows actual workers on the job. Includes secretaries, cashiers, receptionists, bookkeepers and audit clerks, telephone operators, postal clerks/carriers/supervisors, insurance investigators, bank tellers, data entry keyers, and court reporters.

―――――――― Associations ――――――――

★799★
American Bankers Association (ABA)
1120 Connecticut Ave. NW
Washington, DC 20036　　　　　　Phone: (202)663-5000

Membership: Commercial banks and trust companies; combined assets of members represent approximately 95% of the U.S. banking industry. **Purpose:** Seeks to enhance the role of commercial banks as preeminent providers of financial services through communications, research, legal action, lobbying of federal legislative and regulatory bodies, and education and training programs. Serves as spokesperson for the commercial banking industry; facilitates exchange of information among members. Sponsors American Institute of Banking (formerly American Institute of Bank Clerks), which conducts educational and training programs for bank employees and officers through 21 schools of banking. Maintains liaison with federal bank regulators; submits draft legislation and lobbies Congress on issues affecting commercial banks; testifies before congressional committees; represents members in U.S. postal rate proceedings; also represents the U.S. banking industry at the United Nations. Serves as secretariat of the International Money Conference and the Financial Institutions Committee for the American National Standards Institute. Files briefs and lawsuits in major court cases affecting the industry. Conducts teleconferences with state banking associations on such issues as tax reform and compliance; works to build consensus and coordinate activities of leading bank and financial service trade groups. Provides services to members including: television, newspaper, and magazine advertisements promoting full-service banks; insurance program providing directors and officers with liability coverage, financial institution bond, and trust errors and omissions coverage; research service operated through ABA Library and Information Services; fingerprint set processing in conjunction with the Federal Bureau of Investigation. Conducts conferences, forums, and workshops covering subjects including agricultural and community banking, trust management, bank operations, and automation. Sponsors Personal Economics Program, which presents school programs on topics including checking account management and careers in banking. Bestows five Ayres Fellowships annually to academicians; two Hughes Fellowships annually to financial journalists; two Cummings Fellowships annually to professional staff members in the executive or legislative branches of federal or state governments. Maintains library of 60,000 volumes on banking, money, economics, finance, and law. **Publications:** *ABA Bankers Weekly.* • *ABA Banking Journal*, monthly. • *ABA Retail Banker*, monthly. • *The Advisor*, monthly. • *AIB Leaders Letter*, 9/year. • *AIB Student Catalog*, annual. • *Bank Compliance Magazine*, quarterly. • *Bank Personnel News*, monthly. • *Bank Planning News*, bimonthly. • *Commercial Lender Newsletter*, monthly. • *Consumer Banking Digest*, monthly. • *Delinquency Consumer Credit Bulletin*, quarterly. • *Directory*, annual. • *Insurance and Protection Bulletin*, monthly. • *ISO Register*, quarterly. • *Journal of Personal Financial Services*, quarterly. • *Thruput: The ABA Operations/ Automation News Report*, monthly. • *Trust Letter*, monthly. • *Trust Management Update: A Trust Industry Communication on Management, Investments, Marketing, Operations, and Administration*, monthly. • Also issues approximately 400 technical publications, listed in *ABA Catalog*; also produces computer software and video- and audiocassettes. **Toll-free/Additional Phone Number(s):** (202)663-5430 Banker Education Network; (800)872-7747 financial information; (800)424-2871 news service.

★800★
Institute of Financial Education (IFE)
111 E. Wacker Dr.
Chicago, IL 60601-4680   Phone: (312)644-3100
Membership: Nationwide educational organization conducting courses for personnel of savings institutions, commercial banks, and credit unions. **Publications:** *Insider*, monthly. • *Institute of Financial Education—On Track*, bimonthly. **Facsimile Number:** (312)856-0497.

Standards/Certification Agencies

Some banks have their own training programs which result in teller certification. Experienced tellers qualify for certification by taking required courses and passing examinations.

Educational Directories and Programs

★801★
AIB Student Catalog
American Bankers Association (ABA)
1120 Connecticut Ave. NW
Washington, DC 20036   Phone: (202)663-5000
Annual.

Awards, Scholarships, Grants, and Fellowships

★802★
American Institute of Banking Scholarship
American Institute of Banking
c/o Ken Embers
1213 Bakers Way
Manhattan, KS 66502   Phone: (913)537-4750
To be applied to tuition at the American Institute of Banking resident courses lasting 10 or 16 weeks. Applicants must be high school graduates or hold a GED. Scholarships are based on merit (formal education, banking experience, and letters of recommendation).

Basic Reference Guides and Handbooks

★803★
ABA Directory
American Bankers Association (ABA)
1120 Connecticut Ave. NW
Washington, DC 20036   Phone: (202)663-5000
Annual.

★804★
Bank Tellers Do's & Don'ts
American Bankers Association
1120 Connecticut Ave., NW
Washington, DC 20036   Phone: (202)663-7500
Revised edition, 1963. **Facsimile Number:** (202)828-4540.

★805★
The Bank Tellers Job: A Day to Day Reference Guide
American Bankers Association
1120 Connecticut Ave., NW
Washington, DC 20036   Phone: (202)663-7500
American Bankers Association Staff. 1980. **Facsimile Number:** (202)828-4540.

★806★
Teller Operations Manual
Bank Administration Institute
60 Gould Center
Rolling Meadows, IL 60008
1990. **Toll-free/Additional Phone Number(s):** 800-323-8552.

★807★
Teller Performance
Bank Administration Institute
60 Gould Center
Rolling Meadows, IL 60008
1989. **Toll-free/Additional Phone Number(s):** 800-323-8552.

★808★
Teller World
Bank Administration Insitute
60 Gould Center
Rolling Meadows, IL 60008
Third edition, 1989. **Toll-free/Additional Phone Number(s):** 800-323-8552.

Periodicals

★809★
ABA Bankers Weekly
American Bankers Association (ABA)
1120 Connecticut Ave. NW
Washington, DC 20036   Phone: (202)663-5000
Newspaper covering national trends and developments in the banking industry, and federal regulatory action and congressional legislation related to banking.

★810★
ABA Banking Journal
Simmons-Boardman Publishing Corp.
345 Hudson St.
New York, NY 10014   Phone: (212)620-7200
William Streeter, Editor. Monthly. Official magazine of the American Bankers Association. **Facsimile Number:** (212)633-1165.

★811★
The Advisor
American Bankers Association (ABA)
1120 Connecticut Ave. NW
Washington, DC 20036   Phone: (202)663-5000
Monthly.

★812★
Bank Auditing and Accounting Report
Warren, Gorham & Lamont, Inc.
One Penn Plaza
New York, NY 10119   Phone: (212)971-5201
Editor(s): Stephen Collins. Monthly. Provides information on developments, practices, and techniques in bank accounting, auditing, and financial controls. Covers such topics as procedures for preventing embezzlement, improving management information systems, audit planning and supervision, and electronic data processing developments.

★813★
Bank Director's Report
Warren, Gorham & Lamont, Inc.
One Penn Plaza
New York, NY 10119   Phone: (212)971-5000
Editor(s): Margaret Murray. Monthly. Provides information on economics, regulations, law, and competition in the banking industry. Reports on current developments that affect banks, such as interstate banking, competition with nonfinancial institutions, purchasing new banks, and director's liability insurance. Covers the activities of federal financial institutions. Recurring features include news of research and a column titled Bank Director's Legal Report.

★814★
Bank Insurance & Protection Bulletin
American Bankers Association (ABA)
1120 Connecticut Ave. NW
Washington, DC 20036   Phone: (202)663-5305
Editor(s): C. Howie Hodges, II. Monthly. Monitors the latest trends in risk management, insurance, and security for banks. Reports on current bank crime statistics, methods of deterrence, and other "state of the art information.". Recurring features include news of research, notices of publications available, a calendar of events, meeting reports, and news of educational opportunities.

★815★
Bank Operations Report
Warren, Gorham & Lamont, Inc.
One Penn Plaza
New York, NY 10119   Phone: (212)971-5000
Editor(s): Pat Durner. Monthly. Focuses on electronic data processing control, check processing, record keeping, cost control, Federal regulation, credit and debit cards, electronic funds transfer system, physical security, and office automation, computer, and systems applications.

★816★
Bank Security Report
Warren, Gorham & Lamont, Inc.
One Penn Plaza
New York, NY 10119   Phone: (212)971-5000
Editor(s): Pat Durner. Monthly. Compiles news, information, case histories, suggestions, and advice on bank security equipment and procedures, forgeries, check alterations, identifications, kiting, counterfeiting, internal controls, and new federal announcements on bank security.

★817★
Bank Teller's Report
Warren, Gorham & Lamont, Inc.
One Penn Plaza
New York, NY 10119   Phone: (212)971-5000
Editor(s): Joan German. Monthly. Designed to help bank tellers (and also their supervisors) "sharpen their job skills with tips on endorsements, forgeries, kiters, automation, settling, finding errors in computations and various time- and work-savers." Contains articles and briefs that address tellers' concerns and provides them with news, information, and guidance on bank services and customer service. Recurring features include columns titled One of Those Days (where tellers share frustrating or surprising incidents), Tips From Tellers, and Extraordinary Service (in which tellers share instances of service "beyond the call of duty").
Toll-free/Additional Phone Number(s): 800-950-1217.

★818★
The Bankers Magazine
Warren, Gorham and Lamont, Inc.
1 Penn Plaza, 42nd Fl.
New York, NY 10119   Phone: (212)971-5227
Pat Durner and Natalie Baumer, Editors. 6x/yr. Magazine on banking.

★819★
Banking Expansion Reporter
Law and Business, Inc.
Prentice-Hall, Inc.
910 Sylvan Ave.
Englewood Cliffs, NJ 07632   Phone: (201)894-8538
Semimonthly. Discusses new strategies, techniques, and developments in the financial services industry. **Facsimile Number:** (201)894-8666.

★820★
Commercial Lender Newsletter
American Bankers Association (ABA)
1120 Connecticut Ave. NW
Washington, DC 20036   Phone: (202)663-5000
Monthly.

★821★
Consumer Banking Digest
American Bankers Association (ABA)
1120 Connecticut Ave. NW
Washington, DC 20036   Phone: (202)663-5000
Monthly.

★822★
IFE Insider
Institute of Financial Education (IFE)
111 E. Wacker Dr.
Chicago, IL 60601-4680   Phone: (312)644-3100
Monthly. Membership activities newsletter.

★823★
Institute of Financial Education—On Track
Institute of Financial Education (IFE)
111 E. Wacker Dr.
Chicago, IL 60601-4680   Phone: (312)644-3100
Bimonthly. 8/year. Information for financial institution professionals.

★824★
Insurance and Protection Bulletin
American Bankers Association (ABA)
1120 Connecticut Ave. NW
Washington, DC 20036   Phone: (202)663-5000
Monthly.

★825★
ISO Register
American Bankers Association (ABA)
1120 Connecticut Ave. NW
Washington, DC 20036   Phone: (202)663-5000
Quarterly.

★826★
Journal of Personal Financial Services
American Bankers Association (ABA)
1120 Connecticut Ave. NW
Washington, DC 20036   Phone: (202)663-5000
Quarterly.

★827★
Key to Safe Deposit
The American Safe Deposit Association
330 W. Main St.
Greenwood, IN 46142   Phone: (317)888-1118
Editor(s): Joyce McLin. Quarterly. Provides information for the vault area of financial institutions; member state and local associations of banks; trust companies; and other firms engaged in the safe deposit business. Contains suggestions on customer relations and safe deposit operations, as well as notices of relevant workshops and seminars.

★828★
Thruput: The ABA Operations/Automation News Report (ABA)
American Bankers Association (ABA)
1120 Connecticut Ave. NW
Washington, DC 20036   Phone: (202)663-5000
Monthly. Newsletter offering current information on technical advances, legislative and regulatory developments, and the activities of the Federal Communications Commission, U.S. Postal Service, and other federal agencies that affect the operation, data processing, and automation of banks. Includes annual index, calendar of events, and statistics.

★829★
Trust Letter
American Bankers Association (ABA)
1120 Connecticut Ave. NW
Washington, DC 20036   Phone: (202)663-5000
Monthly.

★830★
Trust Management Update: A Trust Industry Communication on Management, Investments, Marketing, Operations, and Administration
American Bankers Association (ABA)
1120 Connecticut Ave. NW
Washington, DC 20036   Phone: (202)663-5000
Monthly. Newsletter including calendar of events and new products and services.

Clerical Supervisors and Managers

Clerical supervisors and managers oversee the general operation of an organization's clerical department. They coordinate the work of individual employees to ensure that projects are completed within their allotted time. They also act as liaisons between the clerical staff and other departments. This may involve clarifying instructions, resolving conflicts, monitoring work progress and quality, and keeping management informed. Clerical supervisors and managers generally interview prospective clerical workers and train new employees. Although clerical workers are found in most industries, the largest number of clerical supervisors and managers are found in government agencies, wholesale trade outlets, banks, business service firms, colleges and universities, hospitals, and telephone companies.

$alaries

Salaries for clerical supervisors and managers are listed below.

Lowest 10 percent	Less than $14,000/year
Middle 50 percent	$17,700-$31,800
Top 10 percent	More than $42,700/year

Employment Outlook

Growth rate until the year 2000: Average.

Clerical Supervisors and Managers

Career Guides

★831★
"Clerical Supervisor and Manager" in *Careers in Banking and Finance* (pp. 33-34)
Rosen Publishing Group, Inc.
29 E. 21st St.
New York, NY 10010   Phone: (212)777-3017
Patricia Haddock. 1990. Describes more than 20 jobs at all levels in banking and finance. Contains information about the types of financial organizations where the jobs are found, educational requirements, job duties, and salaries. Offers advice on job hunting.

★832★
"Clerical Supervisors and Managers" in *Occupational Outlook Handbook* (pp. 250-251)
Superintendent of Documents
U.S. Government Printing Office
Washington, DC 20402   Phone: (202)783-3238
Biennial; latest edition, 1990-91. Encyclopedia of careers describing more than 250 occupations and comprising about 86 percent of all jobs in the economy. Occupations that require lengthy education or training are given the most attention. For each occupation, the handbook describes job duties, working conditions, training, educational preparation, personal qualities, advancement possibilities, job outlook, earnings, and sources of additional information.

★833★
"Clerical Supervisors and Managers" in Volume 3 of *The Encyclopedia of Careers and Vocational Guidance* (pp. 12-15)
J.G. Ferguson Publishing Co.
200 W. Monroe
Chicago, IL 60606   Phone: (312)580-5480
William E. Hopke, editor-in-chief. Eighth edition, 1990. Four-volume set that profiles 500 occupations and describes job trends in 76 industries. Includes career description, educational requirements, history of the job, methods of entry, advancement, employment outlook, earnings, working conditions, social and psychological factors, and sources of additional information.

★834★
"Clerical Supervisors and Managers" in Volume 2 of *Career Discovery Encyclopedia* (pp. 22-23)
J.G. Ferguson Publishing Co.
200 W. Monroe
Chicago, IL 60606   Phone: (312)580-5480
E. Russell Primm, editor-in-chief. 1990. Contains two-page articles on 504 occupations. Each article describes job duties, earnings, and educational and training requirements.

★835★
"Office Manager" in *Administration, Business, and Office*, Volume 1 of *Career Information Center* (pp. 90-91)
Glencoe/Macmillan
15319 Chatsworth St.
Mission Hills, CA 91345   Phone: (818)898-1391
Richard Lidz and Dale Anderson, editorial directors. Fourth edition, 1990. For 600 occupations, describes job duties, entry-level requirements, education and training needed, advancement possibilities, employment outlook, earnings and benefits. The set is divided into 12 volumes. Each volume includes jobs related under a broad career field. Volume 13 is the index. **Facsimile Number:** 818-365-5489.

★836★
"Office Manager" in *Career Opportunities in Art* (pp. 33-34)
Facts on File, Inc.
460 Park Avenue, S.
New York, NY 10016   Phone: (212)683-2244
Susan H. Haubenstock and David Joselit. 1988. Profiles more than 75 art-related jobs. Each occupational profile covers job duties, employment outlook, career paths, salaries, skills, and educational preparation. Offers tips for entering the field.

★837★
"Office Manager" in *Career Opportunities in Television, Cable, and Video* (pp. 168-169)
Facts on File, Inc.
460 Park Avenue, S.
New York, NY 10016   Phone: (212)683-2244
Third edition, 1990. Describes 100 media-related jobs. Each occupational profile covers job duties, employment outlook, career paths, salaries, skills, and educational preparation. Offers tips for entering the field.

★838★
"Office Manager" in *Occu-Facts: Information on 565 Careers in Outline Form* (p. 1.37)
Careers, Inc.
P.O. Box 135
1211 Tenth St., S.W.
Largo, FL 33640　　　　　　　　　Phone: (813)584-7333
Elizabeth Handville. Biennial, 1989-90 edition. Each one-page occupational profile describes duties, working conditions, physical surroundings and demands, aptitudes, temperament, educational requirements, employment outlook, earnings, and places of employment.

★839★
"Office Manager" in *VGM's Careers Encyclopedia* (pp. 312-315)
National Textbook Co.
4255 W. Touhy Ave.
Lincolnwood, IL 60646　　　　　　Phone: (312)679-5500
Third edition, 1991. Contains two- to five-page descriptions of 200 managerial, professional, technical, trade, and service occupations. Each profile includes job duties, places of employment, qualifications, educational preparation, training, employment potential, advancement, income, and additional sources of information.

★840★
"Office Manager" in *VGM's Handbook of Business and Management Careers* (pp. 67-69)
National Textbook Co.
4255 W. Touhy Ave.
Lincolnwood, IL 60646　　　　　　Phone: (312)679-5500
Craig T. Norback, editor. 1990. Contains 43 two-page occupational profiles describing job duties, places of employment, working conditions, qualifications, education, employment outlook, and income.

★841★
Professional Management for First-Line Supervisors
American Management Association
Nine Galen St.
Watertown, MA 02172　　　　　　Phone: (617)926-4600
Videocassette. 1987. ? mins. Management techniques are taught to lower-echelon managers.

★842★
Vocational Visions
Center for Humanities, Inc.
Communications Park
Box 1000
Mount Kisco, NY 10549　　　　　　Phone: (914)666-4100
Videocassette. 1984. 30 mins. This series of programs explains key aspects of actual training and a day in the life of a worker in the specific field mentioned on the videocassette. Occupations include: transportation/mechanics, repair, construction, business/office occupations, health, and agriculture.

───────── Associations ─────────

★843★
American Management Association (AMA)
135 W. 50th St.
New York, NY 10020　　　　　　　Phone: (212)586-8100
Membership: Managers in industry, commerce, and government; charitable and noncommercial organizations; university teachers of management; administrators. **Purpose:** Seeks to broaden members' management knowledge and skills. Awards annual Henry Laurence Gantt Medal, in conjunction with the American Society of Mechanical Engineers, for distinguished achievement in management as a service to the community. Maintains "Correspondent Association" agreements around the world. Operates management centers and offices in North America and, through AMA/International, in Europe and South America. Maintains extensive library, book store, and Management Information Service, which includes films, cassettes, tapes, and records covering all areas of management expertise. Conducts the Extension Institute, a private, self-paced study program and Operation Enterprise, a young adult program for high school/college level students. Other programs include AMA On-Site and Presidents Association. Offers courses, workshops, and briefings. Bestows awards. **Publications:** *Compensation and Benefits Review*, bimonthly. • *CompFlash*, monthly. • *Management Review*, monthly. • *Organizational Dynamics: A Quarterly Review of Organizational Behavior for Professional Managers*. • *Personnel*, monthly. • *The President*, monthly. • *Project Update*, periodic. • *Supervisory Management*, monthly. • *Supervisory Sense*, monthly. • *Trainer's Workshop*, bimonthly. • Also publishes books, management briefings, and survey reports; also produces films and videotapes. **Facsimile Number:** (212)903-8168.

★844★
Association of Management (AM)
PO Box 64841
Virginia Beach, VA 23464-0841　　Phone: (804)479-4473
Membership: Academics and practitioners. **Purpose:** Seeks to align theory and practice in the study of human resources management, information systems management, and organizational behavior. Encourages research in the fields. Maintains 20 divisions. **Publications:** *AM News*, annual. • *AM Proceedings*, annual. • *Journal of Information Technology Management*, annual. • *Journal of Management in Practice*, annual. • *Journal of Management Systems*, periodic.

★845★
Data Entry Management Association (DEMA)
101 Merritt 7, 5th Fl.
Norwalk, CT 06851　　　　　　　Phone: (203)846-3777
Membership: Data entry managers and others involved with the data entry profession. **Purpose:** Promotes the individual development and education of its members through exchange of ideas and discussion of problems and solutions. Conducts seminars and regional workshops and meetings. **Publications:** *Data Entry Management Association-Newsletter*, 10/year. **Facsimile Number:** (203)846-6883.

★846★
Data Processing Management Association (DPMA)
505 Busse Hwy.
Park Ridge, IL 60068　　　　　　Phone: (708)825-8124
Membership: Managerial personnel, staff, educators, and individuals interested in the management of information resources. **Purpose:** Founder of the Certificate in Data Processing examination program, now administered by an intersociety organization. Maintains Legislative Communications Network. Professional education programs include EDP-oriented business and management principles self-study courses and a series of videotaped management development seminars. Sponsors student organizations around the country interested in data processing and encourages members to serve as counselors for the Scout computer merit badge. Conducts research projects, including a business information systems curriculum for two- and four-year colleges. Conducts annual on-site seminar on technical and management subjects. Presents annual Distinguished Information Sciences Award for outstanding contribution to the profession. **Publications:** *Information Executive*, quarterly. • *Inside DAMA*, monthly. **Facsimile Number:** (708)825-1693.

Clerical Supervisors and Managers ★858★

Test Guides

★847★
Key Punch Supervisor
National Learning Corp.
212 Michael Dr.
Syosset, NY 11791   Phone: (516)921-8888
Jack Rudman. Part of the Career Examination Series No. 1. All examination guides in this series contain questions with answers. **Facsimile Number:** (516)921-8743. **Toll-free/Additional Phone Number(s):** 800-645-6337.

★848★
Word Processing Supervisor
National Learning Corp.
212 Michael Dr.
Syosset, NY 11791   Phone: (516)921-8888
Jack Rudman. Part of the Career Examination Series No. 1. All examination guides in this series contain questions with answers. **Facsimile Number:** (516)921-8743. **Toll-free/Additional Phone Number(s):** 800-645-6337.

Educational Directories and Programs

★849★
Clerical Supervisors and Managers
Accrediting Bureau of Health Education
Oak Manor Office
29089 U.S. 20 W.
Elkhart, IN 46514   Phone: (219)293-0124
1991. State-by-state listing of schools offering medical office management training programs. Lists address, phone number, and contact person.

★850★
Industry Directory
Association of Information Systems Professionals
104 Wilmot Rd., Ste. 201
Deerfield, IL 60015-5195   Phone: (708)940-8800
Bea McLean, editor. Irregular; previous edition 1986; new edition possible 1990. Manufacturers of office automation equipment; word processing service bureaus; educational institutions offering office automation and associated software courses or curriculums; personnel agencies serving office automation personnel and users; analysts and counsultants. Entries include: Name, address. Arrangement: Alphabetical within categories above. **Facsimile Number:** (708)940-7218.

Basic Reference Guides and Handbooks

★851★
NOMDA Who's Who
National Office Machine Dealers Association (NOMDA)
12411 Wornall Rd.
Kansas City, MO 64145   Phone: (816)941-3100
Brent Hoskins, editor. Annual. List of 6,000 retailers and 500 manufacturers of typewriters, calculators, word processors, computers, dictation equipment, copying machines, and other office machines. Entries include: Company name, address, phone, names of executives; dealer listings include codes showing products handled. Arrangement: Dealers and manufacturers are geographical and alphabetical. Indexes: Personal name, product. **Facsimile Number:** (816)941-2829.

★852★
Thomas Register's Office Automation Buyer's Guide
Thomas Publishing Company
1 Penn Plaza
New York, NY 10119   Phone: (212)290-7379
Douglas E. Lee, editor. Annual. About 6,000 suppliers of computer and office automation products. Entries include: Company name, address, phone, telex, toll-free phone, fax, names and titles of key personnel, number of employees, financial data, subsidiary and parent company data, description of products. Arrangement: Alphabetical. Indexes: Product/service, trade name.

Periodicals

★853★
Administrative Management
Automated Office Ltd.
1123 Broadway
New York, NY 10010   Phone: (212)924-8989
Don S. Johnson, Editor. Monthly. Managerial magazine containing information on office methods, personnel and business equipment.

★854★
AM News
Association of Management (AM)
PO Box 64841
Virginia Beach, VA 23464-0841   Phone: (804)479-4473
Annual.

★855★
AM Proceedings
Association of Management (AM)
PO Box 64841
Virginia Beach, VA 23464-0841   Phone: (804)479-4473
Annual.

★856★
AMA Project Update
American Management Association (AMA)
135 W. 50th St.
New York, NY 10020   Phone: (212)586-8100
Periodic.

★857★
Compensation and Benefits Review
American Management Association (AMA)
135 W. 50th St.
New York, NY 10020   Phone: (212)586-8100
Bimonthly. Journal including annual index, book reviews, digest service of annotations and selected readings from publications, information on current trends, and calendar of events.

★858★
CompFlash
American Management Association (AMA)
135 W. 50th St.
New York, NY 10020   Phone: (212)586-8100
Monthly. Newsletter featuring new developments in the field, salary and wage surveys, government regulations, pension and benefits news, and available publications.

★859★
DPMA Information Executive
Data Processing Management Association (DPMA)
505 Busse Hwy.
Park Ridge, IL 60068   Phone: (708)825-8124
Quarterly.

★860★
From Nine to Five
Dartnell Corp.
4660 Ravenswood
Chicago, IL 60640   Phone: (312)561-4000
Editor(s): Douglas Leland. Biweekly. Provides "tips, shortcuts, and helpful information for success in the office," particularly secretaries and office workers. Recurring features include columns titled Business Skills Clinic and The Coffee Break. **Toll-free/Additional Phone Number(s):** 800-621-5463. **Facsimile Number:** (312)561-3801.

★861★
Inside DPMA
Data Processing Management Association (DPMA)
505 Busse Hwy.
Park Ridge, IL 60068   Phone: (708)825-8124
Monthly.

★862★
Journal of Information Technology Management
Association of Management (AM)
PO Box 64841
Virginia Beach, VA 23464-0841   Phone: (804)479-4473
Annual. Includes academic research and scholarly articles.

★863★
Journal of Management in Practice
Association of Management (AM)
PO Box 64841
Virginia Beach, VA 23464-0841   Phone: (804)479-4473
Annual. Includes management practice and research briefs, essays, and book reviews.

★864★
Journal of Management Systems
Association of Management (AM)
PO Box 64841
Virginia Beach, VA 23464-0841   Phone: (804)479-4473
Periodic. Includes book and software reviews.

★865★
Management Review
American Management Association (AMA)
135 W. 50th St.
New York, NY 10020   Phone: (212)586-8100
Monthly. Magazine providing information on management trends and techniques. Includes book reviews and case studies.

★866★
Organizational Dynamics: A Quarterly Review of Organizational Behavior for Professional Managers (AMA)
American Management Association (AMA)
135 W. 50th St.
New York, NY 10020   Phone: (212)586-8100
Includes annual index.

★867★
Personnel
American Management Association (AMA)
135 W. 50th St.
New York, NY 10020   Phone: (212)586-8100
Monthly. Magazine for human resources professionals. Includes annual index, editorials, book reviews, and career development calendar.

★868★
The President
American Management Association (AMA)
135 W. 50th St.
New York, NY 10020   Phone: (212)586-8100
Monthly. Newsletter including calendar of events.

★869★
Supervision
National Research Bureau, Inc.
424 N. 3rd St.
Burlington, IA 52601-5224   Phone: (319)752-5415
Barbara Boeding, Editor. Monthly. Magazine for first-line foremen, supervisors, and office managers. **Facsimile Number:** (319)752-3421.

★870★
Supervisory Management
American Management Assn.
135 W. 50th St.
New York, NY 10020   Phone: (212)586-8100
Florence Stone, Editor. Monthly. Newsletter covering management and supervisory topics, including performance appraisals, motivation, and discipline. **Facsimile Number:** (212)903-8168.

★871★
Supervisory Sense
American Management Association (AMA)
135 W. 50th St.
New York, NY 10020   Phone: (212)586-8100
Monthly. Training publication for first- and second-line managers; one subject per issue. Includes case studies.

★872★
Trainer's Workshop
American Management Association (AMA)
135 W. 50th St.
New York, NY 10020   Phone: (212)586-8100
Bimonthly. Magazine for training professionals and managers responsible for training. Contains generic training course including workshop materials.

Meetings and Conventions

★873★
American Management Association Pack Expo (AMA)
135 W. 50th St.
New York, NY 10020   Phone: (212)586-8100
Frequency: Biennial, always held in Chicago, IL. 1992; Nov. 9-13 • 1994; Nov. 14-18 • 1996; Nov. 11-15 • 1998; Nov. 16-20. **Facsimile Number:** (212)903-8168.

Computer and Peripheral Equipment Operators

Computer and peripheral equipment operators oversee the operation of computer hardware systems. Their duties vary depending on the size and type of equipment installed. In organizations with smaller systems, computer and peripheral equipment operators run the computer and all the peripheral equipment such as printers, disk drives, and tape readers. In larger organizations, the computer operator may specialize in console operation, while the peripheral equipment operator runs the related devices. The operators run the equipment, or set the controls, to do a particular job as specified by instructions from a programmer or operations manager. Operators also maintain log books of all computer operations, and resolve problems if error messages occur. Computer and peripheral equipment operators are found in many industries including wholesale trade establishments, manufacturing companies, data processing firms, banks, government agencies, and accounting, auditing, and bookkeeping firms.

$alaries

Salaries for computer and peripheral equipment operators are listed below.

Lowest 10 percent	Less than $10,600/year
Middle 50 percent	$13,500-$23,900/year
Top 10 percent	More than $30,500/year

Employment Outlook

Growth rate until the year 2000: Faster than average.

Computer and Peripheral Equipment Operators

Career Guides

★874★
Career Choices: Computer Science
Walker & Company
720 5th Ave.
New York, NY 10019   Phone: (212)265-3632
1985. **Facsimile Number:** (212)307-1764.

★875★
Careers in Computer Field
Rosen Publishing Group, Inc.
29 E. 21st St.
New York, NY 10010   Phone: (212)777-3017
Joseph Weintraub. 1988. **Toll-free/Additional Phone Number(s):** 800-237-9932. **Facsimile Number:** (212)777-0277.

★876★
Careers in Computers & Data Processing
Petrocelli Books, Inc.
174 Brookstone Dr.
Princeton, NJ 08540-2404   Phone: (609)924-5851
Herman McDaniel. 1978.

★877★
"Careers in Operations and the Information Center" in *Careers in Computers* (pp. 34-41)
National Textbook Co.
4255 W. Touhy Ave.
Lincolnwood, IL 60646   Phone: (312)679-5500
Lila B. Stair. 1991. Describes trends affecting computer careers and explores a wide range of job opportunities from programming to consulting. Provides job qualifications, salary data, job market information, personal and educational requirements, career paths, and the place of the job in the organizational structure. Offers advice on education, certification, and job search.

★878★
The Complete Computer Career Guide
T A B Books
Blue Ridge Summit, PA 17294-0850   Phone: (717)794-2191
Judith Norback. 1987.

★879★
"Computer and Peripheral Equipment Operators" in *America's 50 Fastest Growing Jobs* (pp. 108-109)
JIST Works, Inc.
720 N. Park Ave.
Indianapolis, IN 46202   Phone: (317)264-3720
Michael J. Farr, compiler. 1991. Describes the 50 fastest growing jobs within major career clusters such as technicians, and marketing and sales. Each job profile explains the nature of the work, skills and abilities required, employment outlook, average earnings, related occupations, education and training requirements, and employment opportunities. Also contains career planning information and job search tips.

★880★
"Computer and Peripheral Equipment Operators" in *Occupational Outlook Handbook* (pp. 251-252)
Superintendent of Documents
U.S. Government Printing Office
Washington, DC 20402   Phone: (202)783-3238
Biennial; latest edition, 1990-91. Encyclopedia of careers describing more than 250 occupations and comprising about 86 percent of all jobs in the economy. Occupations that require lengthy education or training are given the most attention. For each occupation, the handbook describes job duties, working conditions, training, educational preparation, personal qualities, advancement possibilities, job outlook, earnings, and sources of additional information.

★881★
"Computer and Peripheral Equipment Operators" in Volume 3 of *The Encyclopedia of Careers and Vocational Guidance* (pp. 19-23)
J.G. Ferguson Publishing Co.
200 W. Monroe
Chicago, IL 60606   Phone: (312)580-5480
William E. Hopke, editor-in-chief. Eighth edition, 1990. Four-volume set that profiles 500 occupations and describes job trends in 76 industries. Includes career description, educational requirements, history of the job, methods of entry, advancement, employment outlook, earnings, working conditions, social and psychological factors, and sources of additional information.

★882★
Computer Careers: The Complete Pocket Guide to America's Fastest-Growing Job Market
Sun Features, Inc.
PO Box 368-P
Cardiff, CA 92007   Phone: (619)753-3489
Joyce L. Kennedy. 1983.

★883★
Computer/Keypunch Operator
Vocational Biographies, Inc.
PO Box 31, Dept. VF10
Sauk Centre, MN 56378   Phone: (612)352-6516

1988. This pamphlet profiles a person working in the job. Includes information about job duties, working conditions, places of employment, educational preparation, labor market outlook, and salaries. **Toll-free/Additional Phone Number(s):** 800-255-0752.

★884★
Computer Numerical Control Machine Operators
Chronicle Guidance Publications, Inc.
PO Box 1190
Moravia, NY 13118-1190   Phone: (315)497-0330

1991. This career brief describes the nature of the work, working conditions, hours and earnings, education and training, licensure, certification, unions, personal qualifications, social and psychological factors, employment outlook, entry methods, advancement, and related occupations. **Toll-free/Additional Phone Number(s):** 800-622-7284.

★885★
"Computer Operating" in *Exploring High Tech Careers* (pp. 56-59)
Rosen Publishing Group, Inc.
29 E. 21st St.
New York, NY 10010   Phone: (212)777-3017

Scott Southworth. Revised edition, 1988. Provides an orientation to the whole area of high tech and surveys jobs such as computer programming, drafting, and technical illustration. Covers educational preparation, advantages and disadvantages, advancement opportunities, and personal characteristics needed. Offers job hunting advice.

★886★
"Computer Operating Personnel" in *The American Almanac of Jobs and Salaries* (pp. 507-509)
Avon Books
105 Madison Avenue
New York, NY 10016   Phone: (212)481-5600

John Wright and Edward J. Dwyer. Revised and updated, 1990. A comprehensive guide to the wages of hundreds of occupations in a wide variety of industries and organizations.

★887★
"Computer Operations" in *Careers in High Tech* (pp. 34-36)
Arco/Prentice Hall Press
1 Gulf & Western Plaza
New York, NY 10023   Phone: (212)373-8500

Connie Winkler. 1987. Surveys career opportunities in data processing, technology, personal computers, telecommunications, manufacturing technology, artificial intelligence, computer graphics, biotechnology, lasers, technical writing, and publishing. Includes information on educational preparation, associations, and periodicals.

★888★
"Computer Operations" in *Opportunities in Information Systems Careers* (p. 25)
National Textbook Co.
4255 W. Touhy Ave.
Lincolnwood, IL 60646   Phone: (312)679-5500

Douglas B. Hoyt. 1991. Provides an overview of information systems with organizational charts and job descriptions. Covers personal characteristics, educational preparation, career paths, places of employment, salaries, and labor market outlook. Offers advice about job hunting and advancement.

★889★
"Computer Operator" in *Administration, Business, and Office*, Volume 1 of *Career Information Center* (pp. 76-77)
Glencoe/Macmillan
15319 Chatsworth St.
Mission Hills, CA 91345   Phone: (818)898-1391

Richard Lidz and Dale Anderson, editorial directors. Fourth edition, 1990. For 600 occupations, describes job duties, entry-level requirements, education and training needed, advancement possibilities, employment outlook, earnings and benefits. The set is divided into 12 volumes. Each volume includes jobs related under a broad career field. Volume 13 is the index. **Facsimile Number:** 818-365-5489.

★890★
"Computer Operator" in *Careers in Banking and Finance* (pp. 39-41)
Rosen Publishing Group, Inc.
29 E. 21st St.
New York, NY 10010   Phone: (212)777-3017

Patricia Haddock. 1990. Describes more than 20 jobs at all levels in banking and finance. Contains information about the types of financial organizations where the jobs are found, educational requirements, job duties, and salaries. Offers advice on job hunting.

★891★
"Computer Operator" in *Exploring Careers in the Computer Field* (pp. 22-23)
Rosen Publishing Group, Inc.
29 E. 21st St.
New York, NY 10010   Phone: (212)777-3017

Joseph Weintraub. 1990. Surveys the newest growth areas in the computer industry including artificial intelligence, desktop publishing, and personal computers. Discusses entry into the field, salaries, future trends and offers job search advice. Contains interviews with five people who describe their real-life experiences working in computer related jobs. Lists organizations and colleges.

★892★
"Computer Operator" in *Guide to Careers Without College* (pp. 51-53)
Franklin Watts, Inc.
387 Park Avenue, S.
New York, NY 10016   Phone: (212)686-7070

Kathleen S. Abrams. 1988. Discusses careers that do not require a college degree in fields such as health care, sales and marketing, and the building trades. Describes the work, employment opportunities, and training.

★893★
"Computer Operator" in *Opportunities in Data Processing Careers* (pp. 49-51)
National Textbook Co.
4255 W. Touhy Ave.
Lincolnwood, IL 60646   Phone: (312)679-5500

Norman N. Noerper. 1989. Provides an overview of the history and development of data processing careers. For each job included, describes responsibilities, salary, and job outlook. Contains separate chapters on educational preparation and job hunting. Lists professional organizations, publications, and schools.

Computer and Peripheral Equipment Operators ★906★

★894★
Computer Operators
Chronicle Guidance Publications, Inc.
PO Box 1190
Moravia, NY 13118-1190　　　　　Phone: (315)497-0330
1988. This career brief describes the nature of the work, working conditions, hours and earnings, education and training, licensure, certification, unions, personal qualifications, social and psychological factors, employment outlook, entry methods, advancement, and related occupations. **Toll-free/Additional Phone Number(s):** 800-622-7284.

★895★
"Computer Operators" in *Jobs! What They Are. . .Where They Are. . .What They Pay* (pp. 64-65)
Simon & Schuster, Inc.
Simon & Schuster Bldg.
1230 Avenue of the Americas
New York, NY 10020　　　　　Phone: (212)698-7000
Robert O. Snelling and Anne M. Snelling. Revised edition, 1989. Profiles 241 occupations, describing duties and responsibilities, educational preparation, earnings, employment opportunities, training, and qualifications.

★896★
"Computer Operators" in *Opportunities in Vocational and Technical Careers* (p. 48)
National Textbook Co.
4255 W. Touhy Ave.
Lincolnwood, IL 60646　　　　　Phone: (312)679-5500
Adrian A. Paradis. 1987. Describes careers which can be prepared for by attending a private vocational or proprietary school—office employee, sales worker, service worker, health services, mechanic, craftworker, and technician. Covers employment outlook, job duties, and salaries. Offers career planning advice.

★897★
"Computer Operators" in *The Complete Computer Career Guide* (pp. 22-26)
Tab Books, Inc.
Blue Ridge Summit, PA 17294-0850　　　　　Phone: (717)794-2191
Judith Norback. 1987. Offers career planning tips and describes the educational preparation needed, employment outlook, industry trends, and certification. Offers job search advice. A separate section includes opportunities for women and minorities.

★898★
"Computer Operators" in Volume 2 of *Career Discovery Encyclopedia* (pp. 44-45)
J G Ferguson Publishing Co.
200 W. Monroe
Chicago, IL 60606　　　　　Phone: (312)580-5480
E. Russell Primm, editor-in-chief. 1990. Contains two-page articles on 504 occupations. Each article describes job duties, earnings, and educational and training requirements.

★899★
"Computer Operators: Keepers of the Machines" in *Careers for Women Without College Degrees* (pp. 189-192)
McGraw-Hill Publishing Co.
11 W. 19th St.
New York, NY 10011　　　　　Phone: (212)337-6010
Beatryce Nivens. 1988. Career planning and job hunting guide containing information on decision-making, skills assessment, and resumes for career changers. Profiles careers with the best occupational outlook. Describes the work, educational preparation, employment outlook, salaries, and required skills.

★900★
Computers - How to Break into the Field
T A B Books
Blue Ridge Summit, PA 17294-0850　　　　　Phone: (717)794-2191
Peter L. Carron, Jr. Second edition. 1983.

★901★
Computing, Operating Personnel, Electronic
Careers, Inc.
PO Box 135
Largo, FL 34649-0135　　　　　Phone: (813)584-7333
1989. Eight-page brief offering the definition, history, duties, working conditions, personal qualifications, educational requirements, earnings, hours, employment outlook, advancement possibilities, and related occupations.

★902★
"Computing or Information Center Operations" in *Opportunities in Computer Science Careers* (pp. 32-33)
National Textbook Co.
4255 W. Touhy Ave.
Lincolnwood, IL 60646　　　　　Phone: (312)679-5500
1991. Surveys careers in the computer field including programming, software development, hardware, research, and technical writing. Profiles five people working in the field. Separate chapters discuss educational preparation and employment outlook. An appendix contains salary information.

★903★
"Electronic Computer Operating Personnel" in *Occu-Facts: Information on 565 Careers in Outline Form* (p. 12.1)
Careers, Inc.
P.O. Box 135
1211 Tenth St., S.W.
Largo, FL 33640　　　　　Phone: (813)584-7333
Elizabeth Handville. Biennial, 1989-90 edition. Each one-page occupational profile describes duties, working conditions, physical surroundings and demands, aptitudes, temperament, educational requirements, employment outlook, earnings, and places of employment.

★904★
Exploring Computer Careers at Home
Rosen Publishing Group, Inc.
29 E. 21st St.
New York, NY 10010　　　　　Phone: (212)777-3017
Scott Southworth. 1986. Part of Careers Series. **Toll-free/Additional Phone Number(s):** 800-237-9932. **Facsimile Number:** (212)777-0277.

★905★
Getting a Job in the Computer Age
Peterson's Guides, Inc.
202 Carnegie Center
PO Box 2123
Princeton, NJ 08543-2123　　　　　Phone: (609)243-9111
1986. **Facsimile Number:** (609)243-9150.

★906★
A Guide to Computer Careers
Free Press
866 3rd Ave.
New York, NY 10022　　　　　Phone: (212)702-3130
Donald D. Spencer. 1985. **Facsimile Number:** (212)605-9364.

VOCATIONAL CAREERS SOURCEBOOK, 1st Edition

★907★
A Guide to Computer Careers
Camelot Publishing Co.
PO Box 1357
Ormond Beach, FL 32175   Phone: (904)672-5672
Donald D. Spencer. 1984.

★908★
Opportunities in Computer Science
National Textbook Co.
4255 W. Touhy Ave.
Lincolnwood, IL 60646-1975   Phone: (708)679-5500
Julie L. Kling. 1987. **Facsimile Number:** (708)679-2494.

★909★
"Peripheral Equipment Operators" in *Careers in High Tech* (pp. 32-34)
Arco/Prentice Hall Press
1 Gulf & Western Plaza
New York, NY 10023   Phone: (212)373-8500
Connie Winkler. 1987. Surveys career opportunities in data processing, technology, personal computers, telecommunications, manufacturing technology, artificial intelligence, computer graphics, biotechnology, lasers, technical writing, and publishing. Includes information on educational preparation, associations, and periodicals.

★910★
Resumes for Computer Personnel
Barron's Educational Series, Inc.
250 Wireless Blvd.
Hauppauge, NY 11788   Phone: (516)434-3311
Adele B. Lewis. 1984.

★911★
Video Career Library - Technical Occupations
Careers, Inc.
1211 10th St., SW
PO Box 135
Largo, FL 34649-0135   Phone: (813)584-7333
Videocassette. 1990. Part of the Video Career Library covering 165 occupations. Shows actual workers on the job. Includes computer and peripheral equipment operators.

★912★
You Don't Have to Be a Computer Genius to Land a Computer Job: How to Find a Career in the World's Fastest Growing Field
Macmillan Publishing Co.
866 3rd Ave.
New York, NY 10022   Phone: (212)702-2000
Jack L. Stone. 1984.

──────── Associations ────────

★913★
Association for Computer Operations Management (AFCOM)
742 E. Chapman Ave.
Orange, CA 92666   Phone: (714)997-7966
Membership: Managers of corporate and institutional computer centers. **Purpose:** Serves as a forum for exchange of ideas and information among members. Promotes continuing professional development of members; seeks to improve members' status and recognition in the computer field. Supports improvements in computer technology; encourages research in the field. Conducts management and technical symposia. **Publications:** *The Communique*, bimonthly. • *The Computer Operations Manager*, bimonthly. • Also publishes *Annual Survey of Data Processing Operations Salaries* and prepares articles for publication in general computer publications. **Facsimile Number:** (714)997-9743; hotline.

──────── Test Guides ────────

★914★
Advanced Placement Examination in Computer Science
Prentice Hall
Rte. 9W
Englewood Cliffs, NJ 07632   Phone: (201)592-2000
Elayne Schulman. Second edition, 1988.

★915★
Chief Data Processing Equipment Operator
National Learning Corp.
212 Michael Dr.
Syosset, NY 11791   Phone: (516)921-8888
Jack Rudman. Part of the Career Examination Series No. 1. All examination guides in this series contain questions with answers. **Facsimile Number:** (516)921-8743. **Toll-free/Additional Phone Number(s):** 800-645-6337.

★916★
Computer Operator
National Learning Corp.
212 Michael Dr.
Syosset, NY 11791   Phone: (516)921-8888
Jack Rudman. Part of the Career Examination Series No. 1.; series also includes a study guide for computer operator trainee. All examination guides in this series contain questions with answers. **Facsimile Number:** (516)921-8743. **Toll-free/Additional Phone Number(s):** 800-645-6337.

★917★
Computer Work & Computer Trainee Exams
Ken-Books
56 Midcrest Way
San Francisco, CA 94131   Phone: (415)826-6550
Harry W. Koch. Second edition, 1987.

★918★
Multi-Keyboard Operator
National Learning Corp.
212 Michael Dr.
Syosset, NY 11791   Phone: (516)921-8888
Jack Rudman. Part of the Career Examination Series No. 1. All examination guides in this series contain questions with answers. **Facsimile Number:** (516)921-8743. **Toll-free/Additional Phone Number(s):** 800-645-6337.

★919★
Principal Data Entry Machine Operator
National Learning Corp.
212 Michael Dr.
Syosset, NY 11791   Phone: (516)921-8888
Jack Rudman. Part of the Career Examination Series No. 1. All examination guides in this series contain questions with answers. **Facsimile Number:** (516)921-8743. **Toll-free/Additional Phone Number(s):** 800-645-6337.

Computer and Peripheral Equipment Operators ★930★

★920★
Senior Business Machine Operator
National Learning Corp.
212 Michael Dr.
Syosset, NY 11791　　　　　　　　Phone: (516)921-8888
Jack Rudman. Part of the Career Examination Series No. 1. All examination guides in this series contain questions with answers. **Facsimile Number:** (516)921-8743. **Toll-free/Additional Phone Number(s):** 800-645-6337.

★921★
Senior Data Processing Control Clerk
National Learning Corp.
212 Michael Dr.
Syosset, NY 11791　　　　　　　　Phone: (516)921-8888
Jack Rudman. Part of the Career Examination Series No. 1. All examination guides in this series contain questions with answers. **Facsimile Number:** (516)921-8743. **Toll-free/Additional Phone Number(s):** 800-645-6337.

★922★
Senior Data Processing Equipment Operator
National Learning Corp.
212 Michael Dr.
Syosset, NY 11791　　　　　　　　Phone: (516)921-8888
Jack Rudman. Part of the Career Examination Series No. 1. All examination guides in this series contain questions with answers. **Facsimile Number:** (516)921-8743. **Toll-free/Additional Phone Number(s):** 800-645-6337.

Basic Reference Guides and Handbooks

★923★
Thomas Register's Office Automation Buyer's Guide
Thomas Publishing Company
1 Penn Plaza
New York, NY 10119　　　　　　　Phone: (212)290-7379
Douglas E. Lee, editor. Annual. About 6,000 suppliers of computer and office automation products. Entries include: Company name, address, phone, telex, toll-free phone, fax, names and titles of key personnel, number of employees, financial data, subsidiary and parent company data, description of products. Arrangement: Alphabetical. Indexes: Product/service, trade name.

Periodicals

★924★
ADAPSO Data
Association of Data Processing Service Organizations, Inc. (ADAPSO)
1300 N. 17th St., Ste. 300
Arlington, VA 22209　　　　　　　Phone: (703)522-5055
Editor(s): Jami Wann amd Cathy Weisbart. Bimonthly. Provides updates on government actions, legal precedents, mergers and acquisitions, and international business developments affecting the computer services and software industry. Recurring features include news of research and news of members.

★925★
Andrew Seybold's Outlook on Professional Computing
Andrew Seybold's Computer Insiders, Inc. (ASCI)
3235 Kifer Rd., Ste. 350
Santa Clara, CA 95051　　　　　　Phone: (408)746-2555
Monthly. Offers news, views, analysis, and informed perspective on issues in the computing industry. Recurring features include new product reviews, interview, a calendar of events, and news of research. **Toll-free/Additional Phone Number(s):** 800-678-0486. **Facsimile Number:** (408)746-2448.

★926★
Apple Library Users Group Newsletter
Apple Computer, Inc.
10381 Bandley Dr.
Cupertino, CA 95014　　　　　　　Phone: (408)974-2552
Editor(s): Monica Ertel. Quarterly. Serves as an exchange for information concerning the use of Apple and Macintosh computers in libraries and information centers of all sizes. Recurring features include news of research, book reviews, news from members, answers to readers' questions, a calendar of events, and columns titled News From/About Apple, Software Reviews, and Information From Our Vendors. **Facsimile Number:** (408)725-8502.

★927★
Ashton-Tate—Update
Ashton-Tate
20101 Hamilton
Torrance, CA 90502-1319　　　　　Phone: (213)204-5570
Editor(s): Randy Rodman. 3/yr. Discusses Ashton-Tate's microcomputer software products,, product capabilities, and how customer needs are addressed by those capabilities. Contains tips and techniques on utilizing software products and articles on competitors.

★928★
The Communique
Association for Computer Operations Management (AFCOM)
742 E. Chapman Ave.
Orange, CA 92666　　　　　　　　Phone: (714)997-7966
Bimonthly. Newsletter containing news items, product announcements, information requests from members, and classified ads.

★929★
Computer Business
Round Table Associates
PO Box 45923
Los Angeles, CA 90045-0923　　　　Phone: (213)649-2846
Editor(s): Abe H. Hassan. Monthly. Provides citations and abstracts of articles on computers and communications appearing in business and technical publications. Reports significant market data, including estimates of market share and industry forecasts. Lists abstracts according to subject in such areas as minicomputers, microcomputers, software, peripherals, data communications, legal and regulatory action, consumer electronics, and human factors.

★930★
Computer Craft
CQ Communications, Inc.
76 N. Broadway
Hicksville, NY 11803　　　　　　　Phone: (516)681-2922
Arthur Salsberg, Editor. Monthly. Magazine covering electronics and computers. **Facsimile Number:** (516)681-2926.

★931★
VOCATIONAL CAREERS SOURCEBOOK, 1st Edition

★931★
Computer Graphics World
PennWell Publishing Co.
1 Technology Park Dr.
PO Box 987
Westford, MA 01886   Phone: (508)692-0700

Philip Lopiccolo, Editor. Monthly. Magazine covering all aspects of computer graphics technology. **Facsimile Number:** (508)692-0525.

★932★
Computer Industry Report
International Data Corp. (IDC)
c/o IDG International News Group
41 West St.
Boston, MA 02111   Phone: (617)423-9030

Editor(s): Doug McLeod. 24/yr. Provides news of all aspects of the electronic data processing industry market. Offers proprietary statistics, forecasts, new product announcements, and relevant legal decisions. Recurring features include five review and forecast issues focusing on a computer market segment. **Facsimile Number:** (617)423-0712.

★933★
Computer Industry Update
IMR, Inc.
PO Box 681
Los Altos, CA 94022   Phone: (415)941-6679

Editor(s): George Weiser. Monthly. Summarizes vendor announcements and articles from the weekly computer trade press. Organizes summaries into six categories: mainframes, minicomputers, terminals, and workstations, peripherals, small business computers, and general.

★934★
The Computer Operations Manager
Association for Computer Operations Management (AFCOM)
742 E. Chapman Ave.
Orange, CA 92666   Phone: (714)997-7966

Bimonthly. Magazine containing feature articles and Washington updates.

★935★
Computer Report and PC Street Price Index
John Murphy
Paint Works Corporate Center
10 Foster Ave., Ste. E-1
Gibbsboro, NJ 08026   Phone: (609)784-8866

Editor(s): John Murphy. Monthly. Concentrates on the latest developments in computer technology and their effects on the corporate end-user. Covers software, personal computers, computer companies, and industry trends.

★936★
Computer Security Products Report
Assets Protection Publishing
PO Box 5323
Madison, WI 53705-0323   Phone: (608)271-6768

Paul Shaw, Editor and Publisher. Quarterly. Magazine featuring equipment for computer protection and security. **Facsimile Number:** (608)271-4520.

★937★
Data Entry Awareness Report
Management Information Corp.
PO Box 5062
Cherry Hill, NJ 08034   Phone: (609)428-1020

Editor(s): Pam Benham. Monthly. Evaluates a data entry system in each issue, including key to disc, intelligent terminals, optical character readers, portable data recorders, and voice data entry. Describes system hardware, software, and pricing, and analyzes the advantages and disadvantages of the system. **Toll-free/Additional Phone Number(s):** 800-678-4642. **Facsimile Number:** (609)428-1683.

★938★
DataWorld
Faulkner Technical Reports, Inc.
114 Cooper Center
7905 Browning Rd.
Pennsauken, NJ 08109-4374   Phone: (609)662-2070

Jan Wright, Mng. Editor. Monthly. Information service describing and evaluating mainframe, mini- and microcomputer hardware and software, as well as communications facilities and equipment. **Facsimile Number:** (609)662-6634.

★939★
Dental Computer Newsletter
Andent, Inc.
1000 North Ave.
Waukegan, IL 60085   Phone: (708)223-5077

Editor(s): Ellis J. Neiburger, D.D.S. Monthly. Emphasizes "practical use of all brands of computers for the professional office." Provides news of the computer industry as well as computer-use tips, information on computer gadgets and systems, and system recommendations. Recurring features include editorials, news of research, letters to the editor, news of members, book reviews, and columns titled Education, Hardware, Software, Specials, and Report on Hardware/Software.

★940★
EDP Weekly
Computer Age
Millin Publishing Group, Inc.
3918 Prosperity Ave.
Ste. 310
Fairfax, VA 22031-3300   Phone: (703)573-8400

Editor(s): Charles Bailey and Mike Cotter. Weekly. Reports news concerning all aspects of the computer industry. Covers standards, licensing agreements, patents issued, industry growth statistics, new technology, and pertinent legislation. Also includes semimonthly features on robotics, electronic funds transfer, mini and micro computers, data communications, and world trade.

———— **Meetings and Conventions** ————

★941★
Association for Computer Operations Management Automated Operations Symposium (AFCOM)
742 E. Chapman Ave.
Orange, CA 92666   Phone: (714)997-7966

Frequency: Annual, usually held in September. **Facsimile Number:** (714)997-9743.

———— **Other Sources of Information** ————

★942★
Annual Survey of Data Processing Operations Salaries (AFCOM)
Association for Computer Operations Management (AFCOM)
742 E. Chapman Ave.
Orange, CA 92666   Phone: (714)997-7966

★943★
Computer Service and Repair Directory
American Business Directories, Inc.
American Business Information, Inc.
5711 S. 86th Circle
Omaha, NE 68127 Phone: (402)593-4600

Annual. 10,207. Entries include: Name, address, phone (including area code), size of advertisement, year first in "Yellow Pages," name of owner or manager, number of employees. Arrangement: Geographical. **Facsimile Number:** (402)331-1505.

★944★
Computers and Computing Information Resources Directory
Gale Research Inc.
835 Penobscot Bldg.
Detroit, MI 48226-4094 Phone: (313)961-2242

Martin Connors and Janice DeMaggio, editor. First edition October 1986; interedition supplement service. Computer-related information sources, including 1,450 consultant and training organizations, 650 trade and professional associations or user groups, 1,000 special libraries and information centers, 900 university computer facilities and research centers; 600 for-profit research services, 240 online services and teleprocessing networks, 1,500 journals, newsletters, and abstracting and indexing services; over 400 trade shows, conventions, and exhibits; 200 publishers, 250 directories; international coverage. Entries include: Name, address, phone, and name of contact; other details (as appropriate), including publications, year founded, target audience, dates and location of exhibit, frequency, price, descriptions of product, service, or area of research. Arrangement: By type of organization or service. Indexes: Organization name/acronym/publication title/keyword, geographical, personal name. **Toll-free/Additional Phone Number(s):** (800)877-GALE. **Facsimile Number:** (313)961-6083.

★945★
Microelectronics & Office Jobs: The Impact of the Chip on Women's Employment
International Labor Office
1828 L St., NW, No. 801
Washington, DC 20036-5104

Diane Werneke. Third edition, 1985.

Credit Clerks and Authorizers

Credit clerks and authorizers review the credit histories of applicants and decide whether or not to approve credit. To obtain the appropriate information, credit clerks contact employers, references, banks, or credit bureaus to verify personal and financial information. Credit authorizers evaluate a customers' computerized credit records and payment histories and make credit decisions. Most charges are automatically approved by computer. The majority of credit clerks and authorizers work in banks or financial institutions, and wholesale and retail trade. Others work for businesses such as credit reporting and collection agencies and computer and data processing services.

$alaries

Salaries for credit clerks and authorizers are listed below.

Credit authorizers	$12,500/year
Beginning credit clerks	$13,000-15,000/year
Senior credit clerks	$20,000-25,000/year

Employment Outlook

Growth rate until the year 2000: Faster than average.

Credit Clerks and Authorizers

Career Guides

★946★
Career Success Series
Cambridge Career Products
90 MacCorkle Ave., SW
South Charleston, WV 25311   Phone: (304)744-9323
Videocassette. 1986. 15 mins. A series, available separately, outlining various career choices for students. Occupations include: flight service, air transportation/ground service, data processing, carpentry, clerk in banking/insurance, commodity sales, cosmetic personal grooming, fire fighting, forestry services, home economics, insulation/roofing, material handling, mechanics, photographic processing, pipefitting and plumbing, police science, printing, secretarial services, and utilities equipment operator.

★947★
"Credit Checker" in *Administration, Business, and Office*, Volume 1 of *Career Information Center* (pp. 49-51)
Glencoe/Macmillan
15319 Chatsworth St.
Mission Hills, CA 91345   Phone: (818)898-1391
Richard Lidz and Dale Anderson, editorial directors. Fourth edition, 1990. For 600 occupations, describes job duties, entry-level requirements, education and training needed, advancement possibilities, employment outlook, earnings and benefits. The set is divided into 12 volumes. Each volume includes jobs related under a broad career field. Volume 13 is the index. **Facsimile Number:** 818-365-5489.

★948★
"Credit Clerks and Authorizers" in *Occupational Outlook Handbook* (pp. 253-254)
Superintendent of Documents
U.S. Government Printing Office
Washington, DC 20402   Phone: (202)783-3238
Biennial; latest edition, 1990-91. Encyclopedia of careers describing more than 250 occupations and comprising about 86 percent of all jobs in the economy. Occupations that require lengthy education or training are given the most attention. For each occupation, the handbook describes job duties, working conditions, training, educational preparation, personal qualities, advancement possibilities, job outlook, earnings, and sources of additional information.

★949★
Credit Workers
Chronicle Guidance Publications, Inc.
PO Box 1190
Moravia, NY 13118-1190   Phone: (315)497-0330
1988. This career brief describes the nature of the work, working conditions, hours and earnings, education and training, licensure, certification, unions, personal qualifications, social and psychological factors, employment outlook, entry methods, advancement, and related occupations. **Toll-free/Additional Phone Number(s):** 800-622-7284.

★950★
Understanding the Lending Process
1st Financial Video Network
1701 East Woodfield Rd.
Suite 412
Schaumburg, IL 60173-5133   Phone: (708)605-0222
Videocassette. 1987. 19 mins. Basic terms and theories of the money lending process are made simple.

Associations

★951★
International Credit Association (ICA)
243 N. Lindbergh Blvd.
St. Louis, MO 63141   Phone: (314)991-3030
Membership: Credit executives. **Purpose:** Conducts educational seminars and conferences; offers group insurance plans. Through its Society of Certified Credit Executives, gives specific designations to members meeting its professional certification program requirements. Sponsors National Credit Education Week. Maintains speakers' bureau. Presents annual Distinguished Service awards, local association awards, and Merit and Pinnacle awards to the top credit executives. **Publications:** *Consumer Trends*, monthly. • *Credit World*, bimonthly. • *Who's Who in Credit Management*, annual. **Facsimile Number:** (314)991-3029.

Standards/Certification Agencies

★952★
International Credit Association (ICA)
243 N. Lindbergh Blvd.
St. Louis, MO 63141   Phone: (314)991-3030
Through its Society of Certified Credit Executives, gives specific designations to members meeting its professional certification program requirements.

Awards, Scholarships, Grants, and Fellowships

★953★
American Institute of Banking Scholarship
American Institute of Banking
c/o Ken Embers
1213 Bakers Way
Manhattan, KS 66502 Phone: (913)537-4750

To be applied to tuition at the American Institute of Banking resident courses lasting 10 or 16 weeks. Applicants must be high school graduates or hold a GED. Scholarships are based on merit (formal education, banking experience, and letters of recommendation).

★954★
Quarter-Century Honor Roll
National Association of Federal Credit Unions
c/o Eric Casey, Director of Marketing
3138 N. 10th St.
Arlington, VA 22201 Phone: (703)522-4770

To recognize individuals, both paid and volunteer, who have dedicated 25 years of service or more to the credit union community. Individuals who have unselfishly contributed much effort to ensure the success of the credit union movement are eligible. Credit Unions can also submit honorees posthumously. A Quarter-Century Honor Roll certificate signed by the president of NAFCU is forwarded to the Board of Directors at the accepted into the Quarter-Century Honor Roll are also acknowledged by NAFCU's bi-monthly magazine, The Federal Credit Union, which periodically publishes an Honor Roll list. Established in 1986.

Periodicals

★955★
Commercial Lenders Alert
Warren, Gorham and Lamont, Inc.
1 Penn Plaza, 40th Fl.
New York, NY 10119 Phone: (212)971-5226

Natalie Baumer, Editor. Monthly. Newsletter for commercial lenders. **Facsimile Number:** (212)971-5025.

★956★
Consumer Credit and Truth-in-Lending Compliance Report
Warren, Gorham & Lamont, Inc.
One Penn Plaza
New York, NY 10119 Phone: (212)971-5591

Editor(s): Earl Phillips. Monthly. Reports on recent changes in the consumer credit field. Acts as a compliance guide on the Equal Credit Opportunity Act, Truth-in-Lending, debt collection practices, credit cards, service contracts, insurance, and related areas. Analyzes significant litigation and current and potential changes in consumer credit legislation. **Facsimile Number:** (212)971-5024.

★957★
Consumer Finance Newsletter
Financial Publishing Company
82 Brookline Ave.
Boston, MA 02215 Phone: (617)262-4040

Editor(s): James C. Senay. Monthly. Provides information on effective and pending credit insurance and installment loan regulations on the state and federal levels. Supplies news about potential state changes in regulations.

★958★
Consumer Trends
International Credit Association (ICA)
243 N. Lindbergh Blvd.
St. Louis, MO 63141 Phone: (314)991-3030
Monthly.

★959★
Cred-Alert
American Collectors Association
4040 W. 70th St.
Minneapolis, MN 55435 Phone: (612)926-6547

Monthly. Monitors credit and collection court decisions, legislative decisions, and other general credit matters of interest to credit grantors and collectors. **Facsimile Number:** (612)926-1624.

★960★
Credit Card Management
Faulkner & Gray, Inc.
106 Fulton St.
New York, NY 10038 Phone: (212)766-7800

John Stewart, Editor. 12x/yr. Magazine covering credit card operations and programs in business; providing pertinent information for bankers, executives, and supervisors. **Facsimile Number:** (212)766-0142.

★961★
Credit Executive
New York Credit & Financial Mgmt. Assn.
520 8th Ave., Ste. 2201
New York, NY 10018 Phone: (212)268-8711

Robert G. Stone, Editor. 6x/yr. Magazine on business and commercial credit and finance. **Facsimile Number:** (212)268-8740.

★962★
Credit Research Center—Monitor
Credit Research Center
Krannert Graduate School of Management
Purdue University
West Lafayette, IN 47907 Phone: (317)494-4380

Editor(s): Robert W. Johnson and Michael E. Staten. Bimonthly. Publishes abstracts of research reports and papers on issues related to consumer and mortgage credit. Covers legislative and regulatory activities, consumer's use of credit and other financial services, and management issues for credit industries.

★963★
Credit World
International Credit Association (ICA)
243 N. Lindbergh Blvd.
St. Louis, MO 63141 Phone: (314)991-3030
Bimonthly.

★964★
ICA's Newsletter
International Credit Association (ICA)
243 N. Lindbergh Blvd.
PO Box 27357
St. Louis, MO 63141-1757 Phone: (314)991-3030

Editor(s): Barbara H. Turner. Bimonthly. Reviews developments in the consumer credit industry. Covers legislation affecting the industry and information on the U.S. consumer installment debt. Recurring features include association news, statistics, and news of research. **Facsimile Number:** (314)991-3029.

★965★
The Journal of Commercial Bank Lending
Robert Morris Associates
1 Liberty Place
1650 Market St., Ste. 2300
Philadelphia, PA 19103-7398   Phone: (215)851-9100
Charlotte Weisman, Editor. Monthly. Magazine for bank loan and credit officers. **Facsimile Number:** (215)851-9206.

★966★
The Journal of Consumer Lending
Faulkner & Gray
106 Fulton St., Ste. 200
New York, NY 10038
David B. Lawrence, Editor-in-Chief. Quarterly

─── **Meetings and Conventions** ───

★967★
National Association of Review Appraisers and Mortgage Underwriters Convention
National Association of Review Appraisers and Mortgage Underwriters
8383 E. Evans Rd.
Scottsdale, AZ 85260   Phone: (602)998-3000
1992. **Facsimile Number:** (602)998-8022.

Financial Records Processors

Financial records processors compute, record, and review financial data in order to maintain systematic records of financial transactions. Some examples of financial records processors are clerks who handle bookkeeping, accounting, billing, payroll, and auditing. In smaller firms, one employee may handle all financial records and transactions. In larger firms, one employee may handle only one area such as accounts payable. Most financial records processors use computers with special software to aid in calculating, recording and storing financial data. Financial records processors are employed in almost every industry including many in wholesale and retail trade, manufacturing, health, education, and business services, and in financial institutions.

$alaries

Salaries for financial records processors vary by occupation.

Lowest 10 percent	Less than $10,500/year
Median	$13,000-20,500
Top 10 percent	More than $25,500/year

Employment Outlook

Growth rate until the year 2000: Employment is expected to remain level.

Financial Records Processors

Career Guides

★968★
Career Success Series
Cambridge Career Products
90 MacCorkle Ave., SW
South Charleston, WV 25311   Phone: (304)744-9323
Videocassette. 1986. 15 mins. A series, available separately, outlining various career choices for students. Occupations include: flight service, air transportation/ground service, data processing, carpentry, clerk in banking/insurance, commodity sales, cosmetic personal grooming, fire fighting, forestry services, home economics, insulation/roofing, material handling, mechanics, photographic processing, pipefitting and plumbing, police science, printing, secretarial services, and utilities equipment operator.

★969★
"Financial Records Processors" in *Occupational Outlook Handbook* (p. 254)
Superintendent of Documents
U.S. Government Printing Office
Washington, DC 20402   Phone: (202)783-3238
Biennial; latest edition, 1990-91. Encyclopedia of careers describing more than 250 occupations and comprising about 86 percent of all jobs in the economy. Occupations that require lengthy education or training are given the most attention. For each occupation, the handbook describes job duties, working conditions, training, educational preparation, personal qualities, advancement possibilities, job outlook, earnings, and sources of additional information.

★970★
Understanding the Lending Process
1st Financial Video Network
1701 East Woodfield Rd.
Suite 412
Schaumburg, IL 60173-5133   Phone: (708)605-0222
Videocassette. 1987. 19 mins. Basic terms and theories of the money lending process are made simple.

Associations

★971★
Association of Independent Colleges and Schools (AICS)
1 Dupont Circle NW, Ste. 350
Washington, DC 20036   Phone: (202)659-2460
Membership: Independent business schools and junior and senior colleges of business. **Purpose:** Sponsors an accrediting commission for postsecondary and collegiate institutions. **Publications:** *AICS Compass*, monthly. • *Capital Comments*, bimonthly. • *Directory of Accredited Institutions*, annual. Facsimile Number: (202)659-2254.

Standards/Certification Agencies

★972★
Association of Independent Colleges and Schools (AICS)
1 Dupont Circle NW, Ste. 350
Washington, DC 20036   Phone: (202)659-2460
Sponsors an accrediting commission for postsecondary and collegiate institutions.

Educational Directories and Programs

★973★
Directory of Accredited Institutions
Association of Independent Colleges and Schools (AICS)
1 Dupont Circle NW, Ste. 350
Washington, DC 20036   Phone: (202)659-2460
Annual.

Basic Reference Guides and Handbooks

★974★
Successfully Managing Your Accounting Career
John Wiley and Sons, Inc.
605 3rd Ave.
New York, NY 10158   Phone: (212)850-6000
Henry Labus. 1988. Facsimile Number: (212)850-6088.

Billing Clerks

Billing clerks compute fees and costs, record data and prepare statements in order to maintain a firm's financial stability. Clerks handling accounts receivable prepare invoices to collect bills from customers. Often they use computers to calculate the amount due from sales tickets, purchase orders or charge slips. Accounts payable clerks verify billing information and handle payment. Billing clerks are employed in banks, insurance companies, health and business services organizations, wholesale and retail establishments, manufacturing, transportation, communications, and utilities.

$alaries
The average salary for billing clerks and related workers is $16,300/year

Employment Outlook
Growth rate until the year 2000: Employment is expected to remain level.

Billing Clerks

Career Guides

★975★
"Billing Clerk" in *Careers in Trucking* (pp. 20-21)
Rosen Publishing Group, Inc.
29 E. 21st St.
New York, NY 10010   Phone: (212)777-3017
Donald D. Schauer. 1987. Describes employment in the trucking industry including driving, operations, sales, and administration. Covers qualifications, training, future outlook, and salaries. Offers career planning and job hunting advice.

★976★
"Billing Clerk" in Volume 1 of *Career Discovery Encyclopedia* (pp. 120-121)
J.G. Ferguson Publishing Co.
200 W. Monroe
Chicago, IL 60606   Phone: (312)580-5480
E. Russell Primm, editor-in-chief. 1990. Contains two-page articles on 504 occupations. Each article describes job duties, earnings, and educational and training requirements.

★977★
Billing Clerks
Chronicle Guidance Publications, Inc.
PO Box 1190
Moravia, NY 13118-1190   Phone: (315)497-0330
1987. This career brief describes the nature of the work, working conditions, hours and earnings, education and training, licensure, certification, unions, personal qualifications, social and psychological factors, employment outlook, entry methods, advancement, and related occupations. **Toll-free/Additional Phone Number(s):** 800-622-7284.

★978★
"Billing Clerks" in *Occupational Outlook Handbook* (p. 255)
Superintendent of Documents
U.S. Government Printing Office
Washington, DC 20402   Phone: (202)783-3238
Biennial; latest edition, 1990-91. Encyclopedia of careers describing more than 250 occupations and comprising about 86 percent of all jobs in the economy. Occupations that require lengthy education or training are given the most attention. For each occupation, the handbook describes job duties, working conditions, training, educational preparation, personal qualities, advancement possibilities, job outlook, earnings, and sources of additional information.

★979★
"Billing Clerks" in Volume 3 of *The Encyclopedia of Careers and Vocational Guidance* (pp. 2-4)
J.G. Ferguson Publishing Co.
200 W. Monroe
Chicago, IL 60606   Phone: (312)580-5480
William E. Hopke, editor-in-chief. Eighth edition, 1990. Four-volume set that profiles 500 occupations and describes job trends in 76 industries. Includes career description, educational requirements, history of the job, methods of entry, advancement, employment outlook, earnings, working conditions, social and psychological factors, and sources of additional information.

★980★
Clerk: Bank, Insurance and Commerce
Morris Video
2730 Monterey St. #105
Monterey Business Park
Torrance, CA 90503   Phone: (213)533-4800
Videocassette. 1981. 15 mins. The many and varied duties of the clerk are examined.

★981★
"Rate Clerk" in *Careers in Trucking* (pp. 65-67)
Rosen Publishing Group, Inc.
29 E. 21st St.
New York, NY 10010   Phone: (212)777-3017
Donald D. Schauer. 1987. Describes employment in the trucking industry including driving, operations, sales, and administration. Covers qualifications, training, future outlook, and salaries. Offers career planning and job hunting advice.

Bookkeeping, Accounting, and Auditing Clerks

Bookkeeping, accounting, and auditing clerks compute and record financial data to develop and maintain financial records. They record debits and credits, compare balance sheets, and monitor accounts payable and receivable. They also verify receipts, prepare bank deposits, and update computer and manual files. Bookkeeping, accounting, and auditing clerks are found in most industries including many in wholesale and retail trade, and organizations providing business, health, educational, and social services.

$alaries

The average salary for bookkeeping, accounting, and auditing clerks is $16,000/year

Employment Outlook

Growth rate until the year 2000: Employment is expected to remain level.

Bookkeeping, Accounting, and Auditing Clerks

Career Guides

★982★
Accounting Clerk
Careers, Inc.
PO Box 135
Largo, FL 34649-0135   Phone: (813)584-7333
1989. Two-page occupational summary card describing duties, working conditions, personal qualifications, training, earnings and hours, employment outlook, places of employment, related careers and where to write for more information.

★983★
Accounting Clerk
Vocational Biographies, Inc.
PO Box 31, Dept. VF10
Sauk Centre, MN 56378   Phone: (612)352-6516
1988. This pamphlet profiles a person working in the job. Includes information about job duties, working conditions, places of employment, educational preparation, labor market outlook, and salaries. **Toll-free/Additional Phone Number(s):** 800-255-0752.

★984★
"Accounting Clerk" in *Occu-Facts: Information on 565 Careers in Outline Form* (p. 12.26)
Careers, Inc.
P.O. Box 135
1211 Tenth St., S.W.
Largo, FL 33640   Phone: (813)584-7333
Elizabeth Handville. Biennial, 1989-90 edition. Each one-page occupational profile describes duties, working conditions, physical surroundings and demands, aptitudes, temperament, educational requirements, employment outlook, earnings, and places of employment.

★985★
"Accounting Clerks and Bookkeepers" in *Opportunities in Vocational and Technical Careers* (pp. 49-50)
National Textbook Co.
4255 W. Touhy Ave.
Lincolnwood, IL 60646   Phone: (312)679-5500
Adrian A. Paradis. 1987. Describes careers which can be prepared for by attending a private vocational or proprietary school—office employee, sales worker, service worker, health services, mechanic, craftworker, and technician. Covers employment outlook, job duties, and salaries. Offers career planning advice.

★986★
"Accounting Clerks" in *The American Almanac of Jobs and Salaries* (p. 507)
Avon Books
105 Madison Avenue
New York, NY 10016   Phone: (212)481-5600
John Wright and Edward J. Dwyer. Revised and updated, 1990. A comprehensive guide to the wages of hundreds of occupations in a wide variety of industries and organizations.

★987★
Bookkeeper
Careers, Inc.
PO Box 135
Largo, FL 34649-0135   Phone: (813)584-7333
1989. Eight-page brief offering the definition, history, duties, working conditions, personal qualifications, educational requirements, earnings, hours, employment outlook, advancement possibilities, and related occupations.

★988★
"Bookkeeper" in *Administration, Business, and Office, Volume 1* of *Career Information Center* (pp. 44-45)
Glencoe/Macmillan
15319 Chatsworth St.
Mission Hills, CA 91345   Phone: (818)898-1391
Richard Lidz and Dale Anderson, editorial directors. Fourth edition, 1990. For 600 occupations, describes job duties, entry-level requirements, education and training needed, advancement possibilities, employment outlook, earnings and benefits. The set is divided into 12 volumes. Each volume includes jobs related under a broad career field. Volume 13 is the index. **Facsimile Number:** 818-365-5489.

★989★
"Bookkeeper" in *Career Opportunities in Television, Cable, and Video* (pp. 20-21)
Facts on File, Inc.
460 Park Avenue, S.
New York, NY 10016   Phone: (212)683-2244
Third edition, 1990. Describes 100 media-related jobs. Each occupational profile covers job duties, employment outlook, career paths, salaries, skills, and educational preparation. Offers tips for entering the field.

★990★
"Bookkeeper" in *Occu-Facts: Information on 565 Careers in Outline Form* (p. 12.27)
Careers, Inc.
P.O. Box 135
1211 Tenth St., S.W.
Largo, FL 33640　　　　　　　　　Phone: (813)584-7333
Elizabeth Handville. Biennial, 1989-90 edition. Each one-page occupational profile describes duties, working conditions, physical surroundings and demands, aptitudes, temperament, educational requirements, employment outlook, earnings, and places of employment.

★991★
"The Bookkeeper-Accountant" in *Opportunities in Office Occupations* (pp. 131-140)
National Textbook Co.
4255 W. Touhy Ave.
Lincolnwood, IL 60646　　　　　　Phone: (312)679-5500
Blanche Ettinger. 1989. Describes factors and trends which will affect office occupations including automation, telecommuting, and unionization. Separate chapters cover clerks, records management, information word processing, the secretary, and the bookkeeper-accountant. Describes job duties, skills needed, educational preparation, job hunting, types of equipment, employment outlook, and salaries.

★992★
"Bookkeeper and Accounting Clerk" in *Careers in Banking and Finance* (pp. 26-27)
Rosen Publishing Group, Inc.
29 E. 21st St.
New York, NY 10010　　　　　　　Phone: (212)777-3017
Patricia Haddock. 1990. Describes more than 20 jobs at all levels in banking and finance. Contains information about the types of financial organizations where the jobs are found, educational requirements, job duties, and salaries. Offers advice on job hunting.

★993★
"Bookkeeper, Secretary, and Clerk" in *Travel & Tourism* (pp. 69-73)
Franklin Watts, Inc.
387 Park Avenue, S.
New York, NY 10016　　　　　　　Phone: (212)686-7070
Marjorie Rittenberg Schulz. 1990. Surveys employment opportunities in the travel and tourism industry. Provides job description, educational preparation, training, salary, employment outlook, and sources of additional information. Offers job hunting advice.

★994★
"Bookkeepers" in Volume 1 of *Career Discovery Encyclopedia* (pp. 134-135)
J.G. Ferguson Publishing Co.
200 W. Monroe
Chicago, IL 60606　　　　　　　　Phone: (312)580-5480
E. Russell Primm, editor-in-chief. 1990. Contains two-page articles on 504 occupations. Each article describes job duties, earnings, and educational and training requirements.

★995★
Bookkeepers and Accounting Clerks
Chronicle Guidance Publications, Inc.
PO Box 1190
Moravia, NY 13118-1190　　　　　Phone: (315)497-0330
1989. This career brief describes the nature of the work, working conditions, hours and earnings, education and training, licensure, certification, unions, personal qualifications, social and psychological factors, employment outlook, entry methods, advancement, and related occupations. **Toll-free/Additional Phone Number(s):** 800-622-7284.

★996★
"Bookkeepers and Accounting Clerks" in *Jobs! What They Are...Where They Are...What They Pay* (pp. 132-133)
Simon & Schuster, Inc.
Simon & Schuster Bldg.
1230 Avenue of the Americas
New York, NY 10020　　　　　　　Phone: (212)698-7000
Robert O. Snelling and Anne M. Snelling. Revised edition, 1989. Profiles 241 occupations, describing duties and responsibilities, educational preparation, earnings, employment opportunities, training, and qualifications.

★997★
"Bookkeeping, Accounting, and Auditing Clerks" in *Occupational Outlook Handbook* (pp. 255-256)
Superintendent of Documents
U.S. Government Printing Office
Washington, DC 20402　　　　　　Phone: (202)783-3238
Biennial; latest edition, 1990-91. Encyclopedia of careers describing more than 250 occupations and comprising about 86 percent of all jobs in the economy. Occupations that require lengthy education or training are given the most attention. For each occupation, the handbook describes job duties, working conditions, training, educational preparation, personal qualities, advancement possibilities, job outlook, earnings, and sources of additional information.

★998★
"Bookkeeping and Accounting" in *The Desk Guide to Training and Work Advisement* (pp. 177-178)
Charles C. Thomas, Publisher
2600 S. First St.
Springfield, IL 62794-9265　　　　Phone: (217)789-8980
Gail Baugher Kuenstler. 1988. Describes alternative methods of gaining entry into an occupation through different types of educational programs, internships and apprenticeships. **Facsimile Number:** (217)789-9130.

★999★
"Bookkeeping and Accounting Clerk" in Volume 3 of *The Encyclopedia of Careers and Vocational Guidance* (pp. 5-8)
J.G. Ferguson Publishing Co.
200 W. Monroe
Chicago, IL 60606　　　　　　　　Phone: (312)580-5480
William E. Hopke, editor-in-chief. Eighth edition, 1990. Four-volume set that profiles 500 occupations and describes job trends in 76 industries. Includes career description, educational requirements, history of the job, methods of entry, advancement, employment outlook, earnings, working conditions, social and psychological factors, and sources of additional information.

★1000★
"Bookkeeping" in *The Career Connection II: A Guide to Technical Majors and Their Related Careers* (pp. 9-10)
ERIS
PO Box 7509
University Station
Provo, UT 84602-0509
Fred A. Rowe. 1988. Contains technical majors, such as automotive technology. Describes the major and the job. Lists high school and postsecondary school courses. Includes

Bookkeeping, Accounting, and Auditing Clerks

occupations related to the major, employment outlook, and starting salary.

★1001★
**"Bookkeeping Systems Operator" in *Occu-Facts:
Information on 565 Careers in Outline Form* (p. 12.28)**
Careers, Inc.
P.O. Box 135
1211 Tenth St., S.W.
Largo, FL 33640 Phone: (813)584-7333

Elizabeth Handville. Biennial, 1989-90 edition. Each one-page occupational profile describes duties, working conditions, physical surroundings and demands, aptitudes, temperament, educational requirements, employment outlook, earnings, and places of employment.

★1002★
Bookkeeping Systems Operators
Careers, Inc.
PO Box 135
Largo, FL 34649-0135 Phone: (813)584-7333

1991. Two-page occupational summary card describing duties, working conditions, personal qualifications, training, earnings and hours, employment outlook, places of employment, related careers and where to write for more information.

★1003★
How to Learn Basic Bookkeeping in Ten Easy Lessons
HarperCollins Publishers, Inc.
10 E. 53rd St.
New York, NY 10022 Phone: (212)207-7000

John Barnes. 1987.

★1004★
Interviewing for a Career in Public Accounting
Hampton Press
PO Box 805
Rochester, MI 48063 Phone: (313)852-0980

John J. Higgins, editor. Second edition, 1990.

★1005★
Opportunities in Accounting Careers
National Textbook Co.
4255 W. Touhy Ave.
Lincolnwood, IL 60646-1975 Phone: (708)679-5500

Arthur Lodge. 1983. **Facsimile Number:** (708)679-2494.

★1006★
Starting & Building Your Own Accounting Business
John Wiley & Sons, Inc.
605 3rd Ave.
New York, NY 10158 Phone: (212)850-6000

Jack Fox. Second edition, 1991. Part of Ronald National Association of Accounting Series. **Facsimile Number:** (212)850-6088.

★1007★
Teach Yourself Bookkeeping
David McKay Co., Inc.
201 E. 50th St.
New York, NY 10022 Phone: (212)751-2600

D. Cousins. 1978. Part of Teach Yourself Series.

★1008★
Video Career Library - Clerical & Administrative Support
Careers, Inc.
1211 10th St., SW
PO Box 135
Largo, FL 34649-0135 Phone: (813)584-7333

Videocassette. 1990. 26 mins. Part of the Video Career Library covering 165 occupations. Shows actual workers on the job. Includes secretaries, cashiers, receptionists, bookkeepers and audit clerks, telephone operators, postal clerks/carriers/supervisors, insurance investigators, bank tellers, data entry keyers, and court reporters.

Associations

★1009★
American Society of Tax Professionals (ASTP)
P.O. Box 1024
Sioux Falls, SD 57101 Phone: (605)335-1185

Membership: Tax preparers, accountants, bookkeepers, accounting services, and public accounting firms seeking to uphold high service standards in professional tax preparation. **Purpose:** Works to enhance the image of tax professionals and make tax practice more profitable; keeps members abreast of tax law and service and delivery changes; promotes networking among members for mutual assistance. Offers continuing education courses and public relations and marketing planning and preparation services. Supports Certified Tax Preparer Program; conducts seminars.

★1010★
Institute of Internal Auditors (IIA)
249 Maitland Ave.
Altamonte Springs, FL 32701-4201 Phone: (407)830-7600

Membership: International professional organization of internal auditors, comptrollers, accountants, educators, and computer specialists in functions of internal auditing in corporations, government agencies, and institutions. **Purpose:** Bestows awards annually for service and accomplishments including the Bradford Cadmus Memorial Award and the Thurston Award; awards doctoral grants for research. Sponsors educational seminars and conferences for all levels of internal audit staff and management and general management; grants professional certification. Maintains library of 2000 volumes.

★1011★
National Association of Accountants (NAA)
10 Paragon Dr.
Montvale, NJ 07645 Phone: (201)573-9000

Membership: Management accountants in industry, public accounting, government, and teaching; other persons interested in internal and management uses of accounting. **Purpose:** Conducts research on accounting methods and procedures and the management purposes served. Established Institute of Certified Management Accountants to implement and administer examinations for the Certificate in Management Accounting. Annually presents medals for manuscripts and Certificate in Management Accounting for the highest examination scores. Offers continuing education programs comprising courses, conferences, and a self-study program in management accounting areas. Maintains 20,000 volume library, placement service, and speakers' bureau. Sponsors the Stuart Cameron McLeod Society and National Junior Achievement Vice President - Finance of the Year. Sponsors competitions.

★1012★
National Society of Public Accountants
1010 N. Fairfax St.
Alexandria, VA 22314 Phone: (703)549-6400
Membership: Practicing accountants and tax practitioners. Represents the independent practitioner. **Purpose:** Conducts correspondence courses and seminars; operates speakers' bureau. Awards 33 scholarships annually to accounting students. Maintains 21 committees.

Standards/Certification Agencies

★1013★
Institute of Internal Auditors (IIA)
249 Maitland Ave.
Altamonte Springs, FL 32701-4201 Phone: (407)830-7600
Grants professional certification.

Test Guides

★1014★
Accounts Payable Practice Set
McGraw-Hill Publishing Co.
1221 Avenue of the Americas
New York, NY 10020 Phone: (212)512-2000
Fred C. Archer. 1969.

★1015★
Accounts Receivable Practice Set
McGraw-Hill Publishing Co.
1221 Avenue of the Americas
New York, NY 10020 Phone: (212)512-2000
Fred C. Archer. 1970.

★1016★
Assistant Accountant
Prentice Hall Press
Simon & Schuster Inc.
200 Old Tappan Rd.
Old Tappan, NJ 07675 Phone: (800)223-2348
Michael McDonough. Third edition, 1984. Includes four sample tests for self-instruction course. Topics include opening and closing books, recording transactions, and compiling balance sheets and income statements.

★1017★
Bookkeeper - Account Clerk
Prentice Hall Press
Simon & Schuster Inc.
200 Old Tappan Rd.
Old Tappan, NJ 07675 Phone: (800)223-2348
Hy Hammer. Sixth edition, 1983. Prepares candidates for the civil service bookkeeper exam at local, state, and federal levels. Includes five actual past exams.

★1018★
Career Examination Series
National Learning Corp.
212 Michael Dr.
Syosset, NY 11791 Phone: (516)921-8888
Jack Rudman. This series from National Learning Corp. includes study guides for careers such as bookkeeper, bookkeeping machine operator, account clerk, clerk-stenographer, clerk-typist, accounting and auditing clerk, and accounting assistant and trainee, among many others. All examination guides in this series contain questions with answers.

Facsimile Number: (516)921-8743. **Toll-free/Additional Phone Number(s):** 800-645-6337.

★1019★
Senior Clerical Series
Prentice Hall Press
Simon & Schuster Inc.
200 Old Tappan Rd.
Old Tappan, NJ 07675 Phone: (800)223-2348
Hy Hammer. Fourth edition, 1983. Complete test preparation for the following senior grade positions: clerk, typist, stenographer, account clerk, file clerk, statistics clerk, stenographer (law), mail and supply clerk, and stores clerk.

Basic Reference Guides and Handbooks

★1020★
Accounting Terms & Bookkeeping Procedures Explained
Gower Publishing Co.
Old Post Rd.
Brookfield, VT 05036 Phone: (802)276-3162
Diane Houghton. 1980.

★1021★
The American System of Practical Bookkeeping: Adapted to the Commerce of the United States
Ayer Company Publishers, Inc.
50 Northwestern Dr., No. 10
PO Box 958
Salem, NH 03079 Phone: (603)898-1200
James A. Bennett. 1976. Part of History of Accounting Series.

★1022★
Basic Bookkeeping
Trans-Atlantic Publications, Inc.
311 Bainbridge St.
Philadelphia, PA 19147 Phone: (215)925-5083
J. O. Magee. 1979. **Facsimile Number:** (215)925-1912.

★1023★
Bookkeeping & Accounts
Butterworths Legal Publishers
289 E. 5th St.
St. Paul, MN 55101 Phone: (612)227-4200
Paul Gee. 20th edition, 1988.

★1024★
Bookkeeping for a Small Business
D B A Books
323 Beacon St.
Boston, MA 02116 Phone: (617)262-0411
Diane Bellavance. Third edition, 1987.

★1025★
Bookkeeping for Beginners
Beekman Publishers, Inc.
Rte. 212
PO Box 888
Woodstock, NY 12498 Phone: (914)679-2300
W. E. Hooper. 1970.

Bookkeeping, Accounting, and Auditing Clerks

★1026★
Bookkeeping for Small Organizations: A Handbook for Treasurers & Finance Committees
Progressive Publisher
401 E. 32nd, No. 1002
Chicago, IL 60616   Phone: (312)225-9181
Kenneth Ives. 1990.

★1027★
Bookkeeping for the Nineteen Nineties
Regal Books
2300 Knoll Dr.
Ventura, CA 93003   Phone: (805)644-9721
Lynn Grobin. 1990.

★1028★
Bookkeeping Made Easy
HarperCollins Publishers, Inc.
10 E. 53rd St.
New York, NY 10022   Phone: (212)207-7000
Alexander L. Sheff. 1971.

★1029★
Bookkeeping Made Simple
Doubleday & Company, Inc.
666 5th Ave.
New York, NY 10103   Phone: (212)765-6500
Louis W. Fields. 1956. Part of Made Simple Series. **Facsimile Number:** (212)492-9700.

★1030★
Bookkeeping: Outline of Double Entry Bookkeeping for Small Business & Co-Operatives
State Mutual Book & Periodical Service, Ltd.
521 5th Ave., 17th Fl.
New York, NY 10175   Phone: (212)682-5844
A. S. Walford. 1982.

★1031★
Bookkeeping the Easy Way
Barron's Eductional Series, Inc.
250 Wireless Blvd.
Hauppauge, NY 11788   Phone: (516)434-3311
Wallace Kravitz. Second edition, 1990. Part of Easy Way Series.

★1032★
Developing Bookkeeping Skills
AMSCO School Publications, Inc.
315 Hudson St.
New York, NY 10013   Phone: (212)675-7000
Wallace W. Kravitz. 1978.

★1033★
Discover Bookkeeping & Accounts
Trans-Atlantic Publications, Inc.
311 Bainbridge St.
Philadelphia, PA 19147   Phone: (215)925-5083
David Spurling. 1988. **Facsimile Number:** (215)925-1912.

★1034★
Double Entry by Single: A New Method of Bookkeeping
Ayer Company Publishers, Inc.
50 Northwestern Dr., No. 10
PO Box 958
Salem, NH 93079   Phone: (603)898-1200
Frederick W. Cronhelm. 1978. Part of Development of Contemporary Accounting Thought Series.

★1035★
Efficient Accounting & Record Keeping
John Wiley, & Sons, Inc.
605 3rd Ave.
New York, NY 10158   Phone: (212)850-6000
Dennis M. Doyle. 1978. Part of Small Business Series. **Facsimile Number:** (212)850-6088.

★1036★
Horsebreeders Bookkeeping System
Printed Horse
PO Box 1908
Fort Collins, CO 80522   Phone: (303)482-2286
1976.

★1037★
Jones's English System of Bookkeeping Single or Double Entry
Ayer Company Publishers, Inc.
50 Northwestern Dr., No. 10
PO Box 958
Salem, NH 03079   Phone: (603)898-1200
Edward T. Jones. 1978. Part of Development of Contemporary Accounting Thought Series.

★1038★
Munro's Bookkeeping & Accountancy
Trans-Atlantic Publications, Inc.
311 Bainbridge St.
Philadelphia, PA 19147   Phone: (215)925-5083
Alfred Palmer. 23rd edition, 1975. **Facsimile Number:** (215)925-1912.

★1039★
A New & Complete System of Bookkeeping by an Improved Method of Double Entry
Ayer Company Publishers, Inc.
50 Northwestern Dr., No. 10
PO Box 958
Salem, NH 03079   Phone: (603)898-1200
William Mitchell. 1978. Part of Development of Contemporary Accounting Thought Series.

★1040★
Record Keeping for Small Rural Businesses
University of Massachusetts, Amherst
Center for International Education
285 Hills House S.
Amherst, MA 01003   Phone: (413)545-0465
Eligia Murcia. Part of Technical Note Series.

★1041★
Schaum's Outline of Bookkeeping & Accounting
McGraw-Hill Publishing Co.
1221 Avenue of the Americas
New York, NY 10020   Phone: (212)512-2000
Joel J. Lerner. Second edition, 1988.

★1042★
Schaum's Outline of Theory & Problems of Bookkeeping
McGraw-Hill Publishing Company
1221 Avenue of the Americas
New York, NY 10020   Phone: (212)512-2000
Joel J. Lerner. 1978.

★1043★
Step-by-Step Bookkeeping
Borgo Press
PO Box 2845
San Bernardino, CA 92406-2845 Phone: (714)884-5813
Robert Ragan. 1989.

★1044★
Step-by-Step Bookkeeping
Sterling Publishing Co., Inc.
387 Park Ave. S.
New York, NY 10016-8810 Phone: (212)532-7160
Robert Ragan. Revised edtion, 1979. **Toll-free/Additional Phone Number(s):** 800-367-9692. **Facsimile Number:** (212)213-2495.

★1045★
Streamlined Bookkeeping for Multi-Level Marketing
Advantage Press
PO Box 51
Rocklin, CA 95677 Phone: (916)652-0185
Audrey A. Scannell. 1985. **Facsimile Number:** (916)652-0539.

★1046★
Successfully Managing Your Accounting Career
John Wiley and Sons, Inc.
605 3rd Ave.
New York, NY 10158 Phone: (212)850-6000
Henry Labus. 1988. **Facsimile Number:** (212)850-6088.

Meetings and Conventions

★1047★
Institute of Internal Auditors Annual Forum (IIA)
249 Maitland Ave.
Altamonte Springs, FL 32701-4201 Phone: (407)830-7600
Frequency: Always held in June. 1992; Jun. 21-24; Phoenix, AZ • 1993; Jun. 20-23; Chicago, IL • 1994; Toronto, ON, Canada. **Toll-free/Additional Phone Number(s):** 800-CIA-DESK. **Facsimile Number:** (407)831-5171.

Other Sources of Information

★1048★
Ancient Double-Entry Bookkeeping
Scholars Book Company
4431 Mt. Vernon
Houston, TX 77006 Phone: (713)528-4395
John B. Geijsbeek. 1975.

★1049★
The Auditor's Guide of Eighteen Sixty-Nine
Garland Publishing, Inc.
136 Madison Ave.
New York, NY 10016 Phone: (212)686-7492
Richard P. Brief, editor. 1988. Part of Foundations of Accounting Series. **Toll-free/Additional Phone Number(s):** 800-627-6273. **Facsimile Number:** (212)889-9399.

★1050★
Four Classics on the Theory of Double Entry Bookkeeping
Garland Publishing, Inc.
136 Madison Ave.
New York, NY 10016 Phone: (212)686-7492
Richard P. Brief, editor. 1982. Part of Accountancy in Transition Series. **Toll-free/Additional Phone Number(s):** 800-627-6273. **Facsimile Number:** (212)889-9399.

★1051★
Robert Oliver & Mercantile Bookkeeping in the Early Nineteenth Century
Ayer Company Publishers, Inc.
50 Northwestern Dr., No. 10
PO Box 958
Salem, NH 03079 Phone: (603)898-1200
Stuart Bruchey. 1976. Part of History of Accounting Series.

Payroll and Timekeeping Clerks

Payroll and timekeeping clerks make sure employees' paychecks are correct and paid on time. Timekeeping clerks distribute and collect timecards each pay period. They review timesheets to verify that the information is correct and properly recorded. Payroll clerks screen the timecards for errors and compute earnings. Payroll clerks also maintain and update employee files when workers resign, retire or transfer. Payroll and timekeeping clerks are found in business, health, education, social services, manufacturing, wholesale and retail trade, and in government.

$alaries
The average salary for payroll and timekeeping clerks is $17,300/year

Employment Outlook
Growth rate until the year 2000: Employment is expected to remain level.

Payroll and Timekeeping Clerks

Career Guides

★1052★
Payroll Accounting
South-Western Publishing Co.
5101 Madison Rd.
Cincinnati, OH 45227　　　　Phone: (513)271-8811
B. Lewis Keeling. 1989.

★1053★
"Payroll and Timekeeping Clerks" in *Occupational Outlook Handbook* (p. 256)
Superintendent of Documents
U.S. Government Printing Office
Washington, DC 20402　　　　Phone: (202)783-3238
Biennial; latest edition, 1990-91. Encyclopedia of careers describing more than 250 occupations and comprising about 86 percent of all jobs in the economy. Occupations that require lengthy education or training are given the most attention. For each occupation, the handbook describes job duties, working conditions, training, educational preparation, personal qualities, advancement possibilities, job outlook, earnings, and sources of additional information.

★1054★
"Payroll Clerk" in *Administration, Business, and Office*, Volume 1 of *Career Information Center* (pp. 63-64)
Glencoe/Macmillan
15319 Chatsworth St.
Mission Hills, CA 91345　　　　Phone: (818)898-1391
Richard Lidz and Dale Anderson, editorial directors. Fourth edition, 1990. For 600 occupations, describes job duties, entry-level requirements, education and training needed, advancement possibilities, employment outlook, earnings and benefits. The set is divided into 12 volumes. Each volume includes jobs related under a broad career field. Volume 13 is the index. **Facsimile Number:** 818-365-5489.

Associations

★1055★
American Payroll Association (APA)
30 E. 33rd St., 5th Fl.
New York, NY 10016　　　　Phone: (212)686-2030
Membership: Payroll employees. **Purpose:** Works to increase members' skills and professionalism through education and mutual support. Represents the interest of members before legislative bodies. Conducts workshops, seminars, and training courses. Administers the certified payroll professional program of recognition. **Publications:** *APA Directory*, annual. • *Payroll Exchange*, monthly. • Also publishes surveys and special reports.

Standards/Certification Agencies

★1056★
American Payroll Association (APA)
30 E. 33rd St., 5th Fl.
New York, NY 10016　　　　Phone: (212)686-2030
Administers the certified payroll professional program of recognition.

Test Guides

★1057★
Head Clerk (Payroll)
National Learning Corp.
212 Michael Dr.
Syosset, NY 11791　　　　Phone: (516)921-8888
Jack Rudman. Part of the Career Examination Series No. 1. All examination guides in this series contain questions with answers. **Facsimile Number:** (516)921-8743. **Toll-free/Additional Phone Number(s):** 800-645-6337.

★1058★
Payroll Clerk
National Learning Corp.
212 Michael Dr.
Syosset, NY 11791　　　　Phone: (516)921-8888
Jack Rudman. Part of the Career Examination Series No. 1. All examination guides in this series contain questions with answers. **Facsimile Number:** (516)921-8743. **Toll-free/Additional Phone Number(s):** 800-645-6337.

★1059★
Senior Payroll Audit Clerk
National Learning Corp.
212 Michael Dr.
Syosset, NY 11791　　　　Phone: (516)921-8888
Jack Rudman. Part of the Career Examination Series No. 1. All examination guides in this series contain questions with answers. **Facsimile Number:** (516)921-8743. **Toll-free/Additional Phone Number(s):** 800-645-6337.

Basic Reference Guides and Handbooks

★1060★
Buying Payroll Software
Cambridge University Press
49 W. 20th St.
New York, NY 10011   Phone: (212)924-3900
British Computer Society Staff. 1985. Part of Software Package Buyer's Guides Series. **Facsimile Number:** (212)691-3239.

★1061★
Payroll Accounting for Microcomputers
South-Western Publishing Co.
5101 Madison Rd.
Cincinnati, OH 45227   Phone: (513)271-8811
B. Lewis Keeling. 1986.

★1062★
Payroll Recordkeeping
McGraw-Hill Publishing Co.
1221 Avenue of the Americas
New York, NY 10020   Phone: (212)512-2000
Hadley Editorial Staff. Seventh edition, 1965.

★1063★
Payroll Systems & Procedures
McGraw-Hill Publishing Co.
1221 Avenue of the Americas
New York, NY 10020   Phone: (212)512-2000
B. F. Wigge. 1970.

★1064★
Principles of Payroll Administration
Prentice Hall
Rte. 9W
Englewood Cliffs, NJ 07632   Phone: (201)592-2000
Debera J. Salam. 1988.

Periodicals

★1065★
Payroll Exchange
American Payroll Association (APA)
30 E. 33rd St., 5th Fl.
New York, NY 10016   Phone: (212)686-2030
Monthly.

Other Sources of Information

★1066★
Available Pay Survey for the U.S.: An Annotated Bibliography
Abbott, Langer & Associates
548 1st St.
Crete, IL 60417   Phone: (708)672-4200
Steven Langer, editor. 1987.

★1067★
Available Pay Survey Reports for Other Countries: An Annotated Bibliography
Abbott, Langer & Associates
548 1st St.
Crete, IL 60417   Phone: (708)672-4200
Steven Langer, editor. 1987.

General Office Clerks

General office clerks do a variety of tasks to support office, business, or administrative operations. Some may specialize in one task such as typing or filing. Others may do many tasks, such as answering phone calls, operating office equipment, or entering data at a computer terminal, depending on the needs of the employer. Experienced employees may handle financial records, inventory, or customer complaints. General office clerks are fairly evenly distributed throughout industry and government.

$alaries

Salaries for general office clerks vary by industry.

Lowest 10 percent	$9,600/year
Median	$12,600-19,800/year
Top 10 percent	More than $26,200
Beginning office clerks in private firms	$10,500/year
Clerks with more responsibilities	$19,300/year

Employment Outlook

Growth rate until the year 2000: Average.

General Office Clerks

Career Guides

★1068★
Clerical Worker
Vocational Biographies, Inc.
PO Box 31, Dept. VF10
Sauk Centre, MN 56378   Phone: (612)352-6516
1988. This pamphlet profiles a person working in the job. Includes information about job duties, working conditions, places of employment, educational preparation, labor market outlook, and salaries. **Toll-free/Additional Phone Number(s):** 800-255-0752.

★1069★
"The Clerk" in *Opportunities in Office Occupations* **(pp. 49-83)**
National Textbook Co.
4255 W. Touhy Ave.
Lincolnwood, IL 60646   Phone: (312)679-5500
Blanche Ettinger. 1989. Describes factors and trends which will affect office occupations including automation, telecommuting, and unionization. Separate chapters cover clerks, records management, information word processing, the secretary, and the bookkeeper-accountant. Describes job duties, skills needed, educational preparation, job hunting, types of equipment, employment outlook, and salaries.

★1070★
Clerk, General Office
Careers, Inc.
PO Box 135
Largo, FL 34649-0135   Phone: (813)584-7333
1990. Eight-page brief offering the definition, history, duties, working conditions, personal qualifications, educational requirements, earnings, hours, employment outlook, advancement possibilities, and related occupations.

★1071★
"General Office Clerk" in *Occu-Facts: Information on 565 Careers in Outline Form* **(p. 12.14)**
Careers, Inc.
P.O. Box 135
1211 Tenth St., S.W.
Largo, FL 33640   Phone: (813)584-7333
Elizabeth Handville. Biennial, 1989-90 edition. Each one-page occupational profile describes duties, working conditions, physical surroundings and demands, aptitudes, temperament, educational requirements, employment outlook, earnings, and places of employment.

★1072★
"General Office Clerks" in *Occupational Outlook Handbook* **(pp. 256-257)**
Superintendent of Documents
U.S. Government Printing Office
Washington, DC 20402   Phone: (202)783-3238
Biennial; latest edition, 1990-91. Encyclopedia of careers describing more than 250 occupations and comprising about 86 percent of all jobs in the economy. Occupations that require lengthy education or training are given the most attention. For each occupation, the handbook describes job duties, working conditions, training, educational preparation, personal qualities, advancement possibilities, job outlook, earnings, and sources of additional information.

★1073★
"General Office Clerks" in Volume 3 of *Career Discovery Encyclopedia* **(pp. 72-73)**
J.G. Ferguson Publishing Co.
200 W. Monroe
Chicago, IL 60606   Phone: (312)580-5480
E. Russell Primm, editor-in-chief. 1990. Contains two-page articles on 504 occupations. Each article describes job duties, earnings, and educational and training requirements.

★1074★
"General Office Clerks" in Volume 3 of *The Encyclopedia of Careers and Vocational Guidance* **(pp. 45-48)**
J.G. Ferguson Publishing Co.
200 W. Monroe
Chicago, IL 60606   Phone: (312)580-5480
William E. Hopke, editor-in-chief. Eighth edition, 1990. Four-volume set that profiles 500 occupations and describes job trends in 76 industries. Includes career description, educational requirements, history of the job, methods of entry, advancement, employment outlook, earnings, working conditions, social and psychological factors, and sources of additional information.

★1075★
"Office Clerk" in *Administration, Business, and Office,* **Volume 1 of** *Career Information Center* **(pp. 60-61)**
Glencoe/Macmillan
15319 Chatsworth St.
Mission Hills, CA 91345   Phone: (818)898-1391
Richard Lidz and Dale Anderson, editorial directors. Fourth edition, 1990. For 600 occupations, describes job duties, entry-level requirements, education and training needed, advancement possibilities, employment outlook, earnings and benefits. The set is divided into 12 volumes. Each volume includes jobs related under a broad career field. Volume 13 is the index. **Facsimile Number:** 818-365-5489.

★1076★
Office Systems & Careers: A Resource for Administrative Assistants
Allyn & Bacon, Inc.
160 Gould St.
Needham Heights, MA 02194
Church. 1981.

★1077★
Vocational Visions
Center for Humanities, Inc.
Communications Park
Box 1000
Mount Kisco, NY 10549   Phone: (914)666-4100

Videocassette. 1984. 30 mins. This series of programs explains key aspects of actual training and a day in the life of a worker in the specific field mentioned on the videocassette. Occupations include: transportation/mechanics, repair, construction, business/office occupations, health, and agriculture.

--- **Test Guides** ---

★1078★
Assistant Clerk
National Learning Corp.
212 Michael Dr.
Syosset, NY 11791   Phone: (516)921-8888

Jack Rudman. Part of the Career Examination Series No. 1. All examination guides in this series contain questions with answers. **Facsimile Number:** (516)921-8743. **Toll-free/Additional Phone Number(s):** 800-645-6337.

★1079★
Beginning Office Worker
National Learning Corp.
212 Michael Dr.
Syosset, NY 11791   Phone: (516)921-8888

Jack Rudman. Part of the Career Examination Series No. 1. All examination guides in this series contain questions with answers. **Facsimile Number:** (516)921-8743. **Toll-free/Additional Phone Number(s):** 800-645-6337.

★1080★
Chief Clerk
National Learning Corp.
212 Michael Dr.
Syosset, NY 11791   Phone: (516)921-8888

Jack Rudman. Part of the Career Examination Series No. 1. All examination guides in this series contain questions with answers. **Facsimile Number:** (516)921-8743. **Toll-free/Additional Phone Number(s):** 800-645-6337.

★1081★
Clerical Careers
National Learning Corp.
212 Michael Dr.
Syosset, NY 11791   Phone: (516)921-8888

Jack Rudman. Part of the Career Examination Series No. 1. All examination guides in this series contain questions with answers. **Facsimile Number:** (516)921-8743. **Toll-free/Additional Phone Number(s):** 800-645-6337.

★1082★
Office Aide
Prentice Hall Press
Simon & Schuster Inc.
200 Old Tappan Rd.
Old Tappan, NJ 07675   Phone: (800)223-2348

Hy Hammer. Second edition, 1985. Contains seven sample exams for the following entry-level civil service postions: clerk, typist, stenographer, receptionist, office machine operator, telephone operator.

★1083★
Practice and Drill for the Clerk, Typist, and Stenographer Examinations
National Learning Corp.
212 Michael Dr.
Syosset, NY 11791   Phone: (516)921-8888

Jack Rudman. Part of the General Aptitude and Abilities Series No. 2. Books in this series provide functional, intensive test practice and drill in the basic skills and areas common to many examinations, as well as general aptitude or achievement necessary for entrance into many occupations or positions. **Facsimile Number:** (516)921-8743. **Toll-free/Additional Phone Number(s):** 800-645-6337.

★1084★
Practice for Clerical, Typing and Stenographic Tests
Prentice Hall Press
Simon & Schuster Inc.
200 Old Tappan Rd.
Old Tappan, NJ 07675   Phone: (800)223-2348

Maryhelen H. Paulick Hoffman. Seventh edition, 1988. Provide preparation for all qualifying tests given by local, state, and federal agencies for all types of clerical positions.

★1085★
Principal Clerk
National Learning Corp.
212 Michael Dr.
Syosset, NY 11791   Phone: (516)921-8888

Jack Rudman. Part of the Career Examination Series No. 1. All examination guides in this series contain questions with answers. **Facsimile Number:** (516)921-8743. **Toll-free/Additional Phone Number(s):** 800-645-6337.

★1086★
Principal Office Assistant
National Learning Corp.
212 Michael Dr.
Syosset, NY 11791   Phone: (516)921-8888

Jack Rudman. Part of the Career Examination Series No. 1. All examination guides in this series contain questions with answers. **Facsimile Number:** (516)921-8743. **Toll-free/Additional Phone Number(s):** 800-645-6337.

★1087★
Senior Clerical Series
National Learning Corp.
212 Michael Dr.
Syosset, NY 11791   Phone: (516)921-8888

Jack Rudman. Part of the Career Examination Series No. 1. All examination guides in this series contain questions with answers. **Facsimile Number:** (516)921-8743. **Toll-free/Additional Phone Number(s):** 800-645-6337.

General Office Clerks

★1088★
Senior Office Assistant
National Learning Corp.
212 Michael Dr.
Syosset, NY 11791   Phone: (516)921-8888
Jack Rudman. Part of the Career Examination Series No. 1. All examination guides in this series contain questions with answers. **Facsimile Number:** (516)921-8743. **Toll-free/Additional Phone Number(s):** 800-645-6337.

★1089★
Senior Office Worker
National Learning Corp.
212 Michael Dr.
Syosset, NY 11791   Phone: (516)921-8888
Jack Rudman. Part of the Career Examination Series No. 1. All examination guides in this series contain questions with answers. **Facsimile Number:** (516)921-8743. **Toll-free/Additional Phone Number(s):** 800-645-6337.

Basic Reference Guides and Handbooks

★1090★
Career Strategies for Secretaries: How to Get Where You Want to Be
Contemporary Books, Inc.
180 N. Michigan Ave.
Chicago, IL 60601   Phone: (312)782-9181
Marie Kisiel. 1982. **Facsimile Number:** (312)782-2157.

★1091★
General Office Procedures for Colleges
South-Western Publishing Co.
5101 Madison Rd.
Cincinnati, OH 45227   Phone: (513)271-8811
Patsy J. Fulton. Ninth edition, 1987.

★1092★
Hotel Front Office Management & Operation
William C. Brown Group
2460 Kerper Blvd.
Dubuque, IA 52001   Phone: (319)588-1451
Peter Dukas. Third edition, 1970. **Facsimile Number:** (319)589-2955.

★1093★
Math on the Job: Secretary/Clerk Typist
National Center for Research in Vocational Education
Ohio State University
1900 Kenry Rd.
Columbus, OH 43210   Phone: (614)292-4353
1985.

★1094★
Office Procedures
McGraw-Hill Publishing Co.
1221 Avenue of the Americas
New York, NY 10020   Phone: (212)512-2000
Jeffrey R. Stewart, Jr. 1980.

★1095★
Procedures for the Office Professional
South-Western Publishing Co.
5101 Madison Rd.
Cincinnati, OH 45227   Phone: (513)271-8811
Patsy J. Fulton. Second edition, 1989.

★1096★
Reference Manual: For the Office
South-Western Publishing Co.
5101 Madison Rd.
Cincinnati, OH 45227   Phone: (513)271-8811
Clifford R. House. Seventh edition, 1988.

★1097★
Technique of Systems & Procedures
Office Research Institute
1517 Sparrow St.
Longwood, FL 32750
John H. Ross.

★1098★
The A to Z Business Office Handbook
Prentice Hall
Rte. 9W
Englewood Cliffs, NJ 07632   Phone: (201)592-2000
Robert E. Swindle. 1984.

Periodicals

★1099★
Bank Operations Report
Warren, Gorham & Lamont, Inc.
One Penn Plaza
New York, NY 10119   Phone: (212)971-5000
Editor(s): Pat Durner. Monthly. Focuses on electronic data processing control, check processing, record keeping, cost control, Federal regulation, credit and debit cards, electronic funds transfer system, physical security, and office automation, computer, and systems applications.

★1100★
From Nine to Five
Dartnell Corp.
4660 Ravenswood
Chicago, IL 60640   Phone: (312)561-4000
Editor(s): Douglas Leland. Biweekly. Provides "tips, shortcuts, and helpful information for success in the office," particularly secretaries and office workers. Recurring features include columns titled Business Skills Clinic and The Coffee Break. **Toll-free/Additional Phone Number(s):** 800-621-5463. **Facsimile Number:** (312)561-3801.

Information Clerks

Information clerks perform a variety of duties related to gathering and providing information in a wide range of employment settings. Many information clerks are employed by hotels and motels to deal directly with the public either by taking reservations, greeting guests, or answering questions. Often they use word processors or personal computers to facilitate their work. Many information clerks are also found in the transportation industry, hospitals, and banks.

$alaries

Salaries for information clerks vary by industry.

Lowest 10 percent	Less than $175/week
Median	$212-350/week
Top 10 percent	More than $479/week

Employment Outlook

Growth rate until the year 2000: Faster than average.

Information Clerks

Career Guides

★1101★
Clerk, Information
Careers, Inc.
PO Box 135
Largo, FL 34649-0135   Phone: (813)584-7333
1990. Two-page job guide card describing duties, working conditions, personal qualifications, training, earnings and hours, employment outlook, places of employment, related careers and where to write for more information.

★1102★
"Information Clerk" in *Occu-Facts: Information on 565 Careers in Outline Form* (p. 12.19)
Careers, Inc.
P.O. Box 135
1211 Tenth St., S.W.
Largo, FL 33640   Phone: (813)584-7333
Elizabeth Handville. Biennial, 1989-90 edition. Each one-page occupational profile describes duties, working conditions, physical surroundings and demands, aptitudes, temperament, educational requirements, employment outlook, earnings, and places of employment.

★1103★
"Information Clerks" in *America's 50 Fastest Growing Jobs* (pp. 109-111)
JIST Works, Inc.
720 N. Park Ave.
Indianapolis, IN 46202   Phone: (317)264-3720
Michael J. Farr, compiler. 1991. Describes the 50 fastest growing jobs within major career clusters such as technicians, and marketing and sales. Each job profile explains the nature of the work, skills and abilities required, employment outlook, average earnings, related occupations, education and training requirements, and employment opportunities. Also contains career planning information and job search tips.

★1104★
"Information Clerks" in *Occupational Outlook Handbook* (pp. 257-259)
Superintendent of Documents
U.S. Government Printing Office
Washington, DC 20402   Phone: (202)783-3238
Biennial; latest edition, 1990-91. Encyclopedia of careers describing more than 250 occupations and comprising about 86 percent of all jobs in the economy. Occupations that require lengthy education or training are given the most attention. For each occupation, the handbook describes job duties, working conditions, training, educational preparation, personal qualities, advancement possibilities, job outlook, earnings, and sources of additional information.

★1105★
The Power of Customer Service
Quiet Advantage
1949 South Manchester St. 34
Anaheim, CA 92802   Phone: (714)748-1840
Videocassette. 1991. 45 mins. Customer oriented service can be the greatest asset for any business. This video discusses the training and building of a service oriented team.

★1106★
"Reservation and Information Clerks" in *Opportunities in Travel Careers* (p. 53)
National Textbook Co.
4255 W. Touhy Ave.
Lincolnwood, IL 60646   Phone: (312)679-5500
Robert Scott Milne. 1991. Explores job opportunities in many travel related fields including the airlines, resorts, travel agencies, recreation, and tourism. Covers the work, salaries, educational preparation and training, and advancement possibilities.

Test Guides

★1107★
Associate Public Information Specialist
National Learning Corp.
212 Michael Dr.
Syosset, NY 11791   Phone: (516)921-8888
Jack Rudman. Part of the Career Examination Series No. 1. All examination guides in this series contain questions with answers. **Facsimile Number:** (516)921-8743. **Toll-free/Additional Phone Number(s):** 800-645-6337.

★1108★
Clerical Careers
National Learning Corp.
212 Michael Dr.
Syosset, NY 11791   Phone: (516)921-8888
Jack Rudman. Part of the Career Examination Series No. 1. All examination guides in this series contain questions with answers. **Facsimile Number:** (516)921-8743. **Toll-free/Additional Phone Number(s):** 800-645-6337.

★1109★
Office Aide
Prentice Hall Press
Simon & Schuster Inc.
200 Old Tappan Rd.
Old Tappan, NJ 07675   Phone: (800)223-2348

Hy Hammer. Second edition, 1985. Contains seven sample exams for the following entry-level civil service postions: clerk, typist, stenographer, receptionist, office machine operator, telephone operator.

★1110★
Public Information Assistant
National Learning Corp.
212 Michael Dr.
Syosset, NY 11791   Phone: (516)921-8888

Jack Rudman. Part of the Career Examination Series No. 1. All examination guides in this series contain questions with answers. **Facsimile Number:** (516)921-8743. **Toll-free/Additional Phone Number(s):** 800-645-6337.

★1111★
Senior Clerical Series
Prentice Hall Press
Simon & Schuster Inc.
200 Old Tappan Rd.
Old Tappan, NJ 07675   Phone: (800)223-2348

Hy Hammer. Fourth edition, 1983. Complete test preparation for the following senior grade positions: clerk, typist, stenographer, account clerk, file clerk, statistics clerk, stenographer (law), mail and supply clerk, and stores clerk.

Hotel and Motel Desk Clerks

Hotel and motel clerks perform a variety of services such as registering guests, assigning rooms, answering questions, and processing payments. In smaller establishments, clerks may also function as bookkeepers, cashiers, or telephone operators. In addition to these duties, clerks keep records of room assignments to maximize profit and coordinate housekeeping and maintenance work. Hotel and motel clerks are in direct contact with the public and, through their attitude, may influence guests positively or negatively about the establishment.

$alaries

The average salary for hotel and motel clerks is $214/week.

Employment Outlook

Growth rate until the year 2000: Faster than average.

Hotel and Motel Desk Clerks

Career Guides

★1112★
Front Desk Courtesy
National Educational Media, Inc.
21601 Devonshire St.
Chatsworth, CA 91311-9962   Phone: (818)709-6009
Videocassette. 1981. 11 mins. A demonstration of the importance of proper guest relations at the hotel front desk in a variety of challenging situations.

★1113★
Hospitality Industry
AIMS Media, Inc.
9710 DeSoto Ave.
Chatsworth, CA 93111-4409   Phone: (818)773-4300
Videocassette. 1988. 40 mins. A section of the "Career Awareness" series which covers the hotel industry.

★1114★
"Hotel and Motel Clerks" in *Occupational Outlook Handbook* (p. 259)
Superintendent of Documents
U.S. Government Printing Office
Washington, DC 20402   Phone: (202)783-3238
Biennial; latest edition, 1990-91. Encyclopedia of careers describing more than 250 occupations and comprising about 86 percent of all jobs in the economy. Occupations that require lengthy education or training are given the most attention. For each occupation, the handbook describes job duties, working conditions, training, educational preparation, personal qualities, advancement possibilities, job outlook, earnings, and sources of additional information.

★1115★
"Hotel and Motel Desk Clerk" in *Hospitality & Recreation* (pp. 15-19)
Franklin Watts, Inc.
387 Park Avenue, S.
New York, NY 10016   Phone: (212)686-7070
Marjorie Rittenberg Schulz. 1990. Provides an overview of jobs in the hotel, motel, food service, fitness, and recreation industries. Covers job duties, educational preparation, salary, and employment outlook. Offers job hunting advice.

★1116★
"Hotel and Motel Front Office Clerks" in *Jobs! What They Are...Where They Are...What They Pay* (pp. 167-168)
Simon & Schuster, Inc.
Simon & Schuster Bldg.
1230 Avenue of the Americas
New York, NY 10020   Phone: (212)698-7000
Robert O. Snelling and Anne M. Snelling. Revised edition, 1989. Profiles 241 occupations, describing duties and responsibilities, educational preparation, earnings, employment opportunities, training, and qualifications.

★1117★
"Hotel Clerks" in Volume 3 of *Career Discovery Encyclopedia* (pp. 120-121)
J.G. Ferguson Publishing Co.
200 W. Monroe
Chicago, IL 60606   Phone: (312)580-5480
E. Russell Primm, editor-in-chief. 1990. Contains two-page articles on 504 occupations. Each article describes job duties, earnings, and educational and training requirements.

★1118★
"Hotel Clerks" in Volume 3 of *The Encyclopedia of Careers and Vocational Guidance* (pp. 48-52)
J.G. Ferguson Publishing Co.
200 W. Monroe
Chicago, IL 60606   Phone: (312)580-5480
William E. Hopke, editor-in-chief. Eighth edition, 1990. Four-volume set that profiles 500 occupations and describes job trends in 76 industries. Includes career description, educational requirements, history of the job, methods of entry, advancement, employment outlook, earnings, working conditions, social and psychological factors, and sources of additional information.

★1119★
"Hotel Desk Clerk" in *Hospitality and Recreation*, Volume 8 of *Career Information Center* (pp. 52-53)
Glencoe/Macmillan
15319 Chatsworth St.
Mission Hills, CA 91345   Phone: (818)898-1391
Richard Lidz and Dale Anderson, editorial directors. Fourth edition, 1990. For 600 occupations, describes job duties, entry-level requirements, education and training needed, advancement possibilities, employment outlook, earnings and benefits. The set is divided into 12 volumes. Each volume includes jobs related under a broad career field. Volume 13 is the index. **Facsimile Number:** 818-365-5489.

★1120★
Hotel/Motel Careers: A World of Opportunities
American Hotel and Motel Association
Educational Institute
1407 S. Harrison Rd.
PO Box 1240
E. Lansing, MI 48826   Phone: (202)289-3100

1990. Booklet providing an overview of the lodging industry and its job opportunities.

★1121★
Hotel/Motel Clerk
Careers, Inc.
PO Box 135
Largo, FL 34649-0135   Phone: (813)584-7333

1990. Two-page occupational summary card describing duties, working conditions, personal qualifications, training, earnings and hours, employment outlook, places of employment, related careers and where to write for more information.

★1122★
"Hotel/Motel Clerk" in Occu-Facts: Information on 565 Careers in Outline Form (p. 12.16)
Careers, Inc.
P.O. Box 135
1211 Tenth St., S.W.
Largo, FL 33640   Phone: (813)584-7333

Elizabeth Handville. Biennial, 1989-90 edition. Each one-page occupational profile describes duties, working conditions, physical surroundings and demands, aptitudes, temperament, educational requirements, employment outlook, earnings, and places of employment.

★1123★
Introduction to Management in the Hospitality Industry
John Wiley & Sons, Inc.
605 3rd Ave.
New York, NY 10158   Phone: (212)850-6000

Tom Powers. Third edition, 1988. **Facsimile Number:** (212)850-6088.

Associations

★1124★
American Hotel & Motel Association (AH&MA)
1201 New York Ave. NW, Ste. 600
Washington, DC 20005   Phone: (202)289-3100

Membership: Federation of 50 state and regional hotel associations, representing over 1.3 million hotel and motel rooms. **Purpose:** Promotes business of hotels and motels through publicity and promotion programs. Works to improve operating methods through dissemination of information on industry methods. Conducts educational institute for training at all levels, through home study, adult education, and colleges. Provides guidance on member and labor relations. Reviews proposed legislation affecting hotels. Sponsors study group programs. Maintains speakers' bureau; conducts research; compiles statistics; sponsors competitions and presents awards. **Publications:** *AH&MA Leadership Directory*, annual. • *Construction and Modernization Report*, monthly. • *Lodging*, monthly. • *Directory of Hotel and Motel Systems*, annual. • Also publishes surveys, guidelines, manuals, brochures, prints of articles and makes available hotel information kits; produces videos and bilingual (English/Spanish) energy conservation reference cards. **Facsimile Number:** (202)289-3199.

★1125★
Hotel-Motel Greeters International (HMGI)
PO Box 20017
El Cajon, CA 92021   Phone: (619)561-5869

Membership: Owners, managers, executives, clerks, and other personnel in hotels, motor hotels, clubs, and apartment hotels. **Purpose:** Provides educational services to members. Offers guest referral service to member hotels and motels. Bestows awards.

Educational Directories and Programs

★1126★
Educational Institute of the American Hotel and Motel Association
PO Box 1240
East Lansing, MI 48826

Provides information on professional development and training programs for careers in the lodging industry.

Awards, Scholarships, Grants, and Fellowships

★1127★
Bellman/Bellwoman of the Year
American Hotel and Motel Association
c/o Mercedes McDonnel
1201 New York Ave., N.W.
Washington, DC 20005-3917   Phone: (202)289-3133

To provide general managers with the opportunity to recognize exceptional service by an employee. Bellmen and bellwomen employed by a hotel or motel that is a member of the Association are eligible. Managers may nominate only one bellman/woman. The entry deadline is November 30. Prizes include a $500 U.S. Savings Bond and travel expenses to the Association's convention. Awarded annually. Established in 1965. Co-sponsored by American Tourister Inc., and Appel-Brooks-Webber.

Basic Reference Guides and Handbooks

★1128★
Directory of Hotel and Motel Systems
American Hotel & Motel Association (AH&MA)
1201 New York Ave. NW, Ste. 600
Washington, DC 20005   Phone: (202)289-3100

Annual. .

★1129★
Hotel Front Office Management & Operation
William C. Brown Group
2460 Kerper Blvd.
Dubuque, IA 52001   Phone: (319)588-1451

Peter Dukas. Third edition, 1970. **Facsimile Number:** (319)589-2955.

Periodicals

★1130★
Construction and Modernization Report
American Hotel & Motel Association (AH&MA)
1201 New York Ave. NW, Ste. 600
Washington, DC 20005   Phone: (202)289-3100
Monthly.

★1131★
Hotel & Motel Management
Edgell Communications, Inc.
7500 Old Oak Blvd.
Cleveland, OH 44130   Phone: (216)243-8100
Robert Nozar, Editor. 18/yr. Magazine (tabloid) covering the lodging industry. **Facsimile Number:** (216)891-2726.

★1132★
Hotels
Cahners Publishing Co.
1350 E. Touhy Ave.
PO Box 5080
Des Plaines, IL 60017-5080   Phone: (708)635-8800
Donald T. Lock, Publisher. Monthly. Magazine covering management and operations as well as foodservice and design in the hospitality industry.

★1133★
Lodging
American Hotel & Motel Association (AH&MA)
1201 New York Ave. NW, Ste. 600
Washington, DC 20005   Phone: (202)289-3100
Monthly.

★1134★
Lodging Industry: National Trend of Business
Laventhol & Horwath
1845 Walnut St.
Philadelphia, PA 19103   Phone: (215)299-1600
Monthly. Compiles statistics and data on the hotel industry. Covers occupancy, room rates, and food and beverage sales, both nationally and by local regions throughout the country. **Facsimile Number:** (215)299-8645.

★1135★
Motel/Hotel Insider
Magna Publishing
2718 Dryden
Madison, WI 53704   Phone: (608)249-2455
Editor(s): Robert Reis. Weekly. Covers motel/hotel management, travel and vacation trends, business travel, new products and services for the hospitality market, motel/hotel chains, and trends and changes in the lodging industry.

★1136★
North American Edition OAG Business Travel Planner
Official Airline Guides
2000 Clearwater Dr.
Oak Brook, IL 60521   Phone: (708)574-6000
Richard A. Nelson, Publisher. Quarterly. Official lodging directory of the American Hotel and Motel Association includes city destination information, hotel listings, airport diagrams, city, metro, resort area and country maps, travel basics, and reservation directories. **Facsimile Number:** (708)574-6667.

★1137★
Prairie Hotelier
Naylor Communications Ltd.
100 Sutherland Ave.
Winnipeg, MB, Canada R2W 3C7   Phone: (204)947-0222
Lisa Kopochinski, Editor. 6x/yr. Hotel industry magazine. **Facsimile Number:** (204)947-2047.

Meetings and Conventions

★1138★
American Hotel and Motel Association Convention
American Hotel and Motel Association
1201 New York Ave., NW, Ste. 600
Washington, DC 20005   Phone: (202)289-3100
1992; Apr. 29-03; Toronto, ON, Canada. **Facsimile Number:** (202)289-3199.

★1139★
American Hotel and Motel Association Fall Conference
American Hotel and Motel Association
1201 New York Ave., NW, Ste. 600
Washington, DC 20005   Phone: (202)289-3100
1992; Toronto, ON, Canada • 1993; Kansas City, MO. **Facsimile Number:** (202)289-3199.

★1140★
Hotel-Motel Greeters International Annual Conference (HMGI)
PO Box 20017
El Cajon, CA 92021   Phone: (619)561-5869
Frequency: Annual.

★1141★
IAHA HITEC-Hospitality Industry Technology Expostion and Conference
International Association of Hospitality Accountants
PO Box 27649
Austin, TX 78755   Phone: (512)346-5680
1992; Jun. 23-25; Baltimore, MD. **Facsimile Number:** (512)346-5760.

Other Sources of Information

★1142★
Hotel & Motel Equipment & Supplies Directory
American Business Directories, Inc.
American Business Information, Inc.
5711 S. 86th Circle
Omaha, NE 68127   Phone: (402)593-4600
Annual. 1,002. Entries include: Name, address, phone, size of advertisement, name of owner or manager, number of employees, year first in "Yellow Pages." Arrangement: Geographical. **Facsimile Number:** (402)331-1505.

Interviewing and New Accounts Clerks

Interviewing clerks gather and process various types of information and assist people in filling out forms. In hospitals, an outpatient admitting clerk gathers the preliminary information necessary for admission and provides general information. Survey workers, sometimes called telemarketers, often conduct telephone interviews to gather information and compile statistics. New accounts clerks interview applicants and help them fill out applications for credit cards or bank accounts. Interviewing and new accounts clerks are often employed by banks, savings and loan associations, firms providing miscellaneous business services, hospitals, and the Federal Government.

$alaries
The average salary for interviewing and new accounts clerks is $288/week

Employment Outlook
Growth rate until the year 2000: Average.

Interviewing and New Accounts Clerks

Career Guides

★1143★
"Admitting Clerk" in *Health Care* (pp. 39-43)
Franklin Watts, Inc.
387 Park Avenue, S.
New York, NY 10016　　　　　Phone: (212)686-7070
Linda Barrett and Galen Guengerich. 1991. Provides an overview of the health care industry. Includes job description, educational preparation, training, salary, and employment outlook. Offers job hunting advice.

★1144★
"Admitting Clerk" in *Health*, Volume 7 of *Career Information Center* (pp. 39-40)
Glencoe/Macmillan
15319 Chatsworth St.
Mission Hills, CA 91345　　　　　Phone: (818)898-1391
Richard Lidz and Dale Anderson, editorial directors. Fourth edition, 1990. For 600 occupations, describes job duties, entry-level requirements, education and training needed, advancement possibilities, employment outlook, earnings and benefits. The set is divided into 12 volumes. Each volume includes jobs related under a broad career field. Volume 13 is the index. **Facsimile Number:** 818-365-5489.

★1145★
"Interviewing and New Accounts Clerks" in *Occupational Outlook Handbook* (pp. 259-260)
Superintendent of Documents
U.S. Government Printing Office
Washington, DC 20402　　　　　Phone: (202)783-3238
Biennial; latest edition, 1990-91. Encyclopedia of careers describing more than 250 occupations and comprising about 86 percent of all jobs in the economy. Occupations that require lengthy education or training are given the most attention. For each occupation, the handbook describes job duties, working conditions, training, educational preparation, personal qualities, advancement possibilities, job outlook, earnings, and sources of additional information.

★1146★
"Tel-a-marketing" in *Careers in Trucking* (p. 39)
Rosen Publishing Group, Inc.
29 E. 21st St.
New York, NY 10010　　　　　Phone: (212)777-3017
Donald D. Schauer. 1987. Describes employment in the trucking industry including driving, operations, sales, and administration. Covers qualifications, training, future outlook, and salaries. Offers career planning and job hunting advice.

★1147★
Telemarketer
Careers, Inc.
PO Box 135
Largo, FL 34649-0135　　　　　Phone: (813)584-7333
1992. Two-page occupational summary card describing duties, working conditions, personal qualifications, training, earnings and hours, employment outlook, places of employment, related careers and where to write for more information.

★1148★
Telemarketer
Vocational Biographies, Inc.
PO Box 31, Dept. VF10
Sauk Centre, MN 56378　　　　　Phone: (612)352-6516
1988. This pamphlet profiles a person working in the job. Includes information about job duties, working conditions, places of employment, educational preparation, labor market outlook, and salaries. **Toll-free/Additional Phone Number(s):** 800-255-0752.

★1149★
"Telemarketer" in *Occu-Facts: Information on 565 Careers in Outline Form* (p. 11.26)
Careers, Inc.
P.O. Box 135
1211 Tenth St., S.W.
Largo, FL 33640　　　　　Phone: (813)584-7333
Elizabeth Handville. Biennial, 1989-90 edition. Each one-page occupational profile describes duties, working conditions, physical surroundings and demands, aptitudes, temperament, educational requirements, employment outlook, earnings, and places of employment.

★1150★
"Telemarketers" in Volume 6 of *Career Discovery Encyclopedia* (pp. 100-101)
J.G. Ferguson Publishing Co.
200 W. Monroe
Chicago, IL 60606　　　　　Phone: (312)580-5480
E. Russell Primm, editor-in-chief. 1990. Contains two-page articles on 504 occupations. Each article describes job duties, earnings, and educational and training requirements.

★1151★
"Telemarketers" in Volume 3 of *The Encyclopedia of Careers and Vocational Guidance* (pp. 110-114)
J.G. Ferguson Publishing Co.
200 W. Monroe
Chicago, IL 60606   Phone: (312)580-5480
William E. Hopke, editor-in-chief. Eighth edition, 1990. Four-volume set that profiles 500 occupations and describes job trends in 76 industries. Includes career description, educational requirements, history of the job, methods of entry, advancement, employment outlook, earnings, working conditions, social and psychological factors, and sources of additional information.

★1152★
"Telemarketing" in *Careers in Marketing* (pp. 57-58)
National Textbook Co.
4255 W. Touhy Ave.
Lincolnwood, IL 60646   Phone: (312)679-5500
Lila B. Stair. 1991. Surveys career opportunities in marketing and related areas such as marketing research, product development, and sales promotion. Includes a description of the work, places of employment, employment outlook, trends, educational preparation, organizational charts, and salaries. Offers job hunting advice.

★1153★
"Telemarketing" in *Opportunities in Telecommunications Careers* (pp. 35-46)
National Textbook Co.
4255 W. Touhy Ave.
Lincolnwood, IL 60646   Phone: (312)679-5500
Jan Bone. 1990. Discusses the many facets of the telecommunications industry including research and development, manufacturing, sales, telecommunications, services, management, telemarketing, electronic mail, networking, and cellular communication. Explores jobs, educational preparation and training requirements, and provides job hunting tips.

★1154★
"Telemarketing Specialist" in *Marketing and Distribution*, Volume 10 of *Career Information Center* (pp. 61-62)
Glencoe/Macmillan
15319 Chatsworth St.
Mission Hills, CA 91345   Phone: (818)898-1391
Richard Lidz and Dale Anderson, editorial directors. Fourth edition, 1990. For 600 occupations, describes job duties, entry-level requirements, education and training needed, advancement possibilities, employment outlook, earnings and benefits. The set is divided into 12 volumes. Each volume includes jobs related under a broad career field. Volume 13 is the index. **Facsimile Number:** 818-365-5489.

★1155★
"Telemarketing: The Fast-Track Medium" in *Marketing and Sales Career Directory* (pp. 68-72)
Career Press, Inc.
PO Box 34
62 Beverly Rd.
Hawthorne, NJ 07507   Phone: (201)427-0229
Ronald W. Fry, editor. Third edition, 1990. Guide to career planning and job hunting in a marketing or sales capacity at a major corporation, market research company, or public relations agency. Lists hundreds of employers seeking entry level employees. Includes job description, work environments, educational preparation, career advancement, earnings, and trends.

★1156★
Telephone Solicitors (Telemarketers)
Chronicle Guidance Publications, Inc.
PO Box 1190
Moravia, NY 13118-1190   Phone: (315)497-0330
1988. This career brief describes the nature of the work, working conditions, hours and earnings, education and training, licensure, certification, unions, personal qualifications, social and psychological factors, employment outlook, entry methods, advancement, and related occupations. **Toll-free/Additional Phone Number(s):** 800-622-7284.

Associations

★1157★
American Bankers Association (ABA)
1120 Connecticut Ave. NW
Washington, DC 20036   Phone: (202)663-5000
Membership: Commercial banks and trust companies; combined assets of members represent approximately 95% of the U.S. banking industry. **Purpose:** Seeks to enhance the role of commercial banks as preeminent providers of financial services through communications, research, legal action, lobbying of federal legislative and regulatory bodies, and education and training programs. Serves as spokesperson for the commercial banking industry; facilitates exchange of information among members. Sponsors American Institute of Banking (formerly American Institute of Bank Clerks), which conducts educational and training programs for bank employees and officers through 21 schools of banking. Maintains liaison with federal bank regulators; submits draft legislation and lobbies Congress on issues affecting commercial banks; testifies before congressional committees; represents members in U.S. postal rate proceedings; also represents the U.S. banking industry at the United Nations. Serves as secretariat of the International Money Conference and the Financial Institutions Committee for the American National Standards Institute. Files briefs and lawsuits in major court cases affecting the industry. Conducts teleconferences with state banking associations on such issues as tax reform and compliance; works to build consensus and coordinate activities of leading bank and financial service trade groups. Provides services to members including: television, newspaper, and magazine advertisements promoting full-service banks; insurance program providing directors and officers with liability coverage, financial institution bond, and trust errors and omissions coverage; research service operated through ABA Library and Information Services; fingerprint set processing in conjunction with the Federal Bureau of Investigation. Conducts conferences, forums, and workshops covering subjects including agricultural and community banking, trust management, bank operations, and automation. Sponsors Personal Economics Program, which presents school programs on topics including checking account management and careers in banking. Bestows five Ayres Fellowships annually to academicians; two Hughes Fellowships annually to financial journalists; two Cummings Fellowships annually to professional staff members in the executive or legislative branches of federal or state governments. Maintains library of 60,000 volumes on banking, money, economics, finance, and law. **Publications:** *ABA Bankers Weekly*. • *ABA Banking Journal*, monthly. • *ABA Retail Banker*, monthly. • *The Advisor*, monthly. • *AIB Leaders Letter*, 9/year. • *AIB Student Catalog*, annual. • *Bank Compliance Magazine*, quarterly. • *Bank Personnel News*, monthly. • *Bank Planning News*, bimonthly. • *Commercial Lender Newsletter*, monthly. • *Consumer Banking Digest*, monthly. • *Delinquency Consumer Credit Bulletin*, quarterly. • *Directory*, annual. • *Insurance and Protection Bulletin*, monthly. • *ISO Register*, quarterly. • *Journal of Personal Financial Services*, quarterly. • *Thruput: The ABA Operations/Automation News Report*, monthly. • *Trust Letter*, monthly. •

Trust Management Update: A Trust Industry Communication on Management, Investments, Marketing, Operations, and Administration, monthly. ● Also issues approximately 400 technical publications, listed in *ABA Catalog*; also produces computer software and video- and audiocassettes. **Toll-free/Additional Phone Number(s):** (202)663-5430 Banker Education Network; (800)872-7747 financial information; (800)424-2871 news service.

Educational Directories and Programs

★1158★
AIB Student Catalog
American Bankers Association (ABA)
1120 Connecticut Ave. NW
Washington, DC 20036   Phone: (202)663-5000
Annual.

Basic Reference Guides and Handbooks

★1159★
ABA Directory
American Bankers Association (ABA)
1120 Connecticut Ave. NW
Washington, DC 20036   Phone: (202)663-5000
Annual.

Periodicals

★1160★
ABA Bankers Weekly
American Bankers Association (ABA)
1120 Connecticut Ave. NW
Washington, DC 20036   Phone: (202)663-5000
Newspaper covering national trends and developments in the banking industry, and federal regulatory action and congressional legislation related to banking.

★1161★
ABA Banking Journal
American Bankers Association (ABA)
1120 Connecticut Ave. NW
Washington, DC 20036   Phone: (202)663-5000
Monthly.

★1162★
The Advisor
American Bankers Association (ABA)
1120 Connecticut Ave. NW
Washington, DC 20036   Phone: (202)663-5000
Monthly.

★1163★
Commercial Lender Newsletter
American Bankers Association (ABA)
1120 Connecticut Ave. NW
Washington, DC 20036   Phone: (202)663-5000
Monthly.

★1164★
Consumer Banking Digest
American Bankers Association (ABA)
1120 Connecticut Ave. NW
Washington, DC 20036   Phone: (202)663-5000
Monthly.

★1165★
Insurance and Protection Bulletin
American Bankers Association (ABA)
1120 Connecticut Ave. NW
Washington, DC 20036   Phone: (202)663-5000
Monthly.

★1166★
ISO Register
American Bankers Association (ABA)
1120 Connecticut Ave. NW
Washington, DC 20036   Phone: (202)663-5000
Quarterly.

★1167★
Journal of Personal Financial Services
American Bankers Association (ABA)
1120 Connecticut Ave. NW
Washington, DC 20036   Phone: (202)663-5000
Quarterly.

★1168★
Thruput: The ABA Operations/Automation News Report (ABA)
American Bankers Association (ABA)
1120 Connecticut Ave. NW
Washington, DC 20036   Phone: (202)663-5000
Monthly. Newsletter offering current information on technical advances, legislative and regulatory developments, and the activities of the Federal Communications Commission, U.S. Postal Service, and other federal agencies that affect the operation, data processing, and automation of banks. Includes annual index, calendar of events, and statistics.

★1169★
Trust Letter
American Bankers Association (ABA)
1120 Connecticut Ave. NW
Washington, DC 20036   Phone: (202)663-5000
Monthly.

★1170★
Trust Management Update: A Trust Industry Communication on Management, Investments, Marketing, Operations, and Administration
American Bankers Association (ABA)
1120 Connecticut Ave. NW
Washington, DC 20036   Phone: (202)663-5000
Monthly. Newsletter including calendar of events and new products and services.

Receptionists

Receptionists greet customers and visitors, determine their needs and refer them to the correct person. This involves daily interaction with people either in person or on the telephone. Depending on where they work, receptionists may schedule appointments, answer questions, open mail, or do bookkeeping. Receptionists often use automated office equipment such as word processors and personal computers to perform their duties. Many receptionists are employed by health care facilities as well as factories, wholesale and retail stores, government agencies, real estate offices, and firms providing business services.

$alaries

The average salary for receptionists is $256/week

Employment Outlook

Growth rate until the year 2000: Faster than average.

Receptionists

Career Guides

★1171★
How to Be a Receptionist
Oddo Publishing, Inc.
PO Box 68
Storybrook Acres
Fayetteville, GA 30214-0068   Phone: (404)461-7627
Johnson.

★1172★
Receptionist
Vocational Biographies, Inc.
PO Box 31, Dept. VF10
Sauk Centre, MN 56378   Phone: (612)352-6516
1990. This pamphlet profiles a person working in the job. Includes information about job duties, working conditions, places of employment, educational preparation, labor market outlook, and salaries. **Toll-free/Additional Phone Number(s):** 800-255-0752.

★1173★
The Receptionist
McGraw-Hill Publishing Co.
1221 Avenue of the Americas
New York, NY 10020   Phone: (212)512-2000
J. W. Twing. 1983.

★1174★
"Receptionist" in *Administration, Business, and Office, Volume 1 of Career Information Center* (pp. 66-67)
Glencoe/Macmillan
15319 Chatsworth St.
Mission Hills, CA 91345   Phone: (818)898-1391
Richard Lidz and Dale Anderson, editorial directors. Fourth edition, 1990. For 600 occupations, describes job duties, entry-level requirements, education and training needed, advancement possibilities, employment outlook, earnings and benefits. The set is divided into 12 volumes. Each volume includes jobs related under a broad career field. Volume 13 is the index. **Facsimile Number:** 818-365-5489.

★1175★
"Receptionist" in *Occu-Facts: Information on 565 Careers in Outline Form* (p. 12.18)
Careers, Inc.
P.O. Box 135
1211 Tenth St., S.W.
Largo, FL 33640   Phone: (813)584-7333
Elizabeth Handville. Biennial, 1989-90 edition. Each one-page occupational profile describes duties, working conditions, physical surroundings and demands, aptitudes, temperament, educational requirements, employment outlook, earnings, and places of employment.

★1176★
"Receptionist/Clerk-Typist" in *Career Opportunities in Television, Cable, and Video* (pp. 22-23)
Facts on File, Inc.
460 Park Avenue, S.
New York, NY 10016   Phone: (212)683-2244
Third edition, 1990. Describes 100 media-related jobs. Each occupational profile covers job duties, employment outlook, career paths, salaries, skills, and educational preparation. Offers tips for entering the field.

★1177★
Receptionists
Chronicle Guidance Publications, Inc.
PO Box 1190
Moravia, NY 13118-1190   Phone: (315)497-0330
1987. This career brief describes the nature of the work, working conditions, hours and earnings, education and training, licensure, certification, unions, personal qualifications, social and psychological factors, employment outlook, entry methods, advancement, and related occupations. **Toll-free/Additional Phone Number(s):** 800-622-7284.

★1178★
"Receptionists" in *Jobs! What They Are...Where They Are...What They Pay* (pp. 210-211)
Simon & Schuster, Inc.
Simon & Schuster Bldg.
1230 Avenue of the Americas
New York, NY 10020   Phone: (212)698-7000
Robert O. Snelling and Anne M. Snelling. Revised edition, 1989. Profiles 241 occupations, describing duties and responsibilities, educational preparation, earnings, employment opportunities, training, and qualifications.

★1179★
"Receptionists" in *Occupational Outlook Handbook* (pp. 260-261)
Superintendent of Documents
U.S. Government Printing Office
Washington, DC 20402   Phone: (202)783-3238
Biennial; latest edition, 1990-91. Encyclopedia of careers describing more than 250 occupations and comprising about 86 percent of all jobs in the economy. Occupations that require lengthy education or training are given the most attention. For each occupation, the handbook describes job duties, working conditions, training, educational preparation, personal qualities,

advancement possibilities, job outlook, earnings, and sources of additional information.

★1180★
"Receptionists" in *Opportunities in Vocational and Technical Careers* (pp. 43-45)
National Textbook Co.
4255 W. Touhy Ave.
Lincolnwood, IL 60646 Phone: (312)679-5500

Adrian A. Paradis. 1987. Describes careers which can be prepared for by attending a private vocational or proprietary school—office employee, sales worker, service worker, health services, mechanic, craftworker, and technician. Covers employment outlook, job duties, and salaries. Offers career planning advice.

★1181★
"Receptionists" in Volume 5 of *Career Discovery Encyclopedia* (pp. 134-135)
J.G. Ferguson Publishing Co.
200 W. Monroe
Chicago, IL 60606 Phone: (312)580-5480

E. Russell Primm, editor-in-chief. 1990. Contains two-page articles on 504 occupations. Each article describes job duties, earnings, and educational and training requirements.

★1182★
"Receptionists" in Volume 3 of *The Encyclopedia of Careers and Vocational Guidance* (pp. 74-77)
J.G. Ferguson Publishing Co.
200 W. Monroe
Chicago, IL 60606 Phone: (312)580-5480

William E. Hopke, editor-in-chief. Eighth edition, 1990. Four-volume set that profiles 500 occupations and describes job trends in 76 industries. Includes career description, educational requirements, history of the job, methods of entry, advancement, employment outlook, earnings, working conditions, social and psychological factors, and sources of additional information.

★1183★
"Receptionists and Switchboard Operators" in *The American Almanac of Jobs and Salaries* (p. 507)
Avon Books
105 Madison Avenue
New York, NY 10016 Phone: (212)481-5600

John Wright and Edward J. Dwyer. Revised and updated, 1990. A comprehensive guide to the wages of hundreds of occupations in a wide variety of industries and organizations.

★1184★
"Receptionists" in *America's 50 Fastest Growing Jobs* (pp. 111-113)
JIST Works, Inc.
720 N. Park Ave.
Indianapolis, IN 46202 Phone: (317)264-3720

Michael J. Farr, compiler. 1991. Describes the 50 fastest growing jobs within major career clusters such as technicians, and marketing and sales. Each job profile explains the nature of the work, skills and abilities required, employment outlook, average earnings, related occupations, education and training requirements, and employment opportunities. Also contains career planning information and job search tips.

★1185★
Telephone Manners
Britannica Films
310 South Michigan Ave.
Chicago, IL 60604 Phone: (312)347-7958

Videocassette. 1989. 11 mins. This program demonstrates every important step in telephone usage including identifying yourself and your organization, personalizing your calls, repeating all instructions given, taking notes of important messages, remembering calls on hold, listening to the caller's mood as well as the message, using common courtesy words and conveying warmth.

★1186★
Video Career Library - Clerical & Administrative Support
Careers, Inc.
1211 10th St., SW
PO Box 135
Largo, FL 34649-0135 Phone: (813)584-7333

Videocassette. 1990. 26 mins. Part of the Video Career Library covering 165 occupations. Shows actual workers on the job. Includes secretaries, cashiers, receptionists, bookkeepers and audit clerks, telephone operators, postal clerks/carriers/supervisors, insurance investigators, bank tellers, data entry keyers, and court reporters.

★1187★
Vocational Visions
Center for Humanities, Inc.
Communications Park
Box 1000
Mount Kisco, NY 10549 Phone: (914)666-4100

Videocassette. 1984. 30 mins. This series of programs explains key aspects of actual training and a day in the life of a worker in the specific field mentioned on the videocassette. Occupations include: transportation/mechanics, repair, construction, business/office occupations, health, and agriculture.

Test Guides

★1188★
Office Aide
Prentice Hall Press
Simon & Schuster Inc.
200 Old Tappan Rd.
Old Tappan, NJ 07675 Phone: (800)223-2348

Hy Hammer. Second edition, 1985. Contains seven sample exams for the following entry-level civil service postions: clerk, typist, stenographer, receptionist, office machine operator, telephone operator.

★1189★
Receptionist
National Learning Corp.
212 Michael Dr.
Syosset, NY 11791 Phone: (516)921-8888

Jack Rudman. Part of the Career Examination Series No. 1. All examination guides in this series contain questions with answers.
Facsimile Number: (516)921-8743. **Toll-free/Additional Phone Number(s):** 800-645-6337.

Receptionists ★1195★

Educational Directories and Programs

★1190★
Industry Directory
Association of Information Systems Professionals
104 Wilmot Rd., Ste. 201
Deerfield, IL 60015-5195 Phone: (708)940-8800
Bea McLean, editor. Irregular; previous edition 1986; new edition possible 1990. Manufacturers of office automation equipment; word processing service bureaus; educational institutions offering office automation and associated software courses or curriculums; personnel agencies serving office automation personnel and users; analysts and counsultants. Entries include: Name, address. Arrangement: Alphabetical within categories above. **Facsimile Number:** (708)940-7218.

★1191★
Receptionists
Accrediting Bureau of Health Education
Oak Manor Office
29089 U.S. 20 W.
Elkhart, IN 46514 Phone: (219)293-0124
1991. State-by-state listing of schools offering medical receptionist training programs. Lists address, phone number, and contact person.

Basic Reference Guides and Handbooks

★1192★
Career Strategies for Secretaries: How to Get Where You Want to Be
Contemporary Books, Inc.
180 N. Michigan Ave.
Chicago, IL 60601 Phone: (312)782-9181
Marie Kisiel. 1982. **Facsimile Number:** (312)782-2157.

★1193★
Math on the Job: Secretary/Clerk Typist
National Center for Research in Vocational Education
Ohio State University
1900 Kenry Rd.
Columbus, OH 43210 Phone: (614)292-4353
1985.

★1194★
Receptionist: A Practical Course in Office Reception Techniques
McGraw-Hill Publishing Co.
1221 Avenue of the Americas
New York, NY 10020 Phone: (212)512-2000
Merle W. Wood. 1966.

Periodicals

★1195★
From Nine to Five
Dartnell Corp.
4660 Ravenswood
Chicago, IL 60640 Phone: (312)561-4000
Editor(s): Douglas Leland. Biweekly. Provides "tips, shortcuts, and helpful information for success in the office," particularly secretaries and office workers. Recurring features include columns titled Business Skills Clinic and The Coffee Break. **Toll-free/Additional Phone Number(s):** 800-621-5463. **Facsimile Number:** (312)561-3801.

Reservation and Transportation Ticket Agents and Travel Clerks

Reservation and transportation ticket agents and travel clerks help passengers plan trips and assist them during travel. Travel clerks gather information on accommodation and transportation rates, make reservations, and calculate expenses. Reservation agents usually work in central offices answering telephone inquiries and booking reservations. They often use computer terminals to quickly access reservation information. Ticket agents sell tickets, answer inquiries, check baggage, examine visas, and ensure passenger seating. Ticket agents, known as gate agents in airports, assist people when boarding. Most ticket agents and travel clerks work for airlines. Others work for automobile clubs, hotels and motels, business firms, and government agencies.

$alaries

The average salary for reservation and transportation ticket agents and travel clerks is $423/week

Employment Outlook

Growth rate until the year 2000: Faster than average.

Reservation and Transportation Ticket Agents and Travel Clerks

Career Guides

★1196★
"Airline Reservations Agent" in *Transportation*, Volume 12 of *Career Information Center* (pp. 36-38)
Glencoe/Macmillan
15319 Chatsworth St.
Mission Hills, CA 91345   Phone: (818)898-1391
Richard Lidz and Dale Anderson, editorial directors. Fourth edition, 1990. For 600 occupations, describes job duties, entry-level requirements, education and training needed, advancement possibilities, employment outlook, earnings and benefits. The set is divided into 12 volumes. Each volume includes jobs related under a broad career field. Volume 13 is the index. **Facsimile Number:** 818-365-5489.

★1197★
"Airline Reservations Agent" in *Travel & Tourism* (pp. 21-25)
Franklin Watts, Inc.
387 Park Avenue, S.
New York, NY 10016   Phone: (212)686-7070
Marjorie Rittenberg Schulz. 1990. Surveys employment opportunities in the travel and tourism industry. Provides job description, educational preparation, training, salary, employment outlook, and sources of additional information. Offers job hunting advice.

★1198★
Airline Reservations Sales Agent
Vocational Biographies, Inc.
PO Box 31, Dept. VF10
Sauk Centre, MN 56378   Phone: (612)352-6516
1990. This pamphlet profiles a person working in the job. Includes information about job duties, working conditions, places of employment, educational preparation, labor market outlook, and salaries. **Toll-free/Additional Phone Number(s):** 800-255-0752.

★1199★
"Airline Sales and Reservations" in *The Travel Agent: Dealer in Dreams* (pp. 113-128)
Prentice Hall Press
1 Gulf & Western Plaza
New York, NY 10023   Phone: (212)373-8500
Aryear Gregory. Third edition, 1989. Comprehensive guide for those interested in the travel industry. Covers the work of the travel agent, agency problems, techniques, and promotion. Describes various jobs within the travel industry including travel consultant, agency manager, and tour operators. Explains the knowledge, skills, training, and educational preparation needed to succeed.

★1200★
Airline Ticket Agent
Careers, Inc.
PO Box 135
Largo, FL 34649-0135   Phone: (813)584-7333
1988. Two-page occupational summary card describing duties, working conditions, personal qualifications, training, earnings and hours, employment outlook, places of employment, related careers and where to write for more information.

★1201★
"Airline Ticket Agent" in *Occu-Facts: Information on 565 Careers in Outline Form* (p. 12.17)
Careers, Inc.
P.O. Box 135
1211 Tenth St., S.W.
Largo, FL 33640   Phone: (813)584-7333
Elizabeth Handville. Biennial, 1989-90 edition. Each one-page occupational profile describes duties, working conditions, physical surroundings and demands, aptitudes, temperament, educational requirements, employment outlook, earnings, and places of employment.

★1202★
"Airline Ticket Agent" in *Transportation*, Volume 12 of *Career Information Center* (pp. 38-39)
Glencoe/Macmillan
15319 Chatsworth St.
Mission Hills, CA 91345   Phone: (818)898-1391
Richard Lidz and Dale Anderson, editorial directors. Fourth edition, 1990. For 600 occupations, describes job duties, entry-level requirements, education and training needed, advancement possibilities, employment outlook, earnings and benefits. The set is divided into 12 volumes. Each volume includes jobs related under a broad career field. Volume 13 is the index. **Facsimile Number:** 818-365-5489.

★1203★
Career in Air Transport Ground Services
Morris Video
2730 Monterey St. #105
Monterey Business Park
Torrance, CA 90503   Phone: (213)533-4800
Videocassette. 198?. 15 mins. Discover the different jobs available in ground services from air traffic controller to ramp attendant.

★1204★
Career Insights
RMI Media Productions, Inc.
2807 West 47th St.
Shawnee Mission, KS 66205   Phone: (913)262-3974

Videocassette series. 1987. This videotape series describes 50 occupations, including skill requirements and interviews with people employed in these fields. Occupations include: flight service, air transportation/ground services, data processing, carpentry, clerk in banking/insurance/business, cosmetic personal grooming, firefighting, roofing, material handling, photographic processing, plumbing, secretarial services, tool and die operations.

★1205★
Careers in Travel
Solitaire Publishing
216 S. Bungalow Park Ave.
Tampa, FL 33609   Phone: (813)876-0286

Claudine Dervaes. 1988. **Toll-free/Additional Phone Number(s):** 800-226-0286.

★1206★
Flying High in Travel: A Complete Guide to Careers in the Travel Industry
John Wiley and Sons, Inc.
605 3rd Ave.
New York, NY 10158   Phone: (212)850-6000

Karen Rubin. 1986. **Facsimile Number:** (212)850-6088.

★1207★
Getting Down to Business: Travel Agency
American Institutes for Research
PO Box 11131
Palo Alto, CA 94302   Phone: (415)493-3550

Rachel L. Rassen. 1981. **Facsimile Number:** (415)858-0958.

★1208★
How to Get a Job with a Cruise Line: Adventure-Travel-Romance - How to Sail Around the World on Cruise Ships & Get Paid for It
Ticket to Adventure, Inc.
PO Box 47622
St. Petersburg, FL 33743   Phone: (813)544-0066

Mary F. Miller. 1990.

★1209★
How to Open and Run a Money-Making Travel Agency
John Wiley and Sons, Inc.
605 3rd Ave.
New York, NY 10158   Phone: (212)850-6000

Pamela Fremont. 1983. **Facsimile Number:** (212)850-6088.

★1210★
"Passenger Agent" in *Opportunities in Airline Careers* (pp. 68-69)
National Textbook Co.
4255 W. Touhy Ave.
Lincolnwood, IL 60646   Phone: (312)679-5500

Adrian A. Paradis. 1987. Surveys trends in the industry and career opportunities with the airlines including management, sales, customer service, flying, and maintenance. Describes pilots' job duties, working conditions, and basic educational and training requirements.

★1211★
"Reservation Agents" in *Travel Agent* (pp. 167-168)
Arco/Prentice Hall Press
1 Gulf & Western Plaza
New York, NY 10023   Phone: (212)373-8500

Wilma Boyd. 1989. Introduction to the travel business. Covers U.S. and foreign travel, time zones, ticketing, world geography, and airline, railroad, and tour bus connections, and accommodations. Outlines entry-level positions in the airline, car rental, and hospitality industries as well as in travel agencies and related travel services. Explains travel agency operations, sales techniques, and the use of computers in travel services. Gives job hunting advice and sales tips.

★1212★
"Reservation and Information Clerks" in *Opportunities in Travel Careers* (p. 53)
National Textbook Co.
4255 W. Touhy Ave.
Lincolnwood, IL 60646   Phone: (312)679-5500

Robert Scott Milne. 1991. Explores job opportunities in many travel related fields including the airlines, resorts, travel agencies, recreation, and tourism. Covers the work, salaries, educational preparation and training, and advancement possibilities.

★1213★
"Reservation and Transportation Ticket Agent" in Volume 5 of *Career Discovery Encyclopedia* (pp. 150-151)
J.G. Ferguson Publishing Co.
200 W. Monroe
Chicago, IL 60606   Phone: (312)580-5480

E. Russell Primm, editor-in-chief. 1990. Contains two-page articles on 504 occupations. Each article describes job duties, earnings, and educational and training requirements.

★1214★
"Reservation and Transportation Ticket Agents" in Volume 3 of *The Encyclopedia of Careers and Vocational Guidance* (pp. 78-81)
J.G. Ferguson Publishing Co.
200 W. Monroe
Chicago, IL 60606   Phone: (312)580-5480

William E. Hopke, editor-in-chief. Eighth edition, 1990. Four-volume set that profiles 500 occupations and describes job trends in 76 industries. Includes career description, educational requirements, history of the job, methods of entry, advancement, employment outlook, earnings, working conditions, social and psychological factors, and sources of additional information.

★1215★
"Reservation and Transportation Ticket Agents and Travel Clerks" in *Occupational Outlook Handbook* (pp. 261-262)
Superintendent of Documents
U.S. Government Printing Office
Washington, DC 20402   Phone: (202)783-3238

Biennial; latest edition, 1990-91. Encyclopedia of careers describing more than 250 occupations and comprising about 86 percent of all jobs in the economy. Occupations that require lengthy education or training are given the most attention. For each occupation, the handbook describes job duties, working conditions, training, educational preparation, personal qualities, advancement possibilities, job outlook, earnings, and sources of additional information.

Reservation and Transportation Ticket Agents and Travel Clerks

★1216★
"Reservationists and Airline Ticket Agents" in *Jobs! What They Are...Where They Are...What They Pay* (pp. 170-171)
Simon & Schuster, Inc.
Simon & Schuster Bldg.
1230 Avenue of the Americas
New York, NY 10020   Phone: (212)698-7000
Robert O. Snelling and Anne M. Snelling. Revised edition, 1989. Profiles 241 occupations, describing duties and responsibilities, educational preparation, earnings, employment opportunities, training, and qualifications.

★1217★
"Reservations Agents" in *Opportunities in Airline Careers* (pp. 65-67)
National Textbook Co.
4255 W. Touhy Ave.
Lincolnwood, IL 60646   Phone: (312)679-5500
Adrian A. Paradis. 1987. Surveys trends in the industry and career opportunities with the airlines including management, sales, customer service, flying, and maintenance. Describes pilots' job duties, working conditions, and basic educational and training requirements.

★1218★
"The Reservations Department" in *Opportunities in Transportation Careers* (pp. 43-44)
National Textbook Co.
4255 W. Touhy Ave.
Lincolnwood, IL 60646   Phone: (312)679-5500
Adrian A. Paradis. 1988. Describes transportation and related employment in driving occupations, the airlines, merchant marine, and travel services. Covers employment outlook, educational and training requirements, wages, and the work itself, and advantages and disadvantages of transportation careers. Offers job hunting advice.

★1219★
"Reservations Sales Agent" in *Opportunities in Aerospace Careers* (pp. 21-25)
National Textbook Co.
4255 W. Touhy Ave.
Lincolnwood, IL 60646   Phone: (312)679-5500
Wallace R. Maples. 1991. Surveys jobs with the airlines, airports, the government, the military, in manufacturing, and in research and development. Describes educational requirements, working conditions, salaries, employment outlook and licensure.

★1220★
"Reservations Sales Agent" in *Travel Agent* (pp. 164-165)
Arco/Prentice Hall Press
1 Gulf & Western Plaza
New York, NY 10023   Phone: (212)373-8500
Wilma Boyd. 1989. Introduction to the travel business. Covers U.S. and foreign travel, time zones, ticketing, world geography, and airline, railroad, and tour bus connections, and accommodations. Outlines entry-level positions in the airline, car rental, and hospitality industries as well as in travel agencies and related travel services. Explains travel agency operations, sales techniques, and the use of computers in travel services. Gives job hunting advice and sales tips.

★1221★
"Ticket Agent" in *Opportunities in Airline Careers* (pp. 67-68)
National Textbook Co.
4255 W. Touhy Ave.
Lincolnwood, IL 60646   Phone: (312)679-5500
Adrian A. Paradis. 1987. Surveys trends in the industry and career opportunities with the airlines including management, sales, customer service, flying, and maintenance. Describes pilots' job duties, working conditions, and basic educational and training requirements.

★1222★
Ticket Agents
Chronicle Guidance Publications, Inc.
PO Box 1190
Moravia, NY 13118-1190   Phone: (315)497-0330
1991. This career brief describes the nature of the work, working conditions, hours and earnings, education and training, licensure, certification, unions, personal qualifications, social and psychological factors, employment outlook, entry methods, advancement, and related occupations. **Toll-free/Additional Phone Number(s):** 800-622-7284.

★1223★
"Ticket Agents, Reservation Agents, and Clerks" in *Opportunities in Travel Careers* (p. 40-42)
National Textbook Co.
4255 W. Touhy Ave.
Lincolnwood, IL 60646   Phone: (312)679-5500
Robert Scott Milne. 1991. Explores job opportunities in many travel related fields including the airlines, resorts, travel agencies, recreation, and tourism. Covers the work, salaries, educational preparation and training, and advancement possibilities.

★1224★
Travel Career Development
Houghton Mifflin Co.
1 Beacon St.
Boston, MA 02108   Phone: (617)725-5000
Nona Starr. Fourth edition, 1990.

★1225★
Travel Free: How to Start and Succeed in Your Own Travel Consultant Business
Prima Publishing and Communications
4970 Topaz Ave., PO Box 1260
Rocklin, CA 95677   Phone: (916)624-5718
Ben Dominitz. 1984.

★1226★
Travel Industry Career Directory
Career Press, Inc.
62 Beverly Rd.
PO Box 34
Hawthorne, NJ 07507   Phone: (201)427-0229
1989. **Facsimile Number:** (201)427-2037.

★1227★
Travel Industry Guidelines for Employment
Travel Text Associates
12605 State Fair
Detroit, MI 48205   Phone: (313)527-6971
Chris Hoosen. 1990. Part of Travel Agent Training Series.

★1228★
Travel Training Workbook, 1991, Section 1: Introduction to Travel & Geography
Solitaire Publishing
216 S. Bungalow Park Ave.
Tampa, FL 33609　　　　　　　　　　Phone: (813)876-0286
Claudine L. Dervaes. Fifth revised edition, 1990. **Toll-free/Additional Phone Number(s):** 800-226-0286.

★1229★
Video Career Library - Marketing and Sales
Careers, Inc.
1211 10th St., SW
PO Box 135
Largo, FL 34649-0135　　　　　　　　Phone: (813)584-7333
Videocassette. 1990. Part of the Video Career Library covering 165 occupations. Shows actual workers on the job. Includes transportation ticket agents.

Associations

★1230★
Air Transport Association of America (ATA)
1709 New York Ave., NW
Washington, DC 20006　　　　　　　Phone: (202)626-4000
Membership: Airlines engaged in transporting persons, goods, and mail by aircraft between fixed terminals on regular schedules. **Purpose:** Maintains resource library of transportation texts and congressional, administrative, and legal histories of civil aviation. **Publications:** *Air Transport*, annual. ● Also publishes fact sheets, press releases, studies, speeches, testimonies, and references.

Test Guides

★1231★
Ticket Agent
National Learning Corp.
212 Michael Dr.
Syosset, NY 11791　　　　　　　　　Phone: (516)921-8888
Jack Rudman. Part of the Career Examination Series No. 1. All examination guides in this series contain questions with answers. **Facsimile Number:** (516)921-8743. **Toll-free/Additional Phone Number(s):** 800-645-6337.

Basic Reference Guides and Handbooks

★1232★
Business of Travel: Agency Operations & Administration
Macmillian Publishing Co.
866 3rd Ave.
New York, NY 10022　　　　　　　　Phone: (212)702-2000
Dennis L. Foster. 1990.

★1233★
Communication Skills
Travel Text Associates
12605 State Fair
Detroit, MI 48205　　　　　　　　　Phone: (313)527-6971
Chris Hoosen. 1989. Part of Travel Agent Training Series.

★1234★
Condominiums for Rent in Resort Areas Database
Information Resource Consultants
12015 Manchester Rd., Ste. 150
St. Louis, MO 63131　　　　　　　　Phone: (314)822-7072
Information on over 1,000 condominiums available for rent in resort areas.

★1235★
Consolidators Handbook: Guide to Low Cost International Travel
Hammond Publishing
PO Box 12924
Gainseville, FL 32604　　　　　　　Phone: (904)378-8780
Kriss Hammond, President, editor. Annual, January. Companies worldwide that offer discount airfare, hotel packages, and tour packages for international travel. Entries include: Company, location, phone. Arrangement: Geographical.

★1236★
Corporate Travel—Directory Issue
Gralla Publications
1515 Broadway, Ste. 3201
New York, NY 10036　　　　　　　　Phone: (212)869-1300
Laurie Berger, editor. Annual, January. Approximately 2,000 airlines, hotels, and other businesses offering travel packages to corporations. Entries include: Company name, address, phone. Arrangement: Geographical. **Facsimile Number:** (212)302-6273.

★1237★
Hotel & Travel Index
500 Plaza Dr.
Secaucus, NJ 07096　　　　　　　　Phone: (201)902-1600
Melinda Bush, Publisher. Quarterly. Magazine serving as a worldwide hotel directory. **Facsimile Number:** (201)319-1628.

Periodicals

★1238★
Air Transport
Air Transport Association of America (ATA)
1709 New York Ave., NW
Washington, DC 20006　　　　　　　Phone: (202)626-4000
Annual.

★1239★
ARTAFACTS
Association of Retail Travel Agents (ARTA)
1745 Jefferson Davis Pkwy., Ste. 300
Arlington, VA 22202-3402　　　　　　Phone: (703)553-7777
Monthly. Reviews developments in the travel industry for retail travel agents. Covers topics such as ethics, tour operations, transportation services, educational opportunities, commissions, and political action in pertinent issues. Includes chapter and association news. **Toll-free/Additional Phone Number(s):** 800-969-6069 **Facsimile Number:** (703)486-0228.

★1240★
Bulletin Voyages
Editions Acra Ltee.
Succursale E.
C.P. 85
Montreal, PQ, Canada H2T 3A5　　　Phone: (514)287-9773
Etienne Ozan-Groulx, Editor. Weekly. Travel trade magazine (French). **Facsimile Number:** (514)842-6180.

Reservation and Transportation Ticket Agents and Travel Clerks

★1241★
CTO News for Travel Agents
Caribbean Tourism Organization (CTO)
20 E. 46th St.
New York, NY 10017   Phone: (212)682-0435
6/yr. Instructs travel agents on how to effectively sell the Caribbean for greater profit. Reviews developments in Caribbean tourism, providing information on air flights, hotels, restaurants, and other attractions. Recurring features include editorials, news of members, and a calendar of events. **Facsimile Number:** (212)697-4258.

★1242★
European Edition OAG Travel Planner Hotel & Motel RedBook
Official Airline Guides
2000 Clearwater Dr.
Oak Brook, IL 60521   Phone: (708)574-6000
Richard A. Nelson, Publisher. Quarterly. Directory containing information on travel to and through Europe, including country basics, city destination data, hotel/motel listings, airport diagrams, city and country maps, and reservation directories. **Facsimile Number:** (708)574-6667.

★1243★
ICTA News
Institute of Certified Travel Agents (ICTA)
148 Linden St.
PO Box 56
Wellesley, MA 02181-0503   Phone: (617)237-0280
Editor(s): Dawn Ringel. 10/yr. Covers the educational activities of the Institute, which grants the Certified Travel Counselor (CTC) designation to travel industry personnel. Offers special news stories on topics relevant to the travel industry. Recurring features include news of members, management tips, and names of newly certified agents. **Toll-free/Additional Phone Number(s):** 800-542-4282 **Facsimile Number:** (617)237-3860.

★1244★
Lodging Briefing
Walter Mathews Associates, Inc.
28 W. 38th St.
New York, NY 10018   Phone: (212)921-4314
Editor(s): Walter Mathews. 10/yr. Remarks on industry developments, consumer trends, and economic performance in the area of travel. Carries information to help travel agents increase their sales, develop their promotional techniques, and to better manage both their employees and finances. Recurring features include travel price indexes. **Facsimile Number:** (212)719-9382.

★1245★
Meetings & Incentive Travel
Maclean Hunter Ltd.
777 Bay St.
Toronto, ON, Canada M5W 1A7   Phone: (416)596-2697
Tommi Lloyd, Editor. 7x/yr. Magazine for corporate meeting planners, incentive travel executives, and travel agents. **Facsimile Number:** (416)596-5810.

★1246★
Motel/Hotel Insider
Magna Publishing
2718 Dryden
Madison, WI 53704   Phone: (608)249-2455
Editor(s): Robert Reis. Weekly. Covers motel/hotel management, travel and vacation trends, business travel, new products and services for the hospitality market, motel/hotel chains, and trends and changes in the lodging industry.

★1247★
North American Edition OAG Business Travel Planner
Official Airline Guides
2000 Clearwater Dr.
Oak Brook, IL 60521   Phone: (708)574-6000
Richard A. Nelson, Publisher. Quarterly. Official lodging directory of the American Hotel and Motel Association includes city destination information, hotel listings, airport diagrams, city, metro, resort area and country maps, travel basics, and reservation directories. **Facsimile Number:** (708)574-6667.

★1248★
Official Airline Guide, Worldwide Edition
Official Airline Guides
2000 Clearwater Dr.
Oak Brook, IL 60521   Phone: (708)574-6000
Richard A. Nelson, Publisher. Monthly. Guide containing schedules of airlines operating throughout the world (excluding North America and Caribbean), published as a service for the airlines, travel agents, and volume users of air transportation. **Facsimile Number:** (708)574-6667.

★1249★
PATA Travel News (Americas Edition)
Baxter Publications, Inc.
310 Dupont St.
Toronto, ON, Canada M5R 1V9   Phone: (416)968-7252
Timothy Baxter, Editor. Monthly. Magazine for the travel trade, emphasizing travel to the Pacific-Asia region. Includes news from the Pacific Asia Travel Association and its 35 chapters in the Americas.

★1250★
Recommend
Worth International Communications Corp.
5979 NW, 151 St., Ste. 120
Miami Lakes, FL 33014   Phone: (305)828-0123
Hal Herman, Pres./Editor-in-Chief. Monthly. Travel industry magazine. **Facsimile Number:** (305)826-6950.

★1251★
Tour & Travel News
CMP Publications, Inc.
600 Community Dr.
Manhasset, NY 11030   Phone: (516)365-4600
Linda Ball, Editor. Weekly Magazine for the travel industry, covering issues of interest to travel agents. ; Jerry Landress, Publisher; Irwin Barnett, Advertising Mgr. **Facsimile Number:** (516)562-5472.

★1252★
TOURISME
Publications TRANSCONTINENTAL Inc.
465, rue St-Jean, 9e etage
Montreal, PQ, Canada H2Y 3S4   Phone: (514)842-6491
Michel Villeneuve, Editor. Weekly. Magazine (tabloid) serving travel industry professionals (French). **Facsimile Number:** (514)842-8557.

★1253★
Travel Agent Magazine
Universal Media
801 2nd Ave.
New York, NY 10017   Phone: (212)370-5050
Irwin M Barnett, Publisher. 2x/wk. Travel industry magazine. **Facsimile Number:** (212)370-4491.

★1254★
Travel Courier East
Baxter Publishing Co.
310 Dupont St.
Toronto, ON, Canada M5R 1V9   Phone: (416)968-7252
Rob Wilson, Editor. Weekly. Magazine (tabloid) serving the travel industry. **Facsimile Number:** (416)968-2377.

★1255★
Travel Digest
1654 SW 28th Ave.
Fort Lauderdale, FL 33312-3949   Phone: (305)792-2234
Jurgen Hartmann, Publisher. Monthly. Magazine for travel agents.

★1256★
Travel News
Travel Agents International, Inc.
111 2nd Ave. NE, 15th Fl.
Box 31005
St. Petersburg, FL 33731-8905   Phone: (813)895-8241
Roger E. Block, Publisher. Monthly Travel publication.

★1257★
Travel People Magazine
CMP Publications, Inc.
600 Community Dr.
Manhasset, NY 11030   Phone: (516)562-5000
Jerry Landress, Group Publisher. Monthly. Lifestyle magazine targeted for travel agents. **Facsimile Number:** (516)562-5472.

★1258★
Travel Trade
15 W. 44th St.
New York, NY 10036   Phone: (212)730-6600
Joel M. Abels, Editor and Publisher. Weekly. Travel industry magazine. **Facsimile Number:** (212)730-7137.

★1259★
Travel Weekly
Reed Travel Group
500 Plaza Dr.
Secaucus, NJ 07096   Phone: (201)902-2000
Alan Fredericks, Editor. 2x/wk. (Mon. and Thurs.). Travel industry magazine. **Facsimile Number:** (201)319-1947.

Meetings and Conventions

★1260★
American Society of Travel Agents World Travel Congress
American Society of Travel Agents
1101 King St.
Alexandria, VA 22314   Phone: (703)739-2782
1992; Sep. 20-26; Cairo, Egypt • 1993; Nov. 07-11; Lisbon, Portugal • 1995; Nov. 12-18. **Facsimile Number:** (703)684-8319.

★1261★
International Travel Industry Expo (ITIX)
The Interface Group, Inc.
300 1st Ave.
Needham, MA 02194   Phone: (617)449-6600
1992. **Facsimile Number:** (617)449-6953.

Mail Clerks and Messengers

Mail clerks serve as the link between the U.S. Postal Service and individual offices and workers. They sort and deliver incoming mail, prepare outgoing mail for delivery to the post office, and contact delivery services to handle important letters or parcels. Mail clerks also operate various machines that facilitate the mailing process. Messengers deliver items for messenger or courier services, as well as private employers such as law firms or financial institutions. Messengers drive vehicles, ride bicycles, or travel by foot.

$alaries

Salaries for mail clerks and messengers are listed below.

Mail clerks	$213-354/week
Messengers	$198-385/week
Beginning messengers in manufacturing, transportation, and utilities	$206/week
Experienced messengers	$233-270/week

Employment Outlook

Growth rate until the year 2000: More slowly than average.

Mail Clerks and Messengers

Career Guides

★1262★
"Mail Clerk" in *Administration, Business, and Office*, Volume 1 of *Career Information Center* (pp. 55-56)
Glencoe/Macmillan
15319 Chatsworth St.
Mission Hills, CA 91345   Phone: (818)898-1391
Richard Lidz and Dale Anderson, editorial directors. Fourth edition, 1990. For 600 occupations, describes job duties, entry-level requirements, education and training needed, advancement possibilities, employment outlook, earnings and benefits. The set is divided into 12 volumes. Each volume includes jobs related under a broad career field. Volume 13 is the index. **Facsimile Number:** 818-365-5489.

★1263★
Mail Clerk, Office
Careers, Inc.
PO Box 135
Largo, FL 34649-0135   Phone: (813)584-7333
1991. Two-page job guide card describing duties, working conditions, personal qualifications, training, earnings and hours, employment outlook, places of employment, related careers and where to write for more information.

★1264★
"Mail Clerks and Messengers" in *Occupational Outlook Handbook* (pp. 262-263)
Superintendent of Documents
U.S. Government Printing Office
Washington, DC 20402   Phone: (202)783-3238
Biennial; latest edition, 1990-91. Encyclopedia of careers describing more than 250 occupations and comprising about 86 percent of all jobs in the economy. Occupations that require lengthy education or training are given the most attention. For each occupation, the handbook describes job duties, working conditions, training, educational preparation, personal qualities, advancement possibilities, job outlook, earnings, and sources of additional information.

★1265★
Mail Clerks (Any Industry)
Chronicle Guidance Publications, Inc.
PO Box 1190
Moravia, NY 13118-1190   Phone: (315)497-0330
1989. This career brief describes the nature of the work, working conditions, hours and earnings, education and training, licensure, certification, unions, personal qualifications, social and psychological factors, employment outlook, entry methods, advancement, and related occupations. **Toll-free/Additional Phone Number(s):** 800-622-7284.

★1266★
"Messenger Service Worker" in *Administration, Business, and Office*, Volume 1 of *Career Information Center* (pp. 58-60)
Glencoe/Macmillan
15319 Chatsworth St.
Mission Hills, CA 91345   Phone: (818)898-1391
Richard Lidz and Dale Anderson, editorial directors. Fourth edition, 1990. For 600 occupations, describes job duties, entry-level requirements, education and training needed, advancement possibilities, employment outlook, earnings and benefits. The set is divided into 12 volumes. Each volume includes jobs related under a broad career field. Volume 13 is the index. **Facsimile Number:** 818-365-5489.

★1267★
"Office Mail Clerk" in *Occu-Facts: Information on 565 Careers in Outline Form* (p. 12.35)
Careers, Inc.
P.O. Box 135
1211 Tenth St., S.W.
Largo, FL 33640   Phone: (813)584-7333
Elizabeth Handville. Biennial, 1989-90 edition. Each one-page occupational profile describes duties, working conditions, physical surroundings and demands, aptitudes, temperament, educational requirements, employment outlook, earnings, and places of employment.

Associations

★1268★
American Postal Workers Union (APWU)
1300 L St. NW
Washington, DC 20005   Phone: (202)842-4200
Membership: Divisions: Clerk; Maintenance; Motor Vehicle; Political Action; Special Delivery Messengers; Support Services. **Publications:** *American Postal Worker*, monthly.

★1269★
Messenger Courier Association of the Americas (MCAA)
10015 Main St.
Fairfax, VA 22031   Phone: (703)385-1389
Membership: Trade organization of local and international messenger courier companies. **Purpose:** Addresses issues facing the industry, including municipal traffic ordinances that impede industry operations. Works to establish driver pools and to develop centralized core computer service bureaus for smaller

★1270★
National Postal Mail Handlers Union (NPMHU)
1 Thomas Circle NW, Ste. 525
Washington, DC 20005   Phone: (202)833-9095

courier companies. Provides training, discount purchasing programs, and group insurance coverage. Bestows awards; conducts educational programs; compiles statistics.

★1270★
National Postal Mail Handlers Union (NPMHU)
1 Thomas Circle NW, Ste. 525
Washington, DC 20005   Phone: (202)833-9095
Operates as a division of Laborers' International Union of North America.

Test Guides

★1271★
Mail & Supply Clerk
National Learning Corp.
212 Michael Dr.
Syosset, NY 11791   Phone: (516)921-8888
Jack Rudman. Part of the Career Examination Series No. 1. All examination guides in this series contain questions with answers. **Facsimile Number:** (516)921-8743. **Toll-free/Additional Phone Number(s):** 800-645-6337.

★1272★
Mail Clerk
National Learning Corp.
212 Michael Dr.
Syosset, NY 11791   Phone: (516)921-8888
Jack Rudman. Part of the Career Examination Series No. 1. All examination guides in this series contain questions with answers. **Facsimile Number:** (516)921-8743. **Toll-free/Additional Phone Number(s):** 800-645-6337.

★1273★
Messenger
National Learning Corp.
212 Michael Dr.
Syosset, NY 11791   Phone: (516)921-8888
Jack Rudman. Part of the Career Examination Series No. 1. All examination guides in this series contain questions with answers. **Facsimile Number:** (516)921-8743. **Toll-free/Additional Phone Number(s):** 800-645-6337.

★1274★
Principal Mail & Supply Clerk
National Learning Corp.
212 Michael Dr.
Syosset, NY 11791   Phone: (516)921-8888
Jack Rudman. Part of the Career Examination Series No. 1. All examination guides in this series contain questions with answers. **Facsimile Number:** (516)921-8743. **Toll-free/Additional Phone Number(s):** 800-645-6337.

★1275★
Senior Clerical Series
Prentice Hall Press
Simon & Schuster Inc.
200 Old Tappan Rd.
Old Tappan, NJ 07675   Phone: (800)223-2348
Hy Hammer. Fourth edition, 1983. Complete test preparation for the following senior grade positions: clerk, typist, stenographer, account clerk, file clerk, statistics clerk, stenographer (law), mail and supply clerk, and stores clerk.

★1276★
Senior Mail Clerk
National Learning Corp.
212 Michael Dr.
Syosset, NY 11791   Phone: (516)921-8888
Jack Rudman. Part of the Career Examination Series No. 1. All examination guides in this series contain questions with answers. **Facsimile Number:** (516)921-8743. **Toll-free/Additional Phone Number(s):** 800-645-6337.

Periodicals

★1277★
The American Postal Worker
American Postal Workers Union, AFL-CIO
1300 L St. NW
Washington, DC 20005   Phone: (202)842-4200
Moe Biller, Editor. Monthly. AFL-CIO postal labor. **Facsimile Number:** (202)842-4297.

Meetings and Conventions

★1278★
Messenger Courier Association of the Americas Conference (MCAA)
10015 Main St.
Fairfax, VA 22031   Phone: (703)385-1389
Frequency: Annual, with exhibits. **Facsimile Number:** (703)273-0456.

★1279★
National Postal Mail Handlers Union (NPMHU)
1 Thomas Circle NW, Ste. 525
Washington, DC 20005   Phone: (202)833-9095
Frequency: Quadrennial assembly - next 1992.

Material Recording, Scheduling, Dispatching, and Distributing Occupations

Material recording, scheduling, dispatching, and distributing occupations involve coordinating, expediting, and keeping track of materials being sent or received. Some dispatchers also receive requests for service, as in the case of medical emergencies, and they coordinate the movement of the vehicles involved. Shipping and receiving clerks keep track of materials being transferred between businesses and their suppliers and customers. Stock clerks receive and issue merchandise or supplies and maintain an inventory of stock. These occupations are found primarily in wholesale and retail establishments, manufacturing, transportation, communications, utilities, and state and local government.

$alaries

Salaries for workers in material recording, scheduling, dispatching, and distributing occupations vary by occupation and industry setting, with dispatchers earning slightly more than average.

Lowest 10 percent	$10,000/year or less
Median	$18,000/year
Top 10 percent	More than $31,000/year
Dispatchers	$18,900/year
Traffic, shipping, receiving, and stock clerks	$16,000-17,000/year

Employment Outlook

Growth rate until the year 2000: Average.

Material Recording, Scheduling, Dispatching, and Distributing Occupations

Career Guides

★1280★
"Material Recording, Scheduling, Dispatching, and Distributing Occupations" in *Occupational Outlook Handbook* (pp. 263-265)
Superintendent of Documents
U.S. Government Printing Office
Washington, DC 20402   Phone: (202)783-3238
Biennial; latest edition, 1990-91. Encyclopedia of careers describing more than 250 occupations and comprising about 86 percent of all jobs in the economy. Occupations that require lengthy education or training are given the most attention. For each occupation, the handbook describes job duties, working conditions, training, educational preparation, personal qualities, advancement possibilities, job outlook, earnings, and sources of additional information.

Test Guides

★1281★
Assistant Stockman
National Learning Corp.
212 Michael Dr.
Syosset, NY 11791   Phone: (516)921-8888
Jack Rudman. Part of the Career Examination Series No. 1. All examination guides in this series contain questions with answers. **Facsimile Number:** (516)921-8743. **Toll-free/Additional Phone Number(s):** 800-645-6337.

★1282★
Stockroom Worker
National Learning Corp.
212 Michael Dr.
Syosset, NY 11791   Phone: (516)921-8888
Jack Rudman. Part of the Career Examination Series No. 1. All examination guides in this series contain questions with answers. **Facsimile Number:** (516)921-8743. **Toll-free/Additional Phone Number(s):** 800-645-6337.

★1283★
Warehouseman
National Learning Corp.
212 Michael Dr.
Syosset, NY 11791   Phone: (516)921-8888
Jack Rudman. Part of the Career Examination Series No. 1. All examination guides in this series contain questions with answers. **Facsimile Number:** (516)921-8743. **Toll-free/Additional Phone Number(s):** 800-645-6337.

Periodicals

★1284★
Supply House Times
Horton Publishing Co.
7574 N. Lincoln Ave.
Skokie, IL 60077   Phone: (708)677-2707
Greg Cassel, Editor. Monthly. Trade magazine for wholesalers in plumbing, heating, cooling, piping, and water systems. Areas of major emphasis include: warehousing, materials handling, inventory control, accounting, data processing, merchandising, salesmanship and general management. **Facsimile Number:** (708)677-5003.

Dispatchers

Dispatchers respond to requests for service and coordinate the appropriate action depending on where they work. Public safety dispatchers, including police, fire, and ambulance dispatchers, are usually the first people called in an emergency. They quickly decide the type and number of units needed and send them to the scene. Truck dispatchers coordinate the movement of trucks and freight between cities. Other dispatchers working in transportation coordinate the movement of trains, buses, taxicabs, or tow trucks. All dispatchers keep records, logs, and schedules of the calls they receive and the actions they take.

$alaries

The median salary for dispatchers is $18,900/year but varies by industry setting.

Taxicab dispatchers	$7,000/year
Bus and emergency vehicle road dispatchers	$11,000/year
Police, fire, and ambulance dispatchers	$17,000/year

Employment Outlook

Growth rate until the year 2000: Average.

Dispatchers

Career Guides

★1285★
Airline Dispatcher
Careers, Inc.
PO Box 135
Largo, FL 34649-0135   Phone: (813)584-7333
1992. Eight-page brief offering the definition, history, duties, working conditions, personal qualifications, educational requirements, earnings, hours, employment outlook, advancement possibilities, and related occupations.

★1286★
"Airline Dispatcher" in *Occu-Facts: Information on 565 Careers in Outline Form* (p. 10.22)
Careers, Inc.
P.O. Box 135
1211 Tenth St., S.W.
Largo, FL 33640   Phone: (813)584-7333
Elizabeth Handville. Biennial, 1989-90 edition. Each one-page occupational profile describes duties, working conditions, physical surroundings and demands, aptitudes, temperament, educational requirements, employment outlook, earnings, and places of employment.

★1287★
"Airline Dispatcher" in *Transportation*, Volume 12 of *Career Information Center* (pp. 122-124)
Glencoe/Macmillan
15319 Chatsworth St.
Mission Hills, CA 91345   Phone: (818)898-1391
Richard Lidz and Dale Anderson, editorial directors. Fourth edition, 1990. For 600 occupations, describes job duties, entry-level requirements, education and training needed, advancement possibilities, employment outlook, earnings and benefits. The set is divided into 12 volumes. Each volume includes jobs related under a broad career field. Volume 13 is the index. **Facsimile Number:** 818-365-5489.

★1288★
Airline Dispatchers
Chronicle Guidance Publications, Inc.
PO Box 1190
Moravia, NY 13118-1190   Phone: (315)497-0330
1991. This career brief describes the nature of the work, working conditions, hours and earnings, education and training, licensure, certification, unions, personal qualifications, social and psychological factors, employment outlook, entry methods, advancement, and related occupations. **Toll-free/Additional Phone Number(s):** 800-622-7284.

★1289★
"Airplane Dispatchers" in Volume 3 of *The Encyclopedia of Careers and Vocational Guidance* (pp. 725-728)
J.G. Ferguson Publishing Co.
200 W. Monroe
Chicago, IL 60606   Phone: (312)580-5480
William E. Hopke, editor-in-chief. Eighth edition, 1990. Four-volume set that profiles 500 occupations and describes job trends in 76 industries. Includes career description, educational requirements, history of the job, methods of entry, advancement, employment outlook, earnings, working conditions, social and psychological factors, and sources of additional information.

★1290★
"Dispatcher" in *Careers in Trucking* (pp. 24-26)
Rosen Publishing Group, Inc.
29 E. 21st St.
New York, NY 10010   Phone: (212)777-3017
Donald D. Schauer. 1987. Describes employment in the trucking industry including driving, operations, sales, and administration. Covers qualifications, training, future outlook, and salaries. Offers career planning and job hunting advice.

★1291★
"Dispatcher and Communications" in *Opportunities in Fire Protection Services* (pp. 28-29)
National Textbook Co.
4255 W. Touhy Ave.
Lincolnwood, IL 60646   Phone: (312)679-5500
Ronny J. Coleman. 1990. Explores firefighting and related jobs with not only local fire departments but also with state and federal governments and private fire departments, fire sprinkler and fire equipment manufacturing companies, and insurance companies. Covers personal qualifications, educational preparation and training, advancement possibilities, and salaries. Offers job hunting advice.

★1292★
"Dispatcher" in *120 Careers in the Health Care Field* (p. 97)
U.S. Directory Service, Publishers
PO Box 68-1700
655 N.W. 128th St.
Miami, FL 33168   Phone: (305)769-1700
Stanley Alperin. Second edition, 1989. Each occupational profile covers job functions and responsibilities, work locations, training requirements, certification, and salaries. Lists community colleges, universities, vocational-technical schools, and other educational institutions that provide accredited training programs.

★1293★
"Dispatchers" in *Occupational Outlook Handbook* (pp. 265-266)
Superintendent of Documents
U.S. Government Printing Office
Washington, DC 20402　　　　　　　Phone: (202)783-3238

Biennial; latest edition, 1990-91. Encyclopedia of careers describing more than 250 occupations and comprising about 86 percent of all jobs in the economy. Occupations that require lengthy education or training are given the most attention. For each occupation, the handbook describes job duties, working conditions, training, educational preparation, personal qualities, advancement possibilities, job outlook, earnings, and sources of additional information.

★1294★
"Flight Dispatcher" in *Opportunities in Airline Careers* (pp. 91-93)
National Textbook Co.
4255 W. Touhy Ave.
Lincolnwood, IL 60646　　　　　　　Phone: (312)679-5500

Adrian A. Paradis. 1987. Surveys trends in the industry and career opportunities with the airlines including management, sales, customer service, flying, and maintenance. Describes pilots' job duties, working conditions, and basic educational and training requirements.

★1295★
"Flight Dispatcher" in *Opportunities in Transportation Careers* (pp. 39-40)
National Textbook Co.
4255 W. Touhy Ave.
Lincolnwood, IL 60646　　　　　　　Phone: (312)679-5500

Adrian A. Paradis. 1988. Describes transportation and related employment in driving occupations, the airlines, merchant marine, and travel services. Covers employment outlook, educational and training requirements, wages, and the work itself, and advantages and disadvantages of transportation careers. Offers job hunting advice.

★1296★
Lifeline—Dispatcher Communications
MTI Teleprograms, Inc.
108 Wilmot Rd.
Deerfield, IL 60015-9990　　　　　　Phone: (708)940-1260

Videocassette. 1977. 16 mins. Designed to impress upon dispatchers the importance and complexity of the police communications job.

★1297★
Radio Dispatchers
Chronicle Guidance Publications, Inc.
PO Box 1190
Moravia, NY 13118-1190　　　　　　Phone: (315)497-0330

1989. This career brief describes the nature of the work, working conditions, hours and earnings, education and training, licensure, certification, unions, personal qualifications, social and psychological factors, employment outlook, entry methods, advancement, and related occupations. **Toll-free/Additional Phone Number(s):** 800-622-7284.

★1298★
"Railroad Signaler, Telegrapher, Telephoner, and Dispatcher" in *Transportation* (pp. 57-61)
Franklin Watts, Inc.
387 Park Avenue, S.
New York, NY 10016　　　　　　　Phone: (212)686-7070

Marjorie Rittenberg Schulz. 1990. Surveys the transportation industry including air, water, and rail services. Provides job description, training, salary, and employment outlook. Offers job hunting advice.

★1299★
State Police Dispatcher
Vocational Biographies, Inc.
PO Box 31, Dept. VF10
Sauk Centre, MN 56378　　　　　　Phone: (612)352-6516

1989. This pamphlet profiles a person working in the job. Includes information about job duties, working conditions, places of employment, educational preparation, labor market outlook, and salaries. **Toll-free/Additional Phone Number(s):** 800-255-0752.

★1300★
"Taxi Dispatcher" in *Travel & Tourism* (pp. 45-49)
Franklin Watts, Inc.
387 Park Avenue, S.
New York, NY 10016　　　　　　　Phone: (212)686-7070

Marjorie Rittenberg Schulz. 1990. Surveys employment opportunities in the travel and tourism industry. Provides job description, educational preparation, training, salary, employment outlook, and sources of additional information. Offers job hunting advice.

★1301★
"Truck and Bus Dispatcher" in *Transportation*, Volume 12 of *Career Information Center* (pp. 116-118)
Glencoe/Macmillan
15319 Chatsworth St.
Mission Hills, CA 91345　　　　　　Phone: (818)898-1391

Richard Lidz and Dale Anderson, editorial directors. Fourth edition, 1990. For 600 occupations, describes job duties, entry-level requirements, education and training needed, advancement possibilities, employment outlook, earnings and benefits. The set is divided into 12 volumes. Each volume includes jobs related under a broad career field. Volume 13 is the index. **Facsimile Number:** 818-365-5489.

Associations

★1302★
American Train Dispatchers Association (ATDA)
The Train Dispatcher Bldg.
1401 S. Harlem Ave.
Berwyn, IL 60402　　　　　　　　　Phone: (708)795-5656

Publications: *The Train Dispatcher*, quarterly. **Facsimile Number:** (708)795-0832.

★1303★
Associated Public-Safety Communications Officers (APCO)
2040 S. Ridgewood
South Daytona, FL 32119　　　　　　Phone: (904)322-2500

Membership: Employees of municipal, county, state, and federal public safety agencies such as 911 emergency phone line, fire, police, highway maintenance, forestry-conservation, civil defense, special emergency, and local government; individuals who sell public safety communication products. **Purpose:** Objectives are to: foster the development and progress of the art of public safety communications; ensure greater cooperation in the correlation of the work and activities of the several town, county, state, and federal agencies; promote cooperation between these agencies and the Federal Communications Commission. Conducts surveys, management and training seminars, and grant-in-aid projects with federal funding agencies. Offers 40-hour and 80-hour training courses for telecommunications and public safety dispatchers; provides

Dispatchers

information service. According to APCO, this is the largest and oldest two-way land mobile radio group in the U.S. and holds the largest annual showing of public safety equipment in the world. Bestows awards; compiles statistics. **Publications:** *APCO Bulletin*, 11/year. • *APCO Membership Directory*, annual. • *APCO Reports*, monthly. • Also publishes operating procedure manual, police telecommunications systems text, coordinators manual, and ten signal cards.

★1304★
CWA/UTW Bargaining Council (Telecommunications)
20525 Center Ridge Rd., Ste. 420
Cleveland, OH 44116   Phone: (216)333-0114
Provides general information and earnings on dispatchers. Founded in 1990 by the merger of Communication Workers of America (founded 1938) and United Telegraph Workers (founded 1902 and formerly, 1968, Commercial Telegraphers' Union). Members: 2500. Local Groups: 40. AFL-CIO. Convention/Meeting: triennial - next 1992.

★1305★
International Municipal Signal Association (IMSA)
1115 N. Main St.
PO Box 539
Newark, NY 14513   Phone: (315)331-2182
Membership: Professional organization of government officials responsible for municipal signaling, fire alarms, traffic signals, radio communication, street lighting, electric inspection, emergency medical service, signs and marking, and other related services. **Purpose:** Sponsors technical seminars. Maintains more than 20 committees including: Emergency Medical Services; Exhibits; Fire/Emergency Communications; Standardization; Street Lighting. **Publications:** *IMSA Journal*, semimonthly. • *IMSA Membership Roster*, annual. • Also publishes *Traffic Signal Manual of Installation and Maintenance Procedures*, *Fire Alarm Manual*, *Microprocessor Manual for Traffic Signals*, and *Wire and Cable Specifications*. **Facsimile Number:** (315)331-8205.

★1306★
Service Employees International Union (SEIU)
1313 L St. NW
Washington, DC 20005   Phone: (202)898-3200
Membership: AFL-CIO; Canadian Labour Congress. **Publications:** *Union*, bimonthly. • *Update*, quarterly.

Standards/Certification Agencies

Police, fire, and ambulance dispatching jobs generally are governed by state or local government civil service regulations. Candidates for these jobs may have to pass written, oral, and performance tests. Although there are no mandatory licensing or certification requirements, some states require that public safety dispatchers possess a certificate to work on a state network such as the Police Information Network. Voluntary certification programs are offered by both APCO and the International Municipal Signal Association.

★1307★
International Municipal Signal Association (IMSA)
1115 N. Main St.
PO Box 539
Newark, NY 14513   Phone: (315)331-2182
Maintains more than 20 committees including Standardization.

Test Guides

★1308★
Assistant Train Dispatcher
National Learning Corp.
212 Michael Dr.
Syosset, NY 11791   Phone: (516)921-8888
Jack Rudman. Part of the Career Examination Series No. 1. All examination guides in this series contain questions with answers. **Facsimile Number:** (516)921-8743. **Toll-free/Additional Phone Number(s):** 800-645-6337.

★1309★
Fire Alarm Dispatcher
National Learning Corp.
212 Michael Dr.
Syosset, NY 11791   Phone: (516)921-8888
Jack Rudman. Part of the Career Examination Series No. 1. All examination guides in this series contain questions with answers. **Facsimile Number:** (516)921-8743. **Toll-free/Additional Phone Number(s):** 800-645-6337.

★1310★
Police Dispatcher
National Learning Corp.
212 Michael Dr.
Syosset, NY 11791   Phone: (516)921-8888
Jack Rudman. Part of the Career Examination Series No. 1. All examination guides in this series contain questions with answers. **Facsimile Number:** (516)921-8743. **Toll-free/Additional Phone Number(s):** 800-645-6337.

★1311★
Public Safety Dispatcher
National Learning Corp.
212 Michael Dr.
Syosset, NY 11791   Phone: (516)921-8888
Jack Rudman. Part of the Career Examination Series No. 1. All examination guides in this series contain questions with answers. **Facsimile Number:** (516)921-8743. **Toll-free/Additional Phone Number(s):** 800-645-6337.

★1312★
Train Dispatcher
National Learning Corp.
212 Michael Dr.
Syosset, NY 11791   Phone: (516)921-8888
Jack Rudman. Part of the Career Examination Series No. 1. All examination guides in this series contain questions with answers. **Facsimile Number:** (516)921-8743. **Toll-free/Additional Phone Number(s):** 800-645-6337.

Awards, Scholarships, Grants, and Fellowships

★1313★
Telecommunication Officer of the Year
Associated Public-Safety Communications Officers
2040 S. Ridgewood
South Daytona, FL 32119   Phone: (904)322-2500
Bestowed to recognize excellence in performance of duties. Local chapters submit nominees; awarded annually.

Basic Reference Guides and Handbooks

★1314★
Fire Alarm Manual (IMSA)
International Municipal Signal Association (IMSA)
1115 N. Main St.
PO Box 539
Newark, NY 14513　　　　　Phone: (315)331-2182

★1315★
Microprocessor Manual for Traffic Signals (IMSA)
International Municipal Signal Association (IMSA)
1115 N. Main St.
PO Box 539
Newark, NY 14513　　　　　Phone: (315)331-2182

★1316★
Traffic Signal Manual of Installation and Maintenance Procedures (IMSA)
International Municipal Signal Association (IMSA)
1115 N. Main St.
PO Box 539
Newark, NY 14513　　　　　Phone: (315)331-2182

Periodicals

★1317★
APCO BULLETIN
APCO, Inc.
2040 S. Ridgewood
South Daytona, FL 32119　　　Phone: (904)322-2500
Alan Chase, Editor. Monthly. Public safety communications magazine. **Facsimile Number:** (904)322-2502.

★1318★
APCO Reports (APCO)
Associated Public-Safety Communications Officers (APCO)
PO Box 669
New Smyrna Beach, FL 32170　Phone: (904)427-3461
Monthly.

★1319★
IMSA Journal (IMSA)
International Municipal Signal Association (IMSA)
1115 N. Main St.
PO Box 539
Newark, NY 14513　　　　　Phone: (315)331-2182
Semimonthly.

★1320★
SEW Update (SEIU)
Service Employees International Union (SEIU)
1313 L St. NW
Washington, DC 20005　　　Phone: (202)898-3200
Quarterly.

★1321★
Union (SEIU)
Service Employees International Union (SEIU)
1313 L St. NW
Washington, DC 20005　　　Phone: (202)898-3200
Bimonthly.

Meetings and Conventions

★1322★
American Train Dispatchers Association (ATDA)
The Train Dispatcher Bldg.
1401 S. Harlem Ave.
Berwyn, IL 60402　　　　　Phone: (708)795-5656
Frequency: Quadrennial general assembly is held, to be held next in 1996.

★1323★
Associated Public-Safety Communications Officers (APCO)
PO Box 669
New Smyrna Beach, FL 32170　Phone: (904)427-3461
1992; Aug. 10-14; Seattle, WA • 1993; Aug. 7-12; New Orleans, LA • 1994; August; Seattle, WA.

★1324★
Service Employees International Union (SEIU)
1313 L St. NW
Washington, DC 20005　　　Phone: (202)898-3200
Frequency: Quadrennial.

Other Sources of Information

★1325★
Wire and Cable Specifications (IMSA)
International Municipal Signal Association (IMSA)
1115 N. Main St.
PO Box 539
Newark, NY 14513　　　　　Phone: (315)331-2182

Stock Clerks

Stock clerks receive, record, and store merchandise or materials. They also organize and label items and report damaged or spoiled goods. Stock clerks sometimes use hand-held scanners connected to computers to keep inventories up to date. In stores, they may be responsible for keeping shelves and racks stocked. Stock clerks are employed by retail and wholesale firms, factories, hospitals, government agencies, schools, and other organizations that keep large quantities of materials and goods on hand.

$alaries

The average salary for stock clerks is $16,000-17,000/year.

Employment Outlook

Growth rate until the year 2000: Average.

Stock Clerks

Career Guides

★1326★
"Average Hourly Wages of Material Movement Workers in Ten Cities" in *The American Almanac of Jobs and Salaries* (p. 521)
Avon Books
105 Madison Avenue
New York, NY 10016   Phone: (212)481-5600
John Wright and Edward J. Dwyer. Revised and updated, 1990. A comprehensive guide to the wages of hundreds of occupations in a wide variety of industries and organizations.

★1327★
Receptionist
Careers, Inc.
PO Box 135
Largo, FL 34649-0135   Phone: (813)584-7333
1990. Two-page occupational summary card describing duties, working conditions, personal qualifications, training, earnings and hours, employment outlook, places of employment, related careers and where to write for more information.

★1328★
Stock Clerk
Careers, Inc.
PO Box 135
Largo, FL 34649-0135   Phone: (813)584-7333
1990. Two-page job guide card describing duties, working conditions, personal qualifications, training, earnings and hours, employment outlook, places of employment, related careers and where to write for more information.

★1329★
"Stock Clerk" in *Marketing and Distribution*, Volume 10 of *Career Information Center* (pp. 58-59)
Glencoe/Macmillan
15319 Chatsworth St.
Mission Hills, CA 91345   Phone: (818)898-1391
Richard Lidz and Dale Anderson, editorial directors. Fourth edition, 1990. For 600 occupations, describes job duties, entry-level requirements, education and training needed, advancement possibilities, employment outlook, earnings and benefits. The set is divided into 12 volumes. Each volume includes jobs related under a broad career field. Volume 13 is the index. **Facsimile Number:** 818-365-5489.

★1330★
"Stock Clerk" in *Occu-Facts: Information on 565 Careers in Outline Form* (p. 12.39)
Careers, Inc.
P.O. Box 135
1211 Tenth St., S.W.
Largo, FL 33640   Phone: (813)584-7333
Elizabeth Handville. Biennial, 1989-90 edition. Each one-page occupational profile describes duties, working conditions, physical surroundings and demands, aptitudes, temperament, educational requirements, employment outlook, earnings, and places of employment.

★1331★
Stock Clerks
Chronicle Guidance Publications, Inc.
PO Box 1190
Moravia, NY 13118-1190   Phone: (315)497-0330
1989. This career brief describes the nature of the work, working conditions, hours and earnings, education and training, licensure, certification, unions, personal qualifications, social and psychological factors, employment outlook, entry methods, advancement, and related occupations. **Toll-free/Additional Phone Number(s):** 800-622-7284.

★1332★
"Stock Clerks" in *Occupational Outlook Handbook* (pp. 266-267)
Superintendent of Documents
U.S. Government Printing Office
Washington, DC 20402   Phone: (202)783-3238
Biennial; latest edition, 1990-91. Encyclopedia of careers describing more than 250 occupations and comprising about 86 percent of all jobs in the economy. Occupations that require lengthy education or training are given the most attention. For each occupation, the handbook describes job duties, working conditions, training, educational preparation, personal qualities, advancement possibilities, job outlook, earnings, and sources of additional information.

★1333★
"Stock Clerks" in Volume 6 of *Career Discovery Encyclopedia* (pp. 68-69)
J.G. Ferguson Publishing Co.
200 W. Monroe
Chicago, IL 60606   Phone: (312)580-5480
E. Russell Primm, editor-in-chief. 1990. Contains two-page articles on 504 occupations. Each article describes job duties, earnings, and educational and training requirements.

★1334★
"Stock Clerks" in Volume 3 of *The Encyclopedia of Careers and Vocational Guidance* (pp. 95-99)
J.G. Ferguson Publishing Co.
200 W. Monroe
Chicago, IL 60606   Phone: (312)580-5480

William E. Hopke, editor-in-chief. Eighth edition, 1990. Four-volume set that profiles 500 occupations and describes job trends in 76 industries. Includes career description, educational requirements, history of the job, methods of entry, advancement, employment outlook, earnings, working conditions, social and psychological factors, and sources of additional information.

★1335★
"Warehouse Worker" in *Marketing and Distribution*, Volume 10 of *Career Information Center* (pp. 64-65)
Glencoe/Macmillan
15319 Chatsworth St.
Mission Hills, CA 91345   Phone: (818)898-1391

Richard Lidz and Dale Anderson, editorial directors. Fourth edition, 1990. For 600 occupations, describes job duties, entry-level requirements, education and training needed, advancement possibilities, employment outlook, earnings and benefits. The set is divided into 12 volumes. Each volume includes jobs related under a broad career field. Volume 13 is the index. **Facsimile Number:** 818-365-5489.

Associations

★1336★
Distributive Education Clubs of America (DECA)
1908 Association Dr.
Reston, VA 22091   Phone: (703)860-5000

Membership: High School juniors and seniors, and junior college students interested in the field of marketing and distribution (retailing and wholesaling) as a vocation.

★1337★
National Retail Federation (NRF)
100 W. 31st. St.
New York, NY 10001   Phone: (212)244-8780

Membership: Department, chain, mass merchandise, and specialty stores retailing men's, women's, and children's apparel and home furnishings. **Purpose:** Conducts conferences and workshops; provides extensive group of manuals, bulletins, promotional materials, and advisory services on all phases of retailing, including financial planning and cash management, taxation, economic forecasting, expense planning, shortage control, credit, electronic data processing, telecommunications, merchandise management, buying, traffic, security, supply, materials handling, store planning and construction, personnel administration, recruitment and training, and advertising and display. Presents awards; maintains a library of 1000 volumes on retail management and fashion merchandising.

Test Guides

★1338★
Shop Clerk
National Learning Corp.
212 Michael Dr.
Syosset, NY 11791   Phone: (516)921-8888

Jack Rudman. Part of the Career Examination Series No. 1. All examination guides in this series contain questions with answers. **Facsimile Number:** (516)921-8743. **Toll-free/Additional Phone Number(s):** 800-645-6337.

★1339★
Stock Clerk
National Learning Corp.
212 Michael Dr.
Syosset, NY 11791   Phone: (516)921-8888

Jack Rudman. Part of the Career Examination Series No. 1. All examination guides in this series contain questions with answers. **Facsimile Number:** (516)921-8743. **Toll-free/Additional Phone Number(s):** 800-645-6337.

Meetings and Conventions

★1340★
Distributive Education Clubs of America Career Development Conference (DECA)
1908 Association Dr.
Reston, VA 22091   Phone: (703)860-5000
Frequency: Annual.

Traffic, Shipping, and Receiving Clerks

Traffic, shipping, and receiving clerks keep records of all materials shipped and received. Traffic clerks record the destination, weight, and charges on all incoming and outgoing freight. Shipping clerks are responsible for all outgoing shipments. They make sure each order is filled correctly, label and address packages, and compute postal rates. Receiving clerks see that incoming orders have been filled correctly, record the shipment and its condition. Most traffic, shipping, and receiving clerks are employed by wholesale establishments, retail stores, and manufacturing firms.

$alaries

The average salary for traffic, shipping, and receiving clerks is $16,000-17,000/year.

Employment Outlook

Growth rate until the year 2000: More slowly than average.

Traffic, Shipping, and Receiving Clerks

Career Guides

★1341★
"Average Hourly Wages of Material Movement Workers in Ten Cities" in *The American Almanac of Jobs and Salaries* (p. 521)
Avon Books
105 Madison Avenue
New York, NY 10016   Phone: (212)481-5600
John Wright and Edward J. Dwyer. Revised and updated, 1990. A comprehensive guide to the wages of hundreds of occupations in a wide variety of industries and organizations.

★1342★
Department Store Receiving and Related Workers
Careers, Inc.
PO Box 135
Largo, FL 34649-0135   Phone: (813)584-7333
1992. Eight-page brief offering the definition, history, duties, working conditions, personal qualifications, educational requirements, earnings, hours, employment outlook, advancement possibilities, and related occupations.

★1343★
"Department Store Receiving, Delivering, & Related Workers" in *Occu-Facts: Information on 565 Careers in Outline Form* (p. 12.37)
Careers, Inc.
P.O. Box 135
1211 Tenth St., S.W.
Largo, FL 33640   Phone: (813)584-7333
Elizabeth Handville. Biennial, 1989-90 edition. Each one-page occupational profile describes duties, working conditions, physical surroundings and demands, aptitudes, temperament, educational requirements, employment outlook, earnings, and places of employment.

★1344★
"Shipping and Receiving Clerk" in *Marketing and Distribution*, Volume 10 of *Career Information Center* (pp. 56-57)
Glencoe/Macmillan
15319 Chatsworth St.
Mission Hills, CA 91345   Phone: (818)898-1391
Richard Lidz and Dale Anderson, editorial directors. Fourth edition, 1990. For 600 occupations, describes job duties, entry-level requirements, education and training needed, advancement possibilities, employment outlook, earnings and benefits. The set is divided into 12 volumes. Each volume includes jobs related under a broad career field. Volume 13 is the index. **Facsimile Number:** 818-365-5489.

★1345★
Shipping and Receiving Clerks
Chronicle Guidance Publications, Inc.
PO Box 1190
Moravia, NY 13118-1190   Phone: (315)497-0330
1987. This career brief describes the nature of the work, working conditions, hours and earnings, education and training, licensure, certification, unions, personal qualifications, social and psychological factors, employment outlook, entry methods, advancement, and related occupations. **Toll-free/Additional Phone Number(s):** 800-622-7284.

★1346★
"Shipping and Receiving Clerks" in Volume 6 of *Career Discovery Encyclopedia* (pp. 24-25)
J.G. Ferguson Publishing Co.
200 W. Monroe
Chicago, IL 60606   Phone: (312)580-5480
E. Russell Primm, editor-in-chief. 1990. Contains two-page articles on 504 occupations. Each article describes job duties, earnings, and educational and training requirements.

★1347★
"Shipping and Receiving Clerks" in Volume 3 of *The Encyclopedia of Careers and Vocational Guidance* (pp. 85-89)
J.G. Ferguson Publishing Co.
200 W. Monroe
Chicago, IL 60606   Phone: (312)580-5480
William E. Hopke, editor-in-chief. Eighth edition, 1990. Four-volume set that profiles 500 occupations and describes job trends in 76 industries. Includes career description, educational requirements, history of the job, methods of entry, advancement, employment outlook, earnings, working conditions, social and psychological factors, and sources of additional information.

★1348★
Shipping Clerk
Careers, Inc.
PO Box 135
Largo, FL 34649-0135   Phone: (813)584-7333
1991. Two-page job guide card describing duties, working conditions, personal qualifications, training, earnings and hours, employment outlook, places of employment, related careers and where to write for more information.

★1349★
"Shipping Clerk" in *Occu-Facts: Information on 565 Careers in Outline Form* (p. 12.38)
Careers, Inc.
P.O. Box 135
1211 Tenth St., S.W.
Largo, FL 33640   Phone: (813)584-7333
Elizabeth Handville. Biennial, 1989-90 edition. Each one-page occupational profile describes duties, working conditions, physical surroundings and demands, aptitudes, temperament, educational requirements, employment outlook, earnings, and places of employment.

★1350★
"Traffic Agents and Clerks" in Volume 6 of *Career Discovery Encyclopedia* (pp. 128-129)
J.G. Ferguson Publishing Co.
200 W. Monroe
Chicago, IL 60606   Phone: (312)580-5480
E. Russell Primm, editor-in-chief. 1990. Contains two-page articles on 504 occupations. Each article describes job duties, earnings, and educational and training requirements.

★1351★
"Traffic Agents and Clerks" in Volume 3 of *The Encyclopedia of Careers and Vocational Guidance* (pp. 121-124)
J.G. Ferguson Publishing Co.
200 W. Monroe
Chicago, IL 60606   Phone: (312)580-5480
William E. Hopke, editor-in-chief. Eighth edition, 1990. Four-volume set that profiles 500 occupations and describes job trends in 76 industries. Includes career description, educational requirements, history of the job, methods of entry, advancement, employment outlook, earnings, working conditions, social and psychological factors, and sources of additional information.

★1352★
"Traffic, Shipping, and Receiving Clerks" in *Occupational Outlook Handbook* (pp. 267-268)
Superintendent of Documents
U.S. Government Printing Office
Washington, DC 20402   Phone: (202)783-3238
Biennial; latest edition, 1990-91. Encyclopedia of careers describing more than 250 occupations and comprising about 86 percent of all jobs in the economy. Occupations that require lengthy education or training are given the most attention. For each occupation, the handbook describes job duties, working conditions, training, educational preparation, personal qualities, advancement possibilities, job outlook, earnings, and sources of additional information.

--- Associations ---

★1353★
American Society of Transportation and Logistics (ASTL)
PO Box 33095
Louisville, KY 40232   Phone: (502)451-8150
Membership: Persons engaged in transportation, traffic, logistics, or physical distribution management. **Purpose:** To establish standards of knowledge, technical training, experience, conduct, and ethics, and to encourage the attainment of high standards of education and technical training requisite for the proper performance of the various functions of traffic, transportation, logistics, and physical distribution management. Conducts regional workshops and extensive educational programs. Presents National Joseph C. Scheleen Award for Excellence, Outstanding Candidate Awards, and chapter and regional awards annually.

★1354★
International Brotherhood of Teamsters, Chauffeurs, Warehousemen and Helpers of America (IBT)
25 Louisiana Ave., NW
Washington, DC 20001   Phone: (202)624-6800
Membership: Formed by merger of Team Drivers International Union and Teamsters National Union. **Purpose:** Maintains DRIVE Political Action committee; maintains 30,000 volume library.

★1355★
National Association of Freight Transportation Consultants (NAFTC)
PO Box 21418
Albuquerque, NM 87154   Phone: (505)275-2046
Membership: Businesses and individuals providing freight transportation consulting services to freight shippers, carriers, and others. **Purpose:** Seeks to enhance the profession through educational programs, information exchange, and communication.

★1356★
National Freight Transportation Association (NFTA)
PO Box 21856
Roanoke, VA 24018   Phone: (703)774-7725
Formerly National Freight Traffic Association.

--- Awards, Scholarships, Grants, and Fellowships ---

★1357★
National Joseph C. Scheleen Award for Excellence
American Society of Transportation and Logistics
PO Box 33095
Louisville, KY 40232   Phone: (502)451-8150

--- Periodicals ---

★1358★
American Shipper
PO Box 4728
Jacksonville, FL 32201   Phone: (904)355-2601
David A. Howard, Editor. Monthly. Transportation and shipping magazine. **Facsimile Number:** (904)791-8836.

★1359★
Drop Shipping News
Consolidated Marketing Services, Inc.
PO Box 1361
New York, NY 10017   Phone: (212)688-8797
Editor(s): Nicholas T. Scheel. Monthly. Supplies data on firms that drop ship their products as a means of distribution. Contains information on sources of consumer and industrial products, formulation of marketing policy, and on the pricing, ordering, packaging, and handling of drop shipments. Includes articles on uses of direct mail and direct-response advertising.

Meetings and Conventions

★1360★
American Society of Transportation and Logistics (ASTL)
PO Box 33095
Louisville, KY 40232　　　　Phone: (502)451-8150
Frequency: Holds annual conference, with a seminar.

★1361★
International Brotherhood of Teamsters, Chauffeurs, Warehousemen and Helpers of America (IBT)
25 Louisiana Ave., NW
Washington, DC 20001　　　　Phone: (202)624-6800
Frequency: Quinquennial - next held in 1996.

Postal Clerks and Mail Carriers

Postal clerks and mail carriers receive, sort, and deliver letters and packages. Postal clerks operate electronic letter-sorting machines and sort odd-sized letters, magazines or newspapers by hand. Clerks at local post offices sort mail for delivery to individual customers, sell stamps, weigh packages, and provide information. City and rural mail carriers travel established routes by vehicle or on foot delivering and collecting mail.

$alaries

Salaries for postal clerks and carriers are listed below.

Beginning postal carriers and clerks	$22,250/year
Postal carriers and clerks after 10 1/2 years of service	$29,385/year
Experienced city delivery mail carriers	$28,056/year
Rural delivery mail carriers	$29,400/year

Employment Outlook

Growth rate until the year 2000: More slowly than average.

Postal Clerks and Mail Carriers

Career Guides

★1362★
The Book of 16,000-60,000 Post Office Jobs: Where They Are, What They Pay, and How to Get Them
Bookhaus Publishers
23323 Teppert
East Detroit, MI 48021   Phone: (313)778-7080
Veltisezar B. Bautista. 1989. Describes a variety of jobs with the U.S. Postal Service such as computer programmer, labor relations manager, and building maintenance supervisor. Many of the jobs listed are available only to current postal employees. Describes qualifications, duties, and salaries, and offers advice about filling out the application and taking the examination. Lists postal service testing centers.

★1363★
Carrying the Mail: A Career in Public Service
National Association of Letter Carriers
100 Indiana Ave., N.W.
Washington, DC 20001   Phone: (202)393-4695
1987. This eight-panel brochure describes job duties, working conditions, earnings, qualifications, and how to apply.

★1364★
How to Get a Job with the Post Office
HarperCollins, Inc.
10 E. 53rd St.
New York, NY 10022   Phone: (212)207-7000
Stephen M. Good. 1985.

★1365★
Mail Carrier
Careers, Inc.
PO Box 135
Largo, FL 34649-0135   Phone: (813)584-7333
1992. Two-page occupational summary card describing duties, working conditions, personal qualifications, training, earnings and hours, employment outlook, places of employment, related careers and where to write for more information.

★1366★
"Mail Carrier" in *Occu-Facts: Information on 565 Careers in Outline Form* (p. 12.34)
Careers, Inc.
P.O. Box 135
1211 Tenth St., S.W.
Largo, FL 33640   Phone: (813)584-7333
Elizabeth Handville. Biennial, 1989-90 edition. Each one-page occupational profile describes duties, working conditions, physical surroundings and demands, aptitudes, temperament, educational requirements, employment outlook, earnings, and places of employment.

★1367★
"Mail Carriers" in Volume 4 of *Career Discovery Encyclopedia* (pp. 46-47)
J.G. Ferguson Publishing Co.
200 W. Monroe
Chicago, IL 60606   Phone: (312)580-5480
E. Russell Primm, editor-in-chief. 1990. Contains two-page articles on 504 occupations. Each article describes job duties, earnings, and educational and training requirements.

★1368★
"Mail Carriers" in Volume 3 of *The Encyclopedia of Careers and Vocational Guidance* (pp. 55-59)
J.G. Ferguson Publishing Co.
200 W. Monroe
Chicago, IL 60606   Phone: (312)580-5480
William E. Hopke, editor-in-chief. Eighth edition, 1990. Four-volume set that profiles 500 occupations and describes job trends in 76 industries. Includes career description, educational requirements, history of the job, methods of entry, advancement, employment outlook, earnings, working conditions, social and psychological factors, and sources of additional information.

★1369★
Mail Handler: U. S. Postal Service
Simon & Schuster, Inc.
Simon & Schuster Bldg.
1230 Avenue of the Americas
New York, NY 10020   Phone: (212)698-7000
Hy Hammer, editor. 1985.

★1370★
"Mail Service Worker" in *Administration, Business, and Office*, Volume 1 of *Career Information Center* (pp. 57-58)
Glencoe/Macmillan
15319 Chatsworth St.
Mission Hills, CA 91345   Phone: (818)898-1391
Richard Lidz and Dale Anderson, editorial directors. Fourth edition, 1990. For 600 occupations, describes job duties, entry-level requirements, education and training needed, advancement possibilities, employment outlook, earnings and benefits. The set is divided into 12 volumes. Each volume includes jobs related under a broad career field. Volume 13 is the index. **Facsimile Number:** 818-365-5489.

★1371★
Post Office Clerk
Careers, Inc.
PO Box 135
Largo, FL 34649-0135 Phone: (813)584-7333
1990. Two-page occupational summary card describing duties, working conditions, personal qualifications, training, earnings and hours, employment outlook, places of employment, related careers and where to write for more information.

★1372★
"Post Office Clerk" in *Occu-Facts: Information on 565 Careers in Outline Form* (p. 12.33)
Careers, Inc.
P.O. Box 135
1211 Tenth St., S.W.
Largo, FL 33640 Phone: (813)584-7333
Elizabeth Handville. Biennial, 1989-90 edition. Each one-page occupational profile describes duties, working conditions, physical surroundings and demands, aptitudes, temperament, educational requirements, employment outlook, earnings, and places of employment.

★1373★
Post Office Clerk-Carrier
Prentice Hall
Rte. 9W
Englewood Cliffs, NJ 07632 Phone: (201)592-2000
Eve P. Steinberg. 1989.

★1374★
"Postal Clerks" in Volume 5 of *Career Discovery Encyclopedia* (pp. 76-77)
J.G. Ferguson Publishing Co.
200 W. Monroe
Chicago, IL 60606 Phone: (312)580-5480
E. Russell Primm, editor-in-chief. 1990. Contains two-page articles on 504 occupations. Each article describes job duties, earnings, and educational and training requirements.

★1375★
"Postal Clerks" in Volume 3 of *The Encyclopedia of Careers and Vocational Guidance* (pp. 62-66)
J.G. Ferguson Publishing Co.
200 W. Monroe
Chicago, IL 60606 Phone: (312)580-5480
William E. Hopke, editor-in-chief. Eighth edition, 1990. Four-volume set that profiles 500 occupations and describes job trends in 76 industries. Includes career description, educational requirements, history of the job, methods of entry, advancement, employment outlook, earnings, working conditions, social and psychological factors, and sources of additional information.

★1376★
"Postal Clerks and Mail Carriers" in *Occupational Outlook Handbook* (pp. 268-270)
Superintendent of Documents
U.S. Government Printing Office
Washington, DC 20402 Phone: (202)783-3238
Biennial; latest edition, 1990-91. Encyclopedia of careers describing more than 250 occupations and comprising about 86 percent of all jobs in the economy. Occupations that require lengthy education or training are given the most attention. For each occupation, the handbook describes job duties, working conditions, training, educational preparation, personal qualities, advancement possibilities, job outlook, earnings, and sources of additional information.

★1377★
"Postal Service Worker" in *Public and Community Services*, Volume 11 of *Career Information Center* (pp. 58-60)
Glencoe/Macmillan
15319 Chatsworth St.
Mission Hills, CA 91345 Phone: (818)898-1391
Richard Lidz and Dale Anderson, editorial directors. Fourth edition, 1990. For 600 occupations, describes job duties, entry-level requirements, education and training needed, advancement possibilities, employment outlook, earnings and benefits. The set is divided into 12 volumes. Each volume includes jobs related under a broad career field. Volume 13 is the index. **Facsimile Number:** 818-365-5489.

★1378★
Postal Service Workers
Chronicle Guidance Publications, Inc.
PO Box 1190
Moravia, NY 13118-1190 Phone: (315)497-0330
1991. This career brief describes the nature of the work, working conditions, hours and earnings, education and training, licensure, certification, unions, personal qualifications, social and psychological factors, employment outlook, entry methods, advancement, and related occupations. **Toll-free/Additional Phone Number(s):** 800-622-7284.

★1379★
Rural Mail Carrier
Vocational Biographies, Inc.
PO Box 31, Dept. VF10
Sauk Centre, MN 56378 Phone: (612)352-6516
1990. This pamphlet profiles a person working in the job. Includes information about job duties, working conditions, places of employment, educational preparation, labor market outlook, and salaries. **Toll-free/Additional Phone Number(s):** 800-255-0752.

★1380★
Video Career Library - Clerical & Administrative Support
Careers, Inc.
1211 10th St., SW
PO Box 135
Largo, FL 34649-0135 Phone: (813)584-7333
Videocassette. 1990. 26 mins. Part of the Video Career Library covering 165 occupations. Shows actual workers on the job. Includes secretaries, cashiers, receptionists, bookkeepers and audit clerks, telephone operators, postal clerks/carriers/supervisors, insurance investigators, bank tellers, data entry keyers, and court reporters.

─────────── Associations ───────────

★1381★
American Postal Workers Union (APWU)
1300 L St. NW
Washington, DC 20005 Phone: (202)842-4200
Membership: Divisions include: Clerk; Maintenance; Motor Vehicle; Political Action; Special Delivery Messengers; Support Services.

★1382★
National Alliance of Postal and Federal Employees (NAPFE)
1628 11th St. NW
Washington, DC 20001 Phone: (202)939-6325
Purpose: Works to eliminate employment discrimination. Bestows scholarship awards to dependent children of members.

Postal Clerks and Mail Carriers

★1383★
National Association of Letter Carriers of the U.S.A. (NALC)
100 Indiana Ave. NW, Ste. 713
Washington, DC 20001   Phone: (202)393-4695
Purpose: Maintains 5000 volume library and information center.

★1384★
National Association of Postal Supervisors (NAPS)
490 L'Enfant Plaza SW, No. 3200
Washington, DC 20024-2120   Phone: (202)484-6070

★1385★
National League of Postmasters of the United States (NLPM)
1023 N. Royal St.
Alexandria, VA 22314   Phone: (703)548-5922
Purpose: Sponsors the Postmasters Benefit Plan. Represents postmasters before Congress. Maintains biographical archives; bestows awards. Conducts semiannual league forum for league officer training.

★1386★
National Postal Mail Handlers Union (NPMHU)
1 Thomas Circle NW, Ste. 525
Washington, DC 20005   Phone: (202)833-9095
Operates as a division of Laborers' International Union of North America.

★1387★
National Star Route Mail Contractors Association (NSRMCA)
324 E. Capitol St.
Washington, DC 20003   Phone: (202)543-1661
Membership: Highway mail contractors with the U.S. Postal Service transporting mail over the highway on authorized schedules. **Publications:** *Star Carrier*, monthly. **Facsimile Number:** (202)543-8863.

★1388★
Third Class Mail Association (TCMA)
1333 F St. NW, Ste. 710
Washington, DC 20004-1108   Phone: (202)347-0055
Membership: Represents producers and users of third class mail and their suppliers. **Purpose:** Seeks to protect interests of members with respect to third class postal rates and services before Congress, the U.S. Postal Service, and the Postal Rate Commission. Is conducting a public relations campaign to persuade mailers to include apartment and suite numbers on address labels. **Publications:** *Membership Directory*, annual. • *TCMA Bulletin*, 50/year. **Toll-free/Additional Phone Number(s):** (202)347-0799 (postal newsline). **Facsimile Number:** (202)347-0789.

Standards/Certification Agencies

Postal clerks and mail carriers must be U.S. citizens or have been granted permanent resident-alien status in the United States. They must be at least 18 years old (or 16, if they have a high school diploma). Qualification is based on a written examination as well as a physical examination. Applicants for jobs as postal clerks operating electronic sorting machines must pass a special examination that includes a machine aptitude test. Applicants for mail carrier positions must have a driver's license, a good driving record, and a passing grade on a road test.

Test Guides

★1389★
Administrative Clerk (USPS)
National Learning Corp.
212 Michael Dr.
Syosset, NY 11791   Phone: (516)921-8888
Jack Rudman. Part of the Career Examination Series No. 1. All examination guides in this series contain questions with answers. **Facsimile Number:** (516)921-8743. **Toll-free/Additional Phone Number(s):** 800-645-6337.

★1390★
Barron's How to Prepare for the U.S. Postal Service Mail Handler - Mail Processor Examination
Barron's Educational Series, Inc.
250 Wireless Blvd.
Hauppauge, NY 11788   Phone: (516)434-3311
Philip Barkus. 1987.

★1391★
Civil Service Arithmetic and Vocabulary
Prentice Hall Press
Simon & Schuster Inc.
200 Old Tappan Rd.
Old Tappan, NJ 07675   Phone: (800)223-2348
Barbara Erdsneker, Margaret A. Haller, and Eve P. Steinberg. Tenth edition, 1991. Practical guide reviews the two subjects most frequently tested on civil service exams. Includes sample questions and answers and test-taking tips and strategies. **Facsimile Number:** (201)767-5852.

★1392★
The Corey Guide to Postal Exams
Prentice Hall
Rte. 9W
Englewood Cliffs, NJ 07632   Phone: (201)592-2000
Richard J. Corey. Third edition, 1988.

★1393★
Distribution Clerk, Machine
Prentice Hall Press
Simon & Schuster Inc.
200 Old Tappan Rd.
Old Tappan, NJ 07675   Phone: (800)223-2348
Eve P. Steinberg. Second edition, 1988. Provides preparation for promotion from Postal Service carrier to distribution clerk. Contains eight sample tests, tips, techniques, and study practice section.

★1394★
Distribution Clerk, Machine: Letter Sorting Machine Operator-U.S. Postal Service
Prentice Hall
Rte. 9W
Englewood Cliffs, NJ 07632   Phone: (201)592-2000
Eve P. Steinberg. Second edition, 1988. Part of ARCO Civil Service Test Tutor Series.

★1395★
Guide to Federal Technical, Trades, and Labor Jobs
Resource Directories
3361 Executive Pkwy., Ste. 302
Toledo, OH 43606   Phone: 800-274-8515
Provides information on written exams and application procedures for postal workers.

★1396★
How to Prepare for a Civil Service Examination (Text)
National Learning Corp.
212 Michael Dr.
Syosset, NY 11791   Phone: (516)921-8888
Jack Rudman. Part of the General Aptitude and Abilities Series No. 2. Books in this series provide functional, intensive test practice and drill in the basic skills and areas common to many examinations, as well as general aptitude or achievement necessary for entrance into many occupations or positions. **Facsimile Number:** (516)921-8743. **Toll-free/Additional Phone Number(s):** 800-645-6337.

★1397★
How to Prepare for the Postal Clerk-Carrier Examination
Barron's Educational Series, Inc.
PO Box 8040
250 Wireless Blvd.
Hauppauge, NY 11788   Phone: (516)434-3311
Philip Barkus. This test guide provides study techniques, test-taking strategies, sample questions with answers, and five timed practice tests. **Toll-free/Additional Phone Number(s):** 800-645-3476 (in NY 800-257-5729).

★1398★
How to Prepare for the U.S. Postal Distribution Machine Clerk Examination
Barron's Educational Series, Inc.
PO Box 8040
250 Wireless Blvd.
Hauppauge, NY 11788   Phone: (516)434-3311
Philip Barkus. Manual provides diagnostic test, followed by address-checking and memory drills. Four additional practice tests are also included, with answers provided. **Toll-free/Additional Phone Number(s):** 800-645-3476 (in NY call 800-257-5729).

★1399★
How to Prepare for the U.S. Postal Service Mailhandler/Mail Processor Examination
Barron's Educational Series, Inc.
PO Box 8040
250 Wireless Blvd.
Hauppauge, NY 11788   Phone: (516)434-3311
Philip Barkus. Manual contains diagnostic test and five model tests, as well as timed practice drills. **Toll-free/Additional Phone Number(s):** 800-645-3476. (In NY call 800-257-5729).

★1400★
Mail Handler
Prentice Hall
Rte. 9W
Englewood Cliffs, NJ 07632   Phone: (201)592-2000
Eve P. Steinberg. Ninth edition, 1988. Part of ARCO Civil Service Test Tutor Series.

★1401★
Mail Handler (USPS)
National Learning Corp.
212 Michael Dr.
Syosset, NY 11791   Phone: (516)921-8888
Jack Rudman. Part of the Career Examination Series No. 1. All examination guides in this series contain questions with answers. **Facsimile Number:** (516)921-8743. **Toll-free/Additional Phone Number(s):** 800-645-6337.

★1402★
Mail Handlers/Mail Processor
Prentice Hall Press
Simon & Schuster Inc.
200 Old Tappan Rd.
Old Tappan, NJ 07675   Phone: (800)223-2348
E.P. Steinberg. Tenth edition, 1991. Provides six full-length sample exams with answers and application information. Also includes tips to improve scores. **Facsimile Number:** (201)767-5852.

★1403★
Mark-up Clerk/Clerk Typist/Clerk Stenographer - U.S. Postal Service
Prentice Hall Press
Simon & Schuster Inc.
200 Old Tappan Rd.
Old Tappan, NJ 07675   Phone: (800)223-2348
Eve P. Steinberg. First edition, 1990. Provides practice exams with explanatory answers.

★1404★
Mark-Up Clerk (USPS)
National Learning Corp.
212 Michael Dr.
Syosset, NY 11791   Phone: (516)921-8888
Jack Rudman. Part of the Career Examination Series No. 1. All examination guides in this series contain questions with answers. **Facsimile Number:** (516)921-8743. **Toll-free/Additional Phone Number(s):** 800-645-6337.

★1405★
Post Office Clerk-Carrier
Prentice Hall Press
Simon & Schuster Inc.
200 Old Tappan Rd.
Old Tappan, NJ 07675   Phone: (800)223-2348
E.P. Steinberg. 16th edition, 1989. Contains 11 complete model exams with answers.

★1406★
Postal Arithmetic
National Learning Corp.
212 Michael Dr.
Syosset, NY 11791   Phone: (516)921-8888
Jack Rudman. Part of the General Aptitude and Abilities Series No. 2. Books in this series provide functional, intensive test practice and drill in the basic skills and areas common to many examinations, as well as general aptitude or achievement necessary for entrance into many occupations or positions. **Facsimile Number:** (516)921-8743. **Toll-free/Additional Phone Number(s):** 800-645-6337.

★1407★
Postal Clerk-Carrier & Mail Handler Exams
Ken-Books
56 Midcrest Way
San Francisco, CA 94131   Phone: (415)826-6550
Harry W. Koch. Fourth edition, 1981.

Postal Clerks and Mail Carriers

★1408★
Postal Exam Handbook
Prentice Hall Press
Simon & Schuster Inc.
200 Old Tappan Rd.
Old Tappan, NJ 07675   Phone: (800)223-2348
E.P. Steinberg. First edition, 1990. Serves as a guide to the tests for the most popular entry-level postal positions, including clerk carrier, mail handler, mark-up clerk, garageman driver, postal police, and more. Contains sample exams and complete information on application procedures.

★1409★
Postal Machines Mechanic (USPS)
National Learning Corp.
212 Michael Dr.
Syosset, NY 11791   Phone: (516)921-8888
Jack Rudman. Part of the Career Examination Series No. 1. All examination guides in this series contain questions with answers. **Facsimile Number:** (516)921-8743. **Toll-free/Additional Phone Number(s):** 800-645-6337.

★1410★
Postal Supervisor (USPS)
National Learning Corp.
212 Michael Dr.
Syosset, NY 11791   Phone: (516)921-8888
Jack Rudman. Part of the Career Examination Series No. 1. All examination guides in this series contain questions with answers. **Facsimile Number:** (516)921-8743. **Toll-free/Additional Phone Number(s):** 800-645-6337.

★1411★
Postal System Examiner (USPS)
National Learning Corp.
212 Michael Dr.
Syosset, NY 11791   Phone: (516)921-8888
Jack Rudman. Part of the Career Examination Series No. 1. All examination guides in this series contain questions with answers. **Facsimile Number:** (516)921-8743. **Toll-free/Additional Phone Number(s):** 800-645-6337.

★1412★
Postal Transportation Clerk (USPS)
National Learning Corp.
212 Michael Dr.
Syosset, NY 11791   Phone: (516)921-8888
Jack Rudman. Part of the Career Examination Series No. 1. All examination guides in this series contain questions with answers. **Facsimile Number:** (516)921-8743. **Toll-free/Additional Phone Number(s):** 800-645-6337.

★1413★
Postmaster (USPS)
National Learning Corp.
212 Michael Dr.
Syosset, NY 11791   Phone: (516)921-8888
Jack Rudman. Part of the Career Examination Series No. 1. Examination guides are available for Postmaster 1st, 2nd, 3rd Classes; and for Postmaster, 4th Class. All examination guides in this series contain questions with answers. **Facsimile Number:** (516)921-8743. **Toll-free/Additional Phone Number(s):** 800-645-6337.

★1414★
Precis of Postal Service Manual
National Learning Corp.
212 Michael Dr.
Syosset, NY 11791   Phone: (516)921-8888
Jack Rudman. Part of the General Aptitude and Abilities Series No. 2. Books in this series provide functional, intensive test practice and drill in the basic skills and areas common to many examinations, as well as general aptitude or achievement necessary for entrance into many occupations or positions. **Facsimile Number:** (516)921-8743. **Toll-free/Additional Phone Number(s):** 800-645-6337.

★1415★
Rural Carrier
Prentice Hall Press
Simon & Schuster Inc.
200 Old Tappan Rd.
Old Tappan, NJ 07675   Phone: (800)223-2348
E.P. Steinberg. First edition, 1989. Prepares applicants for nationwide postal exam; includes three full-length sample exams with answers.

★1416★
Rural Carrier (USPS)
National Learning Corp.
212 Michael Dr.
Syosset, NY 11791   Phone: (516)921-8888
Jack Rudman. Part of the Career Examination Series No. 1. All examination guides in this series contain questions with answers. **Facsimile Number:** (516)921-8743. **Toll-free/Additional Phone Number(s):** 800-645-6337.

★1417★
Test Practice Book for 100 Civil Service Jobs
National Learning Corp.
212 Michael Dr.
Syosset, NY 11791   Phone: (516)921-8888
Jack Rudman. Part of the General Aptitude and Abilities Series No. 2. Books in this series provide functional, intensive test practice and drill in the basic skills and areas common to many examinations, as well as general aptitude or achievement necessary for entrance into many occupations or positions. **Facsimile Number:** (516)921-8743. **Toll-free/Additional Phone Number(s):** 800-645-6337.

★1418★
Video Math and Verbal Review for the Civil Service Exam
Video Aided Instruction, Inc.
182 Village Rd.
East Hills, NY 11577   Phone: (516)621-6176
Videocassette. 1984. 120 mins. A college instructor explains and reviews the basic math skills needed for a civil service exam.

★1419★
Window Clerk (USPS)
National Learning Corp.
212 Michael Dr.
Syosset, NY 11791   Phone: (516)921-8888
Jack Rudman. Part of the Career Examination Series No. 1. All examination guides in this series contain questions with answers. **Facsimile Number:** (516)921-8743. **Toll-free/Additional Phone Number(s):** 800-645-6337.

Basic Reference Guides and Handbooks

★1420★
Mailing Machines & Equipment Directory
American Business Directories, Inc.
American Business Information, Inc.
5711 S. 86th Circle
Omaha, NE 68127   Phone: (402)593-4600
Annual. Entries include: Name, address, phone, size of advertisement, name of owner or manager, number of employees, year first in "Yellow Pages." Arrangement: Geographical. **Facsimile Number:** (402)331-1505.

Periodicals

★1421★
The American Postal Worker
American Postal Workers Union, AFL-CIO
1300 L St. NW
Washington, DC 20005   Phone: (202)842-4200
Moe Biller, Editor. Monthly. AFL-CIO postal labor. **Facsimile Number:** (202)842-4297.

★1422★
National Alliance
National Alliance of Postal and Federal Employees
1628 11th St. NW
Washington, DC 20001   Phone: (202)939-6325
Jacquelyn C. Moore Editor. Monthly. Magazine for postal and federal employees. **Facsimile Number:** (202)939-6389.

★1423★
The National Rural Letter Carrier
National Rural Letter Carriers' Assn.
1630 Duke St., 4th Fl.
Alexandria, VA 22314-3465   Phone: (703)684-5545
William R. Brown, Jr. Editor. Weekly. Magazine covering job developments for members.

★1424★
Postal Bulletin
U.S. Government Printing Office
Superintendent of Documents
Washington, DC 20402   Phone: (202)245-4000
U.S. Postal Service, Directives and Forms Division, Publisher. Biweekly. Bulletin reporting U.S. Postal Service news. **Facsimile Number:** (202)275-0019.

★1425★
Postal Life
475 L'Enfant Plaza SW
Washington, DC 20260
U.S. Postal Service, Dept. of Public and Employee Communications, Publisher. 6x/yr. Magazine for postal employees.

★1426★
Postal Record
National Assn. of Letter Carriers
100 Indiana Ave. NW
Washington, DC 20001-2197   Phone: (202)393-4695
Vincent R. Sombrotto, Editor. Monthly. Magazine for active and retired letter carriers. **Facsimile Number:** (202)737-1540.

★1427★
The Postal Supervisor
490 L'Enfant Plaza SW, Ste. 3200
Washington, DC 20024-2120   Phone: (202)484-6070
Bob McLean, Editor. Quarterly. Postal magazine. **Facsimile Number:** (202)488-7288.

★1428★
Postmasters Gazette
National Assn. of Postmasters
8 Herbert St.
Alexandria, VA 22305-2600   Phone: (703)683-9027
Sally Robinson, Editor. Monthly (combined Oct./Nov.). Postal magazine. **Facsimile Number:** (703)683-6820.

★1429★
TCMA Bulletin
Third Class Mail Association (TCMA)
1333 F St. NW, Ste. 710
Washington, DC 20004-1108   Phone: (202)347-0055
50/year.

Meetings and Conventions

★1430★
American Postal Workers Union (APWU)
1300 L St. NW
Washington, DC 20005   Phone: (202)842-4200
Frequency: Biennial conference. 1992.

★1431★
National Association of Letter Carriers of the U.S.A. (NALC)
100 Indiana Ave. NW, Ste. 713
Washington, DC 20001   Phone: (202)393-4695
Frequency: Biennial. 1992; Jul. or Aug.; St. Louis, MO.

★1432★
National Association of Postmasters of the United States Convention
National Association of Postmasters of the United States
8 Herbert St.
Alexandria, VA 22305-2600   Phone: (703)683-9027
1992; Aug. 22-28; Nashville, TN • 1993; Aug. Boston, MA • 1994; Aug. Albuquerque, NM • 1995; Aug. Chicago, IL. **Facsimile Number:** (703)683-6820.

Other Sources of Information

★1433★
Dames Employees: The Feminization of Postal Workers in Nineteenth-Century France
Haworth Press, Inc.
10 Alice St.
Binghamton, NY 13904   Phone: (607)722-5857
Susan Bachrach. 1984. Part of Women & History Series. **Facsimile Number:** (607)722-1424.

★1434★
The Post Office Worker: A Trade Union & Social History
Unwin Hyman, Inc.
Cambridge, MA 02139-3107
Alan Clinton. 1984. **Toll-free/Additional Phone Number(s):** 800-933-6402.

Record Clerks

Record clerks maintain and update either financial or nonfinancial records for a variety of businesses, government agencies, unions, colleges and universities. Some examples of record clerks include brokerage clerks, file clerks, and library assistants. Most record clerks work in an office setting and have skills in typing and word processing. Interaction with the public is often a basic job element.

$alaries

Salaries for record clerks vary by occupation and employment setting.

Order clerks	$20,100/year
Personnel clerks	$16,700/year
Library assistants and bookmobile drivers	$15,300/year
File clerks	$14,500/year

Employment Outlook

Growth rate until the year 2000: More slowly than average.

Record Clerks

Career Guides

★1435★
"Record Clerks" in *Occupational Outlook Handbook* (pp. 270-272)
Superintendent of Documents
U.S. Government Printing Office
Washington, DC 20402   Phone: (202)783-3238
Biennial; latest edition, 1990-91. Encyclopedia of careers describing more than 250 occupations and comprising about 86 percent of all jobs in the economy. Occupations that require lengthy education or training are given the most attention. For each occupation, the handbook describes job duties, working conditions, training, educational preparation, personal qualities, advancement possibilities, job outlook, earnings, and sources of additional information.

Test Guides

★1436★
Associate Public Records Officer
National Learning Corp.
212 Michael Dr.
Syosset, NY 11791   Phone: (516)921-8888
Jack Rudman. Part of the Career Examination Series No. 1. All examination guides in this series contain questions with answers. **Facsimile Number:** (516)921-8743. **Toll-free/Additional Phone Number(s):** 800-645-6337.

★1437★
Principal Records Center Assistant
National Learning Corp.
212 Michael Dr.
Syosset, NY 11791   Phone: (516)921-8888
Jack Rudman. Part of the Career Examination Series No. 1. All examination guides in this series contain questions with answers. **Facsimile Number:** (516)921-8743. **Toll-free/Additional Phone Number(s):** 800-645-6337.

★1438★
Recording Clerk
National Learning Corp.
212 Michael Dr.
Syosset, NY 11791   Phone: (516)921-8888
Jack Rudman. Part of the Career Examination Series No. 1. All examination guides in this series contain questions with answers. **Facsimile Number:** (516)921-8743. **Toll-free/Additional Phone Number(s):** 800-645-6337.

★1439★
Senior Records Center Assistant
National Learning Corp.
212 Michael Dr.
Syosset, NY 11791   Phone: (516)921-8888
Jack Rudman. Part of the Career Examination Series No. 1. All examination guides in this series contain questions with answers. **Facsimile Number:** (516)921-8743. **Toll-free/Additional Phone Number(s):** 800-645-6337.

Periodicals

★1440★
Bank Operations Report
Warren, Gorham & Lamont, Inc.
One Penn Plaza
New York, NY 10119   Phone: (212)971-5000
Editor(s): Pat Durner. Monthly. Focuses on electronic data processing control, check processing, record keeping, cost control, Federal regulation, credit and debit cards, electronic funds transfer system, physical security, and office automation, computer, and systems applications.

★1441★
Records Management Quarterly
Assn. of Record Managers and Administrators
PO Box 8540
Prairie Village, KS 66208   Phone: (913)341-3808
Ira Penn, Editor and Advertising Manager. Quarterly. Professional journal on records technology and information management. **Facsimile Number:** (913)341-3742.

Brokerage Clerks and Statement Clerks

Brokerage clerks facilitate the sale and purchase of stocks, bonds, commodities, and other types of investments. Some types of brokerage clerks include purchase-and-sale clerks, dividend clerks, transfer clerks, receive-and-deliver clerks, and margin clerks. Purchase-and-sale clerks match orders to buy with orders to sell. Dividend clerks handle the payments of stock or cash dividends to clients. Transfer clerks check stock certificates to see that they adhere to banking regulations. Receive-and-deliver clerks are responsible for receiving and delivering stock certificates. Margin clerks monitor customers' accounts. Statement clerks are employed by banking institutions to process and mail bank statements with the aid of sophisticated machines.

$alaries

The average salary of brokerage clerks is $13,800-26,700/year, with margin clerks, option clerks, and stock loan clerks earning the highest salaries, and transfer clerks, syndicate clerks, registration clerks, and dividend clerks earning the lowest.

Employment Outlook

Growth rate until the year 2000: Employment is expected to remain level.

Brokerage Clerks and Statement Clerks

Career Guides

★1442★
Brokerage Clerk/Sales Assistant
Vocational Biographies, Inc.
PO Box 31, Dept. VF10
Sauk Centre, MN 56378 Phone: (612)352-6516
1988. This pamphlet profiles a person working in the job. Includes information about job duties, working conditions, places of employment, educational preparation, labor market outlook, and salaries. **Toll-free/Additional Phone Number(s):** 800-255-0752.

★1443★
"Brokerage Clerks and Statement Clerks" in
 Occupational Outlook Handbook (p. 272)
Superintendent of Documents
U.S. Government Printing Office
Washington, DC 20402 Phone: (202)783-3238
Biennial; latest edition, 1990-91. Encyclopedia of careers describing more than 250 occupations and comprising about 86 percent of all jobs in the economy. Occupations that require lengthy education or training are given the most attention. For each occupation, the handbook describes job duties, working conditions, training, educational preparation, personal qualities, advancement possibilities, job outlook, earnings, and sources of additional information.

Associations

★1444★
American Stock Exchange (AMEX)
86 Trinity Pl.
New York, NY 10006 Phone: (212)306-1000
Membership: A domestic and international securities and options market organized in the early 19th century, exact year unknown. **Publications:** *American Stock Exchange—Annual Report.* • *American Stock Exchange—Weekly Bulletin.* • *AMEX Fact Book*, annual. • *AMEX Options*, periodic. • Also publishes brochure and index; produces audiovisual material.

Standards/Certification Agencies

Because statement clerks have access to an individual's financial information, they must be bonded.

Periodicals

★1445★
ABA Banking Journal
Simmons-Boardman Publishing Corp.
345 Hudson St.
New York, NY 10014 Phone: (212)620-7200
William Streeter, Editor. Monthly. Official magazine of the American Bankers Association. **Facsimile Number:** (212)633-1165.

★1446★
American Stock Exchange—Weekly Bulletin
American Stock Exchange (AMEX)
86 Trinity Pl.
New York, NY 10006 Phone: (212)306-1000
Reports news of membership changes, new stock exchange and supplemental listings, listing removals, subscription offerings, dividends, and AMEX notices. Also covers stockholder meetings and includes calendar of events.

★1447★
AMEX Options
American Stock Exchange (AMEX)
86 Trinity Pl.
New York, NY 10006 Phone: (212)306-1000
Periodic. Newsletter.

★1448★
Records Management Quarterly
Assn. of Record Managers and Administrators
PO Box 8540
Prairie Village, KS 66208 Phone: (913)341-3808
Ira Penn, Editor and Advertising Manager. Quarterly. Professional journal on records technology and information management. **Facsimile Number:** (913)341-3742.

★1449★
The Speculator
Growth in Funds, Inc.
77 S. Palm Ave.
Sarasota, FL 34236 Phone: (813)954-0330
Byron Sanders, Editor. Biweekly. Stock market advisory magazine. **Facsimile Number:** (813)954-0647.

Other Sources of Information

★1450★
AMEX Fact Book
American Stock Exchange (AMEX)
86 Trinity Pl.
New York, NY 10006   Phone: (212)306-1000

Annual. Statistical reference work including equity trading, options, Market Value Index, new stock listings, and a list of issues on AMEX with trading data. Includes subject index.

File Clerks

File clerks are responsible for maintaining an organized and updated filing system within an organization. They classify, store, update, and retrieve information on request. To keep records updated, file clerks add new material in a timely manner and may have to destroy outdated information or transfer it to a storage system. File clerks may be required to revise the manner of filing to keep pace with the amount of information. Some types of filing systems include file cabinets, microfilm, optical disks, or computerized retrieval systems. In smaller establishments, file clerks sometimes have additional responsibilities such as typing, word processing, or sorting mail. File clerks are found in a wide variety of industries with many employed in finance, insurance, real estate, and government.

$alaries

The average salary for file clerks is $14,500/year

Employment Outlook

Growth rate until the year 2000: More slowly than average.

File Clerks

Career Guides

★1451★
File Clerk
Careers, Inc.
PO Box 135
Largo, FL 34649-0135 Phone: (813)584-7333
1989. Two-page job guide card describing duties, working conditions, personal qualifications, training, earnings and hours, employment outlook, places of employment, related careers and where to write for more information.

★1452★
"File Clerk" in *Administration, Business, and Office, Volume 1 of Career Information Center* (pp. 54-55)
Glencoe/Macmillan
15319 Chatsworth St.
Mission Hills, CA 91345 Phone: (818)898-1391
Richard Lidz and Dale Anderson, editorial directors. Fourth edition, 1990. For 600 occupations, describes job duties, entry-level requirements, education and training needed, advancement possibilities, employment outlook, earnings and benefits. The set is divided into 12 volumes. Each volume includes jobs related under a broad career field. Volume 13 is the index. **Facsimile Number:** 818-365-5489.

★1453★
"File Clerk" in *Careers in Banking and Finance* (pp. 43-45)
Rosen Publishing Group, Inc.
29 E. 21st St.
New York, NY 10010 Phone: (212)777-3017
Patricia Haddock. 1990. Describes more than 20 jobs at all levels in banking and finance. Contains information about the types of financial organizations where the jobs are found, educational requirements, job duties, and salaries. Offers advice on job hunting.

★1454★
"File Clerk" in *Occu-Facts: Information on 565 Careers in Outline Form* (p. 12.24)
Careers, Inc.
P.O. Box 135
1211 Tenth St., S.W.
Largo, FL 33640 Phone: (813)584-7333
Elizabeth Handville. Biennial, 1989-90 edition. Each one-page occupational profile describes duties, working conditions, physical surroundings and demands, aptitudes, temperament, educational requirements, employment outlook, earnings, and places of employment.

★1455★
File Clerk, General Clerk
Prentice Hall
Rte. 9W
Englewood Cliffs, NJ 07632 Phone: (201)592-2000
Hy Hammer. 8th revised edition, 1988. Part of ARCO Civil Service.

★1456★
"File Clerks" in *Jobs! What They Are...Where They Are...What They Pay* (pp. 208-209)
Simon & Schuster, Inc.
Simon & Schuster Bldg.
1230 Avenue of the Americas
New York, NY 10020 Phone: (212)698-7000
Robert O. Snelling and Anne M. Snelling. Revised edition, 1989. Profiles 241 occupations, describing duties and responsibilities, educational preparation, earnings, employment opportunities, training, and qualifications.

★1457★
"File Clerks" in *Occupational Outlook Handbook* (pp. 272-273)
Superintendent of Documents
U.S. Government Printing Office
Washington, DC 20402 Phone: (202)783-3238
Biennial; latest edition, 1990-91. Encyclopedia of careers describing more than 250 occupations and comprising about 86 percent of all jobs in the economy. Occupations that require lengthy education or training are given the most attention. For each occupation, the handbook describes job duties, working conditions, training, educational preparation, personal qualities, advancement possibilities, job outlook, earnings, and sources of additional information.

★1458★
"File Clerks" in Volume 3 of *Career Discovery Encyclopedia* (pp. 24-25)
J.G. Ferguson Publishing Co.
200 W. Monroe
Chicago, IL 60606 Phone: (312)580-5480
E. Russell Primm, editor-in-chief. 1990. Contains two-page articles on 504 occupations. Each article describes job duties, earnings, and educational and training requirements.

★1459★
"File Clerks" in Volume 3 of *The Encyclopedia of Careers and Vocational Guidance* (pp. 33-35)
J.G. Ferguson Publishing Co.
200 W. Monroe
Chicago, IL 60606   Phone: (312)580-5480

William E. Hopke, editor-in-chief. Eighth edition, 1990. Four-volume set that profiles 500 occupations and describes job trends in 76 industries. Includes career description, educational requirements, history of the job, methods of entry, advancement, employment outlook, earnings, working conditions, social and psychological factors, and sources of additional information.

★1460★
"File Clerks" in *The American Almanac of Jobs and Salaries* (pp. 506-507)
Avon Books
105 Madison Avenue
New York, NY 10016   Phone: (212)481-5600

John Wright and Edward J. Dwyer. Revised and updated, 1990. A comprehensive guide to the wages of hundreds of occupations in a wide variety of industries and organizations.

★1461★
Vocational Visions
Center for Humanities, Inc.
Communications Park
Box 1000
Mount Kisco, NY 10549   Phone: (914)666-4100

Videocassette. 1984. 30 mins. This series of programs explains key aspects of actual training and a day in the life of a worker in the specific field mentioned on the videocassette. Occupations include: transportation/mechanics, repair, construction, business/office occupations, health, and agriculture.

Test Guides

★1462★
Chief File Clerk
National Learning Corp.
212 Michael Dr.
Syosset, NY 11791   Phone: (516)921-8888

Jack Rudman. Part of the Career Examination Series No. 1. All examination guides in this series contain questions with answers. **Facsimile Number:** (516)921-8743. **Toll-free/Additional Phone Number(s):** 800-645-6337.

★1463★
File Clerk
National Learning Corp.
212 Michael Dr.
Syosset, NY 11791   Phone: (516)921-8888

Jack Rudman. Part of the Career Examination Series No. 1. All examination guides in this series contain questions with answers. **Facsimile Number:** (516)921-8743. **Toll-free/Additional Phone Number(s):** 800-645-6337.

★1464★
File Clerk - General Clerk
Prentice Hall Press
Simon & Schuster Inc.
200 Old Tappan Rd.
Old Tappan, NJ 07675   Phone: (800)223-2348

Hy Hammer and John Czukor. Provides information on qualifying tests for clerical positions with federal, state, and municipal agencies. Includes sample tests and tips.

★1465★
Principal File Clerk
National Learning Corp.
212 Michael Dr.
Syosset, NY 11791   Phone: (516)921-8888

Jack Rudman. Part of the Career Examination Series No. 1. All examination guides in this series contain questions with answers. **Facsimile Number:** (516)921-8743. **Toll-free/Additional Phone Number(s):** 800-645-6337.

★1466★
Senior Clerical Series
Prentice Hall Press
Simon & Schuster Inc.
200 Old Tappan Rd.
Old Tappan, NJ 07675   Phone: (800)223-2348

Hy Hammer. Fourth edition, 1983. Complete test preparation for the following senior grade positions: clerk, typist, stenographer, account clerk, file clerk, statistics clerk, stenographer (law), mail and supply clerk, and stores clerk.

★1467★
Senior File Clerk
National Learning Corp.
212 Michael Dr.
Syosset, NY 11791   Phone: (516)921-8888

Jack Rudman. Part of the Career Examination Series No. 1. All examination guides in this series contain questions with answers. **Facsimile Number:** (516)921-8743. **Toll-free/Additional Phone Number(s):** 800-645-6337.

★1468★
Workbook Exercises in Alphabetic Filing
McGraw-Hill Publishing Co.
1221 Avenue of the Americas
New York, NY 10020   Phone: (212)512-2000

R. J. Stewart. Third revised edition, 1980.

Basic Reference Guides and Handbooks

★1469★
Alphabetic Filing Rules
Association of Records Managers & Administrators, Inc.
4200 Somerset, Ste. 215
Prairie Village, KS 66208   Phone: (913)341-3808

1986.

★1470★
File Management Techniques
Krieger Publishing Co.
PO Box 9542
Melbourne, FL 32902   Phone: (407)724-9542

Billy G. Claybrook. 1983. **Facsimile Number:** (407)951-3671.

★1471★
File Structure & Design
Krieger Publishing Co.
PO Box 9542
Melbourne, FL 32902   Phone: (407)724-9542

Margaret Cunningham. 1986. **Facsimile Number:** (407)951-3671.

★1472★
Filing & Records Management
Prentice Hall
Rte. 9W
Englewood Cliffs, NJ 07632   Phone: (201)592-2000
Nathan Krevolin. 1986.

★1473★
Filing Procedures Guideline
Association of Records Managers & Administrators
4200 Somerset, Ste. 215
Prairie Village, KS 66208   Phone: (913)341-3808
1989.

★1474★
Filing: Syllabus
National Book Co.
PO Box 8795
Portland, OR 97207-8795   Phone: (503)228-6345
Joanne Piper. Second edition, 1979.

★1475★
Filing Systems & Records Management
McGraw-Hill Publishing Co.
1221 Avenue of the Ameicas
New York, NY 10020   Phone: (212)512-2000
Jeffrey R. Stewart, Jr. Third edition, 1981.

★1476★
Gregg Quick Filing Practice
McGraw-Hill Publishing Co.
1221 Avenue of the Americas
New York, NY 10020   Phone: (212)512-2000
Jeffrey R. Stewart, Jr. Second edition, 1979.

★1477★
How to Set up an Effective Filing System
National Association of Credit Management
8815 Centre Park, Dr., Ste. 200
Columbia, MD 21045   Phone: (301)740-5560
Mary S. Taylor. 1981. **Facsimile Number:** (301)740-5574.

★1478★
Intensive Files Management
South-Western Publishing Co.
5101 Madison Rd.
Cincinnati, OH 45227   Phone: (513)271-8811
Andrea R. Henne. Second edition, 1985.

★1479★
Numeric Filing Guideline
Association of Records Managers & Administrators
4200 Somerset, Ste. 215
Prairie Village, KS 66208   Phone: (913)341-3808
1989.

★1480★
OJT File Clerk Resource Materials
McGraw-Hill Publishing Co.
1221 Avenue of the Americas
New York, NY 10020   Phone: (212)512-2000
Joyce A. Sherster. Second edition, 1981. Part of Gregg Office Job Training Program Series.

★1481★
OJT File Clerk Training Manual
McGraw-Hill, Inc.
1221 Avenue of the Americas
New York, NY 10020   Phone: (212)512-2000
Joyce A. Sherster. Second edition, 1981. Part of Gregg Office Job Training Program Series.

★1482★
Progressive Filing
McGraw-Hill Publishing Co.
1221 Avenue of the Americas
New York, NY 10020   Phone: (212)512-2000
Jeffrey R. Stewart. Ninth edition, 1980.

★1483★
Records & Database Management
McGraw-Hill Publishing Co.
1221 Avenue of the Americas
New York, NY 10020   Phone: (212)512-2000
Jeffrey R. Stewart. Fourth edition, 1989.

★1484★
Records Management
South-Western Publishing Co.
5101 Madison Rd.
Cincinnati, OH 45227   Phone: (513)271-8811
Mina M. Johnson. Fourth edition, 1986.

★1485★
The Vertical File & Its Satellites: A Handbook of Acquisition, Processing, & Organization
Libraries Unlimited, Inc,
6931 S. Yosemite St.
Englewood, CO 80112   Phone: (303)770-1220
Shirley Miller. Second edition, 1979. Part of Library Science Text Series.

———————— Periodicals ————————

★1486★
Records Management Quarterly
Assn. of Record Managers and Administrators
PO Box 8540
Prairie Village, KS 66208   Phone: (913)341-3808
Ira Penn, Editor and Advertising Manager. Quarterly. Professional journal on records technology and information management. **Facsimile Number:** (913)341-3742.

Library Assistants and Bookmobile Drivers

Library assistants help keep library resources in an orderly condition and make sure they are readily available to users. They are responsible for registering patrons and issuing library cards as well as checking out materials and computing overdue fines. Library assistants also sort returned books and periodicals and return them to the shelves. Bookmobile drivers are also employed by many libraries to extend library services by driving a vehicle stocked with books to regular locations. The average salary for library assistants and bookmobile drivers is $15,300/year.

Employment Outlook

Growth rate until the year 2000: More slowly than average.

Library Assistants and Bookmobile Drivers

Career Guides

★1487★
"Library Assistant" in Volume 4 of *Career Discovery Encyclopedia* **(pp. 24-25)**
J.G. Ferguson Publishing Co.
200 W. Monroe
Chicago, IL 60606	Phone: (312)580-5480
E. Russell Primm, editor-in-chief. 1990. Contains two-page articles on 504 occupations. Each article describes job duties, earnings, and educational and training requirements.

★1488★
"Library Assistants and Bookmobile Drivers" in *Occupational Outlook Handbook* **(pp. 273-274)**
Superintendent of Documents
U.S. Government Printing Office
Washington, DC 20402	Phone: (202)783-3238
Biennial; latest edition, 1990-91. Encyclopedia of careers describing more than 250 occupations and comprising about 86 percent of all jobs in the economy. Occupations that require lengthy education or training are given the most attention. For each occupation, the handbook describes job duties, working conditions, training, educational preparation, personal qualities, advancement possibilities, job outlook, earnings, and sources of additional information.

★1489★
Library Clerk
Careers, Inc.
PO Box 135
Largo, FL 34649-0135	Phone: (813)584-7333
1990. Two-page job guide card describing duties, working conditions, personal qualifications, training, earnings and hours, employment outlook, places of employment, related careers and where to write for more information.

★1490★
Library Clerk
Vocational Biographies, Inc.
PO Box 31, Dept. VF10
Sauk Centre, MN 56378	Phone: (612)352-6516
1990. This pamphlet profiles a person working in the job. Includes information about job duties, working conditions, places of employment, educational preparation, labor market outlook, and salaries. **Toll-free/Additional Phone Number(s):** 800-255-0752.

★1491★
"Library Clerk" in *Occu-Facts: Information on 565 Careers in Outline Form* **(p. 12.22)**
Careers, Inc.
P.O. Box 135
1211 Tenth St., S.W.
Largo, FL 33640	Phone: (813)584-7333
Elizabeth Handville. Biennial, 1989-90 edition. Each one-page occupational profile describes duties, working conditions, physical surroundings and demands, aptitudes, temperament, educational requirements, employment outlook, earnings, and places of employment.

★1492★
Library Jobs: How to Fill Them, How to Find Them
Oryx Press
4041 N. Central at Indian School Rd., Ste. 700
Phoenix, AZ 85012-3397	Phone: (602)265-2651
Barbara I. Dewey. 1987. **Toll-free/Additional Phone Number(s):** 800-279-6799. **Facsimile Number:** (602)253-2741.

★1493★
Library Technical Assistant
Careers, Inc.
PO Box 135
Largo, FL 34649-0135	Phone: (813)584-7333
1990. Two-page occupational summary card describing duties, working conditions, personal qualifications, training, earnings and hours, employment outlook, places of employment, related careers and where to write for more information.

★1494★
"Library Technical Assistant" in *Occu-Facts: Information on 565 Careers in Outline Form* **(p. 12.23)**
Careers, Inc.
P.O. Box 135
1211 Tenth St., S.W.
Largo, FL 33640	Phone: (813)584-7333
Elizabeth Handville. Biennial, 1989-90 edition. Each one-page occupational profile describes duties, working conditions, physical surroundings and demands, aptitudes, temperament, educational requirements, employment outlook, earnings, and places of employment.

★1495★
"Library Technical Assistant" in *Opportunities in Vocational and Technical Careers* (pp. 50-52)
National Textbook Co.
4255 W. Touhy Ave.
Lincolnwood, IL 60646   Phone: (312)679-5500

Adrian A. Paradis. 1987. Describes careers which can be prepared for by attending a private vocational or proprietary school—office employee, sales worker, service worker, health services, mechanic, craftworker, and technician. Covers employment outlook, job duties, and salaries. Offers career planning advice.

★1496★
Library Technicians and Assistants
Chronicle Guidance Publications, Inc.
PO Box 1190
Moravia, NY 13118-1190   Phone: (315)497-0330

1988. This career brief describes the nature of the work, working conditions, hours and earnings, education and training, licensure, certification, unions, personal qualifications, social and psychological factors, employment outlook, entry methods, advancement, and related occupations. **Toll-free/Additional Phone Number(s):** 800-622-7284.

★1497★
"Library Technicians and Assistants" in *Jobs! What They Are...Where They Are...What They Pay* (p. 94)
Simon & Schuster, Inc.
Simon & Schuster Bldg.
1230 Avenue of the Americas
New York, NY 10020   Phone: (212)698-7000

Robert O. Snelling and Anne M. Snelling. Revised edition, 1989. Profiles 241 occupations, describing duties and responsibilities, educational preparation, earnings, employment opportunities, training, and qualifications.

─────────── Associations ───────────

★1498★
American Library Association (ALA)
50 E. Huron St.
Chicago, IL 60611   Phone: (312)994-6780

Membership: Librarians, libraries, trustees, friends of libraries, and others interested in the responsibilities of libraries in the educational, social, and cultural needs of society. **Purpose:** Promotes and improves library service and librarianship. Establishes standards of service, support, education, and welfare for libraries and library personnel; promotes the adoption of such standards in libraries of all kinds; safeguards the professional status of librarians; encourages the recruiting of competent personnel for professional careers in librarianship; promotes popular understanding and public acceptance of the value of library service and librarianship; works in liaison with federal agencies to initiate the enactment and administration of legislation that will extend library services. Maintains 24,000 volume library. Sponsors competitions; bestows awards. Offers placement services. **Toll-free/Additional Phone Number(s):** 800-545-2433. **Facsimile Number:** (312)440-9374.

★1499★
Council on Library-Media Technical-Assistants (COLT)
Library/Media Technology Dept., SC 126
2900 Community College Ave.
Cuyahoga Community College
Cleveland, OH 44115   Phone: (216)987-4000

Membership: People involved in two-year associate degree programs for the training of library technical assistants (professional support workers) and graduates of programs employed as library/media technical assistants (B.A. degree holders without M.L.S. degree). Membership includes junior college deans, librarians, curriculum directors, professors, employers, special libraries, university libraries, library schools, publishers, and library technical assistants. **Purpose:** Provides a channel of communication among the institutions and personnel that have developed such training programs; attempts to standardize curriculum offerings; develops educational standards; conducts research on graduates of the programs; represents the interests of library technical assistants and support staff. The council's concerns also include development of clear job descriptions and criteria for employment of technicians and dissemination of information to the public and to prospective students. Sponsors workshops for support staff in areas such as management, supervisory skills, interpersonal communication, business writing, and media center management. Maintains speakers' bureau. Is developing a program for certification of library media technicians and a continuing education program for library support staff.

─────────── Test Guides ───────────

★1500★
Department Library Aide
National Learning Corp.
212 Michael Dr.
Syosset, NY 11791   Phone: (516)921-8888

Jack Rudman. Part of the Career Examination Series No. 1. All examination guides in this series contain questions with answers. **Facsimile Number:** (516)921-8743. **Toll-free/Additional Phone Number(s):** 800-645-6337.

★1501★
Principal Library Clerk
National Learning Corp.
212 Michael Dr.
Syosset, NY 11791   Phone: (516)921-8888

Jack Rudman. Part of the Career Examination Series No. 1. All examination guides in this series contain questions with answers. **Facsimile Number:** (516)921-8743. **Toll-free/Additional Phone Number(s):** 800-645-6337.

★1502★
Senior Library Clerk
National Learning Corp.
212 Michael Dr.
Syosset, NY 11791   Phone: (516)921-8888

Jack Rudman. Part of the Career Examination Series No. 1. All examination guides in this series contain questions with answers. **Facsimile Number:** (516)921-8743. **Toll-free/Additional Phone Number(s):** 800-645-6337.

─────────── Basic Reference Guides and Handbooks ───────────

★1503★
Microcomputer Software for School Library Applications
State Library
South Dakota Department of Education and Cultural Affairs
800 Governors Dr.
Pierre, SD 57501   Phone: (605)773-3131

Donna Gilliland, editor. Latest edition 1984. Publishers of over 125 software packages designed for school library applications such as cataloging, circulation, ordering, inventory of audiovisual equipment, accounting, bibliographies, and word processing. Entries include: Software title, publisher name, address, description, hardware required, price. Arrangement: Classified by library function.

Periodicals

★1504★
The Abbey Newsletter
Abbey Publications, Inc.
320 E. Center St.
Provo, UT 84606　　　　　　　　　Phone: (801)373-1598

Editor(s): Ellen R. McCrady. 8/yr. Encourages the development of library and archival conservation, particularly technical advances and cross-disciplinary research in the field. Covers bookbinding and the conservation of books, papers, photographs, and non-paper materials. Recurring features include book reviews, news of research, job listings, convention reports, letters to the editor, a calendar of events, and a column about equipment and supplies.

★1505★
Apple Library Users Group Newsletter
Apple Computer, Inc.
10381 Bandley Dr.
Cupertino, CA 95014　　　　　　　Phone: (408)974-2552

Editor(s): Monica Ertel. Quarterly. Serves as an exchange for information concerning the use of Apple and Macintosh computers in libraries and information centers of all sizes. Recurring features include news of research, book reviews, news from members, answers to readers' questions, a calendar of events, and columns titled News From/About Apple, Software Reviews, and Information From Our Vendors. **Facsimile Number:** (408)725-8502.

★1506★
CMC News
Computers and the Media Center (CMC)
515 Oak St., N.
Cannon Falls, MN 55009　　　　　Phone: (507)263-3711

Editor(s): Jim Deacon. Quarterly. Acts as a forum where library/media specialists can share information on computer use. Contains reviews of library utility programs on the microcomputer and articles on the management of microcomputers in library/media centers. Recurring features include columns titled Commercially Speaking (information on new computer products) and User Directory (a list of useful computer products and how they are used).

★1507★
ERIC/IR Update
ERIC Clearinghouse on Information Resources
Syracuse University
School of Education
Syracuse, NY 13244-2340　　　　Phone: (315)423-3640

Editor(s): Jane K. Janis. Semiannually. Concentrates on the areas of education technology and library/information science. Offers informational resources and annotated bibliographies on topics of current interest in the areas of bibliographic instruction, microcomputers, computers and libraries, and television, visual literacy, and videotaping. Covers research reports, conference papers, curriculum guides, and trade books, which are available on microfiche and/or photocopy through ERIC.

★1508★
FLICC Newsletter
Federal Library and Information Center Committee (FLICC)
Library of Congress
Washington, DC 20540　　　　　　Phone: (202)707-4800

Editor(s): Darlene J. Dolan. Quarterly. Provides news and items of interest for federal librarians, information specialists, and administrators. Recurring features include minutes of FLICC meetings, descriptions of its programs and projects, and announcements of special training courses for Federal Library and Information Center personnel. **Facsimile Number:** (202)707-4818.

★1509★
Hot Off the Computer
Westchester Library System
8 Westchester Plaza
Elmsford, NY 10523　　　　　　　Phone: (914)592-8214

Editor(s): Diane Courtney. 6/yr. Focuses on administrative and public service applications of microcomputers for public libraries. Includes columns titled Practical uses of Microcomputers, Software Reviews, Database Searches, Book Reviews, and Articles of Interest.

★1510★
IASL Newsletter
International Association of School Librarianship (IASL)
PO Box 1486
Kalamazoo, MI 49005　　　　　　Phone: (716)803-6641

Editor(s): Peter J. Genco. Quarterly. Covers association activities and developments in school library programs. Recurring features include book reviews, a schedule of activities, news of research, and a column titled From the President.

★1511★
Library Times International
Future World Publishing Company
PO Box 15661-0661
Evansville, IN 47716　　　　　　Phone: (812)473-2420

Editor(s): R.N. Sharma. Bimonthly. Monitors international developments and events related to library and information science. Carries items on countries worldwide. Recurring features include interviews, book reviews, a column carrying information science updates, news from library associations and groups, editorials, letters to the editor, listings of new publications, and a calendar of events.

★1512★
The National Librarian: The NLA Newsletter
National Librarians Association (NLA)
PO Box 486
Alma, MI 48801　　　　　　　　　Phone: (517)463-7227

Editor(s): Peter Dollard. Quarterly. Reports on news of concern to professional librarians. Reports on certification, education, relevant legal cases, and news of the Association and related library and educational organizations. Recurring features include book reviews and a section titled Bibliography on Professionalism. **Facsimile Number:** (517)463-8694.

★1513★
OCLC Newsletter
Online Computer Library Center (OCLC)
6565 Frantz Rd.
Dublin, OH 43017　　　　　　　　Phone: (614)764-6000

Editor(s): Philip Schieber and Nita Dean. Bimonthly. Published as a service to users and potential users of automated library and information systems. Includes client news and information on Center activities.

★1514★
Online Libraries and Microcomputers
Information Intelligence, Inc.
PO Box 31098
Phoenix, AZ 85046   Phone: (602)996-2283
Editor(s): George S. Machovec. Monthly, except July and August. Covers new library online and automation applications, library-oriented software and hardware for online and CD-ROM use, library networks, new online and CD-ROM databases, and people in the online/CD-ROM fields. Recurring features include editorials and notices of forthcoming meetings and new publications. **Toll-free/Additional Phone Number(s):** 800-228-9982.

★1515★
Records Management Quarterly
Assn. of Record Managers and Administrators
PO Box 8540
Prairie Village, KS 66208   Phone: (913)341-3808
Ira Penn, Editor and Advertising Manager. Quarterly. Professional journal on records technology and information management. **Facsimile Number:** (913)341-3742.

★1516★
Sipapu
Noel Peattie
23311 County Rd. 88
Winters, CA 95694   Phone: (916)752-1032
Editor(s): Noel Peattie. Semiannually. Serves librarians and others concerned with alternative publications. Contains informal listings, annotation, and articles on small and independent presses; Third World, feminist, underground, counter-culture and radical publications; and dissent literature in general.

★1517★
Technicalities
Media Publishing
2440 O St.
Lincoln, NE 68510-1124   Phone: (402)474-2676
Editor(s): Brian Alley. Monthly. Reports on the field of library and information science, including cataloging, acquisitions, networks and databases, computer operations, serials, preservation and binding, and news of the profession. Recurring features include feature articles with bibliographical notes, interviews with professionals in the field, conference and convention reports, and a section titled Consumer Beware. **Toll-free/Additional Phone Number(s):** 800-627-9919 **Facsimile Number:** (402)474-5104.

★1518★
Wired Librarian's Newsletter
Micro Computer Libraries
297 Hammertown Rd.
Jackson, OH 45640-9093
Editor(s): Eric S. Anderson. Carries news and information on the use of microcomputers for libraries. Covers hardware, software, and library microcomputer user groups. Recurring features include editorials, book reviews, humorous items, listings of related seminars and events.

★1519★
WLW Journal
Women Library Workers (WLW)
2027 Parker St.
Berkeley, CA 94704   Phone: (415)540-5322
Editor(s): Carol Starr. Quarterly. For librarians, library technicians, clerks, and others interested in ending discrimination against women in libraries. Contains in-depth articles on issues affecting women and libraries, feminist management and database building, and feminist presses. Recurring features include reviews of books, films, records, periodicals, pamphlets, and other media; cartoons, editorials, news of members, news of research, letters to the editor, and columns titled Pay Equity for Librarians, Women in Librarianship: Research, and Profiles of Women's Collections.

Meetings and Conventions

★1520★
American Library Association (ALA)
50 E. Huron St.
Chicago, IL 60611   Phone: (312)994-6780
Frequency: Annual conference, with exhibits. 1992; Jun. 27 - Jul. 2; San Francisco, CA • 1993; Jun. 26 - Jul. 1; New Orleans, LA. Also holds annual midwinter meeting, with exhibits. 1992; Jan. 25-30; San Antonio, TX. **Toll-free/Additional Phone Number(s):** 800-545-2433. **Facsimile Number:** (312)440-9374.

★1521★
Council on Library-Media Technical-Assistants (COLT)
Library/Media Technology Dept., SC 126
2900 Community College Ave.
Cuyahoga Community College
Cleveland, OH 44115   Phone: (216)987-4000
Frequency: Annual.

Other Sources of Information

★1522★
A Benefit-Cost Analysis of Alternative Library Delivery Systems
Greenwood Publishing Group, Inc.
88 Post Rd., W.
PO Box 5007
Westport, CT 06881   Phone: (203)226-3571
Teh-Wei Hu. 1975. Part of the Contributions in Librarianship and Information Science Series. **Facsimile Number:** (202)222-1505.

★1523★
Essential Guide to the Library IBM PC: Library Application Software
Meckler Corporation
11 Ferry Ln., W.
Westport, CT 06880   Phone: (203)226-6967
Sara Goodrich Miles, editor. Published 1986. List of suppliers of 100 computer programs suited to the IBM PC with library applications, including audiovisual management, circulation, and serials management. Entries include: Company name, address, phone.

Order Clerks

Order clerks receive and process incoming orders for materials, merchandise, or services. They handle orders for a wide variety of items, with some orders coming from within the organization itself. In large companies, such as automobile manufacturers, parts or equipment need to be ordered from the company's warehouses. Employees in this setting are called "inside order clerks." Order clerks who deal primarily with the public are called "outside order clerks." Many order clerks work on video display terminals, which provide easy access to prices and inventory. Orders are received by telephone, mail, and facsimile machines. Order clerks review incoming orders, enter the information on an order form, and compute the customer's cost. The clerk then routes the order to the department that will send or deliver the item. Order clerks are primarily employed by wholesale and retail establishments and manufacturing firms.

$alaries

The average salary for order clerks is $20,100/year

Employment Outlook

Employment is expected to remain level.

Order Clerks

Career Guides

★1524★
"Catalog Order Clerk" in *Occu-Facts: Information on 565 Careers in Outline Form* (p. 12.21)
Careers, Inc.
P.O. Box 135
1211 Tenth St., S.W.
Largo, FL 33640　　　　　　　　Phone: (813)584-7333
Elizabeth Handville. Biennial, 1989-90 edition. Each one-page occupational profile describes duties, working conditions, physical surroundings and demands, aptitudes, temperament, educational requirements, employment outlook, earnings, and places of employment.

★1525★
"Order Clerks" in *Occupational Outlook Handbook* (pp. 274-275)
Superintendent of Documents
U.S. Government Printing Office
Washington, DC 20402　　　　　Phone: (202)783-3238
Biennial; latest edition, 1990-91. Encyclopedia of careers describing more than 250 occupations and comprising about 86 percent of all jobs in the economy. Occupations that require lengthy education or training are given the most attention. For each occupation, the handbook describes job duties, working conditions, training, educational preparation, personal qualities, advancement possibilities, job outlook, earnings, and sources of additional information.

Periodicals

★1526★
Records Management Quarterly
Assn. of Record Managers and Administrators
PO Box 8540
Prairie Village, KS 66208　　　　Phone: (913)341-3808
Ira Penn, Editor and Advertising Manager. Quarterly. Professional journal on records technology and information management. **Facsimile Number:** (913)341-3742.

Personnel Clerks

Personnel clerks are responsible for maintaining the personnel records of an organization's employees. These records include name, address, job title, earnings, benefits, absences, and information about job performance. Personnel clerks may also be involved in the hiring process. Once new employees begin work, they are greeted by personnel clerks, who provide information about the organization and help them fill out the necessary forms. In temporary help agencies, personnel clerks are known as referral clerks. They match requests for temporary help with qualified applicants. Other personnel clerks may be known as identification clerks and are responsible for security matters. They keep records of all employees and visitors and issue badges, passes and identification cards. Personnel clerks are found in most industries including many in government, colleges and universities, hospitals, department stores, and banks.

$alaries
The average salary for personnel clerks is $16,700/year

Employment Outlook
Growth rate until the year 2000: More slowly than average.

Personnel Clerks

Career Guides

★1527★
The Beginning Consultant Training Program
National Association of Personnel Consultants
3133 Mt. Vernon Ave.
Alexandria, VA 22305   Phone: (703)684-0180

★1528★
Opportunities in Personnel Management
National Textbook Co.
4255 W. Touhy Ave.
Lincolnwood, IL 60646-1975   Phone: (708)679-5500
William J. Traynor. 1983. **Facsimile Number:** (708)679-2494.

★1529★
PAI Career Planning Manual for Human Resource-Personnel: A Guide to the Practice & Accreditation in the Profession
Society for Human Resource Management
606 N. Washington
Alexandria, VA 22314   Phone: (703)548-3440
Personnel Accreditation Institute Staff. 1986. **Facsimile Number:** (703)836-0367.

★1530★
"Personnel Clerk" in *Administration, Business, and Office*, Volume 1 of *Career Information Center* (pp. 64-66)
Glencoe/Macmillan
15319 Chatsworth St.
Mission Hills, CA 91345   Phone: (818)898-1391
Richard Lidz and Dale Anderson, editorial directors. Fourth edition, 1990. For 600 occupations, describes job duties, entry-level requirements, education and training needed, advancement possibilities, employment outlook, earnings and benefits. The set is divided into 12 volumes. Each volume includes jobs related under a broad career field. Volume 13 is the index. **Facsimile Number:** 818-365-5489.

★1531★
"Personnel Clerk" in *Occupational Outlook Handbook* (pp. 275-276)
Superintendent of Documents
U.S. Government Printing Office
Washington, DC 20402   Phone: (202)783-3238
Biennial; latest edition, 1990-91. Encyclopedia of careers describing more than 250 occupations and comprising about 86 percent of all jobs in the economy. Occupations that require lengthy education or training are given the most attention. For each occupation, the handbook describes job duties, working conditions, training, educational preparation, personal qualities, advancement possibilities, job outlook, earnings, and sources of additional information.

★1532★
The Wright Way
Quiet Advantage
1949 South Manchester St. 34
Anaheim, CA 92802   Phone: (714)748-1840
Videocassette. 1991. ? mins. Successful work in the personnel placement field is discussed and defined.

Associations

★1533★
National Association of Personnel Workers (NAPW)
Morehouse Coll.
PO Box 6
Atlanta, GA 30314   Phone: (404)681-2800
Membership: Student affairs personnel at historically black colleges. **Purpose:** Seeks to foster a unified spirit among student affairs personnel at predominantly black universities, colleges, and educational institutions. Works to improve the delivery of student services at black colleges and institutions. Serves as a professional agency for the collection of information and the discussion of scientific studies and problems pertaining to student services administration. Provides professional development for student affairs personnel. Designs projects in accordance with trends in postsecondary education. Monitors legislation that impacts student affairs programs and services. **Publications:** *Journal*, quarterly. • *NAPW Newsletter*, quarterly.

★1534★
Newspaper Personnel Relations Association (NPRA)
11600 Sunrise Valley Dr.
Reston, VA 22091   Phone: (703)648-1000
Membership: International newspaper human resources and labor relations executives; newspaper executives whose companies do not have human resources departments; associate members suppliers. **Purpose:** Seeks to advance human resources and industrial relations by seeking ways for management to make more effective use of people and by educating members in basic methods and techniques. Conducts research on human resource issues at newspapers. Operates speakers' bureau. Sponsors competitions. **Publications:** *Directory*, annual. • *NPRA News*, monthly. **Facsimile Number:** (703)620-4557.

Test Guides

★1535★
Personnel Clerk
National Learning Corp.
212 Michael Dr.
Syosset, NY 11791   Phone: (516)921-8888
Jack Rudman. Part of the Career Examination Series No. 1. All examination guides in this series contain questions with answers. **Facsimile Number:** (516)921-8743. **Toll-free/Additional Phone Number(s):** 800-645-6337.

★1536★
Principal Clerk (Personnel)
National Learning Corp.
212 Michael Dr.
Syosset, NY 11791   Phone: (516)921-8888
Jack Rudman. Part of the Career Examination Series No. 1. All examination guides in this series contain questions with answers. **Facsimile Number:** (516)921-8743. **Toll-free/Additional Phone Number(s):** 800-645-6337.

★1537★
Principal Personnel Clerk
National Learning Corp.
212 Michael Dr.
Syosset, NY 11791   Phone: (516)921-8888
Jack Rudman. Part of the Career Examination Series No. 1. All examination guides in this series contain questions with answers. **Facsimile Number:** (516)921-8743. **Toll-free/Additional Phone Number(s):** 800-645-6337.

★1538★
Senior Personnel Clerk
National Learning Corp.
212 Michael Dr.
Syosset, NY 11791   Phone: (516)921-8888
Jack Rudman. Part of the Career Examination Series No. 1. All examination guides in this series contain questions with answers. **Facsimile Number:** (516)921-8743. **Toll-free/Additional Phone Number(s):** 800-645-6337.

Basic Reference Guides and Handbooks

★1539★
Matching Individuals to Jobs: A Motivational Answer for Personnel & Counseling Professionals
AMACOM
135 W. 50th St.
New York, NY 10020   Phone: (212)903-8089
Leonard H. Chusmir. 1985.

★1540★
NPRA Directory
Newspaper Personnel Relations Association (NPRA)
11600 Sunrise Valley Dr.
Reston, VA 22091   Phone: (703)648-1000
Annual.

Periodicals

★1541★
Compensation and Benefits Review
American Management Assn.
135 W. 50 St.
New York, NY 10020   Phone: (212)586-8100
Hermine Zagat Levine, Editor. 6x/yr. Magazine on employee compensation and benefits. **Facsimile Number:** (212)903-8072.

★1542★
Computers in HR Management
Warren, Gorham & Lamont
One Penn Plaza
New York, NY 10019   Phone: (212)971-5000
Jules Gilder, Editor. Monthly Computer magazine for human resource professionals. William Kutik, Publisher.

★1543★
Current Wage Developments
U.S. Government Printing Office
Superintendent of Documents
Washington, DC 20402   Phone: (202)783-3238
U.S. Bureau of Labor Statistics, Publisher. Monthly. Magazine reporting on wage and benefit changes resulting from collective bargaining settlements and management decisions. Includes statistical summaries and reports on wage trends. **Facsimile Number:** (202)275-0019.

★1544★
EAP Digest
Performance Resource Press
1863 Technology Dr., Ste. 200
Troy, MI 48083   Phone: (313)588-7733
Janet Hearle, Mng. Editor. 6x/yr. Magazine covering planning, development, and administration of employee assistance programs. **Facsimile Number:** (313)588-6633.

★1545★
Employee Benefits Report
Warren, Gorham and Lamont, Inc.
1 Penn Plaza
New York, NY 10119   Phone: (212)971-5234
David Beck, Managing Editor. Monthly. Newsletter presenting articles on benefits and pensions for benefits and personnel specialists. **Facsimile Number:** (212)971-5025.

★1546★
Human Resources Abstracts
Sage Periodicals Press
2455 Teller Rd.
Newbury Park, CA 91320   Phone: (805)499-0721
Paul V. McDowell, Editor. Quarterly. Journal providing abstracts refering to employment and labor relations. **Facsimile Number:** (805)499-0871.

★1547★
NAPW Journal
National Association of Personnel Workers (NAPW)
Morehouse Coll.
PO Box 6
Atlanta, GA 30314   Phone: (404)681-2800
Quarterly.

★1548★
NAPW Newsletter
National Association of Personnel Workers (NAPW)
Morehouse Coll.
PO Box 6
Atlanta, GA 30314　　　　　　　Phone: (404)681-2800
Quarterly.

★1549★
NPRA News
Newspaper Personnel Relations Association (NPRA)
11600 Sunrise Valley Dr.
Reston, VA 22091　　　　　　　Phone: (703)648-1000
Monthly. Newsletter covering trends in human resources and labor, management, training, and legal updates.

★1550★
The Personnel Alert
Alexander Hamilton Institute, Inc.
197 W. Spring Valley Ave.
Maywood, NJ 07607-1700　　　　Phone: (201)587-7050
2x/mo Publication covering legal and legislative developments in the personnel field. **Facsimile Number:** (201)587-7063.

★1551★
Personnel Journal
245 Fischer Ave., B-2
Costa Mesa, CA 92626　　　　　Phone: (714)751-1883
Allan Halcrow, Editor. Monthly. Business magazine for human resources. **Facsimile Number:** (714)751-4106.

★1552★
Personnel Literature
U.S. Government Printing Office
Superintendent of Documents
Washington, DC 20402-9325　　　Phone: (202)783-3238
Monthly (with annual index). Index to publications on personnel issues. Compiled by the Office of Personnel Management Library staff.

★1553★
Personnel Psychology
Personnel Psychology, Inc.
9660 Hillcroft, Ste. 337
Houston, TX 77096　　　　　　Phone: (713)728-3078
Michael A. Campion, PhD, Editor. Quarterly. Journal covering empirical research on personnel, including test validation, selection, labor-management relations, training, compensation, and reward systems. Also publishes related book reviews.

★1554★
Public Personnel Management
International Personnel Management Assn.
1617 Duke St.
Alexandria, VA 22314　　　　　Phone: (703)549-7100
Sarah Shiffert, Editor. Quarterly. Magazine for public personnel administrators responsible for selection, training, and labor relations. **Facsimile Number:** (703)684-0948.

★1555★
Records Management Quarterly
Assn. of Record Managers and Administrators
PO Box 8540
Prairie Village, KS 66208　　　　Phone: (913)341-3808
Ira Penn, Editor and Advertising Manager. Quarterly. Professional journal on records technology and information management. **Facsimile Number:** (913)341-3742.

★1556★
Recruitment Today
245 Fischer Ave., B-2
Costa Mesa, CA 92626　　　　　Phone: (714)751-1883
Allan Halcrow, Editor. 6x/yr. Magazine targeting corporate recruitment executives and covering all aspects of the recruitment process. **Facsimile Number:** (714)751-4106.

Secretaries

Secretaries perform a variety of administrative and clerical duties to help an organization run efficiently. They answer telephone calls, provide information, schedule appointments, maintain files, transcribe dictation, and other related tasks depending on the needs of the employer. There are various types of secretaries who have specified job duties. Administrative secretaries handle everything except dictation and typing. Legal secretaries prepare legal documents for attorneys, while medical secretaries assist physicians and medical scientists. Technical secretaries assist engineers or scientists. In addition to the usual secretarial duties, they prepare much of the correspondence, maintain the technical library, and gather and edit materials for scientific papers. Social secretaries, sometimes called personal secretaries, arrange social functions, answer personal correspondence, and keep employers informed about all social activities. Membership secretaries compile and maintain membership lists, record the receipt of dues and contributions, and give out information to members of organizations and associations. They may also send out newsletters and promotional materials. School secretaries handle secretarial duties in elementary and secondary schools; they may take care of correspondence, prepare bulletins and reports, keep track of money for school supplies and student activities, and maintain a calendar of school events.

$alaries

The average salary for secretaries varies, reflecting differences in skill, experience, level of responsibility, and industry. Salaries of secretaries tend to be highest in transportation and public utilities and lowest in retail trade and finance, insurance, and real estate.

Secretaries	$17,810-29,354/year
Inexperienced secretaries in the federal government	$12,531/year
Secretaries in the federal government	$18,800/year

Employment Outlook

Growth rate until the year 2000: Average.

Secretaries

Career Guides

★1557★
"Administrative Assistants, Clerical Workers, and Secretaries" in *Jobs '91* (pp. 9-13)
Prentice Hall Press
1 Gulf Western Plaza
New York, NY 10023   Phone: (212)373-8500
Kathryn Petras and Ross Petras. Annual, 1991. Discusses employment prospects and trends for 15 professional careers and 29 industries. Lists leading companies, associations, directories, and magazines.

★1558★
The Administrative Secretary
McGraw-Hill Publishing Co.
1221 Avenue of the Americas
New York, NY 10020   Phone: (212)512-2000
R. I. Anderson. Second edition, 1976.

★1559★
Basic Secretarial Skills
Ambrose Video Publishing
1290 Ave. of the Americas
Suite 2245
New York, NY 10104   Phone: (212)696-4545
Videocassette. 1989. 61 mins. A video training course for people who want to be secretaries.

★1560★
"Bookkeeper, Secretary, and Clerk" in *Travel & Tourism* (pp. 69-73)
Franklin Watts, Inc.
387 Park Avenue, S.
New York, NY 10016   Phone: (212)686-7070
Marjorie Rittenberg Schulz. 1990. Surveys employment opportunities in the travel and tourism industry. Provides job description, educational preparation, training, salary, employment outlook, and sources of additional information. Offers job hunting advice.

★1561★
Career Insights
RMI Media Productions, Inc.
2807 West 47th St.
Shawnee Mission, KS 66205   Phone: (913)262-3974
Videocassette series. 1987. This videotape series describes 50 occupations, including skill requirements and interviews with people employed in these fields. Occupations include: flight service, air transportation/ground services, data processing, carpentry, clerk in banking/insurance/business, cosmetic personal grooming, firefighting, roofing, material handling, photographic processing, plumbing, secretarial services, tool and die operations.

★1562★
Career Success Series
Cambridge Career Products
90 MacCorkle Ave., SW
South Charleston, WV 25311   Phone: (304)744-9323
Videocassette. 1986. 15 mins. A series, available separately, outlining various career choices for students. Occupations include: flight service, air transportation/ground service, data processing, carpentry, clerk in banking/insurance, commodity sales, cosmetic personal grooming, fire fighting, forestry services, home economics, insulation/roofing, material handling, mechanics, photographic processing, pipefitting and plumbing, police science, printing, secretarial services, and utilities equipment operator.

★1563★
"Clerical and Secretarial Work" in *Exploring Careers Using Foreign Languages* (pp. 51-52)
Rosen Publishing Group, Inc.
29 E. 21st St.
New York, NY 10010   Phone: (212)777-3017
E. W. Edwards. Revised edition, 1990. Explores careers in teaching, translating, interpreting, business and finance, government, communications, and the media. Covers employment ideas, salaries, job duties, and educational preparation. Contains information on accreditation and job hunting.

★1564★
Complete Secretary's Handbook
Prentice Hall
Rte. 9W
Englewood Cliffs, NJ 07632   Phone: (201)592-2000
Mary A. DeVries, editor. Sixth edition, 1988.

★1565★
Considering a Secretarial Service?: Possibilities for Income
Prosperity & Profits Unlimited
PO Box 570213
Houston, TX 77257   Phone: (713)867-3438
Center for Self-Sufficiency, Research Division Staff. 1983.

★1566★
"Dental and Medical Secretary" in *Health*, Volume 7 of *Career Information Center* (pp. 58-60)
Glencoe/Macmillan
15319 Chatsworth St.
Mission Hills, CA 91345   Phone: (818)898-1391
Richard Lidz and Dale Anderson, editorial directors. Fourth edition, 1990. For 600 occupations, describes job duties, entry-level requirements, education and training needed, advancement possibilities, employment outlook, earnings and benefits. The set is divided into 12 volumes. Each volume includes jobs related under a broad career field. Volume 13 is the index. **Facsimile Number:** 818-365-5489.

★1567★
The Dynamic Secretary: A Practical Guide to Achieving Success as an Executive Assistant
Prentice Hall
Rte. 9W
Englewood Cliffs, NJ 07632   Phone: (201)592-2000
Freida Porat. 1983.

★1568★
Executive Secretary
Vocational Biographies, Inc.
PO Box 31, Dept. VF10
Sauk Centre, MN 56378   Phone: (612)352-6516
1991. This pamphlet profiles a person working in the job. Includes information about job duties, working conditions, places of employment, educational preparation, labor market outlook, and salaries. **Toll-free/Additional Phone Number(s):** 800-255-0752.

★1569★
How to Start You Own Secretarial Services Business at Home
SK Publications
7149 Natalie Blvd.
Northfied Center, OH 44067   Phone: (216)467-8059
Stephen G. Kozlow. 1980.

★1570★
"Information/Word Processing: The Secretary" in *Opportunities in Office Occupations* (pp. 93-115)
National Textbook Co.
4255 W. Touhy Ave.
Lincolnwood, IL 60646   Phone: (312)679-5500
Blanche Ettinger. 1989. Describes factors and trends which will affect office occupations including automation, telecommuting, and unionization. Separate chapters cover clerks, records management, information word processing, the secretary, and the bookkeeper-accountant. Describes job duties, skills needed, educational preparation, job hunting, types of equipment, employment outlook, and salaries.

★1571★
Instant Secretary's Handbook
Dell Publishing Co.
666 5th Ave.
New York, NY 10103   Phone: (212)765-6500
Martha S. Luck. 1988.

★1572★
"Medical Dental Secretary" in *The Career Connection II: A Guide to Technical Majors and Their Related Careers* (pp. 93-94)
ERIS
PO Box 7509
University Station
Provo, UT 84602-0509
Fred A. Rowe. 1988. Contains technical majors, such as automotive technology. Describes the major and the job. Lists high school and postsecondary school courses. Includes occupations related to the major, employment outlook, and starting salary.

★1573★
"Medical or Dental Secretary" in *Health Care* (pp. 51-55)
Franklin Watts, Inc.
387 Park Avenue, S.
New York, NY 10016   Phone: (212)686-7070
Linda Barrett and Galen Guengerich. 1991. Provides an overview of the health care industry. Includes job description, educational preparation, training, salary, and employment outlook. Offers job hunting advice.

★1574★
"Medical Secretary" in *Opportunities in Health and Medical Careers* (pp. 106-107)
National Textbook Co.
4255 W. Touhy Ave.
Lincolnwood, IL 60646   Phone: (312)679-5500
Leo D'Orazio and Donald I. Snook. 1991. Provides an overview of the health care industry with future projections. Describes a wide variety of healthcare jobs covering the nature of the work, educational requirements, employment outlook and salaries. Offers job hunting advice.

★1575★
"Medical Secretary" in *VGM's Careers Encyclopedia* (pp. 279-281)
National Textbook Co.
4255 W. Touhy Ave.
Lincolnwood, IL 60646   Phone: (312)679-5500
Third edition, 1991. Contains two- to five-page descriptions of 200 managerial, professional, technical, trade, and service occupations. Each profile includes job duties, places of employment, qualifications, educational preparation, training, employment potential, advancement, income, and additional sources of information.

★1576★
Not Just a Secretary: Using the Job To Get Ahead
John Wiley & Sons, Inc.
605 3rd Ave.
New York, NY 10158   Phone: (212)850-6000
Jodie B. Morrow. 1984. Part of General Trade Book. **Facsimile Number:** (212)850-6088.

★1577★
Office Systems & Careers: A Resource for Administrative Assistants
Allyn & Bacon, Inc.
160 Gould St.
Needham Heights, MA 02194
Church. 1981.

Secretaries ★1588★

★1578★
Opportunities in Secretarial Careers
National Textbook Co.
4255 W. Touhy Ave.
Lincolnwood, IL 60646-1975   Phone: (708)679-5500
Blanch Ettinger. 1984. **Facsimile Number:** (708)679-2494.

★1579★
Procedures for the Professional Secretary
South-Western Publishing Co.
5101 Madison Rd.
Cincinnati, OH 45227   Phone: (513)271-8811
Patsy J. Fulton. 1984.

★1580★
School Secretary
Vocational Biographies, Inc.
PO Box 31, Dept. VF10
Sauk Centre, MN 56378   Phone: (612)352-6516
1991. This pamphlet profiles a person working in the job. Includes information about job duties, working conditions, places of employment, educational preparation, labor market outlook, and salaries. **Toll-free/Additional Phone Number(s):** 800-255-0752.

★1581★
"Secretarial Science" in *College Majors and Careers: A Resource Guide for Effective Life Planning* (pp. 119-120)
Garrett Park Press
PO Box 190
Garrett Park, MD 20896   Phone: (301)946-2553
Paul Phifer. 1987. Lists 61 college majors. Includes a general definition of the field, related occupations requiring either a bachelor or associate degree, related leisure-time activities denoting personal interest in the field, skills needed, values, and personal attributes. Lists organizations.

★1582★
"Secretarial Science" in *The Career Connection II: A Guide to Technical Majors and Their Related Careers* (pp. 117-118)
ERIS
PO Box 7509
University Station
Provo, UT 84602-0509
Fred A. Rowe. 1988. Contains technical majors, such as automotive technology. Describes the major and the job. Lists high school and postsecondary school courses. Includes occupations related to the major, employment outlook, and starting salary.

★1583★
"Secretaries" in Volume 6 of *Career Discovery Encyclopedia* (pp. 10-11)
J.G. Ferguson Publishing Co.
200 W. Monroe
Chicago, IL 60606   Phone: (312)580-5480
E. Russell Primm, editor-in-chief. 1990. Contains two-page articles on 504 occupations. Each article describes job duties, earnings, and educational and training requirements.

★1584★
"Secretaries" in Volume 3 of *The Encyclopedia of Careers and Vocational Guidance* (pp. 81-85)
J.G. Ferguson Publishing Co.
200 W. Monroe
Chicago, IL 60606   Phone: (312)580-5480
William E. Hopke, editor-in-chief. Eighth edition, 1990. Four-volume set that profiles 500 occupations and describes job trends in 76 industries. Includes career description, educational requirements, history of the job, methods of entry, advancement, employment outlook, earnings, working conditions, social and psychological factors, and sources of additional information.

★1585★
"Secretaries/Administrative Assistants" in *Profitable Careers in Nonprofit* (pp. 149-151)
John Wiley & Sons, Inc.
605 Third Ave.
New York, NY 10158   Phone: (212)850-6000
William Lewis and Carol Milano. 1987. Examines employment opportunities in various types of nonprofit organizations from entry level to high-level executive. Explains the structure of nonprofit corporations, characteristics of employees, the rewards and drawbacks of the work, and offers tips on how to target positions.

★1586★
"Secretaries and Clerical Personnel" in *Opportunities in Real Estate Careers* (pp. 117-118)
National Textbook Co.
4255 W. Touhy Ave.
Lincolnwood, IL 60646   Phone: (312)679-5500
Mariwyn Evans. 1988. Surveys the real estate industry and related careers. Covers the work, academic preparation, employment outlook, licensing, and financial compensation. Offers job hunting information.

★1587★
Secretaries and Stenographers
Chronicle Guidance Publications, Inc.
PO Box 1190
Moravia, NY 13118-1190   Phone: (315)497-0330
1991. This career brief describes the nature of the work, working conditions, hours and earnings, education and training, licensure, certification, unions, personal qualifications, social and psychological factors, employment outlook, entry methods, advancement, and related occupations. **Toll-free/Additional Phone Number(s):** 800-622-7284.

★1588★
"Secretaries and Stenographers" in *Jobs! What They Are...Where They Are...What They Pay* (pp. 211-212)
Simon & Schuster, Inc.
Simon & Schuster Bldg.
1230 Avenue of the Americas
New York, NY 10020   Phone: (212)698-7000
Robert O. Snelling and Anne M. Snelling. Revised edition, 1989. Profiles 241 occupations, describing duties and responsibilities, educational preparation, earnings, employment opportunities, training, and qualifications.

★1589★
"Secretaries" in *America's 50 Fastest Growing Jobs* (pp. 113-116)
JIST Works, Inc.
720 N. Park Ave.
Indianapolis, IN 46202   Phone: (317)264-3720
Michael J. Farr, compiler. 1991. Describes the 50 fastest growing jobs within major career clusters such as technicians, and marketing and sales. Each job profile explains the nature of the work, skills and abilities required, employment outlook, average earnings, related occupations, education and training requirements, and employment opportunities. Also contains career planning information and job search tips.

★1590★
"Secretaries" in *The American Almanac of Jobs and Salaries* (pp. 504-506)
Avon Books
105 Madison Avenue
New York, NY 10016   Phone: (212)481-5600
John Wright and Edward J. Dwyer. Revised and updated, 1990. A comprehensive guide to the wages of hundreds of occupations in a wide variety of industries and organizations.

★1591★
Secretaries, Management & Organizations
Gower Publishing Co.
Old Post Rd.
Brookfield, VT 05036   Phone: (802)276-3162
S. Vinnicombe. 1980.

★1592★
Secretary
Careers, Inc.
PO Box 135
Largo, FL 34649-0135   Phone: (813)584-7333
1989. Eight-page brief offering the definition, history, duties, working conditions, personal qualifications, educational requirements, earnings, hours, employment outlook, advancement possibilities, and related occupations.

★1593★
"Secretary" in *Administration, Business, and Office*, Volume 1 of *Career Information Center* (pp. 94-96)
Glencoe/Macmillan
15319 Chatsworth St.
Mission Hills, CA 91345   Phone: (818)898-1391
Richard Lidz and Dale Anderson, editorial directors. Fourth edition, 1990. For 600 occupations, describes job duties, entry-level requirements, education and training needed, advancement possibilities, employment outlook, earnings and benefits. The set is divided into 12 volumes. Each volume includes jobs related under a broad career field. Volume 13 is the index. **Facsimile Number:** 818-365-5489.

★1594★
Secretary: A Career of Distinction
Professional Secretaries International
10502 N.W. Ambassador Dr.
PO Box 20404
Kansas City, MO 64195-0404   Phone: (816)891-6600
1987. This eight-panel brochure describes educational preparation, travel opportunities, labor market outlook, promotional opportunities, and working conditions.

★1595★
"Secretary" in *Careers in Banking and Finance* (pp. 65-66)
Rosen Publishing Group, Inc.
29 E. 21st St.
New York, NY 10010   Phone: (212)777-3017
Patricia Haddock. 1990. Describes more than 20 jobs at all levels in banking and finance. Contains information about the types of financial organizations where the jobs are found, educational requirements, job duties, and salaries. Offers advice on job hunting.

★1596★
"Secretary" in *Guide to Careers Without College* (pp. 46-49)
Franklin Watts, Inc.
387 Park Avenue, S.
New York, NY 10016   Phone: (212)686-7070
Kathleen S. Abrams. 1988. Discusses careers that do not require a college degree in fields such as health care, sales and marketing, and the building trades. Describes the work, employment opportunities, and training.

★1597★
"Secretary" in *Occu-Facts: Information on 565 Careers in Outline Form* (pp. 1.51, 12.2-12.7)
Careers, Inc.
P.O. Box 135
1211 Tenth St., S.W.
Largo, FL 33640   Phone: (813)584-7333
Elizabeth Handville. Biennial, 1989-90 edition. Each one-page occupational profile describes duties, working conditions, physical surroundings and demands, aptitudes, temperament, educational requirements, employment outlook, earnings, and places of employment.

★1598★
"Secretary" in *Opportunities in Vocational and Technical Careers* (pp. 45-47)
National Textbook Co.
4255 W. Touhy Ave.
Lincolnwood, IL 60646   Phone: (312)679-5500
Adrian A. Paradis. 1987. Describes careers which can be prepared for by attending a private vocational or proprietary school—office employee, sales worker, service worker, health services, mechanic, craftworker, and technician. Covers employment outlook, job duties, and salaries. Offers career planning advice.

★1599★
"Secretary" in *VGM's Careers Encyclopedia* (pp. 424-427)
National Textbook Co.
4255 W. Touhy Ave.
Lincolnwood, IL 60646   Phone: (312)679-5500
Third edition, 1991. Contains two- to five-page descriptions of 200 managerial, professional, technical, trade, and service occupations. Each profile includes job duties, places of employment, qualifications, educational preparation, training, employment potential, advancement, income, and additional sources of information.

★1600★
Secretary, Bilingual
Careers, Inc.
PO Box 135
Largo, FL 34649-0135   Phone: (813)584-7333
1989. Eight-page brief offering the definition, history, duties, working conditions, personal qualifications, educational

Secretaries ★1613★

requirements, earnings, hours, employment outlook, advancement possibilities, and related occupations.

★1601★
Secretary, Executive
Careers, Inc.
PO Box 135
Largo, FL 34649-0135   Phone: (813)584-7333
1991. Eight-page brief offering the definition, history, duties, working conditions, personal qualifications, educational requirements, earnings, hours, employment outlook, advancement possibilities, and related occupations.

★1602★
Secretary, Legal
Careers, Inc.
PO Box 135
Largo, FL 34649-0135   Phone: (813)584-7333
1991. Two-page occupational summary card describing duties, working conditions, personal qualifications, training, earnings and hours, employment outlook, places of employment, related careers and where to write for more information.

★1603★
Secretary on the Job
McGraw-Hill Publishing Co.
1221 Avenue of the Americas
New York, NY 10020   Phone: (212)512-2000
Mary Witherow. 1983.

★1604★
Secretary, Technical
Careers, Inc.
PO Box 135
Largo, FL 34649-0135   Phone: (813)584-7333
1990. Two-page occupational summary card describing duties, working conditions, personal qualifications, training, earnings and hours, employment outlook, places of employment, related careers and where to write for more information.

★1605★
Secretary/Word Processor
Vocational Biographies, Inc.
PO Box 31, Dept. VF10
Sauk Centre, MN 56378   Phone: (612)352-6516
1988. This pamphlet profiles a person working in the job. Includes information about job duties, working conditions, places of employment, educational preparation, labor market outlook, and salaries. **Toll-free/Additional Phone Number(s):** 800-255-0752.

★1606★
Secretary...
Professional Secretaries International
10502 N.W. Ambassador Dr.
PO Box 20404
Kansas City, MO 64195-0404   Phone: (816)891-6600
1990. This pamphlet describes secretarial work, advancement opportunities, and educational preparation.

★1607★
"Skills Analysis: Secretaries" in *The Black Woman's Career Guide* (pp. 52-56)
Doubleday & Co., Inc.
666 Fifth Avenue
New York, NY 10103   Phone: (212)984-7561
Beatryce Nivens. Revised edition, 1987. Offers career planning and job hunting advice. Contains information on 20 different career areas and profiles women working in the field. Each occupational profile describes the work, career paths and earning potential.

★1608★
Starting You Own Secretarial Business
Contemporary Books, Inc.
180 N. Michigan Ave.
Chicago, IL 60601   Phone: (312)782-9181
Betty Lonngren. 1982. **Facsimile Number:** (312)782-2157.

★1609★
Telephone Manners
Britannica Films
310 South Michigan Ave.
Chicago, IL 60604   Phone: (312)347-7958
Videocassette. 1989. 11 mins. This program demonstrates every important step in telephone usage including identifying yourself and your organization, personalizing your calls, repeating all instructions given, taking notes of important messages, remembering calls on hold, listening to the caller's mood as well as the message, using common courtesy words and conveying warmth.

★1610★
"Traveling Secretary/Professional Sports Team" in
   Career Opportunities in the Sports Industry (pp. 43-45)
Facts on File, Inc.
460 Park Avenue, S.
New York, NY 10016   Phone: (212)683-2244
Shelly Field. 1991. Describes various jobs in the sports industry. Each occupational profile covers job duties, employment outlook, career paths, salaries, skills, and educational preparation. Offers tips for entering the field.

★1611★
Video Career Library - Clerical & Administrative Support
Careers, Inc.
1211 10th St., SW
PO Box 135
Largo, FL 34649-0135   Phone: (813)584-7333
Videocassette. 1990. 26 mins. Part of the Video Career Library covering 165 occupations. Shows actual workers on the job. Includes secretaries, cashiers, receptionists, bookkeepers and audit clerks, telephone operators, postal clerks/carriers/supervisors, insurance investigators, bank tellers, data entry keyers, and court reporters.

★1612★
Vocational Visions
Center for Humanities, Inc.
Communications Park
Box 1000
Mount Kisco, NY 10549   Phone: (914)666-4100
Videocassette. 1984. 30 mins. This series of programs explains key aspects of actual training and a day in the life of a worker in the specific field mentioned on the videocassette. Occupations include: transportation/mechanics, repair, construction, business/office occupations, health, and agriculture.

───────── Associations ─────────

★1613★
National Association of Executive Secretaries (NAES)
900 S. Washington St., #G-13
Falls Church, VA 22046   Phone: (703)237-8616
Membership: Professional secretaries united to bring added stature to their profession and to create for members the benefits that are normally limited to members of specialized

professional and fraternal groups. **Purpose:** Sponsors biennial secretarial salary survey. Awards annual scholarship. **Publications:** *Exec-U-Tary*, monthly.

★1614★
National Association of Legal Secretaries (International) (NALS)
2250 E. 73rd St., Ste. 550
Tulsa, OK 74136　　　　　　　　　Phone: (918)493-3540

Membership: Legal secretaries and others employed in work of a legal nature in law offices, banks, and courts. **Purpose:** Sponsors legal secretarial training courses and awards those passing a two-day examination the rating of Certified Professional Legal Secretary. **Publications:** *Docket*, bimonthly. • Also publishes *Career Legal Secretary* and *Manual for the Lawyer's Assistant*. **Facsimile Number:** (918)493-5784.

★1615★
Professional Secretaries International (PSI)
10502 NW Ambassador Dr.
PO Box 20404
Kansas City, MO 64195-0404　　　Phone: (816)891-6600

Membership: Professional organization of secretaries. **Purpose:** Grants CPS (Certified Professional Secretary) Certificate for successful completion of examinations in behavioral science in business, business law, economics and management, accounting, office administration and communication, and office technology; monitors related legislative and governmental activities; sponsors audiovisual productions; provides group insurance plans. Sponsors Professional Secretaries' Week and selects International Secretary of the Year. Has established the PSI Research and Educational Foundation to develop research and educational projects for secretaries, management, and educators. Has also established Professional Secretaries International Retirement Centers Trust to acquire and maintain a home in Albuquerque, NM for needy and elderly secretaries. **Publications:** *The Secretary Magazine*, 9/year. **Facsimile Number:** (816)891-9118.

--- **Standards/Certification Agencies** ---

As secretaries gain experience, they can qualify for the designation Certified Professional Secretary (CPS) by passing a series of examinations given by the Institute for Certifying Secretaries, a department of Professional Secretaries International. This designation is recognized by a growing number of employers as the mark of excellence in the secretarial field. Similarly, a legal secretary with five years' experience may become certified as a Professional Legal Secretary (PLS) by passing an examination administered by the Certifying Board of the National Association of Legal Secretaries.

★1616★
Association of Independent Colleges and Schools (AICS)
1 Dupont Circle NW, Ste. 350
Washington, DC 20036　　　　　Phone: (202)659-2460

Membership: Independent business schools and junior and senior colleges of business. **Purpose:** Sponsors an accrediting commission for postsecondary and collegiate institutions. **Publications:** *AICS Compass*, monthly. • *Capital Comments*, bimonthly. • *Directory of Accredited Institutions*, annual. **Facsimile Number:** (202)659-2254.

★1617★
Association of Independent Colleges and Schools (AICS)
1 Dupont Circle NW, Ste. 350
Washington, DC 20036　　　　　Phone: (202)659-2460

Sponsors an accrediting commission for postsecondary and collegiate institutions.

★1618★
Certified Professional Secretary
Professional Secretaries International
10502 N.W. Ambassador Dr.
PO Box 20404
Kansas City, MO 64195-0404　　　Phone: (816)891-6600

1990. This pamphlet explains the Certified Professional Secretary designation and how to obtain it. Covers eligibility requirements, the examination content, and the application process. Lists examination centers across the United States.

★1619★
National Association of Legal Secretaries (International) (NALS)
2250 E. 73rd St., Ste. 550
Tulsa, OK 74136　　　　　　　　　Phone: (918)493-3540

Sponsors legal secretarial training courses and awards those passing a two-day examination the rating of Certified Professional Legal Secretary.

★1620★
Professional Secretaries International (PSI)
10502 NW Ambassador Dr.
PO Box 20404
Kansas City, MO 64195-0404　　　Phone: (816)891-6600

Grants CPS (Certified Professional Secretary) Certificate for successful completion of examinations in behavioral science in business, business law, economics and management, accounting, office administration and communication, and office technology.

--- **Test Guides** ---

★1621★
Certified Professional Secretary (CPS) Examination Review
Prentice Hall Press
Simon & Schuster Inc.
200 Old Tappan Rd.
Old Tappan, NJ 07675　　　　　Phone: (800)223-2348

Sheryl Lindsell and Stanley Alpert. First edition, 1987. Actual CPS questions are used in this prep guide.

★1622★
Secretarial Assistant
National Learning Corp.
212 Michael Dr.
Syosset, NY 11791　　　　　　　Phone: (516)921-8888

Jack Rudman. Part of the Career Examination Series No. 1. All examination guides in this series contain questions with answers. **Facsimile Number:** (516)921-8743. **Toll-free/Additional Phone Number(s):** 800-645-6337.

★1623★
Secretarial Stenographer
National Learning Corp.
212 Michael Dr.
Syosset, NY 11791　　　　　　　Phone: (516)921-8888

Jack Rudman. Part of the Career Examination Series No. 1. All examination guides in this series contain questions with answers.

Facsimile Number: (516)921-8743. Toll-free/Additional Phone Number(s): 800-645-6337.

★1624★
Secretary
National Learning Corp.
212 Michael Dr.
Syosset, NY 11791   Phone: (516)921-8888
Jack Rudman. Part of the Career Examination Series No. 1. All examination guides in this series contain questions with answers. Facsimile Number: (516)921-8743. Toll-free/Additional Phone Number(s): 800-645-6337.

★1625★
Secretary (Stenography) GS5
National Learning Corp.
212 Michael Dr.
Syosset, NY 11791   Phone: (516)921-8888
Jack Rudman. Part of the Career Examination Series No. 1. All examination guides in this series contain questions with answers. Facsimile Number: (516)921-8743. Toll-free/Additional Phone Number(s): 800-645-6337.

Educational Directories and Programs

★1626★
Directory of Accredited Institutions
Association of Independent Colleges and Schools (AICS)
1 Dupont Circle NW, Ste. 350
Washington, DC 20036   Phone: (202)659-2460
Annual.

★1627★
Industry Directory   Office automation
Association of Information Systems Professionals
104 Wilmot Rd., Ste. 201
Deerfield, IL 60015-5195   Phone: (708)940-8800
Bea McLean, editor. Irregular; previous edition 1986; new edition possible 1990. Manufacturers of office automation equipment; word processing service bureaus; educational institutions offering office automation and associated software courses or curriculums; personnel agencies serving office automation personnel and users; analysts and counsultants. Entries include: Name, address. Arrangement: Alphabetical within categories above. Facsimile Number: (708)940-7218.

★1628★
Secretaries
Accrediting Bureau of Health Education
Oak Manor Office
29089 U.S. 20 W.
Elkhart, IN 46514   Phone: (219)293-0124
1991. State-by-state listing of schools offering secretarial training programs. Lists address, phone number, and contact person.

Awards, Scholarships, Grants, and Fellowships

★1629★
International Secretary of the Year
Professional Secretaries International
10502 NW Ambassador Drive
Kansas City, MO 64195-0404   Phone: (816)891-6600
To pay tribute to an outstanding member secretary and to encourage other secretaries to strive for professionalism. A bronze plaque is awarded annually. Established in 1949.

★1630★
Professional Secretaries Scholarship
Professional Secretaries International
PO Box 20404
Kansas City, MO 64195-0404   Phone: (816)891-6600
To financially aid those interested in postsecondary training in the secretarial sciences. Applicants must be high school students who are interested in studying secretarial sciences on the postsecondary level and must be members of the Future Secretaries Association who plan to attend a 2- or 4-year business/secretarial school. Students should apply by March through one of the 740 chapters in the U.S.A. and Canada. Awarded annually. Loans are also available.

Basic Reference Guides and Handbooks

★1631★
Ansley House Associates: The Executive Secretary - An Office Job Simulation
South-Western Publishing, Co.
5101 Madison Rd.
Cincinnati, OH 45227   Phone: (513)271-8811
Harriet McIntosh. Second edition, 1985.

★1632★
Basic Metric Style Manual for Secretaries
Global Engineering Documents
2805 McGaw Ave.
PO Box 19539
Irvine, CA 92714   Phone: (714)261-1455
John Corbett, editor. 1976. Toll-free/Additional Phone Number(s): 800-854-7179. Facsimile Number: (714)261-7892.

★1633★
The Canadian Secretary's Handbook: An on-the-job Guide for Office Professionals
International Self-Counsel Press
1481 Charlotte Rd.
North Vancouver, BC, Canada V7J 1H1
Anne Morton. 1988. Part of Self-Counsel Reference Series.

★1634★
Career Legal Secretary
National Association of Legal Secretaries (International) (NALS)
2250 E. 73rd St., Ste. 550
Tulsa, OK 74136   Phone: (918)493-3540

★1635★
Career Strategies for Secretaries: How to Get Where You Want to Be
Contemporary Books, Inc.
180 N. Michigan Ave.
Chicago, IL 60601   Phone: (312)782-9181
Marie Kisiel. 1982. **Facsimile Number:** (312)782-2157.

★1636★
Common Secretarial Mistakes & How to Avoid Them
Prentice Hall
Rte. 9W
Englewood Cliffs, NJ 07632   Phone: (201)592-2000
Prentice-Hall Editorial Staff. 1986.

★1637★
Confidential Secretary
National Learning Corp.
212 Michael Dr.
Syosset, NY 11791   Phone: (516)921-8888
Jack Rudman. 1989. Part of Career Examination Series.

★1638★
How to Start a Secretarial & Business Service
Pilot Books
103 Cooper St.
Babylon, NY 11702   Phone: (516)422-2225
Mary Temple. 1989.

★1639★
Instant Secretary's Handbook
Career Publishing, Inc.
905 Allanson Dr.
Mundelein, IL 60060   Phone: (708)949-0011
Martha S. Luck. 1972. Part of Instant Series. **Facsimile Number:** (708)566-8550.

★1640★
Making It Work: The Secretary - Boss Team
Avatar Press
PO Box 77234
Atlanta, GA 30357   Phone: (404)892-8511
Charles E. Kozoll. 1974.

★1641★
Manual for the Lawyer's Assistant
National Association of Legal Secretaries (International) (NALS)
2250 E. 73rd St., Ste. 550
Tulsa, OK 74136   Phone: (918)493-3540

★1642★
Math on the Job: Secretary/Clerk Typist
National Center for Research in Vocational Education
Ohio State University
1900 Kenry Rd.
Columbus, OH 43210   Phone: (614)292-4353
1985.

★1643★
The New Secretary: How to Handle People As Well As You Handled Paper
Facts on File, Inc.
460 Park Ave., S.
New York, NY 10016   Phone: (212)683-2244
Dianna Booher. 1986.

★1644★
NOMDA Who's Who   Office machines
National Office Machine Dealers Association (NOMDA)
12411 Wornall Rd.
Kansas City, MO 64145   Phone: (816)941-3100
Brent Hoskins, editor. Annual. List of 6,000 retailers and 500 manufacturers of typewriters, calculators, word processors, computers, dictation equipment, copying machines, and other office machines. Entries include: Company name, address, phone, names of executives; dealer listings include codes showing products handled. Arrangement: Dealers and manufacturers are geographical and alphabetical. Indexes: Personal name, product. **Facsimile Number:** (816)941-2829.

★1645★
Office Organization & Secretarial Procedures
Trans-Atlantic Publications, Inc.
311 Bainbridge St.
Philadelphia, PA 19147   Phone: (215)925-5083
Helen Harding. 1988. **Facsimile Number:** (215)925-1912.

★1646★
Personal Shorthand for the Executive Secretary: Syllabus
National Book Company
PO Box 8795
Portland, OR 97207-8795   Phone: (503)228-6345
Piper. 1977.

★1647★
Professional Excellence for Secretaries
Crisp Publications, Inc.
95 1st St.
Los Altos, CA 94022   Phone: (415)949-4888
Marilyn Manning. 1988. Part of Fifty Minute Series. **Facsimile Number:** (415)949-1610.

★1648★
Professional Secretary's Handbook
Dartnell Corp.
4660 Ravenswood Ave.
Chicago, IL 60640   Phone: (312)561-4000
Cook. 1988. **Toll-free/Additional Phone Number(s):** 800-621-5463. **Facsimile Number:** (312)561-3801.

★1649★
Secretarial Administration & Management
Prentice Hall
Rte. 9W
Englewood Cliffs, NJ 07632   Phone: (201)592-2000
Daniel R. Boyd. 1985.

★1650★
The Secretarial Handbook on Planning & Organizing Work
Executive Enterprises Publications Co., Inc.
22 W. 21st St.
New York, NY 10010-6904   Phone: (212)645-7880
1975. **Toll-free/Additional Phone Number(s):** 800-332-1105. **Facsimile Number:** (212)645-8689.

★1651★
Secretarial Office Procedures
McGraw-Hill Publishing Co.
1221 Avenue of the Americas
New York, NY 10020   Phone: (212)512-2000
Dorothy E. Lee. Second edition, 1981.

Secretaries

★1652★
Secretarial Practice
Advent Books
141 E. 44th St., Ste. 511
New York, NY 10017   Phone: (212)697-0887
M. C. Kuchhal. Tenth edition, 1984.

★1653★
Secretarial Practice: Syllabus
National Book Co.
PO Box 8795
Portland, OR 97207-8795   Phone: (503)228-6345
Carl Salser. Second edition, 1977.

★1654★
Secretarial Procedures for the Automated Office
Prentice Hall
Rte. 9W
Englewood Cliffs, NJ 07632 Phone: (201)592-2000
Dalton E. McFarland. 1985.

★1655★
Secretarial Procedures in the Electronic Office
Trans-Atlantic Pubications, Inc.
311 Bainbridge St
Philadelphia, PA 19147   Phone: (215)925-5083
Desmond Evans. 1989. **Facsimile Number:** (215)925-1912.

★1656★
The Secretarial Specialist
P.A.R., Inc.
272 W. Exchange St.
Providence, RI 02903-3416   Phone: (401)331-0130
Alfred C. Pascale. 1968.

★1657★
Secretary to Paralegal: A Career Manual & Guide
Prentice Hall
Rte. 9W
Englewood Cliffs, NJ 07632 Phone: (201)592-2000
Lesley J. Prendergast. 1984.

★1658★
The Secretary's Handbook
Macmillan Publishing Co., Inc.
866 3rd Ave.
New York, NY 10022   Phone: (212)702-2000
Sarah A. Taintor. Tenth edition, 1988.

★1659★
The Secretary's Handbook: A Manual for Office Personnel
Academic Press, Inc.
1250 6th Ave.
San Diego, CA 92101   Phone: (619)699-6412
Fourth edition, 1986.

★1660★
Secretary's Problem Solver: Word-for-Word Scripts for Coping with Difficult Situations
Prentice Hall
Rte. 9W
Englewood Cliffs, NJ 07632 Phone: (201)592-2000
Charlotte A. Peterson. 1990.

★1661★
The Secretary's Quick Reference Handbook
Prentice Hall
Rte. 9W
Englewood Cliffs, NJ 07632 Phone: (201)592-2000
Sheryl L. Lindsell. 1989.

★1662★
Senior Secretarial Duties & Office Organization
Trans-Atlantic Publications, Inc.
311 Bainbridge St.
Philadelphia, PA 19147   Phone: (215)925-5083
Evelyn Austin. Third edition, 1983. **Facsimile Number:** (215)925-1912.

★1663★
The Successful Secretary's Handbook
HarperCollins Publisher, Inc.
10 E. 53rd St.
New York, NY 10022   Phone: (212)207-7000
Esther R. Becker. 1984.

★1664★
Technical Secretary: Terminology & Transcription
McGraw-Hill Publishing Co.
1221 Avenue of the Americas
New York, NY 10020   Phone: (212)512-2000
Dorothy Adams. 1967. Part of Diamond Jubilee Series.

★1665★
Thomas Register's Office Automation Buyer's Guide
Thomas Publishing Company
1 Penn Plaza
New York, NY 10119   Phone: (212)290-7379
Douglas E. Lee, editor. Annual. About 6,000 suppliers of computer and office automation products. Entries include: Company name, address, phone, telex, toll-free phone, fax, names and titles of key personnel, number of employees, financial data, subsidiary and parent company data, description of products. Arrangement: Alphabetical. Indexes: Product/service, trade name.

★1666★
Webster's New World Secretarial Handbook
Prentice Hall
Rte. 9W
Englewood Cliffs, NJ 07632 Phone: (201)592-2000
1989.

──────── Periodicals ────────

★1667★
The Corporate Secretary
American Society of Corporate Secretaries, Inc.
1270 Ave. of the Americas
New York, NY 10020   Phone: (212)765-2620
Editor(s): Michael E. Goodman. Bimonthly. Provides legal and legislative news involving corporate secretaries and their executive duties. Recurring features include columns titled SEC Update and Society Notes. **Facsimile Number:** (212)765-8349.

★1668★
Docket (NALS)
National Association of Legal Secretaries (International) (NALS)
2250 E. 73rd St., Ste. 550
Tulsa, OK 74136   Phone: (918)493-3540
Bimonthly.

★1669★
The Exec-U-tary
National Association of Executive Secretaries
900 S. Washington St., No. G13
Falls Church, VA 22046-4020   Phone: (703)237-8616
Editor(s): Ruth Ludeman. Monthly. Provides information pertaining to the business and personal lives of executive secretaries. Recurring features include association news.

★1670★
From Nine to Five
Dartnell Corp.
4660 Ravenswood
Chicago, IL 60640   Phone: (312)561-4000
Editor(s): Douglas Leland. Biweekly. Provides "tips, shortcuts, and helpful information for success in the office," particularly secretaries and office workers. Recurring features include columns titled Business Skills Clinic and The Coffee Break. **Toll-free/Additional Phone Number(s):** 800-621-5463 **Facsimile Number:** (312)561-3801.

Meetings and Conventions

★1671★
National Association of Legal Secretaries (International) (NALS)
2250 E. 73rd St., Ste. 550
Tulsa, OK 74136   Phone: (918)493-3540
Frequency: Annual, always held in July or August. 1992; Los Anglels, CA. **Facsimile Number:** (918)493-5784.

★1672★
National Association of Secretarial Services National Convention
National Association of Secretarial Services
3637 4th St., N., Ste. 330
Saint Petersburg, FL 33704-1336   Phone: (813)823-3646
1992. **Facsimile Number:** (813)894-1277.

★1673★
Professional Secretaries International (PSI)
10502 NW Ambassador Dr.
PO Box 20404
Kansas City, MO 64195-0404   Phone: (816)891-6600
1992; Jul. 19-24; Columbus, OH • 1993; Jul. 25-29; Calgary, AB, Canada • 1994; Jul. 24-28; Orlando, FL • 1995; Jul. 23-26; Seattle, WA • 1996; Jul. 21-24; Des Moines, IA. **Facsimile Number:** (816)891-9118.

Stenographers

Stenographers take dictation using shorthand or a stenotype machine and transcribe spoken communications into a written record. General stenographers take routine dictation in addition to performing other office tasks such as typing or filing. More experienced stenographers may sit in on staff meetings and record the proceedings. Shorthand reporters record all statements at an official proceeding and often work as court reporters. Many other shorthand reporters work as freelance reporters who record out-of-court testimony for attorneys, proceedings of meetings and conventions, and other private activities. Still others record the proceedings in the U.S. Congress, in state and local governing bodies, and in government agencies at all levels. Transcribing-machine operators listen to recordings and transcribe what they hear into the proper format. Sometimes they are called dictating-machine transcribers or dictating-machine typists. Print shop stenographers take dictation and transcribe the dictated material to be used by addressing machines.

$alaries

The average salaries for stenographers are listed below. Salaries for stenographers vary by ability and are slightly higher for shorthand reporters than stenographic office workers.

Stenographers in private industry	$21,528/year
Inexperienced clerk-stenographers in the federal government	$12,531/year
Other clerk-stenographers in the federal government	$15,000/year

Employment Outlook

Growth rate until the year 2000: More slowly than average.

Stenographers

Career Guides

★1674★
Court Reporter
Careers, Inc.
PO Box 135
Largo, FL 34649-0135   Phone: (813)584-7333
1992. Two-page occupational summary card describing duties, working conditions, personal qualifications, training, earnings and hours, employment outlook, places of employment, related careers and where to write for more information.

★1675★
Court Reporter
Vocational Biographies, Inc.
PO Box 31, Dept. VF10
Sauk Centre, MN 56378   Phone: (612)352-6516
1988. This pamphlet profiles a person working in the job. Includes information about job duties, working conditions, places of employment, educational preparation, labor market outlook, and salaries. **Toll-free/Additional Phone Number(s):** 800-255-0752.

★1676★
"Court Reporter" in *Occu-Facts: Information on 565 Careers in Outline Form* (p. 12.8)
Careers, Inc.
P.O. Box 135
1211 Tenth St., S.W.
Largo, FL 33640   Phone: (813)584-7333
Elizabeth Handville. Biennial, 1989-90 edition. Each one-page occupational profile describes duties, working conditions, physical surroundings and demands, aptitudes, temperament, educational requirements, employment outlook, earnings, and places of employment.

★1677★
"Court Reporter (Short Hand Reporter)" in *Career Planning in Criminal Justice* (pp. 59-60)
Anderson Publishing Co.
2035 Reading Rd.
Cincinnati, OH 45202   Phone: (513)421-4142
Robert C. DeLucia and Thomas J. Doyle. 1990. Surveys a wide range of career and employment opportunities in law enforcement, the courts, corrections, forensic science and private security. Contains career planning and job hunting advice. Profiles 77 criminal justice occupations describing job duties, work environments, and educational requirements.

★1678★
Court Reporters
Chronicle Guidance Publications, Inc.
PO Box 1190
Moravia, NY 13118-1190   Phone: (315)497-0330
1987. This career brief describes the nature of the work, working conditions, hours and earnings, education and training, licensure, certification, unions, personal qualifications, social and psychological factors, employment outlook, entry methods, advancement, and related occupations. **Toll-free/Additional Phone Number(s):** 800-622-7284.

★1679★
"Court Reporters" in Volume 3 of *The Encyclopedia of Careers and Vocational Guidance* (pp. 26-28)
J.G. Ferguson Publishing Co.
200 W. Monroe
Chicago, IL 60606   Phone: (312)580-5480
William E. Hopke, editor-in-chief. Eighth edition, 1990. Four-volume set that profiles 500 occupations and describes job trends in 76 industries. Includes career description, educational requirements, history of the job, methods of entry, advancement, employment outlook, earnings, working conditions, social and psychological factors, and sources of additional information.

★1680★
"Court Reporters" in Volume 2 of *Career Discovery Encyclopedia* (pp. 70-71)
J.G. Ferguson Publishing Co.
200 W. Monroe
Chicago, IL 60606   Phone: (312)580-5480
E. Russell Primm, editor-in-chief. 1990. Contains two-page articles on 504 occupations. Each article describes job duties, earnings, and educational and training requirements.

★1681★
"Court Reporters: 40,000-50,000 Recorders" in *Careers for Women Without College Degrees* (pp. 231-233)
McGraw-Hill Publishing Co.
11 W. 19th St.
New York, NY 10011   Phone: (212)337-6010
Beatryce Nivens. 1988. Career planning and job hunting guide containing information on decision-making, skills assessment, and resumes for career changers. Profiles careers with the best occupational outlook. Describes the work, educational preparation, employment outlook, salaries, and required skills.

★1682★
"Court Reporting" in *The Career Connection II: A Guide to Technical Majors and Their Related Careers* (pp. 27-28)
ERIS
PO Box 7509
University Station
Provo, UT 84602-0509

Fred A. Rowe. 1988. Contains technical majors, such as automotive technology. Describes the major and the job. Lists high school and postsecondary school courses. Includes occupations related to the major, employment outlook, and starting salary.

★1683★
Medical Transcriptionist
Vocational Biographies, Inc.
PO Box 31, Dept. VF10
Sauk Centre, MN 56378   Phone: (612)352-6516

1991. This pamphlet profiles a person working in the job. Includes information about job duties, working conditions, places of employment, educational preparation, labor market outlook, and salaries. **Toll-free/Additional Phone Number(s):** 800-255-0752.

★1684★
"Medical Transcriptionist" in *Occu-Facts: Information on 565 Careers in Outline Form* (p. 12.9)
Careers, Inc.
P.O. Box 135
1211 Tenth St., S.W.
Largo, FL 33640   Phone: (813)584-7333

Elizabeth Handville. Biennial, 1989-90 edition. Each one-page occupational profile describes duties, working conditions, physical surroundings and demands, aptitudes, temperament, educational requirements, employment outlook, earnings, and places of employment.

★1685★
"Medical Transcriptionist" in *120 Careers in the Health Care Field* (pp. 257-258)
U.S. Directory Service, Publishers
PO Box 68-1700
655 N.W. 128th St.
Miami, FL 33168   Phone: (305)769-1700

Stanley Alperin. Second edition, 1989. Each occupational profile covers job functions and responsibilities, work locations, training requirements, certification, and salaries. Lists community colleges, universities, vocational-technical schools, and other educational institutions that provide accredited training programs.

★1686★
"Medical Transcriptionist" in *Opportunities in Health and Medical Careers* (p. 122)
National Textbook Co.
4255 W. Touhy Ave.
Lincolnwood, IL 60646   Phone: (312)679-5500

Leo D'Orazio and Donald I. Snook. 1991. Provides an overview of the health care industry with future projections. Describes a wide variety of healthcare jobs covering the nature of the work, educational requirements, employment outlook and salaries. Offers job hunting advice.

★1687★
Secretaries and Stenographers
Chronicle Guidance Publications, Inc.
PO Box 1190
Moravia, NY 13118-1190   Phone: (315)497-0330

1991. This career brief describes the nature of the work, working conditions, hours and earnings, education and training, licensure, certification, unions, personal qualifications, social and psychological factors, employment outlook, entry methods, advancement, and related occupations. **Toll-free/Additional Phone Number(s):** 800-622-7284.

★1688★
"Secretaries and Stenographers" in *Jobs! What They Are...Where They Are...What They Pay* (pp. 211-212)
Simon & Schuster, Inc.
Simon & Schuster Bldg.
1230 Avenue of the Americas
New York, NY 10020   Phone: (212)698-7000

Robert O. Snelling and Anne M. Snelling. Revised edition, 1989. Profiles 241 occupations, describing duties and responsibilities, educational preparation, earnings, employment opportunities, training, and qualifications.

★1689★
"Shorthand Reporter" in *Administration, Business, and Office*, Volume 1 of *Career Information Center* (pp. 80-82)
Glencoe/Macmillan
15319 Chatsworth St.
Mission Hills, CA 91345   Phone: (818)898-1391

Richard Lidz and Dale Anderson, editorial directors. Fourth edition, 1990. For 600 occupations, describes job duties, entry-level requirements, education and training needed, advancement possibilities, employment outlook, earnings and benefits. The set is divided into 12 volumes. Each volume includes jobs related under a broad career field. Volume 13 is the index. **Facsimile Number:** 818-365-5489.

★1690★
Stenographer
Vocational Biographies, Inc.
PO Box 31, Dept. VF10
Sauk Centre, MN 56378   Phone: (612)352-6516

1990. This pamphlet profiles a person working in the job. Includes information about job duties, working conditions, places of employment, educational preparation, labor market outlook, and salaries. **Toll-free/Additional Phone Number(s):** 800-255-0752.

★1691★
"Stenographer and Transcriber" in *Administration, Business, and Office*, Volume 1 of *Career Information Center* (pp. 69-70)
Glencoe/Macmillan
15319 Chatsworth St.
Mission Hills, CA 91345   Phone: (818)898-1391

Richard Lidz and Dale Anderson, editorial directors. Fourth edition, 1990. For 600 occupations, describes job duties, entry-level requirements, education and training needed, advancement possibilities, employment outlook, earnings and benefits. The set is divided into 12 volumes. Each volume includes jobs related under a broad career field. Volume 13 is the index. **Facsimile Number:** 818-365-5489.

Stenographers

★1692★
"Stenographers" in *Occupational Outlook Handbook* (pp. 278-279)
Superintendent of Documents
U.S. Government Printing Office
Washington, DC 20402   Phone: (202)783-3238

Biennial; latest edition, 1990-91. Encyclopedia of careers describing more than 250 occupations and comprising about 86 percent of all jobs in the economy. Occupations that require lengthy education or training are given the most attention. For each occupation, the handbook describes job duties, working conditions, training, educational preparation, personal qualities, advancement possibilities, job outlook, earnings, and sources of additional information.

★1693★
"Stenographers" in Volume 6 of *Career Discovery Encyclopedia* (pp. 62-63)
J.G. Ferguson Publishing Co.
200 W. Monroe
Chicago, IL 60606   Phone: (312)580-5480

E. Russell Primm, editor-in-chief. 1990. Contains two-page articles on 504 occupations. Each article describes job duties, earnings, and educational and training requirements.

★1694★
"Stenographers" in Volume 3 of *The Encyclopedia of Careers and Vocational Guidance* (pp. 92-95)
J.G. Ferguson Publishing Co.
200 W. Monroe
Chicago, IL 60606   Phone: (312)580-5480

William E. Hopke, editor-in-chief. Eighth edition, 1990. Four-volume set that profiles 500 occupations and describes job trends in 76 industries. Includes career description, educational requirements, history of the job, methods of entry, advancement, employment outlook, earnings, working conditions, social and psychological factors, and sources of additional information.

★1695★
A Study of Some Aspects of Satisfaction in the Vocation of Stenography
AMS Press, Inc.
56 E. 13th St.
New York, NY 10003   Phone: (212)777-4700

Margaret S. Quayle. Part of Columbia University Teachers College. Contributions to Education Series. **Facsimile Number:** (212)995-5413

★1696★
Transcriber
Vocational Biographies, Inc.
PO Box 31, Dept. VF10
Sauk Centre, MN 56378   Phone: (612)352-6516

1991. This pamphlet profiles a person working in the job. Includes information about job duties, working conditions, places of employment, educational preparation, labor market outlook, and salaries. **Toll-free/Additional Phone Number(s):** 800-255-0752.

★1697★
Video Career Library - Clerical & Administrative Support
Careers, Inc.
1211 10th St., SW
PO Box 135
Largo, FL 34649-0135   Phone: (813)584-7333

Videocassette. 1990. 26 mins. Part of the Video Career Library covering 165 occupations. Shows actual workers on the job. Includes secretaries, cashiers, receptionists, bookkeepers and audit clerks, telephone operators, postal clerks/carriers/supervisors, insurance investigators, bank tellers, data entry keyers, and court reporters.

★1698★
What Combines Communications, Law, Technology, Finance, Medicine, Engineering...
National Court Reporters Association
8224 Old Courthouse Rd.
Vienna, VA 22182-3808   Phone: (703)556-NCRA

This six-panel brochure describes qualifications, work, future outlook, places of employment, and educational preparation of court reporters.

Associations

★1699★
Association of Independent Colleges and Schools (AICS)
1 Dupont Circle NW, Ste. 350
Washington, DC 20036   Phone: (202)659-2460

Membership: Independent business schools and junior and senior colleges of business. **Purpose:** Sponsors an accrediting commission for postsecondary and collegiate institutions. **Publications:** *AICS Compass*, monthly. • *Capital Comments*, bimonthly. • *Directory of Accredited Institutions*, annual. **Facsimile Number:** (202)659-2254.

★1700★
National Shorthand Reporters Association (NSRA)
118 Park St. SE
Vienna, VA 22180   Phone: (703)281-4677

Membership: Independent state, regional, and local associations. Verbatim shorthand reporters who work as official reporters for courts and government agencies and as freelance reporters for independent contractors, retired reporters, teachers of shorthand reporting, and school officials; student shorthand reporters. **Purpose:** Conducts research; compiles statistics; bestows awards; offers placement service and Registered Professional Reporter Certification program. **Publications:** *Annual Report*. • *The National Shorthand Reporter*, 10/year. • *National Shorthand Reporters Association—Membership Directory and Registry of Professional Reporters*, annual. • Also publishes *Professional Education Series*, convention proceedings, and other guides and booklets.

Standards/Certification Agencies

Some states require each court reporter to be a Certified Shorthand Reporter (CSR). A certification test is administered by a board of examiners in each state that has CSR laws. The National Shorthand Reporters Association confers the designation Registered Professional Reporter (RPR) upon those who pass a two-part examination and participate in continuing education programs. The RPR designation is recognized as the mark of excellence in the profession.

★1701★
About the National Court Reporters Association
National Court Reporters Association
8224 Old Courthouse Rd.
Vienna, VA 22182-3808   Phone: (703)556-NCRA

1991. This six-page pamphlet describes court reporter certification, the work, and the effects of computerization on the profession.

★1702★
Association of Independent Colleges and Schools (AICS)
1 Dupont Circle NW, Ste. 350
Washington, DC 20036 Phone: (202)659-2460
Sponsors an accrediting commission for postsecondary and collegiate institutions.

★1703★
National Shorthand Reporters Association (NSRA)
118 Park St. SE
Vienna, VA 22180 Phone: (703)281-4677
Offers Registered Professional Reporter Certification program.

Test Guides

★1704★
Certified Shorthand Reporter
National Learning Corp.
212 Michael Dr.
Syosset, NY 11791 Phone: (516)921-8888
Jack Rudman. Part of the Career Examination Series No. 1. All examination guides in this series contain questions with answers. **Facsimile Number:** (516)921-8743. **Toll-free/Additional Phone Number(s):** 800-645-6337.

★1705★
Chief Law Stenographer
National Learning Corp.
212 Michael Dr.
Syosset, NY 11791 Phone: (516)921-8888
Jack Rudman. Part of the Career Examination Series No. 1. All examination guides in this series contain questions with answers. **Facsimile Number:** (516)921-8743. **Toll-free/Additional Phone Number(s):** 800-645-6337.

★1706★
Chief of Stenographic Services
National Learning Corp.
212 Michael Dr.
Syosset, NY 11791 Phone: (516)921-8888
Jack Rudman. Part of the Career Examination Series No. 1. All examination guides in this series contain questions with answers. **Facsimile Number:** (516)921-8743. **Toll-free/Additional Phone Number(s):** 800-645-6337.

★1707★
Federal Clerk - Steno - Typist
Prentice Hall Press
Simon & Schuster Inc.
200 Old Tappan Rd.
Old Tappan, NJ 07675 Phone: (800)223-2348
Hy Hammer and John Czukor. Sixth edition, 1988. Coverage includes Federal entry-level clerical positions, including clerk, clerk typist, stenographer, transcriber, office machines operator, and office assistant.

★1708★
Office Aide
Prentice Hall Press
Simon & Schuster Inc.
200 Old Tappan Rd.
Old Tappan, NJ 07675 Phone: (800)223-2348
Hy Hammer. Second edition, 1985. Contains seven sample exams for the following entry-level civil service postions: clerk, typist, stenographer, receptionist, office machine operator, telephone operator.

★1709★
Practice and Drill for the Clerk, Typist, and Stenographer Examinations
National Learning Corp.
212 Michael Dr.
Syosset, NY 11791 Phone: (516)921-8888
Jack Rudman. Part of the General Aptitude and Abilities Series No. 2. Books in this series provide functional, intensive test practice and drill in the basic skills and areas common to many examinations, as well as general aptitude or achievement necessary for entrance into many occupations or positions. **Facsimile Number:** (516)921-8743. **Toll-free/Additional Phone Number(s):** 800-645-6337.

★1710★
Practice & Drill for the Clerk, Typist & Stenographer Examinations
National Learning Corp.
212 Michael Dr.
Syosset, NY 11791 Phone: (516)921-8888
Jack Rudman. 1989. Part of Career Examination Series.

★1711★
Practice for Clerical, Typing and Stenographic Tests
Prentice Hall Press
Simon & Schuster Inc.
200 Old Tappan Rd.
Old Tappan, NJ 07675 Phone: (800)223-2348
Maryhelen H. Paulick Hoffman. Seventh edition, 1988. Provide preparation for all qualifying tests given by local, state, and federal agencies for all types of clerical positions.

★1712★
Principal Clerk/Principal Stenographer
Prentice Hall Press
Simon & Schuster Inc.
200 Old Tappan Rd.
Old Tappan, NJ 07675 Phone: (800)223-2348
Hy Hammer. Third edition, 1983. Contains information to prepare for federal, state, and municipal positions, including five sample exams.

★1713★
Principal Clerk-Stenographer
National Learning Corp.
212 Michael Dr.
Syosset, NY 11791 Phone: (516)921-8888
Jack Rudman. Part of the Career Examination Series No. 1. All examination guides in this series contain questions with answers. **Facsimile Number:** (516)921-8743. **Toll-free/Additional Phone Number(s):** 800-645-6337.

★1714★
Principal Office Stenographer
National Learning Corp.
212 Michael Dr.
Syosset, NY 11791 Phone: (516)921-8888
Jack Rudman. Part of the Career Examination Series No. 1. All examination guides in this series contain questions with answers. **Facsimile Number:** (516)921-8743. **Toll-free/Additional Phone Number(s):** 800-645-6337.

★1715★
Principal Stenographer
National Learning Corp.
212 Michael Dr.
Syosset, NY 11791 Phone: (516)921-8888
Jack Rudman. Part of the Career Examination Series No. 1. All examination guides in this series contain questions with answers.

Stenographers

Facsimile Number: (516)921-8743. **Toll-free/Additional Phone Number(s):** 800-645-6337.

★1716★
Principal Stenographer (Law)
National Learning Corp.
212 Michael Dr.
Syosset, NY 11791   Phone: (516)921-8888

Jack Rudman. Part of the Career Examination Series No. 1. All examination guides in this series contain questions with answers. **Facsimile Number:** (516)921-8743. **Toll-free/Additional Phone Number(s):** 800-645-6337.

★1717★
Senior Clerical Series
Prentice Hall Press
Simon & Schuster Inc.
200 Old Tappan Rd.
Old Tappan, NJ 07675   Phone: (800)223-2348

Hy Hammer. Fourth edition, 1983. Complete test preparation for the following senior grade positions: clerk, typist, stenographer, account clerk, file clerk, statistics clerk, stenographer (law), mail and supply clerk, and stores clerk.

★1718★
Senior Legal Stenographer
National Learning Corp.
212 Michael Dr.
Syosset, NY 11791   Phone: (516)921-8888

Jack Rudman. Part of the Career Examination Series No. 1. All examination guides in this series contain questions with answers. **Facsimile Number:** (516)921-8743. **Toll-free/Additional Phone Number(s):** 800-645-6337.

★1719★
Senior Office Stenographer
National Learning Corp.
212 Michael Dr.
Syosset, NY 11791   Phone: (516)921-8888

Jack Rudman. Part of the Career Examination Series No. 1. All examination guides in this series contain questions with answers. **Facsimile Number:** (516)921-8743. **Toll-free/Additional Phone Number(s):** 800-645-6337.

★1720★
Senior Stenographer
National Learning Corp.
212 Michael Dr.
Syosset, NY 11791   Phone: (516)921-8888

Jack Rudman. Part of the Career Examination Series No. 1. All examination guides in this series contain questions with answers. **Facsimile Number:** (516)921-8743. **Toll-free/Additional Phone Number(s):** 800-645-6337.

★1721★
Shorthand Reporter
National Learning Corp.
212 Michael Dr.
Syosset, NY 11791   Phone: (516)921-8888

Jack Rudman. Part of the Career Examination Series No. 1. All examination guides in this series contain questions with answers. **Facsimile Number:** (516)921-8743. **Toll-free/Additional Phone Number(s):** 800-645-6337.

★1722★
Stenographer
National Learning Corp.
212 Michael Dr.
Syosset, NY 11791   Phone: (516)921-8888

Jack Rudman. Part of the Career Examination Series No. 1. All examination guides in this series contain questions with answers. **Facsimile Number:** (516)921-8743. **Toll-free/Additional Phone Number(s):** 800-645-6337.

★1723★
Stenographer (Law)
National Learning Corp.
212 Michael Dr.
Syosset, NY 11791   Phone: (516)921-8888

Jack Rudman. Part of the Career Examination Series No. 1. All examination guides in this series contain questions with answers. **Facsimile Number:** (516)921-8743. **Toll-free/Additional Phone Number(s):** 800-645-6337.

★1724★
Stenographer-Secretary
National Learning Corp.
212 Michael Dr.
Syosset, NY 11791   Phone: (516)921-8888

Jack Rudman. Part of the Career Examination Series No. 1. All examination guides in this series contain questions with answers. **Facsimile Number:** (516)921-8743. **Toll-free/Additional Phone Number(s):** 800-645-6337.

★1725★
Stenographer-Typist
National Learning Corp.
212 Michael Dr.
Syosset, NY 11791   Phone: (516)921-8888

Jack Rudman. Part of the Career Examination Series No. 1. All examination guides in this series contain questions with answers. **Facsimile Number:** (516)921-8743. **Toll-free/Additional Phone Number(s):** 800-645-6337.

★1726★
Stenographer-Typist GS5-7
National Learning Corp.
212 Michael Dr.
Syosset, NY 11791   Phone: (516)921-8888

Jack Rudman. Part of the Career Examination Series No. 1. All examination guides in this series contain questions with answers. **Facsimile Number:** (516)921-8743. **Toll-free/Additional Phone Number(s):** 800-645-6337.

★1727★
Stenographer-Typist GS1-4
National Learning Corp.
212 Michael Dr.
Syosset, NY 11791   Phone: (516)921-8888

Jack Rudman. Part of the Career Examination Series No. 1. All examination guides in this series contain questions with answers. **Facsimile Number:** (516)921-8743. **Toll-free/Additional Phone Number(s):** 800-645-6337.

★1728★
Stenographic/Secretarial Associate
National Learning Corp.
212 Michael Dr.
Syosset, NY 11791   Phone: (516)921-8888

Jack Rudman. Part of the Career Examination Series No. 1. All examination guides in this series contain questions with answers. **Facsimile Number:** (516)921-8743. **Toll-free/Additional Phone Number(s):** 800-645-6337.

★1729★
Stenographic Secretary
National Learning Corp.
212 Michael Dr.
Syosset, NY 11791   Phone: (516)921-8888
Jack Rudman. Part of the Career Examination Series No. 1. All examination guides in this series contain questions with answers. **Facsimile Number:** (516)921-8743. **Toll-free/Additional Phone Number(s):** 800-645-6337.

★1730★
Stenographic Specialist
National Learning Corp.
212 Michael Dr.
Syosset, NY 11791   Phone: (516)921-8888
Jack Rudman. Part of the Career Examination Series No. 1. All examination guides in this series contain questions with answers. **Facsimile Number:** (516)921-8743. **Toll-free/Additional Phone Number(s):** 800-645-6337.

Educational Directories and Programs

★1731★
Directory of Accredited Institutions
Association of Independent Colleges and Schools (AICS)
1 Dupont Circle NW, Ste. 350
Washington, DC 20036   Phone: (202)659-2460
Annual.

★1732★
NCRA List of Approved Court Reporter Education Programs
National Court Reporters Association
8224 Old Courthouse Rd.
Vienna, VA 22182-3808   Phone: (703)556-NCRA
State-by-state listing of approved court reporter educational programs. Provides address and phone number.

★1733★
NSRA List of Approved Court Reporter Education Programs
National Shorthand Reporters Association
118 Park St., S.E.
Vienna, VA 22180   Phone: (703)281-4677
1990. State-by-state listing of schools meeting minimum standards established by the National Shorthand Reporters Association. Includes address and phone number.

★1734★
Stenographer
Accrediting Bureau of Health Education
Oak Manor Office
29089 U.S. 20 W.
Elkhart, IN 46514   Phone: (219)293-0124
1991. State-by-state listing of schools offering medical transcription training programs. Lists address, phone number, and contact person.

Awards, Scholarships, Grants, and Fellowships

★1735★
Fellow of the Academy of Professional Reporters
National Shorthand Reporters Association
118 Park St., S.E.
Vienna, VA 22180-4689   Phone: (703)281-4677
To recognize outstanding and extraordinary qualifications and experience in the field of shorthand reporting. Professional members who have been in the active practice of shorthand reporting for ten years and who have attained distinction as measured by performance are eligible. A certificate and pin are awarded. Established in 1975.

★1736★
NCRA Heritage Foundation Scholarships
National Court Reporters Association
Director of Professional Development
118 Park St., S.E.
Vienna, VA 22180-4689   Phone: (703)281-4677
Scholarships are offered to students enrolled in NCRA-approved training courses. Candidates must be entering the second year of the program, or equivalent. Each NCRA approved court reporter training program may nominate one outstanding shorthand reporting student on a nomination form which the program must fill out. The nominee must write a one-page essay on a predetermined subject. Awarded annually.

★1737★
NSRA Distinguished Service Award
National Shorthand Reporters Association
118 Park St., S.E.
Vienna, VA 22180-4689   Phone: (703)281-4677
To recognize outstanding service to the profession. Members of the Association are eligible. A bronze scroll/plaque is awarded annually and the recipient's name is added to a silver bowl on display at NSRA headquarters. Established in 1960.

★1738★
NSRA Heritage Foundation Scholarship Fund
National Shorthand Reporters Association
118 Park St., S.E.
Vienna, VA 22180-4689   Phone: (703)281-4677
To recognize outstanding court reporting by students attending NSRA approved court reporter training programs. Students entering the second year of a program who have attained exemplary academic records are eligible to submit essays on a predetermined subject. A $1,000 scholarship is awarded annually. Established in 1982.

Basic Reference Guides and Handbooks

★1739★
Professional Education Series
National Shorthand Reporters Association (NSRA)
118 Park St. SE
Vienna, VA 22180   Phone: (703)281-4677

Periodicals

★1740★
From Nine to Five
Dartnell Corp.
4660 Ravenswood
Chicago, IL 60640   Phone: (312)561-4000

Editor(s): Douglas Leland. Biweekly. Provides "tips, shortcuts, and helpful information for success in the office," particularly secretaries and office workers. Recurring features include columns titled Business Skills Clinic and The Coffee Break. **Toll-free/Additional Phone Number(s):** 800-621-5463 **Facsimile Number:** (312)561-3801.

★1741★
The National Shorthand Reporter (NSRA)
National Shorthand Reporters Association (NSRA)
118 Park St. SE
Vienna, VA 22180   Phone: (703)281-4677

10/year. Magazine for court and freelance shorthand reporters who specialize in hearings, depositions, statements, conferences, and other fields where accurate transcripts are necessary. Includes advertisers', monthly, and annual subject index; also includes book and product reviews, calendar of events, employment opportunities, member profiles, new members, obituaries, and technology updates.

Teacher Aides

Teacher aides assist teachers in a variety of ways to allow them more time for teaching. They help supervise students, record grades, and prepare teaching materials. In some schools, teacher aides perform clerical tasks, while in other districts, they may help instruct students under the guidance of teachers. Many teacher aides work part time during the school year and are concentrated primarily in the lower grades.

$alaries

The average earnings for teacher aides is $6.14-7.05/hour

Employment Outlook

Growth rate until the year 2000: Faster than average.

Teacher Aides

Career Guides

★1742★
"Early Childhood Center Teacher or Aide" in *Exploring Careers in Child Care Services* (pp. 9-21)
Rosen Publishing Group, Inc.
29 E. 21st St.
New York, NY 10010   Phone: (212)777-3017
Jean Ispa, Elizabeth Vemer, and Janis Logan. Revised edition, 1990. Covers occupations working with children including those requiring no education and training to those that require advanced training; from babysitting to program director. Describes the work and a typical work day, employment outlook, advantages and disadvantages, and personal characteristics needed for success in the field. Offers job hunting advice.

★1743★
Teacher Aide
Careers, Inc.
PO Box 135
Largo, FL 34649-0135   Phone: (813)584-7333
1991. Two-page occupational summary card describing duties, working conditions, personal qualifications, training, earnings and hours, employment outlook, places of employment, related careers and where to write for more information.

★1744★
"Teacher Aide" in *Occu-Facts: Information on 565 Careers in Outline Form* (p. 10.30)
Careers, Inc.
P.O. Box 135
1211 Tenth St., S.W.
Largo, FL 33640   Phone: (813)584-7333
Elizabeth Handville. Biennial, 1989-90 edition. Each one-page occupational profile describes duties, working conditions, physical surroundings and demands, aptitudes, temperament, educational requirements, employment outlook, earnings, and places of employment.

★1745★
"Teacher Aides" in *Jobs! What They Are...Where They Are...What They Pay* (pp. 88-89)
Simon & Schuster, Inc.
Simon & Schuster Bldg.
1230 Avenue of the Americas
New York, NY 10020   Phone: (212)698-7000
Robert O. Snelling and Anne M. Snelling. Revised edition, 1989. Profiles 241 occupations, describing duties and responsibilities, educational preparation, earnings, employment opportunities, training, and qualifications.

★1746★
"Teacher Aides" in *Occupational Outlook Handbook* (pp. 279-280)
Superintendent of Documents
U.S. Government Printing Office
Washington, DC 20402   Phone: (202)783-3238
Biennial; latest edition, 1990-91. Encyclopedia of careers describing more than 250 occupations and comprising about 86 percent of all jobs in the economy. Occupations that require lengthy education or training are given the most attention. For each occupation, the handbook describes job duties, working conditions, training, educational preparation, personal qualities, advancement possibilities, job outlook, earnings, and sources of additional information.

★1747★
"Teacher Aides" in *Opportunities in Child Care Careers* (pp. 59-61)
National Textbook Co.
4255 W. Touhy Ave.
Lincolnwood, IL 60646   Phone: (312)679-5500
Renee Wittenberg. 1987. Surveys job opportunities related to child care in child development, child life, health services, and psychology. Covers personal qualifications, training programs, job outlook, and salaries. Offers job hunting advice.

★1748★
"Teacher Aides" in *Opportunities in Teaching Careers* (pp. 37-38)
National Textbook Co.
4255 W. Touhy Ave.
Lincolnwood, IL 60646   Phone: (312)679-5500
Janet Fine. 1989. Describes the teaching profession and related fields. Covers educational preparation, employment conditions and outlook, certification, and salaries. Offers job hunting advice and information about teaching abroad.

★1749★
"Teacher Aides" in Volume 6 of *Career Discovery Encyclopedia* (pp. 94-95)
J.G. Ferguson Publishing Co.
200 W. Monroe
Chicago, IL 60606   Phone: (312)580-5480
E. Russell Primm, editor-in-chief. 1990. Contains two-page articles on 504 occupations. Each article describes job duties, earnings, and educational and training requirements.

★1750★
"Teacher Aides" in Volume 3 of *The Encyclopedia of Careers and Vocational Guidance* (pp. 107-110)
J.G. Ferguson Publishing Co.
200 W. Monroe
Chicago, IL 60606   Phone: (312)580-5480

William E. Hopke, editor-in-chief. Eighth edition, 1990. Four-volume set that profiles 500 occupations and describes job trends in 76 industries. Includes career description, educational requirements, history of the job, methods of entry, advancement, employment outlook, earnings, working conditions, social and psychological factors, and sources of additional information.

★1751★
"Teacher's Aide" in *Public and Community Services, Volume 11 of Career Information Center* (pp. 82-84)
Glencoe/Macmillan
15319 Chatsworth St.
Mission Hills, CA 91345   Phone: (818)898-1391

Richard Lidz and Dale Anderson, editorial directors. Fourth edition, 1990. For 600 occupations, describes job duties, entry-level requirements, education and training needed, advancement possibilities, employment outlook, earnings and benefits. The set is divided into 12 volumes. Each volume includes jobs related under a broad career field. Volume 13 is the index. **Facsimile Number:** 818-365-5489.

★1752★
Teachers Aides
Chronicle Guidance Publications, Inc.
PO Box 1190
Moravia, NY 13118-1190   Phone: (315)497-0330

1988. This career brief describes the nature of the work, working conditions, hours and earnings, education and training, licensure, certification, unions, personal qualifications, social and psychological factors, employment outlook, entry methods, advancement, and related occupations. **Toll-free/Additional Phone Number(s):** 800-622-7284.

★1753★
"Teachers Aides and School Bus Drivers" in *The American Almanac of Jobs and Salaries* (pp. 109-110)
Avon Books
105 Madison Avenue
New York, NY 10016   Phone: (212)481-5600

John Wright and Edward J. Dwyer. Revised and updated, 1990. A comprehensive guide to the wages of hundreds of occupations in a wide variety of industries and organizations.

★1754★
Video Career Library - Education
Careers, Inc.
1211 10th St., SW
PO Box 135
Largo, FL 34649-0135   Phone: (813)584-7333

Videocassette. 1990. Part of the Video Career Library series covering 165 occupations. Shows actual workers on the job. Includes teachers' aides.

Associations

★1755★
American Federation of Teachers (AFT)
555 New Jersey Ave. NW
Washington, DC 20001   Phone: (202)879-4400

Membership: AFL-CIO. **Purpose:** Works with teachers and other educational employees at the state and local level in organizing, collective bargaining, research, educational issues, and public relations. Conducts research in areas such as educational reform, bilingual education, teacher certification, and evaluation. Represents members' concerns through legislative action; offers technical assistance. Seeks to serve professionals with concerns similar to those of teachers, including civil service employees, through the Federation of State Employees, and healthcare workers through the Federation of Nurses and Health Professionals division. Operates Education for Democracy Project. Bestows awards; compiles statistics. **Publications:** *AFT Action: A Newsletter for AFT Leaders*, weekly. ● *American Educator*, quarterly. ● *American Teacher*, 8/year. ● *Healthwire*, 10/year. ● *On Campus*, 9/year. ● *Public Sevice Reporter*, 9/year. **Toll-free/Additional Phone Number(s):** (800)242-5465 (learning activities hot line).

Standards/Certification Agencies

Some states have voluntary certification for general teacher aides. To qualify, an individual may need a high school diploma or general equivalency degree (G.E.D.), or even some college training. Kansas, Louisiana, Texas, and Wisconsin grant permits for paraprofessionals, as some aides are called, in special education.

Test Guides

★1756★
Teaching Assistant
National Learning Corp.
212 Michael Dr.
Syosset, NY 11791   Phone: (516)921-8888

Jack Rudman. Part of the Career Examination Series No. 1. All examination guides in this series contain questions with answers. **Facsimile Number:** (516)921-8743. **Toll-free/Additional Phone Number(s):** 800-645-6337.

Basic Reference Guides and Handbooks

★1757★
Handbook for Teacher Aides
Pendell Publishing Co.
PO Box 2066
Midland, MI 48640   Phone: (517)496-3337

Howard Brighton. 1972.

★1758★
A Handbook of Effective Techniques for Teacher Aides
Charles C. Thomas, Publisher
2600 S. 1st St.
Springfield, IL 62794-9265   Phone: (217)789-8980

Dick B. Clough. 1978. **Facsimile Number:** (217)789-9130.

★1759★
The Teacher Aide in the Instructional Team
McGraw-Hill Publishing Co.
1221 Avenue of the Americas
New York, NY 10020   Phone: (212)512-2000

Don A. Welty. 1976.

Periodicals

★1760★
AFT Public Service Reporter
American Federation of Teachers (AFT)
555 New Jersey Ave. NW
Washington, DC 20001   Phone: (202)879-4400
9/year.

★1761★
American Educator
American Federation of Teachers (AFT)
555 New Jersey Ave. NW
Washington, DC 20001   Phone: (202)879-4400
Quarterly. Magazine.

★1762★
American Teacher
American Federation of Teachers
555 New Jersey Ave. NW
Washington, DC 20001-2079   Phone: (202)879-4430
Trish Gorman, Editor. 8x/yr. Newspaper focusing on issues of education and the labor union. **Facsimile Number:** (202)783-2014.

★1763★
ATEA Journal
American Technical Education Association
North Dakota State College of Science
Wahpeton, ND 58076   Phone: (701)671-2240
Editor(s): Betty Krump and Dr. Charles Losh. Quarterly. Reports on meetings, conferences, and conventions; equipment and teaching aids; news of members in the field of technical education; and reviews of books, pamphlets, and magazine articles. Recurring features include news from industry, U.S. Government publications, and book reviews. **Facsimile Number:** (701)671-2145.

★1764★
Healthwire
American Federation of Teachers (AFT)
555 New Jersey Ave. NW
Washington, DC 20001   Phone: (202)879-4400
10/year. Association and industry newsletter for AFT members involved in health care.

★1765★
On Campus
American Federation of Teachers (AFT)
555 New Jersey Ave. NW
Washington, DC 20001   Phone: (202)879-4400
9/year.

Telephone, Telegraph, and Teletype Operators

Telephone operators help customers with calls that cannot be dialed directly, such as person-to-person calls or collect calls. They also handle special billing requests, such as charging a call to a third number or to a calling card. Directory assistance operators answer customers' inquiries for telephone numbers by accessing computerized alphabetical and geographical directories. Many businesses, such as hotels, employ their own operators to handle house calls. Operators are also found in such settings as answering services and airport communication centers.

$alaries

The average salary for telephone operators is listed below.

Lowest 10 percent	Less than $8,600/year
Median	$15,600/year
Top 10 percent	More than $25,400/year
Starting telephone operators in the federal government	$11,484-14,067/year

Employment Outlook

Growth rate until the year 2000: Average.

Telephone, Telegraph, and Teletype Operators

Career Guides

★1766★
"Dial "O" For Operator" in *Telecommunications Careers* (pp. 54-57)
Franklin Watts, Inc.
387 Park Avenue, S.
New York, NY 10016   Phone: (212)686-7070
James L. Schefter. 1988. Describes the telecommunications industry and profiles jobs in manufacturing, the telephone industry, the military, video communications and television broadcasting. Covers job duties, educational requirements, salaries, and promotional possibilities.

★1767★
"Operator" in *Occu-Facts: Information on 565 Careers in Outline Form* (p. 12.30, 12.31, 12.32)
Careers, Inc.
P.O. Box 135
1211 Tenth St., S.W.
Largo, FL 33640   Phone: (813)584-7333
Elizabeth Handville. Biennial, 1989-90 edition. Each one-page occupational profile describes duties, working conditions, physical surroundings and demands, aptitudes, temperament, educational requirements, employment outlook, earnings, and places of employment.

★1768★
"Radio and Telegraph Operator" in *Telecommunications* (pp. 51-55)
Franklin Watts, Inc.
387 Park Avenue, S.
New York, NY 10016   Phone: (212)686-7070
Linda Barrett and Galen Guengerich. 1991. Surveys opportunities in telecommunications including telephone, radio, telegraph, and television communications. Includes job description, educational preparation, salary, and employment outlook. Offers job hunting advice.

★1769★
"Radio and Telegraph Operators" in Volume 5 of *Career Discovery Encyclopedia* (pp. 118-119)
J.G. Ferguson Publishing Co.
200 W. Monroe
Chicago, IL 60606   Phone: (312)580-5480
E. Russell Primm, editor-in-chief. 1990. Contains two-page articles on 504 occupations. Each article describes job duties, earnings, and educational and training requirements.

★1770★
"Radio and Telegraph Operators" in Volume 2 of *The Encyclopedia of Careers and Vocational Guidance* (pp. 561-564)
J.G. Ferguson Publishing Co.
200 W. Monroe
Chicago, IL 60606   Phone: (312)580-5480
William E. Hopke, editor-in-chief. Eighth edition, 1990. Four-volume set that profiles 500 occupations and describes job trends in 76 industries. Includes career description, educational requirements, history of the job, methods of entry, advancement, employment outlook, earnings, working conditions, social and psychological factors, and sources of additional information.

★1771★
"Receptionists and Switchboard Operators" in *The American Almanac of Jobs and Salaries* (p. 507)
Avon Books
105 Madison Avenue
New York, NY 10016   Phone: (212)481-5600
John Wright and Edward J. Dwyer. Revised and updated, 1990. A comprehensive guide to the wages of hundreds of occupations in a wide variety of industries and organizations.

★1772★
Switchboard Operators
Chronicle Guidance Publications, Inc.
PO Box 1190
Moravia, NY 13118-1190   Phone: (315)497-0330
1988. This career brief describes the nature of the work, working conditions, hours and earnings, education and training, licensure, certification, unions, personal qualifications, social and psychological factors, employment outlook, entry methods, advancement, and related occupations. **Toll-free/Additional Phone Number(s):** 800-622-7284.

★1773★
"Switchboard Operators" in Volume 6 of *Career Discovery Encyclopedia* (pp. 84-85)
J.G. Ferguson Publishing Co.
200 W. Monroe
Chicago, IL 60606   Phone: (312)580-5480
E. Russell Primm, editor-in-chief. 1990. Contains two-page articles on 504 occupations. Each article describes job duties, earnings, and educational and training requirements.

★1774★
"Switchboard Operators" in *The Encyclopedia of Careers and Vocational Guidance* (pp. 99-103)
J.G. Ferguson Publishing Co.
200 W. Monroe
Chicago, IL 60606   Phone: (312)580-5480

William E. Hopke, editor-in-chief. Eighth edition, 1990. Four-volume set that profiles 500 occupations and describes job trends in 76 industries. Includes career description, educational requirements, history of the job, methods of entry, advancement, employment outlook, earnings, working conditions, social and psychological factors, and sources of additional information.

★1775★
"Telephone and PBX Operator" in *Telecommunications* (pp. 15-19)
Franklin Watts, Inc.
387 Park Avenue, S.
New York, NY 10016   Phone: (212)686-7070

Linda Barrett and Galen Guengerich. 1991. Surveys opportunities in telecommunications including telephone, radio, telegraph, and television communications. Includes job description, educational preparation, salary, and employment outlook. Offers job hunting advice.

★1776★
Telephone Answering Service Operator
Careers, Inc.
PO Box 135
Largo, FL 34649-0135   Phone: (813)584-7333

1990. Two-page job guide card describing duties, working conditions, personal qualifications, training, earnings and hours, employment outlook, places of employment, related careers and where to write for more information.

★1777★
Telephone Manners
Britannica Films
310 South Michigan Ave.
Chicago, IL 60604   Phone: (312)347-7958

Videocassette. 1989. 11 mins. This program demonstrates every important step in telephone usage including identifying yourself and your organization, personalizing your calls, repeating all instructions given, taking notes of important messages, remembering calls on hold, listening to the caller's mood as well as the message, using common courtesy words and conveying warmth.

★1778★
Telephone Operator
Careers, Inc.
PO Box 135
Largo, FL 34649-0135   Phone: (813)584-7333

1990. Two-page occupational summary card describing duties, working conditions, personal qualifications, training, earnings and hours, employment outlook, places of employment, related careers and where to write for more information.

★1779★
"Telephone Operator" in *Communications and the Arts*, Volume 3 of *Career Information Center* (pp. 75-77)
Glencoe/Macmillan
15319 Chatsworth St.
Mission Hills, CA 91345   Phone: (818)898-1391

Richard Lidz and Dale Anderson, editorial directors. Fourth edition, 1990. For 600 occupations, describes job duties, entry-level requirements, education and training needed, advancement possibilities, employment outlook, earnings and benefits. The set is divided into 12 volumes. Each volume includes jobs related under a broad career field. Volume 13 is the index. **Facsimile Number:** 818-365-5489.

★1780★
"Telephone Operators" in *Jobs! What They Are...Where They Are...What They Pay* (pp. 212-213)
Simon & Schuster, Inc.
Simon & Schuster Bldg.
1230 Avenue of the Americas
New York, NY 10020   Phone: (212)698-7000

Robert O. Snelling and Anne M. Snelling. Revised edition, 1989. Profiles 241 occupations, describing duties and responsibilities, educational preparation, earnings, employment opportunities, training, and qualifications.

★1781★
"Telephone Operators" in Volume 6 of *Career Discovery Encyclopedia* (pp. 104-105)
J.G. Ferguson Publishing Co.
200 W. Monroe
Chicago, IL 60606   Phone: (312)580-5480

E. Russell Primm, editor-in-chief. 1990. Contains two-page articles on 504 occupations. Each article describes job duties, earnings, and educational and training requirements.

★1782★
"Telephone Operators" in Volume 3 of *The Encyclopedia of Careers and Vocational Guidance* (pp. 115-118)
J.G. Ferguson Publishing Co.
200 W. Monroe
Chicago, IL 60606   Phone: (312)580-5480

William E. Hopke, editor-in-chief. Eighth edition, 1990. Four-volume set that profiles 500 occupations and describes job trends in 76 industries. Includes career description, educational requirements, history of the job, methods of entry, advancement, employment outlook, earnings, working conditions, social and psychological factors, and sources of additional information.

★1783★
Telephone Operators (Central Office)
Chronicle Guidance Publications, Inc.
PO Box 1190
Moravia, NY 13118-1190   Phone: (315)497-0330

1988. This career brief describes the nature of the work, working conditions, hours and earnings, education and training, licensure, certification, unions, personal qualifications, social and psychological factors, employment outlook, entry methods, advancement, and related occupations. **Toll-free/Additional Phone Number(s):** 800-622-7284.

★1784★
"Telephone, Telegraph, and Teletype Operators" in *Occupational Outlook Handbook* (pp. 280-282)
Superintendent of Documents
U.S. Government Printing Office
Washington, DC 20402   Phone: (202)783-3238

Biennial; latest edition, 1990-91. Encyclopedia of careers describing more than 250 occupations and comprising about 86 percent of all jobs in the economy. Occupations that require lengthy education or training are given the most attention. For each occupation, the handbook describes job duties, working conditions, training, educational preparation, personal qualities, advancement possibilities, job outlook, earnings, and sources of additional information.

Telephone, Telegraph, and Teletype Operators

★1785★
Video Career Library - Clerical & Administrative Support
Careers, Inc.
1211 10th St., SW
PO Box 135
Largo, FL 34649-0135   Phone: (813)584-7333
Videocassette. 1990. 26 mins. Part of the Video Career Library covering 165 occupations. Shows actual workers on the job. Includes secretaries, cashiers, receptionists, bookkeepers and audit clerks, telephone operators, postal clerks/carriers/supervisors, insurance investigators, bank tellers, data entry keyers, and court reporters.

★1786★
What Is Telemarketing and How Do I Get Started?
1st Financial Video Network
1701 East Woodfield Rd.
Suite 412
Schaumburg, IL 60173-5133   Phone: (708)605-0222
Videocassette. 1987. 25 mins. Starting a career in telemarketing is explained in this tape.

Associations

★1787★
United States Telephone Association (USTA)
900 19th St. NW, Ste. 800
Washington, DC 20006   Phone: (202)835-3100
Membership: Local operating telephone companies or telephone holding companies. Members represent a total of 114 million access lines. **Purpose:** Presents Distinguished Service Award and Pacesetter Award to outstanding leaders in industry and other fields. Conducts educational and training programs. Maintains 21 committees. **Publications:** *Holding Company Report*, annual. • *Phonefacts*, annual. • *Statistical Volumes*, annual. • *Teletimes*, quarterly. • Also publishes booklets and brochures. **Toll-free/Additional Phone Number(s):** (202)835-3198 telephone news updates on legislative and industry developments.

Test Guides

★1788★
Office Aide
Prentice Hall Press
Simon & Schuster Inc.
200 Old Tappan Rd.
Old Tappan, NJ 07675   Phone: (800)223-2348
Hy Hammer. Second edition, 1985. Contains seven sample exams for the following entry-level civil service positions: clerk, typist, stenographer, receptionist, office machine operator, telephone operator.

★1789★
Police Communications & Teletype Operator
National Learning Corp.
212 Michael Dr.
Syosset, NY 11791   Phone: (516)921-8888
Jack Rudman. Part of the Career Examination Series No. 1. Study guide for the position of Police Communications & Teletype Operator Supervisor is also available. All examination guides in this series contain questions with answers. **Facsimile Number:** (516)921-8743. **Toll-free/Additional Phone Number(s):** 800-645-6337.

★1790★
Principal Telephone Operator
National Learning Corp.
212 Michael Dr.
Syosset, NY 11791   Phone: (516)921-8888
Jack Rudman. Part of the Career Examination Series No. 1. All examination guides in this series contain questions with answers. **Facsimile Number:** (516)921-8743. **Toll-free/Additional Phone Number(s):** 800-645-6337.

★1791★
Radio and Telegraph Operator
National Learning Corp.
212 Michael Dr.
Syosset, NY 11791   Phone: (516)921-8888
Jack Rudman. Part of the Career Examination Series No. 1. All examination guides in this series contain questions with answers. **Facsimile Number:** (516)921-8743. **Toll-free/Additional Phone Number(s):** 800-645-6337.

★1792★
Radio Telephone Operator
National Learning Corp.
212 Michael Dr.
Syosset, NY 11791   Phone: (516)921-8888
Jack Rudman. Part of the Career Examination Series No. 1. All examination guides in this series contain questions with answers. **Facsimile Number:** (516)921-8743. **Toll-free/Additional Phone Number(s):** 800-645-6337.

★1793★
Senior Telephone Operator
National Learning Corp.
212 Michael Dr.
Syosset, NY 11791   Phone: (516)921-8888
Jack Rudman. Part of the Career Examination Series No. 1. All examination guides in this series contain questions with answers. **Facsimile Number:** (516)921-8743. **Toll-free/Additional Phone Number(s):** 800-645-6337.

★1794★
Telephone Operator
National Learning Corp.
212 Michael Dr.
Syosset, NY 11791   Phone: (516)921-8888
Jack Rudman. Part of the Career Examination Series No. 1. All examination guides in this series contain questions with answers. **Facsimile Number:** (516)921-8743. **Toll-free/Additional Phone Number(s):** 800-645-6337.

★1795★
Teletypist
National Learning Corp.
212 Michael Dr.
Syosset, NY 11791   Phone: (516)921-8888
Jack Rudman. Part of the Career Examination Series No. 1. All examination guides in this series contain questions with answers. **Facsimile Number:** (516)921-8743. **Toll-free/Additional Phone Number(s):** 800-645-6337.

Periodicals

★1796★
Dots and Dashes
Morse Telegraph Club
1101 Maplewood Dr.
Normal, IL 61761   Phone: (309)454-2029

Editor(s): W.K. Dunbar. Quarterly. Perpetuates the tradition of the telegraph profession through articles and anecdotes about the use of Morse and International codes and operators, manufacturers, and users of telegraphs. Recurring features include member and chapter news, letters to the editor, and reports of meetings.

★1797★
International PBX/Telecommunicators—Bulletin
International PBX/Telecommunicators
40 Frances Davis
1307 Bellevue
Richmond, VA 23227   Phone: (804)262-0355

Editor(s): Ila Mae Hora and Jean Zurn. Monthly. Carries information for switchboard, Centrex, and Dimension operators in business, industry, education, and the medical field. Acts as a forum for members to share experiences, ideas, and to learn more about telephone equipment and its use. Recurring features include survey results, a calendar of events, and news of educational opportunities.

★1798★
International PBX/Telecommunicators—Newsletter
International PBX/Telecommunicators
2426 Swan Blvd.
Wauwatosa, WI 53226   Phone: (414)771-5336

Editor(s): Ila Mae Hora. Monthly. Furnishes articles and commentary to assist switchboard operators and communication directors to better communicate with customers and government. Recurring features include letters to the editor, interviews, news of research, a calendar of events, reports of meetings, news of educational opportunities, and columns titled President's Message, New Equipment, and Helpful Hints.

★1799★
Telemarketing
Technology Marketing Corp.
1 Technology Plaza
Norwalk, CT 06854   Phone: (203)852-6800

Linda Driscoll, Editor. Monthly. Magazine on telemarketing and business telecommunications technology. **Facsimile Number:** (203)853-2845.

★1800★
Telephone News
Phillips Publishing, Inc.
7811 Montrose Rd.
Potomac, MD 20854   Phone: (301)340-2100

Candace Sams, Editor. Weekly. Telecommunications industry newsletter. **Facsimile Number:** (301)424-4297.

★1801★
Teletimes (USTA)
United States Telephone Association (USTA)
900 19th St. NW, Ste. 800
Washington, DC 20006   Phone: (202)835-3100
Quarterly.

Other Sources of Information

★1802★
Phonefacts
United States Telephone Association (USTA)
900 19th St. NW, Ste. 800
Washington, DC 20006   Phone: (202)835-3100
Annual.

★1803★
Telegraph & Data Transmission over Shortwave Radio Links: Fundamental Principles & Networks
John Wiley & Sons
605 3rd Ave.
New York, NY 10158   Phone: (212)850-6000

Lother Wiesner. Third edition, 1984. **Facsimile Number:** (212)850-6088.

Typists, Word Processors, and Data Entry Keyers

Typists, word processors, and data entry keyers are responsible for the timely processing of information and data. Depending on their experience, typists may prepare simple forms or type technical material from rough drafts. Word processors use word processing equipment to record, edit, store, and revise correspondence, reports, statistical tables, and other materials. Data entry keyers are generally responsible for entering numerical information, such as data from checks or invoices, into computer systems. Typists, word processors, and data entry keyers are employed in a variety of industies, with many found in educational institutions, health care facilities, and firms that provide business services.

$alaries

Average salaries of typists, word processors, and data entry keyers vary by industry.

Typists	$14,612/year
Word processors	$18,148/year
Data entry keyers	$15,002/year

Employment Outlook

Growth rate until the year 2000: More slowly than average.

Typists, Word Processors, and Data Entry Keyers

Basic Reference Guides and Handbooks

★1804★
YARDSTICK
Gartner Group
56 Top Gallant Rd.
Stamford, CT 06904 Phone: (203)967-6855
Randall Brophy, Analyst, editor. Annual, April/June/August; twice quarterly. Top 100 U.S. and worldwide data processing equipment manufacturers, selected on the basis of revenue. Entries include: Company name and financial data in calendar format for prior five years. Quarterly updates on 250 information technology vendors. Arrangement: Ranked by revenues. Indexes: Over 400 charts and tables containing comparative data on revenues, marketing expenses, R&D investment, capital spending, growth, revenues by product segment, profit, etc., each enabling reference to the more extensive profile sheet.

Career Guides

★1805★
Business & Data Processing Machine Operators
Morris Video
2730 Monterey St. #105
Monterey Business Park
Torrance, CA 90503 Phone: (213)533-4800
Videocassette. 1982. 15 mins. Machinery is an integral part of the business world, be it calculator or computer, and women and men are in great demand to operate them.

★1806★
Career Insights
RMI Media Productions, Inc.
2807 West 47th St.
Shawnee Mission, KS 66205 Phone: (913)262-3974
Videocassette series. 1987. This videotape series describes 50 occupations, including skill requirements and interviews with people employed in these fields. Occupations include: flight service, air transportation/ground services, data processing, carpentry, clerk in banking/insurance/business, cosmetic personal grooming, firefighting, roofing, material handling, photographic processing, plumbing, secretarial services, tool and die operations.

★1807★
Career Success Series
Cambridge Career Products
90 MacCorkle Ave., SW
South Charleston, WV 25311 Phone: (304)744-9323
Videocassette. 1986. 15 mins. A series, available separately, outlining various career choices for students. Occupations include: flight service, air transportation/ground service, data processing, carpentry, clerk in banking/insurance, commodity sales, cosmetic personal grooming, fire fighting, forestry services, home economics, insulation/roofing, material handling, mechanics, photographic processing, pipefitting and plumbing, police science, printing, secretarial services, and utilities equipment operator.

★1808★
Computer Program & Systems Analysis
Morris Video
2730 Monterey St. #105
Monterey Business Park
Torrance, CA 90503 Phone: (213)533-4800
Videocassette. 1984. 15 mins. From data processing to program writing, the myriad computer career possibilities are discussed.

★1809★
"Data Entry" in *Careers in High Tech* (pp. 31-32)
Arco/Prentice Hall Press
1 Gulf & Western Plaza
New York, NY 10023 Phone: (212)373-8500
Connie Winkler. 1987. Surveys career opportunities in data processing, technology, personal computers, telecommunications, manufacturing technology, artificial intelligence, computer graphics, biotechnology, lasers, technical writing, and publishing. Includes information on educational preparation, associations, and periodicals.

★1810★
"Data Entry Clerks" in Volume 3 of *The Encyclopedia of Careers and Vocational Guidance* (pp. 29-32)
J.G. Ferguson Publishing Co.
200 W. Monroe
Chicago, IL 60606 Phone: (312)580-5480
William E. Hopke, editor-in-chief. Eighth edition, 1990. Four-volume set that profiles 500 occupations and describes job trends in 76 industries. Includes career description, educational requirements, history of the job, methods of entry, advancement, employment outlook, earnings, working conditions, social and psychological factors, and sources of additional information.

★1811★
"Data Entry Clerks" in Volume 2 of *Career Discovery Encyclopedia* (pp. 87-88)
J.G. Ferguson Publishing Co.
200 W. Monroe
Chicago, IL 60606   Phone: (312)580-5480

E. Russell Primm, editor-in-chief. 1990. Contains two-page articles on 504 occupations. Each article describes job duties, earnings, and educational and training requirements.

★1812★
"Data Entry Keyer" in *Administration, Business, and Office*, Volume 1 of *Career Information Center* (pp. 52-53)
Glencoe/Macmillan
15319 Chatsworth St.
Mission Hills, CA 91345   Phone: (818)898-1391

Richard Lidz and Dale Anderson, editorial directors. Fourth edition, 1990. For 600 occupations, describes job duties, entry-level requirements, education and training needed, advancement possibilities, employment outlook, earnings and benefits. The set is divided into 12 volumes. Each volume includes jobs related under a broad career field. Volume 13 is the index. **Facsimile Number:** 818-365-5489.

★1813★
"Data Entry Keyer" in *Careers in Banking and Finance* (pp. 41-42)
Rosen Publishing Group, Inc.
29 E. 21st St.
New York, NY 10010   Phone: (212)777-3017

Patricia Haddock. 1990. Describes more than 20 jobs at all levels in banking and finance. Contains information about the types of financial organizations where the jobs are found, educational requirements, job duties, and salaries. Offers advice on job hunting.

★1814★
Data Entry Operator
Careers, Inc.
PO Box 135
Largo, FL 34649-0135   Phone: (813)584-7333

1992. Two-page occupational summary card describing duties, working conditions, personal qualifications, training, earnings and hours, employment outlook, places of employment, related careers and where to write for more information.

★1815★
Data Entry Operator
Vocational Biographies, Inc.
PO Box 31, Dept. VF10
Sauk Centre, MN 56378   Phone: (612)352-6516

1988. This pamphlet profiles a person working in the job. Includes information about job duties, working conditions, places of employment, educational preparation, labor market outlook, and salaries. **Toll-free/Additional Phone Number(s):** 800-255-0752.

★1816★
"Data Entry Operator" in *Occu-Facts: Information on 565 Careers in Outline Form* (p. 12.47)
Careers, Inc.
P.O. Box 135
1211 Tenth St., S.W.
Largo, FL 33640   Phone: (813)584-7333

Elizabeth Handville. Biennial, 1989-90 edition. Each one-page occupational profile describes duties, working conditions, physical surroundings and demands, aptitudes, temperament, educational requirements, employment outlook, earnings and places of employment.

★1817★
"Data Entry Operator" in *The Complete Computer Career Guide* (pp. 30-32)
Tab Books, Inc.
Blue Ridge Summit, PA 17294-0850   Phone: (717)794-2191

Judith Norback. 1987. Offers career planning tips and describes the educational preparation needed, employment outlook, industry trends, and certification. Offers job search advice. A separate section includes opportunities for women and minorities.

★1818★
Data Entry Operators
Chronicle Guidance Publications, Inc.
PO Box 1190
Moravia, NY 13118-1190   Phone: (315)497-0330

1989. This career brief describes the nature of the work, working conditions, hours and earnings, education and training, licensure, certification, unions, personal qualifications, social and psychological factors, employment outlook, entry methods, advancement, and related occupations. **Toll-free/Additional Phone Number(s):** 800-622-7284.

★1819★
"Data Entry Specialist" in *Opportunities in Data Processing Careers* (pp. 52-53)
National Textbook Co.
4255 W. Touhy Ave.
Lincolnwood, IL 60646   Phone: (312)679-5500

Norman N. Noerper. 1989. Provides an overview of the history and development of data processing careers. For each job included, describes responsibilities, salary, and job outlook. Contains separate chapters on educational preparation and job hunting. Lists professional organizations, publications, and schools.

★1820★
Data Processing
Gallaudet University Library
Gallaudet Media Distribution
800 Florida Ave. NE
Washington, DC 20002   Phone: (202)651-5579

Videocassette. 1981. 20 mins. A look at areas in the data processing field where deaf people can find jobs.

★1821★
Data Processing: Career Opportunities for Hearing Impaired People
Journal Films, Inc.
930 Pitner Ave.
Evanston, IL 60202   Phone: (708)328-6700

Videocassette. 1982. 11 mins. Hearing impaired people are taught how to enter the field of data processing.

★1822★
Exploring Careers in Word Processing and Desktop Publishing
Rosen Publishing Group, Inc.
29 E. 21st St.
New York, NY 10010   Phone: (212)777-3017

Jean W. Spencer. 1990. Describes past, current and future trends in jobs using word processing. Covers the secretarial, information processing, and desktop publishing fields. Explains training needed, skills needed to succeed on the job, and the equipment used. Lists professional organizations and trade publications.

★1823★
"Information Technology, Data Processing" in *The Career Connection II: A Guide to Technical Majors and Their Related Careers* (pp. 73-74)
ERIS
PO Box 7509
University Station
Provo, UT 84602-0509

Fred A. Rowe. 1988. Contains technical majors, such as automotive technology. Describes the major and the job. Lists high school and postsecondary school courses. Includes occupations related to the major, employment outlook, and starting salary.

★1824★
"Information/Word Processing" in *Opportunities in Office Occupations* (pp. 116-130)
National Textbook Co.
4255 W. Touhy Ave.
Lincolnwood, IL 60646   Phone: (312)679-5500

Blanche Ettinger. 1989. Describes factors and trends which will affect office occupations including automation, telecommuting, and unionization. Separate chapters cover clerks, records management, information word processing, the secretary, and the bookkeeper-accountant. Describes job duties, skills needed, educational preparation, job hunting, types of equipment, employment outlook, and salaries.

★1825★
Office Revolution
NETCHE (Nebraska ETV Council for Higher Education)
Box 83111
Lincoln, NE 68501   Phone: (402)472-3611

Videocassette. 1983. 26 mins. This program is intended as an introduction to word processing.

★1826★
Opportunities in Word Processing Careers
National Textbook Co.
4255 W. Touhy Ave.
Lincolnwood, IL 60646   Phone: (312)679-5500

Marianne Forrester Munday. 1991. Describes the role word processing plays in organizations, career opportunities, and effective training programs. Presents employment outlook, qualifications needed, salaries, working conditions, and what word processors like about their jobs. Provides job huntings tips.

★1827★
Police Department Clerk/Typist
Vocational Biographies, Inc.
PO Box 31, Dept. VF10
Sauk Centre, MN 56378   Phone: (612)352-6516

1990. This pamphlet profiles a person working in the job. Includes information about job duties, working conditions, places of employment, educational preparation, labor market outlook, and salaries. **Toll-free/Additional Phone Number(s):** 800-255-0752.

★1828★
"Receptionist/Clerk-Typist" in *Career Opportunities in Television, Cable, and Video* (pp. 22-23)
Facts on File, Inc.
460 Park Avenue, S.
New York, NY 10016   Phone: (212)683-2244

Third edition, 1990. Describes 100 media-related jobs. Each occupational profile covers job duties, employment outlook, career paths, salaries, skills, and educational preparation. Offers tips for entering the field.

★1829★
Typist
Careers, Inc.
PO Box 135
Largo, FL 34649-0135   Phone: (813)584-7333

1991. Two-page occupational summary card describing duties, working conditions, personal qualifications, training, earnings and hours, employment outlook, places of employment, related careers and where to write for more information.

★1830★
"Typist" in *Occu-Facts: Information on 565 Careers in Outline Form* (p. 12.10, 12.11)
Careers, Inc.
P.O. Box 135
1211 Tenth St., S.W.
Largo, FL 33640   Phone: (813)584-7333

Elizabeth Handville. Biennial, 1989-90 edition. Each one-page occupational profile describes duties, working conditions, physical surroundings and demands, aptitudes, temperament, educational requirements, employment outlook, earnings, and places of employment.

★1831★
"Typist and Word Processors" in *Careers in Banking and Finance* (p. 73)
Rosen Publishing Group, Inc.
29 E. 21st St.
New York, NY 10010   Phone: (212)777-3017

Patricia Haddock. 1990. Describes more than 20 jobs at all levels in banking and finance. Contains information about the types of financial organizations where the jobs are found, educational requirements, job duties, and salaries. Offers advice on job hunting.

★1832★
"Typists" in *Opportunities in Vocational and Technical Careers* (pp. 44-45)
National Textbook Co.
4255 W. Touhy Ave.
Lincolnwood, IL 60646   Phone: (312)679-5500

Adrian A. Paradis. 1987. Describes careers which can be prepared for by attending a private vocational or proprietary school—office employee, sales worker, service worker, health services, mechanic, craftworker, and technician. Covers employment outlook, job duties, and salaries. Offers career planning advice.

★1833★
"Typists" in Volume 6 of *Career Discovery Encyclopedia* (pp. 136-137)
J.G. Ferguson Publishing Co.
200 W. Monroe
Chicago, IL 60606   Phone: (312)580-5480

E. Russell Primm, editor-in-chief. 1990. Contains two-page articles on 504 occupations. Each article describes job duties, earnings, and educational and training requirements.

★1834★
"Typists and Word Processor Operators" in *Jobs! What They Are...Where They Are...What They Pay* (pp. 213-214)
Simon & Schuster, Inc.
Simon & Schuster Bldg.
1230 Avenue of the Americas
New York, NY 10020   Phone: (212)698-7000

Robert O. Snelling and Anne M. Snelling. Revised edition, 1989. Profiles 241 occupations, describing duties and

★1835★ VOCATIONAL CAREERS SOURCEBOOK, 1st Edition

responsibilities, educational preparation, earnings, employment opportunities, training, and qualifications.

★1835★
"Typists and Word Processors" in Volume 3 of *The Encyclopedia of Careers and Vocational Guidance* (pp. 124-129)
J.G. Ferguson Publishing Co.
200 W. Monroe
Chicago, IL 60606   Phone: (312)580-5480
William E. Hopke, editor-in-chief. Eighth edition, 1990. Four-volume set that profiles 500 occupations and describes job trends in 76 industries. Includes career description, educational requirements, history of the job, methods of entry, advancement, employment outlook, earnings, working conditions, social and psychological factors, and sources of additional information.

★1836★
"Typists, Word Processors, and Data Entry Keyers" in *Occupational Outlook Handbook* (pp. 282-284)
Superintendent of Documents
U.S. Government Printing Office
Washington, DC 20402   Phone: (202)783-3238
Biennial; latest edition, 1990-91. Encyclopedia of careers describing more than 250 occupations and comprising about 86 percent of all jobs in the economy. Occupations that require lengthy education or training are given the most attention. For each occupation, the handbook describes job duties, working conditions, training, educational preparation, personal qualities, advancement possibilities, job outlook, earnings, and sources of additional information.

★1837★
Video Career Library - Clerical & Administrative Support
Careers, Inc.
1211 10th St., SW
PO Box 135
Largo, FL 34649-0135   Phone: (813)584-7333
Videocassette. 1990. 26 mins. Part of the Video Career Library covering 165 occupations. Shows actual workers on the job. Includes secretaries, cashiers, receptionists, bookkeepers and audit clerks, telephone operators, postal clerks/carriers/supervisors, insurance investigators, bank tellers, data entry keyers, and court reporters.

★1838★
Vocational Visions
Center for Humanities, Inc.
Communications Park
Box 1000
Mount Kisco, NY 10549   Phone: (914)666-4100
Videocassette. 1984. 30 mins. This series of programs explains key aspects of actual training and a day in the life of a worker in the specific field mentioned on the videocassette. Occupations include: transportation/mechanics, repair, construction, business/office occupations, health, and agriculture.

★1839★
"Word Processing" in *Exploring High Tech Careers* (pp. 60-64)
Rosen Publishing Group, Inc.
29 E. 21st St.
New York, NY 10010   Phone: (212)777-3017
Scott Southworth. Revised edition, 1988. Provides an orientation to the whole area of high tech and surveys jobs such as computer programming, drafting, and technical illustration. Covers educational preparation, advantages and disadvantages, advancement opportunities, vond personal characteristics needed. Offers job hunting advice.

★1840★
Word Processing Machine Operator
Careers, Inc.
PO Box 135
Largo, FL 34649-0135   Phone: (813)584-7333
1988. Two-page occupational summary card describing duties, working conditions, personal qualifications, training, earnings and hours, employment outlook, places of employment, related careers and where to write for more information.

★1841★
"Word Processing Operators" in *The Complete Computer Career Guide* (pp. 75-78)
Tab Books, Inc.
Blue Ridge Summit, PA 17294-0850   Phone: (717)794-2191
Judith Norback. 1987. Offers career planning tips and describes the educational preparation needed, employment outlook, industry trends, and certification. Offers job search advice. A separate section includes opportunities for women and minorities.

★1842★
"Word Processing Personnel" in *The American Almanac of Jobs and Salaries* (pp. 510-516)
Avon Books
105 Madison Avenue
New York, NY 10016   Phone: (212)481-5600
John Wright and Edward J. Dwyer. Revised and updated, 1990. A comprehensive guide to the wages of hundreds of occupations in a wide variety of industries and organizations.

★1843★
"Word Processing Specialists: Information Processors" in *Careers for Women Without College Degrees* (pp. 192-196)
McGraw-Hill Publishing Co.
11 W. 19th St.
New York, NY 10011   Phone: (212)337-6010
Beatryce Nivens. 1988. Career planning and job hunting guide containing information on decision-making, skills assessment, and resumes for career changers. Profiles careers with the best occupational outlook. Describes the work, educational preparation, employment outlook, salaries, and required skills.

★1844★
Word Processing Specialists (Operators)
Chronicle Guidance Publications, Inc.
PO Box 1190
Moravia, NY 13118-1190   Phone: (315)497-0330
1990. This career brief describes the nature of the work, working conditions, hours and earnings, education and training, licensure, certification, unions, personal qualifications, social and psychological factors, employment outlook, entry methods, advancement, and related occupations. **Toll-free/Additional Phone Number(s):** 800-622-7284.

★1845★
"Word Processor" in *Administration, Business, and Office*, Volume 1 of *Career Information Center* (pp. 101-103)
Glencoe/Macmillan
15319 Chatsworth St.
Mission Hills, CA 91345   Phone: (818)898-1391
Richard Lidz and Dale Anderson, editorial directors. Fourth edition, 1990. For 600 occupations, describes job duties, entry-level requirements, education and training needed, advancement possibilities, employment outlook, earnings and benefits. The set is divided into 12 volumes. Each volume

Typists, Word Processors, and Data Entry Keyers

includes jobs related under a broad career field. Volume 13 is the index. **Facsimile Number:** 818-365-5489.

★1846★
"Word Processor" in VGM's Careers Encyclopedia (pp. 489-490)
National Textbook Co.
4255 W. Touhy Ave.
Lincolnwood, IL 60646   Phone: (312)679-5500

Third edition, 1991. Contains two- to five-page descriptions of 200 managerial, professional, technical, trade, and service occupations. Each profile includes job duties, places of employment, qualifications, educational preparation, training, employment potential, advancement, income, and additional sources of information.

★1847★
"Word Processor Operators" in Volume 6 of Career Discovery Encyclopedia (pp. 164-165)
J.G. Ferguson Publishing Co.
200 W. Monroe
Chicago, IL 60606   Phone: (312)580-5480

E. Russell Primm, editor-in-chief. 1990. Contains two-page articles on 504 occupations. Each article describes job duties, earnings, and educational and training requirements.

★1848★
Your Future in Word Processing
Rosen Publishing Group
29 E. 21st St.
New York, NY 10010   Phone: (212)777-3017

Gilbert J. Konkel. First edition, 1981. Discusses a variety of careers in word processing, how to get a job, using word processing as an entry to a specific field, and opportunities of the future. **Toll-free/Additional Phone Number(s):** 800-237-9932. **Facsimile Number:** (212)777-0277.

Associations

★1849★
Data Entry Management Association (DEMA)
101 Merritt 7, 5th Fl.
Norwalk, CT 06851   Phone: (203)846-3777

Membership: Data entry managers and others involved with the data entry profession. **Purpose:** Promotes the individual development and education of its members through exchange of ideas and discussion of problems and solutions. Conducts seminars and regional workshops and meetings. **Publications:** *Data Entry Management Association-Newsletter*, 10/year. **Facsimile Number:** (203)846-6883.

Test Guides

★1850★
Career Examination Series
National Learning Corp.
212 Michael Dr.
Syosset, NY 11791   Phone: (516)921-8888

Jack Rudman. National Learning Corp.'s Career Examination Series No. 1. Contains examination guides for careers in data entry and data processing, including typists, key-punch operators, data entry keyers, word processors, typist-clerks, machine operators, and supervisors. The examination guides in this series contain questions with answers. **Facsimile Number:** (516)921-8743. **Toll-free/Additional Phone Number(s):** 800-645-6337.

★1851★
Federal Clerk - Steno - Typist
Prentice Hall Press
Simon & Schuster Inc.
200 Old Tappan Rd.
Old Tappan, NJ 07675   Phone: (800)223-2348

Hy Hammer and John Czukor. Sixth edition, 1988. Coverage includes Federal entry-level clerical positions, including clerk, clerk typist, stenographer, transcriber, office machines operator, and office assistant.

★1852★
How to Prepare for the Civil Service Examinations for Stenographer, Typist, Clerk, and Office Machine Operator
Barron's Educational Series, Inc.
PO Box 8040
250 Wireless Blvd.
Hauppauge, NY 11788   Phone: (516)434-3311

Jerry Bobrow, Ph.D. Second edition. Test manual includes eleven model tests on verbal and clerical skills, typing, dictation, and office machine operation. All exams have answers explained and each simulates the actual Civil Service Exam. **Toll-free/Additional Phone Number(s):** 800-645-3476 (in NY call 800-257-5729).

★1853★
Office Aide
Prentice Hall Press
Simon & Schuster Inc.
200 Old Tappan Rd.
Old Tappan, NJ 07675   Phone: (800)223-2348

Hy Hammer. Second edition, 1985. Contains seven sample exams for the following entry-level civil service postions: clerk, typist, stenographer, receptionist, office machine operator, telephone operator.

★1854★
Practice and Drill for the Clerk, Typist, and Stenographer Examinations
National Learning Corp.
212 Michael Dr.
Syosset, NY 11791   Phone: (516)921-8888

Jack Rudman. Part of the General Aptitude and Abilities Series No. 2. Books in this series provide functional, intensive test practice and drill in the basic skills and areas common to many examinations, as well as general aptitude or achievement necessary for entrance into many occupations or positions. **Facsimile Number:** (516)921-8743. **Toll-free/Additional Phone Number(s):** 800-645-6337.

★1855★
Practice for Clerical, Typing and Stenographic Tests
Prentice Hall Press
Simon & Schuster Inc.
200 Old Tappan Rd.
Old Tappan, NJ 07675   Phone: (800)223-2348

Maryhelen H. Paulick Hoffman. Seventh edition, 1988. Provide preparation for all qualifying tests given by local, state, and federal agencies for all types of clerical positions.

★1856★
Senior Clerical Series
Prentice Hall Press
Simon & Schuster Inc.
200 Old Tappan Rd.
Old Tappan, NJ 07675   Phone: (800)223-2348

Hy Hammer. Fourth edition, 1983. Complete test preparation for the following senior grade positions: clerk, typist, stenographer, account clerk, file clerk, statistics clerk, stenographer (law), mail and supply clerk, and stores clerk.

Educational Directories and Programs

★1857★
Industry Directory
Association of Information Systems Professionals
104 Wilmot Rd., Ste. 201
Deerfield, IL 60015-5195 Phone: (708)940-8800
Bea McLean, editor. Irregular; previous edition 1986; new edition possible 1990. Manufacturers of office automation equipment; word processing service bureaus; educational institutions offering office automation and associated software courses or curriculums; personnel agencies serving office automation personnel and users; analysts and counsultants. Entries include: Name, address. Arrangement: Alphabetical within categories above. **Facsimile Number:** (708)940-7218.

Awards, Scholarships, Grants, and Fellowships

★1858★
Distinguished Information Sciences Award
Data Processing Management Association
505 Busse Highway
Park Ridge, IL 60068-3191 Phone: (312)825-8124
To recognize an individual for outstanding contributions to the information processing industry. Nominations may be made by DPMA members but the award is not limited to members. The final selection is made by the DPMA Executive Council. A bronze etched plaque and an honorary lifetime membership in the Association are bestowed annually at the DPMA Conference and Business Exposition. Established in 1969.

Basic Reference Guides and Handbooks

★1859★
Busy Person's Guide to Selecting the Right Word Processor: A Visual Shortcut to Understanding & Buying, Complete with Checklist & Prod. Guide
Festival Publications
7944 Capistrano Ave.
West Hills, CA 91304 Phone: (818)340-0175
Alan Gadney. 1984. Part of Busy Person's Computer Buying Guides Series.

★1860★
Choosing & Using a Word Processor
Gower Publishing Co.
Old Post Rd.
Brookfield, VT 05036 Phone: (802)276-3162
Kevin Townsend. 1982.

★1861★
Fullwrite Professional: A User's Guide
Prentice Hall
Rte. 9W
Englewood Cliffs, NJ 07632 Phone: (201)592-2000
Keith Thompson. 1988.

★1862★
How to Buy an Office Computer or Word Processor
Prentice Hall
Rte.9W
Englewood Cliffs, NJ 07632 Phone: (201)592-2000
Brian Donohue. 1983.

★1863★
How to Typeset from a Wordprocessor: An Interfacing Guide
R. R. Bowker, Co.
121 Chanlon Rd.
New Providence, NJ 07974 Phone: (908)464-6800
Ronald A. Labuz. 1984. **Facsimile Number:** (908)464-3553.

★1864★
Low-End Word Processor Market
Frost & Sullivan, Inc.
106 Fulton St.
New York, NY 10038 Phone: (212)233-1080
1984.

★1865★
Math on the Job: Secretary/Clerk Typist
National Center for Research in Vocational Education
Ohio State University
1900 Kenry Rd.
Columbus, OH 43210 Phone: (614)292-4353
1985.

★1866★
Mercury Systems Inc.: Practice Set in Word-Information Processing for Conventional & Text-Editing Typewriters
McGraw-Hill, Inc.
1221 Avenue of the Americas
New York, NY 10020 Phone: (212)512-2000
B. L. Boyce. 1981.

★1867★
Sprint: A Power User's Guide
John Wiley & Sons, Inc.
605 3rd Ave.
New York, NY 10158 Phone: (212)850-6000
Charles Ackerman. 1990. **Facsimile Number:** (212)850-6088.

★1868★
SPRINT Simplified
T A B Books, Inc.
Blue Ridge Summit, PA 17294-0850 Phone: (717)794-2191
Douglas J. Wolf. 1988.

★1869★
Word Magic: A Guide to Understanding & Evaluating Word Processing Equipment
Van Nostrand Reinhold Co., Inc.
115 5th Ave.
New York, NY 10003 Phone: (212)254-3232
Michael Scriven. 1983. **Facsimile Number:** (212)254-9499.

★1870★
Word Processor & Calculator Development System MVP-Forth
Mountain View Press, Inc.
PO Box X
Mountain View, CA 94040 Phone: (415)961-4103
Thomas E. Wempe. 1987. Part of MVP-Forth Books Vol. 9.

Typists, Word Processors, and Data Entry Keyers

★1871★
Word Processor & Calculator Development System Source
Mountain View Press, Inc.
PO Box X
Mountain View, CA 94040 Phone: (415)961-4103
Thomas E. Wempe. 1987. Part of MVP-Forth Series. Vol. 10.

★1872★
Word Processors & Information Processing: What They Are & How to Buy
Para Publishing
PO Box 4232-821
Santa Barbara, CA 93140-4232 Phone: (805)968-7277
Dan Poynter. Second edition, 1982. **Facsimile Number:** (805)968-1379.

★1873★
Word Processors & the Writing Process: An Annotated Bibliography
Greenwood Publishing Group, Inc.
88 Post Rd., W.
PO Box 5007
Westport, CT 06881 Phone: (203)226-3571
Paula R. Nancarrow, editor. 1984. **Facsimile Number:** (202)222-1502.

★1874★
Word Processors & Typewriters Worldwide: Opportunities & Pitfalls
LAAL Companies, Research Group
9 Kaufman Dr.
Westwood, NJ 07675 Phone: (201)664-6222
Villy Diernisse. 1984.

★1875★
You Can Type for Doctors at Home!
Claremont Press
PO Box 177, Cooper Sta.
New York, NY 10003 Phone: (212)260-2812
Ruth de Menezes. 1981.

---------- Periodicals ----------

★1876★
ADAPSO Data
Association of Data Processing Service Organizations, Inc. (ADAPSO)
1300 N. 17th St., Ste. 300
Arlington, VA 22209 Phone: (703)522-5055
Editor(s): Jami Wann amd Cathy Weisbart. Bimonthly. Provides updates on government actions, legal precedents, mergers and acquisitions, and international business developments affecting the computer services and software industry. Recurring features include news of research and news of members.

★1877★
Bank Operations Report
Warren, Gorham & Lamont, Inc.
One Penn Plaza
New York, NY 10119 Phone: (212)971-5000
Editor(s): Pat Durner. Monthly. Focuses on electronic data processing control, check processing, record keeping, cost control, Federal regulation, credit and debit cards, electronic funds transfer system, physical security, and office automation, computer, and systems applications.

★1878★
Data Entry Awareness Report
Management Information Corp.
PO Box 5062
Cherry Hill, NJ 08034 Phone: (609)428-1020
Editor(s): Pam Benham. Monthly. Evaluates a data entry system in each issue, including key to disc, intelligent terminals, optical character readers, portable data recorders, and voice data entry. Describes system hardware, software, and pricing, and analyzes the advantages and disadvantages of the system. **Toll-free/Additional Phone Number(s):** 800-678-4642 **Facsimile Number:** (609)428-1683.

★1879★
From Nine to Five
Dartnell Corp.
4660 Ravenswood
Chicago, IL 60640 Phone: (312)561-4000
Editor(s): Douglas Leland. Biweekly. Provides "tips, shortcuts, and helpful information for success in the office," particularly secretaries and office workers. Recurring features include columns titled Business Skills Clinic and The Coffee Break. **Toll-free/Additional Phone Number(s):** 800-621-5463 **Facsimile Number:** (312)561-3801.

★1880★
Supply House Times
Horton Publishing Co.
7574 N. Lincoln Ave.
Skokie, IL 60077 Phone: (708)677-2707
Greg Cassel, Editor. Monthly. Trade magazine for wholesalers in plumbing, heating, cooling, piping, and water systems. Areas of major emphasis include: warehousing, materials handling, inventory control, accounting, data processing, merchandising, salesmanship and general management. **Facsimile Number:** (708)677-5003.

Service Occupations

Protective Service Occupations

Correction Officers

Corrections officers are responsible for the safety and security of persons who have been arrested, are awaiting trial, or who have been tried and convicted of a crime and sentenced to serve time in a correctional institution. They maintain order and enforce rules within the institution by monitoring inmates' activities, such as working, exercising, eating, and bathing. It may sometimes be necessary to search inmates and their living quarters for drugs or weapons, and to settle disputes between inmates. Corrections officers inspect the facilities for unsanitary conditions, fire hazards, and evidence of infractions by inmates such as lock or window tampering. Counseling and helping inmates with problems are increasingly important parts of the correction officer's job. In some institutions, officers receive specialized training and have a more formal counseling role and may lead or participate in group counseling sessions.

$alaries

Earnings for corrections officers are listed below.

Starting salary at the state level	$17,900/year
Starting salary at the federal level	$15,700/year

Employment Outlook

Growth rate until the year 2000: Faster than average.

Correction Officers

---------- Career Guides ----------

★1881★
Correction Officer
Prentice Hall
Rte. 9W
Englewood Cliffs, NJ 07632   Phone: (201)592-2000
Eve P. Steinberg. 1989.

★1882★
"Correction Officer" in *Public and Community Services, Volume 11 of Career Information Center* (pp. 42-44)
Glencoe/Macmillan
15319 Chatsworth St.
Mission Hills, CA 91345   Phone: (818)898-1391
Richard Lidz and Dale Anderson, editorial directors. Fourth edition, 1990. For 600 occupations, describes job duties, entry-level requirements, education and training needed, advancement possibilities, employment outlook, earnings and benefits. The set is divided into 12 volumes. Each volume includes jobs related under a broad career field. Volume 13 is the index. **Facsimile Number:** 818-365-5489.

★1883★
"Correction Officers" in *Jobs! What They Are...Where They Are...What They Pay* (pp. 189-190)
Simon & Schuster, Inc.
Simon & Schuster Bldg.
1230 Avenue of the Americas
New York, NY 10020   Phone: (212)698-7000
Robert O. Snelling and Anne M. Snelling. Revised edition, 1989. Profiles 241 occupations, describing duties and responsibilities, educational preparation, earnings, employment opportunities, training, and qualifications.

★1884★
"Correction Officers" in *Occupational Outlook Handbook* (pp. 285-286)
Superintendent of Documents
U.S. Government Printing Office
Washington, DC 20402   Phone: (202)783-3238
Biennial; latest edition, 1990-91. Encyclopedia of careers describing more than 250 occupations and comprising about 86 percent of all jobs in the economy. Occupations that require lengthy education or training are given the most attention. For each occupation, the handbook describes job duties, working conditions, training, educational preparation, personal qualities, advancement possibilities, job outlook, earnings, and sources of additional information.

★1885★
"Correction Officers" in *Opportunities in Vocational and Technical Careers* (pp. 73-74)
National Textbook Co.
4255 W. Touhy Ave.
Lincolnwood, IL 60646   Phone: (312)679-5500
Adrian A. Paradis. 1987. Describes careers which can be prepared for by attending a private vocational or proprietary school—office employee, sales worker, service worker, health services, mechanic, craftworker, and technician. Covers employment outlook, job duties, and salaries. Offers career planning advice.

★1886★
"Correction Officers" in Volume 3 of *The Encyclopedia of Careers and Vocational Guidance* (pp. 210-214)
J.G. Ferguson Publishing Co.
200 W. Monroe
Chicago, IL 60606   Phone: (312)580-5480
William E. Hopke, editor-in-chief. Eighth edition, 1990. Four-volume set that profiles 500 occupations and describes job trends in 76 industries. Includes career description, educational requirements, history of the job, methods of entry, advancement, employment outlook, earnings, working conditions, social and psychological factors, and sources of additional information.

★1887★
"Correction Officers" in Volume 2 of *Career Discovery Encyclopedia* (pp. 62-63)
J.G. Ferguson Publishing Co.
200 W. Monroe
Chicago, IL 60606   Phone: (312)580-5480
E. Russell Primm, editor-in-chief. 1990. Contains two-page articles on 504 occupations. Each article describes job duties, earnings, and educational and training requirements.

★1888★
"Correction Officers" in *America's 50 Fastest Growing Jobs* (pp. 116-118)
JIST Works, Inc.
720 N. Park Ave.
Indianapolis, IN 46202   Phone: (317)264-3720
Michael J. Farr, compiler. 1991. Describes the 50 fastest growing jobs within major career clusters such as technicians, and marketing and sales. Each job profile explains the nature of the work, skills and abilities required, employment outlook, average earnings, related occupations, education and training requirements, and employment opportunities. Also contains career planning information and job search tips.

★1889★
Correctional Officer Correspondence Course
American Correctional Association
8025 Laurel Lakes Ct.
Laurel, MD 20707   Phone: (301)206-5100
American Correctional Association Staff. Revised edition, 1990. **Facsimile Number:** (301)206-5061.

★1890★
Correctional Officer Series
AIMS Media, Inc.
9710 DeSoto Ave.
Chatsworth, CA 93111-4409   Phone: (818)773-4300
Videocassette. 198?. 13 mins. This film combines teaching jobs skills, officer self-evaluation, and human understanding. Draws upon experiences of men and women involved in the operation of correctional facilities.

★1891★
Correctional Officers
Chronicle Guidance Publications, Inc.
PO Box 1190
Moravia, NY 13118-1190   Phone: (315)497-0330
1990. This career brief describes the nature of the work, working conditions, hours and earnings, education and training, licensure, certification, unions, personal qualifications, social and psychological factors, employment outlook, entry methods, advancement, and related occupations. **Toll-free/Additional Phone Number(s):** 800-622-7284.

★1892★
"Corrections and Rehabilitation" in *Opportunities in Law Enforcement and Criminal Justice Careers* (pp. 110-124)
National Textbook Co.
4255 W. Touhy Ave.
Lincolnwood, IL 60646   Phone: (312)679-5500
James D. Stinchcomb. 1990. Describes law enforcement and related positions at the city, county, state, and federal levels and in the military. Covers trends, future outlook, personal qualities, selection requirements, salaries, working conditions, and educational preparation.

★1893★
"Corrections Officer" in *Career Planning in Criminal Justice* (pp. 70-72)
Anderson Publishing Co.
2035 Reading Rd.
Cincinnati, OH 45202   Phone: (513)421-4142
Robert C. DeLucia and Thomas J. Doyle. 1990. Surveys a wide range of career and employment opportunities in law enforcement, the courts, corrections, forensic science and private security. Contains career planning and job hunting advice. Profiles 77 criminal justice occupations describing job duties, work environments, and educational requirements.

★1894★
"Corrections Officer" in *VGM's Careers Encyclopedia* (pp. 120-122)
National Textbook Co.
4255 W. Touhy Ave.
Lincolnwood, IL 60646   Phone: (312)679-5500
Third edition, 1991. Contains two- to five-page descriptions of 200 managerial, professional, technical, trade, and service occupations. Each profile includes job duties, places of employment, qualifications, educational preparation, training, employment potential, advancement, income, and additional sources of information.

★1895★
"Corrections Officers" in *The American Almanac of Jobs and Salaries* (pp. 93-95)
Avon Books
105 Madison Avenue
New York, NY 10016   Phone: (212)481-5600
John Wright and Edward J. Dwyer. Revised and updated, 1990. A comprehensive guide to the wages of hundreds of occupations in a wide variety of industries and organizations.

★1896★
Prison Correction Officer
Vocational Biographies, Inc.
PO Box 31, Dept. VF10
Sauk Centre, MN 56378   Phone: (612)352-6516
1988. This pamphlet profiles a person working in the job. Includes information about job duties, working conditions, places of employment, educational preparation, labor market outlook, and salaries. **Toll-free/Additional Phone Number(s):** 800-255-0752.

★1897★
Video Career Library - Public and Personal Services
Careers, Inc.
1211 10th St., SW
PO Box 135
Largo, FL 34649-0135   Phone: (813)584-7333
Videocassette. 1990. 35 mins. Part of the Video Career Library covering 165 occupations. Shows actual workers on the job. Includes firefighters, police officers, correctional officers, bartenders, waiters/waitresses, cooks/chefs, child care workers, flight attendants, barbers/cosmetologists, groundskeepers/gardeners, and butchers/meat cutters.

─────── **Associations** ───────

★1898★
American Correctional Association (ACA)
8025 Laurel Lakes Ct.
Laurel, MD 20707   Phone: (301)206-5100
Membership: Correctional administrators, wardens, superintendents, members of prison and parole boards, probation officers, psychologists, educators, sociologists, and other individuals; institutions and associations involved in the correctional field. **Purpose:** Aims to: improve correctional standards, including selection of personnel, care, supervision, education, training, employment, treatment, and post-release adjustment of inmates; develop adequate physical facilities. Cosponsors voluntary certification of correctional trainers program, with the American Association of Correctional Training Personnel. Administers Correctional Supervisors Correspondence Course, a training program designed exclusively for correctional supervisors in federal, state, or local institutions and agencies. Studies causes of crime and juvenile delinquency and methods of crime control and prevention. Sponsors correctional architecture exhibit/competition. Compiles statistics; bestows awards. Conducts research programs; offers workshops. Maintains 5000 volume library of corrections and criminal justice materials. **Publications:** *Corrections Today*, bimonthly. • *Directory of Institutions*, annual. • *National Jail and Adult Detention Directory*, semiannual. • *On the Line*, 5/year. • *Probation and Parole Directory*, semiannual. • *Proceedings*, annual. • Also publishes books, directories, and standards and guidelines. **Toll-free/Additional Phone Number(s):** (800)ACA-JOIN and (800)825-BOOK. **Facsimile Number:** (301)206-5061.

★1899★
Contact Center
PO Box 81826
Lincoln, NE 68501　　　　　　　　　　　Phone: (402)464-0602

Purpose: Provides referrals to programs that assist with employment, housing, counseling, and other human services in the fields of criminal justice and corrections. **Facsimile Number:** (402)464-5931. **Toll-free/Additional Phone Number(s):** 800-842-2924 (educational services). **Publications:** *Corrections Compendiumd: The National Journal for Corrections Professionals*, monthly; *Corrections International*, quarterly.

Standards/Certification Agencies

★1900★
American Correctional Association (ACA)
8025 Laurel Lakes Ct.
Laurel, MD 20707　　　　　　　　　　　Phone: (301)206-5100

Aims to improve correctional standards, including selection of personnel, care, supervision, education, training, employment, treatment, and post-release adjustment of inmates; develop adequate physical facilities. Cosponsors voluntary certification of correctional trainers program, with the American Association of Correctional Training Personnel. Administers Correctional Supervisors Correspondence Course, a training program designed exclusively for correctional supervisors in federal, state, or local institutions and agencies.

Test Guides

★1901★
Career Examination Series
National Learning Corp.
212 Michael Dr.
Syosset, NY 11791　　　　　　　　　　Phone: (516)921-8888

Jack Rudman. National Learning Corp.'s Career Examination Series No. 1. contains many study guides for careers in the corrections field, including Warden, Deputy Warden, Prison Guard, Jail Guard, Correction Captain, Correction Hospital Officer (men and women), Correction Lieutenant, Correction Matron, Correction Officer, Correction Officer trainee, and Correction Youth Camp Officer. All examination guides in this series contain questions with answers. **Facsimile Number:** (516)921-8743. **Toll-free/Additional Phone Number(s):** 800-645-6337.

★1902★
Correction Officer
Prentice Hall Press
Simon & Schuster Inc.
200 Old Tappan Rd.
Old Tappan, NJ 07675　　　　　　　　Phone: (800)223-2348

Hy Hammer. Eighth edition, 1989. Contains official examination announcements from federal, state, and municipal jurisdictions. Also includes six complete sample practice exams with answers.

★1903★
Correction Officer Promotion Tests
Prentice Hall Press
Simon & Schuster Inc.
200 Old Tappan Rd.
Old Tappan, NJ 07675　　　　　　　　Phone: (800)223-2348

Hugh O'Neill and Hy Hammer. First edition, 1986. Contains seven practice exams with hundreds of actual civil service questions.

★1904★
Correction Promotion Course (One Volume)
National Learning Corp.
212 Michael Dr.
Syosset, NY 11791　　　　　　　　　　Phone: (516)921-8888

Jack Rudman. Part of the General Aptitude and Abilities Series No. 2. Books in this series provide functional, intensive test practice and drill in the basic skills and areas common to many examinations, as well as general aptitude or achievement necessary for entrance into many occupations or positions. **Facsimile Number:** (516)921-8743. **Toll-free/Additional Phone Number(s):** 800-645-6337.

Awards, Scholarships, Grants, and Fellowships

★1905★
Medal of Valor
American Correctional Association
8025 Laurel Lakes Court
Laurel, MD 20707-5075　　　　　　　Phone: (301)699-7600

To recognize corrections professionals who have gone beyond the call of duty and exhibited extreme bravery and courage either on or off the job. Awarded annually at the ACA Winter Conference. Established in 1989.

Basic Reference Guides and Handbooks

★1906★
Burnout in Probation & Corrections
Greenwood Publishing Group, Inc.
88 Post Rd., W.
PO Box 5007
Westport, CT 06881　　　　　　　　　Phone: (203)226-3571

John T. Whitehead. 1989. **Facsimile Number:** (202)222-1502.

★1907★
Correctional Officer Resource Guide
American Correctional Association
8025 Laurel Lakes Ct.
Laurel, MD 20707　　　　　　　　　　Phone: (301)206-5100

Richard L. Phillips, editor. 1989. **Facsimile Number:** (301)206-5061.

★1908★
Correctional Officers: Power, Pressure & Responsibility
American Correctional Association
8025 Laurel Lakes Ct.
Laurel, MD 20707　　　　　　　　　　Phone: (301)206-5100

American Correctional Association Staff. 1983. **Facsimile Number:** (301)206-5061

★1909★
Directory of Institutions
American Correctional Association (ACA)
8025 Laurel Lakes Ct.
Laurel, MD 20707　　　　　　　　　　Phone: (301)206-5100

Annual.

★1910★
Potential Liabilities of Probation & Parole Officers
Anderson Publishing Co.
2035 Reading Rd.
Cincinnati, OH 45202　　　　　　　　Phone: (513)421-4142

Rolando V. Del Carmen. Revised edition, 1986.

★1911★
Practical Law for Jail & Prison Personnel: A Resource Manual & Training Curriculum
American Correctional Association
8025 Laurel Lakes Ct.
Laurel, MD 20707　　　　　　　　Phone: (301)206-5100
1987. **Facsimile Number:** (301)206-5061.

★1912★
Stress Management for Correctional Officers & Their Families
American Correctional Association
8025 Laurel Lakes Ct.
Laurel, MD 20707　　　　　　　　Phone: (301)206-5100
Frances E. Cheek. 1984. **Facsimile Number:** (301)206-5061.

★1913★
Survival Thinking: For Police & Corrections Officers
Charles C. Thomas, Publisher
2600 S. 1st St.
Springfield, IL 62794-9265　　　　Phone: (217)789-8980
James L. Lockard. 1991. **Facsimile Number:** (217)789-9130.

★1914★
Surviving in Corrections: A Guide for Corrections Professionals
Charles C. Thomas, Publisher
2600 S. 1st St.
Springfield, IL 62794-9265　　　　Phone: (217)789-8980
David B. Kalinich. 1984. **Facsimile Number:** (217)789-9130.

——————— Periodicals ———————

★1915★
CEA Newsletter
Correctional Education Association (CEA)
LA County Education Office
9300 E. Imperial Hwy.
Downey, CA 90242　　　　　　　　Phone: (213)803-8204
Editor(s): Heidi Langer. Quarterly. Supports Association efforts "to broaden the professional horizons and equip each member with the support to provide relevant educational programs which focus upon life survival skills for the adult and juvenile offender." Promotes the "importance of interaction between the disciplines and services within (correctional) institutions and agencies, in an attempt to improve the delivery of total treatment services.". Recurring features include association news, practioner-oriented articles, and training news.

★1916★
Corrections Digest
Washington Crime News Service
3918 Prosperity Ave., Ste. 318
Fairfax, VA 22151-4070　　　　　　Phone: (703)573-1600
Editor(s): Betty B. Bosarge. Biweekly. Discusses prison-related issues, including reform, overcrowding, current and pending law, legislation and litigation, commutations, juveniles in adult institutions, individual state issues, budgets, and capital punishment. Provides news of recent publications and job openings. **Facsimile Number:** (703)573-1604.

★1917★
Corrections Today
American Correctional Association (ACA)
8025 Laurel Lakes Ct.
Laurel, MD 20707　　　　　　　　Phone: (301)206-5100
Bimonthly. Journal containing articles about the field of corrections and criminal justice. Contains advertisers and product indexes, book reviews, company profiles, and information on new members.

★1918★
Crime Control Digest
Washington Crime News Service
3918 Prosperity Ave., Ste. 318
Fairfax, VA 22031-3334　　　　　　Phone: (703)573-1600
Editor(s): Betty B. Bosarge. Weekly. Contains articles on all levels of law enforcement in the U.S., including national, state, county, local, and student concerns, though the focus is on matters of national import. Reports on such items as illegal drug trafficking, terrorism, the accreditation of law enforcement agencies, pending legislation, and the implementation of new laws. Recurring features include information on upcoming seminars and conferences, and announcements of awards. **Facsimile Number:** (703)573-1604.

★1919★
Criminal Justice Digest
Washington Crime News Service
3918 Prosperity Ave., Ste. 318
Fairfax, VA 22031-3334　　　　　　Phone: (703)573-1600
Editor(s): Betty B. Bosarge. Monthly. Discusses prevalent managerial problems and solutions in correctional institutions throughout the country. Covers such topics as cost cutting, efficiency improvement, overcrowded prisons, employee motivation, and employer/employee communication. **Facsimile Number:** (703)573-1604.

★1920★
From the State Capitals: Justice Policies
Wakeman/Walworth, Inc.
300 N. Washington St., Ste. 204
Alexandria, VA 22314　　　　　　Phone: (703)549-8606
Editor(s): Keyes Walworth. Weekly. Monitors new state and municipal programs designed to improve court administration in a variety of areas. Covers subjects such as sentencing guidelines; parole programs; public defender systems; court financing and fees; selection of judges; and victim compensation laws. Also reports on developments affecting prison administration: inmate living conditions, alternatives to incarceration, facility financing, and security and staffing. **Facsimile Number:** (703)549-1372.

★1921★
On the Line
American Correctional Association (ACA)
8025 Laurel Lakes Ct.
Laurel, MD 20707　　　　　　　　Phone: (301)206-5100
5/year. Newsletter. Association news. Includes calendar of events, classifieds, and resource information.

Meetings and Conventions

★1922★
American Correctional Association Congress of Correction
American Correctional Association
8025 Laurel Lakes Ct.
Laurel, MD 20707-5075 Phone: (301)206-5100
1992. **Toll-free/Additional Phone Number(s):** 800-888-8784. **Facsimile Number:** (301)206-5061.

★1923★
American Correctional Association Winter Conference
American Correctional Association
8025 Laurel Lakes Ct.
Laurel, MD 20707-5075 Phone: (301)206-5100
Toll-free/Additional Phone Number(s): 800-888-8784. **Facsimile Number:** (301)206-5061.

Other Sources of Information

★1924★
Treatment Custody Role Conflict in Community Based Correctional Workers: Causes & Effects
R & E Publishers
PO Box 2008
Saratoga, CA 95070 Phone: (408)866-6303
Ronald J. Scott. 1977. **Facsimile Number:** (408)866-0825.

Firefighting Occupations

Firefighters work to prevent fires and to save lives and property when fires or other emergencies occur. Firefighters perform a variety of tasks in response to a fire emergency. They rescue victims and administer emergency medical aid, ventilate smoke-filled areas, operate equipment, and salvage contents of buildings. Often firefighters assume additional responsibilities, including natural disaster recovery efforts and emergency rescue and cleanup operations. When not responding to an emergency, on-duty firefighters fill out reports, operate training and public awareness programs, and maintain equipment.

$alaries

Average earnings vary depending on city size and region of the U.S.; although volunteer firefighters make up the majority of firefighters in the U.S., they are not included when determining the average earnings.

>   Beginning firefighters $19,700/year
>   Nonsupervisory firefighters $25,000/year.

Employment Outlook

Growth rate until the year 2000: Slower than average.

Firefighting Occupations

Career Guides

★1925★
American Professionals Series
Cambridge Career Products
90 MacCorkle Ave., SW
South Charleston, WV 25311 Phone: (304)744-9323
Videocassette. 1984. 30 mins. In this series of twenty-one half hour programs, various occupations are examined in depth, including a day in the life of each worker. Included are: fireman, farmer, oil driller, fisherman, horse trainer, and auto assembly repairman.

★1926★
Becoming a Professional Firefighter
International Association of Fire Fighters
1750 New York Ave. NW
Washington, DC 20006-5395 Phone: (202)737-8484
Leaflet covering basic requirements and working conditions.

★1927★
Career Insights
RMI Media Productions, Inc.
2807 West 47th St.
Shawnee Mission, KS 66205 Phone: (913)262-3974
Videocassette series. 1987. This videotape series describes 50 occupations, including skill requirements and interviews with people employed in these fields. Occupations include: flight service, air transportation/ground services, data processing, carpentry, clerk in banking/insurance/business, cosmetic personal grooming, firefighting, roofing, material handling, photographic processing, plumbing, secretarial services, tool and die operations.

★1928★
Career Success Series
Cambridge Career Products
90 MacCorkle Ave., SW
South Charleston, WV 25311 Phone: (304)744-9323
Videocassette. 1986. 15 mins. A series, available separately, outlining various career choices for students. Occupations include: flight service, air transportation/ground service, data processing, carpentry, clerk in banking/insurance, commodity sales, cosmetic personal grooming, fire fighting, forestry services, home economics, insulation/roofing, material handling, mechanics, photographic processing, pipefitting and plumbing, police science, printing, secretarial services, and utilities equipment operator.

★1929★
A Day in the Life of a Firefighter
Troll Associates
100 Corporate Dr.
Mahwah, NJ 07430 Phone: (201)529-4000
Betsy Smith. 1980. **Toll-free/Additional Phone Number(s):** 800-526-5289. **Facsimile Number:** (201)529-9347.

★1930★
"Fire Fighter" in *Action Careers: Employment in the High-Risk Job Market* (pp. 59-75)
Citadel Press/Lyle Stuart Inc.
Carol Publishing Group
120 Enterprise Ave.
Secaucus, NJ 07094 Phone: (201)866-0490
Ragnar Benson. 1988. Describes 24 dangerous careers such as repo man, explosives handler, and river rafting guide. Each profile includes demand for the job, where the jobs can be found, required personal and physical characteristics and training needed.

★1931★
"Fire Fighter" in *Public and Community Services, Volume 11 of Career Information Center* (pp. 50-52)
Glencoe/Macmillan
15319 Chatsworth St.
Mission Hills, CA 91345 Phone: (818)898-1391
Richard Lidz and Dale Anderson, editorial directors. Fourth edition, 1990. For 600 occupations, describes job duties, entry-level requirements, education and training needed, advancement possibilities, employment outlook, earnings and benefits. The set is divided into 12 volumes. Each volume includes jobs related under a broad career field. Volume 13 is the index. **Facsimile Number:** 818-365-5489.

★1932★
"Fire Fighter, Paramedic" in *Straight Talk on Careers: 80 Pros Take You Into Their Professions* (pp. 227-230, 231-232)
Garrett Park Press
PO Box 190
Garrett Park, MD 20896 Phone: (301)946-2553
Mary Barbera-Hogan. 1987. Written for readers in high school and college. Contains candid interviews from professionals who discuss what their days are like and the pros and cons of their occupations.

★1933★
Fire Fighter Professional Qualifications
National Fire Protection Association
1 Batterymarch Park
Quincy, MA 02269-9101   Phone: (617)770-3000
1974. Part of One Thousand Series.

★1934★
Fire Fighters
Scholastic, Inc.
730 Broadway
New York, NY 10003   Phone: (212)505-3000
Robert Maas. 1989.

★1935★
"Fire Fighters" in *Jobs! What They Are...Where They Are...What They Pay* (pp. 112-113)
Simon & Schuster, Inc.
Simon & Schuster Bldg.
1230 Avenue of the Americas
New York, NY 10020   Phone: (212)698-7000
Robert O. Snelling and Anne M. Snelling. Revised edition, 1989. Profiles 241 occupations, describing duties and responsibilities, educational preparation, earnings, employment opportunities, training, and qualifications.

★1936★
"Fire Fighters" in Volume 3 of *Career Discovery Encyclopedia* (pp. 30-31)
J.G. Ferguson Publishing Co.
200 W. Monroe
Chicago, IL 60606   Phone: (312)580-5480
E. Russell Primm, editor-in-chief. 1990. Contains two-page articles on 504 occupations. Each article describes job duties, earnings, and educational and training requirements.

★1937★
Fire Fighters and Inspectors
Chronicle Guidance Publications, Inc.
PO Box 1190
Moravia, NY 13118-1190   Phone: (315)497-0330
1990. This career brief describes the nature of the work, working conditions, hours and earnings, education and training, licensure, certification, unions, personal qualifications, social and psychological factors, employment outlook, entry methods, advancement, and related occupations. **Toll-free/Additional Phone Number(s):** 800-622-7284.

★1938★
"Fire Fighters" in *The American Almanac of Jobs and Salaries* (pp. 96-97)
Avon Books
105 Madison Avenue
New York, NY 10016   Phone: (212)481-5600
John Wright and Edward J. Dwyer. Revised and updated, 1990. A comprehensive guide to the wages of hundreds of occupations in a wide variety of industries and organizations.

★1939★
Fire Prevention & Firefighting
Morris Video
2730 Monterey St. #105
Monterey Business Park
Torrance, CA 90503   Phone: (213)533-4800
Videocassette. 1984. 15 mins. Careers dealing with fire prevention, fighting, and emergency rescue are examined.

★1940★
"Fire Science" in *The Career Connection II: A Guide to Technical Majors and Their Related Careers* (pp. 61-62)
ERIS
PO Box 7509
University Station
Provo, UT 84602-0509
Fred A. Rowe. 1988. Contains technical majors, such as automotive technology. Describes the major and the job. Lists high school and postsecondary school courses. Includes occupations related to the major, employment outlook, and starting salary.

★1941★
Firefighter
Careers, Inc.
PO Box 135
Largo, FL 34649-0135   Phone: (813)584-7333
1991. Two-page occupational summary card describing duties, working conditions, personal qualifications, training, earnings and hours, employment outlook, places of employment, related careers and where to write for more information.

★1942★
"Firefighter" in *Hard Hatted Women: Stories of Struggle and Success in the Trades* (pp. 156-170)
Seal Press
3131 Western Ave., Ste. 410
Seattle, WA 98121   Phone: (206)283-7844
Molly Martin, editor. 1988. Twenty-six women recount their experiences working in blue collar occupations. They describe how they got in, the work they do, their relationships in predominantly male occupations, and their training.

★1943★
"Firefighter" in *Occu-Facts: Information on 565 Careers in Outline Form* (p. 13.3)
Careers, Inc.
P.O. Box 135
1211 Tenth St., S.W.
Largo, FL 33640   Phone: (813)584-7333
Elizabeth Handville. Biennial, 1989-90 edition. Each one-page occupational profile describes duties, working conditions, physical surroundings and demands, aptitudes, temperament, educational requirements, employment outlook, earnings, and places of employment.

★1944★
"Firefighter" in *VGM's Careers Encyclopedia* (pp. 176-178)
National Textbook Co.
4255 W. Touhy Ave.
Lincolnwood, IL 60646   Phone: (312)679-5500
Third edition, 1991. Contains two- to five-page descriptions of 200 managerial, professional, technical, trade, and service occupations. Each profile includes job duties, places of employment, qualifications, educational preparation, training, employment potential, advancement, income, and additional sources of information.

★1945★
"Firefighters" in *Opportunities in Vocational and Technical Careers* (p. 75)
National Textbook Co.
4255 W. Touhy Ave.
Lincolnwood, IL 60646   Phone: (312)679-5500
Adrian A. Paradis. 1987. Describes careers which can be prepared for by attending a private vocational or proprietary school—office employee, sales worker, service worker, health

Firefighting Occupations

services, mechanic, craftworker, and technician. Covers employment outlook, job duties, and salaries. Offers career planning advice.

★1946★
Firefighters: A to Z
Walker & Co.
720 5th Ave.
New York, NY 10019   Phone: (212)265-3632
Jean Johnson. 1985. **Facsimile Number:** (212)307-1764.

★1947★
"Firefighters" in Volume 3 of *The Encyclopedia of Careers and Vocational Guidance* (pp. 242-247)
J.G. Ferguson Publishing Co.
200 W. Monroe
Chicago, IL 60606   Phone: (312)580-5480
William E. Hopke, editor-in-chief. Eighth edition, 1990. Four-volume set that profiles 500 occupations and describes job trends in 76 industries. Includes career description, educational requirements, history of the job, methods of entry, advancement, employment outlook, earnings, working conditions, social and psychological factors, and sources of additional information.

★1948★
"Firefighting Occupations" in *Occupational Outlook Handbook* (pp. 286-288)
Superintendent of Documents
U.S. Government Printing Office
Washington, DC 20402   Phone: (202)783-3238
Biennial; latest edition, 1990-91. Encyclopedia of careers describing more than 250 occupations and comprising about 86 percent of all jobs in the economy. Occupations that require lengthy education or training are given the most attention. For each occupation, the handbook describes job duties, working conditions, training, educational preparation, personal qualities, advancement possibilities, job outlook, earnings, and sources of additional information.

★1949★
Making of a Fire Fighter
Film Communicators
108 Wilmot Rd.
Deerfield, IL 60015-5196   Phone: (708)940-1260
Videocassette. 19??. 16 mins. This film is designed to familiarize prospective recruits and the community with the Fire Service.

★1950★
Opportunities in Fire Protection Services
National Textbook Co.
4255 W. Touhy Ave.
Lincolnwood, IL 60646   Phone: (312)679-5500
Ronny J. Coleman. 1990. Explores firefighting and related jobs with not only local fire departments but also with state and federal governments and private fire departments, fire sprinkler and fire equipment manufacturing companies, and insurance companies. Covers personal qualifications, educational preparation and training, advancement possibilities, and salaries. Offers job hunting advice.

★1951★
Professional Qualifications for Fire Inspector, Fire Investigator, & Fire Prevention Education Officer: NFPA 1031
National Fire Protection Association
1 Batterymarch Park
Quincy, MA 02269-9109   Phone: (617)770-3000
National Fire Protection Association Staff. 1987.

★1952★
Video Career Library - Public and Personal Services
Careers, Inc.
1211 10th St., SW
PO Box 135
Largo, FL 34649-0135   Phone: (813)584-7333
Videocassette. 1990. 35 mins. Part of the Video Career Library covering 165 occupations. Shows actual workers on the job. Includes firefighters, police officers, correctional officers, bartenders, waiters/waitresses, cooks/chefs, child care workers, flight attendants, barbers/cosmetologists, groundskeepers/gardeners, and butchers/meat cutters.

--- Associations ---

★1953★
International Association of Fire Chiefs (IAFC)
1329 18th St., NW
Washington, DC 20036-6516   Phone: (202)833-3420
Membership: Membership in 28 countries includes: fire chiefs in city and state departments, industry, and military installations; equipment manufacturers; individuals interested in fire prevention, fire protection, and fire fighting. **Purpose:** Conducts research and information gathering projects to promote increased fire department efficiency and better public awareness. Presents Benjamin Franklin International Award of Valor to a deserving fire fighter. Maintains library of approximately 5000 volumes on safety, municipal and administrative topics, fire protection, hazardous materials, and labor relations. **Publications:** *IAFC On Scene*, semimonthly. • Also publishes booklets and special reports. **Facsimile Number:** (202)452-0684.

★1954★
International Association of Fire Fighters (IAFF)
1750 New York Ave., NW
Washington, DC 20006   Phone: (202)737-8484
Membership: AFL-CIO, Canadian Labour Congress. **Publications:** *International Fire Fighter*, bimonthly. • *Local Union Officers Directory*, annual.

★1955★
International Fire Service Training Association (IFSTA)
Fire Protection Publications
Oklahoma State Univ.
Stillwater, OK 74078-0118   Phone: (405)744-5723
Purpose: Educational organization formed to develop training materials for the fire service. Members are individuals who represent their respective fire-related fields and are considered leaders or innovators. Association members meet annually to validate training material for publication, add new techniques and developments, delete outmoded methods and equipment, and upgrade fire service training in general; actual publication is done for the association by Fire Protection Publications of Oklahoma State University. Sponsors annual IFSTA Award. Maintains library of 2000 volumes.

★1956★
National Association of Fire Investigators (NAFI)
20 E. Jackson, Ste. 1000
Chicago, IL 60604   Phone: (312)427-6320
Membership: Fire investigators, insurance adjusters, firemen, attorneys, engineers, and members of related professions. **Purpose:** To increase the knowledge and improve the skills of persons engaged in the investigation of fires, explosions, arson, subrogation, and fire prevention. Presents Fire Service Man of the Year Award; compiles statistics on fires, fire fatalities, and fire losses; maintains library.

★1957★
National Fire Protection Association (NFPA)
1 Batterymarch Park
PO Box 9101
Quincy, MA 02269-9101   Phone: (617)770-3000

Membership: Membership drawn from the fire service, business and industry, health care, educational and other institutions, and individuals in the fields of insurance, government, architecture, and engineering. **Purpose:** Develops, publishes, and disseminates standards, prepared by approximately 175 technical committees, intended to minimize the possibility and effects of fire and explosion; conducts fire safety education programs for the general public. Provides information on fire protection, prevention, and suppression; compiles annual statistics on causes and occupancies of fires, large-loss fires (over $1,000,000), fire deaths, and fire fighter casualties. Provides field service by specialists on electricity, flammable liquids and gases, and marine fire problems. Sponsors National Fire Prevention Week each October and public education campaigns featuring Sparky the Fire Dog. Also sponsors seminars on the Life Safety Code, the National Electrical Code, hotel/motel fire safety, shipyard fire protection, fire safety in detention and correctional facilities, and other timely topics. Conducts research projects that apply statistical methods and operations research to develop computer models and data management systems. Maintains 50,000 volume library of books, reports, periodicals, audiovisual materials, and microfiche. **Publications:** *Catalogs of Publications and Visual Aids*, annual (with updates as needed). • *Fire Command*, monthly. • *Fire Journal*, bimonthly. • *Fire News*, bimonthly. • *Fire Protection Reference Directory and Buyer's Guide*, annual. • *Fire Technology*, quarterly. • *National Fire Codes*, annual. • *National Fire Protection Association—Technical Committee Reports/Technical Committee Documentation*, semiannual. • *Yearbook*. • Also publishes *Fire Protection Handbook*, text and reference books, standards, educational booklets, reports, and the *Learn Not to Burn Curriculum*; produces films, videotapes, and slide/tape packages, and issues posters. **Toll-free/Additional Phone Number(s):** (800)344-3555. **Facsimile Number:** (617)770-0700.

Standards/Certification Agencies

Applicants for nonvolunteer firefighting positions usually have to pass written and physical tests administered by the municipality, including tests of physical stamina and agility. Applicants with the highest scores are most likely to be appointed to the position.

★1958★
National Fire Protection Association (NFPA)
1 Batterymarch Park
PO Box 9101
Quincy, MA 02269-9101   Phone: (617)770-3000

Develops, publishes, and disseminates standards intended to minimize the possibility and effects of fire and explosion.

Test Guides

★1959★
Battalion Chief, Fire Dept.
National Learning Corp.
212 Michael Dr.
Syosset, NY 11791   Phone: (516)921-8888

Jack Rudman. Part of the Career Examination Series No. 1. All examination guides in this series contain questions with answers. **Facsimile Number:** (516)921-8743. **Toll-free/Additional Phone Number(s):** 800-645-6337.

★1960★
Captain, Fire Dept.
National Learning Corp.
212 Michael Dr.
Syosset, NY 11791   Phone: (516)921-8888

Jack Rudman. Part of the Career Examination Series No. 1. All examination guides in this series contain questions with answers. **Facsimile Number:** (516)921-8743. **Toll-free/Additional Phone Number(s):** 800-645-6337.

★1961★
Chief Fire Marshal
National Learning Corp.
212 Michael Dr.
Syosset, NY 11791   Phone: (516)921-8888

Jack Rudman. Part of the Career Examination Series No. 1. All examination guides in this series contain questions with answers. **Facsimile Number:** (516)921-8743. **Toll-free/Additional Phone Number(s):** 800-645-6337.

★1962★
Deputy Chief, Fire Dept.
National Learning Corp.
212 Michael Dr.
Syosset, NY 11791   Phone: (516)921-8888

Jack Rudman. Part of the Career Examination Series No. 1. All examination guides in this series contain questions with answers. **Facsimile Number:** (516)921-8743. **Toll-free/Additional Phone Number(s):** 800-645-6337.

★1963★
Deputy Chief Fire Marshal (Uniformed)
National Learning Corp.
212 Michael Dr.
Syosset, NY 11791   Phone: (516)921-8888

Jack Rudman. Part of the Career Examination Series No. 1. All examination guides in this series contain questions with answers. **Facsimile Number:** (516)921-8743. **Toll-free/Additional Phone Number(s):** 800-645-6337.

★1964★
Fire Administration & Supervision
National Learning Corp.
212 Michael Dr.
Syosset, NY 11791   Phone: (516)921-8888

Jack Rudman. Part of the General Aptitude and Abilities Series No. 2. Books in this series provide functional, intensive test practice and drill in the basic skills and areas common to many examinations, as well as general aptitude or achievement necessary for entrance into many occupations or positions. **Facsimile Number:** (516)921-8743. **Toll-free/Additional Phone Number(s):** 800-645-6337.

★1965★
Fire & Safety Representative
National Learning Corp.
212 Michael Dr.
Syosset, NY 11791   Phone: (516)921-8888

Jack Rudman. Part of the Career Examination Series No. 1. All examination guides in this series contain questions with answers. **Facsimile Number:** (516)921-8743. **Toll-free/Additional Phone Number(s):** 800-645-6337.

★1966★
Fire Captain Oral Exam Study Guide
Information Guides
32 18th St.
Hermosa Beach, CA 90254   Phone: (213)374-1914

Arthur R. Couvillon. 1988.

Firefighting Occupations

★1967★
Fire Department Lieutenant/Captain/Battalion Chief
Prentice Hall Press
Simon & Schuster Inc.
200 Old Tappan Rd.
Old Tappan, NJ 07675   Phone: (800)223-2348
Gene Mahony. First edition, 1983. Includes over 600 questions with answers concerning fire department supervision.

★1968★
Fire Department Lieutenant Captain Battalion Chief: Score High on Firefighter Promotion Exams
Prentice Hall
Rte. 9W
Englewood Cliffs, NJ 07632   Phone: (201)592-2000
Gene Maloney. 1983.

★1969★
Fire Engine Driver
National Learning Corp.
212 Michael Dr.
Syosset, NY 11791   Phone: (516)921-8888
Jack Rudman. Part of the Career Examination Series No. 1. All examination guides in this series contain questions with answers. **Facsimile Number:** (516)921-8743. **Toll-free/Additional Phone Number(s):** 800-645-6337.

★1970★
Fire Engineer Written Exam Study Guide
Information Guides
32 18th St.
Hermosa Beach, CA 90254   Phone: (213)374-1914
Arthur R. Couvillon. Second revised edition, 1988.

★1971★
Fire Examinations-All States
National Learning Corp.
212 Michael Dr.
Syosset, NY 11791   Phone: (516)921-8888
Jack Rudman. Part of the Career Examination Series No. 1. All examination guides in this series contain questions with answers. **Facsimile Number:** (516)921-8743. **Toll-free/Additional Phone Number(s):** 800-645-6337.

★1972★
Fire Inspector
National Learning Corp.
212 Michael Dr.
Syosset, NY 11791   Phone: (516)921-8888
Jack Rudman. Part of the Career Examination Series No. 1. All examination guides in this series contain questions with answers. **Facsimile Number:** (516)921-8743. **Toll-free/Additional Phone Number(s):** 800-645-6337.

★1973★
Fire Marshal
National Learning Corp.
212 Michael Dr.
Syosset, NY 11791   Phone: (516)921-8888
Jack Rudman. Part of the Career Examination Series No. 1. All examination guides in this series contain questions with answers. **Facsimile Number:** (516)921-8743. **Toll-free/Additional Phone Number(s):** 800-645-6337.

★1974★
Fire Officer
National Learning Corp.
212 Michael Dr.
Syosset, NY 11791   Phone: (516)921-8888
Jack Rudman. Part of the Career Examination Series No. 1. All examination guides in this series contain questions with answers. **Facsimile Number:** (516)921-8743. **Toll-free/Additional Phone Number(s):** 800-645-6337.

★1975★
Fire Prevention Inspector
National Learning Corp.
212 Michael Dr.
Syosset, NY 11791   Phone: (516)921-8888
Jack Rudman. Part of the Career Examination Series No. 1. All examination guides in this series contain questions with answers. **Facsimile Number:** (516)921-8743. **Toll-free/Additional Phone Number(s):** 800-645-6337.

★1976★
Fire Promotion Course (One Volume)
National Learning Corp.
212 Michael Dr.
Syosset, NY 11791   Phone: (516)921-8888
Jack Rudman. Part of the General Aptitude and Abilities Series No. 2. Books in this series provide functional, intensive test practice and drill in the basic skills and areas common to many examinations, as well as general aptitude or achievement necessary for entrance into many occupations or positions. **Facsimile Number:** (516)921-8743. **Toll-free/Additional Phone Number(s):** 800-645-6337.

★1977★
Fire Protection Specialist
National Learning Corp.
212 Michael Dr.
Syosset, NY 11791   Phone: (516)921-8888
Jack Rudman. Part of the Career Examination Series No. 1. All examination guides in this series contain questions with answers. **Facsimile Number:** (516)921-8743. **Toll-free/Additional Phone Number(s):** 800-645-6337.

★1978★
Fire Safety Officer
National Learning Corp.
212 Michael Dr.
Syosset, NY 11791   Phone: (516)921-8888
Jack Rudman. Part of the Career Examination Series No. 1. All examination guides in this series contain questions with answers. **Facsimile Number:** (516)921-8743. **Toll-free/Additional Phone Number(s):** 800-645-6337.

★1979★
Fire Safety Technician
National Learning Corp.
212 Michael Dr.
Syosset, NY 11791   Phone: (516)921-8888
Jack Rudman. Part of the Career Examination Series No. 1. All examination guides in this series contain questions with answers. **Facsimile Number:** (516)921-8743. **Toll-free/Additional Phone Number(s):** 800-645-6337.

★1980★
Firefighter
Prentice Hall Press
Simon & Schuster Inc.
200 Old Tappan Rd.
Old Tappan, NJ 07675   Phone: (800)223-2348

Robert Andriuolo. Ninth edition, 1990. Includes information on application process, qualifying tests, and preparation needed for physical tests. Written test material includes four sample exams with answers and an actual exam given to New York City firefighter applicants.

★1981★
Firefighter
National Learning Corp.
212 Michael Dr.
Syosset, NY 11791   Phone: (516)921-8888

Jack Rudman. Part of the Career Examination Series No. 1. All examination guides in this series contain questions with answers. **Facsimile Number:** (516)921-8743. **Toll-free/Additional Phone Number(s):** 800-645-6337.

★1982★
Firefighter Entrance Examinations
Ken-Books
56 Midcrest Way
San Francisco, CA 94131   Phone: (415)826-6550

Harry W. Koch. Second edition, 1989.

★1983★
Firehouse Attendant
National Learning Corp.
212 Michael Dr.
Syosset, NY 11791   Phone: (516)921-8888

Jack Rudman. Part of the Career Examination Series No. 1. All examination guides in this series contain questions with answers. **Facsimile Number:** (516)921-8743. **Toll-free/Additional Phone Number(s):** 800-645-6337.

★1984★
Fireman, Fire Dept.
National Learning Corp.
212 Michael Dr.
Syosset, NY 11791   Phone: (516)921-8888

Jack Rudman. Part of the Career Examination Series No. 1. All examination guides in this series contain questions with answers. **Facsimile Number:** (516)921-8743. **Toll-free/Additional Phone Number(s):** 800-645-6337.

★1985★
Fireman-Laborer
National Learning Corp.
212 Michael Dr.
Syosset, NY 11791   Phone: (516)921-8888

Jack Rudman. Part of the Career Examination Series No. 1. All examination guides in this series contain questions with answers. **Facsimile Number:** (516)921-8743. **Toll-free/Additional Phone Number(s):** 800-645-6337.

★1986★
How to Prepare for the Fire Fighter Examinations
Barron's Educational Series, Inc.
PO Box 8040
250 Wireless Blvd.
Hauppauge, NY 11788   Phone: (516)434-3711

Second edition. Guide contains four full-length practice firefighter exams plus one diagnostic exam, with answers explained. Practice exams include two recent New York City Fire Dept. exams and two exams modeled after tests used throughout the U.S. **Toll-free/Additional Phone Number(s):** 800-645-3476 (in NY call 800-257-5729).

Awards, Scholarships, Grants, and Fellowships

★1987★
Fire Fighter of the Year Award
National Association of Professional Insurance Agents
c/o Joan Hoy
400 N. Washington St.
Alexandria, VA 22314   Phone: (703)836-9340

To recognize heroism performed by a fire fighter on or off-duty, or for outstanding community or humanitarian services. The award is meant to honor those brave individuals in the fire service who risk their lives above and beyond the call of duty in the protection of life and property. Fire fighters, paid or volunteer, full or part-time, are eligible. A commemorative plaque and an all expense paid trip to the annual convention to accept the award are presented annually. Established in 1972. Co-sponsored by The International Association of Fire Chiefs.

★1988★
Firehouse Magazine Heroism and Community Service Award
Firehouse
33 Irving Place
New York, NY 10003   Phone: (212)475-5400

For recognition of service above and beyond the call of duty. Members of a professional or volunteer fire service organization may be nominated by December 31. Monetary awards and a plaque are awarded annually. Established in 1977.

★1989★
Fireman of the Year
International Fire Buff Associates
c/o Roman A. Kaminski, Executive Vice President
7509 Chesapeake Ave.
Baltimore, MD 21219   Phone: (301)477-1544

To acknowledge an outstanding fireman serving in the fire department of the city where the group's annual convention is held. The fireman is chosen by the host city Fire Chief. An inscribed plaque and a $100 United States Savings Bond are awarded annually at the convention banquet. Established in 1971.

★1990★
Everett E. Hudiburg Award
International Fire Service Training Association
c/o Carol Smith
Fire Protection Publications
Oklahoma State University
Stillwater, OK 74078-9987   Phone: (405)624-5723

To honor individuals for significant contributions to the training of firefighters. Anyone who works in the fire service field is eligible to submit an application by March 1. Recipients are selected by secret ballot of the Executive Board. A plaque is awarded annually at the Validation Conference in July. Established in 1972 in memory of Everett E. Hudiburg, a past editor.

Firefighting Occupations

★1991★
International Benjamin Franklin Fire Service Award
International Association of Fire Chiefs
c/o Publications Dept., Alice Pottmyer
1329 18th St., N.W.
Washington, DC 20036   Phone: (202)833-3420

To provide worldwide recognition to fire fighters for a life-saving effort involving courage and the demonstration of expert training, professional service and dedication to duty. An active fire fighter of any country may be nominated by his chief for an incident in which he saved a human life. A plaque and medallion are awarded to the individual, and a plaque and a U.S. Savings Bond are awarded to the department. Awarded when merited. Established in 1948. Co-sponsored by the Motorola Corporation.

★1992★
NAFI Man of the Year
National Association of Fire Investigators
20 E. Jackson Blvd., Ste. 1000
Chicago, IL 60604-2210   Phone: (312)939-6050

To recognize significant contributions to the fire investigation profession and NAFI. Firemen, policemen, attorneys, insurance adjusters, claimsmen, fire experts, fire marshals in the military, or full-time fire investigators may be nominated. An engraved plaque is awarded annually when merited. Established in 1969. Formerly: Fire Investigator of the Year.

★1993★
Public Service Award
Scanner Association of North America
P.O. Box 414
Western Springs, IL 60558   Phone: (312)246-4550

To recognize a police, fire, or other public safety volunteer or official for heroic action. Members of the Association may nominate individuals. A monetary prize and a plaque are awarded six times per year. Established in 1978.

Basic Reference Guides and Handbooks

★1994★
Engineers, Pump Operators, Drivers Handbook
Davis Publishing Co.
2015 McFarland Blvd. E.
Tuscaloosa, AL 35405   Phone: (205)759-1508
Robert E. Ford. 1977. **Toll-free/Additional Phone Number(s):** 800-538-0762.

★1995★
Fire Assessment Centers: The New Concept in Promotional Examinations
Davis Publishing Co., Inc.
2015 McFarland Blvd. E.
Tuscaloosa, AL 35405   Phone: (205)759-1508
George Tielsch. 1978. **Toll-free/Additional Phone Number(s):** 800-538-0762.

★1996★
Fire Brigade Training Program: Instructor's Guide
National Fire Protection Association
1 Batterymarch Park
Quincy, MA 02269-9101   Phone: (617)770-3000

★1997★
Fire Brigade Training Program: Student Manual
National Fire Protection Association
1 Batterymarch Park
Quincy, MA 02269-9101   Phone: (616)770-3000

★1998★
Fire Command Officer's Handbook
Davis Publishing Co.
2015 McFarland Blvd. E.
Tuscaloosa, AL 35405   Phone: (205)759-1508
Robert E. Ford. 1978. **Toll-free/Additional Phone Number(s):** 800-538-0762.

★1999★
Fire Department Safety Officer's Reference Guide
National Fire Protection Association
1 Batterymarch Park
Quincy, MA 02269-9101   Phone: (617)770-3000

★2000★
Fire Lieutenant's & Captain's Handbook
Davis Publishing Co.
2015 McFarland Blvd. E.
Tuscaloosa, AL 35405   Phone: (205)759-1508
Robert E. Ford. 1977. **Toll-free/Additional Phone Number(s):** 800-538-0762.

★2001★
Fire Protection Handbook
National Fire Protection Association (NFPA)
1 Batterymarch Park
PO Box 9101
Quincy, MA 02269-9101   Phone: (617)770-3000

★2002★
Firefighter & Paramedic Burnout
Harcourt Brace Jovanovich, Inc.
6277 Sea Harbor Dr.
Orlando, FL 32887   Phone: (407)345-2000
Gerald L. Fishkin. 1990. **Facsimile Number:** (407)345-8388.

★2003★
Firefighter's Entrance Handbook
Davis Publishing Co.
2015 McFarland Blvd. E.
Tuscaloosa, AL 35405   Phone: (205)759-1508
Robert E. Ford. 1977. **Toll-free/Additional Phone Number(s):** 800-538-0762.

★2004★
Industrial Fire Brigades Training Manual
National Fire Protection Association
1 Batterymarch Park
Quincy, MA 02269-9101   Phone: (617)770-3000
Charles A. Tuck, Jr., editor. Fifth edition, 1982.

★2005★
Learn Not to Burn Curriculum
National Fire Protection Association (NFPA)
1 Batterymarch Park
PO Box 9101
Quincy, MA 02269-9101   Phone: (617)770-3000

★2006★
Tentative Standard for Protective Clothing for Fire Fighters
National Fire Protection Association
1 Battertmarch Park
Quincy, MA 02269-9101   Phone: (617)770-3000
1986.

★2007★
Training Reports & Records
National Fire Protection Association
1 Batterymarch Park
Quincy, MA 02269-9101   Phone: (617)770-3000
1970. Part of Zero Series.

★2008★
Winning the Fire Service Leadership Game
Fire Engineering Book Service
Park 80 W., Plaza 2, 7th Fl.
Saddle Brook, NJ 07662   Phone: (212)481-5771
H. Caulfield. 1985.

──────── Periodicals ────────

★2009★
Aerial Applicator Farm, Forest & Fire
Drawer 2263
Santa Fe Springs, CA 90670   Phone: (213)948-3713
Robert G. Rosenblatt, Editor and Publisher. 9x/yr. Aerial agriculture and fire control.

★2010★
American Fire Journal
9072 E. Artesia Blvd., Ste. 7
Bellflower, CA 90706-6299   Phone: (213)866-1664
Carol Carlsen Brooks, Editor. Monthly. Magazine about fire protection.

★2011★
Chief Fire Executive
Firehouse Communications, Inc.
445 Broadhollow Rd., No. 21
Melville, NY 11747-4722
Thomas J. Rahilly, Editor. Quarterly. Magazine on fire service management.

★2012★
Fire Chief
Communication Channels, Inc.
307 N. Michigan Ave.
Chicago, IL 60601-5311   Phone: (312)726-7277
Don Michard, Editor. Monthly. Fire protection magazine. **Facsimile Number:** (312)726-7277.

★2013★
Fire Command
National Fire Protection Association (NFPA)
1 Batterymarch Park
PO Box 9101
Quincy, MA 02269-9101   Phone: (617)770-3000
Monthly. Magazine for fire chiefs and officers. Provides feature articles on tactics, equipment, training, management, rescue, and advances in codes, enforcement, and safety. Includes research reports and new product information.

★2014★
Fire Control Digest
Washington Capital News Reports, Inc.
3918 Prosperity Ave., Ste. 318
Fairfax, VA 22031   Phone: (703)573-1600
Editor(s): Susan Kernus. Monthly. Considers concerns of fire fighting and safety, including arson, construction materials, the toxicity of plastics, fire hazards, emergency medical service (EMS), fire codes, insurance, state concerns, and fire departments that are in the news. Also includes information on seminars and classes. **Facsimile Number:** (703)573-1604.

★2015★
Fire Engineering
Pennwell Publishing Co.
Park 80 West Plaza 2
Saddle Brook, NJ 07662-5612   Phone: (201)845-0800
Bill Manning, Editor. Monthly. Fire suppression, protection, and prevention magazine. **Facsimile Number:** (201)845-6275.

★2016★
Fire Journal
National Fire Protection Association (NFPA)
1 Batterymarch Park
PO Box 9101
Quincy, MA 02269-9101   Phone: (617)770-3000
Bimonthly. Features technical, scientific, and industrial applications of fire protection, suppression, investigations, and education, plus association news. Includes annual and advertisers index, research reports, case histories, and product news.

★2017★
Fire Management Notes
U.S. Government Printing Office
Superintendent of Documents
Washington, DC 20402   Phone: (202)783-3238
David W. Dahl, Editor. Four times/yr. Magazine on forest fire control. **Facsimile Number:** (202)275-0019.

★2018★
Fire News
National Fire Protection Association (NFPA)
1 Batterymarch Park
PO Box 9101
Quincy, MA 02269-9101   Phone: (617)770-3000
Bimonthly. Association and industry newsletter. Features calendar of events and lists job openings.

★2019★
Fire Technology
National Fire Protection Association (NFPA)
1 Batterymarch Park
PO Box 9101
Quincy, MA 02269-9101   Phone: (617)770-3000
Quarterly. Professional journal for the fire safety practitioner and the fire safety researcher. Papers describe advances in fire technology with emphasis on implementation. Includes research reports, book reviews, software reviews, and indexes.

★2020★
Firefighter's News
Lifesaving Communications, Inc.
PO Box 165
Milford, DE 19963-0165   Phone: (302)422-2772
Bill Stevenson, Editor. Six times/yr. Magazine (tabloid) reporting on issues affecting professional and volunteer fire and rescue personnel. **Facsimile Number:** (302)422-0552.

★2021★
Firehouse Magazine
PTN Publishing Co.
445 Broad Hollow Rd.
Melville, NY 11747　　　　　　　Phone: (516)845-2700
Thomas Rahilly, Editor. Monthly. Magazine focusing on fire protection. **Facsimile Number:** (516)845-7109.

★2022★
Grass Roots
National Fire Sprinkler Association (NFSA)
Robin Hill Corporate Park
Rt. 22
Box 1000
Patterson, NY 12563　　　　　　　Phone: (914)878-4200
Monthly. Association and industry newsletter.

★2023★
IAFC On Scene
International Association of Fire Chiefs (IAFC)
1329 18th St., NW
Washington, DC 20036-6516　　　　Phone: (202)833-3420
Semimonthly. Tabloid covering current news of interest to fire and emergency services managers.

★2024★
International Fire Fighter
International Association of Fire Fighters (IAFF)
1750 New York Ave., NW
Washington, DC 20006　　　　　　Phone: (202)737-8484
Bimonthly. Union tabloid; includes IAFF media awards and death and injury survey.

★2025★
ISFSI Instruct-O-Gram
International Society of Fire Service Instructors (ISFSI)
30 Main St.
Ashland, MA 01721　　　　　　　Phone: (617)881-5800
Monthly. Publishes items to be used as a fire training aid.

★2026★
Labor Line
National Fire Sprinkler Association (NFSA)
Robin Hill Corporate Park
Rt. 22
Box 1000
Patterson, NY 12563　　　　　　　Phone: (914)878-4200
Bimonthly. Newsletter reporting to unionized contractors on federal and state labor laws.

★2027★
NPSA Regional Report
National Fire Sprinkler Association (NFSA)
Robin Hill Corporate Park
Rt. 22
Box 1000
Patterson, NY 12563　　　　　　　Phone: (914)878-4200
Monthly. Newsletter.

★2028★
Sprinkler Quarterly
National Fire Sprinkler Association (NFSA)
Robin Hill Corporate Park
Rt. 22
Box 1000
Patterson, NY 12563　　　　　　　Phone: (914)878-4200
Journal providing information on fire sprinkler protection; includes features and technical information for and about the industry. Also covers association news, product and personnel news, codes and standards updates, and new technology information.

★2029★
Sprinkler Technotes
National Fire Sprinkler Association (NFSA)
Robin Hill Corporate Park
Rt. 22
Box 1000
Patterson, NY 12563　　　　　　　Phone: (914)878-4200
Bimonthly. Newsletter listing proposed changes to fire sprinkler codes and standards; also covers developing fire protection technology.

★2030★
Today's Fireman
Towerhigh Publications, Inc.
PO Box 875108
Los Angeles, CA 90087　　　　　　Phone: (213)432-3806
Donald Mack, Editor and Publisher. Quarterly. Fire service magazine.

★2031★
Turn Out
International Fire Buff Associates, Inc.
PO Box 23456
Milwaukee, WI 53223　　　　　　Phone: (414)357-6548
Editor(s): William M. Mokros. Semiannually. Concerned with the firefighting activities of fire departments across the nation. Includes historical accounts and news of association and member activities.

★2032★
The Voice
International Society of Fire Service Instructors (ISFSI)
30 Main St.
Ashland, MA 01721　　　　　　　Phone: (617)881-5800
Editor(s): Ed McCormack. Monthly. Provides professional news for those engaged in fire service instruction in industrial and educational settings. Discusses new products available to fire fighters and safety procedures. Recurring features include book reviews, a calendar of events, and a column titled Across the Country.

Meetings and Conventions

★2033★
Emergency Response Expo
Tower Conference Management Co.
800 Roosevelt Rd., Bldg. E., Ste. 408
Glen Ellyn, IL 60137-5835　　　　Phone: (708)469-3373
1992. **Facsimile Number:** (708)469-7477.

★2034★
Fire and Rescue Educational Conference and Exposition
International Association of Fire Chiefs
1329 18th St., NW
Washington, DC 20036　　　　　　Phone: (202)833-3420
1992; Sep. 12-16; Anaheim, CA. **Facsimile Number:** (202)452-0684.

★2035★
Fire Department Instructors Conference
International Society of Fire Service Instructors
30 Main St.
Ashland, MA 01721　　　　　　　Phone: (502)881-5800
Frequency: Always held at the Convention Center in Cincinnati, Ohio. 1992; Apr. 11-15; Cincinnati, OH • 1993; Apr. 03-07;

Cincinnati, OH • 1994; Mar. 26-30; Cincinnati, OH • 1995; Apr. 08-12; Cincinnati, OH. **Facsimile Number:** (508)881-6829.

★2036★
Great American Firehouse Expo and Muster
PTN Publishing
445 Broad Hollow Rd.
Melville, NY 11747   Phone: (516)845-2700
Frequency: Always held during May at the Convention Center in Baltimore, Maryland. 1992; Jul. 24-26; Baltimore, MD. **Facsimile Number:** (516)496-8013.

★2037★
International Association of Fire Fighters (IAFF)
1750 New York Ave., NW
Washington, DC 20006   Phone: (202)737-8484
Frequency: Biennial, always held in August. 1992 Vancouver, BC, Canada.

★2038★
National Fire Protection Association Annual Meeting
National Fire Protection Association
Batterymarch Park
Quincy, MA 02169   Phone: (617)770-3000
1992; May 17-21; New Orleans, LA. **Toll-free/Additional Phone Number(s):** 800-344-3555. **Facsimile Number:** (617)770-0700.

★2039★
PROTECH - International Exhibition for Protection, Safety, Security, and Fire Prevention
World Access Corp.
15 Bemis Rd.
PO Box 171
Wellesley Hills, MA 02181   Phone: (617)235-8095
1992; Nov. 22-25 • 1993. **Facsimile Number:** (617)235-7360.

——— **Other Sources of Information** ———

★2040★
Fire on the Rim: A Firefighter's Season at the Grand Canyon
Ballantine Books of Canada
1265 Aerowood Dr.
Mississauga, ON, Canada L4W 1B9   Phone: (416)624-0672
Stephen J. Pyne. 1990. **Facsimile Number:** (416)624-6217.

★2041★
Firefighters in Action
State Mutual Book & Periodical Service, Ltd.
521 5th Ave., 17th Fl.
New York, NY 10175   Phone: (212)682-5844
John Creighton. 1985.

★2042★
Firefighters: Their Lives in Their Own Words
Doubleday
666 5th Ave.
New York, NY 10103   Phone: (212)765-6500
Dennis Smith. 1988. **Facsimile Number:** (212)492-9700.

★2043★
Firehouse Trivia
Unlimited Publishing Co.
Box 240, Rte. 17K
Bullville, NY 10915   Phone: (914)361-1299
William J. Geis. 1986.

★2044★
Here Comes the Fireman
Outlet Book Co.
225 Park Ave. S.
New York, NY 10003   Phone: (212)254-1600
1990.

★2045★
Last Alarm
National Fire Protection Association
1 Battertmarch Park
Quincy, MA 02269-9101   Phone: (617)770-3000
Jerry Laughlin. 1986.

★2046★
National Fire Codes
National Fire Protection Association (NFPA)
1 Batterymarch Park
PO Box 9101
Quincy, MA 02269-9101   Phone: (617)770-3000
Annual. Compilation of over 250 fire codes, standards, recommended practices, manuals, and guides on fire protection.

★2047★
National Fire Protection Association—Technical Committee Reports/Technical Committee Documentation
National Fire Protection Association (NFPA)
1 Batterymarch Park
PO Box 9101
Quincy, MA 02269-9101   Phone: (617)770-3000
Semiannual. Committee reports and interim documents on the fire code and standards development process.

Guards

Guards patrol and inspect property against fire, theft, vandalism, and illegal entry. In office buildings, stores, banks, and hospitals, guards protect records, merchandise, money and equipment. At airports and railroads, guards ensure that nothing is stolen while being loaded or unloaded, and screen passengers and visitors for weapons and other forbidden articles. Guards who work in public buildings such as museums or art galleries protect exhibits and may also answer routine questions from visitors. In those places where valuable property or information is kept, such as laboratories or government buildings, guards check the credentials of persons or vehicles entering or leaving the premises. At public gatherings like sporting events, guards maintain order, give information, and watch for persons who may cause trouble. Armored car guards protect money and valuables during transit. Bodyguards protect individuals from bodily injury, kidnapping, or invasion of privacy. Guards usually patrol on foot, but if the property is large, they may make their rounds by car or scooter. As they make their rounds, guards check all doors and windows, see that no unauthorized persons remain after working hours, and ensure that alarms, and other various electrical and plumbing systems are working properly. Guards usually are uniformed and may carry a gun or nightstick. They may also carry a flashlight, whistle, two-way radio, and a watch clock. Industrial security firms and guard agencies employ over 50 percent of all guards. Other guards are employed by banks, building management companies, hotels, hospitals, retail stores, restaurants and bars, schools, colleges and universities, and federal, state, and local government.

$alaries

Earnings vary according to type of guard duty.

Public utilities and transportation	$11.28/hour
Manufacturing	$10.31/hour
Wholesale trade	$8.14/hour
Banking, finance, insurance, and real estate	$7.82/hour
Retail trade	$6.43/hour
Various service industries, including security and guard agencies	$5.04/hour

Employment Outlook

Growth rate until the year 2000: Faster than average.

Guards

Career Guides

★2048★
"Bodyguard" in *Action Careers: Employment in the High-Risk Job Market* (pp. 5-14)
Citadel Press/Lyle Stuart Inc.
Carol Publishing Group
120 Enterprise Ave.
Secaucus, NJ 07094 Phone: (201)866-0490
Ragnar Benson. 1988. Describes 24 dangerous careers such as repo man, explosives handler, and river rafting guide. Each profile includes demand for the job, where the jobs can be found, required personal and physical characteristics and training needed.

★2049★
"Careers in Private Security" in *Career Planning in Criminal Justice* (pp. 91-95)
Anderson Publishing Co.
2035 Reading Rd.
Cincinnati, OH 45202 Phone: (513)421-4142
Robert C. DeLucia and Thomas J. Doyle. 1990. Surveys a wide range of career and employment opportunities in law enforcement, the courts, corrections, forensic science and private security. Contains career planning and job hunting advice. Profiles 77 criminal justice occupations describing job duties, work environments, and educational requirements.

★2050★
Customs Officers
Chronicle Guidance Publications, Inc.
PO Box 1190
Moravia, NY 13118-1190 Phone: (315)497-0330
1989. This career brief describes the nature of the work, working conditions, hours and earnings, education and training, licensure, certification, unions, personal qualifications, social and psychological factors, employment outlook, entry methods, advancement, and related occupations. **Toll-free/Additional Phone Number(s):** 800-622-7284.

★2051★
"Guard" in *Career Opportunities in Art* (pp. 25-26)
Facts on File, Inc.
460 Park Avenue, S.
New York, NY 10016 Phone: (212)683-2244
Susan H. Haubenstock and David Joselit. 1988. Profiles more than 75 art-related jobs. Each occupational profile covers job duties, employment outlook, career paths, salaries, skills, and educational preparation. Offers tips for entering the field.

★2052★
"Guard" in *VGM's Careers Encyclopedia* (pp. 84-86)
National Textbook Co.
4255 W. Touhy Ave.
Lincolnwood, IL 60646 Phone: (312)679-5500
Third edition, 1991. Contains two- to five-page descriptions of 200 managerial, professional, technical, trade, and service occupations. Each profile includes job duties, places of employment, qualifications, educational preparation, training, employment potential, advancement, income, and additional sources of information.

★2053★
Guard, Security
Careers, Inc.
PO Box 135
Largo, FL 34649-0135 Phone: (813)584-7333
1992. Two-page occupational summary card describing duties, working conditions, personal qualifications, training, earnings and hours, employment outlook, places of employment, related careers and where to write for more information.

★2054★
"Guard Supervisor" in *Career Opportunities in Art* (pp. 27-28)
Facts on File, Inc.
460 Park Avenue, S.
New York, NY 10016 Phone: (212)683-2244
Susan H. Haubenstock and David Joselit. 1988. Profiles more than 75 art-related jobs. Each occupational profile covers job duties, employment outlook, career paths, salaries, skills, and educational preparation. Offers tips for entering the field.

★2055★
"Guards" in *Occupational Outlook Handbook* (pp. 288-290)
Superintendent of Documents
U.S. Government Printing Office
Washington, DC 20402 Phone: (202)783-3238
Biennial; latest edition, 1990-91. Encyclopedia of careers describing more than 250 occupations and comprising about 86 percent of all jobs in the economy. Occupations that require lengthy education or training are given the most attention. For each occupation, the handbook describes job duties, working conditions, training, educational preparation, personal qualities, advancement possibilities, job outlook, earnings, and sources of additional information.

★2056★
"Guards" in *America's 50 Fastest Growing Jobs* (pp. 118-120)
JIST Works, Inc.
720 N. Park Ave.
Indianapolis, IN 46202   Phone: (317)264-3720

Michael J. Farr, compiler. 1991. Describes the 50 fastest growing jobs within major career clusters such as technicians, and marketing and sales. Each job profile explains the nature of the work, skills and abilities required, employment outlook, average earnings, related occupations, education and training requirements, and employment opportunities. Also contains career planning information and job search tips.

★2057★
"Guards" in *The American Almanac of Jobs and Salaries* (pp. 531-532)
Avon Books
105 Madison Avenue
New York, NY 10016   Phone: (212)481-5600

John Wright and Edward J. Dwyer. Revised and updated, 1990. A comprehensive guide to the wages of hundreds of occupations in a wide variety of industries and organizations.

★2058★
Health Care Security Training Series
MTI Teleprograms, Inc.
108 Wilmot Rd.
Deerfield, IL 60015-9990   Phone: (708)940-1260

Videocassette. 198?. 15 mins. This series teaches the basic skills needed for working as a security officer in a health care facility.

★2059★
"Security Guard" in *Public and Community Services, Volume 11 of Career Information Center* (pp. 64-66)
Glencoe/Macmillan
15319 Chatsworth St.
Mission Hills, CA 91345   Phone: (818)898-1391

Richard Lidz and Dale Anderson, editorial directors. Fourth edition, 1990. For 600 occupations, describes job duties, entry-level requirements, education and training needed, advancement possibilities, employment outlook, earnings and benefits. The set is divided into 12 volumes. Each volume includes jobs related under a broad career field. Volume 13 is the index. **Facsimile Number:** 818-365-5489.

★2060★
"Security Guards" in *Careers in Law Enforcement and Security* (pp. 81-93)
Rosen Publishing Group, Inc.
29 E. 21st St.
New York, NY 10010   Phone: (212)777-3017

Paul Cohen and Shari Cohen. 1990. Describes jobs such as police, sheriff, detective, FBI, CIA, and Secret Service agents, parole and probation officers, security guards, and private investigators. Covers job duties, qualifications, education, training, income, and advancement possibilities. Offers advice about where and how to apply for jobs.

★2061★
"Security Guards" in Volume 6 of *Career Discovery Encyclopedia* (pp. 14-15)
J.G. Ferguson Publishing Co.
200 W. Monroe
Chicago, IL 60606   Phone: (312)580-5480

E. Russell Primm, editor-in-chief. 1990. Contains two-page articles on 504 occupations. Each article describes job duties, earnings, and educational and training requirements.

★2062★
"Security Guards" in Volume 3 of *The Encyclopedia of Careers and Vocational Guidance* (pp. 308-311)
J.G. Ferguson Publishing Co.
200 W. Monroe
Chicago, IL 60606   Phone: (312)580-5480

William E. Hopke, editor-in-chief. Eighth edition, 1990. Four-volume set that profiles 500 occupations and describes job trends in 76 industries. Includes career description, educational requirements, history of the job, methods of entry, advancement, employment outlook, earnings, working conditions, social and psychological factors, and sources of additional information.

★2063★
Security Officers
Chronicle Guidance Publications, Inc.
PO Box 1190
Moravia, NY 13118-1190   Phone: (315)497-0330

1991. This career brief describes the nature of the work, working conditions, hours and earnings, education and training, licensure, certification, unions, personal qualifications, social and psychological factors, employment outlook, entry methods, advancement, and related occupations. **Toll-free/Additional Phone Number(s):** 800-622-7284.

★2064★
Store Detective
Vocational Biographies, Inc.
PO Box 31, Dept. VF10
Sauk Centre, MN 56378   Phone: (612)352-6516

1988. This pamphlet profiles a person working in the job. Includes information about job duties, working conditions, places of employment, educational preparation, labor market outlook, and salaries. **Toll-free/Additional Phone Number(s):** 800-255-0752.

Associations

★2065★
International Association of Security Service (IASS)
PO Box 8202
Northfield, IL 60093   Phone: (312)973-7712

Membership: Companies providing security services, primarily guard services. **Purpose:** Works to establish standardized licensing and training regulations. Operates research programs; maintains speakers' bureau, hall of fame, museum, and a library of 600 volumes. Plans to conduct seminars and training workshops.

★2066★
International Foundation for Protection Officers (IFPO)
7327 Horne St.
Mission, BC, Canada V2V 3Y5   Phone: (206)733-1571

Purpose: Seeks to: provide for the education, training, and certification of protection officers worldwide; maintain and improve standards of excellence and establish ethical standards within the industry; improve the public perception of protection officers. Interacts with colleges, universities, and other post-secondary educational institutions to facilitate education and certification; conducts research and seminars. Maintains Certified Protection Officer program, which provides professional designation and consists of training in patrols, report writing, crime scenes, interviewing, investigations, public relations, stress management, physical security, VIP protection, and first aid.

Guards

★2067★
International Security Officer's Police and Guard Union (ISOPGU)
321 86th St.
Brooklyn, NY 11209   Phone: (718)836-3508
Membership: Independent. **Facsimile Number:** (718)836-6757.

★2068★
International Union of Security Officers (IUSO)
2404 Merced St.
San Leandro, CA 94577   Phone: (415)895-9905
Membership: Independent. Guards and security officers. **Purpose:** Seeks to improve wages, hours, and working conditions for security officers and guards. Conducts charitable program and shop steward training program. **Publications:** *Newsletter*, 6/year.

★2069★
Security Industry Association (SIA)
2800 28th St., Ste. 101
Santa Monica, CA 90405   Phone: (213)450-4141
Membership: Security equipment manufacturers and distributors. **Purpose:** Seeks advancement of companies in the security products industry. Conducts research programs, educational programs, technical seminars, communications with related industries, and other activities. Maintains speakers' bureau; compiles statistics; sponsors competitions. **Publications:** *Membership Directory*, periodic. • *Security Industry Association —News*, monthly. • Also publishes *National Industry Survey*. **Facsimile Number:** (213)452-7524.

Standards/Certification Agencies

★2070★
International Association of Security Service (IASS)
PO Box 8202
Northfield, IL 60093   Phone: (312)973-7712
Works to establish standardized licensing and training regulations.

★2071★
International Foundation for Protection Officers (IFPO)
7327 Horne St.
Mission, BC, Canada V2V 3Y5   Phone: (206)733-1571
Seeks to provide for the training, and certification of protection officers worldwide; maintain and improve standards of excellence and establish ethical standards within the industry. Maintains Certified Protection Officer program, which provides professional designation and consists of training in patrols, report writing, crime scenes, interviewing, investigations, public relations, stress management, physical security, VIP protection, and first aid.

Test Guides

★2072★
Building Guard
National Learning Corp.
212 Michael Dr.
Syosset, NY 11791   Phone: (516)921-8888
Jack Rudman. Part of the Career Examination Series No. 1. All examination guides in this series contain questions with answers. **Facsimile Number:** (516)921-8743. **Toll-free/Additional Phone Number(s):** 800-645-6337.

★2073★
Guard Patrolman
National Learning Corp.
212 Michael Dr.
Syosset, NY 11791   Phone: (516)921-8888
Jack Rudman. Part of the Career Examination Series No. 1. All examination guides in this series contain questions with answers. **Facsimile Number:** (516)921-8743. **Toll-free/Additional Phone Number(s):** 800-645-6337.

★2074★
Security Guard
National Learning Corp.
212 Michael Dr.
Syosset, NY 11791   Phone: (516)921-8888
Jack Rudman. Part of the Career Examination Series No. 1. All examination guides in this series contain questions with answers. **Facsimile Number:** (516)921-8743. **Toll-free/Additional Phone Number(s):** 800-645-6337.

★2075★
Security Officer
National Learning Corp.
212 Michael Dr.
Syosset, NY 11791   Phone: (516)921-8888
Jack Rudman. Part of the Career Examination Series No. 1. All examination guides in this series contain questions with answers. **Facsimile Number:** (516)921-8743. **Toll-free/Additional Phone Number(s):** 800-645-6337.

★2076★
Senior Building Guard
National Learning Corp.
212 Michael Dr.
Syosset, NY 11791   Phone: (516)921-8888
Jack Rudman. Part of the Career Examination Series No. 1. All examination guides in this series contain questions with answers. **Facsimile Number:** (516)921-8743. **Toll-free/Additional Phone Number(s):** 800-645-6337.

★2077★
Senior Campus Security Officer
National Learning Corp.
212 Michael Dr.
Syosset, NY 11791   Phone: (516)921-8888
Jack Rudman. Part of the Career Examination Series No. 1. All examination guides in this series contain questions with answers. **Facsimile Number:** (516)921-8743. **Toll-free/Additional Phone Number(s):** 800-645-6337.

Awards, Scholarships, Grants, and Fellowships

★2078★
ISDA Special Commendation
International Security and Detective Alliance
c/o Dr. H. Roehm
P.O. Box 6303
Corpus Christi, TX 78466-6303   Phone: (512)888-6164
To honor any individual who significantly promotes the growth and betterment of the private security and investigation professions, or who performs significant acts of heroism, bravery, and/or faithful service. Letters of application with affidavits, statements, etc., as required may be submitted by anyone meeting the above criteria. Certificates are awarded when approved applications are received. Established in 1987.

Basic Reference Guides and Handbooks

★2079★
SIA National Industry Survey
Security Industry Association (SIA)
2800 28th St., Ste. 101
Santa Monica, CA 90405　　　　Phone: (213)450-4141

Periodicals

★2080★
Campus Safety Newsletter
National Safety Council
444 N. Michigan Ave.
Chicago, IL 60611　　　　Phone: (312)527-4800
Editor(s): Katie Kuhfuss. Quarterly. Focuses on safety problems and effective precautions for college and university buildings and campuses. Discusses security patrols, facilities for the handicapped, institutional policies, and similar subjects. Promotes safety education as the direct means of accident prevention.

★2081★
Police & Security News
Days Communications
1690 Quarry Rd.
PO Box 330
Kulpsville, PA 19443　　　　Phone: (215)538-1240
James Devery, Editor. 6x/yr. Tabloid for the law enforcement and private security industries. Includes articles on training, new products, and new technology. **Facsimile Number:** (215)368-9955.

★2082★
Security Industry Association—News
Security Industry Association (SIA)
2800 28th St., Ste. 101
Santa Monica, CA 90405　　　　Phone: (213)450-4141
Monthly. Membership newsletter.

Meetings and Conventions

★2083★
American Correctional Association Congress of Correction
American Correctional Association
8025 Laurel Lakes Ct.
Laurel, MD 20707-5075　　　　Phone: (301)206-5100
1992. **Toll-free/Additional Phone Number(s):** 800-888-8784. **Facsimile Number:** (301)206-5061.

★2084★
American Correctional Association Winter Conference
American Correctional Association
8025 Laurel Lakes Ct.
Laurel, MD 20707-5075　　　　Phone: (301)206-5100
Toll-free/Additional Phone Number(s): 800-888-8784. **Facsimile Number:** (301)206-5061.

★2085★
International Association of Security Service (IASS)
PO Box 8202
Northfield, IL 60093　　　　Phone: (312)973-7712
Frequency: Annual.

★2086★
National Sheriffs' Association Convention
National Sheriffs' Association
1450 Duke St.
Alexandria, VA 22314-3490　　　　Phone: (703)836-7827
1992; Jun. San Diego, CA • 1993; Jun. Salt Lake City, UT • 1994; Jun. Pittsburgh, PA • 1995; Jun. San Antonio, TX. **Toll-free/Additional Phone Number(s):** 800-424-7872. **Facsimile Number:** (703)683-6541.

★2087★
PROTECH - International Exhibition for Protection, Safety, Security, and Fire Prevention
World Access Corp.
15 Bemis Rd.
PO Box 171
Wellesley Hills, MA 02181　　　　Phone: (617)235-8095
1992; Nov. 22-25 • 1993. **Facsimile Number:** (617)235-7360.

Police, Detectives, and Special Agents

Police, detectives, and special agents work to maintain the safety of the nation's cities, towns, and highways. They do this through a variety of activities ranging from controlling traffic to preventing and investigating crimes. Police and detectives who work in small communities may have a wide variety of duties including traffic enforcement, burglary investigations, or giving first aid to an accident victim. In larger areas, officers are usually assigned to a specific type of duty. Detectives and special agents are plainclothes investigators who gather facts and collect evidence for criminal cases. They conduct interviews, examine records, observe the activities of suspects, and participate in raids or arrests. Federal Bureau of Investigation (FBI) special agents investigate violations of federal laws in connection with bank robberies, theft of government property, organized crime, and terrorism. Special agents employed by the U.S. Department of Treasury may work for the U.S. Customs Service where they enforce laws preventing the illegal smuggling of goods across borders; the Bureau of Alcohol, Tobacco, and Firearms where they might investigate illegal sales of guns or the underpayment of taxes by a liquor or cigarette manufacturer; the U.S. Secret Service who protect high ranking government officials; or the Internal Revenue Service which collects evidence of tax evasion. State police officers (sometimes called State troopers or highway patrol officers) patrol highways and enforce laws and regulations that govern their use. In addition to highway responsibilities, state police in the majority of states also enforce criminal laws. About 85 percent of all police, detectives, and special agents are employed by local governments. State police agencies employ about 10 percent; various federal agencies employ an additional 5 percent.

$alaries

Salaries for police, detectives, and special agents vary greatly depending upon region, size of the department, and experience.

Police officers	$20,600-26,700/year
Police and detective sergeants	$17,500-35,300/year
Police chiefs	$19,000 87,000/year
FBI agents	$26,300-41,100/year
Supervisory federal agents	$48,600/year
U.S. Treasury Department agents	$19,500-34,600/year
Supervisory U.S. Treasury Department agents	$41,100

Employment Outlook

Growth rate until the year 2000: Average.

Police, Detectives, and Special Agents

Career Guides

★2088★
Border Patrol Agent
Careers, Inc.
PO Box 135
Largo, FL 34649-0135   Phone: (813)584-7333
1989. Two-page occupational summary card describing duties, working conditions, personal qualifications, training, earnings and hours, employment outlook, places of employment, related careers and where to write for more information.

★2089★
Border Patrol Agent
Vocational Biographies, Inc.
PO Box 31, Dept. VF10
Sauk Centre, MN 56378   Phone: (612)352-6516
1988. This pamphlet profiles a person working in the job. Includes information about job duties, working conditions, places of employment, educational preparation, labor market outlook, and salaries. **Toll-free/Additional Phone Number(s):** 800-255-0752.

★2090★
Career Success Series
Cambridge Career Products
90 MacCorkle Ave., SW
South Charleston, WV 25311   Phone: (304)744-9323
Videocassette. 1986. 15 mins. A series, available separately, outlining various career choices for students. Occupations include: flight service, air transportation/ground service, data processing, carpentry, clerk in banking/insurance, commodity sales, cosmetic personal grooming, fire fighting, forestry services, home economics, insulation/roofing, material handling, mechanics, photographic processing, pipefitting and plumbing, police science, printing, secretarial services, and utilities equipment operator.

★2091★
"Careers in Law Enforcement" in *Career Planning in Criminal Justice* (pp. 19-54)
Anderson Publishing Co.
2035 Reading Rd.
Cincinnati, OH 45202   Phone: (513)421-4142
Robert C. DeLucia and Thomas J. Doyle. 1990. Surveys a wide range of career and employment opportunities in law enforcement, the courts, corrections, forensic science and private security. Contains career planning and job hunting advice. Profiles 77 criminal justice occupations describing job duties, work environments, and educational requirements.

★2092★
County Sheriff
Vocational Biographies, Inc.
PO Box 31, Dept. VF10
Sauk Centre, MN 56378   Phone: (612)352-6516
1991. This pamphlet profiles a person working in the job. Includes information about job duties, working conditions, places of employment, educational preparation, labor market outlook, and salaries. **Toll-free/Additional Phone Number(s):** 800-255-0752.

★2093★
"Customs Worker" in *Occu-Facts: Information on 565 Careers in Outline Form* (p. 1.49)
Careers, Inc.
P.O. Box 135
1211 Tenth St., S.W.
Largo, FL 33640   Phone: (813)584-7333
Elizabeth Handville. Biennial, 1989-90 edition. Each one-page occupational profile describes duties, working conditions, physical surroundings and demands, aptitudes, temperament, educational requirements, employment outlook, earnings, and places of employment.

★2094★
"Customs Worker" in *Public and Community Services, Volume 11* of *Career Information Center* (pp. 94-95)
Glencoe/Macmillan
15319 Chatsworth St.
Mission Hills, CA 91345   Phone: (818)898-1391
Richard Lidz and Dale Anderson, editorial directors. Fourth edition, 1990. For 600 occupations, describes job duties, entry-level requirements, education and training needed, advancement possibilities, employment outlook, earnings and benefits. The set is divided into 12 volumes. Each volume includes jobs related under a broad career field. Volume 13 is the index. **Facsimile Number:** 818-365-5489.

★2095★
Customs Workers
Careers, Inc.
PO Box 135
Largo, FL 34649-0135   Phone: (813)584-7333
1989. Two-page occupational summary card describing duties, working conditions, personal qualifications, training, earnings and hours, employment outlook, places of employment, related careers and where to write for more information.

★2096★

★2096★
A Day in the Life of a Police Detective
Troll Associates
100 Corporate Dr.
Mahwah, NJ 07430   Phone: (201)529-4000
David Paige. 1981. **Toll-free/Additional Phone Number(s):** 800-526-5289. **Facsimile Number:** (201)529-9347.

★2097★
"Detective" in *Public and Community Services*, Volume 11 of *Career Information Center* (pp. 72-73)
Glencoe/Macmillan
15319 Chatsworth St.
Mission Hills, CA 91345   Phone: (818)898-1391
Richard Lidz and Dale Anderson, editorial directors. Fourth edition, 1990. For 600 occupations, describes job duties, entry-level requirements, education and training needed, advancement possibilities, employment outlook, earnings and benefits. The set is divided into 12 volumes. Each volume includes jobs related under a broad career field. Volume 13 is the index. **Facsimile Number:** 818-365-5489.

★2098★
Detective, Police
Careers, Inc.
PO Box 135
Largo, FL 34649-0135   Phone: (813)584-7333
1988. Two-page occupational summary card describing duties, working conditions, personal qualifications, training, earnings and hours, employment outlook, places of employment, related careers and where to write for more information.

★2099★
Face Unique Challenges With the FBI: A Career as a Special Agent
U.S. Department of Justice
Federal Bureau of Investigation
Applicant Recruiting Office
1900 Half St., S.W.
Washington, DC 20535   Phone: (202)324-3000
1989. This eight-page booklet describes the work of an FBI Special Agent. Covers entry requirements, the application process, training, and advancement possibilities. Lists FBI field offices with phone numbers.

★2100★
"FBI Agent" in *Action Careers: Employment in the High-Risk Job Market* (pp. 47-58)
Citadel Press/Lyle Stuart Inc.
Carol Publishing Group
120 Enterprise Ave.
Secaucus, NJ 07094   Phone: (201)866-0490
Ragnar Benson. 1988. Describes 24 dangerous careers such as repo man, explosives handler, and river rafting guide. Each profile includes demand for the job, where the jobs can be found, required personal and physical characteristics and training needed.

★2101★
"FBI Agents" in Volume 3 of *Career Discovery Encyclopedia* (pp. 20-21)
J.G. Ferguson Publishing Co.
200 W. Monroe
Chicago, IL 60606   Phone: (312)580-5480
E. Russell Primm, editor-in-chief. 1990. Contains two-page articles on 504 occupations. Each article describes job duties, earnings, and educational and training requirements.

★2102★
"FBI Agents" in Volume 3 of *The Encyclopedia of Careers and Vocational Guidance* (pp. 236-239)
J.G. Ferguson Publishing Co.
200 W. Monroe
Chicago, IL 60606   Phone: (312)580-5480
William E. Hopke, editor-in-chief. Eighth edition, 1990. Four-volume set that profiles 500 occupations and describes job trends in 76 industries. Includes career description, educational requirements, history of the job, methods of entry, advancement, employment outlook, earnings, working conditions, social and psychological factors, and sources of additional information.

★2103★
"FBI Special Agent" in *Public and Community Services*, Volume 11 of *Career Information Center* (pp. 95-96)
Glencoe/Macmillan
15319 Chatsworth St.
Mission Hills, CA 91345   Phone: (818)898-1391
Richard Lidz and Dale Anderson, editorial directors. Fourth edition, 1990. For 600 occupations, describes job duties, entry-level requirements, education and training needed, advancement possibilities, employment outlook, earnings and benefits. The set is divided into 12 volumes. Each volume includes jobs related under a broad career field. Volume 13 is the index. **Facsimile Number:** 818-365-5489.

★2104★
"FBI Special Agent" in *VGM's Careers Encyclopedia* (pp. 173-175)
National Textbook Co.
4255 W. Touhy Ave.
Lincolnwood, IL 60646   Phone: (312)679-5500
Third edition, 1991. Contains two- to five-page descriptions of 200 managerial, professional, technical, trade, and service occupations. Each profile includes job duties, places of employment, qualifications, educational preparation, training, employment potential, advancement, income, and additional sources of information.

★2105★
FBI Special Agents
Chronicle Guidance Publications, Inc.
PO Box 1190
Moravia, NY 13118-1190   Phone: (315)497-0330
1991. This career brief describes the nature of the work, working conditions, hours and earnings, education and training, licensure, certification, unions, personal qualifications, social and psychological factors, employment outlook, entry methods, advancement, and related occupations. **Toll-free/Additional Phone Number(s):** 800-622-7284.

★2106★
FBI Special Agents
Careers, Inc.
PO Box 135
Largo, FL 34649-0135   Phone: (813)584-7333
1992. Eight-page brief offering the definition, history, duties, working conditions, personal qualifications, educational requirements, earnings, hours, employment outlook, advancement possibilities, and related occupations.

Police, Detectives, and Special Agents

★2107★
"FBI Special Agents" in *Occu-Facts: Information on 565 Careers in Outline Form* (p. 13.6)
Careers, Inc.
P.O. Box 135
1211 Tenth St., S.W.
Largo, FL 33640   Phone: (813)584-7333

Elizabeth Handville. Biennial, 1989-90 edition. Each one-page occupational profile describes duties, working conditions, physical surroundings and demands, aptitudes, temperament, educational requirements, employment outlook, earnings, and places of employment.

★2108★
"Federal Bureau of Investigation" in *Exploring Careers Using Foreign Languages* (pp. 67-69)
Rosen Publishing Group, Inc.
29 E. 21st St.
New York, NY 10010   Phone: (212)777-3017

E. W. Edwards. Revised edition, 1990. Explores careers in teaching, translating, interpreting, business and finance, government, communications, and the media. Covers employment ideas, salaries, job duties, and educational preparation. Contains information on accreditation and job hunting.

★2109★
"Federal Bureau of Investigation" in *Law Enforcement Employment Guide* (pp. 130-131)
Lawman Press
PO Box 1468
Mt. Shasta, CA 96067   Phone: (818)344-6146

Ron Stern. Second edition, 1990. Provides hiring information for 78 federal, state, and local law enforcement agencies across the United States that are currently hiring. Each agency profile contains selection criteria, information about the application and testing process, salaries, benefits, and career ladders. Offers advice on taking tests and interviewing.

★2110★
How to Get a Job With the Police Department: Police Officer
Barnes and Noble Books
10 E. 53rd St.
New York, NY 10022   Phone: (217)207-7000

Stephen M. Good. First edition, 1985.

★2111★
Internal Revenue Agent
Careers, Inc.
PO Box 135
Largo, FL 34649-0135   Phone: (813)584-7333

1988. Eight-page brief offering the definition, history, duties, working conditions, personal qualifications, educational requirements, earnings, hours, employment outlook, advancement possibilities, and related occupations.

★2112★
"Internal Revenue Agent" in *Occu-Facts: Information on 565 Careers in Outline Form* (p. 1.50)
Careers, Inc.
P.O. Box 135
1211 Tenth St., S.W.
Largo, FL 33640   Phone: (813)584-7333

Elizabeth Handville. Biennial, 1989-90 edition. Each one-page occupational profile describes duties, working conditions, physical surroundings and demands, aptitudes, temperament, educational requirements, employment outlook, earnings, and places of employment.

★2113★
"Internal Revenue Agent" in *VGM's Careers Encyclopedia* (pp. 227-229)
National Textbook Co.
4255 W. Touhy Ave.
Lincolnwood, IL 60646   Phone: (312)679-5500

Third edition, 1991. Contains two- to five-page descriptions of 200 managerial, professional, technical, trade, and service occupations. Each profile includes job duties, places of employment, qualifications, educational preparation, training, employment potential, advancement, income, and additional sources of information.

★2114★
Internal Revenue Service Agent
Vocational Biographies, Inc.
PO Box 31, Dept. VF10
Sauk Centre, MN 56378   Phone: (612)352-6516

1988. This pamphlet profiles a person working in the job. Includes information about job duties, working conditions, places of employment, educational preparation, labor market outlook, and salaries. **Toll-free/Additional Phone Number(s):** 800-255-0752.

★2115★
Law Enforcement
AIMS Media, Inc.
9710 DeSoto Ave.
Chatsworth, CA 93111-4409   Phone: (818)773-4300

Videocassette. 1988. 30 mins. This tape from the "Career Awareness" series showcases jobs in law enforcement.

★2116★
Law Enforcement Careers: A Complete Guide from Application to Employment
Lawman Press
PO Box 1468
Mt. Shasta, CA 96067   Phone: (818)344-6146

Ron Stern. 1988. Law enforcement job hunting guide covering the following topics: submitting an application, taking the written examination and oral interview, passing the physical agility test, and going through medical, psychological and polygraph screening. Describes police academy training and life as a police officer. Lists federal and state law enforcement offices.

★2117★
Law Enforcement Employment Guide
Lawman Press
PO Box 1468
Mt. Shasta, CA 96067   Phone: (818)344-6146

Ron Stern. Second edition, 1990. Provides hiring information for 78 federal, state, and local law enforcement agencies across the United States that are currently hiring. Each agency profile contains selection criteria, information about the application and testing process, salaries, benefits, and career ladders. Offers advice on taking tests and interviewing.

★2118★
"Law Enforcement" in *The Career Connection II: A Guide to Technical Majors and Their Related Careers* (pp. 81-82)
ERIS
PO Box 7509
University Station
Provo, UT 84602-0509

Fred A. Rowe. 1988. Contains technical majors, such as automotive technology. Describes the major and the job. Lists high school and postsecondary school courses. Includes occupations related to the major, employment outlook, and starting salary.

★2119★
"Municipal Police Officer" in *VGM's Careers Encyclopedia* (pp. 361-364)
National Textbook Co.
4255 W. Touhy Ave.
Lincolnwood, IL 60646   Phone: (312)679-5500

Third edition, 1991. Contains two- to five-page descriptions of 200 managerial, professional, technical, trade, and service occupations. Each profile includes job duties, places of employment, qualifications, educational preparation, training, employment potential, advancement, income, and additional sources of information.

★2120★
Obtaining Your Private Investigator's License
Paladin Press
PO Box 1307
Boulder, CO 80306   Phone: (303)443-7250

Orion Agency, Inc. Staff. 1986. **Facsimile Number:** (303)442-8741.

★2121★
Opportunities in Law Enforcement and Criminal Justice Careers
National Textbook Co.
4255 W. Touhy Ave.
Lincolnwood, IL 60646   Phone: (312)679-5500

James D. Stinchcomb. 1990. Describes law enforcement and related positions at the city, county, state, and federal levels and in the military. Covers trends, future outlook, personal qualities, selection requirements, salaries, working conditions, and educational preparation.

★2122★
Personal Service Cluster
Center for Humanities, Inc.
Communications Park
Box 1000
Mount Kisco, NY 10549   Phone: (914)666-4100

Videocassette. 1984. 20 mins. Students get to see the day-by-day lives of people who work in the fields of cosmetology, food service and law enforcement.

★2123★
"Police and Detectives" in *Opportunities in Vocational and Technical Careers* (pp. 74-75)
National Textbook Co.
4255 W. Touhy Ave.
Lincolnwood, IL 60646   Phone: (312)679-5500

Adrian A. Paradis. 1987. Describes careers which can be prepared for by attending a private vocational or proprietary school—office employee, sales worker, service worker, health services, mechanic, craftworker, and technician. Covers employment outlook, job duties, and salaries. Offers career planning advice.

★2124★
"Police Detective" in *Occu-Facts: Information on 565 Careers in Outline Form* (p. 13.5)
Careers, Inc.
P.O. Box 135
1211 Tenth St., S.W.
Largo, FL 33640   Phone: (813)584-7333

Elizabeth Handville. Biennial, 1989-90 edition. Each one-page occupational profile describes duties, working conditions, physical surroundings and demands, aptitudes, temperament, educational requirements, employment outlook, earnings, and places of employment.

★2125★
The Police Detective Function
Charles C. Thomas, Publisher
2600 S. 1st St.
Springfield, IL 62794-9265   Phone: (217)789-8980

V. A. Leonard. 1970. **Facsimile Number:** (217)789-9130.

★2126★
"Police Detective" in *Straight Talk on Careers: 80 Pros Take You Into Their Professions* (pp. 236-238)
Garrett Park Press
PO Box 190
Garrett Park, MD 20896   Phone: (301)946-2553

Mary Barbera-Hogan. 1987. Written for readers in high school and college. Contains candid interviews from professionals who discuss what their days are like and the pros and cons of their occupations.

★2127★
"Police, Detectives, and Special Agents" in *Occupational Outlook Handbook* (pp. 290-293)
Superintendent of Documents
U.S. Government Printing Office
Washington, DC 20402   Phone: (202)783-3238

Biennial; latest edition, 1990-91. Encyclopedia of careers describing more than 250 occupations and comprising about 86 percent of all jobs in the economy. Occupations that require lengthy education or training are given the most attention. For each occupation, the handbook describes job duties, working conditions, training, educational preparation, personal qualities, advancement possibilities, job outlook, earnings, and sources of additional information.

★2128★
"Police, Detectives, and Special Agents" in *101 Careers: A Guide to the Fastest-Growing Opportunities* (pp. 140-144)
John Wiley & Sons, Inc.
605 Third Ave.
New York, NY 10158   Phone: (212)850-6000

Michael Harkavy. 1990. Each occupational profile includes a job description, job titles, work environment, employment outlook, qualifications, personal skills, and earnings.

★2129★
"Police" in *The American Almanac of Jobs and Salaries* (pp. 98-102)
Avon Books
105 Madison Avenue
New York, NY 10016   Phone: (212)481-5600

John Wright and Edward J. Dwyer. Revised and updated, 1990. A comprehensive guide to the wages of hundreds of occupations in a wide variety of industries and organizations.

★2130★
Police Officer
Careers, Inc.
PO Box 135
Largo, FL 34649-0135   Phone: (813)584-7333

1990. Two-page occupational summary card describing duties, working conditions, personal qualifications, training, earnings and hours, employment outlook, places of employment, related careers and where to write for more information.

Police, Detectives, and Special Agents ★2142★

★2131★
Police Officer
Vocational Biographies, Inc.
PO Box 31, Dept. VF10
Sauk Centre, MN 56378   Phone: (612)352-6516
1990. This pamphlet profiles a person working in the job. Includes information about job duties, working conditions, places of employment, educational preparation, labor market outlook, and salaries. **Toll-free/Additional Phone Number(s):** 800-255-0752.

★2132★
Police Officer
Prentice Hall
Rte. 9W
Englewood Cliffs, NJ 07632   Phone: (201)592-2000
Robert Panzarella. Tenth edition, 1989.

★2133★
"Police Officer" in *Hard Hatted Women: Stories of Struggle and Success in the Trades* (pp. 71-80)
Seal Press
3131 Western Ave., Ste. 410
Seattle, WA 98121   Phone: (206)283-7844
Molly Martin, editor. 1988. Twenty-six women recount their experiences working in blue collar occupations. They describe how they got in, the work they do, their relationships in predominantly male occupations, and their training.

★2134★
"Police Officer" in *Occu-Facts: Information on 565 Careers in Outline Form* (p. 13.7)
Careers, Inc.
P.O. Box 135
1211 Tenth St., S.W.
Largo, FL 33640   Phone: (813)584-7333
Elizabeth Handville. Biennial, 1989-90 edition. Each one-page occupational profile describes duties, working conditions, physical surroundings and demands, aptitudes, temperament, educational requirements, employment outlook, earnings, and places of employment.

★2135★
"Police Officer" in *Public and Community Services, Volume 11 of Career Information Center* (pp. 57-58)
Glencoe/Macmillan
15319 Chatsworth St.
Mission Hills, CA 91345   Phone: (818)898-1391
Richard Lidz and Dale Anderson, editorial directors. Fourth edition, 1990. For 600 occupations, describes job duties, entry-level requirements, education and training needed, advancement possibilities, employment outlook, earnings and benefits. The set is divided into 12 volumes. Each volume includes jobs related under a broad career field. Volume 13 is the index. **Facsimile Number:** 818-365-5489.

★2136★
"Police Officer" in *Top Professions: The 100 Most Popular, Dynamic, and Profitable Careers in America Today* (pp. 40-41)
Peterson's Guides, Inc.
202 Carnegie Center
PO Box 2123
Princeton, NJ 08543-2123   Phone: (609)243-9111
Nicholas Basta. 1989. Includes occupations requiring a college or advanced degree. Describes job duties, earnings, some typical job titles, career opportunities at different degree levels, and lists related associations.

★2137★
Police Officers
Chronicle Guidance Publications, Inc.
PO Box 1190
Moravia, NY 13118-1190   Phone: (315)497-0330
1991. This career brief describes the nature of the work, working conditions, hours and earnings, education and training, licensure, certification, unions, personal qualifications, social and psychological factors, employment outlook, entry methods, advancement, and related occupations. **Toll-free/Additional Phone Number(s):** 800-622-7284.

★2138★
"Police Officers" in *Jobs! What They Are...Where They Are...What They Pay* (pp. 191-192)
Simon & Schuster, Inc.
Simon & Schuster Bldg.
1230 Avenue of the Americas
New York, NY 10020   Phone: (212)698-7000
Robert O. Snelling and Anne M. Snelling. Revised edition, 1989. Profiles 241 occupations, describing duties and responsibilities, educational preparation, earnings, employment opportunities, training, and qualifications.

★2139★
"Police Officers" in Volume 5 of *Career Discovery Encyclopedia* (pp. 68-69)
J.G. Ferguson Publishing Co.
200 W. Monroe
Chicago, IL 60606   Phone: (312)580-5480
E. Russell Primm, editor-in-chief. 1990. Contains two-page articles on 504 occupations. Each article describes job duties, earnings, and educational and training requirements.

★2140★
"Police Officers" in Volume 3 of *The Encyclopedia of Careers and Vocational Guidance* (pp. 298-302)
J.G. Ferguson Publishing Co.
200 W. Monroe
Chicago, IL 60606   Phone: (312)580-5480
William E. Hopke, editor-in-chief. Eighth edition, 1990. Four-volume set that profiles 500 occupations and describes job trends in 76 industries. Includes career description, educational requirements, history of the job, methods of entry, advancement, employment outlook, earnings, working conditions, social and psychological factors, and sources of additional information.

★2141★
"Police Search & Recovery" in *Footsteps in the Ocean: Careers in Diving* (pp. 109-114)
Lodestar Books
2 Park Avenue
New York, NY 10016   Phone: (212)725-1818
Denise V. Lang. 1987. Explores employment opportunities in sport and commercial diving, science and research, in the military, and police work. Describes the work and training. Lists schools. **Facsimile Number:** (212)532-6568.

★2142★
"Police Sergeant" in *Straight Talk on Careers: 80 Pros Take You Into Their Professions* (pp. 233-235)
Garrett Park Press
PO Box 190
Garrett Park, MD 20896   Phone: (301)946-2553
Mary Barbera-Hogan. 1987. Written for readers in high school and college. Contains candid interviews from professionals who discuss what their days are like and the pros and cons of their occupations.

★2143★
"Secret Service Agent" in *Action Careers: Employment in the High-Risk Job Market* (pp. 211-221)
Citadel Press/Lyle Stuart Inc.
Carol Publishing Group
120 Enterprise Ave.
Secaucus, NJ 07094   Phone: (201)866-0490

Ragnar Benson. 1988. Describes 24 dangerous careers such as repo man, explosives handler, and river rafting guide. Each profile includes demand for the job, where the jobs can be found, required personal and physical characteristics and training needed.

★2144★
"Secret Service Agent" in *VGM's Careers Encyclopedia* (pp. 421-424)
National Textbook Co.
4255 W. Touhy Ave.
Lincolnwood, IL 60646   Phone: (312)679-5500

Third edition, 1991. Contains two- to five-page descriptions of 200 managerial, professional, technical, trade, and service occupations. Each profile includes job duties, places of employment, qualifications, educational preparation, training, employment potential, advancement, income, and additional sources of information.

★2145★
So You Want to Be a Cop
EES Publications
1120 Royal Palm Beach Blvd., No. 216
Royal Palm Beach, FL 33411   Phone: (407)795-7475

Frank Pickens. 1990.

★2146★
State Police/Highway Patrol Officer
Careers, Inc.
PO Box 135
Largo, FL 34649-0135   Phone: (813)584-7333

1990. Two-page occupational summary card describing duties, working conditions, personal qualifications, training, earnings and hours, employment outlook, places of employment, related careers and where to write for more information.

★2147★
"State Police/Highway Patrol Officer" in *Occu-Facts: Information on 565 Careers in Outline Form* (p. 13.8)
Careers, Inc.
P.O. Box 135
1211 Tenth St., S.W.
Largo, FL 33640   Phone: (813)584-7333

Elizabeth Handville. Biennial, 1989-90 edition. Each one-page occupational profile describes duties, working conditions, physical surroundings and demands, aptitudes, temperament, educational requirements, employment outlook, earnings, and places of employment.

★2148★
"State Police Officer" in *Public and Community Services, Volume 11 of Career Information Center* (pp. 66-67)
Glencoe/Macmillan
15319 Chatsworth St.
Mission Hills, CA 91345   Phone: (818)898-1391

Richard Lidz and Dale Anderson, editorial directors. Fourth edition, 1990. For 600 occupations, describes job duties, entry-level requirements, education and training needed, advancement possibilities, employment outlook, earnings and benefits. The set is divided into 12 volumes. Each volume includes jobs related under a broad career field. Volume 13 is the index. **Facsimile Number:** 818-365-5489.

★2149★
"State Police Officer" in *VGM's Careers Encyclopedia* (pp. 364-366)
National Textbook Co.
4255 W. Touhy Ave.
Lincolnwood, IL 60646   Phone: (312)679-5500

Third edition, 1991. Contains two- to five-page descriptions of 200 managerial, professional, technical, trade, and service occupations. Each profile includes job duties, places of employment, qualifications, educational preparation, training, employment potential, advancement, income, and additional sources of information.

★2150★
"State Police Officers" in Volume 6 of *Career Discovery Encyclopedia* (pp. 58-59)
J.G. Ferguson Publishing Co.
200 W. Monroe
Chicago, IL 60606   Phone: (312)580-5480

E. Russell Primm, editor-in-chief. 1990. Contains two-page articles on 504 occupations. Each article describes job duties, earnings, and educational and training requirements.

★2151★
"State Police Officers" in Volume 3 of *The Encyclopedia of Careers and Vocational Guidance* (pp. 316-320)
J.G. Ferguson Publishing Co.
200 W. Monroe
Chicago, IL 60606   Phone: (312)580-5480

William E. Hopke, editor-in-chief. Eighth edition, 1990. Four-volume set that profiles 500 occupations and describes job trends in 76 industries. Includes career description, educational requirements, history of the job, methods of entry, advancement, employment outlook, earnings, working conditions, social and psychological factors, and sources of additional information.

★2152★
State Trooper
Vocational Biographies, Inc.
PO Box 31, Dept. VF10
Sauk Centre, MN 56378   Phone: (612)352-6516

19901 This pamphlet profiles a person working in the job. Includes information about job duties, working conditions, places of employment, educational preparation, labor market outlook, and salaries. **Toll-free/Additional Phone Number(s):** 800-255-0752.

★2153★
"Texas Ranger" in *Offbeat Careers: The Directory of Unusual Work* (pp. 165-166)
Ten Speed Press
PO Box 7123
Berkeley, CA 94707   Phone: (415)845-8414

Al Sacharov. 1988. Profiles eighty-eight unusual careers. Provides job description, history of occupation, salary, and training required. Lists one or more sources of additional information.

★2154★
Traffic Patrol Officer
Vocational Biographies, Inc.
PO Box 31, Dept. VF10
Sauk Centre, MN 56378   Phone: (612)352-6516

1988. This pamphlet profiles a person working in the job. Includes information about job duties, working conditions, places of employment, educational preparation, labor market outlook, and salaries. **Toll-free/Additional Phone Number(s):** 800-255-0752.

Police, Detectives, and Special Agents

★2155★
"United States Customs Service" in *Opportunities in Transportation Careers* (pp. 130-132)
National Textbook Co.
4255 W. Touhy Ave.
Lincolnwood, IL 60646　　　　　Phone: (312)679-5500
Adrian A. Paradis. 1988. Describes transportation and related employment in driving occupations, the airlines, merchant marine, and travel services. Covers employment outlook, educational and training requirements, wages, and the work itself, and advantages and disadvantages of transportation careers. Offers job hunting advice.

★2156★
U.S. Special Agent
Vocational Biographies, Inc.
PO Box 31, Dept. VF10
Sauk Centre, MN 56378　　　　　Phone: (612)352-6516
1989. This pamphlet profiles a person working in the job. Includes information about job duties, working conditions, places of employment, educational preparation, labor market outlook, and salaries. **Toll-free/Additional Phone Number(s):** 800-255-0752.

★2157★
Video Career Library - Public and Personal Services
Careers, Inc.
1211 10th St., SW
PO Box 135
Largo, FL 34649-0135　　　　　Phone: (813)584-7333
Videocassette. 1990. 35 mins. Part of the Video Career Library covering 165 occupations. Shows actual workers on the job. Includes firefighters, police officers, correctional officers, bartenders, waiters/waitresses, cooks/chefs, child care workers, flight attendants, barbers/cosmetologists, groundskeepers/gardeners, and butchers/meat cutters.

Associations

★2158★
American Police Academy (APA)
Lock Box 15350
Chevy Chase, MD 20815　　　　　Phone: (202)293-9088
Membership: Educational arm of the American Federation of Police and International Association of Chiefs of Police. Law enforcement officers who have completed advanced training offered by the academy for on-duty police officers and security personnel. **Purpose:** Establishes professional certification standards for career officers. Conducts workshops and home study programs. Maintains film, slide, and videotape collection, biographical archives, and 600 volume library of law enforcement-related publications. Operates speakers' bureau and placement service; bestows awards; compiles statistics. **Publications:** *Police Times Magazine*, bimonthly. ● *Who's Who in Law Enforcement*, triennial.

★2159★
Association of Federal Investigators (AFI)
3299 K St. NW, 7th Fl.
Washington, DC 20007　　　　　Phone: (202)337-5234
Membership: Persons currently or formerly engaged in investigations, enforcement, security, and related activities for the federal government. **Purpose:** Has established professional standards of work, education, and conduct. Serves as a vehicle for exchange of ideas and broadening of professional contacts; conducts specialized education programs; offers placement service. Addresses such topics as advanced white collar crime investigations, suitability investigations, terrorism, and adjudication standards. Presents awards; annually offers scholarship award. Supports charitable programs. Conducts monthly educational seminars and workshops. **Publications:** *AFI Report*, bimonthly. ● *Association of Federal Investigators—Membership Directory*, annual. ● *The Investigators' Journal*, annual. ● Also published *Investigative and Related Positions in the Federal Government*. **Facsimile Number:** (202)333-5365.

★2160★
Center for Intelligence Studies (CIS)
301 S. Columbus St.
Alexandria, VA 22314　　　　　Phone: (703)684-0625
Membership: Participants contribute to SIF activities in support of the Federal Bureau of Investigation, the National Security Agency, the Defense Intelligence Agency, and the Central Intelligence Agency. **Purpose:** Disseminates information and offers congressional advice on policies, legislation, and activities that affect the capabilities of the FBI, NSA, DIA, or CIA. Maintains extensive files on intelligence group operations and press-related stories. Offers scholarships. Operates placement service and speakers' bureau; conducts research; bestows awards. Holds seminars. **Publications:** *Intelligence Issues*, monthly. ● *Nightwatch*, quarterly. ● Also publishes special reports.

★2161★
International Security and Detective Alliance (ISDA)
PO Box 6303
Corpus Christi, TX 78466-6303　　　　　Phone: (512)888-6164
Membership: Detectives, security and police officers, and investigators; interested others. **Purpose:** Seeks to create a networking and referral system; support the advancement of the security and investigation profession; establish a freelance organization for independent operators, enroll professionals and interested citizens in the field of security and investigation. Provides educational and informational materials and courses. Sets standards for and awards Professional Trade Designations and certifications. Offers training materials, books, information, custom badges, and equipment. Maintains speakers' bureau and library of 300 volumes. Bestows honorary commissioned rank and other awards based on service, life, and work experiences. Sponsors benefit programs including group life, health, and accident insurance. Compiles statistics on state and other government licensure procedures.

★2162★
National Association of Investigative Specialists (NAIS)
PO Box 33244
Austin, TX 78764　　　　　Phone: (512)832-0355
Membership: Private investigators, automobile repossessors, bounty hunters, and law enforcement officers. **Purpose:** Promotes professionalism and provides for information exchange among private investigators. Lobbies for investigative regulations. Offers training programs and issues certificates of completion. Sponsors charitable programs; compiles statistics; maintains speakers' bureau and placement service. Operates 700 volume library, biographical archives, and Investigators' Hall of Fame of Private Investigators. Presents award to outstanding investigators. Offers seminars on cassette tape.

★2163★
National Police Officers Association of America (NPOAA)
1316 Gardiner Ln., Ste. 204
Louisville, KY 40213　　　　　Phone: (502)451-7550
Membership: Professional and fraternal benefit organization of full-time police officers of federal, state, county, and local police departments. **Purpose:** Issues awards for police work including good arrests, bravery, merit, and valor. Offers scholarships. **Publications:** *Enforcement Journal*, quarterly.

★2164★
Society of Professional Investigators (SPI)
239 W. 52 St.
New York, NY 10019　　　　　　　　　Phone: (212)245-8330
Membership: Persons with at least 5 years investigative experience for an official federal, state, or local government agency or for a quasi-official agency formed for law enforcement or related activities. **Purpose:** Seeks to advance knowledge of the science and technology of professional investigation, law enforcement, and police science; maintains high standards and ethics; promotes efficiency of investigators in the services they perform. Grants annual award; Maintains library of books and studies on law enforcement; holds monthly seminar. **Facsimile Number:** (212)581-3217.

Standards/Certification Agencies

★2165★
American Police Academy (APA)
Lock Box 15350
Chevy Chase, MD 20815　　　　　　　Phone: (202)293-9088
Establishes professional certification standards for career officers. Conducts workshops and home study programs.

★2166★
Association of Federal Investigators (AFI)
3299 K St. NW, 7th Fl.
Washington, DC 20007　　　　　　　Phone: (202)337-5234
Has established professional standards of work, education, and conduct.

★2167★
Federal Bureau of Investigation (FBI)
Applicant Recruiting Office
1900 Half St. SW
Washington, DC 20535
Provides information concerning qualifications of FBI special agents.

★2168★
International Security and Detective Alliance (ISDA)
PO Box 6303
Corpus Christi, TX 78466-6303　　　　Phone: (512)888-6164
Sets standards for and awards Professional Trade Designations and certifications.

★2169★
National Association of Investigative Specialists (NAIS)
PO Box 33244
Austin, TX 78764　　　　　　　　　　Phone: (512)832-0355
Offers training programs and issues certificates of completion.

Test Guides

★2170★
Capital Police Officer
National Learning Corp.
212 Michael Dr.
Syosset, NY 11791　　　　　　　　　　Phone: (516)921-8888
Jack Rudman. Part of the Career Examination Series No. 1. All examination guides in this series contain questions with answers. **Facsimile Number:** (516)921-8743. **Toll-free/Additional Phone Number(s):** 800-645-6337.

★2171★
Captain, Police Dept.
National Learning Corp.
212 Michael Dr.
Syosset, NY 11791　　　　　　　　　　Phone: (516)921-8888
Jack Rudman. Part of the Career Examination Series No. 1. All examination guides in this series contain questions with answers. **Facsimile Number:** (516)921-8743. **Toll-free/Additional Phone Number(s):** 800-645-6337.

★2172★
Chief Deputy Sheriff
National Learning Corp.
212 Michael Dr.
Syosset, NY 11791　　　　　　　　　　Phone: (516)921-8888
Jack Rudman. Part of the Career Examination Series No. 1. All examination guides in this series contain questions with answers. **Facsimile Number:** (516)921-8743. **Toll-free/Additional Phone Number(s):** 800-645-6337.

★2173★
Chief of Police
National Learning Corp.
212 Michael Dr.
Syosset, NY 11791　　　　　　　　　　Phone: (516)921-8888
Jack Rudman. Part of the Career Examination Series No. 1. All examination guides in this series contain questions with answers. **Facsimile Number:** (516)921-8743. **Toll-free/Additional Phone Number(s):** 800-645-6337.

★2174★
Chief of Staff (Sheriff)
National Learning Corp.
212 Michael Dr.
Syosset, NY 11791　　　　　　　　　　Phone: (516)921-8888
Jack Rudman. Part of the Career Examination Series No. 1. All examination guides in this series contain questions with answers. **Facsimile Number:** (516)921-8743. **Toll-free/Additional Phone Number(s):** 800-645-6337.

★2175★
Chief Special Investigator
National Learning Corp.
212 Michael Dr.
Syosset, NY 11791　　　　　　　　　　Phone: (516)921-8888
Jack Rudman. Part of the Career Examination Series No. 1. All examination guides in this series contain questions with answers. **Facsimile Number:** (516)921-8743. **Toll-free/Additional Phone Number(s):** 800-645-6337.

★2176★
Deputy Chief Marshal
National Learning Corp.
212 Michael Dr.
Syosset, NY 11791　　　　　　　　　　Phone: (516)921-8888
Jack Rudman. Part of the Career Examination Series No. 1. All examination guides in this series contain questions with answers. **Facsimile Number:** (516)921-8743. **Toll-free/Additional Phone Number(s):** 800-645-6337.

★2177★
Deputy Sheriff
National Learning Corp.
212 Michael Dr.
Syosset, NY 11791　　　　　　　　　　Phone: (516)921-8888
Jack Rudman. Part of the Career Examination Series No. 1. All examination guides in this series contain questions with answers. **Facsimile Number:** (516)921-8743. **Toll-free/Additional Phone Number(s):** 800-645-6337.

Police, Detectives, and Special Agents

★2178★
Detective Investigator
National Learning Corp.
212 Michael Dr.
Syosset, NY 11791 Phone: (516)921-8888
Jack Rudman. Part of the Career Examination Series No. 1. All examination guides in this series contain questions with answers. **Facsimile Number:** (516)921-8743. **Toll-free/Additional Phone Number(s):** 800-645-6337.

★2179★
Drug Enforcement Agent
Prentice Hall Press
Simon & Schuster Inc.
200 Old Tappan Rd.
Old Tappan, NJ 07675 Phone: (800)223-2348
Francis Mullen. First edition, 1989. Includes a complete DEA exam battery, information on firearms tests, and review of drugs of abuse.

★2180★
FBI Entrance Examination
Prentice Hall Press
Simon & Schuster Inc.
200 Old Tappan Rd.
Old Tappan, NJ 07675 Phone: (800)223-2348
John Quirk. First edition, 1988. Provides sample exam, job application information, breakdown of jobs available with the FBI, interview with FBI personnel, and a history of the FBI.

★2181★
How to Prepare for the Police Officer Examination Including Transit and Housing Officer
Barron's Educational Series, Inc.
PO Box 8040
250 Wireless Blvd.
Hauppauge, NY 11788 Phone: (516)434-3311
Donald J. Schroeder and Frank A. Lombardo. Manual offers four full-length practice exams, including the official exams used by the New York City Police Department. Includes answers with explanations and test-taking strategies. **Toll-free/Additional Phone Number(s):** 800-645-3476 (in NY call 800-257-5729).

★2182★
How to Prepare for the Police Sergeant Examination
Barron's Educational Series, Inc.
PO Box 8040
250 Wireless Blvd.
Hauppauge, NY 11788 Phone: (516)434-3311
Donald J. Schroeder and Frank A. Lombardo. Manual presents four diagnostic exams with explained answers. **Toll-free/Additional Phone Number(s):** 800-645-3476 (in NY call 800-257-5729).

★2183★
Police Administration Aide
National Learning Corp.
212 Michael Dr.
Syosset, NY 11791 Phone: (516)921-8888
Jack Rudman. Part of the Career Examination Series No. 1. All examination guides in this series contain questions with answers. **Facsimile Number:** (516)921-8743. **Toll-free/Additional Phone Number(s):** 800-645-6337.

★2184★
Police Administration & Supervision
National Learning Corp.
212 Michael Dr.
Syosset, NY 11791 Phone: (516)921-8888
Jack Rudman. Part of the General Aptitude and Abilities Series No. 2. Books in this series provide functional, intensive test practice and drill in the basic skills and areas common to many examinations, as well as general aptitude or achievement necessary for entrance into many occupations or positions. **Facsimile Number:** (516)921-8743. **Toll-free/Additional Phone Number(s):** 800-645-6337.

★2185★
Police Administrative Aide
Prentice Hall Press
Simon & Schuster Inc.
200 Old Tappan Rd.
Old Tappan, NJ 07675 Phone: (800)223-2348
Hy Hammer. Second edition, 1983. Complete test preparation for the postions of civilian police aide and 911 operator. Covers all major subject areas and includes two practice exams.

★2186★
Police Attendant
National Learning Corp.
212 Michael Dr.
Syosset, NY 11791 Phone: (516)921-8888
Jack Rudman. Part of the Career Examination Series No. 1. All examination guides in this series contain questions with answers. **Facsimile Number:** (516)921-8743. **Toll-free/Additional Phone Number(s):** 800-645-6337.

★2187★
Police Cadet
National Learning Corp.
212 Michael Dr.
Syosset, NY 11791 Phone: (516)921-8888
Jack Rudman. Part of the Career Examination Series No. 1. All examination guides in this series contain questions with answers. **Facsimile Number:** (516)921-8743. **Toll-free/Additional Phone Number(s):** 800-645-6337.

★2188★
Police Captain
National Learning Corp.
212 Michael Dr.
Syosset, NY 11791 Phone: (516)921-8888
Jack Rudman. Part of the Career Examination Series No. 1. All examination guides in this series contain questions with answers. **Facsimile Number:** (516)921-8743. **Toll-free/Additional Phone Number(s):** 800-645-6337.

★2189★
Police Chief
National Learning Corp.
212 Michael Dr.
Syosset, NY 11791 Phone: (516)921-8888
Jack Rudman. Part of the Career Examination Series No. 1. All examination guides in this series contain questions with answers. **Facsimile Number:** (516)921-8743. **Toll-free/Additional Phone Number(s):** 800-645-6337.

★2190★
Police Clerk
National Learning Corp.
212 Michael Dr.
Syosset, NY 11791   Phone: (516)921-8888
Jack Rudman. Part of the Career Examination Series No. 1. All examination guides in this series contain questions with answers. **Facsimile Number:** (516)921-8743. **Toll-free/Additional Phone Number(s):** 800-645-6337.

★2191★
Police Inspector
National Learning Corp.
212 Michael Dr.
Syosset, NY 11791   Phone: (516)921-8888
Jack Rudman. Part of the Career Examination Series No. 1. All examination guides in this series contain questions with answers. **Facsimile Number:** (516)921-8743. **Toll-free/Additional Phone Number(s):** 800-645-6337.

★2192★
Police Lieutenant
National Learning Corp.
212 Michael Dr.
Syosset, NY 11791   Phone: (516)921-8888
Jack Rudman. Part of the Career Examination Series No. 1. All examination guides in this series contain questions with answers. **Facsimile Number:** (516)921-8743. **Toll-free/Additional Phone Number(s):** 800-645-6337.

★2193★
Police Officer
Prentice Hall Press
Simon & Schuster Inc.
200 Old Tappan Rd.
Old Tappan, NJ 07675   Phone: (800)223-2348
Hugh O'Neill, Hy Hammer, and E.P. Steinberg. Tenth edition, 1989. Includes six sample exams with answers. Special feature covers physical, medical, and psychological screening tests.

★2194★
Police Officer
National Learning Corp.
212 Michael Dr.
Syosset, NY 11791   Phone: (516)921-8888
Jack Rudman. Part of the Career Examination Series No. 1. Guides are also available for the positions of police patrolman, police trainee, and policewomen. All examination guides in this series contain questions with answers. **Facsimile Number:** (516)921-8743. **Toll-free/Additional Phone Number(s):** 800-645-6337.

★2195★
Police Officer Exams Review
Video Aided Instruction, Inc.
182 Village Rd.
East Hills, NY 11577   Phone: (516)621-6176
Videocassette. 1990. 120 mins. This video summarizes the mental skills and attitudes necessary for work in the city, county, state, and other police agencies. It includes Test Taking Strategies, Reading Police Materials, Sizing up Suspicious Situations, Information Processing, Police Procedures, Police Reports, Maps and Traffic Diagrams, and Memorizing Faces, Scenes, and Facts.

★2196★
Police Promotion Course (One Volume)
National Learning Corp.
212 Michael Dr.
Syosset, NY 11791   Phone: (516)921-8888
Jack Rudman. Part of the General Aptitude and Abilities Series No. 2. Books in this series provide functional, intensive test practice and drill in the basic skills and areas common to many examinations, as well as general aptitude or achievement necessary for entrance into many occupations or positions. **Facsimile Number:** (516)921-8743. **Toll-free/Additional Phone Number(s):** 800-645-6337.

★2197★
Police Promotion Examinations
Prentice Hall Press
Simon & Schuster Inc.
200 Old Tappan Rd.
Old Tappan, NJ 07675   Phone: (800)223-2348
Hugh O'Neill. First edition, 1983. Provides preparation for the examinations that qualify police officers for promotion to sergeant, lieutenant, and other higher-level positions.

★2198★
Police Reading Comprehension
National Learning Corp.
212 Michael Dr.
Syosset, NY 11791   Phone: (516)921-8888
Jack Rudman. Part of the General Aptitude and Abilities Series No. 2. Books in this series provide functional, intensive test practice and drill in the basic skills and areas common to many examinations, as well as general aptitude or achievement necessary for entrance into many occupations or positions. **Facsimile Number:** (516)921-8743. **Toll-free/Additional Phone Number(s):** 800-645-6337.

★2199★
Principal Special Investigator
National Learning Corp.
212 Michael Dr.
Syosset, NY 11791   Phone: (516)921-8888
Jack Rudman. Part of the Career Examination Series No. 1. All examination guides in this series contain questions with answers. **Facsimile Number:** (516)921-8743. **Toll-free/Additional Phone Number(s):** 800-645-6337.

★2200★
Public Safety Officer
National Learning Corp.
212 Michael Dr.
Syosset, NY 11791   Phone: (516)921-8888
Jack Rudman. Part of the Career Examination Series No. 1. All examination guides in this series contain questions with answers. **Facsimile Number:** (516)921-8743. **Toll-free/Additional Phone Number(s):** 800-645-6337.

★2201★
Secret Service Agent
National Learning Corp.
212 Michael Dr.
Syosset, NY 11791   Phone: (516)921-8888
Jack Rudman. Part of the Career Examination Series No. 1. All examination guides in this series contain questions with answers. **Facsimile Number:** (516)921-8743. **Toll-free/Additional Phone Number(s):** 800-645-6337.

Police, Detectives, and Special Agents

★2202★
Senior Capital Police Officer
National Learning Corp.
212 Michael Dr.
Syosset, NY 11791　　　Phone: (516)921-8888
Jack Rudman. Part of the Career Examination Series No. 1. All examination guides in this series contain questions with answers. **Facsimile Number:** (516)921-8743. **Toll-free/Additional Phone Number(s):** 800-645-6337.

★2203★
Senior Deputy Sheriff
National Learning Corp.
212 Michael Dr.
Syosset, NY 11791　　　Phone: (516)921-8888
Jack Rudman. Part of the Career Examination Series No. 1. All examination guides in this series contain questions with answers. **Facsimile Number:** (516)921-8743. **Toll-free/Additional Phone Number(s):** 800-645-6337.

★2204★
Senior Detective Investigator
National Learning Corp.
212 Michael Dr.
Syosset, NY 11791　　　Phone: (516)921-8888
Jack Rudman. Part of the Career Examination Series No. 1. All examination guides in this series contain questions with answers. **Facsimile Number:** (516)921-8743. **Toll-free/Additional Phone Number(s):** 800-645-6337.

★2205★
Sheriff
National Learning Corp.
212 Michael Dr.
Syosset, NY 11791　　　Phone: (516)921-8888
Jack Rudman. Part of the Career Examination Series No. 1. All examination guides in this series contain questions with answers. **Facsimile Number:** (516)921-8743. **Toll-free/Additional Phone Number(s):** 800-645-6337.

★2206★
Special Agent
Prentice Hall Press
Simon & Schuster Inc.
200 Old Tappan Rd.
Old Tappan, NJ 07675　　　Phone: (800)223-2348
E.P. Steinberg. First edition, 1989. Complete guide to the Treasury Enforcement Agent test that all applicants must take for posts within the U.S. Treasury Department, including the branches of Secret Service, Customs Service, Internal Revenue Service, or Bureau of Alcohol, Tobacco, and Firearms. Contains three full-length sample exams with answers.

★2207★
Special Agent, Department of Justice
National Learning Corp.
212 Michael Dr.
Syosset, NY 11791　　　Phone: (516)921-8888
Jack Rudman. Part of the Career Examination Series No. 1. All examination guides in this series contain questions with answers. **Facsimile Number:** (516)921-8743. **Toll-free/Additional Phone Number(s):** 800-645-6337.

★2208★
Special Agent FBI
National Learning Corp.
212 Michael Dr.
Syosset, NY 11791　　　Phone: (516)921-8888
Jack Rudman. Part of the Career Examination Series No. 1. All examination guides in this series contain questions with answers. **Facsimile Number:** (516)921-8743. **Toll-free/Additional Phone Number(s):** 800-645-6337.

★2209★
Special Agent (INS)
National Learning Corp.
212 Michael Dr.
Syosset, NY 11791　　　Phone: (516)921-8888
Jack Rudman. Part of the Career Examination Series No. 1. All examination guides in this series contain questions with answers. **Facsimile Number:** (516)921-8743. **Toll-free/Additional Phone Number(s):** 800-645-6337.

★2210★
Special Agent (Wildlife)
National Learning Corp.
212 Michael Dr.
Syosset, NY 11791　　　Phone: (516)921-8888
Jack Rudman. Part of the Career Examination Series No. 1. All examination guides in this series contain questions with answers. **Facsimile Number:** (516)921-8743. **Toll-free/Additional Phone Number(s):** 800-645-6337.

★2211★
State Trooper
National Learning Corp.
212 Michael Dr.
Syosset, NY 11791　　　Phone: (516)921-8888
Jack Rudman. Part of the Career Examination Series No. 1. All examination guides in this series contain questions with answers. **Facsimile Number:** (516)921-8743. **Toll-free/Additional Phone Number(s):** 800-645-6337.

★2212★
State Trooper/Highway Patrol Officer/State Traffic Officer
Prentice Hall Press
Simon & Schuster Inc.
200 Old Tappan Rd.
Old Tappan, NJ 07675　　　Phone: (800)223-2348
Hy Hammer and Edward Scheinkman. Ninth edition, 1988. Complete guide to all types of state trooper exams given throughout the country. Includes study sections and five sample exams.

★2213★
Video Review for Police Officer Exams
Video Aided Instruction, Inc.
182 Village Rd.
East Hills, NY 11577　　　Phone: (516)621-6176
Videocassette. 1987. 120 mins. A video primer for police competency test candidates.

Awards, Scholarships, Grants, and Fellowships

★2214★
AFI Honor Roll
Association of Federal Investigators
c/o Leigh Stewart, Executive Director
1612 K St., N.W., Ste. 202
Washington, DC 20006   Phone: (202)466-7288

To recognize individuals who have made the ultimate sacrifice and have given their lives in the line of duty. It is given posthumously each year to those in Federal law enforcement who have made this sacrifice. Their names are added to a special Honor Roll. Established in 1984.

★2215★
Citation for Bravery
National Police Officers Association of America
1316 Gardner Lane, Ste. 204
Louisville, KY 40213   Phone: (502)451-7550

To recognize a law enforcement officer at any time during the year who, by an act of extreme bravery, saves a human life, makes a rescue at great personal peril, or faces great personal danger above and beyond the call of duty.

★2216★
Criminal Investigation Award
American Police Hall of Fame
c/o G.S. Arenberg, Executive Director
1100 N.E. 125th St.
North Miami, FL 33161   Phone: (305)891-1700

To recognize the men and women who quietly work to solve cases through long hours of detective work and for recognition of their talents that lead to the closing of a difficult case. Nominations of any person, any age, are accepted from another person or himself, anytime during the year. A certificate is awarded when warranted.

★2217★
Distinguished Service Award
American Association of Motor Vehicle Administrators
c/o Katherine R. Hutt
4200 Wilson Blvd., Ste. 600
Arlington, VA 22203   Phone: (703)522-4200

To recognize the outstanding services, contributions and accomplishments of individuals in the field of motor vehicle administration and traffic law enforcement. Members of the Association who are employed by a motor vehicle or public safety agency in a U.S. or Canadian jurisdiction are eligible in either of two categories: (1) those who never served on the AAMVA Board; and (2) those who served on the AAMVA Board. A plaque is awarded in each category annually. Established in 1964.

★2218★
Distinguished Service Award
American Police Hall of Fame
c/o G.S. Arenberg, Executive Director
1100 N.E. 125th St.
North Miami, FL 33161   Phone: (305)891-1700

To recognize police officers and high ranking officials who have distinguished themselves with honor in outstanding service to their state and community. Nominations of any person, any age, are accepted from another person or himself, anytime during the year. A certificate is awarded.

★2219★
General Commendation
American Police Hall of Fame
c/o G.S. Arenberg, Executive Director
1100 N.E. 125th St.
North Miami, FL 33161   Phone: (305)891-1700

To recognize officers who have, through an act of service or by professional police work, earned a special commendation on an individual basis. Nominations of any person, any age, are accepted from another person or himself, anytime during the year. Awarded when merited.

★2220★
Good Samaritan Award
American Police Hall of Fame
c/o G.S. Arenberg, Executive Director
1100 N.E. 125th St.
North Miami, FL 33161   Phone: (305)891-1700

To recognize both law enforcement and civilians for an act of charity that aids those less fortunate, thus carrying on the biblical act of the Good Samaritan. Nominations of any person, any age, are accepted from another person or himself, anytime during the year. Awarded when merited.

★2221★
John Edgar Hoover Police Service Award
American Police Hall of Fame
c/o G.S. Arenberg, Executive Director
1100 N.E. 125th St.
North Miami, FL 33161   Phone: (305)891-1700

To honor police and citizens for service and valor nationwide. One award is presented per state. Any person, any age, is and can be nominated either by another person or by himself anytime during the year. The Hoover Trophy is awarded during the Police Memorial Day program. Established in 1966 in honor of police officers and friends of police officers.

★2222★
Human Rights Award
International Association of Official Human Rights Agencies
c/o Executive Director
444 N. Capitol St., N.W., Ste. 249
Washington, DC 20001   Phone: (202)624-5410

To recognize an individual for a contribution to further human rights as it relates to enforcement. Awarded annually.

★2223★
Individual Awards
National Crime Prevention Council
c/o Donna Schulte
1700 K St., N.W., 2nd Fl.
Washington, DC 20006   Phone: (202)466-6272

To recognize individuals, one a volunteer and one a practitioner, who made the greatest contribution to the field of community crime prevention. Although the accomplishments do not have to be of national scope or impact, they must be of an exceptionally meritorious nature. Any organization may initiate a nomination. Applications must be submitted by September 1. Two awards are presented: Individual Practitioner Award and Individual Volunteer Award. The winners receive plaques; awards of merit are sent to screened top nominees, and awards of appreciation are sent to all nominees. Awarded annually. Established in 1980.

Police, Detectives, and Special Agents

★2224★
Investigator of the Year
Association of Federal Investigators
c/o Leigh Stewart, Executive Director
1612 K St., N.W., Ste. 202
Washington, DC 20006   Phone: (202)466-7288

For recognition of significant contributions to the investigative profession. Investigative professionals, public officials, and citizens of the United States are eligible. Nominations are accepted. Awards are given in the following categories: criminal investigator; financial investigator; general investigator; fraud investigator; and security/counterintelligence investigator. A plaque is awarded annually. Established in 1976.

★2225★
ISDA Special Commendation
International Security and Detective Alliance
c/o Dr. H. Roehm
P.O. Box 6303
Corpus Christi, TX 78466-6303   Phone: (512)888-6164

To honor any individual who significantly promotes the growth and betterment of the private security and investigation professions, or who performs significant acts of heroism, bravery, and/or faithful service. Letters of application with affidavits, statements, etc., as required may be submitted by anyone meeting the above criteria. Certificates are awarded when approved applications are received. Established in 1987.

★2226★
Knights of Justice Award
American Police Hall of Fame
c/o G.S. Arenberg, Executive Director
1100 N.E. 125th St.
North Miami, FL 33161   Phone: (305)891-1700

To recognize community service and valor by lawmen who are all "Blue Knights of Justice" and are considered to carry out the work of the world's first police officer, Michael the Archangel. Nominations of any person, any age, are accepted from another person or himself, anytime during the year. An honorary knighthood is awarded as merited.

★2227★
Law Enforcement Leadership Award
Association of Federal Investigators
c/o Leigh Stewart, Executive Director
1612 K St., N.W., Ste. 202
Washington, DC 20006   Phone: (202)466-7288

To recognize individuals in leadership positions in Federal law enforcement who have uniquely provided outstanding leadership contributions towards achieving major law enforcement objectives. A plaque is awarded annually at the awards program. Established in 1966.

★2228★
Man of the Year in Law Enforcement
Society of Professional Investigators
239 W. 52 St.
New York, NY 10019   Phone: (212)245-8330

For recognition of outstanding service rendered in the crusade against crime, racketeering, and corruption in government. Individuals in the investigative area of law enforcement who are nominated by members of the Society are eligible. An engraved plaque is awarded annually. Established in 1957.

★2229★
McDonnell Douglas Law Enforcement Award
Helicopter Association International
c/o Carolyn A. Vujcec, Manager of Communications
1619 Duke St.
Alexandria, VA 22314-3406   Phone: (703)683-4646

To recognize a worthy contribution to the advancement of the crime-suppression concept of helicopter patrol service. The award is limited to anti-crime patrol service and related activities such as surveillance and pursuit, but not limited to pilots or necessarily restricted to law enforcement personnel. Individuals employed by members in good standing of the Association are eligible. An engraved plaque is awarded annually. Established in 1972 by Hughes Helicopter of Culver City, California.

★2230★
Merit Award for Excellent Arrest
American Police Hall of Fame
c/o G.S. Arenberg, Executive Director
1100 N.E. 125th St.
North Miami, FL 33161   Phone: (305)891-1700

For recognition of the apprehension of a felon who was endangering the life and safety of the community. The arrest is considered by the department to be outstanding from the normal arrests day to day. Awarded when merited.

★2231★
NAFI Man of the Year
National Association of Fire Investigators
20 E. Jackson Blvd., Ste. 1000
Chicago, IL 60604-2210   Phone: (312)939-6050

To recognize significant contributions to the fire investigation profession and NAFI. Firemen, policemen, attorneys, insurance adjusters, claimsmen, fire experts, fire marshals in the military, or full-time fire investigators may be nominated. An engraved plaque is awarded annually when merited. Established in 1969. Formerly: Fire Investigator of the Year.

★2232★
Outstanding Law Enforcement Achievement Award
International Association of Fish and Wildlife Agencies
444 N. Capitol St., N.W., Ste. 534
Washington, DC 20001   Phone: (202)624-7890

To recognize outstanding law enforcement efforts in support of wildlife. Individuals and agencies are eligible. Awarded annually. Established in 1982.

★2233★
Parade - IACP Police Service Award
International Association of Chiefs of Police
c/o Jan Sanaie
110 N. Glebe St.
Arlington, VA 22201   Phone: (703)243-6500

To focus attention on the necessary and dedicated role police play. Sworn, operational, full-time police officers of any rank, in any city, federal, county or state police agency, are eligible. A plaque is presented to the winner, with a duplicate given to his department, and ten honorable mentions are awarded annually. Established in 1965 and administered jointly by the IACP and Parade magazine.

★2234★
Patriots Award
American Police Hall of Fame
c/o G.S. Arenberg, Executive Director
1100 N.E. 125th St.
North Miami, FL 33161   Phone: (305)891-1700

For recognition of organizations and individuals whose patriotic acts or service promote liberty and justice in the United States. Nominations of any person, any age, are accepted from another person or himself, anytime during the year. A certificate is awarded when merited.

★2235★
Police Officer of the Year Award
American Police Hall of Fame
c/o G.S. Arenberg, Executive Director
1100 N.E. 125th St.
North Miami, FL 33161   Phone: (305)891-1700

To recognize law enforcement officers who have served above and beyond the line of duty and survived. Any law enforcement officers in the U.S.A. are eligible. A medal, a trophy, and expenses to attend the conference are awarded annually in May. In addition, posthumous awards of valor for officers killed in the line of duty may be presented. Established in 1960.

★2236★
Public Service Award
Scanner Association of North America
P.O. Box 414
Western Springs, IL 60558   Phone: (312)246-4550

To recognize a police, fire, or other public safety volunteer or official for heroic action. Members of the Association may nominate individuals. A monetary prize and a plaque are awarded six times per year. Established in 1978.

★2237★
Recognition Award
International Association of Campus Law Enforcement
    Administrators
c/o Peter Berry
638 Prospect Ave.
Hartford, CT 06105   Phone: (203)233-4531

To recognize individuals who have contributed to or performed outstanding services to make colleges and universities safer places in which to work and study. Any individual who is part of a campus community is eligible. An inscribed pl aque or certificate is awarded annually. Established in 1960.

★2238★
Silver Star for Bravery
American Police Hall of Fame
c/o G.S. Arenberg, Executive Director
1100 N.E. 125th St.
North Miami, FL 33161   Phone: (305)891-1700

To recognize an officer for an act of daring and valor in a life-threatening situation that is above and beyond the line of duty. Nominations by any person, any age, are accepted from another person or himself, anytime during the year. A silver star is awarded as merited.

★2239★
**Sons of the American Revolution Law Enforcement
    Commendation Medal**
National Society - Sons of the American Revolution
c/o Nancy M. Patterson, Staff Secretary
1000 S. Fourth St.
Louisville, KY 40203   Phone: (502)589-1776

To recognize law enforcement officers for outstanding service in the line of duty. A gold filled enamel medal is awarded irregularly. Established in 1968.

★2240★
Special Achievement Awards
Association of Federal Investigators
c/o Leigh Stewart, Executive Director
1612 K St., N.W., Ste. 202
Washington, DC 20006   Phone: (202)466-7288

To recognize an individual for special achievements in federal investigation law enforcement, or the criminal justice system. Investigative professionals, public officials, and citizens of the United States are eligible. Nominations are accepted. A plaque is awarded annually. Established in 1979.

★2241★
VFW J. Edgar Hoover Award
Veterans of Foreign Wars of the U.S.A.
c/o Wade LaDue
V.F.W. Building
Broadway at 34th St.
Kansas City, MO 64111   Phone: (816)756-3390

To recognize an individual for outstanding service in the field of law enforcement. Awarded on recommendation of the National Committee on Awards and Citations and authorization by the Committee on Awards and Citations and authorization by the National Council of Administration. A medal and citation are awarded a nnually at the National Convention. Established in 1966.

★2242★
Woman Officer of the Year
International Association of Women Police
20-25 45th St.
Astoria, NY 11105   Phone: (718)721-6494

To recognize outstanding women of the law enforcement profession by a professional network of peer officers. Women who are sworn law enforcement officers with the power of arrest, and who are currently employed may be nominated with the approval of the highest ranking official of the agency where the woman is employed. Nominations may be made when a woman officer has demonstrated meritorious police service, i.e., has at imminent risk of life performed deeds of valor or has rendered invaluable police service and is dedicated to her daily tasks. Travel and expenses to attend the annual conference are awarded annually in September or October. Established lin 1977.

Basic Reference Guides and Handbooks

★2243★
Detective Work: A Study of Criminal Investigations
Free Press
866 3rd Ave.
New York, NY 10022   Phone: (212)702-3130
William B. Sanders. 1977. **Facsimile Number:** (212)605-9364.

★2244★
Detective's Private Investigation Training Manual
Paladin Press
PO Box 1307
Boulder, CO 80306   Phone: (303)443-7250
William Patterson. 1979. **Facsimile Number:** (303)442-8741.

★2245★
Find 'em Fast: A Private Investigator's Workbook
Paladin Press
PO Box 1307
Boulder, CO 80306   Phone: (303)443-7250
John D. McCann. 1984. **Facsimile Number:** (303)442-8741.

Police, Detectives, and Special Agents

★2246★
Find Them Fast, Find Them Now: Private Investigators Share Their Secrets for Finding Missing Persons
Carol Publishing Group
120 Enterprise Ave.
Secaucus, NJ 07094   Phone: (201)866-0490
Frederick C. Hoyer, Jr. 1988. **Facsimile Number:** (201)866-8159.

★2247★
How to Find Anyone Anywhere
Thomas Publications
202 S. Stratton St.
PO Box 3031
Gettysburg, PA 17325   Phone: (717)334-1921
Ralph D. Thomas. 1986. Part of Private Investigation Series.

★2248★
How to Find Cases Anywhere: P.I.'s Guide to Obtaining Cases, Obtaining Free Publicity & Marketing Investigative Services
Thomas Publications
202 S. Stratton St.
PO Box 3031
Gettysburg, PA 17325   Phone: (717)334-1921
Ralph D. Thomas. 1988.

★2249★
Law Enforcement Career Planning
Charles C. Thomas, Publisher
2600 S. 1st St.
Springfield, IL 62794-9265   Phone: (217)789-8980
Thomas Mahoney. 1989. **Facsimile Number:** (217)789-9130.

★2250★
Police—Buyer's Guide Issue
Hare Publications
6300 Yarrow Dr.
Carlsbad, CA 92009   Phone: (800)854-6449
Sean Hilferty and Robert Shelburne, editor. Annual, September. List of suppliers of police products and services. Entries include: Supplier name, address, phone, products or services supplied. Arrangement: Classified by product or service. **Toll-free/Additional Phone Number(s):** (800)624-6377. **Facsimile Number:** (619)931-5809.

★2251★
The Police Function & the Investigation of Crime
Gower Publishing Co.
Old Post Rd.
Brookfield, VT 05036   Phone: (802)276-3162
Brian J. Morgan. 1990.

★2252★
Police Promotion Manual
Looseleaf Law Publications, Inc.
41-23 150th St.
Flushing, NY 11355
Facsimile Number: (718)539-0941.

★2253★
The Process of Investigation: Concepts & Strategies for the Security Professional
Butterworth-Heinemann
80 Montvale Ave.
Stoneham, MA 02180   Phone: (617)438-8464
Charles A. Sennewald. 1981. **Facsimile Number:** (617)279-4851.

★2254★
Professional Thieves & the Detective
AMS Press, Inc.
56 E. 13th St.
New York, NY 10003   Phone: (212)777-4700
Allan Pinkerton. **Facsimile Number:** (212)995-5413.

★2255★
Shadowing & Surveillance: A Complete Guide Book
Loompanics Unlimited
PO Box 1197
Port Townsend, WA 98368   Phone: (206)385-5087
Burt Rapp. 1985.

★2256★
Top Secret! Codes to Crack
Albert Whitman & Co.
6340 Oakton St.
Morton Grove, IL 60053-2723   Phone: (708)581-0033
Burton Albert, Jr. 1987. **Toll-free/Additional Phone Number(s):** 800-255-7675. **Facsimile Number:** (708)581-0039.

★2257★
Undercover Work: A Complete Handbook
Loompanics Unlimited
PO Box 1197
Port Townsend, WA 98368   Phone: (206)385-5087
Burt Rapp. 1985.

★2258★
Word Detective Picture Word Book
EDC Publishing
10302 E. 55th Pl.
Tulsa, OK 74146   Phone: (918)622-4522
King. 1982.

★2259★
The Young Detective's Handbook
Little, Brown & Co., Inc.
34 Becon St.
Boston, MA 02108   Phone: (617)227-0730
William V. Butler. 1986. **Facsimile Number:** (617)723-9422.

──────────── Periodicals ────────────

★2260★
Action Digest
J. Flores Publications
PO Box 163001
Miami, FL 33116   Phone: (305)559-4652
Eli Flores, Editor. Quarterly Digest featuring articles on guns, self-defense, and law enforcement. Includes crime stories.

★2261★
College of Law Enforcement—Newsletter
College of Law Enforcement
Eastern Kentucky University
105 Stratton
Richmond, KY 40475   Phone: (606)622-1155
Editor(s): Bruce I. Wolford. Biennially. Reports on the activities in the areas of concentration within the College: law enforcement, fire science, security, and traffic safety. Contains articles on criminal justice, public safety, loss prevention, and related subjects. Recurring features include news of members, a calendar of events, and faculty updates. **Toll-free/Additional Phone Number(s):** 800-622-1497 **Facsimile Number:** (606)622-6264.

★2262★
Crime Control Digest
Washington Crime News Service
3918 Prosperity Ave., Ste. 318
Fairfax, VA 22031-3334   Phone: (703)573-1600
Editor(s): Betty B. Bosarge. Weekly. Contains articles on all levels of law enforcement in the U.S., including national, state, county, local, and student concerns, though the focus is on matters of national import. Reports on such items as illegal drug trafficking, terrorism, the accreditation of law enforcement agencies, pending legislation, and the implementation of new laws. Recurring features include information on upcoming seminars and conferences, and announcements of awards. **Facsimile Number:** (703)573-1604.

★2263★
Enforcement Journal
National Police Officers Assn.
1316 Gardiner Ln.
Louisville, KY 40213   Phone: (502)451-7550
John W. Lewis, Editor and Publisher. Quarterly. Magazine serving as a forum for the Police Officers Association of America and Police Reserve Officers Association. Includes articles on new ideas and procedures in law enforcement, reviews of police products and equipment, and association news.

★2264★
First Principles: National Security and Civil Liberties
Center for National Security Studies
122 Maryland Ave. NE
Washington, DC 20002   Phone: (202)544-1681
Editor(s): Gary Stern and Rachel Fischer. 5/yr. Concerned that intelligence agencies, local police, and other government agencies violate the civil liberties of American citizens. Calls for legislative reforms "to prevent further abuses.". Recurring features include reviews of current litigation and legislative activities, and literature in the field.

★2265★
Intelligence Issues
Center for Intelligence Studies (CIS)
301 S. Columbus St.
Alexandria, VA 22314   Phone: (703)684-0625
Monthly.

★2266★
The Investigators' Journal
Association of Federal Investigators (AFI)
3299 K St. NW, 7th Fl.
Washington, DC 20007   Phone: (202)337-5234
Annual. Academic journal on current law enforcement issues and studies.

★2267★
Law and Order
1000 Skokie Blvd.
Wilmette, IL 60091   Phone: (708)256-8555
Bruce Cameron, Editor. Monthly. Law enforcement trade magazine. **Facsimile Number:** (708)256-8574.

★2268★
Law Enforcement Technology
PTN Publishing Co.
445 Broad Hollow Rd., Ste. 21
Melville, NY 11747   Phone: (516)845-2700
Donna Rogers, Editor. 10x/yr. Magazine for police technology and management. **Facsimile Number:** (516)845-2797.

★2269★
Law Officer's Bulletin
Bureau of National Affairs, Inc. (BNA)
1231 25th St. NW
Washington, DC 20037   Phone: (202)452-4200
Editor(s): Robert L. Goebes. Biweekly. Provides an update of court decisions, Justice Department proposals, and congressional actions involving law enforcement officers, describing legal reasoning and explaining the impact on the law enforcement community. Recurring features include the features From the Supreme Court, Trends and Developments, You Be the Judge, Perspective, and Training Calendar. **Toll-free/Additional Phone Number(s):** 800-372-1033 **Facsimile Number:** (202)822-8092.

★2270★
National Disabled Law Officers Association—Newsletter
National Disabled Law Officers Association
75 New St.
Nutley, NJ 07110   Phone: (201)667-9569
Editor(s): Peter A. Frazza. Periodic. Contains news of interest to disabled law officers, including the availability of benefits from federal, state, and local governments. Reports on relevant legislation. Reprints newspaper articles about the association and its members.

★2271★
Nightwatch
Center for Intelligence Studies (CIS)
301 S. Columbus St.
Alexandria, VA 22314   Phone: (703)684-0625
Quarterly.

★2272★
Police
Hare Publications
6300 Yarrow Dr.
Carlsbad, CA 92009   Phone: (619)438-2511
Sean T. Hilferty, Editor. Monthly. Law enforcement magazine. **Facsimile Number:** (619)931-5809.

★2273★
Police & Security News
Days Communications
1690 Quarry Rd.
PO Box 330
Kulpsville, PA 19443   Phone: (215)538-1240
James Devery, Editor. 6x/yr. Tabloid for the law enforcement and private security industries. Includes articles on training, new products, and new technology. **Facsimile Number:** (215)368-9955.

★2274★
The Police Chief
International Assn. of Chiefs of Police
1110 N. Glebe Rd., Ste. 200
Arlington, VA 22201   Phone: (703)243-6500
Charles E. Higginbotham, Editor. Monthly. Law enforcement magazine. **Facsimile Number:** (703)243-0684.

★2275★
Police Times Magazine
American Police Academy (APA)
Lock Box 15350
Chevy Chase, MD 20815   Phone: (202)293-9088
Bimonthly. Tabloid reporting on issues in law enforcement.

Police, Detectives, and Special Agents

★2276★
Sheriff
National Sheriffs' Assn.
1450 Duke St.
Alexandria, VA 22314-3490　　　Phone: (703)836-7827
Julia Stanton Gigante, Editor. 6x/yr. Professional law enforcement magazine. **Facsimile Number:** (703)683-6541.

★2277★
Sheriff and Police Reporter
848 NW 97th St.
Seattle, WA 98117-2211　　　Phone: (206)361-6110
Patrick Murphy, Editor. Quarterly. Law enforcement magazine.

★2278★
Today's Policeman
Towerhigh Publications, Inc.
PO Box 875108
Los Angeles, CA 90087　　　Phone: (213)432-3806
Donald Mack, Editor and Publisher. Quarterly. Law enforcement magazine.

--- Meetings and Conventions ---

★2279★
Annual Associated Public-Safety Communications Officers (APCO) Annual Conference
Associated Public-Safety Communications Officers (APCO)
2040 S. Ridgewood Ave., Ste. 102
South Daytona, FL 32119　　　Phone: (904)322-2500
Frequency: Always held during August. 1992; Aug. 09-14; Seattle, WA ● 1993; Aug. 08-13; New Orleans, LA ● 1994; Aug. 07-12; Pittsburgh, PA. **Toll-free/Additional Phone Number(s):** 800-824-1850. **Facsimile Number:** (904)322-2501.

★2280★
Association of Federal Investigators (AFI)
3299 K St. NW, 7th Fl.
Washington, DC 20007　　　Phone: (202)337-5234
Frequency: Annual conference, with exhibits, is always held in November or December in Washington, DC. **Facsimile Number:** (202)333-5365.

★2281★
Emergency Response Expo
Tower Conference Management Co.
800 Roosevelt Rd., Bldg. E., Ste. 408
Glen Ellyn, IL 60137-5835　　　Phone: (708)469-3373
1992. **Facsimile Number:** (708)469-7477.

★2282★
International Association of Chiefs of Police Annual Conference
International Association of Chiefs of Police
1110 N. Glebe Rd., No. 200
Arlington, VA 22201　　　Phone: (703)243-6500
Frequency: Usually held in October. 1992; Oct. 03-08; San Antonio, TX ● 1993; Oct. 16-21; St. Louis, MO ● 1994; Oct. 15-20; Albuquerque, NM ● 1995; Oct. 14-18; Miami, FL.

★2283★
National Sheriffs' Association Convention
National Sheriffs' Association
1450 Duke St.
Alexandria, VA 22314-3490　　　Phone: (703)836-7827
1992; Jun. San Diego, CA ● 1993; Jun. Salt Lake City, UT ● 1994; Jun. Pittsburgh, PA ● 1995; Jun. San Antonio, TX. **Toll-free/Additional Phone Number(s):** 800-424-7872. **Facsimile Number:** (703)683-6541.

★2284★
PROTECH - International Exhibition for Protection, Safety, Security, and Fire Prevention
World Access Corp.
15 Bemis Rd.
PO Box 171
Wellesley Hills, MA 02181　　　Phone: (617)235-8095
1992; Nov. 22-25 ● 1993. **Facsimile Number:** (617)235-7360.

--- Other Sources of Information ---

★2285★
A Cowboy Detective: A True Story of Twenty-Two Years with a World-Famous Detective Agency
University of Nebraska, Lincoln
University of Nebraska Press
901 N. 17th St.
Lincoln, NE 68588　　　Phone: (402)472-3581
Charles A. Siringo. 1988. **Facsimile Number:** (402)472-6214.

★2286★
Front Page Detective: William J. Burns & the Detective Profession, 1880-1930
Bowling Green State University Popular Press
838 E. Wooster St.
Bowling Green, OH 43403　　　Phone: (419)372-7866
William R. Hunt. 1990. **Facsimile Number:** (419)372-8095.

★2287★
The Idea of Police
Sage Publications, Inc.
2111 W. Hillcrest Dr.
Newbury Park, CA 91320　　　Phone: (805)499-0721
Carl B. Klockars. 1985. Part of Law & Criminal Justice Series. **Facsimile Number:** (805)499-0871.

★2288★
Successful Private Eyes & Private Spies: Private Spies
Thomas Publications
202 S. Stratton St.
PO Box 3031
Gettysburg, PA 17325　　　Phone: (717)334-1921
Barbara L. Thomas. 1986. Part of Private Investigation Series.

Food and Beverage Preparation and Service Occupations

Chefs, Cooks, and Other Kitchen Workers

Chefs and cooks are responsible for preparing meals that are tasty and attractively presented. Typical duties include measuring, mixing, and cooking ingredients, using a variety of pots, pans, cutlery, and equipment including ovens, broilers, grills, and blenders. They often direct the work of other kitchen workers. Many chefs have earned fame for themselves and the eateries they work for because of their skill in artfully preparing traditional favorites and exciting new dishes. The terms chef and cook are sometimes used interchangeably, but chefs are generally the most highly skilled and trained, whereas cooks have more limited skills. Institutional chefs and cooks work in the kitchens of schools, industrial cafeterias, hospitals, and other institutions. They usually prepare a small selection of entrees in large quantities. Restaurant chefs and cooks prepare a wider selection of dishes, cooking individual servings to order. Bread and pastry bakers produce baked goods for restaurants, institutions, and retail bakery shops. Short-order cooks prepare foods to order in eateries that emphasize fast service. Specialty fast-food cooks prepare a limited selection of menu items in fast-food restaurants. Other kitchen workers perform tasks at the direction of chefs and cooks. This may include cleaning and slicing vegetables, and cleaning work areas and equipment.

$alaries

Wages vary depending on region and type of establishment.

Chefs	$9.00-10.00/hour
Cooks	$5.00-6.75/hour
Assistant cooks and short-order cooks	$4.50-5.50/hour
Bread and pastry bakers	$5.50-6.25/hour
Salad preparation workers	$4.25-5.00/hour
Food preparation workers in fast-food restaurants	$3.50-4.75/hour

Employment Outlook

Growth rate until the year 2000: Faster than average.

Chefs, Cooks, and Other Kitchen Workers

Career Guides

★2289★
Bagel Baker
Vocational Biographies, Inc.
PO Box 31, Dept. VF10
Sauk Centre, MN 56378   Phone: (612)352-6516
1990. This pamphlet profiles a person working in the job. Includes information about job duties, working conditions, places of employment, educational preparation, labor market outlook, and salaries. **Toll-free/Additional Phone Number(s):** 800-255-0752.

★2290★
Baker
Careers, Inc.
PO Box 135
Largo, FL 34649-0135   Phone: (813)584-7333
1991. Two-page occupational summary card describing duties, working conditions, personal qualifications, training, earnings and hours, employment outlook, places of employment, related careers and where to write for more information.

★2291★
"Baker" in *Occu-Facts: Information on 565 Careers in Outline Form* (p. 17.30)
Careers, Inc.
P.O. Box 135
1211 Tenth St., S.W.
Largo, FL 33640   Phone: (813)584-7333
Elizabeth Handville. Biennial, 1989-90 edition. Each one-page occupational profile describes duties, working conditions, physical surroundings and demands, aptitudes, temperament, educational requirements, employment outlook, earnings, and places of employment.

★2292★
"Bakers" in Volume 1 of *Career Discovery Encyclopedia* (pp. 102-103)
J.G. Ferguson Publishing Co.
200 W. Monroe
Chicago, IL 60606   Phone: (312)580-5480
E. Russell Primm, editor-in-chief. 1990. Contains two-page articles on 504 occupations. Each article describes job duties, earnings, and educational and training requirements.

★2293★
Bakers and Bakery Products Workers
Chronicle Guidance Publications, Inc.
PO Box 1190
Moravia, NY 13118-1190   Phone: (315)497-0330
1989. This career brief describes the nature of the work, working conditions, hours and earnings, education and training, licensure, certification, unions, personal qualifications, social and psychological factors, employment outlook, entry methods, advancement, and related occupations. **Toll-free/Additional Phone Number(s):** 800-622-7284.

★2294★
"Baking and Pastry" in *Opportunities in Culinary Careers* (pp. 99-106)
National Textbook Co.
4255 W. Touhy Ave.
Lincolnwood, IL 60646   Phone: (312)679-5500
Mary Deirdre Donovan. 1990. Describes the educational preparation and training of chefs and cooks and explores a variety of food service jobs in restaurants, institutions, and research and development. Lists culinary schools and professional organizations.

★2295★
"Becoming a Chef" in *Opportunities in Culinary Careers* (pp. 17-39)
National Textbook Co.
4255 W. Touhy Ave.
Lincolnwood, IL 60646   Phone: (312)679-5500
Mary Deirdre Donovan. 1990. Describes the educational preparation and training of chefs and cooks and explores a variety of food service jobs in restaurants, institutions, and research and development. Lists culinary schools and professional organizations.

★2296★
"Certified Master Chef: the Highest Honor in the Industry" in *Opportunities in Restaurant Careers* (pp. 49-53)
National Textbook Co.
4255 W. Touhy Ave.
Lincolnwood, IL 60646   Phone: (312)679-5500
Carol Ann Caprione Chmelynski. 1990. Provides an overview of the restaurant industry and surveys entry-level, mid-level, and management jobs. Covers working conditions, educational preparation, training, advancement possibilities, employment outlook, and earnings. Lists schools offering programs in hotel, restaurant, and institutional management.

★2297★

"Chef" in *VGM's Careers Encyclopedia* (pp. 84-86)
National Textbook Co.
4255 W. Touhy Ave.
Lincolnwood, IL 60646 Phone: (312)679-5500

Third edition, 1991. Contains two- to five-page descriptions of 200 managerial, professional, technical, trade, and service occupations. Each profile includes job duties, places of employment, qualifications, educational preparation, training, employment potential, advancement, income, and additional sources of information.

★2298★

"Chef/Cook" in *Guide to Careers Without College* (pp. 97-100)
Franklin Watts, Inc.
387 Park Avenue, S.
New York, NY 10016 Phone: (212)686-7070

Kathleen S. Abrams. 1988. Discusses careers that do not require a college degree in fields such as health care, sales and marketing, and the building trades. Describes the work, employment opportunities, and training.

★2299★

Chefs and Cooks
Chronicle Guidance Publications, Inc.
PO Box 1190
Moravia, NY 13118-1190 Phone: (315)497-0330

1988. This career brief describes the nature of the work, working conditions, hours and earnings, education and training, licensure, certification, unions, personal qualifications, social and psychological factors, employment outlook, entry methods, advancement, and related occupations. **Toll-free/Additional Phone Number(s):** 800-622-7284.

★2300★

"Chefs and Cooks" in *Jobs! What They Are...Where They Are...What They Pay* (pp. 164-165)
Simon & Schuster, Inc.
Simon & Schuster Bldg.
1230 Avenue of the Americas
New York, NY 10020 Phone: (212)698-7000

Robert O. Snelling and Anne M. Snelling. Revised edition, 1989. Profiles 241 occupations, describing duties and responsibilities, educational preparation, earnings, employment opportunities, training, and qualifications.

★2301★

"Chefs and Cooks" in *Opportunities in Vocational and Technical Careers* (p. 73)
National Textbook Co.
4255 W. Touhy Ave.
Lincolnwood, IL 60646 Phone: (312)679-5500

Adrian A. Paradis. 1987. Describes careers which can be prepared for by attending a private vocational or proprietary school—office employee, sales worker, service worker, health services, mechanic, craftworker, and technician. Covers employment outlook, job duties, and salaries. Offers career planning advice.

★2302★

"Chefs, Cooks, and Other Kitchen Workers" in *Occupational Outlook Handbook* (pp. 294-296)
Superintendent of Documents
U.S. Government Printing Office
Washington, DC 20402 Phone: (202)783-3238

Biennial; latest edition, 1990-91. Encyclopedia of careers describing more than 250 occupations and comprising about 86 percent of all jobs in the economy. Occupations that require lengthy education or training are given the most attention. For each occupation, the handbook describes job duties, working conditions, training, educational preparation, personal qualities, advancement possibilities, job outlook, earnings, and sources of additional information.

★2303★

"Chefs, Cooks, and Other Kitchen Workers" in *Opportunities in Restaurant Careers* (pp. 22-31)
National Textbook Co.
4255 W. Touhy Ave.
Lincolnwood, IL 60646 Phone: (312)679-5500

Carol Ann Caprione Chmelynski. 1990. Provides an overview of the restaurant industry and surveys entry-level, mid-level, and management jobs. Covers working conditions, educational preparation, training, advancement possibilities, employment outlook, and earnings. Lists schools offering programs in hotel, restaurant, and institutional management.

★2304★

The Choice of the Future
National Restaurant Association
The Educational Foundation
250 S. Wacker Dr., Ste. 1400
Chicago, IL 60606 Phone: (312)715-1010

This 27-page booklet provides an overview of the food service industry and describes jobs, the work, education, training, and advancement possibilities. Contains salary surveys.

★2305★

"Cook and Chef" in *Hospitality and Recreation*, Volume 8 of *Career Information Center* (pp. 76-78)
Glencoe/Macmillan
15319 Chatsworth St.
Mission Hills, CA 91345 Phone: (818)898-1391

Richard Lidz and Dale Anderson, editorial directors. Fourth edition, 1990. For 600 occupations, describes job duties, entry-level requirements, education and training needed, advancement possibilities, employment outlook, earnings and benefits. The set is divided into 12 volumes. Each volume includes jobs related under a broad career field. Volume 13 is the index. **Facsimile Number:** 818-365-5489.

★2306★

"Cook and Chef: The Cornerstones of a Good Restaurant" in *Careers in the Restaurant Industry* (pp. 35-45)
Rosen Publishing Group, Inc.
29 E. 21st St.
New York, NY 10010 Phone: (212)777-3017

Richard S. Lee and Mary Price Lee. Revised edition, 1990. Explores various jobs in the restaurant industry including cooks and chefs, manager, maitre d', bartender, and waiter/waitress. Describes job duties, salaries, educational preparation and job hunting. Contains information about fast food, catering, and small businesses.

★2307★

Cook, Short Order
Careers, Inc.
PO Box 135
Largo, FL 34649-0135 Phone: (813)584-7333

1991. Two-page job guide card describing duties, working conditions, personal qualifications, training, earnings and hours, employment outlook, places of employment, related careers and where to write for more information.

Chefs, Cooks, and Other Kitchen Workers

★2308★
Cooks and Chefs
Careers, Inc.
PO Box 135
Largo, FL 34649-0135	Phone: (813)584-7333
1990. Eight-page brief offering the definition, history, duties, working conditions, personal qualifications, educational requirements, earnings, hours, employment outlook, advancement possibilities, and related occupations.

★2309★
"Cooks and Chefs" in *Occu-Facts: Information on 565 Careers in Outline Form* (p. 13.13)
Careers, Inc.
P.O. Box 135
1211 Tenth St., S.W.
Largo, FL 33640	Phone: (813)584-7333
Elizabeth Handville. Biennial, 1989-90 edition. Each one-page occupational profile describes duties, working conditions, physical surroundings and demands, aptitudes, temperament, educational requirements, employment outlook, earnings, and places of employment.

★2310★
"Cooks and Chefs" in Volume 2 of *Career Discovery Encyclopedia* (pp. 58-59)
J.G. Ferguson Publishing Co.
200 W. Monroe
Chicago, IL 60606	Phone: (312)580-5480
E. Russell Primm, editor-in-chief. 1990. Contains two-page articles on 504 occupations. Each article describes job duties, earnings, and educational and training requirements.

★2311★
"Cooks and Chefs" in *The American Almanac of Jobs and Salaries* (pp. 527-528)
Avon Books
105 Madison Avenue
New York, NY 10016	Phone: (212)481-5600
John Wright and Edward J. Dwyer. Revised and updated, 1990. A comprehensive guide to the wages of hundreds of occupations in a wide variety of industries and organizations.

★2312★
"Cooks, Chefs, and Bakers" in Volume 3 of *The Encyclopedia of Careers and Vocational Guidance* (pp. 204-210)
J.G. Ferguson Publishing Co.
200 W. Monroe
Chicago, IL 60606	Phone: (312)580-5480
William E. Hopke, editor-in-chief. Eighth edition, 1990. Four-volume set that profiles 500 occupations and describes job trends in 76 industries. Includes career description, educational requirements, history of the job, methods of entry, advancement, employment outlook, earnings, working conditions, social and psychological factors, and sources of additional information.

★2313★
"Culinary Arts" in *College Majors and Careers: A Resource Guide for Effective Life Planning* (pp. 45-46)
Garrett Park Press
PO Box 190
Garrett Park, MD 20896	Phone: (301)946-2553
Paul Phifer. 1987. Lists 61 college majors. Includes a general definition of the field, related occupations requiring either a bachelor or associate degree, related leisure-time activities denoting personal interest in the field, skills needed, values, and personal attributes. Lists organizations.

★2314★
Culinary Careers
National Textbook Co.
4255 W. Touhy Ave.
Lincolnwood, IL 60646-1975	Phone: (708)679-5500
Mary D. Donovan. 1990. Part of Opportunities In Career Series. **Facsimile Number:** (708)679-2494.

★2315★
Executive Chef
Culinary Institute of America
The Learning Resources Center
651 South Albany Post Rd.
Hyde Park, NY 12538-1499	Phone: (914)452-9600
Videocassette. 1979. 21 mins. The former executive chef of the Waldorf-Astoria Hotel, Arno Schmidt, tours the kitchen and explains the duties of each department. He discusses the problems and decisions that an executive chef faces daily.

★2316★
Fast Food Services
National Educational Media, Inc.
21601 Devonshire St.
Chatsworth, CA 91311-9962	Phone: (818)709-6009
Videocassette. 1983. 15 mins. This program presents basic job responsibilities of food servers. It gives detailed information on taking and filling orders and keeping work areas clean and properly stocked. It stresses teamwork and includes important information on courtesy and customer relations.

★2317★
Fast Food Workers
Chronicle Guidance Publications, Inc.
PO Box 1190
Moravia, NY 13118-1190	Phone: (315)497-0330
1989. This career brief describes the nature of the work, working conditions, hours and earnings, education and training, licensure, certification, unions, personal qualifications, social and psychological factors, employment outlook, entry methods, advancement, and related occupations. **Toll-free/Additional Phone Number(s):** 800-622-7284.

★2318★
Food Careers
Prentice Hall
Rte. 9W
Englewood Cliffs, NJ 07632	Phone: (201)592-2000
Donna N. Creasy. 1977. Part of Home Economics Careers Series.

★2319★
"Food Service" in *The Career Connection II: A Guide to Technical Majors and Their Related Careers* (pp. 63-64)
ERIS
PO Box 7509
University Station
Provo, UT 84602-0509
Fred A. Rowe. 1988. Contains technical majors, such as automotive technology. Describes the major and the job. Lists high school and postsecondary school courses. Includes occupations related to the major, employment outlook, and starting salary.

★2320★
Food Services
Learning Corporation of America
108 Wilmot Rd.
Deerfield, IL 60015-9990 Phone: (708)940-1260

Videocassette. 1982. 21 mins. Four workers in the food industry offer a look at their jobs: chef, restaurant manager, baker and meat wrapper. From the "Working" series.

★2321★
"Hotel Cook or Chef and Baker" in *Hospitality & Recreation* (pp. 27-31)
Franklin Watts, Inc.
387 Park Avenue, S.
New York, NY 10016 Phone: (212)686-7070

Marjorie Rittenberg Schulz. 1990. Provides an overview of jobs in the hotel, motel, food service, fitness, and recreation industries. Covers job duties, educational preparation, salary, and employment outlook. Offers job hunting advice.

★2322★
Hotel Executive Chef
Vocational Biographies, Inc.
PO Box 31, Dept. VF10
Sauk Centre, MN 56378 Phone: (612)352-6516

1988. This pamphlet profiles a person working in the job. Includes information about job duties, working conditions, places of employment, educational preparation, labor market outlook, and salaries. **Toll-free/Additional Phone Number(s):** 800-255-0752.

★2323★
Introduction to Management in the Hospitality Industry
John Wiley & Sons, Inc.
605 3rd Ave.
New York, NY 10158 Phone: (212)850-6000

Tom Powers. Third edition, 1988. **Facsimile Number:** (212)850-6088.

★2324★
Kitchen Helper
Careers, Inc.
PO Box 135
Largo, FL 34649-0135 Phone: (813)584-7333

1989. Two-page job guide card describing duties, working conditions, personal qualifications, training, earnings and hours, employment outlook, places of employment, related careers and where to write for more information.

★2325★
"Kitchen Helper" in *Occu-Facts: Information on 565 Careers in Outline Form* (p. 13.20)
Careers, Inc.
P.O. Box 135
1211 Tenth St., S.W.
Largo, FL 33640 Phone: (813)584-7333

Elizabeth Handville. Biennial, 1989-90 edition. Each one-page occupational profile describes duties, working conditions, physical surroundings and demands, aptitudes, temperament, educational requirements, employment outlook, earnings, and places of employment.

★2326★
Mise En Place
Culinary Institute of America
The Learning Resources Center
651 South Albany Post Rd.
Hyde Park, NY 12538-1499 Phone: (914)452-9600

Videocassette. 1982. 15 mins. Chef Lyde Buchtenkirch demonstrates simple processes essential for someone who plans to have a career in the kitchen.

★2327★
Opportunities in Culinary Careers
National Textbook Co.
4255 W. Touhy Ave.
Lincolnwood, IL 60646 Phone: (312)679-5500

Mary Deirdre Donovan. 1990. Describes the educational preparation and training of chefs and cooks and explores a variety of food service jobs in restaurants, institutions, and research and development. Lists culinary schools and professional organizations.

★2328★
Opportunities in Restaurant Careers
National Textbook Co.
4255 W. Touhy Ave.
Lincolnwood, IL 60646-1975 Phone: (708)679-5500

1989. **Facsimile Number:** (708)679-2494.

★2329★
"Pastry Chef and Baker" in *Hospitality and Recreation*, Volume 8 of *Career Information Center* (pp. 85-87)
Glencoe/Macmillan
15319 Chatsworth St.
Mission Hills, CA 91345 Phone: (818)898-1391

Richard Lidz and Dale Anderson, editorial directors. Fourth edition, 1990. For 600 occupations, describes job duties, entry-level requirements, education and training needed, advancement possibilities, employment outlook, earnings and benefits. The set is divided into 12 volumes. Each volume includes jobs related under a broad career field. Volume 13 is the index. **Facsimile Number:** 818-365-5489.

★2330★
Personal Service Cluster
Center for Humanities, Inc.
Communications Park
Box 1000
Mount Kisco, NY 10549 Phone: (914)666-4100

Videocassette. 1984. 20 mins. Students get to see the day-by-day lives of people who work in the fields of cosmetology, food service and law enforcement.

★2331★
"Professional Cooking" in *The Desk Guide to Training and Work Advisement* (pp. 77-79)
Charles C. Thomas, Publisher
2600 S. First St.
Springfield, IL 62794-9265 Phone: (217)789-8980

Gail Baugher Kuenstler. 1988. Describes alternative methods of gaining entry into an occupation through different types of educational programs, internships and apprenticeships. **Facsimile Number:** (217)789-9130.

Chefs, Cooks, and Other Kitchen Workers

★2332★
"Restaurant Chef" in *Top Professions: The 100 Most Popular, Dynamic, and Profitable Careers in America Today* (pp. 195-197)
Peterson's Guides, Inc.
202 Carnegie Center
PO Box 2123
Princeton, NJ 08543-2123   Phone: (609)243-9111

Nicholas Basta. 1989. Includes occupations requiring a college or advanced degree. Describes job duties, earnings, some typical job titles, career opportunities at different degree levels, and lists related associations.

★2333★
"Short Order Cook" in *Hospitality and Recreation, Volume 8 of Career Information Center* (pp. 62-64)
Glencoe/Macmillan
15319 Chatsworth St.
Mission Hills, CA 91345   Phone: (818)898-1391

Richard Lidz and Dale Anderson, editorial directors. Fourth edition, 1990. For 600 occupations, describes job duties, entry-level requirements, education and training needed, advancement possibilities, employment outlook, earnings and benefits. The set is divided into 12 volumes. Each volume includes jobs related under a broad career field. Volume 13 is the index. **Facsimile Number:** 818-365-5489.

★2334★
"Short Order Cook" in *Occu-Facts: Information on 565 Careers in Outline Form* (p. 13.14)
Careers, Inc.
P.O. Box 135
1211 Tenth St., S.W.
Largo, FL 33640   Phone: (813)584-7333

Elizabeth Handville. Biennial, 1989-90 edition. Each one-page occupational profile describes duties, working conditions, physical surroundings and demands, aptitudes, temperament, educational requirements, employment outlook, earnings, and places of employment.

★2335★
Video Career Library - Public and Personal Services
Careers, Inc.
1211 10th St., SW
PO Box 135
Largo, FL 34649-0135   Phone: (813)584-7333

Videocassette. 1990. 35 mins. Part of the Video Career Library covering 165 occupations. Shows actual workers on the job. Includes firefighters, police officers, correctional officers, bartenders, waiters/waitresses, cooks/chefs, child care workers, flight attendants, barbers/cosmetologists, groundskeepers/gardeners, and butchers/meat cutters.

★2336★
Waiting Tables
Filmakers Library, Inc.
133 East 58th St.
New York, NY 10022   Phone: (212)355-6545

Videocassette. 1986. 20 mins. An enlightening look at the food service industry where the majority of employees are underpaid, non-unionized women.

Associations

★2337★
American Culinary Federation (ACF)
Ten San Bartola Rd.
PO Box 3466
St. Augustine, FL 32085-3466   Phone: (904)824-4468

Membership: State and local chapters of professional chefs. **Purpose:** Works to advance the culinary profession by sponsoring a continuing education program to keep members informed on food preparation and new equipment, apprenticeship training, and demonstrations for charitable and professional groups. Has sent a United States team of chefs to the International Culinary Olympic Competition in Frankfurt, Federal Republic of Germany since 1960. Sponsors American Academy of Chefs, an honor society that carries out the federation's educational program for the benefit of the food service industry. Sponsors scholarships, culinary competitions, and Chef of the Year Award. Local chapter activities include gourmet dinners "to perpetuate the fine art of dining among the public," and dinners for underprivileged children and hospital patients. Maintains the Educational Institute of the ACF which operates the National Apprenticeship Program for Cooks. **Publications:** *Culinary Review*, monthly. • Also publishes *Culinary Olympic Cookbook*, *Manual for Culinarians*, and accompanying student and teacher guides. **Facsimile Number:** (904)825-4758.

★2338★
Council on Hotel, Restaurant, and Institutional Education (CHRIE)
1200 17th St. NW
Washington, DC 20036-3097   Phone: (202)331-5990

Membership: Schools and colleges offering specialized education and training in cooking, baking, tourism and hotel, restaurant, and institutional administration; individuals, executives, and students. **Purpose:** Sponsors competitions; bestows awards. **Publications:** *CHRIE Communique*, semimonthly. • *Guide to Hospitality Education*, annual. • *Hospitality Education and Research Journal*, 3/year. • *Hospitality and Tourism Educator*, quarterly. **Facsimile Number:** (202)331-2429.

★2339★
National Association of Trade and Technical Schools (NATTS)
2251 Wisconsin Ave. NW
Washington, DC 20007   Phone: (202)333-1021

Membership: Private schools providing career education. **Purpose:** Seeks to inform members of the accreditation process and regulations affecting vocational education. Conducts workshops and institutes for staffs of member schools; provides legislative, administrative, and public relations assistance; serves as federally recognized accrediting agency. Has established Career Training Foundation to support research into private vocational education. Sponsors annual Idea Fair Competition. Presents special awards. Maintains hall of fame; compiles statistics. **Publications:** *Career News Digest*, 3-4/year. • *Career Training*, quarterly. • *Classroom Companion*, quarterly. • *Handbook of Trade and Technical Careers and Training*, annual. • *NATTS News and Views*, bimonthly. • Also publishes *Career Guidance Handouts*.

★2340★
National Restaurant Association (NRA)
1200 17th St. NW
Washington, DC 20036 Phone: (202)331-5900
Membership: Restaurants, cafeterias, clubs, contract foodservice management, drive-ins, caterers, institutional food services, and other members of the foodservice industry; also represents establishments belonging to nonaffiliated state and local restaurant associations in governmental affairs. **Purpose:** Supports foodservice education and research in several educational institutions; conducts traveling management courses and seminars for restaurant personnel. Sponsors the Educational Foundation of the National Restaurant Association to provide training and education for operators, food and equipment manufacturers, distributors, and educators. Offers waiter/waitress training programs. Conducts the Great Menu Contest. Maintains 6000 volume library. **Publications:** *Foodservice Information Abstracts*, biweekly. • *National Restaurant Association—Washington Weekly.* • *Restaurant Industry Operations Report*, annual. • *Restaurants USA*, monthly with combined June/July issue. • *Technical Bulletin*, periodic. • Also publishes educational pamphlets, books, and catalog of publications and statistical reports; makes available films. **Toll-free/Additional Phone Number(s):** (800)424-5156. **Facsimile Number:** (202)331-2429.

Standards/Certification Agencies

★2341★
National Apprenticeship Training Program for Cooks
American Culinary Federation Educational Institute
National Apprenticeship Training Program for Cooks
10 San Bartola Rd.
PO Box 3466
St. Augustine, FL 32085 Phone: (904)824-4468
This six-panel brochure describes the certification process for cooks and chefs. Covers job competencies and future outlook.

★2342★
National Association of Trade and Technical Schools (NATTS)
2251 Wisconsin Ave. NW
Washington, DC 20007 Phone: (202)333-1021
Informs members of the accreditation process and regulations affecting vocational education. Conducts workshops and institutes for staffs of member schools; provides legislative, administrative, and public relations assistance; serves as a federally recognized accrediting agency.

★2343★
The National Certification Program for Cooks and Chefs
American Culinary Federation Educational Institute
National Apprenticeship Training Program for Cooks
10 San Bartola Rd.
PO Box 3466
St. Augustine, FL 32085 Phone: (904)824-4468
This eight-panel pamphlet describes the cook apprenticeship program including the screening process, examinations, basic competencies, and certification.

Test Guides

★2344★
Assistant Cook
National Learning Corp.
212 Michael Dr.
Syosset, NY 11791 Phone: (516)921-8888
Jack Rudman. Part of the Career Examination Series No. 1. All examination guides in this series contain questions with answers. **Facsimile Number:** (516)921-8743. **Toll-free/Additional Phone Number(s):** 800-645-6337.

★2345★
Cook
National Learning Corp.
212 Michael Dr.
Syosset, NY 11791 Phone: (516)921-8888
Jack Rudman. Part of the Career Examination Series No. 1. All examination guides in this series contain questions with answers. **Facsimile Number:** (516)921-8743. **Toll-free/Additional Phone Number(s):** 800-645-6337.

★2346★
Kitchen Supervisor
National Learning Corp.
212 Michael Dr.
Syosset, NY 11791 Phone: (516)921-8888
Jack Rudman. Part of the Career Examination Series No. 1. All examination guides in this series contain questions with answers. **Facsimile Number:** (516)921-8743. **Toll-free/Additional Phone Number(s):** 800-645-6337.

Educational Directories and Programs

★2347★
American Culinary Federation Educational Institute Apprenticeship Programs
American Culinary Federation Educational Institute
National Apprenticeship Training Program for Cooks
10 San Bartola Rd.
PO Box 3466
St. Augustine, FL 32085 Phone: (904)824-4468
State-by-state listing of local culinary associations offering apprenticeship training.

★2348★
Career Guidance Handouts
National Association of Trade and Technical Schools (NATTS)
2251 Wisconsin Ave. NW
Washington, DC 20007 Phone: (202)333-1021

★2349★
Career Training
National Association of Trade and Technical Schools (NATTS)
2251 Wisconsin Ave. NW
Washington, DC 20007 Phone: (202)333-1021
Quarterly.

Chefs, Cooks, and Other Kitchen Workers

★2350★
Classroom Companion
National Association of Trade and Technical Schools (NATTS)
2251 Wisconsin Ave. NW
Washington, DC 20007   Phone: (202)333-1021
Quarterly.

★2351★
College/University Foodservice Who's Who
Information Central, Inc.
Box 3900
Prescott, AZ 86302   Phone: (602)778-1513
Julie G. Woodman, editor. Triennial; latest edition January 1990. Over 2,100 food service programs in colleges and universities. Entries include: Institution name, address, phone, enrollment, total annual food purchases, number of meals served per day; name of management company, principal food service official, services. Arrangement: Geographical. Indexes: Alphabetical.

★2352★
The Guide to Cooking Schools
Shaw Guides, Inc.
625 Biltmore Way, Ste. 1406
Coral Gables, FL 33134   Phone: (305)446-8888
Dorlene V. Shane, editor. Annual, November. Approximately 300 cooking schools including culinary arts colleges, cooking travel programs, institutions offering specialized instruction, and culinary organizations; over 100 cooking programs at vocational/technical schools and junior colleges; international coverage. Entries include: For schools*Name, address, phone, fax, description of program, requirements for admission, faculty credentials, tuition cost. For organizations*Name, address, phone, fax, requirements for admission, services, annual dues. Arrangement: Alphabetical. Indexes: Geographical, type of cuisine, vacation programs. **Facsimile Number:** (305)446-1837.

★2353★
Handbook of Trade and Technical Careers and Training (NATTS)
National Association of Trade and Technical Schools (NATTS)
2251 Wisconsin Ave. NW
Washington, DC 20007   Phone: (202)333-1021
Annual.

Awards, Scholarships, Grants, and Fellowships

★2354★
Culinary Arts Salon
National Restaurant Association
1200 17th St., N.W.
Washington, DC 20036   Phone: (202)331-5900
Recognizes chefs, teams, apprentices, students and culinarians for outstanding food preparation. The event is held at the Association's annual show and is the largest culinary competition of its kind in America. Awards are given in Professional and Student categories. Gold, silver, and bronze medals are awarded. Other awards presented are: Anniversary Cake; Best of Show; Herman Rusch Award; Best Entry for Junior Culinarian; and Judges' Special Awards. Established in 1971. The Culinary Arts Salon is produced by the National Restaurant Association in cooperation with the American Culinary Federation and the ACF, Chicago Chefs of Cuisine.

★2355★
National Restaurant Association Ice Carving Classic
National Restaurant Association
1200 17th St., N.W.
Washington, DC 20036   Phone: (202)331-5900
To recognize three-person teams for transforming huge blocks of ice into magnificent works of art. The competition pits master ice carvers from around the world against one another in three events: compulsory figures, to be completed in one hour; free-style individual blocks, two hours; and team multiple blocks; three hours. Winners are honored at the Association's annual show. Established in 1988 in cooperation with the National Ice Carving Association. Additional information is available from Chuck Wagner in Burr Ridge, IL, phone: (708) 850-3100.

Basic Reference Guides and Handbooks

★2356★
Baking Buyer—Yearbook Issue
Sosland Publishing Company
4800 Main, Ste. 100
Kansas City, MO 64112   Phone: (816)756-1000
Teresa Ahrenholtz, Managing Editor, editor. Annual, June. Lists of approximately 1,000 distributors and 1,000 manufacturers of products and equipment for the baking industry. Entries include: For distributors*Company name, address, phone, fax, name of contact, types of products distributed, geographical area served. For manufacturers*Company name, address, phone, fax. Arrangement: Distributors are geographical. Indexes: Manufacturers*product/service, brand name. **Facsimile Number:** (816)756-0494.

★2357★
Cookbooks by Small Presses
Small Press Center
20 W. 44th St.
New York, NY 10036   Phone: (212)764-7021
Paula Matta, editor. Published 1988. List of more than 350 small presses that publish cookbooks. Entries include: Company name, address, phone. Arrangement: Alphabetical by title. Indexes: Alphabetical by publisher.

★2358★
Culinary Olympic Cookbook
American Culinary Federation (ACF)
Ten San Bartola Rd.
PO Box 3466
St. Augustine, FL 32085-3466   Phone: (904)824-4468

★2359★
Food Distribution Magazine—Food Brokers Directory Issue
Gro Com Group
1002 S. Fort Harrison Ave.
Clearwater, FL 34616   Phone: (813)443-2723
Ann Moore, editor. Annual, December. List of brokers in the food business. Entries include: Company name, address, phone, name and title of contact. **Toll-free/Additional Phone Number(s):** (800)556-7826. **Facsimile Number:** (813)446-1750.

★2360★
Food Professional's Guide
American Showcase
724 5th Ave., 10th Fl.
New York, NY 10019   Phone: (212)245-0981

Irena Chalmers, editor. First edition February 1990. Suppliers, organizations, distributors, manufacturers, cooking schools, food photographers, chef, restaurant owners, specialty food sources, restaurant consultants and designers, supermarket chains, government information sources, and others connected with the food industry. Entries include: Name, address, phone, names and titles of key personnel. Arrangement: Classified by product/service. **Facsimile Number:** (212)265-2247.

★2361★
Guide to Hospitality Education
Council on Hotel, Restaurant, and Institutional Education (CHRIE)
1200 17th St. NW
Washington, DC 20036-3097   Phone: (202)331-5990

Annual.

★2362★
Manual for Culinarians
American Culinary Federation (ACF)
Ten San Bartola Rd.
PO Box 3466
St. Augustine, FL 32085-3466   Phone: (904)824-4468

★2363★
Restaurant Hospitality—Restaurant Industry Almanac Issue
Penton Publishing Company
1100 Superior Ave.
Cleveland, OH 44114   Phone: (216)696-7000

Stephen G. Michaelides, editor. Annual. Lists of manufacturers of foods and beverages, equipment and supplies, and tabletop and decor products; foodservice and restaurant associations; major foodservice events; United States congressmen who are active in legislation related to the foodservice industry; foodservice distributors. Entries include: For manufacturers: Company name, address, phone, products. For foodservice and restaurant associations: Organization name, address, phone. For foodservice events: Name, address, phone, dates. For congressmen:Name, address, phone. For distributors: Company name, address, phone. Arrangement: Manufacturers are classified by product. Indexes: Product, advertisers. **Facsimile Number:** (216)696-8765.

★2364★
Whole Foods—Source Book Issue
Whole Foods Communications, Inc.
3000 Hadley Rd.
South Plainfield, NJ 07080   Phone: (908)769-1160

Dani el McSweeney, editor. Annual, May. Lists of 1,200 manufacturers, 175 wholesalers and distributors, and 65 brokers of natural food products; also 80 publishers of information about natural foods and 50 natural food associations. Entries include: For manufacturers: Company name, address, phone, contact person, line of business. For wholesalers and distributors: Company name, address, phone, toll-free phone, contact, description of products and services, territory covered, shipping company, approximate shipping time, size of sales staff. For brokers: Company name, address, phone, contact, geographic territory covered, firms represented, products. For others: Organization name, address, phone, contact, product or service. Arrangement: Classified by type of business. Indexes: Product/service, brand name, wholesaler/distributor territory. **Toll-free/Additional Phone Number(s):** (908)769-1160. **Facsimile Number:** (908)769-1171.

Periodicals

★2365★
Almost Free Cookbooks and Recipes Update
Update Publicare Company
c/o Prosperity & Profits Unlimited
PO Box 570213
Houston, TX 77257

Editor(s): A.C. Doyle. Annually. Carries information on recipe ingredient substitutions. Recurring features include news of research and lists of "almost free" cookbooks and recipes.

★2366★
Bakers Journal
NCC Publishing
222 Argyle Ave.
Delhi, ON, Canada N4B 2Y2   Phone: (519)582-2510

Ernest Naef, Editor and Publisher. Ten times/yr. Baking and confectionery magazine. **Facsimile Number:** (519)582-4040.

★2367★
Bakery Production and Marketing
Gorman Publishing Co.
Promotion Dept.
8750 W. Bryn Mawr Ave.
Chicago, IL 60631   Phone: (312)693-3200

Ray Lahvic, Editor. 14x/yr. (monthly with two special issues, July and Sept.). Bakery industry magazine. **Facsimile Number:** (312)693-0568.

★2368★
Baking
Putman Publishing Co., Inc.
301 E. Erie St.
Chicago, IL 60611   Phone: (312)644-2020

Jim Kraus, Editor. Monthly. Professional magazine on baking operations and packaging. **Facsimile Number:** (312)644-1131.

★2369★
Baking & Snack
Sosland Publishing Co.
4800 Main, Ste. 100
Kansas City, MO 64112   Phone: (816)756-1000

Laurie Gorton, Editor. Monthly (except March). Equipment and engineering magazine for commercial manufacturers of baked and snack foods. **Facsimile Number:** (816)756-0494.

★2370★
BC&T News
Bakery, Confectionery, and Tobacco Workers International Union
10401 Connecticut Ave.
Kensington, MD 20895-3961   Phone: (301)933-8600

Nine times/yr.

★2371★
Capital News
Snack Food Association (SFA)
1711 King St., Ste. 1
Alexandria, VA 22314   Phone: (703)836-4500

Editor(s): Jim McCarthy. 12/yr. Seeks to disseminate information to those involved in the manufacturing of snack foods. Provides chief executive and government relations officers of snack food companies with reports on legislative and

Chefs, Cooks, and Other Kitchen Workers

regulatory changes of import to the industry. **Facsimile Number:** (703)836-8262.

★2372★
Career News Digest
National Association of Trade and Technical Schools (NATTS)
2251 Wisconsin Ave. NW
Washington, DC 20007   Phone: (202)333-1021
3-4/year.

★2373★
Catering Industry Employee
Hotel Employees and Restaurant Employees International Union
1219 28th St. NW
Washington, DC 20007   Phone: (202)393-4373
Herman Leavitt, Editor. Monthly. Trade journal for culinary and hospitality workers. Official publication of the Hotel Employees and Restaurant Employees International Union. **Facsimile Number:** (202)333-0468.

★2374★
Cheesemakers' Journal
New England Cheesemaking Supply Company
Main St.
PO Box 85
Ashfield, MA 01330   Phone: (413)628-3802
6/yr. Carries information relating to cheese, cheesemaking, and cheesemakers. Contains articles on both small scale commercial and home cheesemaking. Recurring features include recipes, editorials, letters to the editor, news of research, news of members, book reviews, and a calendar of events.

★2375★
Chef Institutional
134 Main St.
New Canaan, CT 06840   Phone: (203)972-3022
George Serra, Publisher. 6x/yr. For the institutional food field.

★2376★
Chile Pepper
Out West Publishing
PO Box 4278
Albuquerque, NM 87196   Phone: (505)266-8322
Dave DeWitt, Editor. 6x/yr. Magazine on spicy cuisine from around the world.

★2377★
CHRIE Communique
Council on Hotel, Restaurant, and Institutional Education (CHRIE)
1200 17th St. NW
Washington, DC 20036-3097   Phone: (202)331-5990
Semimonthly.

★2378★
Cookbook Digest
Park Avenue Publishing
500 5th Ave., Ste. 5423
New York, NY 10036   Phone: (212)575-9420
Robert J. Krefting, Publisher. 6x/yr. Magazine featuring recipes from various cookbooks.

★2379★
Cookies
P. Wetherill
5426 27th St. NW
Washington, DC 20015   Phone: (202)966-0869
Editor(s): P. Wetherill. 6/yr. Focuses on cookies and cookie shaping. Carries historical items on cookie cutters and other shaping devices, and general cookie-related news items. Recurring features include recipes, sources of new cutters and molds, baking tips, news of research, letters to the editor, news of members, book reviews, and a calendar of events.

★2380★
Cooking Contest Chronicle
Karen Martis
PO Box 10792
Merrillville, IN 46411-0792   Phone: (219)887-6983
Editor(s): Karen Martis. 12/yr. Designed to inform readers of cooking contests. Includes entry requirements, closing dates, and news of rapidly changing contest developments. Recurring features include editorials, letters to the editor, news of contestant winners, and cookbook reviews.

★2381★
Cooking For Profit
C P Publishing, Inc.
104 S. Main St.
PO Box 267
Fond du Lac, WI 54936-0267   Phone: (414)923-3700
Colleen Phalen, Editor. Monthly. Magazine providing practical foodservice operation information including recipes, energy conservation, and equipment. Facsimile Number: (414)923-6805.

★2382★
COOK'S
Pennington Publishing, Inc.
4984 Palm Coast Pkwy. W., No. 6
Palm Coast, FL 32137-3620
Deborah S. Hartz, Senior Editor. 10x/yr.

★2383★
Country Chronicle
138 Main St.
PO Box 278
Denmark, WI 54208   Phone: (414)863-2154
Cindy Thompson, Editor. Weekly (Wed.). Rural community newspaper. **Facsimile Number:** (414)863-6102.

★2384★
Culinary Review
American Culinary Federation (ACF)
Ten San Bartola Rd.
PO Box 3466
St. Augustine, FL 32085-3466   Phone: (904)824-4468
Monthly.

★2385★
Dairy-Deli Digest
International Dairy-Deli-Bakery Association
313 Price Pl., Ste. 202
PO Box 5528
Madison, WI 53711   Phone: (608)238-7908
Editor(s): Carol L. Christison. 10/yr. Supports the association, which seeks to increase dairy-deli bakery business and encourage a noncompetitive spirit among all segments of the industry. Focuses on issues of concern to manufacturers, retailers, brokers, distributors, businesses, and organizations involved with the dairy-deli bakery industry. Recurring features include research news, reports of meetings, news of educational opportunities and industrial trends, and notices of publications available.

★2386★
Deli-Bake Advocate
Gro Com Group
1002 S. Ft. Harrison
Clearwater, FL 34616　　　　　　　　Phone: (813)443-2723
Mark Weeks, Co-Publisher. 6x/yr. Trade magazine for the deli and bakery industries (food service and retail). **Facsimile Number:** (813)446-1750.

★2387★
Fast and Light Summer Cooking
GCR Publishing Group, Inc.
888 7th Ave.
New York, NY 10106
Nancy Kalish, Editor. Quarterly Magazine featuring easy to prepare cuisine.

★2388★
Food & Wine
American Express Publishing Corp.
1120 Avenue of the Americas
New York, NY 10036　　　　　　　　Phone: (212)382-5600
Ila Stanger, Editor. Monthly. Magazine devoted to food and wine. **Facsimile Number:** (212)382-5788.

★2389★
Food Chemical News
Louis Rothschild, Jr.
1101 Pennsylvania Ave. SE
Washington, DC 20003　　　　　　　Phone: (202)544-1980
Editor(s): Louis Rothschild, Jr. Weekly. Provides in-depth, timely coverage of the laws affecting food regulation, including additives, colors, pesticides, and allied products. Recurring features include news of research. **Facsimile Number:** (202)546-3890.

★2390★
Food Distribution Research Society—Quarterly Newsletter
Food Distribution Research Society, Inc.
PO Box 441110
Ft. Washington, MD 20744　　　　　　Phone: (301)292-1970
Editor(s): Dale L. Anderson. 3-4/yr. Reports on the actions of government bodies and other developments affecting the food industry. Reprints articles of interest from other publications, with special attention to results of research, surveys, and studies. Recurring features include announcements of conferences, meetings, and educational programs; notices of resource materials available; news of research; statistics; and book reviews. **Facsimile Number:** (301)292-1787.

★2391★
Foodletter
Foodletter
PO Box 204
Mahwah, NJ 07430　　　　　　　　　Phone: (201)529-3835
Editor(s): Doreen Higgins, Evie Bottali, and Louise Weston. 10/yr. Analyzes current trends in foods and beverages, forecasts trends, and gives corresponding ideas for new products and packaging. Recurring features include a column titled Consumer Corner.

★2392★
Foodservice Information Abstracts
National Restaurant Association (NRA)
1200 17th St. NW
Washington, DC 20036　　　　　　　Phone: (202)331-5900
Biweekly. Abstracts from foodservice trade magazines.

★2393★
Foodservice Report
International Foodservice Distributors Association (IFDA)
201 Park Washington Court
Falls Church, VA 22046　　　　　　　Phone: (703)532-940
Editor(s): John D. Thompson. Monthly. Carries news of th food service industry, including activities of manufacturers brokers, and distributors, as well as trends in food servic operation. Recurring features include profiles of food servic distribution companies in the U.S. and Canada, a calendar o events, and reports of conventions and conferences.

★2394★
Fresh Baked
Retail Bakers of America
6525 Belcrest Rd., Ste. 250
Hyattsville, MD 20782　　　　　　　Phone: (301)277-099
Editor(s): Margi Berkowitz. Monthly. Examines trends an issues in the bakery industry. Features items on baker production, marketing, business management, and other topic of interest. Recurring features include news of research meeting reports, a calendar of events, and columns titled Hov to, Ingredient Update, and Donut Directions. **Facsimil Number:** (301)277-2090.

★2395★
Fresh Facts for Foodservice
United Fresh Fruit and Vegetable Association
727 N. Washington St.
Alexandria, VA 22314　　　　　　　Phone: (703)836-341
Editor(s): Elaine McLaughlin. Monthly. Highlights fresh fruit and vegetables that will be in good supply in the coming month and carries articles on food service establishments whicl emphasize fresh items. Recurring features include cooking tips recipes, and notices of promotional materials available.

★2396★
Fresh Off the Vine
California Fresh Market Tomato Advisory Board
2017 N. Gateway Blvd., Ste. 102
Fresno, CA 93727　　　　　　　　　Phone: (209)251-062
Semiannually. Contains "research and crop information handling and storage tips, interviews with chefs and othe foodservice personnel, quantity recipes and use ideas—al geared to help the foodservice operator ultimately increase profits."

★2397★
Hospitality and Tourism Educator
Council on Hotel, Restaurant, and Institutional Education (CHRIE)
1200 17th St. NW
Washington, DC 20036-3097　　　　Phone: (202)331-599
Quarterly.

★2398★
Hospitality Education and Research Journal
Council on Hotel, Restaurant, and Institutional Education (CHRIE)
1200 17th St. NW
Washington, DC 20036-3097　　　　Phone: (202)331-599
3/year.

★2399★
The Hospitality Manager
Cassis Communications
20 Hayward
Ames, IA 50010 Phone: (515)296-2400

Terry Lowman, Editor. Monthly. Trade publication (tabloid) covering restaurant and institutional business in the Midwest. Mailed to restaurants, bars, and institutional food service companies. **Facsimile Number:** (515)296-2405.

★2400★
The Independent
Independent Bakers Association
PO Box 3731
Washington, DC 20007 Phone: (202)333-8190

Editor(s): Robert N. Pyle. Periodic. Carries association news and brief articles on commodities, taxes, labor, and other matters affecting the baking industry. Recurring features include reports of conferences, meetings, and the annual convention; election slates; membership updates; and presidential reports. **Facsimile Number:** (202)337-3809.

★2401★
Kitchen Times
Howard Wilson & Company, Inc.
185 Marlborough St.
Boston, MA 02116 Phone: (617)266-2453

Editor(s): Howard Wilson. Monthly. Contains instructions on buying food and preparing specific dishes. Reviews restaurants, inns, cooks, cookbooks, and wines.

★2402★
Modern Baking
Donohue-Meehan Publishing Co.
2700 River Rd., Ste. 306
Des Plaines, IL 60018 Phone: (708)299-4430

Ed Lee, Editor. Monthly. Magazine on news, products, and trends of the baking industry. **Facsimile Number:** (708)296-1968.

★2403★
Modern Food Service News
Grocers Publishing Co., Inc.
15 Emerald St.
Hackensack, NJ 07601 Phone: (201)488-1800

John Strovinsky, Exec. Editor. Monthly. Magazine for restaurateurs, chefs, caterers, puchasing agents in the food service industry.

★2404★
NACUFS News Wave
National Association of College and University Food Services (NACUFS)
1405 S. Harrison Rd., Ste. 303-304
Manly Miles Bldg.
Michigan State University
East Lansing, MI 48824 Phone: (517)332-2494

Editor(s): Mary Jo Custer. 5/yr. Covers news of interest to food service industry personnel in academic institutions. Also reports on regional association activities. Recurring features include columns titled President's Message, Special Features, and Committee Spotlight.

★2405★
National Nutritional Foods Association—Monitor
National Nutritional Foods Association
150 Paularino Ave., Ste. 285
Costa Mesa, CA 92626 Phone: (714)966-6632

Editor(s): Burton Kallman, Ph.D. Monthly. Supplies professionals in the health foods industry with analysis of business, social, technological, scientific, and economic developments affecting the industry. Provides information and suggestions about marketing, merchandising, public relations, and business management. Recurring features include news of nutrition research, a calendar of events, and columns titled Business Shorts, Science & Technology, and Legal/Legislation. **Facsimile Number:** (714)641-7005.

★2406★
National Restaurant Association—Washington Weekly (NRA)
National Restaurant Association (NRA)
1200 17th St. NW
Washington, DC 20036 Phone: (202)331-5900

Newsletter reporting on legislation and regulatory issues affecting the foodservice industry.

★2407★
Nation's Restaurant News
425 Park Ave.
New York, NY 10022 Phone: (212)371-9400

Charles Bernstein, Editor. Weekly (Mon.). **Facsimile Number:** (212)838-9487.

★2408★
NRA Technical Bulletin
National Restaurant Association (NRA)
1200 17th St. NW
Washington, DC 20036 Phone: (202)331-5900

Periodic.

★2409★
The Practical Gourmet
Healthy Gourmet, Inc.
Gourmet Bldg., No. 102
Seven Putter Lane
Middle Island, NY 11953-0102 Phone: (516)924-8555

Editor(s): Gaylen Andrews, R.N. Monthly. Presents information and ideas for the practical approach to gourmet cooking, emphasizing economy, efficiency, and nutrition. Discusses such topics as general industry trends, new products and processes, entertainment, and health. Recurring features include recipes for various diets, preparation tips, book reviews, letters to the editor, and news of research.

★2410★
Quick 'n Easy Country Cookin'
Parkside Publishing
Box 66
Davis, SD 57021 Phone: (605)238-5704

Zeta Overgard, Editor and Publisher. 6x/yr. Cooking magazine emphasizing meats requiring short preparation times. Includes articles on efficient use of microwave oven, crock pot, and food processor; recipes, food information, craft ideas, poems, and human interest stories.

★2411★
Recipe Ingredient Substitution Update
Update Publicare Company
c/o Prosperity & Profits Unlimited
PO Box 570213
Houston, TX 77257 Phone: (713)867-3438

Editor(s): A.C. Doyle. Annually. Aims to introduce housewives and caterers to new food ideas. Carries recipes and suggestions for ingredient substitutions and recipe variations.

★2412★
Restaurant Business
Biller Communications, Inc.
633 3rd Ave.
New York, NY 10017   Phone: (212)986-4800
Peter R. Berlinski, Editor. 18x/yr. Trade magazine for restaurants and commercial food service. **Facsimile Number:** (212)983-3198.

★2413★
Restaurant Exchange News
PO Box 2655
Greenwich, CT 06836-2655   Phone: (914)638-1108
Robert B. Melton, Editor. Monthly. Food service industry magazine. **Facsimile Number:** (914)638-2549.

★2414★
Restaurant Merchandising News
Mortimer Publishing Co.
53 Sterling Rd.
Trumbull, CT 06611   Phone: (203)261-5506
Dawn Mortimer, Editor. Monthly. Business magazine serving the food service industry.

★2415★
Restaurants & Institutions
Cahners Publishing Co.
1350 E. Touhy Ave.
PO Box 5080
Des Plaines, IL 60018   Phone: (708)635-8800
Mike Bartlett, Editor-in-Chief. 27x/yr. Magazine focusing on foodservice and lodging management. **Facsimile Number:** (708)635-6856.

★2416★
Restaurants USA
National Restaurant Association (NRA)
1200 17th St. NW
Washington, DC 20036   Phone: (202)331-5900
Monthly with combined June/July issue. Magazine to keep foodservice operators and managers abreast of trends and developments in the industry. Contains annual index and calendar of events.

★2417★
Seafood Leader
Waterfront Press Co.
1115 NW 46th St.
Seattle, WA 98107   Phone: (206)789-6506
Peter Redmayne, Editor and Publisher. 6x/yr. Magazine on seafood buying, marketing, and technology. Articles range from seafood processing technology to merchandising to cuisine; featuring seafood from the ocean to the plate. **Facsimile Number:** (206)789-9193.

★2418★
Simple Cooking
Jackdaw Press
PO Box 88
Steuben, ME 04680-0088
Editor(s): John Thorne and Martha Lewis. Quarterly. Discusses culinary subjects, focusing on traditional recipes "requiring the simple preparation of good ingredients." Contains essays on origins, makings, and relevance of recipes. Recurring features include editorials, recipes, and columns titled Table Talk, Kitchen Diary, and Good Things.

Meetings and Conventions

★2419★
American Culinary Federation (ACF)
Ten San Bartola Rd.
PO Box 3466
St. Augustine, FL 32085-3466   Phone: (904)824-4468
Frequency: Annual, with exhibits. 1992; Jul. 26-30; Washington, DC. **Facsimile Number:** (904)825-4758.

★2420★
American School Food Service Association Conference
American School Food Service Association
1600 Duke St., 7th Fl.
Alexandria, VA 22314   Phone: (703)739-3900
1992; Jul. 17-22; Minneapolis, MN ● 1993; Jul. Boston, MA ● 1994; Jul. Anaheim, CA ● 1995; Jul. St. Louis, MO. **Toll-free/Additional Phone Number(s):** 800-877-8822. **Facsimile Number:** (703)739-3915.

★2421★
American Society for Hospital Food Service Administrators Convention
American Hospital Association
Convention and Meetings Division
840 N. Lake Shore Dr.
Chicago, IL 60611   Phone: (312)280-6000
Frequency: Always held in Toronto, Ontario, Canada, at the Harbour Castle Westin. 1992; Toronto, ON, Canada. **Facsimile Number:** (312)280-6462.

★2422★
Council on Hotel, Restaurant, and Institutional Education International Conference (CHRIE)
1200 17th St. NW
Washington, DC 20036-3097   Phone: (202)331-5990
Frequency: Annual. **Facsimile Number:** (202)331-2429.

★2423★
DAIRY-DELI-BAKE
International Dairy-Deli Association
313 Price Pl., Ste. 202
PO Box 5528
Madison, WI 53705-0528   Phone: (608)238-7908
1992; Jun. 07-09; New Orleans, LA ● 1993; Jun. 06-08; Milwaukee, WI.

★2424★
Food and Beverage Show
George Little Management
577 Airport Blvd., Ste. 440
Burlingame, CA 94010-2020   Phone: (415)344-5171
1992. **Facsimile Number:** (415)344-5270.

★2425★
FOODTECH - International Food and Beverage, Catering, Food Production and Processing Equipment, Packaging Machinery and Materials Exhibition
World Access Corp.
15 Bemis Rd.
PO Box 171
Wellesley Hills, MA 02181   Phone: (617)235-8095

★2426★
IFT Annual Meeting and Food Expo
Institute of Food Technologists
221 N. LaSalle
Chicago, IL 60601   Phone: (312)782-8424
1992; Jun. 21-24; New Orleans, LA • 1993; Jul. 11-14; Chicago, IL • 1994; Jun. 26-29; Atlanta, GA • 1995; Jun. 04-07; Anaheim, CA. **Facsimile Number:** (312)782-8348.

★2427★
International Baking Industry Exposition
American Bakers Association
1111 14th St., NW, Ste. 300
Washington, DC 20005   Phone: (202)296-5800
1992. **Facsimile Number:** (202)371-0017.

★2428★
International Caterers' Conference
Helen Brett Enterprises, Inc.
220 S. State St., Ste. 1416
Chicago, IL 60604   Phone: (312)922-0966
1992; San Francisco, CA • 1993; Atlanta, GA • 1994; Mexico City, Mexico. **Facsimile Number:** (312)922-0969.

★2429★
Retail Confectioners International Annual Convention and Exposition
Retail Confectioners International
1807 Glenview Rd., Ste. 204
Glenview, IL 60025   Phone: (708)724-6120
Frequency: Always held in June. 1992; Jun. 18-22; Chicago, IL.

──────── **Other Sources of Information** ────────

★2430★
Commercial Food Equipment Service Association Directory
Commercial Food Equipment Service Association (CFESA)
9240 N. Meridian St., Ste. 355
Indianapolis, IN 46260   Phone: (317)844-4700
Annual. Member foodservice equipment repair technicians.

★2431★
Directory of French-Fry Potatoes
Food Information Services Center
21050 SW 93rd Lane Rd.
Dunnellon, FL 32630   Phone: (904)489-8919
James A. Mixon, editor. Biennial, even years. French-fry potato suppliers and related service companies. Entries include: Company name, address, phone, name and title of contact, subsidiary and branch names and locations, products produced. Arrangement: Classified by product or service. Indexes: Product/service. **Facsimile Number:** (904)489-1872.

★2432★
Directory of Specialty Foods Suppliers
Anderson Publications
230 N. Michigan, 11th Fl., Ste. 1100
Chicago, IL 60601-5910   Phone: (312)726-3268
Mary Jane Anderson, Publisher, editor. Irregular; previous edition July 1988; latest edition January 1991. Specialty food suppliers. Entries include: Company name, address, phone, toll-free phone, fax, name and title of contact, description of products and services provided. Arrangement: Alphabetical. Indexes: Product/service.

★2433★
Frozen Foods—Wholesale Directory
American Business Directories, Inc.
American Business Information, Inc.
5711 S. 86th Circle
Omaha, NE 68127   Phone: (402)593-4600
Annual. 1,768. Entries include: Name, address, phone, size of advertisement, name of owner or manager, number of employees, year first in "Yellow Pages." Arrangement: Geographical. **Facsimile Number:** (402)331-1505.

★2434★
Restaurant Industry Operations Report
National Restaurant Association (NRA)
1200 17th St. NW
Washington, DC 20036   Phone: (202)331-5900
Annual.

Food and Beverage Service Occupations

Food and beverage service workers deal with customers in all manner of dining establishments from small, informal diners to large restaurants. Waiters and waitresses take customers' orders and serve food and beverages. How this is done varies depending on type of establishment. Coffee shops require fast, efficient service, whereas in finer restaurants the service is more formal and personal. Bartenders fill the drink orders given to them by waiters or waitresses. Bartenders must be able to mix drinks accurately and quickly, and may also operate the cash register and clean up. They may also be responsible for ordering and maintaining an inventory of liquor and other bar supplies. Hosts and hostesses welcome guests, take coats, and escort patrons to their tables. They also take reservations and arrange parties. Dining room attendants and bartender helpers keep the serving area stocked, and perform cleaning and maintenance tasks. Counter attendants take orders and serve food at counters. They do food pick-up, prepare short-order items, clean counters and accept payment. Fast-food workers take orders and accept payment from customers standing at counters of fast-food restaurants. They may also cook and package foods.

$alaries

Food and beverage workers derive their earnings from a combination of hourly wages and customer tips. Both vary greatly, depending on type of job and establishment. Median full-time hourly earnings (including tips) are listed below.

Waiters and waitresses	$4.70/hour
Bartenders	$6.00/hour
Dining room attendants and bartender helpers	$4.80/hour
Counter attendants and fast-food workers	$4.00/hour

Employment Outlook

Growth rate until the year 2000: Faster than average.

Food and Beverage Service Occupations

Career Guides

★2435★
"Bartender" in *Hospitality and Recreation*, Volume 8 of *Career Information Center* (pp. 37-38)
Glencoe/Macmillan
15319 Chatsworth St.
Mission Hills, CA 91345   Phone: (818)898-1391
Richard Lidz and Dale Anderson, editorial directors. Fourth edition, 1990. For 600 occupations, describes job duties, entry-level requirements, education and training needed, advancement possibilities, employment outlook, earnings and benefits. The set is divided into 12 volumes. Each volume includes jobs related under a broad career field. Volume 13 is the index. **Facsimile Number:** 818-365-5489.

★2436★
"Bartender" in Volume 1 of *Career Discovery Encyclopedia* (pp. 114-115)
J.G. Ferguson Publishing Co.
200 W. Monroe
Chicago, IL 60606   Phone: (312)580-5480
E. Russell Primm, editor-in-chief. 1990. Contains two-page articles on 504 occupations. Each article describes job duties, earnings, and educational and training requirements.

★2437★
Bartenders
Chronicle Guidance Publications, Inc.
PO Box 1190
Moravia, NY 13118-1190   Phone: (315)497-0330
1991. This career brief describes the nature of the work, working conditions, hours and earnings, education and training, licensure, certification, unions, personal qualifications, social and psychological factors, employment outlook, entry methods, advancement, and related occupations. **Toll-free/Additional Phone Number(s):** 800-622-7284.

★2438★
"Bartenders" in *Opportunities in Restaurant Careers* (pp. 19-22)
National Textbook Co.
4255 W. Touhy Ave.
Lincolnwood, IL 60646   Phone: (312)679-5500
Carol Ann Caprione Chmelynski. 1990. Provides an overview of the restaurant industry and surveys entry-level, mid-level, and management jobs. Covers working conditions, educational preparation, training, advancement possibilities, employment outlook, and earnings. Lists schools offering programs in hotel, restaurant, and institutional management.

★2439★
"Bartenders" in *Opportunities in Vocational and Technical Careers* (pp. 72-73)
National Textbook Co.
4255 W. Touhy Ave.
Lincolnwood, IL 60646   Phone: (312)679-5500
Adrian A. Paradis. 1987. Describes careers which can be prepared for by attending a private vocational or proprietary school—office employee, sales worker, service worker, health services, mechanic, craftworker, and technician. Covers employment outlook, job duties, and salaries. Offers career planning advice.

★2440★
"Bartenders" in Volume 3 of *The Encyclopedia of Careers and Vocational Guidance* (pp. 198-201)
J.G. Ferguson Publishing Co.
200 W. Monroe
Chicago, IL 60606   Phone: (312)580-5480
William E. Hopke, editor-in-chief. Eighth edition, 1990. Four-volume set that profiles 500 occupations and describes job trends in 76 industries. Includes career description, educational requirements, history of the job, methods of entry, advancement, employment outlook, earnings, working conditions, social and psychological factors, and sources of additional information.

★2441★
"Bartenders, Waiters, and Bus Persons" in *The American Almanac of Jobs and Salaries* (pp. 526-527)
Avon Books
105 Madison Avenue
New York, NY 10016   Phone: (212)481-5600
John Wright and Edward J. Dwyer. Revised and updated, 1990. A comprehensive guide to the wages of hundreds of occupations in a wide variety of industries and organizations.

★2442★
Basic Responsibilities of Waiters and Waitresses
National Educational Media, Inc.
21601 Devonshire St.
Chatsworth, CA 91311-9962   Phone: (818)709-6009
Videocassette. 1983. 12 mins. This program is designed to quickly teach students and new employees the basics of day-to-day success as professional food servers.

★2443★
"Cafeteria Attendant" in *Hospitality and Recreation*, Volume 8 of *Career Information Center* (pp. 40-42)
Glencoe/Macmillan
15319 Chatsworth St.
Mission Hills, CA 91345   Phone: (818)898-1391
Richard Lidz and Dale Anderson, editorial directors. Fourth edition, 1990. For 600 occupations, describes job duties, entry-level requirements, education and training needed, advancement possibilities, employment outlook, earnings and benefits. The set is divided into 12 volumes. Each volume includes jobs related under a broad career field. Volume 13 is the index. **Facsimile Number:** 818-365-5489.

★2444★
"Cafeteria Counter Worker" in *Occu-Facts: Information on 565 Careers in Outline Form* (p. 13.15)
Careers, Inc.
P.O. Box 135
1211 Tenth St., S.W.
Largo, FL 33640   Phone: (813)584-7333
Elizabeth Handville. Biennial, 1989-90 edition. Each one-page occupational profile describes duties, working conditions, physical surroundings and demands, aptitudes, temperament, educational requirements, employment outlook, earnings, and places of employment.

★2445★
The Choice of the Future
National Restaurant Association
The Educational Foundation
250 S. Wacker Dr., Ste. 1400
Chicago, IL 60606   Phone: (312)715-1010
This 27-page booklet provides an overview of the food service industry and describes jobs, the work, education, training, and advancement possibilities. Contains salary surveys.

★2446★
College & University Food Service Manual
Colman Publishers
1147 Elmwood
Stockton, CA 95204   Phone: (209)464-9503
Paul Fairbrook. 1979.

★2447★
Culinary Careers
National Textbook Co.
4255 W. Touhy Ave.
Lincolnwood, IL 60646-1975   Phone: (708)679-5500
Mary D. Donovan. 1990. Part of Opportunities In Career Series. **Facsimile Number:** (708)679-2494.

★2448★
Dining Room Attendant
Careers, Inc.
PO Box 135
Largo, FL 34649-0135   Phone: (813)584-7333
1990. Two-page job guide card describing duties, working conditions, personal qualifications, training, earnings and hours, employment outlook, places of employment, related careers and where to write for more information.

★2449★
"Dining Room Attendant" in *Hospitality and Recreation*, Volume 8 of *Career Information Center* (pp. 42-43)
Glencoe/Macmillan
15319 Chatsworth St.
Mission Hills, CA 91345   Phone: (818)898-1391
Richard Lidz and Dale Anderson, editorial directors. Fourth edition, 1990. For 600 occupations, describes job duties, entry-level requirements, education and training needed, advancement possibilities, employment outlook, earnings and benefits. The set is divided into 12 volumes. Each volume includes jobs related under a broad career field. Volume 13 is the index. **Facsimile Number:** 818-365-5489.

★2450★
"Dining Room Attendant" in *Occu-Facts: Information on 565 Careers in Outline Form* (p. 13.18)
Careers, Inc.
P.O. Box 135
1211 Tenth St., S.W.
Largo, FL 33640   Phone: (813)584-7333
Elizabeth Handville. Biennial, 1989-90 edition. Each one-page occupational profile describes duties, working conditions, physical surroundings and demands, aptitudes, temperament, educational requirements, employment outlook, earnings, and places of employment.

★2451★
Efficient Busperson—Assisting the Server
National Educational Media, Inc.
21601 Devonshire St.
Chatsworth, CA 91311-9962   Phone: (818)709-6009
Videocassette. 1981. 10 mins. This program emphasizes the busperson's quiet efficiency and teamwork with servers.

★2452★
"Fast Food Franchise Worker" in *Hospitality and Recreation*, Volume 8 of *Career Information Center* (pp. 47-48)
Glencoe/Macmillan
15319 Chatsworth St.
Mission Hills, CA 91345   Phone: (818)898-1391
Richard Lidz and Dale Anderson, editorial directors. Fourth edition, 1990. For 600 occupations, describes job duties, entry-level requirements, education and training needed, advancement possibilities, employment outlook, earnings and benefits. The set is divided into 12 volumes. Each volume includes jobs related under a broad career field. Volume 13 is the index. **Facsimile Number:** 818-365-5489.

★2453★
Fast Food Jobs: National Study of Fast Foods Employment
National Institute for Work and Learning
1255 23rd St., NW, Ste. 400
Washington, DC 20037   Phone: (202)862-8845
Ivan Charner and Bryna Shore Fraser. 1984.

★2454★
Fast Food Services
National Educational Media, Inc.
21601 Devonshire St.
Chatsworth, CA 91311-9962   Phone: (818)709-6009
Videocassette. 1983. 15 mins. This program presents basic job responsibilities of food servers. It gives detailed information on taking and filling orders and keeping work areas clean and properly stocked. It stresses teamwork and includes important information on courtesy and customer relations.

Food and Beverage Service Occupations

★2455★
"Fast Food Workers" in Volume 3 of *Career Discovery Encyclopedia* (pp. 18-19)
J.G. Ferguson Publishing Co.
200 W. Monroe
Chicago, IL 60606   Phone: (312)580-5480
E. Russell Primm, editor-in-chief. 1990. Contains two-page articles on 504 occupations. Each article describes job duties, earnings, and educational and training requirements.

★2456★
"Fast Food Workers" in Volume 3 of *The Encyclopedia of Careers and Vocational Guidance* (pp. 232-236)
J.G. Ferguson Publishing Co.
200 W. Monroe
Chicago, IL 60606   Phone: (312)580-5480
William E. Hopke, editor-in-chief. Eighth edition, 1990. Four-volume set that profiles 500 occupations and describes job trends in 76 industries. Includes career description, educational requirements, history of the job, methods of entry, advancement, employment outlook, earnings, working conditions, social and psychological factors, and sources of additional information.

★2457★
"Food and Beverage Industry" in *Jobs '91* (pp. 277-286)
Prentice Hall Press
1 Gulf Western Plaza
New York, NY 10023   Phone: (212)373-8500
Kathryn Petras and Ross Petras. Annual, 1991. Discusses employment prospects and trends for 15 professional careers and 29 industries. Lists leading companies, associations, directories, and magazines.

★2458★
"Food and Beverage Service Workers" in *Occupational Outlook Handbook* (pp. 296-298)
Superintendent of Documents
U.S. Government Printing Office
Washington, DC 20402   Phone: (202)783-3238
Biennial; latest edition, 1990-91. Encyclopedia of careers describing more than 250 occupations and comprising about 86 percent of all jobs in the economy. Occupations that require lengthy education or training are given the most attention. For each occupation, the handbook describes job duties, working conditions, training, educational preparation, personal qualities, advancement possibilities, job outlook, earnings, and sources of additional information.

★2459★
Food Careers
Prentice Hall
Rte. 9W
Englewood Cliffs, NJ 07632   Phone: (201)592-2000
Donna N. Creasy. 1977. Part of Home Economics Careers Series.

★2460★
Food Service Careers Guide Book
Educators' Publications, Inc.
1110 S. Pomona Ave.
Fullerton, CA 92632   Phone: (714)871-2950
Joe Witzman. 1987.

★2461★
Food Service Workers
Chronicle Guidance Publications, Inc.
PO Box 1190
Moravia, NY 13118-1190   Phone: (315)497-0330
1987. This career brief describes the nature of the work, working conditions, hours and earnings, education and training, licensure, certification, unions, personal qualifications, social and psychological factors, employment outlook, entry methods, advancement, and related occupations. **Toll-free/Additional Phone Number(s):** 800-622-7284.

★2462★
Food Services
Learning Corporation of America
108 Wilmot Rd.
Deerfield, IL 60015-9990   Phone: (708)940-1260
Videocassette. 1982. 21 mins. Four workers in the food industry offer a look at their jobs: chef, restaurant manager, baker and meat wrapper. From the "Working" series.

★2463★
"Head Waiter and Waitress" in *Hospitality and Recreation*, Volume 8 of *Career Information Center* (pp. 80-81)
Glencoe/Macmillan
15319 Chatsworth St.
Mission Hills, CA 91345   Phone: (818)898-1391
Richard Lidz and Dale Anderson, editorial directors. Fourth edition, 1990. For 600 occupations, describes job duties, entry-level requirements, education and training needed, advancement possibilities, employment outlook, earnings and benefits. The set is divided into 12 volumes. Each volume includes jobs related under a broad career field. Volume 13 is the index. **Facsimile Number:** 818-365-5489.

★2464★
Head Waitress
Vocational Biographies, Inc.
PO Box 31, Dept. VF10
Sauk Centre, MN 56378   Phone: (612)352-6516
1988. This pamphlet profiles a person working in the job. Includes information about job duties, working conditions, places of employment, educational preparation, labor market outlook, and salaries. **Toll-free/Additional Phone Number(s):** 800-255-0752.

★2465★
"Hostessing" in *The Job Hunter's Guide to Japan* (pp. 163-166)
Kodansha International
114 Fifth Ave.
New York, NY 10011   Phone: (212)727-6460
Terra Brockman. 1990. Provides an overview of life in Japan. Describes various types of jobs including hostessing. Outlines necessary qualifications, job hunting strategies, salaries, working hours and conditions, and additional sources of information.

★2466★
Introduction to Management in the Hospitality Industry
John Wiley & Sons, Inc.
605 3rd Ave.
New York, NY 10158   Phone: (212)850-6000
Tom Powers. Third edition, 1988. **Facsimile Number:** (212)850-6088.

★2467★
"Maitre d', Bartender, Waiter/Waitress: The People Who Meet the Public" in *Careers in the Restaurant Industry* (pp. 23-24)
Rosen Publishing Group, Inc.
29 E. 21st St.
New York, NY 10010   Phone: (212)777-3017

Richard S. Lee and Mary Price Lee. Revised edition, 1990. Explores various jobs in the restaurant industry including cooks and chefs, manager, maitre d', bartender, and waiter/waitress. Describes job duties, salaries, educational preparation and job hunting. Contains information about fast food, catering, and small businesses.

★2468★
Opportunities in Food Services
National Textbook Co.
4255 W. Touhy Ave.
Lincolnwood, IL 60646-1975   Phone: (708)679-5500

Carol Caprione. 1983. **Facsimile Number:** (708)679-2494.

★2469★
Opportunities in Restaurant Careers
National Textbook Co.
4255 W. Touhy Ave.
Lincolnwood, IL 60646-1975   Phone: (708)679-5500

1989. **Facsimile Number:** (708)679-2494.

★2470★
Personal Service Cluster
Center for Humanities, Inc.
Communications Park
Box 1000
Mount Kisco, NY 10549   Phone: (914)666-4100

Videocassette. 1984. 20 mins. Students get to see the day-by-day lives of people who work in the fields of cosmetology, food service and law enforcement.

★2471★
"Restaurant Host and Hostess" in *Hospitality and Recreation*, Volume 8 of *Career Information Center* (pp. 60-62)
Glencoe/Macmillan
15319 Chatsworth St.
Mission Hills, CA 91345   Phone: (818)898-1391

Richard Lidz and Dale Anderson, editorial directors. Fourth edition, 1990. For 600 occupations, describes job duties, entry-level requirements, education and training needed, advancement possibilities, employment outlook, earnings and benefits. The set is divided into 12 volumes. Each volume includes jobs related under a broad career field. Volume 13 is the index. **Facsimile Number:** 818-365-5489.

★2472★
Restaurant Host/Hostess
Careers, Inc.
PO Box 135
Largo, FL 34649-0135   Phone: (813)584-7333

1991. Two-page occupational summary card describing duties, working conditions, personal qualifications, training, earnings and hours, employment outlook, places of employment, related careers and where to write for more information.

★2473★
"Restaurant Host/Hostess" in *Occu-Facts: Information on 565 Careers in Outline Form* (p. 13.11)
Careers, Inc.
P.O. Box 135
1211 Tenth St., S.W.
Largo, FL 33640   Phone: (813)584-7333

Elizabeth Handville. Biennial, 1989-90 edition. Each one-page occupational profile describes duties, working conditions, physical surroundings and demands, aptitudes, temperament, educational requirements, employment outlook, earnings, and places of employment.

★2474★
Suggestive Selling for Waiters and Waitresses
National Educational Media, Inc.
21601 Devonshire St.
Chatsworth, CA 91311-9962   Phone: (818)709-6009

Videocassette. 1982. 10 mins. Basic principles of suggestive selling and menu merchandising are demonstrated. Distinguishes the unimaginative order-taker from the profit-producing salesperson.

★2475★
Table Attendant Training
Bergwall Productions
106 Charles Lindbergh Blvd.
Uniondale, NY 11553-3695   Phone: (516)222-1111

Videocassette. 1983. 75 mins. On 5 tapes, the techniques of becoming a good waiter are explained.

★2476★
Video Career Library - Public and Personal Services
Careers, Inc.
1211 10th St., SW
PO Box 135
Largo, FL 34649-0135   Phone: (813)584-7333

Videocassette. 1990. 35 mins. Part of the Video Career Library covering 165 occupations. Shows actual workers on the job. Includes firefighters, police officers, correctional officers, bartenders, waiters/waitresses, cooks/chefs, child care workers, flight attendants, barbers/cosmetologists, groundskeepers/ gardeners, and butchers/meat cutters.

★2477★
"Waiter" in *VGM's Careers Encyclopedia* (pp. 485-487)
National Textbook Co.
4255 W. Touhy Ave.
Lincolnwood, IL 60646   Phone: (312)679-5500

Third edition, 1991. Contains two- to five-page descriptions of 200 managerial, professional, technical, trade, and service occupations. Each profile includes job duties, places of employment, qualifications, educational preparation, training, employment potential, advancement, income, and additional sources of information.

★2478★
"Waiter and Waitress" in *Hospitality and Recreation*, Volume 8 of *Career Information Center* (pp. 70-72)
Glencoe/Macmillan
15319 Chatsworth St.
Mission Hills, CA 91345   Phone: (818)898-1391

Richard Lidz and Dale Anderson, editorial directors. Fourth edition, 1990. For 600 occupations, describes job duties, entry-level requirements, education and training needed, advancement possibilities, employment outlook, earnings and benefits. The set is divided into 12 volumes. Each volume includes jobs related under a broad career field. Volume 13 is the index. **Facsimile Number:** 818-365-5489.

Food and Beverage Service Occupations

★2479★
"Waiter or Waitress and Host or Hostess" in *Hospitality & Recreation* (pp. 39-43)
Franklin Watts, Inc.
387 Park Avenue, S.
New York, NY 10016 Phone: (212)686-7070
Marjorie Rittenberg Schulz. 1990. Provides an overview of jobs in the hotel, motel, food service, fitness, and recreation industries. Covers job duties, educational preparation, salary, and employment outlook. Offers job hunting advice.

★2480★
Waiter-Waitress
Careers, Inc.
PO Box 135
Largo, FL 34649-0135 Phone: (813)584-7333
1989. Two-page occupational summary card describing duties, working conditions, personal qualifications, training, earnings and hours, employment outlook, places of employment, related careers and where to write for more information.

★2481★
"Waiter/Waitress" in *Occu-Facts: Information on 565 Careers in Outline Form* (p. 13.12)
Careers, Inc.
P.O. Box 135
1211 Tenth St., S.W.
Largo, FL 33640 Phone: (813)584-7333
Elizabeth Handville. Biennial, 1989-90 edition. Each one-page occupational profile describes duties, working conditions, physical surroundings and demands, aptitudes, temperament, educational requirements, employment outlook, earnings, and places of employment.

★2482★
Waiters and Waitresses
Chronicle Guidance Publications, Inc.
PO Box 1190
Moravia, NY 13118-1190 Phone: (315)497-0330
1987. This career brief describes the nature of the work, working conditions, hours and earnings, education and training, licensure, certification, unions, personal qualifications, social and psychological factors, employment outlook, entry methods, advancement, and related occupations. **Toll-free/Additional Phone Number(s):** 800-622-7284.

★2483★
"Waiters and Waitresses" in *Opportunities in Restaurant Careers* (p. 10)
National Textbook Co.
4255 W. Touhy Ave.
Lincolnwood, IL 60646 Phone: (312)679-5500
Carol Ann Caprione Chmelynski. 1990. Provides an overview of the restaurant industry and surveys entry-level, mid-level, and management jobs. Covers working conditions, educational preparation, training, advancement possibilities, employment outlook, and earnings. Lists schools offering programs in hotel, restaurant, and institutional management.

★2484★
"Waiters and Waitresses" in Volume 6 of *Career Discovery Encyclopedia* (pp. 150-151)
J.G. Ferguson Publishing Co.
200 W. Monroe
Chicago, IL 60606 Phone: (312)580-5480
E. Russell Primm, editor-in-chief. 1990. Contains two-page articles on 504 occupations. Each article describes job duties, earnings, and educational and training requirements.

★2485★
Waiting Tables
Filmakers Library, Inc.
133 East 58th St.
New York, NY 10022 Phone: (212)355-6545
Videocassette. 1986. 20 mins. An enlightening look at the food service industry where the majority of employees are underpaid, non-unionized women.

★2486★
Who's Hiring in Hospitality
Educator's Pubications, Inc.
1110 S. Pomona Ave.
Fullerton, CA 92632 Phone: (714)871-2950
Joe Witzman. 1987.

--- Associations ---

★2487★
Council on Hotel, Restaurant, and Institutional Education (CHRIE)
1200 17th St. NW
Washington, DC 20036-3097 Phone: (202)331-5990
Membership: Schools and colleges offering specialized education and training in cooking, baking, tourism and hotel, restaurant, and institutional administration; individuals, executives, and students. **Purpose:** Sponsors competitions; bestows awards. **Publications:** *CHRIE Communique*, semimonthly. • *Guide to Hospitality Education*, annual. • *Hospitality Education and Research Journal*, 3/year. • *Hospitality and Tourism Educator*, quarterly. **Facsimile Number:** (202)331-2429.

★2488★
National Association of Trade and Technical Schools (NATTS)
2251 Wisconsin Ave. NW
Washington, DC 20007 Phone: (202)333-1021
Membership: Private schools providing career education. **Purpose:** Seeks to inform members of the accreditation process and regulations affecting vocational education. Conducts workshops and institutes for staffs of member schools; provides legislative, administrative, and public relations assistance; serves as federally recognized accrediting agency. Has established Career Training Foundation to support research into private vocational education. Sponsors annual Idea Fair Competition. Presents special awards. Maintains hall of fame; compiles statistics. **Publications:** *Career News Digest*, 3-4/year. • *Career Training*, quarterly. • *Classroom Companion*, quarterly. • *Handbook of Trade and Technical Careers and Training*, annual. • *NATTS News and Views*, bimonthly. • Also publishes *Career Guidance Handouts*.

★2489★
National Restaurant Association (NRA)
1200 17th St. NW
Washington, DC 20036 Phone: (202)331-5900
Membership: Restaurants, cafeterias, clubs, contract foodservice management, drive-ins, caterers, institutional food services, and other members of the foodservice industry; also represents establishments belonging to nonaffiliated state and local restaurant associations in governmental affairs. **Purpose:** Supports foodservice education and research in several educational institutions; conducts traveling management courses and seminars for restaurant personnel. Sponsors the Educational Foundation of the National Restaurant Association to provide training and education for operators, food and equipment manufacturers, distributors, and educators. Offers

waiter/waitress training programs. Conducts the Great Menu Contest. Maintains 6000 volume library. **Publications:** *Foodservice Information Abstracts*, biweekly. • *National Restaurant Association—Washington Weekly*. • *Restaurant Industry Operations Report*, annual. • *Restaurants USA*, monthly with combined June/July issue. • *Technical Bulletin*, periodic. • Also publishes educational pamphlets, books, and catalog of publications and statistical reports; makes available films. **Toll-free/Additional Phone Number(s):** (800)424-5156. **Facsimile Number:** (202)331-2429.

--- Standards/Certification Agencies ---

★2490★
National Association of Trade and Technical Schools (NATTS)
2251 Wisconsin Ave. NW
Washington, DC 20007   Phone: (202)333-1021
Informs members of the accreditation process and regulations affecting vocational education. Conducts workshops and institutes for staffs of member schools; provides legislative, administrative, and public relations assistance; serves as a federally recognized accrediting agency.

--- Educational Directories and Programs ---

★2491★
Career Guidance Handouts
National Association of Trade and Technical Schools (NATTS)
2251 Wisconsin Ave. NW
Washington, DC 20007   Phone: (202)333-1021

★2492★
Career Training
National Association of Trade and Technical Schools (NATTS)
2251 Wisconsin Ave. NW
Washington, DC 20007   Phone: (202)333-1021
Quarterly.

★2493★
Classroom Companion
National Association of Trade and Technical Schools (NATTS)
2251 Wisconsin Ave. NW
Washington, DC 20007   Phone: (202)333-1021
Quarterly.

★2494★
College/University Foodservice Who's Who
Information Central, Inc.
Box 3900
Prescott, AZ 86302   Phone: (602)778-1513
Julie G. Woodman, editor. Triennial; latest edition January 1990. Over 2,100 food service programs in colleges and universities. Entries include: Institution name, address, phone, enrollment, total annual food purchases, number of meals served per day; name of management company, principal food service official, services. Arrangement: Geographical. Indexes: Alphabetical.

★2495★
Handbook of Trade and Technical Careers and Training (NATTS)
National Association of Trade and Technical Schools (NATTS)
2251 Wisconsin Ave. NW
Washington, DC 20007   Phone: (202)333-1021
Annual.

--- Awards, Scholarships, Grants, and Fellowships ---

★2496★
Salute to Excellence Awards
National Restaurant Association Foundation
c/o Charles Sandler, Director, Public Relations
250 S. Wacker Dr., Ste. 1400
Chicago, IL 60606-5834   Phone: (312)715-1010
To recognize the contributions of foodservice industry leaders and to pay tribute to the professionalism of foodservice operators, employees, students, and suppliers. Awarded annually. Established in 1986.

★2497★
Tony's Food Service Scholarships
American School Food Service Association
c/o Mary Ann Krickus
1600 Duke St., 7th Fl.
Alexandria, VA 22314   Phone: (703)739-3900
Helps needy students pursue additional education and enhances the school food service profession. ASFSA members or their children are eligible. Applicants must be high school graduates or have a GED. College applicants must have a minimum GPA of 2.7. Scholarships are awarded on the basis of school performance, need, and intention to work in school food service. Deadline is April 15.

--- Basic Reference Guides and Handbooks ---

★2498★
Food Service Management by Checklist: A Handbook of Control Techniques
John Wiley & Sons, Inc.
605 3rd Ave.
New York, NY 10158   Phone: (212)850-6000
Herman E. Zaccerelli. 1990. **Facsimile Number:** (212)850-6088.

★2499★
Foodservice Management Study Course
Iowa State University Press
Iowa State University
2121 S. State Ave.
Ames, IA 50010   Phone: (515)292-0140
Shirley Gilmore. Second edition, 1990. **Facsimile Number:** (515)292-3348.

★2500★
Guide to Hospitality Education
Council on Hotel, Restaurant, and Institutional Education (CHRIE)
1200 17th St. NW
Washington, DC 20036-3097   Phone: (202)331-5990
Annual.

Food and Beverage Service Occupations

★2501★
Restaurant Hospitality—Restaurant Industry Almanac Issue
Penton Publishing Company
1100 Superior Ave.
Cleveland, OH 44114   Phone: (216)696-7000
Stephen G. Michaelides, editor. Annual. Lists of manufacturers of foods and beverages, equipment and supplies, and tabletop and decor products; foodservice and restaurant associations; major foodservice events; United States congressmen who are active in legislation related to the foodservice industry; foodservice distributors. Entries include: For manufacturers: Company name, address, phone, products. For foodservice and restaurant associations: Organization name, address, phone. For foodservice events: Name, address, phone, dates. For congressmen:Name, address, phone. For distributors: Company name, address, phone. Arrangement: Manufacturers are classified by product. Indexes: Product, advertisers. **Facsimile Number:** (216)696-8765.

★2502★
Training Programs for Health Care Workers: Food Service Workers
Hospital Research & Educational Trust
840 N. Lake Shore Dr.
Chicago, IL 60611   Phone: (312)280-6000
1967.

Periodicals

★2503★
Atlantic Control States Beverage Journal
Club and Tavern, Inc.
3 Twelfth St.
Wheeling, WV 26003   Phone: (304)232-7620
Arnold Lazarus, Editor. Monthly. Magazine for the alcoholic beverage industry. **Facsimile Number:** (304)232-1236.

★2504★
Bartender
Foley Publishing
PO Box 158
Liberty Corner, NJ 07938   Phone: (908)766-6006
Jaclyn W. Foley, Editor. Four times/yr. Trade magazine. **Facsimile Number:** (908)766-6607.

★2505★
Beverage Alcohol Market Report
Peregrine Communications
160 E. 48th St.
New York, NY 10017   Phone: (212)371-5237
Editor(s): Perry Luntz. 26/yr. Covers beer, wine, and liquor production, importation, marketing, wholesale distribution, and retailing. Recurring features include reports on legislation affecting the industry, news of research, a calendar of events, job changes, and statistics.

★2506★
Beverage Digest
Tomac & Company
PO Box 238
Old Greenwich, CT 06870   Phone: (203)358-8198
Editor(s): Jesse Meyers and Michael Hayes. 22/yr. Focuses primarily on soft drinks. Reports on industry news in relation to pricing, marketing, and competition. **Facsimile Number:** (203)327-9761.

★2507★
Career News Digest
National Association of Trade and Technical Schools (NATTS)
2251 Wisconsin Ave. NW
Washington, DC 20007   Phone: (202)333-1021
3-4/year.

★2508★
Catering Industry Employee
Hotel Employees and Restaurant Employees International Union
1219 28th St. NW
Washington, DC 20007   Phone: (202)393-4373
Herman Leavitt, Editor. Monthly. Trade journal for culinary and hospitality workers. Official publication of the Hotel Employees and Restaurant Employees International Union. **Facsimile Number:** (202)333-0468.

★2509★
Cheers
Jobson Publishing Corp.
352 Park Ave. S.
New York, NY 10010   Phone: (212)685-4848
Bob Keane, Editor. 6x/yr. 8 x 10 7/8 **Facsimile Number:** (212)696-5318.

★2510★
CHRIE Communique
Council on Hotel, Restaurant, and Institutional Education (CHRIE)
1200 17th St. NW
Washington, DC 20036-3097   Phone: (202)331-5990
Semimonthly.

★2511★
Cooking For Profit
C P Publishing, Inc.
104 S. Main St.
PO Box 267
Fond du Lac, WI 54936-0267   Phone: (414)923-3700
Colleen Phalen, Editor. Monthly. Magazine providing practical foodservice operation information including recipes, energy conservation, and equipment. Facsimile Number: (414)923-6805.

★2512★
Food Reviews International
Marcel Dekker, Inc.
270 Madison Ave.
New York, NY 10016   Phone: (212)696-9000
Roy Teranishi, Editor. 4x/yr Journal covering agricultural production, food processing, nutrition, and health. **Facsimile Number:** (212)685-4540.

★2513★
Foodletter
Foodletter
PO Box 204
Mahwah, NJ 07430   Phone: (201)529-3835
Editor(s): Doreen Higgins, Evie Bottali, and Louise Weston. 10/yr. Analyzes current trends in foods and beverages, forecasts trends, and gives corresponding ideas for new products and packaging. Recurring features include a column titled Consumer Corner.

★2514★
Foodservice Information Abstracts
National Restaurant Association (NRA)
1200 17th St. NW
Washington, DC 20036   Phone: (202)331-5900
Biweekly. Abstracts from foodservice trade magazines.

★2515★
Foodservice Product News
Young/Conway Publications, Inc.
104 5th Ave.
New York, NY 10011-6901   Phone: (212)206-7440
Judy Ann Young, Editor. 12x/yr. Tabloid serving the restaurant food service market. **Facsimile Number:** (212)727-0919.

★2516★
Foodservice Report
International Foodservice Distributors Association (IFDA)
201 Park Washington Court
Falls Church, VA 22046   Phone: (703)532-9400
Editor(s): John D. Thompson. Monthly. Carries news of the food service industry, including activities of manufacturers, brokers, and distributors, as well as trends in food service operation. Recurring features include profiles of food service distribution companies in the U.S. and Canada, a calendar of events, and reports of conventions and conferences.

★2517★
Fresh Facts for Foodservice
United Fresh Fruit and Vegetable Association
727 N. Washington St.
Alexandria, VA 22314   Phone: (703)836-3410
Editor(s): Elaine McLaughlin. Monthly. Highlights fresh fruits and vegetables that will be in good supply in the coming months and carries articles on food service establishments which emphasize fresh items. Recurring features include cooking tips, recipes, and notices of promotional materials available.

★2518★
From the State Capitals: Alcoholic Beverage Control
Wakeman/Walworth, Inc.
300 N. Washington St., Ste. 204
Alexandria, VA 22314   Phone: (703)549-8606
Editor(s): Keyes Walworth. Weekly. Provides updates on official and municipal actions affecting the production, marketing, sale, and taxation of alcoholic beverages. Monitors how each state is addressing issues, from advertising to dram shop liability and license regulation. **Facsimile Number:** (703)549-1372.

★2519★
Hospitality and Tourism Educator
Council on Hotel, Restaurant, and Institutional Education (CHRIE)
1200 17th St. NW
Washington, DC 20036-3097   Phone: (202)331-5990
Quarterly.

★2520★
Hospitality Education and Research Journal
Council on Hotel, Restaurant, and Institutional Education (CHRIE)
1200 17th St. NW
Washington, DC 20036-3097   Phone: (202)331-5990
3/year.

★2521★
The Hospitality Manager
Kassis Communications
120 Hayward
Ames, IA 50010   Phone: (515)296-2400
Terry Lowman, Editor. Monthly. Trade publication (tabloid) covering restaurant and institutional business in the Midwest. Mailed to restaurants, bars, and institutional food service companies. **Facsimile Number:** (515)296-2405.

★2522★
Import Statistics
National Association of Beverage Importers, Inc.
1025 Vermont Ave. NW, Ste. 1205
Washington, DC 20005   Phone: (202)638-1617
Monthly. Contains Bureau of Census statistics of beverage imports compiled monthly with cumulative comparisons with the same period of the previous year. Presents statistics by the tariff schedules of beer, wines, and spirits categories. Includes statistics of U.S.-produced beer, wines, and spirits.

★2523★
Kane's Beverage Week
Whitaker Newsletters, Inc.
313 South Ave.
Fanwood, NJ 07023-1324   Phone: (908)889-6336
Editor(s): Joel Whitaker. 47/yr. Presents news items pertaining to the marketing, advertising, and distribution of alcoholic and other types of beverages. Also reports on social, health, and legal issues affecting the beverage industry. Recurring features include interviews, news of research, job listings, notices of publications available, and a calendar of events. **Facsimile Number:** (908)889-6339.

★2524★
Kitchen Times
Howard Wilson & Company, Inc.
185 Marlborough St.
Boston, MA 02116   Phone: (617)266-2453
Editor(s): Howard Wilson. Monthly. Contains instructions on buying food and preparing specific dishes. Reviews restaurants, inns, cooks, cookbooks, and wines.

★2525★
The Liquor Reporter
Smithwrite Communications, Inc.
101 Milwaukee Blvd. S.
Pacific, WA 98047   Phone: (206)833-9642
Robert D. Smith, Editor and Publisher. Monthly. Magazine (tabloid) for Washington's food service and alcohol beverage industry, including food stores, convenience stores, restaurants, and taverns.

★2526★
Mixin'
American Bartenders' Association
PO Box 15527
Sarasota, FL 34277-1527   Phone: (813)922-3316
Editor(s): Douglas Ferguson. Monthly. Supports the Association's dedication to strengthening the position of professional bartenders, bar managers, and bar owners throughout the industry and in the legislature. Includes news of interest to those in the beverage business such as announcements of new products and services, changing prices, alterations in government regulations, and profit-making suggestions. Recurring features include letters to the editor, interviews, news of research, book reviews, notices of publications available, new drink recipes, and a calendar of events. **Toll-free/Additional Phone Number(s):** 800-626-3316 **Facsimile Number:** (813)925-3594.

Food and Beverage Service Occupations

★2527★
Modern Food Service News
Grocers Publishing Co., Inc.
15 Emerald St.
Hackensack, NJ 07601   Phone: (201)488-1800
John Strovinsky, Exec. Editor. Monthly. Magazine for restaurateurs, chefs, caterers, puchasing agents in the food service industry.

★2528★
NACUFS News Wave
National Association of College and University Food Services
    (NACUFS)
1405 S. Harrison Rd., Ste. 303-304
Manly Miles Bldg.
Michigan State University
East Lansing, MI 48824   Phone: (517)332-2494
Editor(s): Mary Jo Custer. 5/yr. Covers news of interest to food service industry personnel in academic institutions. Also reports on regional association activities. Recurring features include columns titled President's Message, Special Features, and Committee Spotlight.

★2529★
National Restaurant Association—Washington Weekly
    (NRA)
National Restaurant Association (NRA)
1200 17th St. NW
Washington, DC 20036   Phone: (202)331-5900
Newsletter reporting on legislation and regulatory issues affecting the foodservice industry.

★2530★
Nation's Restaurant News
425 Park Ave.
New York, NY 10022   Phone: (212)371-9400
Charles Bernstein, Editor. Weekly (Mon.). **Facsimile Number:** (212)838-9487.

★2531★
NATTS News and Views
National Association of Trade and Technical Schools (NATTS)
2251 Wisconsin Ave. NW
Washington, DC 20007   Phone: (202)333-1021
Bimonthly. Newspaper.

★2532★
NRA Technical Bulletin
National Restaurant Association (NRA)
1200 17th St. NW
Washington, DC 20036   Phone: (202)331-5900
Periodic.

★2533★
Restaurant Business
Biller Communications, Inc.
633 3rd Ave.
New York, NY 10017   Phone: (212)986-4800
Peter R. Berlinski, Editor. 18x/yr. Trade magazine for restaurants and commercial food service. **Facsimile Number:** (212)983-3198.

★2534★
Restaurant Exchange News
PO Box 2655
Greenwich, CT 06836-2655   Phone: (914)638-1108
Robert B. Melton, Editor. Monthly. Food service industry magazine. **Facsimile Number:** (914)638-2549.

★2535★
Restaurant Merchandising News
Mortimer Publishing Co.
53 Sterling Rd.
Trumbull, CT 06611   Phone: (203)261-5506
Dawn Mortimer, Editor. Monthly. Business magazine serving the food service industry.

★2536★
Restaurants & Institutions
Cahners Publishing Co.
1350 E. Touhy Ave.
PO Box 5080
Des Plaines, IL 60018   Phone: (708)635-8800
Mike Bartlett, Editor-in-Chief. 27x/yr. Magazine focusing on foodservice and lodging management. **Facsimile Number:** (708)635-6856.

★2537★
Restaurants USA
National Restaurant Association (NRA)
1200 17th St. NW
Washington, DC 20036   Phone: (202)331-5900
Monthly with combined June/July issue. Magazine to keep foodservice operators and managers abreast of trends and developments in the industry. Contains annual index and calendar of events.

★2538★
Top Shelf: Barkeeping at Its Best
Top Shelf, Inc.
199 Ethan Allen Hwy.
Ridgefield, CT 06877   Phone: (203)431-0124
Jack Kenny, Editor. 6x/yr. Trade magazine for bar owners and operators. **Facsimile Number:** (203)431-4461.

───────── Meetings and Conventions ─────────

★2539★
American Deli-Bakery Showcase
International Deli-Bakery Association
PO Box 29632
Atlanta, GA 30359
1992.

★2540★
American School Food Service Association Conference
American School Food Service Association
1600 Duke St., 7th Fl.
Alexandria, VA 22314   Phone: (703)739-3900
1992; Jul. 17-22; Minneapolis, MN ● 1993; Jul. Boston, MA ● 1994; Jul. Anaheim, CA ● 1995; Jul. St. Louis, MO. **Toll-free/Additional Phone Number(s):** 800-877-8822. **Facsimile Number:** (703)739-3915.

★2541★
American Society for Hospital Food Service
    Administrators Convention
American Hospital Association
Convention and Meetings Division
840 N. Lake Shore Dr.
Chicago, IL 60611   Phone: (312)280-6000
Frequency: Always held in Toronto, Ontario, Canada, at the Harbour Castle Westin. 1992; Toronto, ON, Canada. **Facsimile Number:** (312)280-6462.

★2542★
Council on Hotel, Restaurant, and Institutional Education International Conference (CHRIE)
1200 17th St. NW
Washington, DC 20036-3097   Phone: (202)331-5990
Frequency: Annual. **Facsimile Number:** (202)331-2429.

★2543★
Food and Beverage Show
George Little Management
577 Airport Blvd., Ste. 440
Burlingame, CA 94010-2020   Phone: (415)344-5171
1992. **Facsimile Number:** (415)344-5270.

★2544★
FOODTECH - International Food and Beverage, Catering, Food Production and Processing Equipment, Packaging Machinery and Materials Exhibition
World Access Corp.
15 Bemis Rd.
PO Box 171
Wellesley Hills, MA 02181   Phone: (617)235-8095

★2545★
IFT Annual Meeting and Food Expo
Institute of Food Technologists
221 N. LaSalle
Chicago, IL 60601   Phone: (312)782-8424
1992; Jun. 21-24; New Orleans, LA • 1993; Jul. 11-14; Chicago, IL • 1994; Jun. 26-29; Atlanta, GA • 1995; Jun. 04-07; Anaheim, CA. **Facsimile Number:** (312)782-8348.

★2546★
INTERBEV - International Beverage Industry Exhibition and Congress
InterBev, Ltd.
1101 16th St., NW
Washington, DC 20036   Phone: (202)463-6795
Frequency: Always held at the McCormick Place in Chicago, Illinois. 1992; Chicago, IL • 1992; Oct. 24-26; Chicago, IL. **Toll-free/Additional Phone Number(s):** 800-3-INTERBEV. **Facsimile Number:** (202)833-2484.

★2547★
International Caterers' Conference
Helen Brett Enterprises, Inc.
220 S. State St., Ste. 1416
Chicago, IL 60604   Phone: (312)922-0966
1992; San Francisco, CA • 1993; Atlanta, GA • 1994; Mexico City, Mexico. **Facsimile Number:** (312)922-0969.

★2548★
Midway USA Foodservice and Hospitality Exposition
Kansas Restaurant and Hospitality Association
359 S. Hydraulic St.
Wichita, KS 67211   Phone: (316)267-8383
Frequency: Always held at the Century II Expo in Wichita, Kansas. 1992; Oct. 24-25; Wichita, KS • 1993; Oct. 23-24; Wichita, KS • 1994; Oct. 24-25; Wichita, KS • 1995; Oct. 28-29; Wichita, KS. **Facsimile Number:** (316)267-8400.

★2549★
National Food Distributors Association Annual Convention
National Food Distributors Association
401 N. Michigan Ave.
Chicago, IL 60611   Phone: (312)644-6610
1992; Aug. 09-12; Las Vegas, NV. **Facsimile Number:** (312)321-6869.

★2550★
National Restaurant Association Restaurant, Hotel-Motel Show
National Restaurant Association
150 N. Michigan Ave., Ste. 2000
Chicago, IL 60601   Phone: (312)853-2525
Frequency: Dates include weekend before Memorial Day weekend. Always held at McCormick Place in Chicago, Illinois. 1992; May 16-20; Chicago, IL • 1993; May 22-26; Chicago, IL • 1994; May 21-25; Chicago, IL. **Facsimile Number:** (312)853-2548.

★2551★
Northeast Food Service and Lodging Exposition and Conference
Cahners Exposition Group
221 Columbus Ave.
PO Box 35
Boston, MA 02117-0035   Phone: (617)536-8152
Frequency: Always held in Boston, Massachusetts. 1992; Boston, MA. **Toll-free/Additional Phone Number(s):** 800-525-7585. **Facsimile Number:** (617)536-8719.

★2552★
Penna Bakers Show
Pennsylvania Restaurant Association Official Trade Shows
47 W. Main St.
PO Box 2467
Mechanicsburg, PA 17055   Phone: (717)697-4199
Frequency: Always held in August. 1992; Aug. **Toll-free/Additional Phone Number(s):** 800-346-7767. **Facsimile Number:** (717)790-9441.

★2553★
Rocky Mountain Regional Hospitality Convention and Education Exposition - The Restaurant Show
Colorado-Wyoming Restaurant Association
899 Logan St., Ste. 300
Denver, CO 80203   Phone: (303)830-2972
1992. **Facsimile Number:** (303)830-2973.

★2554★
Southeastern Hospitality and Foodservice Show
Cahners Exposition Group (Boston)
221 Columbus Ave.
PO Box 35
Boston, MA 02117-0035   Phone: (617)536-8152
Frequency: Always held during October at the Georgia World Convention Center in Atlanta, Georgia. 1992; Oct. Atlanta, GA. **Facsimile Number:** (617)536-8719.

★2555★
Tri-State Restaurant Food and Equipment Show
Pennsylvania Restaurant Association Official Trade Shows
47 W. Main St.
PO Box 2467
Mechanicsburg, PA 17055   Phone: (717)697-4199
Frequency: Always held in March at the Pittsburgh Expo Mart in Monroeville, Pennsylvania. 1992; Mar. Monroeville, PA.

Food and Beverage Service Occupations

Toll-free/Additional Phone Number(s): 800-346-7767. **Facsimile Number:** (717)790-9441.

★2556★
Upper Midwest Hospitality, Restaurant, and Lodging Show
Minnesota Restaurant, Hotel, and Resort Association
871 Jefferson Ave.
St. Paul, MN 55102   Phone: (612)222-7401
1993; Feb. 23-25; Minneapolis, MN ● 1994; Feb. 22-24; Minneapolis, MN ● 1995; Feb. 21-23; Minneapolis, MN. **Facsimile Number:** (612)222-7347.

——— **Other Sources of Information** ———

★2557★
Catering Today—Buyer's Guide Issue
Pro Tech Publishing
2070 S. Monaco, No. C305
Denver, CO 80224   Phone: (303)758-8022
Ramona Chun, editor. Annual, spring. Lists of manufacturers and suppliers of products to the catering service industry; food associations and organizations. Indexes: Product. **Toll-free/Additional Phone Number(s):** (800)937-4464. **Facsimile Number:** (812)937-4688.

★2558★
Restaurant Industry Operations Report
National Restaurant Association (NRA)
1200 17th St. NW
Washington, DC 20036   Phone: (202)331-5900
Annual.

Health Service Occupations

Dental Assistants

Dental assistants work alongside dentists as they examine and treat patients. Moreover, dental assistants perform a variety of clinical, office, and laboratory duties. Clinical duties include removing sutures, applying anesthetic and caries-preventive agents to the teeth and oral tissue, removing excess cement used in the filling process, and placing rubber dams on the teeth to isolate them for individual treatment. Office duties include arranging and confirming appointments, receiving patients, keeping treatment records, sending bills, receiving payments, and ordering dental supplies and materials. Laboratory duties include casting teeth and the mouth from impressions taken by the dentist. Most dental assistants work in private dental offices. Others work in dental schools, hospital dental departments, state and public health departments, or private clinics. The federal government employs dental assistants in hospitals and dental clinics of the U.S. Public Health Service and the Veterans Administration.

$alaries

Weekly salaries for dental assistants are as follows:

Lowest 10 percent	$180.00/week or less
Median	$267.00/week
Top 10 percent	$407.00/week or more

Employment Outlook

Growth rate until the year 2000: Average.

Dental Assistants

Career Guides

★2559★
Careers in Dental Care
Lerner Publications Co.
241 First Ave., N.
Minneapolis, MN 55401
Joyce Kessel. 1984. Describes fifteen different career possibilities in the dental field. **Toll-free/Additional Phone Number(s):** 800-328-4920. **Facsimile Number:** (612)332-7615

★2560★
Careers in Health Care
Chelsea House Publishers
1974 Sproul Rd., Ste. 400
Broomall, PA 19008   Phone: (215)353-5166
Rachel S. Epstein. 1989. **Facsimile Number:** (215)359-1439.

★2561★
Careers in Health Services: Opportunities for You
Cambridge Career Products
90 MacCorkle Ave., SW
South Charleston, WV 25311   Phone: (304)744-9323
Videocassette. 1989. 30 mins. This program shows the range of career opportunities in health care fields.

★2562★
Comprehensive Review of Dental Assisting
Krieger Publishing Co., Inc.
PO Box 9542
Melbourne, FL 32902   Phone: (407)724-9542
Jacqueline W. Sapp. 1981. **Facsimile Number:** (407)951-3671.

★2563★
"Dental Assistance" in *The Career Connection II: A Guide to Technical Majors and Their Related Careers* (pp. 33-34)
ERIS
PO Box 7509
University Station
Provo, UT 84602-0509
Fred A. Rowe. 1988. Contains technical majors, such as automotive technology. Describes the major and the job. Lists high school and postsecondary school courses. Includes occupations related to the major, employment outlook, and starting salary.

★2564★
Dental Assistant
Careers, Inc.
PO Box 135
Largo, FL 34649-0135   Phone: (813)584-7333
1990. Two-page occupational summary card describing duties, working conditions, personal qualifications, training, earnings and hours, employment outlook, places of employment, related careers and where to write for more information.

★2565★
Dental Assistant
Vocational Biographies, Inc.
PO Box 31, Dept. VF10
Sauk Centre, MN 56378   Phone: (612)352-6516
1989. This pamphlet profiles a person working in the job. Includes information about job duties, working conditions, places of employment, educational preparation, labor market outlook, and salaries. **Toll-free/Additional Phone Number(s):** 800-255-0752.

★2566★
The Dental Assistant
Lea & Febiger
200 Chester Field Pkwy.
Malvern, PA 19355   Phone: (215)251-2230
Roger E. Barton, editor. Sixth edition, 1988. **Facsimile Number:** (215)251-2229.

★2567★
"Dental Assistant" in *Careers in Health Care* (pp. 44-48)
National Textbook Co.
4255 W. Touhy Ave.
Lincolnwood, IL 60646   Phone: (312)679-5500
Barbara M. Swanson. 1989. Discusses 61 health careers, providing information about the history of the occupation, job duties, work environments, salaries, educational preparation, licensure, certification, and employment outlook.

★2568★
"Dental Assistant" in *Health Care* (pp. 57-61)
Franklin Watts, Inc.
387 Park Avenue, S.
New York, NY 10016   Phone: (212)686-7070
Linda Barrett and Galen Guengerich. 1991. Provides an overview of the health care industry. Includes job description, educational preparation, training, salary, and employment outlook. Offers job hunting advice.

★2569★
"Dental Assistant" in *Health*, Volume 7 of *Career Information Center* (pp. 42-43)
Glencoe/Macmillan
15319 Chatsworth St.
Mission Hills, CA 91345   Phone: (818)898-1391
Richard Lidz and Dale Anderson, editorial directors. Fourth edition, 1990. For 600 occupations, describes job duties, entry-level requirements, education and training needed, advancement possibilities, employment outlook, earnings and benefits. The set is divided into 12 volumes. Each volume includes jobs related under a broad career field. Volume 13 is the index. **Facsimile Number:** 818-365-5489.

★2570★
"Dental Assistant" in *Occu-Facts: Information on 565 Careers in Outline Form* (p. 13.21)
Careers, Inc.
P.O. Box 135
1211 Tenth St., S.W.
Largo, FL 33640   Phone: (813)584-7333
Elizabeth Handville. Biennial, 1989-90 edition. Each one-page occupational profile describes duties, working conditions, physical surroundings and demands, aptitudes, temperament, educational requirements, employment outlook, earnings, and places of employment.

★2571★
"Dental Assistant" in *Opportunities in Dental Care Careers* (pp. 17-18, 46-47)
National Textbook Co.
4255 W. Touhy Ave.
Lincolnwood, IL 60646   Phone: (312)679-5500
Bonnie L. Kendall. 1991. Describes the work of dentists and related dental care employees. Covers dental education including admission to dental school, dental specialties, skills, personal qualities, income, and licensure. Lists accredited dental schools, dental hygiene and assisting programs.

★2572★
"Dental Assistant" in *Opportunities in Health and Medical Careers* (p. 15)
National Textbook Co.
4255 W. Touhy Ave.
Lincolnwood, IL 60646   Phone: (312)679-5500
Leo D'Orazio and Donald I. Snook. 1991. Provides an overview of the health care industry with future projections. Describes a wide variety of healthcare jobs covering the nature of the work, educational requirements, employment outlook and salaries. Offers job hunting advice.

★2573★
"Dental Assistant" in *Opportunities in Paramedical Careers* (pp. 37-41)
National Textbook Co.
4255 W. Touhy Ave.
Lincolnwood, IL 60646   Phone: (312)679-5500
Alex Kacen. 1989. Describes paraprofessional careers in the health professions such as physician assistant and mental health technician. Covers job functions, educational preparation, certification, earnings, and job outlook. Lists accredited educational programs.

★2574★
"Dental Assistant" in *VGM's Careers Encyclopedia* (pp. 132-134)
National Textbook Co.
4255 W. Touhy Ave.
Lincolnwood, IL 60646   Phone: (312)679-5500
Third edition, 1991. Contains two- to five-page descriptions of 200 managerial, professional, technical, trade, and service occupations. Each profile includes job duties, places of employment, qualifications, educational preparation, training, employment potential, advancement, income, and additional sources of information.

★2575★
"Dental Assistant" in *120 Careers in the Health Care Field* (pp. 48-63)
U.S. Directory Service, Publishers
PO Box 68-1700
655 N.W. 128th St.
Miami, FL 33168   Phone: (305)769-1700
Stanley Alperin. Second edition, 1989. Each occupational profile covers job functions and responsibilities, work locations, training requirements, certification, and salaries. Lists community colleges, universities, vocational-technical schools, and other educational institutions that provide accredited training programs.

★2576★
The Dental Assistant: Syllabus
National Book Co.
PO Box 8795
Portland, OR 97207-8795   Phone: (503)228-6345
E. A. Jacobson. 1978.

★2577★
Dental Assistants
Chronicle Guidance Publications, Inc.
PO Box 1190
Moravia, NY 13118-1190   Phone: (315)497-0330
1990. This career brief describes the nature of the work, working conditions, hours and earnings, education and training, licensure, certification, unions, personal qualifications, social and psychological factors, employment outlook, entry methods, advancement, and related occupations. **Toll-free/Additional Phone Number(s):** 800-622-7284.

★2578★
"Dental Assistants" in *Occupational Outlook Handbook* (pp. 299-300)
Superintendent of Documents
U.S. Government Printing Office
Washington, DC 20402   Phone: (202)783-3238
Biennial; latest edition, 1990-91. Encyclopedia of careers describing more than 250 occupations and comprising about 86 percent of all jobs in the economy. Occupations that require lengthy education or training are given the most attention. For each occupation, the handbook describes job duties, working conditions, training, educational preparation, personal qualities, advancement possibilities, job outlook, earnings, and sources of additional information.

★2579★
"Dental Assistants" in Volume 3 of *The Encyclopedia of Careers and Vocational Guidance* (pp. 218-221)
J.G. Ferguson Publishing Co.
200 W. Monroe
Chicago, IL 60606   Phone: (312)580-5480
William E. Hopke, editor-in-chief. Eighth edition, 1990. Four-volume set that profiles 500 occupations and describes job

Dental Assistants

trends in 76 industries. Includes career description, educational requirements, history of the job, methods of entry, advancement, employment outlook, earnings, working conditions, social and psychological factors, and sources of additional information.

★2580★
"Dental Assistants" in Volume 2 of *Career Discovery Encyclopedia* (pp. 94-95)
J.G. Ferguson Publishing Co.
200 W. Monroe
Chicago, IL 60606   Phone: (312)580-5480
E. Russell Primm, editor-in-chief. 1990. Contains two-page articles on 504 occupations. Each article describes job duties, earnings, and educational and training requirements.

★2581★
"Dental Assistants and Dental Hygienists" in *The American Almanac of Jobs and Salaries* (pp. 494-495)
Avon Books
105 Madison Avenue
New York, NY 10016   Phone: (212)481-5600
John Wright and Edward J. Dwyer. Revised and updated, 1990. A comprehensive guide to the wages of hundreds of occupations in a wide variety of industries and organizations.

★2582★
"Dental Assistants and Hygienists" in *Jobs! What They Are...Where They Are...What They Pay* (p. 150)
Simon & Schuster, Inc.
Simon & Schuster Bldg.
1230 Avenue of the Americas
New York, NY 10020   Phone: (212)698-7000
Robert O. Snelling and Anne M. Snelling. Revised edition, 1989. Profiles 241 occupations, describing duties and responsibilities, educational preparation, earnings, employment opportunities, training, and qualifications.

★2583★
"Dental Assistants: Chairside Assistants" in *Careers for Women Without College Degrees* (pp. 208-211)
McGraw-Hill Publishing Co.
11 W. 19th St.
New York, NY 10011   Phone: (212)337-6010
Beatryce Nivens. 1988. Career planning and job hunting guide containing information on decision-making, skills assessment, and resumes for career changers. Profiles careers with the best occupational outlook. Describes the work, educational preparation, employment outlook, salaries, and required skills.

★2584★
***Dental Assistants Review*, ARCO**
Appleton & Lange
25 Van Zant St.
East Norwalk, CT 06855   Phone: (203)838-4400
Stuart M. Hirsch. Second edition, 1983.

★2585★
Dental Assisting: Basic & Dental Sciences
Mosby Year Book, Inc.
11830 Westline Industrial Dr.
St. Louis, MO 63146   Phone: (314)872-8370
Leimone. 1987.

★2586★
Dental Technicians
Chronicle Guidance Publications, Inc.
PO Box 1190
Moravia, NY 13118-1190   Phone: (315)497-0330
1990. This career brief describes the nature of the work, working conditions, hours and earnings, education and training, licensure, certification, unions, personal qualifications, social and psychological factors, employment outlook, entry methods, advancement, and related occupations. **Toll-free/Additional Phone Number(s):** 800-622-7284.

★2587★
Have You Considered Dental Assisting?
SELECT
211 E. Chicago Ave., Ste. 1804
Chicago, IL 60611-2678   Phone: (312)440-2500
1990. This eight-page booklet describes what dental assistants do, where they work, educational preparation and certification.

★2588★
Health Career Planning: A Realistic Guide
Human Sciences Press
233 Spring St.
New York, NY 10013   Phone: (212)620-8000
Ellen F. Lederman. 1988.

★2589★
Health Careers Today
C.V. Mosby Co.
11830 Westline Industrial Dr.
St. Louis, MO 63146   Phone: (314)872-8370
Judith A. Gerdin. 1991. Surveys health occupations. Includes information on basic health care skills and careers.

★2590★
Introduction to the Health Professions
Jones and Bartlett Publishers, Inc.
20 Park Plaza
Boston, MA 02116   Phone: (617)482-5243
Peggy Stanfield. 1990.

★2591★
Medical & Dental Associates, P. C.
South-Western Publishing Co.
5101 Madison Rd.
Cincinnati, OH 45227   Phone: (513)271-8811
Kay F. Gow. 1984.

★2592★
120 Careers in the Health Care Field
U.S. Directory Service, Publishers
655 NW 128th St.
PO Box 68-1700
Miami, FL 33168   Phone: (305)769-1700
Stanley Alperin. Second edition, 1989.

★2593★
A Review of Dental Assisting
W. B. Saunders Co.
Curtis Center
Independence Sq. W.
Philadelphia, PA 19106   Phone: (215)238-7800
Hazel O. Torres. 1983.

Associations

★2594★
American Dental Assistants Association (ADAA)
919 N. Michigan Ave., Ste. 3400
Chicago, IL 60611   Phone: (312)664-3327
Membership: Individuals employed as dental assistants in dental offices, clinics, hospitals, or institutions; instructors of dental assistants, and dental students. **Purpose:** Sponsors workshops and seminars; maintains a scholarship fund. Maintains a certifying Board. **Publications:** *The Dental Assistant*, bimonthly journal.

★2595★
American Dental Association (ADA)
211 E. Chicago Ave.
Chicago, IL 60611   Phone: (312)440-2500
Membership: Professional society of dentists. **Purpose:** Encourages the improvement of the health of the public and promotes the art and science of dentistry in matters of legislation and regulations. Inspects and accredits dental schools and schools for dental hygienists, assistants, and laboratory technicians. Conducts research programs at ADA Health Foundation Research Institute. Produces most of the dental health education material used in the U.S. Sponsors National Children's Dental Health Month. Compiles statistics on personnel, practice, and dental care needs and attitudes of patients with regard to dental health. Operates library of 50,000 volumes. Maintains biographical records of U.S. dentists, past and present; and collection of publis hed and original documentary material of historical interest to the profession. Sponsors 11 councils. **Publications:** *American Dental Directory*, annual. • *Index to Dental Literature*, quarterly. • *News*, biweekly.

★2596★
Dental Assisting National Board (DANB)
216 E. Ontario St.
Chicago, IL 60611   Phone: (312)642-3368
Purpose: Certifying agency that administers examinations to dental assistants.

Standards/Certification Agencies

Many dental assistants learn their skills on the job, though some are trained in dental assisting programs offered by community and junior colleges, trade schools, and technical institutes and accredited by the American Dental Association's Commission on Dental Accreditation. Accredited dental assisting programs include classroom, laboratory, and preclinical instruction in dental assisting skills and related theory. In addition, students gain practical experience in affiliated dental schools, local clinics, or selected dental offices. The majority of these programs take one year or less to complete and lead to a certificate or diploma. Graduates of two-year programs offered in community and junior colleges earn an associate degree. Certification is available through the Dental Assisting National Board. Certification is an acknowledgment of an assistant's qualifications and professional competence. In several states that have adopted standards for dental assistants who perform radiologic procedures, completion of the certification examination meets those standards.

★2597★
American Dental Association (ADA)
211 E. Chicago Ave.
Chicago, IL 60611   Phone: (312)440-2500
Promotes the art and science of dentistry in matters of legislation and regulations. Inspects and accredits dental schools and schools for dental hygienists, assistants, and laboratory technicians. Conducts research programs at ADA Health Foundation Research Institute. Produces most of the dental health education material used in the U.S.

★2598★
Are You Known for the Company You Keep?
Dental Assisting National Board
216 E Ontario St.
Chicago, IL 60611   Phone: (312)642-3368
This eight-page booklet describes types of certification and the certification process for dental assistants.

★2599★
Certification for Dental Assistants: Dental Assisting National Board Examinations
Dental Assisting National Board
216 E Ontario St.
Chicago, IL 60611   Phone: (312)642-3368
1991. This 25-page booklet describes the certification process for dental assistants. Covers testing dates, qualifications, and examination contents. Contains a sample test. List testing and educational programs.

★2600★
Dental Assistant Certification
American Medical Technologists
710 Higgins Rd.
Park Ridge, IL 60068-5765   Phone: (708)823-5169
1991. This six-panel brochure describes the requirements for dental assistant certification.

★2601★
Dental Assisting National Board
216 E. Ontario St.
Chicago, IL 60611   Phone: (312)642-3368
Certifying agency that administers examinations to dental assistants; certifying arm of the American Dental Assistants Association.

Test Guides

★2602★
Dental Assistant
National Learning Corp.
212 Michael Dr.
Syosset, NY 11791   Phone: (516)921-8888
Jack Rudman. Part of the Career Examination Series No. 1. All examination guides in this series contain questions with answers.
Facsimile Number: (516)921-8743. **Toll-free/Additional Phone Number(s):** 800-645-6337.

Dental Assistants

★2603★
Essentials of Dental Radiography for Dental Assistants and Dental Hygienists
Appleton & Lange
PO Box 5630
25 Van Zant St.
E. Norwalk, CT 06855 Phone: (516)921-8888
Wolf deLyre and Orlen N. Johnson. Fourth edition, 1989. Contains information needed to pass the licensing, registration, certification, and radiation safety examinations.

★2604★
National Dental Assistant Boards (NDAB)
National Learning Corp.
212 Michael Dr.
Syosset, NY 11791 Phone: (516)921-8888
Jack Rudman. 1989. Part of Admission Test Series.

★2605★
Self-Assessment Questions & Answers for Dental Assistants
Butterworth-Heinemann
80 Montvale Ave.
Stoneham, MA 02180 Phone: (617)438-8464
P. L. Erridge. Second edition, 1988. **Facsimile Number:** (617)279-4851.

Educational Directories and Programs

★2606★
Dental Assistants
Accrediting Bureau of Health Education
Oak Manor Office
29089 U.S. 20 W.
Elkhart, IN 46514 Phone: (219)293-0124
1991. State-by-state listing of schools offering dental assistant training programs. Lists address, phone number, and contact person.

Basic Reference Guides and Handbooks

★2607★
Dental Assistant Techniques
Macmillan Publishing Company, Inc.
866 3rd Ave.
New York, NY 10022 Phone: (212)702-2000
Betty Lorenzen. 1976. Part of Allied Health Series.

★2608★
Dental Assisting Manuals
University of North Carolina Chapel Hill
University of North Carolina Press
116 S. Boundary St.
PO Box 2288
Chapel Hill, NC 27515-2288 Phone: (919)966-3561
Ethel M. Earl. Third edition. **Toll-free/Additional Phone Number(s):** 800-848-6224. **Facsimile Number:** (919)966-3829.

★2609★
Dental Surgical Assistants Handbook
J. B. Lippincott Co.
E. Washington Square.
Philadelphia, PA 19105 Phone: (215)238-4200
Smith. 1987.

★2610★
Effective Dental Assisting
William C. Brown Group
2460 Kerper Blvd.
Dubuque, IA 52001 Phone: (319)588-1451
Shirley Schwarzrock. 1991. **Facsimile Number:** (319)589-2955.

★2611★
Essentials of Clinical Dental Assisting
Mosby Year Book, Inc.
11830 Westline Industrial Dr.
St. Louis, MO 63146 Phone: (314)872-8370
Chasteen. 1989.

★2612★
Handbook of Expanded Dental Auxiliary Practice
J. B. Lippincott Co.
E. Washington Square
Philadelphia, PA 19105 Phone: (215)238-4200
Francis A. Castano. 1973.

★2613★
Modern Dental Assisting
W. B. Saunders, Co.
Curtis Center
Independence Sq. W.
Philadelphia, PA 19106 Phone: (215)238-7800
Hazel O. Torres. Fourth edition, 1990.

★2614★
Patient Management Skills for Dental Assistants
Prentice Hall
Rte. 9W
Englewood Cliffs, NJ 07632 Phone: (201)592-2000
Barbara D. Ingersoll. 1986.

★2615★
Patient Management Skills for Dental Assistants & Hygienist
Appleton & Lange
25 Van Zant St.
East Norwalk, CT 06855 Phone: (203)838-4400
Barbara D. Ingersoll. 1986.

Periodicals

★2616★
ADA News
American Dental Association (ADA)
211 E. Chicago Ave.
Chicago, IL 60611 Phone: (312)440-2500
Biweekly.

★2617★
Clinical Preventive Dentistry
Stevens Publishing Corp.
PO Box 2573
Waco, TX 76702 Phone: (817)776-9000
6x/yr. Journal publishing information on the prevention and control of oral diseases.

★2618★
Corhealth
American Correctional Health Services Association
11 W. Monument Ave., Ste. 510
PO Box 2307
Dayton, OH 45401   Phone: (513)223-9630

Editor(s): Rebecca Craig and Janis James. Bimonthly. "Dedicated to improving correctional health services." Covers news of the association and its chapters and affiliates, who administer and monitor efficiency of health care in correctional institutions. Concerned with the multidisciplinary approach to nursing, dentistry, medicine, surgery, and medical administration. Recurring features include editorials, news of members, statistics, publications available, calls for papers, abstracts, book reviews, and a calendar of events. **Facsimile Number:** (513)223-6307.

★2619★
Current Opinion in Dentistry
Current Science
20 N. 3rd St.
Philadelphia, PA 19106-2113   Phone: (215)574-2266

S.T. Sonis, Editor. 6x/yr Journal for dental professionals. **Facsimile Number:** (215)574-2270.

★2620★
Dental Abstracts
American Dental Assn.
211 E. Chicago Ave., Ste. 2014
Chicago, IL 60611   Phone: (800)621-8099

Tracy A. Briggs, Editor. Monthly. Dentistry professional magazine.

★2621★
The Dental Assistant
American Dental Assistants Assn.
919 N. Michigan, Ste. 3400
Chicago, IL 60611   Phone: (312)664-3327

Elizabeth Sidney, Editor. 6x/yr. **Facsimile Number:** (312)664-5288.

★2622★
Dental Clinics of North America
W.B. Saunders Co.
The Curtis Center
Independence Sq. W.
Philadelphia, PA 19106-3399   Phone: (215)238-7800

Susan C. Short, Editor. Quarterly. Journal reviewing current techniques in dentistry. **Facsimile Number:** (215)238-7883.

★2623★
Dental Office
Stevens Publishing Corp.
225 N. New
PO Box 2573
Waco, TX 76702-2573   Phone: (817)776-9000

Carolyn L. Aydelotte, Editorial Director. 6x/yr Trade magazine for dental assistants. Darrell C. Denny, Publisher.

★2624★
Dental Products Report
7400 Skokie Blvd.
Skokie, IL 60077-3339   Phone: (708)674-0110

Teri Reis-Schmidt, Editor. 11x/yr. Professional tabloid for dentists. Covering new products, new literature, conferences, technical exhibits, esthetic dentistry techniques, and infection-control procedures. **Facsimile Number:** (708)674-2991.

★2625★
Dental Student
Stevens Publishing Corp.
5002 Lakeland Circle
PO Box 7573
Waco, TX 76714   Phone: (817)776-9000

Mark Hartley, Editor. 6x/yr News magazine of the dental profession.

★2626★
DENTIST
Stevens Publishing Corp.
PO Box 7573
Waco, TX 76714   Phone: (817)776-9000

Mark Hartley, Editorial Director. Monthly. News magazine (tabloid) for the dental profession. **Facsimile Number:** (817)776-9018.

★2627★
Dentistry Today
26 Park St.
Montclair, NJ 07042   Phone: (201)783-3935

Jim Roth, Editor. 9x/yr. Dental magazine (tabloid). **Facsimile Number:** (201)783-7112.

★2628★
The Explorer
National Association of Dental Assistants
900 S. Washington St., No. G13
Falls Church, VA 22046-4020   Phone: (703)237-8616

Editor(s): Sue Young. Monthly. Reflects the Association's goal of improving the professional and personal lives of dental assistants and other staff. Provides information relating to the field of dentistry.

★2629★
Healthwire
Federation of Nurses and Health Professionals
American Federation of Teachers
555 New Jersey Ave. NW
Washington, DC 20001   Phone: (202)879-4430

Editor(s): Priscilla M. Nemeth. 6/yr. Explores national news and issues affecting health care workers. Discusses general union developments as well as labor and union concerns specific to the health care field. Recurring features include local member news, book reviews, news of research, and columns titled Clipboard, Pulse Points, Stethoscope, Second Opinion, and Making Rounds.

★2630★
JADA
ADA Publishers Inc.
211 E. Chicago Ave.
Chicago, IL 60611   Phone: (312)440-2740

Dr. William F. Wathan, Editor. Monthly. Dental magazine. **Facsimile Number:** (312)440-2550.

★2631★
Periodicals Digest Dentistry
2236 Chestnut St., Ste. 313
San Francisco, CA 94123   Phone: (415)332-7724

Evelyn F. Hayes, Editor and Publisher. 6x/yr. Bibliographic index covering dental literature.

Dental Assistants

★2632★
Special Care in Dentistry
Federation of Special Care Organizations in Dentistry
211 E. Chicago Ave.
Chicago, IL 60611   Phone: (312)440-2660
Dr. Roseann Mulligan, Editor. 6x/yr. Dental journal. **Facsimile Number:** (312)440-7494.

Meetings and Conventions

★2633★
American Dental Assistants Association (ADAA)
919 N. Michigan Ave., Ste. 3400
Chicago, IL 60611   Phone: (312)664-3327
Frequency: Holds annual session in October or November.

★2634★
American Dental Hygienists' Association Convention
American Dental Hygienists' Association
444 N. Michigan Ave., Ste. 3400
Chicago, IL 60611   Phone: (312)440-8900
1992; Jun. 03-10; Louisville, KY • 1993; Jun. 09-16; Denver, CO. **Facsimile Number:** (312)440-8929.

Medical Assistants

Medical assistants help physicians examine and treat patients. Most medical assistants generalize, handling both clerical and clinical duties and reporting directly to the office manager or physician. Clinical duties include taking and recording vital signs and medical histories; explaining treatment procedures to patients; preparing patients for examination; assisting during the examination; collecting and preparing laboratory specimens or performing basic laboratory tests on the premises; disposing of contaminated supplies; sterilizing medical instruments. Other clinical duties include instructing patients about medication and special diets, authorizing drug refills as directed, telephoning prescriptions to the pharmacy, drawing blood, preparing patients for X-rays, taking EKG's, and applying dressings. They also arrange instruments and equipment in the examining room; check office and laboratory supplies; and maintain the waiting, consulting, and examination rooms in a neat and orderly condition. Administrative duties include answering the telephone, greeting patients, recording and filing patient medical records, filling out insurance forms, handling correspondences, scheduling appointments, arranging for hospital admission and laboratory services, and handling billing and bookkeeping. Some medical assistants specialize. Podiatric medical assistants make castings of the feet, expose and develop X-rays, and assist podiatrists at surgery in addition to handling front office responsibilities. Ophthalmic medical assistants help ophthalmologists provide medical eye care. They take medical histories and use precision instruments to administer diagnostic tests, measure and record vision, and test the functioning of eyes and eye muscles. They also instruct patients in the use of eye dressings, protective shields, and safety glasses, as well as in the insertion, removal, and care of contact lenses. At the direction of the physician, they may administer medications. Their responsibilities may include maintaining optical and surgery instruments and assisting the ophthalmologist in surgery.

$alaries

The average starting salary for graduates of the medical assistant programs is approximately $13,000/year.

Employment Outlook

Growth rate until the year 2000: Faster than average.

Medical Assistants

Career Guides

★2635★
Career in Ophthalmic Medical Assisting
The Joint Commission on Allied Health Personnel in
  Ophthalmology
2025 Woodland Dr.
St. Paul, MN 55125-2995   Phone: (612)731-2944
1991. This six-panel brochure describes the work, qualifications, educational preparation and certification. **Toll-free/Additional Phone Number(s):** 800-284-3937.

★2636★
Careers in Health Care
Chelsea House Publishers
1974 Sproul Rd., Ste. 400
Broomall, PA 19008   Phone: (215)353-5166
Rachel S. Epstein. 1989. **Facsimile Number:** (215)359-1439.

★2637★
Careers in Health Services: Opportunities for You
Cambridge Career Products
90 MacCorkle Ave., SW
South Charleston, WV 25311   Phone: (304)744-9323
Videocassette. 1989. 30 mins. This program shows the range of career opportunities in health care fields.

★2638★
Health Career Planning: A Realistic Guide
Human Sciences Press
233 Spring St.
New York, NY 10013   Phone: (212)620-8000
Ellen F. Lederman. 1988.

★2639★
Health Careers Today
C.V. Mosby Co.
11830 Westline Industrial Dr.
St. Louis, MO 63146   Phone: (314)872-8370
Judith A. Gerdin. 1991. Surveys health occupations. Includes information on basic health care skills and careers.

★2640★
Introduction to the Health Professions
Jones and Bartlett Publishers, Inc.
20 Park Plaza
Boston, MA 02116   Phone: (617)482-5243
Peggy Stanfield. 1990.

★2641★
Make It to the Top: Certify
American Association of Medical Assistants
20 N. Wacker Dr., Ste. 1575
Chicago, IL 60606-2903   Phone: (312)899-1500
This six-panel brochure explains the importance of certification, how to obtain certification, and outlines the contents of the examination. **Toll-free/Additional Phone Number(s):** 800-228-2262.

★2642★
Medical Assistant
Careers, Inc.
PO Box 135
Largo, FL 34649-0135   Phone: (813)584-7333
1990. Two-page occupational summary card describing duties, working conditions, personal qualifications, training, earnings and hours, employment outlook, places of employment, related careers and where to write for more information.

★2643★
Medical Assistant
Vocational Biographies, Inc.
PO Box 31, Dept. VF10
Sauk Centre, MN 56378   Phone: (612)352-6516
1990. This pamphlet profiles a person working in the job. Includes information about job duties, working conditions, places of employment, educational preparation, labor market outlook, and salaries. **Toll-free/Additional Phone Number(s):** 800-255-0752.

★2644★
"Medical Assistant" in *Careers in Health Care* (pp. 114-118)
National Textbook Co.
4255 W. Touhy Ave.
Lincolnwood, IL 60646   Phone: (312)679-5500
Barbara M. Swanson. 1989. Discusses 61 health careers, providing information about the history of the occupation, job duties, work environments, salaries, educational preparation, licensure, certification, and employment outlook.

★2645★
"Medical Assistant" in *Health*, Volume 7 of *Career Information Center* (pp. 68-69)
Glencoe/Macmillan
15319 Chatsworth St.
Mission Hills, CA 91345   Phone: (818)898-1391
Richard Lidz and Dale Anderson, editorial directors. Fourth edition, 1990. For 600 occupations, describes job duties, entry-level requirements, education and training needed,

advancement possibilities, employment outlook, earnings and benefits. The set is divided into 12 volumes. Each volume includes jobs related under a broad career field. Volume 13 is the index. **Facsimile Number:** 818-365-5489.

★2646★
"Medical Assistant" in *Occu-Facts: Information on 565 Careers in Outline Form* (p. 13.22)
Careers, Inc.
P.O. Box 135
1211 Tenth St., S.W.
Largo, FL 33640   Phone: (813)584-7333
Elizabeth Handville. Biennial, 1989-90 edition. Each one-page occupational profile describes duties, working conditions, physical surroundings and demands, aptitudes, temperament, educational requirements, employment outlook, earnings, and places of employment.

★2647★
"Medical Assistant" in *Opportunities in Health and Medical Careers* (p. 17)
National Textbook Co.
4255 W. Touhy Ave.
Lincolnwood, IL 60646   Phone: (312)679-5500
Leo D'Orazio and Donald I. Snook. 1991. Provides an overview of the health care industry with future projections. Describes a wide variety of healthcare jobs covering the nature of the work, educational requirements, employment outlook and salaries. Offers job hunting advice.

★2648★
"Medical Assistant" in *Opportunities in Paramedical Careers* (pp. 27-30)
National Textbook Co.
4255 W. Touhy Ave.
Lincolnwood, IL 60646   Phone: (312)679-5500
Alex Kacen. 1989. Describes paraprofessional careers in the health professions such as physician assistant and mental health technician. Covers job functions, educational preparation, certification, earnings, and job outlook. Lists accredited educational programs.

★2649★
"Medical Assistant" in *VGM's Careers Encyclopedia* (pp. 272-274)
National Textbook Co.
4255 W. Touhy Ave.
Lincolnwood, IL 60646   Phone: (312)679-5500
Third edition, 1991. Contains two- to five-page descriptions of 200 managerial, professional, technical, trade, and service occupations. Each profile includes job duties, places of employment, qualifications, educational preparation, training, employment potential, advancement, income, and additional sources of information.

★2650★
"Medical Assistant" in *120 Careers in the Health Care Field* (pp. 167-185)
U.S. Directory Service, Publishers
PO Box 68-1700
655 N.W. 128th St.
Miami, FL 33168   Phone: (305)769-1700
Stanley Alperin. Second edition, 1989. Each occupational profile covers job functions and responsibilities, work locations, training requirements, certification, and salaries. Lists community colleges, universities, vocational-technical schools, and other educational institutions that provide accredited training programs.

★2651★
"Medical Assistant in Pediatrics" in *Opportunities in Health and Medical Careers* (pp. 17-18)
National Textbook Co.
4255 W. Touhy Ave.
Lincolnwood, IL 60646   Phone: (312)679-5500
Leo D'Orazio and Donald I. Snook. 1991. Provides an overview of the health care industry with future projections. Describes a wide variety of healthcare jobs covering the nature of the work, educational requirements, employment outlook and salaries. Offers job hunting advice.

★2652★
"Medical Assistant" in *The Career Connection II: A Guide to Technical Majors and Their Related Careers* (pp. 91-92)
ERIS
PO Box 7509
University Station
Provo, UT 84602-0509
Fred A. Rowe. 1988. Contains technical majors, such as automotive technology. Describes the major and the job. Lists high school and postsecondary school courses. Includes occupations related to the major, employment outlook, and starting salary.

★2653★
Medical Assistants
Chronicle Guidance Publications, Inc.
PO Box 1190
Moravia, NY 13118-1190   Phone: (315)497-0330
1988. This career brief describes the nature of the work, working conditions, hours and earnings, education and training, licensure, certification, unions, personal qualifications, social and psychological factors, employment outlook, entry methods, advancement, and related occupations. **Toll-free/Additional Phone Number(s):** 800-622-7284.

★2654★
"Medical Assistants" in *Occupational Outlook Handbook* (pp. 300-302)
Superintendent of Documents
U.S. Government Printing Office
Washington, DC 20402   Phone: (202)783-3238
Biennial; latest edition, 1990-91. Encyclopedia of careers describing more than 250 occupations and comprising about 86 percent of all jobs in the economy. Occupations that require lengthy education or training are given the most attention. For each occupation, the handbook describes job duties, working conditions, training, educational preparation, personal qualities, advancement possibilities, job outlook, earnings, and sources of additional information.

★2655★
"Medical Assistants" in Volume 4 of *Career Discovery Encyclopedia* (pp. 76-77)
J.G. Ferguson Publishing Co.
200 W. Monroe
Chicago, IL 60606   Phone: (312)580-5480
E. Russell Primm, editor-in-chief. 1990. Contains two-page articles on 504 occupations. Each article describes job duties, earnings, and educational and training requirements.

Medical Assistants

★2656★
"Medical Assistants" in Volume 3 of *The Encyclopedia of Careers and Vocational Guidance* (pp. 276-279)
J.G. Ferguson Publishing Co.
200 W. Monroe
Chicago, IL 60606   Phone: (312)580-5480
William E. Hopke, editor-in-chief. Eighth edition, 1990. Four-volume set that profiles 500 occupations and describes job trends in 76 industries. Includes career description, educational requirements, history of the job, methods of entry, advancement, employment outlook, earnings, working conditions, social and psychological factors, and sources of additional information.

★2657★
"Medical Assistants" in *America's 50 Fastest Growing Jobs* (pp. 120-121)
JIST Works, Inc.
720 N. Park Ave.
Indianapolis, IN 46202   Phone: (317)264-3720
Michael J. Farr, compiler. 1991. Describes the 50 fastest growing jobs within major career clusters such as technicians, and marketing and sales. Each job profile explains the nature of the work, skills and abilities required, employment outlook, average earnings, related occupations, education and training requirements, and employment opportunities. Also contains career planning information and job search tips.

★2658★
Medical Assisting: A Career for the Future
American Association of Medical Assistants
20 N. Wacker Dr., Ste. 1575
Chicago, IL 60606-2903   Phone: (312)899-1500
This six-panel brochure describes the work, educational preparation, and certification. **Toll-free/Additional Phone Number(s):** 800-228-2262.

★2659★
Medical Assisting - A Career for Today and Tomorrow

Registered Medical Assistants (RMA)
710 Higgins Rd.
Park Ridge, IL 60068-5765   Phone: (708)823-5169

★2660★
Medical Assisting: Today's Career for Tomorrow's Reward
American Association of Medical Assistants
20 N. Wacker Dr., Ste. 1575
Chicago, IL 60606-2903   Phone: (312)899-1500
This six-panel brochure describes the work, educational preparation, and working conditions. **Toll-free/Additional Phone Number(s):** 800-228-2262.

★2661★
"Medical Office Assistants" in *Jobs! What They Are. . .Where They Are. . .What They Pay* (p. 139)
Simon & Schuster, Inc.
Simon & Schuster Bldg.
1230 Avenue of the Americas
New York, NY 10020   Phone: (212)698-7000
Robert O. Snelling and Anne M. Snelling. Revised edition, 1989. Profiles 241 occupations, describing duties and responsibilities, educational preparation, earnings, employment opportunities, training, and qualifications.

★2662★
120 Careers in the Health Care Field
U.S. Directory Service, Publishers
655 NW 128th St.
PO Box 68-1700
Miami, FL 33168   Phone: (305)769-1700
Stanley Alperin. Second edition, 1989.

★2663★
"Ophthalmic Medical Assistant" in *120 Careers in the Health Care Field* (pp. 454-457)
U.S. Directory Service, Publishers
PO Box 68-1700
655 N.W. 128th St.
Miami, FL 33168   Phone: (305)769-1700
Stanley Alperin. Second edition, 1989. Each occupational profile covers job functions and responsibilities, work locations, training requirements, certification, and salaries. Lists community colleges, universities, vocational-technical schools, and other educational institutions that provide accredited training programs.

★2664★
Role of Physician Assistants in Primary Care
Technomic Publishing Co., Inc.
851 Holland Ave.
PO Box 3535
Lancaster, PA 17604-3535   Phone: (717)291-5609
Judith Goodwin Greenwood. 1981. **Facsimile Number:** (717)295-4538.

★2665★
Whatcha Gonna Do Now?
Northern Lights Productions
276 Newbury St.
Boston, MA 02116   Phone: (617)267-0391
Videocassette. 1988. 17 mins. Two high schoolers talk about their future; clips are mixed in that let viewers see the rewards of working as a health care professional.

Associations

★2666★
American Association of Medical Assistants (AAMA)
20 N. Wacker Dr., Ste. 1575
Chicago, IL 60606   Phone: (312)899-1500
Membership: Assistants, receptionists, secretaries, bookkeepers, nurses, and laboratory personnel employed in the offices of physicians and other medical facilities. **Purpose:** Activities include a certification program consisting of study and an examination, passage of which entitles the individual to a certificate as a Certified Medical Assistant. Conducts accreditation of one- and two-year programs in medical assisting in conjunction with the Committee on Allied Health Education and Accreditation and the American Medical Association. Provides assistance and information to institutions of higher learning desirous of initiating courses for medical assistants. Sponsors the Maxine Williams Scholarship program. Offers continuing education to assistants who cannot return to school and guided study courses in human relations and medical law. Awards continuing education units for selected educational programs. Maintains library of textbooks and a reference list. **Publications:** *Network-AAMA*, quarterly. • *Professional Medical Assistant*, bimonthly. • Also publishes brochures and pamphlets.

★2667★
American Medical Technologists (AMT)
710 Higgins Rd.
Park Ridge, IL 60068　　　　　　　　Phone: (708)823-5169
Membership: National professional registry of medical laboratory technologists, technicians, medical assistants, and dental assistants. **Purpose:** Bestows awards in six categories: Distinguished Achievement; Exceptional Merit; Order of the Golden Microscope; Member and Student Writing; President's Award; Technologist of the Year. Maintains placement service. Sponsors AMT Institute for Education, which has developed continuing education programs. **Publications:** *AMT Events and Continuing Education Supplement*, 8/year. • Also publishes *Manual of the Accrediting Bureau of Health Education Schools*. **Facsimile Number:** (708)823-0458.

★2668★
American Society of Podiatric Medical Assistants (ASPMA)
2124 S. Austin Blvd.
Cicero, IL 60650　　　　　　　　Phone: (708)863-6303
Membership: Podiatric assistants. **Purpose:** Purposes are to hold educational seminars and to administer certification examinations. Maintains scholarship trust fund and biographical archives. Holds annual seminar. **Publications:** *Journal*, quarterly. • *Newsletter*, bimonthly. • *Podiatric Assistant*, quarterly.

★2669★
Joint Commission on Allied Health Personnel in Ophthalmology (JCAHPO)
2025 Woodlane Dr.
St. Paul, MN 55125-2995　　　　　　　　Phone: (612)731-2944
Membership: A certifying agency for allied health personnel. **Purpose:** Objectives are: to encourage the establishment of medically oriented programs for training allied health personnel in ophthalmology; to develop standards of education and training in the field; to examine, certify, and recertify ophthalmic medical personnel, and encourage their continued occupational development. Conducts annual national certifying examinations and continuing education programs. **Publications:** *Directory of Certified Ophthalmic Medical Assistants*, annual. • *JCAHPO Outlook*, bimonthly. • *Joint Commission on Allied Health Personnel in Ophthalmology—Annual Report*. **Toll-free/Additional Phone Number(s):** (800)284-3937. **Facsimile Number:** (612)731-0410.

★2670★
Registered Medical Assistants (RMA)
710 Higgins Rd.
Park Ridge, IL 60068-5765　　　　　　　　Phone: (708)823-5169
Membership: A program of the American Medical Technologists. Certified assistants to physicians in office practice, clinics, hospitals, and private health care facilities. Works to establish standards of training; provides continuing education and home study programs; promotes quality care in the allied health field. Works with the Accrediting Bureau of Health Education Schools in regard to certification examinations and student societies. Presents RMA of the Year, Student Writing, Outstanding Student, Best Published Article, Best State Association Publication, Exceptional Merit, Distinguished Achievement, and Medallion of Merit awards. Sponsors annual National Medical Assistant Week. Offers group insurance programs. **Publications:** *Vital Signs*, quarterly. • Also publishes *Medical Assisting - A Career for Today and Tomorrow* (brochure). **Toll-free/Additional Phone Number(s):** (800)229-1268. **Facsimile Number:** (708)823-0458.

Standards/Certification Agencies

It is still often the case that medical assistants are trained on the job. However, formal programs in medical assisting are offered in vocational-technical high schools, and at the postsecondary level by vocational schools, community and junior colleges, and universities and accredited by the American Medical Association's Committee on Allied Health Education and Accreditation (CAHEA) and the Accrediting Bureau of Health Education Schools (ABHES). The medical assisting curriculum consists of courses in the biological sciences and medical terminology as well as typing, transcription, recordkeeping, accounting, and insurance processing. Students also learn laboratory techniques, use of medical equipment, clinical procedures, and first aid; they are also instructed in office practices, patient relations, and medical law and ethics. The American Association of Medical Assistants awards the Certified Medical Assistant credential; the American Medical Technologists awards the Registered Medical Assistant credential; the American Society of Podiatric Assistants awards the Certified Podiatric Assistant credential; and the Joint Commission on Allied Health Personnel in Ophthalmology awards the Ophthalmic Medical Assistant credential at three levels: Certified Ophthalmic Assistant, Certified Ophthalmic Technician, and Certified Ophthalmic Technologist.

★2671★
Accrediting Bureau of Health Education Schools (ABHES)
Oak Manor Office
29089 U.S. 20 W.
Elkhart, IN 46514　　　　　　　　Phone: (219)293-0124
Membership: Independent accrediting agency of the American Medical Technologists. **Purpose:** Serves as a nationally recognized accrediting agency of health education institutions and schools conducting medical laboratory technician and medical assistant education programs. Establishes criteria and standards for the administration and operation of health education institutions. Seeks to enhance the profession through the improvement of schools, courses, and the competence of graduates. Schools must apply voluntarily for accreditation; once accredited, they must report to the bureau annually and be reexamined at least every 6 years. Has accredited 29 programs for medical laboratory technicians, 168 medical assistants, and 118 institutions of allied health. Offers workshops on various accreditation, educational, and school operations. **Publications:** *ABHES News*, periodic. • *Accrediting Bureau of Health Education Schools—Directory of Accredited Schools and Programs*, periodic. **Facsimile Number:** (219)295-8564.

★2672★
American Association of Medical Assistants (AAMA)
20 N. Wacker Dr., Ste. 1575
Chicago, IL 60606　　　　　　　　Phone: (312)899-1500
Activities include a certification program consisting of study and an examination, passage of which entitles the individual to a certificate as a Certified Medical Assistant. Conducts accreditation of one- and two-year programs in medical assisting in conjunction with the Committee on Allied Health Education and Accreditation and the American Medical Association. Provides assistance and information to institutions of higher learning desirous of initiating courses for medical assistants. Sponsors the Maxine Williams Scholarship program. Offers continuing education to assistants who cannot return to school and guided study courses in human relations and medical law. Awards continuing education units for selected educational programs.

Medical Assistants

★2673★
American Society of Podiatric Medical Assistants (ASPMA)
2124 S. Austin Blvd.
Cicero, IL 60650　　　　　　　Phone: (708)863-6303
Holds educational seminars and administers certification examinations.

★2674★
Joint Commission on Allied Health Personnel in Ophthalmology (JCAHPO)
2025 Woodlane Dr.
St. Paul, MN 55125-2995　　　　Phone: (612)731-2944
Develops standards of education and training; examines, certifies, and recertifies ophthalmic medical personnel. Conducts annual national certifying examinations and continuing education programs.

★2675★
Medical Assisting— A Career for Today and Tomorrow
Registered Medical Assistants of American Medical Technologists
710 Higgins Rd.
Park Ridge, IL 60068-5765　　　　Phone: (708)823-5169
1990. This eight-panel brochure describes the registered medical assistant certification process. Covers training and working conditions.

★2676★
Registered Medical Assistants (RMA)
710 Higgins Rd.
Park Ridge, IL 60068-5765　　　　Phone: (708)823-5169
Works to establish standards of training. Works with the Accrediting Bureau of Health Education Schools in regard to certification examinations and student societies.

Test Guides

★2677★
Appleton & Lange's Review for the Surgical Technology Examination, ARCO
Appleton & Lange
PO Box 5630
25 Van Zant St.
E. Norwalk, CT 06855　　　　　Phone: (516)921-8888
Nancy M. Allmers and Joan Ann Verderame. Second edition, 1987. A review for the medical assistant, this title follows the outlines established by the DACUM chart, which defines the entry level skills necessary to function effectively as a medical assistant. The second edition features 1,600 questions with answers and explanations, along with a sample Practice Test simulating the actual exam and test-taking strategies.

★2678★
Career Examination Series
National Learning Corp.
212 Michael Dr.
Syosset, NY 11791　　　　　　Phone: (516)921-8888
Jack Rudman. This series of examination guides from National Learning Corp. includes study guides for many medical positions, including medical aide, medical assistant, medical clerk, medical equipment technician, medical inspector, medical records assistant, medical records clerk, medical stenographer, medical technical assistant, medical technician trainee, medical transcribing machine operator, and medical typist. All examination guides in this series contain questions with answers. **Facsimile Number:** (516)921-8743. **Toll-free/Additional Phone Number(s):** 800-645-6337.

★2679★
Certification Examination for Medical Assistants (CMA)
National Learning Corp.
212 Michael Dr.
Syosset, NY 11791　　　　　　Phone: (516)921-8888
Jack Rudman. Part of the Admission Test Series No. 3. Books in this series provide test practice and drill for actual professional certification and licensure tests. **Facsimile Number:** (516)921-8743. **Toll-free/Additional Phone Number(s):** 800-645-6337.

★2680★
Certification— Why and How
The Joint Commission on Allied Health Personnel in Ophthalmology
2025 Woodland Dr.
St. Paul, MN 55125-2995　　　　Phone: (612)731-2944
Briefly describes certification, qualifications needed, and the certifying examinations. **Toll-free/Additional Phone Number(s):** 800-284-3937.

Educational Directories and Programs

★2681★
JCAHPO Outlook
Joint Commission on Allied Health Personnel in Ophthalmology (JCAHPO)
2025 Woodlane Dr.
St. Paul, MN 55125-2995　　　　Phone: (612)731-2944
Bimonthly. Tabloid including continuing education course listings.

★2682★
Manual of the Accrediting Bureau of Health Education Schools
American Medical Technologists (AMT)
710 Higgins Rd.
Park Ridge, IL 60068　　　　　Phone: (708)823-5169

★2683★
Medical Assistants
Accrediting Bureau of Health Education
Oak Manor Office
29089 U.S. 20 W.
Elkhart, IN 46514　　　　　　Phone: (219)293-0124
1991. State-by-state listing of schools offering medical assistant training programs. Lists address, phone number, and contact person.

Periodicals

★2684★
AMT Events and Continuing Education Supplement

American Medical Technologists (AMT)
710 Higgins Rd.
Park Ridge, IL 60068　　　　　Phone: (708)823-5169
8/year. Journal including book reviews and legislative updates.

★2685★
ASPMA Journal
American Society of Podiatric Medical Assistants (ASPMA)
2124 S. Austin Blvd.
Cicero, IL 60650　　　　　　　Phone: (708)863-6303
Quarterly.

★2686★
ASPMA Newsletter
American Society of Podiatric Medical Assistants (ASPMA)
2124 S. Austin Blvd.
Cicero, IL 60650   Phone: (708)863-6303
Bimonthly.

★2687★
Breathline
American Society of Post Anesthesia Nurses
11512 Allecingie Pkwy.
Richmond, VA 23235   Phone: (804)379-5516
Editor(s): Nancy Burden, R.N. Bimonthly. Publishes news of the Society, which is "an organization of licensed nurses engaged in the practice of post anesthesia patient care." Carries legislative updates, scientific articles, and state component society information. Discusses patient care standards, new drugs and treatments, and clinical issues relating to anesthesia and surgery. Recurring features include a calendar of events and columns titled Comment, Profiles, Keeping Up, Resource Review, President's Message, and Other PACU's. **Facsimile Number:** (804)379-1386.

★2688★
Computers & Medicine
Carol Brierly
PO Box 36
Glencoe, IL 60022   Phone: (708)446-3100
Editor(s): Carol Brierly. Monthly. Contains news and ideas on using computers in the health field for diagnosis, treatment, education, and other purposes. Discusses the social and behavioral implications of computer technology, the utilization of artificial intelligence, and similar considerations. Recurring features include reviews of pertinent articles and books, news of research, and a calendar of events.

★2689★
Convenience Care Update
American Health Consultants, Inc.
67 Peachtree Park Dr. NE
Atlanta, GA 30309   Phone: (404)351-4523
Editor(s): Karen Stephens. Monthly. Reports on issues, trends, and news in the field of emergency medicine, particularly in relation to the operations of hospital emergency departments and freestanding urgent care units. Covers marketing, financial, management, and legal aspects of urgent care. Recurring features include news of research, a calendar of events, and columns titled Sources of Information and Legal Question.

★2690★
Cooperative Connection
Nurse Healers-Professional Associates, Inc.
85 Hawthorne Rd.
Williamstown, MA 01267   Phone: (413)458-9181
Editor(s): Susan Wright. Quarterly. Discusses holistic treatment, healing techniques, and other health issues. Promotes the sharing of healing experiences among health practitioners. Recurring features include news of research, book reviews, news of members, and a calendar of events.

★2691★
Corhealth
American Correctional Health Services Association
11 W. Monument Ave., Ste. 510
PO Box 2307
Dayton, OH 45401   Phone: (513)223-9630
Editor(s): Rebecca Craig and Janis James. Bimonthly. "Dedicated to improving correctional health services." Covers news of the association and its chapters and affiliates, who administer and monitor efficiency of health care in correctional institutions. Concerned with the multidisciplinary approach to nursing, dentistry, medicine, surgery, and medical administration. Recurring features include editorials, news of members, statistics, publications available, calls for papers, abstracts, book reviews, and a calendar of events. **Facsimile Number:** (513)223-6307.

★2692★
Healthwire
Federation of Nurses and Health Professionals
American Federation of Teachers
555 New Jersey Ave. NW
Washington, DC 20001   Phone: (202)879-4430
Editor(s): Priscilla M. Nemeth. 6/yr. Explores national news and issues affecting health care workers. Discusses general union developments as well as labor and union concerns specific to the health care field. Recurring features include local member news, book reviews, news of research, and columns titled Clipboard, Pulse Points, Stethoscope, Second Opinion, and Making Rounds.

★2693★
Network-AAMA
American Association of Medical Assistants (AAMA)
20 N. Wacker Dr., Ste. 1575
Chicago, IL 60606   Phone: (312)899-1500
Quarterly. Newsletter including calendar of events.

★2694★
Podiatric Assistant
American Society of Podiatric Medical Assistants (ASPMA)
2124 S. Austin Blvd.
Cicero, IL 60650   Phone: (708)863-6303
Quarterly.

★2695★
Professional Medical Assistant
American Association of Medical Assistants (AAMA)
20 N. Wacker Dr., Ste. 1575
Chicago, IL 60606   Phone: (312)899-1500
Bimonthly. Journal; includes association news, index of advertisers, book reviews, and calendar of events. Also contains annual directory.

★2696★
Vital Signs
Registered Medical Assistants (RMA)
710 Higgins Rd.
Park Ridge, IL 60068-5765   Phone: (708)823-5169
Quarterly. Newsletter.

Meetings and Conventions

★2697★
American Association of Medical Assistants Regional Conferences
American Association of Medical Assistants
20 N. Wacker Dr., Ste. 1575
Chicago, IL 60606   Phone: (312)899-1500
1992; Oct. 02-07; Seattle, WA • 1993; Oct. Indianapolis, IN.

Medical Assistants

★2698★
Physician Assistants Annual Conference
American Academy of Physician Assistants
950 N. Washington St.
Arlington, VA 22314-1552   Phone: (703)836-2272
1992; May 23-28; Nashville, TN • 1993; Jun. 10-15; Miami, FL • 1994; May 21-26; San Antonio, TX • 1995; May 28-03; Las Vegas, NV • 1996; May 25-30; New York, NY. **Facsimile Number:** (703)684-1924.

★2699★
Registered Medical Assistants (RMA)
710 Higgins Rd.
Park Ridge, IL 60068-5765   Phone: (708)823-5169
Frequency: Annual business meeting, with an educational seminar and exhibits, is always held in July. **Toll-free/Additional Phone Number(s):** (800)229-1268. **Facsimile Number:** (708)823-0458.

Nursing Aides and Psychiatric Aides

Nursing aides and psychiatric aides help care for physically or mentally ill, injured, disabled, or infirm individuals confined to hospitals, long term care facilities such as nursing homes, and mental health settings. Nursing aides are sometimes known as nursing assistants or hospital attendants, and work under the supervision of registered and licensed practical nurses. Nursing aides employed in nursing homes are sometimes called geriatric aides and, like nursing aides, work under the supervision of registered and licensed practical nurses. Psychiatric aides, also known as mental health assistants, psychiatric nursing assistants, or ward attendants, care for mentally impaired or emotionally disturbed individuals. They work under a team that may include psychiatrists, psychologists, psychiatric nurses, social workers, and therapists. Almost half of all nursing aides work in nursing homes, and about 25 percent work in hospitals and state and county mental institutions. Almost all psychiatric aides work in psychiatric hospitals, state and county mental institutions, or private psychiatric facilities.

$alaries

Annual earnings of nursing and psychiatric aides are as follows:

Lowest 10 percent	$7,000/year or less
Middle 50 percent	$8,900—$$15,500/year
Top 10 percent	$21,100/year or more

Employment Outlook

Growth rate until the year 2000: Faster than average.

Nursing Aides and Psychiatric Aides

Career Guides

★2700★
Being a Long-Term Care Nursing Assistant
Prentice Hall
Rte. 9W
Englewood Cliffs, NJ 07632   Phone: (201)592-2000
Connie A. Will. 1983.

★2701★
Careers in Health Care
Chelsea House Publishers
1974 Sproul Rd., Ste. 400
Broomall, PA 19008   Phone: (215)353-5166
Rachel S. Epstein. 1989. **Facsimile Number:** (215)359-1439.

★2702★
Careers in Health Services: Opportunities for You
Cambridge Career Products
90 MacCorkle Ave., SW
South Charleston, WV 25311   Phone: (304)744-9323
Videocassette. 1989. 30 mins. This program shows the range of career opportunities in health care fields.

★2703★
"Geriatric Aide" in *Public and Community Services*, Volume 11 of *Career Information Center* (pp. 52-53)
Glencoe/Macmillan
15319 Chatsworth St.
Mission Hills, CA 91345   Phone: (818)898-1391
Richard Lidz and Dale Anderson, editorial directors. Fourth edition, 1990. For 600 occupations, describes job duties, entry-level requirements, education and training needed, advancement possibilities, employment outlook, earnings and benefits. The set is divided into 12 volumes. Each volume includes jobs related under a broad career field. Volume 13 is the index. **Facsimile Number:** 818-365-5489.

★2704★
Health Assistant
Van Nostrand Reinhold
115 5th Ave.
New York, NY 10003   Phone: (212)254-3232
Esther Caldwell. Third edition, 1981. **Facsimile Number:** (212)254-9499.

★2705★
Health Career Planning: A Realistic Guide
Human Sciences Press
233 Spring St.
New York, NY 10013   Phone: (212)620-8000
Ellen F. Lederman. 1988.

★2706★
Health Careers Today
C.V. Mosby Co.
11830 Westline Industrial Dr.
St. Louis, MO 63146   Phone: (314)872-8370
Judith A. Gerdin. 1991. Surveys health occupations. Includes information on basic health care skills and careers.

★2707★
Hospital Attendant
Careers, Inc.
PO Box 135
Largo, FL 34649-0135   Phone: (813)584-7333
1991. Two-page job guide card describing duties, working conditions, personal qualifications, training, earnings and hours, employment outlook, places of employment, related careers and where to write for more information.

★2708★
"Hospital Attendant" in *Occu-Facts: Information on 565 Careers in Outline Form* (p. 13.25)
Careers, Inc.
P.O. Box 135
1211 Tenth St., S.W.
Largo, FL 33640   Phone: (813)584-7333
Elizabeth Handville. Biennial, 1989-90 edition. Each one-page occupational profile describes duties, working conditions, physical surroundings and demands, aptitudes, temperament, educational requirements, employment outlook, earnings, and places of employment.

★2709★
"Hospital Attendants" in Volume 3 of *Career Discovery Encyclopedia* (pp. 114-115)
J.G. Ferguson Publishing Co.
200 W. Monroe
Chicago, IL 60606   Phone: (312)580-5480
E. Russell Primm, editor-in-chief. 1990. Contains two-page articles on 504 occupations. Each article describes job duties, earnings, and educational and training requirements.

★2710★
Introduction to the Health Professions
Jones and Bartlett Publishers, Inc.
20 Park Plaza
Boston, MA 02116　　　　　　　　　Phone: (617)482-5243
Peggy Stanfield. 1990.

★2711★
"Mental Health Technician/Human Services Technician/ Psychiatric Aide" in *120 Careers in the Health Care Field* **(pp. 260-261)**
U.S. Directory Service, Publishers
PO Box 68-1700
655 N.W. 128th St.
Miami, FL 33168　　　　　　　　　Phone: (305)769-1700
Stanley Alperin. Second edition, 1989. Each occupational profile covers job functions and responsibilities, work locations, training requirements, certification, and salaries. Lists community colleges, universities, vocational-technical schools, and other educational institutions that provide accredited training programs.

★2712★
Nursery and Landscape Workers
Careers, Inc.
PO Box 135
Largo, FL 34649-0135　　　　　　　Phone: (813)584-7333
1990. Two-page occupational summary card describing duties, working conditions, personal qualifications, training, earnings and hours, employment outlook, places of employment, related careers and where to write for more information.

★2713★
Nurse's Aide
Vocational Biographies, Inc.
PO Box 31, Dept. VF10
Sauk Centre, MN 56378　　　　　　Phone: (612)352-6516
1988. This pamphlet profiles a person working in the job. Includes information about job duties, working conditions, places of employment, educational preparation, labor market outlook, and salaries. **Toll-free/Additional Phone Number(s):** 800-255-0752.

★2714★
"Nurse's Aide and Orderly" in *Health,* **Volume 7 of** *Career Information Center* **(pp. 51-52)**
Glencoe/Macmillan
15319 Chatsworth St.
Mission Hills, CA 91345　　　　　　Phone: (818)898-1391
Richard Lidz and Dale Anderson, editorial directors. Fourth edition, 1990. For 600 occupations, describes job duties, entry-level requirements, education and training needed, advancement possibilities, employment outlook, earnings and benefits. The set is divided into 12 volumes. Each volume includes jobs related under a broad career field. Volume 13 is the index. **Facsimile Number:** 818-365-5489.

★2715★
"Nurse's Aide" in *The Career Connection II: A Guide to Technical Majors and Their Related Careers* **(pp. 97-98)**
ERIS
PO Box 7509
University Station
Provo, UT 84602-0509
Fred A. Rowe. 1988. Contains technical majors, such as automotive technology. Describes the major and the job. Lists high school and postsecondary school courses. Includes occupations related to the major, employment outlook, and starting salary.

★2716★
"Nurse's Aide/Psychiatric Aide" in *Careers in Counseling and Human Development* **(pp. 115-116)**
American Association for Counseling and Development
5999 Stevenson Ave.
Alexandria, VA 22304　　　　　　　Phone: (703)823-9800
Brooke B. Collison and Nancy J. Garfield, authors and managing editors. 1990. Surveys jobs in the human services, human development, and counseling fields. Provides an overview of ten different work settings such as private practice, schools, and public agencies. Includes information about certification, credentialing and licensure.

★2717★
"Nurses' Aides and Orderlies" in *The American Almanac of Jobs and Salaries* **(pp. 482-483)**
Avon Books
105 Madison Avenue
New York, NY 10016　　　　　　　Phone: (212)481-5600
John Wright and Edward J. Dwyer. Revised and updated, 1990. A comprehensive guide to the wages of hundreds of occupations in a wide variety of industries and organizations.

★2718★
"Nursing Aide and Psychiatric Aide" in *Careers in Health Care* **(pp. 179-181)**
National Textbook Co.
4255 W. Touhy Ave.
Lincolnwood, IL 60646　　　　　　Phone: (312)679-5500
Barbara M. Swanson. 1989. Discusses 61 health careers, providing information about the history of the occupation, job duties, work environments, salaries, educational preparation, licensure, certification, and employment outlook.

★2719★
"Nursing Aide/Orderly" in *120 Careers in the Health Care Field* **(pp. 288-289)**
U.S. Directory Service, Publishers
PO Box 68-1700
655 N.W. 128th St.
Miami, FL 33168　　　　　　　　　Phone: (305)769-1700
Stanley Alperin. Second edition, 1989. Each occupational profile covers job functions and responsibilities, work locations, training requirements, certification, and salaries. Lists community colleges, universities, vocational-technical schools, and other educational institutions that provide accredited training programs.

★2720★
"Nursing Aides and Psychiatric Aides" in *America's 50 Fastest Growing Jobs* **(pp. 122-123)**
JIST Works, Inc.
720 N. Park Ave.
Indianapolis, IN 46202　　　　　　Phone: (317)264-3720
Michael J. Farr, compiler. 1991. Describes the 50 fastest growing jobs within major career clusters such as technicians, and marketing and sales. Each job profile explains the nature of the work, skills and abilities required, employment outlook, average earnings, related occupations, education and training requirements, and employment opportunities. Also contains career planning information and job search tips.

Nursing Aides and Psychiatric Aides

★2721★
"Nursing Aides and Psychiatric Aides" in *Occupational Outlook Handbook* (pp. 302-303)
Superintendent of Documents
U.S. Government Printing Office
Washington, DC 20402   Phone: (202)783-3238
Biennial; latest edition, 1990-91. Encyclopedia of careers describing more than 250 occupations and comprising about 86 percent of all jobs in the economy. Occupations that require lengthy education or training are given the most attention. For each occupation, the handbook describes job duties, working conditions, training, educational preparation, personal qualities, advancement possibilities, job outlook, earnings, and sources of additional information.

★2722★
"Nursing Aides/Assistants" in *Opportunities in Health and Medical Careers* (pp. 38-39)
National Textbook Co.
4255 W. Touhy Ave.
Lincolnwood, IL 60646   Phone: (312)679-5500
Leo D'Orazio and Donald I. Snook. 1991. Provides an overview of the health care industry with future projections. Describes a wide variety of healthcare jobs covering the nature of the work, educational requirements, employment outlook and salaries. Offers job hunting advice.

★2723★
"Nursing and Psychiatric Aides" in Volume 4 of *Career Discovery Encyclopedia* (pp. 132-133)
J.G. Ferguson Publishing Co.
200 W. Monroe
Chicago, IL 60606   Phone: (312)580-5480
E. Russell Primm, editor-in-chief. 1990. Contains two-page articles on 504 occupations. Each article describes job duties, earnings, and educational and training requirements.

★2724★
"Nursing and Psychiatric Aides" in Volume 3 of *The Encyclopedia of Careers and Vocational Guidance* (pp. 288-291)
J.G. Ferguson Publishing Co.
200 W. Monroe
Chicago, IL 60606   Phone: (312)580-5480
William E. Hopke, editor-in-chief. Eighth edition, 1990. Four-volume set that profiles 500 occupations and describes job trends in 76 industries. Includes career description, educational requirements, history of the job, methods of entry, advancement, employment outlook, earnings, working conditions, social and psychological factors, and sources of additional information.

★2725★
Nursing Assistants
Chronicle Guidance Publications, Inc.
PO Box 1190
Moravia, NY 13118-1190   Phone: (315)497-0330
1987. This career brief describes the nature of the work, working conditions, hours and earnings, education and training, licensure, certification, unions, personal qualifications, social and psychological factors, employment outlook, entry methods, advancement, and related occupations. **Toll-free/Additional Phone Number(s):** 800-622-7284.

★2726★
Nursing Assistants & the Long-Term Health Care Facility
J. B. Lippincott Co.
E. Washington Square
Philadelphia, PA 19105   Phone: (215)238-4200
Lorna Hanebuth. 1977.

★2727★
"Nursing or Psychiatric Aide" in *Health Care* (pp. 21-25)
Franklin Watts, Inc.
387 Park Avenue, S.
New York, NY 10016   Phone: (212)686-7070
Linda Barrett and Galen Guengerich. 1991. Provides an overview of the health care industry. Includes job description, educational preparation, training, salary, and employment outlook. Offers job hunting advice.

★2728★
120 Careers in the Health Care Field
U.S. Directory Service, Publishers
655 NW 128th St.
PO Box 68-1700
Miami, FL 33168   Phone: (305)769-1700
Stanley Alperin. Second edition, 1989.

★2729★
"Orderly" in *Opportunities in Health and Medical Careers* (p. 39)
National Textbook Co.
4255 W. Touhy Ave.
Lincolnwood, IL 60646   Phone: (312)679-5500
Leo D'Orazio and Donald I. Snook. 1991. Provides an overview of the health care industry with future projections. Describes a wide variety of healthcare jobs covering the nature of the work, educational requirements, employment outlook and salaries. Offers job hunting advice.

★2730★
Psychiatric Aide
Careers, Inc.
PO Box 135
Largo, FL 34649-0135   Phone: (813)584-7333
1988. Two-page job guide card describing duties, working conditions, personal qualifications, training, earnings and hours, employment outlook, places of employment, related careers and where to write for more information.

★2731★
"Psychiatric Aide" in *Occu-Facts: Information on 565 Careers in Outline Form* (p. 13.26)
Careers, Inc.
P.O. Box 135
1211 Tenth St., S.W.
Largo, FL 33640   Phone: (813)584-7333
Elizabeth Handville. Biennial, 1989-90 edition. Each one-page occupational profile describes duties, working conditions, physical surroundings and demands, aptitudes, temperament, educational requirements, employment outlook, earnings, and places of employment.

★2732★
Psychiatric Aides and Technicians
Chronicle Guidance Publications, Inc.
PO Box 1190
Moravia, NY 13118-1190   Phone: (315)497-0330
1988. This career brief describes the nature of the work, working conditions, hours and earnings, education and training, licensure, certification, unions, personal qualifications, social and psychological factors, employment outlook, entry methods,

advancement, and related occupations. **Toll-free/Additional Phone Number(s):** 800-622-7284.

★2733★
Whatcha Gonna Do Now?
Northern Lights Productions
276 Newbury St.
Boston, MA 02116   Phone: (617)267-0391

Videocassette. 1988. 17 mins. Two high schoolers talk about their future; clips are mixed in that let viewers see the rewards of working as a health care professional.

Associations

★2734★
American Health Care Association (AHCA)
1201 L St. NW
Washington, DC 20005   Phone: (202)842-4444

Membership: Federation of state associations of long-term health care facilities. **Purpose:** Promotes standards for professionals in long-term health care delivery and quality care for patients and residents in a safe environment. Focuses on issues of availability, quality, affordability, and fair payment. Conducts seminars that provide continuing education for nursing home personnel. Maintains liaison with governmental agencies, Congress, and professional associations. Presents awards; compiles statistics. **Publications:** *AHCA Notes*, biweekly. • *Provider: For Long Term Care Professionals*, monthly. • Also publishes *A Consumer's Guide to Long Term Care*, *Thinking About a Nursing Home?*, *Welcome to Our Nursing Home*, and career information and training manuals; produces audiovisual aids. **Facsimile Number:** (202)842-3860.

★2735★
American Hospital Association (AHA)
840 N. Lake Shore Dr.
Chicago, IL 60611   Phone: (312)280-6000

Membership: Individuals and health care institutions including hospitals, health care systems, and pre- and postacute health care delivery organizations. **Purpose:** Is dedicated to promoting the welfare of the public through its leadership and assistance to its members in the provision of better health services for all people. Carries out research and education projects in such areas as health care administration, hospital economics, and community relations; represents hospitals in national legislation; offers programs for institutional effectiveness review, technology assessment, and hospital administrative services to hospitals; conducts educational programs furthering the in-service education of hospital personnel; collects and analyzes data; furnishes multimedia educational materials; maintains 44,000 volume health care administration library, and biographical archive. Bestows awards. **Publications:** *AHANews*, weekly. • *Guide to the Health Care Field*, annual. • *Hospital Statistics*, annual. • *Hospitals*, biweekly. **Toll-free/Additional Phone Number(s):** (800)621-6712. **Facsimile Number:** (312)280-5979.

Standards/Certification Agencies

★2736★
American Health Care Association (AHCA)
1201 L St. NW
Washington, DC 20005   Phone: (202)842-4444

Promotes standards for professionals in long-term health care delivery and quality care for patients and residents in a safe environment. Conducts seminars that provide continuing education for nursing home personnel. Maintains liaison with governmental agencies, Congress, and professional associations.

Test Guides

★2737★
Career Examination Series
National Learning Corp.
212 Michael Dr.
Syosset, NY 11791   Phone: (516)921-8888

Jack Rudman. This series of examination guides from National Learning Corp. includes study guides for many health-related careers. Guides are available for nurse's aide, nursing assistant, nursing station clerk trainee, nutrition assistant, mental health aide, mental health assistant, mental hygiene therapy aide, mental hygiene therapy assistant, psychology assistant, psychiatric attendant, and psychiatric therapy aide. All examination guides in this series contain questions with answers. **Facsimile Number:** (516)921-8743. **Toll-free/Additional Phone Number(s):** 800-645-6337.

★2738★
Civil Service Tests for Basic Skills Jobs
Prentice Hall Press
Simon & Schuster Inc.
200 Old Tappan Rd.
Old Tappan, NJ 07675   Phone: (800)223-2348

Hy Hammer. First edition, 1985. Contains nine sample examinations to prepare candidates for entry-level positions that include hospital attendant, building groundskeeper, and custodial assistant, among others.

Educational Directories and Programs

★2739★
Guide to the Health Care Field
American Hospital Association (AHA)
840 N. Lake Shore Dr.
Chicago, IL 60611   Phone: (312)280-6000
Annual.

★2740★
Nursing Aides and Psychiatric Aides
Accrediting Bureau of Health Education
Oak Manor Office
29089 U.S. 20 W.
Elkhart, IN 46514   Phone: (219)293-0124

1991. State-by-state listing of schools offering nurse aide training programs. Lists address, phone number, and contact person.

Basic Reference Guides and Handbooks

★2741★
A Clinical Manual for Nursing Assistants
Jones & Bartlett Publishers, Inc.
20 Park Plaza
Boston, MA 02116   Phone: (617)482-5243

Sharon McClelland. 1985.

Nursing Aides and Psychiatric Aides

★2742★
Geriatric Nursing Assistants: An Annotated Bibliography with Models to Enhance Practice
Greenwood Publishing Group, Inc.
88 Post Rd., W.
PO Box 5007
Westport, CT 06881 Phone: (203)226-3571
George H. Weber. 1990. Part of Bibliographies & Indexes in Gerontology Series. **Facsimile Number:** (202)222-1502.

★2743★
Mosby's Textbook for Nursing Assistants
Mosby Year Book, Inc.
11830 Westline Industrial Dr.
St. Louis, MO 63146 Phone: (314)872-8370
Sorrentino. Third edition, 1991.

★2744★
Nurse's Aid Study Manual
W. B. Saunders Co.
Curtis Center
Independence Sq. W.
Philadelphia, PA 19106 Phone: (215)238-7800
Mary E. Mayes. Third edition, 1976.

★2745★
Successful Nurse Aide Management in Nursing Homes
Oryx Press
4041 N. Central at Indian School Rd., Ste. 700
Phoenix, AZ 85012-3397 Phone: (602)265-2651
Joann M. Day, editor. 1989. **Toll-free/Additional Phone Number(s):** 800-279-6799. **Facsimile Number:** (602)253-2741.

★2746★
Textbook for Nursing Assistants
Mosby Year Book, Inc.
11830 Westline Industrial Dr.
St. Louis, MO 63146 Phone: (314)872-8370
Sorretino. Second edition, 1988.

---------- Periodicals ----------

★2747★
AHANews
American Hospital Association (AHA)
840 N. Lake Shore Dr.
Chicago, IL 60611 Phone: (312)280-6000
Weekly.

★2748★
Breathline
American Society of Post Anesthesia Nurses
11512 Allecingie Pkwy.
Richmond, VA 23235 Phone: (804)379-5516
Editor(s): Nancy Burden, R.N. Bimonthly. Publishes news of the Society, which is "an organization of licensed nurses engaged in the practice of post anesthesia patient care." Carries legislative updates, scientific articles, and state component society information. Discusses patient care standards, new drugs and treatments, and clinical issues relating to anesthesia and surgery. Recurring features include a calendar of events and columns titled Comment, Profiles, Keeping Up, Resource Review, President's Message, and Other PACU's. **Facsimile Number:** (804)379-1386.

★2749★
Computers & Medicine
Carol Brierly
PO Box 36
Glencoe, IL 60022 Phone: (708)446-3100
Editor(s): Carol Brierly. Monthly. Contains news and ideas on using computers in the health field for diagnosis, treatment, education, and other purposes. Discusses the social and behavioral implications of computer technology, the utilization of artificial intelligence, and similar considerations. Recurring features include reviews of pertinent articles and books, news of research, and a calendar of events.

★2750★
Convenience Care Update
American Health Consultants, Inc.
67 Peachtree Park Dr. NE
Atlanta, GA 30309 Phone: (404)351-4523
Editor(s): Karen Stephens. Monthly. Reports on issues, trends, and news in the field of emergency medicine, particularly in relation to the operations of hospital emergency departments and freestanding urgent care units. Covers marketing, financial, management, and legal aspects of urgent care. Recurring features include news of research, a calendar of events, and columns titled Sources of Information and Legal Question.

★2751★
Cooperative Connection
Nurse Healers-Professional Associates, Inc.
85 Hawthorne Rd.
Williamstown, MA 01267 Phone: (413)458-9181
Editor(s): Susan Wright. Quarterly. Discusses holistic treatment, healing techniques, and other health issues. Promotes the sharing of healing experiences among health practitioners. Recurring features include news of research, book reviews, news of members, and a calendar of events.

★2752★
Corhealth
American Correctional Health Services Association
11 W. Monument Ave., Ste. 510
PO Box 2307
Dayton, OH 45401 Phone: (513)223-9630
Editor(s): Rebecca Craig and Janis James. Bimonthly. "Dedicated to improving correctional health services." Covers news of the association and its chapters and affiliates, who administer and monitor efficiency of health care in correctional institutions. Concerned with the multidisciplinary approach to nursing, dentistry, medicine, surgery, and medical administration. Recurring features include editorials, news of members, statistics, publications available, calls for papers, abstracts, book reviews, and a calendar of events. **Facsimile Number:** (513)223-6307.

★2753★
Healthwire
Federation of Nurses and Health Professionals
American Federation of Teachers
555 New Jersey Ave. NW
Washington, DC 20001 Phone: (202)879-4430
Editor(s): Priscilla M. Nemeth. 6/yr. Explores national news and issues affecting health care workers. Discusses general union developments as well as labor and union concerns specific to the health care field. Recurring features include local member news, book reviews, news of research, and columns titled Clipboard, Pulse Points, Stethoscope, Second Opinion, and Making Rounds.

★2754★
Hospitals
American Hospital Association (AHA)
840 N. Lake Shore Dr.
Chicago, IL 60611   Phone: (312)280-6000
Biweekly.

★2755★
Men in Nursing
National Male Nurse Association
2309 State St., West Office
Saginaw, MI 48602   Phone: (517)799-8208
Editor(s): Samuel Hart, R.N. Bimonthly. Provides information on nursing and health, particularly as it affects male registered and licensed practical nurses. Recurring features include book reviews, job opportunity notices, and letters to the editor.

★2756★
The Nightingale
National Association of Physician Nurses
900 S. Washington St., No. G13
Falls Church, VA 22046-4020   Phone: (703)237-8616
Editor(s): Sue Young. Monthly. Presents items on "medical and personal subjects pertaining to office nurses and other staff.".

★2757★
Provider: For Long Term Care Professionals
American Health Care Association (AHCA)
1201 L St. NW
Washington, DC 20005   Phone: (202)842-4444
Monthly. Free to long-term health care professionals; Magazine; includes buyers' guide, news reports, advertisers' index, a listing of new products and services, and calendar of events.

★2758★
Quickening
American College of Nurse-Midwives
1522 K St. NW, Ste. 1120
Washington, DC 20005   Phone: (202)347-5445
Editor(s): Mickey G. Nall. Bimonthly. Promotes the training and certification of nurse-midwives. Recurring features include membership, board and convention news, announcements of relevant meetings and workshops, help-wanted items, and lists of significant publications.

- Personal Service and Building and Grounds Service Occupations -

Animal Caretakers, Except Farm

Animal caretakers, sometimes called animal attendants, feed, water, and exercise animals and clean and repair their cages. They also provide social interaction for the animals with play and companionship. Job titles and duties of caretakers vary by employment setting. People who specialize in maintaining dogs' appearance are called dog groomers. Some groomers work in kennels and others operate their own grooming business. Veterinary technicians, also known as animal health technicians, keep records, take specimens, perform laboratory tests, prepare animals and instruments for surgery, take and develop radiographs, dress wounds, and assist the veterinarian with examinations and surgery. Veterinary assistants feed and bathe the animals, administer medication as prescribed by the veterinarian, and assist the veterinarian and veterinary technician in the treatment of the animal. Animal attendants clean cages, exercise the animals, and monitor the animals for symptoms of illnesses. Laboratory animal technologist supervise the daily care and maintenance of animals by a technician and assistant; they may also assist in surgical care and other laboratory procedures. The animal laboratory technician provides the daily care of animals—giving prescribed dosages and medications, taking specimens, performing laboratory tests, and assisting with minor surgery. Technicians also keep daily records of the animals' diets, behavior, and health. The assistant laboratory animal technician sanitizes cages and feeds the animals. Zookeepers prepare the diets, clean the enclosures, and monitor the behavior of exotic animals. Keepers sometimes assist in research studies, train animals, and put on special shows and give lectures to the public. Caretakers are employed at kennels, animal shelters, pet stores, stables, veterinary facilities, laboratories, and zoological parks. Less than 20 percent of all caretakers are self-employed.

$alaries

Annual salaries of caretakers are as follows:

Lowest 10 percent	$7,124/year or less
Middle 50 percent	$8,788—$13,988/year
Top 10 percent	$17,940/year or more

Employment Outlook

Growth rate until the year 2000: Average.

Animal Caretakers, Except Farm

Career Guides

★2759★
Animal Care Attendant
Careers, Inc.
PO Box 135
Largo, FL 34649-0135   Phone: (813)584-7333
1992. Two-page job guide card describing duties, working conditions, personal qualifications, training, earnings and hours, employment outlook, places of employment, related careers and where to write for more information.

★2760★
"Animal Care Attendant" in *Careers for Animal Lovers and Other Zoological Types* (pp. 17-19)
National Textbook Co.
4255 W. Touhy Ave.
Lincolnwood, IL 60646   Phone: (312)679-5500
Louise Miller. 1991. Surveys a wide range of career opportunities working with animals in both the public and profit sectors. Lists job titles and describes qualifications, salaries, benefits, educational requirements, employment outlook, and places of employment. Includes animal trainers and handlers, animal-related businesses, and animal writers, photographers, and illustrators.

★2761★
"Animal Care Attendant" in *Occu-Facts: Information on 565 Careers in Outline Form* (p. 14.14)
Careers, Inc.
P.O. Box 135
1211 Tenth St., S.W.
Largo, FL 33640   Phone: (813)584-7333
Elizabeth Handville. Biennial, 1989-90 edition. Each one-page occupational profile describes duties, working conditions, physical surroundings and demands, aptitudes, temperament, educational requirements, employment outlook, earnings, and places of employment.

★2762★
"Animal Caretaker" in *Hospitality and Recreation, Volume 8 of Career Information Center* (pp. 35-36)
Glencoe/Macmillan
15319 Chatsworth St.
Mission Hills, CA 91345   Phone: (818)898-1391
Richard Lidz and Dale Anderson, editorial directors. Fourth edition, 1990. For 600 occupations, describes job duties, entry-level requirements, education and training needed, advancement possibilities, employment outlook, earnings and benefits. The set is divided into 12 volumes. Each volume includes jobs related under a broad career field. Volume 13 is the index. **Facsimile Number:** 818-365-5489.

★2763★
Animal Caretakers
Chronicle Guidance Publications, Inc.
PO Box 1190
Moravia, NY 13118-1190   Phone: (315)497-0330
1990. This career brief describes the nature of the work, working conditions, hours and earnings, education and training, licensure, certification, unions, personal qualifications, social and psychological factors, employment outlook, entry methods, advancement, and related occupations. **Toll-free/Additional Phone Number(s):** 800-622-7284.

★2764★
"Animal Caretakers, Except Farm" in *Occupational Outlook Handbook* (pp. 304-305)
Superintendent of Documents
U.S. Government Printing Office
Washington, DC 20402   Phone: (202)783-3238
Biennial; latest edition, 1990-91. Encyclopedia of careers describing more than 250 occupations and comprising about 86 percent of all jobs in the economy. Occupations that require lengthy education or training are given the most attention. For each occupation, the handbook describes job duties, working conditions, training, educational preparation, personal qualities, advancement possibilities, job outlook, earnings, and sources of additional information.

★2765★
"Animal Health Technicians" in Volume 4 of *The Encyclopedia of Careers and Vocational Guidance* (pp. 377-381)
J.G. Ferguson Publishing Co.
200 W. Monroe
Chicago, IL 60606   Phone: (312)580-5480
William E. Hopke, editor-in-chief. Eighth edition, 1990. Four-volume set that profiles 500 occupations and describes job trends in 76 industries. Includes career description, educational requirements, history of the job, methods of entry, advancement, employment outlook, earnings, working conditions, social and psychological factors, and sources of additional information.

★2766★
"Animal Health Technicians" in Volume 1 of *Career Discovery Encyclopedia* (pp. 40-41)
J.G. Ferguson Publishing Co.
200 W. Monroe
Chicago, IL 60606   Phone: (312)580-5480
E. Russell Primm, editor-in-chief. 1990. Contains two-page articles on 504 occupations. Each article describes job duties, earnings, and educational and training requirements.

★2767★
Animal Technicians
Chronicle Guidance Publications, Inc.
PO Box 1190
Moravia, NY 13118-1190   Phone: (315)497-0330
1987. This career brief describes the nature of the work, working conditions, hours and earnings, education and training, licensure, certification, unions, personal qualifications, social and psychological factors, employment outlook, entry methods, advancement, and related occupations. **Toll-free/Additional Phone Number(s):** 800-622-7284.

★2768★
"Animal Technicians and Other Paramedical Personnel" in *Opportunities in Veterinary Medicine* (pp. 115-116)
National Textbook Co.
4255 W. Touhy Ave.
Lincolnwood, IL 60646   Phone: (312)679-5500
Robert E. Swope. 1987. Discusses history, educational requirements, and employment opportunities for veterinarians in industry, government, academia, and the military.

★2769★
"Animal Technology" in *120 Careers in the Health Care Field* (pp. 1-6)
U.S. Directory Service, Publishers
PO Box 68-1700
655 N.W. 128th St.
Miami, FL 33168   Phone: (305)769-1700
Stanley Alperin. Second edition, 1989. Each occupational profile covers job functions and responsibilities, work locations, training requirements, certification, and salaries. Lists community colleges, universities, vocational-technical schools, and other educational institutions that provide accredited training programs.

★2770★
Careers at a Zoo
Lerner Publications Co.
241 First Ave., N.
Minneapolis, MN 55401
Mark Lerner. 1980. Describes 15 careers at a zoo, including zoo keeper and animal commissary keeper. **Toll-free/Additional Phone Number(s):** 800-328-4920. **Facsimile Number:** (612)332-7615.

★2771★
The Challenge of a Lifetime: Careers in Animal Science
American Association for Laboratory Animal Science
17 Timber Creek Dr., Ste. 5
Cordova, TN 38018   Phone: (901)754-8620
This 10-page booklet surveys careers in animal laboratory science. Covers entry-level positions and places of employment.

★2772★
Dog Groomer
Careers, Inc.
PO Box 135
Largo, FL 34649-0135   Phone: (813)584-7333
1991. Two-page occupational summary card describing duties, working conditions, personal qualifications, training, earnings and hours, employment outlook, places of employment, related careers and where to write for more information.

★2773★
"Dog Groomer" in *Occu-Facts: Information on 565 Careers in Outline Form* (p. 14.15)
Careers, Inc.
P.O. Box 135
1211 Tenth St., S.W.
Largo, FL 33640   Phone: (813)584-7333
Elizabeth Handville. Biennial, 1989-90 edition. Each one-page occupational profile describes duties, working conditions, physical surroundings and demands, aptitudes, temperament, educational requirements, employment outlook, earnings, and places of employment.

★2774★
Dog Groomers
Chronicle Guidance Publications, Inc.
PO Box 1190
Moravia, NY 13118-1190   Phone: (315)497-0330
1989. This career brief describes the nature of the work, working conditions, hours and earnings, education and training, licensure, certification, unions, personal qualifications, social and psychological factors, employment outlook, entry methods, advancement, and related occupations. **Toll-free/Additional Phone Number(s):** 800-622-7284.

★2775★
"Dog Groomers" in Volume 3 of *The Encyclopedia of Careers and Vocational Guidance* (pp. 341-345)
J.G. Ferguson Publishing Co.
200 W. Monroe
Chicago, IL 60606   Phone: (312)580-5480
William E. Hopke, editor-in-chief. Eighth edition, 1990. Four-volume set that profiles 500 occupations and describes job trends in 76 industries. Includes career description, educational requirements, history of the job, methods of entry, advancement, employment outlook, earnings, working conditions, social and psychological factors, and sources of additional information.

★2776★
"Dog Groomers" in Volume 2 of *Career Discovery Encyclopedia* (pp. 120-121)
J.G. Ferguson Publishing Co.
200 W. Monroe
Chicago, IL 60606   Phone: (312)580-5480
E. Russell Primm, editor-in-chief. 1990. Contains two-page articles on 504 occupations. Each article describes job duties, earnings, and educational and training requirements.

★2777★
"Laboratory Animal Care Worker" in *Health*, Volume 7 of *Career Information Center* (pp. 50-51)
Glencoe/Macmillan
15319 Chatsworth St.
Mission Hills, CA 91345   Phone: (818)898-1391
Richard Lidz and Dale Anderson, editorial directors. Fourth edition, 1990. For 600 occupations, describes job duties, entry-level requirements, education and training needed, advancement possibilities, employment outlook, earnings and

Animal Caretakers, Except Farm ★2787★

benefits. The set is divided into 12 volumes. Each volume includes jobs related under a broad career field. Volume 13 is the index. **Facsimile Number:** 818-365-5489.

★2778★
"Pet Care Worker" in *Consumer, Homemaking, and Personal Services,* Volume 5 of *Career Information Center* (pp. 56-58)
Glencoe/Macmillan
15319 Chatsworth St.
Mission Hills, CA 91345   Phone: (818)898-1391
Richard Lidz and Dale Anderson, editorial directors. Fourth edition, 1990. For 600 occupations, describes job duties, entry-level requirements, education and training needed, advancement possibilities, employment outlook, earnings and benefits. The set is divided into 12 volumes. Each volume includes jobs related under a broad career field. Volume 13 is the index. **Facsimile Number:** 818-365-5489.

★2779★
"Pet Care Worker" in *Personal Services* (pp. 45-49)
Franklin Watts, Inc.
387 Park Avenue, S.
New York, NY 10016   Phone: (212)686-7070
Linda Barrett and Galen Guengerich. 1991. Surveys personal services jobs. Describes job duties, educational preparation, salaries, and employment outlook. Offers job hunting advice.

★2780★
"Pet Grooming" in *Careers for Animal Lovers and Other Zoological Types* (pp. 59-61)
National Textbook Co.
4255 W. Touhy Ave.
Lincolnwood, IL 60646   Phone: (312)679-5500
Louise Miller. 1991. Surveys a wide range of career opportunities working with animals in both the public and profit sectors. Lists job titles and describes qualifications, salaries, benefits, educational requirements, employment outlook, and places of employment. Includes animal trainers and handlers, animal-related businesses, and animal writers, photographers, and illustrators.

★2781★
"Veterinary Technician" in *Careers for Animal Lovers and Other Zoological Types* (pp. 15-17)
National Textbook Co.
4255 W. Touhy Ave.
Lincolnwood, IL 60646   Phone: (312)679-5500
Louise Miller. 1991. Surveys a wide range of career opportunities working with animals in both the public and profit sectors. Lists job titles and describes qualifications, salaries, benefits, educational requirements, employment outlook, and places of employment. Includes animal trainers and handlers, animal-related businesses, and animal writers, photographers, and illustrators.

★2782★
"Veterinary Technician" in *Careers in Veterinary Medicine* (pp. 103-108)
Rosen Publishing Group, Inc.
29 E. 21st St.
New York, NY 10010   Phone: (212)777-3017
Jane Caryl Duncan. 1988. Surveys job opportunities for veterinarians in teaching, private practice, private industry, and zoos. Covers educational preparation, the nature of the work, salaries, licensure, and continuing education.

★2783★
"Veterinary Technicians and Assistants" in *Jobs! What They Are. . . Where They Are. . . What They Pay* (p. 47)
Simon & Schuster, Inc.
Simon & Schuster Bldg.
1230 Avenue of the Americas
New York, NY 10020   Phone: (212)698-7000
Robert O. Snelling and Anne M. Snelling. Revised edition, 1989. Profiles 241 occupations, describing duties and responsibilities, educational preparation, earnings, employment opportunities, training, and qualifications.

★2784★
Your Career in Veterinary Technology
American Veterinary Medical Association
930 N. Mecham Rd.
Schaumburg, IL 60196-1074   Phone: (708)605-8070
1989. This eight-panel brochure describes the work, places of employment, educational preparation, personal attributes, and earnings of veterinary medical technologists.

★2785★
"Zookeeper" in *Careers for Animal Lovers and Other Zoological Types* (pp. 90-93)
National Textbook Co.
4255 W. Touhy Ave.
Lincolnwood, IL 60646   Phone: (312)679-5500
Louise Miller. 1991. Surveys a wide range of career opportunities working with animals in both the public and profit sectors. Lists job titles and describes qualifications, salaries, benefits, educational requirements, employment outlook, and places of employment. Includes animal trainers and handlers, animal-related businesses, and animal writers, photographers, and illustrators.

Associations

★2786★
American Association for Laboratory Animal Science (AALAS)
70 Timber Creek, Ste. 5
Cordova, TN 38018   Phone: (901)754-8620
Membership: Persons and institutions professionally concerned with the production, use, care, and study of laboratory animals. **Purpose:** Serves as clearinghouse for collection and exchange of information on all phases of laboratory animal care and management and on the care, use, and procurement of laboratory animals used in biomedical research. Conducts examinations and certification through its Animal Technician Certification Program. Offers awards that stimulate and encourage research and education. **Publications:** *AALAS Bulletin,* bimonthly. • *American Association for Laboratory Animal Science—Membership Directory,* annual. • *Laboratory Animal Science,* bimonthly. • Also publishes educational material, guides, and list of films and filmstrips.

★2787★
American Association of Zoo Keepers (AAZK)
Topeka Zoological Park
635 Gage Blvd.
Topeka, KS 66606   Phone: (913)272-5821
Membership: Professional members are zoo keepers and aquarists; affiliate members are other zoo employees and volunteers; associate members are students and other interested persons. **Purpose:** Disseminates information about the care of wild animals, birds, reptiles, and marine life found in captivity; fosters a professional attitude in animal keepers by encouraging them to become actively involved in the professional teams at

zoos and aquariums. Maintains library and speakers' bureau. Presents annual Excellence in Zookeeping Award to professionals who have done exemplary work in animal care. Conducts specialized education and research programs; compiles statistics.

★2788★
American Boarding Kennel Association (ABKA)
4575 Galley Rd., #400A
Colorado Springs, CO 80915   Phone: (719)591-1113

Membership: Persons or firms that board pets; kennel suppliers; others interested in the boarding kennel industry. **Purpose:** Seeks to upgrade the industry through educational programs and conventions. Provides insurance plans for members and supplies pet care information to the public. Promotes code of ethics and accreditation program for recognition and training of superior kennel operators. Compiles statistics. **Publications:** *Boarderline*, bimonthly. • *Newsletter*, periodic. • Also publishes brochure and booklets. **Facsimile Number:** (719)597-0006.

★2789★
Humane Society of the United States (HSUS)
2100 L St. NW
Washington, DC 20037   Phone: (202)452-1100

Membership: Promotes public education to foster respect, understanding, and compassion for all creatures. **Purpose:** Programs include: reducing the overbreeding of cats and dogs and promoting responsible pet care; eliminating cruelty in hunting and trapping; exposing and eliminating painful uses of animals in research and testing; eliminating the abuse of animals in movies, television productions, circuses, and competitive events; correcting inhumane conditions for animals in zoos, menageries, pet shops, puppy mills, and kennels; stopping cruelty in the raising, handling, and transporting of animals used for food; protecting endangered wildlife and marine mammals. Campaigns for or against legislation affecting animal protection and monitors enforcement of existing animal protection statutes; works with local agencies to establish effective and humane animal-control programs. Assists local humane societies in improving their administrative, organizational, and sheltering techniques. Sponsors HSUS Animal Control Academy and the National Association for Humane and Environmental Education. Conducts workshops, symposia, and seminars for individuals who work with animals. Maintains nine regional offices. Presents awards. **Publications:** *Animal Activist Alert*, quarterly. • *HSUS Close-Up Reports*, quarterly. • *HSUS News*, quarterly. • *Kind News*, 9/year. • *Kind Teacher*, annual. • *Shelter Sense*, 10/year. • Also publishes pamphlets. **Facsimile Number:** (202)778-6132.

★2790★
National Dog Groomers Association of America (NDGAA)
Box 101
Clark, PA 16113   Phone: (412)962-2711

Membership: Dog groomers and supply distributors organized to upgrade the profession. **Purpose:** Conducts state and local workshops; sponsors competitions. Provides educational information to high school career centers. Makes groomer referrals. **Publications:** *Convention Manual*, annual. • *Dog Breeders List*, annual. • *Groomers Voice*, quarterly. • *Mobile Groomers*, annual. **Facsimile Number:** (412)962-1919.

――― **Standards/Certification Agencies** ―――

Some states require certification of caretakers who put animals to death. Training may be through a veterinarian or a state humane society. Dog groomers may receive professional registration or certification from the National Dog Groomers Association of America. The American Boarding Kennels Association accredits kennels and offers a Certified Kennel Operator program, both of which show professional competency. In veterinary facilities, requirements differ with the type of position. Thirty-five states require veterinary technicians to be licensed; this is the only animal caretaker position requiring licensure. Licensure requirements in most states include graduation from an animal technology program accredited by the American Veterinary Medicine Association. Veterinary technicians with formal training may also obtain certification through state regulatory agencies. Requirements in laboratories also vary with the type of position. The American Association for Laboratory Animal Science (AALS) tests and certifies each level of caretaker.

★2791★
American Association for Laboratory Animal Science (AALAS)
70 Timber Creek, Ste. 5
Cordova, TN 38018   Phone: (901)754-8620

Conducts examinations and certification through its Animal Technician Certification Program. Offers awards that stimulate and encourage research and education.

★2792★
American Boarding Kennel Association (ABKA)
4575 Galley Rd., #400A
Colorado Springs, CO 80915   Phone: (719)591-1113

Promotes code of ethics and accreditation program for recognition and training of superior kennel operators.

――― **Test Guides** ―――

★2793★
Animal Caretaker
National Learning Corp.
212 Michael Dr.
Syosset, NY 11791   Phone: (516)921-8888

Jack Rudman. This series from National Learning Corp. includes study guides for animal caretaker, animal health aide, and animal warden. All examination guides in this series contain questions with answers. **Facsimile Number:** (516)921-8743. **Toll-free/Additional Phone Number(s):** 800-645-6337.

★2794★
Animal Health Aide
National Learning Corp.
212 Michael Dr.
Syosset, NY 11791   Phone: (516)921-8888

Jack Rudman. Part of the Career Examination Series No. 1. All examination guides in this series contain questions with answers. **Facsimile Number:** (516)921-8743. **Toll-free/Additional Phone Number(s):** 800-645-6337.

★2795★
Animal Warden
National Learning Corp.
212 Michael Dr.
Syosset, NY 11791   Phone: (516)921-8888

Jack Rudman. Part of the Career Examination Series No. 1. All examination guides in this series contain questions with answers. **Facsimile Number:** (516)921-8743. **Toll-free/Additional Phone Number(s):** 800-645-6337.

Animal Caretakers, Except Farm

★2796★
Dog Warden
National Learning Corp.
212 Michael Dr.
Syosset, NY 11791 Phone: (516)921-8888
Jack Rudman. Part of the Career Examination Series No. 1. All examination guides in this series contain questions with answers. **Facsimile Number:** (516)921-8743. **Toll-free/Additional Phone Number(s):** 800-645-6337.

★2797★
Menagerie Keeper
National Learning Corp.
212 Michael Dr.
Syosset, NY 11791 Phone: (516)921-8888
Jack Rudman. Part of the Career Examination Series No. 1. All examination guides in this series contain questions with answers. **Facsimile Number:** (516)921-8743. **Toll-free/Additional Phone Number(s):** 800-645-6337.

★2798★
Senior Dog Warden
National Learning Corp.
212 Michael Dr.
Syosset, NY 11791 Phone: (516)921-8888
Jack Rudman. Part of the Career Examination Series No. 1. All examination guides in this series contain questions with answers. **Facsimile Number:** (516)921-8743. **Toll-free/Additional Phone Number(s):** 800-645-6337.

★2799★
Senior Menagerie Keeper
National Learning Corp.
212 Michael Dr.
Syosset, NY 11791 Phone: (516)921-8888
Jack Rudman. Part of the Career Examination Series No. 1. All examination guides in this series contain questions with answers. **Facsimile Number:** (516)921-8743. **Toll-free/Additional Phone Number(s):** 800-645-6337.

Educational Directories and Programs

★2800★
Animal Caretakers, Except Farm
Accrediting Bureau of Health Education
Oak Manor Office
29089 U.S. 20 W.
Elkhart, IN 46514 Phone: (219)293-0124
1991. State-by-state listing of schools offering veterinary assistant training programs. Lists address, phone number, and contact person.

★2801★
Kind Teacher
Humane Society of the United States (HSUS)
2100 L St. NW
Washington, DC 20037 Phone: (202)452-1100
Annual. Contains educational program information and activities for teachers and students.

★2802★
Programs in Veterinary Technology
American Veterinary Medical Association
930 N. Mecham Rd.
Schaumburg, IL 60196-1074 Phone: (708)605-8070
1990. State-by-state listing of accredited veterinary technology educational preparation programs. Lists address, phone number, contact person, and academic award.

Awards, Scholarships, Grants, and Fellowships

★2803★
Excellence in Zookeeping Award
American Association of Zoo Keepers
c/o Barbara Manspeaker, Administrative Secretary
Topeka Zoological Park
635 Gage Blvd.
Topeka, KS 66606

To recognize an individual for achievement and determination in the zookeeping field, and to foster professionalism. Full-time zookeepers employed for at least two years in any North American zoo or aquarium may be nominated by June 1. A certificate, a letter to the institution's director, and national recognition by professional journals are awarded annually at the AAZK Conference. Established in 1974 to honor zoologist R. Marlin Perkins. Formerly: (1984) Marlin Perkins Award.

Basic Reference Guides and Handbooks

★2804★
NDGAA Convention Manual
National Dog Groomers Association of America (NDGAA)
Box 101
Clark, PA 16113 Phone: (412)962-2711
Annual.

Periodicals

★2805★
ABKA Newsletter
American Boarding Kennels Association (ABKA)
4575 Galley Rd., #400A
Colorado Springs, CO 80915 Phone: (719)591-1113
Periodic.

★2806★
Animal Activist Alert
Humane Society of the United States (HSUS)
2100 L St. NW
Washington, DC 20037 Phone: (202)452-1100
Quarterly. Newsletter covering animal legislation.

★2807★
Boarderline
American Boarding Kennels Association (ABKA)
4575 Galley Rd., #400A
Colorado Springs, CO 80915 Phone: (719)591-1113
Bimonthly. Trade journal concerning animal care and business management, with statistics and association news. Includes kennel profiles.

★2808★
Groomers Voice
National Dog Groomers Association of America (NDGAA)
Box 101
Clark, PA 16113 Phone: (412)962-2711
Quarterly. Association and industry newsletter including information on shows, new grooming techniques, and new products. Contains workshop and certification test sites and dates; includes dog breeders' and mobile groomers' lists.

★2809★
HSUS Close-Up Reports
Humane Society of the United States (HSUS)
2100 L St. NW
Washington, DC 20037 Phone: (202)452-1100
Quarterly. Covers critical problems affecting animals.

★2810★
HSUS News (HSUS)
Humane Society of the United States (HSUS)
2100 L St. NW
Washington, DC 20037 Phone: (202)452-1100
Quarterly. Magazine covering society activities.

★2811★
International Society for Animal Rights—Report
International Society for Animal Rights, Inc.
421 S. State St.
Clarks Summit, PA 18411 Phone: (717)586-2200
Editor(s): Nancy Payton. 4-5/yr. Reports on programs undertaken by the Society, on legislative issues affecting animals, and on news of the national and international field of animal rights. **Facsimile Number:** (717)586-9580.

★2812★
Kind News
Humane Society of the United States (HSUS)
2100 L St. NW
Washington, DC 20037 Phone: (202)452-1100
9/year.

★2813★
Laboratory Animal Science
American Association for Laboratory Animal Science (AALAS)
70 Timber Creek, Ste. 5
Cordova, TN 38018 Phone: (901)754-8620
Bimonthly. Journal of scientific papers on topics related to laboratory animal science.

★2814★
Shelter Sense
Humane Society of the United States (HSUS)
5430 Grosvenor Lane, Ste. 100
Bethesda, MD 20814 Phone: (202)571-8989
Editor(s): Rhonda Lucas Donald. 10/yr. Aims to "reduce animal suffering and solve community animal-control problems." Supplies information on animal shelter operation, care of animals, pet adoptions, animal pickup in the field, spay/neuter and public education programs, relevant laws, and cooperation between humane societies and municipal animal-control agencies. Discusses professional qualifications of workers and officers and programs at local humane societies. Recurring features include editorials, news of research, news of awards, and ready-to-copy PSAs.

★2815★
Veterinary Technician
Veterinary Learning Systems
10950 Grandview Drive, No. 458
Overland Park, KS 66210 Phone: (913)451-3475
Dr. Richard B. Ford, Editor. 10x/yr. Official journal of the North American Veterinary Technician Association. Published for veterinary technicians, nurses, and assistants. **Facsimile Number:** (913)451-3929.

——— Meetings and Conventions ———

★2816★
American Animal Hospital Association Annual Meeting
American Animal Hospital Association
PO Box 150899
Denver, CO 80215 Phone: (303)279-2500
Frequency: Always held in March or April. 1992; Apr. 25-01; New Orleans, LA ● 1993; Mar. 13-19; Seattle, WA ● 1994; Mar. 04-11; Boston, MA ● 1995; Mar. 04-10; San Francisco, CA. **Facsimile Number:** (303)279-1816.

★2817★
American Association of Zoo Keepers (AAZK)
Topeka Zoological Park
635 Gage Blvd.
Topeka, KS 66606 Phone: (913)272-5821
Frequency: Annual conference with exhibits. 1991; Toledo, OH ● 1992; San Diego, CA. **Facsimile Number:** (913)272-2539.

★2818★
American Boarding Kennel Association (ABKA)
4575 Galley Rd., #400A
Colorado Springs, CO 80915 Phone: (719)591-1113
Frequency: Annual conference and trade show with exhibits, always fall. **Facsimile Number:** (719)597-0006.

★2819★
American Humane Association Annual Meeting and Training Conference
American Humane Association
63 Inverness Dr., E.
Englewood, CO 80112-5117 Phone: (303)792-9900
1992. **Facsimile Number:** (303)792-5333.

★2820★
National Dog Groomers Association of America Convention
National Dog Groomers Association of America
Box 101
Clark, PA 16113 Phone: (412)962-2711
1992. **Facsimile Number:** (412)962-1919.

★2821★
Western World Pet Supply Association Annual Pet Industry Trade Show
Western World Pet Supply Association, Inc.
406 S. 1st Ave.
Arcadia, CA 91006-3829 Phone: (818)447-2222
Frequency: Held in July at the Convention Center in Long Beach, Califorina. 1992; Jul. 17-19; Long Beach, CA ● 1993; Jul. 16-18; Long Beach, CA ● 1994; Jul. 08-10; Long Beach, CA ● 1995; Jul. 14-16; Long Beach, CA. **Facsimile Number:** (818)447-8350.

Other Sources of Information

★2822★
Mobile Groomers
National Dog Groomers Association of America (NDGAA)
Box 101
Clark, PA 16113 Phone: (412)962-2711
Annual.

Barbers

Barbers cut, trim, shampoo, and style hair; they also offer hair and scalp treatments, shaves, and facial massages. Hairstylists provide additional services, such as hairstyling and permanents. They cut and style hair to suit each customer and may color or straighten hair and fit hairpieces. Most barbers work in barbershops, some work in beauty shops and unisex salons, and a few work in department stores, hotels, hospitals, and prisons. About 75 percent of all barbers operate their own businesses.

$alaries

Barbers generally earn between $300.00 and $500.00/week. Most barbers who are not shopowners normally receive 60 to 70 percent of the money they take in; a few are paid straight salaries.

Employment Outlook

Growth rate until the year 2000: Employment is expected to remain level.

Barbers

Career Guides

★2823★
Barber
Careers, Inc.
PO Box 135
Largo, FL 34649-0135   Phone: (813)584-7333
1990. Two-page occupational summary card describing duties, working conditions, personal qualifications, training, earnings and hours, employment outlook, places of employment, related careers and where to write for more information.

★2824★
Barber
Vocational Biographies, Inc.
PO Box 31, Dept. VF10
Sauk Centre, MN 56378   Phone: (612)352-6516
1988. This pamphlet profiles a person working in the job. Includes information about job duties, working conditions, places of employment, educational preparation, labor market outlook, and salaries. **Toll-free/Additional Phone Number(s):** 800-255-0752.

★2825★
"Barber" in *Occu-Facts: Information on 565 Careers in Outline Form* (p. 13.32)
Careers, Inc.
P.O. Box 135
1211 Tenth St., S.W.
Largo, FL 33640   Phone: (813)584-7333
Elizabeth Handville. Biennial, 1989-90 edition. Each one-page occupational profile describes duties, working conditions, physical surroundings and demands, aptitudes, temperament, educational requirements, employment outlook, earnings, and places of employment.

★2826★
"Barber and Hairstylist" in *Consumer, Homemaking, and Personal Services*, Volume 5 of *Career Information Center* (pp. 66-68)
Glencoe/Macmillan
15319 Chatsworth St.
Mission Hills, CA 91345   Phone: (818)898-1391
Richard Lidz and Dale Anderson, editorial directors. Fourth edition, 1990. For 600 occupations, describes job duties, entry-level requirements, education and training needed, advancement possibilities, employment outlook, earnings and benefits. The set is divided into 12 volumes. Each volume includes jobs related under a broad career field. Volume 13 is the index. **Facsimile Number:** 818-365-5489.

★2827★
Barber-Stylists
Chronicle Guidance Publications, Inc.
PO Box 1190
Moravia, NY 13118-1190   Phone: (315)497-0330
1989. This career brief describes the nature of the work, working conditions, hours and earnings, education and training, licensure, certification, unions, personal qualifications, social and psychological factors, employment outlook, entry methods, advancement, and related occupations. **Toll-free/Additional Phone Number(s):** 800-622-7284.

★2828★
"Barbers" in *Occupational Outlook Handbook* (pp. 306-307)
Superintendent of Documents
U.S. Government Printing Office
Washington, DC 20402   Phone: (202)783-3238
Biennial; latest edition, 1990-91. Encyclopedia of careers describing more than 250 occupations and comprising about 86 percent of all jobs in the economy. Occupations that require lengthy education or training are given the most attention. For each occupation, the handbook describes job duties, working conditions, training, educational preparation, personal qualities, advancement possibilities, job outlook, earnings, and sources of additional information.

★2829★
"Barbers" in *Opportunities in Vocational and Technical Careers* (pp. 76-77)
National Textbook Co.
4255 W. Touhy Ave.
Lincolnwood, IL 60646   Phone: (312)679-5500
Adrian A. Paradis. 1987. Describes careers which can be prepared for by attending a private vocational or proprietary school—office employee, sales worker, service worker, health services, mechanic, craftworker, and technician. Covers employment outlook, job duties, and salaries. Offers career planning advice.

★2830★
"Barbers" in Volume 1 of *Career Discovery Encyclopedia* (pp. 112-113)
J.G. Ferguson Publishing Co.
200 W. Monroe
Chicago, IL 60606   Phone: (312)580-5480
E. Russell Primm, editor-in-chief. 1990. Contains two-page articles on 504 occupations. Each article describes job duties, earnings, and educational and training requirements.

★2831★

"Barbers" in *Volume 3 of The Encyclopedia of Careers and Vocational Guidance* (pp. 195-198)
J.G. Ferguson Publishing Co.
200 W. Monroe
Chicago, IL 60606   Phone: (312)580-5480

William E. Hopke, editor-in-chief. Eighth edition, 1990. Four-volume set that profiles 500 occupations and describes job trends in 76 industries. Includes career description, educational requirements, history of the job, methods of entry, advancement, employment outlook, earnings, working conditions, social and psychological factors, and sources of additional information.

★2832★

"Barbers and Beauticians" in *The American Almanac of Jobs and Salaries* (pp. 529-530)
Avon Books
105 Madison Avenue
New York, NY 10016   Phone: (212)481-5600

John Wright and Edward J. Dwyer. Revised and updated, 1990. A comprehensive guide to the wages of hundreds of occupations in a wide variety of industries and organizations.

★2833★

"Cosmetology, Barbering" in *The Career Connection II: A Guide to Technical Majors and Their Related Careers* (pp. 25-26)
ERIS
PO Box 7509
University Station
Provo, UT 84602-0509

Fred A. Rowe. 1988. Contains technical majors, such as automotive technology. Describes the major and the job. Lists high school and postsecondary school courses. Includes occupations related to the major, employment outlook, and starting salary.

★2834★

Getting Down to Business: Hair Styling Shop
American Institutes for Research
PO Box 11131
Palo Alto, CA   Phone: (415)493-3550

Joyce P. Gall. 1981. **Facsimile Number:** (415)858-0958.

★2835★

Video Career Library - Public and Personal Services
Careers, Inc.
1211 10th St., SW
PO Box 135
Largo, FL 34649-0135   Phone: (813)584-7333

Videocassette. 1990. 35 mins. Part of the Video Career Library covering 165 occupations. Shows actual workers on the job. Includes firefighters, police officers, correctional officers, bartenders, waiters/waitresses, cooks/chefs, child care workers, flight attendants, barbers/cosmetologists, groundskeepers/gardeners, and butchers/meat cutters.

★2836★

Your Career in Professional Barber Styling
National Association of Barber Styling Schools
304 S. 11th St.
Lincoln, NE 68508   Phone: (402)474-4244

This six-panel brochure describes the advantages of working as a barber.

Associations

★2837★

Hair International/Associated Master Barbers and Beauticians of America (HI/AMBBA)
1318 Starbrook Dr.
Charlotte, NC 28210   Phone: (704)552-6233

Membership: Barber styling and cosmetology school and business owners and employees; manufacturers. **Purpose:** Bestows Hair Designer of the Year Award. Operates speakers' bureau; conducts hairstyling show, classes, and seminars. Sponsors hair cutting and styling competitions. **Publications:** *Hair International News*, bimonthly. • *National Bulletin*, quarterly. • Also publishes *Standardized Textbook of Barbering and Styling*.

★2838★

National Association of Barber Styling Schools (NABS)
304 S. 11th St.
Lincoln, NE 68508   Phone: (402)474-4244

Membership: Owners and managers of private barber schools and colleges. **Purpose:** Seeks to improve barber school training and instructor qualifications in an effort to increase professional standards in barbering. Conducts research program on state requirements for barbering; bestows awards. Has instituted Barbering Hall of Fame. Maintains biographical archives; compiles statistics. **Publications:** *NABS News*, quarterly. • *Membership Directory*, annual. • *Research Reports*, annual. • Also publishes *Your Career in Professional Barber Styling*.

Standards/Certification Agencies

All states require barbers to be licensed. Barber training is offered in about 400 schools; nearly 80 percent of all barber schools are private. Barber school programs usually last 9 to 12 months. Students study the basic services; practice on customers, under supervision, in school clinics; attend lectures on barber services, the use and care of instruments, sanitation and hygiene, and recognition of certain skin ailments. Instruction also is given in selling and general business practices. There are also advanced courses for experienced barbers in hairstyling, coloring, and the sale and service of hairpieces.

★2839★

National Association of Barber Styling Schools (NABS)
304 S. 11th St.
Lincoln, NE 68508   Phone: (402)474-4244

Seeks to improve barber school training and instructor qualifications in an effort to increase professional standards in barbering.

★2840★

State Barber Laws
National Association of Barber Styling Schools
304 S. 11th St.
Lincoln, NE 68508   Phone: (402)474-4244

1990. National Association of Barber-Styling Schools Research Report No. 3A. This chart summarizes educational and licensure requirements in the 50 states.

Barbers ★2850★

Test Guides

★2841★
Barber
National Learning Corp.
212 Michael Dr.
Syosset, NY 11791   Phone: (516)921-8888
Jack Rudman. Part of the Career Examination Series No. 1. All examination guides in this series contain questions with answers. **Facsimile Number:** (516)921-8743. **Toll-free/Additional Phone Number(s):** 800-645-6337.

★2842★
Professional Barber Styling State Board Exam Review
Milady Publishing
220 Whie Plains Rd.
Tarrytown, NY 10591   Phone: (914)332-4800
1983. **Facsimile Number:** (212)881-5624.

Educational Directories and Programs

★2843★
Barber Schools in the USA
National Association of Barber Styling Schools
304 S. 11th St.
Lincoln, NE 68508   Phone: (402)474-4244
1990. National Association of Barber-Styling Schools Research Report No. 5A. State-by-state listing of barber styling schools. Indicates private, vocational, or institutional schools and their accreditation.

★2844★
Barber Schools in the USA & PR
National Association of Barber Styling Schools
304 S. 11th St.
Lincoln, NE 68508   Phone: (402)474-4244
Alyce M. Howard, Secretary-Treasurer, editor. Every 2-3 years; latest edition May 1990. 360 barber schools. Entries include: Name, address, type of school, whether nationally accredited. Arrangement: Geographical.

★2845★
Members of the National Association of Barber Styling Schools
National Association of Barber Styling Schools
304 S. 11th St.
Lincoln, NE 68508   Phone: (402)474-4244
1990. Lists schools accredited by the association. Provides address, phone number and contact person.

Awards, Scholarships, Grants, and Fellowships

★2846★
Barbering Hall of Fame
National Association of Barber Styling Schools
c/o Kenneth F. Stone
304 S. 11th St.
Lincoln, NE 68508   Phone: (402)474-4244
To honor those who have made an outstanding contribution in the barber industry. Individuals with 20 years of service to the barber industry are eligible. A plaque, and a picture and accomplishments displayed in the Hall of Fame are awarded annually at the convention. Established in 1966.

Basic Reference Guides and Handbooks

★2847★
Milady's Cosmetology State Board Guide
Milady Publishing Company
220 White Plains Rd.
Tarrytown, NY 10591   Phone: (914)332-4800
Jacob J. Yahm, editor. Annual. State boards for licensing cosmetologists and barbers in the United States and Canada. Entries include: Board name, address, phone, name and title of contact, names and titles of key personnel, outline of requirements to become certified, licensing fees and expiration dates. Arrangement: Geographical. **Toll-free/Additional Phone Number(s):** (800)836-5239. **Facsimile Number:** (518)459-3552.

★2848★
Standardized Textbook of Barbering and Styling

Hair International/Associated Master Barbers and Beauticians of America
1318 Starbrook Dr.
Charlotte, NC 28210   Phone: (704)552-6233

★2849★
Workbook for Professional Barber Styling
Milady Publishing Co.
220 White Plains Rd.
Tarrytown, NY 10591   Phone: (914)332-4800
Milady Editors. 1984. **Facsimile Number:** (212)881-5624.

Periodicals

★2850★
Hair International News
Hair International/Associated Master Barbers and Beauticians of America
1318 Starbrook Dr.
Charlotte, NC 28210   Phone: (704)552-6233
Bimonthly. Magazine.

★2851★
HI/AMBBA National Bulletin
Hair International/Associated Master Barbers and Beauticians of America
1318 Starbrook Dr.
Charlotte, NC 28210   Phone: (704)552-6233
Quarterly.

★2852★
NABS News
National Association of Barber Styling Schools (NABS)
304 S. 11th St.
Lincoln, NE 68508   Phone: (402)474-4244
Quarterly. Provides news, features, and background on the barber industry. Includes calendar of events.

Meetings and Conventions

★2853★
Big Show Expo Beauty and Hair Care Show
Big Show Expo, Inc.
1841 Broadway
New York, NY 10023   Phone: (212)757-7589
Frequency: Three shows per year. 1992.

★2854★
Hair International/Associated Master Barbers and Beauticians of America Conference (HI/AMBBA)
1318 Starbrook Dr.
Charlotte, NC 28210   Phone: (704)552-6233
Frequency: Triennial - next 1994.

★2855★
International Beauty Show
Edgell Expositions
7500 Old Oak Blvd.
Cleveland, OH 44130   Phone: (216)826-2831
1992; Mar. 14-17; New York, NY. **Toll-free/Additional Phone Number(s):** 800-331-5706. **Facsimile Number:** (216)826-2801.

★2856★
National Beauty Show
National Cosmetology Association
3510 Olive St.
St. Louis, MO 63103   Phone: (314)534-7980
Frequency: Always held in January. 1993; Jan. 09-11; Miami, FL • 1994; Jan. 08-10; Miami, FL • 1995; Jan. 07-09; Miami, FL. **Toll-free/Additional Phone Number(s):** 800-527-1683. **Facsimile Number:** (314)534-8618.

★2857★
Salon Fair - The International Beauty Shows
Edgell Expositions
7500 Old Oak Blvd.
Cleveland, OH 44130   Phone: (216)826-2831
1992; Apr. 11-13; Seattle, WA. **Toll-free/Additional Phone Number(s):** 800-331-5706. **Facsimile Number:** (216)826-2801.

★2858★
Salon Focus 2000 - Your Educational Forum
Edgell Expositions (Cleveland)
7500 Old Oak Blvd.
Cleveland, OH 44130   Phone: (216)826-2831
Held as part of the International Beauty Shows. 1992; Nov. 15-16; Dallas, TX. **Facsimile Number:** (216)826-2801.

Other Sources of Information

★2859★
Barbers' Equipment & Supplies—Wholesale Directory
American Business Directories, Inc.
American Business Information, Inc.
5711 S. 86th Circle
Omaha, NE 68127   Phone: (402)593-4600
Annual. 1,728. Entries include: Name, address, phone, size of advertisement, name of owner or manager, number of employees, year first in "Yellow Pages." Arrangement: Geographical. **Facsimile Number:** (402)331-1505.

★2860★
The Journeymen Barbers' International Union of America
AMS Press, Inc.
56 E. 13th St.
New York, NY 10003   Phone: (212)777-4700
William S. Hall. Part of Johns Hopkins University. Studies in the Social Sciences. Fifty-Fourth Series. **Facsimile Number:** (212)995-5413.

★2861★
NABS Research Reports
National Association of Barber Styling Schools (NABS)
304 S. 11th St.
Lincoln, NE 68508   Phone: (402)474-4244
Annual.

★2862★
Your Career in Professional Barber Styling
National Association of Barber Styling Schools (NABS)
304 S. 11th St.
Lincoln, NE 68508   Phone: (402)474-4244

Childcare Workers

Childcare workers look after youngsters whose parents are at work or cannot be with them for other reasons. Workers who care for infants follow a basic routine—feeding, diapering, comforting, and playing and talking with the children. Those who work with preschool children attend to basic needs and, in addition, organize activities that stimulate the children's physical, emotional, intellectual, and social growth. Childcare workers work in daycare centers or in their own homes. In large daycare centers, each worker is in charge of a group of children under the supervision of a director, who lays out specific objectives and activities. Childcare workers, also known as family daycare providers, care for a few children in their own homes. These workers are subject to state licensing requirements that regulate the number of children one worker may care for and the environment in which care is provided. In addition to their childcare duties, they are responsible for all aspects of running a small business. About 70 percent of all childcare workers are self-employed. Most of these are family daycare providers who take care of children in their own homes. The rest work in daycare centers sponsored by a variety of organizations. Many centers are for-profit operations, affiliated in some instances with a local or national chain. Others are run by churches, synagogues, community agencies, school systems, and state and local governments. A small number are operated by business firms for the children of their employees.

$alaries

Annual salaries for childcare workers are as follows:

Middle 50 percent	$7,956—$13,052/year
Top 10 percent	$16,640/year

Employment Outlook

Growth rate until the year 2000: Faster than average.

Childcare Workers

Career Guides

★2863★
Becoming a Helper
Brooks/Cole Publishing Co.
511 Forest Lodge Rd.
Pacific Grove, CA 93950-5098   Phone: (408)373-0728
Marianne Schneider Corey. 1989. **Facsimile Number:** (408)375-6414.

★2864★
Careers in Early Childhood Education
National Association for the Education of Young Children
1834 Connecticut Ave., N.W.
Washington, DC 20009   Phone: (202)232-8777
1990. This six-panel pamphlet covers the work, educational preparation, qualifications, and employment opportunities. **Toll-free/Additional Phone Number(s):** 800-424-2460.

★2865★
"Child Care Assistant" in *Guide to Careers Without College* (pp. 95-97)
Franklin Watts, Inc.
387 Park Avenue, S.
New York, NY 10016   Phone: (212)686-7070
Kathleen S. Abrams. 1988. Discusses careers that do not require a college degree in fields such as health care, sales and marketing, and the building trades. Describes the work, employment opportunities, and training.

★2866★
"Child Care Attendant" in *Occu-Facts: Information on 565 Careers in Outline Form* (p. 13.39)
Careers, Inc.
P.O. Box 135
1211 Tenth St., S.W.
Largo, FL 33640   Phone: (813)584-7333
Elizabeth Handville. Biennial, 1989-90 edition. Each one-page occupational profile describes duties, working conditions, physical surroundings and demands, aptitudes, temperament, educational requirements, employment outlook, earnings, and places of employment.

★2867★
Child Care Worker
Vocational Biographies, Inc.
PO Box 31, Dept. VF10
Sauk Centre, MN 56378   Phone: (612)352-6516
1988. This pamphlet profiles a person working in the job. Includes information about job duties, working conditions, places of employment, educational preparation, labor market outlook, and salaries. **Toll-free/Additional Phone Number(s):** 800-255-0752.

★2868★
"Child Care Workers" in Volume 3 of *The Encyclopedia of Careers and Vocational Guidance* (pp. 201-204)
J.G. Ferguson Publishing Co.
200 W. Monroe
Chicago, IL 60606   Phone: (312)580-5480
William E. Hopke, editor-in-chief. Eighth edition, 1990. Four-volume set that profiles 500 occupations and describes job trends in 76 industries. Includes career description, educational requirements, history of the job, methods of entry, advancement, employment outlook, earnings, working conditions, social and psychological factors, and sources of additional information.

★2869★
Child Care Workers (Institutions)
Chronicle Guidance Publications, Inc.
PO Box 1190
Moravia, NY 13118-1190   Phone: (315)497-0330
1988. This career brief describes the nature of the work, working conditions, hours and earnings, education and training, licensure, certification, unions, personal qualifications, social and psychological factors, employment outlook, entry methods, advancement, and related occupations. **Toll-free/Additional Phone Number(s):** 800-622-7284.

★2870★
"Child Development Associate" in *Exploring Careers in Child Care Services* (pp. 17-18)
Rosen Publishing Group, Inc.
29 E. 21st St.
New York, NY 10010   Phone: (212)777-3017
Jean Ispa, Elizabeth Vemer, and Janis Logan. Revised edition, 1990. Covers occupations working with children including those requiring no education and training to those that require advanced training; from babysitting to program director. Describes the work and a typical work day, employment outlook, advantages and disadvantages, and personal characteristics needed for success in the field. Offers job hunting advice.

★2871★
"Child Development Associate" in *Opportunities in Child Care Careers* (pp. 47-51)
National Textbook Co.
4255 W. Touhy Ave.
Lincolnwood, IL 60646   Phone: (312)679-5500
Renee Wittenberg. 1987. Surveys job opportunities related to child care in child development, child life, health services, and

psychology. Covers personal qualifications, training programs, job outlook, and salaries. Offers job hunting advice.

★2872★
"Childcare" in *How to Get a Job With a Cruise Line* (pp. 7-13)
Ticket to Adventure, Inc.
8800 49th St., N., Ste. 410, Rm. 3
Pinellas Park, FL 34666   Phone: (813)544-0066
Mary Fallon Miller. 1991. Explores jobs with cruise ships, describing duties, responsibilities, benefits, and training. Lists cruise ship lines and schools offering cruise line training. Offers job hunting advice.

★2873★
"Childcare Worker" in *VGM's Careers Encyclopedia* (pp. 91-93)
National Textbook Co.
4255 W. Touhy Ave.
Lincolnwood, IL 60646   Phone: (312)679-5500
Third edition, 1991. Contains two- to five-page descriptions of 200 managerial, professional, technical, trade, and service occupations. Each profile includes job duties, places of employment, qualifications, educational preparation, training, employment potential, advancement, income, and additional sources of information.

★2874★
"Childcare Workers" in *Occupational Outlook Handbook* (pp. 307-308)
Superintendent of Documents
U.S. Government Printing Office
Washington, DC 20402   Phone: (202)783-3238
Biennial; latest edition, 1990-91. Encyclopedia of careers describing more than 250 occupations and comprising about 86 percent of all jobs in the economy. Occupations that require lengthy education or training are given the most attention. For each occupation, the handbook describes job duties, working conditions, training, educational preparation, personal qualities, advancement possibilities, job outlook, earnings, and sources of additional information.

★2875★
"Childcare Workers" in *Opportunities in Vocational and Technical Careers* (pp. 77-78)
National Textbook Co.
4255 W. Touhy Ave.
Lincolnwood, IL 60646   Phone: (312)679-5500
Adrian A. Paradis. 1987. Describes careers which can be prepared for by attending a private vocational or proprietary school—office employee, sales worker, service worker, health services, mechanic, craftworker, and technician. Covers employment outlook, job duties, and salaries. Offers career planning advice.

★2876★
"Childcare Workers" in Volume 2 of *Career Discovery Encyclopedia* (pp. 8-9)
J.G. Ferguson Publishing Co.
200 W. Monroe
Chicago, IL 60606   Phone: (312)580-5480
E. Russell Primm, editor-in-chief. 1990. Contains two-page articles on 504 occupations. Each article describes job duties, earnings, and educational and training requirements.

★2877★
"Childcare Workers" in *America's 50 Fastest Growing Jobs* (pp. 123-125)
JIST Works, Inc.
720 N. Park Ave.
Indianapolis, IN 46202   Phone: (317)264-3720
Michael J. Farr, compiler. 1991. Describes the 50 fastest growing jobs within major career clusters such as technicians, and marketing and sales. Each job profile explains the nature of the work, skills and abilities required, employment outlook, average earnings, related occupations, education and training requirements, and employment opportunities. Also contains career planning information and job search tips.

★2878★
Day Care Provider
Vocational Biographies, Inc.
PO Box 31, Dept. VF10
Sauk Centre, MN 56378   Phone: (612)352-6516
1990. This pamphlet profiles a person working in the job. Includes information about job duties, working conditions, places of employment, educational preparation, labor market outlook, and salaries. **Toll-free/Additional Phone Number(s)**: 800-255-0752.

★2879★
"Day Care Providers" in *Opportunities in Child Care Careers* (pp. 42-43)
National Textbook Co.
4255 W. Touhy Ave.
Lincolnwood, IL 60646   Phone: (312)679-5500
Renee Wittenberg. 1987. Surveys job opportunities related to child care in child development, child life, health services, and psychology. Covers personal qualifications, training programs, job outlook, and salaries. Offers job hunting advice.

★2880★
"Day Care Worker" in *Public and Community Services*, Volume 11 of *Career Information Center* (pp. 70-71)
Glencoe/Macmillan
15319 Chatsworth St.
Mission Hills, CA 91345   Phone: (818)898-1391
Richard Lidz and Dale Anderson, editorial directors. Fourth edition, 1990. For 600 occupations, describes job duties, entry-level requirements, education and training needed, advancement possibilities, employment outlook, earnings and benefits. The set is divided into 12 volumes. Each volume includes jobs related under a broad career field. Volume 13 is the index. **Facsimile Number:** 818-365-5489.

★2881★
"Day-Care Worker" in *The American Almanac of Jobs and Salaries* (pp. 539-540)
Avon Books
105 Madison Avenue
New York, NY 10016   Phone: (212)481-5600
John Wright and Edward J. Dwyer. Revised and updated, 1990. A comprehensive guide to the wages of hundreds of occupations in a wide variety of industries and organizations.

★2882★
Day Care Workers
Chronicle Guidance Publications, Inc.
PO Box 1190
Moravia, NY 13118-1190   Phone: (315)497-0330
1989. This career brief describes the nature of the work, working conditions, hours and earnings, education and training, licensure, certification, unions, personal qualifications, social and psychological factors, employment outlook, entry methods,

Childcare Workers ★2892★

advancement, and related occupations. **Toll-free/Additional Phone Number(s):** 800-622-7284.

★2883★
"Family Day-Care Providers" in *Exploring Careers in Child Care Services* (pp. 22-31)
Rosen Publishing Group, Inc.
29 E. 21st St.
New York, NY 10010   Phone: (212)777-3017

Jean Ispa, Elizabeth Verner, and Janis Logan. Revised edition, 1990. Covers occupations working with children including those requiring no education and training to those that require advanced training; from babysitting to program director. Describes the work and a typical work day, employment outlook, advantages and disadvantages, and personal characteristics needed for success in the field. Offers job hunting advice.

★2884★
"Institutional Child Care Worker" in *Public and Community Services*, Volume 11 of *Career Information Center* (pp. 74-75)
Glencoe/Macmillan
15319 Chatsworth St.
Mission Hills, CA 91345   Phone: (818)898-1391

Richard Lidz and Dale Anderson, editorial directors. Fourth edition, 1990. For 600 occupations, describes job duties, entry-level requirements, education and training needed, advancement possibilities, employment outlook, earnings and benefits. The set is divided into 12 volumes. Each volume includes jobs related under a broad career field. Volume 13 is the index. **Facsimile Number:** 818-365-5489.

★2885★
"Preschool and Childcare Workers" in *101 Careers: A Guide to the Fastest-Growing Opportunities* (pp. 178-181)
John Wiley & Sons, Inc.
605 Third Ave.
New York, NY 10158   Phone: (212)850-6000

Michael Harkavy. 1990. Each occupational profile includes a job description, job titles, work environment, employment outlook, qualifications, personal skills, and earnings.

★2886★
Questions and Answers About Entering the Child Care Profession
Child Care Employee Project
6536 Telegraph Ave., Ste. A-201
Oakland, CA 94609-1114   Phone: (415)653-9889

This one-page leaflet answers questions about training, earnings, employment outlook, and advancement opportunities.

★2887★
Video Career Library - Public and Personal Services
Careers, Inc.
1211 10th St., SW
PO Box 135
Largo, FL 34649-0135   Phone: (813)584-7333

Videocassette. 1990. 35 mins. Part of the Video Career Library covering 165 occupations. Shows actual workers on the job. Includes firefighters, police officers, correctional officers, bartenders, waiters/waitresses, cooks/chefs, child care workers, flight attendants, barbers/cosmetologists, groundskeepers/gardeners, and butchers/meat cutters.

★2888★
Wages and Benefits in Child Care
Child Care Action Campaign
330 Seventh Ave., 18th Fl.
New York, NY 10001   Phone: (212)239-0138

CCAC Information Guide #16. A two-page pamphlet realistically describes the low salaries and few benefits awarded childcare workers.

★2889★
Wages and Benefits in Child Care
Child Care Action Campaign
330 Seventh Ave., 18th Fl.
New York, NY 10001   Phone: (212)239-0138

CCAC Information Guide #3. This five-page leaflet explores employment opportunities for child care workers in various settings such as day care centers, nursery schools, and head start programs. Describes worker qualifications and advancement opportunities.

―――――――― Associations ――――――――

★2890★
Child Care Action Campaign (CCAC)
330 7th Ave., 18th Fl.
New York, NY 10001   Phone: (212)239-0138

Membership: Individuals and organizations interested and active in child care; corporations and financial institutions; labor organizations; editors of leading women's magazines; leaders in government and representatives of religious and civic organizations. **Purpose:** Purposes are to: alert the country to the problems of and need for child care services; prepare and disseminate information responsive to inquiries resulting from publicity; analyze existing services and identify gaps; work directly with communities to stimulate the development of local task forces and long-range plans for improved and coordinated services. Brings pressing legislative action or inaction to public attention. Has worked to help make liability insurance available for child care providers. Compiles statistics. **Publications:** *Childcare ActioNews*, bimonthly. • Also publishes *Child Care: The Bottom Line*, distributes media kit, and produces audio training cassettes for family day care.

★2891★
Child Care Employee Project (CCEP)
6536 Telegraph Ave., Ste. 201A
Oakland, CA 94609   Phone: (415)653-9889

Membership: Child care workers. **Purpose:** Purposes are: to improve salaries, working conditions, and status of child care workers; to increase public awareness about the importance of child care work and the training and skill it demands; to develop resources and create an information sharing network for child care workers nationwide. Gathers current information on salaries and benefits; offers consultation services. Sponsors research projects; compiles statistics. Maintains extensive file of materials on working conditions and research on child care workers. **Publications:** *Child Care Employee News*, quarterly. • Also publishes resource booklets, brochures, curriculum, and occasional articles. **Facsimile Number:** (415)653-8385.

★2892★
Council for Early Childhood Professional Recognition (CECPR)
1718 Connecticut Ave. NW, Ste. 500
Washington, DC 20009   Phone: (202)265-9090

Membership: National credentialing program for child care workers that attempts to improve the quality of child care by developing, evaluating, and recognizing the skills of the child

★2893★

care staff in center-based care facilities. **Purpose:** Awards nationally recognized credential to child care workers based on performance. **Publications:** *Competence*, 3/year. • Also publishes *Improving Child Care Through the Child Development Associate Program* (book). **Toll-free/Additional Phone Number(s):** (800)424-4310. **Facsimile Number:** (202)265-9161.

★2893★
National Association for the Education of Young Children (NAEYC)
1834 Connecticut Ave. NW
Washington, DC 20009   Phone: (202)232-8777

Membership: Teachers and directors of preschool and primary schools, kindergartens, child care centers, cooperatives, church schools, play groups, and groups having similar programs for young children; early childhood education and child development professors, trainers, and researchers. **Purpose:** Open to all individuals interested in serving and acting on behalf of the needs and rights of young children, with primary focus on the provision of educational services and resources. Sponsors a public education campaign entitled "Week of the Young Child." Offers voluntary accreditation for early childhood schools and centers through the National Academy of Early Childhood Programs. **Publications:** *Early Childhood Research Quarterly*. • *Young Children*, bimonthly. • Also publishes books, brochures, and posters. **Toll-free/Additional Phone Number(s):** (800)424-2460. **Facsimile Number:** (202)328-1846.

★2894★
National Child Day Care Association (NCDCA)
1501 Benning Rd. NE
Washington, DC 20002   Phone: (202)397-3800

Membership: A local, nonprofit group. Seeks to provide quality day care services for the Washington, DC area. **Facsimile Number:** (202)399-2666.

─── **Standards/Certification Agencies** ───

The Child Development Associate (CDA) credential program certifies childcare workers. The program is open to anyone 18 years of age or older who has childcare experience and some related classroom, workshop, or other training. A team of childcare professionals helps candidates improve their childcare skills and recommends further training, if necessary. The training is offered in local schools and colleges. When candidates are ready, the team assesses their abilities and performance with young children and decides whether they qualify for the CDA credential.

★2895★
CDA in State Child Care Licensing
Council for Early Childhood Professional Recognition
1718 Connecticut Ave., NW, Ste. 500
Washington, DC 20009-1148   Phone: (202)265-9090

1991. This four-page pamphlet lists 49 states which recognize CDA credentialing as a qualification for child care center teachers and/or directors. **Toll-free/Additional Phone Number(s):** 800-424-4310.

★2896★
The Child Development Associate Credential
Council for Early Childhood Professional Recognition
1718 Connecticut Ave. NW, Ste. 500
Washington, DC 20009-1148   Phone: (202)265-9090

1991. This 13-page booklet describes the Child Development Associate Program. Lists eligibility requirements and explains the assessment process for persons already employed in the field. **Toll-free/Additional Phone Number(s):** 800-424-4210.

★2897★
Council for Early Childhood Professional Recognition
1718 Connecticut Ave., NW, Ste. 500
Washington, DC 20009   Phone: (202)265-9090

National credentialing program for child care workers. Develops, evaluates, and recognizes the skills of the child care staff in center-based facilities. Awards nationally recognized credential to child care workers based on performance. Provides information on eligibility requirements and a description of the Child Development Associate Credential upon request. **Toll-free/Additional Phone Number(s):** 800-424-4310.

★2898★
Improving Child Care Through the Child Development Associate Program
Council for Early Childhood Professional Recognition
1718 Connecticut Ave., NW, Ste. 500
Washington, DC 20009-1148   Phone: (202)265-9090

1990. This eight-page booklet describes the credentialing program for childcare workers. Describes required competencies. **Toll-free/Additional Phone Number(s):** 800-424-4310.

★2899★
National Association for the Education of Young Children (NAEYC)
1834 Connecticut Ave. NW
Washington, DC 20009   Phone: (202)232-8777

Offers voluntary accreditation for early childhood schools and centers through the National Academy of Early Childhood Programs.

─── **Test Guides** ───

★2900★
Day Care Center Aide
National Learning Corp.
212 Michael Dr.
Syosset, NY 11791   Phone: (516)921-8888

Jack Rudman. Part of the Career Examination Series No. 1. All examination guides in this series contain questions with answers. **Facsimile Number:** (516)921-8743. **Toll-free/Additional Phone Number(s):** 800-645-6337.

─── **Educational Directories and Programs** ───

★2901★
CDA Professional Preparation Program
Council for Early Childhood Professional Recognition
1718 Connecticut Ave., NW, Ste. 500
Washington, DC 20009-1148   Phone: (202)265-9090

1991. Brochure that describes the one-year, three-part program for training child care workers. Covers eligibility requirements and the application process. **Toll-free/Additional Phone Number(s):** 8000-424-4210.

Awards, Scholarships, Grants, and Fellowships

★2902★
"CDA Professional Preparation Program Ready for Start-Up" in *Competence*, Vol. 8, No. 2, July 1991
Council for Early Childhood Professional Recognition
1718 Connecticut Ave. NW, Ste. 500
Washington, DC 20009-1148   Phone: (202)265-9090
1991. This issue is devoted to describing the CDAP3 program, an individualized one-year program designed to enable persons to become a Child Development Associate. **Toll-free/Additional Phone Number(s):** 800-424-4210.

★2903★
CDA Scholarship Act Administrative Activities
Council for Early Childhood Professional Recognition
1718 Connecticut Ave. NW, Ste. 500
Washington, DC 20009-1148   Phone: (202)265-9090
1991. State-by-state listing of agencies which administer CDA scholarship funds. **Toll-free/Additional Phone Number(s):** 800-424-4210.

★2904★
CDA Scholarship Act: Executive Summary
Council for Early Childhood Professional Recognition
1718 Connecticut Ave. NW, Ste. 500
Washington, DC 20009-1148   Phone: (202)265-9090
Describes the Child Development Associate Scholarship Program designed to provide candidates with the financial means to complete components of the credentialing process. **Toll-free/Additional Phone Number(s):** 800-424-4210.

Basic Reference Guides and Handbooks

★2905★
Child Care: The Bottom Line
Child Care Action Campaign (CCAC)
330 7th Ave., 18th Fl.
New York, NY 10001   Phone: (212)239-0138

★2906★
Improving Child Care Through the Child Development Associate Program
Council for Early Childhood Professional Recognition (CECPR)
1718 Connecticut Ave. NW, Ste. 500
Washington, DC 20009   Phone: (202)265-9090

Periodicals

★2907★
Ambulatory Pediatric Association—Newsletter
Ambulatory Pediatric Association
6728 Old McLean Village
McLean, VA 22101   Phone: (703)556-9222
Editor(s): John Pascoe, M.D. 3/yr. Publishes news of the members, activities, and concerns of the association, "an organization devoted to promoting the health of children." Provides up-to-date information on efforts in affecting legislation concerned with child abuse, medical care for handicapped newborns, the nuclear arms freeze, and funding for pediatric care. Recurring features include a message from the president and announcements of available financial awards and fellowships.

★2908★
Child Care Employee News
Child Care Employee Project
6536 Telegraph Ave., A201
Oakland, CA 94609-1114   Phone: (415)653-9889
Editor(s): Marcy Whitebook. 4/yr. Serves as "a vehicle for sharing ideas, debating approaches and generally encouraging us all to continue efforts to secure for child care the economic and social resources it deserves." Contains resources, national and legislative news, and news of the Project. Recurring features include editorials, news of research, and book reviews.

★2909★
Childcare ActioNews
Child Care Action Campaign (CCAC)
330 7th Ave., 18th Fl.
New York, NY 10001   Phone: (212)239-0138
Bimonthly. Newsletter on innovations in the field of child care for working parents. Includes calendar of events, legislative update, and resource information.

★2910★
Early Childhood Research Quarterly
National Association for the Education of Young Children (NAEYC)
1834 Connecticut Ave. NW
Washington, DC 20009   Phone: (202)232-8777

★2911★
Family Day Care Bulletin
Children's Foundation
815 15th St. NW, Ste. 928
Washington, DC 20005   Phone: (202)347-3300
Editor(s): Kay Hollestelle. Quarterly. Serves as a national information resource on family day care systems and supports. Covers topics such as government program and legislative developments, day care insurance, day care licensing, and current research concerning child development and behavior. Recurring features include listings of Foundation publications and a calendar of events.

★2912★
Imprints
Birth & Life Bookstore
7001 Alonzo Ave. NW
PO Box 70625
Seattle, WA 98107   Phone: (206)789-4444
3-4/yr. Publishes reviews of books on childbirth, child care, family planning, breastfeeding, and women's health issues. Reports on forthcoming books, new editions, and paperbacks. Contains an annotated list of books available from the Bookstore. Provides an order form and information on book and shipping costs.

★2913★
School Age Notes
Richard T. Scofield
PO Box 40205
Nashville, TN 37204   Phone: (615)242-8464
Editor(s): Richard T. Scofield. Monthly. Carries ideas for activities and games that are developmentally oriented. Offers curricula, advice, news, and think-pieces for improving child care. Recurring features include book reviews, a list of resources, notices of events, and columns titled Director's Corner, Developmental Notes, Activities, Curriculum Corner, and Administrative Notes.

★2914★
Young Children
National Association for the Education of Young Children (NAEYC)
1834 Connecticut Ave. NW
Washington, DC 20009   Phone: (202)232-8777
Bimonthly. Journal covering developments in the practice, research, and theory of early childhood education. Includes book reviews, calendar of events, research reports, and Washington update.

Cosmetologists and Related Workers

Cosmetologists, also called beauty operators, hairstylists, or beauticians, shampoo, cut, and style hair, and advise patrons on how to care for their hair. Related workers include manicurists, who clean, shape, and polish customer's fingernails and toenails; makeup artists, who apply makeup; electrologists, who remove hair from skin by electrolysis; and estheticians, who clean and beautify the skin. Cosmetologists offer all the services that barbers do except men's shaves. Most cosmetologists work in beauty salons, some work in unisex salons, barber shops, or department stores, and a few are employed by hospitals and hotels. About half of all cosmetologists operate their own businesses.

$alaries

Weekly salaries for cosmetologists are as follows:

Lowest 10 percent	$135.00/week or less
Middle 50 percent	$175.00—$320.00/week
Top 10 percent	$420.00/week or more

Employment Outlook

Growth rate until the year 2000: Average.

Cosmetologists and Related Workers

Career Guides

★2915★
Arte and Tecnica (Italy)
Milady Publishing Corporation
3839 White Plains Rd.
Bronx, NY 10467-5394   Phone: (212)881-3000
Videocassette. 1983. 30 mins. Three untitled programs present the art of cutting hair.

★2916★
"Barbers and Beauticians" in *The American Almanac of Jobs and Salaries* (pp. 529-530)
Avon Books
105 Madison Avenue
New York, NY 10016   Phone: (212)481-5600
John Wright and Edward J. Dwyer. Revised and updated, 1990. A comprehensive guide to the wages of hundreds of occupations in a wide variety of industries and organizations.

★2917★
"Beautician" in *How to Get a Job With a Cruise Line* (p. 4)
Ticket to Adventure, Inc.
8800 49th St., N., Ste. 410, Rm. 3
Pinellas Park, FL 34666   Phone: (813)544-0066
Mary Fallon Miller. 1991. Explores jobs with cruise ships, describing duties, responsibilities, benefits, and training. Lists cruise ship lines and schools offering cruise line training. Offers job hunting advice.

★2918★
A Career for Looking Good, Feeling Great
National Association of Accredited Cosmetology Schools
5201 Leesburg Pike, Ste. 205
Falls Church, VA 22041   Phone: (703)845-1333
This six-panel brochure surveys cosmetology related jobs and offers tips on judging the quality of a cosmetology school.

★2919★
Career Insights
RMI Media Productions, Inc.
2807 West 47th St.
Shawnee Mission, KS 66205   Phone: (913)262-3974
Videocassette series. 1987. This videotape series describes 50 occupations, including skill requirements and interviews with people employed in these fields. Occupations include: flight service, air transportation/ground services, data processing, carpentry, clerk in banking/insurance/business, cosmetic personal grooming, firefighting, roofing, material handling, photographic processing, plumbing, secretarial services, tool and die operations.

★2920★
Career Success Series
Cambridge Career Products
90 MacCorkle Ave., SW
South Charleston, WV 25311   Phone: (304)744-9323
Videocassette. 1986. 15 mins. A series, available separately, outlining various career choices for students. Occupations include: flight service, air transportation/ground service, data processing, carpentry, clerk in banking/insurance, commodity sales, cosmetic personal grooming, fire fighting, forestry services, home economics, insulation/roofing, material handling, mechanics, photographic processing, pipefitting and plumbing, police science, printing, secretarial services, and utilities equipment operator.

★2921★
Careers in Beauty Culture
Rosen Publishing Group, Inc.
29 E. 21st St.
New York, NY 10010   Phone: (212)777-3017
Barbara L. Johnson. 1989. Discusses job opportunities for cosmetologists. Describes personal characteristics, training, licensing requirements, working conditions, advancement opportunities, employment outlook, and advantages and disadvantages of the job. Offers advice on job hunting and succeeding on the job. Contains information on owning a salon.

★2922★
Cosmetic and Personal Services
Morris Video
2730 Monterey St. #105
Monterey Business Park
Torrance, CA 90503   Phone: (213)533-4800
Videocassette. 1985. 15 mins. Occupations involving cosmetology, hair styling and manicures are covered.

★2923★
Cosmetologist
Careers, Inc.
PO Box 135
Largo, FL 34649-0135   Phone: (813)584-7333
1990. Two-page occupational summary card describing duties, working conditions, personal qualifications, training, earnings and hours, employment outlook, places of employment, related careers and where to write for more information.

★2924★
Cosmetologist
Vocational Biographies, Inc.
PO Box 31, Dept. VF10
Sauk Centre, MN 56378   Phone: (612)352-6516
1988. This pamphlet profiles a person working in the job. Includes information about job duties, working conditions, places of employment, educational preparation, labor market outlook, and salaries. **Toll-free/Additional Phone Number(s):** 800-255-0752.

★2925★
"Cosmetologist" in *Consumer, Homemaking, and Personal Services*, Volume 5 of *Career Information Center* (pp. 72-74)
Glencoe/Macmillan
15319 Chatsworth St.
Mission Hills, CA 91345   Phone: (818)898-1391
Richard Lidz and Dale Anderson, editorial directors. Fourth edition, 1990. For 600 occupations, describes job duties, entry-level requirements, education and training needed, advancement possibilities, employment outlook, earnings and benefits. The set is divided into 12 volumes. Each volume includes jobs related under a broad career field. Volume 13 is the index. **Facsimile Number:** 818-365-5489.

★2926★
"Cosmetologist" in *Occu-Facts: Information on 565 Careers in Outline Form* (13.33)
Careers, Inc.
P.O. Box 135
1211 Tenth St., S.W.
Largo, FL 33640   Phone: (813)584-7333
Elizabeth Handville. Biennial, 1989-90 edition. Each one-page occupational profile describes duties, working conditions, physical surroundings and demands, aptitudes, temperament, educational requirements, employment outlook, earnings, and places of employment.

★2927★
"Cosmetologist" in *VGM's Careers Encyclopedia* (pp. 122-124)
National Textbook Co.
4255 W. Touhy Ave.
Lincolnwood, IL 60646   Phone: (312)679-5500
Third edition, 1991. Contains two- to five-page descriptions of 200 managerial, professional, technical, trade, and service occupations. Each profile includes job duties, places of employment, qualifications, educational preparation, training, employment potential, advancement, income, and additional sources of information.

★2928★
"Cosmetologist and Related Workers" in *Occupational Outlook Handbook* (pp. 308-310)
Superintendent of Documents
U.S. Government Printing Office
Washington, DC 20402   Phone: (202)783-3238
Biennial; latest edition, 1990-91. Encyclopedia of careers describing more than 250 occupations and comprising about 86 percent of all jobs in the economy. Occupations that require lengthy education or training are given the most attention. For each occupation, the handbook describes job duties, working conditions, training, educational preparation, personal qualities, advancement possibilities, job outlook, earnings, and sources of additional information.

★2929★
Cosmetologists
Chronicle Guidance Publications, Inc.
PO Box 1190
Moravia, NY 13118-1190   Phone: (315)497-0330
1987. This career brief describes the nature of the work, working conditions, hours and earnings, education and training, licensure, certification, unions, personal qualifications, social and psychological factors, employment outlook, entry methods, advancement, and related occupations. **Toll-free/Additional Phone Number(s):** 800-622-7284.

★2930★
"Cosmetologists" in *Opportunities in Vocational and Technical Careers* (pp. 79-80)
National Textbook Co.
4255 W. Touhy Ave.
Lincolnwood, IL 60646   Phone: (312)679-5500
Adrian A. Paradis. 1987. Describes careers which can be prepared for by attending a private vocational or proprietary school—office employee, sales worker, service worker, health services, mechanic, craftworker, and technician. Covers employment outlook, job duties, and salaries. Offers career planning advice.

★2931★
"Cosmetologists" in Volume 3 of *The Encyclopedia of Careers and Vocational Guidance* (pp. 214-218)
J.G. Ferguson Publishing Co.
200 W. Monroe
Chicago, IL 60606   Phone: (312)580-5480
William E. Hopke, editor-in-chief. Eighth edition, 1990. Four-volume set that profiles 500 occupations and describes job trends in 76 industries. Includes career description, educational requirements, history of the job, methods of entry, advancement, employment outlook, earnings, working conditions, social and psychological factors, and sources of additional information.

★2932★
"Cosmetologists" in Volume 2 of *Career Discovery Encyclopedia* (pp. 64-65)
J.G. Ferguson Publishing Co.
200 W. Monroe
Chicago, IL 60606   Phone: (312)580-5480
E. Russell Primm, editor-in-chief. 1990. Contains two-page articles on 504 occupations. Each article describes job duties, earnings, and educational and training requirements.

★2933★
"Cosmetologists: Beauty Preservers" in *Careers for Women Without College Degrees* (pp. 254-257)
McGraw-Hill Publishing Co.
11 W. 19th St.
New York, NY 10011   Phone: (212)337-6010
Beatryce Nivens. 1988. Career planning and job hunting guide containing information on decision-making, skills assessment, and resumes for career changers. Profiles careers with the best occupational outlook. Describes the work, educational preparation, employment outlook, salaries, and required skills.

Cosmetologists and Related Workers

★2934★
"Cosmetology, Barbering" in *The Career Connection II: A Guide to Technical Majors and Their Related Careers* (pp. 25-26)
ERIS
PO Box 7509
University Station
Provo, UT 84602-0509
Fred A. Rowe. 1988. Contains technical majors, such as automotive technology. Describes the major and the job. Lists high school and postsecondary school courses. Includes occupations related to the major, employment outlook, and starting salary.

★2935★
Cosmetology. . .Excellent Opportunities. . .
National Cosmetology Association, Inc.
3510 Olive St.
St. Louis, MO 63103   Phone: (314)534-7980
This two-page leaflet surveys job opportunities for cosmetologists as salon managers, owners and teachers. Outlines preferred personal characteristics and licensure requirements. Offers advice on selecting a cosmetology school.

★2936★
Electrologist
Vocational Biographies, Inc.
PO Box 31, Dept. VF10
Sauk Centre, MN 56378   Phone: (612)352-6516
1988. This pamphlet profiles a person working in the job. Includes information about job duties, working conditions, places of employment, educational preparation, labor market outlook, and salaries. **Toll-free/Additional Phone Number(s):** 800-255-0752.

★2937★
"Electrologist" in *Consumer, Homemaking, and Personal Services*, Volume 5 of *Career Information Center* (pp. 79-81)
Glencoe/Macmillan
15319 Chatsworth St.
Mission Hills, CA 91345   Phone: (818)898-1391
Richard Lidz and Dale Anderson, editorial directors. Fourth edition, 1990. For 600 occupations, describes job duties, entry-level requirements, education and training needed, advancement possibilities, employment outlook, earnings and benefits. The set is divided into 12 volumes. Each volume includes jobs related under a broad career field. Volume 13 is the index. **Facsimile Number:** 818-365-5489.

★2938★
Electrologists
Chronicle Guidance Publications, Inc.
PO Box 1190
Moravia, NY 13118-1190   Phone: (315)497-0330
1991. This career brief describes the nature of the work, working conditions, hours and earnings, education and training, licensure, certification, unions, personal qualifications, social and psychological factors, employment outlook, entry methods, advancement, and related occupations. **Toll-free/Additional Phone Number(s):** 800-622-7284.

★2939★
"Electrologists" in Volume 3 of *The Encyclopedia of Careers and Vocational Guidance* (pp. 229-232)
J.G. Ferguson Publishing Co.
200 W. Monroe
Chicago, IL 60606   Phone: (312)580-5480
William E. Hopke, editor-in-chief. Eighth edition, 1990. Four-volume set that profiles 500 occupations and describes job trends in 76 industries. Includes career description, educational requirements, history of the job, methods of entry, advancement, employment outlook, earnings, working conditions, social and psychological factors, and sources of additional information.

★2940★
Getting Down to Business: Hair Styling Shop
American Institutes for Research
PO Box 11131
Palo Alto, CA   Phone: (415)493-3550
Joyce P. Gall. 1981. **Facsimile Number:** (415)858-0958.

★2941★
"Hair Stylist" in *Career Opportunities in Television, Cable, and Video* (pp. 140-141)
Facts on File, Inc.
460 Park Avenue, S.
New York, NY 10016   Phone: (212)683-2244
Third edition, 1990. Describes 100 media-related jobs. Each occupational profile covers job duties, employment outlook, career paths, salaries, skills, and educational preparation. Offers tips for entering the field.

★2942★
"Hairdressers" in *Jobs! What They Are. . .Where They Are. . .What They Pay* (p. 297)
Simon & Schuster, Inc.
Simon & Schuster Bldg.
1230 Avenue of the Americas
New York, NY 10020   Phone: (212)698-7000
Robert O. Snelling and Anne M. Snelling. Revised edition, 1989. Profiles 241 occupations, describing duties and responsibilities, educational preparation, earnings, employment opportunities, training, and qualifications.

★2943★
"Hairstylist" in *Guide to Careers Without College* (pp. 100-102)
Franklin Watts, Inc.
387 Park Avenue, S.
New York, NY 10016   Phone: (212)686-7070
Kathleen S. Abrams. 1988. Discusses careers that do not require a college degree in fields such as health care, sales and marketing, and the building trades. Describes the work, employment opportunities, and training.

★2944★
Hairstylist Assistant
Vocational Biographies, Inc.
PO Box 31, Dept. VF10
Sauk Centre, MN 56378   Phone: (612)352-6516
1988. This pamphlet profiles a person working in the job. Includes information about job duties, working conditions, places of employment, educational preparation, labor market outlook, and salaries. **Toll-free/Additional Phone Number(s):** 800-255-0752.

★2945★
Makeup Artist
Vocational Biographies, Inc.
PO Box 31, Dept. VF10
Sauk Centre, MN 56378 Phone: (612)352-6516

1989. This pamphlet profiles a person working in the job. Includes information about job duties, working conditions, places of employment, educational preparation, labor market outlook, and salaries. **Toll-free/Additional Phone Number(s):** 800-255-0752.

★2946★
Manicurist
Careers, Inc.
PO Box 135
Largo, FL 34649-0135 Phone: (813)584-7333

1991. Two-page job guide card describing duties, working conditions, personal qualifications, training, earnings and hours, employment outlook, places of employment, related careers and where to write for more information.

★2947★
"Manicurist" in *Occu-Facts: Information on 565 Careers in Outline Form* (p. 13.34)
Careers, Inc.
P.O. Box 135
1211 Tenth St., S.W.
Largo, FL 33640 Phone: (813)584-7333

Elizabeth Handville. Biennial, 1989-90 edition. Each one-page occupational profile describes duties, working conditions, physical surroundings and demands, aptitudes, temperament, educational requirements, employment outlook, earnings, and places of employment.

★2948★
Manicurists and Nail Technicians
Chronicle Guidance Publications, Inc.
PO Box 1190
Moravia, NY 13118-1190 Phone: (315)497-0330

1988. This career brief describes the nature of the work, working conditions, hours and earnings, education and training, licensure, certification, unions, personal qualifications, social and psychological factors, employment outlook, entry methods, advancement, and related occupations. **Toll-free/Additional Phone Number(s):** 800-622-7284.

★2949★
Opportunities in Beauty Culture Careers
National Textbook Co.
4255 W. Touhy Ave.
Lincolnwood, IL 60646 Phone: (312)679-5500

Susan Wood Gearhart. 1989. Describes the work of cosmetologists and related beauty service careers such electrologist and makeup artist. Covers training, licensing, choosing a school and workplace, the curriculum of study, salaries, employment outlook, and working conditions.

★2950★
Personal Service Cluster
Center for Humanities, Inc.
Communications Park
Box 1000
Mount Kisco, NY 10549 Phone: (914)666-4100

Videocassette. 1984. 20 mins. Students get to see the day-by-day lives of people who work in the fields of cosmetology, food service and law enforcement.

★2951★
Video Career Library - Public and Personal Services
Careers, Inc.
1211 10th St., SW
PO Box 135
Largo, FL 34649-0135 Phone: (813)584-7333

Videocassette. 1990. 35 mins. Part of the Video Career Library covering 165 occupations. Shows actual workers on the job. Includes firefighters, police officers, correctional officers, bartenders, waiters/waitresses, cooks/chefs, child care workers, flight attendants, barbers/cosmetologists, groundskeepers/ gardeners, and butchers/meat cutters.

★2952★
Video Tapes for Cosmetology
Golden West College
15744 Golden West St.
Huntington Beach, CA 92647 Phone: (714)892-7711

Videocassette. 1984. 25 mins. This series of six programs is a course in cosmetology from haircutting to manicuring.

─────────── Associations ───────────

★2953★
Hair International/Associated Master Barbers and Beauticians of America (HI/AMBBA)
1318 Starbrook Dr.
Charlotte, NC 28210 Phone: (704)552-6233

Membership: Barber styling and cosmetology school and business owners and employees; manufacturers. **Purpose:** Bestows Hair Designer of the Year Award. Operates speakers' bureau; conducts hairstyling show, classes, and seminars. Sponsors hair cutting and styling competitions. **Publications:** *Hair International News*, bimonthly. ● *National Bulletin*, quarterly. ● Also publishes *Standardized Textbook of Barbering and Styling*.

★2954★
National Association of Accredited Cosmetology Schools (NAACS)
5201 Leesburg Pike, Ste. 205
Falls Church, VA 22041 Phone: (703)845-1333

Membership: Owners and instructors of schools of cosmetology; associate members are manufacturers and jobbers of beauty products and others interested in beauty culture and training. **Purpose:** Presents annual awards; sponsors competitions and seminars. **Publications:** *Membership Directory*, annual. ● *NAACS News*, monthly. ● *Washington Update*, monthly. ● Also publishes *OSHA Hazard Communication Standard: A Compliance Manual for Cosmetology Schools*, salary survey, and brochures. **Facsimile Number:** (703)845-1336.

★2955★
National Beauty Culturists' League
25 Logan Circle NW
Washington, DC 20005 Phone: (202)332-2695

Membership: Beauticians, cosemtologists, and beauty products manufacturers. **Purpose:** Encourages standardized, scientific, and approved methods of hair, scalp, and skin treatments. Offers scholarships and plans to establish a research center. Sponsors: National Institute of Cosmetology, a training course in operating and designing and business techniques; National Beauty Week. Maintains hall of fame; conducts research programs; compiles statistics.

Cosmetologists and Related Workers

★2956★
National Cosmetology Association (NCA)
3510 Olive St.
St. Louis, MO 63103   Phone: (314)534-7980
Membership: Owners of cosmetology salons; cosmetologists. **Purpose:** Sponsors: advanced cosmetology courses at universities throughout the U.S.; National Cosmetology Month; National Beauty Show. Provides special sections for estheticians, school owners, salon owners, and nail technicians. Maintains hall of fame, museum, and biographical archives. **Publications:** *American Images*, semiannual. • *American Salon Magazine*, monthly. • *Association Bulletin*, periodic. **Toll-free/Additional Phone Number(s):** (800)527-1683.

★2957★
World International Nail and Beauty Association (WINBA)
1211 N. Lake View
Anaheim, CA 92807   Phone: (714)779-9883
Membership: Professionals in the nail and skin care industries. **Purpose:** Objectives are to represent the manicure and skin care industry; promote the effective use and application of manicuring and skin care products and equipment; provide a means for mutual communication and joint study; represent the industry before state boards, the Food and Drug Administration, and other regulatory agencies. Conducts seminars; secures discounts on supplies; offers special insurance plans and rates; sponsors competitions and bestows awards in nail art, make-up application, and hair styling; conducts public relations program; sponsors research and educational programs; compiles statistics. Maintains speakers' bureau, placement service, library, and biographical archives.

Standards/Certification Agencies

Although all states require cosmetologists to be licensed, the qualifications necessary to obtain a license vary. Generally, a person must have graduated from a state-licensed cosmetology school, pass a physical examination, and be at least 16 years old. Cosmetology instruction is offered in both public and private vocational schools, in either daytime or evening classes. Many public school programs include cosmetology. An apprenticeship program usually lasts from one to two years. After graduating from a cosmetology program, students take the state licensing examination.

★2958★
National Accrediting Commission of Cosmetology Arts and Sciences (NACCAS)
1333 H St. NW, Ste. 710
Washington, DC 20005   Phone: (202)289-4300
Membership: Accrediting body for schools of cosmetology; presently there are 1900 accredited schools. **Purpose:** Objectives are to: raise standards of cosmetology schools throughout the country; encourage use of modern educational methods and techniques; stimulate self-improvement by the schools. Sponsors standards and professional team training workshops. **Publications:** *Directory of Accredited Cosmetology Schools*, annual. • *NACCAS Review*, quarterly. **Facsimile Number:** (202)789-2964.

★2959★
National Association of Accredited Cosmetology Schools (NAACS)
5201 Leesburg Pike, Ste. 205
Falls Church, VA 22041   Phone: (703)845-1333
Membership: Owners and instructors of schools of cosmetology; associate members are manufacturers and jobbers of beauty products and others interested in beauty culture and training. **Purpose:** Presents annual awards; sponsors competitions and seminars. **Publications:** *Membership Directory*, annual. • *NAACS News*, monthly. • *Washington Update*, monthly. • Also publishes *OSHA Hazard Communication Standard: A Compliance Manual for Cosmetology Schools*, salary survey, and brochures. **Facsimile Number:** (703)845-1336.

Test Guides

★2960★
Cosmetologist
National Learning Corp.
212 Michael Dr.
Syosset, NY 11791   Phone: (516)921-8888
Jack Rudman. Part of the Career Examination Series No. 1. All examination guides in this series contain questions with answers. **Facsimile Number:** (516)921-8743. **Toll-free/Additional Phone Number(s):** 800-645-6337.

★2961★
Cosmetologist's State Board Exam Review in English
Milady Publishing Co
220 White Plains Rd.
Tarrytown, NY 10591   Phone: (914)332-4800
Milady Editors. 1985. **Facsimile Number:** (212)881-5624.

★2962★
State Board Review Examinations In Cosmetology
Keystone Publications, Inc.
1657 Broadway
New York, NY 10019   Phone: (212)582-2254
Anthony B. Colletti. 1976.

Educational Directories and Programs

★2963★
Directory of Accredited Cosmetology Schools
National Accrediting Commission of Cosmetology Arts & Sciences
1333 H St., NW, Ste. 710
Washington, DC 20005   Phone: (202)289-4300
Peggy Smith-Rowland, editor. Annual, July. Over 1,750 accredited cosmetology schools in the United States, Puerto Rico, and Guam. Entries include: School name, address, phone, date accredited, curriculum offered. Arrangement: Geographical. **Facsimile Number:** (202)789-2964.

Awards, Scholarships, Grants, and Fellowships

★2964★
Academy of Legends
Aestheticians International Association
c/o Ron Renee, Editor of Dermascope Magazine
3606 Prescott, Ste. C
Dallas, TX 75219   Phone: (214)526-0752
For recognition of outstanding achievements in the field of skin care, make up and appearance. Nomination is by the Academy of Legends Committee. A trophy is awarded bimonthly and the winner is featured on the cover of DermaScope Magazine. Established in 1986 in memory of Ida Mae Mixon Green.

★2965★
Make-Up Competition
Aestheticians International Association
c/o Ron Renee, Editor of Dermascope Magazine
3606 Prescott, Ste. C
Dallas, TX 75219   Phone: (214)526-0752

For recognition of outstanding make-up artistry, and to encourage personal growth and creativity in make-up. Both professional and student make-up artists may enter. The deadline is usually 30 days prior to show dates. A monetary award and plaque are bestowed for the first, second, and third prizes. Presented annually at the convention.

★2966★
North American Hairstyling Awards
Modern Salon
Vance Publishing Corp.
400 Knightsbridge
Lincolnshire, IL 60069   Phone: (708)634-2600

To recognize creative hairstylists. Non-published hairstyle photographs - 35mm color slide format (professional photography and makeup recommended) - by stylists and students who have not had any of their work published may be entered in any or all of three classifications: (1) Makeover - "Before" and "After" photographs of a single model; (2) Avant Garde - An individual interpretation of fashion-forward hair; and (3) Classic - Photographs of commercial styles designed to flatter and enhance the total look. Published hairstyle photographs which have appeared in the preceding year in any editorial section of a U.S., Canadian or international trade or consumer magazine or newspaper acceptable to contest judges may be entered in any or all of three classifications: (1) North American Stylist of the Year - a complete body of work displaying versatility, creativity and technical expertise; (2) Avant Garde; and (3) Classic. All entries are judged on originality, creativity, style and fashion appeal, overall suitability to model and technical execution. The deadline is January 15. Entry is limited to licensed cosmetologists and licensed men's hairstylists only.

★2967★
Person of the Year Award
American Beauty Association
c/o Fred A. Piattoni, Executive Director
111 E. Wacker Dr., Ste. 600
Chicago, IL 60601   Phone: (312)644-6610

For recognition of an outstanding contribution to the professional salon industry. Selection is by nomination. A plaque is awarded annually at the convention. Established in 1985.

★2968★
WINBA Championship Title
World International Nail and Beauty Association
c/o C. George, Secretary
1221 N. Lakeview
Anaheim, CA 92807   Phone: (714)779-9883

For recognition of achievement and field activity in cosmetology. World Championship Titles are given in the following categories: (1) Student; (2) Nails; (3) Nail Arts; (4) Professional Sculptured Acrylic Nails; (5) U.S. Championship Nails; and (6) Nail Wrapping. Individuals who are 18 years of age, licensed or in a school for nails, and with any citizenship, or association membership in any country may compete. Monetary awards, medallions, jewelry, and travel are awarded annually in each category. Established in 1980 by James George.

Basic Reference Guides and Handbooks

★2969★
Milady's Cosmetology State Board Guide
Milady Publishing Company
220 White Plains Rd.
Tarrytown, NY 10591   Phone: (914)332-4800

Jacob J. Yahm, editor. Annual. State boards for licensing cosmetologists and barbers in the United States and Canada. Entries include: Board name, address, phone, name and title of contact, names and titles of key personnel, outline of requirements to become certified, licensing fees and expiration dates. Arrangement: Geographical. **Toll-free/Additional Phone Number(s):** (800)836-5239. **Facsimile Number:** (518)459-3552.

★2970★
OSHA Hazard Communication Standard: A Compliance Manual for Cosmetology Schools
National Association of Accredited Cosmetology Schools (NAACS)
5201 Leesburg Pike, Ste. 205
Falls Church, VA 22041   Phone: (703)845-1333

★2971★
Standardized Textbook of Barbering and Styling

Hair International/Associated Master Barbers and Beauticians of America
1318 Starbrook Dr.
Charlotte, NC 28210   Phone: (704)552-6233

Periodicals

★2972★
American Images
National Cosmetology Association (NCA)
3510 Olive St.
St. Louis, MO 63103   Phone: (314)534-7980
Semiannual. Magazine.

★2973★
American Salon Magazine
National Cosmetology Association (NCA)
3510 Olive St.
St. Louis, MO 63103   Phone: (314)534-7980
Monthly.

★2974★
Cosmetic Insiders' Report
270 Madison Ave.
New York, NY 10016   Phone: (212)951-6600

Editor(s): Don Davis. Semimonthly. Carries news and current insider views of the cosmetic, toiletries, and fragrance industries. Includes items on marketing, advertising, regulation, technology, consumer buying patterns, new products, company developments, and people in the industry. **Facsimile Number:** (212)481-6562.

Cosmetologists and Related Workers

★2975★
Cosmetics
Clarco Communications Ltd.
227 Front St. E, Ste. 402
Toronto, ON, Canada M5A 1E8   Phone: (416)865-9362
Ronald A. Wood, Editor. 6x/yr. Magazine concerning cosmetics, fragrances, toiletries and personal care. **Facsimile Number:** (416)865-1933.

★2976★
FDC Toiletries, Fragrances and Skin Care - The Rose Sheet
F-D-C Reports, Inc.
5550 Friendship Blvd., Ste. 1
Chevy Chase, MD 20815   Phone: (301)657-9830
Editor(s): Cole Werble and Melissa Carlson. Weekly. "Provides executives in the toiletries, fragrances, skin care and related industries with specialized regulatory, legislative, scientific, financial and legal news." Reports on marketing activities, new product introductions, and line extensions. Also includes a section titled Trademark Review, which lists cosmetics-related product trademarks registered and filed for opposition with the U.S. Patent and Trademark Office. **Facsimile Number:** (301)656-3094.

★2977★
Hair International News
Hair International/Associated Master Barbers and Beauticians of America
1318 Starbrook Dr.
Charlotte, NC 28210   Phone: (704)552-6233
Bimonthly. Magazine.

★2978★
HI/AMBBA National Bulletin
Hair International/Associated Master Barbers and Beauticians of America
1318 Starbrook Dr.
Charlotte, NC 28210   Phone: (704)552-6233
Quarterly.

★2979★
NAACS News
National Association of Accredited Cosmetology Schools
5201 Leesburg Pike, Ste. 205
Falls Church, VA 22041   Phone: (703)845-1333
Monthly. Newsletter.

★2980★
NAACS Washington Update
National Association of Accredited Cosmetology Schools (NAACS)
5201 Leesburg Pike, Ste. 205
Falls Church, VA 22041   Phone: (703)845-1333
Monthly.

★2981★
NACCAS Review
National Accrediting Commission of Cosmetology Arts and Sciences (NACCAS)
1333 H St. NW, Ste. 710
Washington, DC 20005   Phone: (202)289-4300
Quarterly.

★2982★
National Cosmetology Association Bulletin
National Cosmetology Association (NCA)
3510 Olive St.
St. Louis, MO 63103   Phone: (314)534-7980
Periodic.

★2983★
Skin Inc.
Allured Publishing Corp.
PO Box 318
Wheaton, IL 60189   Phone: (708)653-2155
Jean E. Allured, Publisher. 6x/yr. The business magazine for skin care facilities. **Facsimile Number:** (708)653-2192.

★2984★
Soap/Cosmetics/Chemical Specialties
PTN Publishing Co.
445 Broad Hollow Rd.
Melville, NY 11747-3601   Phone: (516)845-2700
Anita Hipius Shaw, Editor-in-Chief. Monthly. Soap, cosmetics, and chemical specialties trade magazine. **Facsimile Number:** (516)845-7109.

Meetings and Conventions

★2985★
Big Show Expo Beauty and Hair Care Show
Big Show Expo, Inc.
1841 Broadway
New York, NY 10023   Phone: (212)757-7589
Frequency: Three shows per year. 1992.

★2986★
Hair International/Associated Master Barbers and Beauticians of America Conference (HI/AMBBA)
1318 Starbrook Dr.
Charlotte, NC 28210   Phone: (704)552-6233
Frequency: Triennial - next 1994.

★2987★
Hawaii and Pacific Basin Nails Expo
Bobit Publishing Co.
49 S. Maple Ave.
Marlton, NJ 08053   Phone: (609)596-0999
1992. **Facsimile Number:** (609)596-0168.

★2988★
International Beauty Show
Edgell Expositions
7500 Old Oak Blvd.
Cleveland, OH 44130   Phone: (216)826-2831
1992; Mar. 14-17; New York, NY. **Toll-free/Additional Phone Number(s):** 800-331-5706. **Facsimile Number:** (216)826-2801.

★2989★
NAILS Magazine Show/Chicago
Bobit Publishing Co.
2512 Artesia Blvd.
Redondo Beach, CA 90278   Phone: (213)376-4001
Frequency: Always held in Chicago, Illinois. 1992; Chicago, IL. **Facsimile Number:** (213)376-9043.

★2990★
NAILS Magazine Show/Dallas
Bobit Publishing Co.
2512 Artesia Blvd.
Redondo Beach, CA 90278   Phone: (213)376-4001
Frequency: Always held in Dallas, Texas. 1992; Dallas, TX. **Facsimile Number:** (213)376-9043.

★2991★
NAILS Magazine Show/Detroit
Bobit Publishing Co.
2512 Artesia Blvd.
Redondo Beach, CA 90278   Phone: (213)376-4001
Frequency: Always held in Detroit, Michigan. 1992; Detroit, MI. **Facsimile Number:** (213)376-9043.

★2992★
NAILS Magazine Show/Hawaii
Bobit Publishing Co.
2512 Artesia Blvd.
Redondo Beach, CA 90278   Phone: (213)376-4001
Frequency: Always held in Hawaii. 1992; HI. **Facsimile Number:** (213)376-9043.

★2993★
NAILS Magazine Show/Las Vegas I
Bobit Publishing Co.
2512 Artesia Blvd.
Redondo Beach, CA 90278   Phone: (213)376-4001
Frequency: Always held in Las Vegas, Nevada. 1992; Las Vegas, NV. **Facsimile Number:** (213)376-9043.

★2994★
NAILS Magazine Show/Las Vegas II
Bobit Publishing Co.
2512 Artesia Blvd.
Redondo, CA 90278   Phone: (213)376-4001
Frequency: Always held in Las Vegas, Nevada. 1992; Las Vegas, NV. **Facsimile Number:** (213)376-9043.

★2995★
NAILS Magazine Show/Los Angeles
Bobit Publishing Co.
2512 Artesia Blvd.
Redondo Beach, CA 90278   Phone: (213)376-4001
Frequency: Always held in Los Angeles, California. 1992; Los Angeles, CA. **Facsimile Number:** (213)376-9043.

★2996★
NAILS Magazine Show/New York
Bobit Publishing Co.
2512 Artesia Blvd.
Redondo Beach, CA 90278   Phone: (213)376-4001
Frequency: Always held in New York, New York. 1992; New York, NY. **Facsimile Number:** (213)376-9043.

★2997★
NAILS Magazine Show/Tampa
Bobit Publishing Co.
2512 Artesia Blvd.
Redondo Beach, CA 90278   Phone: (213)376-4001
Frequency: Always held at the Holiday Inn in Tampa, Florida. 1992; Tampa, FL. **Facsimile Number:** (213)376-9043.

★2998★
NAILS Sunshine Show
Bobit Publishing Co.
49 S. Maple Ave.
Marlton, NJ 08053   Phone: (609)596-0999
1992. **Facsimile Number:** (609)596-0168.

★2999★
National Association of Accredited Cosmetology Schools Annual Convention and Trade Show
Freeman
5201 Leesburg Pke., Ste. 205
Falls Church, VA 22041   Phone: (703)845-1333
1992. **Facsimile Number:** (703)845-1336.

★3000★
National Beauty Show
National Cosmetology Association
3510 Olive St.
St. Louis, MO 63103   Phone: (314)534-7980
Frequency: Always held in January. 1993; Jan. 09-11; Miami, FL • 1994; Jan. 08-10; Miami, FL • 1995; Jan. 07-09; Miami, FL. **Toll-free/Additional Phone Number(s):** 800-527-1683. **Facsimile Number:** (314)534-8618.

★3001★
National Cosmetology Association Convention
National Cosmetology Association
3510 Olive St.
St. Louis, MO 63103   Phone: (314)534-7980
1992; Jul. 18-20; Nashville, TN • 1993; Jul. 17-19; Las Vegas, NV • 1994; • 1995; Jul. 22-24; Chicago, IL. **Toll-free/Additional Phone Number(s):** 800-527-1683. **Facsimile Number:** (314)534-8618.

★3002★
Salon Fair - The International Beauty Shows
Edgell Expositions
7500 Old Oak Blvd.
Cleveland, OH 44130   Phone: (216)826-2831
1992; Apr. 11-13; Seattle, WA. **Toll-free/Additional Phone Number(s):** 800-331-5706. **Facsimile Number:** (216)826-2801.

★3003★
Salon Focus 2000 - Your Educational Forum
Edgell Expositions (Cleveland)
7500 Old Oak Blvd.
Cleveland, OH 44130   Phone: (216)826-2831
Held as part of the International Beauty Shows. 1992; Nov. 15-16; Dallas, TX. **Facsimile Number:** (216)826-2801.

★3004★
USA/Canada Nails Festival
Bobit Publishing Co.
2512 Artesia Blvd.
Redondo Beach, CA 90278   Phone: (213)376-8788
1992.

★3005★
World Champion Beauty Trade Show
World International Nail and Beauty Association (WINBA)
1211 N. Lake View
Anaheim, CA 92807   Phone: (714)779-9883
Frequency: Annual. **Facsimile Number:** (714)779-9971.

Flight Attendants

Flight attendants are aboard all passenger planes to look after the passengers' flight safety and comfort. At least one hour before each flight, the attendants see that the passenger cabin is in order. As the passengers board the plane, attendants assist them. Before the plane takes off, attendants instruct passengers in the use of emergency equipment and check to see that all passengers have their seat belts fastened and seat backs forward. In the air, attendants serve refreshments and, on many flights, heat and distribute precooked meals. After the plane has landed, the flight attendants assist passengers as they leave the plane. Assisting passengers in the rare event of an emergency is the most important function of attendants. Lead or first flight attendants aboard planes oversee the work of the other attendants while performing most of the same duties. Commercial airlines employ the vast majority of all flight attendants. A small number of flight attendants work for large companies that operate their own aircraft for business purposes.

$alaries

Median annual salaries for flight attendants are as follows:

Beginning flight attendants	$12,600/year
Flight attendants with six years of flying experience	$21,500/year
Senior flight attendants	$38,000/year

Employment Outlook

Growth rate until the year 2000: Faster than average.

Flight Attendants

Career Guides

★3006★
Airline Attendants
Chronicle Guidance Publications, Inc.
PO Box 1190
Moravia, NY 13118-1190   Phone: (315)497-0330
1990. This career brief describes the nature of the work, working conditions, hours and earnings, education and training, licensure, certification, unions, personal qualifications, social and psychological factors, employment outlook, entry methods, advancement, and related occupations. **Toll-free/Additional Phone Number(s):** 800-622-7284.

★3007★
"Airline Flight Attendant" in *Transportation*, Volume 12 of *Career Information Center* (pp. 91-92)
Glencoe/Macmillan
15319 Chatsworth St.
Mission Hills, CA 91345   Phone: (818)898-1391
Richard Lidz and Dale Anderson, editorial directors. Fourth edition, 1990. For 600 occupations, describes job duties, entry-level requirements, education and training needed, advancement possibilities, employment outlook, earnings and benefits. The set is divided into 12 volumes. Each volume includes jobs related under a broad career field. Volume 13 is the index. **Facsimile Number:** 818-365-5489.

★3008★
Career in Air Transport Flight Services
Morris Video
2730 Monterey St. #105
Monterey Business Park
Torrance, CA 90503   Phone: (213)533-4800
Videocassette. 198?. 15 mins. Learn what types of jobs are available in flight service from flight attendants to commercial jet pilots. Discover what the educational requirements are and what background skills are needed.

★3009★
Career Insights
RMI Media Productions, Inc.
2807 West 47th St.
Shawnee Mission, KS 66205   Phone: (913)262-3974
Videocassette series. 1987. This videotape series describes 50 occupations, including skill requirements and interviews with people employed in these fields. Occupations include: flight service, air transportation/ground services, data processing, carpentry, clerk in banking/insurance/business, cosmetic personal grooming, firefighting, roofing, material handling, photographic processing, plumbing, secretarial services, tool and die operations.

★3010★
Career Success Series
Cambridge Career Products
90 MacCorkle Ave., SW
South Charleston, WV 25311   Phone: (304)744-9323
Videocassette. 1986. 15 mins. A series, available separately, outlining various career choices for students. Occupations include: flight service, air transportation/ground service, data processing, carpentry, clerk in banking/insurance, commodity sales, cosmetic personal grooming, fire fighting, forestry services, home economics, insulation/roofing, material handling, mechanics, photographic processing, pipefitting and plumbing, police science, printing, secretarial services, and utilities equipment operator.

★3011★
Careers as a Flight Attendant: Flight to the Future
Rosen Publishing Group, Inc.
29 E. 21st St.
New York, NY 10010   Phone: (212)777-3017
Catherine Okray Lobus. 1991. Discusses the work, personal characteristics of successful flight attendants, physical and educational qualifications, the application process, and airline training programs. Lists major airlines and outlines their application processes, policies and benefits, and training programs.

★3012★
Flight Attendant
Arco/Prentice Hall Press
1 Gulf & Western Plaza
New York, NY 10023   Phone: (212)373-8500
Future Aviation Professionals of America; David Massey. 1990. Career planning guide covering the work, pay, benefits, places of employment, training, and employment outlook. Lists major airlines and national airline flight attendant bases. Offers tips about filling out applications, writing resumes, and interviewing.

★3013★
Flight Attendant
Careers, Inc.
PO Box 135
Largo, FL 34649-0135   Phone: (813)584-7333
1989. Eight-page brief offering the definition, history, duties, working conditions, personal qualifications, educational requirements, earnings, hours, employment outlook, advancement possibilities, and related occupations.

★3014★
"Flight Attendant" in *Careers in Aviation* (pp. 15-18)
Rosen Publishing Group, Inc.
29 E. 21st St.
New York, NY 10010   Phone: (212)777-3017

Sharon Carter. 1990. Explores a wide variety of piloting jobs including aerial patrolling, corporate flying, flying for the media, law enforcement, and the airlines, helicopter ambulance flying, and stunt flying. Discusses being licensed, and opportunities for women. Most of the book is based on interviews with people who describe what they do on the job.

★3015★
"Flight Attendant" in *College Board Guide to Jobs and Career Planning* (pp. 80-82)
College Entrance Examination Board
45 Columbus Ave.
New York, NY 10023-6992   Phone: (212)713-8000

Joyce Slayton Mitchell. 1990. Career planning guide written for high school and college students. Covers 100 careers in 15 occupational groups. Provides job description, educational preparation needed, salaries, related careers, and sources of additional information. Includes information about the 90's labor market.

★3016★
"Flight Attendant" in *Occu-Facts: Information on 565 Careers in Outline Form* (p. 13.37)
Careers, Inc.
P.O. Box 135
1211 Tenth St., S.W.
Largo, FL 33640   Phone: (813)584-7333

Elizabeth Handville. Biennial, 1989-90 edition. Each one-page occupational profile describes duties, working conditions, physical surroundings and demands, aptitudes, temperament, educational requirements, employment outlook, earnings, and places of employment.

★3017★
"Flight Attendant" in *Occupational Outlook Handbook* (pp. 310-311)
Superintendent of Documents
U.S. Government Printing Office
Washington, DC 20402   Phone: (202)783-3238

Biennial; latest edition, 1990-91. Encyclopedia of careers describing more than 250 occupations and comprising about 86 percent of all jobs in the economy. Occupations that require lengthy education or training are given the most attention. For each occupation, the handbook describes job duties, working conditions, training, educational preparation, personal qualities, advancement possibilities, job outlook, earnings, and sources of additional information.

★3018★
"Flight Attendant" in *Opportunities in Airline Careers* (pp. 70-75)
National Textbook Co.
4255 W. Touhy Ave.
Lincolnwood, IL 60646   Phone: (312)679-5500

Adrian A. Paradis. 1987. Surveys trends in the industry and career opportunities with the airlines including management, sales, customer service, flying, and maintenance. Describes pilots' job duties, working conditions, and basic educational and training requirements.

★3019★
"Flight Attendant" in *The Complete Aviation/Aerospace Career Guide* (pp. 159-164)
Aero Publishers, Inc.
13311 Monterey Ave.
Blue Ridge Summit, PA 17294   Phone: (717)794-2191

Robert Calderone. 1989. This is a comprehensive guide to hundreds of aviation related jobs. Provides job description, training requirements, advancement opportunities and employment outlook. **Facsimile Number:** (717)794-2080.

★3020★
"Flight Attendant" in *Transportation* (pp. 51-55)
Franklin Watts, Inc.
387 Park Avenue, S.
New York, NY 10016   Phone: (212)686-7070

Marjorie Rittenberg Schulz. 1990. Surveys the transportation industry including air, water, and rail services. Provides job description, training, salary, and employment outlook. Offers job hunting advice.

★3021★
"Flight Attendant" in *VGM's Careers Encyclopedia* (pp. 178-181)
National Textbook Co.
4255 W. Touhy Ave.
Lincolnwood, IL 60646   Phone: (312)679-5500

Third edition, 1991. Contains two- to five-page descriptions of 200 managerial, professional, technical, trade, and service occupations. Each profile includes job duties, places of employment, qualifications, educational preparation, training, employment potential, advancement, income, and additional sources of information.

★3022★
"Flight Attendant" in *The American Almanac of Jobs and Salaries* (pp. 403-404)
Avon Books
105 Madison Avenue
New York, NY 10016   Phone: (212)481-5600

John Wright and Edward J. Dwyer. Revised and updated, 1990. A comprehensive guide to the wages of hundreds of occupations in a wide variety of industries and organizations.

★3023★
Flight Attendant Interview Handbook
State of the Art, Limited
1625 S. Broadway
Denver, CO 80210   Phone: (303)722-7177

Ken Rebalais. 1987. **Facsimile Number:** (303)744-9825.

★3024★
"Flight Attendants" in *Jobs! What They Are...Where They Are...What They Pay* (pp. 165-166)
Simon & Schuster, Inc.
Simon & Schuster Bldg.
1230 Avenue of the Americas
New York, NY 10020   Phone: (212)698-7000

Robert O. Snelling and Anne M. Snelling. Revised edition, 1989. Profiles 241 occupations, describing duties and responsibilities, educational preparation, earnings, employment opportunities, training, and qualifications.

Flight Attendants

★3025★
"Flight Attendants" in *101 Careers: A Guide to the Fastest-Growing Opportunities* (pp. 316-319)
John Wiley & Sons, Inc.
605 Third Ave.
New York, NY 10158   Phone: (212)850-6000
Michael Harkavy. 1990. Each occupational profile includes a job description, job titles, work environment, employment outlook, qualifications, personal skills, and earnings.

★3026★
"Flight Attendants" in *Opportunities in Travel Careers* (pp. 37-39)
National Textbook Co.
4255 W. Touhy Ave.
Lincolnwood, IL 60646   Phone: (312)679-5500
Robert Scott Milne. 1991. Explores job opportunities in many travel related fields including the airlines, resorts, travel agencies, recreation, and tourism. Covers the work, salaries, educational preparation and training, and advancement possibilities.

★3027★
"Flight Attendants" in *Travel Agent* (pp. 165-166)
Arco/Prentice Hall Press
1 Gulf & Western Plaza
New York, NY 10023   Phone: (212)373-8500
Wilma Boyd. 1989. Introduction to the travel business. Covers U.S. and foreign travel, time zones, ticketing, world geography, and airline, railroad, and tour bus connections, and accommodations. Outlines entry-level positions in the airline, car rental, and hospitality industries as well as in travel agencies and related travel services. Explains travel agency operations, sales techniques, and the use of computers in travel services. Gives job hunting advice and sales tips.

★3028★
"Flight Attendants" in Volume 3 of *Career Discovery Encyclopedia* (pp. 36-37)
J.G. Ferguson Publishing Co.
200 W. Monroe
Chicago, IL 60606   Phone: (312)580-5480
E. Russell Primm, editor-in-chief. 1990. Contains two-page articles on 504 occupations. Each article describes job duties, earnings, and educational and training requirements.

★3029★
"Flight Attendants" in Volume 3 of *The Encyclopedia of Careers and Vocational Guidance* (pp. 247-251)
J.G. Ferguson Publishing Co.
200 W. Monroe
Chicago, IL 60606   Phone: (312)580-5480
William E. Hopke, editor-in-chief. Eighth edition, 1990. Four-volume set that profiles 500 occupations and describes job trends in 76 industries. Includes career description, educational requirements, history of the job, methods of entry, advancement, employment outlook, earnings, working conditions, social and psychological factors, and sources of additional information.

★3030★
"Flight Attendants" in *America's 50 Fastest Growing Jobs* (pp. 125-126)
JIST Works, Inc.
720 N. Park Ave.
Indianapolis, IN 46202   Phone: (317)264-3720
Michael J. Farr, compiler. 1991. Describes the 50 fastest growing jobs within major career clusters such as technicians, and marketing and sales. Each job profile explains the nature of the work, skills and abilities required, employment outlook, average earnings, related occupations, education and training requirements, and employment opportunities. Also contains career planning information and job search tips.

★3031★
A Guide to Becoming a Flight Attendant
Bob Adams, Inc.
260 Center St.
Holbrook, MA 02343   Phone: (617)268-9570
Douglas K. Kinan. 1987. Job hunting guide for flight attendants. Describes qualifications. Offers advice on getting an interview, writing resumes and cover letters, filling out the application, and interviewing. Contains 45 sample interview questions with sample "preferred" answers.

★3032★
How You Too Can Become a Flight Attendant!: A Step by Step Guide
Ross Publishing Co.
Rte. 3, 188 Forester Rd.
Slippery Rock, PA 16057   Phone: (412)794-2837
Debby Shearer. 1987.

★3033★
Video Career Library - Public and Personal Services
Careers, Inc.
1211 10th St., SW
PO Box 135
Largo, FL 34649-0135   Phone: (813)584-7333
Videocassette. 1990. 35 mins. Part of the Video Career Library covering 165 occupations. Shows actual workers on the job. Includes firefighters, police officers, correctional officers, bartenders, waiters/waitresses, cooks/chefs, child care workers, flight attendants, barbers/cosmetologists, groundskeepers/gardeners, and butchers/meat cutters.

★3034★
Walking on Air
Aviation Book Co.
25133 Anza Dr., No. E.
Santa Clarita, CA 91355-3412   Phone: (805)294-0101
Helen E. McLaughlin. 1986. **Facsimile Number:** (805)294-0035.

Associations

★3035★
Future Aviation Professionals of America (FAPA)
4959 Massachusetts Blvd.
Atlanta, GA 30337   Phone: (404)997-8097
Membership: Commercial pilots, flight attendants, aviation maintenance personnel, and persons aspiring to careers in those areas. **Purpose:** Purpose is to channel career information to aviation personnel and those seeking careers in aviation. Conducts bimonthly seminar and job fair. **Publications:** *Career Pilot*, monthly. ● Also publishes brochures and flyers. **Facsimile Number:** (404)997-8111.

Test Guides

★3036★
Flight Attendant Skills Test (FAST)
National Learning Corp.
212 Michael Dr.
Syosset, NY 11791 Phone: (516)921-8888
Jack Rudman. Part of the Career Examination Series No. 1. All examination guides in this series contain questions with answers. **Facsimile Number:** (516)921-8743. **Toll-free/Additional Phone Number(s):** 800-645-6337.

Periodicals

★3037★
Air Line Pilot
Air Line Pilots Assn.
535 Herndon Pkwy.
PO Box 1169
Herndon, VA 22070 Phone: (703)689-4176
Esperison Martinez, Jr., Editor. Monthly. Magazine covering industry trends and developments, flight technology, and air safety. **Facsimile Number:** (703)689-4370.

★3038★
Airport Journal
PO Box 273
Clarendon Hills, IL 60514 Phone: (708)318-6872
John Andrews, Editor and Publisher. Monthly. Magazine serving the air transport industry in the Chicago area. **Facsimile Number:** (708)986-5010.

★3039★
Airport Services
Lakewood Publications
50 S. 9th St.
Minneapolis, MN 55402 Phone: (612)333-0471
Patrick Barry, Publisher. 2x/mo. **Facsimile Number:** (612)333-6526.

★3040★
Flightlog
Association of Flight Attendants, AFL-CIO
1625 Massachusetts Ave. NW
Washington, DC 20036 Phone: (202)328-5400
Editor(s): Mary Ann Forbes. Bimonthly. Covers aviation industry news, aviation safety, legislative and government issues affecting flight attendants, union activities, and related topics. **Facsimile Number:** (202)328-5424.

Gardeners and Groundskeepers

Gardeners are responsible for the overall care of the property, ranging from feeding, watering, and pruning the flowering plants and trees to mowing and watering the lawn. Some landscape gardeners, called lawn service workers, specialize in maintaining lawns and shrubs for a fee. Groundskeepers who care for athletic fields keep both natural and artificial turf fields in top condition and mark boundaries and paint team logos and names on the playing fields before each athletic event. Greenskeepers maintain golf courses. In order to keep the putting greens in good condition, greenskeepers periodically relocate the hole. The greenskeepers also must keep golf course equipment in good working order. Cemetery workers prepare graves and maintain cemetery grounds. They dig graves to specified depth. Basic duties of groundskeepers in parks and recreation facilities include caring for lawns, trees, and shrubs, maintaining athletic fields and playgrounds, and keeping parking lots, picnic areas, and other public spaces free of litter. Over 30 percent of all gardeners and groundskeepers work for lawn and garden services and landscape architects. About 10 percent work for private households and estates. Many work for firms that operate real estate; for local government, including parks departments, and recreational facilities. Others are employed by schools, hospitals, cemeteries, hotels, retail nurseries, and garden stores. Approximately 20 percent are self-employed, providing landscape maintenance directly to customers on a contract basis.

$alaries

Weekly earnings for gardeners and groundskeepers are as follows:

Lowest 10 percent	$145.00/year or less
Middle 50 percent	$185.00—$330.00/year
Top 10 percent	$440.00/year or more

Employment Outlook

Growth rate until the year 2000: Faster than average.

Gardeners and Groundskeepers

Career Guides

★3041★
Career Profiles: Environmental Series
Cambridge Career Products
90 MacCorkle Ave., SW
South Charleston, WV 25311   Phone: (304)744-9323
Videocassette. 1989. 15 mins. Environmental careers of all sorts are examined, including grounds and turf management, landscaping, and wastewater treatment plant operator.

★3042★
"Gardener and Grounds Keeper" in *Consumer, Homemaking, and Personal Services*, Volume 5 of *Career Information Center* (pp. 42-44)
Glencoe/Macmillan
15319 Chatsworth St.
Mission Hills, CA 91345   Phone: (818)898-1391
Richard Lidz and Dale Anderson, editorial directors. Fourth edition, 1990. For 600 occupations, describes job duties, entry-level requirements, education and training needed, advancement possibilities, employment outlook, earnings and benefits. The set is divided into 12 volumes. Each volume includes jobs related under a broad career field. Volume 13 is the index. **Facsimile Number:** 818-365-5489.

★3043★
"Gardeners and Groundskeepers" in *Occupational Outlook Handbook* (pp. 311-313)
Superintendent of Documents
U.S. Government Printing Office
Washington, DC 20402   Phone: (202)783-3238
Biennial; latest edition, 1990-91. Encyclopedia of careers describing more than 250 occupations and comprising about 86 percent of all jobs in the economy. Occupations that require lengthy education or training are given the most attention. For each occupation, the handbook describes job duties, working conditions, training, educational preparation, personal qualities, advancement possibilities, job outlook, earnings, and sources of additional information.

★3044★
Grounds Keeper
Careers, Inc.
PO Box 135
Largo, FL 34649-0135   Phone: (813)584-7333
1991. Two-page job guide card describing duties, working conditions, personal qualifications, training, earnings and hours, employment outlook, places of employment, related careers and where to write for more information.

★3045★
"Groundskeeper" in *Occu-Facts: Information on 565 Careers in Outline Form* (p. 14.12)
Careers, Inc.
P.O. Box 135
1211 Tenth St., S.W.
Largo, FL 33640   Phone: (813)584-7333
Elizabeth Handville. Biennial, 1989-90 edition. Each one-page occupational profile describes duties, working conditions, physical surroundings and demands, aptitudes, temperament, educational requirements, employment outlook, earnings, and places of employment.

★3046★
"Groundskeeper and Stadium Worker" in *Hospitality & Recreation* (pp. 57-61)
Franklin Watts, Inc.
387 Park Avenue, S.
New York, NY 10016   Phone: (212)686-7070
Marjorie Rittenberg Schulz. 1990. Provides an overview of jobs in the hotel, motel, food service, fitness, and recreation industries. Covers job duties, educational preparation, salary, and employment outlook. Offers job hunting advice.

★3047★
"Landscapers and Grounds Managers" in Volume 4 of *Career Discovery Encyclopedia* (pp. 10-11)
J.G. Ferguson Publishing Co.
200 W. Monroe
Chicago, IL 60606   Phone: (312)580-5480
E. Russell Primm, editor-in-chief. 1990. Contains two-page articles on 504 occupations. Each article describes job duties, earnings, and educational and training requirements.

★3048★
"Landscapers and Grounds Managers" in Volume 3 of *The Encyclopedia of Careers and Vocational Guidance* (pp. 369-373)
J.G. Ferguson Publishing Co.
200 W. Monroe
Chicago, IL 60606   Phone: (312)580-5480
William E. Hopke, editor-in-chief. Eighth edition, 1990. Four-volume set that profiles 500 occupations and describes job trends in 76 industries. Includes career description, educational requirements, history of the job, methods of entry, advancement, employment outlook, earnings, working conditions, social and psychological factors, and sources of additional information.

★3049★
Lawn Service Technician
Vocational Biographies, Inc.
PO Box 31, Dept. VF10
Sauk Centre, MN 56378   Phone: (612)352-6516

1988. This pamphlet profiles a person working in the job. Includes information about job duties, working conditions, places of employment, educational preparation, labor market outlook, and salaries. **Toll-free/Additional Phone Number(s):** 800-255-0752.

★3050★
"Nursery and Landscape Workers" in Occu-Facts: Information on 565 Careers in Outline Form (p. 14.13)
Careers, Inc.
P.O. Box 135
1211 Tenth St., S.W.
Largo, FL 33640   Phone: (813)584-7333

Elizabeth Handville. Biennial, 1989-90 edition. Each one-page occupational profile describes duties, working conditions, physical surroundings and demands, aptitudes, temperament, educational requirements, employment outlook, earnings, and places of employment.

★3051★
PGMS Job Descriptions Guide
Professional Grounds Management Society (PGMS)
10402 Ridgland Rd., Ste. 4
Cockeysville, MD 21030   Phone: (301)667-1833

★3052★
Video Career Library - Public and Personal Services
Careers, Inc.
1211 10th St., SW
PO Box 135
Largo, FL 34649-0135   Phone: (813)584-7333

Videocassette. 1990. 35 mins. Part of the Video Career Library covering 165 occupations. Shows actual workers on the job. Includes firefighters, police officers, correctional officers, bartenders, waiters/waitresses, cooks/chefs, child care workers, flight attendants, barbers/cosmetologists, groundskeepers/gardeners, and butchers/meat cutters.

——————— Associations ———————

★3053★
American Association of Nurserymen (AAN)
1250 I St. NW, Ste. 500
Washington, DC 20005   Phone: (202)789-2900

Membership: Vertical organization of growers of trees, shrubs, vines, and other landscape plants; wholesalers; landscape nurseries; garden centers; mail order nurseries; suppliers. **Purpose:** Offers management and consulting services and insurance, uniform, and public relations programs. Provides government representation and bank card plan for members. Presents awards; maintains hall of fame; sponsors competitions; compiles statistics.

★3054★
Associated Landscape Contractors of America (ALCA)
405 N. Washington St.
Falls Church, VA 22046   Phone: (703)241-4004

Membership: Landscape contractors. **Purpose:** Provides an exchange of business ideas and information to better serve the American public and to make members of the association better businesspersons and citizens. Holds seminars; maintains industry library. Bestows awards. **Publications:** *Action Letter*, monthly. • *Membership Directory*, annual. • Also publishes technical manuals and management reports. **Facsimile Number:** (703)532-0463.

★3055★
National Landscape Association (NLA)
1250 I St. NW, Ste. 500
Washington, DC 20005   Phone: (202)789-2900

Membership: Landscape firms. **Purpose:** Serves as clearinghouse for managers of firms offering design, planting, and/or maintenance services for landscape sites. Sponsors annual landscape tour in conjunction with American Association of Nurserymen. Presents annual Residential Design Award. **Publications:** *NLA Landscape News*, bimonthly. • Also publishes reports. **Facsimile Number:** (202)789-1893.

★3056★
Professional Grounds Management Society (PGMS)
10402 Ridgland Rd., Ste. 4
Cockeysville, MD 21030   Phone: (301)667-1833

Membership: Professional society of horticulturists and grounds managers of private estates, parks, cemeteries, and institutions; persons engaged in businesses related to gardening. **Purpose:** Purposes are to: establish gardening as a profession; secure opportunities for professional advancement of well-qualified grounds managers; acquaint the public with "the distinction between competent gardeners, equipped through practical experience and systematic study, and self-styled gardeners, lacking these essentials." Original sponsor of International Peace Garden, located in North Dakota on the U.S.-Canadian border. Provides employment referral service to members. Sponsors contests; presents Professional Grounds Maintenance awards. Conducts research and surveys; sponsors certification program for professional grounds managers. Holds seminars. Takes action with the legislative and executive branches of government on issues affecting grounds managers; keeps members informed on matters affecting the profession. **Publications:** *Grounds Maintenance Guidelines*, periodic. • *Grounds Management Forum*, monthly. • *Professional Grounds Management Society—Membership Directory*, annual. • Also publishes *Grounds Manager Certification Program* and *The Professional Grounds Manager* (brochures), *Guide to Grounds Maintenance Estimating*, *Grounds Management Guide*, and *Job Descriptions Guide*. **Facsimile Number:** (301)667-6178.

——————— Standards/Certification Agencies ———————

There are no national standards for gardeners and groundskeepers, but some states require certification for workers involved in the extensive use of chemicals, such as those by chemical lawn services. Certification requirements vary, but usually include passing a test on the proper and safe use of insecticides, pesticides, and fungicides. The Professional Grounds Management Society offers in-house certification to those managers who have a combination of eight years of experience and formal education beyond high school.

★3057★
Professional Grounds Management Society (PGMS)
10402 Ridgland Rd., Ste. 4
Cockeysville, MD 21030   Phone: (301)667-1833

Conducts research and surveys; sponsors certification program for professional grounds managers.

Gardeners and Groundskeepers

Test Guides

★3058★
Assistant Gardener
National Learning Corp.
212 Michael Dr.
Syosset, NY 11791   Phone: (516)921-8888
Jack Rudman. Part of the Career Examination Series No. 1. All examination guides in this series contain questions with answers. **Facsimile Number:** (516)921-8743. **Toll-free/Additional Phone Number(s):** 800-645-6337.

★3059★
Chief Groundskeeper
National Learning Corp.
212 Michael Dr.
Syosset, NY 11791   Phone: (516)921-8888
Jack Rudman. Part of the Career Examination Series No. 1. All examination guides in this series contain questions with answers. **Facsimile Number:** (516)921-8743. **Toll-free/Additional Phone Number(s):** 800-645-6337.

★3060★
Civil Service Tests for Basic Skills Jobs
Prentice Hall Press
Simon & Schuster Inc.
200 Old Tappan Rd.
Old Tappan, NJ 07675   Phone: (800)223-2348
Hy Hammer. First edition, 1985. Contains nine sample examinations to prepare candidates for entry-level positions that include hospital attendant, building groundskeeper, and custodial assistant, among others.

★3061★
Foreman of Gardeners
National Learning Corp.
212 Michael Dr.
Syosset, NY 11791   Phone: (516)921-8888
Jack Rudman. Part of the Career Examination Series No. 1. All examination guides in this series contain questions with answers. **Facsimile Number:** (516)921-8743. **Toll-free/Additional Phone Number(s):** 800-645-6337.

★3062★
Gardener
National Learning Corp.
212 Michael Dr.
Syosset, NY 11791   Phone: (516)921-8888
Jack Rudman. Part of the Career Examination Series No. 1. All examination guides in this series contain questions with answers. **Facsimile Number:** (516)921-8743. **Toll-free/Additional Phone Number(s):** 800-645-6337.

★3063★
Gardener - Grounds Maintenance Worker
Prentice Hall Press
Simon & Schuster Inc.
200 Old Tappan Rd.
Old Tappan, NJ 07675   Phone: (800)223-2348
Hy Hammer. Fourth edition, 1986. Contains eight sample exams with answers for applicants for civil service landscaping and grounds maintenance positions.

★3064★
Greenskeeper
National Learning Corp.
212 Michael Dr.
Syosset, NY 11791   Phone: (516)921-8888
Jack Rudman. Part of the Career Examination Series No. 1. All examination guides in this series contain questions with answers. **Facsimile Number:** (516)921-8743. **Toll-free/Additional Phone Number(s):** 800-645-6337.

★3065★
Groundskeeper
National Learning Corp.
212 Michael Dr.
Syosset, NY 11791   Phone: (516)921-8888
Jack Rudman. Part of the Career Examination Series No. 1. All examination guides in this series contain questions with answers. **Facsimile Number:** (516)921-8743. **Toll-free/Additional Phone Number(s):** 800-645-6337.

★3066★
Principal Groundskeeper
National Learning Corp.
212 Michael Dr.
Syosset, NY 11791   Phone: (516)921-8888
Jack Rudman. Part of the Career Examination Series No. 1. All examination guides in this series contain questions with answers. **Facsimile Number:** (516)921-8743. **Toll-free/Additional Phone Number(s):** 800-645-6337.

★3067★
Senior Groundskeeper
National Learning Corp.
212 Michael Dr.
Syosset, NY 11791   Phone: (516)921-8888
Jack Rudman. Part of the Career Examination Series No. 1. All examination guides in this series contain questions with answers. **Facsimile Number:** (516)921-8743. **Toll-free/Additional Phone Number(s):** 800-645-6337.

Educational Directories and Programs

★3068★
Grounds Manager Certification Program
Professional Grounds Management Society (PGMS)
10402 Ridgland Rd., Ste. 4
Cockeysville, MD 21030   Phone: (301)667-1833

Awards, Scholarships, Grants, and Fellowships

★3069★
AAN American Beautification Award
American Association of Nurserymen
c/o Betsey Lyon
1250 I St., N.W., Ste. 500
Washington, DC 20005   Phone: (202)789-2900
To recognize an outstanding contribution to environmental improvement through the use of living plants. Recipients may be individuals (however, not residential homes), companies, branches of government, churches, clubs, communities, etc. Each AAN Governor is authorized to present one award each year to an outstanding publicly accessible interior or exterior planting. A walnut plaque is presented at a ceremony at the

locale of the planting. Established in 1980. Formerly: Governor's Green Survival Award.

★3070★
W. Allison and Elizabeth Stubbs Davis Award
Municipal Art Society of New York
457 Madison Ave.
New York, NY 10022   Phone: (212)935-3960

To recognize an employee of the Parks Department for exceptional dedication in the service of the city's parks. The recipient is honored with a Certificate of Merit and $500. Established to honor the parents of former Parks Commissioner Gordon J. Davis.

★3071★
Grounds Maintenance Awards
Professional Grounds Management Society
12 Galloway Ave., Ste. 1E
Cockeysville, MD 21030   Phone: (301)667-1833

To recognize outstanding achievement in the grounds maintenance field. Awards are given in the following categories (1) best maintained industrial or office park; (2) best maintained condominium, apartment complex or planned community; (3) best maintained hotel, motel or resort grounds; (4) best maintained golf course; (5) best maintained cemetery or athletic field; (7) best maintained school or university grounds; (8) best maintained government building or complex; (9) best maintained shopping area; (10) best maintained hospital or institution; (11) best maintained small business or residential landscape; and (12) best maintained interior landscape. All entries must include photos and slides with captions, and a brief explanation of the year-round maintenance procedures. Plaques are presented to the grand winners and certificates are presented to honor winners. Awarded annually when merited at the Awards Banquet at the PGMS Annual Conference and trade show in the fall.

★3072★
G.B. Gunlogson Medal
American Horticultural Society
P.O. Box 0105
Mount Vernon, VA 22121   Phone: (703)768-5700

To recognize the creative use of new technology to make home gardening more productive and enjoyable. Selection is based on creativeness and inventiveness in the design, construction and maintenance of home gardens, flower and/or vegetable. A sterling silver medal is awarded annually if merited at the annual meetings. Established in 1974 by G.B. Gunlogson of Racine, Wisconsin.

★3073★
Landscape Manager of the Year
Professional Grounds Management Society
12 Galloway Ave., Ste. 1E
Cockeysville, MD 21030   Phone: (301)667-1833

For recognition of outstanding work performed as a grounds manager. Candidates are chosen by a PGMS committee. A plaque is presented at the Landscape Expo in the spring. The winner is also featured in *Landscape Management* magazine. Established in 1982. Co-sponsored by *Landscape Management* magazine.

★3074★
NLA Residential Landscape Award Program
American Association of Nurserymen
c/o Betsey Lyon
1250 I St., N.W., Ste. 500
Washington, DC 20005   Phone: (202)789-2900

To recognize both those who have created the design and those responsible for its execution and maintenance. Entries are judged on the basis of excellence, as well as practicality of design, selection of plants and materials, execution of the installation, and maintenance of the project. Scope of the project will be considered only in determining the category of entry. Winners are announced at the Landscape/Garden Center Management Clinic in Louisville, Kentucky. Established in 1970.

★3075★
Frances Jones Poetker Award
American Horticultural Society
P.O. Box 0105
Mount Vernon, VA 22121   Phone: (703)768-5700

To recognize a floral artist, either amateur or professional, of national reputation who has, over an extended period of time, generously given inspirational talent which encompasses designing, teaching and/or writing, and has by the use of plant material enhanced the American aesthetic. Established in 1987.

★3076★
Residential Landscape Design Award
National Landscape Association
c/o David L. Peiffer
1250 I St., N.W., Ste. 500
Washington, DC 20005   Phone: (202)789-2900

To recognize professionals who have created outstanding residential landscape designs and those responsible for executing such designs. Awards are presented in the following categories: single-family residence; entrance; active use area; pools, patios, and active recreation areas; public use area; schools, parks, restaurants; and passive use area. A framed certificate is awarded annlually. Established in 1970.

★3077★
Arthur Ross Awards
Classical America
227 E. 50th St.
New York, NY 10108   Phone: (212)753-4376

For recognition of contemporary contributions to the classical tradition in the arts. Painters, sculptors, architects, craftsmen, landscape architects, architectural renderers, gardeners, and patrons who are citizens of the United States are eligible. Mature work that exhibits a continued excellence and integrity in its application of classical ideals and canons is considered. Certificates are awarded annually at the National Academy of Design. Established in 1982 in honor of Arthur Ross.

★3078★
Scottish Gardening Scholarship
c/o Clara Curtis
North Carolina Arboretum
Rt. 3, Box 1249-B
Asheville, NC 28806

To be applied toward a one-year gardening program in Scotland. Applicants must be American students between the ages of 17 and 20 who are high school graduates in good academic standing. At least one full summer's employment in a horticultural activity is required. A letter of application in outline or narrative form must be submitted detailing present occupation; future occupation/vocational plans; horticultural experience; and activities, accomplishments and awards within and outside of the National Junior Horticultural Association (NJHA). A black and white glossy photo should be included. The scholarship is offered annually by the NJHA in conjunction with Longwood Gardens, Inc. and the Scottish-American Heritage.

Gardeners and Groundskeepers

Basic Reference Guides and Handbooks

★3079★
Grounds Maintenance Guidelines
Professional Grounds Management Society (PGMS)
10402 Ridgland Rd., Ste. 4
Cockeysville, MD 21030   Phone: (301)667-1833
Periodic.

★3080★
Grounds Management Guide
Professional Grounds Management Society (PGMS)
10402 Ridgland Rd., Ste. 4
Cockeysville, MD 21030   Phone: (301)667-1833

★3081★
The Grower—Nursery Stock and Seed Directory Issue
Vance Publishing Corp.
7950 College Blvd.
Overland Park, KS 66210   Phone: (913)451-6694
David Ezell, editor. Annual, November. Listing of about 3,500 commercial fruit tree nurseries and seed suppliers. Entries include: Company name, address, phone, variety of product. Arrangement: Alphabetical. Indexes: Product. **Toll-free/Additional Phone Number(s):** (800)255-5113. **Facsimile Number:** (913)451-5821.

★3082★
Guide to Grounds Maintenance Estimating
Professional Grounds Management Society (PGMS)
10402 Ridgland Rd., Ste. 4
Cockeysville, MD 21030   Phone: (301)667-1833

★3083★
Park Maintenance and Grounds Management—Athletic Area and Facilities Buyer's Guide Issue
Madisen Publishing Division
730 W. Frances St.
PO Box 1936
Appleton, WI 54913-1936   Phone: (414)733-2301
Erik Madisen, Jr., editor. Lists of companies and products of interest to managers of parts, campuses, golf courses, or other large grounds areas.

★3084★
The Professional Grounds Manager
Professional Grounds Management Society (PGMS)
10402 Ridgland Rd., Ste. 4
Cockeysville, MD 21030   Phone: (301)667-1833

Periodicals

★3085★
Action Letter
Associated Landscape Contractors of America (ALCA)
405 N. Washington St.
Falls Church, VA 22046   Phone: (703)241-4004
Monthly.

★3086★
American Horticulturist
American Horticultural Society
7931 E. Boulevard Dr.
Alexandria, VA 22308   Phone: (703)768-5700
Editor(s): Kathleen Fisher. Bimonthly. Publishes news of the Society and its interest in gardening and horticulture. Reports on scientific developments, new plants, ecology and environment, and cultivation methods. Recurring features include regional news, a calendar of events, book reviews, and a column titled Plants Wanted. **Toll-free/Additional Phone Number(s):** 800-777-7931 **Facsimile Number:** (703)765-6032.

★3087★
American Nurseryman
American Nurseryman Publishing Co.
111 N. Canal St., Ste. 545
Chicago, IL 60661   Phone: (800)621-5727
Cynthia Champney Urbano, Editor. 2x/mo. Magazine containing information on horticulture and nursery, landscape and garden center management. **Facsimile Number:** (312)782-3232.

★3088★
The American Rose
American Rose Society
PO Box 30,000
Shreveport, LA 71130   Phone: (318)938-5402
Dr. Thomas Cairns, Editor. Monthly. Magazine concerning rose growing.

★3089★
Amerigold Bulletin
Marigold Society of America
PO Box 112
New Britain, PA 18901
Editor(s): Jeannette Lowe and William R. Morris. Quarterly. Highlights events of the Society and discusses topics of interest to horticulturists and marigold lovers. Examines varieties, plant culture, and history of marigold cultivation. Recurring features include convention reports, news of members, commentary, news of upcoming events, a seed exchange, and the column President's Message.

★3090★
The Avant Gardener
Horticultural Data Processors
PO Box 489
New York, NY 10028
Editor(s): Thomas and Betty Powell. Monthly. Contains information on such subjects as indoor and outdoor plants, edible plants, new products, methods of cultivation, breeding and growing techniques, pest control, fertilizers, and landscaping. Recurring features include several special issues per year on specific topics.

★3091★
The Cultivator
Red Butte Gardens and Arboretum
390 Wakara Way
Salt Lake City, UT 84108   Phone: (801)581-5322
Editor(s): Pamela M. Poulson. Quarterly. Covers gardening, general arboreta news, and related items of interest, with particular attention to seasonal information concerning plants and their cultivation. Recurring features include practical gardening tips, book reviews, notices of additions to the library, news of volunteers, reports of field trips and lectures, news of research, and a calendar of events.

★3092★
The Gardener
Men's Garden Clubs of America, Inc.
5560 Merle Hay Rd.
PO Box 241
Johnston, IA 50131　　　　　　　Phone: (515)278-0295
Carol Donovan, Adm. Sec. 6x/yr. Gardening and horticulture magazine.

★3093★
The Gardener's Companion
MLS Publications, Inc.
Division St.
Derby, CT 06418
6x/yr Gardening magazine.

★3094★
Green World News
International Garden Horticultural Industry Association
26 Pine St.
Dover, DE 19901　　　　　　　Phone: (302)736-6781
Editor(s): Virginia Grinse. Monthly. Updates members of the garden horticultural industry on the latest technical information in the field. Reviews new products, growing methods, pertinent regulations, and industry trends. Recurring features include news of research, editorials, news of members, and a calendar of events. **Facsimile Number:** (302)736-6763.

★3095★
Greener Gardening, Easier
E. Dexter Davis
26 Norfolk St.
Holliston, MA 01746　　　　　　　Phone: (508)429-2185
Editor(s): E. Dexter Davis. Monthly. Discusses plants and gardening. Covers topics such as low maintenance plants, choosing and using gardening tools and supplies, vegetable gardening, mulches and efficient watering, and winter protection. Recurring features include news of research, reviews of new books and gardening products, and a calendar of gardening events in the northeast.

★3096★
Grounds Management Forum
Professional Grounds Management Society
10402 Ridgeland Rd., Ste. 4
Cockeysville, MD 21030　　　　　　　Phone: (301)667-1833
Editor(s): Allan Shulder. Monthly. Reports news of the Society and its members. Provides information on upcoming conferences, recent government action, and on current topics of interest to members. Recurring features include book reviews.

★3097★
Harvests
Lawn Institute
PO Box 108
Pleasant Hill, TN 38578　　　　　　　Phone: (615)277-3722
Editor(s): Eliot C. Roberts. Quarterly. Summarizes results of current research on lawns and sports turf. Recurring features include editorials, news of members, book reviews, letters to the editor, reports on turfgrass conferences and field days, and columns titled Lawn Institute Pitch and Director's Dialogue.

★3098★
Horticulture
20 Park Plaza, Ste. 1220
Boston, MA 02116-8241　　　　　　　Phone: (617)482-5600
Thomas C. Cooper, Editor. Monthly. **Facsimile Number:** (617)482-9484.

★3099★
HortIdeas
Greg and Pat Williams
Box 302, Rte. 1
Gravel Switch, KY 40328　　　　　　　Phone: (606)332-7606
Editor(s): Greg and Pat Williams. Monthly. Reviews the latest research on vegetable, fruit, and flower gardening. Provides practical information and tips on growing techniques, tools, plant varieties, and resources in abstract form with full references to original sources. Recurring features include book reviews.

★3100★
Lilacs
International Lilac Society Corp.
Cattle Landing Rd.
RD 1, Box 1344
Meredith, NH 03253　　　　　　　Phone: (603)279-7756
Editor(s): Robert B. Clark. Quarterly. Facilitates an exchange of knowledge, experience, and techniques in the culture and collection of shrubs of the genus syringa (the lilac). Offers information on history, cultivation, varieties, and on the planning of a collection. Recurring features include news of research, announcements of meetings and conventions, and descriptions of attractions and sights involving lilacs.

★3101★
Little Acres
American Farm Publications
PO Box 2026
Easton, MD 21601
Karl Berger, Editor. Monthly. Newspaper (tabloid) featuring articles of interest to small, "sun-down" farmers, gardeners and rural residents.

★3102★
Magnolia: Journal of the Magnolia Society
Magnolia Society, Inc.
1000 Hillcrest Lane
Mobile, AL 36609-5102　　　　　　　Phone: (504)542-9477
Editor(s): Larry W. Langford. Semiannually. Discusses aspects of magnolia culture. Covers hybridization, seed collection, storing, mailing, genetics, the search for new species abroad, and similar subjects. Recurring features include reports of the seed counter program, news of research, book reviews, and Society news.

★3103★
National Gardening
National Gardening Assn.
180 Flynn Ave.
Burlington, VT 05401　　　　　　　Phone: (802)863-1308
Warren Schultz, Editor. Monthly. Magazine covering fruit, vegetable, and ornamental gardening for home and community gardeners. **Facsimile Number:** (802)863-5962.

★3104★
New Horizons
Horticultural Research Institute, Inc.
1250 I St. NW, Ste. 500
Washington, DC 20005　　　　　　　Phone: (202)789-2900
Editor(s): Duane F. Jelinek. 4/yr. Explores research of the science and art of nursery and landscape plant production, marketing, and care. **Facsimile Number:** (202)789-1893.

Gardeners and Groundskeepers

★3105★
NLA Landscape News
National Landscape Association (NLA)
1250 I St. NW, Ste. 500
Washington, DC 20005 Phone: (202)789-2900
Bimonthly. Association and industry newsletter.

★3106★
Organic Gardening
Rodale Press, Inc.
33 E. Minor St.
Emmaus, PA 18098 Phone: (215)967-5171
Stevie Daniels, Editor. Monthly. Horticulture and gardening magazine. **Facsimile Number:** (215)967-3044.

★3107★
Plants & Gardens
Brooklyn Botanic Garden
1000 Washington Ave.
Brooklyn, NY 11225 Phone: (718)622-4433
Barbara Pesch, Editor. Quarterly. Horticultural and botanical magazine. **Facsimile Number:** (718)857-2430.

★3108★
Rocky Mountain Construction
Golden Bell Press
2403 Champa St.
Denver, CO 80205 Phone: (303)295-0630
F. Hol Wagner, Jr., Editor. 2x/mo. Magazine serving the construction industry of America's mountain regions. Covering heavy engineering, building, landscaping, soil conservation, mining, and logging and federal, state, county, and city projects. Includes weekly construction reports. **Facsimile Number:** (303)295-2159.

Meetings and Conventions

★3109★
American Association of Nurserymen Annual Convention and Nursery Industry Exposition
Exhibit Promotions Plus
11620 Vixens Path
Ellicott City, MD 21043 Phone: (301)997-0763
Frequency: Always held in mid-July. 1992; Jul. 23-27; Columbus, OH • 1993; Jul. 15-19; San Antonio, TX • 1994; Jul. 21-25; Salt Lake City, UT. **Facsimile Number:** (301)997-0764.

★3110★
Associated Landscape Contractors of America (ALCA)
405 N. Washington St.
Falls Church, VA 22046 Phone: (703)241-4004
1992; Naples, FL. **Facsimile Number:** (703)532-0463.

★3111★
Eastern Regional Nurserymen Show
Eastern Regional Nurserymen Association
24 West Rd., Ste. 53
Vernon, CT 06066 Phone: (203)872-2095
Frequency: Always held at the Concord Resort Hotel in Kiamesha Lake, New York.

★3112★
International Lawn, Garden, and Power Equipment Expo
Andry Montgomery
Kaden Tower, 6th Fl.
6100 Dutchmans Ln.
Louisville, KY 40205-3284 Phone: (502)473-1992
Frequency: Always held during July at the Kentucky Fair and Exposition Center in Louisville, Kentucky. 1992; Jul. 26-28; Louisville, KY. **Toll-free/Additional Phone Number(s):** 800-558-8767. **Facsimile Number:** (502)473-1999.

★3113★
Mid-Atlantic Nurserymen's Winter Trade Show
Mid-Atlantic Nurserymen's Trade Show, Inc.
PO Box 314
Perry Hall, MD 21128 Phone: (301)256-6474
Frequency: Always held at the Baltimore Convention Center. 1992; Baltimore, MD.

★3114★
National Institute on Park and Grounds Management Convention
National Institute on Park and Grounds Management
Box 1936
Appleton, WI 54913 Phone: (414)733-2301
1992.

★3115★
New England Nurserymen's Annual Trade Show
Connecticut/Eastern Regional Nurserymen's Association
Management Specialties Inc.
288 Walnut St., Ste. 300
Newton, MA 02160 Phone: (617)964-8209
Frequency: Always held in Boston, Massachusetts during January.

★3116★
Penn Allied Nursery Trade Show
Pennsylvania Nurserymen's Association
1924 N. 2nd St.
Harrisburg, PA 17102 Phone: (717)238-1673
Frequency: Always held at the Valley Forge Convention and Exhibit Center in King of Prussia, Pennsylvania. 1992; Jul. 27-30; King of Prussia, PA.

★3117★
Professional Grounds Management Society Trade Show (PGMS)
10402 Ridgland Rd., Ste. 4
Cockeysville, MD 21030 Phone: (301)667-1833
Frequency: Annual - always November. **Facsimile Number:** (301)667-6178.

★3118★
Professional Lawn Care Association of America Annual Conference and Show
Professional Lawn Care Association of America
1225 Johnson Ferry Rd., Ste. B-220
Marietta, GA 30068 Phone: (404)973-2019
1992. **Toll-free/Additional Phone Number(s):** 800-458-3466. **Facsimile Number:** (404)578-6071.

★3119★
Southern Nurserymen Association Horticultural Trade Show
Southern Nurserymen Association
1511 Johnson Ferry Rd., Ste. 115
Marietta, GA 30062-6438   Phone: (404)973-9026
Frequency: Always held during the first weekend in August at the Georgia World Congress Center in Atlanta, Georgia. 1992; Jul. 31-02; Atlanta, GA • 1993; Jul. 30-01; Atlanta, GA • 1994; Aug. 05-07; Atlanta, GA • 1995; Aug. 04-06; Atlanta, GA • 1996; Aug. 02-04; Atlanta, GA • 1997; Aug. 01-03; Atlanta, GA • 1998; Jul. 31-02; Atlanta, GA. **Facsimile Number:** (404)973-9097.

Other Sources of Information

★3120★
Government Product News—Grounds Maintenance Buyers' Guide Issue
Penton, Inc.
1100 Superior Ave.
Cleveland, OH 44114   Phone: (216)696-7000
Leslie A. Drahos, editor. Annual, November. List of over 1,000 manufacturers of grounds maintenance equipment. Entries include: Company name, address, phone, name and title of contact. Arrangement: Alphabetical. Indexes: Manufacturer name, product. **Facsimile Number:** (216)696-7658.

Homemaker-Home Health Aides

Homemaker-home health aides provide home management services, personal care, and emotional support for elderly, disabled, and ill persons. Aides perform management services such as light housekeeping chores. Among the personal care services that aides perform are assisting with bathing or giving a bed bath, shampooing hair, and helping the client move from bed to a chair or another room. Providing emotional support and understanding is a particularly important aspect of the work since a client's progress in regaining strength and independence may be greatly influenced by his or her mental attitude. In agency settings, homemaker-home health aides are assigned specific duties by a supervisor—usually a registered nurse, physical therapist, or social worker.

$alaries

Earnings for homemaker-home health aides vary considerably. Some aides start at the current minimum wage of $4.25/hour. Aides in agencies in large cities that have high living costs generally pay higher wages, up to $8.00/hour to start. Agencies that have union contracts usually pay higher wages and offer more benefits. While some agencies pay the same rate to all aides, most agencies give slight pay increases as aides gain experience and are given more responsibility.

Employment Outlook

Growth rate until the year 2000: Faster than average.

Homemaker-Home Health Aides

Career Guides

★3121★
Becoming a Helper
Brooks/Cole Publishing Co.
511 Forest Lodge Rd.
Pacific Grove, CA 93950-5098   Phone: (408)373-0728
Marianne Schneider Corey. 1989. **Facsimile Number:** (408)375-6414.

★3122★
Careers in Health Services: Opportunities for You
Cambridge Career Products
90 MacCorkle Ave., SW
South Charleston, WV 25311   Phone: (304)744-9323
Videocassette. 1989. 30 mins. This program shows the range of career opportunities in health care fields.

★3123★
Geriatric Aides
Chronicle Guidance Publications, Inc.
PO Box 1190
Moravia, NY 13118-1190   Phone: (315)497-0330
1989. This career brief describes the nature of the work, working conditions, hours and earnings, education and training, licensure, certification, unions, personal qualifications, social and psychological factors, employment outlook, entry methods, advancement, and related occupations. **Toll-free/Additional Phone Number(s):** 800-622-7284.

★3124★
Home Health Aide
Careers, Inc.
PO Box 135
Largo, FL 34649-0135   Phone: (813)584-7333
1991. Two-page job guide card describing duties, working conditions, personal qualifications, training, earnings and hours, employment outlook, places of employment, related careers and where to write for more information.

★3125★
"Home Health Aide" in *Health Care* (pp. 45-49)
Franklin Watts, Inc.
387 Park Avenue, S.
New York, NY 10016   Phone: (212)686-7070
Linda Barrett and Galen Guengerich. 1991. Provides an overview of the health care industry. Includes job description, educational preparation, training, salary, and employment outlook. Offers job hunting advice.

★3126★
"Home Health Aide" in *Health,* Volume 7 of *Career Information Center* (pp. 48-49)
Glencoe/Macmillan
15319 Chatsworth St.
Mission Hills, CA 91345   Phone: (818)898-1391
Richard Lidz and Dale Anderson, editorial directors. Fourth edition, 1990. For 600 occupations, describes job duties, entry-level requirements, education and training needed, advancement possibilities, employment outlook, earnings and benefits. The set is divided into 12 volumes. Each volume includes jobs related under a broad career field. Volume 13 is the index. **Facsimile Number:** 818-365-5489.

★3127★
"Home Health Aide" in *Occu-Facts: Information on 565 Careers in Outline Form* (p. 13.24)
Careers, Inc.
P.O. Box 135
1211 Tenth St., S.W.
Largo, FL 33640   Phone: (813)584-7333
Elizabeth Handville. Biennial, 1989-90 edition. Each one-page occupational profile describes duties, working conditions, physical surroundings and demands, aptitudes, temperament, educational requirements, employment outlook, earnings, and places of employment.

★3128★
Home Health Care Aide
Vocational Biographies, Inc.
PO Box 31, Dept. VF10
Sauk Centre, MN 56378   Phone: (612)352-6516
1988. This pamphlet profiles a person working in the job. Includes information about job duties, working conditions, places of employment, educational preparation, labor market outlook, and salaries. **Toll-free/Additional Phone Number(s):** 800-255-0752.

★3129★
"Home Health Technicians" in Volume 3 of *The Encyclopedia of Careers and Vocational Guidance* (p. 414)
J.G. Ferguson Publishing Co.
200 W. Monroe
Chicago, IL 60606   Phone: (312)580-5480
William E. Hopke, editor-in-chief. Eighth edition, 1990. Four-volume set that profiles 500 occupations and describes job trends in 76 industries. Includes career description, educational requirements, history of the job, methods of entry, advancement, employment outlook, earnings, working conditions, social and psychological factors, and sources of additional information.

★3130★
"Homemaker" in *Consumer, Homemaking, and Personal Services*, Volume 5 of *Career Information Center* (pp. 46-47)
Glencoe/Macmillan
15319 Chatsworth St.
Mission Hills, CA 91345   Phone: (818)898-1391
Richard Lidz and Dale Anderson, editorial directors. Fourth edition, 1990. For 600 occupations, describes job duties, entry-level requirements, education and training needed, advancement possibilities, employment outlook, earnings and benefits. The set is divided into 12 volumes. Each volume includes jobs related under a broad career field. Volume 13 is the index. **Facsimile Number:** 818-365-5489.

★3131★
"Homemaker" in *Opportunities in Home Economics Careers* (pp. 51-52)
National Textbook Co.
4255 W. Touhy Ave.
Lincolnwood, IL 60646   Phone: (312)679-5500
Rhea Shields and Anna K. Williams. 1988. Describes the history of home economics and current trends affecting the field. Explores related careers in interior design, family relations, and home management. Covers the nature of the work, educational preparation, skills, employment outlook, places of employment, and salaries. Lists professional organizations and offers job hunting advice.

★3132★
"Homemaker-Home Health Aide" in *Careers in Health Care* (pp. 103-105)
National Textbook Co.
4255 W. Touhy Ave.
Lincolnwood, IL 60646   Phone: (312)679-5500
Barbara M. Swanson. 1989. Discusses 61 health careers, providing information about the history of the occupation, job duties, work environments, salaries, educational preparation, licensure, certification, and employment outlook.

★3133★
"Homemaker-Home Health Aide" in *120 Careers in the Health Care Field* (pp. 163-165)
U.S. Directory Service, Publishers
PO Box 68-1700
655 N.W. 128th St.
Miami, FL 33168   Phone: (305)769-1700
Stanley Alperin. Second edition, 1989. Each occupational profile covers job functions and responsibilities, work locations, training requirements, certification, and salaries. Lists community colleges, universities, vocational-technical schools, and other educational institutions that provide accredited training programs.

★3134★
"Homemaker Home Health Aide" in *Opportunities in Health and Medical Careers* (pp. 32-33)
National Textbook Co.
4255 W. Touhy Ave.
Lincolnwood, IL 60646   Phone: (312)679-5500
Leo D'Orazio and Donald I. Snook. 1991. Provides an overview of the health care industry with future projections. Describes a wide variety of healthcare jobs covering the nature of the work, educational requirements, employment outlook and salaries. Offers job hunting advice.

★3135★
Homemaker Home Health Aides
Chronicle Guidance Publications, Inc.
PO Box 1190
Moravia, NY 13118-1190   Phone: (315)497-0330
1988. This career brief describes the nature of the work, working conditions, hours and earnings, education and training, licensure, certification, unions, personal qualifications, social and psychological factors, employment outlook, entry methods, advancement, and related occupations. **Toll-free/Additional Phone Number(s):** 800-622-7284.

★3136★
"Homemaker-Home Health Aides" in *America's 50 Fastest Growing Jobs* (pp. 126-129)
JIST Works, Inc.
720 N. Park Ave.
Indianapolis, IN 46202   Phone: (317)264-3720
Michael J. Farr, compiler. 1991. Describes the 50 fastest growing jobs within major career clusters such as technicians, and marketing and sales. Each job profile explains the nature of the work, skills and abilities required, employment outlook, average earnings, related occupations, education and training requirements, and employment opportunities. Also contains career planning information and job search tips.

★3137★
"Homemaker-Home Health Aides" in *Occupational Outlook Handbook* (pp. 313-315)
Superintendent of Documents
U.S. Government Printing Office
Washington, DC 20402   Phone: (202)783-3238
Biennial; latest edition, 1990-91. Encyclopedia of careers describing more than 250 occupations and comprising about 86 percent of all jobs in the economy. Occupations that require lengthy education or training are given the most attention. For each occupation, the handbook describes job duties, working conditions, training, educational preparation, personal qualities, advancement possibilities, job outlook, earnings, and sources of additional information.

★3138★
"Homemaker Home Health Aides" in Volume 3 of *Career Discovery Encyclopedia* (pp. 110-111)
J.G. Ferguson Publishing Co.
200 W. Monroe
Chicago, IL 60606   Phone: (312)580-5480
E. Russell Primm, editor-in-chief. 1990. Contains two-page articles on 504 occupations. Each article describes job duties, earnings, and educational and training requirements.

★3139★
"Homemaker Home Health Aides" in Volume 3 of *The Encyclopedia of Careers and Vocational Guidance* (pp. 259-263)
J.G. Ferguson Publishing Co.
200 W. Monroe
Chicago, IL 60606   Phone: (312)580-5480
William E. Hopke, editor-in-chief. Eighth edition, 1990. Four-volume set that profiles 500 occupations and describes job trends in 76 industries. Includes career description, educational requirements, history of the job, methods of entry, advancement, employment outlook, earnings, working conditions, social and psychological factors, and sources of additional information.

★3140★
Legal Secretary
Vocational Biographies, Inc.
PO Box 31, Dept. VF10
Sauk Centre, MN 56378   Phone: (612)352-6516
1988. This pamphlet profiles a person working in the job. Includes information about job duties, working conditions, places of employment, educational preparation, labor market outlook, and salaries. **Toll-free/Additional Phone Number(s):** 800-255-0752.

Associations

★3141★
National Association for Home Care (NAHC)
519 C St. NE
Stanton Park
Washington, DC 20002   Phone: (202)547-7424
Membership: Providers of home health care, hospice, and homemaker-home health aide services; interested individuals. **Purpose:** Develops and promotes high standards of patient care in home care services. Seeks to affect legislative and regulatory processes concerning home care services; gathers and disseminates home care industry data; develops public relations strategies; works to increase political visibility of home care services. Interprets home care services to governmental and private sector bodies affecting the delivery and financing of such services. Provides legal and accounting consulting services; conducts market research and compiles statistics. Offers members insurance discounts; bestows awards. Sponsors educational programs for organizations and individuals concerned with home care services. **Publications:** *Caring*, monthly. • *Homecare News*, monthly. • *Hospice Forum*, biweekly. • *NAHC Report*, weekly. • *National Home Care and Hospice Directory*, biennial (with alternate year supplement). **Facsimile Number:** (202)547-3540.

Standards/Certification Agencies

★3142★
National Association for Home Care (NAHC)
519 C St. NE
Stanton Park
Washington, DC 20002   Phone: (202)547-7424
Develops and promotes high standards of patient care in home care services. ices. **Publications:** *Caring*, monthly. • *Homecare News*, monthly. • *Hospice Forum*, biweekly. • *NAHC Report*, weekly. • *National Home Care and Hospice Directory*, biennial (with alternate year supplement). **Facsimile Number:** (202)547-3540.

Periodicals

★3143★
AAHA Provider News
American Association of Homes for the Aging (AAHA)
1129 20th St. NW, Ste. 400
Washington, DC 20036-3489   Phone: (202)296-5960
Editor(s): Jean E. Van Ryzin. 12/yr. Discusses topics concerning nonprofit homes and services for the aging, including legislative, regulatory, and judicial developments in long-term care and housing; issues in the field of gerontology; and new developments in alternative services for the aging. Publicizes association events, services and growth, membership accomplishments, and professional opportunities. Recurring features include columns titled Job Mart, Health Issues Conferences, Employer Tips, Trends, and Housing Issues.

★3144★
Adult Day Care Quarterly
National Institute on Adult Daycare (NIAD)
National Council on the Aging
600 Maryland Ave. SW
Washington, DC 20024   Phone: (202)479-1200
Editor(s): Dorothy K. Howe. Quarterly. Meant to assist administrators, planners, and program directors to better serve older, health-impaired adults in day care centers. Supplies programmatic, administrative, and legislative information. Recurring features include Institute news, notices of publications available, news of research and of members, and book reviews.

★3145★
AHEA Action
American Home Economics Assn.
1555 King St.
Alexandria, VA 22314   Phone: (703)706-4600
Marjorie Dahlin, Editor. 5x/yr. Home economics magazine. **Facsimile Number:** (703)706-Home.

★3146★
Caring (NAHC)
National Association for Home Care (NAHC)
519 C St. NE
Stanton Park
Washington, DC 20002   Phone: (202)547-7424
Monthly. Magazine.

★3147★
Home Health Line
Karen #Rak
PO Box 250
Port Republic, MD 20676   Phone: (301)535-4103
Editor(s): Karen Rak. Weekly. Reports on national and state issues, legislation, and regulation affecting home health care. Specifically concerned with federal funding and Medicare programs, hospice care, durable medical equipment, discharge planning, and the home health/home care industry as a business. **Facsimile Number:** (301)535-0632.

★3148★
Homecare News (NAHC)
National Association for Home Care (NAHC)
519 C St. NE
Stanton Park
Washington, DC 20002   Phone: (202)547-7424
Monthly. Tabloid covering association news and serving as an information exchange between state associations and providers and suppliers of products and services to the home health care industry.

★3149★
Hospice Forum (NAHC)
National Association for Home Care (NAHC)
519 C St. NE
Stanton Park
Washington, DC 20002   Phone: (202)547-7424
Biweekly. Newsletter covering legislative and research news.

★3150★
NAHC Report (NAHC)
National Association for Home Care (NAHC)
519 C St. NE
Stanton Park
Washington, DC 20002   Phone: (202)547-7424
Weekly. Newsletter covering legislative and regulatory issues related to the home health care industry. Contains employment opportunity listings.

Meetings and Conventions

★3151★
American Association for Continuity of Care Annual Conference
American Association for Continuity of Care
720 Light St.
Baltimore, MD 21230-3850   Phone: (301)837-1600
Frequency: Always held in September or October. 1992; Sep. 19-23; Las Vegas, NV • 1993; Sep. 22-26; Lake Buena Vista, FL. **Facsimile Number:** (301)752-8295.

★3152★
National Association for Home Care Annual Meeting and Home Care Exhibition
National Association for Home Care
519 C St., NE
Washington, DC 20002   Phone: (202)547-7424
1992; Sep. 30 - Oct. 03; New Orleans, LA • 1993; Oct. 18-23; San Diego, CA • 1994; • 1995; Oct. 07-11; San Francisco, CA. **Facsimile Number:** (202)547-3540.

★3153★
National Home Health Care Exposition
SEMCO Productions
1130 Hightower Trail
Atlanta, GA 30350-2910   Phone: (404)641-8181
Frequency: Always held at the Georgia World Congress Center in Atlanta. 1992; Nov. 19-21; Atlanta, GA • 1993; Nov. 18-20; Atlanta, GA. **Toll-free/Additional Phone Number(s):** 800-635-6657. **Facsimile Number:** (404)642-4715.

Janitors and Cleaners

Janitors or cleaners—also called building custodians—keep office buildings, hospitals, stores, apartment houses, hotels, and other types of buildings clean and in good condition. Some janitors can only do cleaning; others have a wide range of duties. Custodians work in every type of establishment. About 20 percent work in a school, including colleges and universities. Twenty percent work for a firm supplying building maintenance services on a contract basis. Ten percent work in a hotel and another 10 percent in a hospital. Others were employed by restaurants, operators of apartment buildings, office buildings, and other types of real estate, churches and other religious organizations, manufacturing firms, and government agencies.

$alaries

Average weekly earnings of janitors and cleaners are as follows:

Lowest 10 percent	$145.00/week or less
Middle 10 percent	$185.00—$325.00/week
Top 10 percent	$425.00/week or more

Employment Outlook

Growth rate until the year 2000: Average.

Janitors and Cleaners

Career Guides

★3154★
"Building Custodian" in *Exploring Nontraditional Jobs for Women* (pp. 99-105)
Rosen Publishing Group, Inc.
29 E. 21st St.
New York, NY 10010   Phone: (212)777-3017
Rose Neufeld. 1989. Describes blue-collar, male dominated occupations. Discusses what is done on the job, training, where to apply for jobs, tools used, salaries, and advantages and disadvantages. Relates the experiences of women who are working in the field.

★3155★
"Building Custodian" in *Personal Services* (pp. 21-25)
Franklin Watts, Inc.
387 Park Avenue, S.
New York, NY 10016   Phone: (212)686-7070
Linda Barrett and Galen Guengerich. 1991. Surveys personal services jobs. Describes job duties, educational preparation, salaries, and employment outlook. Offers job hunting advice.

★3156★
"Building Custodian" in *Public and Community Services*, Volume 11 of *Career Information Center* (pp. 41-42)
Glencoe/Macmillan
15319 Chatsworth St.
Mission Hills, CA 91345   Phone: (818)898-1391
Richard Lidz and Dale Anderson, editorial directors. Fourth edition, 1990. For 600 occupations, describes job duties, entry-level requirements, education and training needed, advancement possibilities, employment outlook, earnings and benefits. The set is divided into 12 volumes. Each volume includes jobs related under a broad career field. Volume 13 is the index. **Facsimile Number:** 818-365-5489.

★3157★
"Custodial Workers" in *The American Almanac of Jobs and Salaries* (p. 530)
Avon Books
105 Madison Avenue
New York, NY 10016   Phone: (212)481-5600
John Wright and Edward J. Dwyer. Revised and updated, 1990. A comprehensive guide to the wages of hundreds of occupations in a wide variety of industries and organizations.

★3158★
"Custodian" in *Occu-Facts: Information on 565 Careers in Outline Form* (p. 13.28, 13.29)
Careers, Inc.
P.O. Box 135
1211 Tenth St., S.W.
Largo, FL 33640   Phone: (813)584-7333
Elizabeth Handville. Biennial, 1989-90 edition. Each one-page occupational profile describes duties, working conditions, physical surroundings and demands, aptitudes, temperament, educational requirements, employment outlook, earnings, and places of employment.

★3159★
Custodian, Building
Careers, Inc.
PO Box 135
Largo, FL 34649-0135   Phone: (813)584-7333
1990. Two-page job guide card describing duties, working conditions, personal qualifications, training, earnings and hours, employment outlook, places of employment, related careers and where to write for more information.

★3160★
Custodians
Chronicle Guidance Publications, Inc.
PO Box 1190
Moravia, NY 13118-1190   Phone: (315)497-0330
1988. This career brief describes the nature of the work, working conditions, hours and earnings, education and training, licensure, certification, unions, personal qualifications, social and psychological factors, employment outlook, entry methods, advancement, and related occupations. **Toll-free/Additional Phone Number(s):** 800-622-7284.

★3161★
"Hotel, Motel Cleaner" in *Occu-Facts: Information on 565 Careers in Outline Form* (p. 13.27)
Careers, Inc.
P.O. Box 135
1211 Tenth St., S.W.
Largo, FL 33640   Phone: (813)584-7333
Elizabeth Handville. Biennial, 1989-90 edition. Each one-page occupational profile describes duties, working conditions, physical surroundings and demands, aptitudes, temperament, educational requirements, employment outlook, earnings, and places of employment.

★3162★
Inside the Janitorial Business: How to Start from Scratch & Succeed in Professional Cleaning
MBM Books
PO Box 1087
Valley Center, CA 92082   Phone: (619)749-2380

Frederick R. Massey. Second edition, 1989.

★3163★
"Janitor" in *VGM's Careers Encyclopedia* (pp. 235-236)
National Textbook Co.
4255 W. Touhy Ave.
Lincolnwood, IL 60646   Phone: (312)679-5500

Third edition, 1991. Contains two- to five-page descriptions of 200 managerial, professional, technical, trade, and service occupations. Each profile includes job duties, places of employment, qualifications, educational preparation, training, employment potential, advancement, income, and additional sources of information.

★3164★
"Janitors and Cleaners" in *Occupational Outlook Handbook* (pp. 315-316)
Superintendent of Documents
U.S. Government Printing Office
Washington, DC 20402   Phone: (202)783-3238

Biennial; latest edition, 1990-91. Encyclopedia of careers describing more than 250 occupations and comprising about 86 percent of all jobs in the economy. Occupations that require lengthy education or training are given the most attention. For each occupation, the handbook describes job duties, working conditions, training, educational preparation, personal qualities, advancement possibilities, job outlook, earnings, and sources of additional information.

★3165★
"Janitors and Cleaners" in Volume 3 of *Career Discovery Encyclopedia* (pp. 164-165)
J.G. Ferguson Publishing Co.
200 W. Monroe
Chicago, IL 60606   Phone: (312)580-5480

E. Russell Primm, editor-in-chief. 1990. Contains two-page articles on 504 occupations. Each article describes job duties, earnings, and educational and training requirements.

★3166★
"Janitors and Cleaners" in Volume 3 of *The Encyclopedia of Careers and Vocational Guidance* (pp. 271-273)
J.G. Ferguson Publishing Co.
200 W. Monroe
Chicago, IL 60606   Phone: (312)580-5480

William E. Hopke, editor-in-chief. Eighth edition, 1990. Four-volume set that profiles 500 occupations and describes job trends in 76 industries. Includes career description, educational requirements, history of the job, methods of entry, advancement, employment outlook, earnings, working conditions, social and psychological factors, and sources of additional information.

─────────── **Associations** ───────────

★3167★
Building Service Contractors Association International (BSCAI)
10201 Lee Hwy., Ste. 225
Fairfax, VA 22030   Phone: (703)359-7090

Membership: Firms and corporations in 40 countries engaged in contracting building maintenance services including the provision of labor, purchasing materials, and janitorial cleaning and maintenance of a building or its surroundings; associate members are manufacturers of cleaning supplies and equipment. **Purpose:** Seeks to provide a unified voice for building service contractors and to promote increased recognition by government, property owners, and the general business and professional public. Conducts continuing study and action, through committees and special task groups on areas such as public affairs, costs and ratios, uniform accounting, industrial relations and personnel, marketing and sales, contract improvement, research and planning, materials and supplies sources, group insurance, management training, statistics collection, safety, and insurance costs. Has developed a certification program for building service executives, and a registration program for building service managers. **Publications:** *BSCA Insurance Advisor*, quarterly. • *Building Service Contractors Association International—Services*, monthly. • *Information Central Guide*, annual. • *Who's Who in Building Service Contracting*, annual. • Also publishes management and technical monographs; makes available videotape training programs. **Toll-free/Additional Phone Number(s):** (800)368-3414 (United States only). **Facsimile Number:** (703)352-0493.

★3168★
National Executive Housekeepers Association (N.E.H.A.)
1001 Eastwind Dr., Ste. 301
Westerville, OH 43081   Phone: (614)895-7166

Membership: Persons engaged in institutional housekeeping management in hospitals, hotels and motels, schools, and industrial establishments. **Purpose:** Has established educational standards. Sponsors certificate and collegiate degree programs. Holds annual National Housekeepers Week celebration during the second week in September. Created the N.E.H.A. Educational Foundation to allocate financial awards to recognized schools to assist students in institutional housekeeping. Maintains referral service. **Publications:** *Executive Housekeeping Today*, monthly. • *Shop Talk*, quarterly. **Facsimile Number:** (614)895-1248.

─────────── **Standards/Certification Agencies** ───────────

★3169★
Building Service Contractors Association International (BSCAI)
10201 Lee Hwy., Ste. 225
Fairfax, VA 22030   Phone: (703)359-7090

Has developed a certification program for building service executives, and a registration program for building service managers.

★3170★
National Executive Housekeepers Association (N.E.H.A.)
1001 Eastwind Dr., Ste. 301
Westerville, OH 43081   Phone: (614)895-7166

Has established educational standards. Sponsors certificate and collegiate degree programs.

─────────── **Test Guides** ───────────

★3171★
Career Examination Series
National Learning Corp.
212 Michael Dr.
Syosset, NY 11791   Phone: (516)921-8888

Jack Rudman. This study guide series from National Learning Corp. provides practice questions and answers for many

Janitors and Cleaners

occupations, including Assistant Building Custodian, Assistant Custodian, Assistant Head Custodian, Chief Housekeeper, Chief Custodian, Building Maintenance Custodian (USPS), Building Maintenance Foreman, Head Janitor, Housekeeper, Housing Caretaker, Principal Custodial Foreman, Senior Building Custodian, Senior Housekeeper, Window Cleaner, and Custodial Assistants, Laborers, Workers, and Supervisors. All examination guides in this series contain questions with answers. **Facsimile Number:** (516)921-8743. **Toll-free/Additional Phone Number(s):** 800-645-6337.

★3172★
Civil Service Tests for Basic Skills Jobs
Prentice Hall Press
Simon & Schuster Inc.
200 Old Tappan Rd.
Old Tappan, NJ 07675   Phone: (800)223-2348
Hy Hammer. First edition, 1985. Contains nine sample examinations to prepare candidates for entry-level positions that include hospital attendant, building groundskeeper, and custodial assistant, among others.

★3173★
Janitorial & Maintenance Examinations
Ken Books
56 Midcrest Way
San Francisco, CA 94131   Phone: (415)826-6550
Harry W. Koch. Second edition, 1975.

★3174★
Maintenance (Custodial) Branch Initial-Level Supervisor Examination (U.S.P.S.)
National Learning Corp.
212 Michael Dr.
Syosset, NY 11791   Phone: (516)921-8888
Jack Rudman. 1989. Part of Career Examination Series.

Educational Directories and Programs

★3175★
Instructors Guide to Comprehensive Custodial Training Programs
Cleaning Consultant Services, Inc.
1512 Western Ave.
Seattle, WA 98101   Phone: (206)284-9954
William R. Griffin. 1977.

Awards, Scholarships, Grants, and Fellowships

★3176★
Executive Housekeeper of the Year
National Executive Housekeepers Association
1001 Eastwind Dr., Ste. 301
Westerville, OH 43081   Phone: (614)895-7166
For recognition of achievement. Members of the Society are eligible. A plaque and recognition in the national publication are awarded annually in August. Established in 1984 by Zimmerman and Leonard, the Association's publisher.

★3177★
Roomkeeper of the Year
American Hotel and Motel Association
c/o Mercedes McDonnel
1201 New York Ave., N.W.
Washington, DC 20005-3917   Phone: (202)289-3133
To provide managers, owners, and executive housekeepers with the opportunity to reward a staff person for exceptional service that they have rendered to a guest, the management, or the community. The award is limited to non-supervisory (housekeeping) employees of Association member properties. The entry deadline is November 30. Prizes include a commemorative plaque, a U.S. Savings Bond, travel expenses to the Association's convention, and a blazer from the Career Fashions Coordinate Collection, Angelica Uniform Group, Angelica Corporations. Awarded annually. Established in 1976. Sponsored by Angelica Corporations.

Basic Reference Guides and Handbooks

★3178★
BSCAI Information Central Guide (BSCAI)
Building Service Contractors Association International (BSCAI)
10201 Lee Hwy., Ste. 225
Fairfax, VA 22030   Phone: (703)359-7090
Annual.

★3179★
The Complete Custodial Handbook
Prentice Hall
Rte. 9W
Englewood Cliffs, NJ 07632   Phone: (201)592-2000
William R. Griffin. 1989.

★3180★
The Comprehensive Custodial Training Manual
Cleaning Consultant Services, Inc.
1512 Western Ave.
Seattle, WA 98101   Phone: (206)284-9954
Cleaning Consultant Services, Inc. Staff. 1980.

★3181★
Custodial Methods and Procedures Manual
Association of School Business Officials International
11401 N. Shore Dr.
Reston, VA 22090   Phone: (703)478-0405
1986.

★3182★
Supervisors' Guide to Successful Training
Cleaning Consultant Services, Inc.
1512 Western Ave.
Seattle, WA 98101   Phone: (206)284-9954
William R. Griffin. 1977.

★3183★
Vacuum Cleaners Supplies & Parts Directory
American Business Directories, Inc.
American Business Information, Inc.
5711 S. 86th Circle
Omaha, NE 68127   Phone: (402)593-4600
Annual. 1,327. Entries include: Name, address, phone, size of advertisement, name of owner or manager, number of employees, year first in "Yellow Pages." Arrangement: Geographical. **Facsimile Number:** (402)331-1505.

★3184★
Vacuum Cleaning Systems Directory
American Business Directories, Inc.
American Business Information, Inc.
5711 S. 86th Circle
Omaha, NE 68127   Phone: (402)593-4600
Annual. 1,795. Entries include: Name, address, phone, size of advertisement, name of owner or manager, number of employees, year first in "Yellow Pages." Arrangement: Geographical. **Facsimile Number:** (402)331-1505.

Periodicals

★3185★
BSCA Insurance Advisor (BSCAI)
Building Service Contractors Association International (BSCAI)
10201 Lee Hwy., Ste. 225
Fairfax, VA 22030   Phone: (703)359-7090
Quarterly. Membership newsletter covering insurance and risk management.

★3186★
Building Service Contractors Association International—Services (BSCAI)
Building Service Contractors Association International (BSCAI)
10201 Lee Hwy., Ste. 225
Fairfax, VA 22030   Phone: (703)359-7090
Monthly. Trade magazine including calendar of events, classified ads, new product information, new members, industry promotions and appointments, new literature on the industry, legal issues, legislation and regulations, floor and carpet care, and specialty services columns.

★3187★
Building Services Contractor
PTN Publishing Co.
445 Broad Hollow Rd.
Melville, NY 11747-3601
Frank Falcetta, Editor. 6x/yr. Magazine providing information on building cleaning and maintenance.

★3188★
Executive Housekeeping Today (N.E.H.A.)
National Executive Housekeepers Association (N.E.H.A.)
1001 Eastwind Dr., Ste. 301
Westerville, OH 43081   Phone: (614)895-7166
Monthly. Magazine primarily for management executives of the health care and hospitality industries; also includes association news. Contains membership profiles, certification of members, and advertisers index.

★3189★
Installation & Cleaning Specialist
Specialist Publications, Inc.
17835 Ventura Blvd., Ste. 312
Encino, CA 91316   Phone: (818)345-3550
Howard Olansky, Editor and Publisher. Monthly. Trade magazine for floor covering installers, workrooms, contractors, installing retailers, cleaning and maintenance firms, and distributors. **Facsimile Number:** (818)344-9647.

★3190★
Sanitary Maintenance
Trade Press Publishing Corp.
2100 W. Florist Ave.
Milwaukee, WI 53209   Phone: (414)228-7701
Ron Gillette, Mng. Editor. Monthly. Magazine for sanitary supply distributors and building service contracto **Facsimile Number:** (414)228-1134.

★3191★
Services
Building Service Contractors Assn. Int'l.
10201 Lee Hwy., Ste. 225
Fairfax, VA 22030   Phone: (703)359-7090
Robert E. Simanski, Editor. Monthly. Trade journal for maintenance and cleaning contractors. Facsimile Number: (703)352-0493.

★3192★
Shop Talk (N.E.H.A.)
National Executive Housekeepers Association (N.E.H.A.)
1001 Eastwind Dr., Ste. 301
Westerville, OH 43081   Phone: (614)895-7166
Quarterly. Newsletter containing compliance information and news on book sales.

Other Sources of Information

★3193★
An Analysis of Janitor Service in Elementary Schools
AMS Press, Inc.
56 E. 13th St.
New York, NY 10003   Phone: (212)777-4700
Charles E. Reeves. Part of Columbia University. Teachers College. Contributions to Education Series. **Facsimile Number:** (212)995-5413.

Private Household Workers

Most household workers are general houseworkers and usually the only worker performing home management services in the home. Household workers whose primary responsibility is taking care of children are called childcare workers. Those employed on an hourly basis are usually called babysitters. Those who are in charge of infants are sometimes called infant nurses or nannies. Tutors or governesses look after older children. Those who assist elderly, handicapped, or convalescent people are called companions or personal attendants. Households with a large staff may include a housekeeper or a butler, a cook, a caretaker, and a launderer. Housekeepers and butlers hire, supervise, and coordinate the work of the household staff and keep the household running smoothly. Cooks plan and prepare meals, clean the kitchen, order groceries and supplies, and may also serve meals. Caretakers do heavy housework and general home maintenance. More than 50 percent are general houseworkers, mostly dayworkers. About 40 percent are childcare workers, including babysitters. About 6 percent are housekeepers, butlers, cooks, and launderers.

$alaries

Some full-time live-in housekeepers or butlers, nannies, and governesses earn much higher wages than full-time private household workers and cleaners. Median weekly earnings for full-time household workers are as follows:

Private household workers	$140.00/week
Cleaners	$160.00/week
Childcare workers	$119.00/week

Employment Outlook

Growth rate until the year 2000: Slower than average.

Private Household Workers

―――― **Career Guides** ――――

★3194★
American Nanny
TAN Press
PO Box 3721
Georgetown Station
Washington, DC 20007
Robin D. Rice. 1985. Written for the person interested in hiring a nanny. Covers qualifications, job description, employment outlook, and advantages and disadvantages. Lists nanny schools.

★3195★
"Baby-sitting: Caring for Children in Their Home" in *Exploring Careers in Child Care Services* (pp. 1-8)
Rosen Publishing Group, Inc.
29 E. 21st St.
New York, NY 10010   Phone: (212)777-3017
Jean Ispa, Elizabeth Vemer, and Janis Logan. Revised edition, 1990. Covers occupations working with children including those requiring no education and training to those that require advanced training; from babysitting to program director. Describes the work and a typical work day, employment outlook, advantages and disadvantages, and personal characteristics needed for success in the field. Offers job hunting advice.

★3196★
Becoming a Helper
Brooks/Cole Publishing Co.
511 Forest Lodge Rd.
Pacific Grove, CA 93950-5098   Phone: (408)373-0728
Marianne Schneider Corey. 1989. **Facsimile Number:** (408)375-6414.

★3197★
"Companion" in *Consumer, Homemaking, and Personal Services*, Volume 5 of *Career Information Center* (pp. 38-40)
Glencoe/Macmillan
15319 Chatsworth St.
Mission Hills, CA 91345   Phone: (818)898-1391
Richard Lidz and Dale Anderson, editorial directors. Fourth edition, 1990. For 600 occupations, describes job duties, entry-level requirements, education and training needed, advancement possibilities, employment outlook, earnings and benefits. The set is divided into 12 volumes. Each volume includes jobs related under a broad career field. Volume 13 is the index. **Facsimile Number:** 818-365-5489.

★3198★
Cook, Domestic Service
Careers, Inc.
PO Box 135
Largo, FL 34649-0135   Phone: (813)584-7333
1990. Two-page job guide card describing duties, working conditions, personal qualifications, training, earnings and hours, employment outlook, places of employment, related careers and where to write for more information.

★3199★
"Domestic Housekeeper" in *Consumer, Homemaking, and Personal Services*, Volume 5 of *Career Information Center* (pp. 48-49)
Glencoe/Macmillan
15319 Chatsworth St.
Mission Hills, CA 91345   Phone: (818)898-1391
Richard Lidz and Dale Anderson, editorial directors. Fourth edition, 1990. For 600 occupations, describes job duties, entry-level requirements, education and training needed, advancement possibilities, employment outlook, earnings and benefits. The set is divided into 12 volumes. Each volume includes jobs related under a broad career field. Volume 13 is the index. **Facsimile Number:** 818-365-5489.

★3200★
"Domestic Service Cook" in *Occu-Facts: Information on 565 Careers in Outline Form* (p. 13.1)
Careers, Inc.
P.O. Box 135
1211 Tenth St., S.W.
Largo, FL 33640   Phone: (813)584-7333
Elizabeth Handville. Biennial, 1989-90 edition. Each one-page occupational profile describes duties, working conditions, physical surroundings and demands, aptitudes, temperament, educational requirements, employment outlook, earnings, and places of employment.

★3201★
House Cleaner
Vocational Biographies, Inc.
PO Box 31, Dept. VF10
Sauk Centre, MN 56378   Phone: (612)352-6516
1988. This pamphlet profiles a person working in the job. Includes information about job duties, working conditions, places of employment, educational preparation, labor market outlook, and salaries. **Toll-free/Additional Phone Number(s):** 800-255-0752.

★3202★
Household Service Workers
Chronicle Guidance Publications, Inc.
PO Box 1190
Moravia, NY 13118-1190 Phone: (315)497-0330
1987. This career brief describes the nature of the work, working conditions, hours and earnings, education and training, licensure, certification, unions, personal qualifications, social and psychological factors, employment outlook, entry methods, advancement, and related occupations. **Toll-free/Additional Phone Number(s):** 800-622-7284.

★3203★
Household Worker
Careers, Inc.
PO Box 135
Largo, FL 34649-0135 Phone: (813)584-7333
1989. Two-page job guide card describing duties, working conditions, personal qualifications, training, earnings and hours, employment outlook, places of employment, related careers and where to write for more information.

★3204★
"Household Worker" in *Occu-Facts: Information on 565 Careers in Outline Form* (p. 13.2)
Careers, Inc.
P.O. Box 135
1211 Tenth St., S.W.
Largo, FL 33640 Phone: (813)584-7333
Elizabeth Handville. Biennial, 1989-90 edition. Each one-page occupational profile describes duties, working conditions, physical surroundings and demands, aptitudes, temperament, educational requirements, employment outlook, earnings, and places of employment.

★3205★
Houseman
Vocational Biographies, Inc.
PO Box 31, Dept. VF10
Sauk Centre, MN 56378 Phone: (612)352-6516
1988. This pamphlet profiles a person working in the job. Includes information about job duties, working conditions, places of employment, educational preparation, labor market outlook, and salaries. **Toll-free/Additional Phone Number(s):** 800-255-0752.

★3206★
Nannies
Chronicle Guidance Publications, Inc.
PO Box 1190
Moravia, NY 13118-1190 Phone: (315)497-0330
1988. This career brief describes the nature of the work, working conditions, hours and earnings, education and training, licensure, certification, unions, personal qualifications, social and psychological factors, employment outlook, entry methods, advancement, and related occupations. **Toll-free/Additional Phone Number(s):** 800-622-7284.

★3207★
"Nannies" in Volume 4 of *Career Discovery Encyclopedia* (pp. 118-119)
J.G. Ferguson Publishing Co.
200 W. Monroe
Chicago, IL 60606 Phone: (312)580-5480
E. Russell Primm, editor-in-chief. 1990. Contains two-page articles on 504 occupations. Each article describes job duties, earnings, and educational and training requirements.

★3208★
"Nannies" in Volume 3 of *The Encyclopedia of Careers and Vocational Guidance* (pp. 284-288)
J.G. Ferguson Publishing Co.
200 W. Monroe
Chicago, IL 60606 Phone: (312)580-5480
William E. Hopke, editor-in-chief. Eighth edition, 1990. Four-volume set that profiles 500 occupations and describes job trends in 76 industries. Includes career description, educational requirements, history of the job, methods of entry, advancement, employment outlook, earnings, working conditions, social and psychological factors, and sources of additional information.

★3209★
"Nanny" in *Consumer, Homemaking, and Personal Services*, Volume 5 of *Career Information Center* (pp. 87-89)
Glencoe/Macmillan
15319 Chatsworth St.
Mission Hills, CA 91345 Phone: (818)898-1391
Richard Lidz and Dale Anderson, editorial directors. Fourth edition, 1990. For 600 occupations, describes job duties, entry-level requirements, education and training needed, advancement possibilities, employment outlook, earnings and benefits. The set is divided into 12 volumes. Each volume includes jobs related under a broad career field. Volume 13 is the index. **Facsimile Number:** 818-365-5489.

★3210★
"Nanny" in *Offbeat Careers: The Directory of Unusual Work* (pp. 102-103)
Ten Speed Press
PO Box 7123
Berkeley, CA 94707 Phone: (415)845-8414
Al Sacharov. 1988. Profiles eighty-eight unusual careers. Provides job description, history of occupation, salary, and training required. Lists one or more sources of additional information.

★3211★
"Private Child Care Worker" in *Consumer, Homemaking, and Personal Services*, Volume 5 of *Career Information Center* (pp. 36-38)
Glencoe/Macmillan
15319 Chatsworth St.
Mission Hills, CA 91345 Phone: (818)898-1391
Richard Lidz and Dale Anderson, editorial directors. Fourth edition, 1990. For 600 occupations, describes job duties, entry-level requirements, education and training needed, advancement possibilities, employment outlook, earnings and benefits. The set is divided into 12 volumes. Each volume includes jobs related under a broad career field. Volume 13 is the index. **Facsimile Number:** 818-365-5489.

★3212★
"Private Household Worker" in *Personal Services* (pp. 15-19)
Franklin Watts, Inc.
387 Park Avenue, S.
New York, NY 10016 Phone: (212)686-7070
Linda Barrett and Galen Guengerich. 1991. Surveys personal services jobs. Describes job duties, educational preparation, salaries, and employment outlook. Offers job hunting advice.

Private Household Workers

★3213★
"Private Household Workers" in *Occupational Outlook Handbook* (pp. 316-317)
Superintendent of Documents
U.S. Government Printing Office
Washington, DC 20402   Phone: (202)783-3238

Biennial; latest edition, 1990-91. Encyclopedia of careers describing more than 250 occupations and comprising about 86 percent of all jobs in the economy. Occupations that require lengthy education or training are given the most attention. For each occupation, the handbook describes job duties, working conditions, training, educational preparation, personal qualities, advancement possibilities, job outlook, earnings, and sources of additional information.

★3214★
"Private Household Workers" in Volume 5 of *Career Discovery Encyclopedia* (pp. 88-89)
J.G. Ferguson Publishing Co.
200 W. Monroe
Chicago, IL 60606   Phone: (312)580-5480

E. Russell Primm, editor-in-chief. 1990. Contains two-page articles on 504 occupations. Each article describes job duties, earnings, and educational and training requirements.

★3215★
"Private Household Workers" in Volume 3 of *The Encyclopedia of Careers and Vocational Guidance* (pp. 302-305)
J.G. Ferguson Publishing Co.
200 W. Monroe
Chicago, IL 60606   Phone: (312)580-5480

William E. Hopke, editor-in-chief. Eighth edition, 1990. Four-volume set that profiles 500 occupations and describes job trends in 76 industries. Includes career description, educational requirements, history of the job, methods of entry, advancement, employment outlook, earnings, working conditions, social and psychological factors, and sources of additional information.

Associations

★3216★
American Council of Nanny Schools (ACNS)
c/o Joy Shelton
Delta Coll.
University Center, MI 48710   Phone: (517)686-9417

Membership: Schools involved in training programs for nannies. Purposes include: promoting professionalism of nannies and others in the field of child care; compiling information on nanny training programs and placement agencies available; establishing and maintaining a national competency test for nannies; creating standards for schools initiating nanny programs and providing a means for exchanging experiences in the curriculum. Maintains speakers' bureau and placement service; compiles statistics. **Publications:** *ACNewS*, 2/year. • Also publishes brochures on programs and placement.

★3217★
National Academy of Nannies, Inc. (NANI)
3300 E. 1st Ave., Ste. 520
Denver, CO 80206   Phone: (303)333-NANI

Purpose: Private training school for nannies. **Toll-free/Additional Phone Number(s):** (800)222-NANI. **Facsimile Number:** (303)333-9848.

Standards/Certification Agencies

★3218★
American Council of Nanny Schools (ACNS)
c/o Joy Shelton
Delta Coll.
University Center, MI 48710   Phone: (517)686-9417

Maintains a national competency test for nannies, and creates standards for schools initiating nanny programs.

Test Guides

★3219★
Domestic Worker
National Learning Corp.
212 Michael Dr.
Syosset, NY 11791   Phone: (516)921-8888

Jack Rudman. Part of the Career Examination Series No. 1. All examination guides in this series contain questions with answers. **Facsimile Number:** (516)921-8743. **Toll-free/Additional Phone Number(s):** 800-645-6337.

Periodicals

★3220★
ACNewS (ACNS)
American Council of Nanny Schools (ACNS)
c/o Joy Shelton
Delta Coll.
University Center, MI 48710   Phone: (517)686-9417

2/year. Newsletter providing information on child development, nutrition, health care, and other topics.

Meetings and Conventions

★3221★
National Executive Housekeepers Association Exposition
National Executive Housekeepers Association
1001 Eastwind Dr., Ste. 301
Westerville, OH 43081   Phone: (614)895-7166

1992; Aug. 16-20; Nashville, TN • 1994; Orlando, FL. **Facsimile Number:** (614)895-1248.

Agriculture, Forestry, Fishing, and Related Occupations

Farm Operators and Managers

Farm operators and managers in the United States direct the activities of one of the world's largest and most productive agricultural sectors. Farm operators may be farmer owners or tenant farmers (renters). On crop farms, farm operators are responsible for planning, tilling, planting, fertilizing, cultivating, spraying, and harvesting. After the harvest, they make sure that the crops are packaged, loaded, and promptly marketed or stored for resale. On livestock, dairy, and poultry farms, farm operators must plan, feed, and care for the animals and keep barns, pens, coops, and other farm buildings clean and in repair. They also oversee breeding, some slaughtering, and marketing activities. On horticultural specialty farms, farm operators oversee the production of ornamental plants, nursery products, and fruits and vegetables grown in greenhouses. In addition, farm operators must make many managerial decisions and perform tasks ranging from setting up and operating machinery to erecting fences and sheds. Farm managers handle some or all farm operations or oversee tenant operators. Most farm operators and managers handle crop production activities while others manage livestock production activities. A relatively small number are involved in agricultural services such as contract harvesting and farm labor contracting.

$alaries

Incomes vary greatly from year to year, since prices of farm products fluctuate depending upon weather conditions. Farm income also varies greatly depending upon the type and size of farm. Vegetable and melon, cotton, horticultural, specialty, and rice farms generate an average income of over $100,000. Cattle, general crop, corn, tobacco, and other livestock farms generate less than $15,000 in income.

  Farm managers   15,000—$30,000/year.

Employment Outlook

Growth rate until the year 2000: Slower than average.

Farm Operators and Managers

Career Guides

★3222★
Agricultural Cluster
Center for Humanities, Inc.
Communications Park
Box 1000
Mount Kisco, NY 10549   Phone: (914)666-4100
Videocassette. 1984. 20 mins. People who work in agriculture describe their daily work routines for students interested in entering this occupation.

★3223★
American Professionals Series
Cambridge Career Products
90 MacCorkle Ave., SW
South Charleston, WV 25311   Phone: (304)744-9323
Videocassette. 1984. 30 mins. In this series of twenty-one half hour programs, various occupations are examined in depth, including a day in the life of each worker. Included are: fireman, farmer, oil driller, fisherman, horse trainer, and auto assembly repairman.

★3224★
Career Summary: Farm Manager
American Society of Farm Managers and Rural Appriasers
950 S. Cherry St., Ste. 106
Denver, CO 80222   Phone: (303)758-3513
1984. This two-page leaflet describes the work of a farm manager, as well as working conditions, personal qualifications, training, and outlook.

★3225★
Crop Farming Occupations
Chronicle Guidance Publications, Inc.
PO Box 1190
Moravia, NY 13118-1190   Phone: (315)497-0330
1988. This career brief describes the nature of the work, working conditions, hours and earnings, education and training, licensure, certification, unions, personal qualifications, social and psychological factors, employment outlook, entry methods, advancement, and related occupations. **Toll-free/Additional Phone Number(s):** 800-622-7284.

★3226★
Dairy Farmer
Vocational Biographies, Inc.
PO Box 31, Dept. VF10
Sauk Centre, MN 56378   Phone: (612)352-6516
1989. This pamphlet profiles a person working in the job. Includes information about job duties, working conditions, places of employment, educational preparation, labor market outlook, and salaries. **Toll-free/Additional Phone Number(s):** 800-255-0752.

★3227★
Dairy Farmers
Chronicle Guidance Publications, Inc.
PO Box 1190
Moravia, NY 13118-1190   Phone: (315)497-0330
1988. This career brief describes the nature of the work, working conditions, hours and earnings, education and training, licensure, certification, unions, personal qualifications, social and psychological factors, employment outlook, entry methods, advancement, and related occupations. **Toll-free/Additional Phone Number(s):** 800-622-7284.

★3228★
"Dairy Farmers" in Volume 3 of The Encyclopedia of Careers and Vocational Guidance (pp. 338-341)
J.G. Ferguson Publishing Co.
200 W. Monroe
Chicago, IL 60606   Phone: (312)580-5480
William E. Hopke, editor-in-chief. Eighth edition, 1990. Four-volume set that profiles 500 occupations and describes job trends in 76 industries. Includes career description, educational requirements, history of the job, methods of entry, advancement, employment outlook, earnings, working conditions, social and psychological factors, and sources of additional information.

★3229★
"Dairy Farmers" in Volume 2 of Career Discovery Encyclopedia (pp. 78-79)
J.G. Ferguson Publishing Co.
200 W. Monroe
Chicago, IL 60606   Phone: (312)580-5480
E. Russell Primm, editor-in-chief. 1990. Contains two-page articles on 504 occupations. Each article describes job duties, earnings, and educational and training requirements.

★3230★
Employment Opportunities for College Graduates in Food and Agricultural Sciences: Agriculture, Natural Resources, and Veterinary Medicine
U.S. Department of Agriculture
Cooperative State Research Service
Higher Education Programs
Washington, DC 20250   Phone: (202)447-7854
1990. This 26-page booklet describes the labor market outlook for agriculture related careers, including farm operators and managers, from 1990 to 1995.

★3231★

VOCATIONAL CAREERS SOURCEBOOK, 1st Edition

★3231★
Enterprise Farming
Modern Talking Picture Service
5000 Park St. North
St. Petersburg, FL 33709　　　　　Phone: (813)541-7571

Videocassette. 1984. 20 mins. This program offers small entrepreneurial farming as a rewarding alternative occupation.

★3232★
"Farm Management" in *The Career Connection II: A Guide to Technical Majors and Their Related Careers* (pp. 55-56)
ERIS
PO Box 7509
University Station
Provo, UT 84602-0509

Fred A. Rowe. 1988. Contains technical majors, such as automotive technology. Describes the major and the job. Lists high school and postsecondary school courses. Includes occupations related to the major, employment outlook, and starting salary.

★3233★
Farm Manager
Careers, Inc.
PO Box 135
Largo, FL 34649-0135　　　　　Phone: (813)584-7333

1989. Two-page occupational summary card describing duties, working conditions, personal qualifications, training, earnings and hours, employment outlook, places of employment, related careers and where to write for more information.

★3234★
Farm Manager
Vocational Biographies, Inc.
PO Box 31, Dept. VF10
Sauk Centre, MN 56378　　　　　Phone: (612)352-6516

1990. This pamphlet profiles a person working in the job. Includes information about job duties, working conditions, places of employment, educational preparation, labor market outlook, and salaries. **Toll-free/Additional Phone Number(s):** 800-255-0752.

★3235★
"Farm Manager" in *Agribusiness, Environment, and Natural Resources*, Volume 2 of *Career Information Center* (pp. 107-108)
Glencoe/Macmillan
15319 Chatsworth St.
Mission Hills, CA 91345　　　　　Phone: (818)898-1391

Richard Lidz and Dale Anderson, editorial directors. Fourth edition, 1990. For 600 occupations, describes job duties, entry-level requirements, education and training needed, advancement possibilities, employment outlook, earnings and benefits. The set is divided into 12 volumes. Each volume includes jobs related under a broad career field. Volume 13 is the index. **Facsimile Number:** 818-365-5489.

★3236★
"Farm Manager" in *Top Professions: The 100 Most Popular, Dynamic, and Profitable Careers in America Today* (pp. 77-78)
Peterson's Guides, Inc.
202 Carnegie Center
PO Box 2123
Princeton, NJ 08543-2123　　　　　Phone: (609)243-9111

Nicholas Basta. 1989. Includes occupations requiring a college or advanced degree. Describes job duties, earnings, some typical job titles, career opportunities at different degree levels, and lists related associations.

★3237★
"Farm Operatives and Managers" in Volume 3 of *Career Discovery Encyclopedia* (pp. 12-13)
J.G. Ferguson Publishing Co.
200 W. Monroe
Chicago, IL 60606　　　　　Phone: (312)580-5480

E. Russell Primm, editor-in-chief. 1990. Contains two-page articles on 504 occupations. Each article describes job duties, earnings, and educational and training requirements.

★3238★
"Farm Operatives and Managers" in Volume 3 of *The Encyclopedia of Careers and Vocational Guidance* (pp. 350-354)
J.G. Ferguson Publishing Co.
200 W. Monroe
Chicago, IL 60606　　　　　Phone: (312)580-5480

William E. Hopke, editor-in-chief. Eighth edition, 1990. Four-volume set that profiles 500 occupations and describes job trends in 76 industries. Includes career description, educational requirements, history of the job, methods of entry, advancement, employment outlook, earnings, working conditions, social and psychological factors, and sources of additional information.

★3239★
"Farm Operators and Managers" in *Occupational Outlook Handbook* (pp. 318-320)
Superintendent of Documents
U.S. Government Printing Office
Washington, DC 20402　　　　　Phone: (202)783-3238

Biennial; latest edition, 1990-91. Encyclopedia of careers describing more than 250 occupations and comprising about 86 percent of all jobs in the economy. Occupations that require lengthy education or training are given the most attention. For each occupation, the handbook describes job duties, working conditions, training, educational preparation, personal qualities, advancement possibilities, job outlook, earnings, and sources of additional information.

★3240★
"Farmer" in *Agribusiness, Environment, and Natural Resources*, Volume 2 of *Career Information Center* (pp. 76-80, 108-117)
Glencoe/Macmillan
15319 Chatsworth St.
Mission Hills, CA 91345　　　　　Phone: (818)898-1391

Richard Lidz and Dale Anderson, editorial directors. Fourth edition, 1990. For 600 occupations, describes job duties, entry-level requirements, education and training needed, advancement possibilities, employment outlook, earnings and benefits. The set is divided into 12 volumes. Each volume includes jobs related under a broad career field. Volume 13 is the index. **Facsimile Number:** 818-365-5489.

★3241★
"Farmer" in *VGM's Careers Encyclopedia* (pp. 169-171)
National Textbook Co.
4255 W. Touhy Ave.
Lincolnwood, IL 60646　　　　　Phone: (312)679-5500

Third edition, 1991. Contains two- to five-page descriptions of 200 managerial, professional, technical, trade, and service occupations. Each profile includes job duties, places of employment, qualifications, educational preparation, training, employment potential, advancement, income, and additional sources of information.

Farm Operators and Managers

★3242★
Farmer, Cattle
Careers, Inc.
PO Box 135
Largo, FL 34649-0135   Phone: (813)584-7333
1992. Two-page occupational summary card describing duties, working conditions, personal qualifications, training, earnings and hours, employment outlook, places of employment, related careers and where to write for more information.

★3243★
Farmer, Dairy
Careers, Inc.
PO Box 135
Largo, FL 34649-0135   Phone: (813)584-7333
1991. Two-page occupational summary card describing duties, working conditions, personal qualifications, training, earnings and hours, employment outlook, places of employment, related careers and where to write for more information.

★3244★
Farmer, Fruit
Careers, Inc.
PO Box 135
Largo, FL 34649-0135   Phone: (813)584-7333
1989. Two-page occupational summary card describing duties, working conditions, personal qualifications, training, earnings and hours, employment outlook, places of employment, related careers and where to write for more information.

★3245★
Farmer, Poultry
Careers, Inc.
PO Box 135
Largo, FL 34649-0135   Phone: (813)584-7333
1991. Two-page occupational summary card describing duties, working conditions, personal qualifications, training, earnings and hours, employment outlook, places of employment, related careers and where to write for more information.

★3246★
Farmer, Vegetable Crops
Careers, Inc.
PO Box 135
Largo, FL 34649-0135   Phone: (813)584-7333
1992. Two-page occupational summary card describing duties, working conditions, personal qualifications, training, earnings and hours, employment outlook, places of employment, related careers and where to write for more information.

★3247★
Farmers
Careers, Inc.
PO Box 135
Largo, FL 34649-0135   Phone: (813)584-7333
1991. Eight-page brief offering the definition, history, duties, working conditions, personal qualifications, educational requirements, earnings, hours, employment outlook, advancement possibilities, and related occupations.

★3248★
"Farmers" in *Occu-Facts: Information on 565 Careers in Outline Form* (pp. 14.1, 14.2, 14.3, 14.5, 14.6, 14.7, 14.8)
Careers, Inc.
P.O. Box 135
1211 Tenth St., S.W.
Largo, FL 33640   Phone: (813)584-7333
Elizabeth Handville. Biennial, 1989-90 edition. Each one-page occupational profile describes duties, working conditions, physical surroundings and demands, aptitudes, temperament, educational requirements, employment outlook, earnings, and places of employment.

★3249★
"Farmers" in Volume 3 of *Career Discovery Encyclopedia* (pp. 10-11)
J.G. Ferguson Publishing Co.
200 W. Monroe
Chicago, IL 60606   Phone: (312)580-5480
E. Russell Primm, editor-in-chief. 1990. Contains two-page articles on 504 occupations. Each article describes job duties, earnings, and educational and training requirements.

★3250★
"Farmers" in Volume 3 of *The Encyclopedia of Careers and Vocational Guidance* (pp. 345-350)
J.G. Ferguson Publishing Co.
200 W. Monroe
Chicago, IL 60606   Phone: (312)580-5480
William E. Hopke, editor-in-chief. Eighth edition, 1990. Four-volume set that profiles 500 occupations and describes job trends in 76 industries. Includes career description, educational requirements, history of the job, methods of entry, advancement, employment outlook, earnings, working conditions, social and psychological factors, and sources of additional information.

★3251★
"Farmers and Farm Workers" in *The American Almanac of Jobs and Salaries* (pp. 540-542)
Avon Books
105 Madison Avenue
New York, NY 10016   Phone: (212)481-5600
John Wright and Edward J. Dwyer. Revised and updated, 1990. A comprehensive guide to the wages of hundreds of occupations in a wide variety of industries and organizations.

★3252★
Farmers, General
Chronicle Guidance Publications, Inc.
PO Box 1190
Moravia, NY 13118-1190   Phone: (315)497-0330
1987. This career brief describes the nature of the work, working conditions, hours and earnings, education and training, licensure, certification, unions, personal qualifications, social and psychological factors, employment outlook, entry methods, advancement, and related occupations. **Toll-free/Additional Phone Number(s):** 800-622-7284.

★3253★
Grain Farmer
Vocational Biographies, Inc.
PO Box 31, Dept. VF10
Sauk Centre, MN 56378   Phone: (612)352-6516
1990. This pamphlet profiles a person working in the job. Includes information about job duties, working conditions, places of employment, educational preparation, labor market

outlook, and salaries. **Toll-free/Additional Phone Number(s):** 800-255-0752.

★3254★
Stew Leonard's: Creating the Customer's Dream
United Learning, Inc.
6633 West Howard St.
Niles, IL 60648   Phone: (708)647-0600
Videocassette. 1990. 59 mins. Stew Leonard runs a huge dairy in Norwalk, Connecticut, and on this video he attributes his success primarily to the high level of customer service he delivers.

★3255★
There's a New "Challenge in Agriculture"
American Farm Bureau Federation
225 Touhy Ave.
Park Ridge, IL 60068   Phone: (312)399-5700
1991. This booklet surveys opportunities in farming and agriculture. Lists land grant colleges offering degree programs in agriculture. Includes a bibliography of sources for more information about careers in agriculture.

★3256★
Vocational Visions
Center for Humanities, Inc.
Communications Park
Box 1000
Mount Kisco, NY 10549   Phone: (914)666-4100
Videocassette. 1984. 30 mins. This series of programs explains key aspects of actual training and a day in the life of a worker in the specific field mentioned on the videocassette. Occupations include: transportation/mechanics, repair, construction, business/office occupations, health, and agriculture.

★3257★
Vocations U.S.A.
Info-Disc Corporation
4 Professional Dr.
Gaithersburg, MD 20879   Phone: (301)948-2300
Videocassette. 1987. 60 mins. A disc collection outlining the requirements and methods of various career areas. Occupations include: transportation, mechanical/repair, health, agriculture, and construction.

★3258★
When Do You Need a Professional, Accredited Farm Manager?
American Society of Farm Managers and Rural Appraisers
950 S. Cherry St., Ste. 106
Denver, CO 80222   Phone: (303)758-3513
Six-panel brochure describing the job duties and responsibilities of an accredited farm manager.

Associations

★3259★
American Farm Bureau Federation (AFBF)
225 Touhy Ave.
Park Ridge, IL 60068   Phone: (312)399-5700
Membership: Federation of 50 state farm bureaus and the Puerto Rico farm bureau, with membership on a family basis. **Purpose:** Analyzes problems of members and formulates action to achieve educational improvement, economic opportunity, and social advancement. Maintains speakers' bureau; sponsors specialized education program. Operates library. **Publications:** *Farm Bureau News*, weekly. **Facsimile Number:** (312)399-5896.

★3260★
American Forage and Grassland Council (AFGC)
PO Box 891
Georgetown, TX 78627
Membership: Federation of agricultural associations and individuals interested in grassland farming and dedicated to the production and utilization of quality forage. **Purpose:** Coordinates and distributes new information on grassland farming. Sponsors competitions; bestows awards. Maintains speakers' bureau.

★3261★
American Society of Farm Managers and Rural Appraisers (ASFMRA)
950 S. Cherry St., Ste. 106
Denver, CO 80222   Phone: (303)758-3513
Membership: Professional farm managers, appraisers, lenders, and researchers in farm and ranch management and/or rural appraisal. **Purpose:** Bestows registered ARA (Accredited Rural Appraiser) and AFM (Accredited Farm Manager) designations. Operates managing and appraisal schools, seminars, and conferences. Maintains placement service, biographical archives, and library. Presents the D. Howard Doane Award annually to a person who has contributed to agriculture and this profession. **Publications:** *American Society of Farm Managers and Rural Appraisers-General Membership Directory*, annual. ● *FMRA News*, 6/year. ● *Journal of the American Society of Farm Managers and Rural Appraisers*, semiannual. ● Also publishes *Rural Appraisal Manual* and *Farm Management Manual*. Telephone referral services. **Facsimile Number:** (303)758-0190.

★3262★
National FFA Organization (NFFAO)
Natl. FFA Center
Box 15160
5632 Mt. Vernon Memorial Hwy.
Alexandria, VA 22309-0160   Phone: (703)360-3600
Membership: Students of agriculture/agribusiness in public schools. **Purpose:** Organized under the National Vocational Education Act to foster character development, agricultural leadership, and responsible citizenship and to supplement training opportunities for students preparing for careers in farming and agribusiness. Works with youth specialists in approximately 38 countries. Star Farmer of America and Star Agribusinessman of America Awards of $2000 each are presented annually to two outstanding FFA members by the National FFA FND. Maintains Hall of Achievement and 1000 volume library on agricultural education. National FFA Alumni Association is supportive group. Sponsored by Agriculture/ Agribusiness and Natural Resources Staff of the Division of Vocational and Technical Education, U.S. Department of Education. **Publications:** *Between Issues*, bimonthly. ● *FFA Times*, annual. ● *National FFA Organization—Update*, monthly. ● *National FFA Convention Proceedings*, annual. ● *FFA New Horizons Magazine*, bimonthly. ● Also publishes instructional materials. **Facsimile Number:** (703)360-5524.

Standards/Certification Agencies

Professional status can be acquired through certification as an accredited farm manager by the American Society of Farm Managers and Rural Appraisers. Applicants must have several years' farm experience and the appropriate academic background—a bachelor's degree or preferably a master's degree in a field of agricultural science—and must pass courses and examinations relating to business, financial, and legal aspects of farm management.

Farm Operators and Managers

★3263★
American Society of Farm Managers and Rural Appraisers (ASFMRA)
950 S. Cherry St., Ste. 106
Denver, CO 80222   Phone: (303)758-3513
Bestows registered ARA (Accredited Rural Appraiser) and AFM (Accredited Farm Manager) designations. Operates managing and appraisal schools, seminars, and conferences.

★3264★
National Postsecondary Agricultural Student Organization (PAS)
Box 279
Cobleskill, NY 12043   Phone: (518)234-7309
Membership: Two-year agricultural educational institutions (70) and students (1200). **Purpose:** Promotes leadership experiences and assists students in job placement. Sponsors Speakers for Agriculture and Employment Interview and other college bowls and competitions. Bestows Agricultural Machinery Service Technician Award. Conducts Planning for Progress Project to recognize achievement by students. **Publications:** *Newsletter*, 3/year. • Also publishes handbook.

Awards, Scholarships, Grants, and Fellowships

★3265★
Agricultural Hall of Fame
Agricultural Hall of Fame and National Center
c/o Walt Vernon
630 N. 126 St.
Bonner Springs, KS 66012   Phone: (913)721-1075
To honor individuals who have helped make this nation great by their outstanding contributions to the establishment, development, advancement or improvement of agriculture in the United States. Farmers, farm women, farm leaders, teachers, scientists, inventors, governmental leaders and other individuals are eligible. Usually candidates must have been deceased at least ten years. A unanimous vote by the board of governors can declare a living person (or person deceased less than ten years) as an eligible candidate. Portraits of recipients are hung in the Hall of Honorees. Awarded only when merited. Established in 1960.

★3266★
Agricultural Machinery Service Technician Award
National Postsecondary Agricultural Student Organization
Box 279
Cobleskill, NY 12043   Phone: (518)234-7309

★3267★
Distinguished Dairy Cattle Breeder Award
Dairy Shrine
c/o Liz A. Henry
American Breeders Service
P.O. Box 459
DeForest, WI 53532
To recognize an outstanding dairy cattle breeder. Awarded annually. Established in 1973.

★3268★
Distinguished Service to Agriculture
American Society of Farm Managers and Rural Appraisers
c/o Deborah Long Hunt, Publications Editor
950 S. Cherry St., Ste. 106
Denver, CO 80222   Phone: (303)758-3513
To recognize individuals who have made contributions to agriculture. A plaque is awarded annually if merited. Established in 1974.

★3269★
D. Howard Doane Award
American Society of Farm Managers and Rural Appraisers
c/o Deborah Long Hunt, Publications Editor
950 S. Cherry St., Ste. 106
Denver, CO 80222   Phone: (303)758-3513
To recognize an individual who has made an outstanding contribution in the field of agriculture, with emphasis on farm management and rural appraising. Preference is given to members of the Society. A wood and metal plaque are awarded annually if merited. Established in 1951 in honor of D. Howard Doane, first president of the Society.

★3270★
Guest of Honor Award
Dairy Shrine
c/o Liz A. Henry
American Breeders Service
P.O. Box 459
DeForest, WI 53532
To recognize contemporary dairy leaders for outstanding accomplishments and contributions to the dairy industry. One individual is selected annually. Established in 1949.

★3271★
National Award for Agricultural Excellence
National Agri-Marketing Association
c/o Lorie R. North, Communications Manager
12345 W. 95th St., Ste. 204
Shawnee Mission, KS 66215   Phone: (913)492-0220
To recognize members of the agricultural community who have made major contributions to U.S agriculture in the following areas: science, technology, public service, agri-business, and the private sector. A monetary prize and plaque are presented, and the recipients' names are kept in a permanent repository at the University of Missouri-Columbia, Agricultural Building. Awarded annually. Established in 1981.

★3272★
Outstanding Grassland Farmer or Rancher Award
American Forage and Grassland Council
Route 2, Box 129
Belleville, PA 17004-9712   Phone: (717)935-2447
To recognize farmers, farm managers or ranchers who have done an exceptional job of forage crop production or grassland or range management and utilization. The state or Provincial Forage Council is responsible for nominating and selecting the winners. As many as ten farmers or ranchers in each state or province having a Forage Council affiliated with AFGC are eligible. Awarded annually at suitable functions as established by the state or provincial council, where feasible.

★3273★
Outstanding Young Farmer Awards
United States Jaycees
c/o Farren E. Bennett, Public Relations Manager
P.O. Box 7
Tulsa, OK 74121-0007   Phone: (918)584-2481
To foster better urban-rural relations by creating an understanding and interest in today's farmer, his professional

ability, and his problems as a world food supplier. Individuals between the ages of 18 and 35 are eligible. Each state participating in the awards program selects one state winner; the national organization then selects four national winners. Awarded annually. Established in 1954.

★3274★
Pioneer of the Year Award
Northwest Farm Managers Association
c/o David Watt
P.O. Box 5636
Fargo, ND 58105   Phone: (701)237-7466

For recognition of outstanding achievement and lifelong service to agriculture. Nominations are accepted from former winners, and present and former officers of the organization. A plaque is presented annually at the convention in February. Established in 1959.

★3275★
John O. Rowe Citizenship Award
American Milking Shorthorn Society
c/o Wendy Gimler
P.O. Box 449
Beloit, WI 53511-0449   Phone: (608)365-3332

To recognize outstanding service and contributions made by an individual for the Milking Shorthorn breed. Those involved in some way with the dairy industry are eligible. A plaque is awarded at the convention in April. Established in 1983 by Stuart and Lillian Rowe in memory of John O. Rowe, a California Milking Shorthorn breeder who possessed strong dairy skills. Additional information is available from J. Stuart Rowe, Rt. 1, Box 2800, Davis, CA 95616.

★3276★
Star Agribusinessman of America Award
National FFA Organization
Natl. FFA Center
Box 15160
5632 Mt. Vernon Memorial Hwy.
Alexandria, VA 22309-0160   Phone: (703)360-3600

Presented annually to outstanding FFA member by the National FFA Foundation; $2,000 award.

★3277★
Star Farmer of America
National FFA Organization
Natl. FFA Center
Box 15160
5632 Mt. Vernon Memorial Hwy.
Alexandria, VA 22309-0160   Phone: (703)360-3600

Presented annually to outstanding FFA member by the National FFA Foundation; $2,000 award.

★3278★
Wall of Honors
Agricultural Hall of Fame and National Center
c/o Walt Vernon
630 N. 126 St.
Bonner Springs, KS 66012   Phone: (913)721-1075

To honor individuals, clubs, associations and/or businesses that have contributed (financially or otherwise) to the success and development of the Agricultural Hall of Fame. Nominees may or may not have an agricultural background and may or may not be deceased. A certificate or plaque is awarded. A framed portrait and a brief description of the honoree's achievements and contributions are noted on the Wall of Honors, the official name of the place of induction.

Basic Reference Guides and Handbooks

★3279★
American Farmer
ESP, Inc.
1201 E. Johnson
Jonesboro, AR 72401   Phone: (501)935-3533
Ethel Cole. 1976.

★3280★
Conservation Gains in the Tax Reform Act
Natural Resources Defense Council
40 W. 20th St.
New York, NY 10011   Phone: (212)727-4412
Kaid Benfield. 1987.

★3281★
Farm Management Manual (ASFMRA)
American Society of Farm Managers and Rural Appraisers (ASFMRA)
950 S. Cherry St., Ste. 106
Denver, CO 80222   Phone: (303)758-3513

★3282★
Farmers As Hunters: The Implications of Sedentism
Cambridge University Press
40 W. 20th St.
New York, NY 10011   Phone: (212)924-3900
Susan Kent, editor. 1989. Part of New Directions in Archaeology Series. **Facsimile Number:** (212)691-3239.

★3283★
Rural Appraisal Manual (ASFMRA)
American Society of Farm Managers and Rural Appraisers (ASFMRA)
950 S. Cherry St., Ste. 106
Denver, CO 80222   Phone: (303)758-3513

Periodicals

★3284★
Aerial Applicator Farm, Forest & Fire
Drawer 2263
Santa Fe Springs, CA 90670   Phone: (213)948-3713
Robert G. Rosenblatt, Editor and Publisher. 9x/yr. Aerial agriculture and fire control.

★3285★
Ag Alert
California Farm Bureau Federation
1601 Exposition Blvd., No. FB9
Sacramento, CA 95815   Phone: (916)924-4140
Steve Adler, Editor. Weekly. Agricultural magazine (tabloid). **Facsimile Number:** (916)923-5318.

★3286★
AG Consultant
Meister Publishing Co.
37733 Euclid Ave.
Willoughby, OH 44094   Phone: (216)942-2000
Judy Ferguson, Editor. 9x/yr. Crop advisory magazine. **Facsimile Number:** (216)975-3447.

Farm Operators and Managers

★3287★
AG-PILOT International
Graphics Plus
405 Main St.
Mount Vernon, WA 98273   Phone: (206)336-9737
Tom J. Wood, Editor. Monthly. Magazine covering agricultural aviation. **Facsimile Number:** (206)336-2506.

★3288★
Agri-Equipment & Chemical
Columbia Publishing
2809A Fruitvale Blvd.
Yakima, WA 98907-1467   Phone: (509)248-2452
Ken Hodge, Editor. Monthly. Agriculture magazine. **Facsimile Number:** (509)248-4056.

★3289★
Agri Finance
6201 W. Howard St.
Niles, IL 60648   Phone: (708)647-1200
David Pelzer, Editor. 9x/yr. Trade magazine on agriculture banking, professional farm management, and crop consultant news and features. **Facsimile Number:** (708)647-7055.

★3290★
Agri News
PO Box 6118
Rochester, MN 55903-6118   Phone: (507)285-7600
Kelly J. Boldan, Editor. Weekly. Farm newspaper distributed in southern Minnesota, central Minnesota, and northeastern Iowa. **Facsimile Number:** (507)285-7666.

★3291★
Agri-News
Box 30755
Billings, MT 59107-0755   Phone: (406)259-5406
Rebecca K. Tescher, Editor. Weekly. Newspaper covering agriculture in Montana, northern Wyoming, and western North Dakota. **Facsimile Number:** (406)259-6888.

★3292★
Agri-View
700 E. State St.
Iola, WI 54990   Phone: (715)387-6366
Rick Groth, Publisher. 2x/wk. Agricultural newspaper for farmers with 100 acres or more. **Facsimile Number:** (715)387-6369.

★3293★
Agribusiness: An International Journal
John Wiley and Sons, Inc.
605 3rd Ave.
New York, NY 10158   Phone: (212)850-6133
Michael W. Woolverton, Managing Editor (602/978-7150). 6x/yr. International journal focusing on applied research in agribusiness, including agricultural inputs, agricultural production, commodity processing, food manufacturing, and food distribution. **Facsimile Number:** (212)850-6095.

★3294★
Agrichemical Age
ABC Publishing
2300 Clayton Rd., Ste. 1360
Concord, CA 94520   Phone: (415)687-1662
Len Richardson, Editor. Monthly. Magazine providing information on agricultural chemical uses and applications (three regional editions). **Facsimile Number:** (415)687-4945.

★3295★
Agricultural Aviation
National Agricultural Aviation Assn.
1005 E St. SE
Washington, DC 20003   Phone: (202)546-5722
Harold Collins, Editor and Publisher. 10x/yr. Magazine covering trends in the agricultural aviation industry. **Facsimile Number:** (202)546-5726.

★3296★
The Agricultural Education Magazine
1803 Rural Point Rd.
Mechanicsville, VA 23111   Phone: (804)225-2686
Philip Zurbrick, Editor. Monthly. Vocational agriculture education magazine.

★3297★
Agricultural Engineering
American Society of Agricultural Engineers
2950 Niles Rd.
Saint Joseph, MI 49085-9659   Phone: (616)429-0300
Denise Sicking, Editor. 6x/yr. Magazine covering technology for food and agriculture. **Facsimile Number:** (616)429-3852.

★3298★
Agricultural News
Madison County Extension Service
2980 Sentinel Heights Rd.
LaFayette, NY 13084   Phone: (315)677-3852
Robert C. Watson, Publisher and Advertising Manager. Monthly. Agricultural magazine covering farm information and local news. **Facsimile Number:** (315)677-3924.

★3299★
Agriculture & Food: An Abstract Newsletter
National Technical Information Service (NTIS)
U.S. Department of Commerce
5285 Port Royal Rd.
Springfield, VA 22161   Phone: (703)487-4630
Weekly. Publishes abstracts of reports on agricultural chemistry, agricultural equipment, facilities, and operations. Also covers agronomy, horticulture, and plant pathology; fisheries and aquaculture; animal husbandry and veterinary medicine; and food technology.

★3300★
AgriScience
Agrican Publishers, Inc.
151 Slater St., Ste. 907
Ottawa, ON, Canada K1P 5H4   Phone: (613)232-9459
John Watts, Editor/Advertising Manager. Monthly. Technical agriculture magazine. **Facsimile Number:** (619)594-5190.

★3301★
Agronomy Journal
American Society of Agronomy
677 S. Segoe Rd.
Madison, WI 53711   Phone: (608)273-8080
J.L. Hatfield, Editor. 6x/yr. Agriculture science trade journal. **Facsimile Number:** (608)273-2021.

★3302★
AgVenture
Wisconsin Farm Bureau Federation
PO Box 5550
Madison, WI 53705   Phone: (608)833-8070
Joyce Munz Hach, Editor. 6x/yr. Agriculture magazine.

★3303★
Agway Cooperator
Agway, Inc.
PO Box 4933
Syracuse, NY 13221 Phone: (315)449-6231
Jean C. Willis, Editor. 10x/yr. Membership magazine for farm cooperatives.

★3304★
AGWEEK
Grand Forks Herald, Inc.
PO Box 6008
113 N. 3rd St.
Grand Forks, ND 58206 Phone: (701)780-1230
Jim Durkin, Editor. Weekly. News magazine covering markets, prices, and global news affecting American farmers. **Facsimile Number:** (701)780-1188.

★3305★
American Agriculturist
2333 N. Triphammer Rd., No. 202
Ithaca, NY 14850-1011 Phone: (607)273-3507
Gordon L. Conklin, Editor. Monthly. Magazine on agriculture and home-making.

★3306★
American Beef Cattleman
Box 357
Allen, KS 66833 Phone: (316)528-3556
Hayes Walker, Editor and Publisher. Monthly. Newspaper (tabloid) for beef-cow/calf producers including test stations research reports. **Facsimile Number:** (913)841-6468.

★3307★
American Journal of Agricultural Economics
American Agricultural Economics Assn.
Business Office, Iowa State University
80 Heady Hall
Ames, IA 50011-1070 Phone: (515)294-8700
Peter J. Barry, Editor and Publisher. 5x/yr. Magazine on agriculture and resource economics. **Facsimile Number:** (515)294-1234.

★3308★
The Back Forty
Prairie West Publications
601 Dakota Ave.
PO Box 1018
Wahpeton, ND 58075 Phone: (701)642-1501
Patricia Estes, Editor. Monthly. Farm newspaper.

★3309★
BEEF
Webb Division, Intertec Publishing Corp.
7900 International Dr., Ste. 300
Minneapolis, MN 55425 Phone: (612)851-9329
Wayne Bollum, Publisher. Monthly. **Facsimile Number:** (612)851-4600.

★3310★
Beef Today
Farm Journal, Inc.
230 W. Washington Sq.
PO Box 478
Philadelphia, PA 19105 Phone: (215)829-4700
Bill Miller, Editor. Ten times/yr. Magazine for farmers and ranchers raising beef cows, feeders, and backgrounder cattle.

★3311★
Beefweek
Livestock Breeder Journal, Inc.
41A Monroe St.
PO Box 4264
Macon, GA 31208 Phone: (912)746-4465
John Jenkins, Editor. Monthly Livestock magazine.

★3312★
Between Issues (NFFAO)
National FFA Organization (NFFAO)
Natl. FFA Center
Box 15160
5632 Mt. Vernon Memorial Hwy.
Alexandria, VA 22309-0160 Phone: (703)360-3600
Bimonthly. Newsletter.

★3313★
Biodynamics
Biodynamic Farming & Gardening Association
PO Box 550
Kimberton, PA 19442-0550 Phone: (215)935-7797
Joel Morrow, Editor. Quarterly. Magazine on soil conservation, organic agriculture, and goethean science

★3314★
Brahman Journal
Sagebrush Publishing Co., Inc.
PO Box 220
Eddy, TX 76524 Phone: (817)859-5507
Joe Brockett, Editor. Monthly. Livestock and breed journal. **Facsimile Number:** (817)859-5451.

★3315★
Brangus Journal
5750 Epsilon
San Antonio, TX 78249 Phone: (512)696-4343
Ellen H. Godwin, Editor/Mgr. Monthly. Cattle breeding industry magazine. **Facsimile Number:** (512)696-8718.

★3316★
BUFFALO!
National Buffalo Assn.
4 E. Main St.
PO Box 580
Fort Pierre, SD 57532 Phone: (605)223-2829
Kim Dowling, Editor/Adminstrative Dir. Quarterly. Magazine serving ranchers, farmers, and others interested in the American buffalo.

★3317★
Business Farmer-Stockman
1617 Avenue A
Box 770
Scottsbluff, NE 69361 Phone: (308)635-2045
Penny Yekel, Publisher. Weekly (Fri.). Agricultural newspaper. **Facsimile Number:** (308)635-2348.

★3318★
Calavo Newsletter
Calavo Growers of California
PO Box 26081
Santa Ana, CA 92799-6081 Phone: (714)259-1166
Quarterly. Contains news about avocado production and marketing and the Calavo Growers of California. **Facsimile Number:** (714)259-1166.

Farm Operators and Managers

★3319★
CALF News Magazine Ltd.
11477 Hungate Rd.
Colorado Springs, CO 80908   Phone: (719)495-0303
Steve Dittmer, Editor and Publisher. Monthly. Magazine for commercial feedlot operators (1,000 head or more).

★3320★
Cattle Business
Mississippi Cattlemen's Assn.
121 N. Jefferson St.
Jackson, MS 39202   Phone: (601)354-8951
Sarah Groves, Mng. Editor. 10x/yr. Livestock magazine. **Facsimile Number:** (601)355-7128.

★3321★
Cattle Guard
Colorado Cattlemen's Assn.
Livestock Exchange Bldg., Rm. 220
Denver, CO 80216   Phone: (303)296-1114
Lisa Bard Field, Assn. News Editor. Monthly. Magazine covering cattle breeding and feeders. **Facsimile Number:** (303)296-1115.

★3322★
Cattlemen
Public Press
1760 Ellice Ave.
Winnipeg, MB, Canada R3H 0B6   Phone: (204)784-0300
Gren Winslow, Editor. Monthly. Magazine serving commercial beef producers. **Facsimile Number:** (204)775-9052.

★3323★
Charolais Banner
Charolais Banner, Ltd.
101A 1120 53rd Ave. NE
Calgary, AB, Canada T2E 6N9   Phone: (403)295-2292
Mark Kihn, Editor. Monthly. Trade magazine for breeders of purebred Charolais cattle. **Facsimile Number:** (403)275-3089.

★3324★
Citrus and Vegetable Magazine
1819 N. Franklin St.
PO Box 7595
Tampa, FL 33673-7595   Phone: (813)223-7628
E. Shaun Alderman, Editor. Monthly. Magazine serving citrus and vegetable growers, packers, and processors. **Facsimile Number:** (813)223-6878.

★3325★
Cooperative Farmer
Southern States Cooperative, Inc.
PO Box 26234
Richmond, VA 23260   Phone: (804)281-1317
Don R. Tindall, Editor/Advertising Mgr. 9x/yr. Agricultural magazine. **Facsimile Number:** (804)281-1141.

★3326★
Corn Farmer
Meredith Corp.
1716 Locust St.
Des Moines, IA 50336   Phone: (512)284-3000
James Cornick, Publisher. Quarterly. Magazine reporting current information on corn production. **Facsimile Number:** (512)284-2700.

★3327★
Cotton Farming
Little Publications, Inc.
6263 Poplar Ave., Ste. 540
Memphis, TN 38119   Phone: (901)767-4020
Patrick Shepard, Editor. 15x/yr. Agriculture trade magazine. **Facsimile Number:** (901)767-4026.

★3328★
Cotton Grower
7777 Walnut Grove Rd., Ste. OM-38
Memphis, TN 38119   Phone: (901)756-8822
Bill Spencer, Editor. Monthly. Magazine for commercial cotton growers throughout the U.S.

★3329★
Cotton Trade Report
New York Cotton Exchange
Four World Trade Center
New York, NY 10048   Phone: (212)938-7909
Editor(s): Tom Bertolini. Weekly. Contains analyses of conditions, trends, and prospects in the cotton trade; domestic cotton crop progress during the growing season; U.S. Government activities in the cotton trade; and economic conditions affecting the cotton trade and market. Recurring features include charts showing daily and weekly fluctuations of spot and futures cotton prices and a weekly market review. **Facsimile Number:** (212)839-8061.

★3330★
Country Folks
Lee Publications, Inc.
W Grand St.
Box 121
Palatine Bridge, NY 13428   Phone: (518)673-3237
Janice Handy, Editor. Weekly. Farm newspaper. **Facsimile Number:** (518)673-2699.

★3331★
Countryside & Small Stock Journal
Countryside Publications, Ltd.
W8333 Doepke Rd.
Waterloo, WI 53594   Phone: (414)478-3665
Editor(s): Jerome D. Belanger. Bimonthly. Publishes basic and advanced information on all aspects of homesteading and small-scale farming. Carries articles on the selecting and care of livestock, gardening, energy and water conservation, record-keeping, farm incomes, small-scale grain production, and wool production. Recurring features include statistics, book reviews, news of research, letters from readers, and a section on current events titled Spaceship Earth.

★3332★
Crop Science
Crop Science Society of America
677 S. Segoe Rd.
Madison, WI 53711   Phone: (608)273-8080
P.S. Baenziger, Editor. 6x/yr. Agricultural science journal. **Facsimile Number:** (608)273-2021.

★3333★
Dairy and Field Crops Digest
Regional Cooperative Extension Dairy Program
56 Main St.
Owego, NY 13827   Phone: (607)687-4163
William Menzi, Jr., Editor. 6x/yr. Agricultural and dairy magazine.

★3334★
Delta Farm Press
Farm Press Publications, Inc.
PO Box 1420
Intersection Hwy. 61 N.
Clarksdale, MS 38614   Phone: (601)624-8503
Glen Rutz, Editor. Weekly (Fri.). Agriculture tabloid. **Facsimile Number:** (601)627-1977.

★3335★
Doane's Agricultural Report
Doane Information Service
11701 Borman Dr.
St. Louis, MO 63146   Phone: (314)569-2700
Editor(s): Paul Justis. 50/yr. Covers the marketing of commodities (such as cattle, hogs, corn, wheat, and soybeans), as well as providing agricultural, economic, management, and production information. Discusses such topics as profit management, prices, outlook, machinery, buildings, equipment, taxes, social security, law, and government.

★3336★
Experimental Agriculture
Cambridge University Press
40 W. 20th St.
New York, NY 10011   Phone: (914)937-9600
F.G.H. Lupton, Editor. Quarterly Journal publishing research into the agronomy of crops. Also prints related book reviews. Alan Winter, Press Dir., U.S.

★3337★
Farm & Ranch Living
Reiman Publications, Inc.
5400 S. 60th St.
Greendale, WI 53129   Phone: (414)423-0100
Bob Ottum, Editor. 6x/yr. Lifestyle magazine for farmers and ranchers. **Facsimile Number:** (414)423-1143.

★3338★
Farm Economics
Pennsylvania State University Cooperative Extension Service
323 Ag. Admin. Bldg.
University Park, PA 16802   Phone: (814)865-2561
Blair J. Smith, Editor. 6x/yr. Agricultural economics magazine. **Facsimile Number:** (814)865-3746.

★3339★
The Farm Gate
North Waterloo Publishing Ltd.
15 King St.
Elmira, ON, Canada N3B 2R1   Phone: (519)669-5155
J.R. Verdun, Editor and Publisher. Monthly. Agricultural newspaper. **Facsimile Number:** (519)669-5928.

★3340★
Farm News
News Printing Co.
430 S. Adams, Box 1105
Marion, IN 46952   Phone: (317)664-0207
V.O. Pinkerton, Editor. Monthly. Agriculture magazine.

★3341★
Farm/Ranch Exchange
1405 Broadway
PO Box 1709
Scottsbluff, NE 69363-1709   Phone: (308)632-0670
Ken Campbell, Editor. Monthly. Farm newspaper.

★3342★
The Farmers' Advance
Suburban Communications Corp.
130 S. Main St.
Box 8
Camden, MI 49232   Phone: (517)368-5201
John Snyder, Editor. Weekly (Wed.). Agricultural newspaper. **Facsimile Number:** (517)368-5131.

★3343★
Farmer's Exchange
Exchange Publishing Corp.
PO Box 45
New Paris, IN 46553   Phone: (219)831-2138
Paul Hershberger, Editor. Weekly (Fri.). Agricultural newspaper. **Facsimile Number:** (219)831-2131.

★3344★
Farmers Grain and Livestock Corporation—Viewpoint
Farmers Grain and Livestock Corp.
1400 50th St., Ste. 210
PO Box 65537
West Des Moines, IA 50265-0914   Phone: (515)223-2200
Editor(s): Douglas C. Hjort. Weekly. Addresses marketing problems faced by U.S. agricultural producers. Provides marketing recommendations and analysis projecting cash and futures prices activity for agricultural commodities, including corn, soybeans, wheat, feeder cattle, live cattle, hogs, cotton, and sunflowers. Recurring features include statistics and columns titled Fundamentally Speaking, Washington Insight, Weather, and International News. **Toll-free/Additional Phone Number(s):** 800-444-4642 **Facsimile Number:** (515)223-2243.

★3345★
Farmer's Report
211 Hwy. 38E
Rochelle, IL 61068   Phone: (815)562-4171
Laurie Parli, Editor. Monthly. Agricultural publication. **Facsimile Number:** (815)562-7048.

★3346★
Farmland News
104 Depot St.
PO Box 240
Archbold, OH 43502-0240   Phone: (419)445-9456
Jeremy J. Rohrs, Editor. Weekly (Tues.). Agriculture newspaper (tabloid). **Facsimile Number:** (419)445-2077.

★3347★
FFA New Horizons Magazine (NFFAO)
National FFA Organization (NFFAO)
Natl. FFA Center
Box 15160
5632 Mt. Vernon Memorial Hwy.
Alexandria, VA 22309-0160   Phone: (703)360-3600
Bimonthly. Profiles present and former members who have made outstanding contributions to the farming industry. New developments and trends in agriculture and agribusiness are covered along with some technical articles.

★3348★
FFA Times (NFFAO)
National FFA Organization (NFFAO)
Natl. FFA Center
Box 15160
5632 Mt. Vernon Memorial Hwy.
Alexandria, VA 22309-0160   Phone: (703)360-3600
Annual. Tabloid reporting activities of the association's annual convention.

Farm Operators and Managers

★3349★
The Flue Cured Tobacco Farmer
Specialized Agricultural Publications, Inc.
PO Box 95075
Raleigh, NC 27625   Phone: (919)872-5040
Dayton Matlick, Editor and Publisher. 8x/yr. Business magazine for tobacco farmers. **Facsimile Number:** (919)876-6531.

★3350★
FMRA News
American Society of Farm Managers & Rural Appraisers
950 S. Cherry St., Ste. 106
Denver, CO 80222   Phone: (303)758-3513
Editor(s): Deborah Long Hunt. 6/yr. Discusses irrigation, energy problems and developments, food supply, land values, and legislation affecting farm managers and rural appraisers. Recurring features include news of Society activities, a calendar of events, and obituaries.

★3351★
Focus on Farming
6 Central St.
Moravia, NY 13118   Phone: (315)497-1551
Bernard F. McGuerty III, Publisher. Every other week with special issues. Farm oriented newspaper. **Facsimile Number:** (315)497-1551.

★3352★
Fresh Off the Vine
California Fresh Market Tomato Advisory Board
2017 N. Gateway Blvd., Ste. 102
Fresno, CA 93727   Phone: (209)251-0628
Semiannually. Contains "research and crop information, handling and storage tips, interviews with chefs and other foodservice personnel, quantity recipes and use ideas—all geared to help the foodservice operator ultimately increase profits."

★3353★
Gallatin Equipment Company—Newsletter
Gallatin Equipment Company
PO Box 1140
Belgrade, MT 59714   Phone: (406)388-4177
Carries information of interest to users of agricultural equipment.

★3354★
The Giant
Adviser Publications Ltd.
5929 48th Ave.
Bag 5012, Main PO Box
Red Deer, AB, Canada T4N 6R4   Phone: (403)346-3356
Shirley Der, Editor. Monthly. Farm newspaper (tabloid). **Facsimile Number:** (403)347-6620.

★3355★
Grain & Feed Market News
Livestock & Grain Market News Branch
Livestock & Seed Division, AMS
U.S. Department of Agriculture (USDA)
South Bldg., Rm. 2623
Washington, DC 20090-6456   Phone: (202)447-6231
Editor(s): Mike O'Connor. Weekly. Publishes weekly grain and feed marketing statistics. Includes narrative summaries of the grain and feed marketing situation in the U.S. and abroad. **Facsimile Number:** (202)245-4732.

★3356★
Grainews
United Grain Growers
433 Main St.
PO Box 6600
Winnipeg, MB, Canada R3C 3A7   Phone: (204)944-5569
John Clark, Editor and Publisher. 17x/yr. Agricultural information newspaper (tabloid). **Facsimile Number:** (204)944-5416.

★3357★
Grass & Grain
Ag Press, Inc.
16th & Yuma
Box 1009
Manhattan, KS 66502   Phone: (913)539-7558
Steve Suther, Editor. 937-880. Weekly (Tues.). Agricultural tabloid. **Facsimile Number:** (913)539-2679.

★3358★
Hay There!
National Hay Association, Inc.
5445 Mariner St., No. 102
Tampa, FL 33609   Phone: (813)286-3655
Editor(s): Donald F. Kieffer. Monthly. Reports current developments in the hay industry, including marketing and shipping information. **Facsimile Number:** (813)286-1924.

★3359★
High Plains Journal
1500 E. Wyatt Earp
PO Box 760
Dodge City, KS 67801   Phone: (316)227-7171
Galen Hubbs, Editor. Weekly. Agricultural newspaper. **Facsimile Number:** (316)227-7173.

★3360★
International Green Front Report
Friends of the Trees
PO Box 1064
Tonasket, WA 98855   Phone: (509)486-4726
Michael Pilarski, editor. Irregular; previous edition 1988; new edition expected 1991. Organizations and periodicals dealing with sustainable forestry and agriculture and related fields. Entries include: Organization or publisher name, address, phone, description of projects and activities, or description of periodical coverage. Arrangement: Classified by subject. Indexes: Organization name/periodical title. **Facsimile Number:** (509)486-4726.

★3361★
IPPC Infoletter
International Plant Protection Center (IPPC)
Oregon State University
Corvallis, OR 97331   Phone: (503)737-3541
Editor(s): Allan Deutsch. Periodic. Concerned with weed control, especially in less developed countries. Covers small farm agriculture, agricultural equipment and methods, technology transfer, aquatic weeds, and similar subjects of international interest. Recurring features include book reviews, lists of publications available, notices of conferences and courses, and a calendar of events. **Facsimile Number:** (503)737-3080.

★3362★
Journal of the American Society of Farm Managers and Rural Appraisers (ASFMRA)
American Society of Farm Managers and Rural Appraisers (ASFMRA)
950 S. Cherry St., Ste. 106
Denver, CO 80222   Phone: (303)758-3513
Semiannual.

★3363★
Limousin Leader
Bollum Marketing, Inc.
221-18 St. SE
Calgary, AB, Canada T2E 6J5   Phone: (403)248-6760
R. Bollum, Editor. 10x/yr. A trade journal covering the promotion, growth and improvement of Limousin cattle.

★3364★
Limousin World
1241 S. 11th
Yukon, OK 73099   Phone: (405)350-0040
Jim Eischen, Editor. Monthly. Magazine for breeders of Limousin cattle. **Facsimile Number:** (405)350-0054.

★3365★
Little Acres
American Farm Publications
PO Box 2026
Easton, MD 21601
Karl Berger, Editor. Monthly. Newspaper (tabloid) featuring articles of interest to small, "sun-down" farmers, gardeners and rural residents.

★3366★
Livestock Market Digest
PO Box 7458
Albuquerque, NM 87194   Phone: (505)243-9515
Emil Reutzel, Jr., Editor. Weekly. Livestock and agriculture business (tabloid).

★3367★
Livestock, Meat, and Wool Market News
Livestock & Grain Market News Branch
Livestock & Seed Division, AMS
U.S. Department of Agriculture (USDA)
South Bldg., Rm. 2623
Washington, DC 20090-6456   Phone: (202)447-6231
Editor(s): Mike O'Connor. Weekly. Publishes weekly livestock, meat, and wool marketing statistics. Includes narrative summaries of the week's livestock, meat, and wool marketing situation in the United States. **Facsimile Number:** (202)245-4732.

★3368★
Livestock Weekly
Southwest Publishers, Inc.
2601 Sherwood Way
PO Box 3306
San Angelo, TX 76902   Phone: (915)949-4611
Stanley R. Frank, Editor and Publisher. Weekly (Thurs.). Newspaper (tabloid) for the livestock industry.

★3369★
Living Among Nature Daringly
4466 Ike Mooney Rd.
Silverton, OR 97381   Phone: (503)873-8829
Bill Anderson, Editor and Publisher. Five times/yr. Magazine for trappers, farmers, and nature lovers.

★3370★
Monthly Crop and Livestock Report
Ontario Ministry of Agriculture and Food
Queen's Park
Legislative Bldg.
Toronto, ON, Canada M7A 1B6
Bill McGee, editor. 8x/yr. Magazine offering economic information on crops and livestock.

★3371★
National Farm Finance News
Dorset Group, Inc.
212 W. 35th St., 13th floor
New York, NY 10001   Phone: (212)563-4405
Bill Liebtag, Editor. Every other week. Newspaper covering agriculture-related banking, investing, and business. **Facsimile Number:** (212)564-8879.

★3372★
National Farmers Union—Washington Newsletter
National Farmers Union
PO Box 228600
Denver, CO 80251   Phone: (303)337-5500
Editor(s): Milt Hakel. 18/yr. Carries legislative and economic news pertaining to family farm agriculture. Gives explanations for actions taken by the House of Representatives and the Senate, congressional committees, and various agencies of the administration. **Facsimile Number:** (303)368-1390.

★3373★
National FFA Organization—Update (NFFAO)
National FFA Organization (NFFAO)
Natl. FFA Center
Box 15160
5632 Mt. Vernon Memorial Hwy.
Alexandria, VA 22309-0160   Phone: (703)360-3600
Monthly. Newsletter. Includes calendar of events.

★3374★
National Hog Farmer
Webb Division, Intertec Publishing Corp.
7900 International Dr., Ste. 300
Minneapolis, MN 55425   Phone: (612)851-9329
Bill Fleming, Editor. Monthly. Magazine containing articles of interest to hog producers. **Facsimile Number:** (612)851-4600.

★3375★
New England Farm Bulletin & Garden Gazette—Farmer-Consumer Connection Agricultural fairs and farmer markets and museums
Jacob's Meadow, Inc.
Box 147
Cohasset, MA 02025   Phone: (617)383-0158
Valerie A. Lipsett, Max S. Maire, editor. Annual, summer. 1000 suppliers of farm products, farmers' markets, agricultural fairs, and farm museums in New England. Entries include: Name, address, phone, services provided, descriptions of services. Arrangement: Classified by line of service.

★3376★
New England Farm Bulletin & Garden Gazette—NEFB Almanac Issue Agricultural associations
Jacob's Meadow, Inc.
Box 147
Cohasset, MA 02025   Phone: (617)383-0158
Valerie A. Lipsett and Max S. Maire, editor. Annual, January. List of nearly 2,000 farming and gardening organizations in New England. Entries include: Organization name, address, phone,

Farm Operators and Managers ★3391★

name and title of contact. Arrangement: Classified by type of organization.

★3377★
New Farmer
Rodale Press
33 E. Minor St.
Emmaus, PA 18098   Phone: (215)967-5171
George DeVault, Editor and Publisher. 7x/yr. Specialized farming magazine devoted to helping commercial farmers cut production costs and boost profits. **Facsimile Number:** (215)967-3044.

★3378★
The Northern Horizon
Sterling Newspapers Ltd.
901-100th Ave.
Dawson Creek, BC, Canada V1G 1W2   Phone: (604)782-4888
Heinz Goldbach, Editor and Publisher. Every other week. Farm news magazine. **Facsimile Number:** (604)782-6770.

★3379★
Nut Grower
Western Agricultural Publishing Co., Inc.
4974 E. Clinton Way, Ste. 123
Fresno, CA 93727   Phone: (209)252-7000
Harry Cline, Editor. 8x/yr. Magazine on nut growing. **Facsimile Number:** (209)252-7387.

★3380★
Onion World
Columbia Publishing
PO Box 1467
Yakima, WA 98907-1467   Phone: (509)248-2452
D. Brent Clement, Editor and Publisher. 8x/yr. Agricultural magazine. **Facsimile Number:** (509)248-4056.

★3381★
PAS Newsletter (PAS)
National Postsecondary Agriculture Student Organization (PAS)
Box 279
Cobleskill, NY 12043   Phone: (518)234-7309
3/year.

★3382★
The Peanut Farmer
Specialized Agricultural Publications, Inc.
PO Box 95075
Raleigh, NC 27625   Phone: (919)872-5040
Dayton Matlick, Editor and Publisher. 7x/yr. Business magazine for peanut farmers. **Facsimile Number:** (919)876-6531.

★3383★
The Peanut Grower
Agri-Publications, Inc.
PO Box 7026
Tifton, GA 31793   Phone: (912)386-8591
Tyron Spearman, Editor. 6x/yr Magazine on peanut farming. Includes information on production, research, and marketing. **Facsimile Number:** (912)386-9772.

★3384★
Peanut Journal and Nut World
Peanut Journal Publishing Co.
Drawer 347
Suffolk, VA 23434   Phone: (804)484-4804
Terry Reel, Editor. Monthly. Magazine on nut farming and marketing.

★3385★
Pest Alerts
Cooperative Extension Service
Michigan State University
c/o Mark Schriber
Department of Entomology
East Lansing, MI 48824-1115   Phone: (517)353-3890
Weekly during growing season; monthly during off-season. Provides pest predictions and control recommendations in areas including vegetables, fruits, grain, ornamentals, and forestry. Supplies detailed maps and statistics.

★3386★
Premium Grower
Napa Valley Grape Growers Association
4075 Solano Ave.
Napa, CA 94558   Phone: (707)944-8311
Editor(s): Teresa Geremia-Chart. Quarterly. Supplies grape commodity and vineyard news. Carries technical information on grape and wine production, legislative updates,. **Facsimile Number:** (707)224-7836.

★3387★
The Rice World and Soybean News
PO Box 219
Folsom, LA 70437   Phone: (504)796-3012
J.P. Gaines, Editor and Publisher. Monthly. Tabloid reporting information of interest to rice and soybean farmers and processors. **Facsimile Number:** (504)796-3012.

★3388★
Rocky Mountain Union Farmer
Rocky Mountain Farmers Union
10800 E. Bethany Dr., Ste. 450
Aurora, CO 80014   Phone: (303)752-5800
Heidi Hild, Editor. 7x/yr. Agricultural magazine (tabloid) featuring articles on issues affecting family operated farms and ranches. **Facsimile Number:** (303)752-5807.

★3389★
Rural Living
Michigan Farm Bureau
7373 W. Saginaw Hwy.
PO Box 30690
Lansing, MI 48909   Phone: (517)323-7000
Dennis Rudat, Editor/Business Mgr. Quarterly. Regional agriculture lifestyle magazine. **Facsimile Number:** (517)323-6793.

★3390★
San Joaquin Farm Bureau News
San Joaquin Farm Bureau Federation
PO Box 8444
Stockton, CA 95208-0444   Phone: (209)931-4931
Robert J. Cabral, Publisher. Monthly. Agricultural newspaper. **Facsimile Number:** (209)931-1433.

★3391★
Small Farm Advocate
Center for Rural Affairs
PO Box 405
Walthill, NE 68067   Phone: (402)846-5428
Editor(s): Nancy Thompson. Quarterly. "Provides a national overview of regional small farm issues by serving as a clearinghouse for articles prepared by family farm groups across the country." Covers topics such as FmHA loans and foreclosures, U.S. House agriculture subcommittee's programs, women farmers, bankruptcy, lawsuits, and alternative agriculture. Recurring features include columns titled Research

and Extension, Washington Notes, and Family Farm Clearinghouse.

★3392★
Southwest Farm Press
Farm Press Publications, Inc.
PO Box 1420
Clarksdale, MS 38614   Phone: (601)624-8503
James Calvin Pigg, Editor. Weekly. Agriculture tabloid. **Facsimile Number:** (601)627-1977.

★3393★
Spokesman
Iowa Farm Bureau
606 8th St.
Grundy Center, IA 50638   Phone: (319)824-5454
Darryl Jahn, Editor. Weekly. Agricultural newspaper.

★3394★
The Stockman Grass Farmer
Mississippi Valley Publishing Co.
PO Box 9607
Jackson, MS 39206   Phone: (601)483-0633
H. Allan Nation, Editor and Publisher. Monthly. Magazine reporting on livestock and grass farming.

★3395★
The Sugar Producer
520 Park Ave.
Idaho Falls, ID 83402   Phone: (208)524-7000
Steve Janes, Editor. 5x/yr. Magazine for sugar beet growers. **Facsimile Number:** (208)522-5241.

★3396★
The Sunflower
National Sunflower Assn.
4023 N. State St.
Bismarck, ND 58501   Phone: (701)224-3019
Larry Kleingartner, Editor. 5x/yr. Magazine for sunflower producers in the U.S. **Facsimile Number:** (701)224-2798.

★3397★
Times-Plain Dealer
Times-Plain Dealer Publishing, Inc.
Box 350
Cresco, IA 52136   Phone: (319)547-3601
H. Denis Moore, Editor and Publisher. Weekly. Agricultural newspaper. **Facsimile Number:** (319)547-4232.

★3398★
Top Farmer Intelligence
AgriData Resources, Inc.
330 E. Kilbourn Ave.
Milwaukee, WI 53202   Phone: (414)278-7676
Editor(s): Brian J. Basting. 50/yr. Monitors the economic outlook for producers of corn, soybeans, wheat, cotton, cattle, feeder cattle, and hogs. Recurring features include columns titled Cash Market Update and This Week's Strategy Update.

★3399★
Top Farmer Market Insight
Brock & Associates
330 E. Kilbourn Ave.
Milwaukee, WI 53202   Phone: (414)278-7676
Editor(s): Brian J. Basting. 50/yr. Offers "farm market news, cash market information and farm marketing advice." Discusses issues such as "how high a market is likely to go, how low it could drop, and where it is likely to turn." Recurring features include futures price charts. **Toll-free/Additional Phone Number(s):** 800-558-7122.

★3400★
Tree Farmer
1250 Connecticut Ave. NW
Washington, DC 20036   Phone: (202)463-2455
Luke Popovich, Editor. 4x/yr. Forestry journal. **Facsimile Number:** (202)463-2461.

★3401★
Turf News
American Sod Producers Assn.
1855 A Hicks Rd.
Rolling Meadows, IL 60008-1215   Phone: (708)705-9898
Wendell Mathews, Editor. 6x/yr. Trade magazine. **Facsimile Number:** (708)705-8347.

★3402★
Union Farmer
National Farmers Union
250-C 2nd Ave. S.
Saskatoon, SK, Canada S7K 2M1   Phone: (306)652-9465
Terry Pugh, Editor. Monthly. Magazine for farm unions. **Facsimile Number:** (306)664-6226.

★3403★
United Caprine News
PO Drawer A
Rotan, TX 79546   Phone: (915)735-2278
Jeff Klein, Editor. Monthly. Newspaper (tabloid) serving dairy goat producers. **Facsimile Number:** (915)735-2230.

★3404★
U.S. Farm News
U.S. Farmers Assn.
Box 496
Hampton, IA 50441   Phone: (515)456-4470
F.W. Stover, Editor and Publisher. Monthly. Farmers union magazine.

★3405★
The Vealer
Graphicom Inc.
14955 Gulf Blvd.
Madeira Beach, FL 33708-2013
Lee Schultz, Editor. Monthly. Magazine about livestock.

★3406★
Vegetables and Specialties Situation and Outlook Report
Economic Research Service
U.S. Department of Agriculture (USDA)
1301 New York Ave. NW, Rm. 812
Washington, DC 20005-4788   Phone: (202)786-1886
Editor(s): Shannon Hamm. 3/yr. Discusses fresh and processed vegetable crops and products. Provides data on supply, demand, prices, imports and exports for vegetables, including potatoes, sweet potatoes, mushrooms, dried beans, peas, lentils, and specialty vegetables. Carries the official USDA estimate of per capita vegetable utilization in the August issue. **Facsimile Number:** (202)786-1252.

Farm Operators and Managers

★3407★
The Western Producer
Western Producer Publications
2310 Millar Ave.
PO Box 2500
Saskatoon, SK, Canada S7K 2C4   Phone: (306)665-3500
R. Keith Dryden, Editor. Weekly. Agricultural newspaper. **Facsimile Number:** (306)653-1255.

★3408★
The Wheat Grower
415 2nd St. NE, Ste. 300
Washington, DC 20002-4993   Phone: (202)547-7800
Barry Jenkins, Editor and Publisher. 8x/yr. Magazine on growing, harvesting, storing, transporting, and marketing wheat. Covers economic conditions, weather, policies, and politics affecting U.S. and world grain trade. **Facsimile Number:** (202)546-2638.

★3409★
The Wool Sack
North Central Wool Marketing Corp.
PO Box 328
Brookings, SD 57006   Phone: (605)692-2324
Dick Boniface, Editor. 6x/yr. Newspaper about wool marketing and sheep raising. **Facsimile Number:** (605)692-8182.

★3410★
World of Beef
Creative Motion Publishing
200, 807 Manning Rd. NE
Calgary, AB, Canada T2E 7M8   Phone: (403)569-9520
Frankie Thornhill, Editor. Monthly. Trade magazine for cattle producers in Canada and the U.S. **Facsimile Number:** (403)569-9590.

★3411★
Yorkshire Journal
American Yorkshire Club Inc.
1769 U.S. 52 N.
PO Box 2417
West Lafayette, IN 47906   Phone: (317)463-3593
Darrell Anderson, Editor. Monthly Magazine serving breeders of Yorkshire swine. **Facsimile Number:** (317)497-2959.

Meetings and Conventions

★3412★
Ag Expo
South Dakota Fertilizer and Agricultural Chemical Association
121 N. Grand
Pierre, SD 57501   Phone: (605)224-2445
Frequency: Always held during January in Sioux Falls, South Dakota at the Ramkota Exhibition Hall. 1993; Jan. 13-14; Sioux Falls, SD • 1994; Jan. 11-12; Sioux Falls, SD • 1995; Jan. 10-11; Sioux Falls, SD • 1996; Jan. 09-10; Sioux Falls, SD. **Facsimile Number:** (605)224-9913.

★3413★
Agri News Farm Show
Agri News Farm Show
PO Box 6118
Rochester, MN 55903-6110   Phone: (507)285-7600
1992; Mar. 18-20. **Facsimile Number:** (507)283-7772.

★3414★
AGRITECH - International Agriculture, Horticulture, Irrigation and Fisheries Exhibition
World Access Corp.
15 Bemis Rd.
PO Box 171
Wellesley Hills, MA 02181   Phone: (617)235-8095

★3415★
American Farm Bureau Federation Annual Meeting and Trade Show - Farm/Ranch Expo
Marvin Park and Associates
600 Talcott Rd.
Park Ridge, IL 60068   Phone: (708)823-1010
1992; Kansas City, MO. **Facsimile Number:** (708)698-1762.

★3416★
American Feed Industry Association Feed Industries Show
American Feed Industry Association
1501 Wilson Blvd., Ste. 1100
Arlington, VA 22 09   Phone: (703)524-0810
Frequency: Always held during May. 1993; May 17-19; Minneapolis, MN. **Facsimile Number:** (703)524-1921.

★3417★
American Society of Farm Managers and Rural Appraisers Annual Convention
Agri Finance
6201 Howard St.
Niles, IL 60648
1992.

★3418★
American Soybean Association Annual Conference
American Soybean Association
PO Box 27300
St. Louis, MO 63141   Phone: (314)576-1770
Frequency: Always held in late July or early August. 1992; Jul. 24-27; Houston, TX.

★3419★
ARGO-TECHNIKA - Agricultural Machines, Equipment, and Instruments Show
World Access Corp.
15 Bemis Rd.
PO Box 171
Wellesley Hills, MA 02181   Phone: (617)235-8095

★3420★
Electric Power and Farm Equipment Show
Wisconsin Farm Equipment Association
PO Box 44364
Madison, WI 53744-4364   Phone: (608)276-6700
Frequency: Always held at the Dane County Exposition Center in Madison, Wisconsin. 1992; Mar. 18-20; Madison, WI • 1993; Mar. 17-19; Madison, WI. **Facsimile Number:** (608)276-6719.

★3421★
Empire Farm Days
Empire Farm Days
PO Box 566
Stanley, NY 14561   Phone: (716)526-5356
1992; Aug. 04-06; • 1993; Aug. 10-12; • 1994; Aug. 09-11.

★3422★
Farm Progress Show
Farm Progress Companies, Inc.
191 S. Gary Ave.
Carol Stream, IL 60188   Phone: (708)462-2892
1992; Sep. 29-01; IN. **Facsimile Number:** (708)462-2869.

★3423★
International Poultry Trade Show
Southeastern Poultry and Egg Association
1456 Church St.
Decatur, GA 30030   Phone: (404)377-6465
Frequency: Always held during January at the World Congress Center in Atlanta, Georgia. **Facsimile Number:** (404)378-9801.

★3424★
Mid-America Farm Exposition
Salina Area Chamber of Commerce
PO Box 586
Salina, KS 67402-0586   Phone: (913)827-9301
Frequency: Always held during March at Kenwood and Oakdale Parks in Salina, Kansas. 1992; Mar. 24-26; Salina, KS. **Facsimile Number:** (913)827-9758.

★3425★
Mid-South Farm and Gin Supply Exhibit
Southern Cotton Ginners Association
Cotton Gin Pl.
Memphis, TN 38106   Phone: (901)947-3104
Frequency: Always held in Memphis, Tennessee. 1992; Mar. 06-07; Memphis, TN • 1993; Mar. 05-06; Memphis, TN. **Facsimile Number:** (901)947-3103.

★3426★
Midwest Farm Show
American Farm Shows
Box 1
Chippewa Falls, WI 54729   Phone: (715)723-5061
1993; Jan. 20-22; LaCrosse, WI.

★3427★
Midwest Poultry Federation Convention
Midwest Poultry Federation
PO Box 12181
St. Paul, MN 55112   Phone: (612)636-0947
1993; Feb. 17-19; Minneapolis, MN • 1994; Feb. 16-18; Minneapolis, MN.

★3428★
National Association of State Departments of Agriculture National Food and Agriculture Exposition
National Association of State Departments of Agriculture
1616 H St., NW
Washington, DC 20006   Phone: (202)628-1566
1992. **Facsimile Number:** (202)628-9461.

★3429★
National Association of Wheat Growers Convention
National Association of Wheat Growers
415 2nd St., NE, Ste. 300
Washington, DC 20002   Phone: (202)547-7800
1993; Jan. 03-06; Anaheim, CA. **Facsimile Number:** (202)546-2638.

★3430★
National Cattle Congress Fair
National Cattle Congress Fair
PO Box 298
Waterloo, IA 50704   Phone: (319)234-7515
Frequency: Always held in Waterloo, Iowa, at the Cattle Congress Fairgrounds. Starts the second Saturday after Labor Day and runs for 9 days. 1992; Sep. 14-22; Waterloo, IA. **Facsimile Number:** (319)234-8865.

★3431★
National Cattlemen's Association Annual Convention and Trade Show
National Cattlemen's Association
PO Box 3469
Englewood, CO 80155   Phone: (303)694-0305
Facsimile Number: (303)694-0305.

★3432★
National Farm Machinery Show and Championship Tractor Pull
Kentucky State Fair Board
PO Box 37130
Louisville, KY 40233   Phone: (502)366-9592
Frequency: Always held in February at the Kentucky Fair and Exposition Center in Louisville, Kentucky. 1993; Feb. 10-13; Louisville, KY. **Facsimile Number:** (502)368-0574.

★3433★
North American Farm and Power Show
Farm Equipment Association of Minnesota and South Dakota
121 E. Park Sq.
Owatonna, MN 55060   Phone: (507)451-1136
Frequency: Always held at the Convention Center in Minneapolis, Minnesota. 1992; Nov. Minneapolis, MN. **Facsimile Number:** (507)455-5909.

★3434★
Northwest Agricultural Show
Northwest Agricultural Congress
4672 Drift Creek Rd., SE
Sublimity, OR 97385   Phone: (503)769-7120
Frequency: Always held during January at the Multnomah County Expo Center in Portland, Oregon. **Facsimile Number:** (503)769-3549.

★3435★
Society for Range Management Annual Conference
Society for Range Management
1839 York St.
Denver, CO 80206   Phone: (303)355-7070
1992; Spokane, WA • 1993; Albuquerque, NM • 1994; Colorado Springs, CO • 1995; Phoenix, AZ. **Facsimile Number:** (303)355-5059.

★3436★
Southern Farm Show
Southern Shows, Inc.
810 Baxter St.
PO Box 36859
Charlotte, NC 28236   Phone: (704)376-6594
Frequency: Always held at the State Fairgrounds in Raleigh, North Carolina. 1993; Feb. 04-06; Raleigh, NC. **Facsimile Number:** (703)376-6345.

Farm Operators and Managers

★3437★
Triumph of Agriculture Exposition Farm and Ranch Machinery Show
Mid-America Expositions, Inc.
666 Farnam Bldg.
Omaha, NE 68102   Phone: (402)346-8003
Frequency: Always held in March at the Civic Auditorium in Omaha, Nebraska. 1992; Mar. 09-11; Omaha, NE • 1993; Mar. 08-10; Omaha, NE • 1994; Mar. 07-09; Omaha, NE • 1995; Mar. 13-15; Omaha, NE. **Facsimile Number:** (402)346-5412.

★3438★
United Fresh Fruit and Vegetable Association Annual Convention and Exposition
United Fresh Fruit and Vegetable Association
727 N. Washington St.
Alexandria, VA 22314   Phone: (703)836-3410
1993; Feb. 21-23; San Diego, CA • 1994; Jan. 31-01; Las Vegas, NV. **Toll-free/Additional Phone Number(s):** 800-336-3065. **Facsimile Number:** (703)836-7745.

★3439★
Western Farm Show
Western Retail Implement and Hardware Association
638 W. 39th
PO Box 419264
Kansas City, MO 64141   Phone: (816)561-5323
Frequency: Held in February at the American Royal Buildings in Kansas City, Missouri. **Facsimile Number:** (816)561-1249.

★3440★
World Pork Expo
National Pork Producers Council
PO Box 10383
Des Moines, IA 50306   Phone: (515)223-2600
Frequency: Always held during June. 1992; Jun. **Facsimile Number:** (515)223-2646.

Other Sources of Information

★3441★
The Family Farm: Can It Be Saved?
Brethren Press
1451 Dundee Ave.
Elgin, IL 60120   Phone: (708)742-5100
Shantilal P. Bhagat. 1985. **Facsimile Number:** (708)742-6103.

★3442★
Farm: A Year In the Life of an American Farmer
Simon & Schuster Inc.
Simon & Schuster Bldg.
1230 Avenue of the Americas
New York, NY 10020   Phone: (212)698-7000
Richard Rhodes. 1990.

★3443★
Farming Is in Our Blood: Farm Families in Economic Crisis
Iowa State University Press
Iowa State University
2121 S. State Ave.
Ames, IA 50010   Phone: (515)292-0140
Paul C. Rosenblatt. 1990. **Facsimile Number:** (515)292-3348.

★3444★
The Last Farmer
Thorndike Press
PO Box 159
Thorndike, ME 04986   Phone: (207)948-2962
Howard Kohn. 1989. **Toll-free/Additional Phone Number(s):** 800-257-5755. **Facsimile Number:** (207)948-2863.

★3445★
Men of Earth
Ayer Company Publishers, Inc.
50 Northwestern Dr., No. 10
PO Box 958
Salem, NH 03079   Phone: (603)898-1200
Russell Lord. Facsimile edition, 1975. Part of American Farmers & the Rise of Agribusiness Series.

Fishers, Hunters, and Trappers

Fishers, hunters, and trappers gather marine and animal life for human consumption and for animal feed, bait, and other industrial uses, and manage animal life for research and control purposes. Gathering sea life hundreds of miles from shore with vessels requires a crew of up to 30 fishers— captain, or skipper, a first mate and sometimes a second mate, and boatswains and other deckhands. The captain plans and oversees the fishing operation; ensures that the fishing vessel is in suitable condition; oversees the purchase of supplies, gear, and equipment; and hires qualified crew members and assigns their duties. Upon returning to port, the captain arranges for the sale of the catch. The mate— the captain's assistant, who must be familiar with navigation requirements and operation of equipment— assumes control of the vessel when the captain is off duty. The mate's regular duty, with the help of the boatswain and under the captain's oversight, is to direct the fishing operations and sailing responsibilities of the deckhands. Boatswains— highly experienced deckhands with supervisory responsibilities — and other deckhands carry out the sailing and fishing operations. The crew usually includes deckhands who additionally work as a cook or an engineer. The cook is often responsible for the procurement of foodstuffs and supplies and their loading on the vessel. Engineers operate, repair, and maintain the vessel's engines and equipment. Most full-time and virtually all part-time fishers work on motorboats in relatively shallow waters and often in sight of land. Crews are small and collaborate on all aspects of the fishing operation. This includes placing gill nets across the mouths of rivers or inlets, entrapment nets in bays and lakes, and pots and traps for shellfish such as lobsters and crabs. Dredges and scrapes are also used to gather shellfish such as oysters and scallops. In very shallow waters, fish are caught from small boats with an outboard motor, rowboats, or by wading. Fishers use a wide variety of hand-operated equipment— for example, nets, tongs, grabs, rakes, hoes, hooks, and shovels— to gather finfish and shellfish, catch water animals such as frogs and turtles, and harvest marine life such as Irish moss and kelp. Some fishers may use snorkeling equipment while spearing fish. In rare instances, fishers cast lines or nets from the shore, a dock, or a promontory. While most fishers are involved with commercial fishing, some captains and deckhands are primarily involved with recreational fishing. Hunters track, stalk, and kill their quarry. They usually operate alone or as members of a very small hunting party and may use dogs to locate and corner the quarry. They use guns and bows and arrows to hunt predatory animals such as bears, eradicate animal pests such as coyotes, and control the population of large game animals such as deer. Divers hunt fish with spear guns or nets, and alligator hunters shoot their quarry after snaring it with baited hooks. Trappers catch animals or birds using baited, scented, or camouflaged traps, snares, cages, or nets. Many trappers prepare and sell pelts and skins. Many trappers are also involved with animal damage control, wildlife management, disease control, and research activities. The overwhelming majority of fishers, hunters, and trappers work in the fishing, hunting, and trapping industry. Significant numbers of fishers are involved in sport fishing activities while others work for museums— primarily in aquariums, oceanariums, and marine museums.

$alaries

Annual income of most captains range from $20,000 to $80.000. Mates on these vessels generally earn less than one-half of this— slightly more than other crew members. Earnings of fishers on motorboats are substantially lower, on the average. Most hunters and trappers in the federal government start between $16,600 and $21,000 a year. Salaries in state and local governments generally are lower.

Employment Outlook

Growth rate until the year 2000: More slowly than average.

Fishers, Hunters, and Trappers

Career Guides

★3446★
African Campfires
Sportsmen on Film
5038 North Pkwy.
Calabasas, CA 91302 Phone: (818)713-1888
Videocassette. 1987. 60 mins. Peter Capstick discusses his insightful thoughts on professional hunters and other hunting material, including some of his own personal experiences.

★3447★
American Professionals Series
Cambridge Career Products
90 MacCorkle Ave., SW
South Charleston, WV 25311 Phone: (304)744-9323
Videocassette. 1984. 30 mins. In this series of twenty-one half hour programs, various occupations are examined in depth, including a day in the life of each worker. Included are: fireman, farmer, oil driller, fisherman, horse trainer, and auto assembly repairman.

★3448★
"Baitfish Catcher" in *Opportunities in Marine and Maritime Careers* (pp. 110-111)
National Textbook Co.
4255 W. Touhy Ave.
Lincolnwood, IL 60646 Phone: (312)679-5500
William Ray Heitzmann. 1988. Includes careers related by their proximity to water; cruise ships, oceanography, marine sciences, fishing, commercial diving, maritime transportation, shipbuilding, Navy, and Coast Guard. Covers qualifications, job outlook, job duties, educational preparation, and training. Lists associations and schools.

★3449★
"Commercial Diver" in *Occu-Facts: Information on 565 Careers in Outline Form* (p. 15.28)
Careers, Inc.
P.O. Box 135
1211 Tenth St., S.W.
Largo, FL 33640 Phone: (813)584-7333
Elizabeth Handville. Biennial, 1989-90 edition. Each one-page occupational profile describes duties, working conditions, physical surroundings and demands, aptitudes, temperament, educational requirements, employment outlook, earnings, and places of employment.

★3450★
Commercial Fisher
Vocational Biographies, Inc.
PO Box 31, Dept. VF10
Sauk Centre, MN 56378 Phone: (612)352-6516
1990. This pamphlet profiles a person working in the job. Includes information about job duties, working conditions, places of employment, educational preparation, labor market outlook, and salaries. **Toll-free/Additional Phone Number(s):** 800-255-0752.

★3451★
"Commercial Fisher" in *Occu-Facts: Information on 565 Careers in Outline Form* (p. 14.18)
Careers, Inc.
P.O. Box 135
1211 Tenth St., S.W.
Largo, FL 33640 Phone: (813)584-7333
Elizabeth Handville. Biennial, 1989-90 edition. Each one-page occupational profile describes duties, working conditions, physical surroundings and demands, aptitudes, temperament, educational requirements, employment outlook, earnings, and places of employment.

★3452★
"Commercial Fishers" in Volume 3 of *Career Discovery Encyclopedia* (pp. 32-33)
J.G. Ferguson Publishing Co.
200 W. Monroe
Chicago, IL 60606 Phone: (312)580-5480
E. Russell Primm, editor-in-chief. 1990. Contains two-page articles on 504 occupations. Each article describes job duties, earnings, and educational and training requirements.

★3453★
"Commercial Fishers" in Volume 3 of *The Encyclopedia of Careers and Vocational Guidance* (pp. 357-360)
J.G. Ferguson Publishing Co.
200 W. Monroe
Chicago, IL 60606 Phone: (312)580-5480
William E. Hopke, editor-in-chief. Eighth edition, 1990. Four-volume set that profiles 500 occupations and describes job trends in 76 industries. Includes career description, educational requirements, history of the job, methods of entry, advancement, employment outlook, earnings, working conditions, social and psychological factors, and sources of additional information.

★3454★
"Diver" in *Agribusiness, Environment, and Natural Resources*, Volume 2 of *Career Information Center* (pp. 43-45)
Glencoe/Macmillan
15319 Chatsworth St.
Mission Hills, CA 91345   Phone: (818)898-1391
Richard Lidz and Dale Anderson, editorial directors. Fourth edition, 1990. For 600 occupations, describes job duties, entry-level requirements, education and training needed, advancement possibilities, employment outlook, earnings and benefits. The set is divided into 12 volumes. Each volume includes jobs related under a broad career field. Volume 13 is the index. **Facsimile Number:** 818-365-5489.

★3455★
Divers, Commercial
Careers, Inc.
PO Box 135
Largo, FL 34649-0135   Phone: (813)584-7333
1989. Two-page occupational summary card describing duties, working conditions, personal qualifications, training, earnings and hours, employment outlook, places of employment, related careers and where to write for more information.

★3456★
"Diving Technicians" in Volume 4 of *The Encyclopedia of Careers and Vocational Guidance* (pp. 34-41)
J.G. Ferguson Publishing Co.
200 W. Monroe
Chicago, IL 60606   Phone: (312)580-5480
William E. Hopke, editor-in-chief. Eighth edition, 1990. Four-volume set that profiles 500 occupations and describes job trends in 76 industries. Includes career description, educational requirements, history of the job, methods of entry, advancement, employment outlook, earnings, working conditions, social and psychological factors, and sources of additional information.

★3457★
"Diving Technicians" in Volume 2 of *Career Discovery Encyclopedia* (pp. 118-119)
J.G. Ferguson Publishing Co.
200 W. Monroe
Chicago, IL 60606   Phone: (312)580-5480
E. Russell Primm, editor-in-chief. 1990. Contains two-page articles on 504 occupations. Each article describes job duties, earnings, and educational and training requirements.

★3458★
"Fisher" in *Agribusiness, Environment, and Natural Resources*, Volume 2 of *Career Information Center* (pp. 47-49)
Glencoe/Macmillan
15319 Chatsworth St.
Mission Hills, CA 91345   Phone: (818)898-1391
Richard Lidz and Dale Anderson, editorial directors. Fourth edition, 1990. For 600 occupations, describes job duties, entry-level requirements, education and training needed, advancement possibilities, employment outlook, earnings and benefits. The set is divided into 12 volumes. Each volume includes jobs related under a broad career field. Volume 13 is the index. **Facsimile Number:** 818-365-5489.

★3459★
"Fisher" in *Hard Hatted Women: Stories of Struggle and Success in the Trades* (pp. 81-87)
Seal Press
3131 Western Ave., Ste. 410
Seattle, WA 98121   Phone: (206)283-7844
Molly Martin, editor. 1988. Twenty-six women recount their experiences working in blue collar occupations. They describe how they got in, the work they do, their relationships in predominantly male occupations, and their training.

★3460★
Fisher, Commercial
Careers, Inc.
PO Box 135
Largo, FL 34649-0135   Phone: (813)584-7333
1989. Two-page job guide card describing duties, working conditions, personal qualifications, training, earnings and hours, employment outlook, places of employment, related careers and where to write for more information.

★3461★
Fisherman
Morris Video
2730 Monterey St. #105
Monterey Business Park
Torrance, CA 90503   Phone: (213)533-4800
Videocassette. 1982. 30 mins. A North Carolina fisherman discusses the pros and cons of a career in fishing.

★3462★
Fishers, Commercial
Chronicle Guidance Publications, Inc.
PO Box 1190
Moravia, NY 13118-1190   Phone: (315)497-0330
1989. This career brief describes the nature of the work, working conditions, hours and earnings, education and training, licensure, certification, unions, personal qualifications, social and psychological factors, employment outlook, entry methods, advancement, and related occupations. **Toll-free/Additional Phone Number(s):** 800-622-7284.

★3463★
"Fishers, Hunters, and Trappers" in *Occupational Outlook Handbook* (pp. 320-323)
Superintendent of Documents
U.S. Government Printing Office
Washington, DC 20402   Phone: (202)783-3238
Biennial; latest edition, 1990-91. Encyclopedia of careers describing more than 250 occupations and comprising about 86 percent of all jobs in the economy. Occupations that require lengthy education or training are given the most attention. For each occupation, the handbook describes job duties, working conditions, training, educational preparation, personal qualities, advancement possibilities, job outlook, earnings, and sources of additional information.

★3464★
Footsteps in the Ocean: Careers in Diving
Lodestar Books
2 Park Avenue
New York, NY 10016   Phone: (212)725-1818
Denise V. Lang. 1987. Explores employment opportunities in sport and commercial diving, science and research, in the military, and police work. Describes the work and training. Lists schools. **Facsimile Number:** (212)532-6568.

★3465★
Fur Trapping
New Win Publishing, Inc.
PO Box 5159
Clinton, NJ 08809   Phone: (201)735-9701
Bill Musgrove. 1983. **Facsimile Number:** (201)735-9703.

★3466★
Fur Trapping in North America
New Win Publishing, Inc.
PO Box 5159
Clinton, NJ 08809   Phone: (201)735-9701
Steven Geary. Revised and expanded edition, 1985. **Facsimile Number:** (201)735-9703.

★3467★
"Professional Diver" in *Offbeat Careers: The Directory of Unusual Work* (pp. 123-124)
Ten Speed Press
PO Box 7123
Berkeley, CA 94707   Phone: (415)845-8414
Al Sacharov. 1988. Profiles eighty-eight unusual careers. Provides job description, history of occupation, salary, and training required. Lists one or more sources of additional information.

★3468★
Transportation
Learning Corporation of America
108 Wilmot Rd.
Deerfield, IL 60015-9990   Phone: (708)940-1260
Videocassette. 1982. 21 mins. In this program from the "Working" series, we meet five employees in transportation-related jobs: fishing boat captain, auto body repair shop owner, construction equipment operator, air traffic controller and truck driver.

★3469★
"Wildlife Management Trapper" in *Action Careers: Employment in the High-Risk Job Market* (pp. 291-299)
Citadel Press/Lyle Stuart Inc.
Carol Publishing Group
120 Enterprise Ave.
Secaucus, NJ 07094   Phone: (201)866-0490
Ragnar Benson. 1988. Describes 24 dangerous careers such as repo man, explosives handler, and river rafting guide. Each profile includes demand for the job, where the jobs can be found, required personal and physical characteristics and training needed.

Associations

★3470★
American Pilots' Association (APA)
1055 Thomas Jefferson St. NW
Washington, DC 20007   Phone: (202)333-9377
Membership: State associations of licensed state marine pilots representing 1050 members. **Purpose:** Seeks to improve pilotage services. **Publications:** *State Pilotage in America*. **Facsimile Number:** (202)337-6528.

★3471★
Marine Technology Society (MTS)
1825 K St. NW, Ste. 218
Washington, DC 20006   Phone: (202)775-5966
Membership: Scientists, engineers, educators, and others with professional interests in the marine sciences or related fields; includes institutional and corporate members. **Purpose:** To disseminate marine scientific and technical information, including institutional, environmental, physical, and biological aspects; to foster a deeper understanding of the world's seas and attendant technologies. Maintains 14 sections. Operates 500 volume library. Sponsors competitions and bestows awards; conducts tutorials. **Publications:** *Marine Technology Society Journal*, quarterly. • *Newsletter*, bimonthly. • Also publishes transactions of meetings and conference proceedings. **Facsimile Number:** (202)429-9417.

★3472★
National Association of Underwater Instructors (NAUI)
PO Box 14650
Montclair, CA 91763   Phone: (714)621-5801
Membership: Certified instructors of basic, advanced, and specialized courses in underwater diving. **Purpose:** Offers instructor certification programs and training programs. Conducts seminars, workshops, and symposia. Sells diving education books; maintains library of 500 volumes on diving and diving instruction. Sponsors competitions and bestows awards; maintains speakers' bureau and placement service; conducts charitable programs. **Publications:** *Sources: The Journal of Underwater Education*, bimonthly. • Also publishes textbooks. **Toll-free/Additional Phone Number(s):** (800)553-6284. **Facsimile Number:** (714)621-6405.

★3473★
National Oceanic and Atmospheric Administration Office of Public Affairs
1335 East-West Hwy.
Silver Spring, MD 20910
Provides general information on fishing occupations.

★3474★
National Rifle Association of America (NRA)
1600 Rhode Island Ave. NW
Washington, DC 20036   Phone: (202)828-6000
Membership: Target shooters, hunters, gun collectors, gunsmiths, police officers, and others interested in firearms. **Purpose:** Promotes rifle, pistol, and shotgun shooting, hunting, gun collecting, home firearm safety, and wildlife conservation. Encourages civilian marksmanship. Educates police firearms instructors. Maintains national and international records of shooting competitions; sponsors teams to compete in world championships. Also maintains comprehensive collection of antique and modern firearms. Administers the NRA Political Victory Fund. Bestows awards; compiles statistics; sponsors research and education programs; maintains speakers' bureau and museum. Operates library of 1000 volumes; lobbies on firearms issues. **Publications:** *American Hunter*, monthly. • *American Rifleman*, monthly. • *InSights*, monthly. • *Shooting Sports USA*, monthly. • *NRAction*, bimonthly. **Toll-free/Additional Phone Number(s):** (800)368-5714.

★3475★
National Trappers Association (NTA)
PO Box 3667
Bloomington, IL 61702   Phone: (309)829-2422
Membership: Harvesters of furbearers (muskrat, fox, coyote, mink, beaver, raccoon, bobcat, and others) for the purpose of wildlife management, animal damage control, and outdoor recreation. **Purpose:** Promotes sound environmental education programs and conservation of natural resources. Presents Trapper of the Year, Conservationist of the Year, and President's awards annually. Compiles statistics. **Publications:** *American Trapper*, bimonthly. • Also publishes *Facts About Fur*, *Furbearer Management*, *Traps Today*, and other educational materials. **Facsimile Number:** (309)829-7615.

★3476★
Sport Fishing Institute
1010 Massachusetts Ave., NW
Washington, DC 20001

Provides general information on fishing occupations; sponsors symposia on fisheries science and sport fisheries management. Maintains placement service. **Publications:** *SFI Bulletin*, 10/year; *Sportfishing News*, monthly.

Standards/Certification Agencies

★3477★
National Association of Underwater Instructors (NAUI)
PO Box 14650
Montclair, CA 91763   Phone: (714)621-5801

Offers instructor certification programs and training programs.

★3478★
U.S. Coast Guard
Merchant Vessel Personnel Division
2100 Second St., SW
Washington, DC 20593

Provides information on the licensing of captains and mates and requirements for merchant mariner documentation.

Educational Directories and Programs

★3479★
College of Oceaneering
International Diving School
272 S. Fries Ave.
Wilmington, CA 90744

Provides information on training programs to become certified as a professional umbilical diver.

Awards, Scholarships, Grants, and Fellowships

★3480★
Don Harger Memorial Award
Federation of Fly Fishers
P.O. Box 1088
West Yellowstone, MT 59758   Phone: (406)646-9541

To recognize an individual who has been actively engaged or closely related to some aspect of fly fishing as a vocation or avocation. A life membership in the Federation is awarded. Established in 1978 to honor Don Harger, a noted author, photographer and flytier from Salem, Oregon.

Basic Reference Guides and Handbooks

★3481★
Furbearer Management (NTA)
National Trappers Association (NTA)
PO Box 3667
Bloomington, IL 61702   Phone: (309)829-2422

★3482★
Get Set to Trap
Outdoor Empire Publishing, Inc.
PO Box 19000
Seattle, WA 98109   Phone: (206)624-3845
1982.

★3483★
Handy Medical Guide for Seafarers, Fisherman, Trawlermen & Yachtsmen
State Mutual Book & Periodical Service, Ltd.
521 5th Ave., 17th Fl.
New York, NY 10175   Phone: (212)682-5844
R. W. Scott. 1978.

★3484★
Muskrats & Marsh Management
University of Nebraska, Lincoln
University of Nebraska Press
901 N. 17th St.
Lincoln, NE 68588   Phone: (402)472-3581
Paul L. Errington. 1978. **Facsimile Number:** (402)472-6214.

★3485★
NTA Trapping Handbook: A Guide for Better Trapping
National Trappers Association
PO Box 3667
Bloomington, IL 61702   Phone: (309)829-2422
Tom Krause. 1984.

★3486★
Part Time Cash for the Sportsman: Twenty-Five Ways for the Fisherman & Hunter to Earn Extra Money
Northeast Sportsman's Press
PO Box 188
Tarrytown, NY 10591   Phone: (914)762-7193
Jim Capossela. 1984.

★3487★
Ragnar's Ten Best Traps & a Few Others That Are Damn Good, Too
Paladin Press
PO Box 1307
Boulder, CO 80306   Phone: (303)443-7250
Ragnar Benson. 1985. **Facsimile Number:** (303)442-8741.

★3488★
The Trapper's Bible: Traps, Snares, & Pathguards
Paladin Press
PO Box 1307
Boulder, CO 80306   Phone: (303)443-7250
Dale Martin. 1987. **Facsimile Number:** (303)442-8741.

★3489★
Trapper's Handbook
DBI Books, Inc.
4092 Commercial Ave.
Northbrook, IL 60062   Phone: (708)272-6310
Rick Jamison. 1983. **Facsimile Number:** (708)272-2051.

★3490★
Traps Today, (NTA)
National Trappers Association (NTA)
PO Box 3667
Bloomington, IL 61702   Phone: (309)829-2422

Periodicals

★3491★
American Angler
Box 280
Intervale, NH 03845   Phone: (603)356-9425
Jack Russell, Editor. 6x/yr. Fishing magazine.

★3492★
American Hunter
National Rifle Assn. of America
470 Spring Park Pl., Ste. 1000
Herndon, VA 22070   Phone: (703)481-3383
Thomas Fulgham, Editor. Monthly. Hunting magazine emphasizing technique, sportsmanship, and safety. **Facsimile Number:** (703)481-3376.

★3493★
American Rifleman (NRA)
National Rifle Association of America (NRA)
1600 Rhode Island Ave. NW
Washington, DC 20036   Phone: (202)828-6000
Monthly. Magazine containing reports on equipment, tournaments, Olympics, collector items, and NRA news. Also includes book reviews, calendar of events, equipment reviews, shoot results, and shooting range descriptions.

★3494★
American Trapper
National Trappers Assn.
PO Box 3667
Bloomington, IL 61701   Phone: (307)850-3830
Tom Krause, Editor. Bimonthly. Fur trade magazine.

★3495★
Angler & Hunter
Ontario Outdoor Publishing Ltd.
Box 1541
Peterborough, ON, Canada K9J 7H7   Phone: (705)748-3891
Gary Ball, Editor. 10x/yr. Magazine featuring fishing, hunting, and conservation. **Facsimile Number:** (705)748-9577.

★3496★
Atlantic Offshore Fisherman's Association—Newsletter
Atlantic Offshore Fisherman's Association
221 Third St.
PO Box 3001
Newport, RI 02840   Phone: (401)849-3232
Editor(s): Susan Cortis and Richard Allen. Quarterly. Discusses news and concerns of the organization, fishing policies, and trade news affecting the fishing industry. Recurring features include news of members.

★3497★
The Badger Sportsman
19 E. Main St.
Chilton, WI 53014   Phone: (414)849-4551
Tom Woodrow, Editor. Monthly. Hunting, fishing, and camping magazine.

★3498★
Bassin'
NatCom. Inc.
15115 S. 76 E. Ave.
Bixby, OK 74008   Phone: (918)366-4441
Gordon Sprouse, Mng. Editor. Eight times/yr. Bass fishing magazine featuring articles on the proper use of equipment, techniques the experts use, and suggestions for the best locations to fish; including profiles of bass fishermen who have landed a prizewinning catch, product reviews of what's new and old standbys, and regular columns by the experts. **Facsimile Number:** (918)366-4439.

★3499★
Bassmaster Magazine
B.A.S.S., Inc.
PO Box 17900
Montgomery, AL 36117   Phone: (205)272-9530
Dave Precht, Editor. Ten times/yr. Magazine covering boating and freshwater bass fishing. **Facsimile Number:** (205)279-7148.

★3500★
Bowhunter Magazine
Cowles Magazines, Inc.
2245 Kohn Rd.
PO Box 8200
Harrisburg, PA 17105-8200   Phone: (717)657-9555
M.R. James, Editor and Publisher. 8x/yr. Magazine. **Facsimile Number:** (717)657-9526.

★3501★
The Chase
1150 Industry Rd.
Lexington, KY 40505   Phone: (606)254-4262
Jo Ann Stone, Editor/Advertising Mgr. Monthly. Magazine on fox hunting.

★3502★
Commercial Fisheries News
Compass Publications, Inc., Fisheries Division
PO Box 37
Stonington, ME 04681   Phone: (207)367-2396
Robin Alden, Editor and Publisher. Monthly. Magazine for commercial fishermen. **Facsimile Number:** (207)367-2490.

★3503★
Deer & Deer Hunting
The Stump Sitters, Inc.
PO Box 1117
Appleton, WI 54912   Phone: (414)734-0009
R.P. Schwalbach, Mng. Editor. 8x/yr. Magazine devoted to the hunting of white-tailed deer focusing on techniques, deer biology, behavior and management. **Facsimile Number:** (414)734-2919.

★3504★
Delta Pride News
Delta Catfish Processors, Inc.
Industrial Park
PO Box 850
Indianola, MS 38751   Phone: (601)887-5401
Editor(s): Carolyn Ann Sledge. Quarterly. Informs customers and stockholders of new developments and techniques within Delta Catfish Processors and within the fresh fish processing industry. Recurring features include news of research, staff news, items on the annual Brokers' Conference and on awards won by Delta Catfish, new product introductions, information on training materials available, and columns titled A Message

From the President and Outlook on Supply and Demand. **Facsimile Number:** (601)887-5950.

★3505★
Eastern Woods and Waters
James Publications Ltd.
201 Brownlow Ave., Ste. 33
Dartmouth, NS, Canada B2Y 3Y5   Phone: (902)468-2682
Jim Gourlay, Editor. 8x/yr. Magazine featuring articles on hunting, fishing, trapping, environmental concerns, and wildlife management. **Facsimile Number:** (902)468-3996.

★3506★
Field and Stream
Times-Mirror Magazines, Inc.
2 Park Ave.
New York, NY 10016   Phone: (212)779-5000
Duncan Barnes, Editor. Monthly. Magazine focusing on hunting, fishing, camping, and boating. **Facsimile Number:** (212)779-5468.

★3507★
Fins & Feathers
318 Franklin W.
Minneapolis, MN 55404   Phone: (612)874-8001
Dave Greer, Editor. Monthly. Magazine featuring fishing, hunting, and conservation.

★3508★
Fish Boat
Journal Publications
PO Box 1348
Mandeville, LA 70470   Phone: (504)626-0298
Robert Carpenter, Editor. Quarterly. Magazine for the commercial fishing industry. **Facsimile Number:** (504)624-4801.

★3509★
Fish Finder Magazines
Fish Finder Industries
1233 W. Jackson St.
Orlando, FL 32805   Phone: (407)425-0045
Geoff Hall, Editor. Monthly. Magazines covering fishing and hunting markets in 35 states. Published in 25 regional editions. **Facsimile Number:** (407)425-1529.

★3510★
Fish News
New England Fisheries Development Association, Inc.
309 World Trade Center
Boston, MA 02210-2001   Phone: (617)439-5480
Editor(s): Ken Coons. Quarterly. Reports events affecting the fishing and seafood processing and distributing industry in the Northeast U.S. Reports on research and demonstration projects. Recurring features include fisheries statistics and announcements of upcoming meetings and trade shows. **Facsimile Number:** (617)439-5481.

★3511★
The Fisherman
14 Ramsey Rd.
Shirley, NY 11967   Phone: (516)345-5200
Peter Barrett, Editor. Weekly (Thurs.). Not issued last 2 weeks of Dec. Magazine covering local fresh and salt water sportfishing.

★3512★
The Fisherman
The Fisherman Publishing Society
160-111 Victoria Dr.
Vancouver, BC, Canada V5L 4C4   Phone: (604)255-1366
David Lane, Editor. Monthly. Commercial fishing industry newspaper. **Facsimile Number:** (604)255-3162.

★3513★
Fishing
Petersen Publishing Co.
6725 Sunset Blvd.
Los Angeles, CA 90078   Phone: (213)854-2222
Bob Robb, Editor. 6x/yr. Fishing magazine. **Facsimile Number:** (213)854-2718.

★3514★
Fishing & Boating Illustrated
Gallant/Charger Publications, Inc.
34249 Camino Capistrano
Capistrano Beach, CA 92624
Bob Zwirk, Editor. Quarterly Fishing and boating magazine.

★3515★
Fishing and Hunting News
PO Box C-19000
Seattle, WA 98109   Phone: (206)624-3845
Vince Malernee, Editor. Every other week (Thurs.). Hunting, fishing and outdoor sports magazine. **Facsimile Number:** (206)340-9816.

★3516★
Fishing Facts
Northwoods Publishing Co.
PO Box 609
Menomonee Falls, WI 53052-0609   Phone: (414)255-4800
George J. Pazik, Editor and Publisher. Nine times/yr. Magazine on freshwater sport fishing. **Facsimile Number:** (414)255-1694.

★3517★
Flashes
National Fisheries Institute
1525 Wilson Blvd., Ste. 500
Arlington, VA 22209   Phone: (703)524-8880
Editor(s): Emily Holt-Chambers. Monthly. Publishes information on the activities of the Institute and other fishery organizations and on seafood consumption. Covers government actions which affect fishing, such as the National Marine Fisheries Service budget, EPA water quality standards, endangered fishes, fishing rules and regulations, and commercial shipping and trade laws. Recurring features include news of members, news of research, book reviews, and a calendar of events.

★3518★
Fly Fisherman
Cowles Magazines
2245 Kohn Rd.
PO Box 8200
Harrisburg, PA 17105-8200   Phone: (717)657-9555
John Randolph, Editor and Publisher. 6x/yr. Magazine of interest to fly fishermen. **Facsimile Number:** (717)657-9526.

Fishers, Hunters, and Trappers

★3519★
Fly Rod & Reel
Down East Enterprise, Inc.
PO Box 370
Camden, ME 04843   Phone: (207)594-9544
Silvio Calabi, Editor. Six times/yr. **Facsimile Number:** (207)594-7215.

★3520★
Flyfishing
Frank Amato Publications
PO Box 82112
Portland, OR 97282   Phone: (503)653-8151
Marty Sherman, Editor. 5x/yr. Flyfishing magazine. **Facsimile Number:** (503)653-2766.

★3521★
FlyFishing News, Views & Reviews
Bitton Advertising
1387 Cambridge Dr.
Idaho Falls, ID 83401   Phone: (208)523-7300
Dennis Bitton, Editor. Six times/yr. Flyfishing newspaper containing press releases, news stories, and fiction.

★3522★
FUR-FISH-GAME
A.R. Harding Publishing Co.
2878 E. Main St.
Columbus, OH 43209   Phone: (614)231-9585
Mitch Cox, Editor. Monthly. Magazine featuring hunting, trapping, fishing, dogs, and conservation.

★3523★
Game & Fish Magazine
Game & Fish Publications, Inc.
2250 Newmarket Pkwy., Ste. 110
Marietta, GA 30067   Phone: (404)953-9222
David Morris, Editor. Monthly. Magazine with specific state editions providing in-depth information on the wheres, whens, and hows of hunting and fishing in these states.

★3524★
Gray's Sporting Journal
PO Box 130
Lyme, NH 03768   Phone: (603)795-4757
Edward Gray, Editor. 6x/yr. Hunting and fishing magazine. **Facsimile Number:** (603)795-2238.

★3525★
Grit and Steel
De Camp Publishing Co.
Drawer 280
Gaffney, SC 29342   Phone: (803)489-2324
Mary M. Hodge, Editor. Monthly. Game fowl magazine.

★3526★
Hook, Line & Sinker
Rte. 3, Box 337-C
Harrisburg, AR 72432   Phone: (501)578-9501
William J. Beasley, Editor. Quarterly. Fishing magazine. **Facsimile Number:** (501)578-5480.

★3527★
Hooks and Lines
International Women's Fishing Association
P.O. Drawer 3125
Palm Beach, FL 33480
Editor(s): Joan S. Willmott. Bimonthly. Covers the fishing activities of the members, with news items and stories. Recurring features include a calendar of events.

★3528★
The Hospitality Manager
Kassis Communications
120 Hayward
Ames, IA 50010   Phone: (515)296-2400
Terry Lowman, Editor. Monthly. Trade publication (tabloid) covering restaurant and institutional business in the Midwest. Mailed to restaurants, bars, and institutional food service companies. **Facsimile Number:** (515)296-2405.

★3529★
Hunting and Fishing Event Newsletter
Association of American Rod and Gun Clubs, Europe
USAREUR DCSPER
APO
New York, NY 09403
Editor(s): Lee Miethke. Monthly. Offers information on hunting and fishing events and trips throughout Europe. Encourages sportsmanship and game conservation and provides items on hunting and fishing techniques. Recurring features include news of association trips and training programs.

★3530★
The Hunting Report for Big Game Hunters
Oxpecker Enterprises, Inc.
12515 N. Kendall Dr., Ste. 302
Miami, FL 33186-1830   Phone: (305)598-0158
Editor(s): Don Causey. Monthly. Comments on big game hunting conditions, cost, and likelihood of success. Reports recent big game hunting trips by subscribers. **Toll-free/Additional Phone Number(s):** (305)598-0735 **Facsimile Number:** (305)598-0196.

★3531★
IIFET Newsletter
International Institute of Fisheries Economics and Trade (IIFET)
Office of International Research and Development
Oregon State University
Snell Hall 400
Corvallis, OR 97331-1641   Phone: (503)737-2228
Editor(s): Ann L. Shriver. Semiannually. Keeps members abreast of events in the fisheries sectors around the world and facilitates cooperative research in the field. Also covers association workshops, conferences, and training programs. Recurring features include notices of publications available, news of research, and information on new companies and business opportunities. **Facsimile Number:** (503)737-3447.

★3532★
InSights (NRA)
National Rifle Association of America (NRA)
1600 Rhode Island Ave. NW
Washington, DC 20036   Phone: (202)828-6000
Monthly. Magazine including articles on firearm education and safety and hunting tips.

★3533★
The International Angler
International Game Fish Association
3000 E. Las Olas Blvd.
Ft. Lauderdale, FL 33316   Phone: (305)467-0161
Editor(s): Ray Crawford. Bimonthly. Provides information on recreational angling throughout the world. Covers subjects including game fish legislation and conservation efforts, scientific tag and release and other data collection programs, and world record fish catches. Recurring features include information on new fishing areas, new publications, and activities of the association.

★3534★
International Light Tackle Tournament Association— Bulletin
International Light Tackle Tournament Association
2044 Federal Ave.
Costa Mesa, CA 92627   Phone: (714)548-4273
Editor(s): Helen R. Smith. After every tournament. Provides members with detailed formal and informal accounts of light tackle fishing tournaments. **Facsimile Number:** (714)631-7642.

★3535★
Keeping Track
North American Hunting Club
PO Box 3401
Minnetonka, MN 55343   Phone: (612)936-9333
Editor(s): Bill Miller. Bimonthly. Promotes the enjoyment of game animal and bird hunting. Features articles on hunting techniques and equipment. Recurring features include reports on Club activities and programs, news of members, and a calendar of events. **Facsimile Number:** (612)944-2687.

★3536★
Living Among Nature Daringly
4466 Ike Mooney Rd.
Silverton, OR 97381   Phone: (503)873-8829
Bill Anderson, Editor and Publisher. Five times/yr. Magazine for trappers, farmers, and nature lovers.

★3537★
Marine Fish Management
Nautilus Press, Inc.
1201 National Press Bldg.
Washington, DC 20045   Phone: (202)347-6643
Editor(s): John R. Botzum. Monthly. Discusses the organizational, legislative, and ideological issues confronting fisheries management, particularly of the living resources in the U.S. 200-mile fisheries zone. Provides information on aquaculture world fish management news. Recurring features include a calendar of events and news of research.

★3538★
Marine Technology Society Journal (MTS)
Marine Technology Society (MTS)
1825 K St. NW, Ste. 218
Washington, DC 20006   Phone: (202)775-5966
Quarterly. Includes book reviews.

★3539★
MTS Newsletter (MTS)
Marine Technology Society (MTS)
1825 K St. NW, Ste. 218
Washington, DC 20006   Phone: (202)775-5966
Bimonthly.

★3540★
Musky Hunter
ESOX Publishing, Inc.
959 W. Mason St.
Green Bay, WI 54303   Phone: (414)496-0334
Joe Bucher, Editor. 6x/yr. Magazine about musky fishing.

★3541★
National Fisherman
120 Tillson Ave.
PO Box 908
Rockland, ME 04841   Phone: (207)594-6222
James W. Fullilove, Editor. Monthly. Magazine covering the marine industry, including commercial fishing and boat building. **Facsimile Number:** (207)594-8978.

★3542★
Nikon World of Big Game Hunting
Aqua-Field Publications, Inc.
656 Shrewsbury Ave.
Shrewsbury, NJ 07701
Robert Elman, Editor. Magazine providing advice from foremost hunting writers.

★3543★
North American Fisherman
North American Outdoor Group, Inc.
PO Box 3403
Minnetonka, MN 55343   Phone: (612)936-0555
Russ Nolan, Advertising Dir. 6x/yr. Fishing magazine. **Facsimile Number:** (612)936-9755.

★3544★
North American Hunter
North American Hunting Club
12301 Whitewater Drive, Ste. 260
PO Box 3401
Minnetonka, MN 55343   Phone: (612)936-9333
Bill Miller, Editor. 6x/yr. Hunting magazine. **Facsimile Number:** (612)936-9755.

★3545★
North American Journal of Fisheries Management
American Fisheries Society
5410 Grosvenor Ln., Ste. 110
Bethesda, MD 20814-2199   Phone: (301)897-8616
Phyllis Cahn, Editor. 4x/yr. Fisheries management journal. **Facsimile Number:** (301)897-8096.

★3546★
NRAction (NRA)
National Rifle Association of America (NRA)
1600 Rhode Island Ave. NW
Washington, DC 20036   Phone: (202)828-6000
Bimonthly.

★3547★
Outdoor Sports and Recreation
PO Box 5023
Hopkins, MN 55343   Phone: (612)944-1230
Kevin Kennedy, Publisher. 6x/yr. Magazine devoted to fishing, hunting, and outdoor activities in the Midwest.

Fishers, Hunters, and Trappers

★3548★
Pacific Seafood Chronicle
West Coast Fisheries Development Foundation
P.O. Box 38
Portland, OR 97207-0038 Phone: (503)222-3518
Editor(s): Donna O. Reed. Monthly. Focuses on news about fisheries development on the West Coast and Foundation news. Also reports industry and legislative news. Recurring features include interviews, news of research, reports of meetings, and news of educational opportunities.

★3549★
Pacific States Marine Fisheries Commission—Newsletter
Pacific States Marine Fisheries Commission
2501 SW 1st Ave., No. 200
Portland, OR 97201 Phone: (503)326-7025
Editor(s): Russell G. Porter. 3-4/yr. Carries Commission news and articles concerned with Pacific coast fisheries. Reviews Commission activities with U.S. Congress. Recurring features include contract reports, statistics, news of research, and management activities. **Facsimile Number:** (503)326-7033.

★3550★
Petersen's Fishing
Petersen Publishing Co.
8490 Sunset Blvd.
Los Angeles, CA 90069 Phone: (213)854-2222
Bob Sarber, Editor. 6x/yr. Magazine covering fresh- and saltwater fishing.

★3551★
PRODUCT NEWS
Compass Publications, Inc.,-Fisheries Division
PO Box 37
Stonington, ME 04681 Phone: (207)367-2396
Robin Alden, Editor and Publisher. 6x/yr. New product publication for commercial fisherman. **Facsimile Number:** (207)367-2490.

★3552★
Salmon Trout Steelheader
PO Box 82112
Portland, OR 97282 Phone: (503)653-8108
Frank W. Amato, Editor and Publisher. 6x/yr. Magazine featuring salmon, trout, and steelhead sport fishing.

★3553★
Salt Water Sportsman
Times Mirror Magazines, Inc.
280 Summer St.
Boston, MA 02210 Phone: (617)439-9977
Colin M. Cunningham, Jr., Editor-in-Chief. Monthly. Magazine on salt water fishing. **Facsimile Number:** (617)439-9357.

★3554★
Sea Grant Extension Program Newsletter
Sea Grant M.A.P. Extension
University of California, Davis
Davis, CA 95616 Phone: (916)752-1497
Editor(s): Christopher M. Dewees. 6/yr. Discusses commercial fishing, seafood processing, vessel and gear operation and maintenance, recreational fishing, and oceanography. Also examines maritime law, marine education, marine recreation, and government regulations and guidelines affecting marine activity.

★3555★
SFI Bulletin
Sport Fishing Institute (SFI)
1010 Massachusetts Ave. NW, Ste. 320
Washington, DC 20001 Phone: (202)898-0770
Editor(s): Gilbert C. Radonski. 10/yr. Serves as an educational tool regarding the Institute's efforts in fish conservation. Covers fisheries science and management, habitat protection, aquatic ecology and ecosystems management, water pollution control and abatement, and recreational fisheries development. Recurring features include book reviews, editorials, staff commentaries on developments in the field, and coverage of relevant government actions.

★3556★
Shooting Sports USA (NRA)
National Rifle Association of America (NRA)
1600 Rhode Island Ave. NW
Washington, DC 20036 Phone: (202)828-6000
Monthly. Magazine including shooter profiles, shooting results, and how-to articles.

★3557★
Shooting Times
PJS Publications
News Plaza
PO Box 1790
Peoria, IL 61656 Phone: (309)682-6626
Jim Bequette, Editor. Monthly. Magazine focusing on guns and shooting sports. **Facsimile Number:** (309)682-7394.

★3558★
Southeastern Log
Box 7900
Ketchikan, AK 99901 Phone: (907)225-3157
Nikki Murray Jones, Editor. Monthly. Magazine on logging and fishing; also regional human interest articles.

★3559★
Southern Outdoors
B.A.S.S., Inc.
PO Box 17915
Montgomery, AL 36141 Phone: (205)277-3940
Larry Teague, Editor. 9x/yr. Outdoor magazine covering fishing, hunting, camping, and outdoor recreation.

★3560★
Southern Saltwater
B.A.S.S., Inc.
5776 Carmichael Pkwy.
Montgomery, AL 36117 Phone: (205)272-9530
Colin Moore, Editor. Monthly (4 issues); every other month (4 issues). Magazine covering saltwater fishing in coastal southern U.S. **Facsimile Number:** (205)279-7148.

★3561★
The Southwestern Sportsman Magazine
HCR 3045
Winkelman, AZ 85292 Phone: (602)356-6049
Lee Hetrick, Editor. Six times/yr. Magazine for the everyday hunter and fisherman.

★3562★
Sport Fishing
World Publications, Inc.
330 W. Canton Ave.
Winter Park, FL 32789   Phone: (407)628-4802
Pierce Hoover, Editor; Terry Snow, Publisher; Matt Hamill, Advertising Mgr. 6x/yr. Magazine about offshore saltwater fishing.

★3563★
SPORTING CLASSICS
Live Oak Press, Inc.
PO Box 1017
Camden, SC 29020   Phone: (803)425-1003
Charles A. Wechsler, Editor. 6x/yr. Hunting and fishing magazine. **Facsimile Number:** (803)432-8056.

★3564★
The Trapper
McIntosh Publishing Co. Ltd.
PO Box 430
North Battleford, SK, Canada S9A 2Y5   Phone: (306)445-4401
Bill McIntosh, Mng. Editor. 6x/yr. 8 1/4 x 10 1/2 Magazine for the fur trade. **Facsimile Number:** (306)445-1977.

★3565★
The Trapper and Predator Caller
Krause Publications, Inc.
700 E. State St.
Iola, WI 54990   Phone: (715)445-2214
Gordy Krahn, Editor. Monthly. Magazine on hunting, trapping, and predator calling. **Facsimile Number:** (715)445-4087.

★3566★
The Turkey Hunter
Krause Publications, Inc.
700 E. State St.
Iola, WI 54990   Phone: (715)445-2214
Gerry Blair, Editor. 8x/yr. Sportsmen magazine featuring turkey hunting. **Facsimile Number:** (715)445-4087.

★3567★
Waterfowler's World
Waterfowl Publications, Inc.
PO Box 38613
Memphis, TN 38183-0613   Phone: (901)685-8440
Cindy Dixon, Editor. 6x/yr. Hunting magazine.

★3568★
Wildfowl
Stover Publishing Co., Inc.
1901 Bell Ave., Ste. 4
PO Box 35098
Des Moines, IA 50315   Phone: (515)243-2472
Bob Wilbanks, Editor. 6x/yr. **Facsimile Number:** (515)243-0233.

★3569★
Wildlife Crusader
Manitoba Wildlife Federation
1770 Notre-Dame Ave.
Winnipeg, MB, Canada R3E 3K2   Phone: (204)633-5967
Denis C. Corneau, Editor. 6x/yr. Magazine about wildlife and habitat conservation; hunting, fishing, and camping. **Facsimile Number:** (204)632-5200.

★3570★
Wildlife Harvest
Wildlife Harvest Publications
PO Box 96
Goose Lake, IA 52750   Phone: (319)242-3046
John M. Mullin, Editor and Publisher. Monthly. Magazine for hunting resorts, sportsmen's clubs, gun clubs, dog kennels, and commercial gamebird producers.

★3571★
Wing & Shot
Stover Publishing Co., Inc.
1901 Bell Ave., Ste. 4
PO Box 35098
Des Moines, IA 50315   Phone: (515)243-2472
Robert Wilbanks, Editor. 6x/yr. **Facsimile Number:** (515)243-0233.

Meetings and Conventions

★3572★
AGRITECH - International Agriculture, Horticulture, Irrigation and Fisheries Exhibition
World Access Corp.
15 Bemis Rd.
PO Box 171
Wellesley Hills, MA 02181   Phone: (617)235-8095

★3573★
American Convention of Meat Processors
American Association of Meat Processors
PO Box 269
Elizabethtown, PA 17022   Phone: (717)367-1168
1992; Jul. 09-12; Orlando, FL • 1993; Jul. 26-29; Las Vegas, NV • 1994; Aug. 04-07; Milwaukee, WI • 1995; Jul. 20-23; San Antonio, TX. **Facsimile Number:** (717)367-9096.

★3574★
American Fisheries Society Convention
American Fisheries Society
5410 Grosvenor Ln.
Bethesda, MD 20814   Phone: (301)897-8616
1992; Sep. 14-17; Rapid City, SD • 1993; Aug. 26-04; Portland, OR. **Facsimile Number:** (301)897-8096.

★3575★
Fish Expo
National Fisherman Expositions
5 Milk St.
PO Box 7437
Portland, ME 04112   Phone: (207)772-3005
Frequency: Always held in Seattle, Washington, in odd-numbered years and in Boston, Massachusetts, in even-numbered years. 1992; Oct. 15-17; Boston, MA • 1993; Oct. Seattle, WA • 1994; Oct. 13-15; Boston, MA. **Facsimile Number:** (207)772-5059.

★3576★
National Rifle Association of America (NRA)
1600 Rhode Island Ave. NW
Washington, DC 20036   Phone: (202)828-6000
1992; Apr. 24-28; Salt Lake City, UT • 1993; Apr. 23-27; Nashville, TN. **Toll-free/Additional Phone Number(s):** (800)368-5714.

Fishers, Hunters, and Trappers

★3577★
National Trappers Association (NTA)
PO Box 3667
Bloomington, IL 61702   Phone: (309)829-2422
Frequency: Annual - usually third week in August. **Facsimile Number:** (309)829-7615.

Other Sources of Information

★3578★
The Book of the Free Trapper
Pioneer Press
DGW Bldg.
PO Box 684
Union City, TN 38261   Phone: (901)885-0374
Keith Walters. 1981.

★3579★
Distant Water: The Fate of the North Atlantic Fisherman
Viking Penguin
375 Hudson St.
New York, NY 10014   Phone: (212)366-2000
William W. Warner. 1984.

★3580★
Facts About Fur (NTA)
National Trappers Association (NTA)
PO Box 3667
Bloomington, IL 61702   Phone: (309)829-2422

★3581★
Lake Erie Fisherman: Work, Identity & Tradition
University of Illinois, Urbana-Champaign
University of Illinois Press
54 E. Gregory Dr.
Champaign, IL 61820   Phone: (217)333-0950
Timothy C. Lloyd. 1990. **Facsimile Number:** (217)244-8082.

Timber Cutting and Logging Workers

Timber cutting and logging operations are performed by a variety of workers. Fallers cut down trees with chain saws or mechanical felling equipment. Buckers trim off the tops and branches and buck (cut) the resulting logs into specified lengths. These workers usually use gas-powered chain saws. Choker setters fasten chokers (steel cables or chains) around logs to be skidded (dragged) by tractors or forwarded by the cable yarding system to the landing. Included are riggers, who set up and dismantle the cables and guy wires of the cable yarding system. Logging tractor operators drive crawler or wheeled tractors to skid logs from the felling site to the landing. Some operate harvesters— tractors outfitted with specialized equipment that can cut and delimb trees. Others operate forwarders that haul the logs to the landing and load them onto trucks. Log handling equipment operators operate tracked and wheeled equipment to load or unload logs and pulpwood onto or off trucks or gondola railroad cars. Log graders and scalers inspect logs for defects, measure logs to determine their volume, and estimate the marketable content or value of logs or pulpwood. Cruisers hike through forests to assess logging conditions and estimate the volume of marketable timber. Brush clearing laborers clear areas of brush and other growth to prepare for logging activities and to promote growth of desirable species of trees. Tree trimmers prune tree tops and branches, using saws or pruning shears. Pickers select and place logs onto skidders and log blocks onto conveyors to be sent to other machines for further processing. Log markers determine the bucking points at which logs will be sawn into sections. Rivers use sledge hammers, mallets, wedges, and froes (cleaving tools) to split logs to form posts, pickets, shakes, and other objects. Rigging slingers determine the sequence of logs to be yarded by the cable yarding system. Chasers direct the placement of logs at landings and disengage their chokers. Pulp pilers stack pulpwood logs at landings near logging roads. Most salaried timber cutting and logging workers are employed in the logging camps and logging contractors industry. Others work in the sawmills and planing mills and arborist services industries. Although logging operations are found in most states, Oregon and Washington account for about 25 percent of logging workers. About 30 percent of all logging workers are self-employed. While seasonal demand for logging workers varies slightly by region, employment generally is highest in the summer and lowest in the winter.

―――――――――――――― **$alaries** ――――――――――――――

Generally, earnings of more skilled workers are substantially higher than those of less skilled workers.

    Full-time logging workers $17,400/year

―――――――――――― **Employment Outlook** ――――――――――――

Growth rate until the year 2000: Slower than average.

Timber Cutting and Logging Workers

Career Guides

★3582★
Career Success Series
Cambridge Career Products
90 MacCorkle Ave., SW
South Charleston, WV 25311   Phone: (304)744-9323
Videocassette. 1986. 15 mins. A series, available separately, outlining various career choices for students. Occupations include: flight service, air transportation/ground service, data processing, carpentry, clerk in banking/insurance, commodity sales, cosmetic personal grooming, fire fighting, forestry services, home economics, insulation/roofing, material handling, mechanics, photographic processing, pipefitting and plumbing, police science, printing, secretarial services, and utilities equipment operator.

★3583★
Logger
Careers, Inc.
PO Box 135
Largo, FL 34649-0135   Phone: (813)584-7333
1988. Two-page occupational summary card describing duties, working conditions, personal qualifications, training, earnings and hours, employment outlook, places of employment, related careers and where to write for more information.

★3584★
"Logger" in *Agribusiness, Environment, and Natural Resources,* Volume 2 of *Career Information Center* (pp. 51-53)
Glencoe/Macmillan
15319 Chatsworth St.
Mission Hills, CA 91345   Phone: (818)898-1391
Richard Lidz and Dale Anderson, editorial directors. Fourth edition, 1990. For 600 occupations, describes job duties, entry-level requirements, education and training needed, advancement possibilities, employment outlook, earnings and benefits. The set is divided into 12 volumes. Each volume includes jobs related under a broad career field. Volume 13 is the index. **Facsimile Number:** 818-365-5489.

★3585★
"Logger" in *Occu-Facts: Information on 565 Careers in Outline Form* (p. 14.17)
Careers, Inc.
P.O. Box 135
1211 Tenth St., S.W.
Largo, FL 33640   Phone: (813)584-7333
Elizabeth Handville. Biennial, 1989-90 edition. Each one-page occupational profile describes duties, working conditions, physical surroundings and demands, aptitudes, temperament, educational requirements, employment outlook, earnings, and places of employment.

★3586★
Logging Industry Workers
Chronicle Guidance Publications, Inc.
PO Box 1190
Moravia, NY 13118-1190   Phone: (315)497-0330
1990. This career brief describes the nature of the work, working conditions, hours and earnings, education and training, licensure, certification, unions, personal qualifications, social and psychological factors, employment outlook, entry methods, advancement, and related occupations. **Toll-free/Additional Phone Number(s):** 800-622-7284.

★3587★
"Logging Industry Workers" in Volume 4 of *Career Discovery Encyclopedia* (pp. 42-43)
J.G. Ferguson Publishing Co.
200 W. Monroe
Chicago, IL 60606   Phone: (312)580-5480
E. Russell Primm, editor-in-chief. 1990. Contains two-page articles on 504 occupations. Each article describes job duties, earnings, and educational and training requirements.

★3588★
"Logging Industry Workers" in Volume 3 of *The Encyclopedia of Careers and Vocational Guidance* (pp. 373-377)
J.G. Ferguson Publishing Co.
200 W. Monroe
Chicago, IL 60606   Phone: (312)580-5480
William E. Hopke, editor-in-chief. Eighth edition, 1990. Four-volume set that profiles 500 occupations and describes job trends in 76 industries. Includes career description, educational requirements, history of the job, methods of entry, advancement, employment outlook, earnings, working conditions, social and psychological factors, and sources of additional information.

★3589★
Timber & the Forest Service
University of Kansas, Lawrence
University Press of Kansas
Lawrence, KS 66049   Phone: (913)864-4154
David A. Clary. 1986. Part of Development of Western Resources Series. **Facsimile Number:** (913)864-4586.

★3590★
"Timber Cutting and Logging Workers" in *Occupational Outlook Handbook* (pp. 323-325)
Superintendent of Documents
U.S. Government Printing Office
Washington, DC 20402   Phone: (202)783-3238

Biennial; latest edition, 1990-91. Encyclopedia of careers describing more than 250 occupations and comprising about 86 percent of all jobs in the economy. Occupations that require lengthy education or training are given the most attention. For each occupation, the handbook describes job duties, working conditions, training, educational preparation, personal qualities, advancement possibilities, job outlook, earnings, and sources of additional information.

Associations

★3591★
Northeastern Loggers Association (NELA)
PO Box 69
Old Forge, NY 13420   Phone: (315)369-3078

Membership: Timberland owners, independent loggers, professional foresters, and primary wood products industries. **Purpose:** Works to improve the industry in the Northeast and educate the public about the policies, practices, and products of the industry. Maintains Forest Industries Exhibit Hall. Cooperates in research by public and private agencies. Sponsors scholarship competition; bestows awards. **Publications:** *Northern Logger and Timber Processor*, monthly. **Facsimile Number:** (315)369-3736.

★3592★
Pacific Logging Congress (PLC)
2300 SW 6th Ave., Ste. 200
Portland, OR 97201   Phone: (503)224-8406

Membership: Logging firms, manufacturers of wood products and logging equipment, and distributors in Canada, New Zealand, and the United States. **Purpose:** Conducts symposia. **Publications:** *Pacific Logging Journal*, quarterly. **Facsimile Number:** (503)390-3262.

★3593★
Timber Producers Association of Michigan and Wisconsin
PO Box 39
Tomahawk, WI 54487

Provides general information about timber cutting and logging careers, including information on training programs.

Awards, Scholarships, Grants, and Fellowships

★3594★
Northeastern Loggers Association Awards Program
Northeastern Loggers' Association
c/o George Mitchell, Executive Director
P.O. box 69
Old Forge, NY 13420   Phone: (315)369-3078

To recognize significant achievement in forestry and wood utilization during the year in eight major categories: (1) outstanding logging operator; (2) outstanding sawmill operator; (3) outstanding service to the forest industry; (4) outstanding management of resources; (5) outstanding leadership in industry; (6) outstanding contributions to forest industry education; (7) outstanding use of wood; and (8) outstanding contribution to safety. Individuals or organizations need not be members of the Northeastern Loggers' Association. The nominee must reside in or conduct business in the Northeastern or Lake States Region of the United States as delineated by the USFA. The deadline for nominations is January 31. A maximum of one award is given in each category when merited. A plaque is awarded in each of the categories with the exception of the Safety Award. In addition to the plaque, the winner receives a monetary award of $300.

Basic Reference Guides and Handbooks

★3595★
International Tropical Timber Agreement
United Nations Publishing Service
Rm. DC2-0853
New York, NY 10017   Phone: (212)963-8302
1985. **Facsimile Number:** (212)963-3489.

★3596★
Logging & Sawmilling Journal—Guide to Government & Trade Associations
Maclean Hunter Canadian Publishing
700-1111 Melville St.
Vancouver, BC, Canada V6E 3V6   Phone: (604)683-8254

Directory of trade associations, IWA-Canada locals, forest consultants, federal and provincial government departments that are involved with the forest industry or provide a service used by the industry. Entries include: Association, department, or local name, address, phone, and key contact person. **Facsimile Number:** (604)683-4335.

★3597★
Logging Companies Directory
American Business Directories, Inc.
American Business Information, Inc.
5711 S. 86th Circle
Omaha, NE 68127   Phone: (402)593-4600

Annual. 2,236. Entries include: Name, address, phone, size of advertisement, name of owner or manager, number of employees, year first in "Yellow Pages." Arrangement: Geographical. **Facsimile Number:** (402)331-1505.

★3598★
The Practical Design of Structural Elements of Timber
Gower Publishing Co.
Old Post Rd.
Brookfield, VT 05036   Phone: (802)276-3162
John W. Bull. 1989.

★3599★
Promoting Timber Cropping
Gower Publishing Comapany
Old Post Rd.
Brookfield, VT 05036   Phone: (802)276-3162
Paul A. Huber.

★3600★
Timber Cutting Practices
Miller Freeman Publications, Inc.
600 Harrison St.
San Francisco, CA 94105   Phone: (415)397-1881
Steve Conway. Third edtion, 1978.

Timber Cutting and Logging Workers

★3601★
Timber Designer's Manual
Beekman Publishers, Inc.
Rte. 212
PO Box 888
Woodstock, NY 12498   Phone: (914)679-2300
J. A. Baird. Second edition, 1988.

★3602★
Timber: Its Nature & Behavior
Van Nostrand Reinhold Co., Inc.
115 5th Ave.
New York, NY 10003   Phone: (212)254-3232
Dinwoodie. 1981. **Facsimile Number:** (212)254-9499.

★3603★
Timber: Its Structure, Properties & Utilization
Timber Press
9999 SW Wilshire
Portland, OR 97225   Phone: (503)292-0745
H. E. Desch. Sixth edition, 1980. **Facsimile Number:** (503)292-6607.

★3604★
Timber Management: A Quantitative Approach
John Wiley & Sons, Inc.
605 3rd Ave.
New York, NY 10158   Phone: (212)850-6000
Jerome L. Clutter. 1983. **Facsimile Number:** (212)850-6088.

★3605★
Timber!: Problems, Prospects, Policies
Iowa State University Press
Iowa State University
2121 S. State Ave.
Ames, IA 50010   Phone: (515)292-0140
William A. Duerr, editor. 1973. **Facsimile Number:** (515)292-3348.

★3606★
Timber Resources for America's Future: Forest Resource Report No. 14
Ayer Company Publishers, Inc.
50 Northwestern Dr., No. 10
PO Box 958
Salem, NH 03079   Phone: (603)898-1200
U.S. Department of Agriculture, Forest Service Staff. 1972. Part of Use & Abuse of America's Natural Resources Series.

★3607★
Timber Specifier's Guide: Understanding & Specifying Softwoods in Buildings
Blackwell Scientific Publications, Inc.
3 Cambridge Center, Ste. 208
Cambridge, MA 02142   Phone: (617)225-0401
J. A. Baird. 1990. **Facsimile Number:** (617)225-0412.

★3608★
Timber Supply: Issues & Options
Forest Products Research Society
2801 Marshall Ct.
Madison, WI 53705   Phone: (608)231-1361
1979. **Facsimile Number:** (608)231-2152.

★3609★
Vanishing Forest Reserves
Ayer Company Publishers, Inc.
50 Northwestern Dr., No. 10
PO Box 958
Salem, NH 03079   Phone: (603)898-1200
Willard G. Van Name. 1979. Part of Management of Public Lands in the U.S. Series.

--- Periodicals ---

★3610★
Aerial Applicator Farm, Forest & Fire
Drawer 2263
Santa Fe Springs, CA 90670   Phone: (213)948-3713
Robert G. Rosenblatt, Editor and Publisher. 9x/yr. Aerial agriculture and fire control.

★3611★
American Forests
American Forestry Assn.
PO Box 2000
Washington, DC 20013-2000   Phone: (202)667-3300
Bill Rooney, Editor. 6x/yr. Forest conservation magazine. **Facsimile Number:** (202)667-7751.

★3612★
Case 'n Base News
Wood Moulding and Millwork Producers Association
PO Box 25278
Portland, OR 97225   Phone: (503)292-9288
Editor(s): B.J. Tomasko. Monthly. Represents the association, providing members with information concerning the promotion, standardization, and marketing of millwork products. Also provides general news of the industry. Recurring features include news of educational opportunities, job listings, notices of publications available, and a calendar of events. **Facsimile Number:** (503)292-3490.

★3613★
Christmas Trees
Tree Publishers, Inc.
Box 107
Lecompton, KS 66050-0107   Phone: (913)887-6324
Charles (Chuck) W. Wright, Editor. Quarterly. Magazine covering the Christmas tree industry. **Facsimile Number:** (913)887-6734.

★3614★
Crow's Weekly Letter
C.C. Crow Publications, Inc.
PO Box 25749
Portland, OR 97225   Phone: (503)222-9576
Editor(s): Sam Sherrill. Weekly. Serves as a market report on lumber, plywood, and panel wood products, supplying news, analysis, and price information as a guide to sales. Carries market data on the transportation industry as it pertains to the shipment of forest products. Recurring features include housing market updates and news of industry events and personnel.

★3615★
Environmental Report
National Forest Products Association
1250 Connecticut Ave. NW, Ste. 200
Washington, DC 20036   Phone: (202)463-2700
Editor(s): Marilyn Haugen. Monthly. Supplies the paper and forest products industry with information on environmental

issues developments. Includes a 2-page status report on recent regulations, legislation, and litigation.

★3616★
Forest and Conservation History
Forest History Society
701 Vickers Ave.
Durham, NC 27701   Phone: (919)682-9319
David O. Percy, Editor. Quarterly. Journal on the history of forest use and conservation.

★3617★
Forest Conservation
L'Assn. Forestiere Quebecoise Inc.
915, boul. St-Cyrille Ouest, Bureau 110
Sillery, PQ, Canada G1S 1T8   Phone: (418)681-3588
Serge Beaucher, Editor/Dir. 10x/yr. Forest, environment, and natural sciences magazine (French). **Facsimile Number:** (418)681-1670.

★3618★
Forest World
World Forestry Center
4033 SW Canyon Rd.
Portland, OR 97221   Phone: (503)228-1367
John Blackwell, Pres. Quarterly. Magazine covering forest and natural resource issues. **Facsimile Number:** (503)228-3624.

★3619★
The Forestry Chronicle
Canadian Institute of Forestry/Institut Forestier du Canada
151 Slater St., Ste. 1005
Ottawa, ON, Canada K1P 5H3   Phone: (613)234-2242
Dr. I.C.M. Place, Editor. 6x/yr. Forestry journal. **Facsimile Number:** (613)234-6181.

★3620★
Hiballer Forest Magazine
H.B. Publishers
525 Seymour St., Ste. 206
Vancouver, BC, Canada V6B 3H7   Phone: (604)669-7833
Paul Young, Editor and Publisher. 6x/yr. Trade magazine concerning forestry. **Facsimile Number:** (604)669-5910.

★3621★
International Green Front Report ASustainable agriculture resourcesA
Friends of the Trees
PO Box 1064
Tonasket, WA 98855   Phone: (509)486-4726
Michael Pilarski, editor. Irregular; previous edition 1988; new edition expected 1991. Organizations and periodicals dealing with sustainable forestry and agriculture and related fields. Entries include: Organization or publisher name, address, phone, description of projects and activities, or description of periodical coverage. Arrangement: Classified by subject. Indexes: Organization name/periodical title. **Facsimile Number:** (509)486-4726.

★3622★
Log Trucker
Loggers World Publications
4206 Jackson Hwy.
Chehalis, WA 98532   Phone: (206)262-3376
Bill Palmroth, Editor. Monthly Magazine focusing on the transportation of logs from the woods to the mills and sorting yards. **Facsimile Number:** (206)262-3337.

★3623★
Logger and Lumberman
Dixie Publications
210 N. Main St.
Box 489
Wadley, GA 30477   Phone: (912)252-5237
Jack D. Smith, Editor and Publisher. Monthly. Magazine for the forest products industry. **Facsimile Number:** (912)252-1140.

★3624★
Loggers World
Loggers World Publications
4206 Jackson Hwy.
Chehalis, WA 98532   Phone: (206)262-3376
Finley Hays, Editor. Monthly. Trade magazine reporting on the logging industry. **Facsimile Number:** (206)262-3337.

★3625★
Logging and Sawmilling Journal
Maclean Hunter Ltd.
1111 Melville St., Ste. 700
Vancouver, BC, Canada V6E 3V6   Phone: (604)683-8254
Norm Poole, Editor. Monthly. Forest industry trade journal. **Facsimile Number:** (604)683-8202.

★3626★
Modern Woodworking
Target Magazine Group
167 Hwy. 72 E.
Collierville, TN 38027   Phone: (901)853-7720
Joyce Powell, Managing Editor. Monthly Magazine for management in the primary and secondary wood products industry. **Facsimile Number:** (901)853-6437.

★3627★
Monthly F.O.B. Price Summary, Past Sales (Coast Mills)
Western Wood Products Assn.
Yeon Bldg.
522 SW 5th Ave.
Portland, OR 97204-2122   Phone: (503)224-3930
Monthly. Statistical report covering lumber species produced by Coast Mills. **Facsimile Number:** (503)224-3934.

★3628★
Monthly F.O.B. Price Summary, Past Sales (Inland Mills)
Western Wood Products Assn.
Yeon Bldg.
522 SW 5th Ave.
Portland, OR 97204-2122   Phone: (503)224-3930
Monthly. Statistical reports on lumber species produced in the Inland area. **Facsimile Number:** (503)224-3934.

★3629★
National Catholic Forester
National Catholic Society of Foresters
446 E. Ontario
Chicago, IL 60611   Phone: (312)266-6250
Robert Nasenbeny, Editor. Quarterly Magazine informing membership of new products and activities.

★3630★
Northeastern Lumber Manufacturers Association— Information Log
Northeastern Lumber Manufacturers Association
272 Tuttle Rd.
PO Box 87A
Cumberland Center, ME 04021   Phone: (207)829-6901
Editor(s): Donna J. Reynolds. Monthly. Discusses the growth, harvesting, production, and marketing of Northeastern lumber.

Timber Cutting and Logging Workers ★3643★

Includes news of federal and state activities and of business of the association. **Toll-free/Additional Phone Number(s):** (207)829-4293

★3631★
Northern Journal of Applied Forestry
Society of American Foresters
5400 Grosvenor Ln.
Bethesda, MD 20814-2198   Phone: (301)897-8720
Harry V. Wiant, Jr., Editor. 4x/yr. Forestry industry magazine covering an area eastern Kansas and the areas northward and eastward (including all or part of 25 states and 6 provinces of Canada). **Facsimile Number:** (301)897-3690.

★3632★
Northern Logger and Timber Processor
N.L. Publishing, Inc.
PO Box 69
Old Forge, NY 13420   Phone: (315)369-3078
Eric A. Johnson, Editor. Monthly. Magazine for logging and lumber manufacturers. **Facsimile Number:** (315)369-3736.

★3633★
Out of the Woods
Western Forest Industries Association
1500 SW Taylor
Portland, OR 97205   Phone: (503)224-5455
Editor(s): David Ford. Weekly. Covers news of the forest products industry, including significant government and legislative actions and business statistics and trends. Recurring features include reprints of relevant articles from newspapers around the country.

★3634★
Random Lengths
Random Lengths Publications, Inc.
PO Box 867
Eugene, OR 97440-0867   Phone: (503)686-9925
Editor(s): Burrle Elmore. Weekly. Publishes market reports on North American forest products (lumber, softwood panels, shingles, shakes, and particle board) plus an insert listing prices. Contains articles on topics affecting the economy of the industry and analyses of the major North American softwood species. Recurring features include editorials, industry personnel news, and statistics. **Facsimile Number:** (503)686-9629 or 800-874

★3635★
Rocky Mountain Construction
Golden Bell Press
2403 Champa St.
Denver, CO 80205   Phone: (303)295-0630
F. Hol Wagner, Jr., Editor. 2x/mo. Magazine serving the construction industry of America's mountain regions. Covering heavy engineering, building, landscaping, soil conservation, mining, and logging and federal, state, county, and city projects. Includes weekly construction reports. **Facsimile Number:** (303)295-2159.

★3636★
SF Newsletter
Southern Forest Products Association
PO Box 641700
Kenner, LA 70064-1700   Phone: (504)443-4464
Editor(s): David Kellogg. Weekly. Concerned with forest products, timber resources, home building, transportation, lumber manufacturing, and business and association news. **Facsimile Number:** (504)443-6612.

★3637★
Southeastern Log
Box 7900
Ketchikan, AK 99901   Phone: (907)225-3157
Nikki Murray Jones, Editor. Monthly. Magazine on logging and fishing; also regional human interest articles.

★3638★
Southern Journal of Applied Forestry
Society of American Foresters
5400 Grosvenor Ln.
Bethesda, MD 20814-2198   Phone: (301)897-8720
William T. Gladstone, Editor. Quarterly. Forestry industry magazine covering an area south of Maryland and westward into Texas and Oklahoma and other areas with similar conditions. **Facsimile Number:** (301)897-3690.

★3639★
Southern Loggin' Times
Hatton-Brown Publishers, Inc.
225 Hanrick St.
PO Box 2268
Montgomery, AL 36102-2268   Phone: (205)834-1170
D.K. Knight, Publisher. Monthly. Magazine serving the Southern U.S. logging industry. **Facsimile Number:** (205)834-4525.

★3640★
Southern Lumberman
Greysmith Publishing
PO Box 681629
128 Holiday Ct., Ste. 116
Franklin, TN 37068-1629   Phone: (615)791-1961
Nanci P. Gregg, Editor. Monthly. Industry publication for sawmill operators. **Facsimile Number:** (615)790-6188.

★3641★
Stumpage Prices for Sawtimber Sold from National Forests
U.S. Forest Service
PO Box 96090
Washington, DC 20250   Phone: (202)447-7346
U.S. Dept. of Agriculture, Forest Service, Publisher. Quarterly. Bulletin providing information by selected species and region.

★3642★
Supply Post
Ken Kenward Enterprises Ltd.
10819329 Enterprise
Surrey, BC, Canada V35 6J8   Phone: (604)533-5577
Ken Kenward, Editor. Monthly. Magazine dealing with conservation forestry.

★3643★
Timber Equipment Trader
Dixie Publications
210 N. Main St.
PO Box 489
Wadley, GA 30477   Phone: (912)252-5237
David Lumpkin, Advertising Mgr. Monthly. Magazine for buyers and sellers of timber equipment. **Facsimile Number:** (912)252-1140.

★3644★
Timber Harvesting
Hatton-Brown Publishers, Inc.
225 Hanrick St.
PO Box 2268
Montgomery, AL 36102-2268   Phone: (205)834-1170
D.K. Knight, Publisher. Monthly. National magazine for the U.S. logging industry. **Facsimile Number:** (205)834-4525.

★3645★
Timber Mart-South
Timber Marts, Inc.
PO Box 1278
Highlands, NC 28741   Phone: (704)526-3653
Editor(s): Frank Norris. Quarterly. Reports market prices for raw forest products, and provides a finished lumber price index for 13 Southeastern states. Data includes current prices (stumpage) plus current F.O.B. Mill delivered prices actually paid for sawtimber, pulpwood, veneer, chip-n-saw, poles, cross ties, and chips, both pine and hardwood. **Facsimile Number:** (704)526-3683.

★3646★
The Timber Producer
PO Box 39
Tomahawk, WI 54487   Phone: (715)453-5159
Carl F. Theiler, Editor. Monthly. Magazine for timber producers covering production and markets. **Facsimile Number:** (715)453-4177.

★3647★
Timber West
Timber West Publications
PO Box 610
Edmonds, WA 98020   Phone: (206)778-3388
John L. Nederlee, Editor and Publisher. 12x/yr. Logging news. **Facsimile Number:** (206)771-3623.

★3648★
The Truck Logger
The Truck Logger Assn.
518 Beatty St., Ste. 302
Vancouver, BC, Canada V6B 2L3   Phone: (604)682-4080
John Doyle, Editor. 6x/yr. **Facsimile Number:** (604)682-3775.

────── Meetings and Conventions ──────

★3649★
American Forestry Association Convention and Exposition
Offinger Management Co.
1100-H Brandywine Blvd.
PO Box 2188
Zanesville, OH 43702-2188   Phone: (614)452-4541
Frequency: Every two to four. **Facsimile Number:** (614)452-2552.

★3650★
Eastern Region Lumbermen's Association Regional Exposition and Conference
Eastern Building Material Dealers Association
604 E. Baltimore Pke.
Media, PA 19063   Phone: (215)565-6144
Facsimile Number: (215)565-0968.

★3651★
Forest Industries Clinic and Machinery Show
Miller Freeman Expositions
San Francisco Group
600 Harrison St.
San Francisco, CA 94107   Phone: (415)905-2200
Frequency: Always held in March at the Oregon State Convention Center in Portland, Oregon. 1992; Mar. 25-27; Portland, OR • 1993; Mar. 24-26; Portland, OR • 1994; Mar. 23-25; Portland, OR • 1995; Mar. 15-17; Portland, OR • 1996; Mar. 13-15; Portland, OR. **Facsimile Number:** (415)905-2630.

★3652★
Forest Industries Equipment Exhibition
Southex Exhibitions (Don Mills)
1450 Don Mills Rd.
Don Mills, ON, Canada M3B 2X7   Phone: (416)445-6641
1992; • 1994. **Facsimile Number:** (416)442-2207.

★3653★
Forest Products Machinery and Equipment Exposition
Southern Forest Products Association
PO Box 52468
New Orleans, LA 70152   Phone: (504)443-4464
1993; • 1995. **Facsimile Number:** (504)443-6612.

★3654★
Northeastern Loggers Congress and Equipment Exposition
Northeastern Loggers Association
PO Box 69
Old Forge, NY 13420   Phone: (315)369-3078
Frequency: Rotates between Bangor, Maine; Springfield, Massachusetts; and Syracuse, New York. 1992; Apr. 30 - May 02; Bangor, ME • 1993; Apr. 23-24; Springfield, MA. **Facsimile Number:** (315)369-3736.

★3655★
Pacific Logging Congress, Equipment Exhibit, and Working Machinery Demonstration
Pacific Logging Congress
2300 SW 6th, Ste. 200
Portland, OR 97201   Phone: (503)224-8406
1992; Nov. HI. **Facsimile Number:** (503)224-7211.

★3656★
Redwood Region Logging Conference
Redwood Region Logging Conference
PO Box 174
Garberville, CA 95440   Phone: (707)923-3365
1992.

★3657★
Society of American Foresters National Convention
Society of American Foresters
5400 Grosvenor Ln.
Bethesda, MD 20814   Phone: (301)897-8720
1992; Oct. 25-28; Richmond, VA • 1993; Nov. 07-10; Indianapolis, IN • 1994; Sep. 18-21; Anchorage, AK. **Facsimile Number:** (301)897-3690.

Timber Cutting and Logging Workers

★3658★
TIMBER
Hardwood Lumber Manufacturers Association of Pennsylvania
3501 Walnut St.
Harrisburg, PA 17109-3619   Phone: (717)652-0344
Frequency: Always held in August at the Fairgrounds in Bloomsburg, Pennsylvania. 1992; Aug. Bloomsburg, PA. **Facsimile Number:** (717)541-8729.

★3659★
Wood Expo
Southex Exhibitions
4285 Canada Way
Burnaby, BC, Canada V5G 1H2   Phone: (604)433-5121
Frequency: Always held during September at the British Columbia Place Stadium in Vancouver. **Facsimile Number:** (604)433-9549.

―――― **Other Sources of Information** ――――

★3660★
Timbers of the New World
Ayer Company Publishers, Inc.
50 Northwestern Dr., No. 10
PO Box 958
Salem, NH 03079   Phone: (603)898-1200
Samuel J. Record. 1972. Part of Use & Abuse of America's Natural Resources Series.

Mechanics, Installers, and Repairers

Aircraft Mechanics and Engine Specialists

Aircraft mechanics and engine specialists inspect the engine, landing gear, instruments, pressurized sections, accessories, brakes, valves, pumps, and other aircraft equipment and perform the necessary maintenance. Such maintenance usually follows a schedule based on hours flown, calendar days, and cycles of operation. Mechanics specializing in repair work rely on the pilot's description of a problem to find and fix faulty equipment. They may also work on many different types of aircraft, or specialize on one type or one section of aircraft. Technological advancements require aircraft mechanics and engine specialists to spend an increasing amount of time repairing electronic systems and computerized controls. Over 60% of salaried mechanics work for airlines, nearly 20% are employed by aircraft assembly firms, and nearly 16% work for the federal government. Most of the rest are general aviation mechanics that work for independent repair shops or companies. Very few aircraft mechanics are self-employed.

$alaries

The median annual salary of aircraft mechanics is about $26,000.

Beginning aircraft mechanics	$10.00-14.00/hour
Experienced aircraft mechanics	$14.00-23.50/hour

Employment Outlook

Growth rate until the year 2000: Faster than average.

Aircraft Mechanics and Engine Specialists

Career Guides

★3661★
"Aircraft Mechanic" in *Careers in Aviation* (pp. 19-22)
Rosen Publishing Group, Inc.
29 E. 21st St.
New York, NY 10010   Phone: (212)777-3017
Sharon Carter. 1990. Explores a wide variety of piloting jobs including aerial patrolling, corporate flying, flying for the media, law enforcement, and the airlines, helicopter ambulance flying, and stunt flying. Discusses being licensed, and opportunities for women. Most of the book is based on interviews with people who describe what they do on the job.

★3662★
"Aircraft Mechanic" in *Exploring Nontraditional Jobs for Women* (pp. 83-89)
Rosen Publishing Group, Inc.
29 E. 21st St.
New York, NY 10010   Phone: (212)777-3017
Rose Neufeld. 1989. Describes blue-collar, male dominated occupations. Discusses what is done on the job, training, where to apply for jobs, tools used, salaries, and advantages and disadvantages. Relates the experiences of women who are working in the field.

★3663★
"Aircraft Mechanic" in *Occu-Facts: Information on 565 Careers in Outline Form* (p. 15.8)
Careers, Inc.
P.O. Box 135
1211 Tenth St., S.W.
Largo, FL 33640   Phone: (813)584-7333
Elizabeth Handville. Biennial, 1989-90 edition. Each one-page occupational profile describes duties, working conditions, physical surroundings and demands, aptitudes, temperament, educational requirements, employment outlook, earnings, and places of employment.

★3664★
"Aircraft Mechanic" in *Transportation*, Volume 12 of *Career Information Center* (pp. 89-90)
Glencoe/Macmillan
15319 Chatsworth St.
Mission Hills, CA 91345   Phone: (818)898-1391
Richard Lidz and Dale Anderson, editorial directors. Fourth edition, 1990. For 600 occupations, describes job duties, entry-level requirements, education and training needed, advancement possibilities, employment outlook, earnings and benefits. The set is divided into 12 volumes. Each volume includes jobs related under a broad career field. Volume 13 is the index. **Facsimile Number:** 818-365-5489.

★3665★
"Aircraft Mechanics" in *Jobs! What They Are...Where They Are...What They Pay* (pp. 174-175)
Simon & Schuster, Inc.
Simon & Schuster Bldg.
1230 Avenue of the Americas
New York, NY 10020   Phone: (212)698-7000
Robert O. Snelling and Anne M. Snelling. Revised edition, 1989. Profiles 241 occupations, describing duties and responsibilities, educational preparation, earnings, employment opportunities, training, and qualifications.

★3666★
"Aircraft Mechanics" in *101 Careers: A Guide to the Fastest-Growing Opportunities* (pp. 307-310)
John Wiley & Sons, Inc.
605 Third Ave.
New York, NY 10158   Phone: (212)850-6000
Michael Harkavy. 1990. Each occupational profile includes a job description, job titles, work environment, employment outlook, qualifications, personal skills, and earnings.

★3667★
"Aircraft Mechanics" in *Opportunities in Travel Careers* (pp. 37-39)
National Textbook Co.
4255 W. Touhy Ave.
Lincolnwood, IL 60646   Phone: (312)679-5500
Robert Scott Milne. 1991. Explores job opportunities in many travel related fields including the airlines, resorts, travel agencies, recreation, and tourism. Covers the work, salaries, educational preparation and training, and advancement possibilities.

★3668★
"Aircraft Mechanics" in Volume 1 of *Career Discovery Encyclopedia* (pp. 36-37)
J.G. Ferguson Publishing Co.
200 W. Monroe
Chicago, IL 60606   Phone: (312)580-5480
E. Russell Primm, editor-in-chief. 1990. Contains two-page articles on 504 occupations. Each article describes job duties, earnings, and educational and training requirements.

★3669★

★3669★
"Aircraft Mechanics and Engine Specialists" in *Occupational Outlook Handbook* (pp. 326-327)
Superintendent of Documents
U.S. Government Printing Office
Washington, DC 20402   Phone: (202)783-3238

Biennial; latest edition, 1990-91. Encyclopedia of careers describing more than 250 occupations and comprising about 86 percent of all jobs in the economy. Occupations that require lengthy education or training are given the most attention. For each occupation, the handbook describes job duties, working conditions, training, educational preparation, personal qualities, advancement possibilities, job outlook, earnings, and sources of additional information.

★3670★
"Aircraft Mechanics and Engine Specialists" in Volume 3 of *The Encyclopedia of Careers and Vocational Guidance* (pp. 471-475)
J.G. Ferguson Publishing Co.
200 W. Monroe
Chicago, IL 60606   Phone: (312)580-5480

William E. Hopke, editor-in-chief. Eighth edition, 1990. Four-volume set that profiles 500 occupations and describes job trends in 76 industries. Includes career description, educational requirements, history of the job, methods of entry, advancement, employment outlook, earnings, working conditions, social and psychological factors, and sources of additional information.

★3671★
Aircraft Technicians
Chronicle Guidance Publications, Inc.
PO Box 1190
Moravia, NY 13118-1190   Phone: (315)497-0330

1988. This career brief describes the nature of the work, working conditions, hours and earnings, education and training, licensure, certification, unions, personal qualifications, social and psychological factors, employment outlook, entry methods, advancement, and related occupations. **Toll-free/Additional Phone Number(s):** 800-622-7284.

★3672★
"The Airline Mechanic" in *Opportunities in Airline Careers* (pp. 101-105)
National Textbook Co.
4255 W. Touhy Ave.
Lincolnwood, IL 60646   Phone: (312)679-5500

Adrian A. Paradis. 1987. Surveys trends in the industry and career opportunities with the airlines including management, sales, customer service, flying, and maintenance. Describes pilots' job duties, working conditions, and basic educational and training requirements.

★3673★
"Airplane Mechanic" in *VGM's Careers Encyclopedia* (pp. 32-34)
National Textbook Co.
4255 W. Touhy Ave.
Lincolnwood, IL 60646   Phone: (312)679-5500

Third edition, 1991. Contains two- to five-page descriptions of 200 managerial, professional, technical, trade, and service occupations. Each profile includes job duties, places of employment, qualifications, educational preparation, training, employment potential, advancement, income, and additional sources of information.

★3674★
"Airplane Mechanics" in *The American Almanac of Jobs and Salaries* (p. 405)
Avon Books
105 Madison Avenue
New York, NY 10016   Phone: (212)481-5600

John Wright and Edward J. Dwyer. Revised and updated, 1990. A comprehensive guide to the wages of hundreds of occupations in a wide variety of industries and organizations.

★3675★
"Aviation Maintenance" in *The Complete Aviation/Aerospace Career Guide* (pp. 165-169)
Aero Publishers, Inc.
13311 Monterey Ave.
Blue Ridge Summit, PA 17294   Phone: (717)794-2191

Robert Calderone. 1989. This is a comprehensive guide to hundreds of aviation related jobs. Provides job description, training requirements, advancement opportunities and employment outlook. **Facsimile Number:** (717)794-2080.

★3676★
"Aviation Maintenance Technology" in *The Career Connection II: A Guide to Technical Majors and Their Related Careers* (pp. 7-8)
ERIS
PO Box 7509
University Station
Provo, UT 84602-0509

Fred A. Rowe. 1988. Contains technical majors, such as automotive technology. Describes the major and the job. Lists high school and postsecondary school courses. Includes occupations related to the major, employment outlook, and starting salary.

★3677★
Career Success Series
Cambridge Career Products
90 MacCorkle Ave., SW
South Charleston, WV 25311   Phone: (304)744-9323

Videocassette. 1986. 15 mins. A series, available separately, outlining various career choices for students. Occupations include: flight service, air transportation/ground service, data processing, carpentry, clerk in banking/insurance, commodity sales, cosmetic personal grooming, fire fighting, forestry services, home economics, insulation/roofing, material handling, mechanics, photographic processing, pipefitting and plumbing, police science, printing, secretarial services, and utilities equipment operator.

★3678★
Do Your Own Thing in the Mechanical Field
AIMS Media, Inc.
9710 DeSoto Ave.
Chatsworth, CA 93111-4409   Phone: (818)773-4300

Videocassette. 1979. 16 mins. Various job levels in the mechanical field are outlined for students.

★3679★
"Maintenance Technician" in *Opportunities in Aerospace Careers* (pp. 16-21)
National Textbook Co.
4255 W. Touhy Ave.
Lincolnwood, IL 60646   Phone: (312)679-5500

Wallace R. Maples. 1991. Surveys jobs with the airlines, airports, the government, the military, in manufacturing, and in research and development. Describes educational requirements, working conditions, salaries, employment outlook and licensure.

Aircraft Mechanics and Engine Specialists ★3689★

★3680★
Mechanics
Morris Video
2730 Monterey St. #105
Monterey Business Park
Torrance, CA 90503   Phone: (213)533-4800

Videocassette. 1984. 15 mins. Various careers in repair are examined including aircraft, motorcycle, diesel, refrigeration and heavy equipment.

★3681★
"Mechanics" in *Opportunities in Transportation Careers* (pp. 38-39)
National Textbook Co.
4255 W. Touhy Ave.
Lincolnwood, IL 60646   Phone: (312)679-5500

Adrian A. Paradis. 1988. Describes transportation and related employment in driving occupations, the airlines, merchant marine, and travel services. Covers employment outlook, educational and training requirements, wages, and the work itself, and advantages and disadvantages of transportation careers. Offers job hunting advice.

★3682★
"Mechanics: Aircraft and Aircraft Engines" in
Opportunities in Vocational and Technical Careers (p. 106)
National Textbook Co.
4255 W. Touhy Ave.
Lincolnwood, IL 60646   Phone: (312)679-5500

Adrian A. Paradis. 1987. Describes careers which can be prepared for by attending a private vocational or proprietary school—office employee, sales worker, service worker, health services, mechanic, craftworker, and technician. Covers employment outlook, job duties, and salaries. Offers career planning advice.

★3683★
Video Career Library - Mechanical Fields
Careers, Inc.
1211 10th St., SW
PO Box 135
Largo, FL 34649-0135   Phone: (813)584-7333

Videocassette. 1990. 22 mins. Part of the Video Career Library covering 165 occupations. Shows actual workers on the job. Includes automobile mechanics, diesel engine mechanics, aircraft engine mechanics, automobile body repairers, heavy equipment mechanics, heating/air-conditioning/refrigeration mechanics.

★3684★
Vocational Visions
Center for Humanities, Inc.
Communications Park
Box 1000
Mount Kisco, NY 10549   Phone: (914)666-4100

Videocassette. 1984. 30 mins. This series of programs explains key aspects of actual training and a day in the life of a worker in the specific field mentioned on the videocassette. Occupations include: transportation/mechanics, repair, construction, business/office occupations, health, and agriculture.

★3685★
Vocations U.S.A.
Info-Disc Corporation
4 Professional Dr.
Gaithersburg, MD 20879   Phone: (301)948-2300

Videocassette. 1987. 60 mins. A disc collection outlining the requirements and methods of various career areas. Occupations include: transportation, mechanical/repair, health, agriculture, and construction.

★3686★
Your Career in Aviation Maintenance
Professional Aviation Maintenance Association
500 N.W. Plaza, Ste. 809
St. Ann, MO 63074   Phone: (314)739-2580

1991. This 48-page booklet describes the work of airframe and powerplant technicians. Covers eligibility, experience, and knowledge requirements and offers advice for selecting a school. Lists schools nationwide and includes accreditation, programs offered, length of the course of study, and admissions requirements.

Associations

★3687★
Aviation Maintenance Foundation International (AMFI)
PO Box 2826
Redmond, WA 98073   Phone: (206)828-3917

Membership: Trade association consisting of licensed aircraft mechanics, students, and schools as well as companies involved in the aviation maintenance industry. **Purpose:** To promote and improve the industry through education and research. Conducts surveys and market studies. Appoints professional aviation maintenance delegates to foreign countries. Sponsors competitions; bestows awards to individuals who demonstrate service to the industry. Conducts seminars; maintains speakers' bureau and placement service; compiles statistics. Offers scholarships to deserving aircraft mechanics students through the Aviation Maintenance Education Fund; operates charitable program. **Publications:** *AMFI Industry News*, bimonthly. • *Industry Report*, annual. • *Job Opportunities Listing*, monthly. • Also publishes aviation maintenance educational materials. **Facsimile Number:** (206)827-6895.

★3688★
Future Aviation Professionals of America (FAPA)
4959 Massachusetts Blvd.
Atlanta, GA 30337   Phone: (404)997-8097

Membership: Commercial pilots, flight attendants, aviation maintenance personnel, and persons aspiring to careers in those areas. **Purpose:** Purpose is to channel career information to aviation personnel and those seeking careers in aviation. Conducts bimonthly seminar and job fair. **Publications:** *Career Pilot*, monthly. • Also publishes brochures and flyers. **Facsimile Number:** (404)997-8111.

★3689★
Professional Aviation Maintenance Association (PAMA)
500 Northwest Plaza, Ste. 809
St. Ann, MO 63074   Phone: (314)739-2580

Membership: General aviation aircraft (A & P) technicians and aviation industry-related companies. **Purpose:** Purposes are to increase the professionalism of the individual aviation technician through greater technical knowledge and better understanding of safety requirements. Establishes communication among technicians throughout the country. Fosters and improves methods, skills, learning, and achievement in the aviation maintenance field. Promotes education in the aviation field through scholarships and seminars. Donates maintenance manuals, parts catalogs, technical information, tools, and training aids to several aviation technician schools. Presents awards including annual Aviation Technician of the Year Award, Joe Chase Award, and PAMA-ATP Award. Maintains job referral assistance program. **Publications:** *Membership Directory and Information Guide*, annual. • *PAMA News Magazine*, 10/year. • Also publishes *Your Career in Aviation*

Maintenance (booklet), technical reports, and press releases.
Facsimile Number: (314)739-2039.

Standards/Certification Agencies

The majority of mechanics who work on civilian aircraft are certified by the FAA as "airframe mechanic," "powerplant mechanic," or "repairman" after at least 18 months of work experience. Applicants for all certificates must pass written and oral tests and demonstrate that they can do the work authorized by the certificate.

Educational Directories and Programs

★3690★
Your Career in Aviation Maintenance
Professional Aviation Maintenance Association
500 N.W. Plaza, Ste. 809
St. Ann, MO 63074   Phone: (314)739-2580

1991. This 48-page booklet describes the work of airframe and powerplant technicians. Covers eligibility, experience, and knowledge requirements and offers advice for selecting a school. Lists schools nationwide and includes accreditation, programs offered, length of the course of study, and admissions requirements.

Awards, Scholarships, Grants, and Fellowships

★3691★
Helicopter Maintenance Award
Helicopter Association International
c/o Carolyn A. Vujcec, Manager of Communications
1619 Duke St.
Alexandria, VA 22314-3406   Phone: (703)683-4646

To recognize a distinguished contribution to aviation safety through good practice in the field of helicopter maintenance or through significant innovation. Individuals employed by a regular or associate class C member in good standing of the Association are eligible. An engraved plaque commemorating the individual's achievement is awarded annually. Established in 1973.

★3692★
PAMA CareerQuest Scholarship
Professional Aviation Maintenance Association
Scholarship Department
CareerQuest Program
500 Northwest Plaza, Ste. 809
St. Ann, MO 63074   Phone: (314)739-2580

To provide funds to students pursuing Airframe and Powerplant (A&P) Technician certificates through an FAA Part 147 Aviation Maintenance Technician School. Applicants must have completed 25 percent of the required curriculum for A&P eligibility, have a B average or equivalent, show a need for financial aid, be in good standing at an ATEC school, and must be planning for a career in aviation maintenance. Applications must be submitted through a student's school, signed by student and sponsor, and accompanied by written recommendation from an instructor or chapter person. All fund applications must be submitted to PAMA Headquarters on the "PAMA Scholarship Application (Form SCH-880)". Three awards are given in December and three in April.

★3693★
PAMA Technician of the Year Award
Professional Aviation Maintenance Association
c/o Jan Grumke
500 Northwest Plaza, Ste. 401
St. Ann, MO 63074   Phone: (314)739-2580

To recognize the general aviation mechanic who has made an outstanding contribution to air safety through maintenance practices. The following classifications for the selection of winners have been established: (1) for the suggestion of a design or improvement to an aircraft or powerplant; (2) for the suggestion or development of a maintenance and/or inspection procedure that contributed significantly to safety in aviation; or (3) for the consistent demonstration of a high level of professionalism and excellence in the performance of duties as an aviation mechanic that led to, or resulted in, increased reliability and/or safety in aviation. Applications are accepted. The deadline is May 15. A trophy is presented annually in Washington, D.C., by the NBAA, PAMA, FAA, HAI, NATA, AOPA and GAMA. Established in 1963.

Basic Reference Guides and Handbooks

★3694★
Aircraft Cabin Cleaning & Refurbishing Operations
National Fire Protection Association
1 Batterymarch Park
Quincy, MA 02269-9101   Phone: (617)770-3000

1989. Part of Four Hundred Series.

★3695★
Aircraft Cleaning, Painting & Paint Removal
National Fire Protection Association
1 Batterymarch Park
Quincy, MA 02269-9101   Phone: (617)770-3000

1989. Part of Four Hundred Series.

★3696★
Aircraft Fuel System Maintenance
National Fire Protection Association
1 Batterymarch Park
Quincy, MA 02269-9101   Phone: (617)770-3000

★3697★
Aircraft Maintenance & Repair
McGraw-Hill Publishing Co.
1221 Avenue of the Americas
New York, NY 10020   Phone: (212)512-2000

F. Delp. Fifth edition, 1987.

★3698★
Aircraft Mechanics Digest
Palomar Books
PO Box 915
Marquette, MI 49855   Phone: (906)346-6781

Larry Reithmaier, editor. 1982.

★3699★
Aircraft Mechanic's Shop Manual
Palomar Books
PO Box 915
Marquette, MI 49855   Phone: (906)346-6781

Larry Reithmaier. New edition, 1979.

Aircraft Mechanics and Engine Specialists

★3700★
Aircraft Repair Manual
Palomar Books
PO Box 915
Marquette, MI 49855　　　　Phone: (906)346-6781
Larry Reithmaier, editor. 1981.

★3701★
Aviation Maintenance Management
Southern Illinois University, Carbondale
Southern Illinois University Press
PO Box 3697
Carbondale, IL 62902-3697　　　Phone: (618)453-2281
Frank King. 1968. Part of Aviation Management Series. **Facsimile Number:** (618)453-1221.

★3702★
Lightplane Refurbishing Techniques
TAB Books, Inc.
Blue Ridge Summit, PA 17294-0850　　Phone: (717)794-2191
Joe Christy. 1986.

★3703★
Make Your Airplane Last Forever
TAB Books
Blue Ridge Summit, PA 17294-0850　　Phone: (717)794-2191
Nicholas E. Silitch. 1982.

Periodicals

★3704★
Air Line Pilot
Air Line Pilots Assn.
535 Herndon Pkwy.
PO Box 1169
Herndon, VA 22070　　　　Phone: (703)689-4176
Esperison Martinez, Jr., Editor. Monthly. Magazine covering industry trends and developments, flight technology, and air safety. **Facsimile Number:** (703)689-4370.

★3705★
Aircraft Technician
Johnson Hill Press, Inc.
1233 Janesville Ave.
Fort Atkinson, WI 53538　　　Phone: (414)563-6388
Michael Murrell, Publisher. 6x/yr. Magazine addressing the professional and technical needs of the aviation maintenance professional. **Facsimile Number:** (414)563-1702.

★3706★
Airport Journal
PO Box 273
Clarendon Hills, IL 60514　　　Phone: (708)318-6872
John Andrews, Editor and Publisher. Monthly. Magazine serving the air transport industry in the Chicago area. **Facsimile Number:** (708)986-5010.

★3707★
Airport Press
JAJ Publishers, Inc.
PO Box 879
Jamaica, NY 11430-0879　　　Phone: (718)528-8600
Robert Cubbedge, Editor. Monthly. Newspaper for the air transport industry.

★3708★
Aviation Equipment Maintenance
Irving-Cloud Publishing Co.
7300 N. Cicero Ave.
Lincolnwood, IL 60646-1696　　　Phone: (708)674-7300
Paul Berner, Editor. Monthly. Magazine covering aviation maintenance. **Facsimile Number:** (708)674-7015.

★3709★
Aviation Mechanics Bulletin
Flight Safety Foundation, Inc.
2200 Wilson Blvd., Ste. 500
Arlington, VA 22201-3324
Roger Rozelle, Editor. Six times/yr. Aviation magazine.

★3710★
Business & Commercial Aviation
Westchester City Airport Hangar C1
White Plains, NY 10604　　　Phone: (914)939-0300
John Olcott, Editor and Publisher. Monthly. Magazine focusing on operation and maintenance of business and commercial aircraft.

★3711★
FAA Aviation News
DOT/FAA
AFS-20
Washington, DC 20591　　　Phone: (202)267-7953
6x/yr. Magazine containing aviation news. **Facsimile Number:** (202)366-7060.

★3712★
International Aviation Mechanics Journal
I.A.P., Inc.
PO Box 10000
Casper, WY 82602-1000　　　Phone: (307)266-3838
Marlon Atkins, Editor. Monthly. Magazine for professionals responsible for the maintenance of fixed wing and rotory wing aircraft. **Facsimile Number:** (307)472-5106.

★3713★
PAMA News
Professional Aviation Maintenance Association, Inc. (PAMA)
c/o Peter Rohrbach
9609 Barkston Ct.
Potomac, MD 20850　　　Phone: (314)739-2580
Editor(s): Peter Rohrbach. Monthly. Devoted to raising the professional level of the aircraft maintenance technician. Provides practical articles on aviation service problems, discussions of safety standards and procedures, and reports on developments in regulations. Recurring features include news of research, calendars of events, news from members and local chapters, and a column from the executive director's office. **Facsimile Number:** (314)739-2039.

★3714★
PAMA News Magazine (PAMA)
Professional Aviation Maintenance Association (PAMA)
500 Northwest Plaza, Ste. 809
St. Ann, MO 63074　　　Phone: (314)739-2580
10/year. Newsletter covering aviation parts and maintenance and association activities. Includes list of new members and company profiles.

★3715★
ROTOR
Helicopter Assoc. International
1619 Duke St.
Alexandria, VA 22314-3406   Phone: (703)683-4646
Daniel P. Warsley, Editor. Quarterly. Civil helicopter industry magazine. **Facsimile Number:** (703)683-4745.

★3716★
Rotor & Wing International
Phillips Publications, Inc.
7811 Montrose Rd.
Potomac, MD 20854   Phone: (301)340-2100
David Jensen, Editor. Monthly. Magazine covering helicopters. **Facsimile Number:** (301)340-0542.

★3717★
Rotorgram
Helicopter Assn. Intl.
1619 Duke St.
Alexandria, VA 22314-3406   Phone: (703)683-4646
Daniel P. Warsley, Editor. Quarterly. Helicopter industry magazine.

──────── Meetings and Conventions ────────

★3718★
AMTECH - International Aviation Maintenance and Ground Support Equipment Trade Show and Conference
Andry Montgomery
Kaden Tower, 6th Fl.
6100 Dutchmans Ln.
Louisville, KY 40205-3284   Phone: (502)473-1992
1992. **Facsimile Number:** (502)473-1999.

★3719★
Annual Aviation Maintenance Symposium and Trade Show
Professional Aviation Maintenance Association
500 NW Plaza, Ste. 809
St. Ann, MO 63074   Phone: (314)739-2580
1992. **Facsimile Number:** (314)739-2039.

★3720★
Aviation Maintenance Foundation International (AMFI)
PO Box 2826
Redmond, WA 98073   Phone: (206)828-3917
Frequency: Annual symposium, with exhibits. 1992; Oct. 20-22; Seattle, WA. **Facsimile Number:** (206)827-6895.

★3721★
Professional Aviation Maintenance Association (PAMA)
500 Northwest Plaza, Ste. 809
St. Ann, MO 63074   Phone: (314)739-2580
Frequency: Annual. **Facsimile Number:** (314)739-2039.

──────── Other Sources of Information ────────

★3722★
AMFI Industry Report (AMFI)
Aviation Maintenance Foundation International (AMFI)
PO Box 2826
Redmond, WA 98073   Phone: (206)828-3917
Annual.

★3723★
AMFI Job Opportunities Listing (AMFI)
Aviation Maintenance Foundation International (AMFI)
PO Box 2826
Redmond, WA 98073   Phone: (206)828-3917
Monthly. Directory of job listings for aircraft mechanics.

★3724★
Your Career in Aviation Maintenance (PAMA)
Professional Aviation Maintenance Association (PAMA)
500 Northwest Plaza, Ste. 809
St. Ann, MO 63074   Phone: (314)739-2580

Automotive Body Repairers

Automotive body repairers fix motor vehicle bodies that have been damaged in accidents. Often with instructions from supervisors, automotive body repairers restore damaged metal frames and body sections to their original shape and location, and remove badly damaged sections and replace them with new ones. Body repairers also repair or replace the plastic body parts increasingly used on newer model vehicles. They routinely use special tools and machines like alignment machines and hydraulic jacks. In large shops, body repairers may specialize in one type of repair, such as frame straightening or glass installing. Most automotive body repairers work for shops that specialize in body repairs and painting. Others work for trucking companies and automobile rental companies. A few work for motor vehicle manufacturers. About 20% of automotive body repairers are self-employed.

$alaries

Body repairers employed by automobile dealers in 18 large metropolitan areas had average weekly earnings of $683. Helpers and trainees usually earn from 30 to 60 percent of the earnings of skilled workers.

Employment Outlook

Growth rate until the year 2000: Faster than average.

Automotive Body Repairers

---- **Career Guides** ----

★3725★
Auto Assembly Line General Repairman
Morris Video
2730 Monterey St. #105
Monterey Business Park
Torrance, CA 90503   Phone: (213)533-4800
Videocassette. 1982. 30 mins. A fifteen year employee of auto manufacturing offers his insights on the industry for those wishing to pursue such a career.

★3726★
Auto Body Repairer
Careers, Inc.
PO Box 135
Largo, FL 34649-0135   Phone: (813)584-7333
1991. Two-page occupational summary card describing duties, working conditions, personal qualifications, training, earnings and hours, employment outlook, places of employment, related careers and where to write for more information.

★3727★
Auto Body Repairer
Vocational Biographies, Inc.
PO Box 31, Dept. VF10
Sauk Centre, MN 56378   Phone: (612)352-6516
1990. This pamphlet profiles a person working in the job. Includes information about job duties, working conditions, places of employment, educational preparation, labor market outlook, and salaries. **Toll-free/Additional Phone Number(s):** 800-255-0752.

★3728★
"Auto Body Repairer" in *Transportation*, Volume 12 of *Career Information Center* (pp. 92-94)
Glencoe/Macmillan
15319 Chatsworth St.
Mission Hills, CA 91345   Phone: (818)898-1391
Richard Lidz and Dale Anderson, editorial directors. Fourth edition, 1990. For 600 occupations, describes job duties, entry-level requirements, education and training needed, advancement possibilities, employment outlook, earnings and benefits. The set is divided into 12 volumes. Each volume includes jobs related under a broad career field. Volume 13 is the index. **Facsimile Number:** 818-365-5489.

★3729★
Auto Shop Safety
Bergwall Productions
106 Charles Lindbergh Blvd.
Uniondale, NY 11553-3695   Phone: (516)222-1111
Videocassette. 1987. 10 mins. The basics of working safely in an auto shop are given. The entire series is also available as a single tape for the same cost.

★3730★
"Automobile Body Repairers" in *Opportunities in Automotive Service Careers* (pp. 25-30)
National Textbook Co.
4255 W. Touhy Ave.
Lincolnwood, IL 60646   Phone: (312)679-5500
Robert M. Weber. 1989. Describes the work of the automobile mechanic and related occupations such as service station attendant and automobile body repairer. Covers working conditions, places of employment, qualifications, training, apprenticeships, certification, advancement opportunities, employment outlook, tools needed, and earnings.

★3731★
"Automobile Body Repairers" in Volume 1 of *Career Discovery Encyclopedia* (pp. 88-89)
J.G. Ferguson Publishing Co.
200 W. Monroe
Chicago, IL 60606   Phone: (312)580-5480
E. Russell Primm, editor-in-chief. 1990. Contains two-page articles on 504 occupations. Each article describes job duties, earnings, and educational and training requirements.

★3732★
"Automobile Body Repairers" in Volume 3 of *The Encyclopedia of Careers and Vocational Guidance* (pp. 475-479)
J.G. Ferguson Publishing Co.
200 W. Monroe
Chicago, IL 60606   Phone: (312)580-5480
William E. Hopke, editor-in-chief. Eighth edition, 1990. Four-volume set that profiles 500 occupations and describes job trends in 76 industries. Includes career description, educational requirements, history of the job, methods of entry, advancement, employment outlook, earnings, working conditions, social and psychological factors, and sources of additional information.

★3733★
"Automotive Body Repairer" in *Occu-Facts: Information on 565 Careers in Outline Form* (p. 15.7)
Careers, Inc.
P.O. Box 135
1211 Tenth St., S.W.
Largo, FL 33640   Phone: (813)584-7333
Elizabeth Handville. Biennial, 1989-90 edition. Each one-page occupational profile describes duties, working conditions, physical surroundings and demands, aptitudes, temperament, educational requirements, employment outlook, earnings, and places of employment.

★3734★
"Automotive Body Repairer" in *The Career Connection II: A Guide to Technical Majors and Their Related Careers* (pp. 3-4)
ERIS
PO Box 7509
University Station
Provo, UT 84602-0509
Fred A. Rowe. 1988. Contains technical majors, such as automotive technology. Describes the major and the job. Lists high school and postsecondary school courses. Includes occupations related to the major, employment outlook, and starting salary.

★3735★
Automotive Body Repairers
Chronicle Guidance Publications, Inc.
PO Box 1190
Moravia, NY 13118-1190   Phone: (315)497-0330
1987. This career brief describes the nature of the work, working conditions, hours and earnings, education and training, licensure, certification, unions, personal qualifications, social and psychological factors, employment outlook, entry methods, advancement, and related occupations. **Toll-free/Additional Phone Number(s):** 800-622-7284.

★3736★
"Automotive Body Repairers" in *Occupational Outlook Handbook* (pp. 327-329)
Superintendent of Documents
U.S. Government Printing Office
Washington, DC 20402   Phone: (202)783-3238
Biennial; latest edition, 1990-91. Encyclopedia of careers describing more than 250 occupations and comprising about 86 percent of all jobs in the economy. Occupations that require lengthy education or training are given the most attention. For each occupation, the handbook describes job duties, working conditions, training, educational preparation, personal qualities, advancement possibilities, job outlook, earnings, and sources of additional information.

★3737★
Career Opportunities. . .in the Automotive Collision Repair and Refinishing Industry
Automotive Service Association
PO Box 929
Bedford, TX 76095-0929   Phone: (817)283-6205
Booklet describing the work, training, areas of specialization, places of employment, hours, and outlook for automotive repair and refinishing specialists.

★3738★
Transportation
Learning Corporation of America
108 Wilmot Rd.
Deerfield, IL 60015-9990   Phone: (708)940-1260
Videocassette. 1982. 21 mins. In this program from the "Working" series, we meet five employees in transportation-related jobs: fishing boat captain, auto body repair shop owner, construction equipment operator, air traffic controller and truck driver.

★3739★
Transportation/Mechanical Cluster
Center for Humanities, Inc.
Communications Park
Box 1000
Mount Kisco, NY 10549   Phone: (914)666-4100
Videocassette. 1984. 20 mins. The key aspects of working in the fields of Auto Body Repair, Truck Driving, and Auto Mechanics are explained.

★3740★
Video Career Library - Mechanical Fields
Careers, Inc.
1211 10th St., SW
PO Box 135
Largo, FL 34649-0135   Phone: (813)584-7333
Videocassette. 1990. 22 mins. Part of the Video Career Library covering 165 occupations. Shows actual workers on the job. Includes automobile mechanics, diesel engine mechanics, aircraft engine mechanics, automobile body repairers, heavy equipment mechanics, heating/air-conditioning/refrigeration mechanics.

★3741★
Vocational Visions
Center for Humanities, Inc.
Communications Park
Box 1000
Mount Kisco, NY 10549   Phone: (914)666-4100
Videocassette. 1984. 30 mins. This series of programs explains key aspects of actual training and a day in the life of a worker in the specific field mentioned on the videocassette. Occupations include: transportation/mechanics, repair, construction, business/office occupations, health, and agriculture.

★3742★
Vocations U.S.A.
Info-Disc Corporation
4 Professional Dr.
Gaithersburg, MD 20879   Phone: (301)948-2300
Videocassette. 1987. 60 mins. A disc collection outlining the requirements and methods of various career areas. Occupations include: transportation, mechanical/repair, health, agriculture, and construction.

Associations

★3743★
Automotive Service Association (ASA)
1901 Airport Fwy., Ste. 100
PO Box 929
Bedford, TX 76095-0929   Phone: (817)283-6205
Membership: Automotive service businesses (10,100) including body, paint, and trim shops, engine rebuilders, radiator shops, brake and wheel alignment services, transmission shops, tune-up services, and air conditioning services; associate members (320) are manufacturers and wholesalers of automotive parts,

and the trade press. **Purpose:** Represents independent businessmen before private agencies and national and state legislative bodies. Promotes confidence between consumer and automotive technician, safety inspection of motor vehicles, and better highways. Conducts professional training seminars in business management, technical and update training, and other areas. Maintains 130 volume collection of automotive repair videotapes. **Publications:** *AutoInc*, monthly. • *Collision Repair Report*, monthly. • *Mechanical News*, bimonthly. • *TransTechnical News*, monthly. • Also publishes convention brochure, fact sheet, and bylaws. **Facsimile Number:** (817)685-0225.

★3744★
Automotive Service Industry Association (ASIA)
444 N. Michigan Ave.
Chicago, IL 60611-3975   Phone: (312)836-1300
Membership: Executives representing independent automotive wholesalers, warehouse distributors, heavy-duty vehicle and equipment parts distributors, automotive electrical service and supply wholesalers and distributors, manufacturers' representatives, and manufacturers and remanufacturers of replacement parts, tools, equipment, chemicals, refinishing materials, supplies, and accessories. **Purpose:** Operates extensive business management library. Holds seminars; bestows awards; compiles statistics; maintains hall of fame. **Publications:** *Automotive Service Industry Association—Buyers Guide*, periodic. • *Automotive Service Industry Association—Membership Directory*, periodic. • *Automotive Service Industry Association—Product Directory*, periodic. • *Selling Today*, periodic. • *Voice of the Industry*, periodic. **Facsimile Number:** (312)836-1009.

★3745★
National Association of Trade and Technical Schools (NATTS)
2251 Wisconsin Ave. NW
Washington, DC 20007   Phone: (202)333-1021
Membership: Private schools providing career education. **Purpose:** Seeks to inform members of the accreditation process and regulations affecting vocational education. Conducts workshops and institutes for staffs of member schools; provides legislative, administrative, and public relations assistance; serves as federally recognized accrediting agency. Has established Career Training Foundation to support research into private vocational education. Sponsors annual Idea Fair Competition. Presents special awards. Maintains hall of fame; compiles statistics. **Publications:** *Career News Digest*, 3-4/year. • *Career Training*, quarterly. • *Classroom Companion*, quarterly. • *Handbook of Trade and Technical Careers and Training*, annual. • *NATTS News and Views*, bimonthly. • Also publishes *Career Guidance Handouts*.

★3746★
National Institute for Automotive Service Excellence (ASE)
13505 Dulles Technology Dr.
Herndon, VA 22071-3415   Phone: (703)742-3800
Membership: Governed by a 40-member board of directors selected from all sectors of the automotive service industry and from education, government, and consumer groups. **Purpose:** Encourages and promotes the highest standards of automotive service in the public interest. Conducts continuing research to determine the best methods for training automotive technicians; encourages the development of effective training programs. Tests and certifies the competence of automobile, heavy-duty truck, collision repair, and engine machinist technicians. **Publications:** *ASE Test Registration Booklet*, semiannual. • *ASE Training Guide*, annual. • *The Blue Seal*, semiannual. **Facsimile Number:** (703)904-0727.

★3747★
Society of Collision Repair Specialists (SCRS)
PO Box 197
1201 Landmark, Ste. 3
Liberty, MO 64068   Phone: (816)781-5225
Membership: Businesses; associations; individual owners and managers of auto collision repair shops, suppliers, insurance and educational associates. **Purpose:** Distributes technical information; develops and maintains industry standards; works to promote professionalism within the industry. Conducts seminars and workshops, including hands-on demonstrations of technical equipment. Maintains library of periodicals.

Standards/Certification Agencies

Voluntary certification by the National Institute for Automotive Service Excellence (ASE), is recognized as a standard of achievement for automotive body repairers. To be certified, a body repairer must pass a written examination and must have at least two years of experience. Completion of a high school, vocational school, trade school, or community college program in automotive body repair may be substituted for one year of work experience. To retain certification, the exam must be taken at least every five years.

★3748★
Auto Body Repairmen! Painters/Refinishers! Become a Proven Pro: Get ASE Certified
National Institute for Automotive Service Excellence
13505 Dulles Technology Dr.
Herndon, VA 22071-3415   Phone: (703)742-3800
This four-panel brochure describes the examinations for certification for automotive body repairers and painters.

★3749★
National Association of Trade and Technical Schools (NATTS)
2251 Wisconsin Ave. NW
Washington, DC 20007   Phone: (202)333-1021
Informs members of the accreditation process and regulations affecting vocational education. Conducts workshops and institutes for staffs of member schools; provides legislative, administrative, and public relations assistance; serves as a federally recognized accrediting agency.

★3750★
National Institute for Automotive Service Excellence (ASE)
13505 Dulles Technology Dr.
Herndon, VA 22071-3415   Phone: (703)742-3800
Encourages and promotes the highest standards of automotive service in the public interest. Conducts continuing research to determine the best methods for training automotive technicians; encourages the development of effective training programs. Tests and certifies the competence of automobile, heavy-duty truck, collision repair, and engine machinist technicians.

Test Guides

★3751★
ASE Test Registration Booklet (ASE)
National Institute for Automotive Service Excellence (ASE)
13505 Dulles Technology Dr.
Herndon, VA 22071-3415 Phone: (703)742-3800

Semiannual. Registration for technicians who wish to become ASE certified. Provides registration information and sample questions.

★3752★
ASE Training Guide (ASE)
National Institute for Automotive Service Excellence (ASE)
13505 Dulles Technology Dr.
Herndon, VA 22071-3415 Phone: (703)742-3800

Annual. Bibliographic listing of training materials available for upgrading technicians' skills in automotive repair, including sample ASE test questions and test specifications.

★3753★
Auto Body Repair
National Learning Corp.
212 Michael Dr.
Syosset, NY 11791 Phone: (516)921-8888

Jack Rudman. Part of Occupational Competency Examination Series.

★3754★
Auto Body Repairmen
National Learning Corp.
212 Michael Dr.
Syosset, NY 11791 Phone: (516)921-8888

Jack Rudman. Part of the Career Examination Series No. 1. All examination guides in this series contain questions with answers. **Facsimile Number:** (516)921-8743. **Toll-free/Additional Phone Number(s):** 800-645-6337.

★3755★
Body Repair Inspector
National Learning Corp.
212 Michael Dr.
Syosset, NY 11791 Phone: (516)921-8888

Jack Rudman. Part of the Career Examination Series No. 1. All examination guides in this series contain questions with answers. **Facsimile Number:** (516)921-8743. **Toll-free/Additional Phone Number(s):** 800-645-6337.

★3756★
The Official ASE Preparation Guide to ASE Automobile and Body/Paint Tests
National Institute for Automotive Service Excellence
13505 Dulles Technology Dr.
Herndon, VA 22071-3415 Phone: (703)742-3800

Describes the certification process for automobile mechanics and auto body repairers. Offers tips on preparing for the test. Contains sample test questions.

★3757★
Senior Automotive Serviceman
National Learning Corp.
212 Michael Dr.
Syosset, NY 11791 Phone: (516)921-8888

Jack Rudman. Part of the Career Examination Series No. 1. All examination guides in this series contain questions with answers. **Facsimile Number:** (516)921-8743. **Toll-free/Additional Phone Number(s):** 800-645-6337.

Educational Directories and Programs

★3758★
Career Guidance Handouts (NATTS)
National Association of Trade and Technical Schools (NATTS)
2251 Wisconsin Ave. NW
Washington, DC 20007 Phone: (202)333-1021

★3759★
Career Training (NATTS)
National Association of Trade and Technical Schools (NATTS)
2251 Wisconsin Ave. NW
Washington, DC 20007 Phone: (202)333-1021
Quarterly.

★3760★
Classroom Companion (NATTS)
National Association of Trade and Technical Schools (NATTS)
2251 Wisconsin Ave. NW
Washington, DC 20007 Phone: (202)333-1021
Quarterly.

★3761★
Handbook of Trade and Technical Careers and Training (NATTS)
National Association of Trade and Technical Schools (NATTS)
2251 Wisconsin Ave. NW
Washington, DC 20007 Phone: (202)333-1021
Annual.

Basic Reference Guides and Handbooks

★3762★
Advances & Trends in Automotive Sheet Steel Stamping
Society of Automotive Engineers, Inc.
400 Commonwealth Dr.
Warrendale, PA 15096-0001 Phone: (412)776-4841
1988.

★3763★
Advances in Exterior Body Panels
Society of Automotive Engineers
400 Commonwealth Dr.
Warrendale, PA 15096-0001 Phone: (412)776-4841
1987.

★3764★
Auto Body Repairing & Repainting
Goodheart-Willcox Company
123 Taft Dr.
South Holland, IL 60473 Phone: (708)333-7200

Bill Toboldt. Revised edition, 1982. **Facsimile Number:** (708)331-9130.

Automotive Body Repairers

★3765★
Autobody Refinishing Handbook
Prentice Hall
Rte 9W
Englewood Cliffs, NJ 07632   Phone: (201)592-2000
Andre G. Deroche. 1988.

★3766★
Autobody Repair & Refinishing
Prentice Hall
Rte 9W
Englewood Cliffs, NJ 07632   Phone: (201)592-2000
Robert P. Schmidt. 1981.

★3767★
Automotive Chassis & Body
McGraw-Hill Publishing Company
1221 Avenue of the Americas
New York, NY 10020   Phone: (212)512-2000
William H. Crouse. Fifth edition, 1975. Part of Automotive Technology Series.

★3768★
Automotive Exterior Body Panels
Society of Automotive Engineers, Inc.
400 Commonwealth Dr.
Warrendale, PA 15096-0001   Phone: (412)776-4841
1988.

★3769★
Collision Repair Guide
McGraw-Hill Publishing Company
1221 Avenue of the Americas
New York, NY 10020   Phone: (212)512-2000
Robert C. MacPherson. 1971.

★3770★
The Complete Guide to Automotive Refinishing
Prentice Hall
Rte 9W
Englewood Cliffs, NJ 07632   Phone: (201)592-2000
Harry T. Chudy. Second edition, 1988.

★3771★
Directory of Certified Aftermarket Body Parts
    Automotive parts industry
Certified Automotive Parts Association (CAPA)
1518 K St. NW, Ste. 305
Washington, DC 20005   Phone: (202)737-2212
Jack Gillis, editor. Quarterly. Suppliers of about 1,000 aftermarket automotive body parts which meet CAPA certification standards. Entries include: Distributor or manufacturer name, address, phone, telex, name and title of contact, geographical area served, description of products. Arrangement: Classified by vehicle make and model. **Facsimile Number:** (202)737-2214.

★3772★
Exterior Body Panel Developments
Society of Automotive Engineers, Inc.
400 Commonwealth Dr.
Warrendale, PA 15096-0001   Phone: (412)776-4841
1985.

★3773★
Fixing Cars
Rose Pubishing Co.
1148 Holly St.
Alameda, CA 94501   Phone: (415)523-5913
Rick Greenspan. 1974.

★3774★
How to Restore Wooden Body Framing
Motorbooks International Publishers & Wholesalers, Inc.
729 Prospect Ave., Box 2
Osceola, WI 54020   Phone: (715)294-3345
A. Alderwyck. 1984. Part of Osprey Restoration Guide Series.

★3775★
New Polymer Technology for Auto Body Exteriors
American Institute of Chemical Engineers
345 E. 47th St.
New York, NY 10017   Phone: (212)705-7338
W. R. Schmeal, editor. 1988. Part of AIChE Symposium Series.
Facsimile Number: (212)752-3294.

★3776★
Structural Design & Crashworthiness of Automobiles
Springer-Verlag New York, Inc.
175 5th Ave., 19th Fl.
New York, NY 10010   Phone: (212)460-1500
T. K. Murthy, editor. 1987.

★3777★
Total Auto Body Repair
Macmillan Publishing Company, Inc.
866 3rd Ave.
New York, NY 10022   Phone: (212)702-2000
L. C. Rhone. Second edition, 1982.

★3778★
Vehicle Body Building One
State Mutual Book & Periodical Service, Ltd.
521 5th Ave., 17th Fl.
New York, NY 10175   Phone: (212)682-5844

★3779★
Vehicle Body Building Two
State Mutual Book & Periodical Service, Ltd.
521 5th Ave., 17th Fl.
New York, NY 10175   Phone: (212)682-5844

──────────── Periodicals ────────────

★3780★
Auto Inc.
Automotive Service Councils, Inc.
PO Box 929
Bedford, TX 76021-0929   Phone: (817)283-6205
Editor(s): Monica Buchholz. Monthly. Carries automotive technical material, news of the automotive industry, information on relevant legislation, and news of the Automotive Service Association. **Facsimile Number:** (817)685-0225.

★3781★
Auto and Flat Glass Journal
PO Box 12099
Seattle, WA 98102-0099   Phone: (206)322-5120
Burton Winters, Editor. Monthly. Magazine for the auto glass replacement industry.

★3782★
The Auto Index
7 Clinton Pl.
Suffern, NY 10901   Phone: (914)357-3695
6x/yr. Magazine providing a general purpose index to 14 automotive periodicals.

★3783★
AutoGlass Magazine
National Glass Assn.
8200 Greenboro Dr., No. 302
Mclean, VA 22102   Phone: (703)442-4890
Joyce A. Grimely, Publisher. Six times/yr. Trade publication for auto glass manufacturers, distributors, and installers. **Facsimile Number:** (703)442-0630.

★3784★
AutoInc (ASA)
Automotive Service Association (ASA)
1901 Airport Fwy., Ste. 100
PO Box 929
Bedford, TX 76095-0929   Phone: (817)283-6205
Monthly. Journal covering technical and business information of interest to members; contains shop profiles, legislative news, industry events, and descriptions of new products.

★3785★
Automobile International
Johnston International Publishing Corp.
950 Lee St., No. 100
Des Plaines, IL 60016-6588
M. Havis Dawson, Editor. Nine times/yr. International magazine of auto service and repairs. Printed in English and Spanish; published quarterly in Arabic.

★3786★
Automotive Body Repair News
Stanley Publishing Co., Inc.
5 Revere Dr., Ste. 202
Northbrook, IL 60062   Phone: (708)272-0559
Neal Mann, Editor. Monthly. Magazine reporting automotive repair industry news. **Facsimile Number:** (708)272-1088.

★3787★
The Automotive Messenger
Hansen Publishing, Inc.
431 Chez Paree
Hazelwood, MO 63042   Phone: (314)831-4000
B. Hank Hansen, Publisher. Monthly. Automotive magazine. **Facsimile Number:** (314)831-3610.

★3788★
The Blue Seal
National Institute for Automotive Service Excellence
13505 Dulles Technology Dr.
Herndon, VA 22071   Phone: (703)713-3800
Editor(s): Martin Lawson. Semiannually. Covers news of the Institute's efforts to certify auto, H-D truck, engine machinists, and collision repair technicians. Discusses industry trends, vehicle repair tips, and training information, and highlights activities of ASE-certified technicians. **Facsimile Number:** (703)713-0727.

★3789★
Career News Digest (NATTS)
National Association of Trade and Technical Schools (NATTS)
2251 Wisconsin Ave. NW
Washington, DC 20007   Phone: (202)333-1021
3-4/year.

★3790★
Collision Repair Report (ASA)
Automotive Service Association (ASA)
1901 Airport Fwy., Ste. 100
PO Box 929
Bedford, TX 76095-0929   Phone: (817)283-6205
Monthly. Speciality publication for members of the ASA Collision Division.

★3791★
Convenient Automotive Services Retailer
Graphics Concepts
1801 Rockville Pike, Ste. 330
Rockville, MD 20852   Phone: (301)984-4000
Jocklynn Keville, Editor. 6x/yr. Trade magazine for professionals in the automotive services industry.

★3792★
Gasoline and Automotive Service Dealers Association—Bulletin
Gasoline and Automotive Service Dealers Association (GASDA)
6338 Ave. N
Brooklyn, NY 11234   Phone: (718)241-1111
Editor(s): Stanley M. Schuer. Monthly. Reports on industry news, laws, and regulations affecting service station operators in New York. Updates association news and provides general tips on operation. Recurring features include news of research, news of educational opportunities and Association programs, reports of meetings, and a calendar of events.

★3793★
IADA Watchline
Independent Automotive Damage Appraisers Association (IADA)
5151 Belt Line Rd., No. K 1005
Dallas, TX 75240-6738   Phone: (214)702-9022
Editor(s): Norman Wetzel. Quarterly. Informs readers of new methods, techniques, and problems within the automotive repair industry.

★3794★
Import Service
Gemini Communications
306 N. Cleveland Massillon Rd.
Akron, OH 44333   Phone: (216)666-9553
Karl Seyfert, Editor. Monthly. Magazine covering the service and repair of imported cars. **Facsimile Number:** (216)666-8912.

★3795★
Mechanical News (ASA)
Automotive Service Association (ASA)
1901 Airport Fwy., Ste. 100
PO Box 929
Bedford, TX 76095-0929   Phone: (817)283-6205
Bimonthly. Speciality publication for members of the ASA Mechanical Division.

★3796★
Motor Age
Chilton Co.
Chilton Way
Radnor, PA 19089   Phone: (215)964-4000
Stan Stephenson, Editor. Monthly. Trade magazine serving the automotive service industry. **Facsimile Number:** (215)964-4981.

Automotive Body Repairers

★3797★
Motor in Canada
Sanford Evans Communications Ltd.
1077 St. James St.
PO Box 6900
Winnipeg, MB, Canada R3C 3B1   Phone: (204)775-0201
Dan Proudley, Editor. Monthly. Magazine for the auto service industry. **Facsimile Number:** (204)783-7488.

★3798★
Motor Magazine
Hearst Corp.
645 Stewart Ave.
Garden City, NY 11530   Phone: (516)227-1400
Wade Hoyt, Editor. Monthly. Magazine for the automotive aftermarket trade, professional mechanics and shop owners. Facsimile Number: (516)227-1405.

★3799★
Motor Service
Hunter Publishing Ltd. Partnership
950 Lee St.
Des Plaines, IL 60016   Phone: (708)296-0770
Jim Halloran, Editorial Director. Monthly. Magazine for auto repair shops. **Facsimile Number:** (708)803-3328.

★3800★
NATTS News and Views (NATTS)
National Association of Trade and Technical Schools (NATTS)
2251 Wisconsin Ave. NW
Washington, DC 20007   Phone: (202)333-1021
Bimonthly. Newspaper.

★3801★
Selling Today (ASIA)
Automotive Service Industry Association (ASIA)
444 N. Michigan Ave.
Chicago, IL 60611-3975   Phone: (312)836-1300
Periodic.

★3802★
Tech Center News
Monday Morning Newspapers, Inc.
31201 Chicago Rd. S.
B-300
Warren, MI 48093   Phone: (313)939-6800
Peter Salinas, Editor. Weekly. Newspaper containing automotive and business news for the business community, including General Motors Technical Center, Warren, Michigan. **Facsimile Number:** (313)939-5850.

★3803★
TransTechnical News (ASA)
Automotive Service Association (ASA)
1901 Airport Fwy., Ste. 100
PO Box 929
Bedford, TX 76095-0929   Phone: (817)283-6205
Monthly.

★3804★
Voice of the Industry (ASIA)
Automotive Service Industry Association (ASIA)
444 N. Michigan Ave.
Chicago, IL 60611-3975   Phone: (312)836-1300
Periodic.

--- Meetings and Conventions ---

★3805★
Automotive Service Association of Ohio (ASA OH) Industry-Wide Trade Show
Automotive Shows, Inc.
27692 Deputy Cr.
Laguna Hills, CA 92653   Phone: (714)362-9702
1992. **Facsimile Number:** (714)362-9803.

★3806★
Automotive Service Association of Pennsylvania (ASA PA) Industry-Wide Trade Show
Automotive Shows, Inc.
27692 Deputy Cr.
LaGuana Hills, CA 92653   Phone: (714)362-9702
1992. **Facsimile Number:** (714)362-9803.

★3807★
Automotive Service Councils of California (ASC CA-North) Industry-Wide Trade Show
Automotive Shows, Inc.
27692 Deputy Cr.
LaGuana Hills, CA 92653   Phone: (714)362-9702
1992. **Facsimile Number:** (714)362-9803.

★3808★
Automotive Service Councils of California (ASC CA-South) Industry-Wide Trade Show
Automotive Shows, Inc.
27692 Deputy Cr.
Laguna Hills, CA 92653   Phone: (714)362-9702
Frequency: Always held at the Convention Center in Anaheim, California. 1992; Anaheim, CA. **Facsimile Number:** (714)362-9803.

★3809★
Automotive Service Councils of Missouri (ASC MO) Industry-Wide Trade Show
Automotive Shows, Inc.
27692 Deputy Cr.
Laguna Hills, CA 92653   Phone: (714)362-9702

★3810★
Automotive Service Industry Association (ASIA)
444 N. Michigan Ave.
Chicago, IL 60611-3975   Phone: (312)836-1300
Frequency: Annual trade show. 1992; Nov. 16-21; Las Vegas, NV • 1993; Nov. 15-20; Las Vegas, NV. **Facsimile Number:** (312)836-1009.

★3811★
Congress of Automotive Repair and Service
Automotive Service Association (ASA)
1901 Airport Fwy., Ste. 100
PO Box 929
Bedford, TX 76095-0929   Phone: (817)283-6205
Frequency: Annual. **Facsimile Number:** (817)685-0225.

★3812★
Society of Collision Repair Specialists (SCRS)
PO Box 197
1201 Landmark, Ste. 3
Liberty, MO 64068   Phone: (816)781-5225
Frequency: Annual, with exhibits, always held in June.

────── **Other Sources of Information** ──────

★3813★
Automotive Aerodynamics: An Update
Society of Automotive Engineers
400 Commonwealth Dr.
Warrendale, PA 15096-0001   Phone: (412)776-4841
1987.

★3814★
Automotive Instrument Panels: Design, Materials & Manufacturing
Society of Automotive Engineers, Inc.
400 Commonwealth Dr.
Warrendale, PA 15096-0001   Phone: (412)776-4841
1987.

★3815★
Collision Parts Industry Roster & Suppliers Guide
Automotive Body Parts Association
Sarco Management & Publications
2500 Wildcrest Dr., Ste. 510
Houston, TX 77042-2752   Phone: (713)977-5551
Stanley A. Rodman, editor. Annual, spring;first edition 1990. Approximately 2,000 general suppliers, association members, participants in the ADP-Audatex Parts Exchange Program, and prominent members of the automotive aftermarket industry; coverage includes Canada. Entries include: Name, address, phone, fax, geographical area served, product/service. Arrangement: Geographical. **Toll-free/Additional Phone Number(s):** (800)323-5832. **Facsimile Number:** (713)531-9411.

★3816★
Computers in Design Construction & Operation of Automobiles
Springer-Verlag New York, Inc.
175 5th Ave., 19th Fl.
New York, NY 10010   Phone: (212)460-1500
T. K. Murthy, editor. 1987.

★3817★
Racing & Sports Car Chassis Design
Robert Bentley, Inc, Publishers
1000 Massachusetts Ave.
Cambridge, MA 02138   Phone: (617)547-4170
Michael Costin. 1965. **Facsimile Number:** (617)876-9235.

Automotive Mechanics

Automotive mechanics, often called automotive service technicians, repair and service automobiles and occasionally light trucks, with gasoline engines. Based on a description of the symptoms, the mechanic may test drive, or use diagnostic equipment to find the problem. Many mechanics consider the diagnostic process the most challenging and satisfying part of the job. Once the cause of the problem is found, mechanics make adjustments or repairs. If a part is worn or damaged beyond repair, or cannot be fixed at a reasonable cost, they replace it, usually after consultation with the vehicle owner. During routine service, mechanics inspect, lubricate, and adjust various components to prevent breakdowns. A variety of tools are used such as pneumatic wrenches, grinding machines, and a growing variety of electronic and computerized service equipment. In larger shops, specialization is common, including automatic transmission mechanics that work on gear trains and other transmission parts, tune-up mechanics that adjust timing mechanisms and ensure efficient engine performance, brake repairers, and many other specialists. The majority of automotive mechanics work for automotive dealers, independent repair shops, and gasoline service stations. Others are employed at automotive service facilities at department and other stores. Some maintain auto fleets for taxicab and leasing companies, government facilities, and other organizations. Motor vehicle manufacturers may also employ mechanics to make final adjustments and repairs at the end of assembly. Over 20% of automotive mechanics are self-employed.

$alaries

Earnings for automotive mechanics vary with skill level.

Highly skilled mechanics	$17.40/hour
Less skilled mechanics	$12.40/hour
Semi-skilled mechanics	$8.70/hour

Employment Outlook

Growth rate until the year 2000: Average.

Automotive Mechanics

Career Guides

★3818★
Auto Assembly Line General Repairman
Morris Video
2730 Monterey St. #105
Monterey Business Park
Torrance, CA 90503   Phone: (213)533-4800
Videocassette. 1982. 30 mins. A fifteen year employee of auto manufacturing offers his insights on the industry for those wishing to pursue such a career.

★3819★
Auto Brake Specialist
Careers, Inc.
PO Box 135
Largo, FL 34649-0135   Phone: (813)584-7333
1992. Two-page occupational summary card describing duties, working conditions, personal qualifications, training, earnings and hours, employment outlook, places of employment, related careers and where to write for more information.

★3820★
"Auto Mechanic" in *Exploring Nontraditional Jobs for Women* (pp. 89-95)
Rosen Publishing Group, Inc.
29 E. 21st St.
New York, NY 10010   Phone: (212)777-3017
Rose Neufeld. 1989. Describes blue-collar, male dominated occupations. Discusses what is done on the job, training, where to apply for jobs, tools used, salaries, and advantages and disadvantages. Relates the experiences of women who are working in the field.

★3821★
"Auto Mechanic" in *The Desk Guide to Training and Work Advisement* (p. 85)
Charles C. Thomas, Publisher
2600 S. First St.
Springfield, IL 62794-9265   Phone: (217)789-8980
Gail Baugher Kuenstler. 1988. Describes alternative methods of gaining entry into an occupation through different types of educational programs, internships and apprenticeships.
Facsimile Number: (217)789-9130.

★3822★
Auto Shop Safety
Bergwall Productions
106 Charles Lindbergh Blvd.
Uniondale, NY 11553-3695   Phone: (516)222-1111
Videocassette. 1987. 10 mins. The basics of working safely in an auto shop are given. The entire series is also available as a single tape for the same cost.

★3823★
"Automobile Mechanics" in Volume 1 of *Career Discovery Encyclopedia* (pp. 90-91)
J.G. Ferguson Publishing Co.
200 W. Monroe
Chicago, IL 60606   Phone: (312)580-5480
E. Russell Primm, editor-in-chief. 1990. Contains two-page articles on 504 occupations. Each article describes job duties, earnings, and educational and training requirements.

★3824★
"Automobile Mechanics" in Volume 3 of *The Encyclopedia of Careers and Vocational Guidance* (pp. 480-484)
J.G. Ferguson Publishing Co.
200 W. Monroe
Chicago, IL 60606   Phone: (312)580-5480
William E. Hopke, editor-in-chief. Eighth edition, 1990. Four-volume set that profiles 500 occupations and describes job trends in 76 industries. Includes career description, educational requirements, history of the job, methods of entry, advancement, employment outlook, earnings, working conditions, social and psychological factors, and sources of additional information.

★3825★
"Automobile Mechanics" in *The American Almanac of Jobs and Salaries* (pp. 523-524)
Avon Books
105 Madison Avenue
New York, NY 10016   Phone: (212)481-5600
John Wright and Edward J. Dwyer. Revised and updated, 1990. A comprehensive guide to the wages of hundreds of occupations in a wide variety of industries and organizations.

★3826★
Automobile Technicians (Mechanics)
Chronicle Guidance Publications, Inc.
PO Box 1190
Moravia, NY 13118-1190   Phone: (315)497-0330
1989. This career brief describes the nature of the work, working conditions, hours and earnings, education and training,

licensure, certification, unions, personal qualifications, social and psychological factors, employment outlook, entry methods, advancement, and related occupations. **Toll-free/Additional Phone Number(s):** 800-622-7284.

★3827★
"Automotive Brake Specialist" in *Occu-Facts: Information on 565 Careers in Outline Form* (p. 15.2)
Careers, Inc.
P.O. Box 135
1211 Tenth St., S.W.
Largo, FL 33640 Phone: (813)584-7333

Elizabeth Handville. Biennial, 1989-90 edition. Each one-page occupational profile describes duties, working conditions, physical surroundings and demands, aptitudes, temperament, educational requirements, employment outlook, earnings, and places of employment.

★3828★
"Automotive Cooling System Technicians" in Volume 4 of *The Encyclopedia of Careers and Vocational Guidance* (p. 123)
J.G. Ferguson Publishing Co.
200 W. Monroe
Chicago, IL 60606 Phone: (312)580-5480

William E. Hopke, editor-in-chief. Eighth edition, 1990. Four-volume set that profiles 500 occupations and describes job trends in 76 industries. Includes career description, educational requirements, history of the job, methods of entry, advancement, employment outlook, earnings, working conditions, social and psychological factors, and sources of additional information.

★3829★
"Automotive Exhaust Emissions Technicians" in Volume 1 of *Career Discovery Encyclopedia* (pp. 96-97)
J.G. Ferguson Publishing Co.
200 W. Monroe
Chicago, IL 60606 Phone: (312)580-5480

E. Russell Primm, editor-in-chief. 1990. Contains two-page articles on 504 occupations. Each article describes job duties, earnings, and educational and training requirements.

★3830★
Automotive Mechanic
Careers, Inc.
PO Box 135
Largo, FL 34649-0135 Phone: (813)584-7333

1989. Eight-page brief offering the definition, history, duties, working conditions, personal qualifications, educational requirements, earnings, hours, employment outlook, advancement possibilities, and related occupations.

★3831★
"Automotive Mechanic" in *Occu-Facts: Information on 565 Careers in Outline Form* (p. 15.3)
Careers, Inc.
P.O. Box 135
1211 Tenth St., S.W.
Largo, FL 33640 Phone: (813)584-7333

Elizabeth Handville. Biennial, 1989-90 edition. Each one-page occupational profile describes duties, working conditions, physical surroundings and demands, aptitudes, temperament, educational requirements, employment outlook, earnings, and places of employment.

★3832★
"Automotive Mechanic" in *Transportation*, Volume 12 of *Career Information Center* (pp. 94-96)
Glencoe/Macmillan
15319 Chatsworth St.
Mission Hills, CA 91345 Phone: (818)898-1391

Richard Lidz and Dale Anderson, editorial directors. Fourth edition, 1990. For 600 occupations, describes job duties, entry-level requirements, education and training needed, advancement possibilities, employment outlook, earnings and benefits. The set is divided into 12 volumes. Each volume includes jobs related under a broad career field. Volume 13 is the index. **Facsimile Number:** 818-365-5489.

★3833★
"Automotive Mechanic" in *VGM's Careers Encyclopedia* (pp. 54-56)
National Textbook Co.
4255 W. Touhy Ave.
Lincolnwood, IL 60646 Phone: (312)679-5500

Third edition, 1991. Contains two- to five-page descriptions of 200 managerial, professional, technical, trade, and service occupations. Each profile includes job duties, places of employment, qualifications, educational preparation, training, employment potential, advancement, income, and additional sources of information.

★3834★
"Automotive Mechanics" in *Jobs! What They Are...Where They Are...What They Pay* (pp. 175-176)
Simon & Schuster, Inc.
Simon & Schuster Bldg.
1230 Avenue of the Americas
New York, NY 10020 Phone: (212)698-7000

Robert O. Snelling and Anne M. Snelling. Revised edition, 1989. Profiles 241 occupations, describing duties and responsibilities, educational preparation, earnings, employment opportunities, training, and qualifications.

★3835★
"Automotive Mechanics" in *Occupational Outlook Handbook* (pp. 329-331)
Superintendent of Documents
U.S. Government Printing Office
Washington, DC 20402 Phone: (202)783-3238

Biennial; latest edition, 1990-91. Encyclopedia of careers describing more than 250 occupations and comprising about 86 percent of all jobs in the economy. Occupations that require lengthy education or training are given the most attention. For each occupation, the handbook describes job duties, working conditions, training, educational preparation, personal qualities, advancement possibilities, job outlook, earnings, and sources of additional information.

★3836★
Automotive Technician: A Challenging and Changing Career
Automotive Service Association
PO Box 929
Bedford, TX 76095-0929 Phone: (817)283-6205

This eight-page booklet describes the work, job duties, places of employment, labor market outlook, advancement prospects, training, certification, and earnings of the automotive technician.

Automotive Mechanics ★3848★

★3837★
"Automotive Technology" in *The Career Connection II: A Guide to Technical Majors and Their Related Careers* (pp. 5-6)
ERIS
PO Box 7509
University Station
Provo, UT 84602-0509

Fred A. Rowe. 1988. Contains technical majors, such as automotive technology. Describes the major and the job. Lists high school and postsecondary school courses. Includes occupations related to the major, employment outlook, and starting salary.

★3838★
"Brake Specialist" in *Opportunities in Automotive Service Careers* (p. 54)
National Textbook Co.
4255 W. Touhy Ave.
Lincolnwood, IL 60646   Phone: (312)679-5500

Robert M. Weber. 1989. Describes the work of the automobile mechanic and related occupations such as service station attendant and automobile body repairer. Covers working conditions, places of employment, qualifications, training, apprenticeships, certification, advancement opportunities, employment outlook, tools needed, and earnings.

★3839★
Career Success Series
Cambridge Career Products
90 MacCorkle Ave., SW
South Charleston, WV 25311   Phone: (304)744-9323

Videocassette. 1986. 15 mins. A series, available separately, outlining various career choices for students. Occupations include: flight service, air transportation/ground service, data processing, carpentry, clerk in banking/insurance, commodity sales, cosmetic personal grooming, fire fighting, forestry services, home economics, insulation/roofing, material handling, mechanics, photographic processing, pipefitting and plumbing, police science, printing, secretarial services, and utilities equipment operator.

★3840★
Certified Automotive Technician
Vocational Biographies, Inc.
PO Box 31, Dept. VF10
Sauk Centre, MN 56378   Phone: (612)352-6516

1990. This pamphlet profiles a person working in the job. Includes information about job duties, working conditions, places of employment, educational preparation, labor market outlook, and salaries. **Toll-free/Additional Phone Number(s):** 800-255-0752.

★3841★
Do Your Own Thing. in the Mechanical Field
AIMS Media, Inc.
9710 DeSoto Ave.
Chatsworth, CA 93111-4409   Phone: (818)773-4300

Videocassette. 1979. 16 mins. Various job levels in the mechanical field are outlined for students.

★3842★
"Mechanic" in *Guide to Careers Without College* (pp. 92-95)
Franklin Watts, Inc.
387 Park Avenue, S.
New York, NY 10016   Phone: (212)686-7070

Kathleen S. Abrams. 1988. Discusses careers that do not require a college degree in fields such as health care, sales and marketing, and the building trades. Describes the work, employment opportunities, and training.

★3843★
"Mechanics: Automobiles and Motorcycles" in *Opportunities in Vocational and Technical Careers* (pp. 103-104)
National Textbook Co.
4255 W. Touhy Ave.
Lincolnwood, IL 60646   Phone: (312)679-5500

Adrian A. Paradis. 1987. Describes careers which can be prepared for by attending a private vocational or proprietary school—office employee, sales worker, service worker, health services, mechanic, craftworker, and technician. Covers employment outlook, job duties, and salaries. Offers career planning advice.

★3844★
"Mechanics: Automotive Body Repair" in *Opportunities in Vocational and Technical Careers* (p. 105)
National Textbook Co.
4255 W. Touhy Ave.
Lincolnwood, IL 60646   Phone: (312)679-5500

Adrian A. Paradis. 1987. Describes careers which can be prepared for by attending a private vocational or proprietary school—office employee, sales worker, service worker, health services, mechanic, craftworker, and technician. Covers employment outlook, job duties, and salaries. Offers career planning advice.

★3845★
Rewarding Careers in the Automotive Service Industry
Motor Vehicle Manufacturers Association of the United States, Inc.
7430 Second Ave., Ste. 300
Detroit, MI 48202   Phone: (313)872-4311

1990. This 12-page booklet describes the demand for, work, earnings, and training of automotive mechanics.

★3846★
Transportation/Mechanical Cluster
Center for Humanities, Inc.
Communications Park
Box 1000
Mount Kisco, NY 10549   Phone: (914)666-4100

Videocassette. 1984. 20 mins. The key aspects of working in the fields of Auto Body Repair, Truck Driving, and Auto Mechanics are explained.

★3847★
Video Career Library - Mechanical Fields
Careers, Inc.
1211 10th St., SW
PO Box 135
Largo, FL 34649-0135   Phone: (813)584-7333

Videocassette. 1990. 22 mins. Part of the Video Career Library covering 165 occupations. Shows actual workers on the job. Includes automobile mechanics, diesel engine mechanics, aircraft engine mechanics, automobile body repairers, heavy equipment mechanics, heating/air-conditioning/refrigeration mechanics.

★3848★
Vocational Visions
Center for Humanities, Inc.
Communications Park
Box 1000
Mount Kisco, NY 10549   Phone: (914)666-4100

Videocassette. 1984. 30 mins. This series of programs explains key aspects of actual training and a day in the life of a worker in the specific field mentioned on the videocassette. Occupations include: transportation/mechanics, repair, construction, business/office occupations, health, and agriculture.

★3849★
Vocations U.S.A.
Info-Disc Corporation
4 Professional Dr.
Gaithersburg, MD 20879　　　　　Phone: (301)948-2300
Videocassette. 1987. 60 mins. A disc collection outlining the requirements and methods of various career areas. Occupations include: transportation, mechanical/repair, health, agriculture, and construction.

Associations

★3850★
Automotive Service Association (ASA)
1901 Airport Fwy., Ste. 100
PO Box 929
Bedford, TX 76095-0929　　　　　Phone: (817)283-6205
Membership: Automotive service businesses (10,100) including body, paint, and trim shops, engine rebuilders, radiator shops, brake and wheel alignment services, transmission shops, tune-up services, and air conditioning services; associate members (320) are manufacturers and wholesalers of automotive parts, and the trade press. **Purpose:** Represents independent businessmen before private agencies and national and state legislative bodies. Promotes confidence between consumer and automotive technician, safety inspection of motor vehicles, and better highways. Conducts professional training seminars in business management, technical and update training, and other areas. Maintains 130 volume collection of automotive repair videotapes. **Publications:** *AutoInc*, monthly. • *Collision Repair Report*, monthly. • *Mechanical News*, bimonthly. • *TransTechnical News*, monthly. • Also publishes convention brochure, fact sheet, and bylaws. **Facsimile Number:** (817)685-0225.

★3851★
Automotive Service Industry Association (ASIA)
444 N. Michigan Ave.
Chicago, IL 60611-3975　　　　　Phone: (312)836-1300
Membership: Executives representing independent automotive wholesalers, warehouse distributors, heavy-duty vehicle and equipment parts distributors, automotive electrical service and supply wholesalers and distributors, manufacturers' representatives, and manufacturers and remanufacturers of replacement parts, tools, equipment, chemicals, refinishing materials, supplies, and accessories. **Purpose:** Operates extensive business management library. Holds seminars; bestows awards; compiles statistics; maintains hall of fame. **Publications:** *Automotive Service Industry Association—Buyers Guide*, periodic. • *Automotive Service Industry Association—Membership Directory*, periodic. • *Automotive Service Industry Association—Product Directory*, periodic. • *Selling Today*, periodic. • *Voice of the Industry*, periodic. **Facsimile Number:** (312)836-1009.

★3852★
Motor and Equipment Manufacturers Association (MEMA)
300 Sylvan Ave.
PO Box 1638
Englewood Cliffs, NJ 07632-0638　　　　Phone: (201)569-8500
Membership: Manufacturers of automotive and heavy-duty original equipment and replacement components, maintenance equipment, chemicals, accessories, refinishing supplies, tools, and service equipment united for research into all aspects of the automotive and heavy-duty markets. **Purpose:** Provides manufacturer-oriented services and programs including: marketing consultation for the automotive industry; federal and state legal, safety, and legislative representation and consultation; personnel services; manpower development workshops; international information. Maintains credit reporting and collection service covering wholesalers, retailers, chain stores, and warehouse distributors; offers electronic order-entry, price-update, and electronic document exchange services through MEMA/Transnet system; maintains international liaison. Administers U.S. Automotive Parts Industry Japan Office in conjunction with the U.S. Department of Commerce. Conducts seminars on domestic and overseas marketing, federal trade regulations, freight forwarding, and credit and collections. Compiles statistics on automotive service industry for use by members and as a public service. **Publications:** *Automotive Distributor Trends and Financial Analysis*, periodic. • *Credit and Sales Reference Directory*, 2/year. • *International Buyer's Guide of U.S.* • *Marketing Insight*, quarterly. • Also publishes *Japan Automotive Insight*, *Autobody Supply and Equipment Market*, *Automotive Jobbers in the U.S.* **Facsimile Number:** (201)569-0159.

★3853★
National Automotive Technicians Education Foundation (NATEF)
13505 Dulles Technology Dr.
Herndon, VA 22071-3415　　　　　Phone: (703)904-0100
Purpose: Encourages the development of automotive technical education and the maintenance of national standards set by the automotive industry for secondary and postsecondary educational facilities. Evaluates and reviews the structure and resources of automobile training programs in areas such as learning resources, student services, instruction, and facilities. Makes recommendations that lead to program certification by the National Institute of Automotive Service Excellence. **Facsimile Number:** (703)904-0727.

★3854★
National Institute for Automotive Service Excellence (ASE)
13505 Dulles Technology Dr.
Herndon, VA 22071-3415　　　　　Phone: (703)742-3800
Membership: Governed by a 40-member board of directors selected from all sectors of the automotive service industry and from education, government, and consumer groups. **Purpose:** Encourages and promotes the highest standards of automotive service in the public interest. Conducts continuing research to determine the best methods for training automotive technicians; encourages the development of effective training programs. Tests and certifies the competence of automobile, heavy-duty truck, collision repair, and engine machinist technicians. **Publications:** *ASE Test Registration Booklet*, semiannual. • *ASE Training Guide*, annual. • *The Blue Seal*, semiannual. **Facsimile Number:** (703)904-0727.

Standards/Certification Agencies

Voluntary certification by the National Institute for Automotive Service Excellence (ASE) is widely recognized as a standard of achievement for automotive mechanics. Certification, which may be in one or more of eight different service areas, requires at least two years of experience and the passing of a written examination. Completion of an automotive mechanic program in high school, vocational or trade school, or community or junior college may be substituted for one year of experience. Certified mechanics must retake the examination at least every five years.

Automotive Mechanics

★3855★
Certified Advantage for Auto Technicians
National Institute for Automotive Service Excellence
13505 Dulles Technology Dr.
Herndon, VA 22071-3415   Phone: (703)742-3800
This eight-panel brochure describes the testing procedure and explains the advantages of being certified.

★3856★
National Automotive Technicians Education Foundation (NATEF)
13505 Dulles Technology Dr.
Herndon, VA 22071-3415   Phone: (703)904-0100
Makes recommendations that lead to program certification by the National Institute of Automotive Service Excellence.

★3857★
National Institute for Automotive Service Excellence (ASE)
13505 Dulles Technology Dr.
Herndon, VA 22071-3415   Phone: (703)742-3800
Encourages and promotes the highest standards of automotive service in the public interest. Conducts continuing research to determine the best methods for training automotive technicians; encourages the development of effective training programs. Tests and certifies the competence of automobile, heavy-duty truck, collision repair, and engine machinist technicians.

Test Guides

★3858★
ASE Test Registration Booklet (ASE)
National Institute for Automotive Service Excellence (ASE)
13505 Dulles Technology Dr.
Herndon, VA 22071-3415   Phone: (703)742-3800
Semiannual. Registration for technicians who wish to become ASE certified. Provides registration information and sample questions.

★3859★
ASE Training Guide (ASE)
National Institute for Automotive Service Excellence (ASE)
13505 Dulles Technology Dr.
Herndon, VA 22071-3415   Phone: (703)742-3800
Annual. Bibliographic listing of training materials available for upgrading technicians' skills in automotive repair, including sample ASE test questions and test specifications.

★3860★
Auto Engineman
National Learning Corp.
212 Michael Dr.
Syosset, NY 11791   Phone: (516)921-8888
Jack Rudman. Part of the Career Examination Series No. 1. All examination guides in this series contain test questions with answers. **Facsimile Number:** (516)921-8743. **Toll-free/Additional Phone Number(s):** 800-645-6337.

★3861★
Auto Maintenance Coordinator
National Learning Corp.
212 Michael Dr.
Syosset, NY 11791   Phone: (516)921-8888
Jack Rudman. Part of the Career Examination Series No. 1. All examination guides in this series contain test questions with answers. **Facsimile Number:** (516)921-8743. **Toll-free/Additional Phone Number(s):** 800-645-6337.

★3862★
Auto Mechanic
National Learning Corp.
212 Michael Dr.
Syosset, NY 11791   Phone: (516)921-8888
Jack Rudman. Part of the Career Examination Series No. 1. All examination guides in this series contain test questions with answers. **Facsimile Number:** (516)921-8743. **Toll-free/Additional Phone Number(s):** 800-645-6337.

★3863★
Auto Mechanic/Automotive Serviceman
Prentice Hall Press
Simon & Schuster Inc.
200 Old Tappan Rd.
Old Tappan, NJ 07675   Phone: (800)223-2348
Hy Hammer. Sixth edition, 1982. Preparation for the complete civil service exam for journeymen, automobile mechanics, and automotive servicemen. Contains actual past exams given for these positions.

★3864★
Auto Mechanics
National Learning Corp.
212 Michael Dr.
Syosset, NY 11791   Phone: (516)921-8888
Jack Rudman. 1989. Part of Occupational Competency Examination Series.

★3865★
Automobile Mechanic Certification Tests
Prentice Hall Press
Simon & Schuster Inc.
200 Old Tappan Rd.
Old Tappan, NJ 07675   Phone: (800)223-2348
David Sharp. Second edition, 1985. Provides sample tests, basic technical review, glossary of terms, and information on the certification exams and programs of the National Institute for Automotive Service Excellence (NIASE).

★3866★
Automotive Serviceman
National Learning Corp.
212 Michael Dr.
Syosset, NY 11791   Phone: (516)921-8888
Jack Rudman. Part of the Career Examination Series No. 1. All examination guides in this series contain test questions with answers. **Facsimile Number:** (516)921-8743. **Toll-free/Additional Phone Number(s):** 800-645-6337.

★3867★
Certified General Automobile Mechanic (CGAM)
National Learning Corp.
212 Michael Dr.
Syosset, NY 11791   Phone: (516)921-8888
Jack Rudman. Part of the Career Examination Series No. 1. All examination guides in this series contain questions with answers. **Facsimile Number:** (516)921-8743. **Toll-free/Additional Phone Number(s):** 800-645-6337.

★3868★
Foreman Auto Mechanic
National Learning Corp.
212 Michael Dr.
Syosset, NY 11791   Phone: (516)921-8888
Jack Rudman. Part of the Career Examination Series No. 1. All examination guides in this series contain questions with answers. **Facsimile Number:** (516)921-8743. **Toll-free/Additional Phone Number(s):** 800-645-6337.

★3869★
GMC Apprentice Program Battery Tests (GMC)
National Learning Corp.
212 Michael Dr.
Syosset, NY 11791   Phone: (516)921-8888
Jack Rudman. Part of the Admission Test Series No. 3. Books in this series provide test practice and drill for actual professional certification and licensure tests. **Facsimile Number:** (516)921-8743. **Toll-free/Additional Phone Number(s):** 800-645-6337.

★3870★
Head Automotive Mechanic
National Learning Corp.
212 Michael Dr.
Syosset, NY 11791   Phone: (516)921-8888
Jack Rudman. Part of the Career Examination Series No. 1. All examination guides in this series contain questions with answers. **Facsimile Number:** (516)921-8743. **Toll-free/Additional Phone Number(s):** 800-645-6337.

★3871★
The Official ASE Preparation Guide to ASE Automobile and Body/Paint Tests
National Institute for Automotive Service Excellence
13505 Dulles Technology Dr.
Herndon, VA 22071-3415   Phone: (703)742-3800
1990. Describes the certification process for automobile mechanics and auto body repairers. Offers tips on preparing for the test. Contains sample test questions.

★3872★
Senior Automotive Mechanic
National Learning Corp.
212 Michael Dr.
Syosset, NY 11791   Phone: (516)921-8888
Jack Rudman. Part of the Career Examination Series No. 1. All examination guides in this series contain questions with answers. **Facsimile Number:** (516)921-8743. **Toll-free/Additional Phone Number(s):** 800-645-6337.

Educational Directories and Programs

★3873★
ASSET Program
Ford Motor Company
Ford Parts and Service Division, Training Dept.
Dearborn, MI 48121
Automobile manufacturer sponsored 2-year training program in automotive service technology.

★3874★
Chrysler Dealer Apprenticeship Program
c/o National C.A.P. Coordinator
26001 Lawrence Ave.
Center Line, MI 48015
Two-year apprenticeship program in automotive service technology offered by the auto manufacturer.

★3875★
General Motors Automotive Service Educational Program
c/o National College Coordinator
General Motors Technical Service
30501 Van Dyke Ave.
Warren, MI 48090
Automobile manufacturer sponsored training program in auto service technology.

★3876★
Jobber Topics—Aftermarket Training Directory Issue
  AMotor vehicle industryA
Irving-Cloud Publishing Company
7300 N. Cicero Ave.
Lincolnwood, IL 60646-1696   Phone: (312)674-7300
Martin Schultz, editor. Latest edition March 1990. List of companies offering training courses in automotive service. Entries include: Company name, address, phone, name and title of contact, courses offered, duration, costs, usual locations, general comments on additional educational materials offered and quality of the courses. Arrangement: Alphabetical by company name. **Facsimile Number:** (312)674-7015.

Basic Reference Guides and Handbooks

★3877★
Auto Mechanics
National Learning Corp.
212 Michael Dr.
Syosset, NY 11791   Phone: (516)921-8888
Jack Rudman. 1988. Part of DANTES Series.

★3878★
Auto Mechanics for the Complete Dummy
Motormatics Publications
PO Box 91051
Long Beach, CA 90809   Phone: (213)434-6701
Philip R. Martin. Second edition, 1983.

★3879★
Auto Mechanics Refresher Course
H. M. Gousha Co.
2001 The Alameda
San Jose, CA 95126   Phone: (408)296-1060
Chek-Chart Staff.

★3880★
Autobody Supply and Equipment Market (MEMA)
Motor and Equipment Manufacturers Association (MEMA)
300 Sylvan Ave.
PO Box 1638
Englewood Cliffs, NJ 07632-0638   Phone: (201)569-8500

★3881★
Automechanics
Prentice Hall
Rte. 9W
Englewood Cliffs, NJ 07632   Phone: (201)592-2000
Herbert E. Ellinger. Fourth edition, 1988.

Automotive Mechanics

★3882★
Automechanic's Guide to Electronic Instrumentation & Microprocessor
Prentice Hall
Rte. 9W
Englewood Cliffs, NJ 07632　　　Phone: (201)592-2000
Lynn S. Mosher. 1987.

★3883★
Automechanics: Understanding the New Technology
Prentice Hall
Rte. 9W
Englewood Cliffs, NJ 07632　　　Phone: (201)592-2000
Don Knowles. 1987.

★3884★
Automotive Mechanics
McGraw-Hill Publishing Company
1221 Avenue of the Americas
New York, NY 10020　　　Phone: (212)512-2000
William H. Crouse. Ninth edition, 1985.

★3885★
Car Maintenance in the U.S.A. (MEMA)
Motor and Equipment Manufacturers Association (MEMA)
300 Sylvan Ave.
PO Box 1638
Englewood Cliffs, NJ 07632-0638　　　Phone: (201)569-8500

★3886★
Foreign Vehicle Maintenance in the U.S.A. (MEMA)
Motor and Equipment Manufacturers Association (MEMA)
300 Sylvan Ave.
PO Box 1638
Englewood Cliffs, NJ 07632-0638　　　Phone: (201)569-8500

★3887★
Heavy Duty Truck Maintenance in the U.S.A. (MEMA)
Motor and Equipment Manufacturers Association (MEMA)
300 Sylvan Ave.
PO Box 1638
Englewood Cliffs, NJ 07632-0638　　　Phone: (201)569-8500

★3888★
Mathematics for Auto Mechanics
Delmar Publishers, Inc.
PO Box 15015
2 Computer Dr., W.
Albany, NY 12212　　　Phone: (518)459-1150
T. G. Hendrix. 1978. **Facsimile Number:** (518)453-6472.

★3889★
Mercruiser Stern Drive Shop Manual 1964-1987
Clymer Publications
PO Box 120901
Overland Park, KS 66212　　　Phone: (913)541-6752
Kalton Lahue. **Toll-free/Additional Phone Number(s):** 800-633-6219. **Facsimile Number:** (913)541-6769.

★3890★
Motor Service—Tool & Equipment Buyers Guide Issue
Hunter Publishing Company, Inc.
950 Lee St.
Des Plaines, IL 60016　　　Phone: (708)296-0770
Jim Halloran, Editorial Director, editor. Annual, December. Companies that manufacture tools and equipment for the automotive service industry. **Facsimile Number:** (708)803-3328.

Periodicals

★3891★
Auto Inc.
Automotive Service Councils, Inc.
PO Box 929
Bedford, TX 76021-0929　　　Phone: (817)283-6205
Editor(s): Monica Buchholz. Monthly. Carries automotive technical material, news of the automotive industry, information on relevant legislation, and news of the Automotive Service Association. **Facsimile Number:** (817)685-0225.

★3892★
The Auto Index
7 Clinton Pl.
Suffern, NY 10901　　　Phone: (914)357-3695
6x/yr. Magazine providing a general purpose index to 14 automotive periodicals.

★3893★
Auto Mecanico Hispano
Hunter Publishing Ltd. Partnership
950 Lee St.
Des Plaines, IL 60016　　　Phone: (708)296-0770
Jim Halloran, Editor. Quarterly. Magazine specializing in automotive procedures for technicians (English and Spanish). **Facsimile Number:** (708)803-3328.

★3894★
Auto Tech Magazine
Larry Flynt Publications, Inc.
9171 Wilshire Blvd., Ste. 300
Beverly Hills, CA 90210　　　Phone: (213)275-3857
C. Vantune, Editor. Monthly Automotive magazine. ; James Kohls, Publisher.

★3895★
AutoInc (ASA)
Automotive Service Association (ASA)
1901 Airport Fwy., Ste. 100
PO Box 929
Bedford, TX 76095-0929　　　Phone: (817)283-6205
Monthly. Journal covering technical and business information of interest to members; contains shop profiles, legislative news, industry events, and descriptions of new products.

★3896★
Automobile International
Johnston International Publishing Corp.
950 Lee St., No. 100
Des Plaines, IL 60016-6588
M. Havis Dawson, Editor. Nine times/yr. International magazine of auto service and repairs. Printed in English and Spanish; published quarterly in Arabic.

★3897★
Automotive Distributor Trends and Financial Analysis (MEMA)
Motor and Equipment Manufacturers Association (MEMA)
300 Sylvan Ave.
PO Box 1638
Englewood Cliffs, NJ 07632-0638　　　Phone: (201)569-8500
Periodic.

★3898★
Automotive Jobbers in the U.S.A. (MEMA)
Motor and Equipment Manufacturers Association (MEMA)
300 Sylvan Ave.
PO Box 1638
Englewood Cliffs, NJ 07632-0638   Phone: (201)569-8500

★3899★
The Automotive Messenger
Hansen Publishing, Inc.
431 Chez Paree
Hazelwood, MO 63042   Phone: (314)831-4000
B. Hank Hansen, Publisher. Monthly. Automotive magazine. **Facsimile Number:** (314)831-3610.

★3900★
The Blue Seal (ASE)
National Institute for Automotive Service Excellence (ASE)
13505 Dulles Technology Dr.
Herndon, VA 22071-3415   Phone: (703)742-3800
Semiannual. Newsletter providing information on new technologies, training guides, and tips on servicing automobiles for certified technicians and their employers. Also provides information on certified technicians and events.

★3901★
Collision Repair Report (ASA)
Automotive Service Association (ASA)
1901 Airport Fwy., Ste. 100
PO Box 929
Bedford, TX 76095-0929   Phone: (817)283-6205
Monthly. Speciality publication for members of the ASA Collision Division.

★3902★
Convenient Automotive Services Retailer
Graphics Concepts
1801 Rockville Pike, Ste. 330
Rockville, MD 20852   Phone: (301)984-4000
Jocklynn Keville, Editor. 6x/yr. Trade magazine for professionals in the automotive services industry.

★3903★
Exhaust News
PO Box 120937
Arlington, TX 76012   Phone: (817)860-2375
Lee Cruse, Editor and Publisher. Monthly. Automotive magazine.

★3904★
Gasoline and Automotive Service Dealers Association— Bulletin
Gasoline and Automotive Service Dealers Association (GASDA)
6338 Ave. N
Brooklyn, NY 11234   Phone: (718)241-1111
Editor(s): Stanley M. Schuer. Monthly. Reports on industry news, laws, and regulations affecting service station operators in New York. Updates association news and provides general tips on operation. Recurring features include news of research, news of educational opportunities and Association programs, reports of meetings, and a calendar of events.

★3905★
IADA Watchline
Independent Automotive Damage Appraisers Association (IADA)
5151 Belt Line Rd., No. K 1005
Dallas, TX 75240-6738   Phone: (214)702-9022
Editor(s): Norman Wetzel. Quarterly. Informs readers of new methods, techniques, and problems within the automotive repair industry.

★3906★
Import Service
Gemini Communications
306 N. Cleveland Massillon Rd.
Akron, OH 44333   Phone: (216)666-9553
Karl Seyfert, Editor. Monthly. Magazine covering the service and repair of imported cars. **Facsimile Number:** (216)666-8912.

★3907★
Mechanical News (ASA)
Automotive Service Association (ASA)
1901 Airport Fwy., Ste. 100
PO Box 929
Bedford, TX 76095-0929   Phone: (817)283-6205
Bimonthly. Speciality publication for members of the ASA Mechanical Division.

★3908★
MEMA Marketing Insight (MEMA)
Motor and Equipment Manufacturers Association (MEMA)
300 Sylvan Ave.
PO Box 1638
Englewood Cliffs, NJ 07632-0638   Phone: (201)569-8500
Quarterly.

★3909★
Motor Age
Chilton Co.
Chilton Way
Radnor, PA 19089   Phone: (215)964-4000
Stan Stephenson, Editor. Monthly. Trade magazine serving the automotive service industry. **Facsimile Number:** (215)964-4981.

★3910★
Motor in Canada
Sanford Evans Communications Ltd.
1077 St. James St.
PO Box 6900
Winnipeg, MB, Canada R3C 3B1   Phone: (204)775-0201
Dan Proudley, Editor. Monthly. Magazine for the auto service industry. **Facsimile Number:** (204)783-7488.

★3911★
Motor Magazine
Hearst Corp.
645 Stewart Ave.
Garden City, NY 11530   Phone: (516)227-1400
Wade Hoyt, Editor. Monthly. Magazine for the automotive aftermarket trade, professional mechanics and shop owners. Facsimile Number: (516)227-1405.

★3912★
Motor Service
Hunter Publishing Ltd. Partnership
950 Lee St.
Des Plaines, IL 60016   Phone: (708)296-0770
Jim Halloran, Editorial Director. Monthly. Magazine for auto repair shops. **Facsimile Number:** (708)803-3328.

Automotive Mechanics

★3913★
Renews
Kona Communications, Inc.
707 Lake-Cook Rd.
Deerfield, IL 60015   Phone: (708)498-3180
Terry Haller, Editor. 12x/yr. Trade magazine covering rebuilding truck and auto parts.

★3914★
Selling Today (ASIA)
Automotive Service Industry Association (ASIA)
444 N. Michigan Ave.
Chicago, IL 60611-3975   Phone: (312)836-1300
Periodic.

★3915★
Super Automotive Service
Irving-Cloud Publications Co.
7300 N. Cicero Ave.
Lincolnwood, IL 60646   Phone: (708)588-7300
Bob Weber, Editor. Monthly. Trade magazine covering the technical aspects of normal service station/tire dealership/garage repair and service operations. **Facsimile Number:** (708)674-7015.

★3916★
Tech Center News
Monday Morning Newspapers, Inc.
31201 Chicago Rd. S.
B-300
Warren, MI 48093   Phone: (313)939-6800
Peter Salinas, Editor. Weekly. Newspaper containing automotive and business news for the business community, including General Motors Technical Center, Warren, Michigan. **Facsimile Number:** (313)939-5850.

★3917★
TransTechnical News (ASA)
Automotive Service Association (ASA)
1901 Airport Fwy., Ste. 100
PO Box 929
Bedford, TX 76095-0929   Phone: (817)283-6205
Monthly.

★3918★
Undercar Digest
M D Publications, Inc.
PO Box 2210
Springfield, MO 65801-2210   Phone: (417)866-3917
Dan Engler, Editor. Monthly. Magazine for the undercar service and supply industry. **Facsimile Number:** (417)866-2781.

★3919★
Voice of the Industry (ASIA)
Automotive Service Industry Association (ASIA)
444 N. Michigan Ave.
Chicago, IL 60611-3975   Phone: (312)836-1300
Periodic.

Meetings and Conventions

★3920★
Automotive Dealers Business Show and Conference
Flagg Management Inc.
369 Lexington Ave.
New York, NY 10017   Phone: (212)286-0333
1992. **Facsimile Number:** (212)286-0086.

★3921★
Automotive Engine Rebuilders Tech Show
330 Lexington Dr.
Buffalo Grove, IL 60089   Phone: (708)541-6550
1992; Jun. 18-20; Cincinnati, OH • 1993; Jun. 17-19; Las Vegas, NV. **Facsimile Number:** (708)541-5808.

★3922★
Automotive Service Industry Association (ASIA)
444 N. Michigan Ave.
Chicago, IL 60611-3975   Phone: (312)836-1300
Frequency: Annual trade show. 1992; Nov. 16-21; Las Vegas, NV • 1993; Nov. 15-20; Las Vegas, NV. **Facsimile Number:** (312)836-1009.

★3923★
Congress of Automotive Repair and Service
Automotive Service Association (ASA)
1901 Airport Fwy., Ste. 100
PO Box 929
Bedford, TX 76095-0929   Phone: (817)283-6205
Frequency: Annual. **Facsimile Number:** (817)685-0225.

★3924★
National Automotive Radiator Service Association Annual Trade Show and Convention
National Automotive Radiator Service Association
Box 1307
Lansdale, PA 19446   Phone: (215)362-5800
1992; Mar. 18-22; Orlando, FL. **Facsimile Number:** (215)855-7257.

Other Sources of Information

★3925★
ASSET: Q: Where Can You. . .?
Ford Motor Company
Ford Parts and Service Division
Training Department
Dearborn, MI 48121   Phone: (800)392-3673
This eight-page booklet describes the ASSET work-study program to train entry-level automotive service technicians for Ford and Lincoln Mercury dealerships.

★3926★
Automotive Technology Development Contractor's Coordination Meeting, 24th: Proceedings
Society of Automotive Engineers, Inc.
400 Commonwealth Dr.
Warrendale, PA 15096-0001   Phone: (412)776-4841
1987.

★3927★
CAP Orientation Guide
Chryser Corporation
National C.A.P. Development Dept.
Attn.: Rich Hund
26001 Lawrence Ave.
Center Line, MI 48015-1718   Phone: (313)445-7290
1991. This eight-page guide describes the Chrysler Dealer Apprenticeship work-study program designed to train automotive technicians for Chrysler dealerships.

★3928★
Distributors Financial Analysis (MEMA)
Motor and Equipment Manufacturers Association (MEMA)
300 Sylvan Ave.
PO Box 1638
Englewood Cliffs, NJ 07632-0638   Phone: (201)569-8500

Commercial and Industrial Electronic Equipment Repairers

Commercial and industrial electronic equipment repairers, also called industrial electronics technicians, install and repair electronic equipment used in industrial automated equipment controls, missile control systems, radar systems, medical diagnostic equipment, transmitters, and antennas. Preventive maintenance is a major responsibility of electronics repairers. They periodically check, clean, repair, or replace equipment to prevent problems. When an equipment failure does occur, a determination is made as to whether it is an electronic component. If so, diagnostic tests are run, and the problem fixed. About 20% of commercial and industrial electronic repairers are employed by the federal government; the overwhelming majority of these work for the Department of Defense at military installations. Electronic repairers are also employed by electronic and transportation equipment manufacturers, machinery and equipment wholesalers, telephone companies, hospitals, electronic repair shops, and firms that provide maintenance under contract.

$alaries

Earnings for commercial and industrial electronic equipment repairers are listed below.

Beginning repairers	$16,000-20,000/year
Experienced repairers	$20,000-24,000/year
Highly skilled, specialized repairers	$24,000-30,000/year

Employment Outlook

Growth rate until the year 2000: Average.

Commercial and Industrial Electronic Equipment Repairers

Career Guides

★3929★
Careers in the Electronics Industry
International Society of Certified Electronics Technicians
2708 W Berry St.
Fort Worth, TX 76109   Phone: (817)921-9101
This 16-page booklet provides an overview of the electronics industry and describes training and qualifications, employment outlook, earnings, and working conditions. Includes a state-by-state listing of electronic technician training schools.

★3930★
"Commercial and Industrial Electronic Equipment Repairers" in *Occupational Outlook Handbook* (pp. 331-333)
Superintendent of Documents
U.S. Government Printing Office
Washington, DC 20402   Phone: (202)783-3238
Biennial; latest edition, 1990-91. Encyclopedia of careers describing more than 250 occupations and comprising about 86 percent of all jobs in the economy. Occupations that require lengthy education or training are given the most attention. For each occupation, the handbook describes job duties, working conditions, training, educational preparation, personal qualities, advancement possibilities, job outlook, earnings, and sources of additional information.

★3931★
The Complete Electronics Career Guide
TAB Books
Blue Ridge Summit, PA 17294-0850   Phone: (717)794-2191
Joseph A. Risse. First edition, 1989.

★3932★
Electrical Maintenance Training Program
NUS Training Corporation
910 Clopper Rd.
Gaithersburg, MD 20878-1399   Phone: (301)258-8763
Videocassette. 1982. 60 mins. This program is designed to improve the skills of electrical maintenance personnel currently in the field and to train new entrees into the field. Programs available as an entire series or individually.

★3933★
Electronics...Your Bridge to Tomorrow
Modern Talking Picture Service
5000 Park St. North
St. Petersburg, FL 33709   Phone: (813)541-7571
Videocassette. 1981. 16 mins. This program presents opportunities for young people and adults in the growing consumer electronic field.

★3934★
"Industrial Electronic Equipment Repairers" in Volume 3 of *Career Discovery Encyclopedia* (pp. 130-131)
J.G. Ferguson Publishing Co.
200 W. Monroe
Chicago, IL 60606   Phone: (312)580-5480
E. Russell Primm, editor-in-chief. 1990. Contains two-page articles on 504 occupations. Each article describes job duties, earnings, and educational and training requirements.

★3935★
Industrial Electronics Training Program
TPC Training Systems
310 South Michigan Ave.
Chicago, IL 60604   Phone: (312)537-6610
Videocassette. 1982. 15 mins. Five modules of five programs each provide in-depth training for industrial electronics workers. All programs are available individually.

★3936★
"Mechanics: Commercial and Industrial Electronic Equipment" in *Opportunities in Vocational and Technical Careers* (pp. 107-108)
National Textbook Co.
4255 W. Touhy Ave.
Lincolnwood, IL 60646   Phone: (312)679-5500
Adrian A. Paradis. 1987. Describes careers which can be prepared for by attending a private vocational or proprietary school—office employee, sales worker, service worker, health services, mechanic, craftworker, and technician. Covers employment outlook, job duties, and salaries. Offers career planning advice.

★3937★
The Professional Electronics Technician
Electronics Technicians Association
602 N Jackson St.
Greencastle, IN 46135   Phone: (317)653-8262
This six-page brochure describes job duties, training, skills and aptitudes, salaries, employment outlook, and certification.

★3938★
Tools for the Electrical Trades
Bergwall Productions
106 Charles Lindbergh Blvd.
Uniondale, NY 11553-3695　　　　　Phone: (516)222-1111

Videocassette. 1986. 58 mins. A look at various electronic tools; on four tapes.

★3939★
Video Career Library - Repair Fields
Careers, Inc.
1211 10th St., SW
PO Box 135
Largo, FL 34649-0135　　　　　Phone: (813)584-7333

Videocassette. 1990. 23 mins. Part of the Video Career Library covering 165 occupations. Shows actual workers on the job. Includes industrial machinery repairers, communications equipment repairers, data processing equipment repairers, home entertainment equipment repairers, office machine repairers, electrical power installers and repairers, and electrical and electronic repairers.

Associations

★3940★
Electronics Technicians Association, International (ETA-I)
602 N. Jackson
Greencastle, IN 46135　　　　　Phone: (317)653-8262

Membership: Skilled electronics technicians. **Purpose:** Provides placement service; sponsors regional technician training workshops and business management seminars; offers certification examinations for electronics technicians. Compiles wage and manpower statistics. Conducts training seminars in general electronics and specific aspects of the master antenna and satellite television business. Bestows Technician of the Year Award. Offers insurance to members. Maintains 170 volume library on technical and business training and VCR tapes for certification practice exams. **Publications:** *EEA Training Program*, monthly. • *Management Update*, monthly. • *Directory of Professional Electronics Technicians*, annual. • *Technician Association News*, monthly. **Facsimile Number:** (317)653-8262.

★3941★
International Society of Certified Electronics Technicians (ISCET)
2708 W. Berry, Ste. 3
Fort Worth, TX 76109　　　　　Phone: (817)921-9101

Membership: Technicians in 5 countries who have been certified by the society. **Purpose:** Seeks to provide a fraternal bond among certified electronics technicians, raise their public image, and improve the effectiveness of industry education programs for technicians. Offers training programs in new electronics information; presents awards. Maintains library of service literature for consumer electronic equipment, including manuals and schematics for out-of-date equipment. Offers general radiotelephone license. Sponsors testing program for certification of electronics technicians in the fields of audio, communications, computer, consumer, industrial, medical electronics, radar, radio-television, and video. Operates Hall of Fame. **Publications:** *ISCET Update*, quarterly. • *Professional Electronics Magazine*, bimonthly. • *Technical Log*, quarterly. **Facsimile Number:** (817)921-3741.

Standards/Certification Agencies

Repairers who test and repair marine, aviation, and certain other radio transmitting equipment, must hold a General Radiotelephone Operator License from the Federal Communications Commission. The International Society of Certified Electronics Technicians and the Electronics Technicians Association both offer voluntary certification programs. In both programs, electronics repairers with four years of experience may apply for certification as a Certified Electronics Technician.

★3942★
Electronics Technicians Association, International (ETA-I)
602 N. Jackson
Greencastle, IN 46135　　　　　Phone: (317)653-8262

Offers certification examinations for electronics technicians. Maintains VCR tapes for certification practice exams.

★3943★
Federal Communications Commission
1919 M St., NW
Washington, DC 20554

Provides information on the general radiotelephone operator license, upon request.

★3944★
International Society of Certified Electronics Technicians (ISCET)
2708 W. Berry, Ste. 3
Fort Worth, TX 76109　　　　　Phone: (817)921-9101

Sponsors testing program for certification of electronics technicians in the fields of audio, communications, computer, consumer, industrial, medical electronics, radar, radio-television, and video.

★3945★
Professionals. . .Are Certified by the Electronics Technicians Association, International
Electronics Technicians Association
602 N Jackson St.
Greencastle, IN 46135　　　　　Phone: (317)653-8262

This six-panel brochure describes the certification process for electronics technicians. Covers eligibility requirements, examination contents, and specialties.

Test Guides

★3946★
Assistant Electronic Technician
National Learning Corp.
212 Michael Dr.
Syosset, NY 11791　　　　　Phone: (516)921-8888

Jack Rudman. Part of the Career Examination Series No. 1. All examination guides in this series contain questions with answers. **Facsimile Number:** (516)921-8743. **Toll-free/Additional Phone Number(s):** 800-645-6337.

★3947★
Certified Electronic Technician (CET)
National Learning Corp.
212 Michael Dr.
Syosset, NY 11791　　　　　Phone: (516)921-8888

Jack Rudman. Part of the Admission Test Series No. 3. Books in this series provide test practice and drill for actual professional certification and licensure tests. **Facsimile Number:** (516)921-8743. **Toll-free/Additional Phone Number(s):** 800-645-6337.

Commercial and Industrial Electronic Equipment Repairers

★3948★
The CET Exam: ISCET: Certified Electronics Technician
International Society of Certified Electronics Technicians
2708 W. Berry St.
Fort Worth, TX 76109   Phone: (817)921-9101
This six-panel brochure describes certification for electronic technicians. Outlines examination contents.

★3949★
EEA Training Program (ETA-I)
Electronics Technicians Association, International (ETA-I)
602 N. Jackson
Greencastle, IN 46135   Phone: (317)653-8262
Monthly.

★3950★
Electronic Equipment Repairer
National Learning Corp.
212 Michael Dr.
Syosset, NY 11791   Phone: (516)921-8888
Jack Rudman. Part of the Career Examination Series No. 1. All examination guides in this series contain questions with answers. **Facsimile Number:** (516)921-8743. **Toll-free/Additional Phone Number(s):** 800-645-6337.

★3951★
Industrial Electronics
National Learning Corp.
212 Michael Dr.
Syosset, NY 11791   Phone: (516)921-8888
Jack Rudman. 1989. Part of Occupational Competency Examination Series.

Awards, Scholarships, Grants, and Fellowships

★3952★
Electronics Technicians Association, International Technician of the Year
Electronics Technicians Association, International
604 N. Jackson
Greencastle, IN 46135   Phone: (317)653-8262
To honor a practicing electronics technician as an incentive for all other technicians to achieve higher goals. A plaque is awarded annually at the convention. Established in 1979 in memory of Norris R. Browne, CET, Houston, TX.

★3953★
ISCET Tech-of-the-Year Award
International Society of Certified Electronics Technicians
c/o Alice Johnson
2708 W. Berry St.
Fort Worth, TX 76109   Phone: (817)921-9101
To recognize a technician for outstanding work in the field of electronics. Established in 1976.

★3954★
NAPET La Croix Award
National Association of Photo Equipment Technicians
c/o Keith Anderson
Photo Marketing Association International
3000 Picture Place
Jackson, MI 49201   Phone: (517)788-8100
For recognition of achievement or contribution to the photo equipment repair industry. Officers of the Association make nominations and the members vote. A trophy is awarded annually at the convention in the spring. Established in 1976 in honor of George La Croix.

Basic Reference Guides and Handbooks

★3955★
Electronic Maintenance
State Mutual Book & Periodical Service, Ltd.
521 5th Ave., 17th Fl.
New York, NY 10175   Phone: (212)682-5844
1982.

★3956★
Electronic Maintenance Two
State Mutual Book & Periodical Service Ltd.
521 5th Ave., 17th Fl.
New York, NY 10175   Phone: (212)682-5844
1982.

★3957★
Electronics for Industrial Electricians
Delmar Publishers, Inc.
PO Box 15015
2 Computer Dr., W.
Albany, NY 12212   Phone: (518)459-1150
Stephen L. Herman. Second edition, 1985. **Facsimile Number:** (518)453-6472.

★3958★
Electronics in Industry
McGraw-Hill Publishing Company
1221 Avenue of the Americas
New York, NY 10020   Phone: (212)512-2000
George M. Chute. Fifth edition, 1979.

★3959★
The Electronics Manual to Industrial Automation
TAB Books, Inc.
Blue Ridge Summit, PA 17294-0850   Phone: (717)794-2191
G. R. Slone. 1987.

★3960★
Guide to Electronic Components
Van Nostrand Reinhold
115 5th Ave.
New York, NY 10003   Phone: (212)254-3232
Segalis. **Facsimile Number:** (212)254-9499.

★3961★
Handbook of Basic Electronic Troubleshooting
Prentice Hall
Rte. 9W
Englewood Cliffs, NJ 07632   Phone: (201)592-2000
John D. Lenk. 1979.

★3962★
Home Electronics
Time Life Books, Inc.
777 Duke St.
Alexandria, VA 22314   Phone: (703)838-7000
1988. Part of Fix-It-Yourself Series.

★3963★
How to Locate Needed Servicing Information
ARS Enterprises
PO Box 997
Mercer Island, WA 98040   Phone: (206)236-7071

★3964★
The Illustrated Home Electronics Fix-it Book
TAB Books
Blue Ridge Summit, PA 17294-0850   Phone: (717)794-2191
Homer L. Davidson. Second edition, 1988.

★3965★
Industrial Circuits & Automated Manufacturing
Holt, Rinehart & Winston, Inc.
6277 Sea Harbor Dr.
Orlando, FL 32887   Phone: (407)345-2500
Clyde Kale. 1989.

★3966★
Industrial Control Electronics
Prentice Hall
Rte. 9W
Englewood Cliffs, NJ 07632   Phone: (201)592-2000
David P. Beach. 1990.

★3967★
Industrial Electronics: A Text-Lab Manual
McGraw-Hill Publishing Company
1221 Avenue of the Americas
New York, NY 10020   Phone: (212)512-2000
Paul B Zbar. Third edition, 1981.

★3968★
Industrial Electronics and Controls
Prentice Hall
Rte. 9W
Englewood Cliffs, NJ 07632   Phone: (201)592-2000
Martin Newman. 1986. Part of Electronic Technology Series.

★3969★
Industrial Electronics: Devices & Systems
Prentice Hall
Rte. 9W
Englewood Cliffs, NJ 07632   Phone: (201)592-2000
Dale R. Patrick. 1986.

★3970★
Interconnection Products Directory
Connector Study Group, Inc.
104 Wilmot Rd., Ste. 201
Deerfield, IL 60015-5195   Phone: (312)940-8800
Gerald L. Ginsberg, editor. Biennial, November of odd years. More than 500 manufacturers, distributors, representatives, sales offices, and other suppliers to the electrical and electronics industry worldwide, including suppliers of connectors, wire, and cable (part 1); printed circuit products (part 2); circular rack and panel products (part 3); wire and cable products (part 4); materials (part 5); and military products (part 6). Entries include: Name, address, products, whether catalog is available. Arrangement: Classified by product. Indexes: Product.

★3971★
Manual of Electronic Servicing Test & Measurements
Prentice Hall
Rte. 9W
Englewood Cliffs, NJ 07632   Phone: (201)592-2000
Robert C. Genn, Jr. Second edition, 1990.

★3972★
New Manufacturing Technologies
State Mutual Book & Periodical Service, Ltd.
521 5th Ave., 17th Fl.
New York, NY 10175   Phone: (212)682-5844
Network Staff. 1984.

★3973★
New Ways to Use Test Meters: A Modern Guide to Electronic Servicing
Prentice Hall
Rte. 9W
Englewood Cliffs, NJ 07632   Phone: (201)592-2000
Robert G. Middleton. 1986.

★3974★
Repairing Appliances
Time Life Books, Inc.
777 Duke St.
Alexandria, VA 22314   Phone: (703)838-7000
1981. Part of Home Repair & Improvement Series.

★3975★
Troubleshooting Electronics Equipment Without Service Data
Prentice Hall
Rte. 9W
Englewood Cliffs, NJ 07632   Phone: (201)592-2000
Robert G. Middleton. 1989.

──────── Periodicals ────────

★3976★
American Electronics Association—Update
American Electronics Association
5201 Great America Pkwy.
Santa Clara, CA 95054   Phone: (408)987-4234
Editor(s): April Nellson. Carries electronics industry news and statistics. Discusses international trade; federal tax laws; and public affairs, finance, sales and marketing, and management issues facing the electronics industry. Lists association activities and events. Recurring features include a calendar of events. **Facsimile Number:** (408)970-8565.

★3977★
EASA Currents
Electrical Apparatus Service Association, Inc. (EASA)
1331 Baur Blvd.
St. Louis, MO 63132   Phone: (314)993-2220
Editor(s): Carl Fields. Monthly. Provides news of the electric motor sales and repair industry and related topics, including safety, financial management, and market trends. Recurring features include a report from the staff engineer, chapter news, and news of members. **Facsimile Number:** (314)993-1269.

★3978★
Electronic and Electrical Equipment
National Safety Council
444 N. Michigan Ave.
Chicago, IL 60611   Phone: (312)527-4800
Editor(s): Katie Kuhfuss. 6/yr. Provides safety tips for persons who work with electronic and electrical equipment. Promotes and reports on training courses in accident prevention, safety precautions, and compliance with safety regulations. Also carries items on safety awareness off the job.

Commercial and Industrial Electronic Equipment Repairers

★3979★
Electronic Business Forecast
Cahners Economics
Cahners Publishing Company
275 Washington St.
Newton, MA 02158   Phone: (617)630-2119
Editor(s): Madeline Franchi and Julie Handel. Bimonthly. Provides news, analysis, and forecasts of developments in the electronics industry. Recurring features include one page columns on electronic end markets, supply conditions, and international developments. **Facsimile Number:** (617)630-2100.

★3980★
Electronic Industries Association—Executive Report
Electronic Industries Association
2001 Pennsylvania Ave. NW
Washington, DC 20006   Phone: (202)457-4980
Editor(s): Mack V. Rosenker. Bimonthly. Provides news of electronics and the electronics industry, with items on legislative and regulatory developments that affect members. Recurring features include news of association business and membership events, a calendar of events, and announcements of new publications. **Facsimile Number:** (202)457-4985.

★3981★
Electronic Services Update
LINK Resources Corp.
79 Fifth Ave., 12th Fl.
New York, NY 10003   Phone: (212)627-1500
Editor(s): Steven K. Sieck. Monthly. Concerned with interactive communications industry. Covers integrated networks, electronic entertainment and information, videotex, and electronic home offices. Recurring features include a column titled Statistical Spotlight and a calendar of events. **Facsimile Number:** (212)620-3099.

★3982★
Electronic Servicing & Technology
Intertec Publishing Corp.
9221 Quivira Rd.
PO Box 12901
Overland Park, KS 66212-9981   Phone: (913)888-4664
Conrad Persson, Editor. Monthly. Consumer electronics servicing magazine. **Facsimile Number:** (913)541-6697.

★3983★
ETA-I Management Update (ETA-I)
Electronics Technicians Association, International (ETA-I)
602 N. Jackson
Greencastle, IN 46135   Phone: (317)653-8262
Monthly.

★3984★
ETA-I Technician Association News (ETA-I)
Electronics Technicians Association, International (ETA-I)
602 N. Jackson
Greencastle, IN 46135   Phone: (317)653-8262
Monthly. Industry and association journal. Includes book reviews, obituaries, information on new products and new members, and employment listings.

★3985★
ETA Technician Association News
Electronic Technicians Association (ETA)
604 N. Jackson St.
Greencastle, IN 46135   Phone: (317)653-5541
Editor(s): Dick Glass. Monthly. Serves member technicians with news of the association and the electronics industry, including items on service, education, employment, management, and events. Includes sections on membership, management, telecommunications, and business and technical training programs. Recurring features include editorials, news of research, letters to the editor, book reviews, and a calendar of events. **Toll-free/Additional Phone Number(s):** 800-359-6706 **Facsimile Number:** (317)653-8262.

★3986★
International Society of Certified Electronics Technicians —Update
International Society of Certified Electronics Technicians
2708 W. Berry St.
Ft. Worth, TX 76109   Phone: (817)921-9101
Editor(s): Barbara Rubin. Quarterly. Reflects the aims of the Society, which are to raise the public image of certified electronics technicians and to improve the effectiveness of industry education programs for technicians. Recurring features include news of research, a calendar of events, reports of meetings, news of educational opportunities, and job listings.

★3987★
ISCET Update (ISCET)
International Society of Certified Electronics Technicians (ISCET)
2708 W. Berry, Ste. 3
Fort Worth, TX 76109   Phone: (817)921-9101
Quarterly. Society and industry newsletter. Includes job listings.

★3988★
NESSDA Update
National Electronic Sales and Service Dealers Association (NESSDA)
2708 W. Berry
Ft. Worth, TX 76109   Phone: (817)921-9061
Editor(s): Wallace Harrison. Quarterly. Contains NESDA and electronics industry news and information regarding NESDA programs and services. Supplies information as a supplement to Professional Electronics Magazine. Recurring features include news of research, news of members, and computer service news. **Facsimile Number:** (817)921-3741.

★3989★
Professional Electronics Magazine (ISCET)
International Society of Certified Electronics Technicians (ISCET)
2708 W. Berry, Ste. 3
Fort Worth, TX 76109   Phone: (817)921-9101
Bimonthly.

★3990★
Retail News Reporter
739 Main St., Ste. 4
PO Box 830034
Stone Mountain, GA 30083-0001   Phone: (404)879-9682
Byron Hollingsworth, Publisher. Monthly. Newspaper (tabloid) for the electronics and appliances industry. **Facsimile Number:** (404)879-6791.

──────── Meetings and Conventions ────────

★3991★
APEC - Applied Power Electronics Conference and Exposition
Trade Associates, Inc.
6001 Montrose Rd., Ste. 900
Rockville, MD 20852-1608   Phone: (301)468-3210
1992. **Facsimile Number:** (301)468-3662.

★3992★
Electrical/Electronic Supply Trade Show
Electric Association of Missouri and Kansas
1308 Pennsylvania
Kansas City, MO 64105   Phone: (816)221-1808
Frequency: Held every three years in metropolitan Kansas City, Mis. **Facsimile Number:** (816)221-1810.

★3993★
Electronic Technicians Association Annual Convention
Electronic Technicians Association, International
604 N. Jackson St.
Greencastle, IN 46135   Phone: (317)653-5541
1992.

★3994★
International Society of Certified Electronics Technicians (ISCET)
2708 W. Berry, Ste. 3
Fort Worth, TX 76109   Phone: (817)921-9101
Frequency: Annual conference, with exhibits, always held first week in August. Also holds annual Consumers Electronics Instructors Conference and trade shows. **Facsimile Number:** (817)921-3741.

Communications Equipment Mechanics

Communications equipment mechanics install, repair, and maintain an array of complex and sophisticated communications equipment. Most communications equipment mechanics, sometimes referred to as telecommunications technicians, work either in telephone company central offices, or on customers' premises installing and repairing telephone switching and transmission systems. Central office equipment installers set up, rearrange and remove switching and dialing equipment used in central offices. Frame wirers, sometimes referred to as frame workers or frame attendants, connect, disconnect, inspect, and repair wires that run from telephone lines and cables to the central office. Central office repairers, often referred to as central office technicians or switching equipment technicians, test, repair, and maintain all types of local and toll switching equipment that automatically connects lines when customers dial numbers. Trouble locators work at special switchboards to find the source of the problem. PBX installers, often called systems technicians, specialize in complex telephone system installation. They create switchboard systems for businesses with unique communications requirements. PBX repairers, with the assistance of trouble locators, locate the malfunction in customers' PBX, CENTREX, KEY, or other telephone systems and make the necessary repairs. Most communications equipment mechanics work for telephone and telegraph companies. A small number work for cable television and related companies, as well as for railroad companies and electrical repair shops.

$alaries

Wage rates for communications equipment mechanics vary by employer and locality; specific information may be obtained from local telephone companies. Central office installers, and office technicians, and PBX installers employed by AT & T and the Bell Operating Companies and represented by the Communications Workers of America earn an average weekly salary of $650.00. Frame attendants averaged $550.00.

Employment Outlook

Growth rate until the year 2000: Slower than average.

Communications Equipment Mechanics

Career Guides

★3995★
"Avionics and Marine Electronics" in *Electronic Service Careers* (pp. 71-76)
Franklin Watts, Inc.
387 Park Avenue, S.
New York, NY 10016   Phone: (212)686-7070
Robert Laurance. 1987. Discusses the work of an electronic service technician, employment outlook, places of employment, and educational preparation and training. Describes jobs with computers, consumer electronics, industrial electronics and the military.

★3996★
"Avionics Technician" in *Opportunities in Aerospace Careers* (pp. 34-37)
National Textbook Co.
4255 W. Touhy Ave.
Lincolnwood, IL 60646   Phone: (312)679-5500
Wallace R. Maples. 1991. Surveys jobs with the airlines, airports, the government, the military, in manufacturing, and in research and development. Describes educational requirements, working conditions, salaries, employment outlook and licensure.

★3997★
"Avionics Technician" in *Transportation*, Volume 12 of *Career Information Center* (pp. 96-98)
Glencoe/Macmillan
15319 Chatsworth St.
Mission Hills, CA 91345   Phone: (818)898-1391
Richard Lidz and Dale Anderson, editorial directors. Fourth edition, 1990. For 600 occupations, describes job duties, entry-level requirements, education and training needed, advancement possibilities, employment outlook, earnings and benefits. The set is divided into 12 volumes. Each volume includes jobs related under a broad career field. Volume 13 is the index. **Facsimile Number:** 818-365-5489.

★3998★
"Avionics Technicians" in Volume 4 of *The Encyclopedia of Careers and Vocational Guidance* (pp. 131-134)
J.G. Ferguson Publishing Co.
200 W. Monroe
Chicago, IL 60606   Phone: (312)580-5480
William E. Hopke, editor-in-chief. Eighth edition, 1990. Four-volume set that profiles 500 occupations and describes job trends in 76 industries. Includes career description, educational requirements, history of the job, methods of entry, advancement, employment outlook, earnings, working conditions, social and psychological factors, and sources of additional information.

★3999★
"Avionics Technicians" in Volume 1 of *Career Discovery Encyclopedia* (pp. 100-101)
J.G. Ferguson Publishing Co.
200 W. Monroe
Chicago, IL 60606   Phone: (312)580-5480
E. Russell Primm, editor-in-chief. 1990. Contains two-page articles on 504 occupations. Each article describes job duties, earnings, and educational and training requirements.

★4000★
"Central Office Technician" in *Exploring Nontraditional Jobs for Women* (pp. 32-37)
Rosen Publishing Group, Inc.
29 E. 21st St.
New York, NY 10010   Phone: (212)777-3017
Rose Neufeld. 1989. Describes blue-collar, male dominated occupations. Discusses what is done on the job, training, where to apply for jobs, tools used, salaries, and advantages and disadvantages. Relates the experiences of women who are working in the field.

★4001★
"Communications Equipment Mechanic" in *VGM's Careers Encyclopedia* (pp. 111-114)
National Textbook Co.
4255 W. Touhy Ave.
Lincolnwood, IL 60646   Phone: (312)679-5500
Third edition, 1991. Contains two- to five-page descriptions of 200 managerial, professional, technical, trade, and service occupations. Each profile includes job duties, places of employment, qualifications, educational preparation, training, employment potential, advancement, income, and additional sources of information.

★4002★
"Communications Equipment Mechanics" in *Occupational Outlook Handbook* (pp. 333-335)
Superintendent of Documents
U.S. Government Printing Office
Washington, DC 20402   Phone: (202)783-3238
Biennial; latest edition, 1990-91. Encyclopedia of careers describing more than 250 occupations and comprising about 86 percent of all jobs in the economy. Occupations that require lengthy education or training are given the most attention. For each occupation, the handbook describes job duties, working conditions, training, educational preparation, personal qualities, advancement possibilities, job outlook, earnings, and sources of additional information.

★4003★ VOCATIONAL CAREERS SOURCEBOOK, 1st Edition

★4003★
"Communications Equipment Mechanics" in Volume 3 of *The Encyclopedia of Careers and Vocational Guidance* (pp. 640-643)
J.G. Ferguson Publishing Co.
200 W. Monroe
Chicago, IL 60606   Phone: (312)580-5480
William E. Hopke, editor-in-chief. Eighth edition, 1990. Four-volume set that profiles 500 occupations and describes job trends in 76 industries. Includes career description, educational requirements, history of the job, methods of entry, advancement, employment outlook, earnings, working conditions, social and psychological factors, and sources of additional information.

★4004★
"Communications Equipment Mechanics" in Volume 2 of *Career Discovery Encyclopedia* (pp. 40-41)
J.G. Ferguson Publishing Co.
200 W. Monroe
Chicago, IL 60606   Phone: (312)580-5480
E. Russell Primm, editor-in-chief. 1990. Contains two-page articles on 504 occupations. Each article describes job duties, earnings, and educational and training requirements.

★4005★
"Communications Mechanic" in *Opportunities in Electrical Trades* (pp. 83-84)
National Textbook Co.
4255 W. Touhy Ave.
Lincolnwood, IL 60646   Phone: (312)679-5500
Robert Wood. 1990. Provides an overview of the electrical industry describing current trends and future projections. Surveys electrician jobs and covers the nature of the work, working conditions, job outlook, advancement possibilities, education and training, earnings, and specialization. Offers career planning advice.

★4006★
"Communications or Telecommunications" in *Careers in High Tech* (p. 104)
Arco/Prentice Hall Press
1 Gulf & Western Plaza
New York, NY 10023   Phone: (212)373-8500
Connie Winkler. 1987. Surveys career opportunities in data processing, technology, personal computers, telecommunications, manufacturing technology, artificial intelligence, computer graphics, biotechnology, lasers, technical writing, and publishing. Includes information on educational preparation, associations, and periodicals.

★4007★
"Communications Technician" in *VGM's Handbook of Scientific and Technical Careers* (pp. 28-30)
National Textbook Co.
4255 W. Touhy Ave.
Lincolnwood, IL 60646   Phone: (312)679-5500
Craig T. Norback, editor. 1990. Includes 50 occupations in science and technology and describes job duties, qualifications, education, training, potential advancement, income. Lists sources of additional information.

★4008★
Do Your Own Thing. in the Mechanical Field
AIMS Media, Inc.
9710 DeSoto Ave.
Chatsworth, CA 93111-4409   Phone: (818)773-4300
Videocassette. 1979. 16 mins. Various job levels in the mechanical field are outlined for students.

★4009★
The Professional Electronics Technician
Electronics Technicians Association
602 N Jackson St.
Greencastle, IN 46135   Phone: (317)653-8262
This six-page brochure describes job duties, training, skills and aptitudes, salaries, employment outlook, and certification.

★4010★
"Railroad Signaler and Signal Maintainer" in *Transportation*, Volume 12 of *Career Information Center* (pp. 76-78)
Glencoe/Macmillan
15319 Chatsworth St.
Mission Hills, CA 91345   Phone: (818)898-1391
Richard Lidz and Dale Anderson, editorial directors. Fourth edition, 1990. For 600 occupations, describes job duties, entry-level requirements, education and training needed, advancement possibilities, employment outlook, earnings and benefits. The set is divided into 12 volumes. Each volume includes jobs related under a broad career field. Volume 13 is the index. **Facsimile Number:** 818-365-5489.

★4011★
"Signal Mechanics" in Volume 3 of *The Encyclopedia of Careers and Vocational Guidance* (pp. 705-708)
J.G. Ferguson Publishing Co.
200 W. Monroe
Chicago, IL 60606   Phone: (312)580-5480
William E. Hopke, editor-in-chief. Eighth edition, 1990. Four-volume set that profiles 500 occupations and describes job trends in 76 industries. Includes career description, educational requirements, history of the job, methods of entry, advancement, employment outlook, earnings, working conditions, social and psychological factors, and sources of additional information.

★4012★
"Telecommunications Technicians" in Volume 4 of *The Encyclopedia of Careers and Vocational Guidance* (pp. 103-104)
J.G. Ferguson Publishing Co.
200 W. Monroe
Chicago, IL 60606   Phone: (312)580-5480
William E. Hopke, editor-in-chief. Eighth edition, 1990. Four-volume set that profiles 500 occupations and describes job trends in 76 industries. Includes career description, educational requirements, history of the job, methods of entry, advancement, employment outlook, earnings, working conditions, social and psychological factors, and sources of additional information.

★4013★
"Telecommunications Technicians" in Volume 6 of *Career Discovery Encyclopedia* (pp. 98-99)
J.G. Ferguson Publishing Co.
200 W. Monroe
Chicago, IL 60606   Phone: (312)580-5480
E. Russell Primm, editor-in-chief. 1990. Contains two-page articles on 504 occupations. Each article describes job duties, earnings, and educational and training requirements.

Communications Equipment Mechanics ★4023★

★4014★
"Telecommunications Technology" in *The Career Connection II: A Guide to Technical Majors and Their Related Careers* (pp. 123-124)
ERIS
PO Box 7509
University Station
Provo, UT 84602-0509

Fred A. Rowe. 1988. Contains technical majors, such as automotive technology. Describes the major and the job. Lists high school and postsecondary school courses. Includes occupations related to the major, employment outlook, and starting salary.

★4015★
"Telephone and PBX Installers and Repairers" in Volume 3 of *The Encyclopedia of Careers and Vocational Guidance* (pp. 715-718)
J.G. Ferguson Publishing Co.
200 W. Monroe
Chicago, IL 60606   Phone: (312)580-5480

William E. Hopke, editor-in-chief. Eighth edition, 1990. Four-volume set that profiles 500 occupations and describes job trends in 76 industries. Includes career description, educational requirements, history of the job, methods of entry, advancement, employment outlook, earnings, working conditions, social and psychological factors, and sources of additional information.

★4016★
"Telephone Central Office Technician" in *Communications and the Arts*, Volume 3 of *Career Information Center* (pp. 71-73)
Glencoe/Macmillan
15319 Chatsworth St.
Mission Hills, CA 91345   Phone: (818)898-1391

Richard Lidz and Dale Anderson, editorial directors. Fourth edition, 1990. For 600 occupations, describes job duties, entry-level requirements, education and training needed, advancement possibilities, employment outlook, earnings and benefits. The set is divided into 12 volumes. Each volume includes jobs related under a broad career field. Volume 13 is the index. **Facsimile Number:** 818-365-5489.

★4017★
"Telephone Central Office Technician" in *Telecommunications* (pp. 39-43)
Franklin Watts, Inc.
387 Park Avenue, S.
New York, NY 10016   Phone: (212)686-7070

Linda Barrett and Galen Guengerich. 1991. Surveys opportunities in telecommunications including telephone, radio, telegraph, and television communications. Includes job description, educational preparation, salary, and employment outlook. Offers job hunting advice.

★4018★
Video Career Library - Repair Fields
Careers, Inc.
1211 10th St., SW
PO Box 135
Largo, FL 34649-0135   Phone: (813)584-7333

Videocassette. 1990. 23 mins. Part of the Video Career Library covering 165 occupations. Shows actual workers on the job. Includes industrial machinery repairers, communications equipment repairers, data processing equipment repairers, home entertainment equipment repairers, office machine repairers, electrical power installers and repairers, and electrical and electronic repairers.

Associations

★4019★
National Association of Radio and Telecommunications Engineers (NARTE)
PO Box 678
Midway, MA 02053   Phone: (508)533-8333

Membership: Radio and telecommunications engineers and technicians. **Purpose:** Objectives are to: foster professionalism; develop guidelines for certification; promote radio and telecommunications education in colleges and universities. Conducts engineering seminars and symposia. Bestows scholarships to students in the field.

★4020★
United States Telephone Association (USTA)
900 19th St. NW, Ste. 800
Washington, DC 20006   Phone: (202)835-3100

Membership: Local operating telephone companies or telephone holding companies. Members represent a total of 114 million access lines. **Purpose:** Presents Distinguished Service Award and Pacesetter Award to outstanding leaders in industry and other fields. Conducts educational and training programs. Maintains 21 committees. **Publications:** *Holding Company Report*, annual. • *Phonefacts*, annual. • *Statistical Volumes*, annual. • *Teletimes*, quarterly. • Also publishes booklets and brochures. **Toll-free/Additional Phone Number(s):** (202)835-3198. Telephone news updates on legislative and industry developments.

Standards/Certification Agencies

★4021★
National Association of Radio and Telecommunications Engineers (NARTE)
PO Box 678
Midway, MA 02053   Phone: (508)533-8333

Develops guidelines for certification.

Test Guides

★4022★
Police Communications Technician
National Learning Corp.
212 Michael Dr.
Syosset, NY 11791   Phone: (516)921-8888

Jack Rudman. Part of the Career Examination Series No. 1. All examination guides in this series contain questions with answers. **Facsimile Number:** (516)921-8743. **Toll-free/Additional Phone Number(s):** 800-645-6337.

Awards, Scholarships, Grants, and Fellowships

★4023★
NARTE Scholarships
National Association of Radio and Telecommunications Engineers
PO Box 678
Midway, MA 02053   Phone: (508)533-8333

Scholarships awarded to students in the field.

Periodicals

★4024★
Sound & Communications Magazine
25 Willowdale Ave.
Port Washington, NY 11050   Phone: (516)767-2500
Judith Morrison, Editor. Monthly. Magazine focusing on sound and communications systems equipment, installations, and technology. **Facsimile Number:** (516)767-9335.

★4025★
Telecommunications Reports
Business Research Publications, Inc.
1333 H St., NW
Washington, DC 20005   Phone: (202)842-3006
Victoria A. Mason, Editor. Publication tracking all aspects of the telecommunications industry on state, federal, and international levels. Coverage includes the FCC, Congress, state regulatory commissions and legislatures, and federal and state court decisions. Also reports on telecommunications companies and equipment manufacturers, new services and products, personnel changes, and labor union developments. Includes quarterly index. Available online via NewsNet. **Facsimile Number:** (202)842-3047.

★4026★
Telephone News
Phillips Publishing, Inc.
7811 Montrose Rd.
Potomac, MD 20854   Phone: (301)340-2100
Candace Sams, Editor. Weekly. Telecommunications industry newsletter. **Facsimile Number:** (301)424-4297.

★4027★
Teletimes (USTA)
United States Telephone Association (USTA)
900 19th St. NW, Ste. 800
Washington, DC 20006   Phone: (202)835-3100
Quarterly.

Other Sources of Information

★4028★
Phonefacts (USTA)
United States Telephone Association (USTA)
900 19th St. NW, Ste. 800
Washington, DC 20006   Phone: (202)835-3100
Annual.

Computer and Office Machine Repairers

Computer and office machine repairers (often called field engineers, customer service engineers, or service technicians) install, do preventive maintenance, or correct emergency problems on computers and other office equipment. Field technicians visit the offices and stores of customers in their assigned area to perform routine maintenance such as cleaning, oiling, and adjusting parts. In the case of machine breakdown, technicians run special diagnostic programs that pinpoint the malfunction. Once the problem has been located, fixing the equipment may take only a few minutes because most repairs merely involve the replacement of malfunctioning parts. About 75% of repairers are employed by wholesalers of computers and other office equipment and by firms that provide maintenance services for a fee. The remainder work for equipment manufacturers, retail establishments, and organizations with enough equipment and funding to warrant a full-time service staff.

$alaries

Median annual earnings of full-time computer and office machine repairers is about $25,300. The median annual earnings for those who specialize in computer repairs is $26,700, and those in office machine repair $22,400.

Lowest 10 percent	$15,900/year or less
Middle 50 percent	$20,000-33,300/year
Top 10 percent	$40,500/year

Employment Outlook

Growth rate until the year 2000: Faster than average.

Computer and Office Machine Repairers

Career Guides

★4029★
"Business Computers and Office Equipment Service" in *Electronic Service Careers* (pp. 46-56)
Franklin Watts, Inc.
387 Park Avenue, S.
New York, NY 10016   Phone: (212)686-7070
Robert Laurance. 1987. Discusses the work of an electronic service technician, employment outlook, places of employment, and educational preparation and training. Describes jobs with computers, consumer electronics, industrial electronics and the military.

★4030★
"Business Machine Operator" in *Administration, Business, and Office*, Volume 1 of *Career Information Center* (pp. 46-47)
Glencoe/Macmillan
15319 Chatsworth St.
Mission Hills, CA 91345   Phone: (818)898-1391
Richard Lidz and Dale Anderson, editorial directors. Fourth edition, 1990. For 600 occupations, describes job duties, entry-level requirements, education and training needed, advancement possibilities, employment outlook, earnings and benefits. The set is divided into 12 volumes. Each volume includes jobs related under a broad career field. Volume 13 is the index. **Facsimile Number:** 818-365-5489.

★4031★
"Business Machine Repairers" in *Jobs! What They Are...Where They Are...What They Pay* (pp. 206-207)
Simon & Schuster, Inc.
Simon & Schuster Bldg.
1230 Avenue of the Americas
New York, NY 10020   Phone: (212)698-7000
Robert O. Snelling and Anne M. Snelling. Revised edition, 1989. Profiles 241 occupations, describing duties and responsibilities, educational preparation, earnings, employment opportunities, training, and qualifications.

★4032★
"Business Machine Service Technician" in *VGM's Careers Encyclopedia* (pp. 72-73)
National Textbook Co.
4255 W. Touhy Ave.
Lincolnwood, IL 60646   Phone: (312)679-5500
Third edition, 1991. Contains two- to five-page descriptions of 200 managerial, professional, technical, trade, and service occupations. Each profile includes job duties, places of employment, qualifications, educational preparation, training, employment potential, advancement, income, and additional sources of information.

★4033★
"Business Machine Service Technician" in *VGM's Handbook of Scientific and Technical Careers* (pp. 18-19)
National Textbook Co.
4255 W. Touhy Ave.
Lincolnwood, IL 60646   Phone: (312)679-5500
Craig T. Norback, editor. 1990. Includes 50 occupations in science and technology and describes job duties, qualifications, education, training, potential advancement, income. Lists sources of additional information.

★4034★
"Computer and Office Machine Repairers" in *America's 50 Fastest Growing Jobs* (pp. 129-131)
JIST Works, Inc.
720 N. Park Ave.
Indianapolis, IN 46202   Phone: (317)264-3720
Michael J. Farr, compiler. 1991. Describes the 50 fastest growing jobs within major career clusters such as technicians, and marketing and sales. Each job profile explains the nature of the work, skills and abilities required, employment outlook, average earnings, related occupations, education and training requirements, and employment opportunities. Also contains career planning information and job search tips.

★4035★
"Computer and Office Machine Repairers" in *Occupational Outlook Handbook* (pp. 335-337)
Superintendent of Documents
U.S. Government Printing Office
Washington, DC 20402   Phone: (202)783-3238
Biennial; latest edition, 1990-91. Encyclopedia of careers describing more than 250 occupations and comprising about 86 percent of all jobs in the economy. Occupations that require lengthy education or training are given the most attention. For each occupation, the handbook describes job duties, working conditions, training, educational preparation, personal qualities, advancement possibilities, job outlook, earnings, and sources of additional information.

★4036★
"Computer Maintenance" in *The Career Connection II: A Guide to Technical Majors and Their Related Careers* (pp. 21-22)
ERIS
PO Box 7509
University Station
Provo, UT 84602-0509

Fred A. Rowe. 1988. Contains technical majors, such as automotive technology. Describes the major and the job. Lists high school and postsecondary school courses. Includes occupations related to the major, employment outlook, and starting salary.

★4037★
"Computer Service" in *Opportunities in Vocational and Technical Careers* (pp. 108-109)
National Textbook Co.
4255 W. Touhy Ave.
Lincolnwood, IL 60646   Phone: (312)679-5500

Adrian A. Paradis. 1987. Describes careers requiring instruction at a private vocational or proprietary school including office employee, sales worker, service worker, health services, mechanic, craftworker, and technician. Covers employment outlook, job duties and salaries. Offers career planning advice.

★4038★
Computer Service Technician
Careers, Inc.
PO Box 135
Largo, FL 34649-0135   Phone: (813)584-7333

1990. Two-page occupational summary card describing duties, working conditions, personal qualifications, training, earnings and hours, employment outlook, places of employment, related careers and where to write for more information.

★4039★
"Computer Service Technician" in *Occu-Facts: Information on 565 Careers in Outline Form* (p. 15.12)
Careers, Inc.
P.O. Box 135
1211 Tenth St., S.W.
Largo, FL 33640   Phone: (813)584-7333

Elizabeth Handville. Biennial, 1989-90 edition. Each one-page occupational profile describes duties, working conditions, physical surroundings and demands, aptitudes, temperament, educational requirements, employment outlook, earnings, and places of employment.

★4040★
"Computer Service Technician" in *Opportunities in Data Processing Careers* (pp. 66-67)
National Textbook Co.
4255 W. Touhy Ave.
Lincolnwood, IL 60646   Phone: (312)679-5500

Norman N. Noerper. 1989. Provides an overview of the history and development of data processing careers. For each job included, describes responsibilities, salary, and job outlook. Contains separate chapters on educational preparation and job hunting. Lists professional organizations, publications, and schools.

★4041★
"Computer Service Technician" in *VGM's Careers Encyclopedia* (pp. 116-118)
National Textbook Co.
4255 W. Touhy Ave.
Lincolnwood, IL 60646   Phone: (312)679-5500

Third edition, 1991. Contains two- to five-page descriptions of 200 managerial, professional, technical, trade and service occupations. Each profile includes job duties, places of employment, qualifications, educational preparation and job hunting. Lists professional organizations, publications, and schools.

★4042★
"Computer Service Technician" in *VGM's Handbook of Scientific and Technical Careers* (pp. 33-34)
National Textbook Co.
4255 W. Touhy Ave.
Lincolnwood, IL 60646   Phone: (312)679-5500

Craig T. Norback, editor. 1990. Includes 50 occupations in science and technology and describes job duties, qualifications, education, training, potential advancement, and income. Lists sources of additional information.

★4043★
Computer Service Technicians
Chronicle Guidance Publications, Inc.
PO Box 1190
Moravia, NY 13118-1190   Phone: (315)497-0330

1990. This career brief describes the nature of the work, working conditions, hours and earnings, education and training, licensure, certification, unions, personal qualifications, social and psychological factors, employment outlook, entry methods, advancement, and related occupations. **Toll-free/Additional Phone Number(s):** 800-622-7284.

★4044★
"Computer Service Technicians" in *Jobs! What They Are...Where They Are...What They Pay* (pp. 65-66)
Simon & Schuster, Inc.
Simon & Schuster Bldg.
1230 Avenue of the Americas
New York, NY 10020   Phone: (212)698-7000

Robert O. Snelling and Anne M. Snelling. Revised edition, 1989. Profiles 241 occupations, describing duties and responsibilities, educational preparation, earnings, employment opportunities, training, and qualifications.

★4045★
"Computer Service Technicians" in Volume 4 of *The Encyclopedia of Careers and Vocational Guidance* (pp. 21-26)
J.G. Ferguson Publishing Co.
200 W. Monroe
Chicago, IL 60606   Phone: (312)580-5480

William E. Hopke, editor-in-chief. Eighth edition, 1990. Four-volume set that profiles 500 occupations and describes job trends in 76 industries. Includes career description, educational requirements, history of the job, methods of entry, advancement, employment outlook, earnings, working conditions, social and psychological factors, and sources of additional information.

Computer and Office Machine Repairers

★4046★
"Computer Service Technicians" in Volume 2 of *Career Discovery Encyclopedia* **(pp. 48-49)**
J.G. Ferguson Publishing Co.
200 W. Monroe
Chicago, IL 60606   Phone: (312)580-5480
E. Russell Primm, editor-in-chief. 1990. Contains two-page articles on 504 occupations. Each article describes job duties, earnings, and educational and training requirements.

★4047★
"Computer Service Technicians: Troubleshooting in High Tech" in *Careers for Women Without College Degrees* **(pp. 185-189)**
McGraw-Hill Publishing Co.
11 W. 19th St.
New York, NY 10011   Phone: (212)337-6010
Beatryce Nivens. 1988. Career planning and job hunting guide containing information on decision-making, skills assessment, and resumes for career changers. Profiles careers with the best occupational outlook. Describes the work, educational preparation, employment outlook, salaries, and required skills.

★4048★
"Computer Servicer" in *Administration, Business, and Office,* **Volume 1 of** *Career Information Center* **(pp. 79-81)**
Glencoe/Macmillan
15319 Chatsworth St.
Mission Hills, CA 91345   Phone: (818)898-1391
Richard Lidz and Dale Anderson, editorial directors. Fourth edition, 1990. For 600 occupations, describes job duties, entry-level requirements, education and training needed, advancement possibilities, employment outlook, earnings and benefits. The set is divided into 12 volumes. Each volume includes jobs related under a broad career field. Volume 13 is the index. **Facsimile Number:** 818-365-5489.

★4049★
"Computer Servicing and Troubleshooting" in *The Complete Electronics Career Guide* **(pp. 81-86)**
Tab Books, Inc.
Blue Ridge Summit, PA 17294-0850   Phone: (717)794-2191
Joe Risse. 1989. Explores opportunities for electronic technicians in industry, broadcasting, appliance repair, telecommunications, computer servicing, and technical writing. Offers advice on educational preparation, training, finding or changing jobs, and career advancement. Lists trade publications and professional associations.

★4050★
"Computer Technologists and Professionals" in *The American Almanac of Jobs and Salaries* **(pp. 295-312)**
Avon Books
105 Madison Avenue
New York, NY 10016   Phone: (212)481-5600
John Wright and Edward J. Dwyer. Revised and updated, 1990. A comprehensive guide to the wages of hundreds of occupations in a wide variety of industries and organizations.

★4051★
Copier Repair Technician
Vocational Biographies, Inc.
PO Box 31, Dept. VF10
Sauk Centre, MN 56378   Phone: (612)352-6516
1991. This pamphlet profiles a person working in the job. Includes information about job duties, working conditions, places of employment, educational preparation, labor market outlook, and salaries. **Toll-free/Additional Phone Number(s):** 800-255-0752.

★4052★
Exploring Careers as a Computer Technician
Rosen Publishing Group, Inc.
29 E. 21st St.
New York, NY 10010   Phone: (212)777-3017
Jean W. Spencer. Revised edition, 1989. Covers job prospects and duties, educational preparation, equipment, tools, work environment, advancement possibilities, job satisfaction, and salaries. Lists schools, journals and professional associations.

★4053★
Exploring Careers As a Computer Technician
Rosen Publishing Group
29 E. 21st St.
New York, NY 10010   Phone: (212)777-3017
Jean Spencer. Revised edition, 1989. Part of Careers in Depth Series. **Toll-free/Additional Phone Number(s):** 800-237-9932. **Facsimile Number:** (212)777-0277.

★4054★
"Hardware Service Technician" in *The Complete Computer Career Guide* **(pp. 42-47)**
Tab Books, Inc.
Blue Ridge Summit, PA 17294-0850   Phone: (717)794-2191
Judith Norback. 1987. Offers career planning tips and describes the educational preparation needed, employment outlook, industry trends, and certification. Offers job search advice. A separate section includes opportunities for women and minorities.

★4055★
"Mechanics: Cash Register and Office Machine Services" in *Opportunities in Vocational and Technical Careers* **(p. 108)**
National Textbook Co.
4255 W. Touhy Ave.
Lincolnwood, IL 60646   Phone: (312)679-5500
Adrian A. Paradis. 1987. Describes careers which can be prepared for by attending a private vocational or proprietary school—office employee, sales worker, service worker, health services, mechanic, craftworker, and technician. Covers employment outlook, job duties, and salaries. Offers career planning advice.

★4056★
Office Machine Service Technician
Careers, Inc.
PO Box 135
Largo, FL 34649-0135   Phone: (813)584-7333
1989. Eight-page brief offering the definition, history, duties, working conditions, personal qualifications, educational requirements, earnings, hours, employment outlook, advancement possibilities, and related occupations.

★4057★
"Office Machine Service Technician" in *Occu-Facts: Information on 565 Careers in Outline Form* **(p. 15.23)**
Careers, Inc.
P.O. Box 135
1211 Tenth St., S.W.
Largo, FL 33640   Phone: (813)584-7333
Elizabeth Handville. Biennial, 1989-90 edition. Each one-page occupational profile describes duties, working conditions, physical surroundings and demands, aptitudes, temperament, educational requirements, employment outlook, earnings, and places of employment.

★4058★

"Office Machine Servicer" in *Administration, Business, and Office*, Volume 1 of *Career Information Center* (pp. 61-63)
Glencoe/Macmillan
15319 Chatsworth St.
Mission Hills, CA 91345   Phone: (818)898-1391

Richard Lidz and Dale Anderson, editorial directors. Fourth edition, 1990. For 600 occupations, describes job duties, entry-level requirements, education and training needed, advancement possibilities, employment outlook, earnings and benefits. The set is divided into 12 volumes. Each volume includes jobs related under a broad career field. Volume 13 is the index. **Facsimile Number:** 818-365-5489.

★4059★

"Office Machine Servicers" in Volume 4 of *Career Discovery Encyclopedia* (pp. 138-139)
J.G. Ferguson Publishing Co.
200 W. Monroe
Chicago, IL 60606   Phone: (312)580-5480

E. Russell Primm, editor-in-chief. 1990. Contains two-page articles on 504 occupations. Each article describes job duties, earnings, and educational and training requirements.

★4060★

"Office Machine Servicers" in Volume 3 of *The Encyclopedia of Careers and Vocational Guidance* (pp. 545-548)
J.G. Ferguson Publishing Co.
200 W. Monroe
Chicago, IL 60606   Phone: (312)580-5480

William E. Hopke, editor-in-chief. Eighth edition, 1990. Four-volume set that profiles 500 occupations and describes job trends in 76 industries. Includes career description, educational requirements, history of the job, methods of entry, advancement, employment outlook, earnings, working conditions, social and psychological factors, and sources of additional information.

★4061★

Office Machine Technicians
Chronicle Guidance Publications, Inc.
PO Box 1190
Moravia, NY 13118-1190   Phone: (315)497-0330

1988. This career brief describes the nature of the work, working conditions, hours and earnings, education and training, licensure, certification, unions, personal qualifications, social and psychological factors, employment outlook, entry methods, advancement, and related occupations. **Toll-free/Additional Phone Number(s):** 800-622-7284.

★4062★

Opportunities in Computer Maintenance Careers
National Textbook Co.
4255 W. Touhy Ave.
Lincolnwood, IL 60646   Phone: (312)679-5500

Elliott S. Kanter. 1988. Provides an overview of the work of a computer service technician, places of employment, educational preparation, employment outlook, and salaries. Offers job hunting advice. Profiles people working in the field.

★4063★

"PC Technicians" in *Careers in High Tech* (pp. 81-82)
Arco/Prentice Hall Press
1 Gulf & Western Plaza
New York, NY 10023   Phone: (212)373-8500

Connie Winkler. 1987. Surveys career opportunities in data processing, technology, personal computers, telecommunications, manufacturing technology, artificial intelligence, computer graphics, biotechnology, lasers, technical writing, and publishing. Includes information on educational preparation, associations, and periodicals.

★4064★

The Professional Electronics Technician
Electronics Technicians Association
602 N Jackson St.
Greencastle, IN 46135   Phone: (317)653-8262

This six-page brochure describes job duties, training, skills and aptitudes, salaries, employment outlook, and certification.

★4065★

"Service Technician/Customer Service" in *Careers in High Tech* (pp. 65-70)
Arco/Prentice Hall Press
1 Gulf & Western Plaza
New York, NY 10023   Phone: (212)373-8500

Connie Winkler. 1987. Surveys career opportunities in data processing, technology, personal computers, telecommunications, manufacturing technology, artificial intelligence, computer graphics, biotechnology, lasers, technical writing, and publishing. Includes information on educational preparation, associations, and periodicals.

★4066★

Video Career Library - Repair Fields
Careers, Inc.
1211 10th St., SW
PO Box 135
Largo, FL 34649-0135   Phone: (813)584-7333

Videocassette. 1990. 23 mins. Part of the Video Career Library covering 165 occupations. Shows actual workers on the job. Includes industrial machinery repairers, communications equipment repairers, data processing equipment repairers, home entertainment equipment repairers, office machine repairers, electrical power installers and repairers, and electrical and electronic repairers.

── **Associations** ──

★4067★

National Office Machine Dealers Association (NOMDA)
12411 Wornall
Kansas City, MO 64145   Phone: (816)941-3100

Membership: Retailers of office machines including copiers and business systems. **Purpose:** Offers 60 seminars on management, service, and business systems. Conducts research; sponsors Insurance Trust and Scholarship Foundation. **Publications:** *Hotline*, semimonthly. • *NOMDA Spokesman*, monthly. • *Who's Who Directory*, annual. **Facsimile Number:** (816)941-3100.

★4068★

National Office Machine Service Association (NOMSA)
Total Copy System
15544 Minnesota Ave.
Paramount, CA 90723   Phone: (213)633-4724

Membership: Individuals or firms involved directly in office machine service and repair; individuals or firms engaged in areas relating to machine service; parts and supply manufacturers. **Purpose:** Aims to advance the practice of office machine repair and maintenance as a viable, professional service business. Seeks to develop management skills and promote high standards of excellence among members. Conducts meetings, seminars, and workshops. Assists members in locating parts and supplies and in obtaining machine service manuals and repair

Computer and Office Machine Repairers ★4083★

information. **Publications:** *Membership Directory*, annual. • *Newsletter*, bimonthly.

Basic Reference Guides and Handbooks

★4069★
Advances in Cooling Techniques for Computers
Hemisphere Publishing Corp.
1900 Frost Rd., Ste. 101
Bristol, PA 19007　　　　　Phone: (215)785-5800
Win Aung, editor. 1991. **Facsimile Number:** (215)785-5515.

★4070★
Computer Parts and Supplies Directory
American Business Directories, Inc.
American Business Information, Inc.
5711 S. 86th Circle
Omaha, NE 68127　　　　　Phone: (402)593-4600
Annual. 9,594. Entries include: Name, address, phone (including area code), size of advertisement, year first in "Yellow Pages," name of owner or manager, number of employees. Arrangement: Geographical. **Facsimile Number:** (402)331-1505.

★4071★
Computer Technician's Handbook
TAB Books
Blue Ridge Summit, PA 17294-0850　　Phone: (717)794-2191
Art Margolis. Second edition.

★4072★
Computer Troubleshooting & Maintenance
Harcourt Brace Jovanovich, Inc.
6277 Sea Harbor Dr.
Orlando, FL 32887　　　　　Phone: (407)345-2000
Walter J. McBride. 1988. **Facsimile Number:** (407)345-8388.

★4073★
Computerized Maintenance Management Systems
Industrial Press, Inc.
200 Madison Ave.
New York, NY 10016　　　　Phone: (212)889-6330
Terry Wireman. 1986. **Facsimile Number:** (212)545-8327.

★4074★
Handbook of Software Maintenance
John Wiley & Sons, Inc.
605 3rd Ave.
New York, NY 10158　　　　Phone: (212)850-6000
Girish Parikh. 1986. **Facsimile Number:** (212)850-6088.

★4075★
IBM PC Advanced Troubleshooting & Repair
Howard W. Sams & Co., Publishers
2647 Waterfront Pkwy., E. Dr.
Indianapolis, IN 46214-2012
Robert Brenner. **Toll-free/Additional Phone Number(s):** 800-257-5755. **Facsimile Number:** (317)298-5604.

★4076★
Installing Personal Computer
QED Information Sciences, Inc.
Box 82-181
Wellesley, MA 02181　　　　Phone: (617)237-5656
William E. Perry. 1984. Part of QED Personal Computing Series. **Facsimile Number:** (617)235-0826.

★4077★
The Plain English Maintenance & Repair Guide for the IBM PC & PCjr
Simon & Schuster, Inc.
Simon & Schuster Bldg.
1230 Avenue of the Americas
New York, NY 10020　　　　Phone: (212)698-7000
Henry F. Beechhold. 1985.

★4078★
Service Management: Principles & Practices
Instrument Society of America
67 Alexander Dr.
PO Box 12277
Research Triangle Park, NC 27709　　Phone: (919)549-8411
W. H. Bleuel. Second edition, 1986.

★4079★
Troubleshooting & Repairing TVRO Systems
TAB Books
Blue Ridge Summit, PA 17294-0850　　Phone: (717)794-2191
Stan Prentiss. 1988.

Periodicals

★4080★
EDP Weekly
Computer Age
Millin Publishing Group, Inc.
3918 Prosperity Ave.
Ste. 310
Fairfax, VA 22031-3300　　　　Phone: (703)573-8400
Editor(s): Charles Bailey and Mike Cotter. Weekly. Reports news concerning all aspects of the computer industry. Covers standards, licensing agreements, patents issued, industry growth statistics, new technology, and pertinent legislation. Also includes semimonthly features on robotics, electronic funds transfer, mini and micro computers, data communications, and world trade.

★4081★
NOMDA Hotline (NOMDA)
National Office Machine Dealers Association (NOMDA)
12411 Wornall
Kansas City, MO 64145　　　　Phone: (816)941-3100
Semimonthly. Newsletter.

★4082★
NOMDA Spokesman (NOMDA)
National Office Machine Dealers Association (NOMDA)
12411 Wornall
Kansas City, MO 64145　　　　Phone: (816)941-3100
Monthly. Magazine including product stories, industry information, and legal opinions.

★4083★
NOMSA Newsletter (NOMSA)
National Office Machine Service Association (NOMSA)
Total Copy System
15544 Minnesota Ave.
Paramount, CA 90723　　　　Phone: (213)633-4724
Bimonthly.

Meetings and Conventions

★4084★
National Office Machine Service Association (NOMSA)
Total Copy System
15544 Minnesota Ave.
Paramount, CA 90723   Phone: (213)633-4724
Frequency: Annual.

Diesel Mechanics

Diesel mechanics repair and maintain diesel engines that power transportation equipment, such as heavy trucks, buses, and locomotives; construction equipment such as bulldozers, cranes, and road graders; and farm equipment such as tractors and combines. A small number work on diesel-powered automobiles. Diesel mechanics spend much time doing preventive maintenance like brake and steering system inspections. In some shops, mechanics do all kinds of repairs, while in other shops, the mechanics may specialize in one or two types of work, like transmissions or electrical systems. Diesel mechanics use a variety of tools like pneumatic wrenches and grinding machines, and a wide range of testing equipment like ohmmeters and tachometers. Over 30% of diesel mechanics work for vehicle and equipment dealers, leasing companies, and independent automotive repair shops. Nearly 25% are employed by local and long-distance trucking companies, and about 20% for buslines, public transit companies, school systems, and federal, state, and local government. The remainder maintain the fleets of trucks and other equipment of manufacturing, construction, and other companies. A relatively small number are self-employed.

$alaries

Diesel mechanics employed by trucking companies, buslines, and other firms that maintain their own vehicles have average hourly earnings of $13.35.

Transportation	$13.87/hour
Wholesale trade	$13.51/hour
Manufacturing	$12.97/hour
Retail trade	$12.90/hour
Services	$12.05/hour

Employment Outlook

Growth rate until the year 2000: Average.

Diesel Mechanics

---- Career Guides ----

★4085★
"Automotive, Diesel, and Gas Turbine Technicians" in Volume 4 of *The Encyclopedia of Careers and Vocational Guidance* (pp. 124-130)
J.G. Ferguson Publishing Co.
200 W. Monroe
Chicago, IL 60606　　　　　　　Phone: (312)580-5480
William E. Hopke, editor-in-chief. Eighth edition, 1990. Four-volume set that profiles 500 occupations and describes job trends in 76 industries. Includes career description, educational requirements, history of the job, methods of entry, advancement, employment outlook, earnings, working conditions, social and psychological factors, and sources of additional information.

★4086★
Diesel Mechanic
Careers, Inc.
PO Box 135
Largo, FL 34649-0135　　　　　Phone: (813)584-7333
1991. Two-page occupational summary card describing duties, working conditions, personal qualifications, training, earnings and hours, employment outlook, places of employment, related careers and where to write for more information.

★4087★
Diesel Mechanic
Vocational Biographies, Inc.
PO Box 31, Dept. VF10
Sauk Centre, MN 56378　　　　Phone: (612)352-6516
1989. This pamphlet profiles a person working in the job. Includes information about job duties, working conditions, places of employment, educational preparation, labor market outlook, and salaries. **Toll-free/Additional Phone Number(s):** 800-255-0752.

★4088★
"Diesel Mechanic" in *Careers in Trucking* (pp. 40-43)
Rosen Publishing Group, Inc.
29 E. 21st St.
New York, NY 10010　　　　　Phone: (212)777-3017
Donald D. Schauer. 1987. Describes employment in the trucking industry including driving, operations, sales, and administration. Covers qualifications, training, future outlook, and salaries. Offers career planning and job hunting advice.

★4089★
"Diesel Mechanic" in *Occu-Facts: Information on 565 Careers in Outline Form* (p. 15.4)
Careers, Inc.
P.O. Box 135
1211 Tenth St., S.W.
Largo, FL 33640　　　　　　　Phone: (813)584-7333
Elizabeth Handville. Biennial, 1989-90 edition. Each one-page occupational profile describes duties, working conditions, physical surroundings and demands, aptitudes, temperament, educational requirements, employment outlook, earnings, and places of employment.

★4090★
"Diesel Mechanic" in *Transportation*, Volume 12 of *Career Information Center* (pp. 100-102)
Glencoe/Macmillan
15319 Chatsworth St.
Mission Hills, CA 91345　　　　Phone: (818)898-1391
Richard Lidz and Dale Anderson, editorial directors. Fourth edition, 1990. For 600 occupations, describes job duties, entry-level requirements, education and training needed, advancement possibilities, employment outlook, earnings and benefits. The set is divided into 12 volumes. Each volume includes jobs related under a broad career field. Volume 13 is the index. **Facsimile Number:** 818-365-5489.

★4091★
"Diesel Mechanics" in *Occupational Outlook Handbook* (pp. 337-339)
Superintendent of Documents
U.S. Government Printing Office
Washington, DC 20402　　　　Phone: (202)783-3238
Biennial; latest edition, 1990-91. Encyclopedia of careers describing more than 250 occupations and comprising about 86 percent of all jobs in the economy. Occupations that require lengthy education or training are given the most attention. For each occupation, the handbook describes job duties, working conditions, training, educational preparation, personal qualities, advancement possibilities, job outlook, earnings, and sources of additional information.

★4092★
"Diesel Mechanics" in Volume 3 of *The Encyclopedia of Careers and Vocational Guidance* (pp. 499-503)
J.G. Ferguson Publishing Co.
200 W. Monroe
Chicago, IL 60606　　　　　　　Phone: (312)580-5480
William E. Hopke, editor-in-chief. Eighth edition, 1990. Four-volume set that profiles 500 occupations and describes job trends in 76 industries. Includes career description, educational requirements, history of the job, methods of entry,

advancement, employment outlook, earnings, working conditions, social and psychological factors, and sources of additional information.

★4093★
"Diesel Mechanics" in Volume 2 of *Career Discovery Encyclopedia* (pp. 106-107)
J.G. Ferguson Publishing Co.
200 W. Monroe
Chicago, IL 60606   Phone: (312)580-5480

E. Russell Primm, editor-in-chief. 1990. Contains two-page articles on 504 occupations. Each article describes job duties, earnings, and educational and training requirements.

★4094★
"Diesel Technology" in *The Career Connection II: A Guide to Technical Majors and Their Related Careers* (pp. 37-38)
ERIS
PO Box 7509
University Station
Provo, UT 84602-0509

Fred A. Rowe. 1988. Contains technical majors, such as automotive technology. Describes the major and the job. Lists high school and postsecondary school courses. Includes occupations related to the major, employment outlook, and starting salary.

★4095★
Do Your Own Thing. in the Mechanical Field
AIMS Media, Inc.
9710 DeSoto Ave.
Chatsworth, CA 93111-4409   Phone: (818)773-4300

Videocassette. 1979. 16 mins. Various job levels in the mechanical field are outlined for students.

★4096★
Mechanics
Morris Video
2730 Monterey St. #105
Monterey Business Park
Torrance, CA 90503   Phone: (213)533-4800

Videocassette. 1984. 15 mins. Various careers in repair are examined including aircraft, motorcycle, diesel, refrigeration and heavy equipment.

★4097★
"Mechanics: Diesel Engines" in *Opportunities in Vocational and Technical Careers* (pp. 104-105)
National Textbook Co.
4255 W. Touhy Ave.
Lincolnwood, IL 60646   Phone: (312)679-5500

Adrian A. Paradis. 1987. Describes careers which can be prepared for by attending a private vocational or proprietary school—office employee, sales worker, service worker, health services, mechanic, craftworker, and technician. Covers employment outlook, job duties, and salaries. Offers career planning advice.

★4098★
Video Career Library - Mechanical Fields
Careers, Inc.
1211 10th St., SW
PO Box 135
Largo, FL 34649-0135   Phone: (813)584-7333

Videocassette. 1990. 22 mins. Part of the Video Career Library covering 165 occupations. Shows actual workers on the job. Includes automobile mechanics, diesel engine mechanics, aircraft engine mechanics, automobile body repairers, heavy equipment mechanics, heating/air-conditioning/refrigeration mechanics.

★4099★
Vocational Visions
Center for Humanities, Inc.
Communications Park
Box 1000
Mount Kisco, NY 10549   Phone: (914)666-4100

Videocassette. 1984. 30 mins. This series of programs explains key aspects of actual training and a day in the life of a worker in the specific field mentioned on the videocassette. Occupations include: transportation/mechanics, repair, construction, business/office occupations, health, and agriculture.

★4100★
Vocations U.S.A.
Info-Disc Corporation
4 Professional Dr.
Gaithersburg, MD 20879   Phone: (301)948-2300

Videocassette. 1987. 60 mins. A disc collection outlining the requirements and methods of various career areas. Occupations include: transportation, mechanical/repair, health, agriculture, and construction.

Associations

★4101★
Automotive Service Industry Association (ASIA)
444 N. Michigan Ave.
Chicago, IL 60611-3975   Phone: (312)836-1300

Membership: Executives representing independent automotive wholesalers, warehouse distributors, heavy-duty vehicle and equipment parts distributors, automotive electrical service and supply wholesalers and distributors, manufacturers' representatives, and manufacturers and remanufacturers of replacement parts, tools, equipment, chemicals, refinishing materials, supplies, and accessories. **Purpose:** Operates extensive business management library. Holds seminars; bestows awards; compiles statistics; maintains hall of fame. **Publications:** *Automotive Service Industry Association—Buyers Guide*, periodic. • *Automotive Service Industry Association—Membership Directory*, periodic. • *Automotive Service Industry Association—Product Directory*, periodic. • *Selling Today*, periodic. • *Voice of the Industry*, periodic. **Facsimile Number:** (312)836-1009.

★4102★
International Association of Machinists and Aerospace Workers (IAM)
1300 Connecticut Ave.
Washington, DC 20036   Phone: (202)857-5200

Membership: AFL-CIO. **Publications:** *The Machinist*, monthly.

★4103★
Motor and Equipment Manufacturers Association (MEMA)
300 Sylvan Ave.
PO Box 1638
Englewood Cliffs, NJ 07632-0638   Phone: (201)569-8500

Membership: Manufacturers of automotive and heavy-duty original equipment and replacement components, maintenance equipment, chemicals, accessories, refinishing supplies, tools, and service equipment united for research into all aspects of the automotive and heavy-duty markets. **Purpose:** Provides manufacturer-oriented services and programs including: marketing consultation for the automotive industry; federal and state legal, safety, and legislative representation and

Diesel Mechanics ★4110★

consultation; personnel services; manpower development workshops; international information. Maintains credit reporting and collection service covering wholesalers, retailers, chain stores, and warehouse distributors; offers electronic order-entry, price-update, and electronic document exchange services through MEMA/Transnet system; maintains international liaison. Administers U.S. Automotive Parts Industry Japan Office in conjunction with the U.S. Department of Commerce. Conducts seminars on domestic and overseas marketing, federal trade regulations, freight forwarding, and credit and collections. Compiles statistics on automotive service industry for use by members and as a public service. **Publications:** *Automotive Distributor Trends and Financial Analysis*, periodic. • *Credit and Sales Reference Directory*, 2/year. • *International Buyer's Guide of U.S.* • *Marketing Insight*, quarterly. • Also publishes *Japan Automotive Insight*, *Autobody Supply and Equipment Market*, *Automotive Jobbers in the U.S.* **Facsimile Number:** (201)569-0159.

★4104★
National Association of Trade and Technical Schools (NATTS)
2251 Wisconsin Ave. NW
Washington, DC 20007   Phone: (202)333-1021

Membership: Private schools providing career education. **Purpose:** Seeks to inform members of the accreditation process and regulations affecting vocational education. Conducts workshops and institutes for staffs of member schools; provides legislative, administrative, and public relations assistance; serves as federally recognized accrediting agency. Has established Career Training Foundation to support research into private vocational education. Sponsors annual Idea Fair Competition. Presents special awards. Maintains hall of fame; compiles statistics. **Publications:** *Career News Digest*, 3-4/year. • *Career Training*, quarterly. • *Classroom Companion*, quarterly. • *Handbook of Trade and Technical Careers and Training*, annual. • *NATTS News and Views*, bimonthly. • Also publishes *Career Guidance Handouts*.

★4105★
National Institute for Automotive Service Excellence (ASE)
13505 Dulles Technology Dr.
Herndon, VA 22071-3415   Phone: (703)742-3800

Membership: Governed by a 40-member board of directors selected from all sectors of the automotive service industry and from education, government, and consumer groups. **Purpose:** Encourages and promotes the highest standards of automotive service in the public interest. Conducts continuing research to determine the best methods for training automotive technicians; encourages the development of effective training programs. Tests and certifies the competence of automobile, heavy-duty truck, collision repair, and engine machinist technicians. **Publications:** *ASE Test Registration Booklet*, semiannual. • *ASE Training Guide*, annual. • *The Blue Seal*, semiannual. **Facsimile Number:** (703)904-0727.

★4106★
Truck-Frame and Axle Repair Association (TARA)
915 E. 99th St.
Brooklyn, NY 11236   Phone: (212)257-6133

Membership: Owners and operators of heavy-duty truck repair facilities and their mechanics; allied and associate members are manufacturers of heavy-duty trucks and repair equipment, engineers, trade press, and insurance firms. **Purpose:** Seeks to help members share skills and technical knowledge and keep abreast of new developments and technology to better serve customers in areas of minimum downtime, cost, and maximum efficiency. Conducts studies and surveys regarding safety, fuel conservation, and heavy-duty truck maintenance and repairs. Has formed TARA's Young Executives to help make young people at TARA members' repair facilities more proficient in normal business functions and to ensure the future of TARA.

Standards/Certification Agencies

Voluntary certification by the National Institute for Automotive Service Excellence (ASE) is recognized as a standard of achievement for diesel mechanics. Mechanics may be certified as Master Heavy-Duty Truck Technician, or in any one or more of six different areas of heavy-duty truck repair. For certification in each area, mechanics must pass a written examination and have at least two years of experience. High school, vocational or trade school, or community or junior college training in gasoline or diesel engine repair may substitute for up to one year of experience. To retain certification, mechanics must retake the tests at least every five years.

★4107★
National Association of Trade and Technical Schools (NATTS)
2251 Wisconsin Ave. NW
Washington, DC 20007   Phone: (202)333-1021

Informs members of the accreditation process and regulations affecting vocational education. Conducts workshops and institutes for staffs of member schools; provides legislative, administrative, and public relations assistance; serves as a federally recognized accrediting agency.

★4108★
National Institute for Automotive Service Excellence (ASE)
13505 Dulles Technology Dr.
Herndon, VA 22071-3415   Phone: (703)742-3800

Encourages and promotes the highest standards of automotive service in the public interest. Conducts continuing research to determine the best methods for training automotive technicians; encourages the development of effective training programs. Tests and certifies the competence of automobile, heavy-duty truck, collision repair, and engine machinist technicians.

★4109★
Why Should a Heavy Duty Truck Technician be Certified?
National Institute for Automotive Service Excellence
13505 Dulles Technology Dr.
Herndon, VA 22071-3415   Phone: (703)742-3800

This six panel brochure explains certification for heavy duty truck mechanics.

Test Guides

★4110★
ASE Test Registration Booklet (ASE)
National Institute for Automotive Service Excellence (ASE)
13505 Dulles Technology Dr.
Herndon, VA 22071-3415   Phone: (703)742-3800

Semiannual. Registration for technicians who wish to become ASE certified. Provides registration information and sample questions.

★4111★
ASE Training Guide (ASE)
National Institute for Automotive Service Excellence (ASE)
13505 Dulles Technology Dr.
Herndon, VA 22071-3415   Phone: (703)742-3800
Annual. Bibliographic listing of training materials available for upgrading technicians' skills in automotive repair, including sample ASE test questions and test specifications.

★4112★
Auto Mechanic (Diesel)
National Learning Corp.
212 Michael Dr.
Syosset, NY 11791   Phone: (516)921-8888
Jack Rudman. Part of the Career Examination Series No. 1. All examination guides in this series contain questions with answers. **Facsimile Number:** (516)921-8743. **Toll-free/Additional Phone Number(s):** 800-645-6337.

Educational Directories and Programs

★4113★
Career Guidance Handouts (NATTS)
National Association of Trade and Technical Schools (NATTS)
2251 Wisconsin Ave. NW
Washington, DC 20007   Phone: (202)333-1021

★4114★
Career Training (NATTS)
National Association of Trade and Technical Schools (NATTS)
2251 Wisconsin Ave. NW
Washington, DC 20007   Phone: (202)333-1021
Quarterly.

★4115★
Classroom Companion (NATTS)
National Association of Trade and Technical Schools (NATTS)
2251 Wisconsin Ave. NW
Washington, DC 20007   Phone: (202)333-1021
Quarterly.

★4116★
Handbook of Trade and Technical Careers and Training (NATTS)
National Association of Trade and Technical Schools (NATTS)
2251 Wisconsin Ave. NW
Washington, DC 20007   Phone: (202)333-1021
Annual.

Awards, Scholarships, Grants, and Fellowships

★4117★
NATTS Award
National Association of Trade and Technical Schools
2251 Wisconsin Ave., NW
Washington, DC 20007   Phone: (202)333-1021
Bestowed to recognize excellence in the field of training; awarded annually to former student who has gone into a particular field.

★4118★
Silver Spark Plug Award
American Trucking Associations - Maintenance Council
2200 Mill Rd.
Alexandria, VA 22314   Phone: (703)838-1700
To recognize individuals for contributions to the improvement of equipment and its maintenance. Individuals who have a minimum of five years active service with the Council are eligible. A plaque and a certificate are awarded annually. Established about 1960.

Basic Reference Guides and Handbooks

★4119★
Autobody Supply and Equipment Market (MEMA)
Motor and Equipment Manufacturers Association (MEMA)
300 Sylvan Ave.
PO Box 1638
Englewood Cliffs, NJ 07632-0638   Phone: (201)569-8500

★4120★
Car Maintenance in the U.S.A. (MEMA)
Motor and Equipment Manufacturers Association (MEMA)
300 Sylvan Ave.
PO Box 1638
Englewood Cliffs, NJ 07632-0638   Phone: (201)569-8500

★4121★
Foreign Vehicle Maintenance in the U.S.A. (MEMA)
Motor and Equipment Manufacturers Association (MEMA)
300 Sylvan Ave.
PO Box 1638
Englewood Cliffs, NJ 07632-0638   Phone: (201)569-8500

★4122★
Heavy Duty Truck Maintenance in the U.S.A. (MEMA)
Motor and Equipment Manufacturers Association (MEMA)
300 Sylvan Ave.
PO Box 1638
Englewood Cliffs, NJ 07632-0638   Phone: (201)569-8500

Periodicals

★4123★
Automotive Distributor Trends and Financial Analysis (MEMA)
Motor and Equipment Manufacturers Association (MEMA)
300 Sylvan Ave.
PO Box 1638
Englewood Cliffs, NJ 07632-0638   Phone: (201)569-8500
Periodic.

★4124★
Automotive Jobbers in the U.S.A. (MEMA)
Motor and Equipment Manufacturers Association (MEMA)
300 Sylvan Ave.
PO Box 1638
Englewood Cliffs, NJ 07632-0638   Phone: (201)569-8500

★4125★
The Blue Seal (ASE)
National Institute for Automotive Service Excellence (ASE)
13505 Dulles Technology Dr.
Herndon, VA 22071-3415   Phone: (703)742-3800
Semiannual. Newsletter providing information on new technologies, training guides, and tips on servicing automobiles

for certified technicians and their employers. Also provides information on certified technicians and events.

★4126★
Career News Digest (NATTS)
National Association of Trade and Technical Schools (NATTS)
2251 Wisconsin Ave. NW
Washington, DC 20007   Phone: (202)333-1021
3-4/year.

★4127★
Diesel & Gas Turbine Worldwide
Diesel & Gas Turbine Publications
13555 Bishop's Ct.
Brookfield, WI 53005-6286   Phone: (414)784-9177
Joseph M. Kane, Editor. Monthly. (Jan./Feb., July/Aug. issues combined). International magazine covering diesel, natural gas, and gas turbine design and operation. **Facsimile Number:** (414)784-8133.

★4128★
Diesel Progress Engines & Drives
Diesel & Gas Turbine Publications
13555 Bishop's Ct.
Brookfield, WI 53005-6286   Phone: (414)784-9177
Michael J. Osenga, Editor. Monthly. Technical magazine covering engine-powered drive systems in mobile, stationary and marine equipment. **Facsimile Number:** (414)784-8133.

★4129★
MEMA Marketing Insight (MEMA)
Motor and Equipment Manufacturers Association (MEMA)
300 Sylvan Ave.
PO Box 1638
Englewood Cliffs, NJ 07632-0638   Phone: (201)569-8500
Quarterly.

★4130★
NATTS News and Views (NATTS)
National Association of Trade and Technical Schools (NATTS)
2251 Wisconsin Ave. NW
Washington, DC 20007   Phone: (202)333-1021
Bimonthly. Newspaper.

★4131★
Renews
Kona Communications, Inc.
707 Lake-Cook Rd.
Deerfield, IL 60015   Phone: (708)498-3180
Terry Haller, Editor. 12x/yr. Trade magazine covering rebuilding truck and auto parts.

★4132★
Selling Today (ASIA)
Automotive Service Industry Association (ASIA)
444 N. Michigan Ave.
Chicago, IL 60611-3975   Phone: (312)836-1300
Periodic.

★4133★
Voice of the Industry (ASIA)
Automotive Service Industry Association (ASIA)
444 N. Michigan Ave.
Chicago, IL 60611-3975   Phone: (312)836-1300
Periodic.

────── Meetings and Conventions ──────

★4134★
Association of Diesel Specialists International Convention and Exhibit
Association of Diesel Specialists
9140 Ward Pkwy.
Kansas City, MO 64114   Phone: (816)444-3500
1992. **Facsimile Number:** (816)444-0330.

────── Other Sources of Information ──────

★4135★
Distributors Financial Analysis (MEMA)
Motor and Equipment Manufacturers Association (MEMA)
300 Sylvan Ave.
PO Box 1638
Englewood Cliffs, NJ 07632-0638   Phone: (201)569-8500

Electronic Home Entertainment Equipment Repairers

Electronic home entertainment equipment repairers, also called service technicians, repair radios, televisions, stereo systems, home security systems, and video systems. Some may specialize in only one kind of equipment. Repairers conduct routine checks to locate the trouble. When these checks fail to find the problem, the repairers refer to wiring diagrams and service manuals. Repairs usually consist of part replacements or adjustments using tools such as soldering guns, wire cutters, and other handtools. Self-employed electronic home entertainment equipment repairers also have managerial responsibilities, including ordering supplies and keeping records. Nearly 25% of repairers are self-employed, a larger percentage than that of most repair occupations. Most repairers work in electronic repair shops or in stores that sell and service home electronic entertainment products.

$alaries

Repairers earn between $7 and $14 an hour, depending upon skill level, type of employer, and geographic location.

Employment Outlook

Growth rate until the year 2000: Average.

Electronic Home Entertainment Equipment Repairers

Career Guides

★4136★
Aim For A Job As An Electronic Technician
Rosen Publishing Group, Inc.
29 E. 21st St.
New York, NY 10010　　　　Phone: (212)777-3017
John E. Keefe. Revised edition, 1978. Describes the training requirements and the advantages and disadvantages of various jobs available in electronics. **Toll-free/Additional Phone Number(s):** 800-237-9932. **Facsimile Number:** (212)777-0277.

★4137★
Careers in Electronics
RMI Media Productions, Inc.
2807 West 47th St.
Shawnee Mission, KS 66205　　　Phone: (913)262-3974
Videocassette. 1984. 19 mins. This program shows the wide variety of occupations in the electronics field.

★4138★
Careers in the Electronics Industry
International Society of Certified Electronics Technicians
2708 W. Berry St.
Fort Worth, TX 76109　　　　Phone: (817)921-9101
This 16-page booklet provides an overview of the electronics industry and describes training and qualifications, employment outlook, earnings, and working conditions. Includes a state-by-state listing of electronic technician training schools.

★4139★
"Consumer Electronic Services" in *Electronic Service Careers* (pp. 57-62)
Franklin Watts, Inc.
387 Park Avenue, S.
New York, NY 10016　　　　Phone: (212)686-7070
Robert Laurance. 1987. Discusses the work of an electronic service technician, employment outlook, places of employment, and educational preparation and training. Describes jobs with computers, consumer electronics, industrial electronics and the military.

★4140★
"Consumer Electronics" in *The Complete Electronics Career Guide* (pp. 30-32)
Tab Books, Inc.
Blue Ridge Summit, PA 17294-0850　　Phone: (717)794-2191
Joe Risse. 1989. Explores opportunities for electronic technicians in industry, broadcasting, appliance repair, telecommunications, computer servicing, and technical writing. Offers advice on educational preparation, training, finding or changing jobs, and career advancement. Lists trade publications and professional associations.

★4141★
Consumer Electronics Service Technician
Careers, Inc.
PO Box 135
Largo, FL 34649-0135　　　　Phone: (813)584-7333
1988. Two-page occupational summary card describing duties, working conditions, personal qualifications, training, earnings and hours, employment outlook, places of employment, related careers and where to write for more information.

★4142★
Consumer Electronics Technicians
Chronicle Guidance Publications, Inc.
PO Box 1190
Moravia, NY 13118-1190　　　Phone: (315)497-0330
1991. This career brief describes the nature of the work, working conditions, hours and earnings, education and training, licensure, certification, unions, personal qualifications, social and psychological factors, employment outlook, entry methods, advancement, and related occupations. **Toll-free/Additional Phone Number(s):** 800-622-7284.

★4143★
"Consumer Servicing" in *The Complete Electronics Career Guide* (pp. 65-69)
Tab Books, Inc.
Blue Ridge Summit, PA 17294-0850　　Phone: (717)794-2191
Joe Risse. 1989. Explores opportunities for electronic technicians in industry, broadcasting, appliance repair, telecommunications, computer servicing, and technical writing. Offers advice on educational preparation, training, finding or changing jobs, and career advancement. Lists trade publications and professional associations.

★4144★
"Electronic Home Entertainment Equipment Repairers" in *Occupational Outlook Handbook* (pp. 339-341)
Superintendent of Documents
U.S. Government Printing Office
Washington, DC 20402　　　　Phone: (202)783-3238
Biennial; latest edition, 1990-91. Encyclopedia of careers describing more than 250 occupations and comprising about 86 percent of all jobs in the economy. Occupations that require lengthy education or training are given the most attention. For each occupation, the handbook describes job duties, working conditions, training, educational preparation, personal qualities, advancement possibilities, job outlook, earnings, and sources of additional information.

★4145★
"Electronic Organ Technicians" in Volume 4 of *The Encyclopedia of Careers and Vocational Guidance* (pp. 338-341)
J.G. Ferguson Publishing Co.
200 W. Monroe
Chicago, IL 60606 Phone: (312)580-5480
William E. Hopke, editor-in-chief. Eighth edition, 1990. Four-volume set that profiles 500 occupations and describes job trends in 76 industries. Includes career description, educational requirements, history of the job, methods of entry, advancement, employment outlook, earnings, working conditions, social and psychological factors, and sources of additional information.

★4146★
Electronic Service Careers
Franklin Watts, Inc.
387 Park Ave., S.
New York, NY 10016 Phone: (212)686-7070
Robert Laurance. 1987. Describes the career opportunities in electronics and the education and training requirements.
Facsimile Number: (212)213-6435.

★4147★
Electronics Technician: A Career for Tomorrow
Electronic Industries Association
Consumer Electronics Group
2001 Eye St. NW
PO Box 19100
Washington, DC 20006 Phone: (202)457-4919
1987. This eight-panel brochure describes the work, employment outlook, training, earnings, and opportunities for advancement.

★4148★
Electronics. . .Your Bridge to Tomorrow
Modern Talking Picture Service
5000 Park St. North
St. Petersburg, FL 33709 Phone: (813)541-7571
Videocassette. 1981. 16 mins. This program presents opportunities for young people and adults in the growing consumer electronic field.

★4149★
"Home Electronics Repairers" in Volume 3 of *Career Discovery Encyclopedia* (pp. 108-109)
J.G. Ferguson Publishing Co.
200 W. Monroe
Chicago, IL 60606 Phone: (312)580-5480
E. Russell Primm, editor-in-chief. 1990. Contains two-page articles on 504 occupations. Each article describes job duties, earnings, and educational and training requirements.

★4150★
The Professional Electronics Technician
Electronics Technicians Association
602 N Jackson St.
Greencastle, IN 46135 Phone: (317)653-8262
This six-page brochure describes job duties, training, skills and aptitudes, salaries, employment outlook, and certification.

★4151★
"Radio and Television Service Technician" in *Occu-Facts: Information on 565 Careers in Outline Form* (p. 15.13)
Careers, Inc.
P.O. Box 135
1211 Tenth St., S.W.
Largo, FL 33640 Phone: (813)584-7333
Elizabeth Handville. Biennial, 1989-90 edition. Each one-page occupational profile describes duties, working conditions, physical surroundings and demands, aptitudes, temperament, educational requirements, employment outlook, earnings, and places of employment.

★4152★
"Radio and Television Technician" in *Telecommunications* (pp. 63-67)
Franklin Watts, Inc.
387 Park Avenue, S.
New York, NY 10016 Phone: (212)686-7070
Linda Barrett and Galen Guengerich. 1991. Surveys opportunities in telecommunications including telephone, radio, telegraph, and television communications. Includes job description, educational preparation, salary, and employment outlook. Offers job hunting advice.

★4153★
Repair Cluster
Center for Humanities, Inc.
Communications Park
Box 1000
Mount Kisco, NY 10549 Phone: (914)666-4100
Videocassette. 1984. 15 mins. People who work in the fields of Heating/Air Conditioning Repair, and Radio/TV Repair describe what it's like to work at their jobs.

★4154★
"Television and Radio Service Technician" in *Communications and the Arts*, Volume 3 of *Career Information Center* (pp. 80-82)
Glencoe/Macmillan
15319 Chatsworth St.
Mission Hills, CA 91345 Phone: (818)898-1391
Richard Lidz and Dale Anderson, editorial directors. Fourth edition, 1990. For 600 occupations, describes job duties, entry-level requirements, education and training needed, advancement possibilities, employment outlook, earnings and benefits. The set is divided into 12 volumes. Each volume includes jobs related under a broad career field. Volume 13 is the index. **Facsimile Number:** 818-365-5489.

★4155★
"Television and Radio Service Technician" in *VGM's Careers Encyclopedia* (pp. 460-462)
National Textbook Co.
4255 W. Touhy Ave.
Lincolnwood, IL 60646 Phone: (312)679-5500
Third edition, 1991. Contains two- to five-page descriptions of 200 managerial, professional, technical, trade, and service occupations. Each profile includes job duties, places of employment, qualifications, educational preparation, training, employment potential, advancement, income, and additional sources of information.

Electronic Home Entertainment Equipment Repairers ★4164★

★4156★
Television Repairer
Vocational Biographies, Inc.
PO Box 31, Dept. VF10
Sauk Centre, MN 56378   Phone: (612)352-6516
1990. This pamphlet profiles a person working in the job. Includes information about job duties, working conditions, places of employment, educational preparation, labor market outlook, and salaries. **Toll-free/Additional Phone Number(s):** 800-255-0752.

★4157★
Tools for the Electrical Trades
Bergwall Productions
106 Charles Lindbergh Blvd.
Uniondale, NY 11553-3695   Phone: (516)222-1111
Videocassette. 1986. 58 mins. A look at various electronic tools; on four tapes.

★4158★
Video Career Library - Repair Fields
Careers, Inc.
1211 10th St., SW
PO Box 135
Largo, FL 34649-0135   Phone: (813)584-7333
Videocassette. 1990. 23 mins. Part of the Video Career Library covering 165 occupations. Shows actual workers on the job. Includes industrial machinery repairers, communications equipment repairers, data processing equipment repairers, home entertainment equipment repairers, office machine repairers, electrical power installers and repairers, and electrical and electronic repairers.

★4159★
"Video Service Technician" in *Career Opportunities in Television, Cable, and Video* (pp. 196-197)
Facts on File, Inc.
460 Park Avenue, S.
New York, NY 10016   Phone: (212)683-2244
Third edition, 1990. Describes 100 media-related jobs. Each occupational profile covers job duties, employment outlook, career paths, salaries, skills, and educational preparation. Offers tips for entering the field.

Associations

★4160★
Electronic Industries Association (EIA)
2001 Pennsylvania Ave. NW, Ste. 1100
Washington, DC 20006-1813   Phone: (202)457-4900
Membership: Trade organization representing manufacturers of electronic parts, tubes, and solid state components; radio, television, and video systems; audio equipment; government electronic systems; and industrial and communications electronic products. **Purpose:** Sponsors Electronic Industries Foundation. Presents Medal of Honor and Distinguished Service awards for outstanding contributions to the electronic industries. Operates Marketing Research Library. Maintains placement and children's services. Compiles statistics. **Publications:** *EIA Publications Index*, semiannual. **Facsimile Number:** (202)457-4985;

★4161★
Electronics Technicians Association, International (ETA-I)
602 N. Jackson
Greencastle, IN 46135   Phone: (317)653-8262
Membership: Skilled electronics technicians. **Purpose:** Provides placement service; sponsors regional technician training workshops and business management seminars; offers certification examinations for electronics technicians. Compiles wage and manpower statistics. Conducts training seminars in general electronics and specific aspects of the master antenna and satellite television business. Bestows Technician of the Year Award. Offers insurance to members. Maintains 170 volume library on technical and business training and VCR tapes for certification practice exams. **Publications:** *EEA Training Program*, monthly. • *Management Update*, monthly. • *Directory of Professional Electronics Technicians*, annual. • *Technician Association News*, monthly. **Facsimile Number:** (317)653-8262.

★4162★
International Society of Certified Electronics Technicians (ISCET)
2708 W. Berry, Ste. 3
Fort Worth, TX 76109   Phone: (817)921-9101
Membership: Technicians in 5 countries who have been certified by the society. **Purpose:** Seeks to provide a fraternal bond among certified electronics technicians, raise their public image, and improve the effectiveness of industry education programs for technicians. Offers training programs in new electronics information; presents awards. Maintains library of service literature for consumer electronic equipment, including manuals and schematics for out-of-date equipment. Offers general radiotelephone license. Sponsors testing program for certification of electronics technicians in the fields of audio, communications, computer, consumer, industrial, medical electronics, radar, radio-television, and video. Operates Hall of Fame. **Publications:** *ISCET Update*, quarterly. • *Professional Electronics Magazine*, bimonthly. • *Technical Log*, quarterly. **Facsimile Number:** (817)921-3741.

★4163★
National Electronic Sales and Service Dealers Association (NESDA)
2708 W. Berry St., Ste. 3
Ft. Worth, TX 76109   Phone: (817)921-9061
Membership: Local and state electronic service associations and companies representing 4200 individuals. **Purpose:** Provides educational assistance in electronic training to public schools; supplies technical service information on business management training to electronic service dealers. Offers certification, apprenticeship, and training programs through International Society of Certified Electronics Technicians. Compiles statistics on electronics service business; conducts technical service and business management seminars; bestows awards. **Publications:** *National Electronic Sales and Service Dealers Association—Member Memo*, bimonthly. • *National Electronic Sales and Services Dealers Association—Update*, quarterly. • *Professional Electronics*, bimonthly. • *Professional Electronics Yearbook*. **Facsimile Number:** (817)921-3741.

Standards/Certification Agencies

Connecticut, Indiana, Louisiana, Massachusetts, and Oregon require repairers to be certified. Applicants for certification must pass an examination covering electronic circuits and components and the use of test equipment.

★4164★
Electronics Technicians Association, International (ETA-I)
602 N. Jackson
Greencastle, IN 46135   Phone: (317)653-8262
Offers certification examinations for electronics technicians. Maintains VCR tapes for certification practice exams.

★4165★
International Society of Certified Electronics Technicians (ISCET)
2708 W. Berry, Ste. 3
Fort Worth, TX 76109　　　　　Phone: (817)921-9101
Sponsors testing program for certification of electronics technicians in the fields of audio, communications, computer, consumer, industrial, medical electronics, radar, radio-television, and video.

★4166★
National Electronic Sales and Service Dealers Association (NESDA)
2708 W. Berry St., Ste. 3
Ft. Worth, TX 76109　　　　　Phone: (817)921-9061
Offers certification, apprenticeship, and training programs through International Society of Certified Electronics Technicians. L *Professional Electronics Yearbook*. **Facsimile Number:** (817)921-3741.

★4167★
Professionals...Are Certified by the Electronics Technicians Association, International
Electronics Technicians Association
602 N Jackson St.
Greencastle, IN 46135　　　　　Phone: (317)653-8262
This six-panel brochure describes the certification process for electronics technicians. Covers eligibility requirements, examination contents, and specialties.

――――― **Test Guides** ―――――

★4168★
Certified Electronic Technician (CET)
National Learning Corp.
212 Michael Dr.
Syosset, NY 11791　　　　　Phone: (516)921-8888
Jack Rudman. Part of the Admission Test Series No. 3. Books in this series provide test practice and drill for actual professional certification and licensure tests. **Facsimile Number:** (516)921-8743. **Toll-free/Additional Phone Number(s):** 800-645-6337.

★4169★
The CET Exam: ISCET: Certified Electronics Technician
International Society of Certified Electronics Technicians
2708 W. Berry St.
Fort Worth, TX 76109　　　　　Phone: (817)921-9101
This six-panel brochure describes certification for electronic technicians. Outlines examination contents.

★4170★
EEA Training Program (ETA-I)
Electronics Technicians Association, International (ETA-I)
602 N. Jackson
Greencastle, IN 46135　　　　　Phone: (317)653-8262
Monthly.

――――― **Awards, Scholarships, Grants, and Fellowships** ―――――

★4171★
Electronics Technicians Association, International Technician of the Year
Electronics Technicians Association, International
604 N. Jackson
Greencastle, IN 46135　　　　　Phone: (317)653-8262
To honor a practicing electronics technician as an incentive for all other technicians to achieve higher goals. A plaque is awarded annually at the convention. Established in 1979 in memory of Norris R. Browne, CET, Houston, TX.

★4172★
ISCET Tech-of-the-Year Award
International Society of Certified Electronics Technicians
c/o Alice Johnson
2708 W. Berry St.
Fort Worth, TX 76109　　　　　Phone: (817)921-9101
To recognize a technician for outstanding work in the field of electronics. Established in 1976.

――――― **Basic Reference Guides and Handbooks** ―――――

★4173★
Interconnection Products Directory
Connector Study Group, Inc.
104 Wilmot Rd., Ste. 201
Deerfield, IL 60015-5195　　　　　Phone: (312)940-8800
Gerald L. Ginsberg, editor. Biennial, November of odd years. More than 500 manufacturers, distributors, representatives, sales offices, and other suppliers to the electrical and electronics industry worldwide, including suppliers of connectors, wire, and cable (part 1); printed circuit products (part 2); circular rack and panel products (part 3); wire and cable products (part 4); materials (part 5); and military products (part 6). Entries include: Name, address, products, whether catalog is available. Arrangement: Classified by product. Indexes: Product.

★4174★
Professional Electronics Yearbook (NESDA)
National Electronic Sales and Service Dealers Association (NESDA)
2708 W. Berry St., Ste. 3
Ft. Worth, TX 76109　　　　　Phone: (817)921-9061
Compilation of news, professional information, advice, and reference aids for the electronics sales and service dealer, professional electronics technician, and others in the electronics industry. Includes listings of major electronic manufacturers' key contacts for repair parts, listing of parts distributors, and important toll-free numbers.

Electronic Home Entertainment Equipment Repairers ★4187★

Periodicals

★4175★
Electronic and Electrical Equipment
National Safety Council
444 N. Michigan Ave.
Chicago, IL 60611　　　　　Phone: (312)527-4800
Editor(s): Katie Kuhfuss. 6/yr. Provides safety tips for persons who work with electronic and electrical equipment. Promotes and reports on training courses in accident prevention, safety precautions, and compliance with safety regulations. Also carries items on safety awareness off the job.

★4176★
Electronic Servicing & Technology
Intertec Publishing Corp.
9221 Quivira Rd.
PO Box 12901
Overland Park, KS 66212-9981　　Phone: (913)888-4664
Conrad Persson, Editor. Monthly. Consumer electronics servicing magazine. **Facsimile Number:** (913)541-6697.

★4177★
ETA-I Management Update (ETA-I)
Electronics Technicians Association, International (ETA-I)
602 N. Jackson
Greencastle, IN 46135　　　　Phone: (317)653-8262
Monthly.

★4178★
ETA-I Technician Association News (ETA-I)
Electronics Technicians Association, International (ETA-I)
602 N. Jackson
Greencastle, IN 46135　　　　Phone: (317)653-8262
Monthly. Industry and association journal. Includes book reviews, obituaries, information on new products and new members, and employment listings.

★4179★
International Society of Certified Electronics Technicians —Update
International Society of Certified Electronics Technicians
2708 W. Berry St.
Ft. Worth, TX 76109　　　　Phone: (817)921-9101
Editor(s): Barbara Rubin. Quarterly. Reflects the aims of the Society, which are to raise the public image of certified electronics technicians and to improve the effectiveness of industry education programs for technicians. Recurring features include news of research, a calendar of events, reports of meetings, news of educational opportunities, and job listings.

★4180★
ISCET Update (ISCET)
International Society of Certified Electronics Technicians (ISCET)
2708 W. Berry, Ste. 3
Fort Worth, TX 76109　　　　Phone: (817)921-9101
Quarterly. Society and industry newsletter. Includes job listings.

★4181★
National Electronic Sales and Service Dealers Association —Member Memo (NESDA)
National Electronic Sales and Service Dealers Association (NESDA)
2708 W. Berry St., Ste. 3
Ft. Worth, TX 76109　　　　Phone: (817)921-9061
Bimonthly. Association and industry newsletter.

★4182★
National Electronic Sales and Services Dealers Association —Update (NESDA)
National Electronic Sales and Service Dealers Association (NESDA)
2708 W. Berry St., Ste. 3
Ft. Worth, TX 76109　　　　Phone: (817)921-9061
Quarterly. Association newsletter providing information on legislation, regulations, legal, and industry news.

★4183★
NESSDA Update
National Electronic Sales and Service Dealers Association (NESSDA)
2708 W. Berry
Ft. Worth, TX 76109　　　　Phone: (817)921-9061
Editor(s): Wallace Harrison. Quarterly. Contains NESDA and electronics industry news and information regarding NESDA programs and services. Supplies information as a supplement to Professional Electronics Magazine. Recurring features include news of research, news of members, and computer service news. **Facsimile Number:** (817)921-3741.

★4184★
Professional Electronics (NESDA)
National Electronic Sales and Service Dealers Association (NESDA)
2708 W. Berry St., Ste. 3
Ft. Worth, TX 76109　　　　Phone: (817)921-9061
Bimonthly. Journal for owners, operators, and employees of retail electronics sales/service firms. Includes technical articles as well as general interest articles for those in the industry.

★4185★
Professional Electronics Magazine (ISCET)
International Society of Certified Electronics Technicians (ISCET)
2708 W. Berry, Ste. 3
Fort Worth, TX 76109　　　　Phone: (817)921-9101
Bimonthly.

★4186★
Retail News Reporter
739 Main St., Ste. 4
PO Box 830034
Stone Mountain, GA 30083-0001　　Phone: (404)879-9682
Byron Hollingsworth, Publisher. Monthly. Newspaper (tabloid) for the electronics and appliances industry. **Facsimile Number:** (404)879-6791.

Meetings and Conventions

★4187★
International Society of Certified Electronics Technicians (ISCET)
2708 W. Berry, Ste. 3
Fort Worth, TX 76109　　　　Phone: (817)921-9101
Frequency: Annual conference, with exhibits, always held first week in August. Also holds annual Consumers Electronics

Instructors Conference and trade shows. **Facsimile Number:** (817)921-3741.

★4188★
National Professional Electronics Convention and Trade Show
National Electronic Sales and Service Dealers Association
2708 W. Berry St., Ste. 3
Ft. Worth, TX 76109   Phone: (817)921-9061
1992; Aug. 03-08; Ft. Worth, TX. **Facsimile Number:** (817)921-3741.

Elevator Installers and Repairers

Elevator installers and repairers (also called elevator constructors or mechanics) assemble, install, and replace elevators, escalators, and similar equipment in new and old buildings. Once the equipment is in service, they maintain and repair it. These duties require thorough knowledge of electronics, electricity, and hydraulics. Elevator constructors usually specialize in installation, maintenance, or repair work. Maintenance and repair workers generally need more knowledge of electricity and electronics than installers because a large part of maintenance and repair work is troubleshooting. Similarly, construction "adjustors," who fine-tune the newly installed equipment, need a thorough knowledge of electricity, electronics, and computers. Most elevator installers and repairers are employed by field offices of elevator manufacturers; small, local elevator maintenance and repair contractors; or by government agencies or businesses that do their own elevator maintenance and repair.

$alaries

Weekly earnings for elevator installers and repairers are listed below.

Elevator installers and repairers	$670/week
Probationary helpers	$330/week
Non-probationary helpers	$470/week
Mechanics-in-charge	$750/week

Employment Outlook

Growth rate until the year 2000: Average.

Elevator Installers and Repairers

Career Guides

★4189★
"Elevator Constructor and Repair Worker" in *Construction*, Volume 4 of *Career Information Center* (pp. 56-58)
Glencoe/Macmillan
15319 Chatsworth St.
Mission Hills, CA 91345   Phone: (818)898-1391
Richard Lidz and Dale Anderson, editorial directors. Fourth edition, 1990. For 600 occupations, describes job duties, entry-level requirements, education and training needed, advancement possibilities, employment outlook, earnings and benefits. The set is divided into 12 volumes. Each volume includes jobs related under a broad career field. Volume 13 is the index. **Facsimile Number:** 818-365-5489.

★4190★
"Elevator Constructors" in *Opportunities in Building Construction Trades* (p. 52)
National Textbook Co.
4255 W. Touhy Ave.
Lincolnwood, IL 60646   Phone: (312)679-5500
Michael Sumichrast. 1989. Gives an overview of the construction industry and describes the jobs of various craftworkers. Covers different kinds of builders: home, custom; and describes management skills needed and industry trends affecting opportunities.

★4191★
Elevator Constructors (Mechanics)
Chronicle Guidance Publications, Inc.
PO Box 1190
Moravia, NY 13118-1190   Phone: (315)497-0330
1987. This career brief describes the nature of the work, working conditions, hours and earnings, education and training, licensure, certification, unions, personal qualifications, social and psychological factors, employment outlook, entry methods, advancement, and related occupations. **Toll-free/Additional Phone Number(s):** 800-622-7284.

★4192★
"Elevator Installers and Repairers" in *Occupational Outlook Handbook* (pp. 341-342)
Superintendent of Documents
U.S. Government Printing Office
Washington, DC 20402   Phone: (202)783-3238
Biennial; latest edition, 1990-91. Encyclopedia of careers describing more than 250 occupations and comprising about 86 percent of all jobs in the economy. Occupations that require lengthy education or training are given the most attention. For each occupation, the handbook describes job duties, working conditions, training, educational preparation, personal qualities, advancement possibilities, job outlook, earnings, and sources of additional information.

★4193★
"Elevator Installers and Repairers" in Volume 3 of *The Encyclopedia of Careers and Vocational Guidance* (pp. 660-662)
J.G. Ferguson Publishing Co.
200 W. Monroe
Chicago, IL 60606   Phone: (312)580-5480
William E. Hopke, editor-in-chief. Eighth edition, 1990. Four-volume set that profiles 500 occupations and describes job trends in 76 industries. Includes career description, educational requirements, history of the job, methods of entry, advancement, employment outlook, earnings, working conditions, social and psychological factors, and sources of additional information.

★4194★
"Elevator Installers and Repairers" in Volume 2 of *Career Discovery Encyclopedia* (pp. 160-161)
J.G. Ferguson Publishing Co.
200 W. Monroe
Chicago, IL 60606   Phone: (312)580-5480
E. Russell Primm, editor-in-chief. 1990. Contains two-page articles on 504 occupations. Each article describes job duties, earnings, and educational and training requirements.

Associations

★4195★
International Union of Elevator Constructors (IUEC)
Clark Bldg., Ste. 530
5565 Sterrett Pl.
Columbia, MD 21044   Phone: (301)997-9000
Membership: Elevator constructor unions in the U.S. and Canada. **Purpose:** Supplies companies with referrals to elevator installers. **Publications:** *The Constructor*, monthly.

Standards/Certification Agencies

Almost all elevator constructors learn their trade in programs administered by joint committees of employers and local chapters of the International Union of Elevator Constructors. These programs, through which the trainee learns everything from installation to repair, combine on-the-job training with classroom instruction in electrical and electronic theory, mathematics, applications of physics, and safety.

Test Guides

★4196★
Chief Elevator Starter
National Learning Corp.
212 Michael Dr.
Syosset, NY 11791   Phone: (516)921-8888
Jack Rudman. Part of the Career Examination Series No. 1. All examination guides in this series contain questions with answers. **Facsimile Number:** (516)921-8743. **Toll-free/Additional Phone Number(s):** 800-645-6337.

★4197★
Elevator Mechanic
National Learning Corp.
212 Michael Dr.
Syosset, NY 11791   Phone: (516)921-8888
Jack Rudman. Part of the Career Examination Series No. 1. Other guides are available for elevator mechanic's helper, elevator inspector, and elevator starter. All examination guides in this series contain questions with answers. **Facsimile Number:** (516)921-8743. **Toll-free/Additional Phone Number(s):** 800-645-6337.

★4198★
Foreman Elevator Mechanic
National Learning Corp.
212 Michael Dr.
Syosset, NY 11791   Phone: (516)921-8888
Jack Rudman. Part of the Career Examination Series No. 1. All examination guides in this series contain questions with answers. **Facsimile Number:** (516)921-8743. **Toll-free/Additional Phone Number(s):** 800-645-6337.

★4199★
Maintenance Mechanic
Prentice Hall Press
Simon & Schuster Inc.
200 Old Tappan Rd.
Old Tappan, NJ 07675   Phone: (800)223-2348
Hy Hammer. First edition, 1988. Provides information for applicants interested in the following entry-level civil service positions: mason's helper, elevator mechanic's helper, mechanical maintainer's helper, among others.

Basic Reference Guides and Handbooks

★4200★
Elevators & Engineering: An Architectural Guide
Vance Bibliographies
112 N. Charter St.
Monticello, IL 61856   Phone: (217)762-3831
Coppa & Avery Consultants Staff. 1987.

★4201★
Lift Practice
State Mutual Book & Periodical Service, Ltd.
521 5th Ave., 17th Fl.
New York, NY 10175   Phone: (212)682-5844
1982.

★4202★
Lift Servicing & Maintenance
State Mutual Book & Periodical Service, Ltd.
521 5th Ave. 17th Fl.
New York, NY 10175   Phone: (212)682-5844
1982.

★4203★
Safety Code for Elevators & Escalators
American Society of Mechanical Engineers
345 E. 47th St.
New York, NY 10017   Phone: (212)705-7722
1987.

★4204★
Safey Code for Elevators & Escalators: Handbook on A17.1
American Society of Mechanical Engineers
345 E. 47th St.
New York, NY 10017   Phone: (212)705-7722
E. A. Donoghue, editor. 1987.

Periodicals

★4205★
Elevator World, Inc.
354 Morgan Ave.
PO Box 6507
Mobile, AL 36606   Phone: (205)479-4514
W.C. Sturgeon, Editor. Monthly. Magazine for the elevator industry. **Facsimile Number:** (205)479-7043.

Meetings and Conventions

★4206★
International Union of Elevator Constructors (IUEC)
Clark Bldg., Ste. 530
5565 Sterrett Pl.
Columbia, MD 21044   Phone: (301)997-9000
Frequency: Quinquennial.

Other Sources of Information

★4207★
The Elevator
Walker & Company
720 5th Ave.
New York, NY 10019   Phone: (212)265-3632
Barbara Ford. 1982. Part of Inventions that Changed Our Lives Series. **Facsimile Number:** (212)307-1764.

★4208★
Lift Erection
State Mutual Book & Periodical Services, Ltd.
521 5th Ave., 17th Fl.
New York, NY 10175   Phone: (212)682-5844
1982.

★4209★
Vertical Transportation: Elevators & Escalators
John Wiley & Sons, Inc.
605 3rd Ave.
New York, NY 10158   Phone: (212)850-6000
George R. Strakosch. Second edition, 1983. **Facsimile Number:** (212)850-6088.

Farm Equipment Mechanics

Farm equipment mechanics perform preventive maintenance and repair all manners of farm equipment like tractors, combines, planters, and tillage equipment. As farm machinery has grown larger with more electronic and hydraulic controls, farmers have increasingly turned to farm equipment dealers for service and repair of the machines they sell. Therefore, almost every dealer employs farm equipment mechanics, often called service technicians, to do this work. Some mechanics specialize in certain types of work such as hydraulics or transmission repair. A variety of basic handtools are used in addition to sophisticated precision equipment. While most farm equipment mechanics work in service departments of farm equipment dealers, others work in independent repair shops and in shops on large farms. About 10% are self-employed.

$alaries

Farm equipment mechanics have median hourly earnings of about $8.30. The top 10 percent earn over $12.40/hour

Employment Outlook

Growth rate until the year 2000: Employment is expected to remain level.

Farm Equipment Mechanics

Career Guides

★4210★
Careers in Farm Equipment Mechanics
North American Equipment Dealers Association/NAED Foundation
10877 Watson Rd.
St. Louis, MO 63127-1081   Phone: (314)821-7220
This six-panel brochure describes the nature of the work, working conditions, places of employment, training, and advancement opportunities, employment outlook, and earnings.

★4211★
Do Your Own Thing. in the Mechanical Field
AIMS Media, Inc.
9710 DeSoto Ave.
Chatsworth, CA 93111-4409   Phone: (818)773-4300
Videocassette. 1979. 16 mins. Various job levels in the mechanical field are outlined for students.

★4212★
Farm Equipment Mechanic
Careers, Inc.
PO Box 135
Largo, FL 34649-0135   Phone: (813)584-7333
1989. Two-page occupational summary card describing duties, working conditions, personal qualifications, training, earnings and hours, employment outlook, places of employment, related careers and where to write for more information.

★4213★
"Farm Equipment Mechanic" in Occu-Facts: Information on 565 Careers in Outline Form (p. 15.9)
Careers, Inc.
P.O. Box 135
1211 Tenth St., S.W.
Largo, FL 33640   Phone: (813)584-7333
Elizabeth Handville. Biennial, 1989-90 edition. Each one-page occupational profile describes duties, working conditions, physical surroundings and demands, aptitudes, temperament, educational requirements, employment outlook, earnings, and places of employment.

★4214★
Farm Equipment Mechanics
Chronicle Guidance Publications, Inc.
PO Box 1190
Moravia, NY 13118-1190   Phone: (315)497-0330
1988. This career brief describes the nature of the work, working conditions, hours and earnings, education and training, licensure, certification, unions, personal qualifications, social and psychological factors, employment outlook, entry methods, advancement, and related occupations. **Toll-free/Additional Phone Number(s):** 800-622-7284.

★4215★
"Farm Equipment Mechanics" in Occupational Outlook Handbook (pp. 342-344)
Superintendent of Documents
U.S. Government Printing Office
Washington, DC 20402   Phone: (202)783-3238
Biennial; latest edition, 1990-91. Encyclopedia of careers describing more than 250 occupations and comprising about 86 percent of all jobs in the economy. Occupations that require lengthy education or training are given the most attention. For each occupation, the handbook describes job duties, working conditions, training, educational preparation, personal qualities, advancement possibilities, job outlook, earnings, and sources of additional information.

★4216★
"Farm Equipment Mechanics" in Volume 3 of Career Discovery Encyclopedia (pp. 8-9)
J.G. Ferguson Publishing Co.
200 W. Monroe
Chicago, IL 60606   Phone: (312)580-5480
E. Russell Primm, editor-in-chief. 1990. Contains two-page articles on 504 occupations. Each article describes job duties, earnings, and educational and training requirements.

★4217★
"Farm Equipment Mechanics" in Volume 3 of The Encyclopedia of Careers and Vocational Guidance (pp. 503-507)
J.G. Ferguson Publishing Co.
200 W. Monroe
Chicago, IL 60606   Phone: (312)580-5480
William E. Hopke, editor-in-chief. Eighth edition, 1990. Four-volume set that profiles 500 occupations and describes job trends in 76 industries. Includes career description, educational requirements, history of the job, methods of entry, advancement, employment outlook, earnings, working conditions, social and psychological factors, and sources of additional information.

Associations

★4218★
Motor and Equipment Manufacturers Association (MEMA)
300 Sylvan Ave.
PO Box 1638
Englewood Cliffs, NJ 07632-0638   Phone: (201)569-8500

Membership: Manufacturers of automotive and heavy-duty original equipment and replacement components, maintenance equipment, chemicals, accessories, refinishing supplies, tools, and service equipment united for research into all aspects of the automotive and heavy-duty markets. **Purpose:** Provides manufacturer-oriented services and programs including: marketing consultation for the automotive industry; federal and state legal, safety, and legislative representation and consultation; personnel services; manpower development workshops; international information. Maintains credit reporting and collection service covering wholesalers, retailers, chain stores, and warehouse distributors; offers electronic order-entry, price-update, and electronic document exchange services through MEMA/Transnet system; maintains international liaison. Administers U.S. Automotive Parts Industry Japan Office in conjunction with the U.S. Department of Commerce. Conducts seminars on domestic and overseas marketing, federal trade regulations, freight forwarding, and credit and collections. Compiles statistics on automotive service industry for use by members and as a public service. **Publications:** *Automotive Distributor Trends and Financial Analysis*, periodic. • *Credit and Sales Reference Directory*, 2/year. • *International Buyer's Guide of U.S.* • *Marketing Insight*, quarterly. • Also publishes *Japan Automotive Insight*, *Autobody Supply and Equipment Market*, *Automotive Jobbers in the U.S.* **Facsimile Number:** (201)569-0159.

★4219★
North American Equipment Dealers Association (NAEDA)
10877 Watson Rd.
St. Louis, MO 63127   Phone: (314)821-7220

Membership: Retailers of farm machinery, implements, light industrial machinery, tools, vehicles, outdoor power equipment, and related supplies. **Purpose:** Conducts programs on management training, and governmental and trade relations. Sponsors group health and accident insurance program for members and their employees. Compiles statistics. **Publications:** *Cost of Doing Business Study*, annual. • *Farm and Power Equipment Dealer*, monthly. • *Official Guide—Tractors and Farm Equipment*, semiannual. • *Official Industrial Equipment Guide*, semiannual. • *Outdoor Power Equipment Official Guide*, annual. **Facsimile Number:** (314)821-0674.

Basic Reference Guides and Handbooks

★4220★
Autobody Supply and Equipment Market **(MEMA)**
Motor and Equipment Manufacturers Association (MEMA)
300 Sylvan Ave.
PO Box 1638
Englewood Cliffs, NJ 07632-0638   Phone: (201)569-8500

★4221★
Car Maintenance in the U.S.A. **(MEMA)**
Motor and Equipment Manufacturers Association (MEMA)
300 Sylvan Ave.
PO Box 1638
Englewood Cliffs, NJ 07632-0638   Phone: (201)569-8500

★4222★
Foreign Vehicle Maintenance in the U.S.A. **(MEMA)**
Motor and Equipment Manufacturers Association (MEMA)
300 Sylvan Ave.
PO Box 1638
Englewood Cliffs, NJ 07632-0638   Phone: (201)569-8500

★4223★
Heavy Duty Truck Maintenance in the U.S.A. **(MEMA)**
Motor and Equipment Manufacturers Association (MEMA)
300 Sylvan Ave.
PO Box 1638
Englewood Cliffs, NJ 07632-0638   Phone: (201)569-8500

★4224★
Official Guide—Tractors and Farm Equipment **(NAEDA)**
North American Equipment Dealers Association (NAEDA)
10877 Watson Rd.
St. Louis, MO 63127   Phone: (314)821-7220

Semiannual. Guide for evaluating used tractors and other farm equipment.

★4225★
Official Industrial Equipment Guide **(NAEDA)**
North American Equipment Dealers Association (NAEDA)
10877 Watson Rd.
St. Louis, MO 63127   Phone: (314)821-7220

Semiannual. Guide for evaluating used industrial equipment. Includes rental information.

★4226★
Outdoor Power Equipment Official Guide **(NAEDA)**
North American Equipment Dealers Association (NAEDA)
10877 Watson Rd.
St. Louis, MO 63127   Phone: (314)821-7220

Annual. Guide for evaluating used outdoor power equipment. Includes rental information.

★4227★
Tractor Equipment & Parts Directory
American Business Directories, Inc.
American Business Information, Inc.
5711 S. 86th Circle
Omaha, NE 68127   Phone: (402)593-4600

Annual. Entries include: Name, address, phone, size of advertisement, name of owner or manager, number of employees, year first in "Yellow Pages." Arrangement: Geographical. **Facsimile Number:** (402)331-1505.

Periodicals

★4228★
Agri-Equipment & Chemical
Columbia Publishing
2809A Fruitvale Blvd.
Yakima, WA 98907-1467   Phone: (509)248-2452

Ken Hodge, Editor. Monthly. Agriculture magazine. **Facsimile Number:** (509)248-4056.

Farm Equipment Mechanics

★4229★
Automotive Distributor Trends and Financial Analysis (MEMA)
Motor and Equipment Manufacturers Association (MEMA)
300 Sylvan Ave.
PO Box 1638
Englewood Cliffs, NJ 07632-0638   Phone: (201)569-8500
Periodic.

★4230★
Automotive Jobbers in the U.S.A. (MEMA)
Motor and Equipment Manufacturers Association (MEMA)
300 Sylvan Ave.
PO Box 1638
Englewood Cliffs, NJ 07632-0638   Phone: (201)569-8500

★4231★
Cost of Doing Business Study (NAEDA)
North American Equipment Dealers Association (NAEDA)
10877 Watson Rd.
St. Louis, MO 63127   Phone: (314)821-7220
Annual.

★4232★
Farm and Power Equipment Dealer (NAEDA)
North American Equipment Dealers Association (NAEDA)
10877 Watson Rd.
St. Louis, MO 63127   Phone: (314)821-7220
Monthly. Magazine providing management and marketing information for farm, lawn and garden, and industrial equipment dealers. Also includes tax and legislative information, sales tips, and management hints, advertisers index, and statistics.

★4233★
MEMA Marketing Insight (MEMA)
Motor and Equipment Manufacturers Association (MEMA)
300 Sylvan Ave.
PO Box 1638
Englewood Cliffs, NJ 07632-0638   Phone: (201)569-8500
Quarterly.

--- **Other Sources of Information** ---

★4234★
Distributors Financial Analysis (MEMA)
Motor and Equipment Manufacturers Association (MEMA)
300 Sylvan Ave.
PO Box 1638
Englewood Cliffs, NJ 07632-0638   Phone: (201)569-8500

General Maintenance Mechanics

General maintenance mechanics repair and maintain all manner of mechanical equipment, machines, and buildings, as opposed to most craft workers who specialize in one kind of work. They may work on plumbing, electrical, and heating and cooling systems. Other projects may include drywall repairs, and roof, floor, and window maintenance and repairs. They also have knowledge of specialized equipment and machinery often found in cafeterias, laundries, hospitals, and factories. General maintenance mechanics inspect and diagnose problems and plan how the work will be done. They use a variety of common hand and power tools such as drills and wrenches. Nearly 30% of general maintenance mechanics work in service industries; most work for elementary and secondary schools, colleges, and universities, hospitals and nursing homes, and hotels. About 25% are employed by the manufacturing industry. Others work for real estate firms that operate office and apartment buildings and for wholesale and retail firms, government agencies, and gas and electric companies.

$alaries

Earnings vary widely by industry, geographic area, and skill level but generally are between $6.00 and $13.00 an hour.

Employment Outlook

Growth rate until the year 2000: Average.

General Maintenance Mechanics

Career Guides

★4235★
Building Maintenance Management
Sheridan House, Inc.
145 Palisade St.
Dobbs Ferry, NY 10522   Phone: (914)693-2410
Reginald Lee. Third edition, 1987.

★4236★
Career Success Series
Cambridge Career Products
90 MacCorkle Ave., SW
South Charleston, WV 25311   Phone: (304)744-9323
Videocassette. 1986. 15 mins. A series, available separately, outlining various career choices for students. Occupations include: flight service, air transportation/ground service, data processing, carpentry, clerk in banking/insurance, commodity sales, cosmetic personal grooming, fire fighting, forestry services, home economics, insulation/roofing, material handling, mechanics, photographic processing, pipefitting and plumbing, police science, printing, secretarial services, and utilities equipment operator.

★4237★
General and Mechanical Maintenance Training Program
NUS Training Corporation
910 Clopper Rd.
Gaithersburg, MD 20878-1399   Phone: (301)258-8763
Videocassette. 1980. 60 mins. This series is designed to improve the skills of personnel currently assigned to maintenance work or to provide newly assigned personnel with the skills required to become accomplished maintenance personnel. Programs available as a series or individually.

★4238★
"General Maintenance Mechanics" in *Occupational Outlook Handbook* (pp. 344-345)
Superintendent of Documents
U.S. Government Printing Office
Washington, DC 20402   Phone: (202)783-3238
Biennial; latest edition, 1990-91. Encyclopedia of careers describing more than 250 occupations and comprising about 86 percent of all jobs in the economy. Occupations that require lengthy education or training are given the most attention. For each occupation, the handbook describes job duties, working conditions, training, educational preparation, personal qualities, advancement possibilities, job outlook, earnings, and sources of additional information.

★4239★
"General Maintenance Mechanics" in Volume 3 of *Career Discovery Encyclopedia* (pp. 68-69)
J.G. Ferguson Publishing Co.
200 W. Monroe
Chicago, IL 60606   Phone: (312)580-5480
E. Russell Primm, editor-in-chief. 1990. Contains two-page articles on 504 occupations. Each article describes job duties, earnings, and educational and training requirements.

★4240★
"General Maintenance Mechanics" in Volume 3 of *The Encyclopedia of Careers and Vocational Guidance* (pp. 514-518)
J.G. Ferguson Publishing Co.
200 W. Monroe
Chicago, IL 60606   Phone: (312)580-5480
William E. Hopke, editor-in-chief. Eighth edition, 1990. Four-volume set that profiles 500 occupations and describes job trends in 76 industries. Includes career description, educational requirements, history of the job, methods of entry, advancement, employment outlook, earnings, working conditions, social and psychological factors, and sources of additional information.

★4241★
Lawn and Garden Equipment Technicians
Chronicle Guidance Publications, Inc.
PO Box 1190
Moravia, NY 13118-1190   Phone: (315)497-0330
1987. This career brief describes the nature of the work, working conditions, hours and earnings, education and training, licensure, certification, unions, personal qualifications, social and psychological factors, employment outlook, entry methods, advancement, and related occupations. **Toll-free/Additional Phone Number(s):** 800-622-7284.

★4242★
"Maintenance Mechanics" in *The American Almanac of Jobs and Salaries* (pp. 503)
Avon Books
105 Madison Avenue
New York, NY 10016   Phone: (212)481-5600
John Wright and Edward J. Dwyer. Revised and updated, 1990. A comprehensive guide to the wages of hundreds of occupations in a wide variety of industries and organizations.

★4243★
Maintenance Mechanics Qualification Program
Technical Association of the Pulp & Paper Industry
Technology Park/Atlanta
PO Box 105113
Atlanta, GA 30348   Phone: (404)446-1400
Clint C. Bell. Second edition, 1989.

★4244★
Mechanics
Morris Video
2730 Monterey St. #105
Monterey Business Park
Torrance, CA 90503   Phone: (213)533-4800
Videocassette. 1984. 15 mins. Various careers in repair are examined including aircraft, motorcycle, diesel, refrigeration and heavy equipment.

★4245★
Vocations U.S.A.
Info-Disc Corporation
4 Professional Dr.
Gaithersburg, MD 20879   Phone: (301)948-2300
Videocassette. 1987. 60 mins. A disc collection outlining the requirements and methods of various career areas. Occupations include: transportation, mechanical/repair, health, agriculture, and construction.

Associations

★4246★
General Society of Mechanics and Tradesmen (GSMT)
20 W. 44th St.
New York, NY 10036   Phone: (212)840-1840
Purpose: Operates Mechanics Institute, founded in 1820, which offers free evening classes in architectural drafting, mechanical drafting, plumbing and sanitation, and industrial electricity.

Test Guides

★4247★
Building Custodian - Building Superintendent - Custodian Engineer
Prentice Hall Press
Simon & Schuster Inc.
200 Old Tappan Rd.
Old Tappan, NJ 07675   Phone: (800)223-2348
Robert Padula and Hy Hammer. Eighth edition, 1990. Contains past exams with questions on plumbing, electrical, and structural repairs and the operation and maintenance of the heating system, plus material on the effective supervision of maintenance and custodial workers.

★4248★
Electronic Equipment Maintainer
National Learning Corp.
212 Michael Dr.
Syosset, NY 11791   Phone: (516)921-8888
Jack Rudman. Part of the Career Examination Series No. 1. All examination guides in this series contain questions with answers. **Facsimile Number:** (516)921-8743. **Toll-free/Additional Phone Number(s):** 800-645-6337.

★4249★
Foreman of Mechanics
National Learning Corp.
212 Michael Dr.
Syosset, NY 11791   Phone: (516)921-8888
Jack Rudman. Part of the Career Examination Series No. 1. All examination guides in this series contain questions with answers. **Facsimile Number:** (516)921-8743. **Toll-free/Additional Phone Number(s):** 800-645-6337.

★4250★
Foreman (Structures Group A-H)
National Learning Corp.
212 Michael Dr.
Syosset, NY 11791   Phone: (516)921-8888
Jack Rudman. Group of seven study guides that are part of the Career Examination Series No. 1. These guides cover structures foreman examinations in carpentry, masonry, iron work, sheet metal, plumbing, painting, and heating and air conditioning. All examination guides in this series contain questions with answers. **Facsimile Number:** (516)921-8743. **Toll-free/Additional Phone Number(s):** 800-645-6337.

★4251★
Maintenance Mechanic
Prentice Hall Press
Simon & Schuster Inc.
200 Old Tappan Rd.
Old Tappan, NJ 07675   Phone: (800)223-2348
Hy Hammer. First edition, 1988. Provides information for applicants interested in the following entry-level civil service positions: mason's helper, elevator mechanic's helper, mechanical maintainer's helper, among others.

★4252★
Mechanical Maintainer
National Learning Corp.
212 Michael Dr.
Syosset, NY 11791   Phone: (516)921-8888
Jack Rudman. Part of the Career Examination Series No. 1. All examination guides in this series contain questions with answers. **Facsimile Number:** (516)921-8743. **Toll-free/Additional Phone Number(s):** 800-645-6337.

★4253★
Structure Maintainer (Groups A-H)
National Learning Corp.
212 Michael Dr.
Syosset, NY 11791   Phone: (516)921-8888
Jack Rudman. Part of the Career Examination Series No. 1. All examination guides in this series contain questions with answers and include tests for carpentry, masonry, iron work, sheet metal, plumbing, sign painting, painting, air conditioning and heating. **Facsimile Number:** (516)921-8743. **Toll-free/Additional Phone Number(s):** 800-645-6337.

★4254★
Structure Maintainer Trainee (Groups A-H)
National Learning Corp.
212 Michael Dr.
Syosset, NY 11791   Phone: (516)921-8888
Jack Rudman. Part of the Career Examination Series No. 1. All examination guides in this series contain questions with answers and include trainee tests for carpentry, masonry, iron work, plumbing, painting, and air conditioning and heating. **Facsimile Number:** (516)921-8743. **Toll-free/Additional Phone Number(s):** 800-645-6337.

General Maintenance Mechanics

Basic Reference Guides and Handbooks

★4255★
Maintenance Management Handbook
Fairmont Press, Inc.
700 Indian Trail
Lilburn, GA 30247   Phone: (404)925-9388
S. T. Cordero.

★4256★
The Maintenance Mechanic's-Machinist's Toolbox Manual
Prentice Hall
Rte. 9W
Englewood Cliffs, NJ 07632   Phone: (201)592-2000
John D. Bies. 1989.

★4257★
Maintenance Supplies—Buyers' Guide Issue
PTN Publishing Co.
445 Broad Hollow Rd.
Melville, NY 11747   Phone: (516)845-2700
Susan Brady, editor. Annual, December. Approximately 1,000 suppliers and associations for commercial, industrial, and institutional maintenance contractors; international coverage. Entries include: Company name, address, phone, names and titles of key personnel, product/service. Arrangement: Classified by product/service. **Facsimile Number:** (516)845-7109.

★4258★
Planned Maintenance
Didactic Systems, Inc.
PO Box 457
Cranford, NJ 07016   Phone: (201)789-2194
Didactic Systems Staff. 1969. Part of Simulation Game Series.

★4259★
Practical Guide Maintenance Engineering
Butterworth-Heinemann
80 Montvale Ave.
Stoneham, MA 02180   Phone: (617)438-8464
C. Dunlop. 1990. **Facsimile Number:** (617)279-4851

Periodicals

★4260★
Installation & Cleaning Specialist
Specialist Publications, Inc.
17835 Ventura Blvd., Ste. 312
Encino, CA 91316   Phone: (818)345-3550
Howard Olansky, Editor and Publisher. Monthly. Trade magazine for floor covering installers, workrooms, contractors, installing retailers, cleaning and maintenance firms, and distributors. **Facsimile Number:** (818)344-9647.

★4261★
Services
Building Service Contractors Assn. Int'l.
10201 Lee Hwy., Ste. 225
Fairfax, VA 22030   Phone: (703)359-7090
Robert E. Simanski, Editor. Monthly. Trade journal for maintenance and cleaning contractors. Facsimile Number: (703)352-0493.

Meetings and Conventions

★4262★
International Maintenance Institute Show and Technical Conference
International Maintenance Institute
PO Box 266695
Houston, TX 77207   Phone: (713)481-0869
1992; Oct. 01-02; Pasadena, TX. **Facsimile Number:** (713)481-8337.

Heating, Air-Conditioning, and Refrigeration Mechanics

Heating, air-conditioning, and refrigeration mechanics, also known as technicians, install, maintain, and repair heating, air-conditioning and refrigeration systems in residential, commercial, industrial, and other buildings. Mechanics must be able to maintain, diagnose, and correct problems within the entire system. They adjust system controls to recommended settings and test the performance of the entire system using special tools and test equipment. Mechanics may specialize in installation or maintenance and repair. They may also specialize in a particular type of equipment. However, more and more technicians do both installation and servicing, and work with a variety of equipment. Heating equipment technicians, also called furnace installers, follow blueprints or other specifications to install oil, gas, electric, solid-fuel, and multifuel heating systems. After installation, they perform routine maintenance to keep the system operating efficiently. Air-conditioning and refrigeration mechanics install and service central air-conditioning systems and a variety of refrigeration equipment following blueprints, design specifications, and manufacturers' instructions. Once installed, they also perform necessary maintenance. Technicians use a wide range of tools including drills and torches. They also use a variety of testing devices such as voltmeters and pressure gauges. About 50% of the heating, air-conditioning, and refrigeration mechanics work for cooling and heating contractors. The remainder work for fuel oil dealers, utilities, and service and repair shops. Others are employed by the federal government, hospitals, office buildings, and other organizations. About 15% of mechanics are self-employed.

$alaries

Median weekly earnings of air-conditioning, heating, amd refrigeration mechanics who are wage and salary workers is $414.00.

Lowest 10 percent	$265/week or less
Middle 50 percent	$322-567/week
Top 10 percent	$726/week or more

Employment Outlook

Growth rate until the year 2000: Average.

Heating, Air-Conditioning, and Refrigeration Mechanics

Career Guides

★4263★
"Air Conditioning and Heating Technician" in *Construction*, Volume 4 of *Career Information Center* (pp. 91-92)
Glencoe/Macmillan
15319 Chatsworth St.
Mission Hills, CA 91345   Phone: (818)898-1391
Richard Lidz and Dale Anderson, editorial directors. Fourth edition, 1990. For 600 occupations, describes job duties, entry-level requirements, education and training needed, advancement possibilities, employment outlook, earnings and benefits. The set is divided into 12 volumes. Each volume includes jobs related under a broad career field. Volume 13 is the index. **Facsimile Number:** 818-365-5489.

★4264★
Air-Conditioning and Refrigeration
Chronicle Guidance Publications, Inc.
PO Box 1190
Moravia, NY 13118-1190   Phone: (315)497-0330
1990. This career brief describes the nature of the work, working conditions, hours and earnings, education and training, licensure, certification, unions, personal qualifications, social and psychological factors, employment outlook, entry methods, advancement, and related occupations. **Toll-free/Additional Phone Number(s):** 800-622-7284.

★4265★
Air Conditioning and Refrigeration Mechanic
Careers, Inc.
PO Box 135
Largo, FL 34649-0135   Phone: (813)584-7333
1991. Two-page occupational summary card describing duties, working conditions, personal qualifications, training, earnings and hours, employment outlook, places of employment, related careers and where to write for more information.

★4266★
"Air-Conditioning and Refrigeration Mechanic" in *Occu-Facts: Information on 565 Careers in Outline Form* (p. 15.17)
Careers, Inc.
P.O. Box 135
1211 Tenth St., S.W.
Largo, FL 33640   Phone: (813)584-7333
Elizabeth Handville. Biennial, 1989-90 edition. Each one-page occupational profile describes duties, working conditions, physical surroundings and demands, aptitudes, temperament, educational requirements, employment outlook, earnings, and places of employment.

★4267★
"Air Conditioning, Heating, and Refrigeration Mechanic" in *Construction*, Volume 4 of *Career Information Center* (pp. 37-39)
Glencoe/Macmillan
15319 Chatsworth St.
Mission Hills, CA 91345   Phone: (818)898-1391
Richard Lidz and Dale Anderson, editorial directors. Fourth edition, 1990. For 600 occupations, describes job duties, entry-level requirements, education and training needed, advancement possibilities, employment outlook, earnings and benefits. The set is divided into 12 volumes. Each volume includes jobs related under a broad career field. Volume 13 is the index. **Facsimile Number:** 818-365-5489.

★4268★
"Air Conditioning, Heating, and Refrigeration Mechanics" in *The American Almanac of Jobs and Salaries* (p. 522)
Avon Books
105 Madison Avenue
New York, NY 10016   Phone: (212)481-5600
John Wright and Edward J. Dwyer. Revised and updated, 1990. A comprehensive guide to the wages of hundreds of occupations in a wide variety of industries and organizations.

★4269★
Air Conditioning/Heating/Solar Technician
Careers, Inc.
PO Box 135
Largo, FL 34649-0135   Phone: (813)584-7333
1988. Two-page occupational summary card describing duties, working conditions, personal qualifications, training, earnings and hours, employment outlook, places of employment, related careers and where to write for more information.

★4270★
"Air-Conditioning/Heating/Solar Technician" in *Occu-Facts: Information on 565 Careers in Outline Form* (p. 10.6)
Careers, Inc.
P.O. Box 135
1211 Tenth St., S.W.
Largo, FL 33640   Phone: (813)584-7333
Elizabeth Handville. Biennial, 1989-90 edition. Each one-page occupational profile describes duties, working conditions, physical surroundings and demands, aptitudes, temperament, educational requirements, employment outlook, earnings, and places of employment.

★4271★
"Air Conditioning, Refrigeration, and Heating Mechanic" in *Exploring Nontraditional Jobs for Women* (pp. 76-82)
Rosen Publishing Group, Inc.
29 E. 21st St.
New York, NY 10010   Phone: (212)777-3017
Rose Neufeld. 1989. Describes blue-collar, male dominated occupations. Discusses what is done on the job, training, where to apply for jobs, tools used, salaries, and advantages and disadvantages. Relates the experiences of women who are working in the field.

★4272★
"Air-Conditioning, Refrigeration, and Heating Mechanic" in *VGM's Careers Encyclopedia* (pp. 29-32)
National Textbook Co.
4255 W. Touhy Ave.
Lincolnwood, IL 60646   Phone: (312)679-5500
Third edition, 1991. Contains two- to five-page descriptions of 200 managerial, professional, technical, trade, and service occupations. Each profile includes job duties, places of employment, qualifications, educational preparation, training, employment potential, advancement, income, and additional sources of information.

★4273★
"Air-Conditioning, Refrigeration, and Heating Mechanics" in Volume 3 of *The Encyclopedia of Careers and Vocational Guidance* (pp. 466-470)
J.G. Ferguson Publishing Co.
200 W. Monroe
Chicago, IL 60606   Phone: (312)580-5480
William E. Hopke, editor-in-chief. Eighth edition, 1990. Four-volume set that profiles 500 occupations and describes job trends in 76 industries. Includes career description, educational requirements, history of the job, methods of entry, advancement, employment outlook, earnings, working conditions, social and psychological factors, and sources of additional information.

★4274★
Construction: Basic Principles
RMI Media Productions, Inc.
2807 West 47th St.
Shawnee Mission, KS 66205   Phone: (913)262-3974
Videocassette. 1984. 20 mins. This series of five programs of varying lengths covers different aspects of career opportunities in the construction trades. Included are: concrete masonry, carpentry, electrical work, plumbing, and heating and air conditioning.

★4275★
Do Your Own Thing. in the Mechanical Field
AIMS Media, Inc.
9710 DeSoto Ave.
Chatsworth, CA 93111-4409   Phone: (818)773-4300
Videocassette. 1979. 16 mins. Various job levels in the mechanical field are outlined for students.

★4276★
"Heating, Air-Conditioning, and Refrigeration Mechanics" in *Jobs! What They Are...Where They Are...What They Pay* (pp. 176-178)
Simon & Schuster, Inc.
Simon & Schuster Bldg.
1230 Avenue of the Americas
New York, NY 10020   Phone: (212)698-7000
Robert O. Snelling and Anne M. Snelling. Revised edition, 1989. Profiles 241 occupations, describing duties and responsibilities, educational preparation, earnings, employment opportunities, training, and qualifications.

★4277★
"Heating, Air-Conditioning, and Refrigeration Mechanics" in *Occupational Outlook Handbook* (pp. 345-347)
Superintendent of Documents
U.S. Government Printing Office
Washington, DC 20402   Phone: (202)783-3238
Biennial; latest edition, 1990-91. Encyclopedia of careers describing more than 250 occupations and comprising about 86 percent of all jobs in the economy. Occupations that require lengthy education or training are given the most attention. For each occupation, the handbook describes job duties, working conditions, training, educational preparation, personal qualities, advancement possibilities, job outlook, earnings, and sources of additional information.

★4278★
"Heating and Air Conditioning Installers" in *Opportunities in Building Construction Trades* (pp. 57-58)
National Textbook Co.
4255 W. Touhy Ave.
Lincolnwood, IL 60646   Phone: (312)679-5500
Michael Sumichrast. 1989. Gives an overview of the construction industry and describes the jobs of various craftworkers. Covers different kinds of builders: home, custom; and describes management skills needed and industry trends affecting opportunities.

★4279★
"Heating and Cooling Mechanics" in Volume 3 of *Career Discovery Encyclopedia* (pp. 98-99)
J.G. Ferguson Publishing Co.
200 W. Monroe
Chicago, IL 60606   Phone: (312)580-5480
E. Russell Primm, editor-in-chief. 1990. Contains two-page articles on 504 occupations. Each article describes job duties, earnings, and educational and training requirements.

★4280★
Heating and Cooling Service
Vocational Biographies, Inc.
PO Box 31, Dept. VF10
Sauk Centre, MN 56378   Phone: (612)352-6516
1989. This pamphlet profiles a person working in the job. Includes information about job duties, working conditions, places of employment, educational preparation, labor market outlook, and salaries. **Toll-free/Additional Phone Number(s):** 800-255-0752.

Heating, Air-Conditioning, and Refrigeration Mechanics

★4281★
"Heating and Cooling Technicians" in Volume 3 of
Career Discovery Encyclopedia (pp. 100-101)
J.G. Ferguson Publishing Co.
200 W. Monroe
Chicago, IL 60606　　　　　　　　Phone: (312)580-5480
E. Russell Primm, editor-in-chief. 1990. Contains two-page articles on 504 occupations. Each article describes job duties, earnings, and educational and training requirements.

★4282★
"Heating, Cooling, and Refrigeration" in *Opportunities in Plumbing and Pipefitting Careers* (pp. 83-85)
National Textbook Co.
4255 W. Touhy Ave.
Lincolnwood, IL 60646　　　　　　Phone: (312)679-5500
Patrick J. Galvin. 1989. Describes the work, jobs, educational preparation, training, apprenticeships, a typical working day, salaries, future trends, and related fields.

★4283★
"Heating, Ventilation and Air Conditioning" in *The Career Connection II: A Guide to Technical Majors and Their Related Careers* (pp. 67-68)
T
ERIS
PO Box 7509
University Station
Provo, UT 84602-0509
Fred A. Rowe. 1988. Contains technical majors, such as automotive technology. Describes the major and the job. Lists high school and postsecondary school courses. Includes occupations related to the major, employment outlook, and starting salary.

★4284★
Mechanics
Morris Video
2730 Monterey St. #105
Monterey Business Park
Torrance, CA 90503　　　　　　　Phone: (213)533-4800
Videocassette. 1984. 15 mins. Various careers in repair are examined including aircraft, motorcycle, diesel, refrigeration and heavy equipment.

★4285★
"Mechanics: Air-Conditioning, Heating, and Refrigeration" in *Opportunities in Vocational and Technical Careers* (pp. 105-106)
National Textbook Co.
4255 W. Touhy Ave.
Lincolnwood, IL 60646　　　　　　Phone: (312)679-5500
Adrian A. Paradis. 1987. Describes careers which can be prepared for by attending a private vocational or proprietary school—office employee, sales worker, service worker, health services, mechanic, craftworker, and technician. Covers employment outlook, job duties, and salaries. Offers career planning advice.

★4286★
Repair Cluster
Center for Humanities, Inc.
Communications Park
Box 1000
Mount Kisco, NY 10549　　　　　　Phone: (914)666-4100
Videocassette. 1984. 15 mins. People who work in the fields of Heating/Air Conditioning Repair, and Radio/TV Repair describe what it's like to work at their jobs.

★4287★
Video Career Library - Mechanical Fields
Careers, Inc.
1211 10th St., SW
PO Box 135
Largo, FL 34649-0135　　　　　　Phone: (813)584-7333
Videocassette. 1990. 22 mins. Part of the Video Career Library covering 165 occupations. Shows actual workers on the job. Includes automobile mechanics, diesel engine mechanics, aircraft engine mechanics, automobile body repairers, heavy equipment mechanics, heating/air-conditioning/refrigeration mechanics.

★4288★
Would You Like a Career That Pays Well, Helps People, and Provides Exceptional Opportunities?
Air Conditioning and Refrigeration Institute
1501 Wilson Blvd., 6th Fl.
Arlington, VA 22209　　　　　　　Phone: (703)534-8800
An eight-panel brochure describes job opportunities in the air conditioning and refrigeration industry.

★4289★
Your Future in the Plumbing Heating Cooling Industry
National Association of Plumbing, Heating, and Cooling Contractors
P.O. Box 6808
180 S. Washington St.
Washington, DC 20046　　　　　　Phone: (202)331-7675
1988. This eight-panel brochure describes the work, opportunities, working conditions, and entry into the field.

――――――――― **Associations** ―――――――――

★4290★
Associated Builders and Contractors (ABC)
729 15th St. NW
Washington, DC 20005　　　　　　Phone: (202)637-8800
Membership: Construction contractors, subcontractors, suppliers, and associates. **Purpose:** Aim is to foster and perpetuate the principles of rewarding shop construction workers and management on the basis of merit. Sponsors leadership conference and management education programs including Wheels of Learning; also sponsors apprenticeship and skill training programs. Disseminates technological and labor relations information. Maintains biographical archives and placement service. Bestows awards; compiles statistics. **Publications:** *ABC Newsline*, semimonthly. • *The Builder and Contractor*, monthly. • *Classified Membership Directory*, annual. • Also publishes safety manuals.

★4291★
National Association of Home Builders of the U.S. (NAHB)
15th and M Sts. NW
Washington, DC 20005　　　　　　Phone: (202)822-0200
Membership: Single and multifamily home builders, commercial builders, and others associated with the building industry. **Purpose:** Lobbies on behalf of the housing industry and conducts public affairs activities to increase public understanding of housing and the economy. Collects and disseminates data on current developments in home building and home builders' plans through its Economics Department and nationwide Metropolitan Housing Forecast. Maintains NAHB Research Center, which functions as the research arm of the home building industry. Sponsors seminars and workshops on construction, mortgage credit, labor relations, cost reduction, land use, remodeling, and business management. Sponsors competitions; bestows awards; compiles statistics; offers

charitable program, spokesman training, and placement service; maintains speakers' bureau, biographical archives, hall of fame, and extensive library on housing. Subsidiaries include Home Builders Institute and National Council of the Housing Industry. Maintains over 50 committees in many areas of construction; operates National Commercial Builders Council, National Council of the Multifamily Housing Industry, National Remodelers Council, and National Sales and Marketing Council. **Publications:** *Builder Magazine*, monthly. • *Economic News Notes*, monthly. • *Homes and Homebuilding*, annual. • *Library Bulletin*, monthly. • *Nation's Building News*, semimonthly. • Also publishes bibliographies, booklets, and manuals. **Toll-free/Additional Phone Number(s):** (800)221-NAHB Audio Feed Line.

★4292★
National Association of Plumbing-Heating-Cooling Contractors (NAPHCC)
PO Box 6808
180 S. Washington St.
Falls Church, VA 22040 Phone: (703)237-8100

Membership: Federation of state and local associations of plumbing, heating, and cooling contractors. **Purpose:** Seeks to advance sanitation, encourage sanitary laws, and generally improve the plumbing, heating, ventilating, and air conditioning industries. Conducts apprenticeship training programs, workshops, and seminars; cooperates with Plumbing-Heating-Cooling Information Bureau. **Publications:** *Contractor's Connection*, 18/year. • *Leadership Directory*, annual. • *News*, monthly. • Also publishes technical, safety, estimating, and business publications and videotapes. **Toll-free/Additional Phone Number(s):** (800)533-7694. **Facsimile Number:** (703)237-7442.

★4293★
Refrigeration Service Engineers Society (RSES)
1666 Rand Rd.
Des Plaines, IL 60016-3552 Phone: (708)297-6464

Membership: Persons engaged in refrigeration, air-conditioning and heating installation, service, sales, and maintenance. **Purpose:** Conducts training courses. **Publications:** *Refrigeration Service and Contracting*, monthly. • Also publishes service application manual.

── **Standards/Certification Agencies** ──

Some mechanics learn the trade through apprenticeship programs that are frequently run by joint committees representing local chapters of the Air-Conditioning Contractors of America, the Mechanical Contractors Association of America, and the Sheet Metal Workers' International Association, or the United Association of Journeymen and Apprentices of the Plumbing and Pipefitting Industry of the United States and Canada. Other apprenticeship programs are sponsored by local chapters of the Associated Builders and Contractors and the Home Builders Institute of the National Association of Home Builders. These programs generally last three or four years and combine on-the-job training with 144 hours of classroom instruction each year.

── **Test Guides** ──

★4294★
Air Conditioning, Heating & Refrigeration Mechanic
National Learning Corp.
212 Michael Dr.
Syosset, NY 11791 Phone: (516)921-8888

Jack Rudman. Part of the Career Examination Series No. 1. All examination guides in this series contain questions with answers. **Facsimile Number:** (516)921-8743. **Toll-free/Additional Phone Number(s):** 800-645-6337.

★4295★
Automatic Heating
National Learning Corp.
212 Michael Dr.
Syosset, NY 11791 Phone: (516)921-8888

Jack Rudman. 1989. Part of Occupational Competency Examination Series.

★4296★
Refrigerating Machine Mechanic
National Learning Corp.
212 Michael Dr.
Syosset, NY 11791 Phone: (516)921-8888

Jack Rudman. Part of the Career Examination Series No. 1. All examination guides in this series contain questions with answers. **Facsimile Number:** (516)921-8743. **Toll-free/Additional Phone Number(s):** 800-645-6337.

★4297★
What Do You Know about Air Conditioning, Refrigeration & Heating
National Learning Corporation
212 Michael Dr.
Syosset, NY 11791 Phone: (516)921-8888

Jack Rudman. 1990. Part of Test Your Knowledge Series.

── **Educational Directories and Programs** ──

★4298★
New England Fuel Institute
P.O. Box 888
Watertown, MA 02272

Provides information on career opportunities and training in heating, air conditioning and refrigeration mechanics.

── **Basic Reference Guides and Handbooks** ──

★4299★
Air-to-Air Heat Exchangers: Directory and Buyers' Guide
Cutter Information Corporation
37 Broadway
Arlington, MA 02174 Phone: (617)648-8700

J.D. Ned Nisson, editor. Published 1987. Guide that compares various types of air-to-air heat exchangers. Provides purchasing information and a directory section that lists manufacturers and dealers of residential air-to-air heat exchangers. Arrangement:

Heating, Air-Conditioning, and Refrigeration Mechanics ★4315★

Organized into seven tables. **Toll-free/Additional Phone Number(s):** (800)888-8939. **Facsimile Number:** (617)648-8707.

★4300★
ASHRAE Pocket Guide for Air-Conditioning, Heating, Ventilation & Refrigeration
American Society of Heating, Refrigerating & Air Conditioning Engineers
1791 Tullie Circle NE
Atlanta, GA 30329   Phone: (404)636-8400
Carl McPhee, editor. Revised edition, 1989. **Facsimile Number:** (404)321-5478.

★4301★
Combustion Hot Spot Analysis for Fired Process Heaters: Prediction, Control, Troubleshooting
Gulf Publishing Company
PO Box 2608
Houston, TX 77252   Phone: (713)529-4301
E. Talmor. 1982. **Facsimile Number:** (713)520-4438.

★4302★
Faber & Kell's Heating & Air Conditioning of Buildings
Butterworth-Heinemann
80 Montvale Ave.
Stoneham, MA 02180   Phone: (617)438-8464
P. L. Martin. Seventh edition, 1989. **Facsimile Number:** (617)279-4851.

★4303★
Heating, Cooling & Lighting
John Wiley & Sons, Inc.
605 3rd Ave.
New York, NY 10158   Phone: (212)850-6000
Herbert M. Lechner. 1991. **Facsimile Number:** (212)850-6088.

★4304★
Heating System Troubleshooting Handbook
Prentice Hall
Rte. 9W
Englewood Cliffs, NJ 07632   Phone: (201)592-2000
Billy C. Langley. 1988.

★4305★
Heating, Ventilating & Air Conditioning
Prentice Hall
Rte. 9W
Englewoods Cliffs, NJ 07632   Phone: (201)592-2000
George Clifford. 1984.

★4306★
Home Heating & Air Conditioning Systems
TAB Books
Blue Ridge Summit, PA 17294-0850   Phone: (717)794-2191
James L. Kittle. 1989.

★4307★
Homes and Homebuilding (NAHB)
National Association of Home Builders of the U.S. (NAHB)
15th and M Sts. NW
Washington, DC 20005   Phone: (202)822-0200
Annual.

★4308★
IBPAT Directory (IBPAT)
International Brotherhood of Painters and Allied Trades (IBPAT)
United Unions Bldg.
1750 New York Ave., NW
Washington, DC 20006   Phone: (202)637-0720
Annual.

★4309★
Introduction to Air Conditioning, Refrigeration & Heating
National Learning Corp.
212 Michael Dr.
Syosset, NY 11791   Phone: (516)921-8888
Jack Rudman. 1989. Part of DANTES Series.

★4310★
Mathematics for the Heating, Ventilating & Cooling Trades
Prentice Hall
Rte. 9W
Englewoods Cliffs, NJ 07632   Phone: (201)592-2000
David L. Goetsch. 1988.

★4311★
Modern Heating, Ventilating & Air Conditioning
Prentice Hall
Rte. 9W
Englewood Cliffs, NJ 07632   Phone: (201)592-2000
George Clifford. 1990.

★4312★
The News HVAC/R Directory AHeating, ventilation, air conditioning, and refrigeration industriesA
Business News Publishing Co.
755 W. Big Beaver, 10th Fl.
Troy, MI 48084   Phone: (313)362-3700
Carolynn Perucca, editor. Annual, January. Manufacturers, wholesalers, exporters, associations, products, consultants, and manufacturers' representatives. Entries include: Contact name, company, address, phone, fax, and product descriptions. **Facsimile Number:** (313)362-0317.

★4313★
Oil Heat Technician's Manual
Kendall/Hunt Publishing Company
2460 Kerper Blvd.
Dubuque, IA 52001   Phone: (319)588-1451
P.M.E.F. Staff. 1990.

★4314★
Residential Heating Operations & Troubleshooting
Prentice Hall
Rte 9W
Englewood Cliffs, NJ 07632   Phone: (201)592-2000
John E. Traister. 1985.

★4315★
Wholesaler—"Wholesaling 100" Issue APlumbing and heatingA
Delta Communications, Inc.
400 N. Michigan Ave.
Chicago, IL 60611   Phone: (312)222-2000
Mary Ann Falkman, Editorial Director, editor. Annual, July. 100 leading wholesalers of plumbing-heating equipment and supplies. Entries include: Company name, address, phone, telex, names and titles of key personnel, number of employees, business breakdown (percentage). Arrangement: Ranked by sales. **Facsimile Number:** (312)222-2026.

Periodicals

★4316★
ACCA News
Air Conditioning Contractors of America (ACCA)
1513 16th St. NW
Washington, DC 20036   Phone: (202)483-9370
Editor(s): Elaine W. Smith. 10/yr. Reports on ACCA members, activities, and issues. Covers trends in the heating, ventilating, and air conditioning industries that affect contractors. Discusses management, legal issues, and new technology. Recurring features include editorials and a calendar of events. **Facsimile Number:** (202)234-4721.

★4317★
Air Conditioning, Heating and Refrigeration News
Business News Publishing Co.
PO Box 2600
Troy, MI 48007   Phone: (313)362-3700
Thomas A. Mahoney, Editor. Weekly. Tabloid for HVAC and commercial refrigeration contractors, wholesalers, manufacturers, engineers, and owners/managers. **Facsimile Number:** (313)362-0317.

★4318★
Appliance Service News
Gamit Enterprises, Inc.
110 W. St. Charles Rd.
PO Box 789
Lombard, IL 60148   Phone: (708)932-9550
William Wingstedt, Editor and Publisher. Monthly. Magazine for appliance repairmen.

★4319★
ASHRAE Journal
American Society of Heating, Refrigerating and
Air-Conditioning Engineers
1791 Tullie Circle NE
Atlanta, GA 30329   Phone: (404)636-8400
William R. Coker, Editor. Monthly. Magazine for the heating, refrigeration, and air conditioning trade. **Facsimile Number:** (404)321-4578.

★4320★
The Builder and Contractor (ABC)
Associated Builders and Contractors (ABC)
729 15th St. NW
Washington, DC 20005   Phone: (202)637-8800
Monthly.

★4321★
Builder Magazine (NAHB)
National Association of Home Builders of the U.S. (NAHB)
15th and M Sts. NW
Washington, DC 20005   Phone: (202)822-0200
Monthly.

★4322★
Builder's Log
Better Heating-Cooling Council
35 Russo Pl.
PO Box 218
Berkeley Heights, NJ 07922   Phone: (201)464-8200
Editor(s): Richard W. Roth. Quarterly. Provides information about installing and maintaining heating equipment for the home building industry. Discusses complaints against certain systems and cites instances of builder- and utility-company fiascoes.

★4323★
Contractor's Connection (NAPHCC)
National Association of Plumbing-Heating-Cooling Contractors
   (NAPHCC)
PO Box 6808
180 S. Washington St.
Falls Church, VA 22040   Phone: (703)237-8100
18/year.

★4324★
Distributor
Technical Reporting Corp.
651 W. Washington St., Ste. 300
Chicago, IL 60661   Phone: (312)993-0929
Steve Read, Editor. Monthly. Magazine focusing on air conditioning, heating, ventilation, and plumbing. **Facsimile Number:** (312)993-0960.

★4325★
District Heating and Cooling
International District Heating and Cooling Assn.
1101 Connecticut Ave., Ste. 700
Washington, DC 20036   Phone: (202)429-5111
David F. Hobson, Editor. Quarterly. Heating and cooling magazine. **Facsimile Number:** (202)775-2625.

★4326★
Economic News Notes (NAHB)
National Association of Home Builders of the U.S. (NAHB)
15th and M Sts. NW
Washington, DC 20005   Phone: (202)822-0200
Monthly.

★4327★
HVAC Product News
Delta Communications, Inc.
400 N. Michigan
Chicago, IL 60611   Phone: (312)222-2000
Roland Winkler, Editor. 12x/yr. Heating, ventilating, and air conditioning magazine (tabloid). **Facsimile Number:** (312)222-2026.

★4328★
*Industrial Heating Equipment Association—Legislative
   Report*
Industrial Heating Equipment Association (IHEA)
1901 N. Moore St., Ste. 509
Arlington, VA 22209   Phone: (703)525-2513
Editor(s): James J. Houston. Quarterly. Presents news of government legislation of importance to the industrial heat processing industries.

Heating, Air-Conditioning, and Refrigeration Mechanics

★4329★
Koldfax
Air-Conditioning and Refrigeration Institute
1501 Wilson Blvd., Ste. 600
Arlington, VA 22209   Phone: (703)524-8800
Editor(s): Maura Shannon. Monthly. Supplies information on air conditioning and refrigeration for manufacturers of such equipment. Recurring features include statistics, legislative and regulatory news, technical updates, and international trade information.

★4330★
NAHB Library Bulletin (NAHB)
National Association of Home Builders of the U.S. (NAHB)
15th and M Sts. NW
Washington, DC 20005   Phone: (202)822-0200
Monthly.

★4331★
NAPHCC News (NAPHCC)
National Association of Plumbing-Heating-Cooling Contractors (NAPHCC)
PO Box 6808
180 S. Washington St.
Falls Church, VA 22040   Phone: (703)237-8100
Monthly.

★4332★
Nation's Building News (NAHB)
National Association of Home Builders of the U.S. (NAHB)
15th and M Sts. NW
Washington, DC 20005   Phone: (202)822-0200
Semimonthly. Tabloid newsletter providing the latest information concerning the housing industry, including finance, legislation, new technologies, and membership news.

★4333★
Palmetto Piper
Mechanical Contractor's Assn. of South Carolina
1504 Morninghill Dr.
PO Box 384
Columbia, SC 29202   Phone: (803)772-7834
Monthly. Plumbing, heating, air conditioning, and electrical journal.

★4334★
Reeves Journal: Plumbing Heating Cooling
Business News Publishing Co.
23187 La Cadena Dr., Ste. 101
PO Box 30700
Laguna Hills, CA 92654   Phone: (714)830-0881
Larry Dill, Editor. Monthly. Regional plumbing, heating, and cooling magazine. **Facsimile Number:** (714)859-7845.

★4335★
Refrigeration Service and Contracting (RSES)
Refrigeration Service Engineers Society (RSES)
1666 Rand Rd.
Des Plaines, IL 60016-3552   Phone: (708)297-6464
Monthly.

★4336★
RSC (Refrigeration Service and Contracting)
Business News Publishing Co.
PO Box 7021
Troy, MI 48007   Phone: (313)362-3700
Peter Powell, Editor. Monthly. Official magazine of the Refrigeration Service Engineer's Society; reporting on service, repair, installation, and replacement. **Facsimile Number:** (313)362-0317.

★4337★
Service Reporter
651 W. Washington St., Ste. 300
Chicago, IL 60606   Phone: (312)993-0929
Steve Read, Editor. Monthly. Magazine (tabloid) focusing on air conditioning and ventilation, heating, and refrigeration.

★4338★
Snips Magazine
407 Mannheim Rd.
Bellwood, IL 60104-9989   Phone: (708)544-3870
Nick Carter, Editor and Publisher. Monthly. Magazine for the sheet metal, warm-air heating, ventilating, and air conditioning industry. **Facsimile Number:** (708)544-3884.

★4339★
Southern Plumbing, Heating, Cooling
Southern Trade Publications, Inc.
Box 18343
Greensboro, NC 27419   Phone: (919)854-3033
Emmet Atkins, Jr., Publisher. Monthly. Trade magazine covering plumbing, heating, and air conditioning.

★4340★
Supply House Times
Horton Publishing Co.
7574 N. Lincoln Ave.
Skokie, IL 60077   Phone: (708)677-2707
Greg Cassel, Editor. Monthly. Trade magazine for wholesalers in plumbing, heating, cooling, piping, and water systems. Areas of major emphasis include: warehousing, materials handling, inventory control, accounting, data processing, merchandising, salesmanship and general management. **Facsimile Number:** (708)677-5003.

Meetings and Conventions

★4341★
International Air-Conditioning, Heating, Refrigerating Exposition
International Exposition Co.
200 Park Ave.
New York, NY 10166   Phone: (212)986-4232
1993; Jan. 25-28; Chicago, IL • 1994; Jan. 24-26; New Orleans, LA. **Facsimile Number:** (212)682-8982.

★4342★
Mobile Air Conditioning Society Trade Show and Technical Conference
Mobile Air Conditioning Society
1709 N. Broad St.
PO Box 1307
Lansdale, PA 19446   Phone: (215)362-5800
Frequency: Always held during mid-January. **Facsimile Number:** (215)855-7257.

★4343★
National Association of Plumbing-Heating-Cooling Contractors (NAPHCC)
PO Box 6808
180 S. Washington St.
Falls Church, VA 22040   Phone: (703)237-8100
1992; Oct. 20-24; Atlanta, GA • 1993; Oct. 13-17; Anaheim, CA. **Toll-free/Additional Phone Number(s):** (800)533-7694. **Facsimile Number:** (703)237-7442.

★4344★
REVAC - Refrigeration, Ventilation, Air-Conditioning, and Heating Exhibition
World Access Corp.
15 Bemis Rd.
PO Box 171
Wellesley Hills, MA 02181   Phone: (617)235-8095
Facsimile Number: (617)235-7360.

★4345★
Sheet Metal and Air-Conditioning Contractors National Association Convention
Sheet Metal and Air-Conditioning Contractors National Association
PO Box 70
Merrifield, VA 22116   Phone: (703)790-9890
1992; Seattle, WA • 1993; Boston, MA • 1994; Orlando, FL.

Home Appliance and Power Tool Repairers

Home appliance and power tool repairers, sometimes called service technicians, install and service a variety of household labor-saving appliances such as ovens, washers and dryers, vacuum cleaners, lawnmowers and power tools. Repairers in large shops generally specialize. Some may handle small appliances, others may service power tools. To determine why a piece of equipment fails, repairers look for frequent sources of trouble such as faulty wiring, and also consult service manuals. After diagnosing the problem, they make the necessary repairs or replacements. This often involves removing old parts and installing new ones. Common handtools such as soldering guns and screwdrivers, and special tools designed for particular appliances aid in this task. Repairers also answer customers' questions and complaints about appliances, and provide estimates of the cost of repairs. About 70% of repairers in this field work in retail trade establishments such as department stores, household appliance stores, and dealers that sell or service appliances and power tools. Others work for gas and electric utility companies, wholesalers, and electrical repair shops. About 10% of repairers in this field are self-employed.

$alaries

Earnings of home appliance and power tool repairers vary widely according to skill level, geographic location, and the type of equipment serviced. Average annual salaries for experienced technicians ranged from $15,000 to $24,000.

Employment Outlook

Growth rate until the year 2000: Employment is expected to remain level.

Home Appliance and Power Tool Repairers

Career Guides

★4346★
Appliance Repairer
Vocational Biographies, Inc.
PO Box 31, Dept. VF10
Sauk Centre, MN 56378 Phone: (612)352-6516
1990. This pamphlet profiles a person working in the job. Includes information about job duties, working conditions, places of employment, educational preparation, labor market outlook, and salaries. **Toll-free/Additional Phone Number(s):** 800-255-0752.

★4347★
"Appliance Repairer" in *VGM's Careers Encyclopedia* (pp. 44-46)
National Textbook Co.
4255 W. Touhy Ave.
Lincolnwood, IL 60646 Phone: (312)679-5500
Third edition, 1991. Contains two- to five-page descriptions of 200 managerial, professional, technical, trade, and service occupations. Each profile includes job duties, places of employment, qualifications, educational preparation, training, employment potential, advancement, income, and additional sources of information.

★4348★
"Appliance Repairers" in Volume 1 of *Career Discovery Encyclopedia* (pp. 46-47)
J.G. Ferguson Publishing Co.
200 W. Monroe
Chicago, IL 60606 Phone: (312)580-5480
E. Russell Primm, editor-in-chief. 1990. Contains two-page articles on 504 occupations. Each article describes job duties, earnings, and educational and training requirements.

★4349★
"Appliance Repairers" in Volume 3 of *The Encyclopedia of Careers and Vocational Guidance* (pp. 569-573)
J.G. Ferguson Publishing Co.
200 W. Monroe
Chicago, IL 60606 Phone: (312)580-5480
William E. Hopke, editor-in-chief. Eighth edition, 1990. Four-volume set that profiles 500 occupations and describes job trends in 76 industries. Includes career description, educational requirements, history of the job, methods of entry, advancement, employment outlook, earnings, working conditions, social and psychological factors, and sources of additional information.

★4350★
"Appliance Repairers" in *The American Almanac of Jobs and Salaries* (p. 523)
Avon Books
105 Madison Avenue
New York, NY 10016 Phone: (212)481-5600
John Wright and Edward J. Dwyer. Revised and updated, 1990. A comprehensive guide to the wages of hundreds of occupations in a wide variety of industries and organizations.

★4351★
Appliance Service Technician, Electrical
Careers, Inc.
PO Box 135
Largo, FL 34649-0135 Phone: (813)584-7333
1990. Eight-page brief offering the definition, history, duties, working conditions, personal qualifications, educational requirements, earnings, hours, employment outlook, advancement possibilities, and related occupations.

★4352★
"Appliance Service Worker" in *Consumer, Homemaking, and Personal Services*, Volume 5 of *Career Information Center* (pp. 65-66)
Glencoe/Macmillan
15319 Chatsworth St.
Mission Hills, CA 91345 Phone: (818)898-1391
Richard Lidz and Dale Anderson, editorial directors. Fourth edition, 1990. For 600 occupations, describes job duties, entry-level requirements, education and training needed, advancement possibilities, employment outlook, earnings and benefits. The set is divided into 12 volumes. Each volume includes jobs related under a broad career field. Volume 13 is the index. **Facsimile Number:** 818-365-5489.

★4353★
"Electrical Appliance Service Technician" in *Occu-Facts: Information on 565 Careers in Outline Form* (p. 15.14)
Careers, Inc.
P.O. Box 135
1211 Tenth St., S.W.
Largo, FL 33640 Phone: (813)584-7333
Elizabeth Handville. Biennial, 1989-90 edition. Each one-page occupational profile describes duties, working conditions, physical surroundings and demands, aptitudes, temperament, educational requirements, employment outlook, earnings, and places of employment.

★4354★
Gas Appliance Service Technician
Chronicle Guidance Publications, Inc.
PO Box 1190
Moravia, NY 13118-1190 Phone: (315)497-0330
1990. This career brief describes the nature of the work, working conditions, hours and earnings, education and training, licensure, certification, unions, personal qualifications, social and psychological factors, employment outlook, entry methods, advancement, and related occupations. **Toll-free/Additional Phone Number(s):** 800-622-7284.

★4355★
"Home Appliance and Power Tool Repairers" in *Occupational Outlook Handbook* **(pp. 347-348)**
Superintendent of Documents
U.S. Government Printing Office
Washington, DC 20402 Phone: (202)783-3238
Biennial; latest edition, 1990-91. Encyclopedia of careers describing more than 250 occupations and comprising about 86 percent of all jobs in the economy. Occupations that require lengthy education or training are given the most attention. For each occupation, the handbook describes job duties, working conditions, training, educational preparation, personal qualities, advancement possibilities, job outlook, earnings, and sources of additional information.

★4356★
"Home Appliance Repairer" in *Personal Services* **(pp. 51-55)**
Franklin Watts, Inc.
387 Park Avenue, S.
New York, NY 10016 Phone: (212)686-7070
Linda Barrett and Galen Guengerich. 1991. Surveys personal services jobs. Describes job duties, educational preparation, salaries, and employment outlook. Offers job hunting advice.

★4357★
"Mechanics: Home Appliance and Power Tools" in *Opportunities in Vocational and Technical Careers* **(p. 107)**
National Textbook Co.
4255 W. Touhy Ave.
Lincolnwood, IL 60646 Phone: (312)679-5500
Adrian A. Paradis. 1987. Describes careers which can be prepared for by attending a private vocational or proprietary school—office employee, sales worker, service worker, health services, mechanic, craftworker, and technician. Covers employment outlook, job duties, and salaries. Offers career planning advice.

★4358★
"Power Tool Repairer" in *Construction,* **Volume 4 of** *Career Information Center* **(pp. 78-80)**
Glencoe/Macmillan
15319 Chatsworth St.
Mission Hills, CA 91345 Phone: (818)898-1391
Richard Lidz and Dale Anderson, editorial directors. Fourth edition, 1990. For 600 occupations, describes job duties, entry-level requirements, education and training needed, advancement possibilities, employment outlook, earnings and benefits. The set is divided into 12 volumes. Each volume includes jobs related under a broad career field. Volume 13 is the index. **Facsimile Number:** 818-365-5489.

★4359★
Vocations U.S.A.
Info-Disc Corporation
4 Professional Dr.
Gaithersburg, MD 20879 Phone: (301)948-2300
Videocassette. 1987. 60 mins. A disc collection outlining the requirements and methods of various career areas. Occupation include: transportation, mechanical/repair, health, agriculture and construction.

―――― Associations ――――

★4360★
Association of Home Appliance Manufacturers (AHAM)
20 N. Wacker Dr.
Chicago, IL 60606 Phone: (312)984-5800
Membership: Companies manufacturing major and portable appliances; associate members provide products and services to the appliance industry. **Purpose:** Major areas of activity include market research and reporting of industry statistics development of standard methods for measuring appliance performance and certification of certain characteristics of room air conditioners, refrigerators, freezers, humidifiers, dehumidifiers, and room air cleaners; public relations and press relations. Represents the appliance industry before government at the federal, state, and local levels through an office at 200 Daingerfield Rd., Ste. 220, Alexandria, VA 22314. Sponsors the Major Appliance Consumer Action Panel. Maintains committees and boards in communications, engineering, consumer relations, market research, economics, and other service areas. **Publications:** *AHAM Factory Shipment Release,* monthly. • *AHAM Membership Directory,* annual. • *Consumer Selection Guide for Refrigerators and Freezers,* annual. • *Consumer Selection Guide for Room Air Conditioners,* annual. • *Directory of Certified Dehumidifiers,* semiannual. • *Directory of Certified Humidifiers,* semiannual. • *Directory of Certified Refrigerators and Freezers,* semiannual. • *Directory of Certified Room Air Conditioners,* semiannual. • *MACAP Statistical Report,* annual. • *Trends and Forecasts,* quarterly.

★4361★
Power Tool Institute (PTI)
PO Box 818
Yachats, OR 97498 Phone: (503)547-3185
Membership: Manufacturers of portable, lawn and garden, and stationary tools, both electric and battery operated. **Purpose:** Distributes brochures, slides, and cassettes on power tool safety. Offers educational programs. **Publications:** *Directory,* annual. **Facsimile Number:** (503)547-3539.

―――― Standards/Certification Agencies ――――

Some states and areas require repairers who service gas appliances to be licensed or registered. Applicants for licensure must meet certain minimum standards of education, training, and experience. They also must pass an examination, which can be written, practical, or a combination, depending upon the requirements of the licensing authority.

★4362★
Association of Home Appliance Manufacturers (AHAM)
20 N. Wacker Dr.
Chicago, IL 60606 Phone: (312)984-5800
Develops standard methods for measuring appliance performance and certification of certain characteristics of room air conditioners, refrigerators, freezers, humidifiers, dehumidifiers, and room air cleaners. Represents the appliance

Home Appliance and Power Tool Repairers ★4371★

industry before government at the federal, state, and local levels.

Basic Reference Guides and Handbooks

★4363★
Association of Home Appliance Manufacturers—Associates Resource Catalog
Association of Home Appliance Manufacturers (AHAM)
20 N. Wacker Dr.
Chicago, IL 60606   Phone: (312)984-5800
Irregular; latest edition September 1986. Approximately 75 AHAM member manufacturers of products and supplies to the home appliance industry and consumers. Entries include: Company name, address, phone, name and title of contact, branch office, products provided. Arrangement: Alphabetical. Indexes: Product.

★4364★
Power Tool Maintenance
McGraw-Hill Publishing
1221 Avenue of the Americas
New York, NY 10020   Phone: (212)512-2000
D. Irvin. 1971.

★4365★
Shop Savvy
Borgo Press
PO Box 2845
San Bernardino, CA 92406-2845   Phone: (714)884-5813
Roy Moungovan. 1990.

★4366★
Troubleshooting & Repairing Power Tools
TAB Books
Blue Ridge Summit, PA 17294-0850   Phone: (717)794-2191
Homer L. Davidson. 1990.

Periodicals

★4367★
Appliance
Dana Chase Publications, Inc.
1110 Jorie Blvd., CS 9019
Oak Brook, IL 60522-9019   Phone: (708)990-3484
James R. Stevens, V.P./Editor. Monthly. Trade magazine focusing on appliances: commercial, consumer, and business. **Facsimile Number:** (708)990-0078.

★4368★
Appliance Service News
Gamit Enterprises, Inc.
110 W. St. Charles Rd.
PO Box 789
Lombard, IL 60148   Phone: (708)932-9550
William Wingstedt, Editor and Publisher. Monthly. Magazine for appliance repairmen.

★4369★
Retail News Reporter
739 Main St., Ste. 4
PO Box 830034
Stone Mountain, GA 30083-0001   Phone: (404)879-9682
Byron Hollingsworth, Publisher. Monthly. Newspaper (tabloid) for the electronics and appliances industry. **Facsimile Number:** (404)879-6791.

★4370★
Trends and Forecasts (AHAM)
Association of Home Appliance Manufacturers (AHAM)
20 N. Wacker Dr.
Chicago, IL 60606   Phone: (312)984-5800
Quarterly. A one-page tabular statistical report giving trends and forecasts (ten-year) of domestic and export shipments of major appliances.

Meetings and Conventions

★4371★
Association of Home Appliance Manufacturers (AHAM)
20 N. Wacker Dr.
Chicago, IL 60606   Phone: (312)984-5800
Frequency: Annual, always spring.

Industrial Machinery Repairers

Industrial machinery repairers, often called maintenance mechanics, do preventive maintenance and repairs for machinery used in factories and plants. This includes inspecting machinery and spotting and correcting minor problems. Mechanics diagnose major problems, and disassemble the equipment and repair or replace necessary parts. The final step is to test the machine to ensure that it is running smoothly. When repairing electronically controlled machinery, these mechanics may work closely with electronic repairers or electricians who maintain the machine's electric parts. A wide range of tools may be used in doing maintenance and repair work, from a screwdriver to adjust engine parts, to a hoist to lift heavy equipment. Most industrial machinery repairers work in manufacturing industries. Other work for government agencies, public utilities, and mining companies.

$alaries

Industrial machinery repairers median hourly earnings are $11.23.

Lowest 10 percent	$6.95/hour or less
Middle 50 percent	$8.55-14.08/hour
Top 10 percent	$17.35/hour or more.

Employment Outlook

Growth rate until the year 2000: Average.

Industrial Machinery Repairers

Career Guides

★4372★
American Professionals Series
Cambridge Career Products
90 MacCorkle Ave., SW
South Charleston, WV 25311   Phone: (304)744-9323
Videocassette. 1984. 30 mins. In this series of twenty-one half hour programs, various occupations are examined in depth, including a day in the life of each worker. Included are: fireman, farmer, oil driller, fisherman, horse trainer, and auto assembly repairman.

★4373★
Chemical Plant Operations Training Program
NUS Training Corporation
910 Clopper Rd.
Gaithersburg, MD 20878-1399   Phone: (301)258-8763
Videocassette. 1984. 60 mins. A comprehensive view for vocational purposes of industrial chemical plant maintenance, functions, processes and repair.

★4374★
"Industrial Machinery Mechanics" in Volume 3 of *Career Discovery Encyclopedia* (pp. 134-135)
J.G. Ferguson Publishing Co.
200 W. Monroe
Chicago, IL 60606   Phone: (312)580-5480
E. Russell Primm, editor-in-chief. 1990. Contains two-page articles on 504 occupations. Each article describes job duties, earnings, and educational and training requirements.

★4375★
"Industrial Machinery Mechanics" in Volume 3 of *The Encyclopedia of Careers and Vocational Guidance* (pp. 522-524)
J.G. Ferguson Publishing Co.
200 W. Monroe
Chicago, IL 60606   Phone: (312)580-5480
William E. Hopke, editor-in-chief. Eighth edition, 1990. Four-volume set that profiles 500 occupations and describes job trends in 76 industries. Includes career description, educational requirements, history of the job, methods of entry, advancement, employment outlook, earnings, working conditions, social and psychological factors, and sources of additional information.

★4376★
"Industrial Machinery Repairer" in *Manufacturing, Volume 9 of Career Information Center* (pp. 61-62)
Glencoe/Macmillan
15319 Chatsworth St.
Mission Hills, CA 91345   Phone: (818)898-1391
Richard Lidz and Dale Anderson, editorial directors. Fourth edition, 1990. For 600 occupations, describes job duties, entry-level requirements, education and training needed, advancement possibilities, employment outlook, earnings and benefits. The set is divided into 12 volumes. Each volume includes jobs related under a broad career field. Volume 13 is the index. **Facsimile Number:** 818-365-5489.

★4377★
"Industrial Machinery Repairer" in *Occu-Facts: Information on 565 Careers in Outline Form* (p. 15.10)
Careers, Inc.
P.O. Box 135
1211 Tenth St., S.W.
Largo, FL 33640   Phone: (813)584-7333
Elizabeth Handville. Biennial, 1989-90 edition. Each one-page occupational profile describes duties, working conditions, physical surroundings and demands, aptitudes, temperament, educational requirements, employment outlook, earnings, and places of employment.

★4378★
Industrial Machinery Repairers
Chronicle Guidance Publications, Inc.
PO Box 1190
Moravia, NY 13118-1190   Phone: (315)497-0330
1987. This career brief describes the nature of the work, working conditions, hours and earnings, education and training, licensure, certification, unions, personal qualifications, social and psychological factors, employment outlook, entry methods, advancement, and related occupations. **Toll-free/Additional Phone Number(s):** 800-622-7284.

★4379★
"Industrial Machinery Repairers" in *Occupational Outlook Handbook* (pp. 348-349)
Superintendent of Documents
U.S. Government Printing Office
Washington, DC 20402   Phone: (202)783-3238
Biennial; latest edition, 1990-91. Encyclopedia of careers describing more than 250 occupations and comprising about 86 percent of all jobs in the economy. Occupations that require lengthy education or training are given the most attention. For each occupation, the handbook describes job duties, working conditions, training, educational preparation, personal qualities,

advancement possibilities, job outlook, earnings, and sources of additional information.

★4380★
"Industrial Machinery Repairers" in *The American Almanac of Jobs and Salaries* (pp. 524-525)
Avon Books
105 Madison Avenue
New York, NY 10016　　　　　　　　　Phone: (212)481-5600
John Wright and Edward J. Dwyer. Revised and updated, 1990. A comprehensive guide to the wages of hundreds of occupations in a wide variety of industries and organizations.

★4381★
Machinery Repairer, Industrial
Careers, Inc.
PO Box 135
Largo, FL 34649-0135　　　　　　　　Phone: (813)584-7333
1989. Eight-page brief offering the definition, history, duties, working conditions, personal qualifications, educational requirements, earnings, hours, employment outlook, advancement possibilities, and related occupations.

★4382★
"Mechanics: Industrial Machinery" in *Opportunities in Vocational and Technical Careers* (pp. 104, 106-107)
National Textbook Co.
4255 W. Touhy Ave.
Lincolnwood, IL 60646　　　　　　　　Phone: (312)679-5500
Adrian A. Paradis. 1987. Describes careers which can be prepared for by attending a private vocational or proprietary school—office employee, sales worker, service worker, health services, mechanic, craftworker, and technician. Covers employment outlook, job duties, and salaries. Offers career planning advice.

★4383★
Video Career Library - Repair Fields
Careers, Inc.
1211 10th St., SW
PO Box 135
Largo, FL 34649-0135　　　　　　　　Phone: (813)584-7333
Videocassette. 1990. 23 mins. Part of the Video Career Library covering 165 occupations. Shows actual workers on the job. Includes industrial machinery repairers, communications equipment repairers, data processing equipment repairers, home entertainment equipment repairers, office machine repairers, electrical power installers and repairers, and electrical and electronic repairers.

────────── Associations ──────────

★4384★
International Union of Electronic, Electrical, Salaried, Machine, and Furniture Workers (IUE)
1126 16th St., NW
Washington, DC 20036　　　　　　　　Phone: (202)296-1200
Membership: Districts: 6. Locals: 550. AFL-CIO. **Purpose:** Negotiates collective bargaining agreements; bestows awards; maintains apprenticeship programs. Conducts district education directors meeting and training programs. Compiles statistics. **Publications:** *Health and Safety*, 3-4/year. • *International Union of Electronic, Electrical, Salaried, Machine, and Furniture Workers—Convention Proceedings*, biennial. • *IUE News*, monthly. • *Keeping Up With The Law*, 3-4/year. • *Research Information*, monthly. **Facsimile Number:** (202)785-4563. **Boards:** Amalgamated Locals Conference; General Electric Conference; General Motors Conference; Multi-Employer Conference; Professional, Technical and Salaried Conference; Westinghouse Conference.

────────── Standards/Certification Agencies ──────────

Some industrial machinery repairers learn the trade through apprenticeship programs sponsored by the International Association of Machinists and Aerospace Workers, the United Automobile, Aerospace, and Agricultural Implement Workers of America, and the International Union of Electronic, Electrical, Salaried, Machine, and Furniture Workers. This training usually lasts four years and consists of on-the-job training and 144 hours of related classroom instruction each year.

────────── Test Guides ──────────

★4385★
Machinist - Machinist's Helper
Prentice Hall Press
Simon & Schuster Inc.
200 Old Tappan Rd.
Old Tappan, NJ 07675　　　　　　　　Phone: (800)223-2348
Hy Hammer. Fourth edition, 1984. For applicants for civil service entry level and advanced level positions. Includes nine sample exams with answers.

★4386★
Maintenance Worker/Mechanical Maintainer
Prentice Hall Press
Simon & Schuster Inc.
200 Old Tappan Rd.
Old Tappan, NJ 07675　　　　　　　　Phone: (800)223-2348
Hy Hammer. Fourth edition, 1984. Provides information for applicants interested in the following civil service positions: carpenter, mason, plumber, electrician, painter, machinist. Includes eight sample tests.

────────── Periodicals ──────────

★4387★
Health and Safety (IUE)
International Union of Electronic, Electrical, Salaried, Machine, and Furni
ture Workers
1126 16th St., NW
Washington, DC 20036　　　　　　　　Phone: (202)296-1200
3-4/year.

★4388★
IUE News (IUE)
International Union of Electronic, Electrical, Salaried, Machine, and Furni
ture Workers
1126 16th St., NW
Washington, DC 20036　　　　　　　　Phone: (202)296-1200
Monthly. Association newsletter in tabloid form.

★4389★
IUE Research Information (IUE)
Intl. Union of Electronic, Electrical, Salaried, Machine, and
  Furniture Wor
kers
1126 16th St., NW
Washington, DC 20036   Phone: (202)296-1200
Monthly.

★4390★
Keeping Up With The Law (IUE)
International Union of Electronic, Electrical, Salaried, Machine,
  and Furni
ture Workers
1126 16th St., NW
Washington, DC 20036   Phone: (202)296-1200
3-4/year.

Meetings and Conventions

★4391★
**International Union of Electronic, Electrical, Salaried,
  Machine, and Furniture Workers (IUE)**
1126 16th St., NW
Washington, DC 20036   Phone: (202)296-1200
Frequency: Biennial - next held in 1992. **Facsimile Number:** (202)785-4563.

Line Installers and Cable Splicers

Line installers and cable splicers construct and maintain the network of wires and cables that link the electric power produced in generating plants to individual customers, connects telephone central offices to customers' telephones and switchboards, and extends cable TV to residential and commercial customers. In installing new elecric power or telephone lines, line installers, often referred to as outside plant technicians or construction line workers, install poles and terminals and place wires and cables that lead from the source of the transmission to the customers' premises. They also lay cable television lines underground or hang them on poles with the telephone and utility wires. Cable splicers, or cable splicing technicians, complete the line connections after the line installers have done their job. Cable splicers connect individual wires or fibers within the cable and rearrange wires when lines have to be changed. After determining the proper splicing specifications, splices are made by twisting, soldering, or joining wires and cables with small handtools and epoxy. Line installers and cable splicers also maintain and repair telephone, power, and cable TV lines. Preventive maintenance is extremely important, because a single defect may interrupt service for many customers. Nearly all line installers and cable splicers work for telephone companies, cable television companies, power companies, and construction companies.

$alaries

Line installers and repairers earn a median weekly wage of $547.00

Lowest 10 percent	$301/week or less
Middle 50 percent	$419-656/week
Top 10 percent	$721/week or more

Employment Outlook

Growth rate until the year 2000: Slower than average.

Line Installers and Cable Splicers

Career Guides

★4392★
Alive or Dead
American Educational Films
3807 Dickerson Rd.
Nashville, TN 37207   Phone: (800)822-5678
Videocassette. 1983. 26 mins. This tape reviews the precautions that should be taken when working with high voltage power cables.

★4393★
The Cable Job Guide
Cable Television Information Center
1700 Shaker Church Rd., NW
Olympia, WA 98502-9514   Phone: (703)941-1770
Janet Quigley. Second edition, 1985.

★4394★
"Cable Splicer" in *Exploring Nontraditional Jobs for Women* (pp. 26-31)
Rosen Publishing Group, Inc.
29 E. 21st St.
New York, NY 10010   Phone: (212)777-3017
Rose Neufeld. 1989. Describes blue-collar, male dominated occupations. Discusses what is done on the job, training, where to apply for jobs, tools used, salaries, and advantages and disadvantages. Relates the experiences of women who are working in the field.

★4395★
"Cable Splicer" in *Opportunities in Electrical Trades* (pp. 58-60)
National Textbook Co.
4255 W. Touhy Ave.
Lincolnwood, IL 60646   Phone: (312)679-5500
Robert Wood. 1990. Provides an overview of the electrical industry describing current trends and future projections. Surveys electrician jobs and covers the nature of the work, working conditions, job outlook, advancement possibilities, education and training, earnings, and specialization. Offers career planning advice.

★4396★
Cable Television Systems Technicians and Installers
Chronicle Guidance Publications, Inc.
PO Box 1190
Moravia, NY 13118-1190   Phone: (315)497-0330
1989. This career brief describes the nature of the work, working conditions, hours and earnings, education and training, licensure, certification, unions, personal qualifications, social and psychological factors, employment outlook, entry methods, advancement, and related occupations. **Toll-free/Additional Phone Number(s):** 800-622-7284.

★4397★
Careers with an Electric Company
Lerner Publications Co.
241 First Ave., N.
Minneapolis, MN 55401
Pam Fricke. 1984. Describes fifteen career possibilities with an electric company including such jobs as lineman and system operator. **Toll-free/Additional Phone Number(s):** 800-328-4920. **Facsimile Number:** (612)332-7615.

★4398★
The IBEW Leads to Electrifying Careers
International Brotherhood of Electrical Workers
1125 15th St. NW
Washington, DC 20005   Phone: (202)833-7000
1988. This 15-page booklet describes the electrician apprenticeship program and the jobs of electricians, communications, and utility workers and licensure.

★4399★
"Line Installer" in *Exploring Nontraditional Jobs for Women* (pp. 37-43)
Rosen Publishing Group, Inc.
29 E. 21st St.
New York, NY 10010   Phone: (212)777-3017
Rose Neufeld. 1989. Describes blue-collar, male dominated occupations. Discusses what is done on the job, training, where to apply for jobs, tools used, salaries, and advantages and disadvantages. Relates the experiences of women who are working in the field.

★4400★
"Line Installers and Cable Splicers" in *Occupational Outlook Handbook* (pp. 350-352)
Superintendent of Documents
U.S. Government Printing Office
Washington, DC 20402   Phone: (202)783-3238
Biennial; latest edition, 1990-91. Encyclopedia of careers describing more than 250 occupations and comprising about 86 percent of all jobs in the economy. Occupations that require lengthy education or training are given the most attention. For each occupation, the handbook describes job duties, working conditions, training, educational preparation, personal qualities, advancement possibilities, job outlook, earnings, and sources of additional information.

★4401★
"Line Installers and Cable Splicers" in Volume 4 of *Career Discovery Encyclopedia* (pp. 32-33)
J.G. Ferguson Publishing Co.
200 W. Monroe
Chicago, IL 60606　　　　　　　　Phone: (312)580-5480
E. Russell Primm, editor-in-chief. 1990. Contains two-page articles on 504 occupations. Each article describes job duties, earnings, and educational and training requirements.

★4402★
"Line Installers and Cable Splicers" in Volume 3 of *The Encyclopedia of Careers and Vocational Guidance* (pp. 573-676)
J.G. Ferguson Publishing Co.
200 W. Monroe
Chicago, IL 60606　　　　　　　　Phone: (312)580-5480
William E. Hopke, editor-in-chief. Eighth edition, 1990. Four-volume set that profiles 500 occupations and describes job trends in 76 industries. Includes career description, educational requirements, history of the job, methods of entry, advancement, employment outlook, earnings, working conditions, social and psychological factors, and sources of additional information.

★4403★
Line Workers (Electric Power)
Chronicle Guidance Publications, Inc.
PO Box 1190
Moravia, NY 13118-1190　　　　　　Phone: (315)497-0330
1990. This career brief describes the nature of the work, working conditions, hours and earnings, education and training, licensure, certification, unions, personal qualifications, social and psychological factors, employment outlook, entry methods, advancement, and related occupations. **Toll-free/Additional Phone Number(s):** 800-622-7284.

★4404★
Linemen
Film Library
3450 Wilshire Blvd. #700
Los Angeles, CA 90010-2215　　　　Phone: (213)384-8114
Videocassette. 198?. 14 mins. This film shows a group of linemen discussing why they became involved in their profession.

★4405★
"Lineperson" in *Opportunities in Electrical Trades* (p. 56)
National Textbook Co.
4255 W. Touhy Ave.
Lincolnwood, IL 60646　　　　　　Phone: (312)679-5500
Robert Wood. 1990. Provides an overview of the electrical industry describing current trends and future projections. Surveys electrician jobs and covers the nature of the work, working conditions, job outlook, advancement possibilities, education and training, earnings, and specialization. Offers career planning advice.

★4406★
Live Line Maintenance
L & K International Video Training
295 Evans Ave.
Toronto, ON, Canada M8Z 5P9　　　Phone: (416)252-6407
Videocassette. 1984. 60 mins. This program explains the training techniques for Electrical Utility Linemen.

★4407★
"On the Line" in *Telecommunications Careers* (pp. 50-54)
Franklin Watts, Inc.
387 Park Avenue, S.
New York, NY 10016　　　　　　　Phone: (212)686-7070
James L. Schefter. 1988. Describes the telecommunications industry and profiles jobs in manufacturing, the telephone industry, the military, video communications and television broadcasting. Covers job duties, educational requirements, salaries, and promotional possibilities.

★4408★
Our Wiremen
International Brotherhood of Electrical Workers
1125 15th St. NW
Washington, DC 20005　　　　　　Phone: (202)833-7000
Brochure describing the work, skills needed, and training.

★4409★
Telephone Cable Splicing Technician
Vocational Biographies, Inc.
PO Box 31, Dept. VF10
Sauk Centre, MN 56378　　　　　　Phone: (612)352-6516
1988. This pamphlet profiles a person working in the job. Includes information about job duties, working conditions, places of employment, educational preparation, labor market outlook, and salaries. **Toll-free/Additional Phone Number(s):** 800-255-0752.

★4410★
Telephone Line Installers and Cable Splicers
Careers, Inc.
PO Box 135
Largo, FL 34649-0135　　　　　　　Phone: (813)584-7333
1990. Eight-page brief offering the definition, history, duties, working conditions, personal qualifications, educational requirements, earnings, hours, employment outlook, advancement possibilities, and related occupations.

★4411★
"Telephone Line Installers and Cable Splicers" in *Occu-Facts: Information on 565 Careers in Outline Form* (p. 15.15)
Careers, Inc.
P.O. Box 135
1211 Tenth St., S.W.
Largo, FL 33640　　　　　　　　　Phone: (813)584-7333
Elizabeth Handville. Biennial, 1989-90 edition. Each one-page occupational profile describes duties, working conditions, physical surroundings and demands, aptitudes, temperament, educational requirements, employment outlook, earnings, and places of employment.

★4412★
"Telephone Line Worker and Cable Splicer" in *Communications and the Arts*, Volume 3 of *Career Information Center* (pp. 73-75)
Glencoe/Macmillan
15319 Chatsworth St.
Mission Hills, CA 91345　　　　　　Phone: (818)898-1391
Richard Lidz and Dale Anderson, editorial directors. Fourth edition, 1990. For 600 occupations, describes job duties, entry-level requirements, education and training needed, advancement possibilities, employment outlook, earnings and benefits. The set is divided into 12 volumes. Each volume includes jobs related under a broad career field. Volume 13 is the index. **Facsimile Number:** 818-365-5489.

Line Installers and Cable Splicers

★4413★
"Telephone Line Worker and Cable Splicer" in *Telecommunications* (pp. 33-37)
Franklin Watts, Inc.
387 Park Avenue, S.
New York, NY 10016　　　　　Phone: (212)686-7070
Linda Barrett and Galen Guengerich. 1991. Surveys opportunities in telecommunications including telephone, radio, telegraph, and television communications. Includes job description, educational preparation, salary, and employment outlook. Offers job hunting advice.

★4414★
Video Career Library - Repair Fields
Careers, Inc.
1211 10th St., SW
PO Box 135
Largo, FL 34649-0135　　　　　Phone: (813)584-7333
Videocassette. 1990. 23 mins. Part of the Video Career Library covering 165 occupations. Shows actual workers on the job. Includes industrial machinery repairers, communications equipment repairers, data processing equipment repairers, home entertainment equipment repairers, office machine repairers, electrical power installers and repairers, and electrical and electronic repairers.

★4415★
Your Guardian Angel
Film Library
3450 Wilshire Blvd. #700
Los Angeles, CA 90010-2215　　　　　Phone: (213)384-8114
Videocassette. 198?. 15 mins. Harry Sparks, the guardian angel of electrical workers looks at the hazards and characteristics of 600-volt lines and equipment.

Associations

★4416★
International Brotherhood of Electrical Workers (IBEW)
1125 15th St. NW
Washington, DC 20005　　　　　Phone: (202)833-7000
Membership: AFL-CIO. **Publications:** *IBEW Journal*, monthly.

★4417★
United States Telephone Association (USTA)
900 19th St. NW, Ste. 800
Washington, DC 20006　　　　　Phone: (202)835-3100
Membership: Local operating telephone companies or telephone holding companies. Members represent a total of 114 million access lines. **Purpose:** Conducts educational and training programs. Maintains 21 committees. **Publications:** *Holding Company Report*, annual. • *Phonefacts*, annual. • *Statistical Volumes*, annual. • *Teletimes*, quarterly. • Also publishes booklets and brochures. **Toll-free/Additional Phone Number(s):** (202)835-3198 telephone news updates on legislative and industry developments.

Standards/Certification Agencies

Line installers and cable splicers in electric companies and construction firms specializing in cable installation generally complete a formal apprenticeship program. These are administered jointly by the employer and the union representing the workers, either the International Brotherhood of Electrical Workers or the Communications Workers of America. These programs last several years and combine formal instruction with on-the-job training.

Test Guides

★4418★
Foreman Cable Splicer
National Learning Corp.
212 Michael Dr.
Syosset, NY 11791　　　　　Phone: (516)921-8888
Jack Rudman. Part of the Career Examination Series No. 1. All examination guides in this series contain questions with answers. **Facsimile Number:** (516)921-8743. **Toll-free/Additional Phone Number(s):** 800-645-6337.

★4419★
Foreman (Power Cables)
National Learning Corp.
212 Michael Dr.
Syosset, NY 11791　　　　　Phone: (516)921-8888
Jack Rudman. Part of the Career Examination Series No. 1. All examination guides in this series contain questions with answers. **Facsimile Number:** (516)921-8743. **Toll-free/Additional Phone Number(s):** 800-645-6337.

★4420★
Lineman (Electrical Power)
National Learning Corp.
212 Michael Dr.
Syosset, NY 11791　　　　　Phone: (516)921-8888
Jack Rudman. Part of the Career Examination Series No. 1. All examination guides in this series contain questions with answers. **Facsimile Number:** (516)921-8743. **Toll-free/Additional Phone Number(s):** 800-645-6337.

Basic Reference Guides and Handbooks

★4421★
Cable Hardware & Technology
Frost & Sullivan, Inc.
106 Fulton St.
New York, NY 10038　　　　　Phone: (212)233-1080
1987.

★4422★
Cable Television Technology Handbook
Artech House, Inc.
685 Canton St.
Norwood, MA 02062　　　　　Phone: (617)769-9750
Bobby Harrell. 1985. **Facsimile Number:** (617)769-6334.

★4423★
Interconnection Products Directory
Connector Study Group, Inc.
104 Wilmot Rd., Ste. 201
Deerfield, IL 60015-5195　　　　　Phone: (312)940-8800
Gerald L. Ginsberg, editor. Biennial, November of odd years. More than 500 manufacturers, distributors, representatives, sales offices, and other suppliers to the electrical and electronics industry worldwide, including suppliers of connectors, wire, and cable (part 1); printed circuit products (part 2); circular rack and panel products (part 3); wire and cable products (part 4); materials (part 5); and military products (part 6). Entries include: Name, address, products, whether catalog is available. Arrangement: Classified by product. Indexes: Product.

Periodicals

★4424★
The Electricity Journal
2101 4th Ave., Ste. 345
Seattle, WA 98121-2317   Phone: (206)448-4078
Robert O. Marritz, Editor and Publisher. 10x/yr Magazine serving the electric utility industry. **Facsimile Number:** (206)441-7443.

★4425★
Rural Telecommunications
National Telephone Cooperative Assn., Inc.
2626 Pennsylvania Ave. NW
Washington, DC 20037   Phone: (202)298-2300
Ingrid K. Young, Managing Editor. Quarterly. **Facsimile Number:** (202)298-2320.

★4426★
Telecommunications Reports
Business Research Publications, Inc.
1333 H St., NW
Washington, DC 20005   Phone: (202)842-3006
Victoria A. Mason, Editor. Publication tracking all aspects of the telecommunications industry on state, federal, and international levels. Coverage includes the FCC, Congress, state regulatory commissions and legislatures, and federal and state court decisions. Also reports on telecommunications companies and equipment manufacturers, new services and products, personnel changes, and labor union developments. Includes quarterly index. Available online via NewsNet. **Facsimile Number:** (202)842-3047.

★4427★
Telephone News
Phillips Publishing, Inc.
7811 Montrose Rd.
Potomac, MD 20854   Phone: (301)340-2100
Candace Sams, Editor. Weekly. Telecommunications industry newsletter. **Facsimile Number:** (301)424-4297.

★4428★
Teletimes (USTA)
United States Telephone Association (USTA)
900 19th St. NW, Ste. 800
Washington, DC 20006   Phone: (202)835-3100
Quarterly.

Meetings and Conventions

★4429★
Eastern Cable Television Trade Show and Convention
Convention and Show Management Co.
6175 Barfield Rd., Ste. 220
Atlanta, GA 30328   Phone: (404)252-2454
1992.

★4430★
Great Lakes Cable Expo
Great Lakes Cable Expo
300 N. Meridian, Ste. 1800
Indianapolis, IN 46204   Phone: (317)237-3330
1992.

★4431★
Western Cable Television Convention and Exposition
Trade Associates, Inc.
6001 Montrose Rd., Ste. 900
Rockville, MD 20852-1608   Phone: (301)468-3210
Frequency: Always held at the Convention Center in Anaheim, California. 1992; Dec. 02-04; Anaheim, CA. **Facsimile Number:** (301)468-3662.

★4432★
Wire Expo - Wire Association International Annual Meeting and Exposition
Wire Association International
1570 Boston Post Rd.
PO Box H
Guilford, CT 06437   Phone: (203)453-2727
1992; Louisville, KY ● 1994; Detroit, MI. **Facsimile Number:** (203)453-8384.

Other Sources of Information

★4433★
Phonefacts (USTA)
United States Telephone Association (USTA)
900 19th St. NW, Ste. 800
Washington, DC 20006   Phone: (202)835-3100
Annual.

Millwrights

Millwrights install and dismantle the machinery and heavy equipment used in almost every industry. The machinery must be lifted and moved, therefore millwrights use a variety of rigging and hoisting devices. A knowledge of load-bearing properties of ropes, cables, and hoists is essential. New machinery sometimes requires a new foundation and millwrights prepare or supervise the construction. This requires a background on blueprint reading and building materials. When assembling machinery, millwrights fit bearings, align gears and wheels, and connect belts according to the manufacturer's blueprints and drawings. Millwrights are also involved in the installation of industrial robots and other automated equipment. In addition to installing and dismantling machinery, millwrights also repair and maintain equipment. Millwrights employed in factories tend to specialize in the particular types of machinery used by their employers. Those employed by contract installation and construction companies must know how to do a variety of installation work. Almost 75% of millwrights work in manufacturing. Most of the rest are employed by firms involved in construction and those providing millwright services on a contract basis.

$alaries

Full-time millwrights have median hourly earnings of $12.65.

Lowest 10 percent	$7.80/hour or less
Middle 50 percent	$10.10-15.50/hour
Top 10 percent	$19.20/hour or more.

Employment Outlook

Growth rate until the year 2000: Average.

Millwrights

Career Guides

★4434★
Millwright
Careers, Inc.
PO Box 135
Largo, FL 34649-0135   Phone: (813)584-7333

1990. Eight-page brief offering the definition, history, duties, working conditions, personal qualifications, educational requirements, earnings, hours, employment outlook, advancement possibilities, and related occupations.

★4435★
"Millwright" in *Occu-Facts: Information on 565 Careers in Outline Form* (p. 15.25)
Careers, Inc.
P.O. Box 135
1211 Tenth St., S.W.
Largo, FL 33640   Phone: (813)584-7333

Elizabeth Handville. Biennial, 1989-90 edition. Each one-page occupational profile describes duties, working conditions, physical surroundings and demands, aptitudes, temperament, educational requirements, employment outlook, earnings, and places of employment.

★4436★
"Millwright" in *Opportunities in Carpentry Careers* (p. 52)
National Textbook Co.
4255 W. Touhy Ave.
Lincolnwood, IL 60646   Phone: (312)679-5500

Roger Sheldon. 1987. Covers the history of the crafts, a typical carpenter's workday, future opportunities for carpenters, qualifications, training, apprenticeships, and special advice for women and minorities. Surveys various training opportunities.

★4437★
Millwrights
Chronicle Guidance Publications, Inc.
PO Box 1190
Moravia, NY 13118-1190   Phone: (315)497-0330

1987. This career brief describes the nature of the work, working conditions, hours and earnings, education and training, licensure, certification, unions, personal qualifications, social and psychological factors, employment outlook, entry methods, advancement, and related occupations. **Toll-free/Additional Phone Number(s):** 800-622-7284.

★4438★
"Millwrights" in *Occupational Outlook Handbook* (pp. 352-353)
Superintendent of Documents
U.S. Government Printing Office
Washington, DC 20402   Phone: (202)783-3238

Biennial; latest edition, 1990-91. Encyclopedia of careers describing more than 250 occupations and comprising about 86 percent of all jobs in the economy. Occupations that require lengthy education or training are given the most attention. For each occupation, the handbook describes job duties, working conditions, training, educational preparation, personal qualities, advancement possibilities, job outlook, earnings, and sources of additional information.

★4439★
"Millwrights" in Volume 4 of *Career Discovery Encyclopedia* (pp. 96-97)
J.G. Ferguson Publishing Co.
200 W. Monroe
Chicago, IL 60606   Phone: (312)580-5480

E. Russell Primm, editor-in-chief. 1990. Contains two-page articles on 504 occupations. Each article describes job duties, earnings, and educational and training requirements.

★4440★
"Millwrights" in Volume 3 of *The Encyclopedia of Careers and Vocational Guidance* (pp. 542-544)
J.G. Ferguson Publishing Co.
200 W. Monroe
Chicago, IL 60606   Phone: (312)580-5480

William E. Hopke, editor-in-chief. Eighth edition, 1990. Four-volume set that profiles 500 occupations and describes job trends in 76 industries. Includes career description, educational requirements, history of the job, methods of entry, advancement, employment outlook, earnings, working conditions, social and psychological factors, and sources of additional information.

★4441★
Video Career Library - Construction
Careers, Inc.
1211 10th St., SW
PO Box 135
Largo, FL 34649-0135   Phone: (813)584-7333

Videocassette. 1990. 36 mins. Part of the Video Career Library covering 165 occupations. Shows actual workers on the job. Includes millwrights, brickmasons, carpenters, drywall installers, electricians, painters, plumbers and pipefitters, carpenter and soft tile installers, insulation workers, paving equipment operators, and structural metal workers.

Associations

★4442★
Associated General Contractors of America (AGC)
1957 E St. NW
Washington, DC 20006   Phone: (202)393-2040
Membership: General construction contractors; subcontractors; industry suppliers; service firms. **Purpose:** Provides tax services through its divisions. Conducts special conferences and seminars designed specifically for construction firms. Compiles statistics on job accidents reported by member firms. Bestows annual awards for safety and Build/America awards for innovative and outstanding achievements by general contractors. Offers college scholarships through AGC Education and Research Foundation. Maintains 65 committees, including joint cooperative committees with other associations and liaison committees with federal agencies. **Publications:** *AGC Membership Directory and Buyers' Guide*, annual. • *Associated General Contractors of America—National Newsletter*, biweekly. • *Constructor*, monthly. • Also publishes manuals, guides, model contract documents, studies, and checklists. **Facsimile Number:** (202)347-4004.

Periodicals

★4443★
Associated General Contractors of America—National Newsletter (AGC)
Associated General Contractors of America (AGC)
1957 E St. NW
Washington, DC 20006   Phone: (202)393-2040
Biweekly.

★4444★
Constructor (AGC)
Associated General Contractors of America (AGC)
1957 E St. NW
Washington, DC 20006   Phone: (202)393-2040
Monthly. Association magazine for general contractors engaged in construction.

Meetings and Conventions

★4445★
Association of Operative Millers Technical Conference and Trade Show
Association of Operative Millers
4901 Main, Ste. 414
Kansas City, MO 64112   Phone: (816)561-4171
1992; May 23-26; San Diego, CA. **Facsimile Number:** (816)561-8813.

Mobile Heavy Equipment Mechanics

Mobile heavy equipment mechanics service and repair the engines, transmissions, and other components of equipment such as motor graders, trenches and backhoes, crawler-loaders, and stripping and loading shovels that are used at construction sites. Mobile heavy equipment mechanics perform routine maintenance and repairs on the engines of heavy equipment. After diagnosis, they repair, replace, clean, and lubricate parts as necessary. Repairing malfunctioning hydraulic components is one of a mechanic's major responsibilities. Diagnosing and correcting electrical problems is another important task. They use a variety of tools from common handtools to more technical equipment such as dynamometers and voltmeters. Most mechanics work in small repair shops of construction contractors, logging and mining companies, and local government road maintenance departments.

$alaries

Mobile heavy equipment mechanics have median hourly earnings of about $12.00.

Lowest 10 percent	$7.40/hour or less
Middle 50 percent	$9.25-15/hour
Top 10 percent	$19.00/hour or more.

Employment Outlook

Growth rate until the year 2000: Average.

Mobile Heavy Equipment Mechanics

Career Guides

★4446★
"Construction Equipment Mechanic" in *Construction*, Volume 4 of *Career Information Center* (pp. 47-49)
Glencoe/Macmillan
15319 Chatsworth St.
Mission Hills, CA 91345   Phone: (818)898-1391
Richard Lidz and Dale Anderson, editorial directors. Fourth edition, 1990. For 600 occupations, describes job duties, entry-level requirements, education and training needed, advancement possibilities, employment outlook, earnings and benefits. The set is divided into 12 volumes. Each volume includes jobs related under a broad career field. Volume 13 is the index. **Facsimile Number:** 818-365-5489.

★4447★
Do Your Own Thing. in the Mechanical Field
AIMS Media, Inc.
9710 DeSoto Ave.
Chatsworth, CA 93111-4409   Phone: (818)773-4300
Videocassette. 1979. 16 mins. Various job levels in the mechanical field are outlined for students.

★4448★
Mechanics
Morris Video
2730 Monterey St. #105
Monterey Business Park
Torrance, CA 90503   Phone: (213)533-4800
Videocassette. 1984. 15 mins. Various careers in repair are examined including aircraft, motorcycle, diesel, refrigeration and heavy equipment.

★4449★
"Mechanics: Mobile Heavy Equipment" in *Opportunities in Vocational and Technical Careers* (p. 107)
National Textbook Co.
4255 W. Touhy Ave.
Lincolnwood, IL 60646   Phone: (312)679-5500
Adrian A. Paradis. 1987. Describes careers which can be prepared for by attending a private vocational or proprietary school—office employee, sales worker, service worker, health services, mechanic, craftworker, and technician. Covers employment outlook, job duties, and salaries. Offers career planning advice.

★4450★
"Mobile Heavy Equipment Mechanics" in *Occupational Outlook Handbook* (pp. 353-355)
Superintendent of Documents
U.S. Government Printing Office
Washington, DC 20402   Phone: (202)783-3238
Biennial; latest edition, 1990-91. Encyclopedia of careers describing more than 250 occupations and comprising about 86 percent of all jobs in the economy. Occupations that require lengthy education or training are given the most attention. For each occupation, the handbook describes job duties, working conditions, training, educational preparation, personal qualities, advancement possibilities, job outlook, earnings, and sources of additional information.

★4451★
"Mobile Heavy Equipment Mechanics" in Volume 4 of *Career Discovery Encyclopedia* (pp. 100-101)
J.G. Ferguson Publishing Co.
200 W. Monroe
Chicago, IL 60606   Phone: (312)580-5480
E. Russell Primm, editor-in-chief. 1990. Contains two-page articles on 504 occupations. Each article describes job duties, earnings, and educational and training requirements.

★4452★
Video Career Library - Mechanical Fields
Careers, Inc.
1211 10th St., SW
PO Box 135
Largo, FL 34649-0135   Phone: (813)584-7333
Videocassette. 1990. 22 mins. Part of the Video Career Library covering 165 occupations. Shows actual workers on the job. Includes automobile mechanics, diesel engine mechanics, aircraft engine mechanics, automobile body repairers, heavy equipment mechanics, heating/air-conditioning/refrigeration mechanics.

★4453★
Vocations U.S.A.
Info-Disc Corporation
4 Professional Dr.
Gaithersburg, MD 20879   Phone: (301)948-2300
Videocassette. 1987. 60 mins. A disc collection outlining the requirements and methods of various career areas. Occupations include: transportation, mechanical/repair, health, agriculture, and construction.

Associations

★4454★
Motor and Equipment Manufacturers Association (MEMA)
300 Sylvan Ave.
PO Box 1638
Englewood Cliffs, NJ 07632-0638   Phone: (201)569-8500
Membership: Manufacturers of automotive and heavy-duty original equipment and replacement components, maintenance equipment, chemicals, accessories, refinishing supplies, tools, and service equipment united for research into all aspects of the automotive and heavy-duty markets. **Purpose:** Provides manufacturer-oriented services and programs including: marketing consultation for the automotive industry; federal and state legal, safety, and legislative representation and consultation; personnel services; manpower development workshops; international information. Maintains credit reporting and collection service covering wholesalers, retailers, chain stores, and warehouse distributors; offers electronic order-entry, price-update, and electronic document exchange services through MEMA/Transnet system; maintains international liaison. Administers U.S. Automotive Parts Industry Japan Office in conjunction with the U.S. Department of Commerce. Conducts seminars on domestic and overseas marketing, federal trade regulations, freight forwarding, and credit and collections. Compiles statistics on automotive service industry for use by members and as a public service. **Publications:** *Automotive Distributor Trends and Financial Analysis*, periodic. • *Credit and Sales Reference Directory*, 2/year. • *International Buyer's Guide of U.S.* • *Marketing Insight*, quarterly. • Also publishes *Japan Automotive Insight*, *Autobody Supply and Equipment Market*, *Automotive Jobbers in the U.S.* **Facsimile Number:** (201)569-0159.

Test Guides

★4455★
Heavy Equipment Mechanic
National Learning Corp.
212 Michael Dr.
Syosset, NY 11791   Phone: (516)921-8888
Jack Rudman. Part of the Career Examination Series No. 1. All examination guides in this series contain questions with answers. **Facsimile Number:** (516)921-8743. **Toll-free/Additional Phone Number(s):** 800-645-6337.

Basic Reference Guides and Handbooks

★4456★
Autobody Supply and Equipment Market **(MEMA)**
Motor and Equipment Manufacturers Association (MEMA)
300 Sylvan Ave.
PO Box 1638
Englewood Cliffs, NJ 07632-0638   Phone: (201)569-8500

★4457★
Car Maintenance in the U.S.A. **(MEMA)**
Motor and Equipment Manufacturers Association (MEMA)
300 Sylvan Ave.
PO Box 1638
Englewood Cliffs, NJ 07632-0638   Phone: (201)569-8500

★4458★
Foreign Vehicle Maintenance in the U.S.A. **(MEMA)**
Motor and Equipment Manufacturers Association (MEMA)
300 Sylvan Ave.
PO Box 1638
Englewood Cliffs, NJ 07632-0638   Phone: (201)569-8500

★4459★
Heavy Duty Truck Maintenance in the U.S.A. **(MEMA)**
Motor and Equipment Manufacturers Association (MEMA)
300 Sylvan Ave.
PO Box 1638
Englewood Cliffs, NJ 07632-0638   Phone: (201)569-8500

Periodicals

★4460★
Automotive Distributor Trends and Financial Analysis **(MEMA)**
Motor and Equipment Manufacturers Association (MEMA)
300 Sylvan Ave.
PO Box 1638
Englewood Cliffs, NJ 07632-0638   Phone: (201)569-8500
Periodic.

★4461★
Automotive Jobbers in the U.S.A. **(MEMA)**
Motor and Equipment Manufacturers Association (MEMA)
300 Sylvan Ave.
PO Box 1638
Englewood Cliffs, NJ 07632-0638   Phone: (201)569-8500

★4462★
MEMA Marketing Insight **(MEMA)**
Motor and Equipment Manufacturers Association (MEMA)
300 Sylvan Ave.
PO Box 1638
Englewood Cliffs, NJ 07632-0638   Phone: (201)569-8500
Quarterly.

Meetings and Conventions

★4463★
Heating, Ventilation, and Air Conditioning Product and Equipment Show
Institute of Heating and Air Conditioning Industries
606 N. Larchmont Blvd., Ste. 4A
Los Angeles, CA 90004   Phone: (213)467-1158

★4464★
International District Heating and Cooling Association Convention
International District Heating and Cooling Association
1101 Connecticut Ave., NW, Ste. 700
Washington, DC 20036   Phone: (202)429-5111
1992; Jun. 18-22; Danvers, MA. **Facsimile Number:** (204)223-4579.

★4465★
Midwest Specialty Exposition
Kansas Plumbing, Heating, and Cooling Contractors Association
320 Laura St.
Wichita, KS 67211   Phone: (316)262-8860
1992. **Facsimile Number:** (316)265-7381.

★4466★
PHCP EXPO - National Plumbing-Heating-Cooling-Piping Products Exposition
National Association of Plumbing, Heating, and Cooling Contractors
180 S. Washington St.
PO Box 6808
Fall Church, VA 22046   Phone: (703)237-8100
1992; Oct. 20-24; Atlanta, GA ● 1993; Oct. 13-17; Anaheim, CA. **Toll-free/Additional Phone Number(s):** 800-533-7694. **Facsimile Number:** (703)237-7442.

---- Other Sources of Information ----

★4467★
Distributors Financial Analysis (MEMA)
Motor and Equipment Manufacturers Association (MEMA)
300 Sylvan Ave.
PO Box 1638
Englewood Cliffs, NJ 07632-0638   Phone: (201)569-8500

Motorcycle, Boat, and Small-Engine Mechanics

Motorcycle, boat, and small-engine mechanics service power equipment that includes boats, motorcycles, lawn and garden equipment, and occasionally outdoor power equipment. Routine maintenance like adjusting, cleaning, and lubricating parts is a major part of the mechanic's work. When breakdowns do occur, mechanics diagnose the cause and repair or replace the faulty parts. This is accomplished by using common handtools such as pliers and screwdrivers, and a variety of testing devices such as engine analyzers and voltmeters. Mechanics usually specialize in the service and repair of one type of equipment. Motorboat mechanics repair and adjust the engines and electrical and mechanical equipment of inboard and outboard marine engines. Small-engine mechanics service and repair outdoor power equipment such as lawnmowers, garden tractors, and chain saws. 33% of mechanics in this field are self-employed. About 33% work for boat, motorcycle, and miscellaneous vehicle dealers. Others are employed by independent repair shops, marinas, boat yards, hardware and lawn shops, and equipment rental firms.

$alaries

Full-time motorcycle, boat, and small-engine mechanics have median hourly earnings of about $8.10.

Lowest 10 percent	$5.20/hour or less
Middle 50 percent	$6.20-10.50/hour
Highest 10 percent	$14.70/hour or more

Employment Outlook

Growth rate until the year 2000: Average.

Motorcycle, Boat, and Small-Engine Mechanics

Career Guides

★4468★
"Boat Motor Mechanic" in *Transportation*, Volume 12 of *Career Information Center* (pp. 98-100)
Glencoe/Macmillan
15319 Chatsworth St.
Mission Hills, CA 91345 Phone: (818)898-1391
Richard Lidz and Dale Anderson, editorial directors. Fourth edition, 1990. For 600 occupations, describes job duties, entry-level requirements, education and training needed, advancement possibilities, employment outlook, earnings and benefits. The set is divided into 12 volumes. Each volume includes jobs related under a broad career field. Volume 13 is the index. **Facsimile Number:** 818-365-5489.

★4469★
Do Your Own Thing. in the Mechanical Field
AIMS Media, Inc.
9710 DeSoto Ave.
Chatsworth, CA 93111-4409 Phone: (818)773-4300
Videocassette. 1979. 16 mins. Various job levels in the mechanical field are outlined for students.

★4470★
"Marine Engine Mechanic" in *Opportunities in Marine and Maritime Careers* (pp. 105-107)
National Textbook Co.
4255 W. Touhy Ave.
Lincolnwood, IL 60646 Phone: (312)679-5500
William Ray Heitzmann. 1988. Includes careers related by their proximity to water; cruise ships, oceanography, marine sciences, fishing, commercial diving, maritime transportation, shipbuilding, Navy, and Coast Guard. Covers qualifications, job outlook, job duties, educational preparation, and training. Lists associations and schools.

★4471★
"Marine Services Technician" in *Transportation*, Volume 12 of *Career Information Center* (pp. 62-63)
Glencoe/Macmillan
15319 Chatsworth St.
Mission Hills, CA 91345 Phone: (818)898-1391
Richard Lidz and Dale Anderson, editorial directors. Fourth edition, 1990. For 600 occupations, describes job duties, entry-level requirements, education and training needed, advancement possibilities, employment outlook, earnings and benefits. The set is divided into 12 volumes. Each volume includes jobs related under a broad career field. Volume 13 is the index. **Facsimile Number:** 818-365-5489.

★4472★
Mechanics
Morris Video
2730 Monterey St. #105
Monterey Business Park
Torrance, CA 90503 Phone: (213)533-4800
Videocassette. 1984. 15 mins. Various careers in repair are examined including aircraft, motorcycle, diesel, refrigeration and heavy equipment.

★4473★
"Mechanics: Automobiles and Motorcycles" in *Opportunities in Vocational and Technical Careers* (pp. 103-104)
National Textbook Co.
4255 W. Touhy Ave.
Lincolnwood, IL 60646 Phone: (312)679-5500
Adrian A. Paradis. 1987. Describes careers which can be prepared for by attending a private vocational or proprietary school—office employee, sales worker, service worker, health services, mechanic, craftworker, and technician. Covers employment outlook, job duties, and salaries. Offers career planning advice.

★4474★
Motorboat Mechanics
Chronicle Guidance Publications, Inc.
PO Box 1190
Moravia, NY 13118-1190 Phone: (315)497-0330
1988. This career brief describes the nature of the work, working conditions, hours and earnings, education and training, licensure, certification, unions, personal qualifications, social and psychological factors, employment outlook, entry methods, advancement, and related occupations. **Toll-free/Additional Phone Number(s):** 800-622-7284.

★4475★
"Motorcycle, Boat, and Small-Engine Mechanics and Repairers" in *Occupational Outlook Handbook* (pp. 355-357)
Superintendent of Documents
U.S. Government Printing Office
Washington, DC 20402 Phone: (202)783-3238
Biennial; latest edition, 1990-91. Encyclopedia of careers describing more than 250 occupations and comprising about 86 percent of all jobs in the economy. Occupations that require lengthy education or training are given the most attention. For each occupation, the handbook describes job duties, working conditions, training, educational preparation, personal qualities, advancement possibilities, job outlook, earnings, and sources of additional information.

★4476★
Motorcycle Mechanic
Careers, Inc.
PO Box 135
Largo, FL 34649-0135   Phone: (813)584-7333

1991. Two-page occupational summary card describing duties, working conditions, personal qualifications, training, earnings and hours, employment outlook, places of employment, related careers and where to write for more information.

★4477★
"Motorcycle Mechanic" in *Occu-Facts: Information on 565 Careers in Outline Form* (p. 15.6)
Careers, Inc.
P.O. Box 135
1211 Tenth St., S.W.
Largo, FL 33640   Phone: (813)584-7333

Elizabeth Handville. Biennial, 1989-90 edition. Each one-page occupational profile describes duties, working conditions, physical surroundings and demands, aptitudes, temperament, educational requirements, employment outlook, earnings, and places of employment.

★4478★
"Motorcycle Mechanic" in *Transportation*, Volume 12 of *Career Information Center* (pp. 108-109)
Glencoe/Macmillan
15319 Chatsworth St.
Mission Hills, CA 91345   Phone: (818)898-1391

Richard Lidz and Dale Anderson, editorial directors. Fourth edition, 1990. For 600 occupations, describes job duties, entry-level requirements, education and training needed, advancement possibilities, employment outlook, earnings and benefits. The set is divided into 12 volumes. Each volume includes jobs related under a broad career field. Volume 13 is the index. **Facsimile Number:** 818-365-5489.

★4479★
"Motorcycle Mechanics" in *Opportunities in Automotive Service Careers* (p. 59)
National Textbook Co.
4255 W. Touhy Ave.
Lincolnwood, IL 60646   Phone: (312)679-5500

Robert M. Weber. 1989. Describes the work of the automobile mechanic and related occupations such as service station attendant and automobile body repairer. Covers working conditions, places of employment, qualifications, training, apprenticeships, certification, advancement opportunities, employment outlook, tools needed, and earnings.

★4480★
"Motorcycle Mechanics" in Volume 4 of *Career Discovery Encyclopedia* (pp. 108-109)
J.G. Ferguson Publishing Co.
200 W. Monroe
Chicago, IL 60606   Phone: (312)580-5480

E. Russell Primm, editor-in-chief. 1990. Contains two-page articles on 504 occupations. Each article describes job duties, earnings, and educational and training requirements.

★4481★
Motorcycle Technicians
Chronicle Guidance Publications, Inc.
PO Box 1190
Moravia, NY 13118-1190   Phone: (315)497-0330

1988. This career brief describes the nature of the work, working conditions, hours and earnings, education and training, licensure, certification, unions, personal qualifications, social and psychological factors, employment outlook, entry methods, advancement, and related occupations. **Toll-free/Additional Phone Number(s):** 800-622-7284.

———— Associations ————

★4482★
Motor and Equipment Manufacturers Association (MEMA)
300 Sylvan Ave.
PO Box 1638
Englewood Cliffs, NJ 07632-0638   Phone: (201)569-8500

Membership: Manufacturers of automotive and heavy-duty original equipment and replacement components, maintenance equipment, chemicals, accessories, refinishing supplies, tools, and service equipment united for research into all aspects of the automotive and heavy-duty markets. **Purpose:** Provides manufacturer-oriented services and programs including: marketing consultation for the automotive industry; federal and state legal, safety, and legislative representation and consultation; personnel services; manpower development workshops; international information. Maintains credit reporting and collection service covering wholesalers, retailers, chain stores, and warehouse distributors; offers electronic order-entry, price-update, and electronic document exchange services through MEMA/Transnet system; maintains international liaison. Administers U.S. Automotive Parts Industry Japan Office in conjunction with the U.S. Department of Commerce. Conducts seminars on domestic and overseas marketing, federal trade regulations, freight forwarding, and credit and collections. Compiles statistics on automotive service industry for use by members and as a public service. **Publications:** *Automotive Distributor Trends and Financial Analysis*, periodic. • *Credit and Sales Reference Directory*, 2/year. • *International Buyer's Guide of U.S* • *Marketing Insight*, quarterly. • Also publishes *Japan Automotive Insight*, *Autobody Supply and Equipment Market*, *Automotive Jobbers in the U.S.* **Facsimile Number:** (201)569-0159.

———— Test Guides ————

★4483★
Motor Equipment Mechanic
National Learning Corp.
212 Michael Dr.
Syosset, NY 11791   Phone: (516)921-8888

Jack Rudman. Part of the Career Examination Series No. 1. All examination guides in this series contain questions with answers. **Facsimile Number:** (516)921-8743. **Toll-free/Additional Phone Number(s):** 800-645-6337.

———— Basic Reference Guides and Handbooks ————

★4484★
Autobody Supply and Equipment Market (MEMA)
Motor and Equipment Manufacturers Association (MEMA)
300 Sylvan Ave.
PO Box 1638
Englewood Cliffs, NJ 07632-0638   Phone: (201)569-8500

★4485★
Car Maintenance in the U.S.A. (MEMA)
Motor and Equipment Manufacturers Association (MEMA)
300 Sylvan Ave.
PO Box 1638
Englewood Cliffs, NJ 07632-0638   Phone: (201)569-8500

Motorcycle, Boat, and Small-Engine Mechanics

★4486★
The Care & Repair of Small Marine Diesels
International Marine Publishing Company
PO Box 220
Camden, ME 04843 Phone: (207)236-4837
Chris Thompson. 1987. **Facsimile Number:** (207)236-6314.

★4487★
The Complete Guide To Motorcycle Mechanics
Prentice Hall
Rte. 9W
Englewood Cliffs, NJ 07632 Phone: (201)592-2000
Motorcycle Mechanics Institute Staff. 1984.

★4488★
Foreign Vehicle Maintenance in the U.S.A. (MEMA)
Motor and Equipment Manufacturers Association (MEMA)
300 Sylvan Ave.
PO Box 1638
Englewood Cliffs, NJ 07632-0638 Phone: (201)569-8500

★4489★
Heavy Duty Truck Maintenance in the U.S.A. (MEMA)
Motor and Equipment Manufacturers Association (MEMA)
300 Sylvan Ave.
PO Box 1638
Englewood Cliffs, NJ 07632-0638 Phone: (201)569-8500

★4490★
Metal Corrosion in Boats
International Marine Publishing Company
PO Box 220
Camden, ME 04843 Phone: (207)236-4837
Nigel Warren. 1987. **Facsimile Number:** (207)236-6314.

★4491★
Motorcycle Electrics Without Pain
M. Arman Publishing, Inc.
PO Box 785
Ormond Beach, FL 32175 Phone: (904)673-5576
Mike Arman. 1980.

★4492★
Motorcycle Mechanics
McGraw-Hill Publishing Company
1221 Avenue of the Americas
New York, NY 10020 Phone: (212)512-2000
William H. Crouse. 1982.

★4493★
Motorcycle Mechanics
Prentice Hall
Rte. 9W
Englewood Cliffs, NJ 07632 Phone: (201)592-2000
Lynn S. Mosher. 1977.

★4494★
Small Steel Craft: Design, Construction & Maintenance
Sheridan House, Inc.
145 Palisade St.
Dobbs Ferry, NY 10522 Phone: (914)693-2410
Ian Nicolson. Second edition, 1986.

Periodicals

★4495★
ABYC News
American Boat & Yacht Council, Inc. (ABYC)
PO Box 747
Millersville, MD 21108 Phone: (410)923-3932
Editor(s): Louise Lincoln. 1-4/yr. Concerned with voluntary standards in boat and equipment design, construction, service, and repair. Publishes news of Council activities. Recurring features include announcements of new officers and members and project and technical committee news. **Facsimile Number:** (410)923-3988.

★4496★
American Boat Builders & Repairers Association—Bulletin
American Boat Builders & Repairers Association
PO Box 1236
Stamford, CT 06904 Phone: (203)967-4745
Editor(s): Elizabeth Thoresby-Cross. Semimonthly. Covers matters of interest and concern to boatbuilders, boatyards, and marinas. **Facsimile Number:** (203)967-4618.

★4497★
Automotive Distributor Trends and Financial Analysis (MEMA)
Motor and Equipment Manufacturers Association (MEMA)
300 Sylvan Ave.
PO Box 1638
Englewood Cliffs, NJ 07632-0638 Phone: (201)569-8500
Periodic.

★4498★
Automotive Jobbers in the U.S.A. (MEMA)
Motor and Equipment Manufacturers Association (MEMA)
300 Sylvan Ave.
PO Box 1638
Englewood Cliffs, NJ 07632-0638 Phone: (201)569-8500

★4499★
HummerNews
Harley Hummer Club
PO Box 7294
Gaithersburg, MD 20398-7294 Phone: (301)424-6954
Editor(s): David M. Hennessey. Quarterly. Supplies information for persons interested in the preservation and restoration of Harley-Davidson 2-stroke motorcycles made in the U.S. between 1948 and 1966. Carries pictures, technical tips, and reprints of old Harley advertisements. Recurring features include notices of motorcycles and parts wanted and for sale, listings of other collector groups, letters to the editor, and news of members.

★4500★
MEMA Marketing Insight (MEMA)
Motor and Equipment Manufacturers Association (MEMA)
300 Sylvan Ave.
PO Box 1638
Englewood Cliffs, NJ 07632-0638 Phone: (201)569-8500
Quarterly.

Other Sources of Information

★4501★
***Distributors Financial Analysis* (MEMA)**
Motor and Equipment Manufacturers Association (MEMA)
300 Sylvan Ave.
PO Box 1638
Englewood Cliffs, NJ 07632-0638   Phone: (201)569-8500

Musical Instrument Repairers and Tuners

Musical instrument repairers and tuners maintain piano, pipe-organ, brass, wind, and string instruments so they perform properly. Piano tuners adjust piano strings to the proper pitch by setting them in relation to a properly adjusted "A" string. They also diagnose and correct any problems that may affect proper operation. Pipe-organ repairers tune, repair, and install organs that make music by forcing air through flue pipes or reed pipes. Like piano tuners, pipe-organ repairers tune the various pipes in relation to the "A" pipe. Repairers also do maintenance work cleaning the pipes, and may assemble organs onsite in churches and auditoriums. Violin repairers adjust and repair bowed instruments like violins and cellos. Brass and wind instrument repairers clean, adjust, and repair instruments such as flutes, saxophones and trumpets. About 80% of all repairers and tuners work in music stores. The rest work in repair shops or for musical instrument manufacturers. About half of all repairers and tuners are self-employed.

$alaries

Earnings for musical instrument repairers and tuners are listed below.

Apprentices	$8,000-10,000/year
Beginner repairers and tuners	$12,000-18,000/year
Experienced repairers and tuners	$20,000-40,000/year

Employment Outlook

Growth rate until the year 2000: Slower than average.

Musical Instrument Repairers and Tuners

Career Guides

★4502★
"Bow Repairer and Restorer" in *Career Opportunities in the Music Industry* (pp. 131-132)
Facts on File, Inc.
460 Park Avenue, S.
New York, NY 10016   Phone: (212)683-2244
Shelly Field. Second edition, 1991. Describes more than 70 music related jobs. Each occupational profile covers job duties, employment outlook, career paths, salaries, skills, and educational preparation. Offers tips for entering the field.

★4503★
"Instrument Repair & Restoration Specialist" in *Career Opportunities in the Music Industry* (pp. 127-128)
Facts on File, Inc.
460 Park Avenue, S.
New York, NY 10016   Phone: (212)683-2244
Shelly Field. Second edition, 1991. Describes more than 70 music related jobs. Each occupational profile covers job duties, employment outlook, career paths, salaries, skills, and educational preparation. Offers tips for entering the field.

★4504★
Instrument Repairers
Chronicle Guidance Publications, Inc.
PO Box 1190
Moravia, NY 13118-1190   Phone: (315)497-0330
1988. This career brief describes the nature of the work, working conditions, hours and earnings, education and training, licensure, certification, unions, personal qualifications, social and psychological factors, employment outlook, entry methods, advancement, and related occupations. **Toll-free/Additional Phone Number(s):** 800-622-7284.

★4505★
"Musical Instrument Repairers" in Volume 4 of *Career Discovery Encyclopedia* (pp. 112-113)
J.G. Ferguson Publishing Co.
200 W. Monroe
Chicago, IL 60606   Phone: (312)580-5480
E. Russell Primm, editor-in-chief. 1990. Contains two-page articles on 504 occupations. Each article describes job duties, earnings, and educational and training requirements.

★4506★
"Musical Instrument Repairers and Tuners" in *Occupational Outlook Handbook* (pp. 357-358)
Superintendent of Documents
U.S. Government Printing Office
Washington, DC 20402   Phone: (202)783-3238
Biennial; latest edition, 1990-91. Encyclopedia of careers describing more than 250 occupations and comprising about 86 percent of all jobs in the economy. Occupations that require lengthy education or training are given the most attention. For each occupation, the handbook describes job duties, working conditions, training, educational preparation, personal qualities, advancement possibilities, job outlook, earnings, and sources of additional information.

★4507★
"Musical Instrument Repairers and Tuners" in *The Encyclopedia of Careers and Vocational Guidance* (pp. 591-595)
J.G. Ferguson Publishing Co.
200 W. Monroe
Chicago, IL 60606   Phone: (312)580-5480
William E. Hopke, editor-in-chief. Eighth edition, 1990. Four-volume set that profiles 500 occupations and describes job trends in 76 industries. Includes career description, educational requirements, history of the job, methods of entry, advancement, employment outlook, earnings, working conditions, social and psychological factors, and sources of additional information.

★4508★
"Piano and Organ Tuner, Technician" in *Consumer, Homemaking, and Personal Services*, Volume 5 of *Career Information Center* (pp. 91-93)
Glencoe/Macmillan
15319 Chatsworth St.
Mission Hills, CA 91345   Phone: (818)898-1391
Richard Lidz and Dale Anderson, editorial directors. Fourth edition, 1990. For 600 occupations, describes job duties, entry-level requirements, education and training needed, advancement possibilities, employment outlook, earnings and benefits. The set is divided into 12 volumes. Each volume includes jobs related under a broad career field. Volume 13 is the index. **Facsimile Number:** 818-365-5489.

★4509★
"Piano Technicians" in Volume 4 of *The Encyclopedia of Careers and Vocational Guidance* (pp. 358-360)
J.G. Ferguson Publishing Co.
200 W. Monroe
Chicago, IL 60606   Phone: (312)580-5480

William E. Hopke, editor-in-chief. Eighth edition, 1990. Four-volume set that profiles 500 occupations and describes job trends in 76 industries. Includes career description, educational requirements, history of the job, methods of entry, advancement, employment outlook, earnings, working conditions, social and psychological factors, and sources of additional information.

★4510★
"Piano Tuner" in *Offbeat Careers: The Directory of Unusual Work* (pp. 111-112)
Ten Speed Press
PO Box 7123
Berkeley, CA 94707   Phone: (415)845-8414

Al Sacharov. 1988. Profiles eighty-eight unusual careers. Provides job description, history of occupation, salary, and training required. Lists one or more sources of additional information.

★4511★
Piano Tuner-Technician
Careers, Inc.
PO Box 135
Largo, FL 34649-0135   Phone: (813)584-7333

1990. Two-page occupational summary card describing duties, working conditions, personal qualifications, training, earnings and hours, employment outlook, places of employment, related careers and where to write for more information.

★4512★
The Piano Tuner-Technician
Piano Technicians Guild
4510 Belleview, Ste. 100
Kansas City, MO 64111   Phone: (816)753-7747

1984. This pamphlet describes the work, the skills needed, places of employment, and earnings.

★4513★
"Piano Tuner Technician" in *Career Opportunities in the Music Industry* (pp. 129-130)
Facts on File, Inc.
460 Park Avenue, S.
New York, NY 10016   Phone: (212)683-2244

Shelly Field. Second edition, 1991. Describes more than 70 music related jobs. Each occupational profile covers job duties, employment outlook, career paths, salaries, skills, and educational preparation. Offers tips for entering the field.

★4514★
"Piano Tuner-Technician" in *Occu-Facts: Information on 565 Careers in Outline Form* (p. 15.21)
Careers, Inc.
P.O. Box 135
1211 Tenth St., S.W.
Largo, FL 33640   Phone: (813)584-7333

Elizabeth Handville. Biennial, 1989-90 edition. Each one-page occupational profile describes duties, working conditions, physical surroundings and demands, aptitudes, temperament, educational requirements, employment outlook, earnings, and places of employment.

★4515★
Piano Tuners and Technicians
Chronicle Guidance Publications, Inc.
PO Box 1190
Moravia, NY 13118-1190   Phone: (315)497-0330

1991. This career brief describes the nature of the work, working conditions, hours and earnings, education and training, licensure, certification, unions, personal qualifications, social and psychological factors, employment outlook, entry methods, advancement, and related occupations. **Toll-free/Additional Phone Number(s):** 800-622-7284.

★4516★
"Pipe Organ Technicians" in Volume 4 of *The Encyclopedia of Careers and Vocational Guidance* (pp. 361-363)
J.G. Ferguson Publishing Co.
200 W. Monroe
Chicago, IL 60606   Phone: (312)580-5480

William E. Hopke, editor-in-chief. Eighth edition, 1990. Four-volume set that profiles 500 occupations and describes job trends in 76 industries. Includes career description, educational requirements, history of the job, methods of entry, advancement, employment outlook, earnings, working conditions, social and psychological factors, and sources of additional information.

★4517★
"Tuner/Technician" in *Opportunities in Music Careers* (pp. 134-135)
National Textbook Co.
4255 W. Touhy Ave.
Lincolnwood, IL 60646   Phone: (312)679-5500

Second edition, 1991. Covers many aspects of the music business including careers in music performance and publishing, the recording industry, and teaching. Lists resources, associations, and unions.

Associations

★4518★
American Federation of Violin and Bow Makers (AFVBM)
288 Richmond Terrace
Staten Island, NY 10301   Phone: (718)816-7818

Membership: Professionals who make, restore, and repair violins and bows. **Purpose:** To elevate professional standards of craftsmanship and ethical conduct among members. Designs programs to develop members' technical skills and knowledge; aims to establish internship programs to individuals who wish to become violin makers or repair persons. Conducts competitions and annual exhibition; awards prizes to the best instruments displayed. Grants journeyman and master status in the field. Maintains speakers' bureau, museum, and biographical archives. Holds seminars.

★4519★
American Institute of Organbuilders (AIO)
PO Box 130982
Houston, TX 77219   Phone: (713)529-2212

Membership: Professional builders and service technicians of pipe organs. **Purpose:** To advance the art of pipe organ building by encouraging discussion, inquiry, research, and experimentation; to further knowledge regarding pipe organ building through lectures and the exchange of information. Conducts examinations and bestows certification at the journeyman and master levels. Maintains archives.

Musical Instrument Repairers and Tuners

★4520★
Guild of American Luthiers (GAL)
8222 S. Park Ave.
Tacoma, WA 98408   Phone: (206)472-7853
Membership: Luthiers (makers and repairers of stringed instruments such as guitars, violins, lutes, harpsichords, banjos, and dulcimers); suppliers; luthier schools; interested musicians, musicologists, and aficionados. **Purpose:** Disseminates information on instrument building and repair. Seeks to create and sustain an active community of luthiers. Sponsors demonstrations, lectures, and seminars.

★4521★
National Association of Professional Band Instrument Repair Technicians (NAPBIRT)
8 Ardith Dr.
PO Box 51
Normal, IL 61761   Phone: (309)452-4257
Membership: Professional technicians who repair or restore band instruments. **Purpose:** Purpose is to promote technical integrity in the craft. Conducts self-evaluation programs, local parts and services exchange programs, and problem solution services. Surveys tools and procedures to improve work quality. Serves as liaison between manufacturers/suppliers and technicians by providing a technical audience for the introduction and evaluation of new products and policies. Makes available emergency maintenance and repair of band instruments to college and university instructors, thus allowing musicians to continue in concert. Has established a code of ethics; is developing library on the construction, repair, and restoration of band instruments. Bestows Super Boss Award to persons with whom members are associated as employees or subcontractors. Maintains the Tom Chekouras Scholarship Fund for potential band instrument repair technicians. Provides placement service. **Publications:** *Administrative Newsletter*, quarterly. • *Directory*, periodic. • *Regional Newsletter*, quarterly. • *TechniCom* bimonthly.

★4522★
Piano Technicians Guild (PTG)
4510 Belleview, Ste. 100
Kansas City, MO 64111   Phone: (816)753-7747
Membership: Piano tuners and technicians. **Purpose:** Conducts technical institutes at conventions, seminars, and local chapter meetings. Promotes public education in piano care; maintains liaison with piano manufacturers and teachers. Bestows awards; maintains hall of fame. **Publications:** *Members Bulletin*, monthly. • *Official Directory*, annual. • *Piano Technicians Journal*, 13/year. • Has also published *Piano Action Handbook* and *Piano Parts and Their Functions, Illustrated*.

Standards/Certification Agencies

★4523★
American Federation of Violin and Bow Makers (AFVBM)
288 Richmond Terrace
Staten Island, NY 10301   Phone: (718)816-7818
Elevates professional standards of craftsmanship and ethical conduct among members. Grants journeyman and master status in the field.

★4524★
American Institute of Organbuilders (AIO)
PO Box 130982
Houston, TX 77219   Phone: (713)529-2212
Conducts examinations and bestows certification at the journeyman and master levels.

Awards, Scholarships, Grants, and Fellowships

★4525★
Tom Chekouras Scholarship Fund
National Association of Professional Band Instrument Repair Technicians
8 Ardith Dr.
PO Box 51
Normal, IL 61761   Phone: (309)452-4257
Scholarship fund is maintained to support potential band instrument repair technicians.

★4526★
Golden Hammer Award
Piano Technicians Guild
4510 Belleview, Ste. 100
Kansas City, MO 64111   Phone: (816)753-7747
To recognize an individual for exceptional personal service in and to the piano technological profession over many years. Members of the Guild are eligible. A gold-plated tuning hammer displayed in a hand-made case in the shape of a grand piano is awarded annually. Established in 1969.

★4527★
Hall of Fame
Piano Technicians Guild
4510 Belleview, Ste. 100
Kansas City, MO 64111   Phone: (816)753-7747
To perpetuate the memory of piano industry greats and to recognize a lifetime of very special services to the music industry. A wood and lucite Hall of Fame plaque is presented to the honoree, whose picture and resume are in the Hall of Fame at the Home Office. Awarded annually. Established in 1976.

Basic Reference Guides and Handbooks

★4528★
Complete Course in Professional Piano Tuning, Repair & Rebuilding
Nelson-Hall, Inc.
111 N. Canal St.
Chicago, IL 60606   Phone: (312)930-9446
Floyd A. Stevens. 1972.

★4529★
Guitar Repair
Bold Strummer, Ltd
20 Turkey Hill Circle
PO Box 2037
Westport, CT 06880   Phone: (203)259-3021
Irving Sloane. Revised edition, 1989. **Facsimile Number:** (203)259-7369.

★4530★
How to Tune, Repair & Regulate Pianos: A Practical Guide
Hill Springs Publications
5023 Kentucky St.
South Charleston, WV 23509   Phone: (364)768-8223
Jack Bradley. 1986.

★4531★
NAPBIRT Directory (NAPBIRT)
National Association of Professional Band Instrument Repair Technicians
8 Ardith Dr.
PO Box 51
Normal, IL 61761   Phone: (309)452-4257
Periodic.

★4532★
Piano Action Handbook (PTG)
Piano Technicians Guild (PTG)
4510 Belleview, Ste. 100
Kansas City, MO 64111   Phone: (816)753-7747

★4533★
Piano Parts and Their Functions, Illustrated (PTG)
Piano Technicians Guild (PTG)
4510 Belleview, Ste. 100
Kansas City, MO 64111   Phone: (816)753-7747

★4534★
Piano Servicing, Tuning & Rebuilding
Vestal Press, Ltd.
320 N. Jensen Rd.
PO Box 97
Vestal, NY 13851-0097   Phone: (607)797-4872
Arthur A. Reblitz. 1986. **Facsimile Number:** (607)797-4898.

★4535★
Player Piano Servicing & Rebuilding
Vestal Press, Ltd.
320 N. Jensen Rd.
PO Box 97
Vestal, NY 13851-0097   Phone: (607)797-4872
Arthur A. Reblitz. 1985. (607)797-4898.

---------- Periodicals ----------

★4536★
Catgut Acoustical Society—Journal
Catgut Acoustical Society
112 Essex Ave.
Montclair, NJ 07042   Phone: (201)744-4029
Editor(s): Daniel W. Haines. Semiannually. Deals with the practical, technical, and acoustical aspects of musical instrument making. Discusses the history and performance of musical instruments and musical composition. Covers new developments in the field. Recurring features include book reviews and bibliographies.

★4537★
Experimental Musical Instruments
Bart #Hopkin
PO Box 784
Nicasio, CA 94946   Phone: (415)662-2182
Editor(s): Bart Hopkin. Bimonthly. Explores new and unconventional musical instruments and sound sculpture. Covers all types of instruments and musical forms, discussing acoustics, tools and techniques, recording, and composition. Recurring features include news of research, letters to the editor, and reviews of books and recordings.

★4538★
FIGA—Newsletter
Fretted Instrument Guild of America (FIGA)
c/o Ann Pertoney
2344 Oakley Ave.
Chicago, IL 60608   Phone: (312)376-1143
Editor(s): Glen Lemmer. Bimonthly. Publishes news of the Guild and musical pieces for fretted instruments, including the banjo, guitar, violin, fiddle, mandolin, lute, and bass.

★4539★
NAPBIRT Administrative Newsletter (NAPBIRT)
National Association of Professional Band Instrument Repair Technicians
8 Ardith Dr.
PO Box 51
Normal, IL 61761   Phone: (309)452-4257
Quarterly.

★4540★
NAPBIRT Regional Newsletter (NAPBIRT)
National Association of Professional Band Instrument Repair Technicians
8 Ardith Dr.
PO Box 51
Normal, IL 61761   Phone: (309)452-4257
Quarterly.

★4541★
Piano Technicians Journal
Piano Technicians Guild, Inc.
4510 Belleview, Ste. 100
Kansas City, MO 64111   Phone: (816)753-7747
Larry Goldsmith, Editor. Monthly. Magazine for piano technicians. **Facsimile Number:** (816)531-0070.

★4542★
PTG Members Bulletin (PTG)
Piano Technicians Guild (PTG)
4510 Belleview, Ste. 100
Kansas City, MO 64111   Phone: (816)753-7747
Monthly.

★4543★
STRINGS
The String Letter Corp.
412 Red Hill Ave.
PO Box 767
San Anselmo, CA 94960   Phone: (415)485-6946
David M. Brin, Editor. 6x/yr. **Facsimile Number:** (415)485-0831.

★4544★
TECHNICOM
National Association of Professional Band Instrument Repair Technicians
PO Box 51
Normal, IL 61761   Phone: (309)452-4257
Editor(s): Chuck Hagler. 6/yr. Serves as an exchange of information among band instrument repair technicians, providing news of developments in the field and articles by association members. Carries updates on Association activities and profiles of industry professionals.

★4545★
TechniCom (NAPBIRT)
National Association of Professional Band Instrument Repair Technicians
8 Ardith Dr.
PO Box 51
Normal, IL 61761   Phone: (309)452-4257
Bimonthly. Journal.

―――― Meetings and Conventions ――――

★4546★
American Federation of Violin and Bow Makers (AFVBM)
288 Richmond Terrace
Staten Island, NY 10301   Phone: (718)816-7818
Frequency: Holds annual mid-April meeting.

★4547★
American Institute of Organbuilders (AIO)
PO Box 130982
Houston, TX 77219   Phone: (713)529-2212
Frequency: Annual convention, with exhibits, is always held in October.

★4548★
Guild of American Luthiers Conference (GAL)
8222 S. Park Ave.
Tacoma, WA 98408   Phone: (206)472-7853
Frequency: Biennial, with exhibits. 1992; Vermillion, SD.

★4549★
National Association of Professional Band Instrument Repair Technicians Conference (NAPBIRT)
8 Ardith Dr.
PO Box 51
Normal, IL 61761   Phone: (309)452-4257
Frequency: Annual.

★4550★
Piano Manufacturers Association International Semiannual Trade Show
Piano Manufacturers Association International
Don Dillon Associates
4020 McEwen
Dallas, TX 75244   Phone: (214)233-9107
Frequency: Always held during January at the Convention Center in Anaheim, California. 1993; Jan. 15-17; Anaheim, CA.
Facsimile Number: (214)490-4219.

Telephone Installers and Repairers

Telephone installers and repairers install, service, and repair telephones and other communications equipment on customers' property. Telephone installers and repairers, sometimes called station installers or service technicians, relocate telephones or make changes on existing equipment, such as adding extensions or replacing an old phone with a newer model. In homes under construction they may install all necessary wiring and telephone jacks in the desired locations. Installers and technicians connect telephones to outside service wires, sometimes climbing poles or ladders to do so. In diagnosing problems, they work closely with trouble locators in the central office. Repairers find the source of the problem by connecting a test set to the customer's telephone line and then testing in conjunction with the trouble locator. Some experienced service technicians have learned additional skills in line installation and cable splicing. Those with multiple skills and the ability to handle emergencies quickly are considered especially valuable by many small companies.

$alaries

Pay scales vary greatly across the country. Specific information may be obtained from local telephone companies. However, telephone installers and repairers employed by AT & T and the Bell Operating Companies, and represented by the Communications Workers of America, earn an average weekly salary of $640.00.

Employment Outlook

Growth rate until the year 2000: Slower than average.

Telephone Installers and Repairers

Career Guides

★4551★
"Phone Repair Technician" in *Hard Hatted Women: Stories of Struggle and Success in the Trades* (pp. 235-253)
Seal Press
3131 Western Ave., Ste. 410
Seattle, WA 98121   Phone: (206)283-7844
Molly Martin, editor. 1988. Twenty-six women recount their experiences working in blue collar occupations. They describe how they got in, the work they do, their relationships in predominantly male occupations, and their training.

★4552★
"Telephone Installer" in *Exploring Nontraditional Jobs for Women* (pp. 43-48)
Rosen Publishing Group, Inc.
29 E. 21st St.
New York, NY 10010   Phone: (212)777-3017
Rose Neufeld. 1989. Describes blue-collar, male dominated occupations. Discusses what is done on the job, training, where to apply for jobs, tools used, salaries, and advantages and disadvantages. Relates the experiences of women who are working in the field.

★4553★
"Telephone Installer" in *Occu-Facts: Information on 565 Careers in Outline Form* (p. 15.16)
Careers, Inc.
P.O. Box 135
1211 Tenth St., S.W.
Largo, FL 33640   Phone: (813)584-7333
Elizabeth Handville. Biennial, 1989-90 edition. Each one-page occupational profile describes duties, working conditions, physical surroundings and demands, aptitudes, temperament, educational requirements, employment outlook, earnings, and places of employment.

★4554★
Telephone Installer/Repair Technician
Careers, Inc.
PO Box 135
Largo, FL 34649-0135   Phone: (813)584-7333
1988. Two-page occupational summary card describing duties, working conditions, personal qualifications, training, earnings and hours, employment outlook, places of employment, related careers and where to write for more information.

★4555★
"Telephone Installers and Repairers" in *Occupational Outlook Handbook* (pp. 358-360)
Superintendent of Documents
U.S. Government Printing Office
Washington, DC 20402   Phone: (202)783-3238
Biennial; latest edition, 1990-91. Encyclopedia of careers describing more than 250 occupations and comprising about 86 percent of all jobs in the economy. Occupations that require lengthy education or training are given the most attention. For each occupation, the handbook describes job duties, working conditions, training, educational preparation, personal qualities, advancement possibilities, job outlook, earnings, and sources of additional information.

★4556★
"Telephone Installers and Repairers" in Volume 6 of *Career Discovery Encyclopedia* (pp. 102-103)
J.G. Ferguson Publishing Co.
200 W. Monroe
Chicago, IL 60606   Phone: (312)580-5480
E. Russell Primm, editor-in-chief. 1990. Contains two-page articles on 504 occupations. Each article describes job duties, earnings, and educational and training requirements.

★4557★
"Telephone Service Technician" in *Communications and the Arts*, Volume 3 of *Career Information Center* (pp. 79-80)
Glencoe/Macmillan
15319 Chatsworth St.
Mission Hills, CA 91345   Phone: (818)898-1391
Richard Lidz and Dale Anderson, editorial directors. Fourth edition, 1990. For 600 occupations, describes job duties, entry-level requirements, education and training needed, advancement possibilities, employment outlook, earnings and benefits. The set is divided into 12 volumes. Each volume includes jobs related under a broad career field. Volume 13 is the index. **Facsimile Number:** 818-365-5489.

★4558★
"Telephone Service Technician" in *Telecommunications* (pp. 27-31)
Franklin Watts, Inc.
387 Park Avenue, S.
New York, NY 10016   Phone: (212)686-7070
Linda Barrett and Galen Guengerich. 1991. Surveys opportunities in telecommunications including telephone, radio, telegraph, and television communications. Includes job description, educational preparation, salary, and employment outlook. Offers job hunting advice.

★4559★
Telephone Systems Installer
Vocational Biographies, Inc.
PO Box 31, Dept. VF10
Sauk Centre, MN 56378   Phone: (612)352-6516
1989. This pamphlet profiles a person working in the job. Includes information about job duties, working conditions, places of employment, educational preparation, labor market outlook, and salaries. **Toll-free/Additional Phone Number(s):** 800-255-0752.

---------- Associations ----------

★4560★
North American Telecommunications Association (NATA)
2000 M St. NW, Ste. 550
Washington, DC 20036   Phone: (202)296-9800
Membership: Manufacturers and distributors of communications, computer, and office equipment; suppliers, consultants, and users of voice and data technology; related service and information providers. **Purpose:** Provides legal, legislative, public relations, research, and membership services. Maintains the National Telecommunications Education Committee which serves as an information source and liaison between the telecommunications industry and educational institutions with telecommunications programs. Conducts specialized education and research programs. Presents annual exhibition showcase. Maintains library. Compiles statistics. **Publications:** *Directory of Telecommunications and Education Programs*, periodic. • *NATA Communicator*, monthly. • *NATA Sourcebook*, annual. • *Telecom Export Guide*, biennial. • *Telecom Market Review and Forecast*, annual. • *Washington Update*, biweekly. • Also publishes *Sales Agency: A Comparative Analysis* and *Voice Processing Industry Review* (books) and *Industry Basics*. **Facsimile Number:** (202)296-4993.

★4561★
United States Telephone Association (USTA)
900 19th St. NW, Ste. 800
Washington, DC 20006   Phone: (202)835-3100
Membership: Local operating telephone companies or telephone holding companies. Members represent a total of 114 million access lines. **Purpose:** Presents Distinguished Service Award and Pacesetter Award to outstanding leaders in industry and other fields. Conducts educational and training programs. Maintains 21 committees. **Publications:** *Holding Company Report*, annual. • *Phonefacts*, annual. • *Statistical Volumes*, annual. • *Teletimes*, quarterly. • Also publishes booklets and brochures. **Toll-free/Additional Phone Number(s):** (202)835-3198 telephone news updates on legislative and industry developments.

---------- Educational Directories and Programs ----------

★4562★
Directory of Telecommunications and Education Programs (NATA)
North American Telecommunications Association (NATA)
2000 M St. NW, Ste. 550
Washington, DC 20036   Phone: (202)296-9800
Periodic.

---------- Basic Reference Guides and Handbooks ----------

★4563★
NATA Industry Basics (NATA)
North American Telecommunications Association (NATA)
2000 M St. NW, Ste. 550
Washington, DC 20036   Phone: (202)296-9800

★4564★
NATA Sourcebook (NATA)
North American Telecommunications Association (NATA)
2000 M St. NW, Ste. 550
Washington, DC 20036   Phone: (202)296-9800
Annual. Directory.

---------- Periodicals ----------

★4565★
NATA Communicator (NATA)
North American Telecommunications Association (NATA)
2000 M St. NW, Ste. 550
Washington, DC 20036   Phone: (202)296-9800
Monthly.

★4566★
NATA Washington Update (NATA)
North American Telecommunications Association (NATA)
2000 M St. NW, Ste. 550
Washington, DC 20036   Phone: (202)296-9800
Biweekly.

★4567★
Rural Telecommunications
National Telephone Cooperative Assn., Inc.
2626 Pennsylvania Ave. NW
Washington, DC 20037   Phone: (202)298-2300
Ingrid K. Young, Managing Editor. Quarterly. **Facsimile Number:** (202)298-2320.

★4568★
Telecommunications Reports
Business Research Publications, Inc.
1333 H St., NW
Washington, DC 20005   Phone: (202)842-3006
Victoria A. Mason, Editor. Publication tracking all aspects of the telecommunications industry on state, federal, and international levels. Coverage includes the FCC, Congress, state regulatory commissions and legislatures, and federal and state court decisions. Also reports on telecommunications companies and equipment manufacturers, new services and products, personnel changes, and labor union developments. Includes quarterly index. Available online via NewsNet. **Facsimile Number:** (202)842-3047.

★4569★
Telephone News
Phillips Publishing, Inc.
7811 Montrose Rd.
Potomac, MD 20854   Phone: (301)340-2100
Candace Sams, Editor. Weekly. Telecommunications industry newsletter. **Facsimile Number:** (301)424-4297.

★4570★
Teletimes (USTA)
United States Telephone Association (USTA)
900 19th St. NW, Ste. 800
Washington, DC 20006   Phone: (202)835-3100
Quarterly.

——— Meetings and Conventions ———

★4571★
Association of Telemessaging Services International Annual Meeting
Association of Telemessaging Services International
320 King St., Ste. 500
Alexandria, VA 22314   Phone: (703)684-0016
1992. **Facsimile Number:** (703)684-3415.

★4572★
International Customer Service Association Conference
International Customer Service Association
111 E. Wacker Dr., Ste. 600
Chicago, IL 60601   Phone: (312)644-6610
1992; Sep. 20-23; San Antonio, TX • 1993; Sep. 12-15; Toronto, ON, Canada.

★4573★
INTERWIRE
Wire Association International
1570 Boston Post Rd.
PO Box H
Guilford, CT 06437   Phone: (203)453-2777
1993; Apr. Atlanta, GA. **Facsimile Number:** (203)453-8384.

——— Other Sources of Information ———

★4574★
Phonefacts (USTA)
United States Telephone Association (USTA)
900 19th St. NW, Ste. 800
Washington, DC 20006   Phone: (202)835-3100
Annual.

★4575★
Telecom Market Review and Forecast (NATA)
North American Telecommunications Association (NATA)
2000 M St. NW, Ste. 550
Washington, DC 20036   Phone: (202)296-9800
Annual. Statistical review of the telecommunications industry.

★4576★
Voice Processing Industry Review (NATA)
North American Telecommunications Association (NATA)
2000 M St. NW, Ste. 550
Washington, DC 20036   Phone: (202)296-9800

Vending Machine Servicers and Repairers

Vending machine servicers and repairers install, service, and stock vending machines and keep them in good working order. Servicers make sure machines operate correctly by checking that refrigeration and heating units work properly, handles, springs, and merchandise chutes operate, and that coin and change making mechanisms are functional. When installing the machines, they make the necessary water and electrical connections and recheck the machines for proper operation. Another major duty of these workers is preventive maintenance. This involves cleaning and lubrication of various parts and making necessary adjustments. In case of machine breakdown, repairers inspect it for obvious problems, consult troubleshooting manuals and use testing devices to locate the defect. Once the problem is found, they use a variety of tools in repair such as pipe cutters, soldering guns and other power tools. Because many vending machines dispense food, these workers must comply with state and local public health and sanitation standards. They also must comply with local plumbing and electrical codes. Most repairers work for vending companies that sell food and other items through machines. Others work for soft drink bottling companies that have their own coin-operated machines. Some work for companies that own video games, pinball machines, juke boxes, and similar types of amusement equipment.

$alaries

Wage rates for experienced vending machine servicers and repairers range from $7.00-14.00/hour depending on the size of the firm and the region of the country.

Employment Outlook

Growth rate until the year 2000: Employment is expected to remain level.

Vending Machine Servicers and Repairers

Career Guides

★4577★
Vending Machine Mechanic
Careers, Inc.
PO Box 135
Largo, FL 34649-0135   Phone: (813)584-7333

1991. Two-page occupational summary card describing duties, working conditions, personal qualifications, training, earnings and hours, employment outlook, places of employment, related careers and where to write for more information.

★4578★
"Vending Machine Mechanic" in *Occu-Facts: Information on 565 Careers in Outline Form* (p. 15.31)
Careers, Inc.
P.O. Box 135
1211 Tenth St., S.W.
Largo, FL 33640   Phone: (813)584-7333

Elizabeth Handville. Biennial, 1989-90 edition. Each one-page occupational profile describes duties, working conditions, physical surroundings and demands, aptitudes, temperament, educational requirements, employment outlook, earnings, and places of employment.

★4579★
"Vending Machine Mechanics" in Volume 6 of *Career Discovery Encyclopedia* (pp. 144-145)
J.G. Ferguson Publishing Co.
200 W. Monroe
Chicago, IL 60606   Phone: (312)580-5480

E. Russell Primm, editor-in-chief. 1990. Contains two-page articles on 504 occupations. Each article describes job duties, earnings, and educational and training requirements.

★4580★
"Vending Machine Mechanics" in Volume 3 of *The Encyclopedia of Careers and Vocational Guidance* (pp. 565-568)
J.G. Ferguson Publishing Co.
200 W. Monroe
Chicago, IL 60606   Phone: (312)580-5480

William E. Hopke, editor-in-chief. Eighth edition, 1990. Four-volume set that profiles 500 occupations and describes job trends in 76 industries. Includes career description, educational requirements, history of the job, methods of entry, advancement, employment outlook, earnings, working conditions, social and psychological factors, and sources of additional information.

★4581★
Vending Machine Repairers
Chronicle Guidance Publications, Inc.
PO Box 1190
Moravia, NY 13118-1190   Phone: (315)497-0330

1987. This career brief describes the nature of the work, working conditions, hours and earnings, education and training, licensure, certification, unions, personal qualifications, social and psychological factors, employment outlook, entry methods, advancement, and related occupations. **Toll-free/Additional Phone Number(s):** 800-622-7284.

★4582★
Vending Machine Route Driver
Vocational Biographies, Inc.
PO Box 31, Dept. VF10
Sauk Centre, MN 56378   Phone: (612)352-6516

1991. This pamphlet profiles a person working in the job. Includes information about job duties, working conditions, places of employment, educational preparation, labor market outlook, and salaries. **Toll-free/Additional Phone Number(s):** 800-255-0752.

★4583★
"Vending Machine Route Worker" in *Marketing and Distribution*, Volume 10 of *Career Information Center* (pp. 62-63)
Glencoe/Macmillan
15319 Chatsworth St.
Mission Hills, CA 91345   Phone: (818)898-1391

Richard Lidz and Dale Anderson, editorial directors. Fourth edition, 1990. For 600 occupations, describes job duties, entry-level requirements, education and training needed, advancement possibilities, employment outlook, earnings and benefits. The set is divided into 12 volumes. Each volume includes jobs related under a broad career field. Volume 13 is the index. **Facsimile Number:** 818-365-5489.

★4584★
Vending Machine Route Workers
Careers, Inc.
PO Box 135
Largo, FL 34649-0135   Phone: (813)584-7333

1988. Two-page job guide card describing duties, working conditions, personal qualifications, training, earnings and hours, employment outlook, places of employment, related careers and where to write for more information.

★4585★
"Vending Machine Route Workers" in *Occu-Facts: Information on 565 Careers in Outline Form* (p. 19.8)
Careers, Inc.
P.O. Box 135
1211 Tenth St., S.W.
Largo, FL 33640 Phone: (813)584-7333

Elizabeth Handville. Biennial, 1989-90 edition. Each one-page occupational profile describes duties, working conditions, physical surroundings and demands, aptitudes, temperament, educational requirements, employment outlook, earnings, and places of employment.

★4586★
"Vending Machine Servicers and Repairers" in *Occupational Outlook Handbook* (pp. 360-361)
Superintendent of Documents
U.S. Government Printing Office
Washington, DC 20402 Phone: (202)783-3238

Biennial; latest edition, 1990-91. Encyclopedia of careers describing more than 250 occupations and comprising about 86 percent of all jobs in the economy. Occupations that require lengthy education or training are given the most attention. For each occupation, the handbook describes job duties, working conditions, training, educational preparation, personal qualities, advancement possibilities, job outlook, earnings, and sources of additional information.

Associations

★4587★
National Automatic Merchandising Association (NAMA)
20 N. Wacker Dr.
Chicago, IL 60606 Phone: (312)346-0370

Membership: Manufacturing and operating companies in the automatic vending machine industry; food service management firms; office coffee machine operators; suppliers of products and services such as food, candy, beverages, cigarettes, and packaging. **Purpose:** Compiles industry profit ratios; conducts manufacturing census. **Publications:** *Employee Relations Quarterly Bulletin*. • *National Automatic Merchandising Association—Directory of Members*, annual. • *National Automatic Merchandising Association-Newsletter*, bimonthly. • *National Automatic Merchandising Association—State Legislative Review*, periodic. • *Quarterly Labor Relations Comprehensive Bulletin*. **Facsimile Number:** (312)704-4140.

Standards/Certification Agencies

The National Automatic Merchandising Association has established an apprenticeship program whereby apprentices receive 144 hours of home-study instruction in subjects such as basic electricity and electronics, blueprint reading, customer relations, and safety. The program lasts from six months to three years, at the end of which, the employee can earn certification by passing performance and written tests.

Periodicals

★4588★
NAMA Employee Relations Quarterly Bulletin (NAMA)
National Automatic Merchandising Association (NAMA)
20 N. Wacker Dr.
Chicago, IL 60606 Phone: (312)346-0370

★4589★
National Automatic Merchandising Association-Newsletter (NAMA)
National Automatic Merchandising Association (NAMA)
20 N. Wacker Dr.
Chicago, IL 60606 Phone: (312)346-0370

Bimonthly. Association and vending/foodservice management industry newsletter.

★4590★
National Automatic Merchandising Association—State Legislative Review (NAMA)
National Automatic Merchandising Association (NAMA)
20 N. Wacker Dr.
Chicago, IL 60606 Phone: (312)346-0370

Periodic. Newsletter containing state legislation affecting the vending/foodservice management industry.

★4591★
Quarterly Labor Relations Comprehensive Bulletin (NAMA)
National Automatic Merchandising Association (NAMA)
20 N. Wacker Dr.
Chicago, IL 60606 Phone: (312)346-0370

Newsletter concerned with technical-legal aspects of employee relations policies in the vending/foodservice management industry.

Meetings and Conventions

★4592★
National Automatic Merchandising Association (NAMA)
20 N. Wacker Dr.
Chicago, IL 60606 Phone: (312)346-0370

1992; Mar. 27-29; Reno, NV and Nov. 5-8; Washington, DC.
Facsimile Number: (312)704-4140.

Construction Trades and Extractive Occupations

Bricklayers and Stonemasons

Bricklayers build walls, floors, partitions, fireplaces, and other structures with brick, cinder or concrete block, and other masonry materials. They also install firebrick linings in industrial furnaces. Stonemasons build stone walls as well as set stone exteriors and floors. Because stone is expensive, stonemasons work mostly on high-cost buildings, such as churches, hotels, and office buildings. Bricklayers and stonemasons also repair imperfections and cracks or replace broken or missing masonry units in walls and floors. Refractory repairers or masons are bricklayers who install firebrick and refractory tile in high-temperature boilers, furnaces, cupolas, ladles and soaking pits in industrial establishments. Most work in steel mills, where molten materials flow on refractory beds from furnaces to rolling machines.

$alaries

Apprentices or helpers in each trade start at about 50 percent of the wage rate paid to experienced workers. The rate increases as they gain experience. Weekly earnings for bricklayers and stonemasons are as follows:

Lowest 10 percent	$231/week or less
Median	$448/week
Top 10 percent	$694/week or more

Employment Outlook

Growth rate until the year 2000: Average.

Bricklayers and Stonemasons

―――― Career Guides ――――

★4593★
Bricklayer
Careers, Inc.
PO Box 135
Largo, FL 34649-0135   Phone: (813)584-7333
1990. Two-page occupational summary card describing duties, working conditions, personal qualifications, training, earnings and hours, employment outlook, places of employment, related careers and where to write for more information.

★4594★
"Bricklayer" in *Construction*, Volume 4 of *Career Information Center* (pp. 39-41)
Glencoe/Macmillan
15319 Chatsworth St.
Mission Hills, CA 91345   Phone: (818)898-1391
Richard Lidz and Dale Anderson, editorial directors. Fourth edition, 1990. For 600 occupations, describes job duties, entry-level requirements, education and training needed, advancement possibilities, employment outlook, earnings and benefits. The set is divided into 12 volumes. Each volume includes jobs related under a broad career field. Volume 13 is the index. **Facsimile Number:** 818-365-5489.

★4595★
"Bricklayer" in *Occu-Facts: Information on 565 Careers in Outline Form* (p. 16.2)
Careers, Inc.
P.O. Box 135
1211 Tenth St., S.W.
Largo, FL 33640   Phone: (813)584-7333
Elizabeth Handville. Biennial, 1989-90 edition. Each one-page occupational profile describes duties, working conditions, physical surroundings and demands, aptitudes, temperament, educational requirements, employment outlook, earnings, and places of employment.

★4596★
"Bricklayers" in *Opportunities in Building Construction Trades* (pp. 49-52)
National Textbook Co.
4255 W. Touhy Ave.
Lincolnwood, IL 60646   Phone: (312)679-5500
Michael Sumichrast. 1989. Gives an overview of the construction industry and describes the jobs of various craftworkers. Covers different kinds of builders: home, custom; and describes management skills needed and industry trends affecting opportunities.

★4597★
Bricklayers and Stonemasons
Chronicle Guidance Publications, Inc.
PO Box 1190
Moravia, NY 13118-1190   Phone: (315)497-0330
1988. This career brief describes the nature of the work, working conditions, hours and earnings, education and training, licensure, certification, unions, personal qualifications, social and psychological factors, employment outlook, entry methods, advancement, and related occupations. **Toll-free/Additional Phone Number(s):** 800-622-7284.

★4598★
"Bricklayers and Stonemasons" in *Occupational Outlook Handbook* (pp. 362-363)
Superintendent of Documents
U.S. Government Printing Office
Washington, DC 20402   Phone: (202)783-3238
Biennial; latest edition, 1990-91. Encyclopedia of careers describing more than 250 occupations and comprising about 86 percent of all jobs in the economy. Occupations that require lengthy education or training are given the most attention. For each occupation, the handbook describes job duties, working conditions, training, educational preparation, personal qualities, advancement possibilities, job outlook, earnings, and sources of additional information.

★4599★
"Bricklayers and Stonemasons" in Volume 1 of *Career Discovery Encyclopedia* (pp. 138-139)
J.G. Ferguson Publishing Co.
200 W. Monroe
Chicago, IL 60606   Phone: (312)580-5480
E. Russell Primm, editor-in-chief. 1990. Contains two-page articles on 504 occupations. Each article describes job duties, earnings, and educational and training requirements.

★4600★
"Bricklayers and Stonemasons" in Volume 3 of *The Encyclopedia of Careers and Vocational Guidance* (pp. 629-632)
J.G. Ferguson Publishing Co.
200 W. Monroe
Chicago, IL 60606   Phone: (312)580-5480
William E. Hopke, editor-in-chief. Eighth edition, 1990. Four-volume set that profiles 500 occupations and describes job trends in 76 industries. Includes career description, educational requirements, history of the job, methods of entry, advancement, employment outlook, earnings, working conditions, social and psychological factors, and sources of additional information.

★4601★
"Bricklayers" in *The American Almanac of Jobs and Salaries* (pp. 500-501)
Avon Books
105 Madison Avenue
New York, NY 10016   Phone: (212)481-5600
John Wright and Edward J. Dwyer. Revised and updated, 1990. A comprehensive guide to the wages of hundreds of occupations in a wide variety of industries and organizations.

★4602★
Bricklaying
Brick Institute of America
1750 Old Meadow Rd.
McLean, VA 22102   Phone: (703)893-4010
This four-page pamphlet describes skills, benefits, and how to get started as a bricklayer.

★4603★
Construction Cluster
Center for Humanities, Inc.
Communications Park
Box 1000
Mount Kisco, NY 10549   Phone: (914)666-4100
Videocassette. 1984. 15 mins. Construction workers describe what it's like to work at their jobs, and show the special equipment they use in their field.

★4604★
"Marble Setters" in Volume 4 of *Career Discovery Encyclopedia* (pp. 56-57)
J.G. Ferguson Publishing Co.
200 W. Monroe
Chicago, IL 60606   Phone: (312)580-5480
E. Russell Primm, editor-in-chief. 1990. Contains two-page articles on 504 occupations. Each article describes job duties, earnings, and educational and training requirements.

★4605★
"Marble Setters, Tile Setters, and Terrazzo Workers" in Volume 3 of *The Encyclopedia of Careers and Vocational Guidance* (pp. 677-679)
J.G. Ferguson Publishing Co.
200 W. Monroe
Chicago, IL 60606   Phone: (312)580-5480
William E. Hopke, editor-in-chief. Eighth edition, 1990. Four-volume set that profiles 500 occupations and describes job trends in 76 industries. Includes career description, educational requirements, history of the job, methods of entry, advancement, employment outlook, earnings, working conditions, social and psychological factors, and sources of additional information.

★4606★
"Marble, Tile, and Terrazzo Worker" in *Construction*, Volume 4 of *Career Information Center* (pp. 71-72)
Glencoe/Macmillan
15319 Chatsworth St.
Mission Hills, CA 91345   Phone: (818)898-1391
Richard Lidz and Dale Anderson, editorial directors. Fourth edition, 1990. For 600 occupations, describes job duties, entry-level requirements, education and training needed, advancement possibilities, employment outlook, earnings and benefits. The set is divided into 12 volumes. Each volume includes jobs related under a broad career field. Volume 13 is the index. **Facsimile Number:** 818-365-5489.

★4607★
Marble, Tile Setters, Terrazzo, and Stone Workers
Careers, Inc.
PO Box 135
Largo, FL 34649-0135   Phone: (813)584-7333
1989. Eight-page brief offering the definition, history, duties, working conditions, personal qualifications, educational requirements, earnings, hours, employment outlook, advancement possibilities, and related occupations.

★4608★
"Marble, Tile, Terrazzo, and Stone Workers" in *Occu-Facts: Information on 565 Careers in Outline Form* (p. 16.3)
Careers, Inc.
P.O. Box 135
1211 Tenth St., S.W.
Largo, FL 33640   Phone: (813)584-7333
Elizabeth Handville. Biennial, 1989-90 edition. Each one-page occupational profile describes duties, working conditions, physical surroundings and demands, aptitudes, temperament, educational requirements, employment outlook, earnings, and places of employment.

★4609★
Stonemason
Careers, Inc.
PO Box 135
Largo, FL 34649-0135   Phone: (813)584-7333
1991. Two-page occupational summary card describing duties, working conditions, personal qualifications, training, earnings and hours, employment outlook, places of employment, related careers and where to write for more information.

★4610★
"Stonemason" in *Construction*, Volume 4 of *Career Information Center* (pp. 85-87)
Glencoe/Macmillan
15319 Chatsworth St.
Mission Hills, CA 91345   Phone: (818)898-1391
Richard Lidz and Dale Anderson, editorial directors. Fourth edition, 1990. For 600 occupations, describes job duties, entry-level requirements, education and training needed, advancement possibilities, employment outlook, earnings and benefits. The set is divided into 12 volumes. Each volume includes jobs related under a broad career field. Volume 13 is the index. **Facsimile Number:** 818-365-5489.

★4611★
"Stonemason" in *Exploring Nontraditional Jobs for Women* (pp. 11-16)
Rosen Publishing Group, Inc.
29 E. 21st St.
New York, NY 10010   Phone: (212)777-3017
Rose Neufeld. 1989. Describes blue-collar, male dominated occupations. Discusses what is done on the job, training, where to apply for jobs, tools used, salaries, and advantages and disadvantages. Relates the experiences of women who are working in the field.

★4612★
"Stonemason" in *Occu-Facts: Information on 565 Careers in Outline Form* (p. 16.4)
Careers, Inc.
P.O. Box 135
1211 Tenth St., S.W.
Largo, FL 33640   Phone: (813)584-7333
Elizabeth Handville. Biennial, 1989-90 edition. Each one-page occupational profile describes duties, working conditions,

Bricklayers and Stonemasons

physical surroundings and demands, aptitudes, temperament, educational requirements, employment outlook, earnings, and places of employment.

★4613★
"Stonemasons" in *Opportunities in Building Construction Trades* (pp. 70-72)
National Textbook Co.
4255 W. Touhy Ave.
Lincolnwood, IL 60646   Phone: (312)679-5500
Michael Sumichrast. 1989. Gives an overview of the construction industry and describes the jobs of various craftworkers. Covers different kinds of builders: home, custom; and describes management skills needed and industry trends affecting opportunities.

★4614★
The Trowel Trades
International Masonry Institute
823 15th St. NW, Ste. 1001
Washington, DC 20005   Phone: (202)783-3908
This six-panel brochure describes skills, advancement opportunities, and apprentice training.

★4615★
Video Career Library - Construction
Careers, Inc.
1211 10th St., SW
PO Box 135
Largo, FL 34649-0135   Phone: (813)584-7333
Videocassette. 1990. 36 mins. Part of the Video Career Library covering 165 occupations. Shows actual workers on the job. Includes millwrights, brickmasons, carpenters, drywall installers, electricians, painters, plumbers and pipefitters, carpenter and soft tile installers, insulation workers, paving equipment operators, and structural metal workers.

★4616★
Vocational Visions
Center for Humanities, Inc.
Communications Park
Box 1000
Mount Kisco, NY 10549   Phone: (914)666-4100
Videocassette. 1984. 30 mins. This series of programs explains key aspects of actual training and a day in the life of a worker in the specific field mentioned on the videocassette. Occupations include: transportation/mechanics, repair, construction, business/office occupations, health, and agriculture.

★4617★
Vocations U.S.A.
Info-Disc Corporation
4 Professional Dr.
Gaithersburg, MD 20879   Phone: (301)948-2300
Videocassette. 1987. 60 mins. A disc collection outlining the requirements and methods of various career areas. Occupations include: transportation, mechanical/repair, health, agriculture, and construction.

★4618★
You Can Become a Tile, Marble, Terrazzo and Dimensional Stone Installer
United Brotherhood of Carpenters and Joiners of America
101 Constitution Ave., N.W.
Washington, DC 20001   Phone: (202)546-6206
This six-panel brochure describes apprenticeship training, hours, and working conditions.

Associations

★4619★
Associated General Contractors of America (AGC)
1957 E St. NW
Washington, DC 20006   Phone: (202)393-2040
Membership: General construction contractors; subcontractors; industry suppliers; service firms. **Purpose:** Provides tax services through its divisions. Conducts special conferences and seminars designed specifically for construction firms. Compiles statistics on job accidents reported by member firms. Bestows annual awards for safety and Build/America awards for innovative and outstanding achievements by general contractors. Offers college scholarships through AGC Education and Research Foundation. Maintains 65 committees, including joint cooperative committees with other associations and liaison committees with federal agencies. **Publications:** *AGC Membership Directory and Buyers' Guide*, annual. • *Associated General Contractors of America—National Newsletter*, biweekly. • *Constructor*, monthly. • Also publishes manuals, guides, model contract documents, studies, and checklists. **Facsimile Number:** (202)347-4004.

★4620★
Brick Institute of America (BIA)
11490 Commerce Park Dr.
Reston, VA 22091   Phone: (703)620-0010
Membership: Manufacturers of clay brick. **Purpose:** Maintains technical library of 2000 volumes on engineering and ceramics pertinent to masonry construction. **Publications:** *BIA News*, monthly. • *Brick in Architecture*, bimonthly. • *Builder Notes*, bimonthly. • *Directory*, annual. • *Technical Notes*, bimonthly. • Also distributes posters, slides, film, and video presentations. **Facsimile Number:** (703)620-3928.

★4621★
International Union of Bricklayers and Allied Craftsmen (BAC)
815 15th St., NW
Washington, DC 20005   Phone: (202)783-3788
Membership: AFL-CIO. **Publications:** *Chalkline*, periodic. • *Journal*, monthly. **Facsimile Number:** (202)393-0219.

Standards/Certification Agencies

Most bricklayers and stonemasons pick up their skills informally by working as helpers or hod carriers and by observing and learning from experienced workers. The remainder learn their skills through apprenticeship programs, which are usually sponsored by local contractors or by local union-management committees of the International Union of Bricklayers and Allied Craftsmen. The apprenticeship program requires three years of on-the-job training in addition to a minimum 144 hours of classroom instruction each year.

★4622★ VOCATIONAL CAREERS SOURCEBOOK, 1st Edition

site, date, name and title of contact. Arrangement: Geographical, alphabetical. **Toll-free/Additional Phone Number(s):** (800)827-7468. **Facsimile Number:** (317)299-1356.

Test Guides

★4622★
Bricklayer
National Learning Corp.
212 Michael Dr.
Syosset, NY 11791　　　　　　　　　Phone: (516)921-8888

Jack Rudman. Part of the Career Examination Series No. 1. All examination guides in this series contain questions with answers. **Facsimile Number:** (516)921-8743. **Toll-free/Additional Phone Number(s):** 800-645-6337.

★4623★
Foreman Bricklayer
National Learning Corp.
212 Michael Dr.
Syosset, NY 11791　　　　　　　　　Phone: (516)921-8888

Jack Rudman. Part of the Career Examination Series No. 1. All examination guides in this series contain questions with answers. **Facsimile Number:** (516)921-8743. **Toll-free/Additional Phone Number(s):** 800-645-6337.

Basic Reference Guides and Handbooks

★4624★
BIA Directory (BIA)
Brick Institute of America (BIA)
11490 Commerce Park Dr.
Reston, VA 22091　　　　　　　　　Phone: (703)620-0010
Annual.

★4625★
Gauged Brickwork: A Technical Handbook
Gower Publishing Company
Old Post Rd.
Brookfield, VT 05036　　　　　　　　Phone: (802)276-3162
Gerard Lynch. 1990.

★4626★
Intelligent Buildings Institute—Directory of Products and Services
Intelligent Buildings Institute (IBI)
2101 L St., NW, Ste. 300
Washington, DC 20037　　　　　　　Phone: (202)457-1988

S. Hunt, Associate Executive Director, editor. Annual, September. Member consultants, associations, research organizations, and other suppliers of products and services to the construction and building industry. Entries include: Company name, address, phone. Arrangement: Alphabetical. Indexes: Product/service. **Facsimile Number:** (202)457-8468.

★4627★
Mid-West Contractor—Annual Convention Guide and Association Directory AConstruction industryA
Allied Publications, Inc.
7355 N. Woodland Dr.
Box 603
Indianapolis, IN 46278　　　　　　　Phone: (317)297-5500

Jennifer Wynne, editor. Annual. List of 160 construction contracting and architectural associations in the Midwest. Entries include: Association name, address, phone, names and titles of key personnel, description of association; convention

---
Periodicals

★4628★
ABC Newsline
Associated Builders and Contractors, Inc. (ABC)
729 15th St. NW
Washington, DC 20005　　　　　　　Phone: (202)637-8800

Editor(s): Lisa A. Nardone. Semimonthly. Designed to keep readers alerted to important changes within ABC and the construction industry. Reports on legislative issues, construction trends, conferences and meetings, and ABC services. Recurring features include news of members and a column titled Industry Briefs.

★4629★
American Architectural Manufacturers Association— Quarterly Review
American Architectural Manufacturers Association
1540 E. Dundee Rd., Ste. K 310
Palatine, IL 60067-8321　　　　　　Phone: (708)202-1350

Editor(s): Tony Coorlim. Annually. Contains industry news on architectural products. Covers prime and combination storm windows, sliding glass and combination storm doors, window and curtain-walls, store fronts and entrances, siding, soffits, fascia, gutters, downspouts, skylights, space enclosures, and mobile home components. Recurring features include news of research, notices of publications available, and announcements by the association. **Facsimile Number:** (708)202-1480.

★4630★
American Institute of Constructors—Newsletter
American Institute of Constructors
9887 Gandy Blvd. N., No. 104
Saint Petersburg, FL 33702-2451

Editor(s): Ed Freedman. Bimonthly. Concerned with construction practice, design, administration, and teaching. Carries news of members, listings of job opportunities, local chapter reports, and notices of new publications. **Facsimile Number:** (614)464-3226.

★4631★
Associated General Contractors of America—National Newsletter (AGC)
Associated General Contractors of America (AGC)
1957 E St. NW
Washington, DC 20006　　　　　　　Phone: (202)393-2040
Biweekly.

★4632★
BAC Journal (BAC)
International Union of Bricklayers and Allied Craftsmen (BAC)
815 15th St., NW
Washington, DC 20005　　　　　　　Phone: (202)783-3788
Monthly.

★4633★
BIA News (BIA)
Brick Institute of America (BIA)
11490 Commerce Park Dr.
Reston, VA 22091　　　　　　　　　Phone: (703)620-0010
Monthly. Newsletter.

★4634★
Bia Technical Notes (BIA)
Brick Institute of America (BIA)
11490 Commerce Park Dr.
Reston, VA 22091   Phone: (703)620-0010
Bimonthly.

★4635★
Blue Reports, Inc.
Construction News Service
7325 Steel Mill Dr.
Springfield, VA 22050   Phone: (703)644-5884
Editor(s): Calvin S. Oren. Daily. Reports on public and private construction projects in the Washington, DC, Virginia, and Maryland areas. Provides owner's and architect's names, plan status, date bids due, prospective bidders, low bids received, and specification details. **Facsimile Number:** (703)644-1929.

★4636★
Brick in Architecture (BIA)
Brick Institute of America (BIA)
11490 Commerce Park Dr.
Reston, VA 22091   Phone: (703)620-0010
Bimonthly.

★4637★
Builder
Hanley-Wood, Inc.
655 15th St. NW, Ste. 475
Washington, DC 20005   Phone: (202)737-0717
Mitchell Rouda, Editor. Monthly. Magazine covering housing, commercial, and industrial building. **Facsimile Number:** (202)737-2439.

★4638★
Builder and Contractor
Associated Builders and Contractors, Inc.
729 15th St. NW
Washington, DC 20005   Phone: (202)637-8800
Susan Schindler, Mng. Editor. Monthly. Magazine for open shop contractors and subcontractors. Includes articles on national and regional construction news, construction management, project case histories, new products, and building design.

★4639★
Builder Architect
Sunshine Media, Inc.
7500 N. Dreamy Draw, Ste. 111
PO Box 9400
Phoenix, AZ 85068   Phone: (602)943-3575
Marie Vere, Editor. Monthly. Home builders magazine. **Facsimile Number:** (602)371-0241.

★4640★
Builder/Dealer
Peterson Bros. Inc., Publishing
16 1st Ave.
Corry, PA 16407-1894   Phone: (814)664-8624
Charles P. Mancino, Publisher. Monthly. Trade magazine. **Facsimile Number:** (814)664-8506.

★4641★
Builder Insider
Divibest, Inc.
PO Box 191125
Dallas, TX 75219   Phone: (214)871-2913
Michael J. Anderson, Editor and Publisher. Monthly. Magazine (tabloid) for builders, architects, and remodelers.

★4642★
Builder Notes (BIA)
Brick Institute of America (BIA)
11490 Commerce Park Dr.
Reston, VA 22091   Phone: (703)620-0010
Bimonthly.

★4643★
Building Business & Management
Builders Assn. of Southeastern Michigan
30375 Northwestern Hwy.
Farmington Hills, MI 48334   Phone: (313)737-4477
Kathleen M. Eischeid, Editor. Monthly. Construction and apartment industry magazine. **Facsimile Number:** (313)737-5741.

★4644★
Building Concerns
National Association of Minority Contractors (NAMC)
806 15th St. NW, Ste. 340
Washington, DC 20005   Phone: (202)347-8259
Editor(s): Ralph C. Thomas, III. Monthly. Concentrates on national and regional news regarding minority construction contractors. Contains articles on issues generally affecting the industry—especially issues affecting minorities—including topics such as legislative and regulatory activity and reports on major corporation developments. Recurring features include reports of meetings, news of educational opportunities, a calendar of events, and news of NAMC chapters and members.

★4645★
Building Design & Construction
Cahners Publishing Co.
1350 E. Touhy Ave.
PO Box 5080
Des Plaines, IL 60018   Phone: (708)635-8800
Philip G. Schreiner, Editor. Monthly. Magazine on business and technology for commercial, institutional, and industrial buildings. **Facsimile Number:** (708)299-8622.

★4646★
Building Homes & Renovations
Southam Business & Communications, Inc.
1450 Don Mills Rd.
Don Mills, ON, Canada M3B 2X7   Phone: (416)445-6641
Randy Threndyle, Editor. 5x/yr. Building trade and products magazine. **Facsimile Number:** (416)442-2214.

★4647★
Building Industry
Trade Publishing Co.
287 Mokauea St.
Honolulu, HI 96819   Phone: (808)848-0711
Jay McWilliams, Editor. Monthly. Construction and design magazine. **Facsimile Number:** (808)841-3053.

★4648★
Building Industry Technology: An Abstract Newsletter
National Technical Information Service (NTIS)
U.S. Department of Commerce
5285 Port Royal Rd.
Springfield, VA 22161   Phone: (703)487-4630
Weekly. Consists of abstracts of reports on architectural and environmental design, building standards, construction materials and equipment, and structural analyses. Recurring features include a form for ordering reports from NTIS.

★4649★
Buildings
427 6th Ave. SE
PO Box 1888
Cedar Rapids, IA 52406　　　　Phone: (319)364-6167
Linda Monroe, Editor. Monthly. **Facsimile Number:** (319)365-5421.

★4650★
Capital Comments
National Lumber & Building Material Dealers Association
40 Ivy St. SE
Washington, DC 20003　　　　Phone: (202)547-2230
Editor(s): Matt Geitner. Semimonthly. Reports on news of legislation pertaining to lumber, other building materials, and housing. Discusses such issues as lumber subsidies, interest rates on homes, health and safety, and jobs. **Facsimile Number:** (202)547-7640.

★4651★
Chalkline (BAC)
International Union of Bricklayers and Allied Craftsmen (BAC)
815 15th St., NW
Washington, DC 20005　　　　Phone: (202)783-3788
Periodic.

★4652★
ConnStruction
PO Box 9768
Wethersfield, CT 06109　　　　Phone: (203)529-3246
Victor Bonini, Editor. 7x/yr. Magazine for construction industry. **Facsimile Number:** (203)563-0616.

★4653★
CONSTRUCTION
26 Long Hill Rd.
Guilford, CT 06437　　　　Phone: (203)453-3717
Jack C. Lewis, Editor and Publisher. 2x/mo. Journal for the construction industry.

★4654★
Construction Dimensions
Assn. of Wall & Ceiling
PO Box 5504
Washington, DC 20016　　　　Phone: (301)656-7050
Gerald Wykoff, Editor. Monthly. Wall and ceiling industry magazine.

★4655★
Construction Industry International
Maclean Hunter Publishing Co.
29 N. Wacker Dr.
Chicago, IL 60606　　　　Phone: (312)726-2802
Alan Elliott, Editor-in-Chief. Monthly. Trade magazine.

★4656★
Construction News
715 W. 2nd St.
PO Box 2421
Little Rock, AR 72203　　　　Phone: (501)376-1931
Robert Alvey, Editor. Weekly. Construction industry magazine. **Facsimile Number:** (501)375-5831.

★4657★
Construction Newsletter
National Safety Council
444 N. Michigan Ave.
Chicago, IL 60611　　　　Phone: (312)527-4800
6/yr. Focuses on industrial and occupational safety in the construction industry. Carries items on such topics as safe work practices and products, accident prevention, and successful industrial safety programs and policies.

★4658★
Constructor (AGC)
Associated General Contractors of America (AGC)
1957 E St. NW
Washington, DC 20006　　　　Phone: (202)393-2040
Monthly. Association magazine for general contractors engaged in construction.

★4659★
Daily Construction Reporter
4901 Pacific Hwy.
San Diego, CA 92110-4098　　　　Phone: (619)296-0183
Kenneth F. Kerr, Editor and Publisher. Daily. Construction trade newspaper covering jobs that are out for bid, bid results, building permits, and other information. **Facsimile Number:** (619)298-3027.

★4660★
Dimensional Stone
20335 Ventura Blvd., Ste. 400
Woodland Hills, CA 91364　　　　Phone: (818)704-5555
John Maynard, Editor. 10x/yr. Magazine providing information for specifying, cutting, and installing natural stone products. **Facsimile Number:** (818)704-6500.

★4661★
Fine Homebuilding
The Taunton Press, Inc.
63 S. Main St.
PO Box 5506
Newtown, CT 06470　　　　Phone: (203)426-5506
Mark Feirer, Editor. 7x/yr. Magazine for builders, architects, designers, and owner-builders. **Facsimile Number:** (203)426-3434.

★4662★
Home BUILDER Magazine
Work-4 Projects Ltd.
PO Box 400, Victoria Sta.
Westmount, PQ, Canada H3Z 2V8　　　　Phone: (514)489-4941
Nachmi Artzy, Editor and Publisher. 6x/yr. Magazine for home construction industry. **Facsimile Number:** (514)489-5505.

★4663★
The Journal of Light Construction
Hanley-Wood Partners
RR 2, Box 146
Richmond, VT 05477-9607　　　　Phone: (802)864-0091
Steve Bliss, Editor. Monthly. Magazine (tabloid) for residential and light professionals involved in new and rehabilitative construction. Each issue covers a single aspect of construction.

★4664★
Journal of the International ⅝¾Union of Bricklayers & Allied Craftsmen
815 15th St. NW
Washington, DC 20005　　　　Phone: (202)783-3788
Paul Ruffins, Exec. Editor. Monthly. Tabloid for trade union members. **Facsimile Number:** (202)393-0219.

Bricklayers and Stonemasons

★4665★
Nation's Building News
15th & M Sts. NW
Washington, DC 20005   Phone: (202)822-0525
Tim Ahern, Editor. 2x/mo. Trade magazine (tabloid) covering home building and all related industries. **Facsimile Number:** (202)861-2131.

★4666★
Professional Builder
Cahners Publishing Co.
1350 E. Touhy Ave.
Des Plaines, IL 60018   Phone: (708)635-8800
Roy L. Diez, Editor. 19x/yr. **Facsimile Number:** (708)299-8622.

★4667★
The SPEC-DATA Program
Construction Specifications Institute
601 Madison St.
Alexandria, VA 22314   Phone: (703)684-0300
Brenda A. Furiga, Mgr. Quarterly. Magazine (loose-leaf) for the construction industry covering technical and product information. **Facsimile Number:** (703)684-0465.

★4668★
Stone Review
National Stone Assn.
1415 Elliot Pl. NW
Washington, DC 20007-2599   Phone: (202)342-1100
Kash H. McClure, Exec. Editor. Frank E. Atlee, Editor/Advertising Mgr. 6x/yr. Trade magazine for stone producers and suppliers of equipment to the aggregates industry. **Facsimile Number:** (202)342-0702.

★4669★
Stone Through the Ages
Marble Institute of America
33505 State St.
Farmington, MI 48335   Phone: (313)476-5558
Robert Hund, Editor. Quarterly. **Facsimile Number:** (313)476-1630.

★4670★
Stone World
320 Kinderkamack Rd.
Oradell, NJ 07649-2102   Phone: (201)599-0136
Mike Lench, Editor and Publisher. Monthly. Trade magazine on natural stone products. **Facsimile Number:** (201)599-2378.

Meetings and Conventions

★4671★
Brick Institute of America (BIA)
11490 Commerce Park Dr.
Reston, VA 22091   Phone: (703)620-0010
Frequency: Annual. 1992; Oct. 24-27; White Sulphur Springs, WV • 1993; Oct. 24-27; White Sulphur Springs, WV. **Facsimile Number:** (703)620-3928.

★4672★
International Union of Bricklayers and Allied Craftsmen (BAC)
815 15th St., NW
Washington, DC 20005   Phone: (202)783-3788
Frequency: Quinquennial. **Facsimile Number:** (202)393-0219.

★4673★
National Association of Brick Distributors Trade Exhibit
National Association of Brick Distributors
212 S. Henry
Alexandria, VA 22314   Phone: (703)549-2555
1992; Dallas, TX.

Carpenters

Carpenters working on construction projects constitute the largest group of building trade workers. A carpenter employed by a special trade contractor may specialize in setting forms for concrete construction, while one who is employed by a general building contractor may perform many tasks, such as framing walls and partitions, putting in doors and windows, and installing paneling and tile ceilings. Carpenters employed outside the construction industry are involved in a variety of installation and maintenance work. In manufacturing firms, carpenters may assist in moving or installing machinery. Local building codes often dictate where certain materials can and cannot be used, and carpenters have to know these requirements. All carpenters work in teams or are assisted by a helper.

$alaries

Maintenance carpenters, who generally have more steady employment, average $14.00/hour. Weekly salaries for other carpenters who are not self-employed are as follows:

Lowest 10 percent	$215/week or less
Median	$381/week
Top 10 percent	$676/week or more

Employment Outlook

Growth rate until the year 2000: Average.

Carpenters

Career Guides

★4674★
Career Insights
RMI Media Productions, Inc.
2807 West 47th St.
Shawnee Mission, KS 66205   Phone: (913)262-3974

Videocassette series. 1987. This videotape series describes 50 occupations, including skill requirements and interviews with people employed in these fields. Occupations include: flight service, air transportation/ground services, data processing, carpentry, clerk in banking/insurance/business, cosmetic personal grooming, firefighting, roofing, material handling, photographic processing, plumbing, secretarial services, tool and die operations.

★4675★
Career Success Series
Cambridge Career Products
90 MacCorkle Ave., SW
South Charleston, WV 25311   Phone: (304)744-9323

Videocassette. 1986. 15 mins. A series, available separately, outlining various career choices for students. Occupations include: flight service, air transportation/ground service, data processing, carpentry, clerk in banking/insurance, commodity sales, cosmetic personal grooming, fire fighting, forestry services, home economics, insulation/roofing, material handling, mechanics, photographic processing, pipefitting and plumbing, police science, printing, secretarial services, and utilities equipment operator.

★4676★
Carpenter
Vocational Biographies, Inc.
PO Box 31, Dept. VF10
Sauk Centre, MN 56378   Phone: (612)352-6516

1988. This pamphlet profiles a person working in the job. Includes information about job duties, working conditions, places of employment, educational preparation, labor market outlook, and salaries. **Toll-free/Additional Phone Number(s):** 800-255-0752.

★4677★
"Carpenter" in *Construction*, Volume 4 of *Career Information Center* (pp. 41-43)
Glencoe/Macmillan
15319 Chatsworth St.
Mission Hills, CA 91345   Phone: (818)898-1391

Richard Lidz and Dale Anderson, editorial directors. Fourth edition, 1990. For 600 occupations, describes job duties, entry-level requirements, education and training needed, advancement possibilities, employment outlook, earnings and benefits. The set is divided into 12 volumes. Each volume includes jobs related under a broad career field. Volume 13 is the index. **Facsimile Number:** 818-365-5489.

★4678★
"Carpenter" in *Exploring Nontraditional Jobs for Women* (pp. 6-11)
Rosen Publishing Group, Inc.
29 E. 21st St.
New York, NY 10010   Phone: (212)777-3017

Rose Neufeld. 1989. Describes blue-collar, male dominated occupations. Discusses what is done on the job, training, where to apply for jobs, tools used, salaries, and advantages and disadvantages. Relates the experiences of women who are working in the field.

★4679★
"Carpenter" in *Hard Hatted Women: Stories of Struggle and Success in the Trades* (pp. 45-54)
Seal Press
3131 Western Ave., Ste. 410
Seattle, WA 98121   Phone: (206)283-7844

Molly Martin, editor. 1988. Twenty-six women recount their experiences working in blue collar occupations. They describe how they got in, the work they do, their relationships in predominantly male occupations, and their training.

★4680★
"Carpenter" in *Opportunities in Crafts Careers* (pp. 29-30)
National Textbook Co.
4255 W. Touhy Ave.
Lincolnwood, IL 60646   Phone: (312)679-5500

Marianne F. Munday. 1988. Covers crafts such as woodworking, ceramics, and leatherworking, and crafts-related careers such as writing and teaching. Offers advice on planning a career in crafts, starting a crafts business, and selling crafts.

★4681★
"Carpenter" in *VGM's Careers Encyclopedia* (pp. 75-78)
National Textbook Co.
4255 W. Touhy Ave.
Lincolnwood, IL 60646   Phone: (312)679-5500

Third edition, 1991. Contains two- to five-page descriptions of 200 managerial, professional, technical, trade, and service occupations. Each profile includes job duties, places of employment, qualifications, educational preparation, training, employment potential, advancement, income, and additional sources of information.

★4682★
Carpenter, Construction
Careers, Inc.
PO Box 135
Largo, FL 34649-0135   Phone: (813)584-7333
1989. Eight-page brief offering the definition, history, duties, working conditions, personal qualifications, educational requirements, earnings, hours, employment outlook, advancement possibilities, and related occupations.

★4683★
Carpenters
Chronicle Guidance Publications, Inc.
PO Box 1190
Moravia, NY 13118-1190   Phone: (315)497-0330
1989. This career brief describes the nature of the work, working conditions, hours and earnings, education and training, licensure, certification, unions, personal qualifications, social and psychological factors, employment outlook, entry methods, advancement, and related occupations. **Toll-free/Additional Phone Number(s):** 800-622-7284.

★4684★
"Carpenters" in *Occupational Outlook Handbook* (pp. 363-365)
Superintendent of Documents
U.S. Government Printing Office
Washington, DC 20402   Phone: (202)783-3238
Biennial; latest edition, 1990-91. Encyclopedia of careers describing more than 250 occupations and comprising about 86 percent of all jobs in the economy. Occupations that require lengthy education or training are given the most attention. For each occupation, the handbook describes job duties, working conditions, training, educational preparation, personal qualities, advancement possibilities, job outlook, earnings, and sources of additional information.

★4685★
"Carpenters" in *Opportunities in Building Construction Trades* (pp. 23-29)
National Textbook Co.
4255 W. Touhy Ave.
Lincolnwood, IL 60646   Phone: (312)679-5500
Michael Sumichrast. 1989. Gives an overview of the construction industry and describes the jobs of various craftworkers. Covers different kinds of builders: home, custom; and describes management skills needed and industry trends affecting opportunities.

★4686★
"Carpenters" in Volume 1 of *Career Discovery Encyclopedia* (pp. 156-157)
J.G. Ferguson Publishing Co.
200 W. Monroe
Chicago, IL 60606   Phone: (312)580-5480
E. Russell Primm, editor-in-chief. 1990. Contains two-page articles on 504 occupations. Each article describes job duties, earnings, and educational and training requirements.

★4687★
"Carpenters" in Volume 3 of *The Encyclopedia of Careers and Vocational Guidance* (pp. 633-636)
J.G. Ferguson Publishing Co.
200 W. Monroe
Chicago, IL 60606   Phone: (312)580-5480
William E. Hopke, editor-in-chief. Eighth edition, 1990. Four-volume set that profiles 500 occupations and describes job trends in 76 industries. Includes career description, educational requirements, history of the job, methods of entry, advancement, employment outlook, earnings, working conditions, social and psychological factors, and sources of additional information.

★4688★
"Carpenters" in *The American Almanac of Jobs and Salaries* (p. 501)
Avon Books
105 Madison Avenue
New York, NY 10016   Phone: (212)481-5600
John Wright and Edward J. Dwyer. Revised and updated, 1990. A comprehensive guide to the wages of hundreds of occupations in a wide variety of industries and organizations.

★4689★
Carpentry
Morris Video
2730 Monterey St. #105
Monterey Business Park
Torrance, CA 90503   Phone: (213)533-4800
Videocassette. 1984. 15 mins. The various levels of carpentry, plus the tools of the trade, are discussed.

★4690★
"Carpentry and Cabinetmaking" in *The Desk Guide to Training and Work Advisement* (pp. 71-73)
Charles C. Thomas, Publisher
2600 S. First St.
Springfield, IL 62794-9265   Phone: (217)789-8980
Gail Baugher Kuenstler. 1988. Describes alternative methods of gaining entry into an occupation through different types of educational programs, internships and apprenticeships. **Facsimile Number:** (217)789-9130.

★4691★
Carpentry & Construction
TAB Books
Blue Ridge Summit, PA 17294-0850   Phone: (717)794-2191
Rex Miller. Second edition, 1991.

★4692★
"Carpentry" in *The Career Connection II: A Guide to Technical Majors and Their Related Careers* (pp. 19-20)
ERIS
PO Box 7509
University Station
Provo, UT 84602-0509
Fred A. Rowe. 1988. Contains technical majors, such as automotive technology. Describes the major and the job. Lists high school and postsecondary school courses. Includes occupations related to the major, employment outlook, and starting salary.

★4693★
Construction: Basic Principles
RMI Media Productions, Inc.
2807 West 47th St.
Shawnee Mission, KS 66205   Phone: (913)262-3974
Videocassette. 1984. 20 mins. This series of five programs of varying lengths covers different aspects of career opportunities in the construction trades. Included are: concrete masonry, carpentry, electrical work, plumbing, and heating and air conditioning.

Carpenters

★4694★
"Construction Carpenter" in *Occu-Facts: Information on 565 Careers in Outline Form* (p. 16.5)
Careers, Inc.
P.O. Box 135
1211 Tenth St., S.W.
Largo, FL 33640 Phone: (813)584-7333
Elizabeth Handville. Biennial, 1989-90 edition. Each one-page occupational profile describes duties, working conditions, physical surroundings and demands, aptitudes, temperament, educational requirements, employment outlook, earnings, and places of employment.

★4695★
Construction Cluster
Center for Humanities, Inc.
Communications Park
Box 1000
Mount Kisco, NY 10549 Phone: (914)666-4100
Videocassette. 1984. 15 mins. Construction workers describe what it's like to work at their jobs, and show the special equipment they use in their field.

★4696★
Getting Down to Business: Carpentry Business
American Institutes for Research
PO Box 11131
Palo Alto, CA 94302 Phone: (415)493-3550
Joyce P. Gall. 1981. **Facsimile Number:** (415)858-0958.

★4697★
Getting Down to Business: Construction Electrician Business
American Institutes for Research
PO Box 11131
Palo Alto, CA 94302 Phone: (415)493-3550
Joyce P. Gall. 1981. **Facsimile Number:** (415)858-0958.

★4698★
Maintenance Trainee's Introduction to Carpentry
TPC Training Systems
310 South Michigan Ave.
Chicago, IL 60604 Phone: (312)537-6610
Videocassette. 1988. 120 mins. The basics of carpentry are explained. Designed for people who know next to nothing about the subject.

★4699★
Opportunities in Carpentry Careers
National Textbook Co.
4255 W. Touhy Ave.
Lincolnwood, IL 60646 Phone: (312)679-5500
Roger Sheldon. 1987. Covers the history of the crafts, a typical carpenter's workday, future opportunities for carpenters, qualifications, training, apprenticeships, and special advice for women and minorities. Surveys various training opportunities.

★4700★
Video Career Library - Construction
Careers, Inc.
1211 10th St., SW
PO Box 135
Largo, FL 34649-0135 Phone: (813)584-7333
Videocassette. 1990. 36 mins. Part of the Video Career Library covering 165 occupations. Shows actual workers on the job. Includes millwrights, brickmasons, carpenters, drywall installers, electricians, painters, plumbers and pipefitters, carpenter and soft tile installers, insulation workers, paving equipment operators, and structural metal workers.

★4701★
Vocational Visions
Center for Humanities, Inc.
Communications Park
Box 1000
Mount Kisco, NY 10549 Phone: (914)666-4100
Videocassette. 1984. 30 mins. This series of programs explains key aspects of actual training and a day in the life of a worker in the specific field mentioned on the videocassette. Occupations include: transportation/mechanics, repair, construction, business/office occupations, health, and agriculture.

★4702★
Vocations U.S.A.
Info-Disc Corporation
4 Professional Dr.
Gaithersburg, MD 20879 Phone: (301)948-2300
Videocassette. 1987. 60 mins. A disc collection outlining the requirements and methods of various career areas. Occupations include: transportation, mechanical/repair, health, agriculture, and construction.

Associations

★4703★
Associated Builders and Contractors (ABC)
729 15th St. NW
Washington, DC 20005 Phone: (202)637-8800
Membership: Construction contractors, subcontractors, suppliers, and associates. **Purpose:** Aim is to foster and perpetuate the principles of rewarding shop construction workers and management on the basis of merit. Sponsors leadership conference and management education programs including Wheels of Learning; also sponsors apprenticeship and skill training programs. Disseminates technological and labor relations information. Maintains biographical archives and placement service. Bestows awards; compiles statistics. **Publications:** *ABC Newsline*, semimonthly. • *The Builder and Contractor*, monthly. • *Classified Membership Directory*, annual. • Also publishes safety manuals.

★4704★
Associated General Contractors of America (AGC)
1957 E St. NW
Washington, DC 20006 Phone: (202)393-2040
Membership: General construction contractors; subcontractors; industry suppliers; service firms. **Purpose:** Provides tax services through its divisions. Conducts special conferences and seminars designed specifically for construction firms. Compiles statistics on job accidents reported by member firms. Bestows annual awards for safety and Build/America awards for innovative and outstanding achievements by general contractors. Offers college scholarships through AGC Education and Research Foundation. Maintains 65 committees, including joint cooperative committees with other associations and liaison committees with federal agencies. **Publications:** *AGC Membership Directory and Buyers' Guide*, annual. • *Associated General Contractors of America—National Newsletter*, biweekly. • *Constructor*, monthly. • Also publishes manuals, guides, model contract documents, studies, and checklists. **Facsimile Number:** (202)347-4004.

★4705★
National Association of Home Builders of the U.S. (NAHB)
15th and M Sts. NW
Washington, DC 20005 Phone: (202)822-0200
Membership: Single and multifamily home builders, commercial builders, and others associated with the building industry.

Purpose: Lobbies on behalf of the housing industry and conducts public affairs activities to increase public understanding of housing and the economy. Collects and disseminates data on current developments in home building and home builders' plans through its Economics Department and nationwide Metropolitan Housing Forecast. Maintains NAHB Research Center, which functions as the research arm of the home building industry. Sponsors seminars and workshops on construction, mortgage credit, labor relations, cost reduction, land use, remodeling, and business management. Sponsors competitions; bestows awards; compiles statistics; offers charitable program, spokesman training, and placement service; maintains speakers' bureau, biographical archives, hall of fame, and extensive library on housing. Subsidiaries include Home Builders Institute and National Council of the Housing Industry. Maintains over 50 committees in many areas of construction; operates National Commercial Builders Council, National Council of the Multifamily Housing Industry, National Remodelers Council, and National Sales and Marketing Council. **Publications:** *Builder Magazine*, monthly. • *Economic News Notes*, monthly. • *Homes and Homebuilding*, annual. • *Library Bulletin*, monthly. • *Nation's Building News*, semimonthly. • Also publishes bibliographies, booklets, and manuals. **Toll-free/Additional Phone Number(s):** (800)221-NAHB Audio Feed Line.

★4706★
United Brotherhood of Carpenters and Joiners of America (UBC)
101 Constitution Ave. NW
Washington, DC 20001   Phone: (202)546-6206
Membership: AFL-CIO. **Publications:** *Carpenter*, monthly.

Standards/Certification Agencies

Carpenters learn their trade through on-the-job training and through formal training programs. Many pick up skills informally by working under the supervision of experienced workers. Some acquire skills through vocational education. Others participate in employer training programs and apprenticeships. Apprenticeship programs are administered by local chapters of the Associated Builders and Contractors, Inc., and local chapters of the Associated General Contractors, as well as by local joint union-management committees of the United Brotherhood of Carpenters and Joiners of America and the Associated General Contractors or the National Association of Home Builders. These programs combine on-the-job training with related classroom instruction. The length of the program, usually about three to four years, varies with the apprentice's skill.

Test Guides

★4707★
Carpenter
Prentice Hall Press
Simon & Schuster Inc.
200 Old Tappan Rd.
Old Tappan, NJ 07675   Phone: (800)223-2348
Hy Hammer. Fifth edition, 1982. Helps prepare for the civil service exam or to gain employment in the private sector. Includes past exams and answer keys, and glossary of construction terms.

★4708★
Carpenter
National Learning Corp.
212 Michael Dr.
Syosset, NY 11791   Phone: (516)921-8888
Jack Rudman. Part of the Career Examination Series No. 1. All examination guides in this series contain questions with answers. **Facsimile Number:** (516)921-8743. **Toll-free/Additional Phone Number(s):** 800-645-6337.

★4709★
Carpentry
National Learning Corp.
212 Michael Dr.
Syosset, NY 11791   Phone: (516)921-8888
Jack Rudman. 1989. Part of Occupational Competency Examination Series.

★4710★
Foreman Carpenter
National Learning Corp.
212 Michael Dr.
Syosset, NY 11791   Phone: (516)921-8888
Jack Rudman. Part of the Career Examination Series No. 1. All examination guides in this series contain questions with answers. **Facsimile Number:** (516)921-8743. **Toll-free/Additional Phone Number(s):** 800-645-6337.

★4711★
Maintenance Worker/Mechanical Maintainer
Prentice Hall Press
Simon & Schuster Inc.
200 Old Tappan Rd.
Old Tappan, NJ 07675   Phone: (800)223-2348
Hy Hammer. Fourth edition, 1984. Provides information for applicants interested in the following civil service positions: carpenter, mason, plumber, electrician, painter, machinist. Includes eight sample tests.

★4712★
What Do You Know about Carpentry
National Learning Corp.
212 Michael Dr.
Syosset, NY 11791   Phone: (516)291-8888
Jack Rudman. 1990. Part of Test Your Knowledge Series.

Basic Reference Guides and Handbooks

★4713★
The Carpenter's Manifesto
Henry Holt & Company
115 W. 18th St.
New York, NY 10011   Phone: (212)886-9200
Jefferey Ehrlich. 1990.

★4714★
The Carpenter's Toolbox Manual
Prentice Hall
Rte. 9W
Englewoods Cliffs, NJ 07632   Phone: (201)592-2000
Gary D. Meyers. 1989. Part of On-The-Job Reference Series.

Carpenters

★4715★
Carpentry: Framing & Finishing
Prentice Hall
Rte. 9W
Englewood Cliffs, NJ 07632　　Phone: (201)592-2000
Byron W. Maguire. 1989.

★4716★
Finish Carpentry Illustrated
TAB Books
Blue Ridge Summit, PA 17294-0850　　Phone: (717)794-2191
Elizabeth Williams. 1990.

★4717★
Homes and Homebuilding (NAHB)
National Association of Home Builders of the U.S. (NAHB)
15th and M Sts. NW
Washington, DC 20005　　Phone: (202)822-0200
Annual.

★4718★
Intelligent Buildings Institute—Directory of Products and Services
Intelligent Buildings Institute (IBI)
2101 L St., NW, Ste. 300
Washington, DC 20037　　Phone: (202)457-1988
S. Hunt, Associate Executive Director, editor. Annual, September. Member consultants, associations, research organizations, and other suppliers of products and services to the construction and building industry. Entries include: Company name, address, phone. Arrangement: Alphabetical. Indexes: Product/service. **Facsimile Number:** (202)457-8468.

★4719★
Mid-West Contractor—Annual Convention Guide and Association Directory AConstruction industryA
Allied Publications, Inc.
7355 N. Woodland Dr.
Box 603
Indianapolis, IN 46278　　Phone: (317)297-5500
Jennifer Wynne, editor. Annual. List of 160 construction contracting and architectural associations in the Midwest. Entries include: Association name, address, phone, names and titles of key personnel, description of association; convention site, date, name and title of contact. Arrangement: Geographical, alphabetical. **Toll-free/Additional Phone Number(s):** (800)827-7468. **Facsimile Number:** (317)299-1356.

★4720★
Outdoor Structures
Rodale Press, Inc.
33 E. Minor St.
Emmaus, PA 18098　　Phone: (215)967-5171
Nick Engler . 1990. Part of Built-It-Better-Yourself Series. **Toll-free/Additional Phone Number(s):** 800-441-7761. **Facsimile Number:** (215)967-8963.

★4721★
Roof Framing
American Association for Vocational Instructional Materials
745 Goines School Rd.
Athens, GA 30605　　Phone: (404)543-7557
Charley G. Chadwick. 1991. **Facsimile Number:** (404)613-6779.

★4722★
Shelving & Storage
Rodale Press, Inc.
33 E. Minor St.
Emmaus, PA 18098　　Phone: (215)967-5171
Nick Engler. 1989. Part of Build-It-Better-Yourself Series. **Toll-free/Additional Phone Number(s):** 800-441-7761. **Facsimile Number:** (215)967-8963.

★4723★
Trim Carpentry Techniques: Installing Doors, Windows, Base & Crown
Peter Smith Publisher, Inc.
6 Lexington Ave.
Magnolia, MA 01930　　Phone: (617)525-3562
Craig Savage. 1991.

---------- Periodicals ----------

★4724★
ABC Newsline
Associated Builders and Contractors, Inc. (ABC)
729 15th St. NW
Washington, DC 20005　　Phone: (202)637-8800
Editor(s): Lisa A. Nardone. Semimonthly. Designed to keep readers alerted to important changes within ABC and the construction industry. Reports on legislative issues, construction trends, conferences and meetings, and ABC services. Recurring features include news of members and a column titled Industry Briefs.

★4725★
American Architectural Manufacturers Association—Quarterly Review
American Architectural Manufacturers Association
1540 E. Dundee Rd., Ste. K 310
Palatine, IL 60067-8321　　Phone: (708)202-1350
Editor(s): Tony Coorlim. Annually. Contains industry news on architectural products. Covers prime and combination storm windows, sliding glass and combination storm doors, window and curtain-walls, store fronts and entrances, siding, soffits, fascia, gutters, downspouts, skylights, space enclosures, and mobile home components. Recurring features include news of research, notices of publications available, and announcements by the association. **Facsimile Number:** (708)202-1480.

★4726★
American Institute of Constructors—Newsletter
American Institute of Constructors
9887 Gandy Blvd. N., No. 104
Saint Petersburg, FL 33702-2451
Editor(s): Ed Freedman. Bimonthly. Concerned with construction practice, design, administration, and teaching. Carries news of members, listings of job opportunities, local chapter reports, and notices of new publications. **Facsimile Number:** (614)464-3226.

★4727★
Associated General Contractors of America—National Newsletter (AGC)
Associated General Contractors of America (AGC)
1957 E St. NW
Washington, DC 20006　　Phone: (202)393-2040
Biweekly.

★4728★
Blue Reports, Inc.
Construction News Service
7325 Steel Mill Dr.
Springfield, VA 22050   Phone: (703)644-5884
Editor(s): Calvin S. Oren. Daily. Reports on public and private construction projects in the Washington, DC, Virginia, and Maryland areas. Provides owner's and architect's names, plan status, date bids due, prospective bidders, low bids received, and specification details. **Facsimile Number:** (703)644-1929.

★4729★
Builder
Hanley-Wood, Inc.
655 15th St. NW, Ste. 475
Washington, DC 20005   Phone: (202)737-0717
Mitchell Rouda, Editor. Monthly. Magazine covering housing, commercial, and industrial building. **Facsimile Number:** (202)737-2439.

★4730★
Builder and Contractor
Associated Builders and Contractors, Inc.
729 15th St. NW
Washington, DC 20005   Phone: (202)637-8800
Susan Schindler, Mng. Editor. Monthly. Magazine for open shop contractors and subcontractors. Includes articles on national and regional construction news, construction management, project case histories, new products, and building design.

★4731★
The Builder and Contractor (ABC)
Associated Builders and Contractors (ABC)
729 15th St. NW
Washington, DC 20005   Phone: (202)637-8800
Monthly.

★4732★
Builder Architect
Sunshine Media, Inc.
7500 N. Dreamy Draw, Ste. 111
PO Box 9400
Phoenix, AZ 85068   Phone: (602)943-3575
Marie Vere, Editor. Monthly. Home builders magazine. **Facsimile Number:** (602)371-0241.

★4733★
Builder/Dealer
Peterson Bros. Inc., Publishing
16 1st Ave.
Corry, PA 16407-1894   Phone: (814)664-8624
Charles P. Mancino, Publisher. Monthly. Trade magazine. **Facsimile Number:** (814)664-8506.

★4734★
Builder Insider
Divibest, Inc.
PO Box 191125
Dallas, TX 75219   Phone: (214)871-2913
Michael J. Anderson, Editor and Publisher. Monthly. Magazine (tabloid) for builders, architects, and remodelers.

★4735★
Builder Magazine (NAHB)
National Association of Home Builders of the U.S. (NAHB)
15th and M Sts. NW
Washington, DC 20005   Phone: (202)822-0200
Monthly.

★4736★
Building Business & Management
Builders Assn. of Southeastern Michigan
30375 Northwestern Hwy.
Farmington Hills, MI 48334   Phone: (313)737-4477
Kathleen M. Eischeid, Editor. Monthly. Construction and apartment industry magazine. **Facsimile Number:** (313)737-5741.

★4737★
Building Concerns
National Association of Minority Contractors (NAMC)
806 15th St. NW, Ste. 340
Washington, DC 20005   Phone: (202)347-8259
Editor(s): Ralph C. Thomas, III. Monthly. Concentrates on national and regional news regarding minority construction contractors. Contains articles on issues generally affecting the industry—especially issues affecting minorities—including topics such as legislative and regulatory activity and reports on major corporation developments. Recurring features include reports of meetings, news of educational opportunities, a calendar of events, and news of NAMC chapters and members.

★4738★
Building Design & Construction
Cahners Publishing Co.
1350 E. Touhy Ave.
PO Box 5080
Des Plaines, IL 60018   Phone: (708)635-8800
Philip G. Schreiner, Editor. Monthly. Magazine on business and technology for commercial, institutional, and industrial buildings. **Facsimile Number:** (708)299-8622.

★4739★
Building Homes & Renovations
Southam Business & Communications, Inc.
1450 Don Mills Rd.
Don Mills, ON, Canada M3B 2X7   Phone: (416)445-6641
Randy Threndyle, Editor. 5x/yr. Building trade and products magazine. **Facsimile Number:** (416)442-2214.

★4740★
Building Industry
Trade Publishing Co.
287 Mokauea St.
Honolulu, HI 96819   Phone: (808)848-0711
Jay McWilliams, Editor. Monthly. Construction and design magazine. **Facsimile Number:** (808)841-3053.

★4741★
Building Industry Technology: An Abstract Newsletter
National Technical Information Service (NTIS)
U.S. Department of Commerce
5285 Port Royal Rd.
Springfield, VA 22161   Phone: (703)487-4630
Weekly. Consists of abstracts of reports on architectural and environmental design, building standards, construction materials and equipment, and structural analyses. Recurring features include a form for ordering reports from NTIS.

★4742★
Buildings
427 6th Ave. SE
PO Box 1888
Cedar Rapids, IA 52406   Phone: (319)364-6167
Linda Monroe, Editor. Monthly. **Facsimile Number:** (319)365-5421.

★4743★
Capital Comments
National Lumber & Building Material Dealers Association
40 Ivy St. SE
Washington, DC 20003   Phone: (202)547-2230
Editor(s): Matt Geitner. Semimonthly. Reports on news of legislation pertaining to lumber, other building materials, and housing. Discusses such issues as lumber subsidies, interest rates on homes, health and safety, and jobs. **Facsimile Number:** (202)547-7640.

★4744★
The Carpenter
United Brotherhood of Carpenters and Joiners of America, AFL-CIO
101 Constitution Ave. NW
Washington, DC 20001   Phone: (202)546-6206
John S. Rogers, Editor. 6x/yr. Official magazine of the Carpenters' Union. **Facsimile Number:** (202)543-5724.

★4745★
ConnStruction
PO Box 9768
Wethersfield, CT 06109   Phone: (203)529-3246
Victor Bonini, Editor. 7x/yr. Magazine for construction industry. **Facsimile Number:** (203)563-0616.

★4746★
CONSTRUCTION
26 Long Hill Rd.
Guilford, CT 06437   Phone: (203)453-3717
Jack C. Lewis, Editor and Publisher. 2x/mo. Journal for the construction industry.

★4747★
Construction Dimensions
Assn. of Wall & Ceiling
PO Box 5504
Washington, DC 20016   Phone: (301)656-7050
Gerald Wykoff, Editor. Monthly. Wall and ceiling industry magazine.

★4748★
Construction Industry International
Maclean Hunter Publishing Co.
29 N. Wacker Dr.
Chicago, IL 60606   Phone: (312)726-2802
Alan Elliott, Editor-in-Chief. Monthly. Trade magazine.

★4749★
Construction News
715 W. 2nd St.
PO Box 2421
Little Rock, AR 72203   Phone: (501)376-1931
Robert Alvey, Editor. Weekly. Construction industry magazine. **Facsimile Number:** (501)375-5831.

★4750★
Construction Newsletter
National Safety Council
444 N. Michigan Ave.
Chicago, IL 60611   Phone: (312)527-4800
6/yr. Focuses on industrial and occupational safety in the construction industry. Carries items on such topics as safe work practices and products, accident prevention, and successful industrial safety programs and policies.

★4751★
Constructor (AGC)
Associated General Contractors of America (AGC)
1957 E St. NW
Washington, DC 20006   Phone: (202)393-2040
Monthly. Association magazine for general contractors engaged in construction.

★4752★
Daily Construction Reporter
4901 Pacific Hwy.
San Diego, CA 92110-4098   Phone: (619)296-0183
Kenneth F. Kerr, Editor and Publisher. Daily. Construction trade newspaper covering jobs that are out for bid, bid results, building permits, and other information. **Facsimile Number:** (619)298-3027.

★4753★
Economic News Notes (NAHB)
National Association of Home Builders of the U.S. (NAHB)
15th and M Sts. NW
Washington, DC 20005   Phone: (202)822-0200
Monthly.

★4754★
Fine Homebuilding
The Taunton Press, Inc.
63 S. Main St.
PO Box 5506
Newtown, CT 06470   Phone: (203)426-5506
Mark Feirer, Editor. 7x/yr. Magazine for builders, architects, designers, and owner-builders. **Facsimile Number:** (203)426-3434.

★4755★
Home BUILDER Magazine
Work-4 Projects Ltd.
PO Box 400, Victoria Sta.
Westmount, PQ, Canada H3Z 2V8   Phone: (514)489-4941
Nachmi Artzy, Editor and Publisher. 6x/yr. Magazine for home construction industry. **Facsimile Number:** (514)489-5505.

★4756★
The Journal of Light Construction
Hanley-Wood Partners
RR 2, Box 146
Richmond, VT 05477-9607   Phone: (802)864-0091
Steve Bliss, Editor. Monthly. Magazine (tabloid) for residential and light professionals involved in new and rehabilitative construction. Each issue covers a single aspect of construction.

★4757★
NAHB Library Bulletin (NAHB)
National Association of Home Builders of the U.S. (NAHB)
15th and M Sts. NW
Washington, DC 20005   Phone: (202)822-0200
Monthly.

★4758★
Nation's Building News (NAHB)
National Association of Home Builders of the U.S. (NAHB)
15th and M Sts. NW
Washington, DC 20005   Phone: (202)822-0200
Semimonthly. Tabloid newsletter providing the latest information concerning the housing industry, including finance, legislation, new technologies, and membership news.

★4759★
Professional Builder
Cahners Publishing Co.
1350 E. Touhy Ave.
Des Plaines, IL 60018   Phone: (708)635-8800
Roy L. Diez, Editor. 19x/yr. **Facsimile Number:** (708)299-8622.

★4760★
Southwest Contractor
McGraw Hill Publishing Co., Inc.
2050 E. University Dr., Ste. 1
Phoenix, AZ 85034-6731   Phone: (602)230-0598
Elaine Beall, Mng. Editor. Monthly. Regional trade magazine for the contracting industries including highway, municipal, utility, and heavy construction, and mining. **Facsimile Number:** (602)495-9407.

★4761★
The SPEC-DATA Program
Construction Specifications Institute
601 Madison St.
Alexandria, VA 22314   Phone: (703)684-0300
Brenda A. Furiga, Mgr. Quarterly. Magazine (loose-leaf) for the construction industry covering technical and product information. **Facsimile Number:** (703)684-0465.

―――――― Meetings and Conventions ――――――

★4762★
Associated Builders and Contractors (ABC)
729 15th St. NW
Washington, DC 20005   Phone: (202)637-8800
Frequency: Annual.

★4763★
Associated Builders and Contractors Builder and Contractor Convention and Exposition
Associated Builders and Contractors (ABC)
729 15th St., NW
Washington, DC 20005   Phone: (202)637-8800
1992; Mar. 11-15; Orlando, FL.

★4764★
Associated General Contractors National Convention and Constructor Exposition
Associated General Contractors
1957 E St., NW
Washington, DC 20006   Phone: (202)393-2040
1992; Mar. 26-31; Dallas, TX. **Facsimile Number:** (202)347-4004.

★4765★
CONEXPO
Construction Industry Manufacturers Association
111 E. Wisconsin Ave.
Milwaukee, WI 53202   Phone: (414)272-0943
Frequency: Every six years. 1993; Mar. 20-25; Las Vegas, NV • 1999. **Facsimile Number:** (414)272-2672.

★4766★
Eastern Region Lumbermen's Association Regional Exposition and Conference
Eastern Building Material Dealers Association
604 E. Baltimore Pke.
Media, PA 19063   Phone: (215)565-6144
Facsimile Number: (215)565-0968.

★4767★
National Association of Home Builders/The Builders Show
National Association of Home Builders of the United States
15th and M Sts., NW
Washington, DC 20005   Phone: (202)822-0424
Frequency: Usually held in January; location rotates every three years. • 1993; Feb. 19-22; Las Vegas, NV • 1994; Jan. 21-24; Las Vegas, NV. **Toll-free/Additional Phone Number(s):** 800-368-5242. **Facsimile Number:** (202)822-0435.

★4768★
National Frame Builders Association Convention
National Frame Builders Association
872 Rosehill Rd., Ste. 210
Lenexa, KS 66215-4611   Phone: (913)599-0606
1992. **Facsimile Number:** (913)599-6500.

★4769★
Northeastern Retail Lumber Association Annual Convention
Northeastern Retail Lumber Association
339 East Ave.
Rochester, NY 14604   Phone: (716)325-1626
Frequency: Always held in Boston, Massachusetts during January at the Hynes Convention Center. **Facsimile Number:** (716)325-6179.

★4770★
United Brotherhood of Carpenters and Joiners of America (UBC)
101 Constitution Ave. NW
Washington, DC 20001   Phone: (202)546-6206
Frequency: Quinquennial - next held in 1996.

Carpet Installers

Carpet installers measure, cut, and fit carpet materials in homes, offices, stores, restaurants, and other buildings. Many work for flooring contractors or floor covering retailers. Many other carpet installers are self-employed.

$alaries

Carpet installers earn between $25,000 and $50,000/year. Starting wage rates for apprentices and other trainees usually are about half of the experienced worker's rate.

Employment Outlook

Growth rate until the year 2000: Faster than average.

Carpet Installers

Career Guides

★4771★
Carpet Installer
Careers, Inc.
PO Box 135
Largo, FL 34649-0135　　　　Phone: (813)584-7333
1988. Two-page job guide card describing duties, working conditions, personal qualifications, training, earnings and hours, employment outlook, places of employment, related careers and where to write for more information.

★4772★
"Carpet Installer" in *Occu-Facts: Information on 565 Careers in Outline Form* (p. 16.13)
Careers, Inc.
P.O. Box 135
1211 Tenth St., S.W.
Largo, FL 33640　　　　Phone: (813)584-7333
Elizabeth Handville. Biennial, 1989-90 edition. Each one-page occupational profile describes duties, working conditions, physical surroundings and demands, aptitudes, temperament, educational requirements, employment outlook, earnings, and places of employment.

★4773★
"Carpet Installers" in *Occupational Outlook Handbook* (pp. 365-366)
Superintendent of Documents
U.S. Government Printing Office
Washington, DC 20402　　　　Phone: (202)783-3238
Biennial; latest edition, 1990-91. Encyclopedia of careers describing more than 250 occupations and comprising about 86 percent of all jobs in the economy. Occupations that require lengthy education or training are given the most attention. For each occupation, the handbook describes job duties, working conditions, training, educational preparation, personal qualities, advancement possibilities, job outlook, earnings, and sources of additional information.

★4774★
"Floor Covering Installer" in *Construction*, Volume 4 of *Career Information Center* (pp. 58-60)
Glencoe/Macmillan
15319 Chatsworth St.
Mission Hills, CA 91345　　　　Phone: (818)898-1391
Richard Lidz and Dale Anderson, editorial directors. Fourth edition, 1990. For 600 occupations, describes job duties, entry-level requirements, education and training needed, advancement possibilities, employment outlook, earnings and benefits. The set is divided into 12 volumes. Each volume includes jobs related under a broad career field. Volume 13 is the index. **Facsimile Number:** 818-365-5489.

★4775★
"Floor Covering Installer" in Volume 3 of *The Encyclopedia of Careers and Vocational Guidance* (pp. 662-665)
J.G. Ferguson Publishing Co.
200 W. Monroe
Chicago, IL 60606　　　　Phone: (312)580-5480
William E. Hopke, editor-in-chief. Eighth edition, 1990. Four-volume set that profiles 500 occupations and describes job trends in 76 industries. Includes career description, educational requirements, history of the job, methods of entry, advancement, employment outlook, earnings, working conditions, social and psychological factors, and sources of additional information.

★4776★
"Floor Covering Installer (Resilient)" in *Occu-Facts: Information on 565 Careers in Outline Form* (p. 16.12)
Careers, Inc.
P.O. Box 135
1211 Tenth St., S.W.
Largo, FL 33640　　　　Phone: (813)584-7333
Elizabeth Handville. Biennial, 1989-90 edition. Each one-page occupational profile describes duties, working conditions, physical surroundings and demands, aptitudes, temperament, educational requirements, employment outlook, earnings, and places of employment.

★4777★
"Floor Covering Installers" in *Opportunities in Building Construction Trades* (pp. 53-55)
National Textbook Co.
4255 W. Touhy Ave.
Lincolnwood, IL 60646　　　　Phone: (312)679-5500
Michael Sumichrast. 1989. Gives an overview of the construction industry and describes the jobs of various craftworkers. Covers different kinds of builders: home, custom; and describes management skills needed and industry trends affecting opportunities.

★4778★
"Floor Covering Installers" in Volume 3 of *Career Discovery Encyclopedia* (pp. 40-41)
J.G. Ferguson Publishing Co.
200 W. Monroe
Chicago, IL 60606　　　　Phone: (312)580-5480
E. Russell Primm, editor-in-chief. 1990. Contains two-page articles on 504 occupations. Each article describes job duties, earnings, and educational and training requirements.

★4779★
"Resilient Floor Layer" in *Opportunities in Carpentry Careers* (pp. 52-53)
National Textbook Co.
4255 W. Touhy Ave.
Lincolnwood, IL 60646   Phone: (312)679-5500

Roger Sheldon. 1987. Covers the history of the crafts, a typical carpenter's workday, future opportunities for carpenters, qualifications, training, apprenticeships, and special advice for women and minorities. Surveys various training opportunities.

Associations

★4780★
Floor Covering Installation Contractors Association (FCICA)
PO Box 948
Dalton, GA 30722-0948   Phone: (404)226-5488

Membership: Installation contractors, carpet manufacturers, and suppliers to the installation trade. **Purpose:** Goals are to: establish acceptable levels of performance for the carpet installation industry; promote standards of business ethics; encourage quality installations. Represents the interests of the floor covering installation industry by addressing issues such as minimum standards, clear and equitable specifications, uniform training, and quality craftsmanship. Acts as liaison with retailers, manufacturers, and suppliers; represents the industry before government agencies regarding proposed or enacted regulation and legislation. Fosters the sale and use of the industry's products and services. Serves as clearinghouse for resolving problems of mutual interest inside and outside the industry; exchanges information on problems, trends, techniques, and other matters concerning management. Assists local installation workrooms/contractors groups. Sponsors training programs, refresher courses, and workshops; compiles statistics. **Publications:** *Floor Covering Installation Contractors Association—Newsletter*, 3-4/year. • *Membership Directory*, annual. **Facsimile Number:** (404)278-8835.

Standards/Certification Agencies

The majority of carpet installers learn their trade informally on the job as helpers to experienced installers. Informal training programs usually are sponsored by individual contractors and generally last about one to two years. Others learn through formal apprenticeship programs, which include on-the-job training as well as related classroom instruction. Apprenticeship programs and some contractor-sponsored programs provide comprehensive training in all phases of carpet laying. Union-sponsored apprenticeship programs offered by local chapters of the United Brotherhood of Carpenters and Joiners of America and the International Brotherhood of Painters and Allied Trades consist of weekly classes that usually last three years.

Basic Reference Guides and Handbooks

★4781★
Wool Carpet Specification Guide and Resource Directory
Wool Bureau, Inc.
240 Peachtree St., N.W.
Merchandise Mart, 6-F-11
Atlanta, GA 30303   Phone: (404)524-0512

Annual, July. About 220 manufacturers and suppliers of domestic and imported wool and wool blend carpets and rugs. Entries include: Company name, address, phone, name and title of contact, construction specifications of products. Arrangement: Manufacturers are alphabetical. **Facsimile Number:** (404)659-6974.

Periodicals

★4782★
ABC Newsline
Associated Builders and Contractors, Inc. (ABC)
729 15th St. NW
Washington, DC 20005   Phone: (202)637-8800

Editor(s): Lisa A. Nardone. Semimonthly. Designed to keep readers alerted to important changes within ABC and the construction industry. Reports on legislative issues, construction trends, conferences and meetings, and ABC services. Recurring features include news of members and a column titled Industry Briefs.

★4783★
American Architectural Manufacturers Association—Quarterly Review
American Architectural Manufacturers Association
1540 E. Dundee Rd., Ste. K 310
Palatine, IL 60067-8321   Phone: (708)202-1350

Editor(s): Tony Coorlim. Annually. Contains industry news on architectural products. Covers prime and combination storm windows, sliding glass and combination storm doors, window and curtain-walls, store fronts and entrances, siding, soffits, fascia, gutters, downspouts, skylights, space enclosures, and mobile home components. Recurring features include news of research, notices of publications available, and announcements by the association. **Facsimile Number:** (708)202-1480.

★4784★
American Institute of Constructors—Newsletter
American Institute of Constructors
9887 Gandy Blvd. N., No. 104
Saint Petersburg, FL 33702-2451

Editor(s): Ed Freedman. Bimonthly. Concerned with construction practice, design, administration, and teaching. Carries news of members, listings of job opportunities, local chapter reports, and notices of new publications. **Facsimile Number:** (614)464-3226.

★4785★
Blue Reports, Inc.
Construction News Service
7325 Steel Mill Dr.
Springfield, VA 22050   Phone: (703)644-5884

Editor(s): Calvin S. Oren. Daily. Reports on public and private construction projects in the Washington, DC, Virginia, and Maryland areas. Provides owner's and architect's names, plan status, date bids due, prospective bidders, low bids received, and specification details. **Facsimile Number:** (703)644-1929.

★4786★
Building Concerns
National Association of Minority Contractors (NAMC)
806 15th St. NW, Ste. 340
Washington, DC 20005   Phone: (202)347-8259

Editor(s): Ralph C. Thomas, III. Monthly. Concentrates on national and regional news regarding minority construction contractors. Contains articles on issues generally affecting the industry—especially issues affecting minorities—including topics such as legislative and regulatory activity and reports on major corporation developments. Recurring features include reports of meetings, news of educational opportunities, a calendar of events, and news of NAMC chapters and members.

Carpet Installers

★4787★
Building Industry Technology: An Abstract Newsletter
National Technical Information Service (NTIS)
U.S. Department of Commerce
5285 Port Royal Rd.
Springfield, VA 22161 Phone: (703)487-4630
Weekly. Consists of abstracts of reports on architectural and environmental design, building standards, construction materials and equipment, and structural analyses. Recurring features include a form for ordering reports from NTIS.

★4788★
Building Renovation
Maclean Hunter Ltd.
777 Bay St.
Toronto, ON, Canada M5W 1A7 Phone: (416)596-5760
John Fennell, Editor. 6x/yr. Business magazine for professionals in residential and commercial renovation and remodeling. **Facsimile Number:** (416)596-5810.

★4789★
Capital Comments
National Lumber & Building Material Dealers Association
40 Ivy St. SE
Washington, DC 20003 Phone: (202)547-2230
Editor(s): Matt Geitner. Semimonthly. Reports on news of legislation pertaining to lumber, other building materials, and housing. Discusses such issues as lumber subsidies, interest rates on homes, health and safety, and jobs. **Facsimile Number:** (202)547-7640.

★4790★
ConnStruction
PO Box 9768
Wethersfield, CT 06109 Phone: (203)529-3246
Victor Bonini, Editor. 7x/yr. Magazine for construction industry. **Facsimile Number:** (203)563-0616.

★4791★
CONSTRUCTION
26 Long Hill Rd.
Guilford, CT 06437 Phone: (203)453-3717
Jack C. Lewis, Editor and Publisher. 2x/mo. Journal for the construction industry.

★4792★
Construction Dimensions
Assn. of Wall & Ceiling
PO Box 5504
Washington, DC 20016 Phone: (301)656-7050
Gerald Wykoff, Editor. Monthly. Wall and ceiling industry magazine.

★4793★
Construction Industry International
Maclean Hunter Publishing Co.
29 N. Wacker Dr.
Chicago, IL 60606 Phone: (312)726-2802
Alan Elliott, Editor-in-Chief. Monthly. Trade magazine.

★4794★
Construction News
715 W. 2nd St.
PO Box 2421
Little Rock, AR 72203 Phone: (501)376-1931
Robert Alvey, Editor. Weekly. Construction industry magazine. **Facsimile Number:** (501)375-5831.

★4795★
Construction Newsletter
National Safety Council
444 N. Michigan Ave.
Chicago, IL 60611 Phone: (312)527-4800
6/yr. Focuses on industrial and occupational safety in the construction industry. Carries items on such topics as safe work practices and products, accident prevention, and successful industrial safety programs and policies.

★4796★
Daily Construction Reporter
4901 Pacific Hwy.
San Diego, CA 92110-4098 Phone: (619)296-0183
Kenneth F. Kerr, Editor and Publisher. Daily. Construction trade newspaper covering jobs that are out for bid, bid results, building permits, and other information. **Facsimile Number:** (619)298-3027.

★4797★
The Dalton Carpet Journal
The Daily Citizen News
308 S. Thornton Ave.
PO Box 1167
Dalton, GA 30720 Phone: (404)278-1011
Terry Smith, Editor. Monthly. Newspaper (tabloid) covering the carpet and rug industry.

★4798★
Floor Covering Installation Contractors Association—Newsletter (FCICA)
Floor Covering Installation Contractors Association (FCICA)
PO Box 948
Dalton, GA 30722-0948 Phone: (404)226-5488
3-4/year.

★4799★
Floor Covering News
Maclean Hunter Ltd.
777 Bay St.
Toronto, ON, Canada M5W 1A7 Phone: (416)596-5805
Michael Knell, Editor. Ten times/yr. Magazine (tabloid) for the floor covering industry. **Facsimile Number:** (416)593-3189.

★4800★
Floor Covering Weekly
Hearst Business Communications, Inc.
555 W. 57th St., 17th Fl.
New York, NY 10019-2925 Phone: (212)541-4080
Janet Morgan Daly, Editor. Weekly (Mon.). Business newspaper of the floor covering industry. **Facsimile Number:** (212)541-4699.

★4801★
Flooring
Edgerl Communications
7500 Old Oak Blvd.
Cleveland, OH 44140 Phone: (216)243-8100
Mark Kuhar, Editor. Monthly. Magazine on floor coverings. **Facsimile Number:** (216)826-2832.

★4802★
Home BUILDER Magazine
Work-4 Projects Ltd.
PO Box 400, Victoria Sta.
Westmount, PQ, Canada H3Z 2V8 Phone: (514)489-4941
Nachmi Artzy, Editor and Publisher. 6x/yr. Magazine for home construction industry. **Facsimile Number:** (514)489-5505.

★4803★
The Journal of Light Construction
Hanley-Wood Partners
RR 2, Box 146
Richmond, VT 05477-9607   Phone: (802)864-0091

Steve Bliss, Editor. Monthly. Magazine (tabloid) for residential and light professionals involved in new and rehabilitative construction. Each issue covers a single aspect of construction.

★4804★
Nation's Building News
15th & M Sts. NW
Washington, DC 20005   Phone: (202)822-0525

Tim Ahern, Editor. 2x/mo. Trade magazine (tabloid) covering home building and all related industries. **Facsimile Number:** (202)861-2131.

★4805★
Professional Builder
Cahners Publishing Co.
1350 E. Touhy Ave.
Des Plaines, IL 60018   Phone: (708)635-8800

Roy L. Diez, Editor. 19x/yr. **Facsimile Number:** (708)299-8622.

★4806★
Sun Belt Floor Covering
Trade Publications
PO Box 810195
Dallas, TX 75381   Phone: (214)484-4474

Bobbie Carmical, Editor. Monthly. Trade magazine for retail floor covering dealers. **Facsimile Number:** (214)484-4280.

Meetings and Conventions

★4807★
American Floorcovering Association Convention
American Floorcovering Association
13-154 Merchandise Mart
Chicago, IL 60654   Phone: (312)644-1243

Frequency: Usually held in April or May. 1992; Apr. Phoenix, AZ • 1993; May, Marco Island, FL. **Toll-free/Additional Phone Number(s):** 800-776-3566. **Facsimile Number:** (312)644-2787.

★4808★
Carpet and Rugs
World Access Corp.
15 Bemis Rd.
PO Box 171
Wellesley Hills, MA 02181   Phone: (617)235-8095

1992; May 21-24; Singapore. **Facsimile Number:** (617)235-7360.

★4809★
Floor Covering Installation Contractors Association (FCICA)
PO Box 948
Dalton, GA 30722-0948   Phone: (404)226-5488

Frequency: Annual. **Facsimile Number:** (404)278-8835.

★4810★
Home Furnishings and Carpet Market and Floor Coverings
AMC Trade Shows
240 Peachtree St. NW, Ste. 2200
Atlanta, GA 30303   Phone: (404)220-3000

★4811★
Installation Supplies and Ideas Expo
National Association of Floor Covering Distributors
13-126 Merchandise Mart
Chicago, IL 60654   Phone: (708)364-9040

1992; May 09-13; Palm Desert, CA • 1993; Apr. 17-21; Marco Island, FL.

Concrete Masons and Terrazzo Workers

Concrete masons place and finish concrete for such projects as highways, bridges, shopping malls, or large buildings such as factories, schools, and hospitals. They also color concrete surfaces, expose aggregate in walls and sidewalks, or fabricate concrete beams, columns, and panels. Most concrete masons work for concrete contractors or for general contractors; a small number are employed by firms that manufacture concrete products. Terrazzo workers create attractive walkways, floors, patios, and panels by exposing marble chips and other fine aggregates on the surface of finished concrete. They work for special trade contractors who install decorative floors and wall panels. The few concrete masons and terrazzo workers that are self-employed specialize in small jobs, such as driveways, sidewalks, and patios.

$alaries

Nonunion workers generally have lower wage rates than union workers. Apprentices usually start at 50 to 60 percent of the rate paid to experienced workers. Median weekly salaries for concrete masons and terrazzo workers are as follows:

Lowest 10 percent	$224/week or less
Median	$391/year
Top 10 percent	$684/week or more

Employment Outlook

Growth rate until the year 2000: Average.

Concrete Masons and Terrazzo Workers

―――― **Career Guides** ――――

★4812★
Cement Mason
Careers, Inc.
PO Box 135
Largo, FL 34649-0135　　　　Phone: (813)584-7333
1991. Two-page occupational summary card describing duties, working conditions, personal qualifications, training, earnings and hours, employment outlook, places of employment, related careers and where to write for more information.

★4813★
"Cement Mason" in *Construction*, Volume 4 of *Career Information Center* (pp. 43-45)
Glencoe/Macmillan
15319 Chatsworth St.
Mission Hills, CA 91345　　　　Phone: (818)898-1391
Richard Lidz and Dale Anderson, editorial directors. Fourth edition, 1990. For 600 occupations, describes job duties, entry-level requirements, education and training needed, advancement possibilities, employment outlook, earnings and benefits. The set is divided into 12 volumes. Each volume includes jobs related under a broad career field. Volume 13 is the index. **Facsimile Number:** 818-365-5489.

★4814★
"Cement Mason" in *Occu-Facts: Information on 565 Careers in Outline Form* (p. 16.14)
Careers, Inc.
P.O. Box 135
1211 Tenth St., S.W.
Largo, FL 33640　　　　Phone: (813)584-7333
Elizabeth Handville. Biennial, 1989-90 edition. Each one-page occupational profile describes duties, working conditions, physical surroundings and demands, aptitudes, temperament, educational requirements, employment outlook, earnings, and places of employment.

★4815★
Cement Masons
Chronicle Guidance Publications, Inc.
PO Box 1190
Moravia, NY 13118-1190　　　　Phone: (315)497-0330
1988. This career brief describes the nature of the work, working conditions, hours and earnings, education and training, licensure, certification, unions, personal qualifications, social and psychological factors, employment outlook, entry methods, advancement, and related occupations. **Toll-free/Additional Phone Number(s):** 800-622-7284.

★4816★
"Cement Masons" in *Opportunities in Building Construction Trades* (pp. 29-30)
National Textbook Co.
4255 W. Touhy Ave.
Lincolnwood, IL 60646　　　　Phone: (312)679-5500
Michael Sumichrast. 1989. Gives an overview of the construction industry and describes the jobs of various craftworkers. Covers different kinds of builders: home, custom; and describes management skills needed and industry trends affecting opportunities.

★4817★
"Cement Masons" in Volume 3 of *Career Discovery Encyclopedia* (pp. 636-639)
J.G. Ferguson Publishing Co.
200 W. Monroe
Chicago, IL 60606　　　　Phone: (312)580-5480
E. Russell Primm, editor-in-chief. 1990. Contains two-page articles on 504 occupations. Each article describes job duties, earnings, and educational and training requirements.

★4818★
"Cement Masons" in Volume 3 of *The Encyclopedia of Careers and Vocational Guidance* (pp. 636-639)
J.G. Ferguson Publishing Co.
200 W. Monroe
Chicago, IL 60606　　　　Phone: (312)580-5480
William E. Hopke, editor-in-chief. Eighth edition, 1990. Four-volume set that profiles 500 occupations and describes job trends in 76 industries. Includes career description, educational requirements, history of the job, methods of entry, advancement, employment outlook, earnings, working conditions, social and psychological factors, and sources of additional information.

★4819★
"Concrete Masons and Terrazzo Workers" in *Occupational Outlook Handbook* (pp. 366-367)
Superintendent of Documents
U.S. Government Printing Office
Washington, DC 20402　　　　Phone: (202)783-3238
Biennial; latest edition, 1990-91. Encyclopedia of careers describing more than 250 occupations and comprising about 86 percent of all jobs in the economy. Occupations that require lengthy education or training are given the most attention. For each occupation, the handbook describes job duties, working conditions, training, educational preparation, personal qualities, advancement possibilities, job outlook, earnings, and sources of additional information.

★4820★
Construction: Basic Principles
RMI Media Productions, Inc.
2807 West 47th St.
Shawnee Mission, KS 66205   Phone: (913)262-3974

Videocassette. 1984. 20 mins. This series of five programs of varying lengths covers different aspects of career opportunities in the construction trades. Included are: concrete masonry, carpentry, electrical work, plumbing, and heating and air conditioning.

★4821★
Construction Cluster
Center for Humanities, Inc.
Communications Park
Box 1000
Mount Kisco, NY 10549   Phone: (914)666-4100

Videocassette. 1984. 15 mins. Construction workers describe what it's like to work at their jobs, and show the special equipment they use in their field.

★4822★
"Marble Setter, Tilesetters, and Terrazzo Workers" in Opportunities in Building Construction Trades (pp. 63-65)
National Textbook Co.
4255 W. Touhy Ave.
Lincolnwood, IL 60646   Phone: (312)679-5500

Michael Sumichrast. 1989. Gives an overview of the construction industry and describes the jobs of various craftworkers. Covers different kinds of builders: home, custom; and describes management skills needed and industry trends affecting opportunities.

★4823★
Marble Setters, Tile Layers and Terrazzo Workers
Chronicle Guidance Publications, Inc.
PO Box 1190
Moravia, NY 13118-1190   Phone: (315)497-0330

1988. This career brief describes the nature of the work, working conditions, hours and earnings, education and training, licensure, certification, unions, personal qualifications, social and psychological factors, employment outlook, entry methods, advancement, and related occupations. **Toll-free/Additional Phone Number(s):** 800-622-7284.

★4824★
"Marble Setters, Tile Setters, and Terrazzo Workers" in Volume 3 of The Encyclopedia of Careers and Vocational Guidance (pp. 677-679)
J.G. Ferguson Publishing Co.
200 W. Monroe
Chicago, IL 60606   Phone: (312)580-5480

William E. Hopke, editor-in-chief. Eighth edition, 1990. Four-volume set that profiles 500 occupations and describes job trends in 76 industries. Includes career description, educational requirements, history of the job, methods of entry, advancement, employment outlook, earnings, working conditions, social and psychological factors, and sources of additional information.

★4825★
"Marble, Tile, and Terrazzo Worker" in Construction, Volume 4 of Career Information Center (pp. 71-72)
Glencoe/Macmillan
15319 Chatsworth St.
Mission Hills, CA 91345   Phone: (818)898-1391

Richard Lidz and Dale Anderson, editorial directors. Fourth edition, 1990. For 600 occupations, describes job duties, entry-level requirements, education and training needed, advancement possibilities, employment outlook, earnings and benefits. The set is divided into 12 volumes. Each volume includes jobs related under a broad career field. Volume 13 is the index. **Facsimile Number:** 818-365-5489.

★4826★
Marble, Tile Setters, Terrazzo, and Stone Workers
Careers, Inc.
PO Box 135
Largo, FL 34649-0135   Phone: (813)584-7333

1989. Eight-page brief offering the definition, history, duties, working conditions, personal qualifications, educational requirements, earnings, hours, employment outlook, advancement possibilities, and related occupations.

★4827★
"Marble, Tile, Terrazzo, and Stone Workers" in Occu-Facts: Information on 565 Careers in Outline Form (p. 16.3)
Careers, Inc.
P.O. Box 135
1211 Tenth St., S.W.
Largo, FL 33640   Phone: (813)584-7333

Elizabeth Handville. Biennial, 1989-90 edition. Each one-page occupational profile describes duties, working conditions, physical surroundings and demands, aptitudes, temperament, educational requirements, employment outlook, earnings, and places of employment.

★4828★
The Trowel Trades
International Masonry Institute
823 15th St. NW, Ste. 1001
Washington, DC 20005   Phone: (202)783-3908

This six-panel brochure describes skills, advancement opportunities, and apprentice training.

★4829★
Vocational Visions
Center for Humanities, Inc.
Communications Park
Box 1000
Mount Kisco, NY 10549   Phone: (914)666-4100

Videocassette. 1984. 30 mins. This series of programs explains key aspects of actual training and a day in the life of a worker in the specific field mentioned on the videocassette. Occupations include: transportation/mechanics, repair, construction, business/office occupations, health, and agriculture.

★4830★
Vocations U.S.A.
Info-Disc Corporation
4 Professional Dr.
Gaithersburg, MD 20879   Phone: (301)948-2300

Videocassette. 1987. 60 mins. A disc collection outlining the requirements and methods of various career areas. Occupations include: transportation, mechanical/repair, health, agriculture, and construction.

★4831★
You Can Become a Tile, Marble, Terrazzo and Dimensional Stone Installer
United Brotherhood of Carpenters and Joiners of America
101 Constitution Ave., N.W.
Washington, DC 20001   Phone: (202)546-6206

This six-panel brochure describes apprenticeship training, hours, and working conditions.

Concrete Masons and Terrazzo Workers ★4840★

Associations

★4832★
Associated General Contractors of America (AGC)
1957 E St. NW
Washington, DC 20006   Phone: (202)393-2040
Membership: General construction contractors; subcontractors; industry suppliers; service firms. **Purpose:** Provides tax services through its divisions. Conducts special conferences and seminars designed specifically for construction firms. Compiles statistics on job accidents reported by member firms. Bestows annual awards for safety and Build/America awards for innovative and outstanding achievements by general contractors. Offers college scholarships through AGC Education and Research Foundation. Maintains 65 committees, including joint cooperative committees with other associations and liaison committees with federal agencies. **Publications:** *AGC Membership Directory and Buyers' Guide*, annual. • *Associated General Contractors of America—National Newsletter*, biweekly. • *Constructor*, monthly. • Also publishes manuals, guides, model contract documents, studies, and checklists. **Facsimile Number:** (202)347-4004.

★4833★
Concrete Sawing and Drilling Association
6077 Roswell Rd., NE, Ste. 205
Atlanta, GA 30328   Phone: (404)257-1177
Membership: Concrete sawing and drilling contractors and manufacturers. **Purpose:** Seeks to professionalize industry through education and development of standards and procedures. Bestows awards for drilling, flat sawing, wall sawing, and innovative technology.

★4834★
International Union of Bricklayers and Allied Craftsmen (BAC)
815 15th St., NW
Washington, DC 20005   Phone: (202)783-3788
Membership: AFL-CIO. **Publications:** *Chalkline*, periodic. • *Journal*, monthly. **Facsimile Number:** (202)393-0219.

★4835★
National Terrazzo and Mosaic Association (NTMA)
3166 Des Plaines Ave., Ste. 132
Des Plaines, IL 60018   Phone: (708)635-7744
Membership: Contractors who install terrazzo and mosaic work; firms that produce or manufacture materials. **Purpose:** Provides information to building owners, architects, builders, and terrazzo contractors. Conducts research on installation methods. **Publications:** *Directory*, annual. • Also publishes *Terrazzo and Mosaic Catalog*, *Design Book*, technical data, and standard specifications for terrazzo. **Facsimile Number:** (708)635-9127.

★4836★
Operative Plasterers and Cement Masons International Association of U.S. and Canada (OPCMIA)
1125 17th St., NW
Washington, DC 20036   Phone: (202)393-6569
Membership: AFL-CIO. **Publications:** *Plasterer and Cement Mason*, monthly.

★4837★
Portland Cement Association (PCA)
5420 Old Orchard Rd.
Skokie, IL 60077   Phone: (708)966-6200
Membership: Manufacturers and marketers of portland cement in the U.S. and Canada. **Purpose:** Seeks to improve and extend the uses of portland cement and concrete through market promotion, research and development, educational programs, and representation with governmental entities. Conducts research on concrete technology and durability; concrete pavement design; load-bearing capacities, field performance, and fire resistance of concrete; transportation, building, and structural uses of concrete. Operates Construction Technology Laboratories, which conducts research and technical services in construction materials, products, and applications. Sponsors a public affairs program in Washington, DC. Maintains library of 10,000 volumes on cement and concrete technology. **Publications:** *List of Member Companies*, periodic. • Also publishes film and publication catalogs and more than 500 booklets and other materials; issues films and videotapes. **Facsimile Number:** (708)966-9781.

Standards/Certification Agencies

Concrete masons and terrazzo workers learn their trade either through on-the-job training as helpers or through two- or three-year apprenticeship programs. On-the-job training programs consist of informal instruction from experienced workers. Two- and three-year apprenticeship programs, usually jointly sponsored by contractors and local chapters of the Operative Plasterers' and Cement Masons' International Association of the United States and Canada or the International Union of Bricklayers and Allied Craftsmen provide on-the-job training in addition to a recommended minimum of 144 hours of classroom instruction each year. A written test and a physical exam may be required.

★4838★
Concrete Sawing and Drilling Association
6077 Roswell Rd., NE, Ste. 205
Atlanta, GA 30328   Phone: (404)257-1177
Develops standards for products and procedures related to concrete sawing and drilling.

★4839★
National Terrazzo and Mosaic Association (NTMA)
3166 Des Plaines Ave., Ste. 132
Des Plaines, IL 60018   Phone: (708)635-7744
Publishes technical data, and standard specifications for terrazzo.

Test Guides

★4840★
Cement Mason
National Learning Corp.
212 Michael Dr.
Syosset, NY 11791   Phone: (516)921-8888
Jack Rudman. Part of the Career Examination Series No. 1. All examination guides in this series contain questions with answers. **Facsimile Number:** (516)921-8743. **Toll-free/Additional Phone Number(s):** 800-645-6337.

★4841★
Maintenance Mechanic
Prentice Hall Press
Simon & Schuster Inc.
200 Old Tappan Rd.
Old Tappan, NJ 07675　　　　　　　Phone: (800)223-2348

Hy Hammer. First edition, 1988. Provides information for applicants interested in the following entry-level civil service positions: mason's helper, elevator mechanic's helper, mechanical maintainer's helper, among others.

★4842★
Maintenance Worker/Mechanical Maintainer
Prentice Hall Press
Simon & Schuster Inc.
200 Old Tappan Rd.
Old Tappan, NJ 07675　　　　　　　Phone: (800)223-2348

Hy Hammer. Fourth edition, 1984. Provides information for applicants interested in the following civil service positions: carpenter, mason, plumber, electrician, painter, machinist. Includes eight sample tests.

★4843★
Mason
National Learning Corp.
212 Michael Dr.
Syosset, NY 11791　　　　　　　Phone: (516)921-8888

Jack Rudman. Part of the Career Examination Series No. 1. All examination guides in this series contain questions with answers. **Facsimile Number:** (516)921-8743. **Toll-free/Additional Phone Number(s):** 800-645-6337.

★4844★
Mason's Helper
National Learning Corp.
212 Michael Dr.
Syosset, NY 11791　　　　　　　Phone: (516)921-8888

Jack Rudman. Part of the Career Examination Series No. 1. All examination guides in this series contain questions with answers. **Facsimile Number:** (516)921-8743. **Toll-free/Additional Phone Number(s):** 800-645-6337.

Basic Reference Guides and Handbooks

★4845★
Intelligent Buildings Institute—Directory of Products and Services
Intelligent Buildings Institute (IBI)
2101 L St., NW, Ste. 300
Washington, DC 20037　　　　　　　Phone: (202)457-1988

S. Hunt, Associate Executive Director, editor. Annual, September. Member consultants, associations, research organizations, and other suppliers of products and services to the construction and building industry. Entries include: Company name, address, phone. Arrangement: Alphabetical. Indexes: Product/service. **Facsimile Number:** (202)457-8468.

★4846★
Mason Contractors' Equipment & Supplies Directory
American Business Directories, Inc.
American Business Information, Inc.
5711 S. 86th Circle
Omaha, NE 68127　　　　　　　Phone: (402)593-4600

Annual. Entries include: Name, address, phone, size of advertisement, name of owner or manager, number of employees, year first in "Yellow Pages." Arrangement: Geographical. **Facsimile Number:** (402)331-1505.

★4847★
Mid-West Contractor—Annual Convention Guide and Association Directory AConstruction industryA
Allied Publications, Inc.
7355 N. Woodland Dr.
Box 603
Indianapolis, IN 46278　　　　　　　Phone: (317)297-5500

Jennifer Wynne, editor. Annual. List of 160 construction contracting and architectural associations in the Midwest. Entries include: Association name, address, phone, names and titles of key personnel, description of association; convention site, date, name and title of contact. Arrangement: Geographical, alphabetical. **Toll-free/Additional Phone Number(s):** (800)827-7468. **Facsimile Number:** (317)299-1356.

★4848★
NTMA Design Book (NTMA)
National Terrazzo and Mosaic Association (NTMA)
3166 Des Plaines Ave., Ste. 132
Des Plaines, IL 60018　　　　　　　Phone: (708)635-7744

★4849★
NTMA Directory (NTMA)
National Terrazzo and Mosaic Association (NTMA)
3166 Des Plaines Ave., Ste. 132
Des Plaines, IL 60018　　　　　　　Phone: (708)635-7744
Annual. .

Periodicals

★4850★
ABC Newsline
Associated Builders and Contractors, Inc. (ABC)
729 15th St. NW
Washington, DC 20005　　　　　　　Phone: (202)637-8800

Editor(s): Lisa A. Nardone. Semimonthly. Designed to keep readers alerted to important changes within ABC and the construction industry. Reports on legislative issues, construction trends, conferences and meetings, and ABC services. Recurring features include news of members and a column titled Industry Briefs.

★4851★
Aberdeen's Magazine of Masonry Construction
The Aberdeen Group
426 S. Westgate
Addison, IL 60101　　　　　　　Phone: (708)543-0870

Mark Wallace, Editor. Monthly. Trade magazine. **Facsimile Number:** (708)543-3112.

★4852★
ACI Structural Journal
American Concrete Institute
PO Box 19150
Detroit, MI 48219-0150　　　　　　　Phone: (313)532-2600

Robert G. Wiedyke, Director of Journal and Book Publications. 6x/yr. Journal containing information on structural design and analysis of concrete elements and structures; includes design and analysis theory, and related ACI standards and committee reports. **Facsimile Number:** (313)538-0655.

Concrete Masons and Terrazzo Workers ★4864★

★4853★
American Architectural Manufacturers Association—Quarterly Review
American Architectural Manufacturers Association
1540 E. Dundee Rd., Ste. K 310
Palatine, IL 60067-8321
Phone: (708)202-1350
Editor(s): Tony Coorlim. Annually. Contains industry news on architectural products. Covers prime and combination storm windows, sliding glass and combination storm doors, window and curtain-walls, store fronts and entrances, siding, soffits, fascia, gutters, downspouts, skylights, space enclosures, and mobile home components. Recurring features include news of research, notices of publications available, and announcements by the association. **Facsimile Number:** (708)202-1480.

★4854★
American Institute of Constructors—Newsletter
American Institute of Constructors
9887 Gandy Blvd. N., No. 104
Saint Petersburg, FL 33702-2451
Editor(s): Ed Freedman. Bimonthly. Concerned with construction practice, design, administration, and teaching. Carries news of members, listings of job opportunities, local chapter reports, and notices of new publications. **Facsimile Number:** (614)464-3226.

★4855★
Anti-Corrosion Times
Concrete Reinforcing Steel Institute (CRSI)
933 N. Plum Grove Rd.
Schaumburg, IL 60173-4758
Phone: (708)517-1200
Editor(s): Theodore L. Neff. Biennially. Focuses on developments in the reinforced concrete construction industry. Reports on advances and applications of the fusion-bonded coating system for corrosion prevention. Recurring features include profiles of successful construction projects, news of the Institute and its members, and a calendar of events.

★4856★
Associated General Contractors of America—National Newsletter (AGC)
Associated General Contractors of America (AGC)
1957 E St. NW
Washington, DC 20006
Phone: (202)393-2040
Biweekly.

★4857★
BAC Journal (BAC)
International Union of Bricklayers and Allied Craftsmen (BAC)
815 15th St., NW
Washington, DC 20005
Phone: (202)783-3788
Monthly.

★4858★
Blue Reports, Inc.
Construction News Service
7325 Steel Mill Dr.
Springfield, VA 22050
Phone: (703)644-5884
Editor(s): Calvin S. Oren. Daily. Reports on public and private construction projects in the Washington, DC, Virginia, and Maryland areas. Provides owner's and architect's names, plan status, date bids due, prospective bidders, low bids received, and specification details. **Facsimile Number:** (703)644-1929.

★4859★
Building Concerns
National Association of Minority Contractors (NAMC)
806 15th St. NW, Ste. 340
Washington, DC 20005
Phone: (202)347-8259
Editor(s): Ralph C. Thomas, III. Monthly. Concentrates on national and regional news regarding minority construction contractors. Contains articles on issues generally affecting the industry—especially issues affecting minorities—including topics such as legislative and regulatory activity and reports on major corporation developments. Recurring features include reports of meetings, news of educational opportunities, a calendar of events, and news of NAMC chapters and members.

★4860★
Building Industry Technology: An Abstract Newsletter
National Technical Information Service (NTIS)
U.S. Department of Commerce
5285 Port Royal Rd.
Springfield, VA 22161
Phone: (703)487-4630
Weekly. Consists of abstracts of reports on architectural and environmental design, building standards, construction materials and equipment, and structural analyses. Recurring features include a form for ordering reports from NTIS.

★4861★
Building Renovation
Maclean Hunter Ltd.
777 Bay St.
Toronto, ON, Canada M5W 1A7
Phone: (416)596-5760
John Fennell, Editor. 6x/yr. Business magazine for professionals in residential and commercial renovation and remodeling. **Facsimile Number:** (416)596-5810.

★4862★
Capital Comments
National Lumber & Building Material Dealers Association
40 Ivy St. SE
Washington, DC 20003
Phone: (202)547-2230
Editor(s): Matt Geitner. Semimonthly. Reports on news of legislation pertaining to lumber, other building materials, and housing. Discusses such issues as lumber subsidies, interest rates on homes, health and safety, and jobs. **Facsimile Number:** (202)547-7640.

★4863★
Chalkline (BAC)
International Union of Bricklayers and Allied Craftsmen (BAC)
815 15th St., NW
Washington, DC 20005
Phone: (202)783-3788
Periodic.

★4864★
Concrete Abstracts
American Concrete Institute
PO Box 19150
Detroit, MI 48219-0150
Phone: (313)532-2600
Robert G. Wiedyke, Editor. 6x/yr. Magazine summarizing and indexing U.S. and international publications which report developments in concrete and concrete technology. **Facsimile Number:** (313)538-0655.

★4865★
Concrete Construction Magazine
The Aberdeen Group
426 S. Westgate
Addison, IL 60101-9929   Phone: (708)543-0870

Ward R. Malisch, Editor. Monthly. Trade magazine for contractors, subcontractors, and others involved in concrete construction. **Facsimile Number:** (708)543-3112.

★4866★
Concrete International
American Concrete Institute
PO Box 19150
Detroit, MI 48219   Phone: (313)532-2600

William J. Semioli, Editor and Assoc. Publisher. Monthly. Trade magazine covering engineering, construction, structural design, and the technology of concrete. **Facsimile Number:** (313)538-0655.

★4867★
Concrete Masonry News
National Concrete Masonry Association
PO Box 781
Herndon, VA 22070   Phone: (703)435-4900

Editor(s): Scott Ramminger. Monthly. Focuses on the manufacturing and marketing of concrete masonry products and the managment of production plants. Covers fire safety, energy efficiency, pertinent legislative and regulatory developments, production and marketing developments, and new products and services of interest to the industry. Also reports the news and activites of the association. Recurring features include editorials, news of research, news of members, letters to the editor, and a calendar of events. **Facsimile Number:** (703)435-9480.

★4868★
Concrete Producer News
Edgell Communications, Inc.
7500 Old Oak Blvd.
Cleveland, OH 44130   Phone: (216)243-8100

Patrick Hernan, Editor. Monthly. Concrete industry magazine covering new developments, techniques, equipment, and their applications. **Facsimile Number:** (216)891-2726.

★4869★
Concrete Products
Maclean Hunter Publishing Co.
29 N. Wacker Dr.
Chicago, IL 60606   Phone: (312)726-2802

William J. Blaha, Editor. 1XM. Magazine on concrete products and ready-mixed concrete. **Facsimile Number:** (312)726-2574.

★4870★
The Concrete Trader
The Concrete Trader, Inc.
PO Box 660
Dublin, OH 43017-1339   Phone: (614)793-9711

John D. Cowan, Editor and Publisher. Monthly. Magazine (tabloid) serving the concrete products industry. **Facsimile Number:** (614)793-8380.

★4871★
ConnStruction
PO Box 9768
Wethersfield, CT 06109   Phone: (203)529-3246

Victor Bonini, Editor. 7x/yr. Magazine for construction industry. **Facsimile Number:** (203)563-0616.

★4872★
CONSTRUCTION
26 Long Hill Rd.
Guilford, CT 06437   Phone: (203)453-3717

Jack C. Lewis, Editor and Publisher. 2x/mo. Journal for the construction industry.

★4873★
Construction Dimensions
Assn. of Wall & Ceiling
PO Box 5504
Washington, DC 20016   Phone: (301)656-7050

Gerald Wykoff, Editor. Monthly. Wall and ceiling industry magazine.

★4874★
Construction Industry International
Maclean Hunter Publishing Co.
29 N. Wacker Dr.
Chicago, IL 60606   Phone: (312)726-2802

Alan Elliott, Editor-in-Chief. Monthly. Trade magazine.

★4875★
Construction News
715 W. 2nd St.
PO Box 2421
Little Rock, AR 72203   Phone: (501)376-1931

Robert Alvey, Editor. Weekly. Construction industry magazine. **Facsimile Number:** (501)375-5831.

★4876★
Construction Newsletter
National Safety Council
444 N. Michigan Ave.
Chicago, IL 60611   Phone: (312)527-4800

6/yr. Focuses on industrial and occupational safety in the construction industry. Carries items on such topics as safe work practices and products, accident prevention, and successful industrial safety programs and policies.

★4877★
Constructor (AGC)
Associated General Contractors of America (AGC)
1957 E St. NW
Washington, DC 20006   Phone: (202)393-2040

Monthly. Association magazine for general contractors engaged in construction.

★4878★
Daily Construction Reporter
4901 Pacific Hwy.
San Diego, CA 92110-4098   Phone: (619)296-0183

Kenneth F. Kerr, Editor and Publisher. Daily. Construction trade newspaper covering jobs that are out for bid, bid results, building permits, and other information. **Facsimile Number:** (619)298-3027.

★4879★
Home BUILDER Magazine
Work-4 Projects Ltd.
PO Box 400, Victoria Sta.
Westmount, PQ, Canada H3Z 2V8   Phone: (514)489-4941

Nachmi Artzy, Editor and Publisher. 6x/yr. Magazine for home construction industry. **Facsimile Number:** (514)489-5505.

Concrete Masons and Terrazzo Workers ★4893★

★4880★
The Journal of Light Construction
Hanley-Wood Partners
RR 2, Box 146
Richmond, VT 05477-9607 Phone: (802)864-0091
Steve Bliss, Editor. Monthly. Magazine (tabloid) for residential and light professionals involved in new and rehabilitative construction. Each issue covers a single aspect of construction.

★4881★
Journal of the International ⅝¾Union of Bricklayers & Allied Craftsmen
815 15th St. NW
Washington, DC 20005 Phone: (202)783-3788
Paul Ruffins, Exec. Editor. Monthly. Tabloid for trade union members. **Facsimile Number:** (202)393-0219.

★4882★
Masonry
Mason Contractors Assoc. of America
17 W. 601 14th St.
Oakbrook Terrace, IL 60181 Phone: (708)620-6767
Gene Adams, Editor. 6x/yr. Trade magazine on construction, architecture, and engineering. **Facsimile Number:** (708)620-6774.

★4883★
Nation's Building News
15th & M Sts. NW
Washington, DC 20005 Phone: (202)822-0525
Tim Ahern, Editor. 2x/mo. Trade magazine (tabloid) covering home building and all related industries. **Facsimile Number:** (202)861-2131.

★4884★
PCI Journal
Precast/Prestressed Concrete Institute
175 W. Jackson Blvd., Ste. 1859
Chicago, IL 60604 Phone: (312)786-0300
George D. Nasser, Editor. 6x/yr. Concrete engineering journal. **Facsimile Number:** (312)786-0353.

★4885★
Professional Builder
Cahners Publishing Co.
1350 E. Touhy Ave.
Des Plaines, IL 60018 Phone: (708)635-8800
Roy L. Diez, Editor. 19x/yr. **Facsimile Number:** (708)299-8622.

Meetings and Conventions

★4886★
Ceramic Tile Distributors Association Ceramic Tile Exposition
Ceramic Tile Distributors Association
15 Salt Creek Ln., Ste. 422
Hinsdale, IL 60521 Phone: (708)655-3270
1992; Jul. New York, NY.

★4887★
Concrete Industries Exposition
National Concrete Masonry Association
PO Box 781
Herndon, VA 22070 Phone: (703)435-4900
1992.

★4888★
International Concrete and Aggregates Show
National Aggregates Association/National Ready Mixed Concrete Association
900 Spring St.
Silver Spring, MD 20910 Phone: (301)587-1400
1994; Feb. 06-10; Las Vegas, NV • 1996; Jan. 28-01; Atlanta, GA. **Toll-free/Additional Phone Number(s):** 800-233-0823. **Facsimile Number:** (301)587-4260.

★4889★
National Precast Concrete Association Annual Convention and Precast Concrete Industries Exposition
National Precast Concrete Association
825 E. 64th St.
Indianapolis, IN 46220 Phone: (317)253-0486
1993; Feb. 11-16; Tampa, FL • 1994; Feb. 17-22; Nashville, TN • 1995; Feb. 16-21; San Diego, CA • 1996; Feb. 07-13; Denver, CO. **Toll-free/Additional Phone Number(s):** 800-428-5732. **Facsimile Number:** (317)259-7230.

★4890★
National Terrazzo and Mosaic Association (NTMA)
3166 Des Plaines Ave., Ste. 132
Des Plaines, IL 60018 Phone: (708)635-7744
Frequency: Annual. 1992; Tucson, AZ • 1993; Italy. **Facsimile Number:** (708)635-9127.

★4891★
Operative Plasterers and Cement Masons International Association of U.S. and Canada (OPCMIA)
1125 17th St., NW
Washington, DC 20036 Phone: (202)393-6569
Frequency: Quinquennial - next 1994.

★4892★
Prestressed Concrete Institute Convention
Prestressed Concrete Institute
175 W. Jackson Blvd., Ste. 1859
Chicago, IL 60604 Phone: (312)786-0300

★4893★
World of Concrete USA Exposition
The Aberdean Group
426 S. Westgate
Addison, IL 60101 Phone: (708)543-0460
Frequency: Always held during January or February; rotates between Las Vegas, Nevada and Atlanta, Georgia. 1993; Jan. 26-29; Las Vegas, NV • 1994; Mar. 09-12; Las Vegas, NV • 1995; Jan. 29-02; Atlanta, GA • 1996; Jan. 29-02; Las Vegas, NV • 1997; Jan. 28-31; Las Vegas, NV • 1998; Feb. 23-26; Atlanta, GA • 1999; Jan. 26-29; Las Vegas, NV. **Toll-free/Additional Phone Number(s):** 800-323-2576. **Facsimile Number:** (708)543-3112.

Drywall Workers and Lathers

Drywall installers, also called applicators, and drywall finishers, or tapers, work with drywall, a substitute for wet plaster used for walls and ceilings in most buildings. Lathers apply metal or gypsum lath to walls, ceilings, or ornamental frameworks to form the support base for plaster coatings. Most drywall workers and lathers work for contractors who specialize in drywall or lathing installation; others work for contractors who do many kinds of construction.

$alaries

Median weekly earnings for drywall workers and lathers are about $382/week. Trainees start at about half the rate paid to experienced workers.

Employment Outlook

Growth rate until the year 2000: Average.

Drywall Workers and Lathers

Career Guides

★4894★
Big Questions?
National Joint Painting, Decorating and Drywall Apprenticeship and Training Committee
1750 New York Ave., N.W., Lower Level
Washington, DC 20006   Phone: (202)783-7770
This four-page brochure describes requirements, the work, employment opportunities, working conditions, and earnings.

★4895★
"Drywall Installer and Finisher" in *Construction*, Volume 4 of *Career Information Center* (pp. 55-56)
Glencoe/Macmillan
15319 Chatsworth St.
Mission Hills, CA 91345   Phone: (818)898-1391
Richard Lidz and Dale Anderson, editorial directors. Fourth edition, 1990. For 600 occupations, describes job duties, entry-level requirements, education and training needed, advancement possibilities, employment outlook, earnings and benefits. The set is divided into 12 volumes. Each volume includes jobs related under a broad career field. Volume 13 is the index. **Facsimile Number:** 818-365-5489.

★4896★
Drywall Installers and Finishers
Chronicle Guidance Publications, Inc.
PO Box 1190
Moravia, NY 13118-1190   Phone: (315)497-0330
1987. This career brief describes the nature of the work, working conditions, hours and earnings, education and training, licensure, certification, unions, personal qualifications, social and psychological factors, employment outlook, entry methods, advancement, and related occupations. **Toll-free/Additional Phone Number(s):** 800-622-7284.

★4897★
"Drywall Installers and Finishers" in Volume 3 of *The Encyclopedia of Careers and Vocational Guidance* (pp. 647-649)
J.G. Ferguson Publishing Co.
200 W. Monroe
Chicago, IL 60606   Phone: (312)580-5480
William E. Hopke, editor-in-chief. Eighth edition, 1990. Four-volume set that profiles 500 occupations and describes job trends in 76 industries. Includes career description, educational requirements, history of the job, methods of entry, advancement, employment outlook, earnings, working conditions, social and psychological factors, and sources of additional information.

★4898★
"Drywall Installers and Finishers" in Volume 2 of *Career Discovery Encyclopedia* (pp. 130-131)
J.G. Ferguson Publishing Co.
200 W. Monroe
Chicago, IL 60606   Phone: (312)580-5480
E. Russell Primm, editor-in-chief. 1990. Contains two-page articles on 504 occupations. Each article describes job duties, earnings, and educational and training requirements.

★4899★
"Drywall Rocker and Taper" in *Hard Hatted Women: Stories of Struggle and Success in the Trades* (pp. 63-70)
Seal Press
3131 Western Ave., Ste. 410
Seattle, WA 98121   Phone: (206)283-7844
Molly Martin, editor. 1988. Twenty-six women recount their experiences working in blue collar occupations. They describe how they got in, the work they do, their relationships in predominantly male occupations, and their training.

★4900★
"Drywall Workers and Lathers" in *Occupational Outlook Handbook* (pp. 367-369)
Superintendent of Documents
U.S. Government Printing Office
Washington, DC 20402   Phone: (202)783-3238
Biennial; latest edition, 1990-91. Encyclopedia of careers describing more than 250 occupations and comprising about 86 percent of all jobs in the economy. Occupations that require lengthy education or training are given the most attention. For each occupation, the handbook describes job duties, working conditions, training, educational preparation, personal qualities, advancement possibilities, job outlook, earnings, and sources of additional information.

★4901★
Lather
Careers, Inc.
PO Box 135
Largo, FL 34649-0135   Phone: (813)584-7333
1988. Two-page occupational summary card describing duties, working conditions, personal qualifications, training, earnings and hours, employment outlook, places of employment, related careers and where to write for more information.

★4902★
"Lather" in *Construction*, Volume 4 of *Career Information Center* (pp. 68-69)
Glencoe/Macmillan
15319 Chatsworth St.
Mission Hills, CA 91345   Phone: (818)898-1391

Richard Lidz and Dale Anderson, editorial directors. Fourth edition, 1990. For 600 occupations, describes job duties, entry-level requirements, education and training needed, advancement possibilities, employment outlook, earnings and benefits. The set is divided into 12 volumes. Each volume includes jobs related under a broad career field. Volume 13 is the index. **Facsimile Number:** 818-365-5489.

★4903★
"Lather" in *Occu-Facts: Information on 565 Careers in Outline Form* (p. 16.6)
Careers, Inc.
P.O. Box 135
1211 Tenth St., S.W.
Largo, FL 33640   Phone: (813)584-7333

Elizabeth Handville. Biennial, 1989-90 edition. Each one-page occupational profile describes duties, working conditions, physical surroundings and demands, aptitudes, temperament, educational requirements, employment outlook, earnings, and places of employment.

★4904★
Lathers
Chronicle Guidance Publications, Inc.
PO Box 1190
Moravia, NY 13118-1190   Phone: (315)497-0330

1990. This career brief describes the nature of the work, working conditions, hours and earnings, education and training, licensure, certification, unions, personal qualifications, social and psychological factors, employment outlook, entry methods, advancement, and related occupations. **Toll-free/Additional Phone Number(s):** 800-622-7284.

★4905★
"Lathers" in *Opportunities in Building Construction Trades* (pp. 59-61)
National Textbook Co.
4255 W. Touhy Ave.
Lincolnwood, IL 60646   Phone: (312)679-5500

Michael Sumichrast. 1989. Gives an overview of the construction industry and describes the jobs of various craftworkers. Covers different kinds of builders: home, custom; and describes management skills needed and industry trends affecting opportunities.

★4906★
"Lathers" in Volume 3 of *The Encyclopedia of Careers and Vocational Guidance* (pp. 668-670)
J.G. Ferguson Publishing Co.
200 W. Monroe
Chicago, IL 60606   Phone: (312)580-5480

William E. Hopke, editor-in-chief. Eighth edition, 1990. Four-volume set that profiles 500 occupations and describes job trends in 76 industries. Includes career description, educational requirements, history of the job, methods of entry, advancement, employment outlook, earnings, working conditions, social and psychological factors, and sources of additional information.

★4907★
Video Career Library - Construction
Careers, Inc.
1211 10th St., SW
PO Box 135
Largo, FL 34649-0135   Phone: (813)584-7333

Videocassette. 1990. 36 mins. Part of the Video Career Library covering 165 occupations. Shows actual workers on the job. Includes millwrights, brickmasons, carpenters, drywall installers, electricians, painters, plumbers and pipefitters, carpenter and soft tile installers, insulation workers, paving equipment operators, and structural metal workers.

——— Associations ———

★4908★
Associated Builders and Contractors (ABC)
729 15th St. NW
Washington, DC 20005   Phone: (202)637-8800

Membership: Construction contractors, subcontractors, suppliers, and associates. **Purpose:** Aim is to foster and perpetuate the principles of rewarding shop construction workers and management on the basis of merit. Sponsors leadership conference and management education programs including Wheels of Learning; also sponsors apprenticeship and skill training programs. Disseminates technological and labor relations information. Maintains biographical archives and placement service. Bestows awards; compiles statistics. **Publications:** *ABC Newsline*, semimonthly. • *The Builder and Contractor*, monthly. • *Classified Membership Directory*, annual. • Also publishes safety manuals.

★4909★
International Brotherhood of Painters and Allied Trades (IBPAT)
United Unions Bldg.
1750 New York Ave., NW
Washington, DC 20006   Phone: (202)637-0720

Membership: AFL-CIO. **Publications:** *Directory*, annual. • *Painters and Allied Trades Journal*, monthly.

★4910★
National Association of Home Builders of the U.S. (NAHB)
15th and M Sts. NW
Washington, DC 20005   Phone: (202)822-0200

Membership: Single and multifamily home builders, commercial builders, and others associated with the building industry. **Purpose:** Lobbies on behalf of the housing industry and conducts public affairs activities to increase public understanding of housing and the economy. Collects and disseminates data on current developments in home building and home builders' plans through its Economics Department and nationwide Metropolitan Housing Forecast. Maintains NAHB Research Center, which functions as the research arm of the home building industry. Sponsors seminars and workshops on construction, mortgage credit, labor relations, cost reduction, land use, remodeling, and business management. Sponsors competitions; bestows awards; compiles statistics; offers charitable program, spokesman training, and placement service; maintains speakers' bureau, biographical archives, hall of fame, and extensive library on housing. Subsidiaries include Home Builders Institute and National Council of the Housing Industry. Maintains over 50 committees in many areas of construction; operates National Commercial Builders Council, National Council of the Multifamily Housing Industry, National Remodelers Council, and National Sales and Marketing Council. **Publications:** *Builder Magazine*, monthly. • *Economic News Notes*, monthly. • *Homes and Homebuilding*, annual. • *Library Bulletin*, monthly. • *Nation's Building News*, semimonthly. • Also publishes bibliographies, booklets, and manuals. **Toll-free/Additional Phone Number(s):** (800)221-NAHB Audio Feed Line.

★4911★
National Joint Painting, Decorating and Drywall Apprenticeship and Training Committee (NJPDDATC)
1750 New York Ave. NW, Lower Level
Washington, DC 20006   Phone: (202)783-7770
Membership: Sponsored by the National Painting, Decorating and Drywall Apprenticeship and Manpower Training Fund, the committee is composed of representatives of labor and management. **Purpose:** Labor is represented by the International Brotherhood of Painters and Allied Trades; management by Painting and Decorating Contractors of America and the Association of Wall and Ceiling Industries - International. Seeks to increase apprenticeship and training activities so that prospective apprentices can obtain the training necessary to equip themselves and to assume a high level of skill and responsibility. Develops and supplies materials necessary for training tradespersons and journeypersons with emphasis on changing techniques, materials, and tools of the trade. Qualifications, selection, instruction, and terms of apprenticeship are suggested for use as the national standards for painting, decorating, and drywall trades nationally. Also supplies instructional materials for advanced journeyperson programs. Holds workshops and seminars for instructors and coordinators; sponsors National Apprenticeship Panel contests. **Publications:** Brochures, manuals, and instructor guides and test packet; also provides slides, videos, and filmstrips on training.

★4912★
United Brotherhood of Carpenters and Joiners of America (UBC)
101 Constitution Ave. NW
Washington, DC 20001   Phone: (202)546-6206
Membership: AFL-CIO. **Publications:** *Carpenter*, monthly.

Standards/Certification Agencies

Most drywall and lathing workers start as helpers and learn their skills on the job. Some installers and lathers learn their trade in an apprenticeship program. The United Brotherhood of Carpenters and Joiners of America, in cooperation with local contractors, administers an apprenticeship program in carpentry that includes instruction in drywall and lath installation. In addition, local affiliates of the Associated Builders and Contractors conduct a similar training program for nonunion workers. The International Brotherhood of Painters and Allied Trades conducts a 2-year apprenticeship program for drywall finishers.

Basic Reference Guides and Handbooks

★4913★
Homes and Homebuilding
National Association of Home Builders of the U.S. (NAHB)
15th and M Sts. NW
Washington, DC 20005   Phone: (202)822-0200
Annual.

★4914★
IBPAT Directory
International Brotherhood of Painters and Allied Trades (IBPAT)
United Unions Bldg.
1750 New York Ave., NW
Washington, DC 20006   Phone: (202)637-0720
Annual.

Periodicals

★4915★
ABC Newsline
Associated Builders and Contractors, Inc. (ABC)
729 15th St. NW
Washington, DC 20005   Phone: (202)637-8800
Editor(s): Lisa A. Nardone. Semimonthly. Designed to keep readers alerted to important changes within ABC and the construction industry. Reports on legislative issues, construction trends, conferences and meetings, and ABC services. Recurring features include news of members and a column titled Industry Briefs.

★4916★
American Architectural Manufacturers Association—Quarterly Review
American Architectural Manufacturers Association
1540 E. Dundee Rd., Ste. K 310
Palatine, IL 60067-8321   Phone: (708)202-1350
Editor(s): Tony Coorlim. Annually. Contains industry news on architectural products. Covers prime and combination storm windows, sliding glass and combination storm doors, window and curtain-walls, store fronts and entrances, siding, soffits, fascia, gutters, downspouts, skylights, space enclosures, and mobile home components. Recurring features include news of research, notices of publications available, and announcements by the association. **Facsimile Number:** (708)202-1480.

★4917★
American Institute of Constructors—Newsletter
American Institute of Constructors
9887 Gandy Blvd. N., No. 104
Saint Petersburg, FL 33702-2451
Editor(s): Ed Freedman. Bimonthly. Concerned with construction practice, design, administration, and teaching. Carries news of members, listings of job opportunities, local chapter reports, and notices of new publications. **Facsimile Number:** (614)464-3226.

★4918★
Blue Reports, Inc.
Construction News Service
7325 Steel Mill Dr.
Springfield, VA 22050   Phone: (703)644-5884
Editor(s): Calvin S. Oren. Daily. Reports on public and private construction projects in the Washington, DC, Virginia, and Maryland areas. Provides owner's and architect's names, plan status, date bids due, prospective bidders, low bids received, and specification details. **Facsimile Number:** (703)644-1929.

★4919★
Builder
Hanley-Wood, Inc.
655 15th St. NW, Ste. 475
Washington, DC 20005   Phone: (202)737-0717
Mitchell Rouda, Editor. Monthly. Magazine covering housing, commercial, and industrial building. **Facsimile Number:** (202)737-2439.

★4920★
Builder and Contractor
Associated Builders and Contractors, Inc.
729 15th St. NW
Washington, DC 20005   Phone: (202)637-8800
Susan Schindler, Mng. Editor. Monthly. Magazine for open shop contractors and subcontractors. Includes articles on national and regional construction news, construction management, project case histories, new products, and building design.

★4921★
The Builder and Contractor
Associated Builders and Contractors (ABC)
729 15th St. NW
Washington, DC 20005   Phone: (202)637-8800
Monthly.

★4922★
Builder Architect
Sunshine Media, Inc.
7500 N. Dreamy Draw, Ste. 111
PO Box 9400
Phoenix, AZ 85068   Phone: (602)943-3575
Marie Vere, Editor. Monthly. Home builders magazine. **Facsimile Number:** (602)371-0241.

★4923★
Builder/Dealer
Peterson Bros. Inc., Publishing
16 1st Ave.
Corry, PA 16407-1894   Phone: (814)664-8624
Charles P. Mancino, Publisher. Monthly. Trade magazine. **Facsimile Number:** (814)664-8506.

★4924★
Builder Insider
Divibest, Inc.
PO Box 191125
Dallas, TX 75219   Phone: (214)871-2913
Michael J. Anderson, Editor and Publisher. Monthly. Magazine (tabloid) for builders, architects, and remodelers.

★4925★
Builder Magazine
National Association of Home Builders of the U.S. (NAHB)
15th and M Sts. NW
Washington, DC 20005   Phone: (202)822-0200
Monthly.

★4926★
Building Business & Management
Builders Assn. of Southeastern Michigan
30375 Northwestern Hwy.
Farmington Hills, MI 48334   Phone: (313)737-4477
Kathleen M. Eischeid, Editor. Monthly. Construction and apartment industry magazine. **Facsimile Number:** (313)737-5741.

★4927★
Building Concerns
National Association of Minority Contractors (NAMC)
806 15th St. NW, Ste. 340
Washington, DC 20005   Phone: (202)347-8259
Editor(s): Ralph C. Thomas, III. Monthly. Concentrates on national and regional news regarding minority construction contractors. Contains articles on issues generally affecting the industry—especially issues affecting minorities—including topics such as legislative and regulatory activity and reports on major corporation developments. Recurring features include reports of meetings, news of educational opportunities, a calendar of events, and news of NAMC chapters and members.

★4928★
Building Design & Construction
Cahners Publishing Co.
1350 E. Touhy Ave.
PO Box 5080
Des Plaines, IL 60018   Phone: (708)635-8800
Philip G. Schreiner, Editor. Monthly. Magazine on business and technology for commercial, institutional, and industrial buildings. **Facsimile Number:** (708)299-8622.

★4929★
Building Homes & Renovations
Southam Business & Communications, Inc.
1450 Don Mills Rd.
Don Mills, ON, Canada M3B 2X7   Phone: (416)445-6641
Randy Threndyle, Editor. 5x/yr. Building trade and products magazine. **Facsimile Number:** (416)442-2214.

★4930★
Building Industry
Trade Publishing Co.
287 Mokauea St.
Honolulu, HI 96819   Phone: (808)848-0711
Jay McWilliams, Editor. Monthly. Construction and design magazine. **Facsimile Number:** (808)841-3053.

★4931★
Building Industry Technology: An Abstract Newsletter
National Technical Information Service (NTIS)
U.S. Department of Commerce
5285 Port Royal Rd.
Springfield, VA 22161   Phone: (703)487-4630
Weekly. Consists of abstracts of reports on architectural and environmental design, building standards, construction materials and equipment, and structural analyses. Recurring features include a form for ordering reports from NTIS.

★4932★
Buildings
427 6th Ave. SE
PO Box 1888
Cedar Rapids, IA 52406   Phone: (319)364-6167
Linda Monroe, Editor. Monthly. **Facsimile Number:** (319)365-5421.

★4933★
Capital Comments
National Lumber & Building Material Dealers Association
40 Ivy St. SE
Washington, DC 20003   Phone: (202)547-2230
Editor(s): Matt Geitner. Semimonthly. Reports on news of legislation pertaining to lumber, other building materials, and housing. Discusses such issues as lumber subsidies, interest rates on homes, health and safety, and jobs. **Facsimile Number:** (202)547-7640.

★4934★
ConnStruction
PO Box 9768
Wethersfield, CT 06109   Phone: (203)529-3246
Victor Bonini, Editor. 7x/yr. Magazine for construction industry. **Facsimile Number:** (203)563-0616.

Drywall Workers and Lathers

★4935★
CONSTRUCTION
26 Long Hill Rd.
Guilford, CT 06437 Phone: (203)453-3717
Jack C. Lewis, Editor and Publisher. 2x/mo. Journal for the construction industry.

★4936★
Construction Dimensions
Assn. of Wall & Ceiling
PO Box 5504
Washington, DC 20016 Phone: (301)656-7050
Gerald Wykoff, Editor. Monthly. Wall and ceiling industry magazine.

★4937★
Construction Industry International
Maclean Hunter Publishing Co.
29 N. Wacker Dr.
Chicago, IL 60606 Phone: (312)726-2802
Alan Elliott, Editor-in-Chief. Monthly. Trade magazine.

★4938★
Construction News
715 W. 2nd St.
PO Box 2421
Little Rock, AR 72203 Phone: (501)376-1931
Robert Alvey, Editor. Weekly. Construction industry magazine. **Facsimile Number:** (501)375-5831.

★4939★
Construction Newsletter
National Safety Council
444 N. Michigan Ave.
Chicago, IL 60611 Phone: (312)527-4800
6/yr. Focuses on industrial and occupational safety in the construction industry. Carries items on such topics as safe work practices and products, accident prevention, and successful industrial safety programs and policies.

★4940★
Daily Construction Reporter
4901 Pacific Hwy.
San Diego, CA 92110-4098 Phone: (619)296-0183
Kenneth F. Kerr, Editor and Publisher. Daily. Construction trade newspaper covering jobs that are out for bid, bid results, building permits, and other information. **Facsimile Number:** (619)298-3027.

★4941★
Economic News Notes
National Association of Home Builders of the U.S. (NAHB)
15th and M Sts. NW
Washington, DC 20005 Phone: (202)822-0200
Monthly.

★4942★
Fine Homebuilding
The Taunton Press, Inc.
63 S. Main St.
PO Box 5506
Newtown, CT 06470 Phone: (203)426-5506
Mark Feirer, Editor. 7x/yr. Magazine for builders, architects, designers, and owner-builders. **Facsimile Number:** (203)426-3434.

★4943★
Home BUILDER Magazine
Work-4 Projects Ltd.
PO Box 400, Victoria Sta.
Westmount, PQ, Canada H3Z 2V8 Phone: (514)489-4941
Nachmi Artzy, Editor and Publisher. 6x/yr. Magazine for home construction industry. **Facsimile Number:** (514)489-5505.

★4944★
The Journal of Light Construction
Hanley-Wood Partners
RR 2, Box 146
Richmond, VT 05477-9607 Phone: (802)864-0091
Steve Bliss, Editor. Monthly. Magazine (tabloid) for residential and light professionals involved in new and rehabilitative construction. Each issue covers a single aspect of construction.

★4945★
NAHB Library Bulletin
National Association of Home Builders of the U.S. (NAHB)
15th and M Sts. NW
Washington, DC 20005 Phone: (202)822-0200
Monthly.

★4946★
Nation's Building News
National Association of Home Builders of the U.S. (NAHB)
15th and M Sts. NW
Washington, DC 20005 Phone: (202)822-0200
Semimonthly. Tabloid newsletter providing the latest information concerning the housing industry, including finance, legislation, new technologies, and membership news.

★4947★
Painters and Allied Trades Journal
International Brotherhood of Painters and Allied Trades (IBPAT)
United Unions Bldg.
1750 New York Ave., NW
Washington, DC 20006 Phone: (202)637-0720
Monthly.

★4948★
Professional Builder
Cahners Publishing Co.
1350 E. Touhy Ave.
Des Plaines, IL 60018 Phone: (708)635-8800
Roy L. Diez, Editor. 19x/yr. **Facsimile Number:** (708)299-8622.

★4949★
The SPEC-DATA Program
Construction Specifications Institute
601 Madison St.
Alexandria, VA 22314 Phone: (703)684-0300
Brenda A. Furiga, Mgr. Quarterly. Magazine (loose-leaf) for the construction industry covering technical and product information. **Facsimile Number:** (703)684-0465.

★4950★
Walls & Ceilings
LMRector Corp.
8602 N. 40th St.
Tampa, FL 33604 Phone: (813)989-9300
Robert F. Welch, Editor. Monthly. Trade magazine for contractors, suppliers, and distributors of drywall, plaster, stucco, exterior insulation, acoustics, metal framing, and ceilings. **Facsimile Number:** (813)980-3982.

Meetings and Conventions

★4951★
Associated Builders and Contractors (ABC)
729 15th St. NW
Washington, DC 20005   Phone: (202)637-8800
Frequency: Annual.

★4952★
National Association of Home Builders/The Builders Show
National Association of Home Builders of the United States
15th and M Sts., NW
Washington, DC 20005   Phone: (202)822-0424
Frequency: Usually held in January; location rotates every three years. 1993; Feb. 19-22; Las Vegas, NV • 1994; Jan. 21-24; Las Vegas, NV. **Toll-free/Additional Phone Number(s):** 800-368-5242. **Facsimile Number:** (202)822-0435.

★4953★
Western Lath/Plaster/Drywall Industries Association Annual Convention
Western Lath/Plaster/Drywall Industries Association
8635 Navajo Rd.
San Diego, CA 92119   Phone: (619)466-9070
1992; Oct. 07-11; Reno, NV • 1993; Sep. 22-26; Phoenix, AZ • 1994; Sep. 28-01; Reno, NV. **Facsimile Number:** (619)466-9149.

Electricians

Electricians install and maintain electrical systems for climate control, security, and communications purposes. They may also install and maintain the electronic controls for machines in business and industry. Electricians must follow the National Electric Code and comply with state and local building codes when they install these systems. Slightly more than half are employed in the construction industry. Others worked as maintenance electricians and are employed in virtually every industry. In addition, a small percentage of electricians are self-employed.

$alaries

Median weekly salaries for electricians are as follows:

Lowest 10 percent	$254/week or less
Median	$478/week
Top 10 percent	$740/week or more

Employment Outlook

Growth rate until the year 2000: Average.

Electricians

Career Guides

★4954★
Aim For A Job As An Electronic Technician
Rosen Publishing Group, Inc.
29 E. 21st St.
New York, NY 10010   Phone: (212)777-3017
John E. Keefe. Revised edition, 1978. Describes the training requirements and the advantages and disadvantages of various jobs available in electronics. **Toll-free/Additional Phone Number(s):** 800-237-9932. **Facsimile Number:** (212)777-0277.

★4955★
Careers with an Electric Company
Lerner Publications Co.
241 First Ave., N.
Minneapolis, MN 55401
Pam Fricke. 1984. Describes fifteen career possibilities with an electric company including such jobs as lineman and system operator. **Toll-free/Additional Phone Number(s):** 800-328-4920. **Facsimile Number:** (612)332-7615.

★4956★
Construction: Basic Principles
RMI Media Productions, Inc.
2807 West 47th St.
Shawnee Mission, KS 66205   Phone: (913)262-3974
Videocassette. 1984. 20 mins. This series of five programs of varying lengths covers different aspects of career opportunities in the construction trades. Included are: concrete masonry, carpentry, electrical work, plumbing, and heating and air conditioning.

★4957★
Construction Cluster
Center for Humanities, Inc.
Communications Park
Box 1000
Mount Kisco, NY 10549   Phone: (914)666-4100
Videocassette. 1984. 15 mins. Construction workers describe what it's like to work at their jobs, and show the special equipment they use in their field.

★4958★
"Construction Electrician" in *Construction*, Volume 4 of *Career Information Center* (pp. 45-47)
Glencoe/Macmillan
15319 Chatsworth St.
Mission Hills, CA 91345   Phone: (818)898-1391
Richard Lidz and Dale Anderson, editorial directors. Fourth edition, 1990. For 600 occupations, describes job duties, entry-level requirements, education and training needed, advancement possibilities, employment outlook, earnings and benefits. The set is divided into 12 volumes. Each volume includes jobs related under a broad career field. Volume 13 is the index. **Facsimile Number:** 818-365-5489.

★4959★
"Construction Electrician" in *Occu-Facts: Information on 565 Careers in Outline Form* (p. 16.7)
Careers, Inc.
P.O. Box 135
1211 Tenth St., S.W.
Largo, FL 33640   Phone: (813)584-7333
Elizabeth Handville. Biennial, 1989-90 edition. Each one-page occupational profile describes duties, working conditions, physical surroundings and demands, aptitudes, temperament, educational requirements, employment outlook, earnings, and places of employment.

★4960★
"Construction Electrician" in *Opportunities in Electrical Trades* (pp. 44-46)
National Textbook Co.
4255 W. Touhy Ave.
Lincolnwood, IL 60646   Phone: (312)679-5500
Robert Wood. 1990. Provides an overview of the electrical industry describing current trends and future projections. Surveys electricians jobs and covers the nature of the work, working conditions, job outlook, advancement possibilities, education and training, earnings, and specialization. Offers career planning advice.

★4961★
"Electrician" in *Guide to Careers Without College* (pp. 85-86)
Franklin Watts, Inc.
387 Park Avenue, S.
New York, NY 10016   Phone: (212)686-7070
Kathleen S. Abrams. 1988. Discusses careers that do not require a college degree in fields such as health care, sales and marketing, and the building trades. Describes the work, employment opportunities, and training.

★4962★
"Electrician" in *Hard Hatted Women: Stories of Struggle and Success in the Trades* (pp. 216-224)
Seal Press
3131 Western Ave., Ste. 410
Seattle, WA 98121   Phone: (206)283-7844
Molly Martin, editor. 1988. Twenty-six women recount their experiences working in blue collar occupations. They describe

how they got in, the work they do, their relationships in predominantly male occupations, and their training.

★4963★
"Electrician" in *The Career Connection II: A Guide to Technical Majors and Their Related Careers* (pp. 43-44)
ERIS
PO Box 7509
University Station
Provo, UT 84602-0509

Fred A. Rowe. 1988. Contains technical majors, such as automotive technology. Describes the major and the job. Lists high school and postsecondary school courses. Includes occupations related to the major, employment outlook, and starting salary.

★4964★
"Electrician" in *VGM's Careers Encyclopedia* (pp. 155-158)
National Textbook Co.
4255 W. Touhy Ave.
Lincolnwood, IL 60646   Phone: (312)679-5500

Third edition, 1991. Contains two- to five-page descriptions of 200 managerial, professional, technical, trade, and service occupations. Each profile includes job duties, places of employment, qualifications, educational preparation, training, employment potential, advancement, income, and additional sources of information.

★4965★
Electrician, Construction
Careers, Inc.
PO Box 135
Largo, FL 34649-0135   Phone: (813)584-7333

1990. Two-page occupational summary card describing duties, working conditions, personal qualifications, training, earnings and hours, employment outlook, places of employment, related careers and where to write for more information.

★4966★
Electrician, Maintenance
Careers, Inc.
PO Box 135
Largo, FL 34649-0135   Phone: (813)584-7333

1990. Eight-page brief offering the definition, history, duties, working conditions, personal qualifications, educational requirements, earnings, hours, employment outlook, advancement possibilities, and related occupations.

★4967★
"Electricians" in *Occupational Outlook Handbook* (pp. 369-371)
Superintendent of Documents
U.S. Government Printing Office
Washington, DC 20402   Phone: (202)783-3238

Biennial; latest edition, 1990-91. Encyclopedia of careers describing more than 250 occupations and comprising about 86 percent of all jobs in the economy. Occupations that require lengthy education or training are given the most attention. For each occupation, the handbook describes job duties, working conditions, training, educational preparation, personal qualities, advancement possibilities, job outlook, earnings, and sources of additional information.

★4968★
"Electricians" in *Opportunities in Building Construction Trades* (pp. 31-34)
National Textbook Co.
4255 W. Touhy Ave.
Lincolnwood, IL 60646   Phone: (312)679-5500

Michael Sumichrast. 1989. Gives an overview of the construction industry and describes the jobs of various craftworkers. Covers different kinds of builders: home, custom; and describes management skills needed and industry trends affecting opportunities.

★4969★
"Electricians" in Volume 3 of *The Encyclopedia of Careers and Vocational Guidance* (pp. 656-659)
J.G. Ferguson Publishing Co.
200 W. Monroe
Chicago, IL 60606   Phone: (312)580-5480

William E. Hopke, editor-in-chief. Eighth edition, 1990. Four-volume set that profiles 500 occupations and describes job trends in 76 industries. Includes career description, educational requirements, history of the job, methods of entry, advancement, employment outlook, earnings, working conditions, social and psychological factors, and sources of additional information.

★4970★
"Electricians" in Volume 2 of *Career Discovery Encyclopedia* (pp. 146-147)
J.G. Ferguson Publishing Co.
200 W. Monroe
Chicago, IL 60606   Phone: (312)580-5480

E. Russell Primm, editor-in-chief. 1990. Contains two-page articles on 504 occupations. Each article describes job duties, earnings, and educational and training requirements.

★4971★
Electricians, Construction
Chronicle Guidance Publications, Inc.
PO Box 1190
Moravia, NY 13118-1190   Phone: (315)497-0330

1987. This career brief describes the nature of the work, working conditions, hours and earnings, education and training, licensure, certification, unions, personal qualifications, social and psychological factors, employment outlook, entry methods, advancement, and related occupations. **Toll-free/Additional Phone Number(s):** 800-622-7284.

★4972★
"Electricians" in *The American Almanac of Jobs and Salaries* (pp. 501-502)
Avon Books
105 Madison Avenue
New York, NY 10016   Phone: (212)481-5600

John Wright and Edward J. Dwyer. Revised and updated, 1990. A comprehensive guide to the wages of hundreds of occupations in a wide variety of industries and organizations.

★4973★
Electricians, Maintenance
Chronicle Guidance Publications, Inc.
PO Box 1190
Moravia, NY 13118-1190   Phone: (315)497-0330

1990. This career brief describes the nature of the work, working conditions, hours and earnings, education and training, licensure, certification, unions, personal qualifications, social and psychological factors, employment outlook, entry methods, advancement, and related occupations. **Toll-free/Additional Phone Number(s):** 800-622-7284.

Electricians

★4974★
Electronic Service Careers
Franklin Watts, Inc.
387 Park Ave., S.
New York, NY 10016   Phone: (212)686-7070
Robert Laurance. 1987. Describes the career opportunities in electronics and the education and training requirements. **Facsimile Number:** (212)213-6435.

★4975★
Exploring Careers as an Electrician
Rosen Publishing Group, Inc.
29 E. 21st St.
New York, NY 10010   Phone: (212)777-3017
Marilyn Jones. 1987. Electricians in the field describe their work, training, and owning a business. Covers employment outlook.

★4976★
Get Wired for Life as a Construction Electrician
Independent Electrical Contractors, Inc.
PO Box 10379
Alexandria, VA 22310-0379   Phone: (703)549-7351
This six-panel brochure describes high school preparation and minimum qualifications for an electrician's apprenticeship.

★4977★
Getting Down to Business: Construction Electrician Business
American Institutes for Research
PO Box 11131
Palo Alto, CA 94302   Phone: (415)493-3550
Joyce P. Gall. 1981. **Facsimile Number:** (415)858-0958.

★4978★
The IBEW Leads to Electrifying Careers
International Brotherhood of Electrical Workers
1125 15th St. NW
Washington, DC 20005   Phone: (202)833-7000
1988. This 15-page booklet describes the electrician apprenticeship program and the jobs of electricians, communications, and utility workers and licensure.

★4979★
"Maintenance Electrician" in *Construction,* Volume 4 of *Career Information Center* (pp. 104-106)
Glencoe/Macmillan
15319 Chatsworth St.
Mission Hills, CA 91345   Phone: (818)898-1391
Richard Lidz and Dale Anderson, editorial directors. Fourth edition, 1990. For 600 occupations, describes job duties, entry-level requirements, education and training needed, advancement possibilities, employment outlook, earnings and benefits. The set is divided into 12 volumes. Each volume includes jobs related under a broad career field. Volume 13 is the index. **Facsimile Number:** 818-365-5489.

★4980★
"Maintenance Electrician" in *Exploring Nontraditional Jobs for Women* (pp. 118-124)
Rosen Publishing Group, Inc.
29 E. 21st St.
New York, NY 10010   Phone: (212)777-3017
Rose Neufeld. 1989. Describes blue-collar, male dominated occupations. Discusses what is done on the job, training, where to apply for jobs, tools used, salaries, and advantages and disadvantages. Relates the experiences of women who are working in the field.

★4981★
"Maintenance Electrician" in *Occu-Facts: Information on 565 Careers in Outline Form* (p. 15.11)
Careers, Inc.
P.O. Box 135
1211 Tenth St., S.W.
Largo, FL 33640   Phone: (813)584-7333
Elizabeth Handville. Biennial, 1989-90 edition. Each one-page occupational profile describes duties, working conditions, physical surroundings and demands, aptitudes, temperament, educational requirements, employment outlook, earnings, and places of employment.

★4982★
"Maintenance Electrician" in *Opportunities in Electrical Trades* (pp. 46-49)
National Textbook Co.
4255 W. Touhy Ave.
Lincolnwood, IL 60646   Phone: (312)679-5500
Robert Wood. 1990. Provides an overview of the electrical industry describing current trends and future projections. Surveys electricians jobs and covers the nature of the work, working conditions, job outlook, advancement possibilities, education and training, earnings, and specialization. Offers career planning advice.

★4983★
"Marine Electrician" in *Opportunities in Electrical Trades* (pp. 51-53)
National Textbook Co.
4255 W. Touhy Ave.
Lincolnwood, IL 60646   Phone: (312)679-5500
Robert Wood. 1990. Provides an overview of the electrical industry describing current trends and future projections. Surveys electricians jobs and covers the nature of the work, working conditions, job outlook, advancement possibilities, education and training, earnings, and specialization. Offers career planning advice.

★4984★
"Power Plant Maintenance Electrician" in *Opportunities in Electrical Trades* (pp. 54-55)
National Textbook Co.
4255 W. Touhy Ave.
Lincolnwood, IL 60646   Phone: (312)679-5500
Robert Wood. 1990. Provides an overview of the electrical industry describing current trends and future projections. Surveys electricians jobs and covers the nature of the work, working conditions, job outlook, advancement possibilities, education and training, earnings, and specialization. Offers career planning advice.

★4985★
Video Career Library - Construction
Careers, Inc.
1211 10th St., SW
PO Box 135
Largo, FL 34649-0135   Phone: (813)584-7333
Videocassette. 1990. 36 mins. Part of the Video Career Library covering 165 occupations. Shows actual workers on the job. Includes millwrights, brickmasons, carpenters, drywall installers, electricians, painters, plumbers and pipefitters, carpenter and soft tile installers, insulation workers, paving equipment operators, and structural metal workers.

Associations

★4986★
Associated Builders and Contractors (ABC)
729 15th St. NW
Washington, DC 20005   Phone: (202)637-8800
Membership: Construction contractors, subcontractors, suppliers, and associates. **Purpose:** Aim is to foster and perpetuate the principles of rewarding shop construction workers and management on the basis of merit. Sponsors leadership conference and management education programs including Wheels of Learning; also sponsors apprenticeship and skill training programs. Disseminates technological and labor relations information. Maintains biographical archives and placement service; compiles statistics. **Publications:** *ABC Newsline*, semimonthly. • *The Builder and Contractor*, monthly. • *Classified Membership Directory*, annual. • Also publishes safety manuals.

★4987★
Independent Electrical Contractors (IEC)
PO Box 10379
Alexandria, VA 22310-0379   Phone: (703)549-7351
Membership: Independent electrical contractors, small and large, primarily open shop. **Purpose:** Promotes the interests of members regardless of their labor affiliation; works to eliminate "unwise and unfair business practices" and to protect its members against "unfair or unjust taxes and legislative enactments." Sponsors electrical apprenticeship programs; conducts research and educational programs on estimating procedures, cost control, and personnel motivation. Represents independent electrical contractors to the National Electrical Code panel. Conducts surveys on volume of sales and purchases and on type of products used. Sponsors annual legislative workshop. Has formulated National Pattern Standards for Apprentice Training for Electricians. Presents annual awards. **Publications:** *Membership Directory*, annual. • *News Circuit*, quarterly. • Also publishes *Convention Highlights* (pre- and post-convention specials), monographs, and training booklets. **Facsimile Number:** (703)549-7448.

★4988★
International Brotherhood of Electrical Workers (IBEW)
1125 15th St. NW
Washington, DC 20005   Phone: (202)833-7000
Membership: AFL-CIO. **Publications:** *IBEW Journal*, monthly.

★4989★
National Electrical Contractors Association (NECA)
7315 Wisconsin Ave.
Bethesda, MD 20814   Phone: (301)657-3110
Membership: Contractors erecting, installing, repairing, servicing, and maintaining electric wiring, equipment, and appliances. **Purpose:** Provides management services and labor relations programs for electrical contractors; conducts seminars for contractor sales and training. Conducts research and educational programs; compiles statistics. Sponsors honorary society, the Academy of Electrical Contracting. **Publications:** *Electrical Contractor Magazine*, monthly. • *Electro Fact File*, bimonthly. • *NECA News*, weekly. • Also publishes *NECA Standard of Installation* and *Electrical Design Library*. **Facsimile Number:** (301)961-6495.

Standards/Certification Agencies

While some electricians learn their skills informally by working as helpers for experienced electricians and supplementing this training with trade school or correspondence courses, many learn the electrical trade by completing a four-year apprenticeship program. Large apprenticeship programs are usually sponsored by joint committees made up of local unions of the International Brotherhood of Electrical Workers and local chapters of the National Electrical Contractors Association, by company management committees of individual electrical contracting companies, and by local chapters of the Associated Builders and Contractors. The typical program provides at least 150 hours of classroom instruction each year and 8,000 hours of on-the-job training over the course of the apprenticeship. Most localities require electricians to be licensed. Although licensing requirements vary from area to area, electricians generally must pass an examination that tests their knowledge of electrical theory, the National Electrical Code, and local electric and building codes.

★4990★
Independent Electrical Contractors (IEC)
PO Box 10379
Alexandria, VA 22310-0379   Phone: (703)549-7351
Has formulated National Pattern Standards for Apprentice Training for Electricians.

Test Guides

★4991★
Electrician
National Learning Corp.
212 Michael Dr.
Syosset, NY 11791   Phone: (516)921-8888
Jack Rudman. Part of the Career Examination Series No. 1. All examination guides in this series contain questions with answers. **Facsimile Number:** (516)921-8743. **Toll-free/Additional Phone Number(s):** 800-645-6337.

★4992★
Electrician - Electrician's Helper
Prentice Hall Press
Simon & Schuster Inc.
200 Old Tappan Rd.
Old Tappan, NJ 07675   Phone: (800)223-2348
Hy Hammer. Fifth edition, 1982. Provides information on a wide array of electrician tests, including actual previous exams.

★4993★
Electrician's Helper
National Learning Corp.
212 Michael Dr.
Syosset, NY 11791   Phone: (516)921-8888
Jack Rudman. Part of the Career Examination Series No. 1. All examination guides in this series contain questions with answers. **Facsimile Number:** (516)921-8743. **Toll-free/Additional Phone Number(s):** 800-645-6337.

Electricians

★4994★
Foreman Electrician
National Learning Corp.
212 Michael Dr.
Syosset, NY 11791   Phone: (516)921-8888
Jack Rudman. Part of the Career Examination Series No. 1. All examination guides in this series contain questions with answers. **Facsimile Number:** (516)921-8743. **Toll-free/Additional Phone Number(s):** 800-645-6337.

★4995★
Maintenance Worker/Mechanical Maintainer
Prentice Hall Press
Simon & Schuster Inc.
200 Old Tappan Rd.
Old Tappan, NJ 07675   Phone: (800)223-2348
Hy Hammer. Fourth edition, 1984. Provides information for applicants interested in the following civil service positions: carpenter, mason, plumber, electrician, painter, machinist. Includes eight sample tests.

★4996★
Master Electrician
National Learning Corp.
212 Michael Dr.
Syosset, NY 11791   Phone: (516)921-8888
Jack Rudman. Part of the Career Examination Series No. 1. All examination guides in this series contain questions with answers. **Facsimile Number:** (516)921-8743. **Toll-free/Additional Phone Number(s):** 800-645-6337.

★4997★
Special Electrical License
National Learning Corp.
212 Michael Dr.
Syosset, NY 11791   Phone: (516)921-8888
Jack Rudman. Part of the Career Examination Series No. 1. All examination guides in this series contain questions with answers. **Facsimile Number:** (516)921-8743. **Toll-free/Additional Phone Number(s):** 800-645-6337.

Basic Reference Guides and Handbooks

★4998★
Electrical Design Library
National Electrical Contractors Association (NECA)
7315 Wisconsin Ave.
Bethesda, MD 20814   Phone: (301)657-3110

★4999★
The Electrician's Toolbox Manual
Prentice Hall
Rte. 9W
Englewood Ciffs, NJ 07632   Phone: (201)592-2000
Rex Miller. 1989.

★5000★
Intelligent Buildings Institute—Directory of Products and Services
Intelligent Buildings Institute (IBI)
2101 L St., NW, Ste. 300
Washington, DC 20037   Phone: (202)457-1988
S. Hunt, Associate Executive Director, editor. Annual, September. Member consultants, associations, research organizations, and other suppliers of products and services to the construction and building industry. Entries include: Company name, address, phone. Arrangement: Alphabetical. Indexes: Product/service. **Facsimile Number:** (202)457-8468.

★5001★
Interconnection Products Directory
Connector Study Group, Inc.
104 Wilmot Rd., Ste. 201
Deerfield, IL 60015-5195   Phone: (312)940-8800
Gerald L. Ginsberg, editor. Biennial, November of odd years. More than 500 manufacturers, distributors, representatives, sales offices, and other suppliers to the electrical and electronics industry worldwide, including suppliers of connectors, wire, and cable (part 1); printed circuit products (part 2); circular rack and panel products (part 3); wire and cable products (part 4); materials (part 5); and military products (part 6). Entries include: Name, address, products, whether catalog is available. Arrangement: Classified by product. Indexes: Product.

★5002★
Math on the Job: Electrician
National Center for Research in Vocational Education
Ohio State University
1900 Kenry Rd.
Columbus, OH 43210   Phone: (614)292-4353
1985.

★5003★
Mid-West Contractor—Annual Convention Guide and Association Directory
Allied Publications, Inc.
7355 N. Woodland Dr.
Box 603
Indianapolis, IN 46278   Phone: (317)297-5500
Jennifer Wynne, editor. Annual. List of 160 construction contracting and architectural associations in the Midwest. Entries include: Association name, address, phone, names and titles of key personnel, description of association; convention site, date, name and title of contact. Arrangement: Geographical, alphabetical. **Toll-free/Additional Phone Number(s):** (800)827-7468. **Facsimile Number:** (317)299-1356.

Periodicals

★5004★
ABC Newsline
Associated Builders and Contractors, Inc. (ABC)
729 15th St. NW
Washington, DC 20005   Phone: (202)637-8800
Editor(s): Lisa A. Nardone. Semimonthly. Designed to keep readers alerted to important changes within ABC and the construction industry. Reports on legislative issues, construction trends, conferences and meetings, and ABC services. Recurring features include news of members and a column titled Industry Briefs.

★5005★
American Architectural Manufacturers Association— Quarterly Review
American Architectural Manufacturers Association
1540 E. Dundee Rd., Ste. K 310
Palatine, IL 60067-8321   Phone: (708)202-1350
Editor(s): Tony Coorlim. Annually. Contains industry news on architectural products. Covers prime and combination storm windows, sliding glass and combination storm doors, window and curtain-walls, store fronts and entrances, siding, soffits, fascia, gutters, downspouts, skylights, space enclosures, and mobile home components. Recurring features include news of

research, notices of publications available, and announcements by the association. **Facsimile Number:** (708)202-1480.

★5006★
American Institute of Constructors—Newsletter
American Institute of Constructors
9887 Gandy Blvd. N., No. 104
Saint Petersburg, FL 33702-2451

Editor(s): Ed Freedman. Bimonthly. Concerned with construction practice, design, administration, and teaching. Carries news of members, listings of job opportunities, local chapter reports, and notices of new publications. **Facsimile Number:** (614)464-3226.

★5007★
Blue Reports, Inc.
Construction News Service
7325 Steel Mill Dr.
Springfield, VA 22050   Phone: (703)644-5884

Editor(s): Calvin S. Oren. Daily. Reports on public and private construction projects in the Washington, DC, Virginia, and Maryland areas. Provides owner's and architect's names, plan status, date bids due, prospective bidders, low bids received, and specification details. **Facsimile Number:** (703)644-1929.

★5008★
The Builder and Contractor
Associated Builders and Contractors (ABC)
729 15th St. NW
Washington, DC 20005   Phone: (202)637-8800
Monthly.

★5009★
Building Concerns
National Association of Minority Contractors (NAMC)
806 15th St. NW, Ste. 340
Washington, DC 20005   Phone: (202)347-8259

Editor(s): Ralph C. Thomas, III. Monthly. Concentrates on national and regional news regarding minority construction contractors. Contains articles on issues generally affecting the industry—especially issues affecting minorities—including topics such as legislative and regulatory activity and reports on major corporation developments. Recurring features include reports of meetings, news of educational opportunities, a calendar of events, and news of NAMC chapters and members.

★5010★
Building Industry Technology: An Abstract Newsletter
National Technical Information Service (NTIS)
U.S. Department of Commerce
5285 Port Royal Rd.
Springfield, VA 22161   Phone: (703)487-4630

Weekly. Consists of abstracts of reports on architectural and environmental design, building standards, construction materials and equipment, and structural analyses. Recurring features include a form for ordering reports from NTIS.

★5011★
Capital Comments
National Lumber & Building Material Dealers Association
40 Ivy St. SE
Washington, DC 20003   Phone: (202)547-2230

Editor(s): Matt Geitner. Semimonthly. Reports on news of legislation pertaining to lumber, other building materials, and housing. Discusses such issues as lumber subsidies, interest rates on homes, health and safety, and jobs. **Facsimile Number:** (202)547-7640.

★5012★
CEE
InterTech Publishing Co., Inc.
707 Westchester Ave.
White Plains, NY 10604   Phone: (914)949-8500

Stuart M. Lewis, Editor. Monthly. Electrical construction industry magazine. **Facsimile Number:** (914)682-0922.

★5013★
ConnStruction
PO Box 9768
Wethersfield, CT 06109   Phone: (203)529-3246

Victor Bonini, Editor. 7x/yr. Magazine for construction industry. **Facsimile Number:** (203)563-0616.

★5014★
CONSTRUCTION
26 Long Hill Rd.
Guilford, CT 06437   Phone: (203)453-3717

Jack C. Lewis, Editor and Publisher. 2x/mo. Journal for the construction industry.

★5015★
Construction Dimensions
Assn. of Wall & Ceiling
PO Box 5504
Washington, DC 20016   Phone: (301)656-7050

Gerald Wykoff, Editor. Monthly. Wall and ceiling industry magazine.

★5016★
Construction Industry International
Maclean Hunter Publishing Co.
29 N. Wacker Dr.
Chicago, IL 60606   Phone: (312)726-2802

Alan Elliott, Editor-in-Chief. Monthly. Trade magazine.

★5017★
Construction News
715 W. 2nd St.
PO Box 2421
Little Rock, AR 72203   Phone: (501)376-1931

Robert Alvey, Editor. Weekly. Construction industry magazine. **Facsimile Number:** (501)375-5831.

★5018★
Construction Newsletter
National Safety Council
444 N. Michigan Ave.
Chicago, IL 60611   Phone: (312)527-4800

6/yr. Focuses on industrial and occupational safety in the construction industry. Carries items on such topics as safe work practices and products, accident prevention, and successful industrial safety programs and policies.

★5019★
Daily Construction Reporter
4901 Pacific Hwy.
San Diego, CA 92110-4098   Phone: (619)296-0183

Kenneth F. Kerr, Editor and Publisher. Daily. Construction trade newspaper covering jobs that are out for bid, bid results, building permits, and other information. **Facsimile Number:** (619)298-3027.

Electricians

★5020★
Electrical Contractor Magazine
National Electrical Contractors Association (NECA)
7315 Wisconsin Ave.
Bethesda, MD 20814   Phone: (301)657-3110
Monthly.

★5021★
The Electricity Journal
2101 4th Ave., Ste. 345
Seattle, WA 98121-2317   Phone: (206)448-4078
Robert O. Marritz, Editor and Publisher. 10x/yr Magazine serving the electric utility industry. **Facsimile Number:** (206)441-7443.

★5022★
Electro Fact File
National Electrical Contractors Association (NECA)
7315 Wisconsin Ave.
Bethesda, MD 20814   Phone: (301)657-3110
Bimonthly.

★5023★
Electronic and Electrical Equipment
National Safety Council
444 N. Michigan Ave.
Chicago, IL 60611   Phone: (312)527-4800
Editor(s): Katie Kuhfuss. 6/yr. Provides safety tips for persons who work with electronic and electrical equipment. Promotes and reports on training courses in accident prevention, safety precautions, and compliance with safety regulations. Also carries items on safety awareness off the job.

★5024★
Home BUILDER Magazine
Work-4 Projects Ltd.
PO Box 400, Victoria Sta.
Westmount, PQ, Canada H3Z 2V8   Phone: (514)489-4941
Nachmi Artzy, Editor and Publisher. 6x/yr. Magazine for home construction industry. **Facsimile Number:** (514)489-5505.

★5025★
IEC News Circuit
Independent Electrical Contractors (IEC)
PO Box 10379
Alexandria, VA 22310-0379   Phone: (703)549-7351
Quarterly. Newsletter.

★5026★
Interior Construction
Ceilings and Interior Systems Construction Assn.
104 Wilmot, Ste. 201
Deerfield, IL 60015-5195   Phone: (708)940-8800
Sheila Wertz, Editor. 7x/yr. Magazine covering interior finish construction. **Facsimile Number:** (708)940-7218.

★5027★
The Journal of Light Construction
Hanley-Wood Partners
RR 2, Box 146
Richmond, VT 05477-9607   Phone: (802)864-0091
Steve Bliss, Editor. Monthly. Magazine (tabloid) for residential and light professionals involved in new and rehabilitative construction. Each issue covers a single aspect of construction.

★5028★
Nation's Building News
15th & M Sts. NW
Washington, DC 20005   Phone: (202)822-0525
Tim Ahern, Editor. 2x/mo. Trade magazine (tabloid) covering home building and all related industries. **Facsimile Number:** (202)861-2131.

★5029★
NECA News
National Electrical Contractors Association (NECA)
7315 Wisconsin Ave.
Bethesda, MD 20814   Phone: (301)657-3110
Weekly.

★5030★
Palmetto Piper
Mechanical Contractor's Assn. of South Carolina
1504 Morninghill Dr.
PO Box 384
Columbia, SC 29202   Phone: (803)772-7834
Monthly. Plumbing, heating, air conditioning, and electrical journal.

★5031★
Professional Builder
Cahners Publishing Co.
1350 E. Touhy Ave.
Des Plaines, IL 60018   Phone: (708)635-8800
Roy L. Diez, Editor. 19x/yr. **Facsimile Number:** (708)299-8622.

─────── Meetings and Conventions ───────

★5032★
Associated Builders and Contractors (ABC)
729 15th St. NW
Washington, DC 20005   Phone: (202)637-8800
Frequency: Annual.

★5033★
Big Show - Northeast Construction Expo
Slater Expositions
1502 Providence Hwy.
Norwood, MA 02062   Phone: (617)769-7676
Frequency: Always held in Boston, Massachusetts at the World Trade Center. 1992; Mar. 12-19; Boston, MA.

★5034★
Independent Electrical Contractors Convention and Trade Show
Independent Electrical Contractors, Inc.
PO Box 10379
Alexandria, VA 22310-0379   Phone: (703)549-7351
1992; Aug. Atlanta, GA. **Facsimile Number:** (703)549-7448.

★5035★
International Brotherhood of Electrical Workers (IBEW)
1125 15th St. NW
Washington, DC 20005   Phone: (202)833-7000
Frequency: Quadrennial.

★5036★
International Electrical Conference and Exhibition
Kerrwil Publications Ltd.
395 Matheson Blvd., E.
Mississauga, ON, Canada L4Z 2H2   Phone: (416)890-1846
Frequency: Always held in Toronto, Ontario, Canada, at the Metro Toronto Convention Centre. **Facsimile Number:** (416)890-5769.

★5037★
International Electrical Exposition and Congress
Continental Exhibitions, Inc.
370 Lexington Ave., Ste. 902
New York, NY 10017-6578   Phone: (212)370-5005
1992. **Toll-free/Additional Phone Number(s):** 800-222-2596. **Facsimile Number:** (212)370-5699.

★5038★
Midwest Specialty Exposition
Kansas Plumbing, Heating, and Cooling Contractors Association
320 Laura St.
Wichita, KS 67211   Phone: (316)262-8860
1992. **Facsimile Number:** (316)265-7381.

★5039★
National Electrical Equipment Show and Conference
Reed Exhibition Companies (USA)
Cahners Plaza
999 Summer St.
PO Box 3833
Stamford, CT 06905-0833   Phone: (203)964-0000
1992; Chicago, IL. **Facsimile Number:** (203)964-0176.

★5040★
Upper Midwest Electrical Trade Show
North Central Electrical League
4930 77th St., W., Ste. 150
Minneapolis, MN 55435   Phone: (612)835-4808
Frequency: Always held at the Convention Center in Minneapolis, Minnesota. 1992; Apr. 08-09; Minneapolis, MN • 1994; Apr. 20-21; Minneapolis, MN.

★5041★
Wire Expo - Wire Association International Annual Meeting and Exposition
Wire Association International
1570 Boston Post Rd.
PO Box H
Guilford, CT 06437   Phone: (203)453-2727
1992; Louisville, KY • 1994; Detroit, MI. **Facsimile Number:** (203)453-8384.

───── **Other Sources of Information** ─────

★5042★
NECA Standard of Installation
National Electrical Contractors Association (NECA)
7315 Wisconsin Ave.
Bethesda, MD 20814   Phone: (301)657-3110

Glaziers

Glaziers select, cut, install, and remove all types of glass as well as plastics and similar materials. They also install mirrors, shower doors and bathtub enclosures, and glass for table tops and display cases. They may mount steel and aluminum sashes or frames and attach locks and hinges to glass doors. The majority of glaziers work for glazing contractors engaged in new construction, alteration, and repair. Others work for retail glass shops that install or replace glass and wholesale distributors of products containing glass.

$alaries

Apprentice wage rates usually start at 50 to 60 percent of the rate paid to experienced glaziers and increase every six months. Average hourly wages for glaziers vary widely by geographic location.

Average earnings in the South	$12.00 to $18.00/hour
Average earnings in the Northeast and Midwest	$14.00 to $20.00/hour
Average earnings in the West	$13.00 to $24.00/hour

Employment Outlook

Growth rate until the year 2000: Average.

Glaziers

Career Guides

★5043★
Construction Cluster
Center for Humanities, Inc.
Communications Park
Box 1000
Mount Kisco, NY 10549   Phone: (914)666-4100
Videocassette. 1984. 15 mins. Construction workers describe what it's like to work at their jobs, and show the special equipment they use in their field.

★5044★
Glazier
Careers, Inc.
PO Box 135
Largo, FL 34649-0135   Phone: (813)584-7333
1988. Two-page occupational summary card describing duties, working conditions, personal qualifications, training, earnings and hours, employment outlook, places of employment, related careers and where to write for more information.

★5045★
Glazier
Vocational Biographies, Inc.
PO Box 31, Dept. VF10
Sauk Centre, MN 56378   Phone: (612)352-6516
1989. This pamphlet profiles a person working in the job. Includes information about job duties, working conditions, places of employment, educational preparation, labor market outlook, and salaries. **Toll-free/Additional Phone Number(s):** 800-255-0752.

★5046★
"Glazier" in Construction, Volume 4 of Career Information Center (pp. 60-61)
Glencoe/Macmillan
15319 Chatsworth St.
Mission Hills, CA 91345   Phone: (818)898-1391
Richard Lidz and Dale Anderson, editorial directors. Fourth edition, 1990. For 600 occupations, describes job duties, entry-level requirements, education and training needed, advancement possibilities, employment outlook, earnings and benefits. The set is divided into 12 volumes. Each volume includes jobs related under a broad career field. Volume 13 is the index. **Facsimile Number:** 818-365-5489.

★5047★
"Glazier" in Exploring Nontraditional Jobs for Women (pp. 16-20)
Rosen Publishing Group, Inc.
29 E. 21st St.
New York, NY 10010   Phone: (212)777-3017
Rose Neufeld. 1989. Describes blue-collar, male dominated occupations. Discusses what is done on the job, training, where to apply for jobs, tools used, salaries, and advantages and disadvantages. Relates the experiences of women who are working in the field.

★5048★
"Glazier" in Occu-Facts: Information on 565 Careers in Outline Form (p. 16.15)
Careers, Inc.
P.O. Box 135
1211 Tenth St., S.W.
Largo, FL 33640   Phone: (813)584-7333
Elizabeth Handville. Biennial, 1989-90 edition. Each one-page occupational profile describes duties, working conditions, physical surroundings and demands, aptitudes, temperament, educational requirements, employment outlook, earnings, and places of employment.

★5049★
"Glazier" in Occupational Outlook Handbook (pp. 371-372)
Superintendent of Documents
U.S. Government Printing Office
Washington, DC 20402   Phone: (202)783-3238
Biennial; latest edition, 1990-91. Encyclopedia of careers describing more than 250 occupations and comprising about 86 percent of all jobs in the economy. Occupations that require lengthy education or training are given the most attention. For each occupation, the handbook describes job duties, working conditions, training, educational preparation, personal qualities, advancement possibilities, job outlook, earnings, and sources of additional information.

★5050★
Glaziers
Chronicle Guidance Publications, Inc.
PO Box 1190
Moravia, NY 13118-1190   Phone: (315)497-0330
1989. This career brief describes the nature of the work, working conditions, hours and earnings, education and training, licensure, certification, unions, personal qualifications, social and psychological factors, employment outlook, entry methods, advancement, and related occupations. **Toll-free/Additional Phone Number(s):** 800-622-7284.

★5051★
"Glaziers" in *Opportunities in Building Construction Trades* (pp. 55-57)
National Textbook Co.
4255 W. Touhy Ave.
Lincolnwood, IL 60646　　　　Phone: (312)679-5500

Michael Sumichrast. 1989. Gives an overview of the construction industry and describes the jobs of various craftworkers. Covers different kinds of builders: home, custom; and describes management skills needed and industry trends affecting opportunities.

★5052★
"Glaziers" in Volume 3 of *Career Discovery Encyclopedia* (pp. 82-83)
J.G. Ferguson Publishing Co.
200 W. Monroe
Chicago, IL 60606　　　　Phone: (312)580-5480

E. Russell Primm, editor-in-chief. 1990. Contains two-page articles on 504 occupations. Each article describes job duties, earnings, and educational and training requirements.

★5053★
"Glaziers" in Volume 3 of *The Encyclopedia of Careers and Vocational Guidance* (pp. 665-668)
J.G. Ferguson Publishing Co.
200 W. Monroe
Chicago, IL 60606　　　　Phone: (312)580-5480

William E. Hopke, editor-in-chief. Eighth edition, 1990. Four-volume set that profiles 500 occupations and describes job trends in 76 industries. Includes career description, educational requirements, history of the job, methods of entry, advancement, employment outlook, earnings, working conditions, social and psychological factors, and sources of additional information.

Associations

★5054★
International Brotherhood of Painters and Allied Trades (IBPAT)
United Unions Bldg.
1750 New York Ave., NW
Washington, DC 20006　　　　Phone: (202)637-0720

Membership: AFL-CIO. **Publications:** *Directory*, annual. • *Painters and Allied Trades Journal*, monthly.

★5055★
National Glass Association (NGA)
8200 Greensboro Dr., Ste. 302
McLean, VA 22102　　　　Phone: (703)442-4890

Membership: Manufacturers, installers, retailers, distributors, and fabricators of flat, architectural, automotive, and specialty glass and metal products, mirrors, shower and patio doors, windows, and table tops. **Purpose:** Compiles statistics; provides educational and technical services; sponsors competitions and apprenticeship program; presents awards. **Publications:** *Auto Glass Monthly*, biennial. • *Glass Magazine*, monthly. • *Homeowners Guide to Glass*, annual. • *Index of Publications and Resource Catalogue*, annual. • *Membership Directory*, annual. • *National Glass Association—Member Services Catalog*, annual. • Also publishes surveys and reports. **Facsimile Number:** (703)442-0603.

Standards/Certification Agencies

Many glaziers learn the trade informally as helpers that assist experienced workers. Learning the trade this way may not provide training as complete as an apprenticeship program, however, and may take longer. Most employers recommend that glaziers learn the trade through an apprenticeship program that lasts three to four years. Apprenticeship programs, which are administered by the National Glass Association, and local union-management committees of the International Brotherhood of Painters and Allied Trades or local contractors' associations, consist of on-the-job training as well as 144 hours of classroom instruction or home study each year.

Test Guides

★5056★
Glazier
National Learning Corp.
212 Michael Dr.
Syosset, NY 11791　　　　Phone: (516)921-8888

Jack Rudman. Part of the Career Examination Series No. 1. All examination guides in this series contain questions with answers. **Facsimile Number:** (516)921-8743. **Toll-free/Additional Phone Number(s):** 800-645-6337.

Educational Directories and Programs

★5057★
National Glaziers' Architectural Metal and Glassworkers' Industries Apprenticeship Training and Journeymen Education Fund
9030 Red Branch Rd.
Columbia, MD 21045

Provides information on training for glaziers.

Awards, Scholarships, Grants, and Fellowships

★5058★
NGA Awards for Excellence
National Glass Association
8200 Greensboro Dr., Ste. 302
McLean, VA 22102　　　　Phone: (703)442-4890

For recognition of excellence in the use of glass in residential and commercial projects as a building material (design) and excellence in installation skill (craftsmanship). Awards are given in the following two categories: (1) Excellence in Design - Residential and Commercial; and (2) Excellence in Craftsmanship - Residential and Commercial. Entries may be submitted by December 31. The Award for Excellence in Design is chosen by a panel of judges including members of the glazing and architectural industries and is open to all members of the building trade. The Award for Excellence in Craftsmanship is chosen by a panel of judges including members of the glazing industry and is open to all glass companies. Awarded annually.

Basic Reference Guides and Handbooks

★5059★
Intelligent Buildings Institute—Directory of Products and Services
Intelligent Buildings Institute (IBI)
2101 L St., NW, Ste. 300
Washington, DC 20037   Phone: (202)457-1988
S. Hunt, Associate Executive Director, editor. Annual, September. Member consultants, associations, research organizations, and other suppliers of products and services to the construction and building industry. Entries include: Company name, address, phone. Arrangement: Alphabetical. Indexes: Product/service. **Facsimile Number:** (202)457-8468.

★5060★
Mid-West Contractor—Annual Convention Guide and Association Directory
Allied Publications, Inc.
7355 N. Woodland Dr.
Box 603
Indianapolis, IN 46278   Phone: (317)297-5500
Jennifer Wynne, editor. Annual. List of 160 construction contracting and architectural associations in the Midwest. Entries include: Association name, address, phone, names and titles of key personnel, description of association; convention site, date, name and title of contact. Arrangement: Geographical, alphabetical. **Toll-free/Additional Phone Number(s):** (800)827-7468. **Facsimile Number:** (317)299-1356.

★5061★
U.S. Glass, Metal and Glazing—Directory of Suppliers of Machinery & Equipment Issue
U.S. Glass Publications, Inc.
560 Oakwood Ave., Ste. 202
Lake Forest, IL 60045   Phone: (708)295-2900
Sherry Edwards McHone, Managing Editor, editor. Annual, May. List of suppliers of machinery and equipment for the glass, metal, and glazing industry. Entries include: Company name, address, phone, telex, names and titles of key personnel, subsidiary and branch names and locations. Arrangement: Alphabetical. Indexes: Product. **Facsimile Number:** (708)295-2903.

★5062★
U.S. Glass, Metal and Glazing—Directory of Suppliers of Sealants & Glazing Systems Issue
U.S. Glass Publications, Inc.
560 Oakwood Ave., Ste. 202
Lake Forest, IL 60045   Phone: (708)295-2900
Sherry Edwards McHone, Managing Editor, editor. Annual, July. List of about 90 suppliers of sealants and glazing systems for the glass, metal, and glazing industry. Entries include: Company name, address, phone, fax. Arrangement: Classified by product or service. **Facsimile Number:** (708)295-2903.

Periodicals

★5063★
ABC Newsline
Associated Builders and Contractors, Inc. (ABC)
729 15th St. NW
Washington, DC 20005   Phone: (202)637-8800
Editor(s): Lisa A. Nardone. Semimonthly. Designed to keep readers alerted to important changes within ABC and the construction industry. Reports on legislative issues, construction trends, conferences and meetings, and ABC services. Recurring features include news of members and a column titled Industry Briefs.

★5064★
American Architectural Manufacturers Association—Quarterly Review
American Architectural Manufacturers Association
1540 E. Dundee Rd., Ste. K 310
Palatine, IL 60067-8321   Phone: (708)202-1350
Editor(s): Tony Coorlim. Annually. Contains industry news on architectural products. Covers prime and combination storm windows, sliding glass and combination storm doors, window and curtain-walls, store fronts and entrances, siding, soffits, fascia, gutters, downspouts, skylights, space enclosures, and mobile home components. Recurring features include news of research, notices of publications available, and announcements by the association. **Facsimile Number:** (708)202-1480.

★5065★
American Institute of Constructors—Newsletter
American Institute of Constructors
9887 Gandy Blvd. N., No. 104
Saint Petersburg, FL 33702-2451
Editor(s): Ed Freedman. Bimonthly. Concerned with construction practice, design, administration, and teaching. Carries news of members, listings of job opportunities, local chapter reports, and notices of new publications. **Facsimile Number:** (614)464-3226.

★5066★
Auto Glass Monthly
National Glass Association (NGA)
8200 Greensboro Dr., Ste. 302
McLean, VA 22102   Phone: (703)442-4890
Biennial. Magazine containing information on the auto glass industry, including original equipment and after market products.

★5067★
Blue Reports, Inc.
Construction News Service
7325 Steel Mill Dr.
Springfield, VA 22050   Phone: (703)644-5884
Editor(s): Calvin S. Oren. Daily. Reports on public and private construction projects in the Washington, DC, Virginia, and Maryland areas. Provides owner's and architect's names, plan status, date bids due, prospective bidders, low bids received, and specification details. **Facsimile Number:** (703)644-1929.

★5068★
Building Concerns
National Association of Minority Contractors (NAMC)
806 15th St. NW, Ste. 340
Washington, DC 20005   Phone: (202)347-8259
Editor(s): Ralph C. Thomas, III. Monthly. Concentrates on national and regional news regarding minority construction contractors. Contains articles on issues generally affecting the industry—especially issues affecting minorities—including topics such as legislative and regulatory activity and reports on major corporation developments. Recurring features include reports of meetings, news of educational opportunities, a calendar of events, and news of NAMC chapters and members.

★5069★
Building Industry Technology: An Abstract Newsletter
National Technical Information Service (NTIS)
U.S. Department of Commerce
5285 Port Royal Rd.
Springfield, VA 22161   Phone: (703)487-4630
Weekly. Consists of abstracts of reports on architectural and environmental design, building standards, construction materials and equipment, and structural analyses. Recurring features include a form for ordering reports from NTIS.

★5070★
Building Renovation
Maclean Hunter Ltd.
777 Bay St.
Toronto, ON, Canada M5W 1A7   Phone: (416)596-5760
John Fennell, Editor. 6x/yr. Business magazine for professionals in residential and commercial renovation and remodeling. **Facsimile Number:** (416)596-5810.

★5071★
Capital Comments
National Lumber & Building Material Dealers Association
40 Ivy St. SE
Washington, DC 20003   Phone: (202)547-2230
Editor(s): Matt Geitner. Semimonthly. Reports on news of legislation pertaining to lumber, other building materials, and housing. Discusses such issues as lumber subsidies, interest rates on homes, health and safety, and jobs. **Facsimile Number:** (202)547-7640.

★5072★
ConnStruction
PO Box 9768
Wethersfield, CT 06109   Phone: (203)529-3246
Victor Bonini, Editor. 7x/yr. Magazine for construction industry. **Facsimile Number:** (203)563-0616.

★5073★
CONSTRUCTION
26 Long Hill Rd.
Guilford, CT 06437   Phone: (203)453-3717
Jack C. Lewis, Editor and Publisher. 2x/mo. Journal for the construction industry.

★5074★
Construction Dimensions
Assn. of Wall & Ceiling
PO Box 5504
Washington, DC 20016   Phone: (301)656-7050
Gerald Wykoff, Editor. Monthly. Wall and ceiling industry magazine.

★5075★
Construction Industry International
Maclean Hunter Publishing Co.
29 N. Wacker Dr.
Chicago, IL 60606   Phone: (312)726-2802
Alan Elliott, Editor-in-Chief. Monthly. Trade magazine.

★5076★
Construction News
715 W. 2nd St.
PO Box 2421
Little Rock, AR 72203   Phone: (501)376-1931
Robert Alvey, Editor. Weekly. Construction industry magazine. **Facsimile Number:** (501)375-5831.

★5077★
Construction Newsletter
National Safety Council
444 N. Michigan Ave.
Chicago, IL 60611   Phone: (312)527-4800
6/yr. Focuses on industrial and occupational safety in the construction industry. Carries items on such topics as safe work practices and products, accident prevention, and successful industrial safety programs and policies.

★5078★
Daily Construction Reporter
4901 Pacific Hwy.
San Diego, CA 92110-4098   Phone: (619)296-0183
Kenneth F. Kerr, Editor and Publisher. Daily. Construction trade newspaper covering jobs that are out for bid, bid results, building permits, and other information. **Facsimile Number:** (619)298-3027.

★5079★
Glass Magazine
National Glass Association (NGA)
8200 Greensboro Dr., Ste. 302
McLean, VA 22102   Phone: (703)442-4890
Monthly. Magazine. Contains news and information on glass industry management. Topics include architectural glass, storefronts and curtainwall, skylights, greenhouses, sloped glazing, security glazing, insulating glass, windows, doors, hardware, glass equipment and hardware, mirrors, metals, sealants, and tools.

★5080★
Home BUILDER Magazine
Work-4 Projects Ltd.
PO Box 400, Victoria Sta.
Westmount, PQ, Canada H3Z 2V8   Phone: (514)489-4941
Nachmi Artzy, Editor and Publisher. 6x/yr. Magazine for home construction industry. **Facsimile Number:** (514)489-5505.

★5081★
The Journal of Light Construction
Hanley-Wood Partners
RR 2, Box 146
Richmond, VT 05477-9607   Phone: (802)864-0091
Steve Bliss, Editor. Monthly. Magazine (tabloid) for residential and light professionals involved in new and rehabilitative construction. Each issue covers a single aspect of construction.

Glaziers

★5082★
Nation's Building News
15th & M Sts. NW
Washington, DC 20005   Phone: (202)822-0525
Tim Ahern, Editor. 2x/mo. Trade magazine (tabloid) covering home building and all related industries. **Facsimile Number:** (202)861-2131.

★5083★
Painters and Allied Trades Journal
International Brotherhood of Painters and Allied Trades (IBPAT)
United Unions Bldg.
1750 New York Ave., NW
Washington, DC 20006   Phone: (202)637-0720
Monthly.

★5084★
Professional Builder
Cahners Publishing Co.
1350 E. Touhy Ave.
Des Plaines, IL 60018   Phone: (708)635-8800
Roy L. Diez, Editor. 19x/yr. **Facsimile Number:** (708)299-8622.

──────── Meetings and Conventions ────────

★5085★
National Glass Association Annual Convention and National Glass and Machinery Show
National Glass Association
8200 Greensboro Dr., Ste. 302
McLean, VA 22102   Phone: (703)442-4890
1992; Mar. 31-04; San Antonio, TX ● 1993; Apr. 20-24; Los Angeles, CA ● 1994; Apr. 12-16; Miami Beach, FL. **Facsimile Number:** (703)442-0630.

Insulation Workers

Insulation workers install insulation materials. Most work for insulation or other construction contractors. Others work for the federal government, in shipbuilding, and in other manufacturing industries, such as chemicals and petroleum refining.

$alaries

Median hourly salaries for insulation workers are as follows:

Lowest 10 percent	$17.17/hour
Median	$25.08/hour
Top 10 percent	$34.77

Employment Outlook

Growth rate until the year 2000: Average.

Insulation Workers

Career Guides

★5086★
"Asbestos and Insulating Worker" in *Opportunities in Building Construction Trades* (pp. 47-49)
National Textbook Co.
4255 W. Touhy Ave.
Lincolnwood, IL 60646   Phone: (312)679-5500
Michael Sumichrast. 1989. Gives an overview of the construction industry and describes the jobs of various craftworkers. Covers different kinds of builders: home, custom; and describes management skills needed and industry trends affecting opportunities.

★5087★
Career Success Series
Cambridge Career Products
90 MacCorkle Ave., SW
South Charleston, WV 25311   Phone: (304)744-9323
Videocassette. 1986. 15 mins. A series, available separately, outlining various career choices for students. Occupations include: flight service, air transportation/ground service, data processing, carpentry, clerk in banking/insurance, commodity sales, cosmetic personal grooming, fire fighting, forestry services, home economics, insulation/roofing, material handling, mechanics, photographic processing, pipefitting and plumbing, police science, printing, secretarial services, and utilities equipment operator.

★5088★
Construction Cluster
Center for Humanities, Inc.
Communications Park
Box 1000
Mount Kisco, NY 10549   Phone: (914)666-4100
Videocassette. 1984. 15 mins. Construction workers describe what it's like to work at their jobs, and show the special equipment they use in their field.

★5089★
Insulating & Roofing Occupations
Morris Video
2730 Monterey St. #105
Monterey Business Park
Torrance, CA 90503   Phone: (213)533-4800
Videocassette. 1987. 15 mins. A look at the various careers that involve the reduction of the flow of cold, heat or sound.

★5090★
"Insulation Worker" in *Construction*, Volume 4 of *Career Information Center* (pp. 64-65)
Glencoe/Macmillan
15319 Chatsworth St.
Mission Hills, CA 91345   Phone: (818)898-1391
Richard Lidz and Dale Anderson, editorial directors. Fourth edition, 1990. For 600 occupations, describes job duties, entry-level requirements, education and training needed, advancement possibilities, employment outlook, earnings and benefits. The set is divided into 12 volumes. Each volume includes jobs related under a broad career field. Volume 13 is the index. **Facsimile Number:** 818-365-5489.

★5091★
Insulation Workers
Careers, Inc.
PO Box 135
Largo, FL 34649-0135   Phone: (813)584-7333
1988. Two-page occupational summary card describing duties, working conditions, personal qualifications, training, earnings and hours, employment outlook, places of employment, related careers and where to write for more information.

★5092★
"Insulation Workers" in *Occu-Facts: Information on 565 Careers in Outline Form* (p. 16.16)
Careers, Inc.
P.O. Box 135
1211 Tenth St., S.W.
Largo, FL 33640   Phone: (813)584-7333
Elizabeth Handville. Biennial, 1989-90 edition. Each one-page occupational profile describes duties, working conditions, physical surroundings and demands, aptitudes, temperament, educational requirements, employment outlook, earnings, and places of employment.

★5093★
"Insulation Workers" in *Occupational Outlook Handbook* (pp. 372-373)
Superintendent of Documents
U.S. Government Printing Office
Washington, DC 20402   Phone: (202)783-3238
Biennial; latest edition, 1990-91. Encyclopedia of careers describing more than 250 occupations and comprising about 86 percent of all jobs in the economy. Occupations that require lengthy education or training are given the most attention. For each occupation, the handbook describes job duties, working conditions, training, educational preparation, personal qualities, advancement possibilities, job outlook, earnings, and sources of additional information.

★5094★
"Insulation Workers" in Volume 3 of *Career Discovery Encyclopedia* (pp. 150-151)
J.G. Ferguson Publishing Co.
200 W. Monroe
Chicago, IL 60606　　　　　　　　Phone: (312)580-5480
E. Russell Primm, editor-in-chief. 1990. Contains two-page articles on 504 occupations. Each article describes job duties, earnings, and educational and training requirements.

★5095★
Video Career Library - Construction
Careers, Inc.
1211 10th St., SW
PO Box 135
Largo, FL 34649-0135　　　　　　Phone: (813)584-7333
Videocassette. 1990. 36 mins. Part of the Video Career Library covering 165 occupations. Shows actual workers on the job. Includes millwrights, brickmasons, carpenters, drywall installers, electricians, painters, plumbers and pipefitters, carpenter and soft tile installers, insulation workers, paving equipment operators, and structural metal workers.

Associations

★5096★
National Insulation and Abatement Contractors Association (NIAC)
99 Canal Center Plaza, Ste. 222
Alexandria, VA 22314　　　　　　Phone: (703)683-6422
Membership: Insulation and asbestos abatement contractors, distributors, and manufacturers. **Publications:** *Advisor*, monthly. • *Asbestos Abatement Industry Directory*, annual. • *Asbestos Abatement Regulatory Service*, bimonthly. • *First Biannual Commercial and Industrial Insulation Industry Financial Survey*. • *Outlook*, monthly. • Also publishes *Asbestos Abatement Reference Manual*, *Commercial and Industrial Standards Manual*, *Guide to Insulation Product Specifications*, and self-study manuals on commercial and industrial insulation applications. **Facsimile Number:** (703)549-4838.

Standards/Certification Agencies

Most insulation workers learn their trade informally on the job as helpers to experienced insulation workers. On-the-job training can take up to two years, depending on the work. Trainees in formal apprenticeship programs receive in-depth instruction in all phases of insulation. Apprenticeship programs may be provided by a joint committee of local insulation contractors and the local union of the International Association of Heat and Frost Insulators and Asbestos Workers. Programs normally consist of four years of on-the-job training coupled with classroom instruction, and trainees must pass practical and written tests to demonstrate a knowledge of the trade.

Awards, Scholarships, Grants, and Fellowships

★5097★
David P. Ruppert Award
Insulation Contractors Association of America
15819 Crabbs Branch Way
Rockville, MD 20855　　　　　　Phone: (301)590-0030
For recognition of the year's most significant contribution to the insulation industry. The candidate need not be a member of the Association. A plaque is presented at ICAA's annual convention. Established in 1979 in honor of David P. Ruppert, founder of the Association.

Basic Reference Guides and Handbooks

★5098★
Asbestos Abatement Reference Manual
National Insulation and Abatement Contractors Association (NIAC)
99 Canal Center Plaza, Ste. 222
Alexandria, VA 22314　　　　　　Phone: (703)683-6422

★5099★
Guide to Insulation Product Specifications
National Insulation and Abatement Contractors Association (NIAC)
99 Canal Center Plaza, Ste. 222
Alexandria, VA 22314　　　　　　Phone: (703)683-6422

★5100★
Intelligent Buildings Institute—Directory of Products and Services
Intelligent Buildings Institute (IBI)
2101 L St., NW, Ste. 300
Washington, DC 20037　　　　　　Phone: (202)457-1988
S. Hunt, Associate Executive Director, editor. Annual, September. Member consultants, associations, research organizations, and other suppliers of products and services to the construction and building industry. Entries include: Company name, address, phone. Arrangement: Alphabetical. Indexes: Product/service. **Facsimile Number:** (202)457-8468.

★5101★
Mid-West Contractor—Annual Convention Guide and Association Directory
Allied Publications, Inc.
7355 N. Woodland Dr.
Box 603
Indianapolis, IN 46278　　　　　　Phone: (317)297-5500
Jennifer Wynne, editor. Annual. List of 160 construction contracting and architectural associations in the Midwest. Entries include: Association name, address, phone, names and titles of key personnel, description of association; convention site, date, name and title of contact. Arrangement: Geographical, alphabetical. **Toll-free/Additional Phone Number(s):** (800)827-7468. **Facsimile Number:** (317)299-1356.

★5102★
NIAC Commercial and Industrial Standards Manual

National Insulation and Abatement Contractors Association (NIAC)
99 Canal Center Plaza, Ste. 222
Alexandria, VA 22314   Phone: (703)683-6422

Periodicals

★5103★
ABC Newsline
Associated Builders and Contractors, Inc. (ABC)
729 15th St. NW
Washington, DC 20005   Phone: (202)637-8800

Editor(s): Lisa A. Nardone. Semimonthly. Designed to keep readers alerted to important changes within ABC and the construction industry. Reports on legislative issues, construction trends, conferences and meetings, and ABC services. Recurring features include news of members and a column titled Industry Briefs.

★5104★
American Architectural Manufacturers Association—Quarterly Review
American Architectural Manufacturers Association
1540 E. Dundee Rd., Ste. K 310
Palatine, IL 60067-8321   Phone: (708)202-1350

Editor(s): Tony Coorlim. Annually. Contains industry news on architectural products. Covers prime and combination storm windows, sliding glass and combination storm doors, window and curtain-walls, store fronts and entrances, siding, soffits, fascia, gutters, downspouts, skylights, space enclosures, and mobile home components. Recurring features include news of research, notices of publications available, and announcements by the association. **Facsimile Number:** (708)202-1480.

★5105★
American Institute of Constructors—Newsletter
American Institute of Constructors
9887 Gandy Blvd. N., No. 104
Saint Petersburg, FL 33702-2451

Editor(s): Ed Freedman. Bimonthly. Concerned with construction practice, design, administration, and teaching. Carries news of members, listings of job opportunities, local chapter reports, and notices of new publications. **Facsimile Number:** (614)464-3226.

★5106★
Blue Reports, Inc.
Construction News Service
7325 Steel Mill Dr.
Springfield, VA 22050   Phone: (703)644-5884

Editor(s): Calvin S. Oren. Daily. Reports on public and private construction projects in the Washington, DC, Virginia, and Maryland areas. Provides owner's and architect's names, plan status, date bids due, prospective bidders, low bids received, and specification details. **Facsimile Number:** (703)644-1929.

★5107★
Building Concerns
National Association of Minority Contractors (NAMC)
806 15th St. NW, Ste. 340
Washington, DC 20005   Phone: (202)347-8259

Editor(s): Ralph C. Thomas, III. Monthly. Concentrates on national and regional news regarding minority construction contractors. Contains articles on issues generally affecting the industry—especially issues affecting minorities—including topics such as legislative and regulatory activity and reports on major corporation developments. Recurring features include reports of meetings, news of educational opportunities, a calendar of events, and news of NAMC chapters and members.

★5108★
Building Industry Technology: An Abstract Newsletter
National Technical Information Service (NTIS)
U.S. Department of Commerce
5285 Port Royal Rd.
Springfield, VA 22161   Phone: (703)487-4630

Weekly. Consists of abstracts of reports on architectural and environmental design, building standards, construction materials and equipment, and structural analyses. Recurring features include a form for ordering reports from NTIS.

★5109★
Capital Comments
National Lumber & Building Material Dealers Association
40 Ivy St. SE
Washington, DC 20003   Phone: (202)547-2230

Editor(s): Matt Geitner. Semimonthly. Reports on news of legislation pertaining to lumber, other building materials, and housing. Discusses such issues as lumber subsidies, interest rates on homes, health and safety, and jobs. **Facsimile Number:** (202)547-7640.

★5110★
ConnStruction
PO Box 9768
Wethersfield, CT 06109   Phone: (203)529-3246

Victor Bonini, Editor. 7x/yr. Magazine for construction industry. **Facsimile Number:** (203)563-0616.

★5111★
CONSTRUCTION
26 Long Hill Rd.
Guilford, CT 06437   Phone: (203)453-3717

Jack C. Lewis, Editor and Publisher. 2x/mo. Journal for the construction industry.

★5112★
Construction Dimensions
Assn. of Wall & Ceiling
PO Box 5504
Washington, DC 20016   Phone: (301)656-7050

Gerald Wykoff, Editor. Monthly. Wall and ceiling industry magazine.

★5113★
Construction Industry International
Maclean Hunter Publishing Co.
29 N. Wacker Dr.
Chicago, IL 60606   Phone: (312)726-2802

Alan Elliott, Editor-in-Chief. Monthly. Trade magazine.

★5114★
Construction News
715 W. 2nd St.
PO Box 2421
Little Rock, AR 72203   Phone: (501)376-1931

Robert Alvey, Editor. Weekly. Construction industry magazine. **Facsimile Number:** (501)375-5831.

★5115★
Construction Newsletter
National Safety Council
444 N. Michigan Ave.
Chicago, IL 60611   Phone: (312)527-4800
6/yr. Focuses on industrial and occupational safety in the construction industry. Carries items on such topics as safe work practices and products, accident prevention, and successful industrial safety programs and policies.

★5116★
Contractors Guide
6201 Howard St. W.
Niles, IL 60648   Phone: (708)647-7030
Greg Ettling, Editor. Monthly. Trade magazine covering roofing and insulation. **Facsimile Number:** (708)647-7055.

★5117★
Daily Construction Reporter
4901 Pacific Hwy.
San Diego, CA 92110-4098   Phone: (619)296-0183
Kenneth F. Kerr, Editor and Publisher. Daily. Construction trade newspaper covering jobs that are out for bid, bid results, building permits, and other information. **Facsimile Number:** (619)298-3027.

★5118★
Home BUILDER Magazine
Work-4 Projects Ltd.
PO Box 400, Victoria Sta.
Westmount, PQ, Canada H3Z 2V8   Phone: (514)489-4941
Nachmi Artzy, Editor and Publisher. 6x/yr. Magazine for home construction industry. **Facsimile Number:** (514)489-5505.

★5119★
ICAA News
Insulation Contractors Association of America (ICAA)
15819 Crabbs Branch Way
Rockville, MD 20851   Phone: (301)590-0030
Editor(s): R. Hartley Edes. Monthly. Focuses on the insulation industry, including contracting materials, codes and standards, marketing, legislation, and regulation. Promotes professionalism among insulation contractors and quality industry standards. **Facsimile Number:** (301)590-0713.

★5120★
The Journal of Light Construction
Hanley-Wood Partners
RR 2, Box 146
Richmond, VT 05477-9607   Phone: (802)864-0091
Steve Bliss, Editor. Monthly. Magazine (tabloid) for residential and light professionals involved in new and rehabilitative construction. Each issue covers a single aspect of construction.

★5121★
Nation's Building News
15th & M Sts. NW
Washington, DC 20005   Phone: (202)822-0525
Tim Ahern, Editor. 2x/mo. Trade magazine (tabloid) covering home building and all related industries. **Facsimile Number:** (202)861-2131.

★5122★
NIAC Advisor
National Insulation and Abatement Contractors Association (NIAC)
99 Canal Center Plaza, Ste. 222
Alexandria, VA 22314   Phone: (703)683-6422
Monthly.

★5123★
Outlook
National Insulation and Abatement Contractors Assn.
99 Canal Center Plaza, Ste. 222
Alexandria, VA 22314   Phone: (703)683-6480
Judith J. Zwolok, Editor. Monthly. Official publication of the National Insulation Contractors and Abatement Association. **Facsimile Number:** (703)549-4838.

★5124★
Professional Builder
Cahners Publishing Co.
1350 E. Touhy Ave.
Des Plaines, IL 60018   Phone: (708)635-8800
Roy L. Diez, Editor. 19x/yr. **Facsimile Number:** (708)299-8622.

★5125★
RSI (Roofing/Siding/Insulation)
Edgell Communications, Inc.
7500 Old Oak Blvd.
Cleveland, OH 44130   Phone: (216)243-8100
Mike Russo, Editor. Monthly. Magazine containing technical and applications information on roofing, siding, insulation, and related fields.

★5126★
Walls & Ceilings
LMRector Corp.
8602 N. 40th St.
Tampa, FL 33604   Phone: (813)989-9300
Robert F. Welch, Editor. Monthly. Trade magazine for contractors, suppliers, and distributors of drywall, plaster, stucco, exterior insulation, acoustics, metal framing, and ceilings. **Facsimile Number:** (813)980-3982.

――――― Meetings and Conventions ―――――

★5127★
Insulation Contractors Association of America Convention
Insulation Contractors Association of America
15819 Crabbs Branch Way
Rockville, MD 20855   Phone: (301)590-0030
Frequency: Always held in September. 1992; Sep. **Facsimile Number:** (301)590-0713.

★5128★
National Association of Home Builders/The Builders Show
National Association of Home Builders of the United States
15th and M Sts., NW
Washington, DC 20005   Phone: (202)822-0424
Frequency: Usually held in January; location rotates every three years. 1993; Feb. 19-22; Las Vegas, NV • 1994; Jan. 21-24; Las Vegas, NV. **Toll-free/Additional Phone Number(s):** 800-368-5242. **Facsimile Number:** (202)822-0435.

★5129★
National Insulation and Abatement Contractors Association (NIAC)
99 Canal Center Plaza, Ste. 222
Alexandria, VA 22314   Phone: (703)683-6422
1992; Mar. 20-27; Phoenix, AZ • 1993 Mar.; San Diego, CA. **Facsimile Number:** (703)549-4838.

Other Sources of Information

★5130★
First Biannual Commercial and Industrial Insulation Industry Financial Survey
National Insulation and Abatement Contractors Association (NIAC)
99 Canal Center Plaza, Ste. 222
Alexandria, VA 22314   Phone: (703)683-6422
Industry statistics.

Painters and Paperhangers

Painters apply paint, stain, varnish, and other finishes to buildings and other structures. Paperhangers cover walls and ceilings with decorative wall coverings made of paper, vinyl, or fabric. Many painters and paperhangers work for contractors engaged in new construction, repair, restoration, or remodeling work. In addition, organizations that own or manage large buildings, such as hotels, offices, and apartment complexes, employ maintenance painters, as do some schools, hospitals, and factories. Nearly half of painters and paperhangers are self-employed.

$alaries

Median weekly earnings for painters who are not self-employed are as follows:

Lowest 10 percent	$185.00/week or less
Median	$328.00/week
Top 10 percent	$633.00/week or more

Employment Outlook

Growth rate until the year 2000: Average.

Painters and Paperhangers

Career Guides

★5131★
Big Questions?
National Joint Painting, Decorating and Drywall Apprenticeship and Training Committee
1750 New York Ave., N.W., Lower Level
Washington, DC 20006   Phone: (202)783-7770
This four-page brochure describes requirements, the work, employment opportunities, working conditions, and earnings.

★5132★
"Construction Painter" in *Occu-Facts: Information on 565 Careers in Outline Form* (p. 16.8)
Careers, Inc.
P.O. Box 135
1211 Tenth St., S.W.
Largo, FL 33640   Phone: (813)584-7333
Elizabeth Handville. Biennial, 1989-90 edition. Each one-page occupational profile describes duties, working conditions, physical surroundings and demands, aptitudes, temperament, educational requirements, employment outlook, earnings, and places of employment.

★5133★
Paint and Coatings Industry Workers
Chronicle Guidance Publications, Inc.
PO Box 1190
Moravia, NY 13118-1190   Phone: (315)497-0330
1987. This career brief describes the nature of the work, working conditions, hours and earnings, education and training, licensure, certification, unions, personal qualifications, social and psychological factors, employment outlook, entry methods, advancement, and related occupations. **Toll-free/Additional Phone Number(s):** 800-622-7284.

★5134★
"Painter" in *Exploring Nontraditional Jobs for Women* (pp. 20-25)
Rosen Publishing Group, Inc.
29 E. 21st St.
New York, NY 10010   Phone: (212)777-3017
Rose Neufeld. 1989. Describes blue-collar, male dominated occupations. Discusses what is done on the job, training, where to apply for jobs, tools used, salaries, and advantages and disadvantages. Relates the experiences of women who are working in the field.

★5135★
"Painter and Paperhanger" in *Construction*, Volume 4 of *Career Information Center* (pp. 72-74)
Glencoe/Macmillan
15319 Chatsworth St.
Mission Hills, CA 91345   Phone: (818)898-1391
Richard Lidz and Dale Anderson, editorial directors. Fourth edition, 1990. For 600 occupations, describes job duties, entry-level requirements, education and training needed, advancement possibilities, employment outlook, earnings and benefits. The set is divided into 12 volumes. Each volume includes jobs related under a broad career field. Volume 13 is the index. **Facsimile Number:** 818-365-5489.

★5136★
Painter, Construction
Careers, Inc.
PO Box 135
Largo, FL 34649-0135   Phone: (813)584-7333
1990. Eight-page brief offering the definition, history, duties, working conditions, personal qualifications, educational requirements, earnings, hours, employment outlook, advancement possibilities, and related occupations.

★5137★
"Painters" in *Opportunities in Building Construction Trades* (pp. 35-37)
National Textbook Co.
4255 W. Touhy Ave.
Lincolnwood, IL 60646   Phone: (312)679-5500
Michael Sumichrast. 1989. Gives an overview of the construction industry and describes the jobs of various craftworkers. Covers different kinds of builders: home, custom; and describes management skills needed and industry trends affecting opportunities.

★5138★
"Painters and Paperhangers" in *Occupational Outlook Handbook* (pp. 373-375)
Superintendent of Documents
U.S. Government Printing Office
Washington, DC 20402   Phone: (202)783-3238
Biennial; latest edition, 1990-91. Encyclopedia of careers describing more than 250 occupations and comprising about 86 percent of all jobs in the economy. Occupations that require lengthy education or training are given the most attention. For each occupation, the handbook describes job duties, working conditions, training, educational preparation, personal qualities, advancement possibilities, job outlook, earnings, and sources of additional information.

★5139★
"Painters and Paperhangers" in Volume 4 of *Career Discovery Encyclopedia* (pp. 166-167)
J.G. Ferguson Publishing Co.
200 W. Monroe
Chicago, IL 60606   Phone: (312)580-5480
E. Russell Primm, editor-in-chief. 1990. Contains two-page articles on 504 occupations. Each article describes job duties, earnings, and educational and training requirements.

★5140★
"Painters and Paperhangers" in Volume 3 of *The Encyclopedia of Careers and Vocational Guidance* (pp. 682-685)
J.G. Ferguson Publishing Co.
200 W. Monroe
Chicago, IL 60606   Phone: (312)580-5480
William E. Hopke, editor-in-chief. Eighth edition, 1990. Four-volume set that profiles 500 occupations and describes job trends in 76 industries. Includes career description, educational requirements, history of the job, methods of entry, advancement, employment outlook, earnings, working conditions, social and psychological factors, and sources of additional information.

★5141★
Painters (Construction)
Chronicle Guidance Publications, Inc.
PO Box 1190
Moravia, NY 13118-1190   Phone: (315)497-0330
1988. This career brief describes the nature of the work, working conditions, hours and earnings, education and training, licensure, certification, unions, personal qualifications, social and psychological factors, employment outlook, entry methods, advancement, and related occupations. **Toll-free/Additional Phone Number(s):** 800-622-7284.

★5142★
"Painters" in *The American Almanac of Jobs and Salaries* (p. 502)
Avon Books
105 Madison Avenue
New York, NY 10016   Phone: (212)481-5600
John Wright and Edward J. Dwyer. Revised and updated, 1990. A comprehensive guide to the wages of hundreds of occupations in a wide variety of industries and organizations.

★5143★
Paperhanger
Careers, Inc.
PO Box 135
Largo, FL 34649-0135   Phone: (813)584-7333
1990. Two-page occupational summary card describing duties, working conditions, personal qualifications, training, earnings and hours, employment outlook, places of employment, related careers and where to write for more information.

★5144★
"Paperhanger" in *Occu-Facts: Information on 565 Careers in Outline Form* (p. 16.9)
Careers, Inc.
P.O. Box 135
1211 Tenth St., S.W.
Largo, FL 33640   Phone: (813)584-7333
Elizabeth Handville. Biennial, 1989-90 edition. Each one-page occupational profile describes duties, working conditions, physical surroundings and demands, aptitudes, temperament, educational requirements, employment outlook, earnings, and places of employment.

★5145★
Paperhangers
Chronicle Guidance Publications, Inc.
PO Box 1190
Moravia, NY 13118-1190   Phone: (315)497-0330
1991. This career brief describes the nature of the work, working conditions, hours and earnings, education and training, licensure, certification, unions, personal qualifications, social and psychological factors, employment outlook, entry methods, advancement, and related occupations. **Toll-free/Additional Phone Number(s):** 800-622-7284.

★5146★
"Paperhangers" in *Opportunities in Building Construction Trades* (pp. 37-39)
National Textbook Co.
4255 W. Touhy Ave.
Lincolnwood, IL 60646   Phone: (312)679-5500
Michael Sumichrast. 1989. Gives an overview of the construction industry and describes the jobs of various craftworkers. Covers different kinds of builders: home, custom; and describes management skills needed and industry trends affecting opportunities.

★5147★
Video Career Library - Construction
Careers, Inc.
1211 10th St., SW
PO Box 135
Largo, FL 34649-0135   Phone: (813)584-7333
Videocassette. 1990. 36 mins. Part of the Video Career Library covering 165 occupations. Shows actual workers on the job. Includes millwrights, brickmasons, carpenters, drywall installers, electricians, painters, plumbers and pipefitters, carpenter and soft tile installers, insulation workers, paving equipment operators, and structural metal workers.

★5148★
Wallpaper Hanger
Vocational Biographies, Inc.
PO Box 31, Dept. VF10
Sauk Centre, MN 56378   Phone: (612)352-6516
1990. This pamphlet profiles a person working in the job. Includes information about job duties, working conditions, places of employment, educational preparation, labor market outlook, and salaries. **Toll-free/Additional Phone Number(s):** 800-255-0752.

--- Associations ---

★5149★
Associated Builders and Contractors (ABC)
729 15th St. NW
Washington, DC 20005   Phone: (202)637-8800
Membership: Construction contractors, subcontractors, suppliers, and associates. **Purpose:** Aim is to foster and perpetuate the principles of rewarding shop construction workers and management on the basis of merit. Sponsors leadership conference and management education programs including Wheels of Learning; also sponsors apprenticeship and skill training programs. Disseminates technological and labor relations information. Maintains biographical archives and placement service. Bestows awards; compiles statistics. **Publications:** *ABC Newsline*, semimonthly. • *The Builder and Contractor*, monthly. • *Classified Membership Directory*, annual. • Also publishes safety manuals.

Painters and Paperhangers

★5150★
International Brotherhood of Painters and Allied Trades (IBPAT)
United Unions Bldg.
1750 New York Ave., NW
Washington, DC 20006   Phone: (202)637-0720
Membership: AFL-CIO. **Publications:** *Directory*, annual. • *Painters and Allied Trades Journal*, monthly.

Standards/Certification Agencies

Painting and paperhanging are learned through apprenticeship or informal, on-the-job instruction. Under the direction of experienced workers, helpers assist painters and paperhangers for a period of two to three years. However, few opportunities for informal training exist for paperhangers because most do not have a need for helpers. The apprenticeship program for painters and paperhangers is usually administered by local chapters of the International Brotherhood of Painters and Allied Trades and consists of three years of on-the-job training, in addition to 144 hours of related classroom instruction each year.

Test Guides

★5151★
Foreman Painter
National Learning Corp.
212 Michael Dr.
Syosset, NY 11791   Phone: (516)921-8888
Jack Rudman. Part of the Career Examination Series No. 1. All examination guides in this series contain questions with answers. **Facsimile Number:** (516)921-8743. **Toll-free/Additional Phone Number(s):** 800-645-6337.

★5152★
House Painter
National Learning Corp.
212 Michael Dr.
Syosset, NY 11791   Phone: (516)921-8888
Jack Rudman. Part of the Career Examination Series No. 1. All examination guides in this series contain questions with answers. **Facsimile Number:** (516)921-8743. **Toll-free/Additional Phone Number(s):** 800-645-6337.

★5153★
Maintenance Worker/Mechanical Maintainer
Prentice Hall Press
Simon & Schuster Inc.
200 Old Tappan Rd.
Old Tappan, NJ 07675   Phone: (800)223-2348
Hy Hammer. Fourth edition, 1984. Provides information for applicants interested in the following civil service positions: carpenter, mason, plumber, electrician, painter, machinist. Includes eight sample tests.

★5154★
Painter
National Learning Corp.
212 Michael Dr.
Syosset, NY 11791   Phone: (516)921-8888
Jack Rudman. Part of the Career Examination Series No. 1. All examination guides in this series contain questions with answers. **Facsimile Number:** (516)921-8743. **Toll-free/Additional Phone Number(s):** 800-645-6337.

Awards, Scholarships, Grants, and Fellowships

★5155★
"Picture It Painted Professionally" Contest
National Paint and Coatings Association
c/o Katrina L. Norfleet
1500 Rhode Island Ave., N.W.
Washington, DC 20005   Phone: (202)462-6272
To recognize professional painting contractors nationwide for their creative use of paint in residential, commercial and industrial settings. Members of the Painting and Decorating Contractors of America are eligible. A plaque and a certificate are awarded annually.

Basic Reference Guides and Handbooks

★5156★
IBPAT Directory
International Brotherhood of Painters and Allied Trades (IBPAT)
United Unions Bldg.
1750 New York Ave., NW
Washington, DC 20006   Phone: (202)637-0720
Annual.

★5157★
Painters' Equipment & Supplies Directory
American Business Directories, Inc.
American Business Information, Inc.
5711 S. 86th Circle
Omaha, NE 68127   Phone: (402)593-4600
Annual. Entries include: Name, address, phone, size of advertisement, name of owner or manager, number of employees, year first in "Yellow Pages." Arrangement: Geographical. **Facsimile Number:** (402)331-1505.

Periodicals

★5158★
ABC Newsline
Associated Builders and Contractors, Inc. (ABC)
729 15th St. NW
Washington, DC 20005   Phone: (202)637-8800
Editor(s): Lisa A. Nardone. Semimonthly. Designed to keep readers alerted to important changes within ABC and the construction industry. Reports on legislative issues, construction trends, conferences and meetings, and ABC services. Recurring features include news of members and a column titled Industry Briefs.

★5159★
American Architectural Manufacturers Association—Quarterly Review
American Architectural Manufacturers Association
1540 E. Dundee Rd., Ste. K 310
Palatine, IL 60067-8321   Phone: (708)202-1350
Editor(s): Tony Coorlim. Annually. Contains industry news on architectural products. Covers prime and combination storm windows, sliding glass and combination storm doors, window and curtain-walls, store fronts and entrances, siding, soffits, fascia, gutters, downspouts, skylights, space enclosures, and

mobile home components. Recurring features include news of research, notices of publications available, and announcements by the association. **Facsimile Number:** (708)202-1480.

★5160★
American Institute of Constructors—Newsletter
American Institute of Constructors
9887 Gandy Blvd. N., No. 104
Saint Petersburg, FL 33702-2451

Editor(s): Ed Freedman. Bimonthly. Concerned with construction practice, design, administration, and teaching. Carries news of members, listings of job opportunities, local chapter reports, and notices of new publications. **Facsimile Number:** (614)464-3226.

★5161★
American Painting Contractor
American Paint Journal Co.
2911 Washington Ave.
Saint Louis, MO 63103   Phone: (314)534-0301

Paul Stoecklein, Editor. Monthly. Magazine serving paint and wallcovering contractors and in-house maintenance crews. **Facsimile Number:** (314)534-4458.

★5162★
Blue Reports, Inc.
Construction News Service
7325 Steel Mill Dr.
Springfield, VA 22050   Phone: (703)644-5884

Editor(s): Calvin S. Oren. Daily. Reports on public and private construction projects in the Washington, DC, Virginia, and Maryland areas. Provides owner's and architect's names, plan status, date bids due, prospective bidders, low bids received, and specification details. **Facsimile Number:** (703)644-1929.

★5163★
The Builder and Contractor
Associated Builders and Contractors (ABC)
729 15th St. NW
Washington, DC 20005   Phone: (202)637-8800
Monthly.

★5164★
Building Concerns
National Association of Minority Contractors (NAMC)
806 15th St. NW, Ste. 340
Washington, DC 20005   Phone: (202)347-8259

Editor(s): Ralph C. Thomas, III. Monthly. Concentrates on national and regional news regarding minority construction contractors. Contains articles on issues generally affecting the industry—especially issues affecting minorities—including topics such as legislative and regulatory activity and reports on major corporation developments. Recurring features include reports of meetings, news of educational opportunities, a calendar of events, and news of NAMC chapters and members.

★5165★
Building Industry Technology: An Abstract Newsletter
National Technical Information Service (NTIS)
U.S. Department of Commerce
5285 Port Royal Rd.
Springfield, VA 22161   Phone: (703)487-4630

Weekly. Consists of abstracts of reports on architectural and environmental design, building standards, construction materials and equipment, and structural analyses. Recurring features include a form for ordering reports from NTIS.

★5166★
Building Renovation
Maclean Hunter Ltd.
777 Bay St.
Toronto, ON, Canada M5W 1A7   Phone: (416)596-5760

John Fennell, Editor. 6x/yr. Business magazine for professionals in residential and commercial renovation and remodeling. **Facsimile Number:** (416)596-5810.

★5167★
Capital Comments
National Lumber & Building Material Dealers Association
40 Ivy St. SE
Washington, DC 20003   Phone: (202)547-2230

Editor(s): Matt Geitner. Semimonthly. Reports on news of legislation pertaining to lumber, other building materials, and housing. Discusses such issues as lumber subsidies, interest rates on homes, health and safety, and jobs. **Facsimile Number:** (202)547-7640.

★5168★
ConnStruction
PO Box 9768
Wethersfield, CT 06109   Phone: (203)529-3246

Victor Bonini, Editor. 7x/yr. Magazine for construction industry. **Facsimile Number:** (203)563-0616.

★5169★
CONSTRUCTION
26 Long Hill Rd.
Guilford, CT 06437   Phone: (203)453-3717

Jack C. Lewis, Editor and Publisher. 2x/mo. Journal for the construction industry.

★5170★
Construction Dimensions
Assn. of Wall & Ceiling
PO Box 5504
Washington, DC 20016   Phone: (301)656-7050

Gerald Wykoff, Editor. Monthly. Wall and ceiling industry magazine.

★5171★
Construction Industry International
Maclean Hunter Publishing Co.
29 N. Wacker Dr.
Chicago, IL 60606   Phone: (312)726-2802

Alan Elliott, Editor-in-Chief. Monthly. Trade magazine.

★5172★
Construction News
715 W. 2nd St.
PO Box 2421
Little Rock, AR 72203   Phone: (501)376-1931

Robert Alvey, Editor. Weekly. Construction industry magazine. **Facsimile Number:** (501)375-5831.

★5173★
Construction Newsletter
National Safety Council
444 N. Michigan Ave.
Chicago, IL 60611   Phone: (312)527-4800

6/yr. Focuses on industrial and occupational safety in the construction industry. Carries items on such topics as safe work practices and products, accident prevention, and successful industrial safety programs and policies.

Painters and Paperhangers

★5174★
Daily Construction Reporter
4901 Pacific Hwy.
San Diego, CA 92110-4098   Phone: (619)296-0183
Kenneth F. Kerr, Editor and Publisher. Daily. Construction trade newspaper covering jobs that are out for bid, bid results, building permits, and other information. **Facsimile Number:** (619)298-3027.

★5175★
Home BUILDER Magazine
Work-4 Projects Ltd.
PO Box 400, Victoria Sta.
Westmount, PQ, Canada H3Z 2V8   Phone: (514)489-4941
Nachmi Artzy, Editor and Publisher. 6x/yr. Magazine for home construction industry. **Facsimile Number:** (514)489-5505.

★5176★
Interior Construction
Ceilings and Interior Systems Construction Assn.
104 Wilmot, Ste. 201
Deerfield, IL 60015-5195   Phone: (708)940-8800
Sheila Wertz, Editor. 7x/yr. Magazine covering interior finish construction. **Facsimile Number:** (708)940-7218.

★5177★
The Journal of Light Construction
Hanley-Wood Partners
RR 2, Box 146
Richmond, VT 05477-9607   Phone: (802)864-0091
Steve Bliss, Editor. Monthly. Magazine (tabloid) for residential and light professionals involved in new and rehabilitative construction. Each issue covers a single aspect of construction.

★5178★
Nation's Building News
15th & M Sts. NW
Washington, DC 20005   Phone: (202)822-0525
Tim Ahern, Editor. 2x/mo. Trade magazine (tabloid) covering home building and all related industries. **Facsimile Number:** (202)861-2131.

★5179★
Painters and Allied Trades Journal
International Brotherhood of Painters and Allied Trades (IBPAT)
United Unions Bldg.
1750 New York Ave., NW
Washington, DC 20006   Phone: (202)637-0720
Monthly.

★5180★
Painting & Wallcovering Contractor
Finan Publishing Co., Inc.
8730 Big Bend Blvd.
Saint Louis, MO 63119   Phone: (314)961-6644
Jeffery Beckner, Editor. 6x/yr. Magazine covering painting and decorating industry-current research; new trends in techniques and products; and commerical, industrial, institutional, and residential application. **Facsimile Number:** (314)961-4809.

★5181★
Professional Builder
Cahners Publishing Co.
1350 E. Touhy Ave.
Des Plaines, IL 60018   Phone: (708)635-8800
Roy L. Diez, Editor. 19x/yr. **Facsimile Number:** (708)299-8622.

Meetings and Conventions

★5182★
Associated Builders and Contractors (ABC)
729 15th St. NW
Washington, DC 20005   Phone: (202)637-8800
Frequency: Annual.

★5183★
International Brotherhood of Painters and Allied Trades (IBPAT)
United Unions Bldg.
1750 New York Ave., NW
Washington, DC 20006   Phone: (202)637-0720
Frequency: Quinquennial - next held in 1994.

★5184★
National Association of Home Builders/The Builders Show
National Association of Home Builders of the United States
15th and M Sts., NW
Washington, DC 20005   Phone: (202)822-0424
Frequency: Usually held in January; location rotates every three years. 1993; Feb. 19-22; Las Vegas, NV • 1994; Jan. 21-24; Las Vegas, NV. **Toll-free/Additional Phone Number(s):** 800-368-5242. **Facsimile Number:** (202)822-0435.

★5185★
National Guild of Professional Paperhangers Convention
National Guild of Professional Paperhangers
2626 Radcliffe Rd.
Broomall, PA 19008   Phone: (215)353-0300
1992.

★5186★
National Society of Tole and Decorative Painters Annual Meeting and Convention
National Society of Tole and Decorative Painters
PO Box 808
Newton, KS 67114   Phone: (316)283-9665
1992.

★5187★
Paint and Paper Pro Show
Painting and Decorating Contractors of America
3913 Old Lee Hwy., Ste. 33B
Fairfax, VA 22030   Phone: (703)359-0826
1992. **Facsimile Number:** (703)359-2576.

★5188★
Painting and Decorating Contractors of America National Convention and Trade Show
Painting and Decorating Contractors of America
3913 Old Lee Hwy., Ste. 33B
Fairfax, VA 22030   Phone: (703)359-0826
1992; Las Vegas, NV • 1993; Orlando, FL • 1994; Nashville, TN. **Facsimile Number:** (703)359-2576.

Plasterers

Plasterers finish interior walls and ceilings with plaster materials that form fire-resistant and relatively soundproof surfaces. They also apply durable cement plasters, polymer-based acrylic finishes, and stucco to exterior surfaces, and may cast ornamental designs in plaster. Increasingly today, plasterers apply insulation to the exteriors of new and old buildings. Most plasterers work on new construction, particularly where special architectural and lighting effects are part of the work. Some repair and renovate older buildings. Most plasterers work for independent contractors; a small percentage are self-employed.

$alaries

Median hourly earnings for plasterers who belong to a union are $21.98/hour. Apprentice wage rates start at about half the rate paid to experienced plasterers.

Employment Outlook

Growth rate until the year 2000: More slowly than average.

Plasterers

Career Guides

★5189★
Construction Cluster
Center for Humanities, Inc.
Communications Park
Box 1000
Mount Kisco, NY 10549　　　Phone: (914)666-4100
Videocassette. 1984. 15 mins. Construction workers describe what it's like to work at their jobs, and show the special equipment they use in their field.

★5190★
Plasterer
Careers, Inc.
PO Box 135
Largo, FL 34649-0135　　　Phone: (813)584-7333
1991. Two-page occupational summary card describing duties, working conditions, personal qualifications, training, earnings and hours, employment outlook, places of employment, related careers and where to write for more information.

★5191★
"Plasterer" in *Construction*, Volume 4 of *Career Information Center* (pp. 74-76)
Glencoe/Macmillan
15319 Chatsworth St.
Mission Hills, CA 91345　　　Phone: (818)898-1391
Richard Lidz and Dale Anderson, editorial directors. Fourth edition, 1990. For 600 occupations, describes job duties, entry-level requirements, education and training needed, advancement possibilities, employment outlook, earnings and benefits. The set is divided into 12 volumes. Each volume includes jobs related under a broad career field. Volume 13 is the index. **Facsimile Number:** 818-365-5489.

★5192★
"Plasterer" in *Occu-Facts: Information on 565 Careers in Outline Form* (p. 16.10)
Careers, Inc.
P.O. Box 135
1211 Tenth St., S.W.
Largo, FL 33640　　　Phone: (813)584-7333
Elizabeth Handville. Biennial, 1989-90 edition. Each one-page occupational profile describes duties, working conditions, physical surroundings and demands, aptitudes, temperament, educational requirements, employment outlook, earnings, and places of employment.

★5193★
Plasterers
Chronicle Guidance Publications, Inc.
PO Box 1190
Moravia, NY 13118-1190　　　Phone: (315)497-0330
1987. This career brief describes the nature of the work, working conditions, hours and earnings, education and training, licensure, certification, unions, personal qualifications, social and psychological factors, employment outlook, entry methods, advancement, and related occupations. **Toll-free/Additional Phone Number(s):** 800-622-7284.

★5194★
"Plasterers" in *Occupational Outlook Handbook* (pp. 375-376)
Superintendent of Documents
U.S. Government Printing Office
Washington, DC 20402　　　Phone: (202)783-3238
Biennial; latest edition, 1990-91. Encyclopedia of careers describing more than 250 occupations and comprising about 86 percent of all jobs in the economy. Occupations that require lengthy education or training are given the most attention. For each occupation, the handbook describes job duties, working conditions, training, educational preparation, personal qualities, advancement possibilities, job outlook, earnings, and sources of additional information.

★5195★
"Plasterers" in *Opportunities in Building Construction Trades* (pp. 39-41)
National Textbook Co.
4255 W. Touhy Ave.
Lincolnwood, IL 60646　　　Phone: (312)679-5500
Michael Sumichrast. 1989. Gives an overview of the construction industry and describes the jobs of various craftworkers. Covers different kinds of builders: home, custom; and describes management skills needed and industry trends affecting opportunities.

★5196★
"Plasterers" in Volume 5 of *Career Discovery Encyclopedia* (pp. 58-59)
J.G. Ferguson Publishing Co.
200 W. Monroe
Chicago, IL 60606　　　Phone: (312)580-5480
E. Russell Primm, editor-in-chief. 1990. Contains two-page articles on 504 occupations. Each article describes job duties, earnings, and educational and training requirements.

★5197★
"Plasterers" in Volume 3 of *The Encyclopedia of Careers and Vocational Guidance* (pp. 690-692)
J.G. Ferguson Publishing Co.
200 W. Monroe
Chicago, IL 60606 Phone: (312)580-5480
William E. Hopke, editor-in-chief. Eighth edition, 1990. Four-volume set that profiles 500 occupations and describes job trends in 76 industries. Includes career description, educational requirements, history of the job, methods of entry, advancement, employment outlook, earnings, working conditions, social and psychological factors, and sources of additional information.

★5198★
"Plasterers" in *The American Almanac of Jobs and Salaries* (p. 502)
Avon Books
105 Madison Avenue
New York, NY 10016 Phone: (212)481-5600
John Wright and Edward J. Dwyer. Revised and updated, 1990. A comprehensive guide to the wages of hundreds of occupations in a wide variety of industries and organizations.

★5199★
The Trowel Trades
International Masonry Institute
823 15th St. NW, Ste. 1001
Washington, DC 20005 Phone: (202)783-3908
This six-panel brochure describes skills, advancement opportunities, and apprentice training.

Associations

★5200★
International Union of Bricklayers and Allied Craftsmen (BAC)
815 15th St., NW
Washington, DC 20005 Phone: (202)783-3788
Membership: AFL-CIO. **Publications:** *Chalkline*, periodic. • *Journal*, monthly. **Facsimile Number:** (202)393-0219.

★5201★
Operative Plasterers and Cement Masons International Association of U.S. and Canada (OPCMIA)
1125 17th St., NW
Washington, DC 20036 Phone: (202)393-6569
Membership: AFL-CIO. **Publications:** *Plasterer and Cement Mason*, monthly.

Standards/Certification Agencies

Many plasterers learn the trade informally by working as helpers to experienced plasterers. Most employers, however, recommend apprenticeship as the best way to learn plastering. Apprenticeship programs, sponsored by local joint committees of contractors and local chapters of the Operative Plasterers' and Cement Masons' International Association of the United States and Canada, or the International Union of Bricklayers and Allied Craftsmen, generally consist of two to three years of on-the-job training, in addition to at least 144 hours annually of classroom instruction. Some apprenticeship programs also allow individuals to obtain training in related occupations such as cement masonry and bricklaying.

Test Guides

★5202★
Foreman Plasterer
National Learning Corp.
212 Michael Dr.
Syosset, NY 11791 Phone: (516)921-8888
Jack Rudman. Part of the Career Examination Series No. 1. All examination guides in this series contain questions with answers. **Facsimile Number:** (516)921-8743. **Toll-free/Additional Phone Number(s):** 800-645-6337.

★5203★
Plasterer
National Learning Corp.
212 Michael Dr.
Syosset, NY 11791 Phone: (516)921-8888
Jack Rudman. Part of the Career Examination Series No. 1. All examination guides in this series contain questions with answers. **Facsimile Number:** (516)921-8743. **Toll-free/Additional Phone Number(s):** 800-645-6337.

Basic Reference Guides and Handbooks

★5204★
Plastering: A Craftman's Encyclopedia
Blackwell Scientific Publications
3 Cambridge Center, Ste. 208
Cambridge, MA 02142 Phone: (617)225-0401
Don W. Stagg. Second edition, 1989. **Facsimile Number:** (617)225-0412.

Periodicals

★5205★
ABC Newsline
Associated Builders and Contractors, Inc. (ABC)
729 15th St. NW
Washington, DC 20005 Phone: (202)637-8800
Editor(s): Lisa A. Nardone. Semimonthly. Designed to keep readers alerted to important changes within ABC and the construction industry. Reports on legislative issues, construction trends, conferences and meetings, and ABC services. Recurring features include news of members and a column titled Industry Briefs.

★5206★
American Architectural Manufacturers Association—Quarterly Review
American Architectural Manufacturers Association
1540 E. Dundee Rd., Ste. K 310
Palatine, IL 60067-8321 Phone: (708)202-1350
Editor(s): Tony Coorlim. Annually. Contains industry news on architectural products. Covers prime and combination storm windows, sliding glass and combination storm doors, window and curtain-walls, store fronts and entrances, siding, soffits, fascia, gutters, downspouts, skylights, space enclosures, and mobile home components. Recurring features include news of research, notices of publications available, and announcements by the association. **Facsimile Number:** (708)202-1480.

★5207★
American Institute of Constructors—Newsletter
American Institute of Constructors
9887 Gandy Blvd. N., No. 104
Saint Petersburg, FL 33702-2451

Editor(s): Ed Freedman. Bimonthly. Concerned with construction practice, design, administration, and teaching. Carries news of members, listings of job opportunities, local chapter reports, and notices of new publications. **Facsimile Number:** (614)464-3226.

★5208★
BAC Journal
International Union of Bricklayers and Allied Craftsmen (BAC)
815 15th St., NW
Washington, DC 20005   Phone: (202)783-3788
Monthly.

★5209★
Blue Reports, Inc.
Construction News Service
7325 Steel Mill Dr.
Springfield, VA 22050   Phone: (703)644-5884

Editor(s): Calvin S. Oren. Daily. Reports on public and private construction projects in the Washington, DC, Virginia, and Maryland areas. Provides owner's and architect's names, plan status, date bids due, prospective bidders, low bids received, and specification details. **Facsimile Number:** (703)644-1929.

★5210★
Builder
Hanley-Wood, Inc.
655 15th St. NW, Ste. 475
Washington, DC 20005   Phone: (202)737-0717

Mitchell Rouda, Editor. Monthly. Magazine covering housing, commercial, and industrial building. **Facsimile Number:** (202)737-2439.

★5211★
Builder and Contractor
Associated Builders and Contractors, Inc.
729 15th St. NW
Washington, DC 20005   Phone: (202)637-8800

Susan Schindler, Mng. Editor. Monthly. Magazine for open shop contractors and subcontractors. Includes articles on national and regional construction news, construction management, project case histories, new products, and building design.

★5212★
Builder Architect
Sunshine Media, Inc.
7500 N. Dreamy Draw, Ste. 111
PO Box 9400
Phoenix, AZ 85068   Phone: (602)943-3575

Marie Vere, Editor. Monthly. Home builders magazine. **Facsimile Number:** (602)371-0241.

★5213★
Builder/Dealer
Peterson Bros. Inc., Publishing
16 1st Ave.
Corry, PA 16407-1894   Phone: (814)664-8624

Charles P. Mancino, Publisher. Monthly. Trade magazine. **Facsimile Number:** (814)664-8506.

★5214★
Builder Insider
Divibest, Inc.
PO Box 191125
Dallas, TX 75219   Phone: (214)871-2913

Michael J. Anderson, Editor and Publisher. Monthly. Magazine (tabloid) for builders, architects, and remodelers.

★5215★
Building Business & Management
Builders Assn. of Southeastern Michigan
30375 Northwestern Hwy.
Farmington Hills, MI 48334   Phone: (313)737-4477

Kathleen M. Eischeid, Editor. Monthly. Construction and apartment industry magazine. **Facsimile Number:** (313)737-5741.

★5216★
Building Concerns
National Association of Minority Contractors (NAMC)
806 15th St. NW, Ste. 340
Washington, DC 20005   Phone: (202)347-8259

Editor(s): Ralph C. Thomas, III. Monthly. Concentrates on national and regional news regarding minority construction contractors. Contains articles on issues generally affecting the industry—especially issues affecting minorities—including topics such as legislative and regulatory activity and reports on major corporation developments. Recurring features include reports of meetings, news of educational opportunities, a calendar of events, and news of NAMC chapters and members.

★5217★
Building Design & Construction
Cahners Publishing Co.
1350 E. Touhy Ave.
PO Box 5080
Des Plaines, IL 60018   Phone: (708)635-8800

Philip G. Schreiner, Editor. Monthly. Magazine on business and technology for commercial, institutional, and industrial buildings. **Facsimile Number:** (708)299-8622.

★5218★
Building Homes & Renovations
Southam Business & Communications, Inc.
1450 Don Mills Rd.
Don Mills, ON, Canada M3B 2X7   Phone: (416)445-6641

Randy Threndyle, Editor. 5x/yr. Building trade and products magazine. **Facsimile Number:** (416)442-2214.

★5219★
Building Industry
Trade Publishing Co.
287 Mokauea St.
Honolulu, HI 96819   Phone: (808)848-0711

Jay McWilliams, Editor. Monthly. Construction and design magazine. **Facsimile Number:** (808)841-3053.

★5220★
Building Industry Technology: An Abstract Newsletter
National Technical Information Service (NTIS)
U.S. Department of Commerce
5285 Port Royal Rd.
Springfield, VA 22161   Phone: (703)487-4630

Weekly. Consists of abstracts of reports on architectural and environmental design, building standards, construction materials and equipment, and structural analyses. Recurring features include a form for ordering reports from NTIS.

★5221★
Buildings
427 6th Ave. SE
PO Box 1888
Cedar Rapids, IA 52406 Phone: (319)364-6167
Linda Monroe, Editor. Monthly. **Facsimile Number:** (319)365-5421.

★5222★
Capital Comments
National Lumber & Building Material Dealers Association
40 Ivy St. SE
Washington, DC 20003 Phone: (202)547-2230
Editor(s): Matt Geitner. Semimonthly. Reports on news of legislation pertaining to lumber, other building materials, and housing. Discusses such issues as lumber subsidies, interest rates on homes, health and safety, and jobs. **Facsimile Number:** (202)547-7640.

★5223★
Chalkline
International Union of Bricklayers and Allied Craftsmen (BAC)
815 15th St., NW
Washington, DC 20005 Phone: (202)783-3788
Periodic.

★5224★
ConnStruction
PO Box 9768
Wethersfield, CT 06109 Phone: (203)529-3246
Victor Bonini, Editor. 7x/yr. Magazine for construction industry. **Facsimile Number:** (203)563-0616.

★5225★
CONSTRUCTION
26 Long Hill Rd.
Guilford, CT 06437 Phone: (203)453-3717
Jack C. Lewis, Editor and Publisher. 2x/mo. Journal for the construction industry.

★5226★
Construction Dimensions
Assn. of Wall & Ceiling
PO Box 5504
Washington, DC 20016 Phone: (301)656-7050
Gerald Wykoff, Editor. Monthly. Wall and ceiling industry magazine.

★5227★
Construction Industry International
Maclean Hunter Publishing Co.
29 N. Wacker Dr.
Chicago, IL 60606 Phone: (312)726-2802
Alan Elliott, Editor-in-Chief. Monthly. Trade magazine.

★5228★
Construction News
715 W. 2nd St.
PO Box 2421
Little Rock, AR 72203 Phone: (501)376-1931
Robert Alvey, Editor. Weekly. Construction industry magazine. **Facsimile Number:** (501)375-5831.

★5229★
Construction Newsletter
National Safety Council
444 N. Michigan Ave.
Chicago, IL 60611 Phone: (312)527-4800
6/yr. Focuses on industrial and occupational safety in the construction industry. Carries items on such topics as safe work practices and products, accident prevention, and successful industrial safety programs and policies.

★5230★
Daily Construction Reporter
4901 Pacific Hwy.
San Diego, CA 92110-4098 Phone: (619)296-0183
Kenneth F. Kerr, Editor and Publisher. Daily. Construction trade newspaper covering jobs that are out for bid, bid results, building permits, and other information. **Facsimile Number:** (619)298-3027.

★5231★
Fine Homebuilding
The Taunton Press, Inc.
63 S. Main St.
PO Box 5506
Newtown, CT 06470 Phone: (203)426-5506
Mark Feirer, Editor. 7x/yr. Magazine for builders, architects, designers, and owner-builders. **Facsimile Number:** (203)426-3434.

★5232★
Home BUILDER Magazine
Work-4 Projects Ltd.
PO Box 400, Victoria Sta.
Westmount, PQ, Canada H3Z 2V8 Phone: (514)489-4941
Nachmi Artzy, Editor and Publisher. 6x/yr. Magazine for home construction industry. **Facsimile Number:** (514)489-5505.

★5233★
The Journal of Light Construction
Hanley-Wood Partners
RR 2, Box 146
Richmond, VT 05477-9607 Phone: (802)864-0091
Steve Bliss, Editor. Monthly. Magazine (tabloid) for residential and light professionals involved in new and rehabilitative construction. Each issue covers a single aspect of construction.

★5234★
Nation's Building News
15th & M Sts. NW
Washington, DC 20005 Phone: (202)822-0525
Tim Ahern, Editor. 2x/mo. Trade magazine (tabloid) covering home building and all related industries. **Facsimile Number:** (202)861-2131.

★5235★
Professional Builder
Cahners Publishing Co.
1350 E. Touhy Ave.
Des Plaines, IL 60018 Phone: (708)635-8800
Roy L. Diez, Editor. 19x/yr. **Facsimile Number:** (708)299-8622.

★5236★
The SPEC-DATA Program
Construction Specifications Institute
601 Madison St.
Alexandria, VA 22314 Phone: (703)684-0300
Brenda A. Furiga, Mgr. Quarterly. Magazine (loose-leaf) for the construction industry covering technical and product information. **Facsimile Number:** (703)684-0465.

Plasterers

★5237★
Walls & Ceilings
LMRector Corp.
8602 N. 40th St.
Tampa, FL 33604　　　　　　Phone: (813)989-9300

Robert F. Welch, Editor. Monthly. Trade magazine for contractors, suppliers, and distributors of drywall, plaster, stucco, exterior insulation, acoustics, metal framing, and ceilings. **Facsimile Number:** (813)980-3982.

Meetings and Conventions

★5238★
National Association of Home Builders/The Builders Show
National Association of Home Builders of the United States
15th and M Sts., NW
Washington, DC 20005　　　　　　Phone: (202)822-0424

Frequency: Usually held in January; location rotates every three years. 1993; Feb. 19-22; Las Vegas, NV ● 1994; Jan. 21-24; Las Vegas, NV. **Toll-free/Additional Phone Number(s):** 800-368-5242. **Facsimile Number:** (202)822-0435.

★5239★
Operative Plasterers and Cement Masons International Association of U.S. and Canada (OPCMIA)
1125 17th St., NW
Washington, DC 20036　　　　　　Phone: (202)393-6569

Frequency: Quinquennial - next 1994.

★5240★
Western Lath/Plaster/Drywall Industries Association Annual Convention
Western Lath/Plaster/Drywall Industries Association
8635 Navajo Rd.
San Diego, CA 92119　　　　　　Phone: (619)466-9070

1992; Oct. 07-11; Reno, NV ● 1993; Sep. 22-26; Phoenix, AZ ● 1994; Sep. 28-01; Reno, NV. **Facsimile Number:** (619)466-9149.

Plumbers and Pipefitters

Plumbers install and repair the water, waste disposal, drainage, and gas systems in homes and commercial and industrial buildings. They also install plumbing fixtures, such as bathtubs, sinks, and toilets, and appliances such as dishwashers and water heaters. Pipefitters install and repair both high- and low-pressure pipe systems that are used in manufacturing, in the generation of electricity, and in heating and cooling buildings. Some pipefitters specialize in only one type of system. Steamfitters, for example, install pipe systems that move liquids or gases under high pressure. Sprinklerfitters install automatic fire sprinkler systems in buildings. Most plumbers and pipefitters work for mechanical and plumbing contractors engaged in new construction, repair, modernization, or maintenance work. Others do maintenance work for a variety of industrial, commercial, and government employers, such as the petroleum and chemical industries. Only 20 percent of all plumbers and pipefitters are self-employed.

$alaries

Median weekly earnings for plumbers and pipefitters are as follows:

Lowest 10 percent	$248.00/week or less
Median	$461.00/week
Top 10 percent	$787.00/week or more

Employment Outlook

Growth rate until the year 2000: Average.

Plumbers and Pipefitters

Career Guides

★5241★
Career Insights
RMI Media Productions, Inc.
2807 West 47th St.
Shawnee Mission, KS 66205 Phone: (913)262-3974
Videocassette series. 1987. This videotape series describes 50 occupations, including skill requirements and interviews with people employed in these fields. Occupations include: flight service, air transportation/ground services, data processing, carpentry, clerk in banking/insurance/business, cosmetic personal grooming, firefighting, roofing, material handling, photographic processing, plumbing, secretarial services, tool and die operations.

★5242★
Career Opportunities in the Fire Sprinkler Industry
National Fire Sprinkler Association, Inc.
Robin Hill Corporate Park
Route 22
PO Box 1000
Patterson, NY 12563 Phone: (914)878-4200
1991. This eight-page booklet describes the industry, training, earnings, and certification.

★5243★
Career Success Series
Cambridge Career Products
90 MacCorkle Ave., SW
South Charleston, WV 25311 Phone: (304)744-9323
Videocassette. 1986. 15 mins. A series, available separately, outlining various career choices for students. Occupations include: flight service, air transportation/ground service, data processing, carpentry, clerk in banking/insurance, commodity sales, cosmetic personal grooming, fire fighting, forestry services, home economics, insulation/roofing, material handling, mechanics, photographic processing, pipefitting and plumbing, police science, printing, secretarial services, and utilities equipment operator.

★5244★
Construction: Basic Principles
RMI Media Productions, Inc.
2807 West 47th St.
Shawnee Mission, KS 66205 Phone: (913)262-3974
Videocassette. 1984. 20 mins. This series of five programs of varying lengths covers different aspects of career opportunities in the construction trades. Included are: concrete masonry, carpentry, electrical work, plumbing, and heating and air conditioning.

★5245★
Construction Cluster
Center for Humanities, Inc.
Communications Park
Box 1000
Mount Kisco, NY 10549 Phone: (914)666-4100
Videocassette. 1984. 15 mins. Construction workers describe what it's like to work at their jobs, and show the special equipment they use in their field.

★5246★
Getting Down to Business: Plumbing Business
American Institutes for Research
PO Box 11131
Palo Alto, CA 94302 Phone: (415)493-3550
Barbara Sanderson. **Facsimile Number:** (415)858-0958.

★5247★
Pipe Fitters and Steam Fitters
Chronicle Guidance Publications, Inc.
PO Box 1190
Moravia, NY 13118-1190 Phone: (315)497-0330
1988. This career brief describes the nature of the work, working conditions, hours and earnings, education and training, licensure, certification, unions, personal qualifications, social and psychological factors, employment outlook, entry methods, advancement, and related occupations. **Toll-free/Additional Phone Number(s):** 800-622-7284.

★5248★
"Pipe Fitters and Steam Fitters" in Volume 3 of *The Encyclopedia of Careers and Vocational Guidance* (pp. 686-689)
J.G. Ferguson Publishing Co.
200 W. Monroe
Chicago, IL 60606 Phone: (312)580-5480
William E. Hopke, editor-in-chief. Eighth edition, 1990. Four-volume set that profiles 500 occupations and describes job trends in 76 industries. Includes career description, educational requirements, history of the job, methods of entry, advancement, employment outlook, earnings, working conditions, social and psychological factors, and sources of additional information.

★5249★
"Pipefitters and Steamfitters" in Volume 5 of *Career Discovery Encyclopedia* (pp. 54-55)
J.G. Ferguson Publishing Co.
200 W. Monroe
Chicago, IL 60606   Phone: (312)580-5480
E. Russell Primm, editor-in-chief. 1990. Contains two-page articles on 504 occupations. Each article describes job duties, earnings, and educational and training requirements.

★5250★
Pipefitting and Plumbing
Morris Video
2730 Monterey St. #105
Monterey Business Park
Torrance, CA 90503   Phone: (213)533-4800
Videocassette. 1983. 15 mins. A look at the many fields to which plumbing may be applied.

★5251★
Plumber
Vocational Biographies, Inc.
PO Box 31, Dept. VF10
Sauk Centre, MN 56378   Phone: (612)352-6516
1990. This pamphlet profiles a person working in the job. Includes information about job duties, working conditions, places of employment, educational preparation, labor market outlook, and salaries. **Toll-free/Additional Phone Number(s):** 800-255-0752.

★5252★
"Plumber" in *Guide to Careers Without College* (pp. 82-85)
Franklin Watts, Inc.
387 Park Avenue, S.
New York, NY 10016   Phone: (212)686-7070
Kathleen S. Abrams. 1988. Discusses careers that do not require a college degree in fields such as health care, sales and marketing, and the building trades. Describes the work, employment opportunities, and training.

★5253★
"Plumber and Pipe Fitter" in *Construction*, Volume 4 of *Career Information Center* (pp. 76-78)
Glencoe/Macmillan
15319 Chatsworth St.
Mission Hills, CA 91345   Phone: (818)898-1391
Richard Lidz and Dale Anderson, editorial directors. Fourth edition, 1990. For 600 occupations, describes job duties, entry-level requirements, education and training needed, advancement possibilities, employment outlook, earnings and benefits. The set is divided into 12 volumes. Each volume includes jobs related under a broad career field. Volume 13 is the index. **Facsimile Number:** 818-365-5489.

★5254★
"Plumber and Pipefitter" in *VGM's Careers Encyclopedia* (pp. 357-359)
National Textbook Co.
4255 W. Touhy Ave.
Lincolnwood, IL 60646   Phone: (312)679-5500
Third edition, 1991. Contains two- to five-page descriptions of 200 managerial, professional, technical, trade, and service occupations. Each profile includes job duties, places of employment, qualifications, educational preparation, training, employment potential, advancement, income, and additional sources of information.

★5255★
"Plumber" in *The Desk Guide to Training and Work Advisement* (p. 83)
Charles C. Thomas, Publisher
2600 S. First St.
Springfield, IL 62794-9265   Phone: (217)789-8980
Gail Baugher Kuenstler. 1988. Describes alternative methods of gaining entry into an occupation through different types of educational programs, internships and apprenticeships. **Facsimile Number:** (217)789-9130.

★5256★
Plumbers
Chronicle Guidance Publications, Inc.
PO Box 1190
Moravia, NY 13118-1190   Phone: (315)497-0330
1990. This career brief describes the nature of the work, working conditions, hours and earnings, education and training, licensure, certification, unions, personal qualifications, social and psychological factors, employment outlook, entry methods, advancement, and related occupations. **Toll-free/Additional Phone Number(s):** 800-622-7284.

★5257★
"Plumbers" in Volume 5 of *Career Discovery Encyclopedia* (pp. 64-65)
J.G. Ferguson Publishing Co.
200 W. Monroe
Chicago, IL 60606   Phone: (312)580-5480
E. Russell Primm, editor-in-chief. 1990. Contains two-page articles on 504 occupations. Each article describes job duties, earnings, and educational and training requirements.

★5258★
"Plumbers" in Volume 3 of *The Encyclopedia of Careers and Vocational Guidance* (pp. 693-695)
J.G. Ferguson Publishing Co.
200 W. Monroe
Chicago, IL 60606   Phone: (312)580-5480
William E. Hopke, editor-in-chief. Eighth edition, 1990. Four-volume set that profiles 500 occupations and describes job trends in 76 industries. Includes career description, educational requirements, history of the job, methods of entry, advancement, employment outlook, earnings, working conditions, social and psychological factors, and sources of additional information.

★5259★
Plumbers and Pipefitters
Careers, Inc.
PO Box 135
Largo, FL 34649-0135   Phone: (813)584-7333
1990. Eight-page brief offering the definition, history, duties, working conditions, personal qualifications, educational requirements, earnings, hours, employment outlook, advancement possibilities, and related occupations.

★5260★
"Plumbers and Pipefitters" in *Occu-Facts: Information on 565 Careers in Outline Form* (p. 16.11)
Careers, Inc.
P.O. Box 135
1211 Tenth St., S.W.
Largo, FL 33640   Phone: (813)584-7333
Elizabeth Handville. Biennial, 1989-90 edition. Each one-page occupational profile describes duties, working conditions, physical surroundings and demands, aptitudes, temperament, educational requirements, employment outlook, earnings, and places of employment.

Plumbers and Pipefitters

★5261★
"Plumbers and Pipefitters" in *Occupational Outlook Handbook* (pp. 377-378)
Superintendent of Documents
U.S. Government Printing Office
Washington, DC 20402   Phone: (202)783-3238
Biennial; latest edition, 1990-91. Encyclopedia of careers describing more than 250 occupations and comprising about 86 percent of all jobs in the economy. Occupations that require lengthy education or training are given the most attention. For each occupation, the handbook describes job duties, working conditions, training, educational preparation, personal qualities, advancement possibilities, job outlook, earnings, and sources of additional information.

★5262★
"Plumbers and Pipefitters" in *Opportunities in Building Construction Trades* (pp. 41-45)
National Textbook Co.
4255 W. Touhy Ave.
Lincolnwood, IL 60646   Phone: (312)679-5500
Michael Sumichrast. 1989. Gives an overview of the construction industry and describes the jobs of various craftworkers. Covers different kinds of builders: home, custom; and describes management skills needed and industry trends affecting opportunities.

★5263★
"Plumbers" in *The American Almanac of Jobs and Salaries* (pp. 502-503)
Avon Books
105 Madison Avenue
New York, NY 10016   Phone: (212)481-5600
John Wright and Edward J. Dwyer. Revised and updated, 1990. A comprehensive guide to the wages of hundreds of occupations in a wide variety of industries and organizations.

★5264★
"Plumbing" in *The Career Connection II: A Guide to Technical Majors and Their Related Careers* (pp. 107-108)
ERIS
PO Box 7509
University Station
Provo, UT 84602-0509
Fred A. Rowe. 1988. Contains technical majors, such as automotive technology. Describes the major and the job. Lists high school and postsecondary school courses. Includes occupations related to the major, employment outlook, and starting salary.

★5265★
"Sprinkler Fitter" in *Hard Hatted Women: Stories of Struggle and Success in the Trades* (pp. 143-149)
Seal Press
3131 Western Ave., Ste. 410
Seattle, WA 98121   Phone: (206)283-7844
Molly Martin, editor. 1988. Twenty-six women recount their experiences working in blue collar occupations. They describe how they got in, the work they do, their relationships in predominantly male occupations, and their training.

★5266★
"Sprinkler Fitting" in *Opportunities in Plumbing and Pipefitting Careers* (pp. 85-88)
National Textbook Co.
4255 W. Touhy Ave.
Lincolnwood, IL 60646   Phone: (312)679-5500
Patrick J. Galvin. 1989. Describes the work, jobs, educational preparation, training, apprenticeships, a typical working day, salaries, future trends, and related fields.

★5267★
Video Career Library - Construction
Careers, Inc.
1211 10th St., SW
PO Box 135
Largo, FL 34649-0135   Phone: (813)584-7333
Videocassette. 1990. 36 mins. Part of the Video Career Library covering 165 occupations. Shows actual workers on the job. Includes millwrights, brickmasons, carpenters, drywall installers, electricians, painters, plumbers and pipefitters, carpenter and soft tile installers, insulation workers, paving equipment operators, and structural metal workers.

★5268★
Your Future in the Plumbing Heating Cooling Industry
National Association of Plumbing, Heating, and Cooling Contractors
P.O. Box 6808
180 S. Washington St.
Washington, DC 20046   Phone: (202)331-7675
1988. This eight-panel brochure describes the work, opportunities, working conditions, and entry into the field.

─────── Associations ───────

★5269★
Associated Builders and Contractors (ABC)
729 15th St. NW
Washington, DC 20005   Phone: (202)637-8800
Membership: Construction contractors, subcontractors, suppliers, and associates. **Purpose:** Aim is to foster and perpetuate the principles of rewarding shop construction workers and management on the basis of merit. Sponsors leadership conference and management education programs including Wheels of Learning; also sponsors apprenticeship and skill training programs. Disseminates technological and labor relations information. Maintains biographical archives and placement service. Bestows awards; compiles statistics. **Publications:** *ABC Newsline*, semimonthly. • *The Builder and Contractor*, monthly. • *Classified Membership Directory*, annual. • Also publishes safety manuals.

★5270★
Industrial Relations Council for the Plumbing and Pipe Fitting Industry (IRC)
1530 Merchandise Mart
Chicago, IL 60654   Phone: (312)670-6740
Membership: Representatives of employers and employees. **Purpose:** Serves as a voluntary medium for adjudication of local deadlocked disputes in an effort to discourage strikes, lockouts, and work stoppages in the plumbing and pipe fitting industry.

★5271★
Mechanical Contractors Association of America (MCAA)
1385 Piccard Dr.
Rockville, MD 20832   Phone: (301)869-5800
Membership: Contractors who furnish, install, and service piping systems and related equipment for heating, cooling,

refrigeration, ventilating, and air conditioning systems. **Purpose:** Works to standardize materials and methods used in the industry. Conducts business overhead, labor wage, and statistical surveys. Maintains dialogue with key officials in building trade unions. Promotes apprenticeship training programs. Conducts seminars on contracts, labor estimating, job cost control, project management, control law, marketing, collective bargaining, contractor insurance, and other management topics. Promotes methods to conserve energy in new and existing buildings. Sponsors Industrial Relations Council for the Plumbing and Pipe Fitting Industry. **Publications:** *Membership Directory*, annual. • *The Reporter*, monthly. • Also publishes *Labor Estimating Manual*, *Management-Labor Relations Guide*, and management and training aids. **Facsimile Number:** (301)990-9690.

★5272★
National Association of Plumbing-Heating-Cooling Contractors (NAPHCC)
PO Box 6808
180 S. Washington St.
Falls Church, VA 22040   Phone: (703)237-8100

Membership: Federation of state and local associations of plumbing, heating, and cooling contractors. **Purpose:** Seeks to advance sanitation, encourage sanitary laws, and generally improve the plumbing, heating, ventilating, and air conditioning industries. Conducts apprenticeship training programs, workshops, and seminars; cooperates with Plumbing-Heating-Cooling Information Bureau. **Publications:** *Contractor's Connection*, 18/year. • *Leadership Directory*, annual. • *News*, monthly. • Also publishes technical, safety, estimating, and business publications and videotapes. **Toll-free/Additional Phone Number(s):** (800)533-7694. **Facsimile Number:** (703)237-7442.

★5273★
National Fire Sprinkler Association (NFSA)
Robin Hill Corporate Park
Rt. 22
Box 1000
Patterson, NY 12563   Phone: (914)878-4200

Membership: Manufacturers, suppliers, contractors, and installers of fire sprinklers. **Purpose:** Conducts labor negotiations for the industry with 19 local unions. Conducts education program to promote the concept of automatic fire sprinkler protection. Acts as liaison for the industry and participates in fire test research with insurance organizations and fire services. Acts as consultant for building codes; has developed model fire protection codes. **Publications:** *Codewatch*, quarterly. • *Grass Roots*, monthly. • *Labor Line*, bimonthly. • *Membership List*, periodic. • *Regional Report*, monthly. • *Sprinkler Quarterly*. • *Sprinkler Technotes*, bimonthly. • Also publishes technical guides and informational pamphlets. **Facsimile Number:** (914)878-4215.

★5274★
United Association of Journeymen and Apprentices of the Plumbing and Pipe Fitting Industry of the U.S. and Canada
PO Box 37800
Washington, DC 20013   Phone: (202)628-5823

──────── **Standards/Certification Agencies** ────────

Virtually all plumbers undergo some type of apprenticeship training. Some are administered by local union-management committees comprising members of the United Association of Journeyman and Apprentices of the Plumbing and Pipefitting Industry of the United States vond Canada, the Mechanical Contractors Association of America, Inc., the National Association of Plumbing-Heating-Cooling Contractors, or the National Fire Sprinkler Association, Inc. Nonunion apprenticeship programs are administered by local chapters of the Associated Builders and Contractors, the National Association of Plumbing-Heating-Cooling Contractors, and the National Association of Home Builders, Home Builders Institute. Apprenticeships consist of four years on-the-job training, in addition to at least 144 hours annually of related classroom instruction. Although most plumbers are trained through apprenticeship, some still learn their skills informally on the job as helpers to experienced workers. Although there are no uniform national licensing requirements, most communities require plumbers to be licensed. Licensing requirements vary from area to area, but most localities require workers to pass an examination that tests their knowledge of the trade and of local plumbing codes.

★5275★
Mechanical Contractors Association of America (MCAA)
1385 Piccard Dr.
Rockville, MD 20832   Phone: (301)869-5800

Works to standardize materials and methods used in the industry. , annual. • *The Reporter*, monthly. • Also publishes *Labor Estimating Manual*, *Management-Labor Relations Guide*, and management and training aids. **Facsimile Number:** (301)990-9690.

★5276★
National Fire Sprinkler Association (NFSA)
Robin Hill Corporate Park
Rt. 22
Box 1000
Patterson, NY 12563   Phone: (914)878-4200

Acts as consultant for building codes; has developed model fire protection codes.

──────── **Test Guides** ────────

★5277★
Foreman Plumber
National Learning Corp.
212 Michael Dr.
Syosset, NY 11791   Phone: (516)921-8888

Jack Rudman. Part of the Career Examination Series No. 1. All examination guides in this series contain questions with answers. **Facsimile Number:** (516)921-8743. **Toll-free/Additional Phone Number(s):** 800-645-6337.

★5278★
Maintenance Worker/Mechanical Maintainer
Prentice Hall Press
Simon & Schuster Inc.
200 Old Tappan Rd.
Old Tappan, NJ 07675   Phone: (800)223-2348

Hy Hammer. Fourth edition, 1984. Provides information for applicants interested in the following civil service positions: carpenter, mason, plumber, electrician, painter, machinist. Includes eight sample tests.

★5279★
Master Plumber
National Learning Corp.
212 Michael Dr.
Syosset, NY 11791   Phone: (516)921-8888

Jack Rudman. Part of the Career Examination Series No. 1. All examination guides in this series contain questions with answers. **Facsimile Number:** (516)921-8743. **Toll-free/Additional Phone Number(s):** 800-645-6337.

★5280★
Pipefitter
National Learning Corp.
212 Michael Dr.
Syosset, NY 11791   Phone: (516)921-8888
Jack Rudman. Part of the Career Examination Series No. 1. All examination guides in this series contain questions with answers. **Facsimile Number:** (516)921-8743. **Toll-free/Additional Phone Number(s):** 800-645-6337.

★5281★
Plumber
National Learning Corp.
212 Michael Dr.
Syosset, NY 11791   Phone: (516)921-8888
Jack Rudman. Part of the Career Examination Series No. 1. Guides are also available for the plumber's helper, plumbing engineer, plumbing inspector, and plumbing supervisor. All examination guides in this series contain questions with answers. **Facsimile Number:** (516)921-8743. **Toll-free/Additional Phone Number(s):** 800-645-6337.

★5282★
Plumber—Steam Fitter
Prentice Hall Press
Simon & Schuster Inc.
200 Old Tappan Rd.
Old Tappan, NJ 07675   Phone: (800)223-2348
Frank Sparandero. Fourth edition, 1987. Includes 11 practice exams, plus information on plumbing terms, regulations, and mathematical formulas.

Awards, Scholarships, Grants, and Fellowships

★5283★
Award of Merit
American Society of Plumbing Engineers
3617 Thousand Oaks Blvd., Ste. 210
Westlake, CA 91362-3625   Phone: (805)495-7120
To advance the ideals and goals of the Society. A plaque is awarded biannually at the Society's convention.

★5284★
Industry Award
American Society of Plumbing Engineers
3617 Thousand Oaks Blvd., Ste. 210
Westlake, CA 91362-3625   Phone: (805)495-7120
To recognize the advancement of plumbing engineering technology. A plaque is awarded biannually at the Society's convention. Established in 1970.

Basic Reference Guides and Handbooks

★5285★
Basic Plumbing Skills
American Association for Vocational Instructional Materials
745 Goines School Rd.
Athens, GA 30605   Phone: (404)543-7557
William H. Annis. 1990. **Facsimile Number:** (404)613-6779.

★5286★
Blueprint Reading for Plumbers: Residential & Commercial
Delmar Publishers, Inc.
PO Box 15015
2 Computer Dr., W.
Albany, NY 12212   Phone: (518)459-1150
Bartholomew D'Arcangelo. Fifth revised edition, 1989. Part of Blueprint Reading Series. **Facsimile Number:** (518)453-6472.

★5287★
Do-It-Yourself Plumbing
Borgo Press
PO Box 2845
San Bernardino, CA 92406-2845   Phone: (714)884-5813
Max Alth. 1989.

★5288★
Labor Estimating Manual
Mechanical Contractors Association of America (MCAA)
1385 Piccard Dr.
Rockville, MD 20832   Phone: (301)869-5800

★5289★
Math on the Job: Plumber
National Center for Research in Vocational Education
Ohio State University
1900 Kenry Rd.
Columbus, OH 43210   Phone: (614)292-4353
1985.

★5290★
MCAA Management-Labor Relations Guide
Mechanical Contractors Association of America (MCAA)
1385 Piccard Dr.
Rockville, MD 20832   Phone: (301)869-5800

★5291★
Mid-West Contractor—Annual Convention Guide and Association Directory
Allied Publications, Inc.
7355 N. Woodland Dr.
Box 603
Indianapolis, IN 46278   Phone: (317)297-5500
Jennifer Wynne, editor. Annual. List of 160 construction contracting and architectural associations in the Midwest. Entries include: Association name, address, phone, names and titles of key personnel, description of association; convention site, date, name and title of contact. Arrangement: Geographical, alphabetical. **Toll-free/Additional Phone Number(s):** (800)827-7468. **Facsimile Number:** (317)299-1356.

★5292★
Plumbers & Pipefitters Library
Macmillan Publishing Company, Inc.
866 3rd Ave.
New York, NY 10022   Phone: (212)702-2000
Charles N. McConnell. 1990.

★5293★
Plumbers Handbook
Macmillan Publishing Co., Inc.
866 3rd Ave.
New York, NY 10022   Phone: (212)702-2000
Joseph Almond. Eighth edition, 1991.

★5294★
The Plumber's Toolbox Manual
Prentice Hall
Rte. 9W
Englewood Cliffs, NJ 07632   Phone: (201)592-2000
Louis J. Mahiau. 1989. Part of On-the-Job Reference Series.

★5295★
Plumbing
Time-Life Books, Inc.
777 Duke St.
Alexandria, VA 22314   Phone: (703)838-7000
Time-Life Books Editors. Revised edition, 1989. Part of Home Repair & Improvement Series.

★5296★
Plumbing Engineer—Product Directory Issue
TMB Publishing Inc.
1850 Techny Ct.
Northbrook, IL 60062   Phone: (708)564-1127
Arthur Klein, editor. Annual, January. Over 400 plumbing products from approximately 200 manufacturers. Entries include: Company name, phone, fax; name of engineering contact with the firm. **Facsimile Number:** (708)564-1264.

★5297★
Residential Plumbing
Taunton Press, Inc.
63 S. Main St.
Box 5506
Newton, CT 06470-9989   Phone: (203)426-8171
Peter Hemp. 1992. **Toll-free/Additional Phone Number(s):** 800-888-8286. **Facsimile Number:** (203)426-3434.

★5298★
Wholesaler—"Wholesaling 100" Issue   Plumbing and heating
Delta Communications, Inc.
400 N. Michigan Ave.
Chicago, IL 60611   Phone: (312)222-2000
Mary Ann Falkman, Editorial Director, editor. Annual, July. 100 leading wholesalers of plumbing-heating equipment and supplies. Entries include: Company name, address, phone, telex, names and titles of key personnel, number of employees, business breakdown (percentage). Arrangement: Ranked by sales. **Facsimile Number:** (312)222-2026.

Periodicals

★5299★
ABC Newsline
Associated Builders and Contractors, Inc. (ABC)
729 15th St. NW
Washington, DC 20005   Phone: (202)637-8800
Editor(s): Lisa A. Nardone. Semimonthly. Designed to keep readers alerted to important changes within ABC and the construction industry. Reports on legislative issues, construction trends, conferences and meetings, and ABC services. Recurring features include news of members and a column titled Industry Briefs.

★5300★
American Architectural Manufacturers Association—Quarterly Review
American Architectural Manufacturers Association
1540 E. Dundee Rd., Ste. K 310
Palatine, IL 60067-8321   Phone: (708)202-1350
Editor(s): Tony Coorlim. Annually. Contains industry news on architectural products. Covers prime and combination storm windows, sliding glass and combination storm doors, window and curtain-walls, store fronts and entrances, siding, soffits, fascia, gutters, downspouts, skylights, space enclosures, and mobile home components. Recurring features include news of research, notices of publications available, and announcements by the association. **Facsimile Number:** (708)202-1480.

★5301★
American Institute of Constructors—Newsletter
American Institute of Constructors
9887 Gandy Blvd. N., No. 104
Saint Petersburg, FL 33702-2451
Editor(s): Ed Freedman. Bimonthly. Concerned with construction practice, design, administration, and teaching. Carries news of members, listings of job opportunities, local chapter reports, and notices of new publications. **Facsimile Number:** (614)464-3226.

★5302★
ASA News
American Supply Association (ASA)
222 Merchandise Mart Plaza, Ste. 1360
Chicago, IL 60654   Phone: (312)464-0090
Editor(s): Inge Calderon. Bimonthly. Covers association events and news from member companies in the plumbing industry, regional and national industry events, and items of interest. **Facsimile Number:** (312)464-0091.

★5303★
Blue Reports, Inc.
Construction News Service
7325 Steel Mill Dr.
Springfield, VA 22050   Phone: (703)644-5884
Editor(s): Calvin S. Oren. Daily. Reports on public and private construction projects in the Washington, DC, Virginia, and Maryland areas. Provides owner's and architect's names, plan status, date bids due, prospective bidders, low bids received, and specification details. **Facsimile Number:** (703)644-1929.

★5304★
The Builder and Contractor
Associated Builders and Contractors (ABC)
729 15th St. NW
Washington, DC 20005   Phone: (202)637-8800
Monthly.

★5305★
Building Concerns
National Association of Minority Contractors (NAMC)
806 15th St. NW, Ste. 340
Washington, DC 20005   Phone: (202)347-8259
Editor(s): Ralph C. Thomas, III. Monthly. Concentrates on national and regional news regarding minority construction contractors. Contains articles on issues generally affecting the industry—especially issues affecting minorities—including topics such as legislative and regulatory activity and reports on major corporation developments. Recurring features include reports of meetings, news of educational opportunities, a calendar of events, and news of NAMC chapters and members.

Plumbers and Pipefitters

★5306★
Building Industry Technology: An Abstract Newsletter
National Technical Information Service (NTIS)
U.S. Department of Commerce
5285 Port Royal Rd.
Springfield, VA 22161   Phone: (703)487-4630
Weekly. Consists of abstracts of reports on architectural and environmental design, building standards, construction materials and equipment, and structural analyses. Recurring features include a form for ordering reports from NTIS.

★5307★
Capital Comments
National Lumber & Building Material Dealers Association
40 Ivy St. SE
Washington, DC 20003   Phone: (202)547-2230
Editor(s): Matt Geitner. Semimonthly. Reports on news of legislation pertaining to lumber, other building materials, and housing. Discusses such issues as lumber subsidies, interest rates on homes, health and safety, and jobs. **Facsimile Number:** (202)547-7640.

★5308★
Codewatch
National Fire Sprinkler Association (NFSA)
Robin Hill Corporate Park
Rt. 22
Box 1000
Patterson, NY 12563   Phone: (914)878-4200
Quarterly. Newsletter listing changes in model codes and state and local laws and regulations, and amendments to building codes and local ordinances.

★5309★
ConnStruction
PO Box 9768
Wethersfield, CT 06109   Phone: (203)529-3246
Victor Bonini, Editor. 7x/yr. Magazine for construction industry. **Facsimile Number:** (203)563-0616.

★5310★
CONSTRUCTION
26 Long Hill Rd.
Guilford, CT 06437   Phone: (203)453-3717
Jack C. Lewis, Editor and Publisher. 2x/mo. Journal for the construction industry.

★5311★
Construction Dimensions
Assn. of Wall & Ceiling
PO Box 5504
Washington, DC 20016   Phone: (301)656-7050
Gerald Wykoff, Editor. Monthly. Wall and ceiling industry magazine.

★5312★
Construction Industry International
Maclean Hunter Publishing Co.
29 N. Wacker Dr.
Chicago, IL 60606   Phone: (312)726-2802
Alan Elliott, Editor-in-Chief. Monthly. Trade magazine.

★5313★
Construction News
715 W. 2nd St.
PO Box 2421
Little Rock, AR 72203   Phone: (501)376-1931
Robert Alvey, Editor. Weekly. Construction industry magazine. **Facsimile Number:** (501)375-5831.

★5314★
Construction Newsletter
National Safety Council
444 N. Michigan Ave.
Chicago, IL 60611   Phone: (312)527-4800
6/yr. Focuses on industrial and occupational safety in the construction industry. Carries items on such topics as safe work practices and products, accident prevention, and successful industrial safety programs and policies.

★5315★
Contractor's Connection
National Association of Plumbing-Heating-Cooling Contractors (NAPHCC)
PO Box 6808
180 S. Washington St.
Falls Church, VA 22040   Phone: (703)237-8100
18/year.

★5316★
Daily Construction Reporter
4901 Pacific Hwy.
San Diego, CA 92110-4098   Phone: (619)296-0183
Kenneth F. Kerr, Editor and Publisher. Daily. Construction trade newspaper covering jobs that are out for bid, bid results, building permits, and other information. **Facsimile Number:** (619)298-3027.

★5317★
Distributor
Technical Reporting Corp.
651 W. Washington St., Ste. 300
Chicago, IL 60661   Phone: (312)993-0929
Steve Read, Editor. Monthly. Magazine focusing on air conditioning, heating, ventilation, and plumbing. **Facsimile Number:** (312)993-0960.

★5318★
Home BUILDER Magazine
Work-4 Projects Ltd.
PO Box 400, Victoria Sta.
Westmount, PQ, Canada H3Z 2V8   Phone: (514)489-4941
Nachmi Artzy, Editor and Publisher. 6x/yr. Magazine for home construction industry. **Facsimile Number:** (514)489-5505.

★5319★
The Journal of Light Construction
Hanley-Wood Partners
RR 2, Box 146
Richmond, VT 05477-9607   Phone: (802)864-0091
Steve Bliss, Editor. Monthly. Magazine (tabloid) for residential and light professionals involved in new and rehabilitative construction. Each issue covers a single aspect of construction.

★5320★
Mechanical Contractors Association of America— Reporter
Mechanical Contractors Association of America, Inc.
1385 Piccard Dr.
Rockville, MD 20850   Phone: (301)869-5800
Editor(s): Gregory Rosenberg. Monthly. Covers labor issues and government affairs as they affect mechanical contractors in the plumbing and pipefitting industry. Recurring features include reports on the activities of the Association and notices of pertinent seminars and meetings. **Facsimile Number:** (301)990-9630.

★5321★ VOCATIONAL CAREERS SOURCEBOOK, 1st Edition

★5321★
NAPHCC News
National Association of Plumbing-Heating-Cooling Contractors (NAPHCC)
PO Box 6808
180 S. Washington St.
Falls Church, VA 22040   Phone: (703)237-8100
Monthly.

★5322★
Nation's Building News
15th & M Sts. NW
Washington, DC 20005   Phone: (202)822-0525
Tim Ahern, Editor. 2x/mo. Trade magazine (tabloid) covering home building and all related industries. **Facsimile Number:** (202)861-2131.

★5323★
Official Magazine
International Assn. of Plumbing & Mechanical Officials
20001 S. Walnut Dr.
Walnut, CA 91789-2825   Phone: (714)595-8449
E.E. Wachter, Editor. Bimonthly. Trade publication containing articles of interest to plumbing association members about plumbing code matters. **Facsimile Number:** (714)594-3690.

★5324★
Palmetto Piper
Mechanical Contractor's Assn. of South Carolina
1504 Morninghill Dr.
PO Box 384
Columbia, SC 29202   Phone: (803)772-7834
Monthly. Plumbing, heating, air conditioning, and electrical journal.

★5325★
Plumb
Preston Rose Printing
3183 Shallowford Rd.
Atlanta, GA 30341   Phone: (404)458-4414
Dianne Olson, Editor. 6x/yr Plumbing industry magazine.

★5326★
Plumbing Business
Merit Publications, Inc.
18 Perimeter Dr., Ste. 108
Atlanta, GA 30341   Phone: (404)451-4990
James L. Prendergast, Publisher. 6x/yr. Magazine emphasizing plumbing business marketing, merchandising, and management.

★5327★
Plumbing Heating Piping
Delta Communications, Inc.
400 N. Michigan Ave.
Chicago, IL 60611   Phone: (312)222-2000
Cari T. Laird, Editor. Monthly. Magazine on the plumbing, piping, and hydronics industries. **Facsimile Number:** (312)222-2026.

★5328★
Professional Builder
Cahners Publishing Co.
1350 E. Touhy Ave.
Des Plaines, IL 60018   Phone: (708)635-8800
Roy L. Diez, Editor. 19x/yr. **Facsimile Number:** (708)299-8622.

★5329★
Reeves Journal: Plumbing Heating Cooling
Business News Publishing Co.
23187 La Cadena Dr., Ste. 101
PO Box 30700
Laguna Hills, CA 92654   Phone: (714)830-0881
Larry Dill, Editor. Monthly. Regional plumbing, heating, and cooling magazine. **Facsimile Number:** (714)859-7845.

★5330★
The Reporter
Mechanical Contractors Association of America (MCAA)
1385 Piccard Dr.
Rockville, MD 20832   Phone: (301)869-5800
Monthly. Newsletter.

★5331★
Supply House Times
Horton Publishing Co.
7574 N. Lincoln Ave.
Skokie, IL 60077   Phone: (708)677-2707
Greg Cassel, Editor. Monthly. Trade magazine for wholesalers in plumbing, heating, cooling, piping, and water systems. Areas of major emphasis include: warehousing, materials handling, inventory control, accounting, data processing, merchandising, salesmanship and general management. **Facsimile Number:** (708)677-5003.

★5332★
U.A. Journal
United Assn. of Journeymen & Apprentices of the Plumbing & Pipefitting Industry of the U.S. & Canada
901 Massachusetts Ave. NW
Washington, DC 20001   Phone: (202)628-5823
Charles Habig, Editor. Monthly. Labor magazine.

─────── Meetings and Conventions ───────

★5333★
American Society of Plumbing Engineers Convention and Biennial Engineered Plumbing Exposition
National Trade Productions
313 S. Patrick St.
Alexandria, VA 22314
1992; Nov. 17-18; Washington, DC • 1994; Oct. 25-26; Kansas City, MO. **Toll-free/Additional Phone Number(s):** 800-638-8510.

★5334★
Associated Builders and Contractors (ABC)
729 15th St. NW
Washington, DC 20005   Phone: (202)637-8800
Frequency: Annual.

★5335★
Industrial Relations Council for the Plumbing and Pipe Fitting Industry Annual Conference
1530 Merchandise Mart
Chicago, IL 60654   Phone: (312)670-6740
Frequency: Annual conference is always held in February.

★5336★
Industrial Relations Council for the Plumbing and Pipe Fitting Industry Annual Convention
1530 Merchandise Mart
Chicago, IL 60654   Phone: (312)670-6740
Frequency: Always held in February.

Plumbers and Pipefitters

★5337★
Mechanical Contractors Association of America Conference (MCAA)
1385 Piccard Dr.
Rockville, MD 20832   Phone: (301)869-5800
Frequency: Annual. **Facsimile Number:** (301)990-9690.

★5338★
Midwest Specialty Exposition
Kansas Plumbing, Heating, and Cooling Contractors Association
320 Laura St.
Wichita, KS 67211   Phone: (316)262-8860
1992. **Facsimile Number:** (316)265-7381.

★5339★
National Association of Home Builders/The Builders Show
National Association of Home Builders of the United States
15th and M Sts., NW
Washington, DC 20005   Phone: (202)822-0424
Frequency: Usually held in January; location rotates every three years. 1993; Feb. 19-22; Las Vegas, NV • 1994; Jan. 21-24; Las Vegas, NV. **Toll-free/Additional Phone Number(s):** 800-368-5242. **Facsimile Number:** (202)822-0435.

★5340★
National Association of Plumbing-Heating-Cooling Contractors (NAPHCC)
PO Box 6808
180 S. Washington St.
Falls Church, VA 22040   Phone: (703)237-8100
1992; Oct. 20-24; Atlanta, GA • 1993; Oct. 13-17; Anaheim, CA. **Toll-free/Additional Phone Number(s):** (800)533-7694. **Facsimile Number:** (703)237-7442.

★5341★
PHCP EXPO - National Plumbing-Heating-Cooling-Piping Products Exposition
National Association of Plumbing, Heating, and Cooling Contractors
180 S. Washington St.
PO Box 6808
Fall Church, VA 22046   Phone: (703)237-8100
1992; Oct. 20-24; Atlanta, GA • 1993; Oct. 13-17; Anaheim, CA. **Toll-free/Additional Phone Number(s):** 800-533-7694. **Facsimile Number:** (703)237-7442.

★5342★
Plumbing-Heating-Cooling Contractors Convention, Ohio Chapter
Plumbing-Heating-Cooling Contractors, Ohio Chapter
17 S. High St., Ste. 1200
Columbus, OH 43215   Phone: (614)221-1900
1992.

★5343★
Plumbing-Heating-Cooling Contractors Convention, Pennsylvania Chapter
Association of Plumbing-Heating-Cooling Contractors, Pennsylvania Chapter
4015 Jonestown Rd.
Harrisburg, PA 17109   Phone: (717)541-9109
1992; Apr. 30; Philadelphia, PA. **Facsimile Number:** (717)541-9823.

★5344★
Plumbing-Heating-Cooling Contractors Convention, Texas Chapter
Plumbing-Heating-Cooling Contractors, Texas Chapter
1601 Rio Grande, Ste. 440
Austin, TX 78701   Phone: (512)479-0425
1992.

★5345★
United Association of Journeymen and Apprentices of the Plumbing and Pipe Fitting Industry of the U.S. and Canada
PO Box 37800
Washington, DC 20013   Phone: (202)628-5823
Frequency: Quinquennial - next held in 1996. **Facsimile Number:** (202)628-5024.

Roofers

Roofers repair and install roofs of tar or asphalt and gravel, rubber, thermoplastic, and metal; and shingles made of slate, asphalt, fiberglass, wood, or tile. Repair and reroofing provide many work opportunities for these workers. Roofers also may waterproof and dampproof masonry and concrete walls and floors. Most roofers work for roofing contractors. About 30 percent of all roofers are self-employed and specialize in residential work.

$alaries

Median weekly earnings for roofers are as follows:

Lowest 10 percent	$196.00/week or less
Median	$312.00/week
Top 10 percent	$581.00/week or more

Employment Outlook

Growth rate until the year 2000: Average.

Roofers

Career Guides

★5346★
Career Insights
RMI Media Productions, Inc.
2807 West 47th St.
Shawnee Mission, KS 66205   Phone: (913)262-3974
Videocassette series. 1987. This videotape series describes 50 occupations, including skill requirements and interviews with people employed in these fields. Occupations include: flight service, air transportation/ground services, data processing, carpentry, clerk in banking/insurance/business, cosmetic personal grooming, firefighting, roofing, material handling, photographic processing, plumbing, secretarial services, tool and die operations.

★5347★
Career Success Series
Cambridge Career Products
90 MacCorkle Ave., SW
South Charleston, WV 25311   Phone: (304)744-9323
Videocassette. 1986. 15 mins. A series, available separately, outlining various career choices for students. Occupations include: flight service, air transportation/ground service, data processing, carpentry, clerk in banking/insurance, commodity sales, cosmetic personal grooming, fire fighting, forestry services, home economics, insulation/roofing, material handling, mechanics, photographic processing, pipefitting and plumbing, police science, printing, secretarial services, and utilities equipment operator.

★5348★
Construction Cluster
Center for Humanities, Inc.
Communications Park
Box 1000
Mount Kisco, NY 10549   Phone: (914)666-4100
Videocassette. 1984. 15 mins. Construction workers describe what it's like to work at their jobs, and show the special equipment they use in their field.

★5349★
Foreman Roofer
National Learning Corp.
212 Michael Dr.
Syosset, NY 11791   Phone: (516)921-8888
Jack Rudman. 1989. Part of Career Examination Series.

★5350★
Insulating & Roofing Occupations
Morris Video
2730 Monterey St. #105
Monterey Business Park
Torrance, CA 90503   Phone: (213)533-4800
Videocassette. 1987. 15 mins. A look at the various careers that involve the reduction of the flow of cold, heat or sound.

★5351★
Roofer
Careers, Inc.
PO Box 135
Largo, FL 34649-0135   Phone: (813)584-7333
1992. Two-page occupational summary card describing duties, working conditions, personal qualifications, training, earnings and hours, employment outlook, places of employment, related careers and where to write for more information.

★5352★
"Roofer" in *Construction*, Volume 4 of *Career Information Center* (pp. 82-83)
Glencoe/Macmillan
15319 Chatsworth St.
Mission Hills, CA 91345   Phone: (818)898-1391
Richard Lidz and Dale Anderson, editorial directors. Fourth edition, 1990. For 600 occupations, describes job duties, entry-level requirements, education and training needed, advancement possibilities, employment outlook, earnings and benefits. The set is divided into 12 volumes. Each volume includes jobs related under a broad career field. Volume 13 is the index. **Facsimile Number:** 818-365-5489.

★5353★
"Roofer" in *Occu-Facts: Information on 565 Careers in Outline Form* (p. 16.17)
Careers, Inc.
P.O. Box 135
1211 Tenth St., S.W.
Largo, FL 33640   Phone: (813)584-7333
Elizabeth Handville. Biennial, 1989-90 edition. Each one-page occupational profile describes duties, working conditions, physical surroundings and demands, aptitudes, temperament, educational requirements, employment outlook, earnings, and places of employment.

★5354★
Roofers
Chronicle Guidance Publications, Inc.
PO Box 1190
Moravia, NY 13118-1190 Phone: (315)497-0330
1990. This career brief describes the nature of the work, working conditions, hours and earnings, education and training, licensure, certification, unions, personal qualifications, social and psychological factors, employment outlook, entry methods, advancement, and related occupations. **Toll-free/Additional Phone Number(s):** 800-622-7284.

★5355★
"Roofers" in *Occupational Outlook Handbook* (pp. 378-379) IT2
Superintendent of Documents
U.S. Government Printing Office
Washington, DC 20402 Phone: (202)783-3238
Biennial; latest edition, 1990-91. Encyclopedia of careers describing more than 250 occupations and comprising about 86 percent of all jobs in the economy. Occupations that require lengthy education or training are given the most attention. For each occupation, the handbook describes job duties, working conditions, training, educational preparation, personal qualities, advancement possibilities, job outlook, earnings, and sources of additional information.

★5356★
"Roofers" in *Opportunities in Building Construction Trades* (pp. 45-47)
National Textbook Co.
4255 W. Touhy Ave.
Lincolnwood, IL 60646 Phone: (312)679-5500
Michael Sumichrast. 1989. Gives an overview of the construction industry and describes the jobs of various craftworkers. Covers different kinds of builders: home, custom; and describes management skills needed and industry trends affecting opportunities.

★5357★
"Roofers" in Volume 5 of *Career Discovery Encyclopedia* (pp. 164-165)
J.G. Ferguson Publishing Co.
200 W. Monroe
Chicago, IL 60606 Phone: (312)580-5480
E. Russell Primm, editor-in-chief. 1990. Contains two-page articles on 504 occupations. Each article describes job duties, earnings, and educational and training requirements.

★5358★
"Roofers" in Volume 3 of *The Encyclopedia of Careers and Vocational Guidance* (pp. 696-698)
J.G. Ferguson Publishing Co.
200 W. Monroe
Chicago, IL 60606 Phone: (312)580-5480
William E. Hopke, editor-in-chief. Eighth edition, 1990. Four-volume set that profiles 500 occupations and describes job trends in 76 industries. Includes career description, educational requirements, history of the job, methods of entry, advancement, employment outlook, earnings, working conditions, social and psychological factors, and sources of additional information.

★5359★
Roofer's Pitch
International Film Bureau, Inc. (IFB)
332 South Michigan Ave.
Chicago, IL 60604-4382 Phone: (312)427-4545
Videocassette. 198?. 21 mins. This program shows what happens to a roofer when he is not careful on the job and how the crew corrects the problem.

★5360★
Roofing and Waterproofing: A Trade Worth Learning Through Apprenticeship
United Union of Roofers, Waterproofers and Allied Workers
1125 17th St., N.W.
Washington, DC 20036 Phone: (202)638-3228
This eight-panel brochure describes the apprentice roofer program including earnings, the work, and qualifications needed.

—— Associations ——

★5361★
National Roofing Contractors Association (NRCA)
O'Hare Intl. Center
10255 W. Higgins Rd., Ste. 600
Rosemont, IL 60018-5607 Phone: (708)299-9070
Membership: Contractors applying asphalt, cool tar pitch, elasto/plastic, slate, tile, metal, and wood roofs. **Purpose:** Provides instruction to roofing superintendents. Holds management institutes to provide specific information in the field of business management. **Publications:** *Directory*, annual. • *Professional Roofing*, monthly. • Also publishes *Roofing Manual*. **Facsimile Number:** (708)299-1183.

★5362★
United Union of Roofers, Waterproofers and Allied Workers (UURWAW)
1125 17th St. NW
Washington, DC 20036 Phone: (202)638-3228
Membership: AFL-CIO. **Publications:** *Magazine*, quarterly. **Facsimile Number:** (202)737-3621.

—— Standards/Certification Agencies ——

Most roofers acquire their skills informally by working as helpers for roofers. In this manner, it can take five years or more to get experience installing all types of roofing materials. Some roofers train through three-year apprenticeship programs administered by local union-management committees of the United Union of Roofers, Waterproofers and Allied Workers. The apprenticeship program generally consists of a minimum of 1,400 hours of on-the-job training annually, plus 144 hours of classroom instruction per year. On-the-job training for apprentices is similar to that of helpers, except that the apprenticeship program is more structured. Apprentices also learn to dampproof and waterproof walls.

Test Guides

★5363★
Foreman Roofer
National Learning Corp.
212 Michael Dr.
Syosset, NY 11791 Phone: (516)921-8888
Jack Rudman. Part of the Career Examination Series No. 1. All examination guides in this series contain questions with answers. **Facsimile Number:** (516)921-8743. **Toll-free/Additional Phone Number(s):** 800-645-6337.

★5364★
Roofer
National Learning Corp.
212 Michael Dr.
Syosset, NY 11791 Phone: (516)921-8888
Jack Rudman. Part of the Career Examination Series No. 1. All examination guides in this series contain questions with answers. **Facsimile Number:** (516)921-8743. **Toll-free/Additional Phone Number(s):** 800-645-6337.

Basic Reference Guides and Handbooks

★5365★
Intelligent Buildings Institute—Directory of Products and Services
Intelligent Buildings Institute (IBI)
2101 L St., NW, Ste. 300
Washington, DC 20037 Phone: (202)457-1988
S. Hunt, Associate Executive Director, editor. Annual, September. Member consultants, associations, research organizations, and other suppliers of products and services to the construction and building industry. Entries include: Company name, address, phone. Arrangement: Alphabetical. Indexes: Product/service. **Facsimile Number:** (202)457-8468.

★5366★
Mid-West Contractor—Annual Convention Guide and Association Directory
Allied Publications, Inc.
7355 N. Woodland Dr.
Box 603
Indianapolis, IN 46278 Phone: (317)297-5500
Jennifer Wynne, editor. Annual. List of 160 construction contracting and architectural associations in the Midwest. Entries include: Association name, address, phone, names and titles of key personnel, description of association; convention site, date, name and title of contact. Arrangement: Geographical, alphabetical. **Toll-free/Additional Phone Number(s):** (800)827-7468. **Facsimile Number:** (317)299-1356.

★5367★
The NRCA Roofing & Waterproofing Manual
National Roofing Contractors Association
O'Hare Intl. Center
10255 W. Higgins Rd., Ste. 600
Rosemont, IL 60018-5607 Phone: (708)299-9070
Third edition, 1989.

★5368★
NRCA Directory
National Roofing Contractors Association (NRCA)
O'Hare Intl. Center
10255 W. Higgins Rd., Ste. 600
Rosemont, IL 60018-5607 Phone: (708)299-9070
Annual.

★5369★
Roof Framing
American Association for Vocational Instructional Materials
745 Goines School Rd.
Athens, GA 30605 Phone: (404)543-7557
Charley G. Chadwick. 1991. Part of Basic Carpentry Skills Series. **Facsimile Number:** (404)613-6779.

★5370★
Roof Framing
Craftsman Book Company
PO Box 6500
6058 Corte del Cedro
Carlsbad, CA 92009 Phone: (619)438-7828
Marshal Gross. 1989. **Facsimile Number:** (619)438-0398.

★5371★
Roofing: Design Criteria, Options, Selection
R. S. Means Company, Inc.
100 Construction Plaza
Kingston, MA 02364 Phone: (617)585-7880
Robert D. Herbert, III. 1989. **Facsimile Number:** (617)585-7466.

★5372★
Roofing Manual
National Roofing Contractors Association (NRCA)
O'Hare Intl. Center
10255 W. Higgins Rd., Ste. 600
Rosemont, IL 60018-5607 Phone: (708)299-9070

★5373★
Roofing the Right Way
TAB Books
Blue Ridge Summit, PA 17294-0850 Phone: (717)794-2191
Steven Bolt. Second edition, 1990.

Periodicals

★5374★
ABC Newsline
Associated Builders and Contractors, Inc. (ABC)
729 15th St. NW
Washington, DC 20005 Phone: (202)637-8800
Editor(s): Lisa A. Nardone. Semimonthly. Designed to keep readers alerted to important changes within ABC and the construction industry. Reports on legislative issues, construction trends, conferences and meetings, and ABC services. Recurring features include news of members and a column titled Industry Briefs.

★5375★
American Architectural Manufacturers Association—Quarterly Review
American Architectural Manufacturers Association
1540 E. Dundee Rd., Ste. K 310
Palatine, IL 60067-8321 Phone: (708)202-1350
Editor(s): Tony Coorlim. Annually. Contains industry news on architectural products. Covers prime and combination storm

windows, sliding glass and combination storm doors, window and curtain-walls, store fronts and entrances, siding, soffits, fascia, gutters, downspouts, skylights, space enclosures, and mobile home components. Recurring features include news of research, notices of publications available, and announcements by the association. **Facsimile Number:** (708)202-1480.

★5376★
American Institute of Constructors—Newsletter
American Institute of Constructors
9887 Gandy Blvd. N., No. 104
Saint Petersburg, FL 33702-2451
Editor(s): Ed Freedman. Bimonthly. Concerned with construction practice, design, administration, and teaching. Carries news of members, listings of job opportunities, local chapter reports, and notices of new publications. **Facsimile Number:** (614)464-3226.

★5377★
Asphalt Roofing Manufacturers Association—Newsletter
Asphalt Roofing Manufacturers Association
6288 Montrose Rd.
Rockville, MD 20852   Phone: (301)530-5120
Editor(s): Russell K. Snyder. Bimonthly. Reports news and information of interest to professionals in the asphalt roofing industry. Highlights association activities and discusses developments in the industry, including occupational safety and health measures, changes in industry codes and standards, environmental issues, and legislative and regulatory actions. .

★5378★
Blue Reports, Inc.
Construction News Service
7325 Steel Mill Dr.
Springfield, VA 22050   Phone: (703)644-5884
Editor(s): Calvin S. Oren. Daily. Reports on public and private construction projects in the Washington, DC, Virginia, and Maryland areas. Provides owner's and architect's names, plan status, date bids due, prospective bidders, low bids received, and specification details. **Facsimile Number:** (703)644-1929.

★5379★
Builder
Hanley-Wood, Inc.
655 15th St. NW, Ste. 475
Washington, DC 20005   Phone: (202)737-0717
Mitchell Rouda, Editor. Monthly. Magazine covering housing, commercial, and industrial building. **Facsimile Number:** (202)737-2439.

★5380★
Builder and Contractor
Associated Builders and Contractors, Inc.
729 15th St. NW
Washington, DC 20005   Phone: (202)637-8800
Susan Schindler, Mng. Editor. Monthly. Magazine for open shop contractors and subcontractors. Includes articles on national and regional construction news, construction management, project case histories, new products, and building design.

★5381★
Builder Architect
Sunshine Media, Inc.
7500 N. Dreamy Draw, Ste. 111
PO Box 9400
Phoenix, AZ 85068   Phone: (602)943-3575
Marie Vere, Editor. Monthly. Home builders magazine. **Facsimile Number:** (602)371-0241.

★5382★
Builder/Dealer
Peterson Bros. Inc., Publishing
16 1st Ave.
Corry, PA 16407-1894   Phone: (814)664-8624
Charles P. Mancino, Publisher. Monthly. Trade magazine. **Facsimile Number:** (814)664-8506.

★5383★
Builder Insider
Divibest, Inc.
PO Box 191125
Dallas, TX 75219   Phone: (214)871-2913
Michael J. Anderson, Editor and Publisher. Monthly. Magazine (tabloid) for builders, architects, and remodelers.

★5384★
Building Business & Management
Builders Assn. of Southeastern Michigan
30375 Northwestern Hwy.
Farmington Hills, MI 48334   Phone: (313)737-4477
Kathleen M. Eischeid, Editor. Monthly. Construction and apartment industry magazine. **Facsimile Number:** (313)737-5741.

★5385★
Building Concerns
National Association of Minority Contractors (NAMC)
806 15th St. NW, Ste. 340
Washington, DC 20005   Phone: (202)347-8259
Editor(s): Ralph C. Thomas, III. Monthly. Concentrates on national and regional news regarding minority construction contractors. Contains articles on issues generally affecting the industry—especially issues affecting minorities—including topics such as legislative and regulatory activity and reports on major corporation developments. Recurring features include reports of meetings, news of educational opportunities, a calendar of events, and news of NAMC chapters and members.

★5386★
Building Design & Construction
Cahners Publishing Co.
1350 E. Touhy Ave.
PO Box 5080
Des Plaines, IL 60018   Phone: (708)635-8800
Philip G. Schreiner, Editor. Monthly. Magazine on business and technology for commercial, institutional, and industrial buildings. **Facsimile Number:** (708)299-8622.

★5387★
Building Homes & Renovations
Southam Business & Communications, Inc.
1450 Don Mills Rd.
Don Mills, ON, Canada M3B 2X7   Phone: (416)445-6641
Randy Threndyle, Editor. 5x/yr. Building trade and products magazine. **Facsimile Number:** (416)442-2214.

★5388★
Building Industry
Trade Publishing Co.
287 Mokauea St.
Honolulu, HI 96819   Phone: (808)848-0711
Jay McWilliams, Editor. Monthly. Construction and design magazine. **Facsimile Number:** (808)841-3053.

Roofers

★5389★
Building Industry Technology: An Abstract Newsletter
National Technical Information Service (NTIS)
U.S. Department of Commerce
5285 Port Royal Rd.
Springfield, VA 22161   Phone: (703)487-4630
Weekly. Consists of abstracts of reports on architectural and environmental design, building standards, construction materials and equipment, and structural analyses. Recurring features include a form for ordering reports from NTIS.

★5390★
Buildings
427 6th Ave. SE
PO Box 1888
Cedar Rapids, IA 52406   Phone: (319)364-6167
Linda Monroe, Editor. Monthly. **Facsimile Number:** (319)365-5421.

★5391★
Capital Comments
National Lumber & Building Material Dealers Association
40 Ivy St. SE
Washington, DC 20003   Phone: (202)547-2230
Editor(s): Matt Geitner. Semimonthly. Reports on news of legislation pertaining to lumber, other building materials, and housing. Discusses such issues as lumber subsidies, interest rates on homes, health and safety, and jobs. **Facsimile Number:** (202)547-7640.

★5392★
ConnStruction
PO Box 9768
Wethersfield, CT 06109   Phone: (203)529-3246
Victor Bonini, Editor. 7x/yr. Magazine for construction industry. **Facsimile Number:** (203)563-0616.

★5393★
CONSTRUCTION
26 Long Hill Rd.
Guilford, CT 06437   Phone: (203)453-3717
Jack C. Lewis, Editor and Publisher. 2x/mo. Journal for the construction industry.

★5394★
Construction Dimensions
Assn. of Wall & Ceiling
PO Box 5504
Washington, DC 20016   Phone: (301)656-7050
Gerald Wykoff, Editor. Monthly. Wall and ceiling industry magazine.

★5395★
Construction Industry International
Maclean Hunter Publishing Co.
29 N. Wacker Dr.
Chicago, IL 60606   Phone: (312)726-2802
Alan Elliott, Editor-in-Chief. Monthly. Trade magazine.

★5396★
Construction News
715 W. 2nd St.
PO Box 2421
Little Rock, AR 72203   Phone: (501)376-1931
Robert Alvey, Editor. Weekly. Construction industry magazine. **Facsimile Number:** (501)375-5831.

★5397★
Construction Newsletter
National Safety Council
444 N. Michigan Ave.
Chicago, IL 60611   Phone: (312)527-4800
6/yr. Focuses on industrial and occupational safety in the construction industry. Carries items on such topics as safe work practices and products, accident prevention, and successful industrial safety programs and policies.

★5398★
Contractors Guide
6201 Howard St. W.
Niles, IL 60648   Phone: (708)647-7030
Greg Ettling, Editor. Monthly. Trade magazine covering roofing and insulation. **Facsimile Number:** (708)647-7055.

★5399★
Daily Construction Reporter
4901 Pacific Hwy.
San Diego, CA 92110-4098   Phone: (619)296-0183
Kenneth F. Kerr, Editor and Publisher. Daily. Construction trade newspaper covering jobs that are out for bid, bid results, building permits, and other information. **Facsimile Number:** (619)298-3027.

★5400★
Fine Homebuilding
The Taunton Press, Inc.
63 S. Main St.
PO Box 5506
Newtown, CT 06470   Phone: (203)426-5506
Mark Feirer, Editor. 7x/yr. Magazine for builders, architects, designers, and owner-builders. **Facsimile Number:** (203)426-3434.

★5401★
Home BUILDER Magazine
Work-4 Projects Ltd.
PO Box 400, Victoria Sta.
Westmount, PQ, Canada H3Z 2V8   Phone: (514)489-4941
Nachmi Artzy, Editor and Publisher. 6x/yr. Magazine for home construction industry. **Facsimile Number:** (514)489-5505.

★5402★
The Journal of Light Construction
Hanley-Wood Partners
RR 2, Box 146
Richmond, VT 05477-9607   Phone: (802)864-0091
Steve Bliss, Editor. Monthly. Magazine (tabloid) for residential and light professionals involved in new and rehabilitative construction. Each issue covers a single aspect of construction.

★5403★
Journeyman Roofer
Union of Roofers, Waterproofers & Allied Workers
1125 17th St. NW
Washington, DC 20036   Phone: (202)638-3228
John A. McConaty, Editor. Monthly Trade journal. **Facsimile Number:** (202)737-3621.

★5404★
Metal Construction News
Modern Trade Communications
7450 N. Skokie Blvd.
Skokie, IL 60077   Phone: (708)674-2200
Shawn Zuver, Mng. Editor. Monthly. Magazine focusing on metal building, metal roof, and sidewall news. **Facsimile Number:** (708)674-3676.

★5405★
Nation's Building News
15th & M Sts. NW
Washington, DC 20005   Phone: (202)822-0525
Tim Ahern, Editor. 2x/mo. Trade magazine (tabloid) covering home building and all related industries. **Facsimile Number:** (202)861-2131.

★5406★
Professional Builder
Cahners Publishing Co.
1350 E. Touhy Ave.
Des Plaines, IL 60018   Phone: (708)635-8800
Roy L. Diez, Editor. 19x/yr. **Facsimile Number:** (708)299-8622.

★5407★
Professional Roofing
National Roofing Contractors Assn.
10255 W. Higgins Rd., Ste. 600
Rosemont, IL 60018   Phone: (708)299-9070
Monique Mencacci, Sr. Editor. Monthly. Roofing industry magazine. **Facsimile Number:** (708)299-1183.

★5408★
RIEI Information Letter
Roofing Industry Educational Institute (RIEI)
14 Inverness Dr. E., No. H-110
Englewood, CO 80112-5608   Phone: (303)790-7200
Editor(s): Susan E. Mathews. Quarterly. Features technical articles on aspects of the roofing industry. Covers the educational activities of the Institute. Recurring features include a calendar of events. **Facsimile Number:** (303)790-9006.

★5409★
ROOFER Magazine
D & H Publications
12120 Amedicus Ln.
Fort Myers, FL 33907   Phone: (813)275-7663
Kaerrie A. Simons, Editor. 12x/yr. Independent national trade magazine for the roofing industry. **Facsimile Number:** (813)939-0806.

★5410★
RSI (Roofing/Siding/Insulation)
Edgell Communications, Inc.
7500 Old Oak Blvd.
Cleveland, OH 44130   Phone: (216)243-8100
Mike Russo, Editor. Monthly. Magazine containing technical and applications information on roofing, siding, insulation, and related fields.

★5411★
The SPEC-DATA Program
Construction Specifications Institute
601 Madison St.
Alexandria, VA 22314   Phone: (703)684-0300
Brenda A. Furiga, Mgr. Quarterly. Magazine (loose-leaf) for the construction industry covering technical and product information. **Facsimile Number:** (703)684-0465.

─── Meetings and Conventions ───

★5412★
National Association of Home Builders/The Builders Show
National Association of Home Builders of the United States
15th and M Sts., NW
Washington, DC 20005   Phone: (202)822-0424
Frequency: Usually held in January; location rotates every three years. 1993; Feb. 19-22; Las Vegas, NV • 1994; Jan. 21-24; Las Vegas, NV. **Toll-free/Additional Phone Number(s):** 800-368-5242. **Facsimile Number:** (202)822-0435.

★5413★
National Roofing Contractors Association (NRCA)
O'Hare Intl. Center
10255 W. Higgins Rd., Ste. 600
Rosemont, IL 60018-5607   Phone: (708)299-9070
Frequency: Annual. Also holds 3 conferences annually and cosponsors a biennial Conference on Roofing Technology and quinquennial international symposium. **Facsimile Number:** (708)299-1183.

★5414★
National Roofing Contractors Association Annual Convention and Trade Show
National Roofing Contractors Association
O'Hare International Center
10255 W. Higgins Rd., Ste. 600
Rosemont, IL 60018-5607   Phone: (708)299-9070
1993; Feb. 16-29; San Antonio, TX • 1994; Feb. 20-23; San Francisco, CA • 1995; Feb. 19-22; New Orleans, LA • 1996; Feb. 27 - Mar. 01; San Diego, CA • 1997; Feb. 04 - Mar. 07; Orlando, FL • 1998; Feb. 08-11; Las Vegas, NV • 1999; Feb. 07-10; Phoenix, AZ • 2000; Feb. 27 - Mar. 01; Miami, FL. **Facsimile Number:** (708)299-1183.

★5415★
United Union of Roofers, Waterproofers and Allied Workers (UURWAW)
1125 17th St. NW
Washington, DC 20036   Phone: (202)638-3228
Frequency: Quinquennial. **Facsimile Number:** (202)737-3621.

─── Other Sources of Information ───

★5416★
Roofinig Technology Conference, 9th: Proceedings
National Roofing Contractors Association
O'Hare Intl. Center
10255 W. Higgins Rd., Ste. 600
Rosemont, IL 60018-5607   Phone: (708)299-9070
Walter J. Rossiter, Jr., editor. 1989.

★5417★
Standard for Safety for Roof Trusses for Manufactured Homes
Underwriters Laboratories, Inc.
1285 Walt Whitman Rd.
Melville, NY 11747   Phone: (576)271-6200
Third edition, 1990.

Roustabouts

Roustabouts perform much of the routine physical labor and maintenance in and around oil fields and pipelines, such as digging ditches for foundations or for drainage, loading and unloading trucks and boats, and mixing concrete. Roustabouts are employed in the oil and gas field services industry and the contract drilling industry in primarily eight states—Texas, Louisiana, Oklahoma, California, Colorado, Wyoming, Alaska, and New Mexico.

$alaries

Hourly salaries for roustabouts are listed below.

Onshore roustabouts in the oil and gas industry	$11.69/hour
Offshore roustabouts in the oil and gas industry	$13.41/hour
Onshore roustabouts in the contract drilling industry	$9.87/hour
Offshore roustabouts in the contract drilling industry	$9.06/hour

Employment Outlook

Growth rate until the year 2000: Employment is expected to remain level.

Roustabouts

Career Guides

★5418★
American Professionals Series
Cambridge Career Products
90 MacCorkle Ave., SW
South Charleston, WV 25311   Phone: (304)744-9323
Videocassette. 1984. 30 mins. In this series of twenty-one half hour programs, various occupations are examined in depth, including a day in the life of each worker. Included are: fireman, farmer, oil driller, fisherman, horse trainer, and auto assembly repairman.

★5419★
Going Offshore for the First Time
International Training Company
3301 Allen Pkwy.
Post Office Box 3881
Houston, TX 77001   Phone: (713)529-5928
Videocassette. 1984. 50 mins. This program looks at safety procedures for transporting plus orientation to the rig and emergency procedures. This program is part of the "Orientation for New Offshore Personnel" series.

★5420★
The Green Man
Film Library
3450 Wilshire Blvd. #700
Los Angeles, CA 90010-2215   Phone: (213)384-8114
Videocassette. 198?. 20 mins. This film shows how a new employee on a drilling rig is orientated, trained, counselled and begins to gain confidence in himself during his first days on the job.

★5421★
Profile: The Petroleum Industry
University of Texas at Austin
Petroleum Extension Service
10100 Burnet Rd.
Austin, TX 78758   Phone: (512)835-3154
Videocassette. 1981. 30 mins. An overview of the petroleum industry from exploration to refining is provided.

★5422★
Roustabout
Chronicle Guidance Publications, Inc.
PO Box 1190
Moravia, NY 13118-1190   Phone: (315)497-0330
1987. This career brief describes the nature of the work, working conditions, hours and earnings, education and training, licensure, certification, unions, personal qualifications, social and psychological factors, employment outlook, entry methods, advancement, and related occupations. **Toll-free/Additional Phone Number(s):** 800-622-7284.

★5423★
"Roustabout" in *Occupational Outlook Handbook* (pp. 379-381)
Superintendent of Documents
U.S. Government Printing Office
Washington, DC 20402   Phone: (202)783-3238
Biennial; latest edition, 1990-91. Encyclopedia of careers describing more than 250 occupations and comprising about 86 percent of all jobs in the economy. Occupations that require lengthy education or training are given the most attention. For each occupation, the handbook describes job duties, working conditions, training, educational preparation, personal qualities, advancement possibilities, job outlook, earnings, and sources of additional information.

★5424★
"Roustabouts" in Volume 5 of *Career Discovery Encyclopedia* (pp. 166-167)
J.G. Ferguson Publishing Co.
200 W. Monroe
Chicago, IL 60606   Phone: (312)580-5480
E. Russell Primm, editor-in-chief. 1990. Contains two-page articles on 504 occupations. Each article describes job duties, earnings, and educational and training requirements.

★5425★
"Roustabouts" in Volume 3 of *The Encyclopedia of Careers and Vocational Guidance* (pp. 698-702)
J.G. Ferguson Publishing Co.
200 W. Monroe
Chicago, IL 60606   Phone: (312)580-5480
William E. Hopke, editor-in-chief. Eighth edition, 1990. Four-volume set that profiles 500 occupations and describes job trends in 76 industries. Includes career description, educational requirements, history of the job, methods of entry, advancement, employment outlook, earnings, working conditions, social and psychological factors, and sources of additional information.

★5426★
Wellhead Operations
University of Texas at Austin
Petroleum Extension Service
10100 Burnet Rd.
Austin, TX 78758   Phone: (512)835-3154
Videocassette. 1981. 23 mins. This program introduces gas field operators to routine wellhead operations.

★5427★
Work Procedures for a Derrickman
International Training Company
3301 Allen Pkwy.
Post Office Box 3881
Houston, TX 77001　　　　　　　　　Phone: (713)529-5928

Videocassette. 1984. 50 mins. This program discusses job responsibilities of the derrickman, both in the derrick and in the pump room. This program is part of the "Working Offshore" series.

★5428★
Work Procedures for a Roustabout
International Training Company
3301 Allen Pkwy.
Post Office Box 3881
Houston, TX 77001　　　　　　　　　Phone: (713)529-5928

Videocassette. 1984. 50 mins. This program takes a look at the life of a roustabout. This program is part of the "Working Offshore" series.

Associations

★5429★
American Petroleum Institute (API)
1220 L St. NW
Washington, DC 20005　　　　　　　Phone: (202)682-8000

Membership: Corporations in the petroleum and allied products industries, including producers, refiners, marketers, and transporters of crude oil, lubricating oil, gasoline, and natural gas. **Purpose:** Seeks to maintain cooperation between government and industry on all matters of national concern; fosters foreign and domestic trade in American petroleum products; promotes the interests of the petroleum industry; encourages the study of the arts and sciences connected with the petroleum industry. Provides information services; conducts fundamental research on petroleum; maintains large library. Operates functional departments to support the work of the institute including a central abstracting and indexing service in New York City. **Publications:** *American Petroleum Institute—Directory*, annual. • *American Petroleum Institute—Publications and Materials*, annual. • *API Report to the Membership*, annual. • *Basic Petroleum Data Book*, 3 updates/year. • *Imported Crude Oil and Petroleum Products*, monthly. • *Inventories of Natural Gas Liquids and Liquefied Refinery Gases*, monthly. • *Joint Association Survey*, annual. • *Monthly Completion Report*. • *Monthly Statistical Report*. • *Quarterly Completion Report*. • *Weekly Statistical Bulletin*. • Also publishes several hundred manuals, booklets, and other materials on production, refining, marketing, transportation, research, safety and fire protection, standards and codes, and related areas. **Facsimile Number:** (202)682-8030.

★5430★
International Union of Petroleum and Industrial Workers (IUPIW)
8131 E. Rosecrans Ave.
Paramount, CA 90723　　　　　　　Phone: (213)630-6232

Membership: Affiliated with Seafarers' International Union of North America.

Standards/Certification Agencies

Due to keen competition for jobs in recent years, an increasing proportion of entrants to this occupation have previous work experience as a roustabout or a two-year degree in petroleum technology, which provides knowledge of oil field operations and familiarity with automated equipment. Beginning roustabouts without postsecondary training or previous work experience learn through on-the-job training under the supervision of a more skilled worker.

Basic Reference Guides and Handbooks

★5431★
Basic Petroleum Data Book
American Petroleum Institute (API)
1220 L St. NW
Washington, DC 20005　　　　　　　Phone: (202)682-8000

3 updates/year. Domestic and world statistical background data (since 1947) on energy, reserves, exploration and drilling, production, finance, prices, demand, refining, imports, exports, offshore, transportation, natural gas, and the Organization of Petroleum Exporting Countries.

Periodicals

★5432★
ABC Newsline
Associated Builders and Contractors, Inc. (ABC)
729 15th St. NW
Washington, DC 20005　　　　　　　Phone: (202)637-8800

Editor(s): Lisa A. Nardone. Semimonthly. Designed to keep readers alerted to important changes within ABC and the construction industry. Reports on legislative issues, construction trends, conferences and meetings, and ABC services. Recurring features include news of members and a column titled Industry Briefs.

★5433★
Advanced Recovery Week
Pasha Publications, Inc.
2340 Texas Commerce Tower
Houston, TX 77002　　　　　　　　Phone: (713)225-6035

Editor(s): Jerry Grisham. 50/yr. Concentrates on enhanced oil recovery, especially new technology in chemical application, heating, and drilling with the aid of electricity, steam, water, microbes, gasses, polymers, and other techniques. Also covers costs of implementation, government and industry actions affecting oil recovery, market conditions, and tax incentives. **Facsimile Number:** (713)225-6436.

★5434★
API Report to the Membership
American Petroleum Institute (API)
1220 L St. NW
Washington, DC 20005　　　　　　　Phone: (202)682-8000

Annual. Review of API activities.

★5435★
Drilling Contractor
International Assn. of Drilling Contractors
1581 Park 10 Pl., Ste. 222
Houston, TX 77084　　　　　　　　Phone: (713)578-7171

Alvaro Franco, Editor and Publisher. 6x/yr. Magazine covering technical, economic, and political developments affecting the drilling and production segments of the international petroleum industry. **Facsimile Number:** (713)578-0589.

★5436★
IUPIW-Views
International Union of Petroleum & Industrial Workers, SIUNA (IUPIW)
8131 E. Rosecranes
Paramount, CA 90723   Phone: (213)630-6232
Editor(s): Robert Davidson. Bimonthly. Presents labor, safety, and consumer news for petroleum and industrial workers. Recurring features include obituaries, a schedule of activities, editorials, news of research, letters to the editor, news of members, and a calendar of events. **Facsimile Number:** (213)408-1073.

★5437★
Ocean Construction Locator
Offshore Data Services, Inc.
PO Box 19909
Houston, TX 77224-9909   Phone: (713)781-2713
Editor(s): Mark McKee. Monthly. Reports on petroleum-related offshore construction projects worldwide, from the planning stage through final installation. Covers platforms, pipelines, subsea completions, and mooring terminals. Recurring features include sections on construction barge locations and possible areas for future development. **Facsimile Number:** (713)781-9594.

★5438★
Ocean Industry
Gulf Publishing Co.
3301 Allen Pkwy.
PO Box 2608
Houston, TX 77252   Phone: (713)529-4301
Robert Snyder, Editor. 10x/yr. Magazine covering offshore drilling production and pipeline construction projects. **Facsimile Number:** (713)520-4433.

★5439★
Ocean Oil Weekly Report
PennWell Publishing Company
3050 Post Oak, Ste. 200
PO Box 1941
Houston, TX 77251   Phone: (713)621-9720
Editor(s): Michael Crowder. Weekly. Provides weekly news of the offshore oil industry and analysis of significant events. Includes information on offshore concessions, mobile rigs, exploration and productions, pipeline and construction, contractors stock market report, and personnel notes. **Toll-free/Additional Phone Number(s):** 800-874-1510 **Facsimile Number:** (713)963-6285.

★5440★
Offshore Rig Locator
Offshore Data Services, Inc.
PO Box 19909
Houston, TX 77224   Phone: (713)781-2713
Editor(s): John Chadderdon. Monthly. Provides information on the location of offshore drilling rigs. Tracks each of the more than 800 mobile rigs and 400 platform rigs currently operating and under construction, both in the U.S. and in international waters. Categorizes by geographical areas and rig type and includes contract status and major sub-contractors. **Facsimile Number:** (713)781-9594.

★5441★
Offshore Rig Newsletter
Offshore Data Services, Inc.
PO Box 19909
Houston, TX 77224   Phone: (713)781-2713
Editor(s): Richard Maddox. Monthly. Contains information on drilling rigs. Covers performance, design, and new construction of rigs. Discusses insurance, labor problems, costs, accidents, and industry trends. Recurring features include a market outlook each month. **Facsimile Number:** (713)781-9594.

─────── Other Sources of Information ───────

★5442★
API Monthly Statistical Report
American Petroleum Institute (API)
1220 L St. NW
Washington, DC 20005   Phone: (202)682-8000
Summary of the estimated U.S. petroleum balance with analyses of the trends reflected in the *Weekly Statistical Bulletin*.

Sheet-Metal Workers

Sheet-metal workers fabricate, install, and maintain air-conditioning, heating, ventilation, and pollution control duct systems; roofs; siding; rain gutters and downspouts; skylights; restaurant equipment; outdoor signs; and many other building parts and products made from metal sheets. They may also work with fiberglass and plastic materials. Although some workers specialize in fabrication, installation, or maintenance, most do all three jobs. Approximately 75% of sheet-metal workers are employed by plumbing, heating, and air-conditioning contractors; about 20% work for roofing and sheet-metal contractors; and the rest work for general contractors engaged in residential and commercial building. Unlike many other construction trades, very few sheet-metal workers are self-employed.

$alaries

Union sheet-metal workers' average earnings are $18.82/hour. Apprentices generally start at about 40 percent of the rate paid to experienced workers. Thoughout the course of the apprenticeship program, they receive periodic increases as they acquire the skills of the trade.

Employment Outlook

Growth rate until the year 2000: Average.

Sheet-Metal Workers

Career Guides

★5443★
Careers in Sheet Metal
National Training Fund/Sheet Metal
and Air Conditioning Industry
601 N. Fairfax St.
Alexandria, VA 22314

Third edition, 1989. This 24-page booklet describes needed qualities, basic requirements, working conditions, and training. Explains the sheet metal industry's apprenticeship program.

★5444★
Construction Cluster
Center for Humanities, Inc.
Communications Park
Box 1000
Mount Kisco, NY 10549　　　　　Phone: (914)666-4100

Videocassette. 1984. 15 mins. Construction workers describe what it's like to work at their jobs, and show the special equipment they use in their field.

★5445★
"Sheet Metal Duct Systems for Heating and Air Conditioning. . ." in Opportunities in Refrigeration and Air Conditioning Trades (pp. 71-81)
National Textbook Co.
4255 W. Touhy Ave.
Lincolnwood, IL 60646　　　　　Phone: (312)679-5500

Richard Budzik. 1989. Surveys the air conditioning and refrigeration industry. Describes jobs, educational and training requirements, small business opportunities, places of employment, and job outlook. Offers job hunting advice.

★5446★
"Sheet Metal Work" in Opportunities in Plumbing and Pipefitting Careers (pp. 79-82)
National Textbook Co.
4255 W. Touhy Ave.
Lincolnwood, IL 60646　　　　　Phone: (312)679-5500

Patrick J. Galvin. 1989. Describes the work, jobs, educational preparation, training, apprenticeships, a typical working day, salaries, future trends, and related fields.

★5447★
Sheet Metal Worker
Careers, Inc.
PO Box 135
Largo, FL 34649-0135　　　　　Phone: (813)584-7333

1991. Two-page occupational summary card describing duties, working conditions, personal qualifications, training, earnings and hours, employment outlook, places of employment, related careers and where to write for more information.

★5448★
"Sheet Metal Worker" in Construction, **Volume 4 of** *Career Information Center* (pp. 84-85)
Glencoe/Macmillan
15319 Chatsworth St.
Mission Hills, CA 91345　　　　　Phone: (818)898-1391

Richard Lidz and Dale Anderson, editorial directors. Fourth edition, 1990. For 600 occupations, describes job duties, entry-level requirements, education and training needed, advancement possibilities, employment outlook, earnings and benefits. The set is divided into 12 volumes. Each volume includes jobs related under a broad career field. Volume 13 is the index. **Facsimile Number:** 818-365-5489.

★5449★
"Sheet Metal Worker" in Hard Hatted Women: Stories of Struggle and Success in the Trades (pp. 17-32)
Seal Press
3131 Western Ave., Ste. 410
Seattle, WA 98121　　　　　Phone: (206)283-7844

Molly Martin, editor. 1988. Twenty-six women recount their experiences working in blue collar occupations. They describe how they got in, the work they do, their relationships in predominantly male occupations, and their training.

★5450★
"Sheet Metal Worker" in Occu-Facts: Information on 565 Careers in Outline Form (p. 17.10)
Careers, Inc.
P.O. Box 135
1211 Tenth St., S.W.
Largo, FL 33640　　　　　Phone: (813)584-7333

Elizabeth Handville. Biennial, 1989-90 edition. Each one-page occupational profile describes duties, working conditions, physical surroundings and demands, aptitudes, temperament, educational requirements, employment outlook, earnings, and places of employment.

★5451★
Sheet Metal Workers
Chronicle Guidance Publications, Inc.
PO Box 1190
Moravia, NY 13118-1190　　　　　Phone: (315)497-0330

1990. This career brief describes the nature of the work, working conditions, hours and earnings, education and training, licensure, certification, unions, personal qualifications, social and psychological factors, employment outlook, entry methods, advancement, and related occupations. **Toll-free/Additional Phone Number(s):** 800-622-7284.

★5452★

"Sheet Metal Workers" in *Occupational Outlook Handbook* (pp. 381-383)
Superintendent of Documents
U.S. Government Printing Office
Washington, DC 20402　　　　　　Phone: (202)783-3238

Biennial; latest edition, 1990-91. Encyclopedia of careers describing more than 250 occupations and comprising about 86 percent of all jobs in the economy. Occupations that require lengthy education or training are given the most attention. For each occupation, the handbook describes job duties, working conditions, training, educational preparation, personal qualities, advancement possibilities, job outlook, earnings, and sources of additional information.

★5453★

"Sheet Metal Workers" in Volume 6 of *Career Discovery Encyclopedia* (pp. 22-23)
J.G. Ferguson Publishing Co.
200 W. Monroe
Chicago, IL 60606　　　　　　Phone: (312)580-5480

E. Russell Primm, editor-in-chief. 1990. Contains two-page articles on 504 occupations. Each article describes job duties, earnings, and educational and training requirements.

★5454★

"Sheet Metal Workers" in Volume 3 of *The Encyclopedia of Careers and Vocational Guidance* (pp. 702-705)
J.G. Ferguson Publishing Co.
200 W. Monroe
Chicago, IL 60606　　　　　　Phone: (312)580-5480

William E. Hopke, editor-in-chief. Eighth edition, 1990. Four-volume set that profiles 500 occupations and describes job trends in 76 industries. Includes career description, educational requirements, history of the job, methods of entry, advancement, employment outlook, earnings, working conditions, social and psychological factors, and sources of additional information.

★5455★

"Sheet Metal Working" in *Opportunities in Metalworking Careers* (pp. 17-26)
National Textbook Co.
4255 W. Touhy Ave.
Lincolnwood, IL 60646　　　　　　Phone: (312)679-5500

Mark Rowh. 1991. Covers sheet metal work, machining, structural and reinforcing metalworking, and jewelry making. Describes the work performed, skills needed, training and working conditions. Lists unions that sponsor apprenticeship and technical schools which offer training.

★5456★

Technical/Manufacturing Cluster One
Center for Humanities, Inc.
Communications Park
Box 1000
Mount Kisco, NY 10549　　　　　　Phone: (914)666-4100

Videocassette. 1984. 20 mins. An upclose look at people who work in the fields of welding, drafting, and sheet metal.

★5457★

Video Career Library - Production II
Careers, Inc.
1211 10th St., SW
PO Box 135
Largo, FL 34649-0135　　　　　　Phone: (813)584-7333

Videocassette. 1990. 32 mins. Part of the Video Career Library covering 165 occupations. Shows actual workers on the job. Includes tool and die makers, machinists, sheet metal workers, cabinet and bench carpenters, opticians, precision electronic equipment assemblers, industrial machine operators, welders and cutters, and assemblers.

Associations

★5458★

Associated Builders and Contractors (ABC)
729 15th St. NW
Washington, DC 20005　　　　　　Phone: (202)637-8800

Membership: Construction contractors, subcontractors, suppliers, and associates. **Purpose:** Aim is to foster and perpetuate the principles of rewarding shop construction workers and management on the basis of merit. Sponsors leadership conference and management education programs including Wheels of Learning; also sponsors apprenticeship and skill training programs. Disseminates technological and labor relations information. Maintains biographical archives and placement service. Bestows awards; compiles statistics. **Publications:** *ABC Newsline*, semimonthly. • *The Builder and Contractor*, monthly. • *Classified Membership Directory*, annual. • Also publishes safety manuals.

★5459★

National Training Fund for the Sheet Metal and Air Conditioning Industry
Edward F. Carlough Plaza
601 N. Fairfax St., Ste. 240
Alexandria, VA 22314

Provides general information about sheet-metal workers.

★5460★

Sheet Metal and Air Conditioning Contractors' National Association (SMACNA)
PO Box 70
Merrifield, VA 22116　　　　　　Phone: (703)790-9890

Membership: Ventilating, air handling, warm air heating, architectural and industrial sheet metal, kitchen equipment, testing and balancing, siding, and decking and specialty fabrication contractors. **Purpose:** Prepares standards and codes; sponsors research and educational programs on sheet metal duct construction and fire damper (single and multi-blade) construction. Engages in legislative and labor activities; conducts business management and contractor education programs. Maintains 30 committees including: Business Management Education; Codes; Direct Construction Standards; Duct Design; Energy Management; Fibrous Products; Fire and Smoke Control; Future Management Education; SMACPAC. **Publications:** *Annual Report*. • *Membership Directory*, annual. • *SMACNEWS*, bimonthly. • Also publishes *Chaptergram* and materials on standards, specifications, technical books, manuals, and practices and codes covering all phases of the industry. **Facsimile Number:** (703)893-5710.

Standards/Certification Agencies

An apprenticeship program is considered to be the best way to learn the sheet-metal working trade. The program consists of four to five years of on-the-job training and a minimum of 144 hours per year of classroom instruction. It provides comprehensive instruction in both sheet-metal fabrication and installation. The programs are administered by joint committees of locals of the Sheet Metal Workers' International Association and local chapters of the Sheet Metal and Air-Conditioning Contractors' National Association, or by local chapters of the Associated Builders and Contractors. A relatively small number of persons pick up th trade informally, usually by working as

Sheet-Metal Workers

helpers to experienced sheet-metal workers. Those who acquire their skills this way often take vocational school courses in mathematics or sheet metal fabrication to supplement their work experience. Helpers usually must pass an examination to be promoted to the journeyman level.

★5461★
Sheet Metal and Air Conditioning Contractors' National Association (SMACNA)
PO Box 70
Merrifield, VA 22116 Phone: (703)790-9890
Prepares construction standards and codes. bimonthly. • Also publishes *Chaptergram* and materials on standards, specifications, technical books, manuals, and practices and codes covering all phases of the industry. **Facsimile Number:** (703)893-5710.

---------- Test Guides ----------

★5462★
Foreman Sheet Metal Worker
National Learning Corp.
212 Michael Dr.
Syosset, NY 11791 Phone: (516)921-8888
Jack Rudman. Part of the Career Examination Series No. 1. All examination guides in this series contain questions with answers. **Facsimile Number:** (516)921-8743. **Toll-free/Additional Phone Number(s):** 800-645-6337.

★5463★
Sheet Metal Fabrication
National Learning Corp.
212 Michael Dr.
Syosset, NY 11791 Phone: (516)921-8888
Jack Rudman. 1989. Part of Occupational Competency Examination Series.

★5464★
Sheet Metal Worker
National Learning Corp.
212 Michael Dr.
Syosset, NY 11791 Phone: (516)921-8888
Jack Rudman. Part of the Career Examination Series No. 1. All examination guides in this series contain questions with answers. **Facsimile Number:** (516)921-8743. **Toll-free/Additional Phone Number(s):** 800-645-6337.

---------- Basic Reference Guides and Handbooks ----------

★5465★
Intelligent Buildings Institute—Directory of Products and Services
Intelligent Buildings Institute (IBI)
2101 L St., NW, Ste. 300
Washington, DC 20037 Phone: (202)457-1988
S. Hunt, Associate Executive Director, editor. Annual, September. Member consultants, associations, research organizations, and other suppliers of products and services to the construction and building industry. Entries include: Company name, address, phone. Arrangement: Alphabetical. Indexes: Product/service. **Facsimile Number:** (202)457-8468.

★5466★
Mid-West Contractor—Annual Convention Guide and Association Directory
Allied Publications, Inc.
7355 N. Woodland Dr.
Box 603
Indianapolis, IN 46278 Phone: (317)297-5500
Jennifer Wynne, editor. Annual. List of 160 construction contracting and architectural associations in the Midwest. Entries include: Association name, address, phone, names and titles of key personnel, description of association; convention site, date, name and title of contact. Arrangement: Geographical, alphabetical. **Toll-free/Additional Phone Number(s):** (800)827-7468. **Facsimile Number:** (317)299-1356.

---------- Periodicals ----------

★5467★
ABC Newsline
Associated Builders and Contractors, Inc. (ABC)
729 15th St. NW
Washington, DC 20005 Phone: (202)637-8800
Editor(s): Lisa A. Nardone. Semimonthly. Designed to keep readers alerted to important changes within ABC and the construction industry. Reports on legislative issues, construction trends, conferences and meetings, and ABC services. Recurring features include news of members and a column titled Industry Briefs.

★5468★
American Architectural Manufacturers Association— Quarterly Review
American Architectural Manufacturers Association
1540 E. Dundee Rd., Ste. K 310
Palatine, IL 60067-8321 Phone: (708)202-1350
Editor(s): Tony Coorlim. Annually. Contains industry news on architectural products. Covers prime and combination storm windows, sliding glass and combination storm doors, window and curtain-walls, store fronts and entrances, siding, soffits, fascia, gutters, downspouts, skylights, space enclosures, and mobile home components. Recurring features include news of research, notices of publications available, and announcements by the association. **Facsimile Number:** (708)202-1480.

★5469★
American Institute of Constructors—Newsletter
American Institute of Constructors
9887 Gandy Blvd. N., No. 104
Saint Petersburg, FL 33702-2451
Editor(s): Ed Freedman. Bimonthly. Concerned with construction practice, design, administration, and teaching. Carries news of members, listings of job opportunities, local chapter reports, and notices of new publications. **Facsimile Number:** (614)464-3226.

★5470★
Blue Reports, Inc.
Construction News Service
7325 Steel Mill Dr.
Springfield, VA 22050 Phone: (703)644-5884
Editor(s): Calvin S. Oren. Daily. Reports on public and private construction projects in the Washington, DC, Virginia, and Maryland areas. Provides owner's and architect's names, plan status, date bids due, prospective bidders, low bids received, and specification details. **Facsimile Number:** (703)644-1929.

★5471★
The Builder and Contractor
Associated Builders and Contractors (ABC)
729 15th St. NW
Washington, DC 20005			Phone: (202)637-8800
Monthly.

★5472★
Building Concerns
National Association of Minority Contractors (NAMC)
806 15th St. NW, Ste. 340
Washington, DC 20005			Phone: (202)347-8259
Editor(s): Ralph C. Thomas, III. Monthly. Concentrates on national and regional news regarding minority construction contractors. Contains articles on issues generally affecting the industry—especially issues affecting minorities—including topics such as legislative and regulatory activity and reports on major corporation developments. Recurring features include reports of meetings, news of educational opportunities, a calendar of events, and news of NAMC chapters and members.

★5473★
Building Industry Technology: An Abstract Newsletter
National Technical Information Service (NTIS)
U.S. Department of Commerce
5285 Port Royal Rd.
Springfield, VA 22161			Phone: (703)487-4630
Weekly. Consists of abstracts of reports on architectural and environmental design, building standards, construction materials and equipment, and structural analyses. Recurring features include a form for ordering reports from NTIS.

★5474★
Capital Comments
National Lumber & Building Material Dealers Association
40 Ivy St. SE
Washington, DC 20003			Phone: (202)547-2230
Editor(s): Matt Geitner. Semimonthly. Reports on news of legislation pertaining to lumber, other building materials, and housing. Discusses such issues as lumber subsidies, interest rates on homes, health and safety, and jobs. **Facsimile Number:** (202)547-7640.

★5475★
Chaptergram
Sheet Metal and Air Conditioning Contractors' National
  Association (SMACNA
PO Box 70
Merrifield, VA 22116			Phone: (703)790-9890

★5476★
ConnStruction
PO Box 9768
Wethersfield, CT 06109			Phone: (203)529-3246
Victor Bonini, Editor. 7x/yr. Magazine for construction industry. **Facsimile Number:** (203)563-0616.

★5477★
CONSTRUCTION
26 Long Hill Rd.
Guilford, CT 06437			Phone: (203)453-3717
Jack C. Lewis, Editor and Publisher. 2x/mo. Journal for the construction industry.

★5478★
Construction Dimensions
Assn. of Wall & Ceiling
PO Box 5504
Washington, DC 20016			Phone: (301)656-7050
Gerald Wykoff, Editor. Monthly. Wall and ceiling industry magazine.

★5479★
Construction Industry International
Maclean Hunter Publishing Co.
29 N. Wacker Dr.
Chicago, IL 60606			Phone: (312)726-2802
Alan Elliott, Editor-in-Chief. Monthly. Trade magazine.

★5480★
Construction News
715 W. 2nd St.
PO Box 2421
Little Rock, AR 72203			Phone: (501)376-1931
Robert Alvey, Editor. Weekly. Construction industry magazine. **Facsimile Number:** (501)375-5831.

★5481★
Construction Newsletter
National Safety Council
444 N. Michigan Ave.
Chicago, IL 60611			Phone: (312)527-4800
6/yr. Focuses on industrial and occupational safety in the construction industry. Carries items on such topics as safe work practices and products, accident prevention, and successful industrial safety programs and policies.

★5482★
Daily Construction Reporter
4901 Pacific Hwy.
San Diego, CA 92110-4098			Phone: (619)296-0183
Kenneth F. Kerr, Editor and Publisher. Daily. Construction trade newspaper covering jobs that are out for bid, bid results, building permits, and other information. **Facsimile Number:** (619)298-3027.

★5483★
Home BUILDER Magazine
Work-4 Projects Ltd.
PO Box 400, Victoria Sta.
Westmount, PQ, Canada H3Z 2V8			Phone: (514)489-4941
Nachmi Artzy, Editor and Publisher. 6x/yr. Magazine for home construction industry. **Facsimile Number:** (514)489-5505.

★5484★
The Journal of Light Construction
Hanley-Wood Partners
RR 2, Box 146
Richmond, VT 05477-9607			Phone: (802)864-0091
Steve Bliss, Editor. Monthly. Magazine (tabloid) for residential and light professionals involved in new and rehabilitative construction. Each issue covers a single aspect of construction.

★5485★
Nation's Building News
15th & M Sts. NW
Washington, DC 20005			Phone: (202)822-0525
Tim Ahern, Editor. 2x/mo. Trade magazine (tabloid) covering home building and all related industries. **Facsimile Number:** (202)861-2131.

★5486★
Professional Builder
Cahners Publishing Co.
1350 E. Touhy Ave.
Des Plaines, IL 60018   Phone: (708)635-8800
Roy L. Diez, Editor. 19x/yr. **Facsimile Number:** (708)299-8622.

★5487★
SMACNA Newsletter
Sheet Metal and Air Conditioning Contractors' National
   Association (SMACNA)
4201 Layfayette Center Dr.
Chantilly, VA 22021-1209   Phone: (703)803-2980
Editor(s): Rosalind P. Raymond. Semimonthly. Provides information on the sheet metal industry. Covers labor, legislative, and governmental actions affecting the industry. Recurring features include association news and a calendar of events. **Facsimile Number:** (703)803-3732.

★5488★
SMACNEWS
Sheet Metal and Air Conditioning Contractors' National
   Association (SMACNA
PO Box 70
Merrifield, VA 22116   Phone: (703)790-9890
Bimonthly. Newsletter.

★5489★
Snips Magazine
407 Mannheim Rd.
Bellwood, IL 60104-9989   Phone: (708)544-3870
Nick Carter, Editor and Publisher. Monthly. Magazine for the sheet metal, warm-air heating, ventilating, and air conditioning industry. **Facsimile Number:** (708)544-3884.

———— Meetings and Conventions ————

★5490★
Associated Builders and Contractors (ABC)
729 15th St. NW
Washington, DC 20005   Phone: (202)637-8800
Frequency: Annual.

★5491★
Florida Roofing, Sheet Metal, and Air Conditioning Contractors Association Trade Exposition
Florida Roofing, Sheet Metal, and Air Conditioning Contractors
   Association
Drawer 4850
Winter Park, FL 32793   Phone: (407)671-3772
1992. **Toll-free/Additional Phone Number(s):** 800-476-3772. **Facsimile Number:** (407)679-0010.

★5492★
Heating, Ventilation, and Air Conditioning Product and Equipment Show
Institute of Heating and Air Conditioning Industries
606 N. Larchmont Blvd., Ste. 4A
Los Angeles, CA 90004   Phone: (213)467-1158

★5493★
Midwest Specialty Exposition
Kansas Plumbing, Heating, and Cooling Contractors Association
320 Laura St.
Wichita, KS 67211   Phone: (316)262-8860
1992. **Facsimile Number:** (316)265-7381.

★5494★
Sheet Metal and Air-Conditioning Contractors National Association Convention
Sheet Metal and Air-Conditioning Contractors National
   Association
PO Box 70
Merrifield, VA 22116   Phone: (703)790-9890
1992; Seattle, WA • 1993; Boston, MA • 1994; Orlando, FL.

Structural and Reinforcing Ironworkers

Structural and reinforcing ironworkers fabricate, assemble, and install such products as structural steel, reinforced concrete, and ornamental iron. These workers also repair, renovate, and maintain older buildings and structures such as steel mills, utility plants, automobile factories, highways, and bridges. Almost all structural and reinforcing ironworkers are employed in the construction industry. About 50% work for structural steel erection contractors; most of the remainder work for a variety of contractors specializing in the construction of homes, factories, commercial buildings, churches, schools, bridges and tunnels, and water, sewer, communications, and power lines. A few work for government agencies, utilities, and manufacturing firms that do some of their own construction work. Very few are self-employed.

$alaries

Median earnings for ironworkers is about $506/week. Apprentices usually start at 40 to 60 percent of the wages paid to experienced workers.

Employment Outlook

Growth rate until the year 2000: Average.

Structural and Reinforcing Ironworkers

Career Guides

★5495★
Construction Cluster
Center for Humanities, Inc.
Communications Park
Box 1000
Mount Kisco, NY 10549   Phone: (914)666-4100

Videocassette. 1984. 15 mins. Construction workers describe what it's like to work at their jobs, and show the special equipment they use in their field.

★5496★
Construction Ironworkers
Chronicle Guidance Publications, Inc.
PO Box 1190
Moravia, NY 13118-1190   Phone: (315)497-0330

1988. This career brief describes the nature of the work, working conditions, hours and earnings, education and training, licensure, certification, unions, personal qualifications, social and psychological factors, employment outlook, entry methods, advancement, and related occupations. **Toll-free/Additional Phone Number(s):** 800-622-7284.

★5497★
Iron Ore Processing & Blast Furnace Iron Making
South Asia Books
PO Box 502
Columbia, MO 65205   Phone: (314)449-1359

S. K. Gupta, editor. 1990.

★5498★
"Iron Workers" in Occu-Facts: Information on 565 Careers in Outline Form (p. 16.18)
Careers, Inc.
P.O. Box 135
1211 Tenth St., S.W.
Largo, FL 33640   Phone: (813)584-7333

Elizabeth Handville. Biennial, 1989-90 edition. Each one-page occupational profile describes duties, working conditions, physical surroundings and demands, aptitudes, temperament, educational requirements, employment outlook, earnings, and places of employment.

★5499★
Iron Workers (Structural, Ornamental and Reinforcing)
Careers, Inc.
PO Box 135
Largo, FL 34649-0135   Phone: (813)584-7333

1992. Eight-page brief offering the definition, history, duties, working conditions, personal qualifications, educational requirements, earnings, hours, employment outlook, advancement possibilities, and related occupations.

★5500★
"Ironworker" in Hard Hatted Women: Stories of Struggle and Success in the Trades (pp. 102-108)
Seal Press
3131 Western Ave., Ste. 410
Seattle, WA 98121   Phone: (206)283-7844

Molly Martin, editor. 1988. Twenty-six women recount their experiences working in blue collar occupations. They describe how they got in, the work they do, their relationships in predominantly male occupations, and their training.

★5501★
"Ironworkers and Steelworkers" in Opportunities in Building Construction Trades (pp. 68-70)
National Textbook Co.
4255 W. Touhy Ave.
Lincolnwood, IL 60646   Phone: (312)679-5500

Michael Sumichrast. 1989. Gives an overview of the construction industry and describes the jobs of various craftworkers. Covers different kinds of builders: home, custom; and describes management skills needed and industry trends affecting opportunities.

★5502★
Men of Iron
International Film Bureau, Inc. (IFB)
332 South Michigan Ave.
Chicago, IL 60604-4382   Phone: (312)427-4545

Videocassette. 198?. 20 mins. This program follows an apprentice ironworker as he learns the trade and how to do it safely.

★5503★
"Structural and Reinforcing Ironworkers" in Occupational Outlook Handbook (pp. 383-384)
Superintendent of Documents
U.S. Government Printing Office
Washington, DC 20402   Phone: (202)783-3238

Biennial; latest edition, 1990-91. Encyclopedia of careers describing more than 250 occupations and comprising about 86 percent of all jobs in the economy. Occupations that require lengthy education or training are given the most attention. For each occupation, the handbook describes job duties, working conditions, training, educational preparation, personal qualities, advancement possibilities, job outlook, earnings, and sources of additional information.

★5504★

"Structural Steel Workers" in Volume 3 of *The Encyclopedia of Careers and Vocational Guidance* (pp. 708-711)
J.G. Ferguson Publishing Co.
200 W. Monroe
Chicago, IL 60606   Phone: (312)580-5480

William E. Hopke, editor-in-chief. Eighth edition, 1990. Four-volume set that profiles 500 occupations and describes job trends in 76 industries. Includes career description, educational requirements, history of the job, methods of entry, advancement, employment outlook, earnings, working conditions, social and psychological factors, and sources of additional information.

★5505★

Video Career Library - Construction
Careers, Inc.
1211 10th St., SW
PO Box 135
Largo, FL 34649-0135   Phone: (813)584-7333

Videocassette. 1990. 36 mins. Part of the Video Career Library covering 165 occupations. Shows actual workers on the job. Includes millwrights, brickmasons, carpenters, drywall installers, electricians, painters, plumbers and pipefitters, carpenter and soft tile installers, insulation workers, paving equipment operators, and structural metal workers.

Associations

★5506★

Associated General Contractors of America (AGC)
1957 E St. NW
Washington, DC 20006   Phone: (202)393-2040

Membership: General construction contractors; subcontractors; industry suppliers; service firms. **Purpose:** Provides tax services through its divisions. Conducts special conferences and seminars designed specifically for construction firms. Compiles statistics on job accidents reported by member firms. Bestows annual awards for safety and Build/America awards for innovative and outstanding achievements by general contractors. Offers college scholarships through AGC Education and Research Foundation. Maintains 65 committees, including joint cooperative committees with other associations and liaison committees with federal agencies. **Publications:** *AGC Membership Directory and Buyers' Guide*, annual. • *Associated General Contractors of America—National Newsletter*, biweekly. • *Constructor*, monthly. • Also publishes manuals, guides, model contract documents, studies, and checklists. **Facsimile Number:** (202)347-4004.

★5507★

International Association of Bridge, Structural and Ornamental Iron Workers (IABSOIW)
1750 New York Ave. NW
Washington, DC 20006   Phone: (202)383-4810

Membership: AFL-CIO. **Publications:** *Ironworker*, monthly. **Facsimile Number:** (202)638-4856.

★5508★

National Association of Reinforcing Steel Contractors (NARSC)
10382 Main St., Ste. 300
PO Box 280
Fairfax, VA 22030   Phone: (703)591-1870

Membership: Companies engaged primarily in the placing of reinforcing steel and post-tensioning systems; associate members are suppliers of services and materials. **Purpose:** Serves as a unified voice for reinforcing steel contractors. Disseminates information on topics such as trade practices, construction techniques, efficient operation, safety standards, and welfare. Advises members on congressional legislation, wage settlements throughout the country, and other matters. Conducts studies on apprenticeship and training, equal employment, and labor relations. **Publications:** *Membership Roster*, periodic. • *Newsletter*, monthly. **Facsimile Number:** (703)591-1895.

★5509★

National Erectors Association (NEA)
1501 Lee Hwy., No. 202
Arlington, VA 22209   Phone: (703)524-3336

Membership: Active members are erector, ironworking, industrial, and maintenance contracting firms engaged in the erection of steel or allied materials. **Purpose:** Associate members are engaged in the manufacture of products and equipment or providing services generally used in the fabrication, erection, or transportation of structural steel. Objectives include developing industry standards, communicating governmental regulations to members, promoting safe work practices, and expanding opportunities for job training and increasing job skills. Represents the industry engaged in the erection of structural steel, allied work, and industrial maintenance before all divisions of government. Conducts activities with labor organizations to prevent strikes and promote cooperation with labor groups in areas of mutual interest. Conducts research. **Publications:** *I-Beam*, monthly. • *Labor Update*, quarterly. • *Membership Directory*, annual. • *Notes*, monthly. • *Safety Spotlight*, bimonthly. **Facsimile Number:** (703)524-3364.

Standards/Certification Agencies

An apprenticeship program is considered to be the best way to learn the structural and reinforcing ironworking trade. Apprenticeship programs are usually administered by joint union-management committees made up of representatives of local unions of the International Association of Bridge, Structural, and Ornamental Ironworkers and local chapters of contractors's associations. The apprenticeship consists of three years of on-the-job training and a minimum of 144 hours a year of classroom instruction. Some ironworkers learn informally on the job. These workers generally do not receive classroom training, although some large contractors have extensive training programs. They usually begin as helpers assisting experienced ironworkers. Learning through work experience alone may not provide training as complete as an apprenticeship program, however, and generally takes longer.

★5510★

National Association of Reinforcing Steel Contractors (NARSC)
10382 Main St., Ste. 300
PO Box 280
Fairfax, VA 22030   Phone: (703)591-1870

Disseminates information on safety standards.

★5511★

National Erectors Association (NEA)
1501 Lee Hwy., No. 202
Arlington, VA 22209   Phone: (703)524-3336

Develops industry standards, communicates governmental regulations to members, promotes safe work practices, and expands opportunities for job training and increasing job skills. Represents the industry engaged in the erection of structural steel, allied work, and industrial maintenance before all divisions of government.

Basic Reference Guides and Handbooks

★5512★
Intelligent Buildings Institute—Directory of Products and Services
Intelligent Buildings Institute (IBI)
2101 L St., NW, Ste. 300
Washington, DC 20037   Phone: (202)457-1988
S. Hunt, Associate Executive Director, editor. Annual, September. Member consultants, associations, research organizations, and other suppliers of products and services to the construction and building industry. Entries include: Company name, address, phone. Arrangement: Alphabetical. Indexes: Product/service. **Facsimile Number:** (202)457-8468.

★5513★
Mid-West Contractor—Annual Convention Guide and Association Directory
Allied Publications, Inc.
7355 N. Woodland Dr.
Box 603
Indianapolis, IN 46278   Phone: (317)297-5500
Jennifer Wynne, editor. Annual. List of 160 construction contracting and architectural associations in the Midwest. Entries include: Association name, address, phone, names and titles of key personnel, description of association; convention site, date, name and title of contact. Arrangement: Geographical, alphabetical. **Toll-free/Additional Phone Number(s):** (800)827-7468. **Facsimile Number:** (317)299-1356.

Periodicals

★5514★
ABC Newsline
Associated Builders and Contractors, Inc. (ABC)
729 15th St. NW
Washington, DC 20005   Phone: (202)637-8800
Editor(s): Lisa A. Nardone. Semimonthly. Designed to keep readers alerted to important changes within ABC and the construction industry. Reports on legislative issues, construction trends, conferences and meetings, and ABC services. Recurring features include news of members and a column titled Industry Briefs.

★5515★
American Architectural Manufacturers Association—Quarterly Review
American Architectural Manufacturers Association
1540 E. Dundee Rd., Ste. K 310
Palatine, IL 60067-8321   Phone: (708)202-1350
Editor(s): Tony Coorlim. Annually. Contains industry news on architectural products. Covers prime and combination storm windows, sliding glass and combination storm doors, window and curtain-walls, store fronts and entrances, siding, soffits, fascia, gutters, downspouts, skylights, space enclosures, and mobile home components. Recurring features include news of research, notices of publications available, and announcements by the association. **Facsimile Number:** (708)202-1480.

★5516★
American Institute of Constructors—Newsletter
American Institute of Constructors
9887 Gandy Blvd. N., No. 104
Saint Petersburg, FL 33702-2451
Editor(s): Ed Freedman. Bimonthly. Concerned with construction practice, design, administration, and teaching. Carries news of members, listings of job opportunities, local chapter reports, and notices of new publications. **Facsimile Number:** (614)464-3226.

★5517★
Associated General Contractors of America—National Newsletter
Associated General Contractors of America (AGC)
1957 E St. NW
Washington, DC 20006   Phone: (202)393-2040
Biweekly.

★5518★
Blue Reports, Inc.
Construction News Service
7325 Steel Mill Dr.
Springfield, VA 22050   Phone: (703)644-5884
Editor(s): Calvin S. Oren. Daily. Reports on public and private construction projects in the Washington, DC, Virginia, and Maryland areas. Provides owner's and architect's names, plan status, date bids due, prospective bidders, low bids received, and specification details. **Facsimile Number:** (703)644-1929.

★5519★
Building Concerns
National Association of Minority Contractors (NAMC)
806 15th St. NW, Ste. 340
Washington, DC 20005   Phone: (202)347-8259
Editor(s): Ralph C. Thomas, III. Monthly. Concentrates on national and regional news regarding minority construction contractors. Contains articles on issues generally affecting the industry—especially issues affecting minorities—including topics such as legislative and regulatory activity and reports on major corporation developments. Recurring features include reports of meetings, news of educational opportunities, a calendar of events, and news of NAMC chapters and members.

★5520★
Building Industry Technology: An Abstract Newsletter
National Technical Information Service (NTIS)
U.S. Department of Commerce
5285 Port Royal Rd.
Springfield, VA 22161   Phone: (703)487-4630
Weekly. Consists of abstracts of reports on architectural and environmental design, building standards, construction materials and equipment, and structural analyses. Recurring features include a form for ordering reports from NTIS.

★5521★
Capital Comments
National Lumber & Building Material Dealers Association
40 Ivy St. SE
Washington, DC 20003   Phone: (202)547-2230
Editor(s): Matt Geitner. Semimonthly. Reports on news of legislation pertaining to lumber, other building materials, and housing. Discusses such issues as lumber subsidies, interest rates on homes, health and safety, and jobs. **Facsimile Number:** (202)547-7640.

★5522★
ConnStruction
PO Box 9768
Wethersfield, CT 06109　　　　　Phone: (203)529-3246
Victor Bonini, Editor. 7x/yr. Magazine for construction industry. **Facsimile Number:** (203)563-0616.

★5523★
CONSTRUCTION
26 Long Hill Rd.
Guilford, CT 06437　　　　　Phone: (203)453-3717
Jack C. Lewis, Editor and Publisher. 2x/mo. Journal for the construction industry.

★5524★
Construction Dimensions
Assn. of Wall & Ceiling
PO Box 5504
Washington, DC 20016　　　　　Phone: (301)656-7050
Gerald Wykoff, Editor. Monthly. Wall and ceiling industry magazine.

★5525★
Construction Industry International
Maclean Hunter Publishing Co.
29 N. Wacker Dr.
Chicago, IL 60606　　　　　Phone: (312)726-2802
Alan Elliott, Editor-in-Chief. Monthly. Trade magazine.

★5526★
Construction News
715 W. 2nd St.
PO Box 2421
Little Rock, AR 72203　　　　　Phone: (501)376-1931
Robert Alvey, Editor. Weekly. Construction industry magazine. **Facsimile Number:** (501)375-5831.

★5527★
Construction Newsletter
National Safety Council
444 N. Michigan Ave.
Chicago, IL 60611　　　　　Phone: (312)527-4800
6/yr. Focuses on industrial and occupational safety in the construction industry. Carries items on such topics as safe work practices and products, accident prevention, and successful industrial safety programs and policies.

★5528★
Constructor
Associated General Contractors of America (AGC)
1957 E St. NW
Washington, DC 20006　　　　　Phone: (202)393-2040
Monthly. Association magazine for general contractors engaged in construction.

★5529★
Daily Construction Reporter
4901 Pacific Hwy.
San Diego, CA 92110-4098　　　　　Phone: (619)296-0183
Kenneth F. Kerr, Editor and Publisher. Daily. Construction trade newspaper covering jobs that are out for bid, bid results, building permits, and other information. **Facsimile Number:** (619)298-3027.

★5530★
I-Beam
National Erectors Association (NEA)
1501 Lee Hwy., No. 202
Arlington, VA 22209　　　　　Phone: (703)524-3336
Monthly.

★5531★
The Journal of Light Construction
Hanley-Wood Partners
RR 2, Box 146
Richmond, VT 05477-9607　　　　　Phone: (802)864-0091
Steve Bliss, Editor. Monthly. Magazine (tabloid) for residential and light professionals involved in new and rehabilitative construction. Each issue covers a single aspect of construction.

★5532★
Metal Construction News
Modern Trade Communications
7450 N. Skokie Blvd.
Skokie, IL 60077　　　　　Phone: (708)674-2200
Shawn Zuver, Mng. Editor. Monthly. Magazine focusing on metal building, metal roof, and sidewall news. **Facsimile Number:** (708)674-3676.

★5533★
NARSC Newsletter
National Association of Reinforcing Steel Contractors (NARSC)
10382 Main St., Ste. 300
PO Box 280
Fairfax, VA 22030　　　　　Phone: (703)591-1870
Monthly.

★5534★
Nation's Building News
15th & M Sts. NW
Washington, DC 20005　　　　　Phone: (202)822-0525
Tim Ahern, Editor. 2x/mo. Trade magazine (tabloid) covering home building and all related industries. **Facsimile Number:** (202)861-2131.

★5535★
NEA Labor Update
National Erectors Association (NEA)
1501 Lee Hwy., No. 202
Arlington, VA 22209　　　　　Phone: (703)524-3336
Quarterly.

★5536★
NEA Notes
National Erectors Association (NEA)
1501 Lee Hwy., No. 202
Arlington, VA 22209　　　　　Phone: (703)524-3336
Monthly.

★5537★
Professional Builder
Cahners Publishing Co.
1350 E. Touhy Ave.
Des Plaines, IL 60018　　　　　Phone: (708)635-8800
Roy L. Diez, Editor. 19x/yr. **Facsimile Number:** (708)299-8622.

Structural and Reinforcing Ironworkers

★5538★
Roads & Bridges Magazine
Scranton Gillette Communications, Inc.
380 Northwest Hwy.
Des Plaines, IL 60016   Phone: (708)298-6622
Tom Kuennen, Editor. Monthly. Magazine containing information on highway, road, and bridge design, construction, and maintenance for government agencies, contractors, and consulting engineers. **Facsimile Number:** (708)390-0408.

★5539★
Safety Spotlight
National Erectors Association (NEA)
1501 Lee Hwy., No. 202
Arlington, VA 22209   Phone: (703)524-3336
Bimonthly.

Meetings and Conventions

★5540★
International Association of Bridge, Structural and Ornamental Iron Workers (IABSOIW)
1750 New York Ave. NW
Washington, DC 20006   Phone: (202)383-4810
Frequency: Quinquennial. **Facsimile Number:** (202)638-4856.

★5541★
National Association of Home Builders/The Builders Show
National Association of Home Builders of the United States
15th and M Sts., NW
Washington, DC 20005   Phone: (202)822-0424
Frequency: Usually held in January; location rotates every three years. 1993; Feb. 19-22; Las Vegas, NV • 1994; Jan. 21-24; Las Vegas, NV. **Toll-free/Additional Phone Number(s):** 800-368-5242. **Facsimile Number:** (202)822-0435.

★5542★
National Association of Reinforcing Steel Contractors (NARSC)
10382 Main St., Ste. 300
PO Box 280
Fairfax, VA 22030   Phone: (703)591-1870
Frequency: Annual. **Facsimile Number:** (703)591-1895.

★5543★
National Erectors Association Conference (NEA)
1501 Lee Hwy., No. 202
Arlington, VA 22209   Phone: (703)524-3336
Frequency: Annual. Also holds annual midyear conference. **Facsimile Number:** (703)524-3364.

Tilesetters

Tilesetters apply tile to floors, walls, and ceilings. Most are employed by tilesetting contractors who work mainly on nonresidential construction projects, such as schools, hospitals, and office buildings. About 20% of all tilesetters are self-employed.

$alaries

Salaries for journeyman tilesetters range from $11.00/hour to $20.00/hour. Apprentices usually start earning 50% of journeymen's wages.

Employment Outlook

Growth rate until the year 2000: Faster than average.

Tilesetters

Career Guides

★5544★
"Marble Setter, Tilesetters, and Terrazzo Workers" in
  Opportunities in Building Construction Trades (pp. 63-65)
National Textbook Co.
4255 W. Touhy Ave.
Lincolnwood, IL 60646   Phone: (312)679-5500
Michael Sumichrast. 1989. Gives an overview of the construction industry and describes the jobs of various craftworkers. Covers different kinds of builders: home, custom; and describes management skills needed and industry trends affecting opportunities.

★5545★
Marble Setters, Tile Layers and Terrazzo Workers
Chronicle Guidance Publications, Inc.
PO Box 1190
Moravia, NY 13118-1190   Phone: (315)497-0330
1988. This career brief describes the nature of the work, working conditions, hours and earnings, education and training, licensure, certification, unions, personal qualifications, social and psychological factors, employment outlook, entry methods, advancement, and related occupations. **Toll-free/Additional Phone Number(s):** 800-622-7284.

★5546★
"Marble Setters, Tile Setters, and Terrazzo Workers" in
  Volume 3 of The Encyclopedia of Careers and
  Vocational Guidance (677-679)
J.G. Ferguson Publishing Co.
200 W. Monroe
Chicago, IL 60606   Phone: (312)580-5480
William E. Hopke, editor-in-chief. Eighth edition, 1990. Four-volume set that profiles 500 occupations and describes job trends in 76 industries. Includes career description, educational requirements, history of the job, methods of entry, advancement, employment outlook, earnings, working conditions, social and psychological factors, and sources of additional information.

★5547★
"Marble, Tile, and Terrazzo Worker" in Construction,
  Volume 4 of Career Information Center (pp. 71-72)
Glencoe/Macmillan
15319 Chatsworth St.
Mission Hills, CA 91345   Phone: (818)898-1391
Richard Lidz and Dale Anderson, editorial directors. Fourth edition, 1990. For 600 occupations, describes job duties, entry-level requirements, education and training needed, advancement possibilities, employment outlook, earnings and benefits. The set is divided into 12 volumes. Each volume includes jobs related under a broad career field. Volume 13 is the index. **Facsimile Number:** 818-365-5489.

★5548★
Marble, Tile Setters, Terrazzo, and Stone Workers
Careers, Inc.
PO Box 135
Largo, FL 34649-0135   Phone: (813)584-7333
1989. Eight-page brief offering the definition, history, duties, working conditions, personal qualifications, educational requirements, earnings, hours, employment outlook, advancement possibilities, and related occupations.

★5549★
"Marble, Tile, Terrazzo, and Stone Workers" in
  Occu-Facts: Information on 565 Careers in Outline
  Form (p. 16.3)
Careers, Inc.
P.O. Box 135
1211 Tenth St., S.W.
Largo, FL 33640   Phone: (813)584-7333
Elizabeth Handville. Biennial, 1989-90 edition. Each one-page occupational profile describes duties, working conditions, physical surroundings and demands, aptitudes, temperament, educational requirements, employment outlook, earnings, and places of employment.

★5550★
Tile Setter
Vocational Biographies, Inc.
PO Box 31, Dept. VF10
Sauk Centre, MN 56378   Phone: (612)352-6516
1991. This pamphlet profiles a person working in the job. Includes information about job duties, working conditions, places of employment, educational preparation, labor market outlook, and salaries. **Toll-free/Additional Phone Number(s):** 800-255-0752.

★5551★
"Tilesetters" in Occupational Outlook Handbook (pp. 384-385)
Superintendent of Documents
U.S. Government Printing Office
Washington, DC 20402   Phone: (202)783-3238
Biennial; latest edition, 1990-91. Encyclopedia of careers describing more than 250 occupations and comprising about 86 percent of all jobs in the economy. Occupations that require lengthy education or training are given the most attention. For each occupation, the handbook describes job duties, working conditions, training, educational preparation, personal qualities,

advancement possibilities, job outlook, earnings, and sources of additional information.

★5552★
The Trowel Trades
International Masonry Institute
823 15th St. NW, Ste. 1001
Washington, DC 20005   Phone: (202)783-3908

This six-panel brochure describes skills, advancement opportunities, and apprentice training.

★5553★
Video Career Library - Construction
Careers, Inc.
1211 10th St., SW
PO Box 135
Largo, FL 34649-0135   Phone: (813)584-7333

Videocassette. 1990. 36 mins. Part of the Video Career Library covering 165 occupations. Shows actual workers on the job. Includes millwrights, brickmasons, carpenters, drywall installers, electricians, painters, plumbers and pipefitters, carpenter and soft tile installers, insulation workers, paving equipment operators, and structural metal workers.

★5554★
You Can Become a Tile, Marble, Terrazzo and Dimensional Stone Installer
United Brotherhood of Carpenters and Joiners of America
101 Constitution Ave., N.W.
Washington, DC 20001   Phone: (202)546-6206

This six-panel brochure describes apprenticeship training, hours, and working conditions.

Associations

★5555★
International Union of Bricklayers and Allied Craftsmen (BAC)
815 15th St., NW
Washington, DC 20005   Phone: (202)783-3788

Membership: AFL-CIO. **Publications:** *Chalkline*, periodic. ● *Journal*, monthly. **Facsimile Number:** (202)393-0219.

★5556★
United Brotherhood of Carpenters and Joiners of America (UBC)
101 Constitution Ave. NW
Washington, DC 20001   Phone: (202)546-6206

Membership: AFL-CIO. **Publications:** *Carpenter*, monthly.

Standards/Certification Agencies

An apprenticeship program is considered to be the best way to learn the tilesetting trade. The program, which is usually offered by local chapters of the International Union of Bricklayers and Allied Craftsmen and the United Brotherhood of Carpenters and Joiners of America, lasts three years and consists of on-the-job training and related classroom instruction. In practice, however, most tilesetters acquire their skills informally by working as helpers to experienced workers.

Educational Directories and Programs

★5557★
American Ceramic Society Source
American Ceramic Society
757 Brooksedge Plaza Dr.
Westerville, OH 43081   Phone: (614)890-4700

Dr. John B. Wachtman, editor. Annual, September. Directory provides lists of educational institutions, associations, and publications, etc., in the ceramic industry; international coverage. Arrangement: All types of groups listed in single alphabet. Indexes: Product. **Facsimile Number:** (614)899-6109.

Basic Reference Guides and Handbooks

★5558★
Tile Contractors' Association of America—Products and Materials Guide
Tile Contractors' Association of America (TCAA)
112 N. Alfred St.
Alexandria, VA 22314   Phone: (703)836-5995

Biennial, summer of even years.

Periodicals

★5559★
ABC Newsline
Associated Builders and Contractors, Inc. (ABC)
729 15th St. NW
Washington, DC 20005   Phone: (202)637-8800

Editor(s): Lisa A. Nardone. Semimonthly. Designed to keep readers alerted to important changes within ABC and the construction industry. Reports on legislative issues, construction trends, conferences and meetings, and ABC services. Recurring features include news of members and a column titled Industry Briefs.

★5560★
American Architectural Manufacturers Association—Quarterly Review
American Architectural Manufacturers Association
1540 E. Dundee Rd., Ste. K 310
Palatine, IL 60067-8321   Phone: (708)202-1350

Editor(s): Tony Coorlim. Annually. Contains industry news on architectural products. Covers prime and combination storm windows, sliding glass and combination storm doors, window and curtain-walls, store fronts and entrances, siding, soffits, fascia, gutters, downspouts, skylights, space enclosures, and mobile home components. Recurring features include news of research, notices of publications available, and announcements by the association. **Facsimile Number:** (708)202-1480.

★5561★
American Institute of Constructors—Newsletter
American Institute of Constructors
9887 Gandy Blvd. N., No. 104
Saint Petersburg, FL 33702-2451

Editor(s): Ed Freedman. Bimonthly. Concerned with construction practice, design, administration, and teaching. Carries news of members, listings of job opportunities, local chapter reports, and notices of new publications. **Facsimile Number:** (614)464-3226.

★5562★
BAC Journal
International Union of Bricklayers and Allied Craftsmen (BAC)
815 15th St., NW
Washington, DC 20005   Phone: (202)783-3788
Monthly.

★5563★
Blue Reports, Inc.
Construction News Service
7325 Steel Mill Dr.
Springfield, VA 22050   Phone: (703)644-5884
Editor(s): Calvin S. Oren. Daily. Reports on public and private construction projects in the Washington, DC, Virginia, and Maryland areas. Provides owner's and architect's names, plan status, date bids due, prospective bidders, low bids received, and specification details. **Facsimile Number:** (703)644-1929.

★5564★
Building Concerns
National Association of Minority Contractors (NAMC)
806 15th St. NW, Ste. 340
Washington, DC 20005   Phone: (202)347-8259
Editor(s): Ralph C. Thomas, III. Monthly. Concentrates on national and regional news regarding minority construction contractors. Contains articles on issues generally affecting the industry—especially issues affecting minorities—including topics such as legislative and regulatory activity and reports on major corporation developments. Recurring features include reports of meetings, news of educational opportunities, a calendar of events, and news of NAMC chapters and members.

★5565★
Building Industry Technology: An Abstract Newsletter
National Technical Information Service (NTIS)
U.S. Department of Commerce
5285 Port Royal Rd.
Springfield, VA 22161   Phone: (703)487-4630
Weekly. Consists of abstracts of reports on architectural and environmental design, building standards, construction materials and equipment, and structural analyses. Recurring features include a form for ordering reports from NTIS.

★5566★
Building Renovation
Maclean Hunter Ltd.
777 Bay St.
Toronto, ON, Canada M5W 1A7   Phone: (416)596-5760
John Fennell, Editor. 6x/yr. Business magazine for professionals in residential and commercial renovation and remodeling. **Facsimile Number:** (416)596-5810.

★5567★
Capital Comments
National Lumber & Building Material Dealers Association
40 Ivy St. SE
Washington, DC 20003   Phone: (202)547-2230
Editor(s): Matt Geitner. Semimonthly. Reports on news of legislation pertaining to lumber, other building materials, and housing. Discusses such issues as lumber subsidies, interest rates on homes, health and safety, and jobs. **Facsimile Number:** (202)547-7640.

★5568★
Chalkline
International Union of Bricklayers and Allied Craftsmen (BAC)
815 15th St., NW
Washington, DC 20005   Phone: (202)783-3788
Periodic.

★5569★
ConnStruction
PO Box 9768
Wethersfield, CT 06109   Phone: (203)529-3246
Victor Bonini, Editor. 7x/yr. Magazine for construction industry. **Facsimile Number:** (203)563-0616.

★5570★
CONSTRUCTION
26 Long Hill Rd.
Guilford, CT 06437   Phone: (203)453-3717
Jack C. Lewis, Editor and Publisher. 2x/mo. Journal for the construction industry.

★5571★
Construction Dimensions
Assn. of Wall & Ceiling
PO Box 5504
Washington, DC 20016   Phone: (301)656-7050
Gerald Wykoff, Editor. Monthly. Wall and ceiling industry magazine.

★5572★
Construction Industry International
Maclean Hunter Publishing Co.
29 N. Wacker Dr.
Chicago, IL 60606   Phone: (312)726-2802
Alan Elliott, Editor-in-Chief. Monthly. Trade magazine.

★5573★
Construction News
715 W. 2nd St.
PO Box 2421
Little Rock, AR 72203   Phone: (501)376-1931
Robert Alvey, Editor. Weekly. Construction industry magazine. **Facsimile Number:** (501)375-5831.

★5574★
Construction Newsletter
National Safety Council
444 N. Michigan Ave.
Chicago, IL 60611   Phone: (312)527-4800
6/yr. Focuses on industrial and occupational safety in the construction industry. Carries items on such topics as safe work practices and products, accident prevention, and successful industrial safety programs and policies.

★5575★
Daily Construction Reporter
4901 Pacific Hwy.
San Diego, CA 92110-4098   Phone: (619)296-0183
Kenneth F. Kerr, Editor and Publisher. Daily. Construction trade newspaper covering jobs that are out for bid, bid results, building permits, and other information. **Facsimile Number:** (619)298-3027.

★5576★
Home BUILDER Magazine
Work-4 Projects Ltd.
PO Box 400, Victoria Sta.
Westmount, PQ, Canada H3Z 2V8 Phone: (514)489-4941
Nachmi Artzy, Editor and Publisher. 6x/yr. Magazine for home construction industry. **Facsimile Number:** (514)489-5505.

★5577★
The Journal of Light Construction
Hanley-Wood Partners
RR 2, Box 146
Richmond, VT 05477-9607 Phone: (802)864-0091
Steve Bliss, Editor. Monthly. Magazine (tabloid) for residential and light professionals involved in new and rehabilitative construction. Each issue covers a single aspect of construction.

★5578★
Nation's Building News
15th & M Sts. NW
Washington, DC 20005 Phone: (202)822-0525
Tim Ahern, Editor. 2x/mo. Trade magazine (tabloid) covering home building and all related industries. **Facsimile Number:** (202)861-2131.

★5579★
Professional Builder
Cahners Publishing Co.
1350 E. Touhy Ave.
Des Plaines, IL 60018 Phone: (708)635-8800
Roy L. Diez, Editor. 19x/yr. **Facsimile Number:** (708)299-8622.

★5580★
Tile and Decorative Surfaces
20335 Ventura Blvd., No. 400
Woodland Hills, CA 91364 Phone: (818)704-5555
John Maynard, Editor. Monthly. Magazine covering the floor and wall tile industry. **Facsimile Number:** (818)704-6500.

Meetings and Conventions

★5581★
Ceramic Tile Distributors Association Ceramic Tile Exposition
Ceramic Tile Distributors Association
15 Salt Creek Ln., Ste. 422
Hinsdale, IL 60521 Phone: (708)655-3270
1992; Jul. New York, NY.

★5582★
Installation Supplies and Ideas Expo
National Association of Floor Covering Distributors
13-126 Merchandise Mart
Chicago, IL 60654 Phone: (708)364-9040
1992; May 09-13; Palm Desert, CA ● 1993; Apr. 17-21; Marco Island, FL.

★5583★
International Ceramic Tile Exhibit
Tile Contractors Association of America
112 N. Alfred St.
Alexandria, VA 22314 Phone: (703)836-5995
1992; Lake Tahoe, NV ● 1993; Oct. 03-06; New Orleans, LA. **Facsimile Number:** (703)683-3702.

★5584★
International Ceramic Trade Fair
Offinger Management Co.
1100-H Brandywine Blvd.
PO Box 2188
Zanesville, OH 43702-2188 Phone: (614)452-4541
1992. **Facsimile Number:** (614)452-2552.

Production Occupations

Assemblers

Precision Assemblers

Assemblers are workers who put together the parts of manufactured articles. In some instances, hundreds of assemblers work on a single product; in others, a single assembler is responsible for each product. Assembly work varies from simple, repetitive jobs that are relatively easy to learn to those requiring great precision and many months of experience and training. The following industries provide wage and salary jobs for precision assemblers: Electrical and electronic machinery and equipment (38 percent); machinery, except electrical (25 percent); transportation equipment (19 percent); professional and scientific instruments (12 percent); and fabricated metal products (4 percent).

$alaries

Average earnings of assemblers in various industries are as follows:

Full-time workers who assemble electrical and electronic equipment	$214.00—$379.00/week
Union aircraft assemblers	$10.33—$15.38/hour

Employment Outlook

Growth rate until the year 2000: More slowly than average.

Precision Assemblers

Career Guides

★5585★
Aerospace Assembly Worker
Vocational Biographies, Inc.
PO Box 31, Dept. VF10
Sauk Centre, MN 56378   Phone: (612)352-6516
1990. This pamphlet profiles a person working in the job. Includes information about job duties, working conditions, places of employment, educational preparation, labor market outlook, and salaries. **Toll-free/Additional Phone Number(s):** 800-255-0752.

★5586★
"Aircraft Assembler" in *Occu-Facts: Information on 565 Careers in Outline Form* (p. 17.2)
Careers, Inc.
P.O. Box 135
1211 Tenth St., S.W.
Largo, FL 33640   Phone: (813)584-7333
Elizabeth Handville. Biennial, 1989-90 edition. Each one-page occupational profile describes duties, working conditions, physical surroundings and demands, aptitudes, temperament, educational requirements, employment outlook, earnings, and places of employment.

★5587★
Alternatives to Assembly Lines: Modern Times—Revisited
Britannica Films
310 South Michigan Ave.
Chicago, IL 60604   Phone: (312)347-7958
Videocassette. 1988. 29 mins. In this program we visit assembly plants in Sweden and Italy to see how Volvo and Olivetti use self-pacing work teams, replacing the classic assembly line.

★5588★
"Assembler" in *Manufacturing*, Volume 9 of *Career Information Center* (pp. 37-39)
Glencoe/Macmillan
15319 Chatsworth St.
Mission Hills, CA 91345   Phone: (818)898-1391
Richard Lidz and Dale Anderson, editorial directors. Fourth edition, 1990. For 600 occupations, describes job duties, entry-level requirements, education and training needed, advancement possibilities, employment outlook, earnings and benefits. The set is divided into 12 volumes. Each volume includes jobs related under a broad career field. Volume 13 is the index. **Facsimile Number:** 818-365-5489.

★5589★
Assembler, Aircraft
Careers, Inc.
PO Box 135
Largo, FL 34649-0135   Phone: (813)584-7333
1988. Two-page occupational summary card describing duties, working conditions, personal qualifications, training, earnings and hours, employment outlook, places of employment, related careers and where to write for more information.

★5590★
"Assemblers" in Volume 1 of *Career Discovery Encyclopedia* (pp. 62-63)
J.G. Ferguson Publishing Co.
200 W. Monroe
Chicago, IL 60606   Phone: (312)580-5480
E. Russell Primm, editor-in-chief. 1990. Contains two-page articles on 504 occupations. Each article describes job duties, earnings, and educational and training requirements.

★5591★
"Assemblers" in Volume 3 of *The Encyclopedia of Careers and Vocational Guidance* (pp. 573-576)
J.G. Ferguson Publishing Co.
200 W. Monroe
Chicago, IL 60606   Phone: (312)580-5480
William E. Hopke, editor-in-chief. Eighth edition, 1990. Four-volume set that profiles 500 occupations and describes job trends in 76 industries. Includes career description, educational requirements, history of the job, methods of entry, advancement, employment outlook, earnings, working conditions, social and psychological factors, and sources of additional information.

★5592★
Assemblers, Electronics Manufacturing
Careers, Inc.
PO Box 135
Largo, FL 34649-0135   Phone: (813)584-7333
1988. Two-page occupational summary card describing duties, working conditions, personal qualifications, training, earnings and hours, employment outlook, places of employment, related careers and where to write for more information.

★5593★
Automated Factory
Society of Manufacturing Engineers
One SME Dr.
Post Office Box 930
Dearborn, MI 48121-0930   Phone: (313)271-1500

Videocassette. 1987. 60 mins. This series offers a look at the most up-to-date automated factories in the world.

★5594★
"Electronics Assemblers" in *The Complete Electronics Career Guide* (pp. 40-43)
Tab Books, Inc.
Blue Ridge Summit, PA 17294-0850   Phone: (717)794-2191

Joe Risse. 1989. Explores opportunities for electronic technicians in industry, broadcasting, appliance repair, telecommunications, computer servicing, and technical writing. Offers advice on educational preparation, training, finding or changing jobs, and career advancement. Lists trade publications and professional associations.

★5595★
"Electronics Manufacturing Assemblers" in *Occu-Facts: Information on 565 Careers in Outline Form* (p. 18.25)
Careers, Inc.
P.O. Box 135
1211 Tenth St., S.W.
Largo, FL 33640   Phone: (813)584-7333

Elizabeth Handville. Biennial, 1989-90 edition. Each one-page occupational profile describes duties, working conditions, physical surroundings and demands, aptitudes, temperament, educational requirements, employment outlook, earnings, and places of employment.

★5596★
"Precision Assemblers" in *Occupational Outlook Handbook* (pp. 386-387)
Superintendent of Documents
U.S. Government Printing Office
Washington, DC 20402   Phone: (202)783-3238

Biennial; latest edition, 1990-91. Encyclopedia of careers describing more than 250 occupations and comprising about 86 percent of all jobs in the economy. Occupations that require lengthy education or training are given the most attention. For each occupation, the handbook describes job duties, working conditions, training, educational preparation, personal qualities, advancement possibilities, job outlook, earnings, and sources of additional information.

★5597★
"Precision Assemblers" in *The American Almanac of Jobs and Salaries* (pp. 528-529)
Avon Books
105 Madison Avenue
New York, NY 10016   Phone: (212)481-5600

John Wright and Edward J. Dwyer. Revised and updated, 1990. A comprehensive guide to the wages of hundreds of occupations in a wide variety of industries and organizations.

★5598★
"Semi-Skilled Assemblers" in *Occu-Facts: Information on 565 Careers in Outline Form* (p. 18.26)
Careers, Inc.
P.O. Box 135
1211 Tenth St., S.W.
Largo, FL 33640   Phone: (813)584-7333

Elizabeth Handville. Biennial, 1989-90 edition. Each one-page occupational profile describes duties, working conditions, physical surroundings and demands, aptitudes, temperament, educational requirements, employment outlook, earnings, and places of employment.

★5599★
Video Career Library - Production II
Careers, Inc.
1211 10th St., SW
PO Box 135
Largo, FL 34649-0135   Phone: (813)584-7333

Videocassette. 1990. 32 mins. Part of the Video Career Library covering 165 occupations. Shows actual workers on the job. Includes tool and die makers, machinists, sheet metal workers, cabinet and bench carpenters, opticians, precision electronic equipment assemblers, industrial machine operators, welders and cutters, and assemblers.

——————— Associations ———————

★5600★
International Association of Machinists and Aerospace Workers (IAM)
1300 Connecticut Ave.
Washington, DC 20036   Phone: (202)857-5200

Membership: AFL-CIO. **Publications:** *The Machinist*, monthly.

★5601★
International Brotherhood of Electrical Workers (IBEW)
1125 15th St. NW
Washington, DC 20005   Phone: (202)833-7000

Membership: AFL-CIO. **Publications:** *IBEW Journal*, monthly.

★5602★
International Union of Electronic, Electrical, Salaried, Machine, and Furniture Workers (IUE)
1126 16th St., NW
Washington, DC 20036   Phone: (202)296-1200

Membership: Districts: 6. Locals: 550. AFL-CIO. **Purpose:** Negotiates collective bargaining agreements; maintains apprenticeship programs. Conducts district education directors meeting and training programs. Compiles statistics. **Publications:** *Health and Safety*, 3-4/year. • *International Union of Electronic, Electrical, Salaried, Machine, and Furniture Workers—Convention Proceedings*, biennial. • *IUE News*, monthly. • *Keeping Up With The Law*, 3-4/year. • *Research Information*, monthly. **Facsimile Number:** (202)785-4563. **Boards:** Amalgamated Locals Conference; General Electric Conference; General Motors Conference; Multi-Employer Conference; Professional, Technical and Salaried Conference; Westinghouse Conference.

——————— Periodicals ———————

★5603★
Health and Safety (IUE)
International Union of Electronic, Electrical, Salaried, Machine, and Furniture Workers
1126 16th St., NW
Washington, DC 20036   Phone: (202)296-1200

3-4/year.

Precision Assemblers

★5604★
IUE News (IUE)
International Union of Electronic, Electrical, Salaried, Machine, and Furniture Workers
1126 16th St., NW
Washington, DC 20036   Phone: (202)296-1200
Monthly. Association newsletter in tabloid form.

★5605★
IUE Research Information (IUE)
Intl. Union of Electronic, Electrical, Salaried, Machine, and Furniture Workers
1126 16th St., NW
Washington, DC 20036   Phone: (202)296-1200
Monthly.

★5606★
Keeping Up With The Law (IUE)
International Union of Electronic, Electrical, Salaried, Machine, and Furniture Workers
1126 16th St., NW
Washington, DC 20036   Phone: (202)296-1200
3-4/year.

--- Meetings and Conventions ---

★5607★
International Association of Machinists and Aerospace Workers (IAM)
1300 Connecticut Ave.
Washington, DC 20036   Phone: (202)857-5200
Frequency: Quadrennial - next 1992.

★5608★
International Union of Electronic, Electrical, Salaried, Machine, and Furniture Workers (IUE)
1126 16th St., NW
Washington, DC 20036   Phone: (202)296-1200
Frequency: Biennial - next held in 1992. **Facsimile Number:** (202)785-4563.

Blue-Collar Worker Supervisors

Supervisors ensure that workers, equipment, and materials are used properly and efficiently. They make sure machinery is set up correctly and schedule or perform repairs and maintenance work. Supervisors tell other workers what to do and make sure it is done safely, correctly, and on time. Blue-collar worker supervisors may have other titles, such as first-line supervisors, foreman, or forewomen. In the textile industry, they may be referred to as second hands; on ships, boatswains; in the construction industry, they may be called superintendents or crew chiefs; and in oil drilling, toolpushers or gang pushers. Although blue-collar worker supervisors are found in almost all industries, more than 40 percent work in manufacturing; about 15 percent work in the construction industry and 10 percent in wholesale and retail trade. Others were in public utilities, repair shops, transportation, and government agencies.

$alaries

Weekly earnings for blue-collar worker supervisors are as follows:

Lowest 10 percent	$290.00/week or less
Middle 50 percent	$395.00—$705.00/week
Top 10 percent	$895.00/week or more

Employment Outlook

Growth rate until the year 2000: More slowly than average.

Blue-Collar Worker Supervisors

Career Guides

★5609★
"Blue-Collar Worker Supervisors" in *Occupational Outlook Handbook* **(pp. 387-388)**
Superintendent of Documents
U.S. Government Printing Office
Washington, DC 20402   Phone: (202)783-3238

Biennial; latest edition, 1990-91. Encyclopedia of careers describing more than 250 occupations and comprising about 86 percent of all jobs in the economy. Occupations that require lengthy education or training are given the most attention. For each occupation, the handbook describes job duties, working conditions, training, educational preparation, personal qualities, advancement possibilities, job outlook, earnings, and sources of additional information.

★5610★
"Blue Collar Worker Supervisors" in Volume 3 of *The Encyclopedia of Careers and Vocational Guidance* **(pp. 728-731)**
J.G. Ferguson Publishing Co.
200 W. Monroe
Chicago, IL 60606   Phone: (312)580-5480

William E. Hopke, editor-in-chief. Eighth edition, 1990. Four-volume set that profiles 500 occupations and describes job trends in 76 industries. Includes career description, educational requirements, history of the job, methods of entry, advancement, employment outlook, earnings, working conditions, social and psychological factors, and sources of additional information.

★5611★
"Carpenter Foreman" in *Hard Hatted Women: Stories of Struggle and Success in the Trades* **(pp. 122-134)**
Seal Press
3131 Western Ave., Ste. 410
Seattle, WA 98121   Phone: (206)283-7844

Molly Martin, editor. 1988. Twenty-six women recount their experiences working in blue collar occupations. They describe how they got in, the work they do, their relationships in predominantly male occupations, and their training.

★5612★
"Dock Foreman/Supervisor" in *Careers in Trucking* **(pp. 26-28)**
Rosen Publishing Group, Inc.
29 E. 21st St.
New York, NY 10010   Phone: (212)777-3017

Donald D. Schauer. 1987. Describes employment in the trucking industry including driving, operations, sales, and administration. Covers qualifications, training, future outlook, and salaries. Offers career planning and job hunting advice.

★5613★
"Production Supervisor" in *Manufacturing,* **Volume 9 of** *Career Information Center* **(pp. 68-70)**
Glencoe/Macmillan
15319 Chatsworth St.
Mission Hills, CA 91345   Phone: (818)898-1391

Richard Lidz and Dale Anderson, editorial directors. Fourth edition, 1990. For 600 occupations, describes job duties, entry-level requirements, education and training needed, advancement possibilities, employment outlook, earnings and benefits. The set is divided into 12 volumes. Each volume includes jobs related under a broad career field. Volume 13 is the index. **Facsimile Number:** 818-365-5489.

★5614★
Successful Strategies for Manufacturing Management
Deltak, Inc.
East-West Technological Center
1751 Diehl Rd.
Naperville, IL 60566   Phone: (708)369-3000

Videocassette. 1984. 40 mins. This series of programs examines how to plan and design strategies to use the new systems of manufacturing technology.

★5615★
Supervisory Planning and Control
Bureau of Business Practice
24 Rope Ferry Rd.
Waterford, CT 06386   Phone: (203)442-4365

Videocassette. 1986. 21 mins. For businesses, this tape shows how to manage and run a smooth production line.

Associations

★5616★
American Management Association (AMA)
135 W. 50th St.
New York, NY 10020   Phone: (212)586-8100

Membership: Managers in industry, commerce, and government; charitable and noncommercial organizations; university teachers of management; administrators. **Purpose:** Seeks to broaden members' management knowledge and skills. Awards annual Henry Laurence Gantt Medal, in conjunction with the American Society of Mechanical Engineers, for distinguished achievement in management as a service to the community. Maintains "Correspondent Association" agreements around the world. Operates management centers and offices in North America and, through AMA/International, in Europe and South America. Maintains extensive library, book store, and Management Information Service, which includes films, cassettes, tapes, and records covering all areas of management expertise. Conducts the Extension Institute, a private, self-paced study program and Operation Enterprise, a young adult program for high school/college level students. Other programs include AMA On-Site and Presidents Association SSE. Offers courses, workshops, and briefings. Bestows awards. **Publications:** *Compensation and Benefits Review*, bimonthly. • *CompFlash*, monthly. • *Management Review*, monthly. • *Organizational Dynamics: A Quarterly Review of Organizational Behavior for Professional Managers*. • *Personnel*, monthly. • *The President*, monthly. • *Project Update*, periodic. • *Supervisory Management*, monthly. • *Supervisory Sense*, monthly. • *Trainer's Workshop*, bimonthly. • Also publishes books, management briefings, and survey reports; also produces films and videotapes. **Facsimile Number:** (212)903-8168.

Test Guides

★5617★
Assistant Foreman
National Learning Corp.
212 Michael Dr.
Syosset, NY 11791 Phone: (516)921-8888
Jack Rudman. Part of the Career Examination Series No. 1. All examination guides in this series contain questions with answers. **Facsimile Number:** (516)921-8743. **Toll-free/Additional Phone Number(s):** 800-645-6337.

★5618★
Foreman
National Learning Corp.
212 Michael Dr.
Syosset, NY 11791 Phone: (516)921-8888
Jack Rudman. Part of the Career Examination Series No. 1. All examination guides in this series contain questions with answers. **Facsimile Number:** (516)921-8743. **Toll-free/Additional Phone Number(s):** 800-645-6337.

★5619★
Foreman of Laborers
National Learning Corp.
212 Michael Dr.
Syosset, NY 11791 Phone: (516)921-8888
Jack Rudman. Part of the Career Examination Series No. 1. All examination guides in this series contain questions with answers. **Facsimile Number:** (516)921-8743. **Toll-free/Additional Phone Number(s):** 800-645-6337.

Periodicals

★5620★
AMA Project Update
American Management Association (AMA)
135 W. 50th St.
New York, NY 10020 Phone: (212)586-8100
Periodic.

★5621★
Compensation and Benefits Review
American Management Association (AMA)
135 W. 50th St.
New York, NY 10020 Phone: (212)586-8100
Bimonthly. Journal including annual index, book reviews, digest service of annotations and selected readings from publications, information on current trends, and calendar of events.

★5622★
CompFlash
American Management Association (AMA)
135 W. 50th St.
New York, NY 10020 Phone: (212)586-8100
Monthly. Newsletter featuring new developments in the field, salary and wage surveys, government regulations, pension and benefits news, and available publications.

★5623★
Construction Supervision & Safety Letter
Bureau of Business Practice
24 Rope Ferry Rd.
Waterford, CT 06386 Phone: (203)442-4365
Editor(s): DeLoris Lidestri and Winifred Bonney. Semimonthly. Serves supervisors of blue-collar workers with discussion and advice on organizing, planning, and operating. Covers construction safety, the use of communication and motivation as productive management tools, ways to simplify discipline, and building teamwork. Recurring features include interviews with safety professionals, case histories, and cartoons. **Toll-free/Additional Phone Number(s):** 800-243-0876 **Facsimile Number:** (203)434-3341.

★5624★
Management Review
American Management Association (AMA)
135 W. 50th St.
New York, NY 10020 Phone: (212)586-8100
Monthly. Magazine providing information on management trends and techniques. Includes book reviews and case studies.

★5625★
Organizational Dynamics: A Quarterly Review of Organizational Behavior for Professional Managers (AMA)
American Management Association (AMA)
135 W. 50th St.
New York, NY 10020 Phone: (212)586-8100
Includes annual index.

★5626★
Personnel
American Management Association (AMA)
135 W. 50th St.
New York, NY 10020 Phone: (212)586-8100
Monthly. Magazine for human resources professionals. Includes annual index, editorials, book reviews, and career development calendar.

★5627★
The President
American Management Association (AMA)
135 W. 50th St.
New York, NY 10020 Phone: (212)586-8100
Monthly. Newsletter including calendar of events.

★5628★
Supervision
National Research Bureau, Inc.
424 N. 3rd St.
Burlington, IA 52601-5224 Phone: (319)752-5415
Barbara Boeding, Editor. Monthly. Magazine for first-line foremen, supervisors, and office managers. **Facsimile Number:** (319)752-3421.

★5629★
Supervisory Management
American Management Assn.
135 W. 50th St.
New York, NY 10020 Phone: (212)586-8100
Florence Stone, Editor. Monthly. Newsletter covering management and supervisory topics, including performance appraisals, motivation, and discipline. **Facsimile Number:** (212)903-8168.

★5630★
Supervisory Sense
American Management Association (AMA)
135 W. 50th St.
New York, NY 10020 Phone: (212)586-8100
Monthly. Training publication for first- and second-line managers; one subject per issue. Includes case studies.

★5631★
Trainer's Workshop
American Management Association (AMA)
135 W. 50th St.
New York, NY 10020 Phone: (212)586-8100
Bimonthly. Magazine for training professionals and managers responsible for training. Contains generic training course including workshop materials.

Food Processing Occupations

Butchers and Meat, Poultry, and Fish Cutters

Butchers and meat, poultry, and fish cutters reduce animal carcasses into small pieces of meat suitable for sale to consumers. In meatpacking plants, butchers slaughter cattle, hogs, goats, and sheep and cut the carcasses into large wholesale cuts to facilitate handling, distribution, and marketing. Meatcutters separate the wholesale cuts into retail cuts or individual size servings. Poultry cuts slaughter and cut up chickens, turkeys, and other types of poultry. Fish cleaners cut, scale, and dress fish in fish processing plants and wholesale and retail fish markets. Over 80 percent of all butchers and meat, poultry, and fish cutters work in meatpacking and poultry and fish processing plants and retail grocery stores, while others are employed by meat and fish markets, restaurants, hotels, and wholesale establishments.

$alaries

Hourly earnings of butchers and meatcutters are as follows:

Lowest 10 percent	$5.30/hour
Middle 50 percent	$11.10/hour
Top 10 percent	$14.10/hour or more

Employment Outlook

Growth rate until the year 2000: More slowly than average.

Butchers and Meat, Poultry, and Fish Cutters

Career Guides

★5632★
"Butcher or Boucher" in *Opportunities in Culinary Careers* **(pp. 61-62)**
National Textbook Co.
4255 W. Touhy Ave.
Lincolnwood, IL 60646   Phone: (312)679-5500
Mary Deirdre Donovan. 1990. Describes the educational preparation and training of chefs and cooks and explores a variety of food service jobs in restaurants, institutions, and research and development. Lists culinary schools and professional organizations.

★5633★
"Butchers and Meat, Poultry, and Fish Cutters" in *Occupational Outlook Handbook* **(pp. 389-390)**
Superintendent of Documents
U.S. Government Printing Office
Washington, DC 20402   Phone: (202)783-3238
Biennial; latest edition, 1990-91. Encyclopedia of careers describing more than 250 occupations and comprising about 86 percent of all jobs in the economy. Occupations that require lengthy education or training are given the most attention. For each occupation, the handbook describes job duties, working conditions, training, educational preparation, personal qualities, advancement possibilities, job outlook, earnings, and sources of additional information.

★5634★
"Fish Production Technicians" in Volume 4 of *The Encyclopedia of Careers and Vocational Guidance* **(pp. 467-468)**
J.G. Ferguson Publishing Co.
200 W. Monroe
Chicago, IL 60606   Phone: (312)580-5480
William E. Hopke, editor-in-chief. Eighth edition, 1990. Four-volume set that profiles 500 occupations and describes job trends in 76 industries. Includes career description, educational requirements, history of the job, methods of entry, advancement, employment outlook, earnings, working conditions, social and psychological factors, and sources of additional information.

★5635★
"Fish Production Technicians" in Volume 3 of *Career Discovery Encyclopedia* **(pp. 34-35)**
J.G. Ferguson Publishing Co.
200 W. Monroe
Chicago, IL 60606   Phone: (312)580-5480
E. Russell Primm, editor-in-chief. 1990. Contains two-page articles on 504 occupations. Each article describes job duties, earnings, and educational and training requirements.

★5636★
Food Services
Learning Corporation of America
108 Wilmot Rd.
Deerfield, IL 60015-9990   Phone: (708)940-1260
Videocassette. 1982. 21 mins. Four workers in the food industry offer a look at their jobs: chef, restaurant manager, baker and meat wrapper. From the "Working" series.

★5637★
Meat Cutter
Careers, Inc.
PO Box 135
Largo, FL 34649-0135   Phone: (813)584-7333
1991. Two-page occupational summary card describing duties, working conditions, personal qualifications, training, earnings and hours, employment outlook, places of employment, related careers and where to write for more information.

★5638★
"Meat Cutter" in *Occu-Facts: Information on 565 Careers in Outline Form* **(p. 17.28)**
Careers, Inc.
P.O. Box 135
1211 Tenth St., S.W.
Largo, FL 33640   Phone: (813)584-7333
Elizabeth Handville. Biennial, 1989-90 edition. Each one-page occupational profile describes duties, working conditions, physical surroundings and demands, aptitudes, temperament, educational requirements, employment outlook, earnings, and places of employment.

★5639★
"Meat Packing Production Workers" in Volume 4 of *Career Discovery Encyclopedia* **(pp. 66-67)**
J.G. Ferguson Publishing Co.
200 W. Monroe
Chicago, IL 60606   Phone: (312)580-5480
E. Russell Primm, editor-in-chief. 1990. Contains two-page articles on 504 occupations. Each article describes job duties, earnings, and educational and training requirements.

★5640★
"Meat Packing Production Workers" in Volume 3 of *The Encyclopedia of Careers and Vocational Guidance* (pp. 433-436)
J.G. Ferguson Publishing Co.
200 W. Monroe
Chicago, IL 60606   Phone: (312)580-5480
William E. Hopke, editor-in-chief. Eighth edition, 1990. Four-volume set that profiles 500 occupations and describes job trends in 76 industries. Includes career description, educational requirements, history of the job, methods of entry, advancement, employment outlook, earnings, working conditions, social and psychological factors, and sources of additional information.

★5641★
"Meat Packing Worker" in *Agribusiness, Environment, and Natural Resources*, Volume 2 of *Career Information Center* (pp. 55-56)
Glencoe/Macmillan
15319 Chatsworth St.
Mission Hills, CA 91345   Phone: (818)898-1391
Richard Lidz and Dale Anderson, editorial directors. Fourth edition, 1990. For 600 occupations, describes job duties, entry-level requirements, education and training needed, advancement possibilities, employment outlook, earnings and benefits. The set is divided into 12 volumes. Each volume includes jobs related under a broad career field. Volume 13 is the index. **Facsimile Number:** 818-365-5489.

★5642★
"Meat Wrapper (Supermarket)" in *Occu-Facts: Information on 565 Careers in Outline Form* (p. 17.29)
Careers, Inc.
P.O. Box 135
1211 Tenth St., S.W.
Largo, FL 33640   Phone: (813)584-7333
Elizabeth Handville. Biennial, 1989-90 edition. Each one-page occupational profile describes duties, working conditions, physical surroundings and demands, aptitudes, temperament, educational requirements, employment outlook, earnings, and places of employment.

★5643★
Meatcutters
Chronicle Guidance Publications, Inc.
PO Box 1190
Moravia, NY 13118-1190   Phone: (315)497-0330
1988. This career brief describes the nature of the work, working conditions, hours and earnings, education and training, licensure, certification, unions, personal qualifications, social and psychological factors, employment outlook, entry methods, advancement, and related occupations. **Toll-free/Additional Phone Number(s):** 800-622-7284.

★5644★
"Meatcutters" in Volume 4 of *Career Discovery Encyclopedia* (pp. 64-65)
J.G. Ferguson Publishing Co.
200 W. Monroe
Chicago, IL 60606   Phone: (312)580-5480
E. Russell Primm, editor-in-chief. 1990. Contains two-page articles on 504 occupations. Each article describes job duties, earnings, and educational and training requirements.

★5645★
"Meatcutters" in Volume 3 of *The Encyclopedia of Careers and Vocational Guidance* (pp. 273-276)
J.G. Ferguson Publishing Co.
200 W. Monroe
Chicago, IL 60606   Phone: (312)580-5480
William E. Hopke, editor-in-chief. Eighth edition, 1990. Four-volume set that profiles 500 occupations and describes job trends in 76 industries. Includes career description, educational requirements, history of the job, methods of entry, advancement, employment outlook, earnings, working conditions, social and psychological factors, and sources of additional information.

★5646★
"Meatcutters" in *The American Almanac of Jobs and Salaries* (p. 532)
Avon Books
105 Madison Avenue
New York, NY 10016   Phone: (212)481-5600
John Wright and Edward J. Dwyer. Revised and updated, 1990. A comprehensive guide to the wages of hundreds of occupations in a wide variety of industries and organizations.

★5647★
"Retail Butcher" in *Marketing and Distribution*, Volume 10 of *Career Information Center* (pp. 51-52)
Glencoe/Macmillan
15319 Chatsworth St.
Mission Hills, CA 91345   Phone: (818)898-1391
Richard Lidz and Dale Anderson, editorial directors. Fourth edition, 1990. For 600 occupations, describes job duties, entry-level requirements, education and training needed, advancement possibilities, employment outlook, earnings and benefits. The set is divided into 12 volumes. Each volume includes jobs related under a broad career field. Volume 13 is the index. **Facsimile Number:** 818-365-5489.

★5648★
"Seafood Processing and Marketing" in *Opportunities in Marine and Maritime Careers* (pp. 112-113)
National Textbook Co.
4255 W. Touhy Ave.
Lincolnwood, IL 60646   Phone: (312)679-5500
William Ray Heitzmann. 1988. Includes careers related by their proximity to water; cruise ships, oceanography, marine sciences, fishing, commercial diving, maritime transportation, shipbuilding, Navy, and Coast Guard. Covers qualifications, job outlook, job duties, educational preparation, and training. Lists associations and schools.

★5649★
Video Career Library - Public and Personal Services
Careers, Inc.
1211 10th St., SW
PO Box 135
Largo, FL 34649-0135   Phone: (813)584-7333
Videocassette. 1990. 35 mins. Part of the Video Career Library covering 165 occupations. Shows actual workers on the job. Includes firefighters, police officers, correctional officers, bartenders, waiters/waitresses, cooks/chefs, child care workers, flight attendants, barbers/cosmetologists, groundskeepers/gardeners, and butchers/meat cutters.

Butchers and Meat, Poultry, and Fish Cutters

Associations

★5650★
American Association of Meat Processors (AAMP)
PO Box 269
Elizabethtown, PA 17022   Phone: (717)367-1168
Membership: Retail and wholesale operators of meat processing plants, locker plants, frozen food centers, freezer food suppliers and food plants. **Purpose:** Sponsors American Cured Meat Championship and American Meat Platter Competition. Presents achievement award annually. Conducts educational programs; sponsors group insurance program for members.

★5651★
United Food and Commercial Workers International Union (UFCW)
Suffridge Bldg.
1775 K St. NW
Washington, DC 20006   Phone: (202)223-3111
Membership: AFL-CIO. **Purpose:** Maintains 1500 volume library. **Publications:** *UFCW Action*, bimonthly. • *UFCW Leadership Update*, monthly.

Standards/Certification Agencies

Most butchers and meat, poultry, and fish cutters acquire their skills informally on the job or through apprenticeship programs. On-the-job trainees, under the guidance of experienced workers, learn the proper use of tools and equipment and how to prepare various cuts of meat. Meatcutters who learn the trade through apprenticeship programs, which are sponsored by local chapters of the United Food and Commercial Workers International Union, generally complete two years of supervised on-the-job training supplemented by classroom work. At the end of the training period, apprentices must pass a meatcutting test. In some areas, apprentices may become meatcutters without completing the entire training program if they can pass the test.

Test Guides

★5652★
Butcher
National Learning Corp.
212 Michael Dr.
Syosset, NY 11791   Phone: (516)921-8888
Jack Rudman. Part of the Career Examination Series No. 1. All examination guides in this series contain questions with answers. **Facsimile Number:** (516)921-8743. **Toll-free/Additional Phone Number(s):** 800-645-6337.

★5653★
Chief Meat Inspector
National Learning Corp.
212 Michael Dr.
Syosset, NY 11791   Phone: (516)921-8888
Jack Rudman. Part of the Career Examination Series No. 1. All examination guides in this series contain questions with answers. **Facsimile Number:** (516)921-8743. **Toll-free/Additional Phone Number(s):** 800-645-6337.

★5654★
Meat Cutter
National Learning Corp.
212 Michael Dr.
Syosset, NY 11791   Phone: (516)921-8888
Jack Rudman. Part of the Career Examination Series No. 1. All examination guides in this series contain questions with answers. **Facsimile Number:** (516)921-8743. **Toll-free/Additional Phone Number(s):** 800-645-6337.

★5655★
Senior Meat Cutter
National Learning Corp.
212 Michael Dr.
Syosset, NY 11791   Phone: (516)921-8888
Jack Rudman. Part of the Career Examination Series No. 1. All examination guides in this series contain questions with answers. **Facsimile Number:** (516)921-8743. **Toll-free/Additional Phone Number(s):** 800-645-6337.

Periodicals

★5656★
American Meat Institute—Newsletter
American Meat Institute
PO Box 3556
Washington, DC 20007   Phone: (703)841-2400
Editor(s): Rich Parker. Weekly. Contains news about legislative and government regulations and actions relevant to the meat industry. Recurring features include Institute news and livestock slaughter reports. **Facsimile Number:** (703)527-0938.

★5657★
National Broiler Council—Washington Report
National Broiler Council
1155 15th St. NW, Ste. 614
Washington, DC 20005   Phone: (202)296-2622
Editor(s): Margaret Ernst. Weekly. Centers on issues affecting the marketing of poultry for the broiler processing industry. Covers government actions, export markets, and grain supplies. **Facsimile Number:** (202)293-4005.

★5658★
Seafood Leader
Waterfront Press Co.
1115 NW 46th St.
Seattle, WA 98107   Phone: (206)789-6506
Peter Redmayne, Editor and Publisher. 6x/yr. Magazine on seafood buying, marketing, and technology. Articles range from seafood processing technology to merchandising to cuisine; featuring seafood from the ocean to the plate. **Facsimile Number:** (206)789-9193.

★5659★
UFCW Action
United Food and Commercial Workers International Union (UFCW)
Suffridge Bldg.
1775 K St. NW
Washington, DC 20006   Phone: (202)223-3111
Bimonthly. Magazine covering union activities, political and legislative matters, and consumer news.

★5660★
UFCW Leadership Update
United Food and Commercial Workers International Union (UFCW)
Suffridge Bldg.
1775 K St. NW
Washington, DC 20006   Phone: (202)223-3111
Monthly.

★5661★
Western States Meat Association—Bulletin
Western States Meat Association
1615 Broadway, Ste. 900
PO Box 12944
Oakland, CA 94604   Phone: (415)763-1533
Editor(s): JoAnne Mocker. Weekly. Reports news of interest to the protein industry, including government and legislative actions, business trends, price quotations, health and safety procedures, and related topics.

Meetings and Conventions

★5662★
American Convention of Meat Processors
American Association of Meat Processors
PO Box 269
Elizabethtown, PA 17022   Phone: (717)367-1168
1992; Jul. 09-12; Orlando, FL • 1993; Jul. 26-29; Las Vegas, NV • 1994; Aug. 04-07; Milwaukee, WI • 1995; Jul. 20-23; San Antonio, TX. **Facsimile Number:** (717)367-9096.

★5663★
American Meat Institute Exposition
American Meat Institute
PO Box 3556
Washington, DC 20007   Phone: (703)841-2400
Frequency: Exhibits only occur during odd years. 1992; Oct. 08-11; Orlando, FL • 1993; Sep. 30 - Oct. 03; Chicago, IL. **Facsimile Number:** (703)527-0938.

★5664★
Food and Dairy Expo
Dairy and Food Industries Supply Association
6245 Executive Blvd.
Rockville, MD 20852   Phone: (301)984-1444
1993; Oct. 16-20; Atlanta, GA • 1995; Oct. 14-18; Chicago, IL. **Facsimile Number:** (301)881-7832.

★5665★
FOODTECH - International Food and Beverage, Catering, Food Production and Processing Equipment, Packaging Machinery and Materials Exhibition
World Access Corp.
15 Bemis Rd.
PO Box 171
Wellesley Hills, MA 02181   Phone: (617)235-8095

★5666★
IFFA - International Trade Fair for the Meat Industry
German American Chamber of Commerce
666 5th Ave.
New York, NY 10103   Phone: (212)974-8856
Frequency: Every three years. Always held in Frankfurt, Germany. **Facsimile Number:** (212)974-8867.

★5667★
International Exposition for Food Processors
Food Processing Machinery and Supplies Association
200 Daingerfield Rd.
Alexandria, VA 22314   Phone: (703)684-1080
1993; Mar. 07-10; Chicago, IL. **Toll-free/Additional Phone Number(s):** 800-331-8816. **Facsimile Number:** (703)548-6563.

★5668★
International Poultry Trade Show
Southeastern Poultry and Egg Association
1456 Church St.
Decatur, GA 30030   Phone: (404)377-6465
Frequency: Always held during January at the World Congress Center in Atlanta, Georgia. **Facsimile Number:** (404)378-9801.

★5669★
Midwest Poultry Federation Convention
Midwest Poultry Federation
PO Box 12181
St. Paul, MN 55112   Phone: (612)636-0947
1993; Feb. 17-19; Minneapolis, MN • 1994; Feb. 16-18; Minneapolis, MN.

★5670★
SOFFA - Trade Fair for the Butchers' Trade
World Access Corp.
15 Bemis Rd.
PO Box 171
Wellesley Hills, MA 02181   Phone: (617)235-8095
1993; Oct. 17-19. **Facsimile Number:** (617)235-7360.

★5671★
Western States Meat Association Exhibition
Western States Meat Association
PO Box 12944
Oakland, CA 94604   Phone: (415)763-1533

Inspectors, Testers, and Graders

Inspectors, testers, and graders compare products to samples or to specifications in blueprints or graphs to ensure that the products meet quality standards. If the product checks out, inspectors certify it in some manner. They may reject defective items outright, send them for rework, or, in the case of minor problems, fix them themselves. Inspectors, testers, and graders record the results of their inspections, compute the percentage of defects and other statistical parameters, prepare inspection and test reports, notify supervisors of problems, and may help analyze and correct problems. Senior inspectors may also set up tests and test equipment. Over 80 percent of all inspectors, testers, and graders work in manufacturing industries. Some work in wholesale trade, transportation, testing and photofinishing labs, engineering services, and government agencies.

$alaries

Weekly earnings for inspectors, testers, and graders are as follows:

Lowest 10 percent	$235.00/week or less
Middle 50 percent	$310.00—$540.00/week
Top 10 percent	$610.00/week or more

Employment Outlook

Growth rate until the year 2000: Slower than average.

Inspectors, Testers, and Graders

Career Guides

★5672★
Annual Motor Vehicle Inspection
New York State Education Department
Center for Learning Technologies
Media Distribution Network
Room C-7, Concourse Level
Albany, NY 12230   Phone: (518)474-1265

Videocassette. 1983. 15 mins. All aspects of the New York State Motor Vehicle Department's motor vehicle inspection process are explained in this program.

★5673★
"Electronics Inspector" in *Hard Hatted Women: Stories of Struggle and Success in the Trades* (pp. 212-215)
Seal Press
3131 Western Ave., Ste. 410
Seattle, WA 98121   Phone: (206)283-7844

Molly Martin, editor. 1988. Twenty-six women recount their experiences working in blue collar occupations. They describe how they got in, the work they do, their relationships in predominantly male occupations, and their training.

★5674★
"Inspectors, Testers, and Graders" in *Occupational Outlook Handbook* (pp. 390-391)
Superintendent of Documents
U.S. Government Printing Office
Washington, DC 20402   Phone: (202)783-3238

Biennial; latest edition, 1990-91. Encyclopedia of careers describing more than 250 occupations and comprising about 86 percent of all jobs in the economy. Occupations that require lengthy education or training are given the most attention. For each occupation, the handbook describes job duties, working conditions, training, educational preparation, personal qualities, advancement possibilities, job outlook, earnings, and sources of additional information.

★5675★
"Quality Control Inspector" in *Manufacturing*, Volume 9 of *Career Information Center* (pp. 56-58)
Glencoe/Macmillan
15319 Chatsworth St.
Mission Hills, CA 91345   Phone: (818)898-1391

Richard Lidz and Dale Anderson, editorial directors. Fourth edition, 1990. For 600 occupations, describes job duties, entry-level requirements, education and training needed, advancement possibilities, employment outlook, earnings and benefits. The set is divided into 12 volumes. Each volume includes jobs related under a broad career field. Volume 13 is the index. **Facsimile Number:** 818-365-5489.

Associations

★5676★
American Society for Quality Control (ASQC)
310 W. Wisconsin Ave.
Milwaukee, WI 53203   Phone: (414)272-8575

Membership: Society of professionals dedicated to the advancement of quality. **Purpose:** Through its Professional Development Department, offers courses in quality engineering, reliability engineering, managing for quality, management of quality costs, quality audit-development and administration, management of the inspection function, probability and statistics for engineers and scientists, and product liability and prevention. Maintains library of 400 texts and manuals. Offers personnel listing service. Presents annual honors and awards. **Publications:** *Journal of Quality Technology*, quarterly. • *Quality Engineering*, quarterly. • *Quality Progress*, monthly. • *The Quality Review*, quarterly. • *Technical Congress Transactions*, annual. • *Technometrics*, quarterly. **Facsimile Number:** (414)272-1734.

★5677★
National Tooling and Machining Association (NTMA)
9300 Livingston Rd.
Ft. Washington, MD 20744   Phone: (301)248-6200

Membership: Manufacturers of tools, dies, jigs, fixtures, molds, gages, or special machinery; companies that do precision machining on a contract basis; past service and honorary members. **Purpose:** Provides management services; represents members in legislative matters. Promotes apprenticeship programs. Compiles management surveys; conducts management training workshops; maintains speakers' bureau. Has produced motion pictures and videocassettes on tool, die, and precision machining for educational showings. **Publications:** *Business Management Aids*, periodic. • *Buyers Guide of Special Tooling and Precision Machining Services*, annual. • *Catalog of Publications and Training Materials*, periodic. • *Membership Directory*, annual. • *Record*, monthly. • Also publishes handbooks and textbooks. **Toll-free/Additional Phone Number(s):** (800)248-NTMA. **Facsimile Number:** (301)248-7104.

Test Guides

★5678★
Associate Quality Assurance Specialist
National Learning Corp.
212 Michael Dr.
Syosset, NY 11791   Phone: (516)921-8888
Jack Rudman. Part of the Career Examination Series No. 1. All examination guides in this series contain questions with answers. **Facsimile Number:** (516)921-8743. **Toll-free/Additional Phone Number(s):** 800-645-6337.

★5679★
Beverage Control Inspector
National Learning Corp.
212 Michael Dr.
Syosset, NY 11791   Phone: (516)921-8888
Jack Rudman. Part of the Career Examination Series No. 1. All examination guides in this series contain questions with answers. **Facsimile Number:** (516)921-8743. **Toll-free/Additional Phone Number(s):** 800-645-6337.

★5680★
Chief Meat Inspector
National Learning Corp.
212 Michael Dr.
Syosset, NY 11791   Phone: (516)921-8888
Jack Rudman. Part of the Career Examination Series No. 1. All examination guides in this series contain questions with answers. **Facsimile Number:** (516)921-8743. **Toll-free/Additional Phone Number(s):** 800-645-6337.

★5681★
Food Inspector
National Learning Corp.
212 Michael Dr.
Syosset, NY 11791   Phone: (516)921-8888
Jack Rudman. Part of the Career Examination Series No. 1. Study guide is also available for food inspector trainee positions. All examination guides in this series contain questions with answers. **Facsimile Number:** (516)921-8743. **Toll-free/Additional Phone Number(s):** 800-645-6337.

★5682★
Meat Inspector
National Learning Corp.
212 Michael Dr.
Syosset, NY 11791   Phone: (516)921-8888
Jack Rudman. Part of the Career Examination Series No. 1. Study guide for meat inspector trainee also available. All examination guides in this series contain questions with answers. **Facsimile Number:** (516)921-8743. **Toll-free/Additional Phone Number(s):** 800-645-6337.

★5683★
Meat Inspector-Poultry Inspector
National Learning Corp.
212 Michael Dr.
Syosset, NY 11791   Phone: (516)921-8888
Jack Rudman. Part of the Career Examination Series No. 1. All examination guides in this series contain questions with answers. **Facsimile Number:** (516)921-8743. **Toll-free/Additional Phone Number(s):** 800-645-6337.

★5684★
Quality Control Inspector
National Learning Corp.
212 Michael Dr.
Syosset, NY 11791   Phone: (516)921-8888
Jack Rudman. Part of the Career Examination Series No. 1. All examination guides in this series contain questions with answers. **Facsimile Number:** (516)921-8743. **Toll-free/Additional Phone Number(s):** 800-645-6337.

★5685★
Senior Boiler Inspector
National Learning Corp.
212 Michael Dr.
Syosset, NY 11791   Phone: (516)921-8888
Jack Rudman. Part of the Career Examination Series No. 1. All examination guides in this series contain questions with answers. **Facsimile Number:** (516)921-8743. **Toll-free/Additional Phone Number(s):** 800-645-6337.

★5686★
Senior Food Inspector
National Learning Corp.
212 Michael Dr.
Syosset, NY 11791   Phone: (516)921-8888
Jack Rudman. Part of the Career Examination Series No. 1. All examination guides in this series contain questions with answers. **Facsimile Number:** (516)921-8743. **Toll-free/Additional Phone Number(s):** 800-645-6337.

★5687★
Senior Inspector, Meat & Poultry
National Learning Corp.
212 Michael Dr.
Syosset, NY 11791   Phone: (516)921-8888
Jack Rudman. Part of the Career Examination Series No. 1. All examination guides in this series contain questions with answers. **Facsimile Number:** (516)921-8743. **Toll-free/Additional Phone Number(s):** 800-645-6337.

★5688★
Senior Meat Inspector
National Learning Corp.
212 Michael Dr.
Syosset, NY 11791   Phone: (516)921-8888
Jack Rudman. Part of the Career Examination Series No. 1. All examination guides in this series contain questions with answers. **Facsimile Number:** (516)921-8743. **Toll-free/Additional Phone Number(s):** 800-645-6337.

Periodicals

★5689★
Journal of Quality Technology
American Society for Quality Control (ASQC)
310 W. Wisconsin Ave.
Milwaukee, WI 53203   Phone: (414)272-8575
Quarterly.

★5690★
NTMA Business Management Aids
National Tooling and Machining Association (NTMA)
9300 Livingston Rd.
Ft. Washington, MD 20744   Phone: (301)248-6200
Periodic.

Inspectors, Testers, and Graders

★5691★
NTMA Record
National Tooling and Machining Association (NTMA)
9300 Livingston Rd.
Ft. Washington, MD 20744   Phone: (301)248-6200
Monthly.

★5692★
Quality Engineering
American Society for Quality Control (ASQC)
310 W. Wisconsin Ave.
Milwaukee, WI 53203   Phone: (414)272-8575
Quarterly.

★5693★
Quality Progress
American Society for Quality Control (ASQC)
310 W. Wisconsin Ave.
Milwaukee, WI 53203   Phone: (414)272-8575
Monthly.

★5694★
The Quality Review
American Society for Quality Control (ASQC)
310 W. Wisconsin Ave.
Milwaukee, WI 53203   Phone: (414)272-8575
Quarterly.

★5695★
Technometrics
American Society for Quality Control (ASQC)
310 W. Wisconsin Ave.
Milwaukee, WI 53203   Phone: (414)272-8575
Quarterly. Published with American Statistical Association.

──────── Meetings and Conventions ────────

★5696★
American Society for Quality Control Annual Quality Congress
American Society for Quality Control
310 W. Wisconsin Ave., Ste. 500
Milwaukee, WI 53203   Phone: (414)272-8575
1992; May 18-20; Nashville, TN • 1993; May 24-26; Boston, MA • 1994; May 24-26; Las Vegas, NV. **Toll-free/Additional Phone Number(s):** 800-248-1946. **Facsimile Number:** (414)272-1734.

──────── Other Sources of Information ────────

★5697★
Catalog of Publications and Training Materials
National Tooling and Machining Association (NTMA)
9300 Livingston Rd.
Ft. Washington, MD 20744   Phone: (301)248-6200
Periodic.

Metalworking and Plastic-working Occupations

Boilermakers

Boilermakers and boilermaker mechanics construct, assemble, and repair boilers, vats, and other large vessels that hold liquids and gases. In construction and assembly, boilermakers locate reference points for installation, attach rigging, align sections, and attach water tubes, stacks, and other parts. They then test for leaks or other defects. Usually, they assemble large vessels temporarily in a fabrication shop to ensure a proper fit and again on their permanent site. Boilermaker mechanics maintain and repair boilers and similar vessels. They clean and repair various components and replace defective parts. Over 50 percent of all boilermakers work in the construction industry. About 25 percent work in manufacturing, primarily in boiler manufacturing shops, iron and steel plants, petroleum refineries, chemical plants, and shipyards. Some also work for boiler repair firms, railroads, and in Navy shipyards, and federal power facilities.

$alaries

Full-time boilermakers average about $550/week.

Employment Outlook

Growth rate until the year 2000: More slowly than average.

Boilermakers

Career Guides

★5698★
Boilermaker
Careers, Inc.
PO Box 135
Largo, FL 34649-0135   Phone: (813)584-7333
1990. Two-page occupational summary card describing duties, working conditions, personal qualifications, training, earnings and hours, employment outlook, places of employment, related careers and where to write for more information.

★5699★
"Boilermaker" in *Occu-Facts: Information on 565 Careers in Outline Form* (p. 17.5)
Careers, Inc.
P.O. Box 135
1211 Tenth St., S.W.
Largo, FL 33640   Phone: (813)584-7333
Elizabeth Handville. Biennial, 1989-90 edition. Each one-page occupational profile describes duties, working conditions, physical surroundings and demands, aptitudes, temperament, educational requirements, employment outlook, earnings, and places of employment.

★5700★
Boilermakers
Chronicle Guidance Publications, Inc.
PO Box 1190
Moravia, NY 13118-1190   Phone: (315)497-0330
1987. This career brief describes the nature of the work, working conditions, hours and earnings, education and training, licensure, certification, unions, personal qualifications, social and psychological factors, employment outlook, entry methods, advancement, and related occupations. **Toll-free/Additional Phone Number(s):** 800-622-7284.

★5701★
"Boilermakers" in *Occupational Outlook Handbook* (pp. 391-392)
Superintendent of Documents
U.S. Government Printing Office
Washington, DC 20402   Phone: (202)783-3238
Biennial; latest edition, 1990-91. Encyclopedia of careers describing more than 250 occupations and comprising about 86 percent of all jobs in the economy. Occupations that require lengthy education or training are given the most attention. For each occupation, the handbook describes job duties, working conditions, training, educational preparation, personal qualities, advancement possibilities, job outlook, earnings, and sources of additional information.

★5702★
"Boilermaking Occupations" in Volume 3 of *The Encyclopedia of Careers and Vocational Guidance* (pp. 625-629)
J.G. Ferguson Publishing Co.
200 W. Monroe
Chicago, IL 60606   Phone: (312)580-5480
William E. Hopke, editor-in-chief. Eighth edition, 1990. Four-volume set that profiles 500 occupations and describes job trends in 76 industries. Includes career description, educational requirements, history of the job, methods of entry, advancement, employment outlook, earnings, working conditions, social and psychological factors, and sources of additional information.

★5703★
"Boilermaking Worker" in *Manufacturing*, Volume 9 of *Career Information Center* (pp. 42-44)
Glencoe/Macmillan
15319 Chatsworth St.
Mission Hills, CA 91345   Phone: (818)898-1391
Richard Lidz and Dale Anderson, editorial directors. Fourth edition, 1990. For 600 occupations, describes job duties, entry-level requirements, education and training needed, advancement possibilities, employment outlook, earnings and benefits. The set is divided into 12 volumes. Each volume includes jobs related under a broad career field. Volume 13 is the index. **Facsimile Number:** 818-365-5489.

★5704★
"Boilermaking Workers" in Volume 1 of *Career Discovery Encyclopedia* (pp. 132-133)
J.G. Ferguson Publishing Co.
200 W. Monroe
Chicago, IL 60606   Phone: (312)580-5480
E. Russell Primm, editor-in-chief. 1990. Contains two-page articles on 504 occupations. Each article describes job duties, earnings, and educational and training requirements.

Associations

★5705★
International Association of Machinists and Aerospace Workers (IAM)
1300 Connecticut Ave.
Washington, DC 20036   Phone: (202)857-5200
Membership: AFL-CIO. **Publications:** *The Machinist*, monthly.

★5706★
International Brotherhood of Boilermakers, Iron Ship Builders, Blacksmiths, Forgers and Helpers
753 State Ave., Ste. 570
Kansas City, KS 66101 Phone: (913)371-2640
Membership: AFL-CIO, CFL. **Publications:** *Boilermakers-Blacksmiths Reporter*, 6/year. • *Membership Roster*, triennial. • *NTL News*, quarterly. **Facsimile Number:** (913)371-5335.

★5707★
International Union, United Automobile, Aerospace and Agricultural Implement Workers of America (UAW)
8000 E. Jefferson
Detroit, MI 48214 Phone: (313)926-5000
Membership: AFL-CIO. **Publications:** *Ammo*, monthly. • *Skill*, quarterly. • *Solidarity*, 10/year.

★5708★
United Steelworkers of America (USWA)
5 Gateway Center
Pittsburgh, PA 15222 Phone: (412)562-2400
Membership: AFL-CIO. **Publications:** *Steelabor*, 10/year. • *Steelworker Old Time*, quarterly. **Facsimile Number:** (412)562-2445.

Standards/Certification Agencies

Most training authorities recommend a formal apprenticeship to learn this trade. Apprenticeship programs are administered by the joint union-management committees of the International Brotherhood of Boilermakers, Iron Shipbuilders, Blacksmiths, Forgers, and Helpers. Programs usually consist of 4 years of on-the-job training, supplemented by about 48 hours of classroom instruction each year in subjects such as blueprint reading, shop mathematics, and welding.

Test Guides

★5709★
Career Examination Series
National Learning Corp.
212 Michael Dr.
Syosset, NY 11791 Phone: (516)921-8888
Jack Rudman. National Learning Corp.'s Career Examination Series No. 1. contains examination guides for many careers, including boiler inspector, boiler room helper, and boilermaker. All examination guides in this series contain questions with answers. **Facsimile Number:** (516)921-8743. **Toll-free/Additional Phone Number(s):** 800-645-6337.

Awards, Scholarships, Grants, and Fellowships

★5710★
AIRCO Welding Award
American Welding Society
P.O. Box 351040
550 LeJeune Rd., N.W.
Miami, FL 33135 Phone: (305)443-9353
For recognition of distinguished accomplishments in the joining of or severing of metals which have improved and benefited mankind and furthered the welding industry. An honorarium of $1,000 and a certificate are awarded annually. Established in 1967 and sponsored by Airco Welding Products Division of AIRCO, Inc.

Periodicals

★5711★
Ammo
International Union, United Automobile, Aerospace and Agricultural Implement Workers of America
8000 E. Jefferson
Detroit, MI 48214 Phone: (313)926-5000
Monthly. Magazine.

★5712★
Boilermakers-Blacksmiths Reporter
International Brotherhood of Boilermakers, Iron Ship Builders, Blacksmiths, Forgers, and Helpers
753 State Ave., Ste. 570
Kansas City, KS 66101 Phone: (913)371-2640
6/year. Union activities tabloid; includes annual index.

★5713★
NTL News
International Brotherhood of Boilermakers, Iron Ship Builders, Blacksmiths, Forgers, and Helpers
753 State Ave., Ste. 570
Kansas City, KS 66101 Phone: (913)371-2640
Quarterly. Membership activities newsletter.

★5714★
Skill (UAW)
International Union, United Automobile, Aerospace and Agricultural Implement Workers of America
8000 E. Jefferson
Detroit, MI 48214 Phone: (313)926-5000
Quarterly.

★5715★
Solidarity
International Union, United Automobile, Aerospace and Agricultural Implement Workers of America
8000 E. Jefferson
Detroit, MI 48214 Phone: (313)926-5000
10/year. Magazine covering labor, economic, social, and political affairs affecting union members. Includes book and film reviews.

★5716★
Steelabor
United Steelworkers of America (USWA)
5 Gateway Center
Pittsburgh, PA 15222 Phone: (412)562-2400
10/year. News magazine reporting on legislation and regulation affecting the union, union activities at the national and chapter levels, economic developments, pension news, and information on safety and health.

★5717★
Steelworker Old Time
United Steelworkers of America
5 Gateway Center
Pittsburgh, PA 15222 Phone: (412)562-2400
Quarterly.

Meetings and Conventions

★5718★
International Association of Machinists and Aerospace Workers (IAM)
1300 Connecticut Ave.
Washington, DC 20036   Phone: (202)857-5200
Frequency: Quadrennial - next 1992.

★5719★
International Brotherhood of Boilermakers, Iron Ship Builders, Blacksmiths, Forgers and Helpers
753 State Ave., Ste. 570
Kansas City, KS 66101   Phone: (913)371-2640
Frequency: Quinquennial - next 1996. **Facsimile Number:** (913)371-5335.

Jewelers

Jewelers make, repair, and adjust all types of jewelry such as rings, necklaces, and earrings. Using drills, jeweler's soldering torches, and a variety of other handtools, they mold and shape metal, and set precious and semiprecious stones. Jewelers' work varies by the type of establishment in which they work. Those in retail stores and repair shops primarily do adjustments and repairs like resetting stones and replacing broken clasps. Jewelers in manufacturing specialize in a single operation such as engraving. Nearly 50 percent of all salaried jewelers work in retail establishments, while approximately 33 percent are employed in manufacturing plants. About 40 percent of all jewelers are self-employed.

$alaries

Earnings for jewelers vary by type of establishment. Some median salaries are listed below.

Jewelers in retail stores	$22,000/year
Jewelry repair workers	$25,000/year

Employment Outlook

Growth rate until the year 2000: Average.

Jewelers

Career Guides

★5720★
Jeweler
Careers, Inc.
PO Box 135
Largo, FL 34649-0135   Phone: (813)584-7333
1990. Eight-page brief offering the definition, history, duties, working conditions, personal qualifications, educational requirements, earnings, hours, employment outlook, advancement possibilities, and related occupations.

★5721★
Jeweler
Vocational Biographies, Inc.
PO Box 31, Dept. VF10
Sauk Centre, MN 56378   Phone: (612)352-6516
1990. This pamphlet profiles a person working in the job. Includes information about job duties, working conditions, places of employment, educational preparation, labor market outlook, and salaries. **Toll-free/Additional Phone Number(s):** 800-255-0752.

★5722★
"Jeweler" in *Consumer, Homemaking, and Personal Services*, Volume 5 of *Career Information Center* (pp. 82-84)
Glencoe/Macmillan
15319 Chatsworth St.
Mission Hills, CA 91345   Phone: (818)898-1391
Richard Lidz and Dale Anderson, editorial directors. Fourth edition, 1990. For 600 occupations, describes job duties, entry-level requirements, education and training needed, advancement possibilities, employment outlook, earnings and benefits. The set is divided into 12 volumes. Each volume includes jobs related under a broad career field. Volume 13 is the index. **Facsimile Number:** 818-365-5489.

★5723★
"Jeweler" in *Occu-Facts: Information on 565 Careers in Outline Form* (p. 17.9)
Careers, Inc.
P.O. Box 135
1211 Tenth St., S.W.
Largo, FL 33640   Phone: (813)584-7333
Elizabeth Handville. Biennial, 1989-90 edition. Each one-page occupational profile describes duties, working conditions, physical surroundings and demands, aptitudes, temperament, educational requirements, employment outlook, earnings, and places of employment.

★5724★
"Jewelers" in *Jobs! What They Are. . .Where They Are. . .What They Pay* (p. 298)
Simon & Schuster, Inc.
Simon & Schuster Bldg.
1230 Avenue of the Americas
New York, NY 10020   Phone: (212)698-7000
Robert O. Snelling and Anne M. Snelling. Revised edition, 1989. Profiles 241 occupations, describing duties and responsibilities, educational preparation, earnings, employment opportunities, training, and qualifications.

★5725★
"Jewelers" in *Occupational Outlook Handbook* (pp. 392-394)
Superintendent of Documents
U.S. Government Printing Office
Washington, DC 20402   Phone: (202)783-3238
Biennial; latest edition, 1990-91. Encyclopedia of careers describing more than 250 occupations and comprising about 86 percent of all jobs in the economy. Occupations that require lengthy education or training are given the most attention. For each occupation, the handbook describes job duties, working conditions, training, educational preparation, personal qualities, advancement possibilities, job outlook, earnings, and sources of additional information.

★5726★
"Jewelers and Jewelry Repairers" in Volume 3 of *Career Discovery Encyclopedia* (pp. 166-167)
J.G. Ferguson Publishing Co.
200 W. Monroe
Chicago, IL 60606   Phone: (312)580-5480
E. Russell Primm, editor-in-chief. 1990. Contains two-page articles on 504 occupations. Each article describes job duties, earnings, and educational and training requirements.

★5727★
"Jewelers and Jewelry Repairers" in Volume 3 of *The Encyclopedia of Careers and Vocational Guidance* (pp. 584-587)
J.G. Ferguson Publishing Co.
200 W. Monroe
Chicago, IL 60606   Phone: (312)580-5480
William E. Hopke, editor-in-chief. Eighth edition, 1990. Four-volume set that profiles 500 occupations and describes job trends in 76 industries. Includes career description, educational requirements, history of the job, methods of entry, advancement, employment outlook, earnings, working conditions, social and psychological factors, and sources of additional information.

★5728★
"Jewelry Design and Metal Smithing" in *The Career Connection II: A Guide to Technical Majors and Their Related Careers* (pp. 77-78)
ERIS
PO Box 7509
University Station
Provo, UT 84602-0509

Fred A. Rowe. 1988. Contains technical majors, such as automotive technology. Describes the major and the job. Lists high school and postsecondary school courses. Includes occupations related to the major, employment outlook, and starting salary.

★5729★
"Jewelry Making" in *Opportunities in Metalworking Careers* (pp. 59-66)
National Textbook Co.
4255 W. Touhy Ave.
Lincolnwood, IL 60646   Phone: (312)679-5500

Mark Rowh. 1991. Covers sheet metal work, machining, structural and reinforcing metalworking, and jewelry making. Describes the work performed, skills needed, training and working conditions. Lists unions that sponsor apprenticeship and technical schools which offer training.

★5730★
"Jewelry Worker" in *Offbeat Careers: The Directory of Unusual Work* (pp. 83-85)
Ten Speed Press
PO Box 7123
Berkeley, CA 94707   Phone: (415)845-8414

Al Sacharov. 1988. Profiles eighty-eight unusual careers. Provides job description, history of occupation, salary, and training required. Lists one or more sources of additional information.

Associations

★5731★
Jewelers of America (JA)
Time-Life Bldg.
1271 Ave. of the Americas
New York, NY 10020   Phone: (212)489-0023

Membership: Retailers of jewelry, watches, silver, and allied merchandise. **Purpose:** Conducts surveys and compiles statistics. Cosponsors with state affiliates workshops and seminars designed to bring management information to retail jeweler members. **Publications:** *Report*, monthly. • Also publishes manuals and brochures. **Toll-free/Additional Phone Number(s):** (800)223-0673. **Facsimile Number:** (212)586-9396.

Awards, Scholarships, Grants, and Fellowships

★5732★
Boardwalk Art Show
Virginia Beach Center for the Arts
c/o Michael J. marks
2200 Park Ave.
Virginia Beach, VA 23451   Phone: (804)425-0000

To recognize quality artwork at the Boardwalk Show. Awards are given in several categories including jewelry. Slides of a representation of the artist's work of art may be submitted by March 1. The following awards are presented: (1) Best-In-Show Purchase Award - $2,500; (2) Virginia Governor's Trophy - $1,500; (3) Award of Excellence - $1,000; (4) Award of Distinction - $500; (5) ten Awards of Honor - $400 each (6) ten Awards of Merit - $300 each; and (7) ten Sand Dollar Awards - $200 each. Awarded annually. Established in 1956.

★5733★
International Art Competition - New York
International Art Competition - New York
c/o Artitudes
P.O. Box 380
Hartsdale, NY 10538   Phone: (914)633-5333

To recognize artists working in all media and styles. Awards are presented in various categories including jewelry. 35mm slides may be submitted by June 23. The following awards are presented: (1) Purchase prizes totaling $4,800; (2) approximately 40 artists are chosen to exhibit their work at Art 54 Gallery; (3) monetary awards of $2,200 each to selected artists; and (4) Certificates of Merit to ten winners in each category. Awarded annually. Established in 1983.

★5734★
San Mateo County Fair and Floral Fiesta
San Mateo County Fair and Exposition Center
c/o Judy Habel, Assistant Manager
P.O. Box 1027
2495 S. Delaware
San Mateo, CA 94403-0627   Phone: (415)574-FAIR

To recognize outstanding entries in the Fair. The competition is open to anyone, and there are no geographical limitations. Awards are presented in several categories including jewelry. Monetary awards, trophies and ribbons are awarded.

★5735★
Washington Craft Show
Smithsonian Associates Women's Committee
Arts and Industries Building, Room 1278
Smithsonian Institution
Washington, DC 20560   Phone: (202)357-4000

To enable craftsmen to exhibit and sell crafts as fine art. Artisans working in several categories including jewelry are eligible. One hundred exhibitors are selected on the basis of originality, artistic conception, and quality of workmanship. Applications may be submitted by October 13. The following awards are presented to exhibitors in recognition of outstanding work; (1) three awards for excellence - $1,000 each; and (2) a Craftsmen's Choice Award - $300.

Basic Reference Guides and Handbooks

★5736★
Jewelers' Circular/Keystone—Almanac Issue
Chilton Co.
Chilton Way
Radnor, PA 19089   Phone: (215)964-4000

Deborah Holmes, Managing Editor, editor. Annual, July. List of jewelery associations. Entries include: Association name, address, phone. **Facsimile Number:** (215)964-4273.

★5737★
Professional Goldsmithing: A Contemporary Guide to Traditional Jewelry Techniques
Van Nostrand Reinhold
115 5th Ave.
New York, NY 10003   Phone: (212)254-3232

Alan Revere. 1991. **Facsimile Number:** (212)254-9499.

Jewelers ★5750★

Periodicals

★5738★
Accent
Accent Publishing Co., Inc.
60 Chestnut Ave., Ste. 201
Devon, PA 19333   Phone: (215)293-1112
Michelle D. Sterbakov, Editor. Monthly. Fashion jewelry trade magazine. **Facsimile Number:** (215)293-1717.

★5739★
American Jewelry Manufacturer
Chilton Co.
825 7th Ave.
New York, NY 10019   Phone: (212)245-7555
Ellen Berkovitch, Editor. Monthly. Trade magazine. Official publication of Manufacturing Jewelers and Silversmiths of America, Inc. **Facsimile Number:** (212)887-8348.

★5740★
Bijou
Canam Publications Ltd.
8270 Mountain Sights St., Ste. 201
Montreal, PQ, Canada H4P 2B7   Phone: (514)731-9517
Andree Harvey, Editor. 6x/yr. Jewelry and watchmaking magazine (French). Official publication of Corporation des Bijoutiers du Quebec. **Facsimile Number:** (514)731-7459.

★5741★
The Diamond Registry Bulletin
Joseph Schlussel
580 5th Ave., Ste. 806
New York, NY 10036   Phone: (212)575-0444
Editor(s): Joseph Schlussel. Monthly. Supplies current data on the present and future outlook of the diamond market. Provides information concerning trends in jewelry and investment companies and actual wholesale prices by size, quality, and shape for certified and commercial diamonds. Recurring features include reviews of fashion trends, diamond sales boosters, quotes, and anecdotes. **Toll-free/Additional Phone Number(s):** 800-223-7955 **Facsimile Number:** (212)575-0722.

★5742★
Fashion Jewelry Plus
Larkin Publications
485 7th Ave., Ste. 1400
New York, NY 10018   Phone: (212)594-0880
Six times/yr. Jewelry and accessory trade publication. **Facsimile Number:** (212)594-8556.

★5743★
Gem and Jewelry Fact Sheets Quarterly Supplement
American Gem Society
5901 W. Third St.
Los Angeles, CA 90036-2898   Phone: (213)936-4367
Editor(s): Charlotte Preston. Quarterly. Highlights jewelry industry developments. Discusses market projections, new sources of gemstones, and major marketing ideas.

★5744★
Gem Trends
American Gem Society
5901 W. Third St.
Los Angeles, CA 90036-2898   Phone: (213)936-4367
Editor(s): Laurie Hudson. Quarterly. Provides information on various gems, fashion trends, and jewelry buying tips from a retail jeweler's point of view. Educates consumers about how to make wise jewelry purchases and what to look for in a jeweler. Includes a trivia quiz. **Facsimile Number:** (213)936-9629.

★5745★
Gems & Gemology
Gemological Institute of America
1660 Stewart St.
Santa Monica, CA 90404   Phone: (213)829-2991
Alice S. Keller, Editor. Quarterly. Gemology and mineralogy magazine featuring articles on gemstone identification, localities, synthetics, simulants, treatments, and jewelry. **Facsimile Number:** (213)453-4478.

★5746★
The Gemstone Registry Bulletin
Joseph Schlussel
580 5th Ave., Ste. 806
New York, NY 10036   Phone: (212)575-0444
Editor(s): J. Schlussel. Monthly. Supplies data on and analysis of the present and future outlook for the gemstone market. Discusses trends in gemstone jewelry, providing retail surveys, fashion news, market reports, and sales boosters. Recurring features include editorials, news of research, and book reviews.

★5747★
The Goldsmith
Allen-Abernathy
49 E. 21st St., 9th Fl.
New York, NY 10010-6213   Phone: (212)529-5500
Marcie Lynn Avram, Publisher. Monthly. Magazine in five regional editions for jewelry retailers, wholesalers, designers, buyers, and manufacturers. **Facsimile Number:** (212)254-5204.

★5748★
JA Report
Jewelers of America (JA)
Time-Life Bldg.
1271 Ave. of the Americas
New York, NY 10020   Phone: (212)489-0023
Monthly.

★5749★
Jewelers' Circular-Keystone
Chilton Co.
Chilton Way
Radnor, PA 19089   Phone: (215)964-4000
George Holmes, Editor. Monthly. Retail jewelers trade magazine. **Facsimile Number:** (215)964-4100.

★5750★
Jewelry Newsletter International
Newsletters International, Inc.
2600 S. Gessner Rd.
Houston, TX 77063   Phone: (713)783-0100
Editor(s): Len Fox. Monthly. Reports news and developments in the jewelry industry, with brief items on people, companies, products, the changing scene and tastes, retailers, jobbers, and manufacturers. Recurring features include cost-cutting tips, listings of recommended books, professional opportunity notices, and items on economic trends.

★5751★
Lapidary Journal
Lapidary Journal, Inc.
1094 Cudahy Pl., Ste. 316
San Diego, CA 92110　　　　　　　Phone: (619)275-3505
Merle Berk, Editor. Monthly. Magazine for gem cutters, collectors, and jewelry craftsmen. **Facsimile Number:** (215)293-1717.

★5752★
MJSA Benchmark
Manufacturing Jewelers and Silversmiths of America Inc. (MJSA)
100 India St.
Providence, RI 02903　　　　　　Phone: (401)274-3840
Editor(s): Eric Bartheld. Bimonthly. Informs jewelry manufacturers of legislative news concerning their industry, expositions around the country, export news, tax news, and advances in technology. Presents information in the form of brief updates. Recurring features include member profiles and industry news. **Toll-free/Additional Phone Number(s):** 800-444-6572 **Facsimile Number:** (401)274-0265.

★5753★
Modern Jeweler
Vance Publishing Corp.
7950 College Blvd.
PO Box 2939
Shawnee Mission, KS 66201　　　　Phone: (913)451-2200
Joseph Thompson, Editor and Publisher. Monthly. Trade magazine for retail jewelers. **Facsimile Number:** (913)451-5821.

★5754★
National Jeweler
Gralla Publications
1515 Broadway
New York, NY 10036　　　　　　Phone: (212)869-1300
S. Lynn Diamond, Editor-in-Chief and Publisher. 2x/mo. Jewelry industry magazine. **Facsimile Number:** (212)302-6273.

★5755★
Ornament Magazine
PO Box 2349
San Marcos, CA 92079　　　　　Phone: (619)599-0222
4x/yr. Jewelry magazine. **Facsimile Number:** (619)599-0228.

★5756★
Rock & Gem
Miller Magazines, Inc.
2660 E. Main St.
Ventura, CA 93003　　　　　　　Phone: (805)643-3664
W.R.C. Shedenhelm, Sr. Editor. Monthly. Magazine about rocks, gold prosepecting, lapidary, and jewelry making. **Facsimile Number:** (805)643-8351.

★5757★
Spectra
American Gem Society
5901 W. Third
Los Angeles, CA 90036-2898
Editor(s): Charlotte Preston. 9/yr. Informs members of Society activities promoting ethical business standards and professional excellence in the retail jewelry industry. Features articles about technical advances in the field and profiles of members.

Meetings and Conventions

★5758★
American Gem Trade Association Gem Fair and Trade Show
American Gem Trade Association
PO Box 581043
Dallas, TX 75258　　　　　　　Phone: (214)742-4367
Frequency: Always held during February in Tucson, Arizona. **Toll-free/Additional Phone Number(s):** 800-972-1162. **Facsimile Number:** (214)742-7334.

★5759★
International Jewelry Fair
Helen Brett Enterprises Inc.
220 S. State St., Ste. 1416
Chicago, IL 60604　　　　　　　Phone: (312)922-0966
1992. **Facsimile Number:** (312)922-0969.

★5760★
Jewelers International Showcase
Jewelers International Showcase, Inc.
13501 SW 128th St., Ste. 114
Miami, FL 33186-5806　　　　　Phone: (305)253-6160
Frequency: Held 6 times yearly. 1992; Oct. 10-12; Miami Beach, FL. **Facsimile Number:** (305)255-0228.

★5761★
The Jewelry Show/Summer
Jewelers of America
1271 Avenue of the Americas
New York, NY 10020　　　　　　Phone: (212)489-0026
Frequency: Always held at the Jacob K. Javits Convention Center in New York City. 1992; New York, NY.

★5762★
Manufacturing Jewelers and Silversmiths of America Exposition/California
Manufacturing Jewelers and Silversmiths of America
100 India St.
Providence, RI 02903　　　　　　Phone: (401)274-3840
Facsimile Number: (401)274-0265.

★5763★
Manufacturing Jewelers and Silversmiths of America Exposition/New York
Manufacturing Jewelers and Silversmiths of America
100 India St.
Providence, RI 02903　　　　　　Phone: (401)274-3840
Frequency: Always held in March at the Passenger Ship Terminal, Piers 88 and 90 in New York City. 1992; Mar. 01-03; New York, NY. **Facsimile Number:** (401)274-0265.

★5764★
Manufacturing Jewelers and Silversmiths of America Exposition/Providence
Manufacturing Jewelers and Silversmiths of America
100 India St.
Providence, RI 02903　　　　　　Phone: (401)274-3840
Frequency: Always held during March at the Civic Center in Providence, Rhode Island. 1992; Mar. Providence, RI. **Facsimile Number:** (401)274-0265.

★5765★
Mid-American Jewelry Show
Ohio Jewelers Association
50 W. Broad St., Ste. 1616
Columbus, OH 43215   Phone: (614)221-7833
Frequency: Always held during August at the Ohio Center in Columbus. 1992; Aug. 22-23; Columbus, OH. **Facsimile Number:** (614)221-7020.

Machinists

Machinists are skilled workers who produce metal goods that are made in numbers too small to produce with automated machinery. Machinists plan and carry out the operations needed to make machined products that meet precise specifications. They do this by reviewing the specifications for the job, selecting the proper tools and materials, and planning the sequence of cutting and finishing operations. The actual machining operation involves positioning the metal stock on the machine tool, setting the controls, and making the cuts. When the machining operations are completed, machinists use precision instruments, such as micrometers, to make sure their work meets specifications. Then they finish and assemble the pieces. In addition to creating new products, some machinists repair or make new parts for existing machinery. Most precision machinists work in small machining shops or in manufacturing firms that produce durable goods such as metalworking and industrial machinery, aircraft, or motor vehicles. Maintenance machinists are employed in about every industry that uses production machinery, including both wholesale trade and services.

$alaries

The median weekly earnings for machinists is about $435.

Lowest 10 percent	$246/week or less
Middle 50 percent	$331-538/week
Top 10 percent	$663/week or more

Employment Outlook

Growth rate until the year 2000: More slowly than average.

Machinists

Career Guides

★5766★
"All Round Machinist" in *Manufacturing*, Volume 9 of *Career Information Center* (pp. 59-61)
Glencoe/Macmillan
15319 Chatsworth St.
Mission Hills, CA 91345   Phone: (818)898-1391
Richard Lidz and Dale Anderson, editorial directors. Fourth edition, 1990. For 600 occupations, describes job duties, entry-level requirements, education and training needed, advancement possibilities, employment outlook, earnings and benefits. The set is divided into 12 volumes. Each volume includes jobs related under a broad career field. Volume 13 is the index. **Facsimile Number:** 818-365-5489.

★5767★
"All-Round Machinist" in *Occu-Facts: Information on 565 Careers in Outline Form* (p. 17.4)
Careers, Inc.
P.O. Box 135
1211 Tenth St., S.W.
Largo, FL 33640   Phone: (813)584-7333
Elizabeth Handville. Biennial, 1989-90 edition. Each one-page occupational profile describes duties, working conditions, physical surroundings and demands, aptitudes, temperament, educational requirements, employment outlook, earnings, and places of employment.

★5768★
"Average Hourly Wages of Machinists in Ten Cities" in *The American Almanac of Jobs and Salaries* (p. 519)
Avon Books
105 Madison Avenue
New York, NY 10016   Phone: (212)481-5600
John Wright and Edward J. Dwyer. Revised and updated, 1990. A comprehensive guide to the wages of hundreds of occupations in a wide variety of industries and organizations.

★5769★
Career Information for Precision Machining Technology
National Tooling and Machining Association
9300 Livingston Rd.
Ft. Washington, MD 20744   Phone: (301)248-6200
This six-panel brochure lists the advantages of working in the machine tool industry, study course contents, and how to get started.

★5770★
How Valuable is Your Future?
Tooling and Manufacturing Association
1177 S. Dee Rd.
Park Ridge, IL 60068-9809   Phone: (708)825-1120
1989. This ten-panel brochure describes the work of precision metalworkers, the skills, entry into the field, internships, and earnings.

★5771★
"Laser Machinist" in *Opportunities in Laser Technology Careers* (pp. 54-57)
National Textbook Co.
4255 W. Touhy Ave.
Lincolnwood, IL 60646   Phone: (312)679-5500
Jan Bone. 1989. Describes what lasers are, how they work, and their use in health care, manufacturing, the military, space, communications, and research. Lists jobs and covers personal and educational qualifications, salaries, and employment outlook. Offers job hunting advice and lists schools and associations.

★5772★
"Machining and Machinery" in Volume 1 of *The Encyclopedia of Careers and Vocational Guidance* (pp. 269-274)
J.G. Ferguson Publishing Co.
200 W. Monroe
Chicago, IL 60606   Phone: (312)580-5480
William E. Hopke, editor-in-chief. Eighth edition, 1990. Four-volume set that profiles 500 occupations and describes job trends in 76 industries. Includes career description, educational requirements, history of the job, methods of entry, advancement, employment outlook, earnings, working conditions, social and psychological factors, and sources of additional information.

★5773★
"Machinist" in *Hard Hatted Women: Stories of Struggle and Success in the Trades* (pp. 187-191, 254-262)
Seal Press
3131 Western Ave., Ste. 410
Seattle, WA 98121   Phone: (206)283-7844
Molly Martin, editor. 1988. Twenty-six women recount their experiences working in blue collar occupations. They describe how they got in, the work they do, their relationships in predominantly male occupations, and their training.

★5774★ VOCATIONAL CAREERS SOURCEBOOK, 1st Edition

★5774★
"Machinist" in *VGM's Careers Encyclopedia* (pp. 253-255)
National Textbook Co.
4255 W. Touhy Ave.
Lincolnwood, IL 60646   Phone: (312)679-5500
Third edition, 1991. Contains two- to five-page descriptions of 200 managerial, professional, technical, trade, and service occupations. Each profile includes job duties, places of employment, qualifications, educational preparation, training, employment potential, advancement, income, and additional sources of information.

★5775★
Machinist, All-Round
Careers, Inc.
PO Box 135
Largo, FL 34649-0135   Phone: (813)584-7333
1991. Eight-page brief offering the definition, history, duties, working conditions, personal qualifications, educational requirements, earnings, hours, employment outlook, advancement possibilities, and related occupations.

★5776★
Machinists
Chronicle Guidance Publications, Inc.
PO Box 1190
Moravia, NY 13118-1190   Phone: (315)497-0330
1989. This career brief describes the nature of the work, working conditions, hours and earnings, education and training, licensure, certification, unions, personal qualifications, social and psychological factors, employment outlook, entry methods, advancement, and related occupations. **Toll-free/Additional Phone Number(s):** 800-622-7284.

★5777★
"Machinists" in *Jobs! What They Are...Where They Are...What They Pay* (pp. 178-179)
Simon & Schuster, Inc.
Simon & Schuster Bldg.
1230 Avenue of the Americas
New York, NY 10020   Phone: (212)698-7000
Robert O. Snelling and Anne M. Snelling. Revised edition, 1989. Profiles 241 occupations, describing duties and responsibilities, educational preparation, earnings, employment opportunities, training, and qualifications.

★5778★
"Machinists" in *Occupational Outlook Handbook* (pp. 394-396)
Superintendent of Documents
U.S. Government Printing Office
Washington, DC 20402   Phone: (202)783-3238
Biennial; latest edition, 1990-91. Encyclopedia of careers describing more than 250 occupations and comprising about 86 percent of all jobs in the economy. Occupations that require lengthy education or training are given the most attention. For each occupation, the handbook describes job duties, working conditions, training, educational preparation, personal qualities, advancement possibilities, job outlook, earnings, and sources of additional information.

★5779★
"Machinists" in *Opportunities in Metalworking Careers* (pp. 28-29)
National Textbook Co.
4255 W. Touhy Ave.
Lincolnwood, IL 60646   Phone: (312)679-5500
Mark Rowh. 1991. Separate chapters cover sheet metal work, machining, structural and reinforcing metalworking and jewelry making. Describes the work performed, skills needed, training, and working conditions. Lists unions that sponsor apprenticeship, and technical schools and colleges that offer training.

★5780★
"Machinists" in Volume 4 of *Career Discovery Encyclopedia* (pp. 44-45)
J.G. Ferguson Publishing Co.
200 W. Monroe
Chicago, IL 60606   Phone: (312)580-5480
E. Russell Primm, editor-in-chief. 1990. Contains two-page articles on 504 occupations. Each article describes job duties, earnings, and educational and training requirements.

★5781★
"Machinists" in Volume 3 of *The Encyclopedia of Careers and Vocational Guidance* (pp. 538-542)
J.G. Ferguson Publishing Co.
200 W. Monroe
Chicago, IL 60606   Phone: (312)580-5480
William E. Hopke, editor-in-chief. Eighth edition, 1990. Four-volume set that profiles 500 occupations and describes job trends in 76 industries. Includes career description, educational requirements, history of the job, methods of entry, advancement, employment outlook, earnings, working conditions, social and psychological factors, and sources of additional information.

★5782★
Video Career Library - Production II
Careers, Inc.
1211 10th St., SW
PO Box 135
Largo, FL 34649-0135   Phone: (813)584-7333
Videocassette. 1990. 32 mins. Part of the Video Career Library covering 165 occupations. Shows actual workers on the job. Includes tool and die makers, machinists, sheet metal workers, cabinet and bench carpenters, opticians, precision electronic equipment assemblers, industrial machine operators, welders and cutters, and assemblers.

── Associations ──

★5783★
National Screw Machine Products Association (NSMPA)
6700 W. Snowville Rd.
Brecksville, OH 44141   Phone: (216)526-0300
Membership: Manufacturers of component parts to customer's order, machined from rod, bar, or tube stock, of metal, fiber, plastic, or other material, using automatic or hand screw machines, automatic bar machines, and CNC machines.

★5784★
National Tooling and Machining Association (NTMA)
9300 Livingston Rd.
Ft. Washington, MD 20744   Phone: (301)248-6200
Membership: Manufacturers of tools, dies, jigs, fixtures, molds, gages, or special machinery; companies that do precision machining on a contract basis; past service and honorary

Machinists

members. **Purpose:** Provides management services; represents members in legislative matters. Promotes apprenticeship programs. Compiles management surveys; conducts management training workshops; maintains speakers' bureau. Has produced motion pictures and videocassettes on tool, die, and precision machining for educational showings. **Publications:** *Business Management Aids*, periodic. • *Buyers Guide of Special Tooling and Precision Machining Services*, annual. • *Catalog of Publications and Training Materials*, periodic. • *Membership Directory*, annual. • *Record*, monthly. • Also publishes handbooks and textbooks. **Toll-free/Additional Phone Number(s):** (800)248-NTMA. **Facsimile Number:** (301)248-7104.

★5785★
NMTBA - Association for Manufacturing Technology
7901 Westpark Dr.
McLean, VA 22102   Phone: (703)893-2900
Membership: Makers of power driven machines used in the process of transforming man-made materials into durable goods, including machine tools, assembly machines, inspection and testing machinery, robots, parts loaders, and plastics molding machines; associate members are producers of tools and tooling parts and components, attachments and accessories, controls and software, and engineering and systems design services. **Purpose:** Seeks to improve methods of producing and marketing machine tools; promotes research and development in the industry. Sponsors: seminars for training production supervisors, accident prevention and safety, and advertising management; annual competition for excellence in machine tool advertising. Develops and supervises standards for training apprentices. Participates in programs of standardization of design and performance of machine tools and components. Serves as a clearinghouse for technical aspects of the industry. Promotes orderly disposal of government-owned surplus machine tools. Maintains 500 volume library of machine tool publications. **Publications:** *Directories of Machine Tools*, annual. • *Economic Handbook of the Machine Tool Industry*, annual. TO (800)544-3597. **Facsimile Number:** (703)893-1151;

★5786★
The Tooling and Manufacturing Association
1177 S. Dee Rd.
Park Ridge, IL 60068
Provides information on opportunities in high production precision machining.

Standards/Certification Agencies

★5787★
NMTBA - Association for Manufacturing Technology
7901 Westpark Dr.
McLean, VA 22102   Phone: (703)893-2900
Develops and supervises standards for training apprentices. Participates in programs of standardization of design and performance of machine tools and components.

Test Guides

★5788★
Foreman Machinist
National Learning Corp.
212 Michael Dr.
Syosset, NY 11791   Phone: (516)921-8888
Jack Rudman. Part of the Career Examination Series No. 1. All examination guides in this series contain questions with answers. **Facsimile Number:** (516)921-8743. **Toll-free/Additional Phone Number(s):** 800-645-6337.

★5789★
Machinist
National Learning Corp.
212 Michael Dr.
Syosset, NY 11791   Phone: (516)921-8888
Jack Rudman. Part of the Career Examination Series No. 1. All examination guides in this series contain questions with answers. **Facsimile Number:** (516)921-8743. **Toll-free/Additional Phone Number(s):** 800-645-6337.

★5790★
Machinist's Helper
National Learning Corp.
212 Michael Dr.
Syosset, NY 11791   Phone: (516)921-8888
Jack Rudman. Part of the Career Examination Series No. 1. All examination guides in this series contain questions with answers. **Facsimile Number:** (516)921-8743. **Toll-free/Additional Phone Number(s):** 800-645-6337.

Basic Reference Guides and Handbooks

★5791★
Directories of Machine Tools
NMTBA - Association for Manufacturing Technology
7901 Westpark Dr.
McLean, VA 22102   Phone: (703)893-2900
Annual.

★5792★
Economic Handbook of the Machine Tool Industry
NMTBA - Association for Manufacturing Technology
7901 Westpark Dr.
McLean, VA 22102   Phone: (703)893-2900
Annual.

Periodicals

★5793★
Locator
Machinery Information Systems, Inc.
1110 Spring St.
Silver Spring, MD 20910   Phone: (301)585-9498
Rick Shontz, Publisher. Monthly. Magazine on metalworking, plastic and electrical machinery, and power equipment. **Facsimile Number:** (301)585-9460.

★5794★
The Machinist
International Assn. of Machinists & Aerospace Workers
1300 Connecticut Ave. NW
Washington, DC 20036   Phone: (202)857-5200
Robert J. Kalaski, Editor. Monthly. Tabloid containing information on employment and technology.

★5795★
NTMA Business Management Aids
National Tooling and Machining Association (NTMA)
9300 Livingston Rd.
Ft. Washington, MD 20744   Phone: (301)248-6200
Periodic.

★5796★
NTMA Record
National Tooling and Machining Association (NTMA)
9300 Livingston Rd.
Fort Washington, MD 20744 Phone: (301)248-6200
Editor(s): Mark W. Jeschke and Patricia Teets. Monthly. Focuses on business management techniques and government relations for the contract tool, die, and precision machining industry. Supplies information on Association activities. Recurring features include editorials, tax information, and technical notes. **Toll-free/Additional Phone Number(s):** 800-248-6862 **Facsimile Number:** (301)248-7104.

Meetings and Conventions

★5797★
AMB - International Exhibition for Metal Working
World Access Corp.
15 Bemis Rd.
PO Box 171
Wellesley Hills, MA 02181 Phone: (617)235-8095
1992; Sep. 01-05. **Facsimile Number:** (617)235-7360.

★5798★
MAQUINAMEX - Metalworking Machine Tool Expo
Marketing International Corp.
200 N. Glebe Rd., Ste. 900
Arlington, VA 22203 Phone: (703)527-8000
Frequency: Always held during June at the Exhibition Center in Mexico City. 1992; Jun. 17-20; Mexico City, Mexico. **Facsimile Number:** (703)527-8006.

★5799★
Metalform
Precision Metalforming Association
27027 Chardon Rd.
Richmond Heights, OH 44143 Phone: (216)585-8800
Frequency: Always held in Chicago, Illinois at the Rosemont/O'Hare Exposition C. **Facsimile Number:** (216)585-3126.

★5800★
Pacific Coast Industrial and Machine Tool Show
Industrial Shows of America
20 W. Aylesbury Rd.
Timonium, MD 21093 Phone: (301)252-1167
Frequency: Always held in the fall at the Convention Center in Santa Clara, California. 1992; Santa Clara, CA. **Toll-free/Additional Phone Number(s):** 800-638-6396. **Facsimile Number:** (301)560-0477.

★5801★
Tri-State Industrial Show
North American Exposition Co.
33 Rutherford Ave.
Boston, MA 02129 Phone: (617)242-6092
Frequency: Usually held in September or October the Convention Center in Cincinnati, Ohio. 1992; Sep. 29 - Oct. 01; Cincinnati, OH ● 1993; Sep. 21-23; Cincinnati, OH. **Toll-free/Additional Phone Number(s):** 800-225-1577. **Facsimile Number:** (617)242-1817.

Other Sources of Information

★5802★
American Machinist—Buyers' Guide Issue
Penton Publishing Co.
1100 Superior Ave.
Cleveland, OH 44114 Phone: (216)696-7000
Joseph Jablonowski, editor. Annual, April. Guide to over 2,000 manufacturers of products and services used by metalworking industries. Entries include: Company name, address, phone, fax. Arrangement: Separate alphabetical sections for manufacturers and products. **Facsimile Number:** (216)696-4135.

★5803★
Catalog of Publications and Training Materials
National Tooling and Machining Association (NTMA)
9300 Livingston Rd.
Ft. Washington, MD 20744 Phone: (301)248-6200
Periodic.

Metalworking Machine Operators

Metalworking machine operators set up, operate, and tend the machines which form all types of metal parts used in nearly any type of manufactured product. They can be separated into two groups: Those who set up the machine tool for operation and those who tend the machine during operation. Setup workers plan the correct sequence of operations. They adjust speed and other controls, and select the proper tools for each operation. Using micrometers and other measuring instruments, they ensure the completed work meets specifications. Machine tenders perform simple, repetitive tasks like placing metal stock in a machine that is already set up by the setup worker. Others may oversee machines that extrude metal through a die to form slugs or wire. Regardless of the type of machine they operate, machine tenders depend on skilled setup workers for major adjustments when the machines are not operating properly. Most operators work in factories that produce fabricated metal products, nonelectrical machinery, rubber and plastics products, steel products, and transportation equipment.

$alaries

Machine tool operators who work on metal materials have average earnings of $14.61/hour

Employment Outlook

Growth rate until the year 2000: Slower than average.

Metalworking Machine Operators

Career Guides

★5804★
"Machine Tool Operator" in *Manufacturing*, Volume 9 of *Career Information Center* (pp. 51-53)
Glencoe/Macmillan
15319 Chatsworth St.
Mission Hills, CA 91345   Phone: (818)898-1391
Richard Lidz and Dale Anderson, editorial directors. Fourth edition, 1990. For 600 occupations, describes job duties, entry-level requirements, education and training needed, advancement possibilities, employment outlook, earnings and benefits. The set is divided into 12 volumes. Each volume includes jobs related under a broad career field. Volume 13 is the index. **Facsimile Number:** 818-365-5489.

★5805★
Machine Tool Operators
Careers, Inc.
PO Box 135
Largo, FL 34649-0135   Phone: (813)584-7333
1989. Two-page occupational summary card describing duties, working conditions, personal qualifications, training, earnings and hours, employment outlook, places of employment, related careers and where to write for more information.

★5806★
"Machine Tool Operators" in *Occu-Facts: Information on 565 Careers in Outline Form* (p. 18.5)
Careers, Inc.
P.O. Box 135
1211 Tenth St., S.W.
Largo, FL 33640   Phone: (813)584-7333
Elizabeth Handville. Biennial, 1989-90 edition. Each one-page occupational profile describes duties, working conditions, physical surroundings and demands, aptitudes, temperament, educational requirements, employment outlook, earnings, and places of employment.

★5807★
"Machine Tool Operators" in Volume 3 of *The Encyclopedia of Careers and Vocational Guidance* (pp. 535-538)
J.G. Ferguson Publishing Co.
200 W. Monroe
Chicago, IL 60606   Phone: (312)580-5480
William E. Hopke, editor-in-chief. Eighth edition, 1990. Four-volume set that profiles 500 occupations and describes job trends in 76 industries. Includes career description, educational requirements, history of the job, methods of entry, advancement, employment outlook, earnings, working conditions, social and psychological factors, and sources of additional information.

★5808★
"Machining and Machine Operation" in *Opportunities in Metalworking Careers* (pp. 17-27)
National Textbook Co.
4255 W. Touhy Ave.
Lincolnwood, IL 60646   Phone: (312)679-5500
Mark Rowh. 1991. Covers sheet metal work, machining, structural and reinforcing metalworking, and jewelry making. Describes the work performed, skills needed, training and working conditions. Lists unions that sponsor apprenticeship and technical schools which offer training.

★5809★
"Metalworking Machine Operators" in *Occupational Outlook Handbook* (pp. 397-398)
Superintendent of Documents
U.S. Government Printing Office
Washington, DC 20402   Phone: (202)783-3238
Biennial; latest edition, 1990-91. Encyclopedia of careers describing more than 250 occupations and comprising about 86 percent of all jobs in the economy. Occupations that require lengthy education or training are given the most attention. For each occupation, the handbook describes job duties, working conditions, training, educational preparation, personal qualities, advancement possibilities, job outlook, earnings, and sources of additional information.

★5810★
"Milling Machine Operator" in *Occu-Facts: Information on 565 Careers in Outline Form* (p. 18.7)
Careers, Inc.
P.O. Box 135
1211 Tenth St., S.W.
Largo, FL 33640   Phone: (813)584-7333
Elizabeth Handville. Biennial, 1989-90 edition. Each one-page occupational profile describes duties, working conditions, physical surroundings and demands, aptitudes, temperament, educational requirements, employment outlook, earnings, and places of employment.

★5811★
Setup Operators (Machine Shop)
Chronicle Guidance Publications, Inc.
PO Box 1190
Moravia, NY 13118-1190   Phone: (315)497-0330
1988. This career brief describes the nature of the work, working conditions, hours and earnings, education and training, licensure, certification, unions, personal qualifications, social and psychological factors, employment outlook, entry methods,

★5812★
advancement, and related occupations. **Toll-free/Additional Phone Number(s):** 800-622-7284.

★5812★
Stamp of Approval
Michigan Media
University of Michigan
400 Fourth St.
Ann Arbor, MI 48109   Phone: (313)764-8228

Videocassette. 198?. 21 mins. This program documents the process of metal stamping from the time steel is delivered to a modern plant, through cutting, blanking, and forming operations.

★5813★
Vertical Milling Machine Explained
Bergwall Productions
106 Charles Lindbergh Blvd.
Uniondale, NY 11553-3695   Phone: (516)222-1111

Videocassette. 1980. 75 mins. On 6 tapes, here is a look at how milling machines work.

★5814★
Video Career Library - Production II
Careers, Inc.
1211 10th St., SW
PO Box 135
Largo, FL 34649-0135   Phone: (813)584-7333

Videocassette. 1990. 32 mins. Part of the Video Career Library covering 165 occupations. Shows actual workers on the job. Includes tool and die makers, machinists, sheet metal workers, cabinet and bench carpenters, opticians, precision electronic equipment assemblers, industrial machine operators, welders and cutters, and assemblers.

Associations

★5815★
American Foundrymen's Society (AFS)
505 State St.
Des Plaines, IL 60016-8399   Phone: (708)824-0181

Membership: Foundrymen, patternmakers, technologists, and educators. **Purpose:** Sponsors training courses through the Cast Metal Institute; conducts educational and instructional exhibits of foundry industry; sponsors regional conferences, technical meetings, and seminars; maintains a technical information center for literature searches and document retrieval services. **Publications:** *Modern Casting*, monthly.

★5816★
National Tooling and Machining Association (NTMA)
9300 Livingston Rd.
Ft. Washington, MD 20744   Phone: (301)248-6200

Membership: Manufacturers of tools, dies, jigs, fixtures, molds, gages, or special machinery; companies that do precision machining on a contract basis; past service and honorary members. **Purpose:** Provides management services; represents members in legislative matters. Promotes apprenticeship programs. Compiles management surveys; conducts management training workshops; maintains speakers' bureau. Has produced motion pictures and videocassettes on tool, die, and precision machining for educational showings. **Publications:** *Business Management Aids*, periodic. • *Buyers Guide of Special Tooling and Precision Machining Services*, annual. • *Catalog of Publications and Training Materials*, periodic. • *Membership Directory*, annual. • *Record*, monthly. • Also publishes handbooks and textbooks. **Toll-free/Additional Phone Number(s):** (800)248-NTMA. **Facsimile Number:** (301)248-7104.

★5817★
NMTBA - Association for Manufacturing Technology
7901 Westpark Dr.
McLean, VA 22102   Phone: (703)893-2900

Membership: Makers of power driven machines used in the process of transforming man-made materials into durable goods, including machine tools, assembly machines, inspection and testing machinery, robots, parts loaders, and plastics molding machines; associate members are producers of tools and tooling parts and components, attachments and accessories, controls and software, and engineering and systems design services. **Purpose:** Seeks to improve methods of producing and marketing machine tools; promotes research and development in the industry. Sponsors: seminars for training production supervisors, accident prevention and safety, and advertising management; annual competition for excellence in machine tool advertising. Develops and supervises standards for training apprentices. Participates in programs of standardization of design and performance of machine tools and components. Serves as a clearinghouse for technical aspects of the industry. Promotes orderly disposal of government-owned surplus machine tools. Maintains 500 volume library of machine tool publications. **Publications:** *Directories of Machine Tools*, annual. • *Economic Handbook of the Machine Tool Industry*, annual. **Toll-free/Additional Phone Number(s):** (800)544-3597. **Facsimile Number:** (703)893-1151.

★5818★
The Tooling and Manufacturing Association
1177 S. Dee Rd.
Park Ridge, IL 60068

Provides information on opportunities in high production precision machining.

Standards/Certification Agencies

★5819★
NMTBA - Association for Manufacturing Technology
7901 Westpark Dr.
McLean, VA 22102   Phone: (703)893-2900

Develops and supervises standards for training apprentices. Participates in programs of standardization of design and performance of machine tools and components.

Educational Directories and Programs

★5820★
Cast Metals Institute
c/o American Foundrymen's Society
505 State St.
Des Plaines, IL 60016-8399   Phone: (708)824-0181

Conducts foundry training courses on all subjects pertaining to the castings industry.

Basic Reference Guides and Handbooks

★5821★
Directories of Machine Tools
NMTBA - Association for Manufacturing Technology
7901 Westpark Dr.
McLean, VA 22102   Phone: (703)893-2900

Annual.

Metalworking Machine Operators ★5835★

★5822★
Economic Handbook of the Machine Tool Industry
NMTBA - Association for Manufacturing Technology
7901 Westpark Dr.
McLean, VA 22102   Phone: (703)893-2900
Annual.

★5823★
U.S. Glass, Metal and Glazing—Directory of Suppliers of Machinery & Equipment Issue
U.S. Glass Publications, Inc.
560 Oakwood Ave., Ste. 202
Lake Forest, IL 60045   Phone: (708)295-2900
Sherry Edwards McHone, Managing Editor, editor. Annual, May. List of suppliers of machinery and equipment for the glass, metal, and glazing industry. Entries include: Company name, address, phone, telex, names and titles of key personnel, subsidiary and branch names and locations. Arrangement: Alphabetical. Indexes: Product. **Facsimile Number:** (708)295-2903.

★5824★
Western Metalworking Directory
DeRoche Publications
777-W W. 19th St., Ste. W
Costa Mesa, CA 92627   Phone: (714)642-9978
David DeRoche, editor. Annual. Over 1,000 manufacturers and suppliers of metalworking equipment and materials. Entries include: Company name, address, phone, name and title of contact and key personnel, geographical area served, branch/subsidiary offices, product/service provided. Arrangement: Alphabetical. Indexes: Product/service, trade name.

──────── Periodicals ────────

★5825★
Cutting Tool Engineering
CTE Publications, Inc.
464 Central Ave.
Northfield, IL 60093   Phone: (708)441-7520
Don Nelson, Editor. 9x/yr. Metal working and tooling news. **Facsimile Number:** (708)441-8740.

★5826★
Locator
Machinery Information Systems, Inc.
1110 Spring St.
Silver Spring, MD 20910   Phone: (301)585-9498
Rick Shontz, Publisher. Monthly. Magazine on metalworking, plastic and electrical machinery, and power equipment. **Facsimile Number:** (301)585-9460.

★5827★
Machine and Tool Blue Book
Hitchcock Publishing Co.
191 S. Gary Ave.
Carol Stream, IL 60188   Phone: (708)665-1000
James R. Koelsch, Editor. Monthly. Magazine focusing on metalworking manufacturing in large plants and contract manufacturers. **Facsimile Number:** (708)462-2225.

★5828★
Metals Newsletter
National Safety Council
444 N. Michigan Ave.
Chicago, IL 60611   Phone: (312)527-4800
Monthly. Promotes safe work practices and products in the metals industry. Carries accident case histories, items on successful accident prevention programs, and articles on safety at home and elsewhere.

★5829★
NTMA Business Management Aids
National Tooling and Machining Association (NTMA)
9300 Livingston Rd.
Ft. Washington, MD 20744   Phone: (301)248-6200
Periodic.

★5830★
NTMA Record
National Tooling and Machining Association (NTMA)
9300 Livingston Rd.
Ft. Washington, MD 20744   Phone: (301)248-6200
Monthly.

★5831★
Production
Gardner Publications, Inc.
6600 Clough Pike
Cincinnati, OH 45244   Phone: (513)231-8020
Robert F. Huber, Editor-in-Chief. Monthly. Magazine helping managers and executives in the metalworking manufacturing industry interpret, evaluate, and implement new technologies, methods, and equipment. **Facsimile Number:** (513)231-2818.

──────── Meetings and Conventions ────────

★5832★
AMB - International Exhibition for Metal Working
World Access Corp.
15 Bemis Rd.
PO Box 171
Wellesley Hills, MA 02181   Phone: (617)235-8095
1992; Sep. 01-05. **Facsimile Number:** (617)235-7360.

★5833★
American Foundrymen's Society Casting Congress and Cast Expo
American Foundrymen's Society, Inc.
505 State St.
Des Plaines, IL 60016-8399   Phone: (708)824-0181
Frequency: Congress is annual; exposition is held every three years. 1992; May 02-05; Milwaukee, WI. **Toll-free/Additional Phone Number(s):** 800-537-4237. **Facsimile Number:** (708)824-7848.

★5834★
MAQUINAMEX - Metalworking Machine Tool Expo
Marketing International Corp.
200 N. Glebe Rd., Ste. 900
Arlington, VA 22203   Phone: (703)527-8000
Frequency: Always held during June at the Exhibition Center in Mexico City. 1992; Jun. 17-20; Mexico City, Mexico. **Facsimile Number:** (703)527-8006.

★5835★
Metalform
Precision Metalforming Association
27027 Chardon Rd.
Richmond Heights, OH 44143   Phone: (216)585-8800
Frequency: Always held in Chicago, Illinois at the Rosemont/O'Hare Exposition C. **Facsimile Number:** (216)585-3126.

★5836★
Tri-State Industrial Show
North American Exposition Co.
33 Rutherford Ave.
Boston, MA 02129   Phone: (617)242-6092

Frequency: Usually held in September or October the Convention Center in Cincinnati, Ohio. 1992; Sep. 29 - Oct. 01; Cincinnati, OH • 1993; Sep. 21-23; Cincinnati, OH. **Toll-free/Additional Phone Number(s):** 800-225-1577. **Facsimile Number:** (617)242-1817.

Other Sources of Information

★5837★
American Machinist—Buyers' Guide Issue
Penton Publishing Co.
1100 Superior Ave.
Cleveland, OH 44114   Phone: (216)696-7000

Joseph Jablonowski, editor. Annual, April. Guide to over 2,000 manufacturers of products and services used by metalworking industries. Entries include: Company name, address, phone, fax. Arrangement: Separate alphabetical sections for manufacturers and products. **Facsimile Number:** (216)696-4135.

★5838★
Catalog of Publications and Training Materials
National Tooling and Machining Association (NTMA)
9300 Livingston Rd.
Ft. Washington, MD 20744   Phone: (301)248-6200
Periodic.

Plastic-Working Machine Operators

Plastic-working machine operators tend machines that produce a variety of consumer and industrial goods in which plastic is used, from everyday items like soft drink containers to specialized products such as artificial heart valves. Plastic-working machine operators monitor the plastics-forming process which involves setting resin into molds. They check the feed of the materials, temperature and pressure of the machine, and rate at which the piece hardens. They may load plastics material, monitor its transformation, and unload and inspect the finished product. In general, plastic-working machine operators specialize in the operation of one type of machine.

$alaries

Plastics-working machine operators working in plastics plants have average earnings of $14.61/hour

Employment Outlook

Growth rate until the year 2000: Faster than average.

Plastic-Working Machine Operators

Career Guides

★5839★
Opportunities in Plastics Careers
National Textbook Co.
4255 W. Touhy Ave.
Lincolnwood, IL 60646   Phone: (312)679-5500
Jan Bone. 1991. Explores career opportunities for chemists, engineers, machinists, moldmakers, technicians, salespeople, and business executives in plastics manufacturing, research and development, and recycling. Describes educational preparation, preferred personal qualities, job hunting strategies, and continuing education.

★5840★
"Plastic-Working Machine Operators" in *Occupational Outlook Handbook* (pp. 398-399)
Superintendent of Documents
U.S. Government Printing Office
Washington, DC 20402   Phone: (202)783-3238
Biennial; latest edition, 1990-91. Encyclopedia of careers describing more than 250 occupations and comprising about 86 percent of all jobs in the economy. Occupations that require lengthy education or training are given the most attention. For each occupation, the handbook describes job duties, working conditions, training, educational preparation, personal qualities, advancement possibilities, job outlook, earnings, and sources of additional information.

★5841★
"Plastics" in Volume 1 of *The Encyclopedia of Careers and Vocational Guidance* (pp. 362-367)
J.G. Ferguson Publishing Co.
200 W. Monroe
Chicago, IL 60606   Phone: (312)580-5480
William E. Hopke, editor-in-chief. Eighth edition, 1990. Four-volume set that profiles 500 occupations and describes job trends in 76 industries. Includes career description, educational requirements, history of the job, methods of entry, advancement, employment outlook, earnings, working conditions, social and psychological factors, and sources of additional information.

★5842★
"Plastics Industry" in *Manufacturing*, Volume 9 of *Career Information Center* (pp. 132-135)
Glencoe/Macmillan
15319 Chatsworth St.
Mission Hills, CA 91345   Phone: (818)898-1391
Richard Lidz and Dale Anderson, editorial directors. Fourth edition, 1990. For 600 occupations, describes job duties, entry-level requirements, education and training needed, advancement possibilities, employment outlook, earnings and benefits. The set is divided into 12 volumes. Each volume includes jobs related under a broad career field. Volume 13 is the index. **Facsimile Number:** 818-365-5489.

★5843★
"Plastics Products Manufacturing Workers" in Volume 5 of *Career Discovery Encyclopedia* (pp. 60-61)
J.G. Ferguson Publishing Co.
200 W. Monroe
Chicago, IL 60606   Phone: (312)580-5480
E. Russell Primm, editor-in-chief. 1990. Contains two-page articles on 504 occupations. Each article describes job duties, earnings, and educational and training requirements.

★5844★
"Plastics Products Manufacturing Workers" in Volume 3 of *The Encyclopedia of Careers and Vocational Guidance* (pp. 454-457)
J.G. Ferguson Publishing Co.
200 W. Monroe
Chicago, IL 60606   Phone: (312)580-5480
William E. Hopke, editor-in-chief. Eighth edition, 1990. Four-volume set that profiles 500 occupations and describes job trends in 76 industries. Includes career description, educational requirements, history of the job, methods of entry, advancement, employment outlook, earnings, working conditions, social and psychological factors, and sources of additional information.

★5845★
Setup Operators (Machine Shop)
Chronicle Guidance Publications, Inc.
PO Box 1190
Moravia, NY 13118-1190   Phone: (315)497-0330
1988. This career brief describes the nature of the work, working conditions, hours and earnings, education and training, licensure, certification, unions, personal qualifications, social and psychological factors, employment outlook, entry methods, advancement, and related occupations. **Toll-free/Additional Phone Number(s):** 800-622-7284.

★5846★
Video Career Library - Production II
Careers, Inc.
1211 10th St., SW
PO Box 135
Largo, FL 34649-0135   Phone: (813)584-7333
Videocassette. 1990. 32 mins. Part of the Video Career Library covering 165 occupations. Shows actual workers on the job. Includes tool and die makers, machinists, sheet metal workers,

cabinet and bench carpenters, opticians, precision electronic equipment assemblers, industrial machine operators, welders and cutters, and assemblers.

Associations

★5847★
National Tooling and Machining Association (NTMA)
9300 Livingston Rd.
Ft. Washington, MD 20744   Phone: (301)248-6200
Membership: Manufacturers of tools, dies, jigs, fixtures, molds, gages, or special machinery; companies that do precision machining on a contract basis; past service and honorary members. **Purpose:** Provides management services; represents members in legislative matters. Promotes apprenticeship programs. Compiles management surveys; conducts management training workshops; maintains speakers' bureau. Has produced motion pictures and videocassettes on tool, die, and precision machining for educational showings. **Publications:** *Business Management Aids*, periodic. • *Buyers Guide of Special Tooling and Precision Machining Services*, annual. • *Catalog of Publications and Training Materials*, periodic. • *Membership Directory*, annual. • *Record*, monthly. • Also publishes handbooks and textbooks. **Toll-free/Additional Phone Number(s):** (800)248-NTMA. **Facsimile Number:** (301)248-7104.

★5848★
NMTBA - Association for Manufacturing Technology
7901 Westpark Dr.
McLean, VA 22102   Phone: (703)893-2900
Membership: Makers of power driven machines used in the process of transforming man-made materials into durable goods, including machine tools, assembly machines, inspection and testing machinery, robots, parts loaders, and plastics molding machines; associate members are producers of tools and tooling parts and components, attachments and accessories, controls and software, and engineering and systems design services. **Purpose:** Seeks to improve methods of producing and marketing machine tools; promotes research and development in the industry. Sponsors: seminars for training production supervisors, accident prevention and safety, and advertising management; annual competition for excellence in machine tool advertising. Develops and supervises standards for training apprentices. Participates in programs of standardization of design and performance of machine tools and components. Serves as a clearinghouse for technical aspects of the industry. Promotes orderly disposal of government-owned surplus machine tools. Maintains 500 volume library of machine tool publications. **Publications:** *Directories of Machine Tools*, annual. • *Economic Handbook of the Machine Tool Industry*, annual. **Toll-free/Additional Phone Number(s):** (800)544-3597. **Facsimile Number:** (703)893-1151.

★5849★
Society of Plastics Engineers (SPE)
14 Fairfield Dr.
Brookfield, CT 06804-0403   Phone: (203)775-0471
Membership: Professional society of plastics scientists, engineers, educators, students, and others interested in the design, development, production, and utilization of plastics materials, products, and equipment. **Purpose:** Awards plaque, gold medal, and $5000 in recognition of fundamental contributions to the technology of polymer science and engineering, plus seven other awards of $2500 each for achievements in engineering and technology, education, business management, research, production of unique plastic products for consumer and industrial use, and contribution to mankind in the field of plastics. Conducts seminars. Maintains 91 sections. **Publications:** *Journal of Vinyl Technology*, quarterly. • *Plastics Engineering*, monthly. • *Polymer Composites*, bimonthly. • *Polymer Engineering and Science*, semimonthly. • Also publishes *Preprint Volumes* and *Plastics Engineering Series* (books). **Facsimile Number:** (203)775-8490.

★5850★
The Tooling and Manufacturing Association
1177 S. Dee Rd.
Park Ridge, IL 60068
Provides information on opportunities in high production precision machining.

Standards/Certification Agencies

★5851★
NMTBA - Association for Manufacturing Technology
7901 Westpark Dr.
McLean, VA 22102   Phone: (703)893-2900
Develops and supervises standards for training apprentices. Participates in programs of standardization of design and performance of machine tools and components.

Basic Reference Guides and Handbooks

★5852★
Directories of Machine Tools
NMTBA - Association for Manufacturing Technology
7901 Westpark Dr.
McLean, VA 22102   Phone: (703)893-2900
Annual.

★5853★
Economic Handbook of the Machine Tool Industry
NMTBA - Association for Manufacturing Technology
7901 Westpark Dr.
McLean, VA 22102   Phone: (703)893-2900
Annual.

★5854★
Plastics Engineering Series
Society of Plastics Engineers (SPE)
14 Fairfield Dr.
Brookfield, CT 06804-0403   Phone: (203)775-0471

★5855★
Preprint Volumes
Society of Plastics Engineers (SPE)
14 Fairfield Dr.
Brookfield, CT 06804-0403   Phone: (203)775-0471

Periodicals

★5856★
Journal of Vinyl Technology
Society of Plastics Engineers (SPE)
14 Fairfield Dr.
Brookfield, CT 06804-0403   Phone: (203)775-0471
Quarterly. Covers problem solving and use of vinyl polymers in plastics; includes graphs, tables, charts.

Plastic-Working Machine Operators

★5857★
Locator
Machinery Information Systems, Inc.
1110 Spring St.
Silver Spring, MD 20910   Phone: (301)585-9498
Rick Shontz, Publisher. Monthly. Magazine on metalworking, plastic and electrical machinery, and power equipment. **Facsimile Number:** (301)585-9460.

★5858★
Modern Plastics
McGraw-Hill, Inc.
1221 Avenue of the Americas
New York, NY 10020   Phone: (212)512-6241
Robert Martino, Editor. Monthly. Magazine for the plastics industry. **Facsimile Number:** (212)512-6111.

★5859★
NTMA Business Management Aids
National Tooling and Machining Association (NTMA)
9300 Livingston Rd.
Ft. Washington, MD 20744   Phone: (301)248-6200
Periodic.

★5860★
NTMA Record
National Tooling and Machining Association (NTMA)
9300 Livingston Rd.
Ft. Washington, MD 20744   Phone: (301)248-6200
Monthly.

★5861★
Plastics Compounding
Edgell Communications, Inc.
466 Southern Blvd.
PO Box 448
Chatham, NJ 07928   Phone: (201)514-1422
Mary C. McMurrer, Editor. 6x/yr. Magazine on formulation, production, and compounding of plastics, resins, alloys, and blends. **Facsimile Number:** (201)514-1404.

★5862★
Plastics Engineering
Society of Plastics Engineers (SPE)
14 Fairfield Dr.
Brookfield, CT 06804-0403   Phone: (203)775-0471
Monthly.

★5863★
Plastics Machinery & Equipment
Edgell Communications, Inc.
466 Southern Blvd.
PO Box 448
Chatham, NJ 07928   Phone: (201)514-1422
Merle Snyder, Editor (303/832-1022). Monthly. Magazine on plastics machinery and equipment. **Facsimile Number:** (201)514-1404.

★5864★
Plastics Magazine
Western Plastics News, Inc.
1704 Colorado Ave.
Santa Monica, CA 90404   Phone: (213)829-4876
Aida Pavletich, Editor and Advertising Mgr. 6x/yr. Magazine on plastics and polymers.

★5865★
Plastics News
Crain Communications, Inc.
1725 Merriman Rd.
Akron, OH 44313   Phone: (216)836-9180
Robert Grace, Editor. Weekly. Magazine (tabloid) for the plastics industry. **Facsimile Number:** (216)836-2322.

★5866★
Plastics Today
JSD Publishing Co.
5827 Columbia Pike, Ste. 310
Falls Church, VA 22041   Phone: (703)998-7746
Julian Kestler, Editor. 2x/mo. Magazine covering technical innovations in materials and machinery, regulatory issues, pricing and supply, design applications, company and personnel news in the plastics industry.

★5867★
Plastics World
Cahners Publishing Co.
275 Washington St.
Newton, MA 02158-1630   Phone: (617)964-3030
Doug Smock, Editor. Monthly. Plastics magazine. **Facsimile Number:** (617)558-4327.

★5868★
Polymer Engineering and Science
Society of Plastics Engineers (SPE)
14 Fairfield Dr.
Brookfield, CT 06804-0403   Phone: (203)775-0471
Semimonthly. Journal containing symposium papers and translations of foreign technical papers dealing with polymers.

★5869★
Rubber and Plastics Newsletter
National Safety Council
444 N. Michigan Ave.
Chicago, IL 60611   Phone: (312)527-4800
6/yr. Carries accident prevention information and promotes safety awareness in the rubber and plastics industries. Emphasizes safe work practices, conditions, and products and reports on successful industrial safety programs.

──── Other Sources of Information ────

★5870★
Catalog of Publications and Training Materials
National Tooling and Machining Association (NTMA)
9300 Livingston Rd.
Ft. Washington, MD 20744   Phone: (301)248-6200
Periodic.

Steel Workers

Steel workers operate and tend the machinery that produces steel. The process begins when material moving equipment operators load iron ore, coke, and limestone into the top of a blast furnace. Workers called stove tenders operate giant stoves that blow hot air into the bottom of the furnace. This process frees the iron from other elements in the ore. The overall operation of the blast furnace is directed by blowers. These workers are responsible for the quality and quantity of the iron produced and for supervising keepers. Keepers operate the equipment that is used to tap the liquid iron and to remove impurities from the furnace. Melters supervise workers called furnace operators and their assistants. Melters, using information about the raw materials they will be using and the quality of steel they are expected to produce, direct the loading of the furnace and supervise sample taking. This is to ensure the steel has the desired qualities. Furnace operators control the flow of oxygen and other materials into the furnace, and correct any problems that may arise during production. Their assistants, using controls, tilt the furnace to receive the raw materials. They may also take samples to be analyzed. Molding and casting machine operators tend machines that release the molten steel from the ladle into water-cooled molds at a controlled rate. Most steel processed in steel mills is shaped by rolling. Before ingots can be rolled they must be heated in furnaces called soaking pits. Heaters and their helpers control the soaking pit operations. Rollers are workers that operate the equipment that rolls the steel ingots into semifinished shapes. The quality of the ingot depends on the roller's skills.

$alaries

Production workers in steel mills have average earnings of $14.72/hour.

Employment Outlook

Growth rate until the year 2000: Slower than average.

Steel Workers

Career Guides

★5871★
"Iron and Steel Industry" in *Manufacturing*, Volume 9 of *Career Information Center* (pp. 116-119)
Glencoe/Macmillan
15319 Chatsworth St.
Mission Hills, CA 91345   Phone: (818)898-1391
Richard Lidz and Dale Anderson, editorial directors. Fourth edition, 1990. For 600 occupations, describes job duties, entry-level requirements, education and training needed, advancement possibilities, employment outlook, earnings and benefits. The set is divided into 12 volumes. Each volume includes jobs related under a broad career field. Volume 13 is the index. **Facsimile Number:** 818-365-5489.

★5872★
Iron and Steel Industry Workers
Chronicle Guidance Publications, Inc.
PO Box 1190
Moravia, NY 13118-1190   Phone: (315)497-0330
1989. This career brief describes the nature of the work, working conditions, hours and earnings, education and training, licensure, certification, unions, personal qualifications, social and psychological factors, employment outlook, entry methods, advancement, and related occupations. **Toll-free/Additional Phone Number(s):** 800-622-7284.

★5873★
"Iron and Steel Industry Workers" in Volume 3 of *Career Discovery Encyclopedia* (pp. 162-163)
J.G. Ferguson Publishing Co.
200 W. Monroe
Chicago, IL 60606   Phone: (312)580-5480
E. Russell Primm, editor-in-chief. 1990. Contains two-page articles on 504 occupations. Each article describes job duties, earnings, and educational and training requirements.

★5874★
"Iron and Steel Industry Workers" in Volume 3 of *The Encyclopedia of Careers and Vocational Guidance* (pp. 423-426)
J.G. Ferguson Publishing Co.
200 W. Monroe
Chicago, IL 60606   Phone: (312)580-5480
William E. Hopke, editor-in-chief. Eighth edition, 1990. Four-volume set that profiles 500 occupations and describes job trends in 76 industries. Includes career description, educational requirements, history of the job, methods of entry, advancement, employment outlook, earnings, working conditions, social and psychological factors, and sources of additional information.

★5875★
"Steel Workers" in *Occupational Outlook Handbook* (pp. 399-400)
Superintendent of Documents
U.S. Government Printing Office
Washington, DC 20402   Phone: (202)783-3238
Biennial; latest edition, 1990-91. Encyclopedia of careers describing more than 250 occupations and comprising about 86 percent of all jobs in the economy. Occupations that require lengthy education or training are given the most attention. For each occupation, the handbook describes job duties, working conditions, training, educational preparation, personal qualities, advancement possibilities, job outlook, earnings, and sources of additional information.

Associations

★5876★
American Foundrymen's Society (AFS)
505 State St.
Des Plaines, IL 60016-8399   Phone: (708)824-0181
Membership: Foundrymen, patternmakers, technologists, and educators. **Purpose:** Sponsors training courses through the Cast Metal Institute; conducts educational and instructional exhibits of foundry industry; sponsors regional conferences, technical meetings, and seminars; maintains a technical information center for literature searches and document retrieval services. **Publications:** *Modern Casting*, monthly.

★5877★
The Tooling and Manufacturing Association
1177 S. Dee Rd.
Park Ridge, IL 60068
Provides information on opportunities in high production precision machining.

★5878★
United Steelworkers of America (USWA)
5 Gateway Center
Pittsburgh, PA 15222   Phone: (412)562-2400
Membership: AFL-CIO. **Publications:** *Steelabor*, 10/year. • *Steelworker Old Time*, quarterly. **Facsimile Number:** (412)562-2445.

Educational Directories and Programs

★5879★
Cast Metals Institute
c/o American Foundrymen's Society
505 State St.
Des Plaines, IL 60016-8399   Phone: (708)824-0181
Conducts training courses in all subjects pertaining to the castings industries.

Periodicals

★5880★
AISC News
American Institute of Steel Construction, Inc. (AISC)
c/o Publications
PO Box 806276
Chicago, IL 60680-4124   Phone: (312)670-2400
Editor(s): George E. Harper. 5/yr. Provides information about the fabricated structural steel industry. Recurring features include news of the activities of the Institute, reports on promotional and technical meetings, and notices of programs, conferences, conventions, and steel promotion.

★5881★
Industrial Machinery News
Hearst Business Media Corp./IMN Div.
Northfield Plaza II
5700 Crooks Rd., Ste. 219
Troy, MI 48098   Phone: (313)828-7000
Lucky D. Slate, Publisher. Monthly. Magazine reporting on machinery, equipment, and supplies for manufacturing operations in the metal-working industry. **Facsimile Number:** (313)828-7008.

★5882★
Steel Digest
Intersteel Technology, Inc.
3041 Shallowood Ln.
Charlotte, NC 28277   Phone: (704)542-8210
Editor(s): John A. Vallomy. Bimonthly. Highlights new technologies, new equipment, and innovative concepts in the iron and steel industry. Discusses technology pertinent to blast furnaces, oxygen converters, electric arc furnaces, ladle metallury, continuous casting, and general steelmaking. Recurring features include editorials and news of research.

★5883★
Steelabor (USWA)
United Steelworkers of America (USWA)
5 Gateway Center
Pittsburgh, PA 15222   Phone: (412)562-2400
10/year. News magazine reporting on legislation and regulation affecting the union, union activities at the national and chapter levels, economic developments, pension news, and information on safety and health.

★5884★
Steelworker Old Time
United Steelworkers of America
5 Gateway Center
Pittsburgh, PA 15222   Phone: (412)562-2400
Quarterly.

Meetings and Conventions

★5885★
American Foundrymen's Society Casting Congress and Cast Expo
American Foundrymen's Society, Inc.
505 State St.
Des Plaines, IL 60016-8399   Phone: (708)824-0181
Frequency: Congress is annual; exposition is held every three years. 1992; May 02-05; Milwaukee, WI. **Toll-free/Additional Phone Number(s):** 800-537-4237. **Facsimile Number:** (708)824-7848.

★5886★
United Steelworkers of America (USWA)
5 Gateway Center
Pittsburgh, PA 15222   Phone: (412)562-2400
Frequency: Biennial - held in 1992. **Facsimile Number:** (412)562-2445.

Numerical-Control Machine-Tool Operators

Numerical-control machine-tool operators run machine tools that can be programmed to make parts of different dimensions automatically. Working from written instructions or directions from supervisors, operators must load the program into the controller, attach the necessary tools, position the workpiece, and check the coolants and lubricants. The first time a program is run, it must be debugged, or corrected by numerical-control machine-tool operators; in some cases, tool programmers handle the first run. Operators check the finished part using precision inspection equipment to ensure that it meets specifications. Most numerical-control machine-tool operators work in industries that manufacture durable goods, such as aircraft, electrical and metalworking machinery, and construction and general industrial equipment.

$alaries

Numerical-control machine-tool operators earn about $10.50/hour.

Employment Outlook

Growth rate until the year 2000: More slowly than average.

Numerical-Control Machine-Tool Operators

Career Guides

★5887★
A Good Part of Your Life
National Screw Machine Products
6700 W. Snowville Rd.
Brecksville, OH 44141   Phone: (216)526-0300
This six-panel brochure describes the screw machine products industry, workers' skills and earnings.

★5888★
An Important Message To All Mechanical Minded People
National Screw Machine Products
6700 W. Snowville Rd.
Brecksville, OH 44141   Phone: (216)526-0300
This six-panel brochure describes needed skills, the work, and employment opportunities in the screw machine products industry.

★5889★
Machine Tool Operators
Chronicle Guidance Publications, Inc.
PO Box 1190
Moravia, NY 13118-1190   Phone: (315)497-0330
1991. This career brief describes the nature of the work, working conditions, hours and earnings, education and training, licensure, certification, unions, personal qualifications, social and psychological factors, employment outlook, entry methods, advancement, and related occupations. **Toll-free/Additional Phone Number(s):** 800-622-7284.

★5890★
"Numerical Control Machine Operator" in *Careers in High Tech* (pp. 138-139)
Arco/Prentice Hall Press
1 Gulf & Western Plaza
New York, NY 10023   Phone: (212)373-8500
Connie Winkler. 1987. Surveys career opportunities in data processing, technology, personal computers, telecommunications, manufacturing technology, artificial intelligence, computer graphics, biotechnology, lasers, technical writing, and publishing. Includes information on educational preparation, associations, and periodicals.

★5891★
"Numerical Control Machine Operator" in *Manufacturing,* Volume 9 of *Career Information Center* (pp. 53-55)
Glencoe/Macmillan
15319 Chatsworth St.
Mission Hills, CA 91345   Phone: (818)898-1391
Richard Lidz and Dale Anderson, editorial directors. Fourth edition, 1990. For 600 occupations, describes job duties, entry-level requirements, education and training needed, advancement possibilities, employment outlook, earnings and benefits. The set is divided into 12 volumes. Each volume includes jobs related under a broad career field. Volume 13 is the index. **Facsimile Number:** 818-365-5489.

★5892★
"Numerical Control Machine Tool Operator" in *Guide To Careers Without College* (pp. 61-63)
Franklin Watts, Inc.
387 Park Avenue, S.
New York, NY 10016   Phone: (212)686-7070
Kathleen S. Abrams. 1988. Discusses careers that do not require a college degree in fields such as health care, sales and marketing, and the building trades. Describes the work, employment opportunities, and training.

★5893★
"Numerical-Control Machine-Tool Operators" in *Occupational Outlook Handbook* (pp. 401-402)
Superintendent of Documents
U.S. Government Printing Office
Washington, DC 20402   Phone: (202)783-3238
Biennial; latest edition, 1990-91. Encyclopedia of careers describing more than 250 occupations and comprising about 86 percent of all jobs in the economy. Occupations that require lengthy education or training are given the most attention. For each occupation, the handbook describes job duties, working conditions, training, educational preparation, personal qualities, advancement possibilities, job outlook, earnings, and sources of additional information.

Associations

★5894★
National Screw Machine Products Association (NSMPA)
6700 W. Snowville Rd.
Brecksville, OH 44141   Phone: (216)526-0300
Membership: Manufacturers of component parts to customer's order, machined from rod, bar, or tube stock, of metal, fiber,

plastic, or other material, using automatic or hand screw machines, automatic bar machines, and CNC machines.

★5895★
National Tooling and Machining Association (NTMA)
9300 Livingston Rd.
Ft. Washington, MD 20744   Phone: (301)248-6200
Membership: Manufacturers of tools, dies, jigs, fixtures, molds, gages, or special machinery; companies that do precision machining on a contract basis; past service and honorary members. **Purpose:** Provides management services; represents members in legislative matters. Promotes apprenticeship programs. Compiles management surveys; conducts management training workshops; maintains speakers' bureau. Has produced motion pictures and videocassettes on tool, die, and precision machining for educational showings. **Publications:** *Business Management Aids*, periodic. • *Buyers Guide of Special Tooling and Precision Machining Services*, annual. • *Catalog of Publications and Training Materials*, periodic. • *Membership Directory*, annual. • *Record*, monthly. • Also publishes handbooks and textbooks. **Toll-free/Additional Phone Number(s):** (800)248-NTMA. **Facsimile Number:** (301)248-7104.

★5896★
NMTBA - Association for Manufacturing Technology
7901 Westpark Dr.
McLean, VA 22102   Phone: (703)893-2900
Membership: Makers of power driven machines used in the process of transforming man-made materials into durable goods, including machine tools, assembly machines, inspection and testing machinery, robots, parts loaders, and plastics molding machines; associate members are producers of tools and tooling parts and components, attachments and accessories, controls and software, and engineering and systems design services. **Purpose:** Seeks to improve methods of producing and marketing machine tools; promotes research and development in the industry. Sponsors: seminars for training production supervisors, accident prevention and safety, and advertising management; annual competition for excellence in machine tool advertising. Develops and supervises standards for training apprentices. Participates in programs of standardization of design and performance of machine tools and components. Serves as a clearinghouse for technical aspects of the industry. Promotes orderly disposal of government-owned surplus machine tools. Maintains 500 volume library of machine tool publications. **Publications:** *Directories of Machine Tools*, annual. • *Economic Handbook of the Machine Tool Industry*, annual. **Toll-free/Additional Phone Number(s):** (800)544-3597. **Facsimile Number:** (703)893-1151.

★5897★
The Tooling and Manufacturing Association
1177 S. Dee Rd.
Park Ridge, IL 60068
Provides information on opportunities in high production precision machining.

───── **Standards/Certification Agencies** ─────

★5898★
NMTBA - Association for Manufacturing Technology
7901 Westpark Dr.
McLean, VA 22102   Phone: (703)893-2900
Develops and supervises standards for training apprentices. Participates in programs of standardization of design and performance of machine tools and components.

───── **Basic Reference Guides and Handbooks** ─────

★5899★
Directories of Machine Tools
NMTBA - Association for Manufacturing Technology
7901 Westpark Dr.
McLean, VA 22102   Phone: (703)893-2900
Annual.

★5900★
Economic Handbook of the Machine Tool Industry
NMTBA - Association for Manufacturing Technology
7901 Westpark Dr.
McLean, VA 22102   Phone: (703)893-2900
Annual.

★5901★
Tooling and Manufacturing Association—Purchasing Guide
Tooling and Manufacturing Association
1177 Dee Rd.
Park Ridge, IL 60068   Phone: (708)825-1120
Jeff Stollard, editor. Biennial. 1,400 manufacturers and distributors of tools, dies, molds, precision machining, special machines, contract manufacturing services, and related services. Entries include: Company name, address, phone, fax, names and titles of key personnel, products or services, Standard Industrial Classification (SIC) code. Arrangement: Classified by product/service. Indexes: Product/service. **Facsimile Number:** (708)825-1120.

───── **Periodicals** ─────

★5902★
NTMA Business Management Aids
National Tooling and Machining Association (NTMA)
9300 Livingston Rd.
Ft. Washington, MD 20744   Phone: (301)248-6200
Periodic.

★5903★
NTMA Record
National Tooling and Machining Association (NTMA)
9300 Livingston Rd.
Ft. Washington, MD 20744   Phone: (301)248-6200
Monthly.

───── **Meetings and Conventions** ─────

★5904★
Tri-State Industrial Show
North American Exposition Co.
33 Rutherford Ave.
Boston, MA 02129   Phone: (617)242-6092
Frequency: Usually held in September or October the Convention Center in Cincinnati, Ohio. 1992; Sep. 29 - Oct. 01; Cincinnati, OH • 1993; Sep. 21-23; Cincinnati, OH. **Toll-free/Additional Phone Number(s):** 800-225-1577. **Facsimile Number:** (617)242-1817.

Other Sources of Information

★5905★
Catalog of Publications and Training Materials
National Tooling and Machining Association (NTMA)
9300 Livingston Rd.
Ft. Washington, MD 20744   Phone: (301)248-6200
Periodic.

Tool and Die Makers

Tool and die makers are skilled workers who produce tools, dies, and special guiding and holding devices that are used in machines that produce a variety of products. Working from blueprints and instructions, tool and die makers plan the sequence of operations necessary to manufacture the tool or die. They measure and mark the pieces of metal that will be cut or form parts of the final product. They then do the cutting, boring, or drilling that is required. They check the accuracy of what they have done to ensure that the final product will meet specifications. Then they assemble the parts and perform finishing jobs such as filing, grinding, and smoothing surfaces. Most tool and die makers work in industries that manufacture metalworking machinery and equipment, motor vehicles, aircraft, and plastics products.

$alaries

Weekly earnings for tool and die makers are as follows:

Lowest 10 percent	$335.00/week or less
Middle 50 percent	$433.00—$680.00/week
Top 10 percent	$818.00/week or more

Employment Outlook

Growth rate until the year 2000: More slowly than average.

Tool and Die Makers

Career Guides

★5906★
Career Information for Precision Machining Technology
National Tooling and Machining Association
9300 Livingston Rd.
Ft. Washington, MD 20744   Phone: (301)248-6200
This six-panel brochure lists the advantages of working in the machine tool industry, study course contents, and how to get started.

★5907★
Career Insights
RMI Media Productions, Inc.
2807 West 47th St.
Shawnee Mission, KS 66205   Phone: (913)262-3974
Videocassette series. 1987. This videotape series describes 50 occupations, including skill requirements and interviews with people employed in these fields. Occupations include: flight service, air transportation/ground services, data processing, carpentry, clerk in banking/insurance/business, cosmetic personal grooming, firefighting, roofing, material handling, photographic processing, plumbing, secretarial services, tool and die operations.

★5908★
How Valuable is Your Future?
Tooling and Manufacturing Association
1177 S. Dee Rd.
Park Ridge, IL 60068-9809   Phone: (708)825-1120
1989. This ten-panel brochure describes the work of precision metalworkers, the skills, entry into the field, internships, and earnings.

★5909★
"Job and Die Setters" in Volume 3 of *The Encyclopedia of Careers and Vocational Guidance* (pp. 528-530)
J.G. Ferguson Publishing Co.
200 W. Monroe
Chicago, IL 60606   Phone: (312)580-5480
William E. Hopke, editor-in-chief. Eighth edition, 1990. Four-volume set that profiles 500 occupations and describes job trends in 76 industries. Includes career description, educational requirements, history of the job, methods of entry, advancement, employment outlook, earnings, working conditions, social and psychological factors, and sources of additional information.

★5910★
"Tap and Die Maker Technicians" in Volume 4 of *The Encyclopedia of Careers and Vocational Guidance* (pp. 259-260)
J.G. Ferguson Publishing Co.
200 W. Monroe
Chicago, IL 60606   Phone: (312)580-5480
William E. Hopke, editor-in-chief. Eighth edition, 1990. Four-volume set that profiles 500 occupations and describes job trends in 76 industries. Includes career description, educational requirements, history of the job, methods of entry, advancement, employment outlook, earnings, working conditions, social and psychological factors, and sources of additional information.

★5911★
"Tool and Die Design" in *The Career Connection II: A Guide to Technical Majors and Their Related Careers* (pp. 125-126)
ERIS
PO Box 7509
University Station
Provo, UT 84602-0509
Fred A. Rowe. 1988. Contains technical majors, such as automotive technology. Describes the major and the job. Lists high school and postsecondary school courses. Includes occupations related to the major, employment outlook, and starting salary.

★5912★
Tool and Die Maker
Careers, Inc.
PO Box 135
Largo, FL 34649-0135   Phone: (813)584-7333
1990. Two-page occupational summary card describing duties, working conditions, personal qualifications, training, earnings and hours, employment outlook, places of employment, related careers and where to write for more information.

★5913★
"Tool and Die Maker" in *Manufacturing*, Volume 9 of *Career Information Center* (pp. 72-74)
Glencoe/Macmillan
15319 Chatsworth St.
Mission Hills, CA 91345   Phone: (818)898-1391
Richard Lidz and Dale Anderson, editorial directors. Fourth edition, 1990. For 600 occupations, describes job duties, entry-level requirements, education and training needed, advancement possibilities, employment outlook, earnings and benefits. The set is divided into 12 volumes. Each volume includes jobs related under a broad career field. Volume 13 is the index. **Facsimile Number:** 818-365-5489.

★5914★
"Tool and Die Maker" in *Occu-Facts: Information on 565 Careers in Outline Form* (p. 17.1)
Careers, Inc.
P.O. Box 135
1211 Tenth St., S.W.
Largo, FL 33640   Phone: (813)584-7333
Elizabeth Handville. Biennial, 1989-90 edition. Each one-page occupational profile describes duties, working conditions, physical surroundings and demands, aptitudes, temperament, educational requirements, employment outlook, earnings, and places of employment.

★5915★
"Tool and Die Maker" in *VGM's Careers Encyclopedia* (pp. 462-464)
National Textbook Co.
4255 W. Touhy Ave.
Lincolnwood, IL 60646   Phone: (312)679-5500
Third edition, 1991. Contains two- to five-page descriptions of 200 managerial, professional, technical, trade, and service occupations. Each profile includes job duties, places of employment, qualifications, educational preparation, training, employment potential, advancement, income, and additional sources of information.

★5916★
"Tool and Die Makers" in *Jobs! What They Are...Where They Are...What They Pay* (pp. 180-181)
Simon & Schuster, Inc.
Simon & Schuster Bldg.
1230 Avenue of the Americas
New York, NY 10020   Phone: (212)698-7000
Robert O. Snelling and Anne M. Snelling. Revised edition, 1989. Profiles 241 occupations, describing duties and responsibilities, educational preparation, earnings, employment opportunities, training, and qualifications.

★5917★
"Tool and Die Makers" in *Occupational Outlook Handbook* (pp. 402-404)
Superintendent of Documents
U.S. Government Printing Office
Washington, DC 20402   Phone: (202)783-3238
Biennial; latest edition, 1990-91. Encyclopedia of careers describing more than 250 occupations and comprising about 86 percent of all jobs in the economy. Occupations that require lengthy education or training are given the most attention. For each occupation, the handbook describes job duties, working conditions, training, educational preparation, personal qualities, advancement possibilities, job outlook, earnings, and sources of additional information.

★5918★
"Tool and Die Makers" in Volume 6 of *Career Discovery Encyclopedia* (pp. 120-121)
J.G. Ferguson Publishing Co.
200 W. Monroe
Chicago, IL 60606   Phone: (312)580-5480
E. Russell Primm, editor-in-chief. 1990. Contains two-page articles on 504 occupations. Each article describes job duties, earnings, and educational and training requirements.

★5919★
"Tool Design Technician" in *Occu-Facts: Information on 565 Careers in Outline Form* (p. 2.21)
Careers, Inc.
P.O. Box 135
1211 Tenth St., S.W.
Largo, FL 33640   Phone: (813)584-7333
Elizabeth Handville. Biennial, 1989-90 edition. Each one-page occupational profile describes duties, working conditions, physical surroundings and demands, aptitudes, temperament, educational requirements, employment outlook, earnings, and places of employment.

★5920★
"Tool Makers and Die Setters" in Volume 3 of *The Encyclopedia of Careers and Vocational Guidance* (pp. 561-564)
J.G. Ferguson Publishing Co.
200 W. Monroe
Chicago, IL 60606   Phone: (312)580-5480
William E. Hopke, editor-in-chief. Eighth edition, 1990. Four-volume set that profiles 500 occupations and describes job trends in 76 industries. Includes career description, educational requirements, history of the job, methods of entry, advancement, employment outlook, earnings, working conditions, social and psychological factors, and sources of additional information.

★5921★
Toolmakers and Diemakers
Chronicle Guidance Publications, Inc.
PO Box 1190
Moravia, NY 13118-1190   Phone: (315)497-0330
1989. This career brief describes the nature of the work, working conditions, hours and earnings, education and training, licensure, certification, unions, personal qualifications, social and psychological factors, employment outlook, entry methods, advancement, and related occupations. **Toll-free/Additional Phone Number(s):** 800-622-7284.

★5922★
Video Career Library - Production II
Careers, Inc.
1211 10th St., SW
PO Box 135
Largo, FL 34649-0135   Phone: (813)584-7333
Videocassette. 1990. 32 mins. Part of the Video Career Library covering 165 occupations. Shows actual workers on the job. Includes tool and die makers, machinists, sheet metal workers, cabinet and bench carpenters, opticians, precision electronic equipment assemblers, industrial machine operators, welders and cutters, and assemblers.

---- Associations ----

★5923★
National Tooling and Machining Association (NTMA)
9300 Livingston Rd.
Ft. Washington, MD 20744   Phone: (301)248-6200
Membership: Manufacturers of tools, dies, jigs, fixtures, molds, gages, or special machinery; companies that do precision machining on a contract basis; past service and honorary members. **Purpose:** Provides management services; represents members in legislative matters. Promotes apprenticeship programs. Compiles management surveys; conducts management training workshops; maintains speakers' bureau. Has produced motion pictures and videocassettes on tool, die, and precision machining for educational showings. **Publications:**

Tool and Die Makers ★5934★

Business Management Aids, periodic. • *Buyers Guide of Special Tooling and Precision Machining Services*, annual. • *Catalog of Publications and Training Materials*, periodic. • *Membership Directory*, annual. • *Record*, monthly. • Also publishes handbooks and textbooks. **Toll-free/Additional Phone Number(s):** (800)248-NTMA. **Facsimile Number:** (301)248-7104.

★5924★
NMTBA - Association for Manufacturing Technology
7901 Westpark Dr.
McLean, VA 22102   Phone: (703)893-2900

Membership: Makers of power driven machines used in the process of transforming man-made materials into durable goods, including machine tools, assembly machines, inspection and testing machinery, robots, parts loaders, and plastics molding machines; associate members are producers of tools and tooling parts and components, attachments and accessories, controls and software, and engineering and systems design services. **Purpose:** Seeks to improve methods of producing and marketing machine tools; promotes research and development in the industry. Sponsors: seminars for training production supervisors, accident prevention and safety, and advertising management; annual competition for excellence in machine tool advertising. Develops and supervises standards for training apprentices. Participates in programs of standardization of design and performance of machine tools and components. Serves as a clearinghouse for technical aspects of the industry. Promotes orderly disposal of government-owned surplus machine tools. Maintains 500 volume library of machine tool publications. **Publications:** *Directories of Machine Tools*, annual. • *Economic Handbook of the Machine Tool Industry*, annual. **Toll-free/Additional Phone Number(s):** (800)544-3597. **Facsimile Number:** (703)893-1151.

★5925★
The Tooling and Manufacturing Association
1177 S. Dee Rd.
Park Ridge, IL 60068

Provides information on opportunities in high production precision machining.

Standards/Certification Agencies

★5926★
NMTBA - Association for Manufacturing Technology
7901 Westpark Dr.
McLean, VA 22102   Phone: (703)893-2900

Develops and supervises standards for training apprentices. Participates in programs of standardization of design and performance of machine tools and components.

Basic Reference Guides and Handbooks

★5927★
Directories of Machine Tools
NMTBA - Association for Manufacturing Technology
7901 Westpark Dr.
McLean, VA 22102   Phone: (703)893-2900
Annual.

★5928★
Economic Handbook of the Machine Tool Industry
NMTBA - Association for Manufacturing Technology
7901 Westpark Dr.
McLean, VA 22102   Phone: (703)893-2900
Annual.

★5929★
Tooling and Manufacturing Association—Purchasing Guide
Tooling and Manufacturing Association
1177 Dee Rd.
Park Ridge, IL 60068   Phone: (708)825-1120

Jeff Stollard, editor. Biennial. 1,400 manufacturers and distributors of tools, dies, molds, precision machining, special machines, contract manufacturing services, and related services. Entries include: Company name, address, phone, fax, names and titles of key personnel, products or services, Standard Industrial Classification (SIC) code. Arrangement: Classified by product/service. Indexes: Product/service. **Facsimile Number:** (708)825-1120.

Periodicals

★5930★
NTMA Business Management Aids
National Tooling and Machining Association (NTMA)
9300 Livingston Rd.
Ft. Washington, MD 20744   Phone: (301)248-6200
Periodic.

★5931★
NTMA Record
National Tooling and Machining Association (NTMA)
9300 Livingston Rd.
Fort Washington, MD 20744   Phone: (301)248-6200

Editor(s): Mark W. Jeschke and Patricia Teets. Monthly. Focuses on business management techniques and government relations for the contract tool, die, and precision machining industry. Supplies information on Association activities. Recurring features include editorials, tax information, and technical notes. **Toll-free/Additional Phone Number(s):** 800-248-6862 **Facsimile Number:** (301)248-7104.

Meetings and Conventions

★5932★
AMB - International Exhibition for Metal Working
World Access Corp.
15 Bemis Rd.
PO Box 171
Wellesley Hills, MA 02181   Phone: (617)235-8095
1992; Sep. 01-05. **Facsimile Number:** (617)235-7360.

★5933★
International Die Casting Congress and Exposition
Society of Die Casting Engineers
2000 N. 5th Ave.
River Grove, IL 60171   Phone: (708)452-0700
1993; Oct. 18-21; Cleveland, OH.

★5934★
Tri-State Industrial Show
North American Exposition Co.
33 Rutherford Ave.
Boston, MA 02129   Phone: (617)242-6092

Frequency: Usually held in September or October the Convention Center in Cincinnati, Ohio. 1992; Sep. 29 - Oct. 01; Cincinnati, OH • 1993; Sep. 21-23; Cincinnati, OH. **Toll-free/Additional Phone Number(s):** 800-225-1577. **Facsimile Number:** (617)242-1817.

Other Sources of Information

★5935★
Catalog of Publications and Training Materials
National Tooling and Machining Association (NTMA)
9300 Livingston Rd.
Ft. Washington, MD 20744   Phone: (301)248-6200
Periodic.

Welders, Cutters, and Welding Machine Operators

Skilled welders generally plan work from drawings or specifications or by analyzing damaged metal, using their knowledge of welding and metals. They select and set up welding equipment and may also examine welds to ensure they meet standards or specifications. In many production processes, automatic welding machines are used. Welding machine operators set up and operate welding machines as specified by layouts, work orders, or blueprints. Operators set machine controls, place the parts to be joined in fixtures on the machine, and push a button. When the welding operation is completed, operators remove the welded pieces from the machine. About 60 percent of all welders jobs are in plants that manufacture boilers, construction equipment, motor vehicles, machinery, ships, appliances, and other metal products. Most others are in firms that construct bridges, large buildings, pipelines, and other structures or are in repair shops. All welding machine operators are in manufacturing industries, primarily machinery, motor vehicles, and fabricated metal products.

$alaries

Weekly earnings for welders and welding machine operators are as follows:

Lowest 10 percent	$225.00/week or less
Middle 50 percent	$300.00—$500.00/week
Top 10 percent	$615.00/week or more

Employment Outlook

Growth rate until the year 2000: Slower than average.

Welders, Cutters, and Welding Machine Operators

Career Guides

★5936★
Arc Welding Methods
Multi Media Mathematics
11224 Seawind Cove
San Diego, CA 92126   Phone: (619)578-3421
Videocassette. 1987. 28 mins. An introduction for the prospective metal worker on the basics of arc welding.

★5937★
Getting Down to Business: Welding Business
American Institutes for Research
PO Box 11131
Palo Alto, CA 94302   Phone: (415)493-3550
Joyce P. Gall. 1981. **Facsimile Number:** (415)858-0958.

★5938★
Opportunities in Welding Careers
National Textbook Co.
4255 W. Touhy Ave.
Lincolnwood, IL 60646   Phone: (312)679-5500
Mark Rowh. 1990. Describes what welders do, where they work, and the tools they use. Surveys training options and covers certification and salaries. Offers job hunting advice.

★5939★
The Science & Practice of Welding
Cambridge University Press
40 W. 20th St.
New York, NY 10011   Phone: (212)924-3900
A. C. Davies. Ninth edition, 1989. **Facsimile Number:** (212)691-3239.

★5940★
Soldering: Instruction and Vocabulary
RMI Media Productions, Inc.
2807 West 47th St.
Shawnee Mission, KS 66205   Phone: (913)262-3974
Videocassette. 1984. 19 mins. This program provides an introduction to soldering, explaining the terms, materials and tools that relate to the process.

★5941★
Technical/Manufacturing Cluster One
Center for Humanities, Inc.
Communications Park
Box 1000
Mount Kisco, NY 10549   Phone: (914)666-4100
Videocassette. 1984. 20 mins. An upclose look at people who work in the fields of welding, drafting, and sheet metal.

★5942★
Video Career Library - Production II
Careers, Inc.
1211 10th St., SW
PO Box 135
Largo, FL 34649-0135   Phone: (813)584-7333
Videocassette. 1990. 32 mins. Part of the Video Career Library covering 165 occupations. Shows actual workers on the job. Includes tool and die makers, machinists, sheet metal workers, cabinet and bench carpenters, opticians, precision electronic equipment assemblers, industrial machine operators, welders and cutters, and assemblers.

★5943★
"Welder" in *Construction,* **Volume 4 of** *Career Information Center* **(pp. 89-90)**
Glencoe/Macmillan
15319 Chatsworth St.
Mission Hills, CA 91345   Phone: (818)898-1391
Richard Lidz and Dale Anderson, editorial directors. Fourth edition, 1990. For 600 occupations, describes job duties, entry-level requirements, education and training needed, advancement possibilities, employment outlook, earnings and benefits. The set is divided into 12 volumes. Each volume includes jobs related under a broad career field. Volume 13 is the index. **Facsimile Number:** 818-365-5489.

★5944★
"Welder" in *Guide to Careers Without College* **(pp. 67-70)**
Franklin Watts, Inc.
387 Park Avenue, S.
New York, NY 10016   Phone: (212)686-7070
Kathleen S. Abrams. 1988. Discusses careers that do not require a college degree in fields such as health care, sales and marketing, and the building trades. Describes the work, employment opportunities, and training.

★5945★
"Welder" in *Hard Hatted Women: Stories of Struggle and Success in the Trades* **(pp. 33-36)**
Seal Press
3131 Western Ave., Ste. 410
Seattle, WA 98121   Phone: (206)283-7844
Molly Martin, editor. 1988. Twenty-six women recount their experiences working in blue collar occupations. They describe how they got in, the work they do, their relationships in predominantly male occupations, and their training.

★5946★
Welders
Chronicle Guidance Publications, Inc.
PO Box 1190
Moravia, NY 13118-1190   Phone: (315)497-0330

1991. This career brief describes the nature of the work, working conditions, hours and earnings, education and training, licensure, certification, unions, personal qualifications, social and psychological factors, employment outlook, entry methods, advancement, and related occupations. **Toll-free/Additional Phone Number(s):** 800-622-7284.

★5947★
"Welders" in Volume 6 of *Career Discovery Encyclopedia* (pp. 156-157)
J.G. Ferguson Publishing Co.
200 W. Monroe
Chicago, IL 60606   Phone: (312)580-5480

E. Russell Primm, editor-in-chief. 1990. Contains two-page articles on 504 occupations. Each article describes job duties, earnings, and educational and training requirements.

★5948★
"Welders" in Volume 3 of *The Encyclopedia of Careers and Vocational Guidance* (pp. 718-723)
J.G. Ferguson Publishing Co.
200 W. Monroe
Chicago, IL 60606   Phone: (312)580-5480

William E. Hopke, editor-in-chief. Eighth edition, 1990. Four-volume set that profiles 500 occupations and describes job trends in 76 industries. Includes career description, educational requirements, history of the job, methods of entry, advancement, employment outlook, earnings, working conditions, social and psychological factors, and sources of additional information.

★5949★
Welders and Oxygen Cutters
Careers, Inc.
PO Box 135
Largo, FL 34649-0135   Phone: (813)584-7333

1990. Eight-page brief offering the definition, history, duties, working conditions, personal qualifications, educational requirements, earnings, hours, employment outlook, advancement possibilities, and related occupations.

★5950★
"Welders and Oxygen Cutters" in *Occu-Facts: Information on 565 Careers in Outline Form* (p. 18.24)
Careers, Inc.
P.O. Box 135
1211 Tenth St., S.W.
Largo, FL 33640   Phone: (813)584-7333

Elizabeth Handville. Biennial, 1989-90 edition. Each one-page occupational profile describes duties, working conditions, physical surroundings and demands, aptitudes, temperament, educational requirements, employment outlook, earnings, and places of employment.

★5951★
"Welders, Cutters, and Welding Machine Operators" in *Occupational Outlook Handbook* (pp. 404-405)
Superintendent of Documents
U.S. Government Printing Office
Washington, DC 20402   Phone: (202)783-3238

Biennial; latest edition, 1990-91. Encyclopedia of careers describing more than 250 occupations and comprising about 86 percent of all jobs in the economy. Occupations that require lengthy education or training are given the most attention. For each occupation, the handbook describes job duties, working conditions, training, educational preparation, personal qualities, advancement possibilities, job outlook, earnings, and sources of additional information.

★5952★
"Welding" in *Opportunities in Metalworking Careers* (pp. 47-58)
National Textbook Co.
4255 W. Touhy Ave.
Lincolnwood, IL 60646   Phone: (312)679-5500

Mark Rowh. 1991. Covers sheet metal work, machining, structural and reinforcing metalworking, and jewelry making. Describes the work performed, skills needed, training and working conditions. Lists unions that sponsor apprenticeship and technical schools which offer training.

★5953★
Welding and Joining. . .Build a Career to Build a Country
American Welding Society
550 NW LeJeune Rd.
PO Box 351040
Miami, FL 33135   Phone: (305)443-9353

This eight-panel brochure describes required skills and employment opportunities.

★5954★
Welding Careers
National Textbook Company
4255 W. Touhy Ave.
Lincolnwood, IL 60646-1975   Phone: (708)679-5500

Mark Rowh. 1990. Part of Opportunities In Career Series. **Facsimile Number:** (708)679-2494.

★5955★
Welding Machine Operator
Careers, Inc.
PO Box 135
Largo, FL 34649-0135   Phone: (813)584-7333

1989. Two-page job guide card describing duties, working conditions, personal qualifications, training, earnings and hours, employment outlook, places of employment, related careers and where to write for more information.

★5956★
"Welding Machine Operator" in *Occu-Facts: Information on 565 Careers in Outline Form* (p. 18.8)
Careers, Inc.
P.O. Box 135
1211 Tenth St., S.W.
Largo, FL 33640   Phone: (813)584-7333

Elizabeth Handville. Biennial, 1989-90 edition. Each one-page occupational profile describes duties, working conditions, physical surroundings and demands, aptitudes, temperament, educational requirements, employment outlook, earnings, and places of employment.

★5957★
"Welding Technicians" in Volume 4 of *The Encyclopedia of Careers and Vocational Guidance* (pp. 269-273)
J.G. Ferguson Publishing Co.
200 W. Monroe
Chicago, IL 60606   Phone: (312)580-5480

William E. Hopke, editor-in-chief. Eighth edition, 1990. Four-volume set that profiles 500 occupations and describes job trends in 76 industries. Includes career description, educational requirements, history of the job, methods of entry, advancement, employment outlook, earnings, working

Welders, Cutters, and Welding Machine Operators

conditions, social and psychological factors, and sources of additional information.

★5958★
"Welding Technology" in *The Career Connection II: A Guide to Technical Majors and Their Related Careers* (pp. 133-134)
ERIS
PO Box 7509
University Station
Provo, UT 84602-0509

Fred A. Rowe. 1988. Contains technical majors, such as automotive technology. Describes the major and the job. Lists high school and postsecondary school courses. Includes occupations related to the major, employment outlook, and starting salary.

Associations

★5959★
American Welding Society (AWS)
550 LeJeune Rd. NW
PO Box 351040
Miami, FL 33135   Phone: (305)443-9353

Membership: One of several sponsors of the Welding Research Council and the Materials Properties Council. **Purpose:** Professional engineering society in the field of welding. Sponsors seminars. Maintains over 130 technical committees and handbook committees and 144 sections, educational committees, and task forces. **Publications:** *Directory of Technical Council Committees*, annual. • *Welding Handbook*, biennial. • *Welding Journal*, monthly. • Also publishes codes, standards, specifications, and books on welding. **Facsimile Number:** (305)443-7559;

★5960★
National Association of Trade and Technical Schools (NATTS)
2251 Wisconsin Ave. NW
Washington, DC 20007   Phone: (202)333-1021

Membership: Private schools providing career education. **Purpose:** Seeks to inform members of the accreditation process and regulations affecting vocational education. Conducts workshops and institutes for staffs of member schools; provides legislative, administrative, and public relations assistance; serves as federally recognized accrediting agency. Has established Career Training Foundation to support research into private vocational education. Sponsors annual Idea Fair Competition. Presents special awards. Maintains hall of fame; compiles statistics. **Publications:** *Career News Digest*, 3-4/year. • *Career Training*, quarterly. • *Classroom Companion*, quarterly. • *Handbook of Trade and Technical Careers and Training*, annual. • *NATTS News and Views*, bimonthly. • Also publishes *Career Guidance Handouts*.

Standards/Certification Agencies

★5961★
American Welding Society (AWS)
550 LeJeune Rd. NW
PO Box 351040
Miami, FL 33135   Phone: (305)443-9353

Maintains over 130 technical committees and handbook committees and 144 sections, educational committees, and task forces. Publishes codes, standards, specifications, and books on welding.

★5962★
National Association of Trade and Technical Schools (NATTS)
2251 Wisconsin Ave. NW
Washington, DC 20007   Phone: (202)333-1021

Informs members of the accreditation process and regulations affecting vocational education. Conducts workshops and institutes for staffs of member schools; provides legislative, administrative, and public relations assistance; serves as a federally recognized accrediting agency.

Test Guides

★5963★
Gas & Electric Welder
National Learning Corp.
212 Michael Dr.
Syosset, NY 11791   Phone: (516)921-8888

Jack Rudman. Part of the Career Examination Series No. 1. All examination guides in this series contain questions with answers. **Facsimile Number:** (516)921-8743. **Toll-free/Additional Phone Number(s):** 800-645-6337.

★5964★
Structural Welder
National Learning Corp.
212 Michael Dr.
Syosset, NY 11791   Phone: (516)921-8888

Jack Rudman. Part of the Career Examination Series No. 1. All examination guides in this series contain questions with answers. **Facsimile Number:** (516)921-8743. **Toll-free/Additional Phone Number(s):** 800-645-6337.

★5965★
Welder
National Learning Corp.
212 Michael Dr.
Syosset, NY 11791   Phone: (516)921-8888

Jack Rudman. Part of the Career Examination Series No. 1. All examination guides in this series contain questions with answers. **Facsimile Number:** (516)921-8743. **Toll-free/Additional Phone Number(s):** 800-645-6337.

Educational Directories and Programs

★5966★
Career Guidance Handouts
National Association of Trade and Technical Schools (NATTS)
2251 Wisconsin Ave. NW
Washington, DC 20007   Phone: (202)333-1021

★5967★
Career Training
National Association of Trade and Technical Schools (NATTS)
2251 Wisconsin Ave. NW
Washington, DC 20007   Phone: (202)333-1021

Quarterly.

★5968★
Classroom Companion
National Association of Trade and Technical Schools (NATTS)
2251 Wisconsin Ave. NW
Washington, DC 20007   Phone: (202)333-1021

Quarterly.

★5969★
Handbook of Trade and Technical Careers and Training (NATTS)
National Association of Trade and Technical Schools (NATTS)
2251 Wisconsin Ave. NW
Washington, DC 20007 Phone: (202)333-1021
Annual.

★5970★
Welder Education—Today and Tomorrow
American Welding Society
550 NW LeJeune Rd.
PO Box 351040
Miami, FL 33135 Phone: (305)443-9353
This booklet covers welder training needs required by industry and the demand for welders. Profiles five schools offering welding and describes the curriculum and training methods. Reprinted from a series of articles appearing in April, June, and September 1990 issues of Welding Journal.

Awards, Scholarships, Grants, and Fellowships

★5971★
AIRCO Welding Award
American Welding Society
P.O. Box 351040
550 LeJeune Rd., N.W.
Miami, FL 33135 Phone: (305)443-9353
For recognition of distinguished accomplishments in the joining of or severing of metals which have improved and benefited mankind and furthered the welding industry. An honorarium of $1,000 and a certificate are awarded annually. Established in 1967 and sponsored by Airco Welding Products Division of AIRCO, Inc.

Basic Reference Guides and Handbooks

★5972★
AWS Directory of Technical Council Committees (AWS)
American Welding Society (AWS)
550 LeJeune Rd. NW
PO Box 351040
Miami, FL 33135 Phone: (305)443-9353
Annual.

★5973★
Consumable Electrode Processes in Welding Automation
Springer-Verlag New York, Inc.
175 5th Ave., 19th Fl.
New York, NY 10010 Phone: (212)460-1500
J. Cornu. 1989. Part of Advanced Welding Systems Series.

★5974★
Fire Prevention in Use of Cutting & Welding Processes
National Fire Protection Association
1 Batterymarch Park
Quincy, MA 02269-9101 Phone: (617)770-3000
1989. Part of Fifty Series.

★5975★
Guide to Welding
Kendall/Hunt Publishing Co.
2460 Kerper Blvd.
Dubuque, IA 52001 Phone: (319)588-1451
Kenneth Brown. 1990.

★5976★
International Welding Thesaurus
Air Science Company
PO Box 143
Corning, NY 14830 Phone: (607)962-5591
International Institute of Welding Staff. Third edition, 1989. **Facsimile Number:** (607)962-3101.

★5977★
MAN—Modern Applications News—Cutting Tools Directory Issue
Nelson Publishing
2504 N. Tamiami Trail
Nokomis, FL 34275 Phone: (813)966-9521
A. Verner Nelson and Lynda S. Estes, editor. Annual, October. List of manufacturers and distributors of cutting tools. Entries include: Company name, address, phone, name and title of contact, products. Arrangement: Alphabetical. **Facsimile Number:** (813)966-2590.

★5978★
Math for Welders
Goodheart-Willcox Company
123 Taft Dr.
South Holland, IL 60473 Phone: (708)333-7200
Nino Marion. 1990.

★5979★
Practical Problems in Mathematics for Welders
Delmar Publishers, Inc.
PO Box 15015
2 Computer Dr., W.
Albany, NY 12212 Phone: (518)459-1150
Frank R. Schell. Third edition, 1989. Part of Practical Problems in Mathematics Series. **Facsimile Number:** (518)453-6472.

★5980★
Quality Assurance of Welded Construction
Elsevier Science Publishing Company, Inc.
655 Avenue of the Americas
New York, NY 10010 Phone: (212)989-5800
N. T. Burgess. Second edition, 1989.

★5981★
Rational Fabrication Specifications for Steel Structures
Air Science Company
PO Box 143
Corning, NY 14830 Phone: (607)962-5591
Welding Institute Staff. 1989. **Facsimile Number:** (607)962-3101.

★5982★
TIG & Related Processes in Welding Automation
Springer-Verlag New York, Inc.
175 5th Ave., 19th Fl.
New York, NY 10010 Phone: (212)460-1500
J. Cornu. 1989. Part of Advanced Welding Systems Series.

Welders, Cutters, and Welding Machine Operators

★5983★
Tools—Cutting
American Business Directories, Inc.
American Business Information, Inc.
5711 S. 86th Circle
Omaha, NE 68127   Phone: (402)593-4600
Annual. Entries include: Name, address, phone (including area code), size of advertisement, year first in "Yellow Pages." Arrangement: Geographical. **Facsimile Number:** (402)331-1505.

★5984★
Tools—Cutting Directory
American Business Directories, Inc.
American Business Information, Inc.
5711 S. 86th Circle
Omaha, NE 68127   Phone: (402)593-4600
Annual. Entries include: Name, address, phone, size of advertisement, name of owner or manager, number of employees, year first in "Yellow Pages." Arrangement: Geographical. **Facsimile Number:** (402)331-1505.

★5985★
Welding & Cutting: A Guide to Fusion Welding & Associated Cutting Processes
Industrial Press, Inc.
200 Madison Ave.
New York, NY 10016   Phone: (212)889-6330
Peter Houldcroft. 1989. **Facsimile Number:** (212)545-8327.

★5986★
Welding Handbook (AWS)
American Welding Society (AWS)
550 LeJeune Rd. NW
PO Box 351040
Miami, FL 33135   Phone: (305)443-9353
Biennial.

★5987★
Welding: Principles & Applications
Delmar Publishers, Inc.
PO Box 15015
2 Computer Dr., W.
Albany, NY 12212   Phone: (518)459-1150
Larry Jeffus. Second edition, 1989. **Facsimile Number:** (518)453-6472.

★5988★
Welding Technology Fundamentals
Goodheart-Willcox Co.
123 Taft Dr.
South Holland, IL 60473   Phone: (708)333-7200
William A. Bowditch. 1991. **Facsimile Number:** (708)331-9130.

★5989★
Welding Technology Today: Principles & Practices
Prentice Hall
Rte. 9W
Englewood Cliffs, NJ 07632   Phone: (201)592-2000
Craig Stinchcomb. 1989.

Periodicals

★5990★
Career News Digest (NATTS)
National Association of Trade and Technical Schools (NATTS)
2251 Wisconsin Ave. NW
Washington, DC 20007   Phone: (202)333-1021
3-4/year.

★5991★
Modern Blacksmith
National Blacksmiths and Welders Association
PO Box 327
Arnold, NE 69120   Phone: (612)252-4924
Editor(s): Harry Strasil, Jr. Quarterly. Provides news of the association, notices of meetings, profiles of Association members, and information on the welding and repair of equipment.

★5992★
NATTS News and Views
National Association of Trade and Technical Schools (NATTS)
2251 Wisconsin Ave. NW
Washington, DC 20007   Phone: (202)333-1021
Bimonthly. Newspaper.

★5993★
Welding Design & Fabrication
Penton Publishing
1100 Superior Ave.
Cleveland, OH 44114   Phone: (216)696-7000
Rosalie Brosilow, Editor. Monthly. Magazine for the welding and fabricating industry. **Facsimile Number:** (216)696-7648.

★5994★
The Welding Distributor
Penton Publishing
1100 Superior Ave.
Cleveland, OH 44114   Phone: (216)696-7000
Charles Berka, Editor. 6x/yr. Distributors magazine featuring welding and welding safety equipment. **Facsimile Number:** (216)696-7648.

★5995★
Welding Innovation Quarterly
James F. Lincoln Arc Welding Foundation
PO Box 17035
Cleveland, OH 44117   Phone: (216)481-4300
Richard D. Smith, Editor. Quarterly. Magazine covering arc welding design, engineering, and fabrication. **Facsimile Number:** (216)486-1751.

★5996★
Welding Journal (AWS)
American Welding Society (AWS)
550 LeJeune Rd. NW
PO Box 351040
Miami, FL 33135   Phone: (305)443-9353
Monthly. Covers developments in welding technology, the industry, and the society. Includes book reviews, calendar of events, employment listings, new products and literature, and personnel promotions and appointments.

Meetings and Conventions

★5997★
AMB - International Exhibition for Metal Working
World Access Corp.
15 Bemis Rd.
PO Box 171
Wellesley Hills, MA 02181   Phone: (617)235-8095
1992; Sep. 01-05. **Facsimile Number:** (617)235-7360.

★5998★
American Welding Society Welding Show
American Welding Society
PO Box 351040
550 LeJeune Rd., NW
Miami, FL 33135   Phone: (305)443-9353
1992; Mar. 22-27; Chicago, IL ● 1993; Apr. 25-30; Houston, TX ● 1994; Apr. 11-15; Chicago, IL. **Toll-free/Additional Phone Number(s):** 800-443-9353. **Facsimile Number:** (305)443-7559.

★5999★
Trade Fair for Joining and Welding Technology
World Access Corp.
15 Bemis Rd.
PO Box 171
Wellesley Hills, MA 02181   Phone: (617)235-8095
Facsimile Number: (617)235-7360.

★6000★
Tri-State Industrial Show
North American Exposition Co.
33 Rutherford Ave.
Boston, MA 02129   Phone: (617)242-6092
Frequency: Usually held in September or October at the Convention Center in Cincinnati, Ohio. 1992; Sep. 29 - Oct. 01; Cincinnati, OH ● 1993; Sep. 21-23; Cincinnati, OH. **Toll-free/Additional Phone Number(s):** 800-225-1577. **Facsimile Number:** (617)242-1817.

Other Sources of Information

★6001★
Recent Trends in Welding Science & Technology
ASM International
Materials Park, OH 44073   Phone: (216)338-5151
1990. **Facsimile Number:** (216)338-4634.

Plant and Systems Operators

Electric Power Generating Plant Operators and Power Distributors and Dispatchers

Powerplant operators control the machinery that generates electricity. Operators who work in newer plants work mainly in a central control room and usually are called control room operators and control room operator trainees and assistants. Auxiliary equipment operators work throughout the plant, while switchboard operators control the flow of electricity from a central point. NRC-licensed reactor operators are authorized to operate all equipment in a nuclear powerplant. In addition, an NRC-licensed senior reactor operator acts as the supervisor of the plant for each shift. Power distributors and dispatchers, also called load dispatchers or systems operators, oversee the flow of electricity through substations and over a network of transmission and distribution lines to users. Most electric power generating plant operators and power distributors and dispatchers work for electric utility companies and government agencies that produce electricity. Some work for manufacturing establishments that produce electricity for their own use.

$alaries

Median weekly earnings for powerplant operators are about $630.00.

Employment Outlook

Growth rate until the year 2000: Average.

Electric Power Generating Plant Operators and Power Distributors and Dispatchers

---

Career Guides

★6002★
Career Success Series
Cambridge Career Products
90 MacCorkle Ave., SW
South Charleston, WV 25311　　　Phone: (304)744-9323
Videocassette. 1986. 15 mins. A series, available separately, outlining various career choices for students. Occupations include: flight service, air transportation/ground service, data processing, carpentry, clerk in banking/insurance, commodity sales, cosmetic personal grooming, fire fighting, forestry services, home economics, insulation/roofing, material handling, mechanics, photographic processing, pipefitting and plumbing, police science, printing, secretarial services, and utilities equipment operator.

★6003★
Careers in Electricity
RMI Media Productions, Inc.
2807 West 47th St.
Shawnee Mission, KS 66205　　　Phone: (913)262-3974
Videocassette. 1984. 16 mins. This program examines career opportunities in the power field branch of electricity.

★6004★
Careers with an Electric Company
Lerner Publications Co.
241 First Ave., N.
Minneapolis, MN 55401
Pam Fricke. 1984. Describes fifteen career possibilities with an electric company including such jobs as lineman and system operator. **Toll-free/Additional Phone Number(s):** 800-328-4920. **Facsimile Number:** (612)332-7615.

★6005★
"**Electric Power Generating Plant Operators and Power Distributors and Dispatchers**" in *Occupational Outlook Handbook* (pp. 406-407)
Superintendent of Documents
U.S. Government Printing Office
Washington, DC 20402　　　Phone: (202)783-3238
Biennial; latest edition, 1990-91. Encyclopedia of careers describing more than 250 occupations and comprising about 86 percent of all jobs in the economy. Occupations that require lengthy education or training are given the most attention. For each occupation, the handbook describes job duties, working conditions, training, educational preparation, personal qualities, advancement possibilities, job outlook, earnings, and sources of additional information.

★6006★
Electric Power Plant Occupations
Careers, Inc.
PO Box 135
Largo, FL 34649-0135　　　Phone: (813)584-7333
1988. Eight-page brief offering the definition, history, duties, working conditions, personal qualifications, educational requirements, earnings, hours, employment outlook, advancement possibilities, and related occupations.

★6007★
"**Electric Power Plant Occupations**" in *Occu-Facts: Information on 565 Careers in Outline Form* (p. 17.34)
Careers, Inc.
P.O. Box 135
1211 Tenth St., S.W.
Largo, FL 33640　　　Phone: (813)584-7333
Elizabeth Handville. Biennial, 1989-90 edition. Each one-page occupational profile describes duties, working conditions, physical surroundings and demands, aptitudes, temperament, educational requirements, employment outlook, earnings, and places of employment.

★6008★
"**Electric Power Service Worker**" in *Public and Community Services,* Volume 11 of *Career Information Center* (pp. 43-46)
Glencoe/Macmillan
15319 Chatsworth St.
Mission Hills, CA 91345　　　Phone: (818)898-1391
Richard Lidz and Dale Anderson, editorial directors. Fourth edition, 1990. For 600 occupations, describes job duties, entry-level requirements, education and training needed, advancement possibilities, employment outlook, earnings and benefits. The set is divided into 12 volumes. Each volume includes jobs related under a broad career field. Volume 13 is the index. **Facsimile Number:** 818-365-5489.

★6009★
"**Electric Power Transmission, Distribution Worker**" in *Public and Community Service,* Volume 11 of *Career Information Center* (pp. 46-48)
Glencoe/Macmillan
15319 Chatsworth St.
Mission Hills, CA 91345　　　Phone: (818)898-1391
Richard Lidz and Dale Anderson, editorial directors. Fourth edition, 1990. For 600 occupations, describes job duties, entry-level requirements, education and training needed, advancement possibilities, employment outlook, earnings and benefits. The set is divided into 12 volumes. Each volume includes jobs related under a broad career field. Volume 13 is the index. **Facsimile Number:** 818-365-5489.

★6010★
"Electrical Power Worker" in Volume 2 of *Career Discovery Encyclopedia* (pp. 148-149)
J.G. Ferguson Publishing Co.
200 W. Monroe
Chicago, IL 60606   Phone: (312)580-5480

E. Russell Primm, editor-in-chief. 1990. Contains two-page articles on 504 occupations. Each article describes job duties, earnings, and educational and training requirements.

★6011★
Electrical Transmission and Distribution Occupations
Careers, Inc.
PO Box 135
Largo, FL 34649-0135   Phone: (813)584-7333

1989. Eight-page brief offering the definition, history, duties, working conditions, personal qualifications, educational requirements, earnings, hours, employment outlook, advancement possibilities, and related occupations.

★6012★
"Electrical Transmission and Distribution Occupations" in *Occu-Facts: Information on 565 Careers in Outline Form* (p. 17.33)
Careers, Inc.
P.O. Box 135
1211 Tenth St., S.W.
Largo, FL 33640   Phone: (813)584-7333

Elizabeth Handville. Biennial, 1989-90 edition. Each one-page occupational profile describes duties, working conditions, physical surroundings and demands, aptitudes, temperament, educational requirements, employment outlook, earnings, and places of employment.

★6013★
"Nuclear Reactor Operator Technicians" in Volume 4 of *Career Discovery Encyclopedia* (pp. 126-127)
J.G. Ferguson Publishing Co.
200 W. Monroe
Chicago, IL 60606   Phone: (312)580-5480

E. Russell Primm, editor-in-chief. 1990. Contains two-page articles on 504 occupations. Each article describes job duties, earnings, and educational and training requirements.

★6014★
"Nuclear Reactor Operator Technicians" in Volume 4 of *The Encyclopedia of Careers and Vocational Guidance* (pp. 79-84)
J.G. Ferguson Publishing Co.
200 W. Monroe
Chicago, IL 60606   Phone: (312)580-5480

William E. Hopke, editor-in-chief. Eighth edition, 1990. Four-volume set that profiles 500 occupations and describes job trends in 76 industries. Includes career description, educational requirements, history of the job, methods of entry, advancement, employment outlook, earnings, working conditions, social and psychological factors, and sources of additional information.

★6015★
"Power Plant Occupations" in Volume 3 of *The Encyclopedia of Careers and Vocational Guidance* (pp. 766-769)
J.G. Ferguson Publishing Co.
200 W. Monroe
Chicago, IL 60606   Phone: (312)580-5480

William E. Hopke, editor-in-chief. Eighth edition, 1990. Four-volume set that profiles 500 occupations and describes job trends in 76 industries. Includes career description, educational requirements, history of the job, methods of entry, advancement, employment outlook, earnings, working conditions, social and psychological factors, and sources of additional information.

★6016★
"Power Plant Worker" in *Public and Community Services,* Volume 11 of *Career Information Center* (pp. 60-62)
Glencoe/Macmillan
15319 Chatsworth St.
Mission Hills, CA 91345   Phone: (818)898-1391

Richard Lidz and Dale Anderson, editorial directors. Fourth edition, 1990. For 600 occupations, describes job duties, entry-level requirements, education and training needed, advancement possibilities, employment outlook, earnings and benefits. The set is divided into 12 volumes. Each volume includes jobs related under a broad career field. Volume 13 is the index. **Facsimile Number:** 818-365-5489.

★6017★
"Power Plant Workers" in Volume 5 of *Career Discovery Encyclopedia* (pp. 80-81)
J.G. Ferguson Publishing Co.
200 W. Monroe
Chicago, IL 60606   Phone: (312)580-5480

E. Russell Primm, editor-in-chief. 1990. Contains two-page articles on 504 occupations. Each article describes job duties, earnings, and educational and training requirements.

★6018★
"Transmission and Distribution Occupations" in Volume 3 of *The Encyclopedia of Careers and Vocational Guidance* (pp. 790-793)
J.G. Ferguson Publishing Co.
200 W. Monroe
Chicago, IL 60606   Phone: (312)580-5480

William E. Hopke, editor-in-chief. Eighth edition, 1990. Four-volume set that profiles 500 occupations and describes job trends in 76 industries. Includes career description, educational requirements, history of the job, methods of entry, advancement, employment outlook, earnings, working conditions, social and psychological factors, and sources of additional information.

★6019★
"Utility Switch Operator" in *Hard Hatted Women: Stories of Struggle and Success in the Trades* (pp. 150-155)
Seal Press
3131 Western Ave., Ste. 410
Seattle, WA 98121   Phone: (206)283-7844

Molly Martin, editor. 1988. Twenty-six women recount their experiences working in blue collar occupations. They describe how they got in, the work they do, their relationships in predominantly male occupations, and their training.

★6020★
Video Career Library - Production I
Careers, Inc.
1211 10th St., SW
PO Box 135
Largo, FL 34649-0135   Phone: (813)584-7333

Videocassette. 1990. 28 mins. Part of the Video Career Library covering 165 occupations. Shows actual workers on the job. Includes layout workers, precision typesetters, lithographers/photoengravers, bookbinders, hand tailors/dressmakers, upholsterers, water/sewage plant operators, chemical plant operators, and power plant operators.

Electric Power Generating Plant Operators and Power Distributors and Dispatchers ★6031★

★6021★
Your Guardian Angel
Film Library
3450 Wilshire Blvd. #700
Los Angeles, CA 90010-2215   Phone: (213)384-8114
Videocassette. 198?. 15 mins. Harry Sparks, the guardian angel of electrical workers looks at the hazards and characteristics of 600-volt lines and equipment.

Associations

★6022★
Edison Electric Institute (EEI)
701 Pennsylvania Ave. NW
Washington, DC 20004-2696   Phone: (202)508-5000
Membership: Investor-owned electric utility companies operating in the U.S. Has affiliate members in North, Central, and South America. **Purpose:** Maintains library; sponsors educational programs; compiles statistics. Maintains speakers' bureau. **Publications:** *Electric Perspectives*, bimonthly. • *Electrical Reports*, weekly. • *Rate Book*, annual. • *Statistical Reports*, weekly. • *Statistical YearBook*. • Also publishes *Electric Power Surveys*, books, and booklets.

★6023★
Electrical Women's Round Table (EWRT)
PO Box 292793
Nashville, TN 37229-2793   Phone: (615)254-4479
Membership: Women holding positions connected with the electrical industry or allied fields in roles such as communicator, educator, information specialist, and researcher. **Purpose:** To promote knowledge and expertise among members in the fields of electrical energy, energy resources, and energy conservation; increase recognition and encourage upward mobility of women in the electrical industry; advance consumer education. Acts as a forum, promotes research, conducts workshops, and reviews new audiovisual and printed materials. Bestows annual Julia Kiene and Lyle Mamer fellowship awards. **Publications:** *Electrical Women's Round Table—Membership Directory*, annual. • *Electrical Women's Round Table—National Newsletter*, quarterly. • Also publishes promotional brochures.

★6024★
International Brotherhood of Electrical Workers (IBEW)
1125 15th St. NW
Washington, DC 20005   Phone: (202)833-7000
Membership: AFL-CIO. **Publications:** *IBEW Journal*, monthly.

★6025★
Utility Workers Union of America (UWUA)
815 16th St. NW, Ste. 605
Washington, DC 20006   Phone: (202)347-8105
Membership: AFL-CIO. **Purpose:** Sponsors ten educational conferences each year for local officers. Maintains library. **Publications:** *Light*, monthly. **Facsimile Number:** (202)347-4872.

Standards/Certification Agencies

Operators of nuclear powerplants are licensed by the Nuclear Regulatory Commission (NRC). Extensive training and experience are necessary to pass the NRC's examination for licensed reactor operator, including on-the-job training, classroom instruction, and individual study.

Test Guides

★6026★
Assistant Power Plant Operator
National Learning Corp.
212 Michael Dr.
Syosset, NY 11791   Phone: (516)921-8888
Jack Rudman. Part of the Career Examination Series No. 1. All examination guides in this series contain questions with answers. **Facsimile Number:** (516)921-8743. **Toll-free/Additional Phone Number(s):** 800-645-6337.

★6027★
Foreman (Power Distribution)
National Learning Corp.
212 Michael Dr.
Syosset, NY 11791   Phone: (516)921-8888
Jack Rudman. Part of the Career Examination Series No. 1. All examination guides in this series contain questions with answers. **Facsimile Number:** (516)921-8743. **Toll-free/Additional Phone Number(s):** 800-645-6337.

★6028★
High Pressure Plant Tender
National Learning Corp.
212 Michael Dr.
Syosset, NY 11791   Phone: (516)921-8888
Jack Rudman. Part of the Career Examination Series No. 1. All examination guides in this series contain questions with answers. **Facsimile Number:** (516)921-8743. **Toll-free/Additional Phone Number(s):** 800-645-6337.

★6029★
Power Plant Operator
National Learning Corp.
212 Michael Dr.
Syosset, NY 11791   Phone: (516)921-8888
Jack Rudman. Part of the Career Examination Series No. 1. All examination guides in this series contain questions with answers. **Facsimile Number:** (516)921-8743. **Toll-free/Additional Phone Number(s):** 800-645-6337.

★6030★
Stationary Engineer, High Pressure Boiler Operating Engineer, High Pressure Plant Tender
Prentice Hall Press
Simon & Schuster Inc.
200 Old Tappan Rd.
Old Tappan, NJ 07675   Phone: (800)223-2348
Harry Mahler. Sixth edition, 1986. Complete preparation for civil service and certification exams. Includes 12 sample exams and tips to help readers raise their test scores. Includes a special section on boiler operation.

Basic Reference Guides and Handbooks

★6031★
Electric Power Surveys
Edison Electric Institute (EEI)
701 Pennsylvania Ave. NW
Washington, DC 20004-2696   Phone: (202)508-5000

★6032★
Industrial Load Management: Theory, Practice, & Simulations
Elsevier Science Publishing Company, Inc.
655 Avenue of the Americas
New York, NY 10010   Phone: (212)989-5800
C. O. Bjork. 1989. Part of Energy Research Series.

★6033★
Interconnection Products Directory
Connector Study Group, Inc.
104 Wilmot Rd., Ste. 201
Deerfield, IL 60015-5195   Phone: (312)940-8800
Gerald L. Ginsberg, editor. Biennial, November of odd years. More than 500 manufacturers, distributors, representatives, sales offices, and other suppliers to the electrical and electronics industry worldwide, including suppliers of connectors, wire, and cable (part 1); printed circuit products (part 2); circular rack and panel products (part 3); wire and cable products (part 4); materials (part 5); and military products (part 6). Entries include: Name, address, products, whether catalog is available. Arrangement: Classified by product. Indexes: Product.

── Periodicals ──

★6034★
EGSA Powerline
Electrical Generating Systems Association (EGSA)
10251-A W. Sample Rd.
PO Box 9257
Coral Springs, FL 33065   Phone: (305)755-2677
Editor(s): Gordon Johnson. Bimonthly. Contains news of the association and articles on technological and legislative developments, new standards, and unusual applications for generator sets. Recurring features include news of members, news of research, convention and committee reports, and columns titled Industry News and People On the Move. **Facsimile Number:** (305)755-2679.

★6035★
Electric Light & Power
PennWell Publishing Co.
1250 S. Grove Ave., Ste. 302
Barrington, IL 60010   Phone: (708)382-2450
Robert A. Lincicome, Editor. Monthly. Tabloid providing news of electric utility industry developments and activities and coverage of new products and technology. **Facsimile Number:** (708)382-2977.

★6036★
Electric Perspectives (EEI)
Edison Electric Institute (EEI)
701 Pennsylvania Ave. NW
Washington, DC 20004-2696   Phone: (202)508-5000
Bimonthly.

★6037★
Electrical Reports (EEI)
Edison Electric Institute (EEI)
701 Pennsylvania Ave. NW
Washington, DC 20004-2696   Phone: (202)508-5000
Weekly.

★6038★
Electrical Women's Round Table—National Newsletter (EWRT)
Electrical Women's Round Table (EWRT)
PO Box 292793
Nashville, TN 37229-2793   Phone: (615)254-4479
Quarterly. Membership newsletter concerned with efficient use of electrical energy from an administrative standpoint.

★6039★
Electrical World
McGraw-Hill, Inc.
11 W. 19th St.
New York, NY 10011   Phone: (212)337-4072
Robert G. Schwieger, Editorial Director. Monthly. Trade magazine on the business of generating, transmitting, and distributing electric power. **Facsimile Number:** (212)627-3811.

★6040★
Electronic and Electrical Equipment
National Safety Council
444 N. Michigan Ave.
Chicago, IL 60611   Phone: (312)527-4800
Editor(s): Katie Kuhfuss. 6/yr. Provides safety tips for persons who work with electronic and electrical equipment. Promotes and reports on training courses in accident prevention, safety precautions, and compliance with safety regulations. Also carries items on safety awareness off the job.

★6041★
Marketer
Electrical Generating Systems Association (EGSA)
10251-A W. Sample Rd.
Coral Springs, FL 33065   Phone: (305)755-2677
Editor(s): Tony Raucci. Bimonthly. Offers a broad range of technical papers on issues pertaining to the on-site power generation industry and serves as a principal means of communication for the association and its members. Recurring features include letters to the editor, news of members, a calendar of events, and a section titled Industry News.

★6042★
Nuclear Plant Journal
799 Roosevelt Rd., Bldg. 6, Ste. 208
Glen Ellyn, IL 60137   Phone: (708)858-6161
Newal K. Agnihotri, Editor and Publisher. 7x/yr. Magazine focusing on nuclear power plants. **Facsimile Number:** (708)858-8787.

★6043★
Nucleonics Week
McGraw-Hill, Inc.
1120 Vermont Ave. NW, Ste. 1200
Washington, DC 20005   Phone: (202)463-1651
Margaret L. Ryan, Editor. Weekly. Newsletter covering commercial nuclear power business. **Facsimile Number:** (202)463-1611.

★6044★
Rural Electrification Magazine
National Rural Electric Cooperative Assn.
1800 Massachusetts Ave. NW
Washington, DC 20036   Phone: (202)857-9500
J.C. Brown, Jr., Publisher. Monthly. Magazine for directors and employees of rural electric cooperatives. **Facsimile Number:** (202)857-9791.

Electric Power Generating Plant Operators and Power Distributors and Dispatchers ★6049★

★6045★
Ruralite
Ruralite Services, Inc.
PO Box 558
Forest Grove, OR 97116   Phone: (503)357-2105
Rod O'Dell, Editor. Monthly. Magazine serving specific consumer-owned utilities in Alaska, Washington, Oregon, California, Idaho, and Nevada. Published in 52 local editions. **Facsimile Number:** (503)357-8615.

★6046★
Southwest Contractor
McGraw Hill Publishing Co., Inc.
2050 E. University Dr., Ste. 1
Phoenix, AZ 85034-6731   Phone: (602)230-0598
Elaine Beall, Mng. Editor. Monthly. Regional trade magazine for the contracting industries including highway, municipal, utility, and heavy construction, and mining. **Facsimile Number:** (602)495-9407.

─────── Meetings and Conventions ───────

★6047★
Edison Electric Institute (EEI)
701 Pennsylvania Ave. NW
Washington, DC 20004-2696   Phone: (202)508-5000
Frequency: Annual. 1992; Jun. 1-3; Columbus, OH • 1993; Jun. 7-9; Charlotte, NC • 1994 Jun. 13-15; Seattle, WA.

★6048★
POWER-GEN
PennWell Conferences and Exhibitions Co.
3050 Post Oak Blvd., Ste. 200
Houston, TX 77056   Phone: (713)621-9720
• 1992; Orlando, FL • 1993; Nov. Dallas, TX • 1994; Orlando, FL • 1995; Anaheim, CA • 1996; Orlando, FL • 1997; Dallas, TX • 1998; Orlando, FL. **Facsimile Number:** (713)963-6284.

─────── Other Sources of Information ───────

★6049★
Application Procedures for Hydropower Licenses, License Amendments, Exemptions and Preliminary Permits
Public Reference Section
Federal Energy Regulatory Commission
825 N. Capitol St., N.E., Rm. 1000
Washington, DC 20426   Phone: (202)208-0118
Irregular; previous edition summer 1983; latest edition December 1985. List of offices of over 500 governmental agencies at the federal, regional, state, and local levels that may be consulted as part of the application procedure for hydropower licenses. Entries include: Agency name, address, phone, title of contact. Arrangement: By agency, then geographical.

Stationary Engineers

Stationary engineers operate and maintain equipment to provide heating, air-conditioning, and ventilation. This can include boilers, air-conditioning and refrigeration equipment, diesel engines, turbines, generators, pumps, condensers, and compressors. Engineers might also direct the work of assistant stationary engineers, turbine operators, boiler tenders, and air-conditioning and refrigeration operators and mechanics. These workers are called stationary engineers because much of the equipment they operate is similar to the equipment operated by locomotive or marine engineers except that it is not a moving vehicle. They work in a variety of places, including office and apartment buildings, hospitals, schools, factories, shopping malls, and hotels.

$alaries

Weekly earnings for stationary engineers are as follows:

Lowest 10 percent	$271.00/week or less
Middle 50 percent	$374.00—$657.00/week
Top 10 percent	$789.00/week or more

Employment Outlook

Growth rate until the year 2000: Employment is expected to remain level.

Stationary Engineers

Career Guides

★6050★
Stationary Engineer
Careers, Inc.
PO Box 135
Largo, FL 34649-0135   Phone: (813)584-7333
1992. Eight-page brief offering the definition, history, duties, working conditions, personal qualifications, educational requirements, earnings, hours, employment outlook, advancement possibilities, and related occupations.

★6051★
"Stationary Engineer" in *Hard Hatted Women: Stories of Struggle and Success in the Trades* (pp. 37-44)
Seal Press
3131 Western Ave., Ste. 410
Seattle, WA 98121   Phone: (206)283-7844
Molly Martin, editor. 1988. Twenty-six women recount their experiences working in blue collar occupations. They describe how they got in, the work they do, their relationships in predominantly male occupations, and their training.

★6052★
"Stationary Engineer" in *Manufacturing*, Volume 9 of *Career Information Center* (pp. 70-72)
Glencoe/Macmillan
15319 Chatsworth St.
Mission Hills, CA 91345   Phone: (818)898-1391
Richard Lidz and Dale Anderson, editorial directors. Fourth edition, 1990. For 600 occupations, describes job duties, entry-level requirements, education and training needed, advancement possibilities, employment outlook, earnings and benefits. The set is divided into 12 volumes. Each volume includes jobs related under a broad career field. Volume 13 is the index. **Facsimile Number:** 818-365-5489.

★6053★
"Stationary Engineer" in *Occu-Facts: Information on 565 Careers in Outline Form* (p. 17.32)
Careers, Inc.
P.O. Box 135
1211 Tenth St., S.W.
Largo, FL 33640   Phone: (813)584-7333
Elizabeth Handville. Biennial, 1989-90 edition. Each one-page occupational profile describes duties, working conditions, physical surroundings and demands, aptitudes, temperament, educational requirements, employment outlook, earnings, and places of employment.

★6054★
"Stationary Engineers" in *Occupational Outlook Handbook* (pp. 407-408)
Superintendent of Documents
U.S. Government Printing Office
Washington, DC 20402   Phone: (202)783-3238
Biennial; latest edition, 1990-91. Encyclopedia of careers describing more than 250 occupations and comprising about 86 percent of all jobs in the economy. Occupations that require lengthy education or training are given the most attention. For each occupation, the handbook describes job duties, working conditions, training, educational preparation, personal qualities, advancement possibilities, job outlook, earnings, and sources of additional information.

★6055★
"Stationary Engineers" in Volume 3 of *The Encyclopedia of Careers and Vocational Guidance* (pp. 777-780)
J.G. Ferguson Publishing Co.
200 W. Monroe
Chicago, IL 60606   Phone: (312)580-5480
William E. Hopke, editor-in-chief. Eighth edition, 1990. Four-volume set that profiles 500 occupations and describes job trends in 76 industries. Includes career description, educational requirements, history of the job, methods of entry, advancement, employment outlook, earnings, working conditions, social and psychological factors, and sources of additional information.

★6056★
Video Career Library - Production I
Careers, Inc.
1211 10th St., SW
PO Box 135
Largo, FL 34649-0135   Phone: (813)584-7333
Videocassette. 1990. 28 mins. Part of the Video Career Library covering 165 occupations. Shows actual workers on the job. Includes layout workers, precision typesetters, lithographers/photoengravers, bookbinders, hand tailors/dressmakers, upholsterers, water/sewage plant operators, chemical plant operators, and power plant operators.

Associations

★6057★
International Union of Operating Engineers (IUOE)
1125 17th St., NW
Washington, DC 20036   Phone: (202)429-9100
Membership: AFL-CIO. **Publications:** *International Operating Engineer*, monthly.

★6058★
National Association of Power Engineers (NAPE)
2350 E. Devon Ave., Ste. 115
Des Plaines, IL 60018   Phone: (718)298-0600
Membership: Professional society of power and stationary engineers; associate members are sales engineers and teachers of any phase of engineering. **Purpose:** Areas of interest include air conditioning, compressed air, electric power, refrigeration, steam, and water. Promotes education in the power engineering areas. Secures and enforces engineers' license laws to prevent the destruction of life and property in the generation and transmission of power and for the conservation of fuel resources of the nation. **Publications:** *NAPE Directory*, annual. • *National Engineer*, monthly. • Also publishes pamphlets and educational material. **Facsimile Number:** (718)298-1545.

Standards/Certification Agencies

Most stationary engineers acquire their skills through a formal apprenticeship program or through informal on-the-job training which usually is supplemented by courses at trade or technical schools. Apprenticeship programs are sponsored by local labor-management apprenticeship committees of the International Union of Operating Engineers, the principal union to which stationary engineers belong. The apprenticeship usually lasts four years. In addition to on-the-job training, apprentices receive classroom instruction. Those who acquire their skills on the job usually start as helpers to experienced stationary engineers or as boiler tenders. However, becoming a stationary engineer without going through a formal apprenticeship program usually requires many years of work experience. Most states and cities have licensing requirements for stationary engineers. Although requirements differ from place to place, applicants usually must be at least 18 years of age, reside for a specified period in the state or locality, meet the experience requirements for the class of license requested, and pass a written examination. Because of regional differences in licensing requirements, a stationary engineer who moves from one state or city to another may have to pass an examination for a new license. Generally, there are several classes of stationary engineer licenses. Each class specifies the type of equipment or the steam pressure or horsepower of the equipment the engineer can operate without supervision. A first-class license permits the stationary engineer to operate equipment of all types and capacities. Lower class licenses limit the types of capacities of equipment the engineer may operate without the supervision of a higher rated engineer.

Test Guides

★6059★
Chief Stationary Engineer
National Learning Corp.
212 Michael Dr.
Syosset, NY 11791   Phone: (516)921-8888
Jack Rudman. Part of the Career Examination Series No. 1. All examination guides in this series contain questions with answers. **Facsimile Number:** (516)921-8743. **Toll-free/Additional Phone Number(s):** 800-645-6337.

★6060★
Incinerator Stationary Engineer
National Learning Corp.
212 Michael Dr.
Syosset, NY 11791   Phone: (516)921-8888
Jack Rudman. Part of the Career Examination Series No. 1. All examination guides in this series contain questions with answers. **Facsimile Number:** (516)921-8743. **Toll-free/Additional Phone Number(s):** 800-645-6337.

★6061★
Principal Stationary Engineer
National Learning Corp.
212 Michael Dr.
Syosset, NY 11791   Phone: (516)921-8888
Jack Rudman. Part of the Career Examination Series No. 1. All examination guides in this series contain questions with answers. **Facsimile Number:** (516)921-8743. **Toll-free/Additional Phone Number(s):** 800-645-6337.

★6062★
Senior Incinerator Stationary Engineer
National Learning Corp.
212 Michael Dr.
Syosset, NY 11791   Phone: (516)921-8888
Jack Rudman. Part of the Career Examination Series No. 1. All examination guides in this series contain questions with answers. **Facsimile Number:** (516)921-8743. **Toll-free/Additional Phone Number(s):** 800-645-6337.

★6063★
Senior Stationary Engineer
National Learning Corp.
212 Michael Dr.
Syosset, NY 11791   Phone: (516)921-8888
Jack Rudman. Part of the Career Examination Series No. 1. All examination guides in this series contain questions with answers. **Facsimile Number:** (516)921-8743. **Toll-free/Additional Phone Number(s):** 800-645-6337.

★6064★
Senior Stationary Engineer (Electric)
National Learning Corp.
212 Michael Dr.
Syosset, NY 11791   Phone: (516)921-8888
Jack Rudman. Part of the Career Examination Series No. 1. All examination guides in this series contain questions with answers. **Facsimile Number:** (516)921-8743. **Toll-free/Additional Phone Number(s):** 800-645-6337.

★6065★
Stationary Engineer
National Learning Corp.
212 Michael Dr.
Syosset, NY 11791   Phone: (516)921-8888
Jack Rudman. Part of the Career Examination Series No. 1. All examination guides in this series contain questions with answers. **Facsimile Number:** (516)921-8743. **Toll-free/Additional Phone Number(s):** 800-645-6337.

★6066★
Stationary Engineer (Electric)
National Learning Corp.
212 Michael Dr.
Syosset, NY 11791   Phone: (516)921-8888
Jack Rudman. Part of the Career Examination Series No. 1. All examination guides in this series contain questions with answers. **Facsimile Number:** (516)921-8743. **Toll-free/Additional Phone Number(s):** 800-645-6337.

Stationary Engineers

★6067★
Stationary Engineer, High Pressure Boiler Operating Engineer, High Pressure Plant Tender
Prentice Hall Press
Simon & Schuster Inc.
200 Old Tappan Rd.
Old Tappan, NJ 07675   Phone: (800)223-2348
Harry Mahler. Sixth edition, 1986. Complete preparation for civil service and certification exams. Includes 12 sample exams and tips to help readers raise their test scores. Includes a special section on boiler operation.

Periodicals

★6068★
National Engineer **(NAPE)**
National Association of Power Engineers (NAPE)
2350 E. Devon Ave., Ste. 115
Des Plaines, IL 60018   Phone: (718)298-0600
Monthly. Association and industry newsletter.

Meetings and Conventions

★6069★
Heating, Ventilation, and Air Conditioning Product and Equipment Show
Institute of Heating and Air Conditioning Industries
606 N. Larchmont Blvd., Ste. 4A
Los Angeles, CA 90004   Phone: (213)467-1158

★6070★
International Air-Conditioning, Heating, Refrigerating Exposition
International Exposition Co.
200 Park Ave.
New York, NY 10166   Phone: (212)986-4232
1993; Jan. 25-28; Chicago, IL • 1994; Jan. 24-26; New Orleans, LA. **Facsimile Number:** (212)682-8982.

★6071★
International District Heating and Cooling Association Convention
International District Heating and Cooling Association
1101 Connecticut Ave., NW, Ste. 700
Washington, DC 20036   Phone: (202)429-5111
1992; Jun. 18-22; Danvers, MA. **Facsimile Number:** (204)223-4579.

★6072★
REVAC - Refrigeration, Ventilation, Air-Conditioning, and Heating Exhibition
World Access Corp.
15 Bemis Rd.
PO Box 171
Wellesley Hills, MA 02181   Phone: (617)235-8095
Facsimile Number: (617)235-7360.

Water and Wastewater Treatment Plant Operators

Water treatment plant operators treat water so that it is safe to drink. Wastewater treatment plant operators remove harmful domestic and industrial pollution from wastewater. Operators in both types of plants control processes and equipment to remove solid materials, chemicals, and micro-organisms from the water or to render them harmless. By operating and maintaining the pumps, valves, and processing equipment of the treatment facility, operators move the water or wastewater through the various treatment processes. Water and wastewater treatment plant operators work for local governments; some work for private water supply and sanitary services companies, many of which provide operation and management services to local governments on a contract basis.

$alaries

Annual salaries for wastewater treatment plant operators are as follows:

Wastewater treatment plant operators	$21,300/year
Wastewater treatment plant supervisors	$27,200/year

Employment Outlook

Growth rate until the year 2000: Average.

Water and Wastewater Treatment Plant Operators

Career Guides

★6073★
Career Profiles: Environmental Series
Cambridge Career Products
90 MacCorkle Ave., SW
South Charleston, WV 25311   Phone: (304)744-9323
Videocassette. 1989. 15 mins. Environmental careers of all sorts are examined, including grounds and turf management, landscaping, and wastewater treatment plant operator.

★6074★
Video Career Library - Production I
Careers, Inc.
1211 10th St., SW
PO Box 135
Largo, FL 34649-0135   Phone: (813)584-7333
Videocassette. 1990. 28 mins. Part of the Video Career Library covering 165 occupations. Shows actual workers on the job. Includes layout workers, precision typesetters, lithographers/photoengravers, bookbinders, hand tailors/dressmakers, upholsterers, water/sewage plant operators, chemical plant operators, and power plant operators.

★6075★
Wastewater Treatment Plant Operators
Chronicle Guidance Publications, Inc.
PO Box 1190
Moravia, NY 13118-1190   Phone: (315)497-0330
1990. This career brief describes the nature of the work, working conditions, hours and earnings, education and training, licensure, certification, unions, personal qualifications, social and psychological factors, employment outlook, entry methods, advancement, and related occupations. **Toll-free/Additional Phone Number(s):** 800-622-7284.

★6076★
"Wastewater Treatment Plant Operators" in Volume 3 of *The Encyclopedia of Careers and Vocational Guidance* (pp. 797-801)
J.G. Ferguson Publishing Co.
200 W. Monroe
Chicago, IL 60606   Phone: (312)580-5480
William E. Hopke, editor-in-chief. Eighth edition, 1990. Four-volume set that profiles 500 occupations and describes job trends in 76 industries. Includes career description, educational requirements, history of the job, methods of entry, advancement, employment outlook, earnings, working conditions, social and psychological factors, and sources of additional information.

★6077★
"Water and Wastewater-Treatment Plant Operators" in *Occupational Outlook Handbook* (pp. 409-410)
Superintendent of Documents
U.S. Government Printing Office
Washington, DC 20402   Phone: (202)783-3238
Biennial; latest edition, 1990-91. Encyclopedia of careers describing more than 250 occupations and comprising about 86 percent of all jobs in the economy. Occupations that require lengthy education or training are given the most attention. For each occupation, the handbook describes job duties, working conditions, training, educational preparation, personal qualities, advancement possibilities, job outlook, earnings, and sources of additional information.

★6078★
"Water and Wastewater Treatment Plant Operators" in Volume 6 of *Career Discovery Encyclopedia* (pp. 154-155)
J.G. Ferguson Publishing Co.
200 W. Monroe
Chicago, IL 60606   Phone: (312)580-5480
E. Russell Primm, editor-in-chief. 1990. Contains two-page articles on 504 occupations. Each article describes job duties, earnings, and educational and training requirements.

★6079★
Water/Wastewater Operator
Vocational Biographies, Inc.
PO Box 31, Dept. VF10
Sauk Centre, MN 56378   Phone: (612)352-6516
1989. This pamphlet profiles a person working in the job. Includes information about job duties, working conditions, places of employment, educational preparation, labor market outlook, and salaries. **Toll-free/Additional Phone Number(s):** 800-255-0752.

Associations

★6080★
Association of Boards of Certification (ABC)
426 1/2 5th St.
PO Box 786
Ames, IA 50010-0786   Phone: (515)232-3623
Membership: Governmental certification authorities for water utilities and pollution control operating personnel and laboratories, including those that deal with hazardous wastes. **Purpose:** Seeks to strengthen state certification laws, their administration and effectiveness, and to establish uniform certification requirements among members. Promotes

certification as a means to more efficient operation of public utilities; assists newly-created boards in implementing certification programs. Conducts uniform program for reciprocity, wherein certified operators are recognized as such by member boards after passing a standardized test produced by the ABC. Maintains speakers' bureau and biographical archives; compiles statistics; bestows awards. **Publications:** *Certifier*, monthly. • *Directory of Certification and Training Contacts*, periodic. • *Membership Directory*, annual. • Also publishes certification tests, test manuals, and books on water and waste treatment. **Facsimile Number:** (515)232-3778.

★6081★
Water Pollution Control Federation (WPCF)
601 Wythe St.
Alexandria, VA 22314-1994   Phone: (703)684-2400
Membership: Technical societies representing municipal engineers, consulting engineers, public health engineers, water pollution control works superintendents, chemists, operators, educational and research personnel, industrial wastewater engineers, municipal officials, equipment manufacturers, and university professors and students dedicated to the ehancement and preservation of water quality and resources. **Purpose:** Seeks to advance fundamental and practical knowledge concerning the nature, collection, treatment, and disposal of domestic and industrial wastewaters, and the design, construction, operation, and management of facilities for these purposes. Disseminates technical information; promotes good public relations and regulations that improve water pollution control and the status of individuals working in this field. Maintains job bank for wastewater facility employees; conducts educational programs. Sponsors High School Science Fair National Award. Maintains library of 6000 volumes on water pollution and related topics. **Publications:** *The Bench Sheet*, bimonthly. • *Highlights*, monthly. • *Job Bank*, biweekly. • *Literature Review*, annual. • *Operations Forum*, monthly. • *Research Journal Water Pollution Control Federation*, bimonthly. • *Safety and Health Bulletin*, quarterly. • *Washington Bulletin*, monthly. • *Water, Environment, and Technology*, monthly. • Also publishes training materials including *Manuals of Practice*, public education brochures, and a water quality curriculum for schoolchildren. **Toll-free/Additional Phone Number(s):** (800)556-8700 (United States only) **Facsimile Number:** (703)684-2492.

───── **Standards/Certification Agencies** ─────

Some two-year programs leading to an associate degree in wastewater technology and one-year programs leading to a certificate are available; these provide a good general knowledge of water pollution control as well as basic preparation for becoming an operator. In 47 states, operators must pass an examination to certify that they are capable of overseeing wastewater treatment plant operators. Voluntary certification programs are in effect in the remaining states. Water plant operators must be certified in 45 states. Of the remaining states, two have voluntary certification programs, and three do not have any certification requirements. The District of Columbia does not require certification for either water or wastewater treatment plant operators. Typically, there are different classes of certification for different size treatment plants, and certification requirements vary by state. An operator's certification is usually valid for several years; at the end of the time period, the operator must renew the certification. Relocation may mean having to become certified in a new location. However, several states have begun their own reciprocity programs.

★6082★
Association of Boards of Certification (ABC)
426 1/2 5th St.
PO Box 786
Ames, IA 50010-0786   Phone: (515)232-3623
Seeks to strengthen state certification laws, their administration and effectiveness, and to establish uniform certification requirements among members. Promotes certification as a means to more efficient operation of public utilities; assists newly-created boards in implementing certification programs. Conducts uniform program for reciprocity, wherein certified operators are recognized as such by member boards after passing a standardized test produced by the ABC. **Publications:** *Certifier*, monthly. • *Directory of Certification and Training Contacts*, periodic. • *Membership Directory*, annual. • Also publishes certification tests, test manuals, and books on water and waste treatment.

★6083★
Reciprocity Equivalency Chart
Association of Boards of Certification
Environmental Occupations
PO Box 786
Ames, IA 50010-0786   Phone: (515)232-3623
Chart listing states requiring licensing of water and wastewater treatment plant operators.

★6084★
Uniform Program for Reciprocity: Operators
Association of Boards of Certification
Environmental Occupations
PO Box 786
Ames, IA 50010-0786   Phone: (515)232-3623
1991. This two-page pamphlet explains the national certification program for water and wastewater treatment plant operators and certification recognition reciprocity by states belonging to the Association of Boards of Certification.

───── **Test Guides** ─────

★6085★
Assistant Water Maintenance Foreman
National Learning Corp.
212 Michael Dr.
Syosset, NY 11791   Phone: (516)921-8888
Jack Rudman. Part of the Career Examination Series No. 1. All examination guides in this series contain questions with answers. **Facsimile Number:** (516)921-8743. **Toll-free/Additional Phone Number(s):** 800-645-6337.

★6086★
Chief Sewage Treatment Plant Operator
National Learning Corp.
212 Michael Dr.
Syosset, NY 11791   Phone: (516)921-8888
Jack Rudman. Part of the Career Examination Series No. 1. All examination guides in this series contain questions with answers. **Facsimile Number:** (516)921-8743. **Toll-free/Additional Phone Number(s):** 800-645-6337.

★6087★
Chief Water Treatment Plant Operator
National Learning Corp.
212 Michael Dr.
Syosset, NY 11791   Phone: (516)921-8888
Jack Rudman. Part of the Career Examination Series No. 1. All examination guides in this series contain questions with answers.

Water and Wastewater Treatment Plant Operators ★6100★

Facsimile Number: (516)921-8743. **Toll-free/Additional Phone Number(s):** 800-645-6337.

★6088★
Directory of Certification and Training Contacts (ABC)
Association of Boards of Certification (ABC)
426 1/2 5th St.
PO Box 786
Ames, IA 50010-0786   Phone: (515)232-3623
Periodic. Lists state and provincial certification and training contacts in the fields of distribution and collection of water and waste water and industrial waste treatment.

★6089★
Principal Water Plant Supervisor
National Learning Corp.
212 Michael Dr.
Syosset, NY 11791   Phone: (516)921-8888
Jack Rudman. Part of the Career Examination Series No. 1. All examination guides in this series contain questions with answers.
Facsimile Number: (516)921-8743. **Toll-free/Additional Phone Number(s):** 800-645-6337.

★6090★
Sanitation Worker
Prentice Hall Press
Simon & Schuster Inc.
200 Old Tappan Rd.
Old Tappan, NJ 07675   Phone: (800)223-2348
Hy Hammer. Sixth edition, 1983. Contains ten previous tests for practice; includes section on training for physical tests.

★6091★
Senior Sewage Treatment Plant Operator
National Learning Corp.
212 Michael Dr.
Syosset, NY 11791   Phone: (516)921-8888
Jack Rudman. Part of the Career Examination Series No. 1. All examination guides in this series contain questions with answers.
Facsimile Number: (516)921-8743. **Toll-free/Additional Phone Number(s):** 800-645-6337.

★6092★
Senior Sewage Treatment Worker
National Learning Corp.
212 Michael Dr.
Syosset, NY 11791   Phone: (516)921-8888
Jack Rudman. Part of the Career Examination Series No. 1. All examination guides in this series contain questions with answers.
Facsimile Number: (516)921-8743. **Toll-free/Additional Phone Number(s):** 800-645-6337.

★6093★
Senior Water Plant Operator
National Learning Corp.
212 Michael Dr.
Syosset, NY 11791   Phone: (516)921-8888
Jack Rudman. Part of the Career Examination Series No. 1. All examination guides in this series contain questions with answers.
Facsimile Number: (516)921-8743. **Toll-free/Additional Phone Number(s):** 800-645-6337.

★6094★
Senior Water Plant Supervisor
National Learning Corp.
212 Michael Dr.
Syosset, NY 11791   Phone: (516)921-8888
Jack Rudman. Part of the Career Examination Series No. 1. All examination guides in this series contain questions with answers.

Facsimile Number: (516)921-8743. **Toll-free/Additional Phone Number(s):** 800-645-6337.

★6095★
Sewage Plant Operations Supervisor
National Learning Corp.
212 Michael Dr.
Syosset, NY 11791   Phone: (516)921-8888
Jack Rudman. Part of the Career Examination Series No. 1. All examination guides in this series contain questions with answers.
Facsimile Number: (516)921-8743. **Toll-free/Additional Phone Number(s):** 800-645-6337.

★6096★
Sewage Plant Operator
National Learning Corp.
212 Michael Dr.
Syosset, NY 11791   Phone: (516)921-8888
Jack Rudman. Part of the Career Examination Series No. 1. All examination guides in this series contain questions with answers.
Facsimile Number: (516)921-8743. **Toll-free/Additional Phone Number(s):** 800-645-6337.

★6097★
Sewage Pump Operator
National Learning Corp.
212 Michael Dr.
Syosset, NY 11791   Phone: (516)921-8888
Jack Rudman. Part of the Career Examination Series No. 1. All examination guides in this series contain questions with answers.
Facsimile Number: (516)921-8743. **Toll-free/Additional Phone Number(s):** 800-645-6337.

★6098★
Sewage Treatment Operator
National Learning Corp.
212 Michael Dr.
Syosset, NY 11791   Phone: (516)921-8888
Jack Rudman. Part of the Career Examination Series No. 1. All examination guides in this series contain questions with answers.
Facsimile Number: (516)921-8743. **Toll-free/Additional Phone Number(s):** 800-645-6337.

★6099★
Sewage Treatment Operator Trainee
National Learning Corp.
212 Michael Dr.
Syosset, NY 11791   Phone: (516)921-8888
Jack Rudman. Part of the Career Examination Series No. 1. All examination guides in this series contain questions with answers.
Facsimile Number: (516)921-8743. **Toll-free/Additional Phone Number(s):** 800-645-6337.

★6100★
Sewage Treatment Plant Supervisor
National Learning Corp.
212 Michael Dr.
Syosset, NY 11791   Phone: (516)921-8888
Jack Rudman. Part of the Career Examination Series No. 1. All examination guides in this series contain questions with answers.
Facsimile Number: (516)921-8743. **Toll-free/Additional Phone Number(s):** 800-645-6337.

★6101★
Sewage Treatment Worker
National Learning Corp.
212 Michael Dr.
Syosset, NY 11791　　　　　　　Phone: (516)921-8888
Jack Rudman. Part of the Career Examination Series No. 1. All examination guides in this series contain questions with answers. **Facsimile Number:** (516)921-8743. **Toll-free/Additional Phone Number(s):** 800-645-6337.

★6102★
Sewage Treatment Worker Trainee
National Learning Corp.
212 Michael Dr.
Syosset, NY 11791　　　　　　　Phone: (516)921-8888
Jack Rudman. Part of the Career Examination Series No. 1. All examination guides in this series contain questions with answers. **Facsimile Number:** (516)921-8743. **Toll-free/Additional Phone Number(s):** 800-645-6337.

★6103★
Wastewater Treatment Plant Supervisor
National Learning Corp.
212 Michael Dr.
Syosset, NY 11791　　　　　　　Phone: (516)921-8888
Jack Rudman. Part of the Career Examination Series No. 1. All examination guides in this series contain questions with answers. **Facsimile Number:** (516)921-8743. **Toll-free/Additional Phone Number(s):** 800-645-6337.

★6104★
WPCF Manuals of Practice
Water Pollution Control Federation (WPCF)
601 Wythe St.
Alexandria, VA 22314-1994　　　　Phone: (703)684-2400

Awards, Scholarships, Grants, and Fellowships

★6105★
William D. Hatfield Award
Water Pollution Control Federation
c/o Mary C. Smith
601 Wythe St.
Alexandria, VA 22314　　　　　　Phone: (703)684-2400
To recognize outstanding operation of a wastewater treatment plant. Members of the Federation are eligible. A certificate is awarded annually. Established in 1946.

Periodicals

★6106★
The Bench Sheet
Water Pollution Control Federation (WPCF)
601 Wythe St.
Alexandria, VA 22314-1994　　　　Phone: (703)684-2400
Bimonthly. Newsletter.

★6107★
Certifier
Association of Boards of Certification (ABC)
426 1/2 5th St.
PO Box 786
Ames, IA 50010-0786　　　　　　Phone: (515)232-3623
Monthly. Association and industry newsletter for operators and laboratory analysts involved in certification programs for distribution and collection of water and waste water and industrial waste treatment.

★6108★
Clean Water Report
Business Publishers, Inc.
951 Pershing Dr.
Silver Spring, MD 20910　　　　　Phone: (301)587-6300
Editor(s): Elaine Eiserer. Biweekly. Provides information on water pollution control, drinking water supply and safety, and water resources issues. Covers national policy, legislation, regulations, enforcement and litigation, and state and local news.

★6109★
Environmental Science & Engineering
Davcom Communications Inc.
10 Petch Cr.
Aurora, ON, Canada L4G 5N7　　　Phone: (416)727-4666
Tom Davey, Editor. 6x/yr. Magazine on water, sewage, and pollution control. **Facsimile Number:** (416)841-7271.

★6110★
From the State Capitals: Water Supply
Wakeman/Walworth, Inc.
300 N. Washington St., Ste. 204
Alexandria, VA 22314　　　　　　Phone: (703)549-8606
Editor(s): Keyes Walworth. Monthly. Analyzes state and municipal legislative and regulatory trends affecting water supply. Covers subjects such as the construction and financing of reservoirs and treatment plants, pollution controls, water development rights, and irrigation projects. **Facsimile Number:** (703)549-1372.

★6111★
Journal American Water Works Association
American Water Works Assn.
6666 W. Quincy Ave.
Denver, CO 80235　　　　　　　Phone: (303)794-7711
Monthly. Magazine dealing with water supply, treatment, quality, and distribution. **Facsimile Number:** (303)794-7310.

★6112★
Operations Forum
Water Pollution Control Federation
601 Wythe St.
Alexandria, VA 22314-1994　　　　Phone: (703)684-2400
Lisa Preston, Mng. Editor. Monthly. Magazine covering water/wastewater technology for industry professionals.

★6113★
Pollution Engineering
Cahners Publishing Co.
Cahners Plaza
1350 E. Touhy Ave.
PO Box 5080
Des Plaines, IL 60017-5080　　　　Phone: (708)635-8800
Marie Hunter, Production Editor. Monthly. Magazine focusing on pollution control, air, water, solid waste, and toxic/hazardous waste. **Facsimile Number:** (708)390-2636.

★6114★
Research Journal of the Water Pollution Control Federation
Water Pollution Control Federation
601 Wythe St.
Alexandria, VA 22314 Phone: (703)684-2400
Pete R. Piecuch, Editor. 6x/yr. Technical journal covering municipal and industrial water pollution control, water quality, and hazardous wastes. **Facsimile Number:** (703)684-2492.

★6115★
Research Journal Water Pollution Control Federation (WPCF)
Water Pollution Control Federation (WPCF)
601 Wythe St.
Alexandria, VA 22314-1994 Phone: (703)684-2400
Bimonthly.

★6116★
Southwest & Texas Water Works Journal
American Water Works Assn., Southwest Section & Texas Section
306 E. Adams Ave.
PO Box 769
Temple, TX 76503 Phone: (817)778-1313
L.W. Morgan, Editor. Monthly. Magazine serving as forum for water/wastewater utilities organizations in Arkansas, Louisiana, Oklahoma, and Texas. **Facsimile Number:** (817)774-7677.

★6117★
Water & Pollution Control
AIS Communications Ltd.
145 Thames Rd. W.
Exeter, ON, Canada N0M 1S3 Phone: (519)235-2400
Amber Underwood, Editor. Six times/yr. Water, sewage and pollution control market trade magazine with municipal and industrial focus. **Facsimile Number:** (519)235-0795.

★6118★
Water & Wastes Digest
Scranton Gillette Communications, Inc.
380 Northwest Hwy.
Des Plaines, IL 60016 Phone: (312)298-6622
Gail Hanczar, Editor. 6x/yr. Magazine (tabloid) featuring product news for decision makers in the municipal and industrial water and water pollution control industries. **Facsimile Number:** (312)390-0408.

★6119★
Water Conditioning & Purification
Publicom Inc.
4651 N. 1st Ave., Ste. 101
Tucson, AZ 85718 Phone: (602)293-5446
Darlene J. Scheel, Editor. Monthly. Domestic and commercial water conditioning and purification magazine. **Facsimile Number:** (602)887-2383.

★6120★
Water, Environment, and Technology
Water Pollution Control Federation (WPCF)
601 Wythe St.
Alexandria, VA 22314-1994 Phone: (703)684-2400
Monthly.

★6121★
Water Research
Pergamon Press, Inc.
Maxwell House
Fairview Park
Elmsford, NY 10523 Phone: (914)592-7700
K.J. Ives, Editor. 12x/yr. Journal covering research in water pollution. **Facsimile Number:** (914)592-3625.

★6122★
Water Technology
National Trade Publications, Inc.
13 Century Hill Dr.
Latham, NY 12110 Phone: (518)783-1281
Shauwn Tomlinson, Editor. Monthly. Magazine focusing on water treatment. **Facsimile Number:** (518)783-1386.

★6123★
WPCF Highlights
Water Pollution Control Federation (WPCF)
601 Wythe St.
Alexandria, VA 22314-1994 Phone: (703)684-2400
Monthly. Newsletter.

★6124★
WPCF Job Bank
Water Pollution Control Federation (WPCF)
601 Wythe St.
Alexandria, VA 22314-1994 Phone: (703)684-2400
Biweekly.

★6125★
WPCF Safety and Health Bulletin
Water Pollution Control Federation (WPCF)
601 Wythe St.
Alexandria, VA 22314-1994 Phone: (703)684-2400
Quarterly.

★6126★
WPCF Washington Bulletin
Water Pollution Control Federation (WPCF)
601 Wythe St.
Alexandria, VA 22314-1994 Phone: (703)684-2400
Monthly.

―――――― Meetings and Conventions ――――――

★6127★
Annual Meeting and Exhibition of the Air and Waste Management Association
Air and Waste Management Association
PO Box 2861
Pittsburgh, PA 15230 Phone: (412)232-3444
1992; Jun. 21-26; Kansas City, MO • 1993; Jun. 20-25; Denver, CO • 1994; Jun. 19-24; Cincinnati, OH.

★6128★
Association of Boards of Certification (ABC)
426 1/2 5th St.
PO Box 786
Ames, IA 50010-0786 Phone: (515)232-3623
Frequency: Annual conference is always held in March. 1992; Banff, AB, Canada • 1993; Gainesville, FL. **Facsimile Number:** (515)232-3778.

Other Sources of Information

★6129★
WPCF Literature Review
Water Pollution Control Federation (WPCF)
601 Wythe St.
Alexandria, VA 22314-1994   Phone: (703)684-2400
Annual.

Printing Occupations

Bindery Workers

Bookbinding workers specialize in adjusting and preparing equipment to perform a particular task. In firms that do edition binding, workers bind books produced in large numbers or runs, while job binding workers bind books produced in smaller quantities. In firms that specialize in library binding, workers repair books and provide other specialized binding services to libraries. Pamphlet binding workers produce leaflets and folders, while manifold binding workers bind business forms such as ledgers and books of sales receipts. Blankbook binding workers bind blank pages to produce notebooks, checkbooks, address books, diaries, calendars, and note pads. Although some bindery workers are employed by large libraries and others work for book publishers, most jobs are in commercial printing plants. Bindery trade shops, which specialize in binding, are the second largest employer of bindery workers.

$alaries

Hourly earnings for bindery workers are as follows:

Inexperienced bindery workers	$3.35/hour
Journeymen level I bookbinders in unionized firms	$13.70/hour
Journeyman level II bookbinders in unionized firms	$9.65/hour

Employment Outlook

Growth rate until the year 2000: Average.

Bindery Workers

---— Career Guides ———

★6130★
**"Bindery Workers" in *Occupational Outlook Handbook*
 (pp. 411-414)**
Superintendent of Documents
U.S. Government Printing Office
Washington, DC 20402 Phone: (202)783-3238
Biennial; latest edition, 1990-91. Encyclopedia of careers describing more than 250 occupations and comprising about 86 percent of all jobs in the economy. Occupations that require lengthy education or training are given the most attention. For each occupation, the handbook describes job duties, working conditions, training, educational preparation, personal qualities, advancement possibilities, job outlook, earnings, and sources of additional information.

★6131★
**"Bindery Workers" in Volume 1 of *Career Discovery
 Encyclopedia* (pp. 122-123)**
J.G. Ferguson Publishing Co.
200 W. Monroe
Chicago, IL 60606 Phone: (312)580-5480
E. Russell Primm, editor-in-chief. 1990. Contains two-page articles on 504 occupations. Each article describes job duties, earnings, and educational and training requirements.

★6132★
**"Bindery Workers" in Volume 3 of *The Encyclopedia of
 Careers and Vocational Guidance* (pp. 491-495)**
J.G. Ferguson Publishing Co.
200 W. Monroe
Chicago, IL 60606 Phone: (312)580-5480
William E. Hopke, editor-in-chief. Eighth edition, 1990. Four-volume set that profiles 500 occupations and describes job trends in 76 industries. Includes career description, educational requirements, history of the job, methods of entry, advancement, employment outlook, earnings, working conditions, social and psychological factors, and sources of additional information.

★6133★
Book Bindery Worker
Vocational Biographies, Inc.
PO Box 31, Dept. VF10
Sauk Centre, MN 56378 Phone: (612)352-6516
1990. This pamphlet profiles a person working in the job. Includes information about job duties, working conditions, places of employment, educational preparation, labor market outlook, and salaries. **Toll-free/Additional Phone Number(s):** 800-255-0752.

★6134★
**"Bookbinder" in *Communications and the Arts*, Volume 3
 of *Career Information Center* (pp. 51-52)**
Glencoe/Macmillan
15319 Chatsworth St.
Mission Hills, CA 91345 Phone: (818)898-1391
Richard Lidz and Dale Anderson, editorial directors. Fourth edition, 1990. For 600 occupations, describes job duties, entry-level requirements, education and training needed, advancement possibilities, employment outlook, earnings and benefits. The set is divided into 12 volumes. Each volume includes jobs related under a broad career field. Volume 13 is the index. **Facsimile Number:** 818-365-5489.

★6135★
Bookbinder and Bindery Workers
Careers, Inc.
PO Box 135
Largo, FL 34649-0135 Phone: (813)584-7333
1990. Two-page occupational summary card describing duties, working conditions, personal qualifications, training, earnings and hours, employment outlook, places of employment, related careers and where to write for more information.

★6136★
**"Bookbinder and Bindery Workers" in *Occu-Facts:
 Information on 565 Careers in Outline Form* (p. 17.16)**
Careers, Inc.
P.O. Box 135
1211 Tenth St., S.W.
Largo, FL 33640 Phone: (813)584-7333
Elizabeth Handville. Biennial, 1989-90 edition. Each one-page occupational profile describes duties, working conditions, physical surroundings and demands, aptitudes, temperament, educational requirements, employment outlook, earnings, and places of employment.

★6137★
Career Success Series
Cambridge Career Products
90 MacCorkle Ave., SW
South Charleston, WV 25311 Phone: (304)744-9323
Videocassette. 1986. 15 mins. A series, available separately, outlining various career choices for students. Occupations include: flight service, air transportation/ground service, data processing, carpentry, clerk in banking/insurance, commodity sales, cosmetic personal grooming, fire fighting, forestry services, home economics, insulation/roofing, material handling, mechanics, photographic processing, pipefitting and plumbing, police science, printing, secretarial services, and utilities equipment operator.

★6138★
Video Career Library - Production I
Careers, Inc.
1211 10th St., SW
PO Box 135
Largo, FL 34649-0135   Phone: (813)584-7333

Videocassette. 1990. 28 mins. Part of the Video Career Library covering 165 occupations. Shows actual workers on the job. Includes layout workers, precision typesetters, lithographers/photoengravers, bookbinders, hand tailors/dressmakers, upholsterers, water/sewage plant operators, chemical plant operators, and power plant operators.

---------- Associations ----------

★6139★
Graphic Arts Technical Foundation (GATF)
4615 Forbes Ave.
Pittsburgh, PA 15213   Phone: (412)621-6941

Membership: Scientific, technical, and educational organization serving the international graphic communications industries. **Purpose:** Conducts research in all graphic processes and their commercial applications. Conducts seminars, workshops, and forums on graphic arts subjects. Conducts educational programs, including the publishing of graphic arts textbooks and learning modules, audiovisuals, aptitude testing, in-plant and school counseling, scholarship and fellowship program, and national career and manpower recruitment program. Produces test images and quality control devices for the industry. Performs technical services for the graphic arts industry, including problem-solving, material evaluation, and plant audits. Maintains biographical archives and library of over 4000 volumes on printing, graphic arts, and related subjects. Sponsors competitions; bestows awards annually. Compiles statistics. **Publications:** *GATFWORLD*, bimonthly. • *Learning Module Catalog*, annual. • *Product Catalog*, annual. • *Quality Control Device Catalog*, annual. • Also publishes textbooks, conference proceedings, techno-economic forecasts, and special reports. **Facsimile Number:** (412)621-3049.

★6140★
Graphic Communications International Union (GCIU)
1900 L St. NW
Washington, DC 20036   Phone: (202)462-1400

Membership: AFL-CIO; Canadian Labour Congress. **Publications:** *GraphiCommunicator: The Newspaper of the Graphic Communications Union*, 10/year. **Facsimile Number:** (202)331-9516.

---------- Test Guides ----------

★6141★
Journeyman in the Printing Crafts
National Learning Corp.
212 Michael Dr.
Syosset, NY 11791   Phone: (516)921-8888

Jack Rudman. Part of the Career Examination Series No. 1. All examination guides in this series contain questions with answers. **Facsimile Number:** (516)921-8743. **Toll-free/Additional Phone Number(s):** 800-645-6337.

---------- Periodicals ----------

★6142★
American Printer
Maclean Hunter Publishing Co.
29 N. Wacker Dr.
Chicago, IL 60606   Phone: (312)726-2802

Jill Roth, Editorial Director. Monthly. Magazine covering the printing and publishing market. **Facsimile Number:** (312)726-2574.

★6143★
Around the Bargaining Loop
Graphic Arts Employers of America
100 Daingerfield Rd.
Alexandria, VA 22314   Phone: (703)519-8150

Editor(s): Holly T. Kachman. Monthly. Provides "detailed summaries of recent settlements within the printing and other related industries. Wage and fringe benefit provisions are given for both the old and new agreements for quick comparisons." **Facsimile Number:** (703)548-3227.

★6144★
Binders Bulletin
Binding Industries of America
70 E. Lake St.
Chicago, IL 60601   Phone: (312)372-7606

Editor(s): James R. Niesen. 10/yr. Contains management tips and industry news for this association of trade binders and loose leaf manufacturers. Recurring features include a calendar of events, news of members, and listings of equipment wanted or for sale. **Facsimile Number:** (312)704-5025.

★6145★
Binders' Guild—Newsletter
Binders' Guild
Box 289, Rte. 3
Zebulon, NC 27597   Phone: (919)269-6381

Editor(s): Jim Dorsey. 8/yr. Focuses on hand bookbinding. Conveys news of the craft and of persons prominent in the field; describes techniques; and reprints relevant pieces from other publications. Recurring features include announcements of workshops and special courses, book reviews, and occasional inserts of related material.

★6146★
Book Arts Review
Center for Book Arts
626 Broadway
New York, NY 10012   Phone: (212)460-9768

Editor(s): Peter Buck. Quarterly. Promotes the arts of the book: printing, bookbinding, papermaking, calligraphy, and preservation. Composed of interviews with people active in book arts; reviews of exhibitions, lectures, conferences, and books; an international calendar of readings, workshops, and seminars; news of educational programs sponsored by the Center; news of small presses; and book arts suppliers information.

★6147★
GATFWORLD
Graphic Arts Technical Foundation (GATF)
4615 Forbes Ave.
Pittsburgh, PA 15213   Phone: (412)621-6941

Bimonthly. Magazine including technical and research reports.

★6148★
In-Plant Printer & Electronic Publisher
Innes Publishing Co.
PO Box 368
Northbrook, IL 60065　　　　　Phone: (708)564-5940
Andrea Cody, Editor. 6x/yr. Magazine serving printing, graphics, and typesetting facilities located in businesses, industries, hospitals, associations; and educational, government, and, non-profit organizations. **Facsimile Number:** (708)564-8361.

★6149★
Instant and Small Commercial Printer
Innes Publishing Co.
PO Box 368
Northbrook, IL 60065　　　　　Phone: (708)564-5940
Catherine Bazzon, Editor. 10x/yr. Magazine serving the field of instant/quick printers, copy shops, small commercial printers, combination printers, industry suppliers and others allied to the field including typesetters and thermographers.

★6150★
MCBA
Minnesota Center for Book Arts (MCBA)
24 N. Third St.
Minneapolis, MN 55401　　　　　Phone: (612)338-3634
Editor(s): Loring Johnson. Quarterly. Focuses on the field of book arts, including letterpress printing, bookbinding, and papermaking. Reviews current and future.

★6151★
Package Printing and Converting
North American Publishing Co.
401 N. Broad St.
Philadelphia, PA 19108　　　　　Phone: (215)238-5300
David H. Luttenberger, Editor. Monthly. Magazine. **Facsimile Number:** (215)238-5457.

★6152★
Quick Printing
Coast Publishing
1680 SW Bayshore Blvd.
Port Saint Lucie, FL 34984　　　　　Phone: (407)879-6666
Bob Hall, Editor. Monthly. Magazine serving as an equipment information source for commercial copy and printshops. **Facsimile Number:** (407)879-7388.

★6153★
Reproduction Bulletin
Andrews Paper & Chemical Co., Inc.
1 Channel Dr.
PO Box 509
Port Washington, NY 11050　　　　　Phone: (516)767-2800
Peter Muller, Editor. 4x/yr. Magazine focusing on printing. **Facsimile Number:** (516)767-1632.

★6154★
Southern Graphics
Coast Publishing, Inc.
ZedCoast Center
1680 SW Bayshore Blvd.
Port Saint Lucie, FL 34984　　　　　Phone: (407)879-6666
K.J. Moran, Editor. Monthly. Graphic arts magazine serving the printing and graphic arts industry in 14 southern states. **Facsimile Number:** (407)879-7388.

★6155★
Technology Watch
1605 King St.
Alexandria, VA 22314　　　　　Phone: (703)739-5510
Jean Freedman, Editor and Advertising Mgr. Monthly. Printing and graphic arts magazine.

——————— Meetings and Conventions ———————

★6156★
Binding Industries of America (BIA)
70 E. Lake St.
Chicago, IL 60601　　　　　Phone: (312)372-7606
Frequency: Annual, always March. 1992; Mar. 15-19; Palm Beach Gardens, FL • 1993; Mar. 14-18; Tucson, AZ. **Facsimile Number:** (312)704-5025.

——————— Other Sources of Information ———————

★6157★
Learning Module Catalog
Graphic Arts Technical Foundation (GATF)
4615 Forbes Ave.
Pittsburgh, PA 15213　　　　　Phone: (412)621-6941
Annual.

Compositors and Typesetters

Compositors and typesetters set, type, style, and format printing jobs using various forms of technologies: *cold type* technology, *hot type* technology, phototypesetting, and electronic pagination. About 36 percent of all salaried jobs are in newspaper plants, and 29 percent are in commercial printing plants. The remainder are in other kinds of printing and publishing firms; in business firms, including mailing, reproduction, commercial art, and stenographic service establishments; and in a wide range of firms that do their own printing.

$alaries

Weekly earnings for compositors and typesetters are as follows:

Lowest 10 percent	$188.00/week or less
Middle 50 percent	$251.00—$474.00/week
Top 10 percent	$589.00/week or more

Employment Outlook

Growth rate until the year 2000: Employment is expected to remain level.

Compositors and Typesetters

Career Guides

★6158★
A Career in Computer Typesetting
Graphic Arts Technical Foundation
4615 Forbes Ave.
Pittsgurgh, PA 15213-3796   Phone: (412)621-6941
This 12-page booklet describes the work of a computer typesetter and covers the skills required.

★6159★
Career Success Series
Cambridge Career Products
90 MacCorkle Ave., SW
South Charleston, WV 25311   Phone: (304)744-9323
Videocassette. 1986. 15 mins. A series, available separately, outlining various career choices for students. Occupations include: flight service, air transportation/ground service, data processing, carpentry, clerk in banking/insurance, commodity sales, cosmetic personal grooming, fire fighting, forestry services, home economics, insulation/roofing, material handling, mechanics, photographic processing, pipefitting and plumbing, police science, printing, secretarial services, and utilities equipment operator.

★6160★
"Compositors and Typesetters" in *Occupational Outlook Handbook* (pp. 412-414)
Superintendent of Documents
U.S. Government Printing Office
Washington, DC 20402   Phone: (202)783-3238
Biennial; latest edition, 1990-91. Encyclopedia of careers describing more than 250 occupations and comprising about 86 percent of all jobs in the economy. Occupations that require lengthy education or training are given the most attention. For each occupation, the handbook describes job duties, working conditions, training, educational preparation, personal qualities, advancement possibilities, job outlook, earnings, and sources of additional information.

★6161★
"Compositors and Typesetters" in Volume 3 of *The Encyclopedia of Careers and Vocational Guidance* (pp. 495-499)
J.G. Ferguson Publishing Co.
200 W. Monroe
Chicago, IL 60606   Phone: (312)580-5480
William E. Hopke, editor-in-chief. Eighth edition, 1990. Four-volume set that profiles 500 occupations and describes job trends in 76 industries. Includes career description, educational requirements, history of the job, methods of entry, advancement, employment outlook, earnings, working conditions, social and psychological factors, and sources of additional information.

★6162★
Typesetters
Chronicle Guidance Publications, Inc.
PO Box 1190
Moravia, NY 13118-1190   Phone: (315)497-0330
1988. This career brief describes the nature of the work, working conditions, hours and earnings, education and training, licensure, certification, unions, personal qualifications, social and psychological factors, employment outlook, entry methods, advancement, and related occupations. **Toll-free/Additional Phone Number(s):** 800-622-7284.

★6163★
"Typesetters" in Volume 6 of *Career Discovery Encyclopedia* (pp. 134-135)
J.G. Ferguson Publishing Co.
200 W. Monroe
Chicago, IL 60606   Phone: (312)580-5480
E. Russell Primm, editor-in-chief. 1990. Contains two-page articles on 504 occupations. Each article describes job duties, earnings, and educational and training requirements.

★6164★
Typesetting
Quiet Advantage
1949 South Manchester St. 34
Anaheim, CA 92802   Phone: (714)748-1840
Videocassette. 1991. 17 mins. Choosing typefaces and using typesetting techniques.

★6165★
Video Career Library - Production I
Careers, Inc.
1211 10th St., SW
PO Box 135
Largo, FL 34649-0135   Phone: (813)584-7333
Videocassette. 1990. 28 mins. Part of the Video Career Library covering 165 occupations. Shows actual workers on the job. Includes layout workers, precision typesetters, lithographers/photoengravers, bookbinders, hand tailors/dressmakers, upholsterers, water/sewage plant operators, chemical plant operators, and power plant operators.

Associations

★6166★
Graphic Arts Technical Foundation (GATF)
4615 Forbes Ave.
Pittsburgh, PA 15213   Phone: (412)621-6941
Membership: Scientific, technical, and educational organization serving the international graphic communications industries. **Purpose:** Conducts research in all graphic processes and their commercial applications. Conducts seminars, workshops, and forums on graphic arts subjects. Conducts educational programs, including the publishing of graphic arts textbooks and learning modules, audiovisuals, aptitude testing, in-plant and school counseling, scholarship and fellowship program, and national career and manpower recruitment program. Produces test images and quality control devices for the industry. Performs technical services for the graphic arts industry, including problem-solving, material evaluation, and plant audits. Maintains biographical archives and library of over 4000 volumes on printing, graphic arts, and related subjects. Sponsors competitions; bestows awards annually. Compiles statistics. **Publications:** *GATFWORLD*, bimonthly. • *Learning Module Catalog*, annual. • *Product Catalog*, annual. • *Quality Control Device Catalog*, annual. • Also publishes textbooks, conference proceedings, techno-economic forecasts, and special reports. **Facsimile Number:** (412)621-3049.

★6167★
Graphic Communications International Union (GCIU)
1900 L St. NW
Washington, DC 20036   Phone: (202)462-1400
Membership: AFL-CIO; Canadian Labour Congress. **Publications:** *GraphiCommunicator: The Newspaper of the Graphic Communications Union*, 10/year. **Facsimile Number:** (202)331-9516.

★6168★
National Composition and Prepress Association (NCPA)
100 Daingerfield Rd.
Alexandria, VA 22314
Membership: Graphic arts professionals involved in typesetting, electronic composition and prepress, and desktop publishing. **Purpose:** Provides members with information on technologies, management issues, and business opportunities. Sponsors competitions; bestows awards; compiles statistics. Plans to offer data base search of machine and system specifications, online ordering of publications, and text electronic editions of NCPA publications. **Publications:** *Journal*, quarterly. • *Newsline*, monthly. • Also publishes monographs, surveys, and other materials; produces cassettes. **Facsimile Number:** (703)841-8178.

Test Guides

★6169★
Composing Machine Operator
National Learning Corp.
212 Michael Dr.
Syosset, NY 11791   Phone: (516)921-8888
Jack Rudman. Part of the Career Examination Series No. 1. All examination guides in this series contain questions with answers. **Facsimile Number:** (516)921-8743. **Toll-free/Additional Phone Number(s):** 800-645-6337.

★6170★
Journeyman in the Printing Crafts
National Learning Corp.
212 Michael Dr.
Syosset, NY 11791   Phone: (516)921-8888
Jack Rudman. Part of the Career Examination Series No. 1. All examination guides in this series contain questions with answers. **Facsimile Number:** (516)921-8743. **Toll-free/Additional Phone Number(s):** 800-645-6337.

Periodicals

★6171★
American Printer
Maclean Hunter Publishing Co.
29 N. Wacker Dr.
Chicago, IL 60606   Phone: (312)726-2802
Jill Roth, Editorial Director. Monthly. Magazine covering the printing and publishing market. **Facsimile Number:** (312)726-2574.

★6172★
American Typecasting Fellowship—Newsletter
American Typecasting Fellowship
PO Box 263
Terra Alta, WV 26764   Phone: (304)789-2300
Editor(s): Richard L. Hopkins. Periodic. Devoted to conveying information on the preservation of equipment and technology related to metal typecasting. Covers type founding, type design, matrix making, and letterpress printing. Recurring features include letters to the editor and news of members.

★6173★
Around the Bargaining Loop
Graphic Arts Employers of America
100 Daingerfield Rd.
Alexandria, VA 22314   Phone: (703)519-8150
Editor(s): Holly T. Kachman. Monthly. Provides "detailed summaries of recent settlements within the printing and other related industries. Wage and fringe benefit provisions are given for both the old and new agreements for quick comparisons.". **Facsimile Number:** (703)548-3227.

★6174★
Book Arts Review
Center for Book Arts
626 Broadway
New York, NY 10012   Phone: (212)460-9768
Editor(s): Peter Buck. Quarterly. Promotes the arts of the book: printing, bookbinding, papermaking, calligraphy, and preservation. Composed of interviews with people active in book arts; reviews of exhibitions, lectures, conferences, and books; an international calendar of readings, workshops, and seminars; news of educational programs sponsored by the Center; news of small presses; and book arts suppliers information.

★6175★
Compu/Graphics Users Association—Newsletter
Compu/Graphics Users Association
P.O. Drawer 5007
Bend, OR 97708   Phone: (503)382-6978
Editor(s): Kenneth Asher. Monthly. Serves as an exchange of ideas, information, and repair tips for users of compugraphic typesetting equipment.

Compositors and Typesetters

★6176★
GATFWORLD
Graphic Arts Technical Foundation (GATF)
4615 Forbes Ave.
Pittsburgh, PA 15213   Phone: (412)621-6941
Bimonthly. Magazine including technical and research reports.

★6177★
In-Plant Printer & Electronic Publisher
Innes Publishing Co.
PO Box 368
Northbrook, IL 60065   Phone: (708)564-5940
Andrea Cody, Editor. 6x/yr. Magazine serving printing, graphics, and typesetting facilities located in businesses, industries, hospitals, associations; and educational, government, and, non-profit organizations. **Facsimile Number:** (708)564-8361.

★6178★
Instant and Small Commercial Printer
Innes Publishing Co.
PO Box 368
Northbrook, IL 60065   Phone: (708)564-5940
Catherine Bazzon, Editor. 10x/yr. Magazine serving the field of instant/quick printers, copy shops, small commercial printers, combination printers, industry suppliers and others allied to the field including typesetters and thermographers.

★6179★
MCBA
Minnesota Center for Book Arts (MCBA)
24 N. Third St.
Minneapolis, MN 55401   Phone: (612)338-3634
Editor(s): Loring Johnson. Quarterly. Focuses on the field of book arts, including letterpress printing, bookbinding, and papermaking. Reviews current and future.

★6180★
NCPA Journal
National Composition and Prepress Association (NCPA)
100 Daingerfield Rd.
Alexandria, VA 22314
Quarterly.

★6181★
NCPA Newsline
National Composition and Prepress Association (NCPA)
100 Daingerfield Rd.
Alexandria, VA 22314
Monthly. Newsletter.

★6182★
Package Printing and Converting
North American Publishing Co.
401 N. Broad St.
Philadelphia, PA 19108   Phone: (215)238-5300
David H. Luttenberger, Editor. Monthly. Magazine. **Facsimile Number:** (215)238-5457.

★6183★
Quick Printing
Coast Publishing
1680 SW Bayshore Blvd.
Port Saint Lucie, FL 34984   Phone: (407)879-6666
Bob Hall, Editor. Monthly. Magazine serving as an equipment information source for commercial copy and printshops. **Facsimile Number:** (407)879-7388.

★6184★
Reproduction Bulletin
Andrews Paper & Chemical Co., Inc.
1 Channel Dr.
PO Box 509
Port Washington, NY 11050   Phone: (516)767-2800
Peter Muller, Editor. 4x/yr. Magazine focusing on printing. **Facsimile Number:** (516)767-1632.

★6185★
Southern Graphics
Coast Publishing, Inc.
ZedCoast Center
1680 SW Bayshore Blvd.
Port Saint Lucie, FL 34984   Phone: (407)879-6666
K.J. Moran, Editor. Monthly. Graphic arts magazine serving the printing and graphic arts industry in 14 southern states. **Facsimile Number:** (407)879-7388.

★6186★
Technology Watch
1605 King St.
Alexandria, VA 22314   Phone: (703)739-5510
Jean Freedman, Editor and Advertising Mgr. Monthly. Printing and graphic arts magazine.

★6187★
The Typographer
Typographers International Assn.
2233 Wisconsin Ave. NW, Ste. 235
Washington, DC 20007   Phone: (202)965-3400
Xenia Jowyk, Editor/Advertising Mgr. Monthly. Tabloid for commercial typesetting managers features design trends, information on the latest equipment, and management techniques. **Facsimile Number:** (202)965-3522.

─────── Meetings and Conventions ───────

★6188★
Graphic Communications International Union Conference (GCIU)
1900 L St., NW
Washington, DC 20036   Phone: (202)462-1400
Frequency: Annual conference, with exhibits. **Facsimile Number:** (202)331-9516.

★6189★
National Composition and Prepress Association (NCPA)
100 Daingerfield Rd.
Alexandria, VA 22314
Frequency: Annual. **Facsimile Number:** (703)841-8178.

─────── Other Sources of Information ───────

★6190★
Learning Module Catalog
Graphic Arts Technical Foundation (GATF)
4615 Forbes Ave.
Pittsburgh, PA 15213   Phone: (412)621-6941
Annual.

Lithographic and Photoengraving Workers

Lithographers photograph or scan the material to be printed to produce film negatives or positives which are assembled into flats that are used to expose printing plates. Photoengravers etch metal letterpress plates or gravure-etched cylinders for reproduction of copy. Lithographic and photoengraving workers are responsible for a variety of tasks. Camera operators—who are generally classified as line camera operators, halftone operators, or color separation photographers—start the process of making a lithographic plate by photographing and developing negatives of the material to be printed. Scanner operators use computerized equipment to create film negatives or positives of photographs or art. Lithographic dot etchers sharpen or reshape images on the negatives by retouching them. Strippers cut the film to required size and arrange and tape the negatives onto layout sheets used by platemakers to make press plates. Platemakers use a photographic process to make printing plates. Most lithographic and photoengraving jobs are in commercial printing plants, newspapers, printing trade service firms, and *in-plant* operations.

$alaries

Hourly earnings for lithographers and photoengravers are as follows:

Experienced lithographers operating a scanner	$19.80/hour
Color strippers	$16.00/hour

Employment Outlook

Growth rate until the year 2000: Average.

Lithographic and Photoengraving Workers

Career Guides

★6191★
Career Success Series
Cambridge Career Products
90 MacCorkle Ave., SW
South Charleston, WV 25311   Phone: (304)744-9323

Videocassette. 1986. 15 mins. A series, available separately, outlining various career choices for students. Occupations include: flight service, air transportation/ground service, data processing, carpentry, clerk in banking/insurance, commodity sales, cosmetic personal grooming, fire fighting, forestry services, home economics, insulation/roofing, material handling, mechanics, photographic processing, pipefitting and plumbing, police science, printing, secretarial services, and utilities equipment operator.

★6192★
Color Separator Operator/Supervisor
Vocational Biographies, Inc.
PO Box 31, Dept. VF10
Sauk Centre, MN 56378   Phone: (612)352-6516

1989. This pamphlet profiles a person working in the job. Includes information about job duties, working conditions, places of employment, educational preparation, labor market outlook, and salaries. **Toll-free/Additional Phone Number(s):** 800-255-0752.

★6193★
Lithographer
Vocational Biographies, Inc.
PO Box 31, Dept. VF10
Sauk Centre, MN 56378   Phone: (612)352-6516

1988. This pamphlet profiles a person working in the job. Includes information about job duties, working conditions, places of employment, educational preparation, labor market outlook, and salaries. **Toll-free/Additional Phone Number(s):** 800-255-0752.

★6194★
"Lithographic and Photoengraving Workers" in *Occupational Outlook Handbook* (pp. 414-416)
Superintendent of Documents
U.S. Government Printing Office
Washington, DC 20402   Phone: (202)783-3238

Biennial; latest edition, 1990-91. Encyclopedia of careers describing more than 250 occupations and comprising about 86 percent of all jobs in the economy. Occupations that require lengthy education or training are given the most attention. For each occupation, the handbook describes job duties, working conditions, training, educational preparation, personal qualities, advancement possibilities, job outlook, earnings, and sources of additional information.

★6195★
"Lithographic Occupations" in Volume 3 of *The Encyclopedia of Careers and Vocational Guidance* (pp. 748-751)
J.G. Ferguson Publishing Co.
200 W. Monroe
Chicago, IL 60606   Phone: (312)580-5480

William E. Hopke, editor-in-chief. Eighth edition, 1990. Four-volume set that profiles 500 occupations and describes job trends in 76 industries. Includes career description, educational requirements, history of the job, methods of entry, advancement, employment outlook, earnings, working conditions, social and psychological factors, and sources of additional information.

★6196★
"Lithographic Platemaker" in *Occu-Facts: Information on 565 Careers in Outline Form* (p. 17.15)
Careers, Inc.
P.O. Box 135
1211 Tenth St., S.W.
Largo, FL 33640   Phone: (813)584-7333

Elizabeth Handville. Biennial, 1989-90 edition. Each one-page occupational profile describes duties, working conditions, physical surroundings and demands, aptitudes, temperament, educational requirements, employment outlook, earnings, and places of employment.

★6197★
"Lithographic Worker" in *Communications and the Arts*, Volume 3 of *Career Information Center* (pp. 57-59)
Glencoe/Macmillan
15319 Chatsworth St.
Mission Hills, CA 91345   Phone: (818)898-1391

Richard Lidz and Dale Anderson, editorial directors. Fourth edition, 1990. For 600 occupations, describes job duties, entry-level requirements, education and training needed, advancement possibilities, employment outlook, earnings and benefits. The set is divided into 12 volumes. Each volume includes jobs related under a broad career field. Volume 13 is the index. **Facsimile Number:** 818-365-5489.

★6198★
"Lithographic Workers" in Volume 4 of *Career Discovery Encyclopedia* (pp. 36-37)
J.G. Ferguson Publishing Co.
200 W. Monroe
Chicago, IL 60606   Phone: (312)580-5480

E. Russell Primm, editor-in-chief. 1990. Contains two-page articles on 504 occupations. Each article describes job duties, earnings, and educational and training requirements.

★6199★
"Photoengraver" in *Communications and the Arts*, Volume 3 of *Career Information Center* (pp. 62-63)
Glencoe/Macmillan
15319 Chatsworth St.
Mission Hills, CA 91345   Phone: (818)898-1391

Richard Lidz and Dale Anderson, editorial directors. Fourth edition, 1990. For 600 occupations, describes job duties, entry-level requirements, education and training needed, advancement possibilities, employment outlook, earnings and benefits. The set is divided into 12 volumes. Each volume includes jobs related under a broad career field. Volume 13 is the index. **Facsimile Number:** 818-365-5489.

★6200★
"Photoengravers" in Volume 5 of *Career Discovery Encyclopedia* (pp. 32-33)
J.G. Ferguson Publishing Co.
200 W. Monroe
Chicago, IL 60606   Phone: (312)580-5480

E. Russell Primm, editor-in-chief. 1990. Contains two-page articles on 504 occupations. Each article describes job duties, earnings, and educational and training requirements.

★6201★
"Photoengravers" in Volume 3 of *The Encyclopedia of Careers and Vocational Guidance* (pp. 761-763)
J.G. Ferguson Publishing Co.
200 W. Monroe
Chicago, IL 60606   Phone: (312)580-5480

William E. Hopke, editor-in-chief. Eighth edition, 1990. Four-volume set that profiles 500 occupations and describes job trends in 76 industries. Includes career description, educational requirements, history of the job, methods of entry, advancement, employment outlook, earnings, working conditions, social and psychological factors, and sources of additional information.

★6202★
"Platemaker" in *Communications and the Arts*, Volume 3 of *Career Information Center* (pp. 64-65)
Glencoe/Macmillan
15319 Chatsworth St.
Mission Hills, CA 91345   Phone: (818)898-1391

Richard Lidz and Dale Anderson, editorial directors. Fourth edition, 1990. For 600 occupations, describes job duties, entry-level requirements, education and training needed, advancement possibilities, employment outlook, earnings and benefits. The set is divided into 12 volumes. Each volume includes jobs related under a broad career field. Volume 13 is the index. **Facsimile Number:** 818-365-5489.

★6203★
Platemaker, Lithographic
Careers, Inc.
PO Box 135
Largo, FL 34649-0135   Phone: (813)584-7333

1989. Two-page occupational summary card describing duties, working conditions, personal qualifications, training, earnings and hours, employment outlook, places of employment, related careers and where to write for more information.

★6204★
Video Career Library - Production I
Careers, Inc.
1211 10th St., SW
PO Box 135
Largo, FL 34649-0135   Phone: (813)584-7333

Videocassette. 1990. 28 mins. Part of the Video Career Library covering 165 occupations. Shows actual workers on the job. Includes layout workers, precision typesetters, lithographers/photoengravers, bookbinders, hand tailors/dressmakers, upholsterers, water/sewage plant operators, chemical plant operators, and power plant operators.

Associations

★6205★
Graphic Arts Technical Foundation (GATF)
4615 Forbes Ave.
Pittsburgh, PA 15213   Phone: (412)621-6941

Membership: Scientific, technical, and educational organization serving the international graphic communications industries. **Purpose:** Conducts research in all graphic processes and their commercial applications. Conducts seminars, workshops, and forums on graphic arts subjects. Conducts educational programs, including the publishing of graphic arts textbooks and learning modules, audiovisuals, aptitude testing, in-plant and school counseling, scholarship and fellowship program, and national career and manpower recruitment program. Produces test images and quality control devices for the industry. Performs technical services for the graphic arts industry, including problem-solving, material evaluation, and plant audits. Maintains biographical archives and library of over 4000 volumes on printing, graphic arts, and related subjects. Sponsors competitions; bestows awards annually. Compiles statistics. **Publications:** *GATFWORLD*, bimonthly. • *Learning Module Catalog*, annual. • *Product Catalog*, annual. • *Quality Control Device Catalog*, annual. • Also publishes textbooks, conference proceedings, techno-economic forecasts, and special reports. **Facsimile Number:** (412)621-3049.

★6206★
Graphic Communications International Union (GCIU)
1900 L St. NW
Washington, DC 20036   Phone: (202)462-1400

Membership: AFL-CIO; Canadian Labour Congress. **Publications:** *GraphiCommunicator: The Newspaper of the Graphic Communications Union*, 10/year. **Facsimile Number:** (202)331-9516.

Test Guides

★6207★
Journeyman in the Printing Crafts
National Learning Corp.
212 Michael Dr.
Syosset, NY 11791   Phone: (516)921-8888

Jack Rudman. Part of the Career Examination Series No. 1. All examination guides in this series contain questions with answers. **Facsimile Number:** (516)921-8743. **Toll-free/Additional Phone Number(s):** 800-645-6337.

★6208★
Offset Lithography
National Learning Corp.
212 Michael Dr.
Syosset, NY 11791   Phone: (516)921-8888
Jack Rudman. 1989. Part of Occupational Competency Examination Series.

---- Periodicals ----

★6209★
American Printer
Maclean Hunter Publishing Co.
29 N. Wacker Dr.
Chicago, IL 60606   Phone: (312)726-2802
Jill Roth, Editorial Director. Monthly. Magazine covering the printing and publishing market. **Facsimile Number:** (312)726-2574.

★6210★
Around the Bargaining Loop
Graphic Arts Employers of America
100 Daingerfield Rd.
Alexandria, VA 22314   Phone: (703)519-8150
Editor(s): Holly T. Kachman. Monthly. Provides "detailed summaries of recent settlements within the printing and other related industries. Wage and fringe benefit provisions are given for both the old and new agreements for quick comparisons.". **Facsimile Number:** (703)548-3227.

★6211★
Book Arts Review
Center for Book Arts
626 Broadway
New York, NY 10012   Phone: (212)460-9768
Editor(s): Peter Buck. Quarterly. Promotes the arts of the book: printing, bookbinding, papermaking, calligraphy, and preservation. Composed of interviews with people active in book arts; reviews of exhibitions, lectures, conferences, and books; an international calendar of readings, workshops, and seminars; news of educational programs sponsored by the Center; news of small presses; and book arts suppliers information.

★6212★
Flexo
Flexographic Technical Assn.
900 Marconi Ave.
Ronkonkoma, NY 11779   Phone: (516)737-6023
Joel J. Shulman, Editor/Advertising Mgr. Monthly. Magazine covering the flexographic printing method. **Facsimile Number:** (516)737-6813.

★6213★
Flexo Espanol
Flexographic Technical Assn.
900 Marconi Ave.
Ronkonkoma, NY 11779   Phone: (516)737-6023
Graciela I. Gilbride, Editor. Quarterly. Magazine on the flexographic printing method (Spanish). **Facsimile Number:** (516)737-6813.

★6214★
GATFWORLD
Graphic Arts Technical Foundation (GATF)
4615 Forbes Ave.
Pittsburgh, PA 15213   Phone: (412)621-6941
Bimonthly. Magazine including technical and research reports.

★6215★
Graphic Arts Monthly
Cahners Publishing Co.
245 W. 17th St.
New York, NY 10011   Phone: (212)645-0067
Roger Ynostroza, Editor. Monthly (Issued semimonthly in Nov.). Magazine featuring printing and graphic arts. **Facsimile Number:** (212)242-6987.

★6216★
Graphic Arts Product News
Maclean Hunter Publishing, Co.
29 N. Wacker Dr.
Chicago, IL 60606   Phone: (312)726-2802
Keith A. Willis, Publisher. Six times/yr. Magazine (tabloid) covering the newest technology in printing and related industries. **Facsimile Number:** (312)726-2574.

★6217★
In-Plant Printer & Electronic Publisher
Innes Publishing Co.
PO Box 368
Northbrook, IL 60065   Phone: (708)564-5940
Andrea Cody, Editor. 6x/yr. Magazine serving printing, graphics, and typesetting facilities located in businesses, industries, hospitals, associations; and educational, government, and, non-profit organizations. **Facsimile Number:** (708)564-8361.

★6218★
Instant and Small Commercial Printer
Innes Publishing Co.
PO Box 368
Northbrook, IL 60065   Phone: (708)564-5940
Catherine Bazzon, Editor. 10x/yr. Magazine serving the field of instant/quick printers, copy shops, small commercial printers, combination printers, industry suppliers and others allied to the field including typesetters and thermographers.

★6219★
MCBA
Minnesota Center for Book Arts (MCBA)
24 N. Third St.
Minneapolis, MN 55401   Phone: (612)338-3634
Editor(s): Loring Johnson. Quarterly. Focuses on the field of book arts, including letterpress printing, bookbinding, and papermaking. Reviews current and future.

★6220★
Package Printing and Converting
North American Publishing Co.
401 N. Broad St.
Philadelphia, PA 19108   Phone: (215)238-5300
David H. Luttenberger, Editor. Monthly. Magazine. **Facsimile Number:** (215)238-5457.

★6221★
Quick Printing
Coast Publishing
1680 SW Bayshore Blvd.
Port Saint Lucie, FL 34984   Phone: (407)879-6666
Bob Hall, Editor. Monthly. Magazine serving as an equipment information source for commercial copy and printshops. **Facsimile Number:** (407)879-7388.

★6222★
Reproduction Bulletin
Andrews Paper & Chemical Co., Inc.
1 Channel Dr.
PO Box 509
Port Washington, NY 11050   Phone: (516)767-2800
Peter Muller, Editor. 4x/yr. Magazine focusing on printing. **Facsimile Number:** (516)767-1632.

★6223★
Southern Graphics
Coast Publishing, Inc.
ZedCoast Center
1680 SW Bayshore Blvd.
Port Saint Lucie, FL 34984   Phone: (407)879-6666
K.J. Moran, Editor. Monthly. Graphic arts magazine serving the printing and graphic arts industry in 14 southern states. **Facsimile Number:** (407)879-7388.

★6224★
Technology Watch
1605 King St.
Alexandria, VA 22314   Phone: (703)739-5510
Jean Freedman, Editor and Advertising Mgr. Monthly. Printing and graphic arts magazine.

★6225★
Type and Press
24667 Heather Ct.
Hayward, CA 94545   Phone: (415)782-3674
Fred C. Williams, Editor and Publisher. Quarterly. Trade magazine covering letterpress printing.

―――― Meetings and Conventions ――――

★6226★
Graphic Arts Technical Foundation (GATF)
4615 Forbes Ave.
Pittsburgh, PA 15213   Phone: (412)621-6941
Frequency: Annual. **Facsimile Number:** (412)621-3049.

★6227★
Graphic Communications International Union Conference (GCIU)
1900 L St., NW
Washington, DC 20036   Phone: (202)462-1400
Frequency: Annual conference, with exhibits. **Facsimile Number:** (202)331-9516.

★6228★
National Association of Professional Engravers Annual Trade Show and Exhibit
National Association of Professional Engravers
21010 Center Ridge Rd.
Rocky River, OH 44116   Phone: (216)333-7417
1992. **Facsimile Number:** (216)333-1868.

―――― Other Sources of Information ――――

★6229★
Learning Module Catalog
Graphic Arts Technical Foundation (GATF)
4615 Forbes Ave.
Pittsburgh, PA 15213   Phone: (412)621-6941
Annual.

Printing Press Operators

Printing press operators are responsible for the preparation, operation, and maintenance of the press. Preparation involves installing and adjusting the printing plate, mixing fountain solution, adjusting pressure, inking presses, loading paper, and adjusting the press to paper size. Operation involves running the press and maintaining the feeders. Preventive maintenance involves oiling and cleaning the presses and making minor repairs to keep presses running smoothly. Press operators are generally classified according to the type of press they operate—offset, gravure, flexography, screen printing, or letterpress—and duties vary accordingly. Most press operator jobs are in newspaper plants or in firms that handle commercial or business printing. Commercial printing firms print newspaper. Additional jobs are in the *in-plant* section of organizations and businesses that do their own printing—among them, banks, insurance companies, and government agencies.

$alaries

Hourly earnings for printing press operators are as follows:

Two-color sheet-fed press operators	$16.98/hour
Four-color sheet-fed press operators	$18.06/hour

Employment Outlook

Growth rate until the year 2000: Average.

Printing Press Operators

Career Guides

★6230★
Career Success Series
Cambridge Career Products
90 MacCorkle Ave., SW
South Charleston, WV 25311   Phone: (304)744-9323
Videocassette. 1986. 15 mins. A series, available separately, outlining various career choices for students. Occupations include: flight service, air transportation/ground service, data processing, carpentry, clerk in banking/insurance, commodity sales, cosmetic personal grooming, fire fighting, forestry services, home economics, insulation/roofing, material handling, mechanics, photographic processing, pipefitting and plumbing, police science, printing, secretarial services, and utilities equipment operator.

★6231★
Offset Press Operator
Careers, Inc.
PO Box 135
Largo, FL 34649-0135   Phone: (813)584-7333
1990. Eight-page brief offering the definition, history, duties, working conditions, personal qualifications, educational requirements, earnings, hours, employment outlook, advancement possibilities, and related occupations.

★6232★
"Offset Press Operator" in *Occu-Facts: Information on 565 Careers in Outline Form* (p. 18.2)
Careers, Inc.
P.O. Box 135
1211 Tenth St., S.W.
Largo, FL 33640   Phone: (813)584-7333
Elizabeth Handville. Biennial, 1989-90 edition. Each one-page occupational profile describes duties, working conditions, physical surroundings and demands, aptitudes, temperament, educational requirements, employment outlook, earnings, and places of employment.

★6233★
"Printing" in Volume 1 of *The Encyclopedia of Careers and Vocational Guidance* (pp. 375-381)
J.G. Ferguson Publishing Co.
200 W. Monroe
Chicago, IL 60606   Phone: (312)580-5480
William E. Hopke, editor-in-chief. Eighth edition, 1990. Four-volume set that profiles 500 occupations and describes job trends in 76 industries. Includes career description, educational requirements, history of the job, methods of entry, advancement, employment outlook, earnings, working conditions, social and psychological factors, and sources of additional information.

★6234★
Printing Platemakers
Chronicle Guidance Publications, Inc.
PO Box 1190
Moravia, NY 13118-1190   Phone: (315)497-0330
1991. This career brief describes the nature of the work, working conditions, hours and earnings, education and training, licensure, certification, unions, personal qualifications, social and psychological factors, employment outlook, entry methods, advancement, and related occupations. **Toll-free/Additional Phone Number(s):** 800-622-7284.

★6235★
"Printing Press Operator" in *Communications and the Arts*, Volume 3 of *Career Information Center* (pp. 65-67)
Glencoe/Macmillan
15319 Chatsworth St.
Mission Hills, CA 91345   Phone: (818)898-1391
Richard Lidz and Dale Anderson, editorial directors. Fourth edition, 1990. For 600 occupations, describes job duties, entry-level requirements, education and training needed, advancement possibilities, employment outlook, earnings and benefits. The set is divided into 12 volumes. Each volume includes jobs related under a broad career field. Volume 13 is the index. **Facsimile Number:** 818-365-5489.

★6236★
"Printing Press Operator" in *VGM's Careers Encyclopedia* (pp. 368-370)
National Textbook Co.
4255 W. Touhy Ave.
Lincolnwood, IL 60646   Phone: (312)679-5500
Third edition, 1991. Contains two- to five-page descriptions of 200 managerial, professional, technical, trade, and service occupations. Each profile includes job duties, places of employment, qualifications, educational preparation, training, employment potential, advancement, income, and additional sources of information.

★6237★
Printing Press Operators
Chronicle Guidance Publications, Inc.
PO Box 1190
Moravia, NY 13118-1190   Phone: (315)497-0330
1990. This career brief describes the nature of the work, working conditions, hours and earnings, education and training, licensure, certification, unions, personal qualifications, social and psychological factors, employment outlook, entry methods,

★6238★
advancement, and related occupations. **Toll-free/Additional Phone Number(s):** 800-622-7284.

★6238★
"Printing Press Operators" in *Jobs! What They Are...Where They Are...What They Pay* (pp. 179-180)
Simon & Schuster, Inc.
Simon & Schuster Bldg.
1230 Avenue of the Americas
New York, NY 10020   Phone: (212)698-7000

Robert O. Snelling and Anne M. Snelling. Revised edition, 1989. Profiles 241 occupations, describing duties and responsibilities, educational preparation, earnings, employment opportunities, training, and qualifications.

★6239★
"Printing Press Operators" in *Occupational Outlook Handbook* (pp. 416-417)
Superintendent of Documents
U.S. Government Printing Office
Washington, DC 20402   Phone: (202)783-3238

Biennial; latest edition, 1990-91. Encyclopedia of careers describing more than 250 occupations and comprising about 86 percent of all jobs in the economy. Occupations that require lengthy education or training are given the most attention. For each occupation, the handbook describes job duties, working conditions, training, educational preparation, personal qualities, advancement possibilities, job outlook, earnings, and sources of additional information.

★6240★
"Printing Press Operators" in Volume 5 of *Career Discovery Encyclopedia* (pp. 86-87)
J.G. Ferguson Publishing Co.
200 W. Monroe
Chicago, IL 60606   Phone: (312)580-5480

E. Russell Primm, editor-in-chief. 1990. Contains two-page articles on 504 occupations. Each article describes job duties, earnings, and educational and training requirements.

★6241★
"Printing Press Operators and Assistants" in Volume 3 of *The Encyclopedia of Careers and Vocational Guidance* (pp. 555-557)
J.G. Ferguson Publishing Co.
200 W. Monroe
Chicago, IL 60606   Phone: (312)580-5480

William E. Hopke, editor-in-chief. Eighth edition, 1990. Four-volume set that profiles 500 occupations and describes job trends in 76 industries. Includes career description, educational requirements, history of the job, methods of entry, advancement, employment outlook, earnings, working conditions, social and psychological factors, and sources of additional information.

★6242★
"Printing Technology" in *The Career Connection II: A Guide to Technical Majors and Their Related Careers* (pp. 109-110)
ERIS
PO Box 7509
University Station
Provo, UT 84602-0509

Fred A. Rowe. 1988. Contains technical majors, such as automotive technology. Describes the major and the job. Lists high school and postsecondary school courses. Includes occupations related to the major, employment outlook, and starting salary.

★6243★
Video Career Library - Production I
Careers, Inc.
1211 10th St., SW
PO Box 135
Largo, FL 34649-0135   Phone: (813)584-7333

Videocassette. 1990. 28 mins. Part of the Video Career Library covering 165 occupations. Shows actual workers on the job. Includes layout workers, precision typesetters, lithographers/photoengravers, bookbinders, hand tailors/dressmakers, upholsterers, water/sewage plant operators, chemical plant operators, and power plant operators.

── Associations ──

★6244★
Graphic Arts Technical Foundation (GATF)
4615 Forbes Ave.
Pittsburgh, PA 15213   Phone: (412)621-6941

Membership: Scientific, technical, and educational organization serving the international graphic communications industries. **Purpose:** Conducts research in all graphic processes and their commercial applications. Conducts seminars, workshops, and forums on graphic arts subjects. Conducts educational programs, including the publishing of graphic arts textbooks and learning modules, audiovisuals, aptitude testing, in-plant and school counseling, scholarship and fellowship program, and national career and manpower recruitment program. Produces test images and quality control devices for the industry. Performs technical services for the graphic arts industry, including problem-solving, material evaluation, and plant audits. Maintains biographical archives and library of over 4000 volumes on printing, graphic arts, and related subjects. Sponsors competitions; bestows awards annually. Compiles statistics. **Publications:** *GATFWORLD*, bimonthly. • *Learning Module Catalog*, annual. • *Product Catalog*, annual. • *Quality Control Device Catalog*, annual. • Also publishes textbooks, conference proceedings, techno-economic forecasts, and special reports. **Facsimile Number:** (412)621-3049.

★6245★
Graphic Communications International Union (GCIU)
1900 L St. NW
Washington, DC 20036   Phone: (202)462-1400

Membership: AFL-CIO; Canadian Labour Congress. **Publications:** *GraphiCommunicator: The Newspaper of the Graphic Communications Union*, 10/year. **Facsimile Number:** (202)331-9516.

── Test Guides ──

★6246★
Journeyman in the Printing Crafts
National Learning Corp.
212 Michael Dr.
Syosset, NY 11791   Phone: (516)921-8888

Jack Rudman. Part of the Career Examination Series No. 1. All examination guides in this series contain questions with answers. **Facsimile Number:** (516)921-8743. **Toll-free/Additional Phone Number(s):** 800-645-6337.

★6247★
Offset Printing Machine Operator
National Learning Corp.
212 Michael Dr.
Syosset, NY 11791   Phone: (516)921-8888
Jack Rudman. Part of the Career Examination Series No. 1. All examination guides in this series contain questions with answers. **Facsimile Number:** (516)921-8743. **Toll-free/Additional Phone Number(s):** 800-645-6337.

★6248★
Press Operator
National Learning Corp.
212 Michael Dr.
Syosset, NY 11791   Phone: (516)921-8888
Jack Rudman. Part of the Career Examination Series No. 1. All examination guides in this series contain questions with answers. **Facsimile Number:** (516)921-8743. **Toll-free/Additional Phone Number(s):** 800-645-6337.

★6249★
Senior Offset Printing Machine Operator
National Learning Corp.
212 Michael Dr.
Syosset, NY 11791   Phone: (516)921-8888
Jack Rudman. Part of the Career Examination Series No. 1. All examination guides in this series contain questions with answers. **Facsimile Number:** (516)921-8743. **Toll-free/Additional Phone Number(s):** 800-645-6337.

Basic Reference Guides and Handbooks

★6250★
Aligning & Adjusting Cylinders. Instructor Guide
Graphic Arts Technical Foundation
4615 Forbes Ave.
Pittsburgh, PA 15213-3796   Phone: (412)621-6941
Robert J. Schneider, Jr. 1990. **Facsimile Number:** (412)621-3049.

★6251★
Aligning & Adjusting Cylinders on the Sheetfed Offset Press
Graphic Arts Technical Foundation
4615 Forbes Ave.
Pittsburgh, PA 15213-3796   Phone: (412)621-6941
Robert J. Schneider, Jr. 1990. **Facsimile Number:** (412)621-3049.

★6252★
Operating the Dampening System, Instructor Guide
Graphic Arts Technical Foundation
4615 Forbes Ave.
Pittsburgh, PA 15213-3796   Phone: (412)621-6941
Robert J. Schneider, Jr. 1990. **Facsimile Number:** (412)621-3049.

★6253★
Operating the Dampening System on a Sheetfed Offset Press
Graphic Arts Technical Foundation
4615 Forbes Ave.
Pittsburgh, PA 15213-3796   Phone: (412)621-6941
Robert J. Schneider, Jr. 1990. **Facsimile Number:** (412)621-3049.

★6254★
Operating the Inking System. Instructor's Guide
Graphic Arts Technical Foundation
4615 Forbes Ave.
Pittsburgh, PA 15213-3796   Phone: (412)621-6941
Robert J. Schneider, Jr. 1990. **Facsimile Number:** (412)621-3049.

Periodicals

★6255★
American Ink Maker
MacNair-Dorland Co.
445 Broadhollow Rd.
Melville, NY 11747   Phone: (212)279-4456
John Vollmuth, Editor. Monthly. Trade magazine featuring printing inks and pigments.

★6256★
American Printer
Maclean Hunter Publishing Co.
29 N. Wacker Dr.
Chicago, IL 60606   Phone: (312)726-2802
Jill Roth, Editorial Director. Monthly. Magazine covering the printing and publishing market. **Facsimile Number:** (312)726-2574.

★6257★
Around the Bargaining Loop
Graphic Arts Employers of America
100 Daingerfield Rd.
Alexandria, VA 22314   Phone: (703)519-8150
Editor(s): Holly T. Kachman. Monthly. Provides "detailed summaries of recent settlements within the printing and other related industries. Wage and fringe benefit provisions are given for both the old and new agreements for quick comparisons.". **Facsimile Number:** (703)548-3227.

★6258★
Book Arts Review
Center for Book Arts
626 Broadway
New York, NY 10012   Phone: (212)460-9768
Editor(s): Peter Buck. Quarterly. Promotes the arts of the book: printing, bookbinding, papermaking, calligraphy, and preservation. Composed of interviews with people active in book arts; reviews of exhibitions, lectures, conferences, and books; an international calendar of readings, workshops, and seminars; news of educational programs sponsored by the Center; news of small presses; and book arts suppliers information.

★6259★
Flexo
Flexographic Technical Assn.
900 Marconi Ave.
Ronkonkoma, NY 11779   Phone: (516)737-6023
Joel J. Shulman, Editor/Advertising Mgr. Monthly. Magazine covering the flexographic printing method. **Facsimile Number:** (516)737-6813.

★6260★
Flexo Espanol
Flexographic Technical Assn.
900 Marconi Ave.
Ronkonkoma, NY 11779 Phone: (516)737-6023
Graciela I. Gilbride, Editor. Quarterly. Magazine on the flexographic printing method (Spanish). **Facsimile Number:** (516)737-6813.

★6261★
GATFWORLD
Graphic Arts Technical Foundation (GATF)
4615 Forbes Ave.
Pittsburgh, PA 15213 Phone: (412)621-6941
Bimonthly. Magazine including technical and research reports.

★6262★
Graphic Arts Monthly
Cahners Publishing Co.
245 W. 17th St.
New York, NY 10011 Phone: (212)645-0067
Roger Ynostroza, Editor. Monthly (Issued semimonthly in Nov.). Magazine featuring printing and graphic arts. **Facsimile Number:** (212)242-6987.

★6263★
Graphic Arts Product News
Maclean Hunter Publishing, Co.
29 N. Wacker Dr.
Chicago, IL 60606 Phone: (312)726-2802
Keith A. Willis, Publisher. Six times/yr. Magazine (tabloid) covering the newest technology in printing and related industries. **Facsimile Number:** (312)726-2574.

★6264★
In-Plant Printer & Electronic Publisher
Innes Publishing Co.
PO Box 368
Northbrook, IL 60065 Phone: (708)564-5940
Andrea Cody, Editor. 6x/yr. Magazine serving printing, graphics, and typesetting facilities located in businesses, industries, hospitals, associations; and educational, government, and, non-profit organizations. **Facsimile Number:** (708)564-8361.

★6265★
Instant and Small Commercial Printer
Innes Publishing Co.
PO Box 368
Northbrook, IL 60065 Phone: (708)564-5940
Catherine Bazzon, Editor. 10x/yr. Magazine serving the field of instant/quick printers, copy shops, small commercial printers, combination printers, industry suppliers and others allied to the field including typesetters and thermographers.

★6266★
MCBA
Minnesota Center for Book Arts (MCBA)
24 N. Third St.
Minneapolis, MN 55401 Phone: (612)338-3634
Editor(s): Loring Johnson. Quarterly. Focuses on the field of book arts, including letterpress printing, bookbinding, and papermaking. Reviews current and future.

★6267★
Package Printing and Converting
North American Publishing Co.
401 N. Broad St.
Philadelphia, PA 19108 Phone: (215)238-5300
David H. Luttenberger, Editor. Monthly. Magazine. **Facsimile Number:** (215)238-5457.

★6268★
Quick Printing
Coast Publishing
1680 SW Bayshore Blvd.
Port Saint Lucie, FL 34984 Phone: (407)879-6666
Bob Hall, Editor. Monthly. Magazine serving as an equipment information source for commercial copy and printshops. **Facsimile Number:** (407)879-7388.

★6269★
Reproduction Bulletin
Andrews Paper & Chemical Co., Inc.
1 Channel Dr.
PO Box 509
Port Washington, NY 11050 Phone: (516)767-2800
Peter Muller, Editor. 4x/yr. Magazine focusing on printing. **Facsimile Number:** (516)767-1632.

★6270★
Southern Graphics
Coast Publishing, Inc.
ZedCoast Center
1680 SW Bayshore Blvd.
Port Saint Lucie, FL 34984 Phone: (407)879-6666
K.J. Moran, Editor. Monthly. Graphic arts magazine serving the printing and graphic arts industry in 14 southern states. **Facsimile Number:** (407)879-7388.

★6271★
Technology Watch
1605 King St.
Alexandria, VA 22314 Phone: (703)739-5510
Jean Freedman, Editor and Advertising Mgr. Monthly. Printing and graphic arts magazine.

★6272★
Type and Press
24667 Heather Ct.
Hayward, CA 94545 Phone: (415)782-3674
Fred C. Williams, Editor and Publisher. Quarterly. Trade magazine covering letterpress printing.

―――― **Other Sources of Information** ――――

★6273★
Learning Module Catalog
Graphic Arts Technical Foundation (GATF)
4615 Forbes Ave.
Pittsburgh, PA 15213 Phone: (412)621-6941
Annual.

Textile, Apparel, and Furnishings Occupations

Apparel Workers

Various apparel workers transform cloth, as well as leather and fur, into clothing and other consumer products. Patternmakers create pattern pieces from the sample that will complement the fabric and minimize the number of sewing operations. Patternmakers or graders reduce or enlarge the master pattern for different sizes. Layout workers begin the production process. Spreaders, one type of layout worker, spread out layers of material on the cutting table. Other layout workers known as markers must determine the best arrangement of the pattern pieces to minimize waste. After the pattern has been positioned, its outline is drawn with chalk on the top layer of the material. Portable machine cutters cut out the various pieces of material following the outline of the pattern. On especially delicate or valuable items, this may be done by hand cutters. Once the material has been cut, it is ready to be assembled into a product in the sewing room. Garment sewing machine operators sew clothing, usually specializing in a single operation. Nongarment sewing machine operators also specialize in a single operation, but they sew other products, such as towels, sheets, or curtains. Hand sewers are highly skilled workers who may specialize in a particular operation and may work with the designer to make a sample of a new product. Handcutters and trimmers remove loose threads, basting stitching, and lint from the finished product. Hand pressers press the finished product using a hand iron or on pressing machines that are monitored by pressing machine operators. Some pressers specialize in a particular garment part; others are responsible for the final pressing before the product is shipped to the store. Custom tailors and sewers make garments from start to finish and must be knowledgeable in all phases of clothing production. Inspectors are found in all stages of the production process. They may mark defects in uncut fabric so that layout workers can position the pattern to avoid them, or they may mark defects in semifinished garments, which they may repair themselves or send back to be mended by a hand sewer. Most jobs are in the production of apparel or textile products, except for pressers and custom tailors. More than 50 percent of all pressers are employed in the laundry and drycleaning industry. In addition, more than 60 percent of all custom tailors and sewers work in retail clothing establishments; many others are self-employed.

$alaries

Earnings of apparel workers vary by industry and by occupation. Median earnings of apparel workers are as follows:

Production workers in the apparel industry	$6.10/hour
Sewing machine operators	$193.00/week
Pressing machine operators	$190.00/week
Custom tailors	$7.87—$8.82/hour

Employment Outlook

Growth rate until the year 2000: More slowly than average.

Apparel Workers

Career Guides

★6274★
"Apparel" in Volume 1 of *The Encyclopedia of Careers and Vocational Guidance* (pp. 25-32)
J.G. Ferguson Publishing Co.
200 W. Monroe
Chicago, IL 60606   Phone: (312)580-5480
William E. Hopke, editor-in-chief. Eighth edition, 1990. Four-volume set that profiles 500 occupations and describes job trends in 76 industries. Includes career description, educational requirements, history of the job, methods of entry, advancement, employment outlook, earnings, working conditions, social and psychological factors, and sources of additional information.

★6275★
"Apparel Industry" in *Manufacturing*, Volume 9 of *Career Information Center* (pp. 95-98)
Glencoe/Macmillan
15319 Chatsworth St.
Mission Hills, CA 91345   Phone: (818)898-1391
Richard Lidz and Dale Anderson, editorial directors. Fourth edition, 1990. For 600 occupations, describes job duties, entry-level requirements, education and training needed, advancement possibilities, employment outlook, earnings and benefits. The set is divided into 12 volumes. Each volume includes jobs related under a broad career field. Volume 13 is the index. **Facsimile Number:** 818-365-5489.

★6276★
Apparel Industry Workers
Chronicle Guidance Publications, Inc.
PO Box 1190
Moravia, NY 13118-1190   Phone: (315)497-0330
1987. This career brief describes the nature of the work, working conditions, hours and earnings, education and training, licensure, certification, unions, personal qualifications, social and psychological factors, employment outlook, entry methods, advancement, and related occupations. **Toll-free/Additional Phone Number(s):** 800-622-7284.

★6277★
"Apparel Workers" in *Occupational Outlook Handbook* (pp. 418-420)
Superintendent of Documents
U.S. Government Printing Office
Washington, DC 20402   Phone: (202)783-3238
Biennial; latest edition, 1990-91. Encyclopedia of careers describing more than 250 occupations and comprising about 86 percent of all jobs in the economy. Occupations that require lengthy education or training are given the most attention. For each occupation, the handbook describes job duties, working conditions, training, educational preparation, personal qualities, advancement possibilities, job outlook, earnings, and sources of additional information.

★6278★
"Custom Tailor and Dressmaker" in *Consumer, Homemaking, and Personal Services*, Volume 5 of *Career Information Center* (pp. 74-76)
Glencoe/Macmillan
15319 Chatsworth St.
Mission Hills, CA 91345   Phone: (818)898-1391
Richard Lidz and Dale Anderson, editorial directors. Fourth edition, 1990. For 600 occupations, describes job duties, entry-level requirements, education and training needed, advancement possibilities, employment outlook, earnings and benefits. The set is divided into 12 volumes. Each volume includes jobs related under a broad career field. Volume 13 is the index. **Facsimile Number:** 818-365-5489.

★6279★
"Drapery Sewer" in *Occu-Facts: Information on 565 Careers in Outline Form* (p. 18.15)
Careers, Inc.
P.O. Box 135
1211 Tenth St., S.W.
Largo, FL 33640   Phone: (813)584-7333
Elizabeth Handville. Biennial, 1989-90 edition. Each one-page occupational profile describes duties, working conditions, physical surroundings and demands, aptitudes, temperament, educational requirements, employment outlook, earnings, and places of employment.

★6280★
Dressmaker
Careers, Inc.
PO Box 135
Largo, FL 34649-0135   Phone: (813)584-7333
1989. Two-page occupational summary card describing duties, working conditions, personal qualifications, training, earnings and hours, employment outlook, places of employment, related careers and where to write for more information.

★6281★
Dressmakers (Sewing Professionals)
Chronicle Guidance Publications, Inc.
PO Box 1190
Moravia, NY 13118-1190   Phone: (315)497-0330
1988. This career brief describes the nature of the work, working conditions, hours and earnings, education and training, licensure, certification, unions, personal qualifications, social

and psychological factors, employment outlook, entry methods, advancement, and related occupations. **Toll-free/Additional Phone Number(s):** 800-622-7284.

★6282★
"Furniture Upholsterer and Tailor or Dressmaker" in *Personal Services* **(pp. 39-43)**
Franklin Watts, Inc.
387 Park Avenue, S.
New York, NY 10016   Phone: (212)686-7070
Linda Barrett and Galen Guengerich. 1991. Surveys personal services jobs. Describes job duties, educational preparation, salaries, and employment outlook. Offers job hunting advice.

★6283★
Garment Cutter
Careers, Inc.
PO Box 135
Largo, FL 34649-0135   Phone: (813)584-7333
1990. Two-page occupational summary card describing duties, working conditions, personal qualifications, training, earnings and hours, employment outlook, places of employment, related careers and where to write for more information.

★6284★
"Garment Cutter" in *Occu-Facts: Information on 565 Careers in Outline Form* **(p. 18.14)**
Careers, Inc.
P.O. Box 135
1211 Tenth St., S.W.
Largo, FL 33640   Phone: (813)584-7333
Elizabeth Handville. Biennial, 1989-90 edition. Each one-page occupational profile describes duties, working conditions, physical surroundings and demands, aptitudes, temperament, educational requirements, employment outlook, earnings, and places of employment.

★6285★
"Garment Presser" in *Occu-Facts: Information on 565 Careers in Outline Form* **(p. 18.17)**
Careers, Inc.
P.O. Box 135
1211 Tenth St., S.W.
Largo, FL 33640   Phone: (813)584-7333
Elizabeth Handville. Biennial, 1989-90 edition. Each one-page occupational profile describes duties, working conditions, physical surroundings and demands, aptitudes, temperament, educational requirements, employment outlook, earnings, and places of employment.

★6286★
"Hand Sewer" in *Occu-Facts: Information on 565 Careers in Outline Form* **(p. 18.27)**
Careers, Inc.
P.O. Box 135
1211 Tenth St., S.W.
Largo, FL 33640   Phone: (813)584-7333
Elizabeth Handville. Biennial, 1989-90 edition. Each one-page occupational profile describes duties, working conditions, physical surroundings and demands, aptitudes, temperament, educational requirements, employment outlook, earnings, and places of employment.

★6287★
Presser, Garment
Careers, Inc.
PO Box 135
Largo, FL 34649-0135   Phone: (813)584-7333
1989. Two-page job guide card describing duties, working conditions, personal qualifications, training, earnings and hours, employment outlook, places of employment, related careers and where to write for more information.

★6288★
Seamstress
Vocational Biographies, Inc.
PO Box 31, Dept. VF10
Sauk Centre, MN 56378   Phone: (612)352-6516
1991. This pamphlet profiles a person working in the job. Includes information about job duties, working conditions, places of employment, educational preparation, labor market outlook, and salaries. **Toll-free/Additional Phone Number(s):** 800-255-0752.

★6289★
Sewer, Drapery
Careers, Inc.
PO Box 135
Largo, FL 34649-0135   Phone: (813)584-7333
1989. Two-page job guide card describing duties, working conditions, personal qualifications, training, earnings and hours, employment outlook, places of employment, related careers and where to write for more information.

★6290★
Sewer, Hand
Careers, Inc.
PO Box 135
Largo, FL 34649-0135   Phone: (813)584-7333
1992. Two-page job guide card describing duties, working conditions, personal qualifications, training, earnings and hours, employment outlook, places of employment, related careers and where to write for more information.

★6291★
Sewing Machine Operator
Careers, Inc.
PO Box 135
Largo, FL 34649-0135   Phone: (813)584-7333
1988. Two-page occupational summary card describing duties, working conditions, personal qualifications, training, earnings and hours, employment outlook, places of employment, related careers and where to write for more information.

★6292★
"Sewing Machine Operator" in *Occu-Facts: Information on 565 Careers in Outline Form* **(p. 18.16)**
Careers, Inc.
P.O. Box 135
1211 Tenth St., S.W.
Largo, FL 33640   Phone: (813)584-7333
Elizabeth Handville. Biennial, 1989-90 edition. Each one-page occupational profile describes duties, working conditions, physical surroundings and demands, aptitudes, temperament, educational requirements, employment outlook, earnings, and places of employment.

Apparel Workers

★6293★
Sewing Machine Operators (Apparel)
Chronicle Guidance Publications, Inc.
PO Box 1190
Moravia, NY 13118-1190 Phone: (315)497-0330
1989. This career brief describes the nature of the work, working conditions, hours and earnings, education and training, licensure, certification, unions, personal qualifications, social and psychological factors, employment outlook, entry methods, advancement, and related occupations. **Toll-free/Additional Phone Number(s):** 800-622-7284.

★6294★
"Shirt Presser" in Occu-Facts: Information on 565 Careers in Outline Form (p. 18.18)
Careers, Inc.
P.O. Box 135
1211 Tenth St., S.W.
Largo, FL 33640 Phone: (813)584-7333
Elizabeth Handville. Biennial, 1989-90 edition. Each one-page occupational profile describes duties, working conditions, physical surroundings and demands, aptitudes, temperament, educational requirements, employment outlook, earnings, and places of employment.

★6295★
Tailors
Chronicle Guidance Publications, Inc.
PO Box 1190
Moravia, NY 13118-1190 Phone: (315)497-0330
1990. This career brief describes the nature of the work, working conditions, hours and earnings, education and training, licensure, certification, unions, personal qualifications, social and psychological factors, employment outlook, entry methods, advancement, and related occupations. **Toll-free/Additional Phone Number(s):** 800-622-7284.

★6296★
Tailors
Careers, Inc.
PO Box 135
Largo, FL 34649-0135 Phone: (813)584-7333
1991. Eight-page brief offering the definition, history, duties, working conditions, personal qualifications, educational requirements, earnings, hours, employment outlook, advancement possibilities, and related occupations.

★6297★
"Tailors" in Occu-Facts: Information on 565 Careers in Outline Form (p. 17.18)
Careers, Inc.
P.O. Box 135
1211 Tenth St., S.W.
Largo, FL 33640 Phone: (813)584-7333
Elizabeth Handville. Biennial, 1989-90 edition. Each one-page occupational profile describes duties, working conditions, physical surroundings and demands, aptitudes, temperament, educational requirements, employment outlook, earnings, and places of employment.

★6298★
Video Career Library - Production I
Careers, Inc.
1211 10th St., SW
PO Box 135
Largo, FL 34649-0135 Phone: (813)584-7333
Videocassette. 1990. 28 mins. Part of the Video Career Library covering 165 occupations. Shows actual workers on the job. Includes layout workers, precision typesetters, lithographers/photoengravers, bookbinders, hand tailors/dressmakers, upholsterers, water/sewage plant operators, chemical plant operators, and power plant operators.

Associations

★6299★
American Apparel Manufacturers Association (AAMA)
2500 Wilson Blvd., Ste. 301
Arlington, VA 22201 Phone: (703)524-1864
Membership: Manufacturers (434) of infants', children's, boys', girls', juniors', men's, and women's wearing apparel; associate members (381) are suppliers of fabrics, equipment, accessories, and services to the apparel industry. **Purpose:** Conducts seminars. Operates the Apparel Foundation; offers placement service through newsletter; compiles statistics. **Publications:** *AAMA Directory of Members and Associate Members*, annual. ● *AAMA Newsletter*, monthly. ● *Apparel College Directory*, biennial. ● *Apparel Factory Outlet Stores Survey*, annual. ● *Apparel Import Digest*, annual. ● *Apparel Plant Wages Survey*, annual. ● *Apparel Research Notes*, periodic. ● *Apparel Sales/Marketing Compensation Survey*, annual. ● *Comm ittee Manual*, annual. ● *Consumer Affairs Newsletter*, periodic. ● *Economic Profile*, annual. ● *Personnel Policy Survey*, biennial. ● *Technical Advisory Committee Bulletin*, periodic. ● *Technical Advisory Committee Research Paper*, annual. ● *Washington Letter*, every three weeks. **Facsimile Number:** (703)522-6741.

★6300★
National Association of Hosiery Manufacturers (NAHM)
447 S. Sharon Amity Rd.
Charlotte, NC 28211 Phone: (704)365-0913
Membership: Hosiery manufacturers and suppliers. **Purpose:** Develops standards for hosiery measurement. Sponsors annual National Hosiery Week to educate consumers on hosiery varieties. Conducts field visitations for assistance in technical areas. Compiles statistics; maintains library; conducts research programs. **Publications:** *Annual Hosiery Statistics*. ● *Hosiery News*, monthly. ● *NAHM Directory of Hosiery Manufacturers*, periodic. ● *NAHM Directory of Hosiery Mill Suppliers*, periodic. ● Also publishes information on legislation and trade practice rules; disseminates career booklets to high school students. **Facsimile Number:** (704)362-2056.

Standards/Certification Agencies

★6301★
National Association of Hosiery Manufacturers (NAHM)
447 S. Sharon Amity Rd.
Charlotte, NC 28211 Phone: (704)365-0913
Develops standards for hosiery measurement.

Educational Directories and Programs

★6302★
Apparel College Directory (AAMA)
American Apparel Manufacturers Association (AAMA)
2500 Wilson Blvd., Ste. 301
Arlington, VA 22201 Phone: (703)524-1864
Biennial.

Basic Reference Guides and Handbooks

★6303★
Apparel Import Digest
American Apparel Manufacturers Association (AAMA)
2500 Wilson Blvd., Ste. 301
Arlington, VA 22201   Phone: (703)524-1864
Annual.

★6304★
Leather Today—Annual Directory Issue
Fur Publishing Plus, Inc.
19 W. 21 St., No. 403
New York, NY 10010   Phone: (212)727-1210
Annual. Lists of over 1,500 manufacturers, wholesalers, and manufacturers' representatives in the leather apparel industry; approximately 200 tanners and leather dealers; about 30 apparel shows; and about 10 apparel marts; coverage includes Canada. Entries include: company name, address, phone, contact name; some entries include brief description of products. For shows: Event name, date of occurrence, location, phone. For marts: Store name and phone. Arrangement: Companies are geographical; shows and marts are alphabetical. **Facsimile Number:** (212)727-1218.

Periodicals

★6305★
AAMA Committee Manual
American Apparel Manufacturers Association (AAMA)
2500 Wilson Blvd., Ste. 301
Arlington, VA 22201   Phone: (703)524-1864
Annual.

★6306★
AAMA Consumer Affairs Newsletter
American Apparel Manufacturers Association (AAMA)
2500 Wilson Blvd., Ste. 301
Arlington, VA 22201   Phone: (703)524-1864
Periodic.

★6307★
AAMA Newsletter
American Apparel Manufacturers Association (AAMA)
2500 Wilson Blvd., Ste. 301
Arlington, VA 22201   Phone: (703)524-1864
Monthly.

★6308★
AAMA Technical Advisory Committee Bulletin
American Apparel Manufacturers Association (AAMA)
2500 Wilson Blvd., Ste. 301
Arlington, VA 22201   Phone: (703)524-1864
Periodic.

★6309★
Activewear Business News Magazine
Virgo Publishing, Inc.
PO Box C-5400
Scottsdale, AZ 85261   Phone: (602)483-0014
Brent Diamond, Editor. 12x/yr. Apparel trade magazine.

★6310★
Apparel Factory Outlet Stores Survey
American Apparel Manufacturers Association (AAMA)
2500 Wilson Blvd., Ste. 301
Arlington, VA 22201   Phone: (703)524-1864
Annual.

★6311★
Apparel Industry Magazine
Shore Communications, Inc.
180 Allen Rd. NE, Bldg. N, Ste. 300
Atlanta, GA 30328   Phone: (404)252-8831
Larry Shore, Publisher. Monthly. Magazine covering technology, management, and marketing for American apparel manufacturers. **Facsimile Number:** (404)252-4436.

★6312★
Apparel Research Notes (AAMA)
American Apparel Manufacturers Association (AAMA)
2500 Wilson Blvd., Ste. 301
Arlington, VA 22201   Phone: (703)524-1864
Periodic.

★6313★
Clothing Manufacturers Association—News Bulletin
Clothing Manufacturers Association
1290 6th Ave.
New York, NY 10104   Phone: (212)757-6664
Editor(s): Robert A. Kaplan. Disseminates information for the association relating to developments in or affecting the manufacturing of men's and boy's tailored clothing in the U.S. Contains statistics on sales, production, earnings, size, and industry earnings. Recurring features include notices of publications available, labor advisories, import advisories, and news of business opportunities.

★6314★
Economic Profile
American Apparel Manufacturers Association (AAMA)
2500 Wilson Blvd., Ste. 301
Arlington, VA 22201   Phone: (703)524-1864
Annual.

★6315★
Hosiery News
National Association of Hosiery Manufacturers (NAHM)
447 S. Sharon Amity Rd.
Charlotte, NC 28211   Phone: (704)365-0913
Monthly. Trade magazine of the hosiery industry covering legislative and regulatory issues; technology and equipment; new hosiery products at retail; hosiery production, shipments, and foreign trade information; other information of interest to hosiery manufacturers. Includes calendar of events and trademarks entering the field.

★6316★
Justice
International Ladies' Garment and Workers' Union
1710 Broadway
New York, NY 10019   Phone: (212)691-1100
Dwight Burton, Editor. Monthly. Labor magazine.

★6317★
Labor Unity
Amalgamated Clothing & Textile Workers Union
15 Union Sq.
New York, NY 10003   Phone: (212)242-0700
Anne Rivera, Editor. 6x/yr. Tabloid magazine for union members. Contains news of union activities and reports on

organizing, collective bargaining, union policy, and legislative positions. **Facsimile Number:** (212)255-7230.

★6318★
The Needle's Eye
Union Special Corp.
1 Union Special Plaza
Huntley, IL 60142   Phone: (708)699-5101
William H. Christoffersen, Editor. 6x/yr. Sewing industry magazine. **Facsimile Number:** (708)669-3534.

★6319★
Washington Letter
American Apparel Manufacturers Association (AAMA)
2500 Wilson Blvd., Ste. 301
Arlington, VA 22201   Phone: (703)524-1864
Every three weeks.

──────── Meetings and Conventions ────────

★6320★
American Apparel Manufacturers Association (AAMA)
2500 Wilson Blvd., Ste. 301
Arlington, VA 22201   Phone: (703)524-1864
Frequency: Annual, always Atlanta, GA. 1992; Sep. 14-18. Also holds annual spring meeting. **Facsimile Number:** (703)522-6741.

★6321★
Apparel Show of the Americas
Bobbin Blenheim, Inc.
1110 Shop Rd.
PO Box 1986
Columbia, SC 29202   Phone: (803)771-7500
1992; Mar. 25-27; Miami Beach, FL. **Toll-free/Additional Phone Number(s):** 800-845-8820. **Facsimile Number:** (803)799-1461.

★6322★
Industrial Fabric and Equipment Show
Industrial Fabrics Association International
345 Cedar St., Ste. 800
St. Paul, MN 55101   Phone: (612)222-2508
1992; Oct. 03-06; Phoenix, AZ ● 1993; Oct. 16-19; Denver, CO ● 1994; Oct. 29-01; Los Angeles, CA ● 1995; Oct. 27-30; St. Louis, MO. **Toll-free/Additional Phone Number(s):** 800-225-4324. **Facsimile Number:** (612)222-8215.

──────── Other Sources of Information ────────

★6323★
AAMA Technical Advisory Committee Research Paper

American Apparel Manufacturers Association (AAMA)
2500 Wilson Blvd., Ste. 301
Arlington, VA 22201   Phone: (703)524-1864
Annual.

★6324★
Annual Hosiery Statistics
National Association of Hosiery Manufacturers (NAHM)
447 S. Sharon Amity Rd.
Charlotte, NC 28211   Phone: (704)365-0913
Includes information on inventories, per capita consumption, imports/exports, and number of hosiery companies, plants, and employees in the industry. Offers listing of additional sources of information.

★6325★
Apparel Plant Wages Survey
American Apparel Manufacturers Association (AAMA)
2500 Wilson Blvd., Ste. 301
Arlington, VA 22201   Phone: (703)524-1864
Annual.

★6326★
Personnel Policy Survey
American Apparel Manufacturers Association (AAMA)
2500 Wilson Blvd., Ste. 301
Arlington, VA 22201   Phone: (703)524-1864
Biennial.

Shoe and Leather Workers and Repairers

Shoe and leather workers create stylish and durable leather products; shoe and leather repairers keep them in good condition. Among the workers who do leather work and repair are custom luggage makers and orthopedic shoemakers, saddlemakers, and harnessmakers. Self-employed shoe repairers and owners of custom-made shoe and leather shops have managerial responsibilities in addition to their regular duties. They hold over 30 percent of all shoe and leather work and repair jobs. The rest are employed in the manufacture of leather goods. Other areas of employment include large shops operated by shoe stores, department stores, and drycleaning establishments.

$alaries

Average earnings of shoe and leather workers and repairers is $8.00—$11.00/hour. Beginning workers start at $6.00/hour.

Employment Outlook

Growth rate until the year 2000: Employment is expected to remain level.

Shoe and Leather Workers and Repairers

Career Guides

★6327★
Career Information in Shoe Repair
Shoe Service Industry Council
154 W. Hubbard St.
Chicago, IL 60610   Phone: (312)670-3732

This eight-panel brochure describes skills required, job duties, working conditions, places of employment, and earnings. Illustrates the costs of owning a shoe repair business. Includes a state-by-state list of shoe repair schools.

★6328★
Custom Boot Maker
Vocational Biographies, Inc.
PO Box 31, Dept. VF10
Sauk Centre, MN 56378   Phone: (612)352-6516

1989. This pamphlet profiles a person working in the job. Includes information about job duties, working conditions, places of employment, educational preparation, labor market outlook, and salaries. **Toll-free/Additional Phone Number(s):** 800-255-0752.

★6329★
"Leather and Shoe Industries" in *Manufacturing*, Volume 9 of *Career Information Center* (pp. 119-121)
Glencoe/Macmillan
15319 Chatsworth St.
Mission Hills, CA 91345   Phone: (818)898-1391

Richard Lidz and Dale Anderson, editorial directors. Fourth edition, 1990. For 600 occupations, describes job duties, entry-level requirements, education and training needed, advancement possibilities, employment outlook, earnings and benefits. The set is divided into 12 volumes. Each volume includes jobs related under a broad career field. Volume 13 is the index. **Facsimile Number:** 818-365-5489.

★6330★
"Leatherworking" in *Opportunities in Crafts Careers* (p. 61)
National Textbook Co.
4255 W. Touhy Ave.
Lincolnwood, IL 60646   Phone: (312)679-5500

Marianne F. Munday. 1988. Covers crafts such as woodworking, ceramics, and leatherworking, and crafts-related careers such as writing and teaching. Offers advice on planning a career in crafts, starting a crafts business, and selling crafts.

★6331★
Pedorthics: Providing Footwear and Related Services to Aid in the Care of the Foot
Prescription Footwear Association
The Board for Certification in Pedorthics
9861 Broken Land Parkway, Ste. 255
Columbia, MD 21046-1151   Phone: (410)381-7278

1991. This 12-page booklet describes the work of a pedorthist. Covers areas of specialization and certification.

★6332★
"Saddlemaker" in *Offbeat Careers: The Directory of Unusual Work* (pp. 140-141)
Ten Speed Press
PO Box 7123
Berkeley, CA 94707   Phone: (415)845-8414

Al Sacharov. 1988. Profiles eighty-eight unusual careers. Provides job description, history of occupation, salary, and training required. Lists one or more sources of additional information.

★6333★
"Shoe and Leather Workers and Repairers" in *Occupational Outlook Handbook* (pp. 420-421)
Superintendent of Documents
U.S. Government Printing Office
Washington, DC 20402   Phone: (202)783-3238

Biennial; latest edition, 1990-91. Encyclopedia of careers describing more than 250 occupations and comprising about 86 percent of all jobs in the economy. Occupations that require lengthy education or training are given the most attention. For each occupation, the handbook describes job duties, working conditions, training, educational preparation, personal qualities, advancement possibilities, job outlook, earnings, and sources of additional information.

★6334★
"Shoe and Leather Workers and Repairers" in Volume 3 of *The Encyclopedia of Careers and Vocational Guidance* (pp. 311-313)
J.G. Ferguson Publishing Co.
200 W. Monroe
Chicago, IL 60606   Phone: (312)580-5480

William E. Hopke, editor-in-chief. Eighth edition, 1990. Four-volume set that profiles 500 occupations and describes job trends in 76 industries. Includes career description, educational requirements, history of the job, methods of entry, advancement, employment outlook, earnings, working conditions, social and psychological factors, and sources of additional information.

★6335★
Shoe Industry Workers
Chronicle Guidance Publications, Inc.
PO Box 1190
Moravia, NY 13118-1190   Phone: (315)497-0330
1987. This career brief describes the nature of the work, working conditions, hours and earnings, education and training, licensure, certification, unions, personal qualifications, social and psychological factors, employment outlook, entry methods, advancement, and related occupations. **Toll-free/Additional Phone Number(s):** 800-622-7284.

★6336★
"Shoe Industry Workers" in Volume 6 of *Career Discovery Encyclopedia* (pp. 26-27)
J.G. Ferguson Publishing Co.
200 W. Monroe
Chicago, IL 60606   Phone: (312)580-5480
E. Russell Primm, editor-in-chief. 1990. Contains two-page articles on 504 occupations. Each article describes job duties, earnings, and educational and training requirements.

★6337★
"Shoe Industry Workers" in Volume 3 of *The Encyclopedia of Careers and Vocational Guidance* (pp. 599-602)
J.G. Ferguson Publishing Co.
200 W. Monroe
Chicago, IL 60606   Phone: (312)580-5480
William E. Hopke, editor-in-chief. Eighth edition, 1990. Four-volume set that profiles 500 occupations and describes job trends in 76 industries. Includes career description, educational requirements, history of the job, methods of entry, advancement, employment outlook, earnings, working conditions, social and psychological factors, and sources of additional information.

★6338★
Shoe Repairer
Careers, Inc.
PO Box 135
Largo, FL 34649-0135   Phone: (813)584-7333
1990. Two-page occupational summary card describing duties, working conditions, personal qualifications, training, earnings and hours, employment outlook, places of employment, related careers and where to write for more information.

★6339★
"Shoe Repairer" in *Consumer, Homemaking, and Personal Services*, Volume 5 of *Career Information Center* (pp. 59-61)
Glencoe/Macmillan
15319 Chatsworth St.
Mission Hills, CA 91345   Phone: (818)898-1391
Richard Lidz and Dale Anderson, editorial directors. Fourth edition, 1990. For 600 occupations, describes job duties, entry-level requirements, education and training needed, advancement possibilities, employment outlook, earnings and benefits. The set is divided into 12 volumes. Each volume includes jobs related under a broad career field. Volume 13 is the index. **Facsimile Number:** 818-365-5489.

★6340★
"Shoe Repairer" in *Occu-Facts: Information on 565 Careers in Outline Form* (p. 17.20)
Careers, Inc.
P.O. Box 135
1211 Tenth St., S.W.
Largo, FL 33640   Phone: (813)584-7333
Elizabeth Handville. Biennial, 1989-90 edition. Each one-page occupational profile describes duties, working conditions, physical surroundings and demands, aptitudes, temperament, educational requirements, employment outlook, earnings, and places of employment.

★6341★
"Shoe Repairer" in *Personal Services* (pp. 63-67)
Franklin Watts, Inc.
387 Park Avenue, S.
New York, NY 10016   Phone: (212)686-7070
Linda Barrett and Galen Guengerich. 1991. Surveys personal services jobs. Describes job duties, educational preparation, salaries, and employment outlook. Offers job hunting advice.

★6342★
Shoe Repairers
Chronicle Guidance Publications, Inc.
PO Box 1190
Moravia, NY 13118-1190   Phone: (315)497-0330
1987. This career brief describes the nature of the work, working conditions, hours and earnings, education and training, licensure, certification, unions, personal qualifications, social and psychological factors, employment outlook, entry methods, advancement, and related occupations. **Toll-free/Additional Phone Number(s):** 800-622-7284.

★6343★
"Shoe Repairers" in Volume 6 of *Career Discovery Encyclopedia* (pp. 28-29)
J.G. Ferguson Publishing Co.
200 W. Monroe
Chicago, IL 60606   Phone: (312)580-5480
E. Russell Primm, editor-in-chief. 1990. Contains two-page articles on 504 occupations. Each article describes job duties, earnings, and educational and training requirements.

★6344★
"Shoe Repairers" in *The American Almanac of Jobs and Salaries* (pp. 525-526)
Avon Books
105 Madison Avenue
New York, NY 10016   Phone: (212)481-5600
John Wright and Edward J. Dwyer. Revised and updated, 1990. A comprehensive guide to the wages of hundreds of occupations in a wide variety of industries and organizations.

Associations

★6345★
Prescription Footwear Association (PFA)
9861 Broken Land Pkwy.
Columbia, MD 21046   Phone: (301)381-7278
Membership: Manufacturers and retailers of orthopedic footwear; associate members are affiliated branch stores. **Purpose:** Works to enhance and educate retailers in the comfort shoe business to provide for improved customer service. Conducts seminars on orthopedic footwear for adults and children. Provides donations to the Prescription Footwear Research Fund. Maintains library of information on orthopedic

footwear. **Publications:** *Pedoscope*, bimonthly. • *PFA Directory*, annual. **Facsimile Number:** (301)381-1167.

Basic Reference Guides and Handbooks

★6346★
The Complete Handbook of Leathercrafting
Krieger Publishing Company
PO Box 9542
Melbourne, FL 32902 Phone: (407)724-9542
Jane E. Garnes. 1986. **Facsimile Number:** (407)951-3671.

★6347★
Easy-to-Do Leathercraft Projects with Full-Size Templates
Dover Publications, Inc.
31 E. Second St.
Mineola, NY 11501 Phone: (516)294-7000
David Dorne. 1976.

★6348★
Leather Braiding
Cornell Maritime Press, Inc.
PO Box 456
Centreville, MD 21617 Phone: (301)758-1075
Bruce Grant.

★6349★
Leather Makin'
Horizon Publishers & Distributors
PO Box 490
Bountiful, UT 84011-0490 Phone: (801)295-9451
Larry J. Wells. 1985.

★6350★
Leather Today—Annual Directory Issue
Fur Publishing Plus, Inc.
19 W. 21 St., No. 403
New York, NY 10010 Phone: (212)727-1210
Annual. Lists of over 1,500 manufacturers, wholesalers, and manufacturers' representatives in the leather apparel industry; approximately 200 tanners and leather dealers; about 30 apparel shows; and about 10 apparel marts; coverage includes Canada. Entries include: company name, address, phone, contact name; some entries include brief description of products. For shows: Event name, date of occurrence, location, phone. For marts: Store name and phone. Arrangement: Companies are geographical; shows and marts are alphabetical. **Facsimile Number:** (212)727-1218.

★6351★
Leather Tooling & Carving
Dover Publications, Inc.
31 E. Second St.
Mineola, NY 11501 Phone: (516)294-7000
Chris H. Groneman. 1974.

★6352★
PFA Directory
Prescription Footwear Association (PFA)
9861 Broken Land Pkwy.
Columbia, MD 21046 Phone: (301)381-7278
Annual.

★6353★
Projects in Leather
International Specialized Book Services
5602 NE Hassalo St.
Porland, OR 97213 Phone: (503)287-3093
Thor Kristinsson. 1985. **Facsimile Number:** (503)284-8859.

Periodicals

★6354★
American Shoemaking
PO Box 198
Cambridge, MA 02140 Phone: (617)648-8160
James D. Sutton, Editor. Monthly. Magazine reporting on shoe manufacturing. **Facsimile Number:** (617)492-0126.

★6355★
FIA Executive Digest
Footwear Industries of America, Inc. (FIA)
1420 K St. NW, Ste. 600
Washington, DC 20005 Phone: (202)789-1420
Editor(s): Brad Hurlbut. Monthly. Publishes association activities in the areas of footwear technology, finance and management, national affairs, and marketing. Provides current industry statistics.

★6356★
FN (Footwear News)
Fairchild Publications
7 E. 12th St.
New York, NY 10003 Phone: (212)741-4321
Dick Silverman, Editor. Weekly (Mon.). Newspaper covering international footwear, accessories, and leather industries. **Facsimile Number:** (212)337-3224.

★6357★
The Leather Craftsman
Craftsman Publishing Co.
PO Box 1749
Burleson, TX 76028 Phone: (817)295-4695
Nancy Sawyer, Editor. 6x/yr. Magazine for leathercrafters and leather artisans. **Facsimile Number:** (817)295-7413.

★6358★
The Leather Manufacturer
PO Box 198
Cambridge, MA 02140 Phone: (617)648-8160
James Sutton, Editor. Monthly. Magazine on tanning and finishing leather. **Facsimile Number:** (617)492-0126.

★6359★
Pedoscope
Prescription Footwear Association (PFA)
9861 Broken Land Pkwy.
Columbia, MD 21046 Phone: (301)381-7278
Bimonthly. Newsletter.

★6360★
Shoe Service
SSIA Service Corp.
24-R Campbell Blvd.
Baltimore, MD 21236 Phone: (301)931-8100
Mitchell Lebovic, Editor. Monthly. Magazine for the shoe repair industry includes articles detailing modern shoe repair techniques, new technology and products, guides to operating small businesses, industry and convention news, machine

★6361★

maintenance, and features concerning interesting repairers and unique shops. **Facsimile Number:** (301)931-8111.

★6361★
Show Reporter
335 Boylston St.
Newton Center, MA 02159   Phone: (617)965-4577

Irving B. Roberts, Editor and Publisher. 7x/yr. Footwear and related industries publication.

Meetings and Conventions

★6362★
Assembly Technology Expo
Professional Exposition Management Co., Inc. (PEMCO)
2400 E. Devon Ave., Ste. 205
Des Plaines, IL 60018   Phone: (708)299-3131

★6363★
National Shoe Fair of America
National Shoe Fair of America
50 Glen St., 1st Fl.
Glen Cove, NY 11542-2701   Phone: (516)674-0200

1992; Jul. 27-29; Las Vegas, NV. **Facsimile Number:** (516)674-0288.

Textile Machinery Operators

Textile machinery operators tend machines that manufacture textile goods used in all types of consumer and industrial products. There are many phases in the textile production process, and operators' duties and responsibilities depend on the product and the type of machinery in use. Extruding and forming machine operators and tenders maintain the machinery that produces manufactured fiber. Because this fiber is created by a chemical process, the majority of these workers are employed by chemical companies. Textile machine operators and tenders operate the machinery that prepares manufactured or natural fibers for spinning. Textile machine setters and setup operators prepare the machinery prior to a production run and maintain the equipment. Textile bleaching and dyeing machine operators and tenders oversee machines that dye and finish the product either at the textile mill or at a plant specializing in textile finishing. The majority of textile machinery operators are employed in weaving, finishing, yarn, and thread mills. Other significant employers are knitting mills and manufactured fiber producers.

$alaries

Earnings for textile machinery operators vary significantly depending upon the type of mill. The average weekly earnings of production workers in the textile and manufactured fiber industries are as follows:

Organic fibers, noncellulosic	$535.00/week
Miscellaneous textile goods	$358.00/week
Weaving and finishing mills, wool	$335.00/week
Weaving mills, synthetics	$333.00/week
Floor covering mills	$329.00/week
Textile finishing, except wool	$327.00/week
Weaving mills, cotton	$316.00/week
Yarn and thread mills	$288.00/week
Narrow fabric mills	$284.00/week
Knitting mills	$265.00/week

Employment Outlook

Growth rate until the year 2000: Slower than average.

Textile Machinery Operators

Career Guides

★6364★
Fashion & Textile Careers
Prentice Hall
Rte. 9W
Englewood Cliffs, NJ 07632   Phone: (201)592-2000
Martha S. Servian. 1977. Part of Home Economics Careers Series.

★6365★
Staple Yarn Production
North Carolina State University
School of Textiles/ITS
Post Office Box 8301
Raleigh, NC 27695-8301   Phone: (919)737-3231
Videocassette. 1987. 18 mins. A detailed look at the art and machinery of staple yarn production.

★6366★
"Textile Industry" in *Manufacturing*, Volume 9 of *Career Information Center* (pp. 142-144)
Glencoe/Macmillan
15319 Chatsworth St.
Mission Hills, CA 91345   Phone: (818)898-1391
Richard Lidz and Dale Anderson, editorial directors. Fourth edition, 1990. For 600 occupations, describes job duties, entry-level requirements, education and training needed, advancement possibilities, employment outlook, earnings and benefits. The set is divided into 12 volumes. Each volume includes jobs related under a broad career field. Volume 13 is the index. **Facsimile Number:** 818-365-5489.

★6367★
"Textile Machinery Operators" in *Occupational Outlook Handbook* (pp. 421-424)
Superintendent of Documents
U.S. Government Printing Office
Washington, DC 20402   Phone: (202)783-3238
Biennial; latest edition, 1990-91. Encyclopedia of careers describing more than 250 occupations and comprising about 86 percent of all jobs in the economy. Occupations that require lengthy education or training are given the most attention. For each occupation, the handbook describes job duties, working conditions, training, educational preparation, personal qualities, advancement possibilities, job outlook, earnings, and sources of additional information.

★6368★
"Textile Manufacturing Occupations" in Volume 3 of *The Encyclopedia of Careers and Vocational Guidance* (pp. 557-561)
J.G. Ferguson Publishing Co.
200 W. Monroe
Chicago, IL 60606   Phone: (312)580-5480
William E. Hopke, editor-in-chief. Eighth edition, 1990. Four-volume set that profiles 500 occupations and describes job trends in 76 industries. Includes career description, educational requirements, history of the job, methods of entry, advancement, employment outlook, earnings, working conditions, social and psychological factors, and sources of additional information.

★6369★
Textile Mill Worker
Vocational Biographies, Inc.
PO Box 31, Dept. VF10
Sauk Centre, MN 56378   Phone: (612)352-6516
1990. This pamphlet profiles a person working in the job. Includes information about job duties, working conditions, places of employment, educational preparation, labor market outlook, and salaries. **Toll-free/Additional Phone Number(s):** 800-255-0752.

★6370★
Textile Production Workers
Chronicle Guidance Publications, Inc.
PO Box 1190
Moravia, NY 13118-1190   Phone: (315)497-0330
1988. This career brief describes the nature of the work, working conditions, hours and earnings, education and training, licensure, certification, unions, personal qualifications, social and psychological factors, employment outlook, entry methods, advancement, and related occupations. **Toll-free/Additional Phone Number(s):** 800-622-7284.

★6371★
"Textile Workers" in Volume 6 of *Career Discovery Encyclopedia* (pp. 110-111)
J.G. Ferguson Publishing Co.
200 W. Monroe
Chicago, IL 60606   Phone: (312)580-5480
E. Russell Primm, editor-in-chief. 1990. Contains two-page articles on 504 occupations. Each article describes job duties, earnings, and educational and training requirements.

★6372★

★6372★
"Textiles" in Volume 1 of *The Encyclopedia of Careers and Vocational Guidance* (pp. 465-471)
J.G. Ferguson Publishing Co.
200 W. Monroe
Chicago, IL 60606   Phone: (312)580-5480
William E. Hopke, editor-in-chief. Eighth edition, 1990. Four-volume set that profiles 500 occupations and describes job trends in 76 industries. Includes career description, educational requirements, history of the job, methods of entry, advancement, employment outlook, earnings, working conditions, social and psychological factors, and sources of additional information.

---- Associations ----

★6373★
American Fiber Manufacturers Association (AFMA)
1150 17th St. NW
Washington, DC 20036   Phone: (202)296-6508
Membership: Producers of manufactured fibers used in apparel, household goods, industrial materials, and other types of products. **Purpose:** Represents the industry in educational, governmental, and foreign trade matters. Distributes a video depicting production and end uses of manufactured fibers. Bestows research award annually. **Publications:** *Manufactured Fiber Guide*, periodic. • Also publishes *Manufactured Fiber Fact Book*. **Facsimile Number:** (202)296-3052.

★6374★
American Textile Manufacturers Institute (ATMI)
1801 K St. NW, Ste. 900
Washington, DC 20006   Phone: (202)862-0500
Membership: Textile mill firms operating machinery for manufacturing and processing cotton, man-made, wool, and silk textile products; includes spinning, weaving, bleaching, finishing, knitting, and allied plants; does not include manufacturers of hosiery or firms that produce man-made fibers and yarn by a chemical process. **Purpose:** Operates public relations program for the industry, government relations program, textile market program, and statistical and economic information service. Holds seminars and meetings. Maintains 1200 volume library. Sponsors safety contest among textile mills. **Publications:** *Annual Report*. • *ATMI Member Product Directory*, periodic. • *Bulletin*, periodic. • *Official Directory*, annual. • *Textile Hi-Lights*, quarterly. • *Textile Trends*, weekly.

★6375★
National Association of Hosiery Manufacturers (NAHM)
447 S. Sharon Amity Rd.
Charlotte, NC 28211   Phone: (704)365-0913
Membership: Hosiery manufacturers and suppliers. **Purpose:** Develops standards for hosiery measurement. Sponsors annual National Hosiery Week to educate consumers on hosiery varieties. Conducts field visitations for assistance in technical areas. Compiles statistics; maintains library; conducts research programs. **Publications:** *Annual Hosiery Statistics*. • *Hosiery News*, monthly. • *NAHM Directory of Hosiery Manufacturers*, periodic. • *NAHM Directory of Hosiery Mill Suppliers*, periodic. • Also publishes information on legislation and trade practice rules; disseminates career booklets to high school students. **Facsimile Number:** (704)362-2056.

---- Standards/Certification Agencies ----

★6376★
National Association of Hosiery Manufacturers (NAHM)
447 S. Sharon Amity Rd.
Charlotte, NC 28211   Phone: (704)365-0913
Develops standards for hosiery measurement.

---- Basic Reference Guides and Handbooks ----

★6377★
America's Textiles International—Buyer's Guide Issue
Billian Publishing Company
2100 Powers Ferry Rd., Ste. 300
Atlanta, GA 30339   Phone: (404)955-5656
Monte G. Plott and Pat Heller-Bramblett, editor. Annual, July. List of 2,100 suppliers for the textile industry. Entries include: Supplier name, address, phone, telex, fax; separate section lists products for each supplier. Arrangement: Alphabetical. Indexes: Product. **Facsimile Number:** (404)952-0669.

★6378★
Manufactured Fiber Guide
American Fiber Manufacturers Association (AFMA)
1150 17th St. NW
Washington, DC 20036   Phone: (202)296-6508
Periodic.

---- Periodicals ----

★6379★
American Dyestuff Reporter
SAF International Publications, Inc.
Harmon Cove Towers
Promenade A, Ste. 2
Secaucus, NJ 07094   Phone: (201)867-9230
Edward Fox, Editor. Monthly. Magazine covering textile wet-processing. **Facsimile Number:** (201)867-0545.

★6380★
America's Textiles International
Billian Publishing
2100 Powers Ferry NW, Ste. 300
Atlanta, GA 30339   Phone: (404)955-5656
Monte Plott, Editor-in-Chief. Monthly. Magazine for the textile industry; including fiber producers, carpet mills, and dyeing and finishing plants. **Facsimile Number:** (404)952-0669.

★6381★
ATMI Bulletin
American Textile Manufacturers Institute (ATMI)
1801 K St. NW, Ste. 900
Washington, DC 20006   Phone: (202)862-0500
Periodic.

Textile Machinery Operators

★6382★
Clean Scene Magazine
Textile Rental Services Assn. of America
1130 E. Beach Blvd.
Hallandale, FL 33009   Phone: (305)457-7555
Christine Seaman, Editor. Monthly. Magazine featuring how-to information for textile maintenance managers. **Facsimile Number:** (305)457-3890.

★6383★
Hosiery News
National Association of Hosiery Manufacturers (NAHM)
447 S. Sharon Amity Rd.
Charlotte, NC 28211   Phone: (704)365-0913
Monthly. Trade magazine of the hosiery industry covering legislative and regulatory issues; technology and equipment; new hosiery products at retail; hosiery production, shipments, and foreign trade information; other information of interest to hosiery manufacturers. Includes calendar of events and trademarks entering the field.

★6384★
Journal of Coated Fabrics
TECHNOMIC Publishing Co., Inc.
851 New Holland Ave.
PO Box 3535
Lancaster, PA 17604   Phone: (717)291-5609
William C. Smith, Editor. Quarterly. Journal for the coated fabrics and textiles industry. **Facsimile Number:** (717)295-4538.

★6385★
Knitting Times
National Knitwear & Sportswear Assn.
386 Park Ave. S.
New York, NY 10016   Phone: (212)683-7520
David Gross, Editor. Monthly. Magazine for the knit apparel and textile industries. **Facsimile Number:** (212)532-0766.

★6386★
Labor Unity
Amalgamated Clothing & Textile Workers Union
15 Union Sq.
New York, NY 10003   Phone: (212)242-0700
Anne Rivera, Editor. 6x/yr. Tabloid magazine for union members. Contains news of union activities and reports on organizing, collective bargaining, union policy, and legislative positions. **Facsimile Number:** (212)255-7230.

★6387★
Textile Chemist and Colorist
American Assn. of Textile Chemists and Colorists
PO Box 12215
Research Triangle Park, NC 27709   Phone: (919)549-8141
Jack Kissiah, Editor. Monthly. Magazine focusing on dyeing, finishing of fibers and fabrics. **Facsimile Number:** (919)549-8933.

★6388★
Textile Hi-Lights
American Textile Manufacturers Institute (ATMI)
1801 K St. NW, Ste. 900
Washington, DC 20006   Phone: (202)862-0500
Quarterly. Includes monthly supplements.

★6389★
Textile Research Journal
Textile Research Institute
PO Box 625
Princeton, NJ 08542   Phone: (609)924-3150
Richard J. Toner, Editor. Monthly. Scientific journal on the textile and allied industries. **Facsimile Number:** (609)683-7836.

★6390★
Textile Technology Digest
Institute of Textile Technology
PO Box 391
Charlottesville, VA 22902   Phone: (804)296-5511
Dennis Loy, Sr. Editor. Monthly. Textile journal. **Facsimile Number:** (804)977-5400.

★6391★
Textile Trends
American Textile Manufacturers Institute (ATMI)
1801 K St. NW, Ste. 900
Washington, DC 20006   Phone: (202)862-0500
Weekly.

★6392★
Textile World
4170 Ashford Dunwoody Rd., Ste. 520
Atlanta, GA 30319   Phone: (404)847-2770
McAllister Isaacs, Exec. Editor. Monthly. Magazine on textiles and man-made fiber products.

──────── Meetings and Conventions ────────

★6393★
American Fiber Manufacturers Association (AFMA)
1150 17th St. NW
Washington, DC 20036   Phone: (202)296-6508
Frequency: Annual. **Facsimile Number:** (202)296-3052.

★6394★
American Textile Machinery Exhibition International
Textile Hall Corp.
PO Box 5823
Greenville, SC 29606   Phone: (803)233-2562
Always held at the Palmetto International Exposition Center in Greenville, South Carolina. 1992; Oct. 19-23; Greenville, SC • 1993; Apr. 19-23; Greenville, SC. **Facsimile Number:** (803)233-0619.

★6395★
American Textile Manufacturers Institute (ATMI)
1801 K St. NW, Ste. 900
Washington, DC 20006   Phone: (202)862-0500
Frequency: Annual.

★6396★
Industrial Fabric and Equipment Show
Industrial Fabrics Association International
345 Cedar St., Ste. 800
St. Paul, MN 55101   Phone: (612)222-2508
1992; Oct. 03-06; Phoenix, AZ • 1993; Oct. 16-19; Denver, CO • 1994; Oct. 29-01; Los Angeles, CA • 1995; Oct. 27-30; St. Louis, MO. **Toll-free/Additional Phone Number(s):** 800-225-4324. **Facsimile Number:** (612)222-8215.

Other Sources of Information

★6397★
Annual Hosiery Statistics (NAHM)
National Association of Hosiery Manufacturers (NAHM)
447 S. Sharon Amity Rd.
Charlotte, NC 28211   Phone: (704)365-0913
Includes information on inventories, per capita consumption, imports/exports, and number of hosiery companies, plants, and employees in the industry. Offers listing of additional sources of information.

★6398★
Manufactured Fiber Fact Book
American Fiber Manufacturers Association (AFMA)
1150 17th St. NW
Washington, DC 20036   Phone: (202)296-6508

Upholsterers

Upholsterers are skilled craft workers who make new furniture and recondition old furniture. Some repair and replace automobile upholstery and convertible and vinyl tops. Most work in upholstery shops. About 40 percent are self-employed. More than 20 percent are salaried workers in an upholstery repair, auto repair, or furniture store. About 33 percent work in furniture manufacturing.

$alaries

Average weekly earnings for upholsterers are as follows:

Lowest 10 percent	$220.00/week or less
Middle 50 percent	$260.00—$445.00/week
Top 10 percent	$550.00/week or more

Employment Outlook

Growth rate until the year 2000: Average.

Upholsterers

Career Guides

★6399★
"Custom Upholsterer" in *Consumer, Homemaking, and Personal Services,* Volume 5 of *Career Information Center* (pp. 76-77)
Glencoe/Macmillan
15319 Chatsworth St.
Mission Hills, CA 91345 Phone: (818)898-1391
Richard Lidz and Dale Anderson, editorial directors. Fourth edition, 1990. For 600 occupations, describes job duties, entry-level requirements, education and training needed, advancement possibilities, employment outlook, earnings and benefits. The set is divided into 12 volumes. Each volume includes jobs related under a broad career field. Volume 13 is the index. **Facsimile Number:** 818-365-5489.

★6400★
Furniture: An Opportunity Career
American Furniture Manufacturers
PO Box HP-7
High Point, NC 27261 Phone: (202)857-1119
This eight-page booklet briefly describes career opportunities in the furniture manufacturing industry.

★6401★
Furniture Upholsterer
Vocational Biographies, Inc.
PO Box 31, Dept. VF10
Sauk Centre, MN 56378 Phone: (612)352-6516
1988. This pamphlet profiles a person working in the job. Includes information about job duties, working conditions, places of employment, educational preparation, labor market outlook, and salaries. **Toll-free/Additional Phone Number(s):** 800-255-0752.

★6402★
"Furniture Upholsterer" in *Occu-Facts: Information on 565 Careers in Outline Form* (p. 17.19)
Careers, Inc.
P.O. Box 135
1211 Tenth St., S.W.
Largo, FL 33640 Phone: (813)584-7333
Elizabeth Handville. Biennial, 1989-90 edition. Each one-page occupational profile describes duties, working conditions, physical surroundings and demands, aptitudes, temperament, educational requirements, employment outlook, earnings, and places of employment.

★6403★
"Furniture Upholsterer and Tailor or Dressmaker" in *Personal Services* (pp. 39-43)
Franklin Watts, Inc.
387 Park Avenue, S.
New York, NY 10016 Phone: (212)686-7070
Linda Barrett and Galen Guengerich. 1991. Surveys personal services jobs. Describes job duties, educational preparation, salaries, and employment outlook. Offers job hunting advice.

★6404★
"Furniture Upholsterers" in Volume 3 of *Career Discovery Encyclopedia* (pp. 64-65)
J.G. Ferguson Publishing Co.
200 W. Monroe
Chicago, IL 60606 Phone: (312)580-5480
E. Russell Primm, editor-in-chief. 1990. Contains two-page articles on 504 occupations. Each article describes job duties, earnings, and educational and training requirements.

★6405★
"Furniture Upholsterers" in Volume 3 of *The Encyclopedia of Careers and Vocational Guidance* (pp. 579-581)
J.G. Ferguson Publishing Co.
200 W. Monroe
Chicago, IL 60606 Phone: (312)580-5480
William E. Hopke, editor-in-chief. Eighth edition, 1990. Four-volume set that profiles 500 occupations and describes job trends in 76 industries. Includes career description, educational requirements, history of the job, methods of entry, advancement, employment outlook, earnings, working conditions, social and psychological factors, and sources of additional information.

★6406★
"Industrial Upholsterer" in *Manufacturing,* Volume 9 of *Career Information Center* (pp. 63-64)
Glencoe/Macmillan
15319 Chatsworth St.
Mission Hills, CA 91345 Phone: (818)898-1391
Richard Lidz and Dale Anderson, editorial directors. Fourth edition, 1990. For 600 occupations, describes job duties, entry-level requirements, education and training needed, advancement possibilities, employment outlook, earnings and benefits. The set is divided into 12 volumes. Each volume includes jobs related under a broad career field. Volume 13 is the index. **Facsimile Number:** 818-365-5489.

★6407★
Upholsterer, Furniture
Careers, Inc.
PO Box 135
Largo, FL 34649-0135   Phone: (813)584-7333

1991. Two-page occupational summary card describing duties, working conditions, personal qualifications, training, earnings and hours, employment outlook, places of employment, related careers and where to write for more information.

★6408★
"Upholsterers" in *Occupational Outlook Handbook* (pp. 424-425)
Superintendent of Documents
U.S. Government Printing Office
Washington, DC 20402   Phone: (202)783-3238

Biennial; latest edition, 1990-91. Encyclopedia of careers describing more than 250 occupations and comprising about 86 percent of all jobs in the economy. Occupations that require lengthy education or training are given the most attention. For each occupation, the handbook describes job duties, working conditions, training, educational preparation, personal qualities, advancement possibilities, job outlook, earnings, and sources of additional information.

★6409★
Upholsterers (Furniture)
Chronicle Guidance Publications, Inc.
PO Box 1190
Moravia, NY 13118-1190   Phone: (315)497-0330

1988. This career brief describes the nature of the work, working conditions, hours and earnings, education and training, licensure, certification, unions, personal qualifications, social and psychological factors, employment outlook, entry methods, advancement, and related occupations. **Toll-free/Additional Phone Number(s):** 800-622-7284.

★6410★
Video Career Library - Production I
Careers, Inc.
1211 10th St., SW
PO Box 135
Largo, FL 34649-0135   Phone: (813)584-7333

Videocassette. 1990. 28 mins. Part of the Video Career Library covering 165 occupations. Shows actual workers on the job. Includes layout workers, precision typesetters, lithographers/photoengravers, bookbinders, hand tailors/dressmakers, upholsterers, water/sewage plant operators, chemical plant operators, and power plant operators.

Associations

★6411★
Autoleather Guild (AG)
776 Waddington Rd.
Birmingham, MI 48009   Phone: (313)646-5250

Purpose: Promotes the use of genuine leather seating in the automotive industry. Conducts dealer seminars.

★6412★
International Institute of Carpet and Upholstery Certification (IICUC)
2715 E. Mill Plain Blvd.
Vancouver, WA 98661   Phone: (206)693-5675

Membership: Fabric restoration firms (1300) and technicians (3500). **Purpose:** Sets standards of skill and ethics in the fabric restoration industry; works with regulatory bodies to establish proficiency standards. Certifies technicians, firms, and inspectors. **Publications:** *International Directory of Certified Professionals*, annual. **Facsimile Number:** (206)693-4858.

★6413★
National Association of Professional Upholsterers (NAPU)
200 S. Main
PO Box 2754
High Point, NC 27261   Phone: (919)889-0113

Membership: Professional upholsterers, furniture restorers, and custom furniture makers. **Purpose:** Seeks to increase profitability and productivity in the industry; represents members' interests. Provides group health insurance programs and group purchasing system. Conducts job training programs. **Publications:** *Upholstering Today*, periodic. ● Also publishes how-to books.

★6414★
Upholstered Furniture Action Council (UFAC)
PO Box 2436
High Point, NC 27261   Phone: (919)885-5065

Membership: National furniture manufacturers' and retailers' associations. **Purpose:** Conducts research and disseminates information regarding the development and adoption of voluntary guidelines for production of more cigarette-resistant upholstered furniture; educates the public in the safe use of smoking materials. Maintains speakers' bureau; compiles statistics. **Publications:** *UFAC: Important Consumer Safety Information from UFAC*, annual. ● *UFAC Volunteer*, quarterly. ● *Upholstered Furniture Action Council—Directory of Materials Suppliers*, annual. ● Also publishes books, reports, and promotional materials. **Facsimile Number:** (919)884-5303.

Standards/Certification Agencies

★6415★
International Institute of Carpet and Upholstery Certification (IICUC)
2715 E. Mill Plain Blvd.
Vancouver, WA 98661   Phone: (206)693-5675

Sets standards of skill and ethics in the fabric restoration industry; works with regulatory bodies to establish proficiency standards. Certifies technicians, firms, and inspectors.

Basic Reference Guides and Handbooks

★6416★
A Concise Guide to Upholstery Fabrics
State Mutual Book & Periodical Service, Ltd.
521 5th Ave. 17th Fl.
New York, NY 10175   Phone: (212)682-5844
1985.

★6417★
Flammability Regulations & Standards in the United States for Upholstered Furniture
Technomic Publishing Company
851 Holland Ave.
PO Box 3535
Lancaster, PA 17604-3535   Phone: (717)291-5609

Sharon Sue Williams. 1985. **Facsimile Number:** (717)295-4538.

★6418★
Industrial Fabrics in Upholstery
Industrial Fabrics Association International
345 Cedar St.
St. Paul, MN 55101   Phone: (612)222-2508
1981.

★6419★
Machine Developments in Upholstery Sewing
State Mutual Book & Periodical Service, Ltd.
521 5th Ave., 17th Fl.
New York, NY 10175   Phone: (212)682-5844
1985.

★6420★
Professional Upholster Cleaning Techniques: The Basics
Cleaning Consultant Services, Inc.
1512 Western Ave.
Seattle, WA 98101   Phone: (206)284-9954
Roy Moore. Revised edition, 1987.

★6421★
Re-Upholstery Techniques
Little, Brown & Co., Inc.
34 Beacon St.
Boston, MA 02108   Phone: (617)227-0730
Derek Balfour. 1986. **Facsimile Number:** (617)723-9422.

★6422★
Upholsterers' Supplies Directory
American Business Directories, Inc.
American Business Information, Inc.
5711 S. 86th Circle
Omaha, NE 68127   Phone: (402)593-4600
Annual. 1,030. Entries include: Name, address, phone, size of advertisement, name of owner or manager, number of employees, year first in "Yellow Pages." Arrangement: Geographical. **Facsimile Number:** (402)331-1505.

★6423★
Upholstering
Macmillan Publishing Company, Inc.
866 3rd Ave.
New York, NY 10022   Phone: (212)702-2000
James E. Brumbaugh. Second edition, 1984.

★6424★
Upholstering Methods
Goodheart-Willcox Company
123 Taft Dr.
South Holland, IL 60473   Phone: (708)333-7200
Fred W. Zimmerman. 1981. **Facsimile Number:** (708)331-9130.

★6425★
Upholstery
Sterling Publishing Company, Inc.
387 Park Ave. S.
New York, NY 10016-8810   Phone: (212)532-7160
Dorothy Gates. 1990. Part of Living Style Series. **Toll-free/Additional Phone Number(s):** 800-367-9692. **Facsimile Number:** (212)213-2495.

★6426★
Upholstery Styles: A Design Sourcebook
Van Nostrand Reinhold
115 5th Ave.
New York, NY 10003   Phone: (212)254-3232
Gillian Walking. 1989. **Facsimile Number:** (212)254-9499.

★6427★
Upholstery Techniques Illustrated
TAB Books
Blue Ridge Summit, PA 17294-0850   Phone: (717)794-2191
Lloyd W. Gheen. 1986.

Periodicals

★6428★
The Professional Upholsterer
Communications Today Publishing Ltd.
200 S. Main St.
PO Box 2754
High Point, NC 27261-2411   Phone: (919)889-0113
Gary Evans, Group Editor. 6x/yr. Professional upholstering magazine. **Facsimile Number:** (919)841-8256.

★6429★
UFAC Volunteer
Upholstered Furniture Action Council (UFAC)
PO Box 2436
High Point, NC 27261   Phone: (919)885-5065
Quarterly. Newsletter covering industry efforts to develop and promote cigarette-resistant upholstered furniture. Includes member profiles and profiles of Consumer Product Safety Commission employees.

★6430★
Upholstering Today
Communications/Today Ltd.
200 S. Main St.
PO Box 2754
High Point, NC 27261-2411   Phone: (919)889-0113
Gary Evans, Editor. Six times/yr. **Facsimile Number:** (919)841-8256.

★6431★
Upholstering Today
National Association of Professional Upholsterers (NAPU)
200 S. Main
PO Box 2754
High Point, NC 27261   Phone: (919)889-0113
Periodic.

★6432★
Upholstery Manufacturing Management
Delta Communications
PO Box 640
Collierville, TN 38027-0640   Phone: (901)853-7470
Stormy Fitzgerald, Editor. Monthly. Upholstery trade magazine. **Facsimile Number:** (901)853-6437.

Meetings and Conventions

★6433★
Industrial Fabric and Equipment Show
Industrial Fabrics Association International
345 Cedar St., Ste. 800
St. Paul, MN 55101   Phone: (612)222-2508
1992; Oct. 03-06; Phoenix, AZ • 1993; Oct. 16-19; Denver, CO • 1994; Oct. 29-01; Los Angeles, CA • 1995; Oct. 27-30; St. Louis, MO. **Toll-free/Additional Phone Number(s):** 800-225-4324. **Facsimile Number:** (612)222-8215.

Other Sources of Information

★6434★
The Upholstery Fact Book 1986
State Mutal Book & Periodical Service, Ltd.
521 5th Ave., 17th Fl.
New York, NY 10175   Phone: (212)682-5844
1986.

Woodworking Occupations

Woodworkers take raw wood and cut and assemble it to make wooden items. Production woodworkers are found in primary industries such as sawmills and plywood mills, as well as in secondary manufactures such as furniture, kitchen cabinets, musical instruments, and other fabricated wood products. Precision wookworkers, such as cabinetmakers, wood pattern and model makers, wood machinists, and furniture and wood finishers, are found in small shops making architectural woodwork, furniture, and many other specialty firms. They often work on a customized basis, often building one-of-a-kind items. Less skilled workers set up, operate, or tend production equipment or machinery. Wood machine operators in sawmills cut logs into planks, timbers, or boards. In planing mills, they cut veneer sheets from logs for making plywood. And in furniture plants, they make furniture components such as table legs, drawers, rails, and spindles. About 85 percent of all salaried woodworkers work in manufacturing industries. Approximately 24 percent are employed in establishments fabricating household and office furniture; 24 percent are in establishments making millwork, plywood, and structural wood members, used primarily in construction; and 12 percent work in sawmills and planing mills manufacturing a variety of raw, intermediate, and finished woodstock. Woodworkers also are employed by wholesale and retail lumber dealers, furniture stores, reupholstery and furniture repair shops, and construction firms.

$alaries

Median weekly earnings for precision woodworkers and woodworking machine operators are as follows:

Precision woodworkers	$290.00/week
Woodworking machine operators	$270.00/week

Employment Outlook

Growth rate until the year 2000: More slowly than average.

Woodworking Occupations

Career Guides

★6435★
Cabinetmaker
Careers, Inc.
PO Box 135
Largo, FL 34649-0135   Phone: (813)584-7333
1988. Two-page occupational summary card describing duties, working conditions, personal qualifications, training, earnings and hours, employment outlook, places of employment, related careers and where to write for more information.

★6436★
"Cabinetmaker" in *Occu-Facts: Information on 565 Careers in Outline Form* (p. 17.12)
Careers, Inc.
P.O. Box 135
1211 Tenth St., S.W.
Largo, FL 33640   Phone: (813)584-7333
Elizabeth Handville. Biennial, 1989-90 edition. Each one-page occupational profile describes duties, working conditions, physical surroundings and demands, aptitudes, temperament, educational requirements, employment outlook, earnings, and places of employment.

★6437★
"Cabinetmaker" in *Opportunities in Carpentry Careers* (p. 51)
National Textbook Co.
4255 W. Touhy Ave.
Lincolnwood, IL 60646   Phone: (312)679-5500
Roger Sheldon. 1987. Covers the history of the crafts, a typical carpenter's workday, future opportunities for carpenters, qualifications, training, apprenticeships, and special advice for women and minorities. Surveys various training opportunities.

★6438★
"Cabinetmaker" in *Opportunities in Crafts Careers* (pp. 30-31)
National Textbook Co.
4255 W. Touhy Ave.
Lincolnwood, IL 60646   Phone: (312)679-5500
Marianne F. Munday. 1988. Covers crafts such as woodworking, ceramics, and leatherworking, and crafts-related careers such as writing and teaching. Offers advice on planning a career in crafts, starting a crafts business, and selling crafts.

★6439★
"Cabinetmaking" in *The Career Connection II: A Guide to Technical Majors and Their Related Careers* (pp. 17-18)
ERIS
PO Box 7509
University Station
Provo, UT 84602-0509
Fred A. Rowe. 1988. Contains technical majors, such as automotive technology. Describes the major and the job. Lists high school and postsecondary school courses. Includes occupations related to the major, employment outlook, and starting salary.

★6440★
Furniture: An Opportunity Career
American Furniture Manufacturers
PO Box HP-7
High Point, NC 27261   Phone: (202)857-1119
This eight-page booklet briefly describes career opportunities in the furniture manufacturing industry.

★6441★
Furniture Finisher
Careers, Inc.
PO Box 135
Largo, FL 34649-0135   Phone: (813)584-7333
1989. Two-page occupational summary card describing duties, working conditions, personal qualifications, training, earnings and hours, employment outlook, places of employment, related careers and where to write for more information.

★6442★
"Furniture Finisher" in *Occu-Facts: Information on 565 Careers in Outline Form* (p. 17.14)
Careers, Inc.
P.O. Box 135
1211 Tenth St., S.W.
Largo, FL 33640   Phone: (813)584-7333
Elizabeth Handville. Biennial, 1989-90 edition. Each one-page occupational profile describes duties, working conditions, physical surroundings and demands, aptitudes, temperament, educational requirements, employment outlook, earnings, and places of employment.

★6443★
"Furniture Industry" in *Manufacturing*, Volume 9 of *Career Information Center* (pp. 110-111)
Glencoe/Macmillan
15319 Chatsworth St.
Mission Hills, CA 91345 Phone: (818)898-1391

Richard Lidz and Dale Anderson, editorial directors. Fourth edition, 1990. For 600 occupations, describes job duties, entry-level requirements, education and training needed, advancement possibilities, employment outlook, earnings and benefits. The set is divided into 12 volumes. Each volume includes jobs related under a broad career field. Volume 13 is the index. **Facsimile Number:** 818-365-5489.

★6444★
Furniture Manufacturing
L & K International Video Training
295 Evans Ave.
Toronto, ON, Canada M8Z 5P9 Phone: (416)252-6407

Videocassette. 1984. 45 mins. This program is designed for wood-working machine operators in the furniture manufacturing industry.

★6445★
"Furniture Manufacturing Occupations" in Volume 3 of *The Encyclopedia of Careers and Vocational Guidance* (pp. 576-578)
J.G. Ferguson Publishing Co.
200 W. Monroe
Chicago, IL 60606 Phone: (312)580-5480

William E. Hopke, editor-in-chief. Eighth edition, 1990. Four-volume set that profiles 500 occupations and describes job trends in 76 industries. Includes career description, educational requirements, history of the job, methods of entry, advancement, employment outlook, earnings, working conditions, social and psychological factors, and sources of additional information.

★6446★
"Furniture Manufacturing Workers" in Volume 3 of *Career Discovery Encyclopedia* (pp. 60-61)
J.G. Ferguson Publishing Co.
200 W. Monroe
Chicago, IL 60606 Phone: (312)580-5480

E. Russell Primm, editor-in-chief. 1990. Contains two-page articles on 504 occupations. Each article describes job duties, earnings, and educational and training requirements.

★6447★
"Sawmill Workers" in Volume 5 of *Career Discovery Encyclopedia* (pp. 170-171)
J.G. Ferguson Publishing Co.
200 W. Monroe
Chicago, IL 60606 Phone: (312)580-5480

E. Russell Primm, editor-in-chief. 1990. Contains two-page articles on 504 occupations. Each article describes job duties, earnings, and educational and training requirements.

★6448★
Video Career Library - Production II
Careers, Inc.
1211 10th St., SW
PO Box 135
Largo, FL 34649-0135 Phone: (813)584-7333

Videocassette. 1990. 32 mins. Part of the Video Career Library covering 165 occupations. Shows actual workers on the job. Includes tool and die makers, machinists, sheet metal workers, cabinet and bench carpenters, opticians, precision electronic equipment assemblers, industrial machine operators, welders and cutters, and assemblers.

★6449★
"Wood Patternmaker" in *Occu-Facts: Information on 565 Careers in Outline Form* (p. 17.11)
Careers, Inc.
P.O. Box 135
1211 Tenth St., S.W.
Largo, FL 33640 Phone: (813)584-7333

Elizabeth Handville. Biennial, 1989-90 edition. Each one-page occupational profile describes duties, working conditions, physical surroundings and demands, aptitudes, temperament, educational requirements, employment outlook, earnings, and places of employment.

★6450★
Woodworking Machine Operator
Careers, Inc.
PO Box 135
Largo, FL 34649-0135 Phone: (813)584-7333

1989. Two-page occupational summary card describing duties, working conditions, personal qualifications, training, earnings and hours, employment outlook, places of employment, related careers and where to write for more information.

★6451★
"Woodworking Machine Operator" in *Occu-Facts: Information on 565 Careers in Outline Form* (p. 17.13)
Careers, Inc.
P.O. Box 135
1211 Tenth St., S.W.
Largo, FL 33640 Phone: (813)584-7333

Elizabeth Handville. Biennial, 1989-90 edition. Each one-page occupational profile describes duties, working conditions, physical surroundings and demands, aptitudes, temperament, educational requirements, employment outlook, earnings, and places of employment.

★6452★
"Woodworking Occupations" in *Occupational Outlook Handbook* (pp. 425-426)
Superintendent of Documents
U.S. Government Printing Office
Washington, DC 20402 Phone: (202)783-3238

Biennial; latest edition, 1990-91. Encyclopedia of careers describing more than 250 occupations and comprising about 86 percent of all jobs in the economy. Occupations that require lengthy education or training are given the most attention. For each occupation, the handbook describes job duties, working conditions, training, educational preparation, personal qualities, advancement possibilities, job outlook, earnings, and sources of additional information.

─── Associations ───

★6453★
American Furniture Manufacturers Association (AFMA)
PO Box HP-7
High Point, NC 27261 Phone: (919)884-5000

Membership: Furniture manufacturers seeking to provide a unified voice for the furniture industry and to aid in the development of industry personnel. **Purpose:** Provides: market research data; industrial relations services; costs and operating statistics; transportation information; general management and information services. Compiles statistics; develops quarterly Econometric Forecast. **Publications:** *Membership Directory*, annual.

Woodworking Occupations

★6454★
Institute for Woodworking Education
1012 Tenth St.
Manhattan Beach, CA 90266
Provides general information about furniture woodworking occupations.

Awards, Scholarships, Grants, and Fellowships

★6455★
International Art Competition - New York
International Art Competition - New York
c/o Artitudes
P.O. Box 380
Hartsdale, NY 10538   Phone: (914)633-5333
To recognize artists working in all media and styles. Awards are presented in various categories including wood. 35mm slides may be submitted by June 23. The following awards are presented: (1) Purchase prizes totaling $4,800; (2) approximately 40 artists are chosen to exhibit their work at Art 54 Gallery; (3) monetary awards of $2,200 each to selected artists; and (4) Certificates of Merit to ten winners in each category. Awarded annually. Established in 1983.

★6456★
Northeastern Loggers Association Awards Program
Northeastern Loggers' Association
c/o George Mitchell, Executive Director
P.O. box 69
Old Forge, NY 13420   Phone: (315)369-3078
To recognize significant achievement in forestry and wood utilization during the year in eight major categories including "outstanding use of wood." Individuals or organizations need not be members of the Northeastern Loggers' Association. The nominee must reside in or conduct business in the Northeastern or Lake States Region of the United States as delineated by the USFA. The deadline for nominations is January 31. A maximum of one award is given in each category when merited. Winners in the "outstanding use of wood" category receive a plaque and a monetary award of $300.

★6457★
Washington Craft Show
Smithsonian Associates Women's Committee
Arts and Industries Building, Room 1278
Smithsonian Institution
Washington, DC 20560   Phone: (202)357-4000
To enable craftsmen to exhibit and sell crafts as fine art. Artisans working in several categories including wood are eligible. One hundred exhibitors are selected on the basis of originality, artistic conception, and quality of workmanship. Applications may be submitted by October 13. The following awards are presented to exhibitors in recognition of outstanding work; (1) three awards for excellence - $1,000 each; and (2) a Craftsmen's Choice Award - $300.

Basic Reference Guides and Handbooks

★6458★
Artistic Woodturning
Brigham Young University Press
PO Box 7113
University Sta.
Provo, UT 84602   Phone: (801)378-3295
Dale L. Nish. 1980.

★6459★
The Complete Book of Birdhouse Construction for Woodworkers
Dover Publications, Inc.
31 E. Second St.
Mineola, NY 11501   Phone: (516)294-7000
Scott D. Campbell. 1984. Part of Crafts Series.

★6460★
The Conversion & Seasoning of Wood
Linden Publishing Co., Inc.
3845 N. Blackstone
Fresno, CA 93726   Phone: (209)227-2901
William Brown. 1989. **Toll-free/Additional Phone Number(s):** 800-345-4447. **Facsimile Number:** (209)227-3520.

★6461★
Custom Tools for Woodworkers
Stackpole Books
Cameron and Kelker Sts.
Box 1831
Harrisburg, PA 17105   Phone: (717)234-5041
J. Petrovich. 1990. **Facsimile Number:** (717)234-1359.

★6462★
General Woodworking
McGraw-Hill Publishing Company
1221 Avenue of the Americas
New York, NY 10020   Phone: (212)512-2000
Chris H. Groneman. Sixth edition, 1982. Part of Publications in Industrial Education Series.

★6463★
Technical Woodworking
McGraw-Hill Publishing Company
1221 Avenue of the Americas
New York, NY 10020   Phone: (212)512-2000
Chris H. Groneman. Second edition, 1975.

★6464★
Woodworking
Goodheart-Willcox Company
123 Taft Dr.
South Holland, IL 60473   Phone: (708)333-7200
Willis H. Wagner. Revised edition, 1989. Part of Build-a-Course Series. **Facsimile Number:** (708)331-9130.

Periodicals

★6465★
American Woodworker
Rodale Press, Inc.
33 E. Minor St.
Emmaus, PA 18098   Phone: (215)967-5171
James Owens, Advertising Manager. 6x/yr. Magazine devoted to helping woodworkers improve their skills. **Facsimile Number:** (215)965-5670.

★6466★
Bits 'n Chips
Woodworking Machinery Distributors' Association
Adams Bldg., No. 109
251 W. DeKalb Pike
King of Prussia, PA 19406   Phone: (215)265-6658
Editor(s): R. Franklin Brown, Jr. Monthly. Provides news of the woodworking machinery distribution industry. Contains items on pertinent governmental and legislative actions, association activities, and business trends. Recurring features include news of members. **Facsimile Number:** (215)265-3419.

★6467★
Chip Chats
National Wood Carvers Assn.
7424 Miami Ave.
PO Box 43218
Cincinnati, OH 45243   Phone: (513)561-9051
Edward F. Gallenstein, Editor and Publisher. 6x/yr. Journal for amateur and professional wood carvers.

★6468★
Crow's Weekly Letter
C.C. Crow Publications, Inc.
PO Box 25749
Portland, OR 97225   Phone: (503)222-9576
Editor(s): Sam Sherrill. Weekly. Serves as a market report on lumber, plywood, and panel wood products, supplying news, analysis, and price information as a guide to sales. Carries market data on the transportation industry as it pertains to the shipment of forest products. Recurring features include housing market updates and news of industry events and personnel.

★6469★
CWB: Custom Woodworking Business
Vance Publishing Corp.
PO Box 400
Lincolnshire, IL 60069   Phone: (708)634-2600
Helen Kuhl, Exec. Editor. Quarterly. Magazine for custom woodworkers. **Facsimile Number:** (708)634-4379.

★6470★
Modern Woodworking
Target Magazine Group
167 Hwy. 72 E.
Collierville, TN 38027   Phone: (901)853-7720
Joyce Powell, Managing Editor. Monthly Magazine for management in the primary vond secondary wood products industry. **Facsimile Number:** (901)853-6437.

★6471★
Wood & Wood Products
Vance Publishing Corp.
400 Knightsbridge Pkwy.
PO Box 1400
Lincolnshire, IL 60069   Phone: (708)634-4347
Rich Christianson, Editor. Monthly. Magazine for furniture, cabinet, and woodworking industry. **Facsimile Number:** (708)634-4379.

★6472★
Wood Machining News
Wood Machining Institute
PO Box 476
Berkeley, CA 94701   Phone: (510)943-5240
Editor(s): Dr. Ryszard Szymani. Bimonthly. Provides news and technical information on the latest worldwide developments in the field of wood machining. Covers equipment and technology of saws and sawing, planing and sanding operations, and the production of veneer and chips. Recurring features include items on workers' safety and on patents, book reviews, notices of short courses and seminars, editorials, and a calendar of events. **Facsimile Number:** (510)945-0947.

★6473★
Woodshop News
Soundings Publications, Inc.
35 Pratt St.
Essex, CT 06426-1122   Phone: (203)767-8227
Ian Bowen, Editor. Monthly. Trade newspaper (tabloid) focusing on people and businesses involved in woodworking. **Facsimile Number:** (203)767-1048.

★6474★
Woodwork
Ross Periodicals
PO Box 1529
Ross, CA 94957   Phone: (415)382-0580
Jeff Greef, Editor. Quarterly Magazine for professional and nonprofessional woodworkers.

★6475★
The Woodworker's Journal
517 Litchfield Rd.
PO Box 1629
New Milford, CT 06776   Phone: (203)355-2694
Thomas G. Begnal, Editor. 6x/yr. Magazine providing project plans for novice and professional woodworkers; including the basics, special techniques, and shop and finishing tips.

Meetings and Conventions

★6476★
American Furniture Manufacturers Association (AFMA)
PO Box HP-7
High Point, NC 27261   Phone: (919)884-5000
Frequency: Annual.

★6477★
International Woodworking Machinery and Furniture Supply Fair - USA
Reed-Macgregor Exhibitions, Inc.
800 Dennison St., Unit Seven
Markham, ON, Canada L3R 5M9   Phone: (416)479-3939
Frequency: Always held in Atlanta, Georgia during August at the World Congress Center. 1992; Aug. 21-24; Atlanta, GA ● 1994; Aug. 26-29; Atlanta, GA. **Facsimile Number:** (416)479-5144.

★6478★
WOODWORKING - Machinery and Equipment for the Timber and Woodworking Industries
Glahe International, Inc.
1700 K St., NW, Ste. 403
Washington, DC 20006-3824   Phone: (202)659-4557

Other Sources of Information

★6479★
Dimension Purchasing Guide
National Dimension Manufacturers Association (NDMA)
1000 Johnson Ferry Rd., Ste. A-130
Marietta, GA 30068   Phone: (404)565-6660
Annual, summer. Over 100 member manufacturers of wood components. Entries include: Company name, address, phone, fax, name and title of contact, description of products and services. Arrangement: Alphabetical. Indexes: Product.

★6480★
A Reverence for Wood
Henry Holt & Company
115 W. 18th St.
New York, NY 10011   Phone: (212)886-9200
Eric Sloane. 1990.

Miscellaneous Production Occupations

Dental Laboratory Technicians

Dental laboratory technicians are skilled craftworkers that make dentures, bridges, crowns, and other dental prosthetics. Most dental laboratory technicians do not specialize, though some do. Orthodontic technicians make appliances for straightening teeth and treating speech impediments. Removable partial denture technicians make and repair contoured metal frames and retainers for teeth used in removable partial dentures. Most dental laboratory technicians work in commercial dental laboratories. About 12 percent of all technicians work in dentists' offices. Others work for hospitals that provide dental services, including Veterans Administration hospitals and clinics. More than 20 percent of all technicians are self-employed, a higher proportion than in most other occupations.

$alaries

Dental laboratory technicians who work full time in commercial laboratories earn between $15,000 and $25,000/year.

Employment Outlook

Growth rate until the year 2000: More slowly than average.

Dental Laboratory Technicians

Career Guides

★6481★
Dental Laboratory Technician
Careers, Inc.
PO Box 135
Largo, FL 34649-0135   Phone: (813)584-7333
1988. Two-page occupational summary card describing duties, working conditions, personal qualifications, training, earnings and hours, employment outlook, places of employment, related careers and where to write for more information.

★6482★
"Dental Laboratory Technician" in *Careers in Health Care* (pp. 53-56)
National Textbook Co.
4255 W. Touhy Ave.
Lincolnwood, IL 60646   Phone: (312)679-5500
Barbara M. Swanson. 1989. Discusses 61 health careers, providing information about the history of the occupation, job duties, work environments, salaries, educational preparation, licensure, certification, and employment outlook.

★6483★
"Dental Laboratory Technician" in *Health Care* (pp. 63-67)
Franklin Watts, Inc.
387 Park Avenue, S.
New York, NY 10016   Phone: (212)686-7070
Linda Barrett and Galen Guengerich. 1991. Provides an overview of the health care industry. Includes job description, educational preparation, training, salary, and employment outlook. Offers job hunting advice.

★6484★
"Dental Laboratory Technician" in *Health*, Volume 7 of *Career Information Center* (pp. 43-45)
Glencoe/Macmillan
15319 Chatsworth St.
Mission Hills, CA 91345   Phone: (818)898-1391
Richard Lidz and Dale Anderson, editorial directors. Fourth edition, 1990. For 600 occupations, describes job duties, entry-level requirements, education and training needed, advancement possibilities, employment outlook, earnings and benefits. The set is divided into 12 volumes. Each volume includes jobs related under a broad career field. Volume 13 is the index. **Facsimile Number:** 818-365-5489.

★6485★
"Dental Laboratory Technician" in *Occu-Facts: Information on 565 Careers in Outline Form* (p. 17.27)
Careers, Inc.
P.O. Box 135
1211 Tenth St., S.W.
Largo, FL 33640   Phone: (813)584-7333
Elizabeth Handville. Biennial, 1989-90 edition. Each one-page occupational profile describes duties, working conditions, physical surroundings and demands, aptitudes, temperament, educational requirements, employment outlook, earnings, and places of employment.

★6486★
"Dental Laboratory Technician" in *Occupational Outlook Handbook* (pp. 427-428)
Superintendent of Documents
U.S. Government Printing Office
Washington, DC 20402   Phone: (202)783-3238
Biennial; latest edition, 1990-91. Encyclopedia of careers describing more than 250 occupations and comprising about 86 percent of all jobs in the economy. Occupations that require lengthy education or training are given the most attention. For each occupation, the handbook describes job duties, working conditions, training, educational preparation, personal qualities, advancement possibilities, job outlook, earnings, and sources of additional information.

★6487★
"Dental Laboratory Technician" in *120 Careers in the Health Care Field* (pp. 63-67)
U.S. Directory Service, Publishers
PO Box 68-1700
655 N.W. 128th St.
Miami, FL 33168   Phone: (305)769-1700
Stanley Alperin. Second edition, 1989. Each occupational profile covers job functions and responsibilities, work locations, training requirements, certification, and salaries. Lists community colleges, universities, vocational-technical schools, and other educational institutions that provide accredited training programs.

★6488★
"Dental Laboratory Technician" in *Opportunities in Health and Medical Careers* (p. 75)
National Textbook Co.
4255 W. Touhy Ave.
Lincolnwood, IL 60646   Phone: (312)679-5500
Leo D'Orazio and Donald I. Snook. 1991. Provides an overview of the health care industry with future projections. Describes a wide variety of healthcare jobs covering the nature of the work,

★6489★ VOCATIONAL CAREERS SOURCEBOOK, 1st Edition

educational requirements, employment outlook and salaries. Offers job hunting advice.

★6489★
"Dental Laboratory Technicians" in *Jobs! What They Are. . .Where They Are. . .What They Pay* (pp. 151)
Simon & Schuster, Inc.
Simon & Schuster Bldg.
1230 Avenue of the Americas
New York, NY 10020   Phone: (212)698-7000

Robert O. Snelling and Anne M. Snelling. Revised edition, 1989. Profiles 241 occupations, describing duties and responsibilities, educational preparation, earnings, employment opportunities, training, and qualifications.

★6490★
"Dental Laboratory Technicians" in *Opportunities in Dental Care Careers* (pp. 47-49)
National Textbook Co.
4255 W. Touhy Ave.
Lincolnwood, IL 60646   Phone: (312)679-5500

Bonnie L. Kendall. 1991. Describes the work of dentists and related dental care employees. Covers dental education including admission to dental school, dental specialists, skills, personal qualities, income, and licensure. Lists accredited dental schools, dental hygiene, and assisting programs.

★6491★
"Dental Laboratory Technicians" in Volume 4 of *The Encyclopedia of Careers and Vocational Guidance* (pp. 382-386)
J.G. Ferguson Publishing Co.
200 W. Monroe
Chicago, IL 60606   Phone: (312)580-5480

William E. Hopke, editor-in-chief. Eighth edition, 1990. Four-volume set that profiles 500 occupations and describes job trends in 76 industries. Includes career description, educational requirements, history of the job, methods of entry, advancement, employment outlook, earnings, working conditions, social and psychological factors, and sources of additional information.

★6492★
"Dental Laboratory Technicians" in Volume 2 of *Career Discovery Encyclopedia* (pp. 97-98)
J.G. Ferguson Publishing Co.
200 W. Monroe
Chicago, IL 60606   Phone: (312)580-5480

E. Russell Primm, editor-in-chief. 1990. Contains two-page articles on 504 occupations. Each article describes job duties, earnings, and educational and training requirements.

★6493★
Hands That Think: A Word About Careers in Modern Dental Laboratory Technology
National Association of Dental Laboratories
3801 Mt. Vernon Ave.
Alexandria, VA 22305   Phone: (703)683-5263

This six-panel brochure describes the work, employment opportunities, earnings, training, and qualifications for dental laboratory technicians.

★6494★
Have You Considered Dental Laboratory Technology?
SELECT
211 E. Chicago Ave., Ste. 1804
Chicago, IL 60611-2678   Phone: (312)440-2500

1990. This ten-page booklet describes what dental laboratory technicians do, where they work, educational preparation and certification.

★6495★
Video Career Library - Allied Health Fields
Careers, Inc.
1211 10th St., SW
PO Box 135
Largo, FL 34649-0135   Phone: (813)584-7333

Videocassette. 1990. Part of the Video Career Library covering 165 occupations. Shows actual workers on the job. Includes dental laboratory technicians.

──────── Associations ────────

★6496★
American Dental Association (ADA)
211 E. Chicago Ave.
Chicago, IL 60611   Phone: (312)440-2500

Membership: Professional society of dentists. **Purpose:** Encourages the improvement of the health of the public and promotes the art and science of dentistry in matters of legislation and regulations. Inspects and accredits dental schools and schools for dental hygienists, assistants, and laboratory technicians. Conducts research programs at ADA Health Foundation Research Institute. Produces most of the dental health education material used in the U.S. Sponsors National Children's Dental Health Month. Compiles statistics on personnel, practice, and dental care needs and attitudes of patients with regard to dental health. Operates library of 50,000 volumes. Maintains biographical records of U.S. dentists, past and present; and collection of published and original documentary material of historical interest to the profession. Sponsors 11 councils. **Publications:** *American Dental Directory*, annual. • *Index to Dental Literature*, quarterly. • *News*, biweekly.

★6497★
National Association of Dental Laboratories (NADL)
3801 Mt. Vernon Ave.
Alexandria, VA 22305   Phone: (703)683-5263

Membership: Federation of state associations representing 3100 commercial dental laboratories serving the dental profession. **Purpose:** Develops criteria for ethical dental laboratories. Conducts business management seminars; sponsors financial management workshops; offers business and personal insurance programs and Basic Technician's Training Program. Maintains technical videotape lending library; compiles statistics. **Publications:** *Directory of Speakers and Lecturers*, periodic. • *Executive Information Series*, periodic. • *Fabrication Procedures*, periodic. • *Hazard Communication Manual*, periodic. • *Trends and Techniques*, 10/year. • *Who's Who in the Dental Laboratory Industry*, annual. • Also publishes standardized accounting system and *Managing for Profit* (textbook). **Toll-free/Additional Phone Number(s):** (800)950-1150. **Facsimile Number:** (703)549-4788.

──────── Standards/Certification Agencies ────────

Accredited programs in dental laboratory technology are approved by the Commission on Dental Accreditation in

Dental Laboratory Technicians

conjunction with the American Dental Association (ADA). The programs generally take two years to complete and lead to an associate degree, although some lead to a certificate or diploma. Certification, which is voluntary, is offered by the National Board for Certification in five specialty areas: Crown and bridge, ceramics, partial dentures, complete dentures, and orthodontics. Certification is increasingly important as evidence of a technician's competence.

★6498★
American Dental Association (ADA)
211 E. Chicago Ave.
Chicago, IL 60611   Phone: (312)440-2500
Promotes the art and science of dentistry in matters of legislation and regulations. Inspects and accredits dental schools and schools for dental hygienists, assistants, and laboratory technicians. Conducts research programs at ADA Health Foundation Research Institute. Produces most of the dental health education material used in the U.S.

★6499★
National Association of Dental Laboratories (NADL)
3801 Mt. Vernon Ave.
Alexandria, VA 22305   Phone: (703)683-5263
Develops criteria for ethical dental laboratories.
Toll-free/Additional Phone Number(s): (800)950-1150. **Facsimile Number:** (703)549-4788.

Educational Directories and Programs

★6500★
Accredited Dental Assisting, Dental Hygiene and Dental Laboratory Technology Educational Programs
American Dental Association
Commission on Dental Accreditation
211 E. Chicago Ave.
Chicago, IL 60611   Phone: (312)440-2500
1991. State-by-state listing of accredited educational programs.

★6501★
Accredited Dental Laboratory Technology Educational Programs
National Association of Dental Laboratories
3801 Mt. Vernon Ave.
Alexandria, VA 22305   Phone: (703)683-5263
1991. State-by-state listing of dental technology educational programs accredited by the Commission on Dental Accreditation. Includes address, phone number, and contact name.

Basic Reference Guides and Handbooks

★6502★
Complete Handbook for Dental Auxiliaries
Quintessence Publishing Company, Inc.
870 Oak Creek Dr.
Lombard, IL 60148-6405   Phone: (708)620-4443
Charles A. Reap, Jr. 1981. **Toll-free/Additional Phone Number(s):** 800-621-0387. **Facsimile Number:** (708)620-9059.

★6503★
Dental Laboratory Technology
Prentice Hall
Rte. 9W
Englewood Cliffs, NJ 07632   Phone: (201)592-2000
Chester A. Halterman. 1985.

★6504★
Directory of Speakers and Lecturers
National Association of Dental Laboratories (NADL)
3801 Mt. Vernon Ave.
Alexandria, VA 22305   Phone: (703)683-5263
Periodic.

★6505★
Managing for Profit
National Association of Dental Laboratories (NADL)
3801 Mt. Vernon Ave.
Alexandria, VA 22305   Phone: (703)683-5263

★6506★
NADL Hazard Communication Manual
National Association of Dental Laboratories (NADL)
3801 Mt. Vernon Ave.
Alexandria, VA 22305   Phone: (703)683-5263
Periodic.

Periodicals

★6507★
ADA News
American Dental Assn.
211 E. Chicago Ave.
Chicago, IL 60611   Phone: (312)440-2786
James Berry, Editor. Every other week. Dental magazine.

★6508★
Fabrication Procedures
National Association of Dental Laboratories (NADL)
3801 Mt. Vernon Ave.
Alexandria, VA 22305   Phone: (703)683-5263
Periodic.

★6509★
NADL Executive Information Series
National Association of Dental Laboratories (NADL)
3801 Mt. Vernon Ave.
Alexandria, VA 22305   Phone: (703)683-5263
Periodic.

★6510★
Oral Health
Southam Business Communications Inc.
1450 Don Mills Rd.
Don Mills, ON, Canada M3B 2X7   Phone: (416)445-6641
Janet Bonellie, Mng. Editor. Monthly. Journal covering recent clinical advances in dentistry. Offers advice on practice management and personal finance control. **Facsimile Number:** (416)442-2201.

★6511★
Quintessence International
Quintessence Publishing Co., Inc.
870 Oak Creek Dr.
Lombard, IL 60148-6405   Phone: (708)620-4443
Richard J. Simonsen, D.D.S., M.S., Editor-in-Chief. Monthly. Dental journal. **Facsimile Number:** (708)620-9059.

★6512★
Trends and Techniques
National Association of Dental Laboratories (NADL)
3801 Mt. Vernon Ave.
Alexandria, VA 22305 Phone: (703)683-5263
10/year. Magazine.

Other Sources of Information

★6513★
Ethics, Jurisprudence & History for the Dental Hygienist
Lea & Febiger
200 Chester Field Pkwy.
Malvern, PA 19355 Phone: (215)251-2230
Wilma E. Motley. Third edition, 1983. **Facsimile Number:** (215)251-2229.

Ophthalmic Laboratory Technicians

Ophthalmic laboratory technicians—also known as manufacturing opticians, optical mechanics, or optical goods workers—make prescription eyeglass lenses. Ophthalmic laboratory technicians cut, grind, edge, and finish lenses according to specifications provided by dispensing opticians, optometrists, or ophthalmologists, and then assemble the lenses with frames to produce finished glasses. About 50 percent of all ophthalmic laboratory technicians work in retail stores that manufacture prescription glasses, mostly optical goods store chains or independent retailers. Most of the rest work in optical laboratories. A few work for optometrists or ophthalmologists who dispense glasses directly to patients.

$alaries

Most ophthalmic laboratory technicians earn between $10,000—$15,000/year. Trainees are generally paid the minimum wage.

Employment Outlook

Growth rate until the year 2000: Faster than average.

Ophthalmic Laboratory Technicians

Career Guides

★6514★
"Manufacturing Opticians" in *Opportunities in Eye Care Careers* (pp. 79-83)
National Textbook Co.
4255 W. Touhy Ave.
Lincolnwood, IL 60646   Phone: (312)679-5500
Kathleen M. Ahrens. 1991. Explores careers in ophthalmology, optometry, and support positions. Describes the work, working conditions, educational preparation, salary, and employment outlook. Lists accredited educational programs.

★6515★
"Ophthalmic Laboratory Technician" in *Careers in Health Care* (pp. 188-190)
National Textbook Co.
4255 W. Touhy Ave.
Lincolnwood, IL 60646   Phone: (312)679-5500
Barbara M. Swanson 1989. Discusses 61 health careers, providing information about the history of the occupation, job duties, work environments, salaries, educational preparation, licensure, certification, and employment outlook.

★6516★
"Ophthalmic Laboratory Technician" in *Health Care* (pp. 69-73)
Franklin Watts, Inc.
387 Park Avenue, S.
New York, NY 10016   Phone: (212)686-7070
Linda Barrett and Galen Guengerich. 1991. Provides an overview of the health care industry. Includes job description, educational preparation, training, salary, and employment outlook. Offers job hunting advice.

★6517★
"Ophthalmic Laboratory Technician" in *Occupational Outlook Handbook* (pp. 428-429)
Superintendent of Documents
U.S. Government Printing Office
Washington, DC 20402   Phone: (202)783-3238
Biennial; latest edition, 1990-91. Encyclopedia of careers describing more than 250 occupations and comprising about 86 percent of all jobs in the economy. Occupations that require lengthy education or training are given the most attention. For each occupation, the handbook describes job duties, working conditions, training, educational preparation, personal qualities, advancement possibilities, job outlook, earnings, and sources of additional information.

★6518★
"Ophthalmic Laboratory Technician" in *120 Careers in the Health Care Field* (p. 461)
U.S. Directory Service, Publishers
PO Box 68-1700
655 N.W. 128th St.
Miami, FL 33168   Phone: (305)769-1700
Stanley Alperin. Second edition, 1989. Each occupational profile covers job functions and responsibilities, work locations, training requirements, certification, and salaries. Lists community colleges, universities, vocational-technical schools, and other educational institutions that provide accredited training programs.

★6519★
"Ophthalmic Laboratory Technicians" in *Jobs! What They Are...Where They Are...What They Pay* (p. 157)
Simon & Schuster, Inc.
Simon & Schuster Bldg.
1230 Avenue of the Americas
New York, NY 10020   Phone: (212)698-7000
Robert O. Snelling and Anne M. Snelling. Revised edition, 1989. Profiles 241 occupations, describing duties and responsibilities, educational preparation, earnings, employment opportunities, training, and qualifications.

★6520★
"Ophthalmic Laboratory Technicians" in Volume 4 of *Career Discovery Encyclopedia* (pp. 144-145)
J.G. Ferguson Publishing Co.
200 W. Monroe
Chicago, IL 60606   Phone: (312)580-5480
E. Russell Primm, editor-in-chief. 1990. Contains two-page articles on 504 occupations. Each article describes job duties, earnings, and educational and training requirements.

★6521★
"Ophthalmic Laboratory Technicians" in Volume 4 of *The Encyclopedia of Careers and Vocational Guidance* (pp. 426-430)
J.G. Ferguson Publishing Co.
200 W. Monroe
Chicago, IL 60606   Phone: (312)580-5480
William E. Hopke, editor-in-chief. Eighth edition, 1990. Four-volume set that profiles 500 occupations and describes job trends in 76 industries. Includes career description, educational requirements, history of the job, methods of entry, advancement, employment outlook, earnings, working conditions, social and psychological factors, and sources of additional information.

★6522★
"Optical Mechanics" in Volume 4 of *Career Discovery Encyclopedia* (pp. 146-147)
J.G. Ferguson Publishing Co.
200 W. Monroe
Chicago, IL 60606   Phone: (312)580-5480
E. Russell Primm, editor-in-chief. 1990. Contains two-page articles on 504 occupations. Each article describes job duties, earnings, and educational and training requirements.

★6523★
"Opticians and Optical Mechanics" in Volume 3 of *The Encyclopedia of Careers and Vocational Guidance* (pp. 595-598)
J.G. Ferguson Publishing Co.
200 W. Monroe
Chicago, IL 60606   Phone: (312)580-5480
William E. Hopke, editor-in-chief. Eighth edition, 1990. Four-volume set that profiles 500 occupations and describes job trends in 76 industries. Includes career description, educational requirements, history of the job, methods of entry, advancement, employment outlook, earnings, working conditions, social and psychological factors, and sources of additional information.

★6524★
Video Career Library - Technical Occupations
Careers, Inc.
1211 10th St., SW
PO Box 135
Largo, FL 34649-0135   Phone: (813)584-7333
Videocassette. 1990. Part of the Video Career Library covering 165 occupations. Shows actual workers on the job. Includes clinical laboratory technicians.

Associations

★6525★
American Academy of Ophthalmology (AAO)
655 Beach St.
San Francisco, CA 94109   Phone: (415)561-8500
Membership: Ophthalmologists concerned with high-quality eye care and the continuing education of members. **Purpose:** Sponsors Basic and Clinical Science Course for practitioners and residents to maintain current status (includes annual self-assessment); offers information on new techniques. Provides instructional videotapes; maintains 500 volume library and a museum of ophthalmological instruments and artifacts. Operates American Academy of Ophthalmology Government Affairs Office which serves as a liaison between the AAO and the federal government, monitors pending legislation affecting ophthalmology, and prepares statements and testimonies to be presented to congressional committees and regulatory agencies. Also operates Foundation of the American Academy of Ophthalmology, which functions as the charitable arm of the academy. Current activities of the foundation include: National Eye Care Project; Oral Histories Program; Centennial Program. **Publications:** *Argus*, monthly. • *Directory*, biennial. • *Ophthalmology*, monthly. • Also publishes *Basic and Clinical Science Course*, manuals, slide script packages, and study guides. **Facsimile Number:** (415)561-8533.

★6526★
National Society to Prevent Blindness (NSPB)
500 E. Remington Rd.
Schaumburg, IL 60173   Phone: (708)843-2020
Membership: Professional vond laypersons interested in preventing blindness and conserving sight through nationwide comprehensive programs of public and professional education, research, industrial, and community services. **Purpose:** Services include promotion and support of local glaucoma screening programs, preschool vision testing, industrial eye safety, and collection of statistical and other data on nature and extent of causes of blindness and defective vision. Operates National Center for Sight, an information line dealing with eye health and safety topics. In 1968, NSPB transferred its program on the education of partially seeing children to the American Foundation for the Blind. Awards grants for medical research; administers Wellcome Research Fellowship in Ophthalmology sponsored by Burroughs Wellcome Fund. Sponsors Wise Owl Club to promote widespread use of safety eyewear for various occupations. Maintains 3000 volume library; compiles statistics. **Publications:** *Insight/Wise Owl News*, 4/year. • *National Society to Prevent Blindness—Annual Report*. • *National Society to Prevent Blindness—InSight*, quarterly. • Also publishes pamphlets on eye diseases, children's eye care, industrial sports, and school eye safety; distributes home eye tests; issues testing charts, posters, films, and radio and television material. **Toll-free/Additional Phone Number(s):** (800)221-3004. **Facsimile Number:** (708)843-8458.

Standards/Certification Agencies

Formal programs in optical technology are offered by vocational-technical institutes or trade schools. The programs vary in length from six months to one year, and graduates earn certificates or diplomas.

★6527★
Commission on Opticianry Accreditation (COA)
10111 Martin Luther King, Jr. Hwy., No. 100
Bowie, MD 20720   Phone: (301)459-8075
Accrediting agency for ophthalmic dispensing and ophthalmic laboratory technology training programs in postsecondary institutions.

Educational Directories and Programs

★6528★
Commission on Opticianry Accreditation
Commission on Opticianry Accreditation
10111 Martin Luther King Jr. Hwy., #100
Bowie, MD 20720-4299   Phone: (301)459-8075
Brochure that lists accredited opthalmic laboratory technician schools. Provides address, phone number, and contact person.

Periodicals

★6529★
Contact Lens Spectrum
Viscom Publications, Inc.
50 Washington St.
Norwalk, CT 06854   Phone: (203)838-9100
Dr. Joseph T. Barr, Editor. Monthly. Magazine for eye care professionals providing contact lens care and contact lens products. **Facsimile Number:** (203)838-2550.

★6530★
Contemporary Optometry
Academy Professional Information Services, Inc.
116 W. 32nd St.
New York, NY 10001   Phone: (212)736-6688
Garold Edwards, O.D., FAAO, Editor-in-Chief. 2x/yr. Journal containing articles of interest to the professional optometric community. **Facsimile Number:** (212)564-1763.

★6531★
Eye to Eye
Steen-Hall Eye Institute
2611 Greenwood Rd.
Shreveport, LA 71103   Phone: (318)631-2020
Editor(s): Michele R. Taylor. Quarterly. Presents information concerning new ophthalmic developments and the Institute's public service activities. Recurring features include news of research, member news, a calendar of events, news of community projects and programs related to the eye, and human interest stories.

★6532★
Insight/Wise Owl News
National Society to Prevent Blindness (NSPB)
500 E. Remington Rd.
Schaumburg, IL 60173   Phone: (708)843-2020
4/year.

★6533★
National Society to Prevent Blindness—InSight
National Society to Prevent Blindness (NSPB)
500 E. Remington Rd.
Schaumburg, IL 60173   Phone: (708)843-2020
Quarterly. Newsletter on eye health and safety.

★6534★
Ocular Surgery News
Slack, Inc.
6900 Grove Rd.
Thorofare, NJ 08086-9447   Phone: (609)848-1000
Keith Croes, Editor. 2x/mo. Medical newspaper for ophthalmologists. Covering scientific meetings and events, with emphasis on cataract/IOL, glaucoma treatment, laser therapy, clinical anterior segment issues, and legislative and regulatory developments. **Facsimile Number:** (609)853-5991.

★6535★
Ophthalmic Laser Therapy
Mary Ann Liebert, Inc.
1651 Third Ave.
New York, NY 10128   Phone: (212)289-2300
C. Davis Belcher III, M.D., Editor. Quarterly. Medical research journal focusing on advances in opthalmic surgery. **Facsimile Number:** (212)289-4697.

★6536★
Ophthalmic Practice
8200 Decarie Blvd., Ste. 212
Montreal, PQ, Canada H4P 2P5   Phone: (514)340-9157
Inara Gailis, Editor. 6x/yr. Magazine for professionals in ophthalmology. **Facsimile Number:** (514)342-5783.

★6537★
Ophthalmic Research
S. Karger Publishers, Inc.
26 W. Avon Rd.
PO Box 529
Farmington, CT 06085   Phone: (203)675-7834
O. Hockwin, Editor/Advertising Mgr. 6x/yr. **Facsimile Number:** (203)675-7302.

★6538★
Ophthalmic Surgery
Slack, Inc.
6900 Grove Rd.
Thorofare, NJ 08086-9447   Phone: (609)848-1000
George Spaeth, M.D., Editor. Monthly. Journal publishing articles on ophthalmic surgery, research, and clinical approaches. **Facsimile Number:** (609)853-5991.

★6539★
Ophthalmologica
S. Karger Publishers, Inc.
26 W. Avon Rd.
PO Box 529
Farmington, CT 06085   Phone: (203)675-7834
W. Straub, Editor/Advertising Mgr. 8x/yr. Medical research journal (English, French, and German). **Facsimile Number:** (203)675-7302.

★6540★
Ophthalmology Management
Advisory Enterprises, Inc.
1515 Broadway
New York, NY 10036   Phone: (212)869-1300
Herve Byron, M.D., Editor. 10x/yr. Medical professional journal. **Facsimile Number:** (212)302-6273.

★6541★
Ophthalmology Times
Edgell Communications, Inc.
270 Madison Ave.
New York, NY 10016   Phone: (212)951-6600
Dean Celia, Editor. 2x/mo. Tabloid for ophthalmologists. **Facsimile Number:** (212)481-6561.

★6542★
Optometry and Vision Science
Williams & Wilkins
428 E. Preston St.
Baltimore, MD 21202   Phone: (301)528-4068
W.M. Lyle, O.D., Ph.D., Editor. Monthly. Optometry journal. **Facsimile Number:** (301)528-8596.

★6543★
Review of Optometry
Chilton Co.
Chilton Way
Radnor, PA 19089   Phone: (215)964-4376
Richard Guerrein, Publisher. Monthly. Journal for the optometric profession and optical industry. **Facsimile Number:** (215)964-4981.

Painting and Coating Machine Operators

Painting and coating machine operators control the machinery and equipment that applies the many types of paints and coatings to a wide range of manufactured products. Dippers and impregnators immerse racks and baskets of articles in vats of paint, liquid plastic, or other solutions using a power hoist. Tumbling barrel painters deposit articles of porous materials in a barrel of paint, varnish, or other coating, which is then rotated to ensure thorough coverage. Spray-machine operators use equipment with spray guns to coat metal, wood, ceramic, fabric, paper, and even food products with paint and other coating solutions. Paper coating machine operators spray *size,* a coating mixture, on the surface of paper to give it its gloss or finish. Silvering applicators spray silver, tin, and copper solutions on glass in the manufacture of mirrors. Enrobing machine operators coat, or *enrobe,* confectionary, bakery, and other food products with melted chocolate, cheese, oils, sugar, and other substances. Although the majority of painting and coating machine operators are employed in manufacturing, the largest group works in automotive body repair and paint shops. Fewer than 10 percent of all painting and coating machine operators are self-employed; most are automotive painters.

$alaries

Weekly earnings of painting and coating machine operators are as follows:

Lowest 10 percent	$244.00/week or less
Middle 50 percent	$420.00/week
Top 10 percent	$605.00/week or more

Employment Outlook

Growth rate until the year 2000: More slowly than average.

Painting and Coating Machine Operators

Career Guides

★6544★
Auto Painter
Vocational Biographies, Inc.
PO Box 31, Dept. VF10
Sauk Centre, MN 56378   Phone: (612)352-6516
1990. This pamphlet profiles a person working in the job. Includes information about job duties, working conditions, places of employment, educational preparation, labor market outlook, and salaries. **Toll-free/Additional Phone Number(s):** 800-255-0752.

★6545★
"Automobile Painters" in *Opportunities in Automotive Service Careers* (pp. 51-52)
National Textbook Co.
4255 W. Touhy Ave.
Lincolnwood, IL 60646   Phone: (312)679-5500
Robert M. Weber. Describes the work of the automobile mechanic and related occupations such as service station attendant and automobile body repairer. Covers working conditions, places of employment, qualifications, training, apprenticeships, certification, advancement opportunities, employment outlook, tools needed, and earnings.

★6546★
"Automotive Painters" in Volume 1 of *Career Discovery Encyclopedia* (pp. 98-99)
J.G. Ferguson Publishing Co.
200 W. Monroe
Chicago, IL 60606   Phone: (312)580-5480
E. Russell Primm, editor-in-chief. 1990. Contains two-page articles on 504 occupations. Each article describes job duties, earnings, and educational and training requirements.

★6547★
"Automotive Painters" in Volume 3 of *The Encyclopedia of Careers and Vocational Guidance* (pp. 622-625)
J.G. Ferguson Publishing Co.
200 W. Monroe
Chicago, IL 60606   Phone: (312)580-5480
William E. Hopke, editor-in-chief. Eighth edition, 1990. Four-volume set that profiles 500 occupations and describes job trends in 76 industries. Includes career description, educational requirements, history of the job, methods of entry, advancement, employment outlook, earnings, working conditions, social and psychological factors, and sources of additional information.

★6548★
Career Opportunities. . .in the Automotive Collision Repair and Refinishing Industry
Automotive Service Association
PO Box 929
Bedford, TX 76095-0929   Phone: (817)283-6205
This booklet describes the work, training, areas of specialization, places of employment, hours, and outlook.

★6549★
"Paint and Coatings Industry Workers" in Volume 3 of *The Encyclopedia of Careers and Vocational Guidance* (pp. 441-444)
J.G. Ferguson Publishing Co.
200 W. Monroe
Chicago, IL 60606   Phone: (312)580-5480
William E. Hopke, editor-in-chief. Eighth edition, 1990. Four-volume set that profiles 500 occupations and describes job trends in 76 industries. Includes career description, educational requirements, history of the job, methods of entry, advancement, employment outlook, earnings, working conditions, social and psychological factors, and sources of additional information.

★6550★
Painter, Spray
Careers, Inc.
PO Box 135
Largo, FL 34649-0135   Phone: (813)584-7333
1989. Two-page occupational summary card describing duties, working conditions, personal qualifications, training, earnings and hours, employment outlook, places of employment, related careers and where to write for more information.

★6551★
"Painting and Coating Machine Operator" in *Occupational Outlook Handbook* (pp. 430-431)
Superintendent of Documents
U.S. Government Printing Office
Washington, DC 20402   Phone: (202)783-3238
Biennial; latest edition, 1990-91. Encyclopedia of careers describing more than 250 occupations and comprising about 86 percent of all jobs in the economy. Occupations that require lengthy education or training are given the most attention. For each occupation, the handbook describes job duties, working conditions, training, educational preparation, personal qualities, advancement possibilities, job outlook, earnings, and sources of additional information.

★6552★
"Production Painter" in *Manufacturing*, Volume 9 of *Career Information Center* (pp. 55-56)
Glencoe/Macmillan
15319 Chatsworth St.
Mission Hills, CA 91345   Phone: (818)898-1391

Richard Lidz and Dale Anderson, editorial directors. Fourth edition, 1990. For 600 occupations, describes job duties, entry-level requirements, education and training needed, advancement possibilities, employment outlook, earnings and benefits. The set is divided into 12 volumes. Each volume includes jobs related under a broad career field. Volume 13 is the index. **Facsimile Number:** 818-365-5489.

★6553★
"Spray Painter (Production)" in *Occu-Facts: Information on 565 Careers in Outline Form* (p. 18.12)
Careers, Inc.
P.O. Box 135
1211 Tenth St., S.W.
Largo, FL 33640   Phone: (813)584-7333

Elizabeth Handville. Biennial, 1989-90 edition. Each one-page occupational profile describes duties, working conditions, physical surroundings and demands, aptitudes, temperament, educational requirements, employment outlook, earnings, and places of employment.

Associations

★6554★
Automotive Service Association (ASA)
1901 Airport Fwy., Ste. 100
PO Box 929
Bedford, TX 76095-0929   Phone: (817)283-6205

Membership: Automotive service businesses (10,100) including body, paint, and trim shops, engine rebuilders, radiator shops, brake and wheel alignment services, transmission shops, tune-up services, and air conditioning services; associate members (320) are manufacturers and wholesalers of automotive parts, and the trade press. **Purpose:** Represents independent businessmen before private agencies and national and state legislative bodies. Promotes confidence between consumer and automotive technician, safety inspection of motor vehicles, and better highways. Conducts professional training seminars in business management, technical and update training, and other areas. Maintains 130 volume collection of automotive repair videotapes. **Publications:** *AutoInc*, monthly. • *Collision Repair Report*, monthly. • *Mechanical News*, bimonthly. • *TransTechnical News*, monthly. • Also publishes convention brochure, fact sheet, and bylaws. **Facsimile Number:** (817)685-0225.

★6555★
Automotive Service Industry Association (ASIA)
444 N. Michigan Ave.
Chicago, IL 60611-3975   Phone: (312)836-1300

Membership: Executives representing independent automotive wholesalers, warehouse distributors, heavy-duty vehicle and equipment parts distributors, automotive electrical service and supply wholesalers and distributors, manufacturers' representatives, and manufacturers and remanufacturers of replacement parts, tools, equipment, chemicals, refinishing materials, supplies, and accessories. **Purpose:** Operates extensive business management library. Holds seminars; bestows awards; compiles statistics; maintains hall of fame. **Publications:** *Automotive Service Industry Association—Buyers Guide*, periodic. • *Automotive Service Industry Association—Membership Directory*, periodic. • *Automotive Service Industry Association—Product Directory*, periodic. • *Selling Today*, periodic. • *Voice of the Industry*, periodic. **Facsimile Number:** (312)836-1009.

★6556★
International Association of Machinists and Aerospace Workers (IAM)
1300 Connecticut Ave.
Washington, DC 20036   Phone: (202)857-5200

Membership: AFL-CIO. **Publications:** *The Machinist*, monthly.

★6557★
International Brotherhood of Teamsters, Chauffeurs, Warehousemen and Helpers of America (IBT)
25 Louisiana Ave. NW
Washington, DC 20001   Phone: (202)624-6800

Purpose: Maintains 30,000 volume library. **Publications:** *The International Teamster*, monthly.

★6558★
International Union, United Automobile, Aerospace and Agricultural Implement Workers of America (UAW)
8000 E. Jefferson
Detroit, MI 48214   Phone: (313)926-5000

Membership: AFL-CIO. **Publications:** *Ammo*, monthly. • *Skill*, quarterly. • *Solidarity*, 10/year.

★6559★
National Institute for Automotive Service Excellence (ASE)
13505 Dulles Technology Dr.
Herndon, VA 22071-3415   Phone: (703)742-3800

Membership: Governed by a 40-member board of directors selected from all sectors of the automotive service industry and from education, government, and consumer groups. **Purpose:** Encourages and promotes the highest standards of automotive service in the public interest. Conducts continuing research to determine the best methods for training automotive technicians; encourages the development of effective training programs. Tests and certifies the competence of automobile, heavy-duty truck, collision repair, and engine machinist technicians. **Publications:** *ASE Test Registration Booklet*, semiannual. • *ASE Training Guide*, annual. • *The Blue Seal*, semiannual. **Facsimile Number:** (703)904-0727.

Standards/Certification Agencies

Voluntary certification by ASE (the National Institute for Automotive Service Excellence) is recognized as the standard of achievement for automotive painters. For certification, painters must pass a written examination and have at least two years of experience in the field. High school, trade or vocational school, or community or junior college training in automotive painting and refinishing may substitute for up to one year of experience. To retain certification, painters must retake the examination at least every five years.

★6560★
Auto Body Repairmen! Painters/Refinishers! Become a Proven Pro: Get ASE Certified
National Institute for Automotive Service Excellence
13505 Dulles Technology Dr.
Herndon, VA 22071-3415   Phone: (703)742-3800

This four-panel brochure describes the examinations for certification for automotive body repairers and painters.

★6561★
National Institute for Automotive Service Excellence (ASE)
13505 Dulles Technology Dr.
Herndon, VA 22071-3415   Phone: (703)742-3800

Encourages and promotes the highest standards of automotive service in the public interest. Conducts continuing research to determine the best methods for training automotive technicians; encourages the development of effective training programs. Tests and certifies the competence of automobile, heavy-duty truck, collision repair, and engine machinist technicians.

Test Guides

★6562★
ASE Test Registration Booklet
National Institute for Automotive Service Excellence (ASE)
13505 Dulles Technology Dr.
Herndon, VA 22071-3415   Phone: (703)742-3800

Semiannual. Registration for technicians who wish to become ASE certified. Provides registration information and sample questions.

★6563★
ASE Training Guide
National Institute for Automotive Service Excellence (ASE)
13505 Dulles Technology Dr.
Herndon, VA 22071-3415   Phone: (703)742-3800

Annual. Bibliographic listing of training materials available for upgrading technicians' skills in automotive repair, including sample ASE test questions and test specifications.

★6564★
The Official ASE Preparation Guide to ASE Automobile and Body/Paint Tests
National Institute for Automotive Service Excellence
13505 Dulles Technology Dr.
Herndon, VA 22071-3415   Phone: (703)742-3800

Describes the certification process for automobile mechanics and auto body repairers. Offers tips on preparing for the test. Contains sample test questions.

Periodicals

★6565★
Ammo
International Union, United Automobile, Aerospace and
   Agricultural Implement Workers of America
8000 E. Jefferson
Detroit, MI 48214   Phone: (313)926-5000

Monthly. Magazine.

★6566★
AutoInc
Automotive Service Association (ASA)
1901 Airport Fwy., Ste. 100
PO Box 929
Bedford, TX 76095-0929   Phone: (817)283-6205

Monthly. Journal covering technical and business information of interest to members; contains shop profiles, legislative news, industry events, and descriptions of new products.

★6567★
The Blue Seal
National Institute for Automotive Service Excellence (ASE)
13505 Dulles Technology Dr.
Herndon, VA 22071-3415   Phone: (703)742-3800

Semiannual. Newsletter providing information on new technologies, training guides, and tips on servicing automobiles for certified technicians and their employers. Also provides information on certified technicians and events.

★6568★
Collision Repair Report
Automotive Service Association (ASA)
1901 Airport Fwy., Ste. 100
PO Box 929
Bedford, TX 76095-0929   Phone: (817)283-6205

Monthly. Speciality publication for members of the ASA Collision Division.

★6569★
Mechanical News
Automotive Service Association (ASA)
1901 Airport Fwy., Ste. 100
PO Box 929
Bedford, TX 76095-0929   Phone: (817)283-6205

Bimonthly. Speciality publication for members of the ASA Mechanical Division.

★6570★
Selling Today
Automotive Service Industry Association (ASIA)
444 N. Michigan Ave.
Chicago, IL 60611-3975   Phone: (312)836-1300

Periodic.

★6571★
Skill (UAW)
International Union, United Automobile, Aerospace and
   Agricultural Implement Workers of America
8000 E. Jefferson
Detroit, MI 48214   Phone: (313)926-5000

Quarterly.

★6572★
Solidarity (UAW)
International Union, United Automobile, Aerospace and
   Agricultural Implement Workers of America
8000 E. Jefferson
Detroit, MI 48214   Phone: (313)926-5000

10/year. Magazine covering labor, economic, social, and political affairs affecting union members. Includes book and film reviews.

★6573★
TransTechnical News
Automotive Service Association (ASA)
1901 Airport Fwy., Ste. 100
PO Box 929
Bedford, TX 76095-0929   Phone: (817)283-6205

Monthly.

★6574★
Voice of the Industry
Automotive Service Industry Association (ASIA)
444 N. Michigan Ave.
Chicago, IL 60611-3975   Phone: (312)836-1300

Periodic.

Meetings and Conventions

★6575★
International Association of Machinists and Aerospace Workers (IAM)
1300 Connecticut Ave.
Washington, DC 20036   Phone: (202)857-5200
Frequency: Quadrennial - next 1992.

★6576★
International Brotherhood of Teamsters, Chauffeurs, Warehousemen and Helpers of America (IBT)
25 Louisiana Ave., NW
Washington, DC 20001   Phone: (202)624-6800
Frequency: Quinquennial - next held in 1996.

Photographic Process Workers

Photographic process workers in photofinishing or custom photo laboratories develop film, make prints and slides, and do related tasks. All-around darkroom technicians perform delicate tasks by hand. Occupations in this field vary by film development and printing processes. Color film operators use specialized machines to process color film in professional photo processing labs. Developers produce negatives by following a sequence of steps. Printer operators focus light through a negative onto light-sensitive paper in order to make prints. Airbrush artists restore damaged and faded photographs and color drawings to simulate photographs. Photographic retouchers alter photographic negatives and prints to accentuate the desired features of a subject or remove undesirable ones. Colorists apply oil colors to portrait photographs to create a natural, lifelike appearance. Photographic spotters cover or spot out imperfections on photographic prints. Color laboratory technicians produce color prints, negatives, and slides by hand, or operate automated machines. Film developers operate equipment that develops still or motion picture film automatically. Color-printer operators control the equipment used to produce color prints from negatives. Automatic print developers operate machines that develop strips of exposed photographic paper. Takedown sorters sort processed film. Automatic mounters tend the automatic mounting presses that cut slide film into individual transparencies and seal them in mounting frames. About 50 percent of all photo process workers work in large photofinishing laboratories that serve drug stores and grocery stores, or in minilabs that process film at the customer's convenience. Many others work in photo laboratories operated by portrait and commercial art studios or for motion picture producers, photo equipment manufacturers, and other organizations. Some darkroom technicians work in commercial laboratories that specialize in processing the work of professional photographers.

$alaries

Weekly earnings of photo process workers are as follows:

Lowest 10 percent	$177.00/week or less
Middle 50 percent	$207.00—$400.00/week
Top 10 percent	$525.00/week or more

Employment Outlook

Growth rate until the year 2000: Faster than average.

Photographic Process Workers

---- Career Guides ----

★6577★
Career Insights
RMI Media Productions, Inc.
2807 West 47th St.
Shawnee Mission, KS 66205   Phone: (913)262-3974
Videocassette series. 1987. This videotape series describes 50 occupations, including skill requirements and interviews with people employed in these fields. Occupations include: flight service, air transportation/ground services, data processing, carpentry, clerk in banking/insurance/business, cosmetic personal grooming, firefighting, roofing, material handling, photographic processing, plumbing, secretarial services, tool and die operations.

★6578★
Career Success Series
Cambridge Career Products
90 MacCorkle Ave., SW
South Charleston, WV 25311   Phone: (304)744-9323
Videocassette. 1986. 15 mins. A series, available separately, outlining various career choices for students. Occupations include: flight service, air transportation/ground service, data processing, carpentry, clerk in banking/insurance, commodity sales, cosmetic personal grooming, fire fighting, forestry services, home economics, insulation/roofing, material handling, mechanics, photographic processing, pipefitting and plumbing, police science, printing, secretarial services, and utilities equipment operator.

★6579★
"Darkroom Technician" in *Communications and the Arts,* Volume 3 of *Career Information Center* (pp. 55-56)
Glencoe/Macmillan
15319 Chatsworth St.
Mission Hills, CA 91345   Phone: (818)898-1391
Richard Lidz and Dale Anderson, editorial directors. Fourth edition, 1990. For 600 occupations, describes job duties, entry-level requirements, education and training needed, advancement possibilities, employment outlook, earnings and benefits. The set is divided into 12 volumes. Each volume includes jobs related under a broad career field. Volume 13 is the index. **Facsimile Number:** 818-365-5489.

★6580★
"Darkroom Technician" in Volume 2 of *Career Discovery Encyclopedia* (pp. 84-85)
J.G. Ferguson Publishing Co.
200 W. Monroe
Chicago, IL 60606   Phone: (312)580-5480
E. Russell Primm, editor-in-chief. 1990. Contains two-page articles on 504 occupations. Each article describes job duties, earnings, and educational and training requirements.

★6581★
"Darkroom Technicians" in Volume 4 of *The Encyclopedia of Careers and Vocational Guidance* (pp. 334-338)
J.G. Ferguson Publishing Co.
200 W. Monroe
Chicago, IL 60606   Phone: (312)580-5480
William E. Hopke, editor-in-chief. Eighth edition, 1990. Four-volume set that profiles 500 occupations and describes job trends in 76 industries. Includes career description, educational requirements, history of the job, methods of entry, advancement, employment outlook, earnings, working conditions, social and psychological factors, and sources of additional information.

★6582★
"Film Laboratory Technicians" in Volume 4 of *The Encyclopedia of Careers and Vocational Guidance* (pp. 343-344)
J.G. Ferguson Publishing Co.
200 W. Monroe
Chicago, IL 60606   Phone: (312)580-5480
William E. Hopke, editor-in-chief. Eighth edition, 1990. Four-volume set that profiles 500 occupations and describes job trends in 76 industries. Includes career description, educational requirements, history of the job, methods of entry, advancement, employment outlook, earnings, working conditions, social and psychological factors, and sources of additional information.

★6583★
Film Processing Specialist
Careers, Inc.
PO Box 135
Largo, FL 34649-0135   Phone: (813)584-7333
1989. Two-page occupational summary card describing duties, working conditions, personal qualifications, training, earnings and hours, employment outlook, places of employment, related careers and where to write for more information.

★6584★
Industrial Photo Processor
Vocational Biographies, Inc.
PO Box 31, Dept. VF10
Sauk Centre, MN 56378 Phone: (612)352-6516
1988. This pamphlet profiles a person working in the job. Includes information about job duties, working conditions, places of employment, educational preparation, labor market outlook, and salaries. **Toll-free/Additional Phone Number(s):** 800-255-0752.

★6585★
Photofinishing Careers: A Lifelong Commitment to Excellence and Creativity
Photo Marketing Association International
3000 Picture Place
Jackson, MI 49201-8898 Phone: (517)783-2809
This four-page pamphlet describes the work and lists photofinishing schools.

★6586★
Photofinishing Laboratory Technicians
Chronicle Guidance Publications, Inc.
PO Box 1190
Moravia, NY 13118-1190 Phone: (315)497-0330
1988. This career brief describes the nature of the work, working conditions, hours and earnings, education and training, licensure, certification, unions, personal qualifications, social and psychological factors, employment outlook, entry methods, advancement, and related occupations. **Toll-free/Additional Phone Number(s):** 800-622-7284.

★6587★
"Photographic Developer" in *Occu-Facts: Information on 565 Careers in Outline Form* (p. 18.21)
Careers, Inc.
P.O. Box 135
1211 Tenth St., S.W.
Largo, FL 33640 Phone: (813)584-7333
Elizabeth Handville. Biennial, 1989-90 edition. Each one-page occupational profile describes duties, working conditions, physical surroundings and demands, aptitudes, temperament, educational requirements, employment outlook, earnings, and places of employment.

★6588★
"Photographic Process Workers" in *Occupational Outlook Handbook* (pp. 432-433)
Superintendent of Documents
U.S. Government Printing Office
Washington, DC 20402 Phone: (202)783-3238
Biennial; latest edition, 1990-91. Encyclopedia of careers describing more than 250 occupations and comprising about 86 percent of all jobs in the economy. Occupations that require lengthy education or training are given the most attention. For each occupation, the handbook describes job duties, working conditions, training, educational preparation, personal qualities, advancement possibilities, job outlook, earnings, and sources of additional information.

★6589★
Photographic Processing
Morris Video
2730 Monterey St. #105
Monterey Business Park
Torrance, CA 90503 Phone: (213)533-4800
Videocassette. 1987. 15 mins. A guide to photographic and motion picture processing, covering careers such as color timing, printer operating, film mounting, developing and much more.

Associations

★6590★
National Association of Photo Equipment Technicians (NAPET)
3000 Picture Pl.
Jackson, MI 49201 Phone: (517)788-8100
Membership: A division of Photo Marketing Association International. Providers of photo/video repair services. Presents semiannual George LaCroix Award to the member displaying outstanding service to the photo/video repair industry. **Publications:** *NAPET News*, quarterly. • *Who's Who in Photographic Management*, semiannual. • Also publishes marketing surveys and studies.

★6591★
Photo Marketing Association International (PMA)
3000 Picture Pl.
Jackson, MI 49201 Phone: (517)788-8100
Membership: Retailers of photo and video equipment, film, and supplies; firms developing and printing film. **Purpose:** Maintains library on photofinishing and retailing, and hall of fame. Compiles statistics; holds research programs. **Publications:** *Mini Lab Focus*, monthly. • *NAPET News*, quarterly. • *Photo Marketing Association International—Newsline*, semimonthly. • *Photo Marketing Magazine*, monthly. • *Sales Counter*, monthly. • *Specialty Lab Update*, monthly. • *SPFE Newsletter*, bimonthly. • *Who's Who in Photographic Management*, semiannual. • Also publishes financial management tips, surveys, and reports. **Facsimile Number:** (517)788-8371.

Test Guides

★6592★
Senior Photographic Machine Operator
National Learning Corp.
212 Michael Dr.
Syosset, NY 11791 Phone: (516)921-8888
Jack Rudman. Part of the Career Examination Series No. 1. All examination guides in this series contain questions with answers. **Facsimile Number:** (516)921-8743. **Toll-free/Additional Phone Number(s):** 800-645-6337.

Awards, Scholarships, Grants, and Fellowships

★6593★
NAPET La Croix Award
National Association of Photo Equipment Technicians
c/o Keith Anderson
Photo Marketing Association International
3000 Picture Place
Jackson, MI 49201 Phone: (517)788-8100
For recognition of achievement or contribution to the photo equipment repair industry. Officers of the Association make nominations and the members vote. A trophy is awarded annually at the convention in the spring. Established in 1976 in honor of George La Croix.

Basic Reference Guides and Handbooks

★6594★
Basic Guide to Black & White Darkroom Techniques
Price Stern Sloan, Inc.
11150 Olympic Blvd.
Los Angeles, CA 90064   Phone: (213)657-6100
H P Books Staff, editor. 1982. **Facsimile Number:** (213)855-8993.

★6595★
Better Black & White Darkroom Techniques
Prentice Hall
Rte. 9W
Englewood Cliffs, NJ 07632   Phone: (201)592-2000
Robert Casagrande. 1984. Part of Master Class Photography Series.

★6596★
Black & White Darkroom Techniques
Simon & Schuster, Inc.
Simon & Schuster Bldg.
1230 Avenue of the Americas
New York, NY 10020   Phone: (212)698-7000
Eastman Kodak Company Editors. 1986.

★6597★
Carbon & Carbro Tissue: You Can Make It!
Tracy Diers
58-14 84th St.
Elmhurst, NY 11373   Phone: (718)651-2798
Tracy Diers, 1986.

★6598★
Creative Projects & Processes
Embee Press
82 Pine Grove Ave.
Kingston, NY 12401   Phone: (914)338-0427
Mark Baczynsky. 1982.

★6599★
Darkroom
Lustrum Press
PO Box 450
Canal St. Sta.
New York, NY 10013   Phone: (212)254-9692
Eleanor Lewis, editor. 1979.

★6600★
The Darkroom Book
Watson-Guptill Publications, Inc.
1515 Broadway
New York, NY 10036   Phone: (212)764-7300
Jack Schofield, editor. 1985. **Facsimile Number:** (212)536-5359.

★6601★
The Darkroom Handbook
Alfred A. Knopf, Inc.
201 E. 50th St.
New York, NY 10022   Phone: (201)751-2600
Michael Langford. 1984.

★6602★
Darkroom Two
Lustrum Press
PO Box 450
Canal St. Sta.
New York, NY 10013   Phone: (212)254-9692
Jain Kelley. 1979.

★6603★
The Double Exposure Book
Wayne Floyd
1407 Darlene
Arlington, TX 76010   Phone: (817)861-1683
Wayne Floyd. 1985.

★6604★
Elementary Darkroom Practices: A Basic Photography Manual
Kendall/Hunt Publishing Company
2460 Kerper Blvd.
Dubuque, IA 52001   Phone: (319)588-1451
Eugene Groppetti. 1987.

★6605★
The Essential Darkroom Book: A Complete Guide to Black & White Processing
Watson-Guptill Publications, Inc.
1515 Broadway
New York, NY 10036   Phone: (212)764-7300
Tom Grill. 1983. **Facsimile Number:** (212)536-5359.

★6606★
Essential Darkroom Techniques
Sterling Publishing Company, Inc.
387 Park Ave. S.
New York, NY 10016-8810   Phone: (212)532-7160
Jonathan Eastland. 1987. **Toll-free/Additional Phone Number(s):** 800-367-9692. **Facsimile Number:** (212)213-2495.

★6607★
Into Your Darkroom Step-by-Step
Amherst Media
PO Box 645
Calistoga, CA 94515   Phone: (716)883-9220
Dennis Curtin. Revised edition, 1991.

★6608★
John Hedgecoe's Darkroom Techniques
Simon & Schuster
Simon & Schuster Bldg.
1230 Avenue of the Americas
New York, NY 10020   Phone: (212)698-7000
John Hedgecoe. 1988.

★6609★
Society of Photo-technologists—Journal & Service Notes—Parts and Services Directory Issue
Society of Photo-Technologists (SPT)
6535 S. Dayton, Ste. 2000
Englewood, CO 80111   Phone: (303)799-0667
Karen A. Hone, Executive Director, editor. Annual, October. About 300 suppliers of parts and services for camera repair; international coverage. Entries include: Company name, address, phone trade and brand names handled, product or service. Arrangement: Classified by product/brand name. Indexes: Alphabetical. **Toll-free/Additional Phone Number(s):** (800)828-8235. **Facsimile Number:** (303)799-0678.

Periodicals

★6610★
American Photo
1633 Broadway
New York, NY 10019   Phone: (212)767-6273
David Schonauer, Editor. 6x/yr. Photography magazine.

★6611★
Darkroom Photography
LFP
9171 Wilshire Blvd., Ste. 300
Beverly Hills, CA 90210   Phone: (213)858-7100
Thom Harrop, Editor. 12x/yr. Photographic techniques magazine. **Facsimile Number:** (213)275-3857.

★6612★
Mini Lab Focus
Photo Marketing Association International (PMA)
3000 Picture Pl.
Jackson, MI 49201   Phone: (517)788-8100
Monthly. Newsletter providing association mini lab (or one-hour lab) members with information on industry trends and activities, advertising and marketing techniques, business management concepts, financial management, customer relations strategies, and other news of interest.

★6613★
NAPET News
National Association of Photo Equipment Technicians (NAPET)
3000 Picture Pl.
Jackson, MI 49201   Phone: (517)788-8100
Quarterly.

★6614★
Photo Lab Management
PLM Publishing Inc.
1312 Lincoln Blvd.
PO Box 1700
Santa Monica, CA 90406   Phone: (213)451-1344
Carolyn Ryan, Editor. Monthly. Magazine covering photo lab process chemistries, equipment, personnel, and technicians for photo lab owners and managers. **Facsimile Number:** (213)395-9058.

★6615★
Photo Marketing
Photo Marketing Assn. Intl.
3000 Picture Pl.
Jackson, MI 49201   Phone: (517)788-8100
Margaret Hooks, Editor. Monthly. Trade magazine for photo/video dealers and photo finishers. **Facsimile Number:** (517)788-8371.

★6616★
Photo Marketing Association International—Newsline

Photo Marketing Association International (PMA)
3000 Picture Pl.
Jackson, MI 49201   Phone: (517)788-8100
Semimonthly. Newsletter providing a digest of pertinent information about the photo industry. Includes surveys of industry leaders on current topics and people profiles.

★6617★
Photo Marketing Magazine
Photo Marketing Association International (PMA)
3000 Picture Pl.
Jackson, MI 49201   Phone: (517)788-8100
Monthly. Trade magazine featuring articles examining industry issues, product innovations, business management, and interviews with leading industry experts.

★6618★
Photographic Processing
PTN Publishing Co.
445 Broadhollow Rd., No. 21
Melville, NY 11747-4722   Phone: (516)496-8000
Mel Konecoff, Editor. Monthly. Magazine for photo finishers. **Facsimile Number:** (516)496-8013.

★6619★
Photomethods
Photomethods, Inc.
1090 Executive Way
Des Plaines, IL 60018   Phone: (708)299-8161
David Silverman, Editor-in-Chief. Monthly. Technical business magazine. **Facsimile Number:** (708)299-2685.

★6620★
PTN (Photographic Trade News)
PTN Publishing Co.
445 Broad Hollow Rd.
Melville, NY 11747   Phone: (516)845-2700
Bill Schiffner, Editor. 2x/mo. Magazine reporting photo industry products news. **Facsimile Number:** (516)845-7109.

★6621★
Specialty Lab Update
Photo Marketing Association International (PMA)
3000 Picture Pl.
Jackson, MI 49201   Phone: (517)788-8100
Monthly. Newsletter providing information on marketing techniques, business financing and management, government regulations, technical developments in the industry, and other news for in-house, custom, and commercial photo processors.

★6622★
SPFE Newsletter
Photo Marketing Association International (PMA)
3000 Picture Pl.
Jackson, MI 49201   Phone: (517)788-8100
Bimonthly. Newsletter covering society activities, technical developments, and EPA guidelines. Contains information on APFT titles awarded and new products.

Meetings and Conventions

★6623★
National Association of Photo Equipment Technicians Trade Show (NAPET)
3000 Picture Pl.
Jackson, MI 49201   Phone: (517)788-8100
Frequency: Annual.

Other Sources of Information

★6624★
The Keepers of Light: A History & Working Guide to Early Photographic Processes
Morgan & Morgan, Inc.
145 Palisade St.
Dobbs Ferry, NY 10522   Phone: (914)693-0023
William Crawford. 1979.

Transportation and Material Moving Occupations

Busdrivers

Intercity busdrivers transport people between regions of a state or of the country; local transit busdrivers, within a metropolitan area or county; and school busdrivers, to and from schools and related events. They follow time schedules and routes over highways and city and suburban streets to provide passengers with an alternative to other forms of transportation. About 70 percent of all busdrivers work for school systems or companies that provide school bus services under contract. Most of the remainder work for private and local government transit systems; some work for intercity and charter buslines.

$alaries

Weekly earnings for busdrivers are as follows:

Lowest 10 percent	$205.00/week or less
Middle 50 percent	$260.00—$510.00/week
Top 10 percent	$595.00/week or more

Employment Outlook

Growth rate until the year 2000: Average.

Busdrivers

Career Guides

★6625★
"Bus Driver" in *Exploring Nontraditional Jobs for Women* (pp. 63-69)
Rosen Publishing Group, Inc.
29 E. 21st St.
New York, NY 10010 Phone: (212)777-3017
Rose Neufeld. 1989. Describes blue-collar, male dominated occupations. Discusses what is done on the job, training, where to apply for jobs, tools used, salaries, and advantages and disadvantages. Relates the experiences of women who are working in the field.

★6626★
"Bus Driver" in *Transportation* (pp. 27-31)
Franklin Watts, Inc.
387 Park Avenue, S.
New York, NY 10016 Phone: (212)686-7070
Marjorie Rittenberg Schulz. 1990. Surveys the transportation industry including air, water, and rail services. Provides job description, training, salary, and employment outlook. Offers job hunting advice.

★6627★
Bus Drivers
Chronicle Guidance Publications, Inc.
PO Box 1190
Moravia, NY 13118-1190 Phone: (315)497-0330
1988. This career brief describes the nature of the work, working conditions, hours and earnings, education and training, licensure, certification, unions, personal qualifications, social and psychological factors, employment outlook, entry methods, advancement, and related occupations. **Toll-free/Additional Phone Number(s):** 800-622-7284.

★6628★
"Bus Drivers" in Volume 1 of *Career Discovery Encyclopedia* (pp. 140-141)
J.G. Ferguson Publishing Co.
200 W. Monroe
Chicago, IL 60606 Phone: (312)580-5480
E. Russell Primm, editor-in-chief. 1990. Contains two-page articles on 504 occupations. Each article describes job duties, earnings, and educational and training requirements.

★6629★
"Bus Lines" in *Opportunities in Travel Careers* (p. 59-63)
National Textbook Co.
4255 W. Touhy Ave.
Lincolnwood, IL 60646 Phone: (312)679-5500
Robert Scott Milne. 1991. Explores job opportunities in many travel related fields including the airlines, resorts, travel agencies, recreation, and tourism. Covers the work, salaries, educational preparation and training, and advancement possibilities.

★6630★
Busdrivers
Careers, Inc.
PO Box 135
Largo, FL 34649-0135 Phone: (813)584-7333
1989. Two-page occupational summary card describing duties, working conditions, personal qualifications, training, earnings and hours, employment outlook, places of employment, related careers and where to write for more information.

★6631★
"Busdrivers" in *Occu-Facts: Information on 565 Careers in Outline Form* (p. 19.5)
Careers, Inc.
P.O. Box 135
1211 Tenth St., S.W.
Largo, FL 33640 Phone: (813)584-7333
Elizabeth Handville. Biennial, 1989-90 edition. Each one-page occupational profile describes duties, working conditions, physical surroundings and demands, aptitudes, temperament, educational requirements, employment outlook, earnings, and places of employment.

★6632★
"Busdrivers" in *Occupational Outlook Handbook* (pp. 434-436)
Superintendent of Documents
U.S. Government Printing Office
Washington, DC 20402 Phone: (202)783-3238
Biennial; latest edition, 1990-91. Encyclopedia of careers describing more than 250 occupations and comprising about 86 percent of all jobs in the economy. Occupations that require lengthy education or training are given the most attention. For each occupation, the handbook describes job duties, working conditions, training, educational preparation, personal qualities, advancement possibilities, job outlook, earnings, and sources of additional information.

★6633★
"Intercity and Local Transit Bus Drivers" in Volume 3 of
 The Encyclopedia of Careers and Vocational Guidance
 (pp. 733-737)
J.G. Ferguson Publishing Co.
200 W. Monroe
Chicago, IL 60606   Phone: (312)580-5480
William E. Hopke, editor-in-chief. Eighth edition, 1990. Four-volume set that profiles 500 occupations and describes job trends in 76 industries. Includes career description, educational requirements, history of the job, methods of entry, advancement, employment outlook, earnings, working conditions, social and psychological factors, and sources of additional information.

★6634★
"Intercity Bus Driver" in *Transportation*, Volume 12 of
 Career Information Center (pp. 52-54)
Glencoe/Macmillan
15319 Chatsworth St.
Mission Hills, CA 91345   Phone: (818)898-1391
Richard Lidz and Dale Anderson, editorial directors. Fourth edition, 1990. For 600 occupations, describes job duties, entry-level requirements, education and training needed, advancement possibilities, employment outlook, earnings and benefits. The set is divided into 12 volumes. Each volume includes jobs related under a broad career field. Volume 13 is the index. **Facsimile Number:** 818-365-5489.

★6635★
"The Intercity People Movers" in *Opportunities in
 Transportation Careers* (pp. 19-29)
National Textbook Co.
4255 W. Touhy Ave.
Lincolnwood, IL 60646   Phone: (312)679-5500
Adrian A. Paradis. 1988. Describes transportation and related employment in driving occupations, the airlines, merchant marine, and travel services. Covers employment outlook, educational and training requirements, wages, and the work itself, and advantages and disadvantages of transportation careers. Offers job hunting advice.

★6636★
School Bus Driver
Vocational Biographies, Inc.
PO Box 31, Dept. VF10
Sauk Centre, MN 56378   Phone: (612)352-6516
1990. This pamphlet profiles a person working in the job. Includes information about job duties, working conditions, places of employment, educational preparation, labor market outlook, and salaries. **Toll-free/Additional Phone Number(s):** 800-255-0752.

★6637★
"Special Service Bus Driver" in *Transportation*, Volume
 12 of *Career Information Center* (pp. 83-85)
Glencoe/Macmillan
15319 Chatsworth St.
Mission Hills, CA 91345   Phone: (818)898-1391
Richard Lidz and Dale Anderson, editorial directors. Fourth edition, 1990. For 600 occupations, describes job duties, entry-level requirements, education and training needed, advancement possibilities, employment outlook, earnings and benefits. The set is divided into 12 volumes. Each volume includes jobs related under a broad career field. Volume 13 is the index. **Facsimile Number:** 818-365-5489.

★6638★
"Teachers Aides and School Bus Drivers" in *The
 American Almanac of Jobs and Salaries* (pp. 109-110)
Avon Books
105 Madison Avenue
New York, NY 10016   Phone: (212)481-5600
John Wright and Edward J. Dwyer. Revised and updated, 1990. A comprehensive guide to the wages of hundreds of occupations in a wide variety of industries and organizations.

★6639★
"Tour Bus Driver" in *Travel & Tourism* (pp. 35-37)
Franklin Watts, Inc.
387 Park Avenue, S.
New York, NY 10016   Phone: (212)686-7070
Marjorie Rittenberg Schulz. 1990. Surveys employment opportunities in the travel and tourism industry. Provides job description, educational preparation, training, salary, employment outlook, and sources of additional information. Offers job hunting advice.

★6640★
*Video Career Library - Transportation & Materials
 Moving*
Careers, Inc.
1211 10th St., SW
PO Box 135
Largo, FL 34649-0135   Phone: (813)584-7333
Videocassette. 1990. 20 mins. Part of the Video Career Library covering 165 occupations. Shows actual workers on the job. Includes tractor/trailer truck drivers, heavy truck drivers, bus drivers, airplane pilots and navigators, grader/dozer/scraper operators, and forklift operators.

★6641★
Vocational Visions
Center for Humanities, Inc.
Communications Park
Box 1000
Mount Kisco, NY 10549   Phone: (914)666-4100
Videocassette. 1984. 30 mins. This series of programs explains key aspects of actual training and a day in the life of a worker in the specific field mentioned on the videocassette. Occupations include: transportation/mechanics, repair, construction, business/office occupations, health, and agriculture.

★6642★
Vocations U.S.A.
Info-Disc Corporation
4 Professional Dr.
Gaithersburg, MD 20879   Phone: (301)948-2300
Videocassette. 1987. 60 mins. A disc collection outlining the requirements and methods of various career areas. Occupations include: transportation, mechanical/repair, health, agriculture, and construction.

───────────── Associations ─────────────

★6643★
American Bus Association (ABA)
1015 15th St., NW, Ste. 250
Washington, DC 20005   Phone: (202)842-1645
Membership: Primarily privately owned bus operating firms engaged in intercity, local, charter, and tour service; state associations; motor bus manufacturers; oil and gas refiners and distributors; travel/tourism industry organizations; others concerned with the operation of bus service and promotion of motorcoach tours. **Purpose:** Seeks to improve bus service, to

stimulate the establishment of bus terminals and connecting schedules, and to develop and promote increased bus utilization in travel and tourism. Advocates equitable laws and regulations and cooperates with public officials to secure equitable enforcement. Encourages street and highway safety. Operates ABA Institute of Learning; conducts safety seminars; disseminates information to the public. Sponsors competitions; operates speakers' bureau; maintains hall of fame.

★6644★
American Public Transit Association (APTA)
1201 New York Ave. NW, Ste. 400
Washington, DC 20005   Phone: (202)898-4000
Membership: Rapid rail and motor bus transit systems in the U.S., Canada, and Mexico; manufacturers and suppliers of materials and services. **Purpose:** Maintains biographical archives, hall of fame, and 20,000 volume library on urban transportation and related fields. Bestows awards; compiles statistics. Operates placement service and speakers' bureau; conducts seminars. **Publications:** *APTA Directory*, annual. • *Passenger Transport: The Weekly Newspaper of the Transit Industry.* • *Transit Fact Book*, annual. **Facsimile Number:** (202)898-4070.

―――― Standards/Certification Agencies ――――

Busdriver qualifications and standards are established by state and federal regulations. Federal regulations require drivers who operate vehicles designed to transport 16 or more passengers to obtain a Commercial Driver's License (CDL) from the state in which they live. In order to be licensed, applicants for a CDL must take and pass a knowledge test and demonstrate that they have the skills necessary to operate a commercial motor vehicle safely. Trainees must be accompanied by another driver who has a CDL until they are issued a CDL. In addition, interstate busdrivers must meet additional qualifications. State agencies and municipalities may also have additional requirements for drivers who operate within their jurisdictions. School busdrivers are also required to obtain a CDL from the state in which they live.

★6645★
CDL Commercial Driver License: 104 Helpful CDL Facts
Professional Truck Driver Institute of America
8788 Elk Grove Blvd., Ste. 20
Elk Grove, CA 95624   Phone: (916)686-5146
1990. This 32-page booklet explains the Commercial Driver License, a set of minimum standards for licensing and testing commercial drivers established by the federal government. Covers the law, classes of licenses, and test content.

―――――――― Test Guides ――――――――

★6646★
Bus Driver
National Learning Corp.
212 Michael Dr.
Syosset, NY 11791   Phone: (516)921-8888
Jack Rudman. Part of the Career Examination Series No. 1. All examination guides in this series contain questions with answers. **Facsimile Number:** (516)921-8743. **Toll-free/Additional Phone Number(s):** 800-645-6337.

★6647★
Bus Driver's Guide to Commercial Driver Licensing
Prentice Hall Press
Simon & Schuster Inc.
200 Old Tappan Rd.
Old Tappan, NJ 07675   Phone: (800)223-2348
Highway Users Federation for Safety and Mobility. First edition, 1990. Contains information and practice material on new state licensing tests for certification and recertification of all bus drivers.

★6648★
Bus Operator - Conductor
Prentice Hall Press
Simon & Schuster Inc.
200 Old Tappan Rd.
Old Tappan, NJ 07675   Phone: (800)223-2348
Hy Hammer. Sixth edition, 1984. Preparation for the exam given by the New York City Transit Authority; also used for subway conductor positions. Includes past exam and seven practice tests.

★6649★
Head Bus Driver
National Learning Corp.
212 Michael Dr.
Syosset, NY 11791   Phone: (516)921-8888
Jack Rudman. Part of the Career Examination Series No. 1. All examination guides in this series contain questions with answers. **Facsimile Number:** (516)921-8743. **Toll-free/Additional Phone Number(s):** 800-645-6337.

★6650★
Passbooks for Career Opportunities: Transportation Specialist
National Learning Corp.
212 Michael Dr.
Syosset, NY 11791   Phone: (516)921-8888
1980. The Passbook Series.

―――― Awards, Scholarships, Grants, and Fellowships ――――

★6651★
Transportation Man of the Year
Delta Nu Alpha Transportation Fraternity
621 Plainfield, Ste. 308
Willowbrook, IL 60521   Phone: (312)850-7100
To recognize contributions to the field of transportation. A plaque is awarded annually. Established in 1952.

―――――――― Periodicals ――――――――

★6652★
Bus World
Stauss Publications
PO Box 39
Woodland Hills, CA 91367   Phone: (818)710-0208
Ed Stauss, Editor and Publisher. Quarterly. Magazine covering transit and intercity bus systems; provides information on new bus design and technology.

★6653★
Mass Transit
PTN Publishing Co.
445 Broad Hollow Rd.
Melville, NY 11747 Phone: (516)845-2700

Tom Kapinos, Editor. 9x/yr. Urban mass transportation publication.

★6654★
Metro Magazine
Bobit Publishing
2512 Artesia Blvd.
Redondo Beach, CA 90278 Phone: (213)376-8788

Bill Paul, Editor and Publisher. 7x/yr. Magazine on public transportation. **Facsimile Number:** (213)376-9043.

★6655★
National School Bus Report
National School Transportation Assn.
PO Box 2639
Springfield, VA 22152 Phone: (703)644-0700

Karen Finkel, Editor and Publisher. Quarterly. Magazine focusing on the safe transportation of school children and representing the interests of school bus contractors. **Facsimile Number:** (703)644-9385.

★6656★
Passenger Transport
American Public Transit Assn.
1201 New York Ave., Ste. 400
Washington, DC 20005 Phone: (202)898-4119

Dennis Kouba, Editor. Weekly (Mon.). **Facsimile Number:** (202)898-4095.

★6657★
Passenger Transport: The Weekly Newspaper of the Transit Industry
American Public Transit Association (APTA)
1201 New York Ave. NW, Ste. 400
Washington, DC 20005 Phone: (202)898-4000

Tabloid covering the mass transit industry. Contains semiannual index, obituaries, and industry personnel promotions.

★6658★
Russell's Official National Motor Coach Guide
Russell's Guides, Inc.
834 3rd Ave. SE
PO Box 278
Cedar Rapids, IA 52406-0278 Phone: (319)364-6138

Tom Whitters, Editor. Monthly. Magazine providing information about national bus schedules. **Facsimile Number:** (319)364-4853.

★6659★
School Bus Fleet
Bobit Publishing
2512 Artesia Blvd.
Redondo Beach, CA 90278 Phone: (213)376-8788

Bill Paul, Editor and Publisher. 7x/yr. Magazine on pupil transportation. **Facsimile Number:** (213)376-9043.

★6660★
SCTA Hi-Lights
South Carolina Trucking Assoc.
2425 Devine St.
PO Box 50166
Columbia, SC 29250-0166 Phone: (803)799-4306

J. Richards Todd, Editor. Monthly. Newspaper (tabloid) serving South Carolina Trucking Association members, truck operators, bus operators, and fleet owners in South Carolina and adjoining states. **Facsimile Number:** (803)254-7148.

★6661★
Steering Wheel
Texas Motor Transportation Assn.
700 E. 11th St.
PO Box 1669
Austin, TX 78767 Phone: (512)478-2541

Cathy Brandewie, Editor. 6x/yr. Magazine covering the Texas truck and bus industry. **Facsimile Number:** (512)474-6494.

★6662★
Traffic World
Journal of Commerce, Inc.
2 World Trade Center, 27th Fl.
New York, NY 10048 Phone: (212)837-7000

Weekly (Mon.). Transportation trade magazine.

★6663★
Transportation Business
Baxter Publications, Inc.
310 Dupont St.
Toronto, ON, Canada M5R 1V9 Phone: (416)968-7252

Peter Morgan, Editor. Monthly. Transportation industry magazine (tabloid). **Facsimile Number:** (416)968-2377.

★6664★
Transportation Quarterly
Eno Foundation for Transportation
PO Box 2055
Westport, CT 06880 Phone: (203)227-4852

Tracy Dunleavy, Circulation Mgr. Quarterly. Trade magazine on transportation. **Facsimile Number:** (203)227-3928.

★6665★
UTU News
United Transportation Union
14600 Detroit Ave.
Cleveland, OH 44107-4250 Phone: (216)228-9400

Fred Hardin, Editor. 12x/yr. Railroad and bus labor newspaper (tabloid).

―――――― Meetings and Conventions ――――――

★6666★
American Public Transit Association (APTA)
1201 New York Ave. NW, Ste. 400
Washington, DC 20005 Phone: (202)898-4000

Frequency: Holds annual conference, with exhibits. 1992; Oct. 18-22; San Diego, CA • 1993; Oct. 3-6; New Orleans, LA • 1994; Sep. 25-29; Boston, MA • 1995; Oct. 8-12; San Antonio, TX. Also holds triennial international exposition, to be held next in 1993. **Facsimile Number:** (202)898-4070.

★6667★
International Public Transit Expo
American Public Transit Association
1201 New York Ave., NW, Ste. 400
Washington, DC 20005 Phone: (202)898-4000

Frequency: Every three years. 1993; Oct. 04-06; New Orleans, LA • 1996; Oct. 07-09; Anaheim, CA. **Facsimile Number:** (202)898-4070.

★6668★
National School Transportation Association Convention and Trade Show
National School Transportation Association
PO Box 2639
Springfield, VA 22152   Phone: (703)644-0700
1992; Jul. Oak Brook, IL.

——— Other Sources of Information ———

★6669★
Transit Fact Book
American Public Transit Association (APTA)
1201 New York Ave. NW, Ste. 400
Washington, DC 20005   Phone: (202)898-4000
Annual. Statistical data book breaking down the trends of transit finances and operations by modes of travel. Contains glossary of transit terms.

Material Moving Equipment Operators

Material moving equipment operators use machinery to move construction materials and other manufactured goods, earth, logs, petroleum products, grain, coal, and other heavy materials over short distances. Crane and tower operators operate mechanical boom and cable or tower and cable equipment to lift and move materials, machinery, or other heavy objects. Excavation and loading machine operators operate and tend machinery equipped with scoops, shovels, or buckets to excavate earth at construction sites and to load and move loose materials. Grader, dozer, and scraper operators operate vehicles equipped with blades to remove, distribute, level, and grade earth. In addition to the bulldozers, they operate trench excavators, road graders, and similar equipment. Hoist and winch operators operate or tend machines which lift and pull loads using power-operated cable equipment. Most work in loading operations in manufacturing, mining, or logging. Operating engineers are qualified to operate more than one type of the construction equipment. Industrial truck and tractor operators drive and control industrial trucks or tractors, such as a forklift. Nearly 33 percent of all material moving equipment operators work in manufacturing; most of these are industrial truck and tractor operators. More than 20 percent work in the construction industry. Significant numbers work in state and local governments and in the trucking and warehousing, wholesale trade, and mining industries.

$alaries

Weekly median earnings for material moving equipment operators are as follows:

Crane and tower operators	$440.00/week
Excavation and loading machine operators	$430.00/week
Grader, dozer, and scraper operators	$390.00/week
Industrial truck and tractor operators	$340.00/week
Operating engineers	$450.00/week
Other material moving equipment operators	$380.00/week

Employment Outlook

Growth rate until the year 2000: More slowly than average.

Material Moving Equipment Operators

Career Guides

★6670★
"Asphalt Paving Machine Operator" in Volume 1 of *Career Discovery Encyclopedia* (pp. 60-61)
J.G. Ferguson Publishing Co.
200 W. Monroe
Chicago, IL 60606   Phone: (312)580-5480

E. Russell Primm, editor-in-chief. 1990. Contains two-page articles on 504 occupations. Each article describes job duties, earnings, and educational and training requirements.

★6671★
"Asphalt Paving Machine Operators" in Volume 3 of *The Encyclopedia of Careers and Vocational Guidance* (pp. 619-622)
J.G. Ferguson Publishing Co.
200 W. Monroe
Chicago, IL 60606   Phone: (312)580-5480

William E. Hopke, editor-in-chief. Eighth edition, 1990. Four-volume set that profiles 500 occupations and describes job trends in 76 industries. Includes career description, educational requirements, history of the job, methods of entry, advancement, employment outlook, earnings, working conditions, social and psychological factors, and sources of additional information.

★6672★
"Average Hourly Wages of Material Movement Workers in Ten Cities" in *The American Almanac of Jobs and Salaries* (p. 521)
Avon Books
105 Madison Avenue
New York, NY 10016   Phone: (212)481-5600

John Wright and Edward J. Dwyer. Revised and updated, 1990. A comprehensive guide to the wages of hundreds of occupations in a wide variety of industries and organizations.

★6673★
Bulldozer Operator
Careers, Inc.
PO Box 135
Largo, FL 34649-0135   Phone: (813)584-7333

1989. Two-page occupational summary card describing duties, working conditions, personal qualifications, training, earnings and hours, employment outlook, places of employment, related careers and where to write for more information.

★6674★
"Bulldozer Operator" in *Occu-Facts: Information on 565 Careers in Outline Form* (p. 19.17)
Careers, Inc.
P.O. Box 135
1211 Tenth St., S.W.
Largo, FL 33640   Phone: (813)584-7333

Elizabeth Handville. Biennial, 1989-90 edition. Each one-page occupational profile describes duties, working conditions, physical surroundings and demands, aptitudes, temperament, educational requirements, employment outlook, earnings, and places of employment.

★6675★
"Construction Machinery Operator" in *Guide to Careers Without College* (pp. 77-79)
Franklin Watts, Inc.
387 Park Avenue, S.
New York, NY 10016   Phone: (212)686-7070

Kathleen S. Abrams. 1988. Discusses careers that do not require a college degree in fields such as health care, sales and marketing, and the building trades. Describes the work, employment opportunities, and training.

★6676★
Crane Operator
Vocational Biographies, Inc.
PO Box 31, Dept. VF10
Sauk Centre, MN 56378   Phone: (612)352-6516

1990. This pamphlet profiles a person working in the job. Includes information about job duties, working conditions, places of employment, educational preparation, labor market outlook, and salaries. **Toll-free/Additional Phone Number(s):** 800-255-0752.

★6677★
Craneman
Film Library
3450 Wilshire Blvd. #700
Los Angeles, CA 90010-2215   Phone: (213)384-8114

Videocassette. 198?. 20 mins. The basic functions and safe operation of the over head travelling crane are demonstrated in this tape.

★6678★
Forklift Operator Training
Film Library
3450 Wilshire Blvd. #700
Los Angeles, CA 90010-2215   Phone: (213)384-8114

Videocassette. 198?. 14 mins. This course will train forklift operators in OSHA requirements.

★6679★
Forklift Truck: Operator Training
Du Pont Training Services
Barley Mill, P19-1210
Wilmington, DE 19898   Phone: (302)992-3620

Videocassette. 1985. 70 mins. Accompanied by self-study courses for either experienced or novice drivers, this tape outlines the training for forklift handlers.

★6680★
Front-End Loader Operator
Vocational Biographies, Inc.
PO Box 31, Dept. VF10
Sauk Centre, MN 56378   Phone: (612)352-6516

1990. This pamphlet profiles a person working in the job. Includes information about job duties, working conditions, places of employment, educational preparation, labor market outlook, and salaries. **Toll-free/Additional Phone Number(s):** 800-255-0752.

★6681★
"Heavy Equipment Operations" in *The Career Connection II: A Guide to Technical Majors and Their Related Careers* (pp. 69-70)
ERIS
PO Box 7509
University Station
Provo, UT 84602-0509

Fred A. Rowe. 1988. Contains technical majors, such as automotive technology. Describes the major and the job. Lists high school and postsecondary school courses. Includes occupations related to the major, employment outlook, and starting salary.

★6682★
"Heavy Equipment Operator" in *Construction*, Volume 4 of *Career Information Center* (pp. 62-63)
Glencoe/Macmillan
15319 Chatsworth St.
Mission Hills, CA 91345   Phone: (818)898-1391

Richard Lidz and Dale Anderson, editorial directors. Fourth edition, 1990. For 600 occupations, describes job duties, entry-level requirements, education and training needed, advancement possibilities, employment outlook, earnings and benefits. The set is divided into 12 volumes. Each volume includes jobs related under a broad career field. Volume 13 is the index. **Facsimile Number:** 818-365-5489.

★6683★
"Industrial Truck Operator" in *Occu-Facts: Information on 565 Careers in Outline Form* (p. 19.19)
Careers, Inc.
P.O. Box 135
1211 Tenth St., S.W.
Largo, FL 33640   Phone: (813)584-7333

Elizabeth Handville. Biennial, 1989-90 edition. Each one-page occupational profile describes duties, working conditions, physical surroundings and demands, aptitudes, temperament, educational requirements, employment outlook, earnings, and places of employment.

★6684★
"Industrial Truck Operators" in Volume 3 of *Career Discovery Encyclopedia* (pp. 140-141)
J.G. Ferguson Publishing Co.
200 W. Monroe
Chicago, IL 60606   Phone: (312)580-5480

E. Russell Primm, editor-in-chief. 1990. Contains two-page articles on 504 occupations. Each article describes job duties, earnings, and educational and training requirements.

★6685★
"Industrial Truck Operators" in Volume 3 of *The Encyclopedia of Careers and Vocational Guidance* (pp. 746-748)
J.G. Ferguson Publishing Co.
200 W. Monroe
Chicago, IL 60606   Phone: (312)580-5480

William E. Hopke, editor-in-chief. Eighth edition, 1990. Four-volume set that profiles 500 occupations and describes job trends in 76 industries. Includes career description, educational requirements, history of the job, methods of entry, advancement, employment outlook, earnings, working conditions, social and psychological factors, and sources of additional information.

★6686★
"Material Moving Equipment Operators" in *Occupational Outlook Handbook* (pp. 436-437)
Superintendent of Documents
U.S. Government Printing Office
Washington, DC 20402   Phone: (202)783-3238

Biennial; latest edition, 1990-91. Encyclopedia of careers describing more than 250 occupations and comprising about 86 percent of all jobs in the economy. Occupations that require lengthy education or training are given the most attention. For each occupation, the handbook describes job duties, working conditions, training, educational preparation, personal qualities, advancement possibilities, job outlook, earnings, and sources of additional information.

★6687★
Operating Engineer
Careers, Inc.
PO Box 135
Largo, FL 34649-0135   Phone: (813)584-7333

1991. Eight-page brief offering the definition, history, duties, working conditions, personal qualifications, educational requirements, earnings, hours, employment outlook, advancement possibilities, and related occupations.

★6688★
"Operating Engineer" in *Hard Hatted Women: Stories of Struggle and Success in the Trades* (pp. 88-101)
Seal Press
3131 Western Ave., Ste. 410
Seattle, WA 98121   Phone: (206)283-7844

Molly Martin, editor. 1988. Twenty-six women recount their experiences working in blue collar occupations. They describe how they got in, the work they do, their relationships in predominantly male occupations, and their training.

★6689★
"Operating Engineer" in *VGM's Careers Encyclopedia* (pp. 315-317)
National Textbook Co.
4255 W. Touhy Ave.
Lincolnwood, IL 60646   Phone: (312)679-5500

Third edition, 1991. Contains two- to five-page descriptions of 200 managerial, professional, technical, trade, and service

Material Moving Equipment Operators ★6700★

occupations. Each profile includes job duties, places of employment, qualifications, educational preparation, training, employment potential, advancement, income, and additional sources of information.

★6690★
"Operating Engineer" in *VGM's Handbook of Scientific and Technical Careers* (pp. 79-82)
National Textbook Co.
4255 W. Touhy Ave.
Lincolnwood, IL 60646 Phone: (312)679-5500

Craig T. Norback, editor. 1990. Includes 50 occupations in science and technology and describes job duties, qualifications, education, training, potential advancement, and income. Lists sources of additional information.

★6691★
"Operating Engineers" in *Occu-Facts: Information on 565 Careers in Outline Form* (p. 19.18)
Careers, Inc.
P.O. Box 135
1211 Tenth St., S.W.
Largo, FL 33640 Phone: (813)584-7333

Elizabeth Handville. Biennial, 1989-90 edition. Each one-page occupational profile describes duties, working conditions, physical surroundings and demands, aptitudes, temperament, educational requirements, employment outlook, earnings, and places of employment.

★6692★
"Operating Engineers" in *Opportunities in Building Construction Trades* (pp. 66-68)
National Textbook Co.
4255 W. Touhy Ave.
Lincolnwood, IL 60646 Phone: (312)679-5500

Michael Sumichrast. 1989. Gives an overview of the construction industry and describes the jobs of various craftworkers. Covers different kinds of builders: home, custom; and describes management skills needed and industry trends affecting opportunities.

★6693★
"Operating Engineers" in Volume 4 of *Career Discovery Encyclopedia* (pp. 140-141)
J.G. Ferguson Publishing Co.
200 W. Monroe
Chicago, IL 60606 Phone: (312)580-5480

E. Russell Primm, editor-in-chief. 1990. Contains two-page articles on 504 occupations. Each article describes job duties, earnings, and educational and training requirements.

★6694★
"Operating Engineers (Construction Machinery Operators)" in Volume 3 of *The Encyclopedia of Careers and Vocational Guidance* (pp. 680-682)
J.G. Ferguson Publishing Co.
200 W. Monroe
Chicago, IL 60606 Phone: (312)580-5480

William E. Hopke, editor-in-chief. Eighth edition, 1990. Four-volume set that profiles 500 occupations and describes job trends in 76 industries. Includes career description, educational requirements, history of the job, methods of entry, advancement, employment outlook, earnings, working conditions, social and psychological factors, and sources of additional information.

★6695★
"Power Shovel Crane Operator" in *Occu-Facts: Information on 565 Careers in Outline Form* (p. 19.16)
Careers, Inc.
P.O. Box 135
1211 Tenth St., S.W.
Largo, FL 33640 Phone: (813)584-7333

Elizabeth Handville. Biennial, 1989-90 edition. Each one-page occupational profile describes duties, working conditions, physical surroundings and demands, aptitudes, temperament, educational requirements, employment outlook, earnings, and places of employment.

★6696★
"Power Truck Operator" in *Transportation*, Volume 12 of *Career Information Center* (pp. 69-71)
Glencoe/Macmillan
15319 Chatsworth St.
Mission Hills, CA 91345 Phone: (818)898-1391

Richard Lidz and Dale Anderson, editorial directors. Fourth edition, 1990. For 600 occupations, describes job duties, entry-level requirements, education and training needed, advancement possibilities, employment outlook, earnings and benefits. The set is divided into 12 volumes. Each volume includes jobs related under a broad career field. Volume 13 is the index. **Facsimile Number:** 818-365-5489.

★6697★
Shovel-Crave Operator, Power
Careers, Inc.
PO Box 135
Largo, FL 34649-0135 Phone: (813)584-7333

1988. Two-page occupational summary card describing duties, working conditions, personal qualifications, training, earnings and hours, employment outlook, places of employment, related careers and where to write for more information.

★6698★
Transportation
Learning Corporation of America
108 Wilmot Rd.
Deerfield, IL 60015-9990 Phone: (708)940-1260

Videocassette. 1982. 21 mins. In this program from the "Working" series, we meet five employees in transportation-related jobs: fishing boat captain, auto body repair shop owner, construction equipment operator, air traffic controller and truck driver.

★6699★
Truck Operator, Industrial
Careers, Inc.
PO Box 135
Largo, FL 34649-0135 Phone: (813)584-7333

1988. Two-page occupational summary card describing duties, working conditions, personal qualifications, training, earnings and hours, employment outlook, places of employment, related careers and where to write for more information.

★6700★
Video Career Library - Transportation & Materials Moving
Careers, Inc.
1211 10th St., SW
PO Box 135
Largo, FL 34649-0135 Phone: (813)584-7333

Videocassette. 1990. 20 mins. Part of the Video Career Library covering 165 occupations. Shows actual workers on the job. Includes tractor/trailer truck drivers, heavy truck drivers, bus drivers, airplane pilots and navigators, grader/dozer/scraper operators, and forklift operators.

Associations

★6701★
Associated Builders and Contractors (ABC)
729 15th St. NW
Washington, DC 20005   Phone: (202)637-8800

Membership: Construction contractors, subcontractors, suppliers, and associates. **Purpose:** Aim is to foster and perpetuate the principles of rewarding shop construction workers and management on the basis of merit. Sponsors leadership conference and management education programs including Wheels of Learning; also sponsors apprenticeship and skill training programs. Disseminates technological and labor relations information. Maintains biographical archives and placement service. Bestows awards; compiles statistics. **Publications:** *ABC Newsline*, semimonthly. • *The Builder and Contractor*, monthly. • *Classified Membership Directory*, annual. • Also publishes safety manuals.

★6702★
Associated General Contractors of America (AGC)
1957 E St. NW
Washington, DC 20006   Phone: (202)393-2040

Membership: General construction contractors; subcontractors; industry suppliers; service firms. **Purpose:** Provides tax services through its divisions. Conducts special conferences and seminars designed specifically for construction firms. Compiles statistics on job accidents reported by member firms. Bestows annual awards for safety and Build/America awards for innovative and outstanding achievements by general contractors. Offers college scholarships through AGC Education and Research Foundation. Maintains 65 committees, including joint cooperative committees with other associations and liaison committees with federal agencies. **Publications:** *AGC Membership Directory and Buyers' Guide*, annual. • *Associated General Contractors of America—National Newsletter*, biweekly. • *Constructor*, monthly. • Also publishes manuals, guides, model contract documents, studies, and checklists. **Facsimile Number:** (202)347-4004.

★6703★
Industrial Truck Association (ITA)
1750 K St. NW, Ste. 210
Washington, DC 20006   Phone: (202)296-9880

Membership: Manufacturers of powered industrial lift trucks, electric storage batteries, tires, engines, attachments, and hydraulic systems for powered industrial lift trucks.

★6704★
International Union of Operating Engineers (IUOE)
1125 17th St., NW
Washington, DC 20036   Phone: (202)429-9100

Membership: AFL-CIO. **Publications:** *International Operating Engineer*, monthly.

Standards/Certification Agencies

Some construction equipment operators are trained in a three-year apprenticeship program administered by union-management committees of the International Union of Operating Engineers (AFL-CIO) and the Associated General Contractors of America. The programs consist of at least three years of 6,000 hours of on-the-job training and 144 hours a year of related classroom instruction.

Test Guides

★6705★
Crane Operator (Any Motive Power Except Steam)
National Learning Corp.
212 Michael Dr.
Syosset, NY 11791   Phone: (516)921-8888

Jack Rudman. Part of the Career Examination Series No. 1. All examination guides in this series contain questions with answers. **Facsimile Number:** (516)921-8743. **Toll-free/Additional Phone Number(s):** 800-645-6337.

Periodicals

★6706★
ABC Newsline
Associated Builders and Contractors (ABC)
729 15th St. NW
Washington, DC 20005   Phone: (202)637-8800
Semimonthly.

★6707★
American Mover
American Movers Conference
2200 Mill Rd.
Alexandria, VA 22314-4654   Phone: (703)838-1930

Ann S. Dinerman, Editor. Monthly. Magazine for the moving industry. **Facsimile Number:** (703)838-1925.

★6708★
Associated General Contractors of America—National Newsletter
Associated General Contractors of America (AGC)
1957 E St. NW
Washington, DC 20006   Phone: (202)393-2040
Biweekly.

★6709★
The Builder and Contractor
Associated Builders and Contractors (ABC)
729 15th St. NW
Washington, DC 20005   Phone: (202)637-8800
Monthly.

★6710★
Constructor
Associated General Contractors of America (AGC)
1957 E St. NW
Washington, DC 20006   Phone: (202)393-2040

Monthly. Association magazine for general contractors engaged in construction.

★6711★
Rock and Dirt
TAP Publishing Co.
410 W. 4th St.
Crossville, TN 38555   Phone: (615)484-5139

Michael D. Stone, Publisher. 3x/mo. Buy and sell trade newspaper (tabloid) for heavy construction earth moving machinery. **Facsimile Number:** (615)484-2532.

Material Moving Equipment Operators

★6712★
Southwest Contractor
McGraw Hill Publishing Co., Inc.
2050 E. University Dr., Ste. 1
Phoenix, AZ 85034-6731　　　　Phone: (602)230-0598
Elaine Beall, Mng. Editor. Monthly. Regional trade magazine for the contracting industries including highway, municipal, utility, and heavy construction, and mining. **Facsimile Number:** (602)495-9407.

――――― Meetings and Conventions ―――――

★6713★
American Movers Conference Trade Show
American Movers Conference
2200 Mill Rd.
Alexandria, VA 22314　　　　Phone: (703)838-1930
Frequency: Always held in October. 1992; Sep. 30 - Oct. 03; Orlando, FL. **Facsimile Number:** (703)838-1925.

★6714★
IN-DEX - Production Technology, Materials Handling, and Warehousing Exhibition
World Access Corp.
15 Bemis Rd.
PO Box 171
Wellesley Hills, MA 02181　　　　Phone: (617)235-8095
1992; Oct. 04-08. **Facsimile Number:** (617)235-7360.

★6715★
International Brotherhood of Teamsters, Chauffeurs, Warehousemen and Helpers of America (IBT)
25 Louisiana Ave., NW
Washington, DC 20001　　　　Phone: (202)624-6800
Frequency: Quinquennial - next held in 1996.

★6716★
International Materials Handling and Distribution Show
Southex Exhibitions (Don Mills)
1450 Don Mills Rd.
Don Mills, ON, Canada M3B 2X7　　　　Phone: (416)445-6641
1992. **Facsimile Number:** (416)442-2207.

★6717★
NASSTRAC Convention
NASSTRAC
1750 Pennsylvania Ave., Ste. 1105
Washington, DC 20006　　　　Phone: (202)393-5505
1992.

★6718★
Productivity Conference and Distribution/Transportation Exposition
National-American Wholesale Grocers Association
201 Park Washington Ct.
Falls Church, VA 22046　　　　Phone: (703)532-9400
1992; Oct. 27-30; Minneapolis, MN. **Facsimile Number:** (703)538-4673.

Rail Transportation Workers

Rail transportation workers facilitate the movement of passengers and cargo by trains, subways, and streetcars. Locomotive engineers and rail yard engineers operate locomotives in yards, stations, and on the road between stations. Locomotive engineers transport cargo and passengers between stations, while yard engineers move cars within yards to assemble or disassemble trains. Some engineers called dinkey operators work at industrial sites or mines operating engines that help transport coal, rock, or supplies. Road conductors and yard conductors are in charge of train and yard crews. Conductors assigned to freight trains keep records of each car's contents and destination and make sure that cars are added and removed at the proper points along the route. Conductors assigned to passenger trains collect tickets and fares and assist passengers. Yard conductors supervise the crews that assemble and disassemble trains. Brake operators send information to conductors and dispatchers regarding needed repairs while underway or the removal of defective cars at the nearest station or stop. Subway operators guide subway trains, observing the signal system. Streetcar operators drive electric-powered streetcars to transport passengers, collect fares from passengers, and issue change and transfers. Railroads employ about 90 percent of all rail transportation workers. State and local governments and mining and manufacturing establishments that operate their own railroad cars to carry freight employ the remainder.

$alaries

Average annual earnings for rail transportation workers are as follows:

Yard engineers	$41,300/year
Locomotive engineers in passenger service	$54,600/year
Locomotive engineers in freight service	$54,500/year
Conductors in passenger service	$47,200/year
Conductors in freight service	$50,800/year
Brake operators in freight service	$44,700/year
Brake operators in yard service	$34,300/year
Subway operators	$27,000—$31,000/year

Employment Outlook

Growth rate until the year 2000: Employment of railroad transportation workers will grow slower than average; employment of subway operators will grow much faster than average.

Rail Transportation Workers

Career Guides

★6719★
"Brake Operators, Brakers" in Volume 3 of *The Encyclopedia of Careers and Vocational Guidance* (pp. 731-733)
J.G. Ferguson Publishing Co.
200 W. Monroe
Chicago, IL 60606   Phone: (312)580-5480
William E. Hopke, editor-in-chief. Eighth edition, 1990. Four-volume set that profiles 500 occupations and describes job trends in 76 industries. Includes career description, educational requirements, history of the job, methods of entry, advancement, employment outlook, earnings, working conditions, social and psychological factors, and sources of additional information.

★6720★
"Brake Operators or Brakemen" in *The American Almanac of Jobs and Salaries* (p. 465)
Avon Books
105 Madison Avenue
New York, NY 10016   Phone: (212)481-5600
John Wright and Edward J. Dwyer. Revised and updated, 1990. A comprehensive guide to the wages of hundreds of occupations in a wide variety of industries and organizations.

★6721★
"Brakers" in Volume 1 of *Career Discovery Encyclopedia* (pp. 136-137)
J.G. Ferguson Publishing Co.
200 W. Monroe
Chicago, IL 60606   Phone: (312)580-5480
E. Russell Primm, editor-in-chief. 1990. Contains two-page articles on 504 occupations. Each article describes job duties, earnings, and educational and training requirements.

★6722★
"Conductors" in *Opportunities in Travel Careers* (p. 54)
National Textbook Co.
4255 W. Touhy Ave.
Lincolnwood, IL 60646   Phone: (312)679-5500
Robert Scott Milne. 1991. Explores job opportunities in many travel related fields including the airlines, resorts, travel agencies, recreation, and tourism. Covers the work, salaries, educational preparation and training, and advancement possibilities.

★6723★
"Conductors" in *The American Almanac of Jobs and Salaries* (pp. 465-466)
Avon Books
105 Madison Avenue
New York, NY 10016   Phone: (212)481-5600
John Wright and Edward J. Dwyer. Revised and updated, 1990. A comprehensive guide to the wages of hundreds of occupations in a wide variety of industries and organizations.

★6724★
"Engineers and Engineer Helpers" in *Opportunities in Travel Careers* (pp. 54-55)
National Textbook Co.
4255 W. Touhy Ave.
Lincolnwood, IL 60646   Phone: (312)679-5500
Robert Scott Milne. 1991. Explores job opportunities in many travel related fields including the airlines, resorts, travel agencies, recreation, and tourism. Covers the work, salaries, educational preparation and training, and advancement possibilities.

★6725★
The Human Side of Railroading
Association of American Railroads
Information and Public Affairs Department
50 F St., NW
Washington, DC 20001   Phone: (202)639-2100
1987. Booklet describing the jobs of train and engine service workers and track and equipment maintenance workers. Lists headquarters of major railroads.

★6726★
"Locomotive Engineer" in *Occu-Facts: Information on 565 Careers in Outline Form* (p. 19.9)
Careers, Inc.
P.O. Box 135
1211 Tenth St., S.W.
Largo, FL 33640   Phone: (813)584-7333
Elizabeth Handville. Biennial, 1989-90 edition. Each one-page occupational profile describes duties, working conditions, physical surroundings and demands, aptitudes, temperament, educational requirements, employment outlook, earnings, and places of employment.

★6727★
"Locomotive Engineers" in Volume 4 of *Career Discovery Encyclopedia* (pp. 40-41)
J.G. Ferguson Publishing Co.
200 W. Monroe
Chicago, IL 60606   Phone: (312)580-5480
E. Russell Primm, editor-in-chief. 1990. Contains two-page articles on 504 occupations. Each article describes job duties, earnings, and educational and training requirements.

★6728★
"Locomotive Engineers" in Volume 3 of *The Encyclopedia of Careers and Vocational Guidance* (pp. 751-753)
J.G. Ferguson Publishing Co.
200 W. Monroe
Chicago, IL 60606   Phone: (312)580-5480
William E. Hopke, editor-in-chief. Eighth edition, 1990. Four-volume set that profiles 500 occupations and describes job trends in 76 industries. Includes career description, educational requirements, history of the job, methods of entry, advancement, employment outlook, earnings, working conditions, social and psychological factors, and sources of additional information.

★6729★
"Locomotive Engineers" in *The American Almanac of Jobs and Salaries* (pp. 466-467)
Avon Books
105 Madison Avenue
New York, NY 10016   Phone: (212)481-5600
John Wright and Edward J. Dwyer. Revised and updated, 1990. A comprehensive guide to the wages of hundreds of occupations in a wide variety of industries and organizations.

★6730★
"New Horizons for Rail Careers" in *Opportunities in Transportation Careers* (pp. 81-93)
National Textbook Co.
4255 W. Touhy Ave.
Lincolnwood, IL 60646   Phone: (312)679-5500
Adrian A. Paradis. 1988. Describes transportation and related employment in driving occupations, the airlines, merchant marine, and travel services. Covers employment outlook, educational and training requirements, wages, and the work itself, and advantages and disadvantages of transportation careers. Offers job hunting advice.

★6731★
"Rail Transportation Workers" in *Occupational Outlook Handbook* (pp. 438-440)
Superintendent of Documents
U.S. Government Printing Office
Washington, DC 20402   Phone: (202)783-3238
Biennial; latest edition, 1990-91. Encyclopedia of careers describing more than 250 occupations and comprising about 86 percent of all jobs in the economy. Occupations that require lengthy education or training are given the most attention. For each occupation, the handbook describes job duties, working conditions, training, educational preparation, personal qualities, advancement possibilities, job outlook, earnings, and sources of additional information.

★6732★
Railroad Brake Operator
Careers, Inc.
PO Box 135
Largo, FL 34649-0135   Phone: (813)584-7333
1989. Two-page occupational summary card describing duties, working conditions, personal qualifications, training, earnings and hours, employment outlook, places of employment, related careers and where to write for more information.

★6733★
"Railroad Brake Operator" in *Occu-Facts: Information on 565 Careers in Outline Form* (19.10)
Careers, Inc.
P.O. Box 135
1211 Tenth St., S.W.
Largo, FL 33640   Phone: (813)584-7333
Elizabeth Handville. Biennial, 1989-90 edition. Each one-page occupational profile describes duties, working conditions, physical surroundings and demands, aptitudes, temperament, educational requirements, employment outlook, earnings, and places of employment.

★6734★
"Railroad Braker" in *Transportation*, Volume 12 of *Career Information Center* (pp. 71-72)
Glencoe/Macmillan
15319 Chatsworth St.
Mission Hills, CA 91345   Phone: (818)898-1391
Richard Lidz and Dale Anderson, editorial directors. Fourth edition, 1990. For 600 occupations, describes job duties, entry-level requirements, education and training needed, advancement possibilities, employment outlook, earnings and benefits. The set is divided into 12 volumes. Each volume includes jobs related under a broad career field. Volume 13 is the index. **Facsimile Number:** 818-365-5489.

★6735★
"Railroad Braker and Conductor" in *Transportation* (pp. 39-43)
Franklin Watts, Inc.
387 Park Avenue, S.
New York, NY 10016   Phone: (212)686-7070
Marjorie Rittenberg Schulz. 1990. Surveys the transportation industry including air, water, and rail services. Provides job description, training, salary, and employment outlook. Offers job hunting advice.

★6736★
Railroad Conductor
Careers, Inc.
PO Box 135
Largo, FL 34649-0135   Phone: (813)584-7333
1988. Two-page occupational summary card describing duties, working conditions, personal qualifications, training, earnings and hours, employment outlook, places of employment, related careers and where to write for more information.

★6737★
Railroad Conductor
Vocational Biographies, Inc.
PO Box 31, Dept. VF10
Sauk Centre, MN 56378   Phone: (612)352-6516
1989. This pamphlet profiles a person working in the job. Includes information about job duties, working conditions, places of employment, educational preparation, labor market outlook, and salaries. **Toll-free/Additional Phone Number(s):** 800-255-0752.

Rail Transportation Workers

★6738★
"Railroad Conductor" in *Occu-Facts: Information on 565 Careers in Outline Form* (p. 19.1)
Careers, Inc.
P.O. Box 135
1211 Tenth St., S.W.
Largo, FL 33640 Phone: (813)584-7333

Elizabeth Handville. Biennial, 1989-90 edition. Each one-page occupational profile describes duties, working conditions, physical surroundings and demands, aptitudes, temperament, educational requirements, employment outlook, earnings, and places of employment.

★6739★
"Railroad Conductor" in *Transportation*, Volume 12 of *Career Information Center* (pp. 111-113)
Glencoe/Macmillan
15319 Chatsworth St.
Mission Hills, CA 91345 Phone: (818)898-1391

Richard Lidz and Dale Anderson, editorial directors. Fourth edition, 1990. For 600 occupations, describes job duties, entry-level requirements, education and training needed, advancement possibilities, employment outlook, earnings and benefits. The set is divided into 12 volumes. Each volume includes jobs related under a broad career field. Volume 13 is the index. **Facsimile Number:** 818-365-5489.

★6740★
"Railroad Conductors" in Volume 5 of *Career Discovery Encyclopedia* (pp. 128-129)
J.G. Ferguson Publishing Co.
200 W. Monroe
Chicago, IL 60606 Phone: (312)580-5480

E. Russell Primm, editor-in-chief. 1990. Contains two-page articles on 504 occupations. Each article describes job duties, earnings, and educational and training requirements.

★6741★
"Railroad Conductors" in Volume 3 of *The Encyclopedia of Careers and Vocational Guidance* (pp. 129-132)
J.G. Ferguson Publishing Co.
200 W. Monroe
Chicago, IL 60606 Phone: (312)580-5480

William E. Hopke, editor-in-chief. Eighth edition, 1990. Four-volume set that profiles 500 occupations and describes job trends in 76 industries. Includes career description, educational requirements, history of the job, methods of entry, advancement, employment outlook, earnings, working conditions, social and psychological factors, and sources of additional information.

★6742★
"Railroad Engineer" in *Transportation*, Volume 12 of *Career Information Center* (pp. 113-115)
Glencoe/Macmillan
15319 Chatsworth St.
Mission Hills, CA 91345 Phone: (818)898-1391

Richard Lidz and Dale Anderson, editorial directors. Fourth edition, 1990. For 600 occupations, describes job duties, entry-level requirements, education and training needed, advancement possibilities, employment outlook, earnings and benefits. The set is divided into 12 volumes. Each volume includes jobs related under a broad career field. Volume 13 is the index. **Facsimile Number:** 818-365-5489.

★6743★
Railroad Industry Workers
Chronicle Guidance Publications, Inc.
PO Box 1190
Moravia, NY 13118-1190 Phone: (315)497-0330

1991. This career brief describes the nature of the work, working conditions, hours and earnings, education and training, licensure, certification, unions, personal qualifications, social and psychological factors, employment outlook, entry methods, advancement, and related occupations. **Toll-free/Additional Phone Number(s):** 800-622-7284.

★6744★
She's a Railroader
Phoenix/BFA Films
468 Park Ave. South
New York, NY 10016 Phone: (212)684-5910

Videocassette. 1980. 10 mins. This program tells the story of a woman who works on the railroad and how she manages in a traditionally male field.

★6745★
"Subway Conductor" in *Hard Hatted Women: Stories of Struggle and Success in the Trades* (pp. 193-201)
Seal Press
3131 Western Ave., Ste. 410
Seattle, WA 98121 Phone: (206)283-7844

Molly Martin, editor. 1988. Twenty-six women recount their experiences working in blue collar occupations. They describe how they got in, the work they do, their relationships in predominantly male occupations, and their training.

── Associations ──

★6746★
American Public Transit Association (APTA)
1201 New York Ave. NW, Ste. 400
Washington, DC 20005 Phone: (202)898-4000

Membership: Rapid rail and motor bus transit systems in the U.S., Canada, and Mexico; manufacturers and suppliers of materials and services. **Purpose:** Maintains biographical archives, hall of fame, and 20,000 volume library on urban transportation and related fields. Bestows awards; compiles statistics. Operates placement service and speakers' bureau; conducts seminars.

★6747★
Association of American Railroads (AAR)
Amer. Railroads Bldg.
50 F St. NW
Washington, DC 20001 Phone: (202)639-2100

Membership: Coordinating and research agency of the American railway industry. **Purpose:** Fields of interest include railroad operation and maintenance, statistics, medical problems, cooperative advertising and public relations, rates, communications, signals, car exchange rules, safety, police and security matters, and testing of railroad equipment. Maintains library of current and historical volumes and periodicals. **Publications:** *Official Railway Equipment Register*, quarterly. • *Rail News Update*, biweekly. • *Railroad Facts*, periodic. • Also publishes studies, statistical reports, and information publications.

Test Guides

★6748★
Assistant Train Dispatcher
National Learning Corp.
212 Michael Dr.
Syosset, NY 11791   Phone: (516)921-8888
Jack Rudman. Part of the Career Examination Series No. 1. All examination guides in this series contain questions with answers. **Facsimile Number:** (516)921-8743. **Toll-free/Additional Phone Number(s):** 800-645-6337.

★6749★
Foreman (Railroad Watchman)
National Learning Corp.
212 Michael Dr.
Syosset, NY 11791   Phone: (516)921-8888
Jack Rudman. Part of the Career Examination Series No. 1. All examination guides in this series contain questions with answers. **Facsimile Number:** (516)921-8743. **Toll-free/Additional Phone Number(s):** 800-645-6337.

★6750★
Railroad Caretaker
National Learning Corp.
212 Michael Dr.
Syosset, NY 11791   Phone: (516)921-8888
Jack Rudman. Part of the Career Examination Series No. 1. All examination guides in this series contain questions with answers. **Facsimile Number:** (516)921-8743. **Toll-free/Additional Phone Number(s):** 800-645-6337.

★6751★
Railroad Clerk
Prentice Hall Press
Simon & Schuster Inc.
200 Old Tappan Rd.
Old Tappan, NJ 07675   Phone: (800)223-2348
Hy Hammer. Third edition, 1984. Provides seven sample examinations with answers for applicants of the New York City rapid transit system.

★6752★
Railroad Clerk
National Learning Corp.
212 Michael Dr.
Syosset, NY 11791   Phone: (516)921-8888
Jack Rudman. Part of the Career Examination Series No. 1. All examination guides in this series contain questions with answers. **Facsimile Number:** (516)921-8743. **Toll-free/Additional Phone Number(s):** 800-645-6337.

★6753★
Railroad Inspector
National Learning Corp.
212 Michael Dr.
Syosset, NY 11791   Phone: (516)921-8888
Jack Rudman. Part of the Career Examination Series No. 1. All examination guides in this series contain questions with answers. **Facsimile Number:** (516)921-8743. **Toll-free/Additional Phone Number(s):** 800-645-6337.

★6754★
Railroad Porter
National Learning Corp.
212 Michael Dr.
Syosset, NY 11791   Phone: (516)921-8888
Jack Rudman. Part of the Career Examination Series No. 1. All examination guides in this series contain questions with answers. **Facsimile Number:** (516)921-8743. **Toll-free/Additional Phone Number(s):** 800-645-6337.

★6755★
Railroad Signal Specialist
National Learning Corp.
212 Michael Dr.
Syosset, NY 11791   Phone: (516)921-8888
Jack Rudman. Part of the Career Examination Series No. 1. All examination guides in this series contain questions with answers. **Facsimile Number:** (516)921-8743. **Toll-free/Additional Phone Number(s):** 800-645-6337.

★6756★
Railroad Stock Assistant
National Learning Corp.
212 Michael Dr.
Syosset, NY 11791   Phone: (516)921-8888
Jack Rudman. Part of the Career Examination Series No. 1. All examination guides in this series contain questions with answers. **Facsimile Number:** (516)921-8743. **Toll-free/Additional Phone Number(s):** 800-645-6337.

★6757★
Railroad Stockman
National Learning Corp.
212 Michael Dr.
Syosset, NY 11791   Phone: (516)921-8888
Jack Rudman. Part of the Career Examination Series No. 1. All examination guides in this series contain questions with answers. **Facsimile Number:** (516)921-8743. **Toll-free/Additional Phone Number(s):** 800-645-6337.

★6758★
Railroad Track and Structure Inspector
National Learning Corp.
212 Michael Dr.
Syosset, NY 11791   Phone: (516)921-8888
Jack Rudman. Part of the Career Examination Series No. 1. All examination guides in this series contain questions with answers. **Facsimile Number:** (516)921-8743. **Toll-free/Additional Phone Number(s):** 800-645-6337.

★6759★
Track Equipment Maintainer
National Learning Corp.
212 Michael Dr.
Syosset, NY 11791   Phone: (516)921-8888
Jack Rudman. Part of the Career Examination Series No. 1. All examination guides in this series contain questions with answers. **Facsimile Number:** (516)921-8743. **Toll-free/Additional Phone Number(s):** 800-645-6337.

★6760★
Trackman
National Learning Corp.
212 Michael Dr.
Syosset, NY 11791   Phone: (516)921-8888
Jack Rudman. Part of the Career Examination Series No. 1. All examination guides in this series contain questions with answers. **Facsimile Number:** (516)921-8743. **Toll-free/Additional Phone Number(s):** 800-645-6337.

Rail Transportation Workers

★6761★
Train Dispatcher
National Learning Corp.
212 Michael Dr.
Syosset, NY 11791   Phone: (516)921-8888
Jack Rudman. Part of the Career Examination Series No. 1. All examination guides in this series contain questions with answers. **Facsimile Number:** (516)921-8743. **Toll-free/Additional Phone Number(s):** 800-645-6337.

★6762★
Train Operator
National Learning Corp.
212 Michael Dr.
Syosset, NY 11791   Phone: (516)921-8888
Jack Rudman. Part of the Career Examination Series No. 1. All examination guides in this series contain questions with answers. **Facsimile Number:** (516)921-8743. **Toll-free/Additional Phone Number(s):** 800-645-6337.

★6763★
Trainmaster
National Learning Corp.
212 Michael Dr.
Syosset, NY 11791   Phone: (516)921-8888
Jack Rudman. Part of the Career Examination Series No. 1. All examination guides in this series contain questions with answers. **Facsimile Number:** (516)921-8743. **Toll-free/Additional Phone Number(s):** 800-645-6337.

Awards, Scholarships, Grants, and Fellowships

★6764★
Branding Hammer Award
Railway Tie Association
910 Sheraton, Ste. 430
Mars, PA 16046   Phone: (412)772-1790
To recognize an associate member of the Railway Tie Association who is an employee of a railroad and participated over a period of years in the activities and programs of the Association. A crosstie branding hammer mounted on an inscribed plaque is awarded annually. Established in 1975.

★6765★
Broad Axe Award
Railway Tie Association
910 Sheraton, Ste. 430
Mars, PA 16046   Phone: (412)772-1790
To recognize the producer members of the Railway Tie Association for outstanding service over a period of years. Owners or employees of a producer member of the Association are eligible. A miniaturized broad axe on an inscribed plaque is awarded annually. Established in 1974.

★6766★
Distinguished Service Award
American Railway Development Association
c/o G.C. Highfield
Florida Central Railroad Company
P.O. Box 967
Plymouth, FL 32768   Phone: (305)880-8500
To recognize an individual for an outstanding contribution and recognizable achievement in the development field of the railway industry. A plaque is awarded when merited. Established in 1968.

★6767★
Modern Railroad Man of the Year
Modern Railroads
International Thompson Transport Press
20 N. Wacker Dr., Ste. 1725
Chicago, IL 60606   Phone: (312)323-6486
To honor the individual making the greatest contribution to successful railroading. Selection is made by the editors of the magazine. A bronze plaque is awarded annually. Established in 1963.

★6768★
Transportation Man of the Year
Delta Nu Alpha Transportation Fraternity
621 Plainfield, Ste. 308
Willowbrook, IL 60521   Phone: (312)850-7100
To recognize contributions to the field of transportation. A plaque is awarded annually. Established in 1952.

Periodicals

★6769★
American Railway Engineering Association Bulletin
American Railway Engineering Assn.
50 F St. NW, No. 7702
Washington, DC 20001   Phone: (202)639-2190
Louis T. Cerny, Editor. 5x/yr. Magazine of the American Railway Engineering Association. Contains technical committee reports; proposed changes to the Manual for Railway Engineering and Portfolio of Trackwork Plans; reports on railway engineering, construction, and maintenance; results of research investigations and service tests; and proceedings of the Annual Technical Conference. **Facsimile Number:** (202)639-2183.

★6770★
BMWE Journal
Brotherhood of Maintenance of Way Employees
12050 Woodward Ave.
Detroit, MI 48203-3596   Phone: (313)868-0490
Geoffrey N. Zeh, Editor. Monthly. Railroad labor tabloid. **Facsimile Number:** (313)868-5122.

★6771★
Brotherhood of Maintenance of Way Employees Railway Journal
Brotherhood of Maintenance of Way Employees
12050 Woodward Ave.
Highland Park, MI 48203   Phone: (313)868-0490
O.M. Berge, Editor. Monthly Magazine reporting Brotherhood news.

★6772★
Government Tender Report
American Trucking Associations, Inc.
2200 Mill Rd.
Alexandria, VA 22314   Phone: (703)838-1794
Daily, Monday-Friday. Summarizes tenders (except those pertaining to household goods) which have been submitted to the Interstate Commerce Commission by motor and water carriers, rail carriers and bureaus, and freight forwarders in compliance with Section 10721 of the Interstate Commerce Act. Also identifies carriers, tender numbers, effective and expiration dates, commodities, origins, destinations, and rates. Lists and cross-references entries according to regions of origin.

★6773★
Government Traffic Bulletin
American Trucking Associations, Inc.
2200 Mill Rd.
Alexandria, VA 22314　　　　　　　Phone: (703)838-1793
Weekly. Summarizes current traffic requirements of major U.S. Government agencies and reports changes in federal transportation policies, procedures, and personnel. Provides names and phone numbers of individuals who may be contacted for additional information.

★6774★
International Railway Journal
Simmons-Boardman Publishing Corp.
345 Hudson St.
New York, NY 10014　　　　　　　Phone: (212)620-7236
Mike Knutton, Publisher. Monthly. Magazine focusing on railways and rail transit. Summaries in French, German, and Spanish. **Facsimile Number:** (212)633-1165.

★6775★
Locomotive Engineers Journal
Brotherhood of Locomotive Engineers
1370 Ontario St.
Cleveland, OH 44113-1701　　　　　Phone: (216)241-2630
Stephen W. FitzGerald, Public Relations Dir. Quarterly. Railroad industry magazine.

★6776★
Modern Railroads
K-III Press, Inc.
424 W. 33rd St.
New York, NY 10001　　　　　　　Phone: (212)714-3100
Kathy Keeney, Editor. 2x/mo. Magazine covering railroad and rail transit development.

★6777★
Movin'
Canadian National Railways
Public Affairs & Advertising
PO Box 8100 Sta. A
Montreal, PQ, Canada H3C 3N4　　　Phone: (514)399-5822
Lois Caron, Editor. 6x/yr. Rail transportation magazine. **Facsimile Number:** (514)399-5344.

★6778★
NERR Club Official Proceedings
N.E. Railroad Club
PO Box 64
Hanover, MA 02339　　　　　　　Phone: (617)826-0286
J.R. McCombs, Publisher. 4x/yr. Railroad industry proceedings.

★6779★
NITL Notice
National Industrial Transportation League (NITL)
1700 N. Moore St., Ste. 1900
Arlington, VA 22209　　　　　　　Phone: (703)524-5011
Editor(s): James E. Bartley. Weekly. Carries transportation news—railroad, motor carrier, airline, and maritime—in the interest of industrial and commercial shippers. Covers rate-hike proposals, transportation legislation, regulatory agency actions, postal service developments, union actions, and court cases. Recurring features include coverage of the Interstate Commerce Commission, U. **Facsimile Number:** (202)842-3520.

★6780★
The Official Railway Equipment Register
K-III Press, Inc.
424 W. 33rd St.
New York, NY 10001　　　　　　　Phone: (212)714-3100
Bob DeMarco, Publisher. Quarterly. Railroad freight car directory. **Facsimile Number:** (212)695-5025.

★6781★
Official Railway Equipment Register
Association of American Railroads (AAR)
Amer. Railroads Bldg.
50 F St. NW
Washington, DC 20001　　　　　　Phone: (202)639-2100
Quarterly.

★6782★
Passenger Transport
American Public Transit Assn.
1201 New York Ave., Ste. 400
Washington, DC 20005　　　　　　Phone: (202)898-4119
Dennis Kouba, Editor. Weekly (Mon.). **Facsimile Number:** (202)898-4095.

★6783★
Pocket List of Railroad Officials
K-III Press, Inc.
424 W. 33rd St.
New York, NY 10001　　　　　　　Phone: (212)714-3100
Robert DeMarco, Publisher. Quarterly. Comprehensive guide to officials in the freight railroad, rail transit, and rail supply industries. **Facsimile Number:** (212)695-5025.

★6784★
Progressive Railroading
Murphy-Richter Publishing Co.
2 N. Riverside Plaza, No. 1825
Chicago, IL 60606-2784　　　　　　Phone: (312)454-9155
Frank Malone, Editor. Monthly. Railroad magazine. **Facsimile Number:** (312)454-6715.

★6785★
Rail News Update
Association of American Railroads (AAR)
Amer. Railroads Bldg.
50 F St. NW
Washington, DC 20001　　　　　　Phone: (202)639-2100
Biweekly. Newsletter.

★6786★
Railroad Newsletter
National Safety Council
444 N. Michigan Ave.
Chicago, IL 60611　　　　　　　　Phone: (312)527-4800
6/yr. Devoted to accident prevention for railroad personnel. Considers related safety factors, such as noise levels, health hazards, attitudes, and environmental conditions. Provides safety pointers for leisure as well as work activities.

★6787★
Railway Age
345 Hudson St.
New York, NY 10014　　　　　　　Phone: (212)620-7200
Luther Miller, Editor. Monthly. Magazine focusing on railroad and rail transit. **Facsimile Number:** (212)633-1165.

Rail Transportation Workers ★6802★

★6788★
Railway Track and Structures
345 Hudson
New York, NY 10014   Phone: (212)620-7200
Robert E. Tuzik, Editor. Monthly. Magazine focusing on railroad engineering and maintenance. **Facsimile Number:** (212)633-1165.

★6789★
Signalman's Journal
Brotherhood of Railroad Signalmen
601 W. Golf Rd.
PO Box U
Mount Prospect, IL 60056   Phone: (708)439-3732
J. P. Finn, Editor. 6x/yr. Magazine for railroad signalmen. **Facsimile Number:** (708)439-3743.

★6790★
Southern and Southwestern Railway Club Proceedings
Southern and Southwestern Railway Assn.
717 Pinecliffe Dr.
Chesapeake, VA 23320   Phone: (804)547-5891
Quarterly. Railroad magazine.

★6791★
Traffic World
Journal of Commerce, Inc.
2 World Trade Center, 27th Fl.
New York, NY 10048   Phone: (212)837-7000
Weekly (Mon.). Transportation trade magazine.

★6792★
Trains
Kalmbach Publishing Co.
21027 Crossroad Circle
PO Box1612
Waukesha, WI 53187   Phone: (414)796-8776
J.D. Ingles, Editor. Monthly. Magazine featuring railroads past and present. **Facsimile Number:** (414)796-0126.

★6793★
Transport 2000 and Intermodal World
870 Market St., 9th Fl.
San Francisco, CA 94102   Phone: (415)982-6592
Gail E. Neira, Publisher. Quarterly. Magazine on international issues, intermodal trade, and transportation.

★6794★
Transportation: An Abstract Newsletter
National Technical Information Service (NTIS)
U.S. Department of Commerce
5285 Port Royal Rd.
Springfield, VA 22161   Phone: (703)487-4630
Weekly. Provides abstracts of publications in the areas of air, rail, water, pipeline, and road transportation; global navigation systems; and transportation safety.

★6795★
Transportation & Distribution
Penton Publishing
1100 Superior Ave.
Cleveland, OH 44114-4135   Phone: (216)696-7000
Perry Trunick, Editor. Monthly. Magazine covering traffic and physical distribution. **Facsimile Number:** (216)696-8765.

★6796★
Transportation Business
Baxter Publications, Inc.
310 Dupont St.
Toronto, ON, Canada M5R 1V9   Phone: (416)968-7252
Peter Morgan, Editor. Monthly. Transportation industry magazine (tabloid). **Facsimile Number:** (416)968-2377.

★6797★
Transportation Quarterly
Eno Foundation for Transportation
PO Box 2055
Westport, CT 06880   Phone: (203)227-4852
Tracy Dunleavy, Circulation Mgr. Quarterly. Trade magazine on transportation. **Facsimile Number:** (203)227-3928.

★6798★
TWU Express
Transport Workers Union of America
80 West End Ave.
New York, NY 10023   Phone: (212)873-6000
James Gannon, Editor. Monthly. Labor magazine. **Facsimile Number:** (212)721-1431.

★6799★
UTU News
United Transportation Union
14600 Detroit Ave.
Cleveland, OH 44107-4250   Phone: (216)228-9400
Fred Hardin, Editor. 12x/yr. Railroad and bus labor newspaper (tabloid).

★6800★
Weekly Commercial News
C.A. Page Publishing
1117 W. Manchester Blvd., No. A
Inglewood, CA 90301-1500   Phone: (213)608-3350
Mike Richardson, Editor. Weekly (Mon.). Business and transportation industry magazine. **Facsimile Number:** (213)608-3365.

——— Meetings and Conventions ———

★6801★
American Public Transit Association (APTA)
1201 New York Ave. NW, Ste. 400
Washington, DC 20005   Phone: (202)898-4000
Frequency: Holds annual conference, with exhibits. 1992; Oct. 18-22; San Diego, CA ● 1993; Oct. 3-6; New Orleans, LA ● 1994; Sep. 25-29; Boston, MA ● 1995; Oct. 8-12; San Antonio, TX. Also holds triennial international exposition, to be held next in 1993. **Facsimile Number:** (202)898-4070.

——— Other Sources of Information ———

★6802★
Railroad Facts
Association of American Railroads (AAR)
Amer. Railroads Bldg.
50 F St. NW
Washington, DC 20001   Phone: (202)639-2100
Periodic.

Truckdrivers

Long-distance truckdrivers make the initial pickup from factories, consolidate cargo at terminals for intercity shipment, and deliver goods from terminals to stores and homes. Local truckdrivers—called driver-sales workers or route drivers—primarily have sales and customer relations responsibilities. Driver-sales workers, such as wholesale bakery driver-sales workers and vending machine driver-sales workers, mostly have wholesale routes—that is, they deliver to businesses and stores. A few pick up and deliver items to homes, but retail routes are now rare. Trucking companies employ nearly 33 percent of all truckdrivers, and another 33 percent work for companies engaged in wholesale or retail trade. The rest are scattered throughout the economy, including government agencies. Fewer than 10 percent of all truckdrivers are self-employed; of these, a significant number are owner-operators, who either operate independently or lease their services and their trucks to a trucking company.

$alaries

Hourly earnings for truckdrivers, depending on the size of the truck, are as follows:

Medium trucks	$12.38/hour
Tractor-trailers	$12.24/hour
Heavy straight trucks	$10.64/hour
Light trucks	$7.64/hour

Employment Outlook

Growth rate until the year 2000: Average.

Truckdrivers

Career Guides

★6803★
Careers in Truck Driving
American Trucking Association
Office of Public Affairs
2200 Mill Rd.
Alexandria, VA 22314-4677   Phone: (703)838-1873
1990. Eight-panel brochure describing types of truck drivers, required qualifications, training, working conditions, employment outlook, earnings, and advancement opportunities.

★6804★
Careers in Trucking
Rosen Publishing Group, Inc.
29 E. 21st St.
New York, NY 10010   Phone: (212)777-3017
Donald D. Schauer. 1987. Describes employment in the trucking industry including driving, operations, sales, and administration. Covers qualifications, training, future outlook, and salaries. Offers career planning and job hunting advice.

★6805★
Driver, Heavy-Truck
Careers, Inc.
PO Box 135
Largo, FL 34649-0135   Phone: (813)584-7333
1991. Two-page occupational summary card describing duties, working conditions, personal qualifications, training, earnings and hours, employment outlook, places of employment, related careers and where to write for more information.

★6806★
"Heavy Truck Driver" in *Occu-Facts: Information on 565 Careers in Outline Form* (p. 19.3)
Careers, Inc.
P.O. Box 135
1211 Tenth St., S.W.
Largo, FL 33640   Phone: (813)584-7333
Elizabeth Handville. Biennial, 1989-90 edition. Each one-page occupational profile describes duties, working conditions, physical surroundings and demands, aptitudes, temperament, educational requirements, employment outlook, earnings, and places of employment.

★6807★
"Local and Over-the-Road Truck Drivers" in Volume 3 of *The Encyclopedia of Careers and Vocational Guidance* (pp. 793-797)
J.G. Ferguson Publishing Co.
200 W. Monroe
Chicago, IL 60606   Phone: (312)580-5480
William E. Hopke, editor-in-chief. Eighth edition, 1990. Four-volume set that profiles 500 occupations and describes job trends in 76 industries. Includes career description, educational requirements, history of the job, methods of entry, advancement, employment outlook, earnings, working conditions, social and psychological factors, and sources of additional information.

★6808★
"Local Truck Driver" in *Exploring Nontraditional Jobs for Women* (pp. 69-75)
Rosen Publishing Group, Inc.
29 E. 21st St.
New York, NY 10010   Phone: (212)777-3017
Rose Neufeld. 1989. Describes blue-collar, male dominated occupations. Discusses what is done on the job, training, where to apply for jobs, tools used, salaries, and advantages and disadvantages. Relates the experiences of women who are working in the field.

★6809★
"Local Truck Driver" in *Transportation*, Volume 12 of *Career Information Center* (pp. 56-58)
Glencoe/Macmillan
15319 Chatsworth St.
Mission Hills, CA 91345   Phone: (818)898-1391
Richard Lidz and Dale Anderson, editorial directors. Fourth edition, 1990. For 600 occupations, describes job duties, entry-level requirements, education and training needed, advancement possibilities, employment outlook, earnings and benefits. The set is divided into 12 volumes. Each volume includes jobs related under a broad career field. Volume 13 is the index. **Facsimile Number:** 818-365-5489.

★6810★
"Long Distance Truck Drivers" in *Opportunities in Transportation Careers* (pp. 69-72)
National Textbook Co.
4255 W. Touhy Ave.
Lincolnwood, IL 60646   Phone: (312)679-5500
Adrian A. Paradis. 1988. Describes transportation and related employment in driving occupations, the airlines, merchant marine, and travel services. Covers employment outlook, educational and training requirements, wages, and the work

★6811★

itself, and advantages and disadvantages of transportation careers. Offers job hunting advice.

★6811★
"Long Haul Truck Driver" in *Transportation*, Volume 12 of *Career Information Center* (pp. 60-62)
Glencoe/Macmillan
15319 Chatsworth St.
Mission Hills, CA 91345   Phone: (818)898-1391

Richard Lidz and Dale Anderson, editorial directors. Fourth edition, 1990. For 600 occupations, describes job duties, entry-level requirements, education and training needed, advancement possibilities, employment outlook, earnings and benefits. The set is divided into 12 volumes. Each volume includes jobs related under a broad career field. Volume 13 is the index. **Facsimile Number:** 818-365-5489.

★6812★
Standards for Selection of Truck Fleet Personnel: A Guide for Hiring Professional Drivers & Other Employees in the Trucking Industry
American Trucking Associations, Inc.
2200 Mill Rd.
Alexandria, VA 22314-4677   Phone: (703)838-1700

American Trucking Associations Department of Safety. Revised edition, 1885. **Toll-free/Additional Phone Number(s):** 800-225-8382.

★6813★
"Tow Truck Operator" in *Occu-Facts: Information on 565 Careers in Outline Form* (p. 19.4)
Careers, Inc.
P.O. Box 135
1211 Tenth St., S.W.
Largo, FL 33640   Phone: (813)584-7333

Elizabeth Handville. Biennial, 1989-90 edition. Each one-page occupational profile describes duties, working conditions, physical surroundings and demands, aptitudes, temperament, educational requirements, employment outlook, earnings, and places of employment.

★6814★
"Tow Truck Operator" in *Transportation*, Volume 12 of *Career Information Center* (pp. 87-88)
Glencoe/Macmillan
15319 Chatsworth St.
Mission Hills, CA 91345   Phone: (818)898-1391

Richard Lidz and Dale Anderson, editorial directors. Fourth edition, 1990. For 600 occupations, describes job duties, entry-level requirements, education and training needed, advancement possibilities, employment outlook, earnings and benefits. The set is divided into 12 volumes. Each volume includes jobs related under a broad career field. Volume 13 is the index. **Facsimile Number:** 818-365-5489.

★6815★
Transportation
Learning Corporation of America
108 Wilmot Rd.
Deerfield, IL 60015-9990   Phone: (708)940-1260

Videocassette. 1982. 21 mins. In this program from the "Working" series, we meet five employees in transportation-related jobs: fishing boat captain, auto body repair shop owner, construction equipment operator, air traffic controller and truck driver.

★6816★
Transportation/Mechanical Cluster
Center for Humanities, Inc.
Communications Park
Box 1000
Mount Kisco, NY 10549   Phone: (914)666-4100

Videocassette. 1984. 20 mins. The key aspects of working in the fields of Auto Body Repair, Truck Driving, and Auto Mechanics are explained.

★6817★
Truck Driver
Vocational Biographies, Inc.
PO Box 31, Dept. VF10
Sauk Centre, MN 56378   Phone: (612)352-6516

1990. This pamphlet profiles a person working in the job. Includes information about job duties, working conditions, places of employment, educational preparation, labor market outlook, and salaries. **Toll-free/Additional Phone Number(s):** 800-255-0752.

★6818★
"Truck Driver" in *Hard Hatted Women: Stories of Struggle and Success in the Trades* (pp. 225-234)
Seal Press
3131 Western Ave., Ste. 410
Seattle, WA 98121   Phone: (206)283-7844

Molly Martin, editor. 1988. Twenty-six women recount their experiences working in blue collar occupations. They describe how they got in, the work they do, their relationships in predominantly male occupations, and their training.

★6819★
"Truck Driver" in *Transportation* (pp. 21-25)
Franklin Watts, Inc.
387 Park Avenue, S.
New York, NY 10016   Phone: (212)686-7070

Marjorie Rittenberg Schulz. 1990. Surveys the transportation industry including air, water, and rail services. Provides job description, training, salary, and employment outlook. Offers job hunting advice.

★6820★
"Truck Driver" in *VGM's Careers Encyclopedia* (pp. 471-474)
National Textbook Co.
4255 W. Touhy Ave.
Lincolnwood, IL 60646   Phone: (312)679-5500

Third edition, 1991. Contains two- to five-page descriptions of 200 managerial, professional, technical, trade, and service occupations. Each profile includes job duties, places of employment, qualifications, educational preparation, training, employment potential, advancement, income, and additional sources of information.

★6821★
Truck Drivers
Chronicle Guidance Publications, Inc.
PO Box 1190
Moravia, NY 13118-1190   Phone: (315)497-0330

1989. This career brief describes the nature of the work, working conditions, hours and earnings, education and training, licensure, certification, unions, personal qualifications, social and psychological factors, employment outlook, entry methods, advancement, and related occupations. **Toll-free/Additional Phone Number(s):** 800-622-7284.

Truckdrivers

★6822★
"Truck Drivers" in *Jobs! What They Are...Where They Are...What They Pay* (pp. 181-182)
Simon & Schuster, Inc.
Simon & Schuster Bldg.
1230 Avenue of the Americas
New York, NY 10020　　　　　Phone: (212)698-7000
Robert O. Snelling and Anne M. Snelling. Revised edition, 1989. Profiles 241 occupations, describing duties and responsibilities, educational preparation, earnings, employment opportunities, training, and qualifications.

★6823★
"Truck Drivers" in *Opportunities in Vocational and Technical Careers* (pp. 79-80)
National Textbook Co.
4255 W. Touhy Ave.
Lincolnwood, IL 60646　　　　　Phone: (312)679-5500
Adrian A. Paradis. 1987. Describes careers which can be prepared for by attending a private vocational or proprietary school—office employee, sales worker, service worker, health services, mechanic, craftworker, and technician. Covers employment outlook, job duties, and salaries. Offers career planning advice.

★6824★
"Truck Drivers" in Volume 6 of *Career Discovery Encyclopedia* (pp. 132-133)
J.G. Ferguson Publishing Co.
200 W. Monroe
Chicago, IL 60606　　　　　Phone: (312)580-5480
E. Russell Primm, editor-in-chief. 1990. Contains two-page articles on 504 occupations. Each article describes job duties, earnings, and educational and training requirements.

★6825★
"Truck Driving" in *The Career Connection II: A Guide to Technical Majors and Their Related Careers* (pp. 131-132)
ERIS
PO Box 7509
University Station
Provo, UT 84602-0509
Fred A. Rowe. 1988. Contains technical majors, such as automotive technology. Describes the major and the job. Lists high school and postsecondary school courses. Includes occupations related to the major, employment outlook, and starting salary.

★6826★
"Truckdrivers" in *Occupational Outlook Handbook* (pp. 440-442)
Superintendent of Documents
U.S. Government Printing Office
Washington, DC 20402　　　　　Phone: (202)783-3238
Biennial; latest edition, 1990-91. Encyclopedia of careers describing more than 250 occupations and comprising about 86 percent of all jobs in the economy. Occupations that require lengthy education or training are given the most attention. For each occupation, the handbook describes job duties, working conditions, training, educational preparation, personal qualities, advancement possibilities, job outlook, earnings, and sources of additional information.

★6827★
Trucker
Macmillan Publishing Company, Inc.
866 3rd Ave.
New York, NY 10022　　　　　Phone: (212)702-2000
Hope H. Wurmfeld. 1990.

★6828★
Trucksource: Sources of Trucking Industry Information
American Trucking Associations, Inc.
2200 Mill Rd.
Alexandria, VA 22314-4677　　　　　Phone: (703)838-1700
American Trucking Associations. 1991. **Toll-free/Additional Phone Number(s):** 800-225-8382.

★6829★
Video Career Library - Transportation & Materials Moving
Careers, Inc.
1211 10th St., SW
PO Box 135
Largo, FL 34649-0135　　　　　Phone: (813)584-7333
Videocassette. 1990. 20 mins. Part of the Video Career Library covering 165 occupations. Shows actual workers on the job. Includes tractor/trailer truck drivers, heavy truck drivers, bus drivers, airplane pilots and navigators, grader/dozer/scraper operators, and forklift operators.

★6830★
Vocational Visions
Center for Humanities, Inc.
Communications Park
Box 1000
Mount Kisco, NY 10549　　　　　Phone: (914)666-4100
Videocassette. 1984. 30 mins. This series of programs explains key aspects of actual training and a day in the life of a worker in the specific field mentioned on the videocassette. Occupations include: transportation/mechanics, repair, construction, business/office occupations, health, and agriculture.

★6831★
Vocations U.S.A.
Info-Disc Corporation
4 Professional Dr.
Gaithersburg, MD 20879　　　　　Phone: (301)948-2300
Videocassette. 1987. 60 mins. A disc collection outlining the requirements and methods of various career areas. Occupations include: transportation, mechanical/repair, health, agriculture, and construction.

───────── Associations ─────────

★6832★
American Movers Conference (AMC)
2200 Mill Rd.
Alexandria, VA 22314　　　　　Phone: (703)838-1930
Membership: Local, intrastate, interstate, and international movers who transport household goods, office and institutional equipment, and high-value products. Sponsors competition. Presents annual Super Driver Awards. Sponsors Household Goods Dispute Settlement Program which handles consumer complaints between consumers and interstate moving companies.

★6833★
American Trucking Associations (ATA)
2200 Mill Rd.
Alexandria, VA 22314　　　　　　　　Phone: (703)838-1700
Membership: Individuals, state trucking associations, and national conferences of trucking companies. **Purpose:** Sponsors American Trucking Associations Foundation. Operates Motor Carrier Advisory Service, a guide to federal and state regulations; provides quarterly financial and operating statistics service. Offers comprehensive accounting service for all sizes of carriers. Maintains 20,000 volume information center, which provides information services to members and others. Promotes highway and driver safety; supports highway research projects; and studies technical and regulatory problems of the trucking industry. Sponsors competitions; bestows awards; compiles statistics. Maintains numerous programs and services including: Beltway Hotline; Coaching the Professional Truck Driver; Compensation Survey; Computer Hardware/Software Sales and Services; Electronic Data Interchange Standards. **Publications:** Catalog of publications. **Toll-free/Additional Phone Number(s):** (800)ATA-LINE. **Facsimile Number:** (703)684-5720.

★6834★
International Brotherhood of Teamsters, Chauffeurs, Warehousemen and Helpers of America (IBT)
25 Louisiana Ave., NW
Washington, DC 20001　　　　　　　Phone: (202)624-6800
Membership: Formed by merger of Team Drivers International Union and Teamsters National Union. **Purpose:** Maintains DRIVE Political Action committee; maintains 30,000 volume library.

★6835★
Professional Truck Driver Institute of America (PTDIA)
8788 Elk Grove Blvd., Ste. 20
Elk Grove, CA 95624　　　　　　　　Phone: (916)686-5146
Membership: Trade associations, manufacturers, and suppliers to the trucking industry. **Purpose:** Develops professional standards for the certification of truck driver training courses; certifies commercial truck driving training courses. **Facsimile Number:** (916)686-4878.

───── **Standards/Certification Agencies** ─────

All drivers of trucks designed to carry at least 26,000 pounds—which includes most tractor-trailers as well as bigger straight trucks—are required to obtain a special Commercial Driver's License (CDL) from the state in which they live; a regular driver's license will continue to be sufficient for driving light trucks and vans in many states. All truckdrivers who operate trucks that carry hazardous materials also must obtain a CDL. To qualify for a CDL, applicants must pass a knowledge test and demonstrate that they can operate a commercial truck safely. Trainees must be accompanied by a driver with a CDL until they get their own CDL.

★6836★
American Trucking Associations (ATA)
2200 Mill Rd.
Alexandria, VA 22314　　　　　　　　Phone: (703)838-1700
Operates Motor Carrier Advisory Service, a guide to federal and state regulations. Supports highway research projects; and studies technical and regulatory problems of the trucking industry. Maintains numerous programs and services including: Beltway Hotline; Coaching the Professional Truck Driver; Compensation Survey; Computer Hardware/Software Sales and Services; Electronic Data Interchange Standards.

★6837★
CDL Commercial Driver License: 104 Helpful CDL Facts
Professional Truck Driver Institute of America
8788 Elk Grove Blvd., Ste. 20
Elk Grove, CA 95624　　　　　　　　Phone: (916)686-5146
1990. This 32-page booklet explains the Commercial Driver License, a set of minimum standards for licensing and testing commercial drivers established by the federal government. Covers the law, classes of licenses, and test content.

★6838★
Professional Truck Driver Institute of America (PTDIA)
8788 Elk Grove Blvd., Ste. 20
Elk Grove, CA 95624　　　　　　　　Phone: (916)686-5146
Develops professional standards for the certification of truck driver training courses; certifies commercial truck driving training courses.

───── **Test Guides** ─────

★6839★
How to Prepare for the Truck Driver's Commercial Driver's License Test (CDL)
Barron's Educational Series, Inc.
PO Box 8040
250 Wireless Blvd.
Hauppauge, NY 11788　　　　　　　Phone: (516)434-3311
Mike Byrnes, etal. This manual provides information on the Commercial Driver's License tests administered in all 50 states under the same U.S. Department of Transportation standards. Included are model tests with answers, explanations, and diagrams, along with charts and line drawings. **Toll-free/Additional Phone Number(s):** 800-645-3476 (in NY call 800-257-5729).

★6840★
National Highway Traffic Safety Administration's Truck Operator Qualification Examination (NTSATOQ)
National Learning Corp.
212 Michael Dr.
Syosset, NY 11791　　　　　　　　Phone: (516)921-8888
Jack Rudman. Part of the Admission Test Series No. 3. Books in this series provide test practice and drill for actual professional certification and licensure tests. **Facsimile Number:** (516)921-8743. **Toll-free/Additional Phone Number(s):** 800-645-6337.

★6841★
Tractor Operator
National Learning Corp.
212 Michael Dr.
Syosset, NY 11791　　　　　　　　Phone: (516)921-8888
Jack Rudman. Part of the Career Examination Series No. 1. All examination guides in this series contain questions with answers. **Facsimile Number:** (516)921-8743. **Toll-free/Additional Phone Number(s):** 800-645-6337.

★6842★
Tractor-Trailer Operator
National Learning Corp.
212 Michael Dr.
Syosset, NY 11791　　　　　　　　Phone: (516)921-8888
Jack Rudman. Part of the Career Examination Series No. 1. All examination guides in this series contain questions with answers. **Facsimile Number:** (516)921-8743. **Toll-free/Additional Phone Number(s):** 800-645-6337.

Truckdrivers

★6843★
Truck Driver
National Learning Corp.
212 Michael Dr.
Syosset, NY 11791   Phone: (516)921-8888

Jack Rudman. Part of the Career Examination Series No. 1. All examination guides in this series contain questions with answers. **Facsimile Number:** (516)921-8743. **Toll-free/Additional Phone Number(s):** 800-645-6337.

★6844★
Truck Driver's Guide to Commercial Driver Licensing
Prentice Hall Press
Simon & Schuster Inc.
200 Old Tappan Rd.
Old Tappan, NJ 07675   Phone: (800)223-2348

Highway Users Federation for Safety and Mobility. First edition, 1990. Contains information and practice material on new state licensing tests for certification and recertification of all truck drivers.

Educational Directories and Programs

★6845★
Schools With PTDIA Certified Courses Listed by State
Professional Truck Driver Institute of America
8788 Elk Grove Blvd., Ste. 20
Elk Grove, CA 95624   Phone: (916)686-5146

1991. State-by-state listing of schools offering entry-level training. Indicates day or evening courses, part-time or full-time study, and the length of the program.

Awards, Scholarships, Grants, and Fellowships

★6846★
AMC Van Operator Lifetime Achievement Award
American Movers Conference
2200 Mill Road
Alexandria, VA 22314   Phone: (703)838-1930

To recognize veteran drivers for their outstanding careers over many years in the moving industry. The award honors the van operator who consistently achieved excellence during a lifetime of commercial driving.

★6847★
ATA National Truck Driving Championships
American Trucking Associations
c/o Mona B. Heath, Information Center
2200 Mill Rd.
Alexandria, VA 22314   Phone: (703)838-1745

To recognize National Champion Truck Drivers of eight basic types of trucks and combination units. Monetary awards, trophies and plaques are awarded annually. Eligibility is based on one year of accident-free driving, plus one year of continuous employment with the entering driver. Established in 1937. Formerly: ATA National Truck Roadeo.

★6848★
Distinguished Service Award
Towing and Recovery Association of America
c/o Kevin Fritz
417 Whooping Loop, Ste. 1701
Altamonte Springs, FL 32701   Phone: (407)260-0088

For recognition of an individual's outstanding contribution, untiring devotion and dedicated sacrifice to the towing-recovery-storage industry. Individuals who are actively engaged in the towing industry and members of TRAA are eligible. A plaque is awarded annually at the National Convention. Established in 1982.

★6849★
Driver of the Year
Truck Renting and Leasing Association
2011 Eye St., N.W., Ste. 500
Washington, DC 20001   Phone: (202)775-4859

To encourage professional development of all drivers and to promote safe, professional truck driving. Selection is by nomination and application. A plaque and a trip to the annual convention are awarded annually. Established in 1987.

★6850★
Driver of the Year Award
American Trucking Associations
c/o Mona B. Heath, Information Center
2200 Mill Rd.
Alexandria, VA 22314   Phone: (703)838-1745

To recognize the best safety record among truck drivers of the United States and to encourage improved driving performance and a greater appreciation for highway safety. A Driver of the Year pin, a trophy and a certificate are awarded annually. Established in 1947.

★6851★
Safe Worker Award
American Trucking Associations
c/o Mona B. Heath, Information Center
2200 Mill Rd.
Alexandria, VA 22314   Phone: (703)838-1745

To recognize those employees who successfully meet the challenge of working without injury, and to provide incentive to all employees to work in a safe manner. Local drivers, intercity drivers, dockmen, shop employees, working foremen in the above classifications, miscellaneous-custodial employees, watchmen, and spotters are eligible. The award consists of a distinctive pin showing the number of years worked without injury, and a wallet size card attesting to this record, signed by the ATA Director of Safety.

★6852★
Super Van Operator of the Year
American Movers Conference
2200 Mill Rd.
Alexandria, VA 22314   Phone: (703)838-1930

To recognize drivers in the moving industry who have had outstanding driving and service records for the past five years. Both younger and older drivers are considered for the award on an equal basis. Five drivers are chosen as Super Van Operators, and one of the five is named Super Van Operator of the Year.

★6853★
Transportation Man of the Year
Delta Nu Alpha Transportation Fraternity
621 Plainfield, Ste. 308
Willowbrook, IL 60521   Phone: (312)850-7100

To recognize contributions to the field of transportation. A plaque is awarded annually. Established in 1952.

Basic Reference Guides and Handbooks

★6854★
The Art of Giving Quality Service in the Motor Carrier Industry
American Trucking Associations, Inc.
2200 Mill Rd.
Alexandria, VA 22314-4677   Phone: (703)838-1700
Charles W. Clowdis, Jr. 1984. **Toll-free/Additional Phone Number(s):** 800-225-8382.

★6855★
Emergency & Trip Permit Handbook: Important Permit Information for Interstate Trucking Operations in the United States & Canada
J.J. Keller & Associates, Inc.
3003 W. Breezewood
PO Box 368
Neenah, WI 54957-0368   Phone: (414)722-2848
J.J. Keller & Associates, Inc. Fifteenth edition. **Toll-free/Additional Phone Number(s):** 800-327-6868. **Facsimile Number:** (414)727-7516.

★6856★
Federal Motor Carrier Safety Regulations
American Trucking Associations, Inc.
2200 Mill Rd.
Alexandria, VA 22314-4677   Phone: (703)838-1700
American Trucking Associations Safety Department. 1991. **Toll-free/Additional Phone Number(s):** 800-225-8382.

★6857★
Federal Motor Carrier Safety Regulations Pocketbook
J. J. Keller & Associates, Inc.
3003 W. Breezewood
PO Box 368
Neenah, WI 54957-0368   Phone: (414)722-2848
J. J. Keller & Associates, Inc. Staff. Revised edition, 1987. **Toll-free/Additional Phone Number(s):** 800-327-6868. **Facsimile Number:** (414)727-7516.

★6858★
The Hazardous Materials Handbook for Motor Carriers
J.J. Keller & Associates, Inc.
3003 W. Breezewood
PO Box 368
Neenah, WI 54957-0368   Phone: (414)722-2848
1977. **Toll-free/Additional Phone Number(s):** 800-327-6868. **Facsimile Number:** (414)727-7516.

★6859★
Heavy Vehicle Use Tax: Regulations & Instructions
American Trucking Associations, Inc.
2200 Mill Rd.
Alexandria, VA 22314-4677   Phone: (703)838-1700
American Trucking Associations State Laws Department. 1985. **Toll-free/Additional Phone Number(s):** 800-225-8382.

★6860★
How to Achieve a Satisfactory DOT Safety Rating
American Trucking Associations, Inc.
2200 Mill Rd.
Alexandria, VA 22314-4677   Phone: (703)838-1700
1990. **Toll-free/Additional Phone Number(s):** 800-225-8382.

★6861★
Interstate Motor Carrier Forms Manual, 2G: Private, Contract, Exempt
J.J. Keller & Associates, Inc.
3003 W. Breezewood
PO Box 368
Neenah, WI 54957-0368   Phone: (414)722-2848
J.J. Keller & Associates, Inc. Staff. Revised edition, 1987. **Toll-free/Additional Phone Number(s):** 800-327-6868. **Facsimile Number:** (414)727-7516.

★6862★
Managing Your Independent Contractor Fleet Survey: A Nationwide Survey of Trucking Companies Utilizing Owner-Operators
American Trucking Associations, Inc.
2200 Mill Rd.
Alexandria, VA 22314-4677   Phone: (703)838-1700
American Trucking Associations Staff. Sixth edition, 1990. **Toll-free/Additional Phone Number(s):** 800-225-8382.

★6863★
Math on the Job: Local Truck Driver
National Center for Research in Vocational Education
Ohio State University
1900 Kenry Rd.
Columbus, OH 43210   Phone: (614)292-4353
1985.

★6864★
Modern Bulk Transporter—Truck Specifications Directory Issue
Tunnell Publications, Inc.
Box 66010
Houston, TX 77266   Phone: (713)523-8124
Charles Wilson, editor. Annual. Listing of approximately 150 truck models. Entries include: Company name, address, phone, model names and specifications. Arrangement: Classified by product/service. Indexes: Trade name. **Facsimile Number:** (713)523-8384.

★6865★
Motor Carrier Employees Handbook for the Prevention of Freight Loss & Damages
American Trucking Associations, Inc.
2200 Mill Rd.
Alexandria, VA 22313-4677   Phone: (703)838-1700
American Trucking Association, National Freight Claim & Security Council. Revised edition, 1987. **Toll-free/Additional Phone Number(s):** 800-225-8382.

★6866★
Motor Carrier Insurance
American Trucking Associations, Inc.
2200 Mill Rd.
Alexandria, VA 22314-4677   Phone: (703)838-1700
American Trucking Associations, National Accounting & Finance Council. 1986. **Toll-free/Additional Phone Number(s):** 800-255-8382.

Truckdrivers

★6867★
Motor Carrier Management Systems
American Trucking Associations, Inc.
2200 Mill Rd.
Alexandria, VA 22314-4677   Phone: (703)838-1700
Clifford R. Buys. Revised edition, 1987. **Toll-free/Additional Phone Number(s):** 800-225-8382.

★6868★
The Official Directory of Transportation Middlemen
K-III Press, Inc.
424 W. 33rd St.
New York, NY 10001   Phone: (212)714-3100
Carolyn McCoy, editor. Annual. Approximately 2,500 third-party companies in the transportation industry, including brokers, freight forwarders, consultants, and shippers' agents. Entries include: Company name, address, phone, telex, name and title of contact, names and titles of key personnel, number of employees, geographical area served, subsidiary and branch names and locations, description of products or services. Arrangement: Alphabetical. Indexes: Product/service, executive name, geographical. **Toll-free/Additional Phone Number(s):** (800)221-5488. **Facsimile Number:** (212)695-5025.

★6869★
Out of Service Tire Analysis Guide
American Trucking Associations, Inc.
2200 Mill Rd.
Alexandria, VA 22314-4677   Phone: (703)838-1700
American Trucking Association Maintenance Council. 1984. **Toll-free/Additional Phone Number(s):** 800-225-8382.

★6870★
Radial Tire Wear Condition & Causes: A Guide to Wear Pattern Analysis
American Trucking Associations, Inc.
2200 Mill Rd.
Alexandria, VA 22314-4677   Phone: (703)838-1700
American Trucking Association Maintenance Council. 1984. **Toll-free/Additional Phone Number(s):** 800-225-8382.

★6871★
Risk Management Manual for Motor Carriers
American Trucking Associations, Inc.
2200 Mill Rd.
Alexandria, VA 22314-4677   Phone: (703)838-1700
American Trucking Associations National Accounting & Finance Council. 1986. **Toll-free/Additional Phone Number(s):** 800-225-8382.

★6872★
Small Carrier Safety Program
American Trucking Associations, Inc.
2200 Mill Rd.
Alexandria, VA 22314-4677   Phone: (703)838-1700
1982. **Toll-free/Additional Phone Number(s):** 800-225-8382.

★6873★
Summary of Size & Weight Limits
American Trucking Associations, Inc.
2200 Mill Rd.
Alexandria, VA 22314-4677   Phone: (703)838-1700
American Trucking Associations, Inc., Department of State Laws. 1988. **Toll-free/Additional Phone Number(s):** 800-225-8382.

★6874★
Truckers Atlas
American Trucking Associations, Inc.
2200 Mill Rd.
Alexandria, VA 22314-4677   Phone: (703)838-1700
American Trucking Associations & Creative Sales Corporation. 1988. **Toll-free/Additional Phone Number(s):** 800-225-8382.

★6875★
Trucking Permit Guide, 1G: Private, Contract, Common, Exempt
J. J. Keller & Associates, Inc.
3003 W. Breezewood
PO Box 368
Neenah, WI 54957-0368   Phone: (414)722-2848
J.J. Keller & Associates, Inc. Staff, editor. Revised edition, 1987. **Toll-free/Additional Phone Number(s):** 800-327-6868, **Facsimile Number:** (414)727-7516.

★6876★
Wheel & Rim out of Service Guide
American Trucking Associations, Inc.
2200 Mill Rd.
Alexandria, VA 22314-4677   Phone: (703)838-1700
American Trucking Associations, Inc. Maintenance Council. 1987. **Toll-free/Additional Phone Number(s):** 800-225-8382.

---------------- Periodicals ----------------

★6877★
American Trucker Magazine
PO Box 603
Indianapolis, IN 46206   Phone: (317)297-5500
Tom Berg, Editor. Monthly. Magazine for the trucking industry. **Facsimile Number:** (317)299-1356.

★6878★
CALTRUX
California Trucking Association
1251 Beacon Blvd.
PO Box 923
West Sacramento, CA 95691   Phone: (916)373-3531
Editor(s): Jay Van Rein. Weekly. Provides news, commentary, announcements, and advertising of interest to California truck fleet owners and managers. Carries congressional updates, news of developments in the state Public Utilities Commission, a calendar of events, and an industrial relations column.

★6879★
Commercial Carrier Journal
Chilton Co.
Chilton Way
Radnor, PA 19089   Phone: (215)964-4000
Gerald F. Standley, Editor. Monthly. Magazine containing management, maintenance, and operations information for truck and bus fleets. **Facsimile Number:** (215)964-4512.

★6880★
Eastern Trucker
Wadham Publications
1450 Don Mills Rd.
Don Mills, ON, Canada M3B 2X7   Phone: (416)442-2000
Al McCooeye, Publisher. Monthly. Magazine on trucks and truck equipment. **Facsimile Number:** (416)442-2077.

★6881★
Enroute Magazine
2973 Weston Rd.
Weston, ON, Canada M9N 3R3   Phone: (416)741-1112
Steven L. Calitri, Editor. 8x/yr. Trucking magazine.

★6882★
Fleet Product News
Deco Publications, Inc.
510 29th St.
Newport Beach, CA 92663   Phone: (714)675-3225
Dennis O'Connor, Editor and Publisher. 6x/yr. Trade magazine featuring new products, parts, and equipment for the commercial truck market. **Facsimile Number:** (714)675-2767.

★6883★
Fruit and Vegetable Truck Rate Report
Federal-State Market News
630 Sansome St., Rm. 727
San Francisco, CA 94111   Phone: (415)705-1300
Weekly. Lists truck rates per load to selected markets throughout the U.S. Also reports on trucks available in relation to shippers' needs. Recurring features include statistics on the total reported domestic and import truck shipments of fresh fruit and vegetables. **Facsimile Number:** (415)705-1301.

★6884★
Government Tender Report
American Trucking Associations, Inc.
2200 Mill Rd.
Alexandria, VA 22314   Phone: (703)838-1794
Daily, Monday-Friday. Summarizes tenders (except those pertaining to household goods) which have been submitted to the Interstate Commerce Commission by motor and water carriers, rail carriers and bureaus, and freight forwarders in compliance with Section 10721 of the Interstate Commerce Act. Also identifies carriers, tender numbers, effective and expiration dates, commodities, origins, destinations, and rates. Lists and cross-references entries according to regions of origin.

★6885★
Government Traffic Bulletin
American Trucking Associations, Inc.
2200 Mill Rd.
Alexandria, VA 22314   Phone: (703)838-1793
Weekly. Summarizes current traffic requirements of major U.S. Government agencies and reports changes in federal transportation policies, procedures, and personnel. Provides names and phone numbers of individuals who may be contacted for additional information.

★6886★
Heavy Duty Trucking
Newport Publications
Box W
Newport Beach, CA 92658   Phone: (714)261-1636
Doug Condra, Editor. Monthly. Magazine covering long and short haul operations for heavy truck owners and managers. **Facsimile Number:** (714)261-2904.

★6887★
Highway Common Carrier Newsletter
Regular Common Carrier Conference
American Trucking Associations, Inc.
2200 Mill Rd., Ste. 350
Alexandria, VA 22314-4677   Phone: (703)838-1970
Editor(s): Shawn Fields. Biweekly. Focuses on the trucking industry. Covers regulatory, legislative, and judicial matters which affect transportation on the national and state levels. Monitors the activities of the Interstate Commerce Commission and the Department of Transportation. Recurring features include news of the programs of the Conference. **Facsimile Number:** (703)684-4328.

★6888★
Land Line
Owner-Operator Independent Drivers Assn. Inc.
PO Box 26
Oak Grove, MO 64075   Phone: (816)229-5791
Todd Spencer, Editor and Publisher. Six times/yr. **Facsimile Number:** (816)229-0518.

★6889★
Movin' Out
Pollock Enterprises, Ltd.
118 1/2 Franklin St.
PO Box 777
Slippery Rock, PA 16057   Phone: (412)794-6857
Pamela Pollock, Editor. Monthly. Trade magazine. **Facsimile Number:** (412)794-1314.

★6890★
NATSO Truckers News
Newport Publications
1800 E. Deere Ave.
Santa Ana, CA 92705   Phone: (714)261-1636
Tom Stanford, Publisher. Monthly. Magazine (tabloid) for professional truck drivers and owner-operators. Official publication of National Association of Truck Stop Operators. **Facsimile Number:** (714)261-2904.

★6891★
NITL Notice
National Industrial Transportation League (NITL)
1700 N. Moore St., Ste. 1900
Arlington, VA 22209   Phone: (703)524-5011
Editor(s): James E. Bartley. Weekly. Carries transportation news—railroad, motor carrier, airline, and maritime—in the interest of industrial and commercial shippers. Covers rate-hike proposals, transportation legislation, regulatory agency actions, postal service developments, union actions, and court cases. Recurring features include coverage of the Interstate Commerce Commission, U. **Facsimile Number:** (202)842-3520.

★6892★
Owner Operator
Chilton Co.
Chilton Way
Radnor, PA 19089   Phone: (215)964-4000
Leon E. Witconis, Editor. 9x/yr. Magazine. **Facsimile Number:** (215)964-4512.

★6893★
Pro Trucker
Ramp Publishing Group
610 Colonial Park Dr.
Roswell, GA 30075   Phone: (404)587-0311
Carol Prins, Assoc. Editor. Monthly. Trucking industry magazine. **Facsimile Number:** (404)642-8874.

★6894★
Refrigerated Transporter
Tunnell Publications, Inc.
4200 S. Shepherd Dr., Ste. 200
Houston, TX 77098-5354
Gary Macklin, Editor. Monthly. Trade magazine on refrigerated hauling and delivery.

★6895★
Road King Magazine
Union Oil Co. of California
23060 S. Cicero
Richton Park, IL 60471 Phone: (708)481-9240
Richard Vurva, Editor. 6x/yr. Business and leisure reading magazine for over-the-road truck drivers. **Facsimile Number:** (708)481-1063.

★6896★
Rolling Along
North Dakota Motor Carriers Assoc., Inc.
PO Box 874
Bismarck, ND 58502 Phone: (701)223-2700
Leroy H. Ernst, Editor. Quarterly. Motor trucking magazine.

★6897★
SCTA Hi-Lights
South Carolina Trucking Assoc.
2425 Devine St.
PO Box 50166
Columbia, SC 29250-0166 Phone: (803)799-4306
J. Richards Todd, Editor. Monthly. Newspaper (tabloid) serving South Carolina Trucking Association members, truck operators, bus operators, and fleet owners in South Carolina and adjoining states. **Facsimile Number:** (803)254-7148.

★6898★
Southern Motor Cargo
Wallace Witmer Co.
1509 Madison Ave.
Memphis, TN 38104 Phone: (901)276-5424
Randy Duke, Editor. Monthly. Magazine for and about the trucking industry. **Facsimile Number:** (901)276-5400.

★6899★
Steering Wheel
Texas Motor Transportation Assn.
700 E. 11th St.
PO Box 1669
Austin, TX 78767 Phone: (512)478-2541
Cathy Brandewie, Editor. 6x/yr. Magazine covering the Texas truck and bus industry. **Facsimile Number:** (512)474-6494.

★6900★
Tarheel Wheels' Magazine
North Carolina Trucking Assn., Inc.
PO Box 2977
Raleigh, NC 27602 Phone: (919)834-0387
Elbert L. Peters, Jr., Editor. 4x/yr. Magazine on the trucking industry. **Facsimile Number:** (919)832-0390.

★6901★
Traffic World
Journal of Commerce, Inc.
2 World Trade Center, 27th Fl.
New York, NY 10048 Phone: (212)837-7000
Weekly (Mon.). Transportation trade magazine.

★6902★
Transport Fleet News
Transport Publishing Co.
1300 W. Exchange Ave.
Chicago, IL 60609 Phone: (312)523-6669
Phillip Scopelite, Editor and Publisher. Monthly. Trucking magazine. **Facsimile Number:** (312)523-9062.

★6903★
Transport Routier
FCM Communications Inc.
1440 Towers St., Ste. 102
Montreal, PQ, Canada H3H 2C9 Phone: (514)939-3202
Pierre Charette, Editor. Quarterly (March, June, Sept., Dec.). Trucking trade journal (French and English). **Facsimile Number:** (514)939-3170.

★6904★
Transport 2000 and Intermodal World
870 Market St., 9th Fl.
San Francisco, CA 94102 Phone: (415)982-6592
Gail E. Neira, Publisher. Quarterly. Magazine on international issues, intermodal trade, and transportation.

★6905★
Transportation: An Abstract Newsletter
National Technical Information Service (NTIS)
U.S. Department of Commerce
5285 Port Royal Rd.
Springfield, VA 22161 Phone: (703)487-4630
Weekly. Provides abstracts of publications in the areas of air, rail, water, pipeline, and road transportation; global navigation systems; and transportation safety. .

★6906★
Transportation & Distribution
Penton Publishing
1100 Superior Ave.
Cleveland, OH 44114-4135 Phone: (216)696-7000
Perry Trunick, Editor. Monthly. Magazine covering traffic and physical distribution. **Facsimile Number:** (216)696-8765.

★6907★
Transportation Business
Baxter Publications, Inc.
310 Dupont St.
Toronto, ON, Canada M5R 1V9 Phone: (416)968-7252
Peter Morgan, Editor. Monthly. Transportation industry magazine (tabloid). **Facsimile Number:** (416)968-2377.

★6908★
Transportation Quarterly
Eno Foundation for Transportation
PO Box 2055
Westport, CT 06880 Phone: (203)227-4852
Tracy Dunleavy, Circulation Mgr. Quarterly. Trade magazine on transportation. **Facsimile Number:** (203)227-3928.

★6909★
Truck Paper
Peed Corp.
120 W. Harvest St.
PO Box 85010
Lincoln, NE 68501-5010 Phone: (402)477-8900
Lee Chapin, Editor. Weekly (Fri.). Tabloid featuring trucks and trailers for sale. **Facsimile Number:** (402)477-9252.

★6910★
Truck Parts & Service
Kona Communications, Inc.
707 Lake Cook Rd., Ste. 300
Deerfield, IL 60015 Phone: (708)498-3180
David Zaritz, Managing Editor. Monthly. Trade magazine for truck parts and service market. **Facsimile Number:** (708)498-3197.

★6911★

★6911★
Truck World
Truck World Publications Ltd.
No. 3 1610 Kebet Way
Port Coquitlam, BC, Canada V3C 5W9 Phone: (604)942-2305
Rud Kendall, Editor. Monthly. Magazine. **Facsimile Number:** (604)942-4312.

★6912★
TRUCKS Magazine
765 Churchville Rd.
Southampton, PA 18966 Phone: (215)355-1034
John Stevens, Editor and Publisher. 6x/yr. Magazine covering health, safety, image, and profitability for drivers of heavy duty trucks. **Facsimile Number:** (215)355-3931.

★6913★
TWU Express
Transport Workers Union of America
80 West End Ave.
New York, NY 10023 Phone: (212)873-6000
James Gannon, Editor. Monthly. Labor magazine. **Facsimile Number:** (212)721-1431.

★6914★
Weekly Commercial News
C.A. Page Publishing
1117 W. Manchester Blvd., No. A
Inglewood, CA 90301-1500 Phone: (213)608-3350
Mike Richardson, Editor. Weekly (Mon.). Business and transportation industry magazine. **Facsimile Number:** (213)608-3365.

Meetings and Conventions

★6915★
American Trucking Associations (ATA)
2200 Mill Rd.
Alexandria, VA 22314 Phone: (703)838-1700
Frequency: Annual. 1992; New Orleans, LA • 1993; San Francisco, CA. **Toll-free/Additional Phone Number(s):** 800-ATA-LINE. **Facsimile Number:** (703)684-5720.

★6916★
Industrial Truck Association Conference (ITA)
1750 K St. NW, Ste. 210
Washington, DC 20006 Phone: (202)296-9880
Frequency: Annual.

★6917★
International Brotherhood of Teamsters, Chauffeurs, Warehousemen and Helpers of America (IBT)
25 Louisiana Ave., NW
Washington, DC 20001 Phone: (202)624-6800
Frequency: Quinquennial - next held in 1996.

★6918★
International Trucking Show
Independent Trade Show Management
1155A Chess Dr., Ste. C
Foster City, CA 94404 Phone: (415)349-4876
Frequency: Always held during July in Anaheim, California. 1992; Jul. 23-25; Anaheim, CA • 1993; Jul. 22-24; Anaheim, CA. **Toll-free/Additional Phone Number(s):** 800-227-5992. **Facsimile Number:** (415)349-5169.

★6919★
Mid-America Trucking Show
Exhibit Management Associates, Inc.
3701 Taylorville Rd., Ste. 4
Louisville, KY 40220 Phone: (502)458-4487
Frequency: Always held at the Kentucky Fair and Exposition Center in Louisville during March. 1992; Mar. 19-21; Louisville, KY • 1993; Mar. 25-27; Louisville, KY • 1994; Mar. 17-19; Louisville, KY • 1995; Mar. 23-25; Louisville, KY • 1996; Mar. 21-23; Louisville, KY • 1997; Mar. 20-22; Louisville, KY • 1998; Mar. 19-21; Louisville, KY • 1999; Mar. 25-27; Louisville, KY • 2000; Mar. 23-25; Louisville, KY. **Toll-free/Additional Phone Number(s):** 800-626-2370.

★6920★
Mid-West Truck Show
Mid-West Truckers Association
2715 N. Dirksen Pkwy.
Springfield, IL 62702 Phone: (217)525-0310
Frequency: Always held in February at the Prairie Capital Convention Center in Springfield, Illinois. 1993; Feb. 11-13; Springfield, IL. **Facsimile Number:** (217)525-0342.

★6921★
NASSTRAC Convention
NASSTRAC
1750 Pennsylvania Ave., Ste. 1105
Washington, DC 20006 Phone: (202)393-5505
1992.

★6922★
National Tank Truck Carriers Annual Meeting and Tank Equipment Show
National Tank Truck Carriers, Inc.
2200 Mill Rd.
Alexandria, VA 22314 Phone: (703)838-1960
1992; May 18-21; San Francisco, CA • 1993; May 09-12; Boston, MA. **Facsimile Number:** (703)684-5753.

★6923★
National Truck Equipment Association SUPERSHOW
National Truck Equipment Association
38705 7 Mile Rd., Ste. 345
Livonia, MI 48152 Phone: (313)462-2190
Frequency: Always held during even-numbered years. 1992; Mar. 26-28; New Orleans, LA • 1994; Mar. Las Vegas, NV. **Toll-free/Additional Phone Number(s):** 800-866-NTEA. **Facsimile Number:** (313)462-2108.

★6924★
Southwest Trucking Show
Texas Motor Transportation Association
700 E. 11th St.
Austin, TX 78767 Phone: (512)478-2541
1992; Jun. 04-06; Houston, TX • 1993; Jun. 17-19; San Antonio, TX • 1994; Jun. 16-18; Dallas, TX • 1995; Jun. 22-24; Houston, TX • 1996; Jun. 13-15; San Antonio, TX. **Toll-free/Additional Phone Number(s):** 800-876-2161. **Facsimile Number:** (512)474-6494.

Truckdrivers

Other Sources of Information

★6925★
American Trucking Trends, 1990-91
American Trucking Associations, Inc.
2200 Mill Rd.
Alexandria, VA 22314-4677   Phone: (703)838-1700
American Trucking Associations Statistical Analysis Department. 1990. **Toll-free/Additional Phone Number(s):** 800-225-8382.

★6926★
Encouraging Cooperation among Competitors: The Case of Motor Carrier Deregulation & Collective Ratemaking
Greenwood Publishing Group, Inc.
88 Post Rd., W
PO Box 5007
Westport, CT 06881   Phone: (203)226-3571
William B. Tye. 1987. **Facsimile Number:** (202)222-1502.

★6927★
Facts for Consumers From the Federal Trade Commission: Truck-Driving Schools
Federal Trade Commission
Office of Consumer/Business Education
6th & Pennsylvania Ave. NW
Washington, DC 20580   Phone: (202)326-2222
1990. This four-page leaflet offers consumers guidelines for selecting and evaluating a truck-driver training school.

★6928★
Motor Carrier Annual Report
American Trucking Associations, Inc.
2200 Mill Rd.
Alexandria, VA 22314-4677   Phone: (703)838-1700
American Trucking Association, Statistical Analysis Department. 1989. Part of Financial and Operating Statistics Series. **Toll-free/Additional Phone Number(s):** 800-225-8382.

★6929★
Motor Carrier Professional Services Directory
American Trucking Associations, Inc.
2200 Mill Rd.
Alexandria, VA 22314-4677   Phone: (703)838-1700
American Trucking Associations, Inc. 1991. **Toll-free/Additional Phone Number(s):** 800-225-8382.

★6930★
UFAC: Important Consumer Safety Information from UFAC
Upholstered Furniture Action Council (UFAC)
PO Box 2436
High Point, NC 27261   Phone: (919)885-5065
Annual. Guide to UFAC's voluntary program to promote cigarette-resistant upholstered furniture. Includes construction criteria, compliance, and history, plus list of directors, member associations, and supporting organizations.

★6931★
What to Look for in a Truck Driver
American Trucking Association
Office of Public Affairs
2200 Mill Rd.
Alexandria, VA 22314-4677   Phone: (703)838-1873
1990. This six-panel brochure describes truck driver qualifications and offers advice on truck driver training school facilities, curriculum, and instructors. Lists the criteria required for a school to be certified by the Professional Truck Driver Institute of America.

Water Transportation Occupations

Workers in water transportation occupations operate and maintain deep sea merchant ships, tugboats, towboats, ferries, dredges, research vessels, and other waterborne craft on the oceans and the Great Lakes, in harbors, on rivers and canals, and on other waterways. Captains or masters supervise the operation of a vessel and the work of the other officers and the crew. On large vessels, captains are assisted by deck officers or mates; on some inland vessels, they are called pilots. Mates stand watch for specified periods, usually four hours on and eight hours off, overseeing the operation of the vessel. Engineers or marine engineers operate, maintain, and repair propulsion engines, boilers, generators, pumps, and other machinery. Seamen, also called deckhands, particularly on inland waters, help navigate the vessel, operate deck equipment, and keep the nonengineering areas in good condition. Larger vessels have a boatswain or head seaman. Marine oilers lubricate gears, shafts, bearings, and other moving parts of engines and motors, read pressure and temperature gauges and record data, and may repair and adjust machinery. About 33 percent of all water transportation workers are employed on board merchant marine ships or U.S. Navy Military Sealift ships operating on the oceans or Great Lakes. Almost half work on tugs, towboats, ferries, dredges, and other watercraft in harbors, on rivers and canals, and other waterways. Others work in water transportation services such as boatyards and marinas; boat chartering; piloting services; and marine construction, salvaging, and surveying.

$alaries

Annual earnings for water transportation workers are as follows:

Lowest 10 percent	$14,000/year or less
Middle 50 percent	$19,000—$38,000/year
Top 10 percent	$52,000/year or more

Employment Outlook

Growth rate until the year 2000: Slower than average.

Water Transportation Occupations

Career Guides

★6932★
"Able Seaman" in *Occu-Facts: Information on 565 Careers in Outline Form* (p. 19.11)
Careers, Inc.
P.O. Box 135
1211 Tenth St., S.W.
Largo, FL 33640   Phone: (813)584-7333

Elizabeth Handville. Biennial, 1989-90 edition. Each one-page occupational profile describes duties, working conditions, physical surroundings and demands, aptitudes, temperament, educational requirements, employment outlook, earnings, and places of employment.

★6933★
Hanging On
Pennsylvania State University AV Services
University Division of Media & Learning Resources
Special Services Building
Pennsylvania State University
University Park, PA 16802   Phone: (814)865-6314

Videocassette. 1980. 29 mins. Tugboat workers in New York harbor talk about their jobs and their concerns about inflation in this part of the "U.S. Chronicle" series.

★6934★
Longshore Workers
Chronicle Guidance Publications, Inc.
PO Box 1190
Moravia, NY 13118-1190   Phone: (315)497-0330

1988. This career brief describes the nature of the work, working conditions, hours and earnings, education and training, licensure, certification, unions, personal qualifications, social and psychological factors, employment outlook, entry methods, advancement, and related occupations. **Toll-free/Additional Phone Number(s):** 800-622-7284.

★6935★
"Marine Engineer" in *Agribusiness, Environment, and Natural Resources*, Volume 2 of *Career Information Center* (pp. 129-130)
Glencoe/Macmillan
15319 Chatsworth St.
Mission Hills, CA 91345   Phone: (818)898-1391

Richard Lidz and Dale Anderson, editorial directors. Fourth edition, 1990. For 600 occupations, describes job duties, entry-level requirements, education and training needed, advancement possibilities, employment outlook, earnings and benefits. The set is divided into 12 volumes. Each volume includes jobs related under a broad career field. Volume 13 is the index. **Facsimile Number:** 818-365-5489.

★6936★
"Marine Engineer (Shipboard)" in *Occu-Facts: Information on 565 Careers in Outline Form* (p. 19.12)
Careers, Inc.
P.O. Box 135
1211 Tenth St., S.W.
Largo, FL 33640   Phone: (813)584-7333

Elizabeth Handville. Biennial, 1989-90 edition. Each one-page occupational profile describes duties, working conditions, physical surroundings and demands, aptitudes, temperament, educational requirements, employment outlook, earnings, and places of employment.

★6937★
"Marine Engineers" in Volume 4 of *Career Discovery Encyclopedia* (pp. 58-59)
J.G. Ferguson Publishing Co.
200 W. Monroe
Chicago, IL 60606   Phone: (312)580-5480

E. Russell Primm, editor-in-chief. 1990. Contains two-page articles on 504 occupations. Each article describes job duties, earnings, and educational and training requirements.

★6938★
"Marine Engineers" in Volume 3 of *The Encyclopedia of Careers and Vocational Guidance* (pp. 206-207)
J.G. Ferguson Publishing Co.
200 W. Monroe
Chicago, IL 60606   Phone: (312)580-5480

William E. Hopke, editor-in-chief. Eighth edition, 1990. Four-volume set that profiles 500 occupations and describes job trends in 76 industries. Includes career description, educational requirements, history of the job, methods of entry, advancement, employment outlook, earnings, working conditions, social and psychological factors, and sources of additional information.

★6939★
"Marine/Ocean Engineering and Naval Architecture" in *Opportunities in Engineering Careers* (pp. 114-116)
National Textbook Co.
4255 W. Touhy Ave.
Lincolnwood, IL 60646   Phone: (312)679-5500

Nicholas Basta. 1990. Covers the advantages and disadvantages of working as an engineer, employment trends, work environments, and educational preparation.

★6940★
"Maritime Jobs" in *Opportunities in Transportation Careers* (pp. 53-54)
National Textbook Co.
4255 W. Touhy Ave.
Lincolnwood, IL 60646   Phone: (312)679-5500

Adrian A. Paradis. 1988. Describes transportation and related employment in driving occupations, the airlines, merchant marine, and travel services. Covers employment outlook, educational and training requirements, wages, and the work itself, and advantages and disadvantages of transportation careers. Offers job hunting advice.

★6941★
"Merchant Marine Captain" in *Transportation*, Volume 12 of *Career Information Center* (pp. 132-134)
Glencoe/Macmillan
15319 Chatsworth St.
Mission Hills, CA 91345   Phone: (818)898-1391

Richard Lidz and Dale Anderson, editorial directors. Fourth edition, 1990. For 600 occupations, describes job duties, entry-level requirements, education and training needed, advancement possibilities, employment outlook, earnings and benefits. The set is divided into 12 volumes. Each volume includes jobs related under a broad career field. Volume 13 is the index. **Facsimile Number:** 818-365-5489.

★6942★
"Merchant Marine Engineer" in *Transportation* (pp. 63-67)
Franklin Watts, Inc.
387 Park Avenue, S.
New York, NY 10016   Phone: (212)686-7070

Marjorie Rittenberg Schulz. 1990. Surveys the transportation industry including air, water, and rail services. Provides job description, training, salary, and employment outlook. Offers job hunting advice.

★6943★
"Merchant Marine Engineer and Chief Engineer" in *Transportation*, Volume 12 of *Career Information Center* (pp. 104-105)
Glencoe/Macmillan
15319 Chatsworth St.
Mission Hills, CA 91345   Phone: (818)898-1391

Richard Lidz and Dale Anderson, editorial directors. Fourth edition, 1990. For 600 occupations, describes job duties, entry-level requirements, education and training needed, advancement possibilities, employment outlook, earnings and benefits. The set is divided into 12 volumes. Each volume includes jobs related under a broad career field. Volume 13 is the index. **Facsimile Number:** 818-365-5489.

★6944★
Merchant Marine Occupations
Chronicle Guidance Publications, Inc.
PO Box 1190
Moravia, NY 13118-1190   Phone: (315)497-0330

1988. This career brief describes the nature of the work, working conditions, hours and earnings, education and training, licensure, certification, unions, personal qualifications, social and psychological factors, employment outlook, entry methods, advancement, and related occupations. **Toll-free/Additional Phone Number(s):** 800-622-7284.

★6945★
"Merchant Marine Occupations" in Volume 2 of *The Encyclopedia of Careers and Vocational Guidance* (pp. 410-415)
J.G. Ferguson Publishing Co.
200 W. Monroe
Chicago, IL 60606   Phone: (312)580-5480

William E. Hopke, editor-in-chief. Eighth edition, 1990. Four-volume set that profiles 500 occupations and describes job trends in 76 industries. Includes career description, educational requirements, history of the job, methods of entry, advancement, employment outlook, earnings, working conditions, social and psychological factors, and sources of additional information.

★6946★
"Merchant Marine Officers" in *Jobs! What They Are...Where They Are...What They Pay* (pp. 250-251)
Simon & Schuster, Inc.
Simon & Schuster Bldg.
1230 Avenue of the Americas
New York, NY 10020   Phone: (212)698-7000

Robert O. Snelling and Anne M. Snelling. Revised edition, 1989. Profiles 241 occupations, describing duties and responsibilities, educational preparation, earnings, employment opportunities, training, and qualifications.

★6947★
"Merchant Marine Officers" in *Opportunities in Transportation Careers* (pp. 59-60)
National Textbook Co.
4255 W. Touhy Ave.
Lincolnwood, IL 60646   Phone: (312)679-5500

Adrian A. Paradis. 1988. Describes transportation and related employment in driving occupations, the airlines, merchant marine, and travel services. Covers employment outlook, educational and training requirements, wages, and the work itself, and advantages and disadvantages of transportation careers. Offers job hunting advice.

★6948★
"Merchant Marine Unlicensed Sailors" in *Opportunities in Transportation Careers* (pp. 54-58)
National Textbook Co.
4255 W. Touhy Ave.
Lincolnwood, IL 60646   Phone: (312)679-5500

Adrian A. Paradis. 1988. Describes transportation and related employment in driving occupations, the airlines, merchant marine, and travel services. Covers employment outlook, educational and training requirements, wages, and the work itself, and advantages and disadvantages of transportation careers. Offers job hunting advice.

★6949★
"Merchant Sailor" in *Hard Hatted Women: Stories of Struggle and Success in the Trades* (pp. 176-186)
Seal Press
3131 Western Ave., Ste. 410
Seattle, WA 98121   Phone: (206)283-7844

Molly Martin, editor. 1988. Twenty-six women recount their experiences working in blue collar occupations. They describe how they got in, the work they do, their relationships in predominantly male occupations, and their training.

★6950★
Opportunities in Marine and Maritime Careers
National Textbook Co.
4255 W. Touhy Ave.
Lincolnwood, IL 60646   Phone: (312)679-5500
William Ray Heitzmann. 1988. Includes careers related by their proximity to water; cruise ships, oceanography, marine sciences, fishing, commercial diving, maritime transportation, shipbuilding, Navy, and Coast Guard. Covers qualifications, job outlook, job duties, educational preparation, and training. Lists associations and schools.

★6951★
"Ordinary and Able Seaman" in *Transportation*, Volume 12 of *Career Information Center* (pp. 65-67)
Glencoe/Macmillan
15319 Chatsworth St.
Mission Hills, CA 91345   Phone: (818)898-1391
Richard Lidz and Dale Anderson, editorial directors. Fourth edition, 1990. For 600 occupations, describes job duties, entry-level requirements, education and training needed, advancement possibilities, employment outlook, earnings and benefits. The set is divided into 12 volumes. Each volume includes jobs related under a broad career field. Volume 13 is the index. **Facsimile Number:** 818-365-5489.

★6952★
Seaman, Able
Careers, Inc.
PO Box 135
Largo, FL 34649-0135   Phone: (813)584-7333
1988. Two-page occupational summary card describing duties, working conditions, personal qualifications, training, earnings and hours, employment outlook, places of employment, related careers and where to write for more information.

★6953★
"Seaman, Steward, Cook" in *Transportation* (pp. 33-37)
Franklin Watts, Inc.
387 Park Avenue, S.
New York, NY 10016   Phone: (212)686-7070
Marjorie Rittenberg Schulz. 1990. Surveys the transportation industry including air, water, and rail services. Provides job description, training, salary, and employment outlook. Offers job hunting advice.

★6954★
"Tall Ship Crew Member" in *Offbeat Careers: The Directory of Unusual Work* (pp. 161-162)
Ten Speed Press
PO Box 7123
Berkeley, CA 94707   Phone: (415)845-8414
Al Sacharov. 1988. Profiles eighty-eight unusual careers. Provides job description, history of occupation, salary, and training required. Lists one or more sources of additional information.

★6955★
Tugboat Mate
Vocational Biographies, Inc.
PO Box 31, Dept. VF10
Sauk Centre, MN 56378   Phone: (612)352-6516
1989. This pamphlet profiles a person working in the job. Includes information about job duties, working conditions, places of employment, educational preparation, labor market outlook, and salaries. **Toll-free/Additional Phone Number(s):** 800-255-0752.

★6956★
"Water Transportation Occupations" in *Occupational Outlook Handbook* (pp. 442-444)
Superintendent of Documents
U.S. Government Printing Office
Washington, DC 20402   Phone: (202)783-3238
Biennial; latest edition, 1990-91. Encyclopedia of careers describing more than 250 occupations and comprising about 86 percent of all jobs in the economy. Occupations that require lengthy education or training are given the most attention. For each occupation, the handbook describes job duties, working conditions, training, educational preparation, personal qualities, advancement possibilities, job outlook, earnings, and sources of additional information.

★6957★
"Yacht Crew Member" in *Offbeat Careers: The Directory of Unusual Work* (pp. 177-178)
Ten Speed Press
PO Box 7123
Berkeley, CA 94707   Phone: (415)845-8414
Al Sacharov. 1988. Profiles eighty-eight unusual careers. Provides job description, history of occupation, salary, and training required. Lists one or more sources of additional information.

Associations

★6958★
American Institute of Merchant Shipping (AIMS)
1000 16th St., NW, Ste. 511
Washington, DC 20036   Phone: (202)775-4399
Membership: U.S. companies that own and operate tanks, dry bulk carriers, and other oceangoing vessels in U.S. foreign and domestic commerce. **Purpose:** Serves as a spokesperson for the U.S. Merchant Marine industry, with respect to maritime issues and establishment of a strong, well-balanced American flag fleet adequate to meet the national needs for both commerce and defense. Testifies before congressional committees in support of legislation to realize these goals. Keeps in touch with federal and state government agencies concerning maritime matters. Participates in numerous international forums. Cosponsors Ship Safety Achievement Awards; presents Jones F. Devlin awards for accident-free ship operation and sponsors the RADM Halert C. Shepheard Award for achievement in merchant marine safety.

★6959★
Marine Board (MB)
2101 Constitution Ave. NW
Washington, DC 20418   Phone: (202)334-3119
Membership: A section of the National Research Council operating under the council's Commission on Engineering and Technical Systems. **Purpose:** Acts as a study unit for information on U.S. marine engineering and maritime transportation activities. Is concerned with engineering and technology as it affects: coastal and offshore resources development and operations; navigation and commerce of seas and waterways; related human resources and onshore activities including development of public policy. Identifies opportunities and needs for engineering capabilities and for development of new technologies; makes recommendations; promotes multidisciplinary communication and cooperation; acts as a professional forum for the national and professional maritime community.

★6960★
National Waterways Conference (NWC)
1130 17th St. NW, Ste. 200
Washington, DC 20036   Phone: (202)296-4415
Membership: Petroleum, coal, chemical, electric power, building materials, iron steel, and grain companies; industrial development agencies, port authorities, and other governmental bodies; water carriers; companies which build, repair, service, or insure vessels; water resource development associations, banks, chambers of commerce, individuals, and others "joined together to promote a better understanding of the public value of the American waterways system." **Purpose:** Conducts research on the economics of water transportation; sponsors an educational program to publicize the diverse benefits of efficient water transport; keeps members and other waterway proponents posted on developments affecting national waterways policy.

Standards/Certification Agencies

Deck and engineering officers in the merchant marine must be licensed. To qualify for a license, applicants must have graduated from the U.S. Merchant Marine Academy, or one of the six state academies, and pass an exam, or have three years of appropriate sea experience and pass an exam. Since seamen may work six months a year or less, it can take five to eight years to accumulate the necessary experience. Harbor pilot training is usually an apprenticeship with a shipping company or a pilot employees' association.

Test Guides

★6961★
Able Seaman
National Learning Corp.
212 Michael Dr.
Syosset, NY 11791   Phone: (516)921-8888
Jack Rudman. Part of the Career Examination Series No. 1. All examination guides in this series contain questions with answers. **Facsimile Number:** (516)921-8743. **Toll-free/Additional Phone Number(s):** 800-645-6337.

★6962★
Assistant Bridge Operator
National Learning Corp.
212 Michael Dr.
Syosset, NY 11791   Phone: (516)921-8888
Jack Rudman. Part of National Learning Corp.'s Career Examination Series No. 1. All examination guides in this series contain questions with answers. Test guide for assistant bridge operator trainee is also available. **Facsimile Number:** (516)921-8743. **Toll-free/Additional Phone Number(s):** 800-645-6337.

★6963★
Assistant Captain
National Learning Corp.
212 Michael Dr.
Syosset, NY 11791   Phone: (516)921-8888
Jack Rudman. Part of the Career Examination Series No. 1. All examination guides in this series contain questions with answers. **Facsimile Number:** (516)921-8743. **Toll-free/Additional Phone Number(s):** 800-645-6337.

★6964★
Deckhand
National Learning Corp.
212 Michael Dr.
Syosset, NY 11791   Phone: (516)921-8888
Jack Rudman. Part of the Career Examination Series No. 1. All examination guides in this series contain questions with answers. **Facsimile Number:** (516)921-8743. **Toll-free/Additional Phone Number(s):** 800-645-6337.

★6965★
Harbormaster
National Learning Corp.
212 Michael Dr.
Syosset, NY 11791   Phone: (516)921-8888
Jack Rudman. Part of the Career Examination Series No. 1. All examination guides in this series contain questions with answers. **Facsimile Number:** (516)921-8743. **Toll-free/Additional Phone Number(s):** 800-645-6337.

★6966★
Marine Stoker
National Learning Corp.
212 Michael Dr.
Syosset, NY 11791   Phone: (516)921-8888
Jack Rudman. Part of the Career Examination Series No. 1. All examination guides in this series contain questions with answers. **Facsimile Number:** (516)921-8743. **Toll-free/Additional Phone Number(s):** 800-645-6337.

★6967★
Mate
National Learning Corp.
212 Michael Dr.
Syosset, NY 11791   Phone: (516)921-8888
Jack Rudman. Part of the Career Examination Series No. 1. All examination guides in this series contain questions with answers. **Facsimile Number:** (516)921-8743. **Toll-free/Additional Phone Number(s):** 800-645-6337.

★6968★
Merchant Marine Examination Questions—Volume 13: Steam Plants
Superintendent of Documents
U.S. Government Printing Office
Washington, DC 20402   Phone: (202)783-3238
1988. Part of a series of volumes produced by the U.S. government; contains questions used in examinations for merchant marine licenses and documents. Also provides sources and answers.

★6969★
Merchant Marine Examination Questions—Volume 12: Electricity
Superintendent of Documents
U.S. Government Printing Office
Washington, DC 20402   Phone: (202)783-3238
1988. Part of a series of volumes produced by the U.S. government; contains questions used in examinations for merchant marine licenses and documents. Also provides sources and answers.

★6970★
Merchant Marine Examination Questions—Volume 2: Navigation Problems
Superintendent of Documents
U.S. Government Printing Office
Washington, DC 20402　　　　　　　Phone: (202)783-3238

1989. Part of a series of volumes produced by the U.S. government; contains questions used in examinations for merchant marine licenses and documents. Also provides sources and answers.

★6971★
Senior Harbormaster
National Learning Corp.
212 Michael Dr.
Syosset, NY 11791　　　　　　　Phone: (516)921-8888

Jack Rudman. Part of the Career Examination Series No. 1. All examination guides in this series contain questions with answers. **Facsimile Number:** (516)921-8743. **Toll-free/Additional Phone Number(s):** 800-645-6337.

Educational Directories and Programs

★6972★
"Maritime Labor and Training" in *MARAD* (pp. 45-51)
U.S. Department of Transportation
Maritime Administration
Office of External Affairs
400 7th St., S.W.
Washington, DC 20590　　　　　Phone: (202)366-5807

1990. Annual report of the Maritime Administration. Describes state and federal training facilities for the merchant marine. Highlights current events affecting the merchant marine.

Awards, Scholarships, Grants, and Fellowships

★6973★
Transportation Man of the Year
Delta Nu Alpha Transportation Fraternity
621 Plainfield, Ste. 308
Willowbrook, IL 60521　　　　　Phone: (312)850-7100

To recognize contributions to the field of transportation. A plaque is awarded annually. Established in 1952.

Periodicals

★6974★
ABYC News
American Boat & Yacht Council, Inc. (ABYC)
PO Box 747
Millersville, MD 21108　　　　　Phone: (410)923-3932

Editor(s): Louise Lincoln. 1-4/yr. Concerned with voluntary standards in boat and equipment design, construction, service, and repair. Publishes news of Council activities. Recurring features include announcements of new officers and members and project and technical committee news. **Facsimile Number:** (410)923-3988.

★6975★
Cargo Express
Rodney Publications Ltd.
7071 Lawton Blvd.
PO Box 370 Sta. Q
Toronto, ON, Canada M4V 1Z6　　Phone: (416)486-0516

Paul B. Rodney, Editor and Publisher. Monthly. Shipping industry magazine.

★6976★
Government Tender Report
American Trucking Associations, Inc.
2200 Mill Rd.
Alexandria, VA 22314　　　　　Phone: (703)838-1794

Daily, Monday-Friday. Summarizes tenders (except those pertaining to household goods) which have been submitted to the Interstate Commerce Commission by motor and water carriers, rail carriers and bureaus, and freight forwarders in compliance with Section 10721 of the Interstate Commerce Act. Also identifies carriers, tender numbers, effective and expiration dates, commodities, origins, destinations, and rates. Lists and cross-references entries according to regions of origin.

★6977★
Government Traffic Bulletin
American Trucking Associations, Inc.
2200 Mill Rd.
Alexandria, VA 22314　　　　　Phone: (703)838-1793

Weekly. Summarizes current traffic requirements of major U.S. Government agencies and reports changes in federal transportation policies, procedures, and personnel. Provides names and phone numbers of individuals who may be contacted for additional information.

★6978★
MARINE DIGEST and Transportation News
Marine Publishing, Inc.
1201 1st Ave. S, No. 305
PO Box 3905
Seattle, WA 98124　　　　　　Phone: (206)682-3607

Valerie Drogus, Editor. Monthly. Magazine for maritime, shipbuilding, transport, international trade, and allied industries. **Facsimile Number:** (206)682-4023.

★6979★
Marine Log
Simmons-Boardman Publications
345 Hudson St.
New York, NY 10014　　　　　Phone: (212)620-7220

Nicholas Blenkey, Editor. Monthly. Magazine serving ship, boat, and barge owners, builders, and operators, port authorities, and the Navy. **Facsimile Number:** (212)633-1165.

★6980★
Marine Policy Reports
Taylor & Francis
1900 Frost Rd., Ste. 101
Bristol, PA 19007　　　　　　　Phone: (215)785-5800

Gerard J. Mangone, Editor. Quarterly. Journal on naval policies, shipping, fisheries management, and protection of the marine environment. **Facsimile Number:** (215)785-5515.

★6981★
NITL Notice
National Industrial Transportation League (NITL)
1700 N. Moore St., Ste. 1900
Arlington, VA 22209　　　　　Phone: (703)524-5011

Editor(s): James E. Bartley. Weekly. Carries transportation news—railroad, motor carrier, airline, and maritime—in the interest of industrial and commercial shippers. Covers rate-hike proposals, transportation legislation, regulatory agency actions, postal service developments, union actions, and court cases. Recurring features include coverage of the Interstate Commerce Commission, U. **Facsimile Number:** (202)842-3520.

★6982★
Ocean Navigator
18 Danforth St.
Portland, ME 04101   Phone: (207)772-2466
Gregory M. Walsh, Editor and Publisher. 8x/yr. Magazine on Marine navigation and voyaging equipment and techniques.

★6983★
Passenger Transport
American Public Transit Assn.
1201 New York Ave., Ste. 400
Washington, DC 20005   Phone: (202)898-4119
Dennis Kouba, Editor. Weekly (Mon.). **Facsimile Number:** (202)898-4095.

★6984★
Seafarers Log
Seafarers Intl. Union
5201 Auth Way
Camp Springs, MD 20746   Phone: (301)899-0675
Jessica Smith, Communications Dir. Monthly. Monthly tabloid on maritime labor. **Facsimile Number:** (301)899-7355.

★6985★
Seatrade Business Review
Seatrade North America, Inc.
125 Village Blvd., No. 303
Princeton, NJ 08540   Phone: (609)452-9414
Ian Middleton, Editor. 6x/yr. Trade magazine presenting analyses of the business of sea transport. **Facsimile Number:** (609)452-9374.

★6986★
Seaway Review
Harbor House Publishers, Inc.
221 Water St.
Boyne City, MI 49712   Phone: (616)582-2814
Michelle Cortright, Editor. Quarterly. Magazine on maritime transportation, business, and international and economic news and analysis. **Facsimile Number:** (616)582-3392.

★6987★
Southern Shipper Seafarer Magazine, Inc.
PO Box 4728
Jacksonville, FL 32201   Phone: (904)355-2601
Hayes H. Howard, Editor and Publisher. Monthly. Magazine covering transportation and shipping in the Southeast and East Gulf port ranges. **Facsimile Number:** (904)791-8836.

★6988★
Traffic World
Journal of Commerce, Inc.
2 World Trade Center, 27th Fl.
New York, NY 10048   Phone: (212)837-7000
Weekly (Mon.). Transportation trade magazine.

★6989★
Transport 2000 and Intermodal World
870 Market St., 9th Fl.
San Francisco, CA 94102   Phone: (415)982-6592
Gail E. Neira, Publisher. Quarterly. Magazine on international issues, intermodal trade, and transportation.

★6990★
Transportation: An Abstract Newsletter
National Technical Information Service (NTIS)
U.S. Department of Commerce
5285 Port Royal Rd.
Springfield, VA 22161   Phone: (703)487-4630
Weekly. Provides abstracts of publications in the areas of air, rail, water, pipeline, and road transportation; global navigation systems; and transportation safety.

★6991★
Transportation & Distribution
Penton Publishing
1100 Superior Ave.
Cleveland, OH 44114-4135   Phone: (216)696-7000
Perry Trunick, Editor. Monthly. Magazine covering traffic and physical distribution. **Facsimile Number:** (216)696-8765.

★6992★
Transportation Business
Baxter Publications, Inc.
310 Dupont St.
Toronto, ON, Canada M5R 1V9   Phone: (416)968-7252
Peter Morgan, Editor. Monthly. Transportation industry magazine (tabloid). **Facsimile Number:** (416)968-2377.

★6993★
Transportation Quarterly
Eno Foundation for Transportation
PO Box 2055
Westport, CT 06880   Phone: (203)227-4852
Tracy Dunleavy, Circulation Mgr. Quarterly. Trade magazine on transportation. **Facsimile Number:** (203)227-3928.

★6994★
TWU Express
Transport Workers Union of America
80 West End Ave.
New York, NY 10023   Phone: (212)873-6000
James Gannon, Editor. Monthly. Labor magazine. **Facsimile Number:** (212)721-1431.

★6995★
Weekly Commercial News
C.A. Page Publishing
1117 W. Manchester Blvd., No. A
Inglewood, CA 90301-1500   Phone: (213)608-3350
Mike Richardson, Editor. Weekly (Mon.). Business and transportation industry magazine. **Facsimile Number:** (213)608-3365.

★6996★
WWS/World Wide Shipping
World Wide Shipping Guide, Inc.
77 Moehring Dr.
Blauvelt, NY 10913-2093   Phone: (914)359-1934
Ann H. Hagen, Editor. 8x/yr. Magazine reporting trends, developments, and government regulations effecting the shipping business. Serves ports, carriers, shippers, customs brokers, distributors, agents, stevedores, and terminal operators. **Facsimile Number:** (914)359-1938.

Water Transportation Occupations

Meetings and Conventions

★6997★
American Institute of Merchant Shipping (AIMS)
1000 16th St., NW, Ste. 511
Washington, DC 20036   Phone: (202)775-4399
Frequency: Annual.

★6998★
International Work Boat Show
National Fisherman Expositions
5 Milk St.
PO Box 7437 DTS
Portland, ME 04112   Phone: (207)772-3005
1992; Dec. 03-05; New Orleans, LA • 1993; Dec. 02-04; New Orleans, LA. **Facsimile Number:** (207)772-5059.

Handlers, Equipment Cleaners, Helpers, and Laborers

Handlers, Equipment Cleaners, Helpers, and Laborers

Freight, stock, and material movers include stock handlers and baggers, machine feeders and offbearers, stevedores, and related occupations. They move materials to and from storage areas, loading docks, delivery vehicles, ships' holds, machines, and containers either manually or with forklifts, dollies, handtrucks, or carts. Helpers assist construction trades workers, mechanics and repairers, and workers in production and extractive occupations. They aid machine operators and tenders by moving materials, supplies, and tools to and from work areas. Construction laborers provide much of the routine physical labor at building sites. They supply tools, materials, and equipment to carpenters, electricians, masons, plumbers, and other construction workers. Tenders for bricklayers and plasterers mix and supply materials, set up and move scaffolding, and provide other services. Laborers dig trenches, set braces to support the sides of excavations, and clean up rubble and debris. Hand packers and packagers manually package or wrap materials. Refuse collectors collect trash and garbage and drive garbage trucks. Service station attendants conduct various services on automobiles, buses, trucks, and other vehicles. Parking lot attendants assist customers in parking their cars in lots or storage areas and collect fees from customers. Vehicle washers and equipment cleaners clean machinery, vehicles, storage tanks, pipelines, and similar equipment.

$alaries

Weekly earnings for handlers, equipment cleaners, helpers, and laborers are as follows:

Lowest 10 percent	$155.00/week
Middle 50 percent	$200.00—$400.00/week
Top 10 percent	$510.00/week

Employment Outlook

Growth rate until the year 2000: Employment is expected to remain level.

Handlers, Equipment Cleaners, Helpers, and Laborers

Career Guides

★6999★
"Airline Baggage and Freight Handler" in *Transportation*, Volume 12 of *Career Information Center* (pp. 35-36)
Glencoe/Macmillan
15319 Chatsworth St.
Mission Hills, CA 91345   Phone: (818)898-1391
Richard Lidz and Dale Anderson, editorial directors. Fourth edition, 1990. For 600 occupations, describes job duties, entry-level requirements, education and training needed, advancement possibilities, employment outlook, earnings and benefits. The set is divided into 12 volumes. Each volume includes jobs related under a broad career field. Volume 13 is the index. **Facsimile Number:** 818-365-5489.

★7000★
"Airline Freight Handler" in *Transportation* (pp. 15-17)
Franklin Watts, Inc.
387 Park Avenue, S.
New York, NY 10016   Phone: (212)686-7070
Marjorie Rittenberg Schulz. 1990. Surveys the transportation industry including air, water, and rail services. Provides job description, training, salary, and employment outlook. Offers job hunting advice.

★7001★
Airplane Cleaner
Careers, Inc.
PO Box 135
Largo, FL 34649-0135   Phone: (813)584-7333
1989. Two-page job guide card describing duties, working conditions, personal qualifications, training, earnings and hours, employment outlook, places of employment, related careers and where to write for more information.

★7002★
"Airplane Cleaner" in *Occu-Facts: Information on 565 Careers in Outline Form* (p. 20.18)
Careers, Inc.
P.O. Box 135
1211 Tenth St., S.W.
Largo, FL 33640   Phone: (813)584-7333
Elizabeth Handville. Biennial, 1989-90 edition. Each one-page occupational profile describes duties, working conditions, physical surroundings and demands, aptitudes, temperament, educational requirements, employment outlook, earnings, and places of employment.

★7003★
Asphalt Paving Machine Operators
Chronicle Guidance Publications, Inc.
PO Box 1190
Moravia, NY 13118-1190   Phone: (315)497-0330
1987. This career brief describes the nature of the work, working conditions, hours and earnings, education and training, licensure, certification, unions, personal qualifications, social and psychological factors, employment outlook, entry methods, advancement, and related occupations. **Toll-free/Additional Phone Number(s):** 800-622-7284.

★7004★
Auto Body Repair Helper
Careers, Inc.
PO Box 135
Largo, FL 34649-0135   Phone: (813)584-7333
1990. Two-page job guide card describing duties, working conditions, personal qualifications, training, earnings and hours, employment outlook, places of employment, related careers and where to write for more information.

★7005★
"Auto Body Repair Helper" in *Occu-Facts: Information on 565 Careers in Outline Form* (p. 20.2)
Careers, Inc.
P.O. Box 135
1211 Tenth St., S.W.
Largo, FL 33640   Phone: (813)584-7333
Elizabeth Handville. Biennial, 1989-90 edition. Each one-page occupational profile describes duties, working conditions, physical surroundings and demands, aptitudes, temperament, educational requirements, employment outlook, earnings, and places of employment.

★7006★
Automobile Parking Attendant
Careers, Inc.
PO Box 135
Largo, FL 34649-0135   Phone: (813)584-7333
1991. Two-page job guide card describing duties, working conditions, personal qualifications, training, earnings and hours, employment outlook, places of employment, related careers and where to write for more information.

★7007★
Automobile Washer
Careers, Inc.
PO Box 135
Largo, FL 34649-0135   Phone: (813)584-7333
1991. Two-page job guide card describing duties, working conditions, personal qualifications, training, earnings and hours,

employment outlook, places of employment, related careers and where to write for more information.

★7008★
"Automobile Washer" in *Occu-Facts: Information on 565 Careers in Outline Form* (p. 20.20)
Careers, Inc.
P.O. Box 135
1211 Tenth St., S.W.
Largo, FL 33640   Phone: (813)584-7333

Elizabeth Handville. Biennial, 1989-90 edition. Each one-page occupational profile describes duties, working conditions, physical surroundings and demands, aptitudes, temperament, educational requirements, employment outlook, earnings, and places of employment.

★7009★
Automotive Mechanic Helper
Careers, Inc.
PO Box 135
Largo, FL 34649-0135   Phone: (813)584-7333

1991. Two-page job guide card describing duties, working conditions, personal qualifications, training, earnings and hours, employment outlook, places of employment, related careers and where to write for more information.

★7010★
"Automotive Mechanic Helper" in *Occu-Facts: Information on 565 Careers in Outline Form* (p. 20.3)
Careers, Inc.
P.O. Box 135
1211 Tenth St., S.W.
Largo, FL 33640   Phone: (813)584-7333

Elizabeth Handville. Biennial, 1989-90 edition. Each one-page occupational profile describes duties, working conditions, physical surroundings and demands, aptitudes, temperament, educational requirements, employment outlook, earnings, and places of employment.

★7011★
Automotive Service Station Attendant
Careers, Inc.
PO Box 135
Largo, FL 34649-0135   Phone: (813)584-7333

1990. Two-page occupational summary card describing duties, working conditions, personal qualifications, training, earnings and hours, employment outlook, places of employment, related careers and where to write for more information.

★7012★
"Automotive Service Station Attendant" in *Occu-Facts: Information on 565 Careers in Outline Form* (p. 20.16)
Careers, Inc.
P.O. Box 135
1211 Tenth St., S.W.
Largo, FL 33640   Phone: (813)584-7333

Elizabeth Handville. Biennial, 1989-90 edition. Each one-page occupational profile describes duties, working conditions, physical surroundings and demands, aptitudes, temperament, educational requirements, employment outlook, earnings, and places of employment.

★7013★
Bagger, Grocery
Careers, Inc.
PO Box 135
Largo, FL 34649-0135   Phone: (813)584-7333

1990. Two-page job guide card describing duties, working conditions, personal qualifications, training, earnings and hours, employment outlook, places of employment, related careers and where to write for more information.

★7014★
Bricklayer Helper
Careers, Inc.
PO Box 135
Largo, FL 34649-0135   Phone: (813)584-7333

1989. Two-page job guide card describing duties, working conditions, personal qualifications, training, earnings and hours, employment outlook, places of employment, related careers and where to write for more information.

★7015★
"Bricklayer Helper" in *Occu-Facts: Information on 565 Careers in Outline Form* (p. 20.5)
Careers, Inc.
P.O. Box 135
1211 Tenth St., S.W.
Largo, FL 33640   Phone: (813)584-7333

Elizabeth Handville. Biennial, 1989-90 edition. Each one-page occupational profile describes duties, working conditions, physical surroundings and demands, aptitudes, temperament, educational requirements, employment outlook, earnings, and places of employment.

★7016★
Car Wash Attendants
Chronicle Guidance Publications, Inc.
PO Box 1190
Moravia, NY 13118-1190   Phone: (315)497-0330

1989. This career brief describes the nature of the work, working conditions, hours and earnings, education and training, licensure, certification, unions, personal qualifications, social and psychological factors, employment outlook, entry methods, advancement, and related occupations. **Toll-free/Additional Phone Number(s):** 800-622-7284.

★7017★
Car Wash Operator
Vocational Biographies, Inc.
PO Box 31, Dept. VF10
Sauk Centre, MN 56378   Phone: (612)352-6516

1990. This pamphlet profiles a person working in the job. Includes information about job duties, working conditions, places of employment, educational preparation, labor market outlook, and salaries. **Toll-free/Additional Phone Number(s):** 800-255-0752.

★7018★
Career Insights
RMI Media Productions, Inc.
2807 West 47th St.
Shawnee Mission, KS 66205   Phone: (913)262-3974

Videocassette series. 1987. This videotape series describes 50 occupations, including skill requirements and interviews with people employed in these fields. Occupations include: flight service, air transportation/ground services, data processing, carpentry, clerk in banking/insurance/business, cosmetic personal grooming, firefighting, roofing, material handling, photographic processing, plumbing, secretarial services, tool and die operations.

Handlers, Equipment Cleaners, Helpers, and Laborers ★7029★

★7019★
Carpenter Helper
Careers, Inc.
PO Box 135
Largo, FL 34649-0135   Phone: (813)584-7333
1988. Two-page job guide card describing duties, working conditions, personal qualifications, training, earnings and hours, employment outlook, places of employment, related careers and where to write for more information.

★7020★
"Carpenter Helper" in *Occu-Facts: Information on 565 Careers in Outline Form* (p. 20.6)
Careers, Inc.
P.O. Box 135
1211 Tenth St., S.W.
Largo, FL 33640   Phone: (813)584-7333
Elizabeth Handville. Biennial, 1989-90 edition. Each one-page occupational profile describes duties, working conditions, physical surroundings and demands, aptitudes, temperament, educational requirements, employment outlook, earnings, and places of employment.

★7021★
"Construction Electrician Helper" in *Occu-Facts: Information on 565 Careers in Outline Form* (p. 20.7)
Careers, Inc.
P.O. Box 135
1211 Tenth St., S.W.
Largo, FL 33640   Phone: (813)584-7333
Elizabeth Handville. Biennial, 1989-90 edition. Each one-page occupational profile describes duties, working conditions, physical surroundings and demands, aptitudes, temperament, educational requirements, employment outlook, earnings, and places of employment.

★7022★
Construction Helpers
Careers, Inc.
PO Box 135
Largo, FL 34649-0135   Phone: (813)584-7333
1992. Eight-page brief offering the definition, history, duties, working conditions, personal qualifications, educational requirements, earnings, hours, employment outlook, advancement possibilities, and related occupations.

★7023★
"Construction Helpers" in *Occu-Facts: Information on 565 Careers in Outline Form* (p. 20.4)
Careers, Inc.
P.O. Box 135
1211 Tenth St., S.W.
Largo, FL 33640   Phone: (813)584-7333
Elizabeth Handville. Biennial, 1989-90 edition. Each one-page occupational profile describes duties, working conditions, physical surroundings and demands, aptitudes, temperament, educational requirements, employment outlook, earnings, and places of employment.

★7024★
"Construction Laborer" in *Construction*, Volume 4 of *Career Information Center* (pp. 49-51)
Glencoe/Macmillan
15319 Chatsworth St.
Mission Hills, CA 91345   Phone: (818)898-1391
Richard Lidz and Dale Anderson, editorial directors. Fourth edition, 1990. For 600 occupations, describes job duties, entry-level requirements, education and training needed, advancement possibilities, employment outlook, earnings and benefits. The set is divided into 12 volumes. Each volume includes jobs related under a broad career field. Volume 13 is the index. **Facsimile Number:** 818-365-5489.

★7025★
Construction Laborers
Chronicle Guidance Publications, Inc.
PO Box 1190
Moravia, NY 13118-1190   Phone: (315)497-0330
1989. This career brief describes the nature of the work, working conditions, hours and earnings, education and training, licensure, certification, unions, personal qualifications, social and psychological factors, employment outlook, entry methods, advancement, and related occupations. **Toll-free/Additional Phone Number(s):** 800-622-7284.

★7026★
Construction Machine Operators
Chronicle Guidance Publications, Inc.
PO Box 1190
Moravia, NY 13118-1190   Phone: (315)497-0330
1988. This career brief describes the nature of the work, working conditions, hours and earnings, education and training, licensure, certification, unions, personal qualifications, social and psychological factors, employment outlook, entry methods, advancement, and related occupations. **Toll-free/Additional Phone Number(s):** 800-622-7284.

★7027★
"Display Worker Helper" in *Occu-Facts: Information on 565 Careers in Outline Form* (p. 8.8)
Careers, Inc.
P.O. Box 135
1211 Tenth St., S.W.
Largo, FL 33640   Phone: (813)584-7333
Elizabeth Handville. Biennial, 1989-90 edition. Each one-page occupational profile describes duties, working conditions, physical surroundings and demands, aptitudes, temperament, educational requirements, employment outlook, earnings, and places of employment.

★7028★
Divers
Chronicle Guidance Publications, Inc.
PO Box 1190
Moravia, NY 13118-1190   Phone: (315)497-0330
1990. This career brief describes the nature of the work, working conditions, hours and earnings, education and training, licensure, certification, unions, personal qualifications, social and psychological factors, employment outlook, entry methods, advancement, and related occupations. **Toll-free/Additional Phone Number(s):** 800-622-7284.

★7029★
"Dock Worker" in *Transportation*, Volume 12 of *Career Information Center* (pp. 48-50)
Glencoe/Macmillan
15319 Chatsworth St.
Mission Hills, CA 91345   Phone: (818)898-1391
Richard Lidz and Dale Anderson, editorial directors. Fourth edition, 1990. For 600 occupations, describes job duties, entry-level requirements, education and training needed, advancement possibilities, employment outlook, earnings and benefits. The set is divided into 12 volumes. Each volume includes jobs related under a broad career field. Volume 13 is the index. **Facsimile Number:** 818-365-5489.

★7030★
"Dockworker" in *Transportation* (pp. 18-19)
Franklin Watts, Inc.
387 Park Avenue, S.
New York, NY 10016 Phone: (212)686-7070
Marjorie Rittenberg Schulz. 1990. Surveys the transportation industry including air, water, and rail services. Provides job description, training, salary, and employment outlook. Offers job hunting advice.

★7031★
Electrician Helper, Construction
Careers, Inc.
PO Box 135
Largo, FL 34649-0135 Phone: (813)584-7333
1989. Two-page job guide card describing duties, working conditions, personal qualifications, training, earnings and hours, employment outlook, places of employment, related careers and where to write for more information.

★7032★
Electrical Equipment Manufacturing Workers
Chronicle Guidance Publications, Inc.
PO Box 1190
Moravia, NY 13118-1190 Phone: (315)497-0330
1990. This career brief describes the nature of the work, working conditions, hours and earnings, education and training, licensure, certification, unions, personal qualifications, social and psychological factors, employment outlook, entry methods, advancement, and related occupations. **Toll-free/Additional Phone Number(s):** 800-622-7284.

★7033★
"Furnace Cleaner" in *Occu-Facts: Information on 565 Careers in Outline Form* (p. 20.21)
Careers, Inc.
P.O. Box 135
1211 Tenth St., S.W.
Largo, FL 33640 Phone: (813)584-7333
Elizabeth Handville. Biennial, 1989-90 edition. Each one-page occupational profile describes duties, working conditions, physical surroundings and demands, aptitudes, temperament, educational requirements, employment outlook, earnings, and places of employment.

★7034★
Garbage Collector
Careers, Inc.
PO Box 135
Largo, FL 34649-0135 Phone: (813)584-7333
1990. Two-page job guide card describing duties, working conditions, personal qualifications, training, earnings and hours, employment outlook, places of employment, related careers and where to write for more information.

★7035★
"Gasoline Service Station Attendants" in Volume 3 of *The Encyclopedia of Careers and Vocational Guidance* (pp. 743-746)
J.G. Ferguson Publishing Co.
200 W. Monroe
Chicago, IL 60606 Phone: (312)580-5480
William E. Hopke, editor-in-chief. Eighth edition, 1990. Four-volume set that profiles 500 occupations and describes job trends in 76 industries. Includes career description, educational requirements, history of the job, methods of entry, advancement, employment outlook, earnings, working conditions, social and psychological factors, and sources of additional information.

★7036★
"Grocery Bagger" in *Occu-Facts: Information on 565 Careers in Outline Form* (p. 20.13)
Careers, Inc.
P.O. Box 135
1211 Tenth St., S.W.
Largo, FL 33640 Phone: (813)584-7333
Elizabeth Handville. Biennial, 1989-90 edition. Each one-page occupational profile describes duties, working conditions, physical surroundings and demands, aptitudes, temperament, educational requirements, employment outlook, earnings, and places of employment.

★7037★
"Hand Packager" in *Occu-Facts: Information on 565 Careers in Outline Form* (p. 20.22)
Careers, Inc.
P.O. Box 135
1211 Tenth St., S.W.
Largo, FL 33640 Phone: (813)584-7333
Elizabeth Handville. Biennial, 1989-90 edition. Each one-page occupational profile describes duties, working conditions, physical surroundings and demands, aptitudes, temperament, educational requirements, employment outlook, earnings, and places of employment.

★7038★
Lead Parking Attendant
Vocational Biographies, Inc.
PO Box 31, Dept. VF10
Sauk Centre, MN 56378 Phone: (612)352-6516
1989. This pamphlet profiles a person working in the job. Includes information about job duties, working conditions, places of employment, educational preparation, labor market outlook, and salaries. **Toll-free/Additional Phone Number(s):** 800-255-0752.

★7039★
Material Handler
Careers, Inc.
PO Box 135
Largo, FL 34649-0135 Phone: (813)584-7333
1988. Two-page job guide card describing duties, working conditions, personal qualifications, training, earnings and hours, employment outlook, places of employment, related careers and where to write for more information.

★7040★
"Material Handler" in *Occu-Facts: Information on 565 Careers in Outline Form* (p. 20.15)
Careers, Inc.
P.O. Box 135
1211 Tenth St., S.W.
Largo, FL 33640 Phone: (813)584-7333
Elizabeth Handville. Biennial, 1989-90 edition. Each one-page occupational profile describes duties, working conditions, physical surroundings and demands, aptitudes, temperament, educational requirements, employment outlook, earnings, and places of employment.

★7041★
Material Handlers
Chronicle Guidance Publications, Inc.
PO Box 1190
Moravia, NY 13118-1190 Phone: (315)497-0330
1989. This career brief describes the nature of the work, working conditions, hours and earnings, education and training, licensure, certification, unions, personal qualifications, social and psychological factors, employment outlook, entry methods,

Handlers, Equipment Cleaners, Helpers, and Laborers ★7052★

advancement, and related occupations. **Toll-free/Additional Phone Number(s):** 800-622-7284.

★7042★
Packager, Hand
Careers, Inc.
PO Box 135
Largo, FL 34649-0135   Phone: (813)584-7333
1991. Two-page job guide card describing duties, working conditions, personal qualifications, training, earnings and hours, employment outlook, places of employment, related careers and where to write for more information.

★7043★
Parking Attendants
Chronicle Guidance Publications, Inc.
PO Box 1190
Moravia, NY 13118-1190   Phone: (315)497-0330
1990. This career brief describes the nature of the work, working conditions, hours and earnings, education and training, licensure, certification, unions, personal qualifications, social and psychological factors, employment outlook, entry methods, advancement, and related occupations. **Toll-free/Additional Phone Number(s):** 800-622-7284.

★7044★
Plasterer Helper
Careers, Inc.
PO Box 135
Largo, FL 34649-0135   Phone: (813)584-7333
1990. Two-page job guide card describing duties, working conditions, personal qualifications, training, earnings and hours, employment outlook, places of employment, related careers and where to write for more information.

★7045★
"Plasterer Helper" in *Occu-Facts: Information on 565 Careers in Outline Form* (p. 20.8)
Careers, Inc.
P.O. Box 135
1211 Tenth St., S.W.
Largo, FL 33640   Phone: (813)584-7333
Elizabeth Handville. Biennial, 1989-90 edition. Each one-page occupational profile describes duties, working conditions, physical surroundings and demands, aptitudes, temperament, educational requirements, employment outlook, earnings, and places of employment.

★7046★
Plumber Helper
Careers, Inc.
PO Box 135
Largo, FL 34649-0135   Phone: (813)584-7333
1988. Two-page job guide card describing duties, working conditions, personal qualifications, training, earnings and hours, employment outlook, places of employment, related careers and where to write for more information.

★7047★
"Plumber Helper" in *Occu-Facts: Information on 565 Careers in Outline Form* (p. 20.9)
Careers, Inc.
P.O. Box 135
1211 Tenth St., S.W.
Largo, FL 33640   Phone: (813)584-7333
Elizabeth Handville. Biennial, 1989-90 edition. Each one-page occupational profile describes duties, working conditions, physical surroundings and demands, aptitudes, temperament, educational requirements, employment outlook, earnings, and places of employment.

★7048★
Refuse Collectors
Chronicle Guidance Publications, Inc.
PO Box 1190
Moravia, NY 13118-1190   Phone: (315)497-0330
1987. This career brief describes the nature of the work, working conditions, hours and earnings, education and training, licensure, certification, unions, personal qualifications, social and psychological factors, employment outlook, entry methods, advancement, and related occupations. **Toll-free/Additional Phone Number(s):** 800-622-7284.

★7049★
"Refuse Collectors" in Volume 5 of *Career Discovery Encyclopedia* (pp. 142-143)
J.G. Ferguson Publishing Co.
200 W. Monroe
Chicago, IL 60606   Phone: (312)580-5480
E. Russell Primm, editor-in-chief. 1990. Contains two-page articles on 504 occupations. Each article describes job duties, earnings, and educational and training requirements.

★7050★
"Refuse Collectors" in Volume 3 of *The Encyclopedia of Careers and Vocational Guidance* (pp. 770-772)
J.G. Ferguson Publishing Co.
200 W. Monroe
Chicago, IL 60606   Phone: (312)580-5480
William E. Hopke, editor-in-chief. Eighth edition, 1990. Four-volume set that profiles 500 occupations and describes job trends in 76 industries. Includes career description, educational requirements, history of the job, methods of entry, advancement, employment outlook, earnings, working conditions, social and psychological factors, and sources of additional information.

★7051★
"Refuse Worker" in *Public and Community Services,* Volume 11 of *Career Information Center* (pp. 62-64)
Glencoe/Macmillan
15319 Chatsworth St.
Mission Hills, CA 91345   Phone: (818)898-1391
Richard Lidz and Dale Anderson, editorial directors. Fourth edition, 1990. For 600 occupations, describes job duties, entry-level requirements, education and training needed, advancement possibilities, employment outlook, earnings and benefits. The set is divided into 12 volumes. Each volume includes jobs related under a broad career field. Volume 13 is the index. **Facsimile Number:** 818-365-5489.

★7052★
Roofer Helper
Careers, Inc.
PO Box 135
Largo, FL 34649-0135   Phone: (813)584-7333
1991. Two-page job guide card describing duties, working conditions, personal qualifications, training, earnings and hours, employment outlook, places of employment, related careers and where to write for more information.

★7053★
"Roofer Helper" in *Occu-Facts: Information on 565 Careers in Outline Form* (p. 20.11)
Careers, Inc.
P.O. Box 135
1211 Tenth St., S.W.
Largo, FL 33640　　　　　　　　Phone: (813)584-7333
Elizabeth Handville. Biennial, 1989-90 edition. Each one-page occupational profile describes duties, working conditions, physical surroundings and demands, aptitudes, temperament, educational requirements, employment outlook, earnings, and places of employment.

★7054★
"Sanitation Workers" in *The American Almanac of Jobs and Salaries* (pp. 102-103)
Avon Books
105 Madison Avenue
New York, NY 10016　　　　　　Phone: (212)481-5600
John Wright and Edward J. Dwyer. Revised and updated, 1990. A comprehensive guide to the wages of hundreds of occupations in a wide variety of industries and organizations.

★7055★
Service Station Attendants
Chronicle Guidance Publications, Inc.
PO Box 1190
Moravia, NY 13118-1190　　　　Phone: (315)497-0330
1989. This career brief describes the nature of the work, working conditions, hours and earnings, education and training, licensure, certification, unions, personal qualifications, social and psychological factors, employment outlook, entry methods, advancement, and related occupations. **Toll-free/Additional Phone Number(s):** 800-622-7284.

★7056★
"Service Station Attendants" in *Opportunities in Automotive Service Careers* (pp. 25-30)
National Textbook Co.
4255 W. Touhy Ave.
Lincolnwood, IL 60646　　　　　Phone: (312)679-5500
Robert M. Weber. 1989. Describes the work of the automobile mechanic and related occupations such as service station attendant and automobile body repairer. Covers working conditions, places of employment, qualifications, training, apprenticeships, certification, advancement opportunities, employment outlook, tools needed, and earnings.

★7057★
"Service Station Attendants" in Volume 6 of *Career Discovery Encyclopedia* (pp. 20-21)
J.G. Ferguson Publishing Co.
200 W. Monroe
Chicago, IL 60606　　　　　　　Phone: (312)580-5480
E. Russell Primm, editor-in-chief. 1990. Contains two-page articles on 504 occupations. Each article describes job duties, earnings, and educational and training requirements.

★7058★
Sheet Metal Worker Helper
Careers, Inc.
PO Box 135
Largo, FL 34649-0135　　　　　Phone: (813)584-7333
1989. Two-page job guide card describing duties, working conditions, personal qualifications, training, earnings and hours, employment outlook, places of employment, related careers and where to write for more information.

★7059★
"Sheet Metal Worker Helper" in *Occu-Facts: Information on 565 Careers in Outline Form* (p. 20.12)
Careers, Inc.
P.O. Box 135
1211 Tenth St., S.W.
Largo, FL 33640　　　　　　　　Phone: (813)584-7333
Elizabeth Handville. Biennial, 1989-90 edition. Each one-page occupational profile describes duties, working conditions, physical surroundings and demands, aptitudes, temperament, educational requirements, employment outlook, earnings, and places of employment.

★7060★
"Stevedores" in Volume 6 of *Career Discovery Encyclopedia* (pp. 64-65)
J.G. Ferguson Publishing Co.
200 W. Monroe
Chicago, IL 60606　　　　　　　Phone: (312)580-5480
E. Russell Primm, editor-in-chief. 1990. Contains two-page articles on 504 occupations. Each article describes job duties, earnings, and educational and training requirements.

★7061★
"Stevedoring Occupations" in Volume 3 of *The Encyclopedia of Careers and Vocational Guidance* (pp. 783-786)
J.G. Ferguson Publishing Co.
200 W. Monroe
Chicago, IL 60606　　　　　　　Phone: (312)580-5480
William E. Hopke, editor-in-chief. Eighth edition, 1990. Four-volume set that profiles 500 occupations and describes job trends in 76 industries. Includes career description, educational requirements, history of the job, methods of entry, advancement, employment outlook, earnings, working conditions, social and psychological factors, and sources of additional information.

★7062★
"Surveyor Helpers" in *Occu-Facts: Information on 565 Careers in Outline Form* (p. 20.10)
Careers, Inc.
P.O. Box 135
1211 Tenth St., S.W.
Largo, FL 33640　　　　　　　　Phone: (813)584-7333
Elizabeth Handville. Biennial, 1989-90 edition. Each one-page occupational profile describes duties, working conditions, physical surroundings and demands, aptitudes, temperament, educational requirements, employment outlook, earnings, and places of employment.

★7063★
"Surveyor's Helper" in *Construction*, Volume 4 of *Career Information Center* (pp. 87-88)
Glencoe/Macmillan
15319 Chatsworth St.
Mission Hills, CA 91345　　　　Phone: (818)898-1391
Richard Lidz and Dale Anderson, editorial directors. Fourth edition, 1990. For 600 occupations, describes job duties, entry-level requirements, education and training needed, advancement possibilities, employment outlook, earnings and benefits. The set is divided into 12 volumes. Each volume includes jobs related under a broad career field. Volume 13 is the index. **Facsimile Number:** 818-365-5489.

Handlers, Equipment Cleaners, Helpers, and Laborers

Associations

★7064★
International Brotherhood of Teamsters, Chauffeurs, Warehousemen and Helpers of America (IBT)
25 Louisiana Ave., NW
Washington, DC 20001   Phone: (202)624-6800
Membership: Formed by merger of Team Drivers International Union and Teamsters National Union. **Purpose:** Maintains DRIVE Political Action committee; maintains 30,000 volume library.

★7065★
Laborers' International Union of North America (LIUNA)
905 16th St. NW
Washington, DC 20006   Phone: (202)737-8320
Membership: AFL-CIO. **Publications:** *The Laborer*, bimonthly. • *LIUNA - Leadership News*, 10/year. **Facsimile Number:** (202)737-2754.

Test Guides

★7066★
Cleaner-Helper
National Learning Corp.
212 Michael Dr.
Syosset, NY 11791   Phone: (516)921-8888
Jack Rudman. Part of the Career Examination Series No. 1. All examination guides in this series contain questions with answers. **Facsimile Number:** (516)921-8743. **Toll-free/Additional Phone Number(s):** 800-645-6337.

★7067★
Foreman of Laborers
National Learning Corp.
212 Michael Dr.
Syosset, NY 11791   Phone: (516)921-8888
Jack Rudman. Part of the Career Examination Series No. 1. All examination guides in this series contain questions with answers. **Facsimile Number:** (516)921-8743. **Toll-free/Additional Phone Number(s):** 800-645-6337.

★7068★
Stockman
National Learning Corp.
212 Michael Dr.
Syosset, NY 11791   Phone: (516)921-8888
Jack Rudman. Part of the Career Examination Series No. 1. All examination guides in this series contain questions with answers. **Facsimile Number:** (516)921-8743. **Toll-free/Additional Phone Number(s):** 800-645-6337.

★7069★
Warehouseman
National Learning Corp.
212 Michael Dr.
Syosset, NY 11791   Phone: (516)921-8888
Jack Rudman. Part of the Career Examination Series No. 1. All examination guides in this series contain questions with answers. **Facsimile Number:** (516)921-8743. **Toll-free/Additional Phone Number(s):** 800-645-6337.

Awards, Scholarships, Grants, and Fellowships

★7070★
Driver of the Year Award
American Trucking Associations
c/o Mona B. Heath, Information Center
2200 Mill Rd.
Alexandria, VA 22314   Phone: (703)838-1745
To recognize the best safety record among truck drivers of the United States and to encourage improved driving performance and a greater appreciation for highway safety. A Driver of the Year pin, a trophy and a certificate are awarded annually. Established in 1947.

★7071★
Top Job Award
Concrete Sawing and Drilling Association
c/o Edward R. Thorn, Executive Director
6077 Roswell Rd., N.E., Ste. 205
Atlanta, GA 30328   Phone: (404)257-1177
To recognize excellence in sawing and drilling of concrete and to encourage professional development in diamond sawing and drilling. Members of the Association are eligible. A plaque is awarded annually. Established in 1975 by Les Kuzmick.

Periodicals

★7072★
The Laborer
Laborers' International Union of North America (LIUNA)
905 16th St. NW
Washington, DC 20006   Phone: (202)737-8320
Bimonthly.

★7073★
LIUNA - Leadership News
Laborers' International Union of North America (LIUNA)
905 16th St. NW
Washington, DC 20006   Phone: (202)737-8320
10/year. Newsletter.

Meetings and Conventions

★7074★
International Brotherhood of Teamsters, Chauffeurs, Warehousemen and Helpers of America (IBT)
25 Louisiana Ave., NW
Washington, DC 20001   Phone: (202)624-6800
Frequency: Quinquennial - next held in 1996.

★7075★
Laborers' International Union of North America (LIUNA)
905 16th St. NW
Washington, DC 20006   Phone: (202)737-8320
Frequency: Quinquennial - next held in 1996. **Facsimile Number:** (202)737-2754.

Job Opportunities in the Armed Forces

Job Opportunities in the Armed Forces

Military service provides educational opportunities and work experience in literally thousands of occupations. There are more than 2,000 basic and advanced military occupational specialties for enlisted personnel and 1,600 for officers. Over 75 percent of these occupational specialties have civilian counterparts. Those in electrical and mechanical equipment repair occupations maintain aircraft, motor vehicles, and ships. Officers manage the maintenance of aircraft, missiles, conventional and nuclear-powered ships, trucks, earth-moving equipment, and other vehicles. Enlisted personnel serve as mechanics, engine men, and boiler technicians. Infantry, gun crews, and seamanship specialists include both officers and enlisted personnel. Officers plan and direct military operations, oversee security activities, and serve as combat troop leaders. Enlisted personnel serve as infantrymen, gunners' mates, weapons specialists, armored vehicle operators, demolition experts, artillery crew, rocket specialists, special operations forces, and combat engineers. Functional support and administrative jobs in military service also require the support of officers and enlistees. Officers in this category work as directors, executives, adjutants, administrative officers, personnel managers, training administrators, budget officers, finance officers, accountants, hospital administrators, inspectors, computer systems managers, and lawyers. Enlisted personnel in this category work as accounting clerks, payroll clerks, personnel clerks, computer programmers, computer operators, electric accounting machine operators, chaplain assistants, counseling aides, typists, stenographers, storekeepers, and other clerks. Military personnel assigned to electronic equipment repair occupations are responsible for maintaining and repairing many different types of equipment. Officers manage those who repair avionic, communications, radar, and air traffic control equipment. Enlisted personnel repair radio, navigation, and flight control equipment as well as telephone, teletype, and data processing equipment. Communications and intelligence specialists in the military have civilian scientific and engineering counterparts. Officers serve as cryptologists, information analysts, science and engineering researchers, and in related intelligence occupations. Enlisted personnel work as mapping technicians, computer programmers, air traffic controllers, interpreters and translators, and radio and radar operators. Military personnel in service and supply occupations handle food service, security, and personal services and supply. Officers work as logistics officers, supply managers, transportation and traffic managers, and procurement officers. Enlisted personnel include military police, correction specialists, detectives, firefighters, and food preparation and other service workers. Military medical and dental occupations all have civilian counterparts. Holding the rank of medical officer are physicians, dentists, optometrists, nurses, therapists, veterinarians, pharmacists, and others in health diagnosing and treating occupations. Enlisted personnel are trained to work as medical laboratory technologists and technicians, radiologic technologists, emergency medical technicians, dental assistants, pharmaceutical assistants, sanitation specialists, and veterinary assistants. Military personnel assigned to craft occupations are skilled craft workers. Officers serve as civil engineers and architects and manage the work of enlisted personnel who work as carpenters, construction equipment operators, metalworkers, machinists, plumbers, welders, electricians, and heating and air-conditioning specialists. They also work as dental laboratory technicians, opticians, and shipfitters. Other technical and allied specialty occupations also require the joint efforts of officers and enlisted personnel. Officers in this field work as television and motion picture directors, public affairs officers, and band directors. Enlisted personnel are trained to work as musicians, photographers, graphic designers and illustrators, writers and editors, and motion picture camera operators. Of the nearly 2.2 million persons on active duty in the Armed Forces, 31 percent are in the Army, 21 percent in the Air Force, 21 percent in the Navy, 9 percent in the Marine Corps, and 2 percent in the Coast Guard. About 10 percent of those on active duty are women.

$alaries

Military basic pay by grade for active duty personnel with less than two years of service follows:

Enlisted personnel E-1 with less than 4 months of service	$646.20/month
Enlisted personnel E-1	$699.00/month
Enlisted personnel E-2	$783.60/month
Enlisted personnel E-3	$814.20/month
Enlisted personnel E-4	$864.30/month
Warrant officers W-1	$1,195.20/month
Warrant officers W-2	$1,434.30/month
Commissioned officers O-1	$1,338.90/month
Commissioned officers O-2	$1,542.30/month
Commissioned officers O-3	$1,768.80/month
Commisioned officers O-4	$1,903.50/month

Employment Outlook

Growth rate until the year 2000: Faster than average. However, if the Armed Forces are reduced, fewer job opportunities will be available.

Job Opportunities in the Armed Forces

Career Guides

★7076★
Air Force Academy: Commitment to Excellence
Finley-Holiday Film Corporation
Post Office Box 619
Whittier, CA 90608   Phone: (213)945-3325
Videocassette. 19??. 30 mins. Prospective officer candidates for the U.S. Air Force Academy in Colorado Springs will be interested in this informative video, which explores the military college and chronicles the entire academic careers of the airmen and airwomen.

★7077★
Air Force Career Opportunities
Careers, Inc.
PO Box 135
Largo, FL 34649-0135   Phone: (813)584-7333
1988. Eight-page brief offering the definition, history, duties, working conditions, personal qualifications, educational requirements, earnings, hours, employment outlook, advancement possibilities, and related occupations.

★7078★
"Air Force Nurse Corps" in *Opportunities in Nursing Careers* (pp. 112-113)
National Textbook Co.
4255 W. Touhy Ave.
Lincolnwood, IL 60646   Phone: (312)679-5500
Keville Frederickson. 1989. Covers the history and scope of nursing, educational preparation, job hunting, types and places of employment, and nursing organizations. The appendices list state nurses' associations and state boards of nursing.

★7079★
"Air Force Nurse" in *120 Careers in the Health Care Field* (p. 265)
U.S. Directory Service, Publishers
PO Box 68-1700
655 N.W. 128th St.
Miami, FL 33168   Phone: (305)769-1700
Stanley Alperin. Second edition, 1989. Each occupational profile covers job functions and responsibilities, work locations, training requirements, certification, and salaries. Lists community colleges, universities, vocational-technical schools, and other educational institutions that provide accredited training programs.

★7080★
America at Its Best: Opportunities in the National Guard
Rosen Publishing Group, Inc.
29 E. 21st St.
New York, NY 10010   Phone: (212)777-3017
Robert F. Collins. 1989. Describes the purpose of the national guard, enlistment qualifications and procedures, basic training, pay, and daily routines. The appendices list career fields and federal and state military installations.

★7081★
"Armed Forces" in *Opportunities in Business Communication Careers* (pp. 38-39)
National Textbook Co.
4255 W. Touhy Ave.
Lincolnwood, IL 60646   Phone: (312)679-5500
Robert L. Deen. 1987. Describes what business communicators do, the skills they need, and where they work. Covers educational preparation, salaries, entry into the profession, and career paths. Offers job hunting advice and information about freelancing.

★7082★
"Armed Forces" in *Opportunities in Pharmacy Careers* (pp. 115-117)
National Textbook Co.
4255 W. Touhy Ave.
Lincolnwood, IL 60646   Phone: (312)679-5500
Fred B. Gable. 1990. Surveys the wide variety of career options available to pharmacists including community, industrial, and public pharmacy. Covers job duties, licensure, and salaries. Provides in-depth information about pharmaceutical education including high school and college preparation, and pharmacy school admissions and curriculum.

★7083★
"Armed Forces" in *Opportunities in Transportation Careers* (pp. 127-129)
National Textbook Co.
4255 W. Touhy Ave.
Lincolnwood, IL 60646   Phone: (312)679-5500
Adrian A. Paradis. 1988. Describes transportation and related employment in driving occupations, the airlines, merchant marine, and travel services. Covers employment outlook, educational and training requirements, wages, and the work itself, and advantages and disadvantages of transportation careers. Offers job hunting advice.

★7084★
"Armed Forces" in *Opportunities in Vocational and Technical Careers* (pp. 37-41)
National Textbook Co.
4255 W. Touhy Ave.
Lincolnwood, IL 60646   Phone: (312)679-5500
Adrian A. Paradis. 1987. Describes careers which can be prepared for by attending a private vocational or proprietary school—office employee, sales worker, service worker, health services, mechanic, craftworker, and technician. Covers employment outlook, job duties, and salaries. Offers career planning advice.

★7085★
Armed Forces Careers
Chronicle Guidance Publications, Inc.
PO Box 1190
Moravia, NY 13118-1190   Phone: (315)497-0330
1988. This career brief describes the nature of the work, working conditions, hours and earnings, education and training, licensure, certification, unions, personal qualifications, social and psychological factors, employment outlook, entry methods, advancement, and related occupations. **Toll-free/Additional Phone Number(s):** 800-622-7284.

★7086★
"Armed Forces Training" in *Careers With Robots* (pp. 111-115)
Facts on File, Inc.
460 Park Avenue, S.
New York, NY 10016   Phone: (212)683-2244
Texe W. Marrs. 1988. Describes jobs developing from a boom in robotics. Offers career planning advice and covers educational and training requirements, transferable skills, and industries using robots. Includes a state-by-state listing of major robotics employers, and additional sources of information.

★7087★
"Armed Services Careers" in *Public and Community Services*, Volume 11 of *Career Information Center* (pp. 37-39)
Glencoe/Macmillan
15319 Chatsworth St.
Mission Hills, CA 91345   Phone: (818)898-1391
Richard Lidz and Dale Anderson, editorial directors. Fourth edition, 1990. For 600 occupations, describes job duties, entry-level requirements, education and training needed, advancement possibilities, employment outlook, earnings and benefits. The set is divided into 12 volumes. Each volume includes jobs related under a broad career field. Volume 13 is the index. **Facsimile Number:** 818-365-5489.

★7088★
Army Career Opportunities
Careers, Inc.
PO Box 135
Largo, FL 34649-0135   Phone: (813)584-7333
1988. Eight-page brief offering the definition, history, duties, working conditions, personal qualifications, educational requirements, earnings, hours, employment outlook, advancement possibilities, and related occupations.

★7089★
"Army Nurse Corps" in *Opportunities in Nursing Careers* (pp. 110-111)
National Textbook Co.
4255 W. Touhy Ave.
Lincolnwood, IL 60646   Phone: (312)679-5500
Keville Frederickson. 1989. Covers the history and scope of nursing, educational preparation, job hunting, types and places of employment, and nursing organizations. The appendices list state nurses' associations and state boards of nursing.

★7090★
"Army Nurse" in *120 Careers in the Health Care Field* (p. 265)
U.S. Directory Service, Publishers
PO Box 68-1700
655 N.W. 128th St.
Miami, FL 33168   Phone: (305)769-1700
Stanley Alperin. Second edition, 1989. Each occupational profile covers job functions and responsibilities, work locations, training requirements, certification, and salaries. Lists community colleges, universities, vocational-technical schools, and other educational institutions that provide accredited training programs.

★7091★
Basic Training: What to Expect and How to Prepare
Rosen Publishing Group, Inc.
29 E. 21st St.
New York, NY 10010   Phone: (212)777-3017
Robert F. Collins. 1988. Describes basic training in the Army, Navy, Air Force, Marines and Coast Guard. Includes information on enlistment and initial training, processing, and terminology used in each service.

★7092★
Citizen Soldier: Opportunities in the Reserves
Rosen Publishing Group, Inc.
29 E. 21st St.
New York, NY 10010   Phone: (212)777-3017
Carl White. 1990. Describes the function of the armed forces reserve units, pay, retirement income, basic and specialty training, and ROTC programs.

★7093★
"Coast Guard" in *Opportunities in Marine and Maritime Careers* (pp. 97-100)
National Textbook Co.
4255 W. Touhy Ave.
Lincolnwood, IL 60646   Phone: (312)679-5500
William Ray Heitzmann. 1988. Includes careers related by their proximity to water including cruise ships, oceanography, marine sciences, fishing, commercial diving, maritime transportation, shipbuilding, Navy, and Coast Guard. Covers qualifications, job outlook, job duties, educational preparation, and training. Lists associations and schools.

★7094★
Coast Guard Career Opportunities
Careers, Inc.
PO Box 135
Largo, FL 34649-0135   Phone: (813)584-7333
1991. Eight-page brief offering the definition, history, duties, working conditions, personal qualifications, educational requirements, earnings, hours, employment outlook, advancement possibilities, and related occupations.

Job Opportunities in the Armed Forces

★7095★
Coping With Sexism in the Military
Rosen Publishing Group, Inc.
29 E. 21st St.
New York, NY 10010　　　　　Phone: (212)777-3017
Mary V. Stremlow. 1990. Covers the history of women's participation in the armed forces. Describes and defines sexism and sexual harassment and offers advice on how to cope. Discusses the pros and cons of dress, living quarters, physical fitness standards, marriage, pregnancy, and promotional opportunities for women in the armed forces.

★7096★
Exploring Careers in the Military Services
Rosen Publishing Group, Inc.
29 E. 21st St.
New York, NY 10010　　　　　Phone: (212)777-3017
Robert W. Macdonald. 1987. Describes the role of the military services, how to begin a military career, and taking the armed services vocational aptitude battery. Lists military occupations and equivalent civilian jobs. Gives information about the military service academies. A separate chapter covers each branch of the military, what they do, organization, enlistment, training, advancement and career development, and becoming an officer.

★7097★
The Men of Company 208
Centre Productions, Inc.
1800 30th St.
Suite 207
Boulder, CO 80301　　　　　Phone: (303)444-1166
Videocassette. 1986. 28 mins. This video is an informative presentation for young men and women interested or curious about enlisting in the Armed Forces.

★7098★
"Military" in ***College Board Guide to Jobs and Career Planning*** (pp. 208-210)
College Entrance Examination Board
45 Columbus Ave.
New York, NY 10023-6992　　　　　Phone: (212)713-8000
Joyce Slayton Mitchell. 1990. Career planning guide written for high school and college students. Covers 100 careers in 15 occupational groups. Provides job description, educational preparation needed, salaries, related careers, and sources of additional information. Includes information about the 90's labor market.

★7099★
"The Military" in ***Electronic Service Careers*** (pp. 88-99)
Franklin Watts, Inc.
387 Park Avenue, S.
New York, NY 10016　　　　　Phone: (212)686-7070
Robert Laurance. 1987. Discusses the work of an electronic service technician, employment outlook, places of employment, and educational preparation and training. Describes jobs with computers, consumer electronics, industrial electronics and the military.

★7100★
"Military" in ***Footsteps in the Ocean: Careers in Diving*** (pp. 115-122)
Lodestar Books
2 Park Avenue
New York, NY 10016　　　　　Phone: (212)725-1818
Denise V. Lang. 1987. Explores employment opportunities in sport and commercial diving, science and research, in the military, and police work. Describes the work and training. Lists schools. **Facsimile Number:** (212)532-6568.

★7101★
"Military" in ***International Careers: An Insider's Guide, Where to Find Them, How to Build Them*** (pp. 174-176)
Williamson Publishing Co.
185 Church Hill Rd.
Charlotte, VT 05445　　　　　Phone: (802)425-2102
David Win. 1987. Gives an overview of the international business field and its structure. Surveys employment opportunities in government, business, and nonprofit organizations. Offers job hunting advice.

★7102★
"Military Careers" in Volume 4 of ***Career Discovery Encyclopedia*** (pp. 94-95)
J.G. Ferguson Publishing Co.
200 W. Monroe
Chicago, IL 60606　　　　　Phone: (312)580-5480
E. Russell Primm, editor-in-chief. 1990. Contains two-page articles on 504 occupations. Each article describes job duties, earnings, and educational and training requirements.

★7103★
"Military Chaplain" in ***Opportunities in Religious Service Careers*** (pp. 85-87)
National Textbook Co.
4255 W. Touhy Ave.
Lincolnwood, IL 60646　　　　　Phone: (312)679-5500
John Oliver Nelson. 1988. Explores the concept of religious "calling" and offers advice about choosing a career with the clergy in the Protestant, Catholic, or Jewish religions. Surveys many religious related careers including missionary work and education. Covers educational preparation and employment outlook. Lists accredited theological schools in the United States.

★7104★
"Military Counselor" in ***Careers in Counseling and Human Development*** (pp. 102-104)
American Association for Counseling and Development
5999 Stevenson Ave.
Alexandria, VA 22304　　　　　Phone: (703)823-9800
Brooke B. Collison and Nancy J. Garfield, authors and managing editors. 1990. Surveys jobs in the human services, human development, and counseling fields. Provides an overview of ten different work settings such as private practice, schools, and public agencies. Includes information about certification, credentialing and licensure.

★7105★
"Military Fire Protection" in ***Opportunities in Fire Protection Services*** (pp. 32-33)
National Textbook Co.
4255 W. Touhy Ave.
Lincolnwood, IL 60646　　　　　Phone: (312)679-5500
Ronny J. Coleman. 1990. Explores firefighting and related jobs with not only local fire departments but also with state and federal governments and private fire departments, fire sprinkler and fire equipment manufacturing companies, and insurance companies. Covers personal qualifications, educational preparation and training, advancement possibilities, and salaries. Offers job hunting advice.

★7106★
"Military" in *Straight Talk on Careers: 80 Pros Take You Into Their Professions* (pp. 203-224)
Garrett Park Press
PO Box 190
Garrett Park, MD 20896   Phone: (301)946-2553

Mary Barbera-Hogan. 1987. Written for readers in high school and college. Contains candid interviews from professionals who discuss what their days are like and the pros and cons of their occupations.

★7107★
Military Life: the Insider's Guide
Arco/Prentice Hall Press
1 Gulf & Western Plaza
New York, NY 10023   Phone: (212)373-8500

Tod Ensign. 1990. Describes enlistment procedures, basic training, advanced skills training, daily life in the military, and foreign duty. Contains separate chapters for women, minorities, and veterans.

★7108★
"Military Nursing" in *Your Career in Nursing* (pp. 156-160)
National League for Nursing
350 Hudson St.
New York, NY 10014   Phone: (212)989-9393

Lila Anastas. Second edition, 1988. Career planning and information guide. Provides job description, educational preparation, interests, aptitudes and abilities needed, and nursing specialties. Includes an overview of the trends affecting the nursing profession. Explores the differences in diploma, associate degree, and bachelor degree nursing programs.

★7109★
"Military Science" in *College Majors and Careers: A Resource Guide for Effective Life Planning* (pp. 99-100)
Garrett Park Press
PO Box 190
Garrett Park, MD 20896   Phone: (301)946-2553

Paul Phifer. 1987. Lists 61 college majors. Includes a general definition of the field, related occupations requiring either a bachelor or associate degree, related leisure-time activities denoting personal interest in the field, skills needed, values, and personal attributes. Lists organizations.

★7110★
"Military Service" in *Exploring Careers Using Foreign Languages* (pp. 73-74)
Rosen Publishing Group, Inc.
29 E. 21st St.
New York, NY 10010   Phone: (212)777-3017

E. W. Edwards. Revised edition, 1990. Explores careers in teaching, translating, interpreting, business and finance, government, communications, and the media. Covers employment ideas, salaries, job duties, and educational preparation. Contains information on accreditation and job hunting.

★7111★
"Military Service" in Volume 1 of *The Encyclopedia of Careers and Vocational Guidance* (pp. 301-309)
J.G. Ferguson Publishing Co.
200 W. Monroe
Chicago, IL 60606   Phone: (312)580-5480

William E. Hopke, editor-in-chief. Eighth edition, 1990. Four-volume set that profiles 500 occupations and describes job trends in 76 industries. Includes career description, educational requirements, history of the job, methods of entry, advancement, employment outlook, earnings, working conditions, social and psychological factors, and sources of additional information.

★7112★
"Military Services" in *Jobs! What They Are. . .Where They Are. . .What They Pay* (pp. 247-250)
Simon & Schuster, Inc.
Simon & Schuster Bldg.
1230 Avenue of the Americas
New York, NY 10020   Phone: (212)698-7000

Robert O. Snelling and Anne M. Snelling. Revised edition, 1989. Profiles 241 occupations, describing duties and responsibilities, educational preparation, earnings, employment opportunities, training, and qualifications.

★7113★
"The Military Veterinarian" in *Opportunities in Veterinary Medicine* (pp. 107-111)
National Textbook Co.
4255 W. Touhy Ave.
Lincolnwood, IL 60646   Phone: (312)679-5500

Robert E. Swope. 1987. Discusses history, educational requirements, and employment opportunities for veterinarians in industry, government, academia, and the military.

★7114★
Navy Career Opportunities
Careers, Inc.
PO Box 135
Largo, FL 34649-0135   Phone: (813)584-7333

1988. Eight-page brief offering the definition, history, duties, working conditions, personal qualifications, educational requirements, earnings, hours, employment outlook, advancement possibilities, and related occupations.

★7115★
"Navy Military Sealift Command" in *Opportunities in Transportation Careers* (pp. 129-130)
National Textbook Co.
4255 W. Touhy Ave.
Lincolnwood, IL 60646   Phone: (312)679-5500

Adrian A. Paradis. 1988. Describes transportation and related employment in driving occupations, the airlines, merchant marine, and travel services. Covers employment outlook, educational and training requirements, wages, and the work itself, and advantages and disadvantages of transportation careers. Offers job hunting advice.

★7116★
"Navy Nurse Corps" in *Opportunities in Nursing Careers* (pp. 111-112)
National Textbook Co.
4255 W. Touhy Ave.
Lincolnwood, IL 60646   Phone: (312)679-5500

Keville Frederickson. 1989. Covers the history and scope of nursing, educational preparation, job hunting, types and places of employment, and nursing organizations. The appendices list state nurses' associations and state boards of nursing.

★7117★
"Navy Nurse" in *120 Careers in the Health Care Field* (p. 272)
U.S. Directory Service, Publishers
PO Box 68-1700
655 N.W. 128th St.
Miami, FL 33168   Phone: (305)769-1700

Stanley Alperin. Second edition, 1989. Each occupational profile covers job functions and responsibilities, work locations,

Job Opportunities in the Armed Forces ★7128★

training requirements, certification, and salaries. Lists community colleges, universities, vocational-technical schools, and other educational institutions that provide accredited training programs.

★7118★
"Officer, U.S. Armed Forces" in *VGM's Careers Encyclopedia* (pp. 315-317)
National Textbook Co.
4255 W. Touhy Ave.
Lincolnwood, IL 60646　　　　Phone: (312)679-5500
Third edition, 1991. Contains two- to five-page descriptions of 200 managerial, professional, technical, trade, and service occupations. Each profile includes job duties, places of employment, qualifications, educational preparation, training, employment potential, advancement, income, and additional sources of information.

★7119★
Opportunities in Military Careers
National Textbook Co.
4255 W. Touhy Ave.
Lincolnwood, IL 60646　　　　Phone: (312)679-5500
Adrian A. Paradis. 1989. Discusses enlistment in the Armed Services as a career choice. Covers the Army, Navy, Marine Corps, Air Force, and Coast Guard. Describes training opportunities for enlisted men and officers, and related civilian careers. Lists colleges and universities offering ROTC.

★7120★
"Opportunities in the Armed Forces" in *Occupational Outlook Handbook* (pp. 447-451)
Superintendent of Documents
U.S. Government Printing Office
Washington, DC 20402　　　　Phone: (202)783-3238
Biennial; latest edition, 1990-91. Encyclopedia of careers describing more than 250 occupations and comprising about 86 percent of all jobs in the economy. Occupations that require lengthy education or training are given the most attention. For each occupation, the handbook describes job duties, working conditions, training, educational preparation, personal qualities, advancement possibilities, job outlook, earnings, and sources of additional information.

★7121★
"Opportunities in the Armed Services" in *Opportunities in Medical Technology Careers* (pp. 71-83)
National Textbook Co.
4255 W. Touhy Ave.
Lincolnwood, IL 60646　　　　Phone: (312)679-5500
Karen R. Karni and Jane Sidney Oliver. 1990. Defines the field of medical technology and describes trends, employment outlook, salaries, job satisfaction, educational preparation, and opportunities for advancement. Lists associations and accredited educational programs.

★7122★
"Opportunities in the U.S. Armed Forces" in *Opportunities in Refrigeration and Air Conditioning Trades* (pp. 117-122)
National Textbook Co.
4255 W. Touhy Ave.
Lincolnwood, IL 60646　　　　Phone: (312)679-5500
Richard Budzik. 1989. Surveys the air conditioning and refrigeration industry. Describes jobs, educational and training requirements, small business opportunities, places of employment, and job outlook. Offers job hunting advice.

★7123★
The Profession of Arms
National Film Board of Canada
16th Floor
1251 Ave. of the Americas
New York, NY 10020-1173　　　　Phone: (212)586-5131
Videocassette. 1987. 57 mins. Career officers in the military are profiled in this film.

★7124★
Qualifying for Admission to the Service Academies: A Student's Guide
Rosen Publishing Group, Inc.
29 E. 21st St.
New York, NY 10010　　　　Phone: (212)777-3017
Robert F. Collins. 1987. Describes application procedures, academic standards, physical qualifications, and academy life for the five military service academies. Explains the characteristics needed by today's military officers.

★7125★
Soldier Girls
Churchill Films
12210 Nebraska Ave.
Los Angeles, CA 90025　　　　Phone: (213)207-6600
Videocassette. 1981. 87 mins. An account of the experiences of a group of young women newly inducted into the US Army.

★7126★
Sound Off!: American Military Women Speak Out
E.P. Dutton
2 Park Avenue
New York, NY 10016　　　　Phone: (212)725-1818
Dorothy Schneider and Carl J. Schneider. 1988. Includes interviews with 300 women in the five branches of the Armed Services. The women talk about their work, their lives, and their concerns and ideas. Also discusses career opportunities.

★7127★
Transitions: Military Pathways to Civilian Careers
Rosen Publishing Group, Inc.
29 E. 21st St.
New York, NY 10010　　　　Phone: (212)777-3017
Robert W. MacDonald. 1988. Describes how to make the best use of your military service to create a civilian career. Describes skills needed in civilian employment and compares them to skills acquired in the military. Covers career planning, job search, resume writing, and starting a small business. Lists many resources.

★7128★
"United States Navy" in *Opportunities in Marine and Maritime Careers* (pp. 85-97)
National Textbook Co.
4255 W. Touhy Ave.
Lincolnwood, IL 60646　　　　Phone: (312)679-5500
William Ray Heitzmann. 1988. Includes careers related by their proximity to water including cruise ships, oceanography, marine sciences, fishing, commercial diving, maritime transportation, shipbuilding, Navy, and Coast Guard. Covers qualifications, job outlook, job duties, educational preparation, and training. Lists associations and schools.

★7129★
"U.S. Navy Officer" in *Careers for Number Lovers* (pp. 55-57)
The Milbrook Press
2 Old Milford Rd.
Brookfield, CT 06804

Andrew Kaplan. 1991. Contains interviews with 14 people in math related careers. Provides job description, methods of entry into the field, pros and cons, educational preparation, and earnings.

Associations

★7130★
Air Force Association (AFA)
1501 Lee Hwy.
Arlington, VA 22209   Phone: (703)247-5800

★7131★
Association of the United States Army (AUSA)
2425 Wilson Blvd.
Arlington, VA 22201-3385   Phone: (703)841-4300

★7132★
Marine Corps Association (MCA)
Box 1175
Marine Corps Base
Quantico, VA 22134-0775   Phone: (703)640-6161

★7133★
National Association for Uniformed Services (NAUS)
5535 Hempstead Way
Springfield, VA 22151   Phone: (703)750-1342

★7134★
Non-Commissioned Officers Association of the United States of America (NCOA)
10635 IH 35, N.
PO Box 33610
San Antonio, TX 78265   Phone: (800)662-2620

★7135★
United States Naval Institute (USNI)
Annapolis, MD 21402   Phone: (301)268-6110

Test Guides

★7136★
Armed Forces Test (AFT/ASVAB)
National Learning Corp.
212 Michael Dr.
Syosset, NY 11791   Phone: (516)921-8888

Jack Rudman. Part of the Admission Test Series No. 3. Books in this series provide test practice and drill for actual professional certification and licensure tests. **Facsimile Number:** (516)921-8743. **Toll-free/Additional Phone Number(s):** 800-645-6337.

★7137★
ASVAB Basics
Prentice Hall Press
Simon & Schuster Inc.
200 Old Tappan Rd.
Old Tappan, NJ 07675   Phone: (800)223-2348

Ronald Kappraff and Ronald Bronk. First edition, 1990. Provides intensive preparation for the four ASVAB subtests needed to qualify. Includes sample subtests with explanatory answers, basic skills drills, and test-taking tips.

★7138★
ASVAB Review
Careers, Inc.
1211 10th St., SW
PO Box 135
Largo, FL 34649-0135   Phone: (813)584-7333

Videotape (120 mins.) and study guide for the Armed Services Vocational Aptitude Battery test that must be taken when joining the Armed Forces. Areas reviewed include English, technical knowledge, and math skills. **Toll-free/Additional Phone Number(s):** 800-726-0441.

★7139★
Barron's How to Prepare for the Armed Forces Test - ASVAB
Barron's Educational Series, Inc.
PO Box 8040
250 Wireless Blvd.
Hauppauge, NY 11788   Phone: (516)434-3311

Third edition. Manual presents nine complete review courses and features four full-length practice exams with answers and explanations. Applicable for all branches of military service. **Toll-free/Additional Phone Number(s):** 800-645-3476 (in NY call 800-257-5729).

★7140★
Practice for Air Force Placement Tests
Prentice Hall Press
Simon & Schuster Inc.
200 Old Tappan Rd.
Old Tappan, NJ 07675   Phone: (800)223-2348

Solomon Wiener and E.P. Steinberg. Seventh edition, 1989. Complete preparation for the enlistment and placement tests required for Air Force entry. Four practice exams are included.

★7141★
Practice for Army Placement Tests
Prentice Hall Press
Simon & Schuster Inc.
200 Old Tappan Rd.
Old Tappan, NJ 07675   Phone: (800)223-2348

Solomon Wiener and E.P. Steinberg. Fourth edition, 1989. Complete preparation for the enlistment and placement tests required for Army entry. Four practice exams are included.

★7142★
Practice for Navy Placement Tests
Prentice Hall Press
Simon & Schuster Inc.
200 Old Tappan Rd.
Old Tappan, NJ 07675   Phone: (800)223-2348

E.P. Steinberg. Third edition, 1986. Complete practice for the Navy and Marine Corps entrance and placement exams. Four practice tests are included.

★7143★
Practice for the Armed Forces Test - ASVAB
Prentice Hall Press
Simon & Schuster Inc.
200 Old Tappan Rd.
Old Tappan, NJ 07675   Phone: (800)223-2348

Solomon Wiener. 13th edition, 1988. Contains four practice exams with explanations. Reviews all ten subject areas covered on the exam.

★7144★
Video Review for the Armed Forces Exam
Video Aided Instruction, Inc.
182 Village Rd.
East Hills, NY 11577   Phone: (516)621-6176
Videocassette. 1984. 120 mins. A college instructor works out math problems from the Armed Forces exam in this program.

Awards, Scholarships, Grants, and Fellowships

★7145★
Navy-Marine Corps ROTC College Scholarship
Navy-Marine Corps ROTC
College Scholarships Program
PO Box 8205
Gaithersburg, MD 20898-9971   Phone: (800)NAV-ROTC
1992.

Periodicals

★7146★
Air Force Times
Army Times Publishing Co.
6883 Commercial Dr.
Springfield, VA 22159   Phone: (703)750-2000
Lee Ewing, Editor. Weekly. Independent newspaper serving Air Force personnel worldwide. **Facsimile Number:** (703)750-8622.

★7147★
Air University Library Index to Military Periodicals
Government Printing Office
AUL/LSP, Maxwell AFB
Montgomery, AL 36112-5564   Phone: (205)293-2504
Martha M. Stewart, Editor. Quarterly. Subject index to 78 English language journals in the fields of military science, defense, other countries affairs, and aerospace.

★7148★
Airpower Journal
Bldg. 1400, Maxwell Air Force Base
Montgomery, AL 36112-5532   Phone: (205)293-5322
Colonel Keith W. Geiger, Editor. Quarterly. Professional military journal covering the development, fielding, and application of combat power. **Facsimile Number:** (205)293-2593.

★7149★
All Hands
U.S. Government Printing Office
Superintendent of Documents
Washington, DC 20402   Phone: (202)783-3238
Bureau of Navy Personnel, Publisher. Monthly. General interest magazine covering the United States Navy. **Facsimile Number:** (202)275-0019.

★7150★
Armed Forces and Society
Seven Locks Press
PO Box 27
Cabin John, MD 20818   Phone: (301)320-2130
Claude Welch, Editor (716/636-2251). Quarterly. Journal on military institutions, civil-military relations, arms control and peacekeeping, and conflict management, with a focus on historical and comparative writing.

★7151★
Armed Forces Journal International
2000 L St. NW, Ste. 520
Washington, DC 20036   Phone: (202)296-0450
Benjamin F. Schemmer, Editor. Monthly. Magazine concerning the armed services, national security, and defense. **Facsimile Number:** (202)296-5727.

★7152★
Armor
U.S. Army Armor School
HHC 20 Brigade, 1st Armored Division
New York, NY 09066-5000
Major Patrick J. Cooney, Editor. 6x/yr. Military news magazine.

★7153★
Army Aviation Magazine
Army Aviation Publications, Inc.
49 Richmondville Ave.
Westport, CT 06880   Phone: (203)226-8184
William R. Harris, Jr., Editor. 10x/yr. **Facsimile Number:** (203)222-9863.

★7154★
Army Communicator
U.S. Army Signal Corps.
Bldg. 25701
Fort Gordon, GA 30905   Phone: (404)791-7204
Richard Davis, Jr., Editor. Quarterly. Magazine providing information about the Signal Corps. **Facsimile Number:** (404)791-3917.

★7155★
Army Flier
QST Publications, Inc.
905 Rucker Blvd.
Enterprise, AL 36331   Phone: (205)393-2969
Howard Quattlebaum, Publisher. Weekly. Military newspaper. **Facsimile Number:** (205)393-2987.

★7156★
ARMY Magazine
Assn. of the U.S. Army (AUSA)
2425 Wilson Blvd.
Arlington, VA 22201-3385   Phone: (703)841-4300
L. James Binder, Editor-in-Chief. Monthly. Magazine for Regular Army officers, noncommissioned officers, warrant officers, and senior enlisted personnel; industrialists; civilians with an interest in national defense; and members of the Army National Guard and Reserve. **Facsimile Number:** (703)525-9039.

★7157★
Army Reserve Magazine
OCAR, Public Affairs Support Office
1815 N. Fort Myer Dr., Rm. 501
Arlington, VA 22209   Phone: (703)696-3962
Major General William F. Ward, Jr., Publisher. Quarterly. Military magazine. **Facsimile Number:** (703)696-5300.

★7158★
Army Times
Army Times Publishing Co.
6883 Commercial Dr.
Springfield, VA 22159-0225   Phone: (703)750-8699
Tom Donnelly, Editor. Weekly (Mon.). U.S. Army newspaper.

★7159★
Marine Corps Gazette
Marine Corps Assn.
Box 1775
Quantico, VA 22134　　　　　　Phone: (703)640-6161
Col. J.E. Greenwood, USMC (Ret.), Editor. Monthly. **Facsimile Number:** (703)640-0823.

★7160★
Marine Log
Simmons-Boardman Publications
345 Hudson St.
New York, NY 10014　　　　　　Phone: (212)620-7220
Nicholas Blenkey, Editor. Monthly. Magazine serving ship, boat, and barge owners, builders, and operators, port authorities, and the Navy. **Facsimile Number:** (212)633-1165.

★7161★
Military Forum
199 Ethan Allen Hwy.
Richmond, CT 06877　　　　　　Phone: (203)438-4960
Steve Hull, Editor. 9x/yr. Issues-oriented magazine covering the organizations, programs, and people actively engaged in the fields of defense acquisition, readiness, and sustainability.

★7162★
Military Intelligence
U.S. Army Intelligence Center & School
ATSI-TDL-B
Fort Huachuca, AZ 85613-7000　　Phone: (602)538-0674
Captain Linda A. Gorsuch, Editor. Quarterly. **Facsimile Number:** (602)538-6238.

★7163★
Military Lifestyle
Downey Communications, Inc.
4800 Montgomery Ln., Ste. 710
Bethesda, MD 20814　　　　　　Phone: (301)718-7600
Hope M. Daniels, Editor. 10x/yr. Magazine for military families.

★7164★
Military Media Inc.
1 Bushwick Rd.
Poughkeepsie, NY 12603　　　　Phone: (914)454-7900
John Bradbury, Editor. Weekly. Military base newspapers. **Facsimile Number:** (914)454-7987.

★7165★
Military News Recorder-Times
Fisher Publications, Inc.
8603 Botts Ln.
PO Box 17947
San Antonio, TX 78217　　　　　Phone: (512)828-3321
Ed Leal, Editor. Daily. Military community newspaper. **Facsimile Number:** (512)828-3787.

★7166★
Naval Aviation News
U.S. Government Printing Office
Superintendent of Documents
Washington, DC 20402　　　　　Phone: (202)783-3238
Chief of Naval Operations, Publisher. 6x/yr. Magazine presenting articles on all phases of Navy and Marine air activity. **Facsimile Number:** (202)275-0019.

★7167★
Navy News
Orkand Communications, Inc.
2429 Bowland Parkland, Ste. 118
PO Box 8918
Virginia Beach, VA 23450　　　　Phone: (804)486-8000
Robert E. Orkand, Editor and Publisher. Weekly. Navy newspaper (tabloid). **Facsimile Number:** (804)486-8017.

★7168★
Navy Times
Army Times Publishing Co.
6883 Commercial Dr.
Springfield, VA 22159-0225　　　Phone: (703)750-2000
Tom Philpott, Editor. Weekly (Mon.). U.S. Navy newspaper.

★7169★
Officer's Call
Print Media Branch
Command Information Unit
U.S. Department of the Army
Office, Chief of Public Affairs
Washington, DC 20310　　　　　Phone: (202)695-3101
6/yr. Discusses items of interest to Army officers. Carries articles on various aspects of Army life, including professional development and personal affairs.

★7170★
On Target
Public Affairs Office
Newark Air Force Base
Newark, OH 43057-5000　　　　Phone: (614)522-7779
Sandy Layman, Editor. Every other week. Newspaper for Air Force base personnel. **Facsimile Number:** (614)522-7449.

★7171★
Robins Rev-Up
Office of Public Affairs, Robins Air Force Base
1553 Watson Blvd.
PO Box 6129
Warner Robins, GA 31095-6129　　Phone: (912)926-2137
H. Thomas Reed, Editor and Publisher. Weekly. Military newspaper (tabloid). **Facsimile Number:** (912)328-7682.

★7172★
Seabee Coverall
Naval Construction Battalion Center
Public Affairs Office
Port Hueneme, CA 93043-5000　　Phone: (805)982-4493
Kim Taft, Mng. Editor. Monthly. Military and family-interest magazine (tabloid) distributed worldwide to Navy bases and government offices. **Facsimile Number:** (805)982-2471.

★7173★
Sergeants
Air Force Sergeants Assn.
PO Box 50
Temple Hills, MD 20748　　　　　Phone: (301)899-3500
David W. Givans, Editor. Monthly. Military magazine.

★7174★
Sergeants' Business
Print Media Branch
Command Information Unit
U.S. Department of the Army
Office, Chief of Public Affairs
Washington, DC 20310　　　　　Phone: (202)695-7140
Editor(s): W.K. Morris. 6/yr. Aims to contribute to the professional development of Army squad leaders, platoon

sergeants, first sergeants, and sergeants major. Recurring features include a column titled A Sergeant's Viewpoint. **Facsimile Number:** (202)697-5746.

★7175★
Shipmate
U.S. Naval Academy
Alumni House
Annapolis, MD 21402   Phone: (301)263-4469
10x/yr. Magazine on naval and naval alumni interests.

★7176★
SIGNAL
Armed Forces Communications & Electronics Assn. (AFCEA)
4400 Fair Lakes Court
Fairfax, VA 22033   Phone: (703)631-6175
Clarence Robinson, Jr. Editor-in-Chief. Monthly. Magazine on military and industry command, control, communications, intelligence, information systems, and electronics. **Facsimile Number:** (703)631-4693.

★7177★
Soldier Support Journal
U.S. Army Administration Center
Bldg. 600
ATZI-AOJ
Fort Benjamin, IN 46216-5048   Phone: (317)542-4203
Shirley K. Startzman, Editor. Quarterly. U.S. Army magazine containing information about personnel service support Adjutant General and Finance Corps.

★7178★
SOLDIERS
Dept. of the Army
Cameron Sta., Bldg. 2, Door 11
Alexandria, VA 22304-5050   Phone: (703)274-6671
Lt. Col. Robert V. Bryant, Editor. Monthly. Official magazine of the U.S. Army. **Facsimile Number:** (703)274-1896.

★7179★
Soldiers' Scene
Print Media Branch
Command Information Unit
U.S. Department of the Army
Office, Chief of Public Affairs
Washington, DC 20310   Phone: (202)695-7140
Editor(s): W.K. Morris. 6/yr. Informs junior enlisted soldiers of the Army's professional development opportunities and encourages soldiers to take advantage of them. "Provides information on careers, pay and benefits, quality of life, and Army modernization.". **Facsimile Number:** (202)697-5746.

★7180★
Soundoff!
Patuxent Publishing Co.
10750 Little Patuxent Pkwy.
Columbia, MD 21044   Phone: (301)667-6361
K.L. Vantran, Editor. Weekly. Suburban military newspaper. **Facsimile Number:** (301)368-5054.

★7181★
Strategic Review
U.S. Strategic Institute
PO Box 618, Kenmore Sta.
Boston, MA 02215   Phone: (617)353-8700
Dr. Mackubin T. Owens, Editor-in-Chief. Quarterly. Military and political magazine. **Facsimile Number:** (617)353-8707.

★7182★
Surface Warfare Magazine
U.S. Government Printing Office
Superintendent of Documents
Washington, DC 20402   Phone: (202)783-3238
U.S. Department of the Navy, Publisher. 6x/yr. Military magazine. **Facsimile Number:** (202)275-0019.

――――― Meetings and Conventions ―――――

★7183★
Association of the United States Army Annual Convention
Association of the United States Army
2425 Wilson Blvd.
Arlington, VA 22201   Phone: (703)841-4300
Frequency: Always held in Washington, D.C. 1992; Oct. 12-14; Washington, DC • 1993; Oct. 18-20; Washington, DC. **Toll-free/Additional Phone Number(s):** 800-336-4570. **Facsimile Number:** (703)525-9039.

Appendix I: State Occupational and Professional Licensing Agencies

This appendix covers state government agencies responsible for granting professional and occupational licenses. Entries are arranged alphabetically by state and include the state agency's or department's name, address, and phone number.

Appendix 1: State Foundational and Professional Logging Awards

Appendix I: State Occupational and Professional Licensing Agencies

★7184★
Alaska State Department of Commerce and Economic Development
Division of Occupational Licensing
PO Box D
Juneau, AK 99811   Phone: (907)465-2534

★7185★
Arizona State Department of Administration
State Boards Office
1645 W. Jefferson St., Rm. 410
Phoenix, AZ 85007   Phone: (602)542-3095

★7186★
California State and Consumer Services Agency
Department of Consumer Affairs
1020 N St., Rm. 510
Sacramento, CA 95814   Phone: (916)445-1591

★7187★
Colorado State Department of Regulatory Agencies
1525 Sherman St.
Denver, CO 80203   Phone: (303)866-3304

★7188★
Connecticut State Department of Consumer Protection
Division of Licensing and Administration
State Office Bldg.
165 Capitol Ave.
Hartford, CT 06106   Phone: (203)566-7177

★7189★
Delaware State Department of Administrative Services
Division of Professional Regulations
Townsend Bldg.
PO Box 1401
Dover, DE 19903   Phone: (302)736-4522

★7190★
District of Columbia Department of Consumer and Regulatory Affairs
Occupational and Professional Licensing Administration
614 H St. NW
Washington, DC 20001   Phone: (202)727-7480

★7191★
Florida State Department of Professional Regulation
130 N. Monroe St.
Tallahassee, FL 32301   Phone: (904)487-2252

★7192★
Georgia Secretary of State
Professional Examining Boards
166 Pryor St. SW
Atlanta, GA 30303   Phone: (404)656-3900

★7193★
Hawaii State Department of Commerce and Consumer Affairs
Division of Professional and Vocational Licensing
PO Box 3469
Honolulu, HI 96801   Phone: (808)548-6520

★7194★
Idaho State Board of Occupational Licenses
2417 Bank Dr., Rm. 312
Boise, ID 83705   Phone: (208)334-3233

★7195★
Illinois State Department of Registration and Education
Division of Licensing and Testing
320 W. Washington St.
Springfield, IL 62786   Phone: (217)785-0800

★7196★
Indiana State Professional Licensing Agency
State Office Bldg., Rm. 1021
Indianapolis, IN 46204   Phone: (317)232-2980

★7197★
Iowa State Department of Commerce
Professional Licensing and Regulation Division
1918 SE Hulsizer Ave.
Ankney, IA 50021   Phone: (515)281-5596

★7198★
Kentucky State Finance and Administration Cabinet
Occupations and Professions Division
PO Box 456
Frankfort, KY 40602   Phone: (502)564-3296

★7199★
Louisiana State Department of Health and Hospitals
Licensing and Certifications
PO Box 3776
Baton Rouge, LA 70821-3767   Phone: (504)342-5774

★7200★
Maine State Department of Professional and Financial Regulation
Division of Licensing and Enforcement
State House Station 35
Augusta, ME 04333 Phone: (207)289-3671

★7201★
Maryland State Department of Licensing and Regulation
Division of Occupational and Professional Licensing
501 St. Paul Pl., 9th Fl.
Baltimore, MD 21202 Phone: (301)333-6200

★7202★
Massachusetts State Executive Office of Consumer Affairs and Business Regulation
Division of Registration
100 Cambridge St.
Boston, MA 02202 Phone: (617)727-3076

★7203★
Michigan State Department of Licensing and Regulation
PO Box 30018
Lansing, MI 48909 Phone: (517)373-1870

★7204★
Minnesota State Department of Commerce
Division of Registration and Licensing
133 E. 7th St.
St. Paul, MN 55101 Phone: (612)296-6325

★7205★
Mississippi State Board of Medical Licensure
2688-D Insurance Center Dr.
Jackson, MS 39216 Phone: (601)354-6645

★7206★
Missouri State Department of Professional Registration
PO Box 1335
Jefferson City, MO 65102 Phone: (314)751-2334

★7207★
Montana State Department of Commerce
Bureau of Professional and Occupational Licensing
1424 9th Ave.
Helena, MT 59620 Phone: (406)444-3737

★7208★
Nebraska State Bureau of Examining Boards
Department of Health
PO Box 95007
Lincoln, NE 68509-5007 Phone: (402)471-2115

★7209★
New Jersey State Department of Law and Public Safety
Division of Consumer Affairs
1100 Raymond Blvd.
Newark, NJ 07102 Phone: (609)292-4670

★7210★
New Mexico State Department of Regulation and Licensing
Bataan Memorial Bldg.
Santa Fe, NM 87503 Phone: (505)827-6318

★7211★
New York Department of State
Division of Licensing Services
162 Washington Ave.
Albany, NY 12231 Phone: (518)474-3830

★7212★
North Dakota State Licensing Department
Office of the Attorney General
600 E. Blvd.
State Capitol, 17th Fl.
Bismarck, ND 58505 Phone: (701)224-2210

★7213★
Ohio State Department of Commerce
Division of Licensing
77 S. High St., 23rd Fl.
Columbus, OH 43266-0546 Phone: (614)466-4130

★7214★
Oregon State Department of Insurance and Finance
21 Labor and Industries Bldg.
Salem, OR 97310 Phone: (503)378-4100

★7215★
Pennsylvania State Department
Bureau of Professional and Occupational Affairs
Transportation and Safety Bldg., Rm. 618
Harrisburg, PA 17120 Phone: (717)787-8503

★7216★
Puerto Rico Licensing Administration
Minillas Governmental Center
North Tower, Stop 22
Santurce, PR 00940 Phone: (809)721-8282

★7217★
Rhode Island State Department of Labor
Division of Professional Regulation
220 Elmwood Ave.
Providence, RI 02907 Phone: (401)457-1860

★7218★
South Dakota State Department of Commerce and Regulation
Professional and Occupational License Division
910 E. Sioux
Pierre, SD 57501 Phone: (605)773-3177

★7219★
Tennessee State Department of Commerce and Insurance
Regulatory Boards
James Roberston Pkwy., 2nd Fl.
Volunteer Plaza
Nashville, TN 37243-0572 Phone: (615)741-3449

★7220★
Texas State Department of Licensing and Regulation
PO Box 12157
Austin, TX 78711 Phone: (512)463-5520

★7221★
Utah State Department of Business Regulation
Division of Occupational and Professional Licensing
PO Box 45802
Salt Lake City, UT 84145-0801 Phone: (801)530-6628

★7222★
Vermont Secretary of State
Division of Licensing and Registration
Pavillion Office Bldg.
Montpelier, VT 05602   Phone: (802)828-2363

★7223★
Virginia State Department of Social Services
Division of Licensing Programs
8007 Discovery Dr.
Richmond, VA 23229-8699   Phone: (804)662-9025

★7224★
Washington State Department of Licensing
Business and Professions Division
12th & Franklin
Olympia, WA 98504   Phone: (206)753-6918

Appendix II
Employment Growth Rankings and Statistics

This section provides U.S. Bureau of Labor Statistics figures indicating expected employment growth for the occupations covered in this edition of *VCS*.

Appendix B

Longer-term Growth Rank

Bureau of Labor Statistics Occupational Data

Below is an extract from the Bureau of Labor Statistics' Industry-Occupation Matrix (1990). Occupations that appear in *Vocational Careers Sourcebook* are presented two ways: by order of growth and in an alphabetic arrangement. Annual employment figures are in thousands (000s).

Projected Occupational Growth From 1988 to 2000
(Occupations by Percentage of Change)

	1988	2000	%Change
Medical assistants	149	253	70
Homemaker-home health aides	327	534	63
Corrections officers	186	262	41
Receptionists	833	1,164	40
Flight attendants	88	122	39
Computer and office machine repairers	128	172	35
Information clerks	1,316	1,757	34
Guards	795	1,051	32
Nursing aides and psychiatric aides	1,289	1,703	31
Childcare workers	670	856	30
Computer and peripheral equipment operators	316	408	29
Ophthalmic laboratory technicians	25	33.3	28
Reservation and transportation ticket agents and travel clerks	133	170	28
Credit clerks and authorizers	229	290	27
Automotive body repairers	214	270	26
Hotel and motel clerks	113	142	26
Food and beverage service workers	4,458	5,526	24
Gardeners and groundskeepers	760	942	24
Plastic-working machine operators	144	176	22
Tilesetters	26	31.8	22
Chefs, cooks, and other kitchen workers	2,755	3,341	21
Teachers aides	682	827	21
Photographic process workers	67	81	21
Carpet installers	56	68	21
Janitors and cleaners	2,895	3,451	19
General maintenance mechanics	1,080	1,282	19
Dental assistants	166	197	19
Roofers	123	147	19
Sheet-metal workers	97	115	19
Structural and reinforcing ironworkers	91	108	19
Insulation workers	65	77	19
General office clerks	2,519	2,974	18
Adjusters, investigators, and collectors	961	1,133	18
Electricians	542	638	18
Plumbers and pipefitters	396	469	18
Interviewing and new accounts clerks	237	280	18
Lithographic and photoengraving workers	67	79	18
Glaziers	49	57.6	18
Secretaries	3,373	3,944	17
Busdrivers	506	594	17
Heating, air-conditioning, and refrigeration mechanics	225	263	17
Drywall workers and lathers	152	178	17
Concrete masons and terrazzo workers	114	133	17
Commercial and industrial electronic equipment repairers	78.8	91.8	17
Millwrights	77	90	17
Elevators installers and repairers	13	15.3	17
Carpenters	1,106	1,286	16
Automotive mechanics	771	897	16
Industrial machinery repairers	463	538	16
Painter and paperhangers	431	501	16
Diesel mechanics	269	312	16
Bricklayers and stonemasons	167	192	16
Aircraft mechanics and engine specialists	124	144	16
Animal caretakers, except farm	92	106	16
Jewelers	35	40.7	16
Telephone operators	330	378	15
Printing press operators	239	274	15
Truckdrivers	2,641	3,023	14
Dispatchers	202	231	14
Mobile heavy equipment mechanics	108	124	14
Water and wastewater treatment plant operators	76	87	14
Electric power generating plant operators and power distributors and dispatchers	45	51.4	14
Cosmetologists and related workers	649	731	13
Police, detectives, and special agents	515	583	13
Motorcycle, boat, and small-engine mechanics	58	65.7	13
Electric home entertainment equipment repairers	44	49.5	13
Material recording, scheduling, dispatching, and distributing occupations	2,889	3,227	12
Stock clerks	2,152	2,406	12
Clerical supervisors and managers	1,183	1,319	12
Upholsterers	73	81.1	11

	1988	2000	%Change		1988	2000	%Change
Bindery workers	73	80.9	11	Roustabouts	39	<39.5	1
Traffic, shipping, and receiving clerks	535	591	10	Vending machine servicers	27	<27.5	1
Firefighting occupations	291	320	10	Billing clerks and related workers	421	422.4	0
File clerks	263	290	10				
Mail clerks and messengers	259	285	10	Home appliance and power tool repairers	76	<76.5	0
Fishers, hunters, and trappers	54	59.7	10	Barbers	46	<46.5	0
Dental laboratory technicians	51	56.2	10	Shoe and leather workers and repairers	32	<32.5	0
Machinists	397	433	9	Stationary engineers	36	35.5	-1
Woodworking occupations	375	409	9	Order clerks	293	288.6	-2
Personnel clerks	129	141	9	Payroll and timekeeping clerks	176	171.8	-2
Numerical-control machine-tool operators	64	69.9	9	Metalworking and plastic-working machine operators	1,405	1,365	-3
Boilermakers	25	27.2	9				
Butchers and meat, poultry, and fish cutters	368	398	8	Line installers and cable splicers	231	221	-4
Plasterers	27	29.2	8	Private household workers	902	860	-5
Musical instrument repairers and tuners	7.5	8.1	8	Typists, word processors, and data entry keyers	1,416	1,334	-6
Blue-collar worker supervisors	1,797	1,930	7	Metalworking machine operators	1,252	1,182	-6
Postal clerks and mail carriers	665	706	6	Inspectors, testers, and graders	676	634	-6
Library assistants and bookmobile drivers	105	111.1	6	Apparel workers	1,104	1,026	-7
Records clerks	886	930	5	Welders, cutters, and welding machine operators	424	394	-7
Bank tellers	522	546	5				
Painting and coating machine operators	159	167.5	5	Timbers cutting, and logging workers	106	96	-10
Material moving equipment operators	1,010	1,047	4	Textile machinery operators	310	273	-12
Tool and die makers	152	158.8	4	Water transportation occupations	49	43.2	-12
Brokerage clerks and statement clerks	96	98.8	3	Communications equipment mechanics	113	95	-16
Handlers, equipment cleaners, helpers, and laborers	4,894	4,999	2	Railroad transportation workers	106	90	-16
Financial records processors	2,849	2,867	1	Farm operators and managers	1,272	1,035	-19
Bookkeeping, accounting, and auditing clerks	2,252	2,272	1	Steel workers	8.9	7.2	-19
Compositors and typesetters	86	<86.5	1	Telephone installers and repairers	58	46	-20
Farm equipment mechanics	54	54.8	1	Stenographers	159	123	-23
				Precision assemblers	354	344.9	-26

Projected Occupational Growth From 1988 to 2000
(Occupations in Alphabetical Order)

	1988	2000	%Change		1988	2000	%Change
Adjusters, investigators, and collectors	961	1,133	18	Billing clerks and related workers	421	422.4	0
Aircraft mechanics and engine specialists	124	144	16	Bindery workers	73	80.9	11
Animal caretakers, except farm	92	106	16	Blue-collar worker supervisors	1,797	1,930	7
Apparel workers	1,104	1,026	-7	Boilermakers	25	27.2	9
Automotive body repairers	214	270	26	Bookkeeping, accounting, and auditing clerks	2,252	2,272	1
Automotive mechanics	771	897	16	Bricklayers and stonemasons	167	192	16
Bank tellers	552	546	5	Brokerage clerks and statement clerks	96	98.8	3
Barbers	46	<46.5	0	Busdrivers	506	594	17

Appendix II: Employment Growth Rankings and Statistics

	1988	2000	%Change
Butchers and meat, poultry, and fish cutters	368	398	8
Carpenters	1,106	1,286	16
Carpet installers	56	68	21
Chefs, cooks, and other kitchen workers	2,277	3,341	21
Childcare workers	670	856	30
Clerical supervisors and managers	1,183	1,319	12
Commercial and industrial electronic equipment repairers	78.8	91.8	17
Communications equipment mechanics	113	95	-16
Compositors and typesetters	86	<86.5	1
Computer and office machine repairers	128	172	35
Computer and peripheral equipment operators	316	408	29
Concrete masons and terrazzo workers	114	133	17
Corrections officers	186	262	41
Cosmetologists and related workers	649	731	13
Credit clerks and authorizers	229	290	27
Dental assistants	166	197	19
Dental laboratory technicians	51	56.2	10
Diesel mechanics	269	312	16
Dispatchers	202	231	14
Drywall workers and lathers	52	178	17
Electric power generating plant operators and power distributors and dispatchers	45	51.4	14
Electricians	542	638	18
Electronic home entertainment equipment repairers	44	49.5	13
Elevator installers and repairers	13	15.3	17
Farm equipment mechanics	54	54.8	1
Farm operators and managers	1,272	1,035	-19
File clerks	263	290	10
Financial records processors	2,849	2,867	1
Firefighting occupations	291	320	10
Fishers, hunters, and trappers	54	59.7	10
Flight attendants	88	122	39
Food and beverage service workers	4,458	5,526	24
Gardeners and groundkeepers	760	942	24
General maintenance mechanics	1,080	1,282	19
General office clerks	2,519	2,974	18
Glaziers	49	57.6	18
Guards	795	1,051	32
Handlers, equipment cleaners, helpers, and laborers	4,894	4,999	2
Heating, air-conditioning, and refrigeration mechanics	225	263	17
Home appliance and power tool repairers	76	<76.5	0

	1988	2000	%Change
Homemaker-home health aides	327	534	63
Hotel and motel clerks	113	142	26
Industrial machinery repairers	463	538	16
Information clerks	1,316	1,757	34
Inspectors, testers, and graders	676	634	-6
Insulation workers	65	77	19
Interviewing and new accounts clerks	237	280	18
Janitors and cleaners	2,895	3,451	19
Jewelers	35	40.7	16
Library assistants and bookmobile drivers	105	111.1	6
Line installers and cable splicers	231	221	-4
Lithographic and photo-engraving workers	67	79	18
Machinists	397	433	9
Mail clerks and messengers	259	285	10
Material moving equipment operators	1,010	1,047	4
Material recording, scheduling dispatching, and distributing occupations	2,889	3,227	12
Medical assistants	149	253	70
Metalworking and plastic-working machine operators	1,405	1,365	-3
Metalworking machine operators	1,252	1,182	-6
Millwrights	77	90	17
Mobile heavy equipment mechanics	108	124	14
Motorcycle, boat, and small-engine mechanics	58	65.7	13
Musical instrument repairers and tuners	7.5	8.1	8
Nursing aides and psychiatric aides	1,289	1,703	31
Numerical-control machine-tool operators	64	69.9	9
Order clerks	293	288.6	-2
Ophthalmic laboratory technicians	25	33.3	28
Painting and coating machine operators	159	167.5	5
Painters and paperhangers	431	501	16
Payroll and timekeeping clerks	176	171.8	-2
Personnel clerks	129	141	9
Photographic process workers	67	81	21
Plasterers	27	29.2	8
Plastic-working machine operators	144	176	22
Plumbers and pipefitters	396	469	18
Police, detectives, and special agents	515	583	13
Postal clerks and mail carriers	665	706	6
Precision assemblers	354	344.9	-26
Printing press operators	239	274	15
Private household workers	902	860	-5
Railroad transportation workers	106	90	-16
Receptionists	833	1,164	40
Records clerks	886	930	5

	1988	2000	%Change
Reservation and transportation ticket agents and travel clerks	133	170	28
Roofers	123	147	19
Roustabouts	39	<39.5	1
Secretaries	3,373	3,944	17
Sheet-metal workers	97	115	19
Shoe and leather workers and repairers	32	<32.5	0
Stationary engineers	36	35.5	-1
Stenographers	159	123	-23
Steel workers	8.9	7.2	-19
Stock clerks	2,152	2,406	12
Structual and reinforcing ironworkers	91	108	19
Teachers aides	682	827	21
Telephone installers and repairers	58	46	-20
Telephone operators	330	378	15
Textile machinery operators	310	273	-12
Tilesetters	26	31.8	22
Timber cutting and logging workers	106	96	-10
Tool and die makers	152	158.8	4
Traffic, shipping, and receiving clerks	535	591	10
Truckdrivers	2,641	3,023	14
Typists, word processors, and data entry keyers	1,416	1,334	-6
Upholsterers	73	81.1	11
Vending machine servicers and repairers	27	<27.5	1
Water and wastewater treatment plant operators	76	87	14
Water transportation occupations	49	43.2	12
Welders, cutters, and welding machine operators	424	394	-7
Woodworking occupations	375	409	9

Index to Information Sources

A

The A to Z Business Office Handbook 1098
AACS News 610
AAHA Provider News 3143
AAIS Viewpoint 114
AAMA Committee Manual 6305
AAMA Consumer Affairs Newsletter 6306
AAMA Newsletter 6307
AAMA Technical Advisory Committee Bulletin 6308
AAMA Technical Advisory Committee Research Paper 6323
AAN American Beautification Award 3069
ABA Bankers Weekly 809, 1160
ABA Banking Journal 810, 1161, 1445
ABA Directory 803, 1159
The Abbey Newsletter 1504
ABC Newsline 4628, 4724, 4782, 4850, 4915, 5004, 5063, 5103, 5158, 5205, 5299, 5374, 5432, 5467, 5514, 5559, 6706
Aberdeen's Magazine of Masonry Construction 4851
ABKA Newsletter 2805
Able Seaman 6961
"Able Seaman" in *Occu-Facts: Information on 565 Careers in Outline Form* (p. 19.11) 6932
About the National Court Reporters Association 1701
ABYC News 4495, 6974
Academy of Legends 2964
ACCA News 4316
Accent 5738
According to Hoyle 162, 394
Accounting Clerk 982, 983
"Accounting Clerk" in *Occu-Facts: Information on 565 Careers in Outline Form* (p. 12.26) 984
"Accounting Clerks" in *The American Almanac of Jobs and Salaries* (p. 507) 986
"Accounting Clerks and Bookkeepers" in *Opportunities in Vocational and Technical Careers* (pp. 49-50) 985
Accounting Terms & Bookkeeping Procedures Explained 1020
Accounts Payable Practice Set 1014
Accounts Receivable Practice Set 1015
Accredited Dental Assisting, Dental Hygiene and Dental Laboratory Technology Educational Programs 6500
Accredited Dental Laboratory Technology Educational Programs 6501
Accrediting Bureau of Health Education Schools 2671
ACI Structural Journal 4852
ACNewS 3220
Action Digest 2260
Action Letter 3085
Activewear Business News Magazine 6309
Actuarial Clerk 108
ADA News 2616, 6507
ADAPSO Data 924, 1876
"Adjusters" in *Opportunities in Insurance Careers* (pp. 42-43) 714
"Adjusters, Investigators, and Collectors" in *Occupational Outlook Handbook* (pp. 244-248) 715
Adjusters Reference Guide 765
"Administrative Assistants, Clerical Workers, and Secretaries" in *Jobs '91* (pp. 9-13) 1557
Administrative Clerk (USPS) 1389
Administrative Management 853
The Administrative Secretary 1558
"Admitting Clerk" in *Health Care* (pp. 39-43) 1143
"Admitting Clerk" in *Health*, Volume 7 of *Career Information Center* (pp. 39-40) 1144
Adult Day Care Quarterly 3144
Advanced Placement Examination in Computer Science 914
Advanced Recovery Week 5433
Advances & Trends in Automotive Sheet Steel Stamping 3762
Advances in Cooling Techniques for Computers 4069
Advances in Exterior Body Panels 3763
"Advertising Sales" in *Careers in Fashion Retailing* (pp. 80-82) 561
"Advertising Sales Person" in *VGM's Handbook of Business and Management Careers* (pp. 11-14) 562
"Advertising Sales Representatives" in *Jobs! What They Are. . .Where They Are. . .What They Pay* (pp. 275-276) 563
"Advertising Sales, Television" in *Career Choices for the 90's for Students of Communications and Journalism* (pp. 189-191) 564
"Advertising Sales (Television)" in *The Encyclopedia of Career Choices for the 1990s: A Guide to Entry Level Jobs* (pp. 828-830) 565
"Advertising Sales Workers" in Volume 1 of *Career Discovery Encyclopedia* (pp. 20-21) 566
"Advertising Salesperson" in *Career Opportunities in Television, Cable, and Video* (pp. 110-111) 567
"Advertising Space Sales" in *Career Choices for the 90's for Students of Business* (pp. 155-158) 568
"Advertising Space Sales" in *Career Choices for the 90's for Students of Political Science & Government* (pp. 164-167) 569
"Advertising Space Sales" in *The Encyclopedia of Career Choices for the 1990s: A Guide to Entry Level Jobs* (pp. 610-613, 766-769) 570
"Advertising Space Sales, Newspaper Publishing" in *Career Choices for the 90's for Students of Communications and Journalism* (pp. 104-106) 571
"Advertising Space Sales, Newspaper Publishing" in *Career Choices for the 90's for Students of Political Science & Government* (pp. 110-113) 572
"Advertising Space Salesperson" in *Occu-Facts: Information on 565 Careers in Outline Form* (p. 11.7) 573
The Advisor 811, 1162
Aerial Applicator Farm, Forest & Fire 2009, 3284, 3610
Aerospace Assembly Worker 5585
AFI Honor Roll 2214
African Campfires 3446
Africa's Top Wildlife Countries 669
AFT Public Sevice Reporter 1760
Ag Alert 3285
AG Consultant 3286
Ag Expo 3412
AG-PILOT International 3287
Agency Sales Magazine 213
Agents and Brokers 246
Agri-Equipment & Chemical 3288, 4228
Agri Finance 3289
Agri News 3290
Agri-News 3291
Agri News Farm Show 3413
Agri-View 3292
Agribusiness: An International Journal 3293
Agrichemical Age 3294
Agricultural Aviation 3295
Agricultural Cluster 3222
The Agricultural Education Magazine 3296
Agricultural Engineering 3297
Agricultural Hall of Fame 3265
Agricultural Machinery Service Technician Award 3266
Agricultural News 3298
Agriculture & Food: An Abstract Newsletter 3299
AgriScience 3300
AGRITECH - International Agriculture, Horticulture, Irrigation and Fisheries Exhibition 3414, 3572
Agronomy Journal 3301
AgVenture 3302
Agway Cooperator 3303
AGWEEK 3304
AHANews 2747
AHEA Action 3145
AIB Student Catalog 801, 1158
Aim For A Job As An Electronic Technician 4136, 4954
"Air Conditioning and Heating Technician" in *Construction*, Volume 4 of *Career Information Center* (pp. 91-92) 4263
Air-Conditioning and Refrigeration 4264
Air Conditioning and Refrigeration Mechanic 4265
"Air-Conditioning and Refrigeration Mechanic" in *Occu-Facts: Information on 565 Careers in Outline Form* (p. 15.17) 4266
Air Conditioning, Heating & Refrigeration Mechanic 4294
"Air Conditioning, Heating, and Refrigeration Mechanic" in *Construction*, Volume 4 of *Career Information Center* (pp. 37-39) 4267
"Air Conditioning, Heating, and Refrigeration Mechanics" in *The American Almanac of Jobs and Salaries* (p. 522) 4268
Air Conditioning, Heating and Refrigeration News 4317
Air Conditioning/Heating/Solar Technician 4269
"Air-Conditioning/Heating/Solar Technician" in *Occu-Facts: Information on 565 Careers in Outline Form* (p. 10.6) 4270
"Air Conditioning, Refrigeration, and Heating Mechanic" in *Exploring Nontraditional Jobs for Women* (pp. 76-82) 4271
"Air-Conditioning, Refrigeration, and Heating Mechanic" in *VGM's Careers Encyclopedia* (pp. 29-32) 4272
"Air-Conditioning, Refrigeration, and Heating Mechanics" in Volume 3 of *The Encyclopedia of Careers and Vocational Guidance* (pp. 466-470) 4273
Air Force Academy: Commitment to Excellence 7076
Air Force Association 7130
Air Force Career Opportunities 7077
"Air Force Nurse" in *120 Careers in the Health Care Field* (p. 265) 7079

"Air Force Nurse Corps" in *Opportunities in Nursing Careers* (pp. 112-113) **7078**
Air Force Times **7146**
Air Line Pilot **3037, 3704**
Air-to-Air Heat Exchangers: Directory and Buyers' Guide **4299**
Air Transport **1238**
Air Transport Association of America **1230**
Air University Library Index to Military Periodicals **7147**
AIRCO Welding Award **5710, 5971**
"Aircraft Assembler" in *Occu-Facts: Information on 565 Careers in Outline Form* (p. 17.2) **5586**
Aircraft Cabin Cleaning & Refurbishing Operations **3694**
Aircraft Cleaning, Painting & Paint Removal **3695**
Aircraft Fuel System Maintenance **3696**
Aircraft Maintenance & Repair **3697**
"Aircraft Mechanic" in *Careers in Aviation* (pp. 19-22) **3661**
"Aircraft Mechanic" in *Exploring Nontraditional Jobs for Women* (pp. 83-89) **3662**
"Aircraft Mechanic" in *Occu-Facts: Information on 565 Careers in Outline Form* (p. 15.8) **3663**
"Aircraft Mechanic" in *Transportation*, Volume 12 of *Career Information Center* (pp. 89-90) **3664**
"Aircraft Mechanics" in *Jobs! What They Are...Where They Are...What They Pay* (pp. 174-175) **3665**
"Aircraft Mechanics" in *101 Careers: A Guide to the Fastest-Growing Opportunities* (pp. 307-310) **3666**
"Aircraft Mechanics" in *Opportunities in Travel Careers* (pp. 37-39) **3667**
"Aircraft Mechanics" in Volume 1 of *Career Discovery Encyclopedia* (pp. 36-37) **3668**
"Aircraft Mechanics and Engine Specialists" in *Occupational Outlook Handbook* (pp. 326-327) **3669**
"Aircraft Mechanics and Engine Specialists" in Volume 3 of *The Encyclopedia of Careers and Vocational Guidance* (pp. 471-475) **3670**
Aircraft Mechanics Digest **3698**
Aircraft Mechanic's Shop Manual **3699**
Aircraft Repair Manual **3700**
Aircraft Technician **3705**
Aircraft Technicians **3671**
Airline Attendants **3006**
"Airline Baggage and Freight Handler" in *Transportation*, Volume 12 of *Career Information Center* (pp. 35-36) **6999**
Airline Dispatcher **1285**
"Airline Dispatcher" in *Occu-Facts: Information on 565 Careers in Outline Form* (p. 10.22) **1286**
"Airline Dispatcher" in *Transportation*, Volume 12 of *Career Information Center* (pp. 122-124) **1287**
Airline Dispatchers **1288**
"Airline Flight Attendant" in *Transportation*, Volume 12 of *Career Information Center* (pp. 91-92) **3007**
"Airline Freight Handler" in *Transportation* (pp. 15-17) **7000**
"The Airline Mechanic" in *Opportunities in Airline Careers* (pp. 101-105) **3672**
"Airline Reservations Agent" in *Transportation*, Volume 12 of *Career Information Center* (pp. 36-38) **1196**
"Airline Reservations Agent" in *Travel & Tourism* (pp. 21-25) **1197**
Airline Reservations Sales Agent **1198**
"Airline Sales and Reservations" in *The Travel Agent: Dealer in Dreams* (pp. 113-128) **1199**
Airline, Ship & Catering **683**
Airline Ticket Agent **1200**
"Airline Ticket Agent" in *Occu-Facts: Information on 565 Careers in Outline Form* (p. 12.17) **1201**
"Airline Ticket Agent" in *Transportation*, Volume 12 of *Career Information Center* (pp. 38-39) **1202**
Airplane Cleaner **7001**
"Airplane Cleaner" in *Occu-Facts: Information on 565 Careers in Outline Form* (p. 20.18) **7002**
"Airplane Dispatchers" in Volume 3 of *The Encyclopedia of Careers and Vocational Guidance* (pp. 725-728) **1289**
"Airplane Mechanic" in *VGM's Careers Encyclopedia* (pp. 32-34) **3673**
"Airplane Mechanics" in *The American Almanac of Jobs and Salaries* (p. 405) **3674**
Airport Journal **3038, 3706**
Airport Press **3707**
Airport Services **3039**
Airpower Journal **7148**
AISC News **5880**
Alaska State Department of Commerce and Economic Development • Division of Occupational Licensing **7184**
Aligning & Adjusting Cylinders...Instructor Guide **6250**
Aligning & Adjusting Cylinders on the Sheetfed Offset Press **6251**
Alive or Dead **4392**
All Hands **7149**
All Pro **58, 163, 395, 478, 574**
"All Round Machinist" in *Manufacturing*, Volume 9 of *Career Information Center* (pp. 59-61) **5766**
"All-Round Machinist" in *Occu-Facts: Information on 565 Careers in Outline Form* (p. 17.4) **5767**
Alliance of American Insurers **151, 749**
Almost Free Cookbooks and Recipes Update **2365**
Alphabetic Filing Rules **1469**
Alternatives to Assembly Lines: Modern Times—Revisited **5587**
AM News **854**
AM Proceedings **855**
The AMA Handbook of Marketing for the Service Industries **605**
AMA Project Update **856, 5620**
AMA Public Affairs Review **767**
AMB - International Exhibition for Metal Working **5797, 5832, 5932, 5997**
Ambulatory Pediatric Association—Newsletter **2907**
AMC Van Operator Lifetime Achievement Award **6846**
America at Its Best: Opportunities in the National Guard **7080**
American Academy of Ophthalmology **6525**
American Agent & Broker **768**
American Agriculturist **3305**
American Angler **3491**
American Animal Hospital Association Annual Meeting **2816**
American Apparel Manufacturers Association **6299, 6320**
American Architectural Manufacturers Association—Quarterly Review **4629, 4725, 4783, 4853, 4916, 5005, 5064, 5104, 5159, 5206, 5300, 5375, 5468, 5515, 5560**
American Association for Continuity of Care Annual Conference **3151**
American Association for Laboratory Animal Science **2786, 2791**
American Association of Managing General Agents Trade Mart **152**
American Association of Meat Processors **5650**
American Association of Medical Assistants **2666, 2672**
American Association of Medical Assistants Regional Conferences **2697**
American Association of Nurserymen **3053**
American Association of Nurserymen Annual Convention and Nursery Industry Exposition **3109**
American Association of Zoo Keepers **2787, 2817**
American Bankers Association **799, 1157**
American Beef Cattleman **3306**
American Boarding Kennel Association **2788, 2792, 2818**
American Boat Builders & Repairers Association—Bulletin **4496**
American Bus Association **6643**
American Bus Association's Motorcoach Marketer: Complete Directory of the Intercity Bus & Travel/Tourism Industry **670**
American Ceramic Society Source **5557**
American Collectors Association **750**
American Convention of Meat Processors **3573, 5662**
American Correctional Association **1898, 1900**
American Correctional Association Congress of Correction **1922, 2083**
American Correctional Association Winter Conference **1923, 2084**
American Council of Nanny Schools **3216, 3218**
American Culinary Federation **2337, 2419**
American Culinary Federation Educational Institute Apprenticeship Programs **2347**
American Deli-Bakery Showcase **2539**
American Dental Assistants Association **2594, 2633**
American Dental Association **2595, 2597, 6496, 6498**
American Dental Hygienists' Association Convention **2634**
American Dyestuff Reporter **6379**
American Educator **1761**
American Electronics Association—Update **3976**
American Express Pocket Guides **671**
American Farm Bureau Federation **3259**
American Farm Bureau Federation Annual Meeting and Trade Show - Farm/Ranch Expo **3415**
American Farmer **3279**
American Federation of Teachers **1755**
American Federation of Violin and Bow Makers **4518, 4523, 4546**
American Feed Industry Association Feed Industries Show **3416**
American Fiber Manufacturers Association **6373, 6393**
American Fire Journal **2010**
American Fisheries Society Convention **3574**
American Floorcovering Association Convention **4807**
American Forage and Grassland Council **3260**
American Forestry Association Convention and Exposition **3649**
American Forests **3611**
American Foundrymen's Society **5815, 5876**

Index to Information Sources

American Foundrymen's Society Casting Congress and Cast Expo 5833, 5885
American Furniture Manufacturers Association 6453, 6476
American Gem Trade Association Gem Fair and Trade Show 5758
American Health Care Association 2734, 2736
American Horticulturist 3086
American Hospital Association 2735
American Hotel & Motel Association 1124
American Hotel and Motel Association Convention 1138
American Hotel and Motel Association Fall Conference 1139
American Humane Association Annual Meeting and Training Conference 2819
American Hunter 3492
American Images 2972
American Ink Maker 6255
American Institute of Banking Scholarship 802, 953
American Institute of Constructors—Newsletter 4630, 4726, 4784, 4854, 4917, 5006, 5065, 5105, 5160, 5207, 5301, 5376, 5469, 5516, 5561
American Institute of Merchant Shipping 6958, 6997
American Institute of Organbuilders 4519, 4524, 4547
American Jewelry Manufacturer 5739
American Journal of Agricultural Economics 3307
American Library Association 1498, 1520
American Machinist—Buyers' Guide Issue 5802, 5837
American Management Association 843, 5616
American Management Association Pack Expo 873
American Meat Institute Exposition 5663
American Meat Institute—Newsletter 5656
American Medical Technologists 2667
American Mover 6707
American Movers Conference 6832
American Movers Conference Trade Show 6713
American Nanny 3194
American Nurseryman 3087
American Painting Contractor 5161
American Payroll Association 1055, 1056
American Petroleum Institute 5429
American Photo 6610
American Pilots' Association 3470
American Police Academy 2158, 2165
The American Postal Worker 1277, 1421
American Postal Workers Union 1268, 1381, 1430
American Printer 6142, 6171, 6209, 6256
American Professionals Series 164, 1925, 3223, 3447, 4372, 5418
American Public Transit Association 6644, 6666, 6746, 6801
American Railway Engineering Association Bulletin 6769
American Real Estate and Investment Show 384
American Rifleman 3493
The American Rose 3088
American Salesman 115, 214, 460, 537, 611
American Salon Magazine 2973
American School Food Service Association Conference 2420, 2540
American Shipper 1358
American Shoemaking 6354
American Society for Hospital Food Service Administrators Convention 2421, 2541
American Society for Quality Control 5676
American Society for Quality Control Annual Quality Congress 5696
American Society of Appraisers 303, 306, 385
American Society of Chartered Life Underwriters National Conference 153
American Society of CLU and ChFC 101
American Society of Farm Managers and Rural Appraisers 3261, 3263
American Society of Farm Managers and Rural Appraisers Annual Convention 3417
American Society of Plumbing Engineers Convention and Biennial Engineered Plumbing Exposition 5333
American Society of Podiatric Medical Assistants 2668, 2673
American Society of Tax Professionals 1009
American Society of Transportation and Logistics 1353, 1360
American Society of Travel Agents 660, 662
American Society of Travel Agents World Travel Congress 706, 1260
American Soybean Association Annual Conference 3418
American Stock Exchange 1444
American Stock Exchange—Weekly Bulletin 1446
The American System of Practical Bookkeeping: Adapted to the Commerce of the United States 1021
American Teacher 1762
American Textile Machinery Exhibition International 6394
American Textile Manufacturers Institute 6374, 6395
American Train Dispatchers Association 1302, 1322
American Trapper 3494
American Trucker Magazine 6877

American Trucking Associations 6833, 6836, 6915
American Trucking Trends, 1990-91 6925
American Typecasting Fellowship—Newsletter 6172
American Welding Society 5959, 5961
American Welding Society Welding Show 5998
American Woodworker 6465
America's Textiles International 6380
America's Textiles International—Buyer's Guide Issue 6377
Amerigold Bulletin 3089
AMEX Fact Book 1450
AMEX Options 1447
AMFI Industry Report 3722
AMFI Job Opportunities Listing 3723
Ammo 5711, 6565
AMT Events and Continuing Education Supplement 2684
AMTECH - International Aviation Maintenance and Ground Support Equipment Trade Show and Conference 3718
An Analysis of Janitor Service in Elementary Schools 3193
Ancient Double-Entry Bookkeeping 1048
Andrew Seybold's Outlook on Professional Computing 925
Angler & Hunter 3495
Animal Activist Alert 2806
Animal Care Attendant 2759
"Animal Care Attendant" in *Careers for Animal Lovers and Other Zoological Types* (pp. 17-19) 2760
"Animal Care Attendant" in *Occu-Facts: Information on 565 Careers in Outline Form* (p. 14.14) 2761
Animal Caretaker 2793
"Animal Caretaker" in *Hospitality and Recreation*, Volume 8 of *Career Information Center* (pp. 35-36) 2762
Animal Caretakers 2763
Animal Caretakers, Except Farm 2800
"Animal Caretakers, Except Farm" in *Occupational Outlook Handbook* (pp. 304-305) 2764
Animal Health Aide 2794
"Animal Health Technicians" in Volume 4 of *The Encyclopedia of Careers and Vocational Guidance* (pp. 377-381) 2765
"Animal Health Technicians" in Volume 1 of *Career Discovery Encyclopedia* (pp. 40-41) 2766
Animal Technicians 2767
"Animal Technicians and Other Paramedical Personnel" in *Opportunities in Veterinary Medicine* (pp. 115-116) 2768
"Animal Technology" in *120 Careers in the Health Care Field* (pp. 1-6) 2769
Animal Warden 2795
Annual Associated Public-Safety Communications Officers (APCO) Annual Conference 2279
Annual Aviation Maintenance Symposium and Trade Show 3719
Annual Hosiery Statistics 6324, 6397
Annual Meeting and Exhibition of the Air and Waste Management Association 6127
Annual Motor Vehicle Inspection 5672
Annual Survey of Data Processing Operations Salaries 942
Ansley House Associates: The Executive Secretary - An Office Job Simulation 1631
Anti-Corrosion Times 4855
APCO BULLETIN 1317
APCO Reports 1318
APEC - Applied Power Electronics Conference and Exposition 3991
API Monthly Statistical Report 5442
API Report to the Membership 5434
"Apparel" in Volume 1 of *The Encyclopedia of Careers and Vocational Guidance* (pp. 25-32) 6274
Apparel College Directory 6302
Apparel Factory Outlet Stores Survey 6310
Apparel Import Digest 6303
"Apparel Industry" in *Manufacturing*, Volume 9 of *Career Information Center* (pp. 95-98) 6275
Apparel Industry Magazine 6311
Apparel Industry Workers 6276
Apparel Plant Wages Survey 6325
Apparel Research Notes 6312
Apparel Show of the Americas 6321
"Apparel Workers" in *Occupational Outlook Handbook* (pp. 418-420) 6277
Apple Library Users Group Newsletter 926, 1505
Appleton & Lange's Review for the Surgical Technology Examination, ARCO 2677
Appliance 4367
Appliance Repairer 4346
"Appliance Repairer" in *VGM's Careers Encyclopedia* (pp. 44-46) 4347

1085

"Appliance Repairers" in *The American Almanac of Jobs and Salaries* (p. 523) **4350**
"Appliance Repairers" in Volume 1 of *Career Discovery Encyclopedia* (pp. 46-47) **4348**
"Appliance Repairers" in Volume 3 of *The Encyclopedia of Careers and Vocational Guidance* (pp. 569-573) **4349**
Appliance Service News **4318, 4368**
Appliance Service Technician, Electrical **4351**
"Appliance Service Worker" in *Consumer, Homemaking, and Personal Services*, Volume 5 of *Career Information Center* (pp. 65-66) **4352**
Application Procedures for Hydropower Licenses, License Amendments, Exemptions and Preliminary Permits **6049**
"Appraisal" in *Career Choices for the 90's for Students of Mathematics* (pp. 142-144) **247**
"Appraisal" in *Opportunities in Real Estate Careers* (pp. 81-85) **248**
"Appraisal" in *The Encyclopedia of Career Choices for the 1990s: A Guide to Entry Level Jobs* (pp. 750-752) **249**
Appraisal Institute **304, 307, 386**
Appraisal Investigator **310**
The Appraisal Journal **340**
The Appraisal Review **341**
Appraiser **311**
"Appraiser" in *Career Choices for the 90's for Students of Economics* (pp. 130-132) **250**
"Appraiser" in *Consumer, Homemaking, and Personal Services*, Volume 5 of *Career Information Center* (pp. 95-96) **251**
Appraiser Gram **342**
Appraiser News **343**
Arc Welding Methods **5936**
Are You Known for the Company You Keep? **2598**
ARGO-TECHNIKA - Agricultural Machines, Equipment, and Instruments Show **3419**
Arizona State Department of Administration • State Boards Office **7185**
"Armed Forces" in *Opportunities in Business Communication Careers* (pp. 38-39) **7081**
"Armed Forces" in *Opportunities in Pharmacy Careers* (pp. 115-117) **7082**
"Armed Forces" in *Opportunities in Transportation Careers* (pp. 127-129) **7083**
"Armed Forces" in *Opportunities in Vocational and Technical Careers* (pp. 37-41) **7084**
Armed Forces and Society **7150**
Armed Forces Careers **7085**
Armed Forces Journal International **7151**
Armed Forces Test (AFT/ASVAB) **7136**
"Armed Forces Training" in *Careers With Robots* (pp. 111-115) **7086**
"Armed Services Careers" in *Public and Community Services*, Volume 11 of *Career Information Center* (pp. 37-39) **7087**
Armor **7152**
Army Aviation Magazine **7153**
Army Career Opportunities **7088**
Army Communicator **7154**
Army Flier **7155**
ARMY Magazine **7156**
"Army Nurse" in *120 Careers in the Health Care Field* (p. 265) **7090**
"Army Nurse Corps" in *Opportunities in Nursing Careers* (pp. 110-111) **7089**
Army Reserve Magazine **7157**
Army Times **7158**
Around the Bargaining Loop **6143, 6173, 6210, 6257**
The Art of Giving Quality Service in the Motor Carrier Industry **6854**
"Art Supply Salesperson" in *Career Opportunities in Art* (p. 155) **396**
ARTAFACTS **684, 1239**
Arte and Tecnica (Italy) **2915**
Artistic Woodturning **6458**
ARW Counterline **215**
ARW Wholesaler News **216**
ASA Business Valuation **334**
ASA News **5302**
ASA Newsline **344**
Asbestos Abatement Reference Manual **5098**
"Asbestos and Insulating Worker" in *Opportunities in Building Construction Trades* (pp. 47-49) **5086**
ASCLU & ChFC Financial Monitor **116**
ASE Test Registration Booklet **3751, 3858, 4110, 6562**
ASE Training Guide **3752, 3859, 4111, 6563**
ASHRAE Journal **4319**
ASHRAE Pocket Guide for Air-Conditioning, Heating, Ventilation & Refrigeration **4300**
Ashton-Tate—Update **927**
"Asphalt Paving Machine Operator" in Volume 1 of *Career Discovery Encyclopedia* (pp. 60-61) **6670**

Asphalt Paving Machine Operators **7003**
"Asphalt Paving Machine Operators" in Volume 3 of *The Encyclopedia of Careers and Vocational Guidance* (pp. 619-622) **6671**
Asphalt Roofing Manufacturers Association—Newsletter **5377**
ASPMA Journal **2685**
ASPMA Newsletter **2686**
"Assembler" in *Manufacturing*, Volume 9 of *Career Information Center* (pp. 37-39) **5588**
Assembler, Aircraft **5589**
"Assemblers" in Volume 1 of *Career Discovery Encyclopedia* (pp. 62-63) **5590**
"Assemblers" in Volume 3 of *The Encyclopedia of Careers and Vocational Guidance* (pp. 573-576) **5591**
Assemblers, Electronics Manufacturing **5592**
Assembly Technology Expo **6362**
Assessment Assistant **756**
Assessment Clerk **757**
"Assessors and Appraisers" in Volume 1 of *Career Discovery Encyclopedia* (pp. 64-65) **252**
"Assessors and Appraisers" in Volume 2 of *The Encyclopedia of Careers and Vocational Guidance* (pp. 44-48) **253**
ASSET Program **3873**
ASSET: Q: Where Can You. . .? **3925**
Assets: A Business, Tax, and Financial Newsletter **117**
Assistant Accountant **1016**
Assistant Bridge Operator **6962**
Assistant Captain **6963**
Assistant Cashier **17**
Assistant Clerk **1078**
Assistant Cook **2344**
Assistant Electronic Technician **3946**
Assistant Foreman **5617**
Assistant Gardener **3058**
Assistant Power Plant Operator **6026**
Assistant Real Estate Agent **312**
Assistant Real Estate Appraiser **313**
Assistant Stockman **1281**
Assistant Train Dispatcher **1308, 6748**
Assistant Water Maintenance Foreman **6085**
Associate Claim Examiner **758**
Associate Public Information Specialist **1107**
Associate Public Records Officer **1436**
Associate Quality Assurance Specialist **5678**
Associate Real Estate Broker **254**
Associated Builders and Contractors **4290, 4703, 4762, 4908, 4951, 4986, 5032, 5149, 5182, 5269, 5334, 5458, 5490, 6701**
Associated Builders and Contractors Builder and Contractor Convention and Exposition **4763**
Associated General Contractors National Convention and Constructor Exposition **4764**
Associated General Contractors of America **4442, 4619, 4704, 4832, 5506, 6702**
Associated General Contractors of America—National Newsletter **4443, 4631, 4727, 4856, 5517, 6708**
Associated Landscape Contractors of America **3054, 3110**
Associated Public-Safety Communications Officers **1303, 1323**
Association for Computer Operations Management **913**
Association for Computer Operations Management Automated Operations Symposium **941**
Association of American Railroads **6747**
Association of Boards of Certification **6080, 6082, 6128**
Association of Diesel Specialists International Convention and Exhibit **4134**
Association of Federal Investigators **2159, 2166, 2280**
Association of Home Appliance Manufacturers **4360, 4362, 4371**
Association of Home Appliance Manufacturers—Associates Resource Catalog **4363**
Association of Independent Colleges and Schools **971, 972, 1616, 1617, 1699, 1702**
Association of Management **844**
Association of Operative Millers Technical Conference and Trade Show **4445**
Association of Telemessaging Services International Annual Meeting **4571**
Association of the United States Army **7131**
Association of the United States Army Annual Convention **7183**
ASTA Agency Management **685**
ASTA Educational System Catalog **665**
ASTA Officials Directory **672**
ASTA Stat **686**
ASTA Travel Agency Management Magazine **687**
AstaNotes **688**
ASVAB Basics **7137**

Index to Information Sources

ASVAB Review **7138**
ATA National Truck Driving Championships **6847**
ATEA Journal **1763**
Atlantic Control States Beverage Journal **2503**
Atlantic Offshore Fisherman's Association—Newsletter **3496**
ATMI Bulletin **6381**
Atterbury Letter **689**
AudioVideo International **461**
The Auditor's Guide of Eighteen Sixty-Nine **1049**
Auto Inc. **3780, 3891**
"Auto and Car-Parts Sales Representatives" in *Jobs! What They Are. . .Where They Are. . .What They Pay* (pp. 277-278) **397**
Auto and Flat Glass Journal **3781**
Auto Assembly Line General Repairman **3725, 3818**
Auto Body Repair **3753**
Auto Body Repair Helper **7004**
"Auto Body Repair Helper" in *Occu-Facts: Information on 565 Careers in Outline Form* (p. 20.2) **7005**
Auto Body Repairer **3726, 3727**
"Auto Body Repairer" in *Transportation*, Volume 12 of *Career Information Center* (pp. 92-94) **3728**
Auto Body Repairing & Repainting **3764**
Auto Body Repairmen **3754**
Auto Body Repairmen! Painters/Refinishers! Become a Proven Pro: Get ASE Certified **3748, 6560**
Auto Brake Specialist **3819**
Auto Engineman **3860**
Auto Glass Monthly **5066**
The Auto Index **3782, 3892**
Auto Maintenance Coordinator **3861**
Auto Mecanico Hispano **3893**
Auto Mechanic **3862**
"Auto Mechanic" in *Exploring Nontraditional Jobs for Women* (pp. 89-95) **3820**
"Auto Mechanic" in *The Desk Guide to Training and Work Advisement* (p. 85) **3821**
Auto Mechanic/Automotive Serviceman **3863**
Auto Mechanic (Diesel) **4112**
Auto Mechanics **3864, 3877**
Auto Mechanics for the Complete Dummy **3878**
Auto Mechanics Refresher Course **3879**
Auto Painter **6544**
"Auto Parts Counter Worker" in *Marketing and Distribution*, Volume 10 of *Career Information Center* (pp. 37-38) **398**
Auto Rental News **53**
"Auto Sales Worker" in *Marketing and Distribution*, Volume 10 of *Career Information Center* (pp. 39-41) **399**
Auto Shop Safety **3729, 3822**
Auto Tech Magazine **3894**
Autobody Refinishing Handbook **3765**
Autobody Repair & Refinishing **3766**
Autobody Supply and Equipment Market **3880, 4119, 4220, 4456, 4484**
AutoGlass Magazine **3783**
AutoInc **3784, 3895, 6566**
Autoleather Guild **6411**
Automated Factory **5593**
Automatic Heating **4295**
Automechanics **3881**
Automechanic's Guide to Electronic Instrumentation & Microprocessor **3882**
Automechanics: Understanding the New Technology **3883**
"Automobile Body Repairers" in *Opportunities in Automotive Service Careers* (pp. 25-30) **3730**
"Automobile Body Repairers" in Volume 1 of *Career Discovery Encyclopedia* (pp. 88-89) **3731**
"Automobile Body Repairers" in Volume 3 of *The Encyclopedia of Careers and Vocational Guidance* (pp. 475-479) **3732**
Automobile International **3785, 3896**
Automobile Mechanic Certification Tests **3865**
"Automobile Mechanics" in *The American Almanac of Jobs and Salaries* (pp. 523-524) **3825**
"Automobile Mechanics" in Volume 1 of *Career Discovery Encyclopedia* (pp. 90-91) **3823**
"Automobile Mechanics" in Volume 3 of *The Encyclopedia of Careers and Vocational Guidance* (pp. 480-484) **3824**
"Automobile Painters" in *Opportunities in Automotive Service Careers* (pp. 51-52) **6545**
Automobile Parking Attendant **7006**
"Automobile Sales Workers" in Volume 1 of *Career Discovery Encyclopedia* (pp. 92-93) **400**
"Automobile Sales Workers" in Volume 3 of *The Encyclopedia of Careers and Vocational Guidance* (pp. 134-136) **401**
Automobile Salespeople **402**

"Automobile Salesperson" in *College Board Guide to Jobs and Career Planning* (pp. 132-134) **403**
Automobile Technicians (Mechanics) **3826**
Automobile Washer **7007**
"Automobile Washer" in *Occu-Facts: Information on 565 Careers in Outline Form* (p. 20.20) **7008**
Automotive Aerodynamics: An Update **3813**
Automotive Body Repair News **3786**
"Automotive Body Repairer" in *Occu-Facts: Information on 565 Careers in Outline Form* (p. 15.7) **3733**
"Automotive Body Repairer" in *The Career Connection II: A Guide to Technical Majors and Their Related Careers* (pp. 3-4) **3734**
Automotive Body Repairers **3735**
"Automotive Body Repairers" in *Occupational Outlook Handbook* (pp. 327-329) **3736**
"Automotive Brake Specialist" in *Occu-Facts: Information on 565 Careers in Outline Form* (p. 15.2) **3827**
Automotive Chassis & Body **3767**
"Automotive Cooling System Technicians" in Volume 4 of *The Encyclopedia of Careers and Vocational Guidance* (p. 123) **3828**
Automotive Dealers Business Show and Conference **3920**
"Automotive, Diesel, and Gas Turbine Technicians" in Volume 4 of *The Encyclopedia of Careers and Vocational Guidance* (pp. 124-130) **4085**
Automotive Distributor Trends and Financial Analysis **3897, 4123, 4229, 4460, 4497**
Automotive Engine Rebuilders Tech Show **3921**
"Automotive Exhaust Emissions Technicians" in Volume 1 of *Career Discovery Encyclopedia* (pp. 96-97) **3829**
Automotive Exterior Body Panels **3768**
Automotive Instrument Panels: Design, Materials & Manufacturing **3814**
Automotive Jobbers in the U.S.A. **3898, 4124, 4230, 4461, 4498**
Automotive Mechanic **3830**
"Automotive Mechanic" in *Occu-Facts: Information on 565 Careers in Outline Form* (p. 15.3) **3831**
"Automotive Mechanic" in *Transportation*, Volume 12 of *Career Information Center* (pp. 94-96) **3832**
"Automotive Mechanic" in *VGM's Careers Encyclopedia* (pp. 54-56) **3833**
Automotive Mechanic Helper **7009**
"Automotive Mechanic Helper" in *Occu-Facts: Information on 565 Careers in Outline Form* (p. 20.3) **7010**
Automotive Mechanics **3884**
"Automotive Mechanics" in *Jobs! What They Are. . .Where They Are. . .What They Pay* (pp. 175-176) **3834**
"Automotive Mechanics" in *Occupational Outlook Handbook* (pp. 329-331) **3835**
The Automotive Messenger **3787, 3899**
"Automotive Painters" in Volume 1 of *Career Discovery Encyclopedia* (pp. 98-99) **6546**
"Automotive Painters" in Volume 3 of *The Encyclopedia of Careers and Vocational Guidance* (pp. 622-625) **6547**
"Automotive Parts Specialists" in *Opportunities in Automotive Service Careers* (pp. 39-44) **404**
Automotive Service Association **3743, 3850, 6554**
Automotive Service Association of Ohio (ASA OH) Industry-Wide Trade Show **3805**
Automotive Service Association of Pennsylvania (ASA PA) Industry-Wide Trade Show **3806**
Automotive Service Councils of California (ASC CA-North) Industry-Wide Trade Show **3807**
Automotive Service Councils of California (ASC CA-South) Industry-Wide Trade Show **3808**
Automotive Service Councils of Missouri (ASC MO) Industry-Wide Trade Show **3809**
Automotive Service Industry Association **3744, 3810, 3851, 3922, 4101, 6555**
Automotive Service Station Attendant **7011**
"Automotive Service Station Attendant" in *Occu-Facts: Information on 565 Careers in Outline Form* (p. 20.16) **7012**
Automotive Serviceman **3866**
Automotive Technician: A Challenging and Changing Career **3836**
"Automotive Technology" in *The Career Connection II: A Guide to Technical Majors and Their Related Careers* (pp. 5-6) **3837**
Automotive Technology Development Contractor's Coordination Meeting, 24th: Proceedings **3926**
Available Pay Survey for the U.S.: An Annotated Bibliography **1066**
Available Pay Survey Reports for Other Countries: An Annotated Bibliography **1067**
The Avant Gardener **3090**
"Average Hourly Wages of Machinists in Ten Cities" in *The American Almanac of Jobs and Salaries* (p. 519) **5768**

VOCATIONAL CAREERS SOURCEBOOK, 1st Edition

"Average Hourly Wages of Material Movement Workers in Ten Cities" in *The American Almanac of Jobs and Salaries* (p. 521) **1326, 1341, 6672**
Aviation Equipment Maintenance **3708**
"Aviation Maintenance" in *The Complete Aviation/Aerospace Career Guide* (pp. 165-169) **3675**
Aviation Maintenance Foundation International **3687, 3720**
Aviation Maintenance Management **3701**
"Aviation Maintenance Technology" in *The Career Connection II: A Guide to Technical Majors and Their Related Careers* (pp. 7-8) **3676**
Aviation Mechanics Bulletin **3709**
"Avionics and Marine Electronics" in *Electronic Service Careers* (pp. 71-76) **3995**
"Avionics Technician" in *Opportunities in Aerospace Careers* (pp. 34-37) **3996**
"Avionics Technician" in *Transportation*, Volume 12 of *Career Information Center* (pp. 96-98) **3997**
"Avionics Technicians" in Volume 4 of *The Encyclopedia of Careers and Vocational Guidance* (pp. 131-134) **3998**
"Avionics Technicians" in Volume 1 of *Career Discovery Encyclopedia* (pp. 100-101) **3999**
Award of Merit **5283**
AWS Directory of Technical Council Committees **5972**

B

"Baby-sitting: Caring for Children in Their Home" in *Exploring Careers in Child Care Services* (pp. 1-8) **3195**
BAC Journal **4632, 4857, 5208, 5562**
The Back Forty **3308**
The Badger Sportsman **3497**
Bagel Baker **2289**
Bagger, Grocery **7013**
"Baitfish Catcher" in *Opportunities in Marine and Maritime Careers* (pp. 110-111) **3448**
Baker **2290**
"Baker" in *Occu-Facts: Information on 565 Careers in Outline Form* (p. 17.30) **2291**
"Bakers" in Volume 1 of *Career Discovery Encyclopedia* (pp. 102-103) **2292**
Bakers and Bakery Products Workers **2293**
Bakers Journal **2366**
Bakery Production and Marketing **2367**
Baking **2368**
"Baking and Pastry" in *Opportunities in Culinary Careers* (pp. 99-106) **2294**
Baking & Snack **2369**
Baking Buyer—Yearbook Issue **2356**
Bank Auditing and Accounting Report **538, 812**
Bank Director's Report **539, 813**
Bank Insurance & Protection Bulletin **540, 814**
Bank Operations Report **541, 815, 1099, 1440, 1877**
Bank Security Report **542, 816**
Bank Teller **781, 782**
"Bank Teller" in *Administration, Business, and Office*, Volume 1 of *Career Information Center* (pp. 42-44) **783**
"Bank Teller" in *Careers in Banking and Finance* (pp. 21-26) **784**
"Bank Teller" in *Guide to Careers Without College* (pp. 53-56) **785**
"Bank Teller" in *Occu-Facts: Information on 565 Careers in Outline Form* (p. 12.45) **786**
"Bank Teller" in *VGM's Careers Encyclopedia* (pp. 60-61) **787**
"Bank Tellers" in *Jobs! What They Are...Where They Are...What They Pay* (pp. 125-126) **788**
"Bank Tellers" in *Occupational Outlook Handbook* (pp. 248-250) **789**
"Bank Tellers" in Volume 1 of *Career Discovery Encyclopedia* (pp. 110-111) **790**
Bank Tellers Do's & Don'ts **804**
The Bank Tellers Job: A Day to Day Reference Guide **805**
Bank Teller's Report **817**
The Bankers Magazine **818**
"Banking and Financial Services" in Volume 1 of *The Encyclopedia of Careers and Vocational Guidance* (pp. 54-64) **479**
Banking Expansion Reporter **543, 819**
Barber **2823, 2824, 2841**
"Barber" in *Occu-Facts: Information on 565 Careers in Outline Form* (p. 13.32) **2825**
"Barber and Hairstylist" in *Consumer, Homemaking, and Personal Services*, Volume 5 of *Career Information Center* (pp. 66-68) **2826**
Barber Schools in the USA **2843**
Barber Schools in the USA & PR [Puerto Rico] **2844**
Barber-Stylists **2827**
Barbering Hall of Fame **2846**
"Barbers" in *Occupational Outlook Handbook* (pp. 306-307) **2828**
"Barbers" in *Opportunities in Vocational and Technical Careers* (pp. 76-77) **2829**
"Barbers" in Volume 1 of *Career Discovery Encyclopedia* (pp. 112-113) **2830**
"Barbers" in Volume 3 of *The Encyclopedia of Careers and Vocational Guidance* (pp. 195-198) **2831**
"Barbers and Beauticians" in *The American Almanac of Jobs and Salaries* (pp. 529-530) **2832, 2916**
Barbers' Equipment & Supplies—Wholesale Directory **2859**
Barron's How to Prepare for the Armed Forces Test - ASVAB **7139**
Barron's How to Prepare for the U.S. Postal Service Mail Handler - Mail Processor Examination **1390**
Bartender **2504**
"Bartender" in *Hospitality and Recreation*, Volume 8 of *Career Information Center* (pp. 37-38) **2435**
"Bartender" in Volume 1 of *Career Discovery Encyclopedia* (pp. 114-115) **2436**
Bartenders **2437**
"Bartenders" in *Opportunities in Restaurant Careers* (pp. 19-22) **2438**
"Bartenders" in *Opportunities in Vocational and Technical Careers* (pp. 72-73) **2439**
"Bartenders" in Volume 3 of *The Encyclopedia of Careers and Vocational Guidance* (pp. 198-201) **2440**
"Bartenders, Waiters, and Bus Persons" in *The American Almanac of Jobs and Salaries* (pp. 526-527) **2441**
Basic Bookkeeping **1022**
Basic Guide to Black & White Darkroom Techniques **6594**
Basic Metric Style Manual for Secretaries **1632**
Basic Petroleum Data Book **5431**
Basic Plumbing Skills **5285**
Basic Responsibilities of Waiters and Waitresses **2442**
Basic Retail Selling Skills **405, 406**
Basic Secretarial Skills **1559**
Basic Training: What to Expect and How to Prepare **7091**
Bassin' **3498**
Bassmaster Magazine **3499**
Battalion Chief, Fire Dept. **1959**
BC&T News **2370**
"Beautician" in *How to Get a Job With a Cruise Line* (p. 4) **2917**
"Becoming a Chef" in *Opportunities in Culinary Careers* (pp. 17-39) **2295**
Becoming a Helper **2863, 3121, 3196**
Becoming a Professional Firefighter **1926**
BEEF **3309**
Beef Today **3310**
Beefweek **3311**
The Beginning Consultant Training Program **1527**
Beginning Office Worker **1079**
Being a Long-Term Care Nursing Assistant **2700**
Bellman/Bellwoman of the Year **1127**
The Bench Sheet **6106**
A Benefit-Cost Analysis of Alternative Library Delivery Systems **1522**
"Benefits Claims Examiner" in *Opportunities in Insurance Careers* (p. 39) **716**
Better Black & White Darkroom Techniques **6595**
Between Issues **3312**
Beverage Alcohol Market Report **2505**
Beverage Control Inspector **5679**
Beverage Digest **2506**
BIA Directory **4624**
BIA News **4633**
Bia Technical Notes **4634**
Big Questions? **4894, 5131**
Big Show Expo Beauty and Hair Care Show **2853, 2985**
Big Show - Northeast Construction Expo **5033**
Bijou **5740**
Bill Collector **717**
"Bill Collector" in *Occu-Facts: Information on 565 Careers in Outline Form* (p. 12.44) **718**
Bill Collectors **719**
"Billing Clerk" in *Careers in Trucking* (pp. 20-21) **975**
"Billing Clerk" in Volume 1 of *Career Discovery Encyclopedia* (pp. 120-121) **976**
Billing Clerks **977**
"Billing Clerks" in *Occupational Outlook Handbook* (p. 255) **978**
"Billing Clerks" in Volume 3 of *The Encyclopedia of Careers and Vocational Guidance* (pp. 2-4) **979**
Binders Bulletin **6144**
Binders' Guild—Newsletter **6145**
"Bindery Workers" in *Occupational Outlook Handbook* (pp. 411-414) **6130**
"Bindery Workers" in Volume 1 of *Career Discovery Encyclopedia* (pp. 122-123) **6131**

1088

Index to Information Sources

"Bindery Workers" in Volume 3 of *The Encyclopedia of Careers and Vocational Guidance* (pp. 491-495) **6132**
Binding Industries of America **6156**
Biodynamics **3313**
Bits 'n Chips **6466**
Black & White Darkroom Techniques **6596**
"Blue-Collar Worker Supervisors" in *Occupational Outlook Handbook* (pp. 387-388) **5609**
"Blue Collar Worker Supervisors" in Volume 3 of *The Encyclopedia of Careers and Vocational Guidance* (pp. 728-731) **5610**
Blue Reports, Inc. **4635, 4728, 4785, 4858, 4918, 5007, 5067, 5106, 5162, 5209, 5303, 5378, 5470, 5518, 5563**
The Blue Seal **3788, 3900, 4125, 6567**
Blueprint Reading for Plumbers: Residential & Commercial **5286**
BMWE Journal **6770**
Boarderline **2807**
Boardwalk Art Show **5732**
"Boat Motor Mechanic" in *Transportation*, Volume 12 of *Career Information Center* (pp. 98-100) **4468**
Body Repair Inspector **3755**
"Bodyguard" in *Action Careers: Employment in the High-Risk Job Market* (pp. 5-14) **2048**
Boilermaker **5698**
"Boilermaker" in *Occu-Facts: Information on 565 Careers in Outline Form* (p. 17.5) **5699**
Boilermakers **5700**
"Boilermakers" in *Occupational Outlook Handbook* (pp. 391-392) **5701**
Boilermakers-Blacksmiths Reporter **5712**
"Boilermaking Occupations" in Volume 3 of *The Encyclopedia of Careers and Vocational Guidance* (pp. 625-629) **5702**
"Boilermaking Worker" in *Manufacturing*, Volume 9 of *Career Information Center* (pp. 42-44) **5703**
"Boilermaking Workers" in Volume 1 of *Career Discovery Encyclopedia* (pp. 132-133) **5704**
Book Arts Review **6146, 6174, 6211, 6258**
Book Bindery Worker **6133**
The Book of $16,000-$60,000 Post Office Jobs: Where They Are, What They Pay, and How to Get Them **1362**
The Book of the Free Trapper **3578**
"Bookbinder" in *Communications and the Arts*, Volume 3 of *Career Information Center* (pp. 51-52) **6134**
Bookbinder and Bindery Workers **6135**
"Bookbinder and Bindery Workers" in *Occu-Facts: Information on 565 Careers in Outline Form* (p. 17.16) **6136**
Bookkeeper **987**
"Bookkeeper" in *Administration, Business, and Office*, Volume 1 of *Career Information Center* (pp. 44-45) **988**
"Bookkeeper" in *Career Opportunities in Television, Cable, and Video* (pp. 20-21) **989**
"Bookkeeper" in *Occu-Facts: Information on 565 Careers in Outline Form* (p. 12.27) **990**
Bookkeeper - Account Clerk **1017**
"The Bookkeeper-Accountant" in *Opportunities in Office Occupations* (pp. 131-140) **991**
"Bookkeeper and Accounting Clerk" in *Careers in Banking and Finance* (pp. 26-27) **992**
"Bookkeeper, Secretary, and Clerk" in *Travel & Tourism* (pp. 69-73) **993, 1560**
"Bookkeepers" in Volume 1 of *Career Discovery Encyclopedia* (pp. 134-135) **994**
Bookkeepers and Accounting Clerks **995**
"Bookkeepers and Accounting Clerks" in *Jobs! What They Are...Where They Are...What They Pay* (pp. 132-133) **996**
"Bookkeeping" in *The Career Connection II: A Guide to Technical Majors and Their Related Careers* (pp. 9-10) **1000**
"Bookkeeping, Accounting, and Auditing Clerks" in *Occupational Outlook Handbook* (pp. 255-256) **997**
"Bookkeeping and Accounting" in *The Desk Guide to Training and Work Advisement* (pp. 177-178) **998**
"Bookkeeping and Accounting Clerk" in Volume 3 of *The Encyclopedia of Careers and Vocational Guidance* (pp. 5-8) **999**
Bookkeeping & Accounts **1023**
Bookkeeping for a Small Business **1024**
Bookkeeping for Beginners **1025**
Bookkeeping for Small Organizations: A Handbook for Treasurers & Finance Committees **1026**
Bookkeeping for the Nineteen Nineties **1027**
Bookkeeping Made Easy **1028**
Bookkeeping Made Simple **1029**
Bookkeeping: Outline of Double Entry Bookkeeping for Small Business & Co-Operatives **1030**

"Bookkeeping Systems Operator" in *Occu-Facts: Information on 565 Careers in Outline Form* (p. 12.28) **1001**
Bookkeeping Systems Operators **1002**
Bookkeeping the Easy Way **1031**
Border Patrol Agent **2088, 2089**
"Bow Repairer and Restorer" in *Career Opportunities in the Music Industry* (pp. 131-132) **4502**
Bowhunter Magazine **3500**
Brahman Journal **3314**
"Brake Operators, Brakers" in Volume 3 of *The Encyclopedia of Careers and Vocational Guidance* (pp. 731-733) **6719**
"Brake Operators or Brakemen" in *The American Almanac of Jobs and Salaries* (p. 465) **6720**
"Brake Specialist" in *Opportunities in Automotive Service Careers* (p. 54) **3838**
"Brakers" in Volume 1 of *Career Discovery Encyclopedia* (pp. 136-137) **6721**
Branding Hammer Award **6764**
Brangus Journal **3315**
"Breaking into Sales & Trading on Wall Street" in *Internships Volume 3: Accounting, Banking, Brokerage, Finance & Insurance* (pp. 49-53) **480**
Breathline **2687, 2748**
Brick in Architecture **4636**
Brick Institute of America **4620, 4671**
Bricklayer **4593, 4622**
"Bricklayer" in *Construction*, Volume 4 of *Career Information Center* (pp. 39-41) **4594**
"Bricklayer" in *Occu-Facts: Information on 565 Careers in Outline Form* (p. 16.2) **4595**
Bricklayer Helper **7014**
"Bricklayer Helper" in *Occu-Facts: Information on 565 Careers in Outline Form* (p. 20.5) **7015**
"Bricklayers" in *Opportunities in Building Construction Trades* (pp. 49-52) **4596**
"Bricklayers" in *The American Almanac of Jobs and Salaries* (pp. 500-501) **4601**
Bricklayers and Stonemasons **4597**
"Bricklayers and Stonemasons" in *Occupational Outlook Handbook* (pp. 362-363) **4598**
"Bricklayers and Stonemasons" in Volume 1 of *Career Discovery Encyclopedia* (pp. 138-139) **4599**
"Bricklayers and Stonemasons" in Volume 3 of *The Encyclopedia of Careers and Vocational Guidance* (pp. 629-632) **4600**
Bricklaying **4602**
"A Bright Future in Classified Ad Sales" in *Newspapers Career Directory* (pp. 17-19) **575**
Broad Axe Award **6765**
"Broker" in *Careers in Banking and Finance* (pp. 27-33) **481**
Brokerage Clerk/Sales Assistant **1442**
"Brokerage Clerks and Statement Clerks" in *Occupational Outlook Handbook* (p. 272) **1443**
"Brokers" in *The American Almanac of Jobs and Salaries* (pp. 420-421) **482**
"Brokers: Steady As IT Goes" in *Getting Into Money: A Career Guide* (pp. 58-73) **483**
Brotherhood of Maintenance of Way Employees Railway Journal **6771**
BSCA Insurance Advisor **3185**
BSCAI Information Central Guide **3178**
Budget Vacationers Guidebook—Western U.S. **673**
BUFFALO! **3316**
Builder **4637, 4729, 4919, 5210, 5379**
The Builder and Contractor **4320**
Builder and Contractor **4638, 4730**
The Builder and Contractor **4731**
Builder and Contractor **4920**
The Builder and Contractor **4921, 5008, 5163**
Builder and Contractor **5211**
The Builder and Contractor **5304**
Builder and Contractor **5380**
The Builder and Contractor **5471, 6709**
Builder Architect **4639, 4732, 4922, 5212, 5381**
Builder/Dealer **4640, 4733, 4923, 5213, 5382**
Builder Insider **4641, 4734, 4924, 5214, 5383**
Builder Magazine **4321, 4735, 4925**
Builder Notes **4642**
Builder's Log **4322**
Building Business & Management **4643, 4736, 4926, 5215, 5384**
Building Concerns **4644, 4737, 4786, 4859, 4927, 5009, 5068, 5107, 5164, 5216, 5305, 5385, 5472, 5519, 5564**
"Building Custodian" in *Exploring Nontraditional Jobs for Women* (pp. 99-105) **3154**
"Building Custodian" in *Personal Services* (pp. 21-25) **3155**

1089

"Building Custodian" in *Public and Community Services*, Volume 11 of *Career Information Center* (pp. 41-42) **3156**
Building Custodian - Building Superintendent - Custodian Engineer **4247**
Building Design & Construction **4645, 4738, 4928, 5217, 5386**
Building Guard **2072**
Building Homes & Renovations **4646, 4739, 4929, 5218, 5387**
Building Industry **4647, 4740, 4930, 5219, 5388**
Building Industry Technology: An Abstract Newsletter **4648, 4741, 4787, 4860, 4931, 5010, 5069, 5108, 5165, 5220, 5306, 5389, 5473, 5520, 5565**
Building Maintenance Management **4235**
Building Renovation **4788, 4861, 5070, 5166, 5566**
Building Service Contractors Association International **3167, 3169**
Building Service Contractors Association International—Services **3186**
Building Services Contractor **3187**
Buildings **4649, 4742, 4932, 5221, 5390**
Bulldozer Operator **6673**
"Bulldozer Operator" in *Occu-Facts: Information on 565 Careers in Outline Form* (p. 19.17) **6674**
Bulletin Voyages **1240**
Bureau News **217**
Bureau of Wholesale Sales Representatives **208, 240**
Bureau of Wholesale Sales Representatives News **218**
Burnout in Probation & Corrections **1906**
Bus Driver **6646**
"Bus Driver" in *Exploring Nontraditional Jobs for Women* (pp. 63-69) **6625**
"Bus Driver" in *Transportation* (pp. 27-31) **6626**
Bus Drivers **6627**
"Bus Drivers" in Volume 1 of *Career Discovery Encyclopedia* (pp. 140-141) **6628**
Bus Driver's Guide to Commercial Driver Licensing **6647**
"Bus Lines" in *Opportunities in Travel Careers* (p. 59-63) **6629**
Bus Operator - Conductor **6648**
Bus World **6652**
Busdrivers **6630**
"Busdrivers" in *Occu-Facts: Information on 565 Careers in Outline Form* (p. 19.5) **6631**
"Busdrivers" in *Occupational Outlook Handbook* (pp. 434-436) **6632**
Business & Commercial Aviation **3710**
Business & Data Processing Machine Operators **1805**
Business and Finance Career Directory **59, 484**
"Business Computers and Office Equipment Service" in *Electronic Service Careers* (pp. 46-56) **4029**
Business Farmer-Stockman **3317**
Business Insurance: A Sales Skills Introduction **60**
"Business Machine Operator" in *Administration, Business, and Office*, Volume 1 of *Career Information Center* (pp. 46-47) **4030**
"Business Machine Repairers" in *Jobs! What They Are...Where They Are...What They Pay* (pp. 206-207) **4031**
"Business Machine Service Technician" in *VGM's Careers Encyclopedia* (pp. 72-73) **4032**
"Business Machine Service Technician" in *VGM's Handbook of Scientific and Technical Careers* (pp. 18-19) **4033**
Business of Travel: Agency Operations & Administration **674, 1232**
"Business Realtors" in *The New York Times Career Planner* (pp. 139-141) **255**
Busy Person's Guide to Selecting the Right Word Processor: A Visual Shortcut to Understanding & Buying, Complete with Checklist & Prod. Guide **1859**
Butcher **5652**
"Butcher or Boucher" in *Opportunities in Culinary Careers* (pp. 61-62) **5632**
"Butchers and Meat, Poultry, and Fish Cutters" in *Occupational Outlook Handbook* (pp. 389-390) **5633**
Buying Payroll Software **1060**

C

Cabinetmaker **6435**
"Cabinetmaker" in *Occu-Facts: Information on 565 Careers in Outline Form* (p. 17.12) **6436**
"Cabinetmaker" in *Opportunities in Carpentry Careers* (p. 51) **6437**
"Cabinetmaker" in *Opportunities in Crafts Careers* (pp. 30-31) **6438**
"Cabinetmaking" in *The Career Connection II: A Guide to Technical Majors and Their Related Careers* (pp. 17-18) **6439**
Cable Hardware & Technology **4421**
The Cable Job Guide **4393**
"Cable Splicer" in *Exploring Nontraditional Jobs for Women* (pp. 26-31) **4394**
"Cable Splicer" in *Opportunities in Electrical Trades* (pp. 58-60) **4395**
Cable Television Systems Technicians and Installers **4396**

Cable Television Technology Handbook **4422**
"Cafeteria Attendant" in *Hospitality and Recreation*, Volume 8 of *Career Information Center* (pp. 40-42) **2443**
"Cafeteria Counter Worker" in *Occu-Facts: Information on 565 Careers in Outline Form* (p. 13.15) **2444**
Calavo Newsletter **3318**
CALF News Magazine Ltd. **3319**
California State and Consumer Services Agency • Department of Consumer Affairs **7186**
CALTRUX **6878**
Campus Safety Newsletter **2080**
The Canadian Secretary's Handbook: An on-the-job Guide for Office Professionals **1633**
CAP Orientation Guide **3927**
Capital Comments **4650, 4743, 4789, 4862, 4933, 5011, 5071, 5109, 5167, 5222, 5307, 5391, 5474, 5521, 5567**
Capital News **2371**
Capital Police Officer **2170**
Captain, Fire Dept. **1960**
Captain, Police Dept. **2171**
Car Maintenance in the U.S.A. **3885, 4120, 4221, 4457, 4485**
"Car or Truck Rental Agent" in *Transportation* (pp. 69-73) **29**
"Car Rental Agent" in *Transportation*, Volume 12 of *Career Information Center* (pp. 44-46) **30**
Car Rental Agents **31**
"Car Rental Agents" in Volume 1 of *Career Discovery Encyclopedia* (pp. 158-159) **32**
"Car Rental Agents" in Volume 3 of *The Encyclopedia of Careers and Vocational Guidance* (pp. 136-139) **33**
Car Wash Attendants **7016**
Car Wash Operator **7017**
Carbon & Carbro Tissue: You Can Make It! **6597**
The Care & Repair of Small Marine Diesels **4486**
Career Choices: Computer Science **874**
Career Examination Series **1018, 1850, 1901, 2678, 2737, 3171, 5709**
A Career for Looking Good, Feeling Great **2918**
Career Guidance Handouts **2348, 2491, 3758, 4113, 5966**
Career in Air Transport Flight Services **3008**
Career in Air Transport Ground Services **622, 1203**
A Career in Computer Typesetting **6158**
Career in Ophthalmic Medical Assisting **2635**
"A Career in Outdoor Advertising Sales" in *Advertising Career Directory* (pp. 61-64) **576**
Career Information for Precision Machining Technology **5769, 5906**
Career Information in Shoe Repair **6327**
Career Insights **34, 1204, 1561, 1806, 1927, 2919, 3009, 4674, 5241, 5346, 5907, 6577, 7018**
Career Legal Secretary **1634**
Career News Digest **2372, 2507, 3789, 4126, 5990**
Career Opportunities **256**
Career Opportunities in the Fire Sprinkler Industry **5242**
Career Opportunities...in the Automotive Collision Repair and Refinishing Industry **3737, 6548**
"Career Profile: Interview with a Personal Computer Salesman" in *Exploring Careers in the Computer Field* (pp. 95-101) **407**
Career Profiles: Environmental Series **3041, 6073**
Career Strategies for Secretaries: How to Get Where You Want to Be **1090, 1192, 1635**
Career Success Series **61, 165, 408, 791, 946, 968, 1562, 1807, 1928, 2090, 2920, 3010, 3582, 3677, 3839, 4236, 4675, 5087, 5243, 5347, 6002, 6137, 6159, 6191, 6230, 6578**
Career Summary: Farm Manager **3224**
Career Training **2349, 2492, 3759, 4114, 5967**
Careers as a Flight Attendant: Flight to the Future **3011**
Careers at a Zoo **2770**
Careers in a Department Store **409**
Careers in Beauty Culture **2921**
Careers in Computer Field **875**
Careers in Computer Sales **410**
Careers in Computers & Data Processing **876**
Careers in Dental Care **2559**
Careers in Early Childhood Education **2864**
Careers in Electricity **6003**
Careers in Electronics **4137**
Careers in Farm Equipment Mechanics **4210**
Careers in Fashion Retailing **411**
Careers in Health Care **2560, 2636, 2701**
Careers in Health Services: Opportunities for You **2561, 2637, 2702, 3122**
Careers in Insurance: Property and Casualty **62, 720**
"Careers in Law Enforcement" in *Career Planning in Criminal Justice* (pp. 19-54) **2091**
Careers in Life and Health Claims **721**

Index to Information Sources

"Careers in Operations and the Information Center" in *Careers in Computers* (pp. 34-41) 877
"Careers in Private Security" in *Career Planning in Criminal Justice* (pp. 91-95) 2049
Careers in Real Estate 257
Careers in Sheet Metal 5443
Careers in the Electronics Industry 3929, 4138
Careers in the Investment World 485, 792
Careers in Travel 1205
Careers in Truck Driving 6803
Careers in Trucking 6804
Careers with an Electric Company 4397, 4955, 6004
Careers Working With Animals 166
Cargo Express 6975
Caring 3146
Carolinas Association of Professional Insurance Agents Annual Convention 154
Carpenter 4676, 4707, 4708
The Carpenter 4744
"Carpenter" in *Construction*, Volume 4 of *Career Information Center* (pp. 41-43) 4677
"Carpenter" in *Exploring Nontraditional Jobs for Women* (pp. 6-11) 4678
"Carpenter" in *Hard Hatted Women: Stories of Struggle and Success in the Trades* (pp. 45-54) 4679
"Carpenter" in *Opportunities in Crafts Careers* (pp. 29-30) 4680
"Carpenter" in *VGM's Careers Encyclopedia* (pp. 75-78) 4681
Carpenter, Construction 4682
"Carpenter Foreman" in *Hard Hatted Women: Stories of Struggle and Success in the Trades* (pp. 122-134) 5611
Carpenter Helper 7019
"Carpenter Helper" in *Occu-Facts: Information on 565 Careers in Outline Form* (p. 20.6) 7020
Carpenters 4683
"Carpenters" in *Occupational Outlook Handbook* (pp. 363-365) 4684
"Carpenters" in *Opportunities in Building Construction Trades* (pp. 23-29) 4685
"Carpenters" in *The American Almanac of Jobs and Salaries* (p. 501) 4688
"Carpenters" in Volume 1 of *Career Discovery Encyclopedia* (pp. 156-157) 4686
"Carpenters" in Volume 3 of *The Encyclopedia of Careers and Vocational Guidance* (pp. 633-636) 4687
The Carpenter's Manifesto 4713
The Carpenter's Toolbox Manual 4714
Carpentry 4689, 4709
"Carpentry" in *The Career Connection II: A Guide to Technical Majors and Their Related Careers* (pp. 19-20) 4692
"Carpentry and Cabinetmaking" in *The Desk Guide to Training and Work Advisement* (pp. 71-73) 4690
Carpentry & Construction 4691
Carpentry: Framing & Finishing 4715
Carpet and Rugs 4808
Carpet Installer 4771
"Carpet Installer" in *Occu-Facts: Information on 565 Careers in Outline Form* (p. 16.13) 4772
"Carpet Installers" in *Occupational Outlook Handbook* (pp. 365-366) 4773
Carrying the Mail: A Career in Public Service 1363
Case 'n Base News 3612
Cashier 1, 18
"Cashier" in *Marketing and Distribution*, Volume 10 of *Career Information Center* (pp. 41-42) 2
"Cashier" in *Occu-Facts: Information on 565 Careers in Outline Form* (p. 11.22) 3
Cashier-Cashier I 19
Cashier II 20
"Cashiers" in *Occupational Outlook Handbook* (pp. 227-228) 4
"Cashiers" in *Travel Agent* (pp. 171-172) 5
"Cashiers" in Volume 1 of *Career Discovery Encyclopedia* (pp. 164-165) 6
"Cashiers" in Volume 3 of *The Encyclopedia of Careers and Vocational Guidance* (pp. 8-12) 7
Cashiers and Checkers 8
"Cashiers/Retail Clerk" in *The American Almanac of Jobs and Salaries* (p. 531) 9
Cast Metals Institute 5820, 5879
Catalog of Publications and Training Materials 5697, 5803, 5838, 5870, 5905, 5935
"Catalog Order Clerk" in *Occu-Facts: Information on 565 Careers in Outline Form* (p. 12.21) 1524
Catering Industry Employee 2373, 2508
Catering Today—Buyer's Guide Issue 2557

Catgut Acoustical Society—Journal 4536
Cattle Business 3320
Cattle Guard 3321
Cattlemen 3322
CDA in State Child Care Licensing 2895
CDA Professional Preparation Program 2901
"CDA Professional Preparation Program Ready for Start-Up" in *Competence*, Vol. 8, No. 2, July 1991 2902
CDA Scholarship Act Administrative Activities 2903
CDA Scholarship Act: Executive Summary 2904
CDL Commercial Driver License: 104 Helpful CDL Facts 6645, 6837
CEA Newsletter 1915
CEE 5012
Cement Mason 4812, 4840
"Cement Mason" in *Construction*, Volume 4 of *Career Information Center* (pp. 43-45) 4813
"Cement Mason" in *Occu-Facts: Information on 565 Careers in Outline Form* (p. 16.14) 4814
Cement Masons 4815
"Cement Masons" in *Opportunities in Building Construction Trades* (pp. 29-30) 4816
"Cement Masons" in Volume 3 of *Career Discovery Encyclopedia* (pp. 636-639) 4817
"Cement Masons" in Volume 3 of *The Encyclopedia of Careers and Vocational Guidance* (pp. 636-639) 4818
Center for Intelligence Studies 2160
"The Center of the Travel Industry - Getting Started in Car Rental" in *Travel and Hospitality Career Directory* (pp. 41-46) 35
"Central Office Technician" in *Exploring Nontraditional Jobs for Women* (pp. 32-37) 4000
Ceramic Tile Distributors Association Ceramic Tile Exposition 4886, 5581
Certification Examination for Medical Assistants (CMA) 2679
Certification for Dental Assistants: Dental Assisting National Board Examinations 2599
Certification—Why and How 2680
Certified Advantage for Auto Technicians 3855
Certified Automotive Technician 3840
Certified Electronic Technician (CET) 3947, 4168
Certified General Automobile Mechanic (CGAM) 3867
"Certified Master Chef: the Highest Honor in the Industry" in *Opportunities in Restaurant Careers* (pp. 49-53) 2296
Certified Professional Property Appraisers 335
Certified Professional Secretary 1618
Certified Professional Secretary (CPS) Examination Review 1621
Certified Shorthand Reporter 1704
Certifier 6107
The CET Exam: ISCET: Certified Electronics Technician 3948, 4169
Chalkline 4651, 4863, 5223, 5568
The Challenge of a Lifetime: Careers in Animal Science 2771
Chaptergram 5475
Charolais Banner 3323
The Chase 3501
Cheers 2509
Cheesemakers' Journal 2374
"Chef" in *VGM's Careers Encyclopedia* (pp. 84-86) 2297
"Chef/Cook" in *Guide to Careers Without College* (pp. 97-100) 2298
Chef Institutional 2375
Chefs and Cooks 2299
"Chefs and Cooks" in *Jobs! What They Are. . .Where They Are. . .What They Pay* (pp. 164-165) 2300
"Chefs and Cooks" in *Opportunities in Vocational and Technical Careers* (p. 73) 2301
"Chefs, Cooks, and Other Kitchen Workers" in *Occupational Outlook Handbook* (pp. 294-296) 2302
"Chefs, Cooks, and Other Kitchen Workers" in *Opportunities in Restaurant Careers* (pp. 22-31) 2303
Chekouras Scholarship Fund; Tom 4525
Chemical Plant Operations Training Program 4373
Chief Clerk 1080
Chief Data Processing Equipment Operator 915
Chief Deputy Sheriff 2172
Chief Elevator Starter 4196
Chief File Clerk 1462
Chief Fire Executive 2011
Chief Fire Marshal 1961
Chief Groundskeeper 3059
Chief Investigator 759
Chief Law Stenographer 1705
Chief Meat Inspector 5653, 5680
Chief of Police 2173
Chief of Staff (Sheriff) 2174
Chief of Stenographic Services 1706

VOCATIONAL CAREERS SOURCEBOOK, 1st Edition

Chief Sewage Treatment Plant Operator 6086
Chief Special Investigator 2175
Chief Stationary Engineer 6059
Chief Water Treatment Plant Operator 6087
Child Care Action Campaign 2890
"Child Care Assistant" in *Guide to Careers Without College* (pp. 95-97) 2865
"Child Care Attendant" in *Occu-Facts: Information on 565 Careers in Outline Form* (p. 13.39) 2866
Child Care Employee News 2908
Child Care Employee Project 2891
Child Care: The Bottom Line 2905
Child Care Worker 2867
"Child Care Workers" in Volume 3 of *The Encyclopedia of Careers and Vocational Guidance* (pp. 201-204) 2868
Child Care Workers (Institutions) 2869
"Child Development Associate" in *Exploring Careers in Child Care Services* (pp. 17-18) 2870
"Child Development Associate" in *Opportunities in Child Care Careers* (pp. 47-51) 2871
The Child Development Associate Credential 2896
"Childcare" in *How to Get a Job With a Cruise Line* (pp. 7-13) 2872
Childcare ActioNews 2909
"Childcare Worker" in *VGM's Careers Encyclopedia* (pp. 91-93) 2873
"Childcare Workers" in *America's 50 Fastest Growing Jobs* (pp. 123-125) 2877
"Childcare Workers" in *Occupational Outlook Handbook* (pp. 307-308) 2874
"Childcare Workers" in *Opportunities in Vocational and Technical Careers* (pp. 77-78) 2875
"Childcare Workers" in Volume 2 of *Career Discovery Encyclopedia* (pp. 8-9) 2876
Chile Pepper 2376
Chip Chats 6467
The Choice of the Future 2304, 2445
Choosing & Using a Word Processor 1860
Choosing the Right Travel School 709
CHRIE Communique 2377, 2510
Christmas Trees 3613
Chrysler Dealer Apprenticeship Program 3874
Citation for Bravery 2215
Citizen Soldier: Opportunities in the Reserves 7092
Citrus and Vegetable Magazine 3324
Civil Service Arithmetic and Vocabulary 1391
Civil Service Tests for Basic Skills Jobs 2738, 3060, 3172
"Claim Adjuster" in *Administration, Business, and Office*, Volume 1 of *Career Information Center* (pp. 72-74) 722
"Claim Agent" in *Careers in Trucking* (pp. 75-76) 723
"Claim Examiner" in *Administration, Business, and Office*, Volume 1 of *Career Information Center* (pp. 74-75) 724
"Claim Representative" in *VGM's Careers Encyclopedia* (pp. 107-111) 725
"Claim Representative" in *VGM's Handbook of Business and Management Careers* (pp. 31-34) 726
"Claim Representatives" in *Jobs! What They Are...Where They Are...What They Pay* (pp. 129-130) 727
CLAIMS 118
Claims Adjusters (Insurance) 728
Claims Clerk 760
Claims Investigator 761
"Claims Representatives" in *Opportunities in Insurance Careers* (p. 37) 729
Classified Sales Representative 577
Classroom Companion 2350, 2493, 3760, 4115, 5968
Clean Scene Magazine 6382
Clean Water Report 6108
Cleaner-Helper 7066
"Clerical and Secretarial Work" in *Exploring Careers Using Foreign Languages* (pp. 51-52) 1563
Clerical Careers 1081, 1108
"Clerical Supervisor and Manager" in *Careers in Banking and Finance* (pp. 33-34) 831
Clerical Supervisors and Managers 849
"Clerical Supervisors and Managers" in *Occupational Outlook Handbook* (pp. 250-251) 832
"Clerical Supervisors and Managers" in Volume 3 of *The Encyclopedia of Careers and Vocational Guidance* (pp. 12-15) 833
"Clerical Supervisors and Managers" in Volume 2 of *Career Discovery Encyclopedia* (pp. 22-23) 834
Clerical Worker 1068
"The Clerk" in *Opportunities in Office Occupations* (pp. 49-83) 1069
Clerk: Bank, Insurance and Commerce 793, 980
Clerk, General Office 1070

Clerk, Information 1101
Clerks, Insurance 730
A Clinical Manual for Nursing Assistants 2741
Clinical Preventive Dentistry 2617
Clothing Manufacturers Association—News Bulletin 6313
CMC News 1506
"Coast Guard" in *Opportunities in Marine and Maritime Careers* (pp. 97-100) 7093
Coast Guard Career Opportunities 7094
Codewatch 5308
"Collection Workers" in Volume 3 of *The Encyclopedia of Careers and Vocational Guidance* (pp. 15-18) 731
"Collection Workers" in Volume 2 of *Career Discovery Encyclopedia* (pp. 28-29) 732
Collector 769
"Collectors" in *Jobs! What They Are...Where They Are...What They Pay* (pp. 126-127) 733
College & University Food Service Manual 2446
College of Law Enforcement—Newsletter 2261
College of Oceaneering • International Diving School 3479
College/University Foodservice Who's Who 2351, 2494
Collision Parts Industry Roster & Suppliers Guide 3815
Collision Repair Guide 3769
Collision Repair Report 3790, 3901, 6568
Color Separator Operator/Supervisor 6192
Colorado State Department of Regulatory Agencies 7187
Combustion Hot Spot Analysis for Fired Process Heaters: Prediction, Control, Troubleshooting 4301
"Commercial and Industrial Electronic Equipment Repairers" in *Occupational Outlook Handbook* (pp. 331-333) 3930
Commercial Carrier Journal 6879
"Commercial Diver" in *Occu-Facts: Information on 565 Careers in Outline Form* (p. 15.28) 3449
Commercial Fisher 3450
"Commercial Fisher" in *Occu-Facts: Information on 565 Careers in Outline Form* (p. 14.18) 3451
Commercial Fisheries News 3502
"Commercial Fishers" in Volume 3 of *Career Discovery Encyclopedia* (pp. 32-33) 3452
"Commercial Fishers" in Volume 3 of *The Encyclopedia of Careers and Vocational Guidance* (pp. 357-360) 3453
Commercial Food Equipment Service Association Directory 2430
Commercial Investment Real Estate Journal 345
Commercial Lender Newsletter 820, 1163
Commercial Lenders Alert 955
The Commercial Record 346
Commercial Transaction of the Year Award 329
Commission on Opticianry Accreditation 6527
Commission on Opticianry Accreditation 6528
Commodities Trader 486
"Commodities Traders: Upping the Stakes" in *Getting Into Money: A Career Guide* (pp. 91-107) 487
"Commodity Trader" in *Careers in Banking and Finance* (pp. 37-39) 488
Common Secretarial Mistakes & How to Avoid Them 1636
Communication Skills 623, 1233
"Communications Equipment Mechanic" in *VGM's Careers Encyclopedia* (pp. 111-114) 4001
"Communications Equipment Mechanics" in *Occupational Outlook Handbook* (pp. 333-335) 4002
"Communications Equipment Mechanics" in Volume 3 of *The Encyclopedia of Careers and Vocational Guidance* (pp. 640-643) 4003
"Communications Equipment Mechanics" in Volume 2 of *Career Discovery Encyclopedia* (pp. 40-41) 4004
"Communications Mechanic" in *Opportunities in Electrical Trades* (pp. 83-84) 4005
"Communications or Telecommunications" in *Careers in High Tech* (p. 104) 4006
"Communications Technician" in *VGM's Handbook of Scientific and Technical Careers* (pp. 28-30) 4007
The Communique 928
"Companion" in *Consumer, Homemaking, and Personal Services*, Volume 5 of *Career Information Center* (pp. 38-40) 3197
Compensation and Benefits Review 857, 1541, 5621
CompFlash 858, 5622
The Complete Book of Birdhouse Contruction for Woodworkers 6459
The Complete Computer Career Guide 878
Complete Course in Professional Piano Tuning, Repair & Rebuilding 4528
The Complete Custodial Handbook 3179
The Complete Electronics Career Guide 3931
The Complete Guide to Automotive Refinishing 3770

Index to Information Sources

The Complete Guide To Motorcycle Mechanics **4487**
Complete Handbook for Dental Auxiliaries **6502**
The Complete Handbook of Leathercrafting **6346**
Complete Secretary's Handbook **1564**
Composing Machine Operator **6169**
"Compositors and Typesetters" in *Occupational Outlook Handbook* (pp. 412-414) **6160**
"Compositors and Typesetters" in Volume 3 of *The Encyclopedia of Careers and Vocational Guidance* (pp. 495-499) **6161**
The Comprehensive Custodial Training Manual **3180**
Comprehensive Review of Dental Assisting **2562**
Compu/Graphics Users Association—Newsletter **6175**
"Computer and Office Machine Repairers" in *America's 50 Fastest Growing Jobs* (pp. 129-131) **4034**
"Computer and Office Machine Repairers" in *Occupational Outlook Handbook* (pp. 335-337) **4035**
"Computer and Peripheral Equipment Operators" in *America's 50 Fastest Growing Jobs* (pp. 108-109) **879**
"Computer and Peripheral Equipment Operators" in *Occupational Outlook Handbook* (pp. 251-252) **880**
"Computer and Peripheral Equipment Operators" in Volume 3 of *The Encyclopedia of Careers and Vocational Guidance* (pp. 19-23) **881**
Computer Business **929**
Computer Careers: The Complete Pocket Guide to America's Fastest-Growing Job Market **882**
Computer Craft **930**
Computer Graphics World **931**
Computer Industry Report **932**
Computer Industry Update **933**
Computer/Keypunch Operator **883**
"Computer Maintenance" in *The Career Connection II: A Guide to Technical Majors and Their Related Careers* (pp. 21-22) **4036**
Computer Numerical Control Machine Operators **884**
"Computer Operating" in *Exploring High Tech Careers* (pp. 56-59) **885**
"Computer Operating Personnel" in *The American Almanac of Jobs and Salaries* (pp. 507-509) **886**
"Computer Operations" in *Careers in High Tech* (pp. 34-36) **887**
"Computer Operations" in *Opportunities in Information Systems Careers* (p. 25) **888**
The Computer Operations Manager **934**
Computer Operator **916**
"Computer Operator" in *Administration, Business, and Office*, Volume 1 of *Career Information Center* (pp. 76-77) **889**
"Computer Operator" in *Careers in Banking and Finance* (pp. 39-41) **890**
"Computer Operator" in *Exploring Careers in the Computer Field* (pp. 22-23) **891**
"Computer Operator" in *Guide to Careers Without College* (pp. 51-53) **892**
"Computer Operator" in *Opportunities in Data Processing Careers* (pp. 49-51) **893**
Computer Operators **894**
"Computer Operators" in *Jobs! What They Are...Where They Are...What They Pay* (pp. 64-65) **895**
"Computer Operators" in *Opportunities in Vocational and Technical Careers* (p. 48) **896**
"Computer Operators" in *The Complete Computer Career Guide* (pp. 22-26) **897**
"Computer Operators" in Volume 2 of *Career Discovery Encyclopedia* (pp. 44-45) **898**
"Computer Operators: Keepers of the Machines" in *Careers for Women Without College Degrees* (pp. 189-192) **899**
Computer Parts and Supplies Directory **4070**
Computer Program & Systems Analysis **1808**
Computer Report and PC Street Price Index **935**
Computer Security Products Report **936**
"Computer Service" in *Opportunities in Vocational and Technical Careers* (pp. 108-109) **4037**
Computer Service and Repair Directory **943**
Computer Service Technician **4038**
"Computer Service Technician" in *Occu-Facts: Information on 565 Careers in Outline Form* (p. 15.12) **4039**
"Computer Service Technician" in *Opportunities in Data Processing Careers* (pp. 66-67) **4040**
"Computer Service Technician" in *VGM's Careers Encyclopedia* (pp. 116-118) **4041**
"Computer Service Technician" in *VGM's Handbook of Scientific and Technical Careers* (pp. 33-34) **4042**
Computer Service Technicians **4043**
"Computer Service Technicians" in *Jobs! What They Are...Where They Are...What They Pay* (pp. 65-66) **4044**
"Computer Service Technicians" in Volume 4 of *The Encyclopedia of Careers and Vocational Guidance* (pp. 21-26) **4045**
"Computer Service Technicians" in Volume 2 of *Career Discovery Encyclopedia* (pp. 48-49) **4046**
"Computer Service Technicians: Troubleshooting in High Tech" in *Careers for Women Without College Degrees* (pp. 185-189) **4047**
"Computer Servicer" in *Administration, Business, and Office*, Volume 1 of *Career Information Center* (pp. 79-81) **4048**
"Computer Servicing and Troubleshooting" in *The Complete Electronics Career Guide* (pp. 81-86) **4049**
Computer Technician's Handbook **4071**
"Computer Technologists and Professionals" in *The American Almanac of Jobs and Salaries* (pp. 295-312) **4050**
Computer Troubleshooting & Maintenance **4072**
Computer Work & Computer Trainee Exams **917**
Computerized Maintenance Management Systems **4073**
Computers and Computing Information Resources Directory **944**
Computers & Medicine **2688, 2749**
Computers - How to Break into the Field **900**
Computers in Design Construction & Operation of Automobiles **3816**
Computers in HR Management **1542**
Computing, Operating Personnel, Electronic **901**
"Computing or Information Center Operations" in *Opportunities in Computer Science Careers* (pp. 32-33) **902**
A Concise Guide to Upholstery Fabrics **6416**
Concrete Abstracts **4864**
Concrete Construction Magazine **4865**
Concrete Industries Exposition **4887**
Concrete International **4866**
Concrete Masonry News **4867**
"Concrete Masons and Terrazzo Workers" in *Occupational Outlook Handbook* (pp. 366-367) **4819**
Concrete Producer News **4868**
Concrete Products **4869**
Concrete Sawing and Drilling Association **4833, 4838**
The Concrete Trader **4870**
Condominiums for Rent in Resort Areas [Database] **675, 1234**
"Conductors" in *Opportunities in Travel Careers* (p. 54) **6722**
"Conductors" in *The American Almanac of Jobs and Salaries* (pp. 465-466) **6723**
CONEXPO **4765**
Confidential Secretary **1637**
Congress of Automotive Repair and Service **3811, 3923**
Connecticut State Department of Consumer Protection ● Division of Licensing and Administration **7188**
ConnStruction **4652, 4745, 4790, 4871, 4934, 5013, 5072, 5110, 5168, 5224, 5309, 5392, 5476, 5522, 5569**
Conservation Gains in the Tax Reform Act **3280**
Consider a Career as an Insurance Agent **63**
Considering a Secretarial Service?: Possibilities for Income **1565**
Consolidators Handbook: Guide to Low Cost International Travel **1235**
CONSTRUCTION **4653, 4746, 4791, 4872, 4935, 5014, 5073, 5111, 5169, 5225, 5310, 5393, 5477, 5523, 5570**
Construction and Modernization Report **1130**
Construction: Basic Principles **4274, 4693, 4820, 4956, 5244**
"Construction Carpenter" in *Occu-Facts: Information on 565 Careers in Outline Form* (p. 16.5) **4694**
Construction Cluster **4603, 4695, 4821, 4957, 5043, 5088, 5189, 5245, 5348, 5444, 5495**
Construction Dimensions **4654, 4747, 4792, 4873, 4936, 5015, 5074, 5112, 5170, 5226, 5311, 5394, 5478, 5524, 5571**
"Construction Electrician" in *Construction*, Volume 4 of *Career Information Center* (pp. 45-47) **4958**
"Construction Electrician" in *Occu-Facts: Information on 565 Careers in Outline Form* (p. 16.7) **4959**
"Construction Electrician" in *Opportunities in Electrical Trades* (pp. 44-46) **4960**
"Construction Electrician Helper" in *Occu-Facts: Information on 565 Careers in Outline Form* (p. 20.7) **7021**
"Construction Equipment Mechanic" in *Construction*, Volume 4 of *Career Information Center* (pp. 47-49) **4446**
Construction Helpers **7022**
"Construction Helpers" in *Occu-Facts: Information on 565 Careers in Outline Form* (p. 20.4) **7023**
Construction Industry International **4655, 4748, 4793, 4874, 4937, 5016, 5075, 5113, 5171, 5227, 5312, 5395, 5479, 5525, 5572**
Construction Ironworkers **5496**
"Construction Laborer" in *Construction*, Volume 4 of *Career Information Center* (pp. 49-51) **7024**
Construction Laborers **7025**
Construction Machine Operators **7026**
"Construction Machinery Operator" in *Guide to Careers Without College* (pp. 77-79) **6675**

Construction News 4656, 4749, 4794, 4875, 4938, 5017, 5076, 5114, 5172, 5228, 5313, 5396, 5480, 5526, 5573
Construction Newsletter 4657, 4750, 4795, 4876, 4939, 5018, 5077, 5115, 5173, 5229, 5314, 5397, 5481, 5527, 5574
"Construction Painter" in *Occu-Facts: Information on 565 Careers in Outline Form* (p. 16.8) 5132
Construction Supervision & Safety Letter 5623
Constructor 4444, 4658, 4751, 4877, 5528, 6710
Consumable Electrode Processes in Welding Automation 5973
Consumer Banking Digest 821, 1164
Consumer Credit and Truth-in-Lending Compliance Report 956
"Consumer Electronic Services" in *Electronic Service Careers* (pp. 57-62) 4139
"Consumer Electronics" in *The Complete Electronics Career Guide* (pp. 30-32) 4140
Consumer Electronics Service Technician 4141
Consumer Electronics Technicians 4142
Consumer Finance Newsletter 957
"Consumer Servicing" in *The Complete Electronics Career Guide* (pp. 65-69) 4143
Consumer Trends 958
Contact Center 1899
Contact Lens Spectrum 6529
Contemporary Optometry 6530
Contractor's Connection 4323, 5315
Contractors Guide 5116, 5398
Convenience Care Update 2689, 2750
Convenient Automotive Services Retailer 3791, 3902
The Conversion & Seasoning of Wood 6460
Cook 2345
"Cook and Chef" in *Hospitality and Recreation*, Volume 8 of *Career Information Center* (pp. 76-78) 2305
"Cook and Chef: The Cornerstones of a Good Restaurant" in *Careers in the Restaurant Industry* (pp. 35-45) 2306
Cook, Domestic Service 3198
Cook, Short Order 2307
Cookbook Digest 2378
Cookbooks by Small Presses 2357
Cookies 2379
Cooking Contest Chronicle 2380
Cooking For Profit 2381, 2511
COOK'S 2382
Cooks and Chefs 2308
"Cooks and Chefs" in *Occu-Facts: Information on 565 Careers in Outline Form* (p. 13.13) 2309
"Cooks and Chefs" in *The American Almanac of Jobs and Salaries* (pp. 527-528) 2311
"Cooks and Chefs" in Volume 2 of *Career Discovery Encyclopedia* (pp. 58-59) 2310
"Cooks, Chefs, and Bakers" in Volume 3 of *The Encyclopedia of Careers and Vocational Guidance* (pp. 204-210) 2312
Cooperative Connection 2690, 2751
Cooperative Farmer 3325
Copier Repair Technician 4051
Coping With Sexism in the Military 7095
The Corey Guide to Postal Exams 1392
Corhealth 2618, 2691, 2752
Corn Farmer 3326
Corporate Real Estate Executive 347
The Corporate Secretary 1667
Corporate Travel—Directory Issue 1236
Correction Officer 1881, 1902
"Correction Officer" in *Public and Community Services*, Volume 11 of *Career Information Center* (pp. 42-44) 1882
Correction Officer Promotion Tests 1903
"Correction Officers" in *America's 50 Fastest Growing Jobs* (pp. 116-118) 1888
"Correction Officers" in *Jobs! What They Are...Where They Are...What They Pay* (pp. 189-190) 1883
"Correction Officers" in *Occupational Outlook Handbook* (pp. 285-286) 1884
"Correction Officers" in *Opportunities in Vocational and Technical Careers* (pp. 73-74) 1885
"Correction Officers" in Volume 3 of *The Encyclopedia of Careers and Vocational Guidance* (pp. 210-214) 1886
"Correction Officers" in Volume 2 of *Career Discovery Encyclopedia* (pp. 62-63) 1887
Correction Promotion Course (One Volume) 1904
Correctional Officer Correspondence Course 1889
Correctional Officer Resource Guide 1907
Correctional Officer Series 1890
Correctional Officers 1891
Correctional Officers: Power, Pressure & Responsibility 1908

"Corrections and Rehabilitation" in *Opportunities in Law Enforcement and Criminal Justice Careers* (pp. 110-124) 1892
Corrections Digest 1916
"Corrections Officer" in *Career Planning in Criminal Justice* (pp. 70-72) 1893
"Corrections Officer" in *VGM's Careers Encyclopedia* (pp. 120-122) 1894
"Corrections Officers" in *The American Almanac of Jobs and Salaries* (pp. 93-95) 1895
Corrections Today 1917
The Corridor Real Estate Journal 348
Cosmetic and Personal Services 2922
Cosmetic Insiders' Report 2974
Cosmetics 2975
Cosmetologist 2923, 2924, 2960
"Cosmetologist" in *Consumer, Homemaking, and Personal Services*, Volume 5 of *Career Information Center* (pp. 72-74) 2925
"Cosmetologist" in *Occu-Facts: Information on 565 Careers in Outline Form* (13.33) 2926
"Cosmetologist" in *VGM's Careers Encyclopedia* (pp. 122-124) 2927
"Cosmetologist and Related Workers" in *Occupational Outlook Handbook* (pp. 308-310) 2928
Cosmetologists 2929
"Cosmetologists" in *Opportunities in Vocational and Technical Careers* (pp. 79-80) 2930
"Cosmetologists" in Volume 3 of *The Encyclopedia of Careers and Vocational Guidance* (pp. 214-218) 2931
"Cosmetologists" in Volume 2 of *Career Discovery Encyclopedia* (pp. 64-65) 2932
"Cosmetologists: Beauty Preservers" in *Careers for Women Without College Degrees* (pp. 254-257) 2933
Cosmetologist's State Board Exam Review in English 2961
"Cosmetology, Barbering" in *The Career Connection II: A Guide to Technical Majors and Their Related Careers* (pp. 25-26) 2833, 2934
Cosmetology...Excellent Opportunities... 2935
Cost of Doing Business Study 4231
Cotton Farming 3327
Cotton Grower 3328
Cotton Trade Report 3329
Council for Early Childhood Professional Recognition 2892, 2897
Council on Hotel, Restaurant, and Institutional Education 2338, 2487
Council on Hotel, Restaurant, and Institutional Education International Conference 2422, 2542
Council on Library-Media Technical-Assistants 1499, 1521
"Counter and Rental Clerks" in *America's 50 Fastest Growing Jobs* (pp. 100-101) 36
"Counter and Rental Clerks" in *Occupational Outlook Handbook* (pp. 228-230) 37
"Counter and Retail Clerks" in Volume 3 of *The Encyclopedia of Careers and Vocational Guidance* (pp. 23-26) 38
"Counter and Retail Clerks" in Volume 2 of *Career Discovery Encyclopedia* (pp. 68-69) 39
Counter Worker 40
Counterman 54
Country Chronicle 2383
Country Folks 3330
Countryside & Small Stock Journal 3331
County Sheriff 2092
Court Reporter 1674, 1675
"Court Reporter" in *Occu-Facts: Information on 565 Careers in Outline Form* (p. 12.8) 1676
"Court Reporter (Short Hand Reporter)" in *Career Planning in Criminal Justice* (pp. 59-60) 1677
Court Reporters 1678
"Court Reporters" in Volume 3 of *The Encyclopedia of Careers and Vocational Guidance* (pp. 26-28) 1679
"Court Reporters" in Volume 2 of *Career Discovery Encyclopedia*(pp. 70-71) 1680
"Court Reporters: $40,000-$50,000 Recorders" in *Careers for Women Without College Degrees* (pp. 231-233) 1681
"Court Reporting" in *The Career Connection II: A Guide to Technical Majors and Their Related Careers* (pp. 27-28) 1682
A Cowboy Detective: A True Story of Twenty-Two Years with a World-Famous Detective Agency 2285
CPCU Journal 119
Crane Operator 6676
Crane Operator (Any Motive Power Except Steam) 6705
Craneman 6677
Creative Projects & Processes 6598
Cred-Alert 770, 959
Credit 544
Credit and Collection Coordinator 762
Credit Card Management 960

Index to Information Sources

"Credit Checker" in *Administration, Business, and Office*, Volume 1 of *Career Information Center* (pp. 49-51) **947**
"Credit Clerks and Authorizers" in *Occupational Outlook Handbook* (pp. 253-254) **948**
"Credit Collector" in *Administration, Business, and Office*, Volume 1 of *Career Information Center* (pp. 51-52) **734**
Credit Executive **961**
Credit Research Center—Monitor **962**
Credit Workers **949**
Credit World **963**
Crime Control Digest **1918, 2262**
Criminal Investigation Award **2216**
Criminal Justice Digest **1919**
Crop Farming Occupations **3225**
Crop Science **3332**
Crow's Weekly Letter **3614, 6468**
CTCs Newsletter **690**
CTO News for Travel Agents **691, 1241**
"Culinary Arts" in *College Majors and Careers: A Resource Guide for Effective Life Planning* (pp. 45-46) **2313**
Culinary Arts Salon **2354**
Culinary Careers **2314, 2447**
Culinary Olympic Cookbook **2358**
Culinary Review **2384**
The Cultivator **3091**
Current Opinion in Dentistry **2619**
Current Wage Developments **1543**
Custodial Methods and Procedures Manual **3181**
"Custodial Workers" in *The American Almanac of Jobs and Salaries* (p. 530) **3157**
"Custodian" in *Occu-Facts: Information on 565 Careers in Outline Form* (p. 13.28, 13.29) **3158**
Custodian, Building **3159**
Custodians **3160**
Custom Boot Maker **6328**
"Custom Tailor and Dressmaker" in *Consumer, Homemaking, and Personal Services*, Volume 5 of *Career Information Center* (pp. 74-76) **6278**
Custom Tools for Woodworkers **6461**
"Custom Upholsterer" in *Consumer, Homemaking, and Personal Services*, Volume 5 of *Career Information Center* (pp. 76-77) **6399**
"Customer Service Assistant" in *Career Opportunities in Art* (p. 135) **735**
"Customer Service Representative" in *Career Opportunities in Television, Cable, and Video* (pp. 170-171) **736**
"Customer Service Representative" in *Careers in Trucking* (pp. 21-23) **737**
"Customer Service Representative" in *Jobs! What They Are...Where They Are...What They Pay* (pp. 207-208) **738**
"Customer Services Sales" in *Careers in Marketing* (pp. 68-69) **578**
Customs Officers **2050**
"Customs Worker" in *Occu-Facts: Information on 565 Careers in Outline Form* (p. 1.49) **2093**
"Customs Worker" in *Public and Community Services*, Volume 11 of *Career Information Center* (pp. 94-95) **2094**
Customs Workers **2095**
Cutting Tool Engineering **5825**
CWA/UTW Bargaining Council (Telecommunications) **1304**
CWB: Custom Woodworking Business **6469**

D

Daily Construction Reporter **4659, 4752, 4796, 4878, 4940, 5019, 5078, 5117, 5174, 5230, 5316, 5399, 5482, 5529, 5575**
Dairy and Field Crops Digest **3333**
DAIRY-DELI-BAKE **2423**
Dairy-Deli Digest **2385**
Dairy Farmer **3226**
Dairy Farmers **3227**
"Dairy Farmers" in Volume 3 of *The Encyclopedia of Careers and Vocational Guidance* (pp. 338-341) **3228**
"Dairy Farmers" in Volume 2 of *Career Discovery Encyclopedia* (pp. 78-79) **3229**
The Dalton Carpet Journal **4797**
Dames Employees: The Feminization of Postal Workers in Nineteenth-Century France **1433**
Darkroom **6599**
The Darkroom Book **6600**
The Darkroom Handbook **6601**
Darkroom Photography **6611**
"Darkroom Technician" in *Communications and the Arts*, Volume 3 of *Career Information Center* (pp. 55-56) **6579**
"Darkroom Technician" in Volume 2 of *Career Discovery Encyclopedia* (pp. 84-85) **6580**
"Darkroom Technicians" in Volume 4 of *The Encyclopedia of Careers and Vocational Guidance* (pp. 334-338) **6581**
Darkroom Two **6602**
Data Base News **771**
Data Base Reports **772**
"Data Entry" in *Careers in High Tech* (pp. 31-32) **1809**
Data Entry Awareness Report **937, 1878**
"Data Entry Clerks" in Volume 3 of *The Encyclopedia of Careers and Vocational Guidance* (pp. 29-32) **1810**
"Data Entry Clerks" in Volume 2 of *Career Discovery Encyclopedia* (pp. 87-88) **1811**
"Data Entry Keyer" in *Administration, Business, and Office*, Volume 1 of *Career Information Center* (pp. 52-53) **1812**
"Data Entry Keyer" in *Careers in Banking and Finance* (pp. 41-42) **1813**
Data Entry Management Association **845, 1849**
Data Entry Operator **1814, 1815**
"Data Entry Operator" in *Occu-Facts: Information on 565 Careers in Outline Form* (p. 12.47) **1816**
"Data Entry Operator" in *The Complete Computer Career Guide* (pp. 30-32) **1817**
Data Entry Operators **1818**
"Data Entry Specialist" in *Opportunities in Data Processing Careers* (pp. 52-53) **1819**
Data Processing **1820**
Data Processing: Career Opportunities for Hearing Impaired People **1821**
Data Processing Management Association **846**
DataWorld **938**
Davis Award; W. Allison and Elizabeth Stubbs **3070**
Day Care Center Aide **2900**
Day Care Provider **2878**
"Day Care Providers" in *Opportunities in Child Care Careers* (pp. 42-43) **2879**
"Day Care Worker" in *Public and Community Services*, Volume 11 of *Career Information Center* (pp. 70-71) **2880**
"Day-Care Worker" in *The American Almanac of Jobs and Salaries* (pp. 539-540) **2881**
Day Care Workers **2882**
A Day in the Life of a Firefighter **1929**
A Day in the Life of a Police Detective **2096**
DECA Advisor **219**
DECA Guide **212**
Deckhand **6964**
Deer & Deer Hunting **3503**
Defense Science—Directory of Validated Ada Compilers Issue **676**
Degree of Honor Review **120**
Delaware State Department of Administrative Services • Division of Professional Regulations **7189**
Deli-Bake Advocate **2386**
Delta Farm Press **3334**
Delta Pride News **3504**
Dental Abstracts **2620**
"Dental and Medical Secretary" in *Health*, Volume 7 of *Career Information Center* (pp. 58-60) **1566**
"Dental Assistance" in *The Career Connection II: A Guide to Technical Majors and Their Related Careers* (pp. 33-34) **2563**
Dental Assistant **2564, 2565**
The Dental Assistant **2566**
Dental Assistant **2602**
The Dental Assistant **2621**
"Dental Assistant" in *Careers in Health Care* (pp. 44-48) **2567**
"Dental Assistant" in *Health Care* (pp. 57-61) **2568**
"Dental Assistant" in *Health*, Volume 7 of *Career Information Center* (pp. 42-43) **2569**
"Dental Assistant" in *Occu-Facts: Information on 565 Careers in Outline Form* (p. 13.21) **2570**
"Dental Assistant" in *120 Careers in the Health Care Field* (pp. 48-63) **2575**
"Dental Assistant" in *Opportunities in Dental Care Careers* (pp. 17-18, 46-47) **2571**
"Dental Assistant" in *Opportunities in Health and Medical Careers* (p. 15) **2572**
"Dental Assistant" in *Opportunities in Paramedical Careers* (pp. 37-41) **2573**
"Dental Assistant" in *VGM's Careers Encyclopedia* (pp. 132-134) **2574**
Dental Assistant Certification **2600**
The Dental Assistant: Syllabus **2576**
Dental Assistant Techniques **2607**
Dental Assistants **2577, 2606**

VOCATIONAL CAREERS SOURCEBOOK, 1st Edition

"Dental Assistants" in *Occupational Outlook Handbook* (pp. 299-300) **2578**
"Dental Assistants" in Volume 3 of *The Encyclopedia of Careers and Vocational Guidance* (pp. 218-221) **2579**
"Dental Assistants" in Volume 2 of *Career Discovery Encyclopedia* (pp. 94-95) **2580**
"Dental Assistants and Dental Hygienists" in *The American Almanac of Jobs and Salaries* (pp. 494-495) **2581**
"Dental Assistants and Hygienists" in *Jobs! What They Are...Where They Are...What They Pay* (p. 150) **2582**
"Dental Assistants: Chairside Assistants" in *Careers for Women Without College Degrees* (pp. 208-211) **2583**
Dental Assistants Review, ARCO **2584**
Dental Assisting: Basic & Dental Sciences **2585**
Dental Assisting Manuals **2608**
Dental Assisting National Board **2596, 2601**
Dental Clinics of North America **2622**
Dental Computer Newsletter **939**
Dental Laboratory Technician **6481**
"Dental Laboratory Technician" in *Careers in Health Care* (pp. 53-56) **6482**
"Dental Laboratory Technician" in *Health Care* (pp. 63-67) **6483**
"Dental Laboratory Technician" in *Health*, Volume 7 of *Career Information Center* (pp. 43-45) **6484**
"Dental Laboratory Technician" in *Occu-Facts: Information on 565 Careers in Outline Form* (p. 17.27) **6485**
"Dental Laboratory Technician" in *Occupational Outlook Handbook* (pp. 427-428) **6486**
"Dental Laboratory Technician" in *120 Careers in the Health Care Field* (pp. 63-67) **6487**
"Dental Laboratory Technician" in *Opportunities in Health and Medical Careers* (p. 75) **6488**
"Dental Laboratory Technicians" in *Jobs! What They Are...Where They Are...What They Pay* (pp. 151) **6489**
"Dental Laboratory Technicians" in *Opportunities in Dental Care Careers* (pp. 47-49) **6490**
"Dental Laboratory Technicians" in Volume 4 of *The Encyclopedia of Careers and Vocational Guidance* (pp. 382-386) **6491**
"Dental Laboratory Technicians" in Volume 2 of *Career Discovery Encyclopedia* (pp. 97-98) **6492**
Dental Laboratory Technology **6503**
Dental Office **2623**
Dental Products Report **2624**
Dental Student **2625**
Dental Surgical Assistants Handbook **2609**
Dental Technicians **2586**
DENTIST **2626**
Dentistry Today **2627**
Department Library Aide **1500**
Department Store Receiving and Related Workers **1342**
"Department Store Receiving, Delivering, & Related Workers" in *Occu-Facts: Information on 565 Careers in Outline Form* (p. 12.37) **1343**
"Department Store Retailing" in *The Encyclopedia of Career Choices for the 1990s: A Guide to Entry Level Jobs* (pp. 252-272) **412**
Deputy Chief, Fire Dept. **1962**
Deputy Chief Fire Marshal (Uniformed) **1963**
Deputy Chief Marshal **2176**
Deputy Sheriff **2177**
"Detective" in *Public and Community Services*, Volume 11 of *Career Information Center* (pp. 72-73) **2097**
Detective Investigator **2178**
Detective, Police **2098**
Detective Work: A Study of Criminal Investigations **2243**
Detective's Private Investigation Training Manual **2244**
Developing Bookkeeping Skills **1032**
"Dial ''O'' For Operator" in *Telecommunications Careers* (pp. 54-57) **1766**
The Diamond Registry Bulletin **5741**
Diesel & Gas Turbine Worldwide **4127**
Diesel Mechanic **4086, 4087**
"Diesel Mechanic" in *Careers in Trucking* (pp. 40-43) **4088**
"Diesel Mechanic" in *Occu-Facts: Information on 565 Careers in Outline Form* (p. 15.4) **4089**
"Diesel Mechanic" in *Transportation*, Volume 12 of *Career Information Center* (pp. 100-102) **4090**
"Diesel Mechanics" in *Occupational Outlook Handbook* (pp. 337-339) **4091**
"Diesel Mechanics" in Volume 3 of *The Encyclopedia of Careers and Vocational Guidance* (pp. 499-503) **4092**
"Diesel Mechanics" in Volume 2 of *Career Discovery Encyclopedia* (pp. 106-107) **4093**
Diesel Progress Engines & Drives **4128**

"Diesel Technology" in *The Career Connection II: A Guide to Technical Majors and Their Related Careers* (pp. 37-38) **4094**
Dimension Purchasing Guide [Forest products industry] **6479**
Dimensional Stone **4660**
Dining Room Attendant **2448**
"Dining Room Attendant" in *Hospitality and Recreation*, Volume 8 of *Career Information Center* (pp. 42-43) **2449**
"Dining Room Attendant" in *Occu-Facts: Information on 565 Careers in Outline Form* (p. 13.18) **2450**
"Direct Sales Worker" in *Marketing and Distribution*, Volume 10 of *Career Information Center* (pp. 46-48) **413**
Direct Selling: An Income Opportunity for You **414**
Directories of Machine Tools **5791, 5821, 5852, 5899, 5927**
Directory **766**
Directory of Accredited Cosmetology Schools **2963**
Directory of Accredited Institutions **973, 1626, 1731**
Directory of Certification and Training Contacts **6088**
Directory of Certified Aftermarket Body Parts [Automotive parts industry] **3771**
Directory of French-Fry Potatoes **2431**
Directory of Hotel and Motel Systems **1128**
Directory of Institutions **1909**
Directory of Speakers and Lecturers **6504**
Directory of Specialty Foods Suppliers **2432**
Directory of Telecommunications and Education Programs **4562**
Discover Bookkeeping & Accounts **1033**
"Dispatcher" in *Careers in Trucking* (pp. 24-26) **1290**
"Dispatcher" in *120 Careers in the Health Care Field* (p. 97) **1292**
"Dispatcher and Communications" in *Opportunities in Fire Protection Services* (pp. 28-29) **1291**
"Dispatchers" in *Occupational Outlook Handbook* (pp. 265-266) **1293**
"Display Worker Helper" in *Occu-Facts: Information on 565 Careers in Outline Form* (p. 8.8) **7027**
Distant Water: The Fate of the North Atlantic Fisherman **3579**
Distinguished Dairy Cattle Breeder Award **3267**
Distinguished Information Sciences Award **1858**
Distinguished Service Award **330, 2217, 2218, 6766, 6848**
Distinguished Service to Agriculture **3268**
Distribution Clerk, Machine **1393**
Distribution Clerk, Machine: Letter Sorting Machine Operator-U.S. Postal Service **1394**
Distributive Education Clubs of America **209, 1336**
Distributive Education Clubs of America Career Development Conference **241, 1340**
Distributor **4324, 5317**
Distributors Financial Analysis **3928, 4135, 4234, 4467, 4501**
District Heating and Cooling **4325**
District of Columbia Department of Consumer and Regulatory Affairs • Occupational and Professional Licensing Administration **7190**
"Diver" in *Agribusiness, Environment, and Natural Resources*, Volume 2 of *Career Information Center* (pp. 43-45) **3454**
Divers **7028**
Divers, Commercial **3455**
"Diving Technicians" in Volume 4 of *The Encyclopedia of Careers and Vocational Guidance* (pp. 34-41) **3456**
"Diving Technicians" in Volume 2 of *Career Discovery Encyclopedia* (pp. 118-119) **3457**
Do-It-Yourself Plumbing **5287**
Do Your Own Thing... in the Mechanical Field **3678, 3841, 4008, 4095, 4211, 4275, 4447, 4469**
Doane Award; D. Howard **3269**
Doane's Agricultural Report **3335**
"Dock Foreman/Supervisor" in *Careers in Trucking* (pp. 26-28) **5612**
"Dock Worker" in *Transportation*, Volume 12 of *Career Information Center* (pp. 48-50) **7029**
Docket **1668**
"Dockworker" in *Transportation* (pp. 18-19) **7030**
Dog Groomer **2772**
"Dog Groomer" in *Occu-Facts: Information on 565 Careers in Outline Form* (p. 14.15) **2773**
Dog Groomers **2774**
"Dog Groomers" in Volume 3 of *The Encyclopedia of Careers and Vocational Guidance* (pp. 341-345) **2775**
"Dog Groomers" in Volume 2 of *Career Discovery Encyclopedia* (pp. 120-121) **2776**
Dog Warden **2796**
"Domestic Housekeeper" in *Consumer, Homemaking, and Personal Services*, Volume 5 of *Career Information Center* (pp. 48-49) **3199**
"Domestic Service Cook" in *Occu-Facts: Information on 565 Careers in Outline Form* (p. 13.1) **3200**
Domestic Worker **3219**

Index to Information Sources

"Door to Door Sales Workers" in Volume 3 of *The Encyclopedia of Careers and Vocational Guidance* (pp. 140-143) **415**
"Door-to-Door Sales Workers" in Volume 2 of *Career Discovery Encyclopedia* (pp. 122-123) **416**
Dots and Dashes **1796**
Double Entry by Single: A New Method of Bookkeeping **1034**
The Double Exposure Book **6603**
DPMA Information Executive **859**
"Drapery Sewer" in *Occu-Facts: Information on 565 Careers in Outline Form* (p. 18.15) **6279**
Dressmaker **6280**
Dressmakers (Sewing Professionals) **6281**
Drilling Contractor **5435**
Driver, Heavy-Truck **6805**
Driver of the Year **6849**
Driver of the Year Award **6850, 7070**
Drop Shipping News **1359**
Drug Enforcement Agent **2179**
"Drywall Installer and Finisher" in *Construction*, Volume 4 of *Career Information Center* (pp. 55-56) **4895**
Drywall Installers and Finishers **4896**
"Drywall Installers and Finishers" in Volume 3 of *The Encyclopedia of Careers and Vocational Guidance* (pp. 647-649) **4897**
"Drywall Installers and Finishers" in Volume 2 of *Career Discovery Encyclopedia* (pp. 130-131) **4898**
"Drywall Rocker and Taper" in *Hard Hatted Women: Stories of Struggle and Success in the Trades* (pp. 63-70) **4899**
"Drywall Workers and Lathers" in *Occupational Outlook Handbook* (pp. 367-369) **4900**
The Dynamic Secretary: A Practical Guide to Achieving Success as an Executive Assistant **1567**

E

EAP Digest **1544**
"Early Childhood Center Teacher or Aide" in *Exploring Careers in Child Care Services* (pp. 9-21) **1742**
Early Childhood Research Quarterly **2910**
EASA Currents **3977**
Eastern Cable Television Trade Show and Convention **4429**
Eastern Region Lumbermen's Association Regional Exposition and Conference **3650, 4766**
Eastern Regional Nurserymen Show **3111**
Eastern Trucker **6880**
Eastern Woods and Waters **3505**
Easy-to-Do Leathercraft Projects with Full-Size Templates **6347**
Economic Handbook of the Machine Tool Industry **5792, 5822, 5853, 5900, 5928**
Economic News Notes **4326, 4753, 4941**
Economic Profile **6314**
Edison Electric Institute **6022, 6047**
EDP Weekly **940, 4080**
Educational Institute of the American Hotel and Motel Association **1126**
Educators Letter **773**
EEA Training Program **3949, 4170**
Effective Dental Assisting **2610**
Efficient Accounting & Record Keeping **1035**
Efficient Busperson—Assisting the Server **2451**
EGSA Powerline **6034**
Electric Light & Power **6035**
Electric Perspectives **6036**
Electric Power and Farm Equipment Show **3420**
"Electric Power Generating Plant Operators and Power Distributors and Dispatchers" in *Occupational Outlook Handbook* (pp. 406-407) **6005**
Electric Power Plant Occupations **6006**
"Electric Power Plant Occupations" in *Occu-Facts: Information on 565 Careers in Outline Form* (p. 17.34) **6007**
"Electric Power Service Worker" in *Public and Community Services*, Volume 11 of *Career Information Center* (pp. 43-46) **6008**
Electric Power Surveys **6031**
"Electric Power Transmission, Distribution Worker" in *Public and Community Service*, Volume 11 of *Career Information Center* (pp. 46-48) **6009**
Electricain Helper, Construction **7031**
"Electrical Appliance Service Technician" in *Occu-Facts: Information on 565 Careers in Outline Form* (p. 15.14) **4353**
Electrical Contractor Magazine **5020**
Electrical Design Library **4998**
Electrical/Electronic Supply Trade Show **3992**
Electrical Equipment Manufacturing Workers **7032**
Electrical Maintenance Training Program **3932**

"Electrical Power Worker" in Volume 2 of *Career Discovery Encyclopedia* (pp. 148-149) **6010**
Electrical Reports **6037**
Electrical Transmission and Distribution Occupations **6011**
"Electrical Transmission and Distribution Occupations" in *Occu-Facts: Information on 565 Careers in Outline Form* (p. 17.33) **6012**
Electrical Women's Round Table **6023**
Electrical Women's Round Table—National Newsletter **6038**
Electrical World **6039**
Electrician **4991**
"Electrician" in *Guide to Careers Without College* (pp. 85-86) **4961**
"Electrician" in *Hard Hatted Women: Stories of Struggle and Success in the Trades* (pp. 216-224) **4962**
"Electrician" in *The Career Connection II: A Guide to Technical Majors and Their Related Careers* (pp. 43-44) **4963**
"Electrician" in *VGM's Careers Encyclopedia* (pp. 155-158) **4964**
Electrician, Construction **4965**
Electrician - Electrician's Helper **4992**
Electrician, Maintenance **4966**
"Electricians" in *Occupational Outlook Handbook* (pp. 369-371) **4967**
"Electricians" in *Opportunities in Building Construction Trades* (pp. 31-34) **4968**
"Electricians" in *The American Almanac of Jobs and Salaries* (pp. 501-502) **4972**
"Electricians" in Volume 3 of *The Encyclopedia of Careers and Vocational Guidance* (pp. 656-659) **4969**
"Electricians" in Volume 2 of *Career Discovery Encyclopedia* (pp. 146-147) **4970**
Electricians, Construction **4971**
Electrician's Helper **4993**
Electricians, Maintenance **4973**
The Electrician's Toolbox Manual **4999**
The Electricity Journal **4424, 5021**
Electro Fact File **5022**
Electrologist **2936**
"Electrologist" in *Consumer, Homemaking, and Personal Services*, Volume 5 of *Career Information Center* (pp. 79-81) **2937**
Electrologists **2938**
"Electrologists" in Volume 3 of *The Encyclopedia of Careers and Vocational Guidance* (pp. 229-232) **2939**
Electronic and Electrical Equipment **3978, 4175, 5023, 6040**
Electronic Business Forecast **3979**
"Electronic Computer Operating Personnel" in *Occu-Facts: Information on 565 Careers in Outline Form* (p. 12.1) **903**
Electronic Equipment Maintainer **4248**
Electronic Equipment Repairer **3950**
"Electronic Home Entertainment Equipment Repairers" in *Occupational Outlook Handbook* (pp. 339-341) **4144**
Electronic Industries Association **4160**
Electronic Industries Association—Executive Report **3980**
Electronic Maintenance **3955**
Electronic Maintenance Two **3956**
"Electronic Organ Technicians" in Volume 4 of *The Encyclopedia of Careers and Vocational Guidance* (pp. 338-341) **4145**
Electronic Service Careers **4146, 4974**
Electronic Services Update **3981**
Electronic Servicing & Technology **3982, 4176**
Electronic Technicians Association Annual Convention **3993**
"Electronics Assemblers" in *The Complete Electronics Career Guide* (pp. 40-43) **5594**
Electronics for Industrial Electricians **3957**
Electronics in Industry **3958**
"Electronics Inspector" in *Hard Hatted Women: Stories of Struggle and Success in the Trades* (pp. 212-215) **5673**
The Electronics Manual to Industrial Automation **3959**
"Electronics Manufacturing Assemblers" in *Occu-Facts: Information on 565 Careers in Outline Form* (p. 18.25) **5595**
Electronics Technician: A Career for Tomorrow **4147**
Electronics Technicians Association, International **3940, 3942, 4161, 4164**
Electronics Technicians Association, International Technician of the Year **3952, 4171**
Electronics...Your Bridge to Tomorrow **3933, 4148**
Elementary Darkroom Practices: A Basic Photography Manual **6604**
The Elevator **4207**
"Elevator Constructor and Repair Worker" in *Construction*, Volume 4 of *Career Information Center* (pp. 56-58) **4189**
"Elevator Constructors" in *Opportunities in Building Construction Trades* (p. 52) **4190**
Elevator Constructors (Mechanics) **4191**
"Elevator Installers and Repairers" in *Occupational Outlook Handbook* (pp. 341-342) **4192**

"Elevator Installers and Repairers" in Volume 3 of *The Encyclopedia of Careers and Vocational Guidance* (pp. 660-662) 4193
"Elevator Installers and Repairers" in Volume 2 of *Career Discovery Encyclopedia* (pp. 160-161) 4194
Elevator Mechanic 4197
Elevator World, Inc. 4205
Elevators & Engineering: An Architectural Guide 4200
Emergency & Trip Permit Handbook: Important Permit Information for Interstate Trucking Operatiobns in the United States & Canada 6855
Emergency Response Expo 2033, 2281
Empire Farm Days 3421
Employee Benefits Report 1545
Employment Opportunities for College Graduates in Food and Agricultural Sciences: Agriculture, Natural Resources, and Veterinary Medicine 3230
Encouraging Cooperation among Competitors: The Case of Motor Carrier Deregulation & Collective Ratemaking 6926
Enforcement Journal 2263
"Engineers and Engineer Helpers" in *Opportunities in Travel Careers* (pp. 54-55) 6724
Engineers, Pump Operators, Drivers Handbook 1994
Enroute Magazine 6881
Enterprise Farming 3231
Environmental Report 3615
Environmental Science & Engineering 6109
"Equipment Rental and Leasing Service Agent" in *Marketing and Distribution*, Volume 10 of *Career Information Center* (pp. 48-49) 41
ERIC/IR Update 1507
The Essential Darkroom Book: A Complete Guide to Black & White Processing 6605
Essential Darkroom Techniques 6606
Essential Guide to the Library IBM PC: Library Application Software 1523
Essentials of Clinical Dental Assisting 2611
Essentials of Dental Radiography for Dental Assistants and Dental Hygienists 2603
ETA-I Management Update 3983, 4177
ETA-I Technician Association News 3984, 4178
ETA Technician Association News 3985
Ethics, Jurisprudence & History for the Dental Hygienist 6513
Eurail Guide: How to Travel Europe and All the World by Train 710
Europe by Train: The Complete Guide to Inter Railing 711
European Edition OAG Travel Planner Hotel & Motel RedBook 1242
Excellence in Zookeeping Award 2803
Excess Express 121
Exchange of the Year Award 331
The Exec-U-tary 1669
Executive Chef 2315
Executive Housekeeper of the Year 3176
Executive Housekeeping Today 3188
The Executive Officer 349
Executive Secretary 1568
Exhaust News 3903
Existing Home Sales 350
Experimental Agriculture 3336
Experimental Musical Instruments 4537
Explore Your Future: A Career in Life Insurance Sales 64
The Explorer 2628
Exploring Careers as a Computer Technician 4052
Exploring Careers As a Computer Technician 4053
Exploring Careers as an Electrician 4975
Exploring Careers in Computer Sales 579
Exploring Careers in the Military Services 7096
Exploring Careers in the Travel Industry 624
Exploring Careers in Word Processing and Desktop Publishing 1822
Exploring Computer Careers at Home 904
Exterior Body Panel Developments 3772
Eye to Eye 6531

F

FAA Aviation News 3711
Faber & Kell's Heating & Air Conditioning of Buildings 4302
Fabrication Procedures 6508
Face Unique Challenges With the FBI: A Career as a Special Agent 2099
Fact Sheet: Facts About Direct Selling 417
Facts About Fur 3580
Facts for Consumers From the Federal Trade Commission: Truck-Driving Schools 6927
Family Day Care Bulletin 2911
"Family Day-Care Providers" in *Exploring Careers in Child Care Services* (pp. 22-31) 2883

The Family Farm: Can It Be Saved? 3441
Farm: A Year In the Life of an American Farmer 3442
Farm and Power Equipment Dealer 4232
Farm & Ranch Living 3337
Farm Economics 3338
Farm Equipment Mechanic 4212
"Farm Equipment Mechanic" in *Occu-Facts: Information on 565 Careers in Outline Form* (p. 15.9) 4213
Farm Equipment Mechanics 4214
"Farm Equipment Mechanics" in *Occupational Outlook Handbook* (pp. 342-344) 4215
"Farm Equipment Mechanics" in Volume 3 of *Career Discovery Encyclopedia* (pp. 8-9) 4216
"Farm Equipment Mechanics" in Volume 3 of *The Encyclopedia of Careers and Vocational Guidance* (pp. 503-507) 4217
The Farm Gate 3339
"Farm Management" in *The Career Connection II: A Guide to Technical Majors and Their Related Careers* (pp. 55-56) 3232
Farm Management Manual 3281
Farm Manager 3233, 3234
"Farm Manager" in *Agribusiness, Environment, and Natural Resources*, Volume 2 of *Career Information Center* (pp. 107-108) 3235
"Farm Manager" in *Top Professions: The 100 Most Popular, Dynamic, and Profitable Careers in America Today* (pp. 77-78) 3236
Farm News 3340
"Farm Operatives and Managers" in Volume 3 of *Career Discovery Encyclopedia* (pp. 12-13) 3237
"Farm Operatives and Managers" in Volume 3 of *The Encyclopedia of Careers and Vocational Guidance* (pp. 350-354) 3238
"Farm Operators and Managers" in *Occupational Outlook Handbook* (pp. 318-320) 3239
Farm Progress Show 3422
Farm/Ranch Exchange 3341
"Farmer" in *Agribusiness, Environment, and Natural Resources*, Volume 2 of *Career Information Center* (pp. 76-80, 108-117) 3240
"Farmer" in *VGM's Careers Encyclopedia* (pp. 169-171) 3241
Farmer, Cattle 3242
Farmer, Dairy 3243
Farmer, Fruit 3244
Farmer, Poultry 3245
Farmer, Vegetable Crops 3246
Farmers 3247
"Farmers" in *Occu-Facts: Information on 565 Careers in Outline Form* (pp. 14.1, 14.2, 14.3, 14.5, 14.6, 14.7, 14.8) 3248
"Farmers" in Volume 3 of *Career Discovery Encyclopedia* (pp. 10-11) 3249
"Farmers" in Volume 3 of *The Encyclopedia of Careers and Vocational Guidance* (pp. 345-350) 3250
The Farmers' Advance 3342
"Farmers and Farm Workers" in *The American Almanac of Jobs and Salaries* (pp. 540-542) 3251
Farmers As Hunters: The Implications of Sedentism 3282
Farmer's Exchange 3343
Farmers, General 3252
Farmers Grain and Livestock Corporation—Viewpoint 3344
Farmer's Report 3345
Farming Is in Our Blood: Farm Families in Economic Crisis 3443
Farmland News 3346
Fashion & Textile Careers 6364
Fashion Jewelry Plus 5742
Fast and Light Summer Cooking 2387
"Fast Food Franchise Worker" in *Hospitality and Recreation*, Volume 8 of *Career Information Center* (pp. 47-48) 2452
Fast Food Jobs: National Study of Fast Foods Employment 2453
Fast Food Services 2316, 2454
Fast Food Workers 2317
"Fast Food Workers" in Volume 3 of *Career Discovery Encyclopedia* (pp. 18-19) 2455
"Fast Food Workers" in Volume 3 of *The Encyclopedia of Careers and Vocational Guidance* (pp. 232-236) 2456
"FBI Agent" in *Action Careers: Employment in the High-Risk Job Market* (pp. 47-58) 2100
"FBI Agents" in Volume 3 of *Career Discovery Encyclopedia* (pp. 20-21) 2101
"FBI Agents" in Volume 3 of *The Encyclopedia of Careers and Vocational Guidance* (pp. 236-239) 2102
FBI Entrance Examination 2180
"FBI Special Agent" in *Public and Community Services*, Volume 11 of *Career Information Center* (pp. 95-96) 2103
"FBI Special Agent" in *VGM's Careers Encyclopedia* (pp. 173-175) 2104
FBI Special Agents 2105, 2106

Index to Information Sources

"FBI Special Agents" in *Occu-Facts: Information on 565 Careers in Outline Form* (p. 13.6)   **2107**
FDC Toiletries, Fragrances and Skin Care - The Rose Sheet   **2976**
Federal Bureau of Investigation   **2167**
"Federal Bureau of Investigation" in *Exploring Careers Using Foreign Languages* (pp. 67-69)   **2108**
"Federal Bureau of Investigation" in *Law Enforcement Employment Guide* (pp. 130-131)   **2109**
Federal Clerk - Steno - Typist   **1707, 1851**
Federal Communications Commission   **3943**
Federal Motor Carrier Safety Regulations   **6856**
Federal Motor Carrier Safety Regulations Pocketbook   **6857**
Fellow of the Academy of Professional Reporters   **1735**
FFA New Horizons Magazine   **3347**
FFA Times   **3348**
FIA Executive Digest   **6355**
Field and Stream   **3506**
"Field Representatives" in *Opportunities in Insurance Careers* (pp. 42-43)   **739**
FIGA—Newsletter   **4538**
File Clerk   **1451, 1463**
"File Clerk" in *Administration, Business, and Office*, Volume 1 of *Career Information Center* (pp. 54-55)   **1452**
"File Clerk" in *Careers in Banking and Finance* (pp. 43-45)   **1453**
"File Clerk" in *Occu-Facts: Information on 565 Careers in Outline Form* (p. 12.24)   **1454**
File Clerk, General Clerk   **1455**
File Clerk - General Clerk   **1464**
"File Clerks" in *Jobs! What They Are. . .Where They Are. . .What They Pay* (pp. 208-209)   **1456**
"File Clerks" in *Occupational Outlook Handbook* (pp. 272-273)   **1457**
"File Clerks" in *The American Almanac of Jobs and Salaries* (pp. 506-507)   **1460**
"File Clerks" in Volume 3 of *Career Discovery Encyclopedia* (pp. 24-25)   **1458**
"File Clerks" in Volume 3 of *The Encyclopedia of Careers and Vocational Guidance* (pp. 33-35)   **1459**
File Management Techniques   **1470**
File Structure & Design   **1471**
Filing & Records Management   **1472**
Filing Procedures Guideline   **1473**
Filing: Syllabus   **1474**
Filing Systems & Records Management   **1475**
"Film Laboratory Technicians" in Volume 4 of *The Encyclopedia of Careers and Vocational Guidance* (pp. 343-344)   **6582**
Film Processing Specialist   **6583**
"Financial Institution Tellers" in Volume 3 of *The Encyclopedia of Careers and Vocational Guidance* (pp. 41-45)   **794**
"Financial Records Processors" in *Occupational Outlook Handbook* (p. 254)   **969**
"Financial Services" in *Jobs '91* (pp. 269-278)   **489**
Find 'em Fast: A Private Investigator's Workbook   **2245**
Find Them Fast, Find Them Now: Private Investigators Share Their Secrets for Finding Missing Persons   **2246**
Fine Homebuilding   **4661, 4754, 4942, 5231, 5400**
Finish Carpentry Illustrated   **4716**
Fins & Feathers   **3507**
Fire Administration & Supervision   **1964**
Fire Alarm Dispatcher   **1309**
Fire Alarm Manual   **1314**
Fire and Rescue Educational Conference and Exposition   **2034**
Fire & Safety Representative   **1965**
Fire Assessment Centers: The New Concept in Promotional Examinations   **1995**
Fire Brigade Training Program: Instructor's Guide   **1996**
Fire Brigade Training Program: Student Manual   **1997**
Fire Captain Oral Exam Study Guide   **1966**
Fire Chief   **2012**
Fire Command   **2013**
Fire Command Officer's Handbook   **1998**
Fire Control Digest   **2014**
Fire Department Instructors Conference   **2035**
Fire Department Lieutenant/Captain/Battalion Chief   **1967**
Fire Department Lieutenant Captain Battalion Chief: Score High on Firefighter Promotion Exams   **1968**
Fire Department Safety Officer's Reference Guide   **1999**
Fire Engine Driver   **1969**
Fire Engineer Written Exam Study Guide   **1970**
Fire Engineering   **2015**
Fire Examinations-All States   **1971**
"Fire Fighter" in *Action Careers: Employment in the High-Risk Job Market* (pp. 59-75)   **1930**

"Fire Fighter" in *Public and Community Services*, Volume 11 of *Career Information Center* (pp. 50-52)   **1931**
Fire Fighter of the Year Award   **1987**
"Fire Fighter, Paramedic" in *Straight Talk on Careers: 80 Pros Take You Into Their Professions* (pp. 227-230, 231-232)   **1932**
Fire Fighter Professional Qualifications   **1933**
Fire Fighters   **1934**
"Fire Fighters" in *Jobs! What They Are. . .Where They Are. . .What They Pay* (pp. 112-113)   **1935**
"Fire Fighters" in *The American Almanac of Jobs and Salaries* (pp. 96-97)   **1938**
"Fire Fighters" in Volume 3 of *Career Discovery Encyclopedia* (pp. 30-31)   **1936**
Fire Fighters and Inspectors   **1937**
Fire Inspector   **1972**
Fire Journal   **2016**
Fire Lieutenant's & Captain's Handbook   **2000**
Fire Management Notes   **2017**
Fire Marshal   **1973**
Fire News   **2018**
Fire Officer   **1974**
Fire on the Rim: A Firefighter's Season at the Grand Canyon   **2040**
Fire Prevention & Firefighting   **1939**
Fire Prevention in Use of Cutting & Welding Processes   **5974**
Fire Prevention Inspector   **1975**
Fire Promotion Course (One Volume)   **1976**
Fire Protection Handbook   **2001**
Fire Protection Specialist   **1977**
Fire Safety Officer   **1978**
Fire Safety Technician   **1979**
"Fire Science" in *The Career Connection II: A Guide to Technical Majors and Their Related Careers* (pp. 61-62)   **1940**
Fire Technology   **2019**
Firefighter   **1941, 1980, 1981**
"Firefighter" in *Hard Hatted Women: Stories of Struggle and Success in the Trades* (pp. 156-170)   **1942**
"Firefighter" in *Occu-Facts: Information on 565 Careers in Outline Form* (p. 13.3)   **1943**
"Firefighter" in *VGM's Careers Encyclopedia* (pp. 176-178)   **1944**
Firefighter & Paramedic Burnout   **2002**
Firefighter Entrance Examinations   **1982**
"Firefighters" in *Opportunities in Vocational and Technical Careers* (p. 75)   **1945**
Firefighters: A to Z   **1946**
"Firefighters" in Volume 3 of *The Encyclopedia of Careers and Vocational Guidance* (pp. 242-247)   **1947**
Firefighter's Entrance Handbook   **2003**
Firefighters in Action   **2041**
Firefighter's News   **2020**
Firefighters: Their Lives in Their Own Words   **2042**
"Firefighting Occupations" in *Occupational Outlook Handbook* (pp. 286-288)   **1948**
Firehouse Attendant   **1983**
Firehouse Magazine   **2021**
Firehouse Magazine Heroism and Community Service Award   **1988**
Firehouse Trivia   **2043**
Fireman, Fire Dept.   **1984**
Fireman-Laborer   **1985**
Fireman of the Year   **1989**
First Biannual Commercial and Industrial Insulation Industry Financial Survey   **5130**
First Principles: National Security and Civil Liberties   **2264**
Fish Boat   **3508**
Fish Expo   **3575**
Fish Finder Magazines   **3509**
Fish News   **3510**
"Fish Production Technicians" in Volume 4 of *The Encyclopedia of Careers and Vocational Guidance* (pp. 467-468)   **5634**
"Fish Production Technicians" in Volume 3 of *Career Discovery Encyclopedia* (pp. 34-35)   **5635**
"Fisher" in *Agribusiness, Environment, and Natural Resources*, Volume 2 of *Career Information Center* (pp. 47-49)   **3458**
"Fisher" in *Hard Hatted Women: Stories of Struggle and Success in the Trades* (pp. 81-87)   **3459**
Fisher, Commercial   **3460**
Fisherman   **3461**
The Fisherman   **3511, 3512**
Fishers, Commercial   **3462**
"Fishers, Hunters, and Trappers" in *Occupational Outlook Handbook* (pp. 320-323)   **3463**
Fishing   **3513**
Fishing & Boating Illustrated   **3514**
Fishing and Hunting News   **3515**

Fishing Facts 3516
Fixing Cars 3773
Flammability Regulations & Standards in the United States for Upholstered Furniture 6417
Flashes 3517
Fleet Product News 6882
Flexo 6212, 6259
Flexo Espanol 6213, 6260
FLICC Newsletter 1508
Flight Attendant 3012, 3013
"Flight Attendant" in *Careers in Aviation* (pp. 15-18) 3014
"Flight Attendant" in *College Board Guide to Jobs and Career Planning* (pp. 80-82) 3015
"Flight Attendant" in *Occu-Facts: Information on 565 Careers in Outline Form* (p. 13.37) 3016
"Flight Attendant" in *Occupational Outlook Handbook* (pp. 310-311) 3017
"Flight Attendant" in *Opportunities in Airline Careers* (pp. 70-75) 3018
"Flight Attendant" in *The American Almanac of Jobs and Salaries* (pp. 403-404) 3022
"Flight Attendant" in *The Complete Aviation/Aerospace Career Guide* (pp. 159-164) 3019
"Flight Attendant" in *Transportation* (pp. 51-55) 3020
"Flight Attendant" in *VGM's Careers Encyclopedia* (pp. 178-181) 3021
Flight Attendant Interview Handbook 3023
Flight Attendant Skills Test (FAST) 3036
"Flight Attendants" in *America's 50 Fastest Growing Jobs* (pp. 125-126) 3030
"Flight Attendants" in *Jobs! What They Are...Where They Are...What They Pay* (pp. 165-166) 3024
"Flight Attendants" in *101 Careers: A Guide to the Fastest-Growing Opportunities* (pp. 316-319) 3025
"Flight Attendants" in *Opportunities in Travel Careers* (pp. 37-39) 3026
"Flight Attendants" in *Travel Agent* (pp. 165-166) 3027
"Flight Attendants" in Volume 3 of *Career Discovery Encyclopedia* (pp. 36-37) 3028
"Flight Attendants" in Volume 3 of *The Encyclopedia of Careers and Vocational Guidance* (pp. 247-251) 3029
"Flight Dispatcher" in *Opportunities in Airline Careers* (pp. 91-93) 1294
"Flight Dispatcher" in *Opportunities in Transportation Careers* (pp. 39-40) 1295
Flightlog 3040
"Floor Brokers, Traders, and Commodity Traders" in *Jobs! What They Are...Where They Are...What They Pay* (pp. 119-120) 490
Floor Covering Installation Contractors Association 4780, 4809
Floor Covering Installation Contractors Association—Newsletter 4798
"Floor Covering Installer" in *Construction*, Volume 4 of *Career Information Center* (pp. 58-60) 4774
"Floor Covering Installer" in Volume 3 of *The Encyclopedia of Careers and Vocational Guidance* (pp. 662-665) 4775
"Floor Covering Installer (Resilient)" in *Occu-Facts: Information on 565 Careers in Outline Form* (p. 16.12) 4776
"Floor Covering Installers" in *Opportunities in Building Construction Trades* (pp. 53-55) 4777
"Floor Covering Installers" in Volume 3 of *Career Discovery Encyclopedia* (pp. 40-41) 4778
Floor Covering News 4799
Floor Covering Weekly 4800
Flooring 4801
Florida Roofing, Sheet Metal, and Air Conditioning Contractors Association Trade Exposition 5491
Florida State Department of Professional Regulation 7191
The Flue Cured Tobacco Farmer 3349
Fly Fisherman 3518
Fly Rod & Reel 3519
Flyfishing 3520
FlyFishing News, Views & Reviews 3521
Flying High in Travel: A Complete Guide to Careers in the Travel Industry 625, 1206
FMRA News 3350
FN (Footwear News) 6356
Focus on Farming 3351
Fodor's Guides [Travel] 712
"Food and Beverage Industry" in *Jobs '91* (pp. 277-286) 2457
"Food and Beverage Service Workers" in *Occupational Outlook Handbook* (pp. 296-298) 2458
Food and Beverage Show 2424, 2543
Food and Dairy Expo 5664
Food & Wine 2388

Food Careers 2318, 2459
Food Chemical News 2389
Food Distribution Magazine—Food Brokers Directory Issue 2359
Food Distribution Research Society—Quarterly Newsletter 2390
Food Inspector 5681
Food Professional's Guide 2360
Food Reviews International 2512
"Food Service" in *The Career Connection II: A Guide to Technical Majors and Their Related Careers* (pp. 63-64) 2319
Food Service Careers Guide Book 2460
Food Service Management by Checklist: A Handbook of Control Techniques 2498
Food Service Workers 2461
Food Services 2320, 2462, 5636
Foodletter 2391, 2513
Foodservice Information Abstracts 2392, 2514
Foodservice Management Study Course 2499
Foodservice Product News 2515
Foodservice Report 2393, 2516
FOODTECH - International Food and Beverage, Catering, Food Production and Processing Equipment, Packaging Machinery and Materials Exhibition 2425, 2544, 5665
Footsteps in the Ocean: Careers in Diving 3464
Foreign Vehicle Maintenance in the U.S.A. 3886, 4121, 4222, 4458, 4488
Foreman 5618
Foreman Auto Mechanic 3868
Foreman Bricklayer 4623
Foreman Cable Splicer 4418
Foreman Carpenter 4710
Foreman Electrician 4994
Foreman Elevator Mechanic 4198
Foreman Machinist 5788
Foreman of Gardeners 3061
Foreman of Laborers 5619, 7067
Foreman of Mechanics 4249
Foreman Painter 5151
Foreman Plasterer 5202
Foreman Plumber 5277
Foreman (Power Cables) 4419
Foreman (Power Distribution) 6027
Foreman (Railroad Watchman) 6749
Foreman Roofer 5349, 5363
Foreman Sheet Metal Worker 5462
Foreman (Structures Group A-H) 4250
Forest and Conservation History 3616
Forest Conservation 3617
Forest Industries Clinic and Machinery Show 3651
Forest Industries Equipment Exhibition 3652
Forest Products Machinery and Equipment Exposition 3653
Forest World 3618
The Forestry Chronicle 3619
Forklift Operator Training 6678
Forklift Truck: Operator Training 6679
Four Classics on the Theory of Double Entry Bookkeeping 1050
Fresh Baked 2394
Fresh Facts for Foodservice 2395, 2517
Fresh Off the Vine 2396, 3352
From Nine to Five 860, 1100, 1195, 1670, 1740, 1879
From the State Capitals: Alcoholic Beverage Control 2518
From the State Capitals: Justice Policies 1920
From the State Capitals: Water Supply 6110
Front Desk Courtesy 1112
Front-End Loader Operator 6680
Front Page Detective: William J. Burns & the Detective Profession, 1880-1930 2286
Frozen Foods—Wholesale Directory 2433
Fruit and Vegetable Truck Rate Report 6883
Fullwrite Professional: A User's Guide 1861
FUR-FISH-GAME 3522
Fur Trapping 3465
Fur Trapping in North America 3466
Furbearer Management 3481
"Furnace Cleaner" in *Occu-Facts: Information on 565 Careers in Outline Form* (p. 20.21) 7033
Furniture: An Opportunity Career 6400, 6440
Furniture Finisher 6441
"Furniture Finisher" in *Occu-Facts: Information on 565 Careers in Outline Form* (p. 17.14) 6442
"Furniture Industry" in *Manufacturing*, Volume 9 of *Career Information Center* (pp. 110-111) 6443
Furniture Manufacturing 6444

Index to Information Sources

"Furniture Manufacturing Occupations" in Volume 3 of *The Encyclopedia of Careers and Vocational Guidance* (pp. 576-578) **6445**
"Furniture Manufacturing Workers" in Volume 3 of *Career Discovery Encyclopedia* (pp. 60-61) **6446**
Furniture Upholsterer **6401**
"Furniture Upholsterer" in *Occu-Facts: Information on 565 Careers in Outline Form* (p. 17.19) **6402**
"Furniture Upholsterer and Tailor or Dressmaker" in *Personal Services* (pp. 39-43) **6282, 6403**
"Furniture Upholsterers" in Volume 3 of *Career Discovery Encyclopedia* (pp. 64-65) **6404**
"Furniture Upholsterers" in Volume 3 of *The Encyclopedia of Careers and Vocational Guidance* (pp. 579-581) **6405**
Future Aviation Professionals of America **3035, 3688**

G

Gallatin Equipment Company—Newsletter **3353**
Game & Fish Magazine **3523**
Garbage Collector **7034**
Gardener **3062**
The Gardener **3092**
"Gardener and Grounds Keeper" in *Consumer, Homemaking, and Personal Services*, Volume 5 of *Career Information Center* (pp. 42-44) **3042**
Gardener - Grounds Maintenance Worker **3063**
"Gardeners and Groundskeepers" in *Occupational Outlook Handbook* (pp. 311-313) **3043**
The Gardener's Companion **3093**
Garment Cutter **6283**
"Garment Cutter" in *Occu-Facts: Information on 565 Careers in Outline Form* (p. 18.14) **6284**
"Garment Presser" in *Occu-Facts: Information on 565 Careers in Outline Form* (p. 18.17) **6285**
Gas & Electric Welder **5963**
Gas Appliance Service Technician **4354**
Gasoline and Automotive Service Dealers Association—Bulletin **3792, 3904**
"Gasoline Service Station Attendants" in Volume 3 of *The Encyclopedia of Careers and Vocational Guidance* (pp. 743-746) **7035**
GATFWORLD **6147, 6176, 6214, 6261**
Gauged Brickwork: A Technical Handbook **4625**
Gem and Jewelry Fact Sheets Quarterly Supplement **5743**
Gem Trends **5744**
Gems & Gemology **5745**
The Gemstone Registry Bulletin **5746**
General and Mechanical Maintenance Training Program **4237**
General Commendation **2219**
"General Maintenance Mechanics" in *Occupational Outlook Handbook* (pp. 344-345) **4238**
"General Maintenance Mechanics" in Volume 3 of *Career Discovery Encyclopedia* (pp. 68-69) **4239**
"General Maintenance Mechanics" in Volume 3 of *The Encyclopedia of Careers and Vocational Guidance* (pp. 514-518) **4240**
General Motors Automotive Service Educational Program **3875**
"General Office Clerk" in *Occu-Facts: Information on 565 Careers in Outline Form* (p. 12.14) **1071**
"General Office Clerks" in *Occupational Outlook Handbook* (pp. 256-257) **1072**
"General Office Clerks" in Volume 3 of *Career Discovery Encyclopedia* (pp. 72-73) **1073**
"General Office Clerks" in Volume 3 of *The Encyclopedia of Careers and Vocational Guidance* (pp. 45-48) **1074**
General Office Procedures for Colleges **1091**
General Society of Mechanics and Tradesmen **4246**
General Woodworking **6462**
Georgia Secretary of State ● Professional Examining Boards **7192**
"Geriatric Aide" in *Public and Community Services*, Volume 11 of *Career Information Center* (pp. 52-53) **2703**
Geriatric Aides **3123**
Geriatric Nursing Assistants: An Annotated Bibliography with Models to Enhance Practice **2742**
Get Set to Trap **3482**
Get Wired for Life as a Construction Electrician **4976**
Getting a Job in the Computer Age **905**
Getting Down to Business: Carpentry Business **4696**
Getting Down to Business: Construction Electrician Business **4697, 4977**
Getting Down to Business: Hair Styling Shop **2834, 2940**
Getting Down to Business: Plumbing Business **5246**
Getting Down to Business: Travel Agency **626, 1207**

Getting Down to Business: Welding Business **5937**
"Getting Started in Industrial Sales" in *Marketing and Sales Career Directory* (pp. 18-22) **167**
"Getting Started in Retail Ad Sales" in *Newspapers Career Directory* (pp. 21-24) **580**
The Giant **3354**
Glass Magazine **5079**
Glazier **5044, 5045, 5056**
"Glazier" in *Construction*, Volume 4 of *Career Information Center* (pp. 60-61) **5046**
"Glazier" in *Exploring Nontraditional Jobs for Women* (pp. 16-20) **5047**
"Glazier" in *Occu-Facts: Information on 565 Careers in Outline Form* (p. 16.15) **5048**
"Glazier" in *Occupational Outlook Handbook* (pp. 371-372) **5049**
Glaziers **5050**
"Glaziers" in *Opportunities in Building Construction Trades* (pp. 55-57) **5051**
"Glaziers" in Volume 3 of *Career Discovery Encyclopedia* (pp. 82-83) **5052**
"Glaziers" in Volume 3 of *The Encyclopedia of Careers and Vocational Guidance* (pp. 665-668) **5053**
Glossary of Financial Services Terminology **533**
GMC Apprentice Program Battery Tests (GMC) **3869**
Going Offshore for the First Time **5419**
Gold Mining Stock Report **545**
Golden Hammer Award **4526**
The Goldsmith **5747**
A Good Part of Your Life **5887**
Good Samaritan Award **2220**
Government Product News—Grounds Maintenance Buyers' Guide Issue **3120**
Government Tender Report **6772, 6884, 6976**
Government Traffic Bulletin **6773, 6885, 6977**
Grain & Feed Market News **3355**
Grain Farmer **3253**
Grainews **3356**
Graphic Arts Monthly **6215, 6262**
Graphic Arts Product News **6216, 6263**
Graphic Arts Technical Foundation **6139, 6166, 6205, 6226, 6244**
Graphic Communications International Union **6140, 6167, 6206, 6245**
Graphic Communications International Union Conference **6188, 6227**
Grass & Grain **3357**
Grass Roots **2022**
Gray's Sporting Journal **3524**
Great American Firehouse Expo and Muster **2036**
Great Lakes Cable Expo **4430**
The Green Man **5420**
Green World News **3094**
Greener Gardening, Easier **3095**
Greenskeeper **3064**
Gregg Quick Filing Practice **1476**
Grit and Steel **3525**
"Grocery Bagger" in *Occu-Facts: Information on 565 Careers in Outline Form* (p. 20.13) **7036**
Grocery Checker **10**
"Grocery Checker" in *Occu-Facts: Information on 565 Careers in Outline Form* (p. 11.23) **11**
Groomers Voice **2808**
Grounds Keeper **3044**
Grounds Maintenance Awards **3071**
Grounds Maintenance Guidelines **3079**
Grounds Management Forum **3096**
Grounds Management Guide **3080**
Grounds Manager Certification Program **3068**
Groundskeeper **3065**
"Groundskeeper" in *Occu-Facts: Information on 565 Careers in Outline Form* (p. 14.12) **3045**
"Groundskeeper and Stadium Worker" in *Hospitality & Recreation* (pp. 57-61) **3046**
The Grower—Nursery Stock and Seed Directory Issue **3081**
"Guard" in *Career Opportunities in Art* (pp. 25-26) **2051**
"Guard" in *VGM's Careers Encyclopedia* (pp. 84-86) **2052**
Guard Patrolman **2073**
Guard, Security **2053**
"Guard Supervisor" in *Career Opportunities in Art* (pp. 27-28) **2054**
"Guards" in *America's 50 Fastest Growing Jobs* (pp. 118-120) **2056**
"Guards" in *Occupational Outlook Handbook* (pp. 288-290) **2055**
"Guards" in *The American Almanac of Jobs and Salaries* (pp. 531-532) **2057**
Guest of Honor Award **3270**
Guide to Appraising for Federal Agencies [Real estate industry] **391**
A Guide to Becoming a Flight Attendant **3031**

A Guide to Computer Careers 906, 907
The Guide to Cooking Schools 2352
Guide to Electronic Components 3960
Guide to Federal Technical, Trades, and Labor Jobs 1395
Guide to Grounds Maintenance Estimating 3082
Guide to Hospitality Education 2361, 2500
Guide to Insulation Product Specifications 5099
Guide to the Health Care Field 2739
Guide to Welding 5975
Guild of American Luthiers 4520
Guild of American Luthiers Conference 4548
Guitar Repair 4529
Gunlogson Medal; G.B. 3072

H

Hair International/Associated Master Barbers and Beauticians of America 2837, 2953
Hair International/Associated Master Barbers and Beauticians of America Conference 2854, 2986
Hair International News 2850, 2977
"Hair Stylist" in *Career Opportunities in Television, Cable, and Video* (pp. 140-141) 2941
"Hairdressers" in *Jobs! What They Are... Where They Are... What They Pay* (p. 297) 2942
"Hairstylist" in *Guide to Careers Without College* (pp. 100-102) 2943
Hairstylist Assistant 2944
Hall of Fame 4527
"Hand Packager" in *Occu-Facts: Information on 565 Careers in Outline Form* (p. 20.22) 7037
"Hand Sewer" in *Occu-Facts: Information on 565 Careers in Outline Form* (p. 18.27) 6286
Handbook for Teacher Aides 1757
Handbook of Basic Electronic Troubleshooting 3961
A Handbook of Effective Techniques for Teacher Aides 1758
Handbook of Expanded Dental Auxiliary Practice 2612
Handbook of Software Maintenance 4074
Handbook of Trade and Technical Careers and Training 2353, 2495, 3761, 4116, 5969
Hands That Think: A Word About Careers in Modern Dental Laboratory Technology 6493
Handy Medical Guide for Seafarers, Fisherman, Trawlermen & Yachtsmen 3483
Hanging On 6933
Harbormaster 6965
"Hardware Service Technician" in *The Complete Computer Career Guide* (pp. 42-47) 4054
Harger Memorial Award; Don 3480
Harvests 3097
Hatfield Award; William D. 6105
Have You Considered Dental Assisting? 2587
Have You Considered Dental Laboratory Technology? 6494
Hawaii and Pacific Basin Nails Expo 2987
Hawaii State Department of Commerce and Consumer Affairs • Division of Professional and Vocational Licensing 7193
Hay There! 3358
The Hazardous Materials Handbook for Motor Carriers 6858
Head Automotive Mechanic 3870
Head Bus Driver 6649
Head Clerk (Payroll) 1057
"Head Waiter and Waitress" in *Hospitality and Recreation*, Volume 8 of *Career Information Center* (pp. 80-81) 2463
Head Waitress 2464
Health and Disability Insurance Sales Achievement 110
"Health and Fitness Retail Sales" in *Careers in Health and Fitness* (pp. 71-73) 418
Health and Safety 4387, 5603
Health Assistant 2704
Health Care Security Training Series 2058
Health Career Planning: A Realistic Guide 2588, 2638, 2705
Health Careers Today 2589, 2639, 2706
Health Insurance Association of America 102
Health of the Rep Newsletter 220
Healthwire 1764, 2629, 2692, 2753
"Heating, Air-Conditioning, and Refrigeration Mechanics" in *Jobs! What They Are... Where They Are... What They Pay* (pp. 176-178) 4276
"Heating, Air-Conditioning, and Refrigeration Mechanics" in *Occupational Outlook Handbook* (pp. 345-347) 4277
"Heating and Air Conditioning Installers" in *Opportunities in Building Construction Trades* (pp. 57-58) 4278
"Heating and Cooling Mechanics" in Volume 3 of *Career Discovery Encyclopedia* (pp. 98-99) 4279

Heating and Cooling Service 4280
"Heating and Cooling Technicians" in Volume 3 of *Career Discovery Encyclopedia* (pp. 100-101) 4281
Heating, Cooling & Lighting 4303
"Heating, Cooling, and Refrigeration" in *Opportunities in Plumbing and Pipefitting Careers* (pp. 83-85) 4282
Heating System Troubleshooting Handbook 4304
Heating, Ventilating & Air Conditioning 4305
"Heating, Ventilation and Air Conditioning" in *The Career Connection II: A Guide to Technical Majors and Their Related Careers* (pp. 67-68) • T 4283
Heating, Ventilation, and Air Conditioning Product and Equipment Show 4463, 5492, 6069
Heavy Duty Truck Maintenance in the U.S.A. 3887, 4122, 4223, 4459, 4489
Heavy Duty Trucking 6886
Heavy Equipment Mechanic 4455
"Heavy Equipment Operations" in *The Career Connection II: A Guide to Technical Majors and Their Related Careers* (pp. 69-70) 6681
"Heavy Equipment Operator" in *Construction*, Volume 4 of *Career Information Center* (pp. 62-63) 6682
"Heavy Truck Driver" in *Occu-Facts: Information on 565 Careers in Outline Form* (p. 19.3) 6806
Heavy Vehicle Use Tax: Regulations & Instructions 6859
Helicopter Maintenance Award 3691
Here Comes the Fireman 2044
HI/AMBBA National Bulletin 2851, 2978
HIAA Bulletin 122
HIAA Directory 113
HIAA Executive Report 123
Hiballer Forest Magazine 3620
The Hideaway Report 692
High Plains Journal 3359
High Pressure Plant Tender 6028
Highway Common Carrier Newsletter 6887
Hobby Supply Salesperson 419
"Home Appliance and Power Tool Repairers" in *Occupational Outlook Handbook* (pp. 347-348) 4355
"Home Appliance Repairer" in *Personal Services* (pp. 51-55) 4356
Home BUILDER Magazine 4662, 4755, 4802, 4879, 4943, 5024, 5080, 5118, 5175, 5232, 5318, 5401, 5483, 5576
Home Electronics 3962
"Home Electronics Repairers" in Volume 3 of *Career Discovery Encyclopedia* (pp. 108-109) 4149
Home Furnishings and Carpet Market and Floor Coverings 4810
Home Health Aide 3124
"Home Health Aide" in *Health Care* (pp. 45-49) 3125
"Home Health Aide" in *Health*, Volume 7 of *Career Information Center* (pp. 48-49) 3126
"Home Health Aide" in *Occu-Facts: Information on 565 Careers in Outline Form* (p. 13.24) 3127
Home Health Care Aide 3128
Home Health Line 3147
"Home Health Technicians" in Volume 3 of *The Encyclopedia of Careers and Vocational Guidance* (p. 414) 3129
Home Heating & Air Conditioning Systems 4306
Homecare News 3148
"Homemaker" in *Consumer, Homemaking, and Personal Services*, Volume 5 of *Career Information Center* (pp. 46-47) 3130
"Homemaker" in *Opportunities in Home Economics Careers* (pp. 51-52) 3131
"Homemaker-Home Health Aide" in *Careers in Health Care* (pp. 103-105) 3132
"Homemaker-Home Health Aide" in *120 Careers in the Health Care Field* (pp. 163-165) 3133
"Homemaker Home Health Aide" in *Opportunities in Health and Medical Careers* (pp. 32-33) 3134
Homemaker Home Health Aides 3135
"Homemaker-Home Health Aides" in *America's 50 Fastest Growing Jobs* (pp. 126-129) 3136
"Homemaker-Home Health Aides" in *Occupational Outlook Handbook* (pp. 313-315) 3137
"Homemaker Home Health Aides" in Volume 3 of *Career Discovery Encyclopedia* (pp. 110-111) 3138
"Homemaker Home Health Aides" in Volume 3 of *The Encyclopedia of Careers and Vocational Guidance* (pp. 259-263) 3139
Homes and Homebuilding 4307, 4717, 4913
Hook, Line & Sinker 3526
Hooks and Lines 3527
Hoover Police Service Award; John Edgar 2221
Horsebreeders Bookkeeping System 1036
Horticulture 3098
HortIdeas 3099

Index to Information Sources

Hosiery News 6315, 6383
Hospice Forum 3149
Hospital Attendant 2707
"Hospital Attendant" in *Occu-Facts: Information on 565 Careers in Outline Form* (p. 13.25) 2708
"Hospital Attendants" in Volume 3 of *Career Discovery Encyclopedia* (pp. 114-115) 2709
Hospitality and Tourism Educator 2397, 2519
"Hospitality Cashier" in *Hospitality and Recreation*, Volume 8 of *Career Information Center* (pp. 49-50) 12
Hospitality Education and Research Journal 2398, 2520
Hospitality Industry 1113
The Hospitality Manager 2399, 2521, 3528
Hospitals 2754
"Hostessing" in *The Job Hunter's Guide to Japan* (pp. 163-166) 2465
Hot Off the Computer 1509
Hot Tips, Sneaky Tricks, and Last Ditch Tactics: An Insider's Guide to Getting Your First Corporate Job 65, 258
"Hotel and Motel Clerks" in *Occupational Outlook Handbook* (p. 259) 1114
"Hotel and Motel Desk Clerk" in *Hospitality & Recreation* (pp. 15-19) 1115
Hotel & Motel Equipment & Supplies Directory 1142
"Hotel and Motel Front Office Clerks" in *Jobs! What They Are...Where They Are...What They Pay* (pp. 167-168) 1116
Hotel & Motel Management 1131
Hotel & Travel Index 693, 1237
"Hotel Clerks" in Volume 3 of *Career Discovery Encyclopedia* (pp. 120-121) 1117
"Hotel Clerks" in Volume 3 of *The Encyclopedia of Careers and Vocational Guidance* (pp. 48-52) 1118
"Hotel Cook or Chef and Baker" in *Hospitality & Recreation* (pp. 27-31) 2321
"Hotel Desk Clerk" in *Hospitality and Recreation*, Volume 8 of *Career Information Center* (pp. 52-53) 1119
Hotel Executive Chef 2322
Hotel Front Office Management & Operation 1092, 1129
Hotel/Motel Careers: A World of Opportunities 1120
"Hotel, Motel Cleaner" in *Occu-Facts: Information on 565 Careers in Outline Form* (p. 13.27) 3161
Hotel/Motel Clerk 1121
"Hotel/Motel Clerk" in *Occu-Facts: Information on 565 Careers in Outline Form* (p. 12.16) 1122
Hotel-Motel Greeters International 1125
Hotel-Motel Greeters International Annual Conference 1140
Hotels 1132
House Cleaner 3201
House Painter 5152
Household Service Workers 3202
Household Worker 3203
"Household Worker" in *Occu-Facts: Information on 565 Careers in Outline Form* (p. 13.2) 3204
Houseman 3205
How Food Brokers Serve You 168
How to Achieve a Satisfactory DOT Safety Rating 6860
How to Be a Receptionist 1171
How to Buy an Office Computer or Word Processor 1862
How to Find Anyone Anywhere 2247
How to Find Cases Anywhere: P.I.'s Guide to Obtaining Cases, Obtaining Free Publicity & Marketing Investigative Services 2248
How to Get a Job with A Cruise Line: Adventure-Travel-Romance - How to Sail Around the World on Cruise Ships & Get Paid for It 627
How to Get a Job with a Cruise Line: Adventure-Travel-Romance - How to Sail Around the World on Cruise Ships & Get Paid for It 1208
How to Get a Job With the Police Department: Police Officer 2110
How to Get a Job with the Post Office 1364
How to Learn Basic Bookkeeping in Ten Easy Lessons 1003
How to Locate Needed Servicing Information 3963
How to Open and Run a Money-Making Travel Agency 628, 1209
How to Prepare for a Civil Service Examination (Text) 1396
How to Prepare for Real Estate Licensing Examinations—Salesperson and Broker 314
How to Prepare for the Civil Service Examinations for Stenographer, Typist, Clerk, and Office Machine Operator 1852
How to Prepare for the Fire Fighter Examinations 1986
How to Prepare for the Police Officer Examination Including Transit and Housing Officer 2181
How to Prepare for the Police Sergeant Examination 2182
How to Prepare for the Postal Clerk-Carrier Examination 1397
How to Prepare for the Truck Driver's Commercial Driver's License Test (CDL) 6839
How to Prepare for the U.S. Postal Distribution Machine Clerk Examination 1398
How to Prepare for the U.S. Postal Service Mailhandler/Mail Processor Examination 1399
How to Restore Wooden Body Framing 3774
How to Set up an Effective Filing System 1477
How to Start a Secretarial & Business Service 1638
How to Start You Own Secretarial Services Business at Home 1569
How to Succeed As a Real Estate Salesperson: A Comprehensive Training Guide 336
How to Tune, Repair & Regulate Pianos: A Practical Guide 4530
How to Typeset from a Wordprocessor: An Interfacing Guide 1863
How Valuable is Your Future? 5770, 5908
How You Too Can Become a Flight Attendant!: A Step by Step Guide 3032
HSUS Close-Up Reports 2809
HSUS News 2810
Hudiburg Award; Everett E. 1990
Human Resources Abstracts 1546
Human Rights Award 2222
The Human Side of Railroading 6725
Humane Society of the United States 2789
HummerNews 4499
Hunting and Fishing Event Newsletter 3529
The Hunting Report for Big Game Hunters 3530
HVAC Product News 4327

I

I-Beam 5530
IADA Watchline 3793, 3905
IAFC On Scene 2023
IAHA HITEC-Hospitality Industry Technology Expostion and Conference 1141
IASL Newsletter 1510
The IBEW Leads to Electrifying Careers 4398, 4978
IBM PC Advanced Troubleshooting & Repair 4075
IBPAT Directory 4308, 4914, 5156
ICAA News 5119
ICA's Newsletter 964
ICTA News 694, 1243
Idaho State Board of Occupational Licenses 7194
The Idea of Police 2287
Idea Source Guide 221, 612
IEC News Circuit 5025
IFE Insider 822
IFFA - International Trade Fair for the Meat Industry 5666
IFT Annual Meeting and Food Expo 2426, 2545
IIAAction News 124
IIFET Newsletter 3531
III Executive Letter 774
Illinois State Department of Registration and Education ● Division of Licensing and Testing 7195
The Illustrated Home Electronics Fix-it Book 3964
Import Service 3794, 3906
Import Statistics 2522
An Important Message To All Mechanical Minded People 5888
Imprints 2912
Improving Child Care Through the Child Development Associate Program 2898, 2906
IMSA Journal 1319
IN-DEX - Production Technology, Materials Handling, and Warehousing Exhibition 6714
In-Plant Printer & Electronic Publisher 6148, 6177, 6217, 6264
Incinerator Stationary Engineer 6060
The Independent 2400
Independent Agent 125
Independent Electrical Contractors 4987, 4990
Independent Electrical Contractors Convention and Trade Show 5034
Independent Insurance Agents of America 103
Independent Insurance Agents of America Annual Convention and Exhibit 155
Independent Operations 546
Indiana State Professional Licensing Agency 7196
Individual Awards 2223
"Industrial (Business-to-Business) Marketing" in *Opportunities in Marketing Careers* (pp. 36-37) 169
Industrial Circuits & Automated Manufacturing 3965
Industrial Control Electronics 3966
"Industrial Electronic Equipment Repairers" in Volume 3 of *Career Discovery Encyclopedia* (pp. 130-131) 3934
Industrial Electronics 3951
Industrial Electronics: A Text-Lab Manual 3967
Industrial Electronics and Controls 3968
Industrial Electronics: Devices & Systems 3969

1103

Industrial Electronics Training Program **3935**
Industrial Fabric and Equipment Show **6322, 6396, 6433**
Industrial Fabrics in Upholstery **6418**
Industrial Fire Brigades Training Manual **2004**
Industrial Heating Equipment Association—Legislative Report **4328**
Industrial Load Management: Theory, Practice, & Simulations **6032**
"Industrial Machinery Mechanics" in Volume 3 of *Career Discovery Encyclopedia* (pp. 134-135) **4374**
"Industrial Machinery Mechanics" in Volume 3 of *The Encyclopedia of Careers and Vocational Guidance* (pp. 522-524) **4375**
Industrial Machinery News **5881**
"Industrial Machinery Repairer" in *Manufacturing*, Volume 9 of *Career Information Center* (pp. 61-62) **4376**
"Industrial Machinery Repairer" in *Occu-Facts: Information on 565 Careers in Outline Form* (p. 15.10) **4377**
Industrial Machinery Repairers **4378**
"Industrial Machinery Repairers" in *Occupational Outlook Handbook* (pp. 348-349) **4379**
"Industrial Machinery Repairers" in *The American Almanac of Jobs and Salaries* (pp. 524-525) **4380**
Industrial Photo Processor **6584**
Industrial Relations Council for the Plumbing and Pipe Fitting Industry **5270**
Industrial Relations Council for the Plumbing and Pipe Fitting Industry Annual Conference **5335**
Industrial Relations Council for the Plumbing and Pipe Fitting Industry Annual Convention **5336**
"Industrial Sales and Wholesaling" in *Careers in Marketing* (pp. 52-55) **170**
Industrial Truck Association **6703**
Industrial Truck Association Conference **6916**
"Industrial Truck Operator" in *Occu-Facts: Information on 565 Careers in Outline Form* (p. 19.19) **6683**
"Industrial Truck Operators" in Volume 3 of *Career Discovery Encyclopedia* (pp. 140-141) **6684**
"Industrial Truck Operators" in Volume 3 of *The Encyclopedia of Careers and Vocational Guidance* (pp. 746-748) **6685**
"Industrial Upholsterer" in *Manufacturing*, Volume 9 of *Career Information Center* (pp. 63-64) **6406**
Industry Award **5284**
Industry Directory [Office automation] **850, 1190, 1627, 1857**
"Information Clerk" in *Occu-Facts: Information on 565 Careers in Outline Form* (p. 12.19) **1102**
"Information Clerks" in *America's 50 Fastest Growing Jobs* (pp. 109-111) **1103**
"Information Clerks" in *Occupational Outlook Handbook* (pp. 257-259) **1104**
"Information Technology, Data Processing" in *The Career Connection II: A Guide to Technical Majors and Their Related Careers* (pp. 73-74) **1823**
"Information/Word Processing" in *Opportunities in Office Occupations* (pp. 116-130) **1824**
"Information/Word Processing: The Secretary" in *Opportunities in Office Occupations* (pp. 93-115) **1570**
Inside DAMA **861**
Inside Retailing **462**
Inside the Janitorial Business: How to Start from Scratch & Succeed in Professional Cleaning **3162**
Insight/Wise Owl News **6532**
InSights **3532**
"Inspectors, Testers, and Graders" in *Occupational Outlook Handbook* (pp. 390-391) **5674**
Installation & Cleaning Specialist **3189, 4260**
Installation Supplies and Ideas Expo **4811, 5582**
Installing Personal Computer **4076**
Instant and Small Commercial Printer **6149, 6178, 6218, 6265**
Instant Secretary's Handbook **1571, 1639**
Institute for Woodworking Education **6454**
Institute of Certified Travel Agents **661, 663**
Institute of Certified Travel Agents Forum **707**
Institute of Financial Education **800**
Institute of Financial Education—On Track **823**
Institute of Internal Auditors **1010, 1013**
Institute of Internal Auditors Annual Forum **1047**
"Institutional Broker" in *Careers in Banking and Finance* (pp. 54-55) **491**
"Institutional Child Care Worker" in *Public and Community Services*, Volume 11 of *Career Information Center* (pp. 74-75) **2884**
Instructors Guide to Comprehensive Custodial Training Programs **3175**
"Instrument Repair & Restoration Specialist" in *Career Opportunities in the Music Industry* (pp. 127-128) **4503**
Instrument Repairers **4504**

"Instrument Sales Representative" in *Career Opportunities in the Music Industry* (pp. 95-96) **171**
Insulating & Roofing Occupations **5089, 5350**
Insulation Contractors Association of America Convention **5127**
"Insulation Worker" in *Construction*, Volume 4 of *Career Information Center* (pp. 64-65) **5090**
Insulation Workers **5091**
"Insulation Workers" in *Occu-Facts: Information on 565 Careers in Outline Form* (p. 16.16) **5092**
"Insulation Workers" in *Occupational Outlook Handbook* (pp. 372-373) **5093**
"Insulation Workers" in Volume 3 of *Career Discovery Encyclopedia* (pp. 150-151) **5094**
"Insurance" in *Jobs '91* (pp. 309-316) **66**
"Insurance" in *Major Decisions: A Guide to College Majors* (p. 91) **67**
"Insurance" in *The Black Woman's Career Guide* (pp. 288-294) **68**
"Insurance" in Volume 1 of *The Encyclopedia of Careers and Vocational Guidance* (pp. 243-249) **69**
Insurance Accounting and Systems Association Annual Conference and Business Show **156**
Insurance Adjuster **740**
"Insurance Adjuster" in *Occu-Facts: Information on 565 Careers in Outline Form* (p. 12.43) **741**
The Insurance Advocate **126**
"Insurance Agent" in *Top Professions: The 100 Most Popular, Dynamic, and Profitable Careers in America Today* (pp. 8-9) **70**
"Insurance Agent and Broker" in *Marketing and Distribution*, Volume 10 of *Career Information Center* (pp. 71-73) **71**
"Insurance Agent and Broker" in *VGM's Careers Encyclopedia* (pp. 222-225) **72**
"Insurance Agent and Broker" in *VGM's Handbook of Business and Management Careers* (pp. 47-50) **73**
Insurance Agent/Broker, Life **74**
Insurance Agent, Property and Liability **75**
"Insurance Agent/Property & Liability" in *Occu-Facts: Information on 565 Careers in Outline Form* (p. 11.3) **76**
Insurance Agents and Brokers **77**
"Insurance Agents and Brokers" in *Jobs! What They Are...Where They Are...What They Pay* (p. 285) **78**
"Insurance Agents and Brokers" in *101 Careers: A Guide to the Fastest-Growing Opportunities* (pp. 17-20) **79**
"Insurance Agents and Brokers" in Volume 3 of *The Encyclopedia of Careers and Vocational Guidance* (pp. 144-153) **80**
"Insurance Agents and Brokers: Making It in a Premium Career" in *Careers for Women Without College Degrees* (pp. 239-245) **81**
Insurance and Protection Bulletin **824, 1165**
"Insurance Claims Representatives" in Volume 3 of *Career Discovery Encyclopedia* (pp. 152-153) **742**
"Insurance Claims Representatives" in Volume 2 of *The Encyclopedia of Careers and Vocational Guidance* (pp. 323-326) **743**
"Insurance Clerks" in *Occu-Facts: Information on 565 Careers in Outline Form* (p. 12.25) **744**
Insurance Facts **780**
Insurance Industry Newsletter **127**
Insurance Information Institute **751**
"Insurance is Fun!" in *Internships Volume 3: Accounting, Banking, Brokerage, Finance & Insurance* (pp. 55-61) **82**
Insurance Journal **128**
"Insurance Policy Processing Occupations" in Volume 3 of *Career Discovery Encyclopedia* (pp. 154-155) **745**
"Insurance Policy Processing Occupations" in Volume 3 of *The Encyclopedia of Careers and Vocational Guidance* (pp. 52-55) **746**
Insurance Pulse **775**
The Insurance Record **129**
Insurance Review **130, 776**
Insurance Sales **131**
"Insurance, Sales" in *Career Choices for the 90's for Students of Business* (pp. 163-164) **83**
"Insurance Sales" in *Career Choices for the 90's for Students of Communications and Journalism* (pp. 171-172) **84**
"Insurance, Sales" in *Career Choices for the 90's for Students of Economics* (pp. 72-74) **85**
"Insurance, Sales" in *Career Choices for the 90's for Students of Mathematics* (pp. 97-99) **86**
"Insurance Sales" in *Career Choices for the 90's for Students of Political Science & Government* (pp. 172-173) **87**
"Insurance Sales" in *Career Choices for the 90's for Students of Psychology* (pp. 192-193) **88**
"Insurance Sales" in *Fast-Track Careers: A Guide to the Highest-Paying Jobs* (pp. 152-153) **89**
"Insurance Sales" in *Transitions: Military Pathways to Civilian Careers* (pp. 141-142) **90**

Index to Information Sources

"Insurance Sales Workers" in *Occupational Outlook Handbook* (pp. 230-232) **91**
Insurance Salesman **109**
"Insurance Salesperson" in *College Board Guide to Jobs and Career Planning* (pp. 134-136) **92**
"Insurance Salespersons" in *Opportunities in Vocational and Technical Careers* (pp. 61-63) **93**
Insurance Update **777**
Intelligence Issues **2265**
Intelligent Buildings Institute—Directory of Products and Services **4626, 4718, 4845, 5000, 5059, 5100, 5365, 5465, 5512**
Intensive Files Management **1478**
INTERBEV - International Beverage Industry Exhibition and Congress **2546**
"Intercity and Local Transit Bus Drivers" in Volume 3 of *The Encyclopedia of Careers and Vocational Guidance* (pp. 733-737) **6633**
"Intercity Bus Driver" in *Transportation*, Volume 12 of *Career Information Center* (pp. 52-54) **6634**
"The Intercity People Movers" in *Opportunities in Transportation Careers* (pp. 19-29) **6635**
Interconnection Products Directory **3970, 4173, 4423, 5001, 6033**
Interior Construction **5026, 5176**
Internal Revenue Agent **2111**
"Internal Revenue Agent" in *Occu-Facts: Information on 565 Careers in Outline Form* (p. 1.50) **2112**
"Internal Revenue Agent" in *VGM's Careers Encyclopedia* (pp. 227-229) **2113**
Internal Revenue Service Agent **2114**
International Air-Conditioning, Heating, Refrigerating Exposition **4341, 6070**
The International Angler **3533**
International Art Competition - New York **5733, 6455**
International Association of Bridge, Structural and Ornamental Iron Workers **5507, 5540**
International Association of Chiefs of Police Annual Conference **2282**
International Association of Fire Chiefs **1953**
International Association of Fire Fighters **1954, 2037**
International Association of Machinists and Aerospace Workers **4102, 5600, 5607, 5705, 5718, 6556, 6575**
International Association of Security Service **2065, 2070, 2085**
International Aviation Mechanics Journal **3712**
International Baking Industry Exposition **2427**
International Beauty Show **2855, 2988**
International Benjamin Franklin Fire Service Award **1991**
International Brotherhood of Boilermakers, Iron Ship Builders, Blacksmiths, Forgers and Helpers **5706, 5719**
International Brotherhood of Electrical Workers **4416, 4988, 5035, 5601, 6024**
International Brotherhood of Painters and Allied Trades **4909, 5054, 5150, 5183**
International Brotherhood of Teamsters, Chauffeurs, Warehousemen and Helpers of America **1354, 1361, 6557, 6576, 6715, 6834, 6917, 7064, 7074**
International Capital Markets Review **547**
International Caterers' Conference **2428, 2547**
International Ceramic Tile Exhibit **5583**
International Ceramic Trade Fair **5584**
International Concrete and Aggregates Show **4888**
International Credit Association **951, 952**
International Customer Service Association Conference **4572**
International Die Casting Congress and Exposition **5933**
International District Heating and Cooling Association Convention **4464, 6071**
International Electrical Conference and Exhibition **5036**
International Electrical Exposition and Congress **5037**
International Exposition for Food Processors **5667**
International Fire Fighter **2024**
International Fire Service Training Association **1955**
International Foundation for Protection Officers **2066, 2071**
International Green Front Report [Sustainable agriculture resources] **3360, 3621**
International Institute of Carpet and Upholstery Certification **6412, 6415**
International Insurance Monitor **132**
International Jewelry Fair **5759**
International Lawn, Garden, and Power Equipment Expo **3112**
International Light Tackle Tournament Association—Bulletin **3534**
International Maintenance Institute Show and Technical Conference **4262**
International Mass Retail Association Convention and Exhibits **242, 474**
International Materials Handling and Distribution Show **6716**

International Municipal Signal Association **1305, 1307**
International PBX/Telecommunicators—Bulletin **1797**
International PBX/Telecommunicators—Newsletter **1798**
International Poultry Trade Show **3423, 5668**
International Public Transit Expo **6667**
International Railway Journal **6774**
International Real Estate Institute International Real Estate Trade Show and Exhibition **387**
International Secretary of the Year **1629**
International Security and Detective Alliance **2161, 2168**
International Security Officer's Police and Guard Union **2067**
International Society for Animal Rights—Report **2811**
International Society of Certified Electronics Technicians **3941, 3944, 3994, 4162, 4165, 4187**
International Society of Certified Electronics Technicians—Update **3986, 4179**
International Travel Industry Expo **708, 1261**
International Tropical Timber Agreement **3595**
International Trucking Show **6918**
International Union of Bricklayers and Allied Craftsmen **4621, 4672, 4834, 5200, 5555**
International Union of Electronic, Electrical, Salaried, Machine, and Furniture Workers **4384, 4391, 5602, 5608**
International Union of Elevator Constructors **4195, 4206**
International Union of Operating Engineers **6057, 6704**
International Union of Petroleum and Industrial Workers **5430**
International Union of Security Officers **2068**
International Union, United Automobile, Aerospace and Agricultural Implement Workers of America **5707, 6558**
International Welding Thesaurus **5976**
International Woodworking Machinery and Furniture Supply Fair - USA **6477**
International Work Boat Show **6998**
Internships Volume 4: The Travel and Hospitality Industries **42**
Interstate Motor Carrier Forms Manual, 2G: Private, Contract, Exempt **6861**
"Interviewing and New Accounts Clerks" in *Occupational Outlook Handbook* (pp. 259-260) **1145**
Interviewing for a Career in Public Accounting **1004**
INTERWIRE **4573**
Into Your Darkroom Step-by-Step **6607**
Introduction to Air Conditioning, Refrigeration & Heating **4309**
Introduction to Management in the Hospitality Industry **1123, 2323, 2466**
Introduction to the Health Professions **2590, 2640, 2710**
Investigator/Claim Examiner **763**
Investigator of the Year **2224**
The Investigators' Journal **2266**
Investment Vision **548**
Iowa State Department of Commerce • Professional Licensing and Regulation Division **7197**
IPPC Infoletter **3361**
"Iron and Steel Industry" in *Manufacturing*, Volume 9 of *Career Information Center* (pp. 116-119) **5871**
Iron and Steel Industry Workers **5872**
"Iron and Steel Industry Workers" in Volume 3 of *Career Discovery Encyclopedia* (pp. 162-163) **5873**
"Iron and Steel Industry Workers" in Volume 3 of *The Encyclopedia of Careers and Vocational Guidance* (pp. 423-426) **5874**
Iron Ore Processing & Blast Furnace Iron Making **5497**
"Iron Workers" in *Occu-Facts: Information on 565 Careers in Outline Form* (p. 16.18) **5498**
Iron Workers (Structural, Ornamental and Reinforcing) **5499**
"Ironworker" in *Hard Hatted Women: Stories of Struggle and Success in the Trades* (pp. 102-108) **5500**
"Ironworkers and Steelworkers" in *Opportunities in Building Construction Trades* (pp. 68-70) **5501**
ISCET Tech-of-the-Year Award **3953, 4172**
ISCET Update **3987, 4180**
ISDA Special Commendation **2078, 2225**
ISFSI Instruct-O-Gram **2025**
ISO Register **825, 1166**
IUE News **4388, 5604**
IUE Research Information **4389, 5605**
IUPIW-Views **5436**

J

JA Report **5748**
JADA **2630**
"Janitor" in *VGM's Careers Encyclopedia* (pp. 235-236) **3163**
Janitorial & Maintenance Examinations **3173**

"Janitors and Cleaners" in *Occupational Outlook Handbook* (pp. 315-316) **3164**
"Janitors and Cleaners" in Volume 3 of *Career Discovery Encyclopedia* (pp. 164-165) **3165**
"Janitors and Cleaners" in Volume 3 of *The Encyclopedia of Careers and Vocational Guidance* (pp. 271-273) **3166**
JCAHPO Outlook **2681**
Jeweler **5720, 5721**
"Jeweler" in *Consumer, Homemaking, and Personal Services*, Volume 5 of *Career Information Center* (pp. 82-84) **5722**
"Jeweler" in *Occu-Facts: Information on 565 Careers in Outline Form* (p. 17.9) **5723**
"Jewelers" in *Jobs! What They Are... Where They Are... What They Pay* (p. 298) **5724**
"Jewelers" in *Occupational Outlook Handbook* (pp. 392-394) **5725**
"Jewelers and Jewelry Repairers" in Volume 3 of *Career Discovery Encyclopedia* (pp. 166-167) **5726**
"Jewelers and Jewelry Repairers" in Volume 3 of *The Encyclopedia of Careers and Vocational Guidance* (pp. 584-587) **5727**
Jewelers' Circular-Keystone **5749**
Jewelers' Circular/Keystone—Almanac Issue **5736**
Jewelers International Showcase **5760**
Jewelers of America **5731**
"Jewelry Design and Metal Smithing" in *The Career Connection II: A Guide to Technical Majors and Their Related Careers* (pp. 77-78) **5728**
"Jewelry Making" in *Opportunities in Metalworking Careers* (pp. 59-66) **5729**
Jewelry Newsletter International **5750**
The Jewelry Show/Summer **5761**
"Jewelry Worker" in *Offbeat Careers: The Directory of Unusual Work* (pp. 83-85) **5730**
"Job and Die Setters" in Volume 3 of *The Encyclopedia of Careers and Vocational Guidance* (pp. 528-530) **5909**
Jobber Topics—Aftermarket Training Directory Issue [Motor vehicle industry] **3876**
Jobs in Shops & Stores **13, 43, 420**
John Hedgecoe's Darkroom Techniques **6608**
Joint Commission on Allied Health Personnel in Ophthalmology **2669, 2674**
Jones's English System of Bookkeeping Single or Double Entry **1037**
Journal American Water Works Association **6111**
Journal of Coated Fabrics **6384**
The Journal of Commercial Bank Lending **965**
The Journal of Consumer Lending **966**
Journal of Information Technology Management **862**
The Journal of Light Construction **4663, 4756, 4803, 4880, 4944, 5027, 5081, 5120, 5177, 5233, 5319, 5402, 5484, 5531, 5577**
Journal of Management in Practice **863**
Journal of Management Systems **864**
Journal of Personal Financial Services **826, 1167**
The Journal of Portfolio Management **549**
Journal of Property Management **351**
Journal of Quality Technology **5689**
The Journal of Real Estate Development **352**
Journal of Real Estate Taxation **353**
Journal of the American Society of CLU & ChFC **133**
Journal of the American Society of Farm Managers and Rural Appraisers **3362**
Journal of the International — Union of Bricklayers & Allied Craftsmen **4664, 4881**
Journal of Vinyl Technology **5856**
Journeyman in the Printing Crafts **6141, 6170, 6207, 6246**
Journeyman Roofer **5403**
The Journeymen Barbers' International Union of America **2860**
Justice **6316**

K

Kane's Beverage Week **2523**
The Keepers of Light: A History & Working Guide to Early Photographic Processes **6624**
Keeping Current **134**
Keeping Track **3535**
Keeping Up With The Law **4390, 5606**
Kentucky State Finance and Administration Cabinet • Occupations and Professions Division **7198**
Key Punch Supervisor **847**
Key to Safe Deposit **827**
Kind News **2812**
Kind Teacher **2801**
Kitchen Helper **2324**

"Kitchen Helper" in *Occu-Facts: Information on 565 Careers in Outline Form* (p. 13.20) **2325**
Kitchen Supervisor **2346**
Kitchen Times **2401, 2524**
Knights of Justice Award **2226**
Knitting Times **6385**
Koldfax **4329**

L

Labor Estimating Manual **5288**
Labor Line **2026**
Labor Unity **6317, 6386**
"Laboratory Animal Care Worker" in *Health*, Volume 7 of *Career Information Center* (pp. 50-51) **2777**
Laboratory Animal Science **2813**
The Laborer **7072**
Laborers' International Union of North America **7065, 7075**
Lake Erie Fisherman: Work, Identity & Tradition **3581**
Land Line **6888**
Landscape Manager of the Year **3073**
"Landscapers and Grounds Managers" in Volume 4 of *Career Discovery Encyclopedia* (pp. 10-11) **3047**
"Landscapers and Grounds Managers" in Volume 3 of *The Encyclopedia of Careers and Vocational Guidance* (pp. 369-373) **3048**
Lapidary Journal **5751**
"Laser Machinist" in *Opportunities in Laser Technology Careers* (pp. 54-57) **5771**
Last Alarm **2045**
The Last Farmer **3444**
Lather **4901**
"Lather" in *Construction*, Volume 4 of *Career Information Center* (pp. 68-69) **4902**
"Lather" in *Occu-Facts: Information on 565 Careers in Outline Form* (p. 16.6) **4903**
Lathers **4904**
"Lathers" in *Opportunities in Building Construction Trades* (pp. 59-61) **4905**
"Lathers" in Volume 3 of *The Encyclopedia of Careers and Vocational Guidance* (pp. 668-670) **4906**
"Launching a Career on Wall Street" in *Internships Volume 3: Accounting, Banking, Brokerage, Finance & Insurance* (pp. 23-33) **492**
Laundromat Attendant **44**
"Laundromat Attendant" in *Occu-Facts: Information on 565 Careers in Outline Form* (p. 11.21) **45**
Law and Order **2267**
Law Enforcement **2115**
"Law Enforcement" in *The Career Connection II: A Guide to Technical Majors and Their Related Careers* (pp. 81-82) **2118**
Law Enforcement Career Planning **2249**
Law Enforcement Careers: A Complete Guide from Application to Employment **2116**
Law Enforcement Employment Guide **2117**
Law Enforcement Leadership Award **2227**
Law Enforcement Technology **2268**
Law Officer's Bulletin **2269**
Lawn and Garden Equipment Technicians **4241**
Lawn Service Technician **3049**
Lead Parking Attendant **7038**
LeaderLine Newsletter **135**
Learn Not to Burn Curriculum **2005**
Learning Module Catalog **6157, 6190, 6229, 6273**
"Leather and Shoe Industries" in *Manufacturing*, Volume 9 of *Career Information Center* (pp. 119-121) **6329**
Leather Braiding **6348**
The Leather Craftsman **6357**
Leather Makin' **6349**
The Leather Manufacturer **6358**
Leather Today—Annual Directory Issue **6304, 6350**
Leather Tooling & Carving **6351**
"Leatherworking" in *Opportunities in Crafts Careers* (p. 61) **6330**
Legal Secretary **3140**
"Library Assistant" in Volume 4 of *Career Discovery Encyclopedia* (pp. 24-25) **1487**
"Library Assistants and Bookmobile Drivers" in *Occupational Outlook Handbook* (pp. 273-274) **1488**
Library Clerk **1489, 1490**
"Library Clerk" in *Occu-Facts: Information on 565 Careers in Outline Form* (p. 12.22) **1491**
Library Jobs: How to Fill Them, How to Find Them **1492**
Library Manual for Boards of Realtors **337**

Library Technical Assistant **1493**
"Library Technical Assistant" in *Occu-Facts: Information on 565 Careers in Outline Form* (p. 12.23) **1494**
"Library Technical Assistant" in *Opportunities in Vocational and Technical Careers* (pp. 50-52) **1495**
Library Technicians and Assistants **1496**
"Library Technicians and Assistants" in *Jobs! What They Are...Where They Are...What They Pay* (p. 94) **1497**
Library Times International **1511**
Life Association News **136**
"Life Insurance Agent/Broker" in *Occu-Facts: Information on 565 Careers in Outline Form* (p. 11.2) **94**
"Life Insurance Agents and Brokers" in Volume 4 of *Career Discovery Encyclopedia* (pp. 28-29) **95**
Life Office Management Association **752, 754**
Lifeline—Dispatcher Communications **1296**
Lift Erection **4208**
Lift Practice **4201**
Lift Servicing & Maintenance **4202**
Lightplane Refurbishing Techniques **3702**
Lilacs **3100**
Limousin Leader **3363**
Limousin World **3364**
"Line Installer" in *Exploring Nontraditional Jobs for Women* (pp. 37-43) **4399**
"Line Installers and Cable Splicers" in *Occupational Outlook Handbook* (pp. 350-352) **4400**
"Line Installers and Cable Splicers" in Volume 4 of *Career Discovery Encyclopedia* (pp. 32-33) **4401**
"Line Installers and Cable Splicers" in Volume 3 of *The Encyclopedia of Careers and Vocational Guidance* (pp. 573-676) **4402**
Line Workers (Electric Power) **4403**
Lineman (Electrical Power) **4420**
Linemen **4404**
"Lineperson" in *Opportunities in Electrical Trades* (p. 56) **4405**
The Liquor Reporter **2525**
Lithographer **6193**
"Lithographic and Photoengraving Workers" in *Occupational Outlook Handbook* (pp. 414-416) **6194**
"Lithographic Occupations" in Volume 3 of *The Encyclopedia of Careers and Vocational Guidance* (pp. 748-751) **6195**
"Lithographic Platemaker" in *Occu-Facts: Information on 565 Careers in Outline Form* (p. 17.15) **6196**
"Lithographic Worker" in *Communications and the Arts*, Volume 3 of *Career Information Center* (pp. 57-59) **6197**
"Lithographic Workers" in Volume 4 of *Career Discovery Encyclopedia* (pp. 36-37) **6198**
Little Acres **3101, 3365**
LIUNA - Leadership News **7073**
Live Line Maintenance **4406**
Livestock Market Digest **3366**
Livestock, Meat, and Wool Market News **3367**
Livestock Weekly **3368**
Living Among Nature Daringly **3369, 3536**
"Local and Over-the-Road Truck Drivers" in Volume 3 of *The Encyclopedia of Careers and Vocational Guidance* (pp. 793-797) **6807**
"Local Truck Driver" in *Exploring Nontraditional Jobs for Women* (pp. 69-75) **6808**
"Local Truck Driver" in *Transportation*, Volume 12 of *Career Information Center* (pp. 56-58) **6809**
Locator **5793, 5826, 5857**
"Locomotive Engineer" in *Occu-Facts: Information on 565 Careers in Outline Form* (p. 19.9) **6726**
"Locomotive Engineers" in *The American Almanac of Jobs and Salaries* (pp. 466-467) **6729**
"Locomotive Engineers" in Volume 4 of *Career Discovery Encyclopedia* (pp. 40-41) **6727**
"Locomotive Engineers" in Volume 3 of *The Encyclopedia of Careers and Vocational Guidance* (pp. 751-753) **6728**
Locomotive Engineers Journal **6775**
Lodging **1133**
Lodging Briefing **695, 1244**
Lodging Industry: National Trend of Business **1134**
Log Trucker **3622**
Logger **3583**
"Logger" in *Agribusiness, Environment, and Natural Resources*, Volume 2 of *Career Information Center* (pp. 51-53) **3584**
"Logger" in *Occu-Facts: Information on 565 Careers in Outline Form* (p. 14.17) **3585**
Logger and Lumberman **3623**
Loggers World **3624**
Logging and Sawmilling Journal **3625**

Logging & Sawmilling Journal—Guide to Government & Trade Associations **3596**
Logging Companies Directory **3597**
Logging Industry Workers **3586**
"Logging Industry Workers" in Volume 4 of *Career Discovery Encyclopedia* (pp. 42-43) **3587**
"Logging Industry Workers" in Volume 3 of *The Encyclopedia of Careers and Vocational Guidance* (pp. 373-377) **3588**
"Long Distance Truck Drivers" in *Opportunities in Transportation Careers* (pp. 69-72) **6810**
"Long Haul Truck Driver" in *Transportation*, Volume 12 of *Career Information Center* (pp. 60-62) **6811**
Longshore Workers **6934**
Louisiana State Department of Health and Hospitals ● Licensing and Certifications **7199**
Low-End Word Processor Market **1864**

M

Machine and Tool Blue Book **5827**
Machine Developments in Upholstery Sewing **6419**
"Machine Tool Operator" in *Manufacturing*, Volume 9 of *Career Information Center* (pp. 51-53) **5804**
Machine Tool Operators **5805, 5889**
"Machine Tool Operators" in *Occu-Facts: Information on 565 Careers in Outline Form* (p. 18.5) **5806**
"Machine Tool Operators" in Volume 3 of *The Encyclopedia of Careers and Vocational Guidance* (pp. 535-538) **5807**
Machinery Repairer, Industrial **4381**
"Machining and Machine Operation" in *Opportunities in Metalworking Careers* (pp. 17-27) **5808**
"Machining and Machinery" in Volume 1 of *The Encyclopedia of Careers and Vocational Guidance* (pp. 269-274) **5772**
Machinist **5789**
The Machinist **5794**
"Machinist" in *Hard Hatted Women: Stories of Struggle and Success in the Trades* (pp. 187-191, 254-262) **5773**
"Machinist" in *VGM's Careers Encyclopedia* (pp. 253-255) **5774**
Machinist, All-Round **5775**
Machinist - Machinist's Helper **4385**
Machinists **5776**
"Machinists" in *Jobs! What They Are...Where They Are...What They Pay* (pp. 178-179) **5777**
"Machinists" in *Occupational Outlook Handbook* (pp. 394-396) **5778**
"Machinists" in *Opportunities in Metalworking Careers* (pp. 28-29) **5779**
"Machinists" in Volume 4 of *Career Discovery Encyclopedia* (pp. 44-45) **5780**
"Machinists" in Volume 3 of *The Encyclopedia of Careers and Vocational Guidance* (pp. 538-542) **5781**
Machinist's Helper **5790**
"Magazine Advertising Sales" in *Career Choices for the 90's for Students of Business* (pp. 167-169) **581**
"Magazine Advertising Sales" in *Career Choices for the 90's for Students of Political Science & Government* (pp. 176-178) **582**
"Magazine Advertising Sales" in *Career Choices for the 90's for Students of Psychology* (196-198) **583**
"Magazine Advertising Sales" in *The Encyclopedia of Career Choices for the 1990s: A Guide to Entry Level Jobs* (pp. 778-780) **584**
Magnolia: Journal of the Magnolia Society **3102**
The MAI Appraiser **308**
Mail & Supply Clerk **1271**
Mail Carrier **1365**
"Mail Carrier" in *Occu-Facts: Information on 565 Careers in Outline Form* (p. 12.34) **1366**
"Mail Carriers" in Volume 4 of *Career Discovery Encyclopedia* (pp. 46-47) **1367**
"Mail Carriers" in Volume 3 of *The Encyclopedia of Careers and Vocational Guidance* (pp. 55-59) **1368**
Mail Clerk **1272**
"Mail Clerk" in *Administration, Business, and Office*, Volume 1 of *Career Information Center* (pp. 55-56) **1262**
Mail Clerk, Office **1263**
"Mail Clerks and Messengers" in *Occupational Outlook Handbook* (pp. 262-263) **1264**
Mail Clerks (Any Industry) **1265**
Mail Handler **1400**
Mail Handler: U. S. Postal Service **1369**
Mail Handler (USPS) **1401**
Mail Handlers/Mail Processor **1402**
"Mail Service Worker" in *Administration, Business, and Office*, Volume 1 of *Career Information Center* (pp. 57-58) **1370**
Mailing Machines & Equipment Directory **1420**

Maine State Department of Professional and Financial Regulation • Division of Licensing and Enforcement **7200**
Maintenance (Custodial) Branch Initial-Level Supervisor Examination (U.S.P.S.) **3174**
"Maintenance Electrician" in *Construction*, Volume 4 of *Career Information Center* (pp. 104-106) **4979**
"Maintenance Electrician" in *Exploring Nontraditional Jobs for Women* (pp. 118-124) **4980**
"Maintenance Electrician" in *Occu-Facts: Information on 565 Careers in Outline Form* (p. 15.11) **4981**
"Maintenance Electrician" in *Opportunities in Electrical Trades* (pp. 46-49) **4982**
Maintenance Management Handbook **4255**
Maintenance Mechanic **4199, 4251, 4841**
"Maintenance Mechanics" in *The American Almanac of Jobs and Salaries* (pp. 503) **4242**
The Maintenance Mechanic's-Machinist's Toolbox Manual **4256**
Maintenance Mechanics Qualification Program **4243**
Maintenance Supplies—Buyers' Guide Issue **4257**
"Maintenance Technician" in *Opportunities in Aerospace Careers* (pp. 16-21) **3679**
Maintenance Trainee's Introduction to Carpentry **4698**
Maintenance Worker/Mechanical Maintainer **4386, 4711, 4842, 4995, 5153, 5278**
"Maitre d', Bartender, Waiter/Waitress: The People Who Meet the Public" in *Careers in the Restaurant Industry* (pp. 23-24) **2467**
Make It to the Top: Certify **2641**
Make-Up Competition **2965**
Make Your Airplane Last Forever **3703**
Makeup Artist **2945**
Making It Work: The Secretary - Boss Team **1640**
Making of a Fire Fighter **1949**
Making $70,000 Plus a Year as a Self-Employed Manufacturer's Representative **172**
MAN—Modern Applications News—Cutting Tools Directory Issue **5977**
Man of the Year in Law Enforcement **2228**
MANA Agency Sales Magazine **222**
MANA Confidential Newsletter **223**
MANA Financial Fax **224**
Management Review **865, 5624**
Management Service **137**
Managing for Profit **6505**
Managing for Quality in the Service Sector **606**
Managing Your Independent Contractor Fleet Survey: A Nationwide Survey of Trucking Companies Utilizing Owner-Operators **6862**
Manicurist **2946**
"Manicurist" in *Occu-Facts: Information on 565 Careers in Outline Form* (p. 13.34) **2947**
Manicurists and Nail Technicians **2948**
Manual for Culinarians **2362**
Manual for the Lawyer's Assistant **1641**
Manual of Electronic Servicing Test & Measurements **3971**
Manual of the Accrediting Bureau of Health Education Schools **2682**
Manufactured Fiber Fact Book **6398**
Manufactured Fiber Guide **6378**
"Manufactured Products" in *Career Choices for the 90's for Students of Communications and Journalism* (pp. 175-178) **173**
"Manufactured Products" in *Career Choices for the 90's for Students of Political Science & Government* (pp. 178-181) **174**
"Manufactured Products" in *Career Choices for the 90's for Students of Psychology* (pp. 198-201) **175**
"Manufactured Products (Sales)" in *The Encyclopedia of Career Choices for the 1990s: A Guide to Entry Level Jobs* (pp. 780-783) **176**
"Manufactured Sales" in *Career Choices for the 90's for Students of Business* (pp. 169-172) **177**
The Manufacturers' Agent **178**
Manufacturers' Agents National Association **210, 211, 243**
"Manufacturers' and Wholesale Sales Representatives" in *Occupational Outlook Handbook* (pp. 232-234) **179**
Manufacturer's Representative **180**
"Manufacturer's Representative/Sporting Good or Equipment Company" in *Career Opportunities in the Sports Industry* (pp. 172-174) **181**
Manufacturer's Representatives **182**
Manufacturers Representatives of America—Newsline **225**
Manufacturers Sales Representative **183**
"Manufacturer's Sales Representative" in *VGM's Careers Encyclopedia* (pp. 257-259) **184**
"Manufacturer's Sales Representative" in *VGM's Handbook of Business and Management Careers* (pp. 59-61) **185**
"Manufacturers' Sales Representatives" in *Jobs! What They Are...Where They Are...What They Pay* (p. 281) **186**
"Manufacturers' Sales Representatives" in Volume 4 of *Career Discovery Encyclopedia* (pp. 52-53) **187**
"Manufacturers' Sales Worker" in *Marketing and Distribution*, Volume 10 of *Career Information Center* (pp. 73-74) **188**
"Manufacturers' Sales Workers" in *Opportunities in Vocational and Technical Careers* (pp. 68-69) **189**
"Manufacturers' Sales Workers" in Volume 3 of *The Encyclopedia of Careers and Vocational Guidance* (pp. 153-158) **190**
"Manufacturer's Salespeople: Selling Goods" in *Careers for Women Without College Degrees* (pp. 250-253) **191**
"Manufacturer's Salesperson" in *College Board Guide to Jobs and Career Planning* (pp. 137-138) **192**
Manufacturing Jewelers and Silversmiths of America Exposition/California **5762**
Manufacturing Jewelers and Silversmiths of America Exposition/New York **5763**
Manufacturing Jewelers and Silversmiths of America Exposition/Providence **5764**
"Manufacturing Opticians" in *Opportunities in Eye Care Careers* (pp. 79-83) **6514**
"Manufacturing Reps" in *The New York Times Career Planner* (pp. 237-240) **193**
MAQUINAMEX - Metalworking Machine Tool Expo **5798, 5834**
"Marble Setter, Tilesetters, and Terrazzo Workers" in *Opportunities in Building Construction Trades* (pp. 63-65) **4822, 5544**
"Marble Setters" in Volume 4 of *Career Discovery Encyclopedia* (pp. 56-57) **4604**
Marble Setters, Tile Layers and Terrazzo Workers **4823, 5545**
"Marble Setters, Tile Setters, and Terrazzo Workers" in Volume 3 of *The Encyclopedia of Careers and Vocational Guidance* (pp. 677-679) **4605, 4824**
"Marble Setters, Tile Setters, and Terrazzo Workers" in Volume 3 of *The Encyclopedia of Careers and Vocational Guidance* (677-679) **5546**
"Marble, Tile, and Terrazzo Worker" in *Construction*, Volume 4 of *Career Information Center* (pp. 71-72) **4606, 4825, 5547**
Marble, Tile Setters, Terrazzo, and Stone Workers **4607, 4826, 5548**
"Marble, Tile, Terrazzo, and Stone Workers" in *Occu-Facts: Information on 565 Careers in Outline Form* (p. 16.3) **4608, 4827, 5549**
Marine Board **6959**
Marine Corps Association **7132**
Marine Corps Gazette **7159**
MARINE DIGEST and Transportation News **6978**
"Marine Electrician" in *Opportunities in Electrical Trades* (pp. 51-53) **4983**
"Marine Engine Mechanic" in *Opportunities in Marine and Maritime Careers* (pp. 105-107) **4470**
"Marine Engineer" in *Agribusiness, Environment, and Natural Resources*, Volume 2 of *Career Information Center* (pp. 129-130) **6935**
"Marine Engineer (Shipboard)" in *Occu-Facts: Information on 565 Careers in Outline Form* (p. 19.12) **6936**
"Marine Engineers" in Volume 4 of *Career Discovery Encyclopedia* (pp. 58-59) **6937**
"Marine Engineers" in Volume 3 of *The Encyclopedia of Careers and Vocational Guidance* (pp. 206-207) **6938**
Marine Fish Management **3537**
"Marine Insurance Careers" in *Opportunities in Marine and Maritime Careers* (pp. 111-112) **96**
Marine Log **6979, 7160**
"Marine/Ocean Engineering and Naval Architecture" in *Opportunities in Engineering Careers* (pp. 114-116) **6939**
Marine Policy Reports **6980**
"Marine Services Technician" in *Transportation*, Volume 12 of *Career Information Center* (pp. 62-63) **4471**
Marine Stoker **6966**
Marine Technology Society **3471**
Marine Technology Society Journal **3538**
"Maritime Jobs" in *Opportunities in Transportation Careers* (pp. 53-54) **6940**
"Maritime Labor and Training" in *MARAD* (pp. 45-51) **6972**
Mark-up Clerk/Clerk Typist/Clerk Stenographer - U.S. Postal Service **1403**
Mark-Up Clerk (USPS) **1404**
Marketer **6041**
"Marketing and Sales" in *The Encyclopedia of Career Choices for the 1990s: A Guide to Entry Level Jobs* (pp. 407-409) **586**
"Marketing and Sales, Hotel Management" in *Career Choices for the 90's for Students of Psychology* (pp. 101-103) **585**
"Marketing/Sales" in *Career Choices for the 90's for Students of Business* (pp. 99-101) **587**

Index to Information Sources

Marketing Your Services: A Step-by-Step Guide for Small Businesses & Professionals **607**
Maryland State Department of Licensing and Regulation • Division of Occupational and Professional Licensing **7201**
Mason **4843**
Mason Contractors' Equipment & Supplies Directory **4846**
Masonry **4882**
Mason's Helper **4844**
Mass Transit **6653**
Massachusetts State Executive Office of Consumer Affairs and Business Regulation • Division of Registration **7202**
Master Electrician **4996**
Master Plumber **5279**
Matching Individuals to Jobs: A Motivationnal Answer for Personnel & Counseling Professionals **1539**
Mate **6967**
Material Handler **7039**
"Material Handler" in *Occu-Facts: Information on 565 Careers in Outline Form* (p. 20.15) **7040**
Material Handlers **7041**
"Material Moving Equipment Operators" in *Occupational Outlook Handbook* (pp. 436-437) **6686**
"Material Recording, Scheduling, Dispatching, and Distributing Occupations" in *Occupational Outlook Handbook* (pp. 263-265) **1280**
Math for Welders **5978**
Math on the Job: Cashier **25**
Math on the Job: Electrician **5002**
Math on the Job: Local Truck Driver **6863**
Math on the Job: Plumber **5289**
Math on the Job: Secretary/Clerk Typist **1093, 1193, 1642, 1865**
Math Review for Real Estate License Examinations **315**
Mathematics for Auto Mechanics **3888**
Mathematics for the Heating, Ventilating & Cooling Trades **4310**
MCAA Management-Labor Relations Guide **5290**
MCBA **6150, 6179, 6219, 6266**
McDonnell Douglas Law Enforcement Award **2229**
Meat Cutter **5637, 5654**
"Meat Cutter" in *Occu-Facts: Information on 565 Careers in Outline Form* (p. 17.28) **5638**
Meat Inspector **5682**
Meat Inspector-Poultry Inspector **5683**
"Meat Packing Production Workers" in Volume 4 of *Career Discovery Encyclopedia* (pp. 66-67) **5639**
"Meat Packing Production Workers" in Volume 3 of *The Encyclopedia of Careers and Vocational Guidance* (pp. 433-436) **5640**
"Meat Packing Worker" in *Agribusiness, Environment, and Natural Resources*, Volume 2 of *Career Information Center* (pp. 55-56) **5641**
"Meat Wrapper (Supermarket)" in *Occu-Facts: Information on 565 Careers in Outline Form* (p. 17.29) **5642**
Meatcutters **5643**
"Meatcutters" in *The American Almanac of Jobs and Salaries* (p. 532) **5646**
"Meatcutters" in Volume 4 of *Career Discovery Encyclopedia* (pp. 64-65) **5644**
"Meatcutters" in Volume 3 of *The Encyclopedia of Careers and Vocational Guidance* (pp. 273-276) **5645**
"Mechanic" in *Guide to Careers Without College* (pp. 92-95) **3842**
Mechanical Contractors Association of America **5271, 5275**
Mechanical Contractors Association of America Conference **5337**
Mechanical Contractors Association of America—Reporter **5320**
Mechanical Maintainer **4252**
Mechanical News **3795, 3907, 6569**
Mechanics **3680, 4096, 4244, 4284, 4448, 4472**
"Mechanics" in *Opportunities in Transportation Careers* (pp. 38-39) **3681**
"Mechanics: Air-Conditioning, Heating, and Refrigeration" in *Opportunities in Vocational and Technical Careers* (pp. 105-106) **4285**
"Mechanics: Aircraft and Aircraft Engines" in *Opportunities in Vocational and Technical Careers* (p. 106) **3682**
"Mechanics: Automobiles and Motorcycles" in *Opportunities in Vocational and Technical Careers* (pp. 103-104) **3843, 4473**
"Mechanics: Automotive Body Repair" in *Opportunities in Vocational and Technical Careers* (p. 105) **3844**
"Mechanics: Cash Register and Office Machine Services" in *Opportunities in Vocational and Technical Careers* (p. 108) **4055**
"Mechanics: Commercial and Industrial Electronic Equipment" in *Opportunities in Vocational and Technical Careers* (pp. 107-108) **3936**
"Mechanics: Diesel Engines" in *Opportunities in Vocational and Technical Careers* (pp. 104-105) **4097**

"Mechanics: Home Appliance and Power Tools" in *Opportunities in Vocational and Technical Careers* (p. 107) **4357**
"Mechanics: Industrial Machinery" in *Opportunities in Vocational and Technical Careers* (pp. 104, 106-107) **4382**
"Mechanics: Mobile Heavy Equipment" in *Opportunities in Vocational and Technical Careers* (p. 107) **4449**
Medal of Valor **1905**
Medical & Dental Associates, P. C. **2591**
Medical Assistant **2642, 2643**
"Medical Assistant" in *Careers in Health Care* (pp. 114-118) **2644**
"Medical Assistant" in *Health*, Volume 7 of *Career Information Center* (pp. 68-69) **2645**
"Medical Assistant" in *Occu-Facts: Information on 565 Careers in Outline Form* (p. 13.22) **2646**
"Medical Assistant" in *120 Careers in the Health Care Field* (pp. 167-185) **2650**
"Medical Assistant" in *Opportunities in Health and Medical Careers* (p. 17) **2647**
"Medical Assistant" in *Opportunities in Paramedical Careers* (pp. 27-30) **2648**
"Medical Assistant" in *The Career Connection II: A Guide to Technical Majors and Their Related Careers* (pp. 91-92) **2652**
"Medical Assistant" in *VGM's Careers Encyclopedia* (pp. 272-274) **2649**
"Medical Assistant in Pediatrics" in *Opportunities in Health and Medical Careers* (pp. 17-18) **2651**
Medical Assistants **2653, 2683**
"Medical Assistants" in *America's 50 Fastest Growing Jobs* (pp. 120-121) **2657**
"Medical Assistants" in *Occupational Outlook Handbook* (pp. 300-302) **2654**
"Medical Assistants" in Volume 4 of *Career Discovery Encyclopedia* (pp. 76-77) **2655**
"Medical Assistants" in Volume 3 of *The Encyclopedia of Careers and Vocational Guidance* (pp. 276-279) **2656**
Medical Assisting: A Career for the Future **2658**
Medical Assisting - A Career for Today and Tomorrow **2659**
Medical Assisting— A Career for Today and Tomorrow **2675**
Medical Assisting: Today's Career for Tomorrow's Reward **2660**
"Medical Dental Secretary" in *The Career Connection II: A Guide to Technical Majors and Their Related Careers* (pp. 93-94) **1572**
Medical Equipment Sales **194**
"Medical Office Assistants" in *Jobs! What They Are...Where They Are...What They Pay* (p. 139) **2661**
"Medical or Dental Secretary" in *Health Care* (pp. 51-55) **1573**
"Medical Secretary" in *Opportunities in Health and Medical Careers* (pp. 106-107) **1574**
"Medical Secretary" in *VGM's Careers Encyclopedia* (pp. 279-281) **1575**
Medical Transcriptionist **1683**
"Medical Transcriptionist" in *Occu-Facts: Information on 565 Careers in Outline Form* (p. 12.9) **1684**
"Medical Transcriptionist" in *120 Careers in the Health Care Field* (pp. 257-258) **1685**
"Medical Transcriptionist" in *Opportunities in Health and Medical Careers* (p. 122) **1686**
Meetings & Incentive Travel **1245**
MEMA Marketing Insight **3908, 4129, 4233, 4462, 4500**
Members of the National Association of Barber Styling Schools **2845**
Men in Nursing **2755**
The Men of Company 208 **7097**
Men of Earth **3445**
Men of Iron **5502**
Menagerie Keeper **2797**
"Mental Health Technician/Human Services Technician/Psychiatric Aide" in *120 Careers in the Health Care Field* (pp. 260-261) **2711**
"Merchant Marine Captain" in *Transportation*, Volume 12 of *Career Information Center* (pp. 132-134) **6941**
"Merchant Marine Engineer" in *Transportation* (pp. 63-67) **6942**
"Merchant Marine Engineer and Chief Engineer" in *Transportation*, Volume 12 of *Career Information Center* (pp. 104-105) **6943**
Merchant Marine Examination Questions—Volume 13: Steam Plants **6968**
Merchant Marine Examination Questions—Volume 12: Electricity **6969**
Merchant Marine Examination Questions—Volume 2: Navigation Problems **6970**
Merchant Marine Occupations **6944**
"Merchant Marine Occupations" in Volume 2 of *The Encyclopedia of Careers and Vocational Guidance* (pp. 410-415) **6945**
"Merchant Marine Officers" in *Jobs! What They Are...Where They Are...What They Pay* (pp. 250-251) **6946**
"Merchant Marine Officers" in *Opportunities in Transportation Careers* (pp. 59-60) **6947**

1109

"Merchant Marine Unlicensed Sailors" in *Opportunities in Transportation Careers* (pp. 54-58) **6948**
"Merchant Sailor" in *Hard Hatted Women: Stories of Struggle and Success in the Trades* (pp. 176-186) **6949**
Mercruiser Stern Drive Shop Manual 1964-1987 **3889**
Mercury Systems Inc.: Practice Set in Word-Information Processing for Conventional & Text-Editing Typewriters **1866**
Merit Award for Excellent Arrest **2230**
Messenger **1273**
Messenger Courier Association of the Americas **1269**
Messenger Courier Association of the Americas Conference **1278**
"Messenger Service Worker" in *Administration, Business, and Office*, Volume 1 of *Career Information Center* (pp. 58-60) **1266**
Metal Construction News **5404, 5532**
Metal Corrosion in Boats **4490**
Metalform **5799, 5835**
Metals Newsletter **5828**
"Metalworking Machine Operators" in *Occupational Outlook Handbook* (pp. 397-398) **5809**
Metro Magazine **6654**
Michigan State Department of Licensing and Regulation **7203**
Microcomputer Software for School Library Applications **1503**
Microelectronics & Office Jobs: The Impact of the Chip on Women's Employment **945**
Microprocessor Manual for Traffic Signals **1315**
Mid-America Farm Exposition **3424**
Mid-America Trucking Show **6919**
Mid-American Jewelry Show **5765**
Mid-Atlantic Nurserymen's Winter Trade Show **3113**
Mid-South Farm and Gin Supply Exhibit **3425**
Mid-West Contractor—Annual Convention Guide and Association Directory [Construction industry] **4627, 4719, 4847, 5003, 5060, 5101, 5291, 5366, 5466, 5513**
Mid-West Truck Show **6920**
Midway USA Foodservice and Hospitality Exposition **2548**
Midwest Farm Show **3426**
Midwest Poultry Federation Convention **3427, 5669**
Midwest Specialty Exposition **4465, 5038, 5338, 5493**
Milady's Cosmetology State Board Guide **2847, 2969**
"Military" in *College Board Guide to Jobs and Career Planning* (pp. 208-210) **7098**
"The Military" in *Electronic Service Careers* (pp. 88-99) **7099**
"Military" in *Footsteps in the Ocean: Careers in Diving* (pp. 115-122) **7100**
"Military" in *International Careers: An Insider's Guide, Where to Find Them, How to Build Them* (pp. 174-176) **7101**
"Military" in *Straight Talk on Careers: 80 Pros Take You Into Their Professions* (pp. 203-224) **7106**
"Military Careers" in Volume 4 of *Career Discovery Encyclopedia* (pp. 94-95) **7102**
"Military Chaplain" in *Opportunities in Religious Service Careers* (pp. 85-87) **7103**
"Military Counselor" in *Careers in Counseling and Human Development* (pp. 102-104) **7104**
"Military Fire Protection" in *Opportunities in Fire Protection Services* (pp. 32-33) **7105**
Military Forum **7161**
Military Intelligence **7162**
Military Life: the Insider's Guide **7107**
Military Lifestyle **7163**
Military Media Inc. **7164**
Military News Recorder-Times **7165**
"Military Nursing" in *Your Career in Nursing* (pp. 156-160) **7108**
"Military Science" in *College Majors and Careers: A Resource Guide for Effective Life Planning* (pp. 99-100) **7109**
"Military Service" in *Exploring Careers Using Foreign Languages* (pp. 73-74) **7110**
"Military Service" in Volume 1 of *The Encyclopedia of Careers and Vocational Guidance* (pp. 301-309) **7111**
"Military Services" in *Jobs! What They Are...Where They Are...What They Pay* (pp. 247-250) **7112**
"The Military Veterinarian" in *Opportunities in Veterinary Medicine* (pp. 107-111) **7113**
"Milling Machine Operator" in *Occu-Facts: Information on 565 Careers in Outline Form* (p. 18.7) **5810**
Millwright **4434**
"Millwright" in *Occu-Facts: Information on 565 Careers in Outline Form* (p. 15.25) **4435**
"Millwright" in *Opportunities in Carpentry Careers* (p. 52) **4436**
Millwrights **4437**
"Millwrights" in *Occupational Outlook Handbook* (pp. 352-353) **4438**
"Millwrights" in Volume 4 of *Career Discovery Encyclopedia* (pp. 96-97) **4439**

"Millwrights" in Volume 3 of *The Encyclopedia of Careers and Vocational Guidance* (pp. 542-544) **4440**
Mini Lab Focus **6612**
Minnesota State Department of Commerce • Division of Registration and Licensing **7204**
Mise En Place **2326**
Mississippi State Board of Medical Licensure **7205**
Missouri State Department of Professional Registration **7206**
Mixin' **2526**
MJSA Benchmark **5752**
Mobile Air Conditioning Society Trade Show and Technical Conference **4342**
Mobile Groomers **2822**
"Mobile Heavy Equipment Mechanics" in *Occupational Outlook Handbook* (pp. 353-355) **4450**
"Mobile Heavy Equipment Mechanics" in Volume 4 of *Career Discovery Encyclopedia* (pp. 100-101) **4451**
Modern Baking **2402**
Modern Blacksmith **5991**
Modern Bulk Transporter—Truck Specifications Directory Issue **6864**
Modern Dental Assisting **2613**
Modern Food Service News **2403, 2527**
Modern Heating, Ventilating & Air Conditioning **4311**
Modern Jeweler **5753**
Modern Plastics **5858**
Modern Railroad Man of the Year **6767**
Modern Railroads **6776**
Modern Woodworking **3626, 6470**
Montana State Department of Commerce • Bureau of Professional and Occupational Licensing **7207**
Monthly Crop and Livestock Report **3370**
Monthly F.O.B. Price Summary, Past Sales (Coast Mills) **3627**
Monthly F.O.B. Price Summary, Past Sales (Inland Mills) **3628**
Moody's Bond Survey **550**
Mosby's Textbook for Nursing Assistants **2743**
Motel/Hotel Insider **696, 1135, 1246**
Motor Age **3796, 3909**
Motor and Equipment Manufacturers Association **3852, 4103, 4218, 4454, 4482**
Motor Carrier Annual Report **6928**
Motor Carrier Employees Handbook for the Prevention of Freight Loss & Damages **6865**
Motor Carrier Insurance **6866**
Motor Carrier Management Systems **6867**
Motor Carrier Professional Services Directory **6929**
Motor Equipment Mechanic **4483**
Motor in Canada **3797, 3910**
Motor Magazine **3798, 3911**
Motor Service **3799, 3912**
Motor Service—Tool & Equipment Buyers Guide Issue **3890**
Motorboat Mechanics **4474**
"Motorcycle, Boat, and Small-Engine Mechanics and Repairers" in *Occupational Outlook Handbook* (pp. 355-357) **4475**
Motorcycle Electrics Without Pain **4491**
Motorcycle Mechanic **4476**
"Motorcycle Mechanic" in *Occu-Facts: Information on 565 Careers in Outline Form* (p. 15.6) **4477**
"Motorcycle Mechanic" in *Transportation*, Volume 12 of *Career Information Center* (pp. 108-109) **4478**
Motorcycle Mechanics **4492, 4493**
"Motorcycle Mechanics" in *Opportunities in Automotive Service Careers* (p. 59) **4479**
"Motorcycle Mechanics" in Volume 4 of *Career Discovery Encyclopedia* (pp. 108-109) **4480**
Motorcycle Technicians **4481**
Movin' **6777**
Movin' Out **6889**
MTS Newsletter **3539**
Multi-Keyboard Operator **918**
Multinational Service Firms **608**
"Municipal Police Officer" in *VGM's Careers Encyclopedia* (pp. 361-364) **2119**
Munro's Bookkeeping & Accountancy **1038**
"Music Shop Salesperson" in *Career Opportunities in the Music Industry* (pp. 89-90) **421**
"Musical Instrument Repairers" in Volume 4 of *Career Discovery Encyclopedia* (pp. 112-113) **4505**
"Musical Instrument Repairers and Tuners" in *Occupational Outlook Handbook* (pp. 357-358) **4506**
"Musical Instrument Repairers and Tuners" in *The Encyclopedia of Careers and Vocational Guidance* (pp. 591-595) **4507**
Musical Instrument Salesperson **422**
Muskrats & Marsh Management **3484**

Musky Hunter 3540

N

NAACS News 2979
NAACS Washington Update 2980
NABS News 2852
NABS Research Reports 2861
NACCAS Review 2981
NACUFS News Wave 2404, 2528
NADL Executive Information Series 6509
NADL Hazard Communication Manual 6506
NAFI Man of the Year 764, 1992, 2231
NAHB Library Bulletin 4330, 4757, 4945
NAHC Report 3150
NAILS Magazine Show/Chicago 2989
NAILS Magazine Show/Dallas 2990
NAILS Magazine Show/Detroit 2991
NAILS Magazine Show/Hawaii 2992
NAILS Magazine Show/Las Vegas I 2993
NAILS Magazine Show/Las Vegas II 2994
NAILS Magazine Show/Los Angeles 2995
NAILS Magazine Show/New York 2996
NAILS Magazine Show/Tampa 2997
NAILS Sunshine Show 2998
NAMA Employee Relations Quarterly Bulletin 4588
Nannies 3206
"Nannies" in Volume 4 of *Career Discovery Encyclopedia* (pp. 118-119) 3207
"Nannies" in Volume 3 of *The Encyclopedia of Careers and Vocational Guidance* (pp. 284-288) 3208
"Nanny" in *Consumer, Homemaking, and Personal Services*, Volume 5 of *Career Information Center* (pp. 87-89) 3209
"Nanny" in *Offbeat Careers: The Directory of Unusual Work* (pp. 102-103) 3210
NAPBIRT Administrative Newsletter 4539
NAPBIRT Directory 4531
NAPBIRT Regional Newsletter 4540
NAPET La Croix Award 3954, 6593
NAPET News 6613
NAPHCC News 4331, 5321
NAPIA Bulletin 778
NAPW Journal 1547
NAPW Newsletter 1548
NARSC Newsletter 5533
NARTE Scholarships 4023
NASSTRAC Convention 6717, 6921
NATA Communicator 4565
NATA Industry Basics 4563
NATA Sourcebook 4564
NATA Washington Update 4566
National Academy of Nannies, Inc. 3217
National Accrediting Commission of Cosmetology Arts and Sciences 2958
National Agri-Marketing Association Conference 244, 618
National Alliance 1422
National Alliance of Postal and Federal Employees 1382
National Apprenticeship Training Program for Cooks 2341
National Association for Home Care 3141, 3142
National Association for Home Care Annual Meeting and Home Care Exhibition 3152
National Association for Professional Saleswomen 603
National Association for the Education of Young Children 2893, 2899
National Association for Uniformed Services 7133
National Association of Accountants 1011
National Association of Accredited Cosmetology Schools 2954, 2959
National Association of Accredited Cosmetology Schools Annual Convention and Trade Show 2999
National Association of Barber Styling Schools 2838, 2839
National Association of Brick Distributors Trade Exhibit 4673
National Association of Dental Laboratories 6497, 6499
National Association of Executive Secretaries 1613
National Association of Fire Investigators 1956
National Association of Freight Transportation Consultants 1355
National Association of Health Underwriters 104, 107
National Association of Home Builders of the U.S. 4291, 4705, 4910
National Association of Home Builders/The Builders Show 4767, 4952, 5128, 5184, 5238, 5339, 5412, 5541
National Association of Hosiery Manufacturers 6300, 6301, 6375, 6376
National Association of Investigative Specialists 2162, 2169
National Association of Legal Secretaries (International) 1614, 1619, 1671
National Association of Letter Carriers of the U.S.A. 1383, 1431

National Association of Life Underwriters 105, 157
National Association of Personnel Workers 1533
National Association of Photo Equipment Technicians 6590
National Association of Photo Equipment Technicians Trade Show 6623
National Association of Plumbing-Heating-Cooling Contractors 4292, 4343, 5272, 5340
National Association of Postal Supervisors 1384
National Association of Postmasters of the United States Convention 1432
National Association of Power Engineers 6058
National Association of Professional Band Instrument Repair Technicians 4521
National Association of Professional Band Instrument Repair Technicians Conference 4549
National Association of Professional Engravers Annual Trade Show and Exhibit 6228
National Association of Professional Upholsterers 6413
National Association of Public Insurance Adjusters 753, 755
National Association of Radio and Telecommunications Engineers 4019, 4021
National Association of Realtors 305
National Association of Realtors Annual Trade Exposition 388
National Association of Realtors Midyear Trade Exposition 389
National Association of Reinforcing Steel Contractors 5508, 5510, 5542
National Association of Review Appraisers and Mortgage Underwriters Convention 390, 967
National Association of Secretarial Services National Convention 1672
National Association of State Departments of Agriculture National Food and Agriculture Exposition 3428
National Association of Trade and Technical Schools 2339, 2342, 2488, 2490, 3745, 3749, 4104, 4107, 5960, 5962
National Association of Underwater Instructors 3472, 3477
National Association of Wheat Growers Convention 3429
National Automatic Merchandising Association 4587, 4592
National Automatic Merchandising Association-Newsletter 4589
National Automatic Merchandising Association—State Legislative Review 4590
National Automotive Radiator Service Association Annual Trade Show and Convention 3924
National Automotive Technicians Education Foundation 3853, 3856
National Award for Agricultural Excellence 3271
National Beauty Culturists' League 2955
National Beauty Show 2856, 3000
National Broiler Council—Washington Report 5657
National Catholic Forester 3629
National Cattle Congress Fair 3430
National Cattlemen's Association Annual Convention and Trade Show 3431
The National Certification Program for Cooks and Chefs 2343
National Child Day Care Association 2894
National Composition and Prepress Association 6168, 6189
National Cosmetology Association 2956
National Cosmetology Association Bulletin 2982
National Cosmetology Association Convention 3001
National Council of Salesmen's Organizations 604, 619
National Dental Assistant Boards (NDAB) 2604
National Disabled Law Officers Association—Newsletter 2270
National Dog Groomers Association of America 2790
National Dog Groomers Association of America Convention 2820
National Electrical Contractors Association 4989
National Electrical Equipment Show and Conference 5039
National Electronic Sales and Service Dealers Association 4163, 4166
National Electronic Sales and Service Dealers Association—Member Memo 4181
National Electronic Sales and Services Dealers Association—Update 4182
National Engineer 6068
National Erectors Association 5509, 5511
National Erectors Association Conference 5543
National Executive Housekeepers Association 3168, 3170
National Executive Housekeepers Association Exposition 3221
National Farm Finance News 3371
National Farm Machinery Show and Championship Tractor Pull 3432
National Farmers Union—Washington Newsletter 3372
National FFA Organization 3262
National FFA Organization—Update 3373
National Fire Codes 2046
National Fire Protection Association 1957, 1958
National Fire Protection Association Annual Meeting 2038
National Fire Protection Association—Technical Committee Reports/ Technical Committee Documentation 2047

National Fire Sprinkler Association 5273, 5276
National Fisherman 3541
National Food Distributors Association Annual Convention 2549
National Frame Builders Association Convention 4768
National Freight Transportation Association 1356
National Gardening 3103
National Glass Association 5055
National Glass Association Annual Convention and National Glass and Machinery Show 5085
National Glaziers' Architectural Metal and Glassworkers' Industries Apprenticeship Training and Journeymen Education Fund 5057
The National Gleaner Forum 138
National Guild of Professional Paperhangers Convention 5185
National Highway Traffic Safety Administration's Truck Operator Qualification Examination (NTSATOQ) 6840
National Hog Farmer 3374
National Home Health Care Exposition 3153
National Institute for Automotive Service Excellence 3746, 3750, 3854, 3857, 4105, 4108, 6559, 6561
National Institute on Park and Grounds Management Convention 3114
National Insulation and Abatement Contractors Association 5096, 5129
National Jeweler 5754
National Joint Painting, Decorating and Drywall Apprenticeship and Training Committee 4911
National Landscape Association 3055
National League of Postmasters of the United States 1385
The National Librarian: The NLA Newsletter 1512
National Nutritional Foods Association—Monitor 2405
National Oceanic and Atmospheric Administration • Office of Public Affairs 3473
National Office Machine Dealers Association 4067
National Office Machine Service Association 4068, 4084
National Police Officers Association of America 2163
National Postal Mail Handlers Union 1270, 1279, 1386
National Postsecondary Agricultural Student Organization 3264
National Precast Concrete Association Annual Convention and Precast Concrete Industries Exposition 4889
National Professional Electronics Convention and Trade Show 4188
National Quality Award 111
National Real Estate Directory 338
National Real Estate Investor 354
National Relocation and Real Estate 355
National Restaurant Association 2340, 2489
National Restaurant Association Ice Carving Classic 2355
National Restaurant Association Restaurant, Hotel-Motel Show 2550
National Restaurant Association—Washington Weekly 2406, 2529
National Retail Federation 457, 1337
National Retail Federation Convention and Exposition 475
National Rifle Association of America 3474, 3576
National Roofing Contractors Association 5361, 5413
National Roofing Contractors Association Annual Convention and Trade Show 5414
The National Rural Letter Carrier 1423
National Sales Achievement Award 112
National School Bus Report 6655
National School Transportation Association Convention and Trade Show 6668
National Screw Machine Products Association 5783, 5894
National Sheriffs' Association Convention 2086, 2283
National Shoe Fair of America 6363
The National Shorthand Reporter 1741
National Shorthand Reporters Association 1700, 1703
National Society of Public Accountants 1012
National Society of Tole and Decorative Painters Annual Meeting and Convention 5186
National Society to Prevent Blindness 6526
National Society to Prevent Blindness—InSight 6533
National Star Route Mail Contractors Association 1387
National Tank Truck Carriers Annual Meeting and Tank Equipment Show 6922
National Terrazzo and Mosaic Association 4835, 4839, 4890
National Tooling and Machining Association 5677, 5784, 5816, 5847, 5895, 5923
National Training Fund for the Sheet Metal and Air Conditioning Industry 5459
National Trappers Association 3475, 3577
National Truck Equipment Association SUPERSHOW 6923
National Underwriter Property and Casualty/Risk and Benefits Management 139
National Waterways Conference 6960

Nation's Building News 4332, 4665, 4758, 4804, 4883, 4946, 5028, 5082, 5121, 5178, 5234, 5322, 5405, 5485, 5534, 5578
Nation's Restaurant News 2407, 2530
NATSO Truckers News 6890
NATTS Award 4117
NATTS News and Views 2531, 3800, 4130, 5992
Naval Aviation News 7166
Navy Career Opportunities 7114
Navy-Marine Corps ROTC College Scholarship 7145
"Navy Military Sealift Command" in *Opportunities in Transportation Careers* (pp. 129-130) 7115
Navy News 7167
"Navy Nurse" in *120 Careers in the Health Care Field* (p. 272) 7117
"Navy Nurse Corps" in *Opportunities in Nursing Careers* (pp. 111-112) 7116
Navy Times 7168
NAW Report 226
NCPA Journal 6180
NCPA Newsline 6181
NCR No. 3100 Operator 21
NCRA Heritage Foundation Scholarships 1736
NCRA List of Approved Court Reporter Education Programs 1732
The NCRA Roofing & Waterproofing Manual 5367
NDGAA Convention Manual 2804
NEA Labor Update 5535
NEA Notes 5536
Nebraska State Bureau of Examining Boards • Department of Health 7208
NECA News 5029
NECA Standard of Installation 5042
The Needle's Eye 6318
NERR Club Official Proceedings 6778
NESSDA Update 3988, 4183
Network-AAMA 2693
A New & Complete System of Bookkeeping by an Improved Method of Double Entry 1039
New Dimensions 227
New England Farm Bulletin & Garden Gazette—Farmer-Consumer Connection [Agricultural fairs and farmer markets and museums] 3375
New England Farm Bulletin & Garden Gazette—NEFB Almanac Issue [Agricultural associations] 3376
New England Fuel Institute 4298
New England Nurserymen's Annual Trade Show 3115
New Farmer 3377
New Homes Magazine 356
New Horizons 3104
"New Horizons for Rail Careers" in *Opportunities in Transportation Careers* (pp. 81-93) 6730
New Jersey State Department of Law and Public Safety • Division of Consumer Affairs 7209
New Manufacturing Technologies 3972
New Mexico State Department of Regulation and Licensing 7210
New Polymer Technology for Auto Body Exteriors 3775
The New Secretary: How to Handle People As Well As You Handled Paper 1643
New Ways to Use Test Meters: A Modern Guide to Electronic Servicing 3973
New York Department of State • Division of Licensing Services 7211
The News HVAC/R Directory [Heating, ventilation, air conditioning, and refrigeration industries] 4312
"Newspaper and Magazine Advertising Sales Representative" in *Career Opportunities in Advertising and Public Relations* (pp. 224-226) 588
Newspaper Personnel Relations Association 1534
NGA Awards for Excellence 5058
NIAC Advisor 5122
NIAC Commercial and Industrial Standards Manual, 5102
The Nightingale 2756
Nightwatch 2271
Nikon World of Big Game Hunting 3542
NITL Notice 6779, 6891, 6981
NLA Landscape News 3105
NLA Residential Landscape Award Program 3074
NMTBA - Association for Manufacturing Technology 5785, 5787, 5817, 5819, 5848, 5851, 5896, 5898, 5924, 5926
No Experience Necessary: Make $100,000 a Year as a Stockbroker 493
NOMDA Hotline 4081
NOMDA Spokesman 4082
NOMDA Who's Who [Office machines] 851, 1644
NOMSA Newsletter 4083
Non-Commissioned Officers Association of the United States of America 7134
North American Edition OAG Business Travel Planner 697, 1136, 1247

Index to Information Sources

North American Equipment Dealers Association 4219
North American Farm and Power Show 3433
North American Fisherman 3543
North American Hairstyling Awards 2966
North American Hunter 3544
North American Journal of Fisheries Management 3545
North American Telecommunications Association 4560
North Dakota State Licensing Department ● Office of the Attorney General 7212
Northeast Food Service and Lodging Exposition and Conference 2551
Northeastern Loggers Association 3591
Northeastern Loggers Association Awards Program 3594, 6456
Northeastern Loggers Congress and Equipment Exposition 3654
Northeastern Lumber Manufacturers Association—Information Log 3630
Northeastern Retail Lumber Association Annual Convention 4769
The Northern Horizon 3378
Northern Journal of Applied Forestry 3631
Northern Logger and Timber Processor 3632
Northwest Agricultural Show 3434
Not Just a Secretary: Using the Job To Get Ahead 1576
NPRA Directory 1540
NPRA News 1549
NPSA Regional Report 2027
NRA Technical Bulletin 2408, 2532
NRAction 3546
NRCA Directory 5368
NRF Employee Relations Bulletin 463
NRMA Gold Medal Award 459
NSRA Distinguished Service Award 1737
NSRA Heritage Foundation Scholarship Fund 1738
NSRA List of Approved Court Reporter Education Programs 1733
NTA Trapping Handbook: A Guide for Better Trapping 3485
NTL News 5713
NTMA Business Management Aids 5690, 5795, 5829, 5859, 5902, 5930
NTMA Design Book 4848
NTMA Directory 4849
NTMA Record 5691, 5796, 5830, 5860, 5903, 5931
Nuclear Plant Journal 6042
"Nuclear Reactor Operator Technicians" in Volume 4 of *Career Discovery Encyclopedia* (pp. 126-127) 6013
"Nuclear Reactor Operator Technicians" in Volume 4 of *The Encyclopedia of Careers and Vocational Guidance* (pp. 79-84) 6014
Nucleonics Week 6043
Numeric Filing Guideline 1479
"Numerical Control Machine Operator" in *Careers in High Tech* (pp. 138-139) 5890
"Numerical Control Machine Operator" in *Manufacturing*, Volume 9 of *Career Information Center* (pp. 53-55) 5891
"Numerical Control Machine Tool Operator" in *Guide To Careers Without College* (pp. 61-63) 5892
"Numerical-Control Machine-Tool Operators" in *Occupational Outlook Handbook* (pp. 401-402) 5893
Nursery and Landscape Workers 2712
"Nursery and Landscape Workers" in *Occu-Facts: Information on 565 Careers in Outline Form* (p. 14.13) 3050
Nurse's Aid Study Manual 2744
Nurse's Aide 2713
"Nurse's Aide" in *The Career Connection II: A Guide to Technical Majors and Their Related Careers* (pp. 97-98) 2715
"Nurse's Aide and Orderly" in *Health*, Volume 7 of *Career Information Center* (pp. 51-52) 2714
"Nurse's Aide/Psychiatric Aide" in *Careers in Counseling and Human Development* (pp. 115-116) 2716
"Nurses' Aides and Orderlies" in *The American Almanac of Jobs and Salaries* (pp. 482-483) 2717
"Nursing Aide and Psychiatric Aide" in *Careers in Health Care* (pp. 179-181) 2718
"Nursing Aide/Orderly" in *120 Careers in the Health Care Field* (pp. 288-289) 2719
Nursing Aides and Psychiatric Aides 2740
"Nursing Aides and Psychiatric Aides" in *America's 50 Fastest Growing Jobs* (pp. 122-123) 2720
"Nursing Aides and Psychiatric Aides" in *Occupational Outlook Handbook* (pp. 302-303) 2721
"Nursing Aides/Assistants" in *Opportunities in Health and Medical Careers* (pp. 38-39) 2722
"Nursing and Psychiatric Aides" in Volume 4 of *Career Discovery Encyclopedia* (pp. 132-133) 2723
"Nursing and Psychiatric Aides" in Volume 3 of *The Encyclopedia of Careers and Vocational Guidance* (pp. 288-291) 2724
Nursing Assistants 2725
Nursing Assistants & the Long-Term Health Care Facility 2726
"Nursing or Psychiatric Aide" in *Health Care* (pp. 21-25) 2727
Nut Grower 3379

O

Obtaining Your Private Investigator's License 2120
Ocean Construction Locator 5437
Ocean Industry 5438
Ocean Navigator 6982
Ocean Oil Weekly Report 5439
OCLC Newsletter 1513
Ocular Surgery News 6534
Oerating the Dampening System, Instructor Guide 6252
Office Aide 1082, 1109, 1188, 1708, 1788, 1853
"Office Clerk" in *Administration, Business, and Office*, Volume 1 of *Career Information Center* (pp. 60-61) 1075
Office Machine Service Technician 4056
"Office Machine Service Technician" in *Occu-Facts: Information on 565 Careers in Outline Form* (p. 15.23) 4057
"Office Machine Servicer" in *Administration, Business, and Office*, Volume 1 of *Career Information Center* (pp. 61-63) 4058
"Office Machine Servicers" in Volume 4 of *Career Discovery Encyclopedia* (pp. 138-139) 4059
"Office Machine Servicers" in Volume 3 of *The Encyclopedia of Careers and Vocational Guidance* (pp. 545-548) 4060
Office Machine Technicians 4061
"Office Mail Clerk" in *Occu-Facts: Information on 565 Careers in Outline Form* (p. 12.35) 1267
"Office Manager" in *Administration, Business, and Office*, Volume 1 of *Career Information Center* (pp. 90-91) 835
"Office Manager" in *Career Opportunities in Art* (pp. 33-34) 836
"Office Manager" in *Career Opportunities in Television, Cable, and Video* (pp. 168-169) 837
"Office Manager" in *Occu-Facts: Information on 565 Careers in Outline Form* (p. 1.37) 838
"Office Manager" in *VGM's Careers Encyclopedia* (pp. 312-315) 839
"Office Manager" in *VGM's Handbook of Business and Management Careers* (pp. 67-69) 840
Office Organization & Secretarial Procedures 1645
Office Procedures 1094
Office Revolution 1825
Office Systems & Careers: A Resource for Administrative Assistants 1076, 1577
"Officer, U.S. Armed Forces" in *VGM's Careers Encyclopedia* (pp. 315-317) 7118
Officer's Call 7169
Official Airline Guide, Worldwide Edition 698, 1248
The Official ASE Preparation Guide to ASE Automobile and Body/Paint Tests 3756, 3871, 6564
The Official Directory of Transportation Middlemen 6868
Official Guide—Tractors and Farm Equipment 4224
Official Industrial Equipment Guide 4225
Official Magazine 5323
The Official Railway Equipment Register 6780
Official Railway Equipment Register 6781
Official Tour Directory 699
Offset Lithography 6208
Offset Press Operator 6231
"Offset Press Operator" in *Occu-Facts: Information on 565 Careers in Outline Form* (p. 18.2) 6232
Offset Printing Machine Operator 6247
Offshore Rig Locator 5440
Offshore Rig Newsletter 5441
Ohio State Department of Commerce ● Division of Licensing 7213
Oil Heat Technician's Manual 4313
OJT File Clerk Resource Materials 1480
OJT File Clerk Training Manual 1481
On Campus 1765
On Target 7170
On the Line 1921
"On the Line" in *Telecommunications Careers* (pp. 50-54) 4407
120 Careers in the Health Care Field 2592, 2662, 2728
Onion World 3380
Online Libraries and Microcomputers 1514
Operating Engineer 6687
"Operating Engineer" in *Hard Hatted Women: Stories of Struggle and Success in the Trades* (pp. 88-101) 6688
"Operating Engineer" in *VGM's Careers Encyclopedia* (pp. 315-317) 6689
"Operating Engineer" in *VGM's Handbook of Scientific and Technical Careers* (pp. 79-82) 6690
"Operating Engineers" in *Occu-Facts: Information on 565 Careers in Outline Form* (p. 19.18) 6691

"Operating Engineers" in *Opportunities in Building Construction Trades* (pp. 66-68) **6692**
"Operating Engineers" in Volume 4 of *Career Discovery Encyclopedia* (pp. 140-141) **6693**
"Operating Engineers (Construction Machinery Operators)" in Volume 3 of *The Encyclopedia of Careers and Vocational Guidance* (pp. 680-682) **6694**
Operating the Dampening System on a Sheetfed Offset Press **6253**
Operating the Inking System...Instructor's Guide **6254**
Operations Forum **6112**
Operative Plasterers and Cement Masons International Association of U.S. and Canada **4836, 4891, 5201, 5239**
"Operator" in *Occu-Facts: Information on 565 Careers in Outline Form* (p. 12.30, 12.31, 12.32) **1767**
"Ophthalmic Laboratory Technician" in *Careers in Health Care* (pp. 188-190) **6515**
"Ophthalmic Laboratory Technician" in *Health Care* (pp. 69-73) **6516**
"Ophthalmic Laboratory Technician" in *Occupational Outlook Handbook* (pp. 428-429) **6517**
"Ophthalmic Laboratory Technician" in *120 Careers in the Health Care Field* (p. 461) **6518**
"Ophthalmic Laboratory Technicians" in *Jobs! What They Are...Where They Are...What They Pay* (p. 157) **6519**
"Ophthalmic Laboratory Technicians" in Volume 4 of *Career Discovery Encyclopedia* (pp. 144-145) **6520**
"Ophthalmic Laboratory Technicians" in Volume 4 of *The Encyclopedia of Careers and Vocational Guidance* (pp. 426-430) **6521**
Ophthalmic Laser Therapy **6535**
"Ophthalmic Medical Assistant" in *120 Careers in the Health Care Field* (pp. 454-457) **2663**
Ophthalmic Practice **6536**
Ophthalmic Research **6537**
Ophthalmic Surgery **6538**
Ophthalmologica **6539**
Ophthalmology Management **6540**
Ophthalmology Times **6541**
Opportunities in Accounting Careers **1005**
Opportunities in Beauty Culture Careers **2949**
Opportunities in Carpentry Careers **4699**
Opportunities in Computer Maintenance Careers **4062**
Opportunities in Computer Science **908**
Opportunities in Culinary Careers **2327**
Opportunities in Fire Protection Services **1950**
Opportunities in Food Services **2468**
Opportunities in Law Enforcement and Criminal Justice Careers **2121**
Opportunities in Marine and Maritime Careers **6950**
"Opportunities in Marketing & Sales" in *Travel and Hospitality Career Directory* (pp. 66-68) **259, 589**
Opportunities in Military Careers **7119**
Opportunities in Personnel Management **1528**
Opportunities in Plastics Careers **5839**
Opportunities in Real Estate Careers **260**
Opportunities in Restaurant Careers **2328, 2469**
Opportunities in Sales Careers **195**
Opportunities in Secretarial Careers **1578**
"Opportunities in the Armed Forces" in *Occupational Outlook Handbook* (pp. 447-451) **7120**
"Opportunities in the Armed Services" in *Opportunities in Medical Technology Careers* (pp. 71-83) **7121**
"Opportunities in the U.S. Armed Forces" in *Opportunities in Refrigeration and Air Conditioning Trades* (pp. 117-122) **7122**
Opportunities in Welding Careers **5938**
Opportunities in Word Processing Careers **1826**
"Optical Mechanics" in Volume 4 of *Career Discovery Encyclopedia* (pp. 146-147) **6522**
"Opticians and Optical Mechanics" in Volume 3 of *The Encyclopedia of Careers and Vocational Guidance* (pp. 595-598) **6523**
"Options Traders" in *The New York Times Career Planner* (pp. 261-263) **494**
Optometry and Vision Science **6542**
Oral Health **6510**
"Order Clerks" in *Occupational Outlook Handbook* (pp. 274-275) **1525**
"Orderly" in *Opportunities in Health and Medical Careers* (p. 39) **2729**
"Ordinary and Able Seaman" in *Transportation*, Volume 12 of *Career Information Center* (pp. 65-67) **6951**
Oregon State Department of Insurance and Finance **7214**
Organic Gardening **3106**
Organizational Dynamics: A Quarterly Review of Organizational Behavior for Professional Managers **866, 5625**
Ornament Magazine **5755**

OSHA Hazard Communication Standard: A Compliance Manual for Cosmetology Schools, **2970**
OTC Chart Manual **551**
Our Wiremen **4408**
Out of Service Tire Analysis Guide **6869**
Out of the Woods **3633**
Outdoor Power Equipment Official Guide **4226**
Outdoor Sports and Recreation **3547**
Outdoor Structures **4720**
Outlook **5123**
Outstanding Grassland Farmer or Rancher Award **3272**
Outstanding International Travel Agent of the Year **667**
Outstanding Law Enforcement Achievement Award **2232**
Outstanding Young Farmer Awards **3273**
Over-The-Counter Stock Reports **552**
Owner Operator **6892**

P

Pacific Coast Industrial and Machine Tool Show **5800**
Pacific Logging Congress **3592**
Pacific Logging Congress, Equipment Exhibit, and Working Machinery Demonstration **3655**
Pacific Seafood Chronicle **3548**
Pacific States Marine Fisheries Commission—Newsletter **3549**
Package Printing and Converting **6151, 6182, 6220, 6267**
Packager, Hand **7042**
PAI Career Planning Manual for Human Resource-Personnel: A Guide to the Practice & Accreditation in the Profession **1529**
Paint and Coatings Industry Workers **5133**
"Paint and Coatings Industry Workers" in Volume 3 of *The Encyclopedia of Careers and Vocational Guidance* (pp. 441-444) **6549**
Paint and Paper Pro Show **5187**
Painter **5154**
"Painter" in *Exploring Nontraditional Jobs for Women* (pp. 20-25) **5134**
"Painter and Paperhanger" in *Construction*, Volume 4 of *Career Information Center* (pp. 72-74) **5135**
Painter, Construction **5136**
Painter, Spray **6550**
"Painters" in *Opportunities in Building Construction Trades* (pp. 35-37) **5137**
"Painters" in *The American Almanac of Jobs and Salaries* (p. 502) **5142**
Painters and Allied Trades Journal **4947, 5083, 5179**
"Painters and Paperhangers" in *Occupational Outlook Handbook* (pp. 373-375) **5138**
"Painters and Paperhangers" in Volume 4 of *Career Discovery Encyclopedia* (pp. 166-167) **5139**
"Painters and Paperhangers" in Volume 3 of *The Encyclopedia of Careers and Vocational Guidance* (pp. 682-685) **5140**
Painters (Construction) **5141**
Painters' Equipment & Supplies Directory **5157**
"Painting and Coating Machine Operator" in *Occupational Outlook Handbook* (pp. 430-431) **6551**
Painting and Decorating Contractors of America National Convention and Trade Show **5188**
Painting & Wallcovering Contractor **5180**
Palmetto Piper **4333, 5030, 5324**
PAMA CareerQuest Scholarship **3692**
PAMA News **3713**
PAMA News Magazine **3714**
PAMA Technician of the Year Award **3693**
Paperhanger **5143**
"Paperhanger" in *Occu-Facts: Information on 565 Careers in Outline Form* (p. 16.9) **5144**
Paperhangers **5145**
"Paperhangers" in *Opportunities in Building Construction Trades* (pp. 37-39) **5146**
Parade - IACP Police Service Award **2233**
Park Maintenance and Grounds Management—Athletic Area and Facilities Buyer's Guide Issue **3083**
Parking Attendants **7043**
Part Time Cash for the Sportsman: Twenty-Five Ways for the Fisherman & Hunter to Earn Extra Money **3486**
PAS Newsletter **3381**
Passbooks for Career Opportunities: Transportation Specialist **6650**
"Passenger Agent" in *Opportunities in Airline Careers* (pp. 68-69) **1210**
Passenger Transport **6656, 6782, 6983**
Passenger Transport: The Weekly Newspaper of the Transit Industry **6657**

Index to Information Sources

"Pastry Chef and Baker" in *Hospitality and Recreation*, Volume 8 of *Career Information Center* (pp. 85-87)   2329
PATA Travel News (Americas Edition)   700, 1249
Patient Management Skills for Dental Assistants   2614
Patient Management Skills for Dental Assistants & Hygienist   2615
Patriots Award   2234
Payroll Accounting   1052
Payroll Accounting for Microcomputers   1061
"Payroll and Timekeeping Clerks" in *Occupational Outlook Handbook* (p. 256)   1053
Payroll Clerk   1058
"Payroll Clerk" in *Administration, Business, and Office*, Volume 1 of *Career Information Center* (pp. 63-64)   1054
Payroll Exchange   1065
Payroll Recordkeeping   1062
Payroll Systems & Procedures   1063
"PC Technicians" in *Careers in High Tech* (pp. 81-82)   4063
PCI Journal   4884
The Peanut Farmer   3382
The Peanut Grower   3383
Peanut Journal and Nut World   3384
Pedorthics: Providing Footwear and Related Services to Aid in the Care of the Foot   6331
Pedoscope   6359
Penn Allied Nursery Trade Show   3116
Penna Bakers Show   2552
Pennsylvania State Department ● Bureau of Professional and Occupational Affairs   7215
Periodicals Digest Dentistry   2631
"Peripheral Equipment Operators" in *Careers in High Tech* (pp. 32-34)   909
Person of the Year Award   2967
"Personal Computer Salesperson" in *Straight Talk on Careers: 80 Pros Take You Into Their Professions* (pp. 8-10)   423
Personal Selling Power   228, 464, 613
Personal Service Cluster   2122, 2330, 2470, 2950
Personal Shorthand for the Executive Secretary: Syllabus   1646
Personnel   867, 5626
The Personnel Alert   1550
Personnel Clerk   1535
"Personnel Clerk" in *Administration, Business, and Office*, Volume 1 of *Career Information Center* (pp. 64-66)   1530
"Personnel Clerk" in *Occupational Outlook Handbook* (pp. 275-276)   1531
Personnel Journal   1551
Personnel Literature   1552
Personnel Policy Survey   6326
Personnel Psychology   1553
Pest Alerts   3385
"Pet Care Worker" in *Consumer, Homemaking, and Personal Services*, Volume 5 of *Career Information Center* (pp. 56-58)   2778
"Pet Care Worker" in *Personal Services* (pp. 45-49)   2779
"Pet Grooming" in *Careers for Animal Lovers and Other Zoological Types* (pp. 59-61)   2780
Petersen's Fishing   3550
PFA Directory   6352
PGMS Job Descriptions Guide.   3051
"Pharmaceutical Sales Representative" in *Opportunities in Pharmacy Careers* (pp. 106-108)   196
PHCP EXPO - National Plumbing-Heating-Cooling-Piping Products Exposition   4466, 5341
"Phone Repair Technician" in *Hard Hatted Women: Stories of Struggle and Success in the Trades* (pp. 235-253)   4551
Phonefacts   1802, 4028, 4433, 4574
Photo Lab Management   6614
Photo Marketing   6615
Photo Marketing Association International   6591
Photo Marketing Association International—Newsline   6616
Photo Marketing Magazine   6617
"Photoengraver" in *Communications and the Arts*, Volume 3 of *Career Information Center* (pp. 62-63)   6199
"Photoengravers" in Volume 5 of *Career Discovery Encyclopedia* (pp. 32-33)   6200
"Photoengravers" in Volume 3 of *The Encyclopedia of Careers and Vocational Guidance* (pp. 761-763)   6201
Photofinishing Careers: A Lifelong Commitment to Excellence and Creativity   6585
Photofinishing Laboratory Technicians   6586
"Photographic Developer" in *Occu-Facts: Information on 565 Careers in Outline Form* (p. 18.21)   6587
"Photographic Process Workers" in *Occupational Outlook Handbook* (pp. 432-433)   6588
Photographic Processing   6589, 6618

Photomethods   6619
Physician Assistants Annual Conference   2698
PIACTION   140
Piano Action Handbook   4532
"Piano and Organ Tuner, Technician" in *Consumer, Homemaking, and Personal Services*, Volume 5 of *Career Information Center* (pp. 91-93)   4508
Piano Manufacturers Association International Semiannual Trade Show   4550
Piano Parts and Their Functions, Illustrated   4533
Piano Servicing, Tuning & Rebuilding   4534
"Piano Technicians" in Volume 4 of *The Encyclopedia of Careers and Vocational Guidance* (pp. 358-360)   4509
Piano Technicians Guild   4522
Piano Technicians Journal   4541
"Piano Tuner" in *Offbeat Careers: The Directory of Unusual Work* (pp. 111-112)   4510
Piano Tuner-Technician   4511
The Piano Tuner-Technician   4512
"Piano Tuner Technician" in *Career Opportunities in the Music Industry* (pp. 129-130)   4513
"Piano Tuner-Technician" in *Occu-Facts: Information on 565 Careers in Outline Form* (p. 15.21)   4514
Piano Tuners and Technicians   4515
"Picture It Painted Professionally" Contest   5155
Pioneer of the Year Award   3274
Pipe Fitters and Steam Fitters   5247
"Pipe Fitters and Steam Fitters" in Volume 3 of *The Encyclopedia of Careers and Vocational Guidance* (pp. 686-689)   5248
"Pipe Organ Technicians" in Volume 4 of *The Encyclopedia of Careers and Vocational Guidance* (pp. 361-363)   4516
Pipefitter   5280
"Pipefitters and Steamfitters" in Volume 5 of *Career Discovery Encyclopedia* (pp. 54-55)   5249
Pipefitting and Plumbing   5250
The Plain English Maintenance & Repair Guide for the IBM PC & PCjr   4077
Planned Maintenance   4258
Plants & Gardens   3107
Plasterer   5190, 5203
"Plasterer" in *Construction*, Volume 4 of *Career Information Center* (pp. 74-76)   5191
"Plasterer" in *Occu-Facts: Information on 565 Careers in Outline Form* (p. 16.10)   5192
Plasterer Helper   7044
"Plasterer Helper" in *Occu-Facts: Information on 565 Careers in Outline Form* (p. 20.8)   7045
Plasterers   5193
"Plasterers" in *Occupational Outlook Handbook* (pp. 375-376)   5194
"Plasterers" in *Opportunities in Building Construction Trades* (pp. 39-41)   5195
"Plasterers" in *The American Almanac of Jobs and Salaries* (p. 502)   5198
"Plasterers" in Volume 5 of *Career Discovery Encyclopedia* (pp. 58-59)   5196
"Plasterers" in Volume 3 of *The Encyclopedia of Careers and Vocational Guidance* (pp. 690-692)   5197
Plastering: A Craftman's Encyclopedia   5204
"Plastic-Working Machine Operators" in *Occupational Outlook Handbook* (pp. 398-399)   5840
"Plastics" in Volume 1 of *The Encyclopedia of Careers and Vocational Guidance* (pp. 362-367)   5841
Plastics Compounding   5861
Plastics Engineering   5862
Plastics Engineering Series   5854
"Plastics Industry" in *Manufacturing*, Volume 9 of *Career Information Center* (pp. 132-135)   5842
Plastics Machinery & Equipment   5863
Plastics Magazine   5864
Plastics News   5865
"Plastics Products Manufacturing Workers" in Volume 5 of *Career Discovery Encyclopedia* (pp. 60-61)   5843
"Plastics Products Manufacturing Workers" in Volume 3 of *The Encyclopedia of Careers and Vocational Guidance* (pp. 454-457)   5844
Plastics Today   5866
Plastics World   5867
"Platemaker" in *Communications and the Arts*, Volume 3 of *Career Information Center* (pp. 64-65)   6202
Platemaker, Lithographic   6203
Player Piano Servicing & Rebuilding   4535
Plumb   5325
Plumber   5251, 5281

"Plumber" in *Guide to Careers Without College* (pp. 82-85) **5252**
"Plumber" in *The Desk Guide to Training and Work Advisement* (p. 83) **5255**
"Plumber and Pipe Fitter" in *Construction*, Volume 4 of *Career Information Center* (pp. 76-78) **5253**
"Plumber and Pipefitter" in *VGM's Careers Encyclopedia* (pp. 357-359) **5254**
Plumber Helper **7046**
"Plumber Helper" in *Occu-Facts: Information on 565 Careers in Outline Form* (p. 20.9) **7047**
Plumber—Steam Fitter **5282**
Plumbers **5256**
"Plumbers" in *The American Almanac of Jobs and Salaries* (pp. 502-503) **5263**
"Plumbers" in Volume 5 of *Career Discovery Encyclopedia* (pp. 64-65) **5257**
"Plumbers" in Volume 3 of *The Encyclopedia of Careers and Vocational Guidance* (pp. 693-695) **5258**
Plumbers and Pipefitters **5259**
"Plumbers and Pipefitters" in *Occu-Facts: Information on 565 Careers in Outline Form* (p. 16.11) **5260**
"Plumbers and Pipefitters" in *Occupational Outlook Handbook* (pp. 377-378) **5261**
"Plumbers and Pipefitters" in *Opportunities in Building Construction Trades* (pp. 41-45) **5262**
Plumbers & Pipefitters Library **5292**
Plumbers Handbook **5293**
The Plumber's Toolbox Manual **5294**
Plumbing **5295**
"Plumbing" in *The Career Connection II: A Guide to Technical Majors and Their Related Careers* (pp. 107-108) **5264**
Plumbing Business **5326**
Plumbing Engineer—Product Directory Issue **5296**
Plumbing-Heating-Cooling Contractors Convention, Ohio Chapter **5342**
Plumbing-Heating-Cooling Contractors Convention, Pennsylvania Chapter **5343**
Plumbing-Heating-Cooling Contractors Convention, Texas Chapter **5344**
Plumbing Heating Piping **5327**
Pocket List of Railroad Officials **6783**
Podiatric Assistant **2694**
Poetker Award; Frances Jones **3075**
Police **2272**
"Police" in *The American Almanac of Jobs and Salaries* (pp. 98-102) **2129**
Police Administration Aide **2183**
Police Administration & Supervision **2184**
Police Administrative Aide **2185**
"Police and Detectives" in *Opportunities in Vocational and Technical Careers* (pp. 74-75) **2123**
Police & Security News **2081, 2273**
Police Attendant **2186**
Police—Buyer's Guide Issue **2250**
Police Cadet **2187**
Police Captain **2188**
Police Chief **2189**
The Police Chief **2274**
Police Clerk **2190**
Police Communications & Teletype Operator **1789**
Police Communications Technician **4022**
Police Department Clerk/Typist **1827**
"Police Detective" in *Occu-Facts: Information on 565 Careers in Outline Form* (p. 13.5) **2124**
"Police Detective" in *Straight Talk on Careers: 80 Pros Take You Into Their Professions* (pp. 236-238) **2126**
The Police Detective Function **2125**
"Police, Detectives, and Special Agents" in *Occupational Outlook Handbook* (pp. 290-293) **2127**
"Police, Detectives, and Special Agents" in *101 Careers: A Guide to the Fastest-Growing Opportunities* (pp. 140-144) **2128**
Police Dispatcher **1310**
The Police Function & the Investigation of Crime **2251**
Police Inspector **2191**
Police Lieutenant **2192**
Police Officer **2130, 2131, 2132, 2193, 2194**
"Police Officer" in *Hard Hatted Women: Stories of Struggle and Success in the Trades* (pp. 71-80) **2133**
"Police Officer" in *Occu-Facts: Information on 565 Careers in Outline Form* (p. 13.7) **2134**
"Police Officer" in *Public and Community Services*, Volume 11 of *Career Information Center* (pp. 57-58) **2135**
"Police Officer" in *Top Professions: The 100 Most Popular, Dynamic, and Profitable Careers in America Today* (pp. 40-41) **2136**
Police Officer Exams Review **2195**
Police Officer of the Year Award **2235**
Police Officers **2137**
"Police Officers" in *Jobs! What They Are...Where They Are...What They Pay* (pp. 191-192) **2138**
"Police Officers" in Volume 5 of *Career Discovery Encyclopedia* (pp. 68-69) **2139**
"Police Officers" in Volume 3 of *The Encyclopedia of Careers and Vocational Guidance* (pp. 298-302) **2140**
Police Promotion Course (One Volume) **2196**
Police Promotion Examinations **2197**
Police Promotion Manual **2252**
Police Reading Comprehension **2198**
"Police Search & Recovery" in *Footsteps in the Ocean: Careers in Diving* (pp. 109-114) **2141**
"Police Sergeant" in *Straight Talk on Careers: 80 Pros Take You Into Their Professions* (pp. 233-235) **2142**
Police Times Magazine **2275**
Pollution Engineering **6113**
Polymer Engineering and Science **5868**
Portland Cement Association **4837**
Post Office Clerk **1371**
"Post Office Clerk" in *Occu-Facts: Information on 565 Careers in Outline Form* (p. 12.33) **1372**
Post Office Clerk-Carrier **1373, 1405**
The Post Office Worker: A Trade Union & Social History **1434**
Postal Arithmetic **1406**
Postal Bulletin **1424**
Postal Clerk-Carrier & Mail Handler Exams **1407**
"Postal Clerks" in Volume 5 of *Career Discovery Encyclopedia* (pp. 76-77) **1374**
"Postal Clerks" in Volume 3 of *The Encyclopedia of Careers and Vocational Guidance* (pp. 62-66) **1375**
"Postal Clerks and Mail Carriers" in *Occupational Outlook Handbook* (pp. 268-270) **1376**
Postal Exam Handbook **1408**
Postal Life **1425**
Postal Machines Mechanic (USPS) **1409**
Postal Record **1426**
"Postal Service Worker" in *Public and Community Services*, Volume 11 of *Career Information Center* (pp. 58-60) **1377**
Postal Service Workers **1378**
The Postal Supervisor **1427**
Postal Supervisor (USPS) **1410**
Postal System Examiner (USPS) **1411**
Postal Transportation Clerk (USPS) **1412**
Postmaster (USPS) **1413**
Postmasters Gazette **1428**
Potential Liabilities of Probation & Parole Officers **1910**
POWER-GEN **6048**
The Power of Customer Service **1105**
"Power Plant Maintenance Electrician" in *Opportunities in Electrical Trades* (pp. 54-55) **4984**
"Power Plant Occupations" in Volume 3 of *The Encyclopedia of Careers and Vocational Guidance* (pp. 766-769) **6015**
Power Plant Operator **6029**
"Power Plant Worker" in *Public and Community Services*, Volume 11 of *Career Information Center* (pp. 60-62) **6016**
"Power Plant Workers" in Volume 5 of *Career Discovery Encyclopedia* (pp. 80-81) **6017**
"Power Shovel Crane Operator" in *Occu-Facts: Information on 565 Careers in Outline Form* (p. 19.16) **6695**
Power Tool Institute **4361**
Power Tool Maintenance **4364**
"Power Tool Repairer" in *Construction*, Volume 4 of *Career Information Center* (pp. 78-80) **4358**
"Power Truck Operator" in *Transportation*, Volume 12 of *Career Information Center* (pp. 69-71) **6696**
The Practical Design of Structural Elements of Timber **3598**
The Practical Gourmet **2409**
Practical Guide Maintenance Engineering **4259**
Practical Law for Jail & Prison Personnel: A Resource Manual & Training Curriculum **1911**
Practical Problems in Mathematics for Welders **5979**
Practice and Drill for the Clerk, Typist, and Stenographer Examinations **1083, 1709**
Practice & Drill for the Clerk, Typist & Stenographer Examinations **1710**
Practice and Drill for the Clerk, Typist, and Stenographer Examinations **1854**
Practice for Air Force Placement Tests **7140**

Index to Information Sources

Practice for Army Placement Tests **7141**
Practice for Clerical, Typing and Stenographic Tests **1084, 1711, 1855**
Practice for Navy Placement Tests **7142**
Practice for the Armed Forces Test - ASVAB **7143**
Prairie Hotelier **1137**
Precis of Postal Service Manual **1414**
"Precision Assemblers" in *Occupational Outlook Handbook* (pp. 386-387) **5596**
"Precision Assemblers" in *The American Almanac of Jobs and Salaries* (pp. 528-529) **5597**
Premium Grower **3386**
Preprint Volumes **5855**
"Preschool and Childcare Workers" in *101 Careers: A Guide to the Fastest-Growing Opportunities* (pp. 178-181) **2885**
Prescription Footwear Association **6345**
The President **868, 5627**
Press Operator **6248**
Presser, Garment **6287**
Prestressed Concrete Institute Convention **4892**
Prime Real Estate **357**
Principal Cashier **22**
Principal Clerk **1085**
Principal Clerk (Personnel) **1536**
Principal Clerk/Principal Stenographer **1712**
Principal Clerk-Stenographer **1713**
Principal Data Entry Machine Operator **919**
Principal File Clerk **1465**
Principal Groundskeeper **3066**
Principal Library Clerk **1501**
Principal Mail & Supply Clerk **1274**
Principal Office Assistant **1086**
Principal Office Stenographer **1714**
Principal Personnel Clerk **1537**
Principal Records Center Assistant **1437**
Principal Special Investigator **2199**
Principal Stationary Engineer **6061**
Principal Stenographer **1715**
Principal Stenographer (Law) **1716**
Principal Telephone Operator **1790**
Principal Water Plant Supervisor **6089**
Principles of Payroll Administration **1064**
"Printing" in Volume 1 of *The Encyclopedia of Careers and Vocational Guidance* (pp. 375-381) **6233**
Printing Platemakers **6234**
"Printing Press Operator" in *Communications and the Arts*, Volume 3 of *Career Information Center* (pp. 65-67) **6235**
"Printing Press Operator" in *VGM's Careers Encyclopedia* (pp. 368-370) **6236**
Printing Press Operators **6237**
"Printing Press Operators" in *Jobs! What They Are...Where They Are...What They Pay* (pp. 179-180) **6238**
"Printing Press Operators" in *Occupational Outlook Handbook* (pp. 416-417) **6239**
"Printing Press Operators" in Volume 5 of *Career Discovery Encyclopedia* (pp. 86-87) **6240**
"Printing Press Operators and Assistants" in Volume 3 of *The Encyclopedia of Careers and Vocational Guidance* (pp. 555-557) **6241**
"Printing Technology" in *The Career Connection II: A Guide to Technical Majors and Their Related Careers* (pp. 109-110) **6242**
Prison Correction Officer **1896**
"Private Child Care Worker" in *Consumer, Homemaking, and Personal Services*, Volume 5 of *Career Information Center* (pp. 36-38) **3211**
"Private Household Worker" in *Personal Services* (pp. 15-19) **3212**
"Private Household Workers" in *Occupational Outlook Handbook* (pp. 316-317) **3213**
"Private Household Workers" in Volume 5 of *Career Discovery Encyclopedia* (pp. 88-89) **3214**
"Private Household Workers" in Volume 3 of *The Encyclopedia of Careers and Vocational Guidance* (pp. 302-305) **3215**
Pro Trucker **6893**
Procedures for the Office Professional **1095**
Procedures for the Professional Secretary **1579**
The Process of Investigation: Concepts & Strategies for the Security Professional **2253**
PRODUCT NEWS **3551**
Production **5831**
"Production Painter" in *Manufacturing*, Volume 9 of *Career Information Center* (pp. 55-56) **6552**
"Production Supervisor" in *Manufacturing*, Volume 9 of *Career Information Center* (pp. 68-70) **5613**
Productivity Conference and Distribution/Transportation Exposition **6718**

The Profession of Arms **7123**
Professional Agent **141**
Professional Aviation Maintenance Association **3689, 3721**
Professional Barber Styling State Board Exam Review **2842**
Professional Builder **4666, 4759, 4805, 4885, 4948, 5031, 5084, 5124, 5181, 5235, 5328, 5406, 5486, 5537, 5579**
"Professional Cooking" in *The Desk Guide to Training and Work Advisement* (pp. 77-79) **2331**
"Professional Diver" in *Offbeat Careers: The Directory of Unusual Work* (pp. 123-124) **3467**
Professional Education Series **1739**
Professional Electronics **4184**
Professional Electronics Magazine **3989, 4185**
The Professional Electronics Technician **3937, 4009, 4064, 4150**
Professional Electronics Yearbook **4174**
Professional Excellence for Secretaries **1647**
Professional Goldsmithing: A Contemporary Guide to Traditional Jewelry Techniques **5737**
Professional Grounds Management Society **3056, 3057**
Professional Grounds Management Society Trade Show **3117**
The Professional Grounds Manager **3084**
Professional Insurance Agents **106**
Professional Insurance Agents **142**
Professional Insurance Agents Convention and Trade Show **158**
Professional Lawn Care Association of America Annual Conference and Show **3118**
Professional Management for First-Line Supervisors **841**
Professional Medical Assistant **2695**
Professional Qualifications for Fire Inspector, Fire Investigator, & Fire Prevention Education Officer: NFPA 1031 **1951**
Professional Roofing **5407**
Professional Secretaries International **1615, 1620, 1673**
Professional Secretaries Scholarship **1630**
Professional Secretary's Handbook **1648**
Professional Thieves & the Detective **2254**
Professional Truck Driver Institute of America **6835, 6838**
Professional Upholster Cleaning Techniques: The Basics **6420**
The Professional Upholsterer **6428**
"Professionalism - Certified Travel Counselor" in *The Travel Agent: Dealer in Dreams* (pp. 21-22) **629**
Professionals...Are Certified by the Electronics Technicians Association, International **3945, 4167**
Profile: The Petroleum Industry **5421**
Programs in Veterinary Technology **2802**
Progressive Filing **1482**
Progressive Railroading **6784**
Projects in Leather **6353**
Promoting Timber Cropping **3599**
"Property and Casualty Insurance Agents and Brokers" in Volume 5 of *Career Discovery Encyclopedia* (pp. 92-93) **97**
PROTECH - International Exhibition for Protection, Safety, Security, and Fire Prevention **2039, 2087, 2284**
Provider: For Long Term Care Professionals **2757**
Psychiatric Aide **2730**
"Psychiatric Aide" in *Occu-Facts: Information on 565 Careers in Outline Form* (p. 13.26) **2731**
Psychiatric Aides and Technicians **2732**
PTG Members Bulletin **4542**
PTN (Photographic Trade News) **6620**
Public Information Assistant **1110**
Public Personnel Management **1554**
Public Safety Dispatcher **1311**
Public Safety Officer **2200**
Public Service Award **1993, 2236**
Puerto Rico Licensing Administration **7216**

Q

Q & A on the Real Estate License Examinations (RE) **316**
Qualifying for Admission to the Service Academies: A Student's Guide **7124**
Quality Assurance of Welded Construction **5980**
Quality Control Inspector **5684**
"Quality Control Inspector" in *Manufacturing*, Volume 9 of *Career Information Center* (pp. 56-58) **5675**
Quality Engineering **5692**
Quality Progress **5693**
The Quality Review **5694**
Quarter-Century Honor Roll **954**
Quarterly Labor Relations Comprehensive Bulletin **4591**
Query: Questions and Answers About Managing Your Money **143**
Questions and Answers About Entering the Child Care Profession **2886**
Quick 'n Easy Country Cookin' **2410**

Quick Printing   6152, 6183, 6221, 6268
Quickening   2758
Quintessence International   6511

R

Racing & Sports Car Chassis Design   3817
Radial Tire Wear Condition & Causes: A Guide to Wear Pattern Analysis   6870
"Radio Advertising Salesperson" in Career Opportunities in Advertising and Public Relations (pp. 128-130)   590
Radio and Telegraph Operator   1791
"Radio and Telegraph Operator" in Telecommunications (pp. 51-55)   1768
"Radio and Telegraph Operators" in Volume 5 of Career Discovery Encyclopedia (pp. 118-119)   1769
"Radio and Telegraph Operators" in Volume 2 of The Encyclopedia of Careers and Vocational Guidance (pp. 561-564)   1770
"Radio and Television Service Technician" in Occu-Facts: Information on 565 Careers in Outline Form (p. 15.13)   4151
"Radio and Television Technician" in Telecommunications (pp. 63-67)   4152
Radio Dispatchers   1297
Radio Telephone Operator   1792
"Radio, Television, and Print Advertising Sales Workers" in Volume 3 of The Encyclopedia of Careers and Vocational Guidance (pp. 158-162)   591
Ragnar's Ten Best Traps & a Few Others That Are Damn Good, Too   3487
Rail News Update   6785
"Rail Transportation Workers" in Occupational Outlook Handbook (pp. 438-440)   6731
Railroad Brake Operator   6732
"Railroad Brake Operator" in Occu-Facts: Information on 565 Careers in Outline Form (19.10)   6733
"Railroad Braker" in Transportation, Volume 12 of Career Information Center (pp. 71-72)   6734
"Railroad Braker and Conductor" in Transportation (pp. 39-43)   6735
Railroad Caretaker   6750
Railroad Clerk   6751, 6752
Railroad Conductor   6736, 6737
"Railroad Conductor" in Occu-Facts: Information on 565 Careers in Outline Form (p. 19.1)   6738
"Railroad Conductor" in Transportation, Volume 12 of Career Information Center (pp. 111-113)   6739
"Railroad Conductors" in Volume 5 of Career Discovery Encyclopedia (pp. 128-129)   6740
"Railroad Conductors" in Volume 3 of The Encyclopedia of Careers and Vocational Guidance (pp. 129-132)   6741
"Railroad Engineer" in Transportation, Volume 12 of Career Information Center (pp. 113-115)   6742
Railroad Facts   6802
Railroad Industry Workers   6743
Railroad Inspector   6753
Railroad Newsletter   6786
Railroad Porter   6754
Railroad Signal Specialist   6755
"Railroad Signaler and Signal Maintainer" in Transportation, Volume 12 of Career Information Center (pp. 76-78)   4010
"Railroad Signaler, Telegrapher, Telephoner, and Dispatcher" in Transportation (pp. 57-61)   1298
Railroad Stock Assistant   6756
Railroad Stockman   6757
Railroad Track and Structure Inspector   6758
Railway Age   6787
Railway Track and Structures   6788
Random Lengths   3634
"Rate Clerk" in Careers in Trucking (pp. 65-67)   981
Rational Fabrication Specifications for Steel Structures   5981
Re-Upholstery Techniques   6421
"Real Estate" in Career Choices for the 90's for Students of Business (pp. 131-154)   261
"Real Estate" in Career Choices for the 90's for Students of Economics (pp. 122-145)   262
"Real Estate" in Career Choices for the 90's for Students of Mathematics (pp. 134-157)   263
"Real Estate" in Major Decisions: A Guide to College Majors (p. 142)   264
"Real Estate" in The Black Woman's Career Guide (pp. 295-302)   265
"Real Estate" in The Career Connection II: A Guide to Technical Majors and Their Related Careers (pp. 113-114)   290
"Real Estate" in The Encyclopedia of Career Choices for the 1990s: A Guide to Entry Level Jobs (pp. 742-765)   291

"Real Estate" in Volume 1 of The Encyclopedia of Careers and Vocational Guidance (pp. 401-406)   266
Real Estate Agent   317
"Real Estate Agent/Broker" in VGM's Careers Encyclopedia (pp. 395-397)   267
"Real Estate Agent/Broker" in VGM's Handbook of Business and Management Careers (pp. 81-83)   268
"Real Estate Agents" in Opportunities in Home Economics Careers (pp. 95-96)   269
"Real Estate Agents" in Opportunities in Vocational and Technical Careers (pp. 64-66)   270
Real Estate Agents and Brokers   271
"Real Estate Agents and Brokers" in Jobs! What They Are. . .Where They Are. . .What They Pay (p. 286)   272
"Real Estate Agents and Brokers" in 101 Careers: A Guide to the Fastest-Growing Opportunities (pp. 48-51)   273
"Real Estate Agents and Brokers" in The American Almanac of Jobs and Salaries (pp. 552-553)   274
"Real Estate Agents and Brokers" in Volume 5 of Career Discovery Encyclopedia (pp. 132-133)   275
"Real Estate Agents and Brokers" in Volume 3 of The Encyclopedia of Careers and Vocational Guidance (pp. 162-167)   276
"Real Estate Agents and Brokers: Sellers of the Land" in Careers for Women Without College Degrees (pp. 245-250)   277
"Real Estate Agents, Brokers, and Appraisers" in Occupational Outlook Handbook (pp. 234-236)   278
Real Estate Aide   318
"Real Estate and Construction" in Jobs '91 (pp. 349-359)   279
Real Estate Appraiser   280, 319
"Real Estate Appraiser" in Career Choices for the 90's for Students of Business (pp. 139-141)   281
"Real Estate Appraiser" in Marketing and Distribution, Volume 10 of Career Information Center (pp. 98-99)   282
"Real Estate Appraiser" in Occu-Facts: Information on 565 Careers in Outline Form (p. 11.4)   283
"Real Estate Appraiser" in VGM's Careers Encyclopedia (pp. 399-400)   284
"Real Estate Appraiser" in VGM's Handbook of Business and Management Careers (pp. 84-86)   285
Real Estate Appraisers   286
"Real Estate Appraisers" in The New York Times Career Planner (pp. 283-285)   287
Real Estate Assistant   320
Real Estate Broker   321
"Real Estate Broker" in Top Professions: The 100 Most Popular, Dynamic, and Profitable Careers in America Today (pp. 68-69)   288
Real Estate Broker (REB)   322
Real Estate Business   358
"Real Estate Careers" in Transitions: Military Pathways to Civilian Careers (pp. 137-140)   289
Real Estate Center Journal   359
Real Estate Finance   360
The Real Estate Finance Journal   361
Real Estate Finance Today   362
Real Estate Forum   363
The Real Estate Index   392
Real Estate License Examinations   323
Real Estate News   364, 365
Real Estate Outlook   366
Real Estate Record and Builders Guide   367
Real Estate Review   368
"Real Estate Sales" in Career Choices for the 90's for Students of Business (pp. 164-167)   292
"Real Estate Sales" in Career Choices for the 90's for Students of Communications and Journalism (pp. 172-175)   293
"Real Estate Sales" in Opportunities in Property Management Careers (pp. 101-105)   294
"Real Estate Sales" in The Encyclopedia of Career Choices for the 1990s: A Guide to Entry Level Jobs (pp. 775-778)   295
"Real Estate Sales Worker and Broker" in Marketing and Distribution, Volume 10 of Career Information Center (pp. 75-76)   296
Real Estate Salesman (RES)   324
Real Estate Salesperson   297
"Real Estate Salesperson" in College Board Guide to Jobs and Career Planning (pp. 138-140)   298
"Real Estate Salesperson" in Occu-Facts: Information on 565 Careers in Outline Form (p. 11.5)   299
Real Estate Schools Directory   328
Real Estate Today   369
Real Estate Weekly   370
Real Estate West   371
"Real Estate: What's Hot, What's Not" in Fast-Track Careers: A Guide to the Highest-Paying Jobs (pp. 99-121)   300

1118

Index to Information Sources

Realtor News 372
Realtor News - All Member Issue 373
Realtor News-Broker Issue 374
Realtor of the Year 332
REALTORS Land Institute 375
Realty 376
Recent Trends in Welding Science & Technology 6001
Receptionist 1172
The Receptionist 1173
Receptionist 1189, 1327
"Receptionist" in *Administration, Business, and Office*, Volume 1 of *Career Information Center* (pp. 66-67) 1174
"Receptionist" in *Occu-Facts: Information on 565 Careers in Outline Form* (p. 12.18) 1175
Receptionist: A Practical Course in Office Reception Techniques 1194
"Receptionist/Clerk-Typist" in *Career Opportunities in Television, Cable, and Video* (pp. 22-23) 1176, 1828
Receptionists 1177, 1191
"Receptionists" in *America's 50 Fastest Growing Jobs* (pp. 111-113) 1184
"Receptionists" in *Jobs! What They Are...Where They Are...What They Pay* (pp. 210-211) 1178
"Receptionists" in *Occupational Outlook Handbook* (pp. 260-261) 1179
"Receptionists" in *Opportunities in Vocational and Technical Careers* (pp. 43-45) 1180
"Receptionists" in Volume 5 of *Career Discovery Encyclopedia* (pp. 134-135) 1181
"Receptionists" in Volume 3 of *The Encyclopedia of Careers and Vocational Guidance* (pp. 74-77) 1182
"Receptionists and Switchboard Operators" in *The American Almanac of Jobs and Salaries* (p. 507) 1183, 1771
Recipe Ingredient Substitution Update 2411
Reciprocity Equivalency Chart 6083
Recognition Award 2237
Recommend 701, 1250
"Record Clerks" in *Occupational Outlook Handbook* (pp. 270-272) 1435
Record Keeping for Small Rural Businesses 1040
"Record Shop Clerk" in *Career Opportunities in the Music Industry* (pp. 93-94) 424
Recording Clerk 1438
Records & Database Management 1483
Records Management 1484
Records Management Quarterly 1441, 1448, 1486, 1515, 1526, 1555
Recruitment Today 1556
Redwood Region Logging Conference 3656
Reeves Journal: Plumbing Heating Cooling 4334, 5329
Reference Manual: For the Office 1096
Refrigerated Transporter 6894
Refrigerating Machine Mechanic 4296
Refrigeration Service and Contracting 4335
Refrigeration Service Engineers Society 4293
Refuse Collectors 7048
"Refuse Collectors" in Volume 5 of *Career Discovery Encyclopedia* (pp. 142-143) 7049
"Refuse Collectors" in Volume 3 of *The Encyclopedia of Careers and Vocational Guidance* (pp. 770-772) 7050
"Refuse Worker" in *Public and Community Services*, Volume 11 of *Career Information Center* (pp. 62-64) 7051
Registered Medical Assistants 2670, 2676, 2699
Renews 3913, 4131
"Rental Clerk" in *Travel Agent* (p. 168) 46
The Rep Travel Newsletter 229
Rep World 230
Repair Cluster 4153, 4286
Repairing Appliances 3974
RepLetter 231
The Reporter 5330
Reproduction Bulletin 6153, 6184, 6222, 6269
Research Journal of the Water Pollution Control Federation 6114
Research Journal Water Pollution Control Federation 6115
"Reservation Agents" in *Travel Agent* (pp. 167-168) 1211
"Reservation and Information Clerks" in *Opportunities in Travel Careers* (p. 53) 1106, 1212
"Reservation and Transportation Ticket Agent" in Volume 5 of *Career Discovery Encyclopedia* (pp. 150-151) 1213
"Reservation and Transportation Ticket Agents" in Volume 3 of *The Encyclopedia of Careers and Vocational Guidance* (pp. 78-81) 1214
"Reservation and Transportation Ticket Agents and Travel Clerks" in *Occupational Outlook Handbook* (pp. 261-262) 1215
"Reservationists and Airline Ticket Agents" in *Jobs! What They Are...Where They Are...What They Pay* (pp. 170-171) 1216

"Reservations Agents" in *Opportunities in Airline Careers* (pp. 65-67) 1217
"The Reservations Department" in *Opportunities in Transportation Careers* (pp. 43-44) 1218
"Reservations Sales Agent" in *Opportunities in Aerospace Careers* (pp. 21-25) 1219
"Reservations Sales Agent" in *Travel Agent* (pp. 164-165) 1220
Residential Heating Operations & Troubleshooting 4314
Residential Landscape Design Award 3076
Residential Plumbing 5297
"Resilient Floor Layer" in *Opportunities in Carpentry Careers* (pp. 52-53) 4779
Resource 144
Restaurant Business 2412, 2533
"Restaurant Chef" in *Top Professions: The 100 Most Popular, Dynamic, and Profitable Careers in America Today* (pp. 195-197) 2332
Restaurant Exchange News 2413, 2534
Restaurant Hospitality—Restaurant Industry Almanac Issue 2363, 2501
"Restaurant Host and Hostess" in *Hospitality and Recreation*, Volume 8 of *Career Information Center* (pp. 60-62) 2471
Restaurant Host/Hostess 2472
"Restaurant Host/Hostess" in *Occu-Facts: Information on 565 Careers in Outline Form* (p. 13.11) 2473
Restaurant Industry Operations Report 2434, 2558
Restaurant Merchandising News 2414, 2535
Restaurants & Institutions 2415, 2536
Restaurants USA 2416, 2537
Resumes for Computer Personnel 910
"Retail Butcher" in *Marketing and Distribution*, Volume 10 of *Career Information Center* (pp. 51-52) 5647
Retail Confectioners International Annual Convention and Exposition 2429
Retail Control 465
"Retail Industry" in *Footsteps in the Ocean: Careers in Diving* (pp. 37-42) 425
Retail Merchandising 466
Retail News Reporter 3990, 4186, 4369
"Retail Sales" in *Careers in Marketing* (pp. 66-68) 426
Retail Sales Power 427
"Retail Sales Worker" in *VGM's Careers Encyclopedia* (pp. 409-411) 428
"Retail Sales Worker" in Volume 5 of *Career Discovery Encyclopedia* (pp. 156-157) 429
"Retail Sales Workers" in *Occupational Outlook Handbook* (pp. 236-238) 430
"Retail Sales Workers" in *Opportunities in Vocational and Technical Careers* (pp. 63-64) 431
"Retail Sales Workers" in Volume 3 of *The Encyclopedia of Careers and Vocational Guidance* (pp. 167-171) 432
"Retail Salespeople" in *Jobs! What They Are...Where They Are...What They Pay* (pp. 272-273) 433
"Retail Store Sales Worker" in *Marketing and Distribution*, Volume 10 of *Career Information Center* (pp. 53-54) 434
"Retail Store Salesperson" in *The Complete Computer Career Guide* (pp. 57-58) 435
Retailing & Merchandising 47, 436
Retailing News 232, 467, 614
Retirement Housing: Step by Step Guide for Investors, Developers, Accountants, & Other Professionals 339
REVAC - Refrigeration, Ventilation, Air-Conditioning, and Heating Exhibition 4344, 6072
A Reverence for Wood 6480
A Review of Dental Assisting 2593
Review of Optometry 6543
Rewarding Careers in the Automotive Service Industry 3845
Rhode Island State Department of Labor • Division of Professional Regulation 7217
The Rice World and Soybean News 3387
RIEI Information Letter 5408
Right of Way 377
RIS News 468
Risk and Insurance Management Society Annual Conference 159
Risk Management Manual for Motor Carriers 6871
Road King Magazine 6895
Roads & Bridges Magazine 5538
Robert Oliver & Mercantile Bookkeeping in the Early Nineteenth Century 1051
Robins Rev-Up 7171
Rock and Dirt 6711
Rock & Gem 5756
Rocky Mountain Construction 3108, 3635

Rocky Mountain Regional Hospitality Convention and Education Exposition - The Restaurant Show 2553
Rocky Mountain Union Farmer 3388
Role of Physician Assistants in Primary Care 2664
Rolling Along 6896
Roof Framing 4721, 5369, 5370
Roofer 5351, 5364
"Roofer" in Construction, Volume 4 of Career Information Center (pp. 82-83) 5352
"Roofer" in Occu-Facts: Information on 565 Careers in Outline Form (p. 16.17) 5353
Roofer Helper 7052
"Roofer Helper" in Occu-Facts: Information on 565 Careers in Outline Form (p. 20.11) 7053
ROOFER Magazine 5409
Roofers 5354
"Roofers" in Occupational Outlook Handbook (pp. 378-379) IT2 5355
"Roofers" in Opportunities in Building Construction Trades (pp. 45-47) 5356
"Roofers" in Volume 5 of Career Discovery Encyclopedia (pp. 164-165) 5357
"Roofers" in Volume 3 of The Encyclopedia of Careers and Vocational Guidance (pp. 696-698) 5358
Roofer's Pitch 5359
Roofing and Waterproofing: A Trade Worth Learning Through Apprenticeship 5360
Roofing: Design Criteria, Options, Selection 5371
Roofing Manual 5372
Roofing the Right Way 5373
Roofinig Technology Conference, 9th: Proceedings 5416
Roomkeeper of the Year 3177
Rosenbluth Memorial Award; Joseph W. 668
Ross Awards; Arthur 3077
ROTOR 3715
Rotor & Wing International 3716
Rotorgram 3717
Rough Notes 145
Roustabout 5422
"Roustabout" in Occupational Outlook Handbook (pp. 379-381) 5423
"Roustabouts" in Volume 5 of Career Discovery Encyclopedia (pp. 166-167) 5424
"Roustabouts" in Volume 3 of The Encyclopedia of Careers and Vocational Guidance (pp. 698-702) 5425
Rowe Citizenship Award; John O. 3275
RSC (Refrigeration Service and Contracting) 4336
RSI (Roofing/Siding/Insulation) 5125, 5410
Rubber and Plastics Newsletter 5869
Ruppert Award; David P. 5097
Rural Appraisal Manual 3283
Rural Carrier 1415
Rural Carrier (USPS) 1416
Rural Electrification Magazine 6044
Rural Living 3389
Rural Mail Carrier 1379
Rural Telecommunications 4425, 4567
Ruralite 6045
Russell's Official National Motor Coach Guide 6658
RWDSU Record 233, 469

S

S/F (Square Foot) 378
"Saddlemaker" in Offbeat Careers: The Directory of Unusual Work (pp. 140-141) 6332
Safe Worker Award 6851
Safety Code for Elevators & Escalators 4203
Safety Spotlight 5539
Safey Code for Elevators & Escalators: Handbook on A17.1 4204
"Sales" in Opportunities in Insurance Careers (pp. 34-36) 98
Sales and Marketing Show and Conference 245, 620
Sales & Marketing Training 234, 470, 615
"Sales (Insurance)" in The Encyclopedia of Career Choices for the 1990s: A Guide to Entry Level Jobs (pp. 442-444) 99
Sales Management in Financial Services: How to Build a Competitive Sales Team 534
"Sales Opportunities in Service Industries" in Opportunities in Sales Careers (pp. 123-131) 592
"Sales Representative, Wholesale Distribution" in Occu-Facts: Information on 565 Careers in Outline Form (p. 11.13) 197
Sales Representatives, Wholesale Distribution 198
Sales Store Worker 458
"Salesclerk" in Guide to Careers Without College (pp. 20-21) 437
Salesman's Insider 146, 235, 471, 553, 616

Salesmanship 236, 617
Salespeople, Household Appliance 438
Salespeople, Retail 439
"Salesperson" in Occu-Facts: Information on 565 Careers in Outline Form (pp. 11.14, 11.15, 11.16, 11.17, 11.18, 11.19, 11.20, 11.27) 440
Salesperson, Advertising Space 593
Salesperson, Automobile 441
Salesperson, Automotive Parts 442
Salesperson, Camera Store 443
Salesperson, Drugstore 444
Salesperson, Grocery Products 445
Salesperson, Hardware Store 446
Salesperson, Music Store 447
Salesperson, Retail 448
Salesperson, Securities 495
Salmon Trout Steelheader 3552
Salon Fair - The International Beauty Shows 2857, 3002
Salon Focus 2000 - Your Educational Forum 2858, 3003
Salt Water Sportsman 3553
Salute to Excellence Awards 2496
San Joaquin Farm Bureau News 3390
San Mateo County Fair and Floral Fiesta 5734
Sanitary Maintenance 3190
Sanitation Worker 6090
"Sanitation Workers" in The American Almanac of Jobs and Salaries (pp. 102-103) 7054
"Sawmill Workers" in Volume 5 of Career Discovery Encyclopedia (pp. 170-171) 6447
Schaum's Outline of Bookkeeping & Accounting 1041
Schaum's Outline of Theory & Problems of Bookkeeping 1042
Scheleen Award for Excellence; National Joseph C. 1357
School Age Notes 2913
School Bus Driver 6636
School Bus Fleet 6659
School Secretary 1580
Schools With PTDIA Certified Courses Listed by State 6845
The Science & Practice of Welding 5939
Scottish Gardening Scholarship 3078
SCTA Hi-Lights 6660, 6897
Sea Grant Extension Program Newsletter 3554
Sea Shelters 379
Seabee Coverall 7172
Seafarers Log 6984
Seafood Leader 2417, 5658
"Seafood Processing and Marketing" in Opportunities in Marine and Maritime Careers (pp. 112-113) 5648
Seaman, Able 6952
"Seaman, Steward, Cook" in Transportation (pp. 33-37) 6953
Seamstress 6288
Seatrade Business Review 6985
Seaway Review 6986
Secret Service Agent 2201
"Secret Service Agent" in Action Careers: Employment in the High-Risk Job Market (pp. 211-221) 2143
"Secret Service Agent" in VGM's Careers Encyclopedia (pp. 421-424) 2144
Secretarial Administration & Management 1649
Secretarial Assistant 1622
The Secretarial Handbook on Planning & Organizing Work 1650
Secretarial Office Procedures 1651
Secretarial Practice 1652
Secretarial Practice: Syllabus 1653
Secretarial Procedures for the Automated Office 1654
Secretarial Procedures in the Electronic Office 1655
"Secretarial Science" in College Majors and Careers: A Resource Guide for Effective Life Planning (pp. 119-120) 1581
"Secretarial Science" in The Career Connection II: A Guide to Technical Majors and Their Related Careers (pp. 117-118) 1582
The Secretarial Specialist 1656
Secretarial Stenographer 1623
Secretaries 1628
"Secretaries" in America's 50 Fastest Growing Jobs (pp. 113-116) 1589
"Secretaries" in The American Almanac of Jobs and Salaries (pp. 504-506) 1590
"Secretaries" in Volume 6 of Career Discovery Encyclopedia (pp. 10-11) 1583
"Secretaries" in Volume 3 of The Encyclopedia of Careers and Vocational Guidance (pp. 81-85) 1584
"Secretaries/Administrative Assistants" in Profitable Careers in Nonprofit (pp. 149-151) 1585
"Secretaries and Clerical Personnel" in Opportunities in Real Estate Careers (pp. 117-118) 1586
Secretaries and Stenographers 1587, 1687

Index to Information Sources

"Secretaries and Stenographers" in *Jobs! What They Are...Where They Are...What They Pay* (pp. 211-212) **1588, 1688**
Secretaries, Management & Organizations **1591**
Secretary **1592, 1624**
"Secretary" in *Administration, Business, and Office*, Volume 1 of *Career Information Center* (pp. 94-96) **1593**
Secretary: A Career of Distinction **1594**
"Secretary" in *Careers in Banking and Finance* (pp. 65-66) **1595**
"Secretary" in *Guide to Careers Without College* (pp. 46-49) **1596**
"Secretary" in *Occu-Facts: Information on 565 Careers in Outline Form* (pp. 1.51, 12.2-12.7) **1597**
"Secretary" in *Opportunities in Vocational and Technical Careers* (pp. 45-47) **1598**
"Secretary" in *VGM's Careers Encyclopedia* (pp. 424-427) **1599**
Secretary, Bilingual **1600**
Secretary, Executive **1601**
Secretary, Legal **1602**
Secretary on the Job **1603**
Secretary (Stenography) GS5 **1625**
Secretary, Technical **1604**
Secretary to Paralegal: A Career Manual & Guide **1657**
Secretary/Word Processor **1605**
Secretary... **1606**
The Secretary's Handbook **1658**
The Secretary's Handbook: A Manual for Office Personnel **1659**
Secretary's Problem Solver: Word-for-Word Scripts for Coping with Difficult Situations **1660**
The Secretary's Quick Reference Handbook **1661**
Secrets of Locating Past Due Debtors **747**
"Securities" in *Career Choices for the 90's for Students of Business* (pp. 173-193) **496**
"Securities" in *Career Choices for the 90's for Students of Economics* (pp. 146-167) **497**
"Securities" in *Career Choices for the 90's for Students of M.B.A.* (pp. 176-197) **498**
"Securities" in *Career Choices for the 90's for Students of Mathematics* (pp. 158-179) **499**
"Securities" in *The Encyclopedia of Career Choices for the 1990s: A Guide to Entry Level Jobs* (pp. 784-804) **507**
"Securities and Exchange Commission" in *Career Choices for the 90's for Students of Law* (pp. 23-24) **500**
"Securities and Financial Services Sales Representatives" in *America's 50 Fastest Growing Jobs* (pp. 101-104) **501**
"Securities and Financial Services Sales Representatives" in *Occupational Outlook Handbook* (pp. 238-240) **502**
"Securities and Financial Services Sales Representatives" in Volume 3 of *The Encyclopedia of Careers and Vocational Guidance* (pp. 175-177) **503**
"Securities Broker" in *Administration, Business, and Office*, Volume 1 of *Career Information Center* (pp. 139-141) **504**
"Securities Brokerage" in *How to Get the Hot Jobs in Business & Finance* (pp. 117-130) **505**
"Securities Brokers" in *Jobs! What They Are...Where They Are...What They Pay* (p. 121) **506**
Securities Industry Association **532**
Securities Industry Association Sales and Marketing Conference **559**
Securities Industry Institute **560**
Securities Industry Trends **554**
Securities Regulation Law Journal **555**
"Securities Sales" in *Career Choices for the 90's for Students of Business* (pp. 160-163, 180-182) **508**
"Securities Sales" in *Career Choices for the 90's for Students of Communications and Journalism* (pp. 169 171) **509**
"Securities Sales" in *Career Choices for the 90's for Students of Political Science & Government* (pp. 169-172) **510**
"Securities Sales" in *Career Choices for the 90's for Students of Psychology* (pp. 189-191) **511**
"Securities Sales" in *The Encyclopedia of Career Choices for the 1990s: A Guide to Entry Level Jobs* (pp. 771-774) **513**
"Securities Sales Agents" in *Transitions: Military Pathways to Civilian Careers* (pp. 140-141) **512**
Securities Sales Representatives **514**
"Securities Sales Representatives (Stockbrokers)" in *101 Careers: A Guide to the Fastest-Growing Opportunities* (pp. 32-35) **515**
"Securities Sales Worker (Stockbroker)" in *VGM's Careers Encyclopedia* (pp. 427-429) **516**
"Securities Sales Worker (Stockbroker)" in *VGM's Handbook of Business and Management Careers* (pp. 90-92) **517**
"Securities Salesperson" in *Occu-Facts: Information on 565 Careers in Outline Form* (p. 11.6) **518**
Security Guard **2074**
"Security Guard" in *Public and Community Services*, Volume 11 of *Career Information Center* (pp. 64-66) **2059**
"Security Guards" in *Careers in Law Enforcement and Security* (pp. 81-93) **2060**
"Security Guards" in Volume 6 of *Career Discovery Encyclopedia* (pp. 14-15) **2061**
"Security Guards" in Volume 3 of *The Encyclopedia of Careers and Vocational Guidance* (pp. 308-311) **2062**
Security Industry Association **2069**
Security Industry Association—News **2082**
Security Management **556**
Security Officer **2075**
Security Officers **2063**
"Security Sales Workers and Brokers" in *Opportunities in Financial Careers* (pp. 54-61) **519**
Self-Assessment Questions & Answers for Dental Assistants **2605**
Selling Direct: Choosing the Right Opportunity **449**
Selling Services **594**
Selling Today **3801, 3914, 4132, 6570**
"Semi-Skilled Assemblers" in *Occu-Facts: Information on 565 Careers in Outline Form* (p. 18.26) **5598**
Senior Automotive Mechanic **3872**
Senior Automotive Serviceman **3757**
Senior Boiler Inspector **5685**
Senior Building Guard **2076**
Senior Business Machine Operator **920**
Senior Campus Security Officer **2077**
Senior Capital Police Officer **2202**
Senior Cashier **23**
Senior Clerical Series **51, 1019, 1087, 1111, 1275, 1466, 1717, 1856**
Senior Data Processing Control Clerk **921**
Senior Data Processing Equipment Operator **922**
Senior Deputy Sheriff **2203**
Senior Detective Investigator **2204**
Senior Dog Warden **2798**
Senior File Clerk **1467**
Senior Food Inspector **5686**
Senior Groundskeeper **3067**
Senior Harbormaster **6971**
Senior Incinerator Stationary Engineer **6062**
Senior Inspector, Meat & Poultry **5687**
Senior Legal Stenographer **1718**
Senior Library Clerk **1502**
Senior Mail Clerk **1276**
Senior Meat Cutter **5655**
Senior Meat Inspector **5688**
Senior Menagerie Keeper **2799**
Senior Office Assistant **1088**
Senior Office Stenographer **1719**
Senior Office Worker **1089**
Senior Offset Printing Machine Operator **6249**
Senior Payroll Audit Clerk **1059**
Senior Personnel Clerk **1538**
Senior Photographic Machine Operator **6592**
Senior Real Estate Agent **325**
Senior Real Estate Appraiser **326**
Senior Records Center Assistant **1439**
Senior Secretarial Duties & Office Organization **1662**
Senior Sewage Treatment Plant Operator **6091**
Senior Sewage Treatment Worker **6092**
Senior Stationary Engineer **6063**
Senior Stationary Engineer (Electric) **6064**
Senior Stenographer **1720**
Senior Telephone Operator **1793**
Senior Water Plant Operator **6093**
Senior Water Plant Supervisor **6094**
Sergeants **7173**
Sergeants' Business **7174**
Service Employees International Union **1306, 1324**
Service Management: Principles & Practices **4078**
Service Marketing **595**
Service Reporter **4337**
"Service Sales Representatives" in *America's 50 Fastest Growing Jobs* (pp. 104-106) **596**
"Service Sales Representatives" in Volume 3 of *The Encyclopedia of Careers and Vocational Guidance* (pp. 177-181) **597**
Service Station Attendants **7055**
"Service Station Attendants" in *Opportunities in Automotive Service Careers* (pp. 25-30) **7056**
"Service Station Attendants" in Volume 6 of *Career Discovery Encyclopedia* (pp. 20-21) **7057**
"Service Technician/Customer Service" in *Careers in High Tech* (pp. 65-70) **4065**
Services **3191, 4261**

"Services Sales Representatives" in *Occupational Outlook Handbook* (pp. 240-242) **598**
"Services Sales Representatives" in Volume 6 of *Career Discovery Encyclopedia* (pp. 18-19) **520**
Setting Up & Running Financial Systems **535**
Setup Operators (Machine Shop) **5811, 5845**
Seventh Annual Services Marketing Conference Proceedings: Designing a Winning Service Strategy **621**
SEW Update **1320**
Sewage Plant Operations Supervisor **6095**
Sewage Plant Operator **6096**
Sewage Pump Operator **6097**
Sewage Treatment Operator **6098**
Sewage Treatment Operator Trainee **6099**
Sewage Treatment Plant Supervisor **6100**
Sewage Treatment Worker **6101**
Sewage Treatment Worker Trainee **6102**
Sewer, Drapery **6289**
Sewer, Hand **6290**
Sewing Machine Operator **6291**
"Sewing Machine Operator" in *Occu-Facts: Information on 565 Careers in Outline Form* (p. 18.16) **6292**
Sewing Machine Operators (Apparel) **6293**
SF Newsletter **3636**
SFI Bulletin **3555**
Shadowing & Surveillance: A Complete Guide Book **2255**
Sheet Metal and Air Conditioning Contractors' National Association **5460, 5461**
Sheet Metal and Air-Conditioning Contractors National Association Convention **4345, 5494**
"Sheet Metal Duct Systems for Heating and Air Conditioning..." in *Opportunities in Refrigeration and Air Conditioning Trades* (pp. 71-81) **5445**
Sheet Metal Fabrication **5463**
"Sheet Metal Work" in *Opportunities in Plumbing and Pipefitting Careers* (pp. 79-82) **5446**
Sheet Metal Worker **5447, 5464**
"Sheet Metal Worker" in *Construction*, Volume 4 of *Career Information Center* (pp. 84-85) **5448**
"Sheet Metal Worker" in *Hard Hatted Women: Stories of Struggle and Success in the Trades* (pp. 17-32) **5449**
"Sheet Metal Worker" in *Occu-Facts: Information on 565 Careers in Outline Form* (p. 17.10) **5450**
Sheet Metal Worker Helper **7058**
"Sheet Metal Worker Helper" in *Occu-Facts: Information on 565 Careers in Outline Form* (p. 20.12) **7059**
Sheet Metal Workers **5451**
"Sheet Metal Workers" in *Occupational Outlook Handbook* (pp. 381-383) **5452**
"Sheet Metal Workers" in Volume 6 of *Career Discovery Encyclopedia* (pp. 22-23) **5453**
"Sheet Metal Workers" in Volume 3 of *The Encyclopedia of Careers and Vocational Guidance* (pp. 702-705) **5454**
"Sheet Metal Working" in *Opportunities in Metalworking Careers* (pp. 17-26) **5455**
Shelter Sense **2814**
Shelving & Storage **4722**
Sheriff **2205, 2276**
Sheriff and Police Reporter **2277**
She's a Railroader **6744**
Shipmate **7175**
"Shipping and Receiving Clerk" in *Marketing and Distribution*, Volume 10 of *Career Information Center* (pp. 56-57) **1344**
Shipping and Receiving Clerks **1345**
"Shipping and Receiving Clerks" in Volume 6 of *Career Discovery Encyclopedia* (pp. 24-25) **1346**
"Shipping and Receiving Clerks" in Volume 3 of *The Encyclopedia of Careers and Vocational Guidance* (pp. 85-89) **1347**
Shipping Clerk **1348**
"Shipping Clerk" in *Occu-Facts: Information on 565 Careers in Outline Form* (p. 12.38) **1349**
"Shirt Presser" in *Occu-Facts: Information on 565 Careers in Outline Form* (p. 18.18) **6294**
"Shoe and Leather Workers and Repairers" in *Occupational Outlook Handbook* (pp. 420-421) **6333**
"Shoe and Leather Workers and Repairers" in Volume 3 of *The Encyclopedia of Careers and Vocational Guidance* (pp. 311-313) **6334**
Shoe Industry Workers **6335**
"Shoe Industry Workers" in Volume 6 of *Career Discovery Encyclopedia* (pp. 26-27) **6336**
"Shoe Industry Workers" in Volume 3 of *The Encyclopedia of Careers and Vocational Guidance* (pp. 599-602) **6337**
Shoe Repairer **6338**
"Shoe Repairer" in *Consumer, Homemaking, and Personal Services*, Volume 5 of *Career Information Center* (pp. 59-61) **6339**
"Shoe Repairer" in *Occu-Facts: Information on 565 Careers in Outline Form* (p. 17.20) **6340**
"Shoe Repairer" in *Personal Services* (pp. 63-67) **6341**
Shoe Repairers **6342**
"Shoe Repairers" in *The American Almanac of Jobs and Salaries* (pp. 525-526) **6344**
"Shoe Repairers" in Volume 6 of *Career Discovery Encyclopedia* (pp. 28-29) **6343**
Shoe Salesperson **450**
Shoe Service **6360**
Shooting Sports USA **3556**
Shooting Times **3557**
Shop Clerk **1338**
Shop Savvy **4365**
Shop Talk **3192**
"Short Order Cook" in *Hospitality and Recreation*, Volume 8 of *Career Information Center* (pp. 62-64) **2333**
"Short Order Cook" in *Occu-Facts: Information on 565 Careers in Outline Form* (p. 13.14) **2334**
Shorthand Reporter **1721**
"Shorthand Reporter" in *Administration, Business, and Office*, Volume 1 of *Career Information Center* (pp. 80-82) **1689**
Shovel-Crave Operator, Power **6697**
Show Reporter **6361**
SIA National Industry Survey. **2079**
SIA Washington Report **557**
SIGNAL **7176**
"Signal Mechanics" in Volume 3 of *The Encyclopedia of Careers and Vocational Guidance* (pp. 705-708) **4011**
Signalman's Journal **6789**
Silver Spark Plug Award **4118**
Silver Star for Bravery **2238**
Simple Cooking **2418**
Sipapu **1516**
Skill **5714, 6571**
"Skills Analysis: Secretaries" in *The Black Woman's Career Guide* (pp. 52-56) **1607**
Skin Inc. **2983**
SMACNA Newsletter **5487**
SMACNEWS **5488**
Small Carrier Safety Program **6872**
Small Farm Advocate **3391**
Small Steel Craft: Design, Construction & Maintenance **4494**
Smart Selling: Successful Sales Techniques for Bankers **536**
Smart's Insurance Bulletin **147**
Snips Magazine **4338, 5489**
So You Want to Be a Cop **2145**
So You Want to Be a Success at Selling? **451, 599**
Soap/Cosmetics/Chemical Specialties **2984**
Society for Range Management Annual Conference **3435**
Society of Actuaries Convention **160**
Society of American Foresters National Convention **3657**
Society of Chartered Property and Casualty Underwriters Annual Meeting and Seminar **161**
Society of Collision Repair Specialists **3747, 3812**
Society of Photo-technologists—Journal & Service Notes—Parts and Services Directory Issue **6609**
Society of Plastics Engineers **5849**
Society of Professional Investigators **2164**
Society of Real Estate Appraisers—Briefs **380**
Society Page **148**
SOFFA - Trade Fair for the Butchers' Trade **5670**
Soldering: Instruction and Vocabulary **5940**
Soldier Girls **7125**
Soldier Support Journal **7177**
SOLDIERS **7178**
Soldiers' Scene **7179**
Solidarity **5715, 6572**
Sons of the American Revolution Law Enforcement Commendation Medal **2239**
Sound & Communications Magazine **4024**
Sound Off!: American Military Women Speak Out **7126**
Soundoff! **7180**
South Dakota State Department of Commerce and Regulation • Professional and Occupational License Division **7218**
Southeast Real Estate News **381**
Southeast Travel Professional **702**
Southeastern Hospitality and Foodservice Show **2554**
Southeastern Log **3558, 3637**
Southern and Southwestern Railway Club Proceedings **6790**

Southern Apparel Exhibitors Shows 476
Southern Farm Show 3436
Southern Graphics 6154, 6185, 6223, 6270
Southern Insurance 149, 779
Southern Journal of Applied Forestry 3638
Southern Loggin' Times 3639
Southern Lumberman 3640
Southern Motor Cargo 6898
Southern Nurserymen Association Horticultural Trade Show 3119
Southern Outdoors 3559
Southern Plumbing, Heating, Cooling 4339
Southern Saltwater 3560
Southern Shipper Seafarer Magazine, Inc. 6987
Southwest & Texas Water Works Journal 6116
Southwest Contractor 4760, 6046, 6712
Southwest Farm Press 3392
Southwest Real Estate News 382
Southwest Trucking Show 6924
The Southwestern Sportsman Magazine 3561
The SPEC-DATA Program 4667, 4761, 4949, 5236, 5411
Special Achievement Awards 2240
Special Agent 2206
Special Agent, Department of Justice 2207
Special Agent FBI 2208
Special Agent (INS) 2209
Special Agent (Wildlife) 2210
Special Care in Dentistry 2632
Special Electrical License 4997
"Special Service Bus Driver" in *Transportation*, Volume 12 of *Career Information Center* (pp. 83-85) 6637
Specialty Lab Update 6621
Spectra 5757
The Speculator 1449
SPFE Newsletter 6622
Spokesman 3393
Sport Fishing 3562
Sport Fishing Institute 3476
SPORTING CLASSICS 3563
"Sporting Goods Salesperson" in *Career Opportunities in the Sports Industry* (pp. 178-180) 452
"Spray Painter (Production)" in *Occu-Facts: Information on 565 Careers in Outline Form* (p. 18.12) 6553
"Sprinkler Fitter" in *Hard Hatted Women: Stories of Struggle and Success in the Trades* (pp. 143-149) 5265
"Sprinkler Fitting" in *Opportunities in Plumbing and Pipefitting Careers* (pp. 85-88) 5266
Sprinkler Quarterly 2028
Sprinkler Technotes 2029
Sprint: A Power User's Guide 1867
SPRINT Simplified 1868
The SRA Appraiser 309
Stamp of Approval 5812
Standard for Safety for Roof Trusses for Manufactured Homes 5417
Standardized Textbook of Barbering and Styling 2848
Standardized Textbook of Barbering and Styling. 2971
Standards for Selection of Truck Fleet Personnel: A Guide for Hiring Professional Drivers & Other Employees in the Trucking Industry 6812
Staple Yarn Production 6365
Star Agribusinessman of America Award 3276
Star Farmer of America 3277
Starting & Building Your Own Accounting Business 1006
Starting You Own Secretarial Business 1608
State Barber Laws 2840
State Board Review Examinations In Cosmetology 2962
State Police Dispatcher 1299
State Police/Highway Patrol Officer 2146
"State Police/Highway Patrol Officer" in *Occu-Facts: Information on 565 Careers in Outline Form* (p. 13.8) 2147
"State Police Officer" in *Public and Community Services*, Volume 11 of *Career Information Center* (pp. 66-67) 2148
"State Police Officer" in *VGM's Careers Encyclopedia* (pp. 364-366) 2149
"State Police Officers" in Volume 6 of *Career Discovery Encyclopedia* (pp. 58-59) 2150
"State Police Officers" in Volume 3 of *The Encyclopedia of Careers and Vocational Guidance* (pp. 316-320) 2151
State Trooper 2152, 2211
State Trooper/Highway Patrol Officer/State Traffic Officer 2212
Stationary Engineer 6050, 6065
"Stationary Engineer" in *Hard Hatted Women: Stories of Struggle and Success in the Trades* (pp. 37-44) 6051

"Stationary Engineer" in *Manufacturing*, Volume 9 of *Career Information Center* (pp. 70-72) 6052
"Stationary Engineer" in *Occu-Facts: Information on 565 Careers in Outline Form* (p. 17.32) 6053
Stationary Engineer (Electric) 6066
Stationary Engineer, High Pressure Boiler Operating Engineer, High Pressure Plant Tender 6030, 6067
"Stationary Engineers" in *Occupational Outlook Handbook* (pp. 407-408) 6054
"Stationary Engineers" in Volume 3 of *The Encyclopedia of Careers and Vocational Guidance* (pp. 777-780) 6055
Steel Digest 5882
"Steel Workers" in *Occupational Outlook Handbook* (pp. 399-400) 5875
Steelabor 5716, 5883
Steelworker Old Time 5717, 5884
Steering Wheel 6661, 6899
Stenographer 1690, 1722, 1734
"Stenographer and Transcriber" in *Administration, Business, and Office*, Volume 1 of *Career Information Center* (pp. 69-70) 1691
Stenographer (Law) 1723
Stenographer-Secretary 1724
Stenographer-Typist 1725
Stenographer-Typist GS5-7 1726
Stenographer-Typist GS1-4 1727
"Stenographers" in *Occupational Outlook Handbook* (pp. 278-279) 1692
"Stenographers" in Volume 6 of *Career Discovery Encyclopedia* (pp. 62-63) 1693
"Stenographers" in Volume 3 of *The Encyclopedia of Careers and Vocational Guidance* (pp. 92-95) 1694
Stenographic/Secretarial Associate 1728
Stenographic Secretary 1729
Stenographic Specialist 1730
Step-by-Step Bookkeeping 1043, 1044
"Stevedores" in Volume 6 of *Career Discovery Encyclopedia* (pp. 64-65) 7060
"Stevedoring Occupations" in Volume 3 of *The Encyclopedia of Careers and Vocational Guidance* (pp. 783-786) 7061
Stew Leonard's: Creating the Customer's Dream 3254
Stock Clerk 1328, 1339
"Stock Clerk" in *Marketing and Distribution*, Volume 10 of *Career Information Center* (pp. 58-59) 1329
"Stock Clerk" in *Occu-Facts: Information on 565 Careers in Outline Form* (p. 12.39) 1330
Stock Clerks 1331
"Stock Clerks" in *Occupational Outlook Handbook* (pp. 266-267) 1332
"Stock Clerks" in Volume 6 of *Career Discovery Encyclopedia* (pp. 68-69) 1333
"Stock Clerks" in Volume 3 of *The Encyclopedia of Careers and Vocational Guidance* (pp. 95-99) 1334
Stockbroker 521
"Stockbroker" in *College Board Guide to Jobs and Career Planning* (pp. 142-144) 522
"Stockbroker" in *Top Professions: The 100 Most Popular, Dynamic, and Profitable Careers in America Today* (pp. 1-3) 523
"Stockbrokers" in *The New York Times Career Planner* (pp. 308-310) 524
"Stockbrokers" in Volume 6 of *Career Discovery Encyclopedia* (pp. 66-67) 525
Stockman 7068
The Stockman Grass Farmer 3394
Stockroom Worker 1282
Stone Review 4668
Stone Through the Ages 4669
Stone World 4670
Stonemason 4609
"Stonemason" in *Construction*, Volume 4 of *Career Information Center* (pp. 85-87) 4610
"Stonemason" in *Exploring Nontraditional Jobs for Women* (pp. 11-16) 4611
"Stonemason" in *Occu-Facts: Information on 565 Careers in Outline Form* (p. 16.4) 4612
"Stonemasons" in *Opportunities in Building Construction Trades* (pp. 70-72) 4613
Store Detective 2064
Stores Clerk 52
STORES Magazine 472
Strategic Review 7181
Strategic Trends in Services: An Inquiry into the Global Service Economy 609
Streamlined Bookkeeping for Multi-Level Marketing 1045

Stress Management for Correctional Officers & Their Families **1912**
STRINGS **4543**
"Structural and Reinforcing Ironworkers" in *Occupational Outlook Handbook* (pp. 383-384) **5503**
Structural Design & Crashworthiness of Automobiles **3776**
"Structural Steel Workers" in Volume 3 of *The Encyclopedia of Careers and Vocational Guidance* (pp. 708-711) **5504**
Structural Welder **5964**
Structure Maintainer (Groups A-H) **4253**
Structure Maintainer Trainee (Groups A-H) **4254**
A Study of Some Aspects of Satisfaction in the Vocation of Stenography **1695**
Stumpage Prices for Sawtimber Sold from National Forests **3641**
Subject Headings for Real Estate **393**
"Subway Conductor" in *Hard Hatted Women: Stories of Struggle and Success in the Trades* (pp. 193-201) **6745**
Successful Nurse Aide Management in Nursing Homes **2745**
Successful Private Eyes & Private Spies: Private Spies **2288**
The Successful Secretary's Handbook **1663**
Successful Strategies for Manufacturing Management **5614**
Successfully Managing Your Accounting Career **974, 1046**
The Sugar Producer **3395**
Suggestive Selling for Waiters and Waitresses **2474**
Summary of Size & Weight Limits **6873**
Sun Belt Floor Covering **4806**
The Sunflower **3396**
Super Automotive Service **3915**
Super Van Operator of the Year **6852**
SuperCourse for Real Estate Licensing **327**
Supermarket Cashier **14**
Supervising Cashier **24**
Supervision **869, 5628**
Supervisors' Guide to Successful Training **3182**
Supervisory Management **870, 5629**
Supervisory Planning and Control **5615**
Supervisory Sense **871, 5630**
Supply House Times **237, 473, 1284, 1880, 4340, 5331**
Supply Post **3642**
Surface Warfare Magazine **7182**
"Surveyor Helpers" in *Occu-Facts: Information on 565 Careers in Outline Form* (p. 20.10) **7062**
"Surveyor's Helper" in *Construction*, Volume 4 of *Career Information Center* (pp. 87-88) **7063**
Survival Thinking: For Police & Corrections Officers **1913**
Surviving in Corrections: A Guide for Corrections Professionals **1914**
Switchboard Operators **1772**
"Switchboard Operators" in Volume 6 of *Career Discovery Encyclopedia* (pp. 84-85) **1773**
"Switchboard Operators" in Volume 3 of *The Encyclopedia of Careers and Vocational Guidance* (pp. 99-103) **1774**

T

Table Attendant Training **2475**
Tailors **6295, 6296**
"Tailors" in *Occu-Facts: Information on 565 Careers in Outline Form* (p. 17.18) **6297**
Take this Job and Love It! **453**
"Tall Ship Crew Member" in *Offbeat Careers: The Directory of Unusual Work* (pp. 161-162) **6954**
"Tap and Die Maker Technicians" in Volume 4 of *The Encyclopedia of Careers and Vocational Guidance* (pp. 259-260) **5910**
Tarheel Wheels' Magazine **6900**
Tax Briefs from SIA **558**
"Taxi Dispatcher" in *Travel & Tourism* (pp. 45-49) **1300**
TCMA Bulletin **1429**
Teach Yourself Bookkeeping **1007**
Teacher Aide **1743**
"Teacher Aide" in *Occu-Facts: Information on 565 Careers in Outline Form* (p. 10.30) **1744**
The Teacher Aide in the Instructional Team **1759**
"Teacher Aides" in *Jobs! What They Are...Where They Are...What They Pay* (pp. 88-89) **1745**
"Teacher Aides" in *Occupational Outlook Handbook* (pp. 279-280) **1746**
"Teacher Aides" in *Opportunities in Child Care Careers* (pp. 59-61) **1747**
"Teacher Aides" in *Opportunities in Teaching Careers* (pp. 37-38) **1748**
"Teacher Aides" in Volume 6 of *Career Discovery Encyclopedia* (pp. 94-95) **1749**
"Teacher Aides" in Volume 3 of *The Encyclopedia of Careers and Vocational Guidance* (pp. 107-110) **1750**

"Teacher's Aide" in *Public and Community Services*, Volume 11 of *Career Information Center* (pp. 82-84) **1751**
Teachers Aides **1752**
"Teachers Aides and School Bus Drivers" in *The American Almanac of Jobs and Salaries* (pp. 109-110) **1753, 6638**
Teaching Assistant **1756**
Tech Center News **3802, 3916**
Technical/Manufacturing Cluster One **5456, 5941**
Technical Secretary: Terminology & Transcription **1664**
Technical Woodworking **6463**
Technicalities **1517**
TECHNICOM **4544**
TechniCom **4545**
Technique of Systems & Procedures **1097**
Technology Watch **6155, 6186, 6224, 6271**
Technometrics **5695**
"Tel-a-marketing" in *Careers in Trucking* (p. 39) **1146**
Telecom Market Review and Forecast **4575**
Telecommunication Officer of the Year **1313**
Telecommunications Reports **4025, 4426, 4568**
"Telecommunications Technicians" in Volume 4 of *The Encyclopedia of Careers and Vocational Guidance* (pp. 103-104) **4012**
"Telecommunications Technicians" in Volume 6 of *Career Discovery Encyclopedia* (pp. 98-99) **4013**
"Telecommunications Technology" in *The Career Connection II: A Guide to Technical Majors and Their Related Careers* (pp. 123-124) **4014**
Telegraph & Data Transmission over Shortwave Radio Links: Fundamental Principles & Networks **1803**
Telemarketer **1147, 1148**
"Telemarketer" in *Occu-Facts: Information on 565 Careers in Outline Form* (p. 11.26) **1149**
"Telemarketers" in Volume 6 of *Career Discovery Encyclopedia* (pp. 100-101) **1150**
"Telemarketers" in Volume 3 of *The Encyclopedia of Careers and Vocational Guidance* (pp. 110-114) **1151**
Telemarketing **1799**
"Telemarketing" in *Careers in Marketing* (pp. 57-58) **1152**
"Telemarketing" in *Opportunities in Telecommunications Careers* (pp. 35-46) **1153**
"Telemarketing Specialist" in *Marketing and Distribution*, Volume 10 of *Career Information Center* (pp. 61-62) **1154**
"Telemarketing: The Fast-Track Medium" in *Marketing and Sales Career Directory* (pp. 68-72) **1155**
"Telephone and PBX Installers and Repairers" in Volume 3 of *The Encyclopedia of Careers and Vocational Guidance* (pp. 715-718) **4015**
"Telephone and PBX Operator" in *Telecommunications* (pp. 15-19) **1775**
Telephone Answering Service Operator **1776**
Telephone Cable Splicing Technician **4409**
"Telephone Central Office Technician" in *Communications and the Arts*, Volume 3 of *Career Information Center* (pp. 71-73) **4016**
"Telephone Central Office Technician" in *Telecommunications* (pp. 39-43) **4017**
"Telephone Installer" in *Exploring Nontraditional Jobs for Women* (pp. 43-48) **4552**
"Telephone Installer" in *Occu-Facts: Information on 565 Careers in Outline Form* (p. 15.16) **4553**
Telephone Installer/Repair Technician **4554**
"Telephone Installers and Repairers" in *Occupational Outlook Handbook* (pp. 358-360) **4555**
"Telephone Installers and Repairers" in Volume 6 of *Career Discovery Encyclopedia* (pp. 102-103) **4556**
Telephone Line Installers and Cable Splicers **4410**
"Telephone Line Installers and Cable Splicers" in *Occu-Facts: Information on 565 Careers in Outline Form* (p. 15.15) **4411**
"Telephone Line Worker and Cable Splicer" in *Communications and the Arts*, Volume 3 of *Career Information Center* (pp. 73-75) **4412**
"Telephone Line Worker and Cable Splicer" in *Telecommunications* (pp. 33-37) **4413**
Telephone Manners **1185, 1609, 1777**
Telephone News **1800, 4026, 4427, 4569**
Telephone Operator **1778, 1794**
"Telephone Operator" in *Communications and the Arts*, Volume 3 of *Career Information Center* (pp. 75-77) **1779**
"Telephone Operators" in *Jobs! What They Are...Where They Are...What They Pay* (pp. 212-213) **1780**
"Telephone Operators" in Volume 6 of *Career Discovery Encyclopedia* (pp. 104-105) **1781**
"Telephone Operators" in Volume 3 of *The Encyclopedia of Careers and Vocational Guidance* (pp. 115-118) **1782**
Telephone Operators (Central Office) **1783**

Index to Information Sources

"Telephone Service Technician" in *Communications and the Arts*, Volume 3 of *Career Information Center* (pp. 79-80)   **4557**
"Telephone Service Technician" in *Telecommunications* (pp. 27-31)   **4558**
Telephone Solicitors (Telemarketers)   **1156**
Telephone Systems Installer   **4559**
"Telephone, Telegraph, and Teletype Operators" in *Occupational Outlook Handbook* (pp. 280-282)   **1784**
Teletimes   **1801, 4027, 4428, 4570**
Teletypist   **1795**
"Television Advertising Representative" in *Career Opportunities in Advertising and Public Relations* (pp. 137-139)   **600**
"Television Advertising Sales Assistant" in *Career Opportunities in Advertising and Public Relations* (pp. 140-142)   **601**
"Television and Radio Service Technician" in *Communications and the Arts*, Volume 3 of *Career Information Center* (pp. 80-82)   **4154**
"Television and Radio Service Technician" in *VGM's Careers Encyclopedia* (pp. 460-462)   **4155**
Television Repairer   **4156**
Teller Operations Manual   **806**
Teller Performance   **807**
Teller World   **808**
"Tellers and Clerks (Bank)" in *The American Almanac of Jobs and Salaries* (pp. 415-417)   **795**
Tellers, Financial Institution   **796**
Tellers—How Important Are They?   **797**
Tennessee State Department of Commerce and Insurance • Regulatory Boards   **7219**
Tentative Standard for Proctective Clothing for Fire Fighters   **2006**
Test Practice Book for 100 Civil Service Jobs   **1417**
"Texas Ranger" in *Offbeat Careers: The Directory of Unusual Work* (pp. 165-166)   **2153**
Texas State Department of Licensing and Regulation   **7220**
Textbook for Nursing Assistants   **2746**
Textile Chemist and Colorist   **6387**
Textile Hi-Lights   **6388**
"Textile Industry" in *Manufacturing*, Volume 9 of *Career Information Center* (pp. 142-144)   **6366**
"Textile Machinery Operators" in *Occupational Outlook Handbook* (pp. 421-424)   **6367**
"Textile Manufacturing Occupations" in Volume 3 of *The Encyclopedia of Careers and Vocational Guidance* (pp. 557-561)   **6368**
Textile Mill Worker   **6369**
Textile Production Workers   **6370**
Textile Research Journal   **6389**
Textile Technology Digest   **6390**
Textile Trends   **6391**
"Textile Workers" in Volume 6 of *Career Discovery Encyclopedia* (pp. 110-111)   **6371**
Textile World   **6392**
"Textiles" in Volume 1 of *The Encyclopedia of Careers and Vocational Guidance* (pp. 465-471)   **6372**
There's a New "Challenge in Agriculture"   **3255**
Third Class Mail Association   **1388**
Thomas Register's Office Automation Buyer's Guide   **852, 923, 1665**
Thruput: The ABA Operations/Automation News Report   **828, 1168**
Ticket Agent   **1231**
"Ticket Agent" in *Opportunities in Airline Careers* (pp. 67-68)   **1221**
Ticket Agents   **1222**
"Ticket Agents, Reservation Agents, and Clerks" in *Opportunities in Travel Careers* (p. 40-42)   **1223**
TIG & Related Processes in Welding Automation   **5982**
Tile and Decorative Surfaces   **5580**
Tile Contractors' Association of America—Products and Materials Guide   **5558**
Tile Setter   **5550**
"Tilesetters" in *Occupational Outlook Handbook* (pp. 384-385)   **5551**
TIMBER   **3658**
Timber & the Forest Service   **3589**
"Timber Cutting and Logging Workers" in *Occupational Outlook Handbook* (pp. 323-325)   **3590**
Timber Cutting Practices   **3600**
Timber Designer's Manual   **3601**
Timber Equipment Trader   **3643**
Timber Harvesting   **3644**
Timber: Its Nature & Behavior   **3602**
Timber: Its Structure, Properties & Utilization   **3603**
Timber Management: A Quantitative Approach   **3604**
Timber Mart-South   **3645**
Timber!: Problems, Prospects, Policies   **3605**
The Timber Producer   **3646**
Timber Producers Association of Michigan and Wisconsin   **3593**

Timber Resources for America's Future: Forest Resource Report No. 14   **3606**
Timber Specifier's Guide: Understanding & Specifying Softwoods in Buildings   **3607**
Timber Supply: Issues & Options   **3608**
Timber West   **3647**
Timbers of the New World   **3660**
Times-Plain Dealer   **3397**
Today's Fireman   **2030**
Today's Policeman   **2278**
Tony's Food Service Scholarships   **2497**
"Tool and Die Design" in *The Career Connection II: A Guide to Technical Majors and Their Related Careers* (pp. 125-126)   **5911**
Tool and Die Maker   **5912**
"Tool and Die Maker" in *Manufacturing*, Volume 9 of *Career Information Center* (pp. 72-74)   **5913**
"Tool and Die Maker" in *Occu-Facts: Information on 565 Careers in Outline Form* (p. 17.1)   **5914**
"Tool and Die Maker" in *VGM's Careers Encyclopedia* (pp. 462-464)   **5915**
"Tool and Die Makers" in *Jobs! What They Are...Where They Are...What They Pay* (pp. 180-181)   **5916**
"Tool and Die Makers" in *Occupational Outlook Handbook* (pp. 402-404)   **5917**
"Tool and Die Makers" in Volume 6 of *Career Discovery Encyclopedia* (pp. 120-121)   **5918**
"Tool Design Technician" in *Occu-Facts: Information on 565 Careers in Outline Form* (p. 2.21)   **5919**
"Tool Makers and Die Setters" in Volume 3 of *The Encyclopedia of Careers and Vocational Guidance* (pp. 561-564)   **5920**
The Tooling and Manufacturing Association   **5786, 5818, 5850, 5877, 5897, 5925**
Tooling and Manufacturing Association—Purchasing Guide   **5901, 5929**
Toolmakers and Diemakers   **5921**
Tools—Cutting   **5983**
Tools—Cutting Directory   **5984**
Tools for the Electrical Trades   **3938, 4157**
Top Farmer Intelligence   **3398**
Top Farmer Market Insight   **3399**
Top Job Award   **7071**
Top Secret! Codes to Crack   **2256**
Top Shelf: Barkeeping at Its Best   **2538**
Total Auto Body Repair   **3777**
Tour & Travel News   **1251**
"Tour Bus Driver" in *Travel & Tourism* (pp. 35-37)   **6639**
TOURISME   **1252**
"Tow Truck Operator" in *Occu-Facts: Information on 565 Careers in Outline Form* (p. 19.4)   **6813**
"Tow Truck Operator" in *Transportation*, Volume 12 of *Career Information Center* (pp. 87-88)   **6814**
Track Equipment Maintainer   **6759**
Trackman   **6760**
Tractor Equipment & Parts Directory   **4227**
Tractor Operator   **6841**
Tractor-Trailer Operator   **6842**
Trade Fair for Joining and Welding Technology   **5999**
"Trader" in *Careers in Banking and Finance* (pp. 67-72)   **526**
"Traders" in *The American Almanac of Jobs and Salaries* (pp. 421-422)   **527**
"Traders: Dealing With Uncertainty" in *Getting Into Money: A Career Guide* (pp. 74-90)   **528**
Traders: the Jobs, the Products, the Markets   **529**
"Traffic Agents and Clerks" in Volume 6 of *Career Discovery Encyclopedia* (pp. 128-129)   **1350**
"Traffic Agents and Clerks" in Volume 3 of *The Encyclopedia of Careers and Vocational Guidance* (pp. 121-124)   **1351**
Traffic Patrol Officer   **2154**
"Traffic, Shipping, and Receiving Clerks" in *Occupational Outlook Handbook* (pp. 267-268)   **1352**
Traffic Signal Manual of Installation and Maintenance Procedures   **1316**
Traffic World   **6662, 6791, 6901, 6988**
Train Dispatcher   **1312, 6761**
Train Operator   **6762**
Trainer's Workshop   **872, 5631**
Training Programs for Health Care Workers: Food Service Workers   **2502**
Training Reports & Records   **2007**
Trainmaster   **6763**
Trains   **6792**
Transcriber   **1696**
Transit Fact Book   **6669**
Transitions: Military Pathways to Civilian Careers   **7127**

1125

"Transmission and Distribution Occupations" in Volume 3 of *The Encyclopedia of Careers and Vocational Guidance* (pp. 790-793) **6018**
Transport Fleet News **6902**
Transport Routier **6903**
Transport 2000 and Intermodal World **6793, 6904, 6989**
Transportation **3468, 3738, 6698, 6815**
Transportation: An Abstract Newsletter **6794, 6905, 6990**
Transportation & Distribution **6795, 6906, 6991**
Transportation Business **6663, 6796, 6907, 6992**
Transportation Man of the Year **6651, 6768, 6853, 6973**
Transportation/Mechanical Cluster **3739, 3846, 6816**
Transportation Quarterly **6664, 6797, 6908, 6993**
TransTechnical News **3803, 3917, 6573**
The Trapper **3564**
The Trapper and Predator Caller **3565**
The Trapper's Bible: Traps, Snares, & Pathguards **3488**
Trapper's Handbook **3489**
Traps Today, **3490**
"Travel Agencies" in *Opportunities in Travel Careers* (pp. 77-90) **630**
Travel Agency Communications Reports—North American Edition **677**
Travel Agent **631, 632, 633**
"Travel Agent" in *College Board Guide to Jobs and Career Planning* (pp. 144-146) **634**
"Travel Agent" in *Guide to Careers Without College* (pp. 25-26) **635**
"Travel Agent" in *Hospitality and Recreation*, Volume 8 of *Career Information Center* (pp. 118-122) **636**
"Travel Agent" in *Occu-Facts: Information on 565 Careers in Outline Form* (p. 11.28) **637**
"Travel Agent" in *Opportunities in Vocational and Technical Careers* (pp. 59-61) **638**
"Travel Agent" in *Top Professions: The 100 Most Popular, Dynamic, and Profitable Careers in America Today* (pp. 57-59) **639**
"Travel Agent" in *Travel & Tourism* (pp. 27-31) **640**
"Travel Agent" in *VGM's Careers Encyclopedia* (pp. 468-470) **641**
"Travel Agent" in *VGM's Handbook of Business and Management Careers* (pp. 97-99) **642**
The Travel Agent: Dealer in Dreams **643**
Travel Agent—Domestic Tour Manual Issue **678**
Travel Agent—Focus 500 Directory Issue **666**
Travel Agent Magazine **1253**
Travel Agents **644, 664**
"Travel Agents" in *America's 50 Fastest Growing Jobs* (pp. 106-107) **650**
"Travel Agents" in *Jobs! What They Are...Where They Are...What They Pay* (pp. 171-172) **645**
"Travel Agents" in *101 Careers: A Guide to the Fastest-Growing Opportunities* (pp. 319-322) **646**
"Travel Agents" in *The American Almanac of Jobs and Salaries* (pp. 554-556) **647**
"Travel Agents" in Volume 6 of *Career Discovery Encyclopedia* (pp. 130-131) **648**
"Travel Agents" in Volume 3 of *The Encyclopedia of Careers and Vocational Guidance* (pp. 185-189) **649**
"Travel Agents: Plotters of Unforgettable Trips" in *Careers for Women Without College Degrees* (pp. 234-238) **651**
"Travel and Tourism" in *The Career Connection II: A Guide to Technical Majors and Their Related Careers* (pp. 129-130) **652**
Travel and Tourism Research and Marketing Directory **679**
Travel & Vacation Discount Guide **680**
Travel Career Development **653, 1224**
"The Travel Consultant" in *The Travel Agent: Dealer in Dreams* (pp. 13-24) **654**
Travel Courier East **1254**
Travel Digest **1255**
Travel Free: How to Start and Succeed in Your Own Travel Consultant Business **655, 1225**
Travel Industry Association of America—International Travel News Directory **681**
Travel Industry Career Directory **656, 1226**
Travel Industry Guidelines for Employment **657, 1227**
Travel Industry Honors **703**
Travel Industry—Trade Show Directory **713**
Travel News **1256**
Travel People Magazine **1257**
Travel Trade **1258**
Travel Trainers Network **704**
Travel Training Workbook, 1991. Section 1: Introduction to Travel & Geography **658**
Travel Training Workbook, 1991, Section 1: Introduction to Travel & Geography **1228**
Travel Weekly **1259**

"Traveling Secretary/Professional Sports Team" in *Career Opportunities in the Sports Industry* (pp. 43-45) **1610**
Treatment Custody Role Conflict in Community Based Correctional Workers: Causes & Effects **1924**
Tree Farmer **3400**
Trends and Forecasts **4370**
Trends and Techniques **6512**
Tri-State Industrial Show **5801, 5836, 5904, 5934, 6000**
Tri-State Restaurant Food and Equipment Show **2555**
Trim Carpentry Techniques: Installing Doors, Windows, Base & Crown **4723**
Triumph of Agriculture Exposition Farm and Ranch Machinery Show **3437**
Troubleshooting & Repairing Power Tools **4366**
Troubleshooting & Repairing TVRO Systems **4079**
Troubleshooting Electronics Equipment Without Service Data **3975**
The Trowel Trades **4614, 4828, 5199, 5552**
"Truck and Bus Dispatcher" in *Transportation*, Volume 12 of *Career Information Center* (pp. 116-118) **1301**
Truck Driver **6817, 6843**
"Truck Driver" in *Hard Hatted Women: Stories of Struggle and Success in the Trades* (pp. 225-234) **6818**
"Truck Driver" in *Transportation* (pp. 21-25) **6819**
"Truck Driver" in *VGM's Careers Encyclopedia* (pp. 471-474) **6820**
Truck Drivers **6821**
"Truck Drivers" in *Jobs! What They Are...Where They Are...What They Pay* (pp. 181-182) **6822**
"Truck Drivers" in *Opportunities in Vocational and Technical Careers* (pp. 79-80) **6823**
"Truck Drivers" in Volume 6 of *Career Discovery Encyclopedia* (pp. 132-133) **6824**
Truck Driver's Guide to Commercial Driver Licensing **6844**
"Truck Driving" in *The Career Connection II: A Guide to Technical Majors and Their Related Careers* (pp. 131-132) **6825**
Truck-Frame and Axle Repair Association **4106**
The Truck Logger **3648**
Truck Operator, Industrial **6699**
Truck Paper **6909**
Truck Parts & Service **6910**
Truck World **6911**
"Truckdrivers" in *Occupational Outlook Handbook* (pp. 440-442) **6826**
Trucker **6827**
Truckers Atlas **6874**
Trucking Permit Guide, 1G: Private, Contract, Common, Exempt **6875**
TRUCKS Magazine **6912**
Trucksource: Sources of Trucking Industry Information **6828**
Trust Letter **829, 1169**
Trust Management Update: A Trust Industry Communication on Management, Investments, Marketing, Operations, and Administration **830, 1170**
Tugboat Mate **6955**
"Tuner/Technician" in *Opportunities in Music Careers* (pp. 134-135) **4517**
Turf News **3401**
The Turkey Hunter **3566**
Turn Out **2031**
TWU Express **6798, 6913, 6994**
Type and Press **6225, 6272**
Typesetters **6162**
"Typesetters" in Volume 6 of *Career Discovery Encyclopedia* (pp. 134-135) **6163**
Typesetting **6164**
Typist **1829**
"Typist" in *Occu-Facts: Information on 565 Careers in Outline Form* (p. 12.10, 12.11) **1830**
"Typist and Word Processors" in *Careers in Banking and Finance* (p. 73) **1831**
"Typists" in *Opportunities in Vocational and Technical Careers* (pp. 44-45) **1832**
"Typists" in Volume 6 of *Career Discovery Encyclopedia* (pp. 136-137) **1833**
"Typists and Word Processor Operators" in *Jobs! What They Are...Where They Are...What They Pay* (pp. 213-214) **1834**
"Typists and Word Processors" in Volume 3 of *The Encyclopedia of Careers and Vocational Guidance* (pp. 124-129) **1835**
"Typists, Word Processors, and Data Entry Keyers" in *Occupational Outlook Handbook* (pp. 282-284) **1836**
The Typographer **6187**

U

U.A. Journal **5332**

Index to Information Sources

UAMR Confidential Bulletin   238
UAMR Newsletter   239
UFAC: Important Consumer Safety Information from UFAC   6930
UFAC Volunteer   6429
UFCW Action   26, 55, 5659
UFCW Leadership Update   27, 56, 5660
Undercar Digest   3918
Undercover Work: A Complete Handbook   2257
Understanding the Lending Process   950, 970
Uniform Program for Reciprocity: Operators   6084
Union   1321
Union Farmer   3402
United Association of Journeymen and Apprentices of the Plumbing and Pipe Fitting Industry of the U.S. and Canada   5274, 5345
United Brotherhood of Carpenters and Joiners of America   4706, 4770, 4912, 5556
United Caprine News   3403
United Food and Commercial Workers International Union   16, 28, 50, 57, 5651
United Fresh Fruit and Vegetable Association Annual Convention and Exposition   3438
"United States Customs Service" in *Opportunities in Transportation Careers* (pp. 130-132)   2155
United States Naval Institute   7135
"United States Navy" in *Opportunities in Marine and Maritime Careers* (pp. 85-97)   7128
United States Telephone Association   1787, 4020, 4417, 4561
United Steelworkers of America   5708, 5878, 5886
United Union of Roofers, Waterproofers and Allied Workers   5362, 5415
Upholstered Furniture Action Council   6414
Upholsterer, Furniture   6407
"Upholsterers" in *Occupational Outlook Handbook* (pp. 424-425)   6408
Upholsterers (Furniture)   6409
Upholsterers' Supplies Directory   6422
Upholstering   6423
Upholstering Methods   6424
Upholstering Today   6430, 6431
Upholstery   6425
The Upholstery Fact Book 1986   6434
Upholstery Manufacturing Management   6432
Upholstery Styles: A Design Sourcebook   6426
Upholstery Techniques Illustrated   6427
Upper Midwest Electrical Trade Show   5040
Upper Midwest Hospitality, Restaurant, and Lodging Show   2556
U.S. Coast Guard • Merchant Vessel Personnel Division   3478
U.S. Farm News   3404
U.S. Glass, Metal and Glazing—Directory of Suppliers of Machinery & Equipment Issue   5061, 5823
U.S. Glass, Metal and Glazing—Directory of Suppliers of Sealants & Glazing Systems Issue   5062
"U.S. Navy Officer" in *Careers for Number Lovers* (pp. 55-57)   7129
U.S. Special Agent   2156
USA/Canada Nails Festival   3004
Utah State Department of Business Regulation • Division of Occupational and Professional Licensing   7221
"Utility Switch Operator" in *Hard Hatted Women: Stories of Struggle and Success in the Trades* (pp. 150-155)   6019
Utility Workers Union of America   6025
UTU News   6665, 6799

V

Vacuum Cleaners Supplies & Parts Directory   3183
Vacuum Cleaning Systems Directory   3184
Valuation Journal   383
Vanishing Forest Reserves   3609
The Vealer   3405
Vegetables and Specialties Situation and Outlook Report   3406
Vehicle Body Building One   3778
Vehicle Body Building Two   3779
Vehicle Leasing Agent   48
Vending Machine Mechanic   4577
"Vending Machine Mechanic" in *Occu-Facts: Information on 565 Careers in Outline Form* (p. 15.31)   4578
"Vending Machine Mechanics" in Volume 6 of *Career Discovery Encyclopedia* (pp. 144-145)   4579
"Vending Machine Mechanics" in Volume 3 of *The Encyclopedia of Careers and Vocational Guidance* (pp. 565-568)   4580
Vending Machine Repairers   4581
Vending Machine Route Driver   4582

"Vending Machine Route Worker" in *Marketing and Distribution*, Volume 10 of *Career Information Center* (pp. 62-63)   4583
Vending Machine Route Workers   4584
"Vending Machine Route Workers" in *Occu-Facts: Information on 565 Careers in Outline Form* (p. 19.8)   4585
"Vending Machine Servicers and Repairers" in *Occupational Outlook Handbook* (pp. 360-361)   4586
Vermont Secretary of State • Division of Licensing and Registration   7222
The Vertical File & Its Satellites: A Handbook of Acquisition, Processing, & Organization   1485
Vertical Milling Machine Explained   5813
Vertical Transportation: Elevators & Escalators   4209
Veterinary Technician   2815
"Veterinary Technician" in *Careers for Animal Lovers and Other Zoological Types* (pp. 15-17)   2781
"Veterinary Technician" in *Careers in Veterinary Medicine* (pp. 103-108)   2782
"Veterinary Technicians and Assistants" in *Jobs! What They Are. . .Where They Are. . .What They Pay* (p. 47)   2783
VFW J. Edgar Hoover Award   2241
Video Career Library - Allied Health Fields   6495
Video Career Library - Clerical & Administrative Support   15, 748, 798, 1008, 1186, 1380, 1611, 1697, 1785, 1837
Video Career Library - Construction   4441, 4615, 4700, 4907, 4985, 5095, 5147, 5267, 5505, 5553
Video Career Library - Education   1754
Video Career Library - Marketing and Sales   100, 199, 301, 454, 602, 1229
Video Career Library - Mechanical Fields   3683, 3740, 3847, 4098, 4287, 4452
Video Career Library - Production I   6020, 6056, 6074, 6138, 6165, 6204, 6243, 6298, 6410
Video Career Library - Production II   5457, 5599, 5782, 5814, 5846, 5922, 5942, 6448
Video Career Library - Public and Personal Services   1897, 1952, 2157, 2335, 2476, 2835, 2887, 2951, 3033, 3052, 5649
Video Career Library - Repair Fields   3939, 4018, 4066, 4158, 4383, 4414
Video Career Library - Technical Occupations   911, 6524
Video Career Library - Transportation & Materials Moving   6640, 6700, 6829
Video Math and Verbal Review for the Civil Service Exam   1418
Video Review for Police Officer Exams   2213
Video Review for the Armed Forces Exam   7144
"Video Sales Clerk" in *Career Opportunities in Television, Cable, and Video* (pp. 194-195)   455
"Video Service Technician" in *Career Opportunities in Television, Cable, and Video* (pp. 196-197)   4159
Video Tapes for Cosmetology   2952
Virginia State Department of Social Services • Division of Licensing Programs   7223
Vital Signs   2696
Vocational Visions   842, 1077, 1187, 1461, 1612, 1838, 3256, 3684, 3741, 3848, 4099, 4616, 4701, 4829, 6641, 6830
Vocations U.S.A.   3257, 3685, 3742, 3849, 4100, 4245, 4359, 4453, 4617, 4702, 4830, 6642, 6831
The Voice   2032
Voice of the Industry   3804, 3919, 4133, 6574
Voice Processing Industry Review   4576

W

Wages and Benefits in Child Care   2888, 2889
Wagner Award; Percy and Betty   333
"Waiter" in *VGM's Careers Encyclopedia* (pp. 485-487)   2477
"Waiter and Waitress" in *Hospitality and Recreation*, Volume 8 of *Career Information Center* (pp. 70-72)   2478
"Waiter or Waitress and Host or Hostess" in *Hospitality & Recreation* (pp. 39-43)   2479
Waiter-Waitress   2480
"Waiter/Waitress" in *Occu-Facts: Information on 565 Careers in Outline Form* (p. 13.12)   2481
Waiters and Waitresses   2482
"Waiters and Waitresses" in *Opportunities in Restaurant Careers* (p. 10)   2483
"Waiters and Waitresses" in Volume 6 of *Career Discovery Encyclopedia* (pp. 150-151)   2484
Waiting Tables   2336, 2485
Walking on Air   3034
Wall of Honors   3278
"Wall Street Bond Broker" in *Straight Talk on Careers: 80 Pros Take You Into Their Professions* (pp. 21-24)   530

"Wall Street: Building a Career in Finance" in *Fast-Track Careers: A Guide to the Highest-Paying Jobs* (pp. 17-39) 531
Wallpaper Hanger 5148
Walls & Ceilings 4950, 5126, 5237
"Warehouse Worker" in *Marketing and Distribution*, Volume 10 of *Career Information Center* (pp. 64-65) 1335
Warehouseman 1283, 7069
Washington Craft Show 5735, 6457
Washington Letter 6319
Washington State Department of Licensing • Business and Professions Division 7224
Wastewater Treatment Plant Operators 6075
"Wastewater Treatment Plant Operators" in Volume 3 of *The Encyclopedia of Careers and Vocational Guidance* (pp. 797-801) 6076
Wastewater Treatment Plant Supervisor 6103
Water & Pollution Control 6117
Water & Wastes Digest 6118
"Water and Wastewater-Treatment Plant Operators" in *Occupational Outlook Handbook* (pp. 409-410) 6077
"Water and Wastewater Treatment Plant Operators" in Volume 6 of *Career Discovery Encyclopedia* (pp. 154-155) 6078
Water Conditioning & Purification 6119
Water, Environment, and Technology 6120
Water Pollution Control Federation 6081
Water Research 6121
Water Technology 6122
"Water Transportation Occupations" in *Occupational Outlook Handbook* (pp. 442-444) 6956
Water/Wastewater Operator 6079
Waterfowler's World 3567
Webster's New World Secretarial Handbook 1666
Weekly Commercial News 6800, 6914, 6995
The Weekly Insider 150
Welder 5965
"Welder" in *Construction*, Volume 4 of *Career Information Center* (pp. 89-90) 5943
"Welder" in *Guide to Careers Without College* (pp. 67-70) 5944
"Welder" in *Hard Hatted Women: Stories of Struggle and Success in the Trades* (pp. 33-36) 5945
Welder Education—Today and Tomorrow 5970
Welders 5946
"Welders" in Volume 6 of *Career Discovery Encyclopedia* (pp. 156-157) 5947
"Welders" in Volume 3 of *The Encyclopedia of Careers and Vocational Guidance* (pp. 718-723) 5948
Welders and Oxygen Cutters 5949
"Welders and Oxygen Cutters" in *Occu-Facts: Information on 565 Careers in Outline Form* (p. 18.24) 5950
"Welders, Cutters, and Welding Machine Operators" in *Occupational Outlook Handbook* (pp. 404-405) 5951
"Welding" in *Opportunities in Metalworking Careers* (pp. 47-58) 5952
Welding & Cutting: A Guide to Fusion Welding & Associated Cutting Processes 5985
Welding and Joining... Build a Career to Build a Country 5953
Welding Careers 5954
Welding Design & Fabrication 5993
The Welding Distributor 5994
Welding Handbook 5986
Welding Innovation Quarterly 5995
Welding Journal 5996
Welding Machine Operator 5955
"Welding Machine Operator" in *Occu-Facts: Information on 565 Careers in Outline Form* (p. 18.8) 5956
Welding: Principles & Applications 5987
"Welding Technicians" in Volume 4 of *The Encyclopedia of Careers and Vocational Guidance* (pp. 269-273) 5957
"Welding Technology" in *The Career Connection II: A Guide to Technical Majors and Their Related Careers* (pp. 133-134) 5958
Welding Technology Fundamentals 5988
Welding Technology Today: Principles & Practices 5989
Wellhead Operations 5426
Western Cable Television Convention and Exposition 4431
Western Farm Show 3439
Western Lath/Plaster/Drywall Industries Association Annual Convention 4953, 5240
Western Metalworking Directory 5824
The Western Producer 3407
Western States Meat Association—Bulletin 5661
Western States Meat Association Exhibition 5671
Western World Pet Supply Association Annual Pet Industry Trade Show 2821

What Combines Communications, Law, Technology, Finance, Medicine, Engineering... 1698
What Do You Know about Air Conditioning, Refrigeration & Heating 4297
What Do You Know about Carpentry 4712
What is a Travel Agent? 659
What Is Telemarketing and How Do I Get Started? 1786
What to Look for in a Truck Driver 6931
Whatcha Gonna Do Now? 2665, 2733
The Wheat Grower 3408
Wheel & Rim out of Service Guide 6876
When Do You Need a Professional, Accredited Farm Manager? 3258
Whole Foods—Source Book Issue 2364
"Wholesale and Retail Trade" in *The Encyclopedia of Career Choices for the 1990s: A Guide to Entry Level Jobs* (pp. 242-243) 200
"Wholesale Sales Worker" in *Marketing and Distribution*, Volume 10 of *Career Information Center* (pp. 65-67) 201
"Wholesale Sales Workers" in Volume 6 of *Career Discovery Encyclopedia* (pp. 158-159) 202
"Wholesale Trade Sales Representative" in *Guide to Careers Without College* (pp. 23-25) 203
"Wholesale Trade Sales Representatives" in *Jobs! What They Are...Where They Are...What They Pay* (p. 284) 204
"Wholesale Trade Sales Workers" in *Opportunities in Vocational and Technical Careers* (pp. 66-68) 205
"Wholesale Trade Sales Workers" in Volume 3 of *The Encyclopedia of Careers and Vocational Guidance* (pp. 189-193) 206
Wholesaler—"Wholesaling 100" Issue [Plumbing and heating] 4315, 5298
Wholesalers and Distributors 207
Who's Hiring in Hospitality 2486
Who's Who in Direct Selling 477
Why Should a Heavy Duty Truck Technician be Certified? 4109
Wildfowl 3568
Wildlife Crusader 3569
Wildlife Harvest 3570
"Wildlife Management Trapper" in *Action Careers: Employment in the High-Risk Job Market* (pp. 291-299) 3469
WINBA Championship Title 2968
Window Clerk (USPS) 1419
Wing & Shot 3571
Wings and Wheels 49
Winning the Fire Service Leadership Game 2008
Winston's Travel Discoveries 705
Wire and Cable Specifications 1325
Wire Expo - Wire Association International Annual Meeting and Exposition 4432, 5041
Wired Librarian's Newsletter 1518
WLW Journal 1519
Woman Officer of the Year 2242
Wood & Wood Products 6471
Wood Expo 3659
Wood Machining News 6472
"Wood Patternmaker" in *Occu-Facts: Information on 565 Careers in Outline Form* (p. 17.11) 6449
Woodshop News 6473
Woodwork 6474
The Woodworker's Journal 6475
Woodworking 6464
Woodworking Machine Operator 6450
"Woodworking Machine Operator" in *Occu-Facts: Information on 565 Careers in Outline Form* (p. 17.13) 6451
WOODWORKING - Machinery and Equipment for the Timber and Woodworking Industries 6478
"Woodworking Occupations" in *Occupational Outlook Handbook* (pp. 425-426) 6452
Wool Carpet Specification Guide and Resource Directory 4781
The Wool Sack 3409
Word Detective Picture Word Book 2258
Word Magic: A Guide to Understanding & Evaluating Word Processing Equipment 1869
"Word Processing" in *Exploring High Tech Careers* (pp. 60-64) 1839
Word Processing Machine Operator 1840
"Word Processing Operators" in *The Complete Computer Career Guide* (pp. 75-78) 1841
"Word Processing Personnel" in *The American Almanac of Jobs and Salaries* (pp. 510-516) 1842
"Word Processing Specialists: Information Processors" in *Careers for Women Without College Degrees* (pp. 192-196) 1843
Word Processing Specialists (Operators) 1844
Word Processing Supervisor 848
"Word Processor" in *Administration, Business, and Office*, Volume 1 of *Career Information Center* (pp. 101-103) 1845

Index to Information Sources

"Word Processor" in *VGM's Careers Encyclopedia* (pp. 489-490) **1846**
Word Processor & Calculator Development System MVP-Forth **1870**
Word Processor & Calculator Development System Source **1871**
"Word Processor Operators" in Volume 6 of *Career Discovery Encyclopedia* (pp. 164-165) **1847**
Word Processors & Information Processing: What They Are & How to Buy **1872**
Word Processors & the Writing Process: An Annotated Bibliography **1873**
Word Processors & Typewriters Worldwide: Opportunities & Pitfalls **1874**
Work Procedures for a Derrickman **5427**
Work Procedures for a Roustabout **5428**
Workbook Exercises in Alphabetic Filing **1468**
Workbook for Professional Barber Styling **2849**
World Champion Beauty Trade Show **3005**
World International Nail and Beauty Association **2957**
World of Beef **3410**
World of Concrete USA Exposition **4893**
World Pork Expo **3440**
Worldwide Travel Information Contact Book **682**
Would You Like a Career That Pays Well, Helps People, and Provides Exceptional Opportunities? **4288**
WPCF Highlights **6123**
WPCF Job Bank **6124**
WPCF Literature Review **6129**
WPCF Manuals of Practice **6104**
WPCF Safety and Health Bulletin **6125**
WPCF Washington Bulletin **6126**
The Wright Way **1532**
WWS/World Wide Shipping **6996**

Y

"Yacht Crew Member" in *Offbeat Careers: The Directory of Unusual Work* (pp. 177-178) **6957**
YARDSTICK [Data processing] **1804**
Yorkshire Journal **3411**
You Can Become a Tile, Marble, Terrazzo and Dimensional Stone Installer **4618, 4831, 5554**
You Can Type for Doctors at Home! **1875**
You Don't Have to Be a Computer Genius to Land a Computer Job: How to Find a Career in the World's Fastest Growing Field **912**
Young Children **2914**
The Young Detective's Handbook **2259**
Your Career in Aviation Maintenance **3686, 3690, 3724**
Your Career in Business-to-Business Direct Marketing **456**
Your Career in Professional Barber Styling **2836**
Your Career in Professional Barber Styling. **2862**
Your Career in Veterinary Technology **2784**
Your Future in the Plumbing Heating Cooling Industry **4289, 5268**
Your Future in Word Processing **1848**
Your Guardian Angel **4415, 6021**
Your Successful Real Estate Career **302**

Z

"Zookeeper" in *Careers for Animal Lovers and Other Zoological Types* (pp. 90-93) **2785**